PrincetonReview.com

THE BEST 389 COLLEGES

2024 Edition

By Robert Franek, David Soto,
Stephen Koch, Aaron Riccio, Laura Rose,
and The Staff of The Princeton Review

Penguin
Random
House

ACKNOWLEDGMENTS

Each year we assemble an awesomely talented group of colleagues who work together to produce our newest Best Colleges edition. It requires synchronized, Herculean efforts annually to update our college profiles in their component parts—narrative, surveys, rankings, ratings, stats, etc.,—and this, our 32nd edition, is no exception. Everyone involved in this effort—authors, editors, data managers, production specialists, and designers—goes above and beyond to make *The Best 389 Colleges* an exceptional student resource guide. For over 30 years, we've worked to collect and publish what prospective college students really want: The most honest, accessible, and pertinent information about the colleges they are considering attending.

My sincere thanks go to everybody who has contributed to this tremendous project over the course of more than a quarter-century. A special thank you goes to our authors, Jen Adams, Cathy Cuthbertson, Corinne Dolci, Selena Fragassi, Andrea Kornstein, Amanda Krupman, Christine Lindwall, Suzanne McKenzie, Nina Mozes, Hazel Schaffer, Olivia Tejeda, Catherine Thomas, and Tina Tuminaro for their dedication in poring through tens of thousands of surveys to produce the campus culture narratives of each school we profiled. Very special thanks goes to Aaron Riccio and Laura Rose for their editorial commitment and vision, and to Stephen Koch, who continues to work in partnership with school administrators and students. My continued thanks go to our data guru, David Soto, for his successful efforts in collecting and accurately representing the statistical data that appear with each college profile. The scope of this project and its deadline constraints could not have been realized without the calm presence of our director of production, Deborah Weber, and production editor Liz Dacey—their dedication, focus, and attention to detail continue to impress and remind me of what a pleasure it is to work on this project each year. Special thanks also go to Jeanne Krier, my trusted colleague, media advisor, and friend, for the dedicated work she has done on this book and the overall series since its inception. Finally, I would like to make special mention of Tom Russell and Alison Stoltzfus, our Penguin Random House publishing team, for their continuous investment and faith in our ideas.

Robert Franek
Editor-in-Chief
Lead Author—*The Best 389 Colleges*

Contents

Get More (Free) Content
at **PrincetonReview.com/guidebooks**

As easy as 1·2·3

1 Go to PrincetonReview.com/guidebooks or scan the **QR code** and enter the following ISBN for your book: **9780593516867**

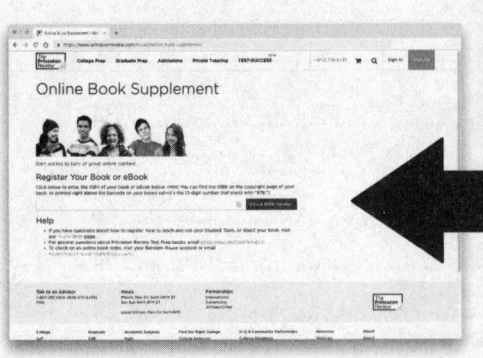

2 Answer a few simple questions to set up an exclusive Princeton Review account. *(If you already have one, you can just log in.)*

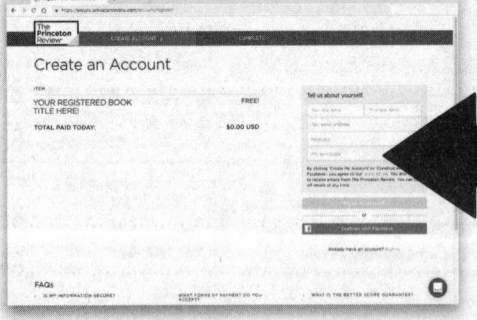

3 Enjoy access to your **FREE** content!

Once you've registered, you can...

- Take a full-length practice SAT® and ACT®

- Get valuable advice about applying to college

- Access a printable copy of the index for ease of use

- Check for any post-print updates or errata

LET'S GO MOBILE! Access all of these free, additional resources by downloading the new Princeton Review app at www.princetonreview.com/mobile/apps/highschool or scan the QR Code to the right.

Need to report a potential **content** issue?

Contact **EditorialSupport@review.com** and include:
- full title of the book
- ISBN
- page number

Need to report a **technical** issue?

Contact **TPRStudentTech@review.com** and provide:
- your full name
- email address used to register the book
- full book title and ISBN
- Operating system (Mac/PC) and browser (Chrome, Firefox, Safari, etc.)

PART 1

Introduction

31 Years of The Princeton Review's College Rankings

1992	Edition	2023
250	Colleges profiled	389
30,000	Student surveys	165,000
120	Average surveys per campus	424
67	Survey questions	85

"There was a void in the college guide market and we have filled it with this book."

Over 30 years ago, The Princeton Review opened the first edition of *The Best Colleges* with this bold statement. In 1992, no other book provided in-depth descriptions of schools alongside statistics covering admissions, financial aid, and student body demographics.

Then, as now, no other guide was based on the input of so many students. Then, as now, we at The Princeton Review believe that current students are the real experts about life at a particular college or university—only they can give you the most candid and informed feedback on what life is really like on campus. More than a million students have participated in our surveys over the past quarter century, and we are pleased to continue to publish what we believe is the most substantive resource you need to find the college that will fit you best.

We've added (and dropped) schools from the book, we've exponentially increased our student survey results, and we've changed or renamed many of the categories in which we've used student feedback to rank 25 top colleges in each of 50 fields. Our guiding conviction, however, remains the same: there is no single "best" college, only the best college for you. The profiles and ranking lists in this book can help you find the school that best fits your unique personality and goals.

What college is right for me?

We encourage students to consider their wants and needs across four categories: academics, campus culture, financial aid, and career services.

Academics

Does the college you're considering offer classes and learning opportunities that interest you? You don't need to declare a college major until your junior year of college—but you're more likely to succeed if you're excited about and engaged by the options available to you. Consider your learning style: Do you prefer informative lectures or lively discussions? Research and analysis, or hands-on experience and practice? Writing papers or working in small groups? Look for the academic experience you'll need to feel challenged and engaged, and what support you'll need for success—peer tutoring, accessible professors, mentorship, and career services are just some of the options you might find on campus. Check out course and program descriptions, reviews of professors, and sit in on some classes if you're able to visit campus.

Campus Culture

Do you want a big school or a small one? A hip urban campus or a verdant quad in the country? A college where everyone cheers on the basketball team, or one where every theater production gets a standing ovation? Every college has its own special vibe.

You can start narrowing down your list by making some decisions about the size of the student body and geographical location, and then move on to aspects you can identify by visiting campus, talking to current students, and trusting your gut instincts: the personalities, politics, and interests of the student body. Take quality of life into account, too, and try to check out the dorms, food, and recreational facilities on campus.

Financial Aid

The cost of college is one of the biggest concerns for students, parents, and counselors. We hear that from the students we work with and see it on our annual College Hopes & Worries Survey. It's important to be realistic about your family's finances and to avoid taking on unreasonable debts in the name of your education—but it's also important not to cross a school off your list because of a scary sticker price.

Many colleges and universities make incredible financial aid offers (sometimes as a combination of grants and scholarships, which means no debt at all!). Raising your grades and your SAT or ACT scores will help you become more eligible for merit-based financial aid. And more and more data on college outcomes—that is, career placement rates and average starting salaries—is becoming available, which can help you assess the value of investing your tuition dollars in a particular college.

You can check out our list of 209 "Best Value" schools in Part 2 of this book, and read more about them in our searchable online listings at https://www.princetonreview.com/college-rankings/best-value-colleges.

Career Development

Visit or contact the career development center at all the schools you're considering. Find out how each supports students in preparing for the professional world. Do they offer résumé writing workshops? Practice interviews? Networking events with alumni? If you foresee yourself in a particular field, location, or specific workplace, ask about past students' track records of finding internships, getting accepted to grad school, or landing entry-level jobs in those areas.

College admission officers and career counselors are more than happy to highlight their institutions' success stories—as well as the unique skill-building programs and experiences their campuses have to offer.

> Our expert admission counselors will help you navigate the college process with less stress and submit stand-out applications to your top-choice schools. Learn more at princetonreview.com/college-admissions/college-counseling.

Getting into Selective Colleges: An Overview for High School Students

6 STEPS TO GETTING INTO COLLEGE

Putting some effort into your schoolwork and extracurricular experiences can make applying to your choice colleges a lot less stressful. Though they might sound obvious, the following steps are extremely important! (Many of these are true even at schools that have adopted Test Optional policies, as submitting a test may help for other considerations, and at a Test Free school, you may want to focus even more on the non-test steps below.)

1. Work hard for good grades.

2. Enroll in challenging courses.

3. Spend time preparing for the ACT® or SAT®.

4. Polish your writing skills.

5. Establish relationships with teachers and advisors who can write strong letters of recommendation for you.

6. Get involved in some activities, community service, or work experiences that will enable you to show your values, talents, and skills.

College admission is all about compatibility. As an applicant, you are looking for an environment where you can thrive academically and personally, and it is the job of an admission officer to identify students who will make great additions to a unique campus community.

Your path to college begins your first year in high school. Grades and test scores are important factors in college admission, but admissions officers are also looking for curious and engaged candidates who will round out a diverse first-year class.

Grades

Most admissions officers report that your GPA and the rigor of your high school curriculum are the most important elements of your college application.

- Choose your high school classes carefully. Challenge yourself with honors, AP®, and IB® courses when they are available.

- Your grades count for all four years of high school. When colleges review your transcript, they often look at grade trends across subjects and course levels.

- Even if you had a rough first year of high school, there's still time to turn your grades around. Many schools will reward your upward trajectory.

Test Scores

SAT and/or ACT scores take the lead, but admissions officers consider your performance on other standardized tests as well.

- The PSAT® is optional your sophomore year, but your junior year PSAT scores can qualify you for scholarship programs such as the National Merit® Scholarship, which can help cover the cost of tuition and get you into a great college. It's also good practice for the SAT. Learning the digital PSAT format will also help prepare you for the SAT (which goes digital in the US in Spring 2024).

- Strong performances on AP Exams can indicate your potential for academic achievement to college admission officers. More than 1,400 colleges and universities accept high scores on AP Exams for course credits.

- Most schools view the ACT and SAT equally, so it's completely up to you which test you take (you can even take both!). The ACT's Writing section is optional, but some colleges may require it.

- Test Optional schools: Schools that are Test Optional do not require standardized test scores as part of a complete application. Since your test scores could qualify you for merit scholarships even at Test Optional schools, it's still a smart idea to take (and prep for!) at least one standardized test.

Extracurriculars

What you do with your time shows colleges who you are and what qualities you'll bring to campus.

- Commitment to a sport, hobby, religious organization, or job over four years of high school is key. Colleges would much rather see you excited about a few worthwhile endeavors than marginally involved with a ton of clubs.

- If an after-school job is cutting into your extracurricular time, don't worry! Work experience demonstrates maturity and responsibility on your college application.

- Make your summer count! Some students enroll in university programs to start earning college credits. Others volunteer or find a summer job. Whatever you do, your experience can make your college application rise to the top of a competitive applicant pool.

What Should You Do This Summer?

Ahhh, summer. The possibilities seem endless. You can get a job, intern, travel, study, volunteer, or do nothing at all. Here are a few ideas to get you started:

- **Go to college:** No, not for real. However, you can participate in summer programs at colleges and universities at home and abroad. Programs can focus on anything from academics (stretch your brain by taking an intensive science or language course) to sports to admissions guidance. This is also a great opportunity to explore college life firsthand, especially if you get to stay in a dorm. Summer is also a time when families on vacations can squeeze in a college visit while they're in "the neighborhood." Even if classes aren't in session when you are able to tour a campus, the more colleges you can visit, the better informed your final college choice will be.

- **Prep for the PSAT, SAT, or ACT:** Even at Test Optional schools—and especially if you're seeking to maximize financial aid—test scores can help to round out your overall application. Getting this valuable prep-work done during a less busy part of your year can also help you to keep your full focus on your grades and extracurriculars when school resumes.

- **Research scholarships:** College is expensive. While you should never rule out a school based on cost, the more scholarship money you can secure beforehand, the more college options you will have. You'll find loads of info on financial aid and scholarships on our site, PrincetonReview.com.

Applying for Financial Aid

The cost of college has been the biggest concern among respondents to our annual College Hopes & Worries survey for the past five years. Educate yourself about the financial aid system before you submit forms to get the best outcome for you and your family.

- Be aware that applying to college and applying for financial aid are two separate processes.

- The U.S. Department of Education (USDOE) requires all schools that offer federal aid to provide a net-price calculator (but does not audit them for accuracy). Use this tool on each prospective school's financial aid website, but be aware that these estimates are non-binding and can be off by $10,000 or more.

- The USDOE has announced that the 2024–2025 version of its Free Application for Federal Student Aid (FAFSA®) will not be released until "sometime in December" due to the tectonic changes involving "FAFSA Simplification." At the time this book went to print, schools were still waiting for guidance from the USDOE, so please visit the websites of the schools to which you are applying for more specific guidance. Do not make the mistake of submitting the 2023–2024 FAFSA.

- In addition to the FAFSA, many schools require the College Board's CSS Profile® and/or their own aid forms to be completed to be considered for institutional aid. The CSS Profile will still be available on October 1. Those applying for Early Decision (and for some schools, Early Action as well), may need to complete this and other aid forms before the FAFSA is released.

- Your financial aid offer is intended to meet your need and can consist of:
  o grants and scholarships (which do not need to be paid back)
  o federal work-study (a job)
  o student loans

- Outside organizations offer scholarships tailored to academic interests, talents, extracurricular activities, career goals, geographic location, and many more factors. Keep an eye on deadlines, which could fall as early as the summer before senior year.

Some of Our Other Helpful Books

The 2024 Edition of The Princeton Review's *Paying for College* contains line-by-line strategies for completing the new-look 2024–2025 FAFSA (as Simplification will not be easy) and 2024–2025 CSS Profile to your best advantage. It explains how the financial aid process works and reveals strategies—all legal—for maximizing your eligibility for aid. Authored by Kal Chany, one of the nation's most widely sourced experts on college funding, it also includes annually updated information on education tax breaks, college savings programs, and student and parent loans. Check out Kal Chany's "26 Tips for Getting Financial Aid . . ." online in your student tools.

College Admission 101 presents simple answers to your toughest questions about the college admissions process, figuring out financial aid, and getting into the school of your choice.

The Complete College Planner provides high-school students with a comprehensive and activity-filled planner to help you map out all the important tasks and information you'll want to gather before and during your college search.

The Complete Guide to College Application Essays recognizes the increasing importance of your personal application statement and walks you through every step of how to prepare, brainstorm, draft, and revise your application essays.

The K&W Guide to Colleges for Students with Learning Differences profiles 360+ schools highly recommended for such students. It includes strategies to help them successfully apply to the best programs for their needs, plus advice from specialists in the field of learning disabilities.

The Ultimate Guide to HBCUs provides a thorough look at all 101 Historically Black Colleges and Universities to make sure that students aren't missing out on a potentially ideal opportunity.

Great Schools for 21 of the Most Popular Undergraduate Majors

Worried about having to declare a major on your college application? Relax. Most colleges won't require you to declare a major until the end of your sophomore year, giving you plenty of time to explore your options. However, problems may arise if you are thinking about majoring in a program that limits its enrollment—meaning that if you don't declare that major early on, you might not get into that program at a later date.

On the flip side, some students declare a major on their application because they believe it will boost their chances of gaining admission. This can be problematic, however, if you later decide to change your major. It involves switching from one school within the college to another (e.g., from the school of arts and sciences to the school of business, for example), which can be difficult.

Never choose a college solely on the prestige of a particular program. College will expose you to new and exciting learning experiences. (Choosing a school based on program availability is a different story.) You may also want to investigate opportunities to design your own major. A commitment to a major would limit you in many ways.

How Did We Compile These Lists?

Each year we collect data from more than 2,000 colleges on the subject of—among many other things—undergraduate academic offerings. We ask colleges to report not only which undergraduate majors they offer, but also which of their majors have the highest enrollment and the number of bachelor's degrees each school awarded in these areas. The list below identifies (in alphabetical order) 21 of the 40 "most popular" majors that the schools responding to our survey reported to us. We also conduct our own research on college majors. We look at institutional data, and we consult with our in-house college admissions experts as well as our National College Counselor Advisory Board (whom we list on pages 847–848) for their input on schools offering great programs in these majors. We thank them and all of the guidance counselors, college admissions counselors, and education experts across the country whose recommendations we considered in developing these lists. Of the nearly 3,000 four-year colleges across the United States, those on these lists represent only a snapshot of the many offering great programs in these majors. Use our lists as a starting point for further research.

Great Schools for Accounting Majors
- Agnes Scott College
- Alfred University
- Assumption University
- Auburn University
- Babson College
- Baylor University
- Bentley University
- Boston College
- Boston University
- Brigham Young University (UT)
- Bryant University
- Bucknell University
- Calvin University
- City University of New York—Baruch College
- City University of New York—Brooklyn College
- City University of New York—Hunter College
- City University of New York—Queens College
- Claremont McKenna College
- Clemson University
- College of Charleston
- Cornell University
- DePaul University
- Drexel University
- Duquesne University
- Elon University
- Emory University
- Fairfield University
- Fordham University
- George Mason University
- Georgetown University
- Hofstra University
- Illinois Wesleyan University
- Indiana University—Bloomington
- Iowa State University
- James Madison University
- Lehigh University
- Le Moyne College
- Marquette University
- Miami University (OH)
- New York University
- Northeastern University
- Pace University
- Penn State University Park
- Pepperdine University
- Rider University
- Rochester Institute of Technology
- St. Bonaventure University
- Seton Hall University
- Siena College
- Southern Methodist University
- Stonehill College
- Suffolk University
- Temple University
- Texas A&M University—College Station
- Transylvania University
- The University of Alabama at Birmingham
- University of Houston
- University of Illinois—Urbana-Champaign
- University of Michigan—Ann Arbor
- University of Mississippi
- University of Oklahoma
- University of Pennsylvania
- University of Southern California
- The University of Texas at Austin
- The University of Texas at Dallas
- Washington & Jefferson College

Great Schools for Agriculture Majors
- Angelo State University
- Auburn University
- Berea College
- Clemson University
- College of the Ozarks
- Colorado State University
- Cornell University
- Illinois Institute of Technology
- Iowa State University
- Kansas State University
- Louisiana State University—Baton Rouge
- Michigan State University
- Middle Tennessee State University
- North Carolina State University
- The Ohio State University–Columbus
- Oregon State University
- Penn State University Park
- Purdue University—West Lafayette
- Texas A&M University—College Station
- Tuskegee University
- University of Arizona
- University of Arkansas—Fayetteville
- University of California—Davis
- University of Connecticut
- University of Florida
- University of Georgia
- University of Hawaii—Manoa
- University of Idaho
- University of Illinois—Urbana-Champaign
- University of Kentucky
- University of Maine
- University of Maryland, College Park
- University of Massachusetts–Amherst
- University of Minnesota—Twin Cities
- University of Missouri—Columbia
- University of Nebraska–Lincoln
- University of Rhode Island
- University of Tennessee—Knoxville
- University of Vermont
- University of Wisconsin—Madison
- University of Wyoming
- Virginia Tech
- Washington State University
- West Virginia University

Great Schools for Biology Majors

- Agnes Scott College
- Albion College
- Allegheny College
- Amherst College
- Appalachian State University
- Auburn University
- Austin College
- Bates College
- Baylor University
- Berea College
- Berry College
- Boston College
- Boston University
- Bowdoin College
- Brandeis University
- Brigham Young University (UT)
- Brown University
- Bryn Mawr College
- Bucknell University
- Carleton College
- Case Western Reserve University
- Centenary College of Louisiana
- Christopher Newport University
- City University of New York—City College
- Clark University
- Clemson University
- Coe College
- Colby College
- Colgate University
- College of Charleston
- The College of New Jersey
- College of Saint Benedict/Saint John's University
- College of Wooster
- Colorado College
- Colorado State University
- Connecticut College
- Cornell University
- Creighton University
- Dartmouth College
- Davidson College
- Denison University
- DePauw University
- Dickinson College
- Drew University
- Drury University
- Duke University
- Duquesne University
- Earlham College
- Eckerd College
- Emory University
- Florida Southern College
- Franklin & Marshall College
- George Mason University
- Gettysburg College
- Gonzaga University
- Gordon College
- Grinnell College
- Hamilton College
- Hampden-Sydney College
- Hampton University
- Hanover College
- Harvard College
- Haverford College
- Hofstra University
- Howard University
- Johns Hopkins University
- Juniata College
- Kalamazoo College
- Knox College
- Lafayette College
- Lake Forest College
- Lawrence University
- Le Moyne College
- Lewis & Clark College
- Louisiana State University—Baton Rouge
- Loyola University of Chicago
- Lycoming College
- Marquette University
- Michigan State University
- Middlebury College
- Millsaps College
- Mount Holyoke College
- Muhlenberg College
- North Carolina State University
- Oberlin College
- Occidental College
- Ohio Wesleyan University
- Pomona College
- Princeton University
- Randolph College
- Randolph-Macon College
- Reed College
- Rhodes College
- Rice University
- Ripon College
- Sacred Heart University
- Saint Louis University
- Saint Michael's College
- Scripps College
- Seton Hall University
- Siena College
- Skidmore College
- Smith College
- Southwestern University
- Spelman College
- St. John's University (NY)
- St. Mary's College of Maryland
- St. Olaf College
- State University of New York—Binghamton University
- State University of New York—College of Environmental Science and Forestry
- State University of New York—Geneseo
- State University of New York—Stony Brook University
- Susquehanna University
- Swarthmore College
- Temple University
- Transylvania University
- Trinity College (CT)
- Trinity University
- Truman State University

- Tufts University
- Tuskegee University
- Union College (NY)
- The University of the South
- University of Alabama at Birmingham
- University of California—Berkeley
- University of California—Davis
- University of California—Irvine
- University of California—Los Angeles
- University of California—Merced
- University of California—Riverside
- University of California—San Diego
- University of California—Santa Barbara
- University of California—Santa Cruz
- The University of Chicago
- University of Colorado Boulder
- University of Dallas
- University of Delaware
- University of Florida
- University of Georgia
- University of Hawaii—Manoa
- University of Houston
- University of Lynchburg
- University of Mary Washington
- University of Maryland, Baltimore County
- University of Massachusetts-Amherst
- University of Miami
- University of Michigan—Ann Arbor
- University of Minnesota—Twin Cities
- University of Montana
- University of New England
- University of New Hampshire
- The University of North Carolina at Chapel Hill
- University of Pittsburgh—Pittsburgh Campus
- University of Rochester
- University of San Diego
- University of Scranton
- University of South Carolina—Columbia
- University of South Florida
- University of Texas at Austin
- The University of Texas at Dallas
- University of Vermont
- University of Washington
- University of Wisconsin-Madison
- Ursinus College
- Vassar College
- Warren Wilson College
- Washington College
- Washington University in St. Louis
- Wellesley College
- Wheaton College (MA)
- Whitman College
- William & Mary
- Wofford College
- Xavier University of Louisiana
- Yale University

Great Schools for Business/Finance Majors

- Alfred University
- Arizona State University
- Babson College
- Bentley University
- Berea College
- Boston College
- Brigham Young University (UT)
- Bradley University
- Bryant University
- Butler University
- California State University, Stanislaus
- Calvin University
- Carnegie Mellon University
- Champlain College
- Chapman University
- Christopher Newport University
- City University of New York—Baruch College
- City University of New York—Brooklyn College
- College of Charleston
- Cornell University
- Creighton University
- DePaul University
- Drexel University
- Elon University
- Emory University
- Fairfield University
- Florida International University
- Florida State University
- Fordham University
- High Point University
- Indiana University—Bloomington
- Iona University
- Iowa State University
- John Carroll University
- Lehigh University
- Lycoming College
- Marquette University
- Massachusetts Institute of Technology
- McDaniel College
- Mercer University
- Miami University (OH)
- Michigan State University
- Middle Tennessee State University
- New York University
- Northwestern University
- Ohio University—Athens
- Oregon State University
- Pace University
- Portland State University
- Rice University
- Roanoke College
- Rollins College
- Rowan University
- Rutgers University—New Brunswick
- Seattle University
- San Diego State University
- Saint Joseph's University (PA)
- Saint Mary's College of California
- Saint Michael's College
- Santa Clara University

- Siena College
- Southwestern University
- Stetson University
- Suffolk University
- Texas State University
- University of Arkansas—Fayetteville
- University of California—Berkeley
- University of California—Irvine
- University of California—Los Angeles
- The University of Chicago
- University of Florida
- University of Houston
- University of Illinois—Urbana-Champaign
- University of Michigan—Ann Arbor
- The University of North Carolina at Greensboro
- University of Notre Dame
- University of Pennsylvania
- University of Richmond
- University of St. Thomas (MN)
- University of San Diego
- University of San Francisco
- University of Southern California
- The University of Texas at Austin
- The University of Texas at Dallas
- The University of Tulsa
- University of Virginia
- Villanova University
- Washington University in St. Louis
- William & Mary
- Wittenberg University

Great Schools for Communications Majors

- American University
- Baylor University
- Boston College
- Boston University
- Bradley University
- Butler University
- City University of New York—City College
- City University of New York—Hunter College
- Clemson University
- College of Charleston
- Cornell University
- Denison University
- DePaul University
- DePauw University
- Duquesne University
- Eckerd College
- Elon University
- Emerson College
- Eugene Lang College of Liberal Arts at The New School
- Fairfield University
- Fordham University
- Gonzaga University
- High Point University
- Hollins University
- Hofstra University
- Howard University
- Indiana University—Bloomington
- Iowa State University
- Ithaca College
- James Madison University
- Lake Forest College
- Loyola University Maryland
- Loyola University New Orleans
- Marist College
- Manhattanville College
- Muhlenberg College
- New York University
- Northwestern University
- Pace University
- Pepperdine University
- Quinnipiac University
- Ripon College
- Salisbury University
- Seton Hall University
- St. Bonaventure University
- St. John's University (NY)
- Stanford University
- State University of New York—Purchase College
- Suffolk University
- Susquehanna University
- Syracuse University
- Texas Christian University
- University of Arizona
- University of California—San Diego
- University of California—Santa Barbara
- University of Iowa
- University of Maryland, College Park
- University of San Diego
- University of Southern California
- University of Tampa
- The University of Texas at Austin
- University of Utah

Great Schools for Computer Science/Computer Engineering Majors

- Arizona State University
- Boston University
- Brown University
- California Institute of Technology
- Carleton College
- Carnegie Mellon University
- Case Western Reserve University
- City University of New York—Brooklyn College
- City University of New York—Hunter College
- Colby College
- Colorado State University
- Columbia University
- DePaul University
- Duke University
- George Mason University
- Georgia Institute of Technology

- Harvey Mudd College
- Harvard College
- Illinois Institute of Technology
- Johns Hopkins University
- Kettering University
- Lehigh University
- Massachusetts Institute of Technology
- Miami University
- Middlebury College
- Missouri University of Science and Technology
- New Jersey Institute of Technology
- Northwestern University
- Oregon State University
- Princeton University
- Purdue University—West Lafayette
- Rice University
- Rensselaer Polytechnic Institute
- Rochester Institute of Technology
- Rose-Hulman Institute of Technology
- Stanford University
- Stevens Institute of Technology
- Swarthmore College
- University of Arizona
- University of California—Berkeley
- University of California—Irvine
- University of California—Los Angeles
- University of California—Riverside
- University of Illinois—Urbana-Champaign
- University of Maryland, Baltimore County
- University of Massachusetts–Amherst
- University of Michigan—Ann Arbor
- The University of Texas at Dallas
- University of Washington
- Washington University in St. Louis
- Worcester Polytechnic Institute

Great Schools for Criminology Majors
- American University
- Angelo State University
- Auburn University
- California State University, Stanislaus
- Champlain College
- Florida State University
- George Mason University
- Indiana University of Pennsylvania
- Loyola University New Orleans
- North Carolina State University
- The Ohio State University—Columbus
- Ohio University—Athens
- Quinnipiac University
- St. John's University (NY)
- Stonehill College
- Suffolk University
- University of California—Irvine
- University of Delaware
- University of Denver
- University of Louisville
- University of Maryland, College Park
- University of Miami
- University of New Hampshire
- University of New Haven
- University of South Carolina—Columbia
- University of South Florida
- University of Tampa
- University of Utah
- Virginia Wesleyan University
- Whittier College

Great Schools for Education Majors
- Alfred University
- Auburn University
- Barnard College
- Bucknell University
- Calvin University
- City University of New York—Brooklyn College
- City University of New York—Hunter College
- Colgate University
- The College of New Jersey
- College of the Ozarks
- Columbia University
- Cornell College
- Cornell University
- Duquesne University
- East Carolina University
- Elmira College
- Elon University
- Gonzaga University
- Goucher College
- Hillsdale College
- Indiana University—Bloomington
- Juniata College
- Knox College
- Loyola Marymount University
- Manhattan College
- Marquette University
- Miami University (OH)
- Monmouth University (NJ)
- Nazareth College
- New York University
- Northeastern University
- Northwestern University
- The Ohio State University—Columbus
- Rider University
- Ripon College
- Rowan University
- St. Bonaventure University
- Salisbury University
- Salve Regina University
- Simmons University
- Skidmore College
- Smith College

- State University of New York—Geneseo
- Trinity University
- University of Louisiana at Lafayette
- University of Maine
- University of Mississippi
- The University of Montana—Missoula
- The University of South Dakota
- Vanderbilt University

- Villanova University
- Wagner College
- Wellesley College
- William Jewell College
- William & Mary
- Wittenberg University
- Xavier University (OH)

Great Schools for Engineering Majors

- California Institute of Technology
- Carnegie Mellon University
- Case Western Reserve University
- Columbia University
- The Cooper Union for the Advancement of Science and Art
- Clarkson University
- Cornell University
- Drexel University
- Duke University
- Franklin W. Olin College of Engineering
- Georgia Institute of Technology
- Harvard College
- Harvey Mudd College
- Illinois Institute of Technology
- Johns Hopkins University
- Kettering University
- Lawrence Technological University
- Manhattan College
- Massachusetts Institute of Technology
- Michigan Technological University
- Missouri University of Science and Technology
- Montana Technological University
- New Jersey Institute of Technology

- Penn State University Park
- Princeton University
- Purdue University—West Lafayette
- Rensselaer Polytechnic Institute
- Rice University
- Rochester Institute of Technology
- Rose-Hulman Institute of Technology
- Stanford University
- Stevens Institute of Technology
- Texas A&M University—College Station
- United States Merchant Marine Academy
- United States Military Academy
- United States Naval Academy
- University of California—Berkeley
- University of California—Los Angeles
- University of California—Merced
- University of Illinois—Urbana-Champaign
- University of Michigan—Ann Arbor
- The University of Texas at Austin
- University of Wisconsin—Madison
- Virginia Tech
- Webb Institute
- Worcester Polytechnic Institute

Great Schools for English Literature and Language Majors

- Alfred University
- Amherst College
- Bard College (NY)
- Barnard College
- Bates College
- Beloit College
- Bennington College
- Bowdoin College
- Brown University
- Bryn Mawr College
- City University of New York—Hunter College
- Colby College
- Colgate University
- Columbia University
- Cornell University
- Dartmouth College
- Davidson College
- Denison University
- DePauw University
- Duke University
- Emerson College
- Emory University
- Eugene Lang College of Liberal Arts at The New School

- Fordham University
- Gettysburg College
- Georgetown University
- Grinnell College
- Harvard College
- Haverford College
- Hanover College
- Hollins University
- Iowa State University
- Johns Hopkins University
- Kalamazoo College
- Kenyon College
- Knox College
- Lawrence University
- Lewis & Clark College
- Oberlin College
- Pitzer College
- Pomona College
- Princeton University
- Reed College
- St. Lawrence University
- St. Olaf College
- Smith College

- Spelman College
- Stanford University
- St. Mary's College of Maryland
- Syracuse University
- Trinity College (CT)
- Truman State University
- Tufts University
- University of California—Berkeley
- The University of Chicago
- University of Michigan—Ann Arbor

- University of North Carolina Asheville
- University of Notre Dame
- The University of the South
- University of Utah
- Vassar College
- Washington University in St. Louis
- Wellesley College
- Wesleyan University
- Williams College
- Yale University

Great Schools for Environmental Studies Majors

- Allegheny College
- Bates College
- Bowdoin College
- Colby College
- College of the Atlantic
- Colorado College
- Dickinson College
- Eckerd College
- Emory University
- The Evergreen State College
- Flagler College
- Harvard College
- Hobart and William Smith Colleges
- Juniata College
- Middlebury College
- New College of Florida
- Northeastern University
- Oberlin College
- Occidental College
- Pitzer College
- Pomona College

- Portland State University
- St. Mary's College of Maryland
- Sonoma State University
- State University of New York—Binghamton University
- State University of New York—College of Environmental Science and Forestry
- University of California—Berkeley
- University of California—Santa Cruz
- University of Colorado Boulder
- University of Idaho
- The University of Montana—Missoula
- University of New Hampshire
- University of North Carolina Asheville
- The University of North Carolina at Chapel Hill
- University of Oregon
- University of Redlands
- The University of the South
- University of Vermont
- Warren Wilson College
- Washington College

Great Schools for Health Services Majors

- Agnes Scott College
- Bellarmine University
- Boston University
- Clemson University
- College of the Ozarks
- Creighton University
- Drexel University
- Duquesne University
- East Carolina University
- Elmira College
- Fairfield University
- Furman University
- Gettysburg College
- Grove City College
- Hampton University
- Howard University
- Iona University
- Ithaca College
- James Madison University
- Johns Hopkins University
- Kalamazoo College
- Loyola University of Chicago
- Manhattanville College

- Mercer University
- Monmouth University (NJ)
- Montana Technological University
- Moravian College
- Nazareth College
- Northeastern University
- Ohio University—Athens
- Purdue University—West Lafayette
- Quinnipiac University
- Sacred Heart University
- Saint Anselm College
- Saint Louis University
- Salve Regina University
- Seton Hall University
- Simmons University
- Spelman College
- State University of New York—Stony Brook University
- Suffolk University
- Texas A&M University—College Station
- Texas Christian University
- Texas State University
- Tulane University
- The University of Alabama at Birmingham

- University of Central Florida
- University of Cincinnati
- University of Delaware
- University of Florida
- University of Houston
- University of Louisville
- University of Lynchburg
- University of Miami
- University of New England
- University of North Dakota
- University of Oklahoma
- University of Portland
- University of Rhode Island
- The University of South Dakota
- University of South Florida
- University of Utah
- University of Wyoming
- Wagner College
- Washington University in St. Louis
- West Virginia University
- Westminster College (UT)
- Wheaton College (IL)
- William Jewell College
- Xavier University (OH)

Great Schools for History Majors

- Bates College
- Bowdoin College
- Brown University
- Centre College
- Colgate University
- College of the Holy Cross
- The College of Wooster
- Columbia University
- Davidson College
- Drew University
- Furman University
- Georgetown University
- Grinnell College
- Hampden-Sydney College
- Harvard College
- Haverford College
- Hillsdale College
- Kenyon College
- Oberlin College
- Princeton University
- Ripon College
- Tulane University
- University of Dallas
- University of Virginia
- Wabash College
- Williams College
- Yale University

Great Schools for International Relations and Affairs Majors

- American University
- Bucknell University
- Claremont McKenna College
- Clark University
- Connecticut College
- George Washington University
- Georgetown University
- Gettysburg College
- Hamilton College
- Harvard College
- Lafayette College
- Lewis & Clark College
- Middlebury College
- Occidental College
- Tufts University
- The University of Chicago
- Yale University

Great Schools for Journalism Majors

- American University
- Arizona State University
- Auburn University
- Boston University
- Carleton College
- Duke University
- Emerson College
- The George Washington University
- Hampton University
- Howard University
- Indiana University—Bloomington
- Iowa State University
- Ithaca College
- Kansas State University
- Loyola University New Orleans
- Michigan State University
- New York University
- Northwestern University
- Ohio University—Athens
- Penn State University Park
- St. Bonaventure University
- State University of New York—Purchase
- State University of New York—Stony Brook University
- Syracuse University
- Temple University
- The University of Alabama—Tuscaloosa
- University of Arizona
- University of Arkansas—Fayetteville
- University of Florida
- University of Georgia
- University of Kansas
- University of Kentucky

- University of Idaho
- University of Illinois—Urbana-Champaign
- University of Iowa
- University of Maryland, College Park
- University of Minnesota—Twin Cities
- University of Mississippi
- University of Missouri—Columbia
- The University of Montana—Missoula
- University of Nebraska–Lincoln
- The University of North Carolina at Chapel Hill
- University of Oklahoma
- University of Oregon
- University of Southern California
- The University of Texas at Austin
- University of Wisconsin—Madison
- Washington State University
- West Virginia University

Great Schools for Marketing and Sales Majors
- Babson College
- Baylor University
- Bentley University
- Bryant University
- Butler University
- DePaul University
- Drury University
- Duquesne University
- Fairfield University
- Hofstra University
- Indiana University—Bloomington
- Iowa State University
- James Madison University
- Loyola Marymount University
- Manhattan College
- Miami University (OH)
- Providence College
- Saint Joseph's University (PA)
- San Diego State University
- Seattle University
- Siena College
- Syracuse University
- Texas A&M University—College Station
- The University of Alabama—Tuscaloosa
- University of Central Florida
- University of Cincinnati
- University of Dayton
- University of Michigan—Ann Arbor
- University of Mississippi
- University of Pennsylvania
- University of South Florida
- The University of Texas at Austin

Great Schools for Mathematics & Statistics Majors
- Amherst College
- Agnes Scott College
- Bowdoin College
- Brown University
- Bryant University
- Bryn Mawr College
- California Institute of Technology
- Carleton College
- Carnegie Mellon University
- College of the Holy Cross
- Grinnell College
- Hamilton College
- Hampton University
- Harvard College
- Harvey Mudd College
- Haverford College
- Macalester College
- Massachusetts Institute of Technology
- Pomona College
- Randolph College
- Reed College
- Rice University
- St. Lawrence University
- St. Olaf College
- United States Coast Guard Academy
- The University of Chicago
- University of Rochester
- Wabash College
- Williams College

Great Schools for Mechanical Engineering Majors
- Auburn University
- Bradley University
- California Institute of Technology
- Case Western Reserve University
- Clarkson University
- Colorado State University
- The Cooper Union for the Advancement of Science and Art
- Drexel University
- Franklin W. Olin College of Engineering
- Georgia Institute of Technology
- Grove City College
- Harvey Mudd College
- Illinois Institute of Technology
- Iowa State University
- Lafayette College
- Lehigh University
- Massachusetts Institute of Technology
- Michigan Technological University
- Missouri University of Science and Technology
- Montana Technological University
- New Jersey Institute of Technology
- North Carolina State University

- Ohio Northern University
- Oregon State University
- Princeton University
- Purdue University—West Lafayette
- Rochester Institute of Technology
- Rose-Hulman Institute of Technology
- Stanford University
- Stevens Institute of Technology
- United States Military Academy
- University of California—Berkeley
- University of Illinois—Urbana-Champaign
- University of Maryland, Baltimore County
- University of Michigan—Ann Arbor
- Virginia Tech
- Worcester Polytechnic Institute

Great Schools for Nursing Majors

- Angelo State University
- Baylor University
- Bellarmine University
- Creighton University
- Calvin University
- The Catholic University of America
- Drexel University
- Duquesne University
- East Carolina University
- Emory University
- Fairfield University
- Florida Southern College
- Indiana University of Pennsylvania
- Loyola University of Chicago
- Montana Technological University
- Ohio Northern University
- Saint Anselm College
- Saint Louis University
- Salve Regina University
- Texas Christian University
- The University of Alabama—Tuscaloosa
- University of Delaware
- University of Louisville
- University of North Dakota
- University of Pennsylvania
- University of Rhode Island
- University of Wyoming
- Villanova University
- Washington State University
- Xavier University (OH)

Great Schools for Political Science/Government Majors

- American University
- Amherst College
- Bard College (NY)
- Bates College
- Bowdoin College
- Brigham Young University (UT)
- Bryn Mawr College
- Bucknell University
- Carleton College
- Claremont McKenna College
- Clark University
- Colby College
- College of the Holy Cross
- Colorado College
- Columbia University
- Connecticut College
- Dartmouth College
- Davidson College
- Dickinson College
- Drew University
- Franklin & Marshall College
- Furman University
- George Mason University
- The George Washington University
- Georgetown University
- Gettysburg College
- Gonzaga University
- Grinnell College
- Harvard College
- Kenyon College
- Macalester College
- Princeton University
- Scripps College
- Skidmore College
- Stanford University
- Swarthmore College
- Syracuse University
- Trinity College (CT)
- University of Arizona
- University of California—Berkeley
- University of California—Los Angeles
- University of Washington
- University of Wisconsin—Madison
- Vassar College
- Wake Forest University
- William & Mary
- Yale University

Great Schools for Psychology Majors

- Agnes Scott College
- Albion College
- Allegheny College
- Assumption University
- Barnard College
- Bates College
- Bucknell University
- Carleton College
- Carnegie Mellon University
- Christopher Newport University
- City University of New York—Brooklyn College
- City University of New York—City College
- City University of New York—Hunter College
- City University of New York—Queens College
- Clark University
- Coe College
- College of the Holy Cross
- Colorado State University
- Columbia University
- Cornell University
- Dartmouth College
- DePaul University
- Duke University
- Earlham College
- Eugene Lang College of Liberal Arts at The New School
- Flagler College
- Florida State University
- Franklin & Marshall College
- George Mason University
- Gettysburg College
- Hampton University
- Hanover College
- Harvard College
- James Madison University
- Le Moyne College
- Lewis & Clark College
- Loyola University New Orleans
- Loyola University of Chicago
- Moravian College
- Mount Holyoke College
- New York University
- The Ohio State University—Columbus
- Ohio Wesleyan University
- Pitzer College
- Portland State University
- Princeton University
- Quinnipiac University
- Randolph College
- Roanoke College
- Rowan University
- St. Mary's College of Maryland
- Siena College
- Simmons University
- Smith College
- Spelman College
- Stanford University
- State University of New York–Geneseo
- Stetson University
- Stonehill College
- Temple University
- Texas A&M University—College Station
- Union College (NY)
- University of Arizona
- University of California—Davis
- University of California—Los Angeles
- University of California—Merced
- University of California—Riverside
- University of California—Santa Barbara
- University of California—Santa Cruz
- University of Connecticut
- University of Florida
- University of Houston
- University of Idaho
- University of Mary Washington
- University of Maryland, College Park
- University of Massachusetts–Amherst
- University of Michigan—Ann Arbor
- University of Minnesota—Twin Cities
- The University of Montana—Missoula
- University of Nebraska–Lincoln
- University of Pittsburgh—Pittsburgh Campus
- University of Puget Sound
- University of San Francisco
- The University of South Dakota
- University of South Florida
- University of Southern California
- University of Tennessee–Knoxville
- The University of Texas at Austin
- University of Utah
- Vassar College
- Washington & Jefferson College
- Washington College
- Washington University in St. Louis
- Wesleyan University
- Xavier University of Louisiana
- Yale University

How We Produce This Book

This Year's Edition

In the 31 years since the first edition of this book, our *Best Colleges* guide has grown considerably. We've added more than 140 colleges to the guide and deleted a fair share along the way. How we choose the schools for the book, and how we produce it, however, has not changed significantly over the years (with the exception of how we conduct our student survey—more on this follows).

To determine which schools will be in each edition, we don't use mathematical calculations or formulas. Instead we rely on a wide range of input, both quantitative and qualitative. Every year we collect data from more than 2,000 colleges that we use for our complete search index of colleges (https://www.princetonreview.com/college-search) and *Best Value Colleges,* this book, and our online profiles of schools. We visit dozens of colleges and meet with their admissions officers, deans, presidents, and college students. We talk with hundreds of high school counselors, parents, and students. Colleges also submit information to us requesting consideration for inclusion in the book. As a result, we are able to maintain a constantly evolving list of colleges to consider adding to the book. Any college we add to the guide, however, must agree to support our efforts to survey its students via our anonymous student survey. (Sometimes a college's administrative protocols will not allow it to participate in our student survey; this has caused some academically outstanding schools to be absent from the guide.) Finally, we work to ensure that our roster of colleges in the book presents a wide representation of institutions by region, character, and type. Here you'll find profiles of public and private schools, Historically Black Colleges and Universities, men's and women's colleges, science- and technology-focused institutions, nontraditional colleges, highly selective schools, and some with virtually open-door admissions policies.

For this year's edition, we added four schools to this guide: Iona University, Rowan University, Trinity College (CT), and University of Portland.

> "We worked to create a guide that would help people who couldn't always get to the campus nonetheless get in-depth campus feedback to find the schools best for them."

The narratives in this edition are based on our surveys of 165,000 students attending the 389 colleges in the book. We surveyed about 424 students per campus on average, though that number varies depending on the size of the student population. We've surveyed in schools like Deep Springs College (almost 100% of the 26-student campus) as well as those like Clemson University, University of Virginia, and United States Naval Academy (more than 1,000 collegians from each).

All of the institutions in this guide are academically terrific in our opinion. The 389 schools featured—our picks of the cream of the crop colleges and universities—comprise only the top 13 percent of the approximately 3,000 four-year colleges in the nation. These are all very different schools with many different and wonderful things to offer. We hope you will use this book as a starting point (it will certainly give you a snapshot of what life is like at these schools), but not as the final word on any one school. Check out other resources. Visit as many colleges as you can. Talk to students at those colleges—ask what they love and what bothers them most about their schools. Finally, form your own opinions about the colleges you are considering. At the end of the day, it's what YOU think about the schools that matters most, and that will enable you to answer that all-important question: "Which college is best for me?"

About Our Student Survey for Our *Best Colleges* Books

Surveying tens of thousands of students on hundreds of campuses is a large undertaking. In 1992, when we published the first edition of this book, we had surveyed an average of 120 students on each of the 250 campuses we profiled. We conducted that survey in person on the college campuses, setting up tables in central locations at which students filled out the surveys. Sometimes in order for us to collect surveys from a wide range of students, first years to seniors, this process took place over several days and at a variety of campus locations.

As you might imagine, today all of our surveys are completed online. The process is more efficient, secure, and representative, and we are able to gather opinions from far more students per college than we had reached previously. The average number of student surveys (per college) upon which our ranking lists are annually tallied is now 424 students per campus (and at some schools we hear from more than 5,000 students).

Our student survey is also now a continuous process. Students submit surveys online from all schools in the book and they can submit their surveys at any time during the academic year at http://survey.review.com. (Our site will accept only one survey from a student per academic year per school.) We also officially conduct surveys of students at each school in the book once every three years, on average, working with administrators to reach out to their students. We conduct these "official" surveys more often than once every three years if the colleges request that we do so (and we can accommodate their request) or if we deem it necessary to capture dramatic changes on a campus. And of course, surveys we receive from students outside of their schools' normal survey cycles are always factored into the subsequent year's ranking calculations, so our pool of student survey data is continuously refreshed.

The survey has more than 80 questions in four main sections: "About Yourself," "Your School's Academics/Administration," "Students," and "Life at Your School." We ask about all sorts of things, from "How many out-of-class hours do you spend studying each day?" to "How do you rate your campus food?" Most questions offer an answer choice on a five-point scale: students fill in one of five boxes on a grid with headers varying by topic (e.g., a range from "Excellent" to "Awful"). Once the surveys have been completed and responses stored in our database, every college is given a score (similar to a GPA) for its students' answers to each question. This score enables us to compare student opinions from college to college and to tally the ranking lists. Most of the lists are based on students' answers to one survey question; some lists are based on answers to several survey questions. But all of our 50 ranking lists are based entirely on our student survey results.

Once we have the student survey information in hand, we write the college profiles. Student quotations in each profile come from our surveys (eight survey questions invite the students to tell us in their own words what they think about various aspects of their student body and campus experiences). We chose quotations that represent sentiments expressed by the majority of survey respondents from the college, or that illustrate one side or another of a mixed bag of student opinion, in which case there will also appear a counterpoint within the text. We send draft profiles to administrative contacts at each school for comments and corrections. We take careful measures to review the school's suggestions against the student survey data we collected and make appropriate changes when warranted.

How This Book Is Organized

Each of the colleges and universities in this book has its own two-page profile. To make it easier to find and compare information about the schools, we've used the same profile format for every school. Look at the sample pages below: each profile has nine major components. First, at the very top of the profile, you will see the school's address, telephone and fax numbers for the admissions office, the telephone number for the financial aid office, and the school's website and/or email address. Second, there are two sidebars (the narrow columns on the outside of each page, which consist mainly of statistics) divided into the categories of Campus Life, Academics, Selectivity, and Financial Facts. Third, there are four sections in the narrative text: Students Say, Admissions, Financial Aid, and From the Admissions Office. Here's what you'll find in each part:

The Sidebars

The sidebars contain various statistics culled from our surveys of students attending the school and from questionnaires that school administrators complete at our request in the fall of each year. Keep

in mind that not every category will appear for every school—in some cases the information is not reported or not applicable. We compile the eight ratings—Quality of Life, Fire Safety, Green Rating, Academic, Profs Interesting, Profs Accessible, Admissions Selectivity, and Financial Aid—listed in the sidebars based on the results from our student surveys and/or institutional data we collect from school administrators.

These ratings are on a scale of 60–99. If a 60* (60 with an asterisk) appears as any rating for any school, it means that the school reported so few of the rating's underlying data points by our deadline that we were unable to calculate an accurate rating for it. (These measures are outlined in the ratings explanation below.) Be advised that because the Admissions Selectivity Rating is a factor in the computation that produces the Academic Rating, a school that has 60* (60 with an asterisk) as its Admissions Selectivity Rating will have an Academic Rating that is lower than it should be. Also bear in mind that each rating places each college on a continuum for purposes of comparing colleges within this edition only. Since our ratings computations may change from year to year, it is invalid to compare the ratings in this edition to those that appear in any prior or future edition.

These ratings are numerical measures that show how a school "sizes up," if you will, on a fixed scale. Here is what each heading in the sidebar tells you, in order of its appearance:

Quality of Life Rating

On a scale of 60–99, this rating is a measure of how happy students are with their campus experiences outside the classroom. To compile this rating, we weighed several factors, all based on students' answers to questions on our survey. They included the students' assessments of their overall happiness; the beauty, safety, and location of the campus; comfort of dorms; quality of food; ease of getting around campus and dealing with administrators; friendliness of fellow students; and the interaction of different student types on campus and within the greater community.

Fire Safety Rating

On a scale of 60–99, this rating measures how well prepared a school is to prevent or respond to campus fires, specifically in residence halls. We asked schools several questions about their efforts to ensure fire safety for campus residents. We developed the questions in consultation with the Center for Campus Fire Safety (https://www.myccfs.org). Each school's responses to seven questions were considered when calculating its Fire Safety Rating. They cover:

1. The percentage of student housing sleeping rooms protected by an automatic fire sprinkler system with a fire sprinkler head located in the individual sleeping rooms

2. The percentage of student housing sleeping rooms equipped with a smoke detector connected to a supervised fire alarm system

3. The number of malicious fire alarms that occur in student housing per year

4. The number of unwanted fire alarms that occur in student housing per year

5. The banning of certain hazardous items and activities in residence halls, like candles, smoking, halogen lamps, etc.

6. The percentage of student housing fire alarm systems that, if activated, result in a signal being transmitted to a monitored location, where security investigates before notifying the fire department

7. The percentage of student housing fire alarm systems that, if activated, result in a signal being transmitted immediately to a continuously monitored location

Schools that did not report answers to a sufficient number of questions receive a Fire Safety Rating of 60* (60 with an asterisk). On page 47 of this book, you'll find a list of the schools with 99 (the highest score) Fire Safety Ratings.

Green Rating

We asked all the schools we collect data from annually to answer a number of questions that evaluate the comprehensive measure of their performance as an environmentally aware and responsible institution. The questions cover 1) whether students have a campus quality of life that is both healthy and sustainable; 2) how well a school is preparing students not only for employment in the clean energy economy of the 21st century, but also for citizenship in a world now defined by environmental challenges; and 3) how environmentally responsible a school's policies are.

Additionally, The Princeton Review and the Association for the Advancement of Sustainability in Higher Education (AASHE) have collaborated on an effort to streamline the reporting process for institutions that choose to participate in various higher education sustainability assessments. The intent of this initiative is to reduce and streamline the amount of time campus staff spend tracking sustainability data and completing related surveys.

Please find more information here:

https://www.princetonreview.com/college-rankings/green-guide/data-partnership

School responses to the following questions were considered when calculating The Princeton Review's Green Rating:

1. What is the percentage of food expenditures that goes toward local, organic or otherwise environmentally preferable food?

2. Does the school offer programs including mass transit programs, bike sharing, facilities for bicyclists, bicycle and pedestrian plans, car sharing, a carpool discount, carpool/van-pool matching, cash-out of parking, prohibiting idling, local housing, telecommuting, and a condensed work week?

3. Does the school have a formal committee with participation from students that is devoted to advancing sustainability on campus?

4. Are school buildings that were constructed or underwent major renovations in the past three years LEED (Leadership in Energy and Environmental Design) certified?

5. What is the school's overall waste-diversion rate?

6. Does the school have an environmental studies major, minor, or concentration?

7. Do the school's students graduate from programs that include sustainability as a required learning outcome or include multiple sustainability learning outcomes?

8. Does the school have a formal plan to mitigate its greenhouse gas emissions?

9. What percentage of the school's energy consumption is derived from renewable resources?

10. Does the school employ a dedicated full-time (or full-time equivalent) sustainability officer?

Colleges that did not supply answers to a sufficient number of the green campus questions for us to fairly compare them to other colleges receive a Green Rating of 60*. On page 47 of this book and on our website at https://www.princetonreview.com/college-rankings/green-guide/green-honor-roll, you'll find a list of the schools with 99 (the highest score) Green Ratings.

> Check out our free resource, The Princeton Review's Guide to Green Colleges at www.princetonreview.com/green-guide.

Type of school
Whether the school is public or private.

Affiliation
Any religious order with which the school is affiliated.

Environment
The type of school environment, based on population and setting.

- Rural (In or near a rural community, pop. under 5,000)
- Village (In a small town, pop. 5,000–24,999, or near a small town)
- Town (In a large town, pop. 25,000–74,999, or near a large town)
- City (In a small/medium city, pop. 75,000–299,999, or within its metropolitan area)
- Metropolis (In a major city, pop. 300,000 or more, or within its metropolitan area)

Total undergrad enrollment
The total number of degree-seeking undergraduates who attend the school.

"% male/female/another gender" through "# countries represented"

Demographic information about the degree-seeking undergraduate student body, including ethnicity and the number of countries represented by the student body. While we have made our male-to-female ratio inclusive of male/female/another gender, because some schools do not track or report this data, the term NR (not reported) may appear in some cases. Also included are the percentages of the student body who are from out of state, attended a public high school, first-year students living on campus, and belong to Greek organizations. Please note that while the data reported in this book tends to be an accurate projection for the coming years, as we went to print, the Supreme Court was in the process of ruling on a case on affirmative action, the results of which may impact future demographics at schools in the 41 states that currently follow this policy.

Survey Says . . .

A snapshot of key results of our student survey. This list names survey topics about which the body of students we surveyed at the school—as a group—showed a statistically higher consensus of opinion in their answers to our questions on those topics (as compared with their answers to questions on other topics). See the end of this section for a detailed explanation of items on the list.

Academic Rating

On a scale of 60–99, this rating is a measure of how hard students work at the school and how much they get back for their efforts. The rating is based on results from our surveys of students and data we collect from administrators. Factors weighed include the number of hours students reported that they study each day outside of class, students' assessments of their professors' teaching abilities and of their accessibility outside the classroom, and the quality of students the school attracts as measured by admissions statistics.

% of students returning for sophomore year

The percentage of degree-seeking first-year students returning for sophomore year.

% of students graduating within 4 years

The percentage of degree-seeking undergraduate students graduating in four years or less.

% of students graduating within 6 years

The percentage of degree-seeking undergraduate students graduating within six years.

Calendar

The school's schedule of academic terms. A "semester" schedule has two long terms, usually starting in September and January. A "trimester" schedule has three terms, one usually beginning before Christmas and two after. A "quarterly" schedule has four terms, which go by very quickly: the entire term, including exams, usually lasts only nine or ten weeks. A "4-1-4" schedule is like a semester schedule, but with a month-long term in between the fall and spring semesters. (Similarly, a "4-4-1" has a short term following two longer semesters.) It is always best to call the admissions office for details.

Student/faculty ratio

The ratio of full-time undergraduate instructional faculty members to all undergraduates.

Profs interesting rating

On a scale of 60–99, this rating is based on levels of surveyed students' agreement or disagreement with this statement: "Your instructors are good teachers."

Profs accessible rating

On a scale of 60–99, this rating is based on levels of surveyed students' agreement or disagreement with this statement: "Your instructors are accessible outside the classroom."

Most common regular class size; Most common lab size

The most commonly occurring class size for regular courses and for labs/discussion sections.

Most popular majors

The majors with the highest enrollments at the school.

Admissions Selectivity Rating

On a scale of 60–99, this rating is a measure of how competitive admission is at the school. This rating is determined by several factors, including the high school class rank of entering first-year students, test scores, and percentage of applicants accepted.

of applicants

The total number of students to apply.

% of applicants accepted

The percentage of applicants to whom the school offered admission.

% of acceptees attending

The percentage of accepted students who eventually enrolled at the school.

applicants offered a place on the wait list

Number of qualified applicants offered a place on waiting list.

% accepting a place on wait list

The percentage of students who decided to take a place on the wait list when offered this option.

% admitted from wait list

The percentage of applicants who opted to take a place on the wait list and were subsequently offered admission. These figures will vary tremendously from college to college, and should be a consideration when deciding whether to accept a place on a college's wait list.

of early decision applicants

The number of students who applied under the college's early decision or early action plan.

% accepted early decision

The percentage of early decision or early action applicants who were admitted under this plan. By the nature of these plans, the vast majority who are admitted ultimately enroll.

Testing policy

Test Flexible allows students to choose which type of test(s) to submit, and you should check with those schools on a case-by-case basis.

Test Free, sometimes referred to as Test Blind, means that the school will not look at or consider your scores in any capacity.

Test Optional means that schools will consider your scores, if you submit them, and we recommend that students do so, as this can sometimes be key in discussions of merit aid.

Test Required means that one of the tests listed is required for your application.

Range SAT EBRW, Range SAT Math, Range ACT Composite

The middle 50 percent range of test scores for entering first-year students.

We made the above information available to contacts at each school for review and approval. You may also cross-reference our print profiles with our online school profiles at PrincetonReview.com, which list the most up-to date data as reported by schools.

Don't be discouraged from applying to the school of your choice even if your combined test scores are below the average, because you may still have a chance of getting in. Remember that many schools value other aspects of your application (e.g., your grades, how good a match you make with the school) more heavily than test scores.

Average HS GPA

The average grade point average of entering first-year students. The majority of schools report this on an unweighted scale of 1.0–4.0, but some have started to report using a weighted scale of 1.0–5.0, so please keep that in mind. (A few schools report averages on a 100 scale, in which case we report those figures.) This is one of the key factors in college admissions.

% graduated top 10%, top 25%, top 50% of class

Of those students for whom class rank was reported, the percentage of entering first-year students who ranked in the top tenth, quarter, and half of their high school classes.

Early decision, early action, priority, and regular admission deadlines

The dates by which all materials must be postmarked (we suggest "received in the office") in order to be considered for admission under each particular admissions option/cycle for matriculation in the fall term. This section also includes, where given, the expected dates for notifications about a decision on your application.

Nonfall registration

Some schools will allow incoming students to register and begin attending classes at times other than the fall term, which is the traditional beginning of the academic calendar year. Other schools will allow you to register for classes only if you can begin in the fall term. A simple "yes" or "no" in this category indicates the school's policy on nonfall registration.

Applicants also look at

These lists are based on information we receive directly from the colleges. Admissions officers are annually given the opportunity to review and suggest alterations to these lists for their schools, as most schools track as closely as they can other schools to which applicants they accepted applied, and whether the applicants chose their school over the other schools, or vice versa.

Financial Aid Rating

On a scale of 60–99, this rating is a measure of the financial aid the school awards and how satisfied students are with the aid they receive. It is based on school-reported data on financial aid and students' responses to the survey question, "If you receive financial aid, how satisfied are you with your financial aid package?" On page 47 of this book you'll find a list of the schools with 99 (the highest score) Financial Aid Ratings.

Annual tuition

The tuition at the school. For public colleges, the cost of tuition is provided for both residents of that school's state and for nonresidents. In-state tuition is typically much lower than out-of-state tuition.

Room and board

Estimated annual room and board costs.

Required fees

Any additional costs students must pay beyond tuition in order to attend the school. These often include fitness center fees and the like. A few state schools may not officially charge in-state students tuition, but those students are still responsible for hefty fees. In a few rare cases, this field may combine tuition and fees, or list a single comprehensive fee that accounts for the total cost of tuition, room and board, and fees. To see how these figures break down, we recommend contacting the school.

Books and supplies

Estimated annual cost of necessary textbooks and/or supplies.

Average frosh/undergraduate need-based scholarship

The average need-based scholarship and grant aid awarded to students with need.

% needy frosh receiving need-based scholarship or grant aid

The percentage of all degree-seeking first-year students who were determined to have need and received any need-based scholarship or grant.

% needy UG receiving need-based scholarship or grant aid

The percentage of all degree-seeking undergraduates who were determined to have need and received any need-based scholarship or grant.

% needy frosh receiving non-need-based scholarship or grant aid

The percentage of all degree-seeking first-year students, determined to have need, receiving any non-need based scholarship or grant aid.

% needy ugrads receiving non-need-based scholarship or grant aid

The percentage of all degree-seeking undergraduates, determined to have need, receiving any non-need based scholarship or grant aid.

% needy frosh receiving need-based self-help aid

The percentage of all degree-seeking first-year students, determined to have need, who received any need-based self-help aid.

% needy ugrads receiving need-based self-help aid

The percentage of all degree-seeking undergraduates, determined to have need, who received any need-based self-help aid.

% frosh receiving any financial aid

The percentage of all degree-seeking first-year students receiving any financial aid (need-based, merit-based, gift aid).

% UG receiving any financial aid

The percentage of all degree-seeking undergraduates receiving any financial aid (need-based, merit-based, gift aid).

% UG borrow to pay for school

The percentage who borrowed at any time through any loan programs (institutional, state, Federal Perkins, Federal Subsidized and Unsubsidized, private loans that were certified by your institution, etc., excluding parent loans). Includes both Federal Direct Student Loans and Federal Family Education Loans.

Average indebtedness

The average per-undergraduate borrower cumulative principal borrowed of those who borrowed at any time through any loan programs (Federal Perkins, Federal Subsidized and Unsubsidized, institutional, state, private loans that institution is aware of, etc.) Includes both Federal Direct Student Loans and Federal Family Education Loans.

Nota Bene: The statistical data reported in this book, unless otherwise noted, was collected from the profiled colleges from the fall of 2022 through the spring of 2023. In some cases, we were unable to publish the most recent data because schools did not report the necessary statistics to us in time, despite our repeated outreach efforts. Because the enrollment and financial statistics, as well as application and financial aid deadlines, fluctuate from one year to another, we recommend that you check with the schools to make sure you have the most current information before applying.

% frosh and ugrad need fully met

The percentage of needy degree-seeking students whose needs were fully met (excludes PLUS loans, unsubsidized loans, and private alternative loans).

Average % of frosh and ugrad need met

On average, the percentage of need that was met of students who were awarded any need-based aid. Excludes any aid that was awarded in excess of need as well as any resources that were awarded to replace EFC (PLUS loans, unsubsidized loans, and private alternative loans).

Students Say

This section shares the straight-from-the-campus feedback we get from the school's most important customers: the students attending them. It summarizes the opinions of first-year students through seniors we've surveyed, and it includes direct quotes from scores of them. When appropriate, it also incorporates statistics provided by the schools. The Students Say section is divided into three subsections: Academics, Life, and Student Body. The Academics section describes how hard students work and how satisfied they are with the education they are getting. It also often tells you which programs or academic departments students rated most favorably and how professors interact with students. Student opinion regarding administrative departments also works its way into this section. The Life section describes life outside the classroom and addresses questions ranging from "How comfortable are the dorms?" to "How popular are fraternities and sororities?" In this section, students describe what they do for entertainment both on-campus and off, providing a clear picture of the social environment at their particular school. The Student Body section will give you the lowdown on the types of students the school attracts and how the students view the level of interaction among various groups, including those of different ethnic, socioeconomic, and religious backgrounds.

All quotations in these sections are from students' responses to open-ended questions on our survey. We select quotations based on the accuracy with which they reflect overall student opinion about the school as conveyed in the survey results.

Admissions

This section lets you know which aspects of your application are most important to the admissions officers at the school. It also lists the high school curricular prerequisites for applicants, which standardized tests (if any) are required, and special information about the school's admissions process (e.g., do minority students and legacies, for example, receive special consideration?). Be aware that as we went to print, the Supreme Court was in the process of ruling on a case on affirmative action, the results of which may impact what schools in the 41 states that currently follow this policy can consider for admission.

Financial Aid

Here you'll find out what you need to know about the financial aid process at the school, namely what forms you need and what types of merit-based aid and loans are available. Information about need-based aid is contained in the financial aid sidebar. This section includes specific deadline dates for submission of materials as reported by the colleges. We strongly encourage students seeking financial aid to file all forms—federal, state, and institutional—carefully, fully, and on time.

The Inside Word

This section gives you the inside scoop on what it takes to gain admission to the school. It reflects our own insights about each school's admissions process and acceptance trends. (We visit scores of colleges each year and talk with hundreds of admissions officers in order to glean this info.) It also incorporates information from institutional data we collect and our surveys over the years of students at the school.

From the Admissions Office

This section presents the key things the school's admissions office would like you to know about the institution as a whole. (This may include information beyond the undergraduate data that is reported in the sidebars.)

Survey Says . . .

Our Survey Says list, located in the Campus Life sidebar on each school's two-page spread, is based entirely on the results of our student survey. In other words, the items on this list are based on the opinions of the students we surveyed at those schools (not on any quantitative analysis of library size, endowment, etc.). These items reveal popular or unpopular trends on campus for the purpose of providing a snapshot of life on that campus only. The appearance of a Survey Says item in the sidebar does not reflect the popularity of that item relative to its popularity among the student bodies at other schools. Some of the terms that appear on the Survey Says list are not entirely self-explanatory. These terms are defined as follows:

Diverse types of students interact: We asked students whether students from different class and ethnic backgrounds interacted frequently and easily. When students' collective response is "yes," the heading "Diverse types of students interact" appears on the list. Note: This topic is not based on demographic data about the student body.

No one cheats: We asked students how prevalent cheating is at their school. If students reported cheating to be rare, the phrase "No one cheats" shows up on the list.

Students are happy: This category reflects student responses to the question "Overall, how happy are you?"

Students are very religious or Students aren't religious: We asked students how religious students are at their school. Their responses are reflected in this category.

Students get along with local community: This category reflects student responses to a question concerning how well the student body gets along with residents of the college town or community.

Career services are great: This category reflects student opinion on the quality of career/job placement services on campus.

About Our College Ranking Lists

Finding a college with terrific academics is easy. Out of the thousands of schools you might attend, there are hundreds that offer high-level courses across the board. Hundreds more have specialized programs that are among the best in their field. Finding those schools is sometimes just a matter of searching out professors that you want to learn from or research with, majors that fascinate you, or unique learning opportunities—such as experiential curricula or studying abroad. Our 389 school profiles in this book note such opportunities—and more. Where those schools differ, however, is in their campus cultures, student bodies, and non-academic offerings. To that end, we feature in this book dozens of unique categories of ranking lists. They reveal distinctions about the colleges in matters that may be vitally important to you.

> Our 50 ranking lists are entirely based on our surveys of 165,000 students at the colleges in our book.

Though some members of the media, the public, and school administrators attribute these rankings to us at The Princeton Review (indeed, we are the company that tallies and reports them), these lists do not reflect our opinion of the schools. It's the way in which students communicate to us what they think of their experiences at their schools that determine on which lists schools appear. Our lists are not based on *our* estimate of how interesting a school's professors are or how generous the school is with financial aid or how good the campus food is.

Our 50 ranking lists are entirely based on our *surveys of the 165,000 students at the colleges* in our book. We ask them 80+ questions about everything from how they rate their campus experiences to their POV about their school's campus culture and student body. (You'll find detailed information about our student survey and the methodology for our ranking lists on our website at https://www.princetonreview.com/college-rankings/ranking-methodology.)

> It is *what their students tell us* about their experiences at these schools that determines on which lists the schools appear.

Note: our *choice* of the 389 schools in this book *is* largely based on our opinion of the schools' academics. Only about 15 percent of the nation's four-year colleges are in the book. *In our view,* every one offers an outstanding undergraduate education. We consider these schools the "best" in the nation—academically (hence the word "Best" in our book's title). It is *what their students tell us* about their experiences at these schools that determines on which lists the schools appear.

The way in which we report our ranking lists has also evolved over time. Based on over 14,000 responses from our annual College Hopes & Worries Surveys, we focused on the 10 campus topics that mattered most to those searching for a best-fit college. The areas they indicated were of highest importance to them were academics, financial aid, amenities and facilities, campus services (including career, health, and wellness), and insights about the campus culture and student body. From that feedback, we have developed two new lists. In 2022, to address the 77% of students who indicated that information about a college's commitment to the environment would affect their decision to attend, we added "Green Matters: Everyone Cares About Conservation," based on student answers to questions about support for conservation and sustainability awareness. This year, we've added "Friendliest Students."

We have also made two significant changes in our remaining ranking lists. First, we trimmed the number of them from 62 to 50 (and renamed some for clarity). Then, for the remaining lists, we increased the number of schools on each from 20 to 25. Because this allowed us to name more schools per category, we were able to better shine a light on some Best schools that hadn't made our previous lists. (More than two-thirds of the 389 schools in this book appear on one of our "top 25" lists in this edition.)

These decisions are compatible with our long-standing commitment to *not* rank the colleges in this book hierarchically on academics or on any other topic (in the case of this edition from 1 to 389). Our fifty categories of lists of top 25 ranking colleges in this book are presented as an alternative to mega-list one-topic-fits-all rankings. As Rob Franek, our editor-in-chief and lead author of this book, has said for many years, hundreds of times in interviews as well as in talks he gives to college applicants and their parents, "It's not, 'Which college is best?' but 'Which college is best for YOU' that matters."

This book exists to give applicants and parents information that goes beyond academics and that provides more focused information about a college's offerings and character to help an applicant decide—on a very personal level—whether it's the right (or wrong!) school for them.

We close with a grateful note to the college officials, counselors, advisors, students, and parents who have made this annual guide possible for thirty-plus years. Our ranking lists, rating scores, and profiles have factored in data from more than 2 million students and tens of thousands of administrators. To all who have completed our past surveys and all who will complete them this year: thanks. Your input is essential to our book. We have heard from many students who told us that without our book, they might never have considered the schools that were their "best fit" colleges, schools which they have since become outstanding applicants to and alumni of!

We wish you all the best *on your* college journey.

> This book exists to give applicants and parents information that goes beyond academics and that provides more focused information about a college's offerings and character to help an applicant decide—on a very personal level—whether it's the right (or wrong!) school for them.

WE WANT TO HEAR FROM YOU

To all of our readers, we welcome your feedback on how we can continue to improve this guide. We hope you will share with us your comments, questions, and suggestions. Please contact us at editorialsupport@review.com. We welcome it.

To college applicants, we wish you all the best in your college search. And when you get to your campuses and settle in to your college life, come back to us online; participate in our survey for this book at https://www.princetonreview.com/college-rankings/student-survey. Let your honest comments about your schools guide prospective students who want your help answering the $64,000 question (goodness knows, the sticker price at some schools may be that high or even higher!): "Which is the best college for me?"

PART 2

School Rankings and Lists

We present our 50 "Top 25" ranking lists in seven categories.

Under each list heading, we tell you the survey question or assessment that we used to tabulate the list. We tally student responses to several questions on our survey for our lists "Best Classroom Experience," "Best Quality of Life," and "Green Matters: Everyone Cares About Conservation." Be aware that these 50 ranking lists are based entirely on student surveys. They do not reflect our opinions of the schools. They are entirely the result of what students attending these schools tell us about them: It's how students rate their own schools and what they report to us about their campus experiences at them that make our ranking lists so unusual. After all, what better way is there to judge a school than by what its customers—its students—say about it?

ACADEMICS/ADMINISTRATION

Best Classroom Experience

Based on student ratings of their professors, lab facilities, the percent of classes they attend, and the amount of in-class discussion.

1. Reed College
2. Franklin W. Olin College of Engineering
3. University of Richmond
4. Wellesley College
5. St. Olaf College
6. Dickinson College
7. Earlham College
8. Emory University
9. Bennington College
10. Grinnell College
11. Thomas Aquinas College (CA)
12. United States Military Academy
13. St. John's College (MD)
14. Wabash College
15. Gettysburg College
16. Denison University
17. Claremont McKenna College
18. Sarah Lawrence College
19. College of Wooster
20. Bucknell University
21. Mount Holyoke College
22. College of the Atlantic
23. Rollins College
24. Hamilton College
25. Bowdoin College

11. Princeton University
12. Wellesley College
13. Carnegie Mellon University
14. Williams College
15. Bowdoin College
16. St. John's College (NM)
17. Bucknell University
18. Amherst College
19. University of Richmond
20. Colby College
21. Washington University in St. Louis
22. Webb Institute
23. Rhodes College
24. St. John's College (MD)
25. Gonzaga University

Students Study the Most

We rank the most studious colleges based on student ratings of how many hours they spend studying outside of class each day.

1. Franklin W. Olin College of Engineering
2. California Institute of Technology
3. Lehigh University
4. College of the Atlantic
5. Massachusetts Institute of Technology
6. Rose-Hulman Institute of Technology
7. Gettysburg College
8. Centre College
9. Grinnell College
10. Reed College

Professors Get High Marks

The students at these schools give their professors high marks.

1. Sarah Lawrence College
2. Wabash College
3. Reed College
4. Franklin W. Olin College of Engineering
5. St. John's College (MD)
6. Mount Holyoke College
7. St. John's College (NM)
8. University of Dallas
9. Washington College
10. Hillsdale College
11. Claremont McKenna College
12. Wellesley College
13. Centre College
14. College of the Atlantic
15. University of Richmond
16. Florida Southern College
17. Dickinson College
18. Thomas Aquinas College (CA)
19. Williams College
20. United States Military Academy
21. Emory University
22. Wheaton College (IL)
23. Scripps College
24. Hobart and William Smith Colleges
25. Bennington College

Professors Get Low Marks

Based on student ratings of their professors' ability to bring their material to life.

1. Kettering University
2. Louisiana State University—Baton Rouge
3. State University of New York at Geneseo
4. Pace University
5. East Carolina University
6. University of Louisville
7. Illinois Institute of Technology
8. University of Delaware
9. State University of New York— Stony Brook University
10. Elmira College
11. University of Hawaii at Manoa
12. University of Central Florida
13. University of Kentucky
14. University of Connecticut
15. University of Cincinnati
16. St. John's University
17. George Mason University
18. University of Pittsburgh—Pittsburgh Campus
19. Florida International University
20. University of Maine
21. University of Rhode Island
22. Michigan State University
23. Xavier University of Louisiana
24. Queens College of the City University of New York
25. University of California—Santa Cruz

Most Accessible Professors

Based on student ratings of how accessible their professors are outside of the classroom.

1. Wabash College
2. College of Wooster
3. Bowdoin College
4. St. Lawrence University
5. University of Richmond
6. Juniata College
7. Coe College
8. Williams College
9. United States Military Academy
10. St. John's College (NM)
11. Webb Institute
12. Whitman College
13. Lake Forest College
14. Franklin W. Olin College of Engineering
15. Reed College
16. Claremont McKenna College
17. Wheaton College (IL)
18. Dickinson College
19. St. John's College (MD)
20. Rose-Hulman Institute of Technology
21. Union College (NY)
22. Furman University
23. Randolph College
24. Centre College
25. Bard College

Best Science Lab Facilities

Based on student ratings of their school's science lab facilities.

1. Union College (NY)
2. Lake Forest College
3. Emory University
4. St. Olaf College
5. Chapman University
6. St. Lawrence University
7. University of Richmond
8. College of Wooster
9. Lehigh University
10. California Institute of Technology
11. Denison University
12. United States Military Academy
13. Carnegie Mellon University
14. Rose-Hulman Institute of Technology
15. Randolph-Macon College
16. William & Mary
17. Washington University in St. Louis
18. University of Scranton
19. Rice University
20. Eckerd College
21. Santa Clara University
22. Wheaton College (MA)
23. Loyola Marymount University
24. United States Naval Academy
25. Vanderbilt University

Best Health Services

Based on student ratings of the health services on campus.

1. University of Virginia
2. Lake Forest College
3. University of Utah
4. Florida International University
5. The University of North Carolina at Asheville
6. Kansas State University
7. Washington State University
8. Bowdoin College
9. United States Air Force Academy
10. United States Military Academy
11. Texas Christian University
12. University of Arizona
13. Wabash College
14. Florida State University
15. Auburn University
16. Angelo State University
17. Emory University
18. University of Wisconsin-Madison
19. The University of Texas at Austin
20. University of Miami
21. University of Denver
22. Randolph College
23. University of San Diego
24. High Point University
25. Rollins College

Best Student Support and Counseling Services
Based on students' assessments of counseling services available on campus.

1. United States Naval Academy
2. Vanderbilt University
3. Lake Forest College
4. Hillsdale College
5. Kansas State University
6. Franklin W. Olin College of Engineering
7. Emory University
8. Virginia Tech
9. United States Military Academy
10. United States Air Force Academy
11. Rose-Hulman Institute of Technology
12. Calvin College
13. Florida State University
14. Angelo State University
15. Agnes Scott College
16. University of Richmond
17. Thomas Aquinas College (CA)
18. Grove City College
19. High Point University
20. Lynchburg College
21. Washington State University
22. Wabash College
23. Texas Christian University
24. University of Denver
25. Rollins College

Best Career Services
Based on student ratings of their school's career and job placement services.

1. Bentley University
2. Wabash College
3. Denison University
4. Claremont McKenna College
5. Southwestern University
6. Franklin W. Olin College of Engineering
7. Clemson University
8. Coe College
9. Kansas State University
10. Rose-Hulman Institute of Technology
11. University of Richmond
12. Hampden-Sydney College
13. High Point University
14. Northeastern University
15. Elon University
16. Hillsdale College
17. Randolph-Macon College
18. Florida Southern College
19. Lake Forest College
20. Texas Christian University
21. St. Olaf College
22. Washington State University
23. University of Denver
24. Hobart and William Smith Colleges
25. St. John's College (NM)

Best College Library
Based on student ratings of their library facilities.

1. Brigham Young University (UT)
2. Hampden-Sydney College
3. University of Denver
4. Mount Holyoke College
5. Columbia University
6. William & Mary
7. University of Utah
8. United States Military Academy
9. Williams College
10. Salisbury University
11. Emory University
12. Reed College
13. Franklin W. Olin College of Engineering
14. University of Richmond
15. Lehigh University
16. Florida State University
17. Loyola Marymount University
18. Ohio State University—Columbus
19. University of Virginia
20. Texas Christian University
21. Washington University in St. Louis
22. Wesleyan University
23. Hollins University
24. Bryant University
25. College of Wooster

Great Financial Aid
Based on real student ratings of overall satisfaction with their financial aid packages.

1. Washington University in St. Louis
2. Thomas Aquinas College (CA)
3. Skidmore College
4. College of the Atlantic
5. Wabash College
6. Emory University
7. St. Olaf College
8. Reed College
9. Williams College
10. Gettysburg College
11. California Institute of Technology
12. University of North Carolina at Chapel Hill
13. Franklin W. Olin College of Engineering
14. Dickinson College
15. Princeton University
16. Union College (NY)
17. Trinity College (CT)
18. Amherst College
19. Vanderbilt University
20. Wellesley College
21. Grinnell College
22. Bowdoin College
23. Rice University
24. Columbia University
25. Juniata College

Financial Aid Not So Great

Based on real student ratings of overall satisfaction with their financial aid packages.

1. Emerson College
2. American University
3. New York University
4. State University of New York—Stony Brook University
5. Spelman College
6. Eugene Lang College of Liberal Arts at The New School
7. University of California—Santa Cruz
8. The College of New Jersey
9. University of Pittsburgh—Pittsburgh Campus
10. University of Massachusetts-Amherst
11. James Madison University
12. East Carolina University
13. Santa Clara University
14. State University of New York—Purchase College
15. State University of New York at Geneseo
16. University of New England
17. Appalachian State University
18. Florida International University
19. George Mason University
20. University of Tennessee—Knoxville
21. University of Delaware
22. Oregon State University
23. University of Cincinnati
24. Elon University
25. University of Maryland, Baltimore County

Best-Run Colleges

Based on student ratings of how smoothly their colleges are run.

1. University of Dayton
2. Rice University
3. University of Richmond
4. Texas Christian University
5. University of Wisconsin-Madison
6. Washington University in St. Louis
7. Brigham Young University (UT)
8. Elon University
9. Angelo State University
10. University of San Diego
11. High Point University
12. Washington State University
13. Claremont McKenna College
14. Emory University
15. Wabash College
16. St. Lawrence University
17. University of St. Thomas (MN)
18. Baylor University
19. Ohio State University—Columbus
20. Bowdoin College
21. Denison University
22. Lake Forest College
23. Vanderbilt University
24. Tulane University
25. The University of Texas at Austin

Green Matters: Everyone Cares About Conservation

Based on students' answers to survey questions, including how they rate administration and student support for environmental awareness and conservation efforts.

1. College of the Atlantic
2. State University of New York—College of Environmental Science and Forestry
3. Pitzer College
4. Dickinson College
5. University of Vermont
6. The University of North Carolina at Asheville
7. Skidmore College
8. Emory University
9. University of San Diego
10. Colby College
11. American University
12. St. Mary's College of Maryland
13. Bennington College
14. University of St. Thomas (MN)
15. University of Denver
16. Washington University in St. Louis
17. Salve Regina University
18. Wesleyan University
19. Bowdoin College
20. Macalester College
21. Ithaca College
22. Hobart and William Smith Colleges
23. Rochester Institute of Technology
24. University of California—Merced
25. Agnes Scott College

Their Students Love These Colleges

Based on student ratings of their overall satisfaction with their schools.

1. Lehigh University
2. Emory University
3. Franklin W. Olin College of Engineering
4. Auburn University
5. Hillsdale College
6. Kansas State University
7. Washington State University
8. Florida State University
9. Vanderbilt University
10. Angelo State University
11. Carnegie Mellon University
12. Washington University in St. Louis
13. University of Denver
14. Hampden-Sydney College
15. University of Wisconsin-Madison
16. College of the Atlantic
17. Claremont McKenna College
18. The University of North Carolina at Chapel Hill
19. William & Mary
20. Tulane University
21. Elon University
22. Rice University
23. Bowdoin College
24. University of Richmond
25. Marist College

QUALITY OF LIFE

Happiest Students
Overall, how happy are you?

1. Texas Christian University
2. Kansas State University
3. Thomas Aquinas College (CA)
4. Washington State University
5. Emory University
6. Auburn University
7. Angelo State University
8. Wheaton College (IL)
9. University of Dallas
10. University of Richmond
11. Skidmore College
12. Hampden-Sydney College
13. Hillsdale College
14. University of San Diego
15. Brown University
16. Rice University
17. University of Denver
18. University of Utah
19. Denison University
20. Williams College
21. Tulane University
22. Vanderbilt University
23. University of Dayton
24. Bowdoin College
25. Marist College

Most Beautiful Campus
Based on real student ratings of the beauty of their campuses.

1. University of Richmond
2. University of San Diego
3. Bryn Mawr College
4. Lewis & Clark College
5. The University of the South
6. Florida Southern College
7. Mount Holyoke College
8. Salve Regina University
9. Thomas Aquinas College (CA)
10. Washington University in St. Louis
11. Rice University
12. Loyola Marymount University
13. Vanderbilt University
14. Reed College
15. Bennington College
16. Texas Christian University
17. Rhodes College
18. Rollins College
19. High Point University
20. University of Puget Sound
21. University of California—Santa Cruz
22. Pepperdine University
23. Berry College
24. Lehigh University
25. St. Olaf College

Best Campus Food
Our best campus food ranking list is based on student ratings of the food at their colleges.

1. University of Massachusetts-Amherst
2. Cornell University
3. Bowdoin College
4. Pitzer College
5. Washington University in St. Louis
6. Vanderbilt University
7. University of Dayton
8. Virginia Tech
9. Kansas State University
10. St. Olaf College
11. University of Richmond
12. Gettysburg College
13. High Point University
14. Wheaton College (IL)
15. James Madison University
16. Scripps College
17. Wesleyan University
18. Rollins College
19. Muhlenberg College
20. Washington State University
21. Mount Holyoke College
22. Elon University
23. Rice University
24. Columbia University
25. Reed College

Campus Food Not So Tasty
Based on student ratings of the food on their campuses.

1. Ohio Wesleyan University
2. Kettering University
3. Lawrence Technological University
4. Hampden-Sydney College
5. Spelman College
6. Sarah Lawrence College
7. William & Mary
8. Providence College
9. University of California—Merced
10. Lycoming College
11. Saint Joseph's University (PA)
12. Florida Southern College
13. Xavier University of Louisiana
14. Salve Regina University
15. Washington & Jefferson College
16. Fordham University
17. Randolph-Macon College
18. Simmons University
19. McDaniel College
20. Siena College
21. John Carroll University
22. Creighton University
23. Transylvania University
24. Clarkson University
25. Warren Wilson College

Best College Dorms

Based on student ratings of their dorms and residence halls.

1. Washington University in St. Louis
2. Franklin W. Olin College of Engineering
3. Emory University
4. High Point University
5. Scripps College
6. Bowdoin College
7. Pitzer College
8. Kansas State University
9. Texas Christian University
10. Reed College
11. University of Kentucky
12. Bryn Mawr College
13. Skidmore College
14. Mount Holyoke College
15. University of Richmond
16. Washington State University
17. Rice University
18. Claremont McKenna College
19. Brigham Young University (UT)
20. Amherst College
21. Marist College
22. Elon University
23. Butler University
24. Bennington College
25. University of Dayton

College Dorms Not So Fancy

Based on student ratings of their dorms and residence halls.

1. Xavier University of Louisiana
2. Simmons University
3. Washington & Jefferson College
4. Siena College
5. Rider University
6. St. John's College (MD)
7. Berry College
8. Mercer University
9. Washington College
10. Ohio Wesleyan University
11. Sarah Lawrence College
12. Lycoming College
13. United States Military Academy
14. Kettering University
15. University of Dallas
16. The University of the South
17. Wagner College
18. City University of New York—Brooklyn College
19. Stevens Institute of Technology
20. Southwestern University
21. State University of New York—Purchase College
22. College of the Ozarks
23. United States Naval Academy
24. Manhattan College
25. Oregon State University

Best Quality of Life

Based on student ratings of the beauty, safety, and friendliness on campus, among other ratings.

1. Vanderbilt University
2. Emory University
3. University of San Diego
4. Kansas State University
5. Wheaton College (IL)
6. Washington State University
7. Texas Christian University
8. Auburn University
9. University of Richmond
10. Washington University in St. Louis
11. Thomas Aquinas College (CA)
12. Rice University
13. Bowdoin College
14. Skidmore College
15. Claremont McKenna College
16. Franklin W. Olin College of Engineering
17. Angelo State University
18. Pitzer College
19. Stonehill College
20. Tulane University
21. Loyola University New Orleans
22. College of the Atlantic
23. Reed College
24. Lake Forest College
25. Colorado State University

Friendliest Students

Based on how strongly students agree that their fellow students are extremely friendly.

1. Kansas State University
2. Hillsdale College
3. Franklin W. Olin College of Engineering
4. Claremont McKenna College
5. Wheaton College (IL)
6. Hampden-Sydney College
7. Auburn University
8. Thomas Aquinas College (CA)
9. Emory University
10. Washington State University
11. Pitzer College
12. Clemson University
13. Washington University in St. Louis
14. College of the Atlantic
15. Carleton College
16. Gordon College
17. Loyola University New Orleans
18. St. Olaf College
19. Creighton University
20. Colby College
21. Randolph-Macon College
22. Lehigh University
23. University of Denver
24. St. Lawrence University
25. University of Vermont

POLITICS

Most Conservative Students

Based on students' assessments of their personal political views.

1. Thomas Aquinas College (CA)
2. College of the Ozarks
3. Hillsdale College
4. Grove City College
5. University of Dallas
6. Hampden-Sydney College
7. United States Air Force Academy
8. University of Utah
9. United States Military Academy
10. Wheaton College (IL)
11. United States Naval Academy
12. Clemson University
13. High Point University
14. Montana Tech of the University of Montana
15. Baylor University
16. Wabash College
17. Auburn University
18. Bentley University
19. Assumption College
20. University of South Carolina—Columbia
21. Gordon College
22. University of North Dakota
23. University of Wyoming
24. Texas Christian University
25. Wofford College

Most Liberal Students

Based on students' assessments of their personal political views.

1. Sarah Lawrence College
2. Reed College
3. Bennington College
4. Lewis & Clark College
5. Mount Holyoke College
6. Eugene Lang College of Liberal Arts at The New School
7. College of the Atlantic
8. Scripps College
9. Grinnell College
10. Warren Wilson College
11. Pitzer College
12. Macalester College
13. Wellesley College
14. Wesleyan University
15. Hollins University
16. Bryn Mawr College
17. Goucher College
18. College of Wooster
19. Seattle University
20. Bowdoin College
21. Princeton University
22. University of California—Santa Cruz
23. Clark University
24. Ithaca College
25. New York University

Most Politically Active Students

Based on student ratings of their own levels of political awareness.

1. Claremont McKenna College
2. Mount Holyoke College
3. Hampden-Sydney College
4. Pitzer College
5. Bennington College
6. The University of North Carolina at Asheville
7. Grinnell College
8. George Washington University
9. Columbia University
10. Sarah Lawrence College
11. Wesleyan University
12. Lewis & Clark College
13. Hillsdale College
14. Eugene Lang College of Liberal Arts at The New School
15. Williams College
16. American University
17. Wellesley College
18. Fordham University
19. William & Mary
20. Brown University
21. Tulane University
22. Warren Wilson College
23. Gonzaga University
24. Reed College
25. Hollins University

Least Politically Active Students

Based on student ratings of their own levels of political awareness.

1. State University of New York at Geneseo
2. University of Denver
3. Stonehill College
4. University of Utah
5. Carnegie Mellon University
6. Iona University
7. City University of New York—Brooklyn College
8. University of California—Merced
9. University of California—Irvine
10. University of Massachusetts-Amherst
11. Rider University
12. Rowan University
13. University of New England
14. Elmira College
15. Sacred Heart University
16. Salisbury University
17. Worcester Polytechnic Institute
18. Juniata College
19. Saint Joseph's University (PA)
20. University of Scranton
21. Moravian University
22. New Jersey Institute of Technology
23. Illinois Institute of Technology
24. Manhattan College
25. City University of New York—Hunter College

CAMPUS LIFE

Lots of Race/Class Interaction
Do different types of students interact frequently and easily?

1. Rice University
2. St. John's College (NM)
3. Lehigh University
4. United States Naval Academy
5. Drury University
6. Emory University
7. Loyola University New Orleans
8. Angelo State University
9. Claremont McKenna College
10. Thomas Aquinas College (CA)
11. United States Military Academy
12. William & Mary
13. Agnes Scott College
14. Reed College
15. St. Bonaventure University
16. University of Houston
17. College of Wooster
18. United States Air Force Academy
19. Hampden-Sydney College
20. Washington State University
21. Wabash College
22. Grinnell College
23. Washington University in St. Louis
24. Drew University
25. Vanderbilt University

Little Race/Class Interaction
Based on how strongly students agree that different types of students interact frequently and easily at their schools.

1. Quinnipiac University
2. Providence College
3. Washington & Jefferson College
4. Fairfield University
5. Bentley University
6. Trinity College (CT)
7. Santa Clara University
8. The Catholic University of America
9. Sarah Lawrence College
10. Simmons University
11. Warren Wilson College
12. University of Notre Dame
13. University of Richmond
14. Manhattan College
15. Bucknell University
16. Connecticut College
17. Moravian University
18. Bowdoin College
19. University of New Hampshire
20. Brigham Young University (UT)
21. Gettysburg College
22. University of Mary Washington
23. George Washington University
24. University of Tennessee—Knoxville
25. University of California—Irvine

LGBTQ-Friendly
Based on how strongly students agree that their fellow students treat all persons equally, regardless of their sexual orientation and gender identity/expression.

1. Reed College
2. Franklin W. Olin College of Engineering
3. College of the Atlantic
4. Pitzer College
5. Wellesley College
6. Bennington College
7. Claremont McKenna College
8. Emerson College
9. Earlham College
10. Emory University
11. Scripps College
12. Wesleyan University
13. Washington University in St. Louis
14. Eugene Lang College of Liberal Arts at The New School
15. Grinnell College
16. Clark University
17. University of California—Merced
18. Simmons University
19. The University of North Carolina at Asheville
20. Columbia University
21. William & Mary
22. Mount Holyoke College
23. Macalester College
24. Sarah Lawrence College
25. Rice University

LGBTQ-Unfriendly
Based on how strongly students disagree that their fellow students treat all persons equally, regardless of their sexual orientation and gender identity/expression.

1. College of the Ozarks
2. Brigham Young University (UT)
3. The Catholic University of America
4. University of Tennessee—Knoxville
5. Indiana University of Pennsylvania
6. University of Dallas
7. Auburn University
8. Baylor University
9. Berry College
10. The University of Alabama—Tuscaloosa
11. Wheaton College (IL)
12. East Carolina University
13. Moravian University
14. Fairfield University
15. Gordon College
16. Providence College
17. Duquesne University
18. Calvin College
19. Bentley University
20. Rowan University
21. Louisiana State University—Baton Rouge
22. Salisbury University
23. Santa Clara University
24. Southwestern University
25. Bucknell University

Most Religious Students

Based on how strongly students agree that their fellow students are very religious.

1. Brigham Young University (UT)
2. Hillsdale College
3. Wheaton College (IL)
4. Thomas Aquinas College (CA)
5. Auburn University
6. Gordon College
7. University of Dallas
8. College of the Ozarks
9. Pepperdine University
10. The Catholic University of America
11. University of Utah
12. Baylor University
13. Saint Anselm College
14. Berry College
15. Kansas State University
16. Creighton University
17. Angelo State University
18. The University of Alabama—Tuscaloosa
19. John Carroll University
20. Saint Louis University
21. Christopher Newport University
22. University of Scranton
23. Sacred Heart University
24. Clemson University
25. Grove City College

Least Religious Students

Based on how strongly students disagree that their fellow students are very religious.

1. Grinnell College
2. Reed College
3. Lewis & Clark College
4. Emerson College
5. Bennington College
6. Sarah Lawrence College
7. Eugene Lang College of Liberal Arts at The New School
8. Wheaton College (MA)
9. Mount Holyoke College
10. Pitzer College
11. Warren Wilson College
12. Wesleyan University
13. Macalester College
14. Brown University
15. University of California—Santa Cruz
16. Claremont McKenna College
17. Clark University
18. Scripps College
19. Connecticut College
20. University of Puget Sound
21. Oregon State University
22. Northeastern University
23. University of New Hampshire
24. Hamilton College
25. Bowdoin College

TOWN LIFE

College City Gets High Marks

Based on student ratings of the towns and cities where their schools are located.

1. Tulane University
2. Columbia University
3. American University
4. Bernard Baruch College of the City University of New York
5. Northeastern University
6. Simmons University
7. University of Denver
8. Vanderbilt University
9. Kansas State University
10. Suffolk University
11. Salve Regina University
12. Emory University
13. Rollins College
14. The Cooper Union for the Advancement of Science and Art
15. College of Charleston
16. University of Vermont
17. Stevens Institute of Technology
18. University of San Diego
19. Loyola University New Orleans
20. Emerson College
21. Eugene Lang College of Liberal Arts at The New School
22. New York University
23. University of Wisconsin-Madison
24. United States Naval Academy
25. George Washington University

Town-Gown Relations Are Great

Based on student ratings of how well they get along with the local community.

1. Kansas State University
2. Auburn University
3. Wheaton College (IL)
4. United States Naval Academy
5. Clemson University
6. Brigham Young University (UT)
7. Vanderbilt University
8. Agnes Scott College
9. Texas Christian University
10. Washington State University
11. Assumption College
12. United States Military Academy
13. Loyola University New Orleans
14. Emory University
15. Suffolk University
16. College of the Atlantic
17. United States Air Force Academy
18. Franklin W. Olin College of Engineering
19. Gordon College
20. St. Olaf College

21. University of Denver
22. Salve Regina University
23. Randolph-Macon College
24. College of the Ozarks
25. Nazareth College

EXTRACURRICULARS

Best Athletic Facilities
Based on student ratings of the recreational and athletic facilities at their schools.

1. Auburn University
2. University of Utah
3. The University of Alabama—Tuscaloosa
4. Claremont McKenna College
5. Kansas State University
6. Washington State University
7. University of Richmond
8. Ohio State University—Columbus
9. Georgia Institute of Technology
10. Gettysburg College
11. Louisiana State University—Baton Rouge
12. James Madison University
13. Texas Christian University
14. Denison University
15. Florida State University
16. Providence College
17. University of Denver
18. Washington University in St. Louis
19. Roanoke College
20. Vanderbilt University
21. University of Puget Sound
22. Butler University
23. Stonehill College
24. Wabash College
25. University of North Dakota

Students Love Their School Teams
Based on student assessments of the popularity of intercollegiate sports at their schools.

1. Gonzaga University
2. Arizona State University at the Tempe campus
3. Auburn University
4. Brigham Young University (UT)
5. Creighton University
6. Xavier University (OH)
7. Wabash College
8. Butler University
9. Hampden-Sydney College
10. University of Wisconsin-Madison
11. Clemson University
12. Syracuse University
13. University of Dayton
14. Florida State University
15. Ohio State University—Columbus
16. University of Tennessee—Knoxville
17. United States Naval Academy
18. Michigan State University

19. University of Nebraska—Lincoln
20. University of Georgia
21. University of Central Florida
22. Bowdoin College
23. University of Notre Dame
24. Bryant University
25. The University of Texas at Austin

Everyone Plays Intramural Sports
Based on student ratings of the popularity of intramural sports at their schools.

1. Gettysburg College
2. Fordham University
3. Texas Christian University
4. The University of Alabama—Tuscaloosa
5. University of Arizona
6. The University of the South
7. Providence College
8. St. John's College (MD)
9. Elon University
10. University of Richmond
11. Washington University in St. Louis
12. Albion College
13. Wabash College
14. Iowa State University
15. Clemson University
16. James Madison University
17. Gonzaga University
18. University of Virginia
19. Brigham Young University (UT)
20. Washington State University
21. Auburn University
22. United States Naval Academy
23. Clarkson University
24. Florida State University
25. Michigan State University

Best College Radio Station
Based on student ratings of their campus radio stations.

1. University of South Florida
2. Emerson College
3. Reed College
4. Arizona State University at the Tempe campus
5. University of Puget Sound
6. Skidmore College
7. Rider University
8. Wellesley College
9. Bowdoin College
10. Hofstra University
11. Denison University
12. Hillsdale College
13. Mount Holyoke College
14. Bennington College
15. Princeton University
16. Ithaca College
17. Washington State University
18. Dickinson College
19. Seton Hall University
20. Hamilton College

21. Macalester College
22. Sarah Lawrence College
23. Fordham University
24. Roanoke College
25. Providence College

Best College Newspaper
Based on student ratings of their campus newspaper.

1. Columbia University
2. Hillsdale College
3. Wabash College
4. Bowdoin College
5. William & Mary
6. Rice University
7. Lehigh University
8. Ithaca College
9. Loyola University New Orleans
10. Mount Holyoke College
11. Wofford College
12. The University of North Carolina at Chapel Hill
13. Hampden-Sydney College
14. Fordham University
15. Vanderbilt University
16. Wellesley College
17. American University
18. Emory University
19. Hamilton College
20. Wesleyan University
21. Lewis & Clark College
22. Gonzaga University
23. Connecticut College
24. Dickinson College
25. University of Virginia

Best College Theater
Based on student ratings of their campus theater productions.

1. Carnegie Mellon University
2. Muhlenberg College
3. Bennington College
4. Emerson College
5. Sarah Lawrence College
6. Skidmore College
7. Wagner College
8. Elon University
9. Wesleyan University
10. Brigham Young University (UT)
11. Denison University
12. Wabash College
13. Columbia University
14. State University of New York—Purchase College
15. Florida Southern College
16. Grinnell College
17. Ithaca College
18. Drew University
19. University of Mary Washington
20. New York University
21. Sacred Heart University
22. Furman University
23. Butler University
24. Loyola Marymount University
25. Pepperdine University

Students Most Engaged in Community Service
Based on how strongly students agree that the students at their schools are committed to community service.

1. Brandeis University
2. Hillsdale College
3. United States Military Academy
4. Brigham Young University (UT)
5. Creighton University
6. Mercer University
7. Pitzer College
8. Wheaton College (IL)
9. Salve Regina University
10. Emory University
11. Xavier University of Louisiana
12. John Carroll University
13. College of the Atlantic
14. The University of North Carolina at Asheville
15. Virginia Tech
16. Marquette University
17. Gonzaga University
18. Hampden-Sydney College
19. Washington State University
20. Clark University
21. Sacred Heart University
22. The Catholic University of America
23. Tulane University
24. United States Naval Academy
25. Saint Louis University

Most Active Student Government
Based on how strongly students agree that their student governments have an active presence and a tremendous impact on campus.

1. Hampden-Sydney College
2. College of the Atlantic
3. Wabash College
4. Claremont McKenna College
5. High Point University
6. Washington State University
7. St. Lawrence University
8. Hollins University
9. Mount Holyoke College
10. Texas Christian University
11. Reed College
12. Bryant University
13. Angelo State University
14. American University
15. Kansas State University
16. Colby College
17. University of Houston
18. William & Mary
19. Pitzer College
20. Franklin W. Olin College of Engineering
21. Wellesley College
22. Middle Tennessee State University
23. Loyola University New Orleans
24. Bernard Baruch College of the City University of New York
25. University of Arizona

SOCIAL SCENE

Lots of Greek Life

Based on student ratings of the popularity of fraternities and sororities at their schools.

1. Wofford College
2. Bucknell University
3. DePauw University
4. Gettysburg College
5. Auburn University
6. Transylvania University
7. The University of Alabama—Tuscaloosa
8. Wabash College
9. University of Tennessee—Knoxville
10. Texas Christian University
11. Creighton University
12. Hampden-Sydney College
13. Kettering University
14. Sacred Heart University
15. Washington State University
16. Baylor University
17. The University of the South
18. Elon University
19. Ripon College
20. Rhodes College
21. Centre College
22. University of Mississippi
23. Florida State University
24. Rose-Hulman Institute of Technology
25. University of Oklahoma

Lots of Beer

Based on student ratings of how widely beer is used at their schools.

1. West Virginia University
2. Colgate University
3. Bucknell University
4. University of Wisconsin-Madison
5. The University of Alabama—Tuscaloosa
6. University of Richmond
7. Providence College
8. Gettysburg College
9. Colby College
10. Eckerd College
11. Syracuse University
12. Claremont McKenna College
13. Ursinus College
14. University of Florida
15. Tulane University
16. The University of the South
17. University of Dayton
18. Hobart and William Smith Colleges
19. Grinnell College
20. University of Oregon
21. Centre College
22. University of Connecticut
23. University of Delaware
24. University of Virginia
25. University of New Hampshire

Cancel the Keg

Based on student ratings of how widely beer is used at their schools.

1. College of the Ozarks
2. City University of New York—Brooklyn College
3. Brigham Young University (UT)
4. Spelman College
5. City University of New York—Hunter College
6. Bernard Baruch College of the City University of New York
7. City University of New York—City College
8. Wheaton College (IL)
9. California State University, Stanislaus
10. Grove City College
11. Calvin College
12. Gordon College
13. Xavier University of Louisiana
14. Thomas Aquinas College (CA)
15. University of California—Merced
16. United States Naval Academy
17. Queens College of the City University of New York
18. Pepperdine University
19. Princeton University
20. Baylor University
21. United States Air Force Academy
22. University of Maryland, Baltimore County
23. Simmons University
24. Iona University
25. University of South Florida

Lots of Hard Liquor

Based on students' answers to the survey question, "How widely is hard liquor used at your school?"

1. Tulane University
2. Colgate University
3. Syracuse University
4. West Virginia University
5. Wake Forest University
6. Grinnell College
7. University of Wisconsin-Madison
8. Providence College
9. Bucknell University
10. Trinity College (CT)
11. University of Mississippi
12. Boston College
13. Penn State University Park
14. Eckerd College
15. Bryant University
16. Gettysburg College
17. Denison University
18. Claremont McKenna College
19. University of Connecticut
20. The University of the South
21. University of Dayton
22. University of Richmond
23. Centre College
24. University of Delaware
25. University of Maine

Scotch and Soda, Hold the Scotch

Based on students' answers to the survey question, "How widely is hard liquor used at your school?"

1. College of the Ozarks
2. City University of New York—Brooklyn College
3. Brigham Young University (UT)
4. Thomas Aquinas College (CA)
5. Bernard Baruch College of the City University of New York
6. City University of New York—Hunter College
7. City University of New York—City College
8. Wheaton College (IL)
9. United States Air Force Academy
10. California State University, Stanislaus
11. Calvin College
12. Grove City College
13. United States Naval Academy
14. Spelman College
15. Gordon College
16. Lawrence Technological University
17. Princeton University
18. Queens College of the City University of New York
19. University of California—Merced
20. Baylor University
21. Pepperdine University
22. Angelo State University
23. University of California--Riverside
24. Illinois Institute of Technology
25. University of Maryland, Baltimore County

Reefer Madness

Based on student ratings concerning the use of marijuana at their schools.

1. Lewis & Clark College
2. Skidmore College
3. Grinnell College
4. Sarah Lawrence College
5. Pitzer College
6. Reed College
7. Warren Wilson College
8. Bennington College
9. Wesleyan University
10. University of Vermont
11. Emerson College
12. State University of New York—Purchase College
13. Denison University
14. Colby College
15. Colorado College
16. University of Rhode Island
17. Clark University
18. University of Colorado Boulder
19. University of Denver
20. University of California—Santa Cruz
21. St. Lawrence University
22. St. John's College (NM)
23. Syracuse University
24. Albion College
25. Pomona College

Pot's Not Hot

Based on student ratings concerning the use of marijuana at their schools.

1. United States Naval Academy
2. Thomas Aquinas College (CA)
3. College of the Ozarks
4. Brigham Young University (UT)
5. United States Air Force Academy
6. Wheaton College (IL)
7. United States Military Academy
8. Princeton University
9. Bernard Baruch College of the City University of New York
10. City University of New York—Brooklyn College
11. Hillsdale College
12. City University of New York—Hunter College
13. City University of New York—City College
14. California State University, Stanislaus
15. Gordon College
16. Calvin College
17. Grove City College
18. Illinois Institute of Technology
19. Spelman College
20. Baylor University
21. Pepperdine University
22. Rose-Hulman Institute of Technology
23. University of Dallas
24. Angelo State University
25. State University of New York—Stony Brook University

THE PRINCETON REVIEW'S HONOR ROLLS

We salute these schools that received a 99 (the highest score) in the tallies for our "Financial Aid," "Fire Safety," and "Green" Ratings—three of eight ratings on some of the school profiles in this book and at PrincetonReview.com. Our school ratings are numerical scores (Note: They are not ranking lists) that show how a school "sizes up" on a fixed scale. They are comparable to grades and based primarily on institutional data we collect directly from the colleges.

Financial Aid Honor Roll
Schools are listed in alphabetical order. See page 26 for information on how our "Financial Aid Rating" is determined.

Bates College
Bowdoin College
Bryn Mawr College
California Institute of Technology
Carleton College
Franklin & Marshall College
Franklin W. Olin College of Engineering
Grinnell College
Haverford College
Kenyon College
Pomona College
Princeton University
Vassar College
Williams College
Yale University

Fire Safety Honor Roll
Schools are listed in alphabetical order. See page 21 for information on how our "Fire Safety Rating" is determined.

Adelphi University*
Bentley University
Brenau University*
Carleton College
Champlain College
The College of New Jersey
Duquesne University
East Carolina University
Emmanuel College*
Fordham University
Georgia College & State University*
Hofstra University
Indiana University South Bend*
Indiana University Southeast*
Johns Hopkins University
Loyola University New Orleans
Manhattanville College
Mount Saint Mary's University*
Mount St. Joseph University*
New Jersey Institute of Technology
New York University
St. John's College (MD)
Stevens Institute of Technology
Suffolk University
Tufts University
United States Air Force Academy
University of Delaware
University of Maine
University of Maryland, Baltimore County
University of North Carolina at Greensboro
University of South Florida
University of St. Francis*
Wagner College
Webb Institute
Wittenberg University
Xavier University of Louisiana

Schools marked with an asterisk do not appear in the *Best 389 Colleges*. You can find those school profiles in our free online listings at https://www.princetonreview.com/college-search.

Green Honor Roll
Schools are listed in alphabetical order. See page 21 for information on how our "Green Rating" is determined.

The American College of Greece*
Arizona State University
Bates College
Bennington College
Bowling Green State University*
Bucknell University
Colby College
Colgate University
College of the Atlantic
Colorado State University
Cornell University
Dickinson College
Emory University
Grand Valley State University*
Lehigh University
Loyola Marymount University
Loyola University Chicago
Middlebury College
New York University
Northeastern University
Northern Arizona University*
Nova Scotia Community College*
Randolph College
Stanford University
State University of New York—University at Buffalo*
Thompson Rivers University*
University of California—Berkeley
University of California—Irvine
University of California—Merced
University of California—Santa Barbara
University of Connecticut
University of Illinois at Urbana-Champaign
University of La Verne*
University of Maryland, College Park
University of Massachusetts-Amherst
University of Miami
University of North Carolina Asheville
University of Victoria*
Vanderbilt University
Williams College

Tuition-Free Schools Honor Roll
The following schools have been excluded from our ranking and ratings dealing with financial aid:

Berea College
College of the Ozarks
Deep Springs College
United States Air Force Academy
United States Coast Guard Academy
United States Merchant Marine Academy
United States Military Academy
United States Naval Academy
Webb Institute

We commend these schools on their ability to do the seemingly impossible: not charge tuition. While some charge students for room and board and other fees, the overall cost of attendance at these schools is very low, and at some schools: free! (Note: We do not include these schools in our ranking lists dealing with financial aid, since they would have an unfair advantage over schools that charge even a moderate tuition.)

THE PRINCETON REVIEW'S 209 BEST VALUE COLLEGES FOR 2023

The Princeton Review released its current list of Best Value Colleges in April 2023. We selected the 209 schools based on 40 weighted data points, including academics, cost, financial aid, and student debt to statistics on graduation rates, alumni salaries, and job satisfaction. Alumni survey information was provided by PayScale.com. For detailed profiles of all these great schools, see www.PrincetonReview.com/best-value-colleges.

Agnes Scott College
Allegheny College
Amherst College
Arizona State University
Babson College
Barnard College
Bates College
Beloit College
Bentley University
Berea College
Bowdoin College
Bradley University
Brandeis University
Brigham Young University (UT)
Brown University
Bryn Mawr College
Bucknell University
California Institute of Technology
California State University, Long Beach
Carleton College
Carnegie Mellon University
Case Western Reserve University
Centre College
Christopher Newport University
City University of New York—Baruch College
City University of New York—Brooklyn College
City University of New York—Hunter College
City University of New York—Queens College
Claremont McKenna College
Clark University
Clarkson University
Clemson University
Coe College
Colby College
Colgate University
The College of New Jersey
College of the Ozarks
College of Wooster
Colorado College
Columbia University
The Cooper Union for the Advancement of
    Science and Art
Cornell University
Creighton University
Dartmouth College
Davidson College
Deep Springs College
Denison University
Dickinson College
Drew University
Duke University
Earlham College

Elon University
Emory University
Fairfield University
Florida State University
Fordham University
Franklin & Marshall College
Franklin W. Olin College of Engineering
Furman University
George Mason University
Georgetown University
Georgia Institute of Technology
Gettysburg College
Gordon College
Grinnell College
Grove City College
Hamilton College
Hampden-Sydney College
Harvard College
Harvey Mudd College
Haverford College
Hobart and William Smith Colleges
Illinois Institute of Technology
Iowa State University
Johns Hopkins University
Kalamazoo College
Kansas State University
Kenyon College
Kettering University
Lafayette College
Lake Forest College
Lawrence University
Lehigh University
Loyola Marymount University
Macalester College
Marquette University
Massachusetts Institute of Technology
McDaniel College
Miami University
Michigan Technological University
Middlebury College
Missouri University of Science and Technology
Montana Technological University
Mount Holyoke College
New College of Florida
New Jersey Institute of Technology
North Carolina State University
Northeastern University
Northwestern University
Occidental College
The Ohio State University—Columbus
Oregon State University
Penn State University Park

Pepperdine University
Pitzer College
Pomona College
Princeton University
Providence College
Purdue University—West Lafayette
Reed College
Rensselaer Polytechnic Institute
Rhodes College
Rice University
Rose-Hulman Institute of Technology
Saint Louis University
San Diego State University
Santa Clara University
Scripps College
Skidmore College
Smith College
Southwestern University
St. John's College (MD)
St. John's College (NM)
St. Lawrence University
St. Mary's College of Maryland
St. Olaf College
Stanford University
State University of New York—Binghamton University
State University of New York—College of Environmental
    Science and Forestry
State University of New York—Geneseo
State University of New York—Stony Brook University
Stevens Institute of Technology
Stonehill College
Swarthmore College
Texas A&M University—College Station
Thomas Aquinas College (CA)
Trinity University
Truman State University
Tufts University
Tulane University
Union College (NY)
United States Air Force Academy
United States Coast Guard Academy
United States Merchant Marine Academy
United States Military Academy
United States Naval Academy
The University of Alabama—Tuscaloosa
University of Arizona
University of California—Berkeley
University of California—Davis
University of California—Irvine
University of California—Los Angeles
University of California—Riverside
University of California—San Diego
University of California—Santa Barbara
University of California—Santa Cruz

University of Central Florida
The University of Chicago
University of Colorado Boulder
University of Connecticut
University of Dallas
University of Dayton
University of Delaware
University of Florida
University of Georgia
University of Houston
University of Idaho
University of Illinois at Urbana-Champaign
University of Massachusetts-Amherst
University of Miami
University of Michigan—Ann Arbor
University of Minnesota—Twin Cities
University of Nebraska—Lincoln
University of North Carolina at Chapel Hill
University of Notre Dame
University of Pennsylvania
University of Pittsburgh—Pittsburgh Campus
University of Puget Sound
University of Richmond
University of Rochester
University of San Diego
University of South Florida
University of Texas at Austin
The University of Texas at Dallas
The University of the South
University of Tulsa
University of Utah
University of Vermont
University of Virginia
University of Washington
University of Wisconsin-Madison
Vanderbilt University
Vassar College
Virginia Tech
Wabash College
Wake Forest University
Washington State University
Washington University in St. Louis
Webb Institute
Wellesley College
Wesleyan University
Wheaton College (IL)
Whitman College
William & Mary
William Jewell College
Williams College
Wofford College
Worcester Polytechnic Institute
Yale University

The Best Value Colleges contains 14 ranking lists, all of which focus on different aspects of financial aid and career preparation. Because this book already contains a Financial Aid Honors Roll, we've included 12 of those lists here.

Top 50 Best Value Colleges (Private Schools)
The fifty private schools that received the highest overall rating used to determine inclusion in *The Best Value Colleges.*

1. Massachusetts Institute of Technology
2. Princeton University
3. California Institute of Technology
4. Stanford University
5. Harvard College
6. Yale University
7. Harvey Mudd College
8. Williams College
9. Dartmouth College
10. Columbia University
11. Claremont McKenna College
12. Rice University
13. Vanderbilt University
14. University of Pennsylvania
15. Pomona College
16. Duke University
17. The University of Chicago
18. Carleton College
19. Bowdoin College
20. Johns Hopkins University
21. Amherst College
22. Brown University
23. The Cooper Union for the Advancement of Science and Art
24. Rose-Hulman Institute of Technology
25. Haverford College
26. Wabash College
27. Cornell University
28. Middlebury College
29. Lehigh University
30. Swarthmore College
31. Carnegie Mellon University
32. University of Notre Dame
33. Emory University
34. Brigham Young University (UT)
35. Grinnell College
36. Wellesley College
37. Washington University in St. Louis
38. Union College (NY)
39. Babson College
40. Case Western Reserve University
41. Northwestern University
42. Colgate University
43. Wesleyan University
44. Hamilton College
45. Worcester Polytechnic Institute
46. St. Olaf College
47. Rhodes College
48. Lawrence University
49. Gettysburg College
50. Bryn Mawr College

Top 50 Best Value Colleges (Public Schools)
The fifty public schools that received the highest overall rating used to determine inclusion in *The Best Value Colleges.*

1. Georgia Institute of Technology
2. University of Virginia
3. University of California—Berkeley
4. City University of New York—Baruch College
5. University of California—Los Angeles
6. University of California—Santa Barbara
7. University of North Carolina at Chapel Hill
8. University of California—San Diego
9. University of California—Irvine
10. University of Michigan—Ann Arbor
11. University of Illinois at Urbana-Champaign
12. University of Florida
13. William & Mary
14. Texas A&M University—College Station
15. University of Texas at Austin
16. North Carolina State University
17. University of California—Davis
18. University of Washington
19. State University of New York—Binghamton University
20. Purdue University—West Lafayette
21. Florida State University
22. Virginia Tech
23. University of California—Riverside
24. Missouri University of Science and Technology
25. State University of New York—Stony Brook University
26. University of Minnesota—Twin Cities
27. New College of Florida
28. Clemson University
29. University of Wisconsin-Madison
30. Truman State University
31. University of California—Santa Cruz
32. Michigan Technological University
33. University of South Florida
34. Miami University
35. New Jersey Institute of Technology
36. University of Utah
37. University of Georgia
38. City University of New York—Hunter College
39. The Ohio State University—Columbus
40. University of Colorado--Boulder
41. San Diego State University
42. City University of New York—Brooklyn College
43. University of Connecticut
44. University of Massachusetts-Amherst
45. University of Houston
46. The College of New Jersey
47. Montana Technological University
48. The University of Texas at Dallas
49. University of Central Florida
50. Washington State University

Top 20 Best Value Colleges for Students With No Demonstrated Need (Private)

To create this list, we used the same methodology for our ROI rating, but removed need-based aid information. If you don't qualify for financial aid, these are your twenty-five best value private schools.

1. Massachusetts Institute of Technology
2. Harvey Mudd College
3. Stanford University
4. California Institute of Technology
5. Brigham Young University (UT)
6. Princeton University
7. Dartmouth College
8. Yale University
9. Claremont McKenna College
10. Williams College
11. Harvard College
12. University of Pennsylvania
13. Duke University
14. Colgate University
15. Rice University
16. Rose-Hulman Institute of Technology
17. Vanderbilt University
18. Columbia University
19. The Cooper Union for the Advancement of Science and Art
20. Johns Hopkins University

Top 20 Best Value Colleges for Students With No Demonstrated Need (Public)

To create this list, we used the same methodology for our ROI rating, but removed need-based aid information. If you don't qualify for financial aid, these are your twenty-five best value public schools.

1. Georgia Institute of Technology
2. University of California—Berkeley
3. University of Virginia
4. City University of New York—Baruch College
5. University of California—Santa Barbara
6. University of California—Los Angeles
7. University of North Carolina at Chapel Hill
8. University of Georgia
9. University of Texas at Austin
10. University of Illinois at Urbana-Champaign
11. University of California—San Diego
12. William & Mary
13. University of Michigan—Ann Arbor
14. University of Florida
15. Texas A&M University—College Station
16. University of California—Irvine
17. Virginia Tech
18. North Carolina State University
19. State University of New York— Binghamton University
20. Purdue University—West Lafayette

Top 20 Best Alumni Network (Private)

These twenty private schools have the strongest and most active alumni networks, based on current students' ratings of alumni activity and visibility on campus.

1. University of Notre Dame
2. Wabash College
3. Hampden-Sydney College
4. St. Lawrence University
5. Massachusetts Institute of Technology
6. Agnes Scott College
7. Wellesley College
8. Stanford University
9. Georgetown University
10. Mount Holyoke College
11. Bryn Mawr College
12. Williams College
13. Wheaton College (IL)
14. Emory University
15. Wofford College
16. The University of the South
17. Cornell University
18. Tulane University
19. Providence College
20. Clarkson University

Top 20 Best Alumni Network (Public)

These twenty public schools have the strongest and most active alumni networks, based on current students' ratings of alumni activity and visibility on campus.

1. Penn State University Park
2. Kansas State University
3. University of Michigan—Ann Arbor
4. University of Virginia
5. Virginia Tech
6. University of Texas at Austin
7. Georgia Institute of Technology
8. New College of Florida
9. University of Florida
10. Clemson University
11. University of Georgia
12. Purdue University—West Lafayette
13. North Carolina State University
14. Washington State University
15. The University of Alabama—Tuscaloosa
16. Florida State University
17. William & Mary
18. University of Wisconsin-Madison
19. University of North Carolina at Chapel Hill
20. City University of New York—Baruch College

Top 20 Best Schools for Internships (Private)

This top twenty private school list is based on students' ratings of accessibility of internships at their school.

1. Rose-Hulman Institute of Technology
2. Franklin W. Olin College of Engineering
3. University of Richmond
4. Wabash College
5. Northeastern University
6. Duke University
7. Harvey Mudd College
8. Hampden-Sydney College
9. Elon University
10. St. Lawrence University
11. Stanford University
12. Coe College
13. The University of the South
14. College of Wooster
15. Wake Forest University
16. Marquette University
17. Vanderbilt University
18. Lake Forest College
19. Bradley University
20. Dartmouth College

Top 20 Best Schools for Internships (Public)

This top twenty public school list is based on students' ratings of accessibility of internships at their school.

1. William & Mary
2. Kansas State University
3. University of Michigan—Ann Arbor
4. Michigan Technological University
5. Penn State University Park
6. Georgia Institute of Technology
7. Christopher Newport University
8. Purdue University—West Lafayette
9. Missouri University of Science and Technology
10. Washington State University
11. University of Washington
12. University of Texas at Austin
13. Miami University
14. Clemson University
15. Florida State University
16. North Carolina State University
17. University of Georgia
18. Virginia Tech
19. The University of Alabama—Tuscaloosa
20. State University of New York—College of Environmental Science and Forestry

Top 20 Best Career Placement (Private)

This top twenty list or private schools is based on students' ratings of career services at their school, and on PayScale.com's median starting and mid-career salary information.

1. Massachusetts Institute of Technology
2. Harvey Mudd College
3. Stanford University
4. Princeton University
5. California Institute of Technology
6. Claremont McKenna College
7. University of Pennsylvania
8. Carnegie Mellon University
9. Rose-Hulman Institute of Technology
10. Harvard College
11. Babson College
12. Dartmouth College
13. Yale University
14. Worcester Polytechnic Institute
15. Colgate University
16. Duke University
17. Stevens Institute of Technology
18. Columbia University
19. Cornell University
20. Rice University

Top 20 Best Career Placement (Public)

This top twenty list or public schools is based on students' ratings of career services at their school, and on PayScale.com's median starting and mid-career salary information.

1. Georgia Institute of Technology
2. University of California—Berkeley
3. Missouri University of Science and Technology
4. University of Virginia
5. University of California—San Diego
6. Michigan Technological University
7. University of Illinois at Urbana-Champaign
8. University of Michigan—Ann Arbor
9. Virginia Tech
10. University of California—Los Angeles
11. New Jersey Institute of Technology
12. Texas A&M University—College Station
13. William & Mary
14. University of California—Santa Barbara
15. University of Washington
16. University of California—Davis
17. University of Texas at Austin
18. Purdue University—West Lafayette
19. State University of New York—Binghamton University
20. University of California—Irvine

Top 20 Best Schools for Making an Impact (Private)

These twenty private schools were selected based on student ratings and responses to our survey questions covering community service opportunities at their school, student government, sustainability efforts, and on-campus student engagement. We also considered PayScale.com's percentage of alumni from each school that reported that they had high job meaning.

1. Pitzer College
2. Agnes Scott College
3. The University of the South
4. Macalester College
5. Clark University
6. Mount Holyoke College
7. Bowdoin College
8. Whitman College
9. Saint Louis University
10. Emory University
11. College of Wooster
12. Furman University
13. Southwestern University
14. Earlham College
15. Brown University
16. Kalamazoo College
17. Swarthmore College
18. Dickinson College
19. St. Lawrence University
20. Wesleyan University

Top 20 Best Schools for Making an Impact (Public)

These twenty public schools were selected based on student ratings and responses to our survey questions covering community service opportunities at their school, student government, sustainability efforts, and on-campus student engagement. We also considered PayScale.com's percentage of alumni from each school that reported that they had high job meaning.

1. State University of New York—College of Environmental Science and Forestry
2. University of California—Santa Cruz
3. University of Vermont
4. New College of Florida
5. William & Mary
6. University of Washington
7. University of Michigan—Ann Arbor
8. University of California—Davis
9. Christopher Newport University
10. Kansas State University
11. St. Mary's College of Maryland
12. University of North Carolina at Chapel Hill
13. San Diego State University
14. Penn State University Park
15. Florida State University
16. University of Idaho
17. Georgia Institute of Technology
18. Virginia Tech
19. University of Texas at Austin
20. University of California—Riverside

Top 50 Undergraduate Colleges for Game Design

We surveyed 150 institutions and ranked the best schools for game design majors in 2023. Below are those Top 50 schools. Please find more information on this project here: www.princetonreview.com/game-design.

1. New York University
2. University of Southern California
3. Rochester Institute of Technology
4. Clark University
5. DigiPen Institute of Technology
6. University of Central Florida
7. University of Utah
8. Vancouver Film School
9. Michigan State University
10. Drexel University
11. Breda University of Applied Sciences
12. Bradley University
13. Champlain College
14. Worcester Polytechnic Institute
15. Shawnee State University
16. Savannah College of Art and Design
17. Full Sail University
18. Quinnipiac University
19. The University of Texas at Dallas
20. University of Silicon Valley
21. La Salle College Vancouver
22. Laguna College of Art + Design
23. Abertay University
24. Falmouth University
25. Rensselaer Polytechnic Institute
26. New England Institute of Technology
27. Miami University
28. Abilene Christian University
29. Howest University of Applied Sciences
30. University of Wisconsin—Stout
31. Oklahoma Christian University
32. Northeastern University
33. DePaul University
34. Marist College
35. Bloomfield College
36. Academy of Art University
37. New York Film Academy
38. University of Michigan-Dearborn
39. ArtCenter College of Design
40. Dakota State University
41. Stetson University
42. Cleveland Institute of Art
43. Ferris State University
44. Kent State University
45. Cornell University
46. University of the Incarnate Word
47. High Point University
48. University of California—Irvine
49. New Jersey Institute of Technology
50. Massachusetts Institute of Technology

Top 50 Undergraduate Colleges for Entrepreneurship

We surveyed nearly 300 schools with entrepreneurship studies so we can tell you which schools have the best opportunities. Below are those Top 50 schools. Please find more information on this project here: www.princetonreview.com/entrepreneur.

1. University of Houston
2. The University of Texas at Austin
3. Babson College
4. Tecnológico de Monterrey
5. The University of Michigan, Ann Arbor
6. Baylor University
7. University of Maryland
8. Washington University in St. Louis
9. Miami University
10. Northeastern University
11. Iowa State University
12. Texas Tech University
13. University of Washington
14. Georgia Institute of Technology
15. Florida Gulf Coast University
16. Drexel University
17. Syracuse University
18. The University of St. Thomas
19. Florida State University
20. NC State University
21. Michigan State University
22. The University of Iowa
23. The Pennsylvania State University
24. University of Utah
25. The University of Texas at Dallas
26. Belmont University
27. Florida Atlantic University
28. Purdue University
29. DePaul University
30. New Jersey Institute of Technology
31. Saint Louis University
32. Florida International University
33. University of Delaware
34. University of Connecticut
35. Loyola Marymount University
36. Texas A&M University—College Station
37. University of Dayton
38. Kettering University
39. The University of Miami
40. East Carolina University
41. Boston University
42. Temple University
43. The University of Oklahoma
44. Rowan University
45. University of Arizona
46. Ball State University
47. Savannah College of Art and Design
48. University at Buffalo
49. Oklahoma State University
50. University of Rochester

PART 3

The Best 389 Colleges

Agnes Scott College

141 E. College Avenue, Decatur, GA 30030-3770 • Admissions: 404-471-6000 • Fax: 404-471-6414

STUDENTS SAY "..."

Academics

Students lucky enough to attend Agnes Scott College, a small liberal arts school within the wide metropolitan Atlanta area, have the opportunity to join a "supportive community of strong women working to create change in the world." Indeed, undergrads here really respect the fact that the college truly "teach[es students] to engage in the social challenges of [their] time." And they love that Agnes Scott provides amazing "network[ing] connections" and "fantastic internship opportunities." What's more, the college is "great about providing financial support, especially to promising students that would not otherwise be able to attend such an institution." Students attend "small classes" which allow them to easily "get to know [their] professors." As one student boasts, "I've had professors write me letters of recommendation, let me know about global programs I'd be good for, and even send me job postings they saw that they know I'd be interested in." Of course, classes are "rigorous" and instructors "expect a lot" from their students. Nevertheless, these dedicated professors make it clear that they "care about you and your success." And more often than not, they are "willing to go that extra mile." As one incredulous student illustrates, "Some of my professors just asked if anyone needed a home to go to for Thanksgiving." All in all, they "want you to be the best you can be." It's really that simple.

Campus Life

At Agnes Scott, academics often take top priority. New students soon discover that the student body is typically "busy with class assignments and reading materials." However, they also carve out time to become "heavily involved with different student organizations." A handful of students can also be found "playing music on the quad," attending "movie showings," or participating in "on-campus activities like trivia and crafts." Of course, the "college itself...invites important speakers—Janet Mock, for example—so we have the opportunity to go to those as well." Some undergrads here do bemoan the fact that the "campus [can be] dead on the weekends." Indeed, lots of students head to other schools like nearby "Georgia Tech...[to have some] fun." And, of course, many individuals love to take advantage of Agnes Scott's fabulous location. "Downtown Decatur...is [only] a quick walk from campus." In addition, Atlanta is quite accessible as well. Agnes Scott "provides a shuttle service" into the city, and is located "very close to a MARTA station," part of metro Atlanta's public transportation system.

Student Body

Students at Agnes Scott speak glowingly of their peers. Indeed, they describe their fellow Scotties as "ambitious" and "well-intentioned" women who hope to "make the world a... better [place]." As such, they are often interested "in a wide variety of social issues and take [any] opportunity...to enact the change they want to see." Undergrads here also proudly report that the student body is "a collection of intelligent and passionate women, trans... and [non-binary] individuals." Moreover, the students here represent "many different nationalities, religions, political opinions, and backgrounds." Students find the environment at Agnes Scott "welcoming" and boast that everyone [has the chance] to flourish in a safe-space feeling environment." As one undergrad further explains, "The uniqueness of this campus is mostly represented in the sense of community and sisterhood we have." Scotties also love that the school maintains a nice combination of "international students, first-generation college students, and a hardy mix of people from all over the United States." We'll give the last word to one Scottie who states, "Many words come to mind when I think about my peers, but the one that best embodies everyone is warmth.... Whenever I need help, my peers are continuously there for me, to answer questions and support the decisions I make. I never feel alone."

AGNES SCOTT COLLEGE

Financial Aid: 404-471-6395 • E-Mail: admission@agnesscott.edu • Website: www.agnesscott.edu

THE PRINCETON REVIEW SAYS

Admissions

The school reports that its standardized testing policy for use in admission for Fall 2024 is Test Optional. The 2024 testing policy will be permanent. The Princeton Review suggests that interested applicants consult with the school for the most up-to-date standardized testing policies. *Very important factors considered include:* rigor of secondary school record, academic GPA. *Important factors considered include:* application essay, recommendation(s), extracurricular activities, talent/ability, volunteer work. *Other factors considered include:* class rank, standardized test scores, interview, character/personal qualities, first generation, alumni/ae relation, geographical residence, state residency, work experience, level of applicant's interest. High school diploma is required and GED is accepted. *Academic units recommended:* 4 English, 4 math, 4 science, 2 science labs, 2 foreign language, 2 social studies.

Financial Aid

Students should submit: FAFSA. Priority filing deadline is 2/15. The Princeton Review suggests that all financial aid forms be submitted as soon as possible (see page 5 for a note on the FAFSA). *Need-based scholarships/grants offered:* College/university scholarship or grant aid from institutional funds; Federal Pell; Private scholarships; SEOG; State scholarships/grants. *Loan aid offered:* Direct PLUS loans; Direct Subsidized Loans; Direct Unsubsidized Loans. Admitted students will be notified of awards on a rolling basis beginning 3/1. Federal Work-Study Program available. Institutional employment available.

The Inside Word

Admissions officers at Agnes Scott College happily take a holistic approach to their process. They seek to create an incoming class that's diverse and reflective of a myriad of interests and ideas. They also realize that potential can be measured in a variety of ways. This college, which has long been Test Optional, allows applicants to submit SAT/ACT scores, a graded writing assignment, or to sit for an evaluative interview with an admissions counselor.

THE SCHOOL SAYS "..."

From the Admissions Office

"This is *your* liberal arts education, reimagined, at Agnes Scott College. During your four years here, you'll grow as a person, a student and a leader. Through SUMMIT, our signature experience for all students, you'll take on a rigorous curriculum focused on leadership, global citizenship and professional success. You will be able to shape your academic experience within your major with experiential opportunities (study abroad, research and internships) to ensure you are learning what you want to learn for your goals.

"Your classrooms will be small but big on community. You will learn from diverse perspectives; there is no racial or ethnic majority on campus. You'll make lifelong friendships in residence halls and while taking part in 60+ clubs and organizations. You will have the chance to explore the Atlanta community, as one of the best southern cities for culture, cuisine and internship opportunities. And you'll explore the world through class experiences and on your own as an informed global citizen.

"Agnes Scott is committed to your success. 100% of our students earn some form of financial aid. 80% of our students choose to complete mentored research or internships during their four years, and 100% work with our Office of Internship & Career Development starting from your first year on campus to prepare you for your future.

"We'd love to meet you and share more. Schedule your visit at agnesscott.edu/visit."

SELECTIVITY

Admissions Rating	88
# of applicants	1,879
% of applicants accepted	67
% of acceptees attending	22
# of early decision applicants	16
% accepted early decision	88

FIRST-YEAR PROFILE

Testing policy	Test Optional
Range SAT composite	1140–1340
Range SAT EBRW	590–700
Range SAT math	540–650
Range ACT composite	24–31
# submitting SAT scores	90
% submitting SAT scores	33
# submitting ACT scores	62
% submitting ACT scores	22
Average HS GPA	3.8
% frosh submitting high school GPA	100
% graduated top 10% of class	29
% graduated top 25% of class	62
% graduated top 50% of class	93

DEADLINES

Early decision	
Deadline	11/1
Notification	12/1
Early action	
Deadline	11/15
Notification	12/15
Regular	
Priority	1/15
Deadline	5/1
Notification	Rolling, 12/15
Nonfall registration?	No

APPLICANTS OFTEN PREFER
Georgia State University; University of Georgia

APPLICANTS SOMETIMES PREFER
Mount Holyoke College

FINANCIAL FACTS

Financial Aid Rating	85
Annual tuition	$47,820
Room and board	$13,375
Required fees	$330
Books and supplies	$1,000
Average frosh need-based scholarship	$34,589
Average UG need-based scholarship	$34,202
% needy frosh rec. need-based scholarship or grant aid	100
% needy UG rec. need-based scholarship or grant aid	100
% needy frosh rec. non-need-based scholarship or grant aid	26
% needy UG rec. non-need-based scholarship or grant aid	24
% needy frosh rec. need-based self-help aid	72
% needy UG rec. need-based self-help aid	75
% frosh rec. any financial aid	100
% UG rec. any financial aid	99
% UG borrow to pay for school	63
Average cumulative indebtedness	$35,702
% frosh need fully met	26
% ugrads need fully met	25
Average % of frosh need met	85
Average % of ugrad need met	85

ALBION COLLEGE

611 East Porter, Albion, MI 49224 • Admissions: 517-629-1000 • Fax: 517-629-0569

CAMPUS LIFE

Quality of Life Rating	**77**
Fire Safety Rating	**87**
Green Rating	**85**
Type of school	Private
Affiliation	No Affiliation
Environment	Village

STUDENTS

Total undergrad enrollment	1,443
% male/female/another gender	48/52/0
% from out of state	24
% frosh live on campus	97
% ugrads live on campus	94
# of fraternities	6
# of sororities	7
% African American	17
% Asian	2
% White	56
% Hispanic	12
% Native American	<1
% Pacific Islander	0
% Two or more races	4
% Race and/or ethnicity unknown	7
% international	3
# of countries represented	20

SURVEY SAYS . . .
Lab facilities are great
Frats and sororities are popular
Students are happy
Intramural sports are popular

ACADEMICS

Academic Rating	**83**
% students returning for sophomore year	73
% students graduating within 4 years	48
% students graduating within 6 years	59
Calendar	Semester
Student/faculty ratio	11:1
Profs interesting rating	92
Profs accessible rating	95

Most classes have 10–19 students.
Most lab/discussion sessions have
10–19 students.

MOST POPULAR MAJORS
Biology/Biological Sciences, General; Exercise
Science and Kinesiology; Research and
Experimental Psychology, Other

STUDENTS SAY " . . . "

Academics

Described as having both a "great reputation" and a "small-town feeling," Albion College provides undergraduates with a "rigorous but rewarding" academic experience replete with "huge opportunities." Students here truly appreciate that Albion works diligently to foster an environment that "encourages questions [and] thinking" all the while aiming to "provide personal attention to each student." While the college certainly offers a "great liberal arts education," undergrads are especially quick to highlight the strong science, premed, and business programs. Indeed, students like to boast that Albion "has a very high rate of students being accepted into medical school." And business majors point to the Gerstacker Institute for Business and Management, which allows students to "gain real-world experience" and even the potential to walk away with "a job offer." Of course, regardless of discipline or department, Albion undergrads are full of praise for their teachers. As one thrilled student eagerly shares, "The professors care about their students' success and are always there to help." Importantly, they are "very knowledgeable in their material and try to make sure you learn as much as possible." Further, they are "easily approachable," "extremely passionate about their work," and always "available for discussions." As one content undergrad sums up, "I would say that the overall experience has been great, and I couldn't be more pleased with my decision to attend Albion College."

Campus Life

While Albion students are often quite "studious" during the week, once the weekend rolls around they certainly know how to get "crazy [and] exciting." Fortunately, there "is almost always something going on on campus." Indeed, the "Union Board plans lots of free activities, concerts, comedians, etc." Moreover, those interested in the party scene will be delighted to discover that fraternities and sororities are very popular at Albion. As one thrilled undergrad notes, "Greek life is fantastic. It really is the cornerstone of our campus. Every weekend there is a party or something going on at the fraternities. Whether you are into drinking or not, the guys there know how to have a good time." While students bemoan the fact that "there's not much to do in the city of Albion," they do take solace in finding other off campus options. As another satisfied student reveals, "Bigger cities like Jackson and Battle Creek are only a 15- or 20-minute drive away, so if you're looking for a day at a mall, that's always an option. Plus, the college sponsors buses and vans to take students to places like Ann Arbor or Lansing. Generally you can find something to do."

Student Body

At first glance, Albion College appears to be "a microcosm of upper-class metro-Detroit and Chicago." Therefore, it's not surprising that a "slightly right-leaning, white, and Greek-loving [student body seems to be] the norm." However, those seeking more diversity should fear not! One student assures us, "I have met anarchists and proud communists. There is a mix, but you have to dig for it." Beyond race and political affiliation, undergrads here find their peers to be "serious about school but also very fun and friendly." Moreover, they are "bright individuals that want to succeed" and certainly people who "value their education." They also seem to have "a million interests," which they vigorously engage through a number of extracurricular activities and programs. As one socially satisfied undergrad sums up, "I think there is a club or niche here where everyone can find a group of people they fit in with. I truthfully would feel comfortable sitting down at a table with any one of my classmates in the cafeteria and having lunch with them."

ALBION COLLEGE

Financial Aid: 517-629-0440 • E-Mail: admission@albion.edu • Website: www.albion.edu

THE PRINCETON REVIEW SAYS

Admissions

The school reports that its standardized testing policy for use in admission for Fall 2024 is Test Optional. It is unknown at this time if the 2024 testing policy will be permanent. The Princeton Review suggests that interested applicants consult with the school for the most up-to-date standardized testing policies. *Important factors considered include:* rigor of secondary school record, class rank, academic GPA. *Other factors considered include:* extracurricular activities, talent/ability, character/personal qualities, first generation, alumni/ae relation, geographical residence, state residency, religious affiliation/commitment, racial/ethnic status, volunteer work, work experience, level of applicant's interest. High school diploma is required and GED is accepted.

Financial Aid

Students should submit: FAFSA. Priority filing deadline is 12/1. The Princeton Review suggests that all financial aid forms be submitted as soon as possible (see page 5 for a note on the FAFSA). *Need-based scholarships/grants offered:* College/university scholarship or grant aid from institutional funds; Federal Pell; Private scholarships; SEOG; State scholarships/grants. *Loan aid offered:* Direct PLUS loans; Direct Subsidized Loans; Direct Unsubsidized Loans. Admitted students will be notified of awards on a rolling basis beginning 12/1. Federal Work-Study Program available. Institutional employment available.

The Inside Word

Albion's growing reputation means that earning a coveted acceptance letter is no easy feat. Academic success takes precedence, and applicants should have taken a challenging high school curriculum including a handful of honors and advanced placement courses. Of course, admissions officers are also concerned about maintaining a vibrant community, so careful attention will also be paid to essays and extracurricular activities.

THE SCHOOL SAYS "..."

From the Admissions Office

"As an Albion student, you'll be equipped to make an impact. You'll be prepared to go on to the nation's top graduate and professional schools and to assume leadership roles in the sciences and medicine, business, law, education, the arts, and social services. To do that, your education will take you beyond the classroom, beyond our campus, and beyond conventional thinking. It will help you discover what you're meant to do with your life. And it will prepare you to live it well.

"You'll identify your goals through a four-year individualized career plan and build a strong foundation in the liberal arts. You'll sharpen your career focus and develop skills through internships and other real-world, hands-on experiences like those in our prestigious institutes in business, public policy and service, sustainability and the environment, education, and pre-medicine and the sciences. Your creativity and curiosity may be satisfied through a multitude of research experiences available as early as your freshman year through our Foundation for Undergraduate Research, Scholarship and Creative Activity and the Prentiss M. Brown Honors Program.

"On our residential campus, you can choose from more than 100 campus organizations catering to a wide range of interests. Our athletic teams regularly head to NCAA Division III postseason play, and our equestrian team members compete regionally and nationally.

"Check us out online at www.albion.edu or visit us to learn if Albion will be right for you."

SELECTIVITY
Admissions Rating	78
# of applicants	6,827
% of applicants accepted	67
% of acceptees attending	9

FIRST-YEAR PROFILE
Testing policy	Test Optional
# submitting SAT scores	52
% submitting SAT scores	12
# submitting ACT scores	5
% submitting ACT scores	1
Average HS GPA	3.5
% frosh submitting high school GPA	93

DEADLINES
Early action	
Deadline	12/1
Nonfall registration?	Yes

APPLICANTS OFTEN PREFER
Hope College; University of Michigan—Ann Arbor

APPLICANTS SOMETIMES PREFER
Alma College; Central Michigan University; Grand Valley State University; Kalamazoo College; Michigan State University

FINANCIAL FACTS
Financial Aid Rating	86
Annual tuition	$54,410
Room and board	$12,470
Required fees	$520
Required fees (first-year)	$705
Books and supplies	$700
Average frosh need-based scholarship	$49,973
Average UG need-based scholarship	$47,289
% needy frosh rec. need-based scholarship or grant aid	100
% needy UG rec. need-based scholarship or grant aid	100
% needy frosh rec. non-need-based scholarship or grant aid	100
% needy UG rec. non-need-based scholarship or grant aid	99
% needy frosh rec. need-based self-help aid	79
% needy UG rec. need-based self-help aid	81
% frosh rec. any financial aid	100
% UG rec. any financial aid	100
% UG borrow to pay for school	74
Average cumulative indebtedness	$36,821
% frosh need fully met	29
% ugrads need fully met	27
Average % of frosh need met	95
Average % of ugrad need met	92

ALFRED UNIVERSITY

One Saxon Drive, Alfred, NY 14802-1205 • Admissions: 607-871-2111 • Fax: 607-871-2198

STUDENTS SAY ". . ."

Academics

Alfred University is a small school with an impressive range of world-class majors. The school is known for its "excellent art program," particularly its ceramics and glass majors, as well as for its engineering and psychology programs. While some students at Alfred focus only on their majors, students happily report that there are a "variety of academic opportunities" and that it's "easy to take subjects outside your major." This is appreciated by many, including one art student who likes that Alfred offers "other majors versus a traditional art [school] setting. If I had decided to change majors, Alfred has almost every opportunity." Alfred's "outstanding, talented, dedicated" faculty is one of its biggest draws. An English writing student gushes that professors "bring a level of vibrancy and academic encouragement through enthusiasm to the classroom." "The professors are always pushing you to reach your full potential" and are "always willing to put time into student independent projects." Students also rave about the small classes sizes. "It is the closest to one-on-one teaching you can get," a clinical and counseling psychology major notes, and "the classroom size is perfect for a more personalized education."

Campus Life

Alfred's "beautiful," "small" campus and its "somewhat rural location" are big draws for students looking for a quieter academic experience with a strong "sense of community." Of course, its location means the weather isn't exactly tropical. One student notes that it can feel like "it's basically winter here for about 80 percent of the school year, and it snows constantly." Luckily, "there is always something to do on weekends and week days," for distraction, such as "student club productions...and fundraisers and an excellent selection of movies shown on campus." On top of that, "there are so many clubs and options that you can find something to do," and "every sports team is supported, and superfans are at every event." "The facilities are amazing," particularly the "great" art buildings and the engineering facilities. Alfred's "strong equestrian program" and barn are also a big draw. Students find some of Alfred's dorms to be "pretty outdated," and there's a bit of grumbling about the "hit-or-miss" and "expensive" dining facilities.

Student Body

Alfred has a "warm" atmosphere, and "You can't go down the street without receiving a smile." Students are "friendly, outgoing, and involved," and many do community service work and are active in one of Alfred's many clubs or organizations. The prominent art school means that there's a large presence of creative types on campus, and the equally prominent engineering school ensures a good mix of personalities. One student notes there is "a pretty significant gap between the prevalent, spunky art students and the more reclusive engineers," but another adds that this means students are "well-acquainted with people from a variety of studies and backgrounds and with a variety of interests." Most people believe that "everyone finds their own little niche," but they appreciate that it "definitely does not mean they stay there—you are allowed to float between everything." In fact, "more often than not, you'll see engineers rubbing elbows with philosophy majors and artists chilling with math and chemistry majors."

ALFRED UNIVERSITY

Financial Aid: 607-871-2159 • E-Mail: admissions@alfred.edu • Website: www.alfred.edu

THE PRINCETON REVIEW SAYS

Admissions

The school reports that its standardized testing policy for use in admission for Fall 2024 is Test Optional. The 2024 testing policy will be temporary. The Princeton Review suggests that interested applicants consult with the school for the most up-to-date standardized testing policies. *Very important factors considered include:* rigor of secondary school record, class rank, academic GPA, extracurricular activities, character/personal qualities. *Important factors considered include:* standardized test scores, application essay, recommendation(s), interview, volunteer work, work experience. *Other factors considered include:* talent/ability, first generation, racial/ethnic status, level of applicant's interest. High school diploma is required and GED is accepted. *Academic units required:* 4 English, 2 math, 2 science, 2 science labs, 2 social studies. *Academic units recommended:* 4 English, 4 math, 3 science, 3 science labs, 1 foreign language, 3 social studies.

Financial Aid

Students should submit: FAFSA; State aid form. Priority filing deadline is 3/15. The Princeton Review suggests that all financial aid forms be submitted as soon as possible (see page 5 for a note on the FAFSA). *Need-based scholarships/grants offered:* College/university scholarship or grant aid from institutional funds; Federal Pell; Private scholarships; SEOG; State scholarships/grants. *Loan aid offered:* Direct PLUS loans; Direct Subsidized Loans; Direct Unsubsidized Loans; College/university loans from institutional funds. Admitted students will be notified of awards on a rolling basis beginning 2/15. Federal Work-Study Program available. Institutional employment available.

The Inside Word

Alfred is a fine university with a solid local reputation. The allure for arts students is obvious—Alfred's programs in the arts are especially well-regarded—and as a result, competition is fiercest among applicants for these programs. A killer portfolio, even more than great grades and standardized test scores, is your most likely ticket in. Competition for the engineering school is also tight. Applicants will need to have thrived in a rigorous high school program.

THE SCHOOL SAYS "..."

From the Admissions Office

"The admissions process at Alfred University is the foundation for the personal attention each student can expect during their time at AU. Each applicant is evaluated individually and receives genuine, individual care and consideration.

"The best way to discover all Alfred University has to offer is to come to campus. We truly have something for everyone with more than forty courses of study, twenty-one NCAA Division III sports and two IHSA sports, and over eighty student-run clubs and organizations. You can tour campus; meet current students, faculty, coaches and staff; attend a class; and eat in our dining hall—experience firsthand what life at AU is like.

"Alfred University is a place where students are free to pursue their interests—all of them—no matter how varied or different. Academics, athletics, co-ops, study abroad, internships, special interests—they're all part of what makes you who you are and who you are going to become."

SELECTIVITY

Admissions Rating	88
# of applicants	7,091
% of applicants accepted	51
% of acceptees attending	10

FIRST-YEAR PROFILE

Testing policy	Test Optional
Range SAT composite	1085–1390
Range SAT EBRW	540–650
Range SAT math	545–640
Range ACT composite	25–30
# submitting SAT scores	108
% submitting SAT scores	29
# submitting ACT scores	11
% submitting ACT scores	3
Average HS GPA	3.4
% frosh submitting high school GPA	12

DEADLINES

Early action	
Deadline	4/15
Regular	
Priority	2/1
Deadline	8/1
Notification	Rolling, 11/15
Nonfall registration?	Yes

APPLICANTS SOMETIMES PREFER
Rochester Institute of Technology; State University of New York—Buffalo State; State University of New York—University at Buffalo; University of Rochester

APPLICANTS RARELY PREFER
St. Ambrose University; St. Lawrence University

FINANCIAL FACTS

Financial Aid Rating	86
Annual tuition	$38,270
Room and board	$13,560
Required fees	$1,260
Books and supplies	$1,300
Average frosh need-based scholarship	$30,951
Average UG need-based scholarship	$28,182
% needy frosh rec. need-based scholarship or grant aid	98
% needy UG rec. need-based scholarship or grant aid	97
% needy frosh rec. non-need-based scholarship or grant aid	92
% needy UG rec. non-need-based scholarship or grant aid	91
% needy frosh rec. need-based self-help aid	81
% needy UG rec. need-based self-help aid	78
% frosh rec. any financial aid	98
% UG rec. any financial aid	98
% UG borrow to pay for school	73
Average cumulative indebtedness	$33,086
% frosh need fully met	48
% ugrads need fully met	35
Average % of frosh need met	93
Average % of ugrad need met	86

ALLEGHENY COLLEGE

520 North Main Street, Meadville, PA 16335 • Admissions: 814-332-3100 • Fax: 814-337-0431

STUDENTS SAY "..."

Academics

Allegheny College, a small liberal arts school located in rural northwest Pennsylvania, has a campus "full of different interests, experiences and talents." Students highlight Allegheny's diversity and stress that they "are engaged in helping our campus community as well as the community of Meadville." In terms of a diverse educational experience, one of the college's draws is students' ability to mix and match majors and minors from different disciplines, leading to Allegheny's motto of "mind over major." This approach "toted by the Allegheny College curriculum board [resounds] not only in the academics but in the people and opportunities that are a part of this unique campus." Professors here are "dedicated to helping [students] succeed and they genuinely want to see [students] do well." With small class sizes and "classes taught by professors," students say the academics are rigorous at Allegheny, but professors "go above and beyond to make themselves available to help them through [difficult times]." The mandatory independent senior research project is "challenging," but it "does a lot to bolster resumes and prep students for graduate schools."

Campus Life

Though some say Allegheny is "the school that studies like an Ivy and parties like a state school," others contend that most students' weeks are full of books and weekends revolve around some sort of on-campus fun. (A few students bristle at Allegheny's four-year residency requirement, but most find ways to stay occupied.) Meadville is a small town but with over 120 school-sponsored clubs and organizations, "everyone can find something [they're] passionate about at Allegheny." Greek life is "an important component of the school, but with only 20 percent of students involved, you'll never feel obligated to participate." The tight-knit school, with roughly 1,600 students, is "small enough that you will see a familiar face wherever you go, without feeling like you know everyone on campus." As one student puts it, Allegheny is "a school with traditions and weirdness," and during a pre-college campus visit it just "felt right." A very liberal campus, students note that while "there is always space for further diversity," the "majority of [the] student body prides itself on social justice and service work."

Student Body

Allegheny has a "very welcoming, judgment-free student body," with students who are "incredibly involved, engaged, and passionate about what they do." While students who hold more conservative viewpoints say that the school's generally liberal stance "may be alienating to conservative students," the majority of Allegheny students seem to applaud the college's emphasis on "welcoming students from different cultures and a general acceptance of varying creeds, sexual orientations, gender identities, and races." On the whole, students describe Allegheny as a "very active campus" and the "vast majority of people are involved with more than one organization on campus and are extremely invested in their studies and the school." Even though some say to "be prepared to have the majority of your life revolve just around what the school provides, which is a lot," adding that "the location is definitely a drawback," others add that students find plenty to do on campus and with off-campus trips to Pittsburgh and Erie, Pennsylvania, when Meadville gets too small.

ALLEGHENY COLLEGE

Financial Aid: 800-835-7780 • E-Mail: admissions@allegheny.edu • Website: https://allegheny.edu

THE PRINCETON REVIEW SAYS

Admissions

The school reports that its standardized testing policy for use in admission for Fall 2024 is Test Optional. The 2024 testing policy will be permanent. The Princeton Review suggests that interested applicants consult with the school for the most up-to-date standardized testing policies. *Very important factors considered include:* rigor of secondary school record, class rank, academic GPA. *Important factors considered include:* recommendation(s), interview, extracurricular activities, character/personal qualities, level of applicant's interest. *Other factors considered include:* standardized test scores, application essay, talent/ability, first generation, alumni/ae relation, geographical residence, racial/ethnic status, volunteer work, work experience. High school diploma is required and GED is accepted. *Academic units required:* 4 English, 3 math, 3 science, 2 foreign language, 3 social studies, 1 academic elective.

Financial Aid

Students should submit: FAFSA. Priority filing deadline is 2/15. The Princeton Review suggests that all financial aid forms be submitted as soon as possible (see page 5 for a note on the FAFSA). *Need-based scholarships/grants offered:* College/university scholarship or grant aid from institutional funds; Federal Pell; Private scholarships; SEOG; State scholarships/grants. *Loan aid offered:* Direct PLUS loans; Direct Subsidized Loans; Direct Unsubsidized Loans; College/university loans from institutional funds. Admitted students will be notified of awards on a rolling basis beginning 11/1. Federal Work-Study Program available. Institutional employment available.

The Inside Word

Over one-third of enrolled Allegheny students have a GPA of 3.75 or higher, with an average GPA of 3.53. In addition to grades, admission officers look hard at recommendation letters, essays, community involvement, and students' other talents that might not show up on a standardized test. The school is Test Optional. The school has two early decision dates, in addition to a regular admissions date.

THE SCHOOL SAYS "..."

From the Admissions Office

"Allegheny College is one of the nation's most prestigious and dynamic institutions of higher education. We believe higher education should aim higher, which is why we're one of the few colleges in the country that asks students to choose both a major and a minor, each in a different academic division. Our major-minor combination and hands-on learning provide students with intellectual and personal growth, helping to cultivate the creative, big-picture thinking most desired by employers and graduate schools. Plus, our undergrads never wait behind graduate students for research positions on faculty-led projects but instead are actively engaged as research collaborators. Allegheny was the first baccalaureate college in the nation to receive the Award for Undergraduate Research Accomplishment from the Council on Undergraduate Research. Our students also connect classroom learning with real-world experience, benefiting from access to career services, pre-professional and graduate advising, internship and service opportunities, research fellowships, and more. At Allegheny, opportunities to pursue one's passions are limited only by the imagination. A diverse campus life, with more than 130 student-led organizations, sets the stage for a vibrant college experience. Our residential campus includes historic architecture interspersed with facilities bristling with the latest communications and research technology. In the classroom, the community, and beyond, Allegheny provides opportunities that can lead students from hard work and dedication to extraordinary outcomes. Allegheny graduates are equipped to meet challenges and solve problems in a rapidly changing world."

SELECTIVITY

Admissions Rating	85
# of applicants	4,667
% of applicants accepted	75
% of acceptees attending	12
# offered a place on the wait list	173
% accepting a place on wait list	20
% admitted from wait list	9
# of early decision applicants	142
% accepted early decision	56

FIRST-YEAR PROFILE

Testing policy	Test Optional
Range SAT composite	1140–1350
Range SAT EBRW	580–680
Range SAT math	560–670
Range ACT composite	23–28
# submitting SAT scores	113
% submitting SAT scores	28
# submitting ACT scores	52
% submitting ACT scores	13
Average HS GPA	3.5
% frosh submitting high school GPA	100
% graduated top 10% of class	30
% graduated top 25% of class	61
% graduated top 50% of class	83

DEADLINES

Early decision	
Deadline	11/15
Notification	11/30
Other ED deadline	2/1
Other ED notification	2/15
Early action	
Deadline	12/1
Notification	1/1
Regular	
Deadline	2/15
Notification	3/15
Nonfall registration?	Yes

APPLICANTS OFTEN PREFER
Kenyon College; Oberlin College

APPLICANTS SOMETIMES PREFER
Dickinson College; Gettysburg College

APPLICANTS RARELY PREFER
Juniata College; Washington & Jefferson College

FINANCIAL FACTS

Financial Aid Rating	87
Annual tuition	$52,950
Room and board	$13,796
Required fees	$660
Books and supplies	$1,000
Average frosh need-based scholarship	$40,288
Average UG need-based scholarship	$39,791
% needy frosh rec. need-based scholarship or grant aid	100
% needy UG rec. need-based scholarship or grant aid	100
% needy frosh rec. non-need-based scholarship or grant aid	26
% needy UG rec. non-need-based scholarship or grant aid	20
% needy frosh rec. need-based self-help aid	70
% needy UG rec. need-based self-help aid	75
% frosh rec. any financial aid	100
% UG rec. any financial aid	99
% frosh need fully met	32
% ugrads need fully met	28
Average % of frosh need met	89
Average % of ugrad need met	88

AMERICAN UNIVERSITY

4400 Massachusetts Ave., NW, Washington, DC 20016-8001 • Admissions: 202-885-1000 • Fax: 202-885-1025

STUDENTS SAY "..."

Academics

"Tucked away in a beautiful part of Northwest D.C.," American University offers students a "campus [that] has a suburban feel." However, being near the nation's capital means they enjoy "the best of both worlds." Here, classes are structured "in a way that not only encourages, but nearly expects students to undertake internships in their field of study." Specifically, students tout the School of International Service (SIS) and the School of Public Affairs (SPA), "both [of which] are among the best in the nation and offer students opportunities to not just learn about but experience their studies." And inside the classroom, students are greeted by professors who are "passionate about [their] subject [matter]" and who tend to have "real-world experience which is helpful for bringing the material to life." Even better, they're "accessible and constantly reach out and encourage students to attend events." Finally, as one student sums it up, "So many of my classes have wound up being better than I ever could have expected, and have launched me down paths I didn't know existed."

Campus Life

Undergrads at American lead busy and involved lives. Outside of class, students "fill their days with internships and extracurricular activities." This includes anything from "Greek life [to] tutoring to [being a] tour guide," or even singing with an a cappella group. Additionally, "there's always one event or another happening on campus, [whether it's] a concert, cultural event, or movie screening." There's a lot to do both on- and off-campus. Great local options include concerts, cultural events, and movie screenings, while in nearby D.C. you'll find undergrads "attending [a] music festival, visiting the National Mall, [or] going to a congressional hearing." In short, "there is always something going on." Students also love "checking out...museums [and] exploring new neighborhoods," which often sends them strolling through "Tenleytown, shopping in Georgetown...[or] walking around the waterfront." When the weather is nice, they also "love going [to] Rock Creek Park...or [the] farmer's markets on Sunday."

Student Body

Students at American are "truly passionate about what they are learning and are interested in exploring what both D.C. and the world have to offer." Indeed, "whenever you ask them what they are studying...they'll light up and talk for hours on end." Many are also "politically active," "knowledgeable about current events," and "convinced that they will save the world" someday. According to some, this mindset can be "pretty homogenous," as "the AU student body tends to be rather liberal-leaning and relatively affluent." However, another counters, "We have an incredibly diverse student body ranging from students from all across the U.S. to all across the world!" And many insist that "there is a place for everybody on campus." What's more, "everyone is friendly and so easy to strike up conversation with." AU undergrads "care about each other's successes and are there to build each other up, not tear each other down." As this grateful individual concludes, "No other student body both supports and challenges you to be the best student one could possibly be. I could not be more proud to call myself an AU student."

AMERICAN UNIVERSITY

Financial Aid: 202-885-6500 • E-Mail: admissions@american.edu • Website: www.american.edu

THE PRINCETON REVIEW SAYS

Admissions

The school reports that its standardized testing policy for use in admission for Fall 2024 is Test Optional. The 2024 testing policy will be permanent. The Princeton Review suggests that interested applicants consult with the school for the most up-to-date standardized testing policies. *Very important factors considered include:* rigor of secondary school record, academic GPA, level of applicant's interest. *Important factors considered include:* application essay, recommendation(s), extracurricular activities, talent/ability, character/personal qualities, volunteer work. *Other factors considered include:* standardized test scores, first generation, alumni/ae relation, geographical residence, racial/ethnic status, work experience. High school diploma is required and GED is accepted. Academic units required: 4 English, 3 math, 3 science, 2 science labs, 2 foreign language, 2 social studies, 3 academic electives. *Academic units recommended:* 4 English, 4 math, 4 science, 3 foreign language, 4 social studies, 4 academic electives.

Financial Aid

Students should submit: CSS/Financial Aid Profile; FAFSA. Priority filing deadline is 11/15. The Princeton Review suggests that all financial aid forms be submitted as soon as possible (see page 5 for a note on the FAFSA). *Need-based scholarships/grants offered:* College/university scholarship or grant aid from institutional funds; Federal Pell; Private scholarships; SEOG; State scholarships/grants. *Loan aid offered:* Direct PLUS loans; Direct Subsidized Loans; Direct Unsubsidized Loans; College/university loans from institutional funds. Admitted students will be notified of awards on or about 4/1. Federal Work-Study Program available. Institutional employment available.

The Inside Word

Admissions officers at American truly have an interest in getting to know each candidate. And they make a point of closely considering all facets of an application, so you can't slack on any aspect. Of course, your transcript will hold the most weight. And you'll need a challenging college prep curriculum to be a strong contender. Finally, if you loathe standardized tests you can rejoice: American is a Test Optional school. Best of all, withholding your scores will not affect your consideration for merit awards or entrance to the Honors Program.

THE SCHOOL SAYS "..."

From the Admissions Office

"At American University, passion inspires meaningful impact, changemakers find community, and the world's greatest challenges meet their match. Our undergraduate experience centers on empowering lives of purpose, advancing knowledge through experiential learning, and partnering with our home city of Washington, DC. Whatever your passion, an AU education is a launching pad for those who want to lead the way toward positive change.

"AU's rigorous curriculum features high-impact educational experiences that combine in-depth theoretical study with meaningful real-world experiences. Regardless of your choice of major, you'll acquire a solid foundation in liberal arts while pursuing thorough study in your chosen field. The flexibility of our programs and the breadth of our faculty expertise help you focus your studies on what drives you.

"Our community is filled with ambitious visionaries and practitioners who use their passion and purpose to make an impact in this changing world. Our students learn outside of the classroom as much as they do inside through experiences made possible in our home city, where pivotal national and global decisions are made. Our network of world-class faculty and visiting scholars bring deep connections to influential companies and organizations in the public, private, and non-profit sectors and enhance the excellence of our programs.

"We are a university driven to make a difference. We step up, we show up, and we say "challenge accepted" to the issues that matter most to us—and our communities. Are you ready to join us?"

SELECTIVITY

Admissions Rating	93
# of applicants	19,510
% of applicants accepted	41
% of acceptees attending	22
# offered a place on the wait list	9,146
% accepting a place on wait list	23
% admitted from wait list	4
# of early decision applicants	868
% accepted early decision	86

FIRST-YEAR PROFILE

Testing policy	Test Optional
Range SAT composite	1290–1420
Range SAT EBRW	660–730
Range SAT math	630–700
Range ACT composite	29–32
# submitting SAT scores	475
% submitting SAT scores	27
# submitting ACT scores	303
% submitting ACT scores	17

DEADLINES

Early decision	
Deadline	11/15
Notification	12/31
Other ED deadline	1/15
Other ED notification	2/15
Regular	
Deadline	1/15
Notification	4/1
Nonfall registration?	Yes

APPLICANTS ALSO LOOK AT

Boston College; Boston University; Fordham University; Georgetown University; New York University; Northeastern University; Syracuse University; The George Washington University

FINANCIAL FACTS

Financial Aid Rating	82
Annual tuition	$55,724
Room and board	$16,520
Required fees	$819
Books and supplies	$800
Average frosh need-based scholarship	$31,335
Average UG need-based scholarship	$29,340
% needy frosh rec. need-based scholarship or grant aid	96
% needy UG rec. need-based scholarship or grant aid	93
% needy frosh rec. non-need-based scholarship or grant aid	46
% needy UG rec. non-need-based scholarship or grant aid	41
% needy frosh rec. need-based self-help aid	86
% needy UG rec. need-based self-help aid	85
% frosh rec. any financial aid	82
% UG rec. any financial aid	70
% frosh need fully met	63
% ugrads need fully met	30
Average % of frosh need met	93
Average % of ugrad need met	77

AMHERST COLLEGE

Amherst College, Amherst, MA 01002 • Admissions: 413-542-2328 • Fax: 413-542-2040

STUDENTS SAY ". . ."

Academics

An open curriculum and a focus on undergraduates are the foundations of the Amherst College education, where approximately 1,850 students choose their own intellectual path from 41 majors, numerous research opportunities, and additional classes and resources available from other members of the Five College Consortium. It's an "academically rigorous undergraduate education," but there are multiple resource centers to foster awareness and help students "continue and worship our identities" as well, including the Center for International Student Engagement, Women's and Gender Center, Multicultural Resource Center, Queer Resource Center, and Center for Diversity & Student Leadership. The "open curriculum offers the student a perfect level of curricular control over their own education," and students can supplement this with "fully-funded field trips or interesting guest lecturers" and a "plethora of research opportunities for undergraduates." Students still need to declare a major and fulfill the requirements, but they find the open curriculum "gives you so much space and freedom to take a variety of classes at this liberal arts college."

Faculty at Amherst "always leave their door open" with "ridiculously extensive and lenient office hours," and small class sizes further encourage "strong relationships with professors." They "help you think of paper topics, read drafts, and give active feedback." One student shares, "My professors have treated me like family—literally, I have been invited over for dinner…and academically and professionally pushed and helped to do my best." Classes are mainly "small group discussions that require students to teach other students," and students have the opportunity to engage in a variety of subjects with "different perspectives through collaboration."

Campus Life

The packed weekdays at Amherst follow a pretty standard formula: "Go to class. Work. Generally participate in at least one activity a day. Study. Socialize. Repeat." That socializing takes many forms: "People see movies, bowl, and hike," but they also just hang out in the campus center. They also fill their time "cooking, spending time in town or in neighboring towns or cities," and going to recitals. Students here "are constantly moving and busy with packed schedules that encompass a variety of activities," and when the weather cooperates, "people will be found lounging in the grassy quads, playing Frisbee, [and] going out to nearby towns or ponds [and] mini-beaches." On the weekends, students attend "parties at night and events during the day, [including] sporting events." Most who attend call the campus home—97 percent of those enrolled live on campus.

Student Body

The people on this "fairly diverse campus" are "a collection of different ethnicities, gender identities, sexual preferences, and various background lives." Students find that "personalities and interests vary widely," but believe "everyone at Amherst has a story" and "everyone has a space." Amherst students are incredibly generous and "help each other because they want the best for one another." Overall, people are "academically and intellectually engaged and curious," and they "collaborate because they know that it's the best way to learn." The busy nature of the school and the "quite varied interests" of the student body naturally create peers who seek eclectic experiences: "No one is just a football player or a violinist; they are also a singer or an [on-campus organization's] senator," one student offers as an example.

AMHERST COLLEGE

Financial Aid: 413-542-2296 • E-Mail: admission@amherst.edu • Website: www.amherst.edu

THE PRINCETON REVIEW SAYS

Admissions

The school reports that its standardized testing policy for use in admission for Fall 2024 is Test Optional. It is unknown at this time if the 2024 testing policy will be permanent. The Princeton Review suggests that interested applicants consult with the school for the most up-to-date standardized testing policies. *Very important factors considered include:* rigor of secondary school record, academic GPA, application essay, recommendation(s), extracurricular activities, talent/ability, character/personal qualities. *Important factors considered include:* class rank, first generation, volunteer work, work experience. *Other factors considered include:* standardized test scores, alumni/ae relation, geographical residence, racial/ethnic status. High school diploma or equivalent is not required. *Academic units required: Academic units recommended:* 4 English, 4 math, 3 science, 2 science labs, 3 foreign language, 2 social studies, 2 history.

Financial Aid

Students should submit: CSS/Financial Aid Profile; FAFSA; Noncustodial Profile. Priority filing deadline is 1/10. The Princeton Review suggests that all financial aid forms be submitted as soon as possible (see page 5 for a note on the FAFSA). *Need-based scholarships/grants offered:* College/university scholarship or grant aid from institutional funds; Federal Pell; Private scholarships; SEOG; State scholarships/grants. *Loan aid offered:* Direct PLUS loans; Direct Subsidized Loans; Direct Unsubsidized Loans; College/university loans from institutional funds. Admitted students will be notified of awards on or about 4/1. Federal Work-Study Program available. Institutional employment available.

The Inside Word

Membership certainly has its benefits at the highly selective Amherst College. For the price of entry to this school, students also gain entrance to the prestigious Five College Consortium, which allows enrolled students to take courses for credit at no additional cost at any of the four other participating consortium members (Hampshire College, Mount Holyoke College, Smith College, and the University of Massachusetts Amherst). And this deal isn't just confined to the classroom: students can use other schools' libraries, eat meals at the other cafeterias, and participate in extracurricular activities offered at the other schools. And don't worry about how you'll get there—your bus fare is covered too.

THE SCHOOL SAYS "..."

From the Admissions Office

"Founded in 1821, Amherst College is considered one of the premier liberal arts colleges in the nation, enrolling 1,800 bright, talented, engaged students, who are broadly diverse across many dimensions—geographic, racial, ethnic, socioeconomic, academic, and extracurricular. Need-blind admission for all applicants (domestic and international) and generous, no-loan financial aid offers ensure that exceptional students from across the country and around the world are admitted to Amherst based on accomplishment and promise, regardless of family income. Located in Amherst, Massachusetts, a town of 35,000 people in an area of great natural beauty, the College's 1,000-acre campus offers top-notch academic, athletic and residential facilities, including a new state-of-the-art science center designed to facilitate interdisciplinary research. Awarding the BA degree in forty-one majors in the humanities, social sciences and natural sciences, Amherst offers an Open Curriculum, allowing students unusual independence and flexibility in designing their educational programs, unconstrained by distribution or area requirements. Through the Five College Consortium, Amherst students can also take courses and participate in activities at Smith College, Mount Holyoke, Hampshire College, and the University of Massachusetts Amherst, providing access to a remarkably broad collection of curricular and extracurricular options. Amherst's small classes and low student-faculty ratio foster close, one-to-one interactions with professors and fellow students and provide exceptional opportunities for undergraduate research with highly talented, accomplished faculty, contributing to an uncommonly engaging intellectual and personal experience within a lively community."

SELECTIVITY
Admissions Rating	98
# of applicants	14,864
% of applicants accepted	7
% of acceptees attending	43
# offered a place on the wait list	1,419
% accepting a place on wait list	64
% admitted from wait list	4
# of early decision applicants	692
% accepted early decision	32

FIRST-YEAR PROFILE
Testing policy	Test Optional
Range SAT composite	1400–1600
Range SAT EBRW	700–800
Range SAT math	700–800
Range ACT composite	30–36
# submitting SAT scores	190
% submitting SAT scores	41
# submitting ACT scores	103
% submitting ACT scores	22
% graduated top 10% of class	90
% graduated top 25% of class	96
% graduated top 50% of class	100

DEADLINES
Early decision	
Deadline	11/1
Notification	12/15
Regular	
Deadline	1/2
Nonfall registration?	No

APPLICANTS ALSO LOOK AT
Brown University; Columbia University; Dartmouth College; Harvard College; Princeton University; Stanford University; University of Pennsylvania; Williams College; Yale University

FINANCIAL FACTS
Financial Aid Rating	97
Annual tuition	$63,500
Room and board	$16,750
Required fees	$600
Books and supplies	$1,000
Average frosh need-based scholarship	$66,930
Average UG need-based scholarship	$66,393
% needy frosh rec. need-based scholarship or grant aid	100
% needy UG rec. need-based scholarship or grant aid	100
% needy frosh rec. non-need-based scholarship or grant aid	0
% needy UG rec. non-need-based scholarship or grant aid	0
% needy frosh rec. need-based self-help aid	75
% needy UG rec. need-based self-help aid	82
% frosh rec. any financial aid	57
% UG rec. any financial aid	56
% UG borrow to pay for school	26
Average cumulative indebtedness	$18,397
% frosh need fully met	100
% ugrads need fully met	100
Average % of frosh need met	100
Average % of ugrad need met	100

ANGELO STATE UNIVERSITY

2601 West Avenue N, San Angelo, TX 76909-1014 • Admissions: 800-946-8627 • Fax: 325-942-2078

CAMPUS LIFE

Quality of Life Rating	95
Fire Safety Rating	89
Green Rating	88
Type of school	Public
Environment	City

STUDENTS

Total undergrad enrollment	5,449
% male/female/another gender	42/58/0
% from out of state	4
% frosh live on campus	70
% ugrads live on campus	33
# of fraternities	5
# of sororities	2
% African American	6
% Asian	1
% White	44
% Hispanic	41
% Native American	<1
% Pacific Islander	<1
% Two or more races	3
% Race and/or ethnicity unknown	1
% international	4
# of countries represented	33

SURVEY SAYS . . .

Lots of conservative students
Students are happy
School is well run
Diverse student types interact on campus
Students are very religious
Students get along with local community
Intramural sports are popular
Active student government

ACADEMICS

Academic Rating	80
% students returning for sophomore year	73
% students graduating within 4 years	30
% students graduating within 6 years	41
Calendar	Semester
Student/faculty ratio	18:1
Profs interesting rating	91
Profs accessible rating	93

Most classes have 20–29 students.
Most lab/discussion sessions have
10–19 students.

MOST POPULAR MAJORS

Multi-/Interdisciplinary Studies, Other; Registered
Nursing/Registered Nurse; Business
Administration and Management, General

STUDENTS SAY ". . ."

Academics

Angelo State University, located in San Angelo, Texas, offers an academic environment that is "small enough to foster a sense of family among its students, but large enough to carry out the usual dealings of universities that have many more students." Among these offerings are "outstanding instructors," "top-rated programs," and a low faculty-to-student ratio—one student says, "the small…ratio is what really drew me to Angelo State." The university puts forth a variety of "resources available to enhance education." These include scholarship opportunities, ROTC programs, counseling services, and a dedicated Student Affairs office. Student advisory services are provided free of charge and make valuable additions to the overall academic experience. Angelo State students describe professors and other faculty members as "always willing to help" in a variety of ways. The university's professionals go above and beyond by "explaining concepts outside of class time, offering advice of which courses to take, or even offering career advice." They take the time to get to know individual students, "provide additional resources," and "encourage the next generation of scholars" by guiding students to think critically and "better understand multiple perspectives." One student raves, saying, "I have had several different majors in my college journey, and in every program…I felt like the professors really cared about teaching."

Campus Life

The average student at Angelo State tends to maintain a healthy balance between schoolwork and leisure. Students see their work as a priority but still find time to socialize with friends and participate in extracurricular activities. "Just hanging out is common," as students enjoy walking around campus, finding a place outdoors to simply relax, "studying around campus, [and talking] to their friends." Many students spend their time either at the library or at the University Center because both places are considered to be "the most calming." Other students use their personal time to visit the recreation center, which has a full gym, equipped with an inside track and a "weight room [that] is amazing," or they can participate in other recreational sports. "When it gets warm outside, the sand volleyball courts always have a good crowd at them," says a student. Those looking for entertainment off-campus will be pleased that the surrounding area of San Angelo includes restaurants, bars, a shopping mall, and other nearby stores, and "the nightlife is pretty solid around town."

Student Body

The students at Angelo State University offer an extraordinarily "friendly and welcoming" atmosphere on campus. It's also a large enough school that "you are constantly meeting new people, but at the same time you get to see the people you are well-acquainted with." Students at the school affectionately refer to fellow members of the university as the "Ram Fam," which "means that everyone is family at the school…because everyone is out to help you." Most students say their peers are the type of people who are "polite," "uplifting," and "have your back." According to one undergraduate, "Everyone has the goals they want to achieve, and the students find support to achieve those goals within the community they build." Students go out of their way to make others feel comfortable and accepted, "offer to help you find your way to class," or even "open doors or greet you." One states, "I can't walk to class without receiving a 'hello' or 'what's up' from other students." And that crowd of friendly faces "seems to grow [in diversity] each year." Overall, students find the climate on campus to be "beyond amazing."

ANGELO STATE UNIVERSITY

Financial Aid: 325-942-2246 • E-Mail: admissions@angelo.edu • Website: www.angelo.edu

THE PRINCETON REVIEW SAYS

Admissions

The school reports that its standardized testing policy for use in admission for Fall 2024 is Test Optional. The 2024 testing policy will be permanent. The Princeton Review suggests that interested applicants consult with the school for the most up-to-date standardized testing policies. *Very important factors considered include:* class rank, standardized test scores. *Important factors considered include:* rigor of secondary school record. *Other factors considered include:* academic GPA, extracurricular activities, talent/ability, character/personal qualities, first generation, geographical residence, state residency, volunteer work, work experience, level of applicant's interest. High school diploma is required and GED is accepted. *Academic units recommended:* 4 English, 4 math, 4 science, 2 foreign language, 4 social studies, 1 visual/performing arts, 6 academic electives.

Financial Aid

Students should submit: FAFSA. Priority filing deadline is 1/15. The Princeton Review suggests that all financial aid forms be submitted as soon as possible (see page 5 for a note on the FAFSA). *Need-based scholarships/grants offered:* College/university scholarship or grant aid from institutional funds; Federal Pell; Private scholarships; SEOG; State scholarships/grants. *Loan aid offered:* Direct PLUS loans; Direct Subsidized Loans; Direct Unsubsidized Loans; College/university loans from institutional funds; State Loans. Admitted students will be notified of awards on a rolling basis beginning 1/15. Federal Work-Study Program available. Institutional employment available.

The Inside Word

When accepting new students to Angelo State University, the admissions department places a strong emphasis on academic achievement and the desire for students to "find what drives" them. The department takes into consideration the high school class rank and college entrance exam score of each of its prospective students. Students who have graduated in the top 25 percent of their class do not require a minimum SAT or ACT score. Students that fall into the next 25 percent of their class require either a minimum ACT score of 17 or a minimum SAT score of 920. Students in the third and fourth quarters of their graduating class are not assured admission but are still encouraged to apply for further review.

THE SCHOOL SAYS "..."

From the Admissions Office

"Angelo State University is widely known as the premier regional university in West Texas. The university maintains a commitment to excellence for our students by providing endless opportunities through hands-on, experiential learning in a small classroom environment. ASU shines with superb records of graduates' acceptance into professional schools. Seventy percent of pre-med students are accepted into medical school, well above the national average of 36 percent. Ninety percent of students who complete the pre-veterinary program and receive the highest recommendations from ASU faculty are accepted into veterinary school. Over 95 percent of agriculture, biology, chemistry, engineering, geology and physics majors who apply are accepted into graduate school. All graduates of ASU's Honors Program who have applied to graduate programs or professional schools (including medicine and law) have been accepted. ASU nursing students have a pass rate of over 92 percent on the NCLEX-RN licensure exam. Pointing to the future, ASU has joined the Southwest Airlines Destination 225 program that provides career pathways for commercial aviation students, and is developing a Cybersecurity and Artificial Intelligence Center of Excellence.

"Annually awarding nearly $12 million in scholarships, ASU remains one of the top educational values in Texas. About 90 percent of ASU students receive some form of financial support, and over 40 percent graduate debt free. ASU also encourages healthy student lifestyles while fostering leadership development through 100-plus student organizations, a thriving intramurals program, and modern recreation and fitness facilities. ASU student-athletes compete in newly-renovated, state-of-the-art facilities."

SELECTIVITY

Admissions Rating	84
# of applicants	4,116
% of applicants accepted	79
% of acceptees attending	38

FIRST-YEAR PROFILE

Testing policy	Test Optional
Range SAT composite	920–1120
Range SAT EBRW	480–570
Range SAT math	450–580
Range ACT composite	17–23
# submitting SAT scores	689
% submitting SAT scores	50
# submitting ACT scores	476
% submitting ACT scores	34
Average HS GPA	3.7
% frosh submitting high school GPA	80
% graduated top 10% of class	11
% graduated top 25% of class	33
% graduated top 50% of class	61

DEADLINES

Regular	
Notification	Rolling, 9/1
Nonfall registration?	Yes

FINANCIAL FACTS

Financial Aid Rating	81
Annual in-state tuition	$5,619
Annual out-of-state tuition	$17,859
Room and board	$10,520
Required fees	$3,691
Books and supplies	$1,200
Average frosh need-based scholarship	$4,278
Average UG need-based scholarship	$3,810
% needy frosh rec. need-based scholarship or grant aid	87
% needy UG rec. need-based scholarship or grant aid	89
% needy frosh rec. non-need-based scholarship or grant aid	68
% needy UG rec. non-need-based scholarship or grant aid	60
% needy frosh rec. need-based self-help aid	45
% needy UG rec. need-based self-help aid	53
% frosh rec. any financial aid	70
% UG rec. any financial aid	65
% UG borrow to pay for school	54
Average cumulative indebtedness	$23,824
% frosh need fully met	16
% ugrads need fully met	13
Average % of frosh need met	72
Average % of ugrad need met	65

APPALACHIAN STATE UNIVERSITY

287 River Street, John Thomas Building, Boone, NC 28608-2004 • Admissions: 828-262-2000 • Fax: 828-262-3296

STUDENTS SAY "..."

Academics

It's easy for Appalachian State University to attract undergraduates. Not only is the school "exceedingly affordable," but it offers "gorgeous scenery" and "a strong sense of community that makes all its students feel like they have found their place." Undergrads also appreciate the resources provided to facilitate everyone's experience, such as the school's textbook rental program, which "saves most students hundreds of dollars per semester" and tries to ensure that students "do not have to stress about purchasing too many books." Additionally, App State provides "great continuing education scholarships."

The university touts a "terrific Honors College" as well as "a wide range of majors." Plus, all undergrads here benefit from "class sizes [that] are small enough to allow a more personal learning experience while remaining large enough to allow all students to get the classes they need." Many applaud the fact that their professors are "all highly educated experts in their respective fields and do not rely on TAs to teach their courses." And speaking of the faculty, students find that most of them "genuinely seem to love teaching." They are also "exceedingly knowledgeable" and provide students with "great resources that really help [them] to understand and apply material." All in all, "App [has] the greatest professional staff that I have ever encountered. From advisors, professors, or even the people working in the kitchen, everyone legitimately wants to see you succeed."

Campus Life

Simply put, you'd have to work really hard to be bored at App State. For starters, "attending football games and tailgating" is always a big draw. "There are [also] many, many clubs you can join and participate in" like the App State Running club, the Finance Student Association, and theater and music group. Students also note that both "Greek life and religious life [are] common, but not overbearing."

App State also has a fair number of students who gravitate toward the outdoors. In the warmer months, you'll find undergrads "lounging in hammocks or playing [various] outdoor sports." Of course, "once the snow falls, kids have snowball fights, or sled down the hills, taking advantage of the winter fun." And for the adventurous type, you can certainly find plenty here. Perhaps unsurprisingly, the university offers robust Outdoor Programs, organizing exciting trips such as "canoeing [and] stand-up paddle boarding" and "skiing and snowboarding in the winter." There are also "many hiking trails a short drive from campus." Given the school's proximity to the Blue Ridge Parkway, it makes sense that "rock climbing is very popular here and you can often hear rock climbers hooting and hollering as you hike a trail."

Student Body

App State seems to attract "laid-back and casual" individuals who typically give off a "relaxed, accepting vibe" peppered with a "tinge…[of] hippie." A large percentage of students "are extremely passionate about sustainability…and their impact on the environment" as well. Moreover, undergrads see their peers as "open-minded" people who "are very accepting of ideas and identities that do not fit the status quo," though some students do report their peers to lean "more on the liberal side" of the political spectrum. Perhaps more critically, students underscore the fact that their classmates are "kind and genuine." Indeed, "if you need help, almost anyone you find walking down the hallway would go out of their way to lend a helping hand." While some say it can feel like "most of the students are white" and a "vast majority of people…com[e] from North Carolina and other southern states," others counter that you can still meet "students from all around the country and world." Overall, "App State truly has such a welcoming and accepting student body that it would be hard to come across someone that you absolutely just didn't like or didn't enjoy talking to."

APPALACHIAN STATE UNIVERSITY

Financial Aid: 828-262-2190 • E-Mail: admissions@appstate.edu • Website: www.AppState.edu

THE PRINCETON REVIEW SAYS

Admissions

The school reports that its standardized testing policy for use in admission for Fall 2024 is Test Optional. It is unknown at this time if the 2024 testing policy will be permanent. The Princeton Review suggests that interested applicants consult with the school for the most up-to-date standardized testing policies. *Very important factors considered include:* rigor of secondary school record, class rank, academic GPA. *Important factors considered include:* standardized test scores, interview, extracurricular activities, talent/ability, racial/ethnic status, volunteer work, work experience. *Other factors considered include:* application essay, character/personal qualities, first generation, level of applicant's interest. High school diploma is required and GED is accepted. *Academic units required:* 4 English, 4 math, 3 science, 1 science lab, 2 foreign language, 1 social studies, 1 history.

Financial Aid

Students should submit: FAFSA. The Princeton Review suggests that all financial aid forms be submitted as soon as possible (see page 5 for a note on the FAFSA). *Need-based scholarships/grants offered:* College/university scholarship or grant aid from institutional funds; Federal Pell; Private scholarships; SEOG; State scholarships/grants. *Loan aid offered:* Direct PLUS loans; Direct Subsidized Loans; Direct Unsubsidized Loans. Admitted students will be notified of awards on a rolling basis beginning 3/15. Federal Work-Study Program available. Institutional employment available.

The Inside Word

The folks in Appalachian State's admissions office are also looking for individuals who want to fully engage with both campus life and the world at large. To find such candidates, they take a holistic approach to their decision making and closely examine all application facets, from academic rigor to leadership roles in extracurriculars. So don't cut any corners! Of course, academics will still take top priority, but the most competitive students will definitely have some honors and advanced placement or IB courses sprinkled throughout their transcript.

THE SCHOOL SAYS "..."

From the Admissions Office

"App State is known as the "premier public undergraduate institution in the state of North Carolina," and is one of 17 campuses in the University of North Carolina System. The university enrolls more than 20,000 students and offers more than 150 undergraduate and graduate majors, but the student-to-faculty ratio is low, so professors also serve as mentors. The university is located in the Blue Ridge Mountains, one of the country's most beautiful locations—and the perfect setting for students to strengthen their academic focus, discover their passions, enhance their leadership skills and take the next step in their life's journey. The vibrant downtown of Boone is just a block from campus, and the town enjoys the ranking of one of the safest cities in the state. From the moment students begin their studies at App State, they are expected to develop as critical and creative thinkers, effective communicators and inquisitive local-to-global learners. App State alumni go on to earn advanced degrees, start businesses, build distinguished military careers, work overseas and develop careers that take them in many directions, all while giving back to the communities in which they live and work."

SELECTIVITY

Admissions Rating	84
# of applicants	22,255
% of applicants accepted	83
% of acceptees attending	21
# offered a place on the wait list	1,350
% accepting a place on wait list	23
% admitted from wait list	62

FIRST-YEAR PROFILE

Testing policy	Test Optional
Range SAT composite	1100–1270
Range SAT EBRW	560–650
Range SAT math	540–620
Range ACT composite	21–27
# submitting SAT scores	471
% submitting SAT scores	12
# submitting ACT scores	1,141
% submitting ACT scores	29
Average HS GPA	4.0
% frosh submitting high school GPA	100
% graduated top 10% of class	13
% graduated top 25% of class	41
% graduated top 50% of class	81

DEADLINES

Early action	
Deadline	11/1
Notification	1/25
Regular	
Priority	11/1
Deadline	2/1
Notification	Rolling, 1/25
Nonfall registration?	Yes

APPLICANTS ALSO LOOK AT

North Carolina State University; University of North Carolina–Chapel Hill

FINANCIAL FACTS

Financial Aid Rating	76
Annual in-state tuition	$4,242
Annual out-of-state tuition	$20,246
Required fees	$3,208
Books and supplies	$800
Average frosh need-based scholarship	$8,548
Average UG need-based scholarship	$8,893
% needy frosh rec. need-based scholarship or grant aid	76
% needy UG rec. need-based scholarship or grant aid	73
% needy frosh rec. non-need-based scholarship or grant aid	5
% needy UG rec. non-need-based scholarship or grant aid	3
% needy frosh rec. need-based self-help aid	60
% needy UG rec. need-based self-help aid	63
% frosh rec. any financial aid	75
% UG rec. any financial aid	66
% UG borrow to pay for school	55
Average cumulative indebtedness	$23,402
% frosh need fully met	5
% ugrads need fully met	4
Average % of frosh need met	57
Average % of ugrad need met	58

ARIZONA STATE UNIVERSITY

Admission Services, PO Box 871004, Tempe, AZ 85287-1004 • Admissions: 480-965-7788 • Fax: 480-965-3610

STUDENTS SAY ". . ."

Academics

Students report that Arizona State University's focus on "innovation" and its "abundance of resources" are major factors in their school choice. ASU is a large university, yet manages to "personalize every student's experience," and offers "endless...opportunities for success." The university has many strong academic departments and programs of study, and students are quick to brag that ASU has "one of the best journalism schools in the nation" as well as a "renowned business school" and "great engineering program." Regardless of the academic discipline you choose, students suggest that you'll find research opportunities.

ASU students praise their "enthusiastic, supportive, and engaged" professors. Undergraduates report that most of the faculty is effective in incorporating "research interests and experiences" into coursework. "Most of my professors would bend over backward to help me out—even when the issue wasn't in their particular class," reports one enthusiastic undergraduate. It's "very easy to get help/make friends with professors." Another student admiringly tells us, "I had a professor who worked for the UN, as well as [one who was] a skateboarding punk music journalist."

Campus Life

It's virtually impossible to be bored on the ASU campuses, as students are incredibly active. "There are always people out at the pools, exercising in the gym, playing sports on the sand volleyball courts or soccer fields, or riding bikes or long boards." If you prefer indoor sports, don't worry: ASU has a "very strong gaming community." Undergraduates can also enjoy "really interesting lectures" and participate in "fun clubs." There is a "programming board which host[s] events every week, including free films and food." Many students "have jobs and internships" as well. Additionally, Greek life is pretty popular at ASU. Students say that it's "really fun [but] not as party-oriented as it used to be. Fraternities and sororities [now] get involved around campus, whether it be [through] community service, philanthropy, or intramural games." Downtown Tempe offers plenty of excitement as well. For example, "there is a thriving alternative music and DIY scene in the Maple-Ash district just off campus with ties to the local arts communities, political activism, and house shows where local bands play."

Student Body

Undergraduates at ASU love the "diversity" of the student body and describe meeting peers "from all different backgrounds, locations and cultures." There is a "large Greek life presence...along with a very serious academic body within Barrett, The Honors College, and a large section of international students." No matter where they come from, ASU undergraduates appreciate the student body's "unique blend of intelligence and fun." They also tend to be "nice and welcoming." One student sums it up: "Every person you meet has a smile on their face, ready to help with whatever problem there is." A number of undergraduates here also report that their peers "are excellent at getting involved in community activities and speaking up for what they believe in...[as well as] spread[ing] awareness about important issues." Thanks to the university's large size, many students insist that "everyone who comes to ASU is absolutely able to find other people with the same interests, passions, beliefs, and world views, as well as countless others who see the world very differently. No matter who you are, you can find a community of peers."

ARIZONA STATE UNIVERSITY

Financial Aid: 855-278-5080 • E-Mail: admissions@asu.edu • Website: www.asu.edu

THE PRINCETON REVIEW SAYS

Admissions

The school reports that its standardized testing policy for use in admission for Fall 2024 is Test Optional. The 2024 testing policy will be permanent. The Princeton Review suggests that interested applicants consult with the school for the most up-to-date standardized testing policies. *Very important factors considered include:* class rank, academic GPA. *Important factors considered include:* rigor of secondary school record. *Other factors considered include:* state residency. High school diploma is required and GED is accepted. *Academic units required:* 4 English, 4 math, 3 laboratory science, 2 foreign language, 1 social studies, 1 American history, 1 fine arts or 1 career/technical.

Financial Aid

Students should submit: FAFSA. Priority filing deadline is 1/15. The Princeton Review suggests that all financial aid forms be submitted as soon as possible (see page 5 for a note on the FAFSA). *Need-based scholarships/grants offered:* College/university scholarship or grant aid from institutional funds; Federal Nursing Scholarships; Federal Pell; Private scholarships; SEOG; State scholarships/grants; United Negro College Fund. *Loan aid offered:* Direct PLUS loans; Direct Subsidized Loans; Direct Unsubsidized Loans; College/university loans from institutional funds; Federal Nursing Loans; State Loans. Admitted students will be notified of awards on a rolling basis beginning 12/1. Federal Work-Study Program available. Institutional employment available.

The Inside Word

Admission officers at Arizona State University have built an incoming class that reflects diverse backgrounds and interests. The school takes a fairly straightforward approach to the admission process. Applicants must have or meet at least one of the following: minimum 3.00 GPA (based upon a 4.00 scale), be in the top 25 percent of their graduating class, or earned a minimum ACT score of 22 (residents) or 24 (nonresidents) or an SAT score of 1120 (residents) or 1180 (nonresidents).

THE SCHOOL SAYS "..."

From the Admissions Office

"ASU is breaking down the walls of the traditional academic experience to increase the impact of education and research in local and global communities. As a New American University, ASU is committed to interdisciplinary connections, academic excellence, and societal impact. We are bold and forward-thinking, and we see challenges as opportunities. With 400+ undergraduate majors, ASU is a learning environment where personal expression is valued as much as research and discovery. ASU champions intellectual and cultural diversity and welcomes students from all 50 states and more than 140 countries. Our distinguished faculty receives prestigious honors including the Nobel Prize, the Pulitzer Prize, and membership in the National Academies. Student achievements include Rhodes, Fulbright, Marshall, Churchill and Goldwater scholars, National Merit Scholars, National Hispanic Scholars, and National Recognition Scholars.

"ASU has four unique campuses in metropolitan Phoenix, and a site in Lake Havasu City. All feature state-of-the-art living and learning facilities. The Downtown Phoenix campus creates strong learning and career connections for more than 11,000 students with media, health care, corporate, and government organizations. The Polytechnic campus, located in Mesa, Arizona, is home to more than 5,800 students who are exploring professional and technical programs. Thousands of square feet of laboratory space make way for project-based learning.

"ASU welcomes more than 57,600 students studying at the historic Tempe campus. The Sun Devils athletic complex, performing arts facilities, and high-tech research spaces create a dynamic and engaging learning environment.

"At the West campus in northwest Phoenix, ASU offers business, education, health, and interdisciplinary arts and science programs to more than 5,000 students. The campus's award-winning architecture and lush landscaping are designed to create a close-knit learning community."

SELECTIVITY

Admissions Rating	81
# of applicants	68,789
% of applicants accepted	90
% of acceptees attending	25

FIRST-YEAR PROFILE

Testing policy	Test Optional
Average HS GPA	3.6
% frosh submitting high school GPA	98
% graduated top 10% of class	27
% graduated top 25% of class	56
% graduated top 50% of class	85

DEADLINES

Regular	
Priority	1/15
Notification	Rolling, 8/1
Nonfall registration?	Yes

FINANCIAL FACTS

Financial Aid Rating	82
Annual in-state tuition	$10,978
Annual out-of-state tuition	$29,952
Room and board	$14,718
Required fees	$640
Books and supplies	$1,320
Average frosh need-based scholarship	$13,527
Average UG need-based scholarship	$12,143
% needy frosh rec. need-based scholarship or grant aid	96
% needy UG rec. need-based scholarship or grant aid	92
% needy frosh rec. non-need-based scholarship or grant aid	13
% needy UG rec. non-need-based scholarship or grant aid	11
% needy frosh rec. need-based self-help aid	39
% needy UG rec. need-based self-help aid	46
% frosh rec. any financial aid	93
% UG rec. any financial aid	87
% UG borrow to pay for school	41
Average cumulative indebtedness	$23,515
% frosh need fully met	19
% ugrads need fully met	18
Average % of frosh need met	63
Average % of ugrad need met	60

ASSUMPTION UNIVERSITY

Assumption University, Worcester, MA 01609-1296 • Admissions: 508-767-7285 • Fax: 508-799-4412

CAMPUS LIFE

Quality of Life Rating	91
Fire Safety Rating	82
Green Rating	60*
Type of school	Private
Affiliation	Roman Catholic
Environment	City

STUDENTS

Total undergrad enrollment	1,677
% male/female	46/54
% from out of state	28
% frosh from public high school	68
% frosh live on campus	82
% ugrads live on campus	74
# of fraternities	0
# of sororities	0
% African American	5
% Asian	3
% White	74
% Hispanic	10
% Native American	<1
% Two or more races	4
% Race and/or ethnicity unknown	2
% international	1
# of countries represented	15

SURVEY SAYS . . .

Students are happy
Internships are widely available
Diverse student types interact on campus
Students get along with local community
Students involved in community service
Easy to get around campus
Everyone loves the Greyhounds
Active student government
Active minority support groups
Lots of conservative students

ACADEMICS

Academic Rating	81
% students returning for sophomore year	83
% students graduating within 4 years	68
% students graduating within 6 years	71
Calendar	Semester
Student/faculty ratio	11:1
Profs interesting rating	88
Profs accessible rating	94

Most classes have 20–29 students.
Most lab/discussion sessions have 10–19 students.

MOST POPULAR MAJORS

Rehabilitation Science; Health Services/Allied Health/Health Sciences, General; Marketing/Marketing Management, General

STUDENTS SAY ". . ."

Academics

Located in the college haven of Worcester, MA, Assumption University is "a tight knit, faith-based community where everyone is part of a family." The small liberal arts school focuses on "educating aware and prospective young adults to become active and productive members of society while maintaining human core values" through "service, meaningful discussions, and liberal arts classes." Assumption is definitely all about education ("especially if you are a science major"), but there is also "a big push for sports" at this Division II school, and perhaps as a result the university's sense of community is "amazing." As one student puts it, "We are one school." The "beyond helpful" professors here are "engaging," "approachable," and "have a diversity of teaching styles," as well as being "willing to talk to you whenever you need it and [caring] about your well-being." They "bring their personal experiences into the classroom" to make studies "interesting and enjoyable," and the application of the liberal arts curriculum to small classes means that students "receive a greater impact" from their learning. "The professors here at Assumption all love what they do and it is obvious in the classroom," says a junior. However, some do admit that the school is "limited on the number of courses offered," which "can make getting into classes a little difficult." This "very welcoming and inclusive institution" focuses on giving its students every resource possible to help them succeed and be happy; tutoring is provided at the academic center, campus jobs are "abundant," and the Career Development & Internship Center admirably aids students in finding jobs after graduation. "Counselors, teachers, [and] coaches are truly a blessing to have at this university," says a student. Overall, Assumption "helps foster well rounded, creative, intelligent and caring young adults to be successful and morally sound in their future endeavors."

Campus Life

Life at Assumption is great. It's "easy to meet new people" and "there is a great sense of belonging." The "beautiful, diverse and secured campus" is "easily recognizable" from brochures, and those who get to take advantage of it "are very invested in academics, sports, extracurriculars, and social experiences." There is always an activity going on and "always something to do if you want to get off campus" in the college town of Worcester. Housing is guaranteed all four years and the majority of students choose to take advantage of this, but "weekends can be dead sometimes" when students leave campus, and students seeking raucous parties should know that the school is "strict as far as drinking goes." That's not to say that students don't still find ways to let off steam, with "upperclassmen flocking to Leits off-campus" on Thursday nights, while Friday and Saturday see a large majority of students going to campus activities "like Bingo Nights, movie nights, trivia, [and] Family Feud." As one student explains, "They are really fun and have some amazing prizes like iPads."

Student Body

Make no mistake, Assumption is "a VERY Catholic school" with "a very conservative feel." But while there's a lack of socioeconomic diversity—"generally middle-class Caucasians [who] are heterosexual"—students can be separated into "student-athletes and non-student-athletes." Most students "come from Catholic upbringings or have attended Catholic school but are not necessarily religious." New England preppy is a classic style; girls are usually seen in "leggings, UGG boots, a North Face jacket." People here are "generally happy" and "very sociable and approachable" in all aspects of the university; everyone is "courteous and [will] hold doors open or lend you a calculator in class if your forgot yours." Overall, the student body "is like no other": people "genuinely care about each other and it makes for a wonderful experience."

ASSUMPTION UNIVERSITY

Financial Aid: 508-767-7158 • E-Mail: admiss@assumption.edu • Website: www.assumption.edu

THE PRINCETON REVIEW SAYS

Admissions

The school reports that its standardized testing policy for use in admission for Fall 2024 is Test Optional. It is unknown at this time if the 2024 testing policy will be permanent. The Princeton Review suggests that interested applicants consult with the school for the most up-to-date standardized testing policies. *Very important factors considered include:* academic GPA, application essay. *Important factors considered include:* rigor of secondary school record, recommendation(s), interview, volunteer work, level of applicant's interest. *Other factors considered include:* class rank, standardized test scores, extracurricular activities, talent/ability, character/personal qualities, first generation, alumni/ae relation, racial/ethnic status. High school diploma is required and GED is accepted. *Academic units required:* 4 English, 3 math, 2 science, 2 foreign language, 2 history, 5 academic electives.

Financial Aid

Students should submit: FAFSA. Priority filing deadline is 3/15. The Princeton Review suggests that all financial aid forms be submitted as soon as possible (see page 5 for a note on the FAFSA). *Need-based scholarships/grants offered:* College/university scholarship or grant aid from institutional funds; Federal Pell; Private scholarships; SEOG; State scholarships/grants. *Loan aid offered:* Direct PLUS loans; Direct Subsidized Loans; Direct Unsubsidized Loans; State Loans. Admitted students will be notified of awards on a rolling basis beginning in early November. Federal Work-Study Program available. Institutional employment available.

The Inside Word

Around three-quarters of those who apply to Assumption are admitted; keeping in mind that the applicant pool is somewhat self-selective, average students shouldn't have a hard time getting in. Assumption uses the Common Application and submitting standardized test scores is optional. Please note that there are two exceptions. Applicants to the nursing program will have to submit scores, and international students who do not have English as a first language will need to provide English proficiency scores (recommended: TOEFL–80 (iBT), IELTS–6.5, Duolingo–1055).

THE SCHOOL SAYS "..."

From the Admissions Office

"Students flourish at Assumption University. The D'Amour College of Liberal Arts and Sciences, the Grenon School of Business, the Froelich School of Nursing, the School of Health Professions, and the School of Graduate Studies offers students many degree options, as well as dual and accelerated bachelor's/master's programs. Established in 1904 by the Augustinians of the Assumption, the University is a Catholic, liberal arts coeducational institution offering an educational experience that cultivates academic excellence and a holistic approach to the formation of the whole person. Approximately 1,700 undergraduates choose from among 35 majors and 50 minors, gaining a foundation for lifelong success. Students engage with highly credentialed faculty and staff in a community that fosters critical intelligence, thoughtful citizenship, and compassionate service. With a student/faculty ratio of just 11:1, Assumption's professors challenge students to ask questions and "seek the truth in the company of friends." In the past six years, 92.4% of Assumption's graduates were employed, enlisted in the military, enrolled in additional education, or participated in post-graduate service opportunities.

"Assumption's beautiful 185-acre campus is situated in a residential neighborhood just minutes from thriving downtown Worcester, Massachusetts. The campus is lively seven days a week with academic programming, activities sponsored by more than 60 student clubs and organizations, community service opportunities, campus ministry programs; and intercollegiate, intramural, and club sports. The University's campus in Rome, Italy, a ranked Top 10 study abroad program in America, utilizes the city as the classroom and enriches students' academic and cultural pursuits."

SELECTIVITY

Admissions Rating	83
# of applicants	4,035
% of applicants accepted	82
% of acceptees attending	11
# offered a place on the wait list	47
% accepting a place on wait list	23
% admitted from wait list	0
# of early decision applicants	36
% accepted early decision	100

FIRST-YEAR PROFILE

Testing policy	Test Optional
Average HS GPA	3.5
% frosh submitting high school GPA	94
% graduated top 10% of class	39
% graduated top 25% of class	36
% graduated top 50% of class	74

DEADLINES

Early decision	
Deadline	11/15
Notification	12/1
Early action	
Deadline	11/15
Notification	12/15
Other EA Deadline	12/15
Other EA Notification	2/15
Regular	
Deadline	3/15
Notification	3/1
Nonfall registration?	Yes

FINANCIAL FACTS

Financial Aid Rating	85
Annual tuition	$48,552
Room and board	$15,146
Required fees	$920
Books and supplies	$1,000
Average frosh need-based scholarship	$30,611
Average UG need-based scholarship	$29,916
% needy frosh rec. need-based scholarship or grant aid	100
% needy UG rec. need-based scholarship or grant aid	100
% needy frosh rec. non-need-based scholarship or grant aid	35
% needy UG rec. non-need-based scholarship or grant aid	27
% needy frosh rec. need-based self-help aid	68
% needy UG rec. need-based self-help aid	74
% frosh rec. any financial aid	99
% UG rec. any financial aid	99
% UG borrow to pay for school	90
Average cumulative indebtedness	$36,015
% frosh need fully met	37
% ugrads need fully met	33
Average % of frosh need met	83
Average % of ugrad need met	81

AUBURN UNIVERSITY

The Quad Center, Auburn, AL 36849-1111 • Admissions: 334-844-4000 • Fax: 334-844-6436

CAMPUS LIFE

Quality of Life Rating	95
Fire Safety Rating	94
Green Rating	91
Type of school	Public
Environment	Town

STUDENTS

Total undergrad enrollment	24,782
% male/female/another gender	50/50/NR
% from out of state	40
% frosh from public high school	86
% frosh live on campus	62
% ugrads live on campus	18
# of fraternities (% join)	21 (25)
# of sororities (% join)	29 (47)
% African American	5
% Asian	2
% White	82
% Hispanic	4
% Native American	<1
% Pacific Islander	<1
% Two or more races	3
% Race and/or ethnicity unknown	1
% international	4
# of countries represented	58

SURVEY SAYS . . .

Lots of conservative students
Students are happy
Great library
Internships are widely available
School is well run
Students are friendly
Students are very religious
Students get along with local community
Students love Auburn, AL
Recreation facilities are great
Everyone loves the Tigers
Intramural sports are popular
Frats and sororities are popular

ACADEMICS

Academic Rating	79
% students returning for sophomore year	93
% students graduating within 4 years	55
% students graduating within 6 years	81
Calendar	Semester
Student/faculty ratio	20:1
Profs interesting rating	86
Profs accessible rating	92

Most classes have 20–29 students.
Most lab/discussion sessions have
20–29 students.

MOST POPULAR MAJORS

Mechanical Engineering; Business Administration
and Management, General; Registered Nursing/
Registered Nurse

STUDENTS SAY "..."

Academics

Located in the heart of Alabama, Auburn University is called home by more than 20,000 undergraduates, making it one of the state's largest universities. Established before the Civil War, the school's environment is "challenging, captivating, unique and yet still timeless," and students say the university "provides you plenty of resources and opportunities to get a top-notch education." The school channels its efforts into developing young professionals through a "nurturing education, extracurricular involvement opportunities, and professional skill development." Classes may not be easy, "but the work pays off." Professors here are "approachable," "go out of their way to help you learn if you ask them," and "bring material to life." As one student puts it, "My professors...make it clear that they are here to teach me." While a few professors are described as difficult to follow or more focused on research than on teaching, "graduate student assistants are helpful in assisting professors in understanding how to make material more exciting to learn." Along with "excellent diversity in courses/majors," students say that Auburn provides solid academic support and a faculty that is "always very intelligent on the subjects at hand." The science and the "very challenging engineering programs" benefit from updated facilities and classrooms (though some say that liberal arts programs "get less attention") with the added bonus of "many internship/co-op opportunities advertised and available." As one contented student puts it, "I believe I have received a wonderful education."

Campus Life

This "welcoming place" has "an Old South small town feeling," beautiful campus, and an "amazing new recreation center," where students can work out. There are more than 300 organizations for students to join, and "student involvement is high." Greek life is big here, but "it's definitely possible to fit in without being a part of Greek life." The city of Auburn "has a safe downtown area where students can go to bars" on weekends, and there is a nearby state park where people go for fun. There's also a "good food atmosphere in the community," and Birmingham and Atlanta are always doable options for travel and concerts. Sports "drive a ton of campus life and help unite the student body." This is as true for spectators—"Football Saturdays at Auburn are second to none"—as it is for athletes: "I was looking for a large school with an SEC football team but also a good academic program." The student voice is also "very respected" among the administration and "can cause tangible change": the Student Government Association "is very strong at Auburn."

Student Body

Many here are "white," "Republican," and "tend to be conservative." The typical student is "friendly," an Alabama native, and "someone who would say 'hello' walking along the concourse to class" or "would lend a hand in a time of need." As students put it, "there is so much school spirit" here and almost everyone is "highly obsessed with football," which makes it easy to connect. "Alabama students love Alabama football; Auburn students love Auburn," says one student of the communal loyalty in which one can rest assured that "the Auburn Family has your back."

AUBURN UNIVERSITY

Financial Aid: 334-844-4634 • E-Mail: admissions@auburn.edu • Website: www.auburn.edu

THE PRINCETON REVIEW SAYS

Admissions

The school reports that its standardized testing policy for use in admission for Fall 2024 is Test Flexible. It is unknown at this time if the 2024 testing policy will be permanent. The Princeton Review suggests that interested applicants consult with the school for the most up-to-date standardized testing policies. *Very important factors considered include:* academic GPA, standardized test scores. *Important factors considered include:* rigor of secondary school record, extracurricular activities, talent/ability, character/personal qualities, first generation, alumni/ae relation, geographical residence, state residency, volunteer work, work experience, level of applicant's interest. *Other factors considered include:* High school diploma is required and GED is accepted. *Academic units required:* 4 English, 3 math, 2 science, 1 science lab, 3 social studies. *Academic units recommended:* 2 science labs, 1 foreign language, 4 social studies.

Financial Aid

Students should submit: FAFSA. Priority filing deadline is 2/1. The Princeton Review suggests that all financial aid forms be submitted as soon as possible (see page 5 for a note on the FAFSA). *Need-based scholarships/grants offered:* College/university scholarship or grant aid from institutional funds; Federal Pell; Private scholarships; SEOG; State scholarships/grants. *Loan aid offered:* Direct PLUS loans; Direct Subsidized Loans; Direct Unsubsidized Loans; College/university loans from institutional funds; Federal Nursing Loans. Admitted students will be notified of awards on a rolling basis beginning 10/1. Federal Work-Study Program available. Institutional employment available.

The Inside Word

Auburn admissions officers have nearly 21,000 applications to sort through each year, and admission here is somewhat selective. Applicants are evaluated as individuals, and those who fall short of the average GPA, curricular, and standardized test score standards for incoming freshmen should know that the admissions committee is also looking for those with unique talents and abilities that will contribute substantially to campus life. Letters of recommendation, essays, and extracurricular activities are the make-or-break point for borderline candidates. Applicants' test scores must be submitted directly from the testing agencies.

THE SCHOOL SAYS "..."

From the Admissions Office

"Auburn University is a comprehensive land, sea, and space-grant university serving Alabama and the nation. The university is especially charged with the responsibility of enhancing the economic, social, and cultural development of the state through its instruction, research, and extension programs. In all of these programs, the university is committed to the pursuit of excellence. The university assumes an obligation to provide an environment of learning in which the individual and society are enriched by the discovery, preservation, transmission, and application of knowledge; in which students grow intellectually as they study and do research under the guidance of competent faculty; and in which the faculty develop professionally and contribute fully to the intellectual life of the institution, community, and state. This obligation unites Auburn University's continuing commitment to its land-grant traditions and the institution's role as a dynamic and complex, comprehensive university."

SELECTIVITY

Admissions Rating	87
# of applicants	27,619
% of applicants accepted	71
% of acceptees attending	27

FIRST-YEAR PROFILE

Testing policy	Test Flexible
Range SAT composite	1180–1330
Range SAT EBRW	590–670
Range SAT math	580–680
Range ACT composite	24–30
# submitting SAT scores	717
% submitting SAT scores	14
# submitting ACT scores	3,988
% submitting ACT scores	75
Average HS GPA	4.0
% frosh submitting high school GPA	100
% graduated top 10% of class	31
% graduated top 25% of class	62
% graduated top 50% of class	90

DEADLINES

Early action	
Deadline	12/1
Notification	1/15
Regular	
Priority	12/1
Deadline	2/1
Nonfall registration?	Yes

APPLICANTS SOMETIMES PREFER

Clemson University; Georgia Institute of Technology; The University of Alabama—Tuscaloosa; University of Florida; University of Georgia; University of Tennessee—Knoxville

FINANCIAL FACTS

Financial Aid Rating	78
Annual in-state tuition	$10,080
Annual out-of-state tuition	$30,240
Room and board	$14,596
Required fees	$1,746
Books and supplies	$1,200
Average frosh need-based scholarship	$9,807
Average UG need-based scholarship	$8,690
% needy frosh rec. need-based scholarship or grant aid	85
% needy UG rec. need-based scholarship or grant aid	75
% needy frosh rec. non-need-based scholarship or grant aid	19
% needy UG rec. non-need-based scholarship or grant aid	13
% needy frosh rec. need-based self-help aid	58
% needy UG rec. need-based self-help aid	72
% frosh rec. any financial aid	51
% UG rec. any financial aid	45
% UG borrow to pay for school	40
Average cumulative indebtedness	$30,857
% frosh need fully met	20
% ugrads need fully met	14
Average % of frosh need met	53
Average % of ugrad need met	45

AUSTIN COLLEGE

900 N. Grand Avenue, Sherman, TX 75090 • Admissions: 903-813-2000 • Fax: 903-813-3198

STUDENTS SAY "..."

Academics

"Individual attention" is the name of the game at Austin College. Indeed, the small size of the school allows for a lot of "one-on-one interaction" and provides students with "many opportunities to get involved on campus." Additionally, students are grateful that Austin seems to maintain a healthy financial aid office. A psychology major concurs stating, "This college was very generous in helping fund my education." Undergrads are also excited about Austin's "excellent study abroad program." As one thrilled biology major brags, "I have already traveled to Trinidad for three weeks and I am planning to study in Cuba for three weeks as well as a semester abroad in Australia." Students also rave about the college's "GREAT pre-medicine program," "strong Japanese program," and excellent five year education program. Importantly, undergrads find their professors to be "very accessible." They are generally "willing to help and give us opportunities to advance ourselves outside the classroom as well as inside the classroom." Moreover, professors are "devoted to teaching their students how to think, not memorize." Finally, they "encourage their students to engage the material and ask meaningful questions."

Campus Life

Despite its small size, Austin College is certainly a hotbed of activity. Truly, there are a myriad of clubs and events from which to choose. As one amazed senior shares, "I have played in a woodwind ensemble, done swing dancing and English country dancing, [attended] theater performances, art displays, choir, band and symphony concerts." She continues gushing, "There [have even been] mini carnivals with rock walls, live music, food, and inflatable race courses." And undergrads here are quick to tip their (metaphorical) hats to the Campus Activities Board (CAB), which "[throws] events almost every day." These might include "making wax hands...[and] pumpkin painting." Additionally, "CAB also hosts bigger events such as Kangapalooza where the college brings in three bands to play for the student body." While there are plenty of school events, a handful of students feel that "house parties sponsored by Greek groups are usually what encompass social life at Austin." Some students itching to get off campus are dismayed by hometown Sherman, which doesn't seem to offer much beyond "Target and a few book stores." However, others insist there is more than meets the eye. As an optimistic international relations major sums up, "At first, Sherman seemed really small to a big city girl like me. But it really grows on you and now I love it! There are lots of great little hole-in-the-wall restaurants with awesome food. And if you need some city time, Dallas is about an hour away!"

Student Body

Undergrads here emphatically insist that "there is no typical student at AC." As one biology major explains, "Personalities range from frat-tastic jock to the gothic president of the English Country Dancing club." Fortunately, most everyone is "very welcoming." Indeed, "the environment here is so warm and friendly that the students easily fit in." Nevertheless, despite the reported uniqueness of the student body, there are some commonalities to be found. For starters, most undergrads here are "motivated in their studies" as well as "engaged in other extracurricular activities." Many students also describe their peers as "laid back," "pretty liberal," and "open minded." Of course, Austin does net "a lot of local Texas kids." However, there are definitely "some foreign students thrown in [there]" and students appreciate the diversity they bring to campus. And if you're still wary, this junior is moved to assuage your fears: "After coming to campus it doesn't take long to realize that even though most of us call Texas home, we are in no way defined by the Texas stereotype. Don't be deceived; the differences in socio-economic status, religion, political beliefs, and general perspective on life could not be more varied."

AUSTIN COLLEGE

Financial Aid: 903-813-2900 • E-Mail: admission@austincollege.edu • Website: www.austincollege.edu

THE PRINCETON REVIEW SAYS

Admissions

The school reports that its standardized testing policy for use in admission for Fall 2024 is Test Optional. The 2024 testing policy will be permanent. The Princeton Review suggests that interested applicants consult with the school for the most up-to-date standardized testing policies. *Very important factors considered include:* rigor of secondary school record, academic GPA, application essay. *Other factors considered include:* class rank, standardized test scores, recommendation(s), interview, extracurricular activities, talent/ability, character/personal qualities, first generation, alumni/ae relation, volunteer work, work experience, level of applicant's interest. High school diploma is required and GED is accepted. *Academic units required:* 4 English, 3 math, 3 science, 1 science lab, 2 foreign language, 2 social studies, 1 visual/performing arts. *Academic units recommended:* 4 English, 4 math, 4 science, 2 science labs, 2 foreign language, 4 social studies, 2 visual/performing arts.

Financial Aid

Students should submit: FAFSA. Priority filing deadline is 3/1. The Princeton Review suggests that all financial aid forms be submitted as soon as possible (see page 5 for a note on the FAFSA). *Need-based scholarships/grants offered:* College/university scholarship or grant aid from institutional funds; Federal Pell; Private scholarships; SEOG; State scholarships/grants. *Loan aid offered:* Direct PLUS loans; Direct Subsidized Loans; Direct Unsubsidized Loans; State Loans. Admitted students will be notified of awards on a rolling basis beginning 12/1. Federal Work-Study Program available. Institutional employment available.

The Inside Word

Austin College takes a holistic approach to the admissions game. Indeed, the school does its best to get a feel for who each applicant is beyond his or her GPA and test scores. Therefore, expect your recommendations, extracurricular activities, and essay to be heavily vetted. Additionally, the college is impressed with students who challenge themselves academically. Admissions officers are frequently more impressed with a B in an honors course than an A in a standard class.

THE SCHOOL SAYS "..."

From the Admissions Office

"If you want to be anonymous, choose a different school. But if you dream of connecting with others, exploring the world, and discovering more about yourself, then Austin College is exactly where you belong.

"Learning happens in classroom discussions led by talented professors, dedicated to teaching and passionate about their work, who act as partners in education with students. Faculty and students often work together in research projects and learning opportunities in which sometimes the answers discovered aren't as important as the process of inquiry and discovery.

"Students come to Austin College for exceptional academic offerings in more than 57 areas of study in the humanities, sciences, and social sciences. Over the past five years, 82 percent of graduates completed an internship as career preparation. 94 percent of our graduates are attending graduate or professional school or are employed within a year of graduation. The highest number of students enroll in medical and law schools. Many graduates receive prestigious honors like Fulbright grants or Teach for America positions."

From Deposit to Your Graduation in Four Years: Our Commitment to Your Success Is Guaranteed.

"We are confident in our academic programs and personalized mentoring; we promise that any full-time student who meets the Finish in Four Guarantee requirements in effect at the time of their enrollment will graduate in four calendar years. And, if you don't, Austin College will waive tuition costs for any courses you need to complete your degree. Guaranteed."

SELECTIVITY

Admissions Rating	89
# of applicants	5,129
% of applicants accepted	55
% of acceptees attending	12
# offered a place on the wait list	0

FIRST-YEAR PROFILE

Testing policy	Test Optional
Range SAT composite	1120–1365
Range SAT EBRW	570–690
Range SAT math	560–670
Range ACT composite	23–29
# submitting SAT scores	99
% submitting SAT scores	30
# submitting ACT scores	49
% submitting ACT scores	15
Average HS GPA	3.6
% frosh submitting high school GPA	98
% graduated top 10% of class	23
% graduated top 25% of class	27
% graduated top 50% of class	83

DEADLINES

Early decision	
Deadline	11/1
Notification	12/4
Early action	
Deadline	12/1
Notification	1/15
Regular	
Priority	3/1
Deadline	7/31
Nonfall registration?	No

APPLICANTS SOMETIMES PREFER

Baylor University; Southwestern University; Texas A&M University—College Station; Texas Christian University

APPLICANTS RARELY PREFER

Hendrix College; Trinity University; University of Dallas

FINANCIAL FACTS

Financial Aid Rating	88
Annual tuition	$46,290
Room and board	$13,494
Required fees	$185
Required fees (first-year)	$210
Books and supplies	$1,250
Average frosh need-based scholarship	$35,312
Average UG need-based scholarship	$34,022
% needy frosh rec. need-based scholarship or grant aid	100
% needy UG rec. need-based scholarship or grant aid	100
% needy frosh rec. non-need-based scholarship or grant aid	25
% needy UG rec. non-need-based scholarship or grant aid	22
% needy frosh rec. need-based self-help aid	60
% needy UG rec. need-based self-help aid	66
% frosh rec. any financial aid	100
% UG rec. any financial aid	99
% UG borrow to pay for school	60
Average cumulative indebtedness	$32,178
% frosh need fully met	43
% ugrads need fully met	42
Average % of frosh need met	89
Average % of ugrad need met	89

BABSON COLLEGE

231 Forest Street, Babson Park, MA 02457 • Admissions: 781-235-1200 • Fax: 781-239-4006

STUDENTS SAY ". . ."

Academics

Babson College is a small private business school in the Boston area renowned for its entrepreneurial focus. As one student claims, "The academics here are second to none if you are interested in business." Founded in 1919 by a Massachusetts economist to provide practical business training for aspiring executives, Babson now offers a Bachelor of Science in business administration with a strong foundation in liberal arts and sciences and over 20 concentrations to choose from, ranging from traditional areas such as finance to modern ones like environmental sustainability. "Babson is incredibly focused on business curriculum, meaning that your general education requirements have a business backdrop." One of the most popular courses at Babson, and one of the school's major draws, is the Foundations of Management and Entrepreneurship program in which professors help first-year students start their own businesses. "Babson allows students to explore their passions, to take up leadership roles, and to be creative…I'm impressed by the freedom students are given to come up with their own business ideas and to pursue their future careers." Babson students speak highly of their professors and value their practical skills, business acumen, and proven success stories as much as their teaching ability. "Professors are entrepreneurs and business professionals with real-world experience. Teaching is not just theory but theory that is matched with application at every single point." Most students praise their professors' enthusiasm and dedication to teaching as well, with many citing a mentor's guidance as indispensable to their achievements. "The professors and academics really help teach a mindset that will help Babson students succeed in leadership."

Life

Babson students consider the wide array of clubs, teams, and structured social groups available on campus to be one of the school's great strengths. Many note that the administration encourages extracurricular pursuits, not only by offering over a hundred student organizations of various types, but also by providing liberal funding for their creation. "I am a part of many extracurriculars at college, from Student Government to Greek Life. I like everything I am a part of, and I like that I am able to diversify my involvement." Choices range from sports teams such as baseball, equestrian, and figure-skating, to marketing and finance groups, to charitable endeavors such as Habitat for Humanity, and particular interests such as theater, chess, and cooking. "Class schedules are very lenient and flexible, so students fill their days with as many extracurricular and career development activities as possible." In addition to the high level of activity on campus, many students also reap the benefits of living in the Boston area. Many routinely spend their weekends browsing the unique shops on historic Newbury Street, taking in an exhibit at the world-famous Museum of Fine Arts, or even cheering a Red Sox game at Boston's famous Fenway Park.

Student Body

The Babson community, while made up of individuals from many countries and very different backgrounds, is frequently described as tight-knit. "The greatest strength is the size of the school. Because it is relatively small, there is a stronger sense of community and it's a lot easier to make friends." As one student explains: "We play together and get along well." Babson students are almost invariably described as being very serious about their academic work and career ambitions. "Students at Babson College are incredibly motivated and visionary individuals. They tend to be confident in who they are, and are determined to achieve whatever life goal they've set." As another observes, "Babson's student body has the smarts of Ivy League students combined with an entrepreneurial mindset unlike most of other top schools." Many note that a good percentage of Babson students come from families that are financially successful and established in the business world, which some believe provides invaluable networking opportunities. "The student body at Babson College is full of ambitious and competitive people. However, there is also a strong sense of community and people love to help others succeed."

BABSON COLLEGE

Financial Aid: 781-239-4219 • E-Mail: ugradadmission@babson.edu • Website: www.babson.edu

THE PRINCETON REVIEW SAYS

Admissions

The school reports that its standardized testing policy for use in admission for Fall 2024 is Test Optional. The 2024 testing policy will be temporary. The Princeton Review suggests that interested applicants consult with the school for the most up-to-date standardized testing policies. *Very important factors considered include:* rigor of secondary school record, class rank, academic GPA, standardized test scores, application essay, recommendation(s), extracurricular activities, character/personal qualities. *Other factors considered include:* interview, talent/ability, first generation, alumni/ae relation, geographical residence, state residency, racial/ethnic status, volunteer work, work experience, level of applicant's interest. High school diploma is required and GED is accepted. *Academic units required:* 4 English, 4 math, 3 science, 4 social studies. *Academic units recommended:* 4 foreign language.

Financial Aid

Students should submit: CSS/Financial Aid Profile; FAFSA; Noncustodial Profile. Priority filing deadline is 2/1. The Princeton Review suggests that all financial aid forms be submitted as soon as possible after October 1. *Need-based scholarships/grants offered:* College/university scholarship or grant aid from institutional funds; Federal Pell; Private scholarships; SEOG; State scholarships/grants. *Loan aid offered:* Direct PLUS loans; Direct Subsidized Loans; Direct Unsubsidized Loans; State Loans. Admitted students will be notified of awards on or about 4/1. Federal Work-Study Program available. Institutional employment available.

The Inside Word

Babson's prominence as a noteworthy undergraduate business school continues to rise. Incoming students are evaluated on their academic performance (high school GPAs and standardized test scores) as well as nonacademic factors including leadership, involvement, and enthusiasm. Writing ability is a valued commodity, and prospective students should be ready for the supplemental writing section of the application. Besides Regular Decision application, Babson offers three fall application plans for first-years—Early Decision I, Early Decision II, and Early Action—in addition to January G.A.P. Enrollment, which allows students to apply for the spring semester.

THE SCHOOL SAYS "..."

From the Admissions Office

"Nationally recognized as the number one school in entrepreneurship for 24 years, Babson College is the premier institution for entrepreneurship education. Through our entrepreneurial thought and action methodology, we teach all of our students to think and act entrepreneurially to pursue their passions and create a path to success, no matter where that path might lead. As a result, Babson graduates are entrepreneurs of all kinds: startup founders, business leaders, corporate innovators, social changemakers, and so much more.

"Our immersive, hands-on curriculum provides students with the ability to adapt to ever-changing business environments, the experience to hit the ground running upon graduation, and the know-how to discover opportunities that will create economic and social value everywhere. With liberal arts and sciences blended with business courses, Babson emphasizes creativity, innovation, and risk-taking as essential to learning the foundation of business.

"Babson's tight-knit community provides students with the opportunity to form close relationships with faculty and staff. An average class has twenty to twenty-nine students and a student/faculty ratio of 16:1 allows faculty to serve as role models and mentors committed to helping our students grow. With about 87 percent holding a doctoral degree, these accomplished business executives, authors, entrepreneurs, scholars, researchers, and artists bring intellectual diversity and real-world experiences that add depth to Babson's programs. Most importantly, faculty members teach 100 percent of the courses.

"At Babson, students receive a world-class education that is innovative and creative, yet practical. They study business, learn about leadership, and undertake a transformative life experience preparing them to create an authentic, powerful brand of success. Our students make friends, find mentors, and develop long-lasting relationships that will thrive long after graduation."

SELECTIVITY

Admissions Rating	96
# of applicants	7,607
% of applicants accepted	22
% of acceptees attending	39
# offered a place on the wait list	2,699
% accepting a place on wait list	48
% admitted from wait list	0
# of early decision applicants	770
% accepted early decision	39

FRESHMAN PROFILE

Testing policy	Test Optional
Range SAT composite	1270–1480
Range SAT EBRW	660–730
Range SAT math	690–780
Range ACT composite	30–33
# submitting SAT scores	212
% submitting SAT scores	32
# submitting ACT scores	52
% submitting ACT scores	8

DEADLINES

Early decision	
Deadline	11/1
Notification	12/15
Other ED deadline	1/2
Other ED notification	2/15
Early action	
Deadline	11/1
Notification	1/1
Regular	
Priority	11/1
Deadline	1/2
Notification	4/1
Nonfall registration?	Yes

APPLICANTS ALSO LOOK AT

Bentley University; Boston College; Boston University; New York University; Northeastern University

FINANCIAL FACTS

Financial Aid Rating	94
Annual tuition	$56,032
Room and board	$19,732
Required fees	$0
Books and supplies	$1,292
Average frosh need-based scholarship	$42,635
Average UG need-based scholarship	$46,062
% needy frosh rec. need-based scholarship or grant aid	91
% needy UG rec. need-based scholarship or grant aid	96
% needy frosh rec. non-need-based scholarship or grant aid	10
% needy UG rec. non-need-based scholarship or grant aid	10
% needy frosh rec. need-based self-help aid	88
% needy UG rec. need-based self-help aid	82
% frosh rec. any financial aid	39
% UG rec. any financial aid	41
% UG borrow to pay for school	37
Average cumulative indebtedness	$39,255
% frosh need fully met	100
% ugrads need fully met	94
Average % of frosh need met	100
Average % of ugrad need met	96

BARD COLLEGE

PO Box 5000, Annandale-on-Hudson, NY 12504 • Admissions: 845-758-6822 • Fax: 845-758-5208

CAMPUS LIFE

Quality of Life Rating	78
Fire Safety Rating	97
Green Rating	92
Type of school	Private
Affiliation	No Affiliation
Environment	Rural

STUDENTS

Total undergrad enrollment	1,804
% male/female/another gender	41/59/0
% from out of state	66
% frosh from public high school	58
% frosh live on campus	99
% ugrads live on campus	75
# of fraternities	0
# of sororities	0
% African American	6
% Asian	4
% White	57
% Hispanic	10
% Native American	<1
% Pacific Islander	0
% Two or more races	5
% Race and/or ethnicity unknown	6
% international	11
# of countries represented	57

SURVEY SAYS . . .

Lots of liberal students
Lab facilities are great
Class discussions encouraged
Students aren't religious
Students environmentally aware
Theater is popular
Active student government
Active minority support groups
Active student-run political groups

ACADEMICS

Academic Rating	90
% students returning for sophomore year	85
% students graduating within 4 years	62
% students graduating within 6 years	74
Calendar	Semester
Student/faculty ratio	10:1
Profs interesting rating	94
Profs accessible rating	96

Most classes have 10–19 students.

MOST POPULAR MAJORS

English Language and Literature, General; Visual and Performing Arts, General; Social Sciences, General

STUDENTS SAY ". . ."

Academics

Bard College is "built on a very unique philosophy of the liberal arts," one that "truly values education for the sake of self-growth." To that end, every student's academic "experience is entirely customizable." Nevertheless, no matter their course load, all undergrads here are taught to think "critically, [to continually ask] questions...and [to follow through on] those questions." But these students wouldn't have it any other way! Certainly, prospective students should take note—the academics here are quite "rigorous." And virtually every major culminates in a massive "senior project" that requires "substantial independent work."

Inside the classroom, students are greeted by "incredible" professors who genuinely "care about teaching and mentoring." They are also "strong researchers as well" and make a concerted effort to "bring their research into [their classes] and into the community." They truly look to "involve students in almost everything they do." As one photography major boasts, "The classes are what make Bard an amazing school. I could not be happier academically."

Campus Life

Though this is a small campus in a small town, there is no lack of engaging activity. For starters, the college itself sponsors "a multitude of cultural events, from having Edward Snowden speak [remotely]...to great bands playing at one of our venues." Bard also has a thriving performing arts scene. "There's probably a student production to see on average every other week or more. Students, [even] as non-majors, can easily produce their own shows. Plus, we have the Fisher Center, a Broadway-sized theatre that often hosts operas, dance troupes, and plays." Undergrads who tend to be more of the outdoorsy type will be thrilled to discover that "Bard is also surrounded by hiking trails, with easy access to our own private waterfall!" Of course, during those cold winter nights, "'Netflix and chill' is a reliable option." Even in inclement weather, "it's generally pretty easy to find people to go build snowmen with or go ice skating." Lastly, for those curious, Bard maintains a "very low-key party scene." A history major further explains, "Most of the larger parties happen at off-campus houses in Red Hook or Tivoli, the two surrounding towns where many students live. It can get repetitive, but I enjoy how you end up seeing/partying with similar people every weekend."

Student Body

When asked to describe their peers, undergrads here are quick to note that their fellow students are "unique, free-spirited, deviant, and epitomize critical thinking." Indeed, the average Bard student loves "intellectual conversations and enjoy[s] rehashing...topics [discussed in class]." An anthropology major further expounds, "We are always critiquing some aspect of the school, then relating this critique to one of the larger societal structures that we live in." Therefore, it's none too surprising when a sociology major tells us that "Bardians are [also] go-getters, self-motivated, driven, and thoughtful. We challenge authority and all social conventions." We've also been assured that "there isn't much competition between students when it comes to grades or classes. People are just supportive of the projects their peers are working on." Many undergrads here readily admit that they "felt in some way like outsiders in high school." Fortunately, once they arrive at Bard, "a lot of people seem to bond over their weirdness." Perhaps this supremely satisfied student puts it best, "I have been spoiled by my friendships here at Bard; I don't know where else I could find people this interesting and relationships this fulfilling."

BARD COLLEGE

Financial Aid: 845-758-7526 • E-Mail: admissions@bard.edu • Website: www.bard.edu

THE PRINCETON REVIEW SAYS

Admissions

The school reports that its standardized testing policy for use in admission for Fall 2024 is Test Optional. It is unknown at this time if the 2024 testing policy will be permanent. The Princeton Review suggests that interested applicants consult with the school for the most up-to-date standardized testing policies. *Very important factors considered include:* rigor of secondary school record, academic GPA, application essay, recommendation(s), extra-curricular activities, talent/ability, character/personal qualities. *Important factors considered include:* volunteer work, work experience. *Other factors considered include:* class rank, stan-dardized test scores, interview, first generation, alumni/ae relation, geographical residence, state residency, religious affiliation/commitment, racial/ethnic status, level of applicant's interest. High school diploma is required and GED is accepted. *Academic units recom-mended:* 4 English, 4 math, 4 science, 3 science labs, 4 foreign language, 4 social studies, 4 history.

Financial Aid

Students should submit: CSS/Financial Aid Profile; FAFSA; Noncustodial Profile. The Princeton Review suggests that all financial aid forms be submitted as soon as possible (see page 5 for a note on the FAFSA). *Need-based scholarships/grants offered:* College/university scholarship or grant aid from institutional funds; Federal Pell; Private scholarships; SEOG; State scholarships/grants. *Loan aid offered:* Direct PLUS loans; Direct Subsidized Loans; Direct Unsubsidized Loans. Admitted students will be notified of awards on or about 3/20. Federal Work-Study Program available. Institutional employment available.

The Inside Word

We won't mince words; gaining admission to Bard is definitely competitive. Successful applicants tend to have high school transcripts rife with honors and advanced placement courses. And a strong college prep curriculum is clearly a must. Beyond that, admissions officers want students who appear to be independent thinkers with a thirst for knowledge. After all, those are the type of individuals who will likely take advantage of all Bard has to offer. Lastly, submitting ACT or SAT scores is optional.

THE SCHOOL SAYS "..."

From the Admissions Office

"An alliance with Rockefeller University, the renowned graduate scientific research institu-tion, gives Bardians access to Rockefeller's professors and laboratories and to places in Rockefeller's Summer Research Fellows Program. Almost all our math and science gradu-ates pursue graduate or professional studies; 90 percent of our applicants to medical and health professional schools are accepted.

"The Globalization and International Affairs (BGIA) Program is a residential program in the heart of New York City that offers undergraduates a unique opportunity to undertake spe-cialized study with leading practitioners and scholars in international affairs and to gain internship experience with international-affairs organizations. Topics in the curriculum include human rights, international economics, global environmental issues, international justice, managing international risk, and writing on international affairs, among others. Internships/tutorials are tailored to students' particular fields of study.

"Civic engagement has become a large and growing part of student life at Bard, with a high percentage of students participating in a wide variety of local, national, and international programs sponsored by the college or initiated by students.

"Beyond the central campus, Bard has created global programs and satellite campuses from Berlin to the West Bank, offering students unique opportunities for study abroad and making Bard's student body strongly international."

SELECTIVITY

Admissions Rating	87
# of applicants	5,141
% of applicants accepted	65
% of acceptees attending	15
# of early decision applicants	46
% accepted early decision	89

FIRST-YEAR PROFILE

Testing policy	Test Optional
Range ACT composite	27–31
# submitting ACT scores	83
% submitting ACT scores	17
% graduated top 10% of class	41
% graduated top 25% of class	69
% graduated top 50% of class	94

DEADLINES

Early decision	
Deadline	11/1
Notification	1/1
Early action	
Deadline	11/1
Notification	1/1
Regular	
Deadline	1/1
Notification	Rolling, 4/1
Nonfall registration?	No

APPLICANTS OFTEN PREFER

Barnard College; Boston University; Columbia University; Johns Hopkins University; New York University; Northeastern University; Oberlin College; Princeton University; Reed College; Sarah Lawrence College; The University of Chicago; Tufts University; University of California—Santa Cruz

APPLICANTS SOMETIMES PREFER

Bates College; Bowdoin College; Brandeis University; Brown University; Connecticut College; Grinnell College; Haverford College; Kenyon College; Macalester College; Occidental College; Scripps College; Swarthmore College; Vassar College; Wesleyan University

APPLICANTS RARELY PREFER

Bennington College; Bryn Mawr College; Colorado College; Hampshire College; Mount Holyoke College; Rhode Island School of Design; Smith College; University of Rochester

FINANCIAL FACTS

Financial Aid Rating	83
Annual tuition	$55,566
Room and board	$15,876
Required fees	$470
Books and supplies	$1,100
Average frosh need-based scholarship	$47,022
Average UG need-based scholarship	$44,444
% needy frosh rec. need-based scholarship or grant aid	97
% needy UG rec. need-based scholarship or grant aid	96
% needy frosh rec. non-need-based scholarship or grant aid	0
% needy UG rec. non-need-based scholarship or grant aid	0
% needy frosh rec. need-based self-help aid	82
% needy UG rec. need-based self-help aid	81
% frosh rec. any financial aid	69
% UG rec. any financial aid	68
% UG borrow to pay for school	57
Average cumulative indebtedness	$27,726
% frosh need fully met	25
% ugrads need fully met	22
Average % of frosh need met	81
Average % of ugrad need met	79

BARNARD COLLEGE

3009 Broadway, New York, NY 10027 • Admissions: 212-854-5262 • Fax: 212-280-8797

STUDENTS SAY "..."

Academics

Barnard is a small school, an urban school, a resource-rich school, a school that "offers so many opportunities." In some ways, Barnard College combines all the desirable traits one would want from an all-women's liberal arts college. Located in New York City, here "you get the best of both worlds," both a "small academic setting" as well as having "full access to the Ivy League institution (Columbia University) right across the street." The school's size means it "provides a small, close community" where students will "see familiar faces often." Among those familiar faces are the professors themselves, who are "really engaging and make the material approachable and interesting." Classes are a mix between lectures and discussions, and even in the larger classes professors "definitely make time for students to come talk to them." Students say educators here are adept at "creating an environment to learn from and be inspired by classmates through the discussions held." The "phenomenal" education experience at Barnard may be "challenging and very stressful" at times, but students are "so grateful" for those challenges. And while the school itself may be small, "you can cross Broadway and feel that large, Ivy League University feel." Graduates from Barnard should expect to experience a "transition from a young female college student to an adjusted global citizen."

Campus Life

Finding things to do at Barnard? "It's easy—we live in New York." When you live in "one of the greatest cities on Earth," you are "open to a wide range of things to do such as shows, film festivals, amazing restaurants, etc." As one student puts it, while there is a thriving party scene on campus, "put down your vodka and go to the Met." Students even enjoy free admission to many such attractions. But while the opportunities for entertainment and cultural activities are limitless in a city like New York—the museums, sports venues, book stores, music venues, cultural centers, and more are too numerous to list—"a lot of fun events take place on campus." There are a number of clubs on campus, busy students often spend time "just chilling" because "everyone is working or going to office hours, or pursuing an internship, a personal job, etc.," and neighboring Columbia offers a "phenomenal Greek life" for those interested in that scene. No matter their chosen form of distraction from school work and extracurriculars, students here "are intensely dedicated to pursuing their interests, whether that be artistic, academic, pre-professional, or athletic ones."

Student Body

Finding a single trait to define a school full of "cool, creative, confident, well-spoken, and determined" women who are "aware that [they are] in the cosmopolitan NYC" may seem difficult, but the repeated refrain of students makes it clear that there is something that unites Barnard students: they are ambitious. These are "driven, intelligent" women who are "extremely interested, dedicated, and passionate about something." What that something may be varies—"biology, dance, theatre, architecture, economics, or international relations" and more—but the "strong, powerful, intelligent personalities" make them who they are. These "motivated individuals" sometimes "have a tendency to overload," but "all Barnard women are very proactive and use all resources available...to achieve their goals." That said, while students here are "ambitious, driven, and hard workers," it is "not at the cost of physical or mental health: they know how to have fun, too." Barnard women tend to be well-dressed and embrace the cosmopolitan side of New York City. One student comments, "I know of very few students here who feel they don't fit in or haven't found their niche," and maybe that is because a Barnard student is one who is "smart, independent, and ready to take on the world."

BARNARD COLLEGE

Financial Aid: 212-854-2154 • E-Mail: admissions@barnard.edu • Website: www.barnard.edu

THE PRINCETON REVIEW SAYS

Admissions

The school reports that its standardized testing policy for use in admission for Fall 2024 is Test Optional. The 2024 testing policy will be temporary. The Princeton Review suggests that interested applicants consult with the school for the most up-to-date standardized testing policies. *Very important factors considered include:* rigor of secondary school record, academic GPA, application essay, recommendation(s), character/personal qualities. *Important factors considered include:* class rank, extracurricular activities, talent/ability, volunteer work, work experience. *Other factors considered include:* standardized test scores, interview, first generation, alumni/ae relation, geographical residence, racial/ethnic status, level of applicant's interest. High school diploma is required and GED is accepted. *Academic units recommended:* 4 English, 3 math, 3 science, 3 foreign language, 3 history.

Financial Aid

Students should submit: CSS/Financial Aid Profile; FAFSA; Noncustodial Profile. The Princeton Review suggests that all financial aid forms be submitted as soon as possible (see page 5 for a note on the FAFSA). *Need-based scholarships/grants offered:* College/university scholarship or grant aid from institutional funds; Federal Pell; Private scholarships; SEOG; State scholarships/grants. *Loan aid offered:* Direct PLUS loans; Direct Subsidized Loans; Direct Unsubsidized Loans. Admitted students will be notified of awards on or about 3/31. Federal Work-Study Program available. Institutional employment available.

The Inside Word

Barnard may have a highly competitive selection process—indeed, early decision applications have increased dramatically in recent years—but you wouldn't know it based on the admissions staff, who are surprisingly open and accessible. It comes as no surprise that the admission committee's expectations are high, given the school's long and impressive tradition of excellence, but those expectations reflect a genuine interest in who potential students are and what's on their minds.

THE SCHOOL SAYS "..."

From the Admissions Office

"Barnard College is a small, distinguished liberal arts college for women that is partnered with Columbia University and located in the heart of New York City. Barnard students are wide ranging in their interests and passions, but they also share in a distinctive experience that creates an enduring bond: they live and learn in an environment where women always come first, where they're surrounded by other smart and inspiring women, and where they have access to a wide array of opportunities, both on and off campus. The Barnard community thrives on high expectations. By setting rigorous academic standards and giving students the support they need to meet those standards, Barnard enables them to discover their own capabilities.

"The college enrolls women from all over the United States and around the world. More than sixty countries, including Australia, Brazil, China, Denmark, France, India, Morocco, Russia, Turkey, and Zimbabwe are represented in the student body. Students pursue their academic studies in more than forty majors, are able to cross register at Columbia University, and have access to several combined 4+1 BA/MA programs at Columbia. Students may participate in Division I Varsity Columbia University athletic teams, in more than thirty club sports, and in a wide variety of intramural sports, and have access to over 500 student clubs and organizations at Barnard and Columbia."

SELECTIVITY

Admissions Rating	97
# of applicants	9,411
% of applicants accepted	14
% of acceptees attending	54
# offered a place on the wait list	2,096
# of early decision applicants	1,234
% accepted early decision	26

FIRST-YEAR PROFILE

Testing policy	Test Optional
Range SAT composite	1370–1500
Range SAT EBRW	680–748
Range SAT math	670–770
Range ACT composite	31–34
# submitting SAT scores	426
% submitting SAT scores	62
# submitting ACT scores	318
% submitting ACT scores	46
% graduated top 10% of class	90
% graduated top 25% of class	98
% graduated top 50% of class	100

DEADLINES

Early decision	
Deadline	11/1
Notification	12/15
Regular	
Deadline	1/1
Notification	4/1
Nonfall registration?	No

APPLICANTS ALSO LOOK AT

Boston University; Brown University; Columbia University; Cornell University; New York University; Northwestern University; Princeton University; The University of Chicago; Wellesley College; Wesleyan University

FINANCIAL FACTS

Financial Aid Rating	95
Annual tuition	$55,781
Room and board	$15,692
Required fees	$1,698
Books and supplies	$1,150
Average frosh need-based scholarship	$47,288
Average UG need-based scholarship	$46,836
% needy frosh rec. need-based scholarship or grant aid	89
% needy UG rec. need-based scholarship or grant aid	92
% needy frosh rec. non-need-based scholarship or grant aid	0
% needy UG rec. non-need-based scholarship or grant aid	0
% needy frosh rec. need-based self-help aid	80
% needy UG rec. need-based self-help aid	88
% UG rec. any financial aid	47
% UG borrow to pay for school	33
Average cumulative indebtedness	$24,438
% frosh need fully met	96
% ugrads need fully met	98
Average % of frosh need met	100
Average % of ugrad need met	100

BATES COLLEGE

2 Andrews Road, Lewiston, ME 04240 • Admissions: 207-786-6255 • Fax: 207-786-6025

STUDENTS SAY "..."

Academics

Located in Lewiston, Maine, Bates College is a small liberal arts college that invites intellectual exploration and tailors every education to the individual student. This "unbelievably tight-knit community" thrives on an "everyone is welcome" atmosphere and an open classroom environment in which everyone is "challenged to express their opinions, try something new and stand up for a cause." "I've honestly never felt competitive in a class at Bates," says a student. Between academic studies, extracurriculars, volunteering, and employment, students here are known for being "well-rounded, curious, and supportive of all aspects of Bates life." Classes are small here which means that students can really take advantage of their professors' time and attention. The "dynamic" teachers here "make you think and come up with your own opinion about issues." They are "incredibly passionate people who are not afraid to stand on a desk, play devil's advocate, and urge you to think critically about the material you are learning." "The most important thing I've learned so far is how to come up with an intelligent stance on an issue or idea," says a student. A Short Term at the end of the year allows students to explore one subject in depth, and the "flexible calendar" also encourages studying abroad (which the majority of students do). The extensive and "helpful" alumni network demonstrates "a fundamental love for the school," and students are given plenty of additional support through "advising and residential life staff, student leadership opportunities, [and] fun and engaging school-wide traditions." "I couldn't ask for more helpful professors, a more helpful administration, or a variety of classes that suit the needs and requirements of my major," sums up a student.

Campus Life

Bates students are a busy group, but they also appreciate the weekends and having fun with friends. There are "dances, theater productions, and a multitude of other events to go to any day of the week"; students also "really enjoy eating out and going to on-campus events like Wind Down Wednesdays," hosted by various student groups," and "the Village Club Series on Thursdays" when musical groups and performers play for campus. Students say that the Bates security plus a "pretty strict no-hard-alcohol policy" is "quite effective" at restricting underage alcohol consumption as well as maintaining a safe campus environment. The food and dining are "absolutely amazing at Bates": fare here is "all extremely healthy, organic, and naturally sourced," plus "there's food for every dietary restriction." Opportunities to serve the community surrounding campus are abundant, and students take advantage of the outdoor activities Maine has to offer. The student-run Outing Club, in particular, "hosts events every weekend, from skiing at our nearby mountains to sunrise paddles to backpacking trips" and "has a room full of gear that's free to check out." The nights start early and end early here, mostly because "students want to get up early the next day to ski, hike, or just do something with their day." With Portland and Boston being so close, "you can always switch up your scenery when you need city life."

Student Body

Bates students have a range of interests and passions—"no student does just one thing"—and "are not a judgmental group." Everyone finds their niche, and there "is a ton of crossover and interaction between different people." In order to "fit in" here, a student "just has to be friendly and willing to make new friends." A normal lunch conversation "will span from the divine cheese quesadillas in Commons to the implications of language-use and its impact on creating a culture of apathy and ableism." Many here are New Englanders, so there are a fair number of "really preppy" students, and everyone "enjoys the great outdoors."

BATES COLLEGE

Financial Aid: 207-786-6096 • E-Mail: admission@bates.edu • Website: www.bates.edu

THE PRINCETON REVIEW SAYS

Admissions

Bates College has been Test Optional since 1984. *Very important factors considered include:* rigor of secondary school record, class rank, academic GPA, application essay, recommendation(s), extracurricular activities, talent/ability, character/personal qualities. *Important factors considered include:* first generation, geographical residence, state residency, level of applicant's interest. *Other factors considered include:* standardized test scores, interview, alumni/ae relation, racial/ethnic status, volunteer work, work experience. High school diploma is required and GED is not accepted. *Academic units required:* 4 English, 3 math, 3 science, 2 science labs, 2 foreign language, 3 social studies, 3 history. *Academic units recommended:* 4 English, 4 math, 4 science, 3 science labs, 4 foreign language, 4 social studies, 4 history.

Financial Aid

Students should submit: CSS/Financial Aid Profile; FAFSA; Noncustodial Profile. The Princeton Review suggests that all financial aid forms be submitted as soon as possible (see page 5 for a note on the FAFSA). *Need-based scholarships/grants offered:* Federal Pell; Private scholarships; SEOG; State scholarships/grants. *Loan aid offered:* Direct PLUS loans; Direct Subsidized Loans; Direct Unsubsidized Loans. Admitted students will be notified of awards on or about 3/15. Federal Work-Study Program available. Institutional employment available.

The Inside Word

Bates looks for students who challenge themselves in the classroom and beyond. A student's academic rigor, essays, and recommendations may be even more important than his or her GPA and test scores. The essay, in particular, is a chance to stand out—Bates is most interested in what has changed and inspired their applicants. Interviews are encouraged, and candidates who opt out of these face-to-face meetings may place themselves at a disadvantage.

THE SCHOOL SAYS "..."

From the Admissions Office

"Bates College is widely recognized as one of the finest liberal arts colleges in the nation. The curriculum and faculty challenge students to develop the essential skills of critical assessment, analysis, expression, aesthetic sensibility, and independent thought. Founded by abolitionists in 1855, Bates graduates have always included men and women from diverse ethnic and religious backgrounds. Bates highly values its study abroad programs, unique calendar (4-4-1), and the many opportunities available for one-on-one collaboration with faculty through seminars, research, service-learning, and the capstone experience of senior thesis. Co-curricular life at Bates is rich; most students participate in club or varsity sports; many participate in performing arts; and almost all students participate in one of more than 110 student-run clubs and organizations. More than two-thirds of alumni enroll in graduate study within ten years.

"The Bates College Admission Staff reads applications very carefully; the high school record and the quality of writing are of particular importance. Applicants are encouraged to have a personal interview, either on campus or with an alumni representative. Students who choose not to interview may place themselves at a disadvantage in the selection process. Bates offers tours, interviews, and information sessions throughout the summer and fall. Drop-ins are welcome for tours and information sessions. Please call ahead to schedule an interview. At Bates, the submission of standardized testing (the SAT or ACT) is not required for admission. After three decades of optional testing, our research shows no differences in academic performance and graduation rates between submitters and nonsubmitters."

SELECTIVITY

Admissions Rating	96
# of applicants	8,273
% of applicants accepted	14
% of acceptees attending	46
# offered a place on the wait list	2,441
% accepting a place on wait list	52
% admitted from wait list	0
# of early decision applicants	657
% accepted early decision	48

FIRST-YEAR PROFILE

Testing policy	Test Optional
Range SAT composite	1340–1500
Range SAT EBRW	660–750
Range SAT math	650–760
Range ACT composite	31–33
# submitting SAT scores	131
% submitting SAT scores	25
# submitting ACT scores	75
% submitting ACT scores	14
% graduated top 10% of class	55
% graduated top 25% of class	89
% graduated top 50% of class	99

DEADLINES

Early decision	
Deadline	11/15
Notification	12/20
Other ED deadline	1/1
Other ED notification	2/15
Regular	
Deadline	1/1
Notification	4/1
Nonfall registration?	No

FINANCIAL FACTS

Financial Aid Rating	99
Annual tuition	$63,478
Room and board	$17,904
Required fees	$400
Books and supplies	$900
Average frosh need-based scholarship	$54,412
Average UG need-based scholarship	$52,925
% needy frosh rec. need-based scholarship or grant aid	100
% needy UG rec. need-based scholarship or grant aid	100
% needy frosh rec. non-need-based scholarship or grant aid	0
% needy UG rec. non-need-based scholarship or grant aid	0
% needy frosh rec. need-based self-help aid	98
% needy UG rec. need-based self-help aid	98
% UG borrow to pay for school	26
Average cumulative indebtedness	$28,397
% frosh need fully met	100
% ugrads need fully met	100
Average % of frosh need met	100
Average % of ugrad need met	100

BAYLOR UNIVERSITY

Baylor University, Waco, TX 76798-7056 • Admissions: 254-710-3435 • Fax: 254-710-3436

CAMPUS LIFE
Quality of Life Rating	86
Fire Safety Rating	91
Green Rating	60*
Type of school	Private
Affiliation	Baptist
Environment	City

STUDENTS
Total undergrad enrollment	15,134
% male/female/another gender	40/60/0
% from out of state	39
% frosh live on campus	99
% ugrads live on campus	29
# of fraternities (% join)	22 (20)
# of sororities (% join)	20 (34)
% African American	5
% Asian	9
% White	61
% Hispanic	16
% Native American	<1
% Pacific Islander	<1
% Two or more races	5
% Race and/or ethnicity unknown	1
% international	3
# of countries represented	62

SURVEY SAYS . . .
Lots of conservative students
Students are happy
Lab facilities are great
Students are very religious
Recreation facilities are great
Frats and sororities are popular
Everyone loves the Bears

ACADEMICS
Academic Rating	82
% students returning for sophomore year	90
% students graduating within 4 years	68
% students graduating within 6 years	81
Calendar	Semester
Student/faculty ratio	15:1
Profs interesting rating	88
Profs accessible rating	92

Most classes have 10–19 students.
Most lab/discussion sessions have
20–29 students.

MOST POPULAR MAJORS
Biology/Biological Sciences, General; Registered
Nursing/Registered Nurse; Communication,
General

STUDENTS SAY "..."
Academics
Academics at Baylor are rigorous and highly personalized. Students attribute that in part to the "much much better student to professor ratio," where both parties hold their academics "to a high standard." Students note that those pursuing a competitive track should "be prepared to be tested to the limit." Despite these high stakes, Baylor's familiar campus vibe extends to the classroom. One sophomore attests that "The professors are there for you and actually care about your academics, and most even about your well-being. Most professors are willing to work with you and so are your classmates." Students also consider Baylor's Christian mission to be uplifting: "My professors are all passionate people and they do not push faith, but they do involve it in the classroom in an inspirational way."

Baylor's courses are also known for innovative approaches, including discussion-based learning and hands-on field trips. One student brags that "In my Introduction to Teaching course, we tutored students in a local elementary school. My environmental science class took field trips to the Waco wetlands." Practical research and volunteer opportunities are particularly useful to those in specialized fields: "I am in a laparoscopy lab that enables pre-med students to learn about the research process. There is also a surgical skills class that allows pre-health students to learn skills often used in the world of healthcare." Liberal arts students enjoy unique projects like the "UnEssay" that give them "a lot of freedom to incorporate things we like into an English class."

Campus Life
Baylor's "beautiful" campus is home to a "very close-knit community where you feel accepted very easily" and offers lots of "opportunities to find groups of people to belong to." One student explains how "at the beginning of the fall semester we have this event called 'Late Night' where all the clubs including, frats, sororities, and sporting clubs enable you to see all [that is] available on campus." As a NCAA Division I school, many students list football and basketball games among their favorite activities. As one first-year student describes it, "Everyone is excited to go to the football and basketball games, and the student section at Baylor is unlike any other." Baylor's "unapologetically Christian" ethos is also celebrated throughout campus life. "Every Monday night there is Vertical, which is an amazing worship and sermon. When I imagined what a Christian college would look like, Vertical is what I imagined," explains one student. Popular school-sponsored events abound throughout the academic year, including All-University Thanksgiving, homecoming, Christmas on 5th Street, and Diadeloso. Students also rave about weekly Dr. Pepper Hour, the rock climbing wall in the student center, and gathering at coffee shops around Waco on the weekends. Finally, professional organizations, like those for the pre-med world, not only provide vital career opportunities but keep the school feeling "more like a community than a competition."

Student Body
"Baylor feels more like a family than a school," raves one Baylor student. "My peers at Baylor University are the kindest and most loving group of people I have ever known," says another first-year student, "When I think of 'southern hospitality,' the way my peers treat one another comes immediately to mind." Baylor students also describe each other as goal-oriented, focused, and engaged with religious and social communities. "Everyone at Baylor is out and about doing things on campus and interacting with the people around them," describes one student. "They aren't walking around like zombies with their AirPods in, they are talking with friends, laughing, and having a good time." Another student boasts that, "Everyone here at Baylor is aiming for success in their own way." Further, many students cherish that "intellectual diversity and open mindedness are abundant" among professors and students. While around 35% of the 2022 first-year class identifies as a minority, and some cite diversity as an area for growth, many make note of the variety of identities celebrated on campus: "The student body at Baylor is generally Christian, but from a diverse selection of denominations. I also have many non-Christian friends. There is lots of ideological diversity as well, including a thriving LGBTQIA+ community that I myself am a part of."

Financial Aid: 254-710-2611 • E-Mail: admissions@baylor.edu • Website: www.baylor.edu

THE PRINCETON REVIEW SAYS

Admissions

The school reports that its standardized testing policy for use in admission for Fall 2024 is Test Optional. It is unknown at this time if the 2024 testing policy will be permanent. The Princeton Review suggests that interested applicants consult with the school for the most up-to-date standardized testing policies. *Very important factors considered include:* rigor of secondary school record, academic GPA, standardized test scores. *Other factors considered include:* class rank, application essay, recommendation(s), extracurricular activities, talent/ability, character/personal qualities, alumni/ae relation, volunteer work, work experience, level of applicant's interest. High school diploma is required and GED is accepted. *Academic units recommended:* 4 English, 4 math, 4 science, 2 science labs, 2 foreign language, 2 social studies, 1 history.

Financial Aid

Students should submit: CSS/Financial Aid Profile. Priority filing deadline is 2/1. The Princeton Review suggests that all financial aid forms be submitted as soon as possible (see page 5 for a note on the FAFSA). *Need-based scholarships/grants offered:* College/university scholarship or grant aid from institutional funds; Federal Pell; Private scholarships; SEOG; State scholarships/grants. *Loan aid offered:* Direct PLUS loans; Direct Subsidized Loans; Direct Unsubsidized Loans; College/university loans from institutional funds; State Loans. Admitted students will be notified of merit-based awards on a rolling basis beginning 12/15; estimated financial aid awards will be sent on a rolling basis beginning early February. Federal Work-Study Program available. Institutional employment available.

The Inside Word

Securing a spot on Baylor's campus doesn't just come down to GPA, class rank, and test scores—it's quite competitive outside of those factors. Prospective students' desire to be a part of a community valuing both faith and personal calling will also be assessed. Admissions officers will consider an essay, recommendation letters, short answer responses, and a résumé to determine which students are a good fit for their mission, also looking for those who express a true interest in becoming a Baylor Bear. Certain majors (such as Engineering and the Baylor Business Fellows program) have additional requirements, and those who plan to apply should investigate requirements thoroughly before doing so.

THE SCHOOL SAYS "..."

From the Admissions Office

"Baylor's mission is to education men and women for worldwide leadership and service by integrating academic excellence and Christian commitment within a caring community. Our professors share a commitment to research and teaching. That means Baylor faculty include some of the nation's foremost scholars who also have a passion for helping you succeed. In 2021, Baylor University was named a Research 1 university by the Carnegie Classification of Institutions of Higher Education, joining the nation's top-tier research institutions as a doctoral university with very high research activity and elevating Baylor as a preeminent Christian research university. What else makes Baylor unique? Our belief that the world needs a preeminent research university that is distinctly Christian. This allows academics, research, and faith to work together. The outcome? Baylor students find both their career and calling in life. Many majors boast a 100 percent 'success rate,' meaning students find jobs or start graduate school within 90 days of graduation. When you become a student, you join the Baylor family. Professors and classmates become lifelong friends and your biggest cheerleaders. They will inspire you. Embolden you. Stretch you and walk with you. And you'll do the same for them because, after all, you're family. Traditions bind generations of Baylor students together by a shared experience that transcends culture, trends and time. That's why after graduation, you'll want to return 'home' each fall for one of our favorite traditions: Baylor Homecoming."

SELECTIVITY

Admissions Rating	89
# of applicants	40,753
% of applicants accepted	46
% of acceptees attending	18

FIRST-YEAR PROFILE

Testing policy	Test Optional
Range SAT composite	1170–1360
Range SAT EBRW	590–680
Range SAT math	580–690
Range ACT composite	26–32
# submitting SAT scores	1,339
% submitting SAT scores	57
# submitting ACT scores	993
% submitting ACT scores	43
% graduated top 10% of class	40
% graduated top 25% of class	72
% graduated top 50% of class	95

DEADLINES

Early decision	
Deadline	11/1
Notification	12/15
Early action	
Deadline	11/1
Notification	1/15
Regular	
Deadline	2/1
Notification	4/10
Nonfall registration?	Yes

FINANCIAL FACTS

Financial Aid Rating	81
Annual tuition	$54,326
Room and board	$15,318
Required fees	$190
Books and supplies	$1,438
Average frosh need-based scholarship	$27,760
Average UG need-based scholarship	$26,583
% needy frosh rec. need-based scholarship or grant aid	99
% needy UG rec. need-based scholarship or grant aid	96
% needy frosh rec. non-need-based scholarship or grant aid	78
% needy UG rec. non-need-based scholarship or grant aid	80
% needy frosh rec. need-based self-help aid	79
% needy UG rec. need-based self-help aid	80
% UG borrow to pay for school	51
Average cumulative indebtedness	$49,610
% frosh need fully met	14
% ugrads need fully met	13
Average % of frosh need met	69
Average % of ugrad need met	66

BELLARMINE UNIVERSITY

2001 Newburg Road, Louisville, KY 40205 • Admissions: 502-272-8000 • Fax: 502-272-8002

STUDENTS SAY "..."

Academics

Located at the edge of Louisville, this small Catholic university offers 50 majors and "seeks to benefit the public interest, to help create the future, and to improve the human condition." A "superb teaching staff," a recently renovated library, and an Academic Resource Center with free tutoring cohere to deliver a "challenging but rewarding" academic experience for students. The nursing program is a big draw here, as are Bellarmine's study abroad programs in 68 countries, which more than one-third of students avail themselves of. Generous financial aid only sweetens the pot. In line with its mission, Bellarmine University "seeks to train its students in the love of truth and equips them with the skills and tools necessary (e.g., critical thinking, problem solving) to live an enriched life."

The "insightful and dedicated" professors are almost always available to answer questions or concerns, and "want their students to pass their class with as much knowledge as possible." Because of the small class sizes ("I have one class with seven students," reports an actuarial science major), students are able to have one-on-one discussions with their professors. Most professors at Bellarmine "even provide their personal cell phones to students on their syllabi." This access to professors "really [establishes] an ability to grow closer to future employers and be willing to open up with them about issues, concerns, or ideas." Material is often taught through real-world applications, and many teachers will even "help you find internships and jobs." Though students admit that some adjunct professors can be below par, "Bellarmine takes their course evaluations pretty seriously and assesses the situation quickly."

Campus Life

People here are "very studious" during the week, but weekends offer plenty of options for socializing. A major hub of the city (Bardstown Road) is nearby, providing lots of little shops, restaurants, and bars, and the campus is close to the Louisville Zoological Garden, a park where students can often be found "playing and hanging out." The university also coordinates off-campus actives such as "Knight at the Movies" (the knight is Bellarmine's mascot), ice skating, and concerts, and students can take advantage of the Louisville Connections program, which offers "free tickets to events or places around Louisville, such as to Dracula at Actors Theatre, a day at Kentucky Kingdom, or a day horseback riding."

On campus, most people "hang around Cafe Ogle in between classes, sipping on coffee and working on their laptops." Bellarmine's men's basketball team draws huge crowds, and the school has "a niche, club, or activity for everyone" (and "encourages and supports any club a student would like to create"). There are also events like "Late Knight Bingo, which is a huge Bingo party where students can win really awesome prizes," Homecoming, and "Ball on the Belle (a Halloween dance on the [steamboat] Belle of Louisville)." The campus itself is both beautiful and "small enough to be easily traversed if you only have 10 minutes between classes and need to be across campus."

Student Body

Though mostly white and from Kentucky and neighboring states, this is a socially wide-ranging group considering the small size of the student body, which naturally allows "blobbing of the social groups." Part of this may come from the way the school handles its strong athletic programs, which are never placed above academics: as a result, "the athletes are also amazing students." The school is "welcoming to every single person and makes an effort to include everyone." Students note that though they are introduced to "different cultures and customs from around the world, seeing that our student body is so diverse," they feel, overall, as if "I can't say I've ever met a stranger." Everyone is always willing to help and "comfort you with just a simple smile on their face."

BELLARMINE UNIVERSITY

Financial Aid: 502-272-4723 • E-Mail: admissions@bellarmine.edu • Website: www.bellarmine.edu

THE PRINCETON REVIEW SAYS

Admissions
The school reports that its standardized testing policy for use in admission for Fall 2024 is Test Optional. The 2024 testing policy will be permanent. The Princeton Review suggests that interested applicants consult with the school for the most up-to-date standardized testing policies. *Very important factors considered include:* rigor of secondary school record, academic GPA, recommendation(s), character/personal qualities, level of applicant's interest. *Important factors considered include:* class rank, extracurricular activities. *Other factors considered include:* standardized test scores, application essay, interview, talent/ability, first generation, alumni/ae relation, geographical residence, state residency, racial/ethnic status, volunteer work, work experience. High school diploma is required and GED is accepted. *Academic units required:* 4 English, 3 math, 3 science, 2 science labs, 2 foreign language, 2 social studies, 1 history, 5 academic electives. *Academic units recommended:* 4 English, 4 math, 4 science, 2 science labs, 2 foreign language, 3 social studies, 2 history, 7 academic electives.

Financial Aid
Students should submit: FAFSA. Priority filing deadline is 11/1. The Princeton Review suggests that all financial aid forms be submitted as soon as possible (see page 5 for a note on the FAFSA). *Need-based scholarships/grants offered:* College/university scholarship or grant aid from institutional funds; Federal Pell; Private scholarships; SEOG; State scholarships/grants. *Loan aid offered:* Direct PLUS loans; Direct Subsidized Loans; Direct Unsubsidized Loans; College/university loans from institutional funds. Admitted students will be notified of awards on a rolling basis beginning 1/31. Federal Work-Study Program available. Institutional employment available.

The Inside Word
Admissions at Bellarmine University is relatively competitive. However, as you would expect from their mission statement, the admissions committee takes a holistic approach to applications, and is looking for a well-rounded candidate whose qualifications reflect more than the sum total of a GPA and test scores. Recommendations and personal statements—which should present a strong picture of the student's educational goals—volunteer experiences, and extracurricular commitments, hold significant weight. Candidates with strong grades and diverse interests are likely to earn acceptance.

THE SCHOOL SAYS "..."

From the Admissions Office
"Bellarmine University prepares students for success through a liberal arts education, combined with training for mastery in a specialized area. We offer more than fifty majors in the arts and sciences, humanities, education, communication, business, environmental studies, nursing and health science, plus graduate programs in nursing, education, physical therapy, business and communication. We engage students in state-of-the-art classrooms and expand their horizons through internship and study abroad opportunities. Bellarmine delivers this world-class education just five miles from downtown Louisville, the nation's sixteenth largest city. The 175-acre campus is set in a safe, historic and eclectic neighborhood, and features a fitness center, tennis courts, athletic fields and two new dining halls. With more than fifty clubs and organizations, twenty NCAA Division II athletic teams, plus Division I men's lacrosse, Bellarmine offers a variety of recreational opportunities for all students. Students who reside on campus also find a Bellarmine difference in the living arrangements. From traditional residence halls to apartment-style and suite living arrangements, students have many housing options to choose from; the newest residence halls surround a Tuscan-style piazza. As Bellarmine attracts more residential students, the university has created more gathering spaces for them, such as the café on the ground floor of the Siena Primo residence hall. New learning communities cater to residents and commuters alike, offering opportunities for focused, collaborative studies on topics such as leadership, healthcare, science and technology."

SELECTIVITY
Admissions Rating	84
# of applicants	4,190
% of applicants accepted	82
% of acceptees attending	17

FIRST-YEAR PROFILE
Testing policy	Test Optional
Range SAT composite	1030–1280
Range SAT EBRW	520–640
Range SAT math	500–640
Range ACT composite	21–28
# submitting SAT scores	101
% submitting SAT scores	18
# submitting ACT scores	529
% submitting ACT scores	92
Average HS GPA	3.4
% frosh submitting high school GPA	100

DEADLINES
Early action	
Deadline	11/1
Notification	11/15
Regular	
Priority	2/1
Deadline	8/15
Notification	Rolling, 9/1
Nonfall registration?	Yes

APPLICANTS OFTEN PREFER
University of Kentucky; University of Louisville

FINANCIAL FACTS
Financial Aid Rating	84
Annual tuition	$42,970
Room and board	$9,030
Required fees	$1,550
Required fees (first-year)	$1,950
Average frosh need-based scholarship	$29,215
Average UG need-based scholarship	$28,033
% needy frosh rec. need-based scholarship or grant aid	99
% needy UG rec. need-based scholarship or grant aid	97
% needy frosh rec. non-need-based scholarship or grant aid	33
% needy UG rec. non-need-based scholarship or grant aid	36
% needy frosh rec. need-based self-help aid	67
% needy UG rec. need-based self-help aid	63
% UG borrow to pay for school	71
Average cumulative indebtedness	$32,606
% frosh need fully met	27
% ugrads need fully met	27
Average % of frosh need met	80
Average % of ugrad need met	81

BELOIT COLLEGE

700 College St., Beloit, WI 53511 • Admissions: 608-363-2000 • Fax: 608-363-2075

CAMPUS LIFE

Quality of Life Rating	84
Fire Safety Rating	84
Green Rating	82
Type of school	Private
Affiliation	No Affiliation
Environment	Town

STUDENTS

Total undergrad enrollment	921
% male/female/another gender	48/52/0
% from out of state	79
% frosh from public high school	64
% frosh live on campus	97
% ugrads live on campus	90
# of fraternities	3
# of sororities	3
% African American	9
% Asian	3
% White	49
% Hispanic	17
% Native American	0
% Pacific Islander	0
% Two or more races	4
% Race and/or ethnicity unknown	3
% international	15
# of countries represented	43

SURVEY SAYS . . .

Lots of liberal students
Lab facilities are great
Class discussions encouraged
Students aren't religious

ACADEMICS

Academic Rating	86
% students returning for sophomore year	82
% students graduating within 4 years	65
% students graduating within 6 years	71
Calendar	Semester
Student/faculty ratio	10:1
Profs interesting rating	94
Profs accessible rating	95
Most classes have 10–19 students.	

MOST POPULAR MAJORS

Environmental Biology; Psychology, General;
Anthropology

STUDENTS SAY "..."

Academics

A small liberal arts college in southern Wisconsin, Beloit College offers students "small class sizes, [and] expansive study abroad opportunities" in an academic environment "that encourages debate and discovery." Beloit "embraces individuality" by giving students "freedom to study what they are passionate about," and so there are student-designed "academic paths [that] can be customized to suit every student's needs, interests, and goals." Whether you're studying journalism or majoring in molecular biology, Beloit cultivates "critical thinkers who can put the liberal arts in practice" and the curriculum stresses "intensive essay writing and an emphasis on self-identity." As one student puts it, at Beloit "there is no such thing as a one-sided problem...we ask the hard questions and approach solutions in a multidisciplinary manner that requires critical thinking, collaboration, and creativity."

Beloiters describe their academic experiences as "nothing short of phenomenal." As one student explains, "My first day of classes, teachers already knew my name by the time I sat down at the desk." Students benefit from "many one-on-one experiences, hands-on classes, and project-based learning," and note that professors "bring unique perspectives to class material, and the small class size allows them the flexibility to tailor the courses to their students." Because of the low student-to-faculty ratio and "motivated student body, it is possible to have close relationships with faculty that make for a more enriching college experience." And students relish those relationships, describing their professors as "easily accessible," "dynamic and knowledgeable," and "generally nice and open." Beloit professors also prove to be "very good resources for helping you with research, internships, and graduate school applications and program decisions."

Campus Life

Beloit is "decorated by its open, welcoming community." Students say that "there is a lot of freedom for students to learn from their mistakes while living on campus and to make their own decisions. Students at Beloit are responsible for taking initiative in their decisions to learn, both in the classroom and out." Students report that there is a fair amount of "drinking on the weekend" but that "it's usually done pretty safely." Even though it is a small school, there is plenty on campus to keep students occupied: "Whether it's a Greek event, Black Lives Matter panel, new movie screenings, school sponsored trip to a haunted house or musical, or our professors' band is playing in the quad, there is always something going on." Sports and extracurricular activities are also popular as "everyone is a part of at least one club, and usually several." As spring rolls around, students look forward "to Spring Day," a day without classes when students enjoy "giant inflatable bouncy houses, caricature artists, free junk food, and the martial arts demonstration."

Student Body

Many students celebrate the "outstanding diversity of the student body," including "a large international student population on campus and domestic students [who] come from all over the United States." Beloiters are predominantly liberal and "very engaged students and citizens, who are passionate about various causes and their academics." Most agree that students aren't afraid to address tough subjects and seek out "different opinions, backgrounds, and ideas that allow [them] to explore things outside of [their] comfort zone socially, personally, and intellectually." Even for "students who have felt out of place before" arriving at college, Beloit provides "a safe space to learn." "Beloit College students are a mixed bunch." One student explains, "[We're] unafraid to be different, and aesthetically unmatched by any other student body."

BELOIT COLLEGE

Financial Aid: 608-363-2663 • E-Mail: admissions@beloit.edu • Website: www.beloit.edu

THE PRINCETON REVIEW SAYS

Admissions

The school reports that its standardized testing policy for use in admission for Fall 2024 is Test Optional. The 2024 testing policy will be permanent. The Princeton Review suggests that interested applicants consult with the school for the most up-to-date standardized testing policies. *Very important factors considered include:* rigor of secondary school record, academic GPA, application essay. *Important factors considered include:* character/personal qualities. *Other factors considered include:* class rank, standardized test scores, recommendation(s), interview, extracurricular activities, talent/ability, first generation, alumni/ae relation, racial/ethnic status, volunteer work, work experience, level of applicant's interest. High school diploma is required and GED is accepted. *Academic units recommended:* 4 English, 3 math, 3 science, 3 science labs, 2 foreign language, 3 social studies.

Financial Aid

Students should submit: FAFSA. Priority filing deadline is 11/1. The Princeton Review suggests that all financial aid forms be submitted as soon as possible (see page 5 for a note on the FAFSA). *Need-based scholarships/grants offered:* College/university scholarship or grant aid from institutional funds; Federal Pell; Private scholarships; SEOG; State scholarships/grants. *Loan aid offered:* Direct PLUS loans; Direct Subsidized Loans; Direct Unsubsidized Loans; College/university loans from institutional funds. Admitted students will be notified of awards on a rolling basis. Federal Work-Study Program available. Institutional employment available.

The Inside Word

Beloit wants to see a rigorous academic transcript but also emphasizes a holistic approach that focuses on getting to know the student behind the application. The admission office prefers to receive a letter of recommendation from a teacher who taught you during your junior year, but it is most important to select someone who can provide the most insight to you as a student. Standardized test scores are optional for most applicants.

THE SCHOOL SAYS "..."

From the Admissions Office

"Through exploring their interests in and outside of the classroom, Beloiters learn to be effective communicators, productive collaborators, creative problem solvers, and intellectually and professionally agile. These skills serve them well in applying their education to meaningful lives and flourishing careers.

"A focus on the purposeful application of a liberal arts and sciences education has long distinguished Beloit and its graduates. Beloit students value learning for its own sake and understand the connection between college and their role as citizens of the world.

"There's a huge difference between getting an education and being so immersed, so transformed, so enthralled with living and learning that your education never really stops. That's Beloit College.

"Often described as 'the most interesting people in the room,' Beloiters thrive on unexpected connections and combinations. Students hail from 43 states and 39 countries and more than 30% double major. Beloiters are united in their uniqueness, believe in the strength of an inclusive community, stay connected for a lifetime, and learn from the world around them.

"Innovation, agility, compassion, and collaboration are part of our culture and reflected in the students who are drawn to Beloit and in the education they receive."

SELECTIVITY

Admissions Rating	89
# of applicants	3,462
% of applicants accepted	66
% of acceptees attending	20
# offered a place on the wait list	20
% accepting a place on wait list	19
% admitted from wait list	100
# of early decision applicants	7
% accepted early decision	43

FIRST-YEAR PROFILE

Testing policy	Test Optional
Range SAT composite	1230–1360
Range SAT EBRW	610–690
Range SAT math	580–670
Range ACT composite	26–31
# submitting SAT scores	26
% submitting SAT scores	11
# submitting ACT scores	30
% submitting ACT scores	13
Average HS GPA	3.4
% frosh submitting high school GPA	100
% graduated top 10% of class	39
% graduated top 25% of class	67
% graduated top 50% of class	88

DEADLINES

Early decision	
Deadline	11/1
Notification	12/1
Early action	
Deadline	11/1
Notification	12/1
Regular	
Priority	1/15
Notification	Rolling, 11/1
Nonfall registration?	Yes

APPLICANTS SOMETIMES PREFER

Carleton College; DePauw University; Earlham College; Grinnell College; Illinois Wesleyan University; Kalamazoo College; Kenyon College; Knox College; Lawrence University; Lewis & Clark College; Macalester College; Oberlin College; St. Olaf College

FINANCIAL FACTS

Financial Aid Rating	89
Annual tuition	$58,042
Room and board	$10,740
Required fees	$512
Books and supplies	$1,134
Average frosh need-based scholarship	$39,493
Average UG need-based scholarship	$37,603
% needy frosh rec. need-based scholarship or grant aid	99
% needy UG rec. need-based scholarship or grant aid	98
% needy frosh rec. non-need-based scholarship or grant aid	47
% needy UG rec. non-need-based scholarship or grant aid	50
% needy frosh rec. need-based self-help aid	80
% needy UG rec. need-based self-help aid	83
% frosh rec. any financial aid	99
% UG rec. any financial aid	99
% UG borrow to pay for school	61
Average cumulative indebtedness	$23,534
% frosh need fully met	32
% ugrads need fully met	31
Average % of frosh need met	96
Average % of ugrad need met	95

BENNINGTON COLLEGE

One College Drive, Bennington, VT 05201 • Admissions: 802-442-5401 • Fax: 802-440-4320

STUDENTS SAY "..."

Academics

Student autonomy and an individualized curriculum are at the heart of a Bennington College education, and some say that the school's "greatest strength is how non-traditional it is." Here, students map out Plans for study and application, rather than adhering to the traditional declaration of a major. "Having access to such interesting and strange subjects is an opportunity unique" to the school, and the one-on-one guidance each student receives is "a game changer in terms of getting experience in your field." With the help of a personal Plan committee, students work toward obtaining several fundamental Capacities such as inquiry, research, and communication. All students also spend six weeks a year in a fieldwork term, completing an internship or experience where the practical outcomes of their education can be seen: "This experience is life changing, and one of the reasons why I wanted to come to Bennington," says a student. "Nothing is handed to you here, but there is freedom to do whatever you want if you have the energy to go out and get it," which students see as a learning experience in and of itself. There is a great "trust in the students to create their own path and make good decisions."

Students and professors "are encouraged to be on a first name basis with each other" and there's an appreciation for how teachers work to "succinctly encapsulate your journey, work, and experience in the course within a paragraph that is archived for futurity." Studies tend to be "very interdisciplinary and focus on a lot of unconventional and experimental ideas," and professors "will also often bring their colleagues in to discuss and connect with students." The "flexibility and nimbleness of the institution allows for maximum creativity and independence," and to many, that makes this a dream school, in that "students can literally dream up their course of study, and do work important to them."

Campus Life

Housing at Bennington is just as untraditional as is its approach to degrees and grading: instead of dorms, there are houses of 30–45 students each, which means leads to "real connections with your housemates instead of just coexisting." The dining hall staff are incredibly accommodating, and there are "food options for vegans, vegetarians, meat eaters, and halal." A shuttle service provides ease for "grocery trips, exploring town, pickup and drop-off to and from the Albany airport and Amtrak train station," and "it's really easy to bike, walk around, and do any outdoor activities safely." As one student says, "If you are inspired by nature, Bennington is the place to be." That said, organized athletics can be hard to find: "There are sometimes sports happening, but not really." Instead, Vermont is "known for natural swimming holes, skiing, and maple syrup tapping which students become involved in seasonally." There are, however, "many opportunities to involve yourself in student leadership if you have the ambition" and "a whole bunch of clubs" for budding improv artists, comic-book fans, creative writers, and Dungeons & Dragons role-players.

Student Body

This is a place that is "full of people open to self-expression and being who you are, whoever you may be," where students are "very, very LGBTQIA+ accepting" and "most people are a part of the community." This "colorful cast of wonderful, intelligent people who question the world around them in very significant ways" are "as 'liberal' as a liberal arts college could get." The campus "is very inclusive and diverse which is astonishing considering the student population is not very big," and there is a "politically conscious student body that is generally very engaged in their areas of interest and work." Almost "the entire student body lives on campus for all four years, meaning communal living on campus is ever adapting and improving."

BENNINGTON COLLEGE

Financial Aid: 800-833-6845 • E-Mail: admissions@bennington.edu • Website: www.bennington.edu

THE PRINCETON REVIEW SAYS

Admissions

The school reports that its standardized testing policy for use in admission for Fall 2024 is Test Optional, as it has been since 2006. *Very important factors considered include:* rigor of secondary school record, academic GPA, application essay, recommendation(s), interview, talent/ability, character/personal qualities. *Other factors considered include:* class rank, standardized test scores, extracurricular activities, first generation, racial/ethnic status, volunteer work, work experience. High school diploma is required and GED is accepted. *Academic units required:* 4 English. *Academic units recommended:* 4 math, 4 science, 3 science labs, 3 foreign language, 3 social studies.

Financial Aid

Students should submit: CSS/Financial Aid Profile; FAFSA; Noncustodial Profile. Priority filing deadline is 1/15. The Princeton Review suggests that all financial aid forms be submitted as soon as possible (see page 5 for a note on the FAFSA). *Need-based scholarships/ grants offered:* College/university scholarship or grant aid from institutional funds; Federal Pell; Private scholarships; SEOG; State scholarships/grants. *Loan aid offered:* Direct PLUS loans; Direct Subsidized Loans; Direct Unsubsidized Loans. Admitted students will be notified of awards on or about 3/20. Federal Work-Study Program available. Institutional employment available.

The Inside Word

Bennington truly seeks a mutual fit in the students it admits, and its somewhat unorthodox admissions is designed to showcase the applicant: new students can choose to either share a collection of their work that reflects their talents and abilities, or can use the Common Application and include supplemental materials such as recommendations. The school works with all admitted students to craft affordable, workable finance plans, and 98 percent of Bennington students receive some form of financial aid.

THE SCHOOL SAYS "..."

From the Admissions Office

"Bennington College's founders referred to it as a bold educational experiment. They dared to imagine what would happen if they freed students to explore their skills and interests, rather than meet the requirements of a core curriculum. We call it The Plan. This self-directed learning model often combines several areas of study in a collaborative process guided by faculty.

"Students put their knowledge to work during the yearly Field Work Term, an opportunity to test knowledge and invigorate their studies with relevant experiences in the United States and abroad. The result is a student-centered, interdisciplinary, creatively rigorous education that is responsive to the world's needs.

"This innovative approach is possible through lots of direct interaction with talented faculty practitioners and a commitment of support that runs throughout the College, including student life, financial aid, and health services. Students find a diverse LGBTQ+-affirming community where individuals shine and strong bonds form.

"On Bennington's beautiful campus, known for vibrant creative energy and dramatic architecture, students thrive. They go on to become Forbes "30 Under 30" honorees, National Endowment for the Arts Fellowship recipients, and Guggenheim Fellows. They have won Oscars, Emmys, MacArthur Fellow "Genius Grants," National Book Awards, and Pulitzer prizes. As Bennington graduates, they are equipped to, as our mission states, make the world more beautiful, sustainable, democratic, and just."

SELECTIVITY

Admissions Rating	92
# of applicants	2,801
% of applicants accepted	45
% of acceptees attending	17
# offered a place on the wait list	88
% accepting a place on wait list	66
% admitted from wait list	40
# of early decision applicants	123
% accepted early decision	30

FIRST-YEAR PROFILE

Testing policy	Test Optional
Range SAT composite	1260–1370
Range SAT EBRW	660–700
Range SAT math	600–670
Range ACT composite	29–33
# submitting SAT scores	27
% submitting SAT scores	13
# submitting ACT scores	11
% submitting ACT scores	5
Average HS GPA	3.6
% frosh submitting high school GPA	67
% graduated top 10% of class	25
% graduated top 25% of class	65
% graduated top 50% of class	96

DEADLINES

Early decision	
Deadline	11/15
Notification	12/15
Other ED deadline	1/15
Other ED notification	2/5
Early action	
Deadline	12/1
Notification	1/31
Regular	
Deadline	1/15
Nonfall registration?	Yes

APPLICANTS ALSO LOOK AT

Bard College; Brandeis University; Emerson College; Eugene Lang College of Liberal Arts at The New School; Hampshire College; Lewis & Clark College; New York University; Oberlin College; Sarah Lawrence College; Skidmore College

FINANCIAL FACTS

Financial Aid Rating	86
Annual tuition	$63,802
Room and board	$18,640
Required fees	$842
Required fees (first-year)	$1,417
Books and supplies	$1,200
Average frosh need-based scholarship	$53,074
Average UG need-based scholarship	$50,754
% needy frosh rec. need-based scholarship or grant aid	99
% needy UG rec. need-based scholarship or grant aid	100
% needy frosh rec. non-need-based scholarship or grant aid	9
% needy UG rec. non-need-based scholarship or grant aid	9
% needy frosh rec. need-based self-help aid	79
% needy UG rec. need-based self-help aid	82
% frosh rec. any financial aid	98
% UG rec. any financial aid	98
% UG borrow to pay for school	52
Average cumulative indebtedness	$19,010
% frosh need fully met	37
% ugrads need fully met	23
Average % of frosh need met	93
Average % of ugrad need met	90

BENTLEY UNIVERSITY

175 Forest Street, Waltham, MA 02452 • Admissions: 781-891-2244 • Fax: 781-891-3414

STUDENTS SAY "..."

Academics

Though Bentley University leads with its reputation as a business school, don't underestimate the breadth of its curriculum, which draws a comprehensive liberal arts element into its advanced business curriculum. The over 4,000 undergraduates who attend this Massachusetts school gain "excellent technical knowledge and skills and [can choose from a] variety of business disciplines." The strong business curriculum (finance and accounting "are Bentley's bread and butter") is "dominated by relevant coursework," and it shows in the placement rates: more than 97 percent of students are employed or in graduate school within six months of graduation. Some classes run in conjunction with each other, "enhancing what students learn and take away from those courses," and many feature supplemental presentations outside of class in which students gain insights from working professionals. There's an academic program for everyone interested in business, with "niches for any unique students" and "plenty of opportunities for students to get involved."

Classrooms and teaching techniques take advantage of advanced technology, and in recent years, Bentley has "focused on growing students' soft skills by incorporating multiple group projects." Professors work hard to teach their subjects well and ensure students understand the topics, and many instructors "[have] industry experience and in-depth education prior to arriving at Bentley." The "above and beyond" Career Services office "does a great job of prepping students for life ahead," and classes are "relevant and feature real learning." To wit: "Even the General Education subjects are designed to be applicable in the corporate world."

Campus Life

Everyone at Bentley has "a strong focus on jobs, internships, and résumé building," so much of students' free time goes to interest-based extracurriculars, which consist of clubs and activities (such as the student-run Bentley Investment Group) that "offer students an opportunity to explore their interests [and] acquire new knowledge and skills." Still, "students are able to prioritize work, but when we are finished up we have some fun." Most students are "part of an organization, whether it be Greek life or a club." On the weekends, there are usually some parties, but "there is no pressure to go. They are fun but not a major part of life on campus." Fraternities are off-campus, and as such, "the frat-mosphere is not nearly as pronounced as the hyper-focus on where [you are] steering your career." "We hang out and discuss a lot of different ideas about business-related externalities.... It's the entire culture," says one student. The campus activities board "makes sure there are events throughout the week and weekends for people to attend that are school-sanctioned," and other fun activities around campus include attending Division I hockey games in the school's brand new sports complex, as well as "events that [the Campus Activities Board] constantly promotes."

Student Body

"Motivated" is the number one way to describe "driven yet collaborative" Bentley students, and most people "take academics extremely seriously" and "spend most of their time at the library or the stock trading room on campus." That said, people here are "very outgoing and involved in a range of activities on campus" and are "diverse in culture and educational experience, with broad perspectives from industries and countries across the world." Regardless of background, "everyone understands the language of business." There are a large number of international students, and "a lot more men than women." The student body is "a little bit cliquey, but alright in general," and there is "a sense of mutual respect among peers."

BENTLEY UNIVERSITY

Financial Aid: 781-891-3441 • E-Mail: ugadmission@bentley.edu • Website: www.bentley.edu

THE PRINCETON REVIEW SAYS

Admissions

The school reports that its standardized testing policy for use in admission for Fall 2024 is Test Optional. It is unknown at this time if the 2024 testing policy will be permanent. The Princeton Review suggests that interested applicants consult with the school for the most up-to-date standardized testing policies. *Very important factors considered include:* rigor of secondary school record. *Important factors considered include:* academic GPA, application essay, recommendation(s), extracurricular activities, talent/ability, character/personal qualities, volunteer work, level of applicant's interest. *Other factors considered include:* class rank, standardized test scores, interview, first generation, alumni/ae relation, geographical residence, state residency, racial/ethnic status, work experience. High school diploma is required and GED is accepted. *Academic units required:* 4 English, 3 math, 2 science, 2 science labs, 3 foreign language, 3 social studies. *Academic units recommended:* 4 English, 4 math, 3 science, 2 science labs, 3 foreign language, 4 social studies.

Financial Aid

Students should submit: Business/Farm Supplement; CSS/Financial Aid Profile; FAFSA; Noncustodial Profile; Parent and student tax returns (W-2 forms and all schedules filed). Priority filing deadline is 11/15. The Princeton Review suggests that all financial aid forms be submitted as soon as possible (see page 5 for a note on the FAFSA). *Need-based scholarships/grants offered:* College/university scholarship or grant aid from institutional funds; Federal Pell; Private scholarships; SEOG; State scholarships/grants. *Loan aid offered:* Direct PLUS loans; Direct Subsidized Loans; Direct Unsubsidized Loans; State Loans. Admitted students will be notified of awards on or about 3/31. Federal Work-Study Program available. Institutional employment available.

The Inside Word

If you're thinking about stacking your senior year electives with business classes in order to impress the Bentley admissions officers, think again. Taking a broad array of classes that challenge your skills, at AP level if possible, is your best approach. Whether in English, history/social sciences, math, lab sciences, and foreign language, the admissions committee wants to see academic diversity. And be sure your grades and test scores are up to snuff, because you'll have plenty of competition.

THE SCHOOL SAYS "..."

From the Admissions Office

"Bentley University is one of the nation's leading business schools, dedicated to preparing graduates who will transform business and the world for better. Students develop well-rounded skills that lead to successful and rewarding careers and become a powerful force in whatever field the choose. Bentley students have the technical skills, global perspective and high ethical standards required for personal and professional success and are highly sought-after by today's leading organizations.

"In 2021, 99% of all Bentley graduates were employed or enrolled in graduate school within six months of graduation. This success is recognized annually by *The Princeton Review*, which has ranked the university's career services office among the top five in the nation for seven consecutive years.

"Approximately 94 percent of freshmen live on campus. Students live and learn in a diverse environment that prepares them to thrive in today's diverse work world. International students representing over 80 countries are part of the Bentley community. There are more than 100 student organizations, as well as abundant intramurals, recreational sports, and over 20 varsity teams in NCAA Divisions I and II. Bentley's location in Waltham, Massachusetts—minutes from Boston—puts the city's many resources within easy reach. Bentley's free shuttle makes regular trips to Harvard Square in Cambridge, just a subway ride from the heart of Boston. Boston also offers students many opportunities for internships and jobs after graduation."

SELECTIVITY

Admissions Rating	90
# of applicants	9,662
% of applicants accepted	58
% of acceptees attending	20
# offered a place on the wait list	1,594
% accepting a place on wait list	25
% admitted from wait list	6
# of early decision applicants	414
% accepted early decision	78

FIRST-YEAR PROFILE

Testing policy	Test Optional
Range SAT composite	1280–1400
Range SAT EBRW	618–690
Range SAT math	640–730
Range ACT composite	28–32
# submitting SAT scores	304
% submitting SAT scores	27
# submitting ACT scores	53
% submitting ACT scores	5
% graduated top 10% of class	34
% graduated top 25% of class	67
% graduated top 50% of class	94

DEADLINES

Early decision	
Deadline	11/15
Notification	12/31
Other ED deadline	1/15
Other ED notification	2/1
Regular	
Priority	11/15
Deadline	1/15
Notification	3/31
Nonfall registration?	Yes

APPLICANTS SOMETIMES PREFER
Babson College; Bryant University; Fairfield University; Fordham University; Indiana University—Bloomington; Northeastern University; Providence College; University of Connecticut; University of Massachusetts Amherst; University of New Hampshire

FINANCIAL FACTS

Financial Aid Rating	85
Annual tuition	$58,150
Room and board	$19,200
Books and supplies	$1,300
Average frosh need-based scholarship	$38,022
Average UG need-based scholarship	$37,341
% needy frosh rec. need-based scholarship or grant aid	100
% needy UG rec. need-based scholarship or grant aid	99
% needy frosh rec. non-need-based scholarship or grant aid	22
% needy UG rec. non-need-based scholarship or grant aid	15
% needy frosh rec. need-based self-help aid	69
% needy UG rec. need-based self-help aid	81
% frosh rec. any financial aid	85
% UG rec. any financial aid	78
% UG borrow to pay for school	51
Average cumulative indebtedness	$34,626
% frosh need fully met	28
% ugrads need fully met	29
Average % of frosh need met	86
Average % of ugrad need met	87

BEREA COLLEGE

101 Chestnut Street, Berea, KY 40404 • Admissions: 859-985-3000 • Fax: 859-985-3512

STUDENTS SAY "..."

Academics

Kentucky's Berea College is one of the nation's few entirely tuition-free private colleges, providing a liberal arts education "to those who otherwise couldn't afford college but who are deserving of the opportunity." Berea is "truly a different world when it comes to the atmosphere of the college," and the "wonderful opportunity" offered to students is truly appreciated. The school takes a "holistic approach" to education and "expects a lot from students both in and outside of class," including labor (everyone is required to work at least 10 hours per week) and convocations.

Professors take an active role in helping students learn: "If you miss a class, professors will email you to find out why." They "care about not just your learning but also about who you are as an individual" and "lively and passionate about their subjects, and it is very evident within their classrooms." "I've never felt more challenged than when I stepped foot in a Berea classroom," says a junior. The small student-to-faculty ratio gives professors the opportunity to get to know their students, and "[allows] them to adapt to their students' needs."

Dating back to 1855, the college is "very deeply rooted in Appalachian culture and history, but unafraid to address issues outside of that." The school gives low-income students the opportunity to obtain a higher education while participating in a labor program, and so "produces well-rounded, hardworking students fully prepared for grad school or the workforce." "If the labor program is used to its fullest extent, each student has the opportunity to graduate with a fantastic résumé and many network connections," says a sophomore. It also offers "a huge scholarship to study abroad," of which many students take advantage.

Campus Life

"Berea is a calm place" and "there isn't much going on unless you make something happen." Students are quite busy with studying and work, so "naps are rare" and "we usually don't sleep in because there is just so much to do." Most students are taking a full course load and then doing at least one or two extracurricular activities as well. While some note that "the town life is simply atrocious," on campus, "student organizations are constantly holding events to keep Berea students occupied and having fun," including "movie nights, game nights, dances, [and] bowling." Heritage activities, such as Contra dancing, are big.

The town of Richmond is just a 15-minute drive away (there is also a campus shuttle, and Lexington is a bit further), so getting out of small town life for some shopping or restaurant dining "is a must" from time to time. It is illegal to sell alcohol in the town of Berea, and it is against school rules to have alcohol on campus, so "there isn't a big party scene." There also happen to be "a lot of couples on campus," and "people take relationships seriously" here.

Student Body

Berea students are "creative" and "incredibly resilient" and almost everyone "comes from the Appalachian region [and] limited resources." Many tend to be first-generation college students, and "most students' priorities are not in having the best material items or joining the best sorority." The most typical thing you'll see is "an overworked, but generally content student shuffling between classes and work." Also, "the one thing that ties us all together is the fact that we had to work so hard to get into Berea," says a first-year student. ("You have to be either an outright nerd or a secret nerd to get [here].") As some have noticed, there "seems to be a great divide between traditional students and non-traditional."

BEREA COLLEGE

Financial Aid: 859-985-3314 • E-Mail: admissions@berea.edu • Website: www.berea.edu

THE PRINCETON REVIEW SAYS

Admissions

The school reports that its standardized testing policy for use in admission for Fall 2024 is Test Optional. It is unknown at this time if the 2024 testing policy will be permanent. The Princeton Review suggests that interested applicants consult with the school for the most up-to-date standardized testing policies. *Very important factors considered include:* interview. *Important factors considered include:* rigor of secondary school record, class rank, academic GPA, standardized test scores, application essay, character/personal qualities. *Other factors considered include:* recommendation(s), extracurricular activities, talent/ability, first generation, geographical residence, state residency, racial/ethnic status, volunteer work, work experience, level of applicant's interest. High school diploma is required and GED is accepted. *Academic units recommended:* 4 English, 3 math, 2 science, 2 science labs, 2 foreign language, 2 social studies.

Financial Aid

Students should submit: FAFSA. Priority filing deadline is 10/31. The Princeton Review suggests that all financial aid forms be submitted as soon as possible (see page 5 for a note on the FAFSA). *Need-based scholarships/grants offered:* College/university scholarship or grant aid from institutional funds; Federal Pell; Private scholarships; SEOG; State scholarships/grants. *Loan aid offered:* Direct PLUS loans; Direct Subsidized Loans; Direct Unsubsidized Loans; College/university loans from institutional funds. Admitted students will be notified of awards on a rolling basis beginning 3/1. Federal Work-Study Program available.

The Inside Word

The Tuition Promise Scholarship that every student receives understandably attracts a lot of applicants. Competition among candidates is intense. It's also important to note, you may be too wealthy to get admitted here. Berea won't admit students whose parents can afford to send them elsewhere. Financially qualified applicants should apply as early as possible.

THE SCHOOL SAYS "..."

From the Admissions Office

"Since its founding in 1855, Berea College has provided a high quality, low-cost education to students of all races. As the first interracial and co-educational college in the South, Berea admits students with great academic promise but limited financial means. Over the past 150 years, Berea has evolved into one of the most distinctive colleges in the United States serving students primarily from the Appalachian region.

"All admitted students receive a Tuition Promise Scholarship, which completely covers the cost of tuition after other forms of grant and scholarship aid are applied. This leaves only minimal expenses for housing, meals, and other expenses. Students graduate with one of the lowest rates of student educational debt in the nation, and one in three students graduate debt free. In addition to the Scholarship, students receive a laptop computer and a paid on-campus job to assist with educational and personal expenses as well as gain valuable work experience before graduation.

"As a result of this combination of academic reputation and generous financial assistance, Berea attracts many more applicants than are able to be accepted, so admission is competitive. The best means of improving the chances for admission is to complete the application process as early as possible, preferably by October 31 of the senior year."

SELECTIVITY

Admissions Rating	96
# of applicants	2,217
% of applicants accepted	25
% of acceptees attending	65

FIRST-YEAR PROFILE

Testing policy	Test Optional
Range SAT composite	1163–1273
Range SAT EBRW	578–673
Range SAT math	558–625
Range ACT composite	23–27
# submitting SAT scores	28
% submitting SAT scores	8
# submitting ACT scores	141
% submitting ACT scores	40
Average HS GPA	3.6
% frosh submitting high school GPA	93
% graduated top 10% of class	31
% graduated top 25% of class	70
% graduated top 50% of class	96

DEADLINES

Regular	
Priority	10/31
Deadline	3/31
Notification	Rolling, 11/15
Nonfall registration?	No

FINANCIAL FACTS

Annual tuition	$0
Room and board	$7,742
Required fees	$726
Books and supplies	$700
Average frosh need-based scholarship	$51,196
Average UG need-based scholarship	$51,676
% needy frosh rec. need-based scholarship or grant aid	100
% needy UG rec. need-based scholarship or grant aid	100
% needy frosh rec. non-need-based scholarship or grant aid	0
% needy UG rec. non-need-based scholarship or grant aid	0
% needy frosh rec. need-based self-help aid	100
% needy UG rec. need-based self-help aid	100
% frosh rec. any financial aid	100
% UG rec. any financial aid	100
% UG borrow to pay for school	39
Average cumulative indebtedness	$5,208
% frosh need fully met	0
% ugrads need fully met	0
Average % of frosh need met	98
Average % of ugrad need met	99

BERRY COLLEGE

2277 Martha Berry Hwy, NW, Mount Berry, GA 30149-0159 • Admissions: 706-232-5374

STUDENTS SAY ". . ."

Academics

Since its founding in 1902, Berry College has dedicated itself to providing a well-rounded liberal arts education and, being "Christian in spirit," the option for religious life. There are over 75 areas of study at Berry, ranging from traditional subjects like physics, French, nursing, art, and psychology, to innovative programs like One Health—a transdisciplinary approach to solving health-related problems—and a career path in professional tennis management. True to its liberal arts mission, Berry encourages students to explore their various academic interests and, above all, acquire a broad-based education. "We are a liberal arts school, so the foundation classes we take are just as important as our classes required for our major." Students speak glowingly of their professors and of the dedication they display. "I truly feel as if my success is their top priority." Students believe that Berry's traditionally small classes and faculty-student ratio (roughly 12 to 1) enhances their learning and the overall quality of the college experience. "I have had many classes where the whole reason I got up in the morning was because of said class and professor." Adds another: "These professors are skilled in their respective fields and bring a level of passion to their classes that is unrivaled." Berry supports students from start to finish, with faculty and peer mentors directly helping first-year students identify and ultimately achieve their academic goals.

Campus Life

Berry's sprawling campus, located at the foot of the Appalachian Mountains, comprises 27,000 acres of mountains, streams, and woodlands, making it the largest contiguous college campus in the world. "My favorite extracurricular activity at Berry College is walking the trails or taking drives around our mountain campus, especially during student-organized midnight/full-moon hikes." Groups of students can often be found scaling Lavender Mountain to reach the House o' Dreams—the founder's quaint stone and board-and-batter cottage from which one can not only see the entire campus, but also Northwest Georgia, Alabama, and Tennessee. "Berry's beautiful campus encourages lots of outdoor activities and engagement." Pickleball is a favorite among students and a social ritual for many, as are the various activities organized by the Krannert Center Activities Board, such as skate nights, concerts, and talent shows, all of which are alcohol-free (as liquor is prohibited on the main Berry campus). Students consider the optional LifeWorks program, which guarantees a paying job for all four years of college, one of the best aspects of campus life. "It's given me the leg up I need by helping me gain professional experience by doing things that actually affect the campus and its brand." Lifeworks jobs cover a broad range of interests, such as arts and theater, animal care, hospitality, athletics, and technology.

Student Body

Students often refer to the "Berry bubble," a term that emphasizes their close fellowship and the strength of their collective identity. "Berry is a tight-knit community and there's a friendly face around every corner." The relatively small student body enhances this sense of unity and school loyalty. "At Berry, no matter what kind of person you come across, everyone is genuine, kind, and helpful." Students praise the college as grounded in Christian principles, but proudly diverse, warmly welcoming members of all faiths. Many students take the school's ministering motto to heart, frequently volunteering to help their fellow students as well as those in need beyond the campus. "Even when it feels like nobody out there cares, some student here is waiting to change your mind." As another observes, "Our community is focused on service and giving back. We do many projects for classes that include serving in the community outside of our school." While all religious life is voluntary at Berry, many choose to attend services regularly and can be seen frequenting the many stunning chapels and other houses of worship that dot the Berry campus.

Financial Aid: 706-236-1714 • E-Mail: admissions@berry.edu • Website: www.berry.edu/

THE PRINCETON REVIEW SAYS

Admissions

The school reports that its standardized testing policy for use in admission for Fall 2024 is Test Optional. The 2024 testing policy will be permanent. The Princeton Review suggests that interested applicants consult with the school for the most up-to-date standardized testing policies. *Very important factors considered include:* rigor of secondary school record, academic GPA. *Important factors considered include:* extracurricular activities. *Other factors considered include:* standardized test scores, application essay, recommendation(s), interview, character/personal qualities, volunteer work, work experience. High school diploma is required and GED is accepted. *Academic units required:* 4 English, 4 math, 3 science, 2 foreign language, 3 social studies, 4 academic electives.

Financial Aid

Students should submit: FAFSA; State aid form. Priority filing deadline is 1/15. The Princeton Review suggests that all financial aid forms be submitted as soon as possible (see page 5 for a note on the FAFSA). *Need-based scholarships/grants offered:* College/university scholarship or grant aid from institutional funds; Federal Pell; Private scholarships; SEOG. *Loan aid offered:* Direct PLUS loans; Direct Subsidized Loans; Direct Unsubsidized Loans; College/university loans from institutional funds; State Loans. Admitted students will be notified of awards on a rolling basis beginning 11/1. Federal Work-Study Program available. Institutional employment available.

The Inside Word

Admissions officers at Berry College do their best to get to know and wholly consider each candidate. Of course, a solid college prep curriculum is a must. Students have the option of submitting either a Common App or using Berry's own application; both are given equal weight. Better yet, both are free. Finally, applicants who are sure that Berry is their top choice are encouraged to apply early decision.

THE SCHOOL SAYS "..."

From the Admissions Office

"Berry College offers approximately 2,000 undergraduates and 100 graduate students a one-of-a-kind educational experience, saying "Comparisons fail. There's no place like Berry." With 27,000 acres set amid multiple ecosystems, it's the largest campus in the world where science students conduct field research alongside professors; animal science majors get hands-on experience on a working farm; and everyone connects to nature whether hiking or biking 88 miles of trails or simply hanging a hammock. Ongoing development of state-of-the-art facilities is a priority, with recent additions such as the 23,000-square-foot animal science building. Ninety-seven percent of students participate in the signature work program—known as LifeWorks—and have access to eight semesters of paid professional development. Through the Center for Personal and Professional Development, they're matched with on-campus positions where they apply classroom knowledge in practical ways; build transferable skills like leadership, teamwork and critical thinking; and connect with a nationwide network of alumni. With rigorous academics across 75+ majors, minors and pre-professional programs, Berry averages 18 students per class; 82% of students complete a significant research or internship experience. Student-faculty interaction was ranked in the top 10% nationally by freshmen completing the National Survey of Student Engagement. Students receive one-on-one mentoring in a committed, caring community of professors, staff, and peers—often forming lifelong relationships. Shaped intellectually, professionally and personally for a life a purpose, 99% of graduates report employment or acceptance to graduate school (including 98% of pre-law and pre-med students and 80% of pre-vet students) within one year of graduation."

SELECTIVITY

Admissions Rating	87
# of applicants	5,643
% of applicants accepted	66
% of acceptees attending	17

FIRST-YEAR PROFILE

Testing policy	Test Optional
Range SAT composite	1110–1290
Range SAT EBRW	570–660
Range SAT math	540–630
Range ACT composite	21–29
# submitting SAT scores	134
% submitting SAT scores	21
# submitting ACT scores	141
% submitting ACT scores	22
Average HS GPA	3.8
% frosh submitting high school GPA	100
% graduated top 10% of class	28
% graduated top 25% of class	63
% graduated top 50% of class	92

DEADLINES

Early action	
Deadline	11/1
Notification	12/1
Regular	
Deadline	1/15
Notification	Rolling, 11/1
Nonfall registration?	Yes

FINANCIAL FACTS

Financial Aid Rating	87
Annual tuition	$40,140
Room and board	$14,230
Required fees	$226
Books and supplies	$1,000
Average frosh need-based scholarship	$32,198
Average UG need-based scholarship	$30,860
% needy frosh rec. need-based scholarship or grant aid	100
% needy UG rec. need-based scholarship or grant aid	100
% needy frosh rec. non-need-based scholarship or grant aid	30
% needy UG rec. non-need-based scholarship or grant aid	31
% needy frosh rec. need-based self-help aid	59
% needy UG rec. need-based self-help aid	62
% frosh rec. any financial aid	100
% UG rec. any financial aid	100
% UG borrow to pay for school	61
Average cumulative indebtedness	$27,775
% frosh need fully met	38
% ugrads need fully met	38
Average % of frosh need met	88
Average % of ugrad need met	87

BOSTON COLLEGE

140 Commonwealth Avenue, Chestnut Hill, MA 02467-3809 • Admissions: 617-552-8000 • Fax: 617-552-0798

STUDENTS SAY "..."

Academics

Boston College, a small Jesuit school on the outskirts of Boston, "is all about educating the person as a whole." Its strong core curriculum ensures all students receive a "well-rounded" liberal arts education regardless of their chosen major. Boston College's well-respected education and business school attract a lot of students, and there are many other strong programs, including English and communication. Students think Boston College is a "great experience academically" and gush about their "phenomenal professors." A secondary education major student says, "Boston College's professors are truly exceptional and are devoted to undergraduate learning." They're "engaging, challenging, and understanding, [and] are genuinely interested in the student as a whole person." Boston College's "prestigious" academics come with "high expectations," but if students need help, professors are "easily accessible outside of classes." Students "feel prepared for whatever is next" and note that their "well-connected" teachers and strong alumni network help with the job search. One student, who was drawn to Boston College because of its stellar reputation, finds it "even better than expected." Another adds, "I have always revered Boston College's academic and athletic reputation, and coming here, I have not been disappointed."

Campus Life

Boston College's "gorgeous campus" and "perfect'" suburban location has created a very rich campus life and given the school a "strong community feel." There's "a superb sense of school spirit, which truly sets it apart." One student raves, "There is just so much school spirit and love for the university!" Boston College's "incredible sports teams" are well-supported by "superfans at every event." "There is also a large service component," to life at Boston College, which allows students "to serve the community in Boston and communities all around the world." Boston College offers a "plethora of extracurricular activities," and students think "there's a club or group for everyone here." The school has "great facilities" and "state-of-the-art resources." Dorms are generally well-reviewed, though students think the housing lottery could be more "fair." Students often go into Boston for all of its entertainment and cultural activities but are happy to return to their "close-knit college" where they "feel very at home."

Student Body

Boston College has gotten some flak for its "preppy," "white," and "homogenous" student body, and a communication student admits, "The school's nickname as 'J. Crew U' isn't entirely unwarranted." Boston College could definitely use "greater racial diversity," but one student says that each year "the student body becomes more and more diverse." A student double-majoring in economics and German says, "Once you've settled in, you'll find that it's not at all difficult to find a group of friends," no matter who you are. "There is a large religious/spiritual community," because of the school's Jesuit affiliation, but "it is only one group of many." Boston College's Division I ranking means there are plenty of athletes and sports fans. Students warn that Boston College is "not the place to go to class in your pajamas." People, particularly women, are "very well-dressed" and "stylish." Students say their peers are "really ambitious" and "hardworking." "The majority of students seem intelligent and academically driven as well as dedicated to and passionate about one or more extracurricular activities." Though people at Boston College are "academically oriented," they're "also into having a good time, and "have a work hard, play hard mentality." There's a moderate amount of drinking on campus and off, but students say that no matter what, everyone "definitely [has] school as a top priority."

BOSTON COLLEGE

Financial Aid: 617-552-3300 • E-Mail: admission@bc.edu • Website: www.bc.edu

THE PRINCETON REVIEW SAYS

Admissions

The school reports that its standardized testing policy for use in admission for Fall 2024 is Test Optional. The 2024 testing policy will be temporary. The Princeton Review suggests that interested applicants consult with the school for the most up-to-date standardized testing policies. *Very important factors considered include:* rigor of secondary school record, academic GPA. *Important factors considered include:* class rank, application essay, recommendation(s), extracurricular activities, talent/ability, character/personal qualities, alumni/ae relation, religious affiliation/commitment, volunteer work. *Other factors considered include:* standardized test scores, first generation, racial/ethnic status, work experience. High school diploma is required and GED is accepted. *Academic units recommended:* 4 English, 4 math, 4 science, 4 science labs, 4 foreign language, 4 social studies, 4 history.

Financial Aid

Students should submit: Business/Farm Supplement; CSS/Financial Aid Profile; FAFSA; Noncustodial Profile. Priority filing deadline is 2/1. The Princeton Review suggests that all financial aid forms be submitted as soon as possible (see page 5 for a note on the FAFSA). *Need-based scholarships/grants offered:* College/university scholarship or grant aid from institutional funds; Federal Pell; Private scholarships; SEOG; State scholarships/grants. *Loan aid offered:* Direct PLUS loans; Direct Subsidized Loans; Direct Unsubsidized Loans; Federal Nursing Loans; State Loans. Admitted students will be notified of awards on or about 4/1. Federal Work-Study Program available. Institutional employment available.

The Inside Word

Boston College is one of many selective schools that eschew set admissions formulae. While a challenging high school curriculum and strong test scores are essential for any serious candidate, the college seeks students who are passionate and make connections between academic pursuits and extracurricular activities. The application process should reveal a distinct, mature voice and a student whose interest in education goes beyond the simple desire to earn an A.

THE SCHOOL SAYS "..."

From the Admissions Office

"Boston College undergraduate students achieve at the highest levels with honors in the past ten years including 1 Rhodes Scholarship winner, 114 Fulbrights, 1 Marshall, 7 Goldwaters, 6 Beckmans, and 6 Truman Postgraduate Fellowship Programs. Junior Year Abroad and Scholar of the College Program offer students flexibility within the curriculum. Facilities opened in the past ten years include: Stokes Hall, Cadigan Alumni Center, Thomas More Apartments, Fish Field House, Margot Connell Recreation Center, and the new Schiller Institute for Integrated Sciences and Society. Students enjoy the vibrant location in Chestnut Hill with easy access to the cultural and historical richness of Boston."

SELECTIVITY

Admissions Rating	97
# of applicants	40,494
% of applicants accepted	17
% of acceptees attending	35
# of early decision applicants	4,428
% accepted early decision	28

FIRST-YEAR PROFILE

Testing policy	Test Optional
Range SAT composite	1450–1520
Range SAT EBRW	705–760
Range SAT math	730–780
Range ACT composite	33–35
# submitting SAT scores	800
% submitting SAT scores	34
# submitting ACT scores	415
% submitting ACT scores	18
% graduated top 10% of class	90
% graduated top 25% of class	98
% graduated top 50% of class	99

DEADLINES

Early decision	
Deadline	11/1
Notification	12/15
Other ED deadline	1/1
Other ED notification	2/15
Regular	
Deadline	1/1
Notification	4/1
Nonfall registration?	Yes

APPLICANTS OFTEN PREFER

Brown University; Columbia University; Cornell University; Dartmouth College; Duke University; Harvard College; Tufts University; University of California—Berkeley; University of California—Los Angeles; University of Michigan—Ann Arbor; University of Notre Dame

APPLICANTS RARELY PREFER

Boston University; College of the Holy Cross; Fordham University; New York University; Northeastern University; Providence College; The George Washington University; University of Massachusetts Amherst; Villanova University

FINANCIAL FACTS

Financial Aid Rating	94
Annual tuition	$62,950
Room and board	$16,120
Required fees	$1,226
Books and supplies	$1,250
Average frosh need-based scholarship	$49,130
Average UG need-based scholarship	$47,465
% needy frosh rec. need-based scholarship or grant aid	89
% needy UG rec. need-based scholarship or grant aid	89
% needy frosh rec. non-need-based scholarship or grant aid	4
% needy UG rec. non-need-based scholarship or grant aid	3
% needy frosh rec. need-based self-help aid	89
% needy UG rec. need-based self-help aid	90
% UG rec. any financial aid	66
% UG borrow to pay for school	46
Average cumulative indebtedness	$23,075
% frosh need fully met	100
% ugrads need fully met	100
Average % of frosh need met	100
Average % of ugrad need met	100

BOSTON UNIVERSITY

One Silber Way, Boston, MA 02215 • Admissions: 617-353-2000

STUDENTS SAY "..."

Academics

Long recognized for offering both the breadth of a large research university and the depth of a private college, the "various schools and colleges within Boston University provide students with access to almost every imaginable program of study." In keeping with this, students report a wide variety of majors and concentrations, naming standout programs in engineering, health sciences, and business administration. Professors are praised as much as is students' ability to choose them: BU professors are both "actively pursuing research in their field" and "engaging partners in my academic experience," and students find that professors' "interesting backgrounds...fuel class discussions in a variety of academic areas." Undergraduates also love the university's "location" as an "urban campus" in Boston's Back Bay, and benefit distinctly from BU's "opportunity access" when it comes to job placement. As a private university with a large student body, BU students also become the beneficiaries of the institution's "wealth," calling the experience one of "big campus resources with a small campus feel." The faculty and administration "are constantly striving to be better for the student's benefit" in delivering BU's unique curriculum, which is "equal parts liberal arts education and pre-professional experience." The university emphasizes "study abroad" and "research opportunities," which further broaden the possibilities of a BU education. Perhaps ideal for the student who desires a wide variety of choices in order to discover what comes next, "the range and diversity of opportunities at Boston University allows you to Be You."

Campus Life

Continuing the theme of wide-ranging options, BU undergraduates divulge that student "life at BU is anything you want it to be." Because of BU's location in "the heart of Boston," "the city itself is like our campus," and BU undergrads can mingle freely with Boston's many other college students in nearby Cambridge, Somerville, Allston, and Brookline. Students are rarely bored because "there's always something interesting going on on- and off-campus": campus life boasts "a lot of clubs and activities to get involved in," as well as "house parties," "BU hockey games," and "frat parties," while students' access to Boston spans everything from "a run along the Charles River" to "shopping on Newbury or in Harvard Square" to frequenting "plays and ballets and museums" and the many local "clubs and bars." Students strive to maximize the best of both sides of BU life, "prid[ing] themselves on being able to find balance in living strong academic lives and exciting social lives as well." Students seem satisfied with the choices they do end up making, reporting that BU life is "wonderful" and that "there is more to do than you will be able to find the time for."

Student Body

"There is a great sense of diversity, yet an overwhelming feeling of unity" within BU's large but closely connected undergraduate population. Students strongly resist the idea of a "typical student," asserting that "originality is valued highly at BU," as is "diversity of thought." "Because we are an international university," many students point out, "the student body is vastly diverse." Students have "a wide range of interests both inside and outside the classroom," and characterize themselves as "motivated, culturally-aware, intelligent, adventurous," "driven and involved," and "very passionate." BU undergrads find their peers "intellectually stimulating in conversations" and tend to group, as in most college experiences, around shared interests and experiences. One student echoes many of her classmates this way: "My life at BU is quite packed because I chose to make it that way."

BOSTON UNIVERSITY

Financial Aid: 617-353-4176 • E-Mail: admissions@bu.edu; intadmis@bu.edu • Website: www.bu.edu

THE PRINCETON REVIEW SAYS

Admissions

The school reports that its standardized testing policy for use in admission for Fall 2024 is Test Optional. The 2024 testing policy will be temporary. The Princeton Review suggests that interested applicants consult with the school for the most up-to-date standardized testing policies. *Very important factors considered include:* rigor of secondary school record, academic GPA. *Important factors considered include:* class rank, application essay, recommendation(s), extracurricular activities, character/personal qualities. *Other factors considered include:* standardized test scores, first generation, alumni/ae relation, geographical residence, state residency, racial/ethnic status, volunteer work, work experience, level of applicant's interest. High school diploma is required and GED is accepted. *Academic units required:* 4 English, 3 math, 3 science, 3 science labs, 2 foreign language, 3 social studies. *Academic units recommended:* 4 English, 4 math, 4 science, 4 science labs, 4 foreign language, 4 social studies.

Financial Aid

Students should submit: CSS/Financial Aid Profile; FAFSA; Noncustodial Profile. The Princeton Review suggests that all financial aid forms be submitted as soon as possible (see page 5 for a note on the FAFSA). *Need-based scholarships/grants offered:* College/university scholarship or grant aid from institutional funds; Federal Pell; Private scholarships; SEOG; State scholarships/grants. *Loan aid offered:* Direct PLUS loans; Direct Subsidized Loans; Direct Unsubsidized Loans; State Loans. Admitted students will be notified of awards on a rolling basis beginning in late March. Federal Work-Study Program available. Institutional employment available.

The Inside Word

BU can afford to stay competitive, and they strongly emphasize high school academic performance as the key indicator of a student's admissibility to the university. BU values students who take on a challenging high school curriculum (especially AP and IB classes, or whatever the most challenging course load available is). The personal essay, recommendations, and extracurricular activities are also important factors in assessing applicants. BU meets full demonstrated need for admitted first-year students who are U.S. citizens or permanent residents.

THE SCHOOL SAYS "..."

From the Admissions Office

"Boston University is a world-recognized, private teaching and research university committed to excellence in undergraduate education. Students study with distinguished faculty that include Fulbright Scholars, Pulitzer Prize winners, a MacArthur Fellow, and a former Poet Laureate. In ten undergraduate schools and colleges, BU offers students more than 300 programs of study, cutting-edge research with faculty mentors, internships in the United States and abroad, and one of the nation's most extensive study abroad programs. Housing is guaranteed for four years in a variety of on-campus residences, including high-rise buildings and historic brownstones. BU students are engaged with their campus community through over 450 student organizations, club and intramural sports, and twenty-three NCAA Division I sports teams. Students experience the city of Boston as an extension of campus for study, internships, employment, and cultural and recreational activities.

"Students also benefit from research and internship opportunities in the United States and abroad and a network of more than 400,000 alumni in 174 countries around the world. With over 70 study abroad opportunities and classmates from over 100 countries, BU is truly a global university."

SELECTIVITY

Admissions Rating	97
# of applicants	80,796
% of applicants accepted	14
% of acceptees attending	31
# offered a place on the wait list	9,643
% accepting a place on wait list	61
% admitted from wait list	0
# of early decision applicants	6,309
% accepted early decision	25

FIRST-YEAR PROFILE

Testing policy	Test Optional
Range SAT composite	1370–1480
Range SAT EBRW	660–730
Range SAT math	690–770
Range ACT composite	31–34
# submitting SAT scores	823
% submitting SAT scores	23
# submitting ACT scores	448
% submitting ACT scores	12
Average HS GPA	3.9
% frosh submitting high school GPA	100
% graduated top 10% of class	87
% graduated top 25% of class	99
% graduated top 50% of class	100

DEADLINES

Early decision	
Deadline	11/1
Notification	12/15
Other ED deadline	1/4
Other ED notification	2/15
Regular	
Deadline	1/1
Notification	4/1
Nonfall registration?	Yes

APPLICANTS ALSO LOOK AT

Boston College; Brown University; Columbia University; Emory University; Johns Hopkins University; New York University; Northeastern University; Northwestern University; The George Washington University; Tufts University

FINANCIAL FACTS

Financial Aid Rating	86
Annual tuition	$61,050
Room and board	$17,400
Required fees	$1,310
Books and supplies	$1,000
Average frosh need-based scholarship	$57,882
Average UG need-based scholarship	$53,029
% needy frosh rec. need-based scholarship or grant aid	100
% needy UG rec. need-based scholarship or grant aid	99
% needy frosh rec. non-need-based scholarship or grant aid	26
% needy UG rec. non-need-based scholarship or grant aid	24
% needy frosh rec. need-based self-help aid	72
% needy UG rec. need-based self-help aid	66
% frosh rec. any financial aid	55
% UG rec. any financial aid	53
% UG borrow to pay for school	36
Average cumulative indebtedness	$38,263
% frosh need fully met	34
% ugrads need fully met	32
Average % of frosh need met	95
Average % of ugrad need met	89

BOWDOIN COLLEGE

255 Maine Street, Brunswick, ME 04011-8441 • Admissions: 207-725-3000 • Fax: 207-725-3101

STUDENTS SAY ". . ."

Academics

Bowdoin College, a liberal arts school on the east coast of Maine, has produced luminary alumni like Nathaniel Hawthorne, Henry Wadsworth Longfellow, and Franklin Pierce. This rich history has shaped its current and traditional academic vision of a well-rounded education. New students are required to take a writing seminar, as well as at least one class in areas such as mathematics, natural science, and visual and performing arts. Sophomores can then choose their majors from a wide variety of over 30 subjects, ranging from traditional fields such as history, physics, and English to modern focuses such as Digital and Computational Studies. Bowdoin encourages academic exploration so that students have the time to take courses outside their main areas of study. This freedom is enhanced by small classes that facilitate thoughtful discussion, with a notable student-faculty ratio of 9 to 1. That ideal class size, according to students, has resulted in one of the college's greatest strengths: excellent and dedicated professors who can provide personalized attention. "I'm really grateful to go to a liberal arts college where I can get so much more attention from professors…they are only here to teach and they love it." As another explains, Bowdoin offers "amazing professors who are passionate and smart and who care deeply about their students."

Campus Life

Bowdoin's eighteenth-century architecture is distinct, a New England campus that stands out whether it is dotted with Maine's celebrated foliage in autumn or dusted with snow in winter. The natural surroundings are a great draw; some students have come to love the outdoors through the Bowdoin Outing Club (BOC), a student organization that hosts over 150 events each year. "I came here without ANY experience in the outdoors at all…but now I've done whitewater canoeing/rafting, mountain biking, skiing, backpacking, etc.!" First-year and second-year students are required to live on campus and most choose to stay until they graduate. As there is no Greek life at Bowdoin, the many clubs and extracurricular activities, which include environmental advocacy, crafts, and the student newspaper, are central to life at the college. "Most students are involved in multiple on-campus activities—I don't know anyone who doesn't do several other things outside of classes." Students can also be found perusing the renowned Bowdoin College Museum of Art, which houses over 20,000 artworks in its collection.

Student Body

The Bowdoin community is known for its camaraderie. "Bowdoin's student body is small enough that walking on campus means saying 'hi' to a lot of familiar faces." The "Bowdoin hello," a longstanding tradition by which students greet each other enthusiastically on campus, represents the sense of unity and friendliness often observed. "One thing I love about Bowdoin, and that drew me to the school in my college search, was the supportive and collaborative atmosphere." This community spirit is reflected in students' support for school athletics, which has a strong presence on campus. Varsity football, baseball, and ice hockey games are routinely filled with groups of Bowdoin "Polar Bears" excitedly cheering in support of their teams.

Students also suggest that their peers "care very strongly about forming community and bridging connections." Many describe their classmates as academically competitive in general, yet extremely supportive. "I appreciate the community here, as people want others to succeed with them and are more than willing to offer help to get you where you want to be." The helpfulness of fellow students is frequently cited as a significant factor in the school's academic success. "I feel I can grow more as a student with collaborative peers rather than [with] peers who are trying to compete with me."

BOWDOIN COLLEGE

Financial Aid: 207-725-3144 • E-Mail: admissions@bowdoin.edu • Website: www.bowdoin.edu

THE PRINCETON REVIEW SAYS

Admissions

The school reports that its standardized testing policy for use in admission for Fall 2024 remains Test Optional, as it has been since 1969. *Very important factors considered include:* rigor of secondary school record, class rank, academic GPA, application essay, recommendation(s), extracurricular activities, talent/ability, character/personal qualities. *Other factors considered include:* standardized test scores (if submitted), interview, first generation, alumni/ae relation, geographical residence, state residency, racial/ethnic status, volunteer work, work experience, level of applicant's interest. High school diploma is required and GED is accepted. *Academic units recommended:* 4 English, 4 math, 4 science, 3 science labs, 4 foreign language, 4 social studies.

Financial Aid

Students should submit: Business/Farm Supplement; CSS/Financial Aid Profile; FAFSA; Noncustodial Profile. The Princeton Review suggests that all financial aid forms be submitted as soon as possible (see page 5 for a note on the FAFSA). *Need-based scholarships/grants offered:* College/university scholarship or grant aid from institutional funds; Federal Pell; Private scholarships; SEOG; State scholarships/grants. *Loan aid offered:* Direct Subsidized Loans; Direct Unsubsidized Loans; State Loans. Admitted students will be notified of awards on or about in mid-March, with the letter of admission. Federal Work-Study Program available. Institutional employment available.

The Inside Word

Admissions officers at Bowdoin emphasize their search for students proving themselves to be curious, thoughtful, and engaged. Bowdoin looks at student grades relative to the respective school's level of difficulty, recommendations from teachers and counselors, writing samples, school and community involvement, character, personality, and overall academic potential. A personal interview isn't required but is recommended. Bowdoin has a Test Optional policy and also provides the opportunity for students to submit a video response, which is optional but allows students to give a two-minute response to a randomly selected question.

THE SCHOOL SAYS "..."

From the Admissions Office

"Bowdoin is a welcoming and diverse community of students, faculty, and staff who care deeply about and support each other through four years of learning, exploration, and growth. We are dedicated to the liberal arts, to deep intellectual inquiry, and to discourse and debate on the toughest issues.

"Bowdoin offers a wide array of curricular and extracurricular opportunities combined with a 221-year tradition of serving the common good. Bowdoin also leads in the study and teaching of the environment, with fifty years of an interdisciplinary approach and an unparalleled collection of facilities and field stations in which to conduct place-based research. Study of the environment at Bowdoin encourages broad environmental literacy through course offerings and activities available to all students—building a solid foundation for the career paths that Bowdoin graduates pursue in all walks of life.

"The College makes a Bowdoin education affordable. We accept students on a need-blind basis with a commitment to meet full demonstrated need for all four years. Nearly half of our students receive scholarship assistance from the College and Bowdoin stands firm in its decision to eliminate loans from aid packages.

"This all takes place in the easily accessible and vibrant town of Brunswick amid one of the most beautiful settings anywhere—the extraordinary coast of Maine. As Bowdoin's seventh president wrote in 'The Offer of the College' in 1906, the Bowdoin experience may very well be '...the best four years of your life.'"

SELECTIVITY

Admissions Rating	98
# of applicants	9,376
% of applicants accepted	9
% of acceptees attending	59
# of early decision applicants	1,009
% accepted early decision	26

FIRST-YEAR PROFILE

Testing policy	Test Optional
Range SAT composite	1340–1520
Range SAT EBRW	670–760
Range SAT math	670–780
Range ACT composite	31–35
# submitting SAT scores	294
% submitting SAT scores	58
# submitting ACT scores	154
% submitting ACT scores	30
% graduated top 10% of class	83
% graduated top 25% of class	95
% graduated top 50% of class	99

DEADLINES

Early decision	
Deadline	11/15
Notification	12/15
Other ED deadline	1/5
Other ED notification	2/15
Regular	
Deadline	1/5
Nonfall registration?	No

APPLICANTS OFTEN PREFER

Brown University; Dartmouth College; Harvard College; Yale University

APPLICANTS SOMETIMES PREFER

Amherst College; Cornell University; Swarthmore College; Williams College

APPLICANTS RARELY PREFER

Middlebury College; Wesleyan University

FINANCIAL FACTS

Financial Aid Rating	99
Annual tuition	$60,952
Room and board	$16,772
Required fees	$576
Books and supplies	$840
Average frosh need-based scholarship	$60,558
Average UG need-based scholarship	$59,010
% needy frosh rec. need-based scholarship or grant aid	100
% needy UG rec. need-based scholarship or grant aid	100
% needy frosh rec. non-need-based scholarship or grant aid	0
% needy UG rec. non-need-based scholarship or grant aid	0
% needy frosh rec. need-based self-help aid	100
% needy UG rec. need-based self-help aid	99
% frosh rec. any financial aid	49
% UG rec. any financial aid	48
% UG borrow to pay for school	23
Average cumulative indebtedness	$20,652
% frosh need fully met	100
% ugrads need fully met	100
Average % of frosh need met	100
Average % of ugrad need met	100

BRADLEY UNIVERSITY

1501 W. Bradley Avenue, Peoria, IL 61625 • Admissions: 309-676-7611 • Fax: 309-677-2797

STUDENTS SAY "..."

Academics

Bradley University in Peoria, Illinois offers students "personal attention and unique opportunities you don't get at big schools," and "everything feels personalized." Students say, "the Engineering program at the university is phenomenal," and boasts "a fabulous new building." Most agree that "the nursing, engineering, and business departments seem to be the crown jewels of the school," also citing that "the communication department and English department are excellent." In class, students can expect to be engaged and challenged no matter your course of study. "Much of my coursework involves discussions and projects to push you outside of your comfort zone," one student explains, but "workload is entirely dependent on the classes you take," and can vary by subject. "The number of credit hours you're taking doesn't necessarily correlate to workload."

Here, "the faculty really care about each student," but still hold them to the "high degree of standard and excellence that is expected of students at Bradley." But undergrads are not alone while working to rise to the challenge, as "the professors strive to help their students meet and exceed those standards." Enrollees largely agree that most professors "are subject matter experts in their field," and "most are willing to work with students inside and outside of the classroom to help them through." When it comes to research opportunities, "students get to work directly with the professors to find academically relevant findings together." Bradley also offers "many services for internship help, career advice, academic tutoring services," as well as a career center that "provide[s] a strong relationship with advisors."

Campus Life

Bradley students spend much of their time socializing on campus, in and out of doors. "There is almost always a large group of people in the non-dining hall eating areas, such as the student center." In nice weather, students "sit outside on the quad chairs and just hang out," or stroll on one of the "long connecting paths that make leisure walking accessible." The library is a popular place to "stay up late studying, complete group work, and socialize." The Markin Recreation Center also has "anything and everything you could want/need," including "the gym, basketball courts, rock climbing, dance rooms, and the pool." The student activities council, ACBU, keeps students busy with "some really great events all through the year," and "Late Night BU" is "a non-alcohol influence activity that happens at least every month." Students are also involved in a myriad of extracurriculars, such as music organizations, the literary journal, and professional Greek organizations. Greek life and "Wags for Mags, an organization that trains service dogs" are also popular. With so many options, the majority feel "it is very easy to get involved on campus."

Student Body

Located in central Illinois, "most of the students here come from Central Illinois, Chicago or St. Louis." At Bradley University, "nearly all on-campus, full-time students are within the same age range, but there are some older online graduate students." In terms of demographics, many say "the student population is primarily white and middle/upper-middle class," but even though "there is not a ton of diversity...there is enough of it that people won't feel alone," one student admits.

In discussing their classmates, many have overwhelmingly positive things to say. "Most all Bradley students I have met over the years are friendly, caring, motivated, and enjoy being at Bradley," another student attests. "Our student body is passionate, excited to learn, and paving the way to a new and accepting generation." Students describe their peers as "inquisitive and thought-provoking," and many are "very career-minded." Being a smaller school, "it's possible to know most people in your major and year," and as a result, "people seem extremely comfortable around each other."

BRADLEY UNIVERSITY

Financial Aid: 309-677-3089 • E-Mail: admissions@bradley.edu • Website: www.bradley.edu

THE PRINCETON REVIEW SAYS

Admissions

The school reports that its standardized testing policy for use in admission for Fall 2024 is Test Optional. The 2024 testing policy will be permanent. The Princeton Review suggests that interested applicants consult with the school for the most up-to-date standardized testing policies. *Very important factors considered include:* rigor of secondary school record, academic GPA. *Other factors considered include:* class rank, standardized test scores, application essay, recommendation(s), interview, extracurricular activities, talent/ability, character/personal qualities, first generation, alumni/ae relation, volunteer work, work experience, level of applicant's interest. High school diploma is required and GED is accepted. *Academic units required:* 4 English, 3 math, 2 science, 2 science labs, 2 social studies. *Academic units recommended:* 4 English, 4 math, 3 science, 3 science labs, 2 foreign language, 3 social studies, 2 history.

Financial Aid

Students should submit: FAFSA. Priority filing deadline is 12/1. The Princeton Review suggests that all financial aid forms be submitted as soon as possible (see page 5 for a note on the FAFSA). *Need-based scholarships/grants offered:* College/university scholarship or grant aid from institutional funds; Federal Pell; Private scholarships; SEOG; State scholarships/grants; United Negro College Fund. *Loan aid offered:* Direct PLUS loans; Direct Subsidized Loans; Direct Unsubsidized Loans; Federal Nursing Loans. Admitted students will be notified of awards on a rolling basis beginning 11/15. Federal Work-Study Program available. Institutional employment available.

The Inside Word

Bradley has a strong regional pull, which leads to an undergraduate population of mostly Illinois residents. However, out-of-staters who dream of attaining their ever-popular business or health care degrees, shouldn't worry! This university has a history of eagerly admitting above-average students who want to get an excellent education, without the grueling admission process other private schools put applicants through. Just make sure you keep your application deadlines straight, as there are three separate application deadlines to choose from (early action, regular, and extended).

THE SCHOOL SAYS "..."

From the Admissions Office

"Bradley offers nearly 6,000 students a broad range of academic programs enhanced by required experiential learning. The university prepares students for immediate and substantial career success by offering resources not found at small colleges and more personalized experiences than large universities. Great academic variety leads to choices of majors, minors and graduate programs that are uncommon at most private universities. More than 185 academic programs are available in business, communications, education, engineering, fine and performing arts, health sciences, liberal arts, science and technology. Unique programs include entrepreneurship, game design, sports communication and physical therapy. Located less than three hours from Chicago, St. Louis and Indianapolis, the eighty-five-acre residential campus is located in a historic neighborhood just one mile from downtown Peoria, the largest metropolitan area in downstate Illinois.

"Bradley students develop leadership skills in more than 240 student organizations, with more than 60 dedicated to student leadership and community service. Students may also participate in the nation's most winning speech team, fraternities and sororities, and NCAA Division I athletics.

"Bradley graduates are well prepared for a career or direct entry to graduate school with 91 percent employed, continuing their education or pursuing other postgraduate experiences within six months of graduation. Eighty-two percent of students reported having at least one career-related work experience before graduating, and 95 percent report having participated in an internship, practicum, undergraduate research, community service or study abroad.

"The Princeton Review rates Bradley's internship opportunities among the top 20 for private schools in the nation, and the video game design program as among the top 20 in the nation."

SELECTIVITY

Admissions Rating	84
# of applicants	11,352
% of applicants accepted	75
% of acceptees attending	12

FIRST-YEAR PROFILE

Testing policy	Test Optional
Range SAT composite	1070–1280
Range SAT EBRW	580–670
Range SAT math	490–610
Range ACT composite	24–30
# submitting SAT scores	416
% submitting SAT scores	40
# submitting ACT scores	143
% submitting ACT scores	14
Average HS GPA	3.8
% frosh submitting high school GPA	100
% graduated top 10% of class	22
% graduated top 25% of class	51
% graduated top 50% of class	85

DEADLINES

Regular	
Priority	11/1
Nonfall registration?	Yes

APPLICANTS OFTEN PREFER
University of Illinois—Urbana-Champaign

APPLICANTS SOMETIMES PREFER
DePaul University; Marquette University

APPLICANTS RARELY PREFER
Augustana College (IL); Illinois State University

FINANCIAL FACTS

Financial Aid Rating	83
Annual tuition	$37,380
Room and board	$12,196
Required fees	$420
Books and supplies	$1,200
Average frosh need-based scholarship	$26,541
Average UG need-based scholarship	$23,160
% needy frosh rec. need-based scholarship or grant aid	100
% needy UG rec. need-based scholarship or grant aid	99
% needy frosh rec. non-need-based scholarship or grant aid	16
% needy UG rec. non-need-based scholarship or grant aid	15
% needy frosh rec. need-based self-help aid	77
% needy UG rec. need-based self-help aid	77
% UG borrow to pay for school	75
Average cumulative indebtedness	$35,603
% frosh need fully met	21
% ugrads need fully met	20
Average % of frosh need met	80
Average % of ugrad need met	75

BRANDEIS UNIVERSITY

415 South St., Waltham, MA 02454-9110 • Admissions: 781-736-2000 • Fax: 781-736-3536

STUDENTS SAY "..."

Academics

Situated just outside of Boston, Brandeis University is a phenomenal school that "teaches... the value of hard work, cultivates curiosity and [an] interest in learning, and introduces one to various perspectives." Importantly, the university offers undergrads "the opportunity to explore every possible interest, from cupcakes to neuroscience, with the overwhelming support of faculty and peers." Because Brandeis embraces a policy of academic "flexibility," students feel free to "to study whatever they want." There's also an "abundance of undergraduate research opportunities in all majors." Overall, undergrads here find their coursework "challenging" and "rewarding." Inside the classroom, they are greeted by "engaging, insightful, and responsive" professors who truly make an effort to "relate to students." As one delighted individual shares, "My current bio teacher is known for using memes in her lectures, and they're usually pretty funny." It's also quite evident that professors "care for their students and want them to be successful." To that end, they strive to make themselves "accessible" and "encourage students coming to talk to them." Perhaps that's why one highly contented undergrad asserts, "I strongly believe the professors are one of Brandeis's most appealing aspects."

Campus Life

At Brandeis, academics often take top priority. And first-year students quickly discover that "on weeknights the library is the most social spot on campus." But fear not; undergrads here still manage to find plenty of time to step away from the books. In fact, we're told that "Brandeis thrives on its campus club and student activities culture," which makes sense given that there are over 200 clubs on campus to join. Many students can be found participating "in community service clubs, cultural clubs, electronics clubs, and religious organizations, do research in labs, perform in musicals and plays, participate in sport events, and play music in ensembles." Undergrads also simply "enjoy the green spaces on campus and have fun connecting [there] with other students." Once the weekend rolls around, "there are always shows going on, whether it's theatre, a cappella, or improv." Additionally, there tend to be "sports events and guest lecturers." Undergrads also frequently attend "Greek life events off campus." However, those gatherings are "not sanctioned by the university." Lastly, students love the school's "[close] proximity" to Cambridge and Boston. And since Brandeis has a commuter rail stop on campus and runs a free shuttle on weekends, both cities are wholly "accessible" and provide a great respite from campus life.

Student Body

It's safe to say that Brandeis students really care for their peers. After all, they rush to describe them as "intelligent, driven, [and] kind-hearted." They also seem to maintain "a diverse range of interests (both academic and extracurricular) and are extremely passionate about everything they are involved in." Moreover, undergrads readily admit that they "do have the tendency to be a little more on the introverted and nerdy side." And they truly love that their classmates are often "quirky and a little weird in the best way possible." As one student explains, "There is no normal Brandeis. I love that I can wear whatever I want because I know there's nowhere where it will be a problem that I don't fit in or feel judged. Everyone's attitude is kind of 'do whatever you want to/need to do.'" Given that openness, it's not too surprising to learn that Brandeis students also report that their classmates are quite "friendly." Indeed, a student reports, "Everyone here is very welcoming and supportive and they push me to try a bit harder every day, while offering support whenever it is needed without even having to be asked to do so."

BRANDEIS UNIVERSITY

Financial Aid: 781-736-3700 • E-Mail: admissions@brandeis.edu • Website: www.brandeis.edu/

THE PRINCETON REVIEW SAYS

Admissions

The school reports that its standardized testing policy for use in admission for Fall 2024 is Test Flexible. It is unknown at this time if the 2024 testing policy will be permanent. The Princeton Review suggests that interested applicants consult with the school for the most up-to-date standardized testing policies. *Very important factors considered include:* rigor of secondary school record, class rank, academic GPA, character/personal qualities. *Important factors considered include:* application essay, recommendation(s), extracurricular activities, talent/ability. *Other factors considered include:* standardized test scores, interview, first generation, alumni/ae relation, geographical residence, state residency, religious affiliation/commitment, racial/ethnic status, volunteer work, work experience, level of applicant's interest. High school diploma is required and GED is accepted. *Academic units recommended:* 4 English, 4 math, 4 science, 2 science labs, 4 foreign language, 4 social studies.

Financial Aid

Students should submit: CSS/Financial Aid Profile; FAFSA; Noncustodial Profile. The Princeton Review suggests that all financial aid forms be submitted as soon as possible (see page 5 for a note on the FAFSA). *Need-based scholarships/grants offered:* College/university scholarship or grant aid from institutional funds; Federal Pell; Private scholarships; SEOG; State scholarships/grants. *Loan aid offered:* Direct PLUS loans; Direct Subsidized Loans; Direct Unsubsidized Loans; College/university loans from institutional funds; State Loans. Admitted students will be notified of awards on or about 4/1. Federal Work-Study Program available. Institutional employment available.

The Inside Word

Admissions to Brandeis is selective. Therefore, it's imperative that applicants have taken a challenging course load that includes a handful of honors, AP, or IB classes (if and when possible). However, admissions officers are also looking for students who will thrive in and contribute to campus life. Hence, personal statements, letters of recommendations, and extracurricular activities also hold some weight. Finally, Brandeis is a Test Flexible school. Students who opt not to submit SAT or ACT scores will have to send in a graded analytical paper (from an 11th or 12th grade class) or three different exams (from an approved list of AP and IB tests) instead.

THE SCHOOL SAYS "..."

From the Admissions Office

"Brandeis was established in 1948 by the American Jewish community at a time when Jews and other ethnic and racial minorities, and women, faced discrimination in higher education. Today, Brandeis is a leading research university for anyone, regardless of background, who wants to use their knowledge, skills and experience to improve the world. Over 3,500 Brandeis undergraduates and 550 faculty members collaborate across disciplines, interests, and perspectives on scholarship that has a positive impact throughout society.

"At the core of our community are values rooted in Jewish history and experience: a reverence for academic excellence, a robust engagement in critical thinking, and a commitment to making the world a better place. Classes are taught by professors who value teaching undergraduates and serve as advisors and mentors. Our flexible curriculum lets students pursue their passions with the ability to double major, study abroad, and engage in research and internships in Waltham, Boston, and beyond.

"Brandeis is a vibrant, free-thinking, intellectual university that values community. Students are actively engaged on campus in pursuits ranging from the arts to athletics and student government to community service.

"Brandeis has an ideal location on the commuter rail right outside of downtown Boston, giving students access to internships, jobs, and research in law, medicine, government, finance, business, and the arts."

SELECTIVITY

Admissions Rating	95
# of applicants	11,343
% of applicants accepted	30
% of acceptees attending	25
# offered a place on the wait list	1,553
% accepting a place on wait list	41
% admitted from wait list	1
# of early decision applicants	953
% accepted early decision	37

FIRST-YEAR PROFILE

Testing policy	Test Flexible
Range SAT composite	1380–1490
Range SAT EBRW	660–730
Range SAT math	690–790
Range ACT composite	30–33
# submitting SAT scores	549
% submitting SAT scores	64
# submitting ACT scores	219
% submitting ACT scores	25
Average HS GPA	3.8
% frosh submitting high school GPA	90
% graduated top 10% of class	56
% graduated top 25% of class	83
% graduated top 50% of class	97

DEADLINES

Early decision	
Deadline	11/1
Notification	12/15
Other ED deadline	1/1
Other ED notification	2/1
Regular	
Deadline	1/1
Notification	4/1
Nonfall registration?	Yes

FINANCIAL FACTS

Financial Aid Rating	94
Annual tuition	$55,340
Room and board	$16,080
Required fees	$2,221
Required fees (first-year)	$2,596
Books and supplies	$1,000
Average frosh need-based scholarship	$44,006
Average UG need-based scholarship	$42,876
% needy frosh rec. need-based scholarship or grant aid	96
% needy UG rec. need-based scholarship or grant aid	95
% needy frosh rec. non-need-based scholarship or grant aid	10
% needy UG rec. non-need-based scholarship or grant aid	6
% needy frosh rec. need-based self-help aid	86
% needy UG rec. need-based self-help aid	92
% frosh rec. any financial aid	65
% UG rec. any financial aid	67
% UG borrow to pay for school	46
Average cumulative indebtedness	$32,158
% frosh need fully met	121
% ugrads need fully met	94
Average % of frosh need met	97
Average % of ugrad need met	97

BRIGHAM YOUNG UNIVERSITY (UT)

Brigham Young University, Provo, UT 84602-1110 • Admissions: 801-422-1211 • Fax: 801-422-0005

CAMPUS LIFE

Quality of Life Rating	90
Fire Safety Rating	75
Green Rating	60*
Type of school	Private
Affiliation	Church of Jesus Christ of Latter-day Saints
Environment	City

STUDENTS

Total undergrad enrollment	31,633
% male/female/another gender	49/51/NR
% from out of state	72
% frosh live on campus	43
% ugrads live on campus	17
# of fraternities	0
# of sororities	0
% African American	0
% Asian	2
% White	79
% Hispanic	7
% Native American	<1
% Pacific Islander	<1
% Two or more races	4
% Race and/or ethnicity unknown	1
% international	5
# of countries represented	121

SURVEY SAYS . . .

Students are happy
Classroom facilities are great
Great library
School is well run
No one cheats
Students are friendly
Students are very religious
Students get along with local community
Students involved in community service
Everyone loves the Cougars
Intramural sports are popular
Theater is popular
Dorms are like palaces

ACADEMICS

Academic Rating	87
% students returning for sophomore year	89
% students graduating within 4 years	8
% students graduating within 6 years	54
Calendar	Semester
Student/faculty ratio	21:1
Profs interesting rating	90
Profs accessible rating	92
Most classes have 10–19 students.	

MOST POPULAR MAJORS

Business/Commerce, General; Elementary Education and Teaching; Exercise Physiology and Kinesiology

STUDENTS SAY ". . ."

Academics

Founded in the tradition of The Church of Jesus Christ of Latter-day Saints, Utah's Brigham Young University has long held a reputation for quality academics and alumni that go on to great things. It has also provided "a spiritual side to our education in addition to all the secular knowledge," which is useful to those of its attendees who are religious: "Some of my best classes here have been ones where the professor ties the subject to religion or God." The school "has clear guidelines and expectations as to the conduct of its students," and, with almost 200 majors to choose from, does "a great job at helping students find their passions and [making] them successful in their careers." The school also embraces innovation and technology to the fullest, supporting students with "virtual spaces where we can interact with TAs and get help."

Within the classroom, student highlight their professors as encouraging, both through the material they hand out—"assignments that enhance my learning instead of just busy work—and in the way they help students "to push themselves and to take advantage of the many internships and research that the school provides." They're also a fan of the approach some teachers take toward "final projects, both in groups and individually, rather than exams" and appreciate that they "consistently looked for feedback from the students throughout the semester to make sure that the class topics were tailored to what the students were interested in." Overall, there are "incredible opportunities to succeed," whether that's from the "guest lecturers from all walks of life" that BYU brings in or the frequent "field trips to places in the area relevant to the subject material," research and study abroad opportunities, and outlets "to display your work throughout campus."

Campus Life

Students suggest that coursework is rigorous and that "most time at BYU is filled by academic studies," but also note that there are "a million different ways to be involved on campus with clubs and events," including "a 'Cougar skate' activity once or twice a month where people can come roller skating" and country swing, which is "a popular activity year round." Just don't expect "a big drinking or partying culture"; look instead to the highly attended "state-wide affair" of sports and note the school's Provo location, which leads to "a big culture of hiking, climbing, camping, and boating in the mountains" or just visits to the "so many national parks nearby." Those looking for more career- or service-related opportunities will find that "church activities are always happening" that give students opportunities to pitch in, and the BYU Student-Alumni program, a huge driver for networking, puts on events each year, "including an etiquette dinner, a food drive, [and] a traditions ball to celebrate the history of the school." There's even an annual "summit retreat featuring TED-talk-style presenters."

Student Body

While many at BYU are a part of the LDS church, "you can still meet a pretty broad sampling of people from within that group," and students are said to maintain a "broad worldview and are interested in learning more about other people's experiences and supporting them in their journeys." It helps that the school has made "diligent efforts" to diversity and bring in "a large international population," such that there is "great diversity regarding culture, political orientation, and extracurricular interests." There is "a good mix of people who like to constantly socialize and also are diligent and serious studying," and "a strong community of service and people who care about one another." This high-achieving group "expect a lot (sometimes too much) of themselves and at times others," but all remain "very kind and considerate" overall, and "for the most part, we are a rule-following community."

BRIGHAM YOUNG UNIVERSITY (UT)

Financial Aid: 801-422-8153 • E-Mail: admissions@byu.edu • Website: www.byu.edu

THE PRINCETON REVIEW SAYS

Admissions

The school reports that its standardized testing policy for use in admission for Fall 2024 is Test Optional. It is unknown at this time if the 2024 testing policy will be permanent. The Princeton Review suggests that interested applicants consult with the school for the most up-to-date standardized testing policies. *Very important factors considered include:* rigor of secondary school record, academic GPA, standardized test scores, application essay, recommendation(s), extracurricular activities, talent/ability, character/personal qualities, religious affiliation/commitment, volunteer work, work experience. *Important factors considered include:* first generation. *Other factors considered include:* level of applicant's interest. High school diploma is required and GED is accepted. *Academic units recommended:* 4 English, 4 math, 3 science, 2 foreign language, 2 history.

Financial Aid

Students should submit: FAFSA. Priority filing deadline is 2/1. The Princeton Review suggests that all financial aid forms be submitted as soon as possible (see page 5 for a note on the FAFSA). *Need-based scholarships/grants offered:* College/university scholarship or grant aid from institutional funds; Federal Pell; Private scholarships; State scholarships/grants. *Loan aid offered:* Direct PLUS loans; Direct Subsidized Loans; Direct Unsubsidized Loans; College/university loans from institutional funds. Admitted students will be notified of awards on a rolling basis.

The Inside Word

Students at Brigham Young University tend to be a self-selecting bunch: more than four-fifths of those who get accepted to the school end up attending. That dedication manifests in many ways throughout the application process, but admissions officers certainly appreciate seeing students who embrace LDS principles. That goes the other way too: the Church of Jesus Christ of Latter-day Saints supports BYU students by helping to subsidize tuition prices, so much so that—per the school—it's as if "each student attending BYU is on scholarship."

THE SCHOOL SAYS "..."

From the Admissions Office

"The mission of Brigham Young University—founded, supported, and guided by The Church of Jesus Christ of Latter-day Saints—is to assist individuals in their quest for perfection and eternal life. That assistance should provide a period of intensive learning in a stimulating setting where a commitment to excellence is expected and the full realization of human potential is pursued. All instruction, programs, and services at BYU, including a wide variety of extracurricular experiences, should make their own contribution toward the balanced development of the total person. Such a broadly prepared individual will not only be capable of meeting personal challenge and change but will also bring strength to others in the tasks of home and family life, social relationships, civic duty, and service to mankind."

SELECTIVITY

Admissions Rating	94
# of applicants	11,608
% of applicants accepted	59
% of acceptees attending	79

FIRST-YEAR PROFILE

Testing policy	Test Optional
Range SAT composite	1230–1420
Range SAT EBRW	620–720
Range SAT math	600–720
Range ACT composite	26–32
# submitting SAT scores	1,101
% submitting SAT scores	20
# submitting ACT scores	4,111
% submitting ACT scores	76
Average HS GPA	3.9
% frosh submitting high school GPA	99

DEADLINES

Regular	
Priority	11/1
Deadline	12/15
Notification	2/18
Nonfall registration?	Yes

FINANCIAL FACTS

Financial Aid Rating	76
Annual tuition	$6,120
Room and board	$8,048
Required fees	$0
Books and supplies	$912
Average frosh need-based scholarship	$5,736
Average UG need-based scholarship	$5,821
% needy frosh rec. need-based scholarship or grant aid	51
% needy UG rec. need-based scholarship or grant aid	76
% needy frosh rec. non-need-based scholarship or grant aid	63
% needy UG rec. non-need-based scholarship or grant aid	53
% needy frosh rec. need-based self-help aid	18
% needy UG rec. need-based self-help aid	18
% frosh rec. any financial aid	27
% UG rec. any financial aid	43
% UG borrow to pay for school	21
Average cumulative indebtedness	$12,627
% frosh need fully met	2
% ugrads need fully met	3
Average % of frosh need met	32
Average % of ugrad need met	35

BROWN UNIVERSITY

One Prospect Street, Providence, RI 02912 • Admissions: 401-863-1000 • Fax: 401-863-9300

CAMPUS LIFE

Quality of Life Rating	**95**
Fire Safety Rating	**88**
Green Rating	**94**
Type of school	Private
Affiliation	No Affiliation
Environment	City

STUDENTS

Total undergrad enrollment	7,222
% male/female/another gender	49/51/<1
% from out of state	94
% frosh from public high school	55
% frosh live on campus	99
% ugrads live on campus	70
# of fraternities (% join)	9 (7)
# of sororities (% join)	7 (4)
% African American	8
% Asian	19
% White	38
% Hispanic	12
% Native American	<1
% Pacific Islander	<1
% Two or more races	8
% Race and/or ethnicity unknown	3
% international	12
# of countries represented	117

SURVEY SAYS . . .

Lots of liberal students
Students always studying
Students are happy
Lab facilities are great
Great library
Career services are great
Internships are widely available
Great financial aid
No one cheats
Students are friendly
Diverse student types interact on campus
Students aren't religious
Students involved in community service
Students environmentally aware
Students love Providence, RI
Easy to get around campus
Recreation facilities are great
Theater is popular
Campus newspaper is popular
Active student government
Active minority support groups
Active student-run political groups

ACADEMICS

Academic Rating	**96**
% students returning for sophomore year	99
% students graduating within 4 years	85
% students graduating within 6 years	95
Calendar	Semester
Student/faculty ratio	6:1
Profs interesting rating	95
Profs accessible rating	95
Most classes have 10–19 students.	

MOST POPULAR MAJORS

Computer and Information Sciences, General;
Biology/Biological Sciences, General; Econometrics
and Quantitative Economics

STUDENTS SAY ". . ."

Academics

Interdisciplinary-focused Brown University, in Providence, Rhode Island, is dedicated to undergraduate freedom, meaning students must take responsibility for designing their own courses of study via the Open Curriculum. Students sing the praises of the academic flexibility at this Ivy League institution and the accompanying emphasis on social action. "We would not be...strong students and teachers without a proper system in place to encourage that," says one undergrad. Those who roam these hallowed halls are "constantly questioning what could make the world and our school a better place." Every person "has their own interests and pursues it without any push from others," which is why Brown can be a "very intense" place to go to school—not because students are competing academically with each other, but "because there are so many people doing so much and fighting so hard for it."

Brown's faculty "are at the top of their fields and are working on research that pushes those fields forward." The "engaging, personal, and incredibly dedicated" professors are "the heart and soul of our strongest departments." They "care so much about what they do and connect with students on a very human level." Undergraduates come first here, and Brown encourages students to "explore their academic interests independently in order to experience everything that academics have to offer." As one enrollee explains it, "No other school I had looked at allowed students to...build their own academic journey without any general requirements." Graduates tend to "not just go to the normative career options," and "career and internship placement has become a top priority of the new university administration."

Campus Life

Students describe a nice balance between work and play at Brown—academia rules during a week that is "filled with countless hours of study," but it's also an "exciting" and "very happy place with many activities and events going on all the time." Some go to parties or "downtown for the weekend," while others make the most of the constant "lectures, movie screenings, improv shows, dance performances, [and] a cappella showcases." Many here also do "intellectual activities or athletics over breaks," and "community clubs and special interest clubs (such as international student groups)" are extremely popular. Students also often go to the lounges in the dorms to watch movies with friends. And, "beautiful" as the campus is, students can easily walk one minute to Thayer Street and "enjoy restaurants and excellent dining" or walk 20 minutes to Providence Place Mall. Boston and New York are very close, but "Providence is busy enough that Brown never completely empties out."

Student Body

This "knowledgeable and inspiring" community is made up of people who are "very intelligent, care about global issues, and possess one or two quirks." The school "has a way of molding people into their best selves," and the most common trait is "a true zeal for whatever it is that we care most about." Although this is a liberal campus, there are "a handful of conservatives," and "the entire body has a general chilled-out vibe." As one student puts it, "I've never experienced so many people willing to have a conversation about topics that usually make people uncomfortable." There is "a prevailing intolerance of intolerance on campus," and the culture of activism "bespeaks an idealism and a strong moral code that drives a lot of the work students do on campus."

Financial Aid: 401-863-2721 • E-Mail: admission@brown.edu • Website: www.brown.edu

THE PRINCETON REVIEW SAYS

Admissions

The school reports that its standardized testing policy for use in admission for Fall 2024 is Test Optional. It is unknown at this time if the 2024 testing policy will be permanent. The Princeton Review suggests that interested applicants consult with the school for the most up-to-date standardized testing policies. *Very important factors considered include:* rigor of secondary school record, class rank, academic GPA, application essay, recommendation(s), talent/ability, character/personal qualities. *Important factors considered include:* extracurricular activities. *Other factors considered include:* standardized test scores, first generation, alumni/ae relation, geographical residence, state residency, racial/ethnic status, volunteer work, work experience. High school diploma is required and GED is accepted. *Academic units required:* 4 English, 4 math, 3 science, 2 science labs, 3 foreign language, 2 history, 1 academic elective. *Academic units recommended:* 4 English, 4 math, 4 science, 3 science labs, 4 foreign language, 1 social studies, 3 history, 1 visual/performing arts, 1 academic elective.

Financial Aid

Students should submit: CSS/Financial Aid Profile; FAFSA; Noncustodial Profile. Priority filing deadline is 2/1. The Princeton Review suggests that all financial aid forms be submitted as soon as possible (see page 5 for a note on the FAFSA). *Need-based scholarships/grants offered:* College/university scholarship or grant aid from institutional funds; Federal Pell; Private scholarships; SEOG; State scholarships/grants. *Loan aid offered:* Direct PLUS loans; Direct Subsidized Loans; Direct Unsubsidized Loans; College/university loans from institutional funds. Admitted students will be notified of awards on or about 4/1. Federal Work-Study Program available. Institutional employment available.

The Inside Word

The cream of just about every crop applies to Brown, and admission is competitive. Gaining admission requires more than just a superior academic profile from high school. Candidates from states that are overrepresented in the applicant pool, such as New York, have to be particularly distinguished in order to have the best chance at admission. Brown accepts the Common Application, with additional writing supplements for all first-year students, and requires some additional statements from students who apply to the Program in Liberal Medical Education or the Dual Degree Program with Rhode Island School of Design.

THE SCHOOL SAYS "..."

From the Admissions Office

"Brown University is the nation's seventh oldest institution and one of eight members of the Ivy League. The University is known for its academic rigor rooted in its "Open Curriculum." Brown has no distribution requirements that students must complete to graduate, which attracts self-motivated students committed to being the architects of their own education. Our students like to say that only Brown gives them the absolute freedom to study what they love, and only what they love. In the process, students are challenged by their own experiences, peers, and advisors to expand their notions of "what they love." Students sample a wide range of courses before immersing themselves in more than 80 academic concentrations, with the option of independent study. Brown offers unparalleled opportunities for research collaboration with faculty who lead in their fields; the best in educational innovation, leading-edge scholarship; and opportunities for community-based service learning. This has contributed to a reputation for graduating entrepreneurial, socially conscious students who make an impact in their communities and the world. Brown has among the highest rates nationally of admission to law school and medical school, and graduates successfully begin careers in areas of science and engineering, the arts, policy, medicine and many other fields. The Warren Alpert Medical School and the Brown University School of Public Health are the only medical school and public health school in the state of Rhode Island, offering medical instruction, clinical training, and leading research into therapies and cures and areas of population health."

SELECTIVITY

Admissions Rating	99
# of applicants	50,649
% of applicants accepted	5
% of acceptees attending	67
# of early decision applicants	6,146
% accepted early decision	15

FIRST-YEAR PROFILE

Testing policy	Test Optional
Range SAT composite	1500–1560
Range SAT EBRW	730–780
Range SAT math	760–800
Range ACT composite	34–36
# submitting SAT scores	923
% submitting SAT scores	54
# submitting ACT scores	456
% submitting ACT scores	27
% graduated top 10% of class	93
% graduated top 25% of class	97
% graduated top 50% of class	100

DEADLINES

Early decision	
Deadline	11/1
Notification	12/15
Regular	
Deadline	1/3
Notification	3/31
Nonfall registration?	No

APPLICANTS ALSO LOOK AT

Columbia University; Cornell University; Dartmouth College; Duke University; Harvard College; Northwestern University; Princeton University; Stanford University; University of Pennsylvania; Yale University

FINANCIAL FACTS

Financial Aid Rating	97
Annual tuition	$65,656
Room and board	$16,598
Required fees	$2,474
Average frosh need-based scholarship	$59,928
Average UG need-based scholarship	$60,190
% needy frosh rec. need-based scholarship or grant aid	100
% needy UG rec. need-based scholarship or grant aid	99
% needy frosh rec. non-need-based scholarship or grant aid	0
% needy UG rec. non-need-based scholarship or grant aid	0
% needy frosh rec. need-based self-help aid	83
% needy UG rec. need-based self-help aid	84
% frosh rec. any financial aid	56
% UG rec. any financial aid	48
% UG borrow to pay for school	21
Average cumulative indebtedness	$26,272
% frosh need fully met	100
% ugrads need fully met	100
Average % of frosh need met	100
Average % of ugrad need met	100

BRYANT UNIVERSITY

1150 Douglas Pike, Smithfield, RI 02917-1291 • Admissions: 401-232-6000 • Fax: 401-232-6741

STUDENTS SAY ". . ."

Academics

Bryant University in Rhode Island prides itself on doing things differently, and they stand by that by encouraging an integrated curriculum of business, liberal arts, and health and behavioral science. It's a combination that students don't seem to mind, citing "phenomenal job placement numbers." One student claims "it is very hard to *not* get a job within six months of graduating." That could be due, in part, to the fact that the school "excels in its ability to provide hands-on academic experiences" that "ensure all students are ready for what the real world will be like." One such initiative is the first-year Bryant IDEA Program, which is "a three-day intensive program that teaches design thinking." Those opportunities don't end on Bryant's campus, though, as students can also take advantage of programs like the one-to-two-week Sophomore International Experience abroad.

Regardless of where Bryant's students are, the "academic experience is always focused on learning rather than getting a grade." and everyone here is "very willing to offer extra help when it is needed," making it "hard [for a student] to fall through the cracks." To that end, faculty here are "professionals in their industry" and are "quite open...about their real-world experiences." Their words "bring great insight into various industries" and "allow students to get in touch with the latest information so they can catch up with the current [trends] in the business world." This also comes with the open style of teaching many classes employ, "which allows for a dialogue and expansion of thoughts and ideas in the classroom." That dialogue also reaches beyond the classroom thanks to an "incredible network of alumni who genuinely care and want to get Bryant students jobs."

Campus Life

For Bryant Bulldogs, weekdays "are filled with class, homework, and group projects," so students are "always busy with group meetings." But when they're not in a meeting or in class, students "normally sit and do homework by the pond—if it is nice out." When they're ready to step away from their studies, there's plenty of school spirit to go around for the NCAA Division I sports: "Everyone goes to...games...dressed in black and gold." Outside of intramurals, "various clubs attract a lot of students," with an assortment of options ranging from those that "promote mental health awareness [to those] that play video games every Friday night." On weekends, students will often "take a trip to Providence for dinner or go on a trip with the Student Programming Board to go bowling, to [see] a play, or to [watch] a Boston sports game." Whatever your tastes may be, this "extremely welcoming" community has the "perfect balance of academics, recreation, and extracurricular activities."

Student Body

At Bryant, "no one is simply looking for a job—everyone is searching for *the* job." This leads to "an air of professionalism here," although students can "be labeled as over-involved" as they do what they can to gain experience and stand out. It's not hard for students to recognize each other at Bryant, though, as it's a "relatively small school in land and in numbers." One student says, "That means we get to know our peers on a more personal level." This familiarity is also helped by the fact that "many choose to double major." Indeed, this group is "driven to succeed in their careers after college," and "almost everyone who can is employed in a summer internship." Overall, campus life is teeming with "different types of leaders who are each striving for their individual goals but are also devoted to maintaining a strong, cohesive student body."

Financial Aid: 401-232-6020 • E-Mail: admission@bryant.edu • Website: www.bryant.edu/

THE PRINCETON REVIEW SAYS

Admissions

The school reports that its standardized testing policy for use in admission for Fall 2024 is Test Optional. The 2024 testing policy will be permanent. The Princeton Review suggests that interested applicants consult with the school for the most up-to-date standardized testing policies. *Very important factors considered include:* rigor of secondary school record, academic GPA. *Important factors considered include:* class rank, standardized test scores, application essay, recommendation(s). *Other factors considered include:* interview, extracurricular activities, talent/ability, character/personal qualities, first generation, alumni/ae relation, geographical residence, state residency, racial/ethnic status, volunteer work, work experience, level of applicant's interest. High school diploma is required and GED is accepted. *Academic units required:* 4 English, 4 math, 2 science, 2 science labs, 2 foreign language, 2 history. *Academic units recommended:* 4 English, 4 math, 3 science, 3 science labs, 2 foreign language, 3 history.

Financial Aid

Students should submit: FAFSA. Priority filing deadline is 2/15. The Princeton Review suggests that all financial aid forms be submitted as soon as possible (see page 5 for a note on the FAFSA). *Need-based scholarships/grants offered:* College/university scholarship or grant aid from institutional funds; Federal Pell; Private scholarships; SEOG; State scholarships/grants. *Loan aid offered:* Direct PLUS loans; Direct Subsidized Loans; Direct Unsubsidized Loans. Admitted students will be notified of awards on or about 3/24. Federal Work-Study Program available. Institutional employment available.

The Inside Word

The admissions process at Bryant University is wholly comprehensive. To begin, the school wants students who have taken a challenging college prep curriculum (including honors, AP, and IB courses when possible). Of course, letters of recommendation and extracurricular involvement are also important. Applicants wary of standardized tests will be delighted to learn that Bryant is a Test Optional school. In lieu of submitting scores, students will have to respond to three short essay questions.

THE SCHOOL SAYS "..."

From the Admissions Office

"At Bryant University, students reach higher and achieve more. You'll belong to a close-knit community with faculty and staff dedicated to helping you create your path to success and reach your fullest potential. Our integrated academic and student life programs deliver superior outcomes and a return on investment among the top 1% in the U.S.

"Bryant students benefit from a career-focused curriculum at the intersection of business, the liberal arts, and health and behavioral sciences. By selecting the combination of studies that interest you most, you'll develop critical 21st-century skills for leadership positions in high-demand fields such as data science, finance, health, marketing, and accounting.

"You'll graduate with the real-world-ready knowledge to excel now and in the future, and you'll gain experience solving real problems for leading companies and organizations, as well as a set of values you can draw upon to make important and complex decisions. Inspired to excel, you'll become a game changer and impact thinker.

"The nationally recognized programs of Bryant's Amica Center for Career Education will help you develop lifelong leadership ability and professional skills to secure the position you want after college. Our 50,000 accomplished alumni provide a powerful professional network that opens doors around the world.

"Bryant's approach prepares you for both personal fulfillment and professional success. Ninety-nine percent of the University's students are employed or enrolled in graduate school within six months of graduation with a median starting salary of $68,000. Most importantly, Bryant prepared them to make a difference in the world."

SELECTIVITY

Admissions Rating	87
# of applicants	8,898
% of applicants accepted	69
% of acceptees attending	16
# offered a place on the wait list	280
% accepting a place on wait list	50
% admitted from wait list	0
# of early decision applicants	153
% accepted early decision	82

FIRST-YEAR PROFILE

Testing policy	Test Optional
Range SAT composite	1180–1320
Range SAT EBRW	580–650
Range SAT math	583–670
Range ACT composite	27–32
# submitting SAT scores	187
% submitting SAT scores	19
# submitting ACT scores	24
% submitting ACT scores	3
Average HS GPA	3.5
% frosh submitting high school GPA	99
% graduated top 10% of class	16
% graduated top 25% of class	45
% graduated top 50% of class	83

DEADLINES

Early decision	
Deadline	11/1
Notification	12/1
Other ED deadline	1/15
Other ED notification	2/15
Early action	
Deadline	11/15
Notification	1/15
Regular	
Deadline	2/15
Notification	3/15
Nonfall registration?	Yes

APPLICANTS OFTEN PREFER

Babson College; Bentley University; Boston College; Boston University; University of Connecticut; University of Massachusetts Amherst

APPLICANTS SOMETIMES PREFER

Fairfield University; Fordham University; Loyola University Maryland; Marist College; Northeastern University; Providence College; University of Vermont

FINANCIAL FACTS

Financial Aid Rating	81
Annual tuition	$50,272
Room and board	$17,258
Required fees	$897
Books and supplies	$1,400
Average frosh need-based scholarship	$24,195
Average UG need-based scholarship	$23,340
% needy frosh rec. need-based scholarship or grant aid	100
% needy UG rec. need-based scholarship or grant aid	100
% needy frosh rec. non-need-based scholarship or grant aid	23
% needy UG rec. non-need-based scholarship or grant aid	17
% needy frosh rec. need-based self-help aid	74
% needy UG rec. need-based self-help aid	80
% frosh rec. any financial aid	98
% UG rec. any financial aid	95
% UG borrow to pay for school	58
Average cumulative indebtedness	$58,086
% frosh need fully met	24
% ugrads need fully met	19
Average % of frosh need met	67
Average % of ugrad need met	65

BRYN MAWR COLLEGE

101 North Merion Avenue, Bryn Mawr, PA 19010-2899 • Admissions: 610-526-5000 • Fax: 610-526-7471

STUDENTS SAY "..."

Academics

A women's liberal arts college founded in 1885 (and the first to offer the PhD), Bryn Mawr College in southeastern Pennsylvania is an "institution with a heart" that fosters "a close-knit community of empowered lifelong learners" who are "committed to striving for social equality and academic excellency." Students enjoy the relaxed and intimate atmosphere of a small college. One student describes "dinner parties in professors' homes, small reading groups that meet once a week, film screenings and weekend outings with my classmates" and shares, "I think I'm lucky to have such open and accessible professors and mentors." Bryn Mawr's low student-to-faculty ratio allows students to get plenty of face time with their professors and peers in during classes, which students describe as "laid back, in that everyone is working hard but does not feel the competitive pressure found at other schools." "It is easy to get a spot in most classes," one student tells us, "so your schedule truly reflects your interests." Bryn Mawr offers other ways for students to personalize their studies, even within the required coursework: "The freshman writing seminar has about 20 different classes, so students get to explore a topic that excites them." Bryn Mawr is also part of the Seven Sister Colleges and the Tri-College Consortium "with Haverford and Swarthmore [which] allows students to explore a range of fields without compromising on the small liberal arts college experience." Overall students are thrilled with their experience at Bryn Mawr and the support they receive, or, as one student puts it: "Bryn Mawr College represents hope and self-empowerment for every student who walks through Pem Arch."

Campus Life

"Bryn Mawr students are serious about classes," but that doesn't mean they don't have a social life. While "most week days people do homework and study in the libraries," students use the weekends to "go into Philadelphia or just go around the area" for "restaurants, concerts, museums, and special events." And there is always something fun to do on campus as well. The "student activities office plans a lot of events like movie screenings, tie dye, concerts, [and] pumpkin decorating" and Bryn Mawr's many clubs and student groups host events as well, "like crafting nights, culture shows, [and] keynote speakers." These socially-minded students can also discuss, plan, and organize within the college's "activist groups with causes ranging from the environment to elder care." The college's rich and storied history means that there are a lot of "traditions and annual parties (e.g., 'East vs. West')" for students to take part in, and for off-campus parties, "We hop on the blue bus and head over to Haverford, which has a better music/party scene," students tell us.

Student Body

"Brilliantly smart, informed and active in the community," Bryn Mawr students show a high regard for one another and value the individual contributions each one of their peers makes. "While there are countless stereotypes about the sort of people who attend a women's college," one student explains, "there's really no one Bryn Mawr type." The college hosts "an incredibly talented and diverse group" of students who are united by "our love of Bryn Mawr and learning in general." Students say the student body is "quite political," and "while straight, cis women can certainly thrive at Bryn Mawr, you should come here prepared for an active and thriving LGBTQIA+ culture. It's a very special part of Bryn Mawr that I wouldn't trade for anything." These "intellectual, accepting, open, kind, inclusive and bright individuals" "are a part of dance groups, singing groups and just about any other activity," and they make sure to "attend each other's performances." Overall, students agree that the student body is a reflection of a BMC culture that thrives to "[help] people achieve their fullest potential without forcing them into a mold."

BRYN MAWR COLLEGE

Financial Aid: 610-526-5245 • E-Mail: admissions@brynmawr.edu • Website: www.brynmawr.edu

THE PRINCETON REVIEW SAYS

Admissions

The school reports that its standardized testing policy for use in admission for Fall 2024 is Test Optional. It is unknown at this time if the 2024 testing policy will be permanent. The Princeton Review suggests that interested applicants consult with the school for the most up-to-date standardized testing policies. *Very important factors considered include:* rigor of secondary school record, application essay, recommendation(s). *Important factors considered include:* class rank, academic GPA, extracurricular activities, character/personal qualities. *Other factors considered include:* standardized test scores, interview, talent/ability, first generation, alumni/ae relation, geographical residence, state residency, racial/ethnic status, volunteer work, work experience. High school diploma is required and GED is accepted. *Academic units recommended:* 4 English, 4 math, 4 science, 1 science lab, 4 foreign language, 2 social studies, 2 history, 2 academic electives.

Financial Aid

Students should submit: CSS/Financial Aid Profile; FAFSA; Noncustodial Profile. The Princeton Review suggests that all financial aid forms be submitted as soon as possible (see page 5 for a note on the FAFSA). *Need-based scholarships/grants offered:* College/university scholarship or grant aid from institutional funds; Federal Pell; Private scholarships; SEOG; State scholarships/grants. *Loan aid offered:* Direct PLUS loans; Direct Subsidized Loans; Direct Unsubsidized Loans; College/university loans from institutional funds. Federal Work-Study Program available. Institutional employment available.

The Inside Word

Bryn Mawr College is among the most academically competitive in the nation. Incoming first-year students need to submit the Common Application or the Coalition Application, a writing supplement, two teacher evaluations, a mid-year report, standardized tests results (see Test Optional policy), and a final report. While not required, students are also encouraged to interview with an alum or admissions officer, and students can also submit art supplements through the Common App as well.

THE SCHOOL SAYS "..."

From the Admissions Office

"Bryn Mawr, a selective women's college with 1,402 undergraduates, is renowned for its academic excellence, diverse and close-knit community, and engagement with the world.

"On an historic campus just outside of Philadelphia, Bryn Mawr students find challenging courses and research; strong bonds with faculty, students, and alumnae/i; innovative programs that connect study with action; and top-tier partnerships that expand options.

"Critical, creative, and collaborative, Bryn Mawr alumnae/i are agents of change in every arena—and forever members of a community founded on respect for individuals.

"Minutes outside of Philadelphia and only two hours by train from New York City and Washington, D.C., Bryn Mawr is recognized by many as one of the most stunning college campuses in the United States.

"Standardized test scores for U.S. applicants or U.S. permanent residents are not required. Non-U.S. citizens and Non-U.S. permanent residents are required to submit standardized test scores (SAT or ACT) as well as either the TOEFL or IELTS if their primary language is not English and/or their language of instruction over the last four years has not been English."

SELECTIVITY

Admissions Rating	94
# of applicants	3,594
% of applicants accepted	31
% of acceptees attending	36

FIRST-YEAR PROFILE

Testing policy	Test Optional
Range SAT composite	1300–1470
Range SAT EBRW	660–750
Range SAT math	620–750
Range ACT composite	29–35
# submitting SAT scores	223
% submitting SAT scores	56
# submitting ACT scores	116
% submitting ACT scores	29
% graduated top 10% of class	63
% graduated top 25% of class	86
% graduated top 50% of class	98

DEADLINES

Early decision	
Deadline	11/15
Other ED deadline	1/1
Regular	
Deadline	1/15
Notification	4/1
Nonfall registration?	No

APPLICANTS ALSO LOOK AT

Barnard College; Boston University; Brown University; Haverford College; Mount Holyoke College; Smith College; Swarthmore College; The University of Chicago; Wellesley College; Wesleyan University

FINANCIAL FACTS

Financial Aid Rating	99
Annual tuition	$61,190
Room and board	$18,690
Required fees	$970
Books and supplies	$1,000
Average frosh need-based scholarship	$52,528
Average UG need-based scholarship	$57,712
% needy frosh rec. need-based scholarship or grant aid	99
% needy UG rec. need-based scholarship or grant aid	99
% needy frosh rec. non-need-based scholarship or grant aid	27
% needy UG rec. non-need-based scholarship or grant aid	27
% needy frosh rec. need-based self-help aid	78
% needy UG rec. need-based self-help aid	85
% UG borrow to pay for school	50
Average cumulative indebtedness	$30,234
% frosh need fully met	100
% ugrads need fully met	100
Average % of frosh need met	100
Average % of ugrad need met	100

BUCKNELL UNIVERSITY

1 Dent Drive, Lewisburg, PA 17837 • Admissions: 570-577-2000 • Fax: 570-577-3538

CAMPUS LIFE

Quality of Life Rating	84
Fire Safety Rating	93
Green Rating	99
Type of school	Private
Affiliation	No Affiliation
Environment	Village

STUDENTS

Total undergrad enrollment	3,732
% male/female/another gender	48/52/NR
% from out of state	76
% frosh from public high school	61
% frosh live on campus	100
% ugrads live on campus	88
# of fraternities (% join)	7 (30)
# of sororities (% join)	9 (41)
% African American	4
% Asian	5
% White	76
% Hispanic	7
% Native American	<1
% Pacific Islander	<1
% Two or more races	4
% Race and/or ethnicity unknown	1
% international	5
# of countries represented	50

SURVEY SAYS . . .

Students always studying
Students are happy
Classroom facilities are great
Lab facilities are great
Great library
Career services are great
Internships are widely available
Easy to get around campus
Recreation facilities are great
Intramural sports are popular
Frats and sororities are popular
Alumni active on campus

ACADEMICS

Academic Rating	90
% students returning for sophomore year	91
% students graduating within 4 years	82
% students graduating within 6 years	87
Calendar	Semester
Student/faculty ratio	9:1
Profs interesting rating	92
Profs accessible rating	94
Most classes have 10–19 students.	
Most lab/discussion sessions have 10–19 students.	

MOST POPULAR MAJORS

Economics, General; Political Science and
Government, General; Psychology, General

STUDENTS SAY "..."

Academics

To students, Bucknell University is a Goldilocks school: not too big or small, but "just right." The 445-acre campus is glowingly, goldenly described as well: "A beautiful campus...the sunset is unbeatable and the buildings are so technologically advanced." Curiosity is a pillar of learning at Bucknell, where the administration "ensure[s] a well-rounded education with experiential learning." Enrollees are welcome "to study far beyond my chosen major" in all three schools—College of Arts & Sciences, College of Engineering, and Freeman College of Management. Biomedical engineers note their work with orthopedic surgeons on device prototypes, Markets, Innovation & Design students examine sustainability for renovations on campus, and management students treat $3 million of Bucknell's endowment like their own investment company. Students feel their education at Bucknell "simulates a real-life work environment while also being centered around serving the Lewisburg community."

Bucknell professors are "all leaders in their field," and devote time to share their expertise: "[They] are very dedicated and willing to engage with students...on an academic level or just grabbing a coffee to chat." The 9:1 student-teacher ratio sets the bar for dynamic discussion in small classes, as one observes, "Get[ting] to know my professors personally...makes me more likely to ask questions." Even with all the attention, students still feel they are allowed the autonomy to learn and make mistakes. They rise to the challenges of "academically rigorous" and "truly stellar" instruction, which fuels the inquisitive mind: "Everyday class life has proved to keep me motivated and constantly trying to learn in different disciplines."

Campus Life

The vibrant campus life at Bucknell "has the perfect balance of challenging academics and a plethora of fun activities [with which] to let off steam." The University hosts weekly activities; some foster arts and entertainment with concerts and gallery shows; others advance education and careers with guest speakers who are often alumni, a network that "genuinely wants to help out the community that helped them." Students embrace the cooperative spirit with their "highly involved" leadership and outreach. Many are "committed to making change," with "amazing research opportunities" starting freshman year, like Bucknell's chapter of "e-NABLE," where students rev up MakerSpace's 3-D printer to fabricate upper limb prosthetics for those in need, and in turn see "a great chance to support and get to know the local community."

On the weekend, students kick back with a movie, break a sweat on a hike, or venture off the quad to "let loose" outside of campus. Many partake in Super Saturday, "an all-day party hosted by the fraternities where everyone is welcome." Bucknellians can "easily walk downtown" for the restaurant and bar scene or go kayaking and biking. Whatever the interest, group camaraderie abounds: "There is always someone who will happily join you."

Student Body

Students at Bucknell work together in a wide variety of ways to study, improve the school, and advance their "collaborative living and learning environment." The collegiate atmosphere, described as "extremely supportive and smart, but not overly competitive," motivates students—"I feel compelled by my peers to work hard"—and the many study groups help to keep "an emphasis on teamwork."

Students also "prioritize health," which means many can be found together on the field, from gym workouts to Division I sports. "Many of my peers are athletes," notes a student; a few have even gone on to become Olympians. A "work hard, play hard" mantra also cultivates a "strong community bond" among students that explains why diversity and equity are so important to students. One student has already taken notice: "I feel...the student body became more diverse...from the time I was a freshman to a senior." Regardless of similarities and differences, Bucknellians are confident about what unites them, declaring, "[We] all share the same goal: to learn."

BUCKNELL UNIVERSITY

Financial Aid: 570-577-1331 • E-Mail: admissions@bucknell.edu • Website: www.bucknell.edu

THE PRINCETON REVIEW SAYS

Admissions

The school reports that its standardized testing policy for use in admission for Fall 2024 is Test Optional. The 2024 testing policy will be temporary. The Princeton Review suggests that interested applicants consult with the school for the most up-to-date standardized testing policies. *Very important factors considered include:* rigor of secondary school record, academic GPA, application essay, extracurricular activities, talent/ability, character/personal qualities. *Important factors considered include:* standardized test scores, recommendation(s), volunteer work, work experience. *Other factors considered include:* class rank, first generation, alumni/ae relation, geographical residence, religious affiliation/commitment, racial/ethnic status, level of applicant's interest. High school diploma is required and GED is accepted. *Academic units required:* 4 English, 3 math, 2 science, 2 foreign language, 2 social studies, 2 history, 1 academic elective. *Academic units recommended:* 4 English, 4 math, 4 science, 2 science labs, 4 foreign language, 2 social studies, 2 history, 1 academic elective.

Financial Aid

Students should submit: CSS/Financial Aid Profile; FAFSA. The Princeton Review suggests that all financial aid forms be submitted as soon as possible (see page 5 for a note on the FAFSA). *Need-based scholarships/grants offered:* College/university scholarship or grant aid from institutional funds; Federal Pell; Private scholarships; SEOG; State scholarships/grants. *Loan aid offered:* Direct PLUS loans; Direct Subsidized Loans; Direct Unsubsidized Loans. Admitted students will be notified of awards on or about 4/1. Federal Work-Study Program available. Institutional employment available.

The Inside Word

A well-rounded, extremely polished application is non-negotiable for the hopeful Bucknell applicant, as the school gets more competitive every year. Admissions officers strive to consider all facets of the applications they receive—test scores, essays, recommendations, transcripts—so make sure you consider all of them carefully. In particular, the admission committee is looking for applicants who can demonstrate how they are bold, thoughtful, and compassionate leaders. Bucknell accepts the Common Application.

THE SCHOOL SAYS "..."

From the Admissions Office

"Bucknell University offers more than 60 majors and 70 minors in the College of Arts & Sciences, College of Engineering and Freeman College of Management. Your professors will be mentors and innovators in their fields who will challenge you to think critically, develop your ideas thoughtfully and apply what you learn. Bucknell is a residential university, so most students live on campus, but learning, service, research and recreation extend off campus. You will have the opportunity to volunteer as close as the local nursing home, community center and sustainable farm, and as far away as New Orleans and Nicaragua. Every year, students also travel off campus to conduct research with faculty mentors. Destinations have included Alaska, Suriname and Australia.

"At Bucknell, you'll take advantage of career services such as advising, networking, mock interviews and employer fairs. You can explore your career options and network with alumni through summer internships with corporations, government organizations and non-profits locally, nationally and internationally. An externship program provides job-shadowing opportunities for sophomores.

"With its green spaces, brick buildings and striking vistas, Bucknell's 450-acre campus is a quintessential college environment in the heart of scenic central Pennsylvania. The restaurants and shops of downtown Lewisburg—including the Barnes & Noble at Bucknell University and the historic Campus Theatre—lie within walking distance of campus. The University is located within three- to four-hours' driving distance of Baltimore, New York City, Philadelphia, Pittsburgh and Washington, D.C."

SELECTIVITY

Admissions Rating	94
# of applicants	11,707
% of applicants accepted	33
% of acceptees attending	27
# offered a place on the wait list	3,463
% accepting a place on wait list	45
% admitted from wait list	1
# of early decision applicants	954
% accepted early decision	54

FIRST-YEAR PROFILE

Testing policy	Test Optional
Range SAT composite	1180–1390
Range SAT EBRW	590–690
Range SAT math	580–710
Range ACT composite	27–32
# submitting SAT scores	722
% submitting SAT scores	70
# submitting ACT scores	269
% submitting ACT scores	26
Average HS GPA	3.6
% frosh submitting high school GPA	100
% graduated top 10% of class	57
% graduated top 25% of class	84
% graduated top 50% of class	99

DEADLINES

Early decision	
Deadline	11/15
Notification	12/15
Other ED deadline	1/15
Other ED notification	2/15
Regular	
Deadline	1/15
Notification	4/1
Nonfall registration?	No

APPLICANTS OFTEN PREFER
Cornell University; Dartmouth College; Tufts University; University of Pennsylvania; University of Virginia

APPLICANTS SOMETIMES PREFER
Boston College; Colgate University; Lehigh University; University of Richmond; Wake Forest University

APPLICANTS RARELY PREFER
Elon University; Lafayette College; Northeastern University; Penn State University Park; Villanova University

FINANCIAL FACTS

Financial Aid Rating	83
Annual tuition	$64,418
Room and board	$16,118
Required fees	$354
Books and supplies	$900
Average frosh need-based scholarship	$43,466
Average UG need-based scholarship	$42,325
% needy frosh rec. need-based scholarship or grant aid	96
% needy UG rec. need-based scholarship or grant aid	97
% needy frosh rec. non-need-based scholarship or grant aid	34
% needy UG rec. non-need-based scholarship or grant aid	35
% needy frosh rec. need-based self-help aid	82
% needy UG rec. need-based self-help aid	83
% frosh rec. any financial aid	69
% UG rec. any financial aid	63
% UG borrow to pay for school	38
Average cumulative indebtedness	$37,632
% frosh need fully met	25
% ugrads need fully met	17
Average % of frosh need met	92
Average % of ugrad need met	85

BUTLER UNIVERSITY

4600 Sunset Avenue, Indianapolis, IN 46208 • Admissions: 800-368-6852 • Fax: 317-940-8150

STUDENTS SAY "..."

Academics

Centrally located in the heart of Indianapolis, Butler University combines city living with a personalized academic experience. Offering "a large mix of majors and minors," the university does a "great job at providing connections and opportunities from undergraduate research...to outstanding internships." Butler's academic excellence can also be seen in programs like Dance, Pharmacy, and Business that are "extremely well done and nationally known." Across departments, many enrollees agree that the school "goes above and beyond to promote an outstanding environment of learning and growing for its students." Undergrads tout the benefits of small classes and a low student-to-faculty ratio, which "create[s] the perfect atmosphere to get one-on-one time with professors" and "develop a greater understanding of the material."

The hands-on educational experience is made more valuable by the "high quality of academic faculty," especially those who "are passionate and have a genuine interest in students' learning." As one enrollee notes, "Professors at Butler care about who you are as a person, not just [as] a student." The "attentive and engaging" faculty "make learning fun" while also being ever-ready to "help a student out and give them support both academically and personally. With "ample opportunity to work with the professors and get great experience for grad school," many enrollees find that the university provides a "high level of education" that they were looking for.

Campus Life

Many students, affectionately known as Bulldogs, consider Butler's 300-acre campus to be "very beautiful, which makes it enjoyable to be outside when the weather is nice." A variety of extracurricular options, including "hundreds of clubs as well as Greek life [helps] keep the whole campus united." In fact, Greek life tops the charts as a "fun way to meet new people and get one's mind off school." Bulldogs also "enjoy participating in intramural sports" and mention that "it's a huge part of Butler culture to attend basketball games." In addition to all of the campus activities, undergrads are all involved with the local community via the university's unique "'Indianapolis Community Requirement' that has students take one class connecting them with the Indianapolis area and often centers around community service." One undergrad sums it up nicely, saying, "everyone is involved in something,"

At Butler, you get the best of both worlds with "great access to a big city while still being far away enough to not be fully encompassed by [it]." Students agree that "Indianapolis itself is very cool to explore," and specifically note enjoying the nice restaurants and gardens, as well as "going to Broad Ripple (a small trendy area of town)." Additionally, "downtown Indy and the river walk are also very common spots on the weekends for students to go and hangout at or visit." As one student puts it, "being so close to Indy gives you a lot of opportunities for fun."

Student Body

"Butler's student population continues to emit Hoosier Hospitality. If any student is ever in need of help, they always have someone to go to." The majority of students agree, describing the university as a "very tight knit community," with one person expressing, "Butler students are very friendly," and "[it's] easier to find a kind student at Butler than an unkind one." In terms of diversity, while some find the student body to be "overwhelming majority white," others feel that "Butler is making an effort to [create] an inclusive and diverse environment." As one student puts it, "Although there are many different political beliefs and divides, my peers all come together to celebrate our school and our community." At Butler, "everyone does a great job of making sure people fit in." That's in large part due to what respondents describe as "Hoosier Hospitality," in that "if any student is ever in need of help, they always have someone to go to."

BUTLER UNIVERSITY

Financial Aid: 317-940-8200 • E-Mail: admission@butler.edu • Website: www.butler.edu

THE PRINCETON REVIEW SAYS

Admissions

The school reports that its standardized testing policy for use in admission for Fall 2024 is Test Optional. The 2024 testing policy will be permanent. The Princeton Review suggests that interested applicants consult with the school for the most up-to-date standardized testing policies. *Very important factors considered include:* rigor of secondary school record, academic GPA, standardized test scores. *Important factors considered include:* application essay, extracurricular activities. *Other factors considered include:* class rank, recommendation(s), talent/ability, character/personal qualities, first generation, volunteer work, work experience, level of applicant's interest. High school diploma is required and GED is accepted. *Academic units required:* 4 English, 3 math, 3 science, 2 social studies. *Academic units recommended:* 2 foreign language.

Financial Aid

Students should submit: FAFSA. Priority filing deadline is 12/1. The Princeton Review suggests that all financial aid forms be submitted as soon as possible (see page 5 for a note on the FAFSA). *Need-based scholarships/grants offered:* College/university scholarship or grant aid from institutional funds; Federal Pell; Private scholarships; SEOG; State scholarships/grants. *Loan aid offered:* Direct PLUS loans; Direct Subsidized Loans; Direct Unsubsidized Loans. Admitted students will be notified of awards on a rolling basis beginning 2/1. Federal Work-Study Program available. Institutional employment available.

The Inside Word

Butler tires to make the application process as easy as possible for potential undergrads. You can choose to apply via their university-specific application or the Common App. Supplemental requirements vary based on if you're a first-year applicant, transfer student, or international student, so make sure you double check the applicable required and optional checklists provided by the university. Additionally, when it comes to test scores, you get to choose whether you apply with or without test scores. Ultimately, the admissions department seeks applicants who are accomplished in their academics, involved in their school or community, and are ambitious about their future endeavors.

SELECTIVITY

Admissions Rating	86
# of applicants	13,386
% of applicants accepted	82
% of acceptees attending	11
# offered a place on the wait list	62
% accepting a place on wait list	19
% admitted from wait list	100

FIRST-YEAR PROFILE

Testing policy	Test Optional
Range SAT composite	1130–1320
Range SAT EBRW	560–660
Range SAT math	550–660
Range ACT composite	24–30
# submitting SAT scores	594
% submitting SAT scores	50
# submitting ACT scores	324
% submitting ACT scores	27
Average HS GPA	3.9
% frosh submitting high school GPA	100
% graduated top 10% of class	41
% graduated top 25% of class	74
% graduated top 50% of class	94

DEADLINES

Early action	
Deadline	11/1
Regular	
Deadline	8/1
Nonfall registration?	Yes

FINANCIAL FACTS

Financial Aid Rating	82
Annual tuition	$44,990
Room and board	$15,350
Required fees	$990
Books and supplies	$1,300
Average frosh need-based scholarship	$27,362
Average UG need-based scholarship	$26,106
% needy frosh rec. need-based scholarship or grant aid	99
% needy UG rec. need-based scholarship or grant aid	94
% needy frosh rec. non-need-based scholarship or grant aid	25
% needy UG rec. non-need-based scholarship or grant aid	21
% needy frosh rec. need-based self-help aid	66
% needy UG rec. need-based self-help aid	69
% frosh rec. any financial aid	98
% UG rec. any financial aid	96
% UG borrow to pay for school	47
Average cumulative indebtedness	$39,506
% frosh need fully met	13
% ugrads need fully met	13
Average % of frosh need met	69
Average % of ugrad need met	73

CALIFORNIA INSTITUTE OF TECHNOLOGY

383 S. Hill Ave, Pasadena, CA 91106 • Admissions: 626-395-6341 • Fax: 626-683-3026

CAMPUS LIFE

Quality of Life Rating	91
Fire Safety Rating	88
Green Rating	60*
Type of school	Private
Affiliation	No Affiliation
Environment	City

STUDENTS

Total undergrad enrollment	982
% male/female	55/45
% from out of state	64
% frosh from public high school	65
% frosh live on campus	100
% ugrads live on campus	93
# of fraternities	0
# of sororities	0
% African American	3
% Asian	34
% White	21
% Hispanic	22
% Native American	<1
% Pacific Islander	<1
% Two or more races	9
% Race and/or ethnicity unknown	1
% international	9
# of countries represented	36

SURVEY SAYS . . .

Students always studying
Lab facilities are great
Great financial aid
No one cheats
Students aren't religious
Students love Pasadena, CA
Dorms are like palaces
Easy to get around campus

ACADEMICS

Academic Rating	90
% students returning for sophomore year	98
% students graduating within 4 years	81
% students graduating within 6 years	94
Calendar	Quarter
Student/faculty ratio	3:1
Profs interesting rating	86
Profs accessible rating	89

Most classes have 10–19 students.
Most lab/discussion sessions have
10–19 students.

MOST POPULAR MAJORS

Computer and Information Sciences, General;
Mechanical Engineering; Physics, General

STUDENTS SAY "..."

Academics

Beyond arguably one of the most rigorous undergraduate educations in science out there, Caltech is a small, tight-knit community that is "geared toward training tomorrow's leaders and pioneers in the field of science." There may be a heavy emphasis on scientific learning and research, but "not to the point where students can do nothing else," as the core curriculum "exposes each student to a broad range of subjects" beyond the stereotypical fare. At Caltech, passionate researchers "work together to solve the problems of tomorrow, while enjoying great weather." Or to put it in the parlance of collegiate times: "Cross collaboration of ideas and ingenuity leads to epic-ness!" Academics are understandably "intense" at Caltech: "The work can be hell but you'll love what you learn." Fortunately, "classes are small and it's often easy to form tight bonds with the professors." The quality of teaching can vary—"just because they're Nobel Prize winners, does not make them good lecturers"—but the extremely low student-to-faculty ratio "makes it easier to interact on a personal basis with professors." "My academic experience here has been an extremely difficult whirlwind of humbling and fascinating knowledge," says a student. Much learning is done through the homework sets, on which students are encouraged to collaborate. The dedication Caltech has for training the researchers of tomorrow is renowned, and is evident in the accessibility to research for all students, even first-years. The academic experience isn't just in the classroom; there are "lots of funding opportunities (for instance, the Housner Fund and the Moore-Hufstedler Fund) for projects outside of the classroom." "One professor took me on for research after [my first] year (we formulated an improved way to rank basketball players and teams), and I'm very good friends with him in what is now my junior year," says a mathematics major. Undergraduate student representation and self-government are happily welcomed here, and the school "really cares about the undergrads and wants to keep us happy." The school also does "a really good job of keeping students occupied and entertained while at the same time cramming a ridiculous amount of information into our heads."

Campus Life

Modeled after the Oxford college system (and "very similar to Harry Potter"), the Caltech house system is the basis for undergraduate life, offering both a place to live and a social center for students. First-years are placed into one of nine residential communities after the first week of school, and "immediately are integrated into a close social network/safety net. Basically each student automatically gets ~100 friends." Each house has "a slightly different culture, and most people find that they identify strongly with at least one of the cultures"; as one student says, "My house has a tool room and turned down the housing office's offer to buy us a TV," says a senior electrical engineering major. In keeping with the one big happy family vibe, "undergraduates and grad students play Frisbee together, students and faculty play together in music groups, grad students go to undergraduate parties...and the students have a lot of unexploited trust from the faculty because of the Honor Code." Caltech has lots of fun traditions such as Halloween, when students "freeze pumpkins in liquid nitrogen and drop them off of [Caltech Hall] as a 'pumpkin-drop experiment.'" However, some feel that some of the new administrators "are trying to circumvent various student traditions and freedoms." The cherry on top of the Caltech sundae is "the fantastic SoCal weather, which is hard to beat anywhere in the world." Time is at a premium, but students "take trips to the beach and LA" over the weekend; during the week, "[problem] sets and extracurriculars keep us pretty close to campus."

Student Body

"Everyone knows each other" at this "beautiful, small campus," and there's "no way around it": students here are "smart" and "nerdier than average," but "there is a wide range in personality within the student body." Almost everyone has "an odd sense of humor and a serious hobby, whether it be Minecraft, building lasers, or rock climbing." There is "complete trust within the student body" at Caltech, and the house system provides "a family-like support network for students," which is a welcome respite from "extreme academic pressures."

CALIFORNIA INSTITUTE OF TECHNOLOGY

Financial Aid: 626-395-6280 • E-Mail: ugadmissions@caltech.edu • Website: www.admissions.caltech.edu

THE PRINCETON REVIEW SAYS

Admissions

The school reports that its standardized testing policy for use in admission for Fall 2024 is Test Free. The 2024 testing policy will be temporary. The Princeton Review suggests that interested applicants consult with the school for the most up-to-date standardized testing policies. *Very important factors considered include:* rigor of secondary school record, application essay, recommendation(s), character/personal qualities. *Important factors considered include:* class rank, academic GPA, extracurricular activities. *Other factors considered include:* talent/ability, first generation, racial/ethnic status, volunteer work, work experience. High school diploma or equivalent is not required. *Academic units required:* 3 English, 4 math, 2 science, 1 science lab, 1 social studies. *Academic units recommended:* 4 English, 4 science, 3 foreign language, 3 social studies.

Financial Aid

Students should submit: Business/Farm Supplement; CSS/Financial Aid Profile; FAFSA; Institution's own financial aid form; Noncustodial Profile; State aid form. Priority filing deadline is 3/15. The Princeton Review suggests that all financial aid forms be submitted as soon as possible (see page 5 for a note on the FAFSA). *Need-based scholarships/grants offered:* College/university scholarship or grant aid from institutional funds; Federal Pell; Private scholarships; SEOG; State scholarships/grants. *Loan aid offered:* Direct PLUS loans; Direct Subsidized Loans; Direct Unsubsidized Loans; College/university loans from institutional funds. Admitted students will be notified of awards on or about 4/15. Federal Work-Study Program available. Institutional employment available.

The Inside Word

The Undergraduate Admissions Committee has faculty on it, so keep that in mind when submitting your application and showcase your creativity and intellect: no student is admitted to the school unless they receive a positive review from a faculty member. Stellar academic credentials are a must, and prospective students must display an aptitude for math and science.

THE SCHOOL SAYS "..."

From the Admissions Office

"Successful applicants to Caltech are multifaceted individuals deeply passionate about STEM, they seek out the most challenging classes available to them, creatively solve problems, and are tenacious every day. Their intrinsic curiosity propels them to explore STEM in and outside of the classroom while also appreciating humanities and social sciences. At Caltech, students do not study just one thing and a passion for all STEM fields is necessary to be successful.

"Applications are reviewed holistically; meaning, each required component of an application is evaluated and used by the admissions committee to reach a decision. Our review process allows multiple admissions officers and faculty committee members to read and discuss the most competitive applications. Admissions officers move the most competitive application onto a faculty review who do a full read of a student's application materials. The context of an applicant's individual circumstances allows us to get to know them and assess their prior attainment and potential. Each applicant is considered as a whole person, therefore, there is no single admissions requirement that is deemed more important than others. Visit our website to learn more about how we review applications, preparing for Caltech, and learn what we look for."

SELECTIVITY

Admissions Rating	99
# of applicants	16,626
% of applicants accepted	3
% of acceptees attending	50
# offered a place on the wait list	195
% accepting a place on wait list	86
% admitted from wait list	8

FIRST-YEAR PROFILE

Testing policy	Test Free
% graduated top 10% of class	96
% graduated top 25% of class	100

DEADLINES

Early action	
Deadline	11/1
Notification	12/15
Regular	
Deadline	1/3
Notification	3/15
Nonfall registration?	No

FINANCIAL FACTS

Financial Aid Rating	99
Annual tuition	$58,479
Room and board	$18,606
Required fees	$2,385
Required fees (first-year)	$2,885
Books and supplies	$1,428
Average frosh need-based scholarship	$63,160
Average UG need-based scholarship	$58,169
% needy frosh rec. need-based scholarship or grant aid	100
% needy UG rec. need-based scholarship or grant aid	100
% needy frosh rec. non-need-based scholarship or grant aid	0
% needy UG rec. non-need-based scholarship or grant aid	0
% needy frosh rec. need-based self-help aid	35
% needy UG rec. need-based self-help aid	44
% frosh rec. any financial aid	56
% UG rec. any financial aid	51
% UG borrow to pay for school	27
Average cumulative indebtedness	$17,219
% frosh need fully met	100
% ugrads need fully met	100
Average % of frosh need met	100
Average % of ugrad need met	100

CALIFORNIA STATE UNIVERSITY, STANISLAUS

One University Circle, Turlock, CA 95382 • Admissions: 209-667-3122 • Fax: 209-667-3788

CAMPUS LIFE

Quality of Life Rating	87
Fire Safety Rating	97
Green Rating	89
Type of school	Public
Environment	City

STUDENTS

Total undergrad enrollment	8,836
% male/female/another gender	33/67/NR
% from out of state	0
% frosh from public high school	95
% frosh live on campus	16
% ugrads live on campus	6
# of fraternities (% join)	3 (2)
# of sororities (% join)	7 (2)
% African American	2
% Asian	9
% White	18
% Hispanic	63
% Native American	<1
% Pacific Islander	<1
% Two or more races	2
% Race and/or ethnicity unknown	4
% international	1
# of countries represented	16

SURVEY SAYS . . .

Active student government
Lab facilities are great
Great library
Students are friendly
College radio is popular
Active minority support groups

ACADEMICS

Academic Rating	75
% students returning for sophomore year	81
% students graduating within 6 years	55
Calendar	Semester
Student/faculty ratio	17:1
Profs interesting rating	85
Profs accessible rating	85

Most classes have 20–29 students.
Most lab/discussion sessions have
10–19 students.

MOST POPULAR MAJORS

Business Administration; Psychology;
Liberal Studies

STUDENTS SAY "..."

Academics

Known familiarly as Stan State, CSU Stanislaus is "an uncut gem," offering what students believe to be "the highest level of university education that you can receive for the smallest amount of money." Particularly, the "good student to teacher ratio" enables undergraduates to have better access to their professors and "allows for students to have more support from the teachers." This support extends into ensuring an inclusive education for all types of enrollees by offering "many resources for minority groups, like disabled students, students of color, low-income students, LGBTQ+ students, etc." Undergrads are eager to learn from their "understanding and professional" instructors. The staff's "passion for what they are teaching" shines through, and that extends to the administrative side, thanks to teachers who are "clear on due dates, deadlines, [and] school schedule[s]." Students in the business and nursing programs especially rave about their professors, saying they "work hard to make sure that the students' needs are met and that they are getting the guidance they need to succeed." Competition for a spot in popular programs can be stiff, as "the number of sections and class size for many classes still remains the same" despite a growing student body. Most students agree, however, that regardless of what you end up taking, "Stan State [is] dedicated to [its] students' education."

Campus Life

CSU Stanislaus' main Turlock campus is "filled with a homey small-town mentality." Undergrads love the "beautiful and peaceful campus" which "helps students to feel less stressed." Despite being "mostly a commuter campus," many find "the college serves as a hub to bring students together who under normal circumstances would probably never meet."

And when they get together, there's a slew of activities, events, and places to choose from, such as the new Student University Center, which boasts "a diner, apparel store, and study spaces for students to go study or just hang out and catch up with others." School spirit is not lacking here, so you might find friends getting together and "go[ing] all out for Warrior Wednesdays," a weekly campus pride event or attending school games. The campus also has "a nice gym with a basketball/volleyball court," and "recreational leagues for tons of different types of sports."

Students looking for non-athletic opportunities can head to Greek Row, where "there are a bunch of booths for various organizations set up that they hang out throughout the day between classes," and "clubs around art and ethnic studies are very interactive and positive with very welcoming energy." One undergrad sums it up nicely, saying, "I do not feel left out because there are so many programs and clubs that interest me and there's something to do for everybody."

Student Body

The student body at Stanislaus State "generally reflects the central valley of California," with "a mix of ages, ethnicities, as well as gender orientations" represented, and "an incredibly high portion of first-generation Latinx students." Many feel that "the student community is a very welcoming and accepting space." Building connections with your fellow peers is one of the best parts of college for many Stan State students. "We spend a lot of time deepening our relationships and ourselves and developing our small overlapping communities." And in getting to know each other, most have only positive things to say about their classmates. "My peers are brilliant; I always enjoyed learning different ways to approach problems," one student writes. Above all, students agree that one of the most special things about their campus is the "diversity among the student body that presents perspectives from hundreds of different life paths, perspectives, and philosophies."

CALIFORNIA STATE UNIVERSITY, STANISLAUS

Financial Aid: 209-667-3336 • E-Mail: Outreach_help_desk@csustan.edu • Website: www.csustan.edu

THE PRINCETON REVIEW SAYS

Admissions

The school reports that its standardized testing policy for use in admission for Fall 2024 is Test Optional. The 2024 testing policy will be permanent. The Princeton Review suggests that interested applicants consult with the school for the most up-to-date standardized testing policies. *Very important factors considered include:* rigor of secondary school record, academic GPA. *Important factors considered include:* class rank. *Other factors considered include:* extracurricular activities, first generation, volunteer work, work experience. High school diploma is required and GED is accepted. *Academic units required:* 4 English, 3 math, 2 science, 2 science labs, 2 foreign language, 1 social studies, 1 history, 1 visual/performing arts, 1 academic elective.

Financial Aid

Students should submit: FAFSA; Institution's own financial aid form; State aid form. Priority filing deadline is 3/2. The Princeton Review suggests that all financial aid forms be submitted as soon as possible (see page 5 for a note on the FAFSA). *Need-based scholarships/grants offered:* College/university scholarship or grant aid from institutional funds; Federal Pell; Private scholarships; SEOG; State scholarships/grants. *Loan aid offered:* Direct PLUS loans; Direct Subsidized Loans; Direct Unsubsidized Loans. Admitted students will be notified of awards on a rolling basis beginning 4/1. Federal Work-Study Program available. Institutional employment available.

The Inside Word

California State University, Stanislaus, accepts students from all kinds of backgrounds with a wide variety of life experiences to bring to the campus. The university is committed to providing an education that is both accessible and outstanding. Hence, it's safe to say that when evaluating potential new students, both strong academics and character play a strong role in admissions. The best contenders will have a strong GPA, challenge themselves academically, and demonstrate what they can bring to the CSU community.

THE SCHOOL SAYS "..."

From the Admissions Office

"For over sixty years, California State University, Stanislaus, has welcomed students from California's Central Valley and worldwide. Stanislaus State continues to distinguish itself as an institution that provides top-quality degree programs with a high level of personal attention, offering forty-five majors, forty-four minors and more than 100 areas of concentration, along with eighteen master's degree programs, six credential programs, and a doctorate in educational leadership. With a student-to-faculty ratio of 17:1, Stanislaus State demonstrates its commitment to individualized instruction over the more common lecture-hall style of many larger universities. The university enjoys an ideal location in the Northern San Joaquin Valley, a short distance from the San Francisco Bay Area, Monterey, Big Sur, the Sierra Nevada Mountains, and the state capital of Sacramento. The main campus is located in the city of Turlock, a community that prides itself on its small town atmosphere, clean living space, excellent schools, and low crime rate. Degree programs in these disciplines have earned specialized accreditation: art, business administration, education, genetic counseling, music, nursing, psychology, public administration, social work, and theater. The College of Business Administration and the College of Education, Kinesiology and Social Work have also earned prestigious state and national accreditation. Over $65 million in merit- and need-based grants and scholarships were awarded for the 2021–22 school year, and over 79 percent of undergraduates receive need-based aid."

SELECTIVITY

Admissions Rating	75
# of applicants	6,345
% of applicants accepted	93
% of acceptees attending	18

FIRST-YEAR PROFILE

Testing policy	Test Optional
Average HS GPA	3.5
% frosh submitting high school GPA	98

DEADLINES

Regular	
Priority	11/30
Deadline	11/30
Notification	Rolling, 11/1
Nonfall registration?	Yes

FINANCIAL FACTS

Financial Aid Rating	87
Annual in-state tuition	$5,742
Annual out-of-state tuition	$17,622
Room and board	$11,828
Required fees	$2,076
Books and supplies	$1,038
Average frosh need-based scholarship	$11,575
Average UG need-based scholarship	$10,756
% needy frosh rec. need-based scholarship or grant aid	92
% needy UG rec. need-based scholarship or grant aid	87
% needy frosh rec. non-need-based scholarship or grant aid	5
% needy UG rec. non-need-based scholarship or grant aid	3
% needy frosh rec. need-based self-help aid	87
% needy UG rec. need-based self-help aid	91
% frosh rec. any financial aid	83
% UG rec. any financial aid	82
% UG borrow to pay for school	39
Average cumulative indebtedness	$16,758
% frosh need fully met	11
% ugrads need fully met	7
Average % of frosh need met	79
Average % of ugrad need met	74

CALVIN UNIVERSITY

3201 Burton Street S.E., Grand Rapids, MI 49546 • Admissions: 616-526-6000

CAMPUS LIFE

Quality of Life Rating	92
Fire Safety Rating	87
Green Rating	90
Type of school	Private
Affiliation	Christian Reformed
Environment	Metropolis

STUDENTS

Total undergrad enrollment	2,963
% male/female/another gender	47/53/0
% from out of state	36
% frosh from public high school	52
% frosh live on campus	93
% ugrads live on campus	57
# of fraternities	0
# of sororities	0
% African American	4
% Asian	5
% White	71
% Hispanic	4
% Native American	<1
% Pacific Islander	0
% Two or more races	3
% Race and/or ethnicity unknown	1
% international	12
# of countries represented	63

SURVEY SAYS . . .

Students are happy
Lab facilities are great
Internships are widely available
Students are very religious
Students environmentally aware
Students love Grand Rapids, MI
Easy to get around campus
Recreation facilities are great

ACADEMICS

Academic Rating	83
% students returning for sophomore year	86
% students graduating within 4 years	66
% students graduating within 6 years	77
Calendar	Semester
Student/faculty ratio	12:1
Profs interesting rating	92
Profs accessible rating	95

Most classes have 20–29 students.
Most lab/discussion sessions have
fewer than 10 students.

MOST POPULAR MAJORS

Engineering, General; Registered Nursing/
Registered Nurse; Business Administration and
Management, General

STUDENTS SAY "..."

Academics

Founded in 1876, Calvin University is a mid-sized Christian liberal arts institution located in Grand Rapids, Michigan that trains students "to think critically and live out their vocation in the world while working to advance God's Kingdom." The prestigious academics (the nursing and honors programs are standouts) feature a high level of integration of faith within the classroom, and "departments teach their specific content in the context of a Christian worldview." The coursework is "difficult and challenging," but faculty "make us feel welcomed and make sure they are available for all of our questions." Not only are their teaching methods stellar, they are "relatable and offer good advice, genuinely wishing the students a good future."

Professors have "a desire to share their wealth of experiences and passions with the students" and are "extremely talented, interesting, and connected in their specific fields." Instructors are also "masters at integration of education and Christianity," making the classes at Calvin less about teaching the requisites for getting a job and "more about how to continue to learn about the field and how Christianity should figure into it." Within courses, there is great opportunity to delve into complicated and often controversial topics "in a way that doesn't ignore culture, science, or social scientific data." Sharing ideas is encouraged between students. "I feel I can appropriately express my opinions and views without the condemnation of others," says one. No matter your passion or career choice, "you will be paired with advisors [who have] similar passions," which "allows freedom to express thoughts and talk openly with willing professors."

Campus Life

"Dorm life is vibrant" and "a big focus" at Calvin. Within the dorms "there is plenty of opportunity for leadership, and everyone is encouraged to grow together." Floor events in the residential halls are huge bonding occasions. The Student Life Division does a good job of organizing events that many students attend, including movies, board game nights, and concerts, and there are also "lots of clubs on campus that you can get involved in." When people aren't studying (studying in the hammocks around campus is popular) or in class, they often go to coffee shops or to get food together. Most work part-time, and there are "many different opportunities for on-campus jobs." Extracurriculars are big, and students "go backpacking, swing dancing...or hiking." There are also lots of things to do in the Grand Rapids area, and "people go out to meals, movies, bowling, sporting events, the downtown market, and other events in the city such as ArtPrize," or will go to Lake Michigan. Chapel is held daily but is not required, and there are a lot of "study groups and Bible studies to help each other grow toward academic and spiritual goals."

Student Body

Calvin's 3,100-strong body of undergrads includes a wide range of students and interests, including a significant number of international students, athletes, those with Dutch heritage, and "valedictorians everywhere." A large percentage of the students "are Christians and come from somewhere in the Midwest," and all are generally "friendly, helpful, outgoing, and hardworking." One student notes, "Some people feel that Calvin University is very diverse and others feel that it is not diverse at all, depending on where they came from." Diversity activities are highly emphasized and encouraged around campus, and the student body is "small enough that Calvin begins to feel like home, but large enough that you don't know everyone." As one student puts it best, "There is a niche for everyone in the social life of the school."

CALVIN UNIVERSITY

Financial Aid: 800-688-0122 • E-Mail: admissions@calvin.edu • Website: www.calvin.edu

THE PRINCETON REVIEW SAYS

Admissions

The school reports that its standardized testing policy for use in admission for Fall 2024 is Test Optional. It is unknown at this time if the 2024 testing policy will be permanent. The Princeton Review suggests that interested applicants consult with the school for the most up-to-date standardized testing policies. *Very important factors considered include:* rigor of secondary school record, academic GPA. *Important factors considered include:* standardized test scores, application essay, recommendation(s), extracurricular activities, character/personal qualities, religious affiliation/commitment. *Other factors considered include:* class rank, alumni/ae relation, volunteer work, work experience, level of applicant's interest. High school diploma is required and GED is accepted. *Academic units required:* 3 English, 2 math, 2 science, 2 social studies, 3 academic electives. *Academic units recommended:* 4 English, 3 math, 2 science, 2 foreign language, 3 social studies, 3 academic electives.

Financial Aid

Students should submit: FAFSA. The Princeton Review suggests that all financial aid forms be submitted as soon as possible (see page 5 for a note on the FAFSA). *Need-based scholarships/grants offered:* College/university scholarship or grant aid from institutional funds; Federal Pell; Private scholarships; SEOG; State scholarships/grants; United Negro College Fund. *Loan aid offered:* Direct PLUS loans; Direct Subsidized Loans; Direct Unsubsidized Loans. Admitted students will be notified of awards on a rolling basis. Federal Work-Study Program available. Institutional employment available.

The Inside Word

Admissions officers at Calvin are interested in candidates who will flourish within the school's academic and social community. Just as importantly, they seek applicants who are looking to deepen and affirm their Christian faith. The college accepts over 75 percent of their applicant pool, so students who maintain solid transcripts should not have too much difficulty getting in. Bear in mind, though, that the high acceptance rate is partially due to the self-selecting nature of Calvin's applicant cohort.

THE SCHOOL SAYS "..."

From the Admissions Office

"Calvin University is a top-ranked Christian liberal arts institution that prepares students to lead with courageous conviction. Through rigorous academic study and intentional Christian community, students learn to think deeply, act justly and live wholeheartedly.

"At Calvin, we dare to pursue excellence in everything we take on. We don't settle for good enough...not in a lab, not in an art show, not even in a jump shot. It's a bold college path, but thousands of alumni will tell you it's a path worth traveling, no matter what sparks your passion.

"Here we believe that no one major has the upper hand in uncovering truths about God and the world. All are invited into the discovery. In fact, Calvin has had a liberal arts bent—a desire to explore all things—since its beginnings in 1876.

"Today's multi-faceted core curriculum allows students to chase the wonderings of philosophy, the intricacies of languages foreign and familiar, and the beauty of the world at a molecular level. Calvin offers 100+ academic options, as well as Graduate programs in accounting, education, geographic information science, media and strategic communication, public health, exercise science, speech pathology and audiology, and a master's in business administration.

"You can start meaningful work in your area of interest right away during your Calvin experience: participate in the innovative career-and-life readiness program, Calvin LifeWork; conduct significant research, present and publish alongside world-class faculty; and make global connections by studying abroad through faculty-led off-campus programs."

SELECTIVITY

Admissions Rating	86
# of applicants	3,985
% of applicants accepted	75
% of acceptees attending	25

FIRST-YEAR PROFILE

Testing policy	Test Optional
Range SAT composite	1130–1330
Range SAT EBRW	560–670
Range SAT math	560–670
Range ACT composite	24–30
# submitting SAT scores	450
% submitting SAT scores	61
# submitting ACT scores	179
% submitting ACT scores	24
Average HS GPA	3.8
% frosh submitting high school GPA	100
% graduated top 10% of class	29
% graduated top 25% of class	59
% graduated top 50% of class	85

DEADLINES

Regular	
Priority	11/1
Deadline	8/15
Notification	Rolling, 11/1
Nonfall registration?	Yes

APPLICANTS OFTEN PREFER
University of Michigan—Ann Arbor; Wheaton College (IL)

APPLICANTS SOMETIMES PREFER
Cedarville University; Central Michigan University; Grand Valley State University; Hope College; Michigan State University; Purdue University—West Lafayette; Taylor University

APPLICANTS RARELY PREFER
Cornerstone University; Indiana Wesleyan University; Olivet Nazarene University; Spring Arbor University; Trinity Christian College; Western Michigan University

FINANCIAL FACTS

Financial Aid Rating	85
Annual tuition	$38,370
Room and board	$10,908
Required fees	$250
Books and supplies	$1,300
Average frosh need-based scholarship	$25,244
Average UG need-based scholarship	$23,259
% needy frosh rec. need-based scholarship or grant aid	100
% needy UG rec. need-based scholarship or grant aid	100
% needy frosh rec. non-need-based scholarship or grant aid	21
% needy UG rec. non-need-based scholarship or grant aid	20
% needy frosh rec. need-based self-help aid	78
% needy UG rec. need-based self-help aid	81
% frosh rec. any financial aid	100
% UG rec. any financial aid	97
% UG borrow to pay for school	56
Average cumulative indebtedness	$29,596
% frosh need fully met	25
% ugrads need fully met	27
Average % of frosh need met	82
Average % of ugrad need met	80

CARLETON COLLEGE

One North College Street, Northfield, MN 55057 • Admissions: 507-222-4000 • Fax: 507-222-4526

STUDENTS SAY "..."

Academics

Carleton College, with its low student-teacher ratio and small-town Minnesota setting, "is a rigorous school full of laid-back, outdoorsy students with a passion for learning and for developing strong community." With a trimester schedule and an emphasis on the liberal arts and interdisciplinary scholarship, Carleton also boasts strong programs in the sciences and social sciences. The school has a reputation for being "highly rigorous without the cut-throat competition that other elite institutions are known for"; many students use the words "challenging" and "collaborative" to describe this tight-knit, highly focused academic community. One student sums it up as an "Ivy League education without all the Ivy League pretensions." While academics are "challenging" and classes are "fairly fast-paced," the work is "worth every ounce of effort" and professors are almost universally praised as "friendly, accessible, supportive, and enthusiastic about teaching." Students "have no qualms about dropping in on office hours to chat" and have "been to many wonderful dinners at professors' homes." "Students help each other out a lot, too (even if it is just emotional support)." One student describes the school accurately with her reasons for choosing to attend: "I wanted to be at a place where I was challenged. I wanted to be surrounded by people who were smarter than me but also wanted to see me succeed." Finally, students report excellent resources for pursuing graduate study, and visible improvements within career services.

Campus Life

Weekends at Carleton bustle with activity to help balance the intellectual challenges of weekday classes. As one student put it, "I often find myself attending a concert at the Cave, the student pub; going to a show one of my friends wrote at the Little Nourse Theater; taking a quick trip to the cities for Mall of America or an uptown excursion; or, most likely, having a surprisingly engaging and deep intellectual discussion with some friends at a party on a Friday night." Intramural sports such as broomball and ultimate Frisbee are "freakishly popular." Outdoor activities are very popular in the Arboretum, "an 800-acre forest where students go for runs, go snow-shoeing, or have camp fires." The campus even features Dacie Moses House, "a house for baking cookies 24/7." If you're looking to unwind with a less structured activity, "the drinking policy throughout Northfield is strict, but...it's relaxed here at Carleton," and most students report that while partying is an option, "there are just as many opportunities for substance-free activities. Even at parties, there is no pressure to drink." As Northfield is small and most students live in the dorms (a few wish for more off-campus living options), Carleton life tends to be campus-centric. "Carls" complain about very few things: the cold Minnesota weather, on-campus food options, and the accessibility of the health center. Overall, though, it's clear that students here feel well cared for.

Student Body

At Carleton, students are, "on the whole, pretty liberal" as well as "politically and environmentally aware," and "are highly interested in activism on the whole." The school has also "been ramping up diversity efforts in recent years." Students note that they "spend the majority of the weekend studying but still find time for socializing and spending time on extracurriculars," though some note they wish they had more downtime, especially since their peers tend to be "very welcoming," "extremely kind," and "kind of dorky" in the best possible sense. "There are so many clubs and organizations to get involved in, and so many people doing really interesting things outside of any structured class or club, that it is incredibly hard to not get involved in something or other." That level of activity extends to hanging out as well: "Everyone loves to have meaningful conversations" and "the best part about that is that they all keep really open minds."

Financial Aid: 507-222-4138 • E-Mail: admissions@carleton.edu • Website: www.carleton.edu

THE PRINCETON REVIEW SAYS

Admissions

The school reports that its standardized testing policy for use in admission for Fall 2024 is Test Optional. The 2024 testing policy will be temporary. The Princeton Review suggests that interested applicants consult with the school for the most up-to-date standardized testing policies. *Very important factors considered include:* rigor of secondary school record, class rank, academic GPA, application essay, recommendation(s), extracurricular activities, talent/ability, character/personal qualities. *Other factors considered include:* standardized test scores, interview, first generation, alumni/ae relation, geographical residence, racial/ethnic status, volunteer work, work experience. High school diploma is required and GED is accepted. *Academic units recommended:* 4 English, 3 math, 3 science, 1 science lab, 3 foreign language, 3 social studies.

Financial Aid

Students should submit: CSS/Financial Aid Profile; FAFSA; Noncustodial Profile. Priority filing deadline is 1/15. The Princeton Review suggests that all financial aid forms be submitted as soon as possible (see page 5 for a note on the FAFSA). *Need-based scholarships/grants offered:* College/university scholarship or grant aid from institutional funds; Federal Pell; Private scholarships; SEOG; State scholarships/grants. *Loan aid offered:* Direct PLUS loans; Direct Subsidized Loans; Direct Unsubsidized Loans; College/university loans from institutional funds; State Loans. Admitted students will be notified of awards on or about 3/31. Federal Work-Study Program available. Institutional employment available.

The Inside Word

Gaining admission to Carleton is highly competitive. While it is possible to get in without stellar high school grades and test scores if you show tremendous promise or have an exceptional talent, most successful applicants demonstrate all of these qualities. High school records are weighed most heavily here; standardized test scores are required, and your personal essay is also very important. Given the importance of community at Carleton, interviews are strongly recommended.

THE SCHOOL SAYS "..."

From the Admissions Office

"While Carleton students are curious and ambitious, they don't take themselves too seriously and are always there to help each other out. Carleton offers 33 majors and 38 minors, and students don't declare a major until spring of their sophomore year. Outside of the classroom, Carleton students are active in over 200 student-led clubs, from KRLX (the student-run radio station) to K-Pop to juggling. About 70% of Carleton students study abroad, 69% participate in community or civic engagement, and 77% are engaged in research. The college is committed to meeting 100% of calculated family financial need and keeping loans to a manageable amount; nearly 3 out of 5 students receive need-based financial aid and 13% are among the first in their families to attend college. Carleton grads go on to success across sectors, whether they become astrophysicists photographing black holes, ecology researchers tracking bird migration, Pulitzer Prize-winning editorial writers, developers at Google, doctors providing care to communities most in need, or Academy Award-winning film directors. Carleton is also a top Fulbright-producing school. You'll find Carleton alumni serving in the Peace Corps, leading Fortune 500 companies, and pursuing grad school (about 70% go on to graduate school). It has a uniquely loyal alumni network of 25,000, and grads are always willing to help other Carls."

SELECTIVITY

Admissions Rating	97
# of applicants	8,583
% of applicants accepted	17
% of acceptees attending	37
# offered a place on the wait list	1,363
% accepting a place on wait list	43
% admitted from wait list	5
# of early decision applicants	1,161
% accepted early decision	23

FIRST-YEAR PROFILE

Testing policy	Test Optional
Range SAT composite	1430–1540
Range SAT EBRW	710–770
Range SAT math	720–780
Range ACT composite	32–35
# submitting SAT scores	191
% submitting SAT scores	36
# submitting ACT scores	149
% submitting ACT scores	28
% graduated top 10% of class	75
% graduated top 25% of class	94
% graduated top 50% of class	99

DEADLINES

Early decision	
Deadline	11/15
Notification	12/15
Other ED deadline	1/15
Other ED notification	2/15
Regular	
Deadline	1/15
Notification	3/31
Nonfall registration?	No

APPLICANTS OFTEN PREFER
Brown University; Pomona College; Williams College; Yale University

APPLICANTS SOMETIMES PREFER
Bowdoin College; Swarthmore College

APPLICANTS RARELY PREFER
Grinnell College; Macalester College; Middlebury College

FINANCIAL FACTS

Financial Aid Rating	99
Annual tuition	$65,043
Room and board	$16,710
Required fees	$414
Average frosh need-based scholarship	$57,346
Average UG need-based scholarship	$53,106
% needy frosh rec. need-based scholarship or grant aid	100
% needy UG rec. need-based scholarship or grant aid	100
% needy frosh rec. non-need-based scholarship or grant aid	13
% needy UG rec. non-need-based scholarship or grant aid	12
% needy frosh rec. need-based self-help aid	96
% needy UG rec. need-based self-help aid	97
% frosh rec. any financial aid	53
% UG rec. any financial aid	58
% UG borrow to pay for school	37
Average cumulative indebtedness	$18,677
% frosh need fully met	100
% ugrads need fully met	100
Average % of frosh need met	100
Average % of ugrad need met	100

CARNEGIE MELLON UNIVERSITY

5000 Forbes Avenue, Pittsburgh, PA 15213 • Admissions: 412-268-2000 • Fax: 412-268-7838

CAMPUS LIFE

Quality of Life Rating	89
Fire Safety Rating	97
Green Rating	98
Type of school	Private
Affiliation	No Affiliation
Environment	Metropolis

STUDENTS

Total undergrad enrollment	7,447
% male/female/another gender	49/51/NR
% from out of state	66
% frosh live on campus	100
% ugrads live on campus	46
# of fraternities (% join)	15 (14)
# of sororities (% join)	10 (11)
% African American	4
% Asian	32
% White	21
% Hispanic	10
% Native American	<1
% Pacific Islander	<1
% Two or more races	5
% Race and/or ethnicity unknown	5
% international	24
# of countries represented	66

SURVEY SAYS . . .

Students always studying
Students are happy
Lab facilities are great
Career services are great
Students love Pittsburgh, PA
Easy to get around campus
Theater is popular
Active minority support groups

ACADEMICS

Academic Rating	90
% students returning for sophomore year	97
% students graduating within 4 years	76
% students graduating within 6 years	92
Calendar	Semester
Student/faculty ratio	6:1
Profs interesting rating	88
Profs accessible rating	93

Most classes have fewer than 10 students.
Most lab/discussion sessions have 20–29 students.

MOST POPULAR MAJORS

Computer Science; Electrical and Electronics Engineering; Business Administration and Management, General

STUDENTS SAY ". . ."

Academics

It's easy to understand why students feel Carnegie Mellon is "one of the brightest universities in the country." After all, the university offers "unlimited opportunities for academic exploration and mastery." Indeed, CMU undergrads value "the interdisciplinary nature of many departments here" as it certainly "enhances [their] education." One individual elaborates, "I like that it allows students of different majors to collaborate and get to know each other, expanding general knowledge" in the process. Academically, the engineering and computer science programs are popular and "rank very highly." Another student shares, "The curriculum is very advanced in all the STEM courses so people graduate with the most up-to-date knowledge and skills." Though the vast majority of classes at CMU are on the smaller side, some students observe that "lower-level classes tend to be large lectures." That said, classes overall put a "huge focus on problem-solving, rather than memorization," which students appreciate. And while some admit there are some courses "incredibly difficult and at many times overwhelming," the overall "academic experience itself [is] enriching." And for many, a few grueling classes is worth it, as "CMU is very well-connected to many industries and organizations, and it is very feasible for CMU students to use the university as a launching pad into their interests."

Campus Life

Life at Carnegie Mellon moves at a frenetic pace. "There's always something to do and experience." As one undergrad explains, "Whether it's programming, singing a cappella, dancing Bhangra, driving in Buggy races, we invest and spend a lot of time in everything we do." Of course, it helps that "the school's extracurriculars are sensational." Many feel "there's such a wide variety of...clubs, events, and traditions" that there's something for everyone. "I have enjoyed academic bowl, model UN, ultimate Frisbee, and the Black student organization. There are also professional and other minority organizations, mock trial, intramural and club sports, a newspaper and other policy magazines," one student notes.

When the weekend rolls around, you can always find "some sort of party" or a handful of students heading "out to bars and clubs," though many people are also content with "movie and game nights." Finally, CMU undergrads also love to experience all that Pittsburgh has to offer. You can often find people "heading into the neighboring areas of Oakland, Squirrel Hill, and Shadyside to grab food and hang out." Plus, the city has tons "of cool museums," and the university is "situated between two nice parks" which are always great for a stroll.

Student Body

Students at Carnegie Mellon immediately note that their peers tend to be incredibly "academically focused" and "set themselves to a very high standard in their work." Fortunately, they still know how to foster "a supportive learning environment where students help each other grow. There's no toxic competition among us." But there is no denying that many are "intensely working for internships and jobs which will carry us in the future." This type of dedication to excellence extends beyond the classroom as well, with students saying their peers are "really passionate about things they do," including their extracurriculars. Though a few individuals do lament that some classmates "find that participating in other organizations is only a means to add things to a resume, rather than have fun in school," most feel it's "more important to have a healthy work-life balance."

Socially, "many people [at CMU] are introverts." Although people like to stick to their groups—like athletes or international students—"the student body can be diverse if you don't stay in your bubble." At CMU, "everyone is a quirky kid" and has "unique interests and hobbies that you wouldn't expect." As one student notes, "You can have a good conversation with almost anyone about their courses, their departments, homework, different professors, etc."

CARNEGIE MELLON UNIVERSITY

Financial Aid: 412-268-8186 • E-Mail: admission@andrew.cmu.edu • Website: www.cmu.edu

THE PRINCETON REVIEW SAYS

Admissions

The school reports that its standardized testing policy for use in admission for Fall 2024 is Test Optional. Due to the COVID-19 pandemic, SAT and ACT scores are currently completely optional. SAT Subject Tests are neither required nor recommended, and aren't considered in our admission process. The Princeton Review suggests that interested applicants consult with the school for the most up-to-date standardized testing policies. *Very important factors considered include:* rigor of secondary school record, class rank, academic GPA, extracurricular activities, character/personal qualities, volunteer work. *Important factors considered include:* application essay, recommendation(s), talent/ability, first generation, racial/ethnic status. *Other factors considered include:* standardized test scores, geographical residence, work experience. High school diploma is required and GED is accepted. *Academic units required:* 4 English, 4 math, 3 science, 2 foreign language, 3 academic electives. *Academic units recommended:* 4 English, 4 math, 3 science, 2 foreign language, 3 academic electives.

Financial Aid

Students should submit: CSS/Financial Aid Profile; FAFSA; Noncustodial Profile. The Princeton Review suggests that all financial aid forms be submitted as soon as possible (see page 5 for a note on the FAFSA). *Need-based scholarships/grants offered:* College/university scholarship or grant aid from institutional funds; Federal Pell; Private scholarships; SEOG; State scholarships/grants. *Loan aid offered:* Direct PLUS loans; Direct Subsidized Loans; Direct Unsubsidized Loans; College/university loans from institutional funds. Admitted students will be notified of awards on or about 4/1. Federal Work-Study Program available. Institutional employment available.

The Inside Word

There's a large, high qualified applicant pool for Carnegie Mellon, which means that it can be challenging to gain admission. Interested students should think about how to best showcase their academic strengths and demonstrate leadership roles and passion, motivation, and perseverance in their extracurriculars. Each individual school at CMU has its own academic requirements, so be sure to check those thresholds and maintain a rigorous course load to ensure that you stand out.

THE SCHOOL SAYS ". . ."

From the Admissions Office

"Carnegie Mellon is a world-class, innovative university, rich with tradition and culture. Our interdisciplinary approach to education sharpens students' problem-solving, critical thinking, analytical and quantitative skills. With more than 90 majors and minors, our premier fine arts, business and humanities programs are equally matched by top-ranked technology, science and computer science programs. Our students and faculty are world changers in problem-solving, leadership and communication. Graduates leave Carnegie Mellon equipped with the skills to impact society in a transformative way.

"We take pride in our academics, but also realize the importance of life outside the classroom. Campus life at Carnegie Mellon is vibrant, with opportunities spanning Fraternity and Sorority life and service, clubs and organizations, and intramurals and athletics. Though we're in the midst of the city of Pittsburgh, we have a 148-acre campus bordered by 500-acre Schenley Park—there's plenty of green space in every direction. With hundreds of ways to spend a study break, students take advantage of our culturally rich surroundings and get involved in the Pittsburgh community. And with three of the best athletic teams around (the Penguins, Pirates and Steelers!) here in our city, we know you'll love being a Pittsburgher as much as we do."

SELECTIVITY

Admissions Rating	98
# of applicants	34,261
% of applicants accepted	11
% of acceptees attending	44
# offered a place on the wait list	8,986
% accepting a place on wait list	52
% admitted from wait list	1
# of early decision applicants	4,528
% accepted early decision	13

FIRST-YEAR PROFILE

Testing policy	Test Optional
Range SAT composite	1500–1560
Range SAT EBRW	720–770
Range SAT math	770–800
Range ACT composite	34–35
# submitting SAT scores	867
% submitting SAT scores	51
# submitting ACT scores	338
% submitting ACT scores	20
Average HS GPA	3.9
% frosh submitting high school GPA	100
% graduated top 10% of class	90
% graduated top 25% of class	100
% graduated top 50% of class	100

DEADLINES

Early decision	
Deadline	11/1
Notification	12/15
Regular	
Deadline	1/1
Notification	4/1
Nonfall registration?	No

APPLICANTS ALSO LOOK AT

Brown University; Cornell University; Georgia Institute of Technology; Harvard College; Massachusetts Institute of Technology; Princeton University; Stanford University; University of California—Berkeley; University of California—Los Angeles

FINANCIAL FACTS

Financial Aid Rating	93
Annual tuition	$62,260
Room and board	$17,158
Required fees	$1,014
Required fees (first-year)	$1,569
Books and supplies	$1,000
Average frosh need-based scholarship	$47,052
Average UG need-based scholarship	$45,245
% needy frosh rec. need-based scholarship or grant aid	97
% needy UG rec. need-based scholarship or grant aid	98
% needy frosh rec. non-need-based scholarship or grant aid	38
% needy UG rec. non-need-based scholarship or grant aid	24
% needy frosh rec. need-based self-help aid	91
% needy UG rec. need-based self-help aid	93
% frosh rec. any financial aid	53
% UG rec. any financial aid	49
% UG borrow to pay for school	34
Average cumulative indebtedness	$30,334
% frosh need fully met	95
% ugrads need fully met	87
Average % of frosh need met	100
Average % of ugrad need met	100

CASE WESTERN RESERVE UNIVERSITY

10900 Euclid Avenue, Cleveland, OH 44106-7055 • Admissions: 216-368-2000 • Fax: 216-368-5111

CAMPUS LIFE

Quality of Life Rating	85
Fire Safety Rating	88
Green Rating	96
Type of school	Private
Affiliation	No Affiliation
Environment	Metropolis

STUDENTS

Total undergrad enrollment	5,697
% male/female/another gender	53/47/0
% from out of state	80
% frosh from public high school	70
% frosh live on campus	90
% ugrads live on campus	70
# of fraternities (% join)	18 (3)
# of sororities (% join)	9 (9)
% African American	5
% Asian	24
% White	39
% Hispanic	10
% Native American	<1
% Pacific Islander	<1
% Two or more races	4
% Race and/or ethnicity unknown	6
% international	13
# of countries represented	46

SURVEY SAYS . . .

Students are happy
Lab facilities are great
Great library
Diverse student types interact on campus
Students environmentally aware
Frats and sororities are popular
Theater is popular
Active minority support groups

ACADEMICS

Academic Rating	86
% students returning for sophomore year	94
% students graduating within 4 years	67
% students graduating within 6 years	84
Calendar	Semester
Student/faculty ratio	9:1
Profs interesting rating	85
Profs accessible rating	90

Most classes have 10–19 students.
Most lab/discussion sessions have 10–19 students.

MOST POPULAR MAJORS

Bioengineering and Biomedical Engineering; Mechanical Engineering; Biology/Biological Sciences, General

STUDENTS SAY "..."

Academics

Located in Cleveland, Ohio, Case Western Reserve University is a mid-sized school that boasts "fantastic research opportunities," "an awesome environment," and "amazing financial aid." CWRU is "known as an outstanding engineering school" and "companies in the engineering field are aware of CWRU's excellence and rigor and are very eager to hire CWRU grads." As one happy student puts it, "our academics and academic reputation is phenomenal." So are the school's services: "We even get free tutoring (up to five hours a week). [The] academic load can be challenging, but if you take advantage of all the available resources around, it's definitely manageable!" The "well-qualified and passionate" professors are "very involved in their fields" and "usually accessible and reasonable about their workload." Moreover, "they all have connections within the research community or the private work sector." A handful of liberal-arts students suggest that their departments may not get as much attention as others; CWRU "is very good at producing students prepared to excel in their career, especially within engineering, medicine, and business." The university "offers great scholarships and has fantastic research opportunities." A finance major reports she decided to attend because "it was affordable, prestigious, in an awesome environment, and the people here were all so genuine when I came to visit." All in all, students really feel that CWRU is a university on the rise. As a cognitive science and psychology student puts it, "If universities were stocks, I'd put all my money into Case Western."

Campus Life

One student sums up the university as "nerdy but a lot of fun." Activities at CWRU reflect this "nerdy" nature. "One of our biggest campus events (which I help run) is a 10-day long game of tag known as Humans vs. Zombies," a sociology and theatre major says. On campus, "Case offers literally everything in the way of clubs, jobs, research, and things to do." There's even a fairly strong Greek presence. Students do, however, note that the school's academic focus leads to somewhat lackluster school spirit: "Few students could tell you the football team's record or who the basketball team is facing this weekend." Off-campus, students have the entire city of Cleveland to explore, with several noting that the area closest to campus "offers great museums and downtown has lots of attractions to check out."

Student Body

At Case Western Reserve University, "you can find all sorts of people" thanks to a student body that is "a quirky mish-mosh of quirky students all engaging with one another and doing their best to advance society in one form or another." Students are high achievers, the sort who typically "works hard [and] studies a lot" yet always makes sure to find "time to socialize and invest their time in numerous groups, activities, and other endeavors." The "best way to fit in" is to get active by "joining student organizations, doing community service, jamming out to music in the residence halls, or doing a group study session."

CASE WESTERN RESERVE UNIVERSITY

Financial Aid: 216-368-4530 • E-Mail: admission@case.edu • Website: www.case.edu

THE PRINCETON REVIEW SAYS

Admissions

The school reports that its standardized testing policy for use in admission for Fall 2024 is Test Optional. The 2024 testing policy will be temporary. The Princeton Review suggests that interested applicants consult with the school for the most up-to-date standardized testing policies. *Very important factors considered include:* rigor of secondary school record, class rank, academic GPA, extracurricular activities. *Important factors considered include:* application essay, recommendation(s), interview, talent/ability, character/personal qualities, racial/ethnic status, volunteer work. *Other factors considered include:* standardized test scores, first generation, alumni/ae relation, work experience, level of applicant's interest. High school diploma is required and GED is accepted. *Academic units required:* 4 English, 3 math, 3 science, 2 science labs, 2 foreign language, 3 social studies. *Academic units recommended:* 4 math, 3 science labs, 3 foreign language, 4 social studies.

Financial Aid

Students should submit: CSS/Financial Aid Profile; FAFSA; Institution's own financial aid form; Noncustodial Profile. Priority filing deadline is 1/15. The Princeton Review suggests that all financial aid forms be submitted as soon as possible (see page 5 for a note on the FAFSA). *Need-based scholarships/grants offered:* College/university scholarship or grant aid from institutional funds; Federal Pell; Private scholarships; SEOG; State scholarships/grants. *Loan aid offered:* Direct PLUS loans; Direct Subsidized Loans; Direct Unsubsidized Loans; College/university loans from institutional funds. Admitted students will be notified of awards on a rolling basis. Federal Work-Study Program available. Institutional employment available.

The Inside Word

CWRU is a school with a growing profile, which means that the number of applications keeps increasing and competition is getting stiffer. CWRU uses a "single-door admission policy," meaning students apply to the whole school rather than individual departments. Once accepted, you can change majors without reapplying. CWRU accepts the Common Application and Coalition with Scoir. Note that through Fall 2024, CWRU is adopting a Test Optional policy.

THE SCHOOL SAYS " . . ."

From the Admissions Office

"Challenging and innovative academic programs, next-level technology, experiential learning, real-world environments, and faculty mentors are at the core of the Case Western Reserve University experience. CWRU's faculty challenges and supports all students, and its partnerships with world-class cultural, educational, and scientific institutions ensure that your education extends beyond the classroom. CWRU offers more than 100 academic programs and a single-door admission policy; once admitted to CWRU, you can major in any of our programs, or double and even triple major in several of them. Our 9:1 student-to-faculty ratio, among the best in the nation, allows students to have close interaction with professors. Co-ops, internships, research, creative endeavors, study abroad, and other opportunities bring theory to life in amazing settings, and 99 percent of students participate in these experiential learning opportunities. With 80 percent of students living on campus, CWRU has a residential feel unique to urban universities. First-year students live together in one of four residential communities. Advisors offer students guidance, helping them learn about and gain access to everything CWRU has to offer, in order to situate students for success."

SELECTIVITY

Admissions Rating	95
# of applicants	33,232
% of applicants accepted	26
% of acceptees attending	18
# offered a place on the wait list	11,494
% accepting a place on wait list	43
% admitted from wait list	7
# of early decision applicants	888
% accepted early decision	36

FIRST-YEAR PROFILE

Testing policy	Test Optional
Range SAT composite	1420–1520
Range SAT EBRW	680–740
Range SAT math	730–790
Range ACT composite	32–35
# submitting SAT scores	626
% submitting SAT scores	39
# submitting ACT scores	434
% submitting ACT scores	27
% graduated top 10% of class	62
% graduated top 25% of class	95
% graduated top 50% of class	100

DEADLINES

Early decision	
Deadline	11/1
Notification	12/5
Other ED deadline	1/15
Other ED notification	2/1
Early action	
Deadline	11/1
Notification	12/21
Regular	
Deadline	1/15
Notification	3/19
Nonfall registration?	Yes

APPLICANTS OFTEN PREFER
Carnegie Mellon University; Washington University in St. Louis

APPLICANTS SOMETIMES PREFER
The Ohio State University—Columbus; University of Michigan—Ann Arbor; University of Pittsburgh—Pittsburgh Campus

FINANCIAL FACTS

Financial Aid Rating	94
Annual tuition	$64,100
Room and board	$18,202
Required fees	$571
Books and supplies	$1,200
Average frosh need-based scholarship	$37,640
Average UG need-based scholarship	$38,481
% needy frosh rec. need-based scholarship or grant aid	97
% needy UG rec. need-based scholarship or grant aid	96
% needy frosh rec. non-need-based scholarship or grant aid	37
% needy UG rec. non-need-based scholarship or grant aid	23
% needy frosh rec. need-based self-help aid	90
% needy UG rec. need-based self-help aid	90
% UG borrow to pay for school	51
Average cumulative indebtedness	$28,085
% frosh need fully met	89
% ugrads need fully met	87
Average % of frosh need met	100
Average % of ugrad need met	97

THE CATHOLIC UNIVERSITY OF AMERICA

620 Michigan Avenue, NE, Washington, DC 20064 • Admissions: 202-319-5000 • Fax: 202-319-6533

STUDENTS SAY ". . ."

Academics

"You know you're at The Catholic University of America when Aristotle, Marx, and Kant are all part of the dinner conversation," say students, noting that their school is "a beacon of where faith and reasoning intersect," especially "for anyone looking to strengthen their Catholic faith." Home to around 5,000 graduate and undergraduate students, "it is a big enough school to accommodate for students of many interests, while still maintaining a strong community." CUA puts a "focus on philosophy," not just requiring it as part of the liberal arts program, but incorporating key concepts into other courses, which students enjoy: "This allows for deep and free thinking, which is exactly what college is for."

Students also highlight advantages of the school's Washington, DC, location with a history class "where the professor takes students off campus to sites around the city," an art class that takes place at the city's National Gallery of Art, or even a chemistry discussion section that used the American Museum of Natural History to host "a scavenger hunt involving chemical formulas and other empirical observations." Activities like these foster "fantastic discussions" and help "connect us with the material in such a profound way." For the career-minded, it's not unusual to hear of "internships with the FBI" or "field trips to CIA Headquarters." And professors are also lauded as being "passionate about what they teach, and they draw me into the topics by encouraging me to share my opinions and going deeper with what has already been said in class."

Campus Life

"You cannot only view yourself as an individual at Catholic because everything about this campus has something to do with community," explains one sophomore. Others agree, noting that most students are "heavily involved in campus life," especially when it comes to the "student-led campus ministry" and the various service projects that showcase how "Catholic is built on student leadership." The on-campus basilica is a highlight—"that place where I go to when I need to reflect and meditate; looking at the art inspires me and uplifts my mood"—but there are plenty of other "picturesque locations" popular for "simply hanging out." As for more direct ways to engage with peers, a member of the women's soccer team suggests that: "All of the sports teams are fun and have a family-like feel to them." Spectating is also popular, so much so that "the party scene on campus revolves around the athletics schedule." In essence, whether you're taking fitness classes or watching trivia nights, there are enough activities such that "any and all people with different interests [can] find something they like to do." Finally, students emphasize that being in DC is "quite a perk," especially as "there is a metro stop right next to campus that takes you into the heart of the city."

Student Body

Given its very strong identity, the Catholic University of America naturally "attracts Catholic students," but is also "welcoming to those of other faith traditions." One senior explains that meeting people from around the world has "expanded my understanding of many different backgrounds and cultures." One student recounts that "it was very easy to make friends, and I continue to have fruitful conversations with classmates, friends, and fellow students across the university." That said, the biggest differences at the school seem to be between those "with vastly differing political views," leading to a mix of "very different social groups, some much more conservative/religious and some … who party frequently." Ultimately, the school's greatest strength—a "sense of community and care that the university fosters for the students"—unites these "very ambitious" enrollees, making it "easy to get involved in student organizations, events, jobs, [and] internships." Overall, the student body is united by its desire to support others: "Whether through service or leadership, my peers are largely involved in helping others."

THE CATHOLIC UNIVERSITY OF AMERICA

Financial Aid: 202-319-5307 • E-Mail: cua-admissions@cua.edu • Website: www.catholic.edu

THE PRINCETON REVIEW SAYS

Admissions

The school reports that its standardized testing policy for use in admission for Fall 2024 is Test Free. The 2024 testing policy will be permanent. The Princeton Review suggests that interested applicants consult with the school for the most up-to-date standardized testing policies. *Very important factors considered include:* rigor of secondary school record, academic GPA, character/personal qualities. *Important factors considered include:* application essay, recommendation(s), extracurricular activities, first generation. *Other factors considered include:* class rank, interview, talent/ability, alumni/ae relation, geographical residence, racial/ethnic status, volunteer work, work experience, level of applicant's interest. High school diploma is required and GED is accepted. *Academic units required: Academic units recommended:* 4 English, 4 math, 3 science, 2 science labs, 3 foreign language, 4 social studies.

Financial Aid

Students should submit: FAFSA; Noncustodial Profile. Priority filing deadline is 2/1. The Princeton Review suggests that all financial aid forms be submitted as soon as possible (see page 5 for a note on the FAFSA). *Need-based scholarships/grants offered:* College/university scholarship or grant aid from institutional funds; Federal Pell; Private scholarships; SEOG; State scholarships/grants. *Loan aid offered:* Direct PLUS loans; Direct Subsidized Loans; Direct Unsubsidized Loans; State Loans. Admitted students will be notified of awards on a rolling basis beginning 2/1. Federal Work-Study Program available. Institutional employment available.

The Inside Word

The Catholic University of America's admission is fairly competitive. Certainly, the admission committee carefully assesses your GPA and the rigor of your course load, but standardized test scores are Test Free. However, you must not slack on the other facets of your application as close attention is given to your personal statement and recommendations. Your extracurricular involvement is also vetted, and the university is especially on the lookout for candidates dedicated to community service.

THE SCHOOL SAYS "..."

From the Admissions Office

"Students at The Catholic University of America have opportunities and advantages unlike anywhere else. Our remarkable combination of outstanding academics, a vibrant residential student life, opportunities for meaningful undergraduate research, competitive athletics, and a rich array of student clubs and organizations is made even more distinctive by our location in Washington, D.C.—a world center for "big ideas" in business, science, politics and government, public policy, health care, the arts, and more. By the time they graduate, more than 75 percent of our students complete internships (more than 60 percent complete two or more) on Capitol Hill, at the Smithsonian, with NASA, the National Institutes of Health, Kennedy Center for the Performing Arts, or any of the hundreds of leading corporations and nonprofit organizations with headquarters in D.C. And when not studying or working, they and their classmates also get to enjoy the scores of museums and galleries, theaters, restaurants, monuments, markets, parks, and historic sites that make the U.S. capital one of the most interesting, dynamic, and influential cities in the world.

"Add to all of this having the largest and greenest campus in the District, our own University center in Rome (among nearly 100 international study programs we offer), rich opportunities for student leadership and community service, and the Office of Academic and Career Success, where dedicated professionals are ready to help guide and support students from the moment they enroll right through graduation and beyond, and you start to realize why the educational experience at Catholic University is unparalleled."

SELECTIVITY

Admissions Rating	83
# of applicants	5,895
% of applicants accepted	86
% of acceptees attending	14
# offered a place on the wait list	48
% accepting a place on wait list	27
% admitted from wait list	15
# of early decision applicants	72
% accepted early decision	76

FIRST-YEAR PROFILE

Testing policy	Test Free
Range SAT EBRW	590–680
Range SAT math	570–670
Range ACT composite	23–31
# submitting SAT scores	158
% submitting SAT scores	23
# submitting ACT scores	49
% submitting ACT scores	7
Average HS GPA	3.5
% frosh submitting high school GPA	98

DEADLINES

Early decision	
Deadline	11/1
Notification	12/15
Other ED deadline	1/15
Other ED notification	2/15
Early action	
Deadline	11/1
Notification	1/15
Regular	
Priority	1/15
Deadline	1/15
Nonfall registration?	Yes

APPLICANTS OFTEN PREFER
Villanova University

APPLICANTS SOMETIMES PREFER
American University; Fordham University; Loyola University Maryland; The George Washington University

APPLICANTS RARELY PREFER
Saint Joseph's University (PA)

FINANCIAL FACTS

Financial Aid Rating	88
Annual tuition	$53,040
Room and board	$16,670
Required fees	$1,146
Books and supplies	$1,000
Average frosh need-based scholarship	$37,885
Average UG need-based scholarship	$35,628
% needy frosh rec. need-based scholarship or grant aid	99
% needy UG rec. need-based scholarship or grant aid	99
% needy frosh rec. non-need-based scholarship or grant aid	0
% needy UG rec. non-need-based scholarship or grant aid	0
% needy frosh rec. need-based self-help aid	72
% needy UG rec. need-based self-help aid	76
% frosh rec. any financial aid	74
% UG rec. any financial aid	93
% UG borrow to pay for school	72
Average cumulative indebtedness	$48,415
% frosh need fully met	47
% ugrads need fully met	47
Average % of frosh need met	85
Average % of ugrad need met	83

CENTRE COLLEGE

625 West Walnut Street, Danville, KY 40422-1394 • Admissions: 859-238-5200 • Fax: 859-238-5373

STUDENTS SAY ". . ."

Academics

Centre College is a school that prides itself on fostering a "tight knit community," one in which "everyone genuinely cares." Undergrads appreciate the college's liberal arts education, which provides them with "substantial freedom to pursue whatever academic experience and career they wish." Additionally, "small class sizes" are the norm at Centre, leading to a very personalized classroom experience and education. "In every class I've ever taken in my four years, the professor has known my name and made an effort to get to know everyone." Of course, individualized attention also means that "you must work hard and you must be ready to learn!" A fellow classmate cautions that at Centre, "You cannot get by with not trying." But don't worry. The Centre faculty consists of "extremely knowledgeable" individuals who maintain "a vested interest in [their students'] success" and are there to support you on your academic journey. As this undergrad sums up, "Even professors that I've had in the past always have their door open, so to speak, to get questions answered or simply talk." Ultimately, students leave these courses well-equipped, quickly stressing that the "academic rigor is great preparation for graduate school and fellowships" along with "the real world." As one individual emphasizes, "I know that I'll have connections for internships and jobs for the remainder of my time here and after I graduate."

Campus Life

Given Centre's rigorous academics, a lot of "students' time is spent studying." But fear not, the college still manages to generate plenty of opportunities for fun. For starters, Greek life is quite popular. Indeed, Centre maintains a "healthy culture of fraternities and sororities, which most students engage in." Additionally, there are numerous career-focused organizations like the investment society that enables students to "manage over $200,000 in stocks [as well as] look for opportunities to grow [their] portfolio and teach others about investing." There are also more traditional clubs such as the college orchestra, garden club, intramural sports, and the Centre Environmental Association. Plus, "every weekend the campus center puts on an event from laser tag to mechanical bull riding." Students also simply "enjoy hanging out and watching shows or movies with friends" or "socializ[ing] during their meals." It is important to acknowledge hometown Danville is "a very small town." Because many feel "there's not much to do for fun" in the small town, most are content taking advantage of all of the built-in fun offered from their college.

Student Body

Centre College does a great job amassing a group of undergraduates who are "hard working, high achieving, and very involved on and off campus." Students here "are always happy to help in any way they can." And while they are undoubtedly "academically motivated," Centre students definitely "know how to have fun" as well. Most people "prioritize studying during the week and social life during the weekends, though the two are often combined."

In terms of diversity, undergrads recognize that the "student body is predominantly white." However, they rush to note that "Centre [is] certainly striv[ing] for a more diverse make up." And many also point out that you'll definitely meet "people from all over the country and the world" here. What's more, students report that their peers are "focus[ed] on [ensuring]...inclusion everywhere on campus in terms of sports, Greek life, academics, and extracurriculars." This undergrad agrees, adding, "Our community is very welcoming and warm to all student[s] whether you [are] international, American, Republican, Democrat, there is something and someone for everyone."

CENTRE COLLEGE

Financial Aid: 800-423-6236 • E-Mail: admission@centre.edu • Website: www.centre.edu

THE PRINCETON REVIEW SAYS

Admissions

The school reports that its standardized testing policy for use in admission for Fall 2024 is Test Optional. It is unknown at this time if the 2024 testing policy will be permanent. The Princeton Review suggests that interested applicants consult with the school for the most up-to-date standardized testing policies. *Very important factors considered include:* rigor of secondary school record, academic GPA. *Important factors considered include:* class rank, standardized test scores, application essay, recommendation(s). *Other factors considered include:* interview, extracurricular activities, talent/ability, character/personal qualities, first generation, alumni/ae relation, geographical residence, racial/ethnic status, volunteer work, work experience. High school diploma is required and GED is not accepted. *Academic units required:* 4 English, 3 math, 2 science, 2 science labs, 2 foreign language, 2 history. *Academic units recommended:* 4 math, 4 science, 4 foreign language, 2 social studies, 2 history, 1 visual/performing arts.

Financial Aid

Students should submit: FAFSA; Institution's own financial aid form. The Princeton Review suggests that all financial aid forms be submitted as soon as possible (see page 5 for a note on the FAFSA). *Need-based scholarships/grants offered:* College/university scholarship or grant aid from institutional funds; Federal Pell; Private scholarships; SEOG; State scholarships/grants. *Loan aid offered:* Direct PLUS loans; Direct Subsidized Loans; Direct Unsubsidized Loans; College/university loans from institutional funds. Admitted students will be notified of awards on or about 12/23 (early decision), 2/7 (early action), 3/15 (regular decision). Federal Work-Study Program available. Institutional employment available.

The Inside Word

Centre College evaluates applicants holistically. Students who have challenged themselves with high-level coursework, earned a solid GPA, and shown improvement throughout their high school career are strong candidates for admissions. Though the school is Test Optional, it still values those scores, and this is a good place for a driven student to get their attention. The college also gives appropriate weight to extracurriculars, letters of recommendations, and personal statements.

THE SCHOOL SAYS "..."

From the Admissions Office

"Centre College offers its students a world of opportunities, highlighted by the nation's premier study abroad program. Approximately 85 percent of students study abroad at least once. CentreTerm programs explore an ever-increasing number of countries. Over the last several years, destinations have included Argentina, Austria, Barbados, Brazil, Costa Rica, Cuba, Ecuador, Egypt, England, Ghana, India, Israel, Italy, Japan, Malaysia, Mexico, Morocco, Myanmar, the Netherlands, New Zealand, Panama, Rwanda, Spain, and Uganda. In addition, there are nine permanent, semester-long residential programs: England, Scotland, Northern Ireland, France, Spain, Yucatan, China, and Japan. Centre's personalized approach means that most international study includes at least one Centre professor. Study abroad is so important that it is a component of the Centre Commitment: study abroad, an internship or research experience, and graduation in four years—guaranteed, or Centre will provide up to one more year of tuition for free. On average, 93 percent of graduates participated in either an internship and/or undergraduate research. Centre's stellar academic reputation and exceptional commitment to remaining affordable lead to extraordinary success for our students: entrance to top graduate and professional schools, prestigious undergraduate and postgraduate fellowships (Rhodes, Fulbright, Goldwater, Rotary, and Gates-Cambridge), and rewarding jobs. (On average, 97 percent are employed or in advanced study within one year of graduation.) Centre is a place where important conversations occur—in and out of the classroom. In 2012, for the second time in a dozen years, Centre's Norton Center for the Arts was the setting for the nation's only vice presidential debate. Annually, the Norton Center features an amazing array of high-profile arts performances and speakers, including the legendary Vienna Philharmonic and Yo-Yo Ma to rock legends Greg Allman and ZZ Top."

SELECTIVITY

Admissions Rating	88
# of applicants	2,212
% of applicants accepted	76
% of acceptees attending	21
# offered a place on the wait list	115
% accepting a place on wait list	15
% admitted from wait list	100
# of early decision applicants	73
% accepted early decision	88

FIRST-YEAR PROFILE

Testing policy	Test Optional
Range SAT composite	1150–1380
Range SAT EBRW	570–650
Range SAT math	560–730
Range ACT composite	26–32
# submitting SAT scores	74
% submitting SAT scores	26
# submitting ACT scores	281
% submitting ACT scores	79
Average HS GPA	3.6
% frosh submitting high school GPA	99
% graduated top 10% of class	52
% graduated top 25% of class	80
% graduated top 50% of class	97

DEADLINES

Early decision	
Deadline	11/15
Notification	12/15
Early action	
Deadline	12/1
Notification	1/15
Regular	
Deadline	1/15
Notification	3/15
Nonfall registration?	No

APPLICANTS OFTEN PREFER
Vanderbilt University

APPLICANTS SOMETIMES PREFER
Denison University; Furman University

APPLICANTS RARELY PREFER
Miami University; The University of the South

FINANCIAL FACTS

Financial Aid Rating	87
Annual tuition	$43,000
Room and board	$10,740
Required fees	$0
Books and supplies	$1,400
Average frosh need-based scholarship	$36,467
Average UG need-based scholarship	$33,652
% needy frosh rec. need-based scholarship or grant aid	100
% needy UG rec. need-based scholarship or grant aid	100
% needy frosh rec. non-need-based scholarship or grant aid	0
% needy UG rec. non-need-based scholarship or grant aid	0
% needy frosh rec. need-based self-help aid	62
% needy UG rec. need-based self-help aid	65
% frosh rec. any financial aid	97
% UG rec. any financial aid	96
% UG borrow to pay for school	51
Average cumulative indebtedness	$27,418
% frosh need fully met	36
% ugrads need fully met	32
Average % of frosh need met	90
Average % of ugrad need met	87

CHAMPLAIN COLLEGE

163 South Willard Street, Burlington, VT 05402-0670 • Admissions: 802-860-2700 • Fax: 802-860-2767

STUDENTS SAY "..."

Academics

The students at Champlain College in Burlington, Vermont, are "professional" and "career-minded," and name Champlain's "career-focused curriculum" as a primary reason for choosing the college. "Networking and the emphasis on internships at Champlain lead to a great deal of job placements relevant to your chosen major after (or before!) graduation," extols one student. Students love the "small class sizes," which "allow your professors and classmates to know, contribute, and follow your success." They're also crazy about Champlain's Upside-Down Curriculum, which uniquely allows undergraduates to jump right into key classes: "I could begin major-related work on the first day." Game design, filmmaking, digital forensics, psychology, and marketing are all offered as majors, distinguishing Champlain's available courses of study to many applicants, with its "strong focus on major-specific skills, and field-applicable classwork." For the most part, students say the professors are "engaging, encouraging, and interesting" and "do all they can to help students understand the material and reach their full potential." Champlain works hard to produce graduates who know "how to survive and thrive in the business world" and "reach their highest level of satisfaction." Champlain is a "career-focused school that gives students the tools to succeed in the professional world." This career-conscious education is animated by Champlain's "engaging, encouraging, and interesting" professors, who "know your name," are "enthusiastic about the students' education," and "come from extremely professional backgrounds and add personal touches to their discussions that make students want to participate." In addition to academic curricula, Champlain's InSight program "readies students for outside life," teaching life skills such as "financial sophistication" and fostering a "strong sense of community." For those interested in the burgeoning gaming industry, "Champlain's game [majors are] also rigorous and unique, bringing students from amateurs to developing a game in a seemingly short four years." Champlain's greatest academic strength lies in "excellent professors, innovative classes," and an "inviting small-classroom environment."

Campus Life

The small liberal arts college in cozy Burlington, Vermont, has a heavy academic focus on the video game industry, and skiing and gaming figure prominently into Champlain's social life. "There is a lot to do in town, and on campus there are often events put on by clubs or the SGA [Student Government Association]. Every Thursday, a bus also takes students from campus to free bowling or to see a free movie at the movie theater." Students love Burlington—"full of endless opportunities for both outside and indoor activities"—and enjoy the shops and nightlife of Church Street. Both Champlain and Burlington "heavily promote sustainable living," and as such, students learn "an incredible amount about how to help and be aware of my community and ecosystem." For the dedicated skier/student, Champlain IDs will nab you discounted ski passes in the area, and "snow dictates class attendance in the spring." Overall, the outdoorsy will find plenty to love about Champlain and the mantra seems to be, "Anything to be outside." Indoors, the "laid-back" social atmosphere tends toward "play[ing] video games rather often," and "there is an excellent music scene here in Burlington."

Student Body

Champlain's student population is summed up by one as "Champlain attracts a certain type: open, artistic, thoughtful, and intelligent," while another student is a little more blunt: "We are all nerdy in our own special way." It's a self-selective, "open-minded" population that's passionately adored by those who know what to expect: students "fit in well if they have researched the college before coming, as it is a small community within a larger community." There is "literally a bit of everything. Nerds, partiers, skiers, snowboarders, skateboarders, and hippies." Another summarizes the Champlain student body as "everyone is incredibly friendly and supportive. I love that it's large enough not to know everyone but small enough that it still feels like family." As a whole, Champlain students are "motivated and engaged." They enjoy the social opportunities afforded by Burlington and Champlain, but "are also serious about doing big things and going far in life."

CHAMPLAIN COLLEGE

Financial Aid: 802-860-2730 • E-Mail: admission@champlain.edu • Website: www.champlain.edu

THE PRINCETON REVIEW SAYS

Admissions

The school reports that its standardized testing policy for use in admission for Fall 2024 is Test Optional. The 2024 testing policy will be permanent. The Princeton Review suggests that interested applicants consult with the school for the most up-to-date standardized testing policies. *Very important factors considered include:* rigor of secondary school record, academic GPA, talent/ability. *Important factors considered include:* application essay, recommendation(s), extracurricular activities, character/personal qualities, level of applicant's interest. *Other factors considered include:* class rank, standardized test scores, interview, first generation, alumni/ae relation, geographical residence, state residency, racial/ethnic status, volunteer work, work experience. High school diploma is required and GED is accepted. *Academic units required:* 4 English, 3 math, 3 science, 2 science labs, 2 foreign language, 3 history, 5 academic electives. *Academic units recommended:* 4 math, 4 science, 3 foreign language, 4 history.

Financial Aid

Students should submit: FAFSA. Priority filing deadline is 1/15. The Princeton Review suggests that all financial aid forms be submitted as soon as possible (see page 5 for a note on the FAFSA). *Need-based scholarships/grants offered:* College/university scholarship or grant aid from institutional funds; Federal Pell; Private scholarships; SEOG; State scholarships/grants. *Loan aid offered:* Direct PLUS loans; Direct Subsidized Loans; Direct Unsubsidized Loans; State Loans. Admitted students will be notified of awards on a rolling basis beginning 12/15. Federal Work-Study Program available. Institutional employment available.

The Inside Word

For the BFA or BS programs in creative media, filmmaking, graphic design and digital media, game art and animation, and game design, prospective students must submit a portfolio of relevant creative work. Strong writing skills are important for all applicants.

THE SCHOOL SAYS "..."

From the Admissions Office

"Champlain combines world-class academics with real-world experience. Our primary mission is to provide students with the most innovative and relevant career-focused education you'll find anywhere. We don't just keep pace with current technology, arts, and social progress—we graduate leaders and influencers in these spheres, ready to tackle complex problems and create meaningful change. Our unique Upside-Down Curriculum allows students to gain more in-depth experience in their fields than they would at nearly any other institution. You'll start taking the classes you are most interested in right away—and spend four years immersed in your field of study.

"Champlain's multidimensional approach includes a liberal arts Core curriculum that helps you develop your communication skills, expand your perspective, and explore science, culture, and other pillars of society. The InSight program, integrated throughout the academic experience, gives you the personal finance, career-planning, and well-being knowledge you'll need to lead a satisfying and successful life.

"Each Champlain curriculum encourages at least one semester of study abroad while ensuring you graduate on time. Our campuses in Dublin, Ireland, and Montreal, Canada, provide seamless options for continuing your studies (and financial aid), while exchange and third-party programs can take you almost anywhere else you'd like to go.

"Our beautiful hilltop campus in Burlington, Vermont overlooks Lake Champlain and the Adirondack Mountains. All first-year students live in one of our 20 beautifully restored Victorian-era mansions, which are just a short walk from the waterfront and city center. Schedule a visit at Champlain: champlain.edu/visit."

SELECTIVITY

Admissions Rating	89
# of applicants	6,766
% of applicants accepted	56
% of acceptees attending	14
# of early decision applicants	410
% accepted early decision	67

FIRST-YEAR PROFILE

Testing policy	Test Optional
Range SAT composite	1170–1340
Range SAT EBRW	603–698
Range SAT math	560–650
Range ACT composite	27–31
# submitting SAT scores	122
% submitting SAT scores	23
# submitting ACT scores	17
% submitting ACT scores	3
Average HS GPA	3.5
% frosh submitting high school GPA	93
% graduated top 10% of class	17
% graduated top 25% of class	47
% graduated top 50% of class	77

DEADLINES

Early decision	
Deadline	11/15
Notification	12/15
Other ED deadline	12/15
Other ED notification	1/15
Regular	
Priority	11/15
Deadline	1/15
Notification	2/15
Nonfall registration?	Yes

APPLICANTS ALSO LOOK AT

Ithaca College; Plymouth State University; Quinnipiac University; Rochester Institute of Technology; Roger Williams University; Saint Michael's College; University of Connecticut; University of Maine; University of New Hampshire; University of Vermont

FINANCIAL FACTS

Financial Aid Rating	83
Annual tuition	$45,100
Room and board	$16,900
Required fees	$450
Books and supplies	$1,000
Average frosh need-based scholarship	$30,358
Average UG need-based scholarship	$29,120
% needy frosh rec. need-based scholarship or grant aid	99
% needy UG rec. need-based scholarship or grant aid	99
% needy frosh rec. non-need-based scholarship or grant aid	17
% needy UG rec. non-need-based scholarship or grant aid	17
% needy frosh rec. need-based self-help aid	69
% needy UG rec. need-based self-help aid	73
% frosh rec. any financial aid	97
% UG rec. any financial aid	97
% UG borrow to pay for school	68
Average cumulative indebtedness	$34,261
% frosh need fully met	23
% ugrads need fully met	22
Average % of frosh need met	79
Average % of ugrad need met	78

CHAPMAN UNIVERSITY

One University Drive, Orange, CA 92866 • Admissions: 714-997-6815 • Fax: 714-997-6711

CAMPUS LIFE

Quality of Life Rating	85
Fire Safety Rating	79
Green Rating	72
Type of school	Private
Affiliation	Disciples of Christ
Environment	Metropolis

STUDENTS

Total undergrad enrollment	7,665
% male/female/another gender	40/60/0
% from out of state	31
% frosh live on campus	89
% ugrads live on campus	47
# of fraternities (% join)	10 (23)
# of sororities (% join)	8 (39)
% African American	2
% Asian	16
% White	49
% Hispanic	18
% Native American	<1
% Pacific Islander	<1
% Two or more races	9
% Race and/or ethnicity unknown	2
% international	3
# of countries represented	64

SURVEY SAYS . . .

Students are happy
Classroom facilities are great
Great library
Internships are widely available
Students aren't religious
Easy to get around campus
Frats and sororities are popular
College radio is popular

ACADEMICS

Academic Rating	80
% students returning for sophomore year	91
% students graduating within 4 years	76
% students graduating within 6 years	84
Calendar	4/1/4
Student/faculty ratio	12:1
Profs interesting rating	86
Profs accessible rating	92

Most classes have 10–19 students.
Most lab/discussion sessions have
  10–19 students.

MOST POPULAR MAJORS

Public Relations/Image Management;
Cinematography and Film/Video Production;
Business Administration and Management,
General

STUDENTS SAY ". . ."

Academics

With its "small school" setting and So-Cal vibe, it's easy to see why students are charmed by Chapman. The university "truly emphasizes personal growth, campus involvement, and global citizenship," factors that undergrads here appreciate. There's also "great technology available" and a "gorgeous campus" to boot. Even better, "research and internship [opportunities]" abound. Chapman students also tend to rave about their "very engaging" professors, who make a concerted effort to "explain complex concepts in an understandable way." As a health sciences major shares, "These teachers aren't out to get you—they challenge you academically but are willing to help you if you're stuck or confused." It's quite obvious that "they're very dedicated and interested in the subject matters that they teach." Most importantly, they strive "to build meaningful relationships with students." And a biochemistry major boasts, "They offer so much help outside of the classroom and want to see you succeed. My overall academic experience has been wonderful."

Campus Life

It's nearly impossible to not lead a "full and engaging" life here at Chapman. After all, there's so many different things to do. To begin with, "the main campus provides concerts, plays, musical performances, art showings, and lectures, which are generally free for students." Additionally, "Dodge Film School has movie screenings...sometimes of movies that haven't come out yet." Chapman hosts plenty of "cool events like 'Yoga on the Lawn,' a winter festival or a chili cook off" as well. And we're also told that there's "a very large Greek presence." In fact, some undergrads insist that "Greek life can be instrumental in finding your group of friends." When the weekend rolls around, "there are usually house parties or people go to the local bars." However, many undergrads do complain that the parties tend to get shut down fairly early. Not surprisingly, students love attending school in Southern California. Chapman itself is located "right next to [Old Towne] Orange, which has many shops and restaurants where students love to walk around." Beyond that, "you can go to Disney, the beach, the Angels stadium, Los Angeles, San Diego, or wherever else tickles your fancy."

Student Body

Chapman undergrads describe their peers as "kind, respectful, artistic, intelligent, and adventurous." A few suggest that the student body also leans toward the "affluent," "attractive," and "conservative," but note that for the most part, the campus is "accepting [of] diversity" and comes together around their common "driven" personalities. As such, Chapman avoids cutthroat competition, and instead is filled with students who "love to work together to understand the subject material." One major notes that "The mood of the student body is very collaborative. Everyone wants to socialize and be friendly and meet new people." As a sociology major puts it, "No matter what the interest is, whether... Greek life, community service, their major, or even their social life, [students here] are motivated to succeed in their endeavors."

CHAPMAN UNIVERSITY

Financial Aid: 714-997-6741 • E-Mail: admit@chapman.edu • Website: www.chapman.edu

THE PRINCETON REVIEW SAYS

Admissions

The school reports that its standardized testing policy for use in admission for Fall 2024 is Test Optional. The 2024 testing policy will be permanent. *Very important factors considered include:* rigor of secondary school record, class rank, academic GPA, application essay, character/personal qualities. *Important factors considered include:* extracurricular activities, talent/ability. *Other factors considered include:* standardized test scores, recommendation(s), interview, first generation, geographical residence, state residency, Film and Television Production, volunteer work, work experience, level of applicant's interest. High school diploma is required and GED is accepted. *Academic units required:* 4 English, 3 math, 2 science, 1 science lab, 2 foreign language, 2 social studies, 2 history. *Academic units recommended:* 4 English, 4 math, 4 science, 2 science labs, 4 foreign language, 2 social studies, 2 history, 2 academic electives.

Financial Aid

Students should submit: FAFSA; State aid form. Priority filing deadline is 3/2. The Princeton Review suggests that all financial aid forms be submitted as soon as possible (see page 5 for a note on the FAFSA). *Need-based scholarships/grants offered:* College/university scholarship or grant aid from institutional funds; Federal Pell; Private scholarships; SEOG; State scholarships/grants. *Loan aid offered:* Direct PLUS loans; Direct Subsidized Loans; Direct Unsubsidized Loans; College/university loans from institutional funds. Admitted students will be notified of awards on a rolling basis beginning 3/15. Federal Work-Study Program available. Institutional employment available.

The Inside Word

Gaining admission to Chapman is certainly competitive. When reviewing applications, admissions officers tend to take a holistic approach. The rigor of an academic curriculum, grade trends, letters of recommendation, extracurricular activities and personal statements will all be closely evaluated. Students intending to study Film and Television Production will need to apply by November 1, and those looking for a degree in Dance, Pre-Pharmacy, Screen Acting, Theatre Performance, and Writing for Film and Television have a priority deadline of November 1.

THE SCHOOL SAYS "..."

From the Admissions Office

"Chapman University provides a personalized and interdisciplinary educational experience to highly qualified students. We offer more than 120 areas of study—options for nearly every interest and passion. Not sure what you want to do? No problem. Entering Undeclared is also a popular option. Our academic plans encourage you to explore across subject areas—something that's supported in and out of class.

- Our average class size is 23; most of your classes will range from 10–19 students.
- There are more than 190 academic, professional, and special-interest clubs on campus.
- We offer 19 intercollegiate athletic teams (NCAA Division III) and 8 club teams.
- You can choose from over 90 semester and academic-year study abroad programs. (More than 40 percent of Chapman students study abroad.)

"With on-campus housing guaranteed for all first-year students and sophomores (more than 90 percent of them live on campus), our university is a vibrant community located in the heart of Orange County. From campus you can walk to Old Town Orange, or drive to nearby attractions, including beaches, mountains, sporting venues, or Disneyland. We invite you to visit Chapman and see what's possible here. In the meantime, our website is a great resource to learn more about the university and schedule a campus tour."

SELECTIVITY

Admissions Rating	87
# of applicants	13,690
% of applicants accepted	73
% of acceptees attending	21
# offered a place on the wait list	992
% accepting a place on wait list	57
% admitted from wait list	0
# of early decision applicants	214
% accepted early decision	61

FIRST-YEAR PROFILE

Testing policy	Test Optional
Range SAT composite	1220–1380
Range SAT EBRW	600–700
Range SAT math	600–700
Range ACT composite	26–31
# submitting SAT scores	524
% submitting SAT scores	25
# submitting ACT scores	252
% submitting ACT scores	12
% graduated top 10% of class	26
% graduated top 25% of class	63
% graduated top 50% of class	91

DEADLINES

Early decision	
Deadline	11/1
Notification	12/20
Early action	
Deadline	11/1
Notification	12/20
Regular	
Priority	11/1
Deadline	1/15
Notification	4/1
Nonfall registration?	Yes

FINANCIAL FACTS

Financial Aid Rating	81
Annual tuition	$62,400
Room and board	$19,954
Required fees	$384
Books and supplies	$1,600
Average frosh need-based scholarship	$23,622
Average UG need-based scholarship	$21,416
% needy frosh rec. need-based scholarship or grant aid	92
% needy UG rec. need-based scholarship or grant aid	90
% needy frosh rec. non-need-based scholarship or grant aid	79
% needy UG rec. non-need-based scholarship or grant aid	75
% needy frosh rec. need-based self-help aid	84
% needy UG rec. need-based self-help aid	87
% frosh rec. any financial aid	89
% UG borrow to pay for school	46
Average cumulative indebtedness	$27,530
% frosh need fully met	19
% ugrads need fully met	15
Average % of frosh need met	77
Average % of ugrad need met	71

CHRISTOPHER NEWPORT UNIVERSITY

1 Avenue of the Arts, Newport News, VA 23606-3072 • Admissions: 757-594-7000 • Fax: 757-594-7333

CAMPUS LIFE

Quality of Life Rating	90
Fire Safety Rating	92
Green Rating	60*
Type of school	Public
Environment	City

STUDENTS

Total undergrad enrollment	4,442
% male/female/another gender	46/54/0
% from out of state	7
% frosh from public high school	80
% frosh live on campus	96
% ugrads live on campus	80
# of fraternities (% join)	11 (21)
# of sororities (% join)	10 (19)
% African American	8
% Asian	4
% White	74
% Hispanic	8
% Native American	<1
% Pacific Islander	<1
% Two or more races	5
% Race and/or ethnicity unknown	1
% international	<1
# of countries represented	27

SURVEY SAYS . . .

Lots of conservative students
Students are happy
Classroom facilities are great
Lab facilities are great
Career services are great
Internships are widely available
School is well run
No one cheats
Students are friendly
Students are very religious
Students involved in community service
Dorms are like palaces
Easy to get around campus
Theater is popular

ACADEMICS

Academic Rating	81
% students returning for sophomore year	86
% students graduating within 4 years	69
% students graduating within 6 years	76
Calendar	Semester
Student/faculty ratio	13:1
Profs interesting rating	88
Profs accessible rating	92

Most classes have 10–19 students.

MOST POPULAR MAJORS

Psychology, General; Business Administration and Management, General; Speech Communication and Rhetoric

STUDENTS SAY "..."

Academics

Christopher Newport University invites students to become part of a "vibrant community," one that's truly "invested in the well-being and growth" of all undergraduates who attend. Indeed, CNU students are privy to both "strong academics and [a] very strong support system." Many individuals here also appreciate that there's a "focus on undergraduate research," noting how easy it is "to ask a professor if you can join them." Additionally, they are quick to mention that "service...and study abroad opportunities" abound as well. And they certainly benefit from "small class sizes" too, which allows "for more personal attention from professors." The faculty here "make a strong effort to get to know you and create a relationship with you while [you're] in their class." In turn, "this... makes it easier to ask for help when you need it and/or gives you a faculty member you can always reach out to." It's also abundantly clear that "their passion is teaching students, and they are very good at it." As this grateful undergrad illustrates, "They get more excited about my accomplishment[s] than I do and are always an ear when needed." Some may even go as far as stating that "professors at CNU are the strongest asset of this university."

Campus Life

Christopher Newport's modest size belies a campus that's always abuzz with activity. "The fact that [it is] a smaller campus does not mean there are fewer opportunities to be involved." With "over 200 clubs and organizations at CNU" and "students are always going to events put on by their student organizations or to ones put on by our Campus Activities Board." Importantly, these clubs run the gamut; there's everything from "the student-run farmers market and sustainability commission" to "CNU *Survivor*...a club [that] mimic[s] the show *Survivor* on [CBS]." There are also many opportunities to "volunteer at local community sites." Moreover, it's common for students to "fill their days by working on campus." One undergrad explains, "CNU has a lot of job opportunities for students that allow us to study and work simultaneously."

Undergrads here love taking advantage of the nice weather as well. In the "warmer seasons a lot of students will fill the many lawns of the campus with frisbees, lacrosse sticks, footballs, etc." Then again, it's easy to get a break from campus life if you need. In fact, it's part of a classic CNU tradition. "One signature activity here at CNU is watching the sunset at a location called Lions Bridge. It's roughly a 30-minute walk from campus and a 10-minute drive to watch the beautiful pinks and oranges set over the coast." No matter on-campus or off, "there always seems to be fun things to do."

Student Body

Students at Christopher Newport speak highly of their "driven and friendly" peers. It's easy to understand why. The vast majority "are super optimistic and outgoing people who love to get involved in organizations both on and off campus." They also tend to be "overwhelmingly kind," but share "a strange unspoken expectation for all students to present themselves as more formal." You'll often see students "go out of their way to open doors and smile at strangers." But don't worry; their kindness is no less authentic! "While walking to class you quickly see friends or classmates, and nobody is afraid to wave or ask how your day is going." Although a few individuals do caution that the university is a "predominantly white institution," and it can feel as though "most students come from the Northern Virginia or Richmond area," rest assured, even if you don't fit that mold, you'll still find everyone is "very respectful" and "welcoming community." As this undergrad sums up, "The student body at Christopher Newport is the...most supportive network any student can ask for. It is truly a community."

CHRISTOPHER NEWPORT UNIVERSITY

Financial Aid: 757-594-7170 • E-Mail: admit@cnu.edu • Website: www.cnu.edu

THE PRINCETON REVIEW SAYS

Admissions

The school reports that its standardized testing policy for use in admission for Fall 2024 is Test Optional. The 2024 testing policy will be permanent. The Princeton Review suggests that interested applicants consult with the school for the most up-to-date standardized testing policies. *Very important factors considered include:* rigor of secondary school record, academic GPA. *Important factors considered include:* class rank, standardized test scores, application essay, recommendation(s), interview, extracurricular activities, talent/ability, character/personal qualities, level of applicant's interest. *Other factors considered include:* first generation, alumni/ae relation, geographical residence, state residency, volunteer work, work experience. High school diploma is required and GED is not accepted. *Academic units required:* 4 English, 4 math, 4 science, 4 science labs, 3 foreign language, 4 social studies, 1 visual/performing arts, 2 academic electives.

Financial Aid

Students should submit: FAFSA. Priority filing deadline is 3/1. The Princeton Review suggests that all financial aid forms be submitted as soon as possible (see page 5 for a note on the FAFSA). *Need-based scholarships/grants offered:* College/university scholarship or grant aid from institutional funds; Federal Pell; Private scholarships; SEOG; State scholarships/grants. *Loan aid offered:* Direct PLUS loans; Direct Subsidized Loans; Direct Unsubsidized Loans. Admitted students will be notified of awards on a rolling basis beginning 3/1. Federal Work-Study Program available. Institutional employment available.

The Inside Word

Christopher Newport values strong academics as well as students whose character and goals are a good fit. Therefore, pay special attention to your application essay, choose your recommenders wisely, and highlight your extracurriculars strategically. That being said, the rigor of your high school curriculum will still take priority. If you're taking a few honors, AP, or IB courses, you will be in good shape. And even though they are now Test Optional, a good SAT or ACT score won't hurt your chances!

THE SCHOOL SAYS "..."

From the Admissions Office

"Christopher Newport University recruits future graduates who will thrive academically and socially on campus, and then go on to lead lives of significance. That's why our undergraduate experience—one that combines cutting-edge research and technology, innovative leadership opportunities, and high-impact service learning initiatives—inspires great leaders for the twenty-first century. Honoring the essential traditions of the liberal arts and sciences, our curriculum challenges hearts, as well as minds. We look for students of honor who will seek to make the world a better place. Fifty percent of our students score between 1130 and 1270 on the SAT (evidence-based reading and writing + math). Students are required to live on campus through their junior year. Our contemporary, state-of-the-art residential facilities win rave reviews from students and parents alike.

"Here you will study alongside distinguished professors, and over the last five years, we have added more than 100 tenure-track PhDs to our faculty. Outside the classroom, you will gain hands-on experience through internships with top organizations like NASA and the Thomas Jefferson National Accelerator Facility.

"At CNU, you will enjoy countless opportunities to develop leadership skills. Make an impact through the President's Leadership Program; design a challenging curriculum in the Honors Program; team with faculty on groundbreaking research; take your studies overseas by studying abroad; and share your talents through 200-plus student organizations. We are also home to one of the most successful NCAA Division III programs in the nation with student-athletes who excel both in the classroom and on the courts and fields of play. Check us out—we offer a truly distinctive student experience on a breathtakingly beautiful campus!"

SELECTIVITY

Admissions Rating	83
# of applicants	7,428
% of applicants accepted	85
% of acceptees attending	18
# offered a place on the wait list	559
% accepting a place on wait list	30
% admitted from wait list	100
# of early decision applicants	253
% accepted early decision	92

FIRST-YEAR PROFILE

Testing policy	Test Optional
Range SAT composite	1120–1280
Range SAT EBRW	560–660
Range SAT math	540–630
Range ACT composite	22–29
# submitting SAT scores	468
% submitting SAT scores	40
# submitting ACT scores	79
% submitting ACT scores	7
Average HS GPA	3.8
% frosh submitting high school GPA	100
% graduated top 10% of class	13
% graduated top 25% of class	38
% graduated top 50% of class	73

DEADLINES

Early decision	
Deadline	11/15
Notification	12/15
Early action	
Deadline	12/1
Notification	1/15
Regular	
Deadline	2/1
Notification	3/15
Nonfall registration?	Yes

APPLICANTS OFTEN PREFER

James Madison University; University of Virginia; William & Mary

APPLICANTS SOMETIMES PREFER

George Mason University; Virginia Commonwealth University; Virginia Tech

APPLICANTS RARELY PREFER

Longwood University; University of Mary Washington

FINANCIAL FACTS

Financial Aid Rating	79
Annual in-state tuition	$15,425
Annual out-of-state tuition	$28,663
Room and board	$11,990
Average frosh need-based scholarship	$9,506
Average UG need-based scholarship	$8,624
% needy frosh rec. need-based scholarship or grant aid	58
% needy UG rec. need-based scholarship or grant aid	61
% needy frosh rec. non-need-based scholarship or grant aid	51
% needy UG rec. non-need-based scholarship or grant aid	40
% needy frosh rec. need-based self-help aid	64
% needy UG rec. need-based self-help aid	66
% frosh rec. any financial aid	75
% UG rec. any financial aid	67
% UG borrow to pay for school	53
Average cumulative indebtedness	$38,174
% frosh need fully met	17
% ugrads need fully met	17
Average % of frosh need met	68
Average % of ugrad need met	64

CITY UNIVERSITY OF NEW YORK—BARUCH COLLEGE

One Bernard Baruch Way, New York, NY 10010 • Admissions: 646-312-1000 • Fax: 646-312-1361

STUDENTS SAY "..."

Academics

One of the City University of New York's senior colleges, Baruch College's schools (Weissman School of Arts and Sciences, Marxe School of Public and International Affairs, and the Zicklin School of Business, which is the largest of the three) are located in Manhattan and take full advantage of being in "the greatest city of the world": students here have access to "internships, big companies, and...Wall Street." Low in-state (as well as reasonable out-of-state) tuition means that many here "go to school while already working in interesting and impressive positions," and have come to Baruch purely "to improve themselves," which increases the level of maturity in the classroom. There is a wide variety of courses ("especially [for] those interested in business"), and the school offers ad-hoc majors, which allows students to design programs that will support their career goals.

Though this is not a research university, there are a "vast amount of resources" that are available to the students here. The education system is "well organized and up to date with the current world," and Baruch is tied with many companies in New York, which "creates even more opportunities for internships as well as job opportunities." "Some of my business professors came from leading huge corporations, and their anecdotes about their prior work help students internalize the material," says one student. There is "an impressive number of career-developing programs on campus that are free of charge and readily available to all students," and "it is clear that the professors at Baruch have first-hand experience in the material they are teaching to students."

Campus Life

As a commuter school, most students go to classes and go home, but "there are great clubs and events always happening" for those that do hang around, and the "lounges are usually packed." "It is all about how much time and effort you put into finding things to do," says a student. Most students are working part-time or full-time while taking courses here, but find plenty to do in between classes, from "hanging out in the club area with the clubs, playing in the game room, working out in the gym, or taking classes in our trading floor." There is so much student activity around Baruch that it is often hard to contain, and "there is always something going on and always free food around campus."

Though most do not get the typical on-campus college experience, all agree that "for the price and the benefits associated with the school, the trade-off is worth it." This is New York City, which means "you can practically do ANYTHING with your day." Museums are free for students, and "of course the shopping and food are amazing." The school's Newman Vertical Campus on Lexington Ave is a hive of activity, and though elevator crowding is a problem, when a student's eyes look at the breathtaking view of the building, "It makes you feel proud to be a Baruchi!"

Student Body

Students come from all over the world and Baruch is "full of bright and ambitious minds"; being a student here "means you learn to interact with peers from all over the world." "My fellow peers have a good sense of where they want to steer their careers and exactly what they want to do after college," says one student. Baruch is "full of first-generation college graduates," and the school is a real microcosm of NYC: "the hustle and bustle, crowds, everyone has somewhere to go, and everyone has a dream they hope will one day be fulfilled." This is a very unique commuter school in that "it has such an involved student body" where "there is a sense of community through clubs and extracurriculars."

CITY UNIVERSITY OF NEW YORK—BARUCH COLLEGE

Financial Aid: 646-312-1390 • E-Mail: admissions@baruch.cuny.edu • Website: www.baruch.cuny.edu

THE PRINCETON REVIEW SAYS

Admissions

The school reports that its standardized testing policy for use in admission for Fall 2024 is Test Optional. The 2024 testing policy will be temporary. The Princeton Review suggests that interested applicants consult with the school for the most up-to-date standardized testing policies. *Very important factors considered include:* rigor of secondary school record, academic GPA. *Important factors considered include:* application essay, recommendation(s). *Other factors considered include:* standardized test scores, interview, extracurricular activities, talent/ability, character/personal qualities, work experience. High school diploma is required and GED is accepted. *Academic units required:* 4 English, 3 math, 2 science, 2 science labs, 2 foreign language, 3 social studies, 1 visual/performing arts. *Academic units recommended:* 4 English, 4 math, 3 science, 2 science labs, 2 foreign language, 4 social studies, 1 visual/performing arts, 1 academic elective.

Financial Aid

Students should submit: FAFSA; State aid form. Priority filing deadline is 6/30. The Princeton Review suggests that all financial aid forms be submitted as soon as possible (see page 5 for a note on the FAFSA). *Need-based scholarships/grants offered:* Federal Pell; SEOG; State scholarships/grants. *Loan aid offered:* Direct PLUS loans; Direct Subsidized Loans; Direct Unsubsidized Loans. Admitted students will be notified of awards on a rolling basis beginning 6/30. Federal Work-Study Program available. Institutional employment available.

The Inside Word

Admissions have grown steadily more competitive in recent years, especially for students seeking undergraduate business degrees. Today, Baruch receives nearly 15 applications for every slot in its freshman class.

THE SCHOOL SAYS ". . ."

From the Admissions Office

"As an undergraduate at Baruch College, you will join a vibrant learning community of students and scholars in the heart of exhilarating, possibility-filled New York City. Baruch is a place where theory meets practice. You can network with city leaders; secure business, cultural, and nonprofit internships; access the music, art, and business scene; and meet experts who visit our campus. You will take classes that bridge business, arts, science, government, political and international affairs, learning from professors who are among the best in their fields. One-third of our freshmen participate in learning communities, which offer incoming students small, interdisciplinary classes and an opportunity to get to know our faculty through classroom discussion and planned field trips throughout the city. Baruch offers 30 majors and 60 minors in three schools: the Marxe School of Public Affairs and International Affairs, the Weissman School of Arts and Science, and the Zicklin School of Business. Highly qualified undergraduates may apply to the Baruch College Honors program, which offers scholarships, small seminars and honors courses. Students may also study abroad through programs in more than 30 countries. Our 17-floor Newman Vertical Campus serves as the college's hub. Here you will find the atmosphere and resources of a traditional college campus, but in a lively urban setting. Our classrooms have state-of-the-art technology, and our library was named the top college library in the nation. Baruch also has a simulated trading floor for students who are interested in Wall Street. You can also enjoy a three-level athletics and recreation complex, which features a twenty-five-meter indoor pool as well as a performing arts complex. The state-of-the-art residences, blocks from Central Park on the Upper East Side, are equipped with a concierge, high tech gym, laundry facility that texts when your clothes are dry, and a very chill lounge to study or relax with your friends. Baruch's selective admission standards, strong academic programs, top national honors, as well as its internship and job-placement opportunities make it an exceptional educational value."

SELECTIVITY

Admissions Rating	86
# of applicants	23,434
% of applicants accepted	51
% of acceptees attending	21

FIRST-YEAR PROFILE

Testing policy	Test Optional
Average HS GPA	3.7
% frosh submitting high school GPA	94
% graduated top 10% of class	60
% graduated top 25% of class	87
% graduated top 50% of class	98

DEADLINES

Regular	
Priority	12/1
Deadline	2/1
Notification	Rolling, 2/1
Nonfall registration?	Yes

APPLICANTS OFTEN PREFER

City University of New York—Brooklyn College; City University of New York—Hunter College; City University of New York—Queens College

APPLICANTS SOMETIMES PREFER

St. John's University (NY); State University of New York—Stony Brook University

FINANCIAL FACTS

Financial Aid Rating	78
Annual in-state tuition	$6,930
Annual out-of-state tuition	$18,600
Required fees	$531
Books and supplies	$1,364
Average frosh need-based scholarship	$10,046
Average UG need-based scholarship	$9,219
% needy frosh rec. need-based scholarship or grant aid	98
% needy UG rec. need-based scholarship or grant aid	96
% needy frosh rec. non-need-based scholarship or grant aid	5
% needy UG rec. non-need-based scholarship or grant aid	5
% needy frosh rec. need-based self-help aid	7
% needy UG rec. need-based self-help aid	12
% UG borrow to pay for school	11
Average cumulative indebtedness	$13,219
% frosh need fully met	3
% ugrads need fully met	3
Average % of frosh need met	41
Average % of ugrad need met	40

CITY UNIVERSITY OF NEW YORK—BROOKLYN COLLEGE

2900 Bedford Avenue, Brooklyn, NY 11210 • Admissions: 718-951-5000 • Fax: 718-951-4506

CAMPUS LIFE

Quality of Life Rating	80
Fire Safety Rating	60*
Green Rating	88
Type of school	Public
Environment	Metropolis

STUDENTS

Total undergrad enrollment	10,785
% male/female/another gender	43/57/<1
% from out of state	2
% frosh live on campus	0
% ugrads live on campus	0
# of fraternities	7
# of sororities	5
% African American	19
% Asian	25
% White	25
% Hispanic	24
% Native American	<1
% Pacific Islander	<1
% Two or more races	3
% Race and/or ethnicity unknown	0
% international	3

SURVEY SAYS ...

Great library
Recreation facilities are great
Easy to get around campus

ACADEMICS

Academic Rating	74
% students returning for sophomore year	77
% students graduating within 4 years	32
% students graduating within 6 years	55
Calendar	Semester
Student/faculty ratio	15:1
Profs interesting rating	81
Profs accessible rating	85

Most classes have 20–29 students.

MOST POPULAR MAJORS
Psychology, General; Accounting; Business Administration and Management, General

STUDENTS SAY "..."

Academics

At Brooklyn College, a key part of the City University of New York system, its more than 13,000 undergraduate "students receive a quality education for a fraction of the price," especially for in-state residents. Autonomy is woven throughout the curricula and activities; one class required students "to input topics we would like to see on the syllabus, creating a more engaged environment," and "there are so many different options of choosing your own schedule." Students can also take part in special programs such as First College Year, which is designed to help students transition to the social and academic aspects of higher education the summer before their first year, or can avail themselves of what one respondent considers "the greatest strength of my school…[the] tons of resources and help throughout the semester" provided by the Magner Career Center. The administration also makes sure that students "can find answers to possibly any and all questions you may have," and provides "resources I can't find anywhere else," such as "advisement, trainings/workshops, [and] work readiness workshops."

Classes are varied and may include fieldwork or interactive labs, which creates "an active learning environment and further learning about what is taught in lectures." An increase in online courses has been said to provide "an innovative way [of] learning without walls." These learning environments succeed in "encouraging students to speak freely and challenge ideas in a respectful way." In addition, "professors…push you in a good way" and are "very kind and understanding as well as extremely knowledgeable in their subjects" and "keep in touch regularly."

Campus Life

The Brooklyn "campus is beautiful [with] lots of space," and since it is located in a mass transit hub, there are "many ways of traveling easily" around New York City. One student says, "I took a class called Arts in NYC and we took many trips outside the classroom to the Metropolitan Opera, various museums, other plays/theater events." Though no dorms are available through the school itself, residences are available through an associated non-profit organization. The campus "closes late, [so] there's lots of access to buildings and rooms on site" for those that need a place (like the library) to study or meet, and there are also "many tables and benches around the campus so we have more than enough space [to] hang around." Activities give a further reason to linger, with plenty of "very diverse and fun" clubs, ranging from badminton to ASL. The student government "[holds] different events that help students communicate and connect with others," and the especially popular movie nights are "usually well-known movies so more students can participate and converse with other students or staff."

Student Body

Students here "come from all different countries, cultures and religions," and "everyone has a place to fit in…no matter what boxes you as a student may or may not tick off." This diversity helps create an environment where students are constantly "learning something new from everyone's own perspectives and shared experiences" and are "welcoming, kind, and always willing to get together to study." Brooklyn College is primarily a commuter school, and everyone "has a common goal and is serious about their future." Students "constantly want the best for each other while also pushing each other to discover their potentials," and "there's an effort to make everyone seen." The strong sense of community means "people aren't shy to help each other out, share views, and create safe spaces for everyone to thrive," and "you will be able to find friends and peers from cultures all over the world." There "are very close-knit relationships among the student body, whether it's between students or with professors as well." Ultimately "everybody gets very comfortable with one another and ends up getting…together at the food plaza right behind the library." One student confirms: "I never feel out of place when I am in school and whenever I need help, someone is always willing to assist me."

CITY UNIVERSITY OF NEW YORK—BROOKLYN COLLEGE

Financial Aid: 718-951-5051 • E-Mail: adminqry@brooklyn.cuny.edu • Website: www.brooklyn.cuny.edu

THE PRINCETON REVIEW SAYS

Admissions

The school reports that its standardized testing policy for use in admission for Fall 2024 is Test Optional. It is unknown at this time if the 2024 testing policy will be permanent. The Princeton Review suggests that interested applicants consult with the school for the most up-to-date standardized testing policies. *Very important factors considered include:* rigor of secondary school record, academic GPA. *Other factors considered include:* High school diploma is required and GED is accepted. *Academic units required:* 4 English, 3 math, 3 science, 3 foreign language, 4 social studies, 2 visual/performing arts.

Financial Aid

Students should submit: FAFSA; State aid form. Priority filing deadline is 5/1. The Princeton Review suggests that all financial aid forms be submitted as soon as possible (see page 5 for a note on the FAFSA). *Need-based scholarships/grants offered:* College/university scholarship or grant aid from institutional funds; Federal Pell; Private scholarships; SEOG; State scholarships/grants. *Loan aid offered:* Direct PLUS loans; Direct Subsidized Loans; Direct Unsubsidized Loans. Admitted students will be notified of awards on a rolling basis. Federal Work-Study Program available. Institutional employment available.

The Inside Word

Brooklyn College doesn't set the bar inordinately high; students with less-than-stellar high school records can receive a chance to prove themselves here. Once they get in, though, they had better be prepared to work; Brooklyn College typically loses about 20 percent of its freshman class each year, and six-year graduation rates are just over 50 percent. Getting into Brooklyn College is one thing; surviving its academic challenges is a whole other thing entirely.

THE SCHOOL SAYS "..."

From the Admissions Office

"Known for its rigorous academics, enormous value, and ability to help students climb the socioeconomic ladder, Brooklyn College is a leading senior college within The City University of New York system that offers a vibrant and supportive student experience on a beautifully landscaped 35-acre campus. Offering more than 100 undergraduate and graduate degree programs in the arts, humanities, sciences, education, and business, the College is also renowned for its diversity, award-winning faculty, distinguished alumni, and community impact.

"The School of Education is ranked nationally in the top 20 for graduates who go on to become some of the top educators in New York City. The Murray Koppelman School of Business is the only program in Brooklyn that is accredited by the prestigious international Association to Advance Collegiate Schools of Business, and it regularly connects students with industry leaders and top-tier business internships.

"Brooklyn College's strong academic reputation has attracted faculty who have been awarded Pulitzer Prizes, Guggenheim Fellowships, Fulbright Awards, National Institutes of Health grants, and other awards. The student body consists of 15,938 students who have been awarded Fulbright, Truman, and Rhodes scholarships, among other awards.

"The College has been repeatedly recognized by *The Princeton Review* as one of America's Best Value Colleges (2019, 2020, 2021), as well as recently being ranked in the top 10 nationwide on the latest Social Mobility Index Report. It was also named the No. 1 College Among North Regional Universities for Campus Ethnic Diversity by *U.S. News and World Report* (2019).

"Recent additions to campus include the Feirstein Graduate School of Cinema—the only film school housed on a working lot—and the Leonard & Claire Tow Center for the Performing Arts."

SELECTIVITY

Admissions Rating	80
# of applicants	28,858
% of applicants accepted	55
% of acceptees attending	11

FIRST-YEAR PROFILE

Testing policy	Test Optional
Average HS GPA	3.4
% frosh submitting high school GPA	98

DEADLINES

Regular	
Priority	2/1
Notification	Rolling, 2/1
Nonfall registration?	Yes

FINANCIAL FACTS

Financial Aid Rating	83
Annual in-state tuition	$6,930
Annual out-of-state tuition	$18,600
Required fees	$510
Average frosh need-based scholarship	$9,404
Average UG need-based scholarship	$9,021
% needy frosh rec. need-based scholarship or grant aid	95
% needy UG rec. need-based scholarship or grant aid	88
% needy frosh rec. non-need-based scholarship or grant aid	84
% needy UG rec. non-need-based scholarship or grant aid	30
% needy frosh rec. need-based self-help aid	10
% needy UG rec. need-based self-help aid	13
% UG borrow to pay for school	7
Average cumulative indebtedness	$12,540
% frosh need fully met	57
% ugrads need fully met	33
Average % of frosh need met	60
Average % of ugrad need met	58

CITY UNIVERSITY OF NEW YORK—CITY COLLEGE

160 Convent Avenue, Wille Admin. Bldg., New York, NY 10031 • Admissions: 212-650-7000 • Fax: 212-650-6417

CAMPUS LIFE

Quality of Life Rating	85
Fire Safety Rating	90
Green Rating	83
Type of school	Public
Environment	Metropolis

STUDENTS

Total undergrad enrollment	11,463
% male/female/another gender	47/53/<1
% from out of state	2
% frosh from public high school	79
% frosh live on campus	5
% ugrads live on campus	2
# of fraternities (% join)	3 (1)
# of sororities (% join)	4 (<1)
% African American	15
% Asian	25
% White	12
% Hispanic	39
% Native American	<1
% Pacific Islander	<1
% Two or more races	3
% Race and/or ethnicity unknown	0
% international	5
# of countries represented	147

SURVEY SAYS . . .

Great library
Diverse student types interact on campus
Students love New York, NY
College radio is popular

ACADEMICS

Academic Rating	76
% students returning for sophomore year	75
% students graduating within 4 years	22
% students graduating within 6 years	58
Calendar	Semester
Student/faculty ratio	13:1
Profs interesting rating	84
Profs accessible rating	86
Most classes have 20–29 students.	
Most lab/discussion sessions have 20–29 students.	

MOST POPULAR MAJORS

Communication and Media Studies, Other;
Psychology, General; Biological and Biomedical
Sciences, Other

STUDENTS SAY ". . ."

Academics

Students searching for a school that offers a "quality and challenging education," may want to consider The City College of New York. Of course, many students are initially drawn in by CCNY's "lower than average tuition," as well as the school's "commitment to provid[e] opportunities to all...students no matter [their] race or background." When it comes to academics, undergrads love that City College offers a "broad curriculum." Additionally, they are quick to mention that the "science[s] at CCNY are rigorous" and boast that "the Engineering School is one of the best public schools." No matter your major, you're likely to have classes led by professors who students say are a "true gift to the school." Most agree that their instructors are good at fostering "discussion and engagement" and "will help you in any way they can to achieve your goals." They truly "go above and beyond for their students in terms of making time and really listening."

Campus Life

There's no denying that CCNY is a "commuter school," so it's common to see "people come, go to class, and leave." Nevertheless, there's plenty to enjoy both on the "beautiful and safe campus" and in the city at large. Undergrads appreciate that many clubs and organizations "offer multiple resources and host seminars to learn about internships and potential research opportunities." Groups range from those interested in sustainability to a pre-law club, salsa club, swimming club, video game club, and so much more. The college itself also hosts numerous events such as the annual CCNY Poetry Festival. Further, it offers a handful of "fun workshops ranging from cooking to arts and crafts" as well as meditation classes. And, of course, CCNY students have all of New York City at their fingertips. As this individual shares, "Exploring the different attractions (such as the pop up stores in Bryant Park or the museums) and various restaurants in NYC with my friends or significant other is my favorite thing to do."

Student Body

Simply put, "CCNY's student body is one of the most diverse in the country." Undergrads here come from "all around the world" and it's rather routine to hear "many languages... spoken on campus." One student heartily agrees "I've met so many peers from so many backgrounds, I've lost count." Many also stress that this diversity extends across all "racial and socioeconomic" lines as well. As another undergrad further explains, "The university draws people of incredible intellect who are maybe economically challenged and allows them to excel." A few undergrads do lament that "most students do not linger on campus when they're finished with their classes" so you really have to "put in the effort to make friends at CCNY." Fortunately, students assure us that "if you join clubs or become more involved with the opportunities the school provides, it's much easier to make meaningful connections." Plus, the consensus is that most people who attend are "very friendly and supportive." This is bolstered by a non-traditional student who concludes, "I was petrified to return and be the oldest in most if not all of my classes. The student body made me feel comfortable from day one.... Everyone has treated me with respect and as a fellow peer."

CITY UNIVERSITY OF NEW YORK—CITY COLLEGE

Financial Aid: 212-650-5824 • E-Mail: admissions@ccny.cuny.edu • Website: www.ccny.cuny.edu

THE PRINCETON REVIEW SAYS

Admissions

The school reports that its standardized testing policy for use in admission for Fall 2024 is Test Optional. The 2024 testing policy will be temporary. The Princeton Review suggests that interested applicants consult with the school for the most up-to-date standardized testing policies. *Very important factors considered include:* academic GPA. *Important factors considered include:* rigor of secondary school record. *Other factors considered include:* standardized test scores. High school diploma is required and GED is accepted. *Academic units required:* 2 English, 2 math. *Academic units recommended:* 4 English, 3 math, 2 science, 3 foreign language, 3 social studies, 3 history, 1 computer science, 1 visual/performing arts, 1 academic elective.

Financial Aid

Students should submit: FAFSA. Priority filing deadline is 3/15. The Princeton Review suggests that all financial aid forms be submitted as soon as possible (see page 5 for a note on the FAFSA). *Need-based scholarships/grants offered:* Federal Pell; SEOG. *Loan aid offered:* Direct PLUS loans; Direct Subsidized Loans; Direct Unsubsidized Loans. Admitted students will be notified of awards on a rolling basis beginning 3/1. Federal Work-Study Program available. Institutional employment available.

Inside Word

The City College of New York has a fairly standard application process, with an emphasis on your academic transcript and GPA. Some majors have unique application requirements, such as an audition or degree-specific writing component. When applying, make sure to confirm your specific program's requirements.

THE SCHOOL SAYS "..."

From the Admissions Office

"The City College of New York is the founding institution of the City University of New York and home to over 100 outstanding undergraduate and graduate programs, and eight schools and divisions, each dedicated to the advancement of research and knowledge. City College is the place where Albert Einstein first presented his theory of general relativity outside of Europe, and where our alumni discovered the polio vaccine, helped build the Internet, and designed the Panama Canal.

"Since 1847, CCNY has provided a high-quality and affordable education to generations of New Yorkers in a wide variety of disciplines. Embracing our position at the forefront of social change we serve more than 15,000 students, representing over 150 nationalities, pursuing undergraduate and graduate degrees driven by significant funded research, creativity, and scholarship. In fact, this year launched the most expansive fundraising campaign in CCNY history titled "Doing Remarkable Things Together" with a goal of raising more than $1 billion in total assets in support of the College mission.

"From architecture, engineering, education, medicine and liberal arts and sciences, CCNY offers programming in emerging fields, such as sonic arts and biomedical engineering.

"City College is located in Harlem. The 37-acre tree-lined campus boasts neo-gothic architecture, complete with gargoyles and grotesques in the North Campus, while modern facilities, including the Spitzer School of Architecture and the Center for Discovery and Innovation occupy the South Campus. City College's downtown campus, the Center for Worker Education, is located in the Wall Street area in the iconic Cunard Building."

SELECTIVITY

Admissions Rating	80
# of applicants	33,651
% of applicants accepted	62
% of acceptees attending	13

FIRST-YEAR PROFILE

Testing policy	Test Optional
Average HS GPA	3.4
% frosh submitting high school GPA	100

DEADLINES

Regular	
Priority	2/1
Notification	Rolling, 2/15
Nonfall registration?	Yes

APPLICANTS SOMETIMES PREFER

City University of New York—John Jay College of Criminal Justice; City University of New York—Baruch College; City University of New York—Brooklyn College; City University of New York—Hunter College; City University of New York—Queens College

FINANCIAL FACTS

Financial Aid Rating	77
Annual in-state tuition	$6,930
Annual out-of-state tuition	$18,600
Required fees	$410
Books and supplies	$1,364
Average frosh need-based scholarship	$8,255
Average UG need-based scholarship	$8,059
% needy frosh rec. need-based scholarship or grant aid	90
% needy UG rec. need-based scholarship or grant aid	87
% needy frosh rec. non-need-based scholarship or grant aid	85
% needy UG rec. non-need-based scholarship or grant aid	76
% needy frosh rec. need-based self-help aid	8
% needy UG rec. need-based self-help aid	10
% frosh rec. any financial aid	89
% UG rec. any financial aid	78
% UG borrow to pay for school	12
Average cumulative indebtedness	$17,106
% frosh need fully met	2
% ugrads need fully met	2
Average % of frosh need met	57
Average % of ugrad need met	55

CITY UNIVERSITY OF NEW YORK—HUNTER COLLEGE

695 Park Ave, Room N203, New York, NY 10065 • Admissions: 212-772-4000

CAMPUS LIFE

Quality of Life Rating	82
Fire Safety Rating	94
Green Rating	87
Type of school	Public
Environment	Metropolis

STUDENTS

Total undergrad enrollment	17,736
% male/female/another gender	33/67/0
% from out of state	3
% frosh from public high school	80
# of fraternities	2
# of sororities	2
% African American	12
% Asian	32
% White	29
% Hispanic	23
% Native American	<1
% Pacific Islander	0
% Two or more races	0
% Race and/or ethnicity unknown	0
% international	5
# of countries represented	158

SURVEY SAYS . . .

Lots of liberal students
Students love New York, NY
College radio is popular

ACADEMICS

Academic Rating	75
% students returning for sophomore year	87
% students graduating within 4 years	25
% students graduating within 6 years	57
Calendar	Semester
Student/faculty ratio	13:1
Profs interesting rating	83
Profs accessible rating	85

Most classes have 30–39 students.

MOST POPULAR MAJORS

Computer Science; Human Biology; Psychology, General

STUDENTS SAY "..."

Academics

The crown jewel of the CUNY system, Hunter College is an institution teeming with "resources" and "endless...opportunities." Of course, many students are drawn to Hunter for its "very affordable" price tag and "prime location." Undergrads also love just how many "great" academic programs the college truly offers, including "nursing," "psychology," "political science," and "education." No matter what you want to study, you can rest assured Hunter will deliver. Students also benefit from the amazing "support systems" that Hunter maintains. Indeed, they can rely on the fact that numerous "advisors are always there to answer questions about careers, classes to take, and graduation needs." This care and concern can be found within the classroom as well. After all, Hunter professors tend to be "passionate about what they teach and prefer for students to be active in class." Moreover, "they are extremely willing to help outside the classroom" as well. And many undergrads simply find their instructors "very nice and knowledgeable." Finally, as this thrilled student boasts, "They keep challenging me to do better with my work and to never stop working at the idea that is in my head to make it a reality. They genuinely believe that the students at Hunter are above others, which gives me a confidence that I chose the right school."

Campus Life

Hunter College doesn't have a sprawling or self-contained campus. And, given that many undergrads here commute, it's quite common for people to pop in "just for classes and are running back to the train when classes are over." Of course, "if there's a break, people often join up with friends to eat, or study together in the library, by the halls, or the digital cafes." And, when time allows, "people often go to the gyms and workout downstairs." A large percentage of undergrads here hold "part-time jobs that offer flexible hours" as well. A decent number also carve out time to "volunteer." Additionally, the college itself "hosts many, many programs and activities all throughout the week." When the weather is nice, many students like to head to "nearby Central Park" to hang out and/or study. Students frequently "explore the city because there is always stuff to do in New York." For example, "there are tons of museums in the area that are free for Hunter students." And undergrads who are of age seem to love checking out the "bars and clubs" the city has to offer.

Student Body

Primarily a "commuter" school, Hunter's student body is dominated by New York City "locals who are trying to get their education in a cost-efficient manner." Fortunately, they are also an extremely "diverse" lot. You can find undergrads of "every culture, religion, race, etc." And since "everyone comes from different walks of life," you will "never feel like an outcast." Indeed, Hunter students are extraordinarily "accepting." Some individuals lament, however, that their peers do tend to "keep to themselves." Others argue that if you take the time to talk to people, you quickly discover that most students are "friendly" and "welcoming." They can also be "very supportive and caring." As one undergrad explains, "We make sure that we help each other out in our studies and teach each other when there is something we do not understand." Additionally, the vast majority of Hunter students are "driven to succeed." They are often "found vigorously studying for their classes and forming networks with people that have similar interests as them." It's quite evident that everyone here really "wants to achieve something in life." And, as this wise undergrad succinctly states, "Being around people with that general same motivation is really good."

CITY UNIVERSITY OF NEW YORK—HUNTER COLLEGE

Financial Aid: 212-772-4820 • E-Mail: admissions@hunter.cuny.edu • Website: www.hunter.cuny.edu/main/

THE PRINCETON REVIEW SAYS

Admissions

The school reports that its standardized testing policy for use in admission for Fall 2024 is Test Optional. It is unknown at this time if the 2024 testing policy will be permanent. The Princeton Review suggests that interested applicants consult with the school for the most up-to-date standardized testing policies. *Very important factors considered include:* rigor of secondary school record, academic GPA. *Other factors considered include:* standardized test scores, application essay, recommendation(s), extracurricular activities, talent/ability, character/personal qualities, geographical residence, state residency, volunteer work, work experience. High school diploma is required and GED is accepted. *Academic units required:* 2 English, 2 math, 1 science, 1 science lab. *Academic units recommended:* 4 English, 3 math, 2 science, 2 foreign language, 4 social studies, 1 visual/performing arts, 1 academic elective.

Financial Aid

Students should submit: FAFSA; State aid form. Priority filing deadline is 5/1. The Princeton Review suggests that all financial aid forms be submitted as soon as possible (see page 5 for a note on the FAFSA). *Need-based scholarships/grants offered:* College/university scholarship or grant aid from institutional funds; Federal Pell; Private scholarships; SEOG; State scholarships/grants. *Loan aid offered:* Direct PLUS loans; Direct Subsidized Loans; Direct Unsubsidized Loans; College/university loans from institutional funds; State Loans. Admitted students will be notified of awards on a rolling basis beginning 5/15. Federal Work-Study Program available. Institutional employment available.

The Inside Word

The admissions process at Hunter College is rather straightforward. Admissions officers do their utmost to take a well-rounded approach, giving all application facets careful consideration. Of course, your high school transcript and GPA will hold the most weight. Hunter wants evidence that you're prepared for college-level courses after all. And, finally, the admissions committee relies on supplemental essays to assess what kind of impact you might have on life at Hunter.

THE SCHOOL SAYS "..."

From the Admissions Office

"Located in the heart of Manhattan, Hunter offers students the stimulating learning environment and career-building opportunities you might expect from a college that's been a part of the world's most exciting city since 1870. The largest senior college in the City University of New York, Hunter pulses with energy. Hunter's vitality stems from a large, highly diverse faculty and student body. Its schools—Arts and Sciences, Education, Nursing, Social Work and Public Health—provide an affordable first-rate education. Undergraduates have extraordinary opportunities to conduct high-level research with renowned faculty, and to participate in credit-bearing internships in media, the arts, government and many other fields. The college's high standards and special programs ensure a challenging education. Specialized programs for first-year students keep classmates together as they pursue courses in the liberal arts, pre-health science, pre-nursing, pre-med, or honors. A range of honors programs is available for students with strong academic records, including the highly competitive Macaulay Honors College for entering freshmen and the Thomas Hunter Honors Program for continuing students. There are also six different freshman scholar programs offered in the arts, sciences, humanities, computer science, public policy, and nursing. All honors programs are accompanied by significant merit scholarship opportunities and feature small classes with personalized mentoring by outstanding faculty members. Qualified students also benefit from Hunter's participation in minority science research and training programs, the prestigious Andrew W. Mellon Minority Undergraduate Program, and many other passports to professional success. Hunter College has four residence halls on Manhattan's east side, housing almost 1,000 students."

SELECTIVITY

Admissions Rating	92
# of applicants	32,287
% of applicants accepted	40
% of acceptees attending	20

FIRST-YEAR PROFILE

Testing policy	Test Optional
Range SAT EBRW	570–650
Range SAT math	580–690
# submitting SAT scores	2,483
% submitting SAT scores	96
Average HS GPA	3.5
% frosh submitting high school GPA	99

DEADLINES

Regular	
Priority	2/1
Notification	Rolling, 1/15
Nonfall registration?	Yes

FINANCIAL FACTS

Financial Aid Rating	88
Annual in-state tuition	$6,930
Annual out-of-state tuition	$18,600
Required fees	$450
Books and supplies	$1,364
Average frosh need-based scholarship	$8,892
Average UG need-based scholarship	$8,142
% needy frosh rec. need-based scholarship or grant aid	89
% needy UG rec. need-based scholarship or grant aid	88
% needy frosh rec. non-need-based scholarship or grant aid	76
% needy UG rec. non-need-based scholarship or grant aid	46
% needy frosh rec. need-based self-help aid	6
% needy UG rec. need-based self-help aid	11
% frosh rec. any financial aid	96
% UG rec. any financial aid	92
% UG borrow to pay for school	15
Average cumulative indebtedness	$16,272
% frosh need fully met	41
% ugrads need fully met	58
Average % of frosh need met	79
Average % of ugrad need met	82

CITY UNIVERSITY OF NEW YORK—QUEENS COLLEGE

65-30 Kissena Blvd, Queens, NY 11367 • Admissions: 718-997-5000 • Fax: 718-997-5605

CAMPUS LIFE

Quality of Life Rating	83
Fire Safety Rating	97
Green Rating	94
Type of school	Public
Environment	Metropolis

STUDENTS

Total undergrad enrollment	13,510
% male/female/another gender	47/53/0
% from out of state	1
% frosh from public high school	91
% frosh live on campus	1
% ugrads live on campus	2
# of fraternities (% join)	6 (1)
# of sororities (% join)	5 (1)
% African American	10
% Asian	32
% White	20
% Hispanic	30
% Native American	<1
% Pacific Islander	<1
% Two or more races	3
% Race and/or ethnicity unknown	0
% international	6
# of countries represented	153

SURVEY SAYS . . .

Students love Queens, NY
Diverse student types interact on campus
Great library

ACADEMICS

Academic Rating	74
% students returning for sophomore year	77
% students graduating within 4 years	30
% students graduating within 6 years	56
Calendar	Semester
Student/faculty ratio	14:1
Profs interesting rating	83
Profs accessible rating	86
Most classes have 20–29 students.	

MOST POPULAR MAJORS

Accounting; Computer Science; Psychology, General

STUDENTS SAY "..."

Academics

Located in New York's "most diverse borough," Queens College "offers high quality academics for a very reasonable price." As one student puts it, "Queens is about getting a valuable and quality education that does not drain you financially for the future." In keeping with the fact that the majority of QC students live off campus in a variety of nearby communities, one of the school's strengths is helping students become "the best you can be so you can give back to the community." One student even goes as far as to say that QC is "considered the Harvard of CUNY." The Macaulay Honors College and the Aaron Copeland School of Music both get high marks, with students saying that QC as a whole "provides a strong liberal arts education to give [students] well-rounded knowledge and skills." Professors generally "genuinely care about [students'] grades and well-being"; as one student puts it, "They won't let me fall behind." But while "most professors genuinely care for [students'] success," it's inevitable that they will "vary in terms of quality." As one student puts it, "Many of my professors just lecture and don't interact too much, however, some are very involved and passionate." Students appreciate the "challenging yet interesting courses" but some lament that for the coveted courses, "you have to really run and register for those classes like it's a competition."

Campus Life

Though the school opened the Summit Apartments, its first residence hall, in 2009, the majority of QC students still commute; as one student observes, "Even though the Summit Apartments can only house 500 students, it still remains pretty empty throughout the semesters." Since "most students come here to go to class and then head home or to their job afterwards," many QC students say that it's difficult to foster much sense of a school community—"the sense of community could use some work." But others counter, saying that, "I would not expect a school composed mostly of commuters to bond as much as we do." Outside of class, it's "very hard to be bored," especially "being so close to the city, there are a lot of activities to do around the area." Many students explore Queens, which is accessible via a free QC shuttle. For those who live on campus, or those commuters who stick around after class, as one student puts it, "We have clubs for everything, and if there isn't a club for something you like, you could always start [one] up." One thing that students agree helps unite QC as a community is student government: "Student government provides us with events and carnivals during both the fall and spring semesters. It brings people together."

Student Body

Diversity is key at Queens College, where, as one student puts it, "We have a very diverse campus, so no minority is really ever a minority." "If one were to ask me to name every ethnicity, nationality, and religious group on campus, I would not even know where to begin," says another. QC "has a very friendly student body" and some says that "the friendships and bonds you make from taking transit together, or sharing stories is special in [its] own way." Others note that "there is not much of an established social life" and that "if you want to make friends here you really have to work for it." Many students "have part-time jobs," some students "are parents, and have to take care of their children"—"Of course, many people are straight out of high school [too], but even these people usually spend a lot of time off campus." Students describe their peers as "career-minded and focused"; they "love to have fun, but they [are] still focused on their studies and their futures."

CITY UNIVERSITY OF NEW YORK—QUEENS COLLEGE

Financial Aid: 718-997-5123 • E-Mail: chelsea.lavington@qc.cuny.edu • Website: www.qc.cuny.edu

THE PRINCETON REVIEW SAYS

Admissions

The school reports that its standardized testing policy for use in admission for Fall 2024 is Test Optional. It is unknown at this time if the 2024 testing policy will be permanent. The Princeton Review suggests that interested applicants consult with the school for the most up-to-date standardized testing policies. *Very important factors considered include:* rigor of secondary school record, academic GPA. *Important factors considered include:* application essay. *Other factors considered include:* recommendation(s). High school diploma is required and GED is accepted. *Academic units required:* 4 English, 3 math, 2 science, 2 science labs, 3 foreign language, 4 social studies. *Academic units recommended:* 4 English, 3 math, 3 science, 3 science labs, 3 foreign language, 4 social studies.

Financial Aid

Students should submit: FAFSA; State aid form. The Princeton Review suggests that all financial aid forms be submitted as soon as possible (see page 5 for a note on the FAFSA). *Need-based scholarships/grants offered:* College/university scholarship or grant aid from institutional funds; Federal Pell; Private scholarships; SEOG; State scholarships/grants. *Loan aid offered:* Direct PLUS loans; Direct Subsidized Loans; Direct Unsubsidized Loans. Admitted students will be notified of awards on a rolling basis beginning 3/1. Federal Work-Study Program available. Institutional employment available.

The Inside Word

Queens College looks for students with a B average (or better) or a GED score of at least 350 to be a strong candidate for admission; the school encourages a high school education that includes a full range of language arts and science courses. Exceptional applicants should look into Macaulay Honors College, which provides free tuition and other benefits (including a study grant and a free laptop).

THE SCHOOL SAYS "..."

From the Admissions Office

"Queens College prepares students to become the leaders of tomorrow by offering a rigorous education in the liberal arts, business, and sciences under the guidance of an outstanding faculty dedicated to teaching and scholarship.

"Queens College has over 170 programs and is recognized nationally for the excellence of its academic offerings. New this year, the Queens College School of Business and School of Arts offer the best of the liberal arts while building on emerging trends and our vast network of business partners and community organizations. These new schools combine coursework in areas such as fintech and studio art with interdisciplinary research and community collaboration, preparing our students to solve real-world problems.

"Our tuition won't break the bank, as it's among the most affordable in the nation. Over 85% of students who enter as freshmen and graduate within four years earn their degrees without taking federal student loans, and we are in the top 1% of colleges nationwide in helping students from lower-income families attain upward social and economic mobility.

"Located in the world's most exciting city, QC provides a vibrant student life experience for students who live on or off campus. We have over 100 student clubs, 15 NCAA Division II teams, and numerous intramural and recreation programs. Our students represent 140 countries, creating an extraordinarily diverse and welcoming campus community. QC is home to the Kupferberg Center for the Arts, which presents a vast amount of programming, and the Godwin-Ternbach Museum, which holds thought-provoking exhibitions."

SELECTIVITY

Admissions Rating	85
# of applicants	22,193
% of applicants accepted	70
% of acceptees attending	15

FIRST-YEAR PROFILE

Testing policy	Test Optional
Average HS GPA	3.4
% frosh submitting high school GPA	100

DEADLINES

Regular	
Priority	2/1
Notification	Rolling, 2/1
Nonfall registration?	Yes

APPLICANTS ALSO LOOK AT

Adelphi University; City University of New York—York College; City University of New York—Baruch College; City University of New York—Brooklyn College; City University of New York—Hunter College; Hofstra University; New York University; St. John's University

FINANCIAL FACTS

Financial Aid Rating	79
Annual in-state tuition	$6,930
Annual out-of-state tuition	$18,600
Required fees	$608
Books and supplies	$1,364
Average frosh need-based scholarship	$8,018
Average UG need-based scholarship	$7,611
% needy frosh rec. need-based scholarship or grant aid	87
% needy UG rec. need-based scholarship or grant aid	84
% needy frosh rec. non-need-based scholarship or grant aid	86
% needy UG rec. non-need-based scholarship or grant aid	72
% needy frosh rec. need-based self-help aid	8
% needy UG rec. need-based self-help aid	12
% frosh rec. any financial aid	84
% UG rec. any financial aid	85
% UG borrow to pay for school	9
Average cumulative indebtedness	$15,767
% frosh need fully met	4
% ugrads need fully met	4
Average % of frosh need met	55
Average % of ugrad need met	52

CLAREMONT MCKENNA COLLEGE

500 E 9th Street, Claremont, CA 91711 • Admissions: 909-621-8000 • Fax: 909-621-8516

STUDENTS SAY "..."

Academics
Claremont McKenna College offers a "very challenging but rewarding" liberal arts education to a focused group of 1,200 students. Its proximity to Los Angeles—just 30 miles away—and joint curriculars with the other six member schools of The Claremont Colleges allows students to tailor their education and access the resources of a large university—over 2,200 classes and activities to choose from—while still building close relationships with faculty. Experiential learning is a keystone of the curriculum, and "there are many opportunities for students to work with professors outside of class on research projects, or in campus research centers"; more than 90 percent of students also complete internships. Guest speakers who are prominent in their field come to students several times a week via the Athenaeum, "the most impressive program for bringing more viewpoints to campus at any liberal arts college." As one student says, "Oftentimes, someone who would be a commencement speaker somewhere else will be a speaker at the Athenaeum on a random Wednesday."

Professors "are very open to seeing us outside of class and facilitating the tough discussions in class that we need to have in order to grow," and "are flexible but also have high expectations that you get motivated to meet." Classes are designed with innovative pedagogy in mind: for example, the Philosophy, Government, and Economics programs have "three courses dedicated to weekly one-on-one debates and paper exchanges in 'tutorials,'" and an economics class uses "a digital simulator where we can simulate economic concepts in class in a game-like interface." The administration is incredibly supportive, and there are "counseling, tutoring, career services, and many resources and locations for students to just go to whenever they need to talk about anything."

Campus Life
There "is a rich social life to be had on campus," and everyone is "very involved and engaged, so when students are not in classes, they're taking meetings for clubs or working at research institutes." CMC has a "very high caliber of student clubs and organizations (especially for its size)"; for instance, the CMC Mock Trial and Model UN teams are nationally lauded, and enrollees note that there "is a dedicated group of welcoming students behind every club and sport." That carries over even outside of official activities: "I can engage in conversations of fin-tech, cryptocurrencies, [and] Western feminism perspectives on IR [international relations] theories all while munching on chips in the lounge with my peers."

The school also knows how to make the most of its beautiful campus and weather that "is almost always sunny." There are "many free day trips and incredible opportunities to see sporting events, concerts, or just get into nature," and one student cites a bunch of fitness classes as well as activities like painting and philosophy journal before summing things up simply as "there's just so [much] offered here." There's also a variety of athletic offerings: "basically our entire campus shows up to big football/water polo games," and there are also intramural sports as well as the fact that "people love getting outside [and] playing casual sports."

Student Body
The "highly intelligent and supportive" students at CMC "are very driven and bring multiple different perspectives to the table," with a "critical thinking mindset and freedom of speech mentality." As one student says, "We pride ourselves on considering a wide variety of opinions as we develop solutions for the modern world." That means that while some think it's "kind of a preppy school," there are also "a lot of opportunities here for first generation or low-income students, and so there is quite a diverse population." Students suggest the overall attitude is "beyond humble" and that they are all "encouraged to think for ourselves, by ourselves, and to carry strategies for doing such with us outside of the classroom." That long-term support can be found in the way that students "continue to receive good support from a strong alumni network after college."

CLAREMONT McKENNA COLLEGE

Financial Aid: 909-621-8356 • E-Mail: admission@cmc.edu • Website: www.claremontmckenna.edu

THE PRINCETON REVIEW SAYS

Admissions

The school reports that its standardized testing policy for use in admission for Fall 2024 is Test Optional. The 2024 testing policy will be temporary. The Princeton Review suggests that interested applicants consult with the school for the most up-to-date standardized testing policies. *Very important factors considered include:* rigor of secondary school record, class rank, academic GPA, recommendation(s), extracurricular activities, character/personal qualities. *Important factors considered include:* application essay, interview, talent/ability. *Other factors considered include:* standardized test scores, first generation, alumni/ae relation, geographical residence, racial/ethnic status, volunteer work, work experience. High school diploma is required and GED is accepted. *Academic units required:* 4 English, 3 math, 2 science, 2 science labs, 3 foreign language, 1 social studies, 1 history. *Academic units recommended:* 4 English, 4 math, 3 science, 3 science labs, 3 foreign language, 1 social studies, 1 history.

Financial Aid

Students should submit: Business/Farm Supplement; CSS/Financial Aid Profile; FAFSA; Noncustodial Profile; State aid form. Priority filing deadline is 1/5. The Princeton Review suggests that all financial aid forms be submitted as soon as possible (see page 5 for a note on the FAFSA). *Need-based scholarships/grants offered:* College/university scholarship or grant aid from institutional funds; Federal Pell; Private scholarships; SEOG; State scholarships/grants. *Loan aid offered:* Direct PLUS loans; Direct Subsidized Loans; Direct Unsubsidized Loans; College/university loans from institutional funds. Admitted students will be notified of awards on or about 4/1. Federal Work-Study Program available. Institutional employment available.

The Inside Word

Experience shows that small, selective schools—CMC accepts only 11% of applicants—are more likely to look beyond your grades, especially since they're currently Test Optional. Claremont McKenna's need-blind admissions process means there are a lot of applicants, and you'll want to have an outstanding academic record to stand out from the crowd. Just be prepared to back that up with a demonstration of how well you'd fit the school.

THE SCHOOL SAYS "..."

From the Admissions Office

"CMC offers a first-rate liberal arts education where students can acquire a broad experience across a range of disciplines from the humanities to the social sciences to the sciences, but where they can also pursue an unusually rich spectrum of courses in economics, public affairs, and international relations. CMC's mission is clear: to educate students for meaningful, productive, and responsible lives of leadership. By combining the intellectual breadth of liberal arts with the more pragmatic concerns of public affairs, CMC students gain the vision, skills, and values necessary for leadership in all sectors of society."

SELECTIVITY

Admissions Rating	98
# of applicants	5,709
% of applicants accepted	10
% of acceptees attending	54
# offered a place on the wait list	850
% accepting a place on wait list	63
% admitted from wait list	2
# of early decision applicants	742
% accepted early decision	30

FIRST-YEAR PROFILE

Testing policy	Test Optional
Range SAT composite	1450–1540
Range SAT EBRW	710–760
Range SAT math	730–790
Range ACT composite	33–35
# submitting SAT scores	90
% submitting SAT scores	28
# submitting ACT scores	56
% submitting ACT scores	17
% graduated top 10% of class	68
% graduated top 25% of class	89
% graduated top 50% of class	100

DEADLINES

Early decision	
Deadline	11/1
Notification	12/15
Other ED deadline	1/10
Other ED notification	2/15
Regular	
Deadline	1/10
Notification	4/1
Nonfall registration?	No

FINANCIAL FACTS

Financial Aid Rating	96
Annual tuition	$64,150
Room and board	$19,650
Books and supplies	$1,200
Average frosh need-based scholarship	$59,387
Average UG need-based scholarship	$58,735
% needy frosh rec. need-based scholarship or grant aid	100
% needy UG rec. need-based scholarship or grant aid	99
% needy frosh rec. non-need-based scholarship or grant aid	79
% needy UG rec. non-need-based scholarship or grant aid	75
% needy frosh rec. need-based self-help aid	94
% needy UG rec. need-based self-help aid	94
% frosh rec. any financial aid	53
% UG rec. any financial aid	48
% UG borrow to pay for school	32
Average cumulative indebtedness	$20,978
% frosh need fully met	100
% ugrads need fully met	100
Average % of frosh need met	100
Average % of ugrad need met	100

CLARKSON UNIVERSITY

8 Clarkson Ave., Potsdam, NY 13699 • Admissions: 315-268-6400 • Fax: 315-268-7647

STUDENTS SAY ". . ."

Academics

Nestled at the northern reaches of New York state (with additional graduate and research facilities in Schenectady, Beacon, Saranac Lake, and New York City), Clarkson University is a science and engineering powerhouse that has consistently turned career-ready, "hardworking and determined" students out into the workforce. The school is known for its excellent job placement rate and "the large number of internship opportunities that Clarkson's connections bring"; "Everyone wants you to succeed and provides the resources for you to do so." One of Clarkson's greatest strengths is that all "come here with the understanding that engineering is one of our main concepts" and are encouraged to work with others. The administration "really stresses on how important your career is," and the curriculum and faculty drive home the fact that "you go to college to eventually one day get a career in what you love." Many courses here are project-based, so students receive "hands-on skills and real world experience that will immediately help in the workforce." Professors become "more engaging the higher level of class you take," and the majority of the harder science classes (such as biology and chemistry) pair each lecture with a lab and a discussion class where students "can get a more in-depth view of the material while working in a smaller classroom." "I have taken trips for my classes to visualize rather than just read," says a student.

Both "hard and soft skills have been developed and grown" at Clarkson, and are soon enough put to use; students rave about the Career Center, which holds two career fairs and "a myriad of workshops" annually to help students find and prepare for co-ops, internships, and jobs. Additionally, Clarkson SPEED (Student Projects for Engineering Experience and Design) teams like Design, Build, Fly "allow students to put their practical engineering knowledge to the test," and Shipley Center for Innovation offers students "a chance to create their own companies."

Campus Life

Potsdam is located close to the Adirondacks and near "some of the best skiing in the Northeast." During the long and very cold winters, "a lot of people go to local mountains to ski/snowboard on their days off." The atmosphere of the small campus is "very comforting" and like a "home away from home," and there are "ample things to do around campus, especially in the winter." The school "hosts numerous events to get students involved in campus life," and there is a wide spread of non-academic interests and clubs such as "the Outing Club, [which] is the biggest club on campus." Schoolwork is "a large portion of any student's life" at Clarkson, but on the weekends students attend hockey games, go to parties, have movie nights, or "go fishing on the Raquette River, which is right next to the college."

Student Body

Clarkson truly acts as "a gathering place for like-minded individuals," where different personalities, ethnicities, majors, and cultures reside, but "no one is afraid of work." Everyone is friendly to each other: "You say hello to someone, and you will get a hello back." Clarkson has "a fair ratio of 'nerds' to 'jocks' due to the recruitment of athletes for teams," and the population also skews heavily male. "Diversity isn't huge at Clarkson, but it is something they are working on." In the end, everyone here "understands how difficult classes can be," and problem-solving together and "working in teams is a big part of being successful here." At Clarkson, "you constantly see students attempting to solve the same task in hundreds of different ways."

CLARKSON UNIVERSITY

Financial Aid: 315-268-6480 • E-Mail: admissions@clarkson.edu • Website: www.clarkson.edu

THE PRINCETON REVIEW SAYS

Admissions

The school reports that its standardized testing policy for use in admission for Fall 2024 is Test Optional. The 2024 testing policy will be temporary. The Princeton Review suggests that interested applicants consult with the school for the most up-to-date standardized testing policies. *Very important factors considered include:* rigor of secondary school record, academic GPA. *Important factors considered include:* class rank, recommendation(s), extracurricular activities, volunteer work. *Other factors considered include:* standardized test scores, application essay, talent/ability, character/personal qualities, first generation, alumni/ae relation, work experience, level of applicant's interest. High school diploma is required and GED is accepted. *Academic units required:* 4 English, 3 math, 3 science, 4 social studies. *Academic units recommended:* 4 English, 4 math, 4 science, 1 foreign language, 4 social studies.

Financial Aid

Students should submit: FAFSA; State aid form. Priority filing deadline is 2/1. The Princeton Review suggests that all financial aid forms be submitted as soon as possible (see page 5 for a note on the FAFSA). *Need-based scholarships/grants offered:* College/university scholarship or grant aid from institutional funds; Federal Pell; Private scholarships; SEOG; State scholarships/grants. *Loan aid offered:* Direct PLUS loans; Direct Subsidized Loans; Direct Unsubsidized Loans; College/university loans from institutional funds. Admitted students will be notified of awards on a rolling basis beginning 2/1. Federal Work-Study Program available. Institutional employment available.

The Inside Word

Clarkson wants students with a strong background in science and math who also have a curiosity for applying technology and science in the real world. Show them that you're interested in being involved outside the classroom. Students with solid transcripts will have a good shot at admission. Serious candidates should take advantage of the interview, as well. If you have a strong application and strong desire to come here, the interview could help you get some scholarship money.

THE SCHOOL SAYS "..."

From the Admissions Office

"Clarkson University is the institution of choice for more than 4,600 undergraduate and graduate students from diverse backgrounds who embrace challenge and thrive in a rigorous, highly collaborative learning environment. Our 640-wooded-acre main campus is adjacent to the six-million-acre Adirondack Park, which offers exceptional outdoor recreation and a living laboratory for field research and environmental studies.

"Clarkson's programs in engineering, business, the sciences, liberal arts, education, and the health professions emphasize team-based learning as well as immersion in sustainability principles, creative problem-solving and leadership skills. Clarkson is also on the leading edge of today's emerging technologies and fields of study offering innovative, boundary-spanning degree programs in engineering and management, digital arts and sciences, environmental science and policy, and the health professions among others.

"At Clarkson, students and faculty work closely together in a supportive and personalized environment. Students are encouraged to participate in faculty-mentored research projects from their first year, and to take advantage of co-ops and study abroad programs. Our collaborative and hands-on approach to education translates into remarkably successful careers and meaningful contributions to society; our placement rates into students' career choice are among the highest in the country. Alumni experience accelerated career growth. One in five alumni is already a CEO, president, or vice president of a company."

SELECTIVITY

Admissions Rating	88
# of applicants	7,011
% of applicants accepted	75
% of acceptees attending	14
# offered a place on the wait list	204
% accepting a place on wait list	13
% admitted from wait list	11
# of early decision applicants	145
% accepted early decision	88

FIRST-YEAR PROFILE

Testing policy	Test Optional
Range SAT composite	1190–1370
Range SAT EBRW	580–680
Range SAT math	600–700
Range ACT composite	25–32
# submitting SAT scores	375
% submitting SAT scores	51
# submitting ACT scores	78
% submitting ACT scores	11
Average HS GPA	3.8
% frosh submitting high school GPA	96
% graduated top 10% of class	44
% graduated top 25% of class	77
% graduated top 50% of class	97

DEADLINES

Early decision	
Deadline	12/1
Notification	1/1
Regular	
Deadline	1/15
Notification	Rolling, 1/18
Nonfall registration?	Yes

APPLICANTS OFTEN PREFER

Rensselaer Polytechnic Institute; Rochester Institute of Technology; Worcester Polytechnic Institute

APPLICANTS SOMETIMES PREFER

Le Moyne College; St. Lawrence University; Syracuse University

APPLICANTS RARELY PREFER

Northeastern University; Siena College; University of Rochester

FINANCIAL FACTS

Financial Aid Rating	86
Annual tuition	$54,960
Room and board	$18,152
Required fees	$1,298
Books and supplies	$1,560
Average frosh need-based scholarship	$39,575
Average UG need-based scholarship	$37,520
% needy frosh rec. need-based scholarship or grant aid	100
% needy UG rec. need-based scholarship or grant aid	100
% needy frosh rec. non-need-based scholarship or grant aid	24
% needy UG rec. non-need-based scholarship or grant aid	22
% needy frosh rec. need-based self-help aid	66
% needy UG rec. need-based self-help aid	71
% frosh rec. any financial aid	98
% UG rec. any financial aid	97
% UG borrow to pay for school	78
Average cumulative indebtedness	$28,000
% frosh need fully met	31
% ugrads need fully met	28
Average % of frosh need met	90
Average % of ugrad need met	90

CLARK UNIVERSITY

950 Main Street, Worcester, MA 01610-1477 • Admissions: 508-793-7711 • Fax: 508-793-8821

STUDENTS SAY "..."

Academics

First established in 1887 in Worcester, Massachusetts, Clark University is notable for being one of the original large-scale research institutes in the country. Clark keeps true to its mission with its numerous research-based science programs. In addition to the sciences, there are over 40 diverse areas of study. Students appreciate that the university is a "true liberal arts" school that puts "an emphasis on learning in multiple disciplines so that you can have a more well-rounded education." In fact, there are a number of unique classes offered at Clark, such as a one-of-a-kind food truck entrepreneurship class, with some students noting, "We are one of the only institutions in the country to offer such a thing."

One of the school's "biggest strengths is its small class size," along with an "abundance of labs…[for] very necessary experience." In fact, it's said that some intermediate-level courses can have as few as 10 students, "which means that you have a close access to the teaching assistants and professors," many of whom are described as "clearly passionate about what they teach." At Clark, "the learning is very hands-on, pushing students to apply what they learn in the classroom to experiences outside of the classroom," such as starting a real business in the entrepreneurship class. There are also innovative opportunities afforded to undergraduates, such as virtual reality courses and attending a forensics lab where the professor "builds whole crime scenes for us to go through as a team and 'solve a crime.'"

Campus Life

Clark University is very supportive of students with many noting the campus "offers lots of opportunities for students to reach their maximum potential [with] a plethora of clubs, educational resources, and easily accessible support." As one student says, "For a small school, we have everything you could imagine when it comes to clubs." Some of the favorites include the "Film Screening Society, which holds lots of fun movie screenings and events," as well as the Clark Musical Theatre club, a Model UN, and the International Game Developers Association. In addition, the sports programs are popular, with many mentioning lacrosse, soccer, tennis, a rowing team, and a swim and dive team as big draws. Wellness opportunities are also abundant on campus—many undergrads attend the various yoga classes and there is a counseling center that offers individual and group counseling. Another popular option is the Clarkies for Kindness organization, that "promotes positivity on campus and makes the environment more friendly and accepting." No matter what students might be interested in, "there is a wide range of ways to fill your days here at Clark."

Beyond the campus itself, many students also love to explore the community of Worcester and nearby Boston, taking in the local parks and attractions as well as "trying new restaurants in the city as often as possible, and hiking and biking the hills in and around Worcester to find good views of the skyline."

Student Body

Clark's motto is, "Challenge convention. Change our world," and the diverse and motivated student body at the university embodies this mission on a daily basis. There is a strong culture of advocacy, and "most students are involved in some sort of activism on campus." Some examples include the FIRM pantry that helps fight food insecurity and Choices, a peer-led sex education resource that helps make the university "a culturally enriching place that fosters positive change."

In general, "Clark students are extremely open-minded, social-justice oriented, and down to earth." And "Clarkies are sensitive to political issues and strive to create a very inclusive space for everyone." The school "truly feels like a community of students who are willing to support and show up for one another." Some other words offered to describe the student body include open-minded, progressive, and accepting. As one student puts it, "No matter who you are, how you identify, or where you're from, the Clark community is one of the most supportive and accepting communities I've ever seen."

CLARK UNIVERSITY

Financial Aid: 508-793-7519 • E-Mail: admissions@clarku.edu • Website: www.clarku.edu

THE PRINCETON REVIEW SAYS

Admissions

The school reports that its standardized testing policy for use in admission for Fall 2024 is Test Optional. It is unknown at this time if the 2024 testing policy will be permanent. The Princeton Review suggests that interested applicants consult with the school for the most up-to-date standardized testing policies. *Very important factors considered include:* rigor of secondary school record, academic GPA, recommendation(s). *Important factors considered include:* application essay, extracurricular activities, talent/ability, character/personal qualities, volunteer work. *Other factors considered include:* class rank, standardized test scores, interview, first generation, alumni/ae relation, geographical residence, racial/ethnic status, work experience, level of applicant's interest. High school diploma is required and GED is accepted. *Academic units recommended:* 4 English, 3 math, 3 science, 2 science labs, 2 foreign language, 2 social studies, 2 history.

Financial Aid

Students should submit: CSS/Financial Aid Profile; FAFSA; Noncustodial Profile. Priority filing deadline is 1/15. The Princeton Review suggests that all financial aid forms be submitted as soon as possible (see page 5 for a note on the FAFSA). *Need-based scholarships/grants offered:* College/university scholarship or grant aid from institutional funds; Federal Pell; SEOG; State scholarships/grants. *Loan aid offered:* Direct PLUS loans; Direct Subsidized Loans; Direct Unsubsidized Loans; State Loans. Admitted students will be notified of awards on or about 3/31. Federal Work-Study Program available. Institutional employment available.

The Inside Word

Admissions officers at Clark want students who want to challenge themselves both in and out of the classroom. Successful applicants tend to have achieved a strong A/B average in demanding honors, AP, or equivalent courses. However, the university also acknowledges and appreciates those candidates who have demonstrated a steady improvement throughout their high school tenure. Since admissions officers aim to take a holistic approach, they also closely assess essays, extracurricular involvement, and letters of recommendations. Clark is a Test Optional school, and that applies to merit aid as well.

THE SCHOOL SAYS "..."

From the Admissions Office

"Clark University prepares students to make a meaningful difference in a world hungry for change. We are a small liberal arts-based research university founded in 1887 and located in the second largest city in New England. Our model of undergraduate education is a hands-on approach to learning that takes students outside of the classroom. Our program will help you find success in all types of learning environments, from the traditional to the non-traditional. An environmental science class might collaborate with a professor on his climate change research, while an art history class could curate an exhibit at the Worcester Art Museum. Our vibrant intellectual life is an outgrowth of a dedicated faculty who are as passionate about teaching and mentoring as they are about generating new knowledge. As undergraduates, Clark students have an array of opportunities to study with award-winning researchers and pursue innovative solutions to real-world problems. Clark University offers a unique opportunity for access to graduate study. Our nationally recognized Accelerated Degree Program allows qualified students to begin graduate level coursework in their senior year and to complete the requirements of a master's degree in a fifth year that is tuition-free. Clark's admissions standards are selective and focused on identifying students who are most likely to thrive in our collaborative learning environment. As a community of individuals, we seek students who will embrace our motto, 'Challenge Convention. Change Our World.'"

SELECTIVITY

Admissions Rating	90
# of applicants	8,787
% of applicants accepted	50
% of acceptees attending	16
# offered a place on the wait list	802
% accepting a place on wait list	39
% admitted from wait list	14
# of early decision applicants	324
% accepted early decision	35

FIRST-YEAR PROFILE

Testing policy	Test Optional
Range SAT composite	1260–1430
Range SAT EBRW	640–720
Range SAT math	610–710
Range ACT composite	28–33
# submitting SAT scores	153
% submitting SAT scores	22
# submitting ACT scores	30
% submitting ACT scores	4
Average HS GPA	3.7
% frosh submitting high school GPA	64
% graduated top 10% of class	37
% graduated top 25% of class	73
% graduated top 50% of class	93

DEADLINES

Early decision	
Deadline	11/15
Notification	12/15
Other ED deadline	1/15
Other ED notification	2/15
Early action	
Deadline	11/15
Notification	1/15
Regular	
Deadline	1/15
Notification	4/1
Nonfall registration?	Yes

APPLICANTS OFTEN PREFER
Boston College; Boston University; Brandeis University

APPLICANTS SOMETIMES PREFER
American University; Connecticut College; Mount Holyoke College; Northeastern University; Skidmore College; Syracuse University; The George Washington University; University of Massachusetts Amherst

FINANCIAL FACTS

Financial Aid Rating	86
Annual tuition	$54,760
Room and board	$11,690
Required fees	$427
Books and supplies	$900
Average frosh need-based scholarship	$38,049
Average UG need-based scholarship	$33,535
% needy frosh rec. need-based scholarship or grant aid	99
% needy UG rec. need-based scholarship or grant aid	99
% needy frosh rec. non-need-based scholarship or grant aid	17
% needy UG rec. non-need-based scholarship or grant aid	16
% needy frosh rec. need-based self-help aid	72
% needy UG rec. need-based self-help aid	70
% frosh rec. any financial aid	97
% UG rec. any financial aid	95
% UG borrow to pay for school	66
Average cumulative indebtedness	$38,035
% frosh need fully met	31
% ugrads need fully met	30
Average % of frosh need met	96
Average % of ugrad need met	87

CLEMSON UNIVERSITY

Clemson University, Clemson, SC 29634-5124 • Admissions: 864-656-3311 • Fax: 864-656-2464

STUDENTS SAY "..."

Academics

If you're looking for an education to prepare you for the post-grad world, look no further. At Clemson University, "academics are definitely not a joke." Some say that "classes and homework and study[ing] take up far more than the majority of [their] time." Many students are quick to highlight Clemson's STEM program, which they note is "rigorous and challenging," but acknowledge the hard work ultimately develops "some of the strongest leaders in research." And although the "majority of classes are lecture based," undergrads say that "professors ask questions and use other methods to keep you engaged." From the student perspective, instructors "seem to genuinely care about their students both personally and academically." Importantly, Clemson professors also tend to be "passionate about what they teach and get really excited about the material." Additionally, they're prone to "push[ing] you, but not to a point you cannot handle." As this undergrad concludes, "They care if I learn the material, but care more about [helping me] grow...personally and shaping [me] into the engineer they see in me."

Campus Life

It's virtually impossible to be bored at Clemson University. "We all have multiple things that we are involved in," says one student, "whether it be clubs or jobs or going to sports games." Just what kind of organizations are available? Undergrads participate in everything from student government and mock trial to wiffleball club and Dance Marathon. Additionally, "intramural sports [are] very popular" with lots of people especially gravitating to spikeball. Greek life also has a large presence on campus, with some mentioning it "made their college experience very unique and made transitioning to college very easy."

When it comes partying, students say that "Clemson has more of a house party scene than a bar scene, especially before students turn 21." One individual further clarifies, "As a freshman, frat parties are the main source of 'going-out,' but this changes...once people live in apartments." Though if you're not a big partier, there's no reason to fret. It's just as common for students "to travel on the weekends, go to the lake or on nearby hikes, or find other activities."

Student Body

You don't have to be on Clemson's campus for very long to recognize the "family atmosphere" that ripples through the entire university. Indeed, although it's a large, public institution, Clemson still manages to generate a "small town feel" and a culture where "everyone has everyone else's backs." Of course, it's also easy to socialize when you have peers who are "extremely nice and polite." One undergrad further explains, "The student body is much more relaxed than most; few political or social controversies are on our campus, and school spirit is high." However, they are serious about their academics with numerous undergrads sharing that their classmates are "dedicated to their studies."

Given that Clemson is located in South Carolina, it's none too surprising to learn that a number of students here have "southern roots." And while many undergrads also acknowledge that their peers are "predominantly white," they are quick to assert that "diversity among races, ethnicities, and genders is growing." This student notices the effort, sharing that his classmates "come from all different places and backgrounds." Despite coming from different backgrounds, what brings these students together is "an abundance of school pride and love for [the] university." One student poetically concludes, "Our differences are strong, but I think it's the love of campus—the way we can see the mountains in the distance and breathe such fresh air, walk everywhere we need to be in 15 minutes or less, and the fierce spirit that we'll always call Clemson home—that unites us and makes us feel like old friends."

CLEMSON UNIVERSITY

Financial Aid: 864-656-2280 • E-Mail: cuadmissions@clemson.edu • Website: www.clemson.edu

THE PRINCETON REVIEW SAYS

Admissions

The school reports that its standardized testing policy for use in admission for Fall 2024 is Test Optional. It is unknown at this time if the 2024 testing policy will be permanent. The Princeton Review suggests that interested applicants consult with the school for the most up-to-date standardized testing policies. *Very important factors considered include:* rigor of secondary school record, class rank, academic GPA, standardized test scores, state residency. *Other factors considered include:* application essay, recommendation(s), extracurricular activities, talent/ability, alumni/ae relation. High school diploma is required and GED is accepted. *Academic units required:* 4 English, 3 math, 3 science, 3 science labs, 3 foreign language, 1 social studies, 1 history, 1 computer science, 1 visual/performing arts, 2 academic electives.

Financial Aid

Students should submit: FAFSA. Priority filing deadline is 1/2. The Princeton Review suggests that all financial aid forms be submitted as soon as possible (see page 5 for a note on the FAFSA). *Need-based scholarships/grants offered:* College/university scholarship or grant aid from institutional funds; Federal Pell; Private scholarships; SEOG; State scholarships/grants. *Loan aid offered:* Direct PLUS loans; Direct Subsidized Loans; Direct Unsubsidized Loans. Admitted students will be notified of awards on a rolling basis beginning 3/1. Federal Work-Study Program available. Institutional employment available.

The Inside Word

Earning admissions to Clemson is challenging and competitive, but not unattainable. Clemson's first and foremost priority is considering students' academic achievements. Candidates will significantly improve their chances of admission with a solid GPA, challenging coursework, and a high SAT or ACT score. The university aims to build a diverse class every year, so they also pay attention to applicants' unique experiences, backgrounds, and community engagement. Therefore, demonstrated involvement in things like clubs, teams, community service, or part-time jobs will help you stand out amongst the crowd.

THE SCHOOL SAYS "..."

From the Admissions Office

"Set in a college town with a beautiful backdrop of lakeshore and mountains, Clemson University attracts students looking for a rigorous academic experience, world-class research opportunities, strong sense of community, and vibrant school spirit.

"One of the country's most selective public research universities, Clemson was founded in 1889 with a mission to be a 'high seminary of learning' dedicated to teaching, research, and service. Today, these three concepts remain at the heart of the University and provide the framework for an exceptional educational experience.

"At Clemson, professors take the time to get to know students and explore innovative ways of teaching. Exceptional teaching is one reason our retention and graduation rates rank among the highest in the country for public universities and why Clemson continues to attract a talented student body.

"Clemson offers over 550 student clubs and organizations; the spirit that students show for this university is unparalleled.

"Midway between Charlotte, North Carolina, and Atlanta, Georgia, Clemson University is located on 1,400 acres of beautiful rolling hills within the foothills of the Blue Ridge Mountains and along the shores of Lake Hartwell.

"Test scores must be submitted electronically by the respective testing agency. Clemson does not require the SAT or ACT essay. Clemson University super-scores both the SAT and the ACT. For the SAT, this means that the overall total SAT score will then be derived by taking the highest of the evidence-based reading and writing/math scores. For the ACT, the super composite ACT score is calculated as the average of the best ACT English, Reading, Math, and Science subject scores."

SELECTIVITY
Admissions Rating	92
# of applicants	47,007
% of applicants accepted	49
% of acceptees attending	20
# offered a place on the wait list	9,865
% accepting a place on wait list	50
% admitted from wait list	0

FIRST-YEAR PROFILE
Testing policy	Test Optional
Range SAT composite	1240–1400
Range SAT EBRW	610–700
Range SAT math	610–720
Range ACT composite	27–32
# submitting SAT scores	1,830
% submitting SAT scores	40
# submitting ACT scores	1,369
% submitting ACT scores	30
Average HS GPA	4.4
% frosh submitting high school GPA	100
% graduated top 10% of class	55
% graduated top 25% of class	87
% graduated top 50% of class	100

DEADLINES
Regular	
Priority	12/1
Deadline	5/1
Notification	Rolling, 2/15
Nonfall registration?	Yes

APPLICANTS ALSO LOOK AT
College of Charleston; Georgia Institute of Technology; North Carolina State University; University of Georgia; University of North Carolina—Chapel Hill; University of South Carolina—Columbia; Winthrop University

FINANCIAL FACTS
Financial Aid Rating	77
Annual in-state tuition	$13,838
Annual out-of-state tuition	$36,430
Required fees	$1,282
Books and supplies	$1,248
Average frosh need-based scholarship	$11,786
Average UG need-based scholarship	$10,628
% needy frosh rec. need-based scholarship or grant aid	80
% needy UG rec. need-based scholarship or grant aid	80
% needy frosh rec. non-need-based scholarship or grant aid	52
% needy UG rec. non-need-based scholarship or grant aid	34
% needy frosh rec. need-based self-help aid	64
% needy UG rec. need-based self-help aid	68
% frosh rec. any financial aid	87
% UG rec. any financial aid	71
% UG borrow to pay for school	48
Average cumulative indebtedness	$32,934
% frosh need fully met	9
% ugrads need fully met	9
Average % of frosh need met	47
Average % of ugrad need met	47

COE COLLEGE

1220 First Avenue NE, Cedar Rapids, IA 52402 • Admissions: 319-399-8000 • Fax: 319-399-8816

STUDENTS SAY "..."

Academics

With "academics [that] are top-notch and tailored to the students' needs," it's no wonder that many say that their education at Coe College "stand[s] out as the biggest strength of the school." This is certainly reflected in the "resources, such as the careers center, writing center, learning commons, and tutoring center [that] are easy to use." There's also a "huge emphasis on getting internships and other opportunities in the field BEFORE you graduate!" And students can easily receive help with "strengthen[ing] job applications, resumes, cover letters, etc."

Another important hallmark of a Coe education? "Small class sizes" that allow students to foster "a more personal connection with their professors and peers." Students rave about them, saying "the small, discussion-based classes and the low student-to-professor ratio is wonderful," as it carves out space for "personalized feedback." And while the "coursework is challenging," professors are typically "very understanding with students." The vast majority of the Coe faculty are "incredibly passionate about what they teach and very accessible." As one undergrad shares, "I've never had to wait more than a day to get an email back or get help with a question. They share their lives with us, and we feel comfortable doing the same." A fellow classmate adds, "They are some of the smartest, most interesting, kindest, and generous people ever."

Campus Life

Undoubtedly, the Coe College experience extends far beyond the classroom. "There [are] so many opportunities on campus that if you asked everyone what they were involved in, they would at least have one thing to mention." After all, undergrads have "a unique and extravagant list of over 100 clubs and organizations to join on campus" like KCOE Radio or Student Senate. Undergrads also mention that there is "a large emphasis on Greek life" as well. Additionally, "Coe does a great job holding events for people to get together and do crafts, watch a comedian [or] do yoga." The Student Activities Club (SAC) also sponsors numerous popular events such as Winter Carnival, which features hot chocolate, snacks, and games to play outside. Sports culture at Coe is a big part of student life. "Students at Coe take sports seriously and it is one of the many things that brings everyone together." In fact, "the games are always filled with fans, cheers, students and even faculty members and alumni." Even if you're "not into sports that much, [you] still feel pumped and excited during the games."

And, of course, once the weekend rolls around, it's common for students to explore downtown Cedar Rapids which has a "lot of cool shops and restaurants." While checking out the scene, some like to "go to bars and others go to boba joints or even fun discount shops. The mall is also a common place to hang out." Undergrads looking to get a little further away can enjoy the "surrounding state parks and forest preserves" or head out to nearby "Iowa City for [a] mini-trip."

Student Body

As soon as you set foot on Coe College's campus, you sense "an atmosphere of community and inclusion." Coe students immediately describe their peers as "caring individuals" who are "friendly and willing to be there for everyone else." As this undergrad immediately illustrates, "Students here go out of their way to hold doors for other students [and] greet each other." Even better, they "are always willing to help others out in classes." The "campus is [also] full of doers" who "are passionate about what they are studying and the activities that they are involved in." What's more, many are pleasantly surprised to discover that "the student body is more diverse than you'd expect," though they also acknowledge that "most of the students are white." Nevertheless, you'll still encounter many individuals "from different socioeconomic backgrounds, cultures, and ideologies." One undergrad elaborates, "I feel [like I am] more likely to bump into a peer from out of state or [abroad] than a fellow Iowan." And you can rest assured that most everyone is "incredibly inclusive and welcoming." Another student agrees with this sentiment and sums up by saying "We somehow all mold together to create a cohesive campus and student body that strives to achieve great things."

COE COLLEGE

Financial Aid: 319-399-8540 • E-Mail: admission@coe.edu • Website: www.coe.edu

THE PRINCETON REVIEW SAYS

Admissions

The school reports that its standardized testing policy for use in admission for Fall 2024 is Test Optional. *Very important factors considered include:* academic GPA, standardized test scores. *Important factors considered include:* rigor of secondary school record, class rank. *Other factors considered include:* application essay, recommendation(s), interview, extracurricular activities, talent/ability, character/personal qualities, first generation, alumni/ae relation, volunteer work, level of applicant's interest. High school diploma is required and GED is accepted. *Academic units recommended:* 4 English, 3 math, 3 science, 1 science lab, 2 foreign language, 3 social studies, 2 academic electives.

Financial Aid

Students should submit: FAFSA. Priority filing deadline is 3/1. The Princeton Review suggests that all financial aid forms be submitted as soon as possible (see page 5 for a note on the FAFSA). *Need-based scholarships/grants offered:* College/university scholarship or grant aid from institutional funds; Federal Pell; Private scholarships; SEOG; State scholarships/grants. *Loan aid offered:* Direct PLUS loans; Direct Subsidized Loans; Direct Unsubsidized Loans; College/university loans from institutional funds. Admitted students will be notified of awards on a rolling basis beginning 12/15. Federal Work-Study Program available. Institutional employment available.

The Inside Word

Students seeking to gain admissions to Coe College should illustrate not only academic excellence with a high GPA and test scores (if submitted), but also be well-rounded, displaying interests and ambitions outside the classroom. Of course, academics comes first, so candidates that have completed challenging curriculum will fare best during the review process. For those of you with an aversion to standardized tests, you'll be happy to know that Coe is a Test Optional school. However, in order to qualify for this policy, you must have a minimum GPA of 3.0 or higher.

THE SCHOOL SAYS "..."

From the Admissions Office

"Across Coe's campus, there is an emphasis on putting student needs first, which extends beyond the classroom and into meaningful hands-on experience and career preparation. It's one of the reasons a Coe education pays off and graduates find success so quickly. In fact, for many years, nearly 100% of reporting graduates have been either employed or in graduate school within one year of graduation. Our C3: Creativity, Careers, Community center maintains connections with alumni and industry experts who inform C3 staff on the types of experience employers are looking for and directly assists students in getting that experience. Across the street the new Center for Health & Society provides pathways into health care careers that match student interests. Coe is one of the few liberal arts institutions in the country to require hands-on learning for graduation, and that can be satisfied through an internship, research, practicum or off-campus study. Many students complete more than one experience. In recent years Coe students have interned at places like the Chicago Board of Trade, Google, Mayo Clinic and NASA. Others have completed research on Coe's campus through the National Science Foundation's Research Experiences for Undergraduates program or the Stead Department of Business Administration & Economics' Spellman Summer Research Program. Still others have combined travel with an internship in South Africa or student teaching in Tanzania for an unforgettable off-campus experience. The flexibility in choosing classes and outside learning opportunities creates well-prepared critical thinkers who are adaptable to changing needs in their field."

SELECTIVITY

Admissions Rating	88
# of applicants	6,725
% of applicants accepted	50
% of acceptees attending	11

FIRST-YEAR PROFILE

Testing policy	Test Optional
Range SAT EBRW	510–620
Range SAT math	510–650
Range ACT composite	22–28
# submitting SAT scores	35
% submitting SAT scores	9
# submitting ACT scores	350
% submitting ACT scores	94
Average HS GPA	3.6
% frosh submitting high school GPA	100
% graduated top 10% of class	30
% graduated top 25% of class	65
% graduated top 50% of class	89

DEADLINES

Early action	
Deadline	12/10
Notification	Within two weeks
Regular	
Priority	12/10
Deadline	3/1
Notification	Rolling, 9/1
Nonfall registration?	Yes

APPLICANTS ALSO LOOK AT

Carthage College; Central College; Iowa State University; Loras College; Mount Mercy University; University of Dubuque; University of Iowa; University of Northern Iowa; Upper Iowa University

FINANCIAL FACTS

Financial Aid Rating	85
Annual tuition	$52,226
Room and board	$11,336
Required fees	$350
Books and supplies	$1,000
Average frosh need-based scholarship	$31,524
Average UG need-based scholarship	$28,610
% needy frosh rec. need-based scholarship or grant aid	100
% needy UG rec. need-based scholarship or grant aid	100
% needy frosh rec. non-need-based scholarship or grant aid	14
% needy UG rec. non-need-based scholarship or grant aid	14
% needy frosh rec. need-based self-help aid	85
% needy UG rec. need-based self-help aid	82
% frosh rec. any financial aid	99
% UG rec. any financial aid	99
% UG borrow to pay for school	82
Average cumulative indebtedness	$35,782
% frosh need fully met	20
% ugrads need fully met	21
Average % of frosh need met	85
Average % of ugrad need met	83

COLBY COLLEGE

4000 Mayflower Hill, Waterville, ME 04901 • Admissions: 207-859-4000 • Fax: 207-859-4828

CAMPUS LIFE

Quality of Life Rating	84
Fire Safety Rating	98
Green Rating	99
Type of school	Private
Affiliation	No Affiliation
Environment	Village

STUDENTS

Total undergrad enrollment	2,299
% male/female/another gender	48/52/0
% from out of state	93
% frosh live on campus	100
% ugrads live on campus	96
# of fraternities	0
# of sororities	0
% African American	5
% Asian	10
% White	56
% Hispanic	8
% Native American	<1
% Pacific Islander	<1
% Two or more races	7
% Race and/or ethnicity unknown	4
% international	10
# of countries represented	60

SURVEY SAYS . . .

Students always studying
Great financial aid
Students aren't religious
Students environmentally aware
Active student government
Active minority support groups
Students are friendly

ACADEMICS

Academic Rating	89
% students returning for sophomore year	93
% students graduating within 4 years	84
% students graduating within 6 years	88
Calendar	4/1/4
Student/faculty ratio	10:1
Profs interesting rating	91
Profs accessible rating	96
Most classes have 10–19 students.	

MOST POPULAR MAJORS

Computer Science; Political Science and Government, General; Econometrics and Quantitative Economics

STUDENTS SAY "..."

Academics

Students at Colby College in Waterville, Maine say "Our greatest strength is our sense of community and collaboration that permeate[s] every aspect of campus life." Enrollees should be prepared to work hard, because "classes are very rigorous and there is a high expectation for reading and work outside class." In the STEM departments, for example, "students spend at least 2–3 hours on homework per hour of lecture material." Regardless of your major, undergrads say, degree "requirements are not overbearing, but provide foundational knowledge in the subject area." Overall, "Most have reasonable syllabi as well, in which assignments are spaced out over the semester." Students also enjoy the freedom of Colby's January exploratory term, which enables students "to focus on one topic, make new friends, travel, and enjoy Maine in the winter."

Instructors are reportedly "excellent, accessible, and really care about making their students successful." There's a consensus among many who feel that "Professors are here because they enjoy teaching, and they are generous with their time and willing to help students as much as possible." As one notes, "Many of my professor[s] do not have explicit office hours, solely because they look to be as open as possible with students." And their creative support doesn't go unnoticed. "Professors do a great job [of] finding interesting ways to teach and incorporating Colby's resources into their curriculum," such as "interdisciplinary teaching tools like the Museum of Art and Computer labs" and "field trip[s] to external museums."

Campus Life

Students at Colby College are an active bunch, as "most people are involved in club or varsity athletics." In fact, "about a third of the student body are student-athletes." Many are "very outdoorsy and love to ski and hike often." But don't worry, "if you don't ski when you get here, you'll learn fast," as "weekends during the winter months are dominated by trips to nearby Sugarloaf Mountain." Many of these excursions are led by the Outing Club, one of the largest clubs on campus. When they're not hitting the slopes, "people at the school love to party." And while "there is also a big drinking culture on campus" many agree that "it is not ever forced on other students."

Given that "Colby is fairly isolated…it is a day trip to do anything off-campus." Many students emphasize that "there aren't many cities nearby," although students often "drive down to Portland and Freeport to shop and hit the towns." However, it's worth noting that these day trips "are impossible without a car." Colby "is good for the outdoor lover and people who don't care about being close to large civilization," one student explains. That's why most "appreciate the focus on on-campus events and programming."

Student Body

"Colby is a tight-knit and inclusive community," and "a place for adventurous, friendly, and hardworking students." Your fellow students at Colby College "are generally curious and intellectually motivated and most have some sort of hobby or activity in the outdoors." Undergrads describe their peers as "a rather liberal and environmentally-conscious group," full of "forward thinkers who demand immediate change to social and academic schools of thought."

While "Colby strives for diversity," many attest it "is still socially dominated by New England prep school students." However, despite the feeling that "many Colby students come from a privileged background, everyone is extremely humble, and is a Colby student before anything else." Such humility is understood in the "collaborative culture here on campus where we all learn from each other and celebrate all of our community's successes."

COLBY COLLEGE

Financial Aid: 207-859-4830 • E-Mail: admissions@colby.edu • Website: www.colby.edu

THE PRINCETON REVIEW SAYS

Admissions

The school reports that its standardized testing policy for use in admission is Test Optional, as it has been since 2018. The Princeton Review suggests that interested applicants consult with the school for the most up-to-date standardized testing policies. *Very important factors considered include:* rigor of secondary school record, academic GPA, recommendation(s), character/personal qualities. *Important factors considered include:* class rank, application essay, extracurricular activities, talent/ability, racial/ethnic status. *Other factors considered include:* standardized test scores, first generation, alumni/ae relation, geographical residence, volunteer work, work experience. High school diploma is required and GED is not accepted. *Academic units recommended:* 4 English, 3 math, 2 science, 2 science labs, 3 foreign language, 2 social studies.

Financial Aid

Students should submit: Business/Farm Supplement; CSS/Financial Aid Profile; FAFSA; tax documents (return, schedules, W-2s). The Princeton Review suggests that all financial aid forms be submitted as soon as possible (see page 5 for a note on the FAFSA). *Need-based scholarships/grants offered:* College/university scholarship or grant aid from institutional funds; Federal Pell; SEOG; State scholarships/grants. *Loan aid offered:* Direct PLUS loans; Direct Subsidized Loans; Direct Unsubsidized Loans. Admitted students will be notified of awards on or about 4/1. Federal Work-Study Program available. Institutional employment available.

The Inside Word

Earning admission to Colby College is no small feat. Most admitted students here are at the top of their class and have equally impressive extracurriculars bolstering their applications. The college has been Test Optional since 2018, so applicants with a strong GPA, several high-level courses like honors, APs, or IBs, and demonstrated commitment to an afterschool activity or something similar that highlights their character are best positioned for acceptance.

THE SCHOOL SAYS "..."

From the Admissions Office

"One of the nation's premier liberal arts colleges, Colby offers 59 majors and 36 minors, close interaction with faculty, and guaranteed opportunities for research, internships, and global learning. Colby's rigorous academic experience is connected to the world's most complex challenges. Partnerships with world-class research institutions provide transformative academic experiences rarely available to undergraduates. Exceptional campus facilities, including one of the finest college art museums in the country, state-of-the-art academic buildings and labs, and a 350,000-square-foot athletics and recreation center are enhanced by Maine's unique natural resources. A national leader in sustainability and environmental education, Colby was one of the first colleges in the country to achieve carbon neutrality. Applying to Colby is straightforward: there is no fee to apply and no extra essays to submit. The College meets 100 percent of demonstrated financial need for all admitted students, without including loans in financial aid packages. Families with a total household income of $75,000 or less with typical assets can expect a parent or guardian contribution of $0. Additionally, these students will receive a one-time Weiland Welcome Grant: $1,250 in addition to financial aid to address unexpected expenses such as technology needs and course materials. Families with a total household income of $150,000 and typical assets can expect a parent or guardian contribution of $15,000 or less. These initiatives position Colby as one of the most affordable four-year colleges in the country."

SELECTIVITY

Admissions Rating	98
# of applicants	16,890
% of applicants accepted	8
% of acceptees attending	52
# offered a place on the wait list	5,130
% accepting a place on wait list	36
% admitted from wait list	2
# of early decision applicants	1,025
% accepted early decision	35

FIRST-YEAR PROFILE

Testing policy	Test Optional
Range SAT composite	1440–1530
Range SAT EBRW	710–750
Range SAT math	720–790
Range ACT composite	32–34
# submitting SAT scores	286
% submitting SAT scores	42
# submitting ACT scores	159
% submitting ACT scores	24
% graduated top 10% of class	82
% graduated top 25% of class	96
% graduated top 50% of class	99

DEADLINES

Early decision	
Deadline	11/15
Notification	12/15
Other ED deadline	1/1
Other ED notification	2/15
Regular	
Deadline	1/1
Notification	4/1
Nonfall registration?	Yes

APPLICANTS ALSO LOOK AT

Amherst College; Bates College; Bowdoin College; Brown University; Carleton College; Hamilton College; Middlebury College; Tufts University; Wesleyan University; Williams College

FINANCIAL FACTS

Financial Aid Rating	98
Annual tuition	$60,840
Room and board	$16,330
Required fees	$2,680
Books and supplies	$850
Average frosh need-based scholarship	$65,004
Average UG need-based scholarship	$63,002
% needy frosh rec. need-based scholarship or grant aid	100
% needy UG rec. need-based scholarship or grant aid	100
% needy frosh rec. non-need-based scholarship or grant aid	0
% needy UG rec. non-need-based scholarship or grant aid	0
% needy frosh rec. need-based self-help aid	100
% needy UG rec. need-based self-help aid	90
% frosh rec. any financial aid	41
% UG rec. any financial aid	40
% UG borrow to pay for school	18
Average cumulative indebtedness	$23,958
% frosh need fully met	100
% ugrads need fully met	100
Average % of frosh need met	100
Average % of ugrad need met	100

COLGATE UNIVERSITY

13 Oak Drive, Hamilton, NY 13346 • Admissions: 315-228-1000 • Fax: 315-228-7524

CAMPUS LIFE

Quality of Life Rating	77
Fire Safety Rating	95
Green Rating	99
Type of school	Private
Affiliation	No Affiliation
Environment	Rural

STUDENTS

Total undergrad enrollment	3,124
% male/female/another gender	45/55/NR
% from out of state	76
% frosh from public high school	60
% frosh live on campus	100
% ugrads live on campus	92
# of fraternities	5
# of sororities	3
% African American	5
% Asian	6
% White	64
% Hispanic	9
% Native American	<1
% Pacific Islander	<1
% Two or more races	5
% Race and/or ethnicity unknown	2
% international	9
# of countries represented	41

SURVEY SAYS . . .

Classroom facilities are great
Lab facilities are great
Great library
Career services are great
Great financial aid
Recreation facilities are great
Alumni active on campus

ACADEMICS

Academic Rating	93
% students returning for sophomore year	94
% students graduating within 4 years	88
% students graduating within 6 years	91
Calendar	Semester
Student/faculty ratio	9:1
Profs interesting rating	93
Profs accessible rating	96
Most classes have 10–19 students.	

MOST POPULAR MAJORS

Economics; Political Science; Psychological Science

STUDENTS SAY "..."

Academics

Colgate University is known for its "very rigorous academic curriculum" and "invaluable" professors who "are the glue that hold the university together." Many students say they chose Colgate because they wanted "a small liberal arts school that had the opportunities and resources of a larger institution" combined with a "heavily involved alumni network" that "makes the Colgate connection a truly valuable resource." All agree that, at Colgate, you're "more than just a number" and that "there is no [shortage] of caring professors that are meaningfully invested in your academic success." As intimidating as it might seem to have, "internationally influential" professors, a history and political science double major assures that "classes are enjoyable and the professors are accessible." A junior adds, "One of the wonderful things about Colgate is that these relationships start as early as freshman year. Students do not have to wait until their senior year to build fantastic relationships with the faculty." However, another student grumbles, "Course selection is very stressful, and freshmen often get slighted." Any complaints about the faculty centered on "teaching styles" not meshing with individual students' "learning style." "However, there are a plethora of resources available to students to succeed despite any of their problems." "Colgate allowed me to become the person I always wanted to be, but didn't know I was capable of being," sings one senior whose sentiment is widely echoed.

Campus Life

Colgate University "has an amazing campus with people who work hard and have goals but also know how to have a really fun time." Students say the campus is "breathtaking," and they value "its small size and intimate nature." A philosophy major says, "Colgate is great because you can't walk 200 feet without a professor, student, or faculty member acknowledging you by name, yet you're constantly meeting new people and having new experiences. There is never a dull moment at Colgate." Students say, "Colgate strives for the perfect combination of academics and extracurriculars," and they feel the university "does a great job at helping us balance those and gives us opportunities to get involved in all the groups and events around campus." In addition to a plethora of clubs, students are actively involved in Greek life and Division I athletics. A junior says, "I loved how Colgate was located in the middle of nowhere" because "everything revolved around the campus," but in case you're worried about isolation, another student adds, "Colgate brings a lot of interesting speakers to the campus, which helps provide for a more rounded liberal arts experience." Students praise the administration, saying, "It is easy for students to contact the administration and thus have their voices directly heard by the community. The president holds drop-in office hours for students every week and takes notes on what students say during the session."

Student Body

Colgate boasts a "happy and enthusiastic student body" with a typical student that "is athletic, smart, engaged, and down to earth." They "enjoy having fun, but spend time in the library as well." Many say "the typical Colgate student is a preppy New Englander, who can be found almost always wearing Patagonia and Sperrys." However, this stereotype seems to be becoming less apt as there is "great diversity under the surface." As long as students are "not afraid to do what they love, they will find their niche and fit in." Fraternities and sororities as well as partying in general are popular: "Greek life does have a huge presence in the social life at Colgate," but "it is not exclusive to just those who are members." Most students mentioned the recent changes in the school's alcohol policies. Some tout it as the impetus for "initiatives to expand the amount of alternatives to partying on weekends." Others cited it as "the biggest issue on campus right now" between the students and administration. Despite the "country club atmosphere," a computer science major says, "When you're stranded in Hamilton, New York, for four years you'll inevitably end up fitting in regardless whether you are the typical student or not."

COLGATE UNIVERSITY

Financial Aid: 315-228-7431 • E-Mail: admission@colgate.edu • Website: www.colgate.edu

THE PRINCETON REVIEW SAYS

Admissions

The school reports that its standardized testing policy for use in admission for Fall 2024 is Test Optional. The 2024 testing policy will be temporary. The Princeton Review suggests that interested applicants consult with the school for the most up-to-date standardized testing policies. *Very important factors considered include:* rigor of secondary school record, class rank, academic GPA. *Important factors considered include:* standardized test scores, application essay, recommendation(s), extracurricular activities, talent/ability, character/personal qualities. *Other factors considered include:* first generation, alumni/ae relation, geographical residence, racial/ethnic status, volunteer work, work experience. High school diploma is required and GED is accepted. *Academic units required:* 4 English, 3 math, 3 science, 2 science labs, 3 foreign language, 3 social studies. *Academic units recommended:* 4 English, 4 math, 4 science, 4 science labs, 4 foreign language, 4 social studies.

Financial Aid

Students should submit: Business/Farm Supplement; CSS/Financial Aid Profile; FAFSA; Noncustodial Profile. Priority filing deadline is 1/15. The Princeton Review suggests that all financial aid forms be submitted as soon as possible (see page 5 for a note on the FAFSA). *Need-based scholarships/grants offered:* College/university scholarship or grant aid from institutional funds; Federal Pell; SEOG. *Loan aid offered:* Direct PLUS loans; Direct Subsidized Loans; Direct Unsubsidized Loans; College/university loans from institutional funds. Admitted students will be notified of awards on or about 3/25. Federal Work-Study Program available. Institutional employment available.

The Inside Word

Admission to this upstate New York gem is some of the most competitive around. You need to prepare yourself with excellent grades, scores, recommendations, and extracurricular activities. However, Colgate is also looking for that extra ingredient which might not translate from the Common App alone and is always seeking increased diversity across the board. Be aware that Colgate has adopted a Test Optional policy for all applicants through 2026. Transfer admission also remains Test Optional. Students who, at their own discretion, wish to submit SAT or ACT scores are welcome to do so, and these scores will be considered as part of the holistic review of the applicant.

THE SCHOOL SAYS "..."

From the Admissions Office

"Colgate provides an intellectually rigorous academic environment on a beautiful 575-acre campus in rural upstate New York. Of the Class of 2023, 22 percent self-identify as domestic students of color and 10 percent are international students. Colgate's student body includes students from 50 states and the District of Columbia, and represents 42 countries. Students and faculty alike are drawn to Colgate by the quality of its academic programs. Faculty initiative has given the university a broad mix of learning opportunities that includes a liberal arts core curriculum, 56 academic concentrations, and a wealth of chances for off-campus study abroad and within the United States, including Colgate faculty-led semester long and briefer programs, as well as approved programs offered by other institutions. The residential commons, Colgate's living and learning program, eases students' academic and social transition to college, and residential life in general includes an array of living options, on a campus described as one of the most beautiful in the country. The Trudy Fitness Center is a popular student destination, and the Shaw Wellness Institute fosters healthy, purposeful, and balanced lifestyles. The Max A. Shacknai Center for Outreach, Volunteerism, and Education builds upon the tradition of Colgate students interacting with the surrounding community in meaningful ways. Colgate students become extraordinarily devoted alumni, contributing significantly to career networking and exploration programs both on and off campus. These and many other points of distinction will be supported and expanded through the *Third-Century Plan,* a strategic framework designed to establish the University as one of the very finest undergraduate institutions in the nation and the world."

SELECTIVITY

Admissions Rating	97
# of applicants	21,109
% of applicants accepted	12
% of acceptees attending	31
# offered a place on the wait list	3,663
% accepting a place on wait list	59
% admitted from wait list	0
# of early decision applicants	1,868
% accepted early decision	26

FIRST-YEAR PROFILE

Testing policy	Test Optional
Range SAT composite	1430–1520
Range SAT EBRW	700–750
Range SAT math	710–780
Range ACT composite	32–34
# submitting SAT scores	252
% submitting SAT scores	31
# submitting ACT scores	184
% submitting ACT scores	23
Average HS GPA	3.9
% frosh submitting high school GPA	100
% graduated top 10% of class	73
% graduated top 25% of class	94
% graduated top 50% of class	99

DEADLINES

Early decision	
Deadline	11/15
Notification	12/15
Other ED deadline	1/15
Other ED notification	3/1
Regular	
Deadline	1/15
Notification	4/1
Nonfall registration?	No

APPLICANTS ALSO LOOK AT

Boston College; Bowdoin College; Brown College; Colby College; Cornell University; Dartmouth College; Georgetown University; Hamilton College; Harvard College; Middlebury College

FINANCIAL FACTS

Financial Aid Rating	97
Annual tuition	$66,622
Room and board	$16,790
Required fees	$402
Books and supplies	$1524
Average frosh need-based scholarship	$62,652
% needy frosh rec. need-based scholarship or grant aid	100
% needy UG rec. need-based scholarship or grant aid	100
% needy frosh rec. non-need-based scholarship or grant aid	24
% needy UG rec. non-need-based scholarship or grant aid	29
% needy frosh rec. need-based self-help aid	74
% needy UG rec. need-based self-help aid	72
% frosh rec. any financial aid	50
% UG rec. any financial aid	50
% UG borrow to pay for school	26
Average cumulative indebtedness	$25,631
% frosh need fully met	91
% UG need fully met	96
Average % of frosh need met	100
Average % of UG need met	100

COLLEGE OF CHARLESTON

66 George Street, Charleston, SC 29424 • Admissions: 843-805-5507 • Fax: 843-953-6322

CAMPUS LIFE

Quality of Life Rating	89
Fire Safety Rating	95
Green Rating	87
Type of school	Public
Environment	City

STUDENTS

Total undergrad enrollment	9,972
% male/female/another gender	33/67/0
% from out of state	44
% frosh from public high school	76
% frosh live on campus	90
% ugrads live on campus	28
# of fraternities (% join)	12 (19)
# of sororities (% join)	14 (17)
% African American	6
% Asian	2
% White	78
% Hispanic	7
% Native American	<1
% Pacific Islander	<1
% Two or more races	4
% Race and/or ethnicity unknown	2
% international	1
# of countries represented	72

SURVEY SAYS . . .

Great library
Students love Charleston, SC
Great off-campus food
Active student government

ACADEMICS

Academic Rating	78
% students returning for sophomore year	80
% students graduating within 4 years	57
% students graduating within 6 years	65
Calendar	Semester
Student/faculty ratio	16:1
Profs interesting rating	87
Profs accessible rating	91

Most classes have 20–29 students.
Most lab/discussion sessions have
 20–29 students.

MOST POPULAR MAJORS

Biology/Biological Sciences, General; Psychology,
General; Business Administration and
Management, General

STUDENTS SAY "..."

Academics

Founded in 1770, the College of Charleston provides its 10,000 undergraduates a mid-sized liberal arts experience within the boundaries of one of the south's most thriving cities. Good academic advising, a strong focus on writing skills and interdisciplinary studies, and a reputable business program are just some of the school's many perks, and many classes incorporate non-traditional types of learning such as "lots of field work and field trips around the city." As one student describes the opportunity to tour the city for a hospitality class, this "really [brings] the material to life." The school "caters to everyone, not just a single department or major," and the quantity and breadth of courses offered is appreciated by students. Academic diversity is a huge boon at the College, and within each major "there are plenty of students from different perspectives and the curriculum in class encourages the sharing of ideas from those perspectives."

Professors "care how well their students perform and help them find opportunities through networking and general encouragement." The ideal size of the school creates "a great student to professor ratio." Faculty are "engaged, knowledgeable, and passionate about the subject matter they teach," and they are "eager to engage with students that are excited to study and learn." The location and the school's reputation make for tons of internship and professional opportunities, and everything the school has to offer is available to all. If you need anything from academic advising to counseling or career planning, there are people here "with the passion and resources to help."

Campus Life

The school has a "love of its own history," as well as one for the "booming" city of Charleston. People enjoy "shopping on King Street or going to events hosted by the city," and on weekends, "many people head to the beach or socialize at parties." In between classes, students are found "grabbing food, studying in the library, or working out," and they often gather at each other's residence halls or apartments to relax and study together at night. There is something for everyone at the college with "tons of different groups on campus," and most students are "extremely involved" and "participate in multiple clubs."

Whether it means having the chance to work near campus or being close enough to walk to class every day, "the location is a perfect fit" for just about every student (particularly the many who love the outdoors). "Just going on a walk around town and seeing all of the beautiful houses and their history is extremely entertaining." The college "really does have a beautiful campus and we take pride in keeping it up," and students can just as easily live on-campus as rent nearby.

Student Body

At Charleston, students "can express themselves freely and openly with little to no judgement." The overall population may lean toward "white" and "middle to upper middle class," but "there are many diverse viewpoints and backgrounds." Charleston may technically be an urban environment, but "the city lends to a cool sort of blending where every group overlaps and coexists." This is a "small school with large school energy," and everyone at the College "is welcoming to new students and freshmen." "People are always willing to help each other out and general class culture is very positive and uplifting."

COLLEGE OF CHARLESTON

Financial Aid: 843-953-5540 • E-Mail: admissions@cofc.edu • Website: http://cofc.edu

THE PRINCETON REVIEW SAYS

Admissions

The school reports that its standardized testing policy for use in admission for Fall 2024 is Test Optional. The Princeton Review suggests that interested applicants consult with the school for the most up-to-date standardized testing policies. *Very important factors considered include:* rigor of secondary school record, academic GPA. *Important factors considered include:* class rank, first generation, geographical residence, state residency. *Other factors considered include:* standardized test scores, application essay, recommendation(s), extracurricular activities, talent/ability, character/personal qualities, first generation, alumni/ae relation, geographical residence, state residency, racial/ethnic status, volunteer work, work experience, level of applicant's interest. High school diploma is required and GED is accepted. *Academic units required:* 4 English, 4 math, 3 science, 3 science labs, 2 foreign language, 2 social studies, 1 history, 1 visual/performing arts, 2 academic electives. *Academic units recommended:* 4 English, 4 math, 2 history, 1 computer science.

Financial Aid

Students should submit: FAFSA. Priority filing deadline is 3/1. The Princeton Review suggests that all financial aid forms be submitted as soon as possible (see page 5 for a note on the FAFSA). *Need-based scholarships/grants offered:* College/university scholarship or grant aid from institutional funds; Federal Pell; Private scholarships; SEOG; State scholarships/grants. *Loan aid offered:* Direct PLUS loans; Direct Subsidized Loans; Direct Unsubsidized Loans. Admitted students will be notified of awards on a rolling basis. Federal Work-Study Program available. Institutional employment available.

The Inside Word

Typical first-year students at the College of Charleston had consistent academic achievement in the A/B range in high school. The admissions committee takes a hard look at high school performance, including the rigor of the pre-college workload, in addition to standardized test scores.

THE SCHOOL SAYS "..."

From the Admissions Office

"To succeed in our increasingly complex world, college graduates must be able to think creatively, explore new ideas, compete, collaborate, and meet the challenges of our global society. At the College of Charleston, students find out about themselves, their lives and the lives of others. They discover how to shape their future, and they prepare to create change and opportunity. Founded in 1770, the College of Charleston's mission is to provide students with a first-class education in the arts and sciences, education and business. Students have 148 majors and minors from which to choose—and they often choose to combine several—and complement their academic courses with overseas study, research and internships for a truly customized education.

"Approximately 10,000 undergraduates choose the college for its small-college feel blended with the advantages and diversity of an urban, mid-sized university. The College, home to students from fifty-three U.S. states/territories and 72 countries, provides a creative and intellectually stimulating environment where students are challenged and guided by a committed and caring full-time faculty of distinguished teacher-scholars, all in an incomparable historic setting. The city of Charleston serves as a living and learning laboratory for student experiences in business, science, engineering, teaching, the humanities, languages and the arts. At the same time, students and faculty are engaged with the community in partnerships to improve education, enhance the business community and enrich the overall quality of life in the region. In the great liberal arts tradition, a College of Charleston education focuses on discovery and personal growth, as well as preparation for life, work and service to our society."

SELECTIVITY

Admissions Rating	84
# of applicants	22,020
% of applicants accepted	76
% of acceptees attending	13
# offered a place on the wait list	2,659
% accepting a place on wait list	40
% admitted from wait list	99
# of early decision applicants	245
% accepted early decision	73

FIRST-YEAR PROFILE

Testing policy	Test Optional
Range SAT composite	1140–1290
Range SAT EBRW	580–660
Range SAT math	550–640
Range ACT composite	24–30
# submitting SAT scores	537
% submitting SAT scores	24
# submitting ACT scores	309
% submitting ACT scores	14
Average HS GPA	4.1
% frosh submitting high school GPA	100
% graduated top 10% of class	20
% graduated top 25% of class	50
% graduated top 50% of class	86

DEADLINES

Early decision	
Deadline	10/15
Notification	12/1
Early action	
Deadline	11/1
Notification	12/15
Regular	
Priority	11/1
Deadline	1/15
Nonfall registration?	Yes

APPLICANTS ALSO LOOK AT

Clemson University; Coastal Carolina University; University of South Carolina—Columbia

FINANCIAL FACTS

Financial Aid Rating	78
Annual in-state tuition	$12,518
Annual out-of-state tuition	$35,338
Required fees	$460
Required fees (first-year)	$320
Books and supplies	$1,345
Average frosh need-based scholarship	$2,685
Average UG need-based scholarship	$2,625
% needy frosh rec. need-based scholarship or grant aid	82
% needy UG rec. need-based scholarship or grant aid	78
% needy frosh rec. non-need-based scholarship or grant aid	64
% needy UG rec. non-need-based scholarship or grant aid	50
% needy frosh rec. need-based self-help aid	75
% needy UG rec. need-based self-help aid	73
% frosh rec. any financial aid	51
% UG rec. any financial aid	44
% UG borrow to pay for school	54
Average cumulative indebtedness	$32,906
% frosh need fully met	18
% ugrads need fully met	18
Average % of frosh need met	53
Average % of ugrad need met	54

THE COLLEGE OF NEW JERSEY

2000 Pennington Road, Ewing, NJ 08628-0718 • Admissions: 609-771-2131 • Fax: 609-637-5174

STUDENTS SAY ". . ."

Academics

A strong liberal arts curriculum forms the core of an education at the beautiful College of New Jersey, where almost 7,000 undergraduates can choose from more than 50 programs spread across the college's seven schools. All courses take "a meticulous approach" to the subject at hand, and the small class sizes "foster close relationships between students and professors," contributing to the college's incredibly high retention rate. The programs here are well-respected and each major provides "a great foundation for people who may look for jobs right out of college." Professional development seminars are "typically packed," and "the competition for on-campus interviews for internships is incredible." TCNJ is a college where students can expect "academic rigor and opportunities to take part in multiple organizations, research, and to grow," but, ultimately, "the college is what a person can make of it."

The professors at TCNJ are "always welcoming and friendly" and "intend to help with any questions or problems a student has." They "put in the effort to help the student succeed," and "programs are very fleshed out and rigorous," as well as being "able to prepare us very well for our careers." Within majors like engineering, nursing, and the sciences, "there is little room to slack off," but all who go here find "a fair balance of academic life with socialness, athletics, or relaxing time." Students also "tend to engage fully in supplementary programs (i.e., lecture, awareness, volunteer, celebratory, or other campus events) often affiliated with their major."

Campus Life

The TCNJ campus is "very beautiful and very unified," and students can walk everywhere (first-years aren't allowed to have cars). Students typically have Wednesdays off, during which time they schedule meetings with professors, attend a study group, or just relax. Students have plenty of activities to fill their day like "going to the gym, fishing, running, sleeping, watching a movie, ice cream party, [visiting] friends, [or] extra readings." Greek life is popular at TCNJ, and "there are always philanthropy events to go to." The College Union Board "does a lot of weekend and daily programming for students," including "Lions Latenight" which hosts weekly movies in the Student Center and "events for students to get free stuff." Though some facilities are in need at least of a face-lift, the "housing has improved in some on-campus residential buildings and more will be renovated in the upcoming several years." The suburban setting means that "many people do go home during the weekend." Campus is only about thirty minutes away from Philadelphia, meaning that those who do stick around on weekends are close to "malls, restaurants, and movie theaters, which are all easily accessible through the highway nearby." Dorm living is popular, and students "often have movie and game board nights in their own dorms/apartments."

Student Body

For the most part, the students here are "very driven to do their work and get good grades." Although students' opinions on how diverse the campus is vary, everyone "still gets along and accepts each other." Students at TCNJ create "a community of support that allow each other to grow academically and socially." There's "a real sense of school spirit and camaraderie" and inclusivity, and "we don't have a cliquey feeling or vibe." The college features "several organizations dedicated to the LGBTQ+ community" as well as organizations supporting "multiple different ethnic communities." While the school has multiple sports teams, the student body is "generally not interested in sports," and "all games, with the exception of Homecoming, are sparsely attended."

Financial Aid: 609-771-2211 • E-Mail: tcnjinfo@tcnj.edu • Website: www.tcnj.edu

THE PRINCETON REVIEW SAYS

Admissions

The school reports that its standardized testing policy for use in admission for Fall 2024 is Test Optional. It is unknown at this time if the 2024 testing policy will be permanent. The Princeton Review suggests that interested applicants consult with the school for the most up-to-date standardized testing policies. *Very important factors considered include:* rigor of secondary school record, class rank, extracurricular activities, volunteer work. *Important factors considered include:* application essay, recommendation(s), talent/ability, character/ personal qualities, geographical residence, state residency, level of applicant's interest. *Other factors considered include:* academic GPA, standardized test scores, first generation, alumni/ae relation, racial/ethnic status, work experience. High school diploma is required and GED is accepted. *Academic units required:* 4 English, 4 math, 4 science, 2 science labs, 2 foreign language, 2 social studies, 2 academic electives. *Academic units recommended:* 4 English, 4 math, 4 science, 2 science labs, 2 foreign language, 2 social studies, 4 academic electives.

Financial Aid

Students should submit: FAFSA. Priority filing deadline is 3/1. The Princeton Review suggests that all financial aid forms be submitted as soon as possible (see page 5 for a note on the FAFSA). *Need-based scholarships/grants offered:* College/university scholarship or grant aid from institutional funds; Federal Nursing Scholarships; Federal Pell; Private scholarships; SEOG; State scholarships/grants. *Loan aid offered:* Direct PLUS loans; Direct Subsidized Loans; Direct Unsubsidized Loans; Federal Nursing Loans; State Loans. Admitted students will be notified of awards on a rolling basis beginning 6/1. Federal Work-Study Program available. Institutional employment available.

The Inside Word

TCNJ accepts a little under half of its 14,000 applicants, but that level of competition is what you might expect at a school that offers state residents a small-college experience and a highly respected degree at bargain prices. TCNJ's admissions staff examines every component of a student's application, but none more carefully than the high school transcript. Students should apply as soon as possible once the application becomes available.

THE SCHOOL SAYS "..."

From the Admissions Office

"The College of New Jersey is one of the United States' great higher education success stories. With a long history as New Jersey's preeminent teacher of teachers, the college has grown into a new role as educator of the nation's best students in a wide range of fields. The College of New Jersey has created a culture of constant questioning—a place where knowledge is not merely received but reconfigured. In small classes, students and faculty members collaborate in a rewarding process: As they seek to understand fundamental principles, apply key concepts, reveal new problems, and pursue new lines of inquiry, students gain a fluency of thought in their disciplines. The college's 289-acre tree-lined campus is a union of vision, engineering, beauty, and functionality. Neoclassical Georgian Colonial architecture, meticulous landscaping, and thoughtful design merge in a dynamic system, constantly evolving to meet the needs of TCNJ students. About half of TCNJ's entering class will be academic scholars, with large numbers of National Merit finalists and semifinalists. The College of New Jersey is bringing together the best ideas from around the nation and building a new model for public undergraduate education on one campus."

SELECTIVITY

Admissions Rating	88
# of applicants	10,302
% of applicants accepted	64
% of acceptees attending	24
# offered a place on the wait list	1,018
% accepting a place on wait list	36
% admitted from wait list	5
# of early decision applicants	354
% accepted early decision	97

FIRST-YEAR PROFILE

Testing policy	Test Optional
Range SAT composite	1160–1330
Range SAT EBRW	570–670
Range SAT math	590–680
Range ACT composite	24–30
# submitting SAT scores	721
% submitting SAT scores	46
# submitting ACT scores	64
% submitting ACT scores	4
% graduated top 10% of class	33
% graduated top 25% of class	67
% graduated top 50% of class	94

DEADLINES

Early decision	
Deadline	11/1
Notification	12/1
Regular	
Deadline	2/1
Notification	4/1
Nonfall registration?	Yes

APPLICANTS OFTEN PREFER

Rutgers University—New Brunswick; Stevens Institute of Technology; University of Delaware

APPLICANTS SOMETIMES PREFER

New Jersey Institute of Technology; Penn State University Park; Seton Hall University; Temple University; University of Maryland, College Park; Villanova University

APPLICANTS RARELY PREFER

Ramapo College of New Jersey; State University of New York—Binghamton University; University of Pittsburgh—Pittsburgh Campus

FINANCIAL FACTS

Financial Aid Rating	72
Annual in-state tuition	$14,140
Annual out-of-state tuition	$19,796
Room and board	$15,112
Required fees	$3,840
Books and supplies	$1,200
Average frosh need-based scholarship	$14,402
Average UG need-based scholarship	$12,960
% needy frosh rec. need-based scholarship or grant aid	57
% needy UG rec. need-based scholarship or grant aid	51
% needy frosh rec. non-need-based scholarship or grant aid	50
% needy UG rec. non-need-based scholarship or grant aid	47
% needy frosh rec. need-based self-help aid	53
% needy UG rec. need-based self-help aid	65
% UG borrow to pay for school	58
Average cumulative indebtedness	$39,795
% frosh need fully met	12
% ugrads need fully met	10
Average % of frosh need met	40
Average % of ugrad need met	41

COLLEGE OF SAINT BENEDICT/SAINT JOHN'S UNIVERSITY

37 South College Ave, St. Joseph, MN 56321-7155 • Admissions: 800-249-9840 • Fax: 320-363-5650

STUDENTS SAY "..."

Academics

Minnesota's College of Saint Benedict (for women) and Saint John's University (for men) are two Catholic liberal arts colleges that share one academic program and classes, but retain separate dorms, campuses, and traditions. Students come to this "beautiful, friendly environment" and leave with "a well-rounded education...ready to take on the world." The Benedictine values "are upheld by every student in everyday life" and help breed graduates that are "all about service and making an impact in the world." Says one junior, "This school is a must for any student who wants to feel accepted and a part of a rich community, while at the same time receiving an education that is second to none." Professors truly take to heart the feedback they receive from their students, are "extremely dedicated and passionate," and "are willing to work...on projects outside of class even if it means extra work for them." They "are interested in us figuring things out for ourselves" and are "big on [students] being prepared for class so more time can be spent discussing or practicing material instead of lecturing." The ultimate testament to faculty involvement: "At CSB and SJU, I have never had a professor that has struggled to know my name (besides the fact that I am a twin)." Discussion is "lively" (particularly in upper division courses), and students "are offered many great opportunities to further our experiences and education." The open environment "does what it can to help students feel comfortable and learn."

The schools provide "excellent scientific and business opportunities" and "endless connections with not only other schools across the nation, but...across the world" that aid in post-undergraduate employment or continued education opportunities. The "incredible" study abroad program sees a large number of students take advantage of it at some point in their college careers.

Campus Life

The schools "really make sure your transition into your first semester runs smoothly" and that students "have a lot of options for meeting new people." The Student Activities and Leadership Development Office plans "large campus events such as orientation and Thanksgiving dinners," and also has an "inspired leaders series" of after-hours classes taught by professors that promote leadership on campus. On weekends, students often take adventure trips (like "California Surfing trips, Boundary Waters canoe trips, and Colorado climbing trips") with the schools' Peer Resource Program.

School pride is "ridiculous" at CSB and SJU and athletic events "are the high points for entertainment," especially against rival St. Thomas. For fun, students take advantage of the school's "rich recreational abilities" both in the arboretum and on nearby waterways, where "ice fishing, fishing, hiking, and hanging out at the beach are popular." "The warm months of the year are awesome with the lake/raft open. It feels like a summer camp," says a student. Many students "do go out on the weekends" to parties or bars, but there is an "outstanding campus programming board" that plans events every weekend on campus as an alternative to drinking. "As long as you can step out that door and make good use of your time, you'll have an amazing time," assures a sophomore.

Student Body

Most of the "Johnnies" and "Bennies" here are "from Minnesota or the surrounding states," are "hard-working, fun-loving," and "believe in the importance of education." Not surprisingly, the majority are Catholic and take "'Minnesota Nice' to a whole new level": "Expect to have doors open for you [and] people smile and greet you on occasion when you're passing by." People have no trouble finding a friend group with related interests via "the many clubs and activities that are offered." "Everyone fits like a puzzle piece" and students "commonly have social issues that they are passionate about, such as gender equality, sustainability, [or] health and wellness."

COLLEGE OF SAINT BENEDICT/SAINT JOHN'S UNIVERSITY

Financial Aid: 320-363-5388 • E-Mail: admissions@csbsju.edu • Website: www.csbsju.edu

THE PRINCETON REVIEW SAYS

Admissions

The school reports that its standardized testing policy for use in admission for Fall 2024 is Test Optional. The 2024 testing policy will be permanent. The Princeton Review suggests that interested applicants consult with the school for the most up-to-date standardized testing policies. *Very important factors considered include:* rigor of secondary school record, academic GPA, extracurricular activities. *Other factors considered include:* standardized test scores, application essay, recommendation(s), interview, talent/ability, character/personal qualities, alumni/ae relation, volunteer work, work experience. High school diploma is required and GED is accepted. *Academic units required:* 4 English, 3 math, 2 science, 2 science labs, 2 social studies, 4 academic electives. *Academic units recommended:* 2 foreign language.

Financial Aid

Students should submit: FAFSA. Priority filing deadline is 3/15. The Princeton Review suggests that all financial aid forms be submitted as soon as possible (see page 5 for a note on the FAFSA). *Need-based scholarships/grants offered:* College/university scholarship or grant aid from institutional funds; Federal Pell; Private scholarships; SEOG; State scholarships/grants. *Loan aid offered:* Direct PLUS loans; Direct Subsidized Loans; Direct Unsubsidized Loans; State Loans. Admitted students will be notified of awards on a rolling basis. Federal Work-Study Program available. Institutional employment available.

The Inside Word

Students with decent grades and a few extracurricular activities that "show promise of community contribution" shouldn't have any problem getting into CSB and SJU. You may apply to CSB and SJU using the Common Application or by using the school's CSBSJU GET INspired application—the school doesn't have a preference.

THE SCHOOL SAYS "..."

From the Admissions Office

"The College of Saint Benedict (CSB), for women, and Saint John's University (SJU), for men, are nationally recognized Catholic liberal arts colleges and ranked as two of the top three Catholic colleges in the nation. They share one academic program, and students attend classes together on both campuses. This integrated learning experience combines a challenging academic program with extensive opportunities for international study, leadership, service learning, spiritual growth, and cultural and athletic involvement. We provide students access to the resources of not one, but two nationally leading liberal arts colleges through a common undergraduate curriculum, identical degree requirements, and a single academic calendar. We are committed to the development of the whole person, meeting the unique needs of both women and men in single-gender and co-educational experiences—experiences that could not be provided by traditional single-sex colleges and would not typically be provided by co-educational colleges. The colleges are part of a centuries-old Benedictine tradition of faith, learning, and community. Hospitality, community, stewardship and service to the common good are bedrock Benedictine values expressed throughout the curriculum and the co-curriculum. We are part of a Catholic intellectual tradition committed to openness, intellectual inquiry, and the lively engagement of faith and reason. The colleges are committed to global learning and connection. We provide international study programs on six continents and are annually ranked among the top three baccalaureate colleges nationally in the number of students completing semester-long study abroad. Two-thirds of all students study abroad before they graduate—an international study participation rate significantly higher than the national average for liberal arts colleges. More than 200 academic courses have an international component or global emphasis. One-third of our faculty has led a study abroad program. We enroll nearly 160 students from more than twenty countries, creating an enriching and culturally diverse global experience on campus. CSB and SJU annually rank first or second among Minnesota's private colleges for the number of undergraduate international students."

SELECTIVITY
Admissions Rating	83
# of applicants	3,281
% of applicants accepted	87
% of acceptees attending	25

FIRST-YEAR PROFILE
Testing policy	Test Optional
Range SAT composite	970–1215
Range SAT EBRW	485–605
Range SAT math	485–598
Range ACT composite	21–27
# submitting SAT scores	26
% submitting SAT scores	4
# submitting ACT scores	333
% submitting ACT scores	47
Average HS GPA	3.6
% frosh submitting high school GPA	99
% graduated top 10% of class	21
% graduated top 25% of class	48
% graduated top 50% of class	80

DEADLINES
Early action	
Deadline	12/15
Notification	1/15
Regular	
Notification	Rolling, 10/1
Nonfall registration?	Yes

APPLICANTS OFTEN PREFER
University of Minnesota—Twin Cities; University of Saint Thomas (MN)

APPLICANTS SOMETIMES PREFER
Gustavus Adolphus College; St. Catherine University; St. Olaf College; University of Minnesota Duluth

APPLICANTS RARELY PREFER
Saint Cloud State University; University of Wisconsin-Eau Claire

FINANCIAL FACTS
Financial Aid Rating	88
Annual tuition	$50,950
Room and board	$11,906
Required fees	$1,186
Books and supplies	$1,000
Average frosh need-based scholarship	$39,737
Average UG need-based scholarship	$37,949
% needy frosh rec. need-based scholarship or grant aid	98
% needy UG rec. need-based scholarship or grant aid	98
% needy frosh rec. non-need-based scholarship or grant aid	96
% needy UG rec. non-need-based scholarship or grant aid	95
% needy frosh rec. need-based self-help aid	95
% needy UG rec. need-based self-help aid	92
% frosh rec. any financial aid	96
% UG rec. any financial aid	97
% UG borrow to pay for school	71
Average cumulative indebtedness	$41,123
% frosh need fully met	48
% ugrads need fully met	40
Average % of frosh need met	94
Average % of ugrad need met	92

COLLEGE OF THE ATLANTIC

105 Eden Street, Bar Harbor, ME 04609 • Admissions: 207-288-5015 • Fax: 207-288-4126

CAMPUS LIFE

Quality of Life Rating	95
Fire Safety Rating	97
Green Rating	99
Type of school	Private
Affiliation	No Affiliation
Environment	Rural

STUDENTS

Total undergrad enrollment	372
% male/female/another gender	32/68/0
% from out of state	85
% frosh from public high school	49
% frosh live on campus	99
% ugrads live on campus	64
% African American	1
% Asian	2
% White	63
% Hispanic	6
% Native American	0
% Pacific Islander	0
% Two or more races	3
% Race and/or ethnicity unknown	1
% international	24
# of countries represented	47

SURVEY SAYS . . .

Lots of liberal students
Students always studying
Students are happy
Internships are widely available
Class discussions encouraged
Great financial aid
No one cheats
Students are friendly
Diverse student types interact on campus
Students aren't religious
Students environmentally aware
Great food on campus
Easy to get around campus
Active student government
Students get along with local community
Students involved in community service
Students love Bar Harbor, ME

ACADEMICS

Academic Rating	91
% students returning for sophomore year	74
% students graduating within 4 years	52
% students graduating within 6 years	58
Calendar	Trimester
Student/faculty ratio	11:1
Profs interesting rating	95
Profs accessible rating	95

Most classes have 10–19 students.
Most lab/discussion sessions have
    10–19 students.

MOST POPULAR MAJORS

Humanities/Humanistic Studies; Ecology; Multi-/
Interdisciplinary Studies, Other

STUDENTS SAY "..."

Academics

Located in beautiful Bar Harbor, Maine, College of the Atlantic is a "really small school" that offers students a strong "interdisciplinary approach to learning." The institution strives to shape its students into "more creative...and critical thinkers" and really allows every undergrad to "construct [their] own unique path." One way they accomplish this is through the school's "inclusive governance system" which lets undergrads "have a say in things going on at the school," including things like approving new classes or reviewing internships. COA undergrads applaud the many different academic opportunities that allow for "hands-on, in the field experience through coursework, work-study, internships, [and the] senior project." Additionally, a number of individuals get to participate in "student research through local lab partners or the islands program" as well. Another advantage of a COA education? The fact that "if you have an interest that there aren't classes in, the school will help you design in-depth independent studies and pair you with knowledgeable mentors." With seemingly endless learning opportunities, it's no wonder many believe they "receive an incredible education beyond [their] expectations."

The professors at COA are "incredibly kind and educated." As this undergrad explains, "All of them are nice and will do their best to help if you ask." Students "get to know [their] professors personally," so it comes as no surprise that many agree "every meeting [and] conversation leaves [them] feeling energized and excited" about what they are studying.

Campus Life

Prepare to be busy if you end up attending College of the Atlantic. After all, "there's always a hundred activities and meetings happening every day." And a good number of undergrads here "spend time serving on committees" as well as "take on jobs on campus." In terms of events and extracurriculars, students "love going to open mics and hearing what [their] peers have created" or checking out the work of the "many artists on campus." Then again, there's no denying that COA students are an incredibly outdoorsy lot and can often be found in places like Acadia National Park, which is "right next to campus." Indeed, the outing club is quite active and students frequently "get to hike, cross country ski, boulder, ice skate, canoe, sea kayak, backpack, camp, and build saunas." And there's a Hiking and Backpacking Outdoor Leadership Program too. One participant reveals that it has "allowed me to lead a week-long freshmen orientation trip on the Appalachian Trail for two years in a row."

And if that weren't enough, there's still plenty of ways to bond with your peers in more casual settings. Undergrads here maintain a "strong culture of cooking and eating together" with many "[spending] most of their time in the dining halls" and "generally hang[ing] out with friends." You're also bound to stumble upon students simply "mak[ing] music [or] watch[ing] movies."

Student Body

The student body at College of the Atlantic is generally composed of a "unique combination of activists, oddballs, nature lovers and otherwise passionate and unusual people." And they certainly come together to form a community that is "welcoming [and] kind" and rooted in "compassion...for people, plants, animals and the planet." COA undergrads also make a point of highlighting how diverse their peers are, "in terms of having [both] international students [and] lots of queer students." One individual highlights that the school is "a very transgender-friendly place" as well. And a classmate quickly adds, "I've never felt more able to freely explore...and find out who I want to be and how I want to express myself. As a queer person coming from a very conservative background, COA was like a breath of fresh air." Beyond background and sexual orientation, many students here are "eager to [learn] more and share their knowledge [with] others." This is underscored by a student who says, "I have met people who are passionate about a million things I'd never even thought to care about, whether than be phylogeny, herring gulls, sewing, or subjectivity." But when it comes down to it, what COA undergrads appreciate most about their peers is the fact that they "pay attention to others and their needs."

COLLEGE OF THE ATLANTIC

Financial Aid: 207-801-5645 • E-Mail: inquiry@coa.edu • Website: www.coa.edu

THE PRINCETON REVIEW SAYS

Admissions

The school reports that its standardized testing policy for use in admission for Fall 2024 is Test Optional. The 2024 testing policy will be permanent. *Very important factors considered include:* rigor of secondary school record, application essay, recommendation(s). *Important factors considered include:* class rank, academic GPA, interview, extracurricular activities, character/personal qualities. *Other factors considered include:* standardized test scores, talent/ability, first generation, alumni/ae relation, racial/ethnic status, volunteer work, work experience, level of applicant's interest. High school diploma is required and GED is accepted. *Academic units required:* 4 English, 3 math, 2 science, 2 science labs, 2 social studies. *Academic units recommended:* 4 math, 3 science, 2 foreign language, 2 history, 1 academic elective.

Financial Aid

Students should submit: Business/Farm Supplement; FAFSA; Institution's own financial aid form; Noncustodial Profile. Priority filing deadline is 2/1. The Princeton Review suggests that all financial aid forms be submitted as soon as possible (see page 5 for a note on the FAFSA). *Need-based scholarships/grants offered:* College/university scholarship or grant aid from institutional funds; Federal Pell; Private scholarships; SEOG; State scholarships/grants. *Loan aid offered:* Direct PLUS loans; Direct Subsidized Loans; Direct Unsubsidized Loans. Admitted students will be notified of awards on or about 4/1. Federal Work-Study Program available. Institutional employment available.

The Inside Word

College of the Atlantic is a very small, tight-knit community, and admissions officers here are incredibly focused on finding candidates who will be a great fit for the school. Successful applicants demonstrate a specific interest in the school and value independent learning, community building, and curiosity. Admission officers look for students who thrive in self-directed settings. Given how important character is to the college, completing an interview is highly suggested.

THE SCHOOL SAYS "..."

From the Admissions Office

"College of the Atlantic is a small, interdisciplinary college on Maine's Mount Desert Island. All students design their own major in human ecology—an educational approach that integrates knowledge from across academic disciplines and personal experience to investigate, and ultimately improve, the relationships between humans and our natural, social, and built environments. COA prepares students to become independent thinkers, challenge conventional wisdom, deal with pressing environmental and social issues, and engage passionately and thoughtfully to transform the world around them into a better place.

"Our campus is located on the shore of Frenchman Bay, a short walk from the mountains and trails of Acadia National Park—an ideal location for learning in the field. Many students spend time working or conducting research in the national park or on the college's two organic farms, forest protectorate, wilderness center, and offshore field research stations on Mount Desert Rock and Great Duck Island. In addition to having numerous opportunities for research and field study, all COA students complete an internship and a capstone senior project.

"We look for students seeking a rigorous, experiential, self-directed academic experience and meaningful engagement in a dynamic community of scholars. The best way to experience COA's unique approach to education, governance, and community life is to visit the campus. While you're here, make time to sit in on classes, explore the national park, connect with faculty and current students, and sample a homemade meal in the dining hall."

SELECTIVITY

Admissions Rating	90
# of applicants	486
% of applicants accepted	60
% of acceptees attending	33
# offered a place on the wait list	47
% accepting a place on wait list	21
% admitted from wait list	10
# of early decision applicants	51
% accepted early decision	80

FIRST-YEAR PROFILE

Testing policy	Test Optional
Range SAT composite	1240–1450
Range SAT EBRW	640–750
Range SAT math	590–710
Range ACT composite	27–32
# submitting SAT scores	24
% submitting SAT scores	23
# submitting ACT scores	10
% submitting ACT scores	10
Average HS GPA	3.8
% frosh submitting high school GPA	65
% graduated top 10% of class	24
% graduated top 25% of class	71
% graduated top 50% of class	100

DEADLINES

Early decision	
Deadline	12/1
Notification	12/15
Other ED deadline	1/15
Other ED notification	1/30
Regular	
Deadline	2/1
Notification	4/1
Nonfall registration?	Yes

APPLICANTS SOMETIMES PREFER
Bennington College; Eckerd College; Hampshire College; University of Maine; University of New England; University of New Hampshire; University of Vermont; Warren Wilson College

APPLICANTS RARELY PREFER
University of Southern Maine

FINANCIAL FACTS

Financial Aid Rating	95
Annual tuition	$45,630
Room and board	$10,101
Required fees	$549
Books and supplies	$600
Average frosh need-based scholarship	$39,148
Average UG need-based scholarship	$37,229
% needy frosh rec. need-based scholarship or grant aid	100
% needy UG rec. need-based scholarship or grant aid	100
% needy frosh rec. non-need-based scholarship or grant aid	1
% needy UG rec. non-need-based scholarship or grant aid	2
% needy frosh rec. need-based self-help aid	91
% needy UG rec. need-based self-help aid	87
% frosh rec. any financial aid	98
% UG rec. any financial aid	98
% UG borrow to pay for school	48
Average cumulative indebtedness	$28,140
% frosh need fully met	47
% ugrads need fully met	83
Average % of frosh need met	96
Average % of ugrad need met	96

COLLEGE OF THE HOLY CROSS

1 College Street, Worcester, MA 01610-2395 • Admissions: 508-793-2443 • Fax: 508-793-3888

STUDENTS SAY "..."

Academics

This small, Jesuit liberal arts school in Massachusetts operates under a selfless mission statement of "men and women for and with others." The school's strong academic tradition marries with "countless opportunities to learn through internships, speaker series," "strong student life," and "small classes" to focus on shaping the student as a whole person. Academics at Holy Cross are "rigorous, and the main priority of students on campus"; a caring faculty and administration foster "an incredible learning environment for students," and through their experiences, students receive "a broad-based foundation to be successful in a variety of careers." "From the acceptance letter alone, I knew that my entire application was read thoroughly and that my character was closely examined," says one happy student. At Holy Cross, "you're more than just a number in the classroom and on the field." Professors here are "dedicated to creating an exciting learning environment." They are "always accessible and more than happy to help," and they "get to know you on an individual and personal level." Students are encouraged "to reflect on their experiences and continue to better himself/herself as a whole person." "There are endless opportunities despite the fact that it is a small college," one student says. "It is a place where like in the parable of the mustard seed one can grow." In addition to a "fantastic alumni network" spread across several fields in various industries, there is a strong science program that includes plenty of research opportunities. The college "demands enormous amounts of work from its students, but puts them in a great position to succeed." "Holy Cross equips their students with an intangible set of skills that not only prepares them for a job, but for life," says a student.

Campus Life

Holy Cross has "a multitude" of groups and activities available to its students, as well as a plethora of community service opportunities. Everyone loves "going to sporting events, especially football and basketball." Though the "exceptionally beautiful" campus has a lot of fans, all agree that the college "could update some of the residence halls." Holy Cross has added new dining venues and was named among Bon Appetit's "healthiest dining halls" for its food fitting all kinds of dietary restrictions. The community among freshman dorms is "outstanding," and "many of the friends you make your first year will stay with you for years to come." During the week and on Sundays, "people take their work very seriously," and the library is generally pretty full, but parties are popular on weekends, and "that nerdy chem major you see working hard all week can turn into the girl riding the mechanical bull at a local bar." For those who choose to abstain from the party circuit, "SGA-sponsored events such as karaoke or dances are a blast." Worcester is a fun little town (and Boston a free weekend shuttle ride away), and the restaurants in the area are "amazing."

Student Body

Many students here are "preppy" and from New England, and most all of this "uncommonly friendly" lot is "studious with an activity or two that defines their interests and what they do during the weekend"; in fact, it is rare "to find someone with no extracurricular responsibilities." Everyone tends to be "very put together" and "generally articulate," and "there is a tremendous sense of community." There is "a diverse set of interests" among the whole student body. In general, "all love being here." "If you want to do well academically, have fun on the weekend...study hard and play hard, then you will fit in at Holy Cross."

COLLEGE OF THE HOLY CROSS

Financial Aid: 508-793-2443 • E-Mail: admissions@holycross.edu • Website: www.holycross.edu

THE PRINCETON REVIEW SAYS

Admissions

The school reports that its standardized testing policy for use in admission for Fall 2024 is Test Optional. The 2024 testing policy will be permanent. The Princeton Review suggests that interested applicants consult with the school for the most up-to-date standardized testing policies. *Very important factors considered include:* rigor of secondary school record, academic GPA, application essay, recommendation(s), interview, character/personal qualities. *Important factors considered include:* extracurricular activities, talent/ability. *Other factors considered include:* class rank, standardized test scores, first generation, alumni/ae relation, geographical residence, state residency, religious affiliation/commitment, racial/ethnic status, volunteer work, work experience, level of applicant's interest. High school diploma is required and GED is accepted. *Academic units recommended:* 4 English, 4 math, 4 science, 2 science labs, 4 foreign language, 2 social studies, 2 history.

Financial Aid

Students should submit: CSS/Financial Aid Profile; FAFSA; Noncustodial Profile. The Princeton Review suggests that all financial aid forms be submitted as soon as possible (see page 5 for a note on the FAFSA). *Need-based scholarships/grants offered:* College/university scholarship or grant aid from institutional funds; Federal Pell; Private scholarships; SEOG; State scholarships/grants. *Loan aid offered:* Direct PLUS loans; Direct Subsidized Loans; Direct Unsubsidized Loans; College/university loans from institutional funds. Admitted students will be notified of awards on or about in late March. Federal Work-Study Program available. Institutional employment available.

The Inside Word

Admission to Holy Cross is competitive; therefore, a demanding high school course load is required to be a viable candidate. The college values effective communication skills—it thoroughly evaluates each applicant's personal statement and short essay responses. Interviews are important, especially for those applying early decision. Students who graduate from a Jesuit high school might find themselves at a slight advantage. Holy Cross meets 100% of an admitted student's demonstrated financial need.

THE SCHOOL SAYS "..."

From the Admissions Office

"When applying to Holy Cross, two areas deserve particular attention. First, the essay should be developed thoughtfully, with correct language and syntax in mind. That essay reflects for the Admissions Committee how you think and how you can express yourself. Second, activity beyond the classroom should be clearly defined. Since Holy Cross has only 3,000 students, the chance for involvement/participation is exceptional. The committee reviews many applications for academically qualified students. A key difference in being accepted is the extent to which a candidate participates in-depth beyond the classroom—don't be modest; define who you are. Interviews are highly recommended and are used as part of the evaluation process.

"Standardized test scores are optional. Students may submit their scores if they believe the results paint a fuller picture of their achievements and potential, but those students who don't submit scores will not be at a disadvantage in admissions decisions."

SELECTIVITY

Admissions Rating	94
# of applicants	7,036
% of applicants accepted	36
% of acceptees attending	35
# offered a place on the wait list	2,005
% accepting a place on wait list	49
% admitted from wait list	0
# of early decision applicants	503
% accepted early decision	81

FIRST-YEAR PROFILE

Testing policy	Test Optional
Range SAT composite	1270–1420
Range SAT EBRW	640–720
Range SAT math	620–710
Range ACT composite	28–32
# submitting SAT scores	313
% submitting SAT scores	35
# submitting ACT scores	173
% submitting ACT scores	19
% graduated top 10% of class	43
% graduated top 25% of class	75
% graduated top 50% of class	98

DEADLINES

Early decision	
Deadline	11/15
Notification	12/15
Other ED deadline	1/15
Other ED notification	2/15
Regular	
Deadline	1/15
Nonfall registration?	No

FINANCIAL FACTS

Financial Aid Rating	94
Annual tuition	$60,050
Room and board	$17,750
Required fees	$800
Books and supplies	$1,000
Average frosh need-based scholarship	$44,560
Average UG need-based scholarship	$42,303
% needy frosh rec. need-based scholarship or grant aid	86
% needy UG rec. need-based scholarship or grant aid	83
% needy frosh rec. non-need-based scholarship or grant aid	16
% needy UG rec. non-need-based scholarship or grant aid	19
% needy frosh rec. need-based self-help aid	67
% needy UG rec. need-based self-help aid	75
% frosh rec. any financial aid	58
% UG rec. any financial aid	61
% UG borrow to pay for school	60
Average cumulative indebtedness	$24,617
% frosh need fully met	100
% ugrads need fully met	100
Average % of frosh need met	100
Average % of ugrad need met	100

COLLEGE OF THE OZARKS

1 Opportunity Ave., Point Lookout, MO 65726 • Admissions: 417-334-6411 • Fax: 417-690-2635

CAMPUS LIFE

Quality of Life Rating	86
Fire Safety Rating	83
Green Rating	77
Type of school	Private
Affiliation	Evangelical Christian Interdenominational
Environment	Rural

STUDENTS

Total undergrad enrollment	1,491
% male/female/another gender	45/55/0
% from out of state	24
% frosh from public high school	78
% frosh live on campus	93
% ugrads live on campus	90
# of fraternities	0
# of sororities	0
% African American	1
% Asian	1
% White	90
% Hispanic	2
% Native American	<1
% Pacific Islander	<1
% Two or more races	2
% Race and/or ethnicity unknown	2
% international	1
# of countries represented	17

SURVEY SAYS . . .

Lots of conservative students
Great financial aid
Students are very religious
Students get along with local community
Theater is popular

ACADEMICS

Academic Rating	81
% students returning for sophomore year	73
Calendar	Semester
Student/faculty ratio	14:1
Profs interesting rating	90
Profs accessible rating	89

Most classes have 10–19 students.
Most lab/discussion sessions have 10–19 students.

MOST POPULAR MAJORS

Elementary Education and Teaching; Business Administration and Management, General

STUDENTS SAY "..."

Academics

Students who attend the College of Ozarks leave feeling academically, spiritually, and monetarily richer, thanks to the solid scholastic programs, Christian beliefs, and "the biggest strength ... [getting] to graduate debt-free." Consensus is that having a combination of scholarships and a work program that requires all undergrads to hold a campus job is a "huge asset" because it fosters a "unique sense of community" and ensures that students have real-world experience: "I personally have jumped around and gained a variety of skills that I can add to my résumé." These benefits do come with a measure of strictness in terms of a dress code and curfew, but attendees largely agree that these make "the work ethic of the student body unbelievable. As a whole, we are unmatched." They're also balanced with the school's Christian background, which "does an amazing job at creating a wonderful environment to grow our relationship with God."

Undergrads are quick to praise their "extremely knowledgeable" professors, and the way in which they can bring "topics to life" and "easily connect with the students." Plus, "most professors have found a strong balance between discussion and lecture to create a positive environment and promote student interaction." Though some undergrads do caution that the "classes and academics are rigorous," they emphasize that "professors do everything they can to help students succeed." That interaction goes a long way: "They have prompted [me] to grow in my writing and analytical skills, and have enriched my understanding of the world."

Campus Life

College of the Ozarks certainly lives up to its nickname, "Hard Work U." Not only are students "very devoted to their studies," they also work "15 hours a week on campus" at one of over 80 work stations. Job placements are wide-ranging and include the Print Shop, the Power Plant, and the school radio station, KCOZ. Of course, these industrious undergrads still manage to make time for extracurriculars, from the "pretty popular" worship nights to intramurals that range from seasons of classic sports and tournaments "between dorm buildings" to "a disc golf team...with a huge course going throughout the campus." Additionally, the Student Union "does a great job of putting on different activities," including the highly anticipated Mudfest, an annual game of tug-of-war over a mud pit. For more relaxing fare, students flock to events where they can indulge in "free coffee, treats, and live music." It's also just as common to find undergrads taking advantage of their beautiful surroundings. This often entails "hammocking,...having picnics, [or simply] strolling around campus." Best of all, your walk can take you right to the school's dairy: "You can go there anytime to pet and feed the calves." One thing students feel worth emphasizing is that all of this is "good, clean, real fun," thanks to a "zero-tolerance policy for drugs and alcohol."

Student Body

A sense of community permeates the College of Ozarks' campus and it's easy to understand why. As one junior explains, "We definitely have a relatively small student body here, which makes everyone feel like family." This runs deeper than casual kindness: "People here are genuinely concerned about you; they take five minutes of their day to listen to you and give advice." One area that could stand a little improvement is diversity, with some undergrads acknowledging that the "student body is fairly homogeneous" and mainly hails from "in/around the Ozarks region." However, they also highlight the fact that the school "has its fair sprinkling of international, transfer, and non-traditional students." Of course, no matter where they're from, the vast majority are "Christians who... desire to grow in their knowledge and love of Jesus Christ." Most importantly, they tend to lead with kindness and are quick to "open doors, walk people back to dorms, and frequently donate time or money." As one senior sums up, "My peers are so life-giving. We laugh, cry, and learn to be better people together."

COLLEGE OF THE OZARKS

Financial Aid: 417-690-3292 • E-Mail: admissions@cofo.edu • Website: www.cofo.edu

THE PRINCETON REVIEW SAYS

Admissions

The school reports that its standardized testing policy for use in admission for Fall 2024 requires applicants to submit either the SAT or ACT. It is unknown at this time if the 2024 testing policy will be permanent. The Princeton Review suggests that interested applicants consult with the school for the most up-to-date standardized testing policies. *Very important factors considered include:* rigor of secondary school record, class rank, interview, character/personal qualities. *Important factors considered include:* academic GPA, standardized test scores, recommendation(s), geographical residence, volunteer work, work experience, level of applicant's interest. *Other factors considered include:* extracurricular activities, talent/ability, first generation, alumni/ae relation, state residency, religious affiliation/commitment. High school diploma is required and GED is accepted. *Academic units required:* 4 English, 3 math, 2 science, 1 science lab, 3 history. *Academic units recommended:* 2 foreign language, 3 social studies.

Financial Aid

Students should submit: FAFSA. Priority filing deadline is 11/15. The Princeton Review suggests that all financial aid forms be submitted as soon as possible (see page 5 for a note on the FAFSA). *Need-based scholarships/grants offered:* College/university scholarship or grant aid from institutional funds; Federal Pell; Private scholarships; SEOG; State scholarships/grants. Admitted students will be notified of awards on or about 7/1. Federal Work-Study Program available. Institutional employment available.

The Inside Word

Admissions officers at College of the Ozarks are generally looking to serve students hailing from the Ozark region. Indeed, they're seeking local applicants in the top half of their class who lack the financial resources to pay for college. Applicants should also be individuals who are specifically looking for a Christian education. Finally, children of alumni in good standing will be given preferential consideration until December 31.

THE SCHOOL SAYS "..."

From the Admissions Office

"College of the Ozarks is unique because of its no-tuition, work-study program, but also because it strives to educate the head, the heart, and the hands. At C of O, there are high expectations of students—the college stresses character development as well as study and work. An education from 'Hard Work U.' offers many opportunities, not the least of which is the chance to graduate debt-free. Life at C of O isn't all hard work and no play, however. There are many opportunities for fun. The nearby resort town of Branson, Missouri, offers ample opportunities for recreation and summer employment, and Table Rock Lake, only a few miles away, is a terrific spot to swim, sun, and relax. Numerous on-campus activities such as Mudfest, Luau Night, dances, and holiday parties give students lots of chances for fun without leaving the college. At 'Hard Work U.,' we work hard, but we know how to have fun too."

SELECTIVITY

Admissions Rating	97
# of applicants	2,879
% of applicants accepted	16
% of acceptees attending	84
# offered a place on the wait list	586
% accepting a place on wait list	100
% admitted from wait list	4

FIRST-YEAR PROFILE

Testing policy	SAT or ACT Required
Range SAT EBRW	560–625
Range SAT math	543–605
Range ACT composite	21–26
# submitting SAT scores	12
% submitting SAT scores	3
# submitting ACT scores	374
% submitting ACT scores	97
Average HS GPA	3.7
% frosh submitting high school GPA	99
% graduated top 10% of class	25
% graduated top 25% of class	62
% graduated top 50% of class	96

DEADLINES

Regular	
Priority	12/31
Notification	Rolling, 12/31
Nonfall registration?	Yes

APPLICANTS ALSO LOOK AT

Evangel University; Missouri State University; Southwest Baptist University; William Jewell College

FINANCIAL FACTS

Annual tuition	$0
Room and board	$7,400
Required fees	$460
Books and supplies	$1,100
Average frosh need-based scholarship	$11,182
Average UG need-based scholarship	$11,182
% needy frosh rec. need-based scholarship or grant aid	100
% needy UG rec. need-based scholarship or grant aid	100
% needy frosh rec. non-need-based scholarship or grant aid	36
% needy UG rec. non-need-based scholarship or grant aid	94
% needy frosh rec. need-based self-help aid	64
% needy UG rec. need-based self-help aid	94
% frosh rec. any financial aid	100
% UG rec. any financial aid	100
% UG borrow to pay for school	0
Average cumulative indebtedness	$0
% frosh need fully met	18
% ugrads need fully met	40
Average % of frosh need met	75
Average % of ugrad need met	81

THE COLLEGE OF WOOSTER

1189 Beall Avenue, Wooster, OH 44691 • Admissions: 330-263-2000 • Fax: 330-263-2621

STUDENTS SAY "..."

Academics

The College of Wooster in Ohio is a small, personable "tight-knit community" that offers "a truly stellar education" to those who attend. Mentoring is a huge focal point of Wooster's academics, and the "resources are endless" for those looking to take advantage of things like "numerous opportunities for research and internships." Independent study is a highlight of the undergraduate experience, and the school "teaches research and how to apply skills learned to the outside world." This "very open school" challenges its students to succeed both in and out of the classroom, and "the staff pushes [the college] to change with the times in the classroom and around the campus."

Professors at Wooster are "hidden gems" who are all "very passionate about their subjects" and their goal "to shape their students into lifelong learners." "It's as if your professor is your colleague on your quest for eternal knowledge," says a freshman. These intimate ties between student and professor are "what makes Wooster such an incredible place." "My professors, both past and present, know more than just my name," says a student. "My success is a product of my professors' enthusiasm toward their subject matter and our futures," says another. The work may be "challenging," but it "teaches students how to write exceptionally," and there is "plenty of help from professors, TAs, [and] peer tutoring." "Collaborative work and experience" are stressed, and classes are set up "in a way that allows people to learn from their peers as well as their professors."

Research plays a "huge" role at Wooster, especially with senior year Independent Study, when students are given the opportunity to work with a faculty mentor on a project in any topic they are passionate about—and "they can do so much with it." The institution is also aware of the effort that students must put in to have success and "is realistic in its expectations for students' learning." As one student best sums it up, "Wooster is a community of learners working together to help one another reach their full potential and goals."

Campus Life

"The character of the campus community is friendly beyond measure" at this "dazzling" campus. People are usually "busy in the library doing homework or working on their Independent Studies," but everyone finds time for (typically multiple) extracurriculars, which "run the gamut of recreational pastimes." "We have just as many students in our music ensembles as we do that play sports," says a student. People enjoy using the weekends to relieve the stress of a rigorous academic schedule, and the majority enjoy "socializing" at the fraternity or program houses, or going to the on-campus club called "the Underground" on Friday nights.

For those who choose not to party, there are "many other recreational activities for those who are not in sports or who do not enjoy drinking," and the college "is very good at bringing in entertainment," such as "comedians, professional music artists, and forum speakers which are all free to students." A student run weekly flyer, *The Pot*, helps "keep students up to date on all of the campus events happening." A lot of the time, though, "students will just hang out together and relax."

Student Body

"The life force of this school is really our fantastic student body," says a student. This "unparalleled" community is made up of "quite a range of people," but most are "quirky," "friendly," "open-minded," and "liberal." It's also a "very involved" student body ("school spirit is huge at Wooster"), so a typical COW kid "tends to be in a hodgepodge of sports, clubs, music groups, etc. that suit their fancy." There are "very few social cliques" and everyone is friendly and "willing to interact with one another." Students here are "very accepting of different personalities, beliefs, and ways of life."

THE COLLEGE OF WOOSTER

Financial Aid: 330-263-2317 • E-Mail: admissions@wooster.edu • Website: www.wooster.edu

THE PRINCETON REVIEW SAYS

Admissions

The school reports that its standardized testing policy for use in admission for Fall 2024 is Test Optional. The 2024 testing policy will be permanent. The Princeton Review suggests that interested applicants consult with the school for the most up-to-date standardized testing policies. *Very important factors considered include:* rigor of secondary school record, academic GPA. *Important factors considered include:* class rank, application essay, recommendation(s), interview, extracurricular activities, character/personal qualities, level of applicant's interest. *Other factors considered include:* standardized test scores, talent/ability, first generation, alumni/ae relation, geographical residence, state residency, racial/ethnic status, volunteer work, work experience. High school diploma is required and GED is accepted. *Academic units required:* 4 English, 3 math, 3 science, 2 science labs, 2 foreign language, 3 social studies, 1 academic elective.

Financial Aid

Students should submit: FAFSA; Institution's own financial aid form. Priority filing deadline is 2/15. The Princeton Review suggests that all financial aid forms be submitted as soon as possible (see page 5 for a note on the FAFSA). *Need-based scholarships/grants offered:* College/university scholarship or grant aid from institutional funds; Federal Pell; Private scholarships; SEOG; State scholarships/grants. *Loan aid offered:* Direct PLUS loans; Direct Subsidized Loans; Direct Unsubsidized Loans. Admitted students will be notified of awards on a rolling basis beginning 1/1. Federal Work-Study Program available. Institutional employment available.

The Inside Word

The College of Wooster is focused on accessibility and finding a diverse student body. If you've got character and think you can add to this community's social, intellectual, and scholastic achievements, admissions officers want to meet you. Don't be discouraged if your grades are a little below the accepted range—especially since standardized tests are currently optional—and check with the school if you've missed the application deadline, as they may still be able to consider you (with no penalty to potential scholarships and other aid).

THE SCHOOL SAYS "..."

From the Admissions Office

"The College of Wooster is America's premier college for mentored undergraduate research. Our mission is to graduate educated, not merely trained, people; to produce responsible, independent thinkers, rather than specialists in any given field. Our commitment to independence is especially evident in IS, the college's distinctive program in which every senior works one-to-one with a faculty mentor to complete a project in the major. IS comes from 'independent study,' but, in reality, it is an intellectual collaboration of the highest order and permits every student the freedom to pursue something in which he or she is passionately interested. IS is the centerpiece of an innovative curriculum. More than just the project itself, the culture that sustains IS—and, in turn, is sustained by IS—is an extraordinary college culture. The same attitudes of student initiative, openness, flexibility, and individual support enrich every aspect of Wooster's vital residential college life."

SELECTIVITY

Admissions Rating	89
# of applicants	7,251
% of applicants accepted	56
% of acceptees attending	15
# of early decision applicants	185
% accepted early decision	56

FIRST-YEAR PROFILE

Testing policy	Test Optional
Range SAT composite	1260–1430
Range SAT EBRW	640–720
Range SAT math	610–730
Range ACT composite	27–32
# submitting SAT scores	177
% submitting SAT scores	31
# submitting ACT scores	144
% submitting ACT scores	25
Average HS GPA	3.7
% frosh submitting high school GPA	100
% graduated top 10% of class	46
% graduated top 25% of class	71
% graduated top 50% of class	90

DEADLINES

Early decision	
Deadline	11/1
Notification	11/15
Other ED deadline	1/15
Other ED notification	2/1
Early action	
Deadline	11/25
Notification	12/31
Regular	
Priority	2/15
Deadline	2/15
Notification	4/1
Nonfall registration?	Yes

APPLICANTS ALSO LOOK AT

Allegheny College; Case Western Reserve University; Denison University; Kenyon College; Miami University; The Ohio State University—Columbus

FINANCIAL FACTS

Financial Aid Rating	90
Annual tuition	$59,050
Room and board	$14,000
Required fees	$500
Books and supplies	$1,250
Average frosh need-based scholarship	$42,878
Average UG need-based scholarship	$41,892
% needy frosh rec. need-based scholarship or grant aid	98
% needy UG rec. need-based scholarship or grant aid	98
% needy frosh rec. non-need-based scholarship or grant aid	41
% needy UG rec. non-need-based scholarship or grant aid	35
% needy frosh rec. need-based self-help aid	58
% needy UG rec. need-based self-help aid	64
% frosh rec. any financial aid	100
% UG rec. any financial aid	99
% UG borrow to pay for school	52
Average cumulative indebtedness	$26,785
% frosh need fully met	70
% ugrads need fully met	61
Average % of frosh need met	96
Average % of ugrad need met	94

COLORADO COLLEGE

14 East Cache la Poudre St., Colorado Springs, CO 80903 • Admissions: 719-389-6000 • Fax: 719-389-6816

CAMPUS LIFE

Quality of Life Rating	83
Fire Safety Rating	97
Green Rating	96
Type of school	Private
Affiliation	No Affiliation
Environment	Metropolis

STUDENTS

Total undergrad enrollment	2,174
% male/female/another gender	44/54/2
% from out of state	78
% frosh live on campus	100
% ugrads live on campus	77
# of fraternities	3
# of sororities	3
% African American	3
% Asian	5
% White	67
% Hispanic	11
% Native American	<1
% Pacific Islander	<1
% Two or more races	7
% Race and/or ethnicity unknown	1
% international	6
# of countries represented	50

SURVEY SAYS . . .

Lots of liberal students
Students are happy
Class discussions encouraged
Great financial aid
Students are friendly
Students aren't religious
Students environmentally aware
Great food on campus
Easy to get around campus
Recreation facilities are great
Intramural sports are popular
Theater is popular

ACADEMICS

Academic Rating	91
% students returning for sophomore year	91
% students graduating within 4 years	83
% students graduating within 6 years	86
Calendar	Other
Student/faculty ratio	10:1
Profs interesting rating	93
Profs accessible rating	96
Most classes have 10–19 students.	

MOST POPULAR MAJORS

Economics, General; Political Science and Government, General; Ecology and Evolutionary Biology

STUDENTS SAY "..."

Academics

Students are drawn to Colorado College for its unique Block Plan, in which students take one intensive class at a time. The academic year is structured as eight blocks of three to five weeks each, punctuated by five-day breaks. Students find the Block Plan empowers them to participate in "a strongly immersive approach to education," reporting that "the classes are very challenging, but after cramming in a semester's worth of calculus in four weeks, you basically feel like you can conquer anything." It's a challenge that students appreciate: "Colorado College abhors mediocrity; either you succeed more than you ever thought possible, or fail in spectacular ways." Academically, students "love the class sizes and classes. I feel fully invested in each class I take here." The "intense and exhausting" pace of block classes provides "more opportunities for growth" and bonds students and professors: "In my last block the professor was spending the whole morning afternoon—and evening—with us!" admires one student, while another adds that, I have been amazed at the extent to which the block plan allows each student to delve into their course material." The small classes "do away with student anonymity" and "foster excellent discussion and intellectual growth." Students also appreciate the "internship opportunities" and "preparation for post-graduation" offered by the school, often in concert with the "ability to study off campus or abroad." Colorado College undergrads see their objective as "pursuing excellence through diverse and rich viewpoints" and "immersion in a dynamic array of intellectual endeavors." "They genuinely value the college's "great support system and connections," which provide for accessible "opportunities to learn off campus." Ultimately, "The shared values of intellectual engagement, physical and mental health, passion, and a sense of adventure define Colorado College's spirit."

Campus Life

"Life at school is very busy," and there's a lot of "focused study" at Colorado College, but one need only look out at Pikes Peak to get "a constant reminder about how beautiful of a state we are in." There's an emphasis on "working diligently, so that free time can be appreciated to its fullest," and students note that "outdoor activities are a big thing here." Indeed, you'll find that "slacklining, doing homework in the sun, and playing guitar on the lawn all happen when it's nice out. Sledding and skiing down campus hills, snowball fights, and fire pits happen in the winter." Despite this athletic emphasis, "people are pretty accepting [of] what you like doing for fun" and "the common slang is 'you do you.' ...Another thing I like is there is no peer pressure to get involved with substances." Students note that "you really don't have to leave campus if you don't want to," but if you do, downtown Colorado Springs "is only about a 10-minute walk from campus, and there are many interesting restaurants to dine at for special occasions or a fun night out." In sum, the Colorado College experience is one of "non-competitive, non-judgmental, intellectual and physical adventure on the Block Plan in the little warm nest of the Rockies."

Student Body

Colorado College undergrads respect each other, saying that "everyone here is very intelligent" to the point at which it seems that "almost everyone was a valedictorian or salutatorian." In equal measure, "CC students have passion for academic and outdoor pursuits," as evidenced by one student's depiction of "intellectual discussion about our impact on nature while rock climbing." Some describe the population as full of "rich hippies," and while that's likely an exaggeration, students do note that they'd like more diversity. That said, students see well beyond themselves: "The typical student is well-traveled, intelligent...quirky, outdoorsy, and a bit of a hipster." CC students "are usually very accepting and friendly," as well as "largely involved with their community, environment and academics" and "very vocal about their opinions."

COLORADO COLLEGE

Financial Aid: 719-389-6779 • E-Mail: admission@coloradocollege.edu • Website: www.coloradocollege.edu

THE PRINCETON REVIEW SAYS

Admissions

The school reports that its standardized testing policy for use in admission for Fall 2024 is Test Optional. It is unknown at this time if the 2024 testing policy will be permanent. The Princeton Review suggests that interested applicants consult with the school for the most up-to-date standardized testing policies. *Very important factors considered include:* rigor of secondary school record. *Important factors considered include:* academic GPA, application essay, recommendation(s), extracurricular activities. *Other factors considered include:* class rank, standardized test scores, interview, talent/ability, character/personal qualities, first generation, alumni/ae relation, geographical residence, state residency, religious affiliation/commitment, racial/ethnic status, volunteer work, work experience, level of applicant's interest. High school diploma or equivalent is not required. *Academic units required:* 4 English.

Financial Aid

Students should submit: CSS/Financial Aid Profile; FAFSA; Noncustodial Profile. Priority filing deadline is 11/1. The Princeton Review suggests that all financial aid forms be submitted as soon as possible (see page 5 for a note on the FAFSA). *Need-based scholarships/grants offered:* College/university scholarship or grant aid from institutional funds; Federal Pell; Private scholarships; SEOG; State scholarships/grants. *Loan aid offered:* Direct PLUS loans; Direct Subsidized Loans; Direct Unsubsidized Loans. Admitted students will be notified of awards on or about 12/20. Federal Work-Study Program available. Institutional employment available.

The Inside Word

Admission at Colorado College is highly competitive, with over 95% of the student body accepted last year coming from the top quarter of their high school class. The rigor of the block program requires students to demonstrate self-motivation and commitment to both academics and extracurriculars, and strong writing skills are considered essential to the application. Interviews and arts supplements are non-required application options; students who feel their strengths will be showcased by these options should carefully consider them.

THE SCHOOL SAYS "..."

From the Admissions Office

"Students enter Colorado College for the opportunity to study intensely in small learning communities. Groups of students work closely with one another and faculty in discussion-based classes and hands-on labs. CC encourages a well-rounded education, combining the academic rigor of a traditional liberal arts college, with the focus and flexibility of the block plan. Rich programs in athletics, community service, student government, and the arts balance an engaged student life. The college encourages students to push themselves academically, and many continue their studies at the best graduate and professional schools in the nation. Because roughly 80 percent of students study abroad while at CC, the college has been recognized as a national leader in international education. The block plan allows classes to incorporate field study into the curriculum, whether studying winter field ecology at the CC Cabin or Dante and Michelangelo in Italy. Its location at the base of the Rockies makes CC a great choice for students who enjoy backpacking, hiking, climbing, and skiing."

SELECTIVITY

Admissions Rating	96
# of applicants	7,846
% of applicants accepted	16
% of acceptees attending	42
# offered a place on the wait list	823
% accepting a place on wait list	23
% admitted from wait list	1
# of early decision applicants	691
% accepted early decision	44

FIRST-YEAR PROFILE

Testing policy	Test Optional
Range SAT composite	1270–1460
Range SAT EBRW	640–730
Range SAT math	620–750
Range ACT composite	29–33
# submitting SAT scores	180
% submitting SAT scores	34
# submitting ACT scores	149
% submitting ACT scores	28
Average HS GPA	3.9
% frosh submitting high school GPA	87
% graduated top 10% of class	72
% graduated top 25% of class	95
% graduated top 50% of class	99

DEADLINES

Early decision	
Deadline	11/1
Notification	12/15
Other ED deadline	1/15
Other ED notification	2/15
Early action	
Deadline	11/1
Notification	12/20
Regular	
Priority	1/15
Deadline	1/15
Notification	3/20
Nonfall registration?	Yes

FINANCIAL FACTS

Financial Aid Rating	97
Annual tuition	$67,458
Room and board	$15,228
Required fees	$474
Books and supplies	$1,240
Average frosh need-based scholarship	$63,059
Average UG need-based scholarship	$60,186
% needy frosh rec. need-based scholarship or grant aid	98
% needy UG rec. need-based scholarship or grant aid	96
% needy frosh rec. non-need-based scholarship or grant aid	7
% needy UG rec. non-need-based scholarship or grant aid	4
% needy frosh rec. need-based self-help aid	100
% needy UG rec. need-based self-help aid	100
% frosh rec. any financial aid	62
% UG rec. any financial aid	57
% UG borrow to pay for school	30
Average cumulative indebtedness	$23,706
% frosh need fully met	100
% ugrads need fully met	100
Average % of frosh need met	100
Average % of ugrad need met	100

COLORADO STATE UNIVERSITY

Colorado State University, Fort Collins, CO 80523-1062 • Admissions: 970-491-1101

CAMPUS LIFE

Quality of Life Rating	95
Fire Safety Rating	90
Green Rating	99
Type of school	Public
Environment	City

STUDENTS

Total undergrad enrollment	25,148
% male/female/another gender	46/54/NR
% from out of state	33
% frosh live on campus	90
% ugrads live on campus	23
# of fraternities (% join)	33 (4)
# of sororities (% join)	23 (5)
% African American	2
% Asian	3
% White	71
% Hispanic	16
% Native American	<1
% Pacific Islander	<1
% Two or more races	5
% Race and/or ethnicity unknown	1
% international	2
# of countries represented	73

SURVEY SAYS . . .

Students are happy
Students environmentally aware
Students love Fort Collins, CO
Great off-campus food
Recreation facilities are great
Campus newspaper is popular

ACADEMICS

Academic Rating	78
% students returning for sophomore year	86
% students graduating within 4 years	48
% students graduating within 6 years	67
Calendar	Semester
Student/faculty ratio	17:1
Profs interesting rating	86
Profs accessible rating	90

Most classes have 10–19 students.
Most lab/discussion sessions have
   20–29 students.

MOST POPULAR MAJORS

Computer Science; Psychology, General; Business
Administration and Management, General

STUDENTS SAY ". . ."

Academics

Colorado State University is "an institution that is determined to engage and challenge its students, preparing them for post-graduate life beyond the university." Despite being a large public research university, CSU does a "phenomenal" job of fostering a "community feel." Students guarantee you won't "feel like just a number" here. Many students tell us that they are drawn to Colorado's "amazing" science and engineering programs and "outstanding" business school. And they really appreciate CSU's commitment to "sustainability." Undergrads here also note that the academics are "both challenging and fun." While you're likely to encounter "some good and some bad professors," the "vast majority are very interested in what they are teaching and very passionate." As one pleased student boasts, "My professors are fantastic, they make everything easy to learn, and teach [in] ways that make classes enjoyable even with large lectures." A fellow student concurs, adding that "they bring the material to life and maintain a comfortable environment for discussion." Moreover, it's clear that not only do they care about each student's academic growth, professors here care about "their personal well-being" as well. All in all, Colorado State provides students with "the resources to succeed in academics, pursue hobbies and interests, and maintain good mental and physical health."

Campus Life

Colorado State seems to attract a lot of outdoor enthusiasts. And with good reason. There are many "opportunities from volunteer cleanups to hiking and fishing all along the Poudre River." And, of course, "you have the Rocky Mountains at your doorstep." Therefore, "rock climbing" and "biking" are also popular activities. Further, many weekends are dedicated to "skiing and snowboarding." Of course, there's plenty happening on campus as well. A number of students participate in "intramural sports or [attend] rec center classes." Additionally, "there's always...a movie showing or a visiting professor lecture." And football games are well attended. Students can also join one of the "500 clubs and organizations at CSU." A handful of undergrads are active in Greek life too. Fraternities and sororities do tend to "throw parties on the weekend"; however, these typically "happen off campus." Students also love exploring downtown Fort Collins. After all, the "restaurants are amazing." Moreover, "there is always a buzz around the square, and often times a local band will be playing." And undergrads that are of age enjoy exploring and partaking in the city's "amazing craft beer culture." Finally, when CSU students are looking to get away, they can easily "travel to Denver or Boulder" for some fun!

Student Body

Colorado State students frequently describe their peers as "down to earth and energetic." They're also "respectful, kind, and full of CSU pride." And although undergrads here might appear "predominantly white" as you stroll through campus, many students assert that it's actually "a pretty diverse place." These undergrads also know how to carve out a good work/life balance. Indeed, "they understand when it is time to sit down and work really hard, but also know when a break from the work is needed." Even better, Colorado State undergrads are "extremely friendly." A pleased student shares, "I am always meeting new people and seeing warm faces." Another undergrad agrees adding, "No one ever hesitates to help out a fellow Ram." They are also highly intellectual and approach learning with "excitement and enthusiasm." Despite being a state school, CSU still manages to have a "good mix of out-of-state students." No matter where they hail from, most undergrads are "liberal and...environmentally focused." Finally, as one thankful student concludes, "It is a great, helpful community that I am so proud to be a part of."

COLORADO STATE UNIVERSITY

Financial Aid: 970-491-6321 • E-Mail: admissions@colostate.edu • Website: www.colostate.edu/

THE PRINCETON REVIEW SAYS

Admissions

The school reports that its standardized testing policy for use in admission for Fall 2024 is Test Optional. The 2024 testing policy will be permanent. The Princeton Review suggests that interested applicants consult with the school for the most up-to-date standardized testing policies. *Very important factors considered include:* rigor of secondary school record, academic GPA. *Important factors considered include:* class rank, standardized test scores, application essay, recommendation(s). *Other factors considered include:* extracurricular activities, talent/ability, character/personal qualities, first generation, alumni/ae relation, geographical residence, volunteer work, work experience. High school diploma is required and GED is accepted. *Academic units required:* 4 English, 4 math, 3 science, 2 science labs, 1 foreign language, 3 social studies, 1 history, 2 academic electives. *Academic units recommended:* 2 foreign language.

Financial Aid

Students should submit: FAFSA; Institution's own financial aid form. Priority filing deadline is 3/1. The Princeton Review suggests that all financial aid forms be submitted as soon as possible (see page 5 for a note on the FAFSA). *Need-based scholarships/grants offered:* College/university scholarship or grant aid from institutional funds; Federal Pell; Private scholarships; SEOG; State scholarships/grants. *Loan aid offered:* Direct PLUS loans; Direct Subsidized Loans; Direct Unsubsidized Loans; College/university loans from institutional funds. Admitted students will be notified of awards on a rolling basis beginning 3/1. Federal Work-Study Program available. Institutional employment available.

The Inside Word

When building their incoming class, Colorado State University seeks out students who will be able to meet the school's high academic standards. To do so, they closely examine the rigor of your high school curriculum. Admissions officers want to see that you've been successful in challenging college prep courses. If submitted, your standardized test scores will also hold weight. The university looks at your extracurricular involvement as well. Finally, the admissions office considers circumstances that might have impacted your course selection or academic performance.

THE SCHOOL SAYS "..."

From the Admissions Office

"As one of the nation's premier research universities, Colorado State offers more than 150 undergraduate programs of study in eight colleges. Students come here from fifty states and eighty-five countries, and they appreciate the quality and breadth of the university's academic offerings. But Colorado State is more than just a place where students can take their scholarship to the highest level. It's also a place where they can gain invaluable experience in the fields of their choice, whether they're immersing themselves in professional internships, studying on the other side of the globe or teaming up with faculty on groundbreaking research projects. In addition to an outstanding experiential learning environment, Colorado State students enjoy a sense of community that's unusual for a large university. They develop meaningful relationships with faculty members who bring out their best work, and they live and learn with diverse peers who value their ideas and expand their perspectives. These types of connections lead to countless opportunities for social networking and professional accomplishments. By the time our students graduate from Colorado State, they have the knowledge, practical experience, and interpersonal skills they need to make a significant contribution to their world.

"Although academic performance is a primary factor in admissions decisions, Colorado State's holistic review process also recognizes personal qualities and experiences that have the potential to enrich the university and the Fort Collins community. Students must submit the Common Application for admission."

SELECTIVITY

Admissions Rating	82
# of applicants	33,122
% of applicants accepted	91
% of acceptees attending	19

FIRST-YEAR PROFILE

Testing policy	Test Optional
Range SAT composite	1080–1280
Range SAT EBRW	540–650
Range SAT math	530–640
Range ACT composite	23–29
# submitting SAT scores	2,397
% submitting SAT scores	43
# submitting ACT scores	861
% submitting ACT scores	16
Average HS GPA	3.7
% frosh submitting high school GPA	100
% graduated top 10% of class	18
% graduated top 25% of class	44
% graduated top 50% of class	77

DEADLINES

Early action	
Deadline	12/1
Notification	1/1
Regular	
Priority	2/1
Deadline	7/1
Notification	Rolling, 9/1
Nonfall registration?	Yes

APPLICANTS ALSO LOOK AT

Arizona State University; California Polytechnic State University; Colorado School of Mines; University of Arizona; University of Colorado at Denver; University of Colorado Boulder; University of Denver; University of Northern Colorado; University of Oregon

FINANCIAL FACTS

Financial Aid Rating	79
Annual in-state tuition	$9,903
Annual out-of-state tuition	$29,861
Room and board	$13,360
Required fees	$2,656
Books and supplies	$1,200
Average frosh need-based scholarship	$10,398
Average UG need-based scholarship	$9,815
% needy frosh rec. need-based scholarship or grant aid	73
% needy UG rec. need-based scholarship or grant aid	71
% needy frosh rec. non-need-based scholarship or grant aid	36
% needy UG rec. non-need-based scholarship or grant aid	10
% needy frosh rec. need-based self-help aid	58
% needy UG rec. need-based self-help aid	60
% frosh rec. any financial aid	76
% UG rec. any financial aid	69
% UG borrow to pay for school	48
Average cumulative indebtedness	$27,363
% frosh need fully met	22
% ugrads need fully met	17
Average % of frosh need met	67
Average % of ugrad need met	66

COLUMBIA UNIVERSITY

212 Hamilton Hall MC 2807, New York, NY 10027 • Admissions: 212-854-1754 • Fax: 212-854-1209

STUDENTS SAY "..."

Academics

Columbia University, the Ivy League's New York City office, has been around for more than 250 years, providing prestige, rigorous academics, a strong alumni network, and a multitude of opportunities to its students. As intimate spaces carved out of the larger university, Columbia College and The Fu Foundation School of Engineering and Applied Science throw a "vast amount of resources" at its students, with benefits that "extend from clubs to study abroad programs [to]...proximity to one of the greatest cities in the world." Columbia is "all about building intelligent [and] confident students who are ready for the workplace," and there are "many opportunities to satiate intellectual curiosity." The school's Core Curriculum ensures students leave with a breadth of knowledge, and "everyone is smart in some way."

Though some students have a bad teacher or two, Columbia professors are "fantastic in both their leadership in their field as well as in their interest in teaching students," and if "students carefully select which classes they will take they can find professors they like." The academics here "are truly great" and students "always know you're being taught by people at the forefront of their fields." Columbia attracts a very specific type of student "who is devoted to receiving a true liberal arts education in a variety of subjects," but those who go here shouldn't expect to have knowledge handed to them on a platter: "It is up to the student to get the most out of a class," says one.

Campus Life

When it comes to free time, there's no question as to where students turn: New York City, where there are "countless things to do for fun." The "clubs downtown are always a late night option as are the Broadway shows and comedy clubs near Times Square" and "from shopping in Soho to visiting museums to trying out a new restaurant in Midtown, there's literally nothing you can't do here." That's not to say that students don't stay on campus; people often hang out in dorms and sometimes this turns into a social event itself. "I can walk into my floor lounge at any moment for homework help on anything from Chinese to econometrics, and upon doing so I inevitably wind up having a mind-blowing intellectual discussion of some sort," says a student. The "Monday to Thursday grind is usually pretty tough": people go to classes, do homework and readings, and "try to fit in time with friends in between all the chaos." Weekends are more fun, and Columbia has "a great arts initiative which is perfect for getting [tickets] cheaper" as well as a World Leaders Forum where speakers historically have included "presidents and prime ministers from countries far and wide."

Student Body

This collection of "very ambitious" students is "not only extremely intelligent, but also passionate about everything they do." This group is "diverse in every sense of the word," from race to sexuality to age, and everyone has "a high awareness of the connections between academic, personal, and social issues." People "aren't afraid to speak out against what they think is wrong"; activism is "essential to the Columbia experience," and in fact, "it is encouraged by the school itself." This go-getting crowd tries to do it all, "taking on 5 to 6 classes per semester and holding multiple jobs and internships and leadership positions"; as a result, Columbia does have a bit of a "stress culture," due to the fact that "everyone here really wants to succeed." While it "can be competitive for programs," most students find people here "to be more kind than shrewd."

COLUMBIA UNIVERSITY

Financial Aid: 212-854-3711 • Website: www.columbia.edu

THE PRINCETON REVIEW SAYS

Admissions

The school reports that its standardized testing policy for use in admission for Fall 2024 is Test Optional. The Princeton Review suggests that interested applicants consult with the school for the most up-to-date standardized testing policies. *Very important factors considered include:* rigor of secondary school record, class rank, academic GPA, application essay, recommendation(s), extracurricular activities, character/personal qualities. *Important factors considered include:* talent/ability. *Other factors considered include:* standardized test scores, interview, first generation, alumni/ae relation, geographical residence, racial/ethnic status, volunteer work, work experience. High school diploma is required and GED is accepted. *Academic units required:* 4 English, 4 math, 3 science, 3 science labs, 3 foreign language, 3 history, 3 academic electives. *Academic units recommended:* 4 English, 4 math, 4 science, 4 science labs, 4 foreign language, 4 history, 4 academic electives.

Financial Aid

Students should submit: FAFSA; Noncustodial Profile; State aid form. The Princeton Review suggests that all financial aid forms be submitted as soon as possible (see page 5 for a note on the FAFSA). *Need-based scholarships/grants offered:* College/university scholarship or grant aid from institutional funds; Federal Pell; Private scholarships; SEOG; State scholarships/grants. *Loan aid offered:* Direct PLUS loans; Direct Subsidized Loans; Direct Unsubsidized Loans; College/university loans from institutional funds. Admitted students will be notified of awards on or about 4/1. Federal Work-Study Program available. Institutional employment available.

The Inside Word

There's no magic formula or pattern to guide students who are seeking admission to Columbia University. Excellent grades in rigorous classes may not be enough, and many great candidates are rejected each year. Admissions officers take a holistic approach to evaluating applications, and they pay extra attention to personal accomplishments in non-academic activities as they look to build a diverse class that will greatly contribute to the university.

THE SCHOOL SAYS "..."

From the Admissions Office

"Columbia maintains an intimate college campus within one of the world's most vibrant cities. After a day exploring New York City you come home to a traditional college campus within an intimate neighborhood. Nobel Prize–winning professors will challenge you in class discussions and meet one-on-one afterward. The Core Curriculum attracts intensely free-minded scholars, and connects all undergraduates. Science and engineering students pursue cutting-edge research in world-class laboratories with faculty members at the forefront of scientific discovery. Classroom discussions are only the beginning of your education. Ideas spill out from the classrooms, electrifying the campus and Morningside Heights. Friendships formed in the residence halls solidify during a game of Frisbee on the South Lawn or over bagels on the steps of Low Library. From your first day on campus, you will be part of our diverse community.

"Columbia offers extensive need-based financial aid and meets the full need of every student admitted as a first-year with grants instead of loans. Parents with calculated incomes below $60,000 are not expected to contribute any income or assets to the cost of attendance, and families with calculated incomes between $60,000 and $100,000 have a significantly reduced contribution. Parents earning over $100,000 can still qualify for significant financial aid. To support students pursuing study abroad, research, internships and community service opportunities, Columbia offers the opportunity to apply for additional funding. A commitment to diversity—of every kind—is a long-standing Columbia hallmark. We believe cost should not be a barrier to pursuing your educational dreams."

SELECTIVITY
Admissions Rating	99
# of applicants	60,374
% of applicants accepted	4
% of acceptees attending	65
# of early decision applicants	6,299
% accepted early decision	12

FIRST-YEAR PROFILE
Testing policy	Test Optional
Range SAT composite	1500–1560
Range SAT EBRW	730–780
Range SAT math	770–800
Range ACT composite	34–35
# submitting SAT scores	654
% submitting SAT scores	45
# submitting ACT scores	348
% submitting ACT scores	24
% graduated top 10% of class	96
% graduated top 25% of class	>99
% graduated top 50% of class	100

DEADLINES
Early decision	
Deadline	11/1
Notification	12/15
Regular	
Deadline	1/1
Notification	4/1
Nonfall registration?	No

APPLICANTS ALSO LOOK AT
Harvard College; Massachusetts Institute of Technology; Princeton University; Stanford University; The University of Chicago; University of Pennsylvania; Yale University

FINANCIAL FACTS
Financial Aid Rating	96
Annual tuition	$62,570
Room and board	$16,212
Required fees	$2,954
Required fees (first-year)	$3,569
Books and supplies	$1,366

CONNECTICUT COLLEGE

270 Mohegan Avenue, New London, CT 06320 • Admissions: 860-447-1911 • Fax: 860-439-4301

CAMPUS LIFE

Quality of Life Rating	78
Fire Safety Rating	62
Green Rating	92
Type of school	Private
Affiliation	No Affiliation
Environment	Town

STUDENTS

Total undergrad enrollment	1,915
% male/female/another gender	38/62/0
% from out of state	86
% frosh live on campus	100
% ugrads live on campus	97
# of fraternities	0
# of sororities	0
% African American	4
% Asian	3
% White	67
% Hispanic	12
% Native American	0
% Pacific Islander	<1
% Two or more races	3
% Race and/or ethnicity unknown	2
% international	8
# of countries represented	50

SURVEY SAYS . . .

Internships are widely available
Great financial aid
No one cheats
Students environmentally aware
Active student government

ACADEMICS

Academic Rating	88
% students returning for sophomore year	87
% students graduating within 4 years	79
% students graduating within 6 years	84
Calendar	Semester
Student/faculty ratio	10:1
Profs interesting rating	92
Profs accessible rating	94

Most classes have 10–19 students.
Most lab/discussion sessions have
    10–19 students.

MOST POPULAR MAJORS

Psychology, General; Economics, General; Political
Science and Government, General

STUDENTS SAY "..."

Academics

Located in eastern Connecticut, the picturesque Connecticut College is a classic private New England liberal arts school that shows a "great commitment to being sustainable, to promoting community service, and to learning." The college provides "great academic, extracurricular, and athletic opportunities to all students," and the "beloved" honor code makes for "a close-knit, supportive community." A strong focus on interdisciplinary education, small classes, and self-scheduled exams gives students the autonomy to truly tailor their learning around their interests. The academics are "rigorous but continuously relevant, interesting, and enlightening." Most classes are discussion-based, which "allows students to express their own opinions while hearing from their fellow students and professors." Though there are a few bad apples, most professors are always accessible ("especially outside of their office hours") and are "constantly bringing learning outside of the classroom, whether it be within a residence hall, a restaurant, museum, or gallery downtown, or within their own homes." "All of my professors are incredibly engaging and obviously here to excite students about their studies," says a student. Other high points include the "approachability of the staff," excellent career office and internship opportunities, and strong residential programs and academic centers that "help students with a myriad of topics." Connecticut College assures that no student will go through school with "your typical major/minor pairing"; with certificate programs, tons of research opportunities, independent studies and more, every student "has a completely unique and entirely interdisciplinary experience here."

Campus Life

"Life as a student is all about balancing your school work with your extracurricular activities and choosing which events you want to attend," says one. The residential programs lay a great groundwork for student life, and much of the fun on campus "is through social events through the dorms." It helps that "everyone knows one another—between offices, custodial staff, campus safety, and students." There are a wide range of activities to get involved with (everything from athletics, to arts, to activism, to community service, etc.), as well as "numerous faculty-led discussions and speakers every week." Most activities that take place on campus make it "lively and interesting." The campus as a whole is "very friendly, and you are always surrounded by familiar faces," though the relationship with the town of New London is "something that can always be improved upon." For fun, students "attend each other's events, attend social functions in the student center, grab some coffee at one of our coffee shops, and generally hang out with each other." The library is "a very social place during the week," and though students work very hard, they "know how to have a good time on the weekends"—every weekend there is a variety of on-campus social events (concerts, dances, spoken-word performances) put on by the Student Activities Council. Day trips to Boston and New York are also common.

Student Body

Students note that Conn "embraces diversity," although that doesn't mean there isn't also a sizable population that some describe as "smart, probably upper-class, well-dressed, and white. The common theme among all Conn students is "their active involvement both on campus and off and their desire to be challenged in all aspects of their educations." Students fit in by "showing an interest in their studies, but also carrying on an active social life." It is fairly easy to find one's niche within the community, and "while it might take a semester to become adjusted, there are many groups, teams, and other resources...that help freshmen find a place here."

Financial Aid: 860-439-2058 • E-Mail: admission@conncoll.edu • Website: www.conncoll.edu

THE PRINCETON REVIEW SAYS

Admissions

The school reports that its standardized testing policy for use in admission for Fall 2024 is Test Optional. The 2024 testing policy will be permanent. The Princeton Review suggests that interested applicants consult with the school for the most up-to-date standardized testing policies. *Very important factors considered include:* rigor of secondary school record, class rank, academic GPA, character/personal qualities. *Important factors considered include:* application essay, recommendation(s), interview, extracurricular activities, talent/ability, racial/ethnic status, volunteer work, work experience. *Other factors considered include:* standardized test scores, first generation, alumni/ae relation, geographical residence, state residency, religious affiliation/commitment, level of applicant's interest. High school diploma is required and GED is accepted.

Financial Aid

Students should submit: CSS/Financial Aid Profile; FAFSA; Noncustodial Profile. Priority filing deadline is 1/15. The Princeton Review suggests that all financial aid forms be submitted as soon as possible (see page 5 for a note on the FAFSA). *Need-based scholarships/grants offered:* College/university scholarship or grant aid from institutional funds; Federal Pell; SEOG; State scholarships/grants. *Loan aid offered:* Direct PLUS loans; Direct Subsidized Loans; Direct Unsubsidized Loans; College/university loans from institutional funds. Admitted students will be notified of awards on or about 4/1. Federal Work-Study Program available. Institutional employment available.

The Inside Word

Connecticut College is the archetypal selective New England college, and admissions officers are judicious in their decisions. Competitive applicants will have undertaken a demanding course load in high school. Admissions officers look for students who are curious and who thrive in challenging academic environments. Since Connecticut College has a close-knit community, personal qualities are also closely evaluated, and interviews are important.

THE SCHOOL SAYS " . . . "

From the Admissions Office

"Connecticut College has all the hallmarks of the best liberal arts colleges: small classes, stellar teaching, close faculty-student relationships, a residential campus and plentiful co-curricular activities. But what sets this college apart is its active, outward-focused vision of 'the liberal arts in action.'

"A rigorous new curriculum, Connections, gives students a chance to tailor their academic experiences around a topic of interest to them, a problem they want to solve. It teaches complex thinking and real-world problem-solving, and ultimately ensures successful lives and careers for students beyond college.

"Students can choose from 14 Integrative Pathways or five centers for interdisciplinary scholarship (our version of an honors college), 42 majors and 47 minors. Students connect theory to the real world through community learning, student-faculty research, international experiences and campus leadership. Ninety-two percent of the Class of 2024 cited Connections as one of the main reasons they chose to enroll at Conn.

"Liberal arts in action also means living under a 96-year-old Honor Code that provides for self-scheduled exams, a student-run Honor Council and a student voice in campus decision-making.

"Our four-year career program puts the liberal arts to work, with courses, programming and funding for career exploration and development, including internships. While at Conn, 95% of students work with the career office.

"More than half of students are athletes competing at the varsity level in the New England Small College Athletic Conference (NCAA Division III) or in club sports. The campus community is close and supportive; there is no Greek life."

SELECTIVITY
Admissions Rating	93
# of applicants	8,744
% of applicants accepted	40
% of acceptees attending	18
# offered a place on the wait list	2,484
% accepting a place on wait list	44
% admitted from wait list	<1
# of early decision applicants	434
% accepted early decision	49

FIRST-YEAR PROFILE
Testing policy	Test Optional
Range SAT composite	1180–1390
Range SAT EBRW	600–710
Range SAT math	560–690
Range ACT composite	28–32
# submitting SAT scores	305
% submitting SAT scores	48
# submitting ACT scores	103
% submitting ACT scores	16
Average HS GPA	3.8
% frosh submitting high school GPA	58
% graduated top 10% of class	35
% graduated top 25% of class	72
% graduated top 50% of class	94

DEADLINES
Early decision	
Deadline	11/15
Notification	12/15
Other ED deadline	1/15
Other ED notification	2/12
Regular	
Deadline	1/15
Notification	3/25
Nonfall registration?	Yes

FINANCIAL FACTS
Financial Aid Rating	96
Comprehensive fee	$79,900
Books and supplies	$1,000
Average frosh need-based scholarship	$42,483
Average UG need-based scholarship	$46,784
% needy frosh rec. need-based scholarship or grant aid	98
% needy UG rec. need-based scholarship or grant aid	97
% needy frosh rec. non-need-based scholarship or grant aid	35
% needy UG rec. non-need-based scholarship or grant aid	30
% needy frosh rec. need-based self-help aid	68
% needy UG rec. need-based self-help aid	72
% UG borrow to pay for school	50
Average cumulative indebtedness	$38,564
% frosh need fully met	100
% ugrads need fully met	100
Average % of frosh need met	100
Average % of ugrad need met	100

THE COOPER UNION FOR THE ADVANCEMENT OF SCIENCE AND ART

41 Cooper Square, New York, NY 10003 • Admissions: 212-353-4120

CAMPUS LIFE

Quality of Life Rating	86
Fire Safety Rating	97
Green Rating	60*
Type of school	Private
Affiliation	No Affiliation
Environment	Metropolis

STUDENTS

Total undergrad enrollment	892
% male/female/another gender	49/49/2
% from out of state	37
% frosh live on campus	80
% ugrads live on campus	20
# of fraternities (% join)	1 (1)
# of sororities	0
% African American	5
% Asian	31
% White	28
% Hispanic	12
% Native American	0
% Pacific Islander	0
% Two or more races	8
% Race and/or ethnicity unknown	6
% international	10
# of countries represented	29

SURVEY SAYS . . .

Students love New York, NY
Easy to get around campus
Active student government

ACADEMICS

Academic Rating	85
% students returning for sophomore year	93
% students graduating within 4 years	52
% students graduating within 6 years	83
Calendar	Semester
Student/faculty ratio	9:1
Profs interesting rating	89
Profs accessible rating	92

Most classes have 10–19 students.
Most lab/discussion sessions have
10–19 students.

MOST POPULAR MAJORS

Electrical and Electronics Engineering; Mechanical
Engineering

STUDENTS SAY "..."

Academics

A truly unique New York City institution, Cooper Union provides grants covering more than half tuition to all students (as well as additional need-based aid). Degree programs focus in art, architecture, or engineering. Academics are "very rigorous, although consistent and achievable with the resources provided," and students are very driven in achieving their coursework, "especially with major projects that offer them a great deal of academic freedom to create their own content." Students are pushed "to achieve the most in a short amount of time" and are well aware of the value they are getting relative to "cost of tuition and good job placement after graduating."

Professors are "generally very knowledgeable in their subject area" and "you're not that likely to have the same professor over and over again," making for a diverse learning experience. The "very focused" engineering program "sets you up to be a functioning member of the engineering community and workforce": "Even as a sophomore I have had the opportunity to take (and understand) graduate level material," says one student. The art school "constructs an art curriculum around the individual practice," and the "caliber of art teachers is unbelievable," with professors that "have exhibited at the MOMA and Guggenheim, just to name a few." Students from all major programs mix in the required humanities courses. Though the school's 2009 addition of a new academic building (housing the engineering and art programs, and bringing the total up to two) increased visibility, the building is "chronically short on space due to its atrium," and the school "could use more classrooms to work with." The academic prestige of the school attracts a high standard all around, and art, architects, and engineers come together "to create a rich environment for scholarly thinking, problem solving, learning, and debate."

Campus Life

Aside from classes, students have "ample opportunity to explore New York City" due to "the abundance of safe public transit and places of interest." The campus is in the heart of the East Village and accessible by two subway lines, so students "will often visit local off-campus businesses such as restaurants, stores, and gyms." The "limited on-campus food service," combined with the availability of stovetops in the residence hall, "encourages students to cook their own food when time permits." Meeting areas within the campus are utilized "for both group study and recreational uses," and the small campus (just two buildings) means students are "always near each other ready to chat and grab a coffee for a little break." The school "requires a lot of time to study in order to pass the courses" and "the life is packed"; many take to a bar on weekends or partake in "healthier activities like the gym; sports or video games (not as healthy) are also stress-management mechanisms."

Student Body

Students at the Cooper Union are "generally stressed and hardworking, but high-spirited." Most are "socially and politically left"; "almost everyone is pretty friendly," and finds their niche within the "small but complex community." These "highly intelligent...and helpful" students are there to succeed, and "school work is valued over social interaction." Many students have part-time jobs, and "the level students are at and their work ethic makes you feel like the people here are destined for success." This "strange and ambitious" group "excels in their field doing extra activities that they don't need to because of the curiosity and fun." "Everyone has their own thing that makes them tick," says a student.

THE COOPER UNION FOR THE ADVANCEMENT OF SCIENCE AND ART

Financial Aid: 212-353-4120 • E-Mail: admissions@cooper.edu • Website: www.cooper.edu

THE PRINCETON REVIEW SAYS

Admissions

The school reports that its standardized testing policy for use in admission for Fall 2024 is Test Optional. It is unknown at this time if the 2024 testing policy will be permanent. The Princeton Review suggests that interested applicants consult with the school for the most up-to-date standardized testing policies. *Very important factors considered include:* academic GPA, talent/ability. *Important factors considered include:* rigor of secondary school record, application essay, recommendation(s), interview, character/personal qualities. *Other factors considered include:* class rank, standardized test scores, extracurricular activities, first generation, alumni/ae relation, racial/ethnic status, volunteer work, work experience, level of applicant's interest. High school diploma is required and GED is accepted. *Academic units required:* 4 English, 1 math, 1 science, 1 social studies, 1 history, 8 academic electives. *Academic units recommended:* 4 English, 4 math, 3 science, 2 science labs, 4 foreign language, 2 social studies, 2 history, 4 computer science, 4 visual/performing arts.

Financial Aid

Students should submit: FAFSA. Priority filing deadline is 3/31. The Princeton Review suggests that all financial aid forms be submitted as soon as possible (see page 5 for a note on the FAFSA). *Need-based scholarships/grants offered:* College/university scholarship or grant aid from institutional funds; Federal Pell; Private scholarships; SEOG; State scholarships/grants. *Loan aid offered:* Direct PLUS loans; Direct Subsidized Loans; Direct Unsubsidized Loans. Admitted students will be notified of awards on a rolling basis beginning 1/5. Federal Work-Study Program available. Institutional employment available.

The Inside Word

The admission rate to Cooper Union is extremely competitive. All Cooper admits must be academically accomplished and top of their high school class, especially with the school taking a Test Optional policy through Fall 2024. That said, specific admissions requirements and application deadlines vary based on major, be it engineering, art, or architecture.

THE SCHOOL SAYS "..."

From the Admissions Office

"The Cooper Union was founded in 1859 in the East Village of Manhattan by inventor, industrialist, and social reformer, Peter Cooper. The Cooper Union is a top-ranked, all-honors college committed to making education fair and accessible to all. Every admitted undergraduate student is granted a half-tuition scholarship as well as need-based aid.

Comprised of three schools specializing in architecture, art, and engineering, The Cooper Union offers small, intimate classes organized around a culture of collaboration led by a faculty of teachers who are also leading practitioners in their fields. Throughout its history, Cooper has been a place where thinkers, builders, artists, activists, and dreamers have thrived and contributed to New York City and the world in large and small ways—being of this world and for this world. The Cooper Union also boasts its historic Great Hall; once the largest meeting space in New York City, the Great Hall has hosted 11 US presidents (from Abraham Lincoln to Barack Obama) as well as other national leaders and thinkers from Susan B. Anthony and Frederick Douglass to Congressman John Lewis, activist Gloria Steinem, and artist Ai Weiwei, among others."

SELECTIVITY

Admissions Rating	97
# of applicants	2,451
% of applicants accepted	14
% of acceptees attending	54
# offered a place on the wait list	96
% accepting a place on wait list	100
% admitted from wait list	25
# of early decision applicants	137
% accepted early decision	33

FIRST-YEAR PROFILE

Testing policy	Test Optional
Range SAT composite	1390–1510
Range SAT EBRW	670–740
Range SAT math	710–790
Range ACT composite	32–35
# submitting SAT scores	81
% submitting SAT scores	41
# submitting ACT scores	24
% submitting ACT scores	12
Average HS GPA	3.7
% frosh submitting high school GPA	92

DEADLINES

Early decision	
Deadline	11/1
Notification	12/15
Other ED deadline	12/1
Other ED notification	2/1
Regular	
Deadline	1/5
Notification	4/1
Nonfall registration?	No

APPLICANTS OFTEN PREFER

California Institute of Technology; Carnegie Mellon University; Cornell University; Johns Hopkins University; Massachusetts Institute of Technology; Princeton University; University of California—Berkeley; University of Pennsylvania; Yale University

APPLICANTS SOMETIMES PREFER

Columbia University; Georgia Institute of Technology; New York University; Rhode Island School of Design

APPLICANTS RARELY PREFER

Maryland Institute College of Art; Pratt Institute; State University of New York—Stony Brook University; State University of New York—Albany

FINANCIAL FACTS

Financial Aid Rating	83
Annual tuition	$44,550
Required fees	$2,270
Books and supplies	$1,800
Average frosh need-based scholarship	$48,165
Average UG need-based scholarship	$47,962
% needy frosh rec. need-based scholarship or grant aid	100
% needy UG rec. need-based scholarship or grant aid	61
% needy frosh rec. non-need-based scholarship or grant aid	100
% needy UG rec. non-need-based scholarship or grant aid	61
% needy frosh rec. need-based self-help aid	15
% needy UG rec. need-based self-help aid	17
% frosh rec. any financial aid	100
% UG rec. any financial aid	99
% UG borrow to pay for school	18
Average cumulative indebtedness	$7,388
% frosh need fully met	98
% ugrads need fully met	97
Average % of frosh need met	98
Average % of ugrad need met	97

CORNELL COLLEGE

600 First Street South West, Mount Vernon, IA 52314-1098 • Admissions: 319-895-4000 • Fax: 319-895-4451

CAMPUS LIFE

Quality of Life Rating	79
Fire Safety Rating	87
Green Rating	60*
Type of school	Private
Affiliation	Methodist
Environment	Rural

STUDENTS

Total undergrad enrollment	1,058
% male/female/another gender	52/44/4
% from out of state	78
% frosh from public high school	87
% frosh live on campus	98
% ugrads live on campus	93
# of fraternities (% join)	5 (8)
# of sororities (% join)	6 (18)
% African American	7
% Asian	4
% White	75
% Hispanic	9
% Native American	<1
% Pacific Islander	<1
% Two or more races	1
% Race and/or ethnicity unknown	1
% international	2
# of countries represented	19

SURVEY SAYS . . .

Class discussions encouraged
Easy to get around campus
Great library

ACADEMICS

Academic Rating	84
% students returning for sophomore year	80
% students graduating within 4 years	60
% students graduating within 6 years	63
Calendar	Other
Student/faculty ratio	13:1
Profs interesting rating	88
Profs accessible rating	94
Most classes have 10–19 students.	

MOST POPULAR MAJORS

Engineering, General; Biochemistry; Computer Science

STUDENTS SAY "..."

Academics

Cornell College, a small liberal arts school in Iowa, employs a unique one-course-at-a-time program, allowing students to focus on just one course (or "block") each month, providing an "intense, thorough, and complete immersion." Though students agree that this "doesn't give you any time to think about anything but the class you're in right then," it allows for personalized curricula design, and areas like the humanities "work perfectly with the block plan." Students also "always know when to find people," which makes it easy to get together. Some classes may not be the most challenging, but "upper-level courses are very engaging and fulfilling." It's very varied, according to one student: "You could have hours and hours of homework one block and practically none the next." The block plan makes it very easy to gain off-campus field experience or do international study, and it's "easier to try off-campus opportunities." Administration is generally "excellent at taking a personal interest in each student," though some note, "There is not much transparency at the administrative level," which can be "out of touch" at times. On the classroom side, professors "know how to motivate and encourage their students," and though "you may get a bad apple maybe once a year," they're "not only knowledgeable but dedicated." As one student puts it, "The personal attention you can receive from any given professor, if you seek them out, is especially rewarding." All in all, students love the block structure and the sense of community it creates, as "no matter what it is you may want to do, you can find someone to do it with you." One student claims he "cannot imagine learning any other way."

Campus Life

Since Cornell is very campus-focused, the school makes sure there's a large variety of campus organizations and "many events going on almost every weekend." Though there's definitely a "small-town quiet," Cedar Rapids and Iowa City are both only a twenty-minute drive away, and "ice climbing, rock-climbing, paddling, and hiking" are popular outdoor pastimes. It's also "fairly easy to start up a new club or group." In addition, the school provides fall, winter, and spring breaks as well as "block breaks," which last four and a half days and give students the opportunity to travel, go skiing or camping, and so on. The cold weather can cause problems here, in both a locked-in feel and the possibility for accidents, and students are encouraged to "bring snow boots!" Many here tend to have a love-hate relationship with sports; while athletics are a huge boon, "the athletes and the non-athletes are seldom friends." Much like the curriculum, lunchtimes are pretty unique, and students all eat in a common cafeteria, naturally falling into a somewhat "high school" habit of eating at the same tables every day. Most people stay on campus for entertainment and socializing, "creating a cohesive community." Parties do take place on weekends, and "drinking is popular on campus but never forced," but in general, "people are more interested in just having a good conversation with their peers."

Student Body

There's "a great diversity of interests" in people who attend Cornell, and the "super busy" students have a hard time defining a more common characteristic than the fact that almost all are driven and involved. Some division into typical groups does occur—"the cafeteria design and Greek life are very conducive to this problem"—but "even group to group there is always mingling because you never know who will be in your next class." Since the classes are so small and "you see the same people four hours a day for three and a half weeks," people are generally accepting, and "you have to be really, really strange here to stick out." As one freshman says, "The only intolerance I've seen is toward the consistently indolent."

CORNELL COLLEGE

Financial Aid: 319-895-4216 • E-Mail: admission@cornellcollege.edu • Website: www.cornellcollege.edu/index.shtml

THE PRINCETON REVIEW SAYS

Admissions

The school reports that its standardized testing policy for use in admission for Fall 2024 is Test Optional. The 2024 testing policy will be permanent. The Princeton Review suggests that interested applicants consult with the school for the most up-to-date standardized testing policies. *Very important factors considered include:* academic GPA. *Important factors considered include:* application essay. *Other factors considered include:* rigor of secondary school record, class rank, recommendation(s), interview, extracurricular activities, character/personal qualities, first generation, alumni/ae relation, geographical residence, state residency, racial/ethnic status, volunteer work, work experience, level of applicant's interest. High school diploma is required and GED is accepted. *Academic units recommended:* 4 English, 3 math, 3 science, 2 science labs, 2 foreign language, 3 social studies.

Financial Aid

Students should submit: FAFSA. Priority filing deadline is 3/1. The Princeton Review suggests that all financial aid forms be submitted as soon as possible (see page 5 for a note on the FAFSA). *Need-based scholarships/grants offered:* College/university scholarship or grant aid from institutional funds; Federal Pell; SEOG; State scholarships/grants. *Loan aid offered:* Direct PLUS loans; Direct Subsidized Loans; Direct Unsubsidized Loans; College/university loans from institutional funds. Admitted students will be notified of awards on a rolling basis beginning 12/15. Federal Work-Study Program available. Institutional employment available.

The Inside Word

Given Cornell's relatively unique approach to study, it's no surprise that the admissions committee here focuses attention on both academic and personal strengths. Cornell's small, highly self-selected applicant pool is chock-full of students with solid self-awareness, motivation, and discipline.

THE SCHOOL SAYS "..."

From the Admissions Office

"Cornell College, a selective liberal arts college in Mount Vernon, Iowa, is one of the colleges featured in *Colleges That Change Lives.* Characterized by the life-changing academic immersion of its One Course At A Time curriculum, this distinctive approach allows students to focus on a single academic subject per eighteen-day block. It lays the foundation for a student's entire Cornell education through transformative intellectual partnerships and close-knit learning communities that bring out the best in our ambitious students. The One Course curriculum mirrors the pace of most working environments where employees are expected to handle tight deadlines and high expectations on every project, every day. Since there is never more than one course to focus on, faculty can take entire classes on field trips for a day or an entire block. Cornell's residential campus attracts a student body from 45 states and 16 foreign countries. Together, they experience a vast array of off-campus opportunities designed to take them into the world to fulfill their academic and personal goals, as well as a lineup of speakers and entertainment options that brings the world to them. Cornell College is frequently cited as a 'Best Buy.' Ninety-three percent of Cornell graduates complete their degrees in four years, and 55 percent go on to complete an advanced degree."

SELECTIVITY

Admissions Rating	88
# of applicants	3,057
% of applicants accepted	79
% of acceptees attending	14
# of early decision applicants	0

FIRST-YEAR PROFILE

Testing policy	Test Optional
Range SAT composite	1210–1320
Range SAT EBRW	600–690
Range SAT math	570–690
Range ACT composite	23–90
# submitting SAT scores	33
% submitting SAT scores	24
# submitting ACT scores	84
% submitting ACT scores	60
Average HS GPA	3.6
% frosh submitting high school GPA	100
% graduated top 10% of class	14
% graduated top 25% of class	47
% graduated top 50% of class	82

DEADLINES

Early action	
Deadline	11/1
Nonfall registration?	Yes

APPLICANTS ALSO LOOK AT

Arizona State University; Iowa State University; St. Olaf College; University of Colorado Boulder; University of Illinois at Chicago; University of Illinois—Urbana-Champaign; University of Iowa; University of Minnesota—Twin Cities

FINANCIAL FACTS

Financial Aid Rating	77
Annual tuition	$49,970
Room and board	$11,198
Required fees	$644
Books and supplies	$1,200
Average frosh need-based scholarship	$36,538
Average UG need-based scholarship	$35,839
% needy frosh rec. need-based scholarship or grant aid	100
% needy UG rec. need-based scholarship or grant aid	100
% needy frosh rec. non-need-based scholarship or grant aid	25
% needy UG rec. non-need-based scholarship or grant aid	22
% needy frosh rec. need-based self-help aid	73
% needy UG rec. need-based self-help aid	73
% frosh rec. any financial aid	100
% UG rec. any financial aid	99
% UG borrow to pay for school	64
Average cumulative indebtedness	$41,124
% frosh need fully met	30
% ugrads need fully met	27
Average % of frosh need met	88
Average % of ugrad need met	86

CORNELL UNIVERSITY

410 Thurston Avenue, Ithaca, NY 14850 • Admissions: 607-255-2000 • Fax: 607-255-0659

STUDENTS SAY "..."

Academics

The westernmost of the Ivies, Cornell University provides its students with a prestigious education, paired with "an unwavering commitment to leave a positive impact on the world." The school is "more than a bunch of books and exams—it's an experience that challenges students to break free from their comfort zones." Seven different undergraduate colleges (including the Cornell SC Johnson College of Business) "really make it feel small and specialized," and provide "top notch faculty." The university is "a place where any person can find instruction in any study (and it won't feel like work)," as it allows its students to explore any kind of interest they may have (ranging from Punk Rock as a literary genre to particle physics) while "also offering an incredible amount of depth within each department." There are endless opportunities to "pursue other topics, enhance your knowledge of things that you're already interested in, and try completely random things that you'd never even heard of before." Professors are "experts in their field, almost always conducting their own research, and are enthusiastic about passing their knowledge on to their students."

"[Since] being in Ithaca, you're kind of in the middle of nowhere," and there are plenty of reasons to focus on your studies, but "Cornell as an administration keeps the faculty, research, and access to the most recent information so up-to-date that this campus is as connected as any place in the world." Between balancing those amazing resources and the community feel, the Cornell bigwigs get a lot of applause, as they have "proven time and time again that they care, both on an individual and system-wide level." Great internships, a strong alumni network, and "boundless opportunities after graduation" round out the "definition of amazing" that is Cornell University. "I was intimidated to go here, but now I will say that I cannot imagine going anywhere else," says a junior.

Campus Life

As they say, "Ithaca is gorges," so hiking and outdoor activities are big pastimes. The "absolutely gorgeous campus" in the Finger Lakes region allows students to "truly, purely enjoy their time here" by "experiencing the natural beauties of Upstate New York, along with the eccentricity of surrounding town." The school's infrastructure is "intense"—"we have our own dairy so that we can make our own milk, for goodness sake"—and "there's just so much going on at every moment [that] the hard part is choosing what it is you want to do." Many admit that various aspects of Cornell life can cause stress—the upperclass housing lottery, course enrollment system, workload, and difficulty studying abroad all get singled out—but students are able to discern when to kick back and enjoy themselves. Fun can range anywhere from "an awesome party in Collegetown to a movie night in the dorm while ordering insomnia cookies," but "it's definitely acceptable to turn down weekend plans because you have too much work to do."

Student Body

With so many different colleges within Cornell, there is "a plethora of diverse students" here, but the underlying commonality between all students is "ambition and ability." "From farm kids and pre-med students to engineers and hoteliers, Cornell is home to all sorts of students," says one. "You'll find yourself with a roommate who was on Team USA, a friend who was a firefighter, and a classmate who's backpacked around the world." The integration of people with eclectic interests "[inspires] others to become active students," which is easily enough done at a university with hundreds upon hundreds of student organizations. "Everyone's smart and that's just accepted," but "a competitive environment isn't created." Cornellians are "very committed to academics but always know how to put books aside and relax." Most do research and volunteer work, and many "are involved in some form of Greek life."

CORNELL UNIVERSITY

Financial Aid: 607-255-5145 • E-Mail: admissions@cornell.edu • Website: www.cornell.edu

THE PRINCETON REVIEW SAYS

Admissions

The school reports that its standardized testing policy for use in admission for Fall 2024 is Test Optional. It is unknown at this time if the 2024 testing policy will be permanent. The Princeton Review suggests that interested applicants consult with the school for the most up-to-date standardized testing policies. *Very important factors considered include:* rigor of secondary school record, academic GPA, application essay, recommendation(s), extra-curricular activities, talent/ability, character/personal qualities. *Important factors considered include:* class rank. *Other factors considered include:* standardized test scores, interview, first generation, alumni/ae relation, geographical residence, state residency, racial/ethnic status, volunteer work, work experience.

Financial Aid

Students should submit: CSS/Financial Aid Profile; FAFSA. The Princeton Review suggests that all financial aid forms be submitted as soon as possible (see page 5 for a note on the FAFSA). *Need-based scholarships/grants offered:* College/university scholarship or grant aid from institutional funds; Federal Pell; Private scholarships; SEOG; State scholarships/grants. *Loan aid offered:* Direct PLUS loans; Direct Subsidized Loans; Direct Unsubsidized Loans; College/university loans from institutional funds. Admitted students will be notified of awards on or about 4/1. Federal Work-Study Program available. Institutional employment available.

The Inside Word

Gaining admission to Cornell is a tough coup regardless of your intended field of study, but some of the university's seven colleges are more competitive than others. If you're thinking of trying to "backdoor" your way into one of the most competitive schools—by gaining admission to a less competitive one, then transferring after one year—be aware that you will have to resubmit the entire application and provide a statement outlining your academic plans. It's not impossible to accomplish, but Cornell works hard to discourage this sort of maneuvering.

THE SCHOOL SAYS "..."

From the Admissions Office

"Cornell University, an Ivy League school and land-grant university located in the scenic Finger Lakes region of central New York, provides an outstanding education to students in seven small to midsize undergraduate colleges: Agriculture and Life Sciences; Architecture, Art, and Planning; Arts and Sciences; Engineering; Cornell SC Johnson College of Business; Human Ecology; and Industrial and Labor Relations. Cornellians come from all fifty states and more than 90 countries, and they pursue their academic goals in more than 100 departments. The College of Arts and Sciences, one of the smallest liberal arts schools in the Ivy League, offers more than forty majors, most of which rank near the top nationwide. Applied programs in the other six colleges also rank among the best in the world. Other special features of the university include a world-renowned faculty; over 4,000 courses available to all students; an extensive undergraduate research program; superb research, teaching, and library facilities; a large, diverse study abroad program; and more than 1,000 student organizations and thirty-six varsity sports. Cornell's campus is one of the most beautiful in the country; students pass streams, rocky gorges, and waterfalls on their way to class. First-year students make their home on North Campus, a living-learning community that features a special advising center, faculty-in-residence, a fitness center, and traditional residence halls as well as theme-centered buildings such as Ecology House. Cornell University invites applications from all interested students and uses the Common Application of the Universal College Application with a short required Cornell Supplement."

SELECTIVITY

Admissions Rating	99
# of applicants	67,380
% of applicants accepted	9
% of acceptees attending	64
# offered a place on the wait list	7,746
% accepting a place on wait list	75
% admitted from wait list	0
# of early decision applicants	6,630
% accepted early decision	24

FIRST-YEAR PROFILE

Testing policy	Test Optional
Range SAT composite	1450–1540
Range SAT EBRW	700–760
Range SAT math	750–800
Range ACT composite	33–35
# submitting SAT scores	1,517
% submitting SAT scores	41
# submitting ACT scores	735
% submitting ACT scores	20
% graduated top 10% of class	84
% graduated top 25% of class	97
% graduated top 50% of class	100

DEADLINES

Early decision	
Deadline	11/1
Notification	12/15
Regular	
Deadline	1/2
Notification	4/1
Nonfall registration?	Yes

FINANCIAL FACTS

Financial Aid Rating	97
Annual tuition	$60,286
Room and board	$16,446
Required fees	$729
Books and supplies	$1,000
Average frosh need-based scholarship	$51,026
Average UG need-based scholarship	$49,390
% needy frosh rec. need-based scholarship or grant aid	98
% needy UG rec. need-based scholarship or grant aid	98
% needy frosh rec. non-need-based scholarship or grant aid	0
% needy UG rec. non-need-based scholarship or grant aid	0
% needy frosh rec. need-based self-help aid	70
% needy UG rec. need-based self-help aid	67
% frosh rec. any financial aid	50
% UG rec. any financial aid	48
% UG borrow to pay for school	38
Average cumulative indebtedness	$26,865
% frosh need fully met	100
% ugrads need fully met	100
Average % of frosh need met	100
Average % of ugrad need met	100

CREIGHTON UNIVERSITY

2500 California Plaza, Omaha, NE 68178 • Admissions: 402-280-2700 • Fax: 402-280-2685

STUDENTS SAY ". . ."

Academics

Omaha's Creighton University is a Jesuit institution that prides itself on "shaping the whole person," which means that students find themselves "extremely involved in academic and extracurricular activities." As for the core class structure, all of its more than four thousand undergraduates must fulfill a set curriculum, with a variety of course options available for all requirements (other than a required one-hour oral communication course). By all accounts, this "sets you up very well for success," with students adding that the process "nearly holds your hand into your first job" and "prepares you for the next step, whether that is medical school, law school, or going out to work in the real world." Creighton "works so hard to make sure their students are successful learners and thinkers" by offering programs like EDGE, an all-inclusive tutoring, academic coaching, and academic counseling service that doubles as "a great platform for advisors to gear students to explore certain classes while remaining on track." All of this helps in "cultivating a safe community where we're encouraged to dive into what we believe, figure out what that is exactly, and serve others."

Creighton boasts an 12:1 student-faculty ratio, which leads to "really awesome relationships with faculty and many opportunities for things like undergraduate research." Professors go above and beyond in all ways, from doing their best "not to make lectures dry and boring" to being super receptive to students. Courses offered "are challenging to say the least," but because teachers are "willing to work on your terms and help at all hours of the day and night," both in and out of the classroom, it's a "very rewarding and manageable" process. Dialogue is also crucial: teachers "love when you ask questions" and many utilize a flipped classroom, where peers teach the rest of the class, which "provides a broken-down and simplified way of explaining difficult topics to provide clarification and insight." Adding to the variety and support offered, there are plenty of "field trips that [are] very interesting and insightful" and opportunities for "many upperclassmen [to] participate in research or internships."

Campus Life

The pace at Creighton tends to be a busy one, and not just because of academic or school-related activities: "A lot of students work." That said, things get a bit more relaxed on weekends, which "consist of sporting events, parties, fraternity events, and the like." Creighton students are "very supportive of one another and go to all the home soccer, basketball, baseball, and volleyball games for both men and women's teams," and "people often take part in sports or group exercise programs on campus." The city setting also means that the "campus is a few blocks away from Old Market and Midtown which are full of activities, shops, and restaurants," and there are "also gorgeous outdoor places to go running/walking near downtown when the weather is nice." Students "are encouraged to form clubs and join organizations," and "the resources available to students are absolutely endless."

Student Body

There's a sense of togetherness at Creighton, to the extent that, because there's an "expectation that you go to class every day and on time...if you don't, people will reach out." In short, the community is "very goal-oriented toward their careers," although not in an oppressive sense. If anything, students describe the atmosphere as "fun and light-hearted" and note that "wherever you go you will find a welcoming environment." (This applies across all grades, with students noting that senior students "work hard to make [first-years] feel at home during the first couple weeks at school.") Students are in it together, according to those who list "service and giving back" as a core value, and there's an eagerness described for all activities: "When it comes to getting involved with student organizations and other things on campus, students will jump at the chance to do so."

CREIGHTON UNIVERSITY

Financial Aid: 402-280-2731 • E-Mail: admissions@creighton.edu • Website: www.creighton.edu

THE PRINCETON REVIEW SAYS

Admissions

The school reports that its standardized testing policy for use in admission for Fall 2024 is Test Optional. The 2024 testing policy will be permanent. The Princeton Review suggests that interested applicants consult with the school for the most up-to-date standardized testing policies. *Very important factors considered include:* rigor of secondary school record, academic GPA. *Important factors considered include:* application essay. *Other factors considered include:* class rank, standardized test scores, recommendation(s), extracurricular activities, talent/ability, character/personal qualities, first generation, racial/ethnic status, volunteer work, level of applicant's interest. High school diploma is required and GED is accepted. *Academic units required:* 4 English, 3 math, 2 science, 1 science lab, 2 foreign language, 2 social studies, 3 academic electives. *Academic units recommended:* 4 English, 4 math, 3 science, 2 science labs, 3 foreign language, 4 social studies, 3 academic electives.

Financial Aid

Students should submit: FAFSA; Institution's own financial aid form. Priority filing deadline is 1/15. The Princeton Review suggests that all financial aid forms be submitted as soon as possible (see page 5 for a note on the FAFSA). *Need-based scholarships/grants offered:* College/university scholarship or grant aid from institutional funds; Federal Pell; Private scholarships; SEOG; State scholarships/grants. *Loan aid offered:* Direct PLUS loans; Direct Subsidized Loans; Direct Unsubsidized Loans; College/university loans from institutional funds; Federal Nursing Loans. Admitted students will be notified of awards on a rolling basis beginning 2/15. Federal Work-Study Program available. Institutional employment available.

The Inside Word

Creighton University proudly takes a holistic approach to the admissions game. The school doesn't maintain any strict standardized test score or GPA minimums. However, the committee does scour transcripts for evidence of academic rigor and intellectual curiosity. Applicants who have taken multiple advanced placement, honors, or IB classes will have a leg up; the school also (optionally) considers superscores for both the SAT and ACT. Moreover, as a Jesuit university, Creighton is partial to students who are committed to making the world a better place. Candidates with a passion for social justice issues will be noted.

THE SCHOOL SAYS "..."

From the Admissions Office

"Students come to Creighton University for the opportunities of a lifetime. Our 9 schools and colleges deliver a powerful education that connects renowned programs in arts and sciences, law and business with 9 health professions programs. We are expanding opportunities for medical and health sciences to our new Phoenix campus. Creighton's rigorous academics and commitment to Jesuit, Catholic values creates an environment that fosters academic excellence, social justice and personal growth. Our 4,000+ undergraduates find new possibilities through personalized advising, a strong focus on leadership skills and undergraduate research. The Center for Undergraduate Research and Scholarship (CURAS) ensures that undergraduates work directly with faculty researchers, present at national conferences and publish in scholarly journals. And not all learning takes place in the classroom or lab. With 4 Fortune 500 company headquarters located close to campus, Creighton business students find more paid internship opportunities than there are students to fill them. Students find life-changing experiences through community service opportunities, contributing more than 1 million hours of service locally, regionally, nationally and internationally each year.

"At Creighton, you get it all—a 99% success rate (graduates employed, enrolled in graduate/professional school or in volunteer programs within 6 months of graduation); an 11:1 student-to-faculty ratio; 60+ undergraduate majors; honors programs; abundant service opportunities; study abroad, including our 4-year educational and professional development Global Scholars Program; BIG EAST athletic competition; 200+ clubs and organizations and more—because Creighton University is the complete package."

SELECTIVITY

Admissions Rating	89
# of applicants	8,681
% of applicants accepted	64
% of acceptees attending	18
# offered a place on the wait list	165
% accepting a place on wait list	28
% admitted from wait list	57

FIRST-YEAR PROFILE

Testing policy	Test Optional
Range SAT composite	1155–1320
Range SAT EBRW	570–670
Range SAT math	570–670
Range ACT composite	24–30
# submitting SAT scores	323
% submitting SAT scores	32
# submitting ACT scores	820
% submitting ACT scores	81
Average HS GPA	3.9
% frosh submitting high school GPA	100
% graduated top 10% of class	43
% graduated top 25% of class	73
% graduated top 50% of class	93

DEADLINES

Early action	
Deadline	11/1
Regular	
Priority	12/1
Notification	Rolling, 11/1
Nonfall registration?	Yes

APPLICANTS OFTEN PREFER
University of Notre Dame

APPLICANTS SOMETIMES PREFER
University of Minnesota—Twin Cities; University of Wisconsin—Madison

APPLICANTS RARELY PREFER
Fordham University; Loyola University of Chicago; Marquette University; University of Kansas

FINANCIAL FACTS

Financial Aid Rating	85
Annual tuition	$42,618
Room and board	$11,700
Required fees	$1,906
Books and supplies	$1,200
Average frosh need-based scholarship	$25,431
Average UG need-based scholarship	$23,895
% needy frosh rec. need-based scholarship or grant aid	99
% needy UG rec. need-based scholarship or grant aid	95
% needy frosh rec. non-need-based scholarship or grant aid	34
% needy UG rec. non-need-based scholarship or grant aid	23
% needy frosh rec. need-based self-help aid	68
% needy UG rec. need-based self-help aid	76
% frosh rec. any financial aid	100
% UG rec. any financial aid	97
% UG borrow to pay for school	55
Average cumulative indebtedness	$40,341
% frosh need fully met	37
% ugrads need fully met	27
Average % of frosh need met	87
Average % of ugrad need met	81

DARTMOUTH COLLEGE

6016 McNutt Hall, Hanover, NH 03755 • Admissions: 603-646-1110 • Fax: 603-646-1216

STUDENTS SAY " . . ."

Academics

Tucked away in bucolic New Hampshire, Dartmouth College manages to strike a nice "balance between the intimacy of a college [and] the opportunity of a university." Students feel fortunate that the administration places an "emphasis on pursuing passions, and making the college experience your own." And while Dartmouth certainly maintains a "competitive" atmosphere, students here truly appreciate that "no one really talks about their grades openly." Indeed, it's "generally understood that everyone is smart." A neuroscience major tells us that academically, "Dartmouth puts a huge focus on the undergraduate students, and I have found my professors to be available and engaging in nearly every instance. My classes are all challenging, but they are very discussion based and tend to be small, which keeps me working hard and interested in the material." And an impressed Middle Eastern studies major interjects, "I came to Dartmouth for the professors, but they were far beyond anything I could have hoped for. Not only are they great lecturers and accomplished scholars, they go out of their way to be available outside of the classroom, and to forge relationships beyond what is expected or necessary." When it comes down to it, "Dartmouth is considered to be a combination of Hogwarts and Disney World because it is known for its community and intelligent students and faculty, who also are personable and know how to have fun."

Campus Life

To instill a sense of community, all students are sorted into one of six houses when they arrive on campus, and that community, including the physical neighborhood, is a constant through a student's four years at the College. At Dartmouth, the "Greek system is the main source of social activity." However, if you're wary of fraternities and sororities, fret not. A biology major reveals that a "very large percentage of students are involved which makes the Greek houses quite diverse and representative of the student body as a whole." Indeed, fraternities "are very inclusive." Further, plenty of social options exist beyond the party scene. "On any given night, you can do anything from see a hockey game to the early premiere of some cool new movie at the Hop[kins Center for the Arts], you can go to a dance party or just play cards or jam out on guitar or something...there are so many options to do whatever you're interested in doing." Dartmouth undergrads also love convening with nature. "Outdoorsy activities are huge here. The Appalachian Trail literally runs right through our campus. The Dartmouth Outing Club is the oldest and largest college outing club, and many students (even students who never did so before college) get involved with hiking, canoeing, rock climbing, and so forth." And a philosophy major concludes, "Whether it's skating on Occom Pond, going on a hike, going kayaking, apple picking, thrift shopping...there are boundless opportunities."

Student Body

Undergrads here emphatically insist that it's "hard to define a typical student because at Dartmouth literally every type of person is represented." Of course, if pressed, they might reluctantly admit that the average student comes across as "preppy, academically goal oriented but also extremely social." And, as you might expect, undergrads also report that their peers are certainly very "smart." Fortunately, they "do not boast about their intellectual capacity." A happy senior tells us that "the common denominator is that Dartmouth students are very involved." Indeed, "whether it's with a club sports team, a cappella group, community service project, academic research, or a Greek house, Dartmouth students manage to do a lot of things in the course of the day." One incredulous sophomore concurs, adding that his friends "are always studying and participating in some extracurricular activity and you wonder how they have time to sleep and then you will see them out at a frat too. Then they show up at class the next morning with all of the work completed and they seem like a magician." Finally a junior concludes, "It's a small enough school that there is a sense of community that's always present, but large enough that everyone can find their own niche and their own area of the school and the community that caters to them perfectly."

DARTMOUTH COLLEGE

Financial Aid: 800-443-3605 • E-Mail: admissions.office@dartmouth.edu • Website: www.dartmouth.edu

THE PRINCETON REVIEW SAYS

Admissions

The school reports that its standardized testing policy for use in admission for Fall 2024 is Test Optional. It is unknown at this time if the 2024 testing policy will be permanent. The Princeton Review suggests that interested applicants consult with the school for the most up-to-date standardized testing policies. *Very important factors considered include:* rigor of secondary school record, class rank, academic GPA, standardized test scores, application essay, recommendation(s), extracurricular activities, character/personal qualities. *Important factors considered include:* talent/ability. *Other factors considered include:* interview, first generation, alumni/ae relation, geographical residence, racial/ethnic status, volunteer work, work experience, level of applicant's interest. High school diploma or equivalent is not required. *Academic units recommended:* 4 English, 4 math, 4 science, 4 foreign language, 4 social studies.

Financial Aid

Students should submit: Business/Farm Supplement; CSS/Financial Aid Profile; FAFSA; Noncustodial Profile. The Princeton Review suggests that all financial aid forms be submitted as soon as possible (see page 5 for a note on the FAFSA). *Need-based scholarships/grants offered:* College/university scholarship or grant aid from institutional funds; Federal Pell; Private scholarships; SEOG; State scholarships/grants. *Loan aid offered:* Direct PLUS loans; Direct Subsidized Loans; Direct Unsubsidized Loans; College/university loans from institutional funds; State Loans. Admitted students will be notified of awards on or about 4/2. Federal Work-Study Program available. Institutional employment available.

The Inside Word

Competition to secure a coveted acceptance letter from Dartmouth is fierce. After all, the majority of admitted students are in the top of their respective high school classes. Therefore, academic success is mandatory for any serious contender as is a schedule chock-full of honors, AP and/or IB courses. Of course, admissions officers are looking for well-rounded students so extracurricular activities, personal statements and recommendations will also be closely assessed. Finally, it's important to know that starting with 2022 high school graduates, Dartmouth will be need blind for all students.

THE SCHOOL SAYS "..."

From the Admissions Office

"Dartmouth College is a fusion of renowned liberal arts college and robust research university, where faculty are scholars who teach, and where students partner with them to take on the world's challenges. All classes are taught by professors who are advancing the frontiers of knowledge teaching, mentoring, and collaborating with undergraduates in and out of class.

"The curriculum and structure of Dartmouth's ten-week terms, the College's extensive foreign study programs, and Dartmouth's revolutionary language-learning model, the Rassias Method, allow students to pursue their research and passions around the world while staying on track with their academic aspirations. Dartmouth graduates enter the world equipped with experience, connections, and opportunities on a global scale.

"With a profound sense of place and powerful sense of community developed over its 253-year history, Dartmouth is home to many beloved traditions, from Winter Carnival to the Homecoming Bonfire. Each season brings a new energy and set of events to campus. The adventuresome spirit of the College permeates its nearly 400 student groups, from the country's oldest outing club to 35 Division I varsity teams and a vibrant arts scene.

"Dartmouth's holistic, need-blind admissions process is designed to identify students who will thrive in this intimate environment of curiosity and creativity. There is no 'typical' Dartmouth student, but all Dartmouth students tend to share a passion for intellectual inquiry, a willingness to embrace adventure, and a desire to build a close-knit community."

SELECTIVITY

Admissions Rating	99
# of applicants	28,356
% of applicants accepted	6
% of acceptees attending	70
# offered a place on the wait list	2,669
% accepting a place on wait list	79
% admitted from wait list	0
# of early decision applicants	2,664
% accepted early decision	25

FIRST-YEAR PROFILE

Testing policy	Test Optional
Range SAT composite	1430–1550
Range SAT EBRW	710–770
Range SAT math	730–790
Range ACT composite	32–35
# submitting SAT scores	605
% submitting SAT scores	57
# submitting ACT scores	452
% submitting ACT scores	43
% graduated top 10% of class	94
% graduated top 25% of class	99
% graduated top 50% of class	100

DEADLINES

Early decision	
Deadline	11/1
Notification	12/23
Regular	
Deadline	1/2
Notification	3/31
Nonfall registration?	No

APPLICANTS OFTEN PREFER

Harvard College; Princeton University; Stanford University; Yale University

APPLICANTS SOMETIMES PREFER

Brown University; Columbia University; Massachusetts Institute of Technology; University of Pennsylvania

APPLICANTS RARELY PREFER

Cornell University; Duke University; Johns Hopkins University; Northwestern University; The University of Chicago; Vanderbilt University

FINANCIAL FACTS

Financial Aid Rating	97
Annual tuition	$58,953
Room and board	$17,361
Required fees	$1,695
Required fees (first-year)	$1,917
Books and supplies	$1,005
Average frosh need-based scholarship	$63,279
Average UG need-based scholarship	$60,490
% needy frosh rec. need-based scholarship or grant aid	98
% needy UG rec. need-based scholarship or grant aid	97
% needy frosh rec. non-need-based scholarship or grant aid	0
% needy UG rec. non-need-based scholarship or grant aid	0
% needy frosh rec. need-based self-help aid	87
% needy UG rec. need-based self-help aid	92
% frosh rec. any financial aid	56
% UG rec. any financial aid	
% UG borrow to pay for school	34
Average cumulative indebtedness	$23,217
% frosh need fully met	100
% ugrads need fully met	100
Average % of frosh need met	100
Average % of ugrad need met	100

DAVIDSON COLLEGE

405 N. Main Street, Davidson, NC 28035-7156 • Admissions: 704-894-2000 • Fax: 704-894-2016

STUDENTS SAY "..."

Academics

This small school north of Charlotte, North Carolina, cultivates an environment "that is very open to change and improvement" and empowers students to "be better people and make a difference in the world." The administration works hard to create an on-campus community and constantly makes efforts "to support and improve Davidson," all while keeping students happy and their minds full. "I have never witnessed people so eager to come do their job every day. [Professors] are almost too willing to help," says a student. There is also a trickle-down effect because even the student body is supportive and "eager to watch you succeed." The school offers a classic liberal arts education, and students suggest that they all "come out smarter than they came in" as a result of the encouragement to take classes in all areas. "If I could spend twenty years being educated by this administration and these professors, I would," says a very happy junior. School is the number one priority for all of the students here, and while academics are all-consuming, time-wise, they are also "fascinating and rewarding." Without a doubt, Davidson is a tough school—"99 percent of us left our 4.0 GPAs back in high school," claims a student—and professors don't believe in grade inflation or curving grades, but they do readily make themselves available outside of class for help or discussion. There is a lot of work, but it "is accompanied by even more resources with which it can be successfully managed." One student testimonial: "My calculus teacher last semester had office hours in the student union, and he invited the whole class over to his house for chicken dinner—twice!" The dedication of the staff is contagious, and "though the work is rigorous, time spent in school never feels wasted."

Campus Life

Davidson "possesses an intense study culture, and people hit the books regularly; it's cool to be smart." One of the many wonderful things about Davidson "is that academics voluntarily leave the classroom." "It's not uncommon to hear people discussing their current academic topics at lunch or in the gym." Basketball is a huge common ground for the student body at large; "Everyone enjoys being a part of the underdog/Cinderella story." Weeks are devoted to study, as well as extracurricular activities—"you see your friends because you are doing homework together or eating meals together, not because you're vegging out." Of course, even Davidson students need to kick back, and there are always plenty of parties to be found on the weekends. Fraternities and eating houses (the Davidson version of sororities) are popular. Fortunately, "there really is no pressure to drink. You can go out and dance and have a great time or have movie nights with friends," says a student. The combination of the idyllic atmosphere and the workload "can make it hard to stay up-to-date on current events, yet most students remain well-informed."

Student Body

Davidson is "an amalgamation of all types of people, religiously, ethnically, politically, economically, etc.," all "united under the umbrella of intellectual curiosity" and their devotion to the school as a community. The typical Davidson student is "probably white," but admissions has been making progress in racially diversifying the campus, which students agree is necessary. Though there are plenty of southern, preppy, athletic types to fit the brochure examples, there are many niches for every type of "atypical" student. "There are enough people that one can find a similar group to connect with, and there are few enough people that one ends up connecting with dissimilar [people] anyway," says a student. Everyone here is smart and well-rounded; admissions "does a good job...so if you're in, you'll probably make the cut all the way through the four years." Most students have several extracurriculars to round out their free time, and they have a healthy desire to enjoy themselves when the books shut. "During the week we work hard. On the weekends we play hard. We don't do anything halfway," says a senior. Though the majority of students lean to the left, there's a strong conservative contingent, and there are no real problems between the two.

DAVIDSON COLLEGE

E-Mail: admission@davidson.edu • Website: www.davidson.edu

THE PRINCETON REVIEW SAYS

Admissions

The school reports that its standardized testing policy for use in admission for Fall 2024 is Test Optional. The testing policy is permanent. The Princeton Review suggests that interested applicants consult with the school for the most up-to-date standardized testing policies. *Very important factors considered include:* rigor of secondary school record, recommendation(s), character/personal qualities, volunteer work. *Important factors considered include:* application essay, extracurricular activities, talent/ability. *Other factors considered include:* class rank, academic GPA, standardized test scores, alumni/ae relation. High school diploma is required and GED is not accepted. *Academic units required:* 4 English, 3 math, 2 science, 2 foreign language. *Academic units recommended:* 4 math, 4 science, 4 foreign language.

Financial Aid

Students should submit: CSS/Financial Aid Profile; FAFSA; Noncustodial Profile. The Princeton Review suggests that all financial aid forms be submitted as soon as possible (see page 5 for a note on the FAFSA). *Need-based scholarships/grants offered:* College/university scholarship or grant aid from institutional funds; Federal Pell; Private scholarships; SEOG; State scholarships/grants. *Loan aid offered:* Direct PLUS loans; Direct Subsidized Loans; Direct Unsubsidized Loans. Admitted students will be notified of awards on or about same as admissions notification. Federal Work-Study Program available. Institutional employment available.

The Inside Word

The combination of Davidson's low acceptance rate and high yield really packs a punch. Prospective applicants beware: securing admission at this prestigious school is no easy feat. Admitted students are typically at the top of their high school classes and, if submitted, have strong standardized test scores. Candidates with leadership experience generally garner the favor of admissions officers. The college takes its honor code seriously and, as a result, seeks out students of demonstrated reputable character.

THE SCHOOL SAYS "..."

From the Admissions Office

"Davidson is a community defined by smart, driven and kind people. The relationships and experiences here cultivate the qualities needed in the world today: curiosity, empathy, integrity and courage. The college merges challenging academics with a distinctly supportive community. Mentors push and counsel. Classmates challenge and collaborate. Davidson students are encouraged to think critically, communicate with audiences from all backgrounds and navigate the unfamiliar through research, internships, a campus-based innovation and entrepreneurship hub, and international experience. A strong honor code means doing right when no one is watching. The Davidson community supports student artists and cheers for Division I athletes who are roommates, classmates and friends. Through The Davidson Trust, the college meets 100 percent of calculated financial need for domestic applicants through grants and student employment. Davidson's financial aid packages do not include student loans."

SELECTIVITY

Admissions Rating	97
# of applicants	6,479
% of applicants accepted	17
% of acceptees attending	49
# of early decision applicants	810
% accepted early decision	43

FIRST-YEAR PROFILE

Testing policy	Test Optional
Range SAT composite	1360–1490
Range SAT EBRW	670–740
Range SAT math	680–760
Range ACT composite	31–33
# submitting SAT scores	181
% submitting SAT scores	33
# submitting ACT scores	162
% submitting ACT scores	30
Average HS GPA	3.8
% frosh submitting high school GPA	100
% graduated top 10% of class	69
% graduated top 25% of class	94
% graduated top 50% of class	99

DEADLINES

Early decision	
Deadline	11/15
Notification	12/15
Other ED deadline	1/7
Other ED notification	2/1
Regular	
Deadline	1/10
Notification	4/1
Nonfall registration?	No

FINANCIAL FACTS

Financial Aid Rating	97
Annual tuition	$58,970
Room and board	$16,400
Required fees	$540
Required fees (first-year)	$790
Books and supplies	$1,000
Average frosh need-based scholarship	$52,871
Average UG need-based scholarship	$52,898
% needy frosh rec. need-based scholarship or grant aid	99
% needy UG rec. need-based scholarship or grant aid	99
% needy frosh rec. non-need-based scholarship or grant aid	38
% needy UG rec. non-need-based scholarship or grant aid	28
% needy frosh rec. need-based self-help aid	59
% needy UG rec. need-based self-help aid	62
% frosh rec. any financial aid	57
% UG rec. any financial aid	56
% UG borrow to pay for school	22
Average cumulative indebtedness	$23,409
% frosh need fully met	100
% ugrads need fully met	100
Average % of frosh need met	100
Average % of ugrad need met	100

DEEP SPRINGS COLLEGE

Deep Springs Ranch Road, Highway 168, Dyer, NV 89010 • Admissions: 760-872-2000

STUDENTS SAY "..."

Academics

The "three pillars" of a Deep Springs education—"labor, academics, and self-governance"—combine to produce "unparalleled challenges" that run the gamut "from fixing a hay baler in the middle of the night to puzzling over a particularly difficult passage of Hegel." That's what those who attend Deep Springs tell us. These unique undergraduates basically run their own school, work the ranch where it is located, and complete a rigorous curriculum, an itinerary that "creates an environment of intense growth and responsibility." Class work occurs in a seminar format in which "teachers participate similarly to students." Classes "aren't so much a transfer of information from professor to student as they are a time for the entire class to push the boundaries of collective thought as far as possible." Composition and public speaking are the only required courses; all others are chosen by the student body and taught by a faculty of three long-term professors (one each in the humanities, social sciences, and natural sciences) and one to three visiting scholars or artists. The system relies on a commitment to self-determination, which means "how successful Deep Springs is as an institution depends upon the manner in which its students are engaging with its project." While the size of the school inevitably means that "lab and library facilities are not what they might be," students tell us that the overall Deep Springs experience compensates for any shortcomings. A student explains: "Mistakes and flaws are seen as pedagogy in action. See a broken fence or heater? Fix it, or learn to fix it. The mechanical skills we pick up during the process of taking responsibility for our livelihood are surely valuable, but the self-confidence and that emerges from learning to do things one never could have thought possible is the essence of a Deep Springer's education."

Campus Life

At Deep Springs, where "the desert sun rises slowly," everyday student life is totally unlike other colleges because "no one drinks, everyone helps run the ranch in some way, and no one can be totally self-absorbed (unless he's out hiking in the desert)." Instead, students immerse themselves in the Deep Springs way. As one student explains, "Life is very intellectual but also in constant relationship to the natural beauty of the desert and the operation of the College's farm and ranch." Conversations tend to revolve around "what work needs to be done, what decisions need to be made, [and] which classes are most interesting," or, as one student puts it, "Sunsets. Hegel. Welding. Jane Austen." Fun at Deep Springs, where days are "marked by an extreme busyness," is "self-generated": "'Fun' is hard to come by, and one has to learn how to enjoy people, work, and engagement." Students do occasionally take a break, however: "Fun just means something a little different...Half-naked dances to Miley Cyrus, fully naked soccer, or fully clothed conversations on anything from Kierkegaard to Kanye West ensure that there really isn't a dull moment in the Valley." Also, occasionally "there are 'boojies'," a kind of hectic dance party in the Rumpus Room of the dorm, " or students will "go to the dunes a valley over for a bit of late-night naked surfing down the sand." Undergrads concede that Deep Springs "life can be intense": There is "a whirlwind of activity from labor to class to meals to labor again to meetings to a few precious hours of sleep. But where many students would find such a lifestyle stressful and unsustainable, we find it meaningful and valuable" and that keeps undergrads energized and motivated."

Student Body

"It is impossible to characterize a 'typical' student," students understandably warn, but they add that "we all are hardworking and are committed to a life of service." Undergrads are also predictably "outdoorsy," "interested in the arts," "motivated, and responsible," as "it takes a unique type of person to even consider Deep Springs, much less succeed and thrive in such an environment." As one student puts it, "The typical student at Deep Springs is committed to the life of the intellect and committed to finding education in our labor program. Most of the students here believe that a life of service, informed by discourse and labor, is a necessary notion to understand in today's world."

DEEP SPRINGS COLLEGE

Financial Aid: 760-872-2000 • E-Mail: apcom@deepsprings.edu • Website: www.deepsprings.edu

THE PRINCETON REVIEW SAYS

Admissions

The school reports that its standardized testing policy for use in admission for Fall 2024 is Test Optional. It is unknown at this time if the 2024 testing policy will be permanent. The Princeton Review suggests that interested applicants consult with the school for the most up-to-date standardized testing policies. *Very important factors considered include:* application essay, interview, character/personal qualities, level of applicant's interest. *Important factors considered include:* rigor of secondary school record, academic GPA, extracurricular activities, volunteer work, work experience. *Other factors considered include:* class rank, standardized test scores, recommendation(s), talent/ability, first generation, racial/ethnic status. High school diploma or equivalent is not required.

Financial Aid

The Princeton Review suggests that all financial aid forms be submitted as soon as possible (see page 5 for a note on the FAFSA).

The Inside Word

Students will be hard-pressed to find a school with a more personal or thorough application process than Deep Springs. Given the intimate and collegial atmosphere of the school, matchmaking is the top priority. Candidates are evaluated by a body composed of students, faculty, and staff members. The application is writing intensive; finalists are expected to spend several days on campus, during which they will undergo a lengthy interview.

THE SCHOOL SAYS "..."

From the Admissions Office

"Founded in 1917, Deep Springs College lies isolated in a high desert valley of eastern California, thirty miles from the nearest town. Its enrollment is limited to twenty-eight students, each of whom receives a full scholarship that covers tuition and room and board, and is valued at more than $50,000 per year. Students engage in rigorous academics, govern themselves, and participate in the operation of our ranch and farm.

"Given our small size, statistics must be viewed with context. Nonetheless, we have compiled data from the past five years to give some perspective on the characteristics of our students.

"The Applications Committee (ApCom) receives between 180 and 250 applications each year. Between thirteen and fifteen applicants are invited to enroll; ten are added to a waitlist. After two years at Deep Springs, students generally transfer to other schools to complete their studies. Students regularly attend Yale, University of Chicago, and Brown, and also have recently chosen several other schools including Cornell, Evergreen, Harvard, Reed, Stanford, Swarthmore, and UC Berkeley.

"Despite its small size, Deep Springs is a diverse community. In the past five years, 30 percent of Deep Springs students have been people of color. More than 11 percent of students have identified as LGBT. International students have made up about 20 percent of the Student Body. In each year, at least one student has spent between one semester and two years enrolled at another college before attending Deep Springs."

SELECTIVITY
Admissions Rating	99
# of applicants	200
% of applicants accepted	10
% of acceptees attending	84
# offered a place on the wait list	5
% accepting a place on wait list	100
% admitted from wait list	100

FIRST-YEAR PROFILE
Testing policy	Test Optional
Range SAT EBRW	740–800
Range SAT math	670–740
# submitting SAT scores	12
% submitting SAT scores	80
# submitting ACT scores	3
% submitting ACT scores	20
% graduated top 10% of class	100
% graduated top 25% of class	100
% graduated top 50% of class	100

DEADLINES
Regular	
Deadline	11/7
Notification	4/15
Nonfall registration?	No

FINANCIAL FACTS
Annual tuition	$0
Room and board	$0
Books and supplies	$1,200
% frosh rec. any financial aid	100
Average % of frosh need met	0
Average % of ugrad need met	0

DENISON UNIVERSITY

100 West College Street, Granville, OH 43023 • Admissions: 740-587-0801 • Fax: 740-587-6306

STUDENTS SAY "..."

Academics

At Denison University, students are encouraged to explore their interests "in and out of the classroom." This is encouraged and enabled by a faculty full of "the most caring, supportive, and knowledgeable human beings" and students having "voting powers on many administrative councils, committees, and task forces," which allows them to help shape the school's decision-making.

That cooperation may explain why, when it comes to academics, undergrads find the coursework "challenging but certainly worth it." It may also be from the presentation of the work itself: "classes are rarely taught in the form of lectures...rather they feel like focus groups dedicated to the pursuit of knowledge." The vast majority praise teachers as "enthusiastic about their area of study" and as "caring, thoughtful, and always [challenging] you without ever letting you fail." The consensus is that they're "truly focused on students' learning and development" and want "to see you succeed and become a better person." As one undergrad concludes, "I have built a team of faculty who I can lean on."

Campus Life

Life at Denison can be hectic. Thankfully, students maintain "a good balance of academics, extracurriculars, and fun." The university itself sponsors plenty of activities including "food trucks, movie nights, [and] trivia nights" along with "guest speakers and performances." You can also find numerous student-run clubs for a variety of interests. Groups range from "the Burpees Improv group, which does lots of great shows with high campus engagement," to Quidditch, ski club, and Habitat for Humanity. Students appreciate the way arts are handled: "unlike bigger schools, it's less competitive and just focused on fostering a community" and resources are generally open to students, like "music facilities that we can use at our own leisure." Those into sports appreciate the way that the school helps them juggle "a competitive, serious career in athletics and a rigorous, rewarding academic experience."

Outside of structured events, "hundreds of students...pass time lounging on the main academic quad between classes." And once the weekend rolls around, there tend to be apartment-based parties on Fridays and frat-based ones on Saturdays, though it's noted that while "students are typically social, [they are] not necessarily party animals." That said, those who want to hang together can do so "regardless of Greek life status, which is cool," and those who need a break from the hustle and bustle of college life can visit the quiet village of Granville or "drive to Columbus and explore the city."

Student Body

Denison students are "both ambitious and also open minded...curious, innovative thinkers that are motivated by making a wise impact." While you can still see "the remnants" of a "predominantly white" and "wealthy East-coaster" background, the overall consensus is that you can now meet "all types of students on campus." One undergrad elaborates further, "As an Ohioan, it is really special to go to an in-state school where I can have roommates, friends, and classmates from Britain, India, and China." Driven and diverse, students agree that it's "great to see people support each other in athletic events, theater performances, and even Bluegrass ensembles," all of which makes the school feel like a real community. Indeed, "it is the type of campus where...you keep your head up and say 'hi' to everyone that you pass." Adds another undergrad, "I feel really safe at Denison because I know that if something were to happen to me, students that I know and don't know would step up to help." Ultimately, when it comes down to it, "There is someone representing every personality, character, experience, and friendship style at Denison, so you are guaranteed to find a great group of friends."

DENISON UNIVERSITY

Financial Aid: 740-587-6279 • E-Mail: admission@denison.edu • Website: denison.edu

THE PRINCETON REVIEW SAYS

Admissions

The school reports that its standardized testing policy for use in admission for Fall 2024 is Test Optional. The 2024 testing policy will be permanent. The Princeton Review suggests that interested applicants consult with the school for the most up-to-date standardized testing policies. *Very important factors considered include:* rigor of secondary school record, academic GPA, application essay, recommendation(s). *Important factors considered include:* interview, extracurricular activities, talent/ability. *Other factors considered include:* class rank, standardized test scores, character/personal qualities, first generation, alumni/ae relation, geographical residence, state residency, racial/ethnic status, volunteer work, work experience, level of applicant's interest. High school diploma is required and GED is accepted. *Academic units recommended:* 4 English, 4 math, 4 science, 4 foreign language, 4 social studies.

Financial Aid

Students should submit: CSS/Financial Aid Profile; FAFSA; Noncustodial Profile. Priority filing deadline is 1/15. The Princeton Review suggests that all financial aid forms be submitted as soon as possible (see page 5 for a note on the FAFSA). *Need-based scholarships/grants offered:* College/university scholarship or grant aid from institutional funds; Federal Pell; Private scholarships; SEOG; State scholarships/grants. *Loan aid offered:* Direct PLUS loans; Direct Subsidized Loans; Direct Unsubsidized Loans; College/university loans from institutional funds. Admitted students will be notified of awards on or about 3/15. Federal Work-Study Program available. Institutional employment available.

The Inside Word

Admission to Denison is pretty straightforward. The school "suggests" an interview, meaning you should do one if at all possible. It's a great way to demonstrate your interest in the school, which improves your chances of admission, especially if your grades, test scores, and overall profile put you on the admit/reject borderline. Students may apply using either the Common Application or the Coalition Application.

THE SCHOOL SAYS "..."

From the Admissions Office

"Denison University is a leading national residential liberal arts college located just outside Columbus, Ohio. The college balances a rigorous and relevant academic experience founded on perceptive mentorship by dedicated faculty at the cutting edge of their research, with robust co-curricular and extra-curricular programming, which includes athletics, performing and fine arts, and more than 170 student-run organizations, providing abundant opportunities for students to develop leadership qualities and nurture friendships that will last throughout their lives. Wellness and academic support programs serve the whole student, promoting academic accomplishment as well as resilience, balance and well-being.

"Denison students are comprehensively prepared for lifetimes of civic and personal success, expanding their skills and expertise through extensive research opportunities and innovative career programming. The college is creating the gold standard in supporting students transitioning to life after college, through meaningful alumni networking, innovative programs that establish discrete capabilities related to vocations, and well-paid summer internships in their field of interest, which help them to establish relationships and forge skills directly related to their future careers. Proof of our student success is provided on an interactive web page, 'The Denison Difference,' which reports graduate placement in careers, graduate schools and service opportunities. Denison students have been granted more than 150 Fulbright and other international post-graduate scholarships, and in recent years have garnered 100 percent acceptance rates to both medical and law school programs. The college's distinguished alumni claim both Rhodes Scholar and a Gates Cambridge Scholar honors."

SELECTIVITY

Admissions Rating	**95**
# of applicants	12,220
% of applicants accepted	22
% of acceptees attending	25
# offered a place on the wait list	1,564
% accepting a place on wait list	36
% admitted from wait list	6
# of early decision applicants	1,122
% accepted early decision	31

FIRST-YEAR PROFILE

Testing policy	Test Optional
Range SAT composite	1290–1440
Range SAT EBRW	630–710
Range SAT math	640–750
Range ACT composite	29–32
# submitting SAT scores	188
% submitting SAT scores	28
# submitting ACT scores	175
% submitting ACT scores	26
% graduated top 10% of class	72
% graduated top 25% of class	85
% graduated top 50% of class	100

DEADLINES

Early decision	
Deadline	11/15
Notification	12/15
Other ED deadline	1/15
Other ED notification	2/15
Regular	
Priority	1/15
Deadline	1/15
Notification	4/1
Nonfall registration?	No

APPLICANTS OFTEN PREFER

Carleton College; Colby College; Colgate University; Hamilton College

APPLICANTS SOMETIMES PREFER

American University; Bates College; Boston College; Bucknell University; Case Western Reserve University; Colorado College; Connecticut College; Dickinson College; Elon University; Franklin & Marshall College; Grinnell College; Kenyon College; Macalester College; Miami University; Southern Methodist University; Texas Christian University; University of Denver; University of Michigan—Ann Arbor; University of Richmond; Wake Forest University

FINANCIAL FACTS

Financial Aid Rating	**96**
Annual tuition	$64,000
Room and board	$15,400
Required fees	$0
Books and supplies	$1,000
Average frosh need-based scholarship	$42,723
Average UG need-based scholarship	$42,799
% needy frosh rec. need-based scholarship or grant aid	99
% needy UG rec. need-based scholarship or grant aid	98
% needy frosh rec. non-need-based scholarship or grant aid	13
% needy UG rec. non-need-based scholarship or grant aid	13
% needy frosh rec. need-based self-help aid	100
% needy UG rec. need-based self-help aid	100
% frosh rec. any financial aid	94
% UG rec. any financial aid	94
% UG borrow to pay for school	44
Average cumulative indebtedness	$31,610
% frosh need fully met	100
% ugrads need fully met	100
Average % of frosh need met	100
Average % of ugrad need met	100

DePaul University

1 East Jackson Boulevard, Chicago, IL 60604-2287 • Admissions: 312-362-8000 • Fax: 312-362-5749

CAMPUS LIFE

Quality of Life Rating	90
Fire Safety Rating	95
Green Rating	60*
Type of school	Private
Affiliation	Roman Catholic
Environment	Metropolis

STUDENTS

Total undergrad enrollment	13,948
% male/female/another gender	45/55/NR
% from out of state	26
% frosh from public high school	82
% frosh live on campus	50
% ugrads live on campus	17
# of fraternities (% join)	10 (4)
# of sororities (% join)	17 (5)
% African American	7
% Asian	12
% White	48
% Hispanic	23
% Native American	<1
% Pacific Islander	<1
% Two or more races	4
% Race and/or ethnicity unknown	2
% international	3
# of countries represented	124

SURVEY SAYS . . .

Lots of conservative students
Students are happy
Classroom facilities are great
Lab facilities are great
Great library
Career services are great
No one cheats
Diverse student types interact on campus
Students love Chicago, IL
Great off-campus food
Recreation facilities are great
Students get along with local community
Easy to get around campus

ACADEMICS

Academic Rating	80
% students returning for sophomore year	84
% students graduating within 4 years	58
% students graduating within 6 years	69
Calendar	Differs By Program
Student/faculty ratio	17:1
Profs interesting rating	90
Profs accessible rating	93

Most classes have 20–29 students.
Most lab/discussion sessions have
20–29 students.

MOST POPULAR MAJORS

Public Relations, Advertising, and Applied
Communication, Other; Accounting; Finance,
General

STUDENTS SAY ". . ."

Academics

DePaul University is the nation's largest Catholic university, offering its 14,500 undergraduate students over 130 majors across two campuses, including the option for combined Bachelor's and Master's degrees. These various programs are anchored by a core curriculum that features over 1,400 course options and a Focal Point Seminar, in which students must investigate a significant person, place, event, or idea. Further supplementing that core is an ever-expanding series of options, as "each year [DePaul] strives to improve and add new programs to suit different future career paths of its students." Such offerings are only enhanced by the school's heart-of-Chicago location, which puts it "close to so many educational and vocational opportunities." There are thousands of internships available, as well as "peer-to-peer study groups" and study abroad programs. The administration rises to the task of "keeping the school's environment safe, clean, and well-educated," and "there are plenty of resources specifically set up to help students with pretty much anything," including "tutoring sessions every day, a writing center to help improve papers, a counseling center, [and] financial aid advisers."

Ninety-eight percent of classes are taught by the "highly professional" faculty, so "instead of only learning from a textbook, I am able to gain real experience from professors who have worked in the field for decades at a time." There's a maximum to each class size as well, which guarantees that "teachers actually get to know the students that are in the class." This also lends itself to an accessibility "like no other and it really helps the students that need extra help outside of the classroom." All in all, professors have so "many years of experience behind them, they are able to transfer all their knowledge to students in an effective and fun way." There "are museums, parks, guest speakers in the city that professors will often take advantage of by taking the class to them allowing us to learn the subject from a real-world perspective."

Campus Life

DePaul has "lots of organizations that cater to different causes and a lot of extracurricular activities," as well as 15 Division I athletic teams that students enjoy watching. The Chicago-based campus also ensures that there's not only a lot to do, but plenty of opportunity to put what's being learned to the test. In particular, students complete "a lot of community service in the neighborhood as well as throughout the USA," but many also just "enjoy going out into the city and trying out new restaurants around the city." That doesn't mean DePaul skimps out on campus offerings! There are "always events happening to increase student interaction," and these are "really creative and interesting." And even though DePaul is spread across two campuses, students note that activities are always planned in such a way "that there is enough time to catch a train to get to the other campus."

Student Body

One in three people at DePaul is a first-generation college student, and the student body as a whole "is pretty diverse when it comes to race, gender, religion, and orientation of each student." Attendees find this to be a bonus, because not only are they learning from the professors, but they're also "gain[ing] considerable knowledge from [their] peers." This is especially true given the warm atmosphere, where it is both "easy to make friends and easy to get engaged with events going on around campus," regardless of socioeconomic background. "The campus is pretty liberal," students observe, but stress that everyone has "freedom and respect of choice for views [and] religion." This ultimately results in "a large sense of belonging in any classroom between all the students," and helps to ensure that everyone remains "very focused."

DePaul University

THE PRINCETON REVIEW SAYS

Admissions

The school reports that its standardized testing policy for use in admission for Fall 2024 is Test Optional. It is unknown at this time if the 2024 testing policy will be permanent. The Princeton Review suggests that interested applicants consult with the school for the most up-to-date standardized testing policies. *Very important factors considered include:* rigor of secondary school record, academic GPA, standardized test scores. *Important factors considered include:* class rank, recommendation(s), extracurricular activities, talent/ability, character/personal qualities, volunteer work, work experience, level of applicant's interest. *Other factors considered include:* application essay, interview, first generation, alumni/ae relation, geographical residence, state residency, religious affiliation/commitment, racial/ethnic status. High school diploma is required and GED is accepted. *Academic units required:* 4 English, 3 math, 3 science, 2 science labs. *Academic units recommended:* 4 English, 3 math, 3 science, 2 science labs, 2 foreign language, 2 social studies.

Financial Aid

Students should submit: FAFSA. Priority filing deadline is 12/1. The Princeton Review suggests that all financial aid forms be submitted as soon as possible (see page 5 for a note on the FAFSA). *Need-based scholarships/grants offered:* College/university scholarship or grant aid from institutional funds; Federal Pell; Private scholarships; SEOG; State scholarships/grants. *Loan aid offered:* Direct PLUS loans; Direct Subsidized Loans; Direct Unsubsidized Loans. Admitted students will be notified of awards on a rolling basis beginning 12/15. Federal Work-Study Program available. Institutional employment available.

The Inside Word

DePaul's reputation as one of the most diverse schools in the country is not mere hyperbole, it's a truth expressed by student after student, and by the actions of the administration itself. The school actively seeks out minority students both as first-years and transfers, and in an effort to surmount tuition-related obstacles works with local community colleges so students can meet their requirements at a lower cost before transferring to DePaul. Based on research and DePaul's student-centered approach to education, DePaul has adopted a Test Optional alternative for first-year admission.

THE SCHOOL SAYS "..."

From the Admissions Office

"The nation's largest Catholic university, DePaul University is nationally recognized for its innovative academic programs that embrace a comprehensive learn-by-doing approach. DePaul has two residential locations. The Lincoln Park Campus is home to the College of Liberal Arts and Social Sciences, the College of Science and Health, the College of Education, the School of Music, The Theatre School and the extensive John T. Richardson Library. The Loop location, located in Chicago's downtown—a world-class center for business, government, law, and culture—is home to DePaul's Driehaus College of Business, College of Communication, College of Law, College of Computing and Digital Media, and School of Continuing & Professional Studies."

SELECTIVITY

Admissions Rating	85
# of applicants	31,785
% of applicants accepted	70
% of acceptees attending	13
# offered a place on the wait list	2,637
% accepting a place on wait list	27
% admitted from wait list	11

FIRST-YEAR PROFILE

Testing policy	Test Optional
Range SAT composite	1090–1290
Range SAT EBRW	550–660
Range SAT math	520–640
# submitting SAT scores	1,274
% submitting SAT scores	43
Average HS GPA	3.8
% frosh submitting high school GPA	97
% graduated top 10% of class	29
% graduated top 25% of class	59
% graduated top 50% of class	87

DEADLINES

Early action	
Deadline	11/15
Notification	12/15
Regular	
Priority	11/15
Deadline	2/1
Notification	3/15
Nonfall registration?	Yes

FINANCIAL FACTS

Financial Aid Rating	82
Annual tuition	$42,189
Room and board	$16,068
Required fees	$651
Books and supplies	$1,104
Average frosh need-based scholarship	$27,286
Average UG need-based scholarship	$24,589
% needy frosh rec. need-based scholarship or grant aid	99
% needy UG rec. need-based scholarship or grant aid	97
% needy frosh rec. non-need-based scholarship or grant aid	12
% needy UG rec. non-need-based scholarship or grant aid	11
% needy frosh rec. need-based self-help aid	56
% needy UG rec. need-based self-help aid	63
% frosh rec. any financial aid	98
% UG rec. any financial aid	90
% UG borrow to pay for school	63
Average cumulative indebtedness	$28,754
% frosh need fully met	13
% ugrads need fully met	12
Average % of frosh need met	73
Average % of ugrad need met	70

DePauw University

313 S. Locust Street, Greencastle, IN 46135 • Admissions: 765-658-4800 • Fax: 765-658-4007

CAMPUS LIFE

Quality of Life Rating	**80**
Fire Safety Rating	**73**
Green Rating	**89**
Type of school	Private
Affiliation	No Affiliation
Environment	Village

STUDENTS

Total undergrad enrollment	1,732
% male/female/another gender	49/51/<1
% from out of state	55
% frosh from public high school	83
% frosh live on campus	100
% ugrads live on campus	97
# of fraternities (% join)	13 (65)
# of sororities (% join)	11 (57)
% African American	6
% Asian	3
% White	59
% Hispanic	8
% Native American	0
% Pacific Islander	0
% Two or more races	2
% Race and/or ethnicity unknown	1
% international	21
# of countries represented	38

SURVEY SAYS . . .

Internships are widely available
Class discussions encouraged
Frats and sororities are popular
Alumni active on campus

ACADEMICS

Academic Rating	**85**
% students returning for sophomore year	92
% students graduating within 6 years	79
Calendar	4/1/4
Student/faculty ratio	9:1
Profs interesting rating	86
Profs accessible rating	92
Most classes have 10–19 students.	
Most lab/discussion sessions have 10–19 students.	

MOST POPULAR MAJORS

Economics, General; Speech Communication and Rhetoric

STUDENTS SAY "..."

Academics

DePauw University has done an incredible job of building a "collaborative community" that prioritizes the needs and desires of its undergraduates. Whether it's cultivating a "truly caring faculty," being wholly "receptive to student feedback" or developing "excellent study abroad options," students here are set up to thrive. Importantly, DePauw "emphasizes [a] well-rounded education" as undergrads are expected to "take classes in nearly all departments over their four years." Inevitably, this allows them to develop "both [a] depth and breadth of knowledge" and also helps ensure that there are "programs and courses for every student." Another great benefit of a DePauw education? The "classes are small so students are able to really engage in discussion." But perhaps the true highlight of studying here are the professors who tend to be "knowledgeable, interesting, empathetic and invested." As this undergrad explains, "My professors do a great job at making sure we don't grow tired of our material. They always switch things up to make sure we are learning and growing as individuals." They're also "eager to tell students about internships or job opportunities, and love connecting students with alumni." As another grateful undergrad simply concludes, "The professors at DePauw University are some of the most phenomenal people I have ever met."

Campus Life

Undergrads at DePauw are "very committed to their academics" and it's common for people to "spend much of the week studying." Nevertheless, there's plenty to enjoy when they want to take a break from their books. To begin with, DePauw maintains a fairly robust fraternity and sorority system. "Many students join Greek life at some point and are involved in [their] philanthropy, academic and social activities including partying. Even those not in the Greek system are likely to attend the Greek parties." Additionally, athletics are "very popular" as well and you'll often see "students [at] football games...during the fall semester, especially when they play our rival team during the Monon Bell game." Of course, the university itself also "hosts many fun events to bring students together, such as food truck Fridays." And there are numerous organizations and clubs to join ranging from the student newspaper and TV station to the future medical professionals club and sustainability leadership program. When wanting to get off outside for a bit, "many students go to the Nature Park (a DePauw owned nature preserve). It is very popular in the spring and fall and many students enjoy hiking, reading, or working on homework [there]."

And if you're venturing off campus, undergrads note that "Greencastle['s] downtown has grown tremendously these past few years, and there are many cute restaurants and bars to visit." Students also like to "go to dinner with friends and go see a movie or go bowling, which are free in the town if you are a student."

Student Body

At first glance, it seems as though DePauw's student body primarily consists of individuals from "well off" families "from the Indianapolis or Chicago area." However, though the "core group [may be] midwestern white students," many undergrads insist that you'll find "divers[ity] in a lot of ways—in terms of ethnicity, sexuality, sexual orientation/identity, thoughts, political viewpoints, country of origin/nationality, etc." This individual concurs noting that "each of my classes has...students from all over the world." Just as critical, DePauw undergrads say that their classmates are "open-minded individuals who are eager to learn about the world around them." Another student further explains, "My peers are often unafraid to stand up for what they believe to be right, and actively work to better the DePauw community." Ultimately, when it comes down to it, "The university has a very social student base that acts as a very tight-knit community."

DePauw University

Financial Aid: 765-658-4030 • E-Mail: admission@depauw.edu • Website: www.depauw.edu

THE PRINCETON REVIEW SAYS

Admissions

The school reports that its standardized testing policy for use in admission for Fall 2024 is Test Optional. It is unknown at this time if the 2024 testing policy will be permanent. The Princeton Review suggests that interested applicants consult with the school for the most up-to-date standardized testing policies. *Very important factors considered include:* rigor of secondary school record, academic GPA. *Important factors considered include:* class rank, application essay, recommendation(s). *Other factors considered include:* standardized test scores, interview, extracurricular activities, talent/ability, character/personal qualities, first generation, alumni/ae relation, geographical residence, state residency, volunteer work, work experience, level of applicant's interest. High school diploma is required and GED is accepted. *Academic units required:* 4 English, 3 math, 2 science, 2 science labs, 2 foreign language, 2 social studies. *Academic units recommended:* 4 English, 4 math, 3 science, 2 science labs, 2 foreign language, 3 social studies, 3 history.

Financial Aid

Students should submit: FAFSA. Priority filing deadline is 12/15. The Princeton Review suggests that all financial aid forms be submitted as soon as possible (see page 5 for a note on the FAFSA). *Need-based scholarships/grants offered:* College/university scholarship or grant aid from institutional funds; Federal Pell; Private scholarships; SEOG; State scholarships/grants. *Loan aid offered:* Direct PLUS loans; Direct Subsidized Loans; Direct Unsubsidized Loans. Admitted students will be notified of awards on a rolling basis beginning 2/1. Federal Work-Study Program available. Institutional employment available.

The Inside Word

Admissions officers at DePauw University consider both students' academic performance and involvement outside the classroom when determining whether or not a student will be admitted. They want candidates who will contribute positively to the campus as a whole. A strong application will demonstrate above average achievement, from high GPAs and challenging coursework to leadership roles in extracurriculars. For admissions in Fall 2022 and beyond, the school is adopting a Test Optional policy.

THE SCHOOL SAYS "..."

From the Admissions Office

"DePauw is a nationally recognized liberal arts university committed to rigorous academics and rich co-curricular opportunities for its students. DePauw encourages all students to discover and explore their passions and, with nearly 100 percent of graduates employed or in grad school within six months of graduation, they can do so in confidence. Graduates are extraordinarily successful, demonstrating "Gold Within" leadership qualities in dozens of fields, among them CEOs, Pulitzer Prize winners, doctors, lawyers, humanitarian and civic leaders, legislators, musicians, entrepreneurs, journalists, news anchors, artists, an astronaut, and a Nobel Laureate scientist. Our students demonstrate academic curiosity, a willingness to explore new avenues not yet discovered, and the courage to question assumptions. Ranked in the top four universities nationally for study abroad, more than 92 percent of DePauw students have at least one semester-long study-away, internship, or other immersive experience, enabling them to connect with individuals from all backgrounds and bring a global perspective to solving difficult issues."

SELECTIVITY

Admissions Rating	89
# of applicants	5,708
% of applicants accepted	66
% of acceptees attending	14

FIRST-YEAR PROFILE

Testing policy	Test Optional
Range SAT composite	1160–1360
Range SAT EBRW	570–670
Range SAT math	570–690
Range ACT composite	24–31
# submitting SAT scores	182
% submitting SAT scores	34
# submitting ACT scores	100
% submitting ACT scores	19
Average HS GPA	3.9
% frosh submitting high school GPA	100
% graduated top 10% of class	45
% graduated top 25% of class	78
% graduated top 50% of class	97

DEADLINES

Early decision	
Deadline	11/15
Notification	12/1
Other ED deadline	1/15
Other ED notification	2/1
Early action	
Deadline	12/1
Notification	1/15
Regular	
Deadline	2/1
Nonfall registration?	Yes

FINANCIAL FACTS

Financial Aid Rating	87
Annual tuition	$52,900
Room and board	$14,098
Required fees	$996
Books and supplies	$900
Average frosh need-based scholarship	$42,644
Average UG need-based scholarship	$42,267
% needy frosh rec. need-based scholarship or grant aid	98
% needy UG rec. need-based scholarship or grant aid	99
% needy frosh rec. non-need-based scholarship or grant aid	35
% needy UG rec. non-need-based scholarship or grant aid	28
% needy frosh rec. need-based self-help aid	70
% needy UG rec. need-based self-help aid	81
% UG borrow to pay for school	75
Average cumulative indebtedness	$24,216
% frosh need fully met	43
% ugrads need fully met	36
Average % of frosh need met	88
Average % of ugrad need met	88

DICKINSON COLLEGE

P.O. Box 1773, Carlisle, PA 17013-2896 • Admissions: 717-245-1231 • Fax: 717-245-1442

STUDENTS SAY ". . ."

Academics
Founded just days after the conclusion of the American Revolution by a signer of the Declaration of Independence, Dickinson College was born with the mission of preparing young people to be active and engaged leaders in society via a "global, sustainable, and pragmatic liberal arts education." This Pennsylvania college's serious focus on global engagement and service seeps into every crevice of its "outstanding," interdisciplinary academics, and it has a support system and "infinite amount of resources and facilities" on offer. For instance, there is "a makery for students to use containing craft supplies and a media center" available to all. There are "ample opportunities to keep your mind engaged" (many study abroad at some point), and Dickinson gives students incredible freedom to study under different disciplines. Even students with a focus on one specific major "are able and required to experience classes in other academic areas." Professors at Dickinson are "incredibly accessible and eager to reach out," and "all have very impressive credentials and connections." They "help students see things from various perspectives and not just their own" and encourage students to keep an open mind. Every course is "elaborately prepared by the department" and deans and advisors are helpful when trying to figure out a major. There's no easy ride at Dickinson; faculty "expect a lot from you, [and] outside work can be 1 to 3 hours per class per day." The school encourages students to be educated in all fields of study, and Dickinson students "are always seeking a new answer, discovery, or understanding in every field." A tight 9:1 student-to-faculty ratio and a wide course selection help make students diverse in background and interests, which can "many times overlap in seemingly opposite majors."

Campus Life
Although a small school, students here are involved in the many different available extracurricular organizations, and "most take leadership roles in at least one if not several." They "take their schoolwork seriously, but they take their other roles at least equally as seriously." Many people have jobs on campus, and "when the weather is nice, most students are outside." The college's student activities board, MOB, is the largest organizer of events, which range "from food- to music- to entertainment-related," and the Clarke Forum regularly brings in guest speakers who talk on a variety of topics. Dickinson's food "is not great," but it does a good job of making sure there are kosher and vegan options at meals, and the town has great restaurants and shops. The weekend party scene is "very inclusive and energetic," but "it's definitely possible to enjoy oneself without drinking." Carlisle, the small town that surrounds the school, "has enough to do that you will be entertained." The local movie theater is a popular attraction (especially for the $6 matinees on Saturday and Sunday afternoons) and during the spring, students also attend Harrisburg Senators games, the local minor-league affiliate of the Washington Nationals.

Student Body
This is an "interesting bunch for sure." "We have people who are ardent defenders of social justice, people concerned with community service, artists, musicians, as well as people who can speak six languages...[or] who came to Dickinson from Carlisle itself." Although the student body "isn't the most diverse" from an ethnic standpoint, everyone here "seems to have an open mind and heart" and is "friendly and involved." "Students' voices are heard" here, and "everyone feels welcome" in this "safe and trustworthy community," which also has a fair number of international students. There is also "a strong activist strain" among Dickinson students, and "most people on campus are very attuned to issues of class, race, sexual orientation, gender, and many other identities."

DICKINSON COLLEGE

Financial Aid: 717-245-1308 • E-Mail: admissions@dickinson.edu • Website: www.dickinson.edu/

THE PRINCETON REVIEW SAYS

Admissions

The school reports that its standardized testing policy for use in admission for Fall 2024 is Test Free. The 2024 testing policy will be temporary. The Princeton Review suggests that interested applicants consult with the school for the most up-to-date standardized testing policies. *Very important factors considered include:* rigor of secondary school record, academic GPA, recommendation(s), extracurricular activities, talent/ability, character/personal qualities, level of applicant's interest. *Important factors considered include:* application essay, interview, geographical residence, state residency, racial/ethnic status, volunteer work, work experience. *Other factors considered include:* class rank, standardized test scores, first generation, alumni/ae relation. High school diploma is required and GED is accepted. *Academic units required:* 4 English, 3 math, 3 science, 2 science labs, 2 foreign language, 2 social studies. *Academic units recommended:* 3 foreign language.

Financial Aid

Students should submit: CSS/Financial Aid Profile; FAFSA; Noncustodial Profile; State aid form. Priority filing deadline is 11/15. The Princeton Review suggests that all financial aid forms be submitted as soon as possible (see page 5 for a note on the FAFSA). *Need-based scholarships/grants offered:* College/university scholarship or grant aid from institutional funds; Federal Pell; Private scholarships; SEOG; State scholarships/grants. *Loan aid offered:* Direct PLUS loans; Direct Subsidized Loans; Direct Unsubsidized Loans; College/university loans from institutional funds; State Loans. Admitted students will be notified of awards on or about in late March. Federal Work-Study Program available. Institutional employment available.

The Inside Word

The applicant pool for small liberal arts colleges has become increasingly competitive in recent years, and Dickinson is no exception. For admission here, you'll want to be the stereotypical well-rounded student, with a solid GPA in challenging classes, and broad extracurricular involvement.

THE SCHOOL SAYS "..."

From the Admissions Office

"Dickinson is a nationally recognized liberal arts college chartered in 1783 in Carlisle, Pennsylvania. Devoted to its revolutionary roots, the college maintains the mission of founder Benjamin Rush—to provide a useful education in the liberal arts and sciences. Dickinson has a robust academic program, offering forty-five majors plus minors, certificates, independent research, and internships. Our innovative programs range from neuroscience to security studies and develop intellectual independence by actively engaging in research, fieldwork, lab work in state-of-the-art science programs, and other experiential opportunities. The newest additions to our curriculum—majors in quantitative economics and data analytics—are evidence of our emphasis on being responsive in today's everchanging economy. Dickinson's global curriculum includes international business & management, international studies, thirteen languages, and many globally oriented courses. Dickinson offers one of the world's most respected study-abroad programs, and about two-thirds of Dickinson's students study in thirty-nine programs in twenty-four countries on six continents. Dickinson is recognized as a leader among educational institutions committed to sustainability and green initiatives. The Center for Sustainability Education integrates sustainability into its academics, facilities, operations, and campus culture. Dickinson has received the highest awards from the Association for the Advancement of Sustainability in Higher Education, Sierra Club, Sustainable Endowments Institute, The Princeton Review, and Second Nature. Dickinson alumni are at the top of their fields as business leaders, professional artists and writers, sports agents and athletes, doctors and researchers. And many of them used their liberal arts foundation to forge their own paths. Our graduate school partnerships enable our students to enter top programs with greater ease and reflect the high regard in which Dickinson is held."

SELECTIVITY

Admissions Rating	**94**
# of applicants	8,261
% of applicants accepted	34
% of acceptees attending	20
# offered a place on the wait list	974
% accepting a place on wait list	32
% admitted from wait list	6
# of early decision applicants	432
% accepted early decision	58

FIRST-YEAR PROFILE

Testing policy	Test Free
Range SAT composite	1288–1413
Range SAT EBRW	640–723
Range SAT math	620–703
Range ACT composite	29–32
# submitting SAT scores	112
% submitting SAT scores	19
# submitting ACT scores	32
% submitting ACT scores	6
% graduated top 10% of class	49
% graduated top 25% of class	82
% graduated top 50% of class	94

DEADLINES

Early decision	
Deadline	11/15
Notification	12/15
Other ED deadline	1/15
Other ED notification	2/15
Regular	
Deadline	1/15
Notification	3/31
Nonfall registration?	No

APPLICANTS OFTEN PREFER
Franklin & Marshall College; Gettysburg College; Lafayette College; Skidmore College; University of Vermont

APPLICANTS SOMETIMES PREFER
American University; Bucknell University; Connecticut College; Denison University; Muhlenberg College

FINANCIAL FACTS

Financial Aid Rating	**94**
Annual tuition	$62,900
Room and board	$16,500
Required fees	$550
Books and supplies	$1,324
Average frosh need-based scholarship	$48,261
Average UG need-based scholarship	$48,199
% needy frosh rec. need-based scholarship or grant aid	99
% needy UG rec. need-based scholarship or grant aid	99
% needy frosh rec. non-need-based scholarship or grant aid	14
% needy UG rec. non-need-based scholarship or grant aid	11
% needy frosh rec. need-based self-help aid	81
% needy UG rec. need-based self-help aid	85
% frosh rec. any financial aid	96
% UG rec. any financial aid	91
% UG borrow to pay for school	63
Average cumulative indebtedness	$27,462
% frosh need fully met	90
% ugrads need fully met	78
Average % of frosh need met	99
Average % of ugrad need met	98

DREW UNIVERSITY

36 Madison Avenue, Madison, NJ 07940-1493 • Admissions: 973-408-3000 • Fax: 973-408-3068

STUDENTS SAY ". . ."

Academics

Located in Madison, New Jersey, Drew University is just a hop-and-a-skip away from the New York City universe, and the school takes full advantage of its proximity to industry hubs. The 1,500 undergraduates have access to more than 60 majors, minors, and dual-degree programs, and thousands of related internships, as well as lots of study abroad options. Drew's seven unique New York Semesters allow students to do coursework with professors and then commute into New York City to learn in the field (for example, on Wall Street, at the United Nations, or in the art, communications, social entrepreneurship and theatre scene). The science departments are standouts—one of its fellows won the Nobel Prize for Medicine in 2015—and its top-ranked theatre program is "comprehensive in such a way that every graduate of the program will have at least tried every single part of the theatrical process."

The "incredibly engaging" professors go "above and beyond the role of just...teacher" and are "very much willing to assist in any way." They "facilitate conversations so that you learn in a way that's not just your average PowerPoint [presentation]" and "invest time in you academically and as a young adult looking for a career." The university does an excellent job of fostering undergraduate student research, and professors "require a level of accountability that motivates a student to perform" both in and out of the classroom. Far and away the things that students appreciate the most about Drew are its small class sizes, which bolster the personal attention from teachers, almost all of whom have PhDs. ("There are no classes taught by TAs, which makes for better quality learning.") This "mentorship with professors" is a lasting benefit to students, who say that "you really get to know your professors in an impactful way."

Campus Life

While the small, wooded town of Madison isn't exactly hopping, students make the most of the "gorgeous" campus (where housing is guaranteed all four years; currently 90 percent of the student body lives on campus) and "tend to be proactive in creating their own recreational experiences." People "are very involved in sports and activities, such as clubs and organizations," and many have jobs or internships. New York City is a short 50-minute train ride away, and nearby Morristown also provides some flavor. Academics "take up a good amount of daytime, but life at school is "always manageable"; "classes are challenging enough and the workload isn't overbearing," so "there is always time to relax if you're responsible and manage your time well." Tuesdays and Thursdays are dollar beer nights, so "many students take time out of studying to go out for a little," but "most free time is spent in friends' rooms, playing video games or watching shows." Though school events aren't terribly well-attended, from time to time there are things which students make sure to have fun at, "such as Bingo night, the holiday ball, and Drewchella (a live music festival)." All in all, "there is a good balance of leisure and education."

Student Body

While about half of the students are from New Jersey, the student body is diverse and includes a large international student population. As a small school, "Everyone at least knows of everyone else and is friendly with them." "Drew students are the type that see a $50 bill in the street and find the person who dropped it," says one student of this group that is "attractive inside and out." There's a large percentage of people actively involved in both the arts and sciences, and the regular cliques—"jocks, theatre kids, science nerds"— all "blend together and overlap so that there are no definite lines separating people." Drew is an eco-friendly campus, and "there is a fairly large number of gluten free/vegetarian students."

DREW UNIVERSITY

Financial Aid: 973-408-3112 • E-Mail: admissions@drew.edu • Website: www.drew.edu

THE PRINCETON REVIEW SAYS

Admissions

The school reports that its standardized testing policy for use in admission for Fall 2024 is Test Optional. The 2024 testing policy will be permanent. The Princeton Review suggests that interested applicants consult with the school for the most up-to-date standardized testing policies. *Very important factors considered include:* rigor of secondary school record, academic GPA, interview. *Important factors considered include:* application essay, recommendation(s), extracurricular activities, talent/ability, character/personal qualities. *Other factors considered include:* class rank, standardized test scores, first generation, alumni/ae relation, racial/ethnic status, volunteer work, work experience, level of applicant's interest. High school diploma is required and GED is accepted. *Academic units recommended:* 4 English, 3 math, 2 science, 2 foreign language, 2 social studies, 2 history, 3 academic electives.

Financial Aid

Students should submit: FAFSA. Priority filing deadline is 1/1. The Princeton Review suggests that all financial aid forms be submitted as soon as possible (see page 5 for a note on the FAFSA). *Need-based scholarships/grants offered:* College/university scholarship or grant aid from institutional funds; Federal Pell; Private scholarships; SEOG; State scholarships/grants. *Loan aid offered:* Direct PLUS loans; Direct Subsidized Loans; Direct Unsubsidized Loans. Admitted students will be notified of awards on or about 3/25. Federal Work-Study Program available. Institutional employment available.

The Inside Word

Drew takes a holistic approach to evaluating applications, so you definitely want to showcase more than just your GPA (though that's also important). Drew's applicant pool has grown significantly in recent years, so presenting yourself as not only a great student but also a great fit with the school will help you stand out from the pack. The university is Test Optional.

THE SCHOOL SAYS "..."

From the Admissions Office

"Drew is all about creating a journey for our students filled with epic experiences, connections, and opportunities. Our students graduate having developed proficiency in sought-after skills, engaged with a network of dedicated mentors, and had hands-on immersive experiences that translate to resumes they're confident in talking about in job and graduate school interviews. Every Drew student is guaranteed at least two immersive experiences (like our seven NYC Semesters) that are résumé ready—an essential part of a Drew degree.

"We are affordable and work to provide great access to the benefits of a Drew education to even more families. The average yearly financial award from Drew is $32,000, and over 85 percent of students received merit or need-based aid. The Princeton Review named Drew among their 200 *Best Value Colleges* and twice saluted it as one of fifty *Colleges that Create Futures.*

"Drew's beautiful campus is located in a charming small town twenty miles from New York City, a region full of leading organizations. Drew students recently interned at employers such as CNN, Goldman Sachs, Michael Kors, the Red Sox, and the United Nations, among others. Ninety percent of recent graduates were working or in graduate school within six months of graduation. They are employed at places such as Google, Bank of America, Lincoln Center, the U.S. Department of State, Morgan Stanley, and Prudential, and they attend graduate programs at Harvard, Stanford, Princeton, Oxford, and Columbia, among others.

"Drew students are part of a powerful community on a lively and diverse campus. Ninety percent live on campus, and housing is guaranteed for four years. Students are active in 90+ student-run clubs and 30 percent are Drew Ranger student-athletes. Located within one hour are a wildlife refuge, ski resorts, beaches, the Meadowlands (home of the Giants and Jets), and the museums, concert venues, sports arenas, clubs, galleries, theaters, etc. of New York City."

SELECTIVITY

Admissions Rating	85
# of applicants	3,855
% of applicants accepted	73
% of acceptees attending	11
# offered a place on the wait list	141
% accepting a place on wait list	95
% admitted from wait list	14
# of early decision applicants	89
% accepted early decision	80

FIRST-YEAR PROFILE

Testing policy	Test Optional
Range SAT composite	1120–1300
Range SAT EBRW	560–660
Range SAT math	540–640
Range ACT composite	24–30
# submitting SAT scores	208
% submitting SAT scores	61
# submitting ACT scores	50
% submitting ACT scores	15
Average HS GPA	3.6
% frosh submitting high school GPA	100
% graduated top 10% of class	26
% graduated top 25% of class	57
% graduated top 50% of class	93

DEADLINES

Early decision	
Deadline	11/1
Notification	12/15
Other ED deadline	1/15
Other ED notification	2/15
Early action	
Deadline	12/1
Notification	1/15
Regular	
Priority	11/1
Deadline	2/1
Notification	3/6
Nonfall registration?	Yes

APPLICANTS ALSO LOOK AT

Drexel University; Ithaca College; Montclair State University; Muhlenberg College; New York University; Rutgers University-Rutgers College; The College of New Jersey

FINANCIAL FACTS

Financial Aid Rating	85
Annual tuition	$43,074
Room and board	$16,402
Required fees	$800
Required fees (first-year)	$1,100
Books and supplies	$1,200
Average frosh need-based scholarship	$31,593
Average UG need-based scholarship	$29,649
% needy frosh rec. need-based scholarship or grant aid	100
% needy UG rec. need-based scholarship or grant aid	100
% needy frosh rec. non-need-based scholarship or grant aid	21
% needy UG rec. non-need-based scholarship or grant aid	16
% needy frosh rec. need-based self-help aid	58
% needy UG rec. need-based self-help aid	64
% frosh rec. any financial aid	99
% UG rec. any financial aid	96
% UG borrow to pay for school	61
Average cumulative indebtedness	$24,362
% frosh need fully met	31
% ugrads need fully met	25
Average % of frosh need met	89
Average % of ugrad need met	86

DREXEL UNIVERSITY

3141 Chestnut Street, Philadelphia, PA 19104 • Admissions: 215-895-2000 • Fax: 215-895-1285

CAMPUS LIFE

Quality of Life Rating	83
Fire Safety Rating	97
Green Rating	92
Type of school	Private
Affiliation	No Affiliation
Environment	Metropolis

STUDENTS

Total undergrad enrollment	13,804
% male/female/another gender	51/48/1
% from out of state	50
% frosh live on campus	82
% ugrads live on campus	21
# of fraternities (% join)	20 (11)
# of sororities (% join)	11 (8)
% African American	8
% Asian	23
% White	45
% Hispanic	8
% Native American	<1
% Pacific Islander	<1
% Two or more races	4
% Race and/or ethnicity unknown	2
% international	9
# of countries represented	115

SURVEY SAYS . . .

Career services are great
Internships are widely available
Students love Philadelphia, PA

ACADEMICS

Academic Rating	78
% students returning for sophomore year	87
% students graduating within 6 years	78
Calendar	Quarter
Student/faculty ratio	9:1
Profs interesting rating	82
Profs accessible rating	85

Most classes have 10–19 students.

MOST POPULAR MAJORS

Business/Commerce, General; Registered Nursing/
Registered Nurse; Mechanical Engineering

STUDENTS SAY "..."

Academics

A large private research university, Philadelphia's Drexel University draws many students through its cooperative education ("co-op") program, in which students take major-oriented classes in their first year and then alternate six-month studies with six-month full-time employment. Drexel "moves fast," and students love the feeling that "our work makes an impact in real companies." As a research-driven university, the school has found a "really strong area within the sciences" and also does very well in challenging students with "a fast-paced curriculum" that prepares them for a working environment and helps them to get "a hands-on look at what [they] can do with [their] degree." Though students find the schedule "very different compared to the normal college experience," they are well-aware of the track they've signed up for: "a lot more challenging and a lot less down time." One student explains, "If you are not a very self-motivated, hard-working student, you'll fall behind."

Most Drexel professors work in the industry that they're teaching and "are beyond knowledgeable on the subject" (a good number of professors are also Drexel alumni). Professors are all "extremely intelligent," but many students admit that "sometimes there is a language barrier." Still, teachers here are "resourceful and ready to help solve a problem or redirect to someone who can." The quarter system keeps students on their toes academically, but it "makes the year go by faster." "I was skeptical at first, but it was worth it," says one quarter-system fan. At the end of the day, students say that you "can't beat 21 months' worth of full-time experiences," and the school succeeds in giving students "a rigorous, great education that almost guarantees a job or place in grad school after graduation."

Campus Life

Students generally spend their days "in class, in our gym, or working on co-op." Everyone here "works extremely hard"; due to the quarter system, "there is never a time where students aren't hitting the library or studying with friends." There are plenty of open areas of the campus that you can find students studying ("especially the quad in the spring or summer"), and though students are "not big on structured extracurricular activities," they "do occasionally party." Food trucks are a very popular source of grub, particularly "the Food Truck Alley" behind the Main Building. For fun, Center City Philadelphia is just a short walk or subway ride away, and has everything from the Philadelphia Orchestra and Pennsylvania Ballet to "a variety of clubs, theaters, and bars." The campus is perfectly placed so that "all the conveniences and exciting things about city life are in your backyard, but all the comforts of being on a college campus (security, familiarity) are also there." In those rare periods without midterms or finals, people also "go to the gym frequently and play intramural sports."

Student Body

This work-oriented university is filled with highly-motivated individuals that "consistently challenge themselves and are willing to push themselves so that they can tap their full potential." Most people at Drexel are pretty transparent about their reasons for being there: They're "looking for a good job." Since the "very stressful" curriculum keeps the pedal to the metal, students "rely on one another to ensure they understand and complete the tasks that are assigned." Everyone here is "generally in a state of caffeination or exhaustion (or both)," depending on their schedule for that day. The student body is very diverse (with a large number of international students), with "lots of colorful and unique characters on campus." The community can be fairly "clique-y," but the suite-style rooming "really helps with making friends."

DREXEL UNIVERSITY

Financial Aid: 215-895-2537 • E-Mail: enroll@drexel.edu • Website: www.drexel.edu

THE PRINCETON REVIEW SAYS

Admissions

The school reports that its standardized testing policy for use in admission for Fall 2024 is Test Optional. It is unknown at this time if the 2024 testing policy will be permanent. The Princeton Review suggests that interested applicants consult with the school for the most up-to-date standardized testing policies. *Very important factors considered include:* rigor of secondary school record, class rank, academic GPA, standardized test scores. *Important factors considered include:* application essay, recommendation(s), character/personal qualities. *Other factors considered include:* interview, extracurricular activities, talent/ability, first generation, alumni/ae relation, volunteer work, work experience, level of applicant's interest. High school diploma is required and GED is accepted. *Academic units required:* 3 math, 1 science, 1 science lab. *Academic units recommended:* 1 foreign language.

Financial Aid

Students should submit: CSS/Financial Aid Profile; FAFSA. The Princeton Review suggests that all financial aid forms be submitted as soon as possible (see page 5 for a note on the FAFSA). *Need-based scholarships/grants offered:* College/university scholarship or grant aid from institutional funds; Federal Pell; Private scholarships; SEOG; State scholarships/grants. *Loan aid offered:* Direct PLUS loans; Direct Subsidized Loans; Direct Unsubsidized Loans; State Loans. Admitted students will be notified of awards on or about 4/1. Federal Work-Study Program available. Institutional employment available.

The Inside Word

Drexel University's nationally recognized co-op program provides unique hands-on experience for students with companies in and around Philadelphia to help them in their post-college employment. Given the current state of the economy, that's a huge boost for prospective applicants, especially in the engineering fields that Drexel still specializes in. Drexel accepts the Common Application for most programs, and takes into consideration a number of criteria when determining admission, including high school performance, letters of recommendation, standardized test scores, and the essay.

THE SCHOOL SAYS "..."

From the Admissions Office

"Drexel University has maintained a reputation for academic excellence since its founding in 1891. Through Drexel Co-op, students have the opportunity to test-drive their degree in paid full-time positions where they can earn up to 18 months of workplace experience before graduation with employers such as *Fortune* 500 companies, major pharmaceutical companies, and top design firms, as well as nonprofit agencies and government organizations. More than 1,600 employers in thirty-two states and forty-six international locations participate in the Drexel Co-op program. The average six-month paid co-op salary is more than $16,000.

"Drexel offers more than 80 undergraduate majors and over twenty accelerated degree programs. Accelerated degree options include the BA/BS/JD in law; BA/BS+MD in medicine; BS/DPT in physical therapy; BS/MS in computing and informatics; and BS/MBA in business.

"Qualified students can apply to the Honors program, which is open to students in every academic discipline. The Honors program offers special living communities designed for the exceptional student and opportunities for social activities, traveling, and independent projects. The STAR (Students Tackling Advanced Research) Scholars program invites qualified students to participate in faculty-mentored research projects in their chosen fields as early as the freshman year. Drexel also has an active Study Abroad program in more than two dozen countries around the world."

SELECTIVITY

Admissions Rating	86
# of applicants	37,040
% of applicants accepted	80
% of acceptees attending	10
# of early decision applicants	392
% accepted early decision	94

FIRST-YEAR PROFILE

Testing policy	Test Optional
Range SAT composite	1240–1420
Range SAT EBRW	610–700
Range SAT math	620–730
Range ACT composite	27–32
# submitting SAT scores	1,196
% submitting SAT scores	41
# submitting ACT scores	202
% submitting ACT scores	7
Average HS GPA	3.8
% frosh submitting high school GPA	94
% graduated top 10% of class	37
% graduated top 25% of class	69
% graduated top 50% of class	93

DEADLINES

Early decision	
Deadline	11/1
Notification	12/15
Early action	
Deadline	11/1
Notification	12/15
Regular	
Deadline	1/15
Notification	4/1
Nonfall registration?	Yes

APPLICANTS ALSO LOOK AT

American University; Boston University; Case Western Reserve University; Fordham University; Hofstra University; Lehigh University; New York University; Penn State University Park; Purdue University-Calumet; Rensselaer Polytechnic Institute

FINANCIAL FACTS

Financial Aid Rating	82
Annual tuition	$58,293
Room and board	$17,550
Required fees	$2,370
Books and supplies	$1,200
% frosh rec. any financial aid	100
% UG rec. any financial aid	94

DRURY UNIVERSITY

900 North Benton Avenue, Springfield, MO 65802-3712 • Admissions: 417-873-7879 • Fax: 417-866-3873

CAMPUS LIFE
Quality of Life Rating	91
Fire Safety Rating	82
Green Rating	76
Type of school	Private
Affiliation	Christian Church
	(Disciples of Christ), UCC
Environment	Metropolis

STUDENTS
Total undergrad enrollment	1,369
% male/female/another gender	46/54/NR
% from out of state	24
% frosh live on campus	95
% ugrads live on campus	67
# of fraternities (% join)	4 (15)
# of sororities (% join)	4 (21)
% African American	3
% Asian	3
% White	75
% Hispanic	2
% Native American	>1
% Pacific Islander	<1
% Two or more races	3
% Race and/or ethnicity unknown	6
% international	6
# of countries represented	49

SURVEY SAYS . . .
Students are happy
Internships are widely available
Diverse student types interact on campus
Intramural sports are popular
Frats and sororities are popular
College radio is popular

ACADEMICS
Academic Rating	85
% students returning for sophomore year	75
% students graduating within 4 years	43
% students graduating within 6 years	60
Calendar	Semester
Student/faculty ratio	12:1
Profs interesting rating	92
Profs accessible rating	95

Most classes have 10–19 students.
Most lab/discussion sessions have
10–19 students.

MOST POPULAR MAJORS
Architectural and Building Sciences/Technology;
Biology/Biological Sciences, General; Psychology,
General

STUDENTS SAY "..."

Academics

There is a lot to admire about "the atmosphere that Drury creates," a "truly beautiful and unique" college in Springfield, Missouri. After all, it provides students with a "well-rounded" education, "close community," and numerous "opportunities [for] leadership." Many undergrads also appreciate Drury's course "flexibility," which allows students to "be involved in non-major-specific courses/organizations." Of course, while the university offers a wide range of disciplines, many students highlight the "pre-health" and "architecture" departments as especially strong. Fortunately, no matter the major, Drury's "small size" lends itself to a "personalized [academic] experience." Indeed, since the "average class...is 12 students," everyone has a "better opportunity to communicate with professors on a one-on-one level." Though this doesn't negate the fact that classes here are rather "rigorous." Nevertheless, "the faculty works closely with students to help them be...successful." One grateful student agrees adding, "[Professors] are always available outside of class and really work with me on topics that I am struggling with." They make it evident that "they really care about what they are teaching." Best of all, Drury professors are "very personable, and always willing to go the extra mile to ensure the best learning experience for their students." Therefore, it comes as no surprise that undergrads here are able to develop "last[ing] relationships" with their professors.

Campus Life

There's plenty of fun to be had at Drury. To begin with, "during the fall semester you can find a lot of activity outside and on the campus green spaces, mostly sporting activities sprinkled with friendly gatherings and discussions." Additionally, a large number of students "volunteer in the community on a weekly basis." And most people "participate in at least one organization on campus." "Greek life is really big here" as are "intramural sports... such as basketball and volleyball." If those activities aren't your thing, fear not. The Student Union Board hosts "a lot of events" and those are typically well attended. Undergrads do note that "there is a party scene," as well, although mostly off-campus. Drury students are also rather adept at making their own fun. As one individual shares, "The students on my hall love to have board game nights, and we also have access to a projector room where we watch movies together." Lastly, the Springfield area offers "plenty of bars and clubs" that become quite popular on the weekends. And there are plenty of "coffee shops, restaurants, bookstores, bakeries, movie theaters, etc." too.

Student Body

When asked to describe their peers, undergrads at Drury immediately boast that they are "very engaging and friendly." One student quickly illustrates, "Walking down Drury Lane you say hello to at least five people, some you may not even really know; however, people are so nice and welcoming here that you don't have to...know [them] to say [hi]." Aside from this gregariousness, Drury undergrads are "bright and ambitious" and filled with "awesome school spirit." Moreover, many students desire to become "informed global citizens." As another undergrad proudly states, "I am surrounded by students who take every opportunity and experience to learn about themselves, their community, and the world." Hence, these undergrads love that the university draws students "from all around the world." In fact, it's not unusual for a person to find himself "sitting next to someone from Springfield (a local) or someone from Germany or Kenya." Perhaps this explains why "acceptance is a big part of [Drury's] campus." Indeed, "everyone tries to be as unified as possible." It helps that Drury's "small" size means that there's "so much room for building friendships and the possibility of knowing a good majority of the students here is most certainly possible." As this satisfied undergrad concludes, "I never imagined a college campus could feel so supportive and connected until I came to Drury."

DRURY UNIVERSITY

Financial Aid: 417-873-7312 • E-Mail: druryad@drury.edu • Website: www.drury.edu

THE PRINCETON REVIEW SAYS

Admissions

The school reports that its standardized testing policy for use in admission for Fall 2024 is Test Optional. The 2024 testing policy will be permanent. The Princeton Review suggests that interested applicants consult with the school for the most up-to-date standardized testing policies. *Very important factors considered include:* rigor of secondary school record, academic GPA. *Important factors considered include:* application essay. *Other factors considered include:* class rank, standardized test scores, extracurricular activities, talent/ability, character/personal qualities, first generation, alumni/ae relation, volunteer work, work experience. High school diploma is required and GED is accepted. *Academic units required:* 4 English, 3 math, 3 science, 2 science labs, 2 foreign language, 4 social studies, 2 history. *Academic units recommended:* 4 English, 4 math, 4 science, 3 science labs, 3 foreign language, 4 social studies, 2 history.

Financial Aid

Students should submit: FAFSA. The Princeton Review suggests that all financial aid forms be submitted as soon as possible (see page 5 for a note on the FAFSA). *Need-based scholarships/grants offered:* College/university scholarship or grant aid from institutional funds; Federal Pell; Private scholarships; SEOG; State scholarships/grants. *Loan aid offered:* Direct PLUS loans; Direct Subsidized Loans; Direct Unsubsidized Loans. Admitted students will be notified of awards on a rolling basis beginning 1/15. Federal Work-Study Program available. Institutional employment available.

The Inside Word

The admissions process at Drury is fairly selective. Admissions officers look for applicants who have taken a challenging college prep curriculum. They also closely evaluate personal statements and each student's extracurricular participation. Finally, Drury operates on a basis of rolling admission. If you're really interested in attending, consider submitting your application as early as possible.

THE SCHOOL SAYS "..."

From the Admissions Office

"From day one, Drury students are engaged in real research and scholarship with faculty mentors. This is a rare advantage; one that speaks to Drury's singular approach to equipping students for leadership in the 21st century. Through its distinctive *Your Drury Fusion* program, the University provides students with an opportunity to blend career, calling, life, community, self and service to gain a broader perspective on the world. It also is a place where students get to really know their professors as well as their classmates, creating a strong sense of culture and community that transcends the classroom.

"Established in 1873, Drury University sits on 90 acres in the heart of Springfield, Missouri. A designated "Tree Campus" by the Arbor Day Foundation, it is an oasis within the city where students are engaged in highly interactive, intellectual exercises that teach them to be flexible, innovative and creative problem solvers.

"The university offers all of the majors you would expect from a top liberal arts university plus majors like architecture, music therapy, software engineering, computer game design and a pre-med program with five pre-acceptance partner medical schools.

"Your Drury Fusion provides all students multiple credentials, holistic advising which combines academic and career planning from day 1, and a minimum of three experiential projects over your four year career. The Drury Difference leads to 97% of graduates employed or in professional or graduate school within six months of graduation."

SELECTIVITY

Admissions Rating	92
# of applicants	2,382
% of applicants accepted	49
% of acceptees attending	35

FIRST-YEAR PROFILE

Testing policy	Test Optional
Range SAT composite	1120–1390
Range SAT EBRW	590–700
Range SAT math	560–660
Range ACT composite	22–28
# submitting SAT scores	18
% submitting SAT scores	4
# submitting ACT scores	274
% submitting ACT scores	64
Average HS GPA	3.8
% frosh submitting high school GPA	100
% graduated top 10% of class	25
% graduated top 25% of class	56
% graduated top 50% of class	87

DEADLINES

Regular	
Priority	2/1
Deadline	8/15
Notification	Rolling, 9/1
Nonfall registration?	Yes

APPLICANTS ALSO LOOK AT

Creighton University; Hendrix College; Missouri State University; The University of Tulsa; Truman State University; University of Missouri

FINANCIAL FACTS

Financial Aid Rating	85
Annual tuition	$33,900
Room and board	$10,760
Required fees	$1,400
Books and supplies	$1,240
Average frosh need-based scholarship	$24,750
Average UG need-based scholarship	$23,808
% needy frosh rec. need-based scholarship or grant aid	100
% needy UG rec. need-based scholarship or grant aid	100
% needy frosh rec. non-need-based scholarship or grant aid	23
% needy UG rec. non-need-based scholarship or grant aid	21
% needy frosh rec. need-based self-help aid	59
% needy UG rec. need-based self-help aid	63
% frosh rec. any financial aid	100
% UG rec. any financial aid	98
% UG borrow to pay for school	60
Average cumulative indebtedness	$30,506
% frosh need fully met	26
% ugrads need fully met	26
Average % of frosh need met	79
Average % of ugrad need met	78

DUKE UNIVERSITY

Chapel Drive, Durham, NC 27708 • Admissions: 919-684-8111 • Fax: 919-668-1661

CAMPUS LIFE

Quality of Life Rating	78
Fire Safety Rating	60*
Green Rating	60*
Type of school	Private
Affiliation	Methodist
Environment	Metropolis

STUDENTS

Total undergrad enrollment	6,596
% male/female/another gender	50/50/0
% from out of state	85
% frosh from public high school	65
% frosh live on campus	100
% ugrads live on campus	85
# of fraternities (% join)	21 (29)
# of sororities (% join)	14 (42)
% African American	10
% Asian	22
% White	42
% Hispanic	9
% Native American	<1
% Pacific Islander	<1
% Two or more races	2
% Race and/or ethnicity unknown	4
% international	10
# of countries represented	89

SURVEY SAYS . . .

Classroom facilities are great
Lab facilities are great
Great library
Internships are widely available
Great financial aid
No one cheats
Recreation facilities are great
Everyone loves the Blue Devils
Active student government

ACADEMICS

Academic Rating	86
% students returning for sophomore year	98
% students graduating within 4 years	87
% students graduating within 6 years	96
Calendar	Semester
Student/faculty ratio	6:1
Profs interesting rating	83
Profs accessible rating	87

Most classes have 10–19 students.
Most lab/discussion sessions have 10–19 students.

MOST POPULAR MAJORS

Public Policy Analysis, General; Economics, General; Psychology, General

STUDENTS SAY "..."

Academics

Duke University is "all about academic excellence complemented by highly competitive Division I sports and an enriching array of extracurricular activities," making the university "an exciting, challenging, and enjoyable place to be." Undergraduates choose Duke because they "are passionate about a wide range of things, including academics, sports, community service, research, and fun." And because the school seems equally committed to accommodating all of those pursuits, as one student puts it, "Duke is for the Ivy League candidate who is a little bit more laid-back about school and overachieving (but just a bit)." There's an "across-the-board excellence in all departments from humanities to engineering." In all areas, there's a "supportive environment in which the faculty, staff, and students are willing to look out for the other person and help them succeed." It's the norm to have large study groups, and "the review sessions, peer tutoring system, writing center, and academic support center are always helpful when students are struggling with anything from math homework to creating a résumé." Professors' "number-one priority is teaching undergraduates," and their love of discussion means they "would rather that the students lead the class as opposed to them leading the class." "There are a few who make me want to stay at Duke forever," says a student. Because "the school has a lot of confidence in its students," it offers them "seemingly limitless opportunities."

Campus Life

Life at Duke "is very relaxed," and "you can either be a part of nothing, or you can be so over-committed that it's not even funny." Because "the student union and other organizations provide entertainment all the time, from movies to shows to campus-wide parties," there's "a wealth of on-campus opportunities to get involved." Indeed, weekends are for relaxing, and "people usually stay on campus for fun," because hometown Durham "has a few quirky streets and squares with restaurants, shops, clubs, etc." Undergrads' fervor for Blue Devils sports, on the other hand, can be boundless; sports, "especially basketball, are a huge deal here," and undergrads "will paint themselves completely blue and wait in line on the sidewalk in K-ville for three days to jump up and down in Cameron Indoor Stadium." Greek life "plays a big role in the social scene here," but "almost all the parties are open, so it definitely isn't hard to get into a party." A lot of people "just do their own thing—have a movie night, go exploring, go skiing or to the beach for a weekend." Still, the social scene can be "a little too intense" at times.

Student Body

The student body "is surprisingly ethnically diverse, with a number of students of Asian, African, and Hispanic descent," and "every type of person finds a welcoming group where he or she fits in." The typical Duke student "is someone who cares a lot about his or her education but at the same time won't sacrifice a social life for it." Life involves "getting a ton of work done first and then finding time to play and have fun." The typical student here is studious but social, athletic but can never be seen in the gym, job hunting but not worrying, and so on and so forth." Everyone is "incredibly focused," but "that includes social success as well." Students tend to be "focused on graduating and obtaining a lucrative and prosperous career," and although they "go out two to three times a week," they're "always looking polished." An "overwhelming number" are athletes, "not just varsity athletes...but athletes in high school or generally active people. Duke's athletic pride attracts this kind of person."

DUKE UNIVERSITY

E-Mail: undergrad-admissions@duke.edu • Website: www.duke.edu

THE PRINCETON REVIEW SAYS

Admissions

The school reports that its standardized testing policy for use in admission for Fall 2024 is Test Optional. It is unknown at this time if the 2024 testing policy will be permanent. The Princeton Review suggests that interested applicants consult with the school for the most up-to-date standardized testing policies. *Very important factors considered include:* rigor of secondary school record, academic GPA, standardized test scores, application essay, recommendation(s), extracurricular activities, talent/ability, character/personal qualities. *Other factors considered include:* interview, first generation, alumni/ae relation, geographical residence, state residency, religious affiliation/commitment, racial/ethnic status, volunteer work, work experience, level of applicant's interest. High school diploma is required and GED is not accepted. *Academic units recommended:* 4 English, 3 math, 3 science, 3 foreign language, 3 social studies.

Financial Aid

Students should submit: Business/Farm Supplement; CSS/Financial Aid Profile; FAFSA; Noncustodial Profile. The Princeton Review suggests that all financial aid forms be submitted as soon as possible (see page 5 for a note on the FAFSA). *Need-based scholarships/grants offered:* College/university scholarship or grant aid from institutional funds; Federal Pell; Private scholarships; SEOG; State scholarships/grants. *Loan aid offered:* Direct PLUS loans; Direct Subsidized Loans; Direct Unsubsidized Loans; College/university loans from institutional funds. Admitted students will be notified of awards on or about 4/1. Federal Work-Study Program available. Institutional employment available.

The Inside Word

Duke is an extremely selective undergraduate institution, which affords the school the luxury of rejecting many qualified applicants. You'll have to present an exceptional record just to be considered; to make the cut, you'll have to impress the admissions office that you can contribute something unique and valuable to the incoming class. Being one of the best basketball players in the nation (male or female) helps a lot, but even athletes have to show academic excellence to get in the door here.

THE SCHOOL SAYS "..."

From the Admissions Office

"From the Admissions Office "Duke University offers a blend of tradition and innovation, undergraduate college and major research university, academic excellence and athletic achievement, and global presence and regional charm. Students come to Duke from all over the United States and the world and from a range of racial, ethnic, and socioeconomic backgrounds. They enjoy contact with a world-class faculty through small classes and independent study. More than forty majors are available in the arts and sciences and engineering; arts and sciences students may also design their own curriculum through Program II. Certificate programs are available in a number of interdisciplinary areas. Special academic opportunities include the Focus Program and seminars for first-year students DukeImmerse, study abroad, domestic study away programs in New York, Los Angeles, Washington, DC, Chicago, Silicon Valley, and Alaska, Bass Connections research programs, and DukeEngage summer service opportunities. While admission to Duke is highly selective, applications of U.S. citizens, permanent residents, and undocumented students are evaluated without regard to financial need and the university pledges to meet 100 percent of the demonstrated need of all admitted U.S. students and permanent residents. A limited amount of financial aid is also available for foreign citizens, and the university will meet the full demonstrated financial need for those admitted students as well.

"Applicants must take either the ACT or the SAT."

SELECTIVITY
Admissions Rating	99
# of applicants	35,767
% of applicants accepted	9
% of acceptees attending	55
# of early decision applicants	4,070
% accepted early decision	22

FIRST-YEAR PROFILE
Testing policy	Test Optional
Range SAT EBRW	710–770
Range SAT math	740–800
Range ACT composite	33–35
# submitting SAT scores	928
% submitting SAT scores	53
# submitting ACT scores	1,252
% submitting ACT scores	72
% graduated top 10% of class	95
% graduated top 25% of class	98
% graduated top 50% of class	100

DEADLINES
Early decision	
Deadline	11/1
Notification	12/15
Regular	
Priority	12/20
Deadline	1/3
Notification	4/1
Nonfall registration?	No

FINANCIAL FACTS
Financial Aid Rating	94
Annual tuition	$55,880
Room and board	$15,588
Required fees	$2,051
Books and supplies	$1,434
Average frosh need-based scholarship	$53,400
Average UG need-based scholarship	$53,214
% needy frosh rec. need-based scholarship or grant aid	94
% needy UG rec. need-based scholarship or grant aid	95
% needy frosh rec. non-need-based scholarship or grant aid	16
% needy UG rec. non-need-based scholarship or grant aid	10
% needy frosh rec. need-based self-help aid	73
% needy UG rec. need-based self-help aid	81
% UG borrow to pay for school	32
Average cumulative indebtedness	$21,525
% frosh need fully met	100
% ugrads need fully met	100
Average % of frosh need met	100
Average % of ugrad need met	100

DUQUESNE UNIVERSITY

600 Forbes Avenue, Pittsburgh, PA 15282 • Admissions: 412-396-6000 • Fax: 412-396-6223

STUDENTS SAY "..."

Academics

Students describe their time at Duquesne University as "beyond satisfying.... I was able to discover new subjects that I love learning about and tailor my academic experience to those interests." In particular, students laud the nursing, education, business, and biomedical engineering fields. On the medical side, the "informative" and "hands-on" clinicals and lab simulation opportunities are seen as some of the campus' best and most "one-of-a-kind" academic features. Across the board, students highlight frequently updated technology and a variety of classroom types as benefits, such as the experience-based style: "We have to do whatever we are learning, and it vastly improves my learning." Enrollees also cite "a good number of guest speakers and experts," all of which "breaks up the heavy lectures."

Professors are passionate about what they teach and "want to see their students succeed in everything that they do later in life. [They] are always willing to meet and discuss material ... possible research experience or anything that the student may need." Along those lines, they also practice a range of teaching methods, which some undergrads suggest offers "new ways [of] engaging us, involving us ... and treating us like adults." Another benefit comes in the small, focused class sizes "in which students can discuss specific topics in depth" and also have "better relationships with professors and classmates." For those looking to get out of the classroom, Duquesne's outdoor classes and study-abroad opportunities are much appreciated.

Campus Life

Either at Duquesne University itself, or from its bustling location in central Pittsburgh, "there is nearly always something to do," and students praise its "incredible night life." Most on-campus activities are "cost-free to students," which is a plus, and there are nearly 300 clubs and a thriving Greek Life system to choose from. "There are more than enough active and very involved clubs to keep one engaged for the entire day, every day of the week." Sports are also a healthy part of campus life, including organized team activities as well as "exercise classes that Duquesne offers for free to all students such as spin class [and] yoga." Pittsburgh itself has plenty to offer, especially if you're into sports; the stadium for the National Hockey League's Penguins is "a 45-second walk from campus and the tickets are discounted for students; this is my favorite thing to do for fun."

Student Body

Duquesne has a long history as a private Catholic research university, but while those traditions remain a part of the school, students emphasize that "this campus is a place for anyone" where "there are people of all religions and walks of life." Spirited discussions in "the welcoming nature of the Duquesne classroom" recognize that those "from different political, social, and financial backgrounds have unique experiences" and make for a more enriched learning experience: "Students enjoy sharing in class, and I love learning from them. My classes have been very supportive environments." Overall, attendees see themselves and their peers united as "dedicated individuals who wish to pursue careers after college while also trying to maintain a fun, involved environment at the school."

DUQUESNE UNIVERSITY

Financial Aid: 412-396-6607 • E-Mail: admissions@duq.edu • Website: www.duq.edu

THE PRINCETON REVIEW SAYS

Admissions

The school reports that its standardized testing policy for use in admission for Fall 2024 is Test Optional. It is unknown at this time if the 2024 testing policy will be permanent. The Princeton Review suggests that interested applicants consult with the school for the most up-to-date standardized testing policies. *Very important factors considered include:* rigor of secondary school record, academic GPA, standardized test scores. *Important factors considered include:* class rank, extracurricular activities, talent/ability, character/personal qualities, volunteer work, work experience. *Other factors considered include:* application essay, recommendation(s), interview, first generation, alumni/ae relation, geographical residence, state residency, religious affiliation/commitment, racial/ethnic status, level of applicant's interest. High school diploma is required and GED is accepted. *Academic units required:* 4 English, 2 math, 2 science, 2 foreign language, 2 social studies, 4 academic electives.

Financial Aid

Students should submit: FAFSA. The Princeton Review suggests that all financial aid forms be submitted as soon as possible (see page 5 for a note on the FAFSA). *Need-based scholarships/grants offered:* College/university scholarship or grant aid from institutional funds; Federal Pell; Private scholarships; SEOG; State scholarships/grants; United Negro College Fund. *Loan aid offered:* Direct PLUS loans; Direct Subsidized Loans; Direct Unsubsidized Loans; Federal Nursing Loans. Admitted students will be notified of awards on a rolling basis beginning 12/1. Federal Work-Study Program available. Institutional employment available.

The Inside Word

Duquesne takes a relatively straightforward approach to the admissions process. That means that your GPA and the rigor of your high school curriculum will be the two most important factors. However, the application process is a little more stringent for individuals applying for health sciences. Academic recommendations, standardized test scores, and personal statements will also play a role. The university is currently Test Optional for all undergraduate students.

THE SCHOOL SAYS "..."

From the Admissions Office

"At Duquesne, you'll gain the professional confidence, impressive experience and powerful networks you need to get a running start on a meaningful career or graduate program. Ranked as a best value university (2023 U.S. News), you'll automatically be considered for scholarships based on your accomplishments when you apply. Choose from 80 future-focused majors in business, education, engineering, health sciences, liberal arts, music, science, nursing and pharmacy; Honors College; pre-medical; pre-law; 3+3 bachelor's/JD law programs; plus 35+ study abroad programs. Take classes on a park-like campus next to downtown Pittsburgh, where students enjoy a short walk or bus ride to Pittsburgh's cultural district, sports stadiums, shopping, dining and parks. Develop friendships that last a lifetime, learning with and from students of diverse cultural, socioeconomic and religious backgrounds from every state and 50 countries. With an average student-faculty ratio of 13:1, your professors will walk beside you to help reach your boldest goals. Duquesne's central location provides invaluable access to community engagement and practical experience through fieldwork, research projects and internships at major corporations, healthcare systems, schools and other organizations. Choose from 275+ student organizations, including academic, social, service, spiritual, Greek, political, performing arts and sports. Duquesne has 17 NCAA Division I men's and women's teams (with 3 more coming soon) plus club and intramural sports. More than 8,500 students attend Duquesne annually, and the alumni network is 100,000+ strong. Drawing on our 145-year Catholic Spiritan heritage, we promise you an education that's exactly what you need and more than you could ever have imagined."

SELECTIVITY

Admissions Rating	83
# of applicants	12,282
% of applicants accepted	88
% of acceptees attending	13
# offered a place on the wait list	999
% accepting a place on wait list	77
% admitted from wait list	36

FIRST-YEAR PROFILE

Testing policy	Test Optional
Range SAT composite	1170–1330
Range SAT EBRW	590–670
Range SAT math	570–660
Range ACT composite	25–31
# submitting SAT scores	399
% submitting SAT scores	28
# submitting ACT scores	106
% submitting ACT scores	7
Average HS GPA	3.9
% frosh submitting high school GPA	98
% graduated top 10% of class	24
% graduated top 25% of class	54
% graduated top 50% of class	86

DEADLINES

Early action	
Deadline	11/1
Notification	12/1
Regular	
Priority	11/1
Deadline	8/15
Notification	Rolling, 9/1
Nonfall registration?	Yes

APPLICANTS OFTEN PREFER
Penn State University Park; Temple University; The University of Scranton; University of Dayton; University of Pittsburgh—Pittsburgh Campus

APPLICANTS SOMETIMES PREFER
Drexel University; Indiana University of Pennsylvania; Robert Morris University; West Chester University of Pennsylvania; West Virginia University

FINANCIAL FACTS

Financial Aid Rating	82
Annual tuition	$47,146
Room and board	$15,620
Books and supplies	$1,440
Average frosh need-based scholarship	$27,415
Average UG need-based scholarship	$25,315
% needy frosh rec. need-based scholarship or grant aid	96
% needy UG rec. need-based scholarship or grant aid	98
% needy frosh rec. non-need-based scholarship or grant aid	93
% needy UG rec. non-need-based scholarship or grant aid	95
% needy frosh rec. need-based self-help aid	70
% needy UG rec. need-based self-help aid	74
% frosh rec. any financial aid	100
% UG rec. any financial aid	99
% UG borrow to pay for school	71
Average cumulative indebtedness	$51,598
% frosh need fully met	19
% ugrads need fully met	19
Average % of frosh need met	74
Average % of ugrad need met	71

THE BEST 389 COLLEGES ■ 223

EARLHAM COLLEGE

801 National Road West, Richmond, IN 47374-4095 • Admissions: 765-983-1200 • Fax: 765-983-1560

CAMPUS LIFE

Quality of Life Rating	83
Fire Safety Rating	96
Green Rating	84
Type of school	Private
Affiliation	Quaker
Environment	Town

STUDENTS

Total undergrad enrollment	590
% male/female/another gender	46/50/4
% from out of state	73
% frosh from public high school	69
% frosh live on campus	88
% ugrads live on campus	90
% African American	8
% Asian	3
% White	57
% Hispanic	9
% Native American	0
% Pacific Islander	0
% Two or more races	4
% Race and/or ethnicity unknown	1
% international	19
# of countries represented	53

SURVEY SAYS . . .

Lots of liberal students
Lab facilities are great
Class discussions encouraged
Students environmentally aware
Active student government
Active minority support groups

ACADEMICS

Academic Rating	89
% students returning for sophomore year	80
% students graduating within 4 years	66
% students graduating within 6 years	75
Calendar	Semester
Student/faculty ratio	6:1
Profs interesting rating	93
Profs accessible rating	96

Most classes have fewer than 10 students.
Most lab/discussion sessions have
10–19 students.

MOST POPULAR MAJORS

Biology/Biological Sciences, General; Research
and Experimental Psychology, Other; Multi-/
Interdisciplinary Studies, General

STUDENTS SAY "..."

Academics

A small school with Quaker roots, Earlham College offers "small class sizes [that allow] faculty to easily connect with students." This is a result of a low student-faculty ratio which means students have plenty of opportunity to "have a strong and close connection with professors." Additionally, faculty are "extremely available and willing to connect" to help their students really understand the subjects they "are passionate in teaching." Those professors are "amazing to work with," says a student. Another gushes, "They are like incredibly knowledgeable friends who have [a] strong interest in your future and helping you succeed." Overall, their courses are described as "rigorous," "interesting," and "engaging," and students also find they can "get the help [they] need" without much trouble. Students here cite the unique academic programs which include Peace and Global Studies as well as a program called EPIC, "which [allots] students funds to...research [or intern] in any place or country of their liking." One student sums up the academic experience at Earlham: "Each professor...has made me care about the subject of their class in a way I never would have expected—whether that's opening up a field I already love or finding ways to connect new material to the subjects that are close to me."

Campus Life

Many undergrads proudly proclaim that the "possibilities are endless" at Earlham when it comes to campus activities. Indeed, it's "a wonderful environment for passionate and self-driven students" who thrive on having "back-to-back commitments." As one enthusiastic individual explains, "I run a club, direct and act in plays, sing in the choir, go to the gym, and still take nineteen credits." It's hard to resist the many school-sponsored activities "such as concerts, bowling, movie night, [and] roller skating." Another popular activity is Dance Alloy, which is a "bi-yearly student choreographed dance performance" that many students join and "spend multiple nights a week practicing and preparing" to get just right. Moreover, "every other Friday night there is an open mic event...[where] everyone is welcome to perform." And when the weekend fully rolls around, you can "usually [find some] house parties or people just [hanging] out with their friends." Those hang-out sessions can include "talking about literature, playing cards, [or having] occasional nights of drinking and video games." And a good number simply love exploring the "large chunk of undeveloped woods behind [the] campus."

Student Body

Despite being a small school, Earlham manages to yield a "diverse population." Indeed, you can find students "from all over the world" who enrich the campus with their "interesting stories and backgrounds." Undergrads seem to mesh well as everyone treats each other "with kindness and compassion." Moreover, many students here are "concerned about social issues and justice" and a large number "seem to be inclined to left-wing policies." Or, as another undergrad puts it, "Earlham is hippies. Earlham is bare feet and climbing trees. Earlhamites are activists. They are earth lovers, peace lovers, and lovers of learning." Therefore, it's not too shocking to learn that many students also describe their peers as "collaborative and encouraging" because of the "close-knit bonds [they have] to the people around them." They "care a lot about [their] community" and "make sure everyone feels welcomed." As one undergrad concludes, "After being on campus for so long, it is easy to realize that everyone here is weird in their own ways, and the great part is that the community is very accepting and less judgmental than most other places."

EARLHAM COLLEGE

Financial Aid: 765-983-1217 • E-Mail: admissions@earlham.edu • Website: www.earlham.edu

THE PRINCETON REVIEW SAYS

Admissions

The school reports that its standardized testing policy for use in admission for Fall 2024 is Test Flexible. The 2024 testing policy will be permanent. The Princeton Review suggests that interested applicants consult with the school for the most up-to-date standardized testing policies. *Very important factors considered include:* rigor of secondary school record, academic GPA. *Important factors considered include:* application essay, extracurricular activities, character/personal qualities. *Other factors considered include:* class rank, standardized test scores, recommendation(s), interview, talent/ability, volunteer work, work experience. High school diploma is required and GED is accepted. *Academic units required:* 4 English, 3 math, 3 science, 2 science labs, 2 foreign language, 2 social studies, 2 history. *Academic units recommended:* 4 English, 4 math, 4 science, 2 science labs, 2 foreign language, 2 social studies, 2 history.

Financial Aid

Students should submit: FAFSA. Priority filing deadline is 11/1. The Princeton Review suggests that all financial aid forms be submitted as soon as possible (see page 5 for a note on the FAFSA). *Need-based scholarships/grants offered:* College/university scholarship or grant aid from institutional funds; Federal Pell; Private scholarships; SEOG; State scholarships/grants. *Loan aid offered:* Direct PLUS loans; Direct Subsidized Loans; Direct Unsubsidized Loans. Admitted students will be notified of awards on a rolling basis beginning 11/15. Federal Work-Study Program available. Institutional employment available.

The Inside Word

Earning admission to Earlham is no easy feat. The application process is competitive, and students must demonstrate that that they are academically prepared and intellectually curious. Therefore, you can expect admissions officers to pay close attention to the rigor of your high school curriculum. Of secondary importance will be your personal statement, recommendations, and extracurricular activities. Lastly, we should mention that Earlham is a Test Flexible school. You don't need to submit your scores unless you're an international student, home-schooled, or you earned a GED.

THE SCHOOL SAYS "..."

From the Admissions Office

"Earlham is an academically distinguished liberal arts college that uniquely equips students for the 21st century. In addition to its programs of study, the College emphasizes hands-on and collaborative learning through the Earlham Advantage Grant, a central feature of the Earlham experience. Thanks to a generous gift from an alumnus, the College funds high-impact, immersive experiences like internships and student-faculty research for all students, making these experiences possible to students regardless of family income. These powerful experiences take place across the United States and the world. The result is transformative and leads to compelling opportunities for graduates. Earlham ranks among the top percent of all colleges for graduates who earn a PhD, and acceptance rates to medical, law, and other professional schools are exceptionally high. Earlham has recently invested more than $60 million in academic facilities, and its professors are known for both their scholarship and innovative teaching. Earlham is renowned as a distinctively welcoming community, embracing both individual and cultural differences. Shaped by Quaker perspectives, Earlham prepares its students to be catalysts for good in a changing world. Earlham enrolls students from almost all fifty states and sixty nations. Students compete in nineteen intercollegiate sports and in an equestrian program. The College's diverse and multi-talented student body brings positive energy to campus life, community service, and a drive to make a difference."

SELECTIVITY

Admissions Rating	86
# of applicants	1,375
% of applicants accepted	73
% of acceptees attending	17

FIRST-YEAR PROFILE

Testing policy	Test Flexible
Range SAT composite	1160–1350
Range SAT EBRW	590–710
Range SAT math	540–670
Range ACT composite	24–32
# submitting SAT scores	43
% submitting SAT scores	24
# submitting ACT scores	33
% submitting ACT scores	19
Average HS GPA	3.7
% frosh submitting high school GPA	100
% graduated top 10% of class	25
% graduated top 25% of class	53
% graduated top 50% of class	95

DEADLINES

Early action	
Deadline	11/1
Notification	11/15
Regular	
Priority	11/1
Deadline	3/1
Notification	4/1
Nonfall registration?	Yes

APPLICANTS OFTEN PREFER
Ball State University; Indiana University—Bloomington

APPLICANTS SOMETIMES PREFER
Indiana University—Purdue University Columbus; Purdue University—West Lafayette; University of Oklahoma

FINANCIAL FACTS

Financial Aid Rating	89
Annual tuition	$48,218
Room and board	$12,448
Required fees	$840
Books and supplies	$1,000
Average frosh need-based scholarship	$23,343
Average UG need-based scholarship	$30,446
% needy frosh rec. need-based scholarship or grant aid	77
% needy UG rec. need-based scholarship or grant aid	85
% needy frosh rec. non-need-based scholarship or grant aid	53
% needy UG rec. non-need-based scholarship or grant aid	34
% needy frosh rec. need-based self-help aid	65
% needy UG rec. need-based self-help aid	71
% frosh rec. any financial aid	78
% UG rec. any financial aid	73
% UG borrow to pay for school	55
Average cumulative indebtedness	$25,821
% frosh need fully met	30
% ugrads need fully met	32
Average % of frosh need met	54
Average % of ugrad need met	65

EAST CAROLINA UNIVERSITY

East 5th Street, Greenville, NC 27858-4353 • Admissions: 252-328-6131 • Fax: 252-737-1192

CAMPUS LIFE

Quality of Life Rating	80
Fire Safety Rating	99
Green Rating	93
Type of school	Public
Environment	City

STUDENTS

Total undergrad enrollment	20,385
% male/female/another gender	43/57/0
% from out of state	9
% frosh live on campus	92
% ugrads live on campus	24
# of fraternities	22
# of sororities	14
% African American	16
% Asian	3
% White	64
% Hispanic	9
% Native American	<1
% Pacific Islander	<1
% Two or more races	4
% Race and/or ethnicity unknown	3
% international	1
# of countries represented	56

SURVEY SAYS . . .
Lots of conservative students
Easy to get around campus
Everyone loves the Pirates
School is well run

ACADEMICS

Academic Rating	73
% students returning for sophomore year	80
% students graduating within 4 years	45
% students graduating within 6 years	65
Calendar	Semester
Student/faculty ratio	18:1
Profs interesting rating	81
Profs accessible rating	84

Most classes have 20–29 students.
Most lab/discussion sessions have
  10–19 students.

MOST POPULAR MAJORS
Accounting and Business/Management; Speech
Communication and Rhetoric; Registered
Nursing/Registered Nurse

STUDENTS SAY "..."

Academic

East Carolina University is a public research university in North Carolina that gives students the chance to participate in cutting-edge research, hybrid online and classroom courses, and hands-on learning. Of particular note are the engineering program, which "offers students an unlimited number of opportunities," and "the nursing school, [which] is second to none." Regardless of the chosen program, professors help students "consider all aspects of the material when learning" so they can gain a deeper understanding, and they will often "come in on Saturday or Sunday to help." One student says, "The passion and enthusiasm they show reflects onto the students," describing teaching methods that include scenario-based learning and an "avoidance of reading PowerPoints word-by-word." Most professors "are very interactive and make a great school environment," but there are "a couple that just lecture the whole time."

Both in and out of the classroom, the number of people at East Carolina "make it possible to make a lot of connections for everything," and there are "endless resources here on campus to utilize and use to your advantage to be advanced in your curriculum and personal life." Those resources include a "huge library, writing center, multiple computer labs and study lounges, career center, organization start up lessons, [and] counseling center." There are "so many different services provided for students to help them succeed" and "the Pirate Academic Success Center is always open for tutoring to give a helping hand."

Campus Life

ECU students are physically active: some "will go to the gym and play basketball after class," and "the rec center provides plenty of things to do in terms of working out and swimming." In all, the "Pirate Nation loves to hang out and support ECU athletics." After, they'll quite often "spend time at home with roommates" or find "a comedy night or karaoke night at some of the restaurants, bars or breweries downtown." There are plenty of on-campus activities too, like talent shows and game nights. In all, students "like to turn up and party," and as a result "pack their class schedule to be in the middle of the day" so they have "time to sleep in not too late but [don't have] to get to those dreadful eight or nine A.M. classes." The campus itself is "sprawling but well-organized" in terms of the main academic buildings and dorms, and "everything is close together." Plus, Greenville is "really a college town" where "you feel like you are with people who are in the same mindset."

Student Body

This "very diverse and unique group of students" primarily hails from North Carolina, and despite the large number of students, "it is a very small and family-oriented campus that does not make you feel small." Extracurriculars help build that community on campus, with many taking part in "at least one extracurricular group or activity, and they wear the shirt to prove it." As one East Carolina Pirate puts it, "the library's group study rooms are always full," because "most students try very hard." That said, there is definitely a range "from the typical hardworking motivated student to the atypical Greek life individual who flunks out after a year or two." Overall, these are "great people," and "there is a crowd for whatever type of experience you are looking for."

EAST CAROLINA UNIVERSITY

Financial Aid: 252-328-4347 • E-mail: admissions@ecu.edu • Website: www.ecu.edu

THE PRINCETON REVIEW SAYS

Admissions

The school reports that its standardized testing policy for use in admission for Fall 2024 is Test Free. It is unknown at this time if the 2024 testing policy will be permanent. The Princeton Review suggests that interested applicants consult with the school for the most up-to-date standardized testing policies. *Very important factors considered include:* rigor of secondary school record, academic GPA, application essay, state residency. *Important factors considered include:* class rank. *Other factors considered include:* extracurricular activities, talent/ability, character/personal qualities, first generation, alumni/ae relation, volunteer work, work experience, level of applicant's interest. High school diploma is required and GED is accepted. *Academic units required:* 4 English, 4 math, 3 science, 1 science lab, 2 foreign language, 1 social studies, 1 history. *Academic units recommended:* 4 English, 4 math, 3 science, 1 science lab, 2 foreign language, 2 social studies, 1 history, 1 visual/performing arts.

Financial Aid

Students should submit: FAFSA. Priority filing deadline is 3/1. The Princeton Review suggests that all financial aid forms be submitted as soon as possible (see page 5 for a note on the FAFSA). *Need-based scholarships/grants offered:* College/university scholarship or grant aid from institutional funds; Federal Nursing Scholarships; Federal Pell; Private scholarships; SEOG; State scholarships/grants. *Loan aid offered:* Direct PLUS loans; Direct Subsidized Loans; Direct Unsubsidized Loans; Federal Nursing Loans; State Loans. Admitted students will be notified of awards on a rolling basis beginning 5/1. Federal Work-Study Program available. Institutional employment available.

The Inside Word

Admissions shouldn't be a problem for B students who have taken a solid roster of college preparatory classes, including four years of math and English, three years of natural sciences, and two years of social studies and a foreign language (a foreign language is also strongly recommended during senior year). If you are applying for in-state tuition, you must visit NCresidency.org and verify your residency first.

SELECTIVITY

Admissions Rating	82
# of applicants	21,383
% of applicants accepted	92
% of acceptees attending	19

FIRST-YEAR PROFILE

Testing policy	Test Free
Range SAT composite	1070–1230
Range SAT EBRW	520–620
Range SAT math	520–620
Range ACT composite	18–24
# submitting SAT scores	227
% submitting SAT scores	6
# submitting ACT scores	502
% submitting ACT scores	13
Average HS GPA	3.3
% frosh submitting high school GPA	100
% graduated top 10% of class	13
% graduated top 25% of class	34
% graduated top 50% of class	69

DEADLINES

Regular	
Deadline	4/1
Notification	Rolling, 9/1
Nonfall registration?	Yes

APPLICANTS OFTEN PREFER

North Carolina State University; University of North Carolina–Chapel Hill

APPLICANTS SOMETIMES PREFER

Appalachian State University; University of North Carolina Wilmington; Western Carolina University

FINANCIAL FACTS

Financial Aid Rating	79
Annual in-state tuition	$4,452
Annual out-of-state tuition	$20,729
Room and board	$10,180
Required fees	$2,873
Books and supplies	$1,654
Average frosh need-based scholarship	$9,334
Average UG need-based scholarship	$9,518
% needy frosh rec. need-based scholarship or grant aid	81
% needy UG rec. need-based scholarship or grant aid	89
% needy frosh rec. non-need-based scholarship or grant aid	16
% needy UG rec. non-need-based scholarship or grant aid	16
% needy frosh rec. need-based self-help aid	70
% needy UG rec. need-based self-help aid	66
% frosh rec. any financial aid	80
% UG rec. any financial aid	63
% UG borrow to pay for school	64
Average cumulative indebtedness	$28,120
% frosh need fully met	6
% ugrads need fully met	6
Average % of frosh need met	63
Average % of ugrad need met	62

ECKERD COLLEGE

4200 54th Avenue South, St. Petersburg, FL 33711 • Admissions: 727-867-1166 • Fax: 727-866-2304

CAMPUS LIFE

Quality of Life Rating	92
Fire Safety Rating	91
Green Rating	87
Type of school	Private
Affiliation	Presbyterian
Environment	City

STUDENTS

Total undergrad enrollment	1,986
% male/female/another gender	30/70/0
% from out of state	79
% frosh live on campus	98
% ugrads live on campus	87
# of fraternities	0
# of sororities	0
% African American	2
% Asian	2
% White	76
% Hispanic	9
% Native American	<1
% Pacific Islander	<1
% Two or more races	6
% Race and/or ethnicity unknown	<1
% international	4
# of countries represented	41

SURVEY SAYS . . .

Lots of liberal students
Students are happy
Lab facilities are great
Great library
Internships are widely available
Students are friendly
Students aren't religious
Students involved in community service
Students environmentally aware
Easy to get around campus
Campus newspaper is popular
Active student government

ACADEMICS

Academic Rating	87
% students returning for sophomore year	77
% students graduating within 4 years	62
% students graduating within 6 years	67
Calendar	4/1/4
Student/faculty ratio	11:1
Profs interesting rating	94
Profs accessible rating	96

Most classes have 20–29 students.
Most lab/discussion sessions have 20–29 students.

MOST POPULAR MAJORS
Environmental Studies; Biology/Biological Sciences, General; Animal Behavior and Ethology

STUDENTS SAY "..."

Academics

Located on Florida's Gulf Coast in St. Petersburg, Eckerd College is a small liberal arts college that prepares students to be "well-rounded, educated people for the 'real world,' rather than for just one job." Indeed, 45 percent of all students will go on to pursue advanced degrees, and the school's "academics are top notch and continue to impress," particularly the constantly expanding, "hands-on" science and art departments. Also of note is the study abroad program, of which most students take advantage.

Eckerd is "all about having small class sizes in order to maximize learning and personal connections to professors." Professors are "always approachable on an academic and personal level" and "make the classes fun and interesting." There is a "level of genuine care" from the teachers; according to a senior, "If I have a question, it gets answered, simple as that." "Not once has an email been ignored that I have sent to a professor," echoes a junior. Class discussion is very important (many classes have a sizable participation grade), and faculty encourages opposing views, creating "an environment where it is easy for everybody to openly express their opinions without judgment."

The Mentor program assigns students to professors of their major(s), their job being "to help guide the student through choosing classes and registration, or anything else." The "quirky" liberal arts curriculum turns out graduates that "are not pigeonholed into the skills associated with their major, but [who] have developed a wide range of abilities which make them attractive to employers."

Campus Life

The school's heart-stoppingly beautiful location on the waterfront gives it a feel of being "like summer camp with an enriching academic experience"; as a senior asks (rhetorically): "How can you beat a dorm that overlooks the bay?" The residence halls "are beautiful so there is no need to live off campus," and the school's Community Bike program allows students to "just pick up the yellow bikes and ride wherever you need" (though some students think there should be "more dedication through internal action to the environmental principles it espouses").

There are "eclectic options of student activities" at Eckerd, and with no Greek life, the Campus Activities crew is allotted "a crazy amount of money to have fun events on campus, such as cookouts, dances, casino nights, and an actual carnival brought onto campus." Obviously marine activities are popular, and for fun, people "go to the beach, go downtown, [and borrow] paddleboards/kayaks at the Waterfront." People love exploring downtown St. Pete, and there are many famous restaurants nearby (good thing, as the cafeteria food is "definitely our weakest point," according to many students).

There's a definite party streak here, and "pot and beer are not strangers to Eckerd parties," which typically take place outdoors. Still, it's "a very no-pressure environment" for those who choose not to partake, and "there is a very 'free as a bird' mentality" here so "people rarely feel trapped." Life at this school is generally relaxed but busy. It matches the atmosphere of the location," says a first-year student.

Student Body

This "barefooted and brainy" brood "has a wide variety of students who all fit different niches." "It isn't unheard of to see people in three-piece suits sitting with what we might call modern-day hippies," says a student. The "very relaxed" crowd adopts a "laid-back Florida attitude," and every student is "friendly, approachable and has a general positive attitude about being here at Eckerd." Almost everyone is "pretty liberal" and "has a strong interest in environmental sustainability."

ECKERD COLLEGE

Financial Aid: 727-864-8854 • E-mail: admissions@eckerd.edu • Website: www.eckerd.edu

THE PRINCETON REVIEW SAYS

Admissions

The school reports that its standardized testing policy for use in admission for Fall 2024 is Test Optional. The 2024 testing policy will be temporary. The Princeton Review suggests that interested applicants consult with the school for the most up-to-date standardized testing policies. *Very important factors considered include:* rigor of secondary school record, academic GPA. *Important factors considered include:* standardized test scores, application essay, recommendation(s), interview, extracurricular activities, talent/ability, character/personal qualities, volunteer work, work experience, level of applicant's interest. *Other factors considered include:* class rank, first generation, alumni/ae relation. High school diploma is required and GED is accepted. *Academic units recommended:* 4 English, 3 math, 3 science, 2 science labs, 2 foreign language, 2 social studies, 1 history, 3 academic electives.

Financial Aid

Students should submit: FAFSA. Priority filing deadline is 2/1. The Princeton Review suggests that all financial aid forms be submitted as soon as possible (see page 5 for a note on the FAFSA). *Need-based scholarships/grants offered:* College/university scholarship or grant aid from institutional funds; Federal Pell; SEOG; State scholarships/grants. *Loan aid offered:* Direct PLUS loans; Direct Subsidized Loans; Direct Unsubsidized Loans; College/university loans from institutional funds. Admitted students will be notified of awards on a rolling basis. Federal Work-Study Program available. Institutional employment available.

The Inside Word

Most of the applicants Eckerd admits come from the top quarter of their high school classes. However, competition from other small liberal arts schools of roughly the same caliber or better is stiff. As a result, Eckerd is a relatively easy admit for B-plus students with decent standardized test scores (the school gives more weight in its decisions to courses and grades than to SAT and ACT scores, however). The admissions process offers Early Action and rolling admission options, meaning that applying early will help your chances. Eckerd can afford to be more selective later on in the admissions cycle, especially for candidates who profess an interest in its most esteemed programs (for example, Marine Science), so those with serious interest should consider Eckerd's early admission policy.

THE SCHOOL SAYS "..."

From the Admissions Office

"Students from 48 states and territories and 39 countries take advantage of our spectacular mile of campus waterfront near the Gulf of Mexico for outdoor laboratories in biology, marine science and environmental studies along with an array of intramural, club and intercollegiate sports and water recreation. Offerings in the arts and humanities inspire creativity and foster critical thinking and self-awareness. Eckerd is dedicated to minimizing its operational footprint and maximizing sustainable practices, and our students are service-oriented—donating over 12,000 hours of service outside of graduation requirements annually. With 180 Eckerd grads having served in the Peace Corps, we're a top producer of volunteers among small colleges in the U.S. and recently joined the nationally recognized Peace Corps Prep undergraduate certificate program. Eckerd's innovative 4-1-4 calendar gives students the opportunity to study abroad during the January Winter Term or semester-long programs. Nearly 70 percent of our graduates have taken classes overseas, many at our London Study Centre. In addition to building the 55,000-square-foot James Center for Molecular and Life Sciences, which opened in 2013, the college significantly upgraded equipment, labs and classrooms for the environmental studies, math, physics, computer science and behavioral sciences departments and in 2018 opened the Nielsen Center for Visual Arts. This state-of-the-art facility provides space and equipment for studying, creating and exhibiting visual art—with student studios for ceramics and sculpture, printmaking, painting, drawing, digital arts, film production, and more. We venture together in the Eckerd experience to think beyond the conventional questions, methods and solutions. At Eckerd College, we ThinkOUTside."

SELECTIVITY

Admissions Rating	87
# of applicants	5,548
% of applicants accepted	65
% of acceptees attending	15
# offered a place on the wait list	385

FIRST-YEAR PROFILE

Testing policy	Test Optional
Range SAT composite	1120–1293
Range SAT EBRW	570–670
Range SAT math	538–630
Range ACT composite	23–29
# submitting SAT scores	174
% submitting SAT scores	29
# submitting ACT scores	122
% submitting ACT scores	20

DEADLINES

Early action	
Deadline	11/15
Notification	12/15
Regular	
Priority	11/15
Deadline	7/25
Notification	Rolling, 12/1
Nonfall registration?	Yes

FINANCIAL FACTS

Financial Aid Rating	88
Annual tuition	$48,220
Room and board	$13,854
Required fees	$680
Books and supplies	$1,350
Average frosh need-based scholarship	$26,842
Average UG need-based scholarship	$26,533
% needy frosh rec. need-based scholarship or grant aid	99
% needy UG rec. need-based scholarship or grant aid	99
% needy frosh rec. non-need-based scholarship or grant aid	13
% needy UG rec. non-need-based scholarship or grant aid	12
% needy frosh rec. need-based self-help aid	69
% needy UG rec. need-based self-help aid	76
% UG borrow to pay for school	63
Average cumulative indebtedness	$40,223
% frosh need fully met	16
% ugrads need fully met	16
Average % of frosh need met	58
Average % of ugrad need met	56

ELMIRA COLLEGE

One Park Place, Elmira, NY 14901 • Admissions: 607-735-1800 • Fax: 607-735-1718

CAMPUS LIFE

Quality of Life Rating	79
Fire Safety Rating	88
Green Rating	60*
Type of school	Private
Affiliation	No Affiliation
Environment	Town

STUDENTS

Total undergrad enrollment	787
% male/female/another gender	32/68/0
% from out of state	34
% frosh live on campus	93
% ugrads live on campus	85
# of fraternities	0
# of sororities	0
% African American	5
% Asian	2
% White	76
% Hispanic	5
% Native American	<1
% Pacific Islander	<1
% Two or more races	2
% Race and/or ethnicity unknown	5
% international	4
# of countries represented	12

SURVEY SAYS . . .

Everyone loves the Soaring Eagles
Intramural sports are popular
Easy to get around campus

ACADEMICS

Academic Rating	79
% students returning for sophomore year	78
% students graduating within 4 years	57
% students graduating within 6 years	60
Calendar	Other
Student/faculty ratio	10:1
Profs interesting rating	82
Profs accessible rating	88

Most classes have 10–19 students.
Most lab/discussion sessions have
  10–19 students.

MOST POPULAR MAJORS

Education, General; Business Administration and Management, General; Psychology, General

STUDENTS SAY ". . ."

Academic

Situated in upstate New York, Elmira College was established in 1855 and has long brought its nearly 1,000 undergraduates a solid liberal arts education grounded in critical thinking and reading. Class sizes are low, "so you are guaranteed a shot at success and a connection with your professors." Terms are also shorter, with the academic year broken up into two twelve-week terms, followed by a third six-week term of special, immersive classes. Not only does this structure give students the opportunity to study abroad—about 40 percent of students choose to do so—but it keeps courses "rigorous and challenging because...the shortened amount of time requires each class to be fast-paced and stimulating."

Those challenges are easily faced, as Elmira professors "are dead-set on providing their students with quality information" and are "engaged and willing to help any student with anything." And thanks to the faculty's different perspectives and backgrounds, "students really do experience a wide span of different people with different ideas and passions." This occurs in the classroom as well: though most classes are in lecture format, professors "make an effort to provide us with interactive activities, videos, and hands-on activities." Many also "use alternative assessments, such as a radio broadcast, creative writing, a debate, or a project of choice for a final," and are often "willing to offer independent and directed study courses if students are looking for different classes to take that are not offered."

Campus Life

Elmira is truly a "picturesque college campus" where "the ground is cobblestone with octagon-shaped bricks" and "the buildings are beautiful...and in a Gothic revival style." As one student describes, "It has an air of elegance and beauty founded on tradition while being fun and quirky as well." That fun is evident since students at Elmira "always find something to do, whether on campus or off," and given the small size of the campus, "everyone is encouraged to cultivate their interests and be as involved and outgoing as possible." This means that while most students eat in the dining halls, some "may drive to nearby Horseheads to go shopping at local stores and eat at name-brand restaurants" or visit nearby Corning and Ithaca on weekends. On this communal campus, students can often be found "in the lounges of the dorms by the fire [telling] stories" and "campus events are brought in regularly" by the college. There is "a good variety in the social scene, so students can partake in what they like best," and "some students hang out and watch movies [while] some students party."

Student Body

Here you'll find a "generous and welcoming" group that "makes the college community a comfortable place to be." Elmira "is its own little bubble" and the "mostly white" student body is "similar to that of a small town high school" in terms of a social breakdown, with athletes, "NARPs (non-athletic regular people)," and "thought-leader" students all involved in many extracurricular activities. A big part of that comes in the form of inter-collegiate athletics, with around one-third of the student body devoting "a huge part of [their] days" to practice and games. That's met with school spirit that pervades even outside of sports: "Elmira College may be small, but we are very proud of our college." One student says, "Just walking through campus you can sense the traditions and how the college values its students."

Financial Aid: 607-735-1728 • E-Mail: admissions@elmira.edu • Website: www.elmira.edu

THE PRINCETON REVIEW SAYS

Admissions

The school reports that its standardized testing policy for use in admission for Fall 2024 is Test Optional. The 2024 testing policy will be permanent. The Princeton Review suggests that interested applicants consult with the school for the most up-to-date standardized testing policies. *Very important factors considered include:* rigor of secondary school record, academic GPA, application essay, character/personal qualities. *Important factors considered include:* class rank, recommendation(s), interview, extracurricular activities, level of applicant's interest. *Other factors considered include:* standardized test scores, talent/ability, alumni/ae relation, geographical residence, state residency, racial/ethnic status, volunteer work, work experience. High school diploma is required and GED is not accepted. *Academic units required:* 4 English, 3 math, 3 science, 2 science labs, 3 social studies, 1 history, 2 academic electives. *Academic units recommended:* 2 foreign language.

Financial Aid

Students should submit: FAFSA; State aid form. Priority filing deadline is 2/1. The Princeton Review suggests that all financial aid forms be submitted as soon as possible (see page 5 for a note on the FAFSA). *Need-based scholarships/grants offered:* College/university scholarship or grant aid from institutional funds; Federal Pell; Private scholarships; SEOG; State scholarships/grants. *Loan aid offered:* Direct PLUS loans; Direct Subsidized Loans; Direct Unsubsidized Loans. Admitted students will be notified of awards on a rolling basis beginning 12/1. Federal Work-Study Program available. Institutional employment available.

The Inside Word

Elmira offers two options for students wishing to apply: Early Action and Regular (rolling) Admission. The school doesn't leave students hanging. Results for both are turned around in about two weeks—after the November 1 deadline for Early Action and after the rolling submission for Regular Admission. Test scores and interviews are optional, but both are encouraged if the student believes it will improve their application. Students wishing to apply to Elmira College and early acceptance to Lake Erie College of Osteopathic Medicine, will be required to submit test scores. With its fairly high acceptance rate, students without any major blemishes on their record have a good shot at admission.

THE SCHOOL SAYS "..."

From the Admissions Office

"Founded in 1855, Elmira College is a private, residential, liberal arts college offering 35-plus majors, an honors program, 17 academic societies, and 18 Division III varsity teams. Located in the Southern Finger Lakes Region of New York, Elmira's undergraduate and graduate student population hails from more than 30 states and nine countries. Elmira is a Phi Beta Kappa College and has been ranked a top college, nationally, for student internships.

"Elmira College has a tradition of offering hands-on, immersive learning experiences with small classes. Alumni report the opportunity to complete research, the development of relationships with faculty, and the lifelong friendships with classmates among their most impactful experiences at Elmira.

"The College offers several opportunities for post-graduate work through partnerships with various graduate schools including Lake Erie College of Osteopathic Medicine. Elmira College students already enjoy reserved, early acceptance spots at LECOM sites for those who meet the LECOM acceptance requirements. The addition of LECOM at Elmira College expands the number of reserved medical spots for EC students to 25, the number of reserved pharmacy spots to 20 and the number of reserved dentistry spots to 5, and provides a seamless transition from undergraduate coursework to medical school.

"The College is also home to the Center for Mark Twain Studies, one of four historically significant Twain heritage sites in the U.S., which attracts Twain scholars and educators from around the world. Proud of its history and tradition, the College is committed to the ideals of community service and intellectual growth."

SELECTIVITY

Admissions Rating	83
# of applicants	2,110
% of applicants accepted	84
% of acceptees attending	12

FIRST-YEAR PROFILE

Testing policy	Test Optional
Range SAT EBRW	530–600
Range SAT math	540–610
Range ACT composite	22–26
# submitting SAT scores	88
% submitting SAT scores	43
# submitting ACT scores	23
% submitting ACT scores	8
Average HS GPA	3.3
% frosh submitting high school GPA	100

DEADLINES

Early action	
Deadline	11/1
Notification	11/15
Regular	
Priority	2/15
Notification	Rolling, 11/15
Nonfall registration?	Yes

APPLICANTS OFTEN PREFER

Hartwick College; St. John Fisher University; SUNY Brockport

APPLICANTS SOMETIMES PREFER

Ithaca College; Le Moyne College; State University of New York–Geneseo

APPLICANTS RARELY PREFER

Alfred University; Houghton College

FINANCIAL FACTS

Financial Aid Rating	83
Annual tuition	$33,900
Room and board	$12,500
Required fees	$1,500
Books and supplies	$600
Average frosh need-based scholarship	$30,508
Average UG need-based scholarship	$29,638
% needy frosh rec. need-based scholarship or grant aid	100
% needy UG rec. need-based scholarship or grant aid	100
% needy frosh rec. non-need-based scholarship or grant aid	20
% needy UG rec. non-need-based scholarship or grant aid	16
% needy frosh rec. need-based self-help aid	77
% needy UG rec. need-based self-help aid	80
% UG rec. any financial aid	99
% UG borrow to pay for school	82
Average cumulative indebtedness	$30,084
% frosh need fully met	24
% ugrads need fully met	20
Average % of frosh need met	80
Average % of ugrad need met	79

ELON UNIVERSITY

100 Campus Drive, Elon, NC 27244-2010 • Admissions: 336-278-2000 • Fax: 336-278-7699

CAMPUS LIFE

Quality of Life Rating	88
Fire Safety Rating	85
Green Rating	93
Type of school	Private
Affiliation	No Affiliation
Environment	Town

STUDENTS

Total undergrad enrollment	6,337
% male/female/another gender	41/59/0
% from out of state	79
% frosh from public high school	65
% frosh live on campus	99
% ugrads live on campus	69
# of fraternities (% join)	12 (23)
# of sororities (% join)	13 (55)
% African American	6
% Asian	2
% White	79
% Hispanic	6
% Native American	<1
% Pacific Islander	<1
% Two or more races	3
% Race and/or ethnicity unknown	1
% international	2
# of countries represented	51

SURVEY SAYS . . .

Students are happy
Classroom facilities are great
Lab facilities are great
Great library
Career services are great
Internships are widely available
School is well run
Dorms are like palaces
Easy to get around campus
Intramural sports are popular
Frats and sororities are popular
Theater is popular
Campus newspaper is popular
Great food on campus

ACADEMICS

Academic Rating	83
% students returning for sophomore year	90
% students graduating within 4 years	79
% students graduating within 6 years	83
Calendar	4/1/4
Student/faculty ratio	11:1
Profs interesting rating	91
Profs accessible rating	94
Most classes have 10–19 students.	

MOST POPULAR MAJORS

Business Administration and Management;
Communication, General; Psychology, General

STUDENTS SAY ". . ."

Academics

The student-centered approach of North Carolina's Elon University is woven throughout the many hallmarks of its education, which include global engagement, service learning, and mentorship. All students are required to complete experiential learning via Elon Experiences, which can include study abroad, internships, or research, and the core curriculum "requires students from all majors to take many different classes outside their major," ensuring that they "have a very high level of openness." This is coupled with "many personalized resources that Elon provides to succeed beyond the classroom," and an "amazing support system of resources for everyone." This extends to career development as well, as Elon provides "massive amounts of leadership opportunities and is very hands-on when it comes to helping students get internships," and there are "many free learning labs and workshops all across campus that allow students to experience new concepts both in and out of the classroom."

Classes here "are enjoyable with a great balance of lecture from the professor and group discussions," and "with the study abroad and great internship programs we really do develop professionally here." Teaching mediums vary and keep students engaged: "For one of my classes we left the classroom to walk around campus and find different sustainable and non-sustainable practices, [and] then presented our findings to the class." Overall, students suggest a high level of engagement during class, as "no one's ever afraid to contribute to a lesson." Faculty "[serve] as teachers, but also as mentors for career and educational aspirations." They "will share their experience, knowledge, and connections with students after they have finished the course...which makes students feel incredibly supported during their four years."

Campus Life

Elon's 690-acre campus is "beautifully maintained...just overall a very pretty campus." That makes it easier for the school to encourage students to live in one of the campus's eight residential neighborhoods, each of which is led by faculty, staff, and student mentors and has an area of focus such as sustainability or civic engagement. This aspect ensures that students are "consistently and effectively pushed to become involved on campus by a faculty that cultivates an environment of inclusiveness and motivation."

There is no shortage of things for students to do when not in the classroom, with more than two hundred student organizations and dozens of intramural and club sports teams, as well as seventeen Division I varsity teams. The Student Union Board "plans nighttime events every Thursday, Friday, and Saturday, such as bingo, karaoke, [and] painting classes," and numerous traditions such as College Coffee and Turning 21 Dinners "make our school special and encourage a connection back to Elon long after graduation." Although this tends to be "a pretty busy student body, there is usually a good balance of work and fun" that students manage practically. "Elon truly offers everything, so it is up to you to choose what you want to do," says a student.

Student Body

This "diverse thinking community filled with every variety of person" tends "to be very self-motivated and have concrete goals and aspirations." There is "a strong emphasis on well-being (mental and physical health), [and] it is common for students to be involved in on-campus jobs, community service, and research or internships." A student says: "If you ask someone, 'What are you involved in on campus?', you may have to ask them to narrow down to their top three involvements." Elon students "are also interested in a myriad of subjects and extracurriculars," so "it's a great place to meet peers in your field, as well as explore new realms with others." As one student says: "My friends and I have nightly 'homework parties' where...even though we are all in such different disciplines, we help each other through topics." Though Greek life is very popular here, students take their studies seriously and "there is a campus-wide excitement to learn and gain knowledge." On the whole, this is "a school full of high-achieving, social, and happy students, who always strive to be involved in as much as possible on campus."

ELON UNIVERSITY

Financial Aid: 336-278-7640 • E-Mail: admissions@elon.edu • Website: www.elon.edu

THE PRINCETON REVIEW SAYS

Admissions

The school reports that its standardized testing policy for use in admission for Fall 2024 is Test Optional. It is unknown at this time if the 2024 testing policy will be permanent. The Princeton Review suggests that interested applicants consult with the school for the most up-to-date standardized testing policies. *Very important factors considered include:* rigor of secondary school record, academic GPA, application essay, recommendation(s). *Important factors considered include:* extracurricular activities, talent/ability, alumni/ae relation, volunteer work, work experience. *Other factors considered include:* class rank, character/personal qualities, first generation, geographical residence, state residency, racial/ethnic status, level of applicant's interest. High school diploma is required and GED is accepted. *Academic units required:* 4 English, 3 math, 3 science, 1 science lab, 2 foreign language, 2 social studies, 1 history. *Academic units recommended:* 4 English, 4 math, 3 science, 1 science lab, 3 foreign language, 2 social studies, 1 history.

Financial Aid

Students should submit: CSS/Financial Aid Profile; FAFSA. Priority filing deadline is 3/15. The Princeton Review suggests that all financial aid forms be submitted as soon as possible (see page 5 for a note on the FAFSA). *Need-based scholarships/grants offered:* College/university scholarship or grant aid from institutional funds; Federal Pell; Private scholarships; SEOG; State scholarships/grants; United Negro College Fund. *Loan aid offered:* Direct PLUS loans; Direct Subsidized Loans; Direct Unsubsidized Loans. Admitted students will be notified of awards on a rolling basis beginning 1/31. Federal Work-Study Program available. Institutional employment available.

The Inside Word

Earning admission to Elon University is no small task. In addition to a strong GPA, applicants should have accomplished lives outside of the classroom, including participation in extracurricular activities and service. Your class ranking is of equal importance to your hours of volunteer work. While standardized test scores are not required while the school is Test Optional, they are considered when it comes to awarding scholarships.

THE SCHOOL SAYS "..."

From the Admissions Office

"Elon offers the resources of a large university in a close-knit community atmosphere. The university's more than 6,300 undergraduates choose from more than 70 majors. Graduate programs are offered in business administration, law, business analytics, accounting, education, higher education, interactive media, physical therapy and physician assistant studies. The National Survey of Student Engagement recognizes Elon among the nation's most effective universities in promoting hands-on learning. Academic and co-curricular activities are seamlessly blended, especially in the Elon Experiences: study abroad, internships, service, leadership and undergraduate research. Participation in global study is among the highest in the nation. In addition, 82 percent of Elon students have internship experiences and 81 percent participate in service. Elon's 4-1-4 academic calendar allows students to devote January to global study or to explore innovative on-campus courses. Elon's historic 690-acre campus is recognized as one of the most beautiful in the country. New additions include the Innovation Quad featuring a workshop that provides students access to the most advanced engineering equipment, labs for design, advanced prototyping, astrophysics, prefabrication, mechatronics and virtual reality; and a building with equipment and research facilities for biomedicine, computer science, physics and robotics. Elon's four-year Bachelor of Science and Accelerated Bachelor of Science in Nursing programs prepare students in an Interprofessional Simulation Center and with virtual- and mixed-reality technology to practice skills in low-stake environments. Financial Technology, one of Elon's newest majors, attracts students with interests in finance, quantitative methods, data analysis and basic programming."

SELECTIVITY

Admissions Rating	86
# of applicants	17,551
% of applicants accepted	74
% of acceptees attending	13
# offered a place on the wait list	2,915
% accepting a place on wait list	27
% admitted from wait list	28
# of early decision applicants	294
% accepted early decision	90

FIRST-YEAR PROFILE

Testing policy	Test Optional
Range SAT composite	1175–1330
Range SAT EBRW	590–680
Range SAT math	580–680
Range ACT composite	25–30
# submitting SAT scores	435
% submitting SAT scores	26
# submitting ACT scores	293
% submitting ACT scores	17
Average HS GPA	4.1
% frosh submitting high school GPA	100
% graduated top 10% of class	20
% graduated top 25% of class	50
% graduated top 50% of class	86

DEADLINES

Early decision	
Deadline	11/1
Notification	12/1
Early action	
Deadline	11/1
Notification	12/20
Regular	
Priority	11/1
Deadline	1/10
Notification	3/20
Nonfall registration?	Yes

APPLICANTS OFTEN PREFER

North Carolina State University; University of North Carolina—Chapel Hill; University of South Carolina; Clemson University; Syracuse University; University of North Carolina—Charlotte; University of Delaware; James Madison University

FINANCIAL FACTS

Financial Aid Rating	81
Annual tuition	$41,734
Required fees	$507
Books and supplies	$900
Average frosh need-based scholarship	$18,212
Average UG need-based scholarship	$18,291
% needy frosh rec. need-based scholarship or grant aid	87
% needy UG rec. need-based scholarship or grant aid	89
% needy frosh rec. non-need-based scholarship or grant aid	66
% needy UG rec. non-need-based scholarship or grant aid	66
% needy frosh rec. need-based self-help aid	75
% needy UG rec. need-based self-help aid	75
% frosh rec. any financial aid	70
% UG rec. any financial aid	70
% UG borrow to pay for school	39
Average cumulative indebtedness	$33,774
% frosh need fully met	21
% ugrads need fully met	20
Average % of frosh need met	63
Average % of ugrad need met	61

EMERSON COLLEGE

120 Boylston Street, Boston, MA 02116-4624 • Admissions: 617-824-8500 • Fax: 617-824-8609

CAMPUS LIFE
Quality of Life Rating	85
Fire Safety Rating	94
Green Rating	95
Type of school	Private
Affiliation	No Affiliation
Environment	Metropolis

STUDENTS
Total undergrad enrollment	4,113
% male/female/another gender	36/64/0
% from out of state	81
% frosh live on campus	97
% ugrads live on campus	65
% join fraternities	2
% join sororities	3
% African American	4
% Asian	6
% White	57
% Hispanic	12
% Native American	<1
% Pacific Islander	<1
% Two or more races	4
% Race and/or ethnicity unknown	2
% international	15
# of countries represented	60

SURVEY SAYS . . .
Lots of liberal students
Class discussions encouraged
Students aren't religious
Students love Boston, MA
Theater is popular
Campus newspaper is popular
College radio is popular
Active minority support groups

ACADEMICS
Academic Rating	78
% students returning for sophomore year	87
% students graduating within 4 years	76
% students graduating within 6 years	79
Calendar	Semester
Student/faculty ratio	15:1
Profs interesting rating	89
Profs accessible rating	89
Most classes have 10–19 students.	

MOST POPULAR MAJORS
Theatre/Theater; Cinematography and Film/Video Production; Journalism

STUDENTS SAY ". . ."

Academics
Emerson College boasts its "urban" Boston location as a solid locus for "networking and career-preparation," including the "amazing alumni network," lovingly referred to as the "Emerson Mafia." In particular, "journalism, writing, film, marketing, and theater programs" are especially "strong," and classes are "taught by industry professionals" who "never fail to enlighten." Most of the classes are focused on job readiness: "You do work with actual organizations rather than discuss theories." There are "impressive" facilities and resources, including "film and TV studio facilities and equipment" with broad "availability to students," and "small class sizes with easy-to-reach professors, specific course material, and no meaningless busy work," that "often work more like collaborations than lectures." "We aren't test takers at Emerson," one student says, "so we don't study. We create projects, videos, presentations, [and so on]." Professors are "passionate about the learning material," and "are in constant discourse with the class," "keen on showcasing global perspectives." Emerson stresses "hands on activities, volunteer opportunities, real-time demonstrations, and frequent class discussions," and classes "integrated with external organizations," means students are often out in the community, "working with local nonprofits," or navigating "creative opportunities through internships in the Boston area." Emerson offers a "wealth of resources" on campus, including the "ArtsEmerson productions," "Bright Lights Film series," "Emerson Channel," and the "EVVY Award" give "media creators" all the immersive experience they need to prepare for post-college professions. The study abroad trips are "phenomenal," with students raving about trips to Cuba, Colombia, and the Netherlands.

Campus Life
Students report that while Boston gives them everything they can hope for in terms of entertainment and culture, the on-campus extracurricular activities at Emerson "are innumerable and invaluable." Emerson provides "enough resources that you can do pretty much anything you want to do": clubs are "largely student run and provide a good amount of field experience for whatever it is you want to do." The campus is located "right on the Boston Common," so students enjoy "taking walks," visiting museums, many with "free entry," and trying out "lots of good food." Many students "work part-time" in the city, and otherwise students "hang out in the common rooms," "spend time working with a number of student organizations," exploring "wonderful Common Park," which is located close to campus. Other students like "watching NCAA games" or "attending interesting plays at the Emerson theatre." "Emerson students are known to overcommit themselves to activities," says one student. Another says, "It is not unusual to hear of students working on...several different shows and organizations while always taking challenging courses. Students, however, rarely complain that this affects the "quality of their lives or academic experience."

Student Body
The student body is described as "small, open-minded, artsy, but with a distinct student-athlete crowd." Emerson students "usually enter the school with a career already in mind" with some having "prior experience." It is "rare to find people who are undeclared." Students describe Emerson as "an art school without the label," attracting "creative forces" who are "ambitious, driven, and self-starters." Students "can be a little pretentious and business oriented" and "casual conversations can sometimes feel like a networking event." Yet others stress that their "peers are collaborative and kind," with most "extremely kind and willing to work with each other." Everybody is generally "open to new ideas and perspectives, very accepting and friendly," and "all very committed to their art." One student comments on diversity: "It's a diverse campus in sexual and gender identity, however, racial diversity is limited. There's a range of interests, but the majority of students at Emerson are here to study some aspect of film, and so life is somewhat dominated by that." The campus tends to be "pro-social justice," with a "great activism community" that is "highly involved in Black Lives Matter," "climate change," and other hot-button political issues.

EMERSON COLLEGE

Financial Aid: 617-824-8655 • E-Mail: admission@emerson.edu • Website: www.emerson.edu

THE PRINCETON REVIEW SAYS

Admissions

The school reports that its standardized testing policy for use in admission for Fall 2024 is Test Optional. The 2024 testing policy will be permanent. The Princeton Review suggests that interested applicants consult with the school for the most up-to-date standardized testing policies. *Very important factors considered include:* academic GPA, application essay. *Important factors considered include:* rigor of secondary school record, class rank, recommendation(s), extracurricular activities, talent/ability, character/personal qualities. *Other factors considered include:* standardized test scores, first generation, alumni/ae relation, geographical residence, racial/ethnic status, volunteer work, work experience. High school diploma is required and GED is accepted. *Academic units required:* 4 English, 3 math, 3 science, 3 foreign language, 3 social studies. *Academic units recommended:* 4 English, 3 math, 3 science, 3 foreign language, 3 social studies, 4 academic electives.

Financial Aid

Students should submit: Business/Farm Supplement; CSS/Financial Aid Profile; FAFSA; Noncustodial Profile. Priority filing deadline is 11/15. The Princeton Review suggests that all financial aid forms be submitted as soon as possible (see page 5 for a note on the FAFSA). *Need-based scholarships/grants offered:* College/university scholarship or grant aid from institutional funds; Federal Pell; Private scholarships; SEOG; State scholarships/grants. *Loan aid offered:* Direct PLUS loans; Direct Subsidized Loans; Direct Unsubsidized Loans; State Loans. Admitted students will be notified of awards on or about 4/1. Federal Work-Study Program available. Institutional employment available.

The Inside Word

Emerson's theater-district location and large alumni network make it perfect for those interested in communications, theater, and television, as jobs and internships abound in those fields. If you are applying in cinematography or the performing arts, be prepared to complete an artistic review with your application. Students who choose not to submit standardized test scores will be required to submit either a "contemplative essay responding to a topic related to communication and the arts" or a "creative sample or portfolio that relates specifically to their chosen major."

THE SCHOOL SAYS "..."

From the Admissions Office

"Emerson College is the nation's only four-year, liberal arts institution devoted exclusively to the study of communication and the arts. For over 130 years Emerson has educated the most innovative and creative minds in the fields of marketing, visual and media arts, entrepreneurship, publishing and writing, journalism, performing arts, and speech pathology and audiology. Guided by an award-winning faculty, Emerson students are provided with the real-world experience, professional-grade facilities, and foundational liberal arts knowledge they need to be at the cutting edge of their ever-changing industries. Located in the heart of Boston's Theatre District, Emerson's main campus is home to award-winning literary journals, sound treated television studios, and several digital editing and audio post-production suites. The Tufte Performance and Production Center houses a theater design/technology center, makeup lab, and costume shop. There are several programs to observe speech and hearing therapy, a professional marketing focus group room, digital newsroom, and the Paramount Center, which includes a sound stage, scene shop, rehearsal studios, black box theatre, and film screening room. Emerson has nearly eighty student organizations and performance groups as well as fourteen NCAA Division III teams. The college also sponsors programs in Los Angeles and Washington, D.C.; study abroad in the Netherlands, Taiwan, and Czech Republic; and course cross-registration with the six-member Boston ProArts Consortium. The tightly-knit network of 51,000 alumni and the connections that Emerson students make on campus follow them into their post-graduate life, paving the way to collaborative projects, internships, and career opportunities across the globe."

SELECTIVITY

Admissions Rating	91
# of applicants	11,568
% of applicants accepted	45
% of acceptees attending	20
# offered a place on the wait list	1,220
% accepting a place on wait list	63
% admitted from wait list	3

FIRST-YEAR PROFILE

Testing policy	Test Optional
Range SAT composite	1230–1390
Range SAT EBRW	620–710
Range SAT math	580–690
Range ACT composite	28–32
# submitting SAT scores	294
% submitting SAT scores	28
# submitting ACT scores	132
% submitting ACT scores	12
Average HS GPA	3.7
% frosh submitting high school GPA	89
% graduated top 10% of class	30
% graduated top 25% of class	68
% graduated top 50% of class	95

DEADLINES

Early decision	
Deadline	11/1
Notification	12/15
Early action	
Deadline	11/1
Notification	12/15
Regular	
Deadline	1/15
Notification	4/1
Nonfall registration?	Yes

APPLICANTS OFTEN PREFER
Boston University; Chapman University; New York University; University of Southern California

APPLICANTS SOMETIMES PREFER
American University; Fordham University; Ithaca College; Northeastern University; Syracuse University

APPLICANTS RARELY PREFER
Pace University

FINANCIAL FACTS

Financial Aid Rating	77
Annual tuition	$51,520
Annual tuition (first-year)	$52,288
Room and board	$19,528
Required fees	$944
Books and supplies	$1,200
Average frosh need-based scholarship	$26,215
Average UG need-based scholarship	$25,139
% needy frosh rec. need-based scholarship or grant aid	96
% needy UG rec. need-based scholarship or grant aid	94
% needy frosh rec. non-need-based scholarship or grant aid	17
% needy UG rec. non-need-based scholarship or grant aid	9
% needy frosh rec. need-based self-help aid	91
% needy UG rec. need-based self-help aid	87
% UG borrow to pay for school	56
Average cumulative indebtedness	$22,070
% frosh need fully met	16
% ugrads need fully met	9
Average % of frosh need met	61
Average % of ugrad need met	53

EMORY UNIVERSITY

201 Dowman Drive, Atlanta, GA 30322 • Admissions: 404-727-6123 • Fax: 404-727-4303

STUDENTS SAY ". . ."

Academics

A top research university in Atlanta, Emory University offers more than eighty undergraduate programs across nine schools, and allows students to perform "some of the most cutting-edge research in disciplines ranging from the humanities to the social sciences." The emphasis here is on a student's academic freedom to customize their own curriculum and pursue multiple programs of study, no matter how unusual the combination might be. "Intramural basketball and intro to theater? Sure. History of the human world and advanced mathematics? Go ahead," says a student. In allowing students the room to create their own experience, Emory is also "constantly testing out new programs that may one day benefit future students" and strengthening the community. Most here are "involved in the real world in some aspect," whether through an internship during the summer, or an actual job during the year, and students "are encouraged to pursue their interests" both in and out of the classroom. All in all, Emory cultivates an atmosphere of "bold, courageous inquiry facilitated by world-renowned professors, state-of-the-art facilities, and an omnipresent desire to learn."

Professors at Emory are "incredibly successful in their fields but believe that you can be too," and "are willing to invest time and effort" into seeing this come true. All have open office hours, are "very feedback-oriented," and "respect what students have to say." There is an emphasis on a collaborative environment here, and the "amazing, smart people who bring their brains to class and help educate us" make sure that this permeates every inch of the classroom. There is a lack of competition on campus, which is "actually really heartening and refreshing because students are being pushed to learn and do well in classes and on their topics of interest." As one student puts it, "I know that I am graduating with a support system behind me and endless opportunities in front of me."

Campus Life

Emory is in the suburbs, but just a scant 15 minutes from downtown Atlanta, and the school's popular "Experience Shuttles" take students out to various attractions in the city on a weekly basis. Much of life at Emory revolves around extracurriculars, and the opportunities to get involved on campus abound, with "many volunteer, Greek, arts, and sports organizations." Outside of these activities, many students "hang out at coffee shops on campus, explore the Atlanta area, hike in Emory's large nature preserve, or go to social events on Greek Row." Greek life is very prominent here, so "there is always something going on, whether it is an open social event, a philanthropy event, or commitments within your organization." While many people go to parties or club meetings during the majority of their free time, everyone is perfectly happy to "just chill in the dorm rooms and watch a movie on the free television Emory provides."

Student Body

The diversity within the student body is a huge draw; not only are students "from all over the United States and from around the globe," but the perspectives represented on this campus are "truly astounding." Many students come here with friends from high school, and a fair number of students are in the business school or are pre-med (due to the noted Emory Healthcare system). Everyone at Emory is "extremely curious about the world around them" and passionate about both their areas of study as well as their extracurricular involvements. There's "a niche for literally anything and everything," and "the mood on campus is overall happy and light-hearted." The spirit of Emory encompasses "a community of care, embracing diversity, and providing a learning environment conducive to academic success."

EMORY UNIVERSITY

Financial Aid: 404-727-6039 • E-Mail: admiss@emory.edu • Website: www.emory.edu

THE PRINCETON REVIEW SAYS
Admissions
The school reports that its standardized testing policy for use in admission for Fall 2024 is Test Optional. It is unknown at this time if the 2024 testing policy will be permanent. The Princeton Review suggests that interested applicants consult with the school for the most up-to-date standardized testing policies. *Very important factors considered include:* rigor of secondary school record, academic GPA, recommendation(s), extracurricular activities, talent/ability, character/personal qualities. *Important factors considered include:* standardized test scores, application essay, volunteer work. *Other factors considered include:* class rank, interview, first generation, alumni/ae relation, geographical residence, state residency, racial/ethnic status, work experience. High school diploma is required and GED is not accepted. *Academic units recommended:* 4 English, 4 math, 4 science, 2 science labs, 4 foreign language, 2 social studies, 2 history, 1 computer science, 1 visual/performing arts.

Financial Aid
Students should submit: CSS/Financial Aid Profile; FAFSA; Noncustodial Profile. Priority filing deadline is 2/15. The Princeton Review suggests that all financial aid forms be submitted as soon as possible (see page 5 for a note on the FAFSA). *Need-based scholarships/grants offered:* College/university scholarship or grant aid from institutional funds; Federal Pell; Private scholarships; SEOG. *Loan aid offered:* Direct PLUS loans; Direct Subsidized Loans; Direct Unsubsidized Loans; College/university loans from institutional funds; Federal Nursing Loans; State Loans. Admitted students will be notified of awards on or about 4/1. Federal Work-Study Program available. Institutional employment available.

The Inside Word
Early decision applications to Emory have surged in the past several years, leading students to question whether they want to join the early word crowd—perhaps increasing the likelihood of admission—or take their chances with regular admission. Those hoping for admission should aim for a 3.75 (or better) GPA and polish up their writing skills and extracurricular activities.

THE SCHOOL SAYS "..."
From the Admissions Office
"One of the most selective and diverse universities in the US, Emory offers a distinctive undergraduate education with programs in the humanities, sciences, business, and nursing on its two campuses. First-year students have the option to apply to either Emory College or Oxford College. Emory College, located in Atlanta and set among the energy and pace of the university's seven graduate and professional schools, offers a rigorous four-year liberal arts education at a research university in a thriving, global city. Students also can choose to spend the first two years of their Emory education at Oxford College, located on Emory's original campus, 38 miles (61 km) from Atlanta, in a close-knit, rigorous, small liberal arts college setting. At both campuses, students are taught by faculty who are experts in their fields and dedicated to creating an enriching academic environment.

"Emory's global community represents more than 100 countries. It is a community that comes together for a shared purpose—helping students to flourish and succeed. Faculty, staff, and alumni work together to support students' academic, personal, and professional development. There are abundant extracurricular activities that give students a chance to perform, lead, and interact meaningfully with one another and with the greater Emory and Atlanta communities. The city of Atlanta offers affordable cultural opportunities for students as well as a booming business climate with numerous opportunities for internships and jobs. Emory's dynamic community life inspires students to do more with what they learn."

SELECTIVITY
Admissions Rating	97
# of applicants	33,179
% of applicants accepted	11
% of acceptees attending	38
# offered a place on the wait list	6,448
% accepting a place on wait list	53
% admitted from wait list	3
# of early decision applicants	3,560
% accepted early decision	26

FIRST-YEAR PROFILE
Testing policy	Test Optional
Range SAT composite	1450–1530
Range SAT EBRW	700–760
Range SAT math	730–790
Range ACT composite	32–34
# submitting SAT scores	587
% submitting SAT scores	41
# submitting ACT scores	335
% submitting ACT scores	23
Average HS GPA	3.8
% frosh submitting high school GPA	97
% graduated top 10% of class	81
% graduated top 25% of class	97
% graduated top 50% of class	100

DEADLINES
Early decision	
Deadline	11/1
Notification	12/15
Other ED deadline	1/1
Other ED notification	2/15
Regular	
Deadline	1/1
Notification	4/1
Nonfall registration?	No

FINANCIAL FACTS
Financial Aid Rating	96
Annual tuition	$57,120
Room and board	$17,016
Required fees	$828
Books and supplies	$1,250
Average frosh need-based scholarship	$52,097
Average UG need-based scholarship	$51,808
% needy frosh rec. need-based scholarship or grant aid	90
% needy UG rec. need-based scholarship or grant aid	92
% needy frosh rec. non-need-based scholarship or grant aid	34
% needy UG rec. non-need-based scholarship or grant aid	22
% needy frosh rec. need-based self-help aid	82
% needy UG rec. need-based self-help aid	82
% frosh rec. any financial aid	55
% UG rec. any financial aid	58
% UG borrow to pay for school	32
Average cumulative indebtedness	$25,895
% frosh need fully met	98
% ugrads need fully met	95
Average % of frosh need met	100
Average % of ugrad need met	98

EUGENE LANG COLLEGE OF LIBERAL ARTS AT THE NEW SCHOOL

72 Fifth Avenue (corner of 13th Street), New York, NY 10011 • Admissions: 212-229-5600 • Fax: 212-229-5355

CAMPUS LIFE

Quality of Life Rating	82
Fire Safety Rating	91
Green Rating	85
Type of school	Private
Affiliation	No Affiliation
Environment	Metropolis

STUDENTS

Total undergrad enrollment	1,677
% male/female/another gender	20/75/5
% from out of state	77
% frosh live on campus	84
% ugrads live on campus	33
% African American	5
% Asian	7
% White	53
% Hispanic	14
% Native American	<1
% Pacific Islander	<1
% Two or more races	8
% Race and/or ethnicity unknown	3
% international	9
# of countries represented	54

SURVEY SAYS . . .
Lots of liberal students
Students aren't religious
Students environmentally aware
Students love New York, NY
Great off-campus food

ACADEMICS

Academic Rating	77
% students returning for sophomore year	75
% students graduating within 4 years	39
% students graduating within 6 years	54
Calendar	Semester
Student/faculty ratio	22:1
Profs interesting rating	91
Profs accessible rating	87

Most classes have 10–19 students.
Most lab/discussion sessions have
20–29 students.

MOST POPULAR MAJORS
Psychology; Journalism + Design;
Literary Studies

STUDENTS SAY ". . ."

Academics
Eugene Lang College is the liberal arts college of New York City's The New School, where students are allowed to customize their curriculum using resources throughout The New School, including Parsons School of Design, The College of Performing Arts, and a range of other colleges and schools. Classes at Lang itself are reading- and writing-intensive and typically conducted seminar-style, with the curriculum inherently cross-disciplinary (dual degrees and cross-university minors are readily available). All students complete a First Year Seminar and writing courses as well as some light general requirements (though "the bare credit minimum to graduate for each kind of course is flexible and forgiving"), and are encouraged to look into study abroad and internships as early as their sophomore year. The school understands that "not everyone learns the same way," and so the highly specific courses on offer "are all unique and crafted with care and deliberateness," and most take high advantage of the locale, with "field trips almost every class around New York City." Career Services also taps into the city to connect students with moments for growth: "internships and opportunities are truly out there."

Professors "put effort into creating comfortable atmospheres for student discussion" and "their knowledge comes from real world experience rather than pure theory." As one student says: "You can tell they always come to class ready and excited (in their own way) to discuss the topic they teach." Unique projects often replace exams and assignments, with students citing "graphic arts or musical pieces or performance art in lieu of written essays," or a class in which "we created a zine which was shared with the Lang community." There's "a level of freedom across all disciplines of study," and students appreciate that the texts used "discuss different perspectives on the topics" come from "authors of all different types of backgrounds, rather sticking to the traditional canon."

Campus Life
When your campus is New York City, the cultural world is your oyster: whether "seeing Broadway shows, visiting parks, going to food festivals," there is enough to do that "it often leads me to forget I am a student." That said, the campus is never overlooked: it has highly enjoyable workshops from people both within and without the campus and clubs often organize events to "bring awareness [to various causes]…or to spread positivity on campus." Upon arriving at Lang, people "throw themselves into the New York experience" and many occupy their time with "personal projects such as theater productions, student films, small businesses, [and] writing books." Nearby Washington Square Park and Union Square are common hangout spots, and many explore further and "find their favorite hole in the wall places and bring their friends with them to enjoy it."

Student Body
The New School offers "a highly creative environment" filled with "incredibly smart, driven and ambitious" people who "genuinely have an academic pursuit they care about strongly." To that, those specifically within the Lang college "usher in a new era of style, intelligence, and swagger," bringing a "progressive,… strong sense of urban sensibility" and enjoyment of "the finer things in life like art, music, and literature." While the student body does tend to skew wealthy, everyone "recognizes the privileges that come with attending a private institution" such as Lang. It is, overall, "a haven for [the] creative, opinionated, [and] LGBTQ," and students—many of whom are "international or have some connection to somewhere outside the United States" are "very open-minded and kind."

EUGENE LANG COLLEGE OF LIBERAL ARTS AT THE NEW SCHOOL

Financial Aid: 212-229-8930 • E-Mail: lang@newschool.edu • Website: www.newschool.edu/lang/

THE PRINCETON REVIEW SAYS

Admissions

The school reports that its standardized testing policy for use in admission for Fall 2024 is Test Free. The 2024 testing policy will be permanent. The Princeton Review suggests that interested applicants consult with the school for the most up-to-date standardized testing policies. *Very important factors considered include:* academic GPA, application essay, extracurricular activities. *Important factors considered include:* rigor of secondary school record, recommendation(s), talent/ability, character/personal qualities. *Other factors considered include:* class rank, interview, first generation, racial/ethnic status, volunteer work, work experience, level of applicant's interest. High school diploma is required and GED is accepted. *Academic units required:* 4 English. *Academic units recommended:* 4 math, 4 science, 4 foreign language, 4 social studies, 4 history.

Financial Aid

Students should submit: FAFSA. Priority filing deadline is 2/1. The Princeton Review suggests that all financial aid forms be submitted as soon as possible (see page 5 for a note on the FAFSA). *Need-based scholarships/grants offered:* College/university scholarship or grant aid from institutional funds; Federal Pell; Private scholarships; SEOG; State scholarships/grants; United Negro College Fund. *Loan aid offered:* Direct PLUS loans; Direct Subsidized Loans; Direct Unsubsidized Loans. Admitted students will be notified of awards on a rolling basis. Federal Work-Study Program available. Institutional employment available.

The Inside Word

Eugene Lang College of Liberal Arts is a Test Free school, so SAT and ACT scores won't help your application. Focus instead on keeping up your academic record and getting glowing recommendation letters: those who apply early action may be shifted to regular decision if the school isn't suitably impressed by your grades or current extracurriculars. Know that the school looks for "commitment, independence, and passion," and you should take advantage of both the New School's and the Common App's essay prompts to help convey that, or anything else the school should know about you, especially since interviews are not conducted. The school is pricey, especially when housing is factored in, but all students are automatically considered for merit scholarships.

SELECTIVITY

Admissions Rating	79
# of applicants	2,643
% of applicants accepted	85
% of acceptees attending	19
# offered a place on the wait list	75
% accepting a place on wait list	60
% admitted from wait list	36

FIRST-YEAR PROFILE

Testing policy	Test Free
Average HS GPA	3.5
% frosh submitting high school GPA	99
% graduated top 10% of class	15
% graduated top 25% of class	35
% graduated top 50% of class	88

DEADLINES

Early action	
Deadline	11/1
Notification	12/20
Regular	
Priority	1/15
Deadline	8/1
Notification	Rolling, 3/16
Nonfall registration?	Yes

APPLICANTS ALSO LOOK AT

Emerson College; Fordham University; New York University

FINANCIAL FACTS

Financial Aid Rating	78
Annual tuition	$53,716
Room and board	$18,100
Required fees	$1,300
Average frosh need-based scholarship	$11,593
Average UG need-based scholarship	$13,711
% needy frosh rec. need-based scholarship or grant aid	67
% needy UG rec. need-based scholarship or grant aid	76
% needy frosh rec. non-need-based scholarship or grant aid	86
% needy UG rec. non-need-based scholarship or grant aid	83
% needy frosh rec. need-based self-help aid	57
% needy UG rec. need-based self-help aid	64
% frosh rec. any financial aid	93
% UG rec. any financial aid	91
% UG borrow to pay for school	50
Average cumulative indebtedness	$35,557
% frosh need fully met	11
% ugrads need fully met	9
Average % of frosh need met	47
Average % of ugrad need met	54

EVERGREEN STATE COLLEGE

2700 Evergreen Pkwy NW, Olympia, WA 98505 • Admissions: 360-867-6170 • Fax: 360-867-5114

CAMPUS LIFE

Quality of Life Rating	79
Fire Safety Rating	90
Green Rating	60*
Type of school	Public
Environment	City

STUDENTS

Total undergrad enrollment	1,811
% male/female/another gender	38/61/<1
% from out of state	14
% frosh live on campus	62
% ugrads live on campus	15
# of fraternities	0
# of sororities	0
% African American	5
% Asian	3
% White	61
% Hispanic	13
% Native American	3
% Pacific Islander	1
% Two or more races	7
% Race and/or ethnicity unknown	7
% international	0
# of countries represented	5

SURVEY SAYS . . .

Lots of liberal students
Internships are widely available
No one cheats
Students aren't religious
Students environmentally aware
Active minority support groups
Active student-run political groups

ACADEMICS

Academic Rating	80
% students returning for sophomore year	65
% students graduating within 4 years	31
% students graduating within 6 years	41
Calendar	Quarter
Student/faculty ratio	17:1
Profs interesting rating	93
Profs accessible rating	89
Most classes have 20–29 students.	

MOST POPULAR MAJORS

Liberal Arts and Sciences/Liberal Studies; Natural Sciences; Social Sciences, Other

STUDENTS SAY ". . ."

Academics

"Keeping education in its purest form alive and well in the heart of the Northwest," The Evergreen State College offers "a unique approach" to academics. The school provides an "interactive environment—with a diverse, enriching learning method," which allows students "to focus on [their] passions and explore them in detail." Everyone creates their own educational paths and directs the pace of their own learning. As a few students say admiringly, "I feel a sense of freedom with the academics at Evergreen." "I have more power as a student." Greatly appreciated is the flexibility found within the curriculum. "I was excited about building my own major." "No self-motivated student will leave Evergreen unsatisfied." Students work collaboratively here and support one another in their endeavors. "It's not about grades or competition; it's about self-improvement and personal fulfillment." Evaluations are used to view student progress, with "interdisciplinary education over declared majors" being the focus. "Your classes are all interconnected, so it's easy to link what you're doing into a defined path." "My transcript says more about me than A's, B's, and C's possibly could." "The philosophy...definitely lowers the stress I experience around academics." Professors assist students in innumerable ways and are "very intimately involved in the education of their students." "At Evergreen, in order to have a great experience, you need to be able to talk to your professors and engage with them." "I have not met a professor yet who was not willing to rework their mode of teaching to better serve the class." The educational atmosphere is highly interactive. Almost every student "actively engages the material with field work, undergraduate research, and extended trips." "Class time is spent doing workshops, seminars, or a led discussion where everyone participates." "Even the science programs involve large portions of discussion and peer collaboration." As one undergraduate describes slyly, "My professors have been A++, if Evergreen assigned grades."

Campus Life

Evergreen has a "booming extracurricular life"; students enjoy the "thriving local art and music scene, very hip and fresh," in Olympia as well as easily accessible Seattle or Portland. "The Flaming Eggplant, the student-run cafe, is simply the cheapest and most delicious place on the planet," as well as a very popular hangout. The Student Activities office has no shortage of options for undergraduates here, with "more than 50 different clubs and student groups." Physical activity is popular, and the recreational center has racquetball, a pool, a rock-climbing wall, and various places to exercise. There is "no shortage of local hiking, backpacking, and biking opportunities." "Hikes in the woods, down to the beach, or up to the bluff are very common as well as late-night stargazing." The physical surroundings are viewed with much admiration at Evergreen. "Our campus is set back in this magical forest with these winding paths down to the beach. There are tree forts, giant sculptures, dream catchers in the trees, hidden drum circles, and music everywhere." As one student describes fondly, "To me, it is reminiscent of Thoreau's solitude in nature."

Student Campus Life

The "kindness and awareness of the community" is frequently said by students to be one of the most valued aspects of their experience here. "Articulate" and "inquisitive" undergraduates are evident in large numbers. "Students tend to be very politically aware and active with very liberal points of view" and are "mostly peaceful relaxed people" amidst an "open-minded social environment." The dorms are divided into different themes, and "the residential staff is professional and keeps the housing community functioning and safe." "The campus police are pretty awesome people," as well. Evergreen is respected by students throughout the college for its "forward-thinking" administration and faculty, with a "dedication to sustainability" being clearly evident around the campus.

EVERGREEN STATE COLLEGE

Financial Aid: 360-867-6205 • E-Mail: admissions@evergreen.edu • Website: www.evergreen.edu

THE PRINCETON REVIEW SAYS

Admissions

The school reports that its standardized testing policy for use in admission for Fall 2024 is Test Optional. It is unknown at this time if the 2024 testing policy will be permanent. The Princeton Review suggests that interested applicants consult with the school for the most up-to-date standardized testing policies. *Very important factors considered include:* rigor of secondary school record, academic GPA. *Important factors considered include:* standardized test scores, level of applicant's interest. *Other factors considered include:* application essay, recommendation(s), interview, extracurricular activities, volunteer work, work experience. High school diploma is required and GED is accepted. *Academic units required:* 4 English, 3 math, 2 science, 2 science labs, 2 foreign language, 3 social studies.

Financial Aid

Students should submit: FAFSA. Priority filing deadline is 2/1. The Princeton Review suggests that all financial aid forms be submitted as soon as possible (see page 5 for a note on the FAFSA). *Need-based scholarships/grants offered:* College/university scholarship or grant aid from institutional funds; Federal Pell; Private scholarships; SEOG; State scholarships/grants. *Loan aid offered:* Direct PLUS loans; Direct Subsidized Loans; Direct Unsubsidized Loans; College/university loans from institutional funds. Admitted students will be notified of awards on a rolling basis beginning 4/1. Federal Work-Study Program available. Institutional employment available.

The Inside Word

Students at Evergreen are commonly some of the strongest performers from their high schools, although the admissions department considers a variety of traits from applicants (including strength of character) when considering prospective undergraduates. The school's unique and self-directed academic curriculum favors those students who can adequately handle the responsibility of creating and developing their own educational path.

THE SCHOOL SAYS "..."

From the Admissions Office

"The Evergreen State College is a public liberal arts college located in Olympia, Washington, between Seattle and Portland. As a public college, Evergreen offers unsurpassed value—the academic and campus environment typical of a private college, for lower tuition.

"Evergreen attracts students inspired by the complexity of the world and those that want to take charge of their education. Rather than checking off lists created by someone else, students create their own path to a Bachelor degree, choosing from among 60 academic fields.

"Evergreen has embraced a different model of liberal arts education since its inception in 1967. Students don't take several unrelated classes each term, instead they register for a single, team-taught, full-time course (a program) that incorporates multiple fields of study and focuses on real-life problems and experiences. Students learn in a truly integrated and interdisciplinary way from faculty with experience in multiple academic fields.

"Evergreen graduates go on to careers ranging from public service and non-profit leadership, business, and the creative arts. They're valued in the workplace for their ability to lead diverse teams, meld together ideas and form divergent points of view, and adapt at the speed of today's world.

"Aligning with our belief that each student is an individual defined by much more than a single letter or number, Evergreen offers Test Optional admission.

"Evergreen is a proud member of Colleges That Changes Lives, the Common Application, Consortium for Innovative Environments in Learning, and Western Undergraduate Exchange."

SELECTIVITY

Admissions Rating	80
# of applicants	1,623
% of applicants accepted	74
% of acceptees attending	23

FIRST-YEAR PROFILE

Testing policy	Test Optional
Range SAT EBRW	510–640
Range SAT math	470–580
Range ACT composite	22–29
# submitting SAT scores	35
% submitting SAT scores	13
# submitting ACT scores	12
% submitting ACT scores	4
Average HS GPA	3.3
% frosh submitting high school GPA	93
% graduated top 25% of class	25
% graduated top 50% of class	50

DEADLINES

Regular	
Priority	2/1
Deadline	Rolling
Notification	Rolling, 11/1
Nonfall registration?	Yes

APPLICANTS OFTEN PREFER

Portland State University; University of California—Santa Cruz; University of Washington; Washington State University; Western Washington University

APPLICANTS SOMETIMES PREFER

California Polytechnic University, Humboldt; Central Washington University; Hampshire College; University of Oregon; University of Puget Sound; Willamette University

APPLICANTS RARELY PREFER

Colorado State University; Eastern Washington University; Lewis & Clark College; Pacific Lutheran University; Seattle University; University of Colorado Boulder

FINANCIAL FACTS

Financial Aid Rating	79
Annual in-state tuition	$8,750
Annual out-of-state tuition	$30,059
Room and board	$13,806
Books and supplies	$900
Average frosh need-based scholarship	$13,556
Average UG need-based scholarship	$13,314
% needy frosh rec. need-based scholarship or grant aid	100
% needy UG rec. need-based scholarship or grant aid	99
% needy frosh rec. non-need-based scholarship or grant aid	4
% needy UG rec. non-need-based scholarship or grant aid	2
% needy frosh rec. need-based self-help aid	61
% needy UG rec. need-based self-help aid	67
% UG borrow to pay for school	61
Average cumulative indebtedness	$23,634
% frosh need fully met	12
% ugrads need fully met	8
Average % of frosh need met	62
Average % of ugrad need met	64

FAIRFIELD UNIVERSITY

1073 North Benson Road, Fairfield, CT 06824 • Admissions: 203-254-4000 • Fax: 203-254-4199

STUDENTS SAY "..."

Academics

Fairfield University is a private Jesuit Catholic school offering its 4,800 undergraduates the choice of more than fifty majors and two dozen interdisciplinary minors as part of a comprehensive education that addresses the student as a whole. Classes feature "lots of interactive approaches to learning with other students due to the emphasis on group work and interaction." Some lauded academic examples include "classes co-taught by professors in different disciplines" and a "structure of classes that revolves around the success of the students rather than how easy it is to teach a topic." Additionally, "there are many great service learning and internship opportunities" and an "alumni network [that] cannot be complimented enough. If there is ever a major that I am curious about, there is an alum that is more than happy to discuss the opportunities... [of that] major."

Professors "are wonderful and supportive people who encourage students to think critically about the world" and "are very knowledgeable about their fields and are easily accessible outside of class." They "teach in engaging ways," meaning that they don't assign busy work so much as they "create lessons that are valuable and seem to care about teaching and the students." Outside of class, teachers offer avenues for career exploration: "[There are] job opportunities that I never would have known about without them." Classes then bolster and encourage those experiences "with simulations and interesting cases that really let you put what you learned into practice" as well as "countless research studies that are going on at any given time."

Campus Life

Fairfield is located on the Connecticut coastline just sixty miles "north of" New York City, providing "a good geographical advantage" for those looking for cultural or internship opportunities. That location also means that "No matter the time of year, winter or summer, EVERYONE goes to the beach—most seniors live on the beach." It's the best of both worlds for some attendees as there are "many beautiful views in the campus" but also plenty to do outside of it, like how "shopping near the campus is convenient." Students say "there are always a handful of events or activities running on campus any given day, whether it be professional opportunities or programs for fun," including a "disc golf setup around campus that people use year-round."

While the "work-life balance is great within campus culture," students keep busy. During the week, students "are on a constant grind studying and completing assignments, applying to jobs and internships, meeting with their career counselors, going to the Rec Plex (gym), attending basketball games, volunteering, and engaging with the Fairfield community through their clubs and activities." Since "community service is a big part of Jesuit values," many here partake in activities and classes that feature "community-engaged learning." Many also participate in the New Student Leader program, wherein they "help students transition to a new community and environment." In short, there is "so much opportunity for involvement in so many different areas."

Student Body

The student body at Fairfield "consists of many people that come from similar upbringings" or "the surrounding areas and are either nursing, bio, or finance majors." But students note "a mix of international and west coast students" and how they "can see how the student body over the past few years has been changing." The size of the school "allows everyone to know everyone, which helps to create a supportive student body," and "it is apparent how much Fairfield University students love where they go to school and love the environment of this university." This is a group of "well-rounded individuals who for the most part are dedicated to succeeding in their studies [and] also to making meaningful connections during their time in college." A student summarizes: "We are like one giant family; the student body is constantly looking out for one another."

FAIRFIELD UNIVERSITY

Financial Aid: 203-254-4125 • E-Mail: admis@fairfield.edu • Website: www.fairfield.edu

THE PRINCETON REVIEW SAYS

Admissions

The school reports that its standardized testing policy for use in admission for Fall 2024 is Test Optional. The 2024 testing policy will be permanent. The Princeton Review suggests that interested applicants consult with the school for the most up-to-date standardized testing policies. *Very important factors considered include:* rigor of secondary school record, academic GPA, application essay, recommendation(s). *Important factors considered include:* interview, extracurricular activities, talent/ability, character/personal qualities, first generation, volunteer work, work experience, level of applicant's interest. *Other factors considered include:* class rank, standardized test scores, alumni/ae relation, geographical residence, racial/ethnic status. High school diploma is required and GED is accepted. *Academic units required:* 4 English, 3 math, 3 science, 2 science labs, 2 foreign language, 2 social studies, 2 history. *Academic units recommended:* 4 English, 4 math, 4 science, 2 science labs, 4 foreign language, 2 social studies, 2 history.

Financial Aid

Students should submit: Business/Farm Supplement; CSS/Financial Aid Profile; FAFSA; Noncustodial Profile. Priority filing deadline is 12/1. The Princeton Review suggests that all financial aid forms be submitted as soon as possible (see page 5 for a note on the FAFSA). *Need-based scholarships/grants offered:* College/university scholarship or grant aid from institutional funds; Federal Pell; SEOG; State scholarships/grants. *Loan aid offered:* Direct PLUS loans; Direct Subsidized Loans; Direct Unsubsidized Loans. Admitted students will be notified of awards on a rolling basis beginning 2/1. Federal Work-Study Program available. Institutional employment available.

The Inside Word

While all facets of the application are critical, there's no denying academic records will be of primary importance. Expect admissions officers to closely assess both grades and the rigor of your curriculum; they are also looking for students who will be successful and reflect their Jesuit ideals. And if you panic at the thought of standardized tests, you can breathe a sigh of relief: Fairfield is Test Optional. However, if you choose not to submit, it's highly recommended you sit for an interview.

THE SCHOOL SAYS "..."

From the Admissions Office

"Fairfield University welcomes students into a learning and living community that will give them a solid intellectual foundation and the confidence they need to reach their individual goals. Students at Fairfield benefit from the deep-rooted Jesuit commitment to education of the whole person—mind, body, and spirit, and our admission policies are consistent with that mission. When considering an applicant, Fairfield looks at measures of academic achievement, students' curricular and extracurricular activities, their life skills and accomplishments, and the degree to which they have an appreciation for Fairfield's mission and outlook. In keeping with its holistic review process, Fairfield is a Test Optional institution. Students choosing not to submit test scores do not have to submit any additional documents but are encouraged to schedule a campus interview. Fairfield University students are challenged to be creative and active members of a community in which diversity is encouraged and honored. The university community is committed to excellence in educating, serving, inspiring and training students in a wide variety of disciplines and fields. Students can complement their classroom performance with a rich array of study abroad, internship and research opportunities. Our location is ideal, offering a picturesque 200-acre campus in the coastal community of Fairfield, Connecticut, just an hour away from the cultural, intellectual and economic opportunities of New York City. On campus, students participate in a vast array of activities, including varsity and intramural athletics, performing arts groups and an extremely active student government. All of this prepares our graduates for a rich and fulfilling future. Six months after graduation, 98 percent of the Class of 2022 is employed full time, in graduate school, or pursuing a service opportunity."

SELECTIVITY

Admissions Rating	90
# of applicants	13,359
% of applicants accepted	52
% of acceptees attending	19
# offered a place on the wait list	4,574
% accepting a place on wait list	28
% admitted from wait list	1
# of early decision applicants	284
% accepted early decision	83

FIRST-YEAR PROFILE

Testing policy	Test Optional
Range SAT composite	1260–1360
Range SAT EBRW	620–680
Range SAT math	620–690
Range ACT composite	28–31
# submitting SAT scores	339
% submitting SAT scores	26
# submitting ACT scores	92
% submitting ACT scores	7
Average HS GPA	3.8
% frosh submitting high school GPA	99
% graduated top 10% of class	30
% graduated top 25% of class	67
% graduated top 50% of class	92

DEADLINES

Early decision	
Deadline	11/15
Notification	12/15
Other ED deadline	1/15
Other ED notification	2/15
Early action	
Deadline	11/1
Notification	1/15
Regular	
Deadline	1/15
Notification	4/1
Nonfall registration?	Yes

APPLICANTS OFTEN PREFER
Boston College; Villanova University

APPLICANTS SOMETIMES PREFER
College of the Holy Cross; Elon University; Fordham University; Northeastern University; Providence College

FINANCIAL FACTS

Financial Aid Rating	84
Annual tuition	$53,630
Room and board	$16,750
Required fees	$825
Books and supplies	$1,150
Average frosh need-based scholarship	$36,180
Average UG need-based scholarship	$34,712
% needy frosh rec. need-based scholarship or grant aid	72
% needy UG rec. need-based scholarship or grant aid	81
% needy frosh rec. non-need-based scholarship or grant aid	95
% needy UG rec. non-need-based scholarship or grant aid	92
% needy frosh rec. need-based self-help aid	72
% needy UG rec. need-based self-help aid	75
% frosh rec. any financial aid	95
% UG rec. any financial aid	94
% UG borrow to pay for school	59
Average cumulative indebtedness	$41,297
% frosh need fully met	40
% ugrads need fully met	39
Average % of frosh need met	86
Average % of ugrad need met	80

FLAGLER COLLEGE

74 King Street, St. Augustine, FL 32084 • Admissions: 904-829-6481 • Fax: 904-819-6466

CAMPUS LIFE

Quality of Life Rating	**85**
Fire Safety Rating	**87**
Green Rating	**60***
Type of school	Private
Affiliation	No Affiliation
Environment	Village

STUDENTS

Total undergrad enrollment	2,591
% male/female/another gender	32/68/<1
% from out of state	41
% frosh live on campus	91
% ugrads live on campus	44
# of fraternities	1
# of sororities	2
% African American	3
% Asian	1
% White	73
% Hispanic	12
% Native American	<1
% Pacific Islander	<1
% Two or more races	4
% Race and/or ethnicity unknown	4
% international	3
# of countries represented	52

SURVEY SAYS . . .
Students are happy
Class discussions encouraged
Students love St. Augustine, FL
Easy to get around campus

ACADEMICS

Academic Rating	**81**
% students returning for sophomore year	69
% students graduating within 4 years	50
% students graduating within 6 years	57
Calendar	Semester
Student/faculty ratio	14:1
Profs interesting rating	91
Profs accessible rating	94

Most classes have 10–19 students.
Most lab/discussion sessions have
10–19 students.

MOST POPULAR MAJORS
Business Administration; Psychology; Criminology

STUDENTS SAY "..."

Academics

For those seeking "an excellent education in a beautiful location," Flagler College is a small comprehensive liberal arts school in Florida that offers a "comfortable atmosphere," "tons of history and culture," and "a perfect ratio of professors to student." The school's strong education program is a huge draw here, but there are plenty of other strong programs in Flagler's 74 available majors. Hard workers get noticed, and there are plenty of opportunities to excel outside of the classroom, which "has been the most valuable aspect," according to one student.

The faculty here is "extremely enthusiastic about their jobs" and "very knowledgeable in their fields," though "there are a few that I don't think have real direction," says a student. Nevertheless, most are "always willing to meet and discuss work outside of the classroom," and the fact that "it is pretty easy to get to know the professors within your major on a personal basis makes things a lot easier and comfortable." This close-knit community breeds an environment where every person actively wants "to share experiences and knowledge with the faculty and other students." Class time is treated as an "intellectual journey," wherein one main question or discussion topic is introduced, and students explore every aspect of it using the professor as the tour guide. "This system the professors at Flagler College have evokes curiosity from all students, leaving very little room for confusion."

Aside from the "ample help from teachers," the "personable" administration is "good at communicating to all students via school email." The best classes are the ones with eight or so people in them, as "you really lean on each other throughout the semester."

Campus Life

Life is "pretty chill at Flagler," where "homework usually isn't too bad most of the time." As far as making friends, this "relaxed," happy lot has no problems. "Attend a few of the many social activities that Flagler College offers. It's really easy to make friends there!" suggests one student. On the first Friday of the month, all the art galleries "throw their doors wide open and serve treats," and the "casual and quaint" tourist-centric town of St. Augustine "is an awesome place to spend your time, walking around, going out to eat, and doing a little bit of shopping." Campus activities tend to "die around 7:00 P.M.," and many students tend to live nearby off campus.

Sunny days mean "the pool and West lawn are the places to be," and on weekends, "many times we drive to Jacksonville and go out at night there." Biking, beach volleyball, and walking along the sand dunes are just some of the beachy pastimes here, where "the beach mentality triumphs, including surfer culture." The campus itself "is beautiful, we sometimes even compare it to Hogwarts," says a student.

Student Body

Your typical Flagler student is "easygoing and very laid-back" ("How can you not be with the beach five miles away?" asks a student) as well as "super nice and friendly." It's not difficult to fit in at Flagler College, because "there is a crowd for everybody, despite the small size of the student body," even if this student body as a whole is a bit "homogenous." All students provide different viewpoints and "seem to be very respectful of others' views." There are quite a few surfers and artistic types, and even these groups are "very motivated and ready to broaden their education."

FLAGLER COLLEGE

Financial Aid: 904-819-6225 • E-Mail: admissions@flagler.edu • Website: www.flagler.edu

THE PRINCETON REVIEW SAYS

Admissions

The school reports that its standardized testing policy for use in admission for Fall 2024 is Test Optional. *Very important factors considered include:* academic GPA. *Important factors considered include:* rigor of secondary school record, standardized test scores, application essay, recommendation(s), first generation, geographical residence. *Other factors considered include:* extracurricular activities, character/personal qualities, alumni/ae relation, volunteer work, work experience, level of applicant's interest. High school diploma is required and GED is accepted. *Academic units recommended:* 4 English, 4 math, 3 science, 1 science lab, 1 social studies, 3 history.

Financial Aid

Students should submit: FAFSA; State aid form. Priority filing deadline is 3/1. The Princeton Review suggests that all financial aid forms be submitted as soon as possible (see page 5 for a note on the FAFSA). *Need-based scholarships/grants offered:* College/university scholarship or grant aid from institutional funds; Federal Pell; Private scholarships; SEOG; State scholarships/grants. *Loan aid offered:* Direct PLUS loans; Direct Subsidized Loans; Direct Unsubsidized Loans; State Loans. Admitted students will be notified of awards on a rolling basis beginning 10/25. Federal Work-Study Program available. Institutional employment available.

The Inside Word

Several high-profile programs, a desirable location, and a small, incoming freshman class all conspire to drive down Flagler's admissions rate. Still, Flagler is not top-tier when it comes to selectivity, and strong candidates should meet little resistance from the admissions office. About half of the incoming freshmen graduated in the top quarter of their classes, so make sure you build a strong application with harder courses and strong grades.

THE SCHOOL SAYS "..."

From the Admissions Office

"Flagler College is an independent, four-year, coeducational, residential institution located in picturesque St. Augustine. A famous historic tourist center in northeast Florida, it is located to the south of Jacksonville and north of Daytona Beach. Flagler students have ample opportunity to explore the rich cultural heritage and international flavor of St. Augustine, and there's always time for a relaxing day at the beach, about four miles from campus. The annual cost for tuition, room, and board at Flagler is typically less expensive than most comparable private schools in Florida. The small student body helps to keep one from becoming `just a number.' Flagler serves a predominately full-time student body and seeks to enroll students who can benefit from the type of educational experience the college offers. Because of the college's mission and distinctive characteristics, some students may benefit more from an educational experience at Flagler than others. The college's admission standards and procedures are designed to select from among the applicants those students most likely to succeed academically, to contribute significantly to the student life program at Flagler, and to become graduates of the college. Flagler College provides an exceptional opportunity for a private education at an extremely affordable cost."

SELECTIVITY

Admissions Rating	78
# of applicants	5,376
% of applicants accepted	81
% of acceptees attending	17
# of early decision applicants	340
% accepted early decision	70

FIRST-YEAR PROFILE

Testing policy	Test Optional

DEADLINES

Early decision	
Deadline	11/1
Regular	
Deadline	3/1
Notification	Rolling, 10/1
Nonfall registration?	Yes

FINANCIAL FACTS

Financial Aid Rating	80
Annual tuition	$25,710
Room and board	$14,350
Required fees	$900
Required fees (first-year)	$1,000
Books and supplies	$1,250
Average frosh need-based scholarship	$12,663
Average UG need-based scholarship	$11,456
% needy frosh rec. need-based scholarship or grant aid	99
% needy UG rec. need-based scholarship or grant aid	99
% needy frosh rec. non-need-based scholarship or grant aid	7
% needy UG rec. non-need-based scholarship or grant aid	8
% needy frosh rec. need-based self-help aid	81
% needy UG rec. need-based self-help aid	78
% UG borrow to pay for school	68
Average cumulative indebtedness	$35,720
% frosh need fully met	11
% ugrads need fully met	12
Average % of frosh need met	55
Average % of ugrad need met	54

FLORIDA INTERNATIONAL UNIVERSITY

11200 SW 8 St., Miami, FL 33199 • Admissions: 305-348-2000 • Fax: 305-348-3648

This narrative, like all others in this book, is based on student responses and data collected prior to the 2023–2024 academic school year. While these profiles strive to be an accurate depiction of what to expect for the upcoming year, recent developments in the Florida state system may change the academic offerings and overall atmosphere at colleges in the system. Students should check the free online tools for this book (see page vi) for any late-breaking administrative news and they should voice any concerns or questions with the colleges directly.

STUDENTS SAY ". . ."

Academics

Those at Florida International University are privy to an affordable and "high standard of education," a "beautiful campus," and a community bursting with "the utmost pride and respect for their school." The institution is also teeming with "many opportunities and flexible resources for its student body, such as the various societies, research opportunities, and career help." When it comes to academics, FIU is home to a wide array of departments, with students agreeing the best of the best are "easily the international business and relations, law, medicine, and biological sciences departments." Inside the classroom, undergrads are greeted by faculty who are known to be "industry experts." Although a handful feel that "some classes are too big for intimate discussions," others insist that their professors "look after their students and take pride in giving them a great education." As this undergrad concludes, "My overall academic experience has been very positive. I have had great professors and mentors who have prepared me for work and study in my field."

Campus Life

Sure, academics take priority at Florida International University. But undergrads still manage to carve out time for fun and for extracurriculars. "They have something to do for everyone, and that is a great strength." To begin with, the student council is always organizing activities be it "movie nights, game nights, yoga for beginners, recipe competitions, [or] prize winning events." What's more, academic "departments will host guest lectures with prominent individuals…[such as] researchers or people with experience in a career related to the field." Undergrads looking to burn off some steam and academic stress love to hit up "the recreation center, as it is nicer than any local private gym," with many saying, "intramural sports [are] a favorite." Lots of FIU undergrads are also "active member[s] in multiple student organizations" with "a myriad of clubs to choose from," ranging from Greek life and theater society to pre-health clubs and the chess team.

Taking "drives to Biscayne Bay [or] Miami Beach and food places around town [are a] favorite pastime," as well as sampling all of the "clubs, restaurants, museums, and beautiful parks" around the city. In short, "Miami always has something happening."

Student Body

When it comes to discussing their peers, undergrads are quick to boast that "the student body at Florida International University is one of the most diverse and unique in all the U.S." Indeed, you can find "people from all over the world who attend this university." A large percentage hail from Spanish-speaking countries such as "Venezuela, Colombia, Puerto Rico, [and] Spain." It's really a "melting pot of cultures and customs." Beyond geographical background, students report that their peers are "a very genuine group of people with very smart minds" and "very helpful to each other." One individual elaborates, "They're so friendly that people will leave their bags with complete strangers at the library while they go to the bathroom because it's just that kind of environment." FIU undergrads also tend to be hardworking and dedicated to their studies. "I have never seen such [an] enthusias[tic] and determined group of people. [We stay] up late nights together in a classroom trying to understand the material." Although a few undergrads note that the student body is "mostly composed of commuters" who "do not live on campus" and have "many responsibilities outside of campus, " most agree that "FIU is like a family. Everyone looks out for each other and finds ways to come together."

FLORIDA INTERNATIONAL UNIVERSITY

Financial Aid: 305-348-7272 • E-Mail: admiss@fiu.edu • Website: www.fiu.edu

THE PRINCETON REVIEW SAYS

Admissions

The school reports that its standardized testing policy for use in admission for Fall 2024 requires applicants to submit either the SAT or ACT. The 2024 testing policy will be permanent. The Princeton Review suggests that interested applicants consult with the school for the most up-to-date standardized testing policies. *Very important factors considered include:* rigor of secondary school record, class rank, academic GPA, standardized test scores. *Other factors considered include:* application essay, recommendation(s), extracurricular activities, talent/ability, character/personal qualities, first generation, alumni/ae relation, geographical residence, state residency, volunteer work, work experience, level of applicant's interest. High school diploma is required and GED is accepted. *Academic units required:* 4 English, 4 math, 3 science, 2 science labs, 2 foreign language, 3 social studies, 2 academic electives.

Financial Aid

Students should submit: FAFSA. Priority filing deadline is 3/1. The Princeton Review suggests that all financial aid forms be submitted as soon as possible (see page 5 for a note on the FAFSA). *Need-based scholarships/grants offered:* College/university scholarship or grant aid from institutional funds; Federal Pell; Private scholarships; SEOG; State scholarships/grants. *Loan aid offered:* Direct PLUS loans; Direct Subsidized Loans; Direct Unsubsidized Loans; College/university loans from institutional funds. Admitted students will be notified of awards on a rolling basis beginning 2/1. Federal Work-Study Program available. Institutional employment available.

Inside Word

Florida International University is a highly selective school. Admissions officers want to be sure that accepted students have what it takes to handle FIU's academics rigors. You'll have a leg up with advanced courses on your high school transcript. FIU is seeking individuals who welcome challenges and strive for greatness when faced with adversity. In addition to an impressive course load, be sure to highlight extracurriculars and community involvement for a well-rounded application. Finally, it's important to know that certain degree programs (like architecture and nursing) maintain more stringent admissions requirements.

THE SCHOOL SAYS "..."

From the Admissions Office

"Florida International University (FIU) is Miami's first and only public research university. With more than 200 bachelor's, master's and doctoral options (many available online) and South Florida's only public colleges of law and medicine, FIU offers a program to fit every passion. FIU is dedicated to enriching the lives of the local and global community. With a student body of nearly 60,000 students, FIU is among the top 10 largest universities in the nation and has graduated more than 200,000 alumni. Diversity and access are essential to FIU's mission. Over 80% of the student body is comprised of minorities and FIU ranks first among U.S. public institutions for granting bachelor's and graduate degrees to Hispanics and ranks in the top 5 for bachelor's and graduate degrees granted to Black/African American students. Additionally, more than 50% of FIU's undergraduates come from low-income households and more than 20% are the first in their family to attend college. Designated as a top-tier research institution, FIU also emphasizes research as a major component in the university's mission. FIU's exploration, research and community engagement is supported by more than 40 centers and institutes. From the sciences to socio-political studies, these centers and institutes serve to further student's pursuit of knowledge and understanding."

SELECTIVITY

Admissions Rating	88
# of applicants	17,343
% of applicants accepted	64
% of acceptees attending	40

FIRST-YEAR PROFILE

Testing policy	SAT or ACT Required
Range SAT composite	1070–1240
Range SAT EBRW	550–640
Range SAT math	510–610
Range ACT composite	21–26
# submitting SAT scores	3,966
% submitting SAT scores	90
# submitting ACT scores	455
% submitting ACT scores	10
Average HS GPA	4.0
% frosh submitting high school GPA	99
% graduated top 10% of class	29
% graduated top 25% of class	49
% graduated top 50% of class	59

DEADLINES

Regular	
Deadline	5/1
Notification	7/1
Nonfall registration?	Yes

FINANCIAL FACTS

Financial Aid Rating	77
Annual in-state tuition	$6,168
Annual out-of-state tuition	$18,566
Room and board	$11,600
Required fees	$398
Books and supplies	$1,350
Average frosh need-based scholarship	$9,270
Average UG need-based scholarship	$7,709
% needy frosh rec. need-based scholarship or grant aid	65
% needy UG rec. need-based scholarship or grant aid	82
% needy frosh rec. non-need-based scholarship or grant aid	74
% needy UG rec. non-need-based scholarship or grant aid	39
% needy frosh rec. need-based self-help aid	12
% needy UG rec. need-based self-help aid	27
% frosh rec. any financial aid	75
% UG rec. any financial aid	65
% UG borrow to pay for school	28
Average cumulative indebtedness	$18,139
% frosh need fully met	10
% ugrads need fully met	8
Average % of frosh need met	55
Average % of ugrad need met	42

FLORIDA SOUTHERN COLLEGE

111 Lake Hollingsworth Drive, Lakeland, FL 33801-5698 • Admissions: 863-680-4111 • Fax: 863-680-4120

CAMPUS LIFE

Quality of Life Rating	86
Fire Safety Rating	89
Green Rating	74
Type of school	Private
Affiliation	United Methodist
Environment	City

STUDENTS

Total undergrad enrollment	2,725
% male/female/another gender	37/63/0
% from out of state	39
% frosh from public high school	77
% frosh live on campus	93
% ugrads live on campus	85
# of fraternities (% join)	6 (23)
# of sororities (% join)	6 (26)
% African American	6
% Asian	3
% White	69
% Hispanic	15
% Native American	<1
% Pacific Islander	<1
% Two or more races	3
% Race and/or ethnicity unknown	1
% international	4
# of countries represented	52

SURVEY SAYS . . .

Lots of conservative students
Class discussions encouraged
Frats and sororities are popular
Theater is popular
Students get along with local community
Intramural sports are popular

ACADEMICS

Academic Rating	82
% students returning for sophomore year	77
% students graduating within 4 years	63
% students graduating within 6 years	68
Calendar	Semester
Student/faculty ratio	13:1
Profs interesting rating	94
Profs accessible rating	95

Most classes have 10–19 students.
Most lab/discussion sessions have 10–19 students.

MOST POPULAR MAJORS

Biology/Biological Sciences, General; Registered Nursing/Registered Nurse; Business Administration and Management, General

This narrative, like all others in this book, is based on student responses and data collected prior to the 2023–2024 academic school year. While these profiles strive to be an accurate depiction of what to expect for the upcoming year, recent developments in the Florida state system may change the academic offerings and overall atmosphere at colleges in the system. Students should check the free online tools for this book (see page vi) for any late-breaking administrative news and they should voice any concerns or questions with the colleges directly.

STUDENTS SAY ". . ."

Academics

Florida Southern College is a school that makes a "lifelong commitment to you as a student in an academic and personal sense." Indeed, undergrads say "the faculty is truly amazing," applauding the personalized attention they receive. As one individual illustrates, "My advisor has helped me get additional scholarships, connections at potential jobs, and gone above and beyond in helping me make my schedule every semester." Students also greatly appreciate Florida Southern's "small size," which helps them "easily...foster relationships with [their] professors." Undergrads are pleased to discover that most professors know how to "bring [their] lectures to life and provide [a lot] of hands on learning." They "work hard to make sure we are not only understanding the material but learning in a way that will help us once we graduate." The college excels at "helping prepare students" for their post collegiate lives. This undergrad explains, "The career center and business school have a four-year plan developed to help students secure careers once they graduate."

Campus Life

Outside of the classroom, students at Florida Southern College "fill their day [with] clubs and organizations." There are lots of non-academic courses for students such as "the Remedy classes…[wherein students] create art in many different ways from painting to crocheting." Additionally, "Greek life here is really strong," and that "it also works doubly because, once you're involved in Greek life, they also require you to be involved in at least one other organization on campus." These organizations include student government, Black student union, and improv comedy among many others. Students also boast that "intramurals are so fun" and that they "offer so many unique ones [like] disc golf [and] beach volleyball." Additionally, it's quite common for undergrads to enjoy their beautiful surroundings. They can even rent "hammocks, kayaks, [and] paddle boards" to use on and around the campus lake. "Taking walks around Lake Hollingsworth or driving "lake laps" are also a favorite."

Students also enjoy their surrounding town of Lakeland, which is "a very up-and-coming town with fun food options and entertainment. When looking for a fun day off campus, "a lot of people like to hit the beach or Disney/Universal on the weekends or other days off because it's so close by."

Student Body

Undergrads at FSC love that it has "a big school feel" while still retaining "the perks of a small school." As one student reflects, "You can't walk across campus without seeing someone you know and smiling and saying hi, without feeling like you're too close with everyone!" And just who are the folks you'd be saying hello to as you stroll along Mr. George's Green? Well, they are likely to be "compassionate, highly involved, self-motivated" individuals who "strive to be the best academically as well as socially." Undergrads do say that the "student body is mostly Caucasian and Christian," but as one individual asserts, "The school has done [a lot] better at recruiting more minority students." And a classmate goes on to add that, "there are a lot of first-generation college students here, which is unique!" No matter your background, it's fairly easy to make friends at Florida Southern. After all, students also report that their peers are "so welcoming and kind." Indeed, "it is truly like a family here and everyone wants to see each other succeed."

FLORIDA SOUTHERN COLLEGE

Financial Aid: 863-680-4140 • E-Mail: fscadm@flsouthern.edu • Website: www.flsouthern.edu

THE PRINCETON REVIEW SAYS

Admissions

The school reports that its standardized testing policy for use in admission for Fall 2024 is Test Optional. *Very important factors considered include:* academic GPA and the rigor of the secondary school curriculum. *Other factors considered include:* standardized test scores (ACT or SAT), if submitted, extracurricular activities including volunteer and work experience, talent/ability, character/leadership qualities, letters of recommendation, application essay, and the level of applicant's interest. Proof of English proficiency is required of all international students. High school diploma is required, and GED is accepted. *Academic units required:* 4 English, 3 math, 2 science, 2 science labs, 3 social studies, 3 history, 1 academic elective. *Academic units recommended:* 2 foreign language.

Financial Aid

Students should submit: FAFSA. The College recommends filing as soon as the FAFSA opens. *Need-based scholarships/grants offered:* College scholarships or grant aid from institutional funds; Federal Pell; Private scholarships; SEOG; State scholarships/grants. *Loan aid offered:* Direct PLUS loans; Direct Subsidized Loans; Direct Unsubsidized Loans; Admitted students will be notified of awards on a rolling basis beginning in December. Federal Work-Study Program available. Institutional employment available.

The Inside Word

Florida Southern College admits students based on the usual mix of GPA, transcript, recommendations, and extracurriculars. Special attention is given to those whose accomplishments include peer-engagement and leadership roles. Because FSC offers early admission, applicants are encouraged to apply before November 1.

THE SCHOOL SAYS "..."

From the Admissions Office

"Florida Southern is a national leader in engaged learning, offering real-world, hands-on experiences that include internships, student-faculty collaborative research, performance, service opportunities, and study abroad. The Junior Journey is an innovative travel program that allows students to study overseas or domestically—often at no additional cost.

"FSC offers over seventy majors from computer science and engineering, chemistry, and nursing to art and museum studies, music, and theater performance." Students looking to enter highly specialized career fields can choose from a range of interdisciplinary minors like ethics and neuroscience; there are also outstanding pre-professional programs in subjects like occupational therapy and veterinary medicine. Students wanting to put their career on the fast track can take advantage of a range of 4+1 options allowing them to earn a master's degree, including an MBA, with an extra year of study. The College also offers doctoral programs in education, nursing, and physical therapy."

"The College is known for its friendly, vibrant, and energetic community. Our involved student population enjoys rich and varied student life programming that includes 20 championship NCAA Division II athletic programs, four club sports (equestrian, esports, ice hockey, and water ski), intramurals, more than 100 clubs and organizations, and 12 national fraternities and sororities. The College's popular lakefront allows for weekend activities like kayaking, canoeing, and paddle boarding.

"The College has a state-of-the-art technology center, as well as contemporary residence halls with scenic views of Lake Hollingsworth. FSC is home to the world's largest single-site collection of Frank Lloyd Wright structures, which provides a stunning setting for living and learning. "Within a year of graduation, 95 percent of students report achieving their post-baccalaureate degree goals by securing employment or beginning an advanced degree program."

SELECTIVITY

Admissions Rating	88
# of applicants	11,121
% of applicants accepted	57
% of acceptees attending	12
# of early decision applicants	69
% accepted early decision	72

FIRST-YEAR PROFILE

Testing policy	Test Optional
Range SAT composite	1100–1280
Range SAT EBRW	560–660
Range SAT math	520–630
Range ACT composite	22–29
# submitting SAT scores	304
% submitting SAT scores	40
# submitting ACT scores	179
% submitting ACT scores	24
Average HS GPA	3.8
% frosh submitting high school GPA	100
% graduated top 10% of class	24
% graduated top 25% of class	36
% graduated top 50% of class	88

DEADLINES

Early decision	
Deadline	11/1
Notification	12/15
Early action	
Deadline	11/1
Notification	12/15
Regular	
Priority	3/1
Deadline	5/1
Notification	Rolling, 8/1
Nonfall registration?	Yes

APPLICANTS SOMETIMES PREFER
Florida State University; University of Florida

APPLICANTS RARELY PREFER
Rollins College; Stetson University; The University of Tampa

FINANCIAL FACTS

Financial Aid Rating	85
Annual tuition	$41,500
Room and board	$12,400
Required fees	$860
Books and supplies	$1,250
Average frosh need-based scholarship	$28,693
Average UG need-based scholarship	$27,763
% needy frosh rec. need-based scholarship or grant aid	100
% needy UG rec. need-based scholarship or grant aid	99
% needy frosh rec. non-need-based scholarship or grant aid	59
% needy UG rec. non-need-based scholarship or grant aid	67
% needy frosh rec. need-based self-help aid	2
% needy UG rec. need-based self-help aid	9
% frosh rec. any financial aid	100
% UG rec. any financial aid	100
% UG borrow to pay for school	83
Average cumulative indebtedness	$27,170
% frosh need fully met	26
% ugrads need fully met	28
Average % of frosh need met	74
Average % of ugrad need met	76

FLORIDA STATE UNIVERSITY

Florida State University, Tallahassee, FL 32306-2400 • Admissions: 850-644-2525 • Fax: 850-644-0197

CAMPUS LIFE

Quality of Life Rating	91
Fire Safety Rating	88
Green Rating	60*
Type of school	Public
Environment	City

STUDENTS

Total undergrad enrollment	32,691
% male/female/another gender	43/57/0
% from out of state	13
% frosh from public high school	79
% frosh live on campus	80
% ugrads live on campus	20
# of fraternities (% join)	24 (17)
# of sororities (% join)	24 (23)
% African American	8
% Asian	3
% White	58
% Hispanic	23
% Native American	<1
% Pacific Islander	<1
% Two or more races	4
% Race and/or ethnicity unknown	1
% international	2
# of countries represented	104

SURVEY SAYS . . .

Students are happy
Great library
Career services are great
Internships are widely available
Recreation facilities are great
Everyone loves the Seminoles
Intramural sports are popular
Frats and sororities are popular
Theater is popular
Alumni active on campus
Active student government
Active minority support groups
Active student-run political groups

ACADEMICS

Academic Rating	82
% students returning for sophomore year	94
% students graduating within 4 years	74
% students graduating within 6 years	85
Calendar	Semester
Student/faculty ratio	21:1
Profs interesting rating	88
Profs accessible rating	92

Most classes have 10–19 students.
Most lab/discussion sessions have
20–29 students.

MOST POPULAR MAJORS
Psychology, General; Criminal Justice/Safety
Studies; Finance, General

STUDENTS SAY "..."

Academics

"Research, service, scholarship, and extracurricular opportunities" are abundant at the "large campus" of Florida State University in Tallahassee. It's rather easy to understand why students are drawn to Florida State. After all, the "campus is gorgeous," "the weather is always nice" and there are an abundance "of resources at your fingertips." What's more, "despite its large size...the community is welcoming and [undergrads] don't feel like an anonymous face in the student body." Incredibly, it's still "easy to feel at home." Much of that can be credited to faculty who "are very willing to help undergraduate students with classes, research, career prospects, and everything in between." Florida State professors also excel at bringing their "courses to life and mak[ing] them interesting enough that [students truly] want to learn." Many are also "experts in their field." And "they make it known that they want students to succeed." To that end, "in addition to making themselves available...for office hours, they [continually] offer to make time for students [beyond those hours]." Perhaps this grateful undergrad says it best, "Their advice has pushed me to be a better student and pushed me to find a great future."

Campus Life

Life at Florida State offers a great "mix of academics, socializing, [and] extracurricular [activities]." To begin with, athletics are fairly popular and you can frequently spot "basketball games and volleyball games" popping up around campus. And during the fall, weekends "are spent [at] football games and tailgates." Aside from sports, we've been informed that the "Student Life Cinema always has cool events going on" and "there are always free concerts at Club Down Under on campus" as well. FSU also has "many organizations that are focused on philanthropy." For example, "Dance Marathon is the largest student run organization on campus and we have one of the largest Dance Marathons in the entire country. We also have a large Relay for Life organization." Moreover, a number of undergrads enjoy FSU's reservation, an "off campus [spot] where students can go swimming, paddle boarding, relaxing, or even [try out a] ropes course." Of course, it's also important to mention that some students feel as though "Greek life dominates" the social scene, even though "less than 50% of the student population [participates]." Finally, undergrads greatly appreciate hometown Tallahassee. The city offers "endless" nightlife along with "many great clubs and places for social events as well as pretty landscapes and historical sites."

Student Body

Florida State manages to attract a student body that's a "unique mixture of south Floridians, crunchy granolas, Northern snowbirds, sorority girls, and good ole boys, with a nice international population mixed in there." Despite these diverse personalities, the university still seems to cultivate a "strong sense of community." Of course, it definitely helps that students are "very friendly and always willing to [strike] up conversation." Even better, "everyone you see seems genuinely happy" and everyone "is pushing for you." People here want to see their peers "succeed." As one impressed student shares, "Everyone is so kind. No one is afraid to ask for help, and if they do most would be more than willing to help you out." Undergrads also applaud FSU for doing "a great job in creating or allowing students to create spaces for all communities, particularly those that are historically marginalized/typically first gen students." And no matter what else, students here come together in their shared "love for FSU." As this satisfied student sums up, "I have never been on a campus with such school spirit, excitement, and motivation to improve."

FLORIDA STATE UNIVERSITY

Financial Aid: 850-644-5716 • E-Mail: admissions@fsu.edu • Website: www.fsu.edu

THE PRINCETON REVIEW SAYS

Admissions

The school reports that its standardized testing policy for use in admission for Fall 2024 requires applicants to submit either the SAT or ACT. It is unknown at this time if the 2024 testing policy will be permanent. The Princeton Review suggests that interested applicants consult with the school for the most up-to-date standardized testing policies. *Very important factors considered include:* rigor of secondary school record. *Important factors considered include:* class rank, academic GPA, standardized test scores, application essay, talent/ability, character/personal qualities, first generation, geographical residence, state residency. *Other factors considered include:* extracurricular activities, volunteer work, work experience. High school diploma is required and GED is accepted. *Academic units required:* 4 English, 4 math, 3 science, 2 science labs, 2 foreign language, 1 social studies, 2 history, 3 academic electives. *Academic units recommended:* 4 English, 4 math, 4 science, 2 science labs, 4 foreign language, 2 social studies, 2 history, 3 academic electives.

Financial Aid

Students should submit: FAFSA; State aid form. The Princeton Review suggests that all financial aid forms be submitted as soon as possible (see page 5 for a note on the FAFSA). *Need-based scholarships/grants offered:* College/university scholarship or grant aid from institutional funds; Federal Pell; Private scholarships; SEOG; State scholarships/grants; United Negro College Fund. *Loan aid offered:* Direct PLUS loans; Direct Subsidized Loans; Direct Unsubsidized Loans. Admitted students will be notified of awards on a rolling basis beginning 4/5. Federal Work-Study Program available. Institutional employment available.

The Inside Word

Aspiring FSU students should be forewarned that admission here is selective. Fortunately, the university does take a holistic approach to the process. And candidates should expect that all facets of their application will be thoroughly reviewed. Of course, admissions officers favor students who have taken a rigorous course-load throughout high school. A solid GPA is also a must. Finally, though the essay section of the application is not required, submission is highly recommended. Students who don't write one may be putting themselves at a disadvantage.

THE SCHOOL SAYS "..."

From the Admissions Office

"Florida State University is one of the top public universities in the world and is proud to be recognized as a Preeminent University by the State of Florida. Designated as a Carnegie Research University (with very high research activity), Florida State offers more than 320 undergraduate, graduate, and professional degree programs, including medicine and law. Our diverse and highly talented student body includes students from all fifty states and more than 130 countries. The university is committed to student success for all students as evidenced by impressive retention and graduation rates that place us it at the highest levels nationally. World class faculty, including Nobel laureates, Pulitzer Prize winners, Guggenheim Fellows, members of the National Academy of Sciences and American Academy of Arts and Sciences, and other globally recognized teachers and researchers, are actively creating the knowledge you will be studying in class. You will be encouraged to become engaged in research, internships, entrepreneurial initiatives and other creative activities. You will be supported by comprehensive and innovative student services. And you will be enriched by the extensive variety of cultural, athletic, and recreational offerings available outside the classroom. Our singular goal is make you better than when you arrived, so that you can make a difference in your community and the world."

SELECTIVITY

Admissions Rating	95
# of applicants	78,088
% of applicants accepted	25
% of acceptees attending	31

FIRST-YEAR PROFILE

Testing policy	SAT or ACT Required
Range SAT composite	1220–1360
Range SAT EBRW	620–690
Range SAT math	590–680
Range ACT composite	26–31
# submitting SAT scores	4,107
% submitting SAT scores	68
# submitting ACT scores	1,926
% submitting ACT scores	32
Average HS GPA	3.7
% frosh submitting high school GPA	100
% graduated top 10% of class	65
% graduated top 25% of class	87
% graduated top 50% of class	99

DEADLINES

Early action	
Deadline	10/15
Notification	12/15
Regular	
Priority	12/1
Deadline	3/1
Notification	Rolling, 4/1
Nonfall registration?	Yes

FINANCIAL FACTS

Financial Aid Rating	83
Annual in-state tuition	$4,640
Annual out-of-state tuition	$19,806
Room and board	$11,472
Required fees	$1,877
Books and supplies	$1,000
Average frosh need-based scholarship	$10,100
Average UG need-based scholarship	$10,180
% needy frosh rec. need-based scholarship or grant aid	92
% needy UG rec. need-based scholarship or grant aid	92
% needy frosh rec. non-need-based scholarship or grant aid	12
% needy UG rec. non-need-based scholarship or grant aid	9
% needy frosh rec. need-based self-help aid	29
% needy UG rec. need-based self-help aid	37
% frosh rec. any financial aid	92
% UG rec. any financial aid	89
% UG borrow to pay for school	36
Average cumulative indebtedness	$18,866
% frosh need fully met	13
% ugrads need fully met	9
Average % of frosh need met	64
Average % of ugrad need met	61

FORDHAM UNIVERSITY

441 East Fordham Road, Bronx, NY 10458 • Admissions: 718-817-4000

STUDENTS SAY "..."

Academics

Fordham University's strong Jesuit mission is focused on "creating the next generation of honorable, caring, and curious people." The New York City setting (divided between midtown Manhattan and the Bronx) offers "access to internships and other educational opportunities" and "a great way to network with other people outside of the school environment," as well as "resources of deeper academic inquiry through various graduate schools, institutes, and centers." Ensuring that students make the most of it is, at heart, "a very strong and interesting liberal arts core curriculum that emphasizes the development of reading, writing, and speaking skills," along with "frequent Socratic seminars [and] opportunities to learn outside of the classroom" that are described as "very interdisciplinary" and feature things like "school-sanctioned field trips."

Whether in a formal classroom or not, professors "truly know how to capture students' attention and engage students' ideas within the lessons." They "have impressive backgrounds in their fields, and make sure that all of their class content is backed up with reputable research." And while the faculty emphasizes on academics, "they also focus on soft skills and developing you as a person by...widening your horizons." A student says: "I've enjoyed being able to take many classes that count for my major while learning about other skills and areas."

Campus Life

As one student puts it, "My school challenges me to think creatively and has encouraged me to regularly explore the city and all it has to offer." With Manhattan just "a twenty-minute train ride away," from the Bronx location, that's a feeling shared by others who take the school up on the plentiful "excursions and cultural engagement (Broadway shows, tours of NYC, etc.) opportunities provided by clubs." These organizations are not only "very rich in their activities and breadth" but also feature professional services that "help students learn and build more connections." Athletics are also fairly popular, especially basketball (though there's also a football team that gets "decent turnouts"). There's no Greek life at Fordham, but the school itself hosts "frequent pop-up events where free food is given, such as coffee and cookies with the deans," and "events organized at school always seem to bring people together."

Student Body

Students at Fordham tend to be "largely wealthy, middle class or higher," and, since "lots of people are from New Jersey, New York, and Connecticut," there's a concentration of commuters. On the whole, everyone "has deep respect and admiration for New York City and wants to take advantage of all of the amazing things the city has to offer," and if you fall into that group, "it's quite easy to make friends." That's not just in terms of entertainment—Fordham "applies its Jesuit tradition well in providing opportunities for students to engage in many social justice fights," and students are "passionate about sparking change and collaborating for positive results." Those interested in giving back or bonding through community service will find activities from "volunteering to set up campus as a trick-or-treating space for Bronx residents and their children [to] assisting at the local soup kitchen." It's a collaborative space in and out of class, such as "helping each other find internship placements."

Those looking for "friendly, interesting, open-minded, intelligent" peers will be fulfilled by the Fordham experience. The "community is close-knit and integrated, [and] there is always a friendly face to see on the walk to class or in the cafeteria."

FORDHAM UNIVERSITY

Financial Aid: 718-817-3800 • E-Mail: enroll@fordham.edu • Website: www.fordham.edu

THE PRINCETON REVIEW SAYS

Admissions

The school reports that its standardized testing policy for use in admission for Fall 2024 is Test Optional. The 2024 testing policy will be temporary. The Princeton Review suggests that interested applicants consult with the school for the most up-to-date standardized testing policies. *Very important factors considered include:* rigor of secondary school record, academic GPA. *Important factors considered include:* application essay, recommendation(s), extracurricular activities, talent/ability, character/personal qualities, volunteer work, work experience. *Other factors considered include:* class rank, standardized test scores, first generation, alumni/ae relation, geographical residence, racial/ethnic status, level of applicant's interest. High school diploma is required and GED is accepted. *Academic units required:* 4 English, 3 math, 3 science, 2 foreign language, 3 social studies. *Academic units recommended:* 4 English, 4 math, 4 science, 4 foreign language, 4 social studies.

Financial Aid

Students should submit: CSS/Financial Aid Profile; FAFSA; Noncustodial Profile; State aid form. Priority filing deadline is 11/15. The Princeton Review suggests that all financial aid forms be submitted as soon as possible (see page 5 for a note on the FAFSA). *Need-based scholarships/grants offered:* College/university scholarship or grant aid from institutional funds; Federal Pell; Private scholarships; SEOG; State scholarships/grants. *Loan aid offered:* Direct PLUS loans; Direct Subsidized Loans; Direct Unsubsidized Loans. Admitted students will be notified of awards by 3/15. Federal Work-Study Program available. Institutional employment available.

The Inside Word

Admissions officers at Fordham are on the search for candidates who would be a good match for the school. And in order to find them, they closely consider all facets of student applications. Demonstrated interest such as online engagement or regional programming can help, and a student's inability to visit would never be a barrier to admission. The application review is holistic, which means that the university seeks evidence of leadership, integrity, and academic excellence. The strongest applicants will have taken a challenging course load in high school. You'll definitely want a transcript laden with honors and AP classes, if possible. Fordham only requires one letter of recommendation, but be sure it comes from an individual who can really speak to who you are as a person and as a student. Fordham is in the process of piloting a Test Optional program, during which time the ACT, with or without the essay, or the SAT, will be accepted, but not required.

THE SCHOOL SAYS "..."

From the Admissions Office

"Fordham University offers a distinctive, values-centered educational experience that is rooted in the Jesuit tradition of intellectual rigor and personal attention. Located in New York City, Fordham offers to students the unparalleled educational, cultural and recreational advantages of one of the world's greatest cities. Fordham has two residential campuses in New York—the tree-lined, eighty-five-acre Rose Hill campus in the Bronx and the cosmopolitan Lincoln Center campus in the heart of Manhattan's performing arts center. The university's state-of-the-art facilities and buildings include one of the most technologically advanced libraries in the country. Fordham offers a variety of majors, concentrations and programs that can be combined with an extensive career planning and placement program. More than 3,500 organizations in the New York metropolitan area offer students internships that provide hands-on experience and valuable networking opportunities in fields such as business, communications, medicine, law and education."

SELECTIVITY

Admissions Rating	91
# of applicants	47,203
% of applicants accepted	54
% of acceptees attending	10
# offered a place on the wait list	10,496
% accepting a place on wait list	28
% admitted from wait list	8
# of early decision applicants	338
% accepted early decision	67

FIRST-YEAR PROFILE

Testing policy	Test Optional
Range SAT composite	1330–1460
Range SAT EBRW	660–730
Range SAT math	660–750
Range ACT composite	30–33
# submitting SAT scores	712
% submitting SAT scores	27
# submitting ACT scores	270
% submitting ACT scores	10
Average HS GPA	3.7
% frosh submitting high school GPA	100
% graduated top 10% of class	37
% graduated top 25% of class	75
% graduated top 50% of class	96

DEADLINES

Early decision	
Deadline	11/1
Notification	12/20
Early action	
Deadline	11/1
Notification	12/20
Regular	
Deadline	1/3
Notification	4/1
Nonfall registration?	Yes

APPLICANTS OFTEN PREFER

Boston College; Boston University; City University of New York—Baruch College; City University of New York—Hunter College; George Washington University; New York University; Northeastern University; Rutgers University—New Brunswick; State University of New York—Binghamton University; State University of New York—Stony Brook; Villanova University

APPLICANTS SOMETIMES PREFER

Cornell University; Penn State; Saint John's University; Syracuse University; University of California—Berkeley; University of California—Los Angeles; University of Connecticut; University of Michigan—Ann Arbor; University of Southern California

FINANCIAL FACTS

Financial Aid Rating	82
Annual tuition	$60,335
Room and board	$22,240
Required fees	$1,232
Required fees (first-year)	$1,640
Books and supplies	$1,080
Average frosh need-based scholarship	$31,974
Average UG need-based scholarship	$30,266
% needy frosh rec. need-based scholarship or grant aid	98
% needy UG rec. need-based scholarship or grant aid	97
% needy frosh rec. non-need-based scholarship or grant aid	16
% needy UG rec. non-need-based scholarship or grant aid	14
% needy frosh rec. need-based self-help aid	71
% needy UG rec. need-based self-help aid	73
% frosh rec. any financial aid	96
% UG rec. any financial aid	89
% UG borrow to pay for school	54
Average cumulative indebtedness	$34,901
% frosh need fully met	22
% ugrads need fully met	21
Average % of frosh need met	72
Average % of ugrad need met	68

FRANKLIN & MARSHALL COLLEGE

College Ave, Lancaster, PA 17604-3003 • Admissions: 717-358-3911 • Fax: 717-358-4389

STUDENTS SAY ". . ."

Academics

Established in 1787, Franklin & Marshall College is a little liberal arts gem located in south central Pennsylvania. With around 2,000 students, F&M offers numerous opportunities for academic exploration and expansion, and there is "a great balance between a strong and competitive academic culture, talented and successful athletic teams, and a vibrant social life." The school offers numerous interdisciplinary majors and minors, "does an excellent job of making sure you know how to write," and a collaborative learning experience that extends beyond the classroom through research opportunities, the College Houses (residential communities), and multiple affiliated study abroad programs.

Academics are "demanding and challenging," and students note that "you'll work hard but you'll learn a lot" from professors who are "esteemed published scholars in their respective fields." Small classes offer plenty of face and advice time with these scholars: "Whether it be for class selection or post graduate paths, they are always there to help." The classroom setting at F&M is completely different from the traditional lecture halls of bigger schools, and students "often have round tables for close discussion with...professors." Students love the fact that academic and personal growth are equally important, and the environment is shaped by "people who are active both in school and extracurriculars, and who get excited about both." As one student puts it, "you're not taking advantage of what F&M has to offer if you haven't been to a professor's office and discussed something other than class." The professors at F&M all have "a certain level of uniqueness" in them, but students appreciate that they all possess a great level of understanding. "My professors have managed to get me engaged in areas that have always seemed like a bore to me."

Campus Life

Athletic teams are "highly competitive and are very active in the local community." There is always something to do on weekends, between "[staying] in or [going] to the cinemas to watch movies with your roommates, [hanging] out in frat parties or [attending] events run by an organization for alternative options for frat parties." Club organizations are wildly popular, and "we all really get into our extracurricular activities." Getting around is remarkably easy—"about ten minutes no matter where you are" when you're on the campus, a mall is just 15 minutes away, and off-campus is downtown Lancaster, which offers plenty of entertainment and dining options (like the Central Market).

Student Body

These "smart overachievers who work hard" are also "some of the nicest people you'll ever meet." With only a slight majority of the student body being white, there is an "amazing diversity" on campus, with a bent toward "slightly preppy, but very open-minded." Many F&M students are on a varsity sports team or a member of a sorority or fraternity, and a typical student "is probably involved in three to five clubs and is trying out for theater, an a cappella group, or another organization." Students categorically study hard, and "fill our free time with fun and meaningful clubs and community service."

FRANKLIN & MARSHALL COLLEGE

Financial Aid: 717-358-3991 • E-Mail: admission@fandm.edu • Website: www.fandm.edu

THE PRINCETON REVIEW SAYS

Admissions

The school reports that its standardized testing policy for use in admission for Fall 2024 remains Test Optional, as it has been for years, and there is no indication of that changing. *Very important factors considered include:* rigor of secondary school record, class rank, academic GPA, character/personal qualities. *Important factors considered include:* standardized test scores, application essay, recommendation(s), interview, extracurricular activities, talent/ability, volunteer work. *Other factors considered include:* alumni/ae relation, geographical residence, racial/ethnic status, work experience, level of applicant's interest. High school diploma is required and GED is accepted. *Academic units required:* 4 English, 3 math, 2 science, 2 science labs, 2 foreign language, 1 social studies, 2 history, 1 visual/performing arts. *Academic units recommended:* 4 math, 3 science, 3 science labs, 4 foreign language, 3 social studies, 3 history.

Financial Aid

Students should submit: CSS/Financial Aid Profile; FAFSA; Noncustodial Profile. Priority filing deadline is 2/1. The Princeton Review suggests that all financial aid forms be submitted as soon as possible (see page 5 for a note on the FAFSA). *Need-based scholarships/grants offered:* College/university scholarship or grant aid from institutional funds; Federal Pell; Private scholarships; SEOG; State scholarships/grants. *Loan aid offered:* Direct PLUS loans; Direct Subsidized Loans; Direct Unsubsidized Loans; College/university loans from institutional funds; State Loans. Admitted students will be notified of awards on or about 4/1. Federal Work-Study Program available.

The Inside Word

While admission at F&M is competitive, the admissions committee does show some flexibility. Students who choose not to submit standardized test scores may want to see if they can submit two graded writing samples. Applicants are also encouraged to include nontraditional materials, such as art portfolios or recordings of musical performances, in their applications.

THE SCHOOL SAYS "..."

From the Admissions Office

"The hallmarks of a Franklin & Marshall education are individual attention and a supportive community. Our faculty members challenge you to achieve your best and engage you personally on a level you will not find at other institutions. We have one professor for every nine students, and forty percent of our students collaborate on a research project or other directed study with a faculty member. Here are four more things you should know about F&M: 1) Our professors do not confine learning to classrooms and labs. They take you into the field and the local community to teach you how to *do* what students at other institutions may only read about. 2) We have College Houses, not dorms. Our five College Houses, which bring together first-year students into smaller groups, are student-governed spaces where you socialize, learn, and stretch your intellect. Based in each house are a faculty mentor and an administrative counselor to guide you. 3) No one gets lost. The depth and breadth of student activities and experiences provide everyone with a place to belong. Our students find a strong sense of self, and they find their 'homes' in clubs, athletic teams, their College Houses, fraternities and sororities, the performing and musical arts, and the other strong communities they have the freedom to create for themselves. 4) Our Office of Student and Post-Graduate Development is committed to your success. Ninety-five percent of 2022 graduates were employed or pursuing further education six months after graduating."

SELECTIVITY

Admissions Rating	94
# of applicants	8,923
% of applicants accepted	36
% of acceptees attending	15
# of early decision applicants	490
% accepted early decision	58

FIRST-YEAR PROFILE

Testing policy	Test Optional
Range SAT composite	1300–1410
Range SAT EBRW	640–710
Range SAT math	633–720
Range ACT composite	29–32
# submitting SAT scores	166
% submitting SAT scores	34
# submitting ACT scores	53
% submitting ACT scores	11
% graduated top 10% of class	52
% graduated top 25% of class	78
% graduated top 50% of class	92

DEADLINES

Early decision	
Deadline	11/15
Notification	12/15
Other ED deadline	1/15
Other ED notification	2/15
Regular	
Deadline	1/15
Notification	4/1
Nonfall registration?	Yes

FINANCIAL FACTS

Financial Aid Rating	99
Annual tuition	$65,652
Room and board	$15,040
Required fees	$192
Required fees (first-year)	$392
Books and supplies	$1,200
Average frosh need-based scholarship	$51,871
Average UG need-based scholarship	$53,945
% needy frosh rec. need-based scholarship or grant aid	100
% needy UG rec. need-based scholarship or grant aid	100
% needy frosh rec. non-need-based scholarship or grant aid	31
% needy UG rec. non-need-based scholarship or grant aid	18
% needy frosh rec. need-based self-help aid	72
% needy UG rec. need-based self-help aid	89
% frosh rec. any financial aid	68
% UG rec. any financial aid	62
% UG borrow to pay for school	54
Average cumulative indebtedness	$29,998
% frosh need fully met	100
% ugrads need fully met	100
Average % of frosh need met	100
Average % of ugrad need met	100

FRANKLIN W. OLIN COLLEGE OF ENGINEERING

1000 Olin Way, Needham, MA 02492-1200 • Admissions: 781-292-2222

STUDENTS SAY "..."

Academics

Franklin W. Olin College of Engineering in Massachusetts is a relatively new school, chartered in 1997, but it has taken the engineering world by storm with its rigorous hands-on program on the "bleeding edge of engineering education." Olin emphasizes creating one's own academic path to its 350 undergraduates: The curriculum focuses on "learning skills through project-based learning in order to use engineering and design for the good of the world." At the end of their time at Olin, students emerge as engineers with "fantastic and practical technical skillsets" that they are able to wield in a variety of settings. Classes are "hard, but interesting and worthwhile," and students are also able to take courses at nearby Babson, Wellesley, and Brandeis. Classes traditionally involve breaking into small groups, and "most problems dividing work in teams have to do with students getting too excited about the work and doing more than their fair share rather than shirking group duties," says one student. Self-directed study is important here, and Olin encourages students to design their own semester-long project on a topic that interests them through the college's Passionate Pursuits program.

Professors are "extremely dedicated" to the work they are doing at Olin. "I have had professors come to campus at 10 P.M. because they heard that students were struggling with homework assignments, and stay until well after midnight," says one. Uniqueness is everywhere: There is a tremendous amount of flexibility in the classroom, with almost no lectures; TAs are referred to as Course Assistants; and most semesters offer at least one new experimental course ("and the classes that aren't new are better than they were last semester"). Faculty are "interested in how their teaching works," and there is "constant improvement in the curriculum and learning styles." At the end of the day, "Olin doesn't create engineers—it prepares them."

Campus Life

There are "lots of things happening for such a small school." For starters, people "work...a lot." Students work all day every day and "all the rest of the time seems to get filled by working on random interests." This quirky and innovative group makes time to go on a quick adventure and "explore the local forest, make a code that does something stupid, or eat chips and watch YouTube videos" in the "hotel-room-sized dorms."

For first-years and sophomores, lounge culture is really big in the dorms, and "if you ever want something to do, just explore the lounges and you will find something." It's easy for students to get to Boston, and "there are always students up for spontaneous fun things" like sudden dodgeball in the dining hall or a random dance party. There's even a mailing list called Carpe Diem in which "people randomly send out info on fun things they are doing all the time so others can join." A lot of the things students do in their spare time are the same things they do for school, because "what we're doing in class is genuinely fun."

Student Body

Olin College hosts an "incredibly intelligent and very motivated" body of individuals that are "not your typical engineer." Because of the nature of the student body, you can join any group of people at any time and know that they will be having an interesting discussion. "If one wants to have a conversation on middle eighteenth-century philosophy or if the Earth suddenly stopped would we go flying off into space, both are easily found in the dining hall," says a student. With 80 or so new students flipping each year, some qualities of the student body are "easily changeable" (athleticism, for instance), but this remains a fun group in which "everybody has something that gets them so excited they could stay up all night working on it."

FRANKLIN W. OLIN COLLEGE OF ENGINEERING

Financial Aid: 781-292-2215 • E-Mail: info@olin.edu • Website: www.olin.edu

THE PRINCETON REVIEW SAYS

Admissions

The school reports that its standardized testing policy for use in admission for Fall 2024 is Test Optional. The 2024 testing policy will be temporary. The Princeton Review suggests that interested applicants consult with the school for the most up-to-date standardized testing policies. *Very important factors considered include:* rigor of secondary school record, academic GPA, application essay, recommendation(s), interview, extracurricular activities, talent/ability, character/personal qualities, level of applicant's interest. *Important factors considered include:* class rank, racial/ethnic status, volunteer work, work experience. *Other factors considered include:* standardized test scores, first generation, alumni/ae relation, geographical residence, state residency. High school diploma is required and GED is accepted. *Academic units recommended:* 4 English, 4 math, 4 science, 3 science labs, 2 foreign language, 2 social studies, 2 history.

Financial Aid

Students should submit: FAFSA. Priority filing deadline is 2/15. The Princeton Review suggests that all financial aid forms be submitted as soon as possible (see page 5 for a note on the FAFSA). *Need-based scholarships/grants offered:* College/university scholarship or grant aid from institutional funds; Federal Pell; SEOG. *Loan aid offered:* Direct PLUS loans; Direct Subsidized Loans; Direct Unsubsidized Loans. Admitted students will be notified of awards on or about 4/1. Institutional employment available.

The Inside Word

Brains alone are not enough to get into Olin. Social skills, depth, and the ability to communicate are taken seriously by admissions. Olin boasts many students who have turned down offers from schools like MIT and Caltech for just this reason. It is a unique school that looks for passion, creativity, and a spirit of adventure in its students. If you're a reclusive genius, you will be at a disadvantage in this pool of applicants.

THE SCHOOL SAYS "..."

From the Admissions Office

"We are a vibrant community of talented, empathetic, energetic students and faculty and we are looking for students who are not only academically accomplished but also like adventure, thrive on creativity and use their engineering skills to make a positive impact on people and the world—and come from every kind of cultural, economic and geographic background imaginable. The Olin Tuition Scholarship, valued at more than $115,000, is awarded to every enrolled student to recognize their achievements and is complemented by our policy of meeting full demonstrated need—meaning finances should never stand in the way of an Olin education.

"Our admission process is, like Olin, unique. It's done in two stages; first students apply using the Common Application; then from our exceptionally talented and academically gifted applicant pool we invite between 225–250 students to attend one of three Candidates' Weekends. We seek to get to know our applicants' personal qualities (like risk-taking, creativity, passion and team spirit) during these weekends of getting acquainted through group activities and interviews. Admission is then offered to candidates who possess the greatest promise of contributing to—and benefiting from—the Olin experience. Following the Candidates' Weekends admission is offered to approximately 125–135 students.

"Olin is not your typical engineering school. We are a creative, collaborative community of team players who want to work hard to solve problems and have some serious fun along the way!"

SELECTIVITY

Admissions Rating	97
# of applicants	862
% of applicants accepted	19
% of acceptees attending	45
# offered a place on the wait list	59
% accepting a place on wait list	81
% admitted from wait list	58

FIRST-YEAR PROFILE

Testing policy	Test Optional
Range SAT composite	1500–1550
Range SAT EBRW	720–770
Range SAT math	770–790
Range ACT composite	35–35
# submitting SAT scores	36
% submitting SAT scores	48
# submitting ACT scores	18
% submitting ACT scores	24
Average HS GPA	3.9
% frosh submitting high school GPA	100

DEADLINES

Regular	
Deadline	1/2
Notification	4/1
Nonfall registration?	No

FINANCIAL FACTS

Financial Aid Rating	99
Annual tuition	$59,972
Room and board	$19,820
Required fees	$1,830
Required fees (first-year)	$4,486
Books and supplies	$216
Average frosh need-based scholarship	$55,978
Average UG need-based scholarship	$54,775
% needy frosh rec. need-based scholarship or grant aid	100
% needy UG rec. need-based scholarship or grant aid	100
% needy frosh rec. non-need-based scholarship or grant aid	100
% needy UG rec. non-need-based scholarship or grant aid	100
% needy frosh rec. need-based self-help aid	51
% needy UG rec. need-based self-help aid	73
% frosh rec. any financial aid	100
% UG rec. any financial aid	100
% UG borrow to pay for school	34
Average cumulative indebtedness	$19,911
% frosh need fully met	100
% ugrads need fully met	99
Average % of frosh need met	99
Average % of ugrad need met	99

FURMAN UNIVERSITY

3300 Poinsett Highway, Greenville, SC 29613 • Admissions: 864-294-2034 • Fax: 864-294-2018

STUDENTS SAY "..."

Academics

Furman University is a school that helps its undergraduates "become the best version[s] of [themselves]." That potentially daunting task is made possible thanks to the school's ample resources ranging from "good study abroad [options]" and "experiential learning" to the "many opportunities for research and internships." One of Furman's top selling points is "the strength of its pre-professional curriculum." The university's "pre-health and pre-law advisors are exceptional, and they greatly help students get into graduate programs, regardless of major." Of course, prospective students should be aware that the academics here "are very difficult, particularly [the] science courses." It's important that you come prepared to study. Fortunately, the "overwhelming majority of professors at Furman are experts in their field and truly care about helping students succeed." They seem to excel at creating a classroom environment wherein undergrads "feel comfortable yet challenged at all times." And it's definitely evident that they "love teaching and instilling a passion for growth, inquiry, and engagement." We'll give the last word to this student who shares, "My professors have changed my life by supporting me and working with me from academic interests to personal crises. They are easily the best part of Furman."

Campus Life

If you're lucky enough to attend Furman, you can expect to maintain a pretty busy schedule. "It is very common for everyone to be involved with many clubs and organizations." After all, there's so much to discover and partake in outside of academics. To begin with, Furman undergrads are an athletic lot and you'll often find "people play[ing] pick-up games on the sports fields" or participating in intramurals and club sports. Plus, "athletic events are very accessible to students and are free." For individuals with an altruistic bent, there are a "variety of community service opportunities." Greek life is also fairly popular at Furman. However, students make a point of mentioning that "party culture isn't extremely prevalent on campus, and the Greek organizations are very welcoming and open to anyone, regardless of appearances, socioeconomic class, or affinity for partying." The university itself hosts numerous "cultural events" where undergrads "can go learn about something new or hear an engaging speaker." And, of course, people can easily join some of the many organizations like Residential Life Council, Eco Reps, and the student run musical theatre group, Pauper Players. Lastly, when undergrads want a respite from campus life, they head into "downtown Greenville and try new restaurants, go to concerts, bar hop and EXPLORE. You can often find students downtown at the various "cute coffee shops [and] farmers markets." Given its proximity to the outdoors, many also like to "get into nature and hike Paris Mountain" or "bik[e] the Swamp Rabbit Trail."

Student Body

Furman seems to attract students who "are very motivated and driven to perform well academically." Thankfully, though most everyone has "high aspirations," this isn't a very competitive student body. Instead, undergrads here simply "push...each other to be the best people possible." Students do readily admit that Furman "generally draws a Southern white demographic" with many kids hailing from "generally wealthy backgrounds." However, they note that the university "has expanded its recruitment initiatives and current on-campus opportunities to invite a greater diversity of individuals especially in regard to race." Students also stress that you'll find plenty of people with "unique talents" and "fairly diverse [interests]" when it comes to hobbies, interests, majors, etc." And they certainly "know how to have a good time" and "enjoy stimulating discussions and new experiences." Best of all, they form a "community of open-minded people" who are "willing to help one another." As this student explains, "I transferred to Furman because of the student body. I was completely taken aback at how genuine and kind the people here are."

FURMAN UNIVERSITY

Financial Aid: 864-294-2030 • E-Mail: admissions@furman.edu • Website: www.furman.edu

THE PRINCETON REVIEW SAYS

Admissions

The school reports that its standardized testing policy for use in admission in Fall 2024 remains Test Optional, as it has been since 2011. *Very important factors considered include:* rigor of secondary school record. *Important factors considered include:* class rank, academic GPA, application essay, extracurricular activities, character/personal qualities. *Other factors considered include:* standardized test scores, recommendation(s), talent/ability, first generation, alumni/ae relation, racial/ethnic status, volunteer work, work experience, level of applicant's interest. High school diploma is required and GED is accepted. *Academic units required:* 4 English, 3 math, 2 science, 2 science labs, 2 foreign language, 3 social studies. *Academic units recommended:* 4 English, 4 math, 3 science, 2 science labs, 3 foreign language, 4 social studies.

Financial Aid

Students should submit: Business/Farm Supplement; CSS/Financial Aid Profile; FAFSA; Noncustodial Profile. Priority filing deadline is 2/15. The Princeton Review suggests that all financial aid forms be submitted as soon as possible (see page 5 for a note on the FAFSA). *Need-based scholarships/grants offered:* College/university scholarship or grant aid from institutional funds; Federal Pell; Private scholarships; SEOG; State scholarships/grants. *Loan aid offered:* Direct PLUS loans; Direct Subsidized Loans; Direct Unsubsidized Loans. Admitted students will be notified of awards on or about 3/15. Federal Work-Study Program available. Institutional employment available.

The Inside Word

Furman University is best known for its outstanding academic program. With that in mind, applicants should present a well-rounded transcript complete with advanced courses to show they are used to a challenging academic environment. Though Furman is Test Optional, having strong standardized test scores will work in your favor. The university is looking for prospective students who thrive in the classroom and are not afraid to get involved in their community. We recommend using your personal statement to address issues that you are passionate about and shine a light on what differentiates you from the other applicants. If Furman is your top choice, we strongly suggest you consider applying early.

THE SCHOOL SAYS "..."

From the Admissions Office

"At Furman, your experience is your education. Through stimulating coursework, combined with relevant, real-world experiences, you will explore your interests and passions to discover what drives you. Guaranteed for every Furman student are opportunities to get involved in internships, study away, research, and community-centered learning experiences that will empower you to apply your classroom learning in a variety of settings and prepare you for success. Furman's highly qualified faculty and dedicated mentors will provide the knowledge, skills, and support you need to achieve your personal and professional goals. Your experience will take place on a stunningly beautiful 750-acre, residential campus in the foothills of the Blue Ridge Mountains, in one of the country's fastest growing and most vibrant cities, Greenville, South Carolina. There will be endless opportunities for outdoor excursions and urban adventures. We strive to give you a well-rounded, once-in-a-lifetime college experience that will prepare you for anything. That's The Furman Advantage.

"Our holistic application review is based on an evaluation of your grades, rigor of curriculum, test scores (optional), essay, extracurricular involvement, and potential contribution to campus. Beyond your application, we value personally connecting with each applicant to learn more about you and your interest in Furman. We invite you to visit campus, connect with students and faculty, and learn more about The Furman Advantage that is awaiting you."

SELECTIVITY

Admissions Rating	88
# of applicants	7,510
% of applicants accepted	67
% of acceptees attending	13
# offered a place on the wait list	769
# of early decision applicants	225
% accepted early decision	41

FIRST-YEAR PROFILE

Testing policy	Test Optional
Range SAT composite	1280–1435
Range SAT EBRW	640–730
Range SAT math	620–725
Range ACT composite	27–32
# submitting SAT scores	187
% submitting SAT scores	29
# submitting ACT scores	198
% submitting ACT scores	31
Average HS GPA	3.7
% frosh submitting high school GPA	100
% graduated top 10% of class	39
% graduated top 25% of class	75
% graduated top 50% of class	93

DEADLINES

Early decision	
Deadline	11/15
Notification	12/1
Other ED deadline	1/15
Other ED notification	2/1
Early action	
Deadline	12/1
Notification	2/15
Regular	
Priority	1/15
Deadline	1/15
Notification	3/1
Nonfall registration?	No

APPLICANTS ALSO LOOK AT

Clemson University; Wake Forest University; Elon University; Richmond University

APPLICANTS OFTEN PREFER

University of North Carolina—Chapel Hill

FINANCIAL FACTS

Financial Aid Rating	88
Annual tuition	$55,392
Room and board	$15,148
Required fees	$380
Books and supplies	$1,000
Average frosh need-based scholarship	$33,266
Average UG need-based scholarship	$34,788
% needy frosh rec. need-based scholarship or grant aid	100
% needy UG rec. need-based scholarship or grant aid	100
% needy frosh rec. non-need-based scholarship or grant aid	68
% needy UG rec. non-need-based scholarship or grant aid	57
% needy frosh rec. need-based self-help aid	57
% needy UG rec. need-based self-help aid	59
% UG borrow to pay for school	35
Average cumulative indebtedness	$34,145
% frosh need fully met	51
% ugrads need fully met	44
Average % of frosh need met	90
Average % of ugrad need met	83

GEORGE MASON UNIVERSITY

4400 University Drive, Fairfax, VA 22030-4444 • Admissions: 703-993-1000 • Fax: 703-993-4622

STUDENTS SAY "..."

Academics

With the "nation's capital in its backyard," George Mason University in Fairfax, Virginia offers "strong academics" combined with proximity to a bustling center of industry and innovation. Mason prepares its students to enter by offering a "large variety of academic programs" and providing a solid infrastructure that is "constantly growing" and "providing many excellent opportunities for students," including research opportunities for undergraduates. The "humanities and economics draw on the local Washington D.C. talent" "and the engineering school has an "advanced" IT program that "Is developed with concentrations in information security, healthcare, networking, and more." Students note that "jobs in all the fields that Mason provides are just within a 10-mile radius of campus," including "top tech companies," which "come to Mason because there is a huge Mason alumni community in the Northern Virginia area." One grateful student notes "it was easy to transfer to with NOVA's Pathway Program" because they had an "easy outline of what classes I needed to take at NOVA to transfer over and pursue a certain degree."

Campus Life

With Washington, D.C. just "a metro ride away," "the majority of students at Mason are commuters," meaning "many of them are not very involved." Even in the "close-knit layout of the main campus," in fact, even for on-campus residents, most campus life happens off campus, including the partying, since fraternities are off-campus. There are many social clubs and organizations, however, with "most students taking part in several." Examples include the a cappella group and swing dancing. Many also "meet to practice for competitions, including the Indian dance troupe." Mason has a "free shuttle bus that takes students to the metro" for activities in D.C. The Johnson Center is another "major place that students spend time: there is a food court, a library, meeting rooms, kiosks, the cinema, and huge study areas." Students will also "go to one of the three gyms on campus and work out; a lot of people bike around campus."

Student Body

This is one school where "diversity" is truly an accurate term in all its breadth. Students choose Mason for this wide representation of culture and experience. "As a first-generation student of color," one student says, "I think representation is integral to creating a sense of belonging. Because I could see myself reflected in the students, I chose Mason because I knew that I wouldn't be bothered or feel like I was the minority." There is a "large population of immigrant-heritage students, international students, and students from almost every state in the United States," and the "littlest differences like different name spellings, accents, dress, and more importantly, different political ideas and perspectives are respected and acknowledged, and even more so, celebrated here at Mason." While there are "many students who entered straight from high school...there are also many students who are already working and are returning to school as well as many international students." The "campus keeps growing, housing over 6,000 residents,"—of the 38,000 or so total students. "Due to the enormous and intimidating physical size of GMU, the school offers many ways for students to feel included and engage themselves in extracurricular activities should they choose to do so," one student offers.

GEORGE MASON UNIVERSITY

Financial Aid: 703-993-2353 • E-Mail: admissions@gmu.edu • Website: www2.gmu.edu

THE PRINCETON REVIEW SAYS

Admissions

The school reports that its standardized testing policy for use in admission for Fall 2024 is Test Optional. It is unknown at this time if the 2024 testing policy will be permanent. The Princeton Review suggests that interested applicants consult with the school for the most up-to-date standardized testing policies. *Very important factors considered include:* rigor of secondary school record, academic GPA. *Important factors considered include:* talent/ability. *Other factors considered include:* standardized test scores, application essay, recommendation(s), extracurricular activities, character/personal qualities, geographical residence, state residency, volunteer work, work experience. High school diploma is required and GED is accepted. *Academic units required:* 4 English, 3 math, 2 science, 2 science labs, 2 foreign language, 3 social studies, 3 academic electives. *Academic units recommended:* 4 English, 4 math, 3 science, 3 science labs, 3 foreign language, 4 social studies, 5 academic electives.

Financial Aid

Students should submit: FAFSA. Priority filing deadline is 1/15. The Princeton Review suggests that all financial aid forms be submitted as soon as possible (see page 5 for a note on the FAFSA). *Need-based scholarships/grants offered:* Federal Pell; Private scholarships; SEOG; State scholarships/grants. *Loan aid offered:* Direct PLUS loans; Direct Subsidized Loans; Direct Unsubsidized Loans. Admitted students will be notified of awards on a rolling basis. Federal Work-Study Program available. Institutional employment available.

The Inside Word

GMU is a popular college choice for two key reasons: its proximity to Washington, D.C., and the fact that its applicant pool isn't as competitive as other universities in the Virginia state system. GMU's quality faculty and impressive facilities make it worth consideration, especially if you're looking for a school in the D.C. area and affordability is a factor.

THE SCHOOL SAYS "..."

From the Admissions Office

"In just 50 years, George Mason University has become Virginia's largest, most diverse, and highest-ranked university for innovation by rejecting the traditional university model of exclusivity.

"Located just outside Washington, D.C., Mason's beautiful 677-acre campus is home to more than 5,800 students living in more than 40 residence halls. They're just a fraction of Mason's student population of more than 39,000, comprising individuals enrolled in more than 210 degree programs at the undergraduate, master's, doctoral, and professional levels. Mason's students hail from all 50 states and 130 countries, representing the broadest spectrum of origins, identities, circumstances, and ideologies.

"As an R1 university, Mason's reputation for innovation is displayed through a diverse portfolio of academic programs intentionally created and shaped to address the world's greatest challenges. Our College of Public Health is the first of its kind in Virginia, established to meet the state's growing need for skilled, interdisciplinary health professionals and research. It joins Mason's growing list of other firsts, including Virginia's first-ever School of Computing and the first dedicated cybersecurity engineering program in the region.

"Our prime location at the crossroads of government, industry, and research attracts dedicated faculty who lead in their fields. This connectivity extends to our students, who have access to unparalleled opportunities at national and international companies and organizations. Nearly nine in ten new Mason alumni report advancing their career within six months of graduation, working with companies like Amazon, Deloitte, and Northrup Grumman, and organizations like the Smithsonian Institution, NASA, and the White House."

SELECTIVITY

Admissions Rating	84
# of applicants	20,001
% of applicants accepted	90
% of acceptees attending	23
# offered a place on the wait list	794
% accepting a place on wait list	56
% admitted from wait list	68

FIRST-YEAR PROFILE

Testing policy	Test Optional
Range SAT composite	1160–1340
Range SAT EBRW	580–670
Range SAT math	560–680
Range ACT composite	25–31
# submitting SAT scores	1,560
% submitting SAT scores	38
# submitting ACT scores	133
% submitting ACT scores	3
Average HS GPA	3.7
% frosh submitting high school GPA	100
% graduated top 10% of class	15
% graduated top 25% of class	43
% graduated top 50% of class	77

DEADLINES

Early action	
Deadline	11/1
Notification	12/15
Regular	
Priority	11/1
Nonfall registration?	Yes

APPLICANTS SOMETIMES PREFER

James Madison University; Old Dominion University; Penn State University Park; The George Washington University; University of Maryland, College Park; University of Virginia; Virginia Commonwealth University; Virginia Tech

FINANCIAL FACTS

Financial Aid Rating	77
Annual in-state tuition	$9,795
Annual out-of-state tuition	$33,959
Room and board	$13,120
Required fees	$3,609
Books and supplies	$1,278
Average frosh need-based scholarship	$7,914
Average UG need-based scholarship	$7,924
% needy frosh rec. need-based scholarship or grant aid	85
% needy UG rec. need-based scholarship or grant aid	89
% needy frosh rec. non-need-based scholarship or grant aid	56
% needy UG rec. non-need-based scholarship or grant aid	26
% needy frosh rec. need-based self-help aid	66
% needy UG rec. need-based self-help aid	62
% frosh rec. any financial aid	74
% UG rec. any financial aid	65
% UG borrow to pay for school	53
Average cumulative indebtedness	$31,190
% frosh need fully met	7
% ugrads need fully met	4
Average % of frosh need met	65
Average % of ugrad need met	57

GEORGETOWN UNIVERSITY

37th and O Streets, Washington, DC 20057 • Admissions: 202-687-0100 • Fax: 202-687-5084

CAMPUS LIFE

Quality of Life Rating	62
Fire Safety Rating	88
Green Rating	60*
Type of school	Private
Affiliation	Roman Catholic
Environment	Metropolis

STUDENTS

Total undergrad enrollment	7,285
% male/female/another gender	42/58/NR
% from out of state	98
% frosh from public high school	41
% frosh live on campus	100
% ugrads live on campus	77
# of fraternities	0
# of sororities	0
% African American	5
% Asian	14
% White	50
% Hispanic	7
% Native American	<1
% Pacific Islander	<1
% Two or more races	6
% Race and/or ethnicity unknown	3
% international	14
# of countries represented	117

SURVEY SAYS . . .

Great financial aid
Alumni active on campus
Students politically aware
Easy to get around campus

ACADEMICS

Academic Rating	78
% students returning for sophomore year	97
% students graduating within 4 years	91
% students graduating within 6 years	96
Calendar	Semester
Student/faculty ratio	11:1
Profs interesting rating	82
Profs accessible rating	86

Most classes have 10–19 students.
Most lab/discussion sessions have
10–19 students.

MOST POPULAR MAJORS

English Language and Literature, General;
International Relations and Affairs; Political
Science and Government, General

STUDENTS SAY "..."

Academics

This moderately sized elite academic establishment stays true to its Jesuit foundations by educating its students with the idea of "cura personalis," or "care for the whole person." The "well-informed" student body perpetuates upon itself, creating an atmosphere full of vibrant intellectual life, that is "also balanced with extracurricular learning and development." "Georgetown is...a place where people work very, very hard without feeling like they are in direct competition," says an international politics major. Located in Washington, D.C., there's a noted School of Foreign Service here, and the access to internships is a huge perk for those in political or government programs. In addition, the proximity to the nation's capital fetches "high-profile guest speakers," with many of the most powerful people in global politics speaking regularly, as well as a large number of adjunct professors who, either are currently working in government, or have retired from high-level positions.

Georgetown offers a "great selection of very knowledgeable professors, split with a good proportion of those who are experienced in realms outside of academia (such as former government officials) and career academics," though there are a few superstars who might be "somewhat less than totally collegial." Professors tend to be "fantastic scholars and teachers" and are "generally available to students," as well as often being "interested in getting to know you as a person (if you put forth the effort to talk to them and go to office hours)." Though Georgetown has a policy of grade deflation, meaning "A's are hard to come by," there are "a ton of interesting courses available," and TAs are used only for optional discussion sessions and help with grading. The academics "can be challenging or they can be not so much (not that they are ever really easy, just easier)"; it all depends on the courses you choose and how much you actually do the work. The school administration is well-meaning and "usually willing to talk and compromise with students," but the process of planning activities can be full of headaches and bureaucracy, and the administration itself "sometimes is overstretched or has trouble transmitting its message." Nevertheless, "a motivated student can get done what he or she wants."

Campus Life

Students are "extremely well aware of the world around them," from government to environment, social to economic, and "Georgetown is the only place where an argument over politics, history, or philosophy is preceded by a keg stand." Hoyas like to have a good time on weekends, and parties at campus and off-campus apartments and townhouses "are generally open to all comers and tend to have a somewhat networking atmosphere; meeting people you don't know is a constant theme." With such a motivated group on such a high-energy campus, "people are always headed somewhere, it seems—to rehearsal, athletic practice, a guest speaker, [or] the gym." Community service and political activism are particularly popular, as is basketball. Everything near Georgetown is in walking distance, including the world of D.C.'s museums, restaurants, and stores, and "grabbing or ordering late night food is a popular option."

Student Body

There are "a lot of wealthy students on campus," and preppy-casual is the fashion de rigueur; this is "definitely not a 'granola' school," but students from diverse backgrounds are typically welcomed by people wanting to learn about different experiences. Indeed, everyone here is well-traveled and well-educated, and there are "a ton of international students." "You better have at least some interest in politics or you will feel out-of-place," says a student. The school can also be "a bit cliquish, with athletes at the top," but there are "plenty of groups for everybody to fit into and find their niche," and "there is much crossover between groups."

GEORGETOWN UNIVERSITY

Financial Aid: 202-687-4547 • E-Mail: guadmiss@georgetown.edu • Website: www.georgetown.edu

THE PRINCETON REVIEW SAYS

Admissions

The school reports that its standardized testing policy for use in admission for Fall 2024 requires applicants to submit either the SAT or ACT. It is unknown at this time if the 2024 testing policy will be permanent. The Princeton Review suggests that interested applicants consult with the school for the most up-to-date standardized testing policies. *Very important factors considered include:* rigor of secondary school record, class rank, academic GPA, standardized test scores, application essay, recommendation(s), talent/ability, character/personal qualities. *Important factors considered include:* interview, extracurricular activities. *Other factors considered include:* first generation, alumni/ae relation, geographical residence, state residency, racial/ethnic status, volunteer work, work experience. High school diploma is required and GED is accepted. *Academic units required:* 4 English, 2 math, 1 science, 2 foreign language, 2 social studies, 2 history.

Financial Aid

Students should submit: Business/Farm Supplement; CSS/Financial Aid Profile; FAFSA. Priority filing deadline is 2/1. The Princeton Review suggests that all financial aid forms be submitted as soon as possible (see page 5 for a note on the FAFSA). *Need-based scholarships/grants offered:* Federal Pell; Private scholarships; SEOG; State scholarships/grants. *Loan aid offered:* Direct PLUS loans; Direct Subsidized Loans; Direct Unsubsidized Loans; Federal Nursing Loans. Admitted students will be notified of awards on or about 4/10. Federal Work-Study Program available. Institutional employment available.

The Inside Word

It was always tough to get admitted to Georgetown, but in the early 1980s Patrick Ewing and the Hoyas created a basketball sensation that catapulted the place into position as one of the most selective universities in the nation. There has been no turning back since. GU receives over 12 applications for every space in the entering class, and the academic strength of the pool is impressive. Virtually 80 percent of the entire student body took AP courses in high school. Candidates who are wait-listed should hold little hope for an offer of admission; over the past several years Georgetown has taken very few off their lists.

THE SCHOOL SAYS "..."

From the Admissions Office

"Georgetown was founded in 1789 by John Carroll, who concurred with his contemporaries Benjamin Franklin and Thomas Jefferson in believing that the success of the young democracy depended upon an educated and virtuous citizenry. Carroll founded the school with the dynamic Jesuit tradition of education, characterized by humanism and committed to the assumption of responsibility and action. Georgetown is a national and international university, enrolling students from all fifty states and over 100 foreign countries. Undergraduate students are enrolled in one of five undergraduate schools: the College of Arts and Sciences, School of Foreign Service, Georgetown School of Business, School of Nursing, and School of Health. All students share a common liberal arts core and have access to the entire university curriculum."

SELECTIVITY

Admissions Rating	98
# of applicants	26,638
% of applicants accepted	12
% of acceptees attending	48
# offered a place on the wait list	2,455
% accepting a place on wait list	73
% admitted from wait list	2

FIRST-YEAR PROFILE

Testing policy	SAT or ACT Required
Range SAT composite	1410–1540
Range SAT EBRW	700–770
Range SAT math	690–790
Range ACT composite	32–35
# submitting SAT scores	1,149
% submitting SAT scores	72
# submitting ACT scores	569
% submitting ACT scores	36
% graduated top 10% of class	84
% graduated top 25% of class	95
% graduated top 50% of class	98

DEADLINES

Early action	
Deadline	11/1
Notification	12/15
Regular	
Deadline	1/10
Notification	4/1
Nonfall registration?	No

FINANCIAL FACTS

Financial Aid Rating	94
Annual tuition	$61,872
Room and board	$19,352
Required fees	$180
Average frosh need-based scholarship	$45,572
Average UG need-based scholarship	$45,585
% needy frosh rec. need-based scholarship or grant aid	93
% needy UG rec. need-based scholarship or grant aid	93
% needy frosh rec. non-need-based scholarship or grant aid	34
% needy UG rec. non-need-based scholarship or grant aid	30
% needy frosh rec. need-based self-help aid	83
% needy UG rec. need-based self-help aid	83
% UG borrow to pay for school	37
Average cumulative indebtedness	$25,726
% frosh need fully met	100
% ugrads need fully met	100
Average % of frosh need met	100
Average % of ugrad need met	100

GEORGE WASHINGTON UNIVERSITY

1918 F Street, NW, Washington, DC 20052 • Admissions: 202-994-1000 • Fax: 202-994-0325

CAMPUS LIFE

Quality of Life Rating	83
Fire Safety Rating	60*
Green Rating	94
Type of school	Private
Affiliation	No Affiliation
Environment	Metropolis

STUDENTS

Total undergrad enrollment	10,798
% male/female/another gender	37/63/0
% from out of state	97
% frosh from public high school	70
% frosh live on campus	97
% ugrads live on campus	58
# of fraternities (% join)	12 (5)
# of sororities (% join)	9 (9)
% African American	8
% Asian	14
% White	50
% Hispanic	13
% Native American	<1
% Pacific Islander	<1
% Two or more races	5
% Race and/or ethnicity unknown	2
% international	9
# of countries represented	122

SURVEY SAYS . . .

Lots of liberal students
Students love Washington, DC
Active student government
Career services are great
Students aren't religious
Students environmentally aware
Great off-campus food
Easy to get around campus
Campus newspaper is popular

ACADEMICS

Academic Rating	80
% students returning for sophomore year	90
% students graduating within 4 years	77
% students graduating within 6 years	84
Calendar	Semester
Student/faculty ratio	12:1
Profs interesting rating	86
Profs accessible rating	87

Most classes have 10–19 students.
Most lab/discussion sessions have
20–29 students.

MOST POPULAR MAJORS

International Relations and Affairs; Business
Administration and Management, General;
Psychology, General

STUDENTS SAY "..."

Academics

Nestled right in the middle of our nation's capital, George Washington University provides students with a wealth of research, non-profit, and career opportunities. It embraces its role at the center of politics, with curriculums that connect the classroom to real-world policies and "to internships, particularly those in international or political fields." The administration "has great communication with its students and professors," and "the school makes it very easy to gain access" to jobs, research assistant positions, and speaking events. "I've heard speeches from the German ambassador, the French ambassador, Supreme Court justices, Bill Gates, and many more," says one student.

Professors have "relevant and current experience in what they're teaching" (for instance, "a large number of history professors work for the Office of the Historian for the State Department") and are "extremely qualified." Where applicable, expect teachers to make the most of on-site learning: "I took a class called The Visual World of Shakespeare. We traveled to art museums and libraries across DC every Friday." For those looking to get even more hands-on, study abroad is a popular option that forty percent of students engage in. Professors also encourage students to pressure themselves less with acing an exam and more on the ability to "understand and ask questions about the material," and students have positively responded: "It's great having access to such experienced resources." In short, the emphasis is on the learning, not the frustration: "If someone is struggling with something, there will always be someone to talk to."

Campus Life

"Part of the appeal of being at GW is the Washington, DC, landscape," and there is no shortage of cultural options like the Smithsonian institutions, the National Mall, and visiting the monuments ("Especially at night, it's so fun!"). Since the university "does not have a traditional campus and is instead integrated with the city, most people just go their own way during the day"; it's not unusual to "find a lot of people at coffee shops getting their caffeine fixes and eating while studying."

Students do acknowledge that "housing and dining are amazing," and point to intramural sports, clubs (more than 400 organizations, all told), and the Greek scene, but at least during the week, the focus is on how "academics are a big part of daily life," so much so that "people go to internships as frequently as they go to class." That can be seen in the more technical clubs—"a really great opportunity to learn in a more hands-on and practical way"—as well as in the number of students actively working, whether that's for the school, through an internship, or professionally. One student describes how a short-term gig "creating a new branding identity and set of materials for their yearly gala" wound up leading to a full summer job. These on-the-go students benefit from the GW SafeRide, a free cab service between academic buildings and residence halls at night. The final consensus is that "being in Foggy Bottom is a unique professional and academic experience that you cannot receive at any other institution."

Student Body

GW's national draw exposes students "to so many people from different states and countries," and "there are so many clubs/organizations that can help you find people with similar interests." People who love GW "are very independent and career driven" and "know exactly what they want." The school is "very LGBT+ friendly" with a sizable contingent on campus—there is also a large international student population—and everyone "is very supportive and helpful." Most here "are involved in political activism on and off campus" and "feel a natural inclination to engage in discourse whenever possible." As one student says, "Not one class goes without the participation of multiple students who are well-informed and well-read on the topics that are being discussed." Students here are "passionate about changing the world and making it a better place" and "provide an interesting array of perspectives, especially in senior seminars." One thing everyone has in common: "Everyone here is very proud to be in DC; we love our city."

GEORGE WASHINGTON UNIVERSITY

E-Mail: gwadm@gwu.edu • Website: www.gwu.edu

THE PRINCETON REVIEW SAYS

Admissions

The school reports that its standardized testing policy for use in admission for Fall 2024 is Test Optional. It is unknown at this time if the 2024 testing policy will be permanent. The Princeton Review suggests that interested applicants consult with the school for the most up-to-date standardized testing policies. *Very important factors considered include:* rigor of secondary school record, academic GPA. *Important factors considered include:* application essay, recommendation(s), extracurricular activities, talent/ability, volunteer work. *Other factors considered include:* standardized test scores, character/personal qualities, first generation, alumni/ae relation, geographical residence, racial/ethnic status, work experience, level of applicant's interest. High school diploma is required and GED is accepted. *Academic units required:* 4 English, 2 math, 2 science, 1 science lab, 2 foreign language, 2 social studies. *Academic units recommended:* 4 English, 4 math, 4 science, 4 foreign language, 4 social studies.

Financial Aid

Students should submit: CSS/Financial Aid Profile; FAFSA; Noncustodial Profile. Priority filing deadline is 2/1. The Princeton Review suggests that all financial aid forms be submitted as soon as possible (see page 5 for a note on the FAFSA). *Need-based scholarships/grants offered:* College/university scholarship or grant aid from institutional funds; Federal Pell; SEOG; State scholarships/grants. *Loan aid offered:* Direct PLUS loans; Direct Subsidized Loans; Direct Unsubsidized Loans. Admitted students will be notified of awards on a rolling basis beginning 3/24. Federal Work-Study Program available. Institutional employment available.

The Inside Word

GW knows that its location and academic offerings make it a highly sought-after institution—each year, more students apply, bringing the current number up to just over 27,000. As a result, it seeks to "enroll a bright, talented, and diverse body of students." The school values diversity in its applicants, with students from every state and more than 120 countries, and it has adapted a Test Optional policy that allows it to look more broadly at each student's background and what they bring to the table. Demonstrate your interest by utilizing any of the school's resources that you're applicable for, like for first-generation students, or by appealing directly to special interest programs like the Cisneros Scholars, which supports the Latino community; don't miss an opportunity to tell your story.

THE SCHOOL SAYS "..."

From the Admissions Office

"Located in the heart of Washington, DC, the George Washington University enrolls a diverse, motivated, and active student body from all 50 states and 122 countries. Our students study, learn, and grow on two fully integrated DC campuses—Foggy Bottom, blocks from the National Mall, and Mount Vernon, in a residential neighborhood.

"As a comprehensive global research university, GW offers more than 75 majors in the arts, business, engineering, international affairs, public health, and social and physical sciences—all taught mere blocks from the White House and amid DC's business and high-tech sectors. Students work closely with well-connected faculty to utilize the many academic and cultural resources of the District. Some classes take field trips to museums to study collections while others welcome guest speakers who are experts in their fields. In addition to dynamic classroom experiences, a GW education allows students the ability to put knowledge in action. Through research, internships, community service, and study abroad, GW students implement classroom learning to change the world and improve the human experience.

"We look for bright and diverse students who are ambitious, energetic, and self-motivated. As a Test Optional school, we believe that the best indicator of success at GW is a student's high school performance. Our holistic review takes all pieces of a student's admission application into consideration. We aim to make a GW education affordable to all admitted students, offering generous scholarships and financial aid."

SELECTIVITY

Admissions Rating	93
# of applicants	27,266
% of applicants accepted	49
% of acceptees attending	22
# offered a place on the wait list	5,098
% accepting a place on wait list	40
% admitted from wait list	1
# of early decision applicants	1,132
% accepted early decision	69

FIRST-YEAR PROFILE

Testing policy	Test Optional
Range SAT composite	1340–1470
Range SAT EBRW	670–740
Range SAT math	660–750
Range ACT composite	30–34
# submitting SAT scores	904
% submitting SAT scores	31
# submitting ACT scores	446
% submitting ACT scores	15
% graduated top 10% of class	44
% graduated top 25% of class	78
% graduated top 50% of class	96

DEADLINES

Early decision	
Deadline	11/1
Notification	12/20
Other ED deadline	1/5
Other ED notification	2/28
Regular	
Deadline	1/5
Notification	4/1
Nonfall registration?	Yes

FINANCIAL FACTS

Financial Aid Rating	89
Annual tuition	$62,110
Room and board	$15,720
Required fees	$90
Books and supplies	$1,400
Average frosh need-based scholarship	$38,701
Average UG need-based scholarship	$36,991
% needy frosh rec. need-based scholarship or grant aid	98
% needy UG rec. need-based scholarship or grant aid	97
% needy frosh rec. non-need-based scholarship or grant aid	65
% needy UG rec. non-need-based scholarship or grant aid	57
% needy frosh rec. need-based self-help aid	74
% needy UG rec. need-based self-help aid	75
% UG borrow to pay for school	47
Average cumulative indebtedness	$32,341
% frosh need fully met	78
% ugrads need fully met	65
Average % of frosh need met	94
Average % of ugrad need met	91

GEORGIA INSTITUTE OF TECHNOLOGY

North Avenue, Atlanta, GA 30332-0450 • Admissions: 404-894-2000

STUDENTS SAY "..."

Academics

A world-renowned public research university, Georgia Institute of Technology has a reputations that "opens many doors" for its students. Undergrads here are quick to sing the praises of the university's "rigorous" and "challenging" engineering, science, and business programs. Students also love Georgia Tech's focus on "innovation and hands-on learning," which leaves them well prepared to face the job market come graduation. For example, "throughout the school year there are plenty of competitions to create startup companies, flesh out innovative ideas, and show off prototypes." As if that wasn't enough, many courses have "a project built-in to force you to apply the material you've been studying." Inside the classroom, undergrads are greeted by professors who are "truly passionate about what they are teaching." One student further explains, "Most of the professors do research and continue learning themselves. This is the sort of environment that they foster." Undergrads further appreciate that their instructors "try and stimulate thinking rather than just letting you regurgitate facts." Another undergrad concurs remarking that her professors "challenge me to grow as an intellectual." Best of all, they frequently demonstrate themselves to be "invested in your success and making their classes interesting and applicable to real life."

Campus Life

Given the academic rigors at Georgia Tech, many students will tell you that "studying" is the number one activity. However, even these hard working undergrads need a break every now and then. And thankfully "there is almost always something going on somewhere on campus." For starters, "there are an abundance of clubs...covering a huge variety of interests, and the majority of students are involved in at least one." Additionally, "during the fall, large numbers of students spend their weekends tailgating and attending football games." Undergrads here also enjoy attending "plays and musical events at the arts center." Moreover, Greek life is extremely popular at Georgia Tech. Fortunately, if you choose not join a sorority or fraternity, your social life won't take a hit. After all, we've been informed that "fraternity parties are generally very welcome...even [to] students who choose not to drink" or "people who are not members." Finally, students also love to take advantage of Georgia Tech's prime Atlanta location. The city offers many things to do "from museums, to concerts, festivals, restaurants, clubs, and every other sort of attraction in between!"

Student Body

When asked about their peers, Georgia Tech students immediately describe them as "smart," "driven, and ambitious." Indeed, it's rare to find an undergrad here who is "slacking off." Fortunately, "there isn't a sense of cut-throat academic rivalry; everyone is much more helpful and supportive of one another." As one relieved student shares, "People will help you if you're struggling on a math problem, or if you can't get your program to function correctly, instead of letting you suffer so that they can get a better grade." Undergrads also report that their fellow students are often quite "passionate." Unsurprisingly, that passion is "usually [connected to something] in the technology field." Indeed, "You walk to campus and you hear kids debating which programming language is better." Another student agrees explaining, "Most of the jokes exchanged seem to be science-related, and every now and then you see remote-controlled drones flying in the air." Aside from the "nerd" exterior, you'll find undergrads that are "witty" and "quirky" as well as "sleep deprived." There's also "a very large foreign component to the student body," which many here appreciate. Finally, we'd be remiss if we didn't mention that Georgia Tech is "not just a bunch of computer geeks sitting in their room all day but a group of people who are out there making a difference."

GEORGIA INSTITUTE OF TECHNOLOGY

Financial Aid: 404-894-4160 • E-Mail: admission@gatech.edu • Website: www.gatech.edu

THE PRINCETON REVIEW SAYS

Admissions

The school reports that its standardized testing policy for use in admission for Fall 2024 requires applicants to submit either the SAT or ACT. The 2024 testing policy will be permanent. The Princeton Review suggests that interested applicants consult with the school for the most up-to-date standardized testing policies. *Very important factors considered include:* rigor of secondary school record, academic GPA, character/personal qualities, state residency. *Important factors considered include:* application essay, extracurricular activities, geographical residence. *Other factors considered include:* standardized test scores, recommendation(s), talent/ability, first generation, racial/ethnic status, volunteer work, work experience. High school diploma is required and GED is not accepted. *Academic units required:* 4 English, 4 math, 4 science, 2 science labs, 2 foreign language, 3 social studies.

Financial Aid

Students should submit: CSS/Financial Aid Profile; FAFSA; Institution's own financial aid form. Priority filing deadline is 1/31. The Princeton Review suggests that all financial aid forms be submitted as soon as possible (see page 5 for a note on the FAFSA). *Need-based scholarships/grants offered:* College/university scholarship or grant aid from institutional funds; Federal Pell; Private scholarships; SEOG; State scholarships/grants. *Loan aid offered:* Direct PLUS loans; Direct Subsidized Loans; Direct Unsubsidized Loans; College/university loans from institutional funds; State Loans. Admitted students will be notified of awards on a rolling basis beginning 4/1. Federal Work-Study Program available. Institutional employment available.

The Inside Word

Gaining admission to Georgia Tech is extremely competitive. Admissions officers here are looking to see how much candidates have pushed and stretched themselves academically throughout high school. They want intellectually curious students who aren't afraid of a challenge. Where possible, take AP and IB classes, and be sure that you're involved in your community.

THE SCHOOL SAYS "..."

From the Admissions Office

"Georgia Tech consistently ranks among the nation's top public universities producing leaders in engineering, computing, business, architecture, and the sciences while remaining one of the best college buys in the country. The 400-acre campus is nestled in the heart of the fun, dynamic and progressive city of Atlanta. Recent campus improvements yielded new state-of-the art academic and research buildings, apartment-style housing, phenomenal social and recreational facilities, and the most extensive fiber-optic cable system on any college campus.

"Georgia Tech has a great academic reputation, and our graduates are well-prepared to meet today's challenges. Georgia Tech places a strong emphasis on undergraduate students, with practical work experience offered through our co-op and internship programs, and research opportunities for freshmen. Students can also gain an international perspective through study abroad, work abroad, or the international plan. There's also the Clough Undergraduate Center, which includes forty-one classrooms, two 300-plus seat auditoriums, group study rooms, presentation rehearsal studios, a rooftop garden, and a café.

"With a Division I ACC sports program and access to Atlanta's music, theater, and other cultural venues, Georgia Tech offers its diverse and passionate student body a unique combination of top academics in a thriving and vibrant setting. We encourage you to come visit campus and see why Georgia Tech continues to attract the nation's most motivated, interesting, and creative students."

SELECTIVITY

Admissions Rating	97
# of applicants	50,610
% of applicants accepted	17
% of acceptees attending	42
# offered a place on the wait list	7,122
% accepting a place on wait list	69
% admitted from wait list	1

FIRST-YEAR PROFILE

Testing policy	SAT or ACT Required
Range SAT composite	1370–1530
Range SAT EBRW	670–760
Range SAT math	700–790
Range ACT composite	31–35
# submitting SAT scores	2,713
% submitting SAT scores	74
# submitting ACT scores	1,397
% submitting ACT scores	38
Average HS GPA	4.3
% frosh submitting high school GPA	72
% graduated top 10% of class	87
% graduated top 25% of class	97
% graduated top 50% of class	99

DEADLINES

Early action	
Deadline	11/1
Notification	1/23
Regular	
Priority	10/15
Deadline	1/4
Notification	3/26
Nonfall registration?	Yes

APPLICANTS ALSO LOOK AT

Carnegie Mellon University; Cornell University; Duke University; Massachusetts Institute of Technology; University of California—Berkeley; University of California—Los Angeles; University of Florida; University of Georgia; University of Michigan—Ann Arbor

FINANCIAL FACTS

Financial Aid Rating	80
Annual in-state tuition	$10,258
Annual out-of-state tuition	$31,370
Room and board	$15,244
Required fees	$1,506
Books and supplies	$800
Average frosh need-based scholarship	$14,927
Average UG need-based scholarship	$13,687
% needy frosh rec. need-based scholarship or grant aid	90
% needy UG rec. need-based scholarship or grant aid	92
% needy frosh rec. non-need-based scholarship or grant aid	76
% needy UG rec. non-need-based scholarship or grant aid	56
% needy frosh rec. need-based self-help aid	39
% needy UG rec. need-based self-help aid	44
% frosh rec. any financial aid	70
% UG rec. any financial aid	82
% UG borrow to pay for school	32
Average cumulative indebtedness	$27,451
% frosh need fully met	23
% ugrads need fully met	20
Average % of frosh need met	57
Average % of ugrad need met	50

GETTYSBURG COLLEGE

300 North Washington Street, Gettysburg, PA 17325-1484 • Admissions: 717-337-6300 • Fax: 717-337-6145

CAMPUS LIFE

Quality of Life Rating	88
Fire Safety Rating	98
Green Rating	90
Type of school	Private
Affiliation	Lutheran
Environment	Village

STUDENTS

Total undergrad enrollment	2,241
% male/female/another gender	49/51/NR
% from out of state	73
% frosh live on campus	99
% ugrads live on campus	95
# of fraternities (% join)	9 (26)
# of sororities (% join)	7 (32)
% African American	5
% Asian	3
% White	67
% Hispanic	12
% Native American	<1
% Pacific Islander	<1
% Two or more races	3
% Race and/or ethnicity unknown	3
% international	8
# of countries represented	49

SURVEY SAYS . . .

Students always studying
Students are happy
Classroom facilities are great
Lab facilities are great
Great library
Internships are widely available
Great financial aid
Great food on campus
Easy to get around campus
Recreation facilities are great
Frats and sororities are popular
Active student government
Active student-run political groups
Intramural sports are popular

ACADEMICS

Academic Rating	91
% students returning for sophomore year	89
% students graduating within 4 years	78
% students graduating within 6 years	82
Calendar	Semester
Student/faculty ratio	10:1
Profs interesting rating	93
Profs accessible rating	95

Most classes have 10–19 students.

MOST POPULAR MAJORS

Political Science and Government, General;
Business/Commerce, General; Health Professions
And Related Programs

STUDENTS SAY " . . ."

Academics

Established in 1832, Pennsylvania's Gettysburg College is a selective college of the liberal arts and sciences that focuses on interdisciplinary study and advanced scholarship. One such example is the school's Eisenhower Institute, which is dedicated to civic engagement and leadership. To "support intellectual curiosity" for the school's 2,400 students, Gettysburg also provides an individualized major option; for instance, the Cross-Disciplinary Science Institute prepares students to answer big questions across subjects. Faculty mentors are also at the ready, and they collaborate with hundreds of students on projects each year. "There are a lot of research opportunities for us even though we are undergraduate students," says one. There are also tons of chances "to present research, field trips, hands-on learning experiences, [and] immersion trips."

Small class sizes—there's a 10:1 student-faculty ratio—provide students with further opportunities to "form close relationships with professors, which makes the education experience personalized and thorough." Professors also take point in encouraging "leadership and involvement in academics through research and presentations," and utilize "discussion-based classes [to] foster a greater sense of investment." In turn, the inquisitive minds at Gettysburg "feel comfortable sharing their perspectives and opinions, which makes classes and discussions on campus much more interesting and eye-opening." Experiential learning also keeps things fresh and active, like "community service, going to see movies pertinent to a course's topic, field trips" or, for example, a German class that "used the rock wall in our gym as a trust exercise and to practice giving commands in German." Whatever the situation, professors "are always willing to help and make time to meet outside of class."

Campus Life

The work week is, in fact, a work week here. "Almost everyone is studying or doing work at their favorite study space," says one student. But while there's a lot of agreement that "Mondays to Fridays are rigorous," there's also consensus that "then the weekend rolls around." With 95 percent of the student body living on campus, there are lots of ways to stay active, "whether it be in a Greek organization, clubs, athletics, or working on-campus." Sports and Greek life may "dominate the social scene," but there are plenty of other entertainment outlets, like "cool reenactment options." Gettysburg also boasts "all the advantages other more rural schools have, like plenty of space to run, bike, and walk, and a quaint town too."

Student Body

Students describe their "very interconnected" community as "unmatched," thanks largely to the smaller size and high levels of sociability. "Everybody knows most of the other students from a class taken together, or a club they both attend, or maybe they just go to the gym at the same time." Diversity is important to both students and the school, and there's a lot of appreciation voiced for how the community is "open to different opinions" and "able to have healthy conversations about hard topics." Perhaps that's because students are all "eager to learn about the world beyond their academic area" or because they're "diligent with work and extracurriculars." Whatever the case, "we all click very well."

GETTYSBURG COLLEGE

Financial Aid: 717-337-6611 • E-Mail: admiss@gettysburg.edu • Website: www.gettysburg.edu

THE PRINCETON REVIEW SAYS

Admissions

The school reports that its standardized testing policy for use in admission for Fall 2024 is Test Optional. The 2024 testing policy will be permanent. The Princeton Review suggests that interested applicants consult with the school for the most up-to-date standardized testing policies. *Very important factors considered include:* rigor of secondary school record, academic GPA, application essay, recommendation(s). *Important factors considered include:* class rank, standardized test scores, interview, extracurricular activities, talent/ability, character/personal qualities, volunteer work. *Other factors considered include:* first generation, alumni/ae relation, geographical residence, work experience, level of applicant's interest. High school diploma is required and GED is accepted. *Academic units required:* 4 English, 3 math, 3 science, 3 science labs, 3 foreign language, 3 social studies, 3 history. *Academic units recommended:* 4 English, 4 math, 4 science, 4 science labs, 4 foreign language, 4 social studies, 4 history.

Financial Aid

Students should submit: CSS/Financial Aid Profile; FAFSA. Priority filing deadline is 1/15. The Princeton Review suggests that all financial aid forms be submitted as soon as possible (see page 5 for a note on the FAFSA). *Need-based scholarships/grants offered:* College/university scholarship or grant aid from institutional funds; Federal Pell; Private scholarships; SEOG; State scholarships/grants. *Loan aid offered:* Direct PLUS loans; Direct Subsidized Loans; Direct Unsubsidized Loans; College/university loans from institutional funds. Admitted students will be notified of awards on or about 3/15. Federal Work-Study Program available. Institutional employment available.

The Inside Word

To really get a feel for Gettysburg, many students say a campus visit is a must. Test scores are optional here, and the school strongly emphasizes its desire for extracurricular involvement and positive contributions to the community, as well as students who have made the most of the academic offerings of their high school.

THE SCHOOL SAYS "..."

From the Admissions Office

"For almost 200 years, Gettysburg College has provided a consequential education to generations of innovative, driven students and encouraged them to Do Great Work in their communities and across the world.

"Gettysburg College provides students with a breadth and depth of knowledge through a rigorous and contemporary education in the liberal arts and sciences. Students choose from 65 majors, minors, and academic programs. Our world-class faculty brings to life the arts, humanities, social sciences, and natural sciences, ensuring that our students are exposed to viewpoints across the disciplines.

"Our students' intellectual growth extends beyond the classroom. Gettysburg is committed to high-impact experiential learning like student-faculty research, study abroad, civic engagement, and leadership development that translate to valuable outcomes and careers for our 2,250 undergraduate students.

"Mentorship is central to the Gettysburg experience. Every student is assigned a personal success team—comprised of a faculty advisor, co-curricular advisor, and career advisor. Our active global community of over 32,000 alumni provides students with a powerful network to tap into even before they graduate. We see the return on investment as 98 percent of our most recent alums are either employed or enrolled in graduate school one year after graduation.

"At Gettysburg, there are no bystanders. With more than 120 clubs and organizations offering a thousand leadership positions and sponsoring more than 800 events on campus each year, Gettysburg students have many avenues to get involved. As a result, our students are prepared to make a difference—here at Gettysburg and in the world after they graduate."

SELECTIVITY

Admissions Rating	91
# of applicants	5,796
% of applicants accepted	56
% of acceptees attending	20
# of early decision applicants	507
% accepted early decision	55

FIRST-YEAR PROFILE

Testing policy	Test Optional
Range SAT EBRW	680–720
Range SAT math	670–720
Range ACT composite	28–32
% graduated top 10% of class	47
% graduated top 25% of class	76
% graduated top 50% of class	99

DEADLINES

Early decision	
Deadline	11/15
Notification	12/15
Other ED deadline	1/15
Other ED notification	2/1
Early action	
Deadline	12/1
Notification	2/1
Regular	
Priority	1/15
Deadline	1/15
Notification	3/15
Nonfall registration?	No

APPLICANTS ALSO LOOK AT

Bucknell University; Dickinson College; Franklin & Marshall College; Lafayette College; University of Richmond

FINANCIAL FACTS

Financial Aid Rating	94
Annual tuition	$61,760
Room and board	$14,930
Books and supplies	$1,000
Average frosh need-based scholarship	$50,404
Average UG need-based scholarship	$48,852
% needy frosh rec. need-based scholarship or grant aid	97
% needy UG rec. need-based scholarship or grant aid	98
% needy frosh rec. non-need-based scholarship or grant aid	90
% needy UG rec. non-need-based scholarship or grant aid	75
% needy frosh rec. need-based self-help aid	82
% needy UG rec. need-based self-help aid	80
% frosh rec. any financial aid	60
% UG rec. any financial aid	61
% UG borrow to pay for school	62
Average cumulative indebtedness	$33,421
% frosh need fully met	90
% ugrads need fully met	90
Average % of frosh need met	90
Average % of ugrad need met	90

GONZAGA UNIVERSITY

502 E Boone Avenue, Spokane, WA 99258 • Admissions: 800-986-9585 • Fax: 509-313-5780

CAMPUS LIFE

Quality of Life Rating	89
Fire Safety Rating	97
Green Rating	98
Type of school	Private
Affiliation	Roman Catholic
Environment	Metropolis

STUDENTS

Total undergrad enrollment	5,018
% male/female/another gender	46/54/0
% from out of state	52
% frosh live on campus	98
% ugrads live on campus	53
# of fraternities	0
# of sororities	0
% African American	1
% Asian	7
% White	65
% Hispanic	13
% Native American	<1
% Pacific Islander	<1
% Two or more races	8
% Race and/or ethnicity unknown	3
% international	4
# of countries represented	40

SURVEY SAYS . . .

Recreation facilities are great
Everyone loves the Bulldogs
Intramural sports are popular
Students involved in community service

ACADEMICS

Academic Rating	84
% students returning for sophomore year	93
% students graduating within 4 years	80
% students graduating within 6 years	88
Calendar	Semester
Student/faculty ratio	12:1
Profs interesting rating	90
Profs accessible rating	93

Most classes have 20–29 students.
Most lab/discussion sessions have
10–19 students.

MOST POPULAR MAJORS

Business/Commerce, General; Psychology, General;
Registered Nursing/Registered Nurse

STUDENTS SAY "..."

Academics

Gonzaga University "does a phenomenal job of preparing their students for the real world." This is in part facilitated by the "supportive, rather than competitive" academic environment that helps this "really tight-knit community" of undergrads succeed in the classroom. "Classes are mostly discussion-based rather than lecture-based," and "the majority...establish very clear expectations, grading criteria, and a regular class culture." Students enjoy small class sizes, which "allow for more one-on-one communication with professors" and provide "a lot of opportunities to ask questions and get personalized help." Professors are largely well-liked, "especially in the STEM and business majors." Students report that most professors are "passionate about their fields," "generally extremely accessible." Most are "easy to build relationships with" and "always happy to engage with students about their subjects." Students can definitely tell their professors have their best interest at heart. "They also care about me as a person and take the time to check up on me individually." While there are a few outliers who "basically just lectured every day and gave tests," one student writes, "My best professors...encouraged us to draw connections on our own, and taught according to what struck us as important."

Campus Life

At GU, students have no shortage of clubs, activities, and events to fill their time. "During the week students are dedicated to their school work, and on weekends they carve out time to party and gather with friends." A "basketball-obsessed school," games "united the student body," and many students attend one "every chance they get." However, being a basketball fan is not necessarily a prerequisite. "A student can absolutely be a die-hard basketball fan and many are, but I also know a strong minority of students who have never been to a basketball game," one student explains.

"A lot of time outside of class is spent with friends in campus buildings like the Hemmingson student center." Other campus groups also do a good job planning events to keep students occupied. For example, "GU Outdoors plans and hosts many outdoor excursions every week," leading students in "activities like skiing and hiking that are available [in] nearby Spokane." Intramural sports are a favorite among students, with frisbee team and "spike ball [being] super popular." Many feel these are "not very serious" ways "to socialize and have fun with other students." There is no Greek system, so "there is no way to have hierarchical groups and cliques." Instead, most people turn to local community service groups. "There are numerous ways to volunteer," one student notes. "Gonzaga has a lot of volunteer oriented clubs like Moment of Magic, Setons, and Campus Kids, and a ton of students sign up." A "very service-oriented school," Gonzaga instills "the value of service and caring for others in its students."

Student Body

The student body at Gonzaga prides itself on its friendliness. "I have felt welcomed and like I can be myself without judgment," says one student. "I never feel like I have to work to 'fit in' because everyone is accepting of one another." On campus, there's a saying, "Zags help Zags," which "every student here takes...to heart in their everyday actions and behaviors." As one undergrad notes, "You really get the feeling everyone around you is looking out for you." Students "apply themselves wholeheartedly to everything that they do" and "are generally respectful and curious." They are also "open to discussion and sharing their honest beliefs and questions." Although GU "could stand to improve upon its diversity initiatives," it "still contains a large number of different viewpoints and ideologies." These ideologies often align with the school's Jesuit background, with an emphasis on "caring for not only their community, but the larger world." Although historically associated with Catholicism, "the Jesuit mission is not super religious itself," and students of other religions "do not feel unwelcome or uncomfortable." Ultimately, undergrads are united by their desire "to do something to help the world." Truly, "It's an engaging community to be a part of."

GONZAGA UNIVERSITY

Financial Aid: 509-313-6582 • E-Mail: admissions@gonzaga.edu • Website: www.gonzaga.edu

THE PRINCETON REVIEW SAYS

Admissions

The school reports that its standardized testing policy for use in admission for Fall 2024 is Test Optional. The Princeton Review suggests that interested applicants consult with the school for the most up-to-date standardized testing policies. *Very important factors considered include:* rigor of secondary school record, academic GPA, character/personal qualities. *Important factors considered include:* application essay, recommendation(s), extracurricular activities, talent/ability. *Other factors considered include:* standardized test scores, interview, first generation, alumni/ae relation, racial/ethnic status, volunteer work, work experience, level of applicant's interest. High school diploma is required and GED is not accepted. *Academic units required:* 4 English, 3 math, 3 science, 3 science labs, 2 foreign language, 3 social studies, 3 history, 2 academic electives. *Academic units recommended:* 4 English, 4 math, 4 science, 4 science labs, 3 foreign language, 3 social studies, 3 history, 3 academic electives.

Financial Aid

Students should submit: FAFSA. Priority filing deadline is 2/1. *Need-based scholarships/grants offered:* College/university scholarship or grant aid from institutional funds; Federal Pell; Private scholarships; SEOG; State scholarships/grants. *Loan aid offered:* Direct PLUS loans; Direct Subsidized Loans; Direct Unsubsidized Loans; College/university loans from institutional funds; Federal Nursing Loans. Admitted students will be notified of offers on a rolling basis beginning 3/1. Federal Work-Study Program available. Institutional employment available.

The Inside Word

When applying to Gonzaga, prospective students should focus on more than just their GPA. Though admissions officers will be interested in seeing your strengths in the classroom, they are also looking for applicants interested and involved with the world around them. Extracurriculars such as volunteer work can only help you. Though Gonzaga has strong Catholic Studies and Theology programs, religious background is not a consideration in applications. Gonzaga's testing policy is Test Optional, which should alleviate some stress and allow you to focus more on community involvement, a topic that Gonzaga cares about deeply.

THE SCHOOL SAYS "..."

From the Admissions Office

"Gonzaga educates students for lives of leadership and service for the common good. We seek motivated students who will benefit from the University's challenging academic programs and will positively contribute to our campus with extracurricular achievement, community involvement, unique experiences, and diverse personal interests. In the application, let us know about your experiences thus far and your goals and hopes for the future. Please note that we are Test Optional. Grades and grade trends, curriculum, and writing in the application will be weighted more heavily for students applying without a test score. If you want to discuss admission to Gonzaga, please contact your admission counselor at www.gonzaga.edu/mycounselor."

SELECTIVITY

Admissions Rating	88
# of applicants	9,886
% of applicants accepted	70
% of acceptees attending	18
# offered a place on the wait list	1,829
% accepting a place on wait list	42
% admitted from wait list	64

FIRST-YEAR PROFILE

Testing policy	Test Optional
Range SAT composite	1210–1400
Range SAT EBRW	610–700
Range SAT math	600–710
Range ACT composite	26–31
# submitting SAT scores	342
% submitting SAT scores	28
# submitting ACT scores	159
% submitting ACT scores	13
Average HS GPA	3.7
% frosh submitting high school GPA	97
% graduated top 10% of class	37
% graduated top 25% of class	74
% graduated top 50% of class	95

DEADLINES

Regular	
Priority	12/1
Deadline	2/1
Nonfall registration?	Yes

APPLICANTS OFTEN PREFER

University of Washington

APPLICANTS SOMETIMES PREFER

Santa Clara University; University of Oregon; Washington State University

FINANCIAL FACTS

Financial Aid Rating	88
Annual tuition	$52,540
Room and board	$15,080
Required fees	$960
Books and supplies	$1,382
Average frosh need-based scholarship	$9,771
Average UG need-based scholarship	$11,221
% needy frosh rec. need-based scholarship or grant aid	95
% needy UG rec. need-based scholarship or grant aid	93
% needy frosh rec. non-need-based scholarship or grant aid	99
% needy UG rec. non-need-based scholarship or grant aid	98
% needy frosh rec. need-based self-help aid	63
% needy UG rec. need-based self-help aid	66
% frosh rec. any financial aid	99
% UG rec. any financial aid	99
% UG borrow to pay for school	50
Average cumulative indebtedness	$28,601
% frosh need fully met	53
% ugrads need fully met	53
Average % of frosh need met	80
Average % of ugrad need met	78

GORDON COLLEGE

255 Grapevine Road, Wenham, MA 01984-1899 • Admissions: 978-927-2300 • Fax: 978-867-4682

CAMPUS LIFE

Quality of Life Rating	90
Fire Safety Rating	97
Green Rating	90
Type of school	Private
Affiliation	Multidenominational - Evangelical
Environment	Village

STUDENTS

Total undergrad enrollment	1,428
% male/female/another gender	39/61/0
% from out of state	64
% frosh from public high school	56
% frosh live on campus	93
% ugrads live on campus	87
# of fraternities	0
# of sororities	0
% African American	5
% Asian	5
% White	67
% Hispanic	11
% Native American	0
% Pacific Islander	<1
% Two or more races	2
% Race and/or ethnicity unknown	1
% international	8
# of countries represented	35

SURVEY SAYS . . .

Lots of conservative students
Students are very religious
Easy to get around campus
Intramural sports are popular
Theater is popular
Active minority support groups
Students are friendly

ACADEMICS

Academic Rating	85
% students returning for sophomore year	84
% students graduating within 4 years	65
% students graduating within 6 years	72
Calendar	Semester
Student/faculty ratio	10:1
Profs interesting rating	91
Profs accessible rating	93

Most classes have 10–19 students.
Most lab/discussion sessions have 10–19 students.

MOST POPULAR MAJORS

Psychology, General; Business Administration, Management and Operations; Biology/Biological Sciences, General

STUDENTS SAY "..."

Academics

Tucked away in beautiful, bucolic Massachusetts, Gordon College is a liberal-arts institution that's built on "Christian values without being unnecessarily strict." Here, students receive a "well-rounded education" that encourages them "to make interdisciplinary connections." There's also an appreciated "emphasis on servant leadership through opportunities like the outdoor education requirement." And while there's no denying that "the school is academically rigorous," students note that "there's so much here for support, so it's hard to do poorly in a course." The faculty is described both as "accomplished" and "extremely passionate about the subjects that they teach." and the majority are "very involved and want to know you personally." Students are proud to share their own relationships: "I'm actually friends with my English professor and I've only been in class with him for a semester so far." Another divulges, "I was struggling financially and had professors email me over the summer to help me find a way to get back." This isn't just an "enjoyable [academic] environment" either; there's a sense that "when people leave here, they are prepared to get a job and do well."

Campus Life

Gordon is a school that's always humming with some sort of activity, especially on Mondays, Wednesdays, and Fridays, where "you can find a good portion of [the] student body in chapel." Outside of that, the college sponsors numerous events like "waffle nights, student hosted dinners, coffeehouses, parties [and] game nights," and "sports are pretty popular on campus." (We've been told that "the quad is great for playing spikeball.") There's also a music department that "is very strong and holds a lot of performances," though it's not uncommon to stumble upon unofficial "chill house concerts or jam sessions." Of course, New England weather plays a fairly big role in dictating the activity schedule. "When it's warm everyone hammocks [and] when it snows everyone has snowball fights and builds snowmen." When the opportunity presents itself, undergrads enjoy exploring the "quaint New England coastal towns" that surround the campus, whether that's "to hike or spend a day at the beach," and of course nearby Boston makes for a good weekend getaway for those seeking out things like "museums or concerts." Overall, though, students note that campus life is "pretty tame": there are "some off-campus parties," but people "who drink [and] do drugs...are the exception and are in the minority."

Student Body

When asked about their peers, many individuals at Gordon gush that their classmates are "genuine and kind people" who really "care about how you are doing socially, academically, and spiritually." According to one undergrad, "I could pull aside any random person, tell them I'm having a bad day, and they would listen to me and care about me." Students also value that many of their peers "have a real, lived-out relationship with God." And though it frequently feels as though most students come from "Massachusetts or New England" and are "majority white, majority Christian," you'll also discover that "there are many countries and nationalities represented" among the student body as well. And while there's "not a lot of middle ground" between the very liberal and conservative points of view on campus, students take pride in everyone's ability to "enter into a curious and respectful conversation" when encountering someone who disagrees with them. Perhaps that's because at the end of the day, students find unity in being "committed to their education and goals" and gladly help "one another achieve academic success."

GORDON COLLEGE

Financial Aid: 978-867-4246 • E-Mail: admissions@gordon.edu • Website: www.gordon.edu

THE PRINCETON REVIEW SAYS

Admissions

The school reports that its standardized testing policy for use in admission for Fall 2024 is Test Optional. The 2024 testing policy will be permanent. The Princeton Review suggests that interested applicants consult with the school for the most up-to-date standardized testing policies. *Very important factors considered include:* rigor of secondary school record, academic GPA, standardized test scores, application essay, recommendation(s), interview, talent/ability, character/personal qualities, religious affiliation/commitment. *Important factors considered include:* class rank, extracurricular activities, volunteer work, work experience, level of applicant's interest. *Other factors considered include:* alumni/ae relation, racial/ethnic status. High school diploma is required and GED is accepted. *Academic units required:* 4 English, 2 math, 2 science, 1 science lab, 2 foreign language, 2 social studies, 5 academic electives. *Academic units recommended:* 4 English, 3 math, 3 science, 1 science lab, 4 foreign language, 2 social studies, 5 academic electives.

Financial Aid

Students should submit: FAFSA. Priority filing deadline is 3/1. The Princeton Review suggests that all financial aid forms be submitted as soon as possible (see page 5 for a note on the FAFSA). *Need-based scholarships/grants offered:* College/university scholarship or grant aid from institutional funds; Federal Pell; Private scholarships; SEOG; State scholarships/grants. *Loan aid offered:* Direct PLUS loans; Direct Subsidized Loans; Direct Unsubsidized Loans; State Loans. Admitted students will be notified of awards on a rolling basis beginning 1/15. Federal Work-Study Program available. Institutional employment available.

The Inside Word

Gordon College seeks applicants who display an intellectual curiosity and excitement for learning. You'll need solid grades and a strong college-prep curriculum to be a contender. Successful students also demonstrate commitment to Christian values and you should sit for an interview if at all possible. This allows the college to get a better sense of who you are and provides you with the opportunity to see if the school is a good fit for you.

THE SCHOOL SAYS "..."

From the Admissions Office

"What if faith and learning were complementary, not contradictory?

"At one of the nation's top Christian colleges, we believe that wrestling with the tough questions transforms faith rather than threatens it. In fact, our Christian faith is exactly what motivates us toward intellectual maturity and propels us to serve and lead. We are serious about science and the arts, about analytical thinking and challenging ideas, about learning how to make a case and persuade others. Faith is the framework through which we foster academic curiosity, build skills and experience, and grow into thoughtful leaders and contributors in the world.

"What if excellence and affordability went hand-in-hand?

"Gordon is leading the way on cost and quality: We are among the top ranked and lowest priced of our competitors, thanks to a tuition reset in 2021. But at Gordon, it's not just numbers that confirm value. It's an unwavering commitment to Jesus Christ and faith-driven learning community marked by excellence. The result is that Gordon students are better prepared for a greater purpose.

"What if the beach and Boston were within reach?

"Gordon students reap the benefits of a big city without the price tag of a downtown school. On an idyllic New England campus just three miles from the ocean and 25 miles north of Boston, the global hub of higher education and talent development, they have access to a wealth of professional development, career opportunities and experiential education, as well as rich history and traditions."

SELECTIVITY

Admissions Rating	86
# of applicants	2,884
% of applicants accepted	68
% of acceptees attending	19

FIRST-YEAR PROFILE

Testing policy	Test Optional
Range SAT composite	1028–1273
Range SAT EBRW	520–660
Range SAT math	500–620
Range ACT composite	20–29
# submitting SAT scores	324
% submitting SAT scores	85
# submitting ACT scores	69
% submitting ACT scores	18
Average HS GPA	3.6
% frosh submitting high school GPA	97
% graduated top 10% of class	24
% graduated top 25% of class	51
% graduated top 50% of class	77

DEADLINES

Early action	
Deadline	11/1
Notification	11/15
Regular	
Priority	12/1
Deadline	8/1
Notification	Rolling, 8/15
Nonfall registration?	Yes

APPLICANTS OFTEN PREFER

Calvin University; Grove City College; Houghton College; Liberty University; Messiah University; University of Massachusetts–Boston; Wheaton College (IL)

APPLICANTS SOMETIMES PREFER

Merrimack College; University of Massachusetts Amherst; University of New Hampshire

FINANCIAL FACTS

Financial Aid Rating	83
Annual tuition	$25,250
Room and board	$11,700
Required fees	$1,000
Books and supplies	$960
Average frosh need-based scholarship	$30,279
Average UG need-based scholarship	$25,522
% needy frosh rec. need-based scholarship or grant aid	100
% needy UG rec. need-based scholarship or grant aid	100
% needy frosh rec. non-need-based scholarship or grant aid	15
% needy UG rec. non-need-based scholarship or grant aid	15
% needy frosh rec. need-based self-help aid	81
% needy UG rec. need-based self-help aid	81
% frosh rec. any financial aid	100
% UG rec. any financial aid	99
% UG borrow to pay for school	61
Average cumulative indebtedness	$40,395
% frosh need fully met	17
% ugrads need fully met	20
Average % of frosh need met	82
Average % of ugrad need met	77

GOUCHER COLLEGE

1021 Dulaney Valley Road, Baltimore, MD 21204-2794 • Admissions: 410-337-6100 • Fax: 410-337-6354

CAMPUS LIFE

Quality of Life Rating	84
Fire Safety Rating	97
Green Rating	98
Type of school	Private
Affiliation	No Affiliation
Environment	City

STUDENTS

Total undergrad enrollment	982
% male/female/another gender	33/67/<1
% from out of state	56
% frosh live on campus	94
% ugrads live on campus	77
# of fraternities	0
# of sororities	0
% African American	26
% Asian	5
% White	51
% Hispanic	5
% Native American	<1
% Pacific Islander	0
% Two or more races	1
% Race and/or ethnicity unknown	9
% international	3
# of countries represented	36

SURVEY SAYS . . .

Lots of liberal students
Great library
Class discussions encouraged
Students environmentally aware
Active minority support groups

ACADEMICS

Academic Rating	82
% students returning for sophomore year	77
% students graduating within 4 years	49
% students graduating within 6 years	60
Calendar	Semester
Student/faculty ratio	8:1
Profs interesting rating	92
Profs accessible rating	91

Most classes have 10–19 students.
Most lab/discussion sessions have 10–19 students.

STUDENTS SAY ". . ."

Academics

The small and innovative Goucher College, located just outside of Baltimore, boasts a welcoming, collaborative learning environment, a 100 percent study abroad rate/requirement, and a liberal arts curriculum that focuses on interdisciplinary complex-problem solving. The foundation for every major is the Goucher Commons curriculum, which creates shared, problem-based learning experiences across disciplines. The school encourages its students to live outside of their comfort zones when it comes to being "mindful" of others "so as to learn from...diverse perspectives." Students here are "curious to learn" and "thrive on engaging in deep conversation, and are not afraid to speak their minds." Small class sizes and a low student-to-faculty ratio promote these conversations, and "discussion and critical thinking skills are built into every class so you learn or formulate an argument around a wide variety of issues."

As a way of easing the transition into college, Goucher also provides a course called First Year Experience (FYE) that every first-year student is required to take. During FYE, first-year students "meet with their mentor who was with them during orientation to talk about certain resources provided [at] Goucher for safety, and other subjects about racial identity and how we're getting acquainted with our new environment." As for regular classes, there are a ton of "very interesting" classes, and "it is easy to enroll in a class that is either full or that you don't have the prerequisites for." Professors receive high marks across the board; they get to know students on a personal level and are "invested in [their] unique reasoning for being a part of the department." They "want everyone to share their opinions and certain personal experiences that go along with the topic" at hand. "I know they see me first as a person, second as a student," says one happy student.

Campus Life

The Goucher campus is "beautiful." When it's sunny, "a lot of students are outside doing homework, socializing, playing Frisbee, or doing various other physical activities." During the week, most people work and study ("lots of people use the library as a common place"), so the weekend "is when people hang out." Not a lot of students go off campus, so a lot of small groups and open mics form. Parties "aren't all that common."

Students subscribe to the idea that "a rising tide lifts all boats." One student explains, "There is no internal competition at Goucher; we all work together." That may be a part of why there's no Greek life on campus, and why sports isn't a major focus (though there are 20 Division III athletic teams, and one co-ed equestrian team). Activism is huge on campus, and if you are passionate about a cause with these seemingly "liberal, outspoken" students, "there is usually a club or student union that is already organized, or students who are more than willing to start a club."

Student Body

The Goucher student body comprises "a symposium [of students] to do Socrates proud." Goucher students are "engaged, trust each other, and are brave enough to dialogue in a way most campuses don't seem to be anymore." The degree of political openness here is "only left-looking," and this "delightfully weird" group tends to include "alternative, creative, artistic people who aren't afraid to express themselves." Students describe their peers as middle to upper-middle class and from the East Coast. Diversity and inclusivity are strong at Goucher with 42 percent of the student population being people of color and the Center for Race, Equity, and Identity supporting the sizable BIPOC and LGBTQ+ communities on campus. Keeping it in their own backyard, students love to help and "do their best to give back to their Baltimore and local community."

GOUCHER COLLEGE

Financial Aid: 410-337-6141 • E-Mail: admissions@goucher.edu • Website: www.goucher.edu

THE PRINCETON REVIEW SAYS

Admissions

The school reports that its standardized testing policy for use in admission for Fall 2024 is Test Optional. The 2024 testing policy will be permanent. The Princeton Review suggests that interested applicants consult with the school for the most up-to-date standardized testing policies. *Very important factors considered include:* rigor of secondary school record, academic GPA. *Important factors considered include:* application essay, recommendation(s), extracurricular activities, talent/ability, volunteer work. *Other factors considered include:* class rank, standardized test scores, interview, character/personal qualities, first generation, alumni/ae relation, geographical residence, state residency, racial/ethnic status, work experience, level of applicant's interest. High school diploma is required and GED is accepted. *Academic units required:* 4 English, 3 math, 2 science, 2 science labs, 2 foreign language, 3 social studies, 2 academic electives. *Academic units recommended:* 4 English, 4 math, 3 science, 3 science labs, 4 foreign language, 3 social studies, 2 academic electives.

Financial Aid

Students should submit: FAFSA. Priority filing deadline is 12/1. The Princeton Review suggests that all financial aid forms be submitted as soon as possible (see page 5 for a note on the FAFSA). *Need-based scholarships/grants offered:* College/university scholarship or grant aid from institutional funds; Federal Pell; Private scholarships; SEOG; State scholarships/grants. *Loan aid offered:* Direct PLUS loans; Direct Subsidized Loans; Direct Unsubsidized Loans. Admitted students will be notified of awards on a rolling basis beginning 11/1. Federal Work-Study Program available. Institutional employment available.

The Inside Word

Goucher College requires all students to participate in a study abroad experience, so make sure you've factored that in before applying. Also note that while early decision is not an option here, early action is, and students who have their application materials ready are encouraged to submit.

THE SCHOOL SAYS "..."

From the Admissions Office

"Goucher College is a private, liberal arts college dedicated to teaching students to be complex problem-solvers prepared for the jobs of the future. Goucher's distinct undergraduate experience, The Goucher Edge, consists of five components: the Commons curriculum, your major, a global experience, an internship accelerator, and a student success team.

"Every Goucher student is supported by their own Success Team. Students are assigned a Success Advisor who monitors a student's progress through graduation along with colleagues in Residential Life, Career Education, and Global Education among others.

"Through Goucher's general education requirement, the Commons, students master a range of skills—critical thinking, problem-solving, collaboration, and communication—the very skills being sought by today's employers. Goucher's 29 majors are rooted in the core principles of interdisciplinary study and range from the sciences, to the social sciences, humanities, education and the arts. The emphasis on global education provides 100% of our students the opportunity to study abroad at no additional charge. Further experiential learning opportunities exist through internships, research with faculty, and community-based learning. With career education integrated throughout the curriculum, Goucher's unique Internship Accelerator provides micro-internships to first year and sophomore students that lead to robust experiences as juniors and seniors. Within one year of graduation, 96% of recent graduates are employed or are enrolled in graduate/professional programs.

"Goucher is committed to creating a unique learning and living environment that exposes students to new experiences and is a proud member of the Colleges That Change Lives organization."

SELECTIVITY

Admissions Rating	84
# of applicants	2,928
% of applicants accepted	81
% of acceptees attending	11

FIRST-YEAR PROFILE

Testing policy	Test Optional
Range SAT composite	1140–1320
Range SAT EBRW	580–688
Range SAT math	533–640
Range ACT composite	26–33
# submitting SAT scores	62
% submitting SAT scores	22
# submitting ACT scores	17
% submitting ACT scores	6
Average HS GPA	3.3
% frosh submitting high school GPA	99
% graduated top 10% of class	19
% graduated top 25% of class	45
% graduated top 50% of class	82

DEADLINES

Early decision	
Deadline	12/1
Notification	12/15
Early action	
Deadline	12/1
Notification	2/1
Regular	
Priority	12/1
Deadline	1/15
Notification	Rolling, 11/15
Nonfall registration?	Yes

APPLICANTS SOMETIMES PREFER

American University; Clark University; Towson University; University of Maryland, Baltimore County; University of Maryland, College Park

FINANCIAL FACTS

Financial Aid Rating	87
Annual tuition	$51,000
Room and board	$16,650
Required fees	$250
Books and supplies	$1,200
Average frosh need-based scholarship	$44,059
Average UG need-based scholarship	$40,368
% needy frosh rec. need-based scholarship or grant aid	100
% needy UG rec. need-based scholarship or grant aid	100
% needy frosh rec. non-need-based scholarship or grant aid	19
% needy UG rec. non-need-based scholarship or grant aid	18
% needy frosh rec. need-based self-help aid	67
% needy UG rec. need-based self-help aid	69
% frosh rec. any financial aid	100
% UG rec. any financial aid	99
% frosh need fully met	29
% ugrads need fully met	24
Average % of frosh need met	89
Average % of ugrad need met	89

GRINNELL COLLEGE

1227 Park Street, 1st Floor, Grinnell, IA 50112 • Admissions: 641-269-4000 • Fax: 641-269-4800

STUDENTS SAY ". . ."

Academics

The unique appeal of Grinnell College, according to students, is that you'll get "elite academics in a small-town environment" and a "great educational experience" that many describe as "the best you can find in the Midwest." The overall sense is that "the students are smart, professors outstanding, and the administration does a good job of bringing the world to Grinnell." That plays out in the "depth at which courses are taught," with some proudly noting that there's an "emphasis on understanding rather than rote learning." Enrollees also benefit greatly from "small classes" and an "open curriculum" that enables students to pursue whatever interests them.

While there's "a lot of reading and assignment," students don't mind that rigor, saying that "it is genuinely enjoyable to learn here" and noting that "academics are intense at Grinnell, but as a result I've learned so much." Much of that can be attributed to professors who, by and large, "welcome questions and critique and genuinely care about learning." They also make it easy to foster "strong relationships" with them: "I've been to so many of their houses for meals with my classes." A classmate concurs, adding, "There are many departments here at the college that have great faculty, and they are usually quite willing to engage with students and help them when they need it."

Campus Life

Grinnell is "very academically oriented" and accordingly, undergrads dedicate a lot of time to schoolwork. But when they want to kick back and relax, the college sponsors numerous events ranging from "All-Campus Parties (which are hosted by the student government)" to bingo, dances, trivia, and more. Many students also participate in clubs and extracurricular activities, and the fact that "you only need five people to start a club" means that "it's very easy to make your own," which goes a long way to explain the range of niches filled by DAG, a club devoted to foam sword-fighting; the fiber arts club; a "low-stakes band class"; GORP (Grinnell Outdoor Recreation Program); mock trial; and so much more. Additionally, "intramural sports are slowly becoming popular again." The most commonly shared concept is that Grinnellians are quite adept at making their own fun, in ways that can be life-changing: "I watched a lunar eclipse with a group of people who I didn't know before 1:00am that night; I still keep up with them." And, of course, plenty of people choose to unwind by simply "watching bad movies on Saturday nights."

Student Body

From the moment you step foot on the campus of Grinnell College, you can sense that this is a "tight-knit community" where students are free "to be whoever [they] want... without judgment or reservation." This results in a lot of "passionate, quirky, [and] curious" individuals who tend to maintain "high standards for themselves." Peers are also described as "really smart and driven," so much so that "I feel like everyone I know is working to achieve some rather impressive goals and are actually making good progress." Students tend to identify as liberal and are "not afraid to challenge the status quo or how things are," especially when it comes to "social issues." Additionally, undergrads note that there's "a higher-than-average percentage of students in the LGBTQ+ community," though some also note that many peers seem to be "white, predominantly middle- and upper-class" kids who "went to quite well-funded high schools." Regardless of background, students mostly agree that on campus, everyone is "down to earth and friendly" or at the very least, benefiting from a "lack of pretentiousness" that fosters a sense of community. As this student concludes, "My favorite thing about the Grinnell student body is inclusivity. I never feel like I am not welcome at an event, and while social groups exist, nothing has ever been cliquey or exclusive to me."

GRINNELL COLLEGE

Financial Aid: 641-269-3250 • E-Mail: admission@grinnell.edu • Website: www.grinnell.edu

THE PRINCETON REVIEW SAYS

Admissions

The school reports that its standardized testing policy for use in admission for Fall 2024 is Test Optional. It is unknown at this time if the 2024 testing policy will be permanent. The Princeton Review suggests that interested applicants consult with the school for the most up-to-date standardized testing policies. *Very important factors considered include:* rigor of secondary school record, class rank, academic GPA, recommendation(s). *Important factors considered include:* standardized test scores, application essay, extracurricular activities, talent/ability. *Other factors considered include:* interview, character/personal qualities, first generation, alumni/ae relation, geographical residence, state residency, racial/ethnic status, volunteer work, work experience, level of applicant's interest. High school diploma is required and GED is accepted. *Academic units recommended:* 4 English, 4 math, 3 science, 3 science labs, 3 foreign language, 3 social studies, 3 history.

Financial Aid

Students should submit: CSS/Financial Aid Profile; FAFSA; Noncustodial Profile; State aid form. Priority filing deadline is 12/1. The Princeton Review suggests that all financial aid forms be submitted as soon as possible (see page 5 for a note on the FAFSA). *Need-based scholarships/grants offered:* College/university scholarship or grant aid from institutional funds; Federal Pell; Private scholarships; SEOG; State scholarships/grants. *Loan aid offered:* Direct PLUS loans; Direct Subsidized Loans; Direct Unsubsidized Loans; College/university loans from institutional funds. Admitted students will be notified of awards on or about 4/1. Federal Work-Study Program available. Institutional employment available.

The Inside Word

Accepting just over 10% of its 10,000+ applicants, if you're serious about becoming a Grinnellian, you'll want to take every opportunity to demonstrate that, especially since, according to the school, "no single factor guarantees admission." Take the school up on its preliminary application, request information about and attend any events it may host in your area, and make sure that you're challenging yourself with your high-school courses and scoring well on either the SAT or ACT if you are submitting your scores.

THE SCHOOL SAYS "..."

From the Admissions Office

"Grinnell College is a place where independence of thought and social conscience are instilled. Grinnell is a college with the resources of a school ten times its size, a faculty that reads like a Who's Who of Teaching, and a learning environment where debate does not end in the classroom and often begins in the dining hall.

"Grinnellians are committed to learning, respect for themselves and others, contributing to global social good, willing collaboration, and the courage to try.

"We look for students who show strong potential, have the courage to try new things, demonstrate a willingness to speak out and share their opinions, and bring different perspectives to our international campus in the middle of Iowa. Grinnell College is filled with students who are serious about learning but are not always serious.

"Students applying for first-year admission are not required to submit an SAT and/or ACT test score. Applicants are required to inform us whether or not they will submit a test score by their respective application deadline. Students are not permitted to change their test score preference after their respective application deadline. Applicants who choose to apply with an SAT and/or ACT test score must submit official test scores to Grinnell College."

SELECTIVITY

Admissions Rating	97
# of applicants	11,658
% of applicants accepted	9
% of acceptees attending	41
# offered a place on the wait list	2,699
% accepting a place on wait list	53
% admitted from wait list	4
# of early decision applicants	553
% accepted early decision	53

FIRST-YEAR PROFILE

Testing policy	Test Optional
Range SAT composite	1410–1510
Range SAT EBRW	680–750
Range SAT math	700–780
Range ACT composite	31–34
# submitting SAT scores	121
% submitting SAT scores	28
# submitting ACT scores	119
% submitting ACT scores	27
% graduated top 10% of class	66
% graduated top 25% of class	24
% graduated top 50% of class	98

DEADLINES

Early decision	
Deadline	11/15
Notification	12/15
Other ED deadline	1/1
Other ED notification	1/31
Regular	
Deadline	1/15
Notification	4/1
Nonfall registration?	No

APPLICANTS ALSO LOOK AT

Amherst College; Brown University; Carleton College; Harvard College; Macalester College

FINANCIAL FACTS

Financial Aid Rating	99
Annual tuition	$64,342
Room and board	$15,878
Required fees	$520
Books and supplies	$900
Average frosh need-based scholarship	$57,342
Average UG need-based scholarship	$56,274
% needy frosh rec. need-based scholarship or grant aid	100
% needy UG rec. need-based scholarship or grant aid	100
% needy frosh rec. non-need-based scholarship or grant aid	27
% needy UG rec. non-need-based scholarship or grant aid	26
% needy frosh rec. need-based self-help aid	100
% needy UG rec. need-based self-help aid	100
% frosh rec. any financial aid	91
% UG rec. any financial aid	90
% UG borrow to pay for school	55
Average cumulative indebtedness	$14,738
% frosh need fully met	100
% ugrads need fully met	100
Average % of frosh need met	100
Average % of ugrad need met	100

GROVE CITY COLLEGE

100 Campus Drive, Grove City, PA 16127-2104 • Admissions: 724-458-2000 • Fax: 724-458-3395

STUDENTS SAY "..."

Academics

Located an hour north of Pittsburgh, Pennsylvania, Grove City College provides a Christ-centered, non-sectarian environment in which students and faculty "create a vibrant and uplifting community that encourages one another to live to the fullest in a Christ-like manner." The school desires to see students excel inside and outside the classroom, integrating Christ "into all aspects of education and a career for the future," and it "challenges...students to grow in all aspects—intellectually, spiritually, emotionally, and athletically." And, this philosophy works: "The majority of the students here apply their spiritual relationship with God to all activities on campus, whether it be academic or social." The low cost of tuition is just gravy, as is the strong alumni network and "really good reputation with employers."

The professors at Grove City "vary from department to department," but on the whole, they are "engaging, approachable, and very knowledgeable about the course material" and "willing to personally invest in the students." Many expect a lot from their students and assign a heavy workload, but people find the academics to be "challenging, but not suffocating." The "very intelligent, friendly, and available" faculty usually "have extensive office hours and are more than willing to help [students]." Current students say their instructors maintain "a very open dialogue about various beliefs," and "challenge [students] to ask hard questions" both in an area of study and on a more personal level.

Campus Life

Since Grove City College is located in a relatively remote area of Western Pennsylvania, most activities are done on-campus, but "for a small town, there's lots to do," including plenty of places to eat, a movie theater, and ice cream shops. Days at Grove City are pretty typical, spent "going to class, studying, catching up with friends over meals, movie and game nights on the weekends, dances, campus ministries, [and] club activities." Many are also on sports teams, especially "intramural sports teams like volleyball, basketball, Frisbee, [and] soccer," plus students also "like to hang out in our recreational room or go bowling." Forget about Footloose: there is actually "a great deal of dancing and singing here," and people like to "go for walks when the weather is nice, play games, watch movies, do sports, and simply talk together." Indeed, many lunches "devolve into an ideological, theological, or philosophical discussion." Grove City students are proud of their involvement in the world around them through "various academic lectures, Warriors (an hour-long worship service), and screenings of political debates"; these events, though not required, are "extremely well-attended." Likewise, there "are many great groups on campus that provide community service or benefit for a good cause." Intervisitation between male and female dorms is "limited," and this is in no way a party school.

Student Body

As might be expected, those who come to Grove City are "largely Christian kids," who are "generally polite and law-abiding," and the student body tends to swing conservative or moderate politically. According to students, the college "avoids being...restrictive or closed-minded." "Grove City students know what they believe, but are open to discussion," a student explains. These students collectively provide "the most friendly atmosphere" many have ever been a part of. "Peers I've never even met smile at me as I pass them on the sidewalk," describes one happy student. The college as a whole "welcomes students with open arms," and it is very easy to find "a community that encourages and inspires one another." There are a fair number of type A personalities here: Grove City students are "hardworking and highly motivated to do well," and "many people over-commit themselves to the various on-campus groups."

GROVE CITY COLLEGE

Financial Aid: 724-458-3300 • E-Mail: admissions@gcc.edu • Website: www.gcc.edu

THE PRINCETON REVIEW SAYS

Admissions

The school reports that its standardized testing policy for use in admission for Fall 2024 is Test Optional. The 2024 testing policy will be permanent. The Princeton Review suggests that interested applicants consult with the school for the most up-to-date standardized testing policies. *Very important factors considered include:* rigor of secondary school record, academic GPA, application essay, interview, character/personal qualities, level of applicant's interest. *Important factors considered include:* recommendation(s), extracurricular activities. *Other factors considered include:* class rank, standardized test scores, talent/ability, first generation, alumni/ae relation, geographical residence, state residency, religious affiliation/commitment, racial/ethnic status, volunteer work, work experience. High school diploma is required and GED is accepted. *Academic units recommended:* 4 English, 3 math, 3 science, 2 science labs, 3 foreign language, 3 social studies, 2 history.

Financial Aid

Students should submit: Institution's own financial aid form. The Princeton Review suggests that all financial aid forms be submitted as soon as possible (see page 5 for a note on the FAFSA). *Need-based scholarships/grants offered:* College/university scholarship or grant aid from institutional funds; Private scholarships; State scholarships/grants. *Loan aid offered:* State Loans. Admitted students will be notified of awards on a rolling basis beginning 2/20. Institutional employment available.

The Inside Word

Gaining entrance to Grove City College is difficult and highly competitive. Students must have outstanding personal characteristics, and they need to be prepared for a strenuous but workable course load. Christian values are of utmost importance at Grove City College, and the school values students who seek out surroundings based on those principles. Interviews and letters of recommendation are highly valued as components of the admission process.

THE SCHOOL SAYS "..."

From the Admissions Office

"Students flourish at Grove City College because faith is its foundation. From the classroom to the practice fields, from the dining halls to the dormitories, students seek to understand how faith influences their daily activities and ultimately how they might use their abilities to serve others. The College equips students to discover and pursue their unique callings through an academically excellent and Christ-centered learning and living experience.

"The cornerstone of our excellent education is our incredible community of learners—students, faculty and staff who are committed to pursuing knowledge and truth for the advancement of the common good. Surrounded by peers and mentors who sharpen them, students develop into leaders of the highest proficiency guided by these core values: faithfulness, excellence, community, stewardship, and independence.

"We offer students and families an amazing value. Tuition and costs run about half the national average before scholarships and financial aid. Unlike the vast majority of colleges and universities, we do not practice tuition discounting—tuition price is the same for every student and no student unwittingly subsidizes another student's tuition through artificial scholarships.

"Our nationally ranked Career Services Office begins working with students before they arrive as freshmen, ensuring that by the time they graduate, they will be prepared not only to pursue a fulfilling career but for a lifetime of professional success."

SELECTIVITY

Admissions Rating	88
# of applicants	2,082
% of applicants accepted	73
% of acceptees attending	41
# offered a place on the wait list	97
% accepting a place on wait list	22
% admitted from wait list	71
# of early decision applicants	311
% accepted early decision	95

FIRST-YEAR PROFILE

Testing policy	Test Optional
Range SAT composite	1137–1368
Range SAT EBRW	571–690
Range SAT math	559–692
Range ACT composite	23–30
# submitting SAT scores	304
% submitting SAT scores	49
# submitting ACT scores	136
% submitting ACT scores	22
Average HS GPA	3.7
% frosh submitting high school GPA	67

DEADLINES

Early decision	
Deadline	11/1
Notification	12/15
Other ED deadline	12/1
Other ED notification	1/15
Regular	
Deadline	3/20
Notification	4/15
Nonfall registration?	Yes

APPLICANTS OFTEN PREFER

Calvin University; Cedarville University; Geneva College; Liberty University; Messiah University; Penn State University Park; Saint Vincent College; University of Pittsburgh—Pittsburgh Campus; Westminster College (PA)

APPLICANTS SOMETIMES PREFER

Allegheny College; Covenant College; Duquesne University; Gordon College; Hillsdale College; Houghton College; John Carroll University; Robert Morris University; Slippery Rock University of Pennsylvania; Wheaton College (IL); Youngstown State University

FINANCIAL FACTS

Financial Aid Rating	80
Annual tuition	$19,990
Room and board	$11,050
Books and supplies	$1,000
Average frosh need-based scholarship	$9,667
Average UG need-based scholarship	$9,247
% needy frosh rec. need-based scholarship or grant aid	100
% needy UG rec. need-based scholarship or grant aid	98
% needy frosh rec. non-need-based scholarship or grant aid	13
% needy UG rec. non-need-based scholarship or grant aid	10
% needy frosh rec. need-based self-help aid	41
% needy UG rec. need-based self-help aid	50
% frosh rec. any financial aid	80
% UG rec. any financial aid	79
% UG borrow to pay for school	51
Average cumulative indebtedness	$49,258
% frosh need fully met	13
% ugrads need fully met	11
Average % of frosh need met	59
Average % of ugrad need met	56

HAMILTON COLLEGE

198 College Hill Road, Clinton, NY 13323 • Admissions: 315-859-4011 • Fax: 315-859-4457

CAMPUS LIFE
Quality of Life Rating	86
Fire Safety Rating	92
Green Rating	60*
Type of school	Private
Affiliation	No Affiliation
Environment	Rural

STUDENTS
Total undergrad enrollment	2,071
% male/female/another gender	45/55/NR
% from out of state	72
% frosh from public high school	72
% frosh live on campus	100
% ugrads live on campus	100
# of fraternities (% join)	5 (20)
# of sororities (% join)	3 (13)
% African American	3
% Asian	9
% White	65
% Hispanic	10
% Native American	<1
% Pacific Islander	0
% Two or more races	5
% Race and/or ethnicity unknown	1
% international	7
# of countries represented	54

SURVEY SAYS . . .
Students always studying
Students are happy
Classroom facilities are great
Lab facilities are great
Great library
Great financial aid
Students aren't religious
Campus newspaper is popular
College radio is popular

ACADEMICS
Academic Rating	90
% students returning for sophomore year	95
% students graduating within 4 years	89
% students graduating within 6 years	92
Calendar	Semester
Student/faculty ratio	9:1
Profs interesting rating	92
Profs accessible rating	94

MOST POPULAR MAJORS
Economics; Biology; Government

STUDENTS SAY "..."

Academics

Hamilton College in upstate New York is steeped in the ideals of intellectual pursuit, allowing students to plot their course of study through an open curriculum under the guidance of multiple advisors. Critical thinking is one core skill developed, though, and that's accomplished through classroom projects and methods like "writing a mock grant proposal for biology" or "student-led discussions where we bring in a topic…and tie it in to the theories being taught in class." Finding topics that are personal draws is a crucial element that makes Hamilton tick, and students often "pursue interests that don't seem traditionally compatible" on the surface. However, this allows students "to enjoy [their] major while being able to supplement [it] with other classes" of interest. "The open curriculum gives you freedom and responsibility over what and how you want to learn," boasts one student. Others say "the ability to mix and match your interests to create your major is incredibly liberating." Hamilton is truly "a living and learning community where learning happens outside the classroom."

The academics at Hamilton would be nothing without professors who are "highly invested in their field and…bring that energy to their classrooms." They "make their expectations clear," "will challenge students to produce reasonable yet impassioned results," and "are open to new opinions and discussions, but obviously have a plan for discussion-based classes." Those discussions are still manageable due to Hamilton's small class sizes—which also means "it's almost impossible to slide under the radar." And there are even more positives to those small classes: They "[give] you such an advantage when taking difficult classes" because students can "get one-on-one interaction during office hours or even during class."

Campus Life

Hamilton's campus is separated into what students call "a Light Side and a Dark Side," and students tend to socially segregate to one or the other. "The Light Side is where the athletes and Greek life participants" can be found, and the Dark Side is where the "artsy, hipster, and alternative" students will hang out. There is "no animosity between lightsiders and darksiders, except for a few jokes here and there," and "most of the time students utilize this dynamic to explore new classes and friends." Opportunities for those new experiences abound here since the school features "an incredible array of student clubs and organizations"—there are "lots of activities happening all the time." On weekends, different student clubs will typically have an all-campus event—"a dance club might have a night where they teach people how to salsa, a Harry Potter club might host a Yule Ball"—and students definitely enjoy a party, although attendance is "pretty optional."

Many students "love the outdoors and that is a huge culture here." When the weather is favorable, students "often sit outside for meals or in Adirondack chairs scattered around campus doing work." Those looking for things to do off campus can rest easy: students (only those sophomore year and above are permitted to have vehicles on campus) who have cars can "go off campus to local restaurants, to see movies, or to go bowling or shopping," whereas those without "can use the jitney [shuttle service] which drives on a loop to all of these places."

Student Body

Hamilton has a "quintessential small, communal, and progressive liberal arts feel" that its students seek out and adore. The "weirdly nice" group here is "predominantly white and from the northeastern area" and has "a healthy sense of irreverence." The open curriculum tends to "attract a diverse set of interests and values among its student body," which makes this a "perpetually stimulating environment" where "everyone wants to contribute to campus." The social aspects of that contribution mean "everyone is looking to make friends" and is "very inclusive and welcoming." Life here is "very balanced" and students "generally know how to take a joke and make a joke." As one student sums it up: People here are "friendly and academic, but not cut-throat or competitive in any way."

Financial Aid: 800-859-4413 • E-Mail: admission@hamilton.edu • Website: www.hamilton.edu

THE PRINCETON REVIEW SAYS

Admissions

The school reports that its standardized testing policy for use in admission for Fall 2024 is Test Optional. It is unknown at this time if the 2024 testing policy will be permanent. The Princeton Review suggests that interested applicants consult with the school for the most up-to-date standardized testing policies. *Very important factors considered include:* rigor of secondary school record, class rank, academic GPA. *Important factors considered include:* application essay, recommendation(s), character/personal qualities. *Other factors considered include:* standardized test scores, interview, extracurricular activities, talent/ability, first generation, alumni/ae relation, geographical residence, state residency, volunteer work, work experience, level of applicant's interest. High school diploma is required and GED is accepted. *Academic units recommended:* 4 English, 4 math, 4 science, 3 foreign language, 3 social studies.

Financial Aid

Students should submit: CSS/Financial Aid Profile; FAFSA; State aid form. The Princeton Review suggests that all financial aid forms be submitted as soon as possible (see page 5 for a note on the FAFSA). *Need-based scholarships/grants offered:* College/university scholarship or grant aid from institutional funds; Federal Pell; Private scholarships; SEOG; State scholarships/grants. *Loan aid offered:* Direct PLUS loans; Direct Subsidized Loans; Direct Unsubsidized Loans; College/university loans from institutional funds. Admitted students will be notified of awards on or about 12/15 for ED1, 2/3 for ED2, 3/23 for regular decision. Federal Work-Study Program available. Institutional employment available.

The Inside Word

Similar to any prestigious liberal arts school, Hamilton takes a well-rounded, personal approach to admissions. Academic achievement and intellectual curiosity are assets, as is fit, so students are advised to demonstrate this with an interview where possible, especially if not taking the standardized tests. To further enhance one's candidacy, use the personalized application portal to submit optional materials.

THE SCHOOL SAYS "..."

From the Admissions Office

"There is no one Hamilton student, just as there is no one Hamilton experience, but the promise we make to our students is the same: at Hamilton, our open curriculum enables you to explore your passions, our welcoming student body from diverse backgrounds will expand your perspectives, and our value of writing and communicating well prepares you to express yourself no matter what path you choose after graduation. Our faculty will expect your full attention and participation academically, and you will embark on a life-long journey to "Know Thyself" (the college's motto).

"We are also committed to ensuring that a Hamilton education is available to all deserving students. We will review your application without considering your financial circumstances (which is known as 'need-blind' admission) and then, once you are admitted, we will meet your full demonstrated need for all four years. Hamilton is one of the few colleges that pledges to do both. Application fees are waived for those who are from the first generation in their family to attend college.

"Two new programs deserve special attention. ALEX (Advise, Learn, EXperience) is Hamilton's new coordinated network of on-campus academic centers, resources, and advisors that work together to support students and offer guidance in areas such as off-campus study, experiential learning, and finding balance in their lives. Digital Hamilton gives students the skills to understand, communicate, and work effectively in an increasingly digital world, no matter their chosen field."

SELECTIVITY

Admissions Rating	97
# of applicants	9,899
% of applicants accepted	12
% of acceptees attending	41
# of early decision applicants	743
% accepted early decision	32

FIRST-YEAR PROFILE

Testing policy	Test Optional
Range SAT composite	1440–1520
Range SAT EBRW	700–760
Range SAT math	720–780
Range ACT composite	33–34
# submitting SAT scores	175
% submitting SAT scores	37
# submitting ACT scores	88
% submitting ACT scores	18
% graduated top 10% of class	86
% graduated top 25% of class	98
% graduated top 50% of class	100

DEADLINES

Early decision	
Deadline	11/15
Notification	12/15
Other ED deadline	1/4
Other ED notification	2/15
Regular	
Deadline	1/4
Notification	4/1*
Nonfall registration?	Yes

APPLICANTS ALSO LOOK AT

Bates College; Colby College; Connecticut College; Trinity College

APPLICANTS OFTEN PREFER

Amherst College; Bowdoin College; Brown University; Dartmouth College; Middlebury College; Princeton University; Williams College

APPLICANTS SOMETIMES PREFER

Colby College; Colgate University; Tufts University; Vassar College; Wesleyan University

FINANCIAL FACTS

Financial Aid Rating	97
Annual tuition	$65,090
Room and board	$16,690
Required fees	$650
Books and supplies	$800
Average frosh need-based scholarship	$54,417
Average UG need-based scholarship	$50,645
% needy frosh rec. need-based scholarship or grant aid	99
% needy UG rec. need-based scholarship or grant aid	99
% needy frosh rec. non-need-based scholarship or grant aid	0
% needy UG rec. non-need-based scholarship or grant aid	0
% needy frosh rec. need-based self-help aid	84
% needy UG rec. need-based self-help aid	81
% frosh rec. any financial aid	51
% UG rec. any financial aid	51
% UG borrow to pay for school	45
Average cumulative indebtedness	$22,699
% frosh need fully met	99
% ugrads need fully met	99
Average % of frosh need met	100
Average % of ugrad need met	100

HAMPDEN-SYDNEY COLLEGE

1 College Road, Hampden-Sydney, VA 23943-0067 • Admissions: 434-223-6000 • Fax: 434-223-6346

STUDENTS SAY "..."

Academics

Virginia's Hampden-Sydney College is the tenth oldest higher education institution in the country, providing young men with a liberal arts education steeped in brotherhood and tradition. A 9:1 student-to-faculty ratio allows for small classes, one-on-one instruction, and scads of experiential learning opportunities such as cooperative learning and student research. The Rhetoric program is the cornerstone of a Hampden-Sydney education, instilling students with the "clear and concise oral and written communication skills" that stand out to employers and graduate schools; it follows that the school emphasizes that "freedom of expression is very important" and ensures that "students are able to ask difficult questions and discuss them honestly." Because of this, the college is "one of the best places to develop one's ability to think" and to "learn how a different lens of study changes how one digests and processes information." The "career center and alumni connections are...outstanding" and "having alumni invested in you and your future really makes a difference."

The student-professor connection at Hampden-Sydney is "the real deal," and students can tell that faculty "invest so much time and care into their students...it is clear that they became professors to teach." It helps that courses also keep things fresh with "whole class debates, demonstrations, and historical games." One student says: "One of my classes was based solely on acting out management positions and seeing the psychology play out in real time." While the core curriculum may feel rigid to a few, most come to appreciate the "wide variety of fields" required and even things like "mandatory attendance policies," as they lead to "more face time between professors and students, which translates to better learning." This also enables each class to have "academically stimulating conversations," also described as "in-depth and purposeful," and helps the professors to "keep the student's interest at the forefront of the lessons."

Campus Life

Classes are typically held back-to-back before lunch, after which students "either head to their dorm, the Rhetoric Center, the library, the Tiger Inn, or some other location to study and/or hang out with friends." Since the dining hall is the only food option on campus and there are only 800 undergraduates, "you are bound to run into someone you know, and it is not uncommon to have ten crowd around a tiny round table." The Union-Philanthropic Literary Society ("more or less a weekly debate society") is a popular club, and "on any given day people can be seen going for runs, playing various sports on the lawns around the college, fishing, and even just sleeping under trees between classes."

Though the campus itself is somewhat isolated and provides "limited options on what you can do... that doesn't mean that we don't have fun." There are "fraternities and parties that are available to anyone who wants to participate," and "intramurals are popular along with varsity athletics" (lacrosse and rugby especially). Since "everyone lives on campus, people have no trouble getting together," and "everyone tailgates football games, which is the highlight of the fall."

Student Body

The promise of brotherhood rings true at Hampden-Sydney, as "everyone watches out for you and there is always someone who is willing to help." This is "a very intellectually stimulating and unfiltered environment" where "anyone can truly say any belief without fear of censorship, provided that the beliefs are extended in good faith." This "group of the most thoughtful young men" all adhere to "an excellent Honor Code and Code of Conduct" and come "from all over the nation with all different backgrounds and upbringings." There are "a good amount of extroverts [and] athletes" in this "very intellectual student body," and enrollees strike "the perfect balance between scholars, athletes, servants of the community, and rowdy college-aged men." A "real great spirit of unity" runs among students, who "make connections with others constantly."

HAMPDEN-SYDNEY COLLEGE

Financial Aid: 434-223-6119 • E-Mail: hsapp@hsc.edu • Website: www.hsc.edu

THE PRINCETON REVIEW SAYS

Admissions

The school reports that its standardized testing policy for use in admission for Fall 2024 is Test Optional. The 2024 testing policy will be temporary. The Princeton Review suggests that interested applicants consult with the school for the most up-to-date standardized testing policies. *Very important factors considered include:* rigor of secondary school record, class rank, academic GPA, application essay, recommendation(s), character/personal qualities. *Important factors considered include:* interview, extracurricular activities. *Other factors considered include:* standardized test scores, talent/ability, first generation, alumni/ae relation, volunteer work, work experience, level of applicant's interest. High school diploma is required and GED is accepted. *Academic units required:* 4 English, 3 math, 2 science, 1 science lab, 2 foreign language, 1 social studies, 1 history, 3 academic electives. *Academic units recommended:* 4 math, 3 science, 3 foreign language.

Financial Aid

Students should submit: FAFSA; State aid form. The Princeton Review suggests that all financial aid forms be submitted as soon as possible (see page 5 for a note on the FAFSA). *Need-based scholarships/grants offered:* College/university scholarship or grant aid from institutional funds; Federal Pell; Private scholarships; SEOG; State scholarships/grants. *Loan aid offered:* Direct PLUS loans; Direct Subsidized Loans; Direct Unsubsidized Loans; College/university loans from institutional funds. Admitted students will be notified of awards on a rolling basis beginning 12/15. Federal Work-Study Program available. Institutional employment available.

The Inside Word

Heed the school's motto—"Forming good men and good citizens"—and make sure you can show yourself to be among that crowd. If you're interested in being a Tiger, consider scheduling a virtual or personal campus visit to help get the ball rolling, and if you're sure this is the school for you, make that commitment clear by applying early. The school is temporarily Test Optional (with a few exceptions for international and homeschooled students), but if you go that route, be sure you submit a powerful college essay and are well-prepared for a live interview.

THE SCHOOL SAYS "..."

From the Admissions Office

"Of the colleges you're considering, this one stands apart. Hampden-Sydney is a close-knit brotherhood of young men on a mission—not simply to get a great college education, but to have a coming-of-age experience that can lead them to more successful, more rewarding, and more joyful lives.

"As a result, our men do well in the world, in a wide range of career fields. In recent years, this small school in Virginia has produced alumni with far-reaching impact, including the director of an Oscar-winning film, a U.S. ambassador, executives with YETI and the Denver Broncos, a leading hedge fund manager and part-owner of the Pittsburgh Steelers, a James Beard Award-winning chef, and many leaders, public servants, and innovators across every industry and field you can imagine.

"How does this happen? Our Rhetoric Program teaches you the art of effective communication. Our expert faculty and experiential-focused liberal arts curriculum instill a wealth of knowledge and skills that make you more competitive for top jobs and graduate programs. And our renowned commitment to honor and character means that others know you're a man to be trusted.

"This is a college for young men searching for something different, an experience that stands apart. They are looking for a richer experience than the usual because they are interested in a richer life than the usual. Through a combination of better learning, stronger character, and a lasting brotherhood, Hampden-Sydney enables young men to emerge more confident and capable than they could have ever dreamed."

SELECTIVITY

Admissions Rating	92
# of applicants	2,911
% of applicants accepted	37
% of acceptees attending	21

FIRST-YEAR PROFILE

Testing policy	Test Optional
Range SAT composite	1090–1210
Range SAT EBRW	550–650
Range SAT math	530–610
Range ACT composite	22–25
# submitting SAT scores	38
% submitting SAT scores	17
# submitting ACT scores	20
% submitting ACT scores	9
Average HS GPA	3.5
% frosh submitting high school GPA	100
% graduated top 10% of class	15
% graduated top 25% of class	44
% graduated top 50% of class	71

DEADLINES

Early decision	
Deadline	11/1
Notification	12/1
Early action	
Deadline	12/15
Notification	1/15
Regular	
Deadline	2/1
Notification	4/15
Nonfall registration?	Yes

APPLICANTS SOMETIMES PREFER
James Madison University; Virginia Tech

APPLICANTS RARELY PREFER
Appalachian State University; Christopher Newport University; The University of the South; Virginia Commonwealth University; Virginia Military Institute

FINANCIAL FACTS

Financial Aid Rating	87
Annual tuition	$48,188
Room and board	$14,270
Required fees	$2,552
Books and supplies	$1,000
Average frosh need-based scholarship	$40,452
Average UG need-based scholarship	$37,355
% needy frosh rec. need-based scholarship or grant aid	99
% needy UG rec. need-based scholarship or grant aid	99
% needy frosh rec. non-need-based scholarship or grant aid	31
% needy UG rec. non-need-based scholarship or grant aid	25
% needy frosh rec. need-based self-help aid	63
% needy UG rec. need-based self-help aid	68
% frosh rec. any financial aid	99
% UG rec. any financial aid	98
% UG borrow to pay for school	66
Average cumulative indebtedness	$37,297
% frosh need fully met	35
% ugrads need fully met	33
Average % of frosh need met	90
Average % of ugrad need met	85

HAMPTON UNIVERSITY

Hampton University, Hampton, VA 23668 • Admissions: 757-727-5000 • Fax: 757-727-5095

STUDENTS SAY "..."

Academics

Virginia's Hampton University is one of the world's top historically Black universities, offering students a progressive education in business, the sciences, and the liberal arts. This "school of tradition, family values, and excellent education" is well-known for its focus on STEM programs and its five-year MBA program, and proudly forces its students to be at the top of their game. "My school exudes and strives for a standard of excellence in any and every aspect," says a junior political science major of the oft-quoted motto "The Standard of Excellence."

Professors "are at the top of their field," and the majority of the faculty members provide office hours "where students can have more one-to-one assistance" on lecture topics on which they may need more clarification. "My professors have not only been teachers in the classroom, but in my personal life as well," says a student. "I have been taught how to use the communication and research skills that I have obtained outside of the classroom." In addition, the university provides "a plethora of outside resources" such as paid internships, undergraduate research, and job shadowing opportunities.

The "historically rich" institution is "supportive of its legacy being upheld by all that pass through" while at the same time making individuals aware of their own legacies and "supporting them in their professional and academic endeavors through all available resources." Alumni connections abound in such an environment, and there are plenty of "excellent career planning tools," internships, and careers available to students "during and after their tenure at Hampton." There is "an immense amount of clout and history behind Hampton University's walls." Though the campus is undoubtedly "beautiful" (and sits right on the water), many agree that some of the facilities (especially the dorms) could use renovation. In recent years, three new dorms were constructed and historic halls were modernized.

Campus Life

Hampton does an excellent job of "blending past traditions with modern times," and Homecoming and Spring Fest are two important events for Hampton. On the "closed" campus, there is an "unlimited [number] of activities for students to participate in." During Organization Week, the student center has a two hour "12–2" period, during which "students are able to be social during the day," and many students love to "catch a Friday movie" night there as well, or hang out with friends in the new waterfront dining hall.

Hampton is small and "not a college town," and since "the University is really the only thing around," having a car is useful. Monday through Friday campus life is "mostly academic and extracurricular," with students mostly focused on class and the various clubs that they may be involved in. On the weekends students attend on- and off-campus parties, or go to "kickbacks," which are "a more low key version of a party." "Student life is lacking as far as dorm life," so many students "often interact with the students from NSU, ODU, and William & Mary." For the most part, "everyone on campus has the same mindset, a unanimous goal, and that's to graduate and strive for a successful life."

Student Body

The typical student here is an African-American "go-getter" who is "trying to make something of themselves." He or she is "poised, considerate, and self-sufficient" and "knows how to act and dress in the appropriate setting and time." "Hampton students have a certain attitude about themselves; you can always tell a Hamptonian. Once you have been Hamptonized, there is no going back," explains one student cryptically. This "driven," "hardworking" crowd gets along fairly well, and there are no issues of isolation "unless one chooses that lifestyle." Students are almost without fail "outgoing and involved in many organizations within the school and the community."

Financial Aid: 757-727-5332 • E-Mail: admit@hamptonu.edu • Website: www.hamptonu.edu

THE PRINCETON REVIEW SAYS

Admissions

The school reports that its standardized testing policy for use in admission for Fall 2024 is Test Optional. It is unknown at this time if the 2024 testing policy will be permanent. The Princeton Review suggests that interested applicants consult with the school for the most up-to-date standardized testing policies. *Very important factors considered include:* rigor of secondary school record, academic GPA, application essay, character/personal qualities. *Important factors considered include:* class rank, recommendation(s). *Other factors considered include:* standardized test scores, interview, extracurricular activities, talent/ability, volunteer work, work experience, level of applicant's interest. High school diploma is required and GED is accepted. *Academic units required:* 4 English, 3 math, 2 science, 2 science labs, 2 social studies, 2 history, 6 academic electives. *Academic units recommended:* 2 foreign language.

Financial Aid

Students should submit: FAFSA. Priority filing deadline is 2/15. The Princeton Review suggests that all financial aid forms be submitted as soon as possible (see page 5 for a note on the FAFSA). *Need-based scholarships/grants offered:* College/university scholarship or grant aid from institutional funds; Federal Nursing Scholarships; Federal Pell; Private scholarships; SEOG; State scholarships/grants. *Loan aid offered:* Direct PLUS loans; Direct Subsidized Loans; Direct Unsubsidized Loans. Admitted students will be notified of awards on a rolling basis beginning 2/16. Federal Work-Study Program available.

The Inside Word

Hampton University allows for early action admissions, meaning that students can receive an early decision without having to commit to attending the school. Around one-quarter of HU's applicant pool pursues this option. You would be wise to follow suit; the school is bound to be more lenient early in the process than later, when it has already admitted many qualified students.

THE SCHOOL SAYS "..."

From the Admissions Office

"Hampton attempts to provide the environment and structures most conducive to the intellectual, emotional, and aesthetic enlargement of the lives of its members. The university gives priority to effective teaching and scholarly research while placing the student at the center of its planning. Hampton will ask you to look inwardly at your own history and culture and examine your relationship to the aspirations and development of the world."

SELECTIVITY

Admissions Rating	83
# of applicants	13,192
% of applicants accepted	80
% of acceptees attending	6

FIRST-YEAR PROFILE

Testing policy	Test Optional
Range SAT composite	990–1170
Range SAT EBRW	500–600
Range SAT math	490–580
Range ACT composite	19–26
# submitting SAT scores	206
% submitting SAT scores	33
# submitting ACT scores	87
% submitting ACT scores	14
Average HS GPA	3.3
% frosh submitting high school GPA	100
% graduated top 10% of class	9
% graduated top 25% of class	19
% graduated top 50% of class	63

DEADLINES

Early action	
Deadline	11/15
Notification	12/31
Regular	
Priority	3/1
Deadline	3/1
Nonfall registration?	Yes

APPLICANTS OFTEN PREFER

Howard University; North Carolina A&T State University; Radford University; University of Richmond

APPLICANTS SOMETIMES PREFER

Old Dominion University; Virginia Commonwealth University; Virginia State University

FINANCIAL FACTS

Financial Aid Rating	82
Annual tuition	$26,198
Room and board	$12,986
Required fees	$3,114
Books and supplies	$1,100
% frosh rec. any financial aid	43
% UG rec. any financial aid	44

HANOVER COLLEGE

517 Ball Drive, Hanover, IN 47243 • Admissions: 812-866-7021 • Fax: 812-866-7098

CAMPUS LIFE

Quality of Life Rating	87
Fire Safety Rating	94
Green Rating	80
Type of school	Private
Affiliation	Presbyterian
Environment	Rural

STUDENTS

Total undergrad enrollment	949
% male/female/another gender	49/50/1
% from out of state	36
% frosh from public high school	85
% frosh live on campus	95
% ugrads live on campus	93
# of fraternities (% join)	4 (42)
# of sororities (% join)	4 (37)
% African American	5
% Asian	1
% White	77
% Hispanic	3
% Native American	1
% Pacific Islander	0
% Two or more races	6
% Race and/or ethnicity unknown	3
% international	5
# of countries represented	17

SURVEY SAYS . . .

Lab facilities are great
Class discussions encouraged
Easy to get around campus
Frats and sororities are popular

ACADEMICS

Academic Rating	86
% students returning for sophomore year	78
% students graduating within 4 years	67
% students graduating within 6 years	69
Calendar	4-4-1
Student/faculty ratio	11:1
Profs interesting rating	91
Profs accessible rating	96
Most classes have 10–19 students.	

MOST POPULAR MAJORS

Economics, General; Psychology, General; Speech Communication and Rhetoric

STUDENTS SAY ". . ."

Academics

Hanover College is a school that is brimming with opportunity. And with its "beautiful" campus and emphasis on "gaining real-life skills and making lifelong connections," it's easy to understand why students are drawn here. The vast majority of classes at Hanover are "small and discussion based," and many also place "a heavy focus on writing." While the academics can be challenging, students eagerly report that "many of the harder classes have tutors for that specific class." Additionally, the Learning Center is always "willing to go over things with you, edit papers and more." Importantly, it's evident that Hanover professors "love what they teach…and that excitement often carries over to the student." Indeed, they excel at "bring[ing] the material to life…and easily keep the attention of the class." Just as essential, Hanover professors are also known to be "caring and down to earth" and "devoted to their students." And, as this ecstatic art history major concludes, "Most of the professors on staff are part of the best people you will ever meet in life."

Campus Life

While some undergrads grumble that "life at Hanover is pretty slow," others steadfastly argue that "there are SO many things [with which] to be involved." For starters, students can participate in "over sixty organizations" including "Adopt A Grandparent, Circle K Community Service, Best Buddies, and so many more." Additionally, individuals who enjoy the arts will be delighted to hear that both "the theater department and the improv group…never disappoint [and] the choir and band concerts [are] always very enjoyable [as well]." For those that are more athletically inclined, we're told that "when it's warm out, students go hiking, play wiffleball, or…sand volleyball." Many undergrads also gravitate to the Student Activities Center which offers "game tables, [a] theater room, televisions [and] study spots." And, in the evenings, "chances are some club always has something planned—be it a movie showing [or] a poetry night!" Hanover also has a relatively robust party scene. Indeed, undergrads inform us that "Greek life is big on…campus." And while there "are only four frats…they are a [major] part of [the] social life." Finally, when students are looking for a break from the campus routine, they often head to nearby Madison or Louisville, which is a mere "forty-minute drive [away]" and the closest major city.

Student Body

Hanover is home to a "small, pretty laid back and surprising[ly] interesting community." Indeed, while undergrads here admit that ethnic diversity "is still an issue," they happily point out that you'll find a wide array of personality types. Of course, the "majority of the students are committed to their academics and [strive to find] a balance between work and play." Many Hanover undergrads "are also extremely passionate about the things in which they invest their time, whatever that may be, and encourage that passion in others." It's important to note that the college's small size does make it "[easy] for cliques…to form." However, we're assured "it is also quite easy to break into the cliques if you are really interested in hanging out with certain groups of people." This social ease can be attributed to the fact that Hanover features some of the "friendliest individuals that Indiana has to offer." In fact, you are virtually guaranteed "to see a smiling face or to get a hello anywhere you walk on campus, whether it be from a fellow student or a faculty member." As one satisfied economics major sums up, "We are all about making everyone feel welcome and making Hanover College home."

HANOVER COLLEGE

Financial Aid: 812-866-7029 • E-Mail: admission@hanover.edu • Website: www.hanover.edu

THE PRINCETON REVIEW SAYS

Admissions

The school reports that its standardized testing policy for use in admission for Fall 2024 is Test Optional. It is unknown at this time if the 2024 testing policy will be permanent. The Princeton Review suggests that interested applicants consult with the school for the most up-to-date standardized testing policies. *Very important factors considered include:* rigor of secondary school record, class rank, academic GPA. *Important factors considered include:* standardized test scores, talent/ability, character/personal qualities. *Other factors considered include:* application essay, recommendation(s), interview, extracurricular activities, first generation, alumni/ae relation, geographical residence, state residency, racial/ethnic status, volunteer work, work experience, level of applicant's interest. High school diploma is required and GED is not accepted. *Academic units required:* 4 English, 3 math, 3 science, 2 science labs, 2 foreign language, 2 social studies, 2 history, 2 academic electives. *Academic units recommended:* 4 English, 4 math, 4 science, 3 science labs, 4 foreign language, 3 social studies, 3 history, 1 visual/performing arts, 3 academic electives.

Financial Aid

Students should submit: FAFSA. The Princeton Review suggests that all financial aid forms be submitted as soon as possible (see page 5 for a note on the FAFSA). *Need-based scholarships/grants offered:* College/university scholarship or grant aid from institutional funds; Federal Pell; Private scholarships; SEOG; State scholarships/grants. *Loan aid offered:* Direct PLUS loans; Direct Subsidized Loans; Direct Unsubsidized Loans; College/university loans from institutional funds. Admitted students will be notified of awards on a rolling basis. Federal Work-Study Program available. Institutional employment available.

The Inside Word

Similar to many liberal arts college, Hanover takes a holistic approach to the admissions process. Certainly, the school closely evaluates your high school curriculum as well as your GPA. Standardized test scores are also considered, though they hold less weight than your transcript. Beyond academics, admissions officers look at your extracurricular participation and community activities. Letters of recommendation and a writing sample will also be important. Further, expect Hanover to assess the strength of your high school. And, lastly, ethnic, cultural and geographic diversity will likely come into play.

THE SCHOOL SAYS "..."

From the Admissions Office

"Since our founding in 1827, we have been committed to providing students with a personal, rigorous, and well-rounded liberal arts education. Part of the college search process is finding that school that proves to be a good match. For those who see the value in an education that demands engagement and who see college as a time for exploration and involvement, they will find that Hanover is all they could hope for and more.

"The admission process serves as an introduction to the personal education that students receive at Hanover College. Every application is considered individually with emphasis being placed on a student's high school curriculum and the student's academic performance in that curriculum. While we realize that not every high school has the same course offerings, we expect students to have selected a college preparatory curriculum as challenging as possible within his or her particular high school or academic setting.

"Hanover College optionally accepts both the SAT and ACT. Students taking the ACT are required to take the optional writing section. For students who have taken one or both of the tests multiple times, we will use the highest sub scores when calculating a student's score on either test for admission and scholarship purposes."

SELECTIVITY

Admissions Rating	84
# of applicants	3,187
% of applicants accepted	74
% of acceptees attending	12
# of early decision applicants	35
% accepted early decision	89

FIRST-YEAR PROFILE

Testing policy	Test Optional
Range SAT composite	1100–1300
Range SAT EBRW	550–650
Range SAT math	540–620
Range ACT composite	24–29
# submitting SAT scores	60
% submitting SAT scores	21
# submitting ACT scores	39
% submitting ACT scores	14
Average HS GPA	3.8
% frosh submitting high school GPA	95
% graduated top 10% of class	23
% graduated top 25% of class	50

DEADLINES

Early decision	
Deadline	11/1
Notification	11/15
Other ED deadline	12/1
Other ED notification	Rolling
Early action	
Deadline	11/1 & 12/1
Notification	Rolling
Regular	
Priority	3/1
Deadline	Last week of August
Notification	Rolling
Nonfall registration?	Yes

FINANCIAL FACTS

Financial Aid Rating	86
Annual tuition	$42,003
Room and board	$13,440
Required fees	$891
Books and supplies	$1,200
Average frosh need-based scholarship	$30,349
Average UG need-based scholarship	$31,704
% needy frosh rec. need-based scholarship or grant aid	100
% needy UG rec. need-based scholarship or grant aid	100
% needy frosh rec. non-need-based scholarship or grant aid	23
% needy UG rec. non-need-based scholarship or grant aid	29
% needy frosh rec. need-based self-help aid	76
% needy UG rec. need-based self-help aid	72
% frosh rec. any financial aid	100
% UG rec. any financial aid	100
% UG borrow to pay for school	79
Average cumulative indebtedness	$23,714
% frosh need fully met	28
% ugrads need fully met	36
Average % of frosh need met	82
Average % of ugrad need met	87

HARVARD COLLEGE

86 Brattle Street, Cambridge, MA 02138 • Admissions: 617-495-1000 • Fax: 617-495-8821

CAMPUS LIFE

Quality of Life Rating	72
Fire Safety Rating	60*
Green Rating	60*
Type of school	Private
Affiliation	No Affiliation
Environment	City

STUDENTS

Total undergrad enrollment	7,178
% male/female/another gender	48/52/0
% from out of state	85
% frosh from public high school	57
% frosh live on campus	100
% ugrads live on campus	97
# of fraternities	0
# of sororities	0
% African American	9
% Asian	23
% White	34
% Hispanic	12
% Native American	<1
% Pacific Islander	<1
% Two or more races	8
% Race and/or ethnicity unknown	1
% international	13
# of countries represented	114

SURVEY SAYS . . .

Great financial aid
Campus newspaper is popular
Students politically aware
Students love Cambridge, MA

ACADEMICS

Academic Rating	83
% students returning for sophomore year	98
% students graduating within 4 years	87
% students graduating within 6 years	98
Calendar	Semester
Student/faculty ratio	7:1
Profs interesting rating	78
Profs accessible rating	86

Most classes have fewer than 10 students.
Most lab/discussion sessions have
  fewer than 10 students.

MOST POPULAR MAJORS

Social Sciences, General; Economics, General;
Computer Science

STUDENTS SAY "..."

Academics

Harvard College students describe the school as a "dynamic universe" and an "amazing irresistible hell" that pushes them to the extremes of their intellect and ability. Unsurprisingly, the legendarily "very difficult" school attracts some of the country's most promising youth, who rise to the occasion in almost every aspect of their life on campus, not just the classroom. Harvard's recent financial aid enhancements have increased the number of applications by a landslide, but even after getting past the admissions hurdle, "people find ways to make everything (especially clubs and even partying) competitive." Happily, this streak is more of a "latent competition," as there are more than enough opportunity and resources to go around. "It is impossible to 'get the most out of Harvard' because Harvard offers so much," says one student. Much like the students, the professors at this "beautiful, fun, historic, and academically alive place" in Cambridge, Massachusetts, are among "the brightest minds in the world," and "the level of achievement is unbelievable." Some of the larger introductory classes are taught by teaching fellows (TFs), meaning "you do have to go to office hours to get to know your big lecture class professors on a personal level," but once your figurative underclass dues are paid, the access to "incredible" and "every so often, fantastic" professors is perfectly within reach. Top it off with Grade-A internship and employment opportunities, a good old alumni network, and a crimson pedigree for your résumé, and you may just end up agreeing with the Harvard student who refers to his experience as "rewarding beyond anything else I've ever done." Though the administration can be "waaaaay out of touch with students" and "reticent to change," it at least "does a good job of watching over its freshmen through extensive advising programs," and students all have faith that their best interests are being kept in mind.

Campus Life

Cambridge and Boston are nothing if not college towns, and students never lack for options if they just want to "go see a play, a concert, hit up a party, go to the movies, or dine out." Students quickly learn when to hit the books and when to hit the streets, so "studying becomes routine." "There is a vibrant social atmosphere on campus and between students and the local community." As one student puts it, "Boredom does not exist here. There are endless opportunities and endless passionate people to do them with." "Basically, if you want to do it, Harvard either has it or has the money to give to you so you can start it." "Partying in a more traditional setting is available at Harvard, but is not a prevalent aspect of the school's social life. While there is a pub on campus that provides an excellent venue to hang out and play a game of pool or have a reasonably priced drink," and parties happen on weekends at Harvard's finals clubs, there's no real pressure for students to partake if they're not interested.

Student Body

Much as you might expect, ambition and achievement are the ties that bind at Harvard, and "Everyone is great for one reason or another," says a student. Almost every student can be summed up with the same statement: "Works really hard. Doesn't sleep. Involved in a million extracurriculars." Diversity is found in all aspects of life, from ethnicities to religion to ideology, and "there is a lot of tolerance and acceptance at Harvard for individuals of all races, religions, socioeconomic backgrounds, life styles, etc."

HARVARD COLLEGE

Financial Aid: 617-495-1581 • E-Mail: college@fas.harvard.edu • Website: www.college.harvard.edu

THE PRINCETON REVIEW SAYS

Admissions

The school reports that its standardized testing policy for use in admission for Fall 2024 is Test Optional. It is unknown at this time if the 2024 testing policy will be permanent. The Princeton Review suggests that interested applicants consult with the school for the most up-to-date standardized testing policies. *Other factors considered include:* rigor of secondary school record, academic GPA, standardized test scores, application essay, recommendation(s), interview, extracurricular activities, talent/ability, character/personal qualities, first generation, alumni/ae relation, geographical residence, racial/ethnic status, volunteer work, work experience. High school diploma or equivalent is not required. *Academic units recommended:* 4 English, 4 math, 4 science, 4 foreign language, 3 social studies, 2 history.

Financial Aid

Students should submit: Business/Farm Supplement; CSS/Financial Aid Profile; FAFSA; Noncustodial Profile. Priority filing deadline is 2/1. The Princeton Review suggests that all financial aid forms be submitted as soon as possible (see page 5 for a note on the FAFSA). *Need-based scholarships/grants offered:* College/university scholarship or grant aid from institutional funds; Federal Pell; Private scholarships; SEOG; State scholarships/grants. *Loan aid offered:* Direct PLUS loans; Direct Subsidized Loans; Direct Unsubsidized Loans; College/university loans from institutional funds; State Loans. Admitted students will be notified of awards on or about 4/1. Federal Work-Study Program available. Institutional employment available.

The Inside Word

It just doesn't get any tougher than this. Candidates to Harvard face dual obstacles—an awe-inspiring applicant pool and, as a result, admissions standards that defy explanation in quantifiable terms. Harvard denies admission to the vast majority, and virtually all of them are top students. (Also, as a result of switching to the Common App, it has never been easier to apply to Harvard, which keeps application numbers high.) It all boils down to splitting hairs, which is quite hard to explain and even harder for candidates to understand: for instance, it has been suggested that applicants from lesser-populated states like South Dakota may have an advantage, but Harvard will neither confirm nor deny their policies. For the classes of '27, '28, '29, and '30, Harvard is Test Optional, and says that those who do not submit will not be at a disadvantage. If you feel strongly that your scores will help to better present you as a whole person, you have nothing to lose by submitting them.

THE SCHOOL SAYS "..."

From the Admissions Office

"The admissions committee looks for energy, ambition, and the capacity to make the most of opportunities. Academic ability and preparation are important, and so is intellectual curiosity—but many of the strongest applicants have significant, non-academic interests and accomplishments, as well. There is no formula for admission, and applicants are considered carefully, with attention to future promise."

SELECTIVITY

Admissions Rating	99
# of applicants	61,221
% of applicants accepted	3
% of acceptees attending	83

FIRST-YEAR PROFILE

Testing policy	Test Optional
Range SAT EBRW	730–780
Range SAT math	760–800
Range ACT composite	34–36
# submitting SAT scores	903
% submitting SAT scores	55
# submitting ACT scores	466
% submitting ACT scores	28
Average HS GPA	4.2
% frosh submitting high school GPA	100
% graduated top 10% of class	92
% graduated top 25% of class	98
% graduated top 50% of class	100

DEADLINES

Early action	
Deadline	11/1
Notification	12/16
Regular	
Deadline	1/1
Notification	4/1
Nonfall registration?	No

APPLICANTS ALSO LOOK AT

Duke University; Massachusetts Institute of Technology; Princeton University; Stanford University; Yale University

FINANCIAL FACTS

Financial Aid Rating	98
Annual tuition	$54,269
Room and board	$20,374
Required fees	$4,807
Books and supplies	$1,000
Average frosh need-based scholarship	$65,595
Average UG need-based scholarship	$61,864
% needy frosh rec. need-based scholarship or grant aid	100
% needy UG rec. need-based scholarship or grant aid	100
% needy frosh rec. non-need-based scholarship or grant aid	0
% needy UG rec. non-need-based scholarship or grant aid	0
% needy frosh rec. need-based self-help aid	73
% needy UG rec. need-based self-help aid	84
% frosh rec. any financial aid	71
% UG rec. any financial aid	64
% UG borrow to pay for school	15
Average cumulative indebtedness	$13,683
% frosh need fully met	100
% ugrads need fully met	100
Average % of frosh need met	100
Average % of ugrad need met	100

HARVEY MUDD COLLEGE

320 E Foothill Boulevard, Claremont, CA 91711 • Admissions: 909-621-8000 • Fax: 909-607-7046

STUDENTS SAY ". . ."

Academics
Harvey Mudd College, according to its mission statement, "seeks to educate engineers, scientists, and mathematicians well versed in all of these areas and in the humanities, social sciences, and the arts so that they may assume leadership in their fields with a clear understanding of the impact of their work on society." As a result, its students "really understand their impact on both their global and campus communities." Breadth is also instilled in a Harvey Mudd education through its membership in the "Claremont Colleges," a seven-member consortium that includes Pomona and Claremont McKenna, and because of this, its "students are more well-rounded than most in the sciences and get to pursue their passions outside of the STEM fields." Students also praise the "broad core curriculum at Harvey Mudd," which "produces scientists who can rise to meet interdisciplinary challenges within the sciences" and facilitates "great post-grad opportunities." Classes are hard but rewarding: "The brutal work fosters an extremely collaborative environment where people focus not on the grade they get but the learning behind it." "Academics are perfect. Could not ask for more rigorous and interesting learning." HMC undergrads demonstrate a "commitment to" Harvey Mudd's "honor code," which requires students "to conduct themselves with honesty and integrity both personally and academically and to respect the rights of others." This ethic, as well as support systems like "the proctor [and] mentor systems in the dorms," which positions RAs to act as resources to students "without all of the policing," creates a "tight community" on campus. "There is no segregation based on class year, major, race, academic ability, dorm or anything. Everyone is respectful, smart, aware, supportive, and unique." Professors are almost universally reported to be "incredible," "truly dedicated to undergraduate teaching," and "always willing to spend hours outside of class answering questions." HMC's small classes and lack of graduate programs focuses faculty attention on undergrads: "My only 'large' class as a freshman is an intro to CS Class of 100 students and by the fifth day the professor knew all 100 names." Overall, "the work at HMC is very challenging, but I have had the best support system; from the Academic Excellence tutors providing help for all required core classes to the professors who are readily accessible and enthusiastic helpers."

Campus Life
Students agree that Harvey Mudd enables tremendous growth, which isn't always easy: "You feel really smart before Mudd, you feel really stupid during Mudd, and after Mudd you feel like a genius." Socially speaking, "conversations at dinner are probably really weird and nerdy from an outsiders point of view," and "people care about...lots of other serious issues along with more frivolous ones." Many appreciate that "campus-wide parties are funded by the college, ensuring that they are safe and well-funded," and these include "a foam party, where a dorm courtyard is filled with soap foam," and "a holiday party where (literally) tons of snow are trucked in." There's plenty to do on campus, but "Claremont Village is within a 20-minute walk," and "it takes about an hour and a half to get to LA's Union Station from Mudd, and downtown LA and Little Tokyo are both accessible from there." "A lot of students do drink, but there is honestly never any pressure. I don't drink at all and I have never felt any pressure to do anything I wasn't comfortable with." One student sums up the HMC life this way: "Work really, really hard, play hard."

Student Body
"Harvey Mudd has a strong community of talented students that build each other up." Many HMC students offer similar praise for the college's "small, tight knit community in which everyone looks after one another." The "typical student is friendly, outgoing, and passionate about their (sometimes slightly weird) interests," and "it's really easy to form close friendships, whether in your dorm or through study groups." "Everyone at the school is extremely enthusiastic about learning," and the college's culture promotes lots of intellectual bonding amongst "nerds, but the kind that can hold conversations." "Most people are top of their class from high school, so freshman year, everyone is a bit cocky (but Mudd humbles you really quickly)." Undergrads value that "the honor code works very well, and students are pretty much always eager to help one another."

HARVEY MUDD COLLEGE

Financial Aid: 909-621-8055 • E-Mail: admission@hmc.edu • Website: www.hmc.edu/

THE PRINCETON REVIEW SAYS

Admissions

The school reports that its standardized testing policy for use in admission for Fall 2024 is Test Optional. The 2024 testing policy will be temporary. The Princeton Review suggests that interested applicants consult with the school for the most up-to-date standardized testing policies. *Very important factors considered include:* rigor of secondary school record, academic GPA, application essay, recommendation(s). *Important factors considered include:* extracurricular activities, character/personal qualities. *Other factors considered include:* class rank, standardized test scores, interview, talent/ability, first generation, alumni/ae relation, geographical residence, state residency, racial/ethnic status, volunteer work, work experience. High school diploma or equivalent is not required. *Academic units recommended:* 4 English, 4 math, 4 science, 2 science labs, 2 foreign language, 2 social studies, 2 history, 2 academic electives.

Financial Aid

Students should submit: Business/Farm Supplement; CSS/Financial Aid Profile; FAFSA; Noncustodial Profile; State aid form. The Princeton Review suggests that all financial aid forms be submitted as soon as possible (see page 5 for a note on the FAFSA). *Need-based scholarships/grants offered:* College/university scholarship or grant aid from institutional funds; Federal Pell; Private scholarships; SEOG; State scholarships/grants. *Loan aid offered:* Direct PLUS loans; Direct Subsidized Loans; Direct Unsubsidized Loans; College/university loans from institutional funds. Admitted students will be notified of awards on or about 4/1. Federal Work-Study Program available. Institutional employment available.

The Inside Word

Harvey Mudd is as rigorous in admissions as it is in its education, so serious applicants are well advised to demonstrate big chops in their high school STEM course load, without sacrificing attention to humanities and extracurriculars. Applicants should carefully review HMC's eligibility requirements for high school transcripts, as well as its standardized testing requirements, and remember that the college is competitive enough that admission is no guarantee even for highly qualified applicants.

THE SCHOOL SAYS "..."

From the Admissions Office

"HMC is a wonderfully unusual combination of a liberal arts college and research institute. Our students love math and science, want to live and learn deeply in an intimate climate of cooperation and trust, thrive on innovation and discovery, and enjoy rigorous coursework in arts, humanities, and social sciences in addition to a technical curriculum. At least a year of research or our innovative Clinic Program is required (or guaranteed, if you prefer). The resources at HMC are astounding, and all are accessible to undergraduates: labs, shops, work areas, and most importantly, faculty. You'll find the professors and student body stimulating and supportive—they'll challenge you inside and outside the classroom, and share your love of learning and collaboration. They'll also share your love of fun and sense of humor (math jokes and all). In addition, we benefit from the unique consortium that is the Claremont Colleges.

"In the final analysis, our graduates are prepared well for whatever their next steps will be. They can see relationships between disparate fields of study and investigation, are resourceful, know how to work in teams, and are able to articulate their ideas to both lay-people and specialized experts. A wide range of companies are eager to hire our seniors, and HMC sends the highest proportion of graduates to PhD programs of any undergraduate college in the country."

SELECTIVITY

Admissions Rating	98
# of applicants	4,737
% of applicants accepted	10
% of acceptees attending	48
# offered a place on the wait list	648
% accepting a place on wait list	67
% admitted from wait list	0
# of early decision applicants	485
% accepted early decision	21

FIRST-YEAR PROFILE

Testing policy	Test Optional
Range SAT composite	1470–1540
Range SAT EBRW	710–760
Range SAT math	770–800
Range ACT composite	34–36
# submitting SAT scores	89
% submitting SAT scores	40
# submitting ACT scores	45
% submitting ACT scores	20

DEADLINES

Early decision	
Deadline	11/15
Notification	12/15
Other ED deadline	1/5
Other ED notification	2/15
Regular	
Deadline	1/5
Notification	4/1
Nonfall registration?	No

APPLICANTS OFTEN PREFER
California Institute of Technology; Massachusetts Institute of Technology; Stanford University

APPLICANTS SOMETIMES PREFER
Brown University; Carnegie Mellon University; University of California—Berkeley

APPLICANTS RARELY PREFER
Rose-Hulman Institute of Technology; The University of Chicago; University of California—Los Angeles

FINANCIAL FACTS

Financial Aid Rating	97
Annual tuition	$60,402
Room and board	$19,333
Required fees	$301
Books and supplies	$800
Average frosh need-based scholarship	$36,829
Average UG need-based scholarship	$37,502
% needy frosh rec. need-based scholarship or grant aid	98
% needy UG rec. need-based scholarship or grant aid	97
% needy frosh rec. non-need-based scholarship or grant aid	48
% needy UG rec. non-need-based scholarship or grant aid	48
% needy frosh rec. need-based self-help aid	53
% needy UG rec. need-based self-help aid	59
% frosh rec. any financial aid	74
% UG rec. any financial aid	71
% UG borrow to pay for school	42
Average cumulative indebtedness	$27,423
% frosh need fully met	100
% ugrads need fully met	100
Average % of frosh need met	100
Average % of ugrad need met	100

HAVERFORD COLLEGE

370 Lancaster Avenue, Haverford, PA 19041 • Admissions: 610-896-1000 • Fax: 610-896-1338

CAMPUS LIFE
Quality of Life Rating	84
Fire Safety Rating	88
Green Rating	96
Type of school	Private
Affiliation	No Affiliation
Environment	Town

STUDENTS
Total undergrad enrollment	1,417
% male/female/another gender	46/54/0
% from out of state	86
% frosh from public high school	60
% frosh live on campus	100
% ugrads live on campus	96
# of fraternities	0
# of sororities	0
% African American	5
% Asian	12
% White	49
% Hispanic	13
% Native American	0
% Pacific Islander	0
% Two or more races	9
% Race and/or ethnicity unknown	1
% international	11

SURVEY SAYS . . .
Lots of liberal students
Students always studying
Lab facilities are great
Great library
Internships are widely available
Class discussions encouraged
Great financial aid
No one cheats
Diverse student types interact on campus
Recreation facilities are great
Active minority support groups

ACADEMICS
Academic Rating	98
% students returning for sophomore year	96
% students graduating within 4 years	83
% students graduating within 6 years	91
Calendar	Semester
Student/faculty ratio	9:1
Profs interesting rating	93
Profs accessible rating	96
Most classes have 10–19 students.	

MOST POPULAR MAJORS
Computer and Information Sciences, General;
Biology/Biological Sciences, General; Psychology,
General

STUDENTS SAY "..."

Academics
Founded in 1833, Haverford College in Pennsylvania is "small, but exceptionally vibrant and engaging," offering a "solid academic experience" under one of the country's oldest honor codes. Though founded by Quakers, the school is nonsectarian, but the community aspect of its founders remains, creating what one student calls "a challenging, interesting environment with the best people I know." The real love affair is with Haverford's "awesome, invested" professors, who "lead a group of idealistic students to point—but never force—us into a better way of thinking." They want to put in the time to get to know you, and the small size of the school "allows for plenty of opportunities for collaborating with faculty and staff and building a relationship." "You are more than just a face in a classroom of many; you are a unique person that has something to offer," says a student. "My 'big intro lecture course' has 41 students," says another. "My professor still knows me by name, and we have long conversations when we pass on Founder's Green." The school's learning environment stresses "engaging in hard and honest conversations with your peers," and "students have a lot of power" through their roles in the administration of the college. "I love the amount of independence and autonomy [the school] gives to its students," says a student. Because of the kind of student this attracts, "we wind up with a really conscientious student body invested in the school." The resources available to students here are incredible, as well. You can get "credit for research" (there is plenty of research here in every department), and if you want to go off campus for research, "you can get funding for that as well."

Campus Life
The culture of "trust, concern, and respect" created by the honor code carries over into the rest of this "awesome, at times idiosyncratic, place where community thrives and cliques are very loose if existent at all." "The honor code unifies everyone." "Being able to take an exam in your own room, sitting relaxed on your bed because your professor trusts you not to look at your books is one of the luxuries of being here," says a student. People study hard here, but they take a break over the weekend at a party or two "before cracking the books again. Athletics are also "really important" for much of the student body—most here are athletic, even if it's not at a varsity level—and some of the male sports teams "function like fraternities" (which do not exist at HC). Because it's a small place, "sometimes it feels like everyone knows your business," but everyone is so insanely nice that "the social scene is great." Students govern themselves and the happenings at the school through the "Plenaries" that happen twice a year, when the majority of the student body must be present. New York and Philadelphia are both easily accessible by train, and "Suburban Square (the local outdoor shopping center) is a great place to hang out, get coffee, or even go shopping."

Student Body
Everyone is "passionate," "people are always up for intellectual discussion," and "everyone works very hard." Students here were all motivated enough to get in and "want to succeed for themselves and not to appease others." Students describe other students as having "hearts of gold and giant brains that they put to use to change the world for the better." "It's a small school full of nice kids—not naive (well, sometimes naive), just genuinely compassionate and interested in other people, whether or not that's 'cool,'" says a student. Though all are bound by "intellectual passion and interests outside of academics," diversity otherwise on campus "lacks a little." Still, "the great thing about Haverford is that, although we have a variety of students from all different social circles, everyone is a touch awkward." This is a fact that the "nerdy and ridiculously friendly" students embrace. "I feel like I could potentially become friends with anyone on campus," says a student.

HAVERFORD COLLEGE

Financial Aid: 610-896-1350 • Website: www.haverford.edu

THE PRINCETON REVIEW SAYS

Admissions

The school reports that its standardized testing policy for use in admission for Fall 2024 is Test Optional. The 2024 testing policy will be temporary. The Princeton Review suggests that interested applicants consult with the school for the most up-to-date standardized testing policies. *Very important factors considered include:* rigor of secondary school record, academic GPA, application essay, recommendation(s), extracurricular activities, character/personal qualities. *Important factors considered include:* class rank, standardized test scores, talent/ability, volunteer work, work experience. *Other factors considered include:* interview, first generation, alumni/ae relation, geographical residence, racial/ethnic status, level of applicant's interest. High school diploma is required and GED is accepted.

Financial Aid

Students should submit: CSS/Financial Aid Profile; FAFSA; Noncustodial Profile. Priority filing deadline is 2/1. The Princeton Review suggests that all financial aid forms be submitted as soon as possible (see page 5 for a note on the FAFSA). *Need-based scholarships/grants offered:* College/university scholarship or grant aid from institutional funds; Federal Pell; Private scholarships; SEOG; State scholarships/grants. *Loan aid offered:* Direct PLUS loans; Direct Subsidized Loans; Direct Unsubsidized Loans; College/university loans from institutional funds; State Loans. Admitted students will be notified of awards on or about 3/15. Federal Work-Study Program available. Institutional employment available.

The Inside Word

Haverford's applicant pool is an impressive and competitive lot (only about 20 percent of applicants get in). Intellectual curiosity is paramount, and applicants are expected to keep a demanding academic schedule in high school. Additionally, the college places a high value on ethics, as evidenced by its honor code. The admissions office seeks students who will reflect and promote Haverford's ideals.

THE SCHOOL SAYS "..."

From the Admissions Office

"Haverford College offers one of the finest liberal arts educations in the world and attracts incredibly bright and dedicated students from nearly every state and 36 foreign countries. Haverford students reap the many benefits of attending an all-undergraduate institution, where all courses are taught by professors, and all resources and facilities are available to undergraduates. Haverford provides a rigorous and intensely personal undergraduate education inspired by intellectual depth, integrity, collaboration, and dedication to improving the human condition.

"Our campus culture engenders an immediate sense of colleagueship between students and faculty and creates a relaxed, personal atmosphere. A philosophy of trust, concern, and respect for every individual guides our community and serves as the basis of our completely student-governed honor code. In addition to governing the honor code, students serve on hiring committees, manage budgets, and run more than 145 clubs and organizations.

"Haverford College meets 100 percent of the demonstrated need of all admitted students and seeks to minimize debt for our graduates. Students with family income below $60,000 will not have any loans included in their financial aid package; students with family income above this level will have loans ranging from $1,500 to $3,000 per year. The Haverford Student Loan Debt Relief Fund, an innovative program to help students who do graduate from Haverford with debt, provides funds to young alumni who are employed in jobs of high social value with low remuneration or who are in transition at some point following graduation."

SELECTIVITY

Admissions Rating	97
# of applicants	5,657
% of applicants accepted	14
% of acceptees attending	45
# offered a place on the wait list	1,742
% accepting a place on wait list	61
% admitted from wait list	1
# of early decision applicants	474
% accepted early decision	41

FIRST-YEAR PROFILE

Testing policy	Test Optional
Range SAT composite	1410–1530
Range SAT EBRW	700–760
Range SAT math	730–780
Range ACT composite	33–35
# submitting SAT scores	157
% submitting SAT scores	43
# submitting ACT scores	67
% submitting ACT scores	19
% graduated top 10% of class	96
% graduated top 25% of class	100
% graduated top 50% of class	100

DEADLINES

Early decision	
Deadline	11/15
Notification	12/15
Other ED deadline	1/5
Other ED notification	2/15
Regular	
Deadline	1/15
Notification	4/1
Nonfall registration?	No

APPLICANTS ALSO LOOK AT

Amherst College; Brown University; Georgetown University; Johns Hopkins University; Swarthmore College; The University of Chicago; University of Pennsylvania; Washington University in St. Louis; Wesleyan University

FINANCIAL FACTS

Financial Aid Rating	99
Annual tuition	$67,522
Room and board	$18,250
Required fees	$498
Required fees (first-year)	$778
Books and supplies	$1,194
Average frosh need-based scholarship	$61,802
Average UG need-based scholarship	$60,937
% needy frosh rec. need-based scholarship or grant aid	96
% needy UG rec. need-based scholarship or grant aid	99
% needy frosh rec. non-need-based scholarship or grant aid	17
% needy UG rec. non-need-based scholarship or grant aid	11
% needy frosh rec. need-based self-help aid	87
% needy UG rec. need-based self-help aid	91
% UG borrow to pay for school	23
Average cumulative indebtedness	$16,354
% frosh need fully met	100
% ugrads need fully met	100
Average % of frosh need met	100
Average % of ugrad need met	100

HIGH POINT UNIVERSITY

One University Parkway, High Point, NC 27268 • Admissions: 336-841-9000 • Fax: 336-888-6382

STUDENTS SAY " . . ."

Academics

High Point University is a school that undoubtedly "put[s] the academic and professional success of each of their students first." To that end, it offers "many resources" including counseling, library services, tutoring options, and "so many more [services] that are ready and willing to help students with their careers." Undergrads also highlight the university's emphasis on "career development," which really "prepares students to find a full-time job after graduation." As this undergrad explains, "They assist with your resume, LinkedIn profile (even the ability to have professional photos taken), [and hold] seminars on everything from how to dress to how to prepare for an interview." Of course, much of this success can also be attributed to a great classroom experience. By and large, High Point students are greeted by professors who "are so passionate about what they do [that] it makes [their courses] much more meaningful and engaging." It's also quite evident that the faculty here want to "build true connections with students." They're also "truly knowledgeable and bring real-world experience to the classroom." In turn, this "makes it so much better to sit through their classes because you are able to really trust what they say." When it comes down to it, "HPU is an extraordinary campus with extraordinary professors [who] put the students first."

Campus Life

There's plenty of fun to be had when High Point students step away from their studies. The "Campus Activities Team puts on several events throughout the week and weekends" including "Food Truck Wednesdays, [which] is amazing." Undergrads can also participate in numerous organizations ranging from investment club and the studio art club to Genesis Gospel Choir and "Wishmakers Club, [a group] devoted to earning money to grant wishes for children with cancer." And prospective students with a hankering for outdoor adventure will be delighted to learn that High Point sponsors an "annual white water rafting and zipline trip in the fall [and an] annual ski trip in the spring." You can also rent bikes (free of charge!) from the rec center or take advantage of the school's ice skating rink, another very popular activity. Additionally, the university maintains "very nice gym facilities" and has "lots of club and intramural sports" including volleyball and rowing. "A large majority are involved in Greek life," which we're told is an "extremely inclusive" scene.

Student Body

Undergrads have seemingly built a "strong community" that's based upon "pride in being a High Point student." Of course, it also helps that most people here are "very welcoming and genuine." As this student demonstrates, "You always see people smiling, holding doors, or speaking when you walk by." Another common attribute of High Point undergrads? They're "hardworking and driven individuals" who are "very passionate about learning." Some students do point out that the university is a "predominantly white school" and one that some feel is "only for the rich kids." Nevertheless, "while there are definitely students who have got loads of money coming into the school, there are still plenty of down to earth individuals who just want the best education they can get." Moreover, students stress "most everyone is very inclusive" regardless of your background. "We are becoming more diverse every year. People from all majors are friends and there is no one that is alone if they do not want to be." As one satisfied student sums up, "My peers are collaborative, outgoing, and some of the most fun people I've met."

HIGH POINT UNIVERSITY

Financial Aid: 336-841-9032 • E-Mail: admiss@highpoint.edu • Website: www.highpoint.edu

THE PRINCETON REVIEW SAYS

Admissions

The school reports that its standardized testing policy for use in admission for Fall 2024 is Test Optional. The 2024 testing policy will be permanent. The Princeton Review suggests that interested applicants consult with the school for the most up-to-date standardized testing policies. *Very important factors considered include:* academic GPA. *Important factors considered include:* rigor of secondary school record, standardized test scores, application essay, recommendation(s), interview, extracurricular activities, talent/ability, character/personal qualities, volunteer work, work experience, level of applicant's interest. *Other factors considered include:* class rank, first generation, alumni/ae relation. High school diploma is required and GED is accepted. *Academic units required:* 4 English, 3 math, 3 science, 1 science lab, 2 foreign language, 3 social studies. *Academic units recommended:* 4 English, 4 math, 3 science, 1 science lab, 3 foreign language, 3 social studies.

Financial Aid

Students should submit: FAFSA; State aid form. Priority filing deadline is 3/1. The Princeton Review suggests that all financial aid forms be submitted as soon as possible (see page 5 for a note on the FAFSA). *Need-based scholarships/grants offered:* College/university scholarship or grant aid from institutional funds; Federal Pell; Private scholarships; SEOG; State scholarships/grants. *Loan aid offered:* Direct PLUS loans; Direct Subsidized Loans; Direct Unsubsidized Loans. Admitted students will be notified of awards on a rolling basis beginning 4/1. Federal Work-Study Program available. Institutional employment available.

The Inside Word

High Point considers a variety of factors when it comes to granting students admission to their university. With that being said, your transcript and GPA will be their primary concern. To stand out, we suggest you focus on taking some advanced courses while in high school to prove you can handle a more rigorous course load. In addition to your grades, admissions officers will also be interested in your community involvement and any extracurriculars you participated in while in school. Interests outside of the classroom will prove that you can balance academic life and the more social aspects of student life, such as involvement in clubs or programs.

THE SCHOOL SAYS "..."

From the Admissions Office

"High Point University is The Premier Life Skills University working to transform the lives of our students. HPU knows a thing or two about transformation because we've transformed our campus and our culture in a compressed amount a time that would usually take decades to achieve. HPU invests in educational opportunities that empower you to craft your character and your career in unison, ensuring you are prepared for the world as it is going to be. Through this journey, you'll develop the life skills needed to thrive in an ever-changing global marketplace. You will constantly be given the opportunity to combine classroom content with real-world context as experiential learning is woven into every major. You will have undergraduate research opportunities and a wide range of learning labs that extend well beyond traditional classroom walls. At HPU, you will receive an education that inspires greatness, instills purpose, fosters faith, family and patriotism, and stimulates the desire to live a life of both success and significance.

"Nationally recognized for innovation, HPU's academic model is based on four pillars: academic innovation, experiential learning, modeling values and building character, and the four-year development of each student's life skills. This educating of the entire person coupled with our four-year Career Development plan best positions our students for success. Ninety-eight percent of HPU graduates launch their careers or begin graduate school within 180 days of graduation.

"At High Point University, every student receives an extraordinary education in an inspiring environment with caring people."

SELECTIVITY

Admissions Rating	84
# of applicants	12,446
% of applicants accepted	79
% of acceptees attending	15
# offered a place on the wait list	473
% accepting a place on wait list	100
% admitted from wait list	11
# of early decision applicants	845
% accepted early decision	79

FIRST-YEAR PROFILE

Testing policy	Test Optional
Range SAT composite	1120–1280
Range SAT EBRW	563–640
Range SAT math	540–640
Range ACT composite	23–29
# submitting SAT scores	378
% submitting SAT scores	25
# submitting ACT scores	254
% submitting ACT scores	17
Average HS GPA	3.4
% frosh submitting high school GPA	98
% graduated top 10% of class	16
% graduated top 25% of class	40
% graduated top 50% of class	75

DEADLINES

Early decision	
Deadline	11/1
Notification	11/22
Other ED deadline	2/1
Other ED notification	2/1
Early action	
Deadline	11/15
Notification	12/16
Regular	
Priority	2/1
Deadline	3/1
Notification	2/1
Nonfall registration?	Yes

APPLICANTS ALSO LOOK AT

Appalachian State University; College of Charleston; East Carolina University; Elon University; North Carolina State University; Penn State University Park; University of North Carolina—Chapel Hill

FINANCIAL FACTS

Financial Aid Rating	80
Annual tuition	$36,636
Room and board	$16,524
Required fees	$5,280
Books and supplies	$1,500
Average frosh need-based scholarship	$22,227
Average UG need-based scholarship	$19,604
% needy frosh rec. need-based scholarship or grant aid	100
% needy UG rec. need-based scholarship or grant aid	98
% needy frosh rec. non-need-based scholarship or grant aid	94
% needy UG rec. non-need-based scholarship or grant aid	89
% needy frosh rec. need-based self-help aid	53
% needy UG rec. need-based self-help aid	64
% frosh rec. any financial aid	95
% UG rec. any financial aid	89
% UG borrow to pay for school	54
Average cumulative indebtedness	$47,721
% frosh need fully met	25
% ugrads need fully met	17
Average % of frosh need met	69
Average % of ugrad need met	61

HILLSDALE COLLEGE

33 East College Street, Hillsdale, MI 49242 • Admissions: 517-437-7341 • Fax: 517-607-2223

STUDENTS SAY "..."

Academics

Founded by abolitionists in 1844, Hillsdale College is a private and conservative Christian college that, by catering to just under 1,500 students, emphasizes "both the classical and Christian traditions in a liberal arts education." Critical thinking and discourse are paramount in classes; by utilizing "ancient philosophers and a wide variety of literature and schools of thought," teachings employ a "think for yourself" approach: The "Socratic method is very popular here. Many professors will rearrange the room into a circle and make discussion a large part of class." Students appreciate how the extensive core curriculum "builds character and community" and "allows students to have a shared foundation [for] friendships and conversations." They also praise the guest lecturers who appear at the Center for Constructive Alternatives (Margaret Thatcher and Tom Wolfe, to name a few).

As for the faculty, they get glowing reports: "The relationship between students and professors is like nowhere else I've seen," says one, and another observes, "They make a conscious effort to engage each student," paying special attention to "teach us how to think, not what to think." Studies and relationships with faculty extend beyond the classroom; professors host dinners, musical get-togethers, and field trips, and one student describes a class that migrated to the outside amphitheater as being like "something from Dead Poets Society." All told, students suggest having found more than one professor who will "go above and beyond to help me plan for life after college."

Campus Life

"Hillsdale College students have a knack for never having an empty moment." Students are already described as "academically rigorous," apt to not only extend their studies to late-night conversations and talking "about theology and philosophy and economics at the lunch table" but also to practicing their values: "I don't know one person that doesn't volunteer." Students are equally as involved in Student Activities Board events, from casual bowling nights to the semi-formal and formal Garden Party and President's Ball, and "Homecoming week competitions bring the entire campus together." Music excites students to groove with swing dancing, listen in awe to jazz band performances, or offer their own voices: "I sing in the Chapel Choir, and that is an enormous privilege and delight." Weather permitting, "there are often students sprawled out on any patch of green, but usually with a book in hand." Others take to the outdoors for soccer matches, mountain bike trails, and Baw Beese Lake, where one can "enjoy small beaches, volleyball courts, and other water activities." On weekends, some students drive to Coldwater and Ann Arbor for a taste of the city. Students at Hillsdale strive to improve with intention: "Rarely do I feel as if my time isn't spent doing worthwhile activities or academics that are furthering me as a human."

Student Body

Students call their peers "a strong community of people that I admire and am able to trust" and who form an "uplifting and character-building environment." Another affirms: "[We] are an inquisitive, active, and kind student body. We sign an honor code to participate in the goodness of this college." Due to the small size, students come to know nearly all of their peers, and rely on one another to stimulate intellectual and personal advancement. "I feel challenged to think deeply and aspire to ever improve myself in order to reach my fullest potential, but I also feel supported and encouraged when I fall short."

There is "plenty of diversity of thought" from this "mostly Christian [and] conservative" body. Students place a premium on discussion and debate, finding that "disagreement...is a reason to improve a friendship, not to disintegrate it." Accordingly, they "voice their opinions on pretty much any topic...from the difference between free will and predestination to whether a brachiosaurus will wear a tie at the top or bottom of his neck." Those conversations pay off, as one student observes: "The friends I have made here and the interpersonal struggles that I have faced have formed me into a better person, because the people here are better too, or at least we're all trying together."

Financial Aid: 517-607-2350 • E-Mail: admissions@hillsdale.edu • Website: www.hillsdale.edu

THE PRINCETON REVIEW SAYS

Admissions

The school reports that its standardized testing policy for use in admission for Fall 2024 is Test Optional. The 2024 testing policy will be temporary. The Princeton Review suggests that interested applicants consult with the school for the most up-to-date standardized testing policies. *Very important factors considered include:* rigor of secondary school record, academic GPA, application essay, extracurricular activities, character/personal qualities. *Important factors considered include:* recommendation(s), interview, volunteer work, work experience, level of applicant's interest. *Other factors considered include:* standardized test scores, talent/ability, alumni/ae relation. High school diploma is required and GED is accepted. *Academic units required:* 4 English. *Academic units recommended:* 4 math, 3 science, 2 science labs, 3 foreign language, 3 social studies, 3 history.

Financial Aid

Students should submit: Institution's own financial aid form. Priority filing deadline is 5/1. The Princeton Review suggests that all financial aid forms be submitted as soon as possible (see page 5 for a note on the FAFSA). *Need-based scholarships/grants offered:* College/university scholarship or grant aid from institutional funds; Private scholarships. *Loan aid offered:* College/university loans from institutional funds. Admitted students will be notified of awards on a rolling basis beginning 12/1. Institutional employment available.

The Inside Word

While the academic profile of incoming students is impressive, the College strongly considers a student's extracurricular activities, character, and ambition as well. In addition to the SAT and ACT, Hillsdale also accepts the Classic Learning Test (CLT). Applicants are encouraged to submit a resume of their extracurricular, leadership, and work experiences along with their applications. Interviews are highly recommended, especially for those seeking a scholarship.

THE SCHOOL SAYS "..."

From the Admissions Office

"The College's strength is found in its mission and curriculum. The core curriculum at Hillsdale contains the essence of the classical liberal arts education. Through it, students are introduced to the history, the philosophical and theological ideas, the works of literature, and the scientific discoveries that set Western Civilization apart. As explained in its mission statement, 'the College also considers itself a trustee of our Western philosophical and theological inheritance tracing to Athens and Jerusalem, a heritage finding its clearest expression in the American experiment of self-government under law.'

"Personal attention is a hallmark at Hillsdale. Small classes are combined with teaching professors who make their students a priority. The academic environment at Hillsdale will actively engage you as a student. Extracurricular activities abound at Hillsdale with more than 100 clubs and organizations that offer excellent leadership opportunities. From athletics and the fine arts, to Greek life and community volunteer programs, you will find it difficult not to be involved in our thriving campus community. In addition, numerous study abroad programs, a 685-acre biological station in northern Michigan, and an internship program in Washington, D.C., are just a few of the unique off-campus opportunities available to students at Hillsdale.

"We seek students who are ambitious, intellectually active and who are ready to become leaders worthy of this heritage in their personal as well as professional lives.

"All students sign and abide by the Honor Code, which says: 'A Hillsdale College student is honorable in conduct, honest in word and deed, dutiful in study and service, and respectful of the rights of other. Through education, the student rises to self-government.'"

SELECTIVITY

Admissions Rating	97
# of applicants	3,017
% of applicants accepted	21
% of acceptees attending	62
# offered a place on the wait list	193
% accepting a place on wait list	49
% admitted from wait list	7
# of early decision applicants	339
% accepted early decision	33

FIRST-YEAR PROFILE

Testing policy	Test Optional
Range SAT composite	1370–1480
Range SAT EBRW	690–760
Range SAT math	670–760
Range ACT composite	30–34
# submitting SAT scores	110
% submitting SAT scores	28
# submitting ACT scores	118
% submitting ACT scores	30
Average HS GPA	3.9
% frosh submitting high school GPA	100

DEADLINES

Early decision	
Deadline	11/1
Notification	12/1
Regular	
Priority	12/15
Deadline	3/15
Notification	Rolling, 12/15
Nonfall registration?	Yes

APPLICANTS ALSO LOOK AT

Adrian College; Albion College; Alma College; Ave Maria University; Baylor University; Benedictine College; Bethel College (IN); Biola University; Calvin University; Cedarville University

FINANCIAL FACTS

Financial Aid Rating	82
Annual tuition	$29,590
Room and board	$12,500
Required fees	$1,312
Books and supplies	$1,200
Average frosh need-based scholarship	$11,798
Average UG need-based scholarship	$11,548
% needy frosh rec. need-based scholarship or grant aid	64
% needy UG rec. need-based scholarship or grant aid	64
% needy frosh rec. non-need-based scholarship or grant aid	99
% needy UG rec. non-need-based scholarship or grant aid	88
% needy frosh rec. need-based self-help aid	42
% needy UG rec. need-based self-help aid	53
% frosh rec. any financial aid	99
% UG rec. any financial aid	99
% UG borrow to pay for school	34
Average cumulative indebtedness	$30,497
% frosh need fully met	47
% ugrads need fully met	42
Average % of frosh need met	72
Average % of ugrad need met	71

HOBART AND WILLIAM SMITH COLLEGES

300 Pulteney Street, Geneva, NY 14456 • Admissions: 315-781-3000 • Fax: 315-781-3914

STUDENTS SAY "..."

Academics

There are opportunities everywhere you look at Hobart and William Smith Colleges, whether in the classroom or in the beautiful setting. Students share stories of taking a "research vessel out on Seneca Lake for lab days [to do] hands-on work in environmental science" and of taking part in a $10,000-prize competition "where students pitch a business idea for actual funding." There are "independent studies with professors, graduate-level honors projects," and a "one-of-a-kind" Global Education program: "Almost every single one of my friends is planning to go or already has studied abroad."

HWS students benefit from "small class sizes [that] make it easy to connect with professors." They also find the faculty "extremely engaging" and emphasize that "they work to help each student understand the depth and breadth of the course material." Indeed, "whether it be in-class debates or the opportunity to choose your own project—such as choosing between an essay, a podcast, or an animation—professors always try their best to accommodate each student's learning styles through innovative approaches." They truly go "far out of their way to make sure each student is reaching their full potential and not slipping between the cracks."

As graduation nears, undergrads enter the job market with confidence. This can partially be attributed to the school's career services programs, which offer "a multitude of resources to aid students in finding internships and jobs as well as offering résumé writing workshops and interview workshops." And, of course, undergrads can rely on the alumni network which is "extremely welcoming and strong."

Campus Life

Students report spending a lot of time in the Hobart and William Smith Colleges library—and not minding, because "it is the perfect mix between a study and social place." A popular offering there five nights a week is the Teaching Fellows, the Center for Teaching and Learning, which is not only an area to work, "but also a place to get together with classmates [in a] social studying space." Beyond the academics, HWS "is very supportive of helping students set up their own clubs," and many students juggle multiple, varied activities: "I'm on the varsity lacrosse team, finance society, investment club, and fishing club." Students also like to "make use of the campus rec center which has basketball courts, squash courts, weights, bikes, yoga and HIIT classes and so much more." Undergrads can also relax with "craft nights, cultural food festivals, food trucks, and more." Once the weekend hits, there are on- and off-campus parties, plus the "beautiful city" of Geneva, conveniently within walking distance, where students "go downtown to eat at the amazing restaurants and go to the bars afterwards." And, weather permitting, students can't wait until "it is warm enough to go down to the docks and swim in Seneca Lake!"

Student Body

Hobart and William Smith fosters "a sense of community that you feel on every corner of campus." This is reflected in the "very supportive student body that genuinely wants to push each other to be the best possible while at college and beyond." Students find their peers to be "welcoming and open-minded" and inclusive of "a very diverse range of students from many different backgrounds and corners of the Earth." One student elaborates, "I have met an incredible amount of international students from all over the world since coming here." Whether they're from Pittsburgh or Paris, HWS students are "highly motivated both in and outside of the classroom." The overall sense is that "people want to be in class, add to discussions, and learn about topics that interest and challenge them" and that peers are "ambitious, passionate, and mission oriented." Undergraduates also find that "most students here tend to be talkative, inquisitive, and amicable." Athletes, artists, intellectuals; they'll all find a place here as part of "a community full of well-rounded and open-minded individuals."

HOBART AND WILLIAM SMITH COLLEGES

Financial Aid: 315-781-3315 • E-Mail: admissions@hws.edu • Website: www.hws.edu

THE PRINCETON REVIEW SAYS

Admissions

The school reports that its standardized testing policy for use in admission for Fall 2024 is Test Optional, as it has been since 2006. *Very important factors considered include:* rigor of secondary school record, academic GPA. *Important factors considered include:* class rank, application essay, recommendation(s), interview, extracurricular activities, character/personal qualities, first generation, volunteer work, work experience. *Other factors considered include:* standardized test scores, talent/ability, alumni/ae relation, geographical residence, state residency, racial/ethnic status, level of applicant's interest. High school diploma is required and GED is accepted. *Academic units required:* 4 English, 3 math, 3 science, 2 science labs, 2 foreign language, 4 social studies, 2 academic electives. *Academic units recommended:* 4 English, 4 math, 4 science, 3 foreign language, 4 social studies, 4 academic electives.

Financial Aid

Students should submit: FAFSA; State aid form. Priority filing deadline is 11/15. The Princeton Review suggests that all financial aid forms be submitted as soon as possible (see page 5 for a note on the FAFSA). *Need-based scholarships/grants offered:* College/university scholarship or grant aid from institutional funds; Federal Pell; Private scholarships; SEOG; State scholarships/grants. *Loan aid offered:* Direct PLUS loans; Direct Subsidized Loans; Direct Unsubsidized Loans. Admitted students will be notified of awards on a rolling basis beginning 12/15. Federal Work-Study Program available. Institutional employment available.

The Inside Word

Hobart and William Smith seeks applicants who want to be challenged both inside and outside the classroom. To find such students, the school takes a holistic approach to the admissions process. Therefore, you can expect that all facets of your application will be carefully assessed. And if you're truly gunning for an acceptance letter, you'll want to make sure you've taken a rigorous curriculum throughout high school. The college also typically favors students who have actively worked to better their community and demonstrate great character.

THE SCHOOL SAYS "..."

From the Admissions Office

"At Hobart and William Smith, you'll be on an adventure and your experience will be entirely your own—full of learning, discovery, surprises and accomplishment.

"You'll make a plan, mentored by caring, expert guides and grounded in experiences that let you test your interests and pave the way to a lifetime of purpose.

"You'll gain significant insights into the emerging challenges of the future world.

"You'll find places to belong within the HWS family. Our community welcomes open-minded people from many and varied backgrounds and perspectives.

"You'll be valued as an ethical person who approaches complex problems with empathy and discernment—and in partnership with others.

"You'll be prepared to lead a life of consequence."

SELECTIVITY

Admissions Rating	87
# of applicants	5,082
% of applicants accepted	68
% of acceptees attending	13
# offered a place on the wait list	227
% accepting a place on wait list	41
% admitted from wait list	<1
# of early decision applicants	223
% accepted early decision	74

FIRST-YEAR PROFILE

Testing policy	Test Optional
Range SAT composite	1230–1390
Range SAT EBRW	610–700
Range SAT math	600–700
Range ACT composite	27–32
# submitting SAT scores	98
% submitting SAT scores	22
# submitting ACT scores	20
% submitting ACT scores	9
Average HS GPA	3.6
% frosh submitting high school GPA	98
% graduated top 10% of class	29
% graduated top 25% of class	53
% graduated top 50% of class	87

DEADLINES

Early decision	
Deadline	11/15
Notification	12/15
Other ED deadline	1/15
Other ED notification	2/15
Early action	
Deadline	11/15
Notification	1/15
Regular	
Deadline	2/1
Notification	4/1
Nonfall registration?	Yes

APPLICANTS OFTEN PREFER
Colgate University; St. Lawrence University

APPLICANTS SOMETIMES PREFER
Connecticut College; Cornell University; Hamilton College; Skidmore College; Syracuse University; Union College (NY); University of Vermont

FINANCIAL FACTS

Financial Aid Rating	85
Annual tuition	$60,350
Room and board	$16,910
Required fees	$1,375
Books and supplies	$1,300
Average frosh need-based scholarship	$47,722
Average UG need-based scholarship	$44,873
% needy frosh rec. need-based scholarship or grant aid	96
% needy UG rec. need-based scholarship or grant aid	98
% needy frosh rec. non-need-based scholarship or grant aid	17
% needy UG rec. non-need-based scholarship or grant aid	18
% needy frosh rec. need-based self-help aid	77
% needy UG rec. need-based self-help aid	80
% frosh rec. any financial aid	90
% UG rec. any financial aid	93
% UG borrow to pay for school	72
Average cumulative indebtedness	$37,668
% frosh need fully met	24
% ugrads need fully met	22
Average % of frosh need met	84
Average % of ugrad need met	84

HOFSTRA UNIVERSITY

100 Hofstra University, Hempstead, NY 11549 • Admissions: 516-463-6600 • Fax: 516-463-5100

STUDENTS SAY "..."

Academics

There's no denying that a strong "sense of community" coupled with a "supportive staff" guarantee that "Hofstra [is] a great place to be." After all, the university really makes it a priority to "listen to students" and ensures that "social, academic, and personal concerns are always validated, addressed, and resolved." Undergrads here greatly benefit from a myriad "of opportunities regarding jobs, internships, and experiential learning." And they love that they have great "flexibility [when it comes to] courses [as well as] the ability to mix and match majors and minors." Though Hofstra has many great academic departments, students especially like to highlight the "dual degree programs and health science fields as they have so many connections to local hospitals and have top of the art equipment and cadaver labs." They also note the "extremely accomplished" School of Communications. With such renowned departments, it's reasonable to expect that your professors here will "do their best to challenge [you] and get [you] ready for the real world by teaching [you] critical thinking skills and giving [you] as many opportunities as possible to apply theory to real-life situations."

Campus Life

Undergraduates at Hofstra lead busy lives. Of course, that's understandable given how much there is to do. The university itself "puts [forth quite an] effort to [offer] fun things for their students." For example, "there is the Fall Fest, a carnival, special occasion meals...and other free activities." Undergrads can also frequently attend "any activity sponsored by the honors college" like open mic nights and alumni talk-backs. Many also like hitting up screenings of "different popular movies every Fri, Sat, and Sun" that are organized for them by another student club. There are numerous additional student-run organizations including the Culinary Club and WRHU—Radio Hofstra University. Particularly impressive is the school's TV network students can join regardless of their major. "We have our own television network called the HEAT Network, which [offers]...student-run shows, including our late-night sketch comedy show TNL, which has won a college Emmy. Hofstra's TV program gives off real world experience that truly isn't available at most collegiate institutions." Additionally, "community service opportunities are easy to come by and are often exciting." This is a popular activity and one that many agree "allow[s] the students to belong to something bigger and more important than their individual selves." Volunteer activities include "cleaning up the streets, raking leaves, [and] food drives." Finally, undergrads love to take advantage of Hofstra's proximity to New York City. "With the Long Island Railroad being 15 minutes away from campus and Manhattan being a 40-minute train ride away from the Long Island, the city is extremely accessible, which makes it possible for students to enjoy a multitude of events and activities held [there]."

Student Body

Incoming undergraduates have no reason to be nervous when starting at Hofstra. That's because the school has "a very welcoming student body," one where "just about everyone is approachable and happy to help you with homework or even directions to a building." As this individual shares, "I was drawn to Hofstra for the people, truly because everyone I met was so relaxed and happy to be here." Most students are also "incredib[ly] hardworking, driven, and passionate about the work they do." Fortunately, they "work together to achieve their goals. It's not a competitive environment." But perhaps what Hofstra undergrads appreciate most about their peers is just how diverse they are. While there are certainly a fair amount "from the Long Island/wider New York area," you'll definitely encounter "students from all 50 states and more than 25 other countries" as well as individuals from "all different ethnicities, cultures, religions." Just as critical, you're bound to discover "all sorts of people with unique interests." Indeed, this student assures us that "no matter what your passion, you can find someone who shares it."

HOFSTRA UNIVERSITY

Financial Aid: 516-463-8000 • E-Mail: admission@hofstra.edu • Website: www.hofstra.edu

THE PRINCETON REVIEW SAYS

Admissions

The school reports that its standardized testing policy for use in admission for Fall 2024 is Test Optional. The 2024 testing policy will be permanent. The Princeton Review suggests that interested applicants consult with the school for the most up-to-date standardized testing policies. *Very important factors considered include:* rigor of secondary school record, class rank, academic GPA, application essay, recommendation(s). *Important factors considered include:* interview, extracurricular activities, talent/ability, character/personal qualities. *Other factors considered include:* standardized test scores, first generation, geographical residence, racial/ethnic status, volunteer work, work experience, level of applicant's interest. High school diploma is required and GED is accepted. *Academic units required:* 4 English, 3 math, 3 science, 1 science lab, 2 foreign language, 3 social studies. *Academic units recommended:* 4 math, 4 science, 2 science labs, 3 foreign language, 4 social studies.

Financial Aid

Students should submit: FAFSA; State aid form. Priority filing deadline is 11/15. The Princeton Review suggests that all financial aid forms be submitted as soon as possible (see page 5 for a note on the FAFSA). *Need-based scholarships/grants offered:* College/university scholarship or grant aid from institutional funds; Federal Pell; Private scholarships; SEOG; State scholarships/grants; United Negro College Fund. *Loan aid offered:* Direct PLUS loans; Direct Subsidized Loans; Direct Unsubsidized Loans; College/university loans from institutional funds; State Loans. Admitted students will be notified of awards on a rolling basis beginning 1/15. Federal Work-Study Program available. Institutional employment available.

The Inside Word

Your high school transcript will likely be the essential piece of your application when applying to Hofstra University. Hofstra places high value on each student's academic record, which is why you may want to consider submitting your standardized test scores, even though the university is Test Optional. Nearly 40% of prospective students decide to submit their scores, so if you score high, don't be afraid to let the school know. The university operates on the basis of rolling admission, meaning the earlier you apply, the better.

THE SCHOOL SAYS "..."

From the Admissions Office

"Hofstra is a dynamic private institution that is internationally recognized for academic excellence, civic engagement and community service.

"We provide you with the resources of a large university, but the personal attention of a small college. Students come from 50 U.S. states and territories and over 77 countries, and can choose from 180 program options. Hofstra is home to schools of engineering, business, communication, education, nursing, medicine and law, as well as 21 Division I sports and 35 residence halls.

"Our 244-acre suburban campus, which is a nationally recognized arboretum, is just 25 miles east of New York City, opening the door to prestigious internships at world-class corporations.

"You'll also benefit from experiential learning on campus in our state-of-the-art facilities, including an academic trading room with 34 Bloomberg terminals; advanced engineering labs; and a cutting-edge converged newsroom and multimedia classroom. More than 200 pre-professional, social and academic clubs provide leadership and community service opportunities. Hofstra also values bringing exclusive learning opportunities to campus, most notably by being the only school to ever host 3 consecutive presidential debates (2008, 2012, and 2016).

"Our faculty are entrepreneurs, scholars, artists, and scientists who are pioneers in their disciplines and mentors in the classroom. They'll invite you to collaborate on research projects and connect you with industry veterans.

"At Hofstra, you will pursue your passion and find your purpose."

SELECTIVITY

Admissions Rating	87
# of applicants	23,577
% of applicants accepted	69
% of acceptees attending	10
# offered a place on the wait list	173
% accepting a place on wait list	87
% admitted from wait list	87

FIRST-YEAR PROFILE

Testing policy	Test Optional
Range SAT composite	1200–1370
Range SAT EBRW	600–680
Range SAT math	590–690
Range ACT composite	26–31
# submitting SAT scores	625
% submitting SAT scores	37
# submitting ACT scores	110
% submitting ACT scores	6
Average HS GPA	3.8
% frosh submitting high school GPA	100
% graduated top 10% of class	32
% graduated top 25% of class	61
% graduated top 50% of class	89

DEADLINES

Early action	
Deadline	11/15
Notification	12/15
Nonfall registration?	Yes

APPLICANTS OFTEN PREFER
Boston University; New York University; Northeastern University; Syracuse University

APPLICANTS SOMETIMES PREFER
Drexel University; Fordham University; Penn State University Park; Rutgers University—New Brunswick; State University of New York—Binghamton University; State University of New York—Stony Brook University; University of Delaware

APPLICANTS RARELY PREFER
Quinnipiac University; St. John's University (NY); University of Connecticut

FINANCIAL FACTS

Financial Aid Rating	82
Annual tuition	$52,215
Room and board	$17,960
Required fees	$1,115
Books and supplies	$1,000
Average frosh need-based scholarship	$27,643
Average UG need-based scholarship	$25,203
% needy frosh rec. need-based scholarship or grant aid	100
% needy UG rec. need-based scholarship or grant aid	98
% needy frosh rec. non-need-based scholarship or grant aid	22
% needy UG rec. non-need-based scholarship or grant aid	19
% needy frosh rec. need-based self-help aid	77
% needy UG rec. need-based self-help aid	78
% UG borrow to pay for school	65
Average cumulative indebtedness	$43,300
% frosh need fully met	24
% ugrads need fully met	24
Average % of frosh need met	68
Average % of ugrad need met	65

HOLLINS UNIVERSITY

7916 Williamson Road, Roanoke, VA 24020 • Admissions: 540-362-6000

STUDENTS SAY ". . ."

Academics

Hollins University is a private liberal arts college in Roanoke, Virginia, that heralds the unique benefits that come with being an all-women's college, which includes a student-to-faculty ratio of 8:1, a relatively low class size, and a global network of alums that connects students to mentors, jobs, and internships. "Our community and traditions help us create connections with students and alumnae that will last well into our adulthood," says a student. As for hands-on experiences, they are guaranteed for every eligible student, and three out of four students complete at least one: "I am currently doing an internship that is completely out of my field, but one class I took intrigued me to do so," reports a student, while another notes "I have done three internships through Hollins and it contributes a lot to my career." The so-called J-Term, or January Short Term, helps free up students to pursue such opportunities, as well as research and study abroad. Students also note that the school has made a serious "investment in the creative fields," with plenty of "readings and Q&A sessions by guest authors," and classes incorporate plenty of hands-on elements, such as a public health class where students had "to complete a field experience assignment where we study a disease, and then interview random students about [it] just as a real epidemiologist would."

The school is "academic and forward-thinking without putting a ton of pressure on students to maintain perfect grades," and creates "a positive intellectual standard that makes me and my peers want to really grow and push our education further." Faculty are "absolutely the backbone of this school and have such a passion to support their students in any way they can, both academically, emotionally, and just in life." They "are more than willing to work with you when life throws you curve balls" and are "very good about answering questions and making themselves available outside of class."

Campus Life

Hollins University is "a beautiful, optimistic place" where almost all first-years live, be that in one of the 10 home-style residences or seven special interest houses and halls, all located "right next to a huge natural preserve and reservoir." (That historical, picturesque quality does come with a bit of a price: several students report a desire for renovations—like air-conditioning—in the oldest dorms, and for a more varied menu in the dining hall.) Given the natural scenery, students appreciate the school's outdoor activities, like "hiking and trail walks they set up" to horseback riding and a climbing team (that can also make use of the gym's rock wall). The student government also works to organize "many great sponsored events that take us out of Hollins and into the city of Roanoke," like basketball games, and "lots of social events, ranging from the little hot chocolate buffet on the quad…to the semi-formal fall dance." (Hollins students do love "a party with a theme, any excuse to dress up.") Students also report a lot of activities ("everything from crafting club to anime club") and note that the school is "really great about making sure everyone can get involved."

Student Body

Despite being a historically women's college, "Hollins students represent a wide range of gender identities," including "AFAB, non-binary, trans-masculine, LGBTQIA+ students, as well as cis-gendered women." There is a "Culture of Care implemented on campus, which makes respect and empathy for one another a conscious mindset throughout all of campus." There are just seven hundred undergraduates, which "makes finding friends and familiar faces easy." As one student says: "I never see a face I've never seen before… I find it comforting." This is "a safe place to express oneself" and "everyone is so open and accepting and the clubs, societies, and traditions give everyone a unique place in the school." Overall, this group of "kind, smart, funny, talented" individuals create "a warm and friendly environment where everyone feels like they belong."

HOLLINS UNIVERSITY

Financial Aid: 540-362-6332 • E-Mail: huadm@hollins.edu • Website: www.hollins.edu

THE PRINCETON REVIEW SAYS

Admissions

The school reports that its standardized testing policy for use in admission for Fall 2024 is Test Optional. The 2024 testing policy will be permanent. The Princeton Review suggests that interested applicants consult with the school for the most up-to-date standardized testing policies. *Very important factors considered include:* academic GPA. *Important factors considered include:* rigor of secondary school record, application essay, recommendation(s). *Other factors considered include:* class rank, standardized test scores, interview, extracurricular activities, talent/ability, character/personal qualities, first generation, alumni/ae relation, geographical residence, state residency, volunteer work, work experience, level of applicant's interest. High school diploma is required and GED is accepted. *Academic units required:* 4 English, 3 math, 3 science, 3 social studies. *Academic units recommended:* 3 foreign language.

Financial Aid

Students should submit: FAFSA; State aid form. Priority filing deadline is 2/1. The Princeton Review suggests that all financial aid forms be submitted as soon as possible (see page 5 for a note on the FAFSA). *Need-based scholarships/grants offered:* College/university scholarship or grant aid from institutional funds; Federal Pell; Private scholarships; SEOG; State scholarships/grants. *Loan aid offered:* Direct PLUS loans; Direct Subsidized Loans; Direct Unsubsidized Loans; College/university loans from institutional funds. Admitted students will be notified of awards on a rolling basis beginning 3/1. Federal Work-Study Program available. Institutional employment available.

The Inside Word

If you've got solid grades and—though submitting them is optional—good test scores, you stand a good chance of being in the 75% of students accepted to Hollins University each year. If you're from the Roanoke area, your chances may be even higher—12% of all students are local—and you may even qualify for a HOPE scholarship that fully covers tuition. If you can manage it, there's a grant provided to those who visit the school (and subsequently enroll), and since the school is looking for best-fit candidates, it's a good idea to take them up on this.

THE SCHOOL SAYS "..."

From the Admissions Office

"Empowering women since 1842, Hollins University unites excellence in liberal arts education with experiential learning opportunities and career preparation to help our students lead lives of consequence.

"Our broad liberal arts curriculum offers strong academic programs and superior teaching that emphasize critical thinking, problem solving, creativity, and collaboration—skills that employers seek. Our top five majors (psychology, biology, English/creative writing, studio art, and business) underscore the breadth and scope of the Hollins experience in the physical sciences, social sciences, arts, and humanities. The university's athletic program is dedicated to the pursuit of academic achievement and athletic excellence, and is committed to the overall success of the student-athlete.

"Experiential learning opportunities include a January Short Term, where students can test drive a career with an internship, take a travel/study course, or conduct research through opportunities supported by the Rutherfoord Center for Experiential Learning, and the Batten Leadership Institute, which teaches students how to understand and navigate feedback, conflict, and negotiation.

"Career preparation is also a hallmark: three out of four Hollins graduates complete at least one internship during their undergraduate careers, and half of those participate in two or more internships. The university places students in companies, nonprofits, museums, law firms, and hospitals, both in the U.S. and abroad. One year after graduation, 95 percent of our students are employed or in graduate school."

HOWARD UNIVERSITY

2400 Sixth Street, NW, Washington, DC 20059 • Admissions: 202-806-6100 • Fax: 202-806-4465

CAMPUS LIFE

Quality of Life Rating	71
Fire Safety Rating	79
Green Rating	60*
Type of school	Private
Affiliation	No Affiliation
Environment	Metropolis

STUDENTS

Total undergrad enrollment	8,700
% male/female/another gender	28/72/0
% from out of state	98
% frosh live on campus	95
% ugrads live on campus	56
# of fraternities (% join)	10 (1)
# of sororities (% join)	8 (1)
% African American	67
% Asian	4
% White	0
% Hispanic	7
% Native American	>1
% Pacific Islander	<1
% Two or more races	4
% Race and/or ethnicity unknown	12
% international	3
# of countries represented	86

SURVEY SAYS . . .

Lots of liberal students
Frats and sororities are popular
Campus newspaper is popular
College radio is popular

ACADEMICS

Academic Rating	74
% students returning for sophomore year	91
% students graduating within 4 years	53
% students graduating within 6 years	64
Calendar	Semester
Student/faculty ratio	13:1
Profs interesting rating	78
Profs accessible rating	82

Most classes have 10–19 students.
Most lab/discussion sessions have
20–29 students.

MOST POPULAR MAJORS

Biology/Biological Sciences, General

STUDENTS SAY "..."

Academics

Noted for "outstanding achievements as an institution as well as the accomplishments of a great majority of its alumni," Howard University takes great pride in preparing students "to compete on a local and global level." With "inspiring faculty and a perspective that cannot be found anywhere else," the school "breeds pride and excellence" and is a "formidable force in producing African American intellectuals." As one appreciative student puts it, "Howard University is more than a place to get an education; it is a once-in-a-lifetime experience that not only strengthens your mind, but also your spirit and pride in who you are as a person and who you have the potential to become." Other undergrads add, "I wanted the experience of attending a Historically Black College," and more specifically, "the sense of being a part of such a tremendous legacy." Students here believe that a Howard education is wonderful preparation for life in today's competitive employment environment. "Howard pushes you and teaches patience." Professors are admired for being able to "bridge the gap between the real world and the textbook," are "supportive and helpful," have "a genuine interest in their subject," and make sure "course material is appropriate." Discussions are encouraged, which "helps to solidify understanding.... I am able to have a voice in the class and share my opinion." Networking opportunities are abundant, and job placement upon graduation is high.

Campus Life

A common theme heard throughout Howard University is how "students are very tight-knit and supportive of one another." You can see that across the whole school, from "lively" dorms to how school events are a "major part of the social calendar," and the way in which students are encouraged "to be involved in campus organizations and student government." While there are many Greeks on campus, "the main focus of our Greek life is community service. Any social event or gathering that is hosted by the Greeks normally has most or all of the proceeds going to a charity or community service project." There are also "student-run organizations that work in the community," providing "opportunities to be a part of something bigger than you." Students obviously love taking advantage of all of the opportunities the Washington, D.C. area provides. The Metro is a popular form of transportation, with the station "very easily accessible from the main Howard University campus." Many locations are Metro-accessible, but you must be cognizant of operating hours.

Student Body

At Howard University, there is at least one commonality everyone can agree on: these "very goal-oriented and driven" students are busy. "At any given time a student at Howard can be found taking a full course load, working, and interning." Extracurricular activities and community service are also on the plate of many Howard undergraduates. Students are often described as "friendly, outgoing, stylish, and fashionable." The campus radiates "a culture of achievement and encouragement" that syncs up well with student goals: "A Howardite is very career-oriented and knows what he or she wants to do after graduation." Students here are also "very socially conscious." Geographic diversity is prevalent, and "Howard students are educated to think on a global scale." As a result, "students are very accepting of each other and their backgrounds" and make for an "ever-changing, comprehensive, innovative, and supportive community." Meaningful conversation is prevalent, with many "discussions surrounding social and political issues." As one undergrad sees it, "Howard represents the best of the educated and progressive African American community."

HOWARD UNIVERSITY

E-Mail: admission@howard.edu • Website: www.howard.edu

THE PRINCETON REVIEW SAYS

Admissions

The school reports that its standardized testing policy for use in admission for Fall 2024 is Test Optional. It is unknown at this time if the 2024 testing policy will be permanent. The Princeton Review suggests that interested applicants consult with the school for the most up-to-date standardized testing policies. *Very important factors considered include:* rigor of secondary school record, academic GPA. *Important factors considered include:* application essay, recommendation(s), character/personal qualities. *Other factors considered include:* class rank, standardized test scores, extracurricular activities, talent/ability, first generation, alumni/ae relation, volunteer work, work experience, level of applicant's interest. High school diploma is required and GED is accepted. *Academic units recommended:* 4 English, 3 math, 2 science, 2 science labs, 2 foreign language, 2 social studies, 4 academic electives.

Financial Aid

Students should submit: FAFSA. Priority filing deadline is 2/1. The Princeton Review suggests that all financial aid forms be submitted as soon as possible (see page 5 for a note on the FAFSA). *Need-based scholarships/grants offered:* College/university scholarship or grant aid from institutional funds; Federal Nursing Scholarships; Federal Pell; Private scholarships; SEOG; State scholarships/grants; United Negro College Fund. *Loan aid offered:* Direct PLUS loans; Direct Subsidized Loans; Direct Unsubsidized Loans; College/university loans from institutional funds; State Loans. Admitted students will be notified of awards on a rolling basis beginning 2/16. Federal Work-Study Program available. Institutional employment available.

The Inside Word

Howard attracts quite a significant number of applicants, and the school maintains a high rate of graduation for those who do gain admittance. While standardized testing is certainly a primary part of evaluating those looking to enroll, this does not preclude other students from seeking entrance; proven ability from high school and the capacity to handle higher learning in a diligent, responsible manner is also highly valued.

THE SCHOOL SAYS ". . ."

From the Admissions Office

"Since its founding, Howard has stood among the few institutions of higher learning where blacks and other minorities have participated freely in a truly comprehensive university experience. Thus, Howard has assumed a special responsibility in preparing its students to exercise leadership wherever their interests and commitments take them. Howard has issued approximately 111,233 degrees, diplomas, and certificates to men and women in the professions, the arts and sciences, and the humanities. The university has produced and continues to produce a high percentage of the nation's African American professionals in the fields of medicine, dentistry, pharmacy, engineering, nursing, architecture, religion, law, music, social work, education, and business. There are more than 10,036 students from across the nation and approximately eighty-six countries and territories attending the university. Their varied customs, cultures, ideas, and interests contribute to Howard's international character and vitality. More than 1,598 faculty members represent the largest concentration of black scholars in any single institution of higher education."

SELECTIVITY

Admissions Rating	92
# of applicants	29,396
% of applicants accepted	35
% of acceptees attending	27
# offered a place on the wait list	2,377
% accepting a place on wait list	100
% admitted from wait list	0
# of early decision applicants	441
% accepted early decision	49

FIRST-YEAR PROFILE

Testing policy	Test Optional
Range SAT composite	1100–1270
Range SAT EBRW	550–650
Range SAT math	530–640
Range ACT composite	21–26
# submitting SAT scores	733
% submitting SAT scores	27
# submitting ACT scores	284
% submitting ACT scores	10
Average HS GPA	3.7
% frosh submitting high school GPA	100
% graduated top 10% of class	18
% graduated top 25% of class	59
% graduated top 50% of class	91

DEADLINES

Early decision	
Deadline	11/1
Notification	12/18
Early action	
Deadline	11/1
Notification	12/18
Regular	
Priority	11/1
Deadline	2/15
Notification	4/15
Nonfall registration?	Yes

FINANCIAL FACTS

Financial Aid Rating	79
Annual tuition	$30,584
Room and board	$15,880
Required fees	$466
Books and supplies	$1,360
Average frosh need-based scholarship	$6,412
Average UG need-based scholarship	$12,351
% needy frosh rec. need-based scholarship or grant aid	74
% needy UG rec. need-based scholarship or grant aid	83
% needy frosh rec. non-need-based scholarship or grant aid	94
% needy UG rec. non-need-based scholarship or grant aid	83
% needy frosh rec. need-based self-help aid	60
% needy UG rec. need-based self-help aid	60
% frosh rec. any financial aid	100
% UG rec. any financial aid	100
% UG borrow to pay for school	73
Average cumulative indebtedness	$28,680
% frosh need fully met	34
% ugrads need fully met	29
Average % of frosh need met	58
Average % of ugrad need met	61

ILLINOIS INSTITUTE OF TECHNOLOGY

10 West 35th Street, Chicago, IL 60616 • Admissions: 312-567-3000

STUDENTS SAY ". . ."

Academics

Minutes from downtown Chicago, Illinois Institute of Technology is a "beautiful green oasis in a bustling city." This career-oriented university prepares students to "[make] the jump from student to professional" with a curriculum "strongly based on applied learning" and access "to student research at all levels." Illinois Tech "caters to those individuals that want to pursue careers in areas of STEM," although the curriculum "puts an equal emphasis on the life sciences and doesn't discount humanities." And while most come for the school's "historic reputation," particularly in engineering and architecture, students don't dismiss the value of the school's diversity. "The size and diversity of Illinois Tech is perfect," one student argues, "small enough for individual attention, but large enough for various resources to be available. Working with students from around the world gives you a unique perspective that is useful after college as well." Students are overall positive on the faculty: "I have had some really fantastic professors who are engaging and make the material genuinely interesting," one student explains. "However, I've had the exact opposite too." Others say that their "professors are very willing to help...but [they] want you to think for yourself." Most agree that Illinois Tech "is a very academic-based institution with mostly excellent professors, especially in upper-level classes. Academics here are challenging but rewarding." Others are quick to point out that many of Illinois Tech professors "also work in the field" and, therefore, they "apply topics studied in the lectures to the real world," and "their lectures are very current with the solutions and technologies that are actually being used."

Campus Life

Students engage in common pastimes like watching movies and playing video games, but report that "life at school is work and study every day with a few breaks in between." That "simple and sorted" lifestyle is appealing to some academically-driven students, while others enjoy playing intramural sports and exploring the many museums, restaurants, and cultural attractions of the city. Students suggest that "there doesn't seem to be much partying going on at this school," given the workload, the "mostly small" residential options "that get packed quickly," and an on-campus alcohol policy that feels "very strict" to respondents. As for Greek life, students describe it as being a "serious life-saver for those struggling socially, mentally, emotionally, and academically."

Student Body

At Illinois Institute of Technology, students pridefully declare that they "study hard, focus for the future, bathe in the diversity of campus life, and are able to enjoy" everything that the school and city have to offer. Many students highlight an interest in "innovation and in aspiring creativity." They are "quiet introverts" who value teamwork and hail from around the world. Roughly half of the total Illinois Tech student body are international students, which "provides a variety of perspectives" and cultures present in classroom discussions and clubs. Students largely describe one another as "warm, accepting, welcoming, and friendly." Overwhelmingly, "Illinois Tech students are serious about their studies, have a great eye for design and architecture, and love to have a good time especially when there is free food involved, which is often the case."

ILLINOIS INSTITUTE OF TECHNOLOGY

Financial Aid: 312-567-7219 • E-Mail: admission@iit.edu • Website: www.iit.edu/

THE PRINCETON REVIEW SAYS

Admissions

The school reports that its standardized testing policy for use in admission for Fall 2024 is Test Optional. It is unknown at this time if the 2024 testing policy will be permanent. The Princeton Review suggests that interested applicants consult with the school for the most up-to-date standardized testing policies. *Very important factors considered include:* rigor of secondary school record, academic GPA, standardized test scores. *Important factors considered include:* class rank, recommendation(s). *Other factors considered include:* application essay, interview, extracurricular activities, talent/ability, character/personal qualities, first generation, alumni/ae relation, volunteer work, work experience, level of applicant's interest. High school diploma is required and GED is accepted. *Academic units required:* 4 English, 4 math, 3 science, 2 social studies. *Academic units recommended:* 2 science labs, 2 foreign language, 2 history, 1 computer science, 1 visual/performing arts.

Financial Aid

Students should submit: FAFSA. Priority filing deadline is 10/1. The Princeton Review suggests that all financial aid forms be submitted as soon as possible (see page 5 for a note on the FAFSA). *Need-based scholarships/grants offered:* College/university scholarship or grant aid from institutional funds; Federal Pell; Private scholarships; SEOG; State scholarships/grants. *Loan aid offered:* Direct PLUS loans; Direct Subsidized Loans; Direct Unsubsidized Loans; College/university loans from institutional funds. Admitted students will be notified of awards on a rolling basis. Federal Work-Study Program available. Institutional employment available.

The Inside Word

Competition to get in includes students worthy of top tech schools like MIT and CalTech, so if the acceptance rate seems good, understand that it might be a slightly self-selecting pool made up of high achievers. Accordingly, it would be smart to emphasize work ethic and career goals to win over admission officers at this academically demanding and career-driven school. Extracurriculars and leadership roles always look good, but you should especially highlight any STEM-based activities outside the classroom.

THE SCHOOL SAYS "..."

From the Admissions Office

"Illinois Tech provides students a distinctive and relevant education through hands-on learning, dedicated teachers, small class sizes, and research opportunities. From high-tech maker spaces to cutting-edge research, we prepare students to think big and lead big like no other university can. Our graduates achieve a career placement rate of 90% or above, and their mean starting salaries are much higher than the national average.

"Classes are taught by senior faculty—not teaching assistants—who foster our culture of innovation with their own research experience. Our one-of-a-kind Elevate program ensures that our students develop the twenty-first century skills that employers seek and that they graduate with career readiness. Elevate guarantees that our students will take part in hands-on experiences such as internships, research, study away, competitions, and short courses, while also receiving personalized academic and career mentorship.

"A thriving ecosystem for startups and for advancements in tech, Chicago is a living lab where Illinois Tech students apply what they learn in the classroom through real-world opportunities. Students also receive a multitude of opportunities for networking, internships, and mentorship, as well as opportunities for job placement.

"Illinois Tech's Accelerated Master's Program allows students to complete both a bachelor's and master's degree in as few as five years. Undergraduate scholarships apply to the fifth year of study, meaning students pay the lower undergraduate tuition rate for graduate courses.

"Illinois Tech strives to make higher education accessible for all. Ninety-eight percent of undergraduates receive some form of financial aid, including merit-based scholarships ranging from $10,000 to full tuition."

SELECTIVITY

Admissions Rating	89
# of applicants	7,243
% of applicants accepted	61
% of acceptees attending	14
# of early decision applicants	119
% accepted early decision	43

FIRST-YEAR PROFILE

Testing policy	Test Optional
Range SAT Comp	1230–1390
Range SAT EBRW	610–680
Range SAT Math	610–730
Range ACT Comp	28–32
# submitting SAT	255
% submitting SAT	41
# submitting ACT	89
% submitting ACT	14
Avg HS GPA	4.2
% frosh submitting HS GPA	91
% graduated top 10%	56
% graduated top 25%	79
% graduated top 50%	99

DEADLINES

Early decision	
Deadline	11/1
Notification	12/15
Other ED deadline	1/15
Other ED notification	3/1
Early Action	
Deadline	11/15
Notification	12/31
Regular	
Priority	11/15
Deadline	8/1
Notification	Rolling, 10/1
Nonfall registration?	Yes

APPLICANTS ALSO LOOK AT

Arizona State University; California Polytechnic Institute of Technology; DePaul University; Iowa State University; Loyola University; Purdue University; Rochester Institute of Technology; University of Illinois Chicago; University of Illinois Urbana-Champaign; University of Michigan

FINANCIAL FACTS

Financial Aid Rating	83
Annual tuition	$48,670
Room & Board	$15,570
Required Fees	$1,620
Required Fees (first-year)	$1,970
Books & Supplies	$1,200
Avg frosh need-based scholarship	$41,320
Avg UG need-based scholarship	$38,797
% needy frosh rec. need-based scholarship or grant aid	100
% needy UG rec. need-based scholarship or grant aid	100
% needy frosh rec. non-need-based scholarship or grant aid	15
% needy UG rec. non-need-based scholarship or grant aid	14
% needy frosh rec. need-based self-help aid	53
% needy UG rec. need-based self-help aid	54
% frosh rec. any financial aid	89
% UG rec. any financial aid	93
% UG borrow to pay for school	60
Avg cumulative indebtedness	$29,690
% frosh need fully met	19
% UG need fully met	16
Average % of frosh need met	85
Average % of ugrad need met	80

ILLINOIS WESLEYAN UNIVERSITY

1312 N. Park St., Bloomington, IL 61702-2900 • Admissions: 309-556-1000 • Fax: 309-556-3820

STUDENTS SAY "..."

Academics

Located in Bloomington, Illinois Wesleyan University is a community that "invites you to make the most of your education and is ready to bend over backwards to ensure you enjoy your experience." Though the school doesn't have that big of a reputation outside the Midwest "despite its excellent education," it is an underrated gem that is "always trying to give students opportunities that are beyond what most schools can give." It truly is "a small school that oozes big opportunities."

Professors are "brilliant and accessible" "insightful" individuals who are "the best in their field." "The exuberance they have for their subject area and their students is very evident." Many of them are involved in research and "often include students in helping them," while others are involved in other ways; for example, "the [former] mayor of Bloomington is also a political science professor—how cool is that!" "There have been a few life-changing professors who I am so grateful to have taken their class," says a business administration major.

Facilities and the career center are excellent, there are numerous opportunities for community engagement and research, and "there are so many resources and programs that help students who are seeking any type of support, whether it be academic, moral, or health." Wesleyan also "does a great job getting students ready for graduate school," and faculty "put [a lot of] effort into the information being taught, and really try and relate it to real life."

The school has a reputation for "overinvolved students who travel abroad, are the president of three clubs, and still maintain excellent grades." "IWU pushes us to excel academically while encouraging us to pursue our passions outside of our schoolwork," says a student. Overall, IWU is "a friendly community where your professors become mentors, your classmates become lifelong friends, and you graduate prepared to make a real difference in the world."

Campus Life

As with many colleges, there's a strong weekday-weekend divide: "There is a fair trade of work and play." Sunday through Wednesday nights, "people are studying, going to meetings for clubs, maybe going to an event or two," but come the weekend, students "will go to parties at fraternity houses or off-campus houses, or go to the bars." Bloomington-Normal also has a variety of "great restaurants" and shopping venues which "are fun places to go to on the weekends," and neighboring ISU offers "some of that big college town culture [that] can be found in the area."

The Office of Student Activities "does a great job having entertainment available for students" and almost every weekend a free event is held in the student center, "whether that be a concert, comedian, movie, or other entertainment." There is a "plethora of study groups" ("People are very receptive to getting work done together"), "great opportunities for intellectual discussions" at the coffee shop, and "students are always in food areas discussing, reading, or doing homework." "We have a weird obsession with the Game Show network as well here," confesses a student. "Buncha dorks. We know it and we own it!"

Student Body

The typical Wesleyan student "has a major that they take great pride in studying" and "often compare workloads to bond." Students here are "very academically focused" ("it's very rare to find students who don't try") but are also aware that "having a social life is important as well." Almost everyone is "very liberal and rather artistic" and "very involved with many different activities." While there are noticeable groups such as "athletes, Greek life, and theater kids" which mainly stick together, "everyone has friends in other departments and organizations." There is "lots of competition on campus for internships and research opportunities," but "everyone is very helpful when it comes to informing others of opportunities." A "large percentage" of the campus is Greek life-affiliated.

ILLINOIS WESLEYAN UNIVERSITY

Financial Aid: 309-556-3096 • E-Mail: iwuadmit@iwu.edu • Website: www.iwu.edu

THE PRINCETON REVIEW SAYS

Admissions

The school reports that its standardized testing policy for use in admission for Fall 2024 is Test Optional. The 2024 testing policy will be permanent. The Princeton Review suggests that interested applicants consult with the school for the most up-to-date standardized testing policies. *Very important factors considered include:* rigor of secondary school record, academic GPA, interview. *Important factors considered include:* class rank, standardized test scores, application essay, extracurricular activities, talent/ability, character/personal qualities. *Other factors considered include:* recommendation(s), first generation, alumni/ae relation, geographical residence, state residency, racial/ethnic status, volunteer work, work experience, level of applicant's interest. High school diploma is required and GED is accepted. *Academic units recommended:* 4 English, 3 math, 3 science, 2 science labs, 3 foreign language, 2 social studies.

Financial Aid

Students should submit: FAFSA. Priority filing deadline is 11/1. The Princeton Review suggests that all financial aid forms be submitted as soon as possible (see page 5 for a note on the FAFSA). *Need-based scholarships/grants offered:* College/university scholarship or grant aid from institutional funds; Federal Pell; SEOG; State scholarships/grants. *Loan aid offered:* Direct PLUS loans; Direct Subsidized Loans; Direct Unsubsidized Loans; College/university loans from institutional funds; Federal Nursing Loans. Federal Work-Study Program available. Institutional employment available.

The Inside Word

There's no application fee at IWU, and the school accepts the Common Application, so there are few reasons not to apply to IWU if you're even slightly interested in attending. Those applying to any of the creative arts school may be required to submit additional materials such as a portfolio. Don't expect to breeze through, though. You won't get into this highly selective college without a solid academic profile or a compelling story.

THE SCHOOL SAYS "..."

From the Admissions Office

"Illinois Wesleyan University attracts a wide variety of students who are interested in pursuing diverse fields such as vocal performance, biology, psychology, political science, physics, or business administration. At IWU, students are not forced into either/or choices. Rather, they are encouraged to pursue multiple interests simultaneously—a philosophy that is in keeping with the spirit and value of a liberal arts education. The distinctive 4-4-1 calendar allows students to follow their interests each school year in two semesters followed by an optional month-long class in May. May Term opportunities include classes on campus; research collaboration with faculty; travel and study in such places as Australia, China, South Africa, and Europe; as well as local, national, and international internships. Study abroad is very popular, with one out of every two students enjoying a travel experience.

"The IWU mission statement reads in part: 'A liberal education at Illinois Wesleyan fosters creativity, critical thinking, effective communication, strength of character, and a spirit of inquiry; it deepens the specialized knowledge of a discipline with a comprehensive world view. It affords the greatest possibilities for realizing individual potential while preparing students for democratic citizenship and life in a global society.... The university, through its policies, programs, and practices, is committed to diversity, social justice, and environmental sustainability. A tightly knit, supportive university community, together with a variety of opportunities for close interaction with excellent faculty, both challenges and supports students in their personal and intellectual development.'"

SELECTIVITY

Admissions Rating	91
# of applicants	4,408
% of applicants accepted	42
% of acceptees attending	21

FIRST-YEAR PROFILE

Testing policy	Test Optional
Range SAT composite	1200–1330
Range SAT EBRW	560–660
Range SAT math	560–670
Range ACT composite	25–30
# submitting SAT scores	171
% submitting SAT scores	45
# submitting ACT scores	83
% submitting ACT scores	22
Average HS GPA	3.8
% frosh submitting high school GPA	92
% graduated top 10% of class	30
% graduated top 25% of class	62
% graduated top 50% of class	85

DEADLINES

Early action	
Deadline	11/15
Notification	12/15
Regular	
Notification	Rolling, 1/15
Nonfall registration?	Yes

APPLICANTS ALSO LOOK AT

Augustana College (IL); Bradley University; DePaul University; DePauw University; Northwestern University; University of Illinois—Urbana-Champaign; University of Notre Dame; Washington University in St. Louis

FINANCIAL FACTS

Financial Aid Rating	85
Annual tuition	$55,486
Room and board	$12,930
Required fees	$204
Books and supplies	$800
Average frosh need-based scholarship	$39,114
Average UG need-based scholarship	$36,919
% needy frosh rec. need-based scholarship or grant aid	100
% needy UG rec. need-based scholarship or grant aid	100
% needy frosh rec. non-need-based scholarship or grant aid	39
% needy UG rec. non-need-based scholarship or grant aid	30
% needy frosh rec. need-based self-help aid	68
% needy UG rec. need-based self-help aid	71
% frosh rec. any financial aid	100
% UG rec. any financial aid	99
% UG borrow to pay for school	73
Average cumulative indebtedness	$38,572
% frosh need fully met	25
% ugrads need fully met	25
Average % of frosh need met	87
Average % of ugrad need met	86

INDIANA UNIVERSITY—BLOOMINGTON

107 S. Indiana Avenue, Bloomington, IN 47405-7000 • Admissions: 812-855-4848 • Fax: 812-855-5102

STUDENTS SAY "..."

Academics
"Academics and school spirit are [the] specialties" of Indiana University Bloomington as it creates well-rounded students who will be successful in and after college. This large state school offers excellent financial aid and numerous opportunities for graduate and undergraduate students across all departments to conduct research, adding to "the perfect combination of excellent undergraduate teaching, Division I athletic teams backed by a passionate sense of school spirit, and a lively social scene." In short, it's an academically challenging institution with "rigorous and competitive" classes that also has a "fun collegiate environment."

Students credit the "many excellent professors" who "really care about what they do" for this, noting that they both "bring their subjects to life" and "clearly want what's best for their students." Students also point to the individualized attention: "the knowledge to be successful in our futures through great faculty, facilities, and tradition." The "world-renowned business program" and the education and media schools are standouts here, but students say that all of the "school systems are great and easy to access," which makes "communicating with students/professors easy." Even with 50,000 people on campus, the administration gives student groups "much freedom of planning," and this warm environment allows students to "collaborate academically and non-academically as one community." This autonomy grants students the chance to explore "anything we want, whenever, but [find] the key thing we'll love through many opportunities and great programs."

Campus Life
This "best-kept secret of the Midwest" is located in "the vibrant city of Bloomington," where "the restaurants off campus are amazing," with "many options to choose from." During the week, people "work really hard," and the campus is very active, with "a good number of students working out or running." There is "always something going on and something to do on campus that will fit the need of any student." Weekends generally start on Thursday night and go through Saturday night, when "house parties are popular," and the Greek system, although it only encompasses roughly 20 percent of the campus, "provides a strong social scene." The legendary IU basketball team is "starting to really rebuild its legacy," and attending games is common. There are also "free movies at the Union on weekends," and just "a very fun social scene" in general. Looking around the "beautiful" campus," you can see people jogging or biking, and if the weather's really nice, you can find people "lying outside on the grass and on benches snoozing."

Student Body
With such a large student body, "You are destined to find someone who you 'click' with." "It's unheard of that a student won't be able to fit in somewhere," says one. Typical is hard to nail down with tens of thousands of people, but many here are "very respectful of one another and ready to help out a fellow Hoosier" and "very lively and fun," and each student manages to have "an equal balance of school and social life." International students (often attracted by the business and music schools) are "accepted and encouraged to attend IU." Most students can be called "hard workers who also know how to have fun on the weekends."

INDIANA UNIVERSITY—BLOOMINGTON

Financial Aid: 812-855-6500 • E-Mail: admissions@indiana.edu • Website: www.indiana.edu/

THE PRINCETON REVIEW SAYS

Admissions

The school reports that its standardized testing policy for use in admission for Fall 2024 is Test Optional. The policy is permanent. Students can elect to self-report test scores; official scores need to be submitted if they are admitted. *Very important factors considered include:* rigor of secondary school record, class rank, academic GPA. *Important factors considered include:* standardized test scores (if applicable), application essay. *Other factors considered include:* recommendation(s), interview, extracurricular activities, talent/ability, character/personal qualities, first generation, geographical residence, state residency, racial/ethnic status, volunteer work, work experience. High school diploma is required and GED is accepted. *Academic units required:* 4 English, 3.5 math, 3 science, 2 science labs, 2 foreign language, 2 social studies, 1 history, 1.5 academic electives.

Financial Aid

Students should submit: FAFSA. Priority filing deadline is 4/15. The Princeton Review suggests that all financial aid forms be submitted as soon as possible (see page 5 for a note on the FAFSA). *Need-based scholarships/grants offered:* College/university scholarship or grant aid from institutional funds; Federal Pell; Private scholarships; SEOG; State scholarships/grants. *Loan aid offered:* Direct PLUS loans; Direct Subsidized Loans; Direct Unsubsidized Loans; College/university loans from institutional funds; Federal Nursing Loans. Admitted students will be notified of awards on a rolling basis beginning 2/15. Federal Work-Study Program available. Institutional employment available.

The Inside Word

Above-average high school performers (defined by grade point average and/or test scores) should meet little resistance from the IU admissions office. Students will have the opportunity to meet admissions representatives at numerous recruiting events held in many locations throughout the country or during a campus visit. Rolling admission favors those who apply early in the process. IU's music program is highly competitive; admission hinges upon a successful audition.

THE SCHOOL SAYS "..."

From the Admissions Office

"Indiana University Bloomington is the ideal college experience in an idyllic campus environment. Students enjoy the advantages, opportunities, and resources of a large school while still receiving personal attention and support. Students come to IU from all fifty states and more than 140 countries, bringing their diverse backgrounds, experiences, and beliefs to provide opportunities to connect with and learn from each other. They converge on one of the most beautiful and inspiring campuses in the country. When visiting campus, students and parents often describe IU as 'what college should be like.' Outstanding academic and cultural resources combine to provide space to grow and a place to excel.

"Indiana University is a top teaching and research university that provides students with countless opportunities to expand knowledge and skills in and out of the classroom. Offering 200+ majors and more than 4,000 courses, students can study the arts, sciences, humanities, social sciences, languages, technology, and engineering to create the perfect academic path to reach their goals. Students engage in real-world experiences to enhance learning and build marketable skills, including internships, research opportunities, mentorships, service learning courses, and study abroad. Those experiences are valuable when students meet with the 1,700 businesses, government agencies, and not-for-profit organizations that come to campus year to recruit.

"Applicants must submit a complete application for admissions, including official transcripts, and SAT/ACT scores (if applicable) by November 1 to receive highest consideration for IU Academic Scholarships."

SELECTIVITY

Admissions Rating	86
# of applicants	50,016
% of applicants accepted	83
% of acceptees attending	24
# offered a place on the wait list	782
% accepting a place on wait list	51
% admitted from wait list	6

FIRST-YEAR PROFILE

Testing policy	Test Optional
Range SAT composite	1180–1390
Range SAT EBRW	590–690
Range SAT math	590–710
Range ACT composite	27–32
# submitting SAT scores	3,721
% submitting SAT scores	38
# submitting ACT scores	2,059
% submitting ACT scores	21
Average HS GPA	3.8
% frosh submitting high school GPA	94
% graduated top 10% of class	31
% graduated top 25% of class	64
% graduated top 50% of class	93

DEADLINES

Early action	
Deadline	11/1
Notification	1/15
Regular	
Priority	2/1
Notification	1/15
Nonfall registration?	Yes

APPLICANTS ALSO LOOK AT

Michigan State University; Penn State University Park; Purdue University—West Lafayette; The Ohio State University—Columbus; University of Illinois—Urbana-Champaign; University of Michigan—Ann Arbor; University of Wisconsin—Madison

FINANCIAL FACTS

Financial Aid Rating	80
Annual in-state tuition	$10,012
Annual out-of-state tuition	$37,685
Room and board	$12,228
Required fees	$1,435
Books and supplies	$900
Average frosh need-based scholarship	$12,683
Average UG need-based scholarship	$13,406
% needy frosh rec. need-based scholarship or grant aid	83
% needy UG rec. need-based scholarship or grant aid	80
% needy frosh rec. non-need-based scholarship or grant aid	15
% needy UG rec. non-need-based scholarship or grant aid	14
% needy frosh rec. need-based self-help aid	48
% needy UG rec. need-based self-help aid	49
% frosh rec. any financial aid	80
% UG rec. any financial aid	75
% UG borrow to pay for school	40
Average cumulative indebtedness	$28,449
% frosh need fully met	22
% ugrads need fully met	22
Average % of frosh need met	64
Average % of ugrad need met	67

INDIANA UNIVERSITY OF PENNSYLVANIA

1011 South Drive, Indiana, PA 15705-1085 • Admissions: 724-357-2100 • Fax: 724-357-6281

STUDENTS SAY ". . ."

Academics

From the first day a student sets foot on the Indiana University of Pennsylvania campus, they receive highly personalized attention and support. Each student is immediately assigned a professional mentor, and students say one of the school's greatest strengths are these "staff and faculty who aim to help the students academically, personally, or professionally." Affirms one student, "they want to ensure we all have a good and safe experience at IUP." Class sizes "are small, so there is more one-on-one time with professors," and "[there are] a lot of resources that you can use if you need help, whether it's with academics or [wellness]." Among students' most appreciated aspects of the school are the "variety of academic choices, the writing center, "and the "state-of-the-art labs with amazing resources." Also, "through the multicultural center there are a lot of programs that focus on leadership and all of the soft skills."

Professors "care a lot about the success of their students and go out of their way to help them to truly understand what is being taught." The amount of work a student puts in shapes the relationship with the teachers, and "you have to try in your classes and be present, [but] they will notice you if you do." Classes can be lecture-style or "very discussion-based, [which] it makes it interesting to know everyone's opinion on a topic," and some incorporate field trips or outdoor classrooms. "For my language development class, we had a project where we had to find a child and do a book reading activity with them in order to practice using book reading as a method of treatment for those with language impairments," says a student.

Campus Life

Students say that even though "most people are in a routine of going to classes, studying, and either balancing work, an extracurricular, or a varsity sport," the "workload [is] challenging but doable." Part of this credit goes to the school itself, which is "good at making sure everyone feels included with the various clubs and activities," features many "organizations to join that are both fun and helpful for jobs outside of school," and is "amazing at communicating these opportunities." The success of these programs also goes to a "special club called STATIC that runs all major events on campus and figures out the artist who comes for [the] homecoming concert every year." Off-campus, the town of Indiana "is small so there is not much to do besides explore Main Street and outdoor hiking/activities," but students agree "it's great to walk around during the fall and spring." All in all, the "opportunity that IUP provides students in terms of activities, networking, and future career guidance" is at a high level, especially for "great on-campus job[s]" and there are "a lot of resources around campus to help you with anything you could think of."

Student Body

The community found at IUP "is widely diverse, yet inclusive, [which] creates a wonderful environment to want to be a part of." Students here are "supportive, collaborative, and unique" and "provide a welcoming environment for [incoming] students" of all kinds, including the "very welcoming" LGBTQIA student body and international population. This is "a group of people that likes to try new things from cooking, workout, intense board games, or watching a sports game on campus," and "everyone has their own style and views," and "seems to be respectful of each other." People here are "very well-rounded along with committed to working together as a whole" and "are attentive in class, make smart [decisions], and are passionate about their futures." This bond transcends academic interests; as a student says, "It is so easy to make friends here, even in classes that don't pertain to your major."

INDIANA UNIVERSITY OF PENNSYLVANIA

Financial Aid: 724-357-2218 • E-Mail: admissions-inquiry@iup.edu • Website: www.iup.edu

THE PRINCETON REVIEW SAYS

Admissions

The school is Test Optional for standardized testing through 2025. It is unknown at this time if that policy will continue beyond 2025. The Princeton Review suggests that interested applicants consult with the school for the most up-to-date standardized testing policies. *Very important factors considered include:* academic GPA. *Important factors considered include:* rigor of secondary school record. *Other factors considered include:* class rank, standardized test scores, application essay, recommendation(s), interview, extracurricular activities, talent/ability, character/personal qualities, first generation. High school diploma is required and GED is accepted. *Academic units required:* 4 English, 3 math, 3 science, 2 science labs. *Academic units recommended:* 2 foreign language, 3 social studies.

Financial Aid

Students should submit: FAFSA; State aid form. Priority filing deadline is 5/1. The Princeton Review suggests that all financial aid forms be submitted as soon as possible (see page 5 for a note on the FAFSA). *Need-based scholarships/grants offered:* College/university scholarship or grant aid from institutional funds; Federal Pell; Private scholarships; SEOG; State scholarships/grants; United Negro College Fund. *Loan aid offered:* Direct PLUS loans; Direct Subsidized Loans; Direct Unsubsidized Loans. Admitted students will be notified of awards on a rolling basis beginning 11/20. Federal Work-Study Program available. Institutional employment available.

The Inside Word

Admissions officers at Indiana University of Pennsylvania pay closest attention to academic preparation and performance when considering applications. Officers typically only consider personal statements, recommendations, and extracurricular participation for applicants on the border of eligibility. Finally, IUP operates on the basis of rolling admissions. Therefore, it is advantageous to apply as early as possible.

THE SCHOOL SAYS "..."

From the Admissions Office

"At IUP, we look at each applicant as an individual, not as a number. That means we'll review your application materials very carefully. When reviewing applications, the admissions committee's primary focus is on the student's high school record. We're always happy to speak with prospective students. E-mail us at admissions-inquiry@iup.edu."

SELECTIVITY

Admissions Rating	81
# of applicants	8,603
% of applicants accepted	92
% of acceptees attending	22

FIRST-YEAR PROFILE

Testing policy	Test Optional
Range SAT composite	960–1140
Range SAT EBRW	480–580
Range SAT math	460–570
Range ACT composite	17–23
# submitting SAT scores	701
% submitting SAT scores	42
# submitting ACT scores	26
% submitting ACT scores	2
Average HS GPA	3.4
% frosh submitting high school GPA	98
% graduated top 10% of class	8
% graduated top 25% of class	30
% graduated top 50% of class	66

DEADLINES

Regular	
Deadline	Rolling
Notification	Rolling, 9/1
Nonfall registration?	Yes

APPLICANTS OFTEN PREFER

Bloomsburg University of Pennsylvania; Penn State University Park; Slippery Rock University of Pennsylvania; University of Pittsburgh—Pittsburgh Campus; West Chester University of Pennsylvania

FINANCIAL FACTS

Financial Aid Rating	78
Annual in-state tuition	$7,716
Annual out-of-state tuition	$13,890
Room and board	$12,570
Required fees	$3,604
Books and supplies	$1,100
Average need-based scholarship	$7,455
Average UG need-based scholarship	$7,136
% needy frosh rec. need-based scholarship or grant aid	67
% needy UG rec. need-based scholarship or grant aid	64
% needy frosh rec. non-need-based scholarship or grant aid	99
% needy UG rec. non-need-based scholarship or grant aid	72
% needy frosh rec. need-based self-help aid	89
% needy UG rec. need-based self-help aid	87
% frosh rec. any financial aid	80
% UG rec. any financial aid	79
% UG borrow to pay for school	82
Average cumulative indebtedness	$45,388
% frosh need fully met	18
% ugrads need fully met	17
Average % of frosh need met	73
Average % of ugrad need met	69

IONA UNIVERSITY

715 North Avenue, New Rochelle, NY 10801-1890 • Admissions: 914-633-2000 • Fax: 914-633-2182

STUDENTS SAY "..."

Academics

From their first to final year at Iona University, students are welcomed into an "inclusive community" that some say has "the feeling of home." Undergraduates appreciate that the school has "a lot of resources available" and "a huge network of support that will allow you to pursue your dreams." They also note that there are "opportunities for internships and job offers since the school works so hard to have companies come in and talk with the students," and that being "so close to the city" helps.

When it comes to academics, undergrads are quick to note that "Iona is renowned for their business school," which gets students early access to real-world companies, doing things like creating "an integrated marketing communication plan. This allowed us to take what we learn in the classroom and apply it to the real world." On the entrepreneurial side, students speak of "being able to formulate our own business with our group members and actually sell the products we obtained and made and gave the money collected to a charity of our choosing!"

Regardless of major, students say that "higher-level courses are more discussion/project based and intro classes more lecture-based." Fortunately, no matter the class, "most of the professors here are passionate about the subject material they are teaching, which makes the classes easy to attend." Additionally, they "do an excellent job at preparing students for their intended field of study and providing a meaningful learning experience." Perhaps most importantly, it's evident that they "really care about their students. They will contact you if you are doing well or if you aren't doing well. They want to see you succeed at Iona."

Campus Life

There's plenty of homework at Iona University, so on both the academic and recreational side, Iona looks to make sure "there is never a boring or dull moment here." You might see this play out in study spaces like the library's "Harry Potter themed room," or the school's daily activity hour, a dedicated period from 12:00 P.M. to 1:00 P.M. that "allows students to take a break from school work, meet new people, and join in on an extracurricular activity." In general, student engagement services offers many clubs and programs—everything from rugby to criminal justice—that are not only "exciting and interactive [but that] bring the student body closer together." For those professionally motivated, students say of clubs in accounting and finance: "I love how they create opportunities...to network with alumni and participate in interesting career chats." And for those looking for a Greek community, there are "fun events" like "Greek week where there's kickball and lip sync [performances]." Of course, even with all these activities, students sometimes need a change of scenery. That's where they can capitalize on the university's "proximity to NYC to spend time in Manhattan to experience the Big Apple nightlife and cultural outlets."

Student Body

At Iona University, "respect and dignity is always a priority," so it's no surprise that undergrads speak very highly of their "warm and welcoming" peers. They see each other as "passionate, involved" individuals who are quick to "flash you a smile or hold open the door for you." One student elaborates, "I've met some of my best friends through asking a friendly face for help in many different areas at Iona. You are rarely judged and people genuinely want what's best for you." As another puts it, "The second I walked onto campus everyone made me feel like I belonged." Enrollees also note that the Catholic university attracts a "diverse range of students from different religious backgrounds" and "a lot of people from all over the world. [It] is nice to know that I can always learn something new about a different country." To those at Iona, the most important factor is how they join together to "care about their community and making a difference in the world." Beliefs like that are what lead some students to say their already impressive peers "are going to go far beyond what they expected."

IONA UNIVERSITY

Financial Aid: 914-633-2497 • E-Mail: admissions@iona.edu • Website: www.iona.edu

THE PRINCETON REVIEW SAYS

Admissions

The school reports that its standardized testing policy for use in admission for Fall 2024 is Test Optional. The 2024 testing policy will be permanent. The Princeton Review suggests that interested applicants consult with the school for the most up-to-date standardized testing policies. *Very important factors considered include:* rigor of secondary school record, academic GPA. *Important factors considered include:* character/personal qualities, level of applicant's interest. *Other factors considered include:* class rank, standardized test scores, application essay, recommendation(s), interview, extracurricular activities, talent/ability, first generation, alumni/ae relation, geographical residence, volunteer work, work experience. High school diploma is required and GED is accepted. *Academic units required:* 4 English, 3 math, 3 science, 2 science labs, 2 foreign language, 2 social studies, 1 history, 1 academic elective. *Academic units recommended:* 4 math, 2 history, 3 academic electives.

Financial Aid

Students should submit: FAFSA; State aid form. Priority filing deadline is 2/15. The Princeton Review suggests that all financial aid forms be submitted as soon as possible (see page 5 for a note on the FAFSA). *Need-based scholarships/grants offered:* College/university scholarship or grant aid from institutional funds; Federal Pell; Private scholarships; SEOG; State scholarships/grants. *Loan aid offered:* Direct PLUS loans; Direct Subsidized Loans; Direct Unsubsidized Loans. Admitted students will be notified of awards on a rolling basis beginning 2/1. Federal Work-Study Program available. Institutional employment available.

The Inside Word

Iona University has a high rate of acceptance, but admission can still be a competitive process. To put your best foot forward, find ways to demonstrate your personality, ethics, and drive for success—on top of having strong high school coursework, of course. Standardized tests are optional, but absolutely considered if submitted.

SELECTIVITY

Admissions Rating	80
# of applicants	6,228
% of applicants accepted	96
% of acceptees attending	13
# of early decision applicants	60
% accepted early decision	95

FIRST-YEAR PROFILE

Testing policy	Test Optional
Range SAT composite	1040–1190
Range SAT EBRW	520–610
Range SAT math	510–600
Range ACT composite	22.5–31
# submitting SAT scores	73
% submitting SAT scores	9
# submitting ACT scores	7
% submitting ACT scores	1
Average HS GPA	3.4
% frosh submitting high school GPA	100
% graduated top 10% of class	9
% graduated top 25% of class	29
% graduated top 50% of class	60

DEADLINES

Early decision	
Deadline	12/1
Early action	
Deadline	12/1
Notification	1/15
Regular	
Deadline	2/15
Notification	Rolling, 1/15
Nonfall registration?	Yes

APPLICANTS ALSO LOOK AT

Adelphi University; City University of New York—Lehman College; Fordham University; Manhattan College; Marist College; Mercy College; Pace University; Sacred Heart University; St. John's University (NY); University at Albany—SUNY

FINANCIAL FACTS

Financial Aid Rating	76
Annual tuition	$42,128
Room and board	$17,200
Required fees	$2,200
Books and supplies	$1,500
Average frosh need-based scholarship	$6,512
Average UG need-based scholarship	$7,390
% needy frosh rec. need-based scholarship or grant aid	44
% needy UG rec. need-based scholarship or grant aid	44
% needy frosh rec. non-need-based scholarship or grant aid	100
% needy UG rec. non-need-based scholarship or grant aid	99
% needy frosh rec. need-based self-help aid	73
% needy UG rec. need-based self-help aid	73
% frosh rec. any financial aid	100
% UG rec. any financial aid	99
% UG borrow to pay for school	73
Average cumulative indebtedness	$34,423
% frosh need fully met	29
% ugrads need fully met	26
Average % of frosh need met	73
Average % of ugrad need met	70

IOWA STATE UNIVERSITY

100 Enrollment Services Center, Ames, IA 50011 • Admissions: 515-294-4111 • Fax: 515-294-2592

STUDENTS SAY "..."

Academics

Iowa State University is the state's largest research university, offering more than 100 majors, most notably in the science and technical fields, including an engineering program which is "practically unrivaled." Other standouts include the aerospace program and the journalism and design schools. The school is "quick to add new courses on developing technology" and even make some courses available online, and an excellent job placement rate means "if you're looking to not just get a job but build a career, you're in the right place." Due to the size of the university, there are a lot of opportunities (such as "getting to tour and even work at some of the cutting edge research locations in the world"), and teachers will bring in people who work in the field "to talk to you about what their job is like so you can network and learn about your opportunities." In addition to all the classroom and professional resources, there is a largely popular campus lecture series on various topics, and the university is also currently building a student innovation center. "If you are willing to work hard, you can accomplish a lot."

The faculty at the school are "outstanding" and "represent some of the best instructors in the country." Professors "have so much knowledge to share" and include "innovative approaches" in which students "use technology and applications to do assignments." "Not only are they great teachers, but they're great people," says one student. Classes are hands-on and coursework is "challenging in a way that helps [students] know that [they] will be prepared to perform well" in their future careers, but for anyone struggling with their work, "there's a lot of help if you look for it." Overall, students find that Iowa State "offers everything a student needs to succeed" and strives to ensure that every student "succeeds and performs at a high level academically, professionally, and in their personal lives."

Campus Life

Ames is "the perfect college town." Since Iowa State is the main focus, "everyone that lives here cheers for the Cyclones." The school as a whole has "Midwest values," as well as "a plethora of extracurricular opportunities to be involved as a leader or for fun." All of the classes and buildings are located in the same area or near each other to help students avoid being late to class and "a walk across campus is usually only 10 minutes." The fun usually happens on the weekends, with students heading to parties, bars, or sporting events, and there are also "great places to go for dinner, movie theaters, and lots of volunteering opportunities" to keep busy. Clubs (over 800!) "are huge here" and "everyone has their niche." One student says, "Living in a dorm is the best choice" you can make as a first-year student. Dorms often host game tournaments, movie nights, and other events. There's a "state of the art" recreation center (and other facilities), and during nice times of the year, people around campus hammock in the trees and go hiking.

Student Body

According to some students, Iowa State University "lacks diversity as a student body." But students consistently feel that their peers are "very kind, hardworking, and smart," and tend to be "generally a mix of engineering, design, and agriculture students," all of whom comprise "a good mix of people having fun and studying." There is a sizable number of international students at Iowa State, and the entire student body "looks after one another and are always very helpful toward newcomers." The "Iowa Nice" idea is "clearly embodied by the students of Iowa State," and this is "a special breed of people displaying hospitality and kindness in any situation."

IOWA STATE UNIVERSITY

Financial Aid: 515-294-2223 • E-Mail: admissions@iastate.edu • Website: www.iastate.edu

THE PRINCETON REVIEW SAYS

Admissions

The school reports that its standardized testing policy for use in admission for Fall 2024 is Test Optional. The 2024 testing policy will be permanent. The Princeton Review suggests that interested applicants consult with the school for the most up-to-date standardized testing policies. *Very important factors considered include:* rigor of secondary school record, academic GPA, standardized test scores. *Other factors considered include:* class rank, application essay, recommendation(s), interview, extracurricular activities, talent/ability, character/personal qualities, geographical residence, state residency, volunteer work, work experience. High school diploma is required and GED is accepted. *Academic units required:* 4 English, 3 math, 3 science, 2 science labs, 2 foreign language, 2 social studies. *Academic units recommended:* 4 English, 4 math, 4 science, 3 science labs, 3 foreign language, 4 social studies.

Financial Aid

Students should submit: FAFSA. Priority filing deadline is 12/1. The Princeton Review suggests that all financial aid forms be submitted as soon as possible (see page 5 for a note on the FAFSA). *Need-based scholarships/grants offered:* College/university scholarship or grant aid from institutional funds; Federal Pell; SEOG. *Loan aid offered:* Direct PLUS loans; Direct Subsidized Loans; Direct Unsubsidized Loans; College/university loans from institutional funds; State Loans. Admitted students will be notified of awards on a rolling basis beginning 1/30. Federal Work-Study Program available. Institutional employment available.

The Inside Word

Admission to Iowa State University has historically been based on the following formula: ACT composite score; high school GPA; high school percentile rank; and number of high school courses completed in core subject areas. The formula, known as the Regent Admission Index (RAI), is as follows: RAI = (2 × ACT composite score) + (1 × percentile high school rank) + (20 × high school grade point average) + (5 × number of years of high school courses completed in the core subject areas). Anyone earning an RAI score of at least 245 is automatically admitted. The admissions office reviews applicants scoring below 245 individually to determine whom among them will also be admitted. An alternate RAI is calculated for schools that do not use class rank.

THE SCHOOL SAYS "..."

From the Admissions Office

"Iowa State University offers all the advantages of a major university along with the friendliness and warmth of a residential campus. There are more than 100 undergraduate programs of study in the Colleges of Agriculture and Life Sciences, Business, Design, Human Sciences, Engineering, Liberal Arts and Sciences, and Veterinary Medicine. Our 1,800 faculty members include Rhodes Scholars, Fulbright Scholars, and National Academy of Sciences and National Academy of Engineering members. Recognized for its high quality of life, Iowa State has taken practical steps to make the university a place where students feel like they belong. Iowa State has been recognized for the high quality of campus life and the exemplary out-of-class experiences offered to its students. Along with a strong academic experience, students also have opportunities for further developing their leadership skills and interpersonal relationships through any of the more than 800 student organizations, sixty intramural sports, and a multitude of arts and recreational activities."

SELECTIVITY

Admissions Rating	83
# of applicants	20,223
% of applicants accepted	88
% of acceptees attending	28

FIRST-YEAR PROFILE

Testing policy	Test Optional
Range SAT composite	1040–1290
Range SAT EBRW	480–630
Range SAT math	530–680
Range ACT composite	21–28
# submitting SAT scores	869
% submitting SAT scores	17
# submitting ACT scores	4,324
% submitting ACT scores	85
Average HS GPA	3.7
% frosh submitting high school GPA	100
% graduated top 10% of class	14
% graduated top 25% of class	28
% graduated top 50% of class	95

DEADLINES

Regular	
Priority	3/1
Nonfall registration?	Yes

FINANCIAL FACTS

Financial Aid Rating	84
Annual in-state tuition	$8,042
Annual out-of-state tuition	$23,230
Room and board	$9,193
Required fees	$1,274
Books and supplies	$1,041
Average frosh need-based scholarship	$9,605
Average UG need-based scholarship	$8,850
% needy frosh rec. need-based scholarship or grant aid	99
% needy UG rec. need-based scholarship or grant aid	98
% needy frosh rec. non-need-based scholarship or grant aid	48
% needy UG rec. non-need-based scholarship or grant aid	44
% needy frosh rec. need-based self-help aid	64
% needy UG rec. need-based self-help aid	69
% frosh rec. any financial aid	93
% UG rec. any financial aid	83
% UG borrow to pay for school	57
Average cumulative indebtedness	$29,289
% frosh need fully met	20
% ugrads need fully met	21
Average % of frosh need met	82
Average % of ugrad need met	79

ITHACA COLLEGE

953 Danby Road, Ithaca, NY 14850-7002 • Admissions: 607-274-3124 • Fax: 607-274-1900

CAMPUS LIFE
Quality of Life Rating	**87**
Fire Safety Rating	**92**
Green Rating	**98**
Type of school	Private
Affiliation	No Affiliation
Environment	Town

STUDENTS
Total undergrad enrollment	4,601
% male/female/another gender	45/54/1
% from out of state	57
% frosh from public high school	82
% frosh live on campus	99
% ugrads live on campus	80
# of fraternities	3
# of sororities	0
% African American	5
% Asian	4
% White	72
% Hispanic	10
% Native American	<1
% Pacific Islander	<1
% Two or more races	4
% Race and/or ethnicity unknown	2
% international	3
# of countries represented	44

SURVEY SAYS . . .
Lots of liberal students
Students are happy
Students love Ithaca, NY
Great off-campus food
Theater is popular
Campus newspaper is popular
College radio is popular

ACADEMICS
Academic Rating	**79**
% students returning for sophomore year	83
% students graduating within 4 years	69
% students graduating within 6 years	74
Calendar	Semester
Student/faculty ratio	11:1
Profs interesting rating	88
Profs accessible rating	89
Most classes have 10–19 students.	

MOST POPULAR MAJORS
Radio and Television; Music, General; Business Administration and Management, General

STUDENTS SAY "..."

Academics

"Small class sizes" that afford plenty of "personal attention," "outstanding" scholarships, and cross-registration with nearby Cornell University are a few great reasons to choose Ithaca College, a smallish school in central New York that offers many of the resources you would expect to find at a much larger university. "You are able to be a part of a community and get the chance to pursue interests that are not necessarily a part of your chosen course of study," relates an English major. "We have loads of opportunities to do and try a wide variety of things." The vast multitude of academic offerings includes "one of the best communication schools in the country." Also notable are "strong" majors in music, business, and drama; a "highly competitive" six-year doctorate program in physical therapy; and the cinema and photography program. Professors are "really engaging and understand how to present the material so that it is relevant and meaningful." On the whole, faculty members are "really passionate about their fields and have a genuine interest in getting students excited about their passions." By far, the most common academic complaint about academics at Ithaca concerns registration, which can be trying. Some say, "the buildings—inside and out—are a bit outdated." Overall the campus is known for its picturesque beauty. "People aren't kidding when they say 'Ithaca is Gorges (gorgeous),'" promises one student.

Campus Campus Life

The number of extracurricular choices is "considerable" at Ithaca College. At the same time, "the school is small enough for anyone to get involved." There are "speakers and events offered on campus." There's also a nearly professional-quality college radio station. Many students "are part of an athletic team or participate in intramural athletics." For relaxation, students often "hang out on the quad," throwing Frisbees or "playing music on the lawns on tie-dye sheets." The social situation at Ithaca is "nothing like the party scene you'd find at a larger university," but "there are some good parties" now and then. While the campus is a little "isolated," students also frequently manage to attend frat parties at Cornell and generally "enjoy the social scene" the nearby Ivy offers. "The town of Ithaca is quaint but lively." There's "a good music scene and a lot of cool stores." When the weather is nice, "there's always some festival," or at least it seems that way. "If you're an outdoorsy person," the wooded and rocky surrounding area is a wonderland of activity. "The hiking here is unbelievable," and few other schools offer the opportunity to "go cliff jumping on a hot Saturday." On the negative side, winters are cold as a matter of course, and "the cold and rain do hinder activities." Students joke, be prepared to get your exercise walking between classes; "the hills here will kill you."

Student Body

The typical undergrad here is "genuine," "easygoing," "always busy," "well-dressed," and has a "sunny disposition despite the gray skies." Beyond those qualities, the population is "a wide mix of hipsters, jocks, theater kids, music students," and "crunchy granola hippies." Cliques are often based loosely on academics, but it's worth noting that "people of all kinds fit in here" and "everyone finds their niche," thanks in part to the way that "each school (music, communications, business, etc.) is its own community." Ethnic diversity and other kinds of diversity are "not entirely unheard of." However, people are "usually from the Northeast," and "the population of students that fit into the typical suburban, upper-middle-class family is definitely significant." Politically, "students at Ithaca tend to be liberal." Some students tell us that you'll find "a lot of people are environmentally and socially conscious" here who want "to change the world."

ITHACA COLLEGE

Financial Aid: 607-274-3131 • E-Mail: admission@ithaca.edu • Website: www.ithaca.edu

THE PRINCETON REVIEW SAYS

Admissions

The school reports that its standardized testing policy for use in admission for Fall 2024 is Test Optional. The 2024 testing policy will be permanent. The Princeton Review suggests that interested applicants consult with the school for the most up-to-date standardized testing policies. *Very important factors considered include:* rigor of secondary school record, academic GPA, level of applicant's interest. *Important factors considered include:* application essay, recommendation(s), extracurricular activities, talent/ability, character/personal qualities. *Other factors considered include:* class rank, standardized test scores, first generation, alumni/ae relation, volunteer work, work experience. High school diploma is required and GED is accepted. *Academic units required:* 4 English, 3 math, 3 science, 2 foreign language, 3 social studies, 1 academic elective. *Academic units recommended:* 4 English, 4 math, 4 science, 3 foreign language, 4 social studies, 1 academic elective.

Financial Aid

Students should submit: FAFSA. Priority filing deadline is 1/15 regular admission and early action, 11/1 early decision. The Princeton Review suggests that all financial aid forms be submitted as soon as possible (see page 5 for a note on the FAFSA). *Need-based scholarships/grants offered:* College/university scholarship or grant aid from institutional funds; Federal Pell; Private scholarships; SEOG; State scholarships/grants. *Loan aid offered:* Direct PLUS loans; Direct Subsidized Loans; Direct Unsubsidized Loans. Admitted students will be notified of awards on a rolling basis beginning 2/15 regular admission, 12/15 early decision. Federal Work-Study Program available. Institutional employment available.

The Inside Word

Ithaca's admissions profile continues to be on the rise with a good deal of highly competitive applicants. Programs requiring an audition (for example, music) are among Ithaca's most demanding for admission. If you want to pursue the six-year clinical doctorate in physical therapy, focus on completing substantial math and science coursework in high school.

THE SCHOOL SAYS "..."

From the Admissions Office

"Ithaca College is a transformative community where progress never stops. IC attracts students who are ready to grow, question the status quo, and evolve their world. Surrounded by 150 waterfalls in the Finger Lakes region of New York State, Ithaca is a student-fueled college town and a thriving city of art, music, and festivals. Ithaca hosts tech startups, a vibrant music scene, Broadway-caliber theater, and alumni-owned businesses—including world-class restaurants and ice cream shops. In addition to its main campus, IC has satellite programs in Los Angeles and London.

"IC students unlock their potential through rigorous study with experts in over 90 majors and 70 minors offered by five schools. Students benefit from small class sizes, personal mentorship, and professional guidance, as well as access to first-rate equipment and facilities typically found at large universities. Students who might be called "undecided" at other institutions chart their own path with expert guidance in IC's distinctive Exploratory Program.

"Founded as a music conservatory in 1892, IC offers students a unique combination of academic theory, hands-on practice, and performance. Students apply what they learn in real time—working through setbacks while making new discoveries—to develop a breakthrough mindset. Through involvement in nearly 200 student-led organizations, students find their people while they create award-winning projects, volunteer, philosophize, and connect.

"Whether they are winning Pulitzers, launching nonprofits, anchoring broadcast news, leading multi-billion-dollar companies, or revolutionizing patient care (among other accomplishments), students who graduate from Ithaca College 'learn different and leave different.'"

SELECTIVITY

Admissions Rating	86
# of applicants	12,446
% of applicants accepted	75
% of acceptees attending	14
# offered a place on the wait list	216
% accepting a place on wait list	37
% admitted from wait list	92
# of early decision applicants	109
% accepted early decision	94

FIRST-YEAR PROFILE

Testing policy	Test Optional
Range SAT composite	1213–1360
Range SAT EBRW	613–700
Range SAT math	590–680
Range ACT composite	28–32
# submitting SAT scores	364
% submitting SAT scores	28
# submitting ACT scores	91
% submitting ACT scores	7
% graduated top 10% of class	23
% graduated top 25% of class	54
% graduated top 50% of class	85

DEADLINES

Early decision	
Deadline	11/1
Notification	12/15
Early action	
Deadline	12/1
Notification	2/1
Regular	
Deadline	2/1
Notification	Rolling, 11/15
Nonfall registration?	Yes

APPLICANTS ALSO LOOK AT

Emerson College; Penn State University Park; Quinnipiac University; State University of New York—Binghamton University; State University of New York—University at Buffalo; Syracuse University; University at Albany - SUNY; University of Delaware; University of Massachusetts Amherst; University of Vermont

FINANCIAL FACTS

Financial Aid Rating	87
Annual tuition	$49,883
Annual tuition (first-year)	$50,510
Room and board	$16,030
Required fees	$0
Books and supplies	$850
Average frosh need-based scholarship	$31,969
Average UG need-based scholarship	$31,497
% needy frosh rec. need-based scholarship or grant aid	100
% needy UG rec. need-based scholarship or grant aid	98
% needy frosh rec. non-need-based scholarship or grant aid	24
% needy UG rec. non-need-based scholarship or grant aid	16
% needy frosh rec. need-based self-help aid	81
% needy UG rec. need-based self-help aid	83
% UG borrow to pay for school	72
Average cumulative indebtedness	$36,314
% frosh need fully met	41
% ugrads need fully met	40
Average % of frosh need met	89
Average % of ugrad need met	88

JAMES MADISON UNIVERSITY

800 South Main Street, Harrisonburg, VA 22807 • Admissions: 540-568-6211 • Fax: 540-568-3332

STUDENTS SAY ". . ."
Academics
James Madison University is a public university in Harrisonburg, Virginia, offering its 20,000 undergraduates the choice of 76 majors and access to an entire catalogue of world-class research and experiential opportunities. Students say there are "plenty of resources for tutoring [and] career development" at the Student Success Center, among other strengths that include "grad prep, career prep, job search, interview help, mental health services, food, [and] atmosphere." There is a great "diversity of professions one can major and minor in," as well as "different tactics to teaching that aren't just lectures. Teachers actively want you to learn, not just spit back information." Students appreciate the results, like "reversed classrooms, where the content is primarily learned at home, and then reviewed in class to ensure understanding" and "a discussion-based simulation class." They also praise the practical aspect of courses in the planetarium or for scuba diving, where it feels as if "every class can lead to certifications."

"Access to faculty is amazing," reports another student, noting how easy it "to speak with professors about classes, careers, research, independent projects, etc. in and out of class." One student says: "They've gone above and beyond to teach me, problem-solve with me, and get me real-world experience." The staff also does well to accommodate students of all levels and needs, with one undergrad noting that they're "attentive and are very willing to do what they can for you," including providing people "to talk to and opportunities to prevent stress and anxiety." All in all, the university's "leadership takes a very active role in the student experience."

Campus Life
Because the James Madison University "campus is scenic," students tend to stay there "throughout the day to do homework and study, go to the gym, and get food." On an average day, you may see "students reading, painting/drawing, or even playing music on the Quad," says one. As far as spending time indoors, "facilities are clean, updated, [and] large enough to support the large student body." Off-campus, people enjoy "walking downtown to Harrisonburg and checking out the little shops and going antiquing." Many also like to "go to football games where we festively throw streams," but there's no one activity you have to do: "some people choose to go out at night and some choose to stay in and watch movies." That goes for the "many ways to get involved with organizations" and the numerous "social activities proctored by the school, too, like quad events, and lawn games...JMU has very strong school spirit." Together, the "gorgeous campus and friendly atmosphere create an environment that helps you stay mentally healthy and motivated to learn." It's a vibe, according to one student: "You can definitely tell that people enjoy their time here."

Student Body
James Madison University "is a diverse community full of the kindest people," specifically the sort who are "very easygoing and inclusive, which makes it super easy to go up to strangers and have a normal conversation." The student body is "largely white, middle-class, East Coast-raised," but as a whole, it's "a combination of people from all over the country that joined together to create an inviting and open community," and "a safe space where students feel comfortable expressing themselves." The rallying cry at JMU is "Dukes hold doors!" which makes sense for this "positive, fun, outgoing group of students, the sort where, "if a student here was in need and asked another student for help, I think 9 [out of] 10 students would drop what they were doing to help them."

JAMES MADISON UNIVERSITY

Financial Aid: 540-568-7820 • E-Mail: admissions@jmu.edu • Website: www.jmu.edu

THE PRINCETON REVIEW SAYS

Admissions

The school reports that its standardized testing policy for use in admission for Fall 2024 is Test Optional. It is unknown at this time if the 2024 testing policy will be permanent. The Princeton Review suggests that interested applicants consult with the school for the most up-to-date standardized testing policies. *Very important factors considered include:* rigor of secondary school record, academic GPA. *Important factors considered include:* first generation, state residency. *Other factors considered include:* standardized test scores, application essay, recommendation(s), extracurricular activities, talent/ability, character/personal qualities, alumni/ae relation, geographical residence, racial/ethnic status, volunteer work, work experience. High school diploma is required and GED is accepted. *Academic units required:* 4 English, 4 math, 3 science, 3 science labs, 3 foreign language, 2 social studies, 2 history.

Financial Aid

Students should submit: FAFSA. Priority filing deadline is 3/1. The Princeton Review suggests that all financial aid forms be submitted as soon as possible (see page 5 for a note on the FAFSA). *Need-based scholarships/grants offered:* Federal Pell; Private scholarships; SEOG; State scholarships/grants. *Loan aid offered:* Direct PLUS loans; Direct Subsidized Loans; Direct Unsubsidized Loans. Admitted students will be notified of awards on a rolling basis beginning 4/1. Federal Work-Study Program available. Institutional employment available.

The Inside Word

At JMU, admissions are competitive, but the admissions staff insists that they're not searching for a "magic combination" of test scores and GPA. Admissions officers review each application individually and are most interested in the quality of an applicant's secondary school education, followed by performance and, optionally, test scores. The personal statement is a vehicle for conveying information an applicant deems important but doesn't appear elsewhere in the application; as such, it's optional.

THE SCHOOL SAYS "..."

From the Admissions Office

"James Madison University's philosophy of inclusiveness—known as 'all together one'—means that students become a part of a real community that nurtures its own to learn, grow, and succeed. Our professors, many of whom have a wealth of real-world experience, pride themselves on making teaching their top priority. We take seriously the responsibility to maintain an environment that fosters learning and encourages students to excel in and out of the classroom. Our rich variety of educational, social, and extracurricular activities includes more than 100 innovative and traditional undergraduate majors and programs, a well-established study abroad program, a cutting-edge information security program, more than 350 student clubs and organizations, and an expanded 280,000-square-foot, state-of-the-art recreation center. The university's picturesque, self-contained campus is located in the heart of the Shenandoah Valley, a four-season area that's easy to call home. Great food, fun times, exciting intercollegiate athletics, and rigorous academics all combine to create the unique James Madison experience. From the library to the residence halls and from our outstanding Honors College to our highly successful career placement program, the university is committed to equipping our students with the tools they need to achieve their dreams."

SELECTIVITY

Admissions Rating	84
# of applicants	21,176
% of applicants accepted	86
% of acceptees attending	26
# offered a place on the wait list	983
% accepting a place on wait list	61
% admitted from wait list	22

FIRST-YEAR PROFILE

Testing policy	Test Optional
Range SAT composite	1150–1300
Range SAT EBRW	580–660
Range SAT math	560–650
Range ACT composite	24–29
# submitting SAT scores	1,231
% submitting SAT scores	25
# submitting ACT scores	251
% submitting ACT scores	5
% graduated top 10% of class	15
% graduated top 25% of class	28
% graduated top 50% of class	85

DEADLINES

Early action	
Deadline	11/1
Notification	1/1
Regular	
Priority	11/1
Deadline	1/15
Nonfall registration?	Yes

APPLICANTS SOMETIMES PREFER

George Mason University; Old Dominion University; University of Virginia; Virginia Commonwealth University; Virginia Tech

FINANCIAL FACTS

Financial Aid Rating	80
Annual in-state tuition	$7,684
Annual out-of-state tuition	$28,848
Room and board	$11,940
Required fees	$5,408
Books and supplies	$1,098
Average frosh need-based scholarship	$9,222
Average UG need-based scholarship	$8,070
% needy frosh rec. need-based scholarship or grant aid	66
% needy UG rec. need-based scholarship or grant aid	61
% needy frosh rec. non-need-based scholarship or grant aid	13
% needy UG rec. non-need-based scholarship or grant aid	11
% needy frosh rec. need-based self-help aid	63
% needy UG rec. need-based self-help aid	56
% frosh rec. any financial aid	62
% UG rec. any financial aid	58
% UG borrow to pay for school	50
Average cumulative indebtedness	$30,524
% frosh need fully met	83
% ugrads need fully met	73
Average % of frosh need met	35
Average % of ugrad need met	37

JOHN CARROLL UNIVERSITY

1 John Carroll Boulevard, University Heights, OH 44118-4581 • Admissions: 888-388-2977 • Fax: 216-397-4981

STUDENTS SAY "..."

Academics

Founded in 1886, John Carroll University is a private Jesuit institution that offers its 3,000 undergraduates the opportunity to study in 60 major fields across the College of Arts & Sciences and the Boler College of Business. Community service is a pillar of a JCU education, required for some core classes, and the "mind-blowing in the best way possible" number of opportunities to "immerse yourself in Cleveland and provide support to struggling community members" often leads them to be "passionate about service and social justice." When it comes to religion and academic pace, the school "gives everyone a chance to test the waters and figure out what works for them," and the workload "is doable with content that is challenging and worthwhile" and which "really helps to teach you time management." Regular open study tables in the library "help to cover anything that is confusing," and the school "has fantastic academic advisors" who make it "clear that they actually care whether or not you succeed." The alumni network is equally as strong, and JCU "has many connections with employers" so that there are "great opportunities to add experience on your resume and to your skill set."

Professors "truly have student interests at heart when designing their courses" and "try to make class entertaining and insightful." They "create environments where people feel comfortable sharing their thoughts and feelings without intimidation or fear" and are "fantastic, captivating, and caring people." Many "devote time to class discussions and applied learning rather than a typical lecture," and student-run research, immersion trips, and lab experience are always a possibility.

Campus Life

Located in the "safe, peaceful residential neighborhood" of University Heights just 10 miles outside of Cleveland, students like to "gather outside to do homework and appreciate our beautiful campus," and nature lovers enjoy "hiking through Cuyahoga Valley National Park or simply hammocking between two sturdy stumps." That said, the "very involved" campus culture—23 Division III sports, numerous intramurals, a "very popular" renovated gym, and more than 90 student organizations—tends to leave "little free time for most students" during the week, and many can be found studying in the library during the day. Weekends may involve trips to downtown Cleveland or participating in some of the "random weekend events that sometimes happen, like mini golf in the gym."

Student Body

This "incredibly welcoming" and "very inclusive" community is "full of genuinely kind people." The campus is "predominately white and of European descent" and, being a Catholic institution, "a large portion of the student body relates with a religious or spiritual identity." Regardless of a student's beliefs, the school's religious values seem well-represented, with reports of "a lot of selflessness" and a suggestion that each student "embodies the Jesuit tradition of being with and for others." This also enables a culture of collaboration at JCU, where "innovative ideas are constantly bouncing from student to student." It helps that the campus's size "allows for everyone to know each other," especially "great if you want to make an impact or be known around campus." As an undergrad puts it, when "every face is a friendly face...that makes it feel like home."

John Carroll University

Financial Aid: 216-397-4248 • E-Mail: admission@jcu.edu • Website: https://jcu.edu/

THE PRINCETON REVIEW SAYS

Admissions

The school reports that its standardized testing policy for use in admission for Fall 2024 is Test Optional. It is unknown at this time if the 2024 testing policy will be permanent. The Princeton Review suggests that interested applicants consult with the school for the most up-to-date standardized testing policies. *Very important factors considered include:* rigor of secondary school record, academic GPA, extracurricular activities. *Important factors considered include:* application essay, talent/ability, character/personal qualities, volunteer work, work experience. *Other factors considered include:* class rank, standardized test scores, recommendation(s), interview, first generation, alumni/ae relation, geographical residence, racial/ethnic status, level of applicant's interest. High school diploma is required and GED is accepted. *Academic units required:* 4 English, 3 math, 2 science, 2 science labs, 2 foreign language, 2 social studies, 3 academic electives. *Academic units recommended:* 4 English, 4 math, 3 science, 3 science labs, 3 foreign language, 4 social studies, 3 academic electives.

Financial Aid

Students should submit: FAFSA. Priority filing deadline is 12/1. The Princeton Review suggests that all financial aid forms be submitted as soon as possible (see page 5 for a note on the FAFSA). *Need-based scholarships/grants offered:* College/university scholarship or grant aid from institutional funds; Federal Pell; Private scholarships; SEOG; State scholarships/grants. *Loan aid offered:* Direct PLUS loans; Direct Subsidized Loans; Direct Unsubsidized Loans. Admitted students will be notified of awards on a rolling basis beginning 2/15. Federal Work-Study Program available. Institutional employment available.

The Inside Word

John Carroll University is open about its core values and tends to have a relatively self-selecting pool of like-minded applicants. As they accept nearly 90% of applicants, you don't have to worry *too* much about standing out from the crowd, especially if your grades are above average. However, note that JCU is Test Optional in 2024, so if you're concerned that your high school transcript won't tell the whole story, consider contacting your school's enrollment manager directly. Also, note that there's a literal financial incentive to submit your application and FAFSA by mid-December (the Early Filer Grant), so if this is the school for you, don't wait.

SELECTIVITY

Admissions Rating	85
# of applicants	4,310
% of applicants accepted	82
% of acceptees attending	16

FIRST-YEAR PROFILE

Testing policy	Test Optional
Range SAT composite	1160–1320
Range SAT EBRW	590–660
Range SAT math	570–660
Range ACT composite	25–30
# submitting SAT scores	99
% submitting SAT scores	18
# submitting ACT scores	133
% submitting ACT scores	24
Average HS GPA	3.8
% frosh submitting high school GPA	100
% graduated top 10% of class	29
% graduated top 25% of class	62
% graduated top 50% of class	87

DEADLINES

Early action	
Deadline	11/15
Notification	12/15
Regular	
Priority	11/15
Notification	Rolling, 11/1
Nonfall registration?	Yes

FINANCIAL FACTS

Financial Aid Rating	86
Annual tuition	$47,300
Room and board	$14,160
Required fees	$1,800
Books and supplies	$1,250
Average frosh need-based scholarship	$31,294
Average UG need-based scholarship	$29,193
% needy frosh rec. need-based scholarship or grant aid	96
% needy UG rec. need-based scholarship or grant aid	98
% needy frosh rec. non-need-based scholarship or grant aid	96
% needy UG rec. non-need-based scholarship or grant aid	98
% needy frosh rec. need-based self-help aid	75
% needy UG rec. need-based self-help aid	76
% frosh rec. any financial aid	99
% UG rec. any financial aid	99
% UG borrow to pay for school	68
Average cumulative indebtedness	$32,346
% frosh need fully met	34
% ugrads need fully met	33
Average % of frosh need met	85
Average % of ugrad need met	84

JOHNS HOPKINS UNIVERSITY

3400 North Charles Street, Baltimore, MD 21218 • Admissions: 410-516-8171

STUDENTS SAY "..."

Academics

Johns Hopkins University in Baltimore might have a rep for STEM, but undergrads say Hopkins offers a diversity of strong programs, including in music and political science, in which students "[can] study anything and still be taught by the highest of experts." Students say that the academics here are "beyond compare" and rave about the interdisciplinary studies, hands-on engagement, and an "availability of resources, research, internship, and job opportunities [that] are unmatched." With 5,300 undergrads, Hopkins is "small enough for strong interactions among students" and large enough for "unparalleled opportunities to pursue research, form strong relationships with professors, and learn from an outstanding group of peers." While most students major in STEM fields, they "come from various backgrounds and have vastly different experiences," and every student here is "overwhelmingly passionate about what they do and aspires to make an impact in their field." Students have the ability to design their own curriculum, and professors "make themselves very accessible to their students for coffee chats, career advice or even just to give life advice." A few exceptions aside, most instructors are described as "more than willing to push class topics beyond the confines of the textbook to expose us to the implications of the topics discussed in class." Students appreciate that Hopkins posts what other students think of courses so each person "can see what classes appear 'better' and so professors can gain feedback and improve." Classes are "rigorous but very cooperative" and teach you "how to approach any problem fearlessly." The strong alumni network helps with job placement, and professors are eager ("almost giddy even") to take undergraduates under their wings and show them how to do research. These opportunities are available regardless of your major: "One of my art history major friends curated his own exhibit in a gallery downtown (with work from several world-renowned artists) as his research project," says a student.

Campus Life

There's a saying about the "Hopkins 500"—that "it's the same 500 people who are social and go out to parties and bars." In reality, "it's probably closer to one thousand but it's always the same people you see out," and the library doesn't necessarily die down just because it's a weekend night; "some of the students prefer to study all the time." Though life can get stressful, "most students at Hopkins are the type that thrive under pressure." The majority of student life "revolves around clubs and organizations," and throughout the week (as well as on weekends), students will also attend "concerts, symposiums with famous guest speakers or explore what Baltimore has to offer, such as its "great music and food scene." Nearby Mount Vernon "has fantastic culture and food," and Fells Point and Federal Hill are known for their nightlife; Orioles and Ravens games are also popular. Thanks to the city's relatively low cost of living, students "tend to go out and eat at nice restaurants without paying too much money." During lacrosse season, some people will go to the games and "get really involved in the season."

Student Body

This group of "ambitious workhorses" is "very intellectually curious and smart" and "want to be on the forefront of innovation." The typical Hopkins student "works really hard, and knows how to cut loose as well." Though many students are interested in the sciences, everyone at Hopkins "brings something unique to the school whether it is their love for art, school spirit at sporting events or their desire to find a cure for cancer." The demographics include "a lot of international people and people from various backgrounds." There may be "a lot of introverts," but "people are very nice and helpful," and everyone is "invested in the livelihood of the Hopkins community."

JOHNS HOPKINS UNIVERSITY

Financial Aid: 410-516-8028 • E-Mail: gotojhu@jhu.edu • Website: apply.jhu.ed

THE PRINCETON REVIEW SAYS

Admissions

The school reports that its standardized testing policy for use in admission for Fall 2024 is Test Optional. Johns Hopkins University is test-optional through 2026. The Princeton Review suggests that interested applicants consult with the school for the most up-to-date standardized testing policies. *Very important factors considered include:* rigor of secondary school record, class rank, academic GPA, standardized test scores, application essay, recommendation(s). *Important factors considered include:* extracurricular activities, talent/ability, character/personal qualities, volunteer work, work experience. *Other factors considered include:* first generation, geographical residence, racial/ethnic status. High school diploma is required and GED is accepted. *Academic units required: Academic units recommended:* 4 English, 4 math, 4 science, 4 foreign language, 2 social studies, 2 history.

Financial Aid

Students should submit: CSS/Financial Aid Profile; FAFSA; Noncustodial Profile. The Princeton Review suggests that all financial aid forms be submitted as soon as possible (see page 5 for a note on the FAFSA). *Need-based scholarships offered:* College/university scholarship or grant aid from institutional funds; Federal Pell; Private scholarships; SEOG; State scholarships/grants. *Loan aid offered:* Direct PLUS loans; Direct Subsidized Loans; Direct Unsubsidized Loans. Admitted students will be notified of awards on or about 3/15. Federal Work-Study Program available. Institutional employment available.

The Inside Word

Top schools like Hopkins receive more and more applications every year and, as a result, grow harder and harder to get into. With over 30,000 applicants, Hopkins can be highly selective and looks for individuals who will thrive in the Hopkins community. Admissions counselors utilize a holistic approach to admissions and in particular are looking for applicants who can demonstrate their academic character, their impact outside of the classroom, and how they engage with their communities. Hopkins is need-blind, meets 100 percent of demonstrated need, and funds financial aid offers with need-based scholarships work opportunities.

THE SCHOOL SAYS "..."

From the Admissions Office

"Johns Hopkins University brings together the brightest minds from all backgrounds who want to make an impact. Our students use the resources and opportunities available to them at the #1 research university to learn from each other, push the boundaries of what's possible, and create a better future.

"Through our flexible, liberal arts-based curriculum, students can combine their interests in creative ways. Their enthusiasm for making connections—between ideas and people—leads 68% of our students to double major or minor."

"Our students create a vibrant community, sharing their interests with one another and actively participating in 450+ student-run groups that range from performing arts and varsity sports to service-based clubs, professional organizations, and identity groups.

"Whether they're going to Orioles games, visiting free museums, attending Artscape, or partnering with local organizations to learn from and contribute to the city we call home, our students are active and engaged citizens of Baltimore.

"The admissions committee looks for students who will take advantage of all our university has to offer. We use a holistic application review process so we can better understand who a student is and consider their academic achievements, community impact, and what they'll bring to our campus. To make a world-class education financially possible, we meet 100% of demonstrated need for every admitted student through need-based scholarships and work-study opportunities—money that doesn't need to be repaid."

SELECTIVITY

Admissions Rating	99
# of applicants	37,826
% of applicants accepted	7
% of acceptees attending	51
# offered a place on the wait list	3,443
% accepting a place on wait list	68
% admitted from wait list	0
# of early decision applicants	5,654
% accepted early decision	15

FIRST-YEAR PROFILE

Testing policy	Test Optional
Range SAT composite	1520–1560
Range SAT EBRW	740–770
Range SAT math	780–800
Range ACT composite	34–35
# submitting SAT scores	625
% submitting SAT scores	44
# submitting ACT scores	217
% submitting ACT scores	15
Average HS GPA	3.9
% frosh submitting high school GPA	97
% graduated top 10% of class	99
% graduated top 25% of class	100
% graduated top 50% of class	100

DEADLINES

Early decision	
Deadline	11/1
Notification	12/10
Other ED deadline	1/3
Other ED notification	2/11
Regular	
Deadline	1/3
Notification	3/15
Nonfall registration?	No

APPLICANTS ALSO LOOK AT

Columbia University; Cornell University; Duke University; Harvard College; Princeton University; University of California—Berkeley; University of Pennsylvania; Yale University

FINANCIAL FACTS

Financial Aid Rating	95
Annual tuition	$62,840
Room and board	$19,840
Required fees	$0
Books and supplies	$1,345
Average frosh need-based scholarship	$62,208
Average UG need-based scholarship	$57,350
% needy frosh rec. need-based scholarship or grant aid	99
% needy UG rec. need-based scholarship or grant aid	99
% needy frosh rec. non-need-based scholarship or grant aid	9
% needy UG rec. non-need-based scholarship or grant aid	7
% needy frosh rec. need-based self-help aid	78
% needy UG rec. need-based self-help aid	83
% UG borrow to pay for school	34
Average cumulative indebtedness	$17,712
% frosh need fully met	95
% ugrads need fully met	94
Average % of frosh need met	99
Average % of ugrad need met	98

JUNIATA COLLEGE

1700 Moore Street, Huntingdon, PA 16652-2119 • Admissions: 814-641-3000

STUDENTS SAY "..."

Academics

Juniata College is a private liberal arts college located in Huntingdon, Pennsylvania. The college is named after the Juniata River. The school has "excellent science programs," and a few students say that there need to be "more resources [for] non-science programs." However, even students not majoring in science get access to some great facilities, with theater students exclaiming, "The theater program is unlike any other in country" and praising their new Halbritter Center for the Performing Arts. At Juniata, students can design their educational plan with the college's Program of Emphasis. Many students do so, about 30 percent. Those interested in a specific established program—something like accounting or chemistry—can use an existing designated Program of Emphasis. All students have the option of working with two faculty advisors. The "outstanding education" is built on a bedrock of strong faculty members who offer "superior education through meaningful personal interaction." Most class sizes tend to be fairly small, and though some classes are "tough to get in to because there is only one professor for a certain subject," many agree that they love the attention that each professor gives and that the teachers "really go out of their way" to help students succeed and "value student success as much as the student does." Success, however, doesn't come without a price at Juniata, with a large amount of the students agreeing that their "good grades do not come without effort," but that the class load is "challenging, but not overwhelming."

Campus Life

Students seem to agree that there "isn't much to do in the town" of Huntingdon, but Juniata College makes up for it by making sure there is "always something to do" on campus. There are so many activities and groups on campus that some say, "It feels like you're missing out if you go home for the weekend." There are a "lot of traditions such as Storming of the Arch, Mountain Day, and Madrigal" that have been around the campus for decades and help bring students together. For instance, during Mountain Day, classes are canceled, and students and faculty are shuttled to a state park near the school where there are lunches, nature walks, and various games being played, and neither group knows when exactly it is going to be until the morning of the event. While there might be a lot of activities to do on campus, "if you want to party you can find one." If you want to just relax with your fellow students, "Raystown Lake is only twenty minutes away," where many students like to go and relax. Back on campus, many students seem to think that the "dorms and food" need improvement, but believe that the academic experience they receive outweighs those drawbacks.

Student Body

Students tend to describe themselves as "driven" and "passionately interested in their subjects," though they also take pride in their "laid-back" attitudes, saying they "know how to balance fun and work." During the week students "tend to buckle down and get their work done." A lot of "exchange students from around the world" come to Juniata College to pursue their education. Students agree that "everyone fits in somewhere" at Juniata College because "people are accepted not despite their differences, but because of them."

JUNIATA COLLEGE

Financial Aid: 814-641-3144 • E-Mail: info@juniata.edu • Website: www.juniata.edu/

THE PRINCETON REVIEW SAYS

Admissions

The school reports that its standardized testing policy for use in admission for Fall 2024 is Test Optional. The 2024 testing policy will be permanent. The Princeton Review suggests that interested applicants consult with the school for the most up-to-date standardized testing policies. *Very important factors considered include:* academic GPA. *Important factors considered include:* rigor of secondary school record, application essay, recommendation(s), extracurricular activities, talent/ability, character/personal qualities. *Other factors considered include:* class rank, standardized test scores, interview, first generation, alumni/ae relation, geographical residence, state residency, racial/ethnic status, volunteer work, work experience. High school diploma is required and GED is accepted. *Academic units required:* 4 English, 1 math, 1 science, 1 science lab, 2 foreign language, 1 social studies, 1 history, 1 academic elective.

Financial Aid

Students should submit: FAFSA. Priority filing deadline is 3/1. The Princeton Review suggests that all financial aid forms be submitted as soon as possible (see page 5 for a note on the FAFSA). *Need-based scholarships/grants offered:* College/university scholarship or grant aid from institutional funds; Federal Pell; Private scholarships; SEOG; State scholarships/grants. *Loan aid offered:* Direct PLUS loans; Direct Subsidized Loans; Direct Unsubsidized Loans; College/university loans from institutional funds. Admitted students will be notified of awards on a rolling basis beginning 1/30. Federal Work-Study Program available. Institutional employment available.

The Inside Word

High school seniors who are interested in Juniata must apply either by November 15 for early decision, January 5 for early action, or March 15 for regular decision. Interested applicants can submit their SAT or ACT scores, but standardized test scores are not required. This is in addition to the required essays that are part of the application process. For those looking to save some money, there is no application fee for anyone who applies to Juniata via the website. They also provide incoming freshman with Inbound Retreats each August, which allows them to sign up for one of 38 different retreats and get an idea of what college life is like, but without having to go to class.

THE SCHOOL SAYS "..."

From the Admissions Office

"Surrounded by stunning natural beauty, Juniata College welcomes inquisitive, talented, and hardworking students who do the work of becoming broadly educated, effective citizens of the world. Students can write their own academic programs based on their interests, talents, and goals. They contribute to a close-knit community of people who support, celebrate, and enjoy one another. Highly focused scholars, Juniata students conduct research, engage in meaningful service, intern on or near campus and across the globe, compete as athletes, and collaborate as artists. All of this happens in a modern oasis seemingly reserved for the purpose of fostering exploration and reflection.

"We firmly believe college years are the time to contemplate individual goals and explore options while enjoying the journey. We encourage students to consider new ideas and perspectives, take risks, push themselves to new experiences. As a result, our students graduate in four years not only with a useful college degree, but also with self-reliance, intellectual dexterity, courage of heart, and a collaborative, compassionate spirit.

"In discussions with their advisers, students choose a single discipline POE or write one that is customized to their interests. Still others become the authors of a POE no student has done before. The POE system at Juniata helps students act upon their deepening understanding of themselves and complete an undergraduate education that prepares them for success as they choose to define it. The true power of the POE, however, is that it provides a foundation upon which layers of experiences and opportunities can be added. The result is meaningful outcomes for individuals of consequence."

SELECTIVITY

Admissions Rating	85
# of applicants	2,563
% of applicants accepted	76
% of acceptees attending	15
# of early decision applicants	46
% accepted early decision	67

FIRST-YEAR PROFILE

Testing policy	Test Optional
Range SAT composite	1120–1340
Range SAT EBRW	570–680
Range SAT math	550–660
Range ACT composite	26–30
# submitting SAT scores	81
% submitting SAT scores	28
# submitting ACT scores	11
% submitting ACT scores	4
Average HS GPA	3.7
% frosh submitting high school GPA	100
% graduated top 10% of class	21
% graduated top 25% of class	49
% graduated top 50% of class	83

DEADLINES

Early decision	
Deadline	11/15
Notification	1/15
Early action	
Deadline	1/15
Notification	2/15
Regular	
Deadline	3/15
Notification	Rolling, 10/30
Nonfall registration?	Yes

APPLICANTS SOMETIMES PREFER

Indiana University of Pennsylvania; Penn State University Park; Susquehanna University; Temple University; University of Pittsburgh—Pittsburgh Campus

APPLICANTS RARELY PREFER

Allegheny College; Bloomsburg University of Pennsylvania; Dickinson College; George Mason University; West Chester University of Pennsylvania

FINANCIAL FACTS

Financial Aid Rating	93
Annual tuition	$55,322
Room and board	$13,346
Required fees	$1,080
Books and supplies	$1,000
Average frosh need-based scholarship	$32,423
Average UG need-based scholarship	$34,815
% needy frosh rec. need-based scholarship or grant aid	100
% needy UG rec. need-based scholarship or grant aid	98
% needy frosh rec. non-need-based scholarship or grant aid	100
% needy UG rec. non-need-based scholarship or grant aid	98
% needy frosh rec. need-based self-help aid	100
% needy UG rec. need-based self-help aid	98
% frosh rec. any financial aid	99
% UG rec. any financial aid	98
% UG borrow to pay for school	65
Average cumulative indebtedness	$37,827
% frosh need fully met	40
% ugrads need fully met	81
Average % of frosh need met	88
Average % of ugrad need met	86

KALAMAZOO COLLEGE

1200 Academy Street, Kalamazoo, MI 49006 • Admissions: 269-337-7000 • Fax: 269-552-5083

STUDENTS SAY ". . ."

Academics

Kalamazoo College, also more familiarly known as K, is private liberal arts college in Michigan that brings a personalized approach to education through a flexible, open curriculum featuring real-world experience, service learning, study abroad, and an independent senior year project. This small, nationally-recognized institution "allows students to really develop personal relationships with their peers and professors" and is "a campus run by and for the students." The open curriculum means "students have more time to explore exactly what they want to learn, rather than being required to take classes in which they have no interest," and the school motto of "More in Four" not only describes how much students will learn in their time at K, but "also that this institution will try as hard as possible to get you to graduate in four years." As for post-graduate plans, alumni are "very easy to contact and willing to help." As one student puts it, "Through alumni interaction and my experiences at Kalamazoo, there is a huge culture of giving back to the school and being there for each other."

Full-time professors here, 94 percent of whom hold a PhD or the highest degree in their field, "present challenging information and generally work to achieve camaraderie with students." They "definitely understand that classes may be difficult and really, truly want to help students learn the best they can," and also view students "as equals and peers, and are open to listening to everyone's ideas in classes." Professors "demand quite a lot, but only from a desire to teach the material effectively"; they also "message their departments with internship opportunities quite regularly." Most students have only three classes at a time (the school is on a quarter system) "because each class here tends to be more intense."

Campus Life

Academics are a universal student priority at Kalamazoo College, and "missing classes or letting work slack for social lives and hangovers doesn't happen often." Many times residence halls will host community building events that provide "good food and fun activities," and the school puts on numerous events for the students such as Friday night movies and "Zoo After Dark," and offers a wide variety of programs and clubs to join, and "all are accessible to students who want to pursue them." There "isn't a lot to do" in the surrounding area, but those that are 21 can hit a few bars or clubs and those with access to a car can drive to nearby malls and cities. There "is not a lot of time to have fun on weekdays since things move quickly," but people make time for hanging out. Athletics are popular and "easy to get into"; some teams are more competitive than others, "but for the most part, if you played in high school, you can play in college." Most students study abroad at some point in their K career (typically junior year).

Student Body

Kalamazoo College students are generally "very open-minded, unique, liberal, and quirky," and "you will never find any two students that are the same here." This is mostly a campus of "socially conscious liberals who are predominantly white," though there are a fair number of people with conservative ideologies. While many admit Kalamazoo "needs more diversity in race," students say it is a "very open campus community for people of different gender identities and sexualities." Each student is able to find their niche quickly due to the small-school environment, thus "everyone is always engaged in some kind of work they truly care about."

KALAMAZOO COLLEGE

Financial Aid: 269-337-7192 • E-Mail: admission@kzoo.edu • Website: www.kzoo.edu

THE PRINCETON REVIEW SAYS

Admissions

The school reports that its standardized testing policy for use in admission for Fall 2024 is Test Optional. The 2024 testing policy will be permanent. The Princeton Review suggests that interested applicants consult with the school for the most up-to-date standardized testing policies. *Very important factors considered include:* rigor of secondary school record, academic GPA, extracurricular activities. *Important factors considered include:* application essay, recommendation(s). *Other factors considered include:* standardized test scores, interview, talent/ability, character/personal qualities, first generation, alumni/ae relation, geographical residence, state residency, racial/ethnic status, volunteer work, work experience, level of applicant's interest. High school diploma is required and GED is accepted. *Academic units required:* 4 English, 3 math, 3 science, 2 foreign language, 2 social studies, 2 history. *Academic units recommended:* 4 English, 4 math, 4 science, 3 foreign language, 2 social studies, 2 history.

Financial Aid

Students should submit: FAFSA. Priority filing deadline is 11/15. The Princeton Review suggests that all financial aid forms be submitted as soon as possible (see page 5 for a note on the FAFSA). *Need-based scholarships/grants offered:* College/university scholarship or grant aid from institutional funds; Federal Pell; Private scholarships; SEOG; State scholarships/grants. *Loan aid offered:* Direct Subsidized Loans; Direct Unsubsidized Loans. Admitted students will be notified of awards on a rolling basis beginning 1/15. Federal Work-Study Program available. Institutional employment available.

The Inside Word

The "K-Plan," which focuses on a broad liberal arts education and engagement with other cultures, is central to the Kalamazoo education. Consequently, college admissions officers are on the lookout for students that show the creativity, ambition, and motivation to thrive at Kalamazoo. Students with artistic backgrounds will want to emphasize that in their application. Admissions are competitive here, so in addition to having high grades from school, it's recommended that you submit strong standardized test scores if you can.

THE SCHOOL SAYS "..."

From the Admissions Office

"At Kalamazoo College, faculty and staff embrace our motto—*More in Four. More in a Lifetime.*—by offering students more opportunities to explore, more mentorship and support, and more preparation for meaningful careers that make a positive impact on the world.

"The *K-Plan* provides an integrated, customizable, and experiential education. The majority of students participate in an immersive, academically focused study abroad program; most participate in career development through internships, career treks or an array of community partnerships and community-based courses; and 100 percent complete a senior project in an area of personal interest. Also, Kalamazoo College is one of the few selective liberal arts colleges to be found in a city—the Kalamazoo metro area has a population of over 260,000 with the advantage of being near a university of nearly 20,000 students. It is a diverse and vibrant community with wonderful access to the arts, athletics, service-learning, and social activism opportunities. *K*'s campus is adjacent to downtown Kalamazoo, which offers shops, restaurants, art galleries, live music and more.

"Kalamazoo College uses a holistic review process to fully assess a student's candidacy for admission. Emphasis is placed on a student's high school experience, including GPA, course selection, application essay, and co-curricular involvement."

SELECTIVITY

Admissions Rating	86
# of applicants	3,702
% of applicants accepted	79
% of acceptees attending	12

FIRST-YEAR PROFILE

Testing policy	Test Optional
Range SAT composite	1200–1370
Range SAT EBRW	610–700
Range SAT math	590–670
Range ACT composite	26–32
# submitting SAT scores	139
% submitting SAT scores	38
# submitting ACT scores	17
% submitting ACT scores	5
Average HS GPA	3.8
% frosh submitting high school GPA	100
% graduated top 10% of class	35
% graduated top 25% of class	67
% graduated top 50% of class	92

DEADLINES

Early decision	
Deadline	11/1
Notification	12/1
Other ED deadline	2/1
Other ED notification	2/15
Early action	
Deadline	11/1
Notification	12/20
Regular	
Priority	11/15
Deadline	1/15
Notification	4/1
Nonfall registration?	No

FINANCIAL FACTS

Financial Aid Rating	88
Annual tuition	$58,185
Room and board	$12,084
Required fees	$429
Books and supplies	$900
Average frosh need-based scholarship	$45,752
Average UG need-based scholarship	$43,793
% needy frosh rec. need-based scholarship or grant aid	98
% needy UG rec. need-based scholarship or grant aid	98
% needy frosh rec. non-need-based scholarship or grant aid	27
% needy UG rec. non-need-based scholarship or grant aid	23
% needy frosh rec. need-based self-help aid	71
% needy UG rec. need-based self-help aid	75
% frosh rec. any financial aid	98
% UG rec. any financial aid	97
% UG borrow to pay for school	51
Average cumulative indebtedness	$28,705
% frosh need fully met	39
% ugrads need fully met	38
Average % of frosh need met	96
Average % of ugrad need met	94

KANSAS STATE UNIVERSITY

110 Anderson Hall, Manhattan, KS 66506 • Admissions: 785-532-6011 • Fax: 785-532-6393

STUDENTS SAY ". . ."

Academics
With more than 150 years of traditions and achievements on the record, Kansas State University is the nation's first operational land-grant university, offering more than 250 undergraduate majors and programs across three campuses, as well as various global online courses. The university's sprawling 2,300-acre main campus in Manhattan, Kansas (nicknamed "The Little Apple") includes comprehensive agricultural and research facilities, while the newest campus, Olathe, is located in the Kansas Biosciences Park and works to expand partnerships between students, researchers, and companies. "Leadership opportunities are always within an arm's length," says a student. On the administration's part, there is excellent "communication of resources available to students," and the school is "very conscious of showing students what they are paying for and listening to student feedback in what prices should be for fees/services." In demonstrating further commitment to quality, "professor performance grades are sent out to students at the end of every semester."

At this research powerhouse, faculty members not only conduct "amazing research that is being nationally recognized" but also strive to do in a way that lets them "pass on their knowledge to the students." Such efforts are also recognized in and out of the classroom, whether that's in the way teachers "are skilled at making classes interesting" or how they lead review sessions "to better help students focus on harder topics." (Students also mention how discussion boards are "largely utilized for engagement.) In general, professors are praised for responding "quickly and well to emails" and overall come across as "approachable and really want to see their students learn and succeed."

Campus Life
The college town of Manhattan "provides those from bigger cities with the pros of a small-town feel (community, laid-back style) while also giving students from rural areas a more city-like lifestyle." As one student puts it: "It is super easy to balance school and a social life here since the majority of the people who live here are students." The bars, restaurants, and shopping in the neighborhood of Aggieville make it "a vibrant hotspot for activity every weekend and even on weekdays." The "gym facilities and hiking trails nearby are beautiful and a great way to get moving," and "the city and university maintain public sidewalks and trails for those wishing to bike/run." All student amenities "are within walking distance," and for fun, "many people attend parties, hang out with friends, and attend events hosted in the student union." Intramurals are wildly popular, and Greek life "is fun but not too overpowering," ensuring that the overall vibe allows students to "focus on their studies and dedicate their daytime hours to ensuring they complete their coursework."

Student Body
K-State is composed of "many international students, first generation students, and students from virtually all race, religion, and age," as well as "many students who grew up on a farm or other rural areas," all of whom contribute to a "wonderful community mindset." Traditions abound here, and "the university instills this very real feeling of belonging and family" known as the Wildcat Way. "Purple pride is taken very seriously" here, so much so that one student notes how "We see that Wildcat, and know we're part of the same family." This is "a big school with a small-town feel," and everyone is "exceedingly friendly and proud of the university." The school itself provides plenty of ways for students to be involved, and there are "a multitude of opportunities for students to find their own space to grow and succeed in."

KANSAS STATE UNIVERSITY

Financial Aid: 785-532-6420 • E-Mail: k-state@k-state.edu • Website: www.k-state.edu

THE PRINCETON REVIEW SAYS

Admissions

The school reports that its standardized testing policy for use in admission for Fall 2024 is Test Optional. It is unknown at this time if the 2024 testing policy will be permanent. The Princeton Review suggests that interested applicants consult with the school for the most up-to-date standardized testing policies. *Very important factors considered include:* academic GPA. *Important factors considered include:* standardized test scores. *Other factors considered include:* application essay, recommendation(s). High school diploma is required and GED is accepted. *Academic units required:* 4 English, 4 math, 3 science, 2 foreign language, 3 social studies.

Financial Aid

Students should submit: FAFSA. Priority filing deadline is 12/1. The Princeton Review suggests that all financial aid forms be submitted as soon as possible (see page 5 for a note on the FAFSA). *Need-based scholarships/grants offered:* College/university scholarship or grant aid from institutional funds; Federal Pell; Private scholarships; SEOG; State scholarships/grants. *Loan aid offered:* Direct PLUS loans; Direct Subsidized Loans; Direct Unsubsidized Loans. Admitted students will be notified of awards on a rolling basis beginning 4/1. Federal Work-Study Program available. Institutional employment available.

The Inside Word

Kansas State is pretty transparent about their admission requirements, and the school is Test Optional. So long as your cumulative high school GPA (weighted or unweighted) is above a 3.25, you should be fine; otherwise, you'll want to include an ACT composite of at least 21 or an SAT total of 1060 or higher. Students who don't meet these standards may appeal and have their application considered on a case-by-case basis, but be aware that this might entail sending in additional documentation or information.

THE SCHOOL SAYS "..."

From the Admissions Office

"Kansas State University is synonymous with community, and its family-like environment is hailed by students past and present. The land-grant university also is home to some of the nation's top academic programs, world-renowned researchers, and unparalleled student support. K-State students have access to first-year programs, free tutoring, research opportunities, career exploration, and much more.

"K-State is rooted in diversity and inclusion with students from all 50 states and 100-plus countries. There are numerous opportunities to explore other cultures through student groups and events, and our Black Student Union has been named No. 1 in the Big 12 almost every year in the last decade. Academic experiences can easily be customized for individual goals with 250-plus majors and options alongside faculty who are committed to helping students find success. Our student experience is one of the best in the nation thanks to programs like K-State First, a first-year experience program helping freshmen connect with the university, and K-State Proud, a student-led philanthropy that has raised more than $1 million for fellow students in need.

"The university awards $38 million in scholarships each year, as well as $248 million in financial aid. Whatever it takes to help students succeed both today and in the future, the K-State family is committed to making it happen."

SELECTIVITY
Admissions Rating	80
# of applicants	9,703
% of applicants accepted	95
% of acceptees attending	32

FIRST-YEAR PROFILE
Testing policy	Test Optional
Range SAT composite	1130–1300
Range ACT composite	20–27
# submitting SAT scores	25
% submitting SAT scores	1
# submitting ACT scores	2,447
% submitting ACT scores	84
Average HS GPA	3.8
% frosh submitting high school GPA	98
% graduated top 10% of class	25
% graduated top 25% of class	49
% graduated top 50% of class	80

DEADLINES
Regular	
Priority	2/1
Nonfall registration?	Yes

FINANCIAL FACTS
Financial Aid Rating	79
Annual in-state tuition	$9,489
Annual out-of-state tuition	$25,560
Room and board	$10,100
Required fees	$959
Books and supplies	$1,010
% needy frosh rec. need-based scholarship or grant aid	47
% needy UG rec. need-based scholarship or grant aid	48
% needy frosh rec. non-need-based scholarship or grant aid	94
% needy UG rec. non-need-based scholarship or grant aid	91
% needy frosh rec. need-based self-help aid	55
% needy UG rec. need-based self-help aid	65
% frosh rec. any financial aid	48
% UG rec. any financial aid	46
% frosh need fully met	26
% ugrads need fully met	21
Average % of frosh need met	76
Average % of ugrad need met	75

KENYON COLLEGE

103 Chase Ave, Gambier, OH 43022 • Admissions: 740-427-5000 • Fax: 740-427-5770

CAMPUS LIFE

Quality of Life Rating	83
Fire Safety Rating	87
Green Rating	93
Type of school	Private
Affiliation	Episcopal
Environment	Rural

STUDENTS

Total undergrad enrollment	1,877
% male/female/another gender	44/56/NR
% from out of state	88
% frosh from public high school	50
% frosh live on campus	100
% ugrads live on campus	99
# of fraternities (% join)	5 (8)
# of sororities (% join)	4 (8)
% African American	3
% Asian	5
% White	66
% Hispanic	8
% Native American	0
% Pacific Islander	<1
% Two or more races	5
% Race and/or ethnicity unknown	1
% international	12
# of countries represented	49

SURVEY SAYS . . .

Lots of liberal students
Students always studying
Students are happy
Classroom facilities are great
Lab facilities are great
Class discussions encouraged
Great financial aid
No one cheats
Students are friendly
Students aren't religious
Recreation facilities are great
Theater is popular
Campus newspaper is popular

ACADEMICS

Academic Rating	98
% students returning for sophomore year	91
% students graduating within 4 years	84
% students graduating within 6 years	87
Calendar	Semester
Student/faculty ratio	10:1
Profs interesting rating	94
Profs accessible rating	98

Most classes have 10–19 students.

MOST POPULAR MAJORS
English Language and Literature, General;
Psychology, General; Economics, General

STUDENTS SAY ". . ."

Academics

This tiny midwestern liberal arts mainstay is Ohio's oldest private college, and is filled with "uniquely quirky and motivated" students and faculty alike. The school's "academic vigor" and intense focus on writing (it is known as "The Writers' College") are two of Kenyon's hallmarks, and the curriculum provides "a well-rounded liberal arts education in which emphasis [is] placed on critical thinking and class discussion." "Even though I don't want to be an English major, I think any college that values writing as much as Kenyon does has its priorities straight," says a student of the highly valued workforce skill.

The school "really knows how to offer a huge diversity of programs and activities to a very small campus," and "it is honestly hard to find a professor who is not thrilled by the content that they are teaching." The faculty is a deeply caring bunch who "love learning just as much as the students" and challenge them to succeed, and they make it known that "your voice is valued in class discussion." "I once met with a professor for an hour every day leading up to the final because I was so nervous about it, and he hardly batted an eye at taking that much time out of his day for only one student," says a sophomore.

"Small, individualized class sizes" make it so that classes are "terrifically interesting," and "out of class work is always meaningful." Students don't compete with each other when it comes to grades so "the cooperative learning environment makes it less stressful," and though "you will spend the vast majority of your time studying...it is also extremely rewarding." The "relatively" open curriculum allows students to take courses that they are truly interested in, and "there is a wide variety of options available in terms of classes" for students to develop new passions.

Campus Life

People come to this "small campus with a big sense of community" because they know it will be a good fit, and it shows in the satisfaction levels here. "I stepped on campus and noticed two things: everyone was happy and the campus was gorgeous," says one of many happy students. The school is a place for "smart, forward-thinking students who study hard but also understand the necessity of taking breaks and having a good time on weekends." People at Kenyon are taught "to see, discuss, and connect the dots"; "Even though I'm not a philosophy major, I feel just as at home in those conversations as I do when I discuss Mahler or the next big party," says a student.

The "utterly pastoral" campus is "absolutely lovely"; "It's like going to school in a Marlowe poem—and with all of the English majors running around, most people know who Marlowe is," says a student. The town of Gambier is "in the middle of nowhere, so campus can get to be claustrophobic at times," but it provides its fair share of entertainment. "Greeks throw great parties [and] intramurals are popular, as are activist groups for everything from gender awareness to Palestine," and the nearby Kokosing Gap Trail is oft-used. The KAC (Kenyon Athletic Center) is unparalleled for a Division III school, and the "dining hall has an amazing commitment to local food." Partying on Wednesdays and the weekends "is a typical activity to unwind after a challenging week of academics."

Student Body

The word most often used to describe Kenyon students in "quirky." There are a variety of types, but "most people have a quirk or five." There are "a lot of hipster students and then a good selection of athletes" at Kenyon, but everyone "tends to be extremely friendly, well-rounded, and smart." Everyone is seriously involved in academics and extracurriculars, and "you're either a jack of all trades here or a master of four." There aren't really many cliques; "someone on the football team could just as easily be in the community choir or quiz bowl club."

KENYON COLLEGE

Financial Aid: 740-427-5240 • E-Mail: admissions@kenyon.edu • Website: www.kenyon.edu

THE PRINCETON REVIEW SAYS

Admissions

The school reports that its standardized testing policy for use in admission for Fall 2024 is Test Optional. It is unknown at this time if the 2024 testing policy will be permanent. The Princeton Review suggests that interested applicants consult with the school for the most up-to-date standardized testing policies. *Very important factors considered include:* rigor of secondary school record, academic GPA, application essay, recommendation(s). *Important factors considered include:* class rank, standardized test scores, interview, extracurricular activities, talent/ability, character/personal qualities, level of applicant's interest. *Other factors considered include:* first generation, alumni/ae relation, geographical residence, state residency, racial/ethnic status, volunteer work, work experience. High school diploma is required and GED is accepted. *Academic units required:* 4 English, 4 math, 3 science, 3 science labs, 3 foreign language, 3 social studies, 3 academic electives. *Academic units recommended:* 4 English, 4 math, 4 science, 3 science labs, 4 foreign language, 3 social studies, 3 academic electives.

Financial Aid

Students should submit: CSS/Financial Aid Profile; FAFSA. Priority filing deadline is 1/15. The Princeton Review suggests that all financial aid forms be submitted as soon as possible (see page 5 for a note on the FAFSA). *Need-based scholarships/grants offered:* College/university scholarship or grant aid from institutional funds; Federal Pell; Private scholarships; SEOG; State scholarships/grants. *Loan aid offered:* Direct PLUS loans; Direct Subsidized Loans; Direct Unsubsidized Loans; College/university loans from institutional funds. Admitted students will be notified of awards on or about 3/20. Federal Work-Study Program available. Institutional employment available.

The Inside Word

In terms of admissions selectivity, Kenyon is of the first order of selective, small, Midwestern, liberal arts schools. Kenyon shares a lot of application and admit overlap with other schools in this niche, and the choice for many students comes down to "best fit." As Kenyon is a writing-intensive institution, applicants should expect that all written material submitted to the school in the admissions process will be scrutinized. Revise and proofread accordingly.

THE SCHOOL SAYS "..."

From the Admissions Office

"Students and alumni alike think of Kenyon as a place that fosters 'learning in the company of friends.' While faculty expectations are rigorous and the work challenging, the academic atmosphere is cooperative, not competitive. Indications of intellectual curiosity and passion for learning, more than just high grades and test scores, are what we look for in applications. Important as well are demonstrated interests in non-academic pursuits, whether in athletics, the arts, writing, or another passion. Life in this small college community is fueled by the talents and enthusiasm of our students, so the admission staff seeks students who have a range of talents and interests.

"The high school transcript, recommendations, and the personal statement are of primary importance in reviewing preparedness and fit."

SELECTIVITY

Admissions Rating	95
# of applicants	8,116
% of applicants accepted	34
% of acceptees attending	19
# offered a place on the wait list	2,165
% accepting a place on wait list	54
% admitted from wait list	2

FIRST-YEAR PROFILE

Testing policy	Test Optional
Range SAT composite	1380–1480
Range SAT EBRW	700–760
Range SAT math	670–760
Range ACT composite	31–34
# submitting SAT scores	149
% submitting SAT scores	28
# submitting ACT scores	142
% submitting ACT scores	27
% graduated top 10% of class	63
% graduated top 25% of class	86
% graduated top 50% of class	97

DEADLINES

Early decision	
Deadline	11/15
Notification	12/15
Other ED deadline	1/15
Other ED notification	2/1
Regular	
Deadline	1/15
Notification	3/23
Nonfall registration?	No

APPLICANTS ALSO LOOK AT

Bowdoin College; Brown University; Carleton College; Colby College; Grinnell College; Hamilton College; Middlebury College; Oberlin College; The Ohio State University—Columbus; University of California—Berkeley

FINANCIAL FACTS

Financial Aid Rating	99
Annual tuition	$69,030
Room and board	$14,410
Required fees	$300
Books and supplies	$1,900
Average frosh need-based scholarship	$53,049
Average UG need-based scholarship	$51,701
% needy frosh rec. need-based scholarship or grant aid	100
% needy UG rec. need-based scholarship or grant aid	100
% needy frosh rec. non-need-based scholarship or grant aid	43
% needy UG rec. non-need-based scholarship or grant aid	43
% needy frosh rec. need-based self-help aid	78
% needy UG rec. need-based self-help aid	82
% frosh rec. any financial aid	47
% UG rec. any financial aid	46
% UG borrow to pay for school	39
Average cumulative indebtedness	$25,146
% frosh need fully met	100
% ugrads need fully met	100
Average % of frosh need met	100
Average % of ugrad need met	100

KETTERING UNIVERSITY

1700 University Ave., Flint, MI 48504-6214 • Admissions: 810-762-9500

STUDENTS SAY "..."

Academics

Students with an interest in business or STEM subjects will be pleased with the offerings of Kettering University, which has a focus not just on those disciplines, but in fostering the next generation of industry leaders. Students attribute some of their success to the institution's "awesome" co-op program, which is "unparalleled in preparing students." The way co-op works is by splitting the academic calendar into four approximately 11-week terms, two of which are for school, and two of which are for work. This means that from their first year on, undergrads "get to make money during school while also getting experience and making industry connections."

A word of warning from students, though: this type of scheduling is quite demanding. "Course loads are high and there is often a lot of homework." This can be compounded by what current enrollees feel is an all-or-nothing split between instructor styles: some "care deeply about the subject and the students" and others who are just plain prickly, or as one puts it, "I have had many professors gladly tell me how many students have failed their class." There are plenty of students who share happy stories of faculty members who are "available almost whenever you need them" or who are "very understanding" and "always willing to help," but "there isn't really an in-between."

Campus Life

Kettering may have an unconventional calendar, and some busy students may quip that "We're all engineers, so we're studying all the time," and yet we heard at length about all the fun activities that students found time to squeeze in. "There is a club for anything and everyone," shares one student, and that doesn't seem to be an exaggeration. In addition to the school's SAE teams, which are among "the best in the country," interest-driven activities like the Financial Club, and popular options like the student-run newspaper or radio station, there's even a blacksmithing club. Students also list a variety of intramural sports like flag football and basketball as a great way to escape academic stress. "We may go out bowling, to play top golf, to catch a movie, [to go] skiing or off-roading." Nearby Detroit and Ann Arbor offer even more events, as does the university itself. Undergrads also share that "Greek life is very popular," although here, too, note that some describe the Greek scene as "completely different at Kettering than it is at other campuses."

Student Body

The "very bright" students at Kettering, despite sometimes feeling "overworked, stressed out, and sleep deprived," overall find themselves "bonded by our struggles in our rigorous coursework." Students stay in good humor and find the silver lining in every experience, or as one colorfully puts it, "We are all...caffeine-fueled sarcasm machines that pump out math and science equations at the drop of a hat." The "personable" atmosphere of this "relatively small" school may help to liven everyone's mood. "Even if you do not know someone's name, you recognize a face in the hallway or in a lecture that you can share a smile with." More importantly, students say that their classmates are "very helpful" and note that "it is easy to join a group who is studying and get to know them." Easy, at least, if you're male—the "vast majority is white male engineering students," and some find that to create "a culture of masculinity" that sometimes offers "very little support for the women." Then again, other enrollees dispute this, suggesting that Kettering is "a very inclusive school" where students "accept and accommodate each other's differences." At the end of the day, all undergrads are "technically minded people" who "want to push boundaries and go further than anyone else," and one notes that "if you love cars, engineering, and the automotive industry, there probably is no better school."

KETTERING UNIVERSITY

Financial Aid: 810-762-7859 • Website: www.kettering.edu

THE PRINCETON REVIEW SAYS

Admissions

The school reports that its standardized testing policy for use in admission for Fall 2024 is Test Optional. The 2024 testing policy will be temporary. The Princeton Review suggests that interested applicants consult with the school for the most up-to-date standardized testing policies. *Very important factors considered include:* rigor of secondary school record, academic GPA. *Other factors considered include:* class rank, standardized test scores, application essay, recommendation(s), extracurricular activities, talent/ability, character/personal qualities, first generation, alumni/ae relation, geographical residence, state residency, racial/ethnic status, volunteer work, work experience, level of applicant's interest. High school diploma is required and GED is not accepted. *Academic units required:* 3 English, 4 math, 2 science, 2 science labs. *Academic units recommended:* 4 English, 4 math, 3 science, 3 science labs, 2 social studies, 2 history, 1 academic elective.

Financial Aid

Students should submit: FAFSA. The Princeton Review suggests that all financial aid forms be submitted as soon as possible (see page 5 for a note on the FAFSA). *Need-based scholarships/grants offered:* College/university scholarship or grant aid from institutional funds; Federal Pell; Private scholarships; SEOG; State scholarships/grants. *Loan aid offered:* Direct PLUS loans; Direct Subsidized Loans; Direct Unsubsidized Loans. Admitted students will be notified of awards on a rolling basis beginning in January. Federal Work-Study Program available. Institutional employment available.

The Inside Word

Kettering aims to find students who will be able to handle the university's demanding curriculum. Given that it's a STEM school, the grades you earned in your math and science classes will need to be high. It's also strongly recommended that you take calculus and any computer or drafting courses available. If for any reason you think your GPA or test scores don't accurately reflect your abilities, you are invited to call the admissions office to discuss your application with one of the school's counselors.

THE SCHOOL SAYS "..."

From the Admissions Office

"Kettering University is recognized as a leader in Engineering, STEM, Computer Engineering, and Business Management. Students spend one term enjoying small classes with technical curricula and hands-on learning in workshops and labs, and the next in a paid professional co-op work experience with one of our 400+ co-op employers in Michigan or nationwide. Kettering degree programs generally require 4-1/2 years to complete, including up to nine rotations of progressively-advancing co-op employment. Our graduates are in high demand and are sought-after by employers and the best graduate programs alike. Most seniors receive full-time employment offers before they even graduate due to the reputation of their degree, tremendous professional experience, and considerable professional networking. Our graduates never start at entry-level, unlike their peers, and are most often on the fast track to leadership in their company and industry. Starting salaries of last year's graduating seniors averaged over $78,000.

"Kettering students recognize the value of campus life involvement, too. Here, they find their people who are highly creative and have fun. Intramurals, Esports, music, community service, and Greek Life are among many ways students keep their outside interests sharp, maintain their own healthy lifestyles, and make lifelong connections. Almost 30% of the student body has participated in competitive robotics at some point. Many volunteer in the Robotics Community Center: home to nine teams, machining space, programming labs, and multiple annual events. Kettering students are passionate problem solvers and entrepreneurs and are changing the world in a million innovative, collaborative ways."

KNOX COLLEGE

2 East South Street, Galesburg, IL 61401 • Admissions: 309-341-7000 • Fax: 309-341-7070

STUDENTS SAY ". . ."

Academics

Students say that Knox College enjoys a "great academic reputation" for its dedication to providing a "well-rounded liberal arts program" that "values independent initiative," while "staying in tune with its roots as a progressive and accessible institution." As one student puts it, "I knew that I would be allowed to be myself, choose the classes that I felt would have the most influence on my education and prepare me for the future." Students are highly encouraged to take classes outside of their majors. Undergraduates are "commonly studying two vastly different subjects and allowing them to merge into one interdisciplinary interest." Knox does have "one of the best creative writing programs in the country," as well as the Peace Corps Preparatory Program—Knox is the first college or university in the country to host the contemporary Peace Corps Preparatory Program. The academic three-term system provides students with "a semester's worth of course work in a ten-week period." Many in the student body believe that this arrangement "promotes better study habits and more attention focused on each class," which are "tough and require a lot of time studying, reading, writing, and thinking." To put it another way, "You don't come to Knox if you want to shy away from class discussion," and professors "concentrate on the student having good critical thinking skills." Students are pleased to find that "you are academically challenged without fierce competition" and genuinely don't mind the challenge: "I've never had an easy professor, but I've always had reasonable ones." Projects and presentations are common; if tests are given, there is an honor code, and "they trust you not to cheat." The faculty and administration are spoken of highly, and they "not only encourage the students to take charge and make change, but they listen and act on the student body's opinions."

Campus Life

Popular manners of relaxation and recreation include intramural sports, campus organizations, and "artistic expression, be it poetry, visual art, performance art, music." Students "go to parties, play games, dance, etc., just like any other college campus. The difference is, our fraternity parties are open to the entire campus and do not serve alcohol." Parties here "are places where you generally know everyone there, you have a good time and no one steals your coat or purse." Undergrads here are also very creative. "When we want to do something fun we typically organize it ourselves." A much-anticipated event is "Flunk Day, a day every spring when classes are canceled and the entire campus goes out on the lawn and plays games, eats great food and enjoys free entertainment." Union Board "brings films, entertainers, concerts, and other groups to campus, including Second City," and the Gizmo is "one of the best places to socialize and eat some late night food." Wandering off-campus a bit is also fun. Undergrads say "Galesburg is a charming town...you just have to look a little bit," for fun affairs such as The Knox Jazz Night. Students enjoy the town's relaxing atmosphere: "Good coffee shops, a really nice park with a lake, and many beautiful old historic buildings," and "an annual Chocolate Festival." A 24-hour diner is nearby, and "students can also drive to Peoria or take the train to Chicago."

Student Body

Knox is praised throughout the campus for its "support for first-generation college students, which really reflects Knox's history and values." Students note that "You'll meet a lot of people very fast, and by the end of your first term you'll already be good friends with a pretty big portion of the student body." Many undergrads portray themselves as "weird," with variations on a common theme of celebrated social "Knoxwardness," that's made up of "the smart but sort of socially awkward kids in high school." It's a unifying sort of difference, where "students fit in by being themselves" because while "everyone at Knox is a little eccentric, we embrace each other's differences." As one student perceptively notes, there is a "highly diverse combination of creative, intellectual minds here. It's as if every person here is some highly distinctive character from an artsy film." Another puts it a bit more succinctly: "Thank you college admission gods."

KNOX COLLEGE

Financial Aid: 309-341-7149 • E-Mail: admission@knox.edu • Website: www.knox.edu

THE PRINCETON REVIEW SAYS

Admissions

The school reports that its standardized testing policy for use in admission for Fall 2024 is Test Optional. It is unknown at this time if the 2024 testing policy will be permanent. The Princeton Review suggests that interested applicants consult with the school for the most up-to-date standardized testing policies. *Very important factors considered include:* rigor of secondary school record, academic GPA. *Important factors considered include:* class rank, application essay, recommendation(s). *Other factors considered include:* standardized test scores, interview, extracurricular activities, talent/ability, character/personal qualities, first generation, alumni/ae relation, geographical residence, state residency, racial/ethnic status, volunteer work, work experience, level of applicant's interest. High school diploma is required and GED is accepted. *Academic units recommended:* 4 English, 4 math, 3 science, 2 science labs, 3 foreign language, 2 social studies, 1 history.

Financial Aid

Students should submit: FAFSA; Institution's own financial aid form. Priority filing deadline is 11/1. The Princeton Review suggests that all financial aid forms be submitted as soon as possible (see page 5 for a note on the FAFSA). *Need-based scholarships/grants offered:* College/university scholarship or grant aid from institutional funds; Federal Pell; Private scholarships; SEOG; State scholarships/grants. *Loan aid offered:* Direct PLUS loans; Direct Subsidized Loans; Direct Unsubsidized Loans; College/university loans from institutional funds. Admitted students will be notified of awards on a rolling basis beginning 12/1. Federal Work-Study Program available. Institutional employment available.

The Inside Word

Knox draws students from nearly 50 countries and almost 50 states—with a student body of only 1,200, diversity is hugely important here. Admission standards are high, and prospective students are viewed both qualitatively and quantitatively. Three out of every four freshman were ranked in the top quarter of their high school classes.

THE SCHOOL SAYS "..."

From the Admissions Office

"We believe that every experience is an education, that every new venture, every fantastic idea, every great journey, is human-powered. We also believe you learn the most from the people least like you. Knox is one of the 50 most diverse campuses in America, with a campus community of 1,200 students from nearly every state and 49 countries, including a wide array of races, ethnicities, ages, cultures, backgrounds, genders and gender identities, sexual orientations, and beliefs. A Knox education is not something you sit and watch—it's something you do. Our students test their knowledge by applying theory to practice both in and out of the classroom. That can take the form of advanced research and creative work, internships, off-campus (sometimes way off-campus) programs, community service, or some combination of your own devising. All students are guaranteed funding—at least $2,000—through Knox's innovative Power of Experience program to make these opportunities available to everyone, typically in the junior or senior year. These experiences, combined with opportunities to live and learn with students from different backgrounds and to develop leadership skills in clubs and organizations, all empower graduates to find success after Knox. Our students become engaged, innovative, and productive global citizens, ready to lead lives of purpose and prepared to work in fields that don't even exist yet. They run Fortune 500 companies and grassroots nonprofits, they conduct major research at sites around the world, they found startups and music festivals, they see a human need and they meet it."

SELECTIVITY

Admissions Rating	86
# of applicants	2,996
% of applicants accepted	73
% of acceptees attending	11
# offered a place on the wait list	8
% accepting a place on wait list	13
% admitted from wait list	100
# of early decision applicants	37
% accepted early decision	70

FIRST-YEAR PROFILE

Testing policy	Test Optional
Range SAT composite	1180–1360
Range SAT EBRW	595–705
Range SAT math	565–680
Range ACT composite	24–31
# submitting SAT scores	63
% submitting SAT scores	26
# submitting ACT scores	33
% submitting ACT scores	13
% frosh submitting high school GPA	66
% graduated top 10% of class	25
% graduated top 25% of class	58
% graduated top 50% of class	92

DEADLINES

Early decision	
Deadline	11/1
Notification	12/15
Early action	
Deadline	11/1
Notification	12/15
Regular	
Priority	11/1
Deadline	1/15
Notification	3/15
Nonfall registration?	Yes

APPLICANTS SOMETIMES PREFER

DePaul University; Lawrence University; St. Olaf College; The University of Chicago; University of Illinois—Urbana-Champaign

APPLICANTS RARELY PREFER

Augustana College (IL); Bradley University; Denison University; DePauw University; Illinois State University; Marquette University; The College of Wooster

FINANCIAL FACTS

Financial Aid Rating	85
Annual tuition	$52,461
Room and board	$10,326
Required fees	$798
Books and supplies	$1,200
Average frosh need-based scholarship	$39,063
Average UG need-based scholarship	$37,416
% needy frosh rec. need-based scholarship or grant aid	100
% needy UG rec. need-based scholarship or grant aid	100
% needy frosh rec. non-need-based scholarship or grant aid	18
% needy UG rec. non-need-based scholarship or grant aid	9
% needy frosh rec. need-based self-help aid	83
% needy UG rec. need-based self-help aid	84
% UG borrow to pay for school	76
Average cumulative indebtedness	$26,649
% frosh need fully met	38
% ugrads need fully met	12
Average % of frosh need met	87
Average % of ugrad need met	85

LAFAYETTE COLLEGE

730 High Street, Easton, PA 18042 • Admissions: 610-330-5000 • Fax: 610-330-5355

STUDENTS SAY "..."

Academics

Lafayette College is "a small, prestigious liberal arts school" that offers a "warm, community feel." Even before you decide to attend, "walking around campus left me with a cozy, at-home feeling," one psychology major gushes. Thanks to the "top-quality engineering education," many students say, "Lafayette is your classic liberal arts college with a twist" and point to the "vast array of research" and "study abroad opportunities" available to undergrads. The college "prides itself on student/faculty relationships." A geology major proclaims when professors are "good, they're great. Even the 'bad' professors, however, take the time to know each student and are usually available outside of class." An international affairs major says, "Whether you're an engineer, a premed student, or an art major, there is a great academic program and an embracing group of people waiting for you at Lafayette." Overall the professors get high marks because "their office doors are always open," and "are invested in seeing [students] not only graduate but also do well." The focus on undergraduate education provides "maximum opportunities and makes resumes and applications for graduate school and jobs look fierce!" Students go so far as to claim, "It's not very common to hear that someone doesn't like one of their professors at Lafayette." Generally, "classes are challenging but manageable, if you put in the time."

Campus Life

At Lafayette, the "campus is gorgeous," and students say you feel the "close atmosphere of the school" after "immediately walking onto the campus." Overall students feel, "the campus community is very supportive," and a civil engineering major says, "The family atmosphere adds to the education and makes Lafayette feel more like home than school." With "over 200 clubs and organizations on campus," there "is something that will fit everyone's lifestyle and hobbies," and when it comes to their Division I athletics, "students radiate school pride." Lafayette boasts a "great career center due to the close ties alumni have with the college," and career services are offered to students during all four years of their undergraduate study. The administration actively requests "student forums and opinions when decisions need to be made." Some say "the facilities are first rate" and improving. A new arts campus opened in 2016, including facilities for the theatre, film, and media studies departments, and a new five-story sciences center opened in 2019.

Student Body

Lafayette students are "passionate and driven" and "tend to be athletic, very preppy, and serious about their education." A sophomore says the typical student is "white middle to upper-middle class students from the tri-state area," but another adds, "Recent years have brought in a number of different types of people." "More lower income, international, and non-white students have joined" the Lafayette community. Regardless, some students point out that it can be "a very self-segregated campus." "These cliques are not unique to Lafayette, but they are present." Just under 30 percent of the student body is "involved with Greek life," and some feel that those "not involved in Greek life or sports can be isolated"; however, many students have felt a change occurring in recent years with Lafayette "trying to add more living learning communities (LLCs) to create a social living space outside the Greek system." On weekends, most students stay on campus, and "very rarely is there a weekend where something isn't going on." Organizations are always "sponsoring fun events, including Condom Bingo, which is a fan favorite. And if you're into the party scene, it isn't too hard to stumble into one."

LAFAYETTE COLLEGE

Financial Aid: 610-330-5055 • E-Mail: admissions@lafayette.edu • Website: www.lafayette.edu/

THE PRINCETON REVIEW SAYS

Admissions

The school reports that its standardized testing policy for use in admission for Fall 2024 is Test Optional. The 2024 testing policy will be permanent. The Princeton Review suggests that interested applicants consult with the school for the most up-to-date standardized testing policies. *Very important factors considered include:* rigor of secondary school record, academic GPA. *Important factors considered include:* class rank, standardized test scores, application essay, recommendation(s), interview, extracurricular activities, talent/ability, character/personal qualities. *Other factors considered include:* first generation, alumni/ae relation, geographical residence, racial/ethnic status, volunteer work, work experience, level of applicant's interest. High school diploma or equivalent is not required. *Academic units recommended:* 4 English, 3 math, 2 science, 2 science labs, 2 foreign language, 5 academic electives.

Financial Aid

Students should submit: CSS/Financial Aid Profile; FAFSA; Noncustodial Profile. Priority filing deadline is 1/15. The Princeton Review suggests that all financial aid forms be submitted as soon as possible (see page 5 for a note on the FAFSA). *Need-based scholarships/grants offered:* College/university scholarship or grant aid from institutional funds; Federal Pell; Private scholarships; SEOG; State scholarships/grants. *Loan aid offered:* Direct PLUS loans; Direct Subsidized Loans; Direct Unsubsidized Loans; College/university loans from institutional funds. Admitted students will be notified of awards on or about 4/1. Federal Work-Study Program available. Institutional employment available.

The Inside Word

Like all elite institutions, Lafayette College takes into account a variety of factors when evaluating prospective students. While emphasis is placed on scores, high school record, rigor of courses, and other numbers, the admissions committee also values a commitment to social awareness and potential for leadership as exhibited through extracurricular activities such as community service. In fact, service is a big part of the Lafayette community.

THE SCHOOL SAYS "..."

From the Admissions Office

"The Marquis de Lafayette, our namesake, was 19 years old when he crossed an ocean to a new world, fought for American independence, forged lasting connections, and altered the course of history.

"Like him, you have choices to make that rely on practical thinking, tactical maneuvers, and sheer brilliance. You stand at the helm, turning a wheel that will direct the first major decision of your adult life. What is your course?

"Cur Non, the motto for the Marquis, means Why Not. His example demonstrates what young people are capable of accomplishing when they dare to ask Why Not. Cur Non is our rally cry. It means anything is possible here.

"Why not have the courage and confidence to take risks? Why not engage in every aspect of learning? Why not use your intellect, energy, and talent to find your place in the world?

"You want an international community where you will learn alongside and from students with different backgrounds and experiences. You want a rigorous curriculum that blends the best of the liberal arts tradition with the latest in technological innovation. You also want a place where a strong career services team and dedicated alumni network will help set you on a path to future success.

"Lafayette is that place. Your journey awaits."

SELECTIVITY

Admissions Rating	94
# of applicants	10,500
% of applicants accepted	34
% of acceptees attending	21
# offered a place on the wait list	2,456
% accepting a place on wait list	40
% admitted from wait list	2
# of early decision applicants	835
% accepted early decision	43

FIRST-YEAR PROFILE

Testing policy	Test Optional
Range SAT composite	1350–1400
Range SAT EBRW	660–730
Range SAT math	670–750
Range ACT composite	30–33
# submitting SAT scores	296
% submitting SAT scores	39
# submitting ACT scores	109
% submitting ACT scores	14
Average HS GPA	3.6
% frosh submitting high school GPA	100
% graduated top 10% of class	53
% graduated top 25% of class	75
% graduated top 50% of class	95

DEADLINES

Early decision	
Deadline	11/15
Notification	12/15
Other ED deadline	2/1
Other ED notification	2/15
Regular	
Deadline	1/15
Notification	4/1
Nonfall registration?	No

APPLICANTS OFTEN PREFER

Cornell College; Princeton University; Tufts University

APPLICANTS SOMETIMES PREFER

Boston College; Brown University; Bucknell University; Colgate University; Dickinson College; Fordham University; Lehigh University; Northeastern University; Villanova University

FINANCIAL FACTS

Financial Aid Rating	97
Annual tuition	$61,482
Room and board	$18,290
Required fees	$342
Books and supplies	$1,000
Average frosh need-based scholarship	$48,662
Average UG need-based scholarship	$47,475
% needy frosh rec. need-based scholarship or grant aid	97
% needy UG rec. need-based scholarship or grant aid	98
% needy frosh rec. non-need-based scholarship or grant aid	23
% needy UG rec. non-need-based scholarship or grant aid	18
% needy frosh rec. need-based self-help aid	66
% needy UG rec. need-based self-help aid	76
% frosh rec. any financial aid	57
% UG rec. any financial aid	63
% UG borrow to pay for school	39
Average cumulative indebtedness	$28,840
% frosh need fully met	100
% ugrads need fully met	100
Average % of frosh need met	100
Average % of ugrad need met	100

LAKE FOREST COLLEGE

555 North Sheridan Road, Lake Forest, IL 60045 • Admissions: 847-234-3100 • Fax: 847-735-6271

STUDENTS SAY ". . ."

Academics

Nestled in the Northern suburbs of Chicago, students at Lake Forest College rave about the "excellent professors, small class sizes, and fantastic financial aid." Dedicated to their studies, students feed off of each other's successes. "Everyone wants to do as well as the next person and hearing that one person did well on a test pushes another person to do better going forward." Behind these driven students are a team of equally supportive professors. "One big strength of Lake Forest College is how accessible professors are even outside class hours." Students describe their instructors as "very easy to talk to and very helpful," and report that they are "challenging and professional, yet maintain a consistent amiability and approachable nature at the same time." As one undergrad elaborates, "The professors are teaching at Lake Forest because they want to teach small classes and connect with undergrad students." Truly, "They take the time to get to know you personally, and they are cheering you on every step of your college career." It's clear to those who attend Lake Forest that "staff work endlessly to develop relationships with students and make it hard for you not to succeed."

Lake Forest College offers 32 majors, and students insist "you will always find something you love" and ways to keep it interesting, even in your first year. For example, students have the opportunity to take field trips into Chicago, only an hour by train, through the "First Year Study Courses," which are "specifically designed to get students interested in Chicago, and show how different areas of study connect to Chicago and the surrounding areas." Such engaging classes are truly reflective of the "high quality" education you receive at Lake Forest.

Campus Life

The weekdays are mostly for study, and you find that many "people will spend time in the library." But in their downtime and on weekends, students love to "go to the beach, hang out in the quad area, take the train to Chicago, [and] attend school events" or go to "parties in dorms on weekend[s]." Greek life and "playing intramural sports or going to sports games" are popular pastimes, as are cultural clubs and service opportunities. "We all participate in a bunch of cultural and academic clubs that help us...establish a healthy relationship/friendship with each other," one student says. These healthy relationships also extend to those between student and staff when undergrads express interest in creating new programming or events for things undergrads are passionate about, like mental health. "We are always looking for new ways to express our interests to administration, and they always work with us to the best of their abilities."

Student Body

Lake Forest College has "a very diverse student body with a large number of international students mixed with students from all over the U.S." Students are "socioeconomically diverse, with many choosing Lake Forest because of the financial aid offer."

Many feel "the sense of community on our campus is extremely strong." Undergrads can be counted on to look out for each other, as Lake Forest College has "a lot [of] student leaders that help the incoming class [adjust to] the college as well as the workload." Indeed, many feel like their peers are "awesome, smart and talented," and "very supportive of each other." Students truly feel invested in their community. "Everyone is so willing to help out with anything, and I have felt so welcomed by my peers in class, intramural, social, and academic environments," one student says. At this small school, "everyone tends to know everyone" and "there's never a time where I don't see someone I know or someone I don't know greets me." It is this "really welcoming" environment and student population that make students feel right at home at Lake Forest.

LAKE FOREST COLLEGE

Financial Aid: 847-725-5103 • E-Mail: admissions@lakeforest.edu • Website: www.lakeforest.edu/

THE PRINCETON REVIEW SAYS

Admissions

The school reports that its standardized testing policy for use in admission for Fall 2024 is Test Optional. The 2024 testing policy will be permanent. The Princeton Review suggests that interested applicants consult with the school for the most up-to-date standardized testing policies. *Very important factors considered include:* rigor of secondary school record, application essay, interview, extracurricular activities, talent/ability, character/personal qualities. *Important factors considered include:* academic GPA. *Other factors considered include:* class rank, standardized test scores, recommendation(s), first generation, alumni/ae relation, geographical residence, volunteer work, work experience, level of applicant's interest. High school diploma is required and GED is accepted. *Academic units required:* 4 English, 3 math, 3 science, 3 science labs, 2 foreign language, 2 social studies, 2 history, 3 academic electives. *Academic units recommended:* 4 English, 4 math, 4 science, 4 science labs, 4 foreign language, 2 social studies, 2 history, 3 academic electives.

Financial Aid

Students should submit: FAFSA. Priority filing deadline is 3/1. The Princeton Review suggests that all financial aid forms be submitted as soon as possible (see page 5 for a note on the FAFSA). *Need-based scholarships/grants offered:* College/university scholarship or grant aid from institutional funds; Federal Pell; Private scholarships; SEOG; State scholarships/grants. *Loan aid offered:* Direct PLUS loans; Direct Subsidized Loans; Direct Unsubsidized Loans. Admitted students will be notified of awards on a rolling basis beginning 12/1. Federal Work-Study Program available. Institutional employment available.

The Inside Word

Given this diverse college's top-notch academic programming, Lake Forest aims to create a class of students with high GPAs, intellectual curiosity, and individuality and character who can have a positive impact on campus. Given that Lake Forest is Test Optional, applicants are reviewed holistically, with most emphasis placed on the rigor of your courses, extracurriculars, application essay, interview, and your personal qualities.

THE SCHOOL SAYS "..."

From the Admissions Office

"Our beautiful 107-acre campus is ideally located on Chicago's North Shore near Lake Michigan. Lake Forest College gives every student direct access to superb faculty and a powerful network of alumni who help our graduates begin careers. This access provides every student with a valuable edge on a bright future.

"Our flexible curriculum supports double majors and minors, and students are also offered unparalleled internships in Chicago, great lab research experiences, championship athletics, and study-abroad opportunities. Students learn in a rigorous academic environment in small class settings where professors do all of the teaching and advising. Career-building internships are plentiful in the Chicago area, and students can pursue up to three for credit. Study abroad is encouraged, and students can also spend a semester living and interning in Chicago.

"The student body comes from nearly every state and 100 countries around the world, forming a diverse learning community that is prepared to succeed in today's global society.

"Developing career goals—and a plan of action to achieve them—is fundamental at Lake Forest College. Students have access to programs, resources, career advisors, and a powerful network of alumni throughout their four years.

"Our outcomes are hard to match: Ninety-seven percent of recent graduates had jobs, graduate school, or other opportunities secured within six to nine months of graduation, well above the national average."

SELECTIVITY
Admissions Rating	88
# of applicants	4,665
% of applicants accepted	60
% of acceptees attending	16
# of early decision applicants	52
% accepted early decision	38

FIRST-YEAR PROFILE
Testing policy	Test Optional
Range SAT composite	1163–1348
Range SAT EBRW	590–670
Range SAT math	563–670
Range ACT composite	26–31
# submitting SAT scores	86
% submitting SAT scores	19
# submitting ACT scores	45
% submitting ACT scores	10
Average HS GPA	3.8
% frosh submitting high school GPA	100
% graduated top 10% of class	43
% graduated top 25% of class	69
% graduated top 50% of class	94

DEADLINES
Early decision	
Deadline	11/1
Notification	12/15
Other ED deadline	1/15
Other ED notification	2/1
Early action	
Deadline	11/1
Notification	12/15
Regular	
Deadline	2/15
Notification	Rolling, 11/1
Nonfall registration?	Yes

APPLICANTS ALSO LOOK AT
Augustana College (IL); Beloit College; Denison University; DePaul University; Hobart and William Smith Colleges; Illinois Wesleyan University; Kalamazoo College; Lawrence University; Loyola University of Chicago; Macalester College

FINANCIAL FACTS
Financial Aid Rating	88
Annual tuition	$52,000
Room and board	$11,898
Required fees	$902
Books and supplies	$1,140
Average frosh need-based scholarship	$46,716
Average UG need-based scholarship	$45,175
% needy frosh rec. need-based scholarship or grant aid	100
% needy UG rec. need-based scholarship or grant aid	100
% needy frosh rec. non-need-based scholarship or grant aid	0
% needy UG rec. non-need-based scholarship or grant aid	0
% needy frosh rec. need-based self-help aid	84
% needy UG rec. need-based self-help aid	86
% frosh rec. any financial aid	100
% UG rec. any financial aid	99
% UG borrow to pay for school	60
Average cumulative indebtedness	$31,412
% frosh need fully met	42
% ugrads need fully met	38
Average % of frosh need met	91
Average % of ugrad need met	90

LAWRENCE TECHNOLOGICAL UNIVERSITY

21000 West Ten Mile Rd., Southfield, MI 48075-1058 • Admissions: 800-225-5588 • Fax: 248-204-3188

CAMPUS LIFE

Quality of Life Rating	84
Fire Safety Rating	95
Green Rating	88
Type of school	Private
Affiliation	No Affiliation
Environment	City

STUDENTS

Total undergrad enrollment	1,863
% male/female/another gender	71/29/0
% from out of state	14
% frosh live on campus	64
% ugrads live on campus	46
# of fraternities (% join)	6 (4)
# of sororities (% join)	5 (7)
% African American	10
% Asian	3
% White	64
% Hispanic	4
% Native American	<1
% Pacific Islander	<1
% Two or more races	3
% Race and/or ethnicity unknown	3
% international	12
# of countries represented	35

SURVEY SAYS . . .
Students are happy
Easy to get around campus
Students are friendly

ACADEMICS

Academic Rating	79
% students returning for sophomore year	70
% students graduating within 4 years	22
% students graduating within 6 years	55
Calendar	Semester
Student/faculty ratio	11:1
Profs interesting rating	84
Profs accessible rating	88

Most classes have 10–19 students.
Most lab/discussion sessions have 10–19 students.

MOST POPULAR MAJORS
Mechanical Engineering; Business Administration and Management, General; Architecture

STUDENTS SAY "..."

Academics
Founded in 1932, Michigan's Lawrence Technological University is based on the simple notion of "Theory and Practice"—taking abstract ideas and applying them to real world problems. The university offers about 100 academic programs across its four colleges, as well as numerous mentorship, internship, and practical research opportunities via the Centrepolis Accelerator, the school's manufacturing business accelerator. Just 2,100 undergraduates means "small class sizes with one-on-one opportunities," and plenty of certification, coaching, and consulting support through "professional programs for helping with future careers." LTU has an excellent reputation with companies that recruit and hire students, and the "potential for high quality jobs after college is very helpful and exciting." Resources are readily available, and all undergraduates receive a laptop or tablet, with over 80 percent of students receiving some form of financial aid.

Professors at LTU "are extremely flexible and truly do want to help you and see you succeed," which can be seen in their willingness "to accommodate special situations." They are also "clearly knowledgeable in their fields and do their best to share that experience with students," running application-based courses with the most "up-to-date labs and tools" that are centered around "creating problems and processes to outline the ever-changing industry standards and practices." One student says: "In my computer networks class the professor brought in material to create our own Ethernet cords." Students feel they leave with a lot of experience, thanks to instructors frequently bringing in "guests from popular companies to explain how our work is tied to real life work scenarios" and working to show "the application of the theory you learned in class."

Campus Life
Most out-of-classroom socializing comes by way of clubs, intramural sports, and "a great array of organizations which allow for anyone to find their interest." At least once a week there is an activity hosted by a student organization "that is fun and interactive to attend," and for those who prefer to "often play games on our computers," the school also coaches across various esports. While there are also "some casual parties surrounding Greek life," on the whole, students here are busy with "lots of studying [and being] devoted to school and a career afterwards."

Student Body
"With having a small campus comes having a close-knit student body," and there is "a strong sense of community" where "everyone really looks out for each other." As one student says: "If you ask for help from any of your peers, you'll receive it or you'll solve the problem together." Despite its small size, this is a "group of diverse students who come from different backgrounds, race, and countries." Students do say that there is "a large percentage of commuters," but the school is working on changing that into a more "typical college on campus student body." Around half of students are athletes and many are also "a part of Greek life or a part-time on-campus job."

LAWRENCE TECHNOLOGICAL UNIVERSITY

Financial Aid: 248-204-2280 • E-Mail: admissions@ltu.edu • Website: www.ltu.edu

THE PRINCETON REVIEW SAYS

Admissions

The school reports that its standardized testing policy for use in admission for Fall 2024 is Test Optional. The 2024 testing policy will be temporary. The Princeton Review suggests that interested applicants consult with the school for the most up-to-date standardized testing policies. *Very important factors considered include:* rigor of secondary school record, academic GPA. *Important factors considered include:* *Other factors considered include:* application essay. High school diploma is required and GED is accepted. *Academic units required:* 4 English, 3 math, 2 science, 3 social studies. *Academic units recommended:* 4 English, 4 math, 4 science, 2 science labs, 2 history.

Financial Aid

Students should submit: FAFSA. Priority filing deadline is 4/1. The Princeton Review suggests that all financial aid forms be submitted as soon as possible (see page 5 for a note on the FAFSA). *Need-based scholarships/grants offered:* College/university scholarship or grant aid from institutional funds; Federal Pell; Private scholarships; SEOG; State scholarships/grants. *Loan aid offered:* Direct PLUS loans; Direct Subsidized Loans; Direct Unsubsidized Loans; State Loans. Admitted students will be notified of awards on a rolling basis beginning 1/1. Federal Work-Study Program available. Institutional employment available.

The Inside Word

While Lawrence Tech values an applicant's academic transcript above all, the admissions office also takes into account all factors which demonstrate an aptitude for successful study. Solid B students who have taken a college preparatory curriculum and shown an interest in extracurriculars should have no problems getting in. There is no formal deadline for applications, but students are advised to apply as early as possible to maximize scholarships and financial aid.

THE SCHOOL SAYS "..."

From the Admissions Office

"Lawrence Technological University is a private, nearly 3,000-student university that offers about 100 innovative programs in Colleges of Architecture and Design, Arts and Sciences, Business and Information Technology, and Engineering.

"Lawrence Technological University is one of only 13 private, technical, comprehensive doctoral universities in the U.S.

"At LTU, you will benefit from small class sizes, taught by faculty with industry savvy, and an exceptional focus on theory and practice, with a hands-on education that begins on day one in programs such as design, engineering, nursing, and business. You will also have access to LTU's well-connected career placement services on a high-tech, wireless 107-acre campus. Lawrence Tech produces leaders with an entrepreneurial spirit and global view—helping LTU grads earn some of the highest alumni salaries in the nation.

"Lawrence Tech's unique Southfield, Michigan location also provides you with opportunities for co-ops, internships, and professional development in a region with one of the largest concentrations of engineering, architecture, and technology jobs in the world. Not only that—you will gain exposure to architecture and design, the sciences, and engineering through interdisciplinary projects, giving you a distinct advantage in today's technologically driven global job market.

"You will also be provided with your own high-end laptop loaded with industry standard software—retailing on average over $75,000—a benefit you'll only get at LTU. And there are plenty of opportunities to get involved with on campus including fraternities, sororities, honor societies and student chapters of professional groups; NAIA men's and women's athletics; and residential living."

SELECTIVITY

Admissions Rating	84
# of applicants	2,537
% of applicants accepted	82
% of acceptees attending	21

FIRST-YEAR PROFILE

Testing policy	Test Optional
Range SAT composite	1050–1150
Range SAT EBRW	510–630
Range SAT math	520–640
Range ACT composite	22–30
# submitting SAT scores	178
% submitting SAT scores	42
# submitting ACT scores	44
% submitting ACT scores	10
Average HS GPA	3.5
% frosh submitting high school GPA	100

DEADLINES

Regular	
Deadline	Rolling
Notification	Rolling
Nonfall registration?	Yes

FINANCIAL FACTS

Financial Aid Rating	82
Annual tuition	$40,672
Room and board	$11,670
Required fees	$1,200
Books and supplies	$1,762
Average frosh need-based scholarship	$20,546
Average UG need-based scholarship	$18,755
% needy frosh rec. need-based scholarship or grant aid	99
% needy UG rec. need-based scholarship or grant aid	98
% needy frosh rec. non-need-based scholarship or grant aid	98
% needy UG rec. non-need-based scholarship or grant aid	91
% needy frosh rec. need-based self-help aid	69
% needy UG rec. need-based self-help aid	75
% frosh rec. any financial aid	96
% UG rec. any financial aid	74
% UG borrow to pay for school	66
Average cumulative indebtedness	$43,498
% frosh need fully met	15
% ugrads need fully met	13
Average % of frosh need met	70
Average % of ugrad need met	71

LAWRENCE UNIVERSITY

711 East Boldt Way, Appleton, WI 54911-5626 • Admissions: 920-832-7000 • Fax: 920-832-6782

CAMPUS LIFE

Quality of Life Rating	88
Fire Safety Rating	87
Green Rating	80
Type of school	Private
Affiliation	No Affiliation
Environment	City

STUDENTS

Total undergrad enrollment	1,426
% male/female/another gender	46/54/NR
% from out of state	76
% frosh live on campus	100
% ugrads live on campus	96
# of fraternities (% join)	3 (8)
# of sororities (% join)	4 (6)
% African American	5
% Asian	5
% White	60
% Hispanic	12
% Native American	<1
% Pacific Islander	<1
% Two or more races	5
% Race and/or ethnicity unknown	1
% international	12
# of countries represented	39

SURVEY SAYS . . .

Lots of liberal students
Students aren't religious
Easy to get around campus
Theater is popular
Active student government
Active minority support groups

ACADEMICS

Academic Rating	88
% students returning for sophomore year	89
% students graduating within 4 years	69
% students graduating within 6 years	80
Calendar	Trimester
Student/faculty ratio	8:1
Profs interesting rating	92
Profs accessible rating	96
Most classes have 10–19 students.	

MOST POPULAR MAJORS

Psychology, General; Music Performance, General;
Biology/Biological Sciences, General

STUDENTS SAY "..."

Academics

Lawrence University is a small liberal arts college in Appleton, Wisconsin, centered entirely around the ethos of Engaged Learning, in which students learn by doing. Beginning with the cornerstone Freshman Studies program, these "crazy smart" students are grouped into course sections of about 15 students, and commence the reading and discussion of great works. Exploration of the mind is stressed, and "even the smallest idea is considered on a grand scale." Tutoring is readily available, and the school "places an incredible focus on mental health issues and counseling." Professors "have great opportunities for help and discussion outside of class," and "there are many opportunities for experiential learning (off-campus study, visits, field trips, grants) that are available to those that work for them, without being too hard to get." Lawrence is especially good at "providing a creative and explorative atmosphere within the college," and structuring itself in a manner that allows for student flexibility, so students "are able to explore and study whatever we are interested in and we are encouraged to do so." A stunning 8:1 student-to-faculty ratio means students have access to their professors at all times, all of whom "are excited to transfer their knowledge to us through various kind of ways." Professors are "upfront with us and treat us more like academic peers," and make time to help students outside of class and connect the course to larger ideas. "To the professors, you are a person and they make sure that they know your name and what you're about," says a student.

Campus Life

One student sums up Lawrentian life: "cheese curds, high stress, ten weeks, snow, repeat." "Study takes big part of people's life," but most are also on many different clubs or committees "whether for the student government, toward our major, or just for fun like long boarding club or painting club." "People are always hoping for more time in a day here," says a student. Admittedly, "there isn't much to do in Appleton," so this entirely residential campus is able "to cultivate a fantastic atmosphere within the college," but "outside of the Lawrence bubble is a mystery to most of us." Many people take advantage of the school's offered activities like dances, comedians, musicians, speakers who are brought to campus, and movies shown in the cinema, and every term has a big event, such as the Fall Festival, Trivia, Winter Carnival, Cabaret, and LU-aroo. On weekends, partying is a popular pastime; underclassmen spend their time at the cafe on campus while upperclassmen "flock to our on-campus bar, where we often see our professors during happy hour." As the university houses a popular music conservatory, "there is ALWAYS a type of concert going on (Monday jazz sessions are highlight)."

Student Body

There's a surprisingly large number of international students at Lawrence University, and people embrace the opportunity to learn about different cultures and topics in general: they are all "exceptionally curious and eager to explore fields outside their own major." "Not only do we yearn for experiences that take us outside what is comfortable and known, it is safe to do so," says one. Students here "are not afraid to show who they really are" and "truly just love expressing how every person is their own and that we all accept it." This "healthy and excellent" social atmosphere is due to the chemistry of the student body, which is a "combination of odd, quirky kids, who are dedicated to music or the arts, but also dedicated student athletes." More than anything, the students here "are kind, funny, intelligent and a little bit wacko—in the best way."

LAWRENCE UNIVERSITY

Financial Aid: 920-832-6583 • E-Mail: admissions@lawrence.edu • Website: www.lawrence.edu

THE PRINCETON REVIEW SAYS

Admissions

The school reports that its standardized testing policy for use in admission for Fall 2024 is Test Optional. The 2024 testing policy will be permanent. The Princeton Review suggests that interested applicants consult with the school for the most up-to-date standardized testing policies. *Very important factors considered include:* rigor of secondary school record, class rank, academic GPA, talent/ability, character/personal qualities. *Important factors considered include:* application essay, interview, extracurricular activities. *Other factors considered include:* standardized test scores, recommendation(s), first generation, alumni/ae relation, geographical residence, racial/ethnic status, volunteer work, work experience, level of applicant's interest. High school diploma is required and GED is accepted. *Academic units recommended:* 4 English, 3 math, 3 science, 2 foreign language, 2 social studies, 2 history.

Financial Aid

Students should submit: CSS/Financial Aid Profile; FAFSA; Institution's own financial aid form; Noncustodial Profile. Priority filing deadline is 12/8. The Princeton Review suggests that all financial aid forms be submitted as soon as possible (see page 5 for a note on the FAFSA). *Need-based scholarships/grants offered:* College/university scholarship or grant aid from institutional funds; Federal Pell; Private scholarships; SEOG; State scholarships/grants. *Loan aid offered:* Direct PLUS loans; Direct Subsidized Loans; Direct Unsubsidized Loans. Admitted students will be notified of awards on a rolling basis beginning 12/15. Federal Work-Study Program available. Institutional employment available.

The Inside Word

Lawrence University takes a holistic approach to the admissions game. The school does its best to look beyond numbers and get a full sense of each applicant. Admissions officers pay close attention to the types of classes candidates have taken and the activities pursued. They also consider a student's background. Interviews are highly important so it would behoove applicants to sit for one. Finally, those who are test-taking averse can breathe a sigh of relief; submitting SAT or ACT scores is optional.

THE SCHOOL SAYS "..."

From the Admissions Office

"Lawrence believes college should not be a one-size-fits-all experience, and that you'll learn best when you're educated as a unique individual. Within our college of liberal arts and sciences and our conservatory of music—both devoted exclusively to undergraduate education—you'll have unparalleled opportunities to collaborate closely with your professors. With one of the smallest student-faculty ratios in the country (8:1) and an average class size of 15, Lawrence is built to deliver a highly individualized, interactive (and challenging) academic experience. Our 1,500 students come from nearly every state and about fifty countries to enjoy the distinctive benefits of this engaged—and engaging—community. It's a welcoming and supportive, residential, 24/7 campus filled with smart and talented people who are pursuing an astonishing variety of academic and extracurricular interests in a collaborative rather than competitive way. Our picturesque, residential campus is nestled on the banks of the Fox River in Appleton, Wisconsin, (metro population: 250,000), one of the fastest growing metropolitan areas in the Midwest. Björklunden, our 441-acre estate on more than one mile of pristine Lake Michigan shoreline (two hours north of campus), provides educational and recreational opportunities for students to enhance their on-campus learning experiences. Lawrentians enjoy 99 percent placement within six months of graduation (73 percent working; 23 percent in graduate/professional school; 4 percent traveling/volunteering)."

SELECTIVITY

Admissions Rating	**88**
# of applicants	2,943
% of applicants accepted	72
% of acceptees attending	22
# offered a place on the wait list	18
% accepting a place on wait list	2
% admitted from wait list	1
# of early decision applicants	56
% accepted early decision	80

FIRST-YEAR PROFILE

Testing policy	Test Optional
Range SAT composite	1200–1440
Range SAT EBRW	610–740
Range SAT math	600–730
Range ACT composite	27–32
# submitting SAT scores	93
% submitting SAT scores	26
# submitting ACT scores	121
% submitting ACT scores	33
Average HS GPA	3.7
% frosh submitting high school GPA	90
% graduated top 10% of class	37
% graduated top 25% of class	65
% graduated top 50% of class	87

DEADLINES

Early decision	
Deadline	11/1
Notification	12/1
Early action	
Deadline	11/1
Notification	12/15
Regular	
Deadline	1/15
Notification	4/1
Nonfall registration?	Yes

APPLICANTS SOMETIMES PREFER
St. Olaf College; University of Wisconsin—Madison

APPLICANTS RARELY PREFER
Denison University; Macalester College

FINANCIAL FACTS

Financial Aid Rating	**90**
Annual tuition	$53,667
Room and board	$11,520
Required fees	$312
Books and supplies	$900
Average frosh need-based scholarship	$39,006
Average UG need-based scholarship	$39,293
% needy frosh rec. need-based scholarship or grant aid	99
% needy UG rec. need-based scholarship or grant aid	99
% needy frosh rec. non-need-based scholarship or grant aid	36
% needy UG rec. non-need-based scholarship or grant aid	28
% needy frosh rec. need-based self-help aid	55
% needy UG rec. need-based self-help aid	65
% frosh rec. any financial aid	100
% UG rec. any financial aid	99
% UG borrow to pay for school	57
Average cumulative indebtedness	$27,239
% frosh need fully met	60
% ugrads need fully met	57
Average % of frosh need met	94
Average % of ugrad need met	94

LEHIGH UNIVERSITY

27 Memorial Drive West, Bethlehem, PA 18015 • Admissions: 610-758-3000 • Fax: 610-758-4361

STUDENTS SAY ". . ."

Academics

Located in Pennsylvania's Lehigh Valley, Lehigh University offers students a long history of traditions, more than 100 majors and programs, and "the ability to collaborate with other students across different fields of study." The coursework here is difficult—"keeping even the brightest students on their toes"—but "the kinship formed through the struggle and triumph is irreplaceable." Research opportunities are abundant, study abroad is wildly popular, and a strong engineering school and business school do "an amazing job making sure everyone gets high-paying internships junior year and jobs after college" (in fact, 95 percent of students are employed or in graduate school within six months of graduation).

The professors are "very intellectual beings who are also very interesting as people." They are incredibly accessible, and "always give students their emails, mail boxes, phone numbers, and sometimes even cell phone numbers." One student strongly urges you to take them up on this: "Get to know them outside of the classroom since they often give out career advice." The cross-disciplinary programs that Lehigh offers (such as the IDEAS program, which integrates arts and engineering) are "beyond what many other institutions provide." Resources are in good supply at Lehigh; for example, there are tutors "consistently available to assist students in any subject they are struggling with." In addition to having world-class facilities, students are "encouraged by those around them to become involved in research," which is just one component in the awesome "return on investment" that so many speak of as the great perk of attending Lehigh.

Campus Life

At the beautiful, compact Lehigh campus, "everyone gets a true college experience." There is "never a dull moment" because everyone here is "always working on a project or a class or something they're independently creating." Over 200 different clubs and organizations make it easy to get involved, and Lehigh is "big into Greek life." There are "so many events, guest speakers, athletic competitions, student groups, and alcohol-free/drug-free After Dark events" that students can't even conceive of doing it all. It's also not unusual for groups of friends to plan activities at this collaborative school: "In the past few weeks, I've had snowball fights, gone hiking, eaten dinner with friends, and gone ice skating."

Lehigh is a both-ends-of-the candle school, and typically students spend "countless hours" in the library and then relax by going out at night; "even the kids who are in the hardest classes and wake up at 7:00 A.M. to study are going hard at these parties." Not only are students double and sometimes triple majors in various fields, but "many are also varsity athletes, have multiple minors, and are heavily involved in some type of organization or club on campus."

Student Body

The student body at Lehigh is "extremely hard-working, both academically and socially." This group is "fairly affluent" and a majority of the students are from New Jersey, New York, and Pennsylvania, but "Lehigh prides itself on its search for diversity." The utter respect that Mountain Hawks have for their fellow students is admirable: "The best part about the people around me is the common bond of intelligence," says a student. "No matter what another student is doing, whether it be marching band, or joining a fraternity or a sorority, I know that every student on this campus is an intellectual."

LEHIGH UNIVERSITY

Financial Aid: 610-758-3181 • E-Mail: admissions@lehigh.edu • Website: www.lehigh.edu

THE PRINCETON REVIEW SAYS

Admissions

The school reports that its standardized testing policy for use in admission for Fall 2024 is Test Optional. The 2024 testing policy will be temporary. The Princeton Review suggests that interested applicants consult with the school for the most up-to-date standardized testing policies. *Very important factors considered include:* rigor of secondary school record, academic GPA. *Important factors considered include:* class rank, standardized test scores, application essay, recommendation(s), extracurricular activities, talent/ability, character/personal qualities, racial/ethnic status, volunteer work, level of applicant's interest. *Other factors considered include:* interview, first generation, alumni/ae relation, geographical residence, state residency, work experience. High school diploma is required and GED is accepted. *Academic units required:* 4 English, 3 math, 3 science, 2 foreign language, 2 social studies, 2 history, 2 academic electives. *Academic units recommended:* 4 English, 4 math, 4 science, 2 foreign language, 2 social studies, 2 history, 1 computer science, 1 visual/performing arts, 2 academic electives.

Financial Aid

Students should submit: Business/Farm Supplement; CSS/Financial Aid Profile; FAFSA; Noncustodial Profile. The Princeton Review suggests that all financial aid forms be submitted as soon as possible (see page 5 for a note on the FAFSA). *Need-based scholarships/grants offered:* College/university scholarship or grant aid from institutional funds; Federal Pell; Private scholarships; State scholarships/grants. *Loan aid offered:* Direct PLUS loans; Direct Subsidized Loans; Direct Unsubsidized Loans. Admitted students will be notified of awards on or about 3/30. Federal Work-Study Program available. Institutional employment available.

The Inside Word

Competition for spots in Lehigh's freshmen class is perennially increasing. Students should be sure to start their applications early, be well prepared with scores and grades, as well as demonstrate their talents and passions through volunteer opportunities, work experience, or extracurricular activities. Prospective students should visit the campus and make contact with the admissions staff. Interviews are recommended but not required.

THE SCHOOL SAYS "..."

From the Admissions Office

"Lehigh is a premier private residential research university. The majority of our students—undergraduate and graduate—live on campus, allowing research and discovery to happen almost anywhere. We are a top tier national research university and have earned a reputation for an entrepreneurial and interdisciplinary approach to learning. This learning is connected to real-world applications and reinforced with cutting edge academic research and hands-on experiences. Lehigh's beautifully wooded campus spans 2,358 acres, making it one of the largest private campuses in the country. More than 7,000 students call this hillside university 'home.' With three distinguished undergraduate colleges (Arts & Sciences, Business, Engineering, and Health), Lehigh strikes the perfect balance: students can expect a personalized experience while benefiting from the resources, opportunities and environment of an internationally recognized research university. The Lehigh community is guided by a common set of core values: integrity, equitable community, academic freedom, intellectual curiosity and leadership.

"Today, our global alumni community includes more than 85,000 loyal graduates. Nearly 95 percent of last year's graduates are employed or in graduate school just six months after leaving campus.

"Located in Pennsylvania's scenic Lehigh Valley, home to about 800,000 people, the campus is in close proximity to both New York City and Philadelphia. Our campus is on South Mountain in Bethlehem and consists of three contiguous areas: Asa Packer Campus (most academic and residential buildings), Mountaintop Campus and the Murray H. Goodman Campus (Division I athletic complex)."

SELECTIVITY

Admissions Rating	94
# of applicants	15,163
% of applicants accepted	37
% of acceptees attending	27
# offered a place on the wait list	5,034
% accepting a place on wait list	50
% admitted from wait list	4
# of early decision applicants	1,303
% accepted early decision	66

FIRST-YEAR PROFILE

Testing policy	Test Optional
Range SAT composite	1350–1480
Range SAT EBRW	660–720
Range SAT math	680–770
Range ACT composite	30–33
# submitting SAT scores	552
% submitting SAT scores	37
# submitting ACT scores	198
% submitting ACT scores	13
% graduated top 10% of class	57
% graduated top 25% of class	87
% graduated top 50% of class	97

DEADLINES

Early decision	
Deadline	11/1
Notification	12/15
Other ED deadline	1/1
Other ED notification	2/15
Regular	
Priority	1/1
Deadline	1/15
Notification	3/25
Nonfall registration?	No

APPLICANTS OFTEN PREFER
Boston College; Cornell University; Northeastern University; University of Maryland, College Park; University of Michigan—Ann Arbor; Villanova University

APPLICANTS SOMETIMES PREFER
Boston University; Bucknell University; Lafayette College; Penn State University Park; Rensselaer Polytechnic Institute; Rutgers University—New Brunswick; University of Delaware; University of Pittsburgh—Pittsburgh Campus

APPLICANTS RARELY PREFER
Drexel University

FINANCIAL FACTS

Financial Aid Rating	95
Annual tuition	$61,180
Room and board	$16,470
Required fees	$1,000
Books and supplies	$1,000
Average frosh need-based scholarship	$50,099
Average UG need-based scholarship	$50,287
% needy frosh rec. need-based scholarship or grant aid	99
% needy UG rec. need-based scholarship or grant aid	98
% needy frosh rec. non-need-based scholarship or grant aid	34
% needy UG rec. non-need-based scholarship or grant aid	28
% needy frosh rec. need-based self-help aid	93
% needy UG rec. need-based self-help aid	94
% frosh rec. any financial aid	64
% UG rec. any financial aid	60
% UG borrow to pay for school	45
Average cumulative indebtedness	$37,147
% frosh need fully met	75
% ugrads need fully met	74
Average % of frosh need met	98
Average % of ugrad need met	98

LE MOYNE COLLEGE

1419 Salt Springs Rd., Syracuse, NY 13214-1301 • Admissions: 315-445-4300

STUDENTS SAY ". . ."

Academics

Le Moyne College is a small private liberal arts college rooted in the Catholic and Jesuit tradition that seeks to provide a full education that will prepare students for a lifetime of leadership and service. Located in upstate New York, Le Moyne's 2,600 undergraduates follow a core curriculum that introduces them to the knowledge and skills that will carry them through their time at the college and beyond, bookended by a first-year Transitions seminar and a senior Transformations capstone course or project. Interdisciplinary learning is encouraged, and most departments put on extra credit lectures with guest speakers that are "always educational but entertaining."

Professors at Le Moyne "ensure that you are actually learning and retaining information, [and] that their course has benefited you in every way." In the classroom, they make "use of real life scenarios or hands-on examples" to demonstrate their lessons, and "frequently mention that they prefer to have a conversation about the material rather than simply talk at the students." Discussion-based exercises are preferred over straight lectures, and many classes incorporate "unique group projects." Faculty work to "establish incredibly close connections with students," which helps to "truly understand and accommodate" students. Smaller class sizes provide "a more personal experience with their professors and peers," and both teachers and staff are "always willing to meet with you and do their best to help you succeed."

Campus Life

Le Moyne is a relatively small school, "which allows for it to feel like home away from home." Around 60 percent of students live on the "very well kept" campus: students note the constant renovations (like that of the library and science buildings) that are "always happening to keep it feeling fresh." No matter where they live, students can be found "studying all over campus, from dorm rooms to the library to outside under the trees," and "when people aren't working they'll typically visit downtown Syracuse." A vehicle is highly recommended for such excursions, particular when it comes to taking advantage of "plenty of outdoor activities such as hiking in the local state park." That said, students say "there is always something to do" on campus, whether that's a club or a school-run event like trivia night, bingo, and Dolphy Day, where "students and faculty gather on the quad for a day of food, drinks, and music." Sports are popular both to play and to watch, and students also go up the road to nearby Syracuse University to attend larger athletic events.

Student Body

Given the school's Jesuit values, it makes sense that people are "committed to helping others and have a tremendous sense of empathy and desire to serve others." One student says, "I am proud of Le Moyne's commitment to promoting good character in addition to academics." Students are also "extremely well driven and dedicated toward their goals." Le Moyne is "really great with diversity and bringing in people from all over the world," forming a very inclusive bunch where "you make friends easy, and they're there for life." Many students come from New York State (especially nearby suburbs), and "it is common to share multiple classes with the same people."

LE MOYNE COLLEGE

Financial Aid: 315-445-4400 • E-Mail: admission@lemoyne.edu • Website: www.lemoyne.edu

THE PRINCETON REVIEW SAYS

Admissions

The school reports that its standardized testing policy for use in admission for Fall 2024 is Test Optional. The 2024 testing policy will be permanent. The Princeton Review suggests that interested applicants consult with the school for the most up-to-date standardized testing policies. *Very important factors considered include:* rigor of secondary school record, academic GPA. *Important factors considered include:* class rank, application essay, recommendation(s), interview, extracurricular activities, talent/ability, work experience. *Other factors considered include:* standardized test scores, character/personal qualities, alumni/ae relation, volunteer work, level of applicant's interest. High school diploma is required and GED is accepted. *Academic units required:* 4 English, 3 math, 3 science, 3 foreign language, 4 social studies. *Academic units recommended:* 4 science, 3 science labs.

Financial Aid

Students should submit: FAFSA; State aid form. Priority filing deadline is 2/15. The Princeton Review suggests that all financial aid forms be submitted as soon as possible (see page 5 for a note on the FAFSA). *Need-based scholarships/grants offered:* College/university scholarship or grant aid from institutional funds; Federal Pell; Private scholarships; SEOG; State scholarships/grants. *Loan aid offered:* Direct PLUS loans; Direct Subsidized Loans; Direct Unsubsidized Loans. Admitted students will be notified of awards on or about 3/1. Federal Work-Study Program available. Institutional employment available.

The Inside Word

As a younger college, Le Moyne sees slightly lower application numbers than many other small private colleges in the Northeast. Those with a decent academic record and a letter of recommendation from a guidance counselor or teacher (or three letters from clergy, coaches, employers, teachers, etc.) should have no trouble getting in, but a stronger college prep record and a good SAT or ACT score will help seal the deal.

THE SCHOOL SAYS "..."

From the Admissions Office

"Learning, leadership and service are the hallmarks of a Le Moyne College education. Those values are evident in the College's Core Curriculum, a series of courses steeped in the Jesuit tradition and designed to develop intellectual skills critical for success in the 21st century. The intent of the Core Curriculum is to do more than provide knowledge in specific disciplines, though. It was created to stretch the minds of our students, to remove barriers to their ways of thinking, and to help them discover new approaches to life's challenges. At the center of the Le Moyne experience is a commitment to social justice and to providing students with the best possible preparation for life and work. A place where Greatness meets Goodness.

"Le Moyne students can choose from 100+ undergraduate majors, minors and special programs, as well as graduate programs in arts administration, business administration, education, nursing, occupational therapy, physician assistant studies, and executive leadership. Whatever field they choose to pursue, Le Moyne graduates are prepared to lead successful lives of leadership and service.

"Beyond academics, Le Moyne students have the opportunity to grow and explore on a campus with dynamic academic, athletic and social spaces at a cost that is remarkably affordable. (More than 95 percent of undergrads receive some form of financial aid). With over eighty clubs and organizations, students are sure to find an activity that interests them while forming life-long friendships. Our picturesque 160-acre campus in the heart of New York state enhances Le Moyne's outstanding programs."

SELECTIVITY

Admissions Rating	84
# of applicants	7,066
% of applicants accepted	78
% of acceptees attending	11
# offered a place on the wait list	102
% accepting a place on wait list	19
% admitted from wait list	16

FIRST-YEAR PROFILE

Testing policy	Test Optional
Range SAT composite	1140–1290
Range SAT EBRW	560–640
Range SAT math	570–650
Range ACT composite	26–31
# submitting SAT scores	145
% submitting SAT scores	24
# submitting ACT scores	25
% submitting ACT scores	4
Average HS GPA	3.6
% frosh submitting high school GPA	99
% graduated top 10% of class	24
% graduated top 25% of class	58
% graduated top 50% of class	89

DEADLINES

Early action	
Deadline	11/15
Notification	12/15
Regular	
Priority	2/1
Notification	Rolling, 1/1
Nonfall registration?	Yes

APPLICANTS SOMETIMES PREFER

Ithaca College; Nazareth University; Siena College; St. John Fisher University; State University of New York at Cortland; State University of New York—Binghamton University; State University of New York—Geneseo; State University of New York--Oswego

FINANCIAL FACTS

Financial Aid Rating	85
Annual tuition	$37,770
Room and board	$15,660
Required fees	$1,200
Books and supplies	$2,690
Average frosh need-based scholarship	$26,350
Average UG need-based scholarship	$25,406
% needy frosh rec. need-based scholarship or grant aid	100
% needy UG rec. need-based scholarship or grant aid	100
% needy frosh rec. non-need-based scholarship or grant aid	26
% needy UG rec. non-need-based scholarship or grant aid	24
% needy frosh rec. need-based self-help aid	69
% needy UG rec. need-based self-help aid	70
% frosh rec. any financial aid	99
% UG rec. any financial aid	86
% UG borrow to pay for school	82
Average cumulative indebtedness	$33,462
% frosh need fully met	32
% ugrads need fully met	33
Average % of frosh need met	84
Average % of ugrad need met	82

LEWIS & CLARK COLLEGE

615 S Palatine Hill Road, Portland, OR 97219-7899 • Admissions: 503-768-7000 • Fax: 503-768-7055

CAMPUS LIFE

Quality of Life Rating	83
Fire Safety Rating	90
Green Rating	97
Type of school	Private
Affiliation	No Affiliation
Environment	Metropolis

STUDENTS

Total undergrad enrollment	2,187
% male/female/another gender	35/65/NR
% from out of state	86
% frosh from public high school	78
% frosh live on campus	97
% ugrads live on campus	68
# of fraternities	0
# of sororities	0
% African American	3
% Asian	5
% White	69
% Hispanic	11
% Native American	<1
% Pacific Islander	<1
% Two or more races	8
% Race and/or ethnicity unknown	1
% international	4
# of countries represented	52

SURVEY SAYS . . .

Lots of liberal students
Classroom facilities are great
Great library
Students aren't religious
Students environmentally aware
Students love Portland, OR

ACADEMICS

Academic Rating	86
% students returning for sophomore year	86
% students graduating within 4 years	67
% students graduating within 6 years	73
Calendar	Semester
Student/faculty ratio	13:1
Profs interesting rating	92
Profs accessible rating	94

Most classes have 10–19 students.
Most lab/discussion sessions have
10–19 students.

MOST POPULAR MAJORS

Psychology, General; Sociology and Anthropology;
Biology/Biological Sciences, General

STUDENTS SAY "..."

Academics

Lewis & Clark College offers students everything they could possibly want: a "sense of community, beautiful campus, great academics, and lots of opportunities to engage in extracurriculars." Indeed, "it is a very welcoming" school, one filled with people who "care about the classes they are taking and the work that they are doing." In particular, students shine a spotlight on the school's "amazing job of engaging students in experiential learning," which includes "service work to underserved communities as well as educational and mentorship opportunities at nearby schools." Undergrads praise being able to "work with incarcerated people to explore topics of historical injustices in the criminal justice system or write expert witness statements for immigrants seeking citizenship in the U.S."

Students note that lower-level classes tend to be "much more lecture based" than many of the seminar-style upper-level classes that feature active group discussion, but are described as "still fascinating," due in large part to the fact that "professors are sure to engage their students by asking questions and encouraging participation." On this, undergraduates are largely unanimous: their teachers "are one of the best things about Lewis & Clark...dedicated to teaching and exclusively focused on the undergraduate experience." As one enrollee puts it, "Not only do they provide great instruction in the classroom, but they are available outside of the classroom to talk about class, life, and your future after college." A classmate concurs, adding, "I have made close connections with professors here—they have me feel like I am valuable, that my voice is important. I am so grateful for this, and I think this is a rare thing."

Campus Life

Lewis & Clark is "a pretty lax place, so you can kind of socialize at your own pace," whether that means partaking in the countless school events or just chilling in one's dorm. It's "really easy to start a club, so there is also something that caters to everyone." This eclectic mix includes "a club dedicated to the art of fire dancing" and a "beekeeping and gardening club," as well as staples like cheer, step, speech and debate, and a radio station. Some students also highlight the international affairs symposium, noting that it's "one of the most special things we have. They bring speakers from all over the world to debate on controversial topics and they are very interdisciplinary." Crafty and creatively inclined undergrads can take advantage of the Platteau, a "student-centered art center with free access to a ceramics studio, dance studio, darkroom, printing press, music studio, and general arts needs." Additionally, the school is a haven for outdoor enthusiasts, with one club providing "affordable weekend trips and free gear...for backpacking, white-water rafting, rock climbing, etc." As for downtown Portland, it offers a nice respite from campus life. It's typical to see students sampling the "cafés, brunch places, and thrift shops, museums, [and] malls."

Student Body

Peers at Lewis & Clark are described as "overwhelmingly white, very liberal, and generally pretty well-off, financially," with many hailing from the Bay Area, Washington, and Oregon. Among this cohort, there is also a group of "tight-knit international students" and "a very large and welcoming queer community." Some of the population describes itself as politically "very radical...compared to other colleges," but the overall consensus is of a student body that is "pretty balanced," particularly when it comes to the partying culture, which "never feels unhealthy or unsafe." The atmosphere, in short, is "very warm, welcoming, and open-minded," the sort of place where "no matter where I go on campus, there is always someone to wave to or stop and chat with." Indeed, "it is a very accepting community where everyone can feel comfortable in being their true selves and it is a place where you'll find your people." In other words, as this classmate sums up, "We form such special bonds at this institution and I can't imagine going to school anywhere else."

LEWIS & CLARK COLLEGE

Financial Aid: 503-768-7090 • E-Mail: admissions@lclark.edu • Website: www.lclark.edu

THE PRINCETON REVIEW SAYS

Admissions

The school reports that its standardized testing policy for use in admission for Fall 2024 is Test Optional. The 2024 testing policy will be permanent. The Princeton Review suggests that interested applicants consult with the school for the most up-to-date standardized testing policies. *Very important factors considered include:* rigor of secondary school record, academic GPA. *Important factors considered include:* application essay, recommendation(s), extracurricular activities, talent/ability, character/personal qualities, volunteer work, work experience. *Other factors considered include:* class rank, standardized test scores, interview, first generation, alumni/ae relation, geographical residence, racial/ethnic status, level of applicant's interest. High school diploma is required and GED is accepted. *Academic units recommended:* 4 English, 4 math, 3 science, 2 science labs, 2 foreign language, 3 social studies, 1 visual/performing arts.

Financial Aid

Students should submit: FAFSA. Priority filing deadline is 1/15. The Princeton Review suggests that all financial aid forms be submitted as soon as possible (see page 5 for a note on the FAFSA). *Need-based scholarships/grants offered:* College/university scholarship or grant aid from institutional funds; Federal Pell; Private scholarships; SEOG; State scholarships/grants. *Loan aid offered:* Direct PLUS loans; Direct Subsidized Loans; Direct Unsubsidized Loans. Admitted students will be notified of awards on a rolling basis beginning 12/20. Federal Work-Study Program available. Institutional employment available.

The Inside Word

If you have your heart set on L&C, make sure you tell that to the admissions committee, because the college is interested in students who will take advantage of the school's unique philosophy and educational environment. So make sure your application essay and interview both emphasize why L&C is the right fit for you. L&C is a Test Optional school, which means that applicants indicate whether they want their scores to be considered as part of the holistic admissions review. Note, however, that these scores play no role in the awarding of merit-based or need-based financial aid.

THE SCHOOL SAYS "..."

From the Admissions Office

"At Lewis & Clark, you will explore the liberal arts in small classes with an average size of 18. No matter which of our 29 majors and 33 minors you choose, you will learn to see connections others miss, creatively pursue the ideas you find most intriguing, and solve complex problems across disciplines. Entering first-year students benefit from our 4-5-6 Commitment, in which professors and professional academic advisors guide you through to a BA in four years, or we pay for your ninth semester. If you want to stay for five years, we have a pathway to our Graduate School of Teaching and Counseling that will get you an MAT + licensure in five years. Or in six years, you can earn your BA + a JD from our School of Law. Our location, just six miles from downtown Portland, offers access to internship and employment opportunities that you can explore with help from our Career Center and Bates Center for Entrepreneurship. Sixty percent of our students participate in our distinctive overseas study programs, the majority of which are led by our faculty and take place in countries outside of Western Europe. Our academics will challenge you. Our professors will mentor you. You'll graduate from Lewis & Clark ready to take on the world!"

SELECTIVITY

Admissions Rating	87
# of applicants	6,663
% of applicants accepted	69
% of acceptees attending	14
# offered a place on the wait list	937
% accepting a place on wait list	38
% admitted from wait list	19

FIRST-YEAR PROFILE

Testing policy	Test Optional
Range SAT composite	1270–1400
Range SAT EBRW	650–720
Range SAT math	610–680
Range ACT composite	29–32
# submitting SAT scores	97
% submitting SAT scores	15
# submitting ACT scores	57
% submitting ACT scores	9
Average HS GPA	3.7
% frosh submitting high school GPA	94

DEADLINES

Early decision	
Deadline	11/1
Notification	12/31
Early action	
Deadline	11/1
Notification	12/31
Regular	
Priority	1/15
Deadline	1/15
Notification	4/1
Nonfall registration?	Yes

APPLICANTS ALSO LOOK AT

Colorado College; Occidental College; Pitzer College; Reed College; University of California—Berkeley; University of California—Davis; University of California—Santa Cruz; University of Oregon; University of Puget Sound; University of Washington

FINANCIAL FACTS

Financial Aid Rating	88
Annual tuition	$59,250
Room and board	$14,384
Required fees	$434
Required fees (first-year)	$614
Books and supplies	$1,050
Average frosh need-based scholarship	$44,726
Average UG need-based scholarship	$44,193
% needy frosh rec. need-based scholarship or grant aid	99
% needy UG rec. need-based scholarship or grant aid	99
% needy frosh rec. non-need-based scholarship or grant aid	19
% needy UG rec. non-need-based scholarship or grant aid	15
% needy frosh rec. need-based self-help aid	80
% needy UG rec. need-based self-help aid	83
% frosh rec. any financial aid	99
% UG rec. any financial aid	99
% UG borrow to pay for school	31
Average cumulative indebtedness	$10,544
% frosh need fully met	38
% ugrads need fully met	41
Average % of frosh need met	91
Average % of ugrad need met	90

LOUISIANA STATE UNIVERSITY—BATON ROUGE

Louisiana State University—Baton Rouge, Baton Rouge, LA 70803 • Admissions: 225-578-1175 • Fax: 225-578-4433

CAMPUS LIFE

Quality of Life Rating	82
Fire Safety Rating	97
Green Rating	91
Type of school	Public
Environment	City

STUDENTS

Total undergrad enrollment	27,729
% male/female/another gender	45/55/0
% from out of state	28
% frosh from public high school	70
% frosh live on campus	82
% ugrads live on campus	30
# of fraternities (% join)	18 (15)
# of sororities (% join)	17 (25)
% African American	17
% Asian	5
% White	63
% Hispanic	9
% Native American	1
% Pacific Islander	<1
% Two or more races	3
% Race and/or ethnicity unknown	1
% international	1
# of countries represented	83

SURVEY SAYS . . .

Recreation facilities are great
College radio is popular
Everyone loves the Tigers
Students are happy
Great off-campus food
Active student government

ACADEMICS

Academic Rating	73
% students returning for sophomore year	84
% students graduating within 4 years	48
% students graduating within 6 years	70
Calendar	Semester
Student/faculty ratio	22:1
Profs interesting rating	81
Profs accessible rating	88
Most classes have 10–19 students.	
Most lab/discussion sessions have 10–19 students.	

MOST POPULAR MAJORS

Mass Communication/Media Studies; Physical Education Teaching and Coaching; Biology/Biological Sciences, General

STUDENTS SAY "..."

Academics

Louisiana State University is heralded by its students for having "tons of different programs to choose from" and "stellar academics." A few that students mention are the strong engineering and mass communications programs. Students also appreciate that they're not just abandoned under a variety of classes and programs. "No matter what issue you're having, there is [someone] whose entire job is to help you deal with it," says a student. "The tutoring centers are beyond helpful," if you need assistance with your studies, and faculty is "always available to help students" outside of class. This extra scaffolding keeps the rigor of academic programs "challenging but not unbearable." Some students recall lectures that are "extremely boring," and cite language barriers they've encountered with a few professors. But undergrads are impressed overall, stating, "Professors at LSU…are passionate about their fields of study" and are "accessible, accommodating, and well-informed."

Campus Life

This "beautiful southern university" offers "the best of both worlds," combining its academics with "so many clubs and groups…for students to join." For fun and fitness, "the weather is beautiful here and [the] campus is located next to large lakes where a lot of people run or walk." If you want to take it indoors, the recreation center is an "amazing facility" that "is great for group classes and working out during the day or relaxing at the pool." Socially, "Greek life is prominent," but if that's not your thing, "there are so many different subgroups, and there's really a place for everyone." No matter where you fit in, "tailgating and football are central to the school." As one student says, "It is [an] absolutely amazing environment [in which] everyone comes together to support the teams." Another adds, "When 'Calling Baton Rouge' gets played at an event you end up singing it and dancing to it with someone new, whoever is next to you, no matter where they are from." That love for Baton Rouge extends off-campus as well, to the city itself, which students call "underrated [and] cool."

Student Body

"Southern hospitality shines through in most" here, as "many students are clearly Louisianans first and students second." While many may be state natives, students frequently comment that "the student body at LSU is very diverse." One adds, "I love being able to walk around campus and see people of all cultures speaking different languages and engaging with one another." Along with cultures, interests vary too: "You have people that are party animals, Christian loyalists, sports enthusiasts, [and] academic maniacs." While students appreciate the diversity, some note that the population "continues to be predominated by white, cisgender, and mostly heterosexual people." Nonetheless, a community atmosphere prevails, allowing students to "really feel like they are a part of something bigger." This camaraderie extends all across campus because "people here care about smiles and friendliness," giving it "a smaller and more intimate atmosphere." As one student puts it, as long as "you're a Tiger, then you're family." As another student observes, "When you mix Louisiana culture with 30,000 students who love their school, you get an amazing combination."

LOUISIANA STATE UNIVERSITY—BATON ROUGE

Financial Aid: 225-578-3103 • E-Mail: admissions@lsu.edu • Website: www.lsu.edu

THE PRINCETON REVIEW SAYS

Admissions

The school reports that its standardized testing policy for use in admission for Fall 2024 is Test Optional. Students can either submit scores or be considered as Test Optional. The Princeton Review suggests that interested applicants consult with the school for the most up-to-date standardized testing policies. *Very important factors considered include:* rigor of secondary school record, academic GPA, standardized test scores, recommendation(s). *Important factors considered include:* talent/ability. *Other factors considered include:* class rank, application essay, interview, extracurricular activities, character/personal qualities, first generation, alumni/ae relation, volunteer work, work experience, level of applicant's interest. High school diploma is required and GED is accepted. *Academic units required:* 4 English, 4 math, 4 science, 2 foreign language, 3 social studies, 1 history, 1 visual/performing arts.

Financial Aid

Students should submit: FAFSA. Priority filing deadline is 2/1. The Princeton Review suggests that all financial aid forms be submitted as soon as possible (see page 5 for a note on the FAFSA). *Need-based scholarships/grants offered:* College/university scholarship or grant aid from institutional funds; Federal Pell; Private scholarships; SEOG; State scholarships/grants. *Loan aid offered:* Direct PLUS loans; Direct Subsidized Loans; Direct Unsubsidized Loans; College/university loans from institutional funds. Admitted students will be notified of awards on a rolling basis beginning 12/15. Federal Work-Study Program available. Institutional employment available.

The Inside Word

When assessing applications, LSU looks at the big picture of a student's educational history. That 71 percent acceptance rate suggests there is some selectivity, and applicants are advised to have a solid curriculum, grades, and courses. Demonstrated academic potential is an important consideration, so although the school is Test Optional, if standardized scores will help to show your ability, submit them.

THE SCHOOL SAYS "..."

From the Admissions Office

"LSU, one of only twenty-one universities nationwide designated as a land-grant, sea-grant, and space-grant institution, also holds the Carnegie Foundation's 'very high research activity' university designation.

"LSU's instructional programs include around 200 undergraduate and graduate or professional degrees. Outside of the classroom, residential colleges, service-learning opportunities, and more than 300 registered student organizations contribute to an exciting and meaningful college experience.

"Louisiana State University offers the Southern hospitality of a small community while providing the benefits of a large, technologically advanced institution.

"First-year applicants have the option of submitting SAT or ACT scores; Honors College applicants are required to demonstrate an example of their writing aptitude through any of the following: ACT or SAT writing scores, AP/IB English or History scores, personal essays, or the Honors College essay prompt. If submitted, LSU will use the best scores from either the SAT or ACT when making admission decisions."

SELECTIVITY

Admissions Rating	87
# of applicants	38,853
% of applicants accepted	76
% of acceptees attending	25

FIRST-YEAR PROFILE

Testing policy	Test Optional
Range SAT composite	1140–1310
Range SAT EBRW	580–660
Range SAT math	560–660
Range ACT composite	23–28
# submitting SAT scores	604
% submitting SAT scores	13
# submitting ACT scores	3,968
% submitting ACT scores	87
Average HS GPA	3.8
% frosh submitting high school GPA	98
% graduated top 10% of class	24
% graduated top 25% of class	50
% graduated top 50% of class	78

DEADLINES

Regular	
Priority	12/15
Deadline	4/15
Notification	Rolling, 10/15
Nonfall registration?	Yes

APPLICANTS ALSO LOOK AT

Louisiana Tech University; The University of Alabama—Tuscaloosa; Tulane University; University of Georgia; University of Louisiana at Lafayette; University of Mississippi

FINANCIAL FACTS

Financial Aid Rating	80
Annual in-state tuition	$8,038
Annual out-of-state tuition	$24,715
Room and board	$13,956
Required fees	$3,916
Books and supplies	$1,084
Average frosh need-based scholarship	$13,916
Average UG need-based scholarship	$13,577
% needy frosh rec. need-based scholarship or grant aid	92
% needy UG rec. need-based scholarship or grant aid	91
% needy frosh rec. non-need-based scholarship or grant aid	4
% needy UG rec. non-need-based scholarship or grant aid	3
% needy frosh rec. need-based self-help aid	44
% needy UG rec. need-based self-help aid	51
% frosh rec. any financial aid	94
% UG rec. any financial aid	80
% UG borrow to pay for school	42
Average cumulative indebtedness	$24,784
% frosh need fully met	13
% ugrads need fully met	12
Average % of frosh need met	55
Average % of ugrad need met	55

LOYOLA MARYMOUNT UNIVERSITY

1 LMU Drive, Los Angeles, CA 90045 • Admissions: 800-568-4636

STUDENTS SAY ". . ."

Academics

Loyola Marymount University's Jesuit traditions lay the foundation for a rigorous education guided by ethical values and philosophical discourse. More than 7,000 undergraduates study across the university's seven colleges and schools, and the main Westchester campus in Los Angeles overlooks the Pacific Ocean with "a beautiful view." Small class sizes and an 11:1 student-to-faculty ratio have been "very helpful for learning about opportunities for research on-campus, summer programs, internships, etc. and for getting really good recommendation letters." As one student states of their teachers, "You get a deeper understanding of their journey and how they can help you shape your own." The administration is "receptive to student wants" and "works so hard to foster a positive environment; you can really see it with their emails, their dedication to service, Wellness Wednesday, and the mental health resources." This temperature check is noticed by students, who say that based on their input "each year different things are added and/or focused on based on how well received it was."

Professors provide a reliable support system, and many "are extremely accessible to answer questions and to help you succeed." Real world experience is an important aspect of a LMU education, and teachers craft activities that "mimic a group in a workplace working on a project in order for students to learn how to work in a professional environment and work in a team." Some of the other more specific approaches taken include: "A class on world religions visits various religious halls in the area as a portion of their grade, [while] a peace in conflict course travels to Ireland." These are complemented by a fluid approach in the classroom, where many professors "choose to run classes in discussion-based ways (supplemented by readings and other media)," and "students engage in class discussions regularly." Students especially appreciate those teachers who flexibly "take advantage of LA's nice weather by sometimes holding class outside."

Campus Life

All students take part in the First Year Experience, which offers programming and resources to ensure a successful transition to college life. "Campus Ministry provides a community for religious students, especially Catholics and Christians," and many here take part in "service organizations, which are groups students can apply to be a part of to do service at LMU and in the greater Los Angeles area," or where they can check out social activities. Given the location, there are "frequent trips to the beach to hangout or surf" or "enjoy the sunset" as well as trips with the hiking club.

There "are plenty of places on campus to congregate and spend time" and the many clubs provide "ample opportunity for students on campus to have fun in their free time." Students also make the most of the school's location, and "getting off campus and exploring LA is easy and fun. There's always a new restaurant, concert, or event that you can go to."

Student Body

Among this "inclusive and intellectual student body," people "are kind, service or outward-looking, and generally perceive the injustices surrounding their communities." This "diverse combination of motivated, creative, and unique individuals" is "open to meeting and getting to know new people" and some say they "could ask anyone on campus for help and they'd give it in a heartbeat." Many LMU students "participate in organizations, athletics, or internships that help them gain the experience and academic training they need to construct their futures," are "extremely hardworking and committed to succeeding in college," and most everyone is "pretty active and involved with the school." The demographic has "some degree of diversity and we have multiple clubs that represent minority groups on campus" and the student body matches the "overall LA environment, [which] is casual and chill." Most students "work a job on campus or participate in clubs or service organizations," and "take the school's mission and values to heart" in their daily life. "Being a part of any Greek life/service org/or job will give you a community that makes college so much more fun," one student says.

LOYOLA MARYMOUNT UNIVERSITY

Financial Aid: 310-338-2753 • E-Mail: admissions@lmu.edu • Website: www.lmu.edu

THE PRINCETON REVIEW SAYS

Admissions

The school reports that its standardized testing policy for use in admission for Fall 2024 is Test Optional. The 2024 testing policy will be permanent. The Princeton Review suggests that interested applicants consult with the school for the most up-to-date standardized testing policies. *Very important factors considered include:* academic GPA. *Important factors considered include:* rigor of secondary school record, application essay, talent/ability, character/personal qualities. *Other factors considered include:* class rank, standardized test scores, recommendation(s), extracurricular activities, first generation, alumni/ae relation, volunteer work, work experience. High school diploma is required and GED is accepted. *Academic units recommended:* 4 English, 3 math, 2 science, 2 science labs, 3 foreign language, 3 social studies, 1 academic elective.

Financial Aid

Students should submit: FAFSA. Priority filing deadline is 2/1. The Princeton Review suggests that all financial aid forms be submitted as soon as possible (see page 5 for a note on the FAFSA). *Need-based scholarships/grants offered:* College/university scholarship or grant aid from institutional funds; Federal Pell; Private scholarships; SEOG; State scholarships/grants. *Loan aid offered:* Direct PLUS loans; Direct Subsidized Loans; Direct Unsubsidized Loans; College/university loans from institutional funds. Admitted students will be notified of awards on a rolling basis beginning in late December (early decision), early February (early action), late February/early March (early decision II), and early April (regular decision). Federal Work-Study Program available. Institutional employment available.

The Inside Word

A selective institution, Loyola Marymount University takes a well-rounded approach to admissions. While each applicant's academic record is of primary importance, LMU also considers everything from writing ability and service-related endeavors to letters of recommendation, artistic and athletic prowess, and even an individual's relationship to the university. It should be noted that requirements can vary depending on the program. For example, business students must have taken elementary algebra, geometry, and intermediate algebra/trigonometry. Arts applicants must audition or submit a portfolio. Please note that LMU is currently Test Optional.

THE SCHOOL SAYS "..."

From the Admissions Office

"Loyola Marymount University (LMU) is a nationally ranked, Jesuit university devoted to undergraduate and graduate academic excellence and *cura personalis,* 'care for the whole person.' LMU strives to develop the whole person in mind, body, and spirit. We commit to providing a launching pad for students to be agile problem-solvers and creative thinkers who become passionate leaders ready to ignite change in the world.

"Curiosity and intellectual exploration are encouraged at LMU. We offer more than 150 undergraduate degrees, certificates, and credentials; along with 4+1 master's degrees and over 90 graduate programs to prepare each individual for lives of meaning, purpose, and professional success. LMU's small-size classes taught by dedicated, award-winning professors result in personal attention and deep intellectual engagement that are the hallmarks of Jesuit education. Nationally-ranked programs in a broad range of areas—including the liberal arts, business, film, communication, fine arts, science and engineering—are paired with a vibrant campus life and innovative career and professional development programs.

"LMU welcomes students to our diverse, scenic, and vibrant campus, which is adjacent to the tech hub of Silicon Beach and in the epicenter of Los Angeles' vibrant art, culture, and business communities. Our LMU Career and Professional development programs help connect you to our impressive alumni and business partners for internships, job opportunities, and special events, ensuring you have the chance to build upon your personal interests and professional network."

SELECTIVITY

Admissions Rating	93
# of applicants	21,695
% of applicants accepted	41
% of acceptees attending	18
# offered a place on the wait list	6,788
% admitted from wait list	1
# of early decision applicants	490
% accepted early decision	61

FIRST-YEAR PROFILE

Testing policy	Test Optional
Range SAT composite	1280–1430
Range SAT EBRW	640–720
Range SAT math	630–730
Range ACT composite	28–32
# submitting SAT scores	354
% submitting SAT scores	22
# submitting ACT scores	197
% submitting ACT scores	12
Average HS GPA	4.0
% frosh submitting high school GPA	100
% graduated top 10% of class	34
% graduated top 25% of class	74
% graduated top 50% of class	94

DEADLINES

Early decision	
Deadline	11/1
Notification	12/17
Early action	
Deadline	11/1
Notification	12/17
Regular	
Deadline	1/15
Notification	Rolling, 11/15
Nonfall registration?	Yes

APPLICANTS OFTEN PREFER

University of California—Berkeley; University of California—Los Angeles; University of Southern California

APPLICANTS SOMETIMES PREFER

California Polytechnic State University; New York University; Santa Clara University; University of California—Santa Barbara

APPLICANTS RARELY PREFER

Chapman University; University of California-Irvine; University of San Diego

FINANCIAL FACTS

Financial Aid Rating	82
Annual tuition	$57,602
Room and board	$19,287
Required fees	$887
Required fees (first-year)	$1,372
Books and supplies	$938
Average frosh need-based scholarship	$25,649
Average UG need-based scholarship	$25,111
% needy frosh rec. need-based scholarship or grant aid	99
% needy UG rec. need-based scholarship or grant aid	97
% needy frosh rec. non-need-based scholarship or grant aid	22
% needy UG rec. non-need-based scholarship or grant aid	21
% needy frosh rec. need-based self-help aid	61
% needy UG rec. need-based self-help aid	62
% frosh rec. any financial aid	100
% UG rec. any financial aid	89
% UG borrow to pay for school	43
Average cumulative indebtedness	$32,828
% frosh need fully met	27
% ugrads need fully met	26
Average % of frosh need met	71
Average % of ugrad need met	68

LOYOLA UNIVERSITY CHICAGO

1032 W. Sheridan Rd., Chicago, IL 60660 • Admissions: 312-915-6000 • Fax: 312-915-7216

STUDENTS SAY ". . ."

Academics

With its main campus standing tall alongside the shore of Lake Michigan and eight miles north of downtown Chicago, Loyola University Chicago "provides the best of both worlds: an integrated campus and a taste of the city life." The Lake Shore Campus and the surrounding area are "gorgeous." The academic programs are "rigorous and fascinating," and the school offers "significant financial assistance and plenty of scholarships." The school's location "allows Loyola to attract top-notch faculty while giving students of all disciplines the opportunity to find something that interests them." Built on strong Jesuit values, Loyola cares deeply about social justice ("Go forth and set the world on fire" is a common credo) and "developing intellectual and socially responsible students." As one student puts it, the school is about "preparing students for careers and being aware of problems around us."

"The majority of the professors [are] excellent" and reportedly "find a good balance in their teaching methods that allows students to engage the material." This includes bringing in "business professionals to relate our classroom material to the real world," and one student notes that these flexible, creative professors are the sort "that one remembers for a long time." Adds another, "I've had several professors who I would go out of my way to take again."

The "well-known academic integrity of the school" provides a great reputation in Chicago, and the "connections and opportunities" the school provides to students seeking jobs and internships are numerous. "The work is challenging, but not overbearing," notes one student, and it pushes students "to be the best they can be, no matter what their major or background is." Because the curriculum is centered on being well rounded, "students can build an education that will serve them well in the future."

Campus Life

"What's great about Loyola is that it is very future focused, but it never forgets about the present either," says a student. Students at this school are quite involved, and they "find a good core group of people that they work together with in classes, clubs, organizations, and/or athletics." There are loads of community service and study abroad opportunities, and students "go on trips that involve doing out-of-the-ordinary activities," including skiing and skydiving.

Chicago is "a gold mine" of recreational opportunities, though students admit that the "social atmosphere of the campus is very dull." As one puts it, "Basically, the biggest hobby around here is exploring Chicago. We go out every weekend, just looking for things to do and always finding them," says a student. "Many students drink, but not all." The campus itself is "very relaxed, a sort of oasis in a bustling city," and there is even a beach right off campus on Lake Michigan, so "clearly, it does not feel much like a city most of the time."

Student Body

This group of "witty, hardworking, smart, and outgoing" people are all "studious and fairly involved but able to have fun." The typical student "comes from an upper-middle-class family, has some faith background, and balances school with social life well." Many are from local suburbs of Chicago, and yet "It is very easy to fit in because of how accepting people are," and "there is a real feel of family." Many students comment that there seem to be a lot of pre-med students here. Almost everyone is "involved in some extracurricular or another," and many students have a job as well.

LOYOLA UNIVERSITY CHICAGO

Financial Aid: 773-508-7704 • E-Mail: admission@luc.edu • Website: www.luc.edu/

THE PRINCETON REVIEW SAYS

Admissions

The school reports that its standardized testing policy for use in admission for Fall 2024 is Test Optional. The 2024 testing policy will be permanent. The Princeton Review suggests that interested applicants consult with the school for the most up-to-date standardized testing policies. *Very important factors considered include:* rigor of secondary school record, academic GPA. *Important factors considered include:* application essay, recommendation(s), extracurricular activities, character/personal qualities, volunteer work, work experience, level of applicant's interest. *Other factors considered include:* class rank, standardized test scores, interview, talent/ability, first generation, alumni/ae relation, geographical residence, state residency. High school diploma is required and GED is accepted. *Academic units required:* 4 English, 3 math, 3 science, 2 foreign language, 2 social studies, 1 history. *Academic units recommended:* 4 English, 4 math, 3 science, 2 foreign language, 2 social studies, 2 history, 3 academic electives.

Financial Aid

Students should submit: FAFSA. Priority filing deadline is 3/1. The Princeton Review suggests that all financial aid forms be submitted as soon as possible (see page 5 for a note on the FAFSA). *Need-based scholarships/grants offered:* College/university scholarship or grant aid from institutional funds; Federal Pell; Private scholarships; SEOG; State scholarships/grants. *Loan aid offered:* Direct PLUS loans; Direct Subsidized Loans; Direct Unsubsidized Loans; Federal Nursing Loans. Admitted students will be notified of awards on a rolling basis beginning 2/15. Federal Work-Study Program available. Institutional employment available.

The Inside Word

Loyola is fairly conventional when it comes to admissions policies. Successful candidates usually have a combination of strong grades, success in a tough college preparatory curriculum, and solid extracurricular activities. The school adheres to Jesuit teaching, so applicants with significant volunteer work should impress admissions officers.

THE SCHOOL SAYS "..."

From the Admissions Office

"As a Jesuit, Catholic university, Loyola University Chicago provides a strong liberal arts education, one that stresses the importance of knowledge, curiosity, global perspectives, and *cura personalis,* which translates to "care for the whole person." Loyola offers more than 80 majors and minors, with extensive program options that allow students to explore and develop their unique talents in a vibrant, urban atmosphere. The core curriculum provides a rich selection of courses with a diverse focus, emphasizing lifelong skills and values. The University continues to enhance its undergraduate academic programming by modifying and adding majors in emerging fields.

"For example, Loyola's new Parkinson School of Health Sciences and Public Health is dedicated to improving patient and population health and minimizing inequities—with degrees in exercise science, health systems management, and dietetics. Loyola's School of Environmental Sustainability offers degree program options in environmental studies, environmental policy, and environmental science with concentrations such as conservation and restoration. Housed in a state-of-the-art and LEED-certified facility, the institute features a greenhouse, a biodiesel lab, collaborative research labs, and one of the largest geothermal facilities in the Chicago region. Loyola continues to open new facilities and renovate existing buildings, including a new freshman residence hall, athletics facility, and engineering lab. Between Loyola's two lakeside campuses, students benefit from a traditional campus feel as well as a downtown that's home to Fortune 500 companies. For more information about undergraduate academics, housing, student life, financial aid, scholarship opportunities, and more, visit LUC.edu/undergrad."

SELECTIVITY

Admissions Rating	85
# of applicants	37,824
% of applicants accepted	77
% of acceptees attending	10

FIRST-YEAR PROFILE

Testing policy	Test Optional
Range SAT composite	1180–1350
Range SAT EBRW	590–690
Range SAT math	570–670
Range ACT composite	27–32
# submitting SAT scores	652
% submitting SAT scores	23
# submitting ACT scores	618
% submitting ACT scores	22
Average HS GPA	3.7
% frosh submitting high school GPA	96
% graduated top 10% of class	29
% graduated top 25% of class	61
% graduated top 50% of class	90

DEADLINES

Regular	
Priority	12/1
Notification	Rolling, 10/15
Nonfall registration?	Yes

APPLICANTS OFTEN PREFER
DePaul University; Indiana University—Bloomington; Marquette University; University of Illinois at Chicago; University of Illinois—Urbana-Champaign; University of Michigan—Ann Arbor; University of Wisconsin—Madison

APPLICANTS SOMETIMES PREFER
Michigan State University; Purdue University—West Lafayette; Saint Louis University

APPLICANTS RARELY PREFER
Hope College; Illinois State University; University of Kentucky; University of Minnesota—Twin Cities; University of Oregon

FINANCIAL FACTS

Financial Aid Rating	83
Annual tuition	$48,100
Room and board	$15,180
Required fees	$1,088
Books and supplies	$1,200
Average frosh need-based scholarship	$26,168
Average UG need-based scholarship	$24,672
% needy frosh rec. need-based scholarship or grant aid	99
% needy UG rec. need-based scholarship or grant aid	94
% needy frosh rec. non-need-based scholarship or grant aid	16
% needy UG rec. non-need-based scholarship or grant aid	14
% needy frosh rec. need-based self-help aid	80
% needy UG rec. need-based self-help aid	76
% frosh rec. any financial aid	99
% UG rec. any financial aid	92
% UG borrow to pay for school	61
Average cumulative indebtedness	$33,674
% frosh need fully met	20
% ugrads need fully met	19
Average % of frosh need met	85
Average % of ugrad need met	85

LOYOLA UNIVERSITY MARYLAND

4501 North Charles Street, Baltimore, MD 21210 • Admissions: 410-617-2000

CAMPUS LIFE

Quality of Life Rating	89
Fire Safety Rating	94
Green Rating	83
Type of school	Private
Affiliation	Roman Catholic
Environment	Metropolis

STUDENTS

Total undergrad enrollment	3,968
% male/female/another gender	45/55/NR
% from out of state	69
% frosh live on campus	92
% ugrads live on campus	79
# of fraternities	0
# of sororities	0
% African American	10
% Asian	4
% White	66
% Hispanic	14
% Native American	<1
% Pacific Islander	<1
% Two or more races	4
% Race and/or ethnicity unknown	1
% international	2
# of countries represented	54

SURVEY SAYS . . .

Lots of conservative students
Classroom facilities are great
Students involved in community service
Dorms are like palaces
Recreation facilities are great
Active student government
Active minority support groups

ACADEMICS

Academic Rating	83
% students returning for sophomore year	85
% students graduating within 4 years	75
% students graduating within 6 years	79
Calendar	Semester
Student/faculty ratio	13:1
Profs interesting rating	88
Profs accessible rating	94
Most classes have 10–19 students.	
Most lab/discussion sessions have 10–19 students.	

MOST POPULAR MAJORS

Business Administration and Management, General; Psychology, General; Communication, General

STUDENTS SAY "..."

Academics

The Jesuits have a long history of excellence in higher education, and that tradition is richly reflected in the academic programs at Loyola University in Maryland. The undergraduate experience is built around Loyola's "fantastic core curriculum," which ensures "a solid foundation in the natural sciences, English, history, philosophy, and theology." Through the core, students across disciplines "take some awesome classes that will completely change your perspective on the world." Jesuit values and philosophy are emphasized in the coursework, yet the school strikes the "right balance between religion, spirituality, and the everyday life of college students." No matter what field you choose to study, "the academics are outstanding and the coursework is challenging." A true teaching university, Loyola professors use "different learning techniques to cater to everyone's different learning styles." Professors "actually know each of their students by name." Serving as both personal and academic mentors, Loyola professors "get to know you personally, take time out of their office hours to have intellectual discussions, show you how to learn and how to teach, and help you out when you are having difficulties." The relationship can even extend off campus, as it's "fairly common for professors to give out their personal cell phone numbers or to even invite the class to their home for dinner." There's extensive "academic support" and tutoring for students in every discipline, and the "Career Center is open for students starting at day one." Though some would like to see a "larger variety of classes" for undergraduates, many praise the "excellent study abroad program," which offers the opportunity to spend a year in one of 14 countries.

Campus Life

Loyola students juggle school, service, spirituality, and social life with extraordinary flair. Monday through Friday, most undergraduates are "insanely busy doing loads of homework, projects, reading, community service, clubs, lectures, [and] sports." Of particular note, Loyola offers "amazing opportunities to get involved in the Baltimore community through service." In fact, the school uses "Baltimore city as an extension of the classroom," where students learn about real life, rather than living in a college bubble. On the weekends, things slow down around campus, though students can partake of the "numerous speakers, movies, events, or sporting events" hosted by the university. In addition, "a lot of people go out to bars on Fridays and Saturdays," because "there is no Greek life" on campus and Loyola's strict alcohol policies make it difficult to throw parties. Loyola students can be found out and about in Baltimore, "going out to eat, catching an Orioles game, attending a concert at the BSO, [or] walking around the harbor." "Most students live on campus" during the school year, enjoying a surprisingly comfortable lifestyle in Loyola's cushy dormitories. If you score a spot in one of the suites, you and your roommates will "have full kitchens in your dorm by sophomore year."

Student Body

In addition to being predominantly Catholic, "many of the students are white, from New York or New Jersey, and come from private high schools." You'll see plenty of "UGGs, North Face, pearls, and J. Crew" around campus. Although "the student body may appear homogenous," students insist that "everyone can fit in well if you get past the initial stereotypes and immerse yourself in the opportunities Loyola has to offer." On that note, students "try to live out the core values of the university and enjoy being a contributing member of school community." Here, students "care about their academics and do well in school, but they also try to balance that with extracurriculars and their spiritual life." On the whole, the campus is "really welcoming and trustworthy," with a "great sense of community." With so many ways to get involved, most students "find their niche at Loyola very quickly."

LOYOLA UNIVERSITY MARYLAND

Financial Aid: 410-617-2576 • E-Mail: admission@loyola.edu • Website: www.loyola.edu

THE PRINCETON REVIEW SAYS

Admissions

The school reports that its standardized testing policy for use in admission for Fall 2024 is Test Optional. The 2024 testing policy will be permanent. The Princeton Review suggests that interested applicants consult with the school for the most up-to-date standardized testing policies. *Very important factors considered include:* rigor of secondary school record, academic GPA, character/personal qualities. *Important factors considered include:* application essay, recommendation(s), extracurricular activities, talent/ability, volunteer work, work experience. *Other factors considered include:* standardized test scores, first generation, alumni/ae relation, geographical residence, racial/ethnic status. High school diploma is required and GED is accepted. *Academic units required:* 4 English, 3 math, 3 science, 3 foreign language, 2 history. *Academic units recommended:* 4 English, 4 math, 4 science, 4 foreign language, 3 history.

Financial Aid

Students should submit: CSS/Financial Aid Profile; FAFSA. Priority filing deadline is 12/1. The Princeton Review suggests that all financial aid forms be submitted as soon as possible (see page 5 for a note on the FAFSA). *Need-based scholarships/grants offered:* College/university scholarship or grant aid from institutional funds; Federal Pell; Private scholarships; SEOG; State scholarships/grants. *Loan aid offered:* Direct PLUS loans; Direct Subsidized Loans; Direct Unsubsidized Loans. Admitted students will be notified of awards on a rolling basis beginning 2/1. Federal Work-Study Program available. Institutional employment available.

The Inside Word

Loyola University in Maryland considers a student's academic record to be among the most important factors in an admissions decision. Successful students usually rank in the top quarter of their classes. Although Loyola will consider standardized test scores if you submit them, the SAT or ACT are optional for all first-year applicants. If you decide to apply without taking a test, Loyola asks that you submit an additional personal essay or recommendation.

THE SCHOOL SAYS "..."

From the Admissions Office

"To make a wise choice about your college plans, you will need to find out more. We extend to you these invitations. Question-and-answer periods with an admissions counselor are helpful to prospective students. An appointment should be made in advance. Admission office hours are 9:00 A.M. to 5:00 P.M., Monday through Friday. College day programs and Saturday information programs are scheduled during the academic year. These programs include a video about Loyola, a general information session, a discussion of various majors, a campus tour, and lunch. Summer information programs can help high school juniors to get a head start on investigating colleges. These programs feature an introductory presentation about the university and a campus tour."

SELECTIVITY

Admissions Rating	85
# of applicants	9,643
% of applicants accepted	83
% of acceptees attending	16
# offered a place on the wait list	526
% accepting a place on wait list	47
% admitted from wait list	0
# of early decision applicants	0

FIRST-YEAR PROFILE

Testing policy	Test Optional
Range SAT composite	1185–1350
Range SAT EBRW	600–690
Range SAT math	580–670
Range ACT composite	26–33
# submitting SAT scores	369
% submitting SAT scores	29
# submitting ACT scores	59
% submitting ACT scores	5
Average HS GPA	3.7
% frosh submitting high school GPA	100
% graduated top 10% of class	25
% graduated top 25% of class	56
% graduated top 50% of class	84

DEADLINES

Early action	
Deadline	11/15
Notification	1/15
Regular	
Priority	11/15
Deadline	1/15
Nonfall registration?	Yes

FINANCIAL FACTS

Financial Aid Rating	85
Annual tuition	$55,480
Required fees	$0
Books and supplies	$1,100
Average frosh need-based scholarship	$15,068
Average UG need-based scholarship	$16,601
% needy frosh rec. need-based scholarship or grant aid	91
% needy UG rec. need-based scholarship or grant aid	84
% needy frosh rec. non-need-based scholarship or grant aid	95
% needy UG rec. non-need-based scholarship or grant aid	91
% needy frosh rec. need-based self-help aid	76
% needy UG rec. need-based self-help aid	78
% UG borrow to pay for school	61
Average cumulative indebtedness	$37,594
% frosh need fully met	28
% ugrads need fully met	28
Average % of frosh need met	85
Average % of ugrad need met	82

LOYOLA UNIVERSITY NEW ORLEANS

6363 St. Charles Avenue, New Orleans, LA 70118-6195 • Admissions: 504-865-3240 • Fax: 504-865-3383

STUDENTS SAY "..."

Academics
A Jesuit institution in the heart of one of the country's most vibrant cities, Loyola University New Orleans "offers students countless opportunities to progress spiritually, academically, and career-wise." When undergraduates enroll, they join a "welcoming [and] warm-hearted" community in which "professors, staff and students alike support each other." Academically, "the university encourages students to explore all areas of course offerings." And given the school's small size, it's safe to assume that "the student to teacher ratio is great." Most courses do a fantastic job of balancing "lectures [with] class discussions." Finally, when it comes to the professors, students find the majority are "amazing teachers [who] really make me want to learn." They "keep me inspired and encouraged beyond the typical academic interaction," explains one student. It's easy to tell they "really care about [the] well-being" of their students. Ultimately, "The effort and commitment from faculty transcends the bounds of a classroom space and [they] genuinely invest their time to ensure student success."

Campus Life
Sure, academics take precedence at Loyola. But there's tons of fun outside of the classroom. On campus, undergrads can choose from offerings "such as movie night, casual musical performances by the students, and activities held by the student government such as 'Bears for Bae' which is kind of like Build a Bear." Additionally, Loyola has a number of artsy students and it's quite common for people to "make music, make music videos and [work] on creative projects in general." There's also a robust theater department and scene that puts on "amazing" performances and allows students to "design or assist in designing every show."

Of course, hometown New Orleans is also a massive draw and "lots of time is spent off campus exploring [the city]." The area is filled with "spectacular cultural traditions" and many flock to "see lots of local bands perform." Moreover it's popular for students to "bike on the Mississippi River Trail, hike in state parks, [and] walk around the French Quarter." And you'll find that "people go out a lot to the local bars because here in New Orleans, the bars are 18+ to get in which means freshman and sophomores party a lot."

Student Body
Loyola University does a great job of attracting "artsy, creative, [and] socially conscious" students who are still "down to earth." Undergrads here "care about their communities and environment" and really "focus on...inclusion." They also have "big hearts [and] pride in their Nola culture." The vast majority agree, "There is a really strong community here." As another student concludes, "I have never once felt unwelcome by a member of the Loyola community and I truly feel like it is a place where any one can feel welcome and accepted."

Many people also take pride in the fact that Loyola has "a beautifully diverse student body" noting that undergrads come "from all over the U.S. and internationally." And although the university is Catholic, undergrads say that they "have met people of all...religions." As one person details, "Loyola is a melting pot, full of students of all backgrounds, races, beliefs, sexualities, and socioeconomic backgrounds." Truly, you can find "every type of person here."

LOYOLA UNIVERSITY NEW ORLEANS

Financial Aid: 504-865-3158 • E-Mail: admit@loyno.edu • Website: www.loyno.edu

THE PRINCETON REVIEW SAYS

Admissions

The school reports that its standardized testing policy for use in admission for Fall 2024 is Test Free. The 2024 testing policy will be permanent. The Princeton Review suggests that interested applicants consult with the school for the most up-to-date standardized testing policies. *Very important factors considered include:* rigor of secondary school record, academic GPA. *Important factors considered include:* application essay, recommendation(s), extracurricular activities, talent/ability. *Other factors considered include:* class rank, interview, character/personal qualities, alumni/ae relation, geographical residence, volunteer work, work experience, level of applicant's interest. High school diploma is required and GED is accepted. *Academic units required:* 4 English, 2 math, 2 science, 2 social studies. *Academic units recommended:* 4 English, 3 math, 3 science, 1 science lab, 2 foreign language, 2 social studies, 2 history.

Financial Aid

Students should submit: FAFSA. Priority filing deadline is 2/15. The Princeton Review suggests that all financial aid forms be submitted as soon as possible (see page 5 for a note on the FAFSA). *Need-based scholarships/grants offered:* College/university scholarship or grant aid from institutional funds; Federal Pell; Private scholarships; SEOG; State scholarships/grants; United Negro College Fund. *Loan aid offered:* Direct PLUS loans; Direct Subsidized Loans; Direct Unsubsidized Loans. Admitted students will be notified of awards on a rolling basis beginning 3/1. Federal Work-Study Program available. Institutional employment available.

The Inside Word

The admission process at Loyola University New Orleans focuses on understanding who each applicant is, not just how they score. Of course, your GPA and high school transcript will still carry weight, so we suggest taking advanced courses to help your transcript stand out. Loyola values community involvement, so be sure to include any community service participation in your application. Students who want to enroll in the theater or music program must also be prepared to audition.

THE SCHOOL SAYS "..."

From the Admissions Office

"Nationally recognized for diversity and inclusion, Loyola University New Orleans celebrates the rich history of a Jesuit education, including the commitment to social justice and education of the whole person—body, mind, and spirit. In 2020, in recognition that students are more than their scores, Loyola became a Test Free institution.

"Loyola is home to three undergraduate colleges, a College of Law, and a College of Nursing and Health, which offers a bachelor's degree. Home to aspiring journalists, filmmakers, musicians, designers, artists, producers and music industry executives, the College of Music and Media fosters cross-collaborative learning and innovative storytelling of all kinds. The College of Business capitalizes on New Orleans' entrepreneurial spirit and burgeoning tech and creativity hubs; its Center for Entrepreneurship provides vital links to the business community. The College of Arts and Sciences is home to the Center for Editing and Publishing, which provides opportunities for students to engage in the creation of books and articles. In 2020, the college created two exciting new programs in neuroscience and cybersecurity, and launched two public health majors and a minor in 2021.

"All first-year students at Loyola receive personalized student success coaching and enjoy a wealth of mentoring, advising and tutoring services in the brand-new Pan-American Student Success Center. In the last five years, Loyola New Orleans has twice been named a Top Producer of Fulbright Students and Scholars, as well as a Top Producer of Peace Corps Volunteers and Top Producer of Teach for America Volunteers, demonstrating the school's commitment to academic excellence and service. The Maroon, Loyola's 100-year-old student newspaper routinely wins top awards in the field."

SELECTIVITY

Admissions Rating	77
# of applicants	7,340
% of applicants accepted	78
% of acceptees attending	14

FIRST-YEAR PROFILE

Testing policy	Test Free
Average HS GPA	3.6
% frosh submitting high school GPA	99

DEADLINES

Early action	
Deadline	11/15
Notification	12/1
Regular	
Priority	11/15
Notification	Rolling, 12/1
Nonfall registration?	Yes

APPLICANTS ALSO LOOK AT

Belmont University; College of Charleston; DePaul University; Florida International University; Florida State University; Howard University; Louisiana State University—Baton Rouge; Loyola University of Chicago; Morehouse College; Saint Louis University

FINANCIAL FACTS

Financial Aid Rating	83
Annual tuition	$45,280
Room and board	$14,330
Required fees	$1,960
Required fees (first-year)	$2,210
Books and supplies	$1,300
Average frosh need-based scholarship	$36,249
Average UG need-based scholarship	$33,167
% needy frosh rec. need-based scholarship or grant aid	100
% needy UG rec. need-based scholarship or grant aid	98
% needy frosh rec. non-need-based scholarship or grant aid	14
% needy UG rec. non-need-based scholarship or grant aid	16
% needy frosh rec. need-based self-help aid	82
% needy UG rec. need-based self-help aid	75
% frosh rec. any financial aid	99
% UG rec. any financial aid	94
% UG borrow to pay for school	69
Average cumulative indebtedness	$28,538
% frosh need fully met	15
% ugrads need fully met	16
Average % of frosh need met	81
Average % of ugrad need met	77

LYCOMING COLLEGE

One College Place, Williamsport, PA 17701-5192 • Admissions: 570-321-4026 • Fax: 570-321-4317

CAMPUS LIFE

Quality of Life Rating	85
Fire Safety Rating	86
Green Rating	87
Type of school	Private
Affiliation	Methodist
Environment	Town

STUDENTS

Total undergrad enrollment	1,055
% male/female/another gender	48/52/0
% from out of state	40
% frosh from public high school	90
% frosh live on campus	89
% ugrads live on campus	85
# of fraternities (% join)	3 (7)
# of sororities (% join)	5 (10)
% African American	13
% Asian	1
% White	61
% Hispanic	14
% Native American	<1
% Pacific Islander	0
% Two or more races	3
% Race and/or ethnicity unknown	4
% international	3
# of countries represented	14

SURVEY SAYS . . .
Students are happy
Internships are widely available
Easy to get around campus
Theater is popular

ACADEMICS

Academic Rating	83
% students returning for sophomore year	72
% students graduating within 4 years	55
% students graduating within 6 years	64
Calendar	Semester
Student/faculty ratio	11:1
Profs interesting rating	91
Profs accessible rating	94

Most classes have 10–19 students.
Most lab/discussion sessions have
  fewer than 10 students.

MOST POPULAR MAJORS
Biology/Biological Sciences, General; Psychology, General; Business Administration and Management, General

STUDENTS SAY ". . ."

Academics
Lycoming College is an institution that's built on "personal connections between [the] administration, faculty, and students." This sentiment is quickly echoed by an undergrad who notes that of the school's many strengths, "the most important one to me is how open and welcoming and accepting it is of everyone." Of course, there's plenty to enjoy in addition to the warm vibes. Indeed, at Lyco, learning opportunities extend far beyond the classroom. For example, "There are weekly colloquium seminars for guest speakers [and] students to present their research to the rest of the department." Undergrads can also make the most of "trips to conferences, as well as internships and study abroad opportunities like our May Term classes [that] allow students to travel to other countries with professors to learn about a subject while immersed in it."

Inside the classroom, undergrads benefit from "small class sizes and great professors." This enables students to "learn on a more individualized scale" and makes it easier for anyone to "address any problems or learning issues 1-on-1." As one undergrad explains, teachers here "take the time to answer questions and make sure students have a solid understanding of the material in a way that is meaningful." Many also appreciate that professors do their utmost to connect them with "opportunities such as faculty research, becoming a TA, peer subject tutor, internships, and more!" And while they do acknowledge that there's "a high expectation for the academics here at Lycoming," many "wouldn't change a thing." Or to put it another way: "I love a good challenge and these classes are pushing me to be my best."

Campus Life
Given that "classes are demanding," Lycoming students devote a substantial amount of time to studying. Nevertheless, there's plenty to enjoy beyond the library walls and undergrads "never [have] to have a dull moment here on campus." For this fairly sporty lot, "whether it be recreational basketball, corn-hole, ping pong, foosball, soccer, flag football, volleyball, [or] spike ball, there [are] always some type of games going on through[out] the year." You can also find undergrads "skiing, biking, [or] on ice wall hikes." On campus, clubs range from "chamber and concert choirs," to "SPS Stargazing" and "French club, where we make different kinds of French foods and do activities such as pétanque and Mardi Gras celebrations." As for Greek life, one sorority sister notes that "We are small [but] we are mighty. We make up about two-thirds of all college-organized community service events." Finally, though it may take them far away from campus, the Outdoor Leadership and Education trips are popular among undergraduates. Here, "students can explore the outdoors or go on trips to national parks." These are sometimes coupled with "the alternative spring break trips where students can go work with Habitat for Humanity."

Student Body
Undergrads at Lycoming explain that there's "a club or group for everyone," which helps to match the fact that "our student body is increasingly becoming more diverse and representative of the U.S. population." That is inclusive of "gender expression and identity [as well as] political and religious views." Regardless of their backgrounds, students feel as though they're part of "a tight knit community," the sort of right-size place that "allows everyone to know everybody in some sort of way." This also means that "when help is needed or you want to know any information about something that is going on, you generally can ask anyone on campus." The result is a "positive environment" where people tend to be "very friendly and often say hello or wave when you walk past." Truly, studying here is an "amazing opportunity to meet so many new and interesting people who will become lifelong friends."

LYCOMING COLLEGE

Financial Aid: 570-321-4040 • E-Mail: admissions@lycoming.edu • Website: www.lycoming.edu

THE PRINCETON REVIEW SAYS

Admissions

The school reports that its standardized testing policy for use in admission for Fall 2024 is Test Optional. The 2024 testing policy will be permanent. The Princeton Review suggests that interested applicants consult with the school for the most up-to-date standardized testing policies. *Very important factors considered include:* rigor of secondary school record, recommendation(s). *Important factors considered include:* class rank, academic GPA, standardized test scores, application essay, interview. *Other factors considered include:* extracurricular activities, talent/ability, character/personal qualities, first generation, alumni/ae relation, geographical residence, state residency, racial/ethnic status, volunteer work, work experience, level of applicant's interest. High school diploma is required and GED is accepted. *Academic units required:* 4 English, 3 math, 3 science, 2 foreign language, 3 social studies, 2 academic electives. *Academic units recommended:* 4 English, 4 math, 3 science, 3 foreign language, 4 social studies, 3 academic electives.

Financial Aid

Students should submit: FAFSA; State aid form. Priority filing deadline is 5/1. The Princeton Review suggests that all financial aid forms be submitted as soon as possible (see page 5 for a note on the FAFSA). *Need-based scholarships/grants offered:* College/university scholarship or grant aid from institutional funds; Federal Pell; Private scholarships; SEOG; State scholarships/grants. *Loan aid offered:* Direct PLUS loans; Direct Subsidized Loans; Direct Unsubsidized Loans; College/university loans from institutional funds. Admitted students will be notified of awards on a rolling basis beginning 12/1. Federal Work-Study Program available. Institutional employment available.

The Inside Word

Admissions officers at Lycoming College consider the whole applicant. To that end, everything from GPA and rigor of your course load to recommendations and personal essays will be closely evaluated. Applicants may be delighted to learn that Lycoming is also a Test Optional school (with exceptions). To be eligible, candidates must be in the top half of their graduating class and submit two graded writing samples that are analytical in nature.

THE SCHOOL SAYS "..."

From the Admissions Office

"Lycoming College takes traditional liberal arts to the next level with cutting-edge programs, experiential learning, and extracurriculars that let students think deeply and act boldly. Students are encouraged to craft customized, cross-disciplinary academic pathways tailored to their unique interests and career goals. Lycoming offers forty-four majors and sixty-four minors, with programs that seek to answer 21st-century questions, such as neuroscience, astrophysics, computer science, energy studies, and entrepreneurship.

"As a solely undergraduate institution, Lycoming is able to give students access to advanced equipment, research opportunities, and fieldwork starting freshman year. Professors are both scholars in their field as well as mentors and regularly include students in their personal research projects. Small class sizes foster workshops, hands-on labs, and discussion-based learning. Professors know students by name and have even been known to invite students to their homes for dinner.

"Unique to Lycoming is the Center for Enhanced Academic Experiences, which offers internships, research, fellowships, and study abroad opportunities as well as subject-specific career advising and pre-professional/graduate school guidance.

"Nestled in the Susquehanna River Valley, the city of Williamsport offers something for everyone: a vibrant entertainment, shopping, and arts scene and a rich, natural landscape that beckons outdoor adventure. On campus, the already tight-knit community is strengthened through a variety of clubs, organizations, and programming. It is often said that at Lycoming, it's not a matter of if you'll get involved, but how much."

SELECTIVITY

Admissions Rating	84
# of applicants	3,039
% of applicants accepted	75
% of acceptees attending	13

FIRST-YEAR PROFILE

Testing policy	Test Optional
Range SAT composite	1060–1250
Range SAT EBRW	530–628
Range SAT math	523–610
Range ACT composite	20–25
# submitting SAT scores	132
% submitting SAT scores	45
# submitting ACT scores	19
% submitting ACT scores	6
Average HS GPA	3.6
% frosh submitting high school GPA	96
% graduated top 10% of class	22
% graduated top 25% of class	49
% graduated top 50% of class	84

DEADLINES

Early decision	
Deadline	11/15
Notification	12/1
Early action	
Deadline	12/1
Notification	12/15
Nonfall registration?	Yes

FINANCIAL FACTS

Financial Aid Rating	88
Annual tuition	$46,720
Room and board	$14,612
Required fees	$730
Required fees (first-year)	$955
Books and supplies	$1,200
Average frosh need-based scholarship	$40,015
Average UG need-based scholarship	$39,206
% needy frosh rec. need-based scholarship or grant aid	100
% needy UG rec. need-based scholarship or grant aid	100
% needy frosh rec. non-need-based scholarship or grant aid	18
% needy UG rec. non-need-based scholarship or grant aid	18
% needy frosh rec. need-based self-help aid	72
% needy UG rec. need-based self-help aid	74
% frosh rec. any financial aid	100
% UG rec. any financial aid	100
% frosh need fully met	26
% ugrads need fully met	26
Average % of frosh need met	90
Average % of ugrad need met	89

MACALESTER COLLEGE

1600 Grand Avenue, St. Paul, MN 55105-1899 • Admissions: 651-696-6357 • Fax: 651-696-6724

STUDENTS SAY "..."

Academics

Located between St. Paul and Minneapolis, students at Macalester College benefit from a liberal arts education amplified by the unique cultural and professional offerings available in the surrounding cities. Many classes work with Twin Cities companies and organizations to incorporate real-world experience into the curriculum, and the school "has set up a lot of technical support to help students get a better work experience." This results in comments such as: "For Mac students, it's not about just learning, it's about using what you are learning and applying it to systemic change." Many say that one of the school's greatest strengths is "its location and its connection to so many great community organizations." Support is universal between faculty and staff, and "people genuinely want to provide assistance." As one student puts it: "I have never experienced difficulty finding information on internships or other career opportunities."

Unique pedagogical methods are present across every course of study, including innovative grading systems that "try to reduce student stress while remaining rigorous," such as "ungrading, in which students design individual grading tracks to ultimately evaluate themselves, with support and feedback from the professor." Other approaches include an open learning system where students "are grouped not by ability, but according to their interests and needs." This results in a variety of learning methods, paces, and content beyond testing alone: "Professors try to design methods of assessment that encourage more creativity and teamwork," and "classroom discussions are lively and intense with the intent to actually better understand the world, class materials, and each other." Students say that "flipped classrooms, with lectures as homework and discussion and working on problems in class, are common."

Campus Life

At Macalester College, "being a smaller community [brings with it] a stronger sense of identity, more access to funding, research opportunities, and internships." Students "love the compact campus that has everything we need: recreational spaces, study spaces, classrooms, cafeteria, religious spaces—and it's all walkable." Activities are less party-driven and most here choose to "engage in relaxed activities like playing board or video games, watching TV, or having intellectual (or fun!) discussions while cooking or eating." More than sixty percent of students study abroad, and the Lealtad-Suzuki Center for Social Justice further broadens students' education and perspectives. As befits a school with "many religions/spiritualities [and] a large LGBTQIA+ population," there are also "many opportunities to join organizations and clubs [from those] different backgrounds."

In their remaining free time, students "take advantage of being in the Twin Cities and go off campus to study and explore as well as eat"; while on campus, "lunch and especially dinner in the dining hall are a large part of the social life." The school itself also plans events "like a crafts night, make your own tote bag, and trivia nights which are open to anyone." Student-run events are extremely successful and contribute to the strong sense of community on campus.

Student Body

In general, these diverse, international, and open-minded students are "extremely liberal and globally aware." As one describes it, "it is not uncommon for students to organize transportation from campus to local events and protests." That's because they're "determined to change the world for the better," so much so that "if you ask anybody on campus what they did over break, they will probably say 'volunteered for a non-profit'." They are "very engaged and interested in academics, smart, [and] dedicated." Additionally, a "large percentage of people are queer," which has come to mean "that anyone and everyone is welcome." The school's "atmosphere is very non-judgmental," so while students "have high standards for themselves, these standards do not breed intense competition—rather it cultivates an environment of collaboration and support."

MACALESTER COLLEGE

Financial Aid: 651-696-6214 • E-Mail: admissions@macalester.edu • Website: www.macalester.edu

THE PRINCETON REVIEW SAYS

Admissions

The school reports that its standardized testing policy for use in admission for Fall 2024 is Test Optional. The 2024 testing policy will be permanent. The Princeton Review suggests that interested applicants consult with the school for the most up-to-date standardized testing policies. *Very important factors considered include:* rigor of secondary school record, academic GPA. *Important factors considered include:* application essay, recommendation(s), extracurricular activities, character/personal qualities. *Other factors considered include:* class rank, standardized test scores, interview, talent/ability, first generation, alumni/ae relation, geographical residence, state residency, racial/ethnic status, volunteer work, work experience. High school diploma or equivalent is not required. *Academic units recommended:* 4 English, 3 math, 3 science, 3 science labs, 3 foreign language, 3 social studies.

Financial Aid

Students should submit: CSS/Financial Aid Profile; FAFSA; Noncustodial Profile. Priority filing deadline is 1/23. The Princeton Review suggests that all financial aid forms be submitted as soon as possible (see page 5 for a note on the FAFSA). *Need-based scholarships/grants offered:* College/university scholarship or grant aid from institutional funds; Federal Pell; Private scholarships; SEOG; State scholarships/grants. *Loan aid offered:* Direct PLUS loans; Direct Subsidized Loans; Direct Unsubsidized Loans; College/university loans from institutional funds; State Loans. Admitted students will be notified of awards on or about 4/1. Federal Work-Study Program available. Institutional employment available.

The Inside Word

The number of applicants to Macalester has been steadily increasing each year. Accordingly, it has grown substantially more difficult to gain admission here. Candidates need to put their best foot forward in their applications; 56 percent of the current first-year class ranked in the top 10 percent of their high school classes.

THE SCHOOL SAYS "..."

From the Admissions Office

"Macalester College is one of very few selective liberal arts colleges located in the heart of a major metropolitan area. The campus sits within a friendly residential neighborhood, surrounded by restaurants, coffee houses, bike paths, and bookstores. Students who thrive at Macalester are curious, highly motivated, serious about their academic pursuits, and supportive of each other; choosing collective success over competition. The demanding academic program and commitments to internationalism, multiculturalism, and service to society are amplified by Macalester's location in the Twin Cities of Saint Paul and Minneapolis. Being in a metropolitan area allows for courses and internships that partner with organizations including nonprofits, government agencies, and Fortune 500 companies. Small class sizes allow for a rich experience with strong faculty partnerships, individual attention, and meaningful connections with classmates from more than 90 countries and all 50 states. Contributing to lasting friendships and a sense of community, there are over 100 student organizations available. These groups reflect the diverse interests of students, ranging from outdoor adventures, gaming, politics, and Quiz Bowl, to rocketry, slam poetry, and ultimate frisbee. Macalester has 19 varsity athletic teams as well as club and intramural sports. More than 60% of students study abroad for 15 weeks or longer, immersing themselves in another culture and widening their global perspective. Macalester provides a financial aid package meeting 100% of demonstrated financial need for every student, and offers a robust merit-based scholarship program. The United Nations flag has flown over campus since 1950, symbolizing Macalester's commitment to world peace and understanding."

SELECTIVITY

Admissions Rating	95
# of applicants	8,434
% of applicants accepted	28
% of acceptees attending	23
# offered a place on the wait list	1,081
% accepting a place on wait list	55
% admitted from wait list	0
# of early decision applicants	335
% accepted early decision	53

FIRST-YEAR PROFILE

Testing policy	Test Optional
Range SAT composite	1350–1490
Range SAT EBRW	670–750
Range SAT math	670–750
Range ACT composite	30–34
# submitting SAT scores	183
% submitting SAT scores	33
# submitting ACT scores	168
% submitting ACT scores	30
% graduated top 10% of class	56
% graduated top 25% of class	90
% graduated top 50% of class	99

DEADLINES

Early decision	
Deadline	11/1
Notification	12/4
Other ED deadline	1/1
Other ED notification	1/29
Early action	
Deadline	11/1
Notification	12/21
Regular	
Deadline	1/15
Notification	3/26
Nonfall registration?	No

APPLICANTS ALSO LOOK AT

Brown University; Carleton College; Grinnell College; New York University; Northwestern University; Oberlin College; Occidental College; St. Olaf College; The University of Chicago; Tufts University; University of California—Berkeley; University of California—Los Angeles; University of Michigan—Ann Arbor; University of Minnesota—Twin Cities; University of Wisconsin—Madison; Vassar College; Washington University in St. Louis; Wesleyan University

FINANCIAL FACTS

Financial Aid Rating	91
Annual tuition	$64,678
Room and board	$14,982
Required fees	$230
Books and supplies	$926
Average frosh need-based scholarship	$52,322
Average UG need-based scholarship	$50,236
% needy frosh rec. need-based scholarship or grant aid	99
% needy UG rec. need-based scholarship or grant aid	99
% needy frosh rec. non-need-based scholarship or grant aid	12
% needy UG rec. non-need-based scholarship or grant aid	9
% needy frosh rec. need-based self-help aid	84
% needy UG rec. need-based self-help aid	88
% frosh rec. any financial aid	67
% UG rec. any financial aid	89
% UG borrow to pay for school	87
Average cumulative indebtedness	$21,841
% frosh need fully met	79
% ugrads need fully met	61
Average % of frosh need met	101
Average % of ugrad need met	99

MANHATTAN COLLEGE

Manhattan College Parkway, Riverdale, NY 10471 • Admissions: 718-862-8000 • Fax: 718-862-8019

CAMPUS LIFE
Quality of Life Rating	83
Fire Safety Rating	83
Green Rating	74
Type of school	Private
Affiliation	Roman Catholic
Environment	Metropolis

STUDENTS
Total undergrad enrollment	3,052
% male/female/another gender	58/42/NR
% from out of state	26
% frosh from public high school	57
% frosh live on campus	62
% ugrads live on campus	43
# of fraternities)	3
# of sororities	1
% African American	6
% Asian	5
% White	46
% Hispanic	28
% Native American	<1
% Pacific Islander	<1
% Two or more races	3
% Race and/or ethnicity unknown	8
% international	3
# of countries represented	46

SURVEY SAYS . . .
Everyone loves the Jaspers
Great library
Students are happy

ACADEMICS
Academic Rating	80
% students returning for sophomore year	76
% students graduating within 4 years	49
% students graduating within 6 years	72
Calendar	Semester
Student/faculty ratio	11:1
Profs interesting rating	88
Profs accessible rating	93

Most classes have 20–29 students.
Most lab/discussion sessions have 20–29 students.

MOST POPULAR MAJORS
Marketing/Marketing Management, General; Special Education and Teaching, Other; Civil Engineering, General

STUDENTS SAY "..."

Academics
Manhattan College isn't actually in Manhattan, but is close enough—a quick 30-minute subway trip from the Riverdale section of the Bronx. A Catholic university, Manhattan honors the "five LaSallian values" of "faith, respect, education, community, and social justice," which shape the culture on campus, primarily in its commitment to "service," but also apparent in the presence of Catholic brothers, who teach some of the courses. Students overwhelmingly praise professors who are "not only outstanding in fields they teach, but [who] also care very deeply for their students." Most "are industry professionals, or PhDs that have a lot of experience in the subject matter that they are teaching," providing "an academic experience where one is able to connect the theory behind a certain subject to practical real world applications." The school "carries prestige" and has "a lot of connections," in the "public sector and private industry," so students have a "greater chance of being placed/connected with an internship that closely relates to their field of choice." This is "especially true for the engineering and education departments." Manhattan "gives you room to take initiative, but also does a good job of keeping students on track." Manhattan has "an outstanding internship program," and "good rates at helping students finding jobs after college," especially with the help of the strong alumni network.

Campus Life
Students say Manhattan College's location—last stop on the 1 train—can't be beat for ease into the more bustling parts of the city, but if you stay on campus, "the size of the school is large enough that there are plenty of people to meet and activities to participate in." In nice weather, "everyone hangs out outside on the Quad" or at "Kelly Commons." "Van Cortlandt Park is also very close so people will hike and just hang out" in the "green spaces" there. Manhattan College "isn't considered a party school; however, most people do party and go out on the weekends," including those thrown by "frats" or a sport's team's house, or they head over to Fordham's college bars. At the end of the night, however, "everyone always ends up at Fenwick's (the only bar at Manhattan College). Dorms are "a pleasure," though students point out that "the campus itself is fairly spread out, with the Engineering building being separated from what is called Main Campus," which effectively "separates the student population." Yet "you seem to meet everyone, whether it's in the small classes or sitting next to them in the student section during a basketball game."

Student Body
Manhattan has "an eclectic mix of students, typical of an institution within…New York City." Many students are "relatives of alumni that have gone here, usually their parents," and many are also "first-generation college students, which is something LaSallian institutions pride themselves on." Students boast of the campus's true diversity and familiarity: "Coming back to school at Manhattan after a break is like going to a family reunion," a student says. "You meet people from NY to Alaska" and "all over the world." Students are "generally engaged in class discussions and are passionate about their studies and extracurricular activities." Students get a chance to "make a ton of friends and build relationships that will last a lifetime." One comment sums up the general student body sentiment: "I am very lucky to call myself a Jasper."

Financial Aid: 718-862-7100 • E-Mail: admit@manhattan.edu • Website: www.manhattan.edu

THE PRINCETON REVIEW SAYS

Admissions

The school reports that its standardized testing policy for use in admission for Fall 2024 is Test Optional. It is unknown at this time if the 2024 testing policy will be permanent. The Princeton Review suggests that interested applicants consult with the school for the most up-to-date standardized testing policies. *Very important factors considered include:* rigor of secondary school record, academic GPA. *Important factors considered include:* application essay, recommendation(s). *Other factors considered include:* class rank, standardized test scores, interview, extracurricular activities, talent/ability, character/personal qualities, alumni/ae relation, volunteer work, work experience, level of applicant's interest. High school diploma is required and GED is accepted. *Academic units required:* 4 English, 3 math, 2 science, 2 science labs, 2 foreign language, 3 social studies. *Academic units recommended:* 4 English, 4 math, 4 science, 4 science labs, 3 foreign language, 4 social studies.

Financial Aid

Students should submit: FAFSA. Priority filing deadline is 2/15. The Princeton Review suggests that all financial aid forms be submitted as soon as possible (see page 5 for a note on the FAFSA). *Need-based scholarships/grants offered:* College/university scholarship or grant aid from institutional funds; Federal Pell; Private scholarships; SEOG; State scholarships/grants. *Loan aid offered:* Direct PLUS loans; Direct Subsidized Loans; Direct Unsubsidized Loans. Admitted students will be notified of awards on a rolling basis beginning 12/1. Federal Work-Study Program available. Institutional employment available.

The Inside Word

Manhattan College admission is all done on a rolling basis, though priority is given to those who apply before March 1. With nearly two-thirds of applicants gaining admission, students with solid, rigorous academics should get in.

THE SCHOOL SAYS "..."

From the Admissions Office

"We are a Lasallian Catholic college offering a transformative education that touches your mind and heart. We strive to promote faith, respect, education, community and social action. Manhattan College promises great value by consistently ranking among schools with the best return on investment and highest graduate salaries. In Riverdale, the greatest city in the world is at the doorstep of campus. In a quiet neighborhood in the Bronx, located ten miles from the bustling streets of midtown Manhattan, students enjoy a traditional college campus that's just a short subway ride from the endless opportunities available in NYC. Our professors often use the city as a classroom with field trips to Wall Street, museums and other world-famous locations.

"We have just under 3,500 students and a student-to-faculty ratio of 11:1, so our students enjoy the benefits of a small college with close faculty interaction. With more than forty majors and twenty graduate programs across six distinct schools, Manhattan College has big academic opportunities. Our students take what they learn in the classroom and apply it to the real world through internships, service-learning projects and study abroad.

"Founded on the principles of John Baptist de La Salle, patron saint of teachers, the College strives to promote faith, respect, quality education, community and social justice in all that we do. One example, The Lasallian Outreach Volunteer Experience (L.O.V.E.), provides service and social-justice travel experiences. Some offer immersion experiences: the chance to live in solidarity with the poor, experience an unfamiliar culture and learn about issues of social justice. Others involve more hands-on service work, such as helping rebuild in New Orleans post-Hurricane Katrina."

SELECTIVITY

Admissions Rating	84
# of applicants	9,930
% of applicants accepted	82
% of acceptees attending	9

FIRST-YEAR PROFILE

Testing policy	Test Optional
Range SAT composite	1140–1330
Range SAT EBRW	570–660
Range SAT math	570–670
Range ACT composite	23–30
# submitting SAT scores	134
% submitting SAT scores	17
# submitting ACT scores	26
% submitting ACT scores	3
Average HS GPA	3.6
% frosh submitting high school GPA	100

DEADLINES

Early decision	
Deadline	11/15
Notification	12/15
Regular	
Priority	3/1
Deadline	8/1
Notification	Rolling, 12/15
Nonfall registration?	Yes

APPLICANTS SOMETIMES PREFER

Fordham University; Pace University; St. John's University (NY)

FINANCIAL FACTS

Financial Aid Rating	77
Annual tuition	$42,800
Room and board	$17,900
Required fees	$2,080
Books and supplies	$1,200
Average frosh need-based scholarship	$16,880
Average UG need-based scholarship	$17,660
% needy frosh rec. need-based scholarship or grant aid	88
% needy UG rec. need-based scholarship or grant aid	84
% needy frosh rec. non-need-based scholarship or grant aid	84
% needy UG rec. non-need-based scholarship or grant aid	73
% needy frosh rec. need-based self-help aid	87
% needy UG rec. need-based self-help aid	81
% frosh rec. any financial aid	88
% UG rec. any financial aid	86
% UG borrow to pay for school	44
Average cumulative indebtedness	$19,588
% frosh need fully met	0
% ugrads need fully met	0
Average % of frosh need met	45
Average % of ugrad need met	50

MANHATTANVILLE COLLEGE

2900 Purchase Street, Purchase, NY 10577 • Admissions: 914-694-2200 • Fax: 914-694-1732

STUDENTS SAY ". . ."

Academics

For students who don't like to limit themselves, Manhattanville College provides "endless opportunities to find your passion and get involved." Undergraduates take comfort from the institution's carefully fostered "communal environment" and the "close-knit relationships" this leads to. They also freely capitalize on the college's "diverse course selection," and the way both the academics and school provide "many connections for internships and jobs" while also serving to "help you build your portfolio as a young professional." Students are fairly quick to give credit where it's due, praising professors who often act as "amazing resources" and generally "bring a lot of expertise into their classrooms." In particular, those at Manhattanville appreciate that professors strive to "teach in a way that makes learning interesting and fun." It's no wonder, then, that students actually seem eager to take difficult courses, knowing they'll be backed up by a faculty member who is "very personable and clearly communicates that they are here to help their students and facilitate their success." Based on the feedback we've seen, it's clear that "no matter what the students need, there is always an office, a person, or department ready, willing, and able to help out." Considering all that, it's no wonder that one undergrad describes time spent at Manhattanville as a "challenging but stressless experience."

Campus Life

At Manhattanville, there's tons of fun to be had both in and out of the classroom. To begin with, sports are certainly very popular, and you'll find that the "majority of students attend athletic events to support their fellow Valiants." Many people also participate in intramurals for rugby, volleyball and dodgeball (among others). But don't fret if you're not particularly sporty; there are plenty of other ways to get involved, whether that's participating in the active student government, joining the Finance Society, working on the Manhattanville Video Project, or joining a cultural institution like the Latin American Student Association. One particular highlight is the Sister Mary T. Clark Center for Religion and Social Justice, "where students often will go just to be around the positive energy." Additionally, "a cappella and performance opportunities [abound]" and the college sponsors numerous events such as Fall Fest, a family weekend "with rides, food, and plenty of entertainment" as well as Quad Jam, a music festival with "food trucks, student performances, and a headliner performance such as We The Kings and Lupe Fiasco." Once the weekend rolls around, it's fairly common for undergrads to head off campus—free transportation both to White Plains and New York City doesn't hurt. "There's something for everyone; you just have to be ambitious enough to find exactly what it is you like to do."

Student Body

Manhattanville undergrads seem to pride themselves on the school's "very diverse" community. As one student immediately explains, "I have made friends from all different backgrounds, states, and countries." Just as critically, people here are "willing to embrace different cultures, ethnicities, sexualities and personality types." While a few individuals do note that the "student body is somewhat divided into athletes and non-athletes," others insist that "it's easy to meet people and make friends." By and large, students say their classmates "genuinely care about everyone's well being" and are "willing to help you when you need." And it's certainly common to encounter a "friendly face" as you walk across campus. The vast majority of students are also "very hardworking" and extremely "passionate about their education and extracurriculars." Indeed, "they know the fields they want to be in and strive to achieve their goals." One individual further elaborates, "I also describe them as warriors who don't give up once they reach a failure; they keep on going no matter the road ahead." As this undergrad concludes, "Everyone I've met is so kind and passionate and talented; it's a great environment to be in."

MANHATTANVILLE COLLEGE

Financial Aid: 914-323-5357 • E-Mail: admissions@mville.edu • Website: www.mville.edu

THE PRINCETON REVIEW SAYS

Admissions

The school reports that its standardized testing policy for use in admission for Fall 2024 is Test Free. It is unknown at this time if the 2024 testing policy will be permanent. The Princeton Review suggests that interested applicants consult with the school for the most up-to-date standardized testing policies. *Very important factors considered include:* rigor of secondary school record, academic GPA, application essay, recommendation(s), extracurricular activities, talent/ability, level of applicant's interest. *Important factors considered include:* geographical residence, volunteer work. *Other factors considered include:* class rank, interview, character/personal qualities, state residency, work experience. High school diploma is required and GED is accepted. *Academic units required:* 4 English, 3 math, 2 science, 2 social studies, 5 academic electives.

Financial Aid

Students should submit: FAFSA; State aid form. Priority filing deadline is 3/1. The Princeton Review suggests that all financial aid forms be submitted as soon as possible (see page 5 for a note on the FAFSA). *Need-based scholarships/grants offered:* College/university scholarship or grant aid from institutional funds; Federal Nursing Scholarships; Federal Pell; Private scholarships; SEOG; State scholarships/grants; United Negro College Fund. *Loan aid offered:* Direct PLUS loans; Direct Subsidized Loans; Direct Unsubsidized Loans. Admitted students will be notified of awards on a rolling basis beginning 10/1. Federal Work-Study Program available. Institutional employment available.

The Inside Word

Earning admission to Manhattanville is certainly competitive. Fortunately, the college takes a straightforward approach when assessing applicants. You can expect your high school transcripts and test scores will be carefully considered along with your personal statement and letters of recommendation. While you are not required to sit for an interview, it is strongly recommended. It's also important to note that Manhattanville operates on the basis of rolling admissions. Therefore, the earlier you apply the better your chances.

THE SCHOOL SAYS "..."

From the Admissions Office

"At Manhattanville College, we believe higher education elevates students' knowledge both academically and practically. That's why we offer more than 55 undergraduate areas of study in three academic schools; Arts and Sciences, Education, and Nursing and Health Sciences, wherein all undergraduate students complete a required internship or experiential learning experience prior to completing their undergraduate degree. We call it outcomes-based learning. Popular majors at Manhattanville include education, business, sport studies, Nursing, psychology, and fine and performing arts. Our Accelerated Bachelor's-Master's degree options in the sciences, education, and business programs have become a popular choice for students, allowing them to complete both a bachelor's and master's degree in 5 years. 84 percent of our full-time faculty hold the highest degree in their field. There are ample opportunities to participate in community service on campus and outside in the community through the Sister Mary T. Clark Center for Religion and Social Justice, the Center for Inclusion, and the more than 70 student clubs and organizations on campus. There are more than 200 outlets for community service available on and off campus and more than 1,000 Manhattanville College students give their time to service projects. With a wide range of academic programs, diverse student population, and community service found at Manhattanville College, we are committed to fulfilling our mission to educate students to be ethical and socially responsible leaders in a global community."

SELECTIVITY

Admissions Rating	82
# of applicants	3,338
% of applicants accepted	84
% of acceptees attending	11
# of early decision applicants	1,059
% accepted early decision	95

FIRST-YEAR PROFILE

Testing policy	Test Free
Range SAT composite	1070–1180
Range SAT EBRW	520–600
Range SAT math	520–590
Range ACT composite	20–26
# submitting SAT scores	26
% submitting SAT scores	8
# submitting ACT scores	7
% submitting ACT scores	2
Average HS GPA	3.3
% frosh submitting high school GPA	99

DEADLINES

Early action	
Deadline	12/1
Notification	1/1
Regular	
Priority	3/1
Notification	Rolling, 12/1
Nonfall registration?	Yes

APPLICANTS SOMETIMES PREFER

Manhattan College; Marist College; Mercy College; Sacred Heart University; St. John's University (NY)

FINANCIAL FACTS

Financial Aid Rating	85
Annual tuition	$40,850
Room and board	$15,540
Required fees	$1,700
Books and supplies	$800
Average frosh need-based scholarship	$3,123
Average UG need-based scholarship	$2,955
% needy frosh rec. need-based scholarship or grant aid	89
% needy UG rec. need-based scholarship or grant aid	78
% needy frosh rec. non-need-based scholarship or grant aid	94
% needy UG rec. non-need-based scholarship or grant aid	88
% needy frosh rec. need-based self-help aid	88
% needy UG rec. need-based self-help aid	86
% frosh rec. any financial aid	100
% UG rec. any financial aid	96
% UG borrow to pay for school	69
Average cumulative indebtedness	$4,943
% frosh need fully met	44
% ugrads need fully met	47
Average % of frosh need met	87
Average % of ugrad need met	84

MARIST COLLEGE

3399 North Road, Poughkeepsie, NY 12601-1387 • Admissions: 845-575-3000 • Fax: 845-575-3215

CAMPUS LIFE

Quality of Life Rating	86
Fire Safety Rating	65
Green Rating	88
Type of school	Private
Affiliation	No Affiliation
Environment	Town

STUDENTS

Total undergrad enrollment	5,069
% male/female/another gender	41/59/0
% from out of state	48
% frosh from public high school	72
% frosh live on campus	94
% ugrads live on campus	62
# of fraternities	3
# of sororities	4
% African American	4
% Asian	3
% White	73
% Hispanic	13
% Native American	<1
% Pacific Islander	<1
% Two or more races	3
% Race and/or ethnicity unknown	1
% international	2
# of countries represented	50

SURVEY SAYS . . .

Students are happy
Great library
Internships are widely available
Intramural sports are popular
Theater is popular

ACADEMICS

Academic Rating	81
% students returning for sophomore year	86
% students graduating within 4 years	73
% students graduating within 6 years	81
Calendar	Semester
Student/faculty ratio	16:1
Profs interesting rating	88
Profs accessible rating	90

Most classes have 20–29 students.

MOST POPULAR MAJORS

Communication, General; Psychology, General;
Business Administration and Management,
General

STUDENTS SAY "..."

Academics

At Marist College, faculty "like to make classes interactive yet challenging in a positive aspect." They also value real-life experience and connections in their classrooms. "I have had faculty...[in contact with] a finance firm...within minutes of me mentioning interest in working there," says a student. Professors are "highly qualified," "diverse in the way they teach," and "always willing to help," both in and out of class. "The academics are the best thing about Marist," says another student. Support staff and advisors are also highly praised for being "some of the most supportive people." The Honors program at Marist is "a huge strength because it unlocks many advantages" by "[exploring] unique perspectives on topics related to all sorts of majors." Honors courses include "a class on the ethical implications of emerging technology [and] an economics course focused on why nations fail." One course even involves "riding a boat up and down the Hudson River" in order to examine the environment of the area.

Campus Life

Marist is near the Hudson River, so students often "fill their days by walking along and laying out...when [the weather] is nice." In the winter, "students may be sledding on snow days or getting together with friends" elsewhere. "A big tradition is jumping into the Hudson River before you graduate," says a student. Indeed, Marist's beauty, which "never fails to amaze" students, offers nearby Rhinebeck and New Paltz for hiking and access to the Walkway Over the Hudson, as well as the chance to just walk around the "rich community." For study time, there are campus cafés, and "there are a lot of cute [off-campus cafés] around Poughkeepsie" too. The library "is a very popular hub for studying, group work, or just [hanging] out." Clubs and intramurals "[give] the campus life after dark." Students also mention that "the student center often holds events like bingo nights, stand-up [comedy nights], and more." Outside of participating either in sports or clubs, many students "intern in NYC several times a week while also maintaining a social life."

Student Body

Students identify the community at Marist as "incredibly friendly," and they point out that students have an unspoken "policy to hold the door open for people," "no matter the weather condition." One student commented: "I've never met so many friendly strangers in New York in my life." Another observes that "nearly everyone...is Catholic, but the majority are not religious." While many students herald Marist for its diversity, others claim that appears more "on paper" than on campus. The dominant groups on campus appear to be "athletes," "in the fashion department," or those "studying computers/technology." "I find that students are very hungry for knowledge," says a student. A large portion of the student body also likes to give back: it's common for students to "participate in two hours of weekly community service...[or] help with one-time community-service events."

MARIST COLLEGE

Financial Aid: 845-575-3230 • E-Mail: admission@marist.edu • Website: www.marist.edu/

THE PRINCETON REVIEW SAYS

Admissions

The school reports that its standardized testing policy for use in admission for Fall 2024 is Test Optional. The 2024 testing policy will be permanent. The Princeton Review suggests that interested applicants consult with the school for the most up-to-date standardized testing policies. *Very important factors considered include:* rigor of secondary school record, academic GPA. *Important factors considered include:* recommendation(s), character/personal qualities. *Other factors considered include:* class rank, standardized test scores, application essay, extracurricular activities, talent/ability, first generation, geographical residence, volunteer work, work experience, level of applicant's interest. High school diploma is required and GED is accepted. *Academic units required:* 4 English, 3 math, 3 science, 2 foreign language, 3 social studies, 3 history, 1 academic elective. *Academic units recommended:* 4 English, 3 math, 3 science, 3 foreign language, 3 social studies, 3 history, 1 academic elective.

Financial Aid

Students should submit: FAFSA. Priority filing deadline is 11/15. The Princeton Review suggests that all financial aid forms be submitted as soon as possible (see page 5 for a note on the FAFSA). *Need-based scholarships/grants offered:* College/university scholarship or grant aid from institutional funds; Federal Pell; Private scholarships; SEOG; State scholarships/grants. *Loan aid offered:* Direct PLUS loans; Direct Subsidized Loans; Direct Unsubsidized Loans. Admitted students will be notified of awards on a rolling basis beginning 1/15. Federal Work-Study Program available. Institutional employment available.

The Inside Word

Students with strong applications (GPA and demonstrated academic rigor) have a decent shot at being accepted to Marist College. Those in the range for standardized tests may benefit from including them; if not, don't sleep on the other considerations: essay, extracurriculars, leadership accomplishments, and recommendation letters.

THE SCHOOL SAYS "..."

From the Admissions Office

"Applications to Marist are up over 50 percent in the last few years. Meanwhile, the number of seats available for the first-year class remains at about 1,100, making for a competitive admission process. Our recommendations: keep your grades up, participate in community service, and exercise leadership in the classroom, extracurricular endeavors, and your community. We encourage a campus visit. When prospective students see Marist—our beautiful location on the Hudson River, top-notch facilities, the close interaction between students and faculty, and the fact that students enjoy their time here—they want to become a part of the Marist community. We'll help you in the transition to college through an innovative first-year program that provides mentors for every student. Whatever field you pursue, Marist's emphasis on industry-specific technology gives students a competitive edge. Marist invests in the student experience. New academic buildings (music, science, art, and fashion) and new residence halls have dramatically improved both academic and social space. Students call the dining hall 'Hogwarts on the Hudson.' Marist main goals are ensuring student success, promoting innovation, and advancing the social good. The College is home to the nationally recognized Marist Poll, which employs hundreds of students each year, offering valuable experience into polling, politics, journalism, and interpretation of data. At Marist, you'll get a premium education, develop skills, have fun and make lifelong friends, have the opportunity to gain valuable experience through internship and study abroad programs, including at our branch campus in Florence, Italy, and be ahead of the competition for graduate school or a career."

SELECTIVITY

Admissions Rating	88
# of applicants	10,966
% of applicants accepted	63
% of acceptees attending	19
# offered a place on the wait list	3,052
% accepting a place on wait list	16
% admitted from wait list	27
# of early decision applicants	219
% accepted early decision	77

FIRST-YEAR PROFILE

Testing policy	Test Optional
Range SAT composite	1220–1350
Range SAT EBRW	610–690
Range SAT math	590–670
Range ACT composite	25–30
# submitting SAT scores	260
% submitting SAT scores	19
# submitting ACT scores	68
% submitting ACT scores	5
Average HS GPA	3.6
% frosh submitting high school GPA	100
% graduated top 10% of class	19
% graduated top 25% of class	48
% graduated top 50% of class	84

DEADLINES

Early decision	
Deadline	11/15
Notification	12/15
Other ED deadline	2/1
Other ED notification	3/1
Early action	
Deadline	11/15
Notification	1/15
Regular	
Deadline	2/15
Notification	3/15
Nonfall registration?	Yes

APPLICANTS OFTEN PREFER

Boston College; Fairfield University; Fordham University; Ithaca College; Loyola University Maryland; New York University; Quinnipiac University; State University of New York—Binghamton University; State University of New York—Stony Brook University; Syracuse University; University of Connecticut; University of Delaware; University of Massachusetts Amherst; Villanova University

FINANCIAL FACTS

Financial Aid Rating	83
Annual tuition	$45,300
Room and board	$18,530
Required fees	$660
Required fees (first-year)	$760
Books and supplies	$2,425
Average frosh need-based scholarship	$24,097
Average UG need-based scholarship	$23,766
% needy frosh rec. need-based scholarship or grant aid	99
% needy UG rec. need-based scholarship or grant aid	98
% needy frosh rec. non-need-based scholarship or grant aid	20
% needy UG rec. non-need-based scholarship or grant aid	14
% needy frosh rec. need-based self-help aid	79
% needy UG rec. need-based self-help aid	78
% frosh rec. any financial aid	93
% UG rec. any financial aid	86
% UG borrow to pay for school	60
Average cumulative indebtedness	$41,731
% frosh need fully met	26
% ugrads need fully met	22
Average % of frosh need met	79
Average % of ugrad need met	74

MARQUETTE UNIVERSITY

1250 W Wisconsin Ave., Milwaukee, WI 53201-1881 • Admissions: 414-288-7302 • Fax: 414-288-3764

STUDENTS SAY "..."

Academics

A highly regarded Jesuit, Catholic school, Marquette University "seeks to provide a well-rounded education based upon excellence, faith, leadership and service." Undergrads here truly value how the university is able to seamlessly integrate "the classroom [with] the greater Milwaukee area through applied programs, service learning, and social activities." Marquette also manages to foster "great relationships with many companies in the area (and in other states) and those companies come [here when] looking for interns to hire." As if that wasn't enough, the university's size is also a fantastic asset. A biomedical science major explains, "There's a real sense of community. It's a big enough school so you don't know everyone, but small enough so that you feel important."

Academically, the school's physical therapy, physician's assistant and business programs are all quite "strong" and very "highly" regarded. Fortunately, no matter your major, Marquette undergrads are privy to "enthusiastic" professors who seem to "genuinely care about [their] students." A nursing student agrees adding, "I've seen professors send students home to rest when they are sick, offer study sessions outside of class, lend students a book if they bought the wrong one, etc." Many professors also have ample professional experience. Therefore, they're able to bring "real world" insight directly into classroom. Overall, though "classes are difficult," professors "push you to do your best and you definitely come out learning a lot."

Campus Life

If there's one notion that undergrads here make abundantly clear, it's that there is never a shortage of fun to be had at Marquette. Whether it's "a sorority or fraternity event, a get-together at your friend's, a concert at the Rave…a school-sponsored event such as discounted tickets to the Broadway musical showing downtown, or free admission to the Olympic training ice rink off campus (skates included!)—there is ALWAYS something to do." Naturally, given that Marquette is part of the Big East Conference, the campus maintains a healthy "basketball culture." Students also love the fact that there are "a multitude of opportunities to get involved with community service." Additionally, Marquette offers groups "for everything from knitting to dancing to sailing…[as well as] club sports…[and] various martial arts and quidditch." During the warmer months, it's not uncommon to see students simply "studying [outside] or playing catch/Frisbee [on] the quad." Finally, undergrads love the fact that the campus is a mere "five minutes away from downtown [Milwaukee]." This makes it easy for students to explore all the city has to offer from restaurants and shops to museums and cultural festivals.

Student Body

Given Marquette's location, it's not surprising that the majority of students hail "from the Midwest" with "a [hefty] number…from the Chicago area" in particular. And though "many students come from wealthy families, there are a large portion of people that attend Marquette due to generous scholarships." Thankfully, no matter your geographic heritage or economic status, undergrads assure us that you'll find a "friendly" student body. And though it's a Jesuit university, "Marquette welcomes students of all backgrounds [and] promotes unity among students of all faiths and cultural communities." More importantly, when pressed to describe and define their peers, undergrads assert that their fellow students are "down to earth, kind, funny [and] hardworking." They are also extremely "concerned about others and about social issues [as well]." Additionally, most students tend to be "very upbeat and passionate about everything that has to do with Marquette." Lastly, a political science major gushes, "This place felt like home right away because of how many genuine people are here."

Financial Aid: 414-288-7390 • E-Mail: admissions@marquette.edu • Website: www.marquette.edu

THE PRINCETON REVIEW SAYS

Admissions

The school reports that its standardized testing policy for use in admission for Fall 2024 is Test Optional. The 2024 testing policy will be permanent. The Princeton Review suggests that interested applicants consult with the school for the most up-to-date standardized testing policies. *Very important factors considered include:* rigor of secondary school record, academic GPA. *Important factors considered include:* standardized test scores, application essay, extracurricular activities, volunteer work. *Other factors considered include:* class rank, recommendation(s), interview, talent/ability, character/personal qualities, first generation, alumni/ae relation, racial/ethnic status, work experience, level of applicant's interest. High school diploma is required and GED is accepted. *Academic units required:* 4 English, 2 math, 2 science, 2 science labs, 2 social studies, 2 academic electives. *Academic units recommended:* 4 English, 4 math, 4 science, 3 science labs, 2 foreign language, 3 social studies, 2 history, 5 academic electives.

Financial Aid

Students should submit: FAFSA. The Princeton Review suggests that all financial aid forms be submitted as soon as possible (see page 5 for a note on the FAFSA). *Need-based scholarships/grants offered:* College/university scholarship or grant aid from institutional funds; Federal Nursing Scholarships; Federal Pell; Private scholarships; SEOG; State scholarships/grants. *Loan aid offered:* Direct PLUS loans; Direct Subsidized Loans; Direct Unsubsidized Loans; College/university loans from institutional funds; Federal Nursing Loans; State Loans. Admitted students will be notified of awards on a rolling basis beginning 2/10. Federal Work-Study Program available. Institutional employment available.

The Inside Word

Marquette's admissions officers do not take their job lightly. Each application is read by an admissions counselor, and most files are read by a second counselor before any decisions are made. When evaluating a candidate, officers first look to assess the high school transcript. They make a note of grade trends and pay close attention to how challenging an applicant's course load was. There is a new Test Optional policy, and those not submitting a test score will not be penalized for making this choice. However, if a student chooses to submit an ACT or SAT score, the counselor will consider it as part of the review. Next, they take into account an applicant's personal statement along with his/her extracurricular activities. Finally, the school weighs the evaluation submitted by the guidance counselor.

SELECTIVITY

Admissions Rating	85
# of applicants	15,883
% of applicants accepted	87
% of acceptees attending	14
# offered a place on the wait list	344
% accepting a place on wait list	100
% admitted from wait list	49

FIRST-YEAR PROFILE

Testing policy	Test Optional
Range SAT composite	1180–1350
Range SAT EBRW	590–670
Range SAT math	580–690
Range ACT composite	26–31
# submitting SAT scores	334
% submitting SAT scores	17
# submitting ACT scores	584
% submitting ACT scores	30
Average HS GPA	3.6
% frosh submitting high school GPA	100
% graduated top 10% of class	29
% graduated top 25% of class	61
% graduated top 50% of class	92

DEADLINES

Regular	
Priority	12/1
Deadline	12/1
Notification	Rolling, 12/21
Nonfall registration?	Yes

FINANCIAL FACTS

Financial Aid Rating	89
Annual tuition	$47,690
Room and board	$15,740
Required fees	$1,010
Books and supplies	$720
Average frosh need-based scholarship	$31,331
Average UG need-based scholarship	$30,225
% needy frosh rec. need-based scholarship or grant aid	99
% needy UG rec. need-based scholarship or grant aid	98
% needy frosh rec. non-need-based scholarship or grant aid	26
% needy UG rec. non-need-based scholarship or grant aid	17
% needy frosh rec. need-based self-help aid	63
% needy UG rec. need-based self-help aid	71
% frosh rec. any financial aid	100
% UG rec. any financial aid	99
% UG borrow to pay for school	57
Average cumulative indebtedness	$26,244
% frosh need fully met	37
% ugrads need fully met	33
Average % of frosh need met	85
Average % of ugrad need met	84

MASSACHUSETTS INSTITUTE OF TECHNOLOGY

77 Massachusetts Avenue, Cambridge, MA 02139 • Admissions: 617-253-1000 • Fax: 617-687-9184

STUDENTS SAY ". . ."

Academics

Massachusetts Institute of Technology, the East Coast mecca of engineering, science, and mathematics, "is the ultimate place for information overload, endless possibilities, and expanding your horizons." The "amazing collection of creative minds" includes enough Nobel laureates to fill a jury box as well as brilliant students who are given substantial control of their educations; one explains, "The administration's attitude toward students is one of respect. As soon as you come on campus, you are bombarded with choices." Students need to be able to manage a workload that "definitely push[es you] beyond your comfort level." A chemical engineering major elaborates: "MIT is different from many schools in that its goal is not to teach you specific facts in each subject. MIT teaches you how to think, not about opinions but about problem solving. Facts and memorization are useless unless you know how to approach a tough problem." Professors here range from "excellent teachers who make lectures fun and exciting" to "dull and soporific" ones, but most "make a serious effort to make the material they teach interesting by throwing in jokes and cool demonstrations." "Access to an amazing number of resources, both academic and recreational," "research opportunities for undergrads with some of the nation's leading professors," and a rock-solid alumni network complete the picture. If you ask "MIT alumni where they went to college, most will immediately stick out their hand and show you their 'brass rat' (the MIT ring, the second most recognized ring in the world)."

Campus Life

At MIT, "it may seem…like there's no life outside problem sets and studying for exams," but "there's always time for extracurricular activities or just relaxing" for those "with good time-management skills" or the "ability to survive on [a] lack of sleep." Options range from "building rides" (recent projects have included a motorized couch and a human-sized hamster wheel) "to partying at fraternities to enjoying the largest collection of science fiction novels in the United States at the MIT Science Fiction Library." Students occasionally find time to "pull a hack," which is a prank, "like the life-size Wright brothers' plane that appeared on top of the Great Dome for the one-hundredth anniversary of flight." Undergrads tell us, "MIT has great parties—a lot of Wellesley, Harvard, and BU students come to them," but also that "there are tons of things to do other than party" here. "Movies, shopping, museums, and plays are all possible with our location near Boston. There are great restaurants only [blocks] away from campus too…. From what I can tell, MIT students have way more fun on the weekends than their Cambridge counterparts [at] Harvard."

Student Body

"There actually isn't one typical student at MIT," students here assure us, explaining that "hobbies range from building robots and hacking to getting wasted and partying every weekend. The one thing students all have in common is that they are insanely smart and love to learn. Pretty much anyone can find the perfect group of friends to hang out with at MIT." "Most students do have some form of 'nerdiness'" (like telling nerdy jokes, being an avid fan of *Star Wars*, etc.), but "contrary to MIT's stereotype, most MIT students are not geeks who study all the time and have no social skills. The majority of the students here are actually quite 'normal.'" The "stereotypical student [who] looks techy and unkempt…only represents about 25 percent of the school." The rest include "multiple-sport standouts, political activists, fraternity and sorority members, hippies, clean-cut business types, LARPers, hackers, musicians, and artisans. There are people who look like they stepped out of an Abercrombie & Fitch catalog and people who dress in all black and carry flashlights and multi-tools. Not everyone relates to everyone else, but most people get along, and it's almost a guarantee that you'll fit in somewhere.

MASSACHUSETTS INSTITUTE OF TECHNOLOGY

Financial Aid: 617-258-8600 • E-Mail: admissions@mit.edu • Website: web.mit.edu

THE PRINCETON REVIEW SAYS

Admissions

The school reports that its standardized testing policy for use in admission for Fall 2024 is SAT or ACT Required. The 2024 testing policy will be permanent. The Princeton Review suggests that interested applicants consult with the school for the most up-to-date standardized testing policies. *Very important factors considered include:* character/personal qualities. *Important factors considered include:* rigor of secondary school record, academic GPA, standardized test scores, application essay, recommendation(s), interview, extracurricular activities, talent/ability. *Other factors considered include:* class rank, first generation, geographical residence, racial/ethnic status, volunteer work, work experience. High school diploma or equivalent is not required. *Academic units recommended:* 4 English, 4 math, 4 science, 2 foreign language, 2 social studies.

Financial Aid

Students should submit: CSS/Financial Aid Profile; FAFSA; Noncustodial Profile. Priority filing deadline is 2/15. The Princeton Review suggests that all financial aid forms be submitted as soon as possible (see page 5 for a note on the FAFSA). *Need-based scholarships/ grants offered:* College/university scholarship or grant aid from institutional funds; Federal Pell; Private scholarships; SEOG; State scholarships/grants; United Negro College Fund. *Loan aid offered:* Direct PLUS loans; Direct Subsidized Loans; Direct Unsubsidized Loans; College/university loans from institutional funds. Admitted students will be notified of awards on or about 3/15. Federal Work-Study Program available. Institutional employment available.

The Inside Word

MIT has one of the nation's most competitive admissions processes. The school's applicant pool is so rich it turns away numerous qualified candidates each year. Put your best foot forward and take consolation in the fact that rejection doesn't necessarily mean that you don't belong at MIT, but only that there wasn't enough room for you the year you applied. Your best chance to get an edge: find ways to stress your creativity.

THE SCHOOL SAYS "..."

From the Admissions Office

"The students who come to the Massachusetts Institute of Technology are some of America's—and the world's—best and most creative. As graduates, they leave here to make real contributions—in science, technology, business, education, politics, architecture, and the arts. From any class, many will go on to do work that is historically significant. These young men and women are leaders, achievers, and producers. Helping such students make the most of their talents and dreams would challenge any educational institution. MIT gives them its best advantages: a world-class faculty, unparalleled facilities, and remarkable opportunities. In turn, these students help to make the institute the vital place it is. They bring fresh viewpoints to faculty research: More than three-quarters participate in the Undergraduate Research Opportunities Program, developing solutions for the world's problems in areas such as energy, the environment, cancer, and poverty. They play on MIT's thirty-three intercollegiate teams as well as in its fifty-plus music, theater, and dance groups. To their classes and to their out-of-class activities, they bring enthusiasm, energy, and individual style."

SELECTIVITY

Admissions Rating	99
# of applicants	33,240
% of applicants accepted	4
% of acceptees attending	86
# offered a place on the wait list	632
% accepting a place on wait list	79
% admitted from wait list	5

FIRST-YEAR PROFILE

Testing policy	SAT or ACT Required
Range SAT composite	1520–1570
Range SAT EBRW	730–780
Range SAT math	780–800
Range ACT composite	34–36
# submitting SAT scores	820
% submitting SAT scores	70
# submitting ACT scores	402
% submitting ACT scores	34
% graduated top 10% of class	99
% graduated top 25% of class	100
% graduated top 50% of class	100

DEADLINES

Early action	
Deadline	11/1
Notification	12/20
Regular	
Deadline	1/1
Notification	3/20
Nonfall registration?	No

APPLICANTS SOMETIMES PREFER

Harvard College; Princeton University; Stanford University; Yale University

APPLICANTS RARELY PREFER

California Institute of Technology; Columbia University; Cornell University; Duke University; University of Pennsylvania

FINANCIAL FACTS

Financial Aid Rating	96
Annual tuition	$57,590
Room and board	$18,790
Required fees	$396
Average frosh need-based scholarship	$57,024
Average UG need-based scholarship	$57,499
% needy frosh rec. need-based scholarship or grant aid	97
% needy UG rec. need-based scholarship or grant aid	98
% needy frosh rec. non-need-based scholarship or grant aid	3
% needy UG rec. non-need-based scholarship or grant aid	1
% needy frosh rec. need-based self-help aid	59
% needy UG rec. need-based self-help aid	64
% frosh rec. any financial aid	81
% UG rec. any financial aid	71
% UG borrow to pay for school	18
Average cumulative indebtedness	$26,399
% frosh need fully met	100
% ugrads need fully met	100
Average % of frosh need met	100
Average % of ugrad need met	100

McDaniel College

2 College Hill, Westminster, MD 21157 • Admissions: 410-848-7000

STUDENTS SAY ". . ."

Academics

A pioneering sensibility led to the founding of McDaniel College in 1867—the first coeducational school south of the Mason-Dixon line—and that same visionary thinking informs the small, private liberal arts college today. Students at McDaniel are treated to a First Year Seminar that hones their written, speaking, and critical thinking skills in preparation for "much more in-depth conversation" and for "students to better connect with each other and the faculty" and the school's flexible core curriculum "prepares you very well for life after college." Other requirements include hands-on practicums and experiential coursework, which left one student planning to continue with her sustainability work long after her course ends: "We didn't just talk about environmental justice, we DID it."

McDaniel's "small class sizes [allow] for close relationships with professors and classmates" and take the form of student-led discussions, flipped classrooms, and other novel formats, like a criminology town hall in which "students were assigned roles from famous cases and the rest of the class had to act as the jury. This was incredibly impactful in learning about these cases and how juries work." Classrooms also take to the field—literally: "Some of my lectures have been held on farms or dairies," says one student, and another notes that "the study abroad program is spectacular." Regardless of one's coordinates, McDaniel students tout the "wide variety of support systems" when it comes to coursework, internships, and career advice: personal advisors and professors are "attentive and passionate," and "always willing to help," and free services like the STEM and Writing Centers have "super nice" tutors available to aid with papers or projects. As one student described her McDaniel education: "[The] professors…have really challenged me to explore my beliefs, challenge how I think, and push me to further my education."

Campus Life

McDaniel students manage a "strong work/life balance" between studying at the Hoover Library, "a fantastic resource with a fire Instagram," and relaxing with friends at the recreation lounge over a game of pool. Club participation ranges from theater to Green Life, a group dedicated to preserving and restoring nature, and "there are groups for basically anything on campus." Students stay active with intramural sports, like lacrosse and field hockey, or cheer on the Green Terror football team with "a lot of school spirit." For those seeking alternative activities—like laser tag—the Office of Student Engagement schedules plenty of fun events like food trucks, ice cream nights, and carnival rides, which are, not surprisingly, "usually big hits." For students looking to explore off campus, it's a five-minute stroll to local shops, and those seeking to go further will find "trips that the school [provides] to students at a discounted price," like the National Aquarium in Baltimore, Hersheypark, and Field of Screams.

Student Body

McDaniel students find each other to be "close-knit and welcoming," an advantage of the student body's small size, which "really allows for everybody to connect." This "increasingly more diverse," focused community of "future leaders who will not hesitate to build others up" enables students to grow culturally: as they put it, "learning about people who do not come from where I do is an eye-opening experience" and getting to know "people from all walks of life…can be quite humbling at times." A few students mention they face challenges with accessibility and equity, but also that McDaniel makes the effort to be "as inclusive in its faculty and students as possible" and that "many student and faculty-run organizations…are working to fix [things]." This emphasis on improving the campus and supporting one's peers has also led to a campus full of students who feel comfortable enough to be "very open about their sexual identity, mental health, [and] cultural identities," and to celebrate their authenticity: "Everybody I know here at McDaniel isn't afraid to be themselves, which is truly a great environment to be in."

McDaniel College

Financial Aid: 410-857-2233 • E-Mail: admissions@mcdaniel.edu • Website: www.mcdaniel.edu

THE PRINCETON REVIEW SAYS

Admissions

The school reports that its standardized testing policy for use in admission for Fall 2024 is Test Optional. The 2024 testing policy will be permanent. The Princeton Review suggests that interested applicants consult with the school for the most up-to-date standardized testing policies. *Very important factors considered include:* rigor of secondary school record, academic GPA. *Important factors considered include:* application essay, recommendation(s). *Other factors considered include:* class rank, interview, extracurricular activities, talent/ability, character/personal qualities, first generation, alumni/ae relation, volunteer work, work experience. High school diploma is required and GED is accepted. *Academic units required:* 4 English, 3 math, 3 science, 3 science labs, 3 foreign language, 3 social studies. *Academic units recommended:* 4 English, 4 math, 4 science, 4 foreign language, 3 social studies.

Financial Aid

Students should submit: FAFSA. Priority filing deadline is 11/15. The Princeton Review suggests that all financial aid forms be submitted as soon as possible (see page 5 for a note on the FAFSA). *Need-based scholarships/grants offered:* College/university scholarship or grant aid from institutional funds; Federal Pell; Private scholarships; SEOG; State scholarships/grants. *Loan aid offered:* Direct PLUS loans; Direct Subsidized Loans; Direct Unsubsidized Loans. Admitted students will be notified of awards on a rolling basis beginning 12/15. Federal Work-Study Program available. Institutional employment available.

The Inside Word

This small liberal arts college is seeking students who challenge themselves academically and personally. McDaniel College values individuality, so we suggest you use your student essay as an opportunity to shine a spotlight on your interests that set you apart from the other applicants. McDaniel is looking for creative individuals who will thrive at a university that allows you to customize your degree while preparing you for life beyond the classroom.

THE SCHOOL SAYS "..."

From the Admissions Office

"McDaniel College is a four-year, independent college of the liberal arts and sciences. Founded in 1867 as one of the first coeducational colleges in the nation and the first south of the Mason-Dixon Line, McDaniel is a diverse, student-centered community of 1,800 undergraduates and 1,400 graduate students. Among "Colleges That Change Lives," McDaniel is committed to access and affordability. More than 90 percent of students receive some type of financial assistance and McDaniel invests over $50 million annually in grants and scholarships. Students choose from more than 70 undergraduate programs of study, including pre-professional specializations and student-designed majors, plus over 20 graduate programs. Academics center on the McDaniel Plan, a customized, interdisciplinary curriculum that emphasizes experiential learning and student-faculty collaboration to develop the unique potential in every student. The McDaniel Commitment guarantees every student two experiential learning opportunities, including service learning, study abroad, student-faculty collaborative research, credit-based internship, or independent study. Students also enroll in first-year seminars and senior capstone projects and can take specially designed courses both on- and off-campus during McDaniel's three-week January Term. Special opportunities abound through McDaniel's Center for Experience and Opportunity, Program in Innovation and Entrepreneurship, Honors Program, National Security Fellows, and Global Fellows. Represented by the Green Terror, its 24 athletic teams compete in the NCAA Division III Centennial Conference. Students are involved in over 80 student organizations, intramural sports, and fraternities and sororities. McDaniel offers access to Baltimore and Washington, D.C., plus a European campus in Budapest, Hungary. McDaniel is proudly Test Optional."

SELECTIVITY

Admissions Rating	83
# of applicants	4,311
% of applicants accepted	82
% of acceptees attending	13
# of early decision applicants	10
% accepted early decision	100

FIRST-YEAR PROFILE

Testing policy	Test Optional
Range SAT composite	1030–1230
Range SAT EBRW	520–645
Range SAT math	500–615
Range ACT composite	23–29
# submitting SAT scores	99
% submitting SAT scores	21
# submitting ACT scores	8
% submitting ACT scores	2
Average HS GPA	3.7
% frosh submitting high school GPA	100
% graduated top 10% of class	22
% graduated top 25% of class	45
% graduated top 50% of class	77

DEADLINES

Early decision	
Deadline	11/1
Notification	12/1
Other ED deadline	1/15
Other ED notification	2/1
Early action	
Deadline	12/15
Notification	1/15
Regular	
Priority	2/1
Nonfall registration?	Yes

FINANCIAL FACTS

Financial Aid Rating	86
Annual tuition	$48,672
Room and board	$13,756
Required fees	$975
Books and supplies	$1,450
Average frosh need-based scholarship	$38,968
Average UG need-based scholarship	$37,687
% needy frosh rec. need-based scholarship or grant aid	100
% needy UG rec. need-based scholarship or grant aid	99
% needy frosh rec. non-need-based scholarship or grant aid	24
% needy UG rec. non-need-based scholarship or grant aid	17
% needy frosh rec. need-based self-help aid	78
% needy UG rec. need-based self-help aid	64
% UG borrow to pay for school	67
Average cumulative indebtedness	$23,983
% frosh need fully met	31
% ugrads need fully met	27
Average % of frosh need met	88
Average % of ugrad need met	86

MERCER UNIVERSITY

1501 Mercer University Drive, Macon, GA 31207-0001 • Admissions: 478-301-2700 • Fax: 478-301-2828

STUDENTS SAY "..."

Academics

Mercer University is a private research university in Macon, Georgia, with satellite campuses located across the state. Its strong engineering program is complemented by an emphasis on the arts and interdisciplinary study, and "the small community coupled with stellar professors and academic support opens opportunities for undergraduate students to experience through research" as soon as they step onto campus. Service learning is integrated into the curriculum, and classes involve a "large degree of group-based projects and assignments to encourage teamwork and leadership skills." As one student says "As part of one of my general Ed classes, we mentored students at a local high school. I got to go to New Hampshire to witness and participate in the political process." Scholarships are awarded generously, and there are "many financial resources for study abroad and internships." Some say the resources are the best part of a Mercer education, via "the student to opportunity ratio. If students apply themselves, they can find opportunities."

This is a school "where professors, students and administrators get to know one another well" and "a great place to get individual attention and experience." Faculty "enjoy the teaching process and want to see students do well" and "really care deeply about the students." The university is well-connected within central Georgia, and "the Mercer name carries weight around the state when looking for job opportunities." There are also many openings for "work-based learning, where course credit is offered for doing research or internships with a certain department."

Campus Life

"Almost every student at Mercer is involved in at least one organization on campus," and intramural sports, group fitness, and outdoors activities (such as rock climbing) are extremely popular. Often "people like to sit on Cruz, the small grassy area on campus to talk with friends or study," and attending sporting events is "always fun and relaxing" at this Division I school. Traditions are valued, and there are "great homecoming activities in the fall, Bearstock (which is a concert every year)," and "a very wide variety of programs and activities" hosted by Quadworks (the campus activities board). A lot of students "like to attend concerts, fairs, and other activities in Atlanta, since it's not too far from Macon," and people also often eat in the city as "food in Macon is incredible." Essentially, "any student can find something that suits them."

Student Body

Students here "want to make change, to do well," and most everyone "is involved in some sort of school activity, business, or community service." These are "generally hardworking students who take pride in their work in and out of the classroom" and "the school is big enough that you do not see the same faces every day, but small enough so that you do not feel lost in the crowd." Mercer's student body "is like its own community," and "are all engulfed in the Mercer community and find ways to reach out and give back." As one student says, "almost everyone you meet on campus has large goals and are involved in many things on campus." Numerous "communities and groups of people are represented here at least to some degree," and all students "work hard to maintain scholarship and earn money to pay for their tuition."

MERCER UNIVERSITY

Financial Aid: 478-301-2670 • E-Mail: admissions@mercer.edu • Website: www.mercer.edu

THE PRINCETON REVIEW SAYS

Admissions

The school reports that its standardized testing policy for use in admission for Fall 2024 is Test Optional. It is unknown at this time if the 2024 testing policy will be permanent. The Princeton Review suggests that interested applicants consult with the school for the most up-to-date standardized testing policies. *Very important factors considered include:* rigor of secondary school record, academic GPA, level of applicant's interest. *Important factors considered include:* application essay, recommendation(s), extracurricular activities, talent/ability, character/personal qualities, volunteer work. *Other factors considered include:* class rank, standardized test scores, interview, work experience. High school diploma is required and GED is accepted. *Academic units required:* 4 English, 4 math, 4 science, 3 science labs, 2 foreign language, 1 social studies, 2 history.

Financial Aid

Students should submit: FAFSA; State aid form. Priority filing deadline is 2/2. The Princeton Review suggests that all financial aid forms be submitted as soon as possible (see page 5 for a note on the FAFSA). *Need-based scholarships/grants offered:* College/university scholarship or grant aid from institutional funds; Federal Pell; Private scholarships; SEOG; State scholarships/grants. *Loan aid offered:* Direct PLUS loans; Direct Subsidized Loans; Direct Unsubsidized Loans; College/university loans from institutional funds; Federal Nursing Loans; State Loans. Admitted students will be notified of awards on a rolling basis. Federal Work-Study Program available.

The Inside Word

Admissions officers at Mercer seek individuals who will both add to the university's vibrant campus life as well as benefit from the myriad of academic opportunities provided. To that end, they carefully consider the rigor of each applicant's high school curriculum and GPA. Standardized test scores, personal statements and teacher recommendations are also heavily weighed. Lastly, officers evaluate extracurricular involvement, paying close attention to any leadership roles attained.

THE SCHOOL SAYS "..."

From the Admissions Office

"Mercer's Office of University Admissions strives to make the college admissions process as clear and easy to navigate as possible. As an admissions counseling team, we are committed to helping each and every student that we meet to identify their best personal 'fit' for a college or university. During this process, many find that Mercer is the right place for their higher education journey. At Mercer, each student is matched with a personal admissions counselor. This counselor remains his or her primary point of contact from application through enrollment. We get to know our applicants through personal contact, high school visits, regional receptions, college fairs, and a variety of campus visit opportunities. Our counselors work closely with students and their families through the application, financial aid, housing, orientation, and other enrollment processes to ensure that students make a smooth transition from high school to college. This makes for a truly enjoyable and informed admissions experience for all involved.

"Mercer University begins accepting applications for undergraduate admission on August 1. We encourage high school seniors to submit their completed applications (including official transcripts, letter of recommendation, and test scores; IELTS or TOEFL for international students) before our Early Action deadline of November 15 to be considered for the University's most prestigious scholarships. Our regular decision deadline is February 1. Following the release of Early Action decisions in early January, we begin evaluating applications on a rolling basis throughout the academic year."

SELECTIVITY
Admissions Rating	86
# of applicants	7,586
% of applicants accepted	74
% of acceptees attending	16

FIRST-YEAR PROFILE
Testing policy	Test Optional
Range SAT composite	1210–1340
Range SAT EBRW	600–680
Range SAT math	590–680
Range ACT composite	26–31
# submitting SAT scores	329
% submitting SAT scores	37
# submitting ACT scores	179
% submitting ACT scores	20
Average HS GPA	3.9
% frosh submitting high school GPA	100
% graduated top 10% of class	37
% graduated top 25% of class	67
% graduated top 50% of class	91

DEADLINES
Early action	
Deadline	11/15
Notification	1/15
Regular	
Priority	2/1
Deadline	7/1
Notification	Rolling, 11/18
Nonfall registration?	Yes

APPLICANTS ALSO LOOK AT
Auburn University; Clemson University; Emory University; Furman University; Georgia Institute of Technology; Samford University; University of Georgia

FINANCIAL FACTS
Financial Aid Rating	86
Annual tuition	$39,408
Room and board	$14,046
Required fees	$300
Books and supplies	$1,200
Average frosh need-based scholarship	$30,271
Average UG need-based scholarship	$28,679
% needy frosh rec. need-based scholarship or grant aid	100
% needy UG rec. need-based scholarship or grant aid	100
% needy frosh rec. non-need-based scholarship or grant aid	28
% needy UG rec. non-need-based scholarship or grant aid	27
% needy frosh rec. need-based self-help aid	52
% needy UG rec. need-based self-help aid	58
% frosh rec. any financial aid	100
% UG rec. any financial aid	97
% UG borrow to pay for school	59
Average cumulative indebtedness	$32,246
% frosh need fully met	34
% ugrads need fully met	32
Average % of frosh need met	86
Average % of ugrad need met	83

MIAMI UNIVERSITY

501 E. High Street, Oxford, OH 45056 • Admissions: 513-529-1809

STUDENTS SAY "..."

Academics

Attending school at Miami University may be "the iconic college experience." Located in Oxford, Ohio, "a quaint college town" with a "beautiful red brick campus," which students describe as "gorgeous" and "astoundingly beautiful," the school "has a rich tradition and history" that "is committed to its image as a premier undergraduate institution." The "prestige" of the business school affords many promising opportunities both during school and after graduation. Students agree, "Miami really prepares students for the real world after college." "A degree from Miami is worth a lot to many employers." "Miami University students are recruited by companies, and that provides great leverage when looking for internships and jobs." The curriculum as a whole offers "a challenging academic workload" that truly tests a student's abilities as well as "prepares students for the workplace after graduation while also giving them the opportunity to thrive while on campus." This "devotion to excellent undergraduate instruction" is backed by "an extremely strong orientation program, a dedicated student affairs department, and an overwhelming amount of student involvement in co-curricular activities." Smaller classrooms that allow for "engaging" discussion are more highly valued than large lectures, which may be "hard to sit through." Professors are a "mixed bag." "If you get the right ones, it makes all the difference." A student in the Honors Program calls the experience "phenomenal. It offers the ability to grow as a student and person through both in and out of class experiences."

Campus Life

Miami University offers "a vibrant social atmosphere." With more than 17,000 undergraduate students on campus Miami may be "the perfect size," where you "can see everyone…but still meet many new people." With a "plethora of student activities," "Miami makes it possible to find groups or organizations that can fit any student's interest, and many tend to help in propelling graduates into jobs or programs once they leave the campus." "Greek life is everywhere you look," according to one student who posits "it often seems as though everyone is [Greek affiliated] because of how visible they are on campus," though statistics indicate only about one-third of undergraduates go Greek. On the partying front, "if you are looking to drink, you will certainly find it here if you want." "Miami students can find a wealth of great bars and clubs uptown—many of which are eighteen-plus, allowing freshmen and sophomores to enjoy the dance floors and bars that make up almost all of the nightlife." The campus also "offers a lot of alternative programs for students who wish to avoid alcohol." "Late night programming is offered through Miami, as well as athletic events and other cultural events." Among sports, "hockey is really popular." Students tend to be happy with life at Miami. "There is a ton to do on and off campus. The town is quaint, but it is mainly a college town, so it's like an extension of the school. Nightlife is pretty big here, but so are academics and activities. Students definitely are actively thinking about their futures, and they take academics seriously."

Student Body

The typical student is "very involved on campus, is concerned about his or her academics, and wants to make a good impression on others. We care about how we present ourselves, but in a good way." Another student says, "The typical student is very academically focused, challenge-driven, competitive, extraverted, and demonstrates a preference for dressing well." Several students commented that students tend to "look and dress alike." "It can be very cliquish, especially in the Greek community." Anyone can fit in though, it's "all about finding your niche on campus, which is generally done through people in your major, and especially student organizations." Miami tends to attract students who are "white, upper-middle-class, and Christian. The campus lacks diversity socioeconomically, ethnically, and religiously; however, the student body is generally accepting of all students no matter the background." One student relishes the challenge "to find diversity even in people who look similar and [has] grown because of it."

MIAMI UNIVERSITY

Financial Aid: 513-529-0001 • E-Mail: admission@miamioh.edu • Website: www.miamioh.edu/

THE PRINCETON REVIEW SAYS

Admissions

The school reports that its standardized testing policy for use in admission for Fall 2024 is Test Optional. It is unknown at this time if the 2024 testing policy will be permanent. The Princeton Review suggests that interested applicants consult with the school for the most up-to-date standardized testing policies. *Very important factors considered include:* rigor of secondary school record, class rank, academic GPA, standardized test scores, application essay, recommendation(s), talent/ability, character/personal qualities. *Other factors considered include:* extracurricular activities, first generation, alumni/ae relation, geographical residence, state residency, volunteer work, work experience. High school diploma is required and GED is accepted. *Academic units recommended:* 4 English, 4 math, 3 science, 2 foreign language, 2 social studies, 1 history, 1 visual/performing arts.

Financial Aid

Students should submit: FAFSA. Priority filing deadline is 2/15. The Princeton Review suggests that all financial aid forms be submitted as soon as possible (see page 5 for a note on the FAFSA). *Need-based scholarships/grants offered:* College/university scholarship or grant aid from institutional funds; Federal Pell; Private scholarships; SEOG; State scholarships/grants. *Loan aid offered:* Direct PLUS loans; Direct Subsidized Loans; Direct Unsubsidized Loans; College/university loans from institutional funds. Admitted students will be notified of awards on a rolling basis beginning 3/20. Federal Work-Study Program available. Institutional employment available.

The Inside Word

Getting into Miami University isn't easy. High grades and test scores are a good start, and there is more you can do to better your odds. Admissions officers favor students who have challenged themselves academically, are active in their schools, lead student organizations or other activities, and volunteer in their community.

THE SCHOOL SAYS "..."

From the Admissions Office

"At Miami, you'll find a level of involvement—in your classes, in your research, in your extracurricular activities—that you won't find at other schools. What sets Miami apart as a Public Ivy is the ability to give students a personalized small-college experience within the reputation, experiences, and opportunities of a large research university, all at a public school cost. With more than 100 majors to choose from, and a liberal arts foundation that allows students to explore different areas of interest, finding your true passion—in and out of the classroom—is at the heart of what the Miami University experience is all about. This deep level of engagement is reflected in the 89 percent freshman to sophomore retention rate and Miami's 73 percent four-year graduation rate, which is among the top for public universities across the country. Miami's reputation for producing outstanding leaders with real-world experience makes us a target school for top global firms, leads to acceptance rates into law and medical school which far exceed the national averages, and result in impressive placement rates for graduates. Students also benefit from small class sizes—most undergraduate classes have fewer than thirty students—and personal attention from faculty members in the classroom, through research opportunities, and through faculty mentoring programs. Outside of the classroom, students can participate in over 500 student organizations, attend social and cultural events, or get involved with one of the most extensive intramural and club sports program in the country."

SELECTIVITY

Admissions Rating	85
# of applicants	29,990
% of applicants accepted	89
% of acceptees attending	17
# of early decision applicants	474
% accepted early decision	95

FIRST-YEAR PROFILE

Testing policy	Test Optional
Range SAT composite	1180–1350
Range SAT EBRW	580–680
Range SAT math	580–690
Range ACT composite	24–30
# submitting SAT scores	836
% submitting SAT scores	18
# submitting ACT scores	2,811
% submitting ACT scores	62
Average HS GPA	3.9
% frosh submitting high school GPA	96
% graduated top 10% of class	36
% graduated top 25% of class	68
% graduated top 50% of class	91

DEADLINES

Early decision	
Deadline	11/15
Notification	12/15
Early action	
Deadline	12/01
Notification	2/1
Regular	
Deadline	2/1
Notification	3/15
Nonfall registration?	Yes

APPLICANTS OFTEN PREFER

Case Western Reserve University; Northwestern University; University of Illinois—Urbana-Champaign; University of Michigan—Ann Arbor; Vanderbilt University; Washington University in St. Louis

APPLICANTS SOMETIMES PREFER

Indiana University—Bloomington; Penn State University Park; Purdue University—West Lafayette; Southern Methodist University; The Ohio State University—Columbus; University of Wisconsin—Madison

APPLICANTS RARELY PREFER

Michigan State University; Ohio University—Athens; Syracuse University; University of Cincinnati; University of Connecticut; University of Dayton

FINANCIAL FACTS

Financial Aid Rating	82
Annual in-state tuition	$12,637
Annual in-state tuition (first-year)	$13,136
Annual out-of-state tuition	$32,464
Annual out-of-state tuition (first-year)	$33,563
Room and board	$14,454
Required fees	$2,984
Required fees (first-year)	$3,087
Books and supplies	$1,240
Average frosh need-based scholarship	$15,013
Average UG need-based scholarship	$14,836
% needy frosh rec. need-based scholarship or grant aid	96
% needy UG rec. need-based scholarship or grant aid	92
% needy frosh rec. non-need-based scholarship or grant aid	26
% needy UG rec. non-need-based scholarship or grant aid	19
% needy frosh rec. need-based self-help aid	59
% needy UG rec. need-based self-help aid	63
% UG borrow to pay for school	45
Average cumulative indebtedness	$28,711
% frosh need fully met	32
% ugrads need fully met	25
Average % of frosh need met	65
Average % of ugrad need met	64

MICHIGAN STATE UNIVERSITY

426 Auditorium Rd, East Lansing, MI 48824 • Admissions: 517-355-1855 • Fax: 517-353-1647

CAMPUS LIFE

Quality of Life Rating	82
Fire Safety Rating	60*
Green Rating	96
Type of school	Public
Environment	City

STUDENTS

Total undergrad enrollment	39,021
% male/female/another gender	48/52/NR
% from out of state	15
% frosh live on campus	95
% ugrads live on campus	43
# of fraternities (% join)	38 (11)
# of sororities (% join)	23 (12)
% African American	7
% Asian	8
% White	67
% Hispanic	6
% Native American	<1
% Pacific Islander	<1
% Two or more races	4
% Race and/or ethnicity unknown	2
% international	6
# of countries represented	123

SURVEY SAYS . . .

Students are happy
Everyone loves the Spartans
Intramural sports are popular
Frats and sororities are popular

ACADEMICS

Academic Rating	75
% students returning for sophomore year	89
% students graduating within 4 years	63
% students graduating within 6 years	82
Calendar	Semester
Student/faculty ratio	17:1
Profs interesting rating	82
Profs accessible rating	86

Most classes have 20–29 students.
Most lab/discussion sessions have 20–29 students.

STUDENTS SAY " . . ."

Academics

Michigan State University reverberates with Spartan pride, and it's easy to understand why. The school maintains "a beautiful campus," has "an insane amount of resources," and provides exciting research opportunities for students. It also offers a "fantastic honors college" along with very strong "agricultural...[and] STEM programs (especially [in] astronomy, animal science, and chemistry)." Labs, hands-on learning, and nontraditional classrooms are very popular with students, and a great example of this is the Burgess Institute for Entrepreneurship and Innovation, which encourages students to solve real-world problems through action and innovation.

Though courses are described as demanding, undergrads assure us that help and support are readily available and the school is invested in student success. Many also stress that it's quite easy to "get help from peers and tutors." Inside the classroom, students find engaged professors who are "very passionate about their subjects" and truly endeavor to make their courses relevant and interesting. Nevertheless, students do speak highly of MSU's faculty. As one student enthuses, "I have not encountered a single individual in a teaching role at this university that has not blown me away with their respect and care for the students, their ability to teach, and their passion in their subjects." Another classmate concurs, adding that professors "are always willing to go the extra mile and make sure you understand the material to its full extent."

Campus Life

Camaraderie is key at MSU. As one student puts it, "Our school has a lot of passion for its school spirit and sports; it's something everyone here bonds over incredibly well." The school's stature in the Big Ten is especially celebrated—"the entire campus gets excited"—come football season, whether that's in the stadium or at a tailgate party—but there are plenty of ways for those not interested in Division I sports to experience the thrill of the game. There are intramural sports, like the popular volleyball league, and recreational facilities, and the university hosts plenty of non-sporting events from trivia nights and karaoke to craft nights and open-mic nights. There are also many clubs to join, from the professional—like MSU Management Consulting Academy, the pre-med club, and the Women in Business Students' Association (WBSA)—to the recreational (anime club; sailing club, Model UN; *VIM*, a student-led fashion magazine; and more). A good number of people participate in Greek life as well and students can generally find fraternity or sorority parties to attend on the weekends.

Student Body

Given the size of Michigan State University, students shouldn't be too surprised to learn that the school has a very diverse community. As one undergrad notes, "I would say that the student body is like the ocean; there are all types of unique people with many interests." Undergrads appreciate the fact that the university manages to attract people from across the globe: it's common here "to have a conversation with someone from Nigeria one day and the next have a conversation with someone from Finland." Just like at any large university, there are "highly motivated individuals who are here to [further] their education and another set who are here to party." But in general, students say that their peers are hard-working and "extremely eager to ask questions and engage" while still managing to be "laid-back...and fun." But perhaps what undergrads here cherish most of all is that their colleagues are friendly and supportive—"always willing to help out a fellow Spartan." As one student says, "It is a very welcoming school, with so many people that you are sure to find your group."

MICHIGAN STATE UNIVERSITY

Financial Aid: 517-353-5940 • E-Mail: admis@msu.edu • Website: www.msu.edu

THE PRINCETON REVIEW SAYS

Admissions

The school reports that its standardized testing policy for use in admission for Fall 2024 is Test Optional. The 2024 testing policy will be temporary. The Princeton Review suggests that interested applicants consult with the school for the most up-to-date standardized testing policies. *Very important factors considered include:* academic GPA, application essay. *Important factors considered include:* rigor of secondary school record, extracurricular activities, talent/ability, character/personal qualities, geographical residence, level of applicant's interest. *Other factors considered include:* class rank, standardized test scores, recommendation(s), interview, first generation, alumni/ae relation, state residency, volunteer work, work experience. High school diploma is required and GED is accepted. *Academic units required:* 3 English, 3 math, 3 science, 2 foreign language, 3 social studies. *Academic units recommended:* 4 English, 3 math, 3 science, 1 science lab, 2 foreign language, 3 social studies.

Financial Aid

Students should submit: FAFSA. The Princeton Review suggests that all financial aid forms be submitted as soon as possible after October 1 (see page 5 for a note on the FAFSA). *Need based scholarships/grants offered:* College/university scholarship or grant aid from institutional funds; Federal Pell; Private scholarships; SEOG; State scholarships/grants. *Loan aid offered:* Direct PLUS loans; Direct Subsidized Loans; Direct Unsubsidized Loans; College/ university loans from institutional funds. Admitted students will be notified of awards on a rolling basis. Federal Work-Study Program available. Institutional employment available.

The Inside Word

Michigan State takes a traditional approach to evaluation: your academic performance in high school, strength and quality of your curriculum, recent trends in your academic performance, class rank, and your leadership, talents, conduct, and diversity of experience are all factors in admission.

THE SCHOOL SAYS "..."

From the Admissions Office

"It's not just what we do that makes us Spartans—but also why and how we do it.

"It's the will to think bigger, work harder, and never give up. "United in our drive to achieve our personal best while together pushing the boundaries of what's possible to make a better world for all.

"Believing we are strong as one and extraordinary together.

"Michigan State University got its start more than 165 years ago when we served as the national model for a new kind of higher education that opened doors and expanded opportunities.

"Today, MSU is a place where you can find your path and your passion and a network of people who will support you along the way. And when you leave here, you will be ready to change the world.

"More than half a million strong worldwide, we proudly call ourselves Spartans. Join us."

SELECTIVITY

Admissions Rating	83
# of applicants	53,341
% of applicants accepted	88
% of acceptees attending	21
# offered a place on the wait list	3,000
% accepting a place on wait list	67
% admitted from wait list	1

FIRST-YEAR PROFILE

Testing policy	Test Optional
Range SAT composite	1110–1320
Range SAT EBRW	550–660
Range SAT math	550–680
Range ACT composite	24–30
# submitting SAT scores	4,974
% submitting SAT scores	51
# submitting ACT scores	1,347
% submitting ACT scores	14
Average HS GPA	3.8
% frosh submitting high school GPA	93
% graduated top 10% of class	26
% graduated top 25% of class	58
% graduated top 50% of class	92

DEADLINES

Early action	
Deadline	11/1
Notification	1/15
Regular	
Priority	11/1
Deadline	4/1
Notification	Rolling, 10/1
Nonfall registration?	Yes

FINANCIAL FACTS

Financial Aid Rating	77
Annual in-state tuition	$16,531
Annual in-state tuition (first-year)	$15,192
Annual out-of-state tuition	$42,427
Annual out-of-state tuition (first-year)	$41,778
Room and board	$10,990
Required fees	$180
Books and supplies	$1,254
Average frosh need-based scholarship	$11,569
Average UG need-based scholarship	$11,341
% needy frosh rec. need-based scholarship or grant aid	93
% needy UG rec. need-based scholarship or grant aid	85
% needy frosh rec. non-need-based scholarship or grant aid	94
% needy UG rec. non-need-based scholarship or grant aid	61
% needy frosh rec. need-based self-help aid	50
% needy UG rec. need-based self-help aid	58
% UG borrow to pay for school	50
Average cumulative indebtedness	$31,591
% frosh need fully met	9
% ugrads need fully met	11
Average % of frosh need met	50
Average % of ugrad need met	57

MICHIGAN TECHNOLOGICAL UNIVERSITY

1400 Townsend Drive, Houghton, MI 49931 • Admissions: 906-487-1885 • Fax: 906-487-2125

CAMPUS LIFE
Quality of Life Rating	87
Fire Safety Rating	96
Green Rating	86
Type of school	Public
Environment	Village

STUDENTS
Total undergrad enrollment	5,643
% male/female/another gender	70/30/NR
% from out of state	22
% frosh live on campus	95
% ugrads live on campus	48
# of fraternities (% join)	11 (10)
# of sororities (% join)	7 (10)
% African American	1
% Asian	2
% White	85
% Hispanic	3
% Native American	<1
% Pacific Islander	<1
% Two or more races	4
% Race and/or ethnicity unknown	4
% international	1
# of countries represented	22

SURVEY SAYS . . .
Lots of conservative students
Students are happy
Lab facilities are great
Great library
Career services are great
Internships are widely available
School is well run
Diverse student types interact on campus
Students get along with local community

ACADEMICS
Academic Rating	83
% students returning for sophomore year	85
% students graduating within 4 years	33
% students graduating within 6 years	68
Calendar	Semester
Student/faculty ratio	13:1
Profs interesting rating	86
Profs accessible rating	90

Most classes have fewer than 10 students.
Most lab/discussion sessions have
10–19 students.

MOST POPULAR MAJORS
Chemical Engineering; Electrical and Electronics
Engineering; Mechanical Engineering

STUDENTS SAY "..."

Academics
Michigan Technological University has "very high standards when it comes to education" and offers "serious study in a beautiful (often snowy) environment." It boasts a "really good reputation as an engineering school," and it's no secret that "engineering is a part of everybody's life." All agree, "Michigan Tech provides an atmosphere that nurtures learning" and "puts students first when it comes to their learning experience by providing hands-on experience." The university offers "lots of internship and co-op opportunities" and "pathways for career development and professional advancement." Students say that the courses are "challenging" and that the university "pushes students to excel academically." Professors are "generally interesting and helpful," but some can be "dull." A junior says, "Concentrated courses are great, but [general education courses] are huge, impersonal, and just plain awful," and another student adds, "The experience gets better with more time you put into your program, the professors become more interactive, and the experience becomes more meaningful."

Campus Life
Michigan Tech "is in a small town in the middle of the deep North woods," which makes "the sense of community remarkable." Students say that campus is "incredibly safe," that "the atmosphere is very friendly," and that "there are a lot of opportunities to get involved." A physics major notes, "You start to see people you know everywhere on campus. It is really easy to find a friend and talk to someone." Enhancing the "strong student community" are "over 200 clubs" and a variety of "winter activities to be a part of." Many students take advantage of "free access to Mont Ripley," the university's own ski hill and the oldest one in Michigan. A freshman says, "We have broomball, Winter Carnival, and lots of campus-wide events!" Many students agree, "The administration in every department works hard to answer questions and help out as much as possible, which is really great when you're a freshman," but some feel there's a "gap between [the] administration and students," particularly when it comes to spending. There are complaints about dorm food, leading a junior to say, "I would like to see some more selection and variation between dining halls," and students feel there's a need for "more parking spots close to campus." While "the library is a great place to study," some "of the classrooms are dated" and could use technological updating.

Student Body
At Michigan Tech, the typical student "is smart and a little more introspective than average," but still "great at balancing school and hanging out." Most students "are looking to get a good education and are fairly laid-back," and the student body consists of "down-to-earth friendly people," who "work hard during the week and look forward to relaxing and having fun on the weekends." It's no secret that "the ratio is a little guy-heavy" and that, because of this, "girls get doors opened for them across campus." Students tend to be "white and male," and a junior acknowledges, "There's little diversity ethnically, but everyone feels welcome." A chemical engineering major says, "You have to be a little bit of a nerd to fit in," and another student agrees, "I think most people think about classes first, hanging out second." It's common for students to "stay in and play video games," but there's also a large contingent of "outdoorsy people." A sophomore says, "Winters are long and cold up here," and students take advantage of the plentiful snow by "hiking, biking, four-wheeling, skiing, [and] snowmobiling." Students look forward to Winter Carnival, "a long weekend off from classes where students build giant, impressive snow sculptures, play broomball, [and] stay out all night," and for fun they enjoy "house parties and moderate drinking/merrymaking [to] warm up the cold winters."

MICHIGAN TECHNOLOGICAL UNIVERSITY

Financial Aid: 906-487-2622 • E-Mail: mtu4u@mtu.edu • Website: www.mtu.edu

THE PRINCETON REVIEW SAYS

Admissions

The school reports that its standardized testing policy for use in admission for Fall 2024 is Test Optional. It is unknown at this time if the 2024 testing policy will be permanent. The Princeton Review suggests that interested applicants consult with the school for the most up-to-date standardized testing policies. *Very important factors considered include:* academic GPA. *Important factors considered include:* rigor of secondary school record, standardized test scores. *Other factors considered include:* application essay, recommendation(s), extracurricular activities, talent/ability, character/personal qualities. High school diploma is required and GED is accepted. *Academic units required:* 3 English, 3 math, 2 science. *Academic units recommended:* 4 English, 4 math, 3 science, 2 foreign language, 3 social studies, 1 computer science, 2 academic electives.

Financial Aid

Students should submit: FAFSA. Priority filing deadline is 3/1. The Princeton Review suggests that all financial aid forms be submitted as soon as possible (see page 5 for a note on the FAFSA). *Need-based scholarships/grants offered:* College/university scholarship or grant aid from institutional funds; Federal Pell; Private scholarships; SEOG; State scholarships/grants. *Loan aid offered:* Direct PLUS loans; Direct Subsidized Loans; Direct Unsubsidized Loans; College/university loans from institutional funds. Admitted students will be notified of awards on a rolling basis beginning 1/1. Federal Work-Study Program available. Institutional employment available.

The Inside Word

Michigan Tech strives to enroll bright, adventurous students. Students aren't required to submit recommendations from teachers, although they may submit a "High School Counselor Information Page" if they would like their counselor to share information regarding their high school performance. Applicants to the Visual and Performing Arts Department degree programs may be required to submit supplemental materials, including an essay.

THE SCHOOL SAYS "..."

From the Admissions Office

"At Michigan Tech, our students know that tomorrow needs talented visionaries and new solutions. They are ready. Our unique Enterprise Program lets students work on real industry projects, from building and launching spacecraft for NASA to designing advanced robotics systems, developing better alternative fuels, and inventing water-rescue devices at our Great Lakes Research Center.

"Students can choose from more than 140 degree programs in engineering; forest resources; technology; business and economics; mathematics; natural, physical and environmental sciences; arts; humanities; health professions and pre-health preparation; and social sciences. We offer degree opportunities in growing fields such as biomedical engineering and wildlife ecology and management, as well as cybersecurity and mechatronics in our College of Computing, the first college of its kind in the state of Michigan.

"Outside of classrooms and labs, students enjoy our golf course, ski hill, recreational trails, and 5,000+ acres of University forests, along with a safe, friendly, small-town atmosphere in beautiful Upper Michigan. Situated on the Keweenaw Waterway, the campus is minutes from Lake Superior. During Winter Carnival, students build huge snow statues and play broomball, the most popular of many intramural sports on campus. The varsity sports line-up includes the first varsity-level esports team at a public university in Michigan, along with football, men's and women's basketball, tennis, cross-country, Nordic skiing, track and field, soccer, volleyball, and NCAA Division I hockey.

"Ready to build, design, code, and lead with Lake Superior all around you? Applying to Michigan Tech is free and easy—and there's no deadline."

SELECTIVITY
Admissions Rating	84
# of applicants	8,569
% of applicants accepted	86
% of acceptees attending	19

FIRST-YEAR PROFILE
Testing policy	Test Optional
Range SAT composite	1140–1330
Range SAT EBRW	560–670
Range SAT math	570–680
Range ACT composite	24–30
# submitting SAT scores	986
% submitting SAT scores	71
# submitting ACT scores	341
% submitting ACT scores	25
Average HS GPA	3.8
% frosh submitting high school GPA	100
% graduated top 10% of class	31
% graduated top 25% of class	61
% graduated top 50% of class	89

DEADLINES
Regular	
Priority	1/15
Notification	Rolling, 6/15
Nonfall registration?	Yes

APPLICANTS SOMETIMES PREFER
Grand Valley State University; Michigan State University; Milwaukee School of Engineering; Northern Michigan University; Purdue University—West Lafayette; University of Illinois—Urbana-Champaign; University of Michigan—Ann Arbor; University of Minnesota—Twin Cities; University of Wisconsin—Madison; Western Michigan University

FINANCIAL FACTS
Financial Aid Rating	83
Annual in-state tuition	$17,296
Annual out-of-state tuition	$39,256
Room and board	$12,058
Required fees	$318
Books and supplies	$1,200
Average frosh need-based scholarship	$9,382
Average UG need-based scholarship	$8,808
% needy frosh rec. need-based scholarship or grant aid	81
% needy UG rec. need-based scholarship or grant aid	76
% needy frosh rec. non-need-based scholarship or grant aid	98
% needy UG rec. non-need-based scholarship or grant aid	91
% needy frosh rec. need-based self-help aid	65
% needy UG rec. need-based self-help aid	73
% frosh rec. any financial aid	99
% UG rec. any financial aid	93
% UG borrow to pay for school	66
Average cumulative indebtedness	$36,513
% frosh need fully met	44
% ugrads need fully met	30
Average % of frosh need met	90
Average % of ugrad need met	79

MIDDLEBURY COLLEGE

Middlebury College, Middlebury, VT 05753 • Admissions: 802-443-5000 • Fax: 802-443-2056

STUDENTS SAY "..."

Academics

One of the most highly regarded liberal arts colleges in the United States, Middlebury College in Vermont is about "creating a person both socially and intellectually prepared for the world." The school has "a high level of global thinking and language acquisition in such a rural place," and there is an "emerging focus on creativity and entrepreneurship." When teaching students to develop communication, writing, creativity, and critical thinking skills, the school "allows you to develop these skills in whatever subject or subjects that one is most passionate about." Students' needs and choices are "of very high priority" to the administration, and there is "institutional support for whatever absurd idea might strike you." Professors are, on the whole, "truly top-notch"; not only are they "brilliant academics, but they are also adept teachers and classroom leaders." They come here because they want to teach undergraduates and conduct research; "Middlebury expects both; most professors deliver." "Several of my professors have given out their cell phone numbers after particularly difficult lectures to make sure that students can figure things out," says one. "It's almost impossible to actually be 'invisible.'" The overall academic experience is "very intense" ("If you haven't done the reading, prepare to be called out for it"), but "students reliably enjoy their classes."

Campus Life

Empty hours at Middlebury are in short supply: "If you've got free time in your day at Middlebury, you're doing something wrong," says a student. However, after all that reading, "at the end of the day, we all just like to get together and hit up the Snow Bowl to go skiing." "Vermont does make a difference," says one student of Middlebury's location near mountains, lakes, and ski trails, and its focus on "how important the outdoor experience is for the school." Drinking is "fairly prevalent" on Fridays and Saturdays, but "not during the week." It's a healthy culture, and "public safety does a good job of keeping things safe while not being overly intrusive." The dorms are "gorgeous," and there is even one called the Chateau, modeled after the largest chateau in Fontainebleau, France. The number of activities available are admirable, and "most people actually choose not to go into cities on weekends because they would hate to miss what's going on on-campus that weekend."

Student Body

The pervasive atmosphere at Middlebury is "super friendly and caring," and there is not only the pressure to work hard, but "also the encouragement to make sure students succeed." Students "compete with themselves, not their classmates." With a happy population, beautiful environs, and not a single student going unchallenged, the school encompasses "a perfect blend of intellectual curiosity, responsible living, and fun." As one student eloquently puts it, it's a bunch of "bright kids doing too many things—all of them good, none related to sleep." This "engaged, active," "preppy" student body "doesn't take themselves too seriously but do take serious initiative." A typical go-getter student "pursues at least one major, a minor, and is the star of at least one sports team or special interest group, but usually more." Social life can be "very centered around athletic teams," but these "well-read, outgoing," and "well-rounded students from stable backgrounds" always end up connecting with people they can relate with easily. "You will struggle to find time to spend with all the different friends you will make," says a student. Social ease is a common trait among MiddKids, and most students "know how to hold a conversation and [are] open to new experiences."

MIDDLEBURY COLLEGE

Financial Aid: 802-443-5158 • E-Mail: admissions@middlebury.edu • Website: www.middlebury.edu

THE PRINCETON REVIEW SAYS

Admissions

The school reports that its standardized testing policy for use in admission for Fall 2024 is Test Optional. It is unknown at this time if the 2024 testing policy will be permanent. The Princeton Review suggests that interested applicants consult with the school for the most up-to-date standardized testing policies. *Very important factors considered include:* rigor of secondary school record, class rank, academic GPA, extracurricular activities, talent/ability, character/personal qualities. *Important factors considered include:* standardized test scores, application essay, recommendation(s), racial/ethnic status. *Other factors considered include:* first generation, alumni/ae relation, geographical residence, volunteer work, work experience, level of applicant's interest. High school diploma or equivalent is not required. *Academic units recommended:* 4 English, 4 math, 3 science, 3 science labs, 4 foreign language, 3 social studies.

Financial Aid

Students should submit: CSS/Financial Aid Profile; FAFSA; Noncustodial Profile. Priority filing deadline is 11/15. The Princeton Review suggests that all financial aid forms be submitted as soon as possible (see page 5 for a note on the FAFSA). *Need-based scholarships/grants offered:* College/university scholarship or grant aid from institutional funds; Federal Pell; Private scholarships; SEOG; State scholarships/grants. *Loan aid offered:* Direct PLUS loans; Direct Subsidized Loans; Direct Unsubsidized Loans; College/university loans from institutional funds. Admitted students will be notified of awards on or about 4/1. Federal Work-Study Program available. Institutional employment available.

The Inside Word

Middlebury is extremely competitive; improve your chances of admission by submitting materials that paint you in the best possible light.

THE SCHOOL SAYS "..."

From the Admissions Office

"The successful Middlebury candidate excels in a variety of areas including academics, athletics, the arts, leadership, and service to others. These strengths and interests permit students to grow beyond their traditional 'comfort zones' and conventional limits. Our classrooms are as varied as the Green Mountains, the Metropolitan Museum of Art, or the great cities of Russia and Japan. Outside the classroom, students informally interact with professors in activities such as intramural basketball games and community service. At Middlebury, students develop critical-thinking skills, enduring bonds of friendship, and the ability to challenge themselves.

"Middlebury has more than 60 on-campus buildings for student housing. First-year students are housed within designated first-year communities. Sophomores have the opportunity to select housing with friends in sophomore residential communities. Juniors and seniors live together with friends and can choose from a wide variety of Junior/Senior housing options available across campus.

"Middlebury offers majors and programs in forty-six different fields, with particular strengths in languages, international studies, environmental studies, literature and creative writing, and the sciences. Opportunities for engaging in individual research with faculty abound at Middlebury."

SELECTIVITY

Admissions Rating	97
# of applicants	13,028
% of applicants accepted	15
% of acceptees attending	32
# offered a place on the wait list	2,259
% accepting a place on wait list	98
% admitted from wait list	1
# of early decision applicants	1,039
% accepted early decision	42

FIRST-YEAR PROFILE

Testing policy	Test Optional
Range SAT composite	1420–1520
Range SAT EBRW	700–760
Range SAT math	710–780
Range ACT composite	33–35
# submitting SAT scores	195
% submitting SAT scores	31
# submitting ACT scores	117
% submitting ACT scores	18

DEADLINES

Early decision	
Deadline	11/1
Notification	12/15
Other ED deadline	1/1
Other ED notification	2/1
Regular	
Deadline	1/1
Notification	3/31
Nonfall registration?	Yes

FINANCIAL FACTS

Financial Aid Rating	97
Annual tuition	$62,000
Room and board	$17,800
Required fees	$460
Books and supplies	$1,000
Average frosh need-based scholarship	$60,444
Average UG need-based scholarship	$58,084
% needy frosh rec. need-based scholarship or grant aid	95
% needy UG rec. need-based scholarship or grant aid	97
% needy frosh rec. non-need-based scholarship or grant aid	0
% needy UG rec. non-need-based scholarship or grant aid	0
% needy frosh rec. need-based self-help aid	82
% needy UG rec. need-based self-help aid	86
% frosh rec. any financial aid	57
% UG rec. any financial aid	49
% UG borrow to pay for school	48
Average cumulative indebtedness	$17,792
% frosh need fully met	95
% ugrads need fully met	97
Average % of frosh need met	100
Average % of ugrad need met	100

MIDDLE TENNESSEE STATE UNIVERSITY

1301 East Main Street, Murfreesboro, TN 37132 • Admissions: 615-898-2000 • Fax: 615-898-5478

STUDENTS SAY "..."

Academics

Middle Tennessee State University has become a go-to choice for those wishing to receive a quality and affordable education close to home. The school offers more than 140 degree programs for undergraduates—some "that are not seen in other universities, like animation." One student says, "You can literally major in fermentation and learn about the process of brewing beer." Students find these "highly specialized programs are closely tied to their industry, which means really good job placement." The on-campus growth doesn't stop there: "A staggering amount of resources [are] available to students, [ranging] from research programs to counseling services to 3D printing." Furthermore, students cite "pretty good technology [being] available for students to use or borrow, with updated versions of most programs."

As far as professors go, they "like to be on a first name basis" with students and often "make it a point to get to know you." Students call faculty "very helpful and fair" and "thorough in every aspect of the subject matter." One student shares, "A professor of mine teaches by walking around to every individual student and making sure they understand the subject matter." They're also "willing to circle back around if anyone in the class gets off track." Students who do find themselves needing extra assistance with coursework or concepts can rest easy: "There are a lot of programs in place to help you, such as free tutoring," and students also have "plenty of opportunities to gain a mentor" for more focused guidance during their college careers. Many say this "advising is top notch," and that MTSU takes the time to "foster an environment of care for each and every student." Overall, students agree: "This school is amazing, and it is such a hidden gem."

Campus Life

"The campus is big" but feels like a "comfortable and home-like school" environment where people "sit on the quad by the library and talk with their friends, play music, and skateboard." This type of campus takes advantage of the other outdoor areas of campus too, and students like to "hang hammocks on trees to sit and read and study." One student comments, "There are also many different parks and greenways that we enjoy visiting." For on-campus events, the school is always offering things "like art classes, study groups, or simply a movie showing." Those looking to spend a little time elsewhere, though, will turn to nearby Murfreesboro, where they can hang out at the "plethora of restaurants and bars." Nashville isn't far, either, and students will often "go out to...clubs or arcades" there on weekends. Overall, students find themselves to be quite busy, but the good kind of busy—as one student puts it: "Despite how busy I am, I am happy doing it."

Student Body

"At a school as large as MTSU, you see all types [of students] from different ends of the spectrum" as everyone "is very open to whoever comes into the school." Here you'll find "a mixed bag of fresh-out-of-high-school students,...parents,...returning military veterans, and foreign students." No matter who they are, people at Middle Tennessee are "extremely friendly and inclusive," "pretty laid back," and "nice, courteous and really helpful." "Though everyone is different here, it is still easy to find people like yourself [who are] studying the same things or taking similar classes," says a student.

MIDDLE TENNESSEE STATE UNIVERSITY

Financial Aid: 615-898-2111 • E-Mail: admissions@mtsu.edu • Website: www.mtsu.edu

THE PRINCETON REVIEW SAYS

Admissions

The school reports that its standardized testing policy for use in admission for Fall 2024 is SAT or ACT Required. The Princeton Review suggests that interested applicants consult with the school for the most up-to-date standardized testing policies. *Very important factors considered include:* academic GPA, standardized test scores. *Other factors considered include:* rigor of secondary school record, application essay, recommendation(s), extracurricular activities, talent/ability, character/personal qualities, volunteer work, work experience, level of applicant's interest. High school diploma is required and GED is accepted. *Academic units required:* 4 English, 4 math, 3 science, 1 science lab, 2 foreign language, 1 social studies, 1 history, 1 visual/performing arts.

Financial Aid

Students should submit: FAFSA. Priority filing deadline is 2/1. The Princeton Review suggests that all financial aid forms be submitted as soon as possible (see page 5 for a note on the FAFSA). *Need-based scholarships/grants offered:* College/university scholarship or grant aid from institutional funds; Federal Pell; Private scholarships; SEOG; State scholarships/grants. *Loan aid offered:* Direct PLUS loans; Direct Subsidized Loans; Direct Unsubsidized Loans. Admitted students will be notified of awards on a rolling basis beginning 2/15. Federal Work-Study Program available. Institutional employment available.

The Inside Word

Middle Tennessee State University is very transparent about what guarantees admission for first-year students: Anyone who has completed the recommended college prep classes with a 3.0 GPA will be admitted, as will anyone with a minimum composite ACT score of 22. Additionally, a combination of a 19 composite ACT score and a 2.7 GPA or higher will be admitted. Students who do not meet any these requirements can still be considered for conditional admission, but they must submit a personal statement and are subjected to an individual review process.

SELECTIVITY

Admissions Rating	86
# of applicants	12,868
% of applicants accepted	73
% of acceptees attending	30

FIRST-YEAR PROFILE

Testing policy	SAT or ACT Required
Range SAT composite	1020–1220
Range SAT EBRW	520–630
Range SAT math	500–600
Range ACT composite	19–26
# submitting SAT scores	216
% submitting SAT scores	8
# submitting ACT scores	2,524
% submitting ACT scores	90
Average HS GPA	3.6
% frosh submitting high school GPA	99

DEADLINES

Regular	
Priority	7/1
Deadline	8/15
Notification	Rolling
Nonfall registration?	Yes

APPLICANTS ALSO LOOK AT

Austin Peay State University; Motlow State Community College; Tennessee State University; Tennessee Technological University; The University of Memphis; University of Tennessee-Chattanooga; University of Tennessee—Knoxville

FINANCIAL FACTS

Financial Aid Rating	77
Annual in-state tuition	$9,694
Annual out-of-state tuition	$29,858
Room and board	$11,518
Books and supplies	$1,260
Average frosh need-based scholarship	$7,589
Average UG need-based scholarship	$7,030
% needy frosh rec. need-based scholarship or grant aid	56
% needy UG rec. need-based scholarship or grant aid	59
% needy frosh rec. non-need-based scholarship or grant aid	100
% needy UG rec. non-need-based scholarship or grant aid	100
% needy frosh rec. need-based self-help aid	42
% needy UG rec. need-based self-help aid	46
% frosh rec. any financial aid	86
% UG rec. any financial aid	96
% UG borrow to pay for school	54
Average cumulative indebtedness	$23,722
% frosh need fully met	20
% ugrads need fully met	18
Average % of frosh need met	72
Average % of ugrad need met	69

MILLSAPS COLLEGE

1701 North State Street, Jackson, MS 39210 • Admissions: 601-974-1000 • Fax: 601-974-1059

STUDENTS SAY ". . ."

Academics

Millsaps is a small college, so students "get a lot of personal attention." It is a "school where everybody knows your name," as well as "a place where every student has to work hard to stay above water; excellence is the norm, not the exception." What makes Millsaps unique is how it "breaks the mold by providing superb education as well as fun, combining the two in ways so subtle that a student may not even realize they're learning!" The school "offers great courses taught by charismatic professors" who "bring the material to life...through their innovative teaching methods." "Classes are not easy, but the quality of learning is top notch." "Professors always encourage students to discuss class material and voice their opinions and questions about it. They encourage you to form your own ideas." These "friendly and approachable" professors "continue to teach outside of the classroom." "They welcome one-on-one time...to further develop understanding." Students have praise for the education they are receiving saying, "coming out of Millsaps I will be fully prepared for grad school. My professors not only lecture, but they turn the material into hands-on learning opportunities," and "I seriously respect my school's standard of excellence in hiring people who are wonderful at their jobs." Besides "great professors," the school offers "a prestigious business school," "abundant study abroad programs," and "strong Southern hospitality and heritage." The school's small size provides opportunities to receive "a top-notch education, while also getting to play sports and be in clubs." Although Millsaps may not be affordable for everyone, it "strives to be generous with scholarships." One student was pleased to report, "They offered the most financial assistance by far." Although student surveys were mostly positive, like this one: "Millsaps College provides the ideal learning atmosphere for liberal arts studies where they teach us how to think and not what to think," there were complaints about "the Internet and networking capabilities," and "the cafeteria is an area where great improvement is needed."

Campus Life

"Students at Millsaps think about their classwork first and foremost. After that, we think about hanging out with friends and having fun." The campus is "so beautiful and filled with cozy spots that many students spend a lot of their time outside." "While most schools have 'the quad' where students hang out between classes, Millsaps has 'The Bowl.' It is a beautiful area of grass and trees in the center of campus." But one student notes that there is still room for improvement. "The campus is beautiful, but the insides of the buildings need a serious upgrade. Every time I walk into a building, I feel like I've been transported back to the seventies." Although "most of the upperclassmen dorms are amazing," the "freshman dorms are a little sketchy." On campus "there are concerts and fun days all throughout the semester." "There are parties at the fraternity houses, and...some really cool things to do from concerts to oxygen bars to laser tag." "I would definitely call it a 'party school,' despite the tough academics." "There is a lot of partying on the weekends but almost everyone still manages to get studying finished." Students also point out, "We don't have to drink to have fun at Millsaps, though. You can always find a friend to hang out with, go to the movies, shop, or find a new great place to eat. The Millsaps curriculum even makes study groups fun (for the most part), believe it or not." Off campus, students venture into Jackson where "there are great restaurants."

Student Body

Is there a typical Millsaps student? Some students think so: "The typical student at Millsaps was an over-involved, cool nerd in high school. We throw ourselves into sports, clubs, Greek life, and community service like it's our job. It's how we thrive." "Students fit in by being involved in Greek life and other organizations." "A typical student is involved in many activities from sports to community service clubs. Student interests are diverse, and the student body in general is very friendly and interactive." Another student disagrees, "There is no 'typical student' really—the most common thread is a desire to change the world (usually, with a stop at graduate school)."

MILLSAPS COLLEGE

Financial Aid: 800-352-1050 • E-Mail: admissions@millsaps.edu • Website: www.millsaps.edu

THE PRINCETON REVIEW SAYS

Admissions

The school reports that its standardized testing policy for use in admission for Fall 2024 is Test Optional. It is unknown at this time if the 2024 testing policy will be permanent. The Princeton Review suggests that interested applicants consult with the school for the most up-to-date standardized testing policies. *Very important factors considered include:* rigor of secondary school record, academic GPA. *Important factors considered include:* character/personal qualities. *Other factors considered include:* class rank, standardized test scores, application essay, recommendation(s), extracurricular activities, talent/ability, first generation, alumni/ae relation, volunteer work, level of applicant's interest. High school diploma is required and GED is accepted. *Academic units required:* 4 English, 3 math, 2 science, 2 foreign language, 2 social studies. *Academic units recommended:* 4 English, 3 math, 2 science, 2 science labs, 2 foreign language, 2 social studies, 2 visual/performing arts.

Financial Aid

Students should submit: FAFSA. Priority filing deadline is 3/1. The Princeton Review suggests that all financial aid forms be submitted as soon as possible (see page 5 for a note on the FAFSA). *Need-based scholarships/grants offered:* College/university scholarship or grant aid from institutional funds; Federal Pell; Private scholarships; SEOG; State scholarships/grants. *Loan aid offered:* Direct PLUS loans; Direct Subsidized Loans; Direct Unsubsidized Loans. Admitted students will be notified of awards on a rolling basis beginning in January. Federal Work-Study Program available. Institutional employment available.

The Inside Word

Millsaps' trademark friendliness begins during the admissions process. The school encourages prospective students to get in touch with an admissions counselor to ask questions, arrange a visit, or connect you with a current student. For early action admission or scholarships, students need to apply by November 15. After that, the school admits students on a rolling basis.

THE SCHOOL SAYS "..."

From the Admissions Office

"Small classes lead to big opportunities.

"Students at Millsaps College choose their own paths, but they do so with support from the college's new Pathways Program, which helps them develop the holistic connections between their interests and their chosen vocation. Supported and taught by both faculty and staff, the program is designed to help students figure out who they want to be, and not just what they want to do. The process begins with coursework for all first-year students, in which they are taught to be successful students and leaders while leaning into their own personal values and interests. By the end of their first semester, students choose one of six Pathways based on their interests and values: arts, culture and communication; business; exploratory; health; law, politics and social leadership; and STEM and data science.

"Recognized as having one of top study abroad programs in the country, Millsaps students find themselves helping to excavate Maya ruins in the college's 4,500 acre biocultural reserve in the heart of the Yucatán Peninsula, meeting with members of Parliament in the United Kingdom, painting in the heart of Spain, or immersing themselves in Asian cultures.

"Millsaps boasts the highest graduation rate of any four-year college or university in Mississippi, and its graduates have the highest median earnings of any college or university in the state ten years after starting school. These statistics reveal a strong return on investment, as students complete school in four years and enter the market to begin their chosen career."

SELECTIVITY

Admissions Rating	87
# of applicants	2,220
% of applicants accepted	68
% of acceptees attending	17

FIRST-YEAR PROFILE

Testing policy	Test Optional
Range SAT composite	1135–1355
Range SAT EBRW	610–700
Range SAT math	525–655
Range ACT composite	21–28
# submitting SAT scores	21
% submitting SAT scores	13
# submitting ACT scores	153
% submitting ACT scores	93
Average HS GPA	3.7
% frosh submitting high school GPA	57

DEADLINES

Early action	
Deadline	11/15
Notification	12/1
Regular	
Priority	3/1
Notification	Rolling, 8/1
Nonfall registration?	Yes

FINANCIAL FACTS

Financial Aid Rating	84
Annual tuition	$40,940
Room and board	$15,784
Required fees	$2,875
Books and supplies	$650
Average frosh need-based scholarship	$32,456
Average UG need-based scholarship	$30,749
% needy frosh rec. need-based scholarship or grant aid	100
% needy UG rec. need-based scholarship or grant aid	100
% needy frosh rec. non-need-based scholarship or grant aid	16
% needy UG rec. non-need-based scholarship or grant aid	16
% needy frosh rec. need-based self-help aid	82
% needy UG rec. need-based self-help aid	80
% frosh rec. any financial aid	100
% UG rec. any financial aid	98
% UG borrow to pay for school	60
Average cumulative indebtedness	$33,332
% frosh need fully met	17
% ugrads need fully met	22
Average % of frosh need met	78
Average % of ugrad need met	77

MISSOURI UNIVERSITY OF SCIENCE AND TECHNOLOGY

1870 Miner Circle, Rolla, MO 65409-0910 • Admissions: 573-341-4111 • Fax: 573-341-4082

STUDENTS SAY "..."

Academics

Top performers in science and technology will find a home at Missouri S&T, because here "students are exposed to just about every different type of engineering," making it "one of the best universities that prepares engineers for industry." Unsurprisingly, this does not come without challenge. Classes can be "very tough and intimidating," where "it's not uncommon to have a 55 percent or less average on a test." Students ready for the rigorous academics should "not expect to be babied at all" because "the professors are there to challenge you." The aim is to "prepare students to find a job in the real world and help us to get the experience to succeed in it." Students who have run the gauntlet say "the quality of education and availability of resources here is second to none." That education comes via "hands-on learning, small class sizes, and caring professors" who are "some of the smartest professors in the world." Though they challenge their students, they don't leave them out to dry. "All of the professors have office hours, whether open or by appointment," students note. Indeed, "the accessibility of instructors and other faculty/staff" at this school is seen as a strength. Yes, "this school definitely is willing to challenge their students," but numbers-crunching engineers will find value in their education, because S&T "comes in the top three schools in average starting salary for graduates, and won't guarantee a huge debt burden."

Campus Life

Missouri University of Science and Technology may be "a small school in the middle of Missouri," but "our range of student organizations is mind-boggling." You name the club and it probably exists, as well as school activities ranging from "scavenger hunts, video game nights, cooking classes, viewing parties, dance lessons, and much more." Of course, in a school where "all of the students are always worrying about that next exam in calculus or dreading their lab in the afternoon," it is not surprising that studying is as big a pastime as hanging out. Here, "academics are everyone's top priority." When not studying, "drinking is pretty big on weekends." Other activities include "playing sports, video games, and working out." Downtown Rolla isn't a thriving Mecca of activity because "there's not so much to do in the town"; however, "someone always has something going on." St. Louis is close enough for day trips, and there are a slew of student organizations to occupy downtime. "Virtually every student is either heavily involved in a diverse group of these student organizations or devotes much of their time to design teams or research." Generally, if you're at S&T and are not kept busy, it's probably because you don't want to be busy.

Student Body

Imagine a less stereotypical Big Bang Theory and you're close to the mark. The typical student may be "a little nerdy," "those kids that didn't fit in during high school" but who "now can be themselves." A typical S&T student "is someone who never really had to study in high school to get good grades, but they are working hard here to maintain that standard." While most S&T students are smart—"we came here primarily to learn," one attendee notes—they are not introverted or antisocial. The "very friendly" people on campus "live together in harmony." Indeed, "everyone can find a place to fit in" thanks to the "over 212 student organizations." While about half of the students here are from Missouri or nearby states, the others "are from the edges of the nation and even some foreign countries, which is astounding considering our small enrollment size." Education is the priority for those who attend, so meeting people is simple because "it is really easy just to strike up a conversation with someone." The like-minded atmosphere makes socializing easy. "We are all nerds, so we adapt to the social environment once we are introduced."

MISSOURI UNIVERSITY OF SCIENCE AND TECHNOLOGY

Financial Aid: 573-341-4282 • E-Mail: admissions@mst.edu • Website: www.mst.edu

THE PRINCETON REVIEW SAYS

Admissions

The school reports that its standardized testing policy for use in admission for Fall 2024 is Test Optional. It is unknown at this time if the 2024 testing policy will be permanent. The Princeton Review suggests that interested applicants consult with the school for the most up-to-date standardized testing policies. *Very important factors considered include:* rigor of secondary school record, class rank, academic GPA, standardized test scores. *Important factors considered include:* recommendation(s). *Other factors considered include:* application essay, interview, extracurricular activities, talent/ability, character/personal qualities, volunteer work, work experience, level of applicant's interest. High school diploma is required and GED is accepted. *Academic units required:* 4 English, 4 math, 3 science, 1 science lab, 2 foreign language, 3 social studies, 1 visual/performing arts.

Financial Aid

Students should submit: FAFSA. Priority filing deadline is 2/1. The Princeton Review suggests that all financial aid forms be submitted as soon as possible (see page 5 for a note on the FAFSA). *Need-based scholarships/grants offered:* College/university scholarship or grant aid from institutional funds; Federal Pell; Private scholarships; SEOG; State scholarships/grants. *Loan aid offered:* College/university loans from institutional funds; State Loans. Admitted students will be notified of awards on a rolling basis beginning 4/1. Federal Work-Study Program available. Institutional employment available.

The Inside Word

Winning admission to Missouri University of Science and Technology is largely a numbers game, as it often is with other leading public universities. Expect to have to meet class rank and standardized test cutoffs, along with general education requirements, in order to be granted admission. And apply early if possible. The pool of applicants is competitive, and is made up of students of similar caliber. Get off to an early start and you'll have an advantage.

THE SCHOOL SAYS "..."

From the Admissions Office

"Missouri University of Science and Technology is one of the nation's top technological universities and offers strong academics in humanities, social sciences, education, business and other degree programs. Our fifteen engineering programs and computing and science programs are nationally and internationally renowned. With 7,645 students from the U.S. and around the globe, Missouri S&T provides a 'big campus' feel of diversity and student engagement on a medium-sized campus.

"S&T offers rigorous academics, exceptional graduation and placement rates, excellent access to co-ops and internships, experiential learning for all undergraduates, affordable tuition combined with generous scholarship programs, and a 3.4 percent loan default rate as a result of superior career outcomes for our students. The average starting salary for S&T graduates in 2022 was $69,033.

"S&T students are successful due to a combination of outstanding academics and easy access to personal and professional growth. The vast majority of courses are taught by tenured professors engaged in relevant research and scholarship, in a faculty culture that values undergraduate education and hands-on learning and personal attention, which extends back to our founding in 1870. S&T sponsors over 250 student clubs, and students enjoy outdoor activities among the area's scenic parks, lakes and riverways.

"Widely recognized as one of the nation's best universities, Missouri S&T provides an outstanding education, at an affordable cost with exceptional student outcomes."

SELECTIVITY

Admissions Rating	86
# of applicants	3,876
% of applicants accepted	84
% of acceptees attending	44

FIRST-YEAR PROFILE

Testing policy	Test Optional
Range SAT EBRW	520–640
Range SAT math	580–700
Range ACT composite	25–31
# submitting SAT scores	21
% submitting SAT scores	2
# submitting ACT scores	1,387
% submitting ACT scores	97
Average HS GPA	3.6
% frosh submitting high school GPA	100
% graduated top 10% of class	39
% graduated top 25% of class	72
% graduated top 50% of class	94

DEADLINES

Regular	
Priority	12/1
Deadline	7/1
Notification	Rolling, 10/1

FINANCIAL FACTS

Financial Aid Rating	80
Annual in-state tuition	$13,000
Annual out-of-state tuition	$30,400
Room and board	$11,792
Required fees	$1,462
Books and supplies	$886
Average frosh need-based scholarship	$10,079
Average UG need-based scholarship	$7,978
% needy frosh rec. need-based scholarship or grant aid	94
% needy UG rec. need-based scholarship or grant aid	91
% needy frosh rec. non-need-based scholarship or grant aid	30
% needy UG rec. non-need-based scholarship or grant aid	40
% needy frosh rec. need-based self-help aid	100
% needy UG rec. need-based self-help aid	100
% frosh rec. any financial aid	95
% UG rec. any financial aid	88
% UG borrow to pay for school	66
Average cumulative indebtedness	$27,500
% frosh need fully met	14
% ugrads need fully met	30
Average % of frosh need met	40
Average % of ugrad need met	48

MONMOUTH UNIVERSITY (NJ)

400 Cedar Avenue, West Long Branch, NJ 07764-1898 • Admissions: 732-571-3400 • Fax: 732-263-5166

STUDENTS SAY ". . ."

Academics

Monmouth University, just an hour or so away from both New York City and Philadelphia, wants to be your future home away from home. It's far more than a "beautiful" campus—though that's the way many attendees happily describe it—it's also "great at opening new doors for students." That comes from the institution's responsiveness, such that "if there is a problem, Monmouth staff is quick to resolve it and come to your aid." It also comes from their foresight, with numerous career- and success-minded initiatives and resources, particularly when it comes to tutoring or writing services. There are also a lot of popular volunteering opportunities, with "service trips to Haiti and Guatemala."

The meat-and-potatoes coursework is also praised by undergrads, who note there's a "great variety of course offerings and programs," many of which prioritize "hands-on experience." Additionally, students say that "small class sizes help the learning experience" and "allow you to develop a good rapport with your professors." Don't underestimate the small things either: "Teachers actually knowing your name means a lot." While "some professors are more dedicated than others," many are "wonderful and truly invested in helping you do well." They tend to be "passionate about the subject they teach and make it interesting for the students." Overall, "they're here to push you, but also make it clear that they will be more than willing to meet with you outside of class." Perhaps best of all, professors often strive "to connect what we learn in class to the real world."

Campus Life

If you're into the Greek scene or athletics, Monmouth may be the perfect place for you, as students say that the scene is "dominated" by those two factions. Students mean this in the most fun and flattering light: "Greek life is the best experience of my college career. I was able to make amazing connections and develop leadership skills." There's plenty of opportunity to connect with students outside of the classroom given that "people work out a lot" at facilities like "basketball courts, a swimming pool, and a bowling alley," or just plain attend the athletic events, where there "is always a great, energized student crowd." Of course, there's far more than just athletics here, and as examples of how you can find "a club for most interests," students list things from debate and model UN to the 5678 Dance Club, psychology club, and even a "student-run record label." The school also sponsors a variety of events, from "craft fairs and bonfires" as do the individual residence halls, which have things like "painting night." And should you need a breather from campus life, the surrounding area offers many options. "We are right near the beach, and [an] hour's drive from [New York City]."

Student Body

Undergrads note that at Monmouth University, the "student body is heavily white and rich," and a place where "diversity only exists in small pockets" because most "tend to be from New Jersey." And yet, there's far more beneath the surface, because peers are overall described as "motivated and creative people" and one attendee notes that "the community at Monmouth is more inclusive than any I have ever seen." Friendliness abounds, such that "everyone is always saying hello to each other on their ways to class" and it's rather commonplace to have someone "hold the doors open for you." In short, there's a "very chill beach vibe," which can be refreshing during one's downtime, given the general bustle of those who are "academically driven and work hard to be involved in many things on campus." All in all, "Everyone at Monmouth has something unique to offer, and everyone has their own interests and beliefs, which makes it exciting to meet new people."

MONMOUTH UNIVERSITY (NJ)

Financial Aid: 732-571-3463 • E-Mail: admission@monmouth.edu • Website: www.monmouth.edu

THE PRINCETON REVIEW SAYS

Admissions

The school reports that its standardized testing policy for use in admission for Fall 2024 is Test Optional. The 2024 testing policy will be permanent. The Princeton Review suggests that interested applicants consult with the school for the most up-to-date standardized testing policies. *Very important factors considered include:* rigor of secondary school record, academic GPA. *Important factors considered include:* application essay, recommendation(s). *Other factors considered include:* standardized test scores, extracurricular activities, character/personal qualities, alumni/ae relation, volunteer work, work experience. High school diploma is required and GED is accepted. *Academic units required:* 4 English, 3 math, 2 science, 1 science lab, 2 history, 5 academic electives. *Academic units recommended:* 2 foreign language, 2 social studies.

Financial Aid

Students should submit: FAFSA. Priority filing deadline is 12/15. The Princeton Review suggests that all financial aid forms be submitted as soon as possible (see page 5 for a note on the FAFSA). *Need-based scholarships/grants offered:* College/university scholarship or grant aid from institutional funds; Federal Pell; Private scholarships; SEOG; State scholarships/grants. *Loan aid offered:* Direct PLUS loans; Direct Subsidized Loans; Direct Unsubsidized Loans; College/university loans from institutional funds; State Loans. Admitted students will be notified of awards on a rolling basis beginning 12/15. Federal Work-Study Program available. Institutional employment available.

The Inside Word

Monmouth University takes a fairly standard approach to the admissions process: your cumulative GPA is the most critical factor. Letters of recommendation and extracurricular activities will be of secondary importance, and although the school is Test Optional, they will review your SAT and ACT scores if provided. Undergrads interested in transferring to Monmouth can take advantage of Personalized Transfer Appointments wherein they meet with an admissions counselor to discuss enrollment potential, the university experience, and scholarship opportunities.

THE SCHOOL SAYS "..."

From the Admissions Office

"As one of the nation's top universities providing access and excellence, Monmouth University attracts students looking for a personalized learning environment that will ignite their curiosity and prepare them for life after graduation.

"Students benefit from an intellectually challenging academic experience built on a strong liberal arts foundation and learning experiences that are both high impact and immersive, extending beyond the classroom. Small class sizes foster collaborative learning and research opportunities with faculty and peers who know you by name. Our breathtaking coastal campus provides a safe, suburban setting in one of the world's largest metropolitan regions, ideally positioned to help our students develop and pursue their career interests while enjoying rich cultural opportunities.

"Monmouth's student life features active student clubs and organizations, including eight sororities and six fraternities, and dozens of academic/leadership honor societies. Monmouth's 24 Division I athletic teams attract lively support from students and other members of the campus and local communities while instilling university pride.

"There is a real spirit of entrepreneurship on campus that comes to life through activities like Blue Hawk Records, our student-run record label, and the student-managed investment fund, Hawk Capital. For those adventurers interested in extending their experiences beyond campus, Monmouth encourages students to take part in service projects, study abroad programs, and community-building activities in locales around the globe. Monmouth University is committed to graduating people of purpose with the critical thinking skills required for global relevance and impact."

SELECTIVITY

Admissions Rating	82
# of applicants	7,937
% of applicants accepted	91
% of acceptees attending	12
# of early decision applicants	56
% accepted early decision	79

FIRST-YEAR PROFILE

Testing policy	Test Optional
Range SAT composite	1110–1300
Range SAT EBRW	560–660
Range SAT math	550–640
Range ACT composite	22–30
# submitting SAT scores	206
% submitting SAT scores	23
# submitting ACT scores	16
% submitting ACT scores	2
Average HS GPA	3.6
% frosh submitting high school GPA	100
% graduated top 10% of class	15
% graduated top 25% of class	44
% graduated top 50% of class	80

DEADLINES

Early decision	
Deadline	11/15
Notification	12/15
Early action	
Deadline	12/1
Notification	1/15
Regular	
Notification	4/1
Nonfall registration?	Yes

FINANCIAL FACTS

Financial Aid Rating	80
Annual tuition	$44,098
Room and board	$17,738
Required fees	$752
Books and supplies	$1,000
Average frosh need-based scholarship	$12,847
Average UG need-based scholarship	$13,989
% needy frosh rec. need-based scholarship or grant aid	66
% needy UG rec. need-based scholarship or grant aid	77
% needy frosh rec. non-need-based scholarship or grant aid	96
% needy UG rec. non-need-based scholarship or grant aid	94
% needy frosh rec. need-based self-help aid	83
% needy UG rec. need-based self-help aid	78
% frosh rec. any financial aid	99
% UG rec. any financial aid	96
% UG borrow to pay for school	75
Average cumulative indebtedness	$36,587
% frosh need fully met	19
% ugrads need fully met	17
Average % of frosh need met	73
Average % of ugrad need met	70

Montana Technological University

1300 West Park Street, Butte, MT 59701 • Admissions: 406-496-4256 • Fax: 406-496-4710

CAMPUS LIFE

Quality of Life Rating	83
Fire Safety Rating	83
Green Rating	60*
Type of school	Public
Environment	Town

STUDENTS

Total undergrad enrollment	1,779
% male/female/another gender	61/39/NR
% from out of state	15
% frosh live on campus	61
% ugrads live on campus	17
# of fraternities	0
# of sororities	0
% African American	1
% Asian	1
% White	82
% Hispanic	4
% Native American	3
% Pacific Islander	0
% Two or more races	1
% Race and/or ethnicity unknown	6
% international	2
# of countries represented	10

SURVEY SAYS . . .

Lots of conservative students
Frats and sororities are popular
Internships are widely available

ACADEMICS

Academic Rating	79
% students returning for sophomore year	76
% students graduating within 6 years	57
Calendar	Semester
Student/faculty ratio	13:1
Profs interesting rating	85
Profs accessible rating	89

Most classes have fewer than 10 students.
Most lab/discussion sessions have
10–19 students.

MOST POPULAR MAJORS

Mechanical Engineering; Registered Nursing/
Registered Nurse; Management Information
Systems and Services, Other

STUDENTS SAY "..."

Academics

Located in the foothills of the Rocky Mountains, Montana Technological University is about "science," "engineering," and "getting students ready for a career in high-paying fields." With its "strong STEM programs," the focus is certainly on the technical side of education, and students praise Tech's engineering program and "connection to industry." The relatively small campus creates a "home-like atmosphere where everyone has a sense of community," as well as "the opportunity to really get to know professors." Looking beyond college, "Montana Tech's Career Fair almost guarantees an internship to anyone who is serious about their career." Several students who choose majors outside the popular STEM degrees do wish that the school would "[treat] our non-engineering degrees as part of the school and not [as] second-rate." Tech's nursing program is growing in popularity, and the school is known to "produce compassionate, intelligent nurses." Professors generally earn high marks, as "most of them come from industry backgrounds before they started teaching; therefore, the quality of the material brought to the classroom is top notch." Many professors are "actual engineers with real world experience," and while "Tech is not an easy school," students say that with "the help provided by the professors and the other facilities available on campus," it is possible for "anyone with the work ethic [to] meet their goals."

Campus Life

Life in Montana Tech's hometown of Butte is oriented around the outdoors, and students flock to activities like " skiing, biking, camping, [and] fishing" when they're not buried in schoolwork. Beyond the great outdoors, students say that Butte is "pretty quiet with mostly bars and churches around town," so a lot of time is spent on campus or at off-campus residences (only roughly 12 percent of undergraduates live on campus). The rigorous curriculum means most students study during the week and let loose during the weekend. As one student puts it, "You have to be willing to search for things to do outside of class, [other than] drinking." There are intramural sports and Tech-sponsored events, and "sporting events are very popular activities at Montana Tech."

Student Body

There's no question that men outnumber women at Montana Tech, though the ratio is improving. While some say, "It isn't a problem being a woman here," others counter that Tech "is an unfriendly place for women." In general, the student body "is extremely focused and pushes each other to do better. With such a small campus, the students know each other quite well and want to see their classmates succeed." While some describe their fellow students as "lots of Canadians and cowboys," others say that there is "a very diverse population here at Montana Tech, everyone from transfer students to international students from Saudi Arabia." Even with a competitive atmosphere, students say that at Montana Tech the "clubs are active, the Student Senate genuinely cares about the happiness of their students, and the faculty [do] whatever they can to bring a smile to your face, especially during difficult days of midterms, flu season, and cold weather."

MONTANA TECHNOLOGICAL UNIVERSITY

Financial Aid: 406-496-4223 • E-Mail: admissions@mtech.edu • Website: www.mtech.edu

THE PRINCETON REVIEW SAYS

Admissions

The school reports that its standardized testing policy for use in admission for Fall 2024 is Test Optional. It is unknown at this time if the 2024 testing policy will be permanent. The Princeton Review suggests that interested applicants consult with the school for the most up-to-date standardized testing policies. *Very important factors considered include:* class rank, academic GPA. *Other factors considered include:* High school diploma is required and GED is accepted. *Academic units required:* 4 English, 3 math, 2 science, 2 science labs, 3 social studies. *Academic units recommended:* 4 math.

Financial Aid

Students should submit: FAFSA. Priority filing deadline is 12/1. The Princeton Review suggests that all financial aid forms be submitted as soon as possible (see page 5 for a note on the FAFSA). *Need-based scholarships/grants offered:* College/university scholarship or grant aid from institutional funds; Federal Pell; Private scholarships; SEOG; State scholarships/grants. *Loan aid offered:* Direct PLUS loans; Direct Subsidized Loans; Direct Unsubsidized Loans. Admitted students will be notified of awards on a rolling basis beginning 2/1. Federal Work-Study Program available. Institutional employment available.

The Inside Word

For those leaning toward a technical career, Montana Tech is the place to go. Strong academics are important, but the school can be a place for students that may not be offered a spot at one of the country's larger tech schools. The acceptance rate is high, and admitted students generally having a high school GPA around 3.48. Transcripts are important as well as high school class rank. Though the school is Test Optional, standardized test scores can still be useful if trying to impress the admission team. There are a variety of math and writing proficiency requirements students must meet and the school looks for a high school course load that includes a full range of college prep classes.

THE SCHOOL SAYS "..."

From the Admissions Office

"Characterize Montana Tech by listening to what employers say. They tell us Tech graduates stand out with an incredible work ethic and top-notch technical skills. Last year, 68 organizations held on-campus interviews and 120 companies attended Montana Tech career fairs competing for our students and graduates. The beneficiaries: the students! Montana Tech has a five-year average career outcomes rate of 91 percent and a 92 percent acceptance into professional and graduate programs. Learning takes place in a personalized environment, in first-class academic facilities, and in the heart of the Rocky Mountains. Outdoor recreation provides a great balance to the rigors of the course work at Montana Tech. We are a small school where our students receive a terrific education, and in the end, get great jobs! The SAT (or the ACT with the writing section) is currently optional, but recommended for all students applying for admission. Students who do not take the tests with the writing component may be required to take an additional English placement test from college before they enroll."

SELECTIVITY

Admissions Rating	83
# of applicants	1,952
% of applicants accepted	88
% of acceptees attending	25

FIRST-YEAR PROFILE

Testing policy	Test Optional
Range SAT EBRW	540–660
Range SAT math	550–630
Range ACT composite	20–27
# submitting SAT scores	27
% submitting SAT scores	10
# submitting ACT scores	245
% submitting ACT scores	93
Average HS GPA	3.5
% frosh submitting high school GPA	94
% graduated top 10% of class	21
% graduated top 25% of class	49
% graduated top 50% of class	81

DEADLINES

Nonfall registration?	Yes

APPLICANTS ALSO LOOK AT

Carroll College (MT); Colorado School of Mines; Missouri Tech; Montana State University; New Mexico Institute of Mining and Technology; South Dakota School of Mines and Technology; The University of Montana—Missoula; The University of Montana-Western

FINANCIAL FACTS

Financial Aid Rating	80
Annual in-state tuition	$7,397
Annual out-of-state tuition	$22,561
Room and board	$10,170
Books and supplies	$1,320
Average frosh need-based scholarship	$6,588
Average UG need-based scholarship	$6,379
% needy frosh rec. need-based scholarship or grant aid	87
% needy UG rec. need-based scholarship or grant aid	84
% needy frosh rec. non-need-based scholarship or grant aid	16
% needy UG rec. non-need-based scholarship or grant aid	9
% needy frosh rec. need-based self-help aid	59
% needy UG rec. need-based self-help aid	68
% frosh rec. any financial aid	93
% UG rec. any financial aid	73
% UG borrow to pay for school	51
Average cumulative indebtedness	$21,939
% frosh need fully met	21
% ugrads need fully met	16
Average % of frosh need met	66
Average % of ugrad need met	62

MORAVIAN UNIVERSITY

1200 Main Street, Bethlehem, PA 18018 • Admissions: 610-861-1300 • Fax: 610-625-7930

STUDENTS SAY "..."

Academics

Moravian University's holistic undergraduate experience (named Elevate) is designed with one goal in mind: ensuring that "students feel empowered to learn." This comes through a wide "variety of resources and support for anything that they may need," like getting a MacBook Pro and iPad upon enrollment and having the free opportunity to study abroad with faculty. Resources like Student Opportunities for Academic Research (SOAR) help connect students with undergraduate research under a faculty mentor. Academic and mental support can be found at the counseling center, writing center, or in Peer-Assisted Study Sessions, in which "each class has an assigned student mentor who has taken the class or knows the material [and] can tutor students, hold group study sessions, or even work on study habits for the material." The school also brings in "a lot of guest speakers and hands-on activities that occur outside of just lectures," such as "visiting local museums that have importance to the history of the Moravians and to the city of Bethlehem" for a public history class.

"Small class sizes allow you to get to know your professors well," and many are discussion-based, which "encourages you to think and relate the material to life outside of the class, reminding you that you are not just a student, but you are an individual with your own ideas, goals, and perspective." For those more traditional classes, professors "utilized real-life examples in their lectures." Faculty are also "very supportive, and always offer time to help provide more resources for all students, especially those who are struggling," as well as being "very helpful when it comes to eligibility and making up work/exams." A student says: "If you make an effort to talk to your teacher, they will always be willing to help you out."

Campus Life

Moravian "has a lot of student committees that are very involved with the students on campus"; for example, the Moravian Activities Council (MAC) hosts regular events from crafts (making stuffed animals or potting plants) to activities like scavenger hunts, all of which "get students involved and give them something to look forward to on campus." Many here take part in sports, which means "there are lots of lifting and training sessions for the student-athletes each week, [and] students also play recreational sports on Makuvek Field or in the gymnasium." Spectating is also its own activity at this Division III school. Bethlehem, Pennsylvania "is a nice area with a low crime rate which makes it a great and safe city," and "Main Street is very close so it's nice to go there to take a break and shop/get something to eat." Students find that there are "countless opportunities to get involved, grow, and take on leadership roles."

Student Body

This "tight-knit community [is] filled with highly motivated, outgoing, and passionate students" who are "a mix of local students and students from further away, as well as from many races, ethnicities, faiths, and backgrounds." People here "support and value one another, [and] you can feel the friendly atmosphere whenever you step on campus." Since Moravian is a smaller school, "you see the same faces when walking around campus, which breeds familiarity and a sense of belonging." While "a lot of students are involved in sports...all have different experiences to talk about and what they have learned from playing those sports," and social groups tend to arise from "sports, [dormitory] floors, and relationships build outside of college." Community service is also popular among this group who have "high emotional intelligence and strive to be great citizens." One student describes their spring break staycation as an opportunity "stay on campus and serve the community all week." On the whole, "the student body at Moravian University is very welcoming and accommodating to ensure that everyone feels included" and everyone is "easy to talk to and presents themselves in a good manner throughout campus."

MORAVIAN UNIVERSITY

Financial Aid: 610-861-1330 • E-Mail: admission@moravian.edu • Website: www.moravian.edu

THE PRINCETON REVIEW SAYS

Admissions

The school reports that its standardized testing policy for use in admission for Fall 2024 is Test Optional. The policy is permanent. The Princeton Review suggests that interested applicants consult with the school for the most up-to-date standardized testing policies. *Very important factors considered include:* rigor of secondary school record, extracurricular activities, character/personal qualities. *Important factors considered include:* class rank, academic GPA, application essay, recommendation(s), interview, talent/ability, volunteer work, level of applicant's interest. *Other factors considered include:* standardized test scores, first generation, alumni/ae relation, work experience. High school diploma is required and GED is accepted. *Academic units required:* 4 English, 3 math, 3 science, 2 science labs, 2 foreign language, 4 social studies. *Academic units recommended:* 4 math.

Financial Aid

Students should submit: FAFSA. The Princeton Review suggests that all financial aid forms be submitted as soon as possible (see page 5 for a note on the FAFSA). *Need-based scholarships/grants offered:* College/university scholarship or grant aid from institutional funds; Federal Pell; Private scholarships; SEOG; State scholarships/grants. *Loan aid offered:* Direct PLUS loans; Direct Subsidized Loans; Direct Unsubsidized Loans; Federal Nursing Loans. Admitted students will be notified of awards on a rolling basis beginning 11/15. Federal Work-Study Program available. Institutional employment available.

The Inside Word

Admissions officers seek applicants who will best complement life at Moravian. The school is looking for students who have taken a challenging college prep curriculum and have demonstrated that they're ready for collegiate level coursework. Importantly, Moravian is Test Optional and you will not be at a disadvantage if you choose not to submit scores. However, it is highly recommended that you schedule an interview with an admissions counselor if at all possible.

THE SCHOOL SAYS "..."

From the Admissions Office

"America's sixth-oldest university, Moravian University emphasizes the deliberate integration of a broad-based liberal arts curriculum with hands-on learning experiences to effectively prepare its students, not just for jobs, but for successful careers. Moravian University excels at transforming good students into highly competent graduates that are ready to enter the workplace with confidence or shine in graduate school. Students benefit from Moravian University's strong academic majors, opportunities for internships, undergraduate research and scholarship, and programs that foster a deeper enjoyment of life. The 11:1 student-faculty ratio means students get personal attention from a scholarly and dedicated faculty who ensure their success. The proof is in the results, 97 percent of students who earn a bachelor's degree do so in four years. Moravian University issues a MacBook Pro laptop and an iPad to all incoming freshmen to enhance learning and help students gain the 21st-century knowledge and skills that will be transferable over numerous careers. The university offers fifty programs of study; business, education, health professions, social and biological sciences are among the most popular. Moravian University's strong athletics, music, and art programs, and more than eighty clubs and organizations offer healthy physical and creative outlets for every student.

"Located in historic Bethlehem, PA, Moravian University has long history of educating and developing leaders in many fields. Students leave Moravian University with the skills, knowledge, and support necessary to more deeply enjoy life, work, and their role in the world. More than 95 percent of its graduates are employed or attending graduate school within ten months of graduation."

SELECTIVITY

Admissions Rating	84
# of applicants	3,284
% of applicants accepted	67
% of acceptees attending	19
# of early decision applicants	34
% accepted early decision	76

FIRST-YEAR PROFILE

Testing policy	Test Optional
Range SAT composite	1060–1250
Range SAT EBRW	530–630
Range SAT math	530–620
Range ACT composite	21–26
# submitting SAT scores	128
% submitting SAT scores	30
# submitting ACT scores	12
% submitting ACT scores	3
Average HS GPA	3.6
% frosh submitting high school GPA	99
% graduated top 10% of class	21
% graduated top 25% of class	48
% graduated top 50% of class	83

DEADLINES

Early decision	
Deadline	11/15
Notification	12/1
Regular	
Priority	3/1
Deadline	3/1
Notification	Rolling, 11/1
Nonfall registration?	Yes

APPLICANTS OFTEN PREFER
Lehigh University; Penn State University Park; Temple University

APPLICANTS SOMETIMES PREFER
Kutztown University of Pennsylvania; The College of New Jersey; The University of Scranton

APPLICANTS RARELY PREFER
Albright College; Misericordia University; Ramapo College of New Jersey

FINANCIAL FACTS

Financial Aid Rating	83
Annual tuition	$50,069
Room and board	$15,351
Required fees	$1,931
Required fees (first-year)	$2,431
Books and supplies	$1,284
Average frosh need-based scholarship	$34,795
Average UG need-based scholarship	$31,563
% needy frosh rec. need-based scholarship or grant aid	100
% needy UG rec. need-based scholarship or grant aid	96
% needy frosh rec. non-need-based scholarship or grant aid	14
% needy UG rec. non-need-based scholarship or grant aid	15
% needy frosh rec. need-based self-help aid	85
% needy UG rec. need-based self-help aid	84
% frosh rec. any financial aid	100
% UG rec. any financial aid	99
% UG borrow to pay for school	84
Average cumulative indebtedness	$52,504
% frosh need fully met	16
% ugrads need fully met	17
Average % of frosh need met	78
Average % of ugrad need met	76

MOUNT HOLYOKE COLLEGE

50 College Street, South Hadley, MA 01075 • Admissions: 413-538-2000 • Fax: 413-538-2409

CAMPUS LIFE

Quality of Life Rating	88
Fire Safety Rating	91
Green Rating	60*
Type of school	Private
Affiliation	No Affiliation
Environment	Town

STUDENTS

Total undergrad enrollment	2,183
% male/female/another gender	0/100/0
% from out of state	77
% frosh from public high school	66
% frosh live on campus	99
% ugrads live on campus	95
# of sororities	0
% African American	5
% Asian	7
% White	51
% Hispanic	9
% Native American	<1
% Pacific Islander	<1
% Two or more races	5
% Race and/or ethnicity unknown	1
% international	23
# of countries represented	81

SURVEY SAYS . . .

Lots of liberal students
Students always studying
Students are happy
Classroom facilities are great
Lab facilities are great
Great library
Internships are widely available
Great financial aid
No one cheats
Students are friendly
Diverse student types interact on campus
Students environmentally aware
Students aren't religious
Great food on campus
Dorms are like palaces
Theater is popular
Campus newspaper is popular
College radio is popular
Alumni active on campus
Active student government
Active minority support groups
Active student-run political groups
Great food on campus

ACADEMICS

Academic Rating	89
% students returning for sophomore year	90
% students graduating within 4 years	82
% students graduating within 6 years	85
Calendar	Semester
Student/faculty ratio	9:1
Profs interesting rating	95
Profs accessible rating	96

Most classes have 10–19 students.
Most lab/discussion sessions have
   10–19 students.

MOST POPULAR MAJORS
Biology/Biological Sciences, General; Psychology,
General

STUDENTS SAY ". . ."

Academics

The oldest of the Seven Sisters colleges, Mount Holyoke College is a Western Massachusetts private liberal arts college for female, transgender, and nonbinary students. There is "an incredibly wide range of classes and activities at the school," and with such a diverse selection of classes "even if it's a 'traditional' class, it doesn't feel traditional." Forty percent of students are STEM majors, and more than a third of students choose an interdisciplinary major. "Office hours and professor-student relationships are generally excellent and prioritized," and students say that "working closely with faculty is highly encouraged and accessible." There are "lots of great programs, research opportunities, and connections," and "self-scheduled final exams are innovative because they are also student-run and give the students taking finals freedom to decide when they want to go home (if they are leaving campus after finals), how much time they need to study, and what time…works best for them."

Professors "are extremely passionate and respectful of students, often encouraging them to take risks and promoting opportunities." They help students to "engage in collaborative efforts" with project-heavy classes that range from "creating a board game for an anthropology of play class to creating short films for language classes." As one student puts it, "You get the sense that not only are you learning from your professors, but that your professors are also learning from you." Immersive learning is common, and "this happens through field trips to local spots, or through use of our many campus facilities, particularly the art museum, maker space, and library."

Campus Life

At Mount Holyoke College almost all students live on campus in one of eighteen residence halls, and can focus their stay in a Living Learning Community with others who share their academic or extracurricular interests. This produces "a very peaceful environment" where "people like to hang out with friends in low-key settings." There "are an overwhelming number of activities to do," but in a good way; students say "it's easy to get involved AND to have a leadership position." Though you can find off-campus trips and events, students love staying on site: "People spend a lot of time outside here because the campus is just gorgeous. There's often local vendors or college-sponsored events on the green." It helps, too, that "the dining hall is delicious and there is always a variety of many foods." Those looking for a party school should note that's not the vibe here: "students find more entertainment by going thrifting, to a coffee shop, seeing movies, or picnicking" and the "walking paths on campus are very popular."

Student Body

Mount Holyoke has a "culture of smart women and people," and most here "are very studious overall. People are mostly just focused on their studies and then hang out in smallish groups for socialization." There "is a close sense of community amongst Mount Holyoke students," and "you can ask peers you don't know for help and they will do their best for you." Almost a quarter of students are international, and students agree that "college is a great time to get exposed to other parts of the world and other people's experiences." Many here are "outspoken and social justice-oriented" and "Mount Holyoke really helps students build their confidence and hone their unique voices, including their capacity for activism." As a women's college that is gender diverse, Mount Holyoke provides "a very safe queer space and also a very inclusive and welcoming community towards anyone." This open environment makes it so "people are very comfortable to express themselves the way they like, from the way they dress [to] the way they talk, the way they act, and [the way they] stay true to their own values."

MOUNT HOLYOKE COLLEGE

Financial Aid: 413-538-2291 • Website: www.mtholyoke.edu

THE PRINCETON REVIEW SAYS

Admissions

The school reports that its standardized testing policy for use in admission for Fall 2024 is Test Optional. The 2024 testing policy will be permanent. The Princeton Review suggests that interested applicants consult with the school for the most up-to-date standardized testing policies. *Very important factors considered include:* rigor of secondary school record, academic GPA, application essay, recommendation(s). *Important factors considered include:* class rank, interview, extracurricular activities, talent/ability, character/personal qualities, volunteer work, work experience. *Other factors considered include:* standardized test scores, first generation, alumni/ae relation, geographical residence, racial/ethnic status, level of applicant's interest. High school diploma is required and GED is accepted. *Academic units recommended:* 4 English, 3 math, 3 science, 3 science labs, 3 foreign language, 3 history, 1 academic elective.

Financial Aid

Students should submit: CSS/Financial Aid Profile; FAFSA; Noncustodial Profile. Priority filing deadline is 2/1. The Princeton Review suggests that all financial aid forms be submitted as soon as possible (see page 5 for a note on the FAFSA). *Need-based scholarships/grants offered:* College/university scholarship or grant aid from institutional funds; Federal Pell; Private scholarships; SEOG; State scholarships/grants. *Loan aid offered:* Direct PLUS loans; Direct Subsidized Loans; Direct Unsubsidized Loans; College/university loans from institutional funds; State Loans. Admitted students will be notified of awards on or about 4/1. Federal Work-Study Program available. Institutional employment available.

The Inside Word

Competition to gain admission to Mount Holyoke is tight but there are no defined cutoffs or scores; therefore, a strong academic record is a must. Transcripts are evaluated first for performance over time, and candidates should have taken a rigorous course load, complete with honors, AP, and/or IB classes. The college also values strong writing skills, so expect essays/personal statements and short answers to be closely assessed. While interviews are not required they are strongly recommended. Standardized tests are optional, but homeschooled and other students who feel that their application may need more traditional measurements are encouraged to submit scores.

THE SCHOOL SAYS "..."

From the Admissions Office

"The majority of students who choose Mount Holyoke do so because it is an outstanding research liberal arts college. After a semester or two, they start to appreciate the distinctive advantages of a women's college, even though most never thought they'd attend a women's college when they started their college search. They appreciate the remarkable array of opportunities that are available—for academic achievement, career exploration, internships, study abroad, and leadership—and the impressive, creative accomplishments of their peers. If you're looking for a college that will challenge you to be your best, most powerful self and to fulfill your potential, Mount Holyoke should be at the top of your list.

"Submission of standardized test scores is optional for most applicants to Mount Holyoke College. However, the TOEFL is required of students whose primary language is not English."

SELECTIVITY

Admissions Rating	94
# of applicants	4,894
% of applicants accepted	40
% of acceptees attending	28
# offered a place on the wait list	1,085
% accepting a place on wait list	42
% admitted from wait list	2
# of early decision applicants	393
% accepted early decision	62

FIRST-YEAR PROFILE

Testing policy	Test Optional
Range SAT composite	1370–1500
Range SAT EBRW	690–770
Range SAT math	660–770
Range ACT composite	30–34
# submitting SAT scores	233
% submitting SAT scores	43
# submitting ACT scores	106
% submitting ACT scores	19
Average HS GPA	3.9
% frosh submitting high school GPA	84
% graduated top 10% of class	57
% graduated top 25% of class	76
% graduated top 50% of class	99

DEADLINES

Early decision	
Deadline	11/15
Notification	1/1
Other ED deadline	1/1
Other ED notification	2/1
Regular	
Deadline	1/15
Notification	4/1
Nonfall registration?	Yes

APPLICANTS SOMETIMES PREFER

Barnard College; Brandeis University; Bryn Mawr College; New York University; Oberlin College; Smith College; University of California—Berkeley; University of Massachusetts Amherst; University of Vermont; Wellesley College

APPLICANTS RARELY PREFER

American University; Boston University; Clark University; Northeastern University; Scripps College; Skidmore College; University of California—Los Angeles; University of Connecticut; Vassar College; Wesleyan University

FINANCIAL FACTS

Financial Aid Rating	96
Annual tuition	$63,904
Room and board	$18,838
Required fees	$218
Books and supplies	$1,000
Average frosh need-based scholarship	$48,041
Average UG need-based scholarship	$46,978
% needy frosh rec. need-based scholarship or grant aid	100
% needy UG rec. need-based scholarship or grant aid	100
% needy frosh rec. non-need-based scholarship or grant aid	13
% needy UG rec. non-need-based scholarship or grant aid	9
% needy frosh rec. need-based self-help aid	85
% needy UG rec. need-based self-help aid	87
% frosh rec. any financial aid	85
% UG rec. any financial aid	91
% UG borrow to pay for school	59
Average cumulative indebtedness	$23,715
% frosh need fully met	100
% ugrads need fully met	100
Average % of frosh need met	100
Average % of ugrad need met	100

MUHLENBERG COLLEGE

2400 West Chew Street, Allentown, PA 18104-5596 • Admissions: 484-664-3200 • Fax: 484-664-3032

STUDENTS SAY "..."

Academics

Students who attend Muhlenberg College in Allentown, Pennsylvania are welcomed into a "close-knit" community and are privy to "a well-rounded liberal arts education." And while the academics are certainly "rigorous," undergraduates here love the fact it's "[not] a cutthroat atmosphere." Importantly, students have their pick of many terrific disciplines, from the "amazing theater department" to the "extremely strong" business and science programs. Undergrads are also happy to champion their "dedicated" professors who understand how to create and foster "engaging courses." They also value the fact that Muhlenberg instructors "really take the time to get to know you and answer your questions." As one satisfied student interjects, "My professors so far have all been amazing and truly want me to succeed." Finally, as an international studies and Spanish double major sums up, "Muhlenberg is a place where someone can pursue theater AND chemistry, play a varsity sport, AND lead a volunteer organization, work individually with a professor, AND befriend a dining services worker."

Campus Life

It's quite easy to lead a full and fulfilling life at Muhlenberg. To begin with, the "school offers tons of free activities over the weekends, from movie showings to Stuff-A-Plush." Undergrads here also love to take advantage of the college's strong performing arts scene. Indeed, "a cappella groups are very popular at Muhlenberg." Additionally, given "the large theater department," it's virtually guaranteed that "there's always a show in production." Sports are equally popular and we're told that "football and basketball games have good attendance records." While there's a modest amount of drinking, the college doesn't have a crazy party scene. As a biology major shares, "There's a few bars and clubs in the area that offer college nights on Thursdays, which is fun. From time to time, the school hosts theme parties "like flapper-era zombies or a speakeasy (with a live jazz band!)" as well. Lastly, undergrads enjoy Allentown's public parks which provide "great areas to hike, explore, bird-watch, read or take a jog." And they periodically capitalize on Muhlenberg's relatively close proximity to both Philadelphia and New York.

Student Body

Students at Muhlenberg College are described as extremely "hardworking" and "friendly." A French and education double-major explains, "Most people are involved with many different aspects of campus life, and these aspects tend not to be 'cliquey' because of the crossover. For example, there are many football players who are members of a cappella groups or who take dance." Importantly, we're also told that "being nice is kind of important" at Muhlenberg. An English major somewhat sarcastically qualifies, "If someone doesn't hold the door open for the person behind them, they're basically made to wear a scarlet letter and deemed a pariah." The overall demographics have been changing over the last two years, but some students still describe a number of their peers as "white, upper-middle class, [and] from New Jersey." That said, students agree that there's no one fixed type; in fact: "There is a place for everyone on campus. We have a huge theater program, yet almost 30 percent of our school participates in athletics, so you can see there are all extremes and everything in between."

MUHLENBERG COLLEGE

Financial Aid: 484-664-3175 • E-Mail: admissions@muhlenberg.edu • Website: www.muhlenberg.edu

THE PRINCETON REVIEW SAYS

Admissions

The school reports that its standardized testing policy for use in admission for Fall 2024 remains Test Optional, as it has been since 1996. *Very important factors considered include:* rigor of secondary school record, academic GPA, character/personal qualities. *Important factors considered include:* standardized test scores (if applicable), application essay, recommendation(s), interview, extracurricular activities, talent/ability, volunteer work, work experience. *Other factors considered include:* class rank, first generation, alumni/ae relation, geographical residence, racial/ethnic status, level of applicant's interest. High school diploma is required and GED is accepted. *Academic units required:* 4 English, 3 math, 2 science, 2 science labs, 2 foreign language, 2 history, 1 academic elective. *Academic units recommended:* 4 English, 4 math, 3 science, 3 science labs, 2 foreign language, 2 social studies, 2 history, 1 academic elective.

Financial Aid

Students should submit: FAFSA. The Princeton Review suggests that all financial aid forms be submitted as soon as possible (see page 5 for a note on the FAFSA). *Need-based scholarships/grants offered:* College/university scholarship or grant aid from institutional funds; Federal Pell; Private scholarships; SEOG; State scholarships/grants. *Loan aid offered:* Direct PLUS loans; Direct Subsidized Loans; Direct Unsubsidized Loans. Admitted students will be notified of awards shortly after their admissions decision. Federal Work-Study Program available. Institutional employment available.

The Inside Word

Admissions officers at Muhlenberg endeavor to get a strong sense of each candidate. After all, they are seeking students who will thrive at and complement the college. Of course, that being said, academic records are of primary concern. And a strong performance in college prep courses is a must. Applicants wary of standardized tests rejoice; submission of ACT or SAT scores is optional here. Individual interviews are required for academic partnership programs (UPenn Dental and SUNY Optometry), however, we highly recommend interviews for all applicants so that we may get a strong personal sense of each candidate.

THE SCHOOL SAYS "..."

From the Admissions Office

"Listening to our own students, we've learned that most picked Muhlenberg mainly because it has a long-standing reputation for being academically challenging on one hand but personally supportive on the other. We expect a lot from our students, but we also expect a lot from ourselves in providing the challenge and support they need to stretch, grow, and succeed. It's not unusual for professors to put their cell numbers on the course syllabus and encourage students to call them with questions. 'We really know about collegiality here,' says an alumna who now works at Muhlenberg. 'It's that kind of place.' The supportive atmosphere and strong work ethic produce lots of successes. The pre-med and pre-law programs are very strong, as are programs in theatre arts, English, psychology, the sciences, business, and accounting."

NAZARETH UNIVERSITY

4245 East Avenue, Rochester, NY 14618-3790 • Admissions: 585-389-2525 • Fax: 585-586-2452

CAMPUS LIFE

Quality of Life Rating	89
Fire Safety Rating	93
Green Rating	84
Type of school	Private
Affiliation	No Affiliation
Environment	Village

STUDENTS

Total undergrad enrollment	1,978
% male/female/another gender	28/72/0
% from out of state	15
% frosh from public high school	90
% frosh live on campus	89
% ugrads live on campus	55
# of fraternities	0
# of sororities	0
% African American	5
% Asian	2
% White	79
% Hispanic	7
% Native American	<1
% Pacific Islander	0
% Two or more races	3
% Race and/or ethnicity unknown	2
% international	1
# of countries represented	12

SURVEY SAYS . . .
Students are happy
Lab facilities are great
Internships are widely available
Students get along with local community
Students love Rochester, NY
Easy to get around campus
Theater is popular

ACADEMICS

Academic Rating	83
% students returning for sophomore year	82
% students graduating within 4 years	62
% students graduating within 6 years	69
Calendar	Semester
Student/faculty ratio	9:1
Profs interesting rating	89
Profs accessible rating	92

Most classes have 10–19 students.
Most lab/discussion sessions have
10–19 students.

MOST POPULAR MAJORS
Education, General; Physical Therapy/Therapist;
Business Administration, Management and
Operations, Other

STUDENTS SAY "..."

Academics

Nazareth University's four academic colleges are celebrated for their small class sizes and emphasis on social justice. With a low average class size and student to teacher ratio, "everyone can actually work together and hold intellectual conversation that pushes everyone forward." It helps that "the super supportive and open staff makes it easy to communicate and makes you feel free to express yourself entirely." In addition to classes that prioritize dialogue over traditional lectures, education at Nazareth occurs through "hands-on learning and asking lots of questions based off of knowledge that we are collecting on our own as students." One student speaks of creating workshops for local organizations, writing movie reviews, and attending guest lectures for course credit. Another student appreciates feeling like a "person rather than just a number. It is easier to have one-on-one time with peers and professors to get the help I may need." Academic clubs and organizations also aid in this: "I love the amount of help we can receive here."

In line with "preparing students for lives of meaning and purpose," students feel "the school has a commitment to supporting social justice issues and provides many opportunities for students to get real world experiences." Two popular programs are Partners for Serving and Partners for Learning, where students "go out and volunteer at different organizations or schools in the community. This strengthens community ties while also giving students experience outside."

Campus Life

Affectionately known as "Naz," Nazareth offers students a thriving community centered around sports and service. Students love to attend the NCAA Division III soccer and basketball games, along with watching or participating in JV and intramural sports. Students rave about on-campus yoga and Zumba, as well as nearby golf courses. To further support students' emotional well-being, Naz offers Wellness Wednesday and Relaxation Night: "These events help the students grab something to eat and keep them relaxed during stressful times."

Service also factors prominently in students' extracurricular activities. "Helping Hands Club is a volunteer club that meets bi-weekly to participate in a service-based project, such as making dog toys for a local pet shelter or making cards for seniors in a nearby residential home," explains one student. Students also love to enjoy the beauty of their brick, neo-gothic campus, explore nearby Rochester, and stroll along the Erie Canal. "When the weather is nice, there are a lot of very pretty parts of campus to breathe fresh air and study or hang out with friends."

Student Body

"I love my peers," raves one sophomore. "Inside and outside my classes they have always been kind and helpful." Others enthuse that the students at Naz are "kind-hearted, approachable, [and] welcoming." Many students point out that the population is largely—just over 70%—female and some note that groups can feel "segmented" or "cliquey." However, others are quick to point out that everyone is "always wanting to let anyone and everyone know how they are accepted and welcome here."

Student bonds are formed through informal campus events and during classes themselves. One student describes a "broad mix of dance, theater, music, athletes, science, business, and sporty students." One transfer student enjoys that professors foster a close-knit campus community during class, as well: "The professors encourage us to talk in small groups, one-on-one, or to the whole class about ourselves, our worries, our strengths, and our goals. I think this helps us all support each other in our endeavors."

NAZARETH UNIVERSITY

Financial Aid: 585-389-2310 • E-Mail: admissions@naz.edu • Website: www.naz.edu

THE PRINCETON REVIEW SAYS

Admissions

The school reports that its standardized testing policy for use in admission for Fall 2024 is Test Optional. The 2024 testing policy will be permanent. The Princeton Review suggests that interested applicants consult with the school for the most up-to-date standardized testing policies. *Very important factors considered include:* rigor of secondary school record, class rank, academic GPA, application essay, recommendation(s). *Important factors considered include:* interview, extracurricular activities, talent/ability, character/personal qualities, geographical residence, state residency, racial/ethnic status, volunteer work, work experience, level of applicant's interest. *Other factors considered include:* standardized test scores, first generation, alumni/ae relation. High school diploma is required and GED is accepted. *Academic units required:* 4 English, 3 math, 3 science, 1 science lab, 3 foreign language, 3 social studies. *Academic units recommended:* 4 English, 4 math, 4 science, 4 foreign language, 4 social studies.

Financial Aid

Students should submit: FAFSA; State aid form. Priority filing deadline is 2/15. The Princeton Review suggests that all financial aid forms be submitted as soon as possible (see page 5 for a note on the FAFSA). *Need-based scholarships/grants offered:* College/university scholarship or grant aid from institutional funds; Federal Pell; Private scholarships; SEOG; State scholarships/grants. *Loan aid offered:* Direct PLUS loans; Direct Subsidized Loans; Direct Unsubsidized Loans; Federal Nursing Loans. Admitted students will be notified of awards on a rolling basis beginning 2/1. Federal Work-Study Program available. Institutional employment available.

The Inside Word

Applicants to Nazareth are evaluated on a holistic model. Working hard to earn good grades and participating in extracurriculars or being involved with your community will help you stand out and move your application toward the "accepted" pile. The college has been Test Optional since 2008, but submitted scores will be considered alongside other components if you choose to send them along. They may also be used for scholarship opportunities.

THE SCHOOL SAYS "..."

From the Admissions Office

"Nazareth University is the place to become a brave, bold changemaker, committed to progress and growth—within ourselves, within our professions, and for the good of our world. That is why our collective community is known for its strength of impact.

"Located on 150 wooded acres in the village of Pittsford, just outside Rochester, New York, we offer 60 programs of study in sought-after fields, including health professions, business, and the performing arts. We're proud to have 25 Division III athletic teams, over 400 student activities and events yearly, more than 50 student organizations, a 9:1 student-to-faculty ratio, and 39,000 vibrant alumni making a difference across the globe.

"Nazareth Golden Flyers believe in possibility and hope in their studies. It is the pursuit of ideas that propels our students forward, ever learning, ever innovating, until the passion behind those ideas makes us all feel unstoppable.

"Then, as our graduates charge into the world, there's a new and larger community where they will make a mark and give their all, with a confidence that can only come from clarity of task and superb preparation. We encourage everyone on campus to listen, learn, advocate, and innovate to create action constantly. Our students will actively bridge the world's differences and fractures and lead progress by inspiring people's life's work, no matter where it takes them.

"This is Nazareth University. Where changemakers learn to evolve and thrive."

SELECTIVITY

Admissions Rating	85
# of applicants	3,911
% of applicants accepted	84
% of acceptees attending	14
# offered a place on the wait list	36
% accepting a place on wait list	6
% admitted from wait list	0
# of early decision applicants	140
% accepted early decision	91

FIRST-YEAR PROFILE

Testing policy	Test Optional
Range SAT composite	1150–1310
Range SAT EBRW	570–660
Range SAT math	570–660
Range ACT composite	24–28
# submitting SAT scores	136
% submitting SAT scores	29
# submitting ACT scores	26
% submitting ACT scores	6
Average HS GPA	90.4
% frosh submitting high school GPA	100
% graduated top 10% of class	37
% graduated top 25% of class	69
% graduated top 50% of class	92

DEADLINES

Early decision	
Deadline	11/15
Notification	12/1
Regular	
Priority	1/1
Deadline	2/1
Notification	Rolling, 1/1
Nonfall registration?	Yes

APPLICANTS OFTEN PREFER

Ithaca College; St. John Fisher University

APPLICANTS SOMETIMES PREFER

Hobart and William Smith Colleges; Siena College

FINANCIAL FACTS

Financial Aid Rating	86
Annual tuition	$34,850
Room and board	$15,770
Required fees	$1,660
Required fees (first-year)	$1,885
Books and supplies	$1,000
Average frosh need-based scholarship	$22,047
Average UG need-based scholarship	$20,041
% needy frosh rec. need-based scholarship or grant aid	100
% needy UG rec. need-based scholarship or grant aid	100
% needy frosh rec. non-need-based scholarship or grant aid	51
% needy UG rec. non-need-based scholarship or grant aid	41
% needy frosh rec. need-based self-help aid	89
% needy UG rec. need-based self-help aid	91
% frosh rec. any financial aid	100
% UG rec. any financial aid	99
% UG borrow to pay for school	83
Average cumulative indebtedness	$44,804
% frosh need fully met	47
% ugrads need fully met	39
Average % of frosh need met	85
Average % of ugrad need met	83

NEW COLLEGE OF FLORIDA

5800 Bay Shore Rd, Sarasota, FL 34243-2109 • Admissions: 941-487-5000 • Fax: 941-487-5001

This narrative, like all others in this book, is based on student responses and data collected prior to the 2023–2024 academic school year. While these profiles strive to be an accurate depiction of what to expect for the upcoming year, recent developments in the Florida state system may change the academic offerings and overall atmosphere at colleges in the system. Students should check the free online tools for this book (see page vi) for any late-breaking administrative news and they should voice any concerns or questions with the colleges directly.

STUDENTS SAY ". . ."
Academics
New College of Florida, a uniquely small and unconventional public institution, "provides challenging courses for highly self-motivated students who want a large amount of control over their academic choices." It's all about "self-directed learning" here (working closely with faculty advisers, "the student decides what he or she is going to learn and how she is going to learn it"). Those who can balance the intellectual freedom New College offers with the academic accountability it demands, wind up with "a rounded education that enables them to critically and pragmatically examine and understand the world in which we live." The academics "are undeniably awesome" at New College, while the small-school setting and the student body "encourage a love of learning, whether it be academic, political, or hobby-related." It's the sort of school where "it is very popular for groups of students to get together to talk about class readings outside of the classroom." New College undergrads receive "narrative evaluations instead of grades. These evaluations give advice and help us to become better students." Many here "love having written evaluations in which our process and progress are documented, not only the final outcome. The evaluations force students to fully participate and the professors to pay close attention." All students must write a senior thesis to graduate; reports one undergrad, "recently we had a survey…on which one of the sections dealt with the possibility of making the senior thesis optional. There was an overwhelming response that this was unacceptable. I think that says a lot about how proud we are of our academic standards."

Campus Life
Having fun "in a glorified retirement community requires ingenuity of the New College student population," but "thankfully, most grew up in suburban Florida" and so are used to a slower pace. It helps that the campus is near Lido and Siesta Beaches, "where [students] enjoy unlimited swimming, sunning, and Frisbee playing," and that "downtown Sarasota isn't that bad either," since it's home to a number of "ethnic eateries. Thai food, in particular, seems to have a cult following on campus—with constant debate as to which restaurant is the best or most authentic and student events that advertise Thai food are bound to pull in dozens of followers." On campus, students enjoy everything "from club meetings to public speakers to 'hip' bands playing shows. There's usually something to do and usually free food to be found!" There are also "school-wide parties…in a courtyard outside of the dorms. Different students get to decide the theme of each dance party and the music to be played. Most on-campus students never leave campus during the weekend because of these dance parties."

Student Body
New College students share "a few things in common: Most…are friendly, passionate about the things they believe in, very hard workers, liberal, and most of all, try to be open to new experiences." Thirty percent of the population are students of color. You'll find that students on campus are "largely…liberal." There are of course exceptions, but the school is rather small and there is "a fairly strong [LGBTQ] community here, and many transgendered people who have decided to make New College their coming-out grounds. The student body is generally aware of gender issues and respectful of {LGBTQ} people of all types."

NEW COLLEGE OF FLORIDA

Financial Aid: 941-487-5000 • E-Mail: admissions@ncf.edu • Website: www.ncf.edu

THE PRINCETON REVIEW SAYS

Admissions

The school reports that its standardized testing policy for use in admission for Fall 2024 is SAT or ACT Required. The 2024 testing policy will be permanent. The Princeton Review suggests that interested applicants consult with the school for the most up-to-date standardized testing policies. *Very important factors considered include:* rigor of secondary school record, academic GPA. *Important factors considered include:* class rank, standardized test scores, application essay, character/personal qualities. *Other factors considered include:* recommendation(s), extracurricular activities, talent/ability, first generation, alumni/ae relation, geographical residence, state residency, volunteer work, work experience, level of applicant's interest. High school diploma is required and GED is accepted. *Academic units required:* 4 English, 4 math, 3 science, 2 science labs, 2 foreign language, 3 social studies, 2 academic electives. *Academic units recommended:* 4 English, 4 math, 4 science, 4 science labs, 4 foreign language, 4 social studies, 1 computer science, 2 visual/performing arts, 2 academic electives.

Financial Aid

Students should submit: FAFSA. Priority filing deadline is 11/1. The Princeton Review suggests that all financial aid forms be submitted as soon as possible (see page 5 for a note on the FAFSA). *Need-based scholarships/grants offered:* College/university scholarship or grant aid from institutional funds; Federal Pell; Private scholarships; SEOG; State scholarships/grants. *Loan aid offered:* Direct PLUS loans; Direct Subsidized Loans; Direct Unsubsidized Loans. Admitted students will be notified of awards on a rolling basis beginning 1/15. Federal Work-Study Program available. Institutional employment available.

The Inside Word

New College isn't your typical public school. Freethinking students tend to thrive here, and the admissions staff knows that. Don't be afraid to showcase your individuality; it won't get you in here if your academics aren't top flight, but it certainly won't hurt you either.

THE SCHOOL SAYS "..."

From the Admissions Office

"Deep curiosity, inspired individualism, civic-mindedness, and a dash of quirkiness. New College students collaborate with their professors to build a program of courses, seminars, and independent and group projects to meet their individual needs and interests. The result? A remarkably rigorous and engaging education (with highly affordable tuition). New College students apply theories and methods they learn in the classroom to research and creative work of their own design. While learning to organize and execute large projects, they sharpen their critical thinking—a skill set that serves them well in grad school and the world beyond higher education. The social atmosphere is relaxed and intellectually playful; the campus celebrates creativity, service, and the value of the individual. New College welcomes admitted students to visit "in depth"—arrange to talk and tour, attend a class, perhaps lunch with a current student before making the decision to enroll. Application Materials (November 1 Priority Deadline): Common Application (with fee/fee waiver), Self-Reported Student Academic Report (SSAR), and SAT or ACT scores. Some college transfers can have exam scores waived—please inquire. International applicants and applicants with materials from abroad, should inquire about additional materials needed. Financial Aid (November 1 Priority FAFSA Deadline): If you seek need-based grants and/or federal student loans, please complete the Free Application for Federal Student Aid. In addition to packaging need-based aid, the College offers scholarship funding to nearly all of its entering students."

SELECTIVITY

Admissions Rating	85
# of applicants	1,830
% of applicants accepted	75
% of acceptees attending	14
# offered a place on the wait list	1

FIRST-YEAR PROFILE

Testing policy	SAT or ACT Required
Range SAT composite	1123–1340
Range SAT EBRW	580–710
Range SAT math	523–650
Range ACT composite	24–31
# submitting SAT scores	140
% submitting SAT scores	74
# submitting ACT scores	65
% submitting ACT scores	35
Average HS GPA	4.0
% frosh submitting high school GPA	98
% graduated top 10% of class	29
% graduated top 25% of class	56
% graduated top 50% of class	93

DEADLINES

Early action	
Deadline	12/1
Notification	12/15
Regular	
Priority	11/1
Deadline	4/15
Nonfall registration?	No

APPLICANTS ALSO LOOK AT

Eckerd College; Florida International University; Florida State University; Mount Holyoke College; Rollins College; St. John's College (NM); University of Central Florida; University of Florida; University of North Florida; University of South Florida

FINANCIAL FACTS

Financial Aid Rating	88
Annual in-state tuition	$6,916
Annual out-of-state tuition	$29,944
Room and board	$10,291
Books and supplies	$1,200
Average frosh need-based scholarship	$13,540
Average UG need-based scholarship	$12,831
% needy frosh rec. need-based scholarship or grant aid	99
% needy UG rec. need-based scholarship or grant aid	97
% needy frosh rec. non-need-based scholarship or grant aid	26
% needy UG rec. non-need-based scholarship or grant aid	20
% needy frosh rec. need-based self-help aid	51
% needy UG rec. need-based self-help aid	58
% frosh rec. any financial aid	99
% UG rec. any financial aid	95
% UG borrow to pay for school	37
Average cumulative indebtedness	$15,113
% frosh need fully met	44
% ugrads need fully met	37
Average % of frosh need met	96
Average % of ugrad need met	90

NEW JERSEY INSTITUTE OF TECHNOLOGY

University Heights, Newark, NJ 07102 • Admissions: 973-596-3000 • Fax: 973-596-3300

STUDENTS SAY "..."

Academics

At the New Jersey Institute of Technology, students are "learning on an ivy league level," getting "practical career-focused education" at "a fairly affordable price." Known for their "very rigorous" general education requirements, "particularly [in] math," NJIT specializes in STEM, engineering, and architecture programs. Undergrads should be prepared to put the time in, as "their programs are increasingly difficult and challenging," but these efforts pay off, as "everything [students] learn is applied and tangible." Most majors allow soon-to-be graduates to put their academics into practice with a senior capstone, "where students are connected to companies or professors and given the opportunity to apply their skills over the course of a semester or a whole year." The architecture program, which focuses on innovation and research, encourages "using and learning new programs to portray ideas...trying new apps, sites, or methods of doing your work." It is "one of a select few colleges where students can get an architecture license in New Jersey," and it rounds their program out with site visits and a "Makerspace" facility "dedicated to student projects and research." Given the innovative approach to education, it's no wonder many feel like NJIT is setting them up to be "the best they can be."

Campus Life

"Most if not all of the student body is actively involved in some type of club, research, or studying. It is an academically brilliant campus and even the extracurriculars reflect that." At NJIT, "there are an abundance of clubs and research opportunities to apply what you've learned, so everything comes around full-circle." Particularly popular are "major related clubs that allow us to branch and do more hands-on learning and experience the field in [the] real world." Many students also share "standard nerd interests and hobbies" like video games, anime, and e-sports. Among NJIT's roster of extracurriculars are also Greek life, student government, "where we can actually make a difference as students," cultural clubs, environmental clubs, professional business and architecture organizations, and community service opportunities. "For freshmen orientation, they took us around Newark and we actually helped repair and set up schools," one student recounts.

While on campus, students like to "spend time in lounges in the dorm buildings or academic buildings," but say "campus culture is a little sparse." NJIT's "campus definitely has an urban feel and there is not much green space." Students don't have to rush to class, though, as "[t]he campus is very small and compact, you can walk across in less than 10 minutes." Although the surrounding city of "Newark itself is a pretty rough city," it is "safe during the day," and students don't worry for their safety, as "campus is patrolled very well." Students also enjoy the proximity to New York City, which is "about half an hour away by train."

Student Body

The New Jersey Institute of Technology harbors an "extremely diverse student body" which is "unified by their focus on finding professional success after graduation." Although "predominantly male," NJIT remains "ethnically and culturally diverse" with "many international students as well as a wide variety of people with different interests, hobbies, majors, and backgrounds" and "many coming as first-generation college students."

As "a very competitive group of people," it comes as no surprise that "most students are academically oriented." However, this doesn't mean that undergrads don't get along. "My peers have always been nice, funny, and cool," one student writes. "The student body at NJIT are some of the brightest inquisitive minds I've ever come across," says another. "Everyone is either engrossed in research, club teams, or studying diligently...the students here genuinely want to make a difference in the world." Although "the majority are commuters," this continually inventive student body has no trouble connecting with each other. "The norm is for students to connect through social media apps for support through classes." With the rest of the student body often just a text away, one student says, "I have never felt alone in any of my course[s]."

NEW JERSEY INSTITUTE OF TECHNOLOGY

Financial Aid: 973-596-3479 • E-Mail: admissions@njit.edu • Website: www.njit.edu

THE PRINCETON REVIEW SAYS

Admissions

The school reports that its standardized testing policy for use in admission for Fall 2024 is Test Optional. It is unknown at this time if the 2024 testing policy will be permanent. The Princeton Review suggests that interested applicants consult with the school for the most up-to-date standardized testing policies. *Very important factors considered include:* rigor of secondary school record, class rank. *Important factors considered include:* academic GPA. *Other factors considered include:* standardized test scores, recommendation(s), extracurricular activities, talent/ability, character/personal qualities, alumni/ae relation, geographical residence, state residency, level of applicant's interest. High school diploma is required and GED is accepted. *Academic units required:* 4 English, 4 math, 2 science, 2 science labs. *Academic units recommended:* 2 foreign language, 1 social studies, 1 history, 2 academic electives.

Financial Aid

Students should submit: FAFSA. Priority filing deadline is 2/15. The Princeton Review suggests that all financial aid forms be submitted as soon as possible (see page 5 for a note on the FAFSA). *Need-based scholarships/grants offered:* College/university scholarship or grant aid from institutional funds; Federal Pell; Private scholarships; SEOG; State scholarships/grants. *Loan aid offered:* Direct PLUS loans; Direct Subsidized Loans; Direct Unsubsidized Loans; State Loans. Admitted students will be notified of awards on a rolling basis. Federal Work-Study Program available. Institutional employment available.

The Inside Word

Admission officers at NJIT look for innovative applicants who are committed to not only their academic success but have dreams of a compelling future career. A solid GPA, improved grade trends, and advanced coursework will help make your case. Additionally, while the school remains Test Optional for Fall 2024, good test scores can also assist you on your road to acceptance. Equally important are your extracurriculars. Those who also pursue their passions, illustrate a go-getter attitude, and get involved stand the best chance of admission.

THE SCHOOL SAYS "..."

From the Admissions Office

"Talented high school graduates from across the nation come to NJIT to prepare for leadership roles in architecture, business, engineering, medical, legal, science, and technological fields. Students experience a public research university conducting over $160 million in research that maintains a small-college atmosphere at a modest cost. Our attractive forty-five-acre campus is just minutes from New York City and less than an hour from the Jersey shore. Students find an outstanding faculty and a safe, diverse, and caring learning and residential community. NJIT's academic environment challenges and prepares students for rewarding careers and full-time advanced study after graduation. The campus is computing-intensive."

SELECTIVITY
Admissions Rating	88
# of applicants	13,010
% of applicants accepted	66
% of acceptees attending	18

FIRST-YEAR PROFILE
Testing policy	Test Optional
Range SAT composite	1220–1460
Range SAT EBRW	580–700
Range SAT math	610–700
Range ACT composite	27–33
# submitting SAT scores	633
% submitting SAT scores	40
# submitting ACT scores	61
% submitting ACT scores	4
Average HS GPA	3.8
% frosh submitting high school GPA	87
% graduated top 10% of class	15
% graduated top 25% of class	29
% graduated top 50% of class	40

DEADLINES
Early action	
Deadline	11/15
Notification	12/15
Regular	
Priority	12/15
Deadline	3/1
Notification	Rolling, 11/15
Nonfall registration?	Yes

FINANCIAL FACTS
Financial Aid Rating	79
Annual in-state tuition	$14,448
Annual out-of-state tuition	$30,160
Room and board	$13,900
Required fees	$3,226
Books and supplies	$2,900
Average frosh need-based scholarship	$15,098
Average UG need-based scholarship	$13,390
% needy frosh rec. need-based scholarship or grant aid	96
% needy UG rec. need-based scholarship or grant aid	96
% needy frosh rec. non-need-based scholarship or grant aid	7
% needy UG rec. non-need-based scholarship or grant aid	5
% needy frosh rec. need-based self-help aid	44
% needy UG rec. need-based self-help aid	55
% frosh rec. any financial aid	89
% UG rec. any financial aid	69
% UG borrow to pay for school	53
Average cumulative indebtedness	$28,089
% frosh need fully met	11
% ugrads need fully met	8
Average % of frosh need met	57
Average % of ugrad need met	51

NEW YORK UNIVERSITY

70 Washington Square South, New York, NY 10012 • Admissions: 212-998-1212 • Fax: 212-995-4902

CAMPUS LIFE

Quality of Life Rating	**85**
Fire Safety Rating	**99**
Green Rating	**99**
Type of school	Private
Affiliation	No Affiliation
Environment	Metropolis

STUDENTS

Total undergrad enrollment	29,136
% male/female/another gender	41/59/NR
% from out of state	67
% frosh live on campus	83
% ugrads live on campus	40
# of fraternities (% join)	12 (1)
# of sororities (% join)	12 (3)
% African American	8
% Asian	20
% White	22
% Hispanic	17
% Native American	<1
% Pacific Islander	<1
% Two or more races	4
% Race and/or ethnicity unknown	4
% international	26
# of countries represented	156

SURVEY SAYS . . .

Internships are widely available
Students love New York, NY
Theater is popular
Active student government
Active student-run political groups

ACADEMICS

Academic Rating	**84**
% students returning for sophomore year	95
% students graduating within 4 years	78
% students graduating within 6 years	87
Calendar	Semester
Student/faculty ratio	8:1
Profs interesting rating	87
Profs accessible rating	89

Most classes have 10–19 students.
Most lab/discussion sessions have
  10–19 students.

MOST POPULAR MAJORS

Business/Commerce, General; Liberal Arts and
Sciences/Liberal Studies; Drama and Dramatics/
Theatre Arts, General

STUDENTS SAY "..."

Academics

Students speak highly of the opportunities to be found at New York University, where "there are no limits to what kind of career you can pursue." From career fairs to tech panels, industry nights, and corporate visits, undergrads are always building toward tangible goals, sometimes literally so, as with the school's Vertically Integrated Projects (VIPs)—"the exact answer to the demands of experiential learning outside of the classroom"—one of which had students working as a team to build a steel bridge capable of supporting 2,500 pounds. Even the most standard lectures often benefit from "new media tech being integrated into classrooms" and there are plenty of "mandatory labs that allow for more hands-on learning," as well as "some sort of out-of-classroom element [like] trips to the [Metropolitan Museum of Art], viewing apartment listings as part of a Financial Engineering course, and so on!" Additionally, "there are various seminars that are constantly held where students can see the important work their professors are doing in engineering, medicine, science, and much more. For example, I have a professor who conducts research testing out different nanotechnology to assist in the process of drug delivery."

Undergrads gush that "professors for the most part are top notch and seem to genuinely care about their students." They also tend to be "very well-educated" and "experts in their field," with "real work experiences in the content that they teach that significantly improves the classroom discussions and interactions." Assignments are "challenging yet manageable," and students feel their professors are "making sure that everyone has the opportunity to do well in their classes."

Campus Life

NYU students recognize that "our campus is [New York City,] so there is always something to keep us busy." For instance, "We can go to fashion or literary related events, attend demonstrations for justice…or just relax in one of the many parks." The university itself also manages to captivate undergrads with exciting extracurricular options that allow respondents to compete or "connect with students outside of my major and have great fun." From K-pop dance groups to snowboarding clubs and a space exploration society, there are also numerous "volunteer clubs, including one that delivers leftover food from the NYU dining halls to homeless shelters." Given all that, "Greek life exists, but it's not big on campus." One undergrad elaborates, "There are not a lot of frat parties, but people like to have parties in their apartments or go out to bars in the city." And of course, nothing beats simply "sitting in Washington Square Park on a nice day and just people watching."

Student Body

Like the city it calls home, the university is "a real mixing pot of cultures of people from different backgrounds…both socially and geographically." With over twenty percent of students coming from international backgrounds, it's not unusual to report that "more of my friends are from outside of the country than from the U.S." Of course, while they might have grown up under vastly different circumstances, one thing that unites them is that they're "very career and passion oriented; the student community isn't afraid to say what their dreams are." Indeed, "it's rare to meet so many academically driven students who are genuinely special and unique in their creative ambitions, which is what sets the NYU student body apart from most other top universities." Undergrads also applaud their peers for being "incredibly curious about how the world works," emphasizing that "they're always looking for ways to improve and connect the community." Some students feel that NYU is "more disconnected than other universities" and find themselves looking for more of an athletic presence beyond the standard NCAA Division III offerings, but others note that "there are so many opportunities to make friends through [school] events" that it doesn't matter. As one puts it, "NYU students are all welcoming and are friendly to anyone."

NEW YORK UNIVERSITY

Financial Aid: 212-998-4444 • E-Mail: admissions@nyu.edu • Website: www.nyu.edu

THE PRINCETON REVIEW SAYS

Admissions

The school reports that its standardized testing policy for use in admission for Fall 2024 is Test Flexible. The 2024 testing policy will be temporary. The Princeton Review suggests that interested applicants consult with the school for the most up-to-date standardized testing policies. *Very important factors considered include:* rigor of secondary school record, class rank, academic GPA, standardized test scores, talent/ability. *Important factors considered include:* application essay, recommendation(s), extracurricular activities, character/personal qualities. *Other factors considered include:* interview, first generation, alumni/ae relation, geographical residence, racial/ethnic status, volunteer work, work experience, level of applicant's interest. High school diploma is required and GED is accepted. *Academic units required:* 4 English, 3 math, 3 science, 3 science labs, 3 foreign language, 3 social studies, 3 history. *Academic units recommended:* 4 English, 4 math, 4 science, 4 science labs, 4 foreign language, 4 social studies, 4 history.

Financial Aid

Students should submit: CSS/Financial Aid Profile; FAFSA; Noncustodial Profile. The Princeton Review suggests that all financial aid forms be submitted as soon as possible (see page 5 for a note on the FAFSA). *Need-based scholarships/grants offered:* College/university scholarship or grant aid from institutional funds; Federal Nursing Scholarships; Federal Pell; Private scholarships; SEOG; State scholarships/grants. *Loan aid offered:* Direct PLUS loans; Direct Subsidized Loans; Direct Unsubsidized Loans; College/university loans from institutional funds; Federal Nursing Loans. Admitted students will be notified of awards on or about 4/15. Federal Work-Study Program available. Institutional employment available.

The Inside Word

Undergraduates can apply to more than one of NYU's degree-granting campuses. If you are interested in the New York Campus, you must also apply to one of NYU's undergraduate schools and colleges: the College of Arts and Science; the Tandon School of Engineering; the Liberal Studies Program; the Stern School of Business; Meyers College of Nursing; the Gallatin School of Individualized Study; the Silver School of Social Work; the Steinhardt School of Culture, Education, and Human Development; the Tisch School of the Arts; or the School of Professional Studies. This is different from the application process at some universities and obviously requires some forethought. Remember that this is a highly competitive university; if your application doesn't reflect a serious interest in your intended area of study, your chances of gaining admission will be diminished. NYU has a flexible testing policy that includes SAT or ACT, IB, AP, and many international examinations; in some cases an audition or portfolio can be submitted in lieu of standardized testing.

THE SCHOOL SAYS "..."

From the Admissions Office

"NYU is the University without walls. We remove the boundary between your classroom and the real world to open limitless opportunities. That's why NYU has become one of the most influential universities in the world with campuses in 15 major cities across the globe including New York, Abu Dhabi, Shanghai, London, Madrid, and Washington, D.C. Our expansive global network directly serves our students by allowing a uniquely rich academic experience led by renowned faculty with accolades ranging from the Nobel Prize and MacArthur Genius Grant to Emmy, Oscar, and Grammy Awards. But our community is more than a list of cities and fancy awards. Since our beginning in 1831, we've been champions of diversity, access, and inclusion, creating one of the most diverse student bodies on Earth with no single ethnic majority and students from over 150 countries. NYU is for risk-takers; for the bold, the curious, the innovative, for those that see a problem and find the solution simply because "we have to." For more than 180 years, we have produced some of the brightest minds, ground-breaking research, and most influential people capable of being comfortable anywhere and effective everywhere."

SELECTIVITY

Admissions Rating	98
# of applicants	100,662
% of applicants accepted	12
% of acceptees attending	49

FIRST-YEAR PROFILE

Testing policy	Test Flexible
Range SAT composite	1470–1560
Range SAT EBRW	720–770
Range SAT math	750–800
Range ACT composite	33–35
# submitting SAT scores	1,627
% submitting SAT scores	26
# submitting ACT scores	688
% submitting ACT scores	11
Average HS GPA	3.8
% frosh submitting high school GPA	99

DEADLINES

Early decision	
Deadline	11/1
Notification	12/15
Other ED deadline	1/1
Other ED notification	2/15
Regular	
Deadline	1/5
Notification	4/1
Nonfall registration?	Yes

FINANCIAL FACTS

Financial Aid Rating	79
Annual tuition	$58,128
Room and board	$20,272
Books and supplies	$1,494
Average frosh need-based scholarship	$53,790
Average UG need-based scholarship	$43,939
% needy frosh rec. need-based scholarship or grant aid	100
% needy UG rec. need-based scholarship or grant aid	93
% needy frosh rec. non-need-based scholarship or grant aid	12
% needy UG rec. non-need-based scholarship or grant aid	3
% needy frosh rec. need-based self-help aid	82
% needy UG rec. need-based self-help aid	83
% UG borrow to pay for school	33
Average cumulative indebtedness	$26,388
% frosh need fully met	96
% ugrads need fully met	29
Average % of frosh need met	99
Average % of ugrad need met	65

NORTH CAROLINA STATE UNIVERSITY

Box 7001, Raleigh, NC 27695 • Admissions: 919-515-2011 • Fax: 919-515-5039

STUDENTS SAY "..."

Academics

The "largest and most diverse" of North Carolina's public university system, NC State provides undergrads with a "high-level education" and "great value." The campus rings with a "welcoming, down-to-earth" vibe and "Wolfpack pride" is certainly infectious. Moreover, the university maintains "opportunities to fit every single type of person no matter their interest." Academically, NC State is home to a stellar engineering school that students contend is "the best engineering program in the state of North Carolina." It offers "world-renowned faculty who conduct innovative and cutting edge research in a plethora of scientific fields." Undergrads also like to emphasize the "exceptionally rigorous" design program, which is "small and personal." And we'd certainly be remiss if we didn't mention the "fantastic business school" and "great entrepreneurship program" it has developed. Inside the classroom, students find their professors to be "very enthusiastic about what they teach" and appreciate that they truly "challenge you to think." As one satisfied junior adds, "My professors are extremely knowledgeable about the course material and bring in practical demonstrations to bring the lecture to life." And just as important, "professors love to discuss future professional development plans with undergraduate students." All in all, it's highly evident that "professors and TAs here love their jobs." Simply put, "they want you to succeed."

Campus Life

Students proffer that NC State's campus is always abuzz with activity. Athletics are extremely popular here, and it often feels as though "basketball games and football games are almost required [viewing]." And, naturally, these contests are accompanied by "a large tailgate culture." Additionally, the university "sponsors many different programs, ranging from concerts to a movie at the campus cinema every weekend." And there are "quite a few service and community-oriented activities that go on around campus, such as Shack-A-Thon for Habitat for Humanity and the Krispy Kreme Challenge for children's hospitals." Students also love to take advantage of the surrounding area. As one first-year tells us, "Hillsborough Street has a lot of fun restaurants to go to when we want to go out and do things. Also, there [are] lots of [places] to go to the movies and shop right outside of campus." Indeed, the "Raleigh-area is full of things to do from concerts, bars, shows, restaurants, museums, malls, etc." As another first-year sums up life at NC State, "The problem isn't finding something to do, it is finding time to do it all [while] manag[ing] to stay on task and put aside time to study."

Student Body

When you first step onto the campus of NC State, "first impressions might make it seem like everyone there is a sorority girl or a frat guy who all wear cowboy boots and come from rural NC." However, "if you look closely, [you'll see a] very diverse campus with lots of opportunities." Indeed, you'll find a range from "hipster to farm boy" and everything in between. Of course, no matter the easy or convenient characterization, most undergrads agree that their peers are "welcoming" and "friendly." Students tell us that "fitting in is super easy and getting involved with any of the many programs on campus help[s] with meeting new people and making friends!" And while most students are "devoted to academics," they all still manage to "go out and have fun." Additionally, undergrads say their peers "are service oriented and always think of creative ways to give back." Finally, as one junior reveals, "NCSU is huge, so every person can find a spot—and when you do, you find a family. To me, it doesn't feel like a large school. I see someone I know walking on campus every day. I don't know anyone, particularly those that began their education living on campus, that hasn't found their niche."

NORTH CAROLINA STATE UNIVERSITY

Financial Aid: 919-515-2421 • E-Mail: undergrad-admissions@ncsu.edu • Website: www.ncsu.edu/

THE PRINCETON REVIEW SAYS

Admissions

The school reports that its standardized testing policy for use in admission for Fall 2024 is Test Optional. The 2024 testing policy will be temporary. The Princeton Review suggests that interested applicants consult with the school for the most up-to-date standardized testing policies. *Very important factors considered include:* rigor of secondary school record, class rank, academic GPA. *Other factors considered include:* standardized test scores, application essay, recommendation(s), extracurricular activities, talent/ability, character/personal qualities, first generation, alumni/ae relation, geographical residence, state residency, racial/ethnic status, volunteer work, work experience, level of applicant's interest. High school diploma is required and GED is accepted. *Academic units required:* 4 English, 4 math, 3 science, 1 science lab, 2 foreign language, 1 social studies, 1 U.S. history. *Academic units recommended:* 4 English, 4 math, 3 science, 1 science lab, 2 foreign language, 1 social studies, 1 U.S. history.

Financial Aid

Students should submit: FAFSA. Priority filing deadline is 3/1. The Princeton Review suggests that all financial aid forms be submitted as soon as possible (see page 5 for a note on the FAFSA). *Need-based scholarships/grants offered:* College/university scholarship or grant aid from institutional funds; Federal Pell; Private scholarships; SEOG; State scholarships/grants; United Negro College Fund. *Loan aid offered:* Direct PLUS loans; Direct Subsidized Loans; Direct Unsubsidized Loans; College/university loans from institutional funds; State Loans. Admitted students will be notified of awards on a rolling basis beginning 4/1. Federal Work-Study Program available. Institutional employment available.

The Inside Word

As one of the nation's top research universities, NC State maintains a competitive admissions process. Successful applicants take a rigorous course load and often have a B-plus average or better. Admissions officers also closely weigh GPA, class rank and rigor of secondary school record. Extracurricular activities are of secondary importance.

THE SCHOOL SAYS "..."

From the Admissions Office

"Students choose NC State University for its strong and varied academic programs, national reputation for excellence and friendly atmosphere. Consistently rated best value in North Carolina, NC State is located in Raleigh, the capital of the state, and is minutes away from nationally known Research Triangle Park, providing access to unlimited internships and co-op opportunities. NC State degrees earn the top return on student investment among North Carolina's public universities, and job recruiters rate our alumni among the top 20 most attractive job candidates in the country. Our students thrive with the benefits of a large school, but love the tight-knit feel of our community. NC State offers more than 100 majors and 120 minors, over 600 clubs and organizations, the opportunity to study abroad and engage in research so students have the opportunity to explore all their interests. Members of the Wolfpack aren't only successful—they're passionate. With 23 Division I sports and lifelong traditions, NC State students feel the power of the Pack from the roaring stadiums to the support on campus to the strong network of alumni. Once you're part of the Pack, you're a member for life."

SELECTIVITY

Admissions Rating	93
# of applicants	35,420
% of applicants accepted	47
% of acceptees attending	33
# offered a place on the wait list	7,439
% accepting a place on wait list	36
% admitted from wait list	0

FIRST-YEAR PROFILE

Testing policy	Test Optional
Range SAT composite	1260–1420
Range SAT EBRW	620–700
Range SAT math	625–674
Range ACT composite	24–31
# submitting SAT scores	1,664
% submitting SAT scores	30
# submitting ACT scores	2,194
% submitting ACT scores	40
Average HS GPA	3.8
% frosh submitting high school GPA	97
% graduated top 10% of class	46
% graduated top 25% of class	85
% graduated top 50% of class	99

DEADLINES

Early action	
Deadline	11/1
Notification	1/30
Regular	
Deadline	1/15
Notification	3/30
Nonfall registration?	Yes

APPLICANTS ALSO LOOK AT

Appalachian State University; Clemson University;
University of North Carolina—Chapel Hill;
Virginia Tech

FINANCIAL FACTS

Financial Aid Rating	85
Annual in-state tuition	$6,535
Annual out-of-state tuition	$28,276
Room and board	$12,748
Required fees	$2,593
Books and supplies	$854
Average frosh need-based scholarship	$11,526
Average UG need-based scholarship	$10,883
% needy frosh rec. need-based scholarship or grant aid	97
% needy UG rec. need-based scholarship or grant aid	94
% needy frosh rec. non-need-based scholarship or grant aid	22
% needy UG rec. non-need-based scholarship or grant aid	19
% needy frosh rec. need-based self-help aid	66
% needy UG rec. need-based self-help aid	65
% frosh rec. any financial aid	66
% UG rec. any financial aid	66
% UG borrow to pay for school	47
Average cumulative indebtedness	$24,042
% frosh need fully met	26
% ugrads need fully met	27
Average % of frosh need met	76
Average % of ugrad need met	76

NORTHEASTERN UNIVERSITY

360 Huntington Avenue, Boston, MA 02115 • Admissions: 617-373-2000 • Fax: 617-373-8780

STUDENTS SAY "..."

Academics

Founded in 1898, Northeastern University is an old Boston stalwart, but its "globally-minded and career-focused" approach to education is as current as ever. The school's focus on experiential learning is never more apparent than in the co-op programs, which have been around for more than 100 years. In these, students alternate rigorous classes with full-time work in career-related jobs for six months (during which they do not pay tuition and are often paid), providing "an open-minded, explorative environment where real-life work experience...combined with top-level academics to provide the best preparation possible for students post-college." Often, students receive job offers from previous co-op employers upon graduation. "My overall academic experience has been pretty grueling but completely worth it," says one satisfied student of the "strong academics in conjunction with a reasonable and healthy atmosphere."

On top of the "strong academic pipeline to university-cultivated co-ops and jobs," students benefit from professors who are "passionate about the subject and about you learning the subject." While students admit that there are a handful of "not-so-great professors," they say "the ones that are great, however, are fabulous," elaborating that "they always offer help or ways to give you experience, are there for you in and outside the classroom, and are extremely intelligent." Students love how encouraging both the university and the faculty are, pushing students to study abroad, do a dialogue (a Northeastern global/international summer program that focuses on critical current issues), or complete an international co-op—"anything to experience another culture and be fully emerged in it," one student notes. Different majors benefit from unique integration of their programs with co-op learning, and the way that Northeastern "[marries] theory with practicality," no matter the course of study, is a huge benefit to students throughout their post-graduate lives.

Campus Life

There is certainly no lack of activities in which to participate in nearby Boston (there are four T stops on campus), from movie theaters, museums, restaurants, and shopping malls to the Prudential Center and the Charles River, which "provides opportunities for running, walking, biking, [and] kayaking." One student happily notes that "our location means that I can get dumplings in Chinatown, see a show, or attend the Christmas tree lighting without much effort to get off campus." Weekends are traditionally for city exploring, and weekdays usually are filled with people participating in one of the many clubs the school offers. Plus, Northeastern has "a ton of amazing events and programs on campus that make the campus feel like a community." Students on co-op "tend to have a lot more free time at night and on the weekends, allowing them to get more involved and spend more time with friends." Still, life outside of school is "pretty substantial" for this "extremely social" crowd: Mission Hill is a popular spot for a Friday and Saturday night activities. Greek life is small but "becoming more popular" on campus.

Student Body

Northeastern is "both incredibly diverse as well as being a quintessential New England school." This environment is filled with many people from different backgrounds (including a sizable international population), and "it's not unusual to hear ten languages in ten minutes walking across campus." People are "motivated and passionate about the issues or projects they care about" and "are implementing and rolling with those ideas." No one here is cookie-cutter in any way, as "everyone has their quirks and qualities that shine through." All are "very supportive and seem to genuinely care about each other," which is useful since the nature of the school requires quite a few independent student decisions and those who go here "quickly have to become an adult and take charge of [their] life."

NORTHEASTERN UNIVERSITY

Financial Aid: 617-373-3190 • E-Mail: admissions@northeastern.edu • Website: www.northeastern.edu/

THE PRINCETON REVIEW SAYS

Admissions

The school reports that its standardized testing policy for use in admission for Fall 2024 is Test Optional. It is unknown at this time if the 2024 testing policy will be permanent. The Princeton Review suggests that interested applicants consult with the school for the most up-to-date standardized testing policies. *Very important factors considered include:* rigor of secondary school record, academic GPA, standardized test scores, application essay, recommendation(s). *Important factors considered include:* extracurricular activities, talent/ability, character/personal qualities, volunteer work, work experience. *Other factors considered include:* class rank, first generation, geographical residence, racial/ethnic status, level of applicant's interest. High school diploma is required and GED is accepted. *Academic units required:* 4 English, 3 math, 3 science, 2 science labs, 2 foreign language, 3 social studies, 2 history. *Academic units recommended:* 4 math, 4 science, 4 science labs, 4 foreign language, 4 social studies.

Financial Aid

Students should submit: CSS/Financial Aid Profile; FAFSA; Noncustodial Profile. Priority filing deadline is 2/15. The Princeton Review suggests that all financial aid forms be submitted as soon as possible (see page 5 for a note on the FAFSA). *Need-based scholarships/grants offered:* College/university scholarship or grant aid from institutional funds; Federal Pell; Private scholarships; SEOG; State scholarships/grants. *Loan aid offered:* Direct PLUS loans; Direct Subsidized Loans; Direct Unsubsidized Loans; College/university loans from institutional funds; Federal Nursing Loans; State Loans. Admitted students will be notified of awards on or about 4/1. Federal Work-Study Program available. Institutional employment available.

The Inside Word

Applicants to Northeastern are evaluated based on their secondary school performance, with emphasis given to the difficulty of courses you pursued, and you should go beyond minimum high school graduation requirements to show broad intellectual curiosity. The admission committee recommends having strong standardized test scores. Both the Common Application and the Coalition Application are accepted.

THE SCHOOL SAYS "..."

From the Admissions Office

"There's a certain energy about Northeastern University. It comes from our bright, ambitious students, exhibiting a strong sense of purpose in the classroom and while working or studying abroad. In the heart of Boston—the ultimate college city—and across the globe, Northeastern students challenge themselves intellectually, investigate career options, participate in community service, and graduate both personally and professionally prepared for their future careers and graduate school. A Northeastern education is like no other, integrating rigorous classroom learning with real-world experiences—through opportunities to study, work, research, and serve on seven continents. Our students learn how to apply their knowledge, to solve problems, and to make a difference in the world—before they graduate."

SELECTIVITY

Admissions Rating	98
# of applicants	91,000
% of applicants accepted	7
% of acceptees attending	41
# of early decision applicants	2,707
% accepted early decision	33

FIRST-YEAR PROFILE

Testing policy	Test Optional
Range SAT composite	1450–1535
Range SAT EBRW	700–760
Range SAT math	740–790
Range ACT composite	33–35
# submitting SAT scores	827
% submitting SAT scores	33
# submitting ACT scores	282
% submitting ACT scores	11
% graduated top 10% of class	71
% graduated top 25% of class	93
% graduated top 50% of class	99

DEADLINES

Early decision	
Deadline	11/1
Notification	12/15
Other ED deadline	1/1
Other ED notification	2/15
Early action	
Deadline	11/1
Notification	2/1
Regular	
Deadline	1/1
Notification	4/1
Nonfall registration?	Yes

FINANCIAL FACTS

Financial Aid Rating	87
Annual tuition	$59,100
Room and board	$18,440
Required fees	$1,092
Books and supplies	$1,000
Average frosh need-based scholarship	$50,325
Average UG need-based scholarship	$39,017
% needy frosh rec. need-based scholarship or grant aid	99
% needy UG rec. need-based scholarship or grant aid	97
% needy frosh rec. non-need-based scholarship or grant aid	52
% needy UG rec. non-need-based scholarship or grant aid	48
% needy frosh rec. need-based self-help aid	82
% needy UG rec. need-based self-help aid	76
% UG borrow to pay for school	50
Average cumulative indebtedness	$30,624
% frosh need fully met	100
% ugrads need fully met	49
Average % of frosh need met	100
Average % of ugrad need met	88

NORTHWESTERN UNIVERSITY

633 Clark Street, Evanston, IL 60208 • Admissions: 847-491-3741

STUDENTS SAY " . . ."
Academics
"The strength of the school is its range." Northwestern students agree, vowing their school "has everything": "Intelligent but laid-back students, excel[lence] in academic fields," "great extracurriculars and good parties," "strong [Big Ten] sports spirit," and "so many connections and opportunities during and after graduation." Undergrads here brag of "nationally acclaimed programs for almost anything anyone could be interested in, from engineering to theater to journalism to music," and report "everything is given fairly equal weight. Northwestern students and faculty do not show a considerable bias" toward specific fields. The school accomplishes all this while maintaining a manageable scale. While its relatively small size allows for good student-professor interaction, it has "all the perks" of a big school, including "many opportunities" for research and internships. Be aware, however, "Northwestern is not an easy school. It takes hard work to be average here." If you "learn from your failures quickly and love to learn for the sake of learning rather than the grade," students say it is quite possible to stay afloat and even to excel. Helping matters are numerous resources established by administrators and professors, including tutoring programs such as Northwestern's Gateway Science Workshop. Those who take advantage of these opportunities find the going much easier than those who don't.

Campus Life
There are two distinct sections of the Northwestern campus. The North Campus is where "you can find a party every night of the week," and "the Greek scene is strong." The South Campus, about a one-mile trek from the action to the north, is "more artsy and has minimal partying on weeknights," but is closer to town so "it is easy" to "buy dinner, see a show at the movies, and go shopping. People who live on North Campus have a harder time getting motivated to go into Evanston and tap into all that is offered." As one South Campus resident puts it, "South Campus is nice and quiet in its own way. I enjoy reading and watching movies here, and the quietude is appreciated when study time rolls around. But for more exciting fun, a trip north is a must." Regardless of where students live, extracurriculars are "incredible here. There is a group for every interest, and the groups are amazingly well-managed by students alone. This goes hand-in-hand with how passionate students at Northwestern are about what they love." Many students "are involved in plays, a cappella groups, comedy troupes, and other organizations geared toward the performing arts. Activism is also very popular, with many involved in political groups, human-rights activism, and volunteering." In addition, Northwestern's membership in the Big Ten means students "attend some of the best sporting events in the country." Chicago, of course, "is a wonderful resource. People go into the city for a wide variety of things—daily excursions, jobs, internships, nights out, parties, etc."

Student Body
The typical Northwestern student "was high school class president with a 4.0, swim team captain, and on the chess team." So it makes sense everyone here "is an excellent student who works hard" and "has a leadership position in at least two clubs, plus an on-campus job." Students also tell us "there's [a] great separation between North Campus (think: fraternities, engineering, state school mentality) and South Campus (think: closer to Chicago and its culture, arts and letters, liberal arts school mentality). Students segregate themselves depending on background and interests, and it's rare for these two groups to interact beyond a superficial level." The student body here includes sizable Jewish, Indian, and East-Asian populations.

NORTHWESTERN UNIVERSITY

Financial Aid: 847-491-7400 • E-Mail: ug-admission@northwestern.edu • Website: www.northwestern.edu

THE PRINCETON REVIEW SAYS

Admissions

The school reports that its standardized testing policy for use in admission for Fall 2024 is Test Optional. It is unknown at this time if the 2024 testing policy will be permanent. The Princeton Review suggests that interested applicants consult with the school for the most up-to-date standardized testing policies. *Very important factors considered include:* rigor of secondary school record, class rank, academic GPA, application essay, recommendation(s), extracurricular activities, talent/ability, character/personal qualities. *Other factors considered include:* standardized test scores, interview, first generation, alumni/ae relation, racial/ethnic status, volunteer work, work experience, level of applicant's interest. High school diploma is required and GED is accepted. *Academic units recommended:* 4 English, 3 math, 2 science, 2 science labs, 2 foreign language, 2 social studies, 2 history, 1 academic elective.

Financial Aid

Students should submit: CSS/Financial Aid Profile; FAFSA; Noncustodial Profile. Priority filing deadline is 2/1. The Princeton Review suggests that all financial aid forms be submitted as soon as possible (see page 5 for a note on the FAFSA). *Need-based scholarships/grants offered:* College/university scholarship or grant aid from institutional funds; Federal Pell; SEOG; State scholarships/grants. *Loan aid offered:* Direct PLUS loans; Direct Subsidized Loans; Direct Unsubsidized Loans. Admitted students will be notified of awards on or about 4/15. Federal Work-Study Program available. Institutional employment available.

The Inside Word

Northwestern is among the nation's most expensive undergraduate institutions, a fact that dissuades some qualified students from applying. The school is working to attract more low-income applicants by increasing the number of full scholarships available for students whose family income is less than $45,000. Low-income students who score well on the ACT may receive a letter from the school encouraging them to apply. Even if you don't receive this letter, you should consider applying if you've got the goods—you may be pleasantly surprised by the offer you receive from the financial aid office.

THE SCHOOL SAYS "..."

From the Admissions Office

"Consistent with its dedication to excellence, Northwestern provides both an educational and an extracurricular environment that enables its undergraduate students to become accomplished individuals and informed and responsible citizens. To the students in all its undergraduate schools, Northwestern offers liberal learning and professional education to help them gain the depth of knowledge that will empower them to become leaders in their professions and communities. Furthermore, Northwestern fosters in its students a broad understanding of the world in which we live as well as excellence in the competencies that transcend any particular field of study: writing and oral communication, analytical and creative thinking and expression, and quantitative and qualitative methods of thinking."

SELECTIVITY
Admissions Rating	99
# of applicants	51,259
% of applicants accepted	7
% of acceptees attending	55
# of early decision applicants	5,037
% accepted early decision	23

FIRST-YEAR PROFILE
Testing policy	Test Optional
Range SAT composite	1500–1560
Range SAT EBRW	730–770
Range SAT math	760–800
Range ACT composite	33–35
# submitting SAT scores	965
% submitting SAT scores	47
# submitting ACT scores	638
% submitting ACT scores	31
% graduated top 10% of class	96
% graduated top 25% of class	100
% graduated top 50% of class	100

DEADLINES
Early decision	
Deadline	11/1
Notification	12/15
Regular	
Deadline	1/2
Notification	4/1
Nonfall registration?	No

FINANCIAL FACTS
Financial Aid Rating	95
Annual tuition	$62,391
Room and board	$19,440
Required fees	$1,077
Books and supplies	$1,590
Average frosh need-based scholarship	$62,898
Average UG need-based scholarship	$60,889
% needy frosh rec. need-based scholarship or grant aid	97
% needy UG rec. need-based scholarship or grant aid	97
% needy frosh rec. non-need-based scholarship or grant aid	0
% needy UG rec. non-need-based scholarship or grant aid	0
% needy frosh rec. need-based self-help aid	69
% needy UG rec. need-based self-help aid	67
% UG borrow to pay for school	29
Average cumulative indebtedness	$34,309
% frosh need fully met	100
% ugrads need fully met	100
Average % of frosh need met	100
Average % of ugrad need met	100

OBERLIN COLLEGE

173 West Lorain Street, Oberlin, OH 44074 • Admissions: 440-775-8411 • Fax: 440-775-6905

CAMPUS LIFE

Quality of Life Rating	70
Fire Safety Rating	91
Green Rating	60*
Type of school	Private
Affiliation	No Affiliation
Environment	Village

STUDENTS

Total undergrad enrollment	2,986
% male/female/another gender	41/59/0
% from out of state	93
% frosh from public high school	71
% frosh live on campus	100
% ugrads live on campus	91
# of fraternities	0
# of sororities	0
% African American	5
% Asian	5
% White	61
% Hispanic	8
% Native American	0
% Pacific Islander	0
% Two or more races	10
% Race and/or ethnicity unknown	1
% international	10
# of countries represented	61

SURVEY SAYS . . .

Lots of liberal students
Great financial aid
Students environmentally aware
Theater is popular

ACADEMICS

Academic Rating	80
% students returning for sophomore year	87
% students graduating within 4 years	62
% students graduating within 6 years	83
Calendar	4/1/4
Student/faculty ratio	9:1
Profs interesting rating	87
Profs accessible rating	86

Most classes have fewer than 10 students.
Most lab/discussion sessions have
 fewer than 10 students.

MOST POPULAR MAJORS

Environmental Studies; Political Science and
Government; Economics

STUDENTS SAY " . . ."

Academics

Oberlin College, a school "for laid-back people who enjoy learning and expanding social norms, allows each and every student to have the undergrad experience for which he or she is looking, all the while challenging the students to change themselves and the world for the better." Oberlin is a place where students "focus on learning for learning's sake rather than making money in a career." As one student explains, "I didn't plan on becoming a scholar when I entered Oberlin.... As fate would have it, I ended up loving my college classes and professors. Now I hope to be a professor of religion." At Oberlin, "academics are very highly valued, but balanced with a strong interest in the arts and a commitment to society." Some might suggest Oberlin puts the "liberal" in "liberal arts," and the school's staunchest supporters agree, stressing the school's emphasis on open-mindedness and the belief that "one person can change the world." Among the school's offerings, "the sciences, English, politics, religion, music, environmental studies, and East-Asian studies are particularly noteworthy." The presence of a prestigious music school imbues the entire campus community. One undergrad writes, "Oberlin's greatest strength is the combination of the college and the conservatory. They are not separated, so students mix with each other all the time." Professors here—the "heart and soul of the school"—are dedicated teachers who "treat you more like collaborators and realize that even with their PhDs, they can learn and grow from you, as well as you from them." They are "excellent instructors and fantastic people" who are "focused on learning instead of deadlines." Undergrads also appreciate "a cooperative learning environment" in which "students bond over studying together for difficult exams."

Campus Life

Life during the week at Oberlin can be "pretty bland," as "almost everyone has to crack the books and study it up." It's not always bland, though. Some here manage to find time for the many "events [going on] each weekend—operas, plays, organ pumps, etc.," or "rally to stage to help the oppressed." Thursday afternoons at Oberlin mean "Classical Thursdays," an event during which "you get free beer [or soda] from the college if you bring a professor to the on-campus pub." Another feature of campus life is "the musical scene, which has its heart in the conservatory. All of the other arts—performing, studio, whatever—are intertwined with the talent in the conservatory." On weekends, "people let loose and drink beer. Not everyone does this every weekend. Some don't do it at all," and "there is absolutely no pressure on those who don't." There are also "tons of student-produced social events like parties, fundraisers, concerts, dances, etc.," keeping students "very connected to each other and to what's going on in the community." Hometown Oberlin "is a small town, and about all there is to do there is go out for pizza or Chinese, see a movie for two or three dollars at the Apollo, or go to the Feve, the bar in town."

Student Body

"If you're a liberal, artsy, indie loner who likes to throw around the phrase 'heteronormative white privilege,'" then Oberlin might be the place for you. "We're like the Island of Misfit Toys, but together we make a great toy chest." "We're all different and unusual, which creates a common bond between students." "Musicians, jocks, science geeks, creative writing majors, straight, bi, questioning, queer, and trans [students]," all have their place here, alongside "straight-edge, international, local, and joker students." Oberlin has a reputation for a left-leaning and active student body. One undergrad observes, "They are less active politically than they would like to think, but still more active than most people elsewhere." Another adds, "Most students are very liberal, but the moderates and (few) Republicans have a fine time of it. Every student has different interests and isn't afraid to talk about them." Some here worry, "Oberlin's student body is becoming more and more mainstream each year."

OBERLIN COLLEGE

Financial Aid: 440-775-8142 • E-Mail: college.admissions@oberlin.edu • Website: www.oberlin.edu

THE PRINCETON REVIEW SAYS

Admissions

Oberlin implemented a Test Optional policy starting with the 2020–2021 admissions cycle, which will continue as a pilot program through the 2025–2026 application year. *Very important factors considered include:* rigor of secondary school record, class rank, academic GPA. *Important factors considered include:* application essay, recommendation(s), talent/ability, character/personal qualities, first generation. *Other factors considered include:* standardized test scores, interview, extracurricular activities, alumni/ae relation, racial/ethnic status, volunteer work, work experience. High school diploma is required and GED is accepted. *Academic units recommended:* 4 English, 3 math, 3 science, 3 science labs, 3 foreign language, 3 social studies.

Financial Aid

Students should submit: CSS/Financial Aid Profile; FAFSA; Institution's own financial aid form; Noncustodial Profile. Priority filing deadline is 1/15. The Princeton Review suggests that all financial aid forms be submitted as soon as possible (see page 5 for a note on the FAFSA). *Need-based scholarships/grants offered:* College/university scholarship or grant aid from institutional funds; Federal Pell; Private scholarships; SEOG; State scholarships/grants. *Loan aid offered:* Direct PLUS loans; Direct Subsidized Loans; Direct Unsubsidized Loans. Admitted students will be notified of awards on or about 4/1. Federal Work-Study Program available. Institutional employment available.

The Inside Word

Oberlin's music conservatory is one of the most elite programs in the nation. Aspiring music students should expect stiff competition for one of the 600 available slots. Other applicants won't have a much easier time of it. Oberlin is a highly selective institution that attracts a highly competitive applicant pool. Your personal statement could be the make-or-break factor here.

THE SCHOOL SAYS "..."

From the Admissions Office

"Ranked among the nation's top liberal arts institutions, Oberlin College and Conservatory is known for its exemplary academic and musical pedagogy and its commitment to social justice, sustainability, and creative entrepreneurship. Located in Oberlin, Ohio, about 40 minutes from Cleveland, Oberlin offers one of the world's great undergraduate educations, with a long tradition of educating top scholars and musicians. Founded in 1833, it holds a distinguished place among American colleges and universities as the first to grant bachelor's degrees to women in a coeducational environment and the first to adopt a policy to admit African Americans. Its 2900 students pursue multiple passions and interests within a supportive, collaborative community. The College of Arts and Sciences focuses on undergraduate teaching, hands-on research, culturally immersive study away experiences, and world-class music opportunities. The innovative Conservatory of Music, a recipient of the National Medal of Arts, was founded in 1865, making it the oldest continuously operating conservatory in the United States. In the last century, Oberlin alumni have gone on to earn more PhDs than graduates of any other liberal arts institution. In nearly every career field, Oberlin graduates are making an impact and improving our world."

SELECTIVITY

Admissions Rating	94
# of applicants	11,066
% of applicants accepted	35
% of acceptees attending	23
# offered a place on the wait list	1,691
% accepting a place on wait list	76
% admitted from wait list	9
# of early decision applicants	651
% accepted early decision	43

FIRST-YEAR PROFILE

Testing policy	Test Optional
Range SAT EBRW	690–760
Range SAT math	670–770
Range ACT composite	30–33
# submitting SAT scores	329
% submitting SAT scores	37
# submitting ACT scores	190
% submitting ACT scores	23
Average HS GPA	3.7
% frosh submitting high school GPA	92
% graduated top 10% of class	53
% graduated top 25% of class	79
% graduated top 50% of class	96

DEADLINES

Early decision	
Deadline	11/15
Notification	12/15
Other ED deadline	1/2
Other ED notification	2/1
Regular	
Deadline	1/15
Notification	4/1
Nonfall registration?	No

APPLICANTS ALSO LOOK AT

Brown University; Carleton College; Kenyon College; Macalester College; New York University; University of Michigan—Ann Arbor; Vassar College; Wesleyan University

FINANCIAL FACTS

Financial Aid Rating	97
Annual tuition	$61,106
Room and board	$18,390
Required fees	$918
Books and supplies	$930
Average frosh need-based scholarship	$48,246
Average UG need-based scholarship	$46,359
% needy frosh rec. need-based scholarship or grant aid	99
% needy UG rec. need-based scholarship or grant aid	99
% needy frosh rec. non-need-based scholarship or grant aid	97
% needy UG rec. non-need-based scholarship or grant aid	87
% needy frosh rec. need-based self-help aid	82
% needy UG rec. need-based self-help aid	85
% UG borrow to pay for school	45
Average cumulative indebtedness	$30.446
% frosh need fully met	100
% ugrads need fully met	100
Average % of frosh need met	100
Average % of ugrad need met	100

OCCIDENTAL COLLEGE

1600 Campus Road, Los Angeles, CA 90041-3314 • Admissions: 323-259-2500 • Fax: 323-341-4875

CAMPUS LIFE

Quality of Life Rating	84
Fire Safety Rating	65
Green Rating	86
Type of school	Private
Affiliation	No Affiliation
Environment	Metropolis

STUDENTS

Total undergrad enrollment	1,935
% male/female/another gender	41/59/0
% from out of state	59
% frosh live on campus	100
% ugrads live on campus	80
# of fraternities	2
# of sororities	3
% African American	4
% Asian	13
% White	49
% Hispanic	17
% Native American	0
% Pacific Islander	0
% Two or more races	11
% Race and/or ethnicity unknown	1
% international	5
# of countries represented	23

SURVEY SAYS . . .

Lots of liberal students
Great financial aid
Students are friendly
Diverse student types interact on campus
Great off-campus food

ACADEMICS

Academic Rating	89
% students returning for sophomore year	89
% students graduating within 4 years	77
% students graduating within 6 years	83
Calendar	Semester
Student/faculty ratio	9:1
Profs interesting rating	92
Profs accessible rating	96

Most classes have 10–19 students.
Most lab/discussion sessions have
10–19 students.

MOST POPULAR MAJORS

Biology/Biological Sciences, General; Econometrics
and Quantitative Economics; International
Relations and Affairs

STUDENTS SAY " . . ."

Academics

An "intellectual, accepting, beautiful" liberal arts college in northeast Los Angeles, Occidental is "perfect for hard-working and involved students who not only want to be challenged academically, but also want to be pushed to learn more about the world around them." At this small school, classes are "intellectually stimulating," spearheaded by professors who "encourage critical analysis, ask interesting questions, and allow students to create informed opinions about the subject." The faculty and staff "really encourage students to take a proactive role in their education," giving them the freedom to "experiment with a wide range of courses." A current undergrad enthuses, "I love the interdisciplinary aspect of academics. I can really tailor my coursework to what I am interested in." In the classroom, Oxy professors "find ways to connect the lectures to the real world," and many are "very willing to have students help them with their research," providing valuable hands-on experience to undergraduates. Students further augment their coursework through numerous extracurricular and off-campus opportunities, including study abroad, academic conferences, and the school's popular "UN internship program." "Courses are challenging," but Oxy "professors want to see you succeed," and the favorably low student-to-faculty ratio means "there are plenty of opportunities to get extra help on the tough material." In fact, most professors "go the extra mile to make themselves available" and "are invested in cultivating real relationships with students."

Campus Life

"People are really passionate about their extracurricular activities and internships" at Occidental, where most students are "busy from dawn to dusk, and loving it." Clubs and intramural sports, "from quidditch to women's rugby," are popular across campus, and "Greek life is getting bigger and bigger every year." On campus, "there are frequently guest speakers, dialogues, and workshops," and on the weekends, the school organizes "dances, trivia nights, movie screenings, fashion shows, concerts, food tastings, beer gardens, and many other events." When it comes to parties, the alcohol policy is "strict" (even students of legal age are "forbidden from drinking in their dorms"), so most campus get-togethers are small and subdued. Off campus, "house parties are a huge source of fun on the weekends," as are "music shows, bars, and clubs" in surrounding L.A. When they don't have anything planned, students "listen to and make music, watch movies, have impromptu dance parties, and do wacky things." You can't beat having the "intimacy of a small college with Los Angeles as your backyard," and students love the fact that Oxy is "not isolated from the surrounding community like many other college campuses." In their free time, many take advantage of the Southern California setting to "go to the beach, go shopping in L.A., go out to eat in Eagle Rock, [and] go hiking." "Having a car definitely helps" if you want to explore the surrounding city, though "the school has a 'Bengal Bus' system that provides free rides to areas close to campus."

Students

Oxy students are "well rounded," "socially and politically conscious," and "excited to be at Occidental." Though they take academics seriously, "people at Oxy are concerned with much, much more than their education. They are focused on academically succeeding, sure, but they are also concerned with social issues, identity, meeting new people, having fun, and gathering a variety of other skills to help them succeed in life outside of Oxy." Many note the "overwhelmingly left-wing atmosphere" on campus, admitting that the people and their viewpoints can feel a little "homogeneous" at times. However, "every student at Oxy treats all persons equally, regardless of sexual orientation, gender identity, or religious views," and most are readily "accepting of different opinions." With such a tiny enrollment, it's easy to find "a good niche of close friends at Oxy," and "if you're involved on campus, expect your friend group to continually grow." Despite the rigors of the academic program, "there is a communal desire to help each other succeed."

OCCIDENTAL COLLEGE

Financial Aid: 323-259-2548 • E-Mail: admission@oxy.edu • Website: www.oxy.edu

THE PRINCETON REVIEW SAYS

Admissions

The school reports that its standardized testing policy for use in admission for Fall 2024 is Test Optional. The 2024 testing policy will be continued indefinitely. The Princeton Review suggests that interested applicants consult with the school for the most up-to-date standardized testing policies. *Very important factors considered include:* rigor of secondary school record, academic GPA, application essay. *Important factors considered include:* class rank, recommendation(s), extracurricular activities, character/personal qualities, volunteer work, work experience. *Other factors considered include:* standardized test scores, interview, talent/ability, first generation, alumni/ae relation, geographical residence, level of applicant's interest. High school diploma is required and GED is accepted. *Academic units recommended:* 4 English, 4 math, 3 science, 3 foreign language, 3 social studies.

Financial Aid

Students should submit: CSS/Financial Aid Profile; FAFSA; Noncustodial Profile; State aid form. Priority filing deadline is 1/10. The Princeton Review suggests that all financial aid forms be submitted as soon as possible (see page 5 for a note on the FAFSA). *Need-based scholarships/grants offered:* College scholarship or grant aid from institutional funds; Federal Pell; Private scholarships; SEOG; State scholarships/grants. *Loan aid offered:* Direct PLUS loans; Direct Subsidized Loans; Direct Unsubsidized Loans; College loans from institutional funds. Admitted students will be notified of awards on 3/20. Federal Work-Study Program available. Institutional employment available.

The Inside Word

The admissions team at Occidental does not use any minimums or formulas when evaluating an applicant's eligibility for the incoming class. In addition to academic achievement, they place a lot of weight on essays and recommendations in their mission to create a diverse incoming class. A demanding course load in high school is essential for competitive candidates, but successful applicants will also show what makes them distinct, from volunteer experiences to artistic talent.

THE SCHOOL SAYS "..."

From the Admissions Office

"Here's what our students tell us:

'The professors have all been just amazing. They're all very willing to coordinate times to meet and discuss how you feel about a class and what you want to get out of it.'

'I realize the caliber of discussion that occurs at Oxy is not easily matched. I've developed very strong relationships with many professors, and that's something I believe is unique to Oxy.'

'The program has been awesome. Whether you want to go to med school or grad school, it's a great experience. The professors really want you to succeed.'

'I've been working with postdoctoral researchers as an undergraduate. It's very rewarding. Oxy challenges me both inside and outside the classroom.'

'Occidental opened my eyes to different beliefs, values, and ideas. Discussions in class are much more interesting, because you consider things you might not have thought about before.'

'Oxy's close-knit community and its size make me feel this is a place I can call home.'

'Oxy instills curiosity and makes students want to go out and learn a subject on their own. I've gotten a broader sense of self and have been able to fulfill my learning goals.'"

SELECTIVITY

Admissions Rating	**94**
# of applicants	6,305
% of applicants accepted	39
% of acceptees attending	21
# offered a place on the wait list	1,470
% accepting a place on wait list	43
% admitted from wait list	2
# of early decision applicants	407
% accepted early decision	59

FIRST-YEAR PROFILE

Testing policy	Test Optional
Range SAT composite	1380–1490
Range SAT EBRW	690–750
Range SAT math	680–760
Range ACT composite	31–34
# submitting SAT scores	136
% submitting SAT scores	26
# submitting ACT scores	82
% submitting ACT scores	15
Average HS GPA	3.7
% frosh submitting high school GPA	99
% graduated top 10% of class	54
% graduated top 25% of class	83
% graduated top 50% of class	100

DEADLINES

Early decision	
Deadline	11/15
Notification	12/15
Other ED deadline	1/10
Other ED notification	2/1
Regular	
Deadline	1/10
Notification	3/20
Nonfall registration?	No

APPLICANTS OFTEN PREFER

Pomona College; University of California—Berkeley; University of California—Los Angeles; University of Southern California

APPLICANTS SOMETIMES PREFER

Claremont McKenna College; Macalester College; New York University; Scripps College

FINANCIAL FACTS

Financial Aid Rating	**97**
Annual tuition	$59,970
Room and board	$17,330
Required fees	$596
Books and supplies	$1,240
Average frosh need-based scholarship	$42,893
Average UG need-based scholarship	$43,535
% needy frosh rec. need-based scholarship or grant aid	99
% needy UG rec. need-based scholarship or grant aid	99
% needy frosh rec. non-need-based scholarship or grant aid	60
% needy UG rec. non-need-based scholarship or grant aid	60
% needy frosh rec. need-based self-help aid	79
% needy UG rec. need-based self-help aid	84
% frosh rec. any financial aid	79
% UG rec. any financial aid	77
% UG borrow to pay for school	49
Average cumulative indebtedness	$27,879
% frosh need fully met	99
% ugrads need fully met	100
Average % of frosh need met	100
Average % of ugrad need met	100

OHIO NORTHERN UNIVERSITY

525 South Main Street, Ada, OH 45810 • Admissions: 419-772-2125 • Fax: 419-772-2313

STUDENTS SAY "..."

Academics

Many students are attracted to Ohio Northern University's "prestigious" Raabe College of Pharmacy, a "six-year program" that "is focused on developing the next generation of clinical pharmacists who are well rounded leaders, clinicians, and members of society." But this comprehensive university offers its 2,900 students lots of other outstanding academic options: "The accounting program is highly ranked," "it has a great political science program that has sent many students to graduate school and politics," and "the engineering college is great." An ONU education provides practical applications for knowledge as well as theoretical ones, with a "wonderful incorporation of current events and timeless business principles." Students are also drawn to ONU's "good financial aid" and "varsity sports," with one athlete noting that ONU "was my most affordable option of Division III schools where I could play soccer and receive a quality education." Undergrads feel that their "renowned faculty" "are outstanding and all influential in the field," but also that their "professors are very friendly and down to earth" and that they "are real and treat students like people not as if they are beneath them, so it is easier to understand material." In addition to academic performance, "professors care about the student's well-being and future endeavors" and "they are always available to help." "It's great that even though there are 170-plus senior pharmacy majors, the professors still know my name." ONU's "classes are tough, no doubt about it," but "my overall academic experience has been above and beyond anything I could've expected." As a whole, students call ONU "a top-notch education with a family-like atmosphere that is very conducive for learning and excelling in many disciplines."

Campus Life

ONU's hometown of Ada, OH, is a "small town," but one with "good places to eat and a movie theatre." There's also a "big town," Columbus, 90 minutes away "with a lot of attractions so always something to do if you have the time to drive." "Because we are in a small town, the students bond together to find fun things to do," including D3 athletics and "pick-up sports games," "fraternity house parties and local bars (The Regal Beagle and The Cask Room)," as well as "several university-sponsored events throughout the year." Socializing and academics mix freely: "People love hanging out with each other, especially when they are trying to get things done." Social life can be a "mixed bag" of "students who spend all of their time focused on school" and "a good number of students who enjoy having a good time and hanging out with friends"; still "people here are very relaxed—you do what you want and everyone is fine with you being who you are." "Students usually party on the weekends," but "hard drugs are rare." Dorm life is also popular: "It's easy to have fun in the dorms, especially during winter."

Student Body

As you might expect, "in a small town, students must get along because there are high chances they will see one another again," so at ONU, "everyone is very caring toward each other." The typical ONU student "is committed to academics, to service, and has leadership potential," and students appreciate that "everyone here finds a supportive group of friends." Many students are Midwestern and "some denomination of Christian," with a majority of ONU's population hailing from "in-state, some surrounding states, and internationals." Students see themselves as involved and conscientious: ONU students often belong to "several clubs and organizations," are "always willing to help or mentor younger students, and very concerned about academic success." One undergrad offers this bit of advice: "Most students are friends with other people in the same activities that they're involved in, so join something you're interested in and don't be shy!"

OHIO NORTHERN UNIVERSITY

Financial Aid: 419-772-2272 • E-Mail: admissions-ug@onu.edu • Website: www.onu.edu

THE PRINCETON REVIEW SAYS

Admissions

The school reports that its standardized testing policy for use in admission for Fall 2024 is Test Optional. It is unknown at this time if the 2024 testing policy will be permanent. The Princeton Review suggests that interested applicants consult with the school for the most up-to-date standardized testing policies. *Very important factors considered include:* rigor of secondary school record, academic GPA, standardized test scores. *Important factors considered include:* class rank, interview, extracurricular activities. *Other factors considered include:* application essay, recommendation(s), talent/ability, character/personal qualities, first generation, alumni/ae relation, volunteer work, level of applicant's interest. High school diploma is required and GED is accepted. *Academic units required:* 4 English, 2 math, 2 science, 2 science labs, 2 social studies, 2 history, 4 academic electives. *Academic units recommended:* 4 English, 4 math, 3 science, 2 science labs, 2 foreign language, 3 social studies, 2 history, 1 computer science, 1 visual/performing arts, 4 academic electives.

Financial Aid

Students should submit: FAFSA. Priority filing deadline is 3/1. The Princeton Review suggests that all financial aid forms be submitted as soon as possible (see page 5 for a note on the FAFSA). *Need-based scholarships/grants offered:* College/university scholarship or grant aid from institutional funds; Federal Pell; Private scholarships; SEOG; State scholarships/grants. *Loan aid offered:* Direct PLUS loans; Direct Subsidized Loans; Direct Unsubsidized Loans. Admitted students will be notified of awards on a rolling basis beginning 12/1. Federal Work-Study Program available. Institutional employment available.

The Inside Word

ONU's well-regarded pharmacy school has stricter requirements, so be sure to check with the school directly if that's your area of interest. All applications are rolling, however, which means that the earlier you submit, the better. Strong high school transcripts and standardized test scores will assist any application, and particularly those seeking merit-based financial aid. Applicants are evaluated holistically, so in addition to GPAs and test scores, admissions counselors will also consider high school leadership and community service activities. Applicants are eligible for academic scholarships without an ACT or SAT.

THE SCHOOL SAYS "..."

From the Admissions Office

"The purpose of Ohio Northern is to help students develop into self-reliant, mature men and women capable of clear and logical thinking and sensitive to the higher values of truth, beauty, and goodness. ONU selects its student body from among those students possessing characteristics congruent with the institution's objectives. Generally, a student must be prepared to use the resources of the institution to achieve personal and educational goals.

"The Office of Admissions highly encourages a campus visit. To schedule a visit, please go to www.onu.edu/visit or call 888-408-4668."

SELECTIVITY

Admissions Rating	86
# of applicants	5,205
% of applicants accepted	69
% of acceptees attending	21

FIRST-YEAR PROFILE

Testing policy	Test Optional
Range SAT composite	1130–1330
Range SAT EBRW	540–640
Range SAT math	550–660
Range ACT composite	21–28
# submitting SAT scores	114
% submitting SAT scores	15
# submitting ACT scores	532
% submitting ACT scores	72
Average HS GPA	3.8
% frosh submitting high school GPA	99

DEADLINES

Nonfall registration?	Yes

FINANCIAL FACTS

Financial Aid Rating	86
Annual tuition	$35,480
Room and board	$12,900
Required fees	$1,050
Books and supplies	$1,800
Average frosh need-based scholarship	$28,304
Average UG need-based scholarship	$27,692
% needy frosh rec. need-based scholarship or grant aid	100
% needy UG rec. need-based scholarship or grant aid	100
% needy frosh rec. non-need-based scholarship or grant aid	0
% needy UG rec. non-need-based scholarship or grant aid	0
% needy frosh rec. need-based self-help aid	54
% needy UG rec. need-based self-help aid	62
% UG borrow to pay for school	76
Average cumulative indebtedness	$39,688
% frosh need fully met	35
% ugrads need fully met	31
Average % of frosh need met	81
Average % of ugrad need met	81

THE OHIO STATE UNIVERSITY—COLUMBUS

Student Academic Services Building, Columbus, OH 43210 • Admissions: 614-292-OHIO • Fax: 614-292-3980

CAMPUS LIFE

Quality of Life Rating	90
Fire Safety Rating	87
Green Rating	89
Type of school	Public
Environment	Metropolis

STUDENTS

Total undergrad enrollment	45,140
% male/female/another gender	50/50/NR
% from out of state	20
% frosh from public high school	84
% frosh live on campus	92
% ugrads live on campus	32
# of fraternities (% join)	37 (8)
# of sororities (% join)	27 (11)
% African American	8
% Asian	9
% White	63
% Hispanic	5
% Native American	<1
% Pacific Islander	<1
% Two or more races	4
% Race and/or ethnicity unknown	3
% international	7
# of countries represented	75

SURVEY SAYS . . .

Students are happy
Great library
Students love Columbus, OH
Recreation facilities are great
Everyone loves the Buckeyes

ACADEMICS

Academic Rating	80
% students returning for sophomore year	93
% students graduating within 4 years	69
% students graduating within 6 years	88
Calendar	Semester
Student/faculty ratio	17:1
Profs interesting rating	85
Profs accessible rating	89

Most classes have 10–19 students.
Most lab/discussion sessions have
  20–29 students.

MOST POPULAR MAJORS

Psychology, General; Finance, General;
Communication, General

STUDENTS SAY "..."

Academics

Ohio State, one of the Midwest's premier universities, is a school with "strong name-brand recognition." Of course, it also has a massive student population, which makes the "campus feel like its own city." Nevertheless, OSU does an admirable job of "handling the large number of students that attend and creating opportunities for over 40,000 undergraduates." As one impressed student explains, "Every single student feels personally attended to and not [like] a number in the crowd of Buckeyes." Many undergrads here also appreciate that "the college is very research-based, which allows students to fully discover what exactly they want to do, and to also build connections with faculty." And while there are many great academic programs, a number of undergrads specifically highlight the "very strong business school, medical program, and engineering school." Moreover, students generally give high marks to their "friendly and approachable" professors. Though you might encounter a "couple of duds...depend[ing] on the department," OSU's faculty are usually "very passionate about the material they teach," which even makes for "very interesting general education classes." They're also "more than willing to meet outside of their designated office hours to help a student struggling with course materials or even just to get coffee and chat." Best of all, "they truly seem to have a genuine interest in the students' academic and career success."

Campus Life

OSU students boast that "it's impossible to be bored here" given that the university provides "thousands of opportunities" for extracurricular involvement. For starters, undergrads can participate in "countless intramural or club sport[s]," including volleyball, basketball and rock climbing. "When it's football season, game days are always the best," says a student. They go on to add, "Experiencing the atmosphere of the entire Ohio State campus in one stadium is amazing." Aside from athletics, students can join a number of clubs like "Dungeons and Dragons...student leadership, [and even] small [music] ensembles that don't require auditions." Buckeyes also quickly find that "going out on Thursdays, Fridays, and Saturdays is extremely popular, whether [to] the bars or frat parties." Nevertheless, one student assures that "although partying is common, there is absolutely no pressure to partake in any of it." In fact, "there are an abundance of [alternative] options [like] weekly karaoke and trivia." Finally, should you need a breather from all that campus excitement, downtown Columbus is a "great place...[filled with] art galleries, coffee shops," and "top-notch" restaurants.

Student Body

Undergrads at Ohio State love that their peers come "from quite a range of backgrounds." Indeed, you can just as easily "find yourself meeting an individual from a very remote city in the state...[as you can] an out of state or international student from places...you'd think [the school] wouldn't have a reach." Thankfully, no matter where they grew up, these Buckeyes are typically "down-to-earth and have a strong desire to succeed." They also comprise "some of the most spirited fans" you'll ever meet. And while students here "take their academics quite seriously," there's still "a very friendly [and] cooperative atmosphere." As one undergrad shares, "I've never encountered anybody that didn't want to work on... homework or [study] for an exam due to selfish competitive reasons." Students also greatly appreciate the fact that "there are so many people here that every social group is well represented." For example, "there's a party scene, a big Esports scene, a lot of gym rats, [and] a lot Christian[s] [and representatives from] other religious groups." In other words, rest assured that "there's a place for everyone" at Ohio State.

THE OHIO STATE UNIVERSITY—COLUMBUS

Financial Aid: 614-292-0300 • E-Mail: askabuckeye@osu.edu • Website: www.osu.edu

THE PRINCETON REVIEW SAYS

Admissions

At the time this book went to print, the school was still reviewing its standardized testing policy for Fall 2024. Please check with the school for its most up-to-date standardized testing policy. *Very important factors considered include:* rigor of secondary school record, class rank, academic GPA, standardized test scores. *Important factors considered include:* application essay, extracurricular activities, talent/ability, first generation, volunteer work, work experience. *Other factors considered include:* recommendation(s), character/personal qualities, geographical residence, state residency, racial/ethnic status. High school diploma is required and GED is accepted. *Academic units required:* 4 English, 3 math, 3 science, 3 science labs, 2 foreign language, 2 social studies, 1 visual/performing arts, 1 academic elective. *Academic units recommended:* 4 English, 4 math, 3 science, 3 science labs, 3 foreign language, 3 social studies, 1 visual/performing arts, 1 academic elective.

Financial Aid

Students should submit: FAFSA. Priority filing deadline is 2/1. The Princeton Review suggests that all financial aid forms be submitted as soon as possible (see page 5 for a note on the FAFSA). *Need-based scholarships/grants offered:* College/university scholarship or grant aid from institutional funds; Federal Pell; Private scholarships; SEOG; State scholarships/grants. *Loan aid offered:* Direct PLUS loans; Direct Subsidized Loans; Direct Unsubsidized Loans; College/university loans from institutional funds; Federal Nursing Loans; State Loans. Admitted students will be notified of awards beginning in late Feb. Federal Work-Study Program available. Institutional employment available.

The Inside Word

Despite being a huge state university, OSU truly strives to evaluate applications holistically. The school endeavors to build an incoming class filled with intellectually curious individuals who have proven leadership skills. To that end, admissions officers review all academic achievement, paying close attention to whether applicants have challenged themselves with honors, AP, or IB courses. They also consider level of extracurricular involvement, outstanding talent in a particular area, desire to engage with a diverse campus community, and whether a candidate is a first-generation college student.

THE SCHOOL SAYS "..."

From the Admissions Office

"You are the focus at Ohio State. Your experiences. Your ideas. Your potential. It's that potential we empower. How? By welcoming you into a community that sparks the discoveries you'll make and supports your growth—as a person, as a student. You'll have access to renowned faculty who welcome and challenge you, instilling you with confidence. You'll do research that solves urgent problems. You'll hang out in one of the best student unions in the nation, home to more than 1,400 student organizations that enable you to find your niche. You'll study in libraries that offer deep resources and breathtaking views. Throughout campus, you'll find a supportive community that encourages and challenges you to become your best self."

SELECTIVITY

Admissions Rating	93
# of applicants	65,189
% of applicants accepted	53
% of acceptees attending	23
# offered a place on the wait list	3,236
% accepting a place on wait list	22
% admitted from wait list	66

FIRST-YEAR PROFILE

Testing policy	To Be Announced
Range SAT composite	1270–1430
Range SAT EBRW	610–710
Range SAT math	640–750
Range ACT composite	27–32
# submitting SAT scores	1,956
% submitting SAT scores	24
# submitting ACT scores	4,255
% submitting ACT scores	53
% graduated top 10% of class	70
% graduated top 25% of class	97
% graduated top 50% of class	99

DEADLINES

Early action	
Deadline	11/1
Notification	1/31
Regular	
Deadline	2/1
Notification	3/31
Nonfall registration?	Yes

APPLICANTS OFTEN PREFER
University of Michigan—Ann Arbor; University of Wisconsin—Madison

APPLICANTS SOMETIMES PREFER
Case Western Reserve University; Indiana University—Bloomington; Penn State University Park; Purdue University—West Lafayette; University of Cincinnati

APPLICANTS RARELY PREFER
Miami University; Ohio University—Athens; University of Dayton

FINANCIAL FACTS

Financial Aid Rating	81
Annual in-state tuition	$12,485
Annual out-of-state tuition	$36,722
Room and board	$13,966
Books and supplies	$1,012
Average frosh need-based scholarship	$14,466
Average UG need-based scholarship	$14,002
% needy frosh rec. need-based scholarship or grant aid	85
% needy UG rec. need-based scholarship or grant aid	84
% needy frosh rec. non-need-based scholarship or grant aid	8
% needy UG rec. non-need-based scholarship or grant aid	5
% needy frosh rec. need-based self-help aid	70
% needy UG rec. need-based self-help aid	76
% frosh rec. any financial aid	81
% UG rec. any financial aid	76
% UG borrow to pay for school	44
Average cumulative indebtedness	$25,599
% frosh need fully met	26
% ugrads need fully met	25
Average % of frosh need met	69
Average % of ugrad need met	74

OHIO UNIVERSITY—ATHENS

1 Ohio University, Athens, OH 45701 • Admissions: 740-593-1000 • Fax: 740-593-0560

STUDENTS SAY ". . ."

Academics

"Academically, OHIO has something for everyone, from astrophysics to the history of rock and roll," students at this large state-run university boast. And students have an equally wide range of choices when it comes to committing themselves to academics; "You can take advantage of the vast amount of knowledge and resources directly available, or you can forget studies and party," students tell us. Those seeking a challenge will have no trouble finding it here, however; OHIO boasts "a strong engineering faculty," a noteworthy aviation program offered within the university's demanding college of engineering and technology, an "excellent and very selective early childhood education program," and "one of the best journalism schools in the country"—the E.W. Scripps School of Journalism—which offers "frequent opportunities to learn and grow outside the classroom with guest speakers and special events." The Scripps College houses "a great communications school" offering great hands-on experience; one student informs us that "Southeast Ohio depends on our college television and radio station for their news, weather, and high school sports." As at any large university, unassertive students are in danger of getting lost in the crowd, but those who make the effort to seek out faculty and administrators assure us that "the school is very supportive of the students. I have close relationships with multiple professors, and I think that they generally take a strong interest in the students."

Campus Life

"Ohio University has a beautiful campus with lots of character, both in academia and nightlife," students here report. Though most students remain independent, Greek organizations play a role in the life of the campus, providing service to the community and serving as a social catalyst. Some undergraduates note that the school holds true to its "reputation as a party school." One says, "It is never hard to find a party on any given night, whether in the dorms or off campus." One undergrad writes, "A nationwide reputation as a party school is not something I'm proud of," but most accept things as they are, noting that "Ohio University is a school where everyone can find a group of people doing whatever they're particularly interested in," which is to say that partying is hardly the only option here. College athletics are a big draw (especially football, men's basketball, and women's volleyball), as are such annual events as Homecoming, and the school is host to literally hundreds of student clubs and organizations serving interests of every variety. Hometown Athens is a typical small college town with access to a wide variety of outdoor activities. The closest cities of note—Columbus, Ohio, and Charleston, West Virginia—are each about a 90-minute drive from the OHIO campus.

Student Body

The OHIO student body "is pretty homogenous," with a large contingent of undergrads who are "white, middle- to upper-class, and from Ohio." "We have a small minority population, especially in the undergraduate programs," one student concedes, "but it's easy to interact with other cultures if you seek them out." Students here "try to get involved in community service, especially those involved in Greek life," and they are "generally friendly." One student observes that "students totally devoted to their schoolwork are atypical here." Yet, it should be noted that OHIO students have succeeded in claiming a number of nationally competitive academic awards in recent years, with *The Chronicle of Higher Education* having recognized Ohio University as being among the nation's top producers of U.S. Fulbright Students.

OHIO UNIVERSITY—ATHENS

Financial Aid: 740-593-4141 • E-Mail: admissions@ohio.edu • Website: www.ohio.edu

THE PRINCETON REVIEW SAYS

Admissions

The school reports that its standardized testing policy for use in admission for Fall 2024 is Test Optional. The 2024 testing policy will be permanent. The Princeton Review suggests that interested applicants consult with the school for the most up-to-date standardized testing policies. *Very important factors considered include:* rigor of secondary school record, academic GPA. *Important factors considered include:* class rank. *Other factors considered include:* standardized test scores, application essay, recommendation(s), extracurricular activities, talent/ability, character/personal qualities, first generation, alumni/ae relation, geographical residence, state residency, volunteer work, work experience. High school diploma is required and GED is accepted. *Academic units required:* 4 English, 4 math, 3 science, 2 foreign language, 3 social studies, 4 academic electives. *Academic units recommended:* 1 visual/performing arts.

Financial Aid

Students should submit: FAFSA. The Princeton Review suggests that all financial aid forms be submitted as soon as possible (see page 5 for a note on the FAFSA). *Need-based scholarships/grants offered:* College/university scholarship or grant aid from institutional funds; Federal Pell; Private scholarships; SEOG; State scholarships/grants. *Loan aid offered:* Direct PLUS loans; Direct Subsidized Loans; Direct Unsubsidized Loans. Admitted students will be notified of awards on a rolling basis. Federal Work-Study Program available. Institutional employment available.

The Inside Word

Admissions requirements vary from school to school at Ohio University. The Honors Tutorial College is most selective (top 10 percent of your graduating class), followed by the journalism school (top 15 percent), the business college (top 20 percent), media arts and studies, engineering, and visual communication. Admissions decisions are made through holistic review; those on the cusp should get in if they've demonstrated academic improvement during their junior and senior years and show evidence of academic preparation.

THE SCHOOL SAYS "..."

From the Admissions Office

"Ohio University offers a welcoming campus and more than 240 outstanding academic programs. Our dedicated professors do more than just teach—they serve as mentors and advisors who prepare students for success. Ohio University's recently launched initiative, The OHIO Guarantee, may be of particular interest to families facing budgetary challenges: It enables undergraduate students to pay a single "fixed" rate that covers tuition, room and meal plan, and most fees for four years. In addition, Ohio University is home to an Honors Tutorial College that offers high-ability students distinctive, tutorial-based learning opportunities that mirror the instructional model used for centuries at British universities such as Cambridge and Oxford. Students can enhance their educational experiences with adventures beyond the classroom. Opportunities can range from studying the plays of Shakespeare in London to retail merchandising in China. Students also can participate in meaningful research and internships, community service, and 530 student organizations. OHIO's picturesque campus—among the most beautiful in the nation—features learning communities that create a welcoming environment for first-year students. Friendships are forged as students with diverse backgrounds study, learn, and socialize together. Many students proudly cheer on Ohio University's athletics teams. The Bobcats have garnered consistent national attention in recent years, with the football team earning multiple bowl game experiences and the men's and women's basketball teams excelling in the Mid-American Conference and playing in post-season tournaments. All told, OHIO sponsors 16 varsity sports. Many non-varsity students participate in club and intramural sports or learn to rappel, kayak, or canoe through OHIO's Outdoor Pursuits Program."

SELECTIVITY

Admissions Rating	83
# of applicants	22,518
% of applicants accepted	87
% of acceptees attending	16

FIRST-YEAR PROFILE

Testing policy	Test Optional
Range SAT EBRW	530–630
Range SAT math	520–620
Range ACT composite	21–26
# submitting SAT scores	788
% submitting SAT scores	25
# submitting ACT scores	2,771
% submitting ACT scores	89
Average HS GPA	3.6
% frosh submitting high school GPA	100
% graduated top 10% of class	20
% graduated top 25% of class	49
% graduated top 50% of class	82

DEADLINES

Early action	
Deadline	11/15
Regular	
Priority	11/15
Deadline	2/1
Notification	Rolling, 9/15
Nonfall registration?	Yes

APPLICANTS OFTEN PREFER
Miami University; The Ohio State University—Columbus; University of Cincinnati

APPLICANTS SOMETIMES PREFER
Bowling Green State University; Kent State University; University of Dayton

APPLICANTS RARELY PREFER
University of Akron Wayne College

FINANCIAL FACTS

Financial Aid Rating	77
Annual in-state tuition	$13,352
Annual out-of-state tuition	$23,720
Room and board	$13,656
Books and supplies	$840
Average frosh need-based scholarship	$8,644
Average UG need-based scholarship	$7,355
% needy frosh rec. need-based scholarship or grant aid	95
% needy UG rec. need-based scholarship or grant aid	83
% needy frosh rec. non-need-based scholarship or grant aid	19
% needy UG rec. non-need-based scholarship or grant aid	10
% needy frosh rec. need-based self-help aid	65
% needy UG rec. need-based self-help aid	75
% frosh rec. any financial aid	95
% UG rec. any financial aid	92
% UG borrow to pay for school	69
Average cumulative indebtedness	$28,747
% frosh need fully met	25
% ugrads need fully met	14
Average % of frosh need met	69
Average % of ugrad need met	56

OHIO WESLEYAN UNIVERSITY

61 South Sandusky Street, Delaware, OH 43015 • Admissions: 800-922-8953 • Fax: 740-368-3314

STUDENTS SAY " . . ."

Academics

To some, Ohio Wesleyan University offers the best of both worlds: the "smaller school" experience of a "liberal arts education" along with the "fantastic financial aid," "scholarship money," and "opportunity to play a collegiate sport" available at a "global" university. OWU offers pre-professional majors in areas like pre-medicine, pre-engineering, and pre-law, along with "enriching" programs called out by students in "psychology," "economics," "Black World Studies," and others. In addition, the university facilitates special programs like "the undergraduate research program, SSRP, which allows only Ohio Wesleyan students to work with a professor over the summer," and which entrusts undergrads with "a rare opportunity to get paid to do research almost always one-on-one with a PhD, where at any other school you'll be working with lab techs and graduate students." Connection Grants challenge students to design their own project applications "for grants through the school that allow you to do your own research [and] travel to gain new experience." Similarly, OWU's "Travel-Learning Courses" create "many opportunities to go abroad" for students with intellectual wanderlust, and with such a global focus, OWU also attracts "many international students" to its Ohio campus. The faculty participates in this global citizenship as well: "The professors are very diverse, like the students here, bringing different perspectives and knowledge to campus." They're also committed to their students, who find that professors are "good at engaging the student in classroom discussions" and "will go out of their way to help you. I have had numerous professors support me in applying for grants, applying for research experiences at other universities, as well as jobs." Students report that "a major benefit of going to a smaller school is that I am on a first-name basis with multiple professors, and even text them if I need help with something," and that they've "had professors stay until 6pm just to make sure I understood a concept." An OWU education also builds a foundation for the future: the university boasts "strong career services," and "OWU alums are very dedicated to helping provide employment to students post-graduation."

Campus Life

OWU's "close knit community" is forged through common-interest bonds: "Most students are nerds/passionate about something. They usually fit in by finding people interested in the same things they are." The prototypical OWU student is "extremely involved in clubs/organizations," but has lots of choices of what to join: there's an "amazing club and Greek life," "varsity sports," "jobs on campus," and "SLUs (small living units)," described as "intentional communities centered around various mission statements." All of this adds up to a robust "overall community" and "great campus culture" that "make OWU an even better school to attend. The majority of students stay on campus because of the community and friendships that they have formed." That said, a lot of students "go to class and study during the week like its [their] job," "and every night do homework followed by Netflix." "In general, everyone is in study groups during the week and watching movies with friends when free"; then "weekends are spent with friends at a frat, sorority, or sport house." "Drinking does occur, as does drug usage," but "it's not a huge party school," and "many people are devoted strongly to their academics."

Student Body

OWU is populated by enthusiastic joiners of all different stripes, and students love the "very culturally diverse" atmosphere of the school. "I've never met so many people that are religiously and culturally different in a single place. It's amazing!" Because "students and faculty alike push for acceptance of everyone," it's "very easy to make friends in this type of environment." Students extol each other as "friendly and smart," as well as "outgoing, overcommitted in student organizations, and driven," and love that "it is impossible to judge or peg people" because "everyone here is from all over with different backgrounds." At OWU, "everyone fits in somewhere."

OHIO WESLEYAN UNIVERSITY

Financial Aid: 740-368-3050 • E-Mail: owuadmit@owu.edu • Website: www.owu.edu

THE PRINCETON REVIEW SAYS

Admissions

The school reports that its standardized testing policy for use in admission for Fall 2024 is Test Optional. The Princeton Review suggests that interested applicants consult with the school for the most up-to-date standardized testing policies. *Very important factors considered include:* rigor of secondary school record, academic GPA. *Important factors considered include:* application essay, recommendation(s), character/personal qualities. *Other factors considered include:* class rank, interview, extracurricular activities, talent/ability, first generation, alumni/ae relation, geographical residence, state residency, religious affiliation/commitment, volunteer work, work experience, level of applicant's interest. High school diploma is required and GED is accepted. *Academic units required:* 4 English, 3 math, 3 science, 2 science labs, 3 social studies. *Academic units recommended:* 2 foreign language.

Financial Aid

Students should submit: FAFSA. The Princeton Review suggests that all financial aid forms be submitted as soon as possible (after the FAFSA is available). *Need-based scholarships/grants offered:* College/university scholarship or grant aid from institutional funds; Federal Pell; Private scholarships; SEOG; State scholarships/grants. *Loan aid offered:* Direct PLUS loans; Direct Subsidized Loans; Direct Unsubsidized Loans. Admitted students will be notified of awards on a rolling basis once their FAFSA data has been received. Federal Work-Study Program available. Institutional employment available.

The Inside Word

OWU is test optional. While students are welcome to submit test scores, they will not be used in admission, academic program and/or scholarship decisions. Well-roundedness is a must for any serious applicant. OWU offers Early Decision, Early Action and Regular Decision options.

THE SCHOOL SAYS "..."

From the Admissions Office

"Ohio Wesleyan University is a national liberal arts university with a strong international presence. OWU is distinctive for offering the personal attention of a college with a student-to-faculty ratio of less than 11 to 1, combined with opportunities of a larger university, including more than 70 academic majors.

"Ohio Wesleyan's unique OWU Connection program guides every student to "think big, do good, go global, and get real." The program begins with individual guidance from faculty and advisers to help students find their passion and develop a personalized four-year program that can combine mentored research, travel-learning courses, semester-abroad programs, university-funded Connection grants, interdisciplinary programs, service-learning, creative projects, work in a public-private entrepreneurship center, community and overseas service programs, and internships across the nation. Every student is guaranteed Connection experiences proven to give them real-world experience and help them prepare for the causes, careers, and graduate school opportunities they want to pursue.

"Ohio Wesleyan offers 24 varsity athletic teams, including men's wrestling. The university boasts a vibrant visual and performing arts program, and OWU's 100-plus clubs and activities include marching band. The residential campus features a variety of living options, from traditional residence halls to themed houses. About 70% of all campus housing is newly built or renovated in the past 10 years, including renovated housing for all first-years and apartment-style housing for seniors. As of 2018, OWU students have access to 24/7 dining."

SELECTIVITY
Admissions Rating	83
# of applicants	5,324
% of applicants accepted	52
% of acceptees attending	16
# of early decision applicants	40
% accepted early decision	45

FIRST-YEAR PROFILE
Testing policy	Test Optional
# submitting SAT scores	66
% submitting SAT scores	15
# submitting ACT scores	147
% submitting ACT scores	33
Average HS GPA	3.7
% frosh submitting high school GPA	100
% graduated top 10% of class	29
% graduated top 25% of class	25
% graduated top 50% of class	85

DEADLINES
Early decision	
Deadline	11/15
Notification	Rolling, 12/1
Early action	
Deadline	12/1
Notification	Rolling, 12/15
Regular	
Priority	12/1
Deadline	3/1
Notification	Rolling, 11/1
Nonfall registration?	Yes

APPLICANTS ALSO LOOK AT

Ohio State University; Miami University; Ohio University; Kent State University; University of Cincinnati; Otterbein University; Wittenberg University; Capital University; The College of Wooster; Denison University; Allegheny College; University of Dayton; John Carroll University

FINANCIAL FACTS
Financial Aid Rating	87
Annual tuition	$51,711
Room and board	$14,832
Required fees	$586
Books and supplies	$1,000
Average frosh need-based scholarship	$43,683
Average UG need-based scholarship	$40,507
% needy frosh rec. need-based scholarship or grant aid	100
% needy UG rec. need-based scholarship or grant aid	100
% needy frosh rec. non-need-based scholarship or grant aid	29
% needy UG rec. non-need-based scholarship or grant aid	25
% needy frosh rec. need-based self-help aid	63
% needy UG rec. need-based self-help aid	69
% frosh rec. any financial aid	100
% UG rec. any financial aid	99
% UG borrow to pay for school	70
Average cumulative indebtedness	$35,222
% frosh need fully met	44
% ugrads need fully met	35
Average % of frosh need met	93
Average % of ugrad need met	89

OREGON STATE UNIVERSITY

1500 SW Jefferson Ave., Corvallis, OR 97331 • Admissions: 541-737-1000 • Fax: 541-737-2482

CAMPUS LIFE

Quality of Life Rating	85
Fire Safety Rating	92
Green Rating	92
Type of school	Public
Environment	Town

STUDENTS

Total undergrad enrollment	25,298
% male/female/another gender	53/47/0
% from out of state	34
% frosh live on campus	91
% ugrads live on campus	17
# of fraternities (% join)	27 (11)
# of sororities (% join)	22 (15)
% African American	1
% Asian	8
% White	64
% Hispanic	10
% Native American	<1
% Pacific Islander	<1
% Two or more races	7
% Race and/or ethnicity unknown	2
% international	7
# of countries represented	81

SURVEY SAYS . . .

Intramural sports are popular
Frats and sororities are popular
Recreation facilities are great
Students aren't religious

ACADEMICS

Academic Rating	77
% students returning for sophomore year	84
Calendar	Quarter
Student/faculty ratio	17:1
Profs interesting rating	83
Profs accessible rating	87

Most classes have 20–29 students.
Most lab/discussion sessions have
20–29 students.

MOST POPULAR MAJORS

Computer Science; Mechanical Engineering;
Business Administration and Management,
General

STUDENTS SAY "..."

Academics

It's not just that Oregon State University seems to have it all, from "amazing research programs" to an "incredibly beautiful" campus and "inviting community." It's also that the administration does its utmost to ensure undergrads feel supported from the moment their first semester begins. This includes sending "frequent emails to check in on students' progress" and weekly "updates on career development, research, and community building" initiatives. Students praise many of OSU's offerings, from technology—and specifically engineering, given that the school has "an on-campus nuclear reactor"—to "excellent wildlife, ecology, and natural resources" programs. The hands-on nature of business classes also stood out to this first-year student: "We had to create microbusinesses with teams and sell products we made. It gave me a lot of insight and experience." No matter the course of study, undergrads generally receive a nice balance between "discussion-based classes and experiential learning." Moreover, "there are so many innovative peer education programs that supplement traditional lecture classes and give students another way to learn."

Though "experience varies quite drastically from professor to professor," students say that most of their instructors are "accessible, knowledgeable, and engaging." Indeed, "it's pretty rare that I have a class that feels like a drag." Overall, professors seem to be "very understanding of personal issues and are willing to be flexible and work with individual students to be sure that they succeed." As one enrollee concludes, "I have been blessed with some fantastic professors who have gone above and beyond in the time they put into me and my learning goals."

Campus Life

For the hardworking students of Oregon State who need a break from their studies, "the massive amount of extracurricular clubs and activities is amazing. Anyone can find a group of people with...similar interests." That's great, whether you're into formula racing, bouldering, or drag; there's even stuff like "Concrete Canoe (the civil engineering club where we build a canoe out of concrete, then race it against other school's concrete canoe teams)." There are even non-credited courses like a "bushcraft class." As this individual boasts, "I slept out in the woods for two nights in a tarp shelter using my skills!" For more traditional entertainments, students can "enjoy the active Greek life surrounding the campus." Students also note that because "the beach and mountains are both only an hour away... outdoor recreation is abundant."

Student Body

If Oregon State University were "the set of a movie, then it is very fair to say that we have a very diverse cast that come from all kinds of ethnic backgrounds." A wide variety of personality types as well, united by being "very smart and having fun quirks" from magnetics to country dancing. Students suggest that "the majority are very welcoming and nice and helpful" and that "I never had trouble starting conversations with anyone." Students note that while their classmates are "driven" they also manage to give off a "relaxed" vibe. Case in point: "You'll see multiple people wearing pajamas to class." This all makes it easy to recognize that most "everyone is down to have a really good time." Indeed, "I believe that everyone feels a sense of belonging here because of that."

OREGON STATE UNIVERSITY

Financial Aid: 541-737-2241 • E-Mail: osuadmit@oregonstate.edu • Website: http://oregonstate.edu/

THE PRINCETON REVIEW SAYS

Admissions

The school reports that its standardized testing policy for use in admission for Fall 2024 is Test Optional. It is unknown at this time if the 2024 testing policy will be permanent. The Princeton Review suggests that interested applicants consult with the school for the most up-to-date standardized testing policies. *Very important factors considered include:* academic GPA. *Important factors considered include:* rigor of secondary school record, application essay, talent/ability, character/personal qualities, volunteer work, work experience. *Other factors considered include:* class rank, standardized test scores, recommendation(s), extracurricular activities, level of applicant's interest. High school diploma is required and GED is accepted. *Academic units required:* 4 English, 3 math, 3 science, 2 science labs, 2 foreign language, 3 social studies. *Academic units recommended:* 3 science labs.

Financial Aid

Students should submit: FAFSA. Priority filing deadline is 2/28. The Princeton Review suggests that all financial aid forms be submitted as soon as possible (see page 5 for a note on the FAFSA). *Need-based scholarships/grants offered:* College/university scholarship or grant aid from institutional funds; Federal Pell; Private scholarships; SEOG; State scholarships/grants. *Loan aid offered:* Direct PLUS loans; Direct Subsidized Loans; Direct Unsubsidized Loans; College/university loans from institutional funds. Admitted students will be notified of awards on a rolling basis beginning 4/1. Federal Work-Study Program available. Institutional employment available.

The Inside Word

Oregon State University duly notes that academic performance and test scores are not the only criteria for admission. A broad range of characteristics and perspectives are taken into consideration during the university's admissions process to determine if prospective students are able to succeed here. OSU wants to understand you as a unique, contributing individual.

THE SCHOOL SAYS "..."

From the Admissions Office

"Since 1868, Oregon State University's mission has been to conduct world-leading research and provide a high-quality, relevant, and affordable education for the people of Oregon and beyond.

"We are Oregon's leading public research university with two welcoming campuses, 11 colleges, 200 academic programs, and excellent and inspiring faculty committed to the success of each student.

"Oregon State is one of only two universities in the U.S. to have land, sea, space and sun grant designations, and we take seriously our responsibility to serve the people of Oregon, the nation and the world. Our impact resounds around the globe because we are out there, addressing the most pressing challenges and providing discoveries that improve the health and prosperity of society, the economy and our planet.

"We are known for offering some of the top programs in the world, including forestry (No. 2), oceanography (No. 3) and agriculture (No. 13). Nationally, Oregon State is among the nation's academic leaders in robotics, creative writing and innovative on-line learning. In the classroom, in laboratories and in the community, we provide students the opportunities and the tools necessary to succeed, including exposure to innovations in educational technology and access to opportunities for experiential learning and discovery.

"Our students learn by doing. And what students experience at Oregon State University not only shapes their own lives, it prepares them to transform a future that is smarter, healthier, more prosperous and just."

SELECTIVITY
Admissions Rating	85
# of applicants	14,890
% of applicants accepted	81
% of acceptees attending	31

FIRST-YEAR PROFILE
Testing policy	Test Optional
Range SAT EBRW	540–650
Range SAT math	540–660
Range ACT composite	22–28
# submitting SAT scores	2,547
% submitting SAT scores	69
# submitting ACT scores	1,661
% submitting ACT scores	45
Average HS GPA	3.6
% frosh submitting high school GPA	100
% graduated top 10% of class	28
% graduated top 25% of class	58
% graduated top 50% of class	89

DEADLINES
Early action	
Deadline	11/1
Notification	12/15
Regular	
Priority	2/1
Deadline	9/1
Notification	Rolling, 10/15
Nonfall registration?	Yes

APPLICANTS OFTEN PREFER
University of California—Davis; University of Washington

APPLICANTS SOMETIMES PREFER
University of Oregon; Washington State University; Willamette University

APPLICANTS RARELY PREFER
Portland State University; Western Oregon University

FINANCIAL FACTS
Financial Aid Rating	79
Annual in-state tuition	$9,390
Annual out-of-state tuition	$28,365
Room and board	$12,855
Required fees	$1,776
Books and supplies	$1,200
Average frosh need-based scholarship	$8,662
Average UG need-based scholarship	$7,682
% needy frosh rec. need-based scholarship or grant aid	83
% needy UG rec. need-based scholarship or grant aid	77
% needy frosh rec. non-need-based scholarship or grant aid	3
% needy UG rec. non-need-based scholarship or grant aid	2
% needy frosh rec. need-based self-help aid	96
% needy UG rec. need-based self-help aid	96
% frosh rec. any financial aid	76
% UG rec. any financial aid	69
% UG borrow to pay for school	56
Average cumulative indebtedness	$28,482
% frosh need fully met	14
% ugrads need fully met	11
Average % of frosh need met	71
Average % of ugrad need met	68

PACE UNIVERSITY

One Pace Plaza, New York, NY 10038 • Admissions: 866-722-3338 • Fax: 212-346-1040

CAMPUS LIFE

Quality of Life Rating	82
Fire Safety Rating	92
Green Rating	88
Type of school	Private
Affiliation	No Affiliation
Environment	Metropolis

STUDENTS

Total undergrad enrollment	7,766
% male/female/another gender	33/67/0
% from out of state	50
% frosh live on campus	71
% ugrads live on campus	42
# of fraternities (% join)	7 (4)
# of sororities (% join)	8 (4)
% African American	10
% Asian	8
% White	48
% Hispanic	21
% Native American	<1
% Pacific Islander	<1
% Two or more races	5
% Race and/or ethnicity unknown	1
% international	6
# of countries represented	75

SURVEY SAYS . . .

Students love New York, NY
College radio is popular
Theater is popular
Active student government
Theater is popular

ACADEMICS

Academic Rating	74
% students returning for sophomore year	72
% students graduating within 4 years	50
% students graduating within 6 years	61
Calendar	Semester
Student/faculty ratio	14:1
Profs interesting rating	81
Profs accessible rating	84

Most classes have 10–19 students.
Most lab/discussion sessions have
20–29 students.

MOST POPULAR MAJORS

Research and Experimental Psychology, Other;
Registered Nursing/Registered Nurse; Finance

STUDENTS SAY "..."

Academics

With an emphasis on student-centered learning and close mentorship, Pace University offers students a liberal arts education in two New York locations. With opportunities in close proximity to the theaters of Broadway, students describe the performing arts department at Pace as "its own entity. Everyone is very creative and talented, [and] passionate about what they do." One student particularly enjoys the firsthand experiences offered at Pace: "I take a lot of studio classes for my major, so while they are three hours long ... I get to have fun learning with hands-on experience." Other programs also earn raves, with one student enthusing: "As a nursing major, we utilize the simulation lab often and when I go there, I am able to practice certain skills ... and gets me excited to eventually become [a nurse]." Professional experiences are a favorite across majors on campus, whether that's "advertising with a real world client" or "at an on-campus business run by students."

While faculty on campus do "an incredible job setting students up for success and igniting passions within their field," students appreciate that many of them are also "working professionals, [which adds] so much extra knowledge to courses." A second-year student agrees, saying "Our professors all reference their own experience in the field to teach us 'insider information.' This is exceptionally helpful in my health science/public health major, since I get to hear a lot of what these professors had wished they knew going into the field."

Campus Life

With two relatively close undergraduate campuses—one in Westchester and the other in downtown Manhattan—Pace students can pick between the bucolic university setting and the heart of a thriving city. The 200-acre Westchester campus offers a range of outdoor activities such as hiking and skiing. Students love that "We have lots of different clubs to ensure that there is a chance for everyone to be included," like writing for the school newspaper, singing in the *a capella* club, or moving with the dance and hip hop groups. Westchester students particularly enjoy "watching the basketball and football games, and interacting all around campus, especially during spring semester."

Students at the NYC campus enjoy all the city has to offer, including "going to parks, visiting museums, [and] finding new places to eat." Students list drag brunches and food truck days as favorite events, and Greek life and cultural groups such as Hillel are also popular on campus. To the delight of many students, "Pace gives cheap tickets to Broadway shows [and] sports games."

Student Body

To describe the diverse, inclusive atmosphere at Pace that they love so much, a third-year student notes "Walking around the campus, you can see everyone...being themselves: dressed in a riot of different colors, styles, personalities coming together in different groups, forming bonds in their differences." Another senior characterizes the atmosphere as "a diverse group of students from all over the world. This makes the community lively, culturally diverse, and exciting." It also makes for an exciting and open place for these "creative, individualistic artists... the talents are limitless." Both Pace campuses are described as "welcoming" environments where students "take care of each other" students appreciate the "growing LGBTQIA+ voice at my campus" and the overall friendliness shown across the school. In essence, Pace offers a "tight-knit atmosphere...Students are willing to connect due to our intimate population. You can't go anywhere without exchanging a hello or a smile with someone you know."

PACE UNIVERSITY

Financial Aid: 212-346-1309 • E-Mail: undergradadmission@pace.edu • Website: www.pace.edu

THE PRINCETON REVIEW SAYS

Admissions

The school reports that its standardized testing policy for use in admission for Fall 2024 is Test Optional. The 2024 testing policy will be permanent. The Princeton Review suggests that interested applicants consult with the school for the most up-to-date standardized testing policies. *Very important factors considered include:* rigor of secondary school record, application essay. *Important factors considered include:* class rank, academic GPA, recommendation(s). *Other factors considered include:* standardized test scores, interview, extracurricular activities, talent/ability, character/personal qualities, alumni/ae relation, volunteer work, work experience. High school diploma is required and GED is accepted. *Academic units required:* 4 English, 3 math, 2 science labs, 2 foreign language, 3 history, 2 academic electives.

Financial Aid

Students should submit: FAFSA; State aid form. Priority filing deadline is 11/15. The Princeton Review suggests that all financial aid forms be submitted as soon as possible (see page 5 for a note on the FAFSA). *Need-based scholarships/grants offered:* College/university scholarship or grant aid from institutional funds; Federal Nursing Scholarships; Federal Pell; Private scholarships; SEOG; State scholarships/grants. *Loan aid offered:* Direct PLUS loans; Direct Subsidized Loans; Direct Unsubsidized Loans; Federal Nursing Loans. Admitted students will be notified of awards on a rolling basis beginning 12/1. Federal Work-Study Program available. Institutional employment available.

The Inside Word

Certainly, gaining admission to Pace is competitive. But you can take comfort in knowing that the university takes a holistic approach when reviewing candidates. Therefore, it's important not to slack on any facet of your application. When choosing teachers and mentors for your letters of recommendation, make sure they can really speak to your character and academic potential. Finally, we should note that auditions and/or interviews are required for any student who wants to enroll in the School of Performing Arts.

THE SCHOOL SAYS "..."

From the Admissions Office

"Pace University is at the forefront of creating opportunity. Through the convergence of strong academics, experiential learning, and dedicated advising, we empower our students and positively impact our communities. We develop and launch programs that are relevant, focused, and forward-looking to meet the needs of the workforce of the future. We harness the world-class energy and talent of New York City and Westchester County and leverage the unparalleled access to internship and job opportunities. We champion diversity, equity, and inclusion and celebrate the innate potential of learners of all ages to achieve success.

"Currently, Pace University enrolls more than 13,000 diverse individuals, including first-generation, international, and non-traditional students (both undergrad and grad). Pace combines the benefits and resources of a large university with the personalized attention and focus associated with a small college. Dedicated full-time and adjunct faculty members balance academic preparation with professional experience, bringing a unique dynamic to the classroom. They are practitioners, consultants, advisors, and mentors to our students.

"Pace's signature program, the Pace Path, empowers students to succeed in their fields by combining powerful academics, dedicated mentoring, and immersive experiences including research, clinicals, civic engagement, study abroad, and internships. Pace University has one of the largest internship programs of any college in the New York metropolitan area. Last year, Pace students engaged in more than 8,900 internships, co-ops, field experiences, and clinicals with more than 1,200 different employers. That's why within one year of graduation, Pace students are employed at a rate almost 20% ahead of the national average."

SELECTIVITY

Admissions Rating	82
# of applicants	26,613
% of applicants accepted	83
% of acceptees attending	10
# of early decision applicants	88
% accepted early decision	97

FIRST-YEAR PROFILE

Testing policy	Test Optional
Range SAT composite	1140–1290
Range SAT EBRW	580–670
Range SAT math	540–630
Range ACT composite	24–29
# submitting SAT scores	377
% submitting SAT scores	18
# submitting ACT scores	111
% submitting ACT scores	5
Average HS GPA	3.4
% frosh submitting high school GPA	100
% graduated top 10% of class	19
% graduated top 25% of class	48
% graduated top 50% of class	81

DEADLINES

Early decision	
Deadline	11/1
Notification	12/1
Early action	
Deadline	11/15
Notification	12/1
Regular	
Priority	2/15
Deadline	2/15
Notification	Rolling
Nonfall registration?	Yes

APPLICANTS ALSO LOOK AT

City University of New York—Baruch College;
City University of New York–City College;
City University of New York—Hunter College; Fordham
University; New York University;
Rutgers University—New Brunswick;
Saint John's University

FINANCIAL FACTS

Financial Aid Rating	82
Annual tuition	$48,152
Room and board	$20,480
Required fees	$1,874
Books and supplies	$800
Average frosh need-based scholarship	$35,380
Average UG need-based scholarship	$32,513
% needy frosh rec. need-based scholarship or grant aid	100
% needy UG rec. need-based scholarship or grant aid	98
% needy frosh rec. non-need-based scholarship or grant aid	15
% needy UG rec. non-need-based scholarship or grant aid	14
% needy frosh rec. need-based self-help aid	75
% needy UG rec. need-based self-help aid	75
% frosh rec. any financial aid	100
% UG rec. any financial aid	96
% UG borrow to pay for school	64
Average cumulative indebtedness	$36,501
% frosh need fully met	17
% ugrads need fully met	17
Average % of frosh need met	75
Average % of ugrad need met	72

PENN STATE UNIVERSITY PARK

201 Old Main, University Park, PA 16802 • Admissions: 814-865-4700 • Fax: 814-863-7590

CAMPUS LIFE

Quality of Life Rating	87
Fire Safety Rating	98
Green Rating	98
Type of school	Public
Environment	Town

STUDENTS

Total undergrad enrollment	40,286
% male/female/another gender	53/47/NR
% from out of state	34
% ugrads live on campus	25
# of fraternities	45
# of sororities	26
% African American	4
% Asian	7
% White	65
% Hispanic	8
% Native American	<1
% Pacific Islander	<1
% Two or more races	4
% Race and/or ethnicity unknown	2
% international	10
# of countries represented	124

SURVEY SAYS . . .

Students are happy
Classroom facilities are great
Lab facilities are great
Great library
Career services are great
Internships are widely available
School is well run
Students are friendly
Students get along with local community
Great off-campus food
Recreation facilities are great
Everyone loves the Nittany Lions
Intramural sports are popular
Campus newspaper is popular
Alumni active on campus

ACADEMICS

Academic Rating	82
% students returning for sophomore year	93
% students graduating within 4 years	69
% students graduating within 6 years	85
Calendar	Semester
Student/faculty ratio	15:1
Profs interesting rating	87
Profs accessible rating	92

Most classes have 20–29 students.
Most lab/discussion sessions have
20–29 students.

STUDENTS SAY "..."

Academics

Immense "pride and a sense of community" pervade every aspect of life at Penn State. Students love the remarkable "school spirit" and "strong family feel" on this vibrant campus, and they are equally proud of the "quality education" they receive. An affordable public institution, PSU offers "highly regarded programs across a wide range of academic colleges," including a "prestigious undergrad business school," top engineering and education majors, and the competitive Schreyer Honors College, which participants describe as "the finest honors program in the nation." "Classes freshman year are mostly lectures," which can be "intimidating" for new students. Fortunately, "even in lectures with hundreds of students, many professors still make an effort to get to know their class and have plenty of office hours to make themselves more accessible." Plus, the academic experience becomes more individualized as you move through the system. A current student shares, "As I have gotten into my majors, my classes are down to about 15 to 40 people and there are a lot more discussions. I know all of my professors personally now." Academics are often described as "rigorous" and "competitive," but most students are able to stay afloat; here, "professors will challenge you, but it's nothing that a hard-working student can't handle." Job-seeking seniors praise the career center, as well as the school's fantastic alumni connections, saying, "The Penn State networking web is incredible!" Not to mention, the school's enviable "location within driving distance to Philadelphia, Washington, and New York" makes it easier to score a job at graduation.

Campus Life

If you are looking for the "full college experience," you'll find "the perfect mix of great academics, social life, and sports" at Penn State. While "the library is usually filled with students" during the week, "everyone counts down the days till the weekend, then its party, party, party." Throughout fall semester, football is a campus-wide obsession; "game days are super exciting and unifying for the student population," which turns out in large numbers to tailgate and cheer at Beaver Stadium. In addition to sports, "Greek life dominates the social scene," though students also flock to the many bars in downtown State College. A current student jokes, "Nothing brings the Penn State community together like stumbling around downtown with 3,000 other drunken students." Those looking for a mellower night out will find "on-campus concerts, stand-up comedians, craft nights, sporting events, and other ways of having fun without drugs or alcohol." Others like to "go out to the local avenue and try new eateries, and walk around campus and enjoy the scenery." In addition to the "killer social life," there are hundreds of clubs and student groups; of particular note, many students "fit in by joining THON, the largest student-run philanthropy in the world, that raises money for children with pediatric cancer." No matter what your interests, "between football games, Late Nights at the HUB, festivities downtown, movies, shows at Eisenhower Auditorium or the Penn State Theatre, concerts at the BJC…there is something for everyone."

Student Body

With a total enrollment of more than 45,000, "Penn State is the passion and pride of a large and diverse student body." Demographically, the school draws heavily from the Northeast; in particular, there are "lots of kids from the tristate area," and most could be described as "athletic, suburban, and friendly middle-class." While some note that "the percentage of minorities and foreign students is low," they also say, "pretty much every student will find somewhere to fit in." Especially during the first year, "there are many opportunities to meet new people," and almost "everyone is friendly," making it easy to form bonds and build relationships. The best way to make friends is to "try different clubs and find your niche"; from Greek organizations to sports, most Penn Staters have "a great enthusiasm for extracurricular and philanthropic involvement." On that note, most undergrads "take their education seriously," but achieve a "good balance of school and social life."

PENN STATE UNIVERSITY PARK

Financial Aid: 814-865-6301 • E-Mail: admissions@psu.edu • Website: www.psu.edu

THE PRINCETON REVIEW SAYS

Admissions

The school reports that its standardized testing policy for use in admission for Fall 2024 is Test Optional. It is unknown at this time if the 2024 testing policy will be permanent. The Princeton Review suggests that interested applicants consult with the school for the most up-to-date standardized testing policies. *Very important factors considered include:* academic GPA. *Important factors considered include:* rigor of secondary school record. *Other factors considered include:* standardized test scores, talent/ability, alumni/ae relation, geographical residence, state residency, racial/ethnic status. High school diploma is required and GED is accepted. *Academic units required:* 4 English, 3 math, 3 science, 2 foreign language, 3 social studies. *Academic units recommended:* 3 foreign language.

Financial Aid

Students should submit: FAFSA. Priority filing deadline is 2/15. The Princeton Review suggests that all financial aid forms be submitted as soon as possible (see page 5 for a note on the FAFSA). *Need-based scholarships/grants offered:* College/university scholarship or grant aid from institutional funds; Federal Pell; Private scholarships; SEOG; State scholarships/grants; United Negro College Fund. *Loan aid offered:* Direct PLUS loans; Direct Subsidized Loans; Direct Unsubsidized Loans; College/university loans from institutional funds. Admitted students will be notified of awards on a rolling basis beginning in March. Federal Work-Study Program available. Institutional employment available.

The Inside Word

Though the school does not have any minimum requirements for an incoming student's GPA or standardized test scores, high school GPA is by far the most important factor in PSU admissions. In the absence of a test score, Penn State will continue to look at all factors of a student's application, including grades earned in academic coursework; performance in honors, International Baccalaureate and Advanced Placement courses; a student's essay/personal statement; involvement in activities; and other achievements. PSU is a popular choice for Pennsylvania residents and admits on a rolling basis; prospective students should submit their applications as early as possible.

THE SCHOOL SAYS "..."

From the Admissions Office

"Founded in 1855, Penn State is a world-class public research university with a broad mission of teaching, research and public service. Ranked as one of the world's top universities, Penn State serves a total of nearly 100,000 students through its 24 campuses, which include a medical college, two law schools, an online World Campus and a school of graduate professional studies. As Pennsylvania's sole land-grant institution, Penn State educates nearly 100,000 students each year in more than 160 undergraduate and more than 160 graduate degree programs.

"Ranging in size from 600 to 4,000 students, most of Penn State's residential and commuter locations offer the first two years of baccalaureate instruction as well as a limited number of two- and four-year degree programs. These small-college settings focus on the needs of new students by offering smaller classes and close interaction with faculty. More than half of the undergraduates who complete their studies at University Park start at another Penn State campus.

"Applicants are qualified for review for any of Penn State's campuses, with preferences considered in the order requested. Choice of location and entrance difficulty are based, in part, on demand. Due to its popularity, the University Park campus is the most competitive for admission. Freshman applicants may submit the results from the SAT or the ACT with the writing component.

"Visit http://www.psu.edu for more information."

SELECTIVITY

Admissions Rating	89
# of applicants	78,508
% of applicants accepted	58
% of acceptees attending	19
# offered a place on the wait list	2,481
% accepting a place on wait list	61
% admitted from wait list	96

FIRST-YEAR PROFILE

Testing policy	Test Optional
Range SAT EBRW	600–690
Range SAT math	600–710
Range ACT composite	26–32
# submitting SAT scores	3,148
% submitting SAT scores	37
# submitting ACT scores	697
% submitting ACT scores	8

DEADLINES

Early action	
Deadline	11/1
Notification	12/24
Regular	
Notification	Rolling, 10/1
Nonfall registration?	Yes

APPLICANTS ALSO LOOK AT

Rutgers University–Camden; Temple University; University of Delaware; University of Maryland, College Park; University of Pittsburgh—Pittsburgh Campus

FINANCIAL FACTS

Financial Aid Rating	76
Annual in-state tuition	$18,368
Annual out-of-state tuition	$35,946
Room and board	$12,744
Required fees	$530
Books and supplies	$1,840
Average frosh need-based scholarship	$7,621
Average UG need-based scholarship	$7,906
% needy frosh rec. need-based scholarship or grant aid	33
% needy UG rec. need-based scholarship or grant aid	42
% needy frosh rec. non-need-based scholarship or grant aid	52
% needy UG rec. non-need-based scholarship or grant aid	56
% needy frosh rec. need-based self-help aid	68
% needy UG rec. need-based self-help aid	72
% frosh rec. any financial aid	64
% UG rec. any financial aid	65
% UG borrow to pay for school	55
Average cumulative indebtedness	$43,359
% frosh need fully met	28
% ugrads need fully met	29
Average % of frosh need met	61
Average % of ugrad need met	63

PEPPERDINE UNIVERSITY

24255 Pacific Coast Highway, Malibu, CA 90263 • Admissions: 310-506-4000 • Fax: 310-506-4861

STUDENTS SAY "..."

Academics

Pepperdine University is a Christian liberal arts school situated in picturesque Malibu, California. Many students say the "professors are the greatest strength of Pepperdine," citing "mentorship [and] research collaboration" opportunities thanks to the small classes. Faculty "genuinely care about your individual success, both personally and academically." One student says that it's normal for "them to invite students to their homes for dinner or to host a Bible study group." Professors are lauded as "very passionate" and "successful in their field." Many professors take advantage of Pepperdine's location with "field trips to the beach, lagoon, waste treatment plant, museums, and organizations in Los Angeles." The great scenery doesn't just include California: Pepperdine's "absolutely fantastic" international programs are a draw for many, sending students to destinations like Argentina, Italy, Germany, Switzerland, and England. "The Church of Christ mission is prevalent," as all undergrads are required to take three religion courses.

Campus Life

Students take pride in their "academically rigorous and beautiful school." They find Pepperdine's campus to be "drop dead gorgeous" with an "amazing ocean view." Its prime location in Southern California means there are plenty of options for activities outside of the classroom: students "surf, hike, [and visit] museums." Of course, church is prominent here too. "We are...allowed to freely incorporate our faith into our education," one student says. The school also features a Convocation Series, although some express concerns about that since it "is required [and] factors into [students'] GPA." They still find other ways to connect with religious communities, though, often "doing [community] service in an off-campus location" with a religious affiliation. Evenings bring "a lot of events on campus either sponsored by clubs, athletics, [or] the student programming board," but one thing undergrads would like to see more of is "school spirit at the athletic games." Pepperdine has a dry campus, so students looking for that kind of nightlife spend "weekends...[taking] trips into L.A. [or attending] parties off campus."

Student Body

Pepperdine students rave about their "welcoming," "caring," and "tight-knit" community. "Everyone is genuinely interested in how to make the world better and people take up a real interest in each other," says a student. "Everyone always has a smile on their face" and "in times of crisis the support system is tremendously helpful." "Even though there is a large group of both the left and right," one student says this is "the most open-minded student body." Students find "diverse...personalities and ideas" but say the school would benefit from attracting more students who don't exactly fit the "Christian, white, conservative," and affluent background. Students are "taught to live life with purpose, service, and leadership." Overall there's a "mix of driven entrepreneurs and chill surfers," and "you have your partiers and then you have the very religious" students.

PEPPERDINE UNIVERSITY

Financial Aid: 310-506-4301 • E-Mail: admission-seaver@pepperdine.edu • Website: www.pepperdine.edu

THE PRINCETON REVIEW SAYS

Admissions

The school reports that its standardized testing policy for use in admission for Fall 2024 is Test Optional. The 2024 testing policy will be temporary. The Princeton Review suggests that interested applicants consult with the school for the most up-to-date standardized testing policies. *Very important factors considered include:* rigor of secondary school record, academic GPA, application essay, extracurricular activities, talent/ability, character/personal qualities, religious affiliation/commitment. *Important factors considered include:* recommendation(s), volunteer work. *Other factors considered include:* standardized test scores, interview, first generation, alumni/ae relation, racial/ethnic status, work experience. High school diploma is required and GED is accepted.

Financial Aid

Students should submit: FAFSA. Priority filing deadline is 2/15. The Princeton Review suggests that all financial aid forms be submitted as soon as possible (see page 5 for a note on the FAFSA). *Need-based scholarships/grants offered:* College/university scholarship or grant aid from institutional funds; Federal Pell; Private scholarships; SEOG; State scholarships/grants; United Negro College Fund. *Loan aid offered:* Direct PLUS loans; Direct Subsidized Loans; Direct Unsubsidized Loans; College/university loans from institutional funds. Admitted students will be notified of awards on or about 4/5. Federal Work-Study Program available. Institutional employment available.

The Inside Word

Admission to Pepperdine is highly selective. Decisions are made based on a student's academic record, standardized test scores (if submitted), an academic letter of recommendation, and personal statements. Applicant's demonstrated character and leadership and service experience are also factors. Students affiliated with the Church of Christ are eligible for special Church of Christ scholarships; to be considered, applicants must submit a letter of recommendation from a church leader.

THE SCHOOL SAYS "..."

From the Admissions Office

"Pepperdine's curriculum emphasizes the broad discovery of all disciplines and is at the forefront of holistically developing the next generation of global leaders through rigorous curriculum, faculty mentorship, internship experiences, and tailored research opportunities. With its renowned Malibu campus, facilities throughout California and in Washington, D.C., and six international campuses in South America and Europe, the University is a point of convergence for scholars, believers, artists, athletes, and innovators. We seek students who show promise of academic achievement at the collegiate level. We also look for students who are committed to serving others and demonstrate the potential of emerging as a leader in our community."

SELECTIVITY

Admissions Rating	92
# of applicants	11,466
% of applicants accepted	49
% of acceptees attending	17
# offered a place on the wait list	1,651
% accepting a place on wait list	60
% admitted from wait list	0

FIRST-YEAR PROFILE

Testing policy	Test Optional
Range SAT composite	1290–1460
Range SAT EBRW	650–730
Range SAT math	635–750
Range ACT composite	28–32
# submitting SAT scores	152
% submitting SAT scores	16
# submitting ACT scores	127
% submitting ACT scores	13
Average HS GPA	3.8
% frosh submitting high school GPA	97

DEADLINES

Early action	
Deadline	11/1
Notification	1/10
Regular	
Deadline	1/15
Notification	4/1
Nonfall registration?	Yes

APPLICANTS ALSO LOOK AT

University of California—Berkeley; University of California-Irvine; University of California—Los Angeles; University of California—San Diego; University of California—Santa Barbara; University of Southern California

FINANCIAL FACTS

Financial Aid Rating	83
Annual tuition	$65,990
Room and board	$23,270
Required fees	$752
Books and supplies	$1,000
Average frosh need-based scholarship	$42,983
Average UG need-based scholarship	$42,822
% needy frosh rec. need-based scholarship or grant aid	99
% needy UG rec. need-based scholarship or grant aid	99
% needy frosh rec. non-need-based scholarship or grant aid	0
% needy UG rec. non-need-based scholarship or grant aid	0
% needy frosh rec. need-based self-help aid	63
% needy UG rec. need-based self-help aid	63
% frosh rec. any financial aid	94
% UG rec. any financial aid	92
% UG borrow to pay for school	47
Average cumulative indebtedness	$28,962
% frosh need fully met	17
% ugrads need fully met	19
Average % of frosh need met	78
Average % of ugrad need met	76

PITZER COLLEGE

1050 North Mills Avenue, Claremont, CA 91711-6101 • Admissions: 909-621-8000 • Fax: 909-621-8770

CAMPUS LIFE

Quality of Life Rating	95
Fire Safety Rating	60*
Green Rating	95
Type of school	Private
Affiliation	No Affiliation
Environment	Town

STUDENTS

Total undergrad enrollment	1,212
% male/female/another gender	40/58/2
% from out of state	57
% frosh live on campus	100
% ugrads live on campus	75
# of fraternities	0
# of sororities	0
% African American	5
% Asian	12
% White	49
% Hispanic	13
% Native American	<1
% Pacific Islander	<1
% Two or more races	9
% Race and/or ethnicity unknown	4
% international	7
# of countries represented	28

SURVEY SAYS . . .

Lots of liberal students
Students are happy
Great financial aid
No one cheats
Students are friendly
Students aren't religious
Students involved in community service
Students environmentally aware
Great food on campus
Dorms are like palaces
Easy to get around campus
College radio is popular
Active student government
Active minority support groups
Active student-run political groups

ACADEMICS

Academic Rating	89
% students returning for sophomore year	89
% students graduating within 4 years	57
% students graduating within 6 years	86
Calendar	Semester
Student/faculty ratio	10:1
Profs interesting rating	92
Profs accessible rating	95
Most classes have 10–19 students.	

MOST POPULAR MAJORS

Psychology; Environmental Analysis/Studies;
Political Studies

STUDENTS SAY "..."

Academics

Just outside of Los Angeles, Pitzer College is a "socially responsible and progressive" liberal arts and sciences college with "great academics" and "active students" and that "feels like a second home." Students prize Pitzer's "flexible graduation requirements," especially "the ability to create your own major," and "the options and resources offered throughout the Claremont Consortium," which includes the ability to take classes at any of the other five Claremont Colleges. Because the school is so small, with an enrollment of just under 1,100 undergrads, students feel they belong to a close and caring community: "Pitzer College is basically a year-round summer camp where people go to grow as individuals through liberal arts studies and through relationships that they build." Current students praise the school's "interdisciplinary focus and non-Western centric studies." Furthermore, students say they "love the academic support" they receive at Pitzer, especially the professors, who are "well connected but incredibly caring." "All my professors know me by name," students tell us, "even in introductory courses. [Instructors] all have PhDs from prestigious universities and demonstrate love for teaching." Experiential learning opportunities "[extend] far beyond the classroom to community service projects, the dorms, and abroad," and, because of the school's size, students often get the chance to conduct research with their professors as well. "By my second semester of my first year a professor offered me a research position," one student tells us, which "is typical for many students since class sizes are small, so we get to create intimate relationships and have direct discussions with professors."

Campus Life

Because of the mild southern California climate, Pitzer students can be found "around the pool or in the Grove House" (a student center), as well as enjoying other idyllic locations. "I manage the school garden and care for chickens," one student tells us. "I spend a lot of afternoons just hanging out in the garden doing homework or talking to friends." Weekends are spent taking advantage of the surrounding landscapes by "hiking in the mountains by the school or [driving] into L.A. to shop or go to the beach." Students here are serious about their academics, but they do "study together and mix chatting in with homework." They also take a lot of ownership over how the campus is run: "We sit on hiring committees and our Student Senate has more power than the administration." "Multiple student-run eateries [and] strong student organizations" create a "collaborative atmosphere." On-campus there is "a very active party scene," and "on weekends, [themed] parties are usually hosted by the school." Students "love that Pitzer provides a super progressive environment."

Student Body

While Pitzer's student body contains diverse personalities and backgrounds, in one respect these Sagehens are the same: "Everyone is passionate about something. You won't find a single student who isn't somehow involved on campus outside of the classroom." At Pitzer, "most students tend to lean far left in ideology," and they are generally "outspoken about their views...but open-minded students of any political ideology should not fear the liberal environment." "I cannot count the number of nights I have stayed up until 2:00 A.M. discussing issues ranging from Middle Eastern politics to growing up in the inner-cities," one student tells us. Students speak highly of one another and judge that their peers "are sincerely pursuing passions that they believe are reflective of themselves, as opposed to doing things for jobs/other forms of external validation." Many students are focused on "social justice" and environmental issues, though some reject the "Pitzer hippy stereotype." More than anything, they seem to agree that Pitzer students are "intellectual, and seeking to use that intellect to do good in the world."

PITZER COLLEGE

Financial Aid: 909-621-8208 • E-Mail: admission@pitzer.edu • Website: www.pitzer.edu

THE PRINCETON REVIEW SAYS

Admissions

The school reports that its standardized testing policy for use in admission for Fall 2024 is Test Optional. It is unknown at this time if the 2024 testing policy will be permanent. The Princeton Review suggests that interested applicants consult with the school for the most up-to-date standardized testing policies. *Very important factors considered include:* rigor of secondary school record, academic GPA, application essay, character/personal qualities. *Important factors considered include:* recommendation(s), extracurricular activities, talent/ability, volunteer work. *Other factors considered include:* class rank, standardized test scores, interview, first generation, alumni/ae relation, geographical residence, state residency, racial/ethnic status, work experience, level of applicant's interest. High school diploma is required and GED is accepted. *Academic units recommended:* 4 English, 3 math, 3 science, 3 foreign language, 3 social studies.

Financial Aid

Students should submit: CSS/Financial Aid Profile; FAFSA; Noncustodial Profile; State aid form. Priority filing deadline is 1/7. The Princeton Review suggests that all financial aid forms be submitted as soon as possible (see page 5 for a note on the FAFSA). *Need-based scholarships/grants offered:* College/university scholarship or grant aid from institutional funds; Federal Pell; Private scholarships; SEOG; State scholarships/grants. *Loan aid offered:* Direct PLUS loans; Direct Subsidized Loans; Direct Unsubsidized Loans; College/university loans from institutional funds. Admitted students will be notified of awards on or about 4/1. Federal Work-Study Program available. Institutional employment available.

The Inside Word

Prospective students will use the Common Application with the addition of a Pitzer Writing Supplement to apply for admission. Use the Writing Supplement to demonstrate not only your writing ability but your passion and creativity. It is the admission office's way to see if you would be a good fit on campus, so get to know the school's values (social responsibility, intercultural understanding, interdisciplinary learning, student engagement, and environmental sustainability), and make sure they are reflected in what you write.

THE SCHOOL SAYS "..."

From the Admissions Office

"Pitzer is about opportunities. It's about possibilities. The students who come here are looking for something different from the usual 'take two courses from column A, two courses from column B, and two courses from column C.' That kind of arbitrary selection doesn't make a satisfying education at Pitzer. So we look for students who want to have an impact on their own education, who want the chief responsibility—with help from their faculty advisors—in designing their own futures."

SELECTIVITY

Admissions Rating	97
# of applicants	3,500
% of applicants accepted	18
% of acceptees attending	48
# offered a place on the wait list	775
% accepting a place on wait list	36
% admitted from wait list	<1
# of early decision applicants	406
% accepted early decision	40

FIRST-YEAR PROFILE

Testing policy	Test Optional
Average HS GPA	4.0
% frosh submitting high school GPA	92
% graduated top 10% of class	52
% graduated top 25% of class	76
% graduated top 50% of class	100

DEADLINES

Early decision	
Deadline	11/15
Notification	12/18
Other ED deadline	1/1
Other ED notification	2/15
Regular	
Deadline	1/1
Notification	4/1
Nonfall registration?	No

APPLICANTS ALSO LOOK AT

Occidental College; Pomona College; University of California—Berkeley; University of California—Davis; University of California—San Diego; University of California—Santa Barbara; Wesleyan University

FINANCIAL FACTS

Financial Aid Rating	95
Annual tuition	$62,392
Room and board	$21,374
Required fees	$300
Books and supplies	$1,100
Average frosh need-based scholarship	$51,504
Average UG need-based scholarship	$49,525
% needy frosh rec. need-based scholarship or grant aid	72
% needy UG rec. need-based scholarship or grant aid	84
% needy frosh rec. non-need-based scholarship or grant aid	3
% needy UG rec. non-need-based scholarship or grant aid	1
% needy frosh rec. need-based self-help aid	75
% needy UG rec. need-based self-help aid	84
% frosh rec. any financial aid	75
% UG rec. any financial aid	84
% UG borrow to pay for school	36
Average cumulative indebtedness	$19,715
% frosh need fully met	100
% ugrads need fully met	100
Average % of frosh need met	100
Average % of ugrad need met	100

POMONA COLLEGE

333 N. College Way, Claremont, CA 91711 • Admissions: 909-621-8000 • Fax: 909-621-8952

STUDENTS SAY "..."

Academics

At Pomona College in Claremont, you can get "an academically rigorous education" in a "low-stress California atmosphere." At this prestigious liberal arts school, "The professors are, for the most part, fantastic—engaging, creative, and sharp," and "all classes are taught by professors, not grad students or TAs." With small class sizes in every department, "there is an emphasis on collaborative learning," and "many professors are great discussion leaders and really motivate students to get involved in class." Students have the advantage of "getting to know professors outside the classroom, in any setting, from office hours, to Thanksgiving dinner at their homes." Illustrating how personal the experience can be, a student tells us, "Today, I had a class with seven people in it, then lunch with a physics professor, and then a personal tutorial with a philosophy professor." Another student adds, "Between department barbecues, parties, and weekend retreats, by the time you're an upperclassman, you will know most of the professors in your major department quite well." In complement to the intimate academic atmosphere, Pomona "offers the resources of a large university" through The Claremont College consortium, which offers joint events and cross-registration with four adjoining colleges. Among other programs, "Pomona pays for students to take otherwise unpaid internship positions." Students praise Pomona's "efficiency in taking care of administrative tasks such as financial aid and registration," adding that the administration "is very good at responding to what students want."

Campus Life

Pomona students are "ridiculously happy" about their lot in life, and why shouldn't they be? They're living in a "perfect world full of intelligent, engaging, and open individuals, amazing academics, brilliant opportunities to get involved in, and enough sunshine to make anyone happy to be alive." The weather is a key aspect of the experience, and "on a nice day, everyone heads outside in shorts and T-shirts to do their class work." On any given day, "you'll see people setting up telescopes outside the dorms at night to try to get a glimpse of the stars, you'll find people practicing ukulele on our quad, you'll see students filming for a project in the dining halls, [or] you'll see someone riding around campus on a bamboo bike." This attitude extends to athletics, as "many people are involved in intramural sports," and students love "hiking, skiing, and going to the beach year round." For those seeking out lower-key outdoors activities, "Joshua Tree is only an hour and a half away, so there are camping trips there just about every weekend." Though the school is small, there are four other undergraduate colleges in the Claremont Consortium, and Pomona students can "take their classes, eat at their dining halls, go to their parties, swim in their pools, and generally share in a great experience." When it's time to blow off steam, "there are large 5C-sponsored parties that people go to and enjoy."

Student Body

At Pomona, only one-quarter or so of students are from California, yet the California attitude reigns supreme. "Flip-flops, polo, or tank tops and shorts" are the unofficial uniform—and the overall vibe some get is that of the "liberal, upper-middle-class, hipster athlete." Don't, however, judge a book by its cover: "You will meet the football player who got a perfect score on his SAT or the dreadlocked hippie who took multivariable calculus when he was 16." Students report a "decent level of diversity and a strong international community." Studious and talented, Pomona undergraduates "excel in the classroom and usually have some sort of passion that they pursue outside of the classroom." As one puts it, "underneath our sundresses and rainbow flip-flops—everybody is really passionate about something or other."

POMONA COLLEGE

Financial Aid: 909-621-8205 • E-Mail: admissions@pomona.edu • Website: www.pomona.edu

THE PRINCETON REVIEW SAYS

Admissions

The school reports that its standardized testing policy for use in admission for Fall 2024 is Test Optional. It is unknown at this time if the 2024 testing policy will be permanent. The Princeton Review suggests that interested applicants consult with the school for the most up-to-date standardized testing policies. *Very important factors considered include:* rigor of secondary school record, class rank, academic GPA, application essay, recommendation(s), extracurricular activities, talent/ability, character/personal qualities. *Other factors considered include:* standardized test scores, interview, first generation, geographical residence, racial/ethnic status, volunteer work, work experience. High school diploma or equivalent is not required. *Academic units required:* 4 English, 3 math, 2 science, 2 science labs, 3 foreign language, 2 social studies. *Academic units recommended:* 4 English, 4 math, 4 science, 3 science labs, 3 foreign language, 3 social studies.

Financial Aid

Students should submit: CSS/Financial Aid Profile; FAFSA; Noncustodial Profile. Priority filing deadline is 1/15. The Princeton Review suggests that all financial aid forms be submitted as soon as possible (see page 5 for a note on the FAFSA). *Need-based scholarships/grants offered:* College/university scholarship or grant aid from institutional funds; Federal Pell; Private scholarships; SEOG; State scholarships/grants. *Loan aid offered:* Direct PLUS loans; Direct Subsidized Loans; Direct Unsubsidized Loans; College/university loans from institutional funds. Admitted students will be notified of awards on or about 4/1. Federal Work-Study Program available. Institutional employment available.

The Inside Word

For first-year applicants, Pomona College offers regular decision admissions, as well as two binding early decision programs. Admissions officials evaluate a student's academic record carefully, examining the rigor of high school coursework, class rank, and grade point average. Ninety-one percent of Pomona admits rank in the top 10 percent of their class. Students are strongly encouraged to visit campus and meet with admissions staff, though it's not required.

THE SCHOOL SAYS "..."

From the Admissions Office

"Pomona College is a place for ambitious, creative students who are prepared to dream big, who value diverse learning environments, and who are eager to collaborate across differences as they seek to make an impact on the world. Students enjoy a broad, liberal arts curriculum and ultimately choose among 48 majors.

"At Pomona, professors teach every class (with an average class size of 15). Yet, students enjoy the opportunities and resources of a larger university, with more than 6,000 undergraduates at The Claremont Colleges consortium.

"As the founding member of The Claremont Colleges, Pomona is one of five adjacent undergraduate colleges and two graduate institutions that make up this unique consortium. Students may take classes at any of the other Claremont Colleges, each no more than a few minutes' walk away. Athletics, clubs and organizations, dining and social opportunities are all 5-college strong.

"Located in Southern California, near Los Angeles, Pomona provides students with opportunities for scientific and community-based research, internships with major global companies and local start-ups, countless options to engage with diverse urban communities and natural environments, as well as a stellar range of arts and entertainment options."

SELECTIVITY

Admissions Rating	99
# of applicants	10,666
% of applicants accepted	7
% of acceptees attending	55
# offered a place on the wait list	866
% accepting a place on wait list	71
% admitted from wait list	2
# of early decision applicants	1,596
% accepted early decision	16

FIRST-YEAR PROFILE

Testing policy	Test Optional
Range SAT composite	1480–1540
Range SAT EBRW	730–770
Range SAT math	750–790
Range ACT composite	33–35
# submitting SAT scores	145
% submitting SAT scores	35
# submitting ACT scores	76
% submitting ACT scores	18
% graduated top 10% of class	91
% graduated top 25% of class	98
% graduated top 50% of class	100

DEADLINES

Early decision	
Deadline	11/15
Notification	12/15
Other ED deadline	1/8
Other ED notification	2/15
Regular	
Deadline	1/8
Notification	4/1
Nonfall registration?	No

FINANCIAL FACTS

Financial Aid Rating	99
Annual tuition	$58,818
Room and Board	$19,358
Required Fees	$420
Books and Supplies	$1,100
Average frosh need-based scholarship	$59,843
Average UG need-based scholarship	$59,117
% needy frosh rec. need-based scholarship or grant aid	100
% needy UG rec. need-based scholarship or grant aid	99
% needy frosh rec. non-need-based scholarship or grant aid	0
% needy UG rec. non-need-based scholarship or grant aid	1
% needy frosh rec. need-based self-help aid	100
% needy UG rec. need-based self-help aid	100
% frosh rec. any financial aid	47
% UG rec. any financial aid	52
% UG borrow to pay for school	26
Average cumulative indebtedness	$20,181
% frosh need fully met	100
% ugrads need fully met	99
Average % of frosh need met	100
Average % of ugrad need met	100

PORTLAND STATE UNIVERSITY

P.O. Box 751, Portland, OR 97207-0751 • Admissions: 503-725-3000 • Fax: 503-725-5525

CAMPUS LIFE

Quality of Life Rating	78
Fire Safety Rating	88
Green Rating	98
Type of school	Public
Environment	Metropolis

STUDENTS

Total undergrad enrollment	15,676
% male/female/another gender	44/56/<1
% from out of state	16
% frosh live on campus	61
% ugrads live on campus	9
# of fraternities	3
# of sororities	3
% African American	4
% Asian	10
% White	50
% Hispanic	20
% Native American	>1
% Pacific Islander	<1
% Two or more races	7
% Race and/or ethnicity unknown	3
% international	3
# of countries represented	70

SURVEY SAYS . . .

Lots of liberal students
Students environmentally aware
Recreation facilities are great

ACADEMICS

Academic Rating	77
% students returning for sophomore year	73
% students graduating within 4 years	29
% students graduating within 6 years	54
Calendar	Quarter
Student/faculty ratio	16:1
Profs interesting rating	85
Profs accessible rating	86

Most classes have 10–19 students.
Most lab/discussion sessions have
10–19 students.

MOST POPULAR MAJORS

Computer Science; Biomedical Sciences, General;
Psychology, General

STUDENTS SAY "..."

Academics

Portland State University's motto is "let knowledge serve the city," and students echo this philosophy, saying their school "has a strong focus on civic engagement and sustainability." "PSU is a great learning environment in the heart of the city" and a "good value" for your tuition dollars. It's also "a green-minded urban school" that's "training students to be good community members." The university offers "a wealth of courses," with degrees in social work, a range of business majors, and the hard sciences all receiving praise. "Classes are usually pretty small," and professors "promote lots of in-class discussion and are readily available to meet outside of class as well." "They really care about the student's success, and they really help broaden our scope of learning [and] thinking critically." Adjunct professors are "very connected to the community and their particular areas of expertise." Overall, students are happy with their instructors, saying, "Most professors are engaging and truly want to challenge you and help you succeed." They "are well-educated [and] well-versed in current issues and research." There's "the occasional dud thrown into the mix," though. Generally, "they are prepared and are passionate about the classes they teach. They have a wealth of experiences to bring to classroom," and they're "easily accessible for questions or further assistance; students just need to reach out."

Campus Life

The city of Portland is a big draw for PSU students. "The campus is extraordinarily beautiful and ideally located." Outdoor activities are big here: "There's skiing, hiking, camping, [and] fishing." "The downtown area has plenty of microbrew pubs, nightlife, eateries, and theaters." "The people are friendly, and the city is gorgeous and easy to navigate. You can go to the beach or to the mountain in about two hours, and there are many things to do outdoors. There are great parks throughout the city." "The public transportation is outstanding." It's bike- and vegan-friendly. "There are lots of activist and awareness-raising events going on all the time, and lots of students are involved in volunteering (on and off campus)." Because PSU has a large nontraditional undergraduate population and the majority of students live off campus, the sense of community extends beyond the school and into the city. "There are a lot of things to do on campus, and there are different groups on campus that promote going out into the community at large and helping out." "Because the student body is so big and really diverse, PSU has tons of programs/clubs/groups that help make you feel more involved with your school. PSU is also committed to sustainability: Any new buildings are made with the latest green technology, and recycling is a big deal."

Student Body

"It is difficult to define the typical PSU student, because there are so many of us from so many different backgrounds," one student says, and diversity does indeed seem to be the name of the game at PSU. Students describe themselves as "environmentally aware, hip," and "very liberal." Overall, people at PSU are "invested in their education and are friendly." There's a large population of nontraditional undergraduates, so students are "either typical college-age…or people in their thirties and forties with kids and full-time job trying to juggle everything." Even within this large, diverse student body, "everyone finds a niche pretty quickly." As one student notes, "It's easy to find people you get along with, but it's also easy to find people who are completely different from you, which makes school a lot more interesting."

PORTLAND STATE UNIVERSITY

Financial Aid: 800-547-8887 • E-Mail: admissions@pdx.edu • Website: www.pdx.edu/

THE PRINCETON REVIEW SAYS

Admissions

The school reports that its standardized testing policy for use in admission for Fall 2024 is Test Optional. It is unknown at this time if the 2024 testing policy will be permanent. The Princeton Review suggests that interested applicants consult with the school for the most up-to-date standardized testing policies. *Very important factors considered include:* academic GPA. *Other factors considered include:* standardized test scores, recommendation(s). High school diploma is required and GED is accepted. *Academic units required:* 4 English, 3 math, 3 science, 2 foreign language, 3 social studies. *Academic units recommended:* 1 science lab.

Financial Aid

Students should submit: FAFSA. The Princeton Review suggests that all financial aid forms be submitted as soon as possible (see page 5 for a note on the FAFSA). *Need-based scholarships/grants offered:* College/university scholarship or grant aid from institutional funds; Federal Pell; Private scholarships; SEOG; State scholarships/grants. *Loan aid offered:* Direct PLUS loans; Direct Subsidized Loans; Direct Unsubsidized Loans. Admitted students will be notified of awards on a rolling basis. Federal Work-Study Program available. Institutional employment available.

The Inside Word

PSU offers a range of admission options for new freshmen, transfers, students enrolled at local community colleges, continuing students, and those with nontraditional high school backgrounds. Regardless of an applicant's status, admissions officers look for a secondary school GPA of at least 3.0, though high test scores can make up for a lower average.

THE SCHOOL SAYS "..."

From the Admissions Office

"Portland State University is Oregon's most diverse public university located in the heart of one of America's most progressive cities. It offers more than sixty undergraduate and forty graduate programs in fine and performing arts, liberal arts and sciences, business administration, education, urban and public affairs, social work, engineering, and computer science. PSU offers more than 120 bachelor's, master's, and doctoral degrees.

"The forty-nine-acre downtown campus—whose motto is 'Let Knowledge Serve the City'—places students in a vibrant center of culture, business, and technology. Portland State's urban mission offers opportunities for every student to participate in internships and community-based projects in business, education, social services, government, technology, and the arts and sciences.

"The award-winning University Studies curriculum provides small class sizes and mentoring for undergraduates and culminates in Senior Capstone, which takes students out of the classroom and into the field, where they utilize their knowledge and skills to develop community projects.

"Portland State has taken aggressive steps to enhance the student experience and campus life, with new student housing and a comprehensive recreation complex and remodeled science and performing arts facilities. The university also has hired more academic and career advisers and created new programs to support students. Sustainability—initiatives that balance environmental, economic, and social concerns—is incorporated throughout the curriculum and across the campus."

SELECTIVITY

Admissions Rating	82
# of applicants	7,925
% of applicants accepted	93
% of acceptees attending	22

FIRST-YEAR PROFILE

Testing policy	Test Optional
Range SAT composite	1080–1290
Range SAT EBRW	550–680
Range SAT math	520–620
Range ACT composite	18–27
# submitting SAT scores	70
% submitting SAT scores	4
# submitting ACT scores	71
% submitting ACT scores	4

DEADLINES

Nonfall registration?	Yes

APPLICANTS ALSO LOOK AT

Oregon State University; University of Oregon

FINANCIAL FACTS

Financial Aid Rating	77
Annual in-state tuition	$9,000
Annual out-of-state tuition	$27,900
Room and board	$10,947
Required fees	$1,806
Books and supplies	$888
Average frosh need-based scholarship	$10,128
Average UG need-based scholarship	$9,284
% needy frosh rec. need-based scholarship or grant aid	83
% needy UG rec. need-based scholarship or grant aid	80
% needy frosh rec. non-need-based scholarship or grant aid	3
% needy UG rec. non-need-based scholarship or grant aid	2
% needy frosh rec. need-based self-help aid	53
% needy UG rec. need-based self-help aid	55
% frosh rec. any financial aid	82
% UG rec. any financial aid	69
% UG borrow to pay for school	50
Average cumulative indebtedness	$22,621
% frosh need fully met	8
% ugrads need fully met	5
Average % of frosh need met	64
Average % of ugrad need met	56

PRINCETON UNIVERSITY

Princeton University, Princeton, NJ 08544 • Admissions: 609-258-3000 • Fax: 609-258-6743

CAMPUS LIFE

Quality of Life Rating	85
Fire Safety Rating	94
Green Rating	94
Type of school	Private
Affiliation	No Affiliation
Environment	Town

STUDENTS

Total undergrad enrollment	5,527
% male/female/another gender	50/50/NR
% from out of state	82
% frosh live on campus	100
% ugrads live on campus	95
# of fraternities	0
# of sororities	0
% African American	8
% Asian	24
% White	38
% Hispanic	10
% Native American	<1
% Pacific Islander	<1
% Two or more races	7
% Race and/or ethnicity unknown	2
% international	12
# of countries represented	110

SURVEY SAYS . . .

Students always studying
Classroom facilities are great
Lab facilities are great
Great library
School is well run
Great financial aid
No one cheats
Theater is popular
Campus newspaper is popular
College radio is popular

ACADEMICS

Academic Rating	87
% students returning for sophomore year	97
% students graduating within 4 years	88
% students graduating within 6 years	98
Calendar	Semester
Student/faculty ratio	5:1
Profs interesting rating	84
Profs accessible rating	86

Most classes have 10–19 students.
Most lab/discussion sessions have
10–19 students.

MOST POPULAR MAJORS

Computer Science; Economics; Public &
International Affairs

STUDENTS SAY "..."

Academics

As a member of the grand old Ivy League, Princeton University has long maintained a "sterling reputation" for quality academics; however, students say Princeton's "unique focus on the undergraduate experience" is what makes their school stand out among institutions. It attracts "really experienced and big-name professors, who actually want to teach undergraduates." Introductory lecture classes can be rather large, but "once you take upper-level courses, you'll have a lot of chances to work closely with professors and study what you are most interested in." A current undergrad enthuses, "The discussions I have in seminar are the reason I get out of bed in the morning; after a great class, I feel incredibly invigorated." Though all Princeton professors are "leading scholars in their field," students admit that some classes can be "dry." Fortunately, "the overwhelming majority of professors are wonderful, captivating lecturers" who are "dedicated to their students." While you may be taking a class from a Nobel laureate, "the humility and accessibility of world-famous researchers and public figures is always remarkable." At Princeton, "there are so many chances to meet writers, performers, and professionals you admire." A student details, "The two years I've been here, I've been in discussions with Frank Gehry, David Sedaris, Peter Hessler, John McPhee, Jeff Koons, Chang-rae Lee, Joyce Carol Oates, W.S. Merwin, and on and on." No matter what you study, Princeton is an "intellectually challenging place," and the student experience is "intense in almost every way." Hard work pays off, though "the academic caliber of the school is unparalleled," and a Princeton education is "magnificently rewarding."

Campus Life

Princeton students "tend to participate in a lot of different activities, from varsity sports (recruits), intramural sports (high school athletes), and more academically restricted activities like autonomous vehicle design club, Engineers Without Borders, and the literary magazine." In and out of the classroom, there are a "billion opportunities to do what you know you love" on the Princeton campus, from performance to sports to research. "Princeton offers a lot of different opportunities to relax and de-stress," including "sporting events, concerts, recreational facilities," "a movie theater that frequently screens current films for free," and "arts and crafts at the student center." For some, social life is centered along Prospect Avenue, where "Princeton's eating clubs are lined up like ten booze-soaked ducklings in a row." These eating clubs—private houses that serve as social clubs and cafeterias for upperclassmen—"play a large role in the social scene at the university." On the weekends, "the eating clubs are extremely popular for partying, chatting, drinking, and dancing"—not to mention, "free beer." Though students gush that "the campus is gorgeous year round," when students need a break from the college atmosphere, "there's NJ Transit if you want to go to New York, Philly, or even just the local mall."

Student Body

It's not surprising that most undergraduates are "driven, competitive, and obsessed with perfection." That's because Princeton students emphasize that "Academics come first," which is typified by "a tendency to overwork" and dedication to studying. "Almost everyone at Princeton is involved with something other than school about which they are extremely passionate," and most have "at least one distinct, remarkable talent." This variety means that it's actually "fairly easy for most people to find a good group of friends with whom they have something in common," and many students get involved in one of the "infinite number of clubs" on campus. Superficially, "the preppy Ivy League stereotype" is reflected in the student population, and many students are "well-spoken," "dress nicely," and stay in shape. A student jokes, "Going to Princeton is like being in a contest to see who can be the biggest nerd while simultaneously appearing least nerdy."

PRINCETON UNIVERSITY

Financial Aid: 609-258-3330 • E-Mail: uaoffice@princeton.edu • Website: www.princeton.edu

THE PRINCETON REVIEW SAYS

Admissions

The school reports that its standardized testing policy for use in admission for Fall 2024 is Test Optional. The 2024 testing policy will be temporary. The Princeton Review suggests that interested applicants consult with the school for the most up-to-date standardized testing policies. *Very important factors considered include:* rigor of secondary school record, class rank, academic GPA, standardized test scores, application essay, recommendation(s), extracurricular activities, talent/ability, character/personal qualities. *Other factors considered include:* interview, first generation, alumni/ae relation, geographical residence, racial/ethnic status, volunteer work, work experience. High school diploma or equivalent is not required. *Academic units recommended:* 4 English, 4 math, 4 science, 2 science labs, 4 foreign language, 2 social studies, 2 history, 1 visual/performing arts.

Financial Aid

Students should submit: FAFSA; Institution's own financial aid form. Priority filing deadline is 2/1. The Princeton Review suggests that all financial aid forms be submitted as soon as possible (see page 5 for a note on the FAFSA). *Need-based scholarships/grants offered:* College/university scholarship or grant aid from institutional funds; Federal Pell; Private scholarships; SEOG; State scholarships/grants. *Loan aid offered:* Direct PLUS loans; Direct Subsidized Loans; Direct Unsubsidized Loans; College/university loans from institutional funds. Admitted students will be notified of awards on or about 4/1. Federal Work-Study Program available. Institutional employment available.

The Inside Word

Not surprisingly, admission to Princeton is highly selective. Only about 7 percent of applicants are accepted, and these students usually rank at the top of their high school class. Prospective students should prepare for Princeton by excelling in honors, AP, and upper-level course work during high school. The application materials and personal essays are carefully read and evaluated, so students should also allocate time to prepare their applications. Admission to Princeton comes with a great deal of prestige, and to make the deal even sweeter, Princeton's remarkable no-loan financial aid program means that every student has 100 percent of their financial need met, without student loans.

THE SCHOOL SAYS "..."

From the Admissions Office

"Methods of instruction at Princeton vary widely, but common to all areas is a strong emphasis on individual responsibility and the free interchange of ideas. This is displayed most notably in the wide use of preceptorials and seminars, in the provision of independent study for all upperclass students, and in the availability of a series of special programs to meet a range of individual interests. The undergraduate college encourages the student to be an independent seeker of information and to assume responsibility for gaining both knowledge and judgment that will strengthen later contributions to society. Two hallmarks of the academic experience are the junior paper and senior thesis, which allow students the opportunity to pursue original research and scholarship in a field of their choosing. "Princeton offers a distinctive financial aid program that provides grants, which do not have to be repaid. Princeton meets the full demonstrated financial need of all students offered admission, including international students. Beginning fall 2023, most families earning up to $100,000 a year will pay nothing."

SELECTIVITY

Admissions Rating	99
# of applicants	38,019
% of applicants accepted	6
% of acceptees attending	69
# offered a place on the wait list	1,710
% accepting a place on wait list	79
% admitted from wait list	0

FIRST-YEAR PROFILE

Testing policy	Test Optional
Range SAT composite	1500–1560
Range SAT EBRW	730–780
Range SAT math	760–800
Range ACT composite	33–35
# submitting SAT scores	956
% submitting SAT scores	64
# submitting ACT scores	398
% submitting ACT scores	27
Average HS GPA	4.0
% frosh submitting high school GPA	99

DEADLINES

Early action	
Deadline	11/1
Notification	12/15
Regular	
Deadline	1/1
Notification	4/1
Nonfall registration?	No

FINANCIAL FACTS

Financial Aid Rating	99
Annual tuition	$59,710
Room and board	$19,380
Required fees	$0
Books and supplies	$4,040
Average frosh need-based scholarship	$62,844
Average UG need-based scholarship	$62,876
% needy frosh rec. need-based scholarship or grant aid	100
% needy UG rec. need-based scholarship or grant aid	100
% needy frosh rec. non-need-based scholarship or grant aid	0
% needy UG rec. non-need-based scholarship or grant aid	0
% needy frosh rec. need-based self-help aid	30
% needy UG rec. need-based self-help aid	27
% frosh rec. any financial aid	61
% UG rec. any financial aid	61
% UG borrow to pay for school	17
Average cumulative indebtedness	$12,500
% frosh need fully met	100
% ugrads need fully met	100
Average % of frosh need met	100
Average % of ugrad need met	100

PROVIDENCE COLLEGE

1 Cunningham Square, Providence, RI 02918 • Admissions: 401-865-1000 • Fax: 401-865-2826

STUDENTS SAY "..."

Academics

A "small" Catholic college in Rhode Island, Providence College offers students a "strong" liberal arts curriculum and a "fun and flourishing social environment." Academically, many undergrads point to Providence's "Western Civilization program" as a highlight of their collegiate experience. This interdisciplinary series exposes students to art, literature, philosophy, and theology and shapes undergrads into "well-rounded and deep thinkers." Students are also quick to highlight Providence's "strong business school" as well. And they certainly appreciate that they are "taught to think on our feet and to apply what we have learned in the classroom to real life situations." "Small classes" are another hallmark of a Providence education. In turn, this enables students to develop "great relationships" with their professors. And speaking of professors, undergrads here happily report that their teachers are "phenomenal." Not only are they "extremely knowledgeable," they also "have a real passion for teaching." As one thankful student boasts, "My professors have met with me on the weekends, over the summer, and responded to text messages/emails/phone calls. We have gone off campus just to chat and keep up to date on how things are going." Indeed, these professors might just be Providence's "biggest asset."

Campus Life

Life at Providence can aptly be described as a "whirlwind." This is due to the myriad of "recreational activities," "school sponsored trips," and "programmed nights" the college offers. Additionally, school spirit abounds and students are "very enthusiastic" about attending sporting events, "especially men's basketball and hockey." Students do admit that "partying is a pretty large part of the social life." And on the weekends you'll find that lots of people "go out, either to bars/clubs or senior off-campus housing." One student shares, "People will sit out on the quad on nice sunny days and play catch. We have many activities such as dances and cookouts that the school holds year round." Moreover, there are "two concerts each year where [basically] the entire school attends." Many individuals are also "highly involved in intramural sports" as well as a club or two "aligning with social, political and relig[ious] interests." Of course, students here love exploring the city of Providence too, "which is a short car ride or public bus trip [away]." And undergrads "can [check out] activities around Brown University/Thayer Street, as well as DownCity where there are many shops and a large artistic influence."

Student Body

Students at Providence attest that the college is "very homogenous in regards to race and socioeconomic status," noting that most undergrads are "white" and come from "upper middle class families." Additionally, a large percentage hail from "New England, New York, [or] New Jersey." And many don "preppy" clothing; you frequently "see backwards hats, Vineyard Vines, Patagonia, and bean boots or boat shoes." Thankfully, Providence has grown "increasingly diverse" in the last few years. On top of that, undergrads gush that their peers are "genuinely nice" and quite "inclusive" regardless of background. Students are also quite impressed with how "polite" everyone seems to be. As one undergrad explains, "Doors are held, everyone thanks the professor after class, people say hello as you walk by—it's phenomenal!" Moreover, as a Catholic institution, you do find "kids who take their faith seriously." However, "you do not need to be religious to feel welcomed here." Indeed, "the college preaches about the Friar Family which the students are supposed to embody. When I first started here, I thought that this motto was quite ludicrous, but it honestly seems as though it is true. The way everyone acts is just so kind toward one another. The students here really do treat everyone like family."

PROVIDENCE COLLEGE

Financial Aid: 401-865-2286 • E-Mail: pcadmiss@providence.edu • Website: www.providence.edu

THE PRINCETON REVIEW SAYS

Admissions

The school reports that its standardized testing policy for use in admission for Fall 2024 is Test Optional. It is unknown at this time if the 2024 testing policy will be permanent. The Princeton Review suggests that interested applicants consult with the school for the most up-to-date standardized testing policies. *Very important factors considered include:* rigor of secondary school record, academic GPA, application essay. *Important factors considered include:* recommendation(s), extracurricular activities, character/personal qualities. *Other factors considered include:* class rank, standardized test scores, talent/ability, first generation, alumni/ae relation, geographical residence, racial/ethnic status, volunteer work, work experience, level of applicant's interest. High school diploma is required and GED is not accepted. *Academic units required:* 4 English, 4 math, 3 science, 2 science labs, 3 foreign language, 2 social studies, 2 history. *Academic units recommended:* 4 English, 4 math, 4 science, 2 science labs, 4 foreign language, 2 social studies, 2 history.

Financial Aid

Students should submit: CSS/Financial Aid Profile; FAFSA. Priority filing deadline is 2/1. The Princeton Review suggests that all financial aid forms be submitted as soon as possible (see page 5 for a note on the FAFSA). *Need-based scholarships/grants offered:* College/university scholarship or grant aid from institutional funds; Federal Pell; Private scholarships; SEOG; State scholarships/grants; United Negro College Fund. *Loan aid offered:* Direct PLUS loans; Direct Subsidized Loans; Direct Unsubsidized Loans; State Loans. Admitted students will be notified of awards on or about 11/30. Federal Work-Study Program available. Institutional employment available.

The Inside Word

Applicants to Providence College can rest assured that the school takes a holistic approach to the admissions game. Of course, your high school transcript will still hold the most weight. And given that admission is selective, the strongest candidates have taken several honors or advanced placement classes. Beyond that, the college closely evaluates personal statements, recommendations and extracurricular involvement. Interested students should know that Providence is a Test Optional school.

THE SCHOOL SAYS "..."

From the Admissions Office

"A Providence College education challenges students to find commonality among topics that seem, on the surface, to be opposites. 'Or' often becomes 'and.' There are shared academic experiences such as the Core Curriculum and the distinctive Development of Western Civilization sequence, but the college also encourages students to explore differences of opinion and unfamiliar lines of thought. PC's Catholic and Dominican identity fuels intellectual, spiritual, and emotional growth by encouraging students to view subjects through the complementary lenses of faith and reason. It also fosters a respectful, supportive community that feels like home.

"Submission of standardized test scores is optional for students applying for admission. This policy change allows each student to decide whether they wish to have their standardized test results considered as part of their application for admission. Students who choose not to submit SAT or ACT test scores will not be penalized in the review for admission. Additional details about the Test Optional policy can be found on our website at https://admission.providence.edu/apply/standardized-testing/."

SELECTIVITY

Admissions Rating	88
# of applicants	11,129
% of applicants accepted	53
% of acceptees attending	20
# offered a place on the wait list	3,005
% accepting a place on wait list	35
% admitted from wait list	<1
# of early decision applicants	373
% accepted early decision	87

FIRST-YEAR PROFILE

Testing policy	Test Optional
Range SAT composite	1130–1330
Range SAT EBRW	570–670
Range SAT math	550–670
Range ACT composite	25–31
# submitting SAT scores	652
% submitting SAT scores	56
# submitting ACT scores	149
% submitting ACT scores	13
Average HS GPA	3.6
% frosh submitting high school GPA	100
% graduated top 10% of class	39
% graduated top 25% of class	77
% graduated top 50% of class	95

DEADLINES

Early decision	
Deadline	11/1
Notification	12/1
Other ED deadline	1/15
Other ED notification	2/15
Early action	
Deadline	11/1
Notification	1/1
Regular	
Deadline	1/15
Notification	4/1
Nonfall registration?	Yes

APPLICANTS OFTEN PREFER
Boston College; College of the Holy Cross

APPLICANTS SOMETIMES PREFER
Villanova University

APPLICANTS RARELY PREFER
Fairfield University; Loyola University Maryland

FINANCIAL FACTS

Financial Aid Rating	88
Annual tuition	$59,830
Room and board	$17,150
Required fees	$880
Average frosh need-based scholarship	$35,179
Average UG need-based scholarship	$35,600
% needy frosh rec. need-based scholarship or grant aid	100
% needy UG rec. need-based scholarship or grant aid	100
% needy frosh rec. non-need-based scholarship or grant aid	11
% needy UG rec. non-need-based scholarship or grant aid	6
% needy frosh rec. need-based self-help aid	90
% needy UG rec. need-based self-help aid	89
% frosh rec. any financial aid	70
% UG rec. any financial aid	64
% UG borrow to pay for school	72
Average cumulative indebtedness	$41,907
% frosh need fully met	43
% ugrads need fully met	33
Average % of frosh need met	92
Average % of ugrad need met	90

PURDUE UNIVERSITY—WEST LAFAYETTE

Financial Aid: 765-494-0998 • E-Mail: admissions@purdue.edu • Website: www.purdue.edu

THE PRINCETON REVIEW SAYS

Admissions

The school reports that its standardized testing policy for use in admission for Fall 2024 is Test Optional. It is unknown at this time if the 2024 testing policy will be permanent. The Princeton Review suggests that interested applicants consult with the school for the most up-to-date standardized testing policies. *Very important factors considered include:* rigor of secondary school record, academic GPA, standardized test scores. *Important factors considered include:* application essay, recommendation(s), extracurricular activities, character/personal qualities, first generation. *Other factors considered include:* class rank, talent/ability, geographical residence, state residency, racial/ethnic status, volunteer work, work experience, level of applicant's interest. High school diploma is required and GED is accepted. *Academic units required:* 4 English, 4 math, 3 science, 3 science labs, 2 foreign language, 3 social studies.

Financial Aid

Students should submit: FAFSA. Priority filing deadline is 4/15. The Princeton Review suggests that all financial aid forms be submitted as soon as possible after October 1. The Princeton Review suggests that all financial aid forms be submitted as soon as possible (see page 5 for a note on the FAFSA). *Need-based scholarships/grants offered:* College/ university scholarship or grant aid from institutional funds; Federal Pell; Private scholarships; SEOG; State scholarships/grants. *Loan aid offered:* Direct PLUS loans; Direct Subsidized Loans; Direct Unsubsidized Loans; College/university loans from institutional funds. Admitted students will be notified of awards on or about 3/15. Federal Work-Study Program available. Institutional employment available.

The Inside Word

Purdue looks at student applications holistically. Having said that, Purdue does have minimum high school course requirements, so make sure you have met or exceeded all of those requirements before applying.

THE SCHOOL SAYS "..."

From the Admissions Office

"Although it is one of America's largest universities, Purdue does not 'feel' big to its students. The campus is very compact when compared to universities with similar enrollment. Purdue is a comprehensive university with an international reputation in a wide range of academic fields. A strong work ethic prevails at Purdue. As a member of the Big Ten, Purdue has a strong and diverse athletic program. Purdue offers more than 1,000 clubs and organizations. The residence halls and Greek community offer many participatory activities for students. Numerous convocations and lectures are presented each year. Purdue is all about people, and allowing students to grow academically as well as socially, preparing them for the real world.

"To be considered for the full range of merit-based scholarships, students must complete their admission application by November 1.

"Purdue is a member of the Common Application and the Coalition Application."

SELECTIVITY

Admissions Rating	89
# of applicants	59,173
% of applicants accepted	69
% of acceptees attending	25
# offered a place on the wait list	6,048
% accepting a place on wait list	57
% admitted from wait list	0

FIRST-YEAR PROFILE

Testing policy	Test Optional
Range SAT EBRW	590–690
Range SAT math	600–740
Range ACT composite	26–33
# submitting SAT scores	6,335
% submitting SAT scores	62
# submitting ACT scores	3,152
% submitting ACT scores	31
Average HS GPA	3.7
% frosh submitting high school GPA	96
% graduated top 10% of class	48
% graduated top 25% of class	77
% graduated top 50% of class	96

DEADLINES

Early action	
Deadline	11/1
Notification	12/12
Nonfall registration?	Yes

APPLICANTS OFTEN PREFER
Indiana University—Bloomington; University of Illinois—Urbana-Champaign

APPLICANTS SOMETIMES PREFER
Georgia Institute of Technology; Penn State University Park; The Ohio State University—Columbus; The University of Texas at Austin; University of California—Berkeley; University of California—Davis; University of California—San Diego; University of Michigan—Ann Arbor; University of Wisconsin—Madison

APPLICANTS RARELY PREFER
Ball State University; Boston University; Butler University; California Polytechnic State University; Colorado State University; Cornell University; Drake University; Embry-Riddle Aeronautical University (FL); Illinois State University

FINANCIAL FACTS

Financial Aid Rating	83
Annual in-state tuition	$9,208
Annual out-of-state tuition	$28,010
Room and board	$10,030
Required fees	$784
Books and supplies	$1,160
Average frosh need-based scholarship	$11,985
Average UG need-based scholarship	$12,378
% needy frosh rec. need-based scholarship or grant aid	79
% needy UG rec. need-based scholarship or grant aid	82
% needy frosh rec. non-need-based scholarship or grant aid	15
% needy UG rec. non-need-based scholarship or grant aid	13
% needy frosh rec. need-based self-help aid	52
% needy UG rec. need-based self-help aid	49
% UG borrow to pay for school	40
Average cumulative indebtedness	$40,490
% frosh need fully met	14
% ugrads need fully met	17
Average % of frosh need met	64
Average % of ugrad need met	65

QUINNIPIAC UNIVERSITY

275 Mount Carmel Avenue, Hamden, CT 06518-1940 • Admissions: 203-582-8600 • Fax: 203-582-8906

CAMPUS LIFE

Quality of Life Rating	81
Fire Safety Rating	98
Green Rating	84
Type of school	Private
Affiliation	No Affiliation
Environment	Town

STUDENTS

Total undergrad enrollment	6,021
% male/female/another gender	38/62/0
% from out of state	65
% frosh from public high school	78
% frosh live on campus	93
% ugrads live on campus	63
# of fraternities (% join)	7 (12)
# of sororities (% join)	13 (20)
% African American	4
% Asian	4
% White	74
% Hispanic	11
% Native American	<1
% Pacific Islander	<1
% Two or more races	3
% Race and/or ethnicity unknown	2
% international	2
# of countries represented	52

SURVEY SAYS . . .

Campus newspaper is popular
Frats and sororities are popular
Students are happy
Dorms are like palaces

ACADEMICS

Academic Rating	78
% students returning for sophomore year	88
% students graduating within 4 years	73
% students graduating within 6 years	77
Calendar	Semester
Student/faculty ratio	11:1
Profs interesting rating	86
Profs accessible rating	89

Most classes have 10–19 students.
Most lab/discussion sessions have
10–19 students.

MOST POPULAR MAJORS

Psychology, General; Registered Nursing/
Registered Nurse; Business/Commerce, General

STUDENTS SAY "..."

Academics

Quinnipiac University is not only found in the heart of New England but, some would argue, also *the* heart of New England, a thriving, beating mid-size school that provides students with a dynamic education, especially in the School of Health Sciences and School of Computing and Engineering. Additionally, the university offers a "wide variety of dual-degree and accelerated programs," which many see as a "huge selling point [since] getting more than one degree in an accelerated timeline is a huge deal on a résumé." There's also a much-appreciated "special emphasis...on career development," with "career staff and advisors work[ing] very closely with students to help them get in the best position possible for job recruiting." Indeed, when it comes down to it, there's no denying that "a Quinnipiac degree can take you a long way."

QU's highly involved teaching methods also go the distance with students who note how "the School of Nursing brings in actors and actresses to act as patients...so we can perfect our skills before doing the real thing." These methods are available to all students in all schools, like this first year who got to roleplay the origins of democracy in Ancient Greece: "Actually debating these ideas was far more effective than simply reading about them in a book or watching a slideshow." No matter the chosen method, students are greeted by "super passionate" professors who "take time to make sure each student, not just the class, understands the material." They also ask questions designed to "make us think critically [and] dive deeper in every answer." And they "are always there when [you] need them." As one undergrad explains, "I often email professors and stop by their office, they are always happy to answer questions and prove to me that my education is their priority."

Campus Life

Quinnipiac makes it "so easy to get involved and become a leader in the community." Of course, it certainly helps that "there's a club for practically everything," which students back up by referencing MMA, the Asian Student Alliance, and their "statewide award-winners" *The Qunnipiac Chronicle* newspaper and Q30 television station. There are also school-wide community drives, like "the Big Event...where a large portion of the student body go out for roughly 4 hours on a specific day to do community service for the Hamden area." Students also benefit from the "brand new fitness and wellness center," a popular place: "people love to go there to hangout and workout with friends." The weekends are filled with events, either by the student programming board or, for the roughly 26% of school that participates, Greek activities (some of which are "fun events like kickball or volleyball to raise money for their philanthropic cause"). Overall, sports are lauded, but with special emphasis on the men's hockey games, which "have an electric energy; I would argue they are better than professional games I've been to." Students can also make the most of the natural, surrounding area, "whether it be hiking on Sleeping Giant or biking from Hamden to Southington on the Farmington Canal Rail Trail."

Student Body

Quinnipiac University fans have great pride in their "diversity, equity, and inclusion, and the measures we've taken to diversify our student body shows...our campus [has] turn[ed] into a little melting pot of a community." A number of students describe some sort of split in their peers between those who are "very party-centered or very education-focused." The overall impression, however, is that even if there are "high-end vehicles and expensive bags throughout campus," there's plenty of common ground to be found between students based on how "dedicated and motivated [they are] in the majors they've chosen." Some "even go above and beyond; for example, I've met students who have started actual businesses, or have had their short films accepted in professional film festivals." Best of all, they tend to be "incredibly warm-hearted, welcoming, and helpful." As this undergrad sums up, "I truly believe every[one] finds their place and home at Quinnipiac."

QUINNIPIAC UNIVERSITY

Financial Aid: 203-582-8750 • E-Mail: admissions@qu.edu • Website: www.qu.edu

THE PRINCETON REVIEW SAYS

Admissions

The school reports that its standardized testing policy for use in admission for Fall 2024 is Test Optional. The Princeton Review suggests that interested applicants consult with the school for the most up-to-date standardized testing policies. *Very important factors considered include:* rigor of secondary school record, academic GPA, character/personal qualities. *Important factors considered include:* standardized test scores, application essay, recommendation(s), interview, extracurricular activities, first generation, alumni/ae relation, geographical residence, state residency, volunteer work, level of applicant's interest. *Other factors considered include:* work experience. High school diploma is required and GED is accepted. *Academic units required:* 4 English, 3 math, 3 science, 2 foreign language, 2 social studies, 3 academic electives.

Financial Aid

Students should submit: FAFSA. Priority filing deadline is 3/1. The Princeton Review suggests that all financial aid forms be submitted as soon as possible (see page 5 for a note on the FAFSA). *Need-based scholarships/grants offered:* College/university scholarship or grant aid from institutional funds; Federal Pell; Private scholarships; SEOG; State scholarships/grants. *Loan aid offered:* Direct PLUS loans; Direct Subsidized Loans; Direct Unsubsidized Loans; State Loans. Admitted students will be notified of awards on a rolling basis beginning 12/15. Federal Work-Study Program available. Institutional employment available.

The Inside Word

Quinnipiac University has a variety of admissions options, and students are encouraged to take advantage of those they feel will best favor them. Early Action is strongly recommended for those applying to the competitive programs of physical therapy, nursing, occupational therapy, and physician assistant. The school recommends that students file their applications early in the fall of their senior year and provide supporting transcripts and test scores (as applicable) when available.

THE SCHOOL SAYS "..."

From the Admissions Office

"You bring the passion. Together, we'll unleash it. An education at Quinnipiac embodies the university's commitment to deliver innovative programming that anticipates the future, while developing enlightened global citizens eager to make an impact in their communities.

"Quinnipiac's mission is to fuel the ambition that moves the world forward. The university provides a supportive and stimulating environment for the intellectual and personal growth of its approximately 6,800 undergraduate and 3,000 graduate, law, and medical students.

"The university offers a welcoming community where everyone can thrive—individually and together. The Mount Carmel Campus is the academic home to all undergraduates with traditional, suite, and apartment housing for first-year and sophomore students located on 250 picturesque acres adjacent to Sleeping Giant State Park. The nearby 250-acre York Hill Campus is home to juniors and seniors in apartment-style residences with panoramic views, a lodge-style student center, pub and grill, and the M&T Bank Arena with twin arenas for hockey and basketball. The 100-acre North Haven Campus, just five miles away, is home to graduate programs in Health Sciences, Nursing, Education, Law, Social Work, and Medicine.

"Immersive learning experiences both inside and outside the classroom help prepare students for the evolving careers of the 21st century. Academic initiatives such as the honors program, 'writing across the curriculum,' QU seminar series, extensive internship experiences, study abroad opportunities, and a highly regarded emerging leaders student-life program form the foundation for excellence in business, communications, health sciences, nursing, computing and engineering, education, liberal arts, law, and medicine."

SELECTIVITY

Admissions Rating	83
# of applicants	18,668
% of applicants accepted	84
% of acceptees attending	10
# offered a place on the wait list	1,043
% accepting a place on wait list	41
% admitted from wait list	59
# of early decision applicants	108
% accepted early decision	84

FIRST-YEAR PROFILE

Testing policy	Test Optional
Range SAT composite	1130–1300
Range SAT EBRW	570–650
Range SAT math	550–650
Range ACT composite	24–29
# submitting SAT scores	443
% submitting SAT scores	28
# submitting ACT scores	78
% submitting ACT scores	5
Average HS GPA	3.54
% frosh submitting high school GPA	99
% graduated top 10% of class	19
% graduated top 25% of class	46
% graduated top 50% of class	80

DEADLINES

Early decision	
Deadline	11/1
Notification	12/15
Early action	
Deadline	11/15
Notification	1/15
Regular	
Deadline	2/1
Notification	Rolling
Nonfall registration?	Yes

APPLICANTS ALSO LOOK AT

Bryant University; Fairfield University; Marist College; Penn State University Park; Sacred Heart University; Southern Connecticut State University; Syracuse University; University of Connecticut; University of Delaware; University of Massachusetts Amherst; University of New Hampshire; University of Rhode Island

FINANCIAL FACTS

Financial Aid Rating	81
Annual tuition	$50,400
Room and board	$16,910
Required fees	$2,690
Books and supplies	$1,100
Average frosh need-based scholarship	$30,089
Average UG need-based scholarship	$29,272
% needy frosh rec. need-based scholarship or grant aid	99
% needy UG rec. need-based scholarship or grant aid	98
% needy frosh rec. non-need-based scholarship or grant aid	54
% needy UG rec. non-need-based scholarship or grant aid	52
% needy frosh rec. need-based self-help aid	83
% needy UG rec. need-based self-help aid	86
% frosh rec. any financial aid	100
% UG rec. any financial aid	95
% frosh need fully met	17
% ugrads need fully met	13
Average % of frosh need met	66
Average % of ugrad need met	63

RANDOLPH COLLEGE

2500 Rivermont Avenue, Lynchburg, VA 24503-1555 • Admissions: 434-947-8000 • Fax: 434-947-8996

STUDENTS SAY "..."

Academics

Rest assured, at Randolph College, "You're not just a number; you matter as an individual." Indeed, this "small, tight-knit community" instantly "makes you feel welcome." Additionally, students at Randolph are grateful they attend a college that "promotes self-discovery, personal growth, and individuality." Further, "small class sizes" allow for an "emphasis on student-professor relationships," a hallmark of a Randolph education. One undergrad happily confirms, "My academic experience has been challenging, there's no doubt, but the professor support has made that challenge enjoyable and exciting." A fellow student agrees, sharing, "My professors are excellent. Everyone I have had here has been supremely knowledgeable, understanding, and helpful to students. The number one goal is always to make students better thinkers." Finally, as this student gushes, "My professors are amazing! Their passion for the subject matter and course content is infectious. I look forward to each class each day and feel confident in my education. Learning is interesting and fun here, and professors are eager to answer questions and provide resources to supplement lectures and experiments. Often professors list their home phone numbers on syllabi to allow students to contact them outside of office hours. Every professor replies to email quickly, and professors are all very easy to communicate with in the classroom and one-on-one."

Campus Life

According to many undergrads, "life at Randolph is always busy and exciting." As one ecstatic student quickly asserts, "I don't think I have [been] bored [since] the day I stepped foot on this campus." And why would you be? Indeed, there are "a wide variety of clubs and organizations [in which] to become involved." Moreover, there are "many sports teams and exciting competitions to watch" as well as intramurals, which "offer a chance for non-athletes to" participate. In addition, there are a myriad of "parties and dances...sponsored by various organizations." These events are typically well-attended by students, as "they never disappoint." And for those undergrads looking for an activity a little more out of the box, there's "even a game called Humans vs. Zombies where students dress up and try to 'turn people into zombies' with Nerf guns. It's a lot of fun." Randolph is also home to many proud traditions and students love to partake. An insider reveals, "The even-odd class rivalry is definitely one popular school tradition. Skeller Sings are one of the events where the even spirit society (ETAs) and odd spirit society (Gammas) will sing (read: shout) songs at each other and try to create distractions while the other group sings." Finally, when students want to look beyond the campus for fun, they can "go hiking, swimming, and boating at all the lakes, rivers, and trails. [Indeed] there is a lot of nature and history surrounding the Lynchburg area."

Student Body

Undergrads at Randolph emphatically state that there's no typical student to be found wandering around campus. As one knowing undergrad shares, "Students vary widely in background and personality, preferences, [and] habits." Additionally, a "considerable percentage of the student body is comprised of international students," which certainly adds to the diversity of the school. Of course, if pressed to throw out some adjectives, Randolph undergrads will likely say that their peers are "hardworking, artistic, and caring." They are also "intelligent," "unafraid to speak their minds," and "committed to doing excellent work." Fortunately, "being such a small campus, it is hard not [to] develop lots of friends from several different social groups," and certainly, "campus traditions help form a very strong sense of community here." Or, as one content undergrad simply states, "Everyone gets along fairly well and it's not too hard to fit in when there aren't really any labels for people."

RANDOLPH COLLEGE

Financial Aid: 434-947-8128 • E-Mail: admissions@randolphcollege.edu • Website: www.randolphcollege.com

THE PRINCETON REVIEW SAYS

Admissions

The school reports that its standardized testing policy for use in admission for Fall 2024 is Test Optional. The 2024 testing policy will be permanent. The Princeton Review suggests that interested applicants consult with the school for the most up-to-date standardized testing policies. *Very important factors considered include:* academic GPA. *Important factors considered include:* rigor of secondary school record, extracurricular activities, alumni/ae relation, level of applicant's interest. *Other factors considered include:* class rank, standardized test scores, application essay, recommendation(s), interview, talent/ability, character/personal qualities, first generation, volunteer work, work experience. High school diploma is required and GED is accepted. *Academic units required:* 4 English, 3 math, 3 science, 2 science labs, 2 history, 1 academic elective. *Academic units recommended:* 4 math, 4 foreign language, 3 academic electives.

Financial Aid

Students should submit: FAFSA; State aid form. The Princeton Review suggests that all financial aid forms be submitted as soon as possible (see page 5 for a note on the FAFSA). *Need-based scholarships/grants offered:* College/university scholarship or grant aid from institutional funds; Federal Pell; Private scholarships; SEOG; State scholarships/grants. *Loan aid offered:* Direct PLUS loans; Direct Subsidized Loans; Direct Unsubsidized Loans; College/university loans from institutional funds. Admitted students will be notified of awards on a rolling basis beginning 11/15. Federal Work-Study Program available. Institutional employment available.

The Inside Word

Traditionally, your transcript holds the most weight at Randolph College. However, recommendations, personal essays, and extracurricular activities are also considered.

THE SCHOOL SAYS ". . ."

From the Admissions Office

"Nationally ranked for its academic programs and affordability, Randolph College offers students the best features of breadth—including a comprehensive general education curriculum and a wide range of majors—as well as specialization. Embedded within a liberal arts framework are ample opportunities for study abroad, leadership roles, research partnerships with faculty, and practical experience through internships and service learning. Students are encouraged to pursue academic goals that are personalized and meaningful to them.

"In Fall 2021, Randolph College launched its new "TAKE2" curriculum. This unique curricular model splits the semester into two seven-week sessions. During each one, students concentrate on two courses at a time. Believed to be the only permanent one of its kind in the nation, TAKE2 was designed by faculty to enable a more successful, enjoyable, and rewarding academic experience. Students focus on two courses, rather than several, at a time, in extended class sessions that allow for more applied activities and group interaction. No classes are held on Wednesdays, allowing for a cognitive break to study and prepare for classes, as well as extracurricular activities, community engagement, field trips, and internships.

"A graduate of Randolph College understands the intellectual foundations of the arts, sciences, and humanities while developing critical skills to learn, adapt, and succeed in a rapidly changing global environment. The college's strong emphasis on writing enables students to communicate clearly and persuasively, and the diverse student population and study abroad programs enable students to expand their horizons. The distinctive student-led honor system has long been a central part of daily life at Randolph and adds to the cohesive community feel.

"A member of the Old Dominion Athletic Conference, Randolph's holistic approach to student development enables scholar-athletes to excel in a variety of sports while focusing on academic excellence. Located in the heart of Virginia near the Blue Ridge Mountains, Randolph College's campus is part of the multi-college town of Lynchburg, with abundant cultural, entertainment, and recreational opportunities."

SELECTIVITY
Admissions Rating	80
# of applicants	1,602
% of applicants accepted	95
% of acceptees attending	10

FIRST-YEAR PROFILE
Testing policy	Test Optional
Range SAT composite	1000–1140
Range SAT EBRW	490–570
Range SAT math	440–570
Range ACT composite	22–30
# submitting SAT scores	21
% submitting SAT scores	14
# submitting ACT scores	11
% submitting ACT scores	8
Average HS GPA	3.3
% frosh submitting high school GPA	100
% graduated top 10% of class	5
% graduated top 25% of class	29
% graduated top 50% of class	86

DEADLINES
Early action	
Deadline	11/15
Regular	
Deadline	Rolling
Notification	Rolling, 9/1
Nonfall registration?	Yes

APPLICANTS SOMETIMES PREFER
George Mason University; James Madison University; Randolph-Macon College; University of Virginia; Virginia Commonwealth University; Virginia Tech

FINANCIAL FACTS
Financial Aid Rating	84
Annual tuition	$27,270
Room and board	$11,430
Required fees	$660
Books and supplies	$1,280
Average frosh need-based scholarship	$23,249
Average UG need-based scholarship	$21,693
% needy frosh rec. need-based scholarship or grant aid	100
% needy UG rec. need-based scholarship or grant aid	100
% needy frosh rec. non-need-based scholarship or grant aid	14
% needy UG rec. non-need-based scholarship or grant aid	16
% needy frosh rec. need-based self-help aid	82
% needy UG rec. need-based self-help aid	78
% frosh rec. any financial aid	100
% UG rec. any financial aid	99
% UG borrow to pay for school	82
Average cumulative indebtedness	$12,478
% frosh need fully met	16
% ugrads need fully met	19
Average % of frosh need met	7,778
Average % of ugrad need met	77

RANDOLPH-MACON COLLEGE

202 Henry Street, Ashland, VA 23005-5505 • Admissions: 800-888-1762 • Fax: 804-752-4707

CAMPUS LIFE

Quality of Life Rating	88
Fire Safety Rating	92
Green Rating	60*
Type of school	Private
Affiliation	Methodist
Environment	Village

STUDENTS

Total undergrad enrollment	1,476
% male/female/another gender	45/55/0
% from out of state	21
% frosh from public high school	77
% frosh live on campus	90
% ugrads live on campus	75
# of fraternities	7
# of sororities	4
% African American	9
% Asian	2
% White	75
% Hispanic	5
% Native American	<1
% Pacific Islander	<1
% Two or more races	5
% Race and/or ethnicity unknown	1
% international	2
# of countries represented	25

SURVEY SAYS . . .
Students are happy
Lab facilities are great
Career services are great
Internships are widely available
Students are friendly
Easy to get around campus
Alumni active on campus
Students get along with local community
Everyone loved the Yellow Jackets
Frats and sororities are popular

ACADEMICS

Academic Rating	82
% students returning for sophomore year	81
% students graduating within 4 years	68
% students graduating within 6 years	74
Calendar	4/1/4
Student/faculty ratio	10:1
Profs interesting rating	88
Profs accessible rating	94
Most classes have 10–19 students.	

MOST POPULAR MAJORS
Communication, General; Biology/Biological
Sciences, General; Business/Commerce, General

STUDENTS SAY "..."

Academics

The focused 1,500 undergraduates at Virginia's Randolph-Macon College are treated to an exceptional liberal arts education on the Edge, the school's name for its four-year career preparation program. Across more than 55 areas of study via majors, minors, and pre-professional programs, the college's focus is on producing successful, well-rounded students: "We are all seen and heard at this school." RMC accomplishes this task with a purposeful general education curriculum that requires courses across many subject areas, and a "capstone" experience that shows students to be ready for employment or graduate school. Along the way, the Edge Career Center provides advising, career roadmaps, and internship opportunities, and classes incorporate innovative pedagogy—a hallmark of an RMC education—in the form of "activities, group projects, lab work, guest speakers, and…field trips." Experiential learning is also key, in that "laboratory classes are very hands-on, and most classes make an effort to have discussions," and small class sizes ensure that students "have the opportunity to create strong friendships and relationships." This is especially true of the honors program, which "provides very interesting and different courses," and provides extra attention that goes above and beyond.

Professors help to shake things up by bringing "their own quirks to their classes to make it not as traditional" or by operating flipped classrooms "where the students do the research for the class and teach it for the day." RMC is also "very accommodating," and not just in how "faculty and staff are welcoming and supportive." Says one student, there "plenty of opportunities to explore whatever you want and if the school can't offer what you're looking for in an internship or experience, they'll help you find what you're looking for in the community."

Campus Life

Eighty-five percent of students live on campus "so we really have the opportunity to get to know one another and become closer." People usually "spend half of their days in their classes" and then take to the dining hall—"great for a small school"—and studying at night. On weekends, students "explore Ashland and downtown Richmond" and "fill their days by hanging out on campus lawn chairs, hammocking, or playing around on the football field." A lot of the buildings are new and the layout "is very compact, which makes travelling across campus very nice."

"There are plenty of ways to be active on campus," including participation in the more than 100 student organizations and clubs. The numerous intramural sports "allow you to connect with new people and have physical activity at the same time," and "on varsity sport game days, you can find a good number of students at those games, especially men's basketball." Community service is a facet of the RMC experience, and many students participate in service learning opportunities.

Student Body

The overall vibe of Randolph-Macon College is familial—it's "a home where current students, previous students, and community members gather to celebrate being Yellow Jackets." Along those lines, school spirit is a big part of the culture, with "a large athletic student population" and where "many students spend their time doing activities related to their team." But it's also an emphatically "welcoming community in a cute little town" where "no one seems to be disrespectful to anyone who affiliates differently than someone else." Perhaps that's because the school is "small enough that you'll almost always see someone you know in your short walk to classes," but however you put it, "the courtesy is endless." For those looking beyond their college years, students note that many here "have jobs or internships and everyone is able to have a car on campus if they want," and the alumni network is incredibly supportive.

RANDOLPH-MACON COLLEGE

Financial Aid: 804-752-7259 • E-Mail: admissions@rmc.edu • Website: www.rmc.edu

THE PRINCETON REVIEW SAYS

Admissions

The school reports that its standardized testing policy for use in admission for Fall 2024 is Test Optional. The 2024 testing policy will be temporary. The Princeton Review suggests that interested applicants consult with the school for the most up-to-date standardized testing policies. *Very important factors considered include:* rigor of secondary school record, academic GPA. *Important factors considered include:* class rank, standardized test scores, application essay, recommendation(s). *Other factors considered include:* interview, extracurricular activities, talent/ability, character/personal qualities, first generation, alumni/ae relation, racial/ethnic status, volunteer work, work experience, level of applicant's interest. High school diploma is required and GED is accepted. *Academic units required:* 4 English, 3 math, 2 science, 2 science labs, 2 foreign language, 3 academic electives. *Academic units recommended:* 4 English, 4 math, 4 science, 4 science labs, 3 foreign language, 5 academic electives.

Financial Aid

Students should submit: FAFSA; State aid form. Priority filing deadline is 2/15. The Princeton Review suggests that all financial aid forms be submitted as soon as possible (see page 5 for a note on the FAFSA). *Need-based scholarships/grants offered:* College/university scholarship or grant aid from institutional funds; Federal Pell; Private scholarships; SEOG; State scholarships/grants. *Loan aid offered:* Direct PLUS loans; Direct Subsidized Loans; Direct Unsubsidized Loans. Admitted students will be notified of awards on or about 3/1. Federal Work-Study Program available. Institutional employment available.

The Inside Word

Randolph-Macon College prefers "and over or," so the more that you can show their admissions team—like honors classes or extracurriculars—the better your chances. A few major exceptions to that more-is-better mentality: the school states that there is no special preference given to early action applicants over regular decision ones, and the holistic admissions process won't penalize you for choosing not to submit standardized test scores or for choosing the Common Application over the school's.

THE SCHOOL SAYS "..."

From the Admissions Office

"A Randolph-Macon College education begins with your future in mind. RMC integrates an extraordinary education and pairs it with faculty, staff, coaches and alumni that provide you with a campus-wide support system to help you make the most of your RMC experience. Campus life offers over one hundred organizations, including eSports, an equestrian program, and 18 varsity sports, to provide a dynamic event schedule that enriches your experience. Our challenging curriculum, national and global opportunities through internships and study abroad programs, which include our unique January Term experience, make Randolph-Macon students competitive for any career or academic pursuit post-graduation. This, paired with Randolph-Macon's four-year career preparation program, The Edge, gives students a distinct, competitive advantage after graduation in reaching their career or graduate school goals. Ideally located just outside of Richmond, Virginia and 90 miles from Washington, D.C., RMC offers a wide range of educational and career possibilities, partnerships with prestigious medical institutions, including guaranteed admissions to qualified students to medical or nursing school. The college also offers a new Bachelor of Science in Nursing with a direct entry option for qualified students. Our Four-Year-Degree Guarantee program promises that freshmen who meet the necessary requirements will graduate within four years, which ninety-five percent of Randolph-Macon College students achieve. RMC's loyal alumni rank in the top 25 in the nation for alumni giving, a true testament to their love of, and gratitude for, their Randolph-Macon experience. Randolph-Macon gets you up close and future ready."

SELECTIVITY

Admissions Rating	83
# of applicants	2,446
% of applicants accepted	85
% of acceptees attending	23
# offered a place on the wait list	37
% accepting a place on wait list	19
% admitted from wait list	14
# of early decision applicants	41
% accepted early decision	95

FIRST-YEAR PROFILE

Testing policy	Test Optional
Range SAT composite	1020–1210
Range SAT EBRW	520–630
Range SAT math	500–590
Range ACT composite	23–27
# submitting SAT scores	188
% submitting SAT scores	45
# submitting ACT scores	24
% submitting ACT scores	6
Average HS GPA	3.7
% frosh submitting high school GPA	100
% graduated top 10% of class	11
% graduated top 25% of class	40
% graduated top 50% of class	75

DEADLINES

Early decision	
Deadline	11/1
Notification	11/15
Early action	
Deadline	11/15
Notification	1/1
Regular	
Priority	2/1
Deadline	3/1
Notification	4/1
Nonfall registration?	Yes

FINANCIAL FACTS

Financial Aid Rating	86
Annual tuition	$46,278
Room and board	$14,630
Required fees	$1,724
Required fees (first-year)	$1,828
Books and supplies	$1,000
Average frosh need-based scholarship	$33,692
Average UG need-based scholarship	$32,476
% needy frosh rec. need-based scholarship or grant aid	100
% needy UG rec. need-based scholarship or grant aid	100
% needy frosh rec. non-need-based scholarship or grant aid	24
% needy UG rec. non-need-based scholarship or grant aid	23
% needy frosh rec. need-based self-help aid	81
% needy UG rec. need-based self-help aid	83
% frosh rec. any financial aid	100
% UG rec. any financial aid	98
% UG borrow to pay for school	63
Average cumulative indebtedness	$33,213
% frosh need fully met	29
% ugrads need fully met	29
Average % of frosh need met	76
Average % of ugrad need met	75

REED COLLEGE

3203 SE Woodstock Boulevard, Portland, OR 97202-8199 • Admissions: 503-771-1112 • Fax: 503-777-7553

CAMPUS LIFE

Quality of Life Rating	95
Fire Safety Rating	96
Green Rating	60*
Type of school	Private
Affiliation	No Affiliation
Environment	Metropolis

STUDENTS

Total undergrad enrollment	1,494
% male/female	42/58
% from out of state	93
% frosh from public high school	59
% frosh live on campus	100
% ugrads live on campus	67
# of fraternities	0
# of sororities	0
% African American	4
% Asian	13
% White	59
% Hispanic	10
% Native American	2
% Pacific Islander	<1
% Race and/or ethnicity unknown	1
% international	9
# of countries represented	46

SURVEY SAYS . . .

Lots of liberal students
Students always studying
Students are happy
Classroom facilities are great
Lab facilities are great
Great library
Class discussions encouraged
Great financial aid
No one cheats
Students aren't religious
Students environmentally aware
Students love Portland, OR
Great off-campus food
Dorms are like palaces
Easy to get around campus
Theater is popular
Campus newspaper is popular
College radio is popular
Diverse student types interact on campus
Active student government
Active minority support groups

ACADEMICS

Academic Rating	98
% students returning for sophomore year	86
% students graduating within 4 years	67
% students graduating within 6 years	80
Calendar	Semester
Student/faculty ratio	10:1
Profs interesting rating	98
Profs accessible rating	97

Most classes have 10–19 students.
Most lab/discussion sessions have
fewer than 10 students.

MOST POPULAR MAJORS

English Language and Literature, General;
Psychology, General; Anthropology, General

STUDENTS SAY ". . ."

Academics

Reed College in Portland, Oregon, is a private liberal arts institution known for its devotion to intellectual inquiry and critical thought. Academics are "quite challenging and rigorous," and "there can be heavy reading assignments, lengthy lab reports, and exams all in the same week." That said, none of this is seen as "busy work," but rather as an integral part of the community, which "is generally centered around the passion to learn and gain more knowledge." Reed's structure is designed to focus "on learning significantly more than grades," so much so that unless directly requested, students don't receive grades, preferring instead to let students "self-assess" or focus on specific feedback from their teachers. To help, there are "many networks of support" available, including a peer tutoring program used by more than half of all students.

Unsurprisingly, the faculty-student bond is the foundation of a Reed education, and most classes are conference style, "meaning the students all read the material before the class and come to class to ask questions and discuss with the professor." This interruptible format "pushes us to use our brains and think critically about the readings we have done" and "places responsibility on the individual to do their work." Professors "have such a mastery of their material that they're able to let discussions go and let students explore material on their own," and they will "excitedly jump in the conversation just like a peer and make wonderful co-learners." It's a street that runs both ways, at least in some departments; one student "finds it awesome" that the school invites them to attend lectures by potential professors: "In this way, I have learned a lot about topics related to my major."

Campus Life

If "you are looking to party or become enthralled in a sports culture" or Greek life, Reed is not the school for you, as students here "pride themselves on the amount of work they have to do." That said, "Reedies are also very laid-back, making sure that time for work has corresponding times for play." That's how you wind up with traditions like the Thesis Parade, in which costumed seniors burn their notes and drafts in a bonfire, or "themed dances where you get to dress up, dance, and let loose." The college has "a program called 'The Gray Fund' which helps fund all types of activities that are completely outside of academics," and these "can be as extensive as weeklong trips, or as simple as visits to the local cat café." The pool hall is a massively popular meeting space, and there are weekly events "where students gather for pool tournaments and hanging out." Since this bunch is generally creative, many here "play a lot of board games, have radio shows at the station, knit or crochet, or play musical instruments." Downtown Portland "is very easily accessed by bus" and students also "take day trips to the Oregon coast and go into the mountains near the city."

Student Body

First and foremost, "Reedies are invested in the learning process," so be prepared to meet plenty of students who "are often taking very niche classes that don't pertain to their own major" and who subsequently have "something they could talk your ear off about." This is a group of "academically driven, extremely progressive, friendly, inclusive, and uniquely talented" individuals who are also "colorful, eccentric, and out-there at times." Gender minorities and LGBTQIA+ students find that the school "feels incredibly welcoming and nurturing," and "the social scene of Reed is closely tied to an 'alternative' aesthetic and very niche interests." As one student puts it: "Our motley of student-run clubs and work activities and school-supported extracurriculars end up forming hundreds of mini-communities across campus that give many a chance to be a part of something."

THE PRINCETON REVIEW SAYS

Admissions

The school reports that its standardized testing policy for use in admission for Fall 2024 is Test Blind. The Princeton Review suggests that interested applicants consult with the school for the most up-to-date standardized testing policies. *Very important factors considered include:* rigor of secondary school record, academic GPA, application essay. *Important factors considered include:* class rank, recommendation(s), interview, character/personal qualities. *Other factors considered include:* extracurricular activities, talent/ability, first generation, alumni/ae relation, geographical residence, racial/ethnic status, volunteer work, work experience, level of applicant's interest. High school diploma is required and GED is accepted. *Academic units recommended:* 4 English, 4 math, 4 science, 4 foreign language, 4 social studies.

Financial Aid

Students should submit: CSS/Financial Aid Profile; FAFSA; Noncustodial Profile. Priority filing deadline is 1/15. The Princeton Review suggests that all financial aid forms be submitted as soon as possible (see page 5 for a note on the FAFSA). *Need-based scholarships/grants offered:* College/university scholarship or grant aid from institutional funds; Federal Pell; Private scholarships; SEOG; State scholarships/grants. *Loan aid offered:* Direct PLUS loans; Direct Subsidized Loans; Direct Unsubsidized Loans; College/university loans from institutional funds. Admitted students will be notified of awards on or about 4/1. Federal Work-Study Program available. Institutional employment available.

The Inside Word

Students at Reed are valued for being unconventional, and that's why applicants can choose either the Common or Coalition Application, with the latter allowing students to submit "a personal passion in the media that feels authentic to you." Heed this advice, as this rigorous academic school is, unsurprisingly, competitive and selective, accepting fewer than half of those who apply. Standardized testing is not considered, so if you're determined to get an edge, know that early decision candidates are much more likely to get in.

THE SCHOOL SAYS "..."

From the Admissions Office

"One of the most distinctive colleges in the nation, Reed provides a singular example of the liberal arts experience: a structured curriculum with an emphasis on personal inquiry; extensive written and in-person feedback from professors on assignments; and a deeply collaborative academic environment. Classes are small, faculty members are highly accessible, and students are active participants in the production of new knowledge.

"The Reed community is guided by the Honor Principle. The commitment to the independence of thought and mutual trust and respect helps to create an environment in which students feel connected, challenged, and fulfilled. Reed students are culturally diverse and hail from 49 states. In fact, Reedies travel the farthest to attend Reed out of any school in the nation. The student body is also composed of 9 percent international students.

"The breadth, depth, and rigor of the curriculum provide excellent preparation for nearly any career. Reed is ranked second in the nation in the percentage of graduates who earn PhDs in the humanities, third in the nation in the percentage who earn PhDs in the physical sciences, and fourth across all disciplines. Many Reed alumni win major graduate fellowships, found or lead companies and organizations, and earn medical, business, or law degrees."

SELECTIVITY

Admissions Rating	94
# of applicants	9,023
% of applicants accepted	31
% of acceptees attending	14
# offered a place on the wait list	5,317
% accepting a place on wait list	32
% admitted from wait list	5
# of early decision applicants	281
% accepted early decision	43

FIRST-YEAR PROFILE

Testing policy	Test Blind
Range SAT composite	1320–1500
Range SAT EBRW	690–750
Range SAT math	630–750
Range ACT composite	30–33
# submitting SAT scores	185
% submitting SAT scores	47
# submitting ACT scores	105
% submitting ACT scores	27
Average HS GPA	4.0
% frosh submitting high school GPA	90
% graduated top 10% of class	62
% graduated top 25% of class	81
% graduated top 50% of class	98

DEADLINES

Early decision	
Deadline	11/15
Notification	12/20
Other ED deadline	12/20
Other ED notification	2/15
Early action	
Deadline	11/15
Notification	2/15
Regular	
Notification	2/15
Nonfall registration?	No

FINANCIAL FACTS

Financial Aid Rating	98
Annual tuition	$64,450
Room and board	$15,950
Required fees	$310
Books and supplies	$1,050
Average frosh need-based scholarship	$47,265
Average UG need-based scholarship	$46,643
% needy frosh rec. need-based scholarship or grant aid	100
% needy UG rec. need-based scholarship or grant aid	100
% needy frosh rec. non-need-based scholarship or grant aid	0
% needy UG rec. non-need-based scholarship or grant aid	0
% needy frosh rec. need-based self-help aid	79
% needy UG rec. need-based self-help aid	84
% frosh rec. any financial aid	53
% UG rec. any financial aid	55
% UG borrow to pay for school	52
Average cumulative indebtedness	$22,941
% frosh need fully met	100
% ugrads need fully met	100
Average % of frosh need met	100
Average % of ugrad need met	100

RENSSELAER POLYTECHNIC INSTITUTE

110 Eighth Street, Troy, NY 12180-3590 • Admissions: 518-276-6000 • Fax: 518-276-4072

STUDENTS SAY "..."

Academics

As the 200th anniversary of upstate New York's Rensselaer Polytechnic Institute's founding approaches, RPI looks to use new technologies and tools to address large-scale global issues across an entire range of disciplines and perspectives. Enrollees note how quickly this has been integrated into their education, with engineering programs all including "mandatory project-based courses in each program [so students can] practice working on their teamwork and communication," and Humanities, Arts, and Social Science classes having "a STEM component intertwined." Other celebrated mainstays at RPI are its "rigorous classes and fair expectations" and "comfortable learning environment," as well as the ways in which classes are scheduled in time- and location-based clusters, so as to create smaller communities and frameworks for support and leadership. There are "some truly great resources" available to undergrads, including more than 30 research centers and over 700 labs, studios, and technology spaces on campus, as well as "plenty of opportunities for tutoring and meeting new students." In accordance with its "outstanding return on investment" and placement rate in grad schools, there is also a post-graduate development series that "helps students work toward achieving their desired career through interview preparation and other general professional skills."

Professors at RPI "are constantly looking for applications and real examples of the concepts we learn, such as companies or inventions," and "present the material in clear and convincing ways." They are "beyond accessible and willing to sit with you for hours to help in their office" and "devoted to giving the best education they can and [facilitating] meaningful discussions in the classroom." Hands-on experience is highly valued, such that "a lot of professors will encourage mini field trips to see engineering principles in action" and "very few 'lecture' classes are truly lecture classes."

Campus Life

RPI has more than 200 clubs and organizations, including affiliations for the career-minded as well as "niche clubs for various interests [like] a Cheese Club." Though studying takes up most of the time, the school is an hour or less "from any imaginable outdoor activity possible, [including] rock climbing, kayaking, hiking, skiing, [and] mountain biking." There is also an "extremely big gaming community at RPI," and "Greek life is very strong" as well. Intramural sports are common ways to blow off steam, and "hockey and football games are highly attended."

First-years live with each other on campus, while juniors and seniors have the option of living off-campus. Clubs "are always hosting social events, from ice-cream socials to winter carnivals to musical performances and competitions," and while most students "would rather stay on campus and support one another than leave to find something to do elsewhere," many do pop over to Troy or Albany to explore bars, restaurants, and larger cultural institutions. The campus has plenty of spaces for study and hanging out, and "people can be found in every nook and cranny of campus from dawn to sunset."

Student Body

Despite the workload, there is a kind of united front and "fun camaraderie that comes from everyone having really hard classes," with everyone here "constantly collaborating and helping each other study." RPI is a STEM school, so "most students are math- and science-oriented, but pretty much everyone has interests outside of their major," and there is "a good mix of overachievers…and relaxed students just trying to graduate with a decent GPA." Students know what they're getting into at RPI—"There is a general understanding that this school is very hard and everyone is just a little worn down all of the time." But it's a decision most make with a clear and eager heart, for the environment is known to be "nerdy with the best of people," so much so that it has a distinct culture and vocabulary.

RENSSELAER POLYTECHNIC INSTITUTE

Financial Aid: 518-276-6813 • E-Mail: Admissions@rpi.edu • Website: www.rpi.edu

THE PRINCETON REVIEW SAYS

Admissions

The school reports that its standardized testing policy for use in admission for Fall 2024 is Test Optional. The 2024 testing policy will be temporary. The Princeton Review suggests that interested applicants consult with the school for the most up-to-date standardized testing policies. *Very important factors considered include:* rigor of secondary school record, class rank, academic GPA. *Important factors considered include:* application essay, recommendation(s), extracurricular activities, character/personal qualities. *Other factors considered include:* standardized test scores, talent/ability, first generation, alumni/ae relation, racial/ethnic status, volunteer work, work experience, level of applicant's interest. High school diploma is required and GED is accepted. *Academic units required:* 4 English, 4 math, 3 science, 3 social studies. *Academic units recommended:* 4 science.

Financial Aid

Students should submit: CSS/Financial Aid Profile; FAFSA. Priority filing deadline is 12/1. The Princeton Review suggests that all financial aid forms be submitted as soon as possible (see page 5 for a note on the FAFSA). *Need-based scholarships/grants offered:* College/university scholarship or grant aid from institutional funds; Federal Pell; Private scholarships; SEOG; State scholarships/grants. *Loan aid offered:* Direct PLUS loans; Direct Subsidized Loans; Direct Unsubsidized Loans; State Loans. Admitted students will be notified of awards on or about 3/6. Federal Work-Study Program available. Institutional employment available.

The Inside Word

Outstanding test scores and grades are pretty much a must for any applicant hopeful of impressing the RPI admissions committee. Cohorts of underrepresented minorities and women are increasing each year. The school is unlikely to admit anyone who lacks the skills and background to survive here. While students can change their major option after matriculation, students are encouraged to be as specific as possible when indicating their intended major (or school) on their application.

THE SCHOOL SAYS "..."

From the Admissions Office

"The oldest degree-granting technological research university in the U.S., Rensselaer was founded in 1824 to instruct students to apply 'science to the common purposes of life.' Students immerse themselves in course work that combines theory with learning by experience in unparalleled facilities, using advanced technology. Rensselaer offers more than 140 programs and 1,000 courses leading to bachelor's, master's, and doctoral degrees. Undergraduates pursue studies in architecture; engineering; humanities, arts, and social sciences; business; science; and information technology (web science). A pioneer in interactive learning, Rensselaer provides real-world, hands-on educational opportunities that cut across academic disciplines. The Rensselaer student experience, or CLASS (Clustered Learning, Advocacy, and Support for Students) provides programs and support for students that begins even before they arrive on campus. Students have ready access to laboratories and classes involving lively discussion, problem solving, and faculty mentoring. Students are able to take full advantage of Rensselaer's unique research platforms: the Center for Biotechnology and Interdisciplinary Studies; one of the world's most powerful academic supercomputers, the Center for Computational Innovations; and the Experimental Media and Performing Arts Center, which encourages students to explore the intersection of science, technology, and the arts. Newly renovated residence halls, wireless computing network, and studio classrooms create a fertile environment for study and learning. Rensselaer offers recreational and fitness facilities plus numerous student-run organizations and activities, including fraternities and sororities, newspaper, television and radio station, drama and musical groups, and more than 200 clubs. In addition to intramural sports, NCAA varsity sports include Division I men's and women's ice hockey teams and twenty-one Division III men's and women's teams in thirteen sports. The East Campus Athletic Village raises the bar for student athletic facilities for varsity and non-varsity athletes alike, and includes a football arena, basketball stadium, and sports medicine and training complex."

SELECTIVITY

Admissions Rating	93
# of applicants	17,484
% of applicants accepted	53
% of acceptees attending	14
# offered a place on the wait list	4,474
% accepting a place on wait list	62
% admitted from wait list	9
# of early decision applicants	371
% accepted early decision	63

FIRST-YEAR PROFILE

Testing policy	Test Optional
Range SAT composite	1360–1520
Range SAT EBRW	660–740
Range SAT math	700–780
Range ACT composite	32–34
# submitting SAT scores	571
% submitting SAT scores	43
# submitting ACT scores	199
% submitting ACT scores	15
Average HS GPA	3.9
% frosh submitting high school GPA	93
% graduated top 10% of class	55
% graduated top 25% of class	88
% graduated top 50% of class	97

DEADLINES

Early decision	
Deadline	11/1
Notification	12/11
Other ED deadline	12/15
Other ED notification	1/15
Early action	
Deadline	12/1
Notification	1/29
Regular	
Priority	12/15
Deadline	1/15
Notification	3/12
Nonfall registration?	Yes

APPLICANTS ALSO LOOK AT

Carnegie Mellon University; Cornell University; Georgia Institute of Technology; Massachusetts Institute of Technology; Worcester Polytechnic Institute

FINANCIAL FACTS

Financial Aid Rating	84
Annual tuition	$58,600
Room and board	$16,996
Required fees	$1,451
Books and supplies	$1,260
Average frosh need-based scholarship	$23,080
Average UG need-based scholarship	$20,968
% needy frosh rec. need-based scholarship or grant aid	99
% needy UG rec. need-based scholarship or grant aid	84
% needy frosh rec. non-need-based scholarship or grant aid	25
% needy UG rec. non-need-based scholarship or grant aid	28
% needy frosh rec. need-based self-help aid	100
% needy UG rec. need-based self-help aid	84
% frosh rec. any financial aid	77
% UG rec. any financial aid	98
% UG borrow to pay for school	44
Average cumulative indebtedness	$13,759
% frosh need fully met	34
% ugrads need fully met	36
Average % of frosh need met	85
Average % of ugrad need met	79

RHODES COLLEGE

2000 North Parkway, Memphis, TN 38112 • Admissions: 901-843-3700 • Fax: 901-843-3631

STUDENTS SAY ". . ."

Academics
Rhodes College is a small, appealing southern institution that produces "graduates that have lots of knowledge and experience." To say that the program is "academically very strong" or "unparalleled, especially in the sciences" might actually be somewhat of an understatement, considering feedback from some students who began working before even matriculating. "I was granted a position in a research lab prior to even starting my first semester as a freshman." Early opportunities like these are a common refrain from undergrads, who also talk up the school's "infinite resources," which include academic coaches, peer and professor tutors, advisors for classes and health, and many more. Rhodes also allows students to access their strong alumni network, which provides an "immense array of career opportunities," and there's also a "well-developed study abroad program."

But perhaps the highest praise is reserved for Rhodes' faculty and staff, whom many say are the school's "greatest strength." Students love that their professors "each retain their unique styles, with accessibility being the only common factor." Many "go above and beyond to help students succeed," which is apparent from the way office hours are utilized, not just for help "but for lively discussions on papers…, for finding research opportunities, or just to chat, because they're great humans." And a classmate simply sums up by saying, "Professors have challenged me, and through it all, I have learned more than I ever thought possible."

Campus Life
Undergrads at Rhodes tend to be serious about their academics and students certainly "study very hard throughout the week." Nevertheless, there's plenty to enjoy and experience beyond classwork. For starters, undergrads can join groups as disparate as the board game club and bee-keeping club, get involved with mock trials and student government, or try out for the "really great intramural frisbee team." A number of people also like to participate in the "Rhodes Outdoor Organization, which provides totally free trips to go camping, hiking, and climbing out of Memphis, as well as trips to more local sites to rock climb indoors." Additionally, "Greek life is very big" and we're told that "frat parties are common on Saturday and Friday night." Students also make the most of the city of Memphis, whether that's heading to "Beale Street for night life" going on a taste-test of new restaurants because "the food is amazing" or "attending music and arts fests in Cooper-Young neighborhood."

Student Body
The "great community feel" at Rhodes comes down to the unifying desire to learn. "Students WANT to come to class and complete assignments, because they truly care about the work they are doing." Unsurprisingly, peers describe one another as "very motivated," "intelligent," and "extremely hardworking." Admittedly, students also state that "the campus still feels very white," but qualify this by calling out the fact that they've "met people with diverse perspectives, cultures, and interests that have allowed me to learn more about the world beyond the classroom." Regardless of background, students appraise one another as "genuine, kind, and respectful of others," and one adds that "I'm amazed by how inclusive the student body is and the opportunities they create to ensure the acceptance and safety of everyone." All in all, "finding 'your group' of people is very easy, and not difficult at all because everyone just bonds easily."

RHODES COLLEGE

Financial Aid: 901-843-3810 • E-Mail: adminfo@rhodes.edu • Website: www.rhodes.edu

THE PRINCETON REVIEW SAYS

Admissions

The school reports that its standardized testing policy for use in admission for Fall 2024 requires applicants to submit either the SAT or ACT. It is unknown at this time if the 2024 testing policy will be permanent. The Princeton Review suggests that interested applicants consult with the school for the most up-to-date standardized testing policies. *Very important factors considered include:* rigor of secondary school record, class rank, academic GPA. *Important factors considered include:* standardized test scores, application essay, recommendation(s), extracurricular activities, character/personal qualities, racial/ethnic status. *Other factors considered include:* interview, talent/ability, first generation, alumni/ae relation, geographical residence, state residency, volunteer work, work experience, level of applicant's interest. High school diploma is required and GED is accepted. *Academic units required:* 4 English, 3 math, 2 science, 2 science labs, 2 foreign language, 2 social studies, 3 academic electives.

Financial Aid

Students should submit: CSS/Financial Aid Profile; FAFSA; Noncustodial Profile. Priority filing deadline is 11/15. The Princeton Review suggests that all financial aid forms be submitted as soon as possible (see page 5 for a note on the FAFSA). *Need-based scholarships/grants offered:* College/university scholarship or grant aid from institutional funds; Federal Pell; Private scholarships; SEOG; State scholarships/grants. *Loan aid offered:* Direct PLUS loans; Direct Subsidized Loans; Direct Unsubsidized Loans. Admitted students will be notified of awards on or about 1/15 (early action) or 3/15 (regular decision). Federal Work-Study Program available. Institutional employment available.

The Inside Word

Admissions officers at Rhodes make it their mission to find candidates who will be a great fit for the school. This means that you can expect all facets of your application to be carefully considered: from your GPA to your letters of recommendation and extracurricular involvement. And if you're confident Rhodes is your top choice, we recommend applying early decision. The school gives priority consideration to these candidates with regards to both admission and financial aid.

THE SCHOOL SAYS "..."

From the Admissions Office

"Rhodes is a residential college committed to liberal arts and sciences. Our highest priorities are intellectual engagement, service to others, and honor among ourselves. We live this life on one of the country's most beautiful campuses in the heart of Memphis, Tennessee, an economic, political, and cultural center, making Rhodes one of a handful of top-tier, liberal arts colleges in a major metropolitan area.

"Rhodes has the soul of a liberal arts college coupled with a real-world mindset. Our students put their liberal arts knowledge to work in the world starting their first year. You'll be encouraged to engage in research, leadership and service opportunities—and to take responsibility for shaping your educational experience to meet your personal interests and goals. Memphis is a thriving city right on Rhodes' doorstep, with spectacular resources for students, and the college has pioneered the establishment of programs with world-class institutions and companies, including St. Jude Children's Research Hospital, FedEx and the Memphis Zoo, which take advantage of the college's metropolitan location and provide students with real-world opportunities for academic and personal growth."

SELECTIVITY

Admissions Rating	92
# of applicants	5,253
% of applicants accepted	54
% of acceptees attending	17
# offered a place on the wait list	1,187
% accepting a place on wait list	57
% admitted from wait list	1
# of early decision applicants	261
% accepted early decision	58

FIRST-YEAR PROFILE

Testing policy	SAT or ACT Required
Range SAT composite	1315–1450
Range SAT EBRW	655–725
Range SAT math	650–740
Range ACT composite	28–32
# submitting SAT scores	54
% submitting SAT scores	11
# submitting ACT scores	146
% submitting ACT scores	31
Average HS GPA	3.7
% frosh submitting high school GPA	99
% graduated top 10% of class	54
% graduated top 25% of class	81
% graduated top 50% of class	98

DEADLINES

Early decision	
Deadline	11/1
Notification	11/15
Other ED deadline	1/15
Other ED notification	2/1
Early action	
Deadline	11/15
Notification	1/15
Regular	
Priority	1/15
Deadline	7/1
Notification	4/1
Nonfall registration?	Yes

APPLICANTS OFTEN PREFER
Washington and Lee University; Washington University in St. Louis

APPLICANTS SOMETIMES PREFER
Davidson College; Furman University; The University of the South; Vanderbilt University

FINANCIAL FACTS

Financial Aid Rating	90
Annual tuition	$52,000
Room and board	$12,296
Required fees	$310
Books and supplies	$1,125
Average frosh need-based scholarship	$38,141
Average UG need-based scholarship	$36,842
% needy frosh rec. need-based scholarship or grant aid	98
% needy UG rec. need-based scholarship or grant aid	98
% needy frosh rec. non-need-based scholarship or grant aid	54
% needy UG rec. non-need-based scholarship or grant aid	44
% needy frosh rec. need-based self-help aid	45
% needy UG rec. need-based self-help aid	49
% frosh rec. any financial aid	96
% UG rec. any financial aid	95
% UG borrow to pay for school	39
Average cumulative indebtedness	$21,967
% frosh need fully met	62
% ugrads need fully met	52
Average % of frosh need met	95
Average % of ugrad need met	92

RICE UNIVERSITY

6100 Main Street, Houston, TX 77251-1892 • Admissions: 713-348-0000 • Fax: 713-348-5952

STUDENTS SAY "..."

Academics

According to students, Rice University's greatest strengths "are its academic integrity and quality." That's borne out in the way that science labs "are generally taught with a genuinely unknown problem being presented at the beginning of the semester and students being trained in the methods to explore that problem." Or it's shown by how the Oshman Engineering Design Kitchen "really supports projects and prototyping...as an undergraduate I've learned to design through hands-on, project-based classes." The collaborative spirit is alive and well in offerings like the Academic Fellows Program, which offers free tutoring sessions for and by students. There's also an outside-the-box thinking when it comes to assessments, like "the option to make a 30 minute scientific podcast instead of taking the final," explains one sophomore. This isn't unusual for first-years either; one notes that "instead of doing a bunch of writing and essays, I was tasked with creating...a TED Talk, which really lit a creative flame in me." Outside the classroom, "immersive internships" at places like NASA, State Farm, and Exxon are made possible by Rice's prime location in Houston, Texas.

One of the major drivers of that success, according to students, is the accessibility of the faculty on campus. "Professors will host talks outside of class" and "can also be found eating among students." One student enjoys going to German Table, "a meal held on Mondays by the German department for German speakers. It's a place for people to have natural conversations in German." Another, studying Jewish Immigration, is excited that they will be "traveling to New York City over spring break to interact directly with historical sites." Overall, professors are well-respected for "offering extra office hours, giving extensions on assignments, or just being someone to talk to."

Campus Life

Undergrads praise Rice for doing "an amazing job of assimilating students," noting that a convivial vibe is generated by the way in which students are sorted into one of 11 colleges, in short, creating "a new home, a new family, and a brand-new experience that everyone should enjoy." One sophomore feels "so grateful to have a community of people that unconditionally support my academic and personal success." The school's "emphasis on community" is further developed through the active club scene, with figure skating, crochet, K-pop dance, and even a rocket-building group listed as favorite activities. Additionally, residential advisors and college magisters "act as a support system. Students can reach out to them for academic advice, career advice, life advice, or even recommendations for fun things to do around Houston." Not that it's particularly difficult to find things on-campus: students so often "picnic in the Central Quad" or hang out in residential areas that they happily self-describe themselves as "within the hedges." Rice also hosts campus-wide parties, as well as Beer Bike, a "combination intramural bicycle race and drinking competition." As one third-year student puts it, "People work on the weekdays and during the day on weekends, and then on Friday and Saturday everyone does something fun, whether partying or spending time with friends."

Student Body

Rice students are a multifaceted bunch: "Everyone has their interest in their major, of course, but there's no person not involved in something else too. I know a guy majoring in math who wants to write poetry. My roommate studies civil engineering but does South Asian dance." Another third-year student agrees, saying, "People are highly motivated in different ways, some in arts, others in engineering, and others in athletics; however, all of them interact with each other and share their passions."

Many students appreciate that the "student body is very diverse," and the campus maintains "a large sense of community on all levels, whether it is in the residential colleges, the classroom or on campus in general." Students enjoy that the "typical Rice student is academically focused, but is willing to have a good time." Perhaps most importantly, "We all take pride in our 'Culture of Care,' in which we all take care of each other mentally, academically, and socially."

RICE UNIVERSITY

Financial Aid: 713-348-4958 • E-Mail: admission@rice.edu • Website: www.rice.edu

THE PRINCETON REVIEW SAYS

Admissions

The school reports that its standardized testing policy for use in admission for Fall 2024 requires applicants to submit either the SAT or ACT. It is unknown at this time if the 2024 testing policy will be permanent. The Princeton Review suggests that interested applicants consult with the school for the most up-to-date standardized testing policies. *Very important factors considered include:* rigor of secondary school record, class rank, academic GPA, standardized test scores, application essay, recommendation(s), extracurricular activities, talent/ability, character/personal qualities. *Other factors considered include:* interview, first generation, alumni/ae relation, geographical residence, state residency, racial/ethnic status, volunteer work, work experience, level of applicant's interest. High school diploma is required and GED is accepted. *Academic units required:* 4 English, 3 math, 2 science, 2 foreign language, 2 social studies, 3 academic electives.

Financial Aid

Students should submit: CSS/Financial Aid Profile; FAFSA; Noncustodial Profile; State aid form. Priority filing deadline is 2/1. The Princeton Review suggests that all financial aid forms be submitted as soon as possible (see page 5 for a note on the FAFSA). *Need-based scholarships/grants offered:* College/university scholarship or grant aid from institutional funds; Federal Pell; Private scholarships; SEOG; State scholarships/grants; United Negro College Fund. *Loan aid offered:* Direct PLUS loans; Direct Subsidized Loans; Direct Unsubsidized Loans; State Loans. Admitted students will be notified of awards on or about 4/1. Federal Work-Study Program available. Institutional employment available.

The Inside Word

Gaining admission to Rice University isn't easy. That being said, no one metric in particular holds the most weight. The university considers everything from academic prowess and special talents to creativity, life experiences, and leadership. It should be noted that applicants must apply to one of seven schools—humanities, engineering, natural sciences, architecture, music, social sciences, or business. The school you select is not binding but should reflect your skills and interests. For "high achieving, low-income students" Rice is a participating college in QuestBridge, which provides financial aid packages that include tuition and fees, room and board, books and supplies, and personal and travel expenses.

THE SCHOOL SAYS " . . ."

From the Admissions Office

"What if your next four years exceeded all expectations? Rice University sits in the heart of Houston on a 300-acre, tree-lined campus next to the Texas Medical Center and the Houston Museum District. As a top-tier research institution, we offer more than 50 majors across seven schools of study where students have the freedom and ability to choose their own path. From your first semester on campus, no matter your major, you'll have the opportunity to conduct research alongside experts. You'll be able to apply your skills, gain valuable professional experience, and interact with industry leaders as you address real-world issues. Bright, curious, and diverse, our students have a thirst for knowledge and a desire to shape the world around them.

"Our student life begins with our residential colleges, where we randomly sort new students and where they stay throughout their time at Rice. Because each student is randomly assigned and stays in the same college throughout their undergraduate years, the diversity of our student body creates a rich tapestry of traditions, culture, and, most importantly, community. And by focusing on a culture of care, students find support from their peers resulting in an environment of collaboration over competition.

"This combination of excellence in academics, a vibrant and caring student life and our commitment to access and affordability forms the heart of Rice University."

SELECTIVITY

Admissions Rating	98
# of applicants	31,443
% of applicants accepted	9
% of acceptees attending	44
# offered a place on the wait list	4,244
% accepting a place on wait list	73
% admitted from wait list	0
# of early decision applicants	2,725
% accepted early decision	19

FIRST-YEAR PROFILE

Testing policy	SAT or ACT Required
Range SAT composite	1500–1560
Range SAT EBRW	730–770
Range SAT math	760–800
Range ACT composite	34–36
# submitting SAT scores	635
% submitting SAT scores	53
# submitting ACT scores	281
% submitting ACT scores	23
% graduated top 10% of class	89
% graduated top 25% of class	97
% graduated top 50% of class	100

DEADLINES

Early decision	
Deadline	11/1
Notification	12/15
Regular	
Deadline	1/4
Notification	4/1
Nonfall registration?	No

APPLICANTS ALSO LOOK AT

Cornell University; Duke University; Harvard College; Massachusetts Institute of Technology; Stanford University; The University of Chicago; The University of Texas at Austin; University of California—Berkeley; Vanderbilt University

FINANCIAL FACTS

Financial Aid Rating	97
Annual tuition	$54,100
Room and board	$15,000
Required fees	$860
Books and supplies	$1,350
Average frosh need-based scholarship	$58,740
Average UG need-based scholarship	$57,380
% needy frosh rec. need-based scholarship or grant aid	98
% needy UG rec. need-based scholarship or grant aid	98
% needy frosh rec. non-need-based scholarship or grant aid	9
% needy UG rec. non-need-based scholarship or grant aid	9
% needy frosh rec. need-based self-help aid	23
% needy UG rec. need-based self-help aid	28
% frosh rec. any financial aid	58
% UG rec. any financial aid	57
% UG borrow to pay for school	18
Average cumulative indebtedness	$19,623
% frosh need fully met	100
% ugrads need fully met	99
Average % of frosh need met	100
Average % of ugrad need met	100

RIDER UNIVERSITY

2083 Lawrenceville Road, Lawrenceville, NJ 08648-3099 • Admissions: 609-896-5000 • Fax: 609-895-6645

STUDENTS SAY ". . ."

Academics

Rider University is dedicated to the success of its undergraduates and "has made strong strides in recent years to improve facilities and provide new opportunities." From the get-go, students have access accessibility and support services, including the career center's help with résumés and interview skills. Enrollees also mention how "the Engaged Learning Program is a great part of Rider's commitment" in that it makes clear to students not just how they're doing academically but in skills translatable to a real-world setting. This, in turn, is backed up by the Cranberry Investment, which "guarantees a job, internship, or graduate program acceptance within 1 year of graduation…[or post-graduate] assistance and courses to help you attain this goal."

Students note that this isn't just scaffolding—classes offer unique learning opportunities that go beyond textbooks and lectures, like the Business in Action Program: "I was placed in a group of four of my peers and we were tasked with creating a business idea and executing it from start to finish." Another undergrad adds that they were "able to go out on campus and film things for an assignment" and really enjoyed "being given creative freedom to complete projects." The focused class sizes come in handy here, as they "allow for a more personal connection with professors." And speaking of the faculty, they are typically "very engaged in the class material and willing to help students, inside and outside of the classroom." They also "really do seem to love their job and motivate kids to actually learn to expand their knowledge, not just do the work for a grade." Indeed, they understand how to foster "a safe learning space for students."

Campus Life

At first glance, Rider's campus may appear quiet, given that "a decent portion of the student body commutes." But students list countless "amazing extracurriculars like a table top club, a dance ensemble, a student-directed theatre company, and more. There is truly something for everyone!" Additionally, students say that intramurals are "a lot of fun" and that "Greek life is a big way for students to become more involved and engaged." The school also hosts "many events that bring students together," including their twist on the X Factor television show, R Factor, and sometimes works with clubs to expand offerings like a beach cleanup. Students note that you can participate at your own pace, and appreciate that they can "easily get together to hang out or work on projects, go to the SRC to attend a fitness class, [or head] to our on-campus pub to watch sports games."

Student Body

Rider University's student body "is very small, yet welcoming." Many undergrads say it's "so easy to make connections with people," noting that everyone is "friendly and willing to help you with anything…academic or personal." That doesn't mean the school is without cliques that "tend to stick together as they share most of their classes," but it's not seen as a negative. Rider is also seen as a haven for "many different people here who didn't know if they would be able to go to college," and it shows—individuals work to make the most of this opportunity. "I haven't met one person at this school who hasn't been hardworking or determined with a set of goals in mind." A classmate adds, "I have had an amazing experience with everyone that I have met here at Rider and am really looking forward to seeing where life takes me."

RIDER UNIVERSITY

Financial Aid: 609-896-5360 • E-Mail: admissions@rider.edu • Website: www.rider.edu

THE PRINCETON REVIEW SAYS

Admissions

The school reports that its standardized testing policy for use in admission for Fall 2024 is Test Optional. The 2024 testing policy will be permanent. The Princeton Review suggests that interested applicants consult with the school for the most up-to-date standardized testing policies. *Very important factors considered include:* rigor of secondary school record, academic GPA, application essay, recommendation(s). *Other factors considered include:* standardized test scores, interview, extracurricular activities, talent/ability, character/personal qualities, geographical residence, state residency, volunteer work, work experience, level of applicant's interest. High school diploma is required and GED is accepted. *Academic units required:* 4 English, 3 math. *Academic units recommended:* 4 science, 4 science labs, 2 foreign language, 2 social studies, 2 history, 1 academic elective.

Financial Aid

Students should submit: FAFSA. Priority filing deadline is 2/1. The Princeton Review suggests that all financial aid forms be submitted as soon as possible (see page 5 for a note on the FAFSA). *Need-based scholarships/grants offered:* College/university scholarship or grant aid from institutional funds; Federal Pell; Private scholarships; SEOG; State scholarships/grants. *Loan aid offered:* Direct PLUS loans; Direct Subsidized Loans; Direct Unsubsidized Loans; State Loans. Admitted students will be notified of awards on a rolling basis. Federal Work-Study Program available. Institutional employment available.

The Inside Word

To prepare for college, Rider University suggests that high school students follow a rigorous curriculum of college prep courses, including AP and honors classes. Students need at least four years of high school English and three years of math (including Algebra 2) to be considered for admission to Rider. The most recent incoming class had an average high school GPA of 3.32. Although most students major in the liberal arts and sciences, more than one-quarter of undergraduates are enrolled in the business school. Rider University accepts applications on a rolling basis.

THE SCHOOL SAYS "..."

From the Admissions Office

"At Rider University, your future is wide open.

"Whether you know exactly what your future holds, or are still figuring it out, Rider provides the support to follow your drive and the freedom to explore our 70+ majors and minors.

"The majors at Rider open a world of possibility from internships, to grad school, to career opportunities and new passions you may have not discovered yet! Our Engaged Learning Program combines your academics, career goals and personal interests to guide you through eye-opening, life-changing opportunities.

"Rider is a beautiful campus, but the connections, lessons and sense of community you find here will follow you anywhere. So if you can't come to us, don't worry. Through video calls, photo galleries, texting, live chat—you name it—we'll bring the spirit of Rider to you.

"The Rider experience is an investment in your growth and potential. We're committed to making Rider affordable for all our students, and that begins with exceptional financial aid options. We encourage you to invest in yourself, and our financial aid counselors are here to answer any questions, and guide you, every step of the way.

"Whether you know exactly what you want to do or aren't yet sure where you're headed, let's figure it out together."

SELECTIVITY

Admissions Rating	83
# of applicants	9,340
% of applicants accepted	84
% of acceptees attending	10
# offered a place on the wait list	98
% accepting a place on wait list	49
% admitted from wait list	71

FIRST-YEAR PROFILE

Testing policy	Test Optional
Range SAT composite	1090–1310
Range SAT EBRW	560–650
Range SAT math	540–650
Range ACT composite	21–29
# submitting SAT scores	131
% submitting SAT scores	17
# submitting ACT scores	14
% submitting ACT scores	2
Average HS GPA	3.5
% frosh submitting high school GPA	100
% graduated top 10% of class	21
% graduated top 25% of class	48
% graduated top 50% of class	77

DEADLINES

Early action	
Deadline	11/15
Notification	12/20
Regular	
Priority	1/15
Notification	Rolling, 12/15
Nonfall registration?	Yes

APPLICANTS ALSO LOOK AT

Rutgers University—New Brunswick; Montclair State University; The College of New Jersey; Rowan University; Kean University; Stockton University; Seton Hall University; Rutgers University—Newark; Monmouth University; Temple University

FINANCIAL FACTS

Financial Aid Rating	85
Annual tuition	$37,500
Room and board	$16,730
Required fees	$1,200
Required fees (first-year)	$1,475
Books and supplies	$1,500
Average frosh need-based scholarship	$28,276
Average UG need-based scholarship	$28,255
% needy frosh rec. need-based scholarship or grant aid	100
% needy UG rec. need-based scholarship or grant aid	99
% needy frosh rec. non-need-based scholarship or grant aid	20
% needy UG rec. non-need-based scholarship or grant aid	18
% needy frosh rec. need-based self-help aid	75
% needy UG rec. need-based self-help aid	76
% frosh rec. any financial aid	100
% UG rec. any financial aid	95
% UG borrow to pay for school	78
Average cumulative indebtedness	$34,314
% frosh need fully met	18
% ugrads need fully met	19
Average % of frosh need met	84
Average % of ugrad need met	82

RIPON COLLEGE

300 W. Seward St., Ripon, WI 54971 • Admissions: 920-748-8115 • Fax: 920-748-8335

STUDENTS SAY "..."

Academics

Described as a "close-knit community," "Ripon is a place where a student's best interest matters; all other agendas are secondary." One student chose Ripon because, "I was looking for a liberal arts school that allowed me to do the things I like, namely, be involved in multiple student groups, study abroad, and take classes in different fields, all of which I have been able to do at Ripon." The "quiet beauty," "welcoming nature of the campus," along with "small class sizes and a lot of personal attention from professors" create a "friendly, home-away-from-home atmosphere." Students appreciate the education they are receiving and how it prepares them for a productive life after college. The school's motto, "more together" "is exactly what our school is all about; becoming something more with the help of those here to guide us." "Ripon College prepares students to be productive, service-minded leaders who are ready and willing to influence the direction of our nation's future." "Ripon College is not all about sitting in a classroom listening to lectures and taking notes; it's about teaching us to become more educated in the world around us and helping us to develop the skills needed to succeed." "The hands-on, experiential, service-learning projects have been particularly valuable for my own personal growth and for preparing me for life after college." Another student agrees, saying, "Ripon is a prime example of a college with a positive and supportive living and learning community." "Ripon professors provide an interesting and intellectually challenging environment for students to discuss and to learn." Students say, Ripon is an "amazing community of learners and educators who support one another" and a "unique institution that helps ordinary people uncover their extraordinary potential to do great things." Professors "are not just teachers, but mentors!" Scholarships make a Ripon College education possible for some that otherwise could not attend. One student says, "They offered me a great scholarship and were really willing to work with me to make my college education affordable."

Campus Life

With its "tight-knit and welcoming community," Ripon conveys "a friendly environment conducive to learning, fun, and overall personal growth." It is "not uncommon to sit down to lunch with a professor, or even go over to their house for tea." Life at Ripon has proven blissful for one student who now says, "I cannot remember a time when I wanted to be anywhere else." Besides a "strong academic core," Ripon College has "many successful sports teams," and Greek life "is abundant." Greeks host events and are a big part of many students' life. Partying "is evident but not huge by any respect." "Since Ripon College is in a small town, the college sets up a lot of events on weekends for us to take part in!" "The small-town feel of Ripon forces you sometimes to create your own fun, which usually makes for the best memories." "Being close to several metropolitan areas (Chicago, Milwaukee, Madison, and the Twin Cities), there is rarely a weekend when people are not getting off campus to go explore." But if you are looking for snow days to figure into your schedule, then Ripon may not be for you "because most professors will keep classes going even in negative temperatures with two feet of snow."

Student Body

A typical Ripon student is described as "laid-back and friendly." One student cautions, "You have to plan extra time in between classes because you're guaranteed to be stopped by someone you know along the way to talk for a few minutes." Students are "outgoing, personable, and motivated," "involved in multiple clubs," and may "hold more than one internship at a time. From Student Senate to Ultimate Frisbee to volunteering in the community, there is never a lack of activities in which one can participate." Students are "always looking for something new and exciting to do, and [are] ready to volunteer their time and energy to someone in need."

RIPON COLLEGE

Financial Aid: 920-748-8301 • E-Mail: adminfo@ripon.edu • Website: www.ripon.edu

THE PRINCETON REVIEW SAYS

Admissions

The school reports that its standardized testing policy for use in admission for Fall 2024 is Test Optional. The 2024 testing policy will be permanent. The Princeton Review suggests that interested applicants consult with the school for the most up-to-date standardized testing policies. *Very important factors considered include:* rigor of secondary school record, interview. *Important factors considered include:* class rank, academic GPA, extracurricular activities, character/personal qualities. *Other factors considered include:* standardized test scores, application essay, recommendation(s), talent/ability, volunteer work. High school diploma is required and GED is accepted. *Academic units required:* 4 English, 2 math, 2 science, 2 social studies. *Academic units recommended:* 4 math, 4 science, 2 foreign language, 4 social studies.

Financial Aid

Students should submit: FAFSA. Priority filing deadline is 3/1. The Princeton Review suggests that all financial aid forms be submitted as soon as possible (see page 5 for a note on the FAFSA). *Need-based scholarships/grants offered:* College/university scholarship or grant aid from institutional funds; Federal Pell; Private scholarships; SEOG; State scholarships/grants. *Loan aid offered:* Direct PLUS loans; Direct Subsidized Loans; Direct Unsubsidized Loans; State Loans. Admitted students will be notified of awards on a rolling basis beginning 11/1. Federal Work-Study Program available. Institutional employment available.

The Inside Word

Ripon seeks accomplished high school students who have challenged themselves in and out of the classroom. Solid performers—those earning a B-plus average in a college-prep curriculum and exceeding 1100 SAT/22 ACT (though these tests are currently optional)—should find a clear path awaiting them, although the school does also consider such peripherals as potential contribution to extracurricular life and the likelihood a candidate will flourish in a small-school environment.

THE SCHOOL SAYS "..."

From the Admissions Office

"Since its founding in 1851, Ripon College has adhered to the philosophy that the liberal arts offer the richest foundation for intellectual, cultural, social, and spiritual growth. Academic strength is a 150-year tradition at Ripon. We attract excellent professors who are dedicated to their disciplines; they in turn attract bright, committed students. Together with the other members of our tightly knit learning community, students at Ripon learn more deeply, live more fully, and achieve more success. Students are surprised to discover that here there are more opportunities—to be involved, to lead, to speak out, to make a difference, to explore new interests—than at a college ten times our size. Through collaborative learning, group living, teamwork, and networking, students tap into the power of a community where we all work together to ensure success—at Ripon and beyond.

"All of the best residential liberal arts colleges strive to be true learning communities like Ripon. We succeed better than most because our enrollment of about 1,000 students is perfect for fostering connections inside and outside the classroom. Our students flourish in this environment of mutual respect, where shared values are elevated and diverse ideas are valued. If you are seeking academic challenge and want to benefit from an environment of personal attention and support—then you should take a closer look at Ripon."

SELECTIVITY

Admissions Rating	82
# of applicants	2,142
% of applicants accepted	81
% of acceptees attending	11

FIRST-YEAR PROFILE

Testing policy	Test Optional
Range SAT EBRW	510–580
Range SAT math	480–590
Range ACT composite	19–23
% submitting SAT scores	14
% submitting ACT scores	50
Average HS GPA	3.4
% frosh submitting high school GPA	100
% graduated top 10% of class	17
% graduated top 25% of class	45
% graduated top 50% of class	84

DEADLINES

Regular	
Priority	3/15
Notification	Rolling, 9/15
Nonfall registration?	Yes

FINANCIAL FACTS

Financial Aid Rating	88
Annual tuition	$50,400
Room and board	$10,190
Required fees	$300
Books and supplies	$750
Average frosh need-based scholarship	$37,882
Average UG need-based scholarship	$36,821
% needy frosh rec. need-based scholarship or grant aid	100
% needy UG rec. need-based scholarship or grant aid	100
% needy frosh rec. non-need-based scholarship or grant aid	22
% needy UG rec. non-need-based scholarship or grant aid	22
% needy frosh rec. need-based self-help aid	75
% needy UG rec. need-based self-help aid	75
% frosh rec. any financial aid	90
% UG rec. any financial aid	83
% UG borrow to pay for school	82
Average cumulative indebtedness	$36,593
% frosh need fully met	31
% ugrads need fully met	32
Average % of frosh need met	87
Average % of ugrad need met	88

ROANOKE COLLEGE

221 College Lane, Salem, VA 24153-3794 • Admissions: 540-375-2500 • Fax: 540-375-2267

STUDENTS SAY ". . ."

Academics

Founded in 1842, Roanoke College is a private Lutheran school that wants students to leverage all of the academic, cultural, and practical resources the school has to offer. Real-world experiences such as "field trips, service components, [and interacting with guest] speakers" are encouraged, and there are also study abroad opportunities available in 50 different countries. The school's unique core curriculum allows students to pick classes from a portfolio of interesting topics, such as Statistics and the Sports Industry or Chemistry and Crime. The curriculum includes project-based capstone courses as well as courses that ensure that students truly understand the topics by the end of the course. There is a three-week Intensive Learning Program (also called May Term) that is a focused learning experience in which students participate in activities surrounding a single topic, ranging from debates to travel to student reenactments. Students value the flexibility of an academic format that allows them "to find their purpose on campus and explore several different fields of interest at once."

On the whole, professors strive to engage their students and focus on critical thinking. "Some [professors] even encourage respectful arguments to show different views to get students thinking about [what] they are learning." Many students relate that the professors are what they like most about the college. As one student puts it, "I always feel welcomed and listened to by my professors." Another says, "I think it's rare to have this many professors that truly care about your success and well-being." At Roanoke, "many classes are discussion-based and there are a lot of opportunities for students to ask questions and work together." As one student explains, "professors want students involved because it helps us learn better."

Campus Life

There is a "strong community both within and outside of the campus," and the school does "an amazing job of emphasizing the 'family' aspect of what it means to be a Maroon." Typical days involve some combination of the following: going to class, working out, eating with friends, doing homework, and hanging out on the Quad. Many students remark that they would like more on-campus dining options but note that there is a coffee shop just off campus that many students frequent. Students can also participate in campus activities such as Friday on the Quad, which includes "live music, food trucks, and fun events such as ax throwing and fire juggling." Athletic games (especially basketball) are highly attended, and students enjoy spending time outside playing games like spikeball or relaxing in hammocks. On Mondays, "most students go to Theology on Tap, which provides free food and is hosted by the chaplain." Roanoke is located "in a beautiful area filled with hiking and kayaking nearby," and "there are lots of hiking trips on the weekends." In any time not spent studying, there "are always people hosting hangouts from Greek life" and people going into the towns of Salem and Roanoke to "take advantage of the things like outdoor gear rentals and movie ticket discounts." A lot of people "like to participate in many clubs whether it is the Beekeeping Society or the Cheese Club," or "Toy Like Me, which is a club that modifies toys for children with disabilities and gifts [them] to children and the local hospital system."

Student Body

This "smaller, community-like college" has nearly 1,900 undergraduates, which "allows for relationships between students and faculty," but it's still large enough that "you can walk across campus and say hi to five people you know and still see five people you don't." Though most here are "white and come from [an] affluent background," the school is "steadily working toward a reflection of the diverse population of Virginia," and students themselves strive "toward building a diverse, welcoming community for fellow peers on campus." And as another student says, "Everybody is unique in their own way and makes you feel welcome." Roanoke attracts "smart, kind people who are genuine and excited to get to know each other," and even in class, students "are very open in sharing their opinion and personal life when it is relevant to the lecture." The overall sentiment is that "the students are caring, determined, and outgoing."

Financial Aid: 540-375-2235 • E-Mail: admissions@roanoke.edu • Website: www.roanoke.edu

THE PRINCETON REVIEW SAYS

Admissions

The school reports that its standardized testing policy for use in admission for Fall 2024 is Test Optional. The 2024 testing policy will be permanent. The Princeton Review suggests that interested applicants consult with the school for the most up-to-date standardized testing policies. *Very important factors considered include:* rigor of secondary school record, academic GPA, character/personal qualities. *Important factors considered include:* class rank, interview, extracurricular activities, level of applicant's interest. *Other factors considered include:* standardized test scores, application essay, recommendation(s), talent/ability, alumni/ae relation, racial/ethnic status, volunteer work, work experience. High school diploma is required and GED is accepted. *Academic units required:* 4 English, 3 math, 2 science, 2 science labs, 2 foreign language, 2 social studies, 5 academic electives. *Academic units recommended:* 2 foreign language.

Financial Aid

Students should submit: FAFSA; State aid form. The Princeton Review suggests that all financial aid forms be submitted as soon as possible (see page 5 for a note on the FAFSA). *Need-based scholarships/grants offered:* College/university scholarship or grant aid from institutional funds; Federal Pell; Private scholarships; SEOG; State scholarships/grants. *Loan aid offered:* Direct PLUS loans; Direct Subsidized Loans; Direct Unsubsidized Loans; College/university loans from institutional funds. Admitted students will be notified of awards on a rolling basis beginning 11/15. Federal Work-Study Program available. Institutional employment available.

The Inside Word

Each part of a student's application to Roanoke is important, as the College takes a holistic approach to admission, considering the whole student, not just a string of numbers. That said, the average admitted student comes to Roanoke with a 3.6 high school GPA and nearly 40 percent of admitted applicants have a high school GPA of 3.75 or higher. The optional admissions essay should be seen as required: it gives the school a chance to get to know the real you and the reasons you think Roanoke is the best fit for you and your talents.

THE SCHOOL SAYS "..."

From the Admissions Office

"The Roanoke College experience is a full one. When enrolled students arrive, they embark on a rich personal and academic journey. They discover how to think deeply about their choices, their skills and their contributions to the world. They discover a community of people dedicated to helping them find high-value careers and lives with meaning and purpose"

"The College is nationally recognized for its innovative core curriculum and majors that allow for depth of study and research. All of Roanoke's core introductory courses are topic-based. For example, instead of Statistics 101, students might choose 'Statistics and the Weather,' and discover how statistical analysis is used in weather forecasting."

"Over 95 percent of surveyed Roanoke alumni received job offers or entered graduate school within six months of graduation. The College is also a top producer of academic scholars, including Fulbright, Goldwater and Truman awardees."

"The Cregger Center is the newest addition to campus. The 155,000-square-foot complex features an indoor track, fitness center, academic spaces and 2,500-seat arena. Ten residence halls have been constructed or renovated in the past decade, featuring a mix of traditional double rooms, singles, suites and apartment-style living."

"The College campus is known for its beautiful, lush grounds. Roanoke received 2019 Tree Campus USA recognition for promoting healthy trees, and engaging students and staff in the spirit of conservation. Not surprisingly, the College, minutes away from the Blue Ridge Mountains, has a vibrant outdoor adventures program."

SELECTIVITY

Admissions Rating	83
# of applicants	4,953
% of applicants accepted	80
% of acceptees attending	12
# offered a place on the wait list	167
# of early decision applicants	162
% accepted early decision	77

FIRST-YEAR PROFILE

Testing policy	Test Optional
Range SAT composite	1080–1210
Range SAT EBRW	550–630
Range SAT math	530–600
Range ACT composite	22–27
# submitting SAT scores	162
% submitting SAT scores	35
# submitting ACT scores	45
% submitting ACT scores	10
Average HS GPA	3.6
% frosh submitting high school GPA	99
% graduated top 10% of class	16
% graduated top 25% of class	33
% graduated top 50% of class	67

DEADLINES

Early decision	
Deadline	11/15
Notification	11/5
Early action	
Deadline	10/18
Notification	11/5
Regular	
Deadline	3/15
Notification	Rolling, 11/5
Nonfall registration?	Yes

APPLICANTS OFTEN PREFER
James Madison University; University of Virginia; William & Mary

APPLICANTS SOMETIMES PREFER
Christopher Newport University; University of Lynchburg; University of Richmond; Virginia Tech

FINANCIAL FACTS

Financial Aid Rating	84
Annual tuition	$33,510
Room and board	$15,366
Required fees	$1,690
Required fees (first-year)	$1,840
Books and supplies	$1,000
Average frosh need-based scholarship	$34,774
Average UG need-based scholarship	$34,086
% needy frosh rec. need-based scholarship or grant aid	99
% needy UG rec. need-based scholarship or grant aid	99
% needy frosh rec. non-need-based scholarship or grant aid	99
% needy UG rec. non-need-based scholarship or grant aid	98
% needy frosh rec. need-based self-help aid	74
% needy UG rec. need-based self-help aid	78
% frosh rec. any financial aid	100
% UG rec. any financial aid	97
% UG borrow to pay for school	74
Average cumulative indebtedness	$35,452
% frosh need fully met	18
% ugrads need fully met	19
Average % of frosh need met	84
Average % of ugrad need met	84

ROCHESTER INSTITUTE OF TECHNOLOGY

One Lomb Memorial Drive, Rochester, NY 14623 • Admissions: 585-475-6631 • Fax: 585-475-7424

STUDENTS SAY "..."

Academics

This western New York academic stalwart boasts one of the country's oldest (and largest) co-op programs and regularly turns out job-ready students from its business, computing, and engineering programs alike. Rochester Institute of Technology is laser-focused on "creating students that are more than prepared to enter the job force," and faculty "bring the material to life" by keeping lectures work-related and placing emphasis on "how you would use what we are learning on the job site." "Professors work with the students and see them as equals," says one mechanical engineering major. "When I'm in the classroom, I feel like I'm learning and that I have a voice."

The workload is legendarily daunting and "you will have to reach out and form study groups and pull all-nighters," but professors are "more than happy to help their students" and "truly take pride in helping their students become successful." While the material may be difficult, faculty "are willing to stay after hours, meet with the student, and hold group study/review sessions to help their students understand the material." The easy A is "not very common, especially in engineering classes," but "if you work hard, you will be recognized and grades will reflect that."

The opportunity for students to dip their toes into real-world experience abounds throughout the college, and the paid co-op program (mandatory for most majors) is considered by many to be "the best thing anyone could ever choose to go through if you are a career-driven individual." Additionally, there are "plenty of materials and machines students can use for free where in other schools you still have to pay."

Campus Life

While schoolwork takes up the majority of students' time, outside the classroom they "are constantly doing something to keep busy," whether that's joining one of the 300-plus clubs or chilling at the lab. "RIT has a culture for everybody," so if you are interested in a broad topic like computing, "there are a dozen different clubs/societies that you can join to learn more about whatever niche topic interests you."

Students cop to their being "a large gamer population" at RIT, and both electronic and tabletop gaming clubs and tournaments are wildly popular, as is anime. Hockey is a huge part of RIT and "it is very common to see a large number of students at the games." People also "go to the free on-campus movies, see guest speakers, listen to comedians, and attend events hosted by the College Activities Board."

The atmosphere and layout of the campus are beautifully balanced in that "it is not very spread out but not very small at the same time." More than half of the growing population of students live in on-campus, meaning housing "is not always available for everyone who applies" and dorms can be crowded. While one student notes that "the existing infrastructure is okay at best," the school is currently adding a new 120,000-square-foot maker space, a performing arts center, and upgrading its athletic facilities.

Student Body

RIT is a place "where diversity is highlighted [and] academics are prominent," and the population is "as unique and diverse as they come." This environment "allows for a good [facsimile] of the real world." The school's internationally recognized National Technical Institute for the Deaf means there are "amazing accommodations for deaf and hard of hearing students that attend the university," including "note-taking, interpreters, [and C Print® technology]," and a vibrant LGBT+ community also exists on campus. "Video games are a way of life" and students tend to have a nerdy streak ("We are geeky and we love it"). Large groups and clubs for "anime, World of Warcraft, [and] chain mail" happily thrive among students that are all "very accepting of each other's interests." "This is where students are able to create what their minds generate. It's like teenager's dream," says one.

ROCHESTER INSTITUTE OF TECHNOLOGY

Financial Aid: 585-475-2186 • E-Mail: admissions@rit.edu • Website: www.rit.edu

THE PRINCETON REVIEW SAYS

Admissions

The school reports that its standardized testing policy for use in admission for Fall 2024 is Test Optional. It is unknown at this time if the 2024 testing policy will be permanent. The Princeton Review suggests that interested applicants consult with the school for the most up-to-date standardized testing policies. *Very important factors considered include:* rigor of secondary school record, academic GPA. *Important factors considered include:* class rank, character/personal qualities, level of applicant's interest. *Other factors considered include:* standardized test scores, application essay, recommendation(s), interview, extracurricular activities, talent/ability, first generation, alumni/ae relation, racial/ethnic status, volunteer work, work experience. High school diploma is required and GED is accepted. *Academic units required:* 4 English, 3 math, 2 science, 2 science labs, 1 social studies, 3 history. *Academic units recommended:* 4 English, 3 math, 3 science, 3 science labs, 1 foreign language, 1 social studies, 3 history, 3 academic electives.

Financial Aid

Students should submit: FAFSA; State aid form. Priority filing deadline is 2/15. The Princeton Review suggests that all financial aid forms be submitted as soon as possible (see page 5 for a note on the FAFSA). *Need-based scholarships/grants offered:* College/university scholarship or grant aid from institutional funds; Federal Pell; Private scholarships; SEOG; State scholarships/grants. *Loan aid offered:* Direct PLUS loans; Direct Subsidized Loans; Direct Unsubsidized Loans. Admitted students will be notified of awards on a rolling basis beginning 3/1. Federal Work-Study Program available. Institutional employment available.

The Inside Word

Competition to gain admission into Rochester Institute of Technology is tough. The admissions committee is on the lookout for bright, highly motivated students who will make the most out of the university's experiential learning opportunities, and the majority of students must choose their intended course of study during the admissions process. In addition to a sense of direction, you'll need a transcript that reflects a rigorous high school curriculum (including APs and honors classes) to have a shot at admission here.

THE SCHOOL SAYS "..."

From the Admissions Office

"RIT is a kaleidoscope of curious minds working together through creativity and innovation to find new ways to move the world forward. As one of the world's leading technological institutions, we provide socially conscious, and intellectually curious individuals with a wide range of academic programs, expansive experiential learning opportunities, a leading research program, and an internationally recognized education for deaf and hard-of-hearing students.

"RIT offers undergraduate and graduate programs in areas such as engineering, computing, engineering technology, business, hospitality, science, visual arts, biomedical sciences, game design and development, psychology, advertising, public relations, and public policy. Students may choose from more than 80 different minors to develop personal and professional interests.

"RIT attracts students from every state and nearly 2,000 international students from more than 100 countries. Embodying our commitment to diversity, more than 3,900 students of color have elected to study at RIT. Adding a social and educational dynamic not found at any other university are nearly 1,000 deaf and hard-of-hearing students supported by RIT's National Technical Institute for the Deaf.

"Experiential learning has been a hallmark of an RIT education since 1912. Every academic program offers some form of experiential education opportunity, which may include cooperative education, internships, study abroad, and undergraduate research.

"Students work hard, but learning is complemented with plenty of organized and spontaneous events and activities. RIT is a unique blend of rigor and fun, creativity and specialization, intellect and practice. It is a launching pad for a brilliant career, and a highly unique state of mind. It is a perfect environment in which to pursue your passion."

SELECTIVITY

Admissions Rating	89
# of applicants	23,763
% of applicants accepted	67
% of acceptees attending	19
# offered a place on the wait list	2,115
% accepting a place on wait list	37
% admitted from wait list	27
# of early decision applicants	1,690
% accepted early decision	79

FIRST-YEAR PROFILE

Testing policy	Test Optional
Range SAT composite	1280–1430
Range SAT EBRW	630–710
Range SAT math	640–740
Range ACT composite	29–33
# submitting SAT scores	1,445
% submitting SAT scores	47
# submitting ACT scores	334
% submitting ACT scores	11
Average HS GPA	3.7
% frosh submitting high school GPA	95
% graduated top 10% of class	44
% graduated top 25% of class	79
% graduated top 50% of class	95

DEADLINES

Early decision	
Deadline	11/1
Notification	12/1
Other ED deadline	1/1
Other ED notification	1/15
Regular	
Priority	1/15
Notification	Rolling, 2/15
Nonfall registration?	Yes

APPLICANTS OFTEN PREFER
Carnegie Mellon University; Cornell University

APPLICANTS SOMETIMES PREFER
Penn State University Park; Rensselaer Polytechnic Institute; State University of New York - Buffalo State; State University of New York—Binghamton University; Syracuse University; Worcester Polytechnic Institute

APPLICANTS RARELY PREFER
Clarkson University; Drexel University

FINANCIAL FACTS

Financial Aid Rating	92
Annual tuition	$46,964
Annual tuition (first-year)	$50,564
Room and board	$13,976
Required fees	$676
Books and supplies	$1,088
Average frosh need-based scholarship	$29,745
Average UG need-based scholarship	$28,045
% needy frosh rec. need-based scholarship or grant aid	83
% needy UG rec. need-based scholarship or grant aid	94
% needy frosh rec. non-need-based scholarship or grant aid	20
% needy UG rec. non-need-based scholarship or grant aid	33
% needy frosh rec. need-based self-help aid	78
% needy UG rec. need-based self-help aid	88
% frosh rec. any financial aid	77
% UG rec. any financial aid	77
% UG borrow to pay for school	75
Average cumulative indebtedness	$41,202
% frosh need fully met	67
% ugrads need fully met	80
Average % of frosh need met	87
Average % of ugrad need met	85

ROLLINS COLLEGE

1000 Holt Avenue, Winter Park, FL 32789-4499 • Admissions: 407-646-2000 • Fax: 407-646-1502

STUDENTS SAY "..."

Academics

Rollins College, a private school in Orlando, offers an academic experience that engages students with "local organizations and charities to bring the work we discuss in class into actual action." Such opportunities include "working with community members on development projects, working with policy-makers to present and enact change, [and] working in the museum to curate collections of artifacts." Some majors particularly appreciate that the on-campus child development center allows "hands-on experience for education majors as well as help with research for our psychology program." Driving that is the way in which "professors get to know students...and pass along wonderful educational opportunities." The best teachers at the school are especially lauded for the way they "capture the classes attention with their wit, and transfer their wit to the content." The school also offers financial aid to support studying abroad. This means that all students at Rollins can benefit from "access to summer or winter break study abroad experiences that count towards college credit...[in] amazing places like Singapore, Costa Rica, and London." The even more specifically "free or low-cost" immersion program further "allows students to go off campus around Florida or other parts of the United States to learn about racial justice, personal wellness, or environmental justice." Regardless of the setting, this student sums up the general vibe: "almost every single class I have taken has felt like it has a purpose and taught me things that I will be able to utilize in the real world."

Campus Life

The "beautiful lakeside campus"—which one student describes as "breathtaking" and like a "country club"—is one of the main draws at Rollins. The campus offers students three pools and a host of "free lake activities." Rowing is one of the popular sports on campus, and many students unwind by renting a paddleboard or kayak for a few hours.

Students love the "really nice housing" on campus and appreciate that "the quality and options for dining," particularly "the amazing take-as-much-as-you-need dining hall, which is included with the meal plan." The school also hosts events like movie nights and trivia; the Christmas Party in particular is referenced as "a very memorable night [that] helped destress me before finals." For those willing to walk off-campus, downtown Park Avenue provides restaurants and nightlife to explore. And, of course, the prime Florida setting brings with it "warm weather, hundreds of miles of beaches, and close proximity to theme parks."

Student Body

From the moment students arrive at Rollins College, they're meeting people who are "inspiring and are doing big things with their lives." This stems from a population of "inquirers seeking to gain a better understanding of their surrounding world" and is aided by having "many thriving international exchange outlets [and] so much culture and diversity in every aspect of campus." It's also helped by having students from all backgrounds: "I have not met such a diverse group of people from all over the world." The friendliness goes a long way to make bridges between groups—"No matter where you walk at Rollins you receive smiles"—even with how "prominent" and consequentially "cliquey" Greek life can be or for those students who feel "a lack of diversity." Overall, the consensus is that students "are very welcoming and it really feels like a community."

ROLLINS COLLEGE

Financial Aid: 407-646-2395 • E-Mail: admission@rollins.edu • Website: www.rollins.edu

THE PRINCETON REVIEW SAYS

Admissions

The school reports that its standardized testing policy for use in admission for Fall 2024 is Test Optional. The 2024 testing policy will be permanent. The Princeton Review suggests that interested applicants consult with the school for the most up-to-date standardized testing policies. *Very important factors considered include:* rigor of secondary school record, academic GPA. *Important factors considered include:* standardized test scores, application essay, recommendation(s), extracurricular activities, talent/ability. *Other factors considered include:* class rank, character/personal qualities, first generation, alumni/ae relation, volunteer work, work experience, level of applicant's interest. High school diploma is required and GED is accepted. *Academic units required:* 4 English, 3 math, 2 science, 2 foreign language, 2 social studies, 2 history, 2 academic electives. *Academic units recommended:* 4 English, 4 math, 4 science, 3 foreign language, 3 social studies, 3 history, 3 academic electives.

Financial Aid

Students should submit: FAFSA. Priority filing deadline is 12/1. The Princeton Review suggests that all financial aid forms be submitted as soon as possible (see page 5 for a note on the FAFSA). *Need-based scholarships/grants offered:* College/university scholarship or grant aid from institutional funds; Federal Pell; Private scholarships; SEOG; State scholarships/grants. *Loan aid offered:* Direct PLUS loans; Direct Subsidized Loans; Direct Unsubsidized Loans. Admitted students will be notified of awards on a rolling basis. Federal Work-Study Program available. Institutional employment available.

The Inside Word

Rollins is a Test Optional school, and both academic and need-based scholarships are available to students who choose to not submit standardized test scores. It's the school's way of creating another opportunity for students whose test results do not match their overall academic performance, and it's characteristic of the individualized approach taken here (about 10 percent of applicants opt for this method). Each applicant is assigned an admissions officer who acts as his or her liaison, ensuring a personalized admissions experience. Early decision applicants are given priority in admissions as well as in considerations for merit-based scholarships and need-based financial aid.

THE SCHOOL SAYS "..."

From the Admissions Office

"Rollins' mission is to nurture global citizens and responsible leaders as they chart their own course to a meaningful life and productive career. We believe an education is about more than a degree or that first job after graduation. It's about empowering students to discover what they truly care about and preparing them to pursue that passion with all their might. As you begin the college selection process, remember that you are in control of your destiny. Your academic record—course load, grades earned, test scores—is the most important part of your application credentials. But Rollins also pays close attention to your personal dimension—interests, strengths, values, and potential to contribute to college life. Don't sell yourself short in the application process. Be proud of what you've accomplished and who you are, and be honest when you describe yourself. Finally, the admission committee always likes to see candidates who express interest in the college. If we're your first choice, apply early decision. Each year we admit approximately one-third of the entering class through the early decision process. We encourage you to visit us here on America's most beautiful campus, meet with an admission counselor, and sit in on a class so you can see for yourself what Rollins is all about."

SELECTIVITY

Admissions Rating	85
# of applicants	9,022
% of applicants accepted	50
% of acceptees attending	14
# offered a place on the wait list	902
% admitted from wait list	15
# of early decision applicants	509
% accepted early decision	54

FIRST-YEAR PROFILE

Testing policy	Test Optional
Range SAT composite	1180–1330
Range SAT EBRW	590–690
Range SAT math	560–660
Range ACT composite	25–29
# submitting SAT scores	200
% submitting SAT scores	32
# submitting ACT scores	126
% submitting ACT scores	20
Average HS GPA	3.5
% frosh submitting high school GPA	100
% graduated top 10% of class	28
% graduated top 25% of class	65
% graduated top 50% of class	91

DEADLINES

Early decision	
Deadline	11/15
Notification	12/15
Other ED deadline	1/5
Other ED notification	2/1
Regular	
Deadline	2/1
Notification	4/1
Nonfall registration?	Yes

APPLICANTS ALSO LOOK AT

Eckerd College; Florida State University; Furman University; Stetson University; The University of Tampa; University of Central Florida; University of Florida; University of Miami; University of South Florida

FINANCIAL FACTS

Financial Aid Rating	87
Annual tuition	$58,300
Room and board	$16,190
Required fees	$0
Books and supplies	$760
Average frosh need-based scholarship	$38,231
Average UG need-based scholarship	$39,148
% needy frosh rec. need-based scholarship or grant aid	99
% needy UG rec. need-based scholarship or grant aid	99
% needy frosh rec. non-need-based scholarship or grant aid	20
% needy UG rec. non-need-based scholarship or grant aid	16
% needy frosh rec. need-based self-help aid	69
% needy UG rec. need-based self-help aid	71
% frosh rec. any financial aid	78
% UG rec. any financial aid	79
% UG borrow to pay for school	50
Average cumulative indebtedness	$32,795
% frosh need fully met	36
% ugrads need fully met	32
Average % of frosh need met	83
Average % of ugrad need met	84

ROSE-HULMAN INSTITUTE OF TECHNOLOGY

5500 Wabash Avenue, Terre Haute, IN 47803-3999 • Admissions: 812-877-1511

STUDENTS SAY "..."

Academics

Rose-Hulman Institute of Technology, a celebrated STEM school in Indiana, "does a great job of developing well-rounded engineers." One senior explains that "we truly not only build strong foundations of knowledge as students but are great problem solvers and don't shy away from challenges." Students rave about getting to put principles immediately into practice, given that "nearly every class has a lab associated with it, usually built into the class. From the minute students walk through the door they are already doing labs and getting to use equipment." Students also list a ton of beloved academic projects, like a "biology lab where we got to find our own sample and then do tests to find antibody-producing bacteria and identify it," an in-class competition where they programmed robots to "autonomously navigate a maze," and building the "capstone design projects for seniors."

Students commend the school's flexibility when it comes to switching or doubling STEM majors and applaud the support systems: "They have tutors who are in the basement study rooms of the biggest sophomore dorm every night until about 2 A.M.!" Students also enjoy that "career services" at Rose are "a powerhouse." The overall sense is that "students have a chance to participate in anything that they are interested in" and "the sheer amount of extracurriculars and elective classes in anything from neuroprosthetics to building race cars" backs that up.

Campus Life

Many students share that "we fill our days with studying and homework," yet "the culture on campus is very active, with residence halls and floors hosting movie nights or activities." Those who participate in Greek life say they "love the atmosphere" it offers: "It's a great support system, both socially and academically." Other favorite extracurriculars at Rose include intramural sports, participating in one of the many clubs on campus—drama, student leadership, and pre-professional organizations are popular—and gaming. One third-year student loves being able to switch between "intellectual conversations" and talking about "a new game mechanic in Call of Duty or a Minecraft update."

Attendees note that they felt "immediately welcomed into the community," which might have something to do with the structure of its collaboratively minded residential halls (and the assistants and advisors there to provide support): "Every night my floor will be doing something together...and I can count on our open door policy to collaborate on some homework or have a new conversation at nearly any time of day."

Student Body

The sense of "closeness and trustworthiness" at Rose comes from everyone's passion for STEM: "Since we only have STEM majors, you always have something in common." Students are "highly focused, taking challenging courses," and "driven to make a mark in [their] industry." Within those shared areas, Rose students also celebrate their differences. "I would describe my peers as very unique as most people I meet come from different places and backgrounds," explains one junior. The school's collaborative spirit helps students to observe: "that people are conversational and love to bring others into study groups." Many students point out the gender imbalance at Rose, as the student population is roughly 75% male and 25% female. However, many women find community through organizations such as the Society of Women Engineers, the Association of Women in Mathematics, Women of Like Fields Passionate About Computing, sororities, and women's sports. Overall, this "dynamic and bustling community," makes for "a warm and welcoming home, and while some may underestimate our small size, there's always something new and exciting going on."

ROSE-HULMAN INSTITUTE OF TECHNOLOGY

Financial Aid: 812-877-8259 • E-Mail: admissions@rose-hulman.edu • Website: www.rose-hulman.edu

THE PRINCETON REVIEW SAYS

Admissions

The school reports that its standardized testing policy for use in admission for Fall 2024 is Test Flexible. The 2024 testing policy will be temporary. The Princeton Review suggests that interested applicants consult with the school for the most up-to-date standardized testing policies. *Very important factors considered include:* rigor of secondary school record, academic GPA. *Important factors considered include:* recommendation(s), extracurricular activities. *Other factors considered include:* class rank, standardized test scores, application essay, interview, talent/ability, character/personal qualities, first generation, alumni/ae relation, geographical residence, racial/ethnic status, volunteer work, work experience, level of applicant's interest. High school diploma is required and GED is not accepted. *Academic units required:* 4 English, 4 math, 3 science, 3 science labs, 2 social studies. *Academic units recommended:* 5 math, 4 science, 4 academic electives.

Financial Aid

Students should submit: FAFSA. The Princeton Review suggests that all financial aid forms be submitted as soon as possible (see page 5 for a note on the FAFSA). *Need-based scholarships/grants offered:* College/university scholarship or grant aid from institutional funds; Federal Pell; Private scholarships; SEOG; State scholarships/grants. *Loan aid offered:* Direct PLUS loans; Direct Subsidized Loans; Direct Unsubsidized Loans. Admitted students will be notified of awards on or about 01/15 (early action) 03/15 (regular decision). Federal Work-Study Program available.

The Inside Word

Admission to Rose-Hulman is selective, and the admissions committee isn't shy about the fact that they are looking for the best and the brightest. They expect students to be in the top 25 percent of their graduating class (but will look at other factors like the rigor of your classes if your high school doesn't rank). It's a fantastic idea to apply sooner rather than later: Rose-Hulman's Early Action is non-binding, so you can find out if you were admitted sooner in the process without having to commit to attending.

THE SCHOOL SAYS "..."

From the Admissions Office

"Imagine a college where your classes are taught by professors who know you by name and who also happen to be among the best in the world; a place with a rigorous curriculum that prepares you for today's jobs and for careers that don't yet exist; a place where you have access to state-of-the-art labs, equipment, and research opportunities that are off-limits to undergrads at most schools; a friendly, safe, and collaborative place where you're surrounded by people who love science, engineering, and math as much as you do; and a place where everyone on campus, from your residence hall housekeeper to your academic adviser, will take the time to help you when needed.

"That place is Rose-Hulman, and our culture is the secret to our success.

"Here, your STEM education isn't just about getting a degree, or even a job. It's about taking what you learn and applying it to match your passions. You'll be the center of your experience; not stuck with a one-size-fits-all college career.

"Rose-Hulman has been recognized for more than two decades as the best undergraduate engineering school in the U.S., and we have a track record of excelling at career placement rate—averaging 98 percent—with some of the best-known companies in the world seeking out our students for paid internships and full-time employment.

"There are many more accomplishments we're proud of, but we're prouder of *why* we're so highly regarded. To fully appreciate that, schedule a visit and come see for yourself."

SELECTIVITY

Admissions Rating	91
# of applicants	5,011
% of applicants accepted	73
% of acceptees attending	16
# offered a place on the wait list	230
% accepting a place on wait list	40
% admitted from wait list	18

FIRST-YEAR PROFILE

Testing policy	Test Flexible
Range SAT composite	1310–1470
Range SAT EBRW	620–720
Range SAT math	670–763
Range ACT composite	27–33
# submitting SAT scores	248
% submitting SAT scores	42
# submitting ACT scores	183
% submitting ACT scores	31
Average HS GPA	4.1
% frosh submitting high school GPA	96
% graduated top 10% of class	60
% graduated top 25% of class	89
% graduated top 50% of class	100

DEADLINES

Early action	
Deadline	11/1
Notification	12/15
Regular	
Priority	11/1
Deadline	2/1
Notification	3/15
Nonfall registration?	Yes

APPLICANTS SOMETIMES PREFER
Colorado School of Mines; Purdue University—West Lafayette

APPLICANTS RARELY PREFER
Carnegie Mellon University; Illinois Institute of Technology; Rochester Institute of Technology

FINANCIAL FACTS

Financial Aid Rating	85
Annual tuition	$50,961
Room and board	$16,647
Required fees	$1,158
Books and supplies	$1,500
Average frosh need-based scholarship	$36,683
Average UG need-based scholarship	$36,627
% needy frosh rec. need-based scholarship or grant aid	99
% needy UG rec. need-based scholarship or grant aid	99
% needy frosh rec. non-need-based scholarship or grant aid	68
% needy UG rec. non-need-based scholarship or grant aid	98
% needy frosh rec. need-based self-help aid	67
% needy UG rec. need-based self-help aid	63
% frosh rec. any financial aid	100
% UG rec. any financial aid	99
% UG borrow to pay for school	50
Average cumulative indebtedness	$55,774
% frosh need fully met	31
% ugrads need fully met	32
Average % of frosh need met	73
Average % of ugrad need met	72

ROWAN UNIVERSITY

201 Mullica Hill Road, Glassboro, NJ 08028-1701 • Admissions: 856-256-4200 • Fax: 856-256-4430

CAMPUS LIFE

Quality of Life Rating	**80**
Fire Safety Rating	**91**
Green Rating	**82**
Type of school	Public
Environment	Town

STUDENTS

Total undergrad enrollment	14,914
% male/female/another gender	52/48/0
% from out of state	3
% frosh from public high school	88
% frosh live on campus	72
% ugrads live on campus	35
# of fraternities (% join)	24 (8)
# of sororities (% join)	16 (8)
% African American	11
% Asian	6
% White	64
% Hispanic	13
% Native American	<1
% Pacific Islander	<1
% Two or more races	4
% Race and/or ethnicity unknown	1
% international	2
# of countries represented	41

SURVEY SAYS . . .
Great library
Students are happy
Intramural sports are popular

ACADEMICS

Academic Rating	**76**
% students returning for sophomore year	84
% students graduating within 4 years	49
% students graduating within 6 years	68
Calendar	Semester
Student/faculty ratio	16:1
Profs interesting rating	85
Profs accessible rating	88
Most classes have 20–29 students.	
Most lab/discussion sessions have 20–29 students.	

MOST POPULAR MAJORS
Psychology, General; Business Admin & Mgmt, General; Biology/Biological Sciences, General

STUDENTS SAY "..."

Academics
Rowan University is a large and prominent public research university located in the heart of South Jersey. Students emphatically cite quality teaching, made possible by the ardent dedication of an accomplished faculty, as Rowan's greatest strength. "The professors absolutely make Rowan. Every single one genuinely cares about his or her students and has a passion to teach." That extra mile of interest does not go unnoticed: "I love the way my ... professors supported me through this journey." Rowan offers over 90 majors, not just in the traditional areas of study, but also innovative fields such as bioinformatics, supply chain and logistics systems, jazz studies, inclusive education, and exercise science. For those still undecided, the Exploratory Studies Program offers personalized attention, advice, and assistance from faculty and staff as students explore their academic and career options. Rowan prides itself on such support, which also ranges from tutoring to success coaching to the ASCEND program, which caters to students who are challenged by educational, cultural, or economic circumstances. "Being an international student sometimes can be difficult, but having the confidence that your school has your back and understands you is the best feeling and helps you to keep going and give your best."

Campus Life
Students describe the large suburban Rowan campus as "always buzzing with events" and full of people who like to have fun. There are innumerable student resources and activities, clubs and organizations, and opportunities to socialize: "There is a club out there for every student on campus," with examples ranging from e-sports to parkour and a thriving Greek life scene. The school also matches the needs of its majority commuting students: "I really appreciate that Rowan provides child care." On- and off-campus students alike love to engage with the cultural benefits of being between three major cities—20 minutes from Philadelphia and two hours from both New York City and Washington, D.C.

Student Body
At Rowan University, "Everywhere you look, there is an interesting person with a different story," and these backgrounds are found to enhance the overall educational experience without hindering school unity. "My peers vary in age, gender and demographics, yet through our courses we find commonality." The university greatly values inclusivity and the ideal of providing a welcoming environment for all. "Rowan really has striven to accomplish such a harmonious atmosphere here, and they've done a good job." As another student observes, "It is truly a comfortable campus to be on and everyone is genuine and welcoming." Students speak glowingly of their peers and note a work ethic that creates a supportive and collaborative sentiment on campus. "All students that I have come to meet in my years at Rowan University are friendly, have a passion for learning, and are always willing to help other students as needed."

ROWAN UNIVERSITY

Financial Aid: (856) 256-4250 • E-Mail: admissions@rowan.edu • Website: www.rowan.edu

THE PRINCETON REVIEW SAYS

Admissions

The school reports that its standardized testing policy for use in admission for Fall 2024 is Test Optional. The 2024 testing policy will be permanent. The Princeton Review suggests that interested applicants consult with the school for the most up-to-date standardized testing policies. *Very important factors considered include:* academic GPA. *Important factors considered include:* rigor of secondary school record. *Other factors considered include:* standardized test scores, application essay, recommendation(s), talent/ability. High school diploma is required and GED is accepted. *Academic units required:* 4 English, 3 math, 2 science, 2 science labs, 2 foreign language, 2 social studies, 1 history, 2 academic electives. *Academic units recommended:* 4 math, 3 science, 3 science labs.

Financial Aid

Students should submit: FAFSA. The Princeton Review suggests that all financial aid forms be submitted as soon as possible (see page 5 for a note on the FAFSA). *Need-based scholarships/grants offered:* College/university scholarship or grant aid from institutional funds; Federal Pell; Private scholarships; SEOG; State scholarships/grants; United Negro College Fund. *Loan aid offered:* Direct PLUS loans; Direct Subsidized Loans; Direct Unsubsidized Loans; State Loans. Admitted students will be notified of awards on a rolling basis beginning in January. Federal Work-Study Program available. Institutional employment available.

The Inside Word

This quality New Jersey state school gets a solid number of applicants each year, especially from residents who would pay a reduced in-state tuition. A decent percentage of them are accepted, but that's likely due to self-selection on the student side—the average GPA is in the B+ territory, and those with the best shot of acceptance come from the top 25 percent of their class. Because standardized test scores are optional, it's likely a good idea to submit if your scores are on the higher end of their previously recorded ranges, or if you're seeking some form of scholarship.

THE SCHOOL SAYS "..."

From the Admissions Office

"Since its founding in 1923, Rowan University has evolved from a teacher preparation college to a public research institution ranked among the top in the nation. Rowan offers bachelor's through doctoral degrees and professional certificates in-person and online to 22,000 students through its main campus in Glassboro, N.J., its medical school campuses in Camden, Stratford and Sewell, and on the campuses of partner community colleges. Rowan focuses on practical research at the intersection of engineering, medicine, science, business, and liberal arts while ensuring excellence in undergraduate education. Rowan has earned national recognition for innovation; commitment to high-quality, affordable education; and the development of public-private partnerships. A Carnegie-classified R2 (high research activity) institution, Rowan is the nation's third fastest-growing public research university, as reported by The Chronicle of Higher Education.

"Rowan is one of two public universities in the nation to offer M.D. and D.O. degree programs. Rowan recently partnered with Virtua Health, South Jersey's largest health system, to further establish the region's reputation for health care education and biomedical research. Rowan will soon open New Jersey's first veterinary medical school. Rowan is also designated as a military-friendly school and has an active Army ROTC program.

"The Rowan University community is a vibrant one, with students participating in wide-ranging opportunities. Rowan encourages healthy life choices, multicultural competency, personal and professional growth, campus and community involvement, civic responsibility, and leadership development. Our student-centered approach promotes the education of the whole person, helping students prepare for life after Rowan."

SELECTIVITY

Admissions Rating	85
# of applicants	16,907
% of applicants accepted	77
% of acceptees attending	20

FIRST-YEAR PROFILE

Testing policy	Test Optional
Range SAT composite	1100–1290
Range SAT EBRW	550–650
Range SAT math	540–650
Range ACT composite	23–31
# submitting SAT scores	922
% submitting SAT scores	36
# submitting ACT scores	70
% submitting ACT scores	3
Average HS GPA	3.4
% frosh submitting high school GPA	100
% graduated top 10% of class	14
% graduated top 25% of class	37
% graduated top 50% of class	71

DEADLINES

Regular	
Priority	1/31
Deadline	7/15
Notification	Rolling, 10/15
Nonfall registration?	Yes

FINANCIAL FACTS

Financial Aid Rating	76
Annual in-state tuition	$10,715
Annual out-of-state tuition	$20,108
Room and board	$15,956
Required fees	$4,237
Books and supplies	$1,120
Average frosh need-based scholarship	$12,854
Average UG need-based scholarship	$10,900
% needy frosh rec. need-based scholarship or grant aid	88
% needy UG rec. need-based scholarship or grant aid	82
% needy frosh rec. non-need-based scholarship or grant aid	0
% needy UG rec. non-need-based scholarship or grant aid	0
% needy frosh rec. need-based self-help aid	64
% needy UG rec. need-based self-help aid	71
% frosh rec. any financial aid	65
% UG rec. any financial aid	61
% UG borrow to pay for school	67
Average cumulative indebtedness	$35,245
% frosh need fully met	14
% ugrads need fully met	10
Average % of frosh need met	54
Average % of ugrad need met	48

RUTGERS UNIVERSITY—NEW BRUNSWICK

Rutgers University–New Brunswick, New Brunswick, NJ 08901 • Admissions: 848-445-4636

STUDENTS SAY "..."

Academics

Rutgers is "a big school with many different types of people," a "diverse university in all aspects of the word—academically, culturally, politically, ethnically, linguistically, and socially," which offers "opportunities around every corner." No matter what students seek from their educations, they're likely to find it here, from engineering to business to pharmacy programs and more. That kind of all-encompassing diversity means the school "offers everyone the opportunity to pursue anything they're interested in." It also means, however, that your instructors will run the gamut "from vivacious to narcoleptic"; students will have their "fair share of great professors, average professors, and bad professors." However, for every professor who is "rude when dealing with students," there are 10 who are "intelligent people who have a lot of information to share and a lot of experience that allows them to elaborate on many topics." The best of these professors are "experienced, intelligent, and helpful," as well as "diverse, accessible, proactive, involved in research, and interested in students who take initiative." These educators know how to make learning "enjoyable and informative." Most classes employ a traditional lecture format, but many elective classes "are much smaller and thus much more open to discussion and student presentation." Even more attractive for many, Rutgers' status as a research university means there are ample opportunities for undergraduates "to conduct research and work with professors in any number of fields."

Campus Life

A big campus, "awesome" public transportation, and activities of every type mean staying active at Rutgers is easy. There is certainly no lack of things to do. "There is always something going on," students boast, with sports, "movie screenings, arcade games at the RutgersZone, performing arts, local theaters, university-sponsored concerts, free food events, community service days, Greek life," and more filling whatever down time students might have. Local restaurants abound. School clubs and organizations exist by the hundreds, including those dedicated to theater, music, dance, and community service. "The party scene is definitely present, more so in the warmer months," and there are plenty of bars popular with students. The on-campus party scene tends to be safe, since the school "sends out (campus) police to patrol around the campus twenty-four hours to ensure student safety." Maybe most popular of all is rooting for the scarlet. "During football season...everyone can be found cheering in the student section at the games." For those who need to get off campus, New York City and Philadelphia are both a modest train or bus drive away. With so many opportunities, "Rutgers allows students to do well in school, be a part of an organization, have relationships with friends, and even have a job." Here, "there's rarely a dull moment."

Student Body

Typical student? Not here. The universal refrain from Rutgers students is there is no such thing. "The one common thread most students have is that they are from New Jersey, since it is a state school." Other than that, "Rutgers is truly a melting pot of people from all over the world of all different backgrounds with different interests." Rather than making it more difficult to fit in, students say this melting pot makes it easier because "no matter what you're interested in, there is a group of students here who share the same exact interests. It's really easy to find your own niche." Most students are "dedicated to academics and community service and also to having fun," students who, no matter which group they fall in with, are "very friendly, funny, and nice." Notice the combination of strong academics and a dedication to fun? That, too, is a frequently cited trait common at Rutgers. Even though "there is not one typical student," at the very least, most are "serious about their work and studying but know how to party and have fun." With a large, diverse campus having more than 50,000 students, it doesn't matter the kind of person you are. "It is not uncommon to meet someone new weekly.... With so many students here, everyone is able to find someone to befriend and interact with."

RUTGERS UNIVERSITY—NEW BRUNSWICK

Financial Aid: 848-932-7057 • E-Mail: admissions@ugadm.rutgers.edu • Website: www.newbrunswick.rutgers.edu

THE PRINCETON REVIEW SAYS

Admissions

The school recommends applicants submit either the SAT or ACT for admission for Fall 2024. If you are unable to submit a test score, or choose not to, you will still receive full admission consideration. *Very important factors considered include:* rigor of secondary school record and academic GPA. *Important factors considered include:* application essay, extracurricular activities, and character/personal qualities. *Other factors considered include:* class rank, standardized test scores, interview, talent/ability, first generation status, geographical residence, state residency, racial/ethnic status, volunteer work, and work experience. High school diploma is required and GED is accepted. *Academic units required:* 16 total with 4 English, 3 math, 2 science, 2 foreign language, 5 academic electives. *Academic units recommended:* 20 total.

Financial Aid

Students should submit: FAFSA. Priority filing deadline is 12/1. The Princeton Review suggests that all financial aid forms be submitted as soon as possible (see page 5 for a note on the FAFSA). *Need-based scholarships/grants offered:* College/university scholarship or grant aid from institutional funds; Federal Nursing Scholarships; Federal Pell; SEOG; State scholarships/grants. *Loan aid offered:* Direct PLUS loans; Direct Subsidized Loans; Direct Unsubsidized Loans; College/university loans from institutional funds; Federal Nursing Loans; State Loans. Admitted students will be notified of awards on a rolling basis beginning 2/15. Federal Work-Study Program available. Institutional employment available.

The Inside Word

One does not need to jump through hoops to get into Rutgers. Because of the vast number of applications the university gets each year, applicants will be reviewed based on the standard criteria—grades, the quality of your high school curriculum, standardized test scores, and your student essay—without much beyond that. Solid students should find acceptance into Rutgers a relatively painless process.

THE SCHOOL SAYS "..."

From the Admissions Office

"Standing as one of the nation's leading research universities, Rutgers University–New Brunswick is acclaimed for the excellent achievements of our people and for their contributions to society in the pursuit of education, research, and health care.

"With a diverse student body, prestigious faculty, vast resources, the champion Scarlet Knights, and a national rank among the top 20 public schools, Rutgers is the ideal destination for your curiosity and perseverance.

"Take a closer look:

- At the doorsteps of New York City and Philadelphia, Rutgers–New Brunswick is the flagship location with 2,656 acres—spanning five campuses that together form a single community.
- With 120+ undergraduate majors, 19 schools and colleges, and a 15:1 student-to-faculty ratio to deliver a more personalized learning experience, your Rutgers education transcends the theoretical and puts your coursework into practice.
- 81% of students report positive career outcomes within six months of graduation with top employers including Amazon, Google, RWJ Barnabas Health, and PWC.
- With a global reach, 1000+ students participate annually in study and service-learning abroad programs with access to 120+ programs in 50+ countries.
- Whether you're cheering on our beloved Scarlet Knights at a Big Ten football game or joining one of the 750+ student organizations, there are endless opportunities.
- #1 in diversity among Big Ten schools, with students from all 50 states and 120+ countries.

"From rich academic offerings to a vibrant community and a robust range of global opportunities, Rutgers–New Brunswick ignites purpose and is the ultimate beginning to a remarkable future."

SELECTIVITY
Admissions Rating	89
# of applicants	41,654
% of applicants accepted	66
% of acceptees attending	28

FIRST-YEAR PROFILE
Testing policy	Test Optional
Range SAT EBRW	630–720
Range SAT math	640–760
Range ACT composite	28–33
# submitting SAT scores	3,906
% submitting SAT scores	50
# submitting ACT scores	450
% submitting ACT scores	6
% graduated top 10% of class	29
% graduated top 25% of class	62
% graduated top 50% of class	91

DEADLINES
Early action	
Deadline	11/1
Notification	1/31
Regular	
Priority	12/1
Notification	2/28
Nonfall registration?	Yes

APPLICANTS OFTEN PREFER
Cornell University; Princeton University; University of Pennsylvania

APPLICANTS SOMETIMES PREFER
Boston University; New York University; Penn State University Park; University of Maryland, College Park

FINANCIAL FACTS
Financial Aid Rating	71
Annual in-state tuition	$12,900
Annual out-of-state tuition	$30,600
Room and board	$13,909
Required fees	$3,363
Books and supplies	$1,350
Average frosh need-based scholarship	$13,566
Average UG need-based scholarship	$12,235
% needy frosh rec. need-based scholarship or grant aid	76
% needy UG rec. need-based scholarship or grant aid	80
% needy frosh rec. non-need-based scholarship or grant aid	34
% needy UG rec. non-need-based scholarship or grant aid	22
% needy frosh rec. need-based self-help aid	76
% needy UG rec. need-based self-help aid	75
% frosh rec. any financial aid	64
% UG rec. any financial aid	58
% UG borrow to pay for school	74
Average cumulative indebtedness	$20,979

SACRED HEART UNIVERSITY

5151 Park Avenue, Fairfield, CT 06825 • Admissions: 203-371-7999 • Fax: 203-365-7607

CAMPUS LIFE

Quality of Life Rating	**86**
Fire Safety Rating	**94**
Green Rating	**60***
Type of school	Private
Affiliation	Roman Catholic
Environment	Town

STUDENTS

Total undergrad enrollment	6,729
% male/female/another gender	33/67/0
% from out of state	71
% frosh from public high school	69
% frosh live on campus	91
% ugrads live on campus	51
# of fraternities (% join)	6 (18)
# of sororities (% join)	8 (40)
% African American	4
% Asian	2
% White	77
% Hispanic	12
% Native American	<1
% Pacific Islander	<1
% Two or more races	2
% Race and/or ethnicity unknown	2
% international	1
# of countries represented	33

SURVEY SAYS . . .

Lots of conservative students
Students are happy
Classroom facilities are great
Lab facilities are great
Students involved in community service
Students are friendly
Recreation facilities are great
Everyone loves the Pioneers
Frats and sororities are popular
Theater is popular
Great off-campus food
Active student government

ACADEMICS

Academic Rating	**78**
% students returning for sophomore year	85
% students graduating within 4 years	69
% students graduating within 6 years	73
Calendar	Differs By Program
Student/faculty ratio	16:1
Profs interesting rating	85
Profs accessible rating	88

Most classes have 20–29 students.

MOST POPULAR MAJORS
Psychology, General; Registered Nursing/
Registered Nurse; Marketing/Marketing
Management, General

STUDENTS SAY "..."

Academics

Carrying on Catholic traditions and teachings for 60 years, Sacred Heart University is beloved by students for its high levels of engagement with students, the community, and with hands-on work in the classroom. For instance, in biology and anatomy labs, one student had to "train [a fish] in order to apply what I was learning in class," and exercise science labs feature advanced equipment like BioDex (a robotic measuring instrument that measures muscle strength) and Bod Pods (to measure body fat and lean body mass) "that allow you a unique lab experience." Students praise the experience: "I've learned multiple clinical skills...that I know I will use during my career." They also get a kick out of the experiential learning emphasized in study abroad programs: "Rather than sitting in a classroom and learning about ancient burial tombs, we actually took a scenic walking trip up the green hills of Ireland and saw the tombs in person."

Many students have favorable opinions regarding the faculty at Sacred Heart. Professors are "very passionate about teaching and always want their students to succeed." And they earn kudos for compassion. As one student attests, "My questions are always answered and my professors are very understanding when I have personal situations in my own life."

Campus Life

Students at Sacred Heart continually mention opportunity, whether that's being active in recreational or intramural sports, getting involved in the mentorship of younger students and high-schoolers through programs like Best Buddies or buildOn, or pursuing additional academic interests like the new neuroscience club or SHU Innovate, which helps students discover technology and its social and ethical implications. It's rare to find a program that students aren't enthusiastic about, no matter how specific: "I am on the Irish Dance Ensemble, one of the greatest teams I've been a part of." And of course, there's a strong ministry outreach, described by some as "the soul and heart of campus," which "makes every single person feel welcome." In short, "SHU is fun. Class, work, fraternity. I love it here."

Student Body

At Sacred Heart, "Everyone here welcomes you like family!" This sentiment stems from a variety of students who attribute it to a close-knit "community of peers" and a willingness to be "very accepting...even if there are differences." They also chalk it up to an overall outgoing demeanor and suggest that the school's medium size might actually drive students to participate in order to have "a big campus community" because when you "get involved and meet people [it makes] it seem bigger." Other words frequently used to describe the student body include its "positive attitude" and good manners—"We are a door-holding campus"—and motivation to get involved in "loving and helpful" ways. As one student describes it, "I believe that no institution has students that love their school more than we do," a sentiment that's seemingly only grown in response to the pandemic. "Students have been even more kind and understanding of each other. It is a great community!"

SACRED HEART UNIVERSITY

Financial Aid: 203-371-7980 • E-Mail: enroll@sacredheart.edu • Website: www.sacredheart.edu

THE PRINCETON REVIEW SAYS

Admissions

The school reports that its standardized testing policy for use in admission for Fall 2024 is Test Optional. The 2024 testing policy will be permanent. The Princeton Review suggests that interested applicants consult with the school for the most up-to-date standardized testing policies. *Very important factors considered include:* rigor of secondary school record, academic GPA, volunteer work, work experience, level of applicant's interest. *Important factors considered include:* class rank, application essay, recommendation(s), interview, extracurricular activities, talent/ability, character/personal qualities. *Other factors considered include:* standardized test scores, alumni/ae relation. High school diploma is required and GED is accepted. *Academic units required:* 4 English, 3 math, 3 science, 1 science lab, 2 foreign language, 3 social studies, 3 history, 3 academic electives. *Academic units recommended:* 4 English, 4 math, 4 science, 2 science labs, 4 foreign language, 4 social studies, 4 history, 4 academic electives.

Financial Aid

Students should submit: CSS/Financial Aid Profile; FAFSA. The Princeton Review suggests that all financial aid forms be submitted as soon as possible (see page 5 for a note on the FAFSA). *Need-based scholarships/grants offered:* College/university scholarship or grant aid from institutional funds; Federal Pell; Private scholarships; SEOG; State scholarships/grants. *Loan aid offered:* Direct PLUS loans; Direct Subsidized Loans; Direct Unsubsidized Loans; State Loans. Admitted students will be notified of awards on a rolling basis beginning 3/1. Federal Work-Study Program available. Institutional employment available.

The Inside Word

Sacred Heart takes a holistic approach to the admissions process and the school aims to get a sense of every candidate beyond their quantitative metrics. Nevertheless, while recommendation letters and extracurricular participation are important, academic achievement still carries the most weight. To be seen as a competitive candidate, you should take several honors or advanced placement courses during high school. It's also important to note that Sacred Heart is a Test Optional school.

THE SCHOOL SAYS "..."

From the Admissions Office

"Sacred Heart University is recognized for cutting-edge technology, academic programs with excellent career outcomes, championship Division I athletic programs, and its beautiful suburban campus, with many new facilities and features. Along with exceptional growth in enrollment, academic programs continue to expand and include new majors in engineering, technology, education, business, communications, and the sciences. The physical campus includes the former world headquarters of General Electric, now SHU's West Campus, which houses the IDEA Lab; NeXReality AR/VR/XR labs; the iHub powered by Verizon co-working and incubator space; and the Finance Lab. New campus buildings also include the Center for Healthcare Education, a health and recreation center, dining halls and new residence halls known as Pioneer Village. With an ideal New England location 55 miles from New York City in Fairfield County, Connecticut, plentiful undergraduate research and internship experiences are in place for all majors, the career center works with students as soon as they arrive as freshmen. Students also gain real-world experience taking a wide variety of courses at SHU's international campus in Dingle, Ireland, and study abroad locations around the globe. On campus, an exciting student life program for both residential and commuter students offers more than 100 student organizations, including strong performing arts programs in dance, theater arts, band, orchestra, and choral; fraternity & sorority life; media clubs; community service organizations; 33 Division I varsity sports; and 39 club sports teams."

SELECTIVITY

Admissions Rating	87
# of applicants	13,316
% of applicants accepted	66
% of acceptees attending	20
# of early decision applicants	230
% accepted early decision	93

FIRST-YEAR PROFILE

Testing policy	Test Optional
Range SAT composite	1140–1280
Range SAT EBRW	580–640
Range SAT math	560–640
Range ACT composite	26–29
# submitting SAT scores	303
% submitting SAT scores	17
# submitting ACT scores	64
% submitting ACT scores	4
Average HS GPA	3.7
% frosh submitting high school GPA	100
% graduated top 10% of class	14
% graduated top 25% of class	41
% graduated top 50% of class	76

DEADLINES

Early decision	
Deadline	11/15
Notification	12/1
Other ED deadline	1/15
Other ED notification	2/1
Early action	
Deadline	12/1
Notification	1/15
EA II deadline	2/1
EA II notification	2/15
Regular	
Deadline	Rolling
Notification	Rolling

APPLICANTS SOMETIMES PREFER

Fairfield University; Marist College; Quinnipiac University; University of Connecticut; University of Delaware

FINANCIAL FACTS

Financial Aid Rating	81
Annual tuition	$46,310
Room and board	$17,520
Required fees	$270
Books and supplies	$1,200
Average frosh need-based scholarship	$21,390
Average UG need-based scholarship	$20,450
% needy frosh rec. need-based scholarship or grant aid	100
% needy UG rec. need-based scholarship or grant aid	99
% needy frosh rec. non-need-based scholarship or grant aid	18
% needy UG rec. non-need-based scholarship or grant aid	17
% needy frosh rec. need-based self-help aid	74
% needy UG rec. need-based self-help aid	78
% frosh rec. any financial aid	67
% UG rec. any financial aid	59
% UG borrow to pay for school	71
Average cumulative indebtedness	$46,866
% frosh need fully met	20
% ugrads need fully met	19
Average % of frosh need met	60
Average % of ugrad need met	59

SAINT ANSELM COLLEGE

100 Saint Anselm Drive, Manchester, NH 03102-1310 • Admissions: 603-641-7000 • Fax: 603-641-7550

STUDENTS SAY "..."

Academics

Saint Anselm College is a Benedictine Catholic liberal arts school, a "welcoming, safe place where students can receive an amazing education" within the surroundings of a quintessential New England setting. Adhering to the school's service roots, the monks "are a huge part of life on campus, and even teach some classes" and "any courses that fulfill your civic requirement have an aspect called Community Engaged Learning where you volunteer in the surrounding towns as a part of your grade." To help bridge its 2,000 students into the discussion-based, inquisitive learning of its core curriculum, all first-year students take the two-part *Conversatio* class, where students "explore the connection between ourselves, the world, and the divine through many pieces of historical literature" and "spend most of the time outside lecture talking to classmates and leading discussions on the literature we study."

A student-to-faculty ratio of 11:1 makes it easier to form personal relationships with the "very caring and knowledgeable" professors, who "are always willing to meet with students to help them." There's also an Academic Resource Center that offers further workshops, writing assistance, and peer tutoring. And while some classes may lean heavily on lectures, teachers are praised for bringing in guests who are professionals in their fields to help illustrate the concepts being taught, and the school has a popular study abroad program that seeks to give students first-hand research opportunities. Ultimately, students applaud the Saint Anselm experience, as "no matter what your major is, you will experience a little bit of everything."

Campus Life

The average Saint Anselm enrollee is constantly on the move, "going from meeting to meeting, class to class, club to club." Still, "while everyone is busy, no one is overwhelmed," and students can slow down to enjoy the simple pleasures of "spending time with friends at the dining hall and taking long walks throughout campus." During the day, it tends to be all business: "you will often see people working on their laptops in common areas, the student center, library, even at the dining hall." However, after the books are closed, "people love to spend time outside, whether it's sledding, playing KanJam, cornhole, [or] hiking." Almost all students live on campus for their four years (in single-gender buildings and apartments), and "the campus events clubs try to have events or food trucks as much as possible to make an average day just a little more special."

Student Body

People at Saint Anselm are "easy to get to know," with "a large student athlete population and campus ministry/service population," and everyone tries to "embrace the community as much as we can, and cherish all of the time that we have here." As one student says, "The people who go to Saint Anselm College genuinely love the school and want to be at 'the Hilltop' [the affectionate name for the school campus] as much as possible." While "ethnic and racial diversity is not entirely large" here, this group of "warm-hearted welcoming individuals" say that "no matter your background, you'll find your niche here." To better understand the vibe, know that students commonly say things like "That was [or wasn't] very Anselmian of you," as they expect their peers to be "kind, respectful, and compassionate."

SAINT ANSELM COLLEGE

Financial Aid: 603-641-7110 • E-Mail: admission@anselm.edu • Website: www.anselm.edu

THE PRINCETON REVIEW SAYS

Admissions

The school reports that its standardized testing policy for use in admission for Fall 2024 is Test Optional. It is unknown at this time if the 2024 testing policy will be permanent. The Princeton Review suggests that interested applicants consult with the school for the most up-to-date standardized testing policies. *Very important factors considered include:* academic GPA. *Important factors considered include:* recommendation(s). *Other factors considered include:* rigor of secondary school record, class rank, standardized test scores, application essay, interview, extracurricular activities, talent/ability, character/personal qualities, first generation, alumni/ae relation, geographical residence, racial/ethnic status, volunteer work, work experience, level of applicant's interest. High school diploma is required and GED is accepted. *Academic units required:* 4 English, 3 math, 3 science, 2 science labs, 2 foreign language, 2 social studies. *Academic units recommended:* 4 English, 4 math, 4 science, 2 science labs, 4 foreign language, 4 social studies.

Financial Aid

Students should submit: FAFSA. Priority filing deadline is 12/1. The Princeton Review suggests that all financial aid forms be submitted as soon as possible (see page 5 for a note on the FAFSA). *Need-based scholarships/grants offered:* College/university scholarship or grant aid from institutional funds; Federal Pell; Private scholarships; SEOG; State scholarships/grants. *Loan aid offered:* Direct PLUS loans; Direct Subsidized Loans; Direct Unsubsidized Loans. Admitted students will be notified of awards on a rolling basis beginning 12/1. Federal Work-Study Program available. Institutional employment available.

The Inside Word

Students can submit the Common Application or the Saint Anselm Application, but on either form, you'll want to highlight personal character and community service. Applicants who feel their grades are not as high as they'd like should make sure to emphasize their out-of-class skills and experiences in their application. Note that nursing applicants must apply early action or early decision.

THE SCHOOL SAYS "..."

From the Admissions Office

"Saint Anselm is New England's only Benedictine College, a place where a 1,500 year tradition that values a love of learning and a balanced life is coupled with a contemporary liberal arts education. The college offers over 100 academic programs and is particularly well-known for nursing, politics, business, criminal justice, and psychology. Located in the first in the nation primary state, Saint Anselm is the home of the New Hampshire Institute of Politics, which hosts national debates and provides opportunities for students of any major to engage with candidates, journalists, and elected officials. A student who wants to meet the next President of the United States has a good chance of doing so here. Saint Anselm has been ranked 18th nationally for student engagement in community service by the Princeton Review, hailed by the Carnegie Foundation with Classification in both Curricular Engagement and Outreach and Partnerships, and recognized as a first tier best national liberal arts college by U.S. News & World Report. Faculty from many departments teach in the seminar-based program where students contemplate questions of value and moral choice. The college's Dana Center for the Humanities, used by students and the public, hosts a broad range of theater programming including contemporary dance and music. The Alva De Mars Megan Chapel Art Center provides an extraordinary array of art exhibitions from classic to contemporary. Eighty-five percent of the college's students participates in athletics, intramurals, and club sports. The college also offers fifty student organizations, study abroad, and community service."

SELECTIVITY
Admissions Rating	84
# of applicants	3,514
% of applicants accepted	82
% of acceptees attending	18
# offered a place on the wait list	190
% accepting a place on wait list	43
% admitted from wait list	10
# of early decision applicants	42
% accepted early decision	90

FIRST-YEAR PROFILE
Testing policy	Test Optional
Range SAT composite	1140–1300
Range SAT EBRW	560–650
Range SAT math	560–640
Range ACT composite	26–30
# submitting SAT scores	105
% submitting SAT scores	20
# submitting ACT scores	11
% submitting ACT scores	2
Average HS GPA	3.4
% frosh submitting high school GPA	100
% graduated top 10% of class	19
% graduated top 25% of class	44
% graduated top 50% of class	81

DEADLINES
Early decision	
Deadline	12/1
Notification	1/1
Early action	
Deadline	11/15
Notification	1/15
Regular	
Priority	2/1
Nonfall registration?	Yes

APPLICANTS OFTEN PREFER
Boston College; Colby College; College of the Holy Cross; Villanova University

APPLICANTS SOMETIMES PREFER
Fairfield University; Fordham University; Providence College; Quinnipiac University; Sacred Heart University; Saint Michael's College; Salve Regina University; Stonehill College; Wheaton College (MA)

APPLICANTS RARELY PREFER
Assumption University; Emmanuel College; Merrimack College; Regis College; Saint Joseph's College of Maine; Siena College; Simmons University; University of Massachusetts Amherst; University of Massachusetts Lowell; University of New Hampshire

FINANCIAL FACTS
Financial Aid Rating	87
Annual tuition	$45,360
Room and board	$16,520
Required fees	$1,440
Required fees (first year)	$1,765
Books and supplies	$1,000
Average frosh need-based scholarship	$28,993
Average UG need-based scholarship	$28,859
% needy frosh rec. need-based scholarship or grant aid	100
% needy UG rec. need-based scholarship or grant aid	100
% needy frosh rec. non-need-based scholarship or grant aid	29
% needy UG rec. non-need-based scholarship or grant aid	26
% needy frosh rec. need-based self-help aid	69
% needy UG rec. need-based self-help aid	73
% UG borrow to pay for school	73
Average cumulative indebtedness	$30,398
% frosh need fully met	34
% ugrads need fully met	34
Average % of frosh need met	82
Average % of ugrad need met	82

ST. BONAVENTURE UNIVERSITY

3261 West State Road, St. Bonaventure, NY 14778 • Admissions: 716-375-2000 • Fax: 716-375-4005

STUDENTS SAY "..."

Academics

St. Bonaventure University is a small Franciscan school of around 1,800 undergraduates. It provides "a well-rounded college experience that allows [students] to feel confident after graduation," great academic programs, and "an enormously huge heart." St. Bonaventure University is "very responsive to the need of having small class sizes to improve education outcomes" and the 12:1 student-faculty ratio guarantees personal relationships with the professors and thoughtful discussions with peers. Students "know just about everyone. You go through the same classes with the same students throughout [your] career, and it makes it easier to work in groups and get help," says a student. This is a group of eager learners who have a drive to learn and succeed not only in the classroom but "beyond, in meaningful applications to current and future employment endeavors."

The faculty comes equipped with real-world experience and sparks students' interests in a variety of academic disciplines, and "every single teacher goes out of their way to help students in any way they can." If students need help and show that they really want to learn the material, "[the faculty] will devote so much time to you." Professors "really work hard to make their classes better" and "really take our teacher evaluations to heart." Bonaventure's small size provides each student with "the opportunity to tutor, teach, do research and lead during their undergrad," and the school shows excellent career placement rates.

Campus Life

Between the great people and gorgeous scenery, "it's not that hard to go to school in the middle of nowhere." During the week, the most popular place to be between classes is "either the dining hall or the library." The small campus means students "can roll out of bed 10 minutes before class and still make it on time," and it features "a beautiful trail to walk." Division I athletics at SBU receive a lot of accolades, and students say there's nothing better than cheering for Bona basketball in the Reilly Center. "You can always tell when game day is for the men's basketball team just by walking through campus; it gets pretty crazy." Extracurricular clubs are extremely popular, as is spending time in the Rathskeller, "an on campus bar that features two pool tables, ping-pong, multiple TVs, a dance floor with a DJ usually, [and] other games." Off campus parties are "very common" on weekends. Everyone pretty much sticks to campus or hometown Olean, but for those that do want to venture further (and have access to a car), they can always "spend the day exploring the nearby national forest, or take a trip to Buffalo or Erie."

Student Body

Here in the Bona Bubble, students "look out for each other both during and after our collegiate careers." The campus culture encourages students "to be respectful with each other." "All of my peers know that the bubble we have on campus is unquestionably unique," says one. Besides holding the doors for each other all around campus ("If door holding was an Olympic sport we would win gold"), these "unfailingly kind" students "bond and form a group passionate for their small-town school." "Once a Bonnie, always a Bonnie," says a student. The familial atmosphere that students revel in here often keeps people so tightly knit "that going home for break can be difficult because you miss them so much."

ST. BONAVENTURE UNIVERSITY

Financial Aid: 716-375-2020 • E-Mail: admissions@sbu.edu • Website: www.sbu.edu

THE PRINCETON REVIEW SAYS

Admissions

The school reports that its standardized testing policy for use in admission for Fall 2024 is Test Optional. The 2024 testing policy will be permanent. The Princeton Review suggests that interested applicants consult with the school for the most up-to-date standardized testing policies. *Very important factors considered include:* rigor of secondary school record, academic GPA, recommendation(s), character/personal qualities. *Important factors considered include:* application essay, extracurricular activities, talent/ability, volunteer work. *Other factors considered include:* class rank, standardized test scores, interview, first generation, alumni/ae relation, geographical residence, state residency, work experience, level of applicant's interest. High school diploma is required and GED is accepted. *Academic units recommended:* 4 English, 3 math, 3 science, 3 science labs, 2 foreign language, 4 social studies.

Financial Aid

Students should submit: FAFSA; State aid form. Priority filing deadline is 2/1. The Princeton Review suggests that all financial aid forms be submitted as soon as possible (see page 5 for a note on the FAFSA). *Need-based scholarships/grants offered:* College/university scholarship or grant aid from institutional funds; Federal Pell; Private scholarships; SEOG; State scholarships/grants. *Loan aid offered:* Direct PLUS loans; Direct Subsidized Loans; Direct Unsubsidized Loans; College/university loans from institutional funds. Admitted students will be notified of awards on a rolling basis beginning 1/1. Federal Work-Study Program available. Institutional employment available.

The Inside Word

Prospective students at Bonaventure are evaluated individually and accepted based on their capacity for success in college. St. Bonaventure recommends that applicants submit academic transcripts, standardized test scores, recommendations, and a personal essay, and the admissions committee will consider any other supporting materials that prove a student's overall eligibility for admission. St. Bonaventure has a rolling admissions program, so applications are reviewed as soon as they arrive at the admissions office, and encouraged to apply early in the admission cycle.

THE SCHOOL SAYS "..."

From the Admissions Office

"For more than 160 years, St. Bonaventure University has been dedicated to education excellence as informed by our Franciscan and liberal arts traditions. We seek to transform the lives of our students, inspiring in them a lifelong commitment to service and citizenship.

"The charm of our campus and the inspirational beauty of the surrounding hills provide a special place where growth in learning and living is abundantly realized. St. Bonaventure establishes pathways to internships, graduate schools and careers through its innovate Career and Professional Readiness Center, which engages students from the time they step onto campus. The Richter Recreation Center provides all students with state-of-the-art facilities for athletics and wellness. As a student at one of the smallest Division I schools in the country, you get the benefits of big-time sports along with those of a small, student-centered university. St. Bonaventure is a member of the Atlantic 10.

"Academics at St. Bonaventure are challenging. Small classes and personalized attention encourage individual growth and development. St. Bonaventure's schools of Arts and Sciences, Business, (Jandoli School of) Communications, Education and Health Professions offer fifty majors. The School of Graduate Studies also offers several programs —on-ground, on-line and hybrid formats—leading to the master's degree.

"While St. Bonaventure has adopted a Test Optional policy for standardized tests (ACT and SAT), such scores will still be required for some specific majors, and to be eligible for the university's top three scholarship levels."

SELECTIVITY

Admissions Rating	84
# of applicants	3,330
% of applicants accepted	78
% of acceptees attending	19

FIRST-YEAR PROFILE

Testing policy	Test Optional
Range SAT composite	1080–1280
Range SAT EBRW	530–630
Range SAT math	540–640
Range ACT composite	21–27
# submitting SAT scores	197
% submitting SAT scores	41
# submitting ACT scores	44
% submitting ACT scores	9
Average HS GPA	3.5
% frosh submitting high school GPA	100
% graduated top 10% of class	13
% graduated top 25% of class	39
% graduated top 50% of class	80

DEADLINES

Regular	
Priority	2/15
Deadline	8/15
Notification	Rolling, 10/15
Nonfall registration?	Yes

APPLICANTS ALSO LOOK AT

Niagara University; St. John Fisher University; State University of New York—Buffalo State; State University of New York—Geneseo

FINANCIAL FACTS

Financial Aid Rating	83
Annual tuition	$37,620
Room and board	$14,450
Required fees	$1,150
Books and supplies	$800
Average frosh need-based scholarship	$25,428
Average UG need-based scholarship	$24,575
% needy frosh rec. need-based scholarship or grant aid	99
% needy UG rec. need-based scholarship or grant aid	100
% needy frosh rec. non-need-based scholarship or grant aid	96
% needy UG rec. non-need-based scholarship or grant aid	92
% needy frosh rec. need-based self-help aid	80
% needy UG rec. need-based self-help aid	83
% frosh rec. any financial aid	99
% UG rec. any financial aid	96
% UG borrow to pay for school	84
Average cumulative indebtedness	$33,984
% frosh need fully met	19
% ugrads need fully met	23
Average % of frosh need met	72
Average % of ugrad need met	68

ST. JOHN'S COLLEGE (MD)

60 College Avenue, Annapolis, MD 21401 • Admissions: 410-263-2371 • Fax: 410-269-7916

STUDENTS SAY ". . ."

Academics

At St. John's College in Maryland, the "great books," or texts commonly viewed as the foundation of Western culture, form the backbone of the unique curriculum. St. John's is a liberal arts college with two campuses that encourages exploration and dissection of original, foundational texts so that students may develop critical analysis skills within a "safe and prosperous learning environment." "The teaching of St. John's College is all about allowing individuals to collectively discover the essence of being a human being," sums up one student. Classes are pretty straightforward: "We read, and we talk about what we read." The curriculum includes obscure texts as well as the major classic players, and one of the greatest things about studying here is "engaging with difficult and renowned texts without worrying about impressing others or having to show off."

The "largely brilliant and caring" faculty members at St. John's are "some of the most wonderful and interesting people," and are "willing to meet for coffee or lunch to discuss essays, questions from class, concerns, and even non-program texts." They are "engaged and enthralled by the learning process at St. John's, just as the students are." The college has a unique evaluation system in place, so students at St. John's "are faced with reports not just on their academic success, but also on the way that they treat and interact with their peers, via classroom dynamic." The college has made academic rigor an "overwhelmingly social issue," and the "'too cool for school' attitude is not socially rewarded" here. Not only do students discuss the same works and questions, "they do so in a respectful, tactful manner." In any classroom "you get the sense of togetherness" where everyone listens and "no one's points are any more or less important to the discussion than any other's."

Campus Life

There are "no two Johnnies that are alike" and students at St. John's display a wide range of interests. Most participate in "a study group of some sort, at least one artistic extracurricular, and an intramural sport." St. John's "robust intramural program" is a major component of campus social life, and creates a "fantastic" community in which students are alphabetically sorted onto teams "where anyone can participate in various seasonal sports." "Although I have never been athletic, this is a very welcoming group regardless of ability, and playing intramural sports here has given me a lot of confidence," says one student. A large amount of extracurricular time is spent studying and reading, but there are also "very many popular club options," including "swing dance lessons, fencing, the croquet team, student play productions, orchestra, various choral groups, community service, [and the] environmental club." St. John's also offers students spots in classes run by non-faculty members of the Annapolis community, including "writing classes, poetry, watercolor, and sculpture." Off campus, people often go out to eat at many of the great restaurants in Annapolis, or head to the museums and monuments in Washington, D.C., which is "just a short train ride away." Students can also transfer between the Annapolis or the Santa Fe campuses, and many in Maryland spend a year studying in New Mexico.

Student Body

The student body at St. John's is "intellectual, but far from pretentious," and given that all students go through the same academic program "there is a strong and warm sense of camaraderie." Upperclassmen "couldn't care less that you're a freshmen," and people "who would have never become friends anywhere else are able to come together here and form bonds that start in the classroom but continue into life outside the academics." The curiosity students develop here extends to outside the program as well, so while the program at St. John's is classically oriented, students at the college "are aware of pop culture, current events, and politics." The bubble at St. John's is "real, but in no way impenetrable."

ST. JOHN'S COLLEGE (MD)

Financial Aid: 410-626-2502 • E-Mail: Annapolis.Admissions@sjc.edu • Website: www.sjc.edu

THE PRINCETON REVIEW SAYS

Admissions

The school reports that its standardized testing policy for use in admission for Fall 2024 is Test Optional. The 2024 testing policy will be permanent. The Princeton Review suggests that interested applicants consult with the school for the most up-to-date standardized testing policies. *Very important factors considered include:* application essay. *Important factors considered include:* rigor of secondary school record, recommendation(s), character/personal qualities, level of applicant's interest. *Other factors considered include:* class rank, academic GPA, standardized test scores, interview, extracurricular activities, talent/ability, first generation, geographical residence, volunteer work, work experience. High school diploma is required and GED is accepted. *Academic units required:* 3 math, 2 foreign language. *Academic units recommended:* 4 English, 4 math, 3 science, 3 science labs, 4 foreign language, 2 history.

Financial Aid

Students should submit: FAFSA. The Princeton Review suggests that all financial aid forms be submitted as soon as possible (see page 5 for a note on the FAFSA). *Need-based scholarships/grants offered:* College/university scholarship or grant aid from institutional funds; Federal Pell; Private scholarships; SEOG; State scholarships/grants. *Loan aid offered:* Direct PLUS loans; Direct Subsidized Loans; Direct Unsubsidized Loans; State Loans. Admitted students will be notified of awards on a rolling basis beginning 12/15. Federal Work-Study Program available. Institutional employment available.

The Inside Word

St. John's is a unique environment, best suited to students of a quirky yet serious intellectual predilection. To test the waters before you jump in, consider taking a campus tour or even sitting in on an active tutorial session with students. You can also send your questions about academics and life on campus to a current student through the St. John website. Each applicant is evaluated individually for potential success in the program, and submitting standardized test scores is optional. St. John's also features rolling admission beginning 2/15 with notification within three weeks of completing the application.

THE SCHOOL SAYS "..."

From the Admissions Office

"St. John's College is centered on reading and discussing the greatest books in history. With teachers such as Plato, Shakespeare, Euclid, Nietzsche, Einstein, Austen, and Du Bois, students at St. John's are original and unconventional, love big questions and discussion, and are excited to join an intellectual community of thinkers and seekers.

"All students at St. John's explore our great books curriculum in interdisciplinary classes focused on philosophy, classics, literature, politics, religion, biology, chemistry, physics, mathematics, music, history, language, and more. With a 8:1 student to faculty ratio, every class is a discussion led by one or two faculty members. Instead of choosing a major, all students graduate with a BA in the Liberal Arts. The college regularly ranks among the best for undergraduate teaching and student-faculty relationships.

"Over 70% of Johnnies attend graduate school, particularly in law, business, and journalism, and the college is among the best for students receiving PhDs in the humanities and sciences. Students are free to transfer between the campuses in Annapolis, MD, and Santa Fe, NM.

"On the Annapolis campus, 500 students experience an idyllic college town along the Chesapeake Bay. Annapolis is close to Washington, DC, with dozens of nearby museums and cultural offerings. The college was founded here in 1696, and students embrace long-held traditions such as waltz parties, intramural sports, and the annual croquet match against the Naval Academy. Popular student groups include musical ensembles, community service organizations, and the college's theatrical troupe, King Williams Players."

SELECTIVITY

Admissions Rating	93
# of applicants	983
% of applicants accepted	50
% of acceptees attending	26
# offered a place on the wait list	39
% accepting a place on wait list	100
% admitted from wait list	0
# of early decision applicants	15
% accepted early decision	67

FIRST-YEAR PROFILE

Testing policy	Test Optional
Range SAT composite	1260–1440
Range SAT EBRW	660–740
Range SAT math	590–720
Range ACT composite	30–33
# submitting SAT scores	56
% submitting SAT scores	43
# submitting ACT scores	23
% submitting ACT scores	18
Average HS GPA	3.8
% frosh submitting high school GPA	81
% graduated top 10% of class	33
% graduated top 25% of class	50
% graduated top 50% of class	79

DEADLINES

Early decision	
Deadline	11/1
Notification	12/1
Other ED deadline	1/15
Other ED notification	2/1
Early action	
Deadline	11/15
Notification	12/15
Regular	
Priority	1/15
Deadline	Rolling
Notification	Rolling
Nonfall registration?	Yes

APPLICANTS OFTEN PREFER
Brown University; Harvard College; The University of Chicago

APPLICANTS SOMETIMES PREFER
Bard College; Reed College; William & Mary

APPLICANTS RARELY PREFER
University of Maryland, College Park

FINANCIAL FACTS

Financial Aid Rating	84
Annual tuition	$37,842
Room and board	$14,984
Required fees	$1,284
Books and supplies	$680
Average frosh need-based scholarship	$29,115
Average UG need-based scholarship	$28,017
% needy frosh rec. need-based scholarship or grant aid	100
% needy UG rec. need-based scholarship or grant aid	99
% needy frosh rec. non-need-based scholarship or grant aid	16
% needy UG rec. non-need-based scholarship or grant aid	14
% needy frosh rec. need-based self-help aid	70
% needy UG rec. need-based self-help aid	74
% UG borrow to pay for school	69
Average cumulative indebtedness	$26,265
% frosh need fully met	29
% ugrads need fully met	24
Average % of frosh need met	84
Average % of ugrad need met	80

ST. JOHN'S COLLEGE (NM)

1160 Camino Cruz Blanca, Santa Fe, NM 87505 • Admissions: 505-984-6000

STUDENTS SAY ". . ."

Academics

At St. John's College in Santa Fe, students read and explore a common body of "great books"—including many of the most important books in history—in close partnership with their classmates and teachers. Every professor "must teach (learn) Euclid, Plato, and Darwin, whether he or she has a PhD in mathematics, classics, or biology." This common curriculum and dedication to the liberal arts means that "students are respected for what they can bring, and need never feel self-conscious about whether they're 'smart enough.'" Everywhere you look, there is a "commitment, sincerity, and passion for learning of the community and the faculty." This truly is an academic community that sincerely loves "the journey in its pursuit of knowledge, not simply the destination." The "liberation of the mind" at SJC comes primarily by means of the Socratic Method. SJC does not have professors, but tutors, who are there not to lecture, but to "help lead the class through the curriculum." The tutors are "very different in personality," but also "very knowledgeable and excitable about what we do." As experienced academics, they are "skillful when it comes to managing the classroom discussions and helping students articulate their thoughts" and are "truly open-minded and give everyone a chance to participate." "They really care about their students and treat us as peers in the classroom since they consider themselves also to be constantly learning." "Everyone shares fundamental values of how to treat others in the classroom," says a student. The greatest asset of SJC is the community; with everyone on board this nontraditional learning train, it's hard not to be at your best. "You're thinking nonstop at SJC," says a student. Though the self-selecting student body pretty much ensures success, students can choose how connected they wish to be to the rest of the school. "You can go four years without having an interaction with the president of the college, or you can see him every Tuesday at the Foreign Relations study group," says a student.

Campus Life

At St. John's, "you have to work intensely and relax intensely. Life is more distilled, here." "Is it hard work?" asks a student. "Yes and no. Does staying up until 1:00 A.M. reading Shakespeare or Darwin sound like work?" Santa Fe is "stunning," and the proximity of the mountains (for hiking and skiing) is more than welcome. Though each week is "epic" in its schoolwork, there are dozens of clubs and activities to take part in, from "dance (beginners always welcome) to search and rescue to astronomy to rock-climbing." If you're artsy, there are many galleries in Santa Fe, or "you can stay on campus, join a study group or sports team, or go to the gym." The student government is also responsible for dispersing several thousand dollars to support student clubs annually, so "if you can get signatures to show support, you can probably get funding for snacks or supplies." Many say that food services could have better hours and prices. There are "frequent" field trips to some of the extraordinary places in New Mexico.

Student Body

Most of the 350 undergrads at St. John's are "friendly," "big readers," and "interested in discussions." It's easy to find commonalities, since "you're always able to discuss the program as long as they're the same year or lower." All are here "because we have a genuine interest in the larger questions that are posed in life through academia," and "that's enough for most of us to feel like we're 'fitting in,' however that may be defined." Johnnies are "fascinated with learning in a way different from most schools" and "thrive on epiphanies through the 'great books,' especially ones shared with others."

ST. JOHN'S COLLEGE (NM)

Financial Aid: 505-984-6058 • E-Mail: SantaFe.Admissions@sjc.edu • Website: www.sjc.edu

THE PRINCETON REVIEW SAYS

Admissions

The school reports that its standardized testing policy for use in admission for Fall 2024 is Test Optional. The 2024 testing policy will be permanent. The Princeton Review suggests that interested applicants consult with the school for the most up-to-date standardized testing policies. *Very important factors considered include:* application essay. *Important factors considered include:* rigor of secondary school record, recommendation(s), character/personal qualities, level of applicant's interest. *Other factors considered include:* class rank, academic GPA, standardized test scores, interview, extracurricular activities, talent/ability, first generation, geographical residence, volunteer work, work experience. High school diploma is required and GED is accepted. *Academic units required:* 3 math, 2 foreign language. *Academic units recommended:* 4 English, 4 math, 3 science, 3 science labs, 4 foreign language, 2 history.

Financial Aid

Students should submit: FAFSA. The Princeton Review suggests that all financial aid forms be submitted as soon as possible (see page 5 for a note on the FAFSA). *Need-based scholarships/grants offered:* College/university scholarship or grant aid from institutional funds; Federal Pell; Private scholarships; SEOG; State scholarships/grants. *Loan aid offered:* Direct PLUS loans; Direct Subsidized Loans; Direct Unsubsidized Loans; State Loans. Admitted students will be notified of awards on a rolling basis beginning 12/1. Federal Work-Study Program available. Institutional employment available.

The Inside Word

Self-selection drives this admissions process—more than one-half of the entire applicant pool each year indicates that St. John's is their first choice, and half of those admitted send in tuition deposits. Even so, no one in admissions takes things for granted, and neither should any student considering an application. The admissions process is highly personal on both sides of the coin. Only the intellectually curious and highly motivated need apply. St. John's also features rolling admission beginning 2/15 with notification within three weeks of completing the application.

THE SCHOOL SAYS "..."

From the Admissions Office

"St. John's College is centered on reading and discussing the greatest books in history. With teachers such as Plato, Shakespeare, Euclid, Nietzsche, Einstein, Austen, and Du Bois, students at St. John's are original and unconventional, love big questions and discussion, and are excited to join an intellectual community of thinkers and seekers.

"All students at St. John's explore our great books curriculum in interdisciplinary classes focused on philosophy, classics, literature, politics, religion, biology, chemistry, physics, mathematics, music, history, language, and more. With a 8:1 student to faculty ratio, every class is a discussion led by one or two faculty members. Instead of choosing a major, all students graduate with a BA in the Liberal Arts. The college regularly ranks among the best for undergraduate teaching and student-faculty relationships.

"Over 70% of Johnnies attend graduate school, particularly in law, business, and journalism, and the college is among the best for students receiving PhDs in the humanities and sciences. Students are free to transfer between the campuses in Annapolis, MD, and Santa Fe, NM.

"The Santa Fe campus, in the foothills of the Rocky Mountains, is a one-minute walk to the best hiking, biking, and skiing in the southwest. Santa Fe is also home to more than 250 art galleries, great food, and live music. Nearly 400 Johnnies embrace the stunning natural environment and rich cultural heritage of New Mexico while reading great books on the placita, hiking 12,000-foot mountains, sculpting in the pottery studio, or socializing in the student-run coffee shop."

SELECTIVITY

Admissions Rating	91
# of applicants	452
% of applicants accepted	54
% of acceptees attending	36
# offered a place on the wait list	4
% accepting a place on wait list	100
% admitted from wait list	25
# of early decision applicants	15
% accepted early decision	67

FIRST-YEAR PROFILE

Testing policy	Test Optional
Range SAT composite	1290–1460
Range SAT EBRW	670–750
Range SAT math	620–720
Range ACT composite	30–32
# submitting SAT scores	27
% submitting SAT scores	23
# submitting ACT scores	8
% submitting ACT scores	7
Average HS GPA	3.7
% frosh submitting high school GPA	72
% graduated top 10% of class	44
% graduated top 25% of class	72
% graduated top 50% of class	84

DEADLINES

Early decision	
Deadline	11/1
Notification	12/1
Other ED deadline	1/15
Other ED notification	2/1
Early action	
Deadline	11/15
Notification	12/15
Regular	
Priority	1/15
Deadline	Rolling
Notification	Rolling, 2/15
Nonfall registration?	Yes

APPLICANTS OFTEN PREFER
Colorado College; Reed College; University of California—Berkeley

APPLICANTS SOMETIMES PREFER
Kenyon College; Thomas Aquinas College; University of Puget Sound

APPLICANTS RARELY PREFER
University of New Mexico

FINANCIAL FACTS

Financial Aid Rating	84
Annual tuition	$37,842
Room and board	$15,468
Required fees	$1,514
Books and supplies	$410
Average frosh need-based scholarship	$29,781
Average UG need-based scholarship	$30,001
% needy frosh rec. need-based scholarship or grant aid	100
% needy UG rec. need-based scholarship or grant aid	99
% needy frosh rec. non-need-based scholarship or grant aid	28
% needy UG rec. non-need-based scholarship or grant aid	22
% needy frosh rec. need-based self-help aid	82
% needy UG rec. need-based self-help aid	82
% UG borrow to pay for school	42
Average cumulative indebtedness	$25,727
% frosh need fully met	38
% ugrads need fully met	28
Average % of frosh need met	87
Average % of ugrad need met	86

ST. JOHN'S UNIVERSITY (NY)

8000 Utopia Parkway, Queens, NY 11439 • Admissions: 718-990-6161 • Fax: 718-990-2096

STUDENTS SAY "..."

Academics

St. John's University upholds the Catholic and Vincentian traditions set forth at its founding in 1870. At the residential Queens, New York, campus, located in a suburban area (as well as at the two additional New York City campuses found in Staten Island and Manhattan), students receive "a well-nurtured education that can help one turn into a specialist in whatever field they desire." A wide range of support systems, such as career services, campus ministry, the writing center, and a focus on mentoring ensure that "every student has a safe, healthy, and challenging academic career" while at St. John's.

Most professors are generous "when it comes to providing help and any aids for you to succeed" and "are here to help you and prepare you for the rest of your life." "Almost all my experiences with professors have been positive. If you are willing to put in the work they are willing to work with you," says one actuarial science major. They are very helpful "in making sure you actually understand the information rather than memorize it and not use it outside the classroom," and "provide guidance with classwork, finding jobs and internships, and more." On top of faculty help, the career services office is "amazing." "They help you with your résumé, cover letter, [telling] you when there are career fairs, picking graduate schools, [and] finding internships."

Classes are "easy to follow and there are never any surprises from the professors," and most are discussion-based. Students in all majors find that "the workload is not overwhelming and the assignments are helpful and relevant to the subjects." For commuter and non-commuter students alike, the Monday and Thursday afternoon common hour provides a universal time for most social and academic clubs to meet.

Campus Life

From athletics to coffeehouse shows and cultural events, there are "multiple things to do on campus every day." Many people take advantage of the gym and the classes it offers, or "hang out on the Great Lawn and play Frisbee and other similar games." Students "sometimes have to wait a long time for their next class" so the school provides "too many extracurricular activities to count" to help time pass. There are clubs to represent "almost every racial, religious and interest group" and "there's never a day where there isn't anything to do." Basketball season is a huge rally booster (the men's team plays some games at Madison Square Garden), and St. John's also hosts "many great events on off days such as family day, picnics, barbecues, and more." There are a fair number of commuters, and those who live on campus often venture into the city to "enjoy the fast pace and vibrant life of New York City." Between "the spring carnival, the free commuter breakfasts, and reduced prices on movie tickets, [and] Broadway shows, St. John's wants their students' experience to be unforgettable."

Student Body

This "very diverse" group has students from all over the country and world (it "falls perfectly into place with the diversity of the New York City area as a whole"), which "exposes everyone to new ideas and helps us better define where we stand on our own views." "There's an atmosphere of the core staples of the University: Catholic, Vincentian, and metropolitan," says a student. People speak of the sense of unity that comes from everyone being "more than happy to be here, excited to learn, and [willing to] participate in campus activities." There is a lot of collaboration when it comes to student organizations, and students also "have great initiative when it comes to getting their voice heard."

ST. JOHN'S UNIVERSITY (NY)

Financial Aid: 718-990-2000 • E-Mail: admhelp@stjohns.edu • Website: www.stjohns.edu

THE PRINCETON REVIEW SAYS

Admissions

The school reports that its standardized testing policy for use in admission for Fall 2024 is Test Optional. The 2024 testing policy will be permanent. The Princeton Review suggests that interested applicants consult with the school for the most up-to-date standardized testing policies. *Very important factors considered include:* academic GPA. *Important factors considered include:* rigor of secondary school record, standardized test scores. *Other factors considered include:* class rank, application essay, recommendation(s), extracurricular activities, talent/ability, character/personal qualities, alumni/ae relation, volunteer work, work experience, level of applicant's interest. High school diploma is required and GED is accepted. *Academic units recommended:* 4 English, 3 math, 3 science, 2 foreign language, 2 social studies, 2 history.

Financial Aid

Students should submit: FAFSA. Priority filing deadline is 12/15. The Princeton Review suggests that all financial aid forms be submitted as soon as possible (see page 5 for a note on the FAFSA). *Need-based scholarships/grants offered:* College/university scholarship or grant aid from institutional funds; Federal Pell; Private scholarships; SEOG; State scholarships/grants. *Loan aid offered:* Direct PLUS loans; Direct Subsidized Loans; Direct Unsubsidized Loans. Admitted students will be notified of awards on a rolling basis. Federal Work-Study Program available. Institutional employment available.

The Inside Word

The admissions process at St. John's doesn't include many surprises. High school grades are undoubtedly the most important factors, though volunteer work and extracurricular activities are also highly regarded. The university doesn't consider religious affiliation at all when making admissions decisions; there are students of every religious stripe here.

THE SCHOOL SAYS "..."

From the Admissions Office

"Founded in 1870, St. John's is a Catholic and Vincentian University that prepares students for personal and professional success—and emphasizes academic excellence without bounds—by providing talented students with an outstanding education that builds upon their abilities and aspirations. On the playing courts and athletic fields, St. John's is New York City's team, with 17 NCAA Division I men's and women's athletic teams.

"St. John's offers more than 100 associate, bachelor's, master's, and doctoral degrees in areas including the arts, business, communication arts, education, law, pharmacy, and the natural and applied sciences. More than 94 percent of our full-time professors hold a PhD or comparable terminal degree in their field. Our 16:1 student/faculty ratio ensures personal attention.

"Faith, service, and student success are central to a St. John's education. Each year, students perform more than 100,000 service hours. With world-class academics, renowned professors, outstanding resources, and a storied tradition of academic excellence and service, St. John's prepares you to change the world for the better.

"Our students enjoy both a metropolitan and global experience that starts at our three New York City campuses—in Queens, on Staten Island, and in Manhattan; an international campus in Rome, Italy; and study abroad locations in Paris, France, and Limerick, Ireland, and around the world. Enhancing the University's cosmopolitan character, students come from nearly 50 states and 118 foreign countries—all of them benefiting from the University's network of more than 195,000 alumni."

SELECTIVITY

Admissions Rating	84
# of applicants	24,607
% of applicants accepted	85
% of acceptees attending	14
# offered a place on the wait list	1,624
# of early decision applicants	81
% accepted early decision	63

FIRST-YEAR PROFILE

Testing policy	Test Optional
Range SAT composite	1120–1310
Range SAT EBRW	560–650
Range SAT math	550–660
Range ACT composite	24–29
# submitting SAT scores	880
% submitting SAT scores	30
# submitting ACT scores	99
% submitting ACT scores	3
Average HS GPA	3.5
% frosh submitting high school GPA	100
% graduated top 10% of class	17
% graduated top 25% of class	42
% graduated top 50% of class	72

DEADLINES

Early decision	
Deadline	11/15
Notification	12/15
Early action	
Deadline	12/1
Notification	1/1
Regular	
Notification	Rolling, 12/1
Nonfall registration?	Yes

APPLICANTS ALSO LOOK AT

Fordham University; Hofstra University; New York University; State University of New York—Stony Brook University

FINANCIAL FACTS

Financial Aid Rating	79
Annual tuition	$46,230
Room and board	$18,790
Required fees	$1,350
Required fees (first-year)	$1,600
Books and supplies	$720
Average frosh need-based scholarship	$10,799
Average UG need-based scholarship	$9,247
% needy frosh rec. need-based scholarship or grant aid	73
% needy UG rec. need-based scholarship or grant aid	71
% needy frosh rec. non-need-based scholarship or grant aid	84
% needy UG rec. non-need-based scholarship or grant aid	98
% needy frosh rec. need-based self-help aid	48
% needy UG rec. need-based self-help aid	52
% frosh rec. any financial aid	100
% UG rec. any financial aid	99
% UG borrow to pay for school	54
Average cumulative indebtedness	$29,617
% frosh need fully met	18
% ugrads need fully met	15
Average % of frosh need met	74
Average % of ugrad need met	69

SAINT JOSEPH'S UNIVERSITY (PA)

5600 City Avenue, Philadelphia, PA 19131 • Admissions: 610-660-1000 • Fax: 610-660-1314

CAMPUS LIFE

Quality of Life Rating	83
Fire Safety Rating	90
Green Rating	81
Type of school	Private
Affiliation	Roman Catholic-Jesuit
Environment	Metropolis

STUDENTS

Total undergrad enrollment	5,073
% male/female/another gender	45/55/0
% from out of state	44
% frosh from public high school	56
% frosh live on campus	89
% ugrads live on campus	47
# of fraternities (% join)	4 (10)
# of sororities (% join)	5 (20)
% African American	7
% Asian	11
% White	66
% Hispanic	9
% Native American	<1
% Pacific Islander	<1
% Two or more races	3
% Race and/or ethnicity unknown	2
% international	2
# of countries represented	45

SURVEY SAYS . . .

Students are happy
Intramural sports are popular
Students love Philadelphia, PA

ACADEMICS

Academic Rating	77
% students returning for sophomore year	86
% students graduating within 4 years	76
% students graduating within 6 years	82
Calendar	Semester
Student/faculty ratio	10:1
Profs interesting rating	83
Profs accessible rating	88

Most classes have 10–19 students.
Most lab/discussion sessions have
   10–19 students.

MOST POPULAR MAJORS

Pharmacy (PharmD Direct Entry);
Finance; Marketing

STUDENTS SAY "..."

Academics

Students at Saint Joseph's University find that the school "prepares you for an amazing career ahead," especially if you're focusing on its well-known business school or science/healthcare programs. "They have an amazing network," enthuses one B-school enrollee, adding that "they prepare you for having a great job and being an ethical person." For science majors, students praise the Phage Lab, which offers first-year students an early opportunity to get into research and appreciate the real-world experience they can earn in courses: "We volunteered at the local elementary school, and it was a great way to practice my science communication skills in real life." This seems to be a theme across all subjects, from Irish Literature and Culture ("We got to hurl with each other and, through playing the National sport of Ireland, we came to understand more about [their] national identity") to a class in which "students were instructed to interview farmer's market vendors to learn about their experience in opening up a stand and their visions [and] worries." Students also feel positively toward "the small classroom sizes because I am able to make a connection with the professor and other classmates." And when it comes to accommodating students with special needs, students refer to the way the Kinney Center enables them to "participate in college life, activities, courses, and even aspects of independent living."

Campus Life

Many students agree that SJU's two campus locations—downtown Philadelphia and suburban Hawk Hill—are "perfect because you are not in the crowded city but you're still really close by." While students in the city love exploring Philadelphia, "sports and studies encompass most of a student's daily life at the University City campus." Meanwhile, the "Hawk Hill campus is beautiful...[and] has a large offering of student clubs and activities" for students to enjoy. As one third-year student puts it, there are "many opportunities for people to really find their niche, whether it be with campus ministry or a club team." Karaoke, Hawk Pep Band, and the popular Hawk City Productions are just a few of the extracurricular opportunities "that allow students to unwind and take their minds off school and focus on enjoying their time in college and living their life to the fullest." The "date parties and formals" that make up a part of Greek life also rank among campus favorites, as does "the sheer importance of volunteerism—it seems as if it is present in almost every club on campus." Perhaps most importantly, students appreciate the SJU's priorities: "My school is aware of mental health and stress for students, which is why there are many stress relief events for students near exam weeks or in the middle of the semester."

Student Body

"The community, first and foremost, is amazing. We are a very happy campus and a very friendly one," enthuses one first-year student. This is true even for the most rigorous majors, who note that "every individual is strong, passionate, open, and positive, as we all race to achieve our dreams." Another student describing healthcare classes as being filled with "a lot of critical thinkers and people that are driven by the goal of helping others."

Some students on campus mention that it can feel "like there are two distinct student bodies: those at the [Hawk Hill] campus, and those at the...University City campus." Nevertheless, many contend that "we are a close-knit and collaborative community, and we are proud of our school." And though students perceive their peers as "very regional"—from Pennsylvania and nearby states—they also note "there is no one, cookie-cutter type of student" and that SJU has "a diverse student body in terms of life experience." All in all, SJU is "a great place to make connections and get out into the real world."

SAINT JOSEPH'S UNIVERSITY (PA)

Financial Aid: 610-660-1556 • E-Mail: admit@sju.edu • Website: www.sju.edu

THE PRINCETON REVIEW SAYS

Admissions

The school reports that its standardized testing policy for use in admission for Fall 2024 is Test Optional. It is unknown at this time if the 2024 testing policy will be permanent. The Princeton Review suggests that interested applicants consult with the school for the most up-to-date standardized testing policies. *Very important factors considered include:* rigor of secondary school record, class rank, academic GPA. *Important factors considered include:* standardized test scores, application essay, recommendation(s). *Other factors considered include:* interview, extracurricular activities, talent/ability, character/personal qualities, first generation, alumni/ae relation, geographical residence, racial/ethnic status, volunteer work, work experience, level of applicant's interest. High school diploma is required and GED is accepted. *Academic units required:* 4 English, 3 math, 2 science, 2 science labs, 2 foreign language, 2 history. *Academic units recommended:* 4 English, 4 math, 4 science, 4 science labs, 4 foreign language, 4 history.

Financial Aid

Students should submit: FAFSA. Priority filing deadline is 12/1. The Princeton Review suggests that all financial aid forms be submitted as soon as possible (see page 5 for a note on the FAFSA). *Need-based scholarships/grants offered:* College/university scholarship or grant aid from institutional funds; Federal Pell; Private scholarships; SEOG; State scholarships/grants. *Loan aid offered:* Direct PLUS loans; Direct Subsidized Loans; Direct Unsubsidized Loans. Admitted students will be notified of awards on a rolling basis beginning 3/31. Federal Work-Study Program available. Institutional employment available.

The Inside Word

Saint Joseph's University is on the lookout for applicants that are serious about their education and excited for learning. And they certainly want students who have found success in the classroom. After all, GPAs for admitted students range from 3.27–3.92 (on a 4.0 scale). Fortunately, individuals who dread standardized tests can rejoice; both the ACT and SAT are optional at Saint Joseph's. Beyond academics, admissions officers also look for community involvement and service.

THE SCHOOL SAYS "..."

From the Admissions Office

"Founded in 1851 as Philadelphia's Jesuit university, Saint Joseph's University prepares students for a rapidly changing world by focusing on academic excellence and courageous exploration.

"With an intellectual tradition distinguished by a liberal arts core curriculum and diversified with strong professional programs in education, business, health and science, Saint Joseph's students are empowered, challenged and supported by exceptional faculty members to chart their own path. They have the ability to choose from over 200 academic programs, dozens of co-op and internship opportunities and over 90 student organizations to personalize their college experience.

"Students study in the University's four schools and colleges—College of Arts and Sciences, Erivan K. Haub School of Business, School of Education and Human Development and School of Health Professions. A new School of Nursing and Allied Health will open in 2024, pending government, regulatory and accreditation approvals.

"To complement their studies, 87% of students complete at least one experiential learning opportunity during their time on Hawk Hill. With academic offerings in the most sought-after majors and leading programs in the first-in-the-nation Philadelphia College of Pharmacy, nearly 100% of students are employed, pursuing advanced degrees or volunteering in prestigious service programs upon graduation.

"And the University's network of nearly 100,000 proud alumni keep alive the rallying cry—The Hawk Will Never Die."

SELECTIVITY

Admissions Rating	84
# of applicants	9,708
% of applicants accepted	88
% of acceptees attending	13
# offered a place on the wait list	255
% accepting a place on wait list	29
% admitted from wait list	18
# of early decision applicants	103
% accepted early decision	63

FIRST-YEAR PROFILE

Testing policy	Test Optional
Range SAT composite	1130–1300
Range SAT EBRW	570–660
Range SAT math	560–660
Range ACT composite	26–31
# submitting SAT scores	446
% submitting SAT scores	41
# submitting ACT scores	64
% submitting ACT scores	6
Average HS GPA	3.7
% frosh submitting high school GPA	94
% graduated top 10% of class	28
% graduated top 25% of class	52
% graduated top 50% of class	80

DEADLINES

Early decision	
Deadline	11/15
Notification	12/20
Other ED deadline	1/15
Other ED notification	2/15
Early action	
Deadline	11/15
Notification	12/20
Regular	
Deadline	3/1
Notification	Rolling, 3/15
Nonfall registration?	Yes

APPLICANTS ALSO LOOK AT

Boston College; Drexel University; Fairfield University; Fordham University; James Madison University; La Salle University; Loyola University Maryland; Marist College; Penn State University Park; Providence College

FINANCIAL FACTS

Financial Aid Rating	84
Annual tuition	$51,140
Room and board	$15,740
Required fees	$200
Books and supplies	$1,050
Average frosh need-based scholarship	$27,585
Average UG need-based scholarship	$25,794
% needy frosh rec. need-based scholarship or grant aid	98
% needy UG rec. need-based scholarship or grant aid	97
% needy frosh rec. non-need-based scholarship or grant aid	25
% needy UG rec. non-need-based scholarship or grant aid	21
% needy frosh rec. need-based self-help aid	65
% needy UG rec. need-based self-help aid	69
% frosh rec. any financial aid	97
% UG rec. any financial aid	92
% frosh need fully met	33
% ugrads need fully met	30
Average % of frosh need met	82
Average % of ugrad need met	78

ST. LAWRENCE UNIVERSITY

23 Romoda Drive, Canton, NY 13617 • Admissions: 315-229-5011 • Fax: 315-229-5818

CAMPUS LIFE

Quality of Life Rating	91
Fire Safety Rating	81
Green Rating	78
Type of school	Private
Affiliation	No Affiliation
Environment	Village

STUDENTS

Total undergrad enrollment	2,145
% male/female/another gender	46/54/NR
% from out of state	59
% frosh from public high school	63
% frosh live on campus	100
% ugrads live on campus	99
# of fraternities (% join)	2 (18)
# of sororities (% join)	4 (16)
% African American	3
% Asian	2
% White	76
% Hispanic	6
% Native American	<1
% Pacific Islander	<1
% Two or more races	2
% Race and/or ethnicity unknown	1
% international	10
# of countries represented	70

SURVEY SAYS . . .

Students are happy
Lab facilities are great
Great library
Career services are great
Internships are widely available
No one cheats
School is well run
Students are friendly
Students environmentally aware
Easy to get around campus
Everyone loves the Saints
Alumni active on campus
Active student government
Active student-run political groups
Students aren't religious
Students involved in community service

ACADEMICS

Academic Rating	89
% students returning for sophomore year	85
% students graduating within 4 years	80
% students graduating within 6 years	84
Calendar	Semester
Student/faculty ratio	11:1
Profs interesting rating	94
Profs accessible rating	98

Most classes have 10–19 students.
Most lab/discussion sessions have
10–19 students.

MOST POPULAR MAJORS

Biology/Biological Sciences, General; Psychology,
General; Economics, General

STUDENTS SAY "..."

Academics

Nestled in the uppermost reaches of New York State on a scenic one thousand-acre campus, St. Lawrence University is a vibrant liberal arts institution of around 2,200 undergraduates and a very long reach. The "alumni network is super active," students have "lots of opportunities for hands-on research" and nearly two-thirds of SLU undergrads study abroad. With 75 majors to choose from, and the option to design one's own course of study in the multi-field major program, there are "a plethora of options for one's academic path." Small class sizes—an average of 16 students in each—further focus those options, as enrollees note that they "feel more comfortable asking questions and having conversation," which "fosters learning." Adding to that comfort is a First-Year Program that helps with the transition to college and which is described as "a great way to bond" through living-learning communities in the dorms. The school also offers Community-Based Learning (CBL) courses that immerse students in the real world: "I am currently taking a CBL course at the local correctional facility that allows me to take a philosophy course in a classroom at the jail with ten SLU students and ten inmates as my classmates."

As for the staff, "I've never felt so supported and believed in." Students specifically note that the "compassion professors have for individual success is incredible," particularly in the way that they "know people have different styles of learning" and so "are responsive to questions and always try to make the class [as] interactive as possible." Their classes work "to deliver a well-rounded education and develop our interpersonal skills," and "a lot of the intro classes are very reasonable and give you the right amount of work." And for those interested, you can dive into research from your very first year: "I was offered an opportunity to study and train wildlife detection dogs with a focus on locating amphibians, all thanks to my professors." Overall, students suggest that "St. Lawrence is a place for students to explore past thinkers and ideas while also conversing with their peers to help them establish their own thoughts and views."

Campus Life

Ninety-eight percent of students live on this "walking campus" and "have the opportunity to live in theme houses or Greek houses, which support high-quality residential communities." There are over 150 clubs and organizations, and "skiing, hiking, rock climbing, and other outdoor activities are popular" among this nature-loving group. "The incredible outdoors that SLU has around us is [wonderful]," says a student. And while remote Canton "is a small and rural town" where "there is not a hopping night scene," students actually appreciate knowing "where everyone is going to be on a Saturday night." This means that "sports events are popular," as is "spend[ing] time in the student center to talk and grab coffee, go outside and sit in hammocks if the weather is permitting, and do homework in the library."

Student Body

St. Lawrence students "wear many different hats and are involved in almost all aspects of the school community and culture," including the "large student-athlete population." Undergrads describe this society as "tight knit," such that "even if you don't know someone, you treat them as if you do," and they speak warmly of the "extremely positive and loving" atmosphere this creates. Peers are seen as "a welcoming family in which everybody can find friends," something that's only enhanced by "very low-key people who work very hard in the classroom as well as [at] athletics, but [who] treat it like it is no big deal." One student posits that it might be the cold of being so close to Canada, which "brings a level of closeness and different atmosphere," but based on responses, we think SLU just chooses warm students.

ST. LAWRENCE UNIVERSITY

Financial Aid: 315-229-5266 • E-Mail: admissions@stlawu.edu • Website: www.stlawu.edu

THE PRINCETON REVIEW SAYS

Admissions

The school reports that its standardized testing policy for use in admission for Fall 2024 is Test Optional. The 2024 testing policy will be permanent. The Princeton Review suggests that interested applicants consult with the school for the most up-to-date standardized testing policies. *Very important factors considered include:* rigor of secondary school record, academic GPA, application essay, recommendation(s), character/personal qualities. *Important factors considered include:* class rank, interview, extracurricular activities. *Other factors considered include:* standardized test scores, talent/ability, first generation, alumni/ae relation, geographical residence, volunteer work, work experience. High school diploma is required and GED is accepted. *Academic units recommended:* 4 English, 3 math, 3 science, 3 foreign language, 3 social studies, 2 history.

Financial Aid

Students should submit: FAFSA. Priority filing deadline is 2/1. The Princeton Review suggests that all financial aid forms be submitted as soon as possible (see page 5 for a note on the FAFSA). *Need-based scholarships/grants offered:* College/university scholarship or grant aid from institutional funds; Federal Pell; Private scholarships; SEOG; State scholarships/grants. *Loan aid offered:* Direct PLUS loans; Direct Subsidized Loans; Direct Unsubsidized Loans; College/university loans from institutional funds. Admitted students will be notified of awards on a rolling basis. Federal Work-Study Program available. Institutional employment available.

The Inside Word

At St. Lawrence, you're not required to submit scores from the SAT or the ACT, but that means your high school transcript and teacher recommendations are that much more important during the application review. Merit scholarships selection is based on your overall academic profile.

THE SCHOOL SAYS "..."

From the Admissions Office

"Nestled in the heart of New York's scenic North Country region, St. Lawrence University is a diverse liberal arts learning community of talented students and inspiring faculty. We're proud of the traditions that bring us together and are guided by our enduring spirit of collaboration and curiosity as we focus on the future. Our students, faculty, and staff value thought and action. Here, you'll tap into your full potential as you embrace the natural environment, engage with global challenges, and leverage your liberal arts education to tackles challenges in our complex and changing world.

"Our faculty has chosen St. Lawrence intentionally because they know there is institutional commitment to support great teaching. They are dedicated to making each student's experience challenging and rewarding. Every student has diverse opportunities to connect classroom theory to hands-on, real-world experience through internships, international study, and community projects. Faculty know their students and act as their mentors, guides, and colleagues on their journeys.

"Our graduates make up one of the strongest alumni networks in the country. They're ready, willing, and excited to connect with students and help them succeed. Creative degree paths and comprehensive career preparation programs—including alumni mentoring, career courses, one-on-one coaching, individualized planning, networking trips, and internship opportunities—allow students to discover their passions and turn them into careers of impact.

"Our location on the edge of the Adirondack Mountains gives us easy access to enviable outdoor spaces to learn, to practice environmental sustainability, and to participate year-round in all things outdoors. You must visit and meet our students to get a sense of the energy on campus. Only then can you begin to understand just what makes St. Lawrence University a place our students, faculty, staff, and alumni call home."

SELECTIVITY
Admissions Rating	89
# of applicants	5,172
% of applicants accepted	63
% of acceptees attending	16
# offered a place on the wait list	304
% accepting a place on wait list	21
% admitted from wait list	30
# of early decision applicants	272
% accepted early decision	73

FIRST-YEAR PROFILE
Testing policy	Test Optional
Range SAT composite	1270–1380
Range SAT EBRW	630–700
Range SAT math	610–710
Range ACT composite	29–32
# submitting SAT scores	102
% submitting SAT scores	19
# submitting ACT scores	29
% submitting ACT scores	5
Average HS GPA	3.7
% frosh submitting high school GPA	100
% graduated top 10% of class	37
% graduated top 25% of class	70
% graduated top 50% of class	96

DEADLINES
Early decision	
Deadline	11/1
Other ED deadline	2/1
Regular	
Deadline	2/1
Notification	3/15
Nonfall registration?	Yes

APPLICANTS ALSO LOOK AT
Colby College; Hamilton College; Hobart and William Smith Colleges; Union College (NY); University of Vermont

FINANCIAL FACTS
Financial Aid Rating	88
Annual tuition	$63,450
Room and board	$16,480
Required fees	$420
Books and supplies	$750
Average frosh need-based scholarship	$46,751
Average UG need-based scholarship	$45,157
% needy frosh rec. need-based scholarship or grant aid	99
% needy UG rec. need-based scholarship or grant aid	99
% needy frosh rec. non-need-based scholarship or grant aid	31
% needy UG rec. non-need-based scholarship or grant aid	23
% needy frosh rec. need-based self-help aid	75
% needy UG rec. need-based self-help aid	77
% frosh rec. any financial aid	98
% UG rec. any financial aid	97
% UG borrow to pay for school	62
Average cumulative indebtedness	$35,064
% frosh need fully met	35
% ugrads need fully met	36
Average % of frosh need met	91
Average % of ugrad need met	88

THE BEST 389 COLLEGES ■ 495

SAINT LOUIS UNIVERSITY

One N. Grand Boulevard, Saint Louis, MO 63103 • Admissions: 800-758-3678 • Fax: 314-977-7136

CAMPUS LIFE
Quality of Life Rating	89
Fire Safety Rating	60*
Green Rating	60*
Type of school	Private
Affiliation	Roman Catholic-Jesuit
Environment	Metropolis

STUDENTS
Total undergrad enrollment	7,332
% male/female/another gender	39/61/NR
% from out of state	59
% frosh live on campus	88
% ugrads live on campus	53
# of fraternities	0
# of sororities	0
% African American	8
% Asian	14
% White	60
% Hispanic	8
% Native American	<1
% Pacific Islander	<1
% Two or more races	5
% Race and/or ethnicity unknown	1
% international	4

SURVEY SAYS . . .
Students are happy
Great library
Students are very religious
Students involved in community service
Active student government
Active minority support groups

ACADEMICS
Academic Rating	82
% students returning for sophomore year	87
% students graduating within 4 years	73
% students graduating within 6 years	81
Calendar	Semester
Student/faculty ratio	9:1
Profs interesting rating	88
Profs accessible rating	91

Most classes have 20–29 students.
Most lab/discussion sessions have 20–29 students.

MOST POPULAR MAJORS
Registered Nursing/Registered Nurse; Biology/Biological Sciences, General; Exercise Science and Kinesiology

STUDENTS SAY "..."

Academics

As one of the first institutions of higher learning west of the Mississippi River, Saint Louis University lives up to its over 200-year academic legacy: "At SLU, there is a lot of emphasis on academic success, and the very rigorous classes make it imperative that you focus." This mid-sized university offers a whopping 97 bachelor degree programs, each featuring a variety of large-lecture and small-discussion based formats, and even hybrids of the two. Impressively, students suggest that even in large courses, they were "able to connect with not only other classmates and teaching assistants, but...with my professors." Other students revel in the way programs make learning concrete, whether that's from a nursing student getting "so many clinical hours in very diverse fields" or "lots of opportunities to perform independent guided research as an undergraduate." The list goes on, citing classes that utilize "flight simulators" and backing up the study of world religions by visiting "a Hindu temple, Muslim mosque, and Buddhist meditation center."

Courses may be challenging, but students point to the personal support they receive from their instructors: "I truly believe that the professors I've encountered at Saint Louis University want their students to succeed. The Dean of Students is a wonderful individual and a great resource, and SLU's President is incredible," raves one second-year student. "I have never felt more supported by academic staff ever," adds another. "I have always felt like a student AND a person in my classrooms, and teachers are always one email or text away." As one third-year puts it, "SLU actively does its best to ensure that students succeed academically, professionally, and personally." This extends not just to the academics to but also to "generous financial aid" and professional resources in tutoring, time-management, and career: "With these, I could handle anything that college would throw at me."

Campus Life

Saint Louis University looks for well-rounded students, and to that end offers a robust suite of extracurricular activities and opportunities for service. Among student favorites are the theater program, music program, mock trial, sporting events, and student government. One student enjoys the Micah Program "where we serve [the] community as tutors for elementary-aged kids," and the Billiken Success Program "where we help with new-student events." Warm weather brings even more opportunities for students to come together, "When the weather is nice students will hang hammocks from the trees on campus... They'll play frisbee on the quad or sit with friends and talk in the shade. Our campus comes alive when the weather is warm." Students also remind us that "Saint Louis University is known not only for its large STEM programs, but for having ... great soccer and basketball teams."

Student Body

The SLU community hails from 87 different countries, and many students take pride in the diversity celebrated on the SLU campus: "We host a lot of international students as well as students from different socioeconomic, cultural, and geographical backgrounds. I love getting to learn about other students' experiences and how they differ from mine." Even with so many different backgrounds, a shared passion for enriching the "mind, body, heart, and spirit" unites the student body. "I've found that the overwhelming majority of my peers are supportive of me as an academic and as a whole person, emotionally and spiritually." One first-year student explains, "My peers are helpful, friendly, positive, happy, and ignited with a passion for social justice." Overall, these ambitious students "are here to create a better future."

SAINT LOUIS UNIVERSITY

Financial Aid: 314-977-2350 • E-Mail: admission@slu.edu • Website: www.slu.edu

THE PRINCETON REVIEW SAYS

Admissions

The school reports that its standardized testing policy for use in admission for Fall 2024 is Test Optional. It is unknown at this time if the 2024 testing policy will be permanent. The Princeton Review suggests that interested applicants consult with the school for the most up-to-date standardized testing policies. *Very important factors considered include:* academic GPA. *Important factors considered include:* rigor of secondary school record, application essay, extracurricular activities, talent/ability, character/personal qualities, volunteer work. *Other factors considered include:* standardized test scores, recommendation(s), interview, work experience. High school diploma is required and GED is accepted. *Academic units required:* 4 English, 4 math, 3 science, 3 foreign language, 3 social studies, 3 academic electives. *Academic units recommended:* 4 English, 4 math, 3 science, 3 foreign language, 3 social studies, 3 academic electives.

Financial Aid

Students should submit: FAFSA. Priority filing deadline is 2/1. The Princeton Review suggests that all financial aid forms be submitted as soon as possible (see page 5 for a note on the FAFSA). *Need-based scholarships/grants offered:* College/university scholarship or grant aid from institutional funds; Federal Nursing Scholarships; Federal Pell; Private scholarships; SEOG; State scholarships/grants. *Loan aid offered:* Direct PLUS loans; Direct Subsidized Loans; Direct Unsubsidized Loans; Federal Nursing Loans. Admitted students will be notified of awards on a rolling basis. Federal Work-Study Program available. Institutional employment available.

The Inside Word

Despite being known for mostly drawing its students from the immediate region, SLU continues to expand its range and now 61 percent of students are from out of state. The average high school GPA for admitted first-year is 3.95, with 71 percent of accepted students coming to SLU with a GPA of 3.75 or higher. In addition to grades, the university also weighs each applicant's commitment to the Jesuit ideals of service to the community, so volunteering for Habitat for Humanity can be just as important as scoring off the charts.

THE SCHOOL SAYS "..."

From the Admissions Office

"Saint Louis University gives students the knowledge, skills, and values to build a successful career and make a difference in the lives of those around them. Students live and learn in a safe and attractive campus environment. The beautiful urban residential campus offers many internship, outreach, and recreational opportunities. Ranked as one of the best educational values in the country, the university welcomes students—from all 50 states and 82 foreign countries—who pursue rigorous majors that invite individualization. Accessible faculty, study abroad opportunities, and many small, interactive classes make SLU a great place to learn.

"Founded in 1818, Saint Louis University is one of the nation's oldest and most prestigious Catholic institutions. Rooted in Jesuit values and its pioneering history as the first university west of the Mississippi River, SLU offers nearly 13,000 students a rigorous, transformative education of the whole person. At the core of the University's diverse community of scholars is SLU's service-focused mission, which challenges and prepares students to make the world a better, more just place. Saint Louis University's admission process is standardized-Test Optional for all undergraduate programs. Applicants may submit ACT or SAT test scores, but those who choose not to will not be disadvantaged in the admission process."

SELECTIVITY

Admissions Rating	87
# of applicants	12,986
% of applicants accepted	85
% of acceptees attending	15
# of early decision applicants	69
% accepted early decision	77

FIRST-YEAR PROFILE

Testing policy	Test Optional
Range SAT composite	1158–1333
Range SAT EBRW	570–680
Range SAT math	570–680
Range ACT composite	24–30
# submitting SAT scores	208
% submitting SAT scores	13
# submitting ACT scores	796
% submitting ACT scores	48
Average HS GPA	3.9
% frosh submitting high school GPA	100
% graduated top 10% of class	33
% graduated top 25% of class	65
% graduated top 50% of class	89

DEADLINES

Early decision	
Deadline	11/1
Notification	12/1
Other ED deadline	1/13
Other ED notification	2/1
Early action	
Deadline	12/01
Notification	2/1
Regular	
Deadline	Rolling
Notification	Rolling
Nonfall registration?	Yes

FINANCIAL FACTS

Financial Aid Rating	84
Annual tuition	$49,800
Room and board	$13,890
Required fees	$844
Required fees (first-year)	$1,044
Books and supplies	$1,070
Average frosh need-based scholarship	$38,383
Average UG need-based scholarship	$35,768
% needy frosh rec. need-based scholarship or grant aid	96
% needy UG rec. need-based scholarship or grant aid	97
% needy frosh rec. non-need-based scholarship or grant aid	20
% needy UG rec. non-need-based scholarship or grant aid	21
% needy frosh rec. need-based self-help aid	54
% needy UG rec. need-based self-help aid	56
% UG borrow to pay for school	57
Average cumulative indebtedness	$32,529
% frosh need fully met	26
% ugrads need fully met	25
Average % of frosh need met	85
Average % of ugrad need met	79

SAINT MARY'S COLLEGE OF CALIFORNIA

1928 St. Marys Road, PMB 4433, Moraga, CA 94575 • Admissions: 925-631-4000 • Fax: 925-376-7193

STUDENTS SAY "..."

Academics

Saint Mary's College of California takes a Lasallian approach to service and learning, using the study of the liberal arts to produce students who are both passionate learners and committed citizens. The diverse core curriculum is centered around the Collegiate Seminar, a series of courses in which undergrads read, dissect, discuss, and live the ideas behind major works of Western civilization. This foundation of "interesting texts...allows for students to bring in real world experiences," and encourages the "student-based discussions rather than professor lectures" that are a key aspect of a SMC education. The academic calendar also includes January Term, a month-long course in which enrollees deep dive into one single topic, which many agree is "a fun and exciting way to keep students engaged." Undergrads can choose from one of the many robust study-abroad programs to gain valuable experience (and college credit) while immersed in a different culture. Students also have access to a plethora of academic support services, including tutoring, mental health counseling, and the Center for Writing Across the Curriculum. And if there's anything that attendees need, the administration is committed to listening to student needs: "The staff have been here for all of us students every step of the way."

There are 44 majors offered across four schools, and a student-to-faculty ratio of 14:1 that allows "amazing relationships with professors thanks to the small classroom sizes." Faculty "makes sure that you know everything that you need to prepare you for life," and are "always accessible for meetings and office hours because they want their students to succeed." Additionally, teachers are "an incredible resource for internships, grad school, [and] jobs," and "are always trying to get us involved in outside events."

Campus Life

According to students, this is most definitely "a calm campus," one that goes hand-in-hand with the chill vibe of the San Francisco Bay and the student population, most of which leads a laid-back life when not engrossed in studying: "People walk around campus, occasionally work out, and get food from local places." Cooking and watching Netflix are classic pastimes, and "people spend a lot of time exploring the Bay Area," as the campus is close to Walnut Creek, Oakland, and San Francisco, where the weather is reportedly "beautiful no matter [the] time of year." In fact, the Campus Activities Board "frequently gives BART tickets for students to take public transportation to go to events." Game days are some of the biggest of the year, and "basketball is huge here."

On-campus housing is guaranteed for the first two years, but students may choose to live off-campus their sophomore year. The tight-knit nature of the school creates a "communal, friendly, and intimate" sense of familiarity, as does its modest population of under 2,500 undergraduates: "I enjoy walking to class and knowing eighty percent of the people I pass on the way there."

Student Body

There is "diversity both ethnically and intellectually," and since one-third of Saint Mary's College's students are the first in their families to attend college, there is a "great alumni network" that understands the remarkability of what many students have achieved in order to attend SMC, as well as the school's "ability to produce well-rounded students through a well-designed curriculum." There's also a strong "emphasis on culture and ethic identities" throughout every aspect of the school, which students find desirable on account of the way it "fosters a sense of community." This isn't a gradual effect, either—students agree with the idea that "From the first day of orientation I knew that the student body was very accepting."

SAINT MARY'S COLLEGE OF CALIFORNIA

Financial Aid: 925-631-4370 • E-Mail: smcadmit@stmarys-ca.edu • Website: www.stmarys-ca.edu

THE PRINCETON REVIEW SAYS

Admissions

The school reports that its standardized testing policy for use in admission for Fall 2024 and beyond is Test Optional. *Very important factors considered include:* rigor of secondary school record, academic GPA. *Important factors considered include:* first generation. *Other factors considered include:* class rank, standardized test scores, application essay, recommendation(s), interview, extracurricular activities, talent/ability, character/personal qualities, alumni/ae relation, geographical residence, volunteer work, work experience, level of applicant's interest. High school diploma is required and GED is accepted. *Academic units required:* 4 English, 3 math, 2 science, 1 science lab, 2 foreign language, 2 social studies, 1 U.S. history. *Academic units recommended:* 4 English, 4 math, 2 science, 1 science lab, 3 foreign language, 2 social studies, 1 U.S. history.

Financial Aid

Students should submit: FAFSA. Priority filing deadline is 2/1. The Princeton Review suggests that all financial aid forms be submitted as soon as possible (see page 5 for a note on the FAFSA). *Need-based scholarships/grants offered:* College/university scholarship or grant aid from institutional funds; Federal Pell; Private scholarships; SEOG; State scholarships/grants. *Loan aid offered:* Direct PLUS loans; Direct Subsidized Loans; Direct Unsubsidized Loans. Admitted students will be notified of awards on a rolling basis beginning 2/1. Federal Work-Study Program available. Institutional employment available.

The Inside Word

Saint Mary's has a deep commitment to serving underprivileged students and offering opportunities for low-income students with strong academic potential, which is why the school sets aside a portion of its undergraduate population for low economic status students. That core philosophy of the school won't be changing anytime soon, so students with economic difficulties should not hesitate to apply if their academics are strong.

THE SCHOOL SAYS "..."

From the Admissions Office

"At Saint Mary's College of California, we inspire minds, engage the world, and transform lives. With small class sizes and professors who know you by name, the Saint Mary's experience enables students to thrive—in the classroom, in careers, and beyond.

"From a stunning campus in the San Francisco Bay Area, Saint Mary's offers boundless opportunities in California and around the globe. That includes careers and internships in Silicon Valley and a unique Jan Term program through which students work with faculty in dozens of locations locally, regionally, and internationally. And with knowledge and skills, confidence and support from the Gael community, you'll imagine, discover, and make a lasting impact…Wherever you're at…Whatever you set your heart to become.

"Founded in 1863 with a commitment to making an exemplary education accessible to all, Saint Mary's lives out its Catholic, Lasallian values that embody compassion, dignity, and social justice. We are a community of scholars committed to cultivating leaders who are eager to be agents of change in business, politics, the arts, science, and more.

"Undergraduate research programs provide students a rare opportunity to do hands-on work with real-world applications. Collegiate Seminar brings a rigorous approach to asking big questions—and to understanding diverse perspectives. The High Potential program ensures first-generation and low-income college students have the support they need to succeed.

"At Saint Mary's, our students break the mold by expanding their intellect, fostering innovation, growing their spirit, and embracing the 'Gael Force' attributes of enthusiasm, diversity, belonging, service, passion, and pride."

SELECTIVITY
Admissions Rating	76
# of applicants	3,353
% of applicants accepted	88
% of acceptees attending	15

FIRST-YEAR PROFILE
Testing policy	Test Optional
Average HS GPA	3.7
% frosh submitting high school GPA	98

DEADLINES
Early action	
Deadline	11/11
Notification	12/1
Regular	
Priority	11/15
Deadline	1/15
Notification	Rolling, 2/1
Nonfall registration?	Yes

APPLICANTS OFTEN PREFER
California Polytechnic State University; University of California—Davis; University of California—Santa Cruz

APPLICANTS SOMETIMES PREFER
San Jose State University; Santa Clara University; University of California—Berkeley; University of California—Santa Barbara; University of San Francisco

APPLICANTS RARELY PREFER
Chapman University; San Diego State University; University of California-Irvine; University of California—Los Angeles; University of San Diego

FINANCIAL FACTS
Financial Aid Rating	78
Annual tuition	$53,372
Room and board	$16,300
Required fees	$200
Books and supplies	$1,152
Average frosh need-based scholarship	$18,150
Average UG need-based scholarship	$17,422
% needy frosh rec. need-based scholarship or grant aid	61
% needy UG rec. need-based scholarship or grant aid	71
% needy frosh rec. non-need-based scholarship or grant aid	102
% needy UG rec. non-need-based scholarship or grant aid	82
% needy frosh rec. need-based self-help aid	71
% needy UG rec. need-based self-help aid	76
% frosh rec. any financial aid	100
% UG rec. any financial aid	94
% UG borrow to pay for school	85
% frosh need fully met	1
% ugrads need fully met	0
Average % of frosh need met	72
Average % of ugrad need met	70

St. Mary's College of Maryland

18952 E. Fisher Road, St. Mary's City, MD 20686 • Admissions: 240-895-2000

STUDENTS SAY "..."

Academics

Students fortunate enough to attend St. Mary's College of Maryland receive a "top tier education" wherein they have ample "opportunity to try new things and explore their interests." That extends beyond the applauded "research-based curriculum" to the environment—"the campus is absolutely gorgeous"—and even the food in the "great dining hall." Where St. Mary's shines most, however, is in its academic offerings, which "reflect the challenges that [students] will face in the workplace," particularly for those in the STEM field who "can really get a leg up by doing publishable work even prior to grad school." In this, the faculty are routinely praised for "always [being] super helpful," noting that they "care about your experience and want you to understand the material" and "genuinely try to engage students during lectures." Enrollees feel they're able to properly assess their teachers because of the "small class sizes," which truly allow "you get to know your professors really well, and build relationships and networks with them." This sort of backing makes the rigor tolerable, at least according to those who say "I've...definitely had to work hard but also had the support of professors when I needed it" and note that "They are willing to work with you, to enable and encourage you to have the best academic experience possible!"

Campus Life

There's never a dull moment at St. Mary's thanks to an "extremely active" campus life (and the potential for getaways to nearby DC). Undergrads have the opportunity to participate in "a wide range of clubs from windsurfing to student government to theater and sword fighting." Moreover, "there are multiple events on campus each week including guest magicians, comedians, and musicians," as well as "a murder mystery." The quality of those events has recently improved, as well, with the addition of "a brand-new stadium" which has led to an increasing number of students attending sporting events. And those looking to see a sillier side of their faculty appreciate the various "social events where you can play a game of Cornhole with your professors and get to know them more." St. Mary's gorgeous waterfront location also gets a lot of love: "During the warmer months the river center has free kayak and boat and paddleboard rentals for students and many students go swimming in the river or just sit on the docks." As for weekend-specific activities, it's not only common to find "parties [happening] all over campus," but "most of the time you can just walk [in]...and join...without an invitation."

Student Body

Though the St. Mary's community isn't the most diverse campus around, students emphasize that they are very proud of the diversity they do have, describing their "very creative" and "unique" peers as "extremely accepting." Undergrads are quick to note that "minority communities [are] visible and present" and that the school is "super inclusive [with regards to] LGBT+ students." This applies to personal opinions as well; while many individuals identify as "fairly liberal," classmates are described as "very open to different cultural viewpoints." In fact, some even refer to the friendliness as "quite bold" in that "I've never been at a place where more people will randomly walk up to you and just start a conversation." Indeed, "You can't walk for five minutes in any direction without getting a friendly greeting from someone." Of course, you'll definitely find a range of personality types, "from the athletes to dancers to light-saber fighters" as well as "hippie/hipsters, and nerdy academic students." Ultimately, when it comes down to it, there "seems to be a place for everyone to fit into at St. Mary's."

St. Mary's College of Maryland

Financial Aid: 240-895-3000 • E-Mail: admissions@smcm.edu • Website: www.smcm.edu

THE PRINCETON REVIEW SAYS

Admissions

The school reports that its standardized testing policy for use in admission for Fall 2024 is Test Optional. The 2024 testing policy will be permanent. The Princeton Review suggests that interested applicants consult with the school for the most up-to-date standardized testing policies. *Very important factors considered include:* rigor of secondary school record, academic GPA, application essay, recommendation(s), extracurricular activities, talent/ability, character/personal qualities. *Important factors considered include:* class rank, volunteer work, level of applicant's interest. *Other factors considered include:* standardized test scores, interview, first generation, alumni/ae relation, geographical residence, state residency, racial/ethnic status, work experience. High school diploma is required and GED is accepted. *Academic units required:* 4 English, 3 math, 3 science, 2 science labs, 2 social studies, 1 history. *Academic units recommended:* 4 math, 4 foreign language, 3 social studies.

Financial Aid

Students should submit: FAFSA. Priority filing deadline is 2/28. The Princeton Review suggests that all financial aid forms be submitted as soon as possible (see page 5 for a note on the FAFSA). *Need-based scholarships/grants offered:* College/university scholarship or grant aid from institutional funds; Federal Pell; Private scholarships; SEOG; State scholarships/grants. *Loan aid offered:* Direct PLUS loans; Direct Subsidized Loans; Direct Unsubsidized Loans. Admitted students will be notified of awards on a rolling basis beginning 1/15. Federal Work-Study Program available. Institutional employment available.

The Inside Word

St. Mary's is a public honors college, which means earning admission is no easy feat. The school is looking for intellectually curious students who will be thoroughly engaged in the classroom as well as campus life. Top candidates tend to have taken a rigorous course-load in high school, so you'll want to load up on honors and AP classes. And if you're test-averse, you'll be delighted to hear that St. Mary's is a Test Optional school (with the exception of home-school applicants and students who must demonstrate proficiency with English).

THE SCHOOL SAYS "..."

From the Admissions Office

"St. Mary's College of Maryland, The National Public Honors College, features a stunning, waterfront campus adjacent to historic St. Mary's City, located about 90 minutes from Washington, D.C. As the designated public honors college for the state of Maryland, we offer a prestigious and affordable honors-level liberal arts and sciences education for every member of our diverse community. You will be encouraged to strive higher as you motivate others to set their own bar. Along the way we'll support you on your journey, because to us, honors is about where you are going, not where you are from.

"Our award-winning Learning through Experiential and Applied Discovery (LEAD) curriculum blends rigorous academics with professional skill development, in which you will learn how disciplines connect, the power of collaboration, critical thinking skills, multiple ways to approach problems, and so much more. We believe that the best learning springs from the rich human exchange that takes place in our challenging and engaging small classes, in one-on-one interactions, and even on the walking paths that cross campus. This promotes learning on a personalized level as our faculty, coaches, advisors, and staff play a role in your college career. Through the Honors College Promise, you are guaranteed the opportunity to apply your learning through internships, faculty-guided research, or international experiences. You'll be prepared for a world of possibilities.

"It is this mix of academic excellence, experiential learning, campus environment, and affordability that makes St. Mary's College an education that is uncommonly worth it."

SELECTIVITY

Admissions Rating	85
# of applicants	2,934
% of applicants accepted	77
% of acceptees attending	18
# offered a place on the wait list	242
% accepting a place on wait list	24
% admitted from wait list	16
# of early decision applicants	39
% accepted early decision	90

FIRST-YEAR PROFILE

Testing policy	Test Optional
Range SAT composite	1130–1350
Range SAT EBRW	590–710
Range SAT math	540–660
Range ACT composite	28–30
# submitting SAT scores	134
% submitting SAT scores	33
# submitting ACT scores	16
% submitting ACT scores	4
Average HS GPA	3.5
% frosh submitting high school GPA	100
% graduated top 10% of class	21
% graduated top 25% of class	47
% graduated top 50% of class	83

DEADLINES

Early decision	
Deadline	11/1
Notification	12/1
Early action	
Deadline	11/1
Notification	1/1
Regular	
Priority	11/1
Deadline	1/15
Notification	4/1
Nonfall registration?	Yes

APPLICANTS SOMETIMES PREFER

McDaniel College; Montgomery College—Rockville Campus; Salisbury University; Towson University; University of Maryland, Baltimore County; University of Maryland, College Park

FINANCIAL FACTS

Financial Aid Rating	81
Annual in-state tuition	$12,116
Annual out-of-state tuition	$28,192
Room and board	$14,264
Required fees	$3,064
Books and supplies	$900
Average frosh need-based scholarship	$10,585
Average UG need-based scholarship	$10,502
% needy frosh rec. need-based scholarship or grant aid	91
% needy UG rec. need-based scholarship or grant aid	86
% needy frosh rec. non-need-based scholarship or grant aid	85
% needy UG rec. non-need-based scholarship or grant aid	78
% needy frosh rec. need-based self-help aid	52
% needy UG rec. need-based self-help aid	58
% frosh rec. any financial aid	97
% UG rec. any financial aid	92
% UG borrow to pay for school	62
Average cumulative indebtedness	$27,476
% frosh need fully met	19
% ugrads need fully met	15
Average % of frosh need met	84
Average % of ugrad need met	78

SAINT MICHAEL'S COLLEGE

One Winooski Park, Colchester, VT 05439 • Admissions: 802-654-2000 • Fax: 802-654-2906

STUDENTS SAY ". . ."

Academics

"At Saint Michael's College, small classes" help to ensure that "you are not just another number in a lecture hall." Indeed, the college "really wants to help its students realize their full potential." Many tout the "strong academics" and highlight the education, biology, and religion departments in particular (while a few note that the school "could improve" Digital Media and Communications). Classes are often "discussion-based" and "require a conscientious student who will actively participate in discussion." If there's any negative, it's that some students observe that there are sometimes "not enough seats in popular or required classes." Moreover, undergrads here speak effusively about their professors. As one Biology major shares, "Regardless of which class you're in, you can tell that each professor's #1 priority is that the students succeed." Students agree that these "lifelong teachers" go the extra mile: "I've had professors set up weekend study sessions before exams, bring in donuts for 8:00 A.M. classes, and invite students over for dinner or out for coffee. My professors have also really helped me in beginning my career—setting up research studies in my field of interest, writing incredible letters of recommendation for grad school, or networking to get me internships."

Campus Life

Burlington, Vermont (less than 10 minutes from campus minutes by bus) is "one of the greatest places to be in this part of the country. There is so much to do in such a small, convenient area." Of Burlington, students say that "Church Street is crowded with unique shops, fantastic restaurants, and interesting people," which is nice because a few students observe—as is common of many undergrad dining halls—that on-campus food sometimes "lacks flavor." Many also love to take advantage of Vermont's outdoor recreational options and the school counts many avid skiers, snowboarders, and hikers among it ranks. In fact, "Saint Michael's provides amazing ski pass deals and transportation to amazing ski resorts in the area." St. Mike's campus is "tiny, but in the cold months of winter, five-minute walks to class are a godsend." It's a "pretty chill" atmosphere at St. Mike's, which means that "If a student is one that likes to party, they are able to find it on campus. If a person is more reserved, there are thousands of other things that that person can do."

Student Body

The typical student is self-described as "upper-middle class, environmentally and politically aware, and always says 'Hi,'" and the sort of person who quickly dons "North Faces and UGGs during the cold Vermont winters." Although St. Mike's is a Catholic school, students "are all different in regards to religions, races, sexual orientations and genders." The most frequent comment made by first-years "is that they were shocked when a student held the door open for them." Giving back to the community is a main theme in terms of the typical student here at St. Mike's, as exemplified by the statement that "nearly all students participate in at least one service project during their four years here. Most students are concerned about the environment and social justice." Students are "very relaxed for the most part" and enjoy "the outdoors that this great state provides for us." The overall consensus is that "If you're genuine and true to who you are, you're bound to do well at St. Mike's."

SAINT MICHAEL'S COLLEGE

Financial Aid: 802-654-3243 • E-Mail: admission@smcvt.edu • Website: www.smcvt.edu

THE PRINCETON REVIEW SAYS

Admissions

The school reports that its standardized testing policy for use in admission for Fall 2024 is Test Optional. The 2024 testing policy will be permanent. The Princeton Review suggests that interested applicants consult with the school for the most up-to-date standardized testing policies. *Very important factors considered include:* rigor of secondary school record, class rank, academic GPA, application essay. *Important factors considered include:* recommendation(s), extracurricular activities, talent/ability, character/personal qualities, volunteer work, work experience. *Other factors considered include:* standardized test scores, first generation, racial/ethnic status, level of applicant's interest. High school diploma is required and GED is accepted. *Academic units required:* 4 English, 3 math, 3 science, 2 science labs, 3 foreign language, 3 social studies, 3 history. *Academic units recommended:* 4 English, 4 math, 4 science, 3 science labs, 4 foreign language, 4 social studies, 4 history.

Financial Aid

Students should submit: FAFSA; State aid form. The Princeton Review suggests that all financial aid forms be submitted as soon as possible (see page 5 for a note on the FAFSA). *Need-based scholarships/grants offered:* College/university scholarship or grant aid from institutional funds; Federal Pell; Private scholarships; SEOG; State scholarships/grants. *Loan aid offered:* Direct PLUS loans; Direct Subsidized Loans; Direct Unsubsidized Loans. Admitted students will be notified of awards on a rolling basis beginning in December. Federal Work-Study Program available. Institutional employment available.

The Inside Word

Applicants to St. Mike's are more than just a number, and admissions officers do their utmost to consider candidates in their entirety. Officers consider everything from essays to extracurricular activities, though most weight is given to academic record. The College has been standardized Test Optional for over a decade, and applicants are not penalized in the admission or scholarship process if they choose not to submit their scores.

THE SCHOOL SAYS "..."

From the Admissions Office

"A residential Catholic college welcoming to all, Saint Michael's is steeped in the spirit of our founders, the Society of Saint Edmund. Their example inspires our community to embrace the values of intellectual inquiry, peace, justice, and service to others. Students at St. Mike's are challenged to do well and driven to do good.

"Choosing a major is not always easy. At St. Mike's, students can take advantage of the flexible structure of their majors and our liberal arts core to explore then pursue more than one academic interest. In fact, over 80 percent of our students complete more than just their major, with over 40 percent completing at least a double major or double minor. We help students find and follow their passions and excel at them.

"Outside the classroom, students grow into impressive leaders through their experiences with the Adventure Sports Center, Fire & Rescue, our MOVE service work program, varsity and club athletics, a uniquely active student government, our student run radio station WWPV, the student paper, the College farm, the Center for the Environment, and numerous other opportunities.

"Named among the 'best college towns' in the country, nearby Burlington is a vibrant city with a wealth of professional experiences, arts, and culture. Campus is also located just ninety minutes from the multicultural center of Montreal, Canada. Students enjoy a deeply discounted season's pass to Sugarbush, access to our campus and 440-acre Natural Area for research and recreation, and meaningful internships at top companies.

"St. Mike's will take you wherever you want to go."

SELECTIVITY

Admissions Rating	83
# of applicants	2,629
% of applicants accepted	85
% of acceptees attending	12
# offered a place on the wait list	79
% accepting a place on wait list	34
% admitted from wait list	26

FIRST-YEAR PROFILE

Testing policy	Test Optional
Range SAT composite	1160–1320
Range SAT EBRW	600–680
Range SAT math	560–640
Range ACT composite	26–30
# submitting SAT scores	50
% submitting SAT scores	19
# submitting ACT scores	11
% submitting ACT scores	4

DEADLINES

Early action	
Deadline	11/1
Notification	12/21
Regular	
Priority	11/1
Deadline	2/1
Notification	4/12
Nonfall registration?	Yes

APPLICANTS OFTEN PREFER
University of Massachusetts Amherst; University of New Hampshire; University of Vermont

APPLICANTS SOMETIMES PREFER
Fairfield University; Providence College; Saint Anselm College; St. Lawrence University; Stonehill College; University of Connecticut; University of Maine; University of Rhode Island

APPLICANTS RARELY PREFER
Assumption University; Salve Regina University

FINANCIAL FACTS

Financial Aid Rating	87
Annual tuition	$47,640
Room and board	$16,495
Required fees	$2,400
Books and supplies	$1,000
Average frosh need-based scholarship	$33,770
Average UG need-based scholarship	$34,876
% needy frosh rec. need-based scholarship or grant aid	100
% needy UG rec. need-based scholarship or grant aid	100
% needy frosh rec. non-need-based scholarship or grant aid	35
% needy UG rec. non-need-based scholarship or grant aid	21
% needy frosh rec. need-based self-help aid	61
% needy UG rec. need-based self-help aid	75
% frosh rec. any financial aid	100
% UG rec. any financial aid	100
% UG borrow to pay for school	70
Average cumulative indebtedness	$40,336
% frosh need fully met	37
% ugrads need fully met	27
Average % of frosh need met	87
Average % of ugrad need met	85

ST. OLAF COLLEGE

1520 St. Olaf Avenue, Northfield, MN 55057 • Admissions: 507-786-2222 • Fax: 507-786-3832

STUDENTS SAY "..."

Academics

Founded in 1874, St. Olaf College is a Lutheran liberal arts college that views the entire undergraduate experience as an education. The college establishes a set of goals (called "STOGoals") that all students must achieve regardless of major, including self-development, civic and global engagement, and critical thinking and inquiry, and students have numerous opportunities to fulfill these goals through coursework and co-curricular activities. The Piper Center for Vocation and Career "constantly has new opportunities available for students in any field of study," science classes offer students the chance "to dip their toes in research," and nearly two-thirds of students participate in the "second to none" study abroad programs. There are endless resources in support of students, and "if you need something, St. Olaf will do everything in their power to accommodate."

Professors at St. Olaf are universally beloved, helping with "everything from a mistake on a homework assignment, a course concept that is confusing, writing a thesis for a paper, planning course schedules, and advising students on how to reach their long term goals." The best classes "tend to include a lot of discussion and focus on the process of learning rather than the graded outcome"; indeed, academic innovation thrives at St. Olaf, with courses featuring "conversation dinners for language classes, exploratory field trips, exhibition tours for art courses, guest speakers, and interactive seminars." Professors also organize "panels of people to share their expertise and perspectives (such as a panel of local farmers when studying environmental science)." Academics are "challenging with enough resources that they're manageable," and the school "gets students ready to apply to jobs, internships, and graduate school all over the course of four years."

Campus Life

Though St. Olaf is only located 45 minutes from the bustling Twin Cities, 95 percent of students live on the beautiful, dry campus, a "marvel" that leads to "a lot of school programming with relatively high attendance." This is especially true of extracurriculars: students describe being "very involved at high levels" in things like music ensembles and sports. Academics are equally taken seriously, such that "studying is also a form of hanging out for many people." That said, students do find time for relaxing, especially on weekends, which are filled with seasonal activities like "going to the pumpkin patch or apple orchard ten minutes from campus," and a main student pastime is simply "going to dinner and seeing all of their friends and then going to each other's rooms afterwards." Oles are an outdoorsy bunch, and students "have access to hundreds of acres of forest and prairie on campus to run, bike, and cross-country ski," and "the natural lands and hiking trails are often used."

Student Body

St. Olaf College is entirely welcome to all students and faiths: "the chapel and college pastors, rabbi, [and] Muslim chaplain are very inclusive." Students feel that their peers tend to be at least one of these three things—Minnesotan, conservative, and/or white—but they are all united by "an interest and desire to learn" that often manifests itself "in deep discussions in and out of the classroom." Moreover, because the school is interdisciplinary, you're likely to get exposure to a wider variety of perspectives, as "it is not uncommon to be in a philosophy class full of biology and music majors." On the whole, Oles are "generally kind and cheerful, and with an unmatched respect for others and their property."

ST. OLAF COLLEGE

Financial Aid: 507-786-3019 • E-Mail: admissions@stolaf.edu • Website: wp.stolaf.edu

THE PRINCETON REVIEW SAYS

Admissions

The school reports that its standardized testing policy for use in admission for Fall 2024 is Test Optional. The 2024 testing policy will be permanent. The Princeton Review suggests that interested applicants consult with the school for the most up-to-date standardized testing policies. *Very important factors considered include:* rigor of secondary school record, academic GPA, application essay. *Important factors considered include:* class rank, recommendation(s), interview, extracurricular activities, talent/ability, character/personal qualities, level of applicant's interest. *Other factors considered include:* standardized test scores, first generation, alumni/ae relation, geographical residence, state residency, religious affiliation/commitment, racial/ethnic status, volunteer work, work experience. High school diploma is required and GED is accepted. *Academic units recommended:* 4 English, 4 math, 4 science, 2 science labs, 4 foreign language, 4 social studies.

Financial Aid

Students should submit: CSS/Financial Aid Profile; FAFSA; Noncustodial Profile. Priority filing deadline is 11/1. The Princeton Review suggests that all financial aid forms be submitted as soon as possible (see page 5 for a note on the FAFSA). *Need-based scholarships/grants offered:* College/university scholarship or grant aid from institutional funds; Federal Pell; Private scholarships; SEOG; State scholarships/grants. *Loan aid offered:* Direct PLUS loans; Direct Subsidized Loans; Direct Unsubsidized Loans; College/university loans from institutional funds; State Loans. Admitted students will be notified of awards on or about 3/15. Federal Work-Study Program available. Institutional employment available.

The Inside Word

As St. Olaf's academic reputation steadily rises, so too does competition to gain admission. First and foremost, admissions officers here assess the rigor of each applicant's course load (and subsequent success in the classroom), though there is no minimum GPA threshold and test scores are optional. Of course, as a tight-knit community, the college also looks to admit students who will complement St. Olaf's ethos. To that end, admissions officers also closely analyze personal essays, recommendations, and participation in extracurricular activities.

THE SCHOOL SAYS "..."

From the Admissions Office

"With so many great liberal arts colleges, how do you choose? What makes St. Olaf stand apart? We think it's this: St. Olaf doesn't produce ordinary college grads. It turns out Oles (Oh-Lees). Oles are the people that companies want, because they know how to get stuff done. They think harder, approach problems differently, persevere with enthusiasm. Oles are born of St. Olaf's intense academic program—an academic program that hones minds, while its emphasis on global engagement helps broaden perspectives. Oles aren't necessarily religious, but our religious tradition encourages deep self-reflection. Most important, perhaps, is the Ole community—a vibrant community that accepts, supports and encourages, generating lifelong friendships and invaluable business connections. Today more than ever, the world needs idealistic, tireless problem solvers. In other words, Oles.

"Facts about Oles: St. Olaf's 3,000 students come from 80 countries, every state, and a variety of religious and non-religious backgrounds. Oles choose from more than 85 majors, concentrations, and pre-professional tracks. 95 percent of Oles live on campus or in college-owned houses nearby. Two-thirds of Oles study abroad. Oles participate on 26 varsity teams, numerous club sports and intramurals. They belong to 200 student organizations and have countless opportunities to get involved."

SELECTIVITY

Admissions Rating	92
# of applicants	5,524
% of applicants accepted	56
% of acceptees attending	28
# offered a place on the wait list	883
% accepting a place on wait list	35
% admitted from wait list	5
# of early decision applicants	334
% accepted early decision	72

FIRST-YEAR PROFILE

Testing policy	Test Optional
Range SAT composite	1300–1460
Range SAT EBRW	660–730
Range SAT math	640–750
Range ACT composite	28–33
# submitting SAT scores	129
% submitting SAT scores	15
# submitting ACT scores	319
% submitting ACT scores	37
Average HS GPA	3.7
% frosh submitting high school GPA	92
% graduated top 10% of class	39
% graduated top 25% of class	69
% graduated top 50% of class	94

DEADLINES

Early decision	
Deadline	11/1
Notification	12/10
Other ED deadline	1/15
Other ED notification	2/1
Early action	
Deadline	11/1
Notification	12/23
Regular	
Deadline	1/15
Notification	3/15
Nonfall registration?	No

APPLICANTS OFTEN PREFER
Carleton College; Oberlin College

APPLICANTS SOMETIMES PREFER
Grinnell College; Lawrence University; Macalester College; University of Minnesota—Twin Cities; University of Wisconsin—Madison

APPLICANTS RARELY PREFER
Gustavus Adolphus College; Luther College; University of Saint Thomas (MN)

FINANCIAL FACTS

Financial Aid Rating	94
Annual tuition	$56,970
Room and board	$13,000
Required fees	$0
Books and supplies	$1,000
Average frosh need-based scholarship	$46,115
Average UG need-based scholarship	$44,362
% needy frosh rec. need-based scholarship or grant aid	100
% needy UG rec. need-based scholarship or grant aid	100
% needy frosh rec. non-need-based scholarship or grant aid	75
% needy UG rec. non-need-based scholarship or grant aid	68
% needy frosh rec. need-based self-help aid	88
% needy UG rec. need-based self-help aid	94
% frosh rec. any financial aid	98
% UG rec. any financial aid	97
% UG borrow to pay for school	63
Average cumulative indebtedness	$27,797
% frosh need fully met	100
% ugrads need fully met	85
Average % of frosh need met	100
Average % of ugrad need met	95

SALISBURY UNIVERSITY

1101 Camden Avenue, Salisbury, MD 21801 • Admissions: 410-543-6000 • Fax: 410-546-6016

STUDENTS SAY "..."

Academics

Salisbury University brings a little bit of everything to the university system of Maryland, with students singling out the healthcare, business, and arts programs. The hands-on focus is a major draw, whether that's "getting to be in the hospital working with patients," working directly "with Bloomberg terminals [and meeting] with employers, CEOs, and entrepreneurs," or getting to "make our own claybodies, glazes, and even kilns." There's also appreciation for all the "facilities and technologies that are being upgraded right now." On the art front, students love that the teachers "are all working artists, so I've never felt more capable that I too can become [one]."

Across disciplines, students at Salisbury are empowered to direct their own educational development: "I worked closely with the Spanish department and created a new internship experience for future students where I aided a local hospital with vaccinations and Spanish translations." This sometimes even extends into summer classes, like a "month-long kayaking and camping class ... that focused on the local Maryland and Chesapeake Bay environment and ecosystems." Students note that whatever the course, "I know that if I'm struggling with something, even if it's not related to school, or if I just want to talk to someone, my professors are always there and they offer the best conversations and advice that I've ever had."

Campus Life

Many students "love attending" events from the Student Organization for Activity Planning (SOAP), the engine of student life on campus. Favorite events include bingo and trivia nights, as well as craft nights and SOAP Spa days: "I think SOAP activities help me since they have events that help students here relax." Students also enjoy the Division III athletics and sporting events: "We have a lot of spirit...A lot of people show up to the sporting events and they are...so fun." One student counts *The Flyer*, the campus newspaper, as "the best way to integrate myself in campus life and into the weeds of how the University runs. I've learned more about fellow students, their thoughts, events in and around campus, and just the campus in general." Many Salisbury students also stay busy with service organizations on campus: "This semester I recently joined the non-profit Relay For Life here on campus. I also have had the opportunity to help out at the local women's shelter. Next semester I am planning on joining more extracurricular activities such as CRU, which is the university's Christian service group."

Student Body

"Every semester I reevaluate how I see the world because of my fellow classmates' opinions and perspectives," explains one senior student. Some attribute this confluence of new ideas to the fact that "students from all over come together to create a safe and inclusive environment for those from many different backgrounds." Others suggest that it comes from the colonial-style campus's vibe: "Everyone here is very welcoming ... and help [make it] feel like it's home." In short, these "smart and easy-going people" make room for and are accepting of all extracurricular interests, like a lightsaber dueling club. When reflecting on their experience in class with peers, one senior recalls that "every class I've taken and every club I've been a part of has been filled with people who have a deep love for whatever their major is. Not only are they passionate but they're also incredibly intelligent."

SALISBURY UNIVERSITY

Financial Aid: 410-543-6165 • Website: www.salisbury.edu/

THE PRINCETON REVIEW SAYS

Admissions

The school reports that its standardized testing policy for use in admission for Fall 2024 is Test Optional. It is unknown at this time if the 2024 testing policy will be permanent. The Princeton Review suggests that interested applicants consult with the school for the most up-to-date standardized testing policies. *Very important factors considered include:* rigor of secondary school record, academic GPA. *Important factors considered include:* class rank, standardized test scores. *Other factors considered include:* application essay, recommendation(s), interview, extracurricular activities, talent/ability, character/personal qualities, first generation, alumni/ae relation, geographical residence, state residency, volunteer work, work experience, level of applicant's interest. High school diploma is required and GED is accepted. *Academic units required:* 4 English, 4 math, 3 science, 2 science labs, 2 foreign language, 3 social studies. *Academic units recommended:* 4 English, 4 math, 4 science, 3 science labs, 3 foreign language, 3 social studies, 3 academic electives.

Financial Aid

Students should submit: FAFSA. Priority filing deadline is 3/1. The Princeton Review suggests that all financial aid forms be submitted as soon as possible (see page 5 for a note on the FAFSA). *Need-based scholarships/grants offered:* College/university scholarship or grant aid from institutional funds; Federal Pell; Private scholarships; SEOG; State scholarships/ grants. *Loan aid offered:* Direct PLUS loans; Direct Subsidized Loans; Direct Unsubsidized Loans. Admitted students will be notified of awards on a rolling basis beginning 2/24. Federal Work-Study Program available. Institutional employment available.

The Inside Word

The SU Admissions Office takes a comprehensive view of a student's application and puts top priority on the academic record, including curriculum and performance. Preference is for a college preparatory curriculum and a strong history of leadership experience and community service. The university has an SAT/ACT optional admissions policy for students with a GPA of 3.5 or above. Test scores are required for scholarship consideration. Other requirements include recommendations and a personal essay. Portfolio required for Bachelor of Fine Arts applicants.

THE SCHOOL SAYS "..."

From the Admissions Office

"Salisbury University sets success in motion with a welcoming, "just right" size campus and a culture where students are seen, heard, supported, and challenged. The University is a must-see, with flowering trees, green spaces, and traditional red brick echoing the natural beauty of coastal Maryland. Its location in Salisbury offers restaurants, shops and a historic downtown—and provides the friendly ambiance of nearby beach communities. SU's high-impact, student-focused academic programs, taught by world-class educators, provide the perfect environment for students to develop a liberal arts foundation, hone their communication and entrepreneurship skills, conduct research, and engage in public service, especially education and health care. A top producer of student and faculty Fulbright awards, SU offers access to research in the first semester. Faculty mentors coach students toward opportunities for study abroad, experiential learning (required for all students), and national fellowships. Expansive facilities include the Guerrieri Academic Commons—a state-of-the-art "library of the future" and the hub of academic life. With strong job and graduate school placements, SU offers students a return on investment that pays back a lifetime of possibilities. Academic success is matched by a spirit of community involvement through over 100 student clubs and service projects; a continual commitment to inclusion, diversity, opportunity and equity; and the cultivation of a sense of belonging. Students cheer on SU's Division III athletic programs (with 46 team and individual national championships) in new facilities. The campus also is known nationally for sustainability. SU seeks students who want to shape tomorrow."

SALVE REGINA UNIVERSITY

100 Ochre Point Avenue, Newport, RI 02840-4192 • Admissions: 401-847-6650 • Fax: 401-848-2823

CAMPUS LIFE

Quality of Life Rating	89
Fire Safety Rating	94
Green Rating	94
Type of school	Private
Affiliation	Roman Catholic
Environment	Town

STUDENTS

Total undergrad enrollment	2,190
% male/female/another gender	31/69/0
% from out of state	84
% frosh from public high school	71
% frosh live on campus	97
% ugrads live on campus	57
# of fraternities	0
# of sororities	0
% African American	2
% Asian	1
% White	80
% Hispanic	9
% Native American	<1
% Pacific Islander	<1
% Two or more races	3
% Race and/or ethnicity unknown	3
% international	2
# of countries represented	19

SURVEY SAYS . . .

Classroom facilities are great
Lab facilities are great
Great library
Students get along with local community
Students involved in community service
Students environmentally aware
Students love, Newport RI
Great off-campus food
Everyone loves the Seahawks
Active minority support groups

ACADEMICS

Academic Rating	83
% students returning for sophomore year	82
% students graduating within 4 years	70
% students graduating within 6 years	76
Calendar	Semester
Student/faculty ratio	13:1
Profs interesting rating	91
Profs accessible rating	91

Most classes have 20–29 students.
Most lab/discussion sessions have
10–19 students.

MOST POPULAR MAJORS

Elementary Education and Teaching; Registered
Nursing/Registered Nurse; Business
Administration and Management, General

STUDENTS SAY ". . ."

Academics

Salve Regina University in Newport, Rhode Island, is a liberal arts institution that embraces service and produces conscientious, ambitious learners who work to "become more informed citizen[s]…responsible for making the world a better place." Set on seven connected 19th-century estates overlooking the Atlantic, the school offers 48 undergraduate majors, including 11 combined bachelor's/master's programs, as well as 200 study abroad programs in 45 countries. Classes at Salve do an excellent job of incorporating the unique location, including "walking tours of Newport for various history classes" and "using the proximity to aquatic life and water" in environmental studies classes, the marine biology course, and other classes. There are "incredible research and internship opportunities" available to students, and the Academic Excellence Center is "an excellent resource" and offers tutoring, learning and study strategies, and peer academic coaching.

Students appreciate the small class sizes and the "caring and involved" professors and faculty. Professors are "visibly passionate about their disciplines and the material they teach" and "encourage class discussion and participation." As one student says, "We have…professors who are very encouraging and genuinely want all students to succeed." Finals are sometimes "creative projects that allow students to expand their knowledge in certain subjects that they feel passionate about," including "a short film, poem, short story, [or] video essay," and "it really allows students to be passionate about what they are learning and dive into aspects of larger topics that they love."

Campus Life

There are "an abundance of extracurricular activities and clubs for students to join," and most students are involved in clubs, athletics, or both. Varsity sports "are incredibly well run and receive tons of support." There "are so many opportunities to meet everyone and make new friends." The school places a high priority on student engagement, and as such, "Salve always has an event happening." Salve also "brings in lots of speakers and hosts other events…to provide student[s] with opportunities to immerse themselves in the community." The Mission of Mercy is central to the school, and students "spend time in community service…and helping [others]." Although the school has Catholic roots, "Salve does not pressure students to participate in religious activities if that isn't their thing." As one student observes, "Overall, it is clear that Salve really cares about their students and ensures that we are a community."

More than half of all students live on-campus, and the beautiful surroundings mean the student body spends plenty of time on the weekends enjoying Newport—"whether that's sailing, taking the famous Newport Cliff Walk, or going downtown to seek out "amazing spots to eat, socialize, shop, and enjoy the beautiful oceans and sunsets." The "nightlife and restaurant scene is awesome and there are countless things to do on the island," and "multicultural events are frequent and provide inclusivity to all cultures."

Student Body

This is "a small, tight-knit community" where "the vibe on campus is warm and welcoming." One of the benefits of a smaller campus is that "you really have the opportunity to shine," and "it is rare that you'll be in a class where you don't know anyone." As one student adds, "Being that it is a small school, it's almost like a small town where everybody knows everybody." A small campus is not for everyone, though—"those who seek crazy action and Greek life would not fit in here [well]." Many students have found a healthy work-life balance at the school. "Students here care a lot about what they are studying… [but] we're also a campus that…is extremely balanced—people study, but they also have other…pastimes." In this "relaxed environment," the overall feeling is that the majority of the student body is very open and accepting.

SALVE REGINA UNIVERSITY

Financial Aid: 401-341-2140 • E-Mail: admissions@salve.edu • Website: www.salve.edu

THE PRINCETON REVIEW SAYS

Admissions

The school reports that its standardized testing policy for use in admission for Fall 2024 is Test Optional. It is unknown at this time if the 2024 testing policy will be permanent. The Princeton Review suggests that interested applicants consult with the school for the most up-to-date standardized testing policies. *Very important factors considered include:* rigor of secondary school record, class rank, academic GPA. *Important factors considered include:* application essay, recommendation(s). *Other factors considered include:* standardized test scores, extracurricular activities, talent/ability, character/personal qualities, first generation, alumni/ae relation, racial/ethnic status, volunteer work, work experience, level of applicant's interest. High school diploma is required and GED is accepted. *Academic units required:* 4 English, 3 math, 2 science, 2 science labs, 2 foreign language, 1 social studies, 4 academic electives.

Financial Aid

Students should submit: FAFSA. Priority filing deadline is 3/1. The Princeton Review suggests that all financial aid forms be submitted as soon as possible (see page 5 for a note on the FAFSA). *Need-based scholarships/grants offered:* College/university scholarship or grant aid from institutional funds; Federal Pell; Private scholarships; SEOG; State scholarships/grants. *Loan aid offered:* Direct PLUS loans; Direct Subsidized Loans; Direct Unsubsidized Loans; Federal Nursing Loans. Admitted students will be notified of awards on a rolling basis beginning 1/3. Federal Work-Study Program available. Institutional employment available.

The Inside Word

Ideal candidates, per the school, "will contribute to our campus community, grow as compassionate individuals, and embrace the mission of the university." Admission is lightly competitive—roughly 3,800 applicants were accepted out of the 5,500 total—and because the school assesses each student holistically, being able to demonstrate extracurricular interests that coincide with its goals will help, especially since SAT/ACT scores are optional in 2024. Note that your GPA is recalculated by the admissions team to more heavily weigh rigorous honors and AP courses and core academic subjects.

THE SCHOOL SAYS "..."

From the Admissions Office

"Salve Regina University offers students the opportunity to experience a transformative educational experience through a rigorous curriculum and supportive mentorship from dedicated faculty. It also allows them to discover their place in today's complicated world and work to make a positive contribution to improving society. The small, close-knit campus community encourages the development of close relationships amongst students as they work together to come to a greater understanding of how the world works and how they may impact it, as informed by our Mercy mission imparted from the founding order, the Sisters of Mercy.

"Students benefit from Salve's unique, historic campus, which overlooks the ocean on the famed Cliff Walk of Newport, Rhode Island. Through the Salve Compass—a bold, bright thread running through every undergraduate student's Salve education—theory and practice are integrated to connect curriculum to career through experiences like Sophomore Summer where students experience Newport through an engagement that highlights professional competency development. They also participate in a robust offering of clubs, activities, sports, and enrichment opportunities including speakers sponsored by Salve's Pell Center for International Relations and Public Policy, the on campus 'think tank.' The measure of Salve's strength is the success of students who graduate at rates far exceeding national averages, complete their degrees on time in four years, and demonstrate lifetime ROI as measured by salaries that put Salve in the top 5% of all colleges and universities in the U.S., per a study by the Georgetown Center on Education and the Workforce."

SELECTIVITY

Admissions Rating	86
# of applicants	5,562
% of applicants accepted	70
% of acceptees attending	15
# offered a place on the wait list	448
% accepting a place on wait list	15
% admitted from wait list	42
# of early decision applicants	34
% accepted early decision	88

FIRST-YEAR PROFILE

Testing policy	Test Optional
Range SAT composite	1140–1290
Range SAT EBRW	580–660
Range SAT math	550–620
Range ACT composite	25–29
# submitting SAT scores	116
% submitting SAT scores	20
# submitting ACT scores	19
% submitting ACT scores	3
Average HS GPA	3.6
% frosh submitting high school GPA	100
% graduated top 10% of class	15
% graduated top 25% of class	49
% graduated top 50% of class	83

DEADLINES

Early decision	
Deadline	11/1
Notification	12/15
Early action	
Deadline	11/1
Notification	12/25
EA II deadline	1/5
EA II notification	2/15
Regular	
Priority	2/1
Notification	Rolling, 12/25
Nonfall registration?	Yes

APPLICANTS ALSO LOOK AT

Assumption University; Bryant University; College of Charleston; Endicott College; Fairfield University; Fordham University; Loyola University Maryland; Marist College; Providence College; Quinnipiac University

FINANCIAL FACTS

Financial Aid Rating	83
Annual tuition	$45,250
Room and board	$16,500
Required fees	$750
Books and supplies	$1,550
Average frosh need-based scholarship	$30,009
Average UG need-based scholarship	$26,342
% needy frosh rec. need-based scholarship or grant aid	100
% needy UG rec. need-based scholarship or grant aid	100
% needy frosh rec. non-need-based scholarship or grant aid	18
% needy UG rec. non-need-based scholarship or grant aid	15
% needy frosh rec. need-based self-help aid	76
% needy UG rec. need-based self-help aid	82
% frosh rec. any financial aid	100
% UG rec. any financial aid	100
% UG borrow to pay for school	80
Average cumulative indebtedness	$52,001
% frosh need fully met	21
% ugrads need fully met	18
Average % of frosh need met	75
Average % of ugrad need met	71

SAN DIEGO STATE UNIVERSITY

5500 Campanile Drive, San Diego, CA 92182-7455 • Admissions: 619-594-5200

STUDENTS SAY "..."

Academics

Students lucky enough to attend San Diego State University receive a "quality, affordable education," all while they soak up that brilliant "San Diego sun!" And with a "wide array [of] majors and minors" along with a good deal of "flexibility in course choices," it's understandable why individuals are drawn to this institution. Speaking of majors (and minors), undergrads at SDSU rush to underscore a handful of really stellar academic departments. For starters, the "science programs have vigorous requirements that [truly] prepare you for grad school or medical school." Additionally, the "music program strives to create the best educators and performers." The nursing school is also "amazing" and really works to "accommodate...each individual." And the international business program is considered "one of the top...in the nation."

When it comes to professors, the vast majority at SDSU are "dedicated and eager to teach." Moreover, they typically approach their time in the classroom with "enthusiasm" and manage to "bring life to every lecture." Indeed, they "make learning the material easy and fun." It's also quite apparent that they "care about their students," taking the time to "check in with them" and making themselves "accessible outside of the classroom." And, as a grateful religious studies major explains, they often "inspire [you] to become a more intellectual person and involved student."

Campus Life

Simply put, life at San Diego State is "wonderful." And, no matter whether you opt to participate in "Greek life, a student organization, or a sport, everyone [finds] something to do." Additionally, SDSU's Associated Students is great about sponsoring a number of "fun" events such as Aztec Nights, which in past years have included "Distress Fest, Haunted Montezuma, and the Polar Plunge." A thrilled speech pathology major rushes to brag, "Every Thursday, there is a farmer's market on campus where students can enjoy a wide array of international cuisines prepared by local restaurants. SDSU also has "amazing athletics" and undergrads love "attending football [games], basketball [games] and other sporting events." Of course, given that San Diego has "[beautiful] weather year round," you won't catch SDSU students...spend[ing] much time indoors." It's quite common to see students riding "bikes or skateboards across campus." And a business administration major pipes in, "The beach is a huge draw for people whether you like surfing, paddle boarding, or just swimming." Additionally, the "campus is located 10 minutes from Fashion Valley or Balboa Park, and there are tons of good restaurants around. It is also very close to the Mexican border for easy day trips."

Student Body

San Diego State is comprised of a "diverse community of students who are as laid-back as they are hard-working." Indeed, the university does a great job of attracting undergrads "from all over the world and all walks of life." Students happily report that their peers are both "social" and "academically driven." Even better, "they are supportive and seem to always be open to help others who are struggling." Undergrads also appreciate that there are "endless opportunities to meet new people because the campus is swarming with students." And, for the most part, San Diego undergrads are "very accepting of one another and open minded." Of course, all of this goodwill can partially be attributed to the lovely surroundings. As one business students sums up, "It's hard not to be happy when living in beautiful San Diego."

SAN DIEGO STATE UNIVERSITY

Website: www.sdsu.edu

THE PRINCETON REVIEW SAYS

Admissions

The school reports that its standardized testing policy for use in admission for Fall 2024 is Test Free. The 2024 testing policy will be permanent. The Princeton Review suggests that interested applicants consult with the school for the most up-to-date standardized testing policies. *Very important factors considered include:* rigor of secondary school record, academic GPA. *Important factors considered include:* geographical residence, state residency. *Other factors considered include:* extracurricular activities. High school diploma is required and GED is accepted. *Academic units required:* 4 English, 3 math, 2 science, 2 science labs, 2 foreign language, 1 social studies, 1 history, 1 visual/performing arts, 1 academic elective. *Academic units recommended:* 4 math, 3 science, 3 science labs.

Financial Aid

Students should submit: FAFSA; State aid form. Priority filing deadline is 4/1. The Princeton Review suggests that all financial aid forms be submitted as soon as possible (see page 5 for a note on the FAFSA). *Need-based scholarships/grants offered:* College/university scholarship or grant aid from institutional funds; Federal Pell; Private scholarships; SEOG; State scholarships/grants. *Loan aid offered:* Direct PLUS loans; Direct Subsidized Loans; Direct Unsubsidized Loans; College/university loans from institutional funds. Admitted students will be notified of awards on a rolling basis beginning 3/15. Federal Work-Study Program available. Institutional employment available.

The Inside Word

The admissions process at San Diego State is very by the book. Similar to other universities within the California State system, San Diego relies on the eligibility index as the crux of their decision making. Hence, your GPA will be critical. Moreover, the application is major specific; candidates will be ranked against all other individuals applying to that particular major. You will not be able to change your major during this process (though, aside from nursing, you will once you arrive on campus). Finally, all music, dance, and/or theater candidates will have to audition as well.

THE SCHOOL SAYS " . . ."

From the Admissions Office

"Founded in 1897, San Diego State University is a major public research institution that provides transformative experiences for its more than 36,000 students. SDSU ranks as the number 1 California State University in federal research support, is a long-standing Hispanic-Serving Institution (HSI) and resides on Kumeyaay land.

"The university is known for offering transformational research, international experiences, sustainability and entrepreneurship initiatives, internships and mentoring, and a broad range of student life and leadership opportunities. SDSU is committed to excellence and known for its efforts advancing diversity and inclusion.

"SDSU is nationally recognized for its study abroad initiatives, veterans' programs and support of LGBTQA+ students, as well as its powerhouse Division I Athletics Program. Recognized as a national leader in higher education, students have access to more than 400 student clubs and organizations and an inclusive environment with a diverse range of programs and offerings.

"About 54% of SDSU's undergraduates and graduates are students of color. The university's rich campus life and ideal location offers opportunities for students to lead and engage with the creative and performing arts, career and internship opportunities with SDSU's more than 400,000 living alumni, and the vibrant cultural life of the greater San Diego and U.S.–Mexico region."

SELECTIVITY

Admissions Rating	92
# of applicants	77,250
% of applicants accepted	39
% of acceptees attending	22
# offered a place on the wait list	8,585
% accepting a place on wait list	47
% admitted from wait list	0

FIRST-YEAR PROFILE

Testing policy	Test Free
Range SAT composite	1130–1340
Range SAT EBRW	560–670
Range SAT math	560–670
Range ACT composite	23–29
# submitting SAT scores	664
% submitting SAT scores	10
# submitting ACT scores	272
% submitting ACT scores	4
Average HS GPA	3.9
% frosh submitting high school GPA	100
% graduated top 10% of class	27
% graduated top 25% of class	64
% graduated top 50% of class	92

DEADLINES

Regular	
Deadline	11/30
Notification	5/1
Nonfall registration?	No

FINANCIAL FACTS

Financial Aid Rating	77
Annual in-state tuition	$5,742
Annual out-of-state tuition	$17,622
Room and board	$20,500
Required fees	$2,432
Books and supplies	$908
Average frosh need-based scholarship	$10,714
Average UG need-based scholarship	$10,575
% needy frosh rec. need-based scholarship or grant aid	61
% needy UG rec. need-based scholarship or grant aid	70
% needy frosh rec. non-need-based scholarship or grant aid	26
% needy UG rec. non-need-based scholarship or grant aid	18
% needy frosh rec. need-based self-help aid	90
% needy UG rec. need-based self-help aid	88
% frosh rec. any financial aid	54
% UG rec. any financial aid	59
% UG borrow to pay for school	35
Average cumulative indebtedness	$21,212
% frosh need fully met	3
% ugrads need fully met	2
Average % of frosh need met	68
Average % of ugrad need met	74

SANTA CLARA UNIVERSITY

500 El Camino Real, Santa Clara, CA 95053 • Admissions: 408-554-4700 • Fax: 408-554-5255

STUDENTS SAY "..."

Academics

Situated "at the heart of Silicon Valley," Santa Clara University is a Jesuit school with "rigorous but rewarding [courses]," a place where "you'll never meet more passionate, more intelligent, and often down-to-earth professors." Thanks to small class sizes, professors remain "accessible"; as one student puts it: "I have had a real relationship with every one of my professors at SCU." Meanwhile, the school administration is "great at listening to and implementing student feedback" and "welcomes students to talk with people in high positions of power." There's also an appreciated "openness of the students and faculty to consider new possibilities in academia" and one student notes being "challenged to extend my thinking in every class."

Of the various majors, students speak fondly of the "massive array of classes and professors" in the business school, and the many connections offered from faculty "[that] are CEOs and founders that relate the material we learn to their experiences." Other programs students spoke affectionately of are those for "top tier" accounting, "amazing" public health, and both computer and environmental science. Enrollees appreciate that the school is keeping with the times—a 2021 science building is described as having "awesome, state-of-the-art equipment"—and overall sum up their experience as "perfect, I love it."

Campus Life

Many students sum up the vibe at Santa Clara University as "work hard, play hard." On evenings and weekends, "Santa Clara students can be seen at local restaurants, bars, parties, golfing, or just having fun with friends." Fraternities and sororities—both pre-professional and social—are "huge" and "everywhere" on campus, perhaps contributing to the "big party culture at SCU." Additionally, "there are multiple social activities and events hosted by clubs and other organizations on campus almost every day of the week, and clubs do their best to be readily accessible to nonmembers." One student particularly loves the Investment Fund, "a student-led club that invests a portion of the university's endowment." There's also plenty to do even from the comfort of a residence hall, from pool to ping pong and foosball.

Students rave about the intramural sports available on SCU's "gorgeous" campus, including soccer, volleyball, flag football, and water polo. Though some admit it can be challenging to explore neighboring areas without a car, many value both the urban and wilderness adventures SCU's northern California location provides. "I love the hiking and backpacking club called 'Into the Wild,' which takes students to local scenery," says one student. Others share that weekend adventures to the beach in Santa Cruz or enjoying the nightlife in San Francisco make for excellent SCU memories.

Student Body

Santa Clara University attracts students that are "smart, dedicated, funny, committed, [and] intelligent." While students are "focused on academics"—as one puts it, "People like to have fun, but only after the work is finished"— they "definitely prioritize having a good time." There is a "good sense of community" on campus, but also "enough harmless shenanigans (lightsaber fights in the cafeteria, Shakespeare flash mobs, etc.)" to ensure you're "having a really fun college experience."

"Everyone here is quite relaxed and happy," explains one student. It's not that people aren't academically focused, "they just know how to balance work and school well." The school is fairly diverse in ethnicity, but some students note an "overwhelmingly upper-middle class" vibe. This may just be part of the easy-going atmosphere, however, given that 74% of students are reported to receive aid. At any rate, these "hardworking [students are] always open to help someone," so much so that a first-year "automatically felt at home at Santa Clara because of the warm and welcoming community."

SANTA CLARA UNIVERSITY

Financial Aid: 408-551-1000 • E-Mail: Admission@scu.edu • Website: www.scu.edu

THE PRINCETON REVIEW SAYS

Admissions

The school reports that its standardized testing policy for use in admission for Fall 2024 is Test Optional. It is unknown at this time if the 2024 testing policy will be permanent. The Princeton Review suggests that interested applicants consult with the school for the most up-to-date standardized testing policies. *Very important factors considered include:* rigor of secondary school record, academic GPA, application essay. *Important factors considered include:* class rank, recommendation(s), extracurricular activities, talent/ability, character/personal qualities, first generation, racial/ethnic status, volunteer work. *Other factors considered include:* standardized test scores, alumni/ae relation, geographical residence, state residency, religious affiliation/commitment, work experience, level of applicant's interest. High school diploma is required and GED is accepted. *Academic units required:* 4 English, 3 math, 2 science, 2 foreign language, 3 social studies. *Academic units recommended:* 4 English, 4 math, 3 science, 3 foreign language, 3 social studies, 1 visual/performing arts.

Financial Aid

Students should submit: CSS/Financial Aid Profile; FAFSA. Priority filing deadline is 2/1. The Princeton Review suggests that all financial aid forms be submitted as soon as possible (see page 5 for a note on the FAFSA). *Need-based scholarships/grants offered:* College/university scholarship or grant aid from institutional funds; Federal Pell; Private scholarships; SEOG; State scholarships/grants; United Negro College Fund. *Loan aid offered:* Direct PLUS loans; Direct Subsidized Loans; Direct Unsubsidized Loans; College/university loans from institutional funds. Admitted students will be notified of awards on or about 4/1. Federal Work-Study Program available. Institutional employment available.

The Inside Word

Applications for Santa Clara University come mostly from within California, and although an acceptance rate of slightly over 50 percent might not seem as competitive, admissions criteria is stringent and growing tougher. The number of applications has been increasing over the last few years, and the university's Silicon Valley address ensures even more attention is coming the school's way. Admissions officers consider high school transcripts, standardized test scores, as well as community service and involvement. Applicants apply to one of SCU's three schools and colleges: Arts and Sciences, School of Business, and School of Engineering. School visits are available. There are no admissions interviews offered.

THE SCHOOL SAYS "..."

From the Admissions Office

"Santa Clara University is a comprehensive Jesuit Catholic university located forty miles south of San Francisco in Silicon Valley. We'll challenge you to think critically, take risks, and take charge within a dynamic and caring community, with more than fifty majors, numerous interdisciplinary programs, and over 3,600 courses from which to choose. There's something special about living and learning in one of the most innovative places on Earth, where more than 80 percent of our students have at least one internship before graduating and undergraduates conduct important research alongside professors in a way that is usually reserved for graduate students. The University blends a sense of tradition and history—as the oldest college in California—with a vision that values innovation and a deep commitment to social justice. We offer an experience so great that 92 percent of first-year students return for their sophomore year. People of all backgrounds flourish here. One thing they have in common? They want to make a difference. Santa Clara students are driven to build a better, kinder, more humane, and more sustainable planet. Distinguished nationally by one of the highest graduation rates, SCU provides rigorous undergraduate curricula in the arts and sciences, business, and engineering. Invent the life you want to lead. Find out why SCU is the right fit for you at scu.edu."

SELECTIVITY

Admissions Rating	91
# of applicants	16,650
% of applicants accepted	52
% of acceptees attending	19
# offered a place on the wait list	4,009
% accepting a place on wait list	62
% admitted from wait list	0
# of early decision applicants	456
% accepted early decision	83

FIRST-YEAR PROFILE

Testing policy	Test Optional
Range SAT composite	1300–1470
Range SAT EBRW	640–720
Range SAT math	650–760
Range ACT composite	29–33
# submitting SAT scores	558
% submitting SAT scores	34
# submitting ACT scores	278
% submitting ACT scores	17
Average HS GPA	3.7
% frosh submitting high school GPA	100
% graduated top 10% of class	39
% graduated top 25% of class	74
% graduated top 50% of class	96

DEADLINES

Early decision	
Deadline	11/1
Notification	12/31
Other ED deadline	1/7
Other ED notification	2/15
Early action	
Deadline	11/1
Notification	12/31
Regular	
Deadline	1/7
Notification	3/31
Nonfall registration?	Yes

APPLICANTS ALSO LOOK AT

Boston College; California Polytechnic State University; Gonzaga University; Loyola Marymount University; Stanford University; University of California—Berkeley; University of California—Davis; University of California—Irvine; University of California—Los Angeles; University of San Diego, University of Southern California

FINANCIAL FACTS

Financial Aid Rating	81
Annual tuition	$58,587
Room and board	$17,967
Required fees	$654
Books and supplies	$939
Average frosh need-based scholarship	$35,551
Average UG need-based scholarship	$33,465
% needy frosh rec. need-based scholarship or grant aid	86
% needy UG rec. need-based scholarship or grant aid	71
% needy frosh rec. non-need-based scholarship or grant aid	44
% needy UG rec. non-need-based scholarship or grant aid	41
% needy frosh rec. need-based self-help aid	41
% needy UG rec. need-based self-help aid	38
% frosh rec. any financial aid	75
% UG rec. any financial aid	74
% UG borrow to pay for school	35
Average cumulative indebtedness	$25,193
% frosh need fully met	34
% ugrads need fully met	28
Average % of frosh need met	79
Average % of ugrad need met	76

SARAH LAWRENCE COLLEGE

1 Mead Way, Bronxville, NY 10708-5999 • Admissions: 914-337-0700 • Fax: 914-395-2515

STUDENTS SAY "..."

Academics

"The greatest strengths" at Sarah Lawrence College "are the small class sizes, the high-quality of …relationships between students and professors, and the freedom to create an academic major." Students attribute this to SLC's seminar-conference courses, which "allow students to endlessly customize their academic experience, as independent study is required of every student every semester." Beloved examples include "a literature class on disability that incorporates community service at a local elder care center" or being able to write a paper "in my calculus class about connecting calculus to crochet."

Students also take pride in the close relationships fostered by one-on-one conference courses. "Professors treat us as academic colleagues," explains one senior. "One professor, in a class on Roman and early Medieval art history, regularly brought his own actual artifacts to class" raves another fourth-year." While coursework at Sarah Lawrence often comes down to "research and analysis," students value both their creative control and outside-the-classroom experiences. "I took a class called 'Pattern' that explored the geometry within art and patterns. It was technically a math class, but we took a trip to a gallery and I was able to assemble a portfolio for my final project."

Campus Life

Just a 40-minute train ride from Manhattan, Sarah Lawrence students can enjoy their intimate, liberal arts college setting as well as the thrills of the big city. It's an "intellectual's school," without a huge party scene, but "there is usually plenty to do if you keep your finger on the pulse." This seems especially true for creative students, as the "literary journals are fabulous" and events like The Poetry Festival and Free-Write Fridays offer a chance to exercise one's creativity. On the theatrical side, groups like The Burlesque Troupe, Half-Naked Shakespeare, Melancholy Players, and the annual Rocky Horror Picture Shadow Showcase keep audiences entertained. Many work by day, converse during lunch and then go off "working on your film or choreography piece or manuscript with your friends." Sometimes, it's fun to just "go into New York City to have fun, see shows, and shop."

Student Body

Sarah Lawrence students are "intellectual, ever-curious, open-minded, and autodidactic," says one third-year student, "My peers don't require hand holding. They know what they want to study and how they want to study it." The school's independent student body reflects its self-directed academics: "Everyone cares about something: their music, their art, their friends, their academics, social and political causes and would defend it with their life." One student brags, "A friend of mine can wax poetically on quarks and leptons as much as she can deconstruct Fellini's oeuvre. A uniting factor of the campus is that none of us are looking for a traditional undergraduate academic experience. Above all we value choice." As for diversity on campus, students point to THRIVE, a mentorship program for students of color, which one sophomore notes "made a huge difference in my social life on campus and I am thankful for the connections it allowed me to make." There's also a "historically" huge LGBTQIA+ scene—"as a queer person myself, I have never felt this comfortable anywhere else."

SARAH LAWRENCE COLLEGE

Financial Aid: 914-395 2570 • E-Mail: slcadmit@sarahlawrence.edu • Website: www.sarahlawrence.edu

THE PRINCETON REVIEW SAYS

Admissions

The school reports that its standardized testing policy for use in admission for Fall 2024 is Test Optional. The 2024 testing policy will be permanent. The Princeton Review suggests that interested applicants consult with the school for the most up-to-date standardized testing policies. *Very important factors considered include:* rigor of secondary school record, application essay, recommendation(s). *Important factors considered include:* academic GPA, extracurricular activities, talent/ability, character/personal qualities. *Other factors considered include:* class rank, standardized test scores, interview, first generation, alumni/ae relation, geographical residence, racial/ethnic status, volunteer work, work experience, level of applicant's interest. High school diploma is required and GED is accepted. *Academic units required:* 2 English, 2 math, 2 science, 2 foreign language, 2 history. *Academic units recommended:* 4 English, 4 math, 4 science, 4 foreign language, 4 social studies, 4 history.

Financial Aid

Students should submit: FAFSA; State aid form. Priority filing deadline is 1/15. The Princeton Review suggests that all financial aid forms be submitted as soon as possible (see page 5 for a note on the FAFSA). *Need-based scholarships/grants offered:* College/university scholarship or grant aid from institutional funds; Federal Pell; Private scholarships; SEOG; State scholarships/grants. *Loan aid offered:* Direct PLUS loans; Direct Subsidized Loans; Direct Unsubsidized Loans. Admitted students will be notified of awards on or about 4/1. Federal Work-Study Program available. Institutional employment available.

The Inside Word

Gaining admission to Sarah Lawrence is certainly competitive. Thankfully, admissions officers take a well-rounded approach. Of course, a strong college prep curriculum and solid GPA are of utmost importance, though submitting standardized test scores is optional. Candidates are encouraged to submit scores only if it will enhance their application. Additionally, interviews are optional, but may offer an opportunity to demonstrate what you can bring to this unique community.

THE SCHOOL SAYS " . . ."

From the Admissions Office

"Students who come to Sarah Lawrence are curious about the world, and they have an ardent desire to satisfy that curiosity. Sarah Lawrence offers such students two innovative academic structures: the seminar/conference system and the arts components. Courses in the humanities, social sciences, natural sciences, and mathematics are taught in the seminar/conference style. The seminars enroll an average of eleven students and consist of lecture, discussion, readings, and assigned papers. For each seminar, students also meet one-on-one in biweekly conferences, for which they conceive of individualized projects and shape them under the direction of professors. Arts components let students combine history and theory with practice. Painters, printmakers, photographers, sculptors, filmmakers, composers, musicians, choreographers, dancers, actors, and directors work in readily available studios, editing facilities, and darkrooms, guided by accomplished professionals. The suburban, wooded campus is thirty minutes from midtown Manhattan, and the diversity of people and ideas at Sarah Lawrence make it an extraordinary educational environment.

"Sarah Lawrence College is Test Optional, accepting and reviewing standardized test scores if they are submitted; however, they are not required as part of the admission application."

SELECTIVITY

Admissions Rating	91
# of applicants	5,186
% of applicants accepted	50
% of acceptees attending	15
# offered a place on the wait list	1,241
% accepting a place on wait list	35
% admitted from wait list	7
# of early decision applicants	127
% accepted early decision	59

FIRST-YEAR PROFILE

Testing policy	Test Optional
Range SAT composite	1280–1430
Range SAT EBRW	660–740
Range SAT math	600–710
Range ACT composite	29–33
# submitting SAT scores	58
% submitting SAT scores	15
# submitting ACT scores	22
% submitting ACT scores	6
Average HS GPA	3.8
% frosh submitting high school GPA	84
% graduated top 10% of class	29
% graduated top 25% of class	55
% graduated top 50% of class	88

DEADLINES

Early decision	
Deadline	11/1
Notification	12/15
Other ED deadline	1/15
Other ED notification	2/15
Early action	
Deadline	11/1
Notification	12/15
Regular	
Deadline	1/15
Nonfall registration?	No

APPLICANTS ALSO LOOK AT

Bard College; Barnard College; Brown University; Fordham University; New York University; Oberlin College; Reed College; Smith College; University of California—Los Angeles; Vassar College

FINANCIAL FACTS

Financial Aid Rating	84
Annual tuition	$63,128
Room and board	$17,546
Required fees	$550
Books and supplies	$600
Average frosh need-based scholarship	$40,349
Average UG need-based scholarship	$35,307
% needy frosh rec. need-based scholarship or grant aid	100
% needy UG rec. need-based scholarship or grant aid	98
% needy frosh rec. non-need-based scholarship or grant aid	20
% needy UG rec. non-need-based scholarship or grant aid	18
% needy frosh rec. need-based self-help aid	78
% needy UG rec. need-based self-help aid	80
% frosh rec. any financial aid	84
% UG rec. any financial aid	82
% UG borrow to pay for school	57
Average cumulative indebtedness	$31,901
% frosh need fully met	22
% ugrads need fully met	21
Average % of frosh need met	86
Average % of ugrad need met	80

SCRIPPS COLLEGE

1030 Columbia Avenue, Claremont, CA 91711-3948 • Admissions: 909-621-8000

CAMPUS LIFE
Quality of Life Rating	91
Fire Safety Rating	96
Green Rating	60*
Type of school	Private
Affiliation	No Affiliation
Environment	Town

STUDENTS
Total undergrad enrollment	1,073
% male/female/another gender	0/100/NR
% from out of state	57
% frosh from public high school	55
% frosh live on campus	100
% ugrads live on campus	97
# of fraternities	0
# of sororities	0
% African American	4
% Asian	13
% White	54
% Hispanic	13
% Native American	0
% Pacific Islander	0
% Two or more races	11
% Race and/or ethnicity unknown	1
% international	3
# of countries represented	21

SURVEY SAYS . . .
Lots of liberal students
Students always studying
Students are happy
Classroom facilities are great
Lab facilities are great
Great library
Career services are great
Internships are widely available
Class discussions encouraged
Great financial aid
No one cheats
Students are friendly
Students aren't religious
Students environmentally aware
Great food on campus
Dorms are like palaces
Recreation facilities are great
Campus newspaper is popular
Active minority support groups
Students love Claremont, CA

ACADEMICS
Academic Rating	89
% students returning for sophomore year	91
% students graduating within 4 years	77
% students graduating within 6 years	84
Calendar	Semester
Student/faculty ratio	10:1
Profs interesting rating	95
Profs accessible rating	95
Most classes have 10–19 students.	

MOST POPULAR MAJORS
Research and Experimental Psychology, Other;
Political Science and Government, General

STUDENTS SAY ". . ."

Academics
Scripps College has an "absolutely gorgeous" campus and terrific Southern California vibes, but the reason applicants clamor to attend is because of its "dedication to empowering female voices and education." The focus may be on its "supportive, small community of women who want to fight to make the world a better place," but students won't have to worry about missing out on the resources often attributed to larger institutions, as Scripps is part of the Claremont Colleges, a consortium that grants undergraduates access "to all of the benefits and resources within [four] other colleges."

Access is key across the "challenging and engaging" academic offerings at Scripps, whether that's one-on-one time with professors or simply having opportunity for undergraduate research. This extends to "discussion-based [classes], which allows students to raise questions..., [gain] a better understanding of the course, and connect to the subject more intimately." It helps, too, that professors "are very good at creating interesting courses," and are "generally accepting of a wide range of student opinions, " though students should be aware that these freedoms come with "high expectations." Ultimately, what undergrads appreciate the most is that it's "very easy to form close connections with professors both in class and out of class."

Campus Life
Scripps students are fairly studious, and during the week you'll often find them congregating in one of the "many outdoor study spaces, such as courtyards, lawns, or the lounge chairs by the pool." Of course, there's lots of fun to be had beyond academics. For example, undergrads can take advantage of "a ton of free fitness courses on campus like CrossFit, yoga, and Zumba" as well as unique "intramural sports like inner-tube water polo." Additionally, "there are hundreds of clubs to join that are both specific to Scripps and also across all the Claremont Colleges" as well as school-sponsored "speakers, screenings, presentations, workshops, [and] de-stress activities." Should you need a respite from that overflowing campus life, the surrounding area provides many options. "The train to downtown Los Angeles is about a ten-minute walk away, Mt. Baldy is about a 20-minute drive, and the village in Claremont is filled with shops and eateries."

Student Body
When asked to describe their peers, Scripps undergrads are prone to using effusive adjectives such as "passionate, driven, [and] creative." Many students also "identify as liberal, feminist, [and] social-justice oriented." As one individual explains, "From reproductive rights, prison abolition, racial justice, everyone you talk to has the desire to change the world." Indeed, they are certainly "not afraid to let their voices be heard." A number of undergrads appreciate that the college attracts "many transgender and non-binary students, which creates a very open and safe environment." However, a few do caution that there is a little "tension between white feminism and intersectionality" on campus. Fortunately, most everyone enjoys the fact their classmates are often "intelligent and ready to have in-depth conversations about topics from politics to *The Bachelor* to data on climate change." Undergrads here also tend to be "very supportive of one another" and "very accepting" as well. In fact, when strolling through campus, it's even common to "receive smiles from students [you] don't know." All in all, the Scripps student body offers the "type of community that will cheer with and for you when you succeed and be a shoulder to cry on when needed."

SCRIPPS COLLEGE

Financial Aid: 909-621-8275 • E-Mail: admission@scrippscollege.edu • Website: www.scrippscollege.edu

THE PRINCETON REVIEW SAYS

Admissions

The school reports that its standardized testing policy for use in admission for Fall 2024 is Test Optional. The 2024 testing policy will be permanent. The Princeton Review suggests that interested applicants consult with the school for the most up-to-date standardized testing policies. *Very important factors considered include:* rigor of secondary school record, class rank, academic GPA, application essay, character/personal qualities. *Important factors considered include:* recommendation(s). *Other factors considered include:* standardized test scores, interview, extracurricular activities, talent/ability, first generation, alumni/ae relation, geographical residence, racial/ethnic status, volunteer work, work experience. High school diploma is required and GED is accepted. *Academic units required:* 4 English, 3 math, 3 science, 3 foreign language, 3 social studies.

Financial Aid

Students should submit: Business/Farm Supplement; CSS/Financial Aid Profile; FAFSA; Noncustodial Profile; State aid form. Priority filing deadline is 2/1. The Princeton Review suggests that all financial aid forms be submitted as soon as possible (see page 5 for a note on the FAFSA). *Need-based scholarships/grants offered:* College/university scholarship or grant aid from institutional funds; Federal Pell; Private scholarships; SEOG; State scholarships/grants. *Loan aid offered:* Direct PLUS loans; Direct Subsidized Loans; Direct Unsubsidized Loans; College/university loans from institutional funds. Admitted students will be notified of awards on or about 3/20. Federal Work-Study Program available. Institutional employment available.

The Inside Word

Admissions officers at Scripps truly strive to get to know each applicant. After all, they are looking for the students who will best complement the college and take advantage of the opportunities offered. Therefore, expect every part of your application to be carefully vetted. Your academic achievements will still hold the most weight, but your recommendations, personal statement, and extracurriculars are of great importance. Your scores, thanks to Scripps being Test Optional, should not affect your chances of gaining admission.

THE SCHOOL SAYS "..."

From the Admissions Office

"Scripps College, a top liberal arts college, offers students an experience that combines strong academic rigor in a powerful women's college community. At Scripps, students thrive in an intellectually challenging yet collaborative environment where undergraduate research and critical thinking are top priorities. Scripps' faculty are distinguished teachers and leaders who are experts in their field, and classes are purposefully small (an average of sixteen students or fewer) to promote discussion and debate. The College's Core Curriculum in Interdisciplinary Humanities is a three-semester interdisciplinary program that provides a common academic experience for students. As they explore provocative and relevant topics, Scripps students gain a foundation for critical thinking, writing, and dialogue. Students have access to more than sixty majors, including a number of joint and intercollegiate programs, and all Scripps students complete a semester- or year-long senior thesis project. Sixty percent of students study abroad, more than 80 percent hold at least one internship, and students can participate in eleven NCAA Division III sports. Scripps is a member of The Claremont Colleges, a consortium of five prestigious undergraduate institutions all located within walking distance, and two distinguished graduate institutions. The Claremont Colleges provide an integrated academic and residential experience with many shared clubs and organizations, student services, and facilities. Scripps College meets 100 percent of demonstrated financial need for admitted students who submit the FAFSA and CSS/Profile and all first-year applicants are considered for scholarships ranging from $15,000–$30,000 annually."

SELECTIVITY

Admissions Rating	95
# of applicants	3,099
% of applicants accepted	28
% of acceptees attending	30
# offered a place on the wait list	722
% accepting a place on wait list	50
% admitted from wait list	2
# of early decision applicants	265
% accepted early decision	40

FIRST-YEAR PROFILE

Testing policy	Test Optional
Range SAT composite	1410–1510
Range SAT EBRW	710–760
Range SAT math	680–750
Range ACT composite	32–34
# submitting SAT scores	83
% submitting SAT scores	32
# submitting ACT scores	41
% submitting ACT scores	16
Average HS GPA	4.3
% frosh submitting high school GPA	100
% graduated top 10% of class	70
% graduated top 25% of class	94
% graduated top 50% of class	100

DEADLINES

Early decision	
Deadline	11/15
Notification	12/15
Other ED deadline	1/5
Other ED notification	2/15
Regular	
Deadline	1/5
Notification	4/1
Nonfall registration?	No

APPLICANTS ALSO LOOK AT

Pomona College; Smith College; University of California—Berkeley; University of California—Los Angeles; University of California—San Diego; University of Southern California; Wellesley College

FINANCIAL FACTS

Financial Aid Rating	96
Annual tuition	$60,494
Room and board	$19,818
Required fees	$218
Books and supplies	$800
Average frosh need-based scholarship	$43,073
Average UG need-based scholarship	$44,533
% needy frosh rec. need-based scholarship or grant aid	100
% needy UG rec. need-based scholarship or grant aid	100
% needy frosh rec. non-need-based scholarship or grant aid	0
% needy UG rec. non-need-based scholarship or grant aid	0
% needy frosh rec. need-based self-help aid	67
% needy UG rec. need-based self-help aid	72
% UG borrow to pay for school	28
Average cumulative indebtedness	$17,171
% frosh need fully met	100
% ugrads need fully met	100
Average % of frosh need met	100
Average % of ugrad need met	100

SEATTLE UNIVERSITY

901 12th Ave, Seattle, WA 98122-1090 • Admissions: 206-296-6000 • Fax: 206-296-5656

STUDENTS SAY "..."

Academics

Seattle University is renowned for its excellent academics and programs, particularly its nursing program, and its Jesuit philosophy of holistic education underscores the mission of the university. The 4,100 undergraduates are required to take a collection of Core classes that are more than "just a random collection of math, writing, and social science classes. There's a lot more philosophy, theology, psychology, ethics, and actual service learning" involved, and students say that "often times the Core classes that [they are] required to take ended up being the most memorable classes." The dynamic professors "ensure the students have a chance not only to digest and memorize the information but also a chance to critically think about it and discuss different viewpoints." The university's commitment to social justice is "more than just rhetoric—there are classes structured around specific kinds of service learning." There is a growing sentiment "that SU is increasingly known for the Albers School of Business [and Economics]." Overall, students feel that Seattle U "is about finding community in a large city, and being able to discuss and have deep meaningful conversations about the issues we encounter in our everyday lives."

Campus Life

It's "very much a city lifestyle" at Seattle U; "however, the mountains are not too far away." Here "you have the best of both worlds. You can go to happy hours, brunch, clubs, bars and restaurants, hiking, skiing, canoeing, and swimming in the summer. There is a lot to do in the area." In fact, "as soon as you step off campus, you are in the hustle and bustle of Capitol Hill, a booming, youthful neighborhood that is LGBT friendly. There are coffee shops... concert venues, and parks within a two-block radius." It's "a quick bus ride to downtown and Pike Place Market or a nice half-hour walk. [The International District] is nearby too." And it's fine if you don't feel like walking because "the university loans out bus passes free of charge." Living in the heart of Seattle means that you can never run out of fun things to do on weekends. You could "see plays, go to the Seattle Art Museum, eat all sorts of different types of food, hang out in the International District, [or] attend film festivals. You name it, Seattle has it!" The campus is "super green," providing students with "composting and recycling options in every location possible." The food is not only "delicious," but is largely "locally grown, organic, and well-prepared."

Student Body

As "one of the most liberal Catholic schools," Seattle University is a place where "all faiths are not only accepted, but they are welcomed and encouraged." The "majority of students are liberal," and "everyone is aware of social issues." There is a "very large LGBTQ community" on campus, as well as "lots of international students." At Seattle U, students "frequently discuss gender norms, privilege, and how race influences identity. Identity is a popular topic of discussion—how we all use who we are to impact how we interact in the world." Here, "students are creative, insightful, and dedicated to making their educational experience unique and personal. Community is strongly felt [among] students and staff."

SEATTLE UNIVERSITY

Financial Aid: 206-296-8020 • E-Mail: admissions@seattleu.edu • Website: www.seattleu.edu

THE PRINCETON REVIEW SAYS

Admissions

The school reports that its standardized testing policy for use in admission for Fall 2024 is Test Optional. It is unknown at this time if the 2024 testing policy will be permanent. The Princeton Review suggests that interested applicants consult with the school for the most up-to-date standardized testing policies. *Very important factors considered include:* rigor of secondary school record, academic GPA, character/personal qualities. *Important factors considered include:* application essay, recommendation(s), extracurricular activities, level of applicant's interest. *Other factors considered include:* class rank, standardized test scores, interview, talent/ability, first generation, alumni/ae relation, geographical residence, state residency, religious affiliation/commitment, racial/ethnic status, volunteer work, work experience. High school diploma is required and GED is accepted. *Academic units required:* 4 English, 3 math, 2 science, 2 science labs, 2 foreign language, 3 social studies, 1 history, 2 academic electives.

Financial Aid

Students should submit: FAFSA. Priority filing deadline is 2/1. The Princeton Review suggests that all financial aid forms be submitted as soon as possible (see page 5 for a note on the FAFSA). *Need-based scholarships/grants offered:* College/university scholarship or grant aid from institutional funds; Federal Nursing Scholarships; Federal Pell; Private scholarships; SEOG; State scholarships/grants. *Loan aid offered:* Direct PLUS loans; Direct Subsidized Loans; Direct Unsubsidized Loans; Federal Nursing Loans. Admitted students will be notified of awards on a rolling basis beginning 3/1. Federal Work-Study Program available. Institutional employment available.

The Inside Word

At this Jesuit Catholic school, admissions officers tend to value community service as well as overall "life experience." Those who demonstrate a significant commitment to volunteerism will find themselves at an advantage, as will those who convey a clear sense of their academic and career goals. Applicants should keep in mind that Seattle University has more stringent course work requirements for certain majors.

THE SCHOOL SAYS "..."

From the Admissions Office

"Students who are adventurous, forward-thinking, creative, and have an interest in social justice are drawn to Seattle University, located in the heart of a city with unparalleled access to innovation, technology, the arts and culture. Personalized learning—with an 11:1 student-faculty ratio—provides opportunities for research alongside accomplished faculty. Internships and community engagement give students relevant experience for their resumes and the chance to be noticed by some of the world's most influential nonprofits and companies that call the Seattle area home, such as Microsoft, the Gates Foundation, Starbucks, Amazon, Boeing and Costco. Seattle U is a school of action with an ever-growing impact on the city, the region and throughout the world. In Washington state, where dozens of different languages are spoken and every race, religion and perspective is represented, Seattle U's nearly 4,100 undergraduate students from 53 states and territories and 89 nations fit right in. Service is a cornerstone of the Seattle U experience with four out of five students participating in some form of service learning—that's nearly 3× the national average. That spirit is especially visible in the Seattle University Youth Initiative. As the university's largest-ever community engagement project, the Youth Initiative is transforming lives of Seattle's underserved children while becoming a model of service.

"Discover Seattle University's sustainable campus, which is pesticide-free and wins top awards for its environmental leadership and energy conservation. The urban campus is woven into Seattle's thriving Capitol Hill neighborhood, which abounds with culture and entertainment options."

SELECTIVITY

Admissions Rating	84
# of applicants	7,934
% of applicants accepted	85
% of acceptees attending	15
# offered a place on the wait list	309
% accepting a place on wait list	39
% admitted from wait list	100

FIRST-YEAR PROFILE

Testing policy	Test Optional
Range SAT composite	1160–1360
Range SAT EBRW	580–690
Range SAT math	570–690
Range ACT composite	24–30
# submitting SAT scores	240
% submitting SAT scores	24
# submitting ACT scores	103
% submitting ACT scores	11
Average HS GPA	3.6
% frosh submitting high school GPA	100
% graduated top 10% of class	20
% graduated top 25% of class	53
% graduated top 50% of class	85

DEADLINES

Early action	
Deadline	11/15
Notification	12/23
Regular	
Priority	11/15
Deadline	1/15
Notification	Rolling, 3/1
Nonfall registration?	Yes

FINANCIAL FACTS

Financial Aid Rating	83
Annual tuition	$50,328
Room and board	$13,524
Required fees	$946
Books and supplies	$900
Average frosh need-based scholarship	$44,319
Average UG need-based scholarship	$35,046
% needy frosh rec. need-based scholarship or grant aid	53
% needy UG rec. need-based scholarship or grant aid	75
% needy frosh rec. non-need-based scholarship or grant aid	98
% needy UG rec. non-need-based scholarship or grant aid	95
% needy frosh rec. need-based self-help aid	69
% needy UG rec. need-based self-help aid	68
% frosh rec. any financial aid	98
% UG rec. any financial aid	86
% UG borrow to pay for school	74
Average cumulative indebtedness	$24,995
% frosh need fully met	28
% ugrads need fully met	27
Average % of frosh need met	82
Average % of ugrad need met	80

SETON HALL UNIVERSITY

400 South Orange Avenue, South Orange, NJ 07079 • Admissions: 973-313-6146 • Fax: 973-313-2321

CAMPUS LIFE

Quality of Life Rating	84
Fire Safety Rating	91
Green Rating	60*
Type of school	Private
Affiliation	Roman Catholic
Environment	Village

STUDENTS

Total undergrad enrollment	5,874
% male/female/another gender	45/55/NR
% from out of state	24
% frosh live on campus	61
% ugrads live on campus	36
# of fraternities (% join)	12 (5)
# of sororities (% join)	12 (8)
% African American	10
% Asian	11
% White	47
% Hispanic	23
% Native American	<1
% Pacific Islander	<1
% Two or more races	4
% Race and/or ethnicity unknown	2
% international	1
# of countries represented	65

SURVEY SAYS . . .

Easy to get around campus
College radio is popular
Everyone loves the Pirates

ACADEMICS

Academic Rating	80
% students returning for sophomore year	83
% students graduating within 4 years	66
% students graduating within 6 years	72
Calendar	Semester
Student/faculty ratio	14:1
Profs interesting rating	87
Profs accessible rating	91

Most classes have 10–19 students.
Most lab/discussion sessions have
  10–19 students.

MOST POPULAR MAJORS

Biology/Biological Sciences, General; Registered
Nursing/Registered Nurse; Finance, General

STUDENTS SAY ". . ."

Academics

Founded in 1856, New Jersey's Seton Hall University is a Catholic school offering students "a chance at an affordable, quality college education" composed of challenging coursework and a "diversity of programming." The school "has a very high employment rate," and "the financial aid is wonderful." Seton Hall also features an "excellent career center," making for a good return on investment. Building on that, the proximity to New York City (about 15 miles away) helps in the "abundance of available internships" and "the opportunity to network with Seton Hall alumni [who] are now business professionals." The Honors Program "is very thorough and well put together," the business and nursing schools are notably strong, and the school has done its share of innovating by adding features such as "one-day classes for credit, tech courses online, and money management courses," as well as group-oriented sessions where students "are allowed to stand up and freely discuss the topic at hand" rather than "being bound to a desk."

Professors are "usually experts [in] their fields" who "bring their experience into the classroom," although some students note there are a handful of "weaker professors." Accessibility is important to the faculty, and "if their office hours don't work for you, they'll come up with an alternate time or even give out their cell or suggest a Skype session." There are also "plenty of opportunities to connect with peers and find the academic help that you need" via the Academic Resource Center (ARC) and the Writing Center.

Campus Life

This is an academically serious group that also makes time for "lots of outings to NYC and events on campus." The "environment and energy" at athletic games "draws people together," and the school "has extensive programming that allows opportunities for cultural, social, and service oriented events" while "always [providing] fun things to do on the green when the weather is nice." After class ends, many students "meet up together for lunch on or off campus" or work out; "the Rec Center is always bustling with yoga classes or intramural sports." People generally "fill their days by hanging out in various spots on campus like lounges in the dorms, the dining hall, The Cove, the Living Room, or the library." Some mention the areas around campus "can make students feel unsafe traveling off campus," but note that it's "not unsafe as long as [you are] using common sense." Weekends can involve "various social activities exclusive to Greek life, trips hosted by the Student Activities Board into New York City, as well as club events hosted on campus." In addition, "there are so many different clubs or organizations that allow each student to find their place on campus."

Student Body

This is a "big name and small community atmosphere" in which the "empowered and ambitious students" are "fairly diverse in regards to race" and "eager to jump start their careers." "Christianity is the dominant faith" and Seton Hall's "Catholic values bring in a large range of religious students." One student adds, "It is very easy to build relationships and make connections with people outside your particular field of study." Another goes on to describe the overall feel of campus: "There's never a time I'm on campus where I don't see a friendly face," says a student, and others note that "there's a general familial air around campus." Since the campus draws many students, "there is a heavy commuter population," but those living on campus "are often members of Greek life or have a leadership position in clubs."

SETON HALL UNIVERSITY

Financial Aid: 800-222-7183 • E-Mail: thehall@shu.edu • Website: admissions.shu.edu/

THE PRINCETON REVIEW SAYS

Admissions

The school reports that its standardized testing policy for use in admission for Fall 2024 is Test Optional. The policy will be in place through 2026. The Princeton Review suggests that interested applicants consult with the school for the most up-to-date standardized testing policies. *Very important factors considered include:* rigor of secondary school record, academic GPA, application essay, recommendation(s), level of applicant's interest. *Important factors considered include:* extracurricular activities. *Other factors considered include:* class rank, standardized test scores, interview, talent/ability, character/personal qualities, alumni/ae relation. High school diploma is required and GED is accepted. *Academic units required:* 4 English, 3 math, 1 science, 1 science lab, 2 foreign language, 2 social studies, 4 academic electives.

Financial Aid

Students should submit: FAFSA. The Princeton Review suggests that all financial aid forms be submitted as soon as possible (see page 5 for a note on the FAFSA). *Need-based scholarships/grants offered:* . *Loan aid offered:* . Admitted students will be notified of awards on a rolling basis. Federal Work-Study Program available. Institutional employment available.

The Inside Word

Seton Hall accepts both its own online application and the Common Application. Students with reasonably solid high school transcripts and strong recommendations won't have trouble getting in, and Seton Hall makes an effort to sweeten the deal financially for standout students: generally, the higher a student's academic standing, the higher the scholarship award.

THE SCHOOL SAYS "..."

From the Admissions Office

"A leading Catholic university since 1856, Seton Hall educates great minds like in a challenging, supportive and rigorous environment. With approximately 6,000 undergraduate students and a 14:1 student to faculty ratio, students develop a mentoring relationship with faculty. At Seton Hall, students have unprecedented access to research, conferences, clinicals, corporate mentors, internships, study abroad and many other hands-on learning opportunities as early as freshman year. Located just 14 miles from New York City in suburban South Orange, New Jersey, Seton Hall benefits from all the opportunities the Big Apple has to offer. Seton Hall is ranked No. 4 in the nation for providing internships by *The International Business Times*. Graduates also have 50 percent higher mid-career earnings than the national average. Seton Hall offers over 17,000 internships. Students have found internships or employment upon graduation at Goldman Sachs, CNN, Pfizer, Google, the United Nations, ABC, NBC, CBS, Lockheed Martin, Morgan Stanley, *The Wall Street Journal*, HBO, Amazon, Prudential, Lincoln Center, Standard and Poor's, The State Department and *The New York Times*, as well as acclaimed hospitals, schools and nonprofit organizations. Seton Hall has been rated as one of the best schools for a return on investment and for having the highest paid graduates for the investment. Seton Hall also provides more than $130 million dollars a year in scholarships and grants to students; 98 percent of students receive some form of financial assistance from the University."

SELECTIVITY

Admissions Rating	86
# of applicants	25,732
% of applicants accepted	75
% of acceptees attending	8
# offered a place on the wait list	4,991
% admitted from wait list	26

FIRST-YEAR PROFILE

Testing policy	Test Optional
Range SAT composite	1240–1380
Range SAT EBRW	620–700
Range SAT math	610–690
Range ACT composite	28–31
# submitting SAT scores	363
% submitting SAT scores	24
# submitting ACT scores	82
% submitting ACT scores	5
Average HS GPA	3.7
% frosh submitting high school GPA	100
% graduated top 10% of class	31
% graduated top 25% of class	57
% graduated top 50% of class	86

DEADLINES

Early action	
Deadline	12/15
Notification	1/31
Regular	
Priority	12/15
Deadline	3/1
Nonfall registration?	Yes

APPLICANTS OFTEN PREFER

Kean University; Montclair State University; Pennsylvania State University - McKeesport Campus; Rutgers University—New Brunswick; The College of New Jersey

APPLICANTS SOMETIMES PREFER

Fordham University; Monmouth University (NJ); New York University; Ramapo College of New Jersey; William Paterson University

APPLICANTS RARELY PREFER

Felician University; Saint Joseph's University (PA); The George Washington University

FINANCIAL FACTS

Financial Aid Rating	64
Annual tuition	$46,380
Room and board	$17,482
Required fees	$2,580
Books and supplies	$1,000

SIENA COLLEGE

515 Loudon Road, Loudonville, NY 12211-1462 • Admissions: 518-783-2300 • Fax: 518-783-2436

STUDENTS SAY "..."

Academics

There are multiple pathways to success for students at Siena College, as evidenced by the nursing program's BS and dual RN/BS options. The school also boasts a career-oriented focus that is aided by the school's easy access to Albany, the capital of New York State. Students in the well-regarded pre-law program, for instance, appreciate "getting to hear from attorneys in the Capital Region." Students also speak to the school's inclusive attitude, which presents valuable viewpoints, like "an LGBTQIA+ seminar on...trans individuals in medicine that I thought was really insightful." Having opportunities to "work outside in a garden collecting and harvesting our own herbs to use in an infusion" creates hands-on experiences, and, according to one student, allows them "to be impartial in the decision making of my patients."

Academic choice extends to the "phenomenal" study abroad options: "There is an extremely wide array of programs to choose from, and the staff at Siena helps and encourages you every step of the way." Even those normally outside of traditional study abroad programs have opportunities to travel: "I took a travel course to Ireland. We learned all about Irish literature and history and traveled to places that represented our studies over the course of ten days." In all, Siena helps students to practice and succeed.

Campus Life

"We have a saying that 'Siena Saints don't sit on the sidelines,'" says one senior. "This means that we are active in making our school and community a better and safer place to live, play, and learn." Saints play within 22 Division I athletic programs, and basketball games are a campus favorite. "I love to go to the basketball games with my friends," raves one third year student. Siena even provides transportation to home basketball games in downtown Albany through a popular on-campus club, Dog Pound. "Sports, whether playing for the school or club, are...very popular to play and watch!" explains one sophomore.

Outside of athletics, Saints enjoy being of service to the greater Albany community. Habitat for Humanity and the Bonner Service Leaders Program, where students' academic work is matched with nonprofit organizations in Albany, are common favorites. At Siena, "students can participate in volunteer work, service trips, and community service projects, which provide them with opportunities to make a positive impact on their community." Given the student involvement, it is unsurprising—but satisfying—to hear Siena described as a "really beautiful campus" filled with "green spaces" where "the energy is always positive." One student offers the perfect glimpse of Siena in a nutshell: "the Student Union is always full of peers studying, chatting or grabbing food, and it's very easy to make friends!"

Student Body

"The small size of the student population creates a tight-knit and supportive community," agree many students on campus. Notes another, "there is a diverse community supported by the [Franciscan] Friars." To help support bonds with the "large commuter population," the school also hosts regular on-campus events, such as monthly lunches. Not that students need the help! Many note that "holding doors, smiling at people, and...saying hello" are common courtesies on campus. And one senior fondly recalls that "one of the first things I noticed ... is that when one of my peers saw me carrying large boxes to move in, they held the door for me even though I was far away. The "thoughtful actions, kind hearts, and warm smiles" of the student body are just a few of the reasons why students say things like, "I wake up each day and am grateful that I decided to go to Siena College."

SIENA COLLEGE

Financial Aid: 518-783-2427 • E-Mail: admissions@siena.edu • Website: www.siena.edu/

THE PRINCETON REVIEW SAYS

Admissions

The school reports that its standardized testing policy for use in admission for Fall 2024 is Test Optional. The 2024 testing policy will be permanent. The Princeton Review suggests that interested applicants consult with the school for the most up-to-date standardized testing policies. *Very important factors considered include:* rigor of secondary school record, academic GPA. *Important factors considered include:* recommendation(s), interview. *Other factors considered include:* class rank, standardized test scores, application essay, extracurricular activities, talent/ability, character/personal qualities, first generation, alumni/ae relation, geographical residence, racial/ethnic status, volunteer work, work experience, level of applicant's interest. High school diploma is required and GED is accepted. *Academic units required:* 4 English, 3 math, 3 science, 3 science labs, 2 foreign language, 2 social studies, 2 history. *Academic units recommended:* 4 English, 4 math, 4 science, 4 science labs, 3 foreign language, 2 social studies, 2 history.

Financial Aid

Students should submit: FAFSA; State aid form. Priority filing deadline is 11/15. The Princeton Review suggests that all financial aid forms be submitted as soon as possible (see page 5 for a note on the FAFSA). *Need-based scholarships/grants offered:* College/university scholarship or grant aid from institutional funds; Federal Pell; Private scholarships; SEOG; State scholarships/grants. *Loan aid offered:* Direct PLUS loans; Direct Subsidized Loans; Direct Unsubsidized Loans. Admitted students will be notified of awards on a rolling basis beginning 12/1. Federal Work-Study Program available. Institutional employment available.

The Inside Word

The admissions process at Siena is fairly stringent. With a 81 percent acceptance rate and an average SAT score of 1160 (currently optional) for incoming first years, admissions officers look for a strong academic record. Academic interests and extracurricular activities also play a role. Prior to applying, a campus tour or participation in an admissions program is strongly encouraged.

THE SCHOOL SAYS "..."

From the Admissions Office

"Located in Loudonville, New York—just 10 minutes from the state capital of Albany —the Siena experience is built for a new generation of leaders. The College offers a wide range of scholarship and financial aid opportunities, as well as customized internships. After all, a Siena education isn't something you get, it's something you get to do. Our 3,500 Saints have endless ways to reach their personal and professional goals and engage personally with top professors in a dynamic, customized learning environment. From internships to research to service, they get real world experience now, not later. The result: sought-after graduates prepared to succeed in an ever-changing global society. Hundreds of student life options ranging from Red Cross to rugby join with Siena's Division I athletic program to provide students the opportunity to get in the game, whatever their interests may be. Extensive study abroad programs and immersive service programs allow for discovery and reflection. Saints learn to lead by putting others first, thinking creatively, and developing innovative solutions in pursuit of the greater good. And it's what connects them to Siena, and each other, forever."

SELECTIVITY
Admissions Rating	85
# of applicants	9,466
% of applicants accepted	71
% of acceptees attending	13
# offered a place on the wait list	214
% accepting a place on wait list	95
% admitted from wait list	1

FIRST-YEAR PROFILE
Testing policy	Test Optional
Range SAT composite	1050–1260
Range SAT EBRW	525–640
Range SAT math	520–630
Range ACT composite	22–31
# submitting SAT scores	265
% submitting SAT scores	31
# submitting ACT scores	33
% submitting ACT scores	4
Average HS GPA	3.5
% frosh submitting high school GPA	100
% graduated top 10% of class	17
% graduated top 25% of class	46
% graduated top 50% of class	80

DEADLINES
Early decision	
Deadline	12/1
Notification	1/1
Early action	
Deadline	10/15
Notification	1/7
Regular	
Priority	10/15
Deadline	2/15
Notification	3/15
Nonfall registration?	Yes

APPLICANTS OFTEN PREFER
Marist College; Sacred Heart University; State University of New York—Binghamton University; State University of New York--University at Buffalo; University at Albany - SUNY; University of Connecticut

APPLICANTS SOMETIMES PREFER
Le Moyne College; State University of New York at Cortland; SUNY College at Oneonta

APPLICANTS RARELY PREFER
Quinnipiac University; St. John's University (NY); State University of New York at New Paltz; State University of New York—Stony Brook University

FINANCIAL FACTS
Financial Aid Rating	85
Annual tuition	$42,580
Room and board	$16,705
Required fees	$300
Required fees (first-year)	$1,075
Books and supplies	$1,293
Average frosh need-based scholarship	$27,218
Average UG need-based scholarship	$25,705
% needy frosh rec. need-based scholarship or grant aid	100
% needy UG rec. need-based scholarship or grant aid	99
% needy frosh rec. non-need-based scholarship or grant aid	97
% needy UG rec. non-need-based scholarship or grant aid	94
% needy frosh rec. need-based self-help aid	69
% needy UG rec. need-based self-help aid	70
% frosh rec. any financial aid	98
% UG rec. any financial aid	94
% UG borrow to pay for school	73
Average cumulative indebtedness	$39,057
% frosh need fully met	37
% ugrads need fully met	36
Average % of frosh need met	73
Average % of ugrad need met	72

SIMMONS UNIVERSITY

300 The Fenway, Boston, MA 02115 • Admissions: 617-521-2000

STUDENTS SAY ". . ."

Academics

Located in the middle of Boston, the women's-centered Simmons University is a liberal arts center, offering its 1,800 undergraduates more than sixty majors and programs, including a well-known nursing school. Some courses require field trips and city exploration or internships relevant to the course, while others involve projects that "place students in volunteering jobs to work with the surrounding communities." "Classes involve significant amounts of discussions and presentations," and with small class sizes, students generally get to know all of their peers. Similarly, students enjoy "the ability to create strong personal relationships with professors and advisors" and say that teachers "truly are there for you as human beings, not just professors."

The workload is "heavy, but always doable" at Simmons, and clinicals tend to let students in earlier than many other schools would. "Labs go above and beyond" here, and the school incorporates video lectures into its courses "so that class periods can be more discussion-based." One student says, "Even as a first-year I have already been given multiple research opportunities that amaze and excite me." There are many accelerated programs to which undergraduate students can apply in order to achieve a graduate degree at a faster rate (many at Simmons go on to graduate school), and employers are well-aware of the school's curriculum, which requires every student to partake in "at least one internship, clinical, research [project], or other type of real-world learning." "When I say I attend Simmons, people know I have received a quality education," says a student.

Campus Life

There are two campuses at Simmons: academic and residential. The academic campus has "lots of places to study," such as the library, multicultural center, and cafés, but most students stay on the residential campus when classes aren't going on, and more than half live there. Most in this "nomadic bunch" like to use their free time to explore Boston and surrounding neighborhoods, including nearby Fenway Park. "I spend my days living my best city life," says a student. There are no parties on this "very academics-oriented" campus, especially given the "strict drug and alcohol policy." This is a campus of "all-around intellectuals who are serious about their careers after university [who] will more likely be found studying than partying." A lot of students work "either on campus or in hospitals or restaurants." Boston sporting events are popular pastimes, as is going to the gym, and "there is always something to do off campus." Almost all students go out into the city only on weekends, as "there usually isn't anything going on on-campus," and they get discounts or free admission to many events or institutions, like the Museum of Fine Arts and the Isabella Stewart Gardener Museum, "both of which are right down the street from campus."

Student Body

The women here are "generally highly liberal and outspoken," and "you have to find your niche." Students at Simmons are typically "advocates for a number of causes" and are extremely political. A huge number are healthcare majors, and everyone is "incredibly passionate and intelligent [and] invested in the community." This group is "very centered around acceptance of various identities as well as female empowerment," and "there is a theme of personal growth reflected in the gender identity."

Financial Aid: 617-521-2037 • E-Mail: ugadm@simmons.edu • Website: www.simmons.edu

THE PRINCETON REVIEW SAYS

Admissions

The school reports that its standardized testing policy for use in admission for Fall 2024 is Test Optional. It is unknown at this time if the 2024 testing policy will be permanent. The Princeton Review suggests that interested applicants consult with the school for the most up-to-date standardized testing policies. *Very important factors considered include:* rigor of secondary school record, academic GPA, application essay, recommendation(s). *Other factors considered include:* class rank, standardized test scores, interview, extracurricular activities, volunteer work, work experience. High school diploma is required and GED is accepted. *Academic units required:* 4 English, 4 math, 3 science, 3 foreign language, 3 social studies, 3 history.

Financial Aid

Students should submit: FAFSA. Priority filing deadline is 12/1. The Princeton Review suggests that all financial aid forms be submitted as soon as possible (see page 5 for a note on the FAFSA). *Need-based scholarships/grants offered:* College/university scholarship or grant aid from institutional funds; Federal Pell; Private scholarships; SEOG; State scholarships/grants. *Loan aid offered:* Direct PLUS loans; Direct Subsidized Loans; Direct Unsubsidized Loans; College/university loans from institutional funds. Admitted students will be notified of awards on a rolling basis. Federal Work-Study Program available. Institutional employment available.

The Inside Word

Simmons evaluates prospective students on both academic strength and personal qualities, including community involvement or leadership. Applicants to Simmons should use their personal essays, letters of recommendation, and applications to show the admissions committee who they are as a person. Although a personal interview isn't required, it can be a great way to augment your application, as well as a chance to experience the unique environment at Simmons.

THE SCHOOL SAYS "..."

From the Admissions Office

"Simmons University offers a transformative education that combines liberal arts, science, and the professions. We empower students who are intellectually curious, ambitious, and socially conscious to become everyday leaders in their careers, communities, and beyond.

"Located in the heart of Boston, Simmons is best known for its small classes, access to faculty, and internship and research opportunities. Students say that Simmons's location offers the best of both worlds—an intimate college experience in the heart of a vibrant city. Simmons's nearly 2,000 undergraduates love the fact that they can easily access the city's rich social and cultural resources but also come home to a safe, friendly campus.

"Simmons offers a learning experience that is highly collaborative and much more personal than that of large universities. Simmons professors include distinguished researchers, published authors, Fulbright scholars, health professionals, and community leaders. Seventy percent of faculty are women, and nearly 100 percent hold a terminal degree. They advise numerous government, nonprofit, and corporate organizations in the United States and in the world.

"To help students succeed, career support starts as soon as students step on campus and continues as an ongoing, lifelong service. Ninety-one percent of Simmons graduates are employed or in graduate school within six months of graduation. As the only women's university in Boston, employers see Simmons as a beacon of leadership with a reputation for professionalism and well-prepared graduates."

SELECTIVITY

Admissions Rating	86
# of applicants	4,001
% of applicants accepted	76
% of acceptees attending	13

FIRST-YEAR PROFILE

Testing policy	Test Optional
Range SAT composite	1190–1350
Range SAT EBRW	610–700
Range SAT math	590–690
Range ACT composite	28–35.25
# submitting SAT scores	67
% submitting SAT scores	17
# submitting ACT scores	16
% submitting ACT scores	4
Average HS GPA	3.8
% frosh submitting high school GPA	100
% graduated top 10% of class	24
% graduated top 25% of class	60
% graduated top 50% of class	90

DEADLINES

Early action	
Deadline	11/1
Notification	12/15
Regular	
Priority	2/1
Notification	Rolling, 12/15
Nonfall registration?	Yes

APPLICANTS OFTEN PREFER

Boston University; Mount Holyoke College; Northeastern University

APPLICANTS SOMETIMES PREFER

Regis College; Stonehill College; University of Massachusetts—Boston; Wheaton College (MA)

FINANCIAL FACTS

Financial Aid Rating	85
Annual tuition	$43,060
Room and board	$16,368
Required fees	$5,561
Books and supplies	$1,280
Average frosh need-based scholarship	$36,044
Average UG need-based scholarship	$35,179
% needy frosh rec. need-based scholarship or grant aid	100
% needy UG rec. need-based scholarship or grant aid	99
% needy frosh rec. non-need-based scholarship or grant aid	17
% needy UG rec. non-need-based scholarship or grant aid	12
% needy frosh rec. need-based self-help aid	80
% needy UG rec. need-based self-help aid	83
% frosh rec. any financial aid	100
% UG rec. any financial aid	99
% UG borrow to pay for school	69
Average cumulative indebtedness	$36,358
% frosh need fully met	23
% ugrads need fully met	21
Average % of frosh need met	87
Average % of ugrad need met	87

SKIDMORE COLLEGE

815 North Broadway, Saratoga Springs, NY 12866-1632 • Admissions: 518-580-5000 • Fax: 518-580-5584

CAMPUS LIFE

Quality of Life Rating	95
Fire Safety Rating	98
Green Rating	97
Type of school	Private
Affiliation	No Affiliation
Environment	Town

STUDENTS

Total undergrad enrollment	2,744
% male/female/another gender	41/59/NR
% from out of state	66
% frosh from public high school	57
% frosh live on campus	99
% ugrads live on campus	87
# of fraternities	0
# of sororities	0
% African American	4
% Asian	6
% White	63
% Hispanic	10
% Native American	<1
% Pacific Islander	<1
% Two or more races	6
% Race and/or ethnicity unknown	2
% international	9
# of countries represented	65

SURVEY SAYS . . .

Lots of liberal students
Students are happy
Great library
Internships are widely available
Great financial aid
Students aren't religious
Students environmentally aware
Students love Saratoga Springs, NY
Great food on campus
Great off-campus food
Dorms are like palaces
Easy to get around campus
Theater is popular
College radio is popular

ACADEMICS

Academic Rating	89
% students returning for sophomore year	88
% students graduating within 4 years	81
% students graduating within 6 years	84
Calendar	Semester
Student/faculty ratio	8:1
Profs interesting rating	92
Profs accessible rating	95

Most classes have 10–19 students.
Most lab/discussion sessions have
10–19 students.

MOST POPULAR MAJORS

Psychology, General; Business/Commerce, General;
Political Science and Government, General

STUDENTS SAY "..."

Academics

Just 30 miles north of Albany lies Skidmore College, a small liberal arts school that is home to around 2,500 students. Skidmore thrives on combining academics with creative expression, and the school works to cultivate students who want to explore ideas across traditional disciplinary boundaries. "The pursuit of knowledge is valued here," says a student, so "you won't be barred from an academic department just because you aren't enrolled in it." Another student states that the school is "excellent when it comes to every path or field of study," and "you can pursue everything you are interested in." This all happens in classrooms run by "very helpful, understanding, motivating," and "understanding faculty who know that we are human beings before we are students." Students also enjoy "small class sizes [that] allow for the formation of impactful and lasting relationships." Furthermore, "all teachers are accessible outside the classroom," which helps teaching extend beyond the traditional four walls. Other examples of this include "environmental studies [classes that] take place in the North Woods" and an artist interview class "in which each student chooses an artist they admire and [interview] that artist." One student sums up the Skidmore academic experience by saying, "Learning feels important and productive toward society."

Campus Life

People "are constantly on the go at Skidmore," but this "doesn't mean that students…don't take care of themselves." A typical day involves "going to classes, eating meals with friends,…meeting for a group project, studying in the library, maybe [taking] a nap, and getting outdoors." The outdoorsy crowd finds great joy with the Adirondack Mountains and Lake George being just about an hour away. Those looking to stay a little closer to campus also have options: Saratoga Springs, which some call "an amazing town" to be near, is just a ten-minute walk from campus. And Boston, New York City, and Montreal are just a few hours away as well. Regardless of whether they're spent on campus or off, days are "always full of activity and connection," and there are more than 100 student clubs and organizations, making it "easy to integrate and be part of the community." Those clubs "host tons of lectures and events for students," and "the arts are a huge strength at Skidmore." Anywhere you look, "students are constantly collaborating and playing shows," and there is "a good culture of attending events on campus and supporting the student body."

Student Body

This is an "active and involved" student body, with the average Skidmore student having "at least a major and a minor [and getting] involved in multiple clubs, [while] probably working more than one job as well." One member of this "well-rounded and over accomplished" group says, "Skidmore is the school for students who want to do it all." Plus, it's a place where everyone is "super welcoming and friendly" with a student body that "puts the 'liberal' in liberal arts." That's all representative of the "drive for creativity" on campus and the fact that students "support creativity in one another." As one student jokes, "there are more shades of hair here (mostly unnatural) than there are people." But despite any differences, everyone at Skidmore "has 'their people' and is welcome in many other circles and friend groups as well."

SKIDMORE COLLEGE

Financial Aid: 518-580-5750 • E-Mail: admissions@skidmore.edu • Website: www.skidmore.edu

THE PRINCETON REVIEW SAYS

Admissions

The school reports that its standardized testing policy for use in admission for Fall 2024 is Test Optional. The 2024 testing policy will be permanent. The Princeton Review suggests that interested applicants consult with the school for the most up-to-date standardized testing policies. *Very important factors considered include:* rigor of secondary school record. *Important factors considered include:* class rank, academic GPA, application essay, recommendation(s), extracurricular activities, talent/ability, character/personal qualities, volunteer work, work experience, level of applicant's interest. *Other factors considered include:* standardized test scores, interview, first generation, alumni/ae relation, geographical residence, racial/ethnic status. High school diploma is required and GED is accepted. *Academic units recommended:* 4 English, 4 math, 4 science, 3 science labs, 4 foreign language, 4 social studies.

Financial Aid

Students should submit: CSS/Financial Aid Profile; Noncustodial Profile. The Princeton Review suggests that all financial aid forms be submitted as soon as possible (see page 5 for a note on the FAFSA). *Need-based scholarships/grants offered:* College/university scholarship or grant aid from institutional funds; Federal Pell; Private scholarships; SEOG; State scholarships/grants. *Loan aid offered:* Direct PLUS loans; Direct Subsidized Loans; Direct Unsubsidized Loans; State Loans. Admitted students will be notified of awards on or about 4/1. Federal Work-Study Program available. Institutional employment available.

The Inside Word

Admission to Skidmore is highly competitive, and the admissions staff carefully considers each applicant's academic background. Consistent with their motto ("Creative Thought Matters"), Skidmore carefully reviews a student's extracurricular talents, achievements, and passions when making decisions. Standardized tests are optional in most cases, and students should check with the school for exceptions. While admissions interviews aren't a requirement for Skidmore applicants, students may request a personal interview on campus or with an alum in their area.

THE SCHOOL SAYS "..."

From the Admissions Office

"At Skidmore, we believe a great education is about putting academic theory and creative expression into practice; hence, our belief that creative thought matters. It's a place where faculty and students work together, then figure out how to use what they've learned to make a difference. This often leads to multidisciplinary approaches, where students carry more than one major, student-faculty research is common, most students study abroad, and service-learning courses, internships and community service are standard. Skidmore students develop into independent, creative problem-solvers who aren't restricted to looking at things in traditional ways. This personal journey starts with the First-Year Experience—forty seminars from which to choose, faculty and peer mentors and planned gatherings beyond the classroom. It's meant to ensure that first-year students hit the ground running on day one, connected and involved. When it comes to your major, you can choose from 44 offerings in the sciences, social sciences, arts and humanities, as well as pre-professional fields like management and business. Since we have no fraternities or sororities, student life centers on the 120 student clubs and organizations, which range from the Environmental Action Club to a cappella groups to snowboarding. Add to this the prominence of the arts, which has long set Skidmore apart. When they're not doing lab work in our new Center for Integrated Sciences, science classes can be found collaborating on exhibits at the Tang Museum. Hundreds of students perform, often in the Zankel Music Center. Enroll in dance courses. Participate in theater performances. Most are not even arts majors. Saratoga Springs offers a downtown brimming with shops, galleries, coffeehouses, and great restaurants. Boston, New York City, and Montreal are a three-hour car ride from campus. The Adirondacks, Berkshires, and Green Mountains provide opportunities for skiing, mountain biking, hiking, rock-climbing, and kayaking."

SELECTIVITY

Admissions Rating	95
# of applicants	13,183
% of applicants accepted	26
% of acceptees attending	23
# offered a place on the wait list	3,023
% accepting a place on wait list	44
% admitted from wait list	0
# of early decision applicants	804
% accepted early decision	51

FIRST-YEAR PROFILE

Testing policy	Test Optional
Range SAT composite	1320–1440
Range SAT EBRW	650–740
Range SAT math	650–720
Range ACT composite	30–33
# submitting SAT scores	203
% submitting SAT scores	26
# submitting ACT scores	94
% submitting ACT scores	12
% graduated top 10% of class	36
% graduated top 25% of class	79
% graduated top 50% of class	93

DEADLINES

Early decision	
Deadline	11/15
Notification	12/15
Other ED deadline	1/15
Other ED notification	2/15
Regular	
Deadline	1/15
Notification	4/1
Nonfall registration?	No

APPLICANTS OFTEN PREFER
Bowdoin College; Connecticut College; Vassar College; Wesleyan College

APPLICANTS SOMETIMES PREFER
Boston College; Colby College; Colgate University; Hamilton College; Middlebury College; New York University; Tufts University; University of Vermont

FINANCIAL FACTS

Financial Aid Rating	96
Annual tuition	$61,132
Room and board	$16,632
Required fees	$1,116
Required fees (first-year)	$1,266
Books and supplies	$1,300
Average frosh need-based scholarship	$49,300
Average UG need-based scholarship	$50,000
% needy frosh rec. need-based scholarship or grant aid	100
% needy UG rec. need-based scholarship or grant aid	100
% needy frosh rec. non-need-based scholarship or grant aid	5
% needy UG rec. non-need-based scholarship or grant aid	4
% needy frosh rec. need-based self-help aid	90
% needy UG rec. need-based self-help aid	90
% frosh rec. any financial aid	50
% UG rec. any financial aid	53
% UG borrow to pay for school	38
Average cumulative indebtedness	$29,389
% frosh need fully met	100
% ugrads need fully met	87
Average % of frosh need met	100
Average % of ugrad need met	98

SMITH COLLEGE

Elm St., Northampton, MA 01063 • Admissions: 413-584-2700 • Fax: 413-585-2527

STUDENTS SAY "..."

Academics

Smith College is "an incredibly prestigious, diverse, academically rigorous, socially liberal, and well-respected institution," located in the consummate college town of Northampton, Massachusetts. A Smith education is all about "finding and pursuing your passions." Offering "academic freedom," "Smith doesn't have course requirements" beyond the major, other than a writing-intensive course for first-years, and "self-scheduled finals" allow students to take exam week at their own pace. "One of the most prominent women's colleges in the country," Smith "builds the self-confidence of smart women," and "most classes, even in math and sciences, are very interdisciplinary and often have a feminist bias." Classes are "engaging and promote critical thought," and professors are "inspiring, dynamic, accessible, and brilliant." Smith professors "care deeply about students" and "take the time to get to know you on a first-name basis." Smith also offers fabulous academic facilities and "countless resources" to augment your education, including a "wonderful study abroad department" and ample opportunities for research. There's "a large number of undergrads doing serious scientific research" in addition to course work. If they can't find what they need amid Smith's ample course selection, students "can take classes at the other four schools nearby (UMass Amherst, Amherst College, Hampshire College, and Mount Holyoke College)" through the Five College Consortium. When graduation approaches, Smith students benefit from the school's "excellent alumnae network." "The Career Development Office will do everything in its power to help you get a job."

Campus Life

Smith attracts hardworking and idealistic students, who are "striving to succeed in our classes, as well as make a difference in the Smith College community and the outside community." There's a decided "focus on academics" at Smith, and most students "study, write papers, rehearse, or practice the majority of the time." Students augment course work with "lectures and symposium on campus," as well as "involvement in community service and activism for global issues, women's rights, LGBTQ rights, the environment, and pretty much anything that fights oppression." When they want to relax, Smithies can attend "free movies and concerts, plays, speakers, sports events, and dances," as well as "school-sponsored house parties almost every weekend." When they want to branch out or rub elbows with the opposite sex, students "go to other college parties at surrounding campuses," or head out in Northampton, which is "always bustling" with "concerts, restaurants, and cute shops." The "quality of life is outstanding" on campus, where "the dorms are not dorms but beautiful houses," and cafeteria food is a cut above the average.

Student Body

"Smithies are passionate about everything they do," especially academics. Throughout the semester, undergraduates are known to "study hard" and get "ridiculously stressed" about course work. "It's the nature of Smithies to be driven, but we all want to see our friends and housemates succeed as well." Smith's unique environment attracts "a great mix of nerdy, edgy, [and] traditional" students, including "hipsters, WASPs, crazy partiers, international students, and the average New Englander." Fortunately, there's a "strong sense of community," and "students fit in easily, even if they have different interests." Despite diversity, "one thing all students have in common here is the will for women's empowerment and acceptance of any gender or sexual preference." On that note, many students "love the queer life on campus," where some students are either gay or have "a fluid perception of sexuality." Though there's some political diversity on campus, most Smithies hold "very liberal views," and many are "very conscious and aware, not only of their community but the world in general."

SMITH COLLEGE

Financial Aid: 413-585-2530 • E-Mail: admission@smith.edu • Website: www.smith.edu

THE PRINCETON REVIEW SAYS

Admissions

The school reports that its standardized testing policy for use in admission for Fall 2024 is Test Optional. It is unknown at this time if the 2024 testing policy will be permanent. The Princeton Review suggests that interested applicants consult with the school for the most up-to-date standardized testing policies. *Very important factors considered include:* rigor of secondary school record, academic GPA, application essay, recommendation(s), character/personal qualities. *Important factors considered include:* class rank, interview, extracurricular activities, talent/ability. *Other factors considered include:* standardized test scores, first generation, alumni/ae relation, racial/ethnic status, volunteer work, work experience. High school diploma or equivalent is not required. *Academic units recommended:* 4 English, 3 math, 3 science, 3 science labs, 3 foreign language, 2 history, 1 academic elective.

Financial Aid

Students should submit: CSS/Financial Aid Profile; FAFSA; Institution's own financial aid form; Noncustodial Profile. Priority filing deadline is 1/25. The Princeton Review suggests that all financial aid forms be submitted as soon as possible (see page 5 for a note on the FAFSA). *Need-based scholarships/grants offered:* College/university scholarship or grant aid from institutional funds; Federal Pell; Private scholarships; SEOG; State scholarships/grants. *Loan aid offered:* Direct PLUS loans; Direct Subsidized Loans; Direct Unsubsidized Loans; College/university loans from institutional funds. Admitted students will be notified of awards on or about 3/19. Federal Work-Study Program available. Institutional employment available.

The Inside Word

Every prospective Smithie is carefully evaluated by at least two members of the admissions staff. No hard numbers guarantee admission: Smith is looking for students who will succeed academically and socially in college, evaluating each applicant for both personal and intellectual qualities. To best prepare for admission, Smith recommends that students follow a rigorous college prep curriculum in high school. If you're feeling particularly enthused about your future at Smith, you can become a fan of the admissions department on Facebook, take the online tour, or read student blogs on the admission page.

THE SCHOOL SAYS "..."

From the Admissions Office

"Smith students choose from 1,000 courses in more than fifty areas of study. There are no specific course requirements outside the major; students meet individually with faculty advisers to plan a balanced curriculum. Smith programs offer unique opportunities, including interdisciplinary concentrations, the chance to study abroad, or at another college in the United States, and a semester in Washington, D.C. The Ada Comstock Scholars Program encourages women beyond the traditional age to return to college and complete their undergraduate studies. Smith is located in the scenic Connecticut River valley of western Massachusetts near a number of other outstanding educational institutions. Through the Five College Consortium, Smith, Amherst, Hampshire, and Mount Holyoke colleges, and the University of Massachusetts enrich their academic, social, and cultural offerings by means of joint faculty appointments, joint courses, student and faculty exchanges, shared facilities, and other cooperative arrangements. Smith has the largest and oldest women-only ABET-accredited engineering program in the country; it's also the only college in the country that offers a guaranteed paid internship program ('Praxis')."

SELECTIVITY

Admissions Rating	96
# of applicants	6,064
% of applicants accepted	30
% of acceptees attending	37
# offered a place on the wait list	1,717
% accepting a place on wait list	52
% admitted from wait list	0
# of early decision applicants	513
% accepted early decision	58

FIRST-YEAR PROFILE

Testing policy	Test Optional
Range SAT composite	1390–1510
Range SAT EBRW	690–760
Range SAT math	680–770
Range ACT composite	31–34
# submitting SAT scores	230
% submitting SAT scores	34
# submitting ACT scores	134
% submitting ACT scores	20
Average HS GPA	4.0
% frosh submitting high school GPA	67
% graduated top 10% of class	74
% graduated top 25% of class	93
% graduated top 50% of class	100

DEADLINES

Early decision	
Deadline	11/15
Notification	12/15
Other ED deadline	1/1
Other ED notification	1/31
Regular	
Deadline	1/15
Notification	3/31
Nonfall registration?	Yes

FINANCIAL FACTS

Financial Aid Rating	95
Annual tuition	$55,830
Room and board	$19,420
Required fees	$284
Books and supplies	$800
Average frosh need-based scholarship	$55,032
Average UG need-based scholarship	$53,152
% needy frosh rec. need-based scholarship or grant aid	99
% needy UG rec. need-based scholarship or grant aid	99
% needy frosh rec. non-need-based scholarship or grant aid	2
% needy UG rec. non-need-based scholarship or grant aid	2
% needy frosh rec. need-based self-help aid	90
% needy UG rec. need-based self-help aid	91
% frosh rec. any financial aid	70
% UG rec. any financial aid	71
% UG borrow to pay for school	54
Average cumulative indebtedness	$19,182
% frosh need fully met	100
% ugrads need fully met	100
Average % of frosh need met	100
Average % of ugrad need met	100

SONOMA STATE UNIVERSITY

1801 East Cotati Avenue, Rohnert Park, CA 94928 • Admissions: 707-664-2880 • Fax: 707-664-2060

STUDENTS SAY "..."

Academics

A member of the reputable California state university system, Sonoma State University distinguishes itself from similar institutions through its low-key atmosphere and strong "focus on undergraduates." Employing "teachers who are willing to take the time to make a difference in students' lives," SSU limits most classes to fewer than 50, giving students the opportunity to "develop close and meaningful relationships with professors and classmates that will continue even after graduation." During class time, professors often "allow open discussions and emphasize a comfortable, safe environment to express oneself." After class, they "are always available through email or in person during their office hours." Most SSU instructors are excellent in the classroom, but the school is big enough that you'll find "a wide variety of professors, ranging from spectacular to pretty poor." Fortunately, professors are generally "experts in their field" and "stay up to date on current events that affect our field of study." While students benefit from a very low in-state tuition, SSU has been affected by California budget cuts, and the resulting unit cap "makes it almost impossible to graduate in four years." Students have historically suggested that the bureaucratic process could use some improvements, most notably that the class "registration process is notoriously buggy," and the college has recently done so. For those hoping to stay in California after graduation, "Sonoma County and the city of San Francisco are two places very rich in career opportunities for Sonoma State students."

Campus Life

SSU boasts a "gorgeous campus" and "impressive" facilities, including "incredible" dormitories and "a new rec center with [a] climbing wall and indoor courts, as well as outside fields." A current student enthuses, "Just come look at the housing and you realize that Sonoma is trying to make everyone as comfortable as possible." With its "beautiful setting in the heart of wine country," "the pace here seems to be a slower one, which creates a peaceful and calm environment to take classes and study in; the stress level here is relatively low." After class, students might "hang out by the pools" or study in the "many little redwood groves" around campus. "There are hundreds of clubs" on campus, including many popular Greek organizations, and, for those with a little initiative, "the leadership opportunities are endless." Off campus, surrounding Rohnert Park is a "more suburban" environment, so "it is difficult to go anywhere unless you have a car." With a set of wheels, students love to take day trips to San Francisco, or go miniature golfing, hiking, and bowling nearby. "Outdoor activities are abundant year-round" and, for those of legal drinking age, "there are also a lot of wineries and vineyards to go wine tasting!" Come the weekend, "a lot of students like to party," while others "enjoy on-campus activities like midnight improv and free movies."

Students

"Many students pick Sonoma because it is close to home," whether they live on campus or commute. Southern Californians and other in-staters round out the largely "Bay Area" crowd, and there are a number of older students mixed in with traditional undergrads. In broad strokes, "most students here come from middle- to upper-class backgrounds, and they are all fairly down to earth and really very nice and socially aware." More superficially, you'll notice "a lot of white girls wearing yoga pants, Nike shocks, and drinking Starbucks coffee." That said, "everyone has their own thing" at SSU. Though the school is "not really racially diverse" there is an "eclectic group of students," making it easy to fit in. A wise junior advises, "The important thing is to find your passions, your niche, and pursue it. In the process, you'll come upon like-minded students who share the same interests." "Most of the students here are part of the Greek life," telling us that fraternities and sororities are the best way to make friends and have fun (though others complain that "Greeks feel like they run the school," to the detriment of non-affiliated students). Even if you don't pledge, "the residential community helps build great friendships" for those who live on campus, and "because everyone is friendly most people find it easy to make friends."

SONOMA STATE UNIVERSITY

Financial Aid: 707-664-2389 • E-Mail: student.outreach@sonoma.edu • Website: www.sonoma.edu

THE PRINCETON REVIEW SAYS

Admissions

The school reports that its standardized testing policy for use in admission for Fall 2024 is Test Free. The Princeton Review suggests that interested applicants consult with the school for the most up-to-date standardized testing policies. *Very important factors considered include:* academic GPA, standardized test scores. *Other factors considered include:* geographical residence. High school diploma is required and GED is accepted. *Academic units required:* 4 English, 3 math, 2 science, 1 science lab, 2 foreign language, 2 history, 1 visual/performing arts, 1 academic elective.

Financial Aid

Students should submit: FAFSA. Priority filing deadline is 3/2. The Princeton Review suggests that all financial aid forms be submitted as soon as possible (see page 5 for a note on the FAFSA). *Need-based scholarships/grants offered:* College/university scholarship or grant aid from institutional funds; Federal Pell; Private scholarships; SEOG; State scholarships/grants; United Negro College Fund. *Loan aid offered:* Direct PLUS loans; Direct Subsidized Loans; Direct Unsubsidized Loans. Admitted students will be notified of awards on a rolling basis beginning 3/25. Federal Work-Study Program available. Institutional employment available.

The Inside Word

SSU makes admissions decisions based on an "eligibility index" number, which is calculated using a student's high school GPA; note that honors and advanced placement course work is weighted more heavily than regular courses in calculating a grade point average. Certain majors require a higher index number for admission; those include kinesiology, nursing, and psychology.

THE SCHOOL SAYS "..."

From the Admissions Office

"Sonoma State University occupies 269 acres in the beautiful wine country of Sonoma county, in northern California. Located at the foot of the Sonoma hills, the campus is an hour's drive north of San Francisco and centrally located between the Pacific Ocean to the west and the wine country to the north and east. SSU is deeply committed to the teaching of the liberal arts and sciences with selected professional programs. Within its thirty-four academic departments, SSU awards bachelor's degrees in forty-six areas of specialization and master's degrees in fifteen areas. In addition, the university offers a joint master's degree in mathematics with San Francisco State University and a joint Ed.D. with UC Davis. Sonoma State offers one of the only wine business programs in the country."

SELECTIVITY

Admissions Rating	81
# of applicants	14,129
% of applicants accepted	92
% of acceptees attending	14

FIRST-YEAR PROFILE

Testing policy	Test Free
Average HS GPA	3.2
% frosh submitting high school GPA	100

DEADLINES

Regular	
Priority	3/1
Deadline	11/30
Notification	Rolling, 11/1
Nonfall registration?	Yes

FINANCIAL FACTS

Financial Aid Rating	77
Annual in-state tuition	$8,190
Annual out-of-state tuition	$20,070
Room and board	$16,020
Books and supplies	$1,916
Average frosh need-based scholarship	$10,887
Average UG need-based scholarship	$10,192
% needy frosh rec. need-based scholarship or grant aid	71
% needy UG rec. need-based scholarship or grant aid	73
% needy frosh rec. non-need-based scholarship or grant aid	36
% needy UG rec. non-need-based scholarship or grant aid	36
% needy frosh rec. need-based self-help aid	54
% needy UG rec. need-based self-help aid	55
% frosh rec. any financial aid	59
% UG rec. any financial aid	51
% UG borrow to pay for school	
Average cumulative indebtedness	
% frosh need fully met	6
% ugrads need fully met	5
Average % of frosh need met	57
Average % of ugrad need met	55

SOUTHERN METHODIST UNIVERSITY

6425 Boaz Lane, Dallas, TX 75275-0181 • Admissions: 214-768-2000 • Fax: 214-768-0103

STUDENTS SAY "..."

Academics

Located on a tree-lined, "beautiful campus" in the heart of Dallas, Southern Methodist University is a mid-size private university with a lot going on. The school has a "unique culture" that relies on "top academics" and a "long-standing history of strong traditions" to build "incredible alumni support," which in turn brings students excellent internship and job opportunities. SMU offers everything "from a great social life and extracurricular activities to fun and interesting classes," including a "phenomenal business school" and "amazing" facilities. The school prides itself on being "a close-knit community of the intellectually elite," and this translates into "a wealth of academic resources [with which] to be successful, a flood of opportunities for those who want them, and thus a community of intellectuals who happen to genuinely care about each other." Professors are "incredibly gifted in their fields and exceptional communicators." They "love interacting with students" and "are willing to put in extra time to convey the material accurately to students." "If their office hours don't match yours, they will change their schedule to accommodate people," says a student. Most have worked in the industry that they teach in, and therefore they "can offer real-life connections to the material we learn." The syllabus is also modeled "to what you'll face in the real world." The legion of SMU alumni provides excellent connections into the business world (among others), and three "dedicated career services centers" only sweetens the employment pot. Since many attend SMU for the Cox School of Business, it helps that the school is in the ideal location "to secure great jobs with Fortune 500 companies right here in Dallas." The school's administration also "understands that studying abroad, internships, extracurriculars, etc., also play a crucial role in developing students into the adults and professionals they want to become." "SMU puts the 'classy' back in classical education," says a student.

Campus Life

Despite the fact it is located in the heart of Dallas, "the atmosphere is very calm and relaxing." SMU students frequently head to uptown Dallas "for fine dining and dancing" and often see movies, shop, and attend concerts and sports games. Everyone is always on campus for the football games for "boulevarding" ("basically tailgating but on steroids"), and "we love to have alums come visit us for the tailgate," says a student. Students generally fit in with this "vibrant social life" best once they have found an extracurricular organization that is right for them, and oftentimes "sororities and fraternities tend to be this venue." However, some wish there was "less emphasis on Greek life," since "if you're not Greek, you can sometimes feel left out or looked down on." Students devote a large portion of their time to their studies, but "there is always a social event every weekend night to blow off steam." This heavy concentration on future careers means that most here are "definitely wanting to become leaders in their field or profession," so "fraternity parties and formals are popular, but at the same time, so are speeches from prominent members of the community and theatrical performances."

Student Body

This student body is "happy and leads a balanced life" at a school that it loves. Some students at SMU "tend to be a bit preppy," "polite," and may come from "influential backgrounds." Many "work a lot for pay or do internships," take a lot of class hours, "are involved...and have fun a lot." "They are very busy people, and they prefer it that way," says one student. All of these "motivated, outgoing," people "thrive on leadership" and are "dedicated to academics and involvement, both at SMU and in the greater community." Fashion "is a big part of SMU culture." This group is "very social" and frequently interacts with the Dallas community and "amazing arts and restaurant scene around campus."

SOUTHERN METHODIST UNIVERSITY

Financial Aid: 214-768-3417 • E-Mail: ugadmission@smu.edu • Website: www.smu.edu

THE PRINCETON REVIEW SAYS

Admissions

The school reports that its standardized testing policy for use in admission for Fall 2024 and beyond is Test Optional. The Princeton Review suggests that interested applicants consult with the school for the most up-to-date standardized testing policies. *Very important factors considered include:* rigor of secondary school record, academic GPA, application essay, recommendation(s). *Important factors considered include:* class rank, standardized test scores, extracurricular activities, talent/ability, character/personal qualities. *Other factors considered include:* first generation, alumni/ae relation, lived experiences, volunteer work, work experience, level of applicant's interest. High school diploma is required and GED is not accepted. *Academic units required:* 4 English, 3 math, 3 science, 2 science labs, 2 foreign language, 3 social studies. *Academic units recommended:* 4 English, 4 math, 3 science, 2 science labs, 3 foreign language, 3 history, 3 academic electives.

Financial Aid

Students should submit: CSS/Financial Aid Profile; FAFSA; Noncustodial Profile. Priority filing deadline is 11/1. The Princeton Review suggests that all financial aid forms be submitted as soon as possible (see page 5 for a note on the FAFSA). *Need-based scholarships/grants offered:* College/university scholarship or grant aid from institutional funds; Federal Pell; Private scholarships; SEOG; State scholarships/grants. *Loan aid offered:* Direct PLUS loans; Direct Subsidized Loans; Direct Unsubsidized Loans; College/university loans from institutional funds; State Loans. Admitted students will be notified of awards on a rolling basis. Federal Work-Study Program available. Institutional employment available.

The Inside Word

SMU boasts a potent combination: high-caliber academics, a desirable location, and a beautiful campus. No surprise then that gaining admission is challenging, and growing more so all the time. Solid high school grades and a compelling list of extracurricular activities will usually do the trick. "Special talent" students—artists and athletes in particular—can make up for academic deficiencies; those in the arts must undergo an audition/portfolio review, while promising athletes are scouted. Except for those in the performing arts, all admitted students enter as "pre-majors" in the Dedman College of Humanities and Sciences.

THE SCHOOL SAYS "..."

From the Admissions Office

"At SMU, we seek bright, hardworking students. We match our rigorous academics, powerful opportunities and incredible classroom-to-career experiences with access to outstanding financial resources. We want students to achieve their goals regardless of financial need. When students apply to SMU, they are automatically considered for generous academic awards, many of which can be combined. About 74% of first-years are awarded grants and/or scholarships. We respond to what employers want. The flexibility of our curriculum and our vibrant community in the global gateway of Dallas offer students robust preparation for the demands of a rapidly changing world. All students have the chance to pursue career-boosting internships. SMU students who choose to double or triple major graduate with the ability to demonstrate expertise in different disciplines. Employers tell us that SMU graduates are creative, ethical and critical thinkers who hit the ground running faster because they know how to lead, solve problems and communicate with emotional and cultural intelligence. Students often partner with our professors as co-creators of knowledge, thriving on personal attention in small classes. They can participate in undergraduate research as early as their first year. Our enterprising spirit has long been part of our DNA. The SMU Incubator is a dedicated campus space where entrepreneurial students and faculty work on generating business-friendly solutions. The George W. Bush Presidential Center and renowned Tate Lecture Series offer students access to dignitaries ranging from former presidents to Nobel Laureates."

SELECTIVITY

Admissions Rating	92
# of applicants	16,150
% of applicants accepted	52
% of acceptees attending	19
# offered a place on the wait list	1,547
% accepting a place on wait list	48
% admitted from wait list	0
# of early decision applicants	587
% accepted early decision	71

FIRST-YEAR PROFILE

Testing policy	Test Optional
Range SAT composite	1390–1500
Range SAT EBRW	680–740
Range SAT math	690–770
Range ACT composite	31–34
# submitting SAT scores	272
% submitting SAT scores	17
# submitting ACT scores	342
% submitting ACT scores	21
Average HS GPA	3.7
% frosh submitting high school GPA	100
% graduated top 10% of class	52
% graduated top 25% of class	82
% graduated top 50% of class	98

DEADLINES

Early decision	
Deadline	11/1
Notification	12/31
Other ED deadline	1/15
Other ED notification	3/1
Early action	
Deadline	11/1
Notification	12/31
Regular	
Priority	1/15
Deadline	7/31
Notification	4/1
Nonfall registration?	Yes

APPLICANTS OFTEN PREFER
Duke University; New York University; University of Southern California

APPLICANTS SOMETIMES PREFER
Boston University; Vanderbilt University

APPLICANTS RARELY PREFER
Texas Christian University; Tulane University

FINANCIAL FACTS

Financial Aid Rating	87
Annual tuition	$57,212
Room and board	$18,230
Required fees	$7,248
Books and supplies	$800
Average frosh need-based scholarship	$44,517
Average UG need-based scholarship	$40,975
% needy frosh rec. need-based scholarship or grant aid	97
% needy UG rec. need-based scholarship or grant aid	96
% needy frosh rec. non-need-based scholarship or grant aid	25
% needy UG rec. non-need-based scholarship or grant aid	22
% needy frosh rec. need-based self-help aid	71
% needy UG rec. need-based self-help aid	72
% frosh rec. any financial aid	78
% UG rec. any financial aid	74
% UG borrow to pay for school	25
Average cumulative indebtedness	$38,298
% frosh need fully met	42
% ugrads need fully met	38
Average % of frosh need met	86
Average % of ugrad need met	85

SOUTHWESTERN UNIVERSITY

1001 East University Avenue, Georgetown, TX 78627-0770 • Admissions: 512-863-6511 • Fax: 512-863-9601

STUDENTS SAY ". . ."

Academics

Located just north of Austin, Southwestern University may be the oldest institution of higher learning in Texas, but it prides itself on providing a modern, relevant education that prepares students for dynamic careers. Southwestern's liberal arts education emphasizes the Paideia system of learning, such that students come to identify interdisciplinary relationships between what they are studying and how it relates to the world in terms of understanding and problem-solving. This approach often combines subjects that wouldn't normally be thought of as connected. For example, writing a children's book to improve nutrition in lower socioeconomic communities. Critical and dynamic thinking are emphasized, and students are encouraged to "think and develop a stance every chance they get." With the Paideia approach, classes tend to be more interactive and unique, regardless of the subject. Class discussion "is definitely held in high esteem" and it creates a constructive learning environment. On the whole, professors "go out of the teaching norm to engage students, from having classes outside to creating activities and assignments...[for] students to have a more hands-on and memorable experience." The school is "academically driven to produce not just educated people to work in various fields, but future academics."

The closeness of faculty and students "creates a wonderful learning environment in which students are comfortable asking questions, going to office hours, and getting the specific help that they need." Faculty "are very supportive and tend to be understanding when it comes to accommodations and late work, and it's easy to build a relationship with them." Research and practical experience are valued and there are many opportunities available to students throughout their college career. One example of this is student teaching, which "is an amazing opportunity as most schools only offer it your senior year." The school and faculty facilitate experiential learning; "the Center for Professional Development is very helpful for student internships, networking, and jobs post-graduation," and professors often "have incredible connections in their fields," which can also result in internships and valuable career connections.

Campus Life

More than three-quarters of Southwestern University students live on-campus, and to make getting around easier, everyone has access to Pirate Bikes, the rideshare program that provides green transport on campus. The school provides plenty of social opportunities for students. In addition to clubs, organizations, and athletics, the RAs in the residence halls "put on great events such as Just Dance nights, ping pong tournaments, and craft nights," and the university itself "is good with hosting events open to all of the student body" such as the weekly Friday events that include "comedy, magic, trivia, and roller skating." Greek life and varsity athletics (both playing and attending games) are both strong here. While there is a lot of fun to be had, students take their academics seriously. On the whole, students are very busy and most "try to get their social time while being productive (studying at the same time, club activities)," which is made easier by the good weather and green outdoor common spaces like the quad, and most people "go out on the weekends, but chiefly are here to study." The campus is quite self-contained, but when they want to get away, some students "make the drive into the big city that's 30 minutes away for more choices or events."

Student Body

This is an "involved, communicative, productive, and supportive" student body where most people "join a lot of extracurriculars and quite a few people have on-campus jobs." While it is not a very racially diverse school, it is an inclusive one, and students are "pretty progressive or cool with everyone and their identity." People may have different ideologies, beliefs, and aspirations "yet we all work successfully in the same setting." Everyone at Southwestern "is seen and heard, and resources can be devoted to every student in need." This is a generally laid-back, well-balanced place where "the vibe on the campus is fun and happy."

SOUTHWESTERN UNIVERSITY

Financial Aid: 512-863-1259 • E-Mail: admission@southwestern.edu • Website: www.southwestern.edu

THE PRINCETON REVIEW SAYS

Admissions

The school reports that its standardized testing policy for use in admission for Fall 2024 is Test Optional. The 2024 testing policy will be permanent. The Princeton Review suggests that interested applicants consult with the school for the most up-to-date standardized testing policies. *Very important factors considered include:* rigor of secondary school record, class rank, academic GPA, standardized test scores, application essay, recommendation(s). *Important factors considered include:* interview, extracurricular activities, talent/ability, character/personal qualities, first generation, alumni/ae relation, geographical residence, state residency, racial/ethnic status, volunteer work. *Other factors considered include:* religious affiliation/commitment, work experience, level of applicant's interest. High school diploma is required and GED is accepted. *Academic units required:* 4 English, 4 math, 3 science, 2 science labs, 2 foreign language, 2 social studies, 1 history, 1 academic elective. *Academic units recommended:* 4 English, 4 math, 4 science, 3 science labs, 3 foreign language, 3 social studies, 1 history, 1 academic elective.

Financial Aid

Students should submit: FAFSA. Priority filing deadline is 3/1. The Princeton Review suggests that all financial aid forms be submitted as soon as possible (see page 5 for a note on the FAFSA). *Need-based scholarships/grants offered:* College/university scholarship or grant aid from institutional funds; Federal Pell; Private scholarships; SEOG; State scholarships/grants. *Loan aid offered:* Direct PLUS loans; Direct Subsidized Loans; Direct Unsubsidized Loans; College/university loans from institutional funds; State Loans. Admitted students will be notified of awards on a rolling basis beginning 12/2. Federal Work-Study Program available. Institutional employment available.

The Inside Word

Successful applicants to Southwestern University demonstrate intellectual curiosity and a strong desire to participate in an active collegiate community. Students need to be well-rounded and highly motivated. The vast majority of those who receive the coveted thick envelope are in the top quarter of their class and have above-average standardized test scores.

THE SCHOOL SAYS "..."

From the Admissions Office

"For nearly two centuries Southwestern University has stood proudly as one of the nation's oldest and finest liberal arts institutions. Our beautiful, tree-lined residential campus encompasses more than 700 acres featuring spacious sports and recreational facilities, multiple research laboratories, two live-performance theaters, and countless outdoor places to study, relax or socialize. Recognized for our commitment to sustainable, eco-friendly practices, our campus was one of the first in the nation to meet 100 percent of its electric needs from renewable wind power, and since 1972 we've nourished our landscapes and athletic fields with recycled water.

"Throughout campus and in the world beyond our students make meaningful connections across disciplines, cultures, and experiences through our unique Paideia approach—a curriculum that allows to students to chart a course that best suits their passions and life goals as they develop creative, critical thinking skills that make them adaptable to any challenge or opportunity. The results are impressive: less than a year after graduation, 98 percent of Southwestern students are either employed, attending a professional school or pursuing advanced studies. But while you're at Southwestern you should also know you have the best of all worlds for some good times, whether it's a relaxing stroll through Georgetown's historic town square, spending a day on the crystal-clear San Gabriel River, or enjoying an evening reveling in Austin's live music scene. A bright future begins here, right in the heart of Texas."

SELECTIVITY

Admissions Rating	91
# of applicants	5,557
% of applicants accepted	45
% of acceptees attending	18
# offered a place on the wait list	90
% accepting a place on wait list	18
% admitted from wait list	56
# of early decision applicants	64
% accepted early decision	34

FIRST-YEAR PROFILE

Testing policy	Test Optional
Range SAT composite	1140–1320
Range SAT EBRW	570–690
Range SAT math	550–670
Range ACT composite	24–30
# submitting SAT scores	187
% submitting SAT scores	43
# submitting ACT scores	73
% submitting ACT scores	17
Average HS GPA	3.5
% frosh submitting high school GPA	100
% graduated top 10% of class	25
% graduated top 25% of class	62
% graduated top 50% of class	89

DEADLINES

Early decision	
Deadline	11/1
Notification	12/1
Early action	
Deadline	12/1
Notification	3/1
Regular	
Priority	2/1
Deadline	2/1
Notification	4/1
Nonfall registration?	No

APPLICANTS OFTEN PREFER
Texas A&M University—College Station; The University of Texas at Austin; Trinity University

APPLICANTS SOMETIMES PREFER
Austin College; Baylor University

FINANCIAL FACTS

Financial Aid Rating	86
Annual tuition	$50,558
Room and board	$14,726
Required fees	$200
Books and supplies	$1,300
Average frosh need-based scholarship	$39,049
Average UG need-based scholarship	$37,117
% needy frosh rec. need-based scholarship or grant aid	99
% needy UG rec. need-based scholarship or grant aid	99
% needy frosh rec. non-need-based scholarship or grant aid	98
% needy UG rec. non-need-based scholarship or grant aid	98
% needy frosh rec. need-based self-help aid	70
% needy UG rec. need-based self-help aid	80
% frosh rec. any financial aid	98
% UG rec. any financial aid	98
% UG borrow to pay for school	56
Average cumulative indebtedness	$30,497
% frosh need fully met	35
% ugrads need fully met	28
Average % of frosh need met	94
Average % of ugrad need met	86

SPELMAN COLLEGE

350 Spelman Lane, Atlanta, GA 30314 • Admissions: 404-681-3643 • Fax: 404-270-5201

STUDENTS SAY "..."

Academics

A historically Black women's institution, Spelman College has built a strong reputation for "molding intelligent, goal-oriented young ladies into determined, successful, free-thinking women." Many prospective students are attracted to the school's "powerful history," including the "long list of successful, educated, strong, Black women who have attended Spelman College" during the century since its founding. Once on campus, students are happy to report that Spelman's "professors are committed to the mission of the school," and they really "bring out the best" in their students. In the classroom, students are "encouraged to state our opinions," and professors "allow room for us to challenge and discuss what they present." You'll definitely work hard to stay afloat in this "challenging academic environment," because professors "do not allow for even a minute amount of slacking when it comes to completing assignments and being on time for class." Fortunately, there are "many academic resources available to help us, such as tutoring services and a writing center." Plus, the majority of Spelman professors "take additional time outside of instructional time to assist their students" with course work. Of particular note, Spelman is "very focused on the sciences and improving the number of African-American women in this field, and they offer many facilities, faculty, and opportunities" for advanced study. As graduation approaches, the "Career Counseling Center is extremely strong and has helped numerous students find employment and graduate school placements." While the future looks bright for Spelman grads, many say this private institution could better serve its students by providing "more money for scholarships and financial aid."

Campus Life

There's a "strong sense of tradition and loyalty" on the Spelman campus, and most students are deeply involved in the community. From service groups to sororities, "there are so many organizations and clubs that you're bound to find one that fits you." There are tons of "opportunities to obtain leadership positions" outside the classroom, and many students are "very involved in campus life." A first-year student details, "In my freshman year already, I've walked in a fashion show, I was crowned Miss Glee Club, I write for the campus newspaper." There's a constant buzz of activity on campus, and "informational forums, career fairs, college fairs, performances, and sporting events are at the forefront of everyone's campus life." Socially, "Greek life is quite important at Spelman College, but isn't a must." Even if you don't join a sorority, "there are a lot of social events on campus," and two other historically Black colleges, Clark Atlanta and Morehouse, "are only inches away." Spelman undergrads say, "The camaraderie between the schools is great," and "joint homecoming with Morehouse is the highlight of the entire year." Off campus, students "go skating, bowling, and to Six Flags Over Georgia, as well as to Atlanta Falcons, Hawks, and Braves [games]." Nearby, Atlantic Station is home to "a major movie theater, shopping, [and] restaurants."

Student Body

Spelman College is "full of warm, welcoming, sisterly, and highly educated African-American women." A unique environment, "Spelman College offers a chance for African-American women to be the majority," and students appreciate being "surrounded and empowered by other young, intelligent, and goal-oriented women like myself." At the same time, "the institution promotes diversity within the student body," and Spelman women "come in all shapes and sizes and from all walks of life, though linked by our African descent. Anyone can find their place here." Confidence and individuality are prized at Spelman, and the typical undergraduate "speaks her mind, wears what she wants, [and] is comfortable in her own skin, yet she has empathy and a strong sense of social justice." Many students "love to do service for the community" and are involved in philanthropic projects around Atlanta. Spelman women are "hardworking and focused on academics." However, most are "excellent at balancing a full course load and an active social life."

SPELMAN COLLEGE

Financial Aid: 404-270-5212 • E-Mail: admiss@spelman.edu • Website: www.spelman.edu

THE PRINCETON REVIEW SAYS

Admissions

The school reports that its standardized testing policy for use in admission for Fall 2024 is Test Optional. It is unknown at this time if the 2024 testing policy will be permanent. The Princeton Review suggests that interested applicants consult with the school for the most up-to-date standardized testing policies. *Very important factors considered include:* rigor of secondary school record, academic GPA, application essay, extracurricular activities. *Important factors considered include:* recommendation(s), character/personal qualities, volunteer work. *Other factors considered include:* class rank, standardized test scores, talent/ability, first generation, alumni/ae relation, work experience. High school diploma is required and GED is accepted. *Academic units required:* 4 English, 2 math, 3 science, 1 science lab, 2 foreign language, 2 social studies, 2 history. *Academic units recommended:* 4 English, 4 math, 6 science, 1 science lab, 2 foreign language, 3 social studies, 2 history, 7 academic electives.

Financial Aid

Students should submit: FAFSA. Priority filing deadline is 2/1. The Princeton Review suggests that all financial aid forms be submitted as soon as possible (see page 5 for a note on the FAFSA). *Need-based scholarships/grants offered:* College/university scholarship or grant aid from institutional funds; Federal Pell; Private scholarships; SEOG; State scholarships/grants; United Negro College Fund. *Loan aid offered:* Direct PLUS loans; Direct Subsidized Loans; Direct Unsubsidized Loans; State Loans. Admitted students will be notified of awards on a rolling basis beginning 12/15. Federal Work-Study Program available. Institutional employment available.

The Inside Word

The best way to prepare for admission to Spelman is to pursue a strong, precollege academic curriculum during high school: the average GPA is around 3.8. Students who are particularly interested in Spelman have two early application options: early decision, which is binding, and early action, which is nonbinding, but allows students to receive a response more quickly.

THE SCHOOL SAYS "..."

From the Admissions Office

"As an outstanding Historically Black College for women, Spelman strives for academic excellence in liberal arts education. This predominantly residential private college provides students with an academic climate conducive to the full development of their intellectual and leadership potential. The college is a member of the Atlanta University Center Consortium, and Spelman students enjoy the benefits of a small college while having access to the resources of the other three participating institutions. The purpose extends beyond intellectual development and professional career preparation of students. It seeks to develop the total person. The college provides an academic and social environment that strengthens those qualities that enable women to be self-confident as well as culturally and spiritually enriched. This environment attempts to instill in students both an appreciation for the multicultural communities of the world and a sense of responsibility for bringing about positive change in those communities."

SELECTIVITY

Admissions Rating	93
# of applicants	13,649
% of applicants accepted	28
% of acceptees attending	15
# offered a place on the wait list	1,314
# of early decision applicants	200
% accepted early decision	29

FIRST-YEAR PROFILE

Testing policy	Test Optional
Range SAT composite	1100–1290
Range SAT EBRW	570–670
Range SAT math	520–630
Range ACT composite	22–27
# submitting SAT scores	176
% submitting SAT scores	30
# submitting ACT scores	106
% submitting ACT scores	18
Average HS GPA	3.9
% frosh submitting high school GPA	99
% graduated top 10% of class	35
% graduated top 25% of class	69
% graduated top 50% of class	94

DEADLINES

Early decision	
Deadline	11/1
Notification	12/31
Early action	
Deadline	11/1
Notification	12/31
Regular	
Deadline	2/1
Notification	4/1
Nonfall registration?	Yes

APPLICANTS OFTEN PREFER

Clark Atlanta University; Georgia State University; Hampton University; Howard University; North Carolina A&T State University; Xavier University of Louisiana

FINANCIAL FACTS

Financial Aid Rating	81
Annual tuition	$25,880
Room and board	$15,666
Required fees	$3,005
Required fees (first-year)	$3,265
Books and supplies	$1,500
Average frosh need-based scholarship	$15,592
Average UG need-based scholarship	$15,959
% needy frosh rec. need-based scholarship or grant aid	100
% needy UG rec. need-based scholarship or grant aid	97
% needy frosh rec. non-need-based scholarship or grant aid	14
% needy UG rec. non-need-based scholarship or grant aid	11
% needy frosh rec. need-based self-help aid	80
% needy UG rec. need-based self-help aid	81
% frosh rec. any financial aid	100
% UG rec. any financial aid	91
% UG borrow to pay for school	67
Average cumulative indebtedness	$32,004
% frosh need fully met	65
% ugrads need fully met	62
Average % of frosh need met	24
Average % of ugrad need met	24

STANFORD UNIVERSITY

450 Jane Stanford Way, Stanford, CA 94305 • Admissions: 650-723-2300 • Fax: 650-723-6050

CAMPUS LIFE

Quality of Life Rating	88
Fire Safety Rating	89
Green Rating	99
Type of school	Private
Affiliation	No Affiliation
Environment	City

STUDENTS

Total undergrad enrollment	7,761
% male/female/another gender	48/52/0
% from out of state	59
% frosh from public high school	58
% frosh live on campus	100
% ugrads live on campus	94
# of fraternities (% join)	16 (18)
# of sororities (% join)	12 (23)
% African American	7
% Asian	26
% White	26
% Hispanic	18
% Native American	1
% Pacific Islander	<1
% Two or more races	10
% Race and/or ethnicity unknown	<1
% international	11
# of countries represented	104

SURVEY SAYS . . .

Students are happy
Classroom facilities are great
Lab facilities are great
Great library
Career services are great
Internships are widely available
School is well run
Great financial aid
No one cheats
Students are friendly
Diverse student types interact on campus
Great food on campus
Recreation facilities are great
Everyone loves the Cardinal
Alumni active on campus
Active minority support groups

ACADEMICS

Academic Rating	91
% students returning for sophomore year	98
% students graduating within 4 years	73
% students graduating within 6 years	95
Calendar	Quarter
Student/faculty ratio	6:1
Profs interesting rating	89
Profs accessible rating	94

Most classes have 10–19 students.
Most lab/discussion sessions have
fewer than 10 students.

MOST POPULAR MAJORS

Computer Science; Economics; Engineering

STUDENTS SAY ". . ."

Academics

There are few universities that can match the prestige and caliber of Stanford University. At "the forefront of [nearly] every field of study," it's easy to understand why so many students are attracted to the school. Of course, far more than simply offering access to highly rated departments, Stanford strives to "expand your creativity, challenge and deepen your world view, and make you a passionate and informed citizen of the world." Moreover, the opportunities for research "are incredible" and "the support for students (residential, emotional, academic) is unrivaled." And while the university is certainly "academically rigorous," it is "without the competitive edge that many top-tier institutions are known for." Inside the classroom, undergrads are privy to "dynamic" professors who easily "draw [students] into the material because they are so excited to share their passion for the subject." Though instructors are "at the top of their respective fields," most are also "engaging and approachable." A mechanical engineering major supports this sentiment sharing, "I play basketball on Friday mornings with my major adviser and will often bring my homework with me in order to talk to him about problems I'm stuck on afterward." Ultimately, as this senior boasts, "At Stanford, anything is possible; I've lived on a schooner with faculty studying sharks, snorkeled on the Great Barrier Reef, hiked in the Australian rainforest, studied Antarctic phytoplankton with world-class scientists, and spent countless nights discussing philosophy, politics, film, and art until sunrise."

Campus Life

Undergrads agree that "it's pretty much impossible to be bored" at Stanford. Though students "work insanely hard during the week," they "also make it a priority to have a great time." And with so much to take advantage of, having fun is pretty easy. For example, the university sponsors "Cardinal Nights," a non-alcoholic program that hosts a number of events including "trips to Great America, a local amusement park, [a] movie pre-screening, and Stanford's Got Talent. All of the events are either free or extremely cheap for students." Undergrads also look forward to "special dinners...a common event in upper class housing." These are "nice on-campus dinners that are catered by house chefs. The meals usually have themes, such as Saturday Night Live or Moulin Rouge." Moreover, while there is certainly a drinking scene, it's pretty laid back. A sophomore explains, "you can find as much or as little of a party culture here as you're looking for. There's always a frat party to attend on the weekends, and there's always people to just hang out with at the dorm." Finally, students love the fact that hometown Palo Alto leaves them in close proximity to San Francisco. "A trip to the city is a short train-ride or car-ride away, so going to concerts and events in the city is always a fun option. Same goes for the nearby beaches." However, "there's always so much going on on-campus that sometimes it's hard to leave!"

Student Body

Stanford undergrads speak glowingly of their peers: "Everyone here is smart and has some story that will blow you out of the water if you ask, but are very humble and really just looking to have a good time." They also steadfastly assert, "There really is no typical Stanford student." And, thankfully, that "makes it easy to be an integrated and diverse student body." That being said, most Stanford undergrads are "very driven, independently motivated and willing to seek out opportunities." One senior elaborates by sharing, "Everyone fits in because we're united by a fire that drives us all to be excited about what we do. The trends you'll see will be along the lines of leadership and crazy intellect." Ultimately, students at Stanford are "ridiculously friendly and you can meet new people all over campus at almost every type of event."

STANFORD UNIVERSITY

Financial Aid: 650-723-3058 • E-Mail: admission@stanford.edu • Website: www.stanford.edu

THE PRINCETON REVIEW SAYS

Admissions

The school reports that its standardized testing policy for use in admission for Fall 2024 is Test Optional. It is unknown at this time if the 2024 testing policy will be permanent. The Princeton Review suggests that interested applicants consult with the school for the most up-to-date standardized testing policies. *Very important factors considered include:* rigor of secondary school record, academic GPA, class standing, standardized test scores, application essay, recommendation(s), extracurricular activities, talent/ability, character/personal qualities. *Other factors considered include:* interview, first generation, alumni/ae relation, geographical residence, racial/ethnic status, volunteer work, work experience. High school diploma is required and GED is accepted. *Academic units recommended:* 4 English, 4 math, 3 science, 3 science labs, 3 foreign language, 3 social studies.

Financial Aid

Students should submit: CSS/Financial Aid Profile; FAFSA; Noncustodial Profile. Priority filing deadline is 2/15. The Princeton Review suggests that all financial aid forms be submitted as soon as possible (see page 5 for a note on the FAFSA). *Need-based scholarships/grants offered:* College/university scholarship or grant aid from institutional funds; Federal Pell; Private scholarships; SEOG; State scholarships/grants. *Loan aid offered:* Direct PLUS loans; Direct Subsidized Loans; Direct Unsubsidized Loans. Admitted students will be notified of awards on a rolling basis beginning 4/1. Federal Work-Study Program available. Institutional employment available.

The Inside Word

Receiving a highly coveted acceptance letter from Stanford is no easy feat! Indeed, competition to gain admission is fierce. And, unfortunately, there is no magic formula. Clearly, a stellar academic record is a must. Beyond strong transcripts and test scores, successful applicants readily display intellectual curiosity and vigor, commitment to the topics and activities they are passionate about and initiative in seeking out opportunity.

THE SCHOOL SAYS "..."

From the Admissions Office

"Stanford looks for distinctive students who exhibit energy, personality, a sense of intellectual vitality and extraordinary impact outside the classroom. While there is no minimum grade point average, class rank, or test score one needs to be admitted to Stanford, the vast majority of successful applicants will be among the strongest students (academically) in their secondary schools. We want to understand the impact you have had at your job, in your family, in a club, in your school, or in the larger community, and we want to learn of the impact that experience has had on you. By focusing on your achievements in context, we evaluate how you have excelled in your school environment and how you have taken advantage of what is available to you in your school and community.

"The Common Application *and* Stanford Writing Supplement are both required and must be submitted online. In the Stanford Writing Supplement, accessed at www.commonapp.org, candidates write about an idea or experience important to their intellectual development, as well as a note to their future roommate. In the final essay, candidates are asked to write about something meaningful to them and why.

"Tuition charges are covered for undergrads with family incomes below $150,000. Zero parent contribution for undergrads with family incomes below $100,000."

SELECTIVITY

Admissions Rating	99
# of applicants	56,378
% of applicants accepted	4
% of acceptees attending	84
# offered a place on the wait list	553
% accepting a place on wait list	457
% admitted from wait list	8

FIRST-YEAR PROFILE

Testing policy	Test Optional
Range SAT composite	1500–1570
Range SAT EBRW	730–780
Range SAT math	770–800
Range ACT composite	33–35
# submitting SAT scores	855
% submitting SAT scores	49
# submitting ACT scores	405
% submitting ACT scores	23
Average HS GPA	3.95
% frosh submitting high school GPA	76
% graduated top 10% of class	94
% graduated top 25% of class	100
% graduated top 50% of class	100

DEADLINES

Early action	
Deadline	11/1
Notification	12/15
Regular	
Deadline	1/2
Notification	4/1
Nonfall registration?	No

APPLICANTS ALSO LOOK AT

Brown University; California Institute of Technology; Columbia University; Duke University; Harvard College; Massachusetts Institute of Technology; Princeton University; University of California—Los Angeles; University of Southern California; Yale University

FINANCIAL FACTS

Financial Aid Rating	97
Annual tuition	$57,693
Room and board	$18,619
Required fees	$723
Books and supplies	$1,350
Average frosh need-based scholarship	$63,208
Average UG need-based scholarship	$61,412
% needy frosh rec. need-based scholarship or grant aid	100
% needy UG rec. need-based scholarship or grant aid	99
% needy frosh rec. non-need-based scholarship or grant aid	2
% needy UG rec. non-need-based scholarship or grant aid	2
% needy frosh rec. need-based self-help aid	73
% needy UG rec. need-based self-help aid	80
% frosh rec. any financial aid	100
% UG rec. any financial aid	100
% UG borrow to pay for school	14
Average cumulative indebtedness	$20,691
% frosh need fully met	97
% ugrads need fully met	93
Average % of frosh need met	100
Average % of ugrad need met	100

STATE UNIVERSITY OF NEW YORK—BINGHAMTON UNIVERSITY

4400 Vestal Parkway East, Binghamton, NY 13902-6000 • Admissions: 607-777-2000 • Fax: 607-777-4445

STUDENTS SAY "..."

Academics

As one of the central institutions in one of the country's strongest public university systems, Binghamton University upholds rigorous academic, cultural, and engagement standards. The research university's six schools are spread across 930 acres of the beautiful upstate Susquehanna Valley. The nursing, business, and engineering schools are three standouts, but no matter what course a student chooses to study, you're sure to get the "best bang for your buck." Binghamton's multi-disciplinary education "prepares you not only for your career, but for the rest of your life," by instilling students with leadership, academic and social skills, and "employers rave about the school, especially if you are applying to jobs in New York City or on Long Island." In essence, "Binghamton is all about giving students many options to do what they want," and the career services office is an excellent complement to that; fellow students and alums are also "very willing to give out information that will benefit others, such as an internship or winter program."

Faculty members here are "dedicated and willing to invest in the university," and hold regular office hours, though students "have so many places to go if they are not available." As students get into their major-specific courses, "there is more discussion and less lecturing." Professors are "supportive, reasonable, accessible, clear and fair," and "as long as you are genuinely interested in the subject and willing to put in the work, you will succeed." High-quality research endeavors are available to all (especially those in the sciences), through programs like First-year Research Immersion, which provides first-year students with a three semester-long research experience in sciences, engineering, and public health. The Source Project provides similar research experiences for students in the humanities and social sciences.

Campus Life

The "excellent student board" organizes tons of events throughout the week and is "keen on getting the students...involved and [making] a difference." The university's 450+ organizations carry various roles "from community service to professionalism," and it has "almost any kind of club out there," from club sports to the hula hoop club to L.O.C.K.S. (Ladies Owning their Curls Kinks and Straights). The school's residential college system is modeled after the one at Oxford University, with students living in six different communities, each with its own personality. The living communities "really help break it up and make it feel smaller," and "there are a lot of study spaces and a lot of places to spend time." Though academics take priority, when students do leave their books, "Binghamton offers so many activities to do on campus that it is hard to ever be bored."

The town of Vestal is small and quiet, and there is a 190-acre nature preserve on campus that is frequently hiked by students. The nearby city and communities of greater Binghamton are constantly improving: "Change happens all of the time and the students are getting ready for it." People here do like to party on the weekends, and "going out into downtown Binghamton on Friday and Saturday nights to hit up the bars is popular." For those who prefer to keep it more low-key, the University Union always has "games, arts and crafts, free bowling (with free shoe rentals), ping pong (you do have to rent the paddles if you don't bring your own), billiards, and movie rentals," and there are often performances or movies shown on campus.

Student Body

A high proportion of students are from Long Island or Westchester, but they do report "a surprising amount of diversity" on campus, and students are "happy to step outside of their comfort zones and learn about different cultures." The majority of students "worked hard to afford school and to get into a school as intense as Binghamton" and there is "a very friendly and homey atmosphere at the school." This "extremely loving and generous" group is "multi-disciplined" and "involved in many organizations, leadership roles, jobs, internships, or research."

STATE UNIVERSITY OF NEW YORK—BINGHAMTON UNIVERSITY

Financial Aid: 607-777-2428 • E-Mail: admit@binghamton.edu • Website: www.binghamton.edu

THE PRINCETON REVIEW SAYS

Admissions

The school reports that its standardized testing policy for use in admission for Fall 2024 is Test Optional. It is unknown at this time if the 2024 testing policy will be permanent. The Princeton Review suggests that interested applicants consult with the school for the most up-to-date standardized testing policies. *Very important factors considered include:* rigor of secondary school record, academic GPA. *Important factors considered include:* class rank, application essay, extracurricular activities. *Other factors considered include:* standardized test scores, recommendation(s), talent/ability, character/personal qualities, first generation, alumni/ae relation, geographical residence, state residency, racial/ethnic status, volunteer work, work experience, level of applicant's interest. High school diploma is required and GED is accepted. *Academic units required:* 4 English, 3 math, 2 science, 3 foreign language, 2 social studies. *Academic units recommended:* 4 math, 4 science, 4 social studies, 4 history.

Financial Aid

Students should submit: FAFSA; State aid form. Priority filing deadline is 1/15. The Princeton Review suggests that all financial aid forms be submitted as soon as possible (see page 5 for a note on the FAFSA). *Need-based scholarships/grants offered:* College/university scholarship or grant aid from institutional funds; Federal Pell; Private scholarships; SEOG; State scholarships/grants. *Loan aid offered:* Direct PLUS loans; Direct Subsidized Loans; Direct Unsubsidized Loans; College/university loans from institutional funds; Federal Nursing Loans. Admitted students will be notified of awards on a rolling basis beginning 1/31. Federal Work-Study Program available. Institutional employment available.

The Inside Word

Like the vast majority of New York state schools, Binghamton accepts the single-apply SUNY application. Binghamton also accepts the Common Application, making it easy to apply to Binghamton University and other schools at the same time. Binghamton is one of the top public universities in the country—it's often referred to as a "public Ivy"—so expect competition to be stiff.

THE SCHOOL SAYS "..."

From the Admissions Office

"Binghamton has established itself as the premier public university in the Northeast, because of our outstanding undergraduate programs, vibrant campus culture, and committed faculty. Students are academically motivated, but there is a great deal of mutual help as they compete against the standard of a class rather than each other. Faculty and students work side by side in research labs or on artistic pursuits. Achievement, exploration, and leadership are hallmarks of a Binghamton education. Add to that a campus-wide commitment to internationalization that includes a robust education abroad program, cultural offerings, languages and international studies, and you have a place where graduates leave prepared for success. Binghamton University graduates lead the nation in top starting salaries among public universities, demonstrating that our students are recognized by employers and recruiters for having strong abilities to be leaders, critical thinkers, decision makers, analysts, and researchers in many fields and industries."

SELECTIVITY

Admissions Rating	93
# of applicants	31,642
% of applicants accepted	42
% of acceptees attending	18
# offered a place on the wait list	7,669
% accepting a place on wait list	40
% admitted from wait list	4

FIRST-YEAR PROFILE

Testing policy	Test Optional
Range SAT composite	1340–1510
Range SAT EBRW	650–730
Range SAT math	690–780
Range ACT composite	29–34
# submitting SAT scores	1,673
% submitting SAT scores	54
# submitting ACT scores	358
% submitting ACT scores	12
Average HS GPA	3.9
% frosh submitting high school GPA	100
% graduated top 10% of class	52
% graduated top 25% of class	87
% graduated top 50% of class	98

DEADLINES

Early action	
Deadline	11/1
Notification	1/15
Regular	
Priority	1/15
Nonfall registration?	Yes

APPLICANTS OFTEN PREFER
Cornell University

APPLICANTS SOMETIMES PREFER
Boston University; New York University

APPLICANTS RARELY PREFER
Rutgers University–Newark; State University of New York—Stony Brook University

FINANCIAL FACTS

Financial Aid Rating	80
Annual in-state tuition	$7,070
Annual out-of-state tuition	$24,910
Room and board	$17,064
Required fees	$3,320
Books and supplies	$1,000
Average frosh need-based scholarship	$11,637
Average UG need-based scholarship	$10,848
% needy frosh rec. need-based scholarship or grant aid	89
% needy UG rec. need-based scholarship or grant aid	73
% needy frosh rec. non-need-based scholarship or grant aid	6
% needy UG rec. non-need-based scholarship or grant aid	4
% needy frosh rec. need-based self-help aid	48
% needy UG rec. need-based self-help aid	58
% frosh rec. any financial aid	51
% UG rec. any financial aid	78
% UG borrow to pay for school	51
Average cumulative indebtedness	$25,975
% frosh need fully met	8
% ugrads need fully met	7
Average % of frosh need met	68
Average % of ugrad need met	68

STATE UNIVERSITY OF NEW YORK—COLLEGE OF ENVIRONMENTAL SCIENCE AND FORESTRY

1 Forestry Drive, Syracuse, NY 13210-2779 • Admissions: 315-470-6500 • Fax: 315-470-6933

CAMPUS LIFE
Quality of Life Rating	87
Fire Safety Rating	98
Green Rating	97
Type of school	Public
Environment	City

STUDENTS
Total undergrad enrollment	1,587
% male/female/another gender	50/49/<1
% from out of state	33
% frosh from public high school	90
% frosh live on campus	3
% ugrads live on campus	29
# of fraternities	26
# of sororities	21
% African American	2
% Asian	1
% White	79
% Hispanic	7
% Native American	<1
% Pacific Islander	<1
% Two or more races	3
% Race and/or ethnicity unknown	5
% international	2
# of countries represented	7

SURVEY SAYS . . .
Students environmentally aware
Dorms are like palaces
Active student government
Students involved in community service

ACADEMICS
Academic Rating	79
% students returning for sophomore year	74
% students graduating within 6 years	77
Calendar	Semester
Student/faculty ratio	14:1
Profs interesting rating	88
Profs accessible rating	89

Most classes have fewer than 10 students.
Most lab/discussion sessions have
10–19 students.

MOST POPULAR MAJORS
Environmental Biology; Landscape Architecture;
Environmental Science

STUDENTS SAY ". . ."

Academics
The State University of New York—College of Environmental Science and Forestry is the country's oldest college dedicated entirely to environmental discovery, learning, and sustainability. Campus occupies 12 acres in Syracuse and the institution uses 25,000 acres located across central New York and the Adirondacks as a "living laboratory" for hands-on projects and research. ESF's 1,600 undergrads choose from 27 majors (as well as plenty of specialized courses) and are able to take classes and use facilities and resources at neighboring Syracuse University. The school reports an excellent job placement rate, and students tell us "the student body and faculty care about each other and help everyone get the most out of the experience."

The professors here are "so down to earth and passionate." They "seem to love what they do, and they are all conducting their own research," and this research "is sprinkled into the undergraduate experience." Every class "is applied directly to your major and field of interest." Be it paper engineering and renewable materials science, forest resources, or environmental interpretation, "ESF will cater to your specific needs." The small campus size allows plentiful opportunities for students to gain close relationships with professors, often eventually leading to projects or teaching assistant positions." When it comes to jobs in the environmental field, ESF is well recognized, and "the name alone will likely set you ahead in your career." The school "truly does provide you with the necessary experience for your field with challenging courses and endless volunteer, research, and internship opportunities throughout your time at ESF."

Campus Campus Life
ESF is home to is an extremely active student body, with "students participating in several clubs at a time and holding several leadership positions at a time." There are a lot of wonderful organizations on campus to get involved in, but when students are tired of those things, "the school shares a border with a 160 acre forested cemetery and it is a very popular place for students to explore and hang out." Central New York is also filled with things to do for students with cars, mostly parks and waterfalls. "Here at 'tree school,' we spend most of our time studying, chilling with pals, or appreciating nature," says one student, adding that students looking for a more active social life enjoy "using Syracuse University facilities and attending their parties." ESF students have the option of pledging Greek organizations at Syracuse, as well. ESF is a smaller school so "everyone really does know everyone." The off-campus housing situation illustrates this pretty well; "most of the students from our school live along this one street."

Student Body
Students describe ESF as "fostering a community that uses the knowledge it gains through schooling to make real changes to our world." Though "everyone takes a different path toward the end goal of helping our planet prosper, it's a main concern for all of us," according to one student. With this common goal, students feel "an almost instantaneous camaraderie." This is "one of the most accepting groups of students" out there, and students here "are free to rock their own styles." As one enrollee puts it, "No one is afraid to be themselves, and it is a very open...environment." While some are more focused on wildlife and others on timber resources, "everyone enjoys being outdoors," and students are "often caught discussing class or lab topics in their free time."

STATE UNIVERSITY OF NEW YORK—COLLEGE OF ENVIRONMENTAL SCIENCE AND FORESTRY

Financial Aid: 315-470-6706 • E-Mail: esfinfo@esf.edu • Website: www.esf.edu

THE PRINCETON REVIEW SAYS

Admissions

The school reports that its standardized testing policy for use in admission for Fall 2024 is Test Optional. It is unknown at this time if the 2024 testing policy will be permanent. The Princeton Review suggests that interested applicants consult with the school for the most up-to-date standardized testing policies. *Very important factors considered include:* rigor of secondary school record, academic GPA, standardized test scores, application essay, level of applicant's interest. *Important factors considered include:* class rank, recommendation(s), extracurricular activities, talent/ability. *Other factors considered include:* interview, character/personal qualities, first generation, alumni/ae relation, geographical residence, state residency, racial/ethnic status, volunteer work, work experience. High school diploma is required and GED is accepted. *Academic units required:* 4 English, 3 math, 3 science, 3 social studies, 1 history. *Academic units recommended:* 4 math, 4 science, 3 science labs, 3 foreign language.

Financial Aid

Students should submit: FAFSA; State aid form. Priority filing deadline is 2/1. The Princeton Review suggests that all financial aid forms be submitted as soon as possible (see page 5 for a note on the FAFSA). *Need-based scholarships/grants offered:* College/university scholarship or grant aid from institutional funds; Federal Pell; Private scholarships; SEOG; State scholarships/grants. *Loan aid offered:* Direct PLUS loans; Direct Subsidized Loans; Direct Unsubsidized Loans. Admitted students will be notified of awards on a rolling basis beginning 2/1. Federal Work-Study Program available. Institutional employment available.

The Inside Word

"ESF is an excellent value even for students hailing from outside the Empire State. While there are many specialized bachelor of science degrees, there are also coordinated programs between the college and the Upstate Medical University, as well as a host of pre-professional programs. GPA is an important factor in ESF's admission calculus, but level of demonstrated interest carries as much weight as statistical information. Aspiring Mighty Oaks should make their interest known early and often."

THE SCHOOL SAYS "..."

From the Admissions Office

"ESF is a small college with big ideas. We make a global impact improving and sustaining the environment. We offer a world-class education among a close-knit community of scholars with common values and a shared sense of purpose.

"ESF offers a variety of academic programs leading to Associate, Bachelor's, Master's, and Doctorate degrees, for students interested in sustainability and the science, engineering, design, and management of natural resources and the environment.

"At ESF, students are part of one of the world's largest college campuses which spans from Syracuse, New York, across more than 25,000 acres of forests and wetlands at our field stations throughout Central New York and in the Adirondack Park.

"ESF is a small, specialized college community. Through our long-standing partnership with Syracuse University (SU), which is located right next door, students have access to big university benefits—including classes, student activities and organizations, and recreational facilities.

"Students leave ESF well-trained to execute on improving the world—and their expertise has never been more in demand."

SELECTIVITY

Admissions Rating	85
# of applicants	2,250
% of applicants accepted	68
% of acceptees attending	20
# offered a place on the wait list	101
% accepting a place on wait list	100

FIRST-YEAR PROFILE

Testing policy	Test Optional
Range SAT composite	1140–1297
Range ACT composite	28–31
# submitting SAT scores	110
% submitting SAT scores	36
# submitting ACT scores	23
% submitting ACT scores	7
Average HS GPA	3.7
% frosh submitting high school GPA	100

DEADLINES

Early decision	
Deadline	12/1
Notification	1/15
Regular	
Priority	2/1
Notification	Rolling, 2/1
Nonfall registration?	Yes

FINANCIAL FACTS

Financial Aid Rating	82
Annual in-state tuition	$7,070
Annual out-of-state tuition	$16,980
Room and board	$16,270
Required fees	$2,146
Books and supplies	$1,200
Average frosh need-based scholarship	$7,027
Average UG need-based scholarship	$6,388
% needy frosh rec. need-based scholarship or grant aid	100
% needy UG rec. need-based scholarship or grant aid	96
% needy frosh rec. non-need-based scholarship or grant aid	64
% needy UG rec. non-need-based scholarship or grant aid	58
% needy frosh rec. need-based self-help aid	66
% needy UG rec. need-based self-help aid	63
% frosh rec. any financial aid	91
% UG rec. any financial aid	93
% frosh need fully met	25
% ugrads need fully met	28
Average % of frosh need met	63
Average % of ugrad need met	65

STATE UNIVERSITY OF NEW YORK AT GENESEO

1 College Circle, Geneseo, NY 14454 • Admissions: 585-245-5000 • Fax: 585-245-5550

STUDENTS SAY "..."

Academics

As a public liberal arts college, State University of New York at Geneseo attracts students searching for a "quality education at an affordable price." Undergrads say this academics-focused college provides "challenging but rewarding" courses taught by faculty who are "here to teach and prepare students for the real world." Students find professors to be "fair in terms of tests and expectations," and note that they "really push the students." While most professors use traditional teaching methods, "giving very interesting lectures or leading good group discussions," other notable forms of learning include "live experiments in class," labs that "develop skills necessary for future studies...as well as for general team work," and "counseling services for local businesses." Some classes seem needlessly difficult to students, with the sole purpose of "weeding people out" of competitive majors, but thankfully there are "great resources available to anyone who needs help regardless of the subject matter." Professors provide generous office hours and are mostly "accommodating as long as you reach out to them" and students can "seek help and work with peers through challenging material and problems" at the tutoring centers. Students seeking a challenging liberal arts college environment with a state school price are pleased with the choice to attend Geneseo.

Campus Life

At Geneseo, which sits on a "gorgeous campus [with] beautiful sunsets," students "focus on their academics," but they also make time for clubs or athletics—hockey games in particular bring out school spirit. In addition to team sports, undergrads stay active by "going to the gym or various classes offered by [the] school such as spin, yoga, or Zumba." On warm days, students love to "hang out and do work on the quad, put up a hammock between two trees, or throw a Frisbee around...with friends." Greek life is a big part of the Geneseo experience for some students, as are college sponsored events by the organization Geneseo Late Knight, which "puts on events every single weekend that are free for students." The weekends are also when "students definitely like to party," and they spend time at nearby bars. For those looking to get outside, the "scenery of the Geneseo area" has much more to offer: Students mention it's also great for hiking. Despite this, they note that "the town around us is small so there's not a lot to do," which makes trips to Rochester popular: "it's a short drive away" and reachable via a bus shuttle on the weekends.

Student Body

With its small campus, Geneseo is a "tightly knit community" of "intelligent and kind individuals" where "all members support each other." Students value the "strong sense of community" and say all types of people can be found at Geneseo, although some do claim that their peers are "mostly white," however, students come from "very different upbringings and are from different social classes." One student describes her friends as a mix of "some quiet, some outgoing, some party-animals, and some bookworms." Regardless of this broad range, almost everyone is there to "receive a higher education and be successful." Campus culture is generally liberal, featuring "inclusivity involving ethnicity, religion, and sexuality," but some describe social life as cliquey, noting "it is much harder to make friends if you are not in Greek life." On a final note, one student reassures us, "once you find your people, you will feel right at home."

STATE UNIVERSITY OF NEW YORK AT GENESEO

Financial Aid: 585-245-5731 • E-Mail: admissions@geneseo.edu • Website: www.geneseo.edu

THE PRINCETON REVIEW SAYS

Admissions

The school reports that its standardized testing policy for use in admission for Fall 2024 is Test Optional. The 2024 testing policy will be permanent. The Princeton Review suggests that interested applicants consult with the school for the most up-to-date standardized testing policies. *Very important factors considered include:* rigor of secondary school record, standardized test scores. *Important factors considered include:* class rank, academic GPA, application essay, recommendation(s), extracurricular activities, talent/ability, racial/ethnic status. *Other factors considered include:* character/personal qualities, first generation, alumni/ae relation, state residency, volunteer work, work experience, level of applicant's interest. High school diploma is required and GED is accepted. *Academic units required: Academic units recommended:* 4 English, 4 math, 4 science, 4 foreign language, 4 social studies.

Financial Aid

Students should submit: FAFSA; State aid form. The Princeton Review suggests that all financial aid forms be submitted as soon as possible (see page 5 for a note on the FAFSA). *Need-based scholarships/grants offered:* College/university scholarship or grant aid from institutional funds; Federal Pell; SEOG; State scholarships/grants. *Loan aid offered:* Direct PLUS loans; Direct Subsidized Loans; Direct Unsubsidized Loans. Admitted students will be notified of awards on a rolling basis. Federal Work-Study Program available. Institutional employment available.

The Inside Word

While the current acceptance rate is high, the applicant pool for SUNY Geneseo grows increasingly competitive each year. Grades and rigor of study carry the most weight with the admissions committee here, followed by the rigor of an applicant's high school classes. The personal essay, résumé of co-curricular activities, and recommendations round out the holistic application review.

THE SCHOOL SAYS "..."

From the Admissions Office

"SUNY Geneseo fills a distinct niche among the nation's premier public liberal arts colleges, allowing it to attract highly motivated and talented students from diverse backgrounds. Its highly regarded professional programs, and its cultural, social, recreational, and volunteer opportunities, provide Geneseo's students with the opportunity and tools to become service-minded global citizens. Geneseo is the only SUNY undergraduate college with a chapter of Phi Beta Kappa, the nation's most prestigious academic honor society, further solidifying the college's reputation as a community of outstanding scholars. Inspired by a transformative core curriculum and extraordinary active learning opportunities, Geneseo students can pursue independent study, take advantage of global experiences and get involved in undergraduate research with faculty who value close working relationships with exceptional students. And for savvy students who recognize Geneseo's value and the financial advantage it affords, the College is a smart investment. Founded in 1871, Geneseo celebrated its 150th anniversary in 2021. The College occupies a beautiful 220-acre campus in the historic Village of Geneseo, contributing to its inclusive sense of community. This intellectual and supportive environment is a hallmark of the Geneseo honors college experience that successfully inspires students to pursue life and career goals. Over 40 percent of students pursue graduate study immediately upon graduation, making Geneseo among the country's top 10 master's-awarding colleges for the number of doctorates earned, and in the top seven for those who earn doctorates in STEM fields."

SELECTIVITY

Admissions Rating	86
# of applicants	9,068
% of applicants accepted	75
% of acceptees attending	13
# offered a place on the wait list	1,095
% accepting a place on wait list	27
# of early decision applicants	146
% accepted early decision	97

FIRST-YEAR PROFILE

Testing policy	Test Optional
Range SAT composite	1170–1310
Range SAT EBRW	580–660
Range SAT math	580–660
Range ACT composite	25–31
# submitting SAT scores	238
% submitting SAT scores	27
# submitting ACT scores	30
% submitting ACT scores	3
Average HS GPA	93
% frosh submitting high school GPA	100
% graduated top 10% of class	29
% graduated top 25% of class	62
% graduated top 50% of class	91

DEADLINES

Early decision	
Deadline	11/15
Notification	12/15
Regular	
Deadline	2/1
Notification	3/1
Nonfall registration?	Yes

APPLICANTS OFTEN PREFER

State University of New York—Binghamton University; State University of New York—Stony Brook University; State University of New York—University at Buffalo; University at Albany—SUNY

APPLICANTS SOMETIMES PREFER

City University of New York—Baruch College; City University of New York—Hunter College; State University of New York at Cortland; State University of New York at New Paltz; State University of New York—Oswego; SUNY College at Oneonta

FINANCIAL FACTS

Financial Aid Rating	79
Annual in-state tuition	$7,070
Annual out-of-state tuition	$16,980
Room and board	$14,280
Required fees	$1,857
Books and supplies	$1,000
Average frosh need-based scholarship	$9,464
Average UG need-based scholarship	$8,681
% needy frosh rec. need-based scholarship or grant aid	96
% needy UG rec. need-based scholarship or grant aid	89
% needy frosh rec. non-need-based scholarship or grant aid	13
% needy UG rec. non-need-based scholarship or grant aid	9
% needy frosh rec. need-based self-help aid	90
% needy UG rec. need-based self-help aid	91
% frosh rec. any financial aid	89
% UG rec. any financial aid	74
% UG borrow to pay for school	94
Average cumulative indebtedness	$15,988
% frosh need fully met	23
% ugrads need fully met	23
Average % of frosh need met	63
Average % of ugrad need met	60

STATE UNIVERSITY OF NEW YORK—PURCHASE COLLEGE

735 Anderson Hill Road, Purchase, NY 10577 • Admissions: 914-251-6000 • Fax: 914-251-6314

CAMPUS LIFE

Quality of Life Rating	79
Fire Safety Rating	60*
Green Rating	88
Type of school	Public
Environment	Town

STUDENTS

Total undergrad enrollment	3,145
% male/female/another gender	41/59/0
% from out of state	14
% frosh live on campus	83
% ugrads live on campus	70
# of fraternities	0
# of sororities	0
% African American	13
% Asian	4
% White	49
% Hispanic	26
% Native American	<1
% Pacific Islander	<1
% Two or more races	6
% Race and/or ethnicity unknown	1
% international	1
# of countries represented	54

SURVEY SAYS . . .

Lots of liberal students
Students aren't religious
Theater is popular
Active student government

ACADEMICS

Academic Rating	77
% students returning for sophomore year	78
Calendar	Semester
Student/faculty ratio	11:1
Profs interesting rating	87
Profs accessible rating	88

Most classes have 10–19 students.
Most lab/discussion sessions have
  10–19 students.

MOST POPULAR MAJORS

Psychology, General; Communication, Journalism,
And Related Programs; Playwriting and
Screenwriting

STUDENTS SAY "..."

Academics

Its motto "Think Wide Open" perfectly sums up Purchase College, SUNY, long the artsy lodestone in the SUNY system: the conservatory here "deserves and receives the highest respect." Between the School of the Arts and the School of Liberal Arts & Sciences, there are over 40 majors to choose (and, if those don't suit you, a rarely chosen option to design your own). Nearly all bachelor's students must complete a senior project in which they devote two semesters to in-depth, original, and creative study, and students welcome the chance to explore. "We're all about finding new ways to think about things, from science to art to management," says one.

Classes tend to be about "learning through discussion" rather than lecture, and professors "go out of their way to make sure that everyone is on the same page, and don't leave any-one behind." They often actively work in the field in which they teach, and therefore "bring the material life and take learning outside the classroom." Classes in both the creative arts and general education are "rich and exciting," such as the professor who "teaches classes about Jack Kerouac on a train and walks the path of *On the Road*." Students benefit from the school's proximity to New York City (less than an hour away), where auditions, showcases, and a fertile alumni network thrive, and "some of the best artists in the NY area become adjunct faculty at this school at some point."

Campus Life

For fun, there's "a TON of things going on": weekly dance parties and concerts, student clubs, lectures, an on-campus museum, free yoga classes, Zumba, and tons of festivals. People "pay a lot of money to see bands and they support music and musicians here," and theatre is also "very, very big and popular." Though there are 17 Division III athletics teams, students feel that they get less emphasis, and Greek life is non-existent. Students receive email digests of all the events on campus, and for those who want to get off cam-pus, it's easy to take a bus into White Plains or take the train into Manhattan. "The ques-tion isn't 'What to do for fun?' but rather 'Where do you even start?'" Professors usually "know a lot about what's going on" and will often get free tickets to performances for students. While the Student Center (Stood) and library facilities are admittedly great ("there are different levels, so students never have to be isolated in one spot"), many dorms are still on the older side and "need to be updated badly." To its credit, Purchase has been making yearly renovations and in 2019 introduced the brand-new Wayback residence hall for upperclass students.

Student Body

Students at Purchase describe the school as a place for everyone, particularly the "artsy, unique, passionate, [and] intelligent." The overall "sense of unity and acceptance" means that students are free to be themselves and can "walk around confident in who they are and they aren't afraid to show their unique styles and personalities." There are a lot of "free spirits" and the atmosphere is "filled with liberal ideologies," and the high concentration of visual/multi-media artists, musicians, and dancers means that "creativity and the arts flourish." The decent number of commuters don't have any real problem integrating with the resident population, and "you can always incorporate your craft into whatever you create at Purchase."

STATE UNIVERSITY OF NEW YORK—PURCHASE COLLEGE

E-Mail: admissions@purchase.edu • Website: www.purchase.edu

THE PRINCETON REVIEW SAYS

Admissions

The school reports that its standardized testing policy for use in admission for Fall 2024 is Test Optional. The 2024 testing policy will be permanent. The Princeton Review suggests that interested applicants consult with the school for the most up-to-date standardized testing policies. *Very important factors considered include:* academic GPA, application essay, talent/ability. *Important factors considered include:* rigor of secondary school record, class rank, character/personal qualities. *Other factors considered include:* standardized test scores, recommendation(s), interview, extracurricular activities, first generation, alumni/ae relation, geographical residence, state residency, racial/ethnic status, volunteer work, work experience, level of applicant's interest. High school diploma is required and GED is accepted. *Academic units required:* 4 English, 4 math, 3 science, 1 science lab, 3 foreign language, 4 social studies, 2 academic electives.

Financial Aid

Students should submit: FAFSA; State aid form. Priority filing deadline is 2/1. The Princeton Review suggests that all financial aid forms be submitted as soon as possible (see page 5 for a note on the FAFSA). *Need-based scholarships/grants offered:* College/university scholarship or grant aid from institutional funds; Federal Pell; Private scholarships; SEOG; State scholarships/grants. *Loan aid offered:* Direct PLUS loans; Direct Subsidized Loans; Direct Unsubsidized Loans. Admitted students will be notified of awards on a rolling basis beginning 3/1. Federal Work-Study Program available. Institutional employment available.

The Inside Word

Almost 40 percent of Purchase students are enrolled in the highly selective School of the Arts. Arts applicants should know that to apply to the programs in dance, theatre arts, music, School of Art+Design, or School of Film and Media Studies—the audition, portfolio, or other applicable work samples in addition to academic performance are of paramount importance. Purchase College is Test Optional, and standardized test scores will only be reviewed if a student chooses to submit them.

THE SCHOOL SAYS "..."

From the Admissions Office

"Whether for our top-ranked and innovative liberal arts majors or our world-class arts programs, Purchase attracts students from around the globe seeking to cultivate their intellectual identity, develop their talents, expand their minds and transform their passions into action. By choosing Purchase, students make a conscious decision to join an intense community with a deep respect for individuality and diversity and an unparalleled environment of creativity and innovation.

"Our dynamic faculty are not only among the most accomplished in their fields but also partner with students on research projects and work tirelessly to ensure students succeed in their chosen fields of study or career. The intimate classroom setting and engaged faculty inspire lively classroom discussion and debate, critical thinking, originality, and discovery and invention.

"Purchase students represent a broad spectrum of familial, social, ethnic, economic, and geographical backgrounds. The student body is also diverse in terms of gender identity and sexual orientation. Highly talented, motivated, and entrepreneurial, Purchase students strive to impact our society through civic and cultural engagement.

"Still a relatively young college, Purchase offers students an opportunity to build upon established campus traditions as well as create new ones. Our proximity to New York City provides students access to outstanding cultural and career-related opportunities. On campus, students can see world-class performances at the PAC and notable exhibitions at the Neuberger Museum.

"We seek to enroll highly motivated, hard-working and academically strong students with a consistent record of achievement in a challenging high school curriculum. Admission criteria vary amongst programs."

SELECTIVITY

Admissions Rating	85
# of applicants	5,528
% of applicants accepted	78
% of acceptees attending	16

FIRST-YEAR PROFILE

Testing policy	Test Optional
Range SAT composite	1190–1350
Range SAT EBRW	620–700
Range SAT math	570–650
Range ACT composite	28.5–31
# submitting SAT scores	75
% submitting SAT scores	11
# submitting ACT scores	12
% submitting ACT scores	2
Average HS GPA	3.4
% frosh submitting high school GPA	98

DEADLINES

Early action	
Deadline	11/15
Notification	1/1
Regular	
Priority	3/1
Deadline	7/1
Notification	Rolling, 7/1
Nonfall registration?	Yes

FINANCIAL FACTS

Financial Aid Rating	78
Annual in-state tuition	$7,070
Annual out-of-state tuition	$16,980
Room and board	$14,548
Required fees	$1,883
Books and supplies	$1,240
Average frosh need-based scholarship	$11,697
Average UG need-based scholarship	$11,611
% needy frosh rec. need-based scholarship or grant aid	98
% needy UG rec. need-based scholarship or grant aid	98
% needy frosh rec. non-need-based scholarship or grant aid	22
% needy UG rec. non-need-based scholarship or grant aid	22
% needy frosh rec. need-based self-help aid	83
% needy UG rec. need-based self-help aid	86
% frosh rec. any financial aid	
% UG rec. any financial aid	
% UG borrow to pay for school	
Average cumulative indebtedness	
% frosh need fully met	6
% ugrads need fully met	4
Average % of frosh need met	58
Average % of ugrad need met	54

STATE UNIVERSITY OF NEW YORK—STONY BROOK UNIVERSITY

Office of Admissions, Stony Brook, NY 11794-1901 • Admissions: 631-632-6000 • Fax: 631-632-9898

CAMPUS LIFE

Quality of Life Rating	81
Fire Safety Rating	90
Green Rating	96
Type of school	Public
Environment	Town

STUDENTS

Total undergrad enrollment	17,406
% male/female/another gender	49/51/0
% from out of state	7
% frosh from public high school	90
% frosh live on campus	77
% ugrads live on campus	50
# of fraternities (% join)	11 (3)
# of sororities (% join)	12 (3)
% African American	6
% Asian	34
% White	27
% Hispanic	15
% Native American	<1
% Pacific Islander	<1
% Two or more races	3
% Race and/or ethnicity unknown	6
% international	10
# of countries represented	119

SURVEY SAYS . . .

Lab facilities are great
Everyone loves the Seawolves
Active minority support groups

ACADEMICS

Academic Rating	78
% students returning for sophomore year	88
% students graduating within 4 years	65
% students graduating within 6 years	78
Calendar	Semester
Student/faculty ratio	19:1
Profs interesting rating	84
Profs accessible rating	86

Most classes have 20–29 students.
Most lab/discussion sessions have 20–29 students.

MOST POPULAR MAJORS

Biology/Biological Sciences, General; Health Services/Allied Health/Health Sciences, General; Business Administration and Management, General

STUDENTS SAY "..."

Academics

SUNY Stony Brook is "on par with the best of the country," according to one student. This public "research-intensive" institution uses its large size to offer a wide range of cross-curricular opportunities at both the undergrad and graduate levels. As one enrollee in a part-time MBA program puts it, having "met people with engineering, medical, business, and liberal arts backgrounds…is a fun experience." A third-year also lauds the school's connections to Stony Brook University Hospital, which helps those studying for medical professions, and others point to a wealth of similar opportunities by association: "scholarships, fellowships, job opportunities, or even workshops held by different organizations on a variety of topics."

Even without external offerings, students would still appreciate that professors on campus "are professional and experienced in their own area and are capable of providing us with knowledge and insights in class" and "dedicated to students' development." One sophomore notes that an "algorithm teacher used the New York train system to explain many concepts which are going to stay with me for many years." And for those students following a research track, the Undergraduate Research and Creative Activities (URECA) program helps students take the next steps with faculty, making sure that no opportunities are lost.

Campus Life

From stargazing with the astronomy club to raising puppies for the Guide Dog Foundation, Stony Brook offers "a wide range of clubs and organizations for students to join." Attending cultural club events, participating in Greek life, and watching the "various fantastic shows at the Staller Center for the Arts" are also favorite activities on campus. Meanwhile, those with athletic goals benefit from "a variety of recreational facilities, such as fitness centers, swimming pools, and sports fields."

Some students note that the social life can be "very conservative," given that so many are "focused on excellent grades and performance," particularly at the graduate level. But students do manage to fit in activities: "We typically hang out with friends, chill at the dining halls or library, play frisbee when it's hot, [and] throw snowballs when it snows." And if the campus sometimes feels empty on the weekends, that's only because students venture to nearby New York City or enjoy "visiting the beaches, hiking trails, parks, and many other outdoor activities" available on Long Island.

Student Body

"Students from around the world come to Stony Brook for a variety of interests from medical to science to research," raves one first-year student. Accordingly, there's an array of "diverse cultural and academic backgrounds"—though no shortage of community given the shared enthusiasm: "I feel lucky to meet a group of classmates who share the same passion for Economics!" That common focus delights students who explain that even on online discussion boards, "everyone is very nice and asks good intellectual questions." It also means that regardless of backgrounds, there's an overall bunch of students who are "knowledgeable, and they propel you to do more and achieve more."

STATE UNIVERSITY OF NEW YORK—STONY BROOK UNIVERSITY

Financial Aid: 631-632-6840 • E-Mail: enroll@stonybrook.edu • Website: www.stonybrook.edu/

THE PRINCETON REVIEW SAYS

Admissions

The school reports that its standardized testing policy for use in admission for Fall 2024 is Test Optional. It is unknown at this time if the 2024 testing policy will be permanent. The Princeton Review suggests that interested applicants consult with the school for the most up-to-date standardized testing policies. *Very important factors considered include:* rigor of secondary school record, academic GPA, standardized test scores. *Important factors considered include:* application essay, recommendation(s). *Other factors considered include:* class rank, interview, extracurricular activities, talent/ability, character/personal qualities, first generation, alumni/ae relation, geographical residence, state residency, volunteer work, work experience, level of applicant's interest. High school diploma is required and GED is accepted. *Academic units required:* 4 English, 3 math, 3 science, 4 social studies. *Academic units recommended:* 4 English, 4 math, 4 science, 3 foreign language, 4 social studies.

Financial Aid

Students should submit: FAFSA; State aid form. Priority filing deadline is 1/15. The Princeton Review suggests that all financial aid forms be submitted as soon as possible (see page 5 for a note on the FAFSA). *Need-based scholarships/grants offered:* College/university scholarship or grant aid from institutional funds; Federal Pell; Private scholarships; SEOG; State scholarships/grants. *Loan aid offered:* Direct PLUS loans; Direct Subsidized Loans; Direct Unsubsidized Loans. Admitted students will be notified of awards on a rolling basis. Federal Work-Study Program available. Institutional employment available.

The Inside Word

Admission to Stony Brook University is competitive. Successful applicants for the freshman class will have typically followed a rigorous college prep curriculum in high school and have strong standardized test scores, and the university will also give special consideration to leadership experience or talents demonstrated through extracurricular activities or volunteer work. Students with a particularly strong academic record may be considered for the university's special programs, including the Honors College, the University Scholars program, and Women in Science and Engineering.

THE SCHOOL SAYS "..."

From the Admissions Office

"Stony Brook's designation as a flagship of the State University of New York (SUNY) system reflects the preeminent role that the university plays statewide, nationally, and internationally as a model of research and academic excellence. With more than 200 majors, minors, and combined-degree programs, Stony Brook offers students an elite education with an outstanding return on investment. Among our innovative programs are a fast-track MBA program and the award-winning Undergraduate Research and Creative Activities (URECA) program. Unique research opportunities abound at our medical center, in our marine sciences program, and at nearby Brookhaven National Laboratory, which Stony Brook has a role in running.

"Admission to Stony Brook University is competitive. Successful applicants will have typically followed a rigorous college prep curriculum in high school, and we also consider leadership experience or talents demonstrated through extracurricular activities or volunteer work. We offer a variety of honors programs—such as University Scholars, Honors College, and Women in Science and Engineering, as well as honors tracks in Computer Science and Business—to challenge and inspire our most gifted students. Faculty include Nobel laureates, MacArthur grant recipients, Fields medalists and Pulitzer Prize winners. Stony Brook offers unique study abroad programs on six continents in nearly 30 different countries.

"Students enjoy a dynamic first-year experience in one of three small undergraduate communities, reside in comfortable campus housing, and have access to outstanding recreational facilities, including a 12,300-seat stadium, a sports complex housing a 4,000-seat arena, and a state-of-the art campus recreation center devoted entirely to the health and well-being of the campus community."

SELECTIVITY

Admissions Rating	92
# of applicants	40,513
% of applicants accepted	49
% of acceptees attending	17
# offered a place on the wait list	4,253
% accepting a place on wait list	55
% admitted from wait list	44

FIRST-YEAR PROFILE

Testing policy	Test Optional
Range SAT composite	1320–1480
Range SAT EBRW	640–720
Range SAT math	680–780
Range ACT composite	28–34
# submitting SAT scores	1,368
% submitting SAT scores	41
# submitting ACT scores	157
% submitting ACT scores	5
Average HS GPA	94.2
% frosh submitting high school GPA	100
% graduated top 10% of class	47
% graduated top 25% of class	78
% graduated top 50% of class	96

DEADLINES

Regular	
Priority	1/15
Deadline	1/15
Notification	4/1
Nonfall registration?	Yes

APPLICANTS OFTEN PREFER

Cornell University; New York University; Rensselaer Polytechnic Institute; State University of New York—Binghamton University

APPLICANTS SOMETIMES PREFER

Penn State University Park; Rutgers University—New Brunswick; State University of New York—Geneseo; State University of New York--University at Buffalo; University of Connecticut

APPLICANTS RARELY PREFER

Adelphi University; Hofstra University; Pace University

FINANCIAL FACTS

Financial Aid Rating	80
Annual in-state tuition	$7,070
Annual out-of-state tuition	$24,990
Room and board	$16,408
Required fees	$3,490
Books and supplies	$900
Average frosh need-based scholarship	$11,511
Average UG need-based scholarship	$9,848
% needy frosh rec. need-based scholarship or grant aid	91
% needy UG rec. need-based scholarship or grant aid	86
% needy frosh rec. non-need-based scholarship or grant aid	9
% needy UG rec. non-need-based scholarship or grant aid	8
% needy frosh rec. need-based self-help aid	90
% needy UG rec. need-based self-help aid	89
% frosh rec. any financial aid	88
% UG rec. any financial aid	78
% UG borrow to pay for school	46
Average cumulative indebtedness	$23,899
% frosh need fully met	11
% ugrads need fully met	14
Average % of frosh need met	65
Average % of ugrad need met	63

STETSON UNIVERSITY

421 N. Woodland Boulevard, DeLand, FL 32723 • Admissions: 386-822-7000 • Fax: 386-822-7112

CAMPUS LIFE

Quality of Life Rating	88
Fire Safety Rating	81
Green Rating	84
Type of school	Private
Affiliation	No Affiliation
Environment	Town

STUDENTS

Total undergrad enrollment	2,517
% male/female/another gender	43/56/<1
% from out of state	25
% frosh from public high school	77
% frosh live on campus	80
% ugrads live on campus	65
# of fraternities (% join)	9 (22)
# of sororities (% join)	6 (15)
% African American	12
% Asian	2
% White	53
% Hispanic	20
% Native American	<1
% Pacific Islander	<1
% Two or more races	6
% Race and/or ethnicity unknown	1
% international	7
# of countries represented	54

SURVEY SAYS . . .

Students are happy
Great library
Frats and sororities are popular
Intramural sports are popular
Easy to get around campus
Students environmentally aware
Great off-campus food

ACADEMICS

Academic Rating	82
% students returning for sophomore year	68
% students graduating within 4 years	59
% students graduating within 6 years	64
Calendar	Semester
Student/faculty ratio	11:1
Profs interesting rating	91
Profs accessible rating	94

Most classes have 10–19 students.
Most lab/discussion sessions have 10–19 students.

MOST POPULAR MAJORS

Health Sciences; Psychology; Business Administration and Management

STUDENTS SAY "..."

Academics

Stetson University in Central Florida may offer more than 55 majors to more than 2,500 undergraduate students, but students say the focus remains on the individual. Between "small class sizes," "readily available" technology (like a 3-D printer), numerous "opportunities for involvement and learning," and a "multitude of hands-on activities," the institution not only works to cater to each enrollee, but seeks to engage them in the world with "classes where we spend time in the classroom working on community and global problems and then address them...through volunteering." Stetson never limits itself or its students, which is why those in the Honors Program can design a class of their choice, "which gives students the opportunity to explore something not otherwise offered at Stetson," and offers "countless opportunities to study abroad."

Professors "inherently care about our paths and experiences and always want to enhance them in the best way possible," which often means that they "encourage outdoor activity rather than remaining in one environment to learn." As one student puts it, "They truly care about making sure that students understand the material, and are willing to go out of their way to make that happen." This extra layer of focus on student well-being isn't just because of the low student-to-faculty ratio, though respondents note that this feature is "allowing me to work closely with my professors and developing a unique relationship with some of the best professionals in my field of study." Rather, this level of individualized aid is built into university life, with the school offering "so much support to [its] students. Between one-on-one tutoring, career counseling, the Writing Center, and professors who want to know their students, Stetson does an amazing job making sure we are never alone."

Campus Life

Stetson highly encourages involvement out of the classroom as well, and students suggest that many are "very engaged in campus activities." Some programs, such as mixers and social networking events, are even "specifically catered toward commuters that make you engage with campus and other students." That vibe extends beyond school-sanctioned meetings as well, with undergrads noting that "there are always on-campus events going on, which are generally very well-attended." Even weekdays are busy—"the outside of the student union is filled with tabling events," notes one student, and others add that "there are clubs and organizations to support all religions, faiths, races, and orientations." There's a lot of emphasis on the outdoors as well, whether that comes from the Hollis Center (the on-campus gym), which "has a program called SOAR where they organize outdoor activities" or just from students in general: "If it's a nice day out, I and other students typically grab lunch and eat under the trees." As for the weekend, nearby Downtown DeLand is known for having a "nice nightlife that's fun, even if low-key," and of course, there's always room to "take trips to the beach together."

Student Body

The general consensus is that "Stetson is a place where genuine, lifelong friendships develop." Students feel that the school's relatively smaller size makes it "easier to make connections and friends, especially in classes," but also note that the general culture "is inviting, accessible, and open." All of the opportunities to engage and get involved result in an "incredibly driven group of people" and what some positively describe as "a dynamic vibe on campus." As one puts it, "everyone is a leader in some form on campus." And most importantly about the school to some is not only that there is "a wide range of diversity in its students' background and experience," but that this so often tends to lead to a place where "people are supportive of one another, like a family."

STETSON UNIVERSITY

Financial Aid: 386-822-7100 • E-Mail: admissions@stetson.edu • Website: stetson.edu

THE PRINCETON REVIEW SAYS

Admissions

The school reports that its standardized testing policy for use in admission for Fall 2024 is Test Optional. The 2024 testing policy will be permanent. The Princeton Review suggests that interested applicants consult with the school for the most up-to-date standardized testing policies. *Very important factors considered include:* rigor of secondary school record, academic GPA. *Important factors considered include:* class rank, application essay, recommendation(s), interview, extracurricular activities, talent/ability, character/personal qualities, volunteer work, work experience. *Other factors considered include:* standardized test scores, alumni/ae relation, geographical residence, state residency, racial/ethnic status. High school diploma is required and GED is accepted. *Academic units required:* 4 English, 3 math, 3 science, 2 foreign language, 2 social studies. *Academic units recommended:* 4 English, 4 math, 4 science, 2 foreign language, 4 social studies.

Financial Aid

Students should submit: CSS/Financial Aid Profile; FAFSA. Priority filing deadline is 11/1. The Princeton Review suggests that all financial aid forms be submitted as soon as possible (see page 5 for a note on the FAFSA). *Need-based scholarships/grants offered:* College/university scholarship or grant aid from institutional funds; Federal Pell; Private scholarships; SEOG; State scholarships/grants. *Loan aid offered:* Direct PLUS loans; Direct Subsidized Loans; Direct Unsubsidized Loans. Admitted students will be notified of awards on a rolling basis beginning 12/17. Federal Work-Study Program available. Institutional employment available.

The Inside Word

Stetson University operates with several application deadlines. Applicants are required to submit an official transcript, at least one letter of recommendation, and a writing sample, with standardized test scores being optional but considered if submitted. Stetson's acceptance rate is deceptively high: this school attracts go-getters, and each year's freshman class profile is more impressive than the last.

THE SCHOOL SAYS "..."

From the Admissions Office

"Stetson University offers academic excellence in more than 100 areas of study with small class sizes and a world-class faculty. The average undergraduate receives a financial aid package worth $48,478, and its 2022 graduates enjoyed a 91% success rate, securing meaningful employment or graduate school admission.

"Located in sunny Central Florida near beaches and theme parks, Stetson has been named a top pet-friendly campus in America and one of the most beautiful college campuses in the South.

"At Stetson, students are immersed in hands-on learning outside of the classroom with opportunities to study abroad, obtain internships and conduct research in collaboration with professors.

"Stetson's academic rigor helps students thrive in a creative community that nurtures personal growth, intellectual development and global citizenship. This vibrant and diverse campus is home to more than 100 student organizations, 18 NCAA Division I athletic teams and students from around the world.

"A proud member of Phi Beta Kappa, America's most prestigious academic honor society, Stetson joins only 10% of U.S. colleges and universities with a chapter on campus. The university also belongs to an elite number of schools worldwide with both its Business and Accounting programs accredited by AACSB. And Stetson is one of the oldest colleges in Florida and the first to open schools of business, law and music.

"Stetson requires no application fee, and submitting SAT/ACT test scores is optional. No new essay is required (submit a previously graded paper instead). At Stetson, you will be seen for your talent and your potential."

SELECTIVITY

Admissions Rating	81
# of applicants	7,340
% of applicants accepted	94
% of acceptees attending	10
# offered a place on the wait list	284
% accepting a place on wait list	98
% admitted from wait list	12
# of early decision applicants	128
% accepted early decision	98

FIRST-YEAR PROFILE

Testing policy	Test Optional
Range SAT composite	1055–1260
Range SAT EBRW	540–650
Range SAT math	505–620
Range ACT composite	20–27
# submitting SAT scores	265
% submitting SAT scores	40
# submitting ACT scores	129
% submitting ACT scores	19
Average HS GPA	3.8
% frosh submitting high school GPA	97
% graduated top 10% of class	16
% graduated top 25% of class	45
% graduated top 50% of class	80

DEADLINES

Early decision	
Deadline	11/1
Notification	12/7
Early action	
Deadline	11/1
Notification	12/17
Regular	
Priority	11/1
Nonfall registration?	Yes

APPLICANTS OFTEN PREFER
Florida State University; University of Central Florida; University of Florida

APPLICANTS SOMETIMES PREFER
Rollins College; The University of Tampa

APPLICANTS RARELY PREFER
Elon University; Florida Southern College; University of Miami

FINANCIAL FACTS

Financial Aid Rating	86
Annual tuition	$54,820
Room and board	$16,030
Required fees	$400
Books and supplies	$1,200
Average frosh need-based scholarship	$45,283
Average UG need-based scholarship	$40,145
% needy frosh rec. need-based scholarship or grant aid	99
% needy UG rec. need-based scholarship or grant aid	99
% needy frosh rec. non-need-based scholarship or grant aid	27
% needy UG rec. non-need-based scholarship or grant aid	27
% needy frosh rec. need-based self-help aid	65
% needy UG rec. need-based self-help aid	66
% frosh rec. any financial aid	100
% UG rec. any financial aid	98
% UG borrow to pay for school	57
Average cumulative indebtedness	$23,989
% frosh need fully met	38
% ugrads need fully met	36
Average % of frosh need met	93
Average % of ugrad need met	88

STEVENS INSTITUTE OF TECHNOLOGY

1 Castle Point on Hudson, Hoboken, NJ 07030 • Admissions: 201-216-5000 • Fax: 201-216-8348

STUDENTS SAY ". . ."

Academics

It's no surprise that students at Stevens Institute of Technology feel as if they're receiving an "Ivy League caliber education at a more affordable" price. Indeed, there's much talk of the "high job placement rate" and overall "return on investment," particularly within the "rigorous but fair" physics classes and the "strong engineering department." But under-grads also find the school itself to be "very collaborative and supportive," with plenty of attention given to teaching about the "work ethic and moving past perceived failures." That means that there's room to foster relationships with professors, which can "lead to hands-on, paid research positions and connections to the professional world." As for the faculty, students describe a decent percentage as being "very enthusiastic about their material" and who "look to pass on their knowledge as best they can." If anything, "many professors are so qualified that they begin teaching the material at a level slightly above a beginner's understanding," which can sometimes be demanding, but the overall impression is that there are some great opportunities to learn from experienced mentors.

Campus Life

Life at Stevens can be hectic in the best way, which is to say that there's so much to take advantage of. Students are often "running around to different events, club meetings, eboard meetings, study groups, classes, etc.," and you'll likely find every sort of topic covered, whether it's the poker or anime club, the society of women engineers, or intramural sports like floor hockey. According to some proud undergrads, "We are definitely a nerdy school with some of our most popular events being Lan Parties and the Epic Lans where people can play video games and board games and compete in friendly Melee and Ultimate tournaments." Greek life provides a nice counter-balance for some students and many find themselves busy with "service trips [and] rush events" along with the occasional party. Additionally, there are "a ton of great restaurants on the main street right next to campus." There's also the affordable PATH train just "a 10-minute walk away from campus," which means that "New York City is so close," and a frequent weekend getaway for students looking for even more to do.

Student Body

Some students may throw around terms for their peers like "very ambitious and driven" in a negative light, but not so at Stevens. Here, "nearly everyone is very smart and intelligent without being snobby or arrogant." More importantly, they're also quite supportive of one another. "If you have a huge assignment due and are stressing over it, your friends motivate you by cheering you on and checking up on your progress." A few do complain that "there is a large chunk of students that are very quiet and won't do anything besides schoolwork and video games," but that doesn't lead a negative impact. "Everyone finds a friend group no matter what." It does, however, leave the school "almost split between the Greek community and the non-Greek community." While some students observe that the student body's "diversity is lacking," with a population that's 68% male and where many hail from New Jersey, Stevens undergrads do have varied interests and you're bound to encounter "artistic students, gamers, athletes, and pretty much every other kind." Best of all, you'll discover that "a great sense of community" permeates the campus.

STEVENS INSTITUTE OF TECHNOLOGY

Financial Aid: 201-216-8142 • E-Mail: admissions@stevens.edu • Website: www.stevens.edu/

THE PRINCETON REVIEW SAYS

Admissions

The school reports that its standardized testing policy for use in admission for Fall 2024 is Test Optional. It is unknown at this time if the 2024 testing policy will be permanent. The Princeton Review suggests that interested applicants consult with the school for the most up-to-date standardized testing policies. *Very important factors considered include:* rigor of secondary school record, academic GPA, standardized test scores. *Important factors considered include:* talent/ability, character/personal qualities. *Other factors considered include:* class rank, application essay, recommendation(s), interview, extracurricular activities, first generation, alumni/ae relation, geographical residence, state residency, racial/ethnic status, volunteer work, work experience, level of applicant's interest. High school diploma is required and GED is accepted. *Academic units required:* 4 English, 4 math, 3 science, 3 science labs, 2 foreign language, 2 history. *Academic units recommended:* 4 science, 4 science labs, 4 foreign language, 4 history.

Financial Aid

Students should submit: CSS/Financial Aid Profile; FAFSA. The Princeton Review suggests that all financial aid forms be submitted as soon as possible (see page 5 for a note on the FAFSA). *Need-based scholarships/grants offered:* College/university scholarship or grant aid from institutional funds; Federal Pell; Private scholarships; SEOG; State scholarships/ grants; United Negro College Fund. *Loan aid offered:* Direct PLUS loans; Direct Subsidized Loans; Direct Unsubsidized Loans. Federal Work-Study Program available. Institutional employment available.

The Inside Word

The admissions process at Stevens Institute of Technology is definitely competitive. To be a serious contender, you will need a strong GPA and solid standardized test scores if you submit them. Most highly qualified applicants also have plenty of honors, advanced placement or IB classes on their transcript. And given that Stevens is a tech school, your science and math courses will be closely evaluated. Finally, if you think the college is your top choice, it's a good idea to take advantage of applying early decision.

THE SCHOOL SAYS "..."

From the Admissions Office

"Whether they're designing an award-winning solar-powered home for the future, launching the next great technology startup or performing innovative research, Stevens Institute of Technology students and faculty collaborate in an interdisciplinary, student-centric, entrepreneurial environment to confront global challenges. Leading-edge programs in more than 30 undergraduate majors in business, computer science, arts, humanities, engineering, systems and the sciences teach students how to create and leverage technology in ways that matter to today's society. Tying education to a career path is a long-standing tradition at Stevens, which is why the university is consistently ranked among the nation's elite for student ROI, career services and mid-career salaries of alumni. Stevens' location in Hoboken, New Jersey, minutes from New York City and the surrounding metro area, cultivates unmatched internship, cooperative education and other real-world and hands-on work and research experiences so that when students graduate from Stevens, they are ready to hit the ground running. Stevens' Class of 2022 is the most recent proof, as 97.3% achieved their desired outcome—employment or graduate school—within six months of graduation and had an average starting salary of $84,700.

"Entrepreneurship programs encourage students to think creatively and to pursue big ideas. The annual Innovation Expo is a celebration of interdisciplinary senior capstone projects, mentored by faculty and sponsored by industry partners. A robust student life, a diverse and supportive community, an exciting college town, and more than 150 student organizations and 23 NCAA Division III athletics teams add to an enriching student experience."

SELECTIVITY

Admissions Rating	93
# of applicants	12,500
% of applicants accepted	46
% of acceptees attending	17
# offered a place on the wait list	2,173
% accepting a place on wait list	45
% admitted from wait list	17
# of early decision applicants	713
% accepted early decision	59

FIRST-YEAR PROFILE

Testing policy	Test Optional
Range SAT composite	1380–1510
Range SAT EBRW	670–730
Range SAT math	710–780
Range ACT composite	31–34
# submitting SAT scores	461
% submitting SAT scores	46
# submitting ACT scores	82
% submitting ACT scores	8
Average HS GPA	3.9
% frosh submitting high school GPA	100
% graduated top 10% of class	58
% graduated top 25% of class	88
% graduated top 50% of class	98

DEADLINES

Early decision	
Deadline	11/15
Notification	12/15
Other ED deadline	1/15
Other ED notification	2/15
Regular	
Deadline	1/15
Notification	4/1
Nonfall registration?	No

APPLICANTS ALSO LOOK AT
Carnegie Mellon University; New York University; Northeastern University; Rensselaer Polytechnic Institute; Rutgers University—New Brunswick; Worcester Polytechnic Institute

FINANCIAL FACTS

Financial Aid Rating	82
Annual tuition	$56,680
Room and board	$18,650
Required fees	$2,272
Books and supplies	$1,200
Average frosh need-based scholarship	$33,597
Average UG need-based scholarship	$31,878
% needy frosh rec. need-based scholarship or grant aid	100
% needy UG rec. need-based scholarship or grant aid	99
% needy frosh rec. non-need-based scholarship or grant aid	17
% needy UG rec. non-need-based scholarship or grant aid	15
% needy frosh rec. need-based self-help aid	70
% needy UG rec. need-based self-help aid	71
% UG borrow to pay for school	70
Average cumulative indebtedness	$41,574
% frosh need fully met	18
% ugrads need fully met	17
Average % of frosh need met	74
Average % of ugrad need met	69

STONEHILL COLLEGE

Stonehill College, Easton, MA 02357 • Admissions: 508-565-1000

CAMPUS LIFE

Quality of Life Rating	95
Fire Safety Rating	90
Green Rating	91
Type of school	Private
Affiliation	Roman Catholic
Environment	Village

STUDENTS

Total undergrad enrollment	2,503
% male/female/another gender	45/55/0
% from out of state	33
% frosh from public high school	64
% frosh live on campus	93
% ugrads live on campus	84
# of fraternities	0
# of sororities	0
% African American	5
% Asian	3
% White	78
% Hispanic	7
% Native American	<1
% Pacific Islander	0
% Two or more races	3
% Race and/or ethnicity unknown	3
% international	2
# of countries represented	18

SURVEY SAYS . . .

Students are happy
Lab facilities are great
Great library
Career services are great
Internships are widely available
Students are friendly
Students involved in community service
Easy to get around campus
Recreation facilities are great
Active student government

ACADEMICS

Academic Rating	88
% students returning for sophomore year	89
% students graduating within 4 years	75
% students graduating within 6 years	79
Calendar	Semester
Student/faculty ratio	11:1
Profs interesting rating	92
Profs accessible rating	96

Most classes have 10–19 students.
Most lab/discussion sessions have
   10–19 students.

MOST POPULAR MAJORS

Psychology, General; Finance, General; Criminology

STUDENTS SAY "..."

Academics

Founded in 1948, Stonehill College is located an hour's drive south of Boston and prides itself on a fresh approach to the intersection of education and faith. Offering programs that span everything from Arts to Business to STEM, the Roman Catholic Liberal Arts school is known for its "strong academics" and tailored approach to education. Students have the opportunity to complete an independent major or minor "where you can create your own degree from scratch," as well as participate in IDEAS (Integrating Democratic Education at Stonehill). This "experience central and only available at Stonehill" is "a program through which students can apply to design their own 1-credit, multimodal, discussion-based courses, and then teach them to their peers." Indeed, Stonehill's "academics are challenging but those who work hard are successful," and the institution is known for "helping students reach their full potential academically and guiding [them] toward what [they] might want in [their] future."

When it comes to the professors, students "cannot speak highly enough about the faculty," with many seeing the academic instruction as "the most compelling strength at Stonehill." Professors are "passionate about their subject matter" and "make learning interesting and engaging," which helps to "transfer that passion to their students." Some undergrads note the use of adjunct professors for smaller majors, with one student expressing, "As an education major, I have only had two professors over the course of three years that have been full time." In spite of this, students report building strong relationships with faculty members, using these connections "as a resource as well as a way to make learning better and more meaningful." As one enrollee puts it, "I feel like I have learned the most in my entire life in my four years at Stonehill."

Campus Life

Outside of the classroom, students love "enjoy[ing] the beautiful campus." Staying active is a priority, with "a lot of athletes that dominant most of the social life on campus." Many undergrads devote time to working out at the gym, and "a majority of people are involved" with a team. "The intramural sports and club sports are also awesome to play in," one student notes. For those who prefer less formal activity, "many go to socialize and play catch on the quad" when the weather is nice.

But there's more to Stonehill activities beyond athletics. Undergrads can choose from a "wide variety of clubs and societies to join." Clubs like the school newspaper are "wonderful and very informative" and groups like "physics and engineering club [do] a lot of really fun events like building solar panels from scratch." There are also "a lot of programs out of the Office of Student Engagement, so there is always something to do on weekends and weekdays!" Word is, their "food truck days on the quad with corn hole and other cookout games are awesome." In general, people love "just walking around campus" or "hanging out with friends outside." By the time the weekend rolls around, "if partying is your thing, then there's definitely a party culture on campus." If not, there's always a group that's down to "go off campus for food" or and "go for hikes on the weekends."

Student Body

"The students on campus are by far the friendliest, most welcoming, kind, and caring people I know," says one enrollee. Many agree, describing their peers as "respectful of each other" and the thing that "truly [makes] Stonehill a great place to be." United in their values, the student body is "built on a structure of community rather than looking out for yourself." Just walking around, you're "constantly seeing friendly faces around the close-knit campus," and it's clear that people are "have a sense of curiosity that sets them apart." While some report that "the school significantly lacks diversity," others feel that the community is "heading in a more diverse direction." Regardless of your background, rest assured that "a large portion of the student body...works to foster inclusive environments."

STONEHILL COLLEGE

Financial Aid: 508-565-1088 • E-Mail: admission@stonehill.edu • Website: www.stonehill.edu

THE PRINCETON REVIEW SAYS

Admissions
The school reports that its standardized testing policy for use in admission for Fall 2024 is Test Free. It is unknown at this time if the 2024 testing policy will be permanent. The Princeton Review suggests that interested applicants consult with the school for the most up-to-date standardized testing policies. *Very important factors considered include:* rigor of secondary school record, class rank, academic GPA, talent/ability. *Important factors considered include:* application essay, recommendation(s), extracurricular activities. *Other factors considered include:* interview, character/personal qualities, first generation, alumni/ae relation, geographical residence, religious affiliation/commitment, racial/ethnic status, volunteer work, work experience, level of applicant's interest. High school diploma is required and GED is accepted. *Academic units required:* 4 English, 3 math, 3 science, 3 science labs, 3 foreign language, 3 history. *Academic units recommended:* 4 English, 4 math, 4 science, 3 science labs, 4 foreign language, 4 history.

Financial Aid
Students should submit: CSS/Financial Aid Profile; FAFSA; Noncustodial Profile. Priority filing deadline is 11/15 EA, 12/1 ED, 2/15 RD. The Princeton Review suggests that all financial aid forms be submitted as soon as possible (see page 5 for a note on the FAFSA). *Need-based scholarships/grants offered:* College/university scholarship or grant aid from institutional funds; Federal Pell; Private scholarships; SEOG; State scholarships/grants. *Loan aid offered:* Direct PLUS loans; Direct Subsidized Loans; Direct Unsubsidized Loans; State Loans. Admitted students will be notified of awards on or about 3/15. Federal Work-Study Program available. Institutional employment available.

The Inside Word
Stonehill's admissions team of course takes GPA and academic record into consideration while evaluating applicants, but demonstrated interest, student activities, and the application essay are also weighted heavily, perhaps even more so because the school is Test Free and will not accept standardized test scores. Applicants eager for admission should consider a virtual or in-person campus visit or informational sessions when possible.

THE SCHOOL SAYS " . . ."

From the Admissions Office
"Founded by the Congregation of Holy Cross, Stonehill is a Catholic college that values integrity, tradition, diversity, and the rewards that come when you pair rigorous academics with committed, world-class faculty. Our distinctive approach to liberal arts education melds challenging courses, nationally recognized experiential learning, and life-changing service opportunities to shape compassionate leaders and global thinkers.

"Stonehill is on a beautiful 384-acre campus with architecture ranging from traditional brick-and-ivy academic buildings to our new May School of Arts & Sciences and Meehan School of Business. With its ideal location between Boston and Providence, Stonehill is perfectly situated for internships, professional networking, cultural experiences, pro sports and countless entertainment options.

"More than 90 percent of our students study abroad, complete an internship or perform field research before graduation. Such experiences along with 49 majors and 54 minors in the liberal arts, sciences and business prepare them for productive careers or lives of leadership and service. Our students are also active outside of class. Whether its Ultimate Disc, dance or one of our Division II varsity teams, most participate in some form of athletics. With a student/faculty ratio of 11:1 and an average class size of nineteen, individual attention is a Stonehill hallmark. Whether collaborating on research or mentoring students on careers and graduate school, our faculty puts students first: 94 percent of alumni respondents report being in careers, top graduate programs, or volunteer positions within six months of graduation."

SELECTIVITY

Admissions Rating	79
# of applicants	7,269
% of applicants accepted	73
% of acceptees attending	14
# offered a place on the wait list	1,164
% accepting a place on wait list	23
% admitted from wait list	15

FIRST-YEAR PROFILE

Testing policy	Test Free
Average HS GPA	3.4
% frosh submitting high school GPA	100
% graduated top 10% of class	15
% graduated top 25% of class	40
% graduated top 50% of class	82

DEADLINES

Early decision	
Deadline	12/1
Notification	12/31
Other ED deadline	2/1
Other ED notification	2/15
Early action	
Deadline	11/1
Notification	1/1
Regular	
Deadline	2/15
Notification	3/15
Nonfall registration?	Yes

APPLICANTS OFTEN PREFER
Boston College; College of the Holy Cross

APPLICANTS SOMETIMES PREFER
Assumption University; Bentley University; Boston University; Bryant University; Fairfield University; Fordham University; Loyola University Maryland; Merrimack College; Northeastern University; Providence College; Quinnipiac University; ; Saint Anselm College; Saint Michael's College; University of Connecticut; University of Massachusetts Amherst; University of New Hampshire

FINANCIAL FACTS

Financial Aid Rating	90
Annual tuition	$50,000
Annual tuition (first-year)	$52,000
Room and board	$17,100
Books and supplies	$893
Average frosh need-based scholarship	$39,000
Average UG need-based scholarship	$35,518
% needy frosh rec. need-based scholarship or grant aid	97
% needy UG rec. need-based scholarship or grant aid	98
% needy frosh rec. non-need-based scholarship or grant aid	34
% needy UG rec. non-need-based scholarship or grant aid	38
% needy frosh rec. need-based self-help aid	67
% needy UG rec. need-based self-help aid	63
% frosh rec. any financial aid	99
% UG rec. any financial aid	98
% UG borrow to pay for school	69
Average cumulative indebtedness	$42,318
% frosh need fully met	59
% ugrads need fully met	58
Average % of frosh need met	94
Average % of ugrad need met	93

SUFFOLK UNIVERSITY

73 Tremont St, Boston, MA 02108 • Admissions: 617-573-8460 • Fax: 617-557-1574

STUDENTS SAY ". . ."

Academics

Suffolk University in downtown Boston offers a "very interactive and hands-on" academic experience accompanied by all the benefits of big city life. Incoming freshmen can choose from more than 60 programs of study and complete a set of core curriculum. Luckily, these "Gen Ed's aren't boring, they are tailored to specific majors and have fun ways of teaching projects." While some undergrads think "final projects are difficult and put you out of your comfort zone," many feel the "small classroom experience" and professors who "demonstrate and explain the content well" helps them feel confident in their mastery over the content.

Overall, students say their professors are "genuinely impactful" and "truly care about their students." If one of their methods isn't quite working, undergrads aren't afraid to speak up, as they know their instructors "are always looking to improve." In addition to the network built in the classroom with professors and "a lot of speakers in the fields and industries that [students] are studying," the urban campus allows "for greater job and internship opportunities that you may not be able to find anywhere else." Many appreciate this web of resources and feel they are well-qualified for the "many opportunities for students looking to work in the city after graduation."

Campus Life

One of Suffolk's greatest selling points is that it's located "in the heart of Boston." Many rave about the "great places to eat" and "museums to sight-see." Plus, university-offered perks like "discounted sports tickets" provide the student body with ample opportunity for off-campus entertainment. Some say that "Without a real campus, they are thrown directly into the city full of strangers and real working people." While this can make it "more difficult to make…friends," most find it to be "a great environment despite the unique campus set-up." That doesn't mean school-sponsored activities are lacking. In fact, "students are very involved with student groups and clubs." Greek life is popular, with one student crediting her sorority with providing her with a sense of "having a community on campus." The Queer Student Union is a "small comfortable community," and the Asian American Association is widely recognized as a "safe place for all students to learn more about culture." The school "excels at being actively inclusive," making a point to "[pay] attention to the voice of what the students want." When it comes to social justice issues, the school makes sure to "clarify their stance" while "[explaining] how they value equal rights."

Student Body

Suffolk University is "full of very creative and intelligent people," who are known to be "very adventurous" when it comes to exploring the city around them. At Suffolk, you can expect to meet individuals from "all different walks of life with many different experiences" and a "great mix of economic backgrounds." Many find that "most students are friendly" and "try to listen [to] and respect one another." Peers bond by trying "to be as active and united as possible through various events, be it online or on campus." And despite its non-traditional campus, "still have a level of school spirit." With undergrads coming from so many backgrounds, there are "more chances for networking," which fosters a general sense of community, with one enrollee commenting, "[Suffolk students] want everyone in their class to succeed, not just themselves."

SUFFOLK UNIVERSITY

THE PRINCETON REVIEW SAYS

Admissions

The school reports that its standardized testing policy for use in admission for Fall 2024 will remain Test Optional, as it has been since 2019. The Princeton Review suggests that interested applicants consult with the school for the most up-to-date standardized testing policies. *Very important factors considered include:* rigor of secondary school record, academic GPA. *Important factors considered include:* application essay, recommendation(s), extracurricular activities, talent/ability, character/personal qualities. *Other factors considered include:* class rank, standardized test scores, interview, first generation, alumni/ae relation, volunteer work, work experience, level of applicant's interest. High school diploma is required and GED or HiSET exam is accepted. *Academic units required:* 4 English, 3 math, 2 science, 1 science lab, 2 foreign language, 1 social studies, 1 history, 4 academic electives. *Academic units recommended:* 4 English, 4 math, 3 science, 2 science labs, 2 foreign language, 1 social studies, 2 history, 4 academic electives.

Financial Aid

Students should submit: FAFSA. Priority filing deadline is 3/1. The Princeton Review suggests that all financial aid forms be submitted as soon as possible (see page 5 for a note on the FAFSA). *Need-based scholarships/grants offered:* College/university scholarship or grant aid from institutional funds; Federal Pell; Private scholarships; SEOG; State scholarships/grants. *Loan aid offered:* Direct PLUS loans; Direct Subsidized Loans; Direct Unsubsidized Loans; College/university loans from institutional funds. Admitted students will be notified of awards on a rolling basis beginning 1/15. Federal Work-Study Program available. Institutional employment available.

The Inside Word

The admissions team at Suffolk is looking for applicants who are ambitious, motivated, and passionate. The institution takes a comprehensive look at potential undergrads, evaluating everything from their academic history and GPA to their out-of-classroom experiences. The school's emphasis on overall uniqueness over a single test score led them to adopt a Test Optional policy for students here on out. Applicants will have the choice to submit their SAT or ACT score if they feel it will enhance their application.

THE SCHOOL SAYS "..."

From the Admissions Office

"Located in the heart of downtown Boston, Suffolk University gives students unparalleled access to this dynamic city and transforms their lives. Suffolk offers more than 60 undergraduate programs and over 50 graduate degree programs, including our doctoral program in clinical psychology and numerous certificate options. Students in our College of Arts & Sciences, Sawyer Business School, and Law School come to Suffolk to gain the knowledge and hands-on experiential learning they need to become leaders in their chosen fields. We take pride in being a personal, student-centered university, where faculty members lead small classes and nurture their students' success. Suffolk offers a 14:1 student-faculty ratio and the average undergraduate class size is 23 students. Undergraduates may study at both our flagship Boston campus and our campus in Madrid, Spain. We are steps—or a short T ride—away from Boston's top employers, and we prepare students for professional success from day one. Our partnerships with myriad institutions in Boston, across Massachusetts, and around the world grant Suffolk students a wealth of choices when it comes to internships and co-op experiences. Indeed, 98 percent of recent graduates are employed or enrolled in graduate school."

SELECTIVITY

Admissions Rating	83
# of applicants	9,699
% of applicants accepted	87
% of acceptees attending	15

FIRST-YEAR PROFILE

Testing policy	Test Optional
Range SAT composite	1090–1273
Range SAT EBRW	550–670
Range SAT math	530–630
Range ACT composite	24–30
# submitting SAT scores	268
% submitting SAT scores	21
# submitting ACT scores	46
% submitting ACT scores	4
Average HS GPA	3.4
% frosh submitting high school GPA	95
% graduated top 10% of class	12
% graduated top 25% of class	36
% graduated top 50% of class	74

DEADLINES

Early action	
Deadline	11/15
Notification	12/15
Regular	
Priority	2/15
Notification	Rolling, 1/15
Nonfall registration?	Yes

APPLICANTS ALSO LOOK AT

Bentley University; Boston University; Bridgewater State University; Bryant University; Bunker Hill Community College; Emerson College; Emmanuel College; Fordham University; MCPHS University; Merrimack College

FINANCIAL FACTS

Financial Aid Rating	82
Annual tuition	$44,812
Room and board	$20,360
Required fees	$568
Required fees (first-year)	$851
Books and supplies	$1,200
Average frosh need-based scholarship	$32,214
Average UG need-based scholarship	$28,597
% needy frosh rec. need-based scholarship or grant aid	98
% needy UG rec. need-based scholarship or grant aid	98
% needy frosh rec. non-need-based scholarship or grant aid	7
% needy UG rec. non-need-based scholarship or grant aid	8
% needy frosh rec. need-based self-help aid	89
% needy UG rec. need-based self-help aid	86
% frosh rec. any financial aid	98
% UG rec. any financial aid	94
% UG borrow to pay for school	81
Average cumulative indebtedness	$30,329
% frosh need fully met	12
% ugrads need fully met	17
Average % of frosh need met	78
Average % of ugrad need met	74

SUSQUEHANNA UNIVERSITY

514 University Avenue, Selinsgrove, PA 17870 • Admissions: 570-374-0101 • Fax: 570-372-2722

STUDENTS SAY "..."

Academics

Susquehanna University is an institution that "thrives on building strong leaders and independent thinkers." The school's "small" size means undergrads are joining a "close-knit community" replete with a "strong alumni network." Perhaps more importantly, it's evident that the school "is invested...in the success of their students." While Susquehanna offers a variety of great majors, students are prone to highlight the "top-notch creative writing program," "outstanding music education program," and "strong" science departments. Undergrads also praise a more unique aspect of a Susquehanna education—mandatory study off campus in a culture different from one's own (95 percent of students choose to go abroad). One senior elated about this requirement shares, "I believe that every young adult should have access to a cross-cultural experience and I value Susquehanna for making such an experience a priority for its students." Thankfully, for the most part, undergrads enjoy their on-campus education as well. By and large, this can be attributed to "fantastic" professors who "take a personal interest in their students." Indeed, the "friendly" teachers here really strive to make themselves "accessible." And, as one impressed creative writing major adds, a handful "often invite [students] up to their houses for dinner and discussion." However, one neuroscience major does caution that "you usually have to fight to get into a class with a 'good' professor and the registration process is always a hassle."

Campus Life

There is always something exciting to seek out at Susquehanna! To begin with, "there are over [150] clubs and organizations (academic, cultural, religious, arts, service, special interest, etc.)" in which students can participate. Additionally, "the Student Activities Committee [sponsors] a lot of free events—including the occasional trapeze and gyroscope!" Many undergrads also enjoy the "on-campus nightclub [which] hosts free dances on the weekends." Moreover, Susquehanna is a fairly athletic school. Indeed, "varsity sports are huge on campus; we have a large number of athletic teams for such a small school. Students love "tailgating [at] sporting events" as well. Undergrads also flock to "Charlie's Coffeehouse to watch movies or hang out with friends during the week." And, for students looking to unwind, "every Wednesday, Friday, and Saturday night there is usually off campus partying happening." If students are itching to escape for a bit, they can take advantage of several "recreational places off campus (Bounce Plex, bowling alley, racetrack, rock climbing, hiking, etc.)." And though Selinsgrove "is a small town, it's got everything you need." A senior confidently proclaims that "there are plenty of places to eat and shop!"

Student Body

It can easily feel as though most Susquehanna students hail from "upper-middle class" homes located in either the "Mid-Atlantic [region or] New England." Fortunately, to the delight of many students, the "campus has been steadily diversifying over the years." And besides, these "outgoing" undergrads are able to forge bonds that go well beyond geography. After all, this is the type of student body that "will hold the door for you, even if you are 100 feet away." However, there are a handful of students who feel that, to fully fit in, you have to be "part of either Greek life or a sport." Naturally, other undergrads vehemently disagree, emphatically stating that "students find their niche quickly and make friends easily." A history major helps clarify by relaying that "roughly 25 percent of students are athletes and 17 percent are involved in Greek life. However, for the most part students from every range of the spectrum interact and support each other." As one immensely proud student triumphantly sums up, "We are all awesome. There's no other way to describe it besides awesomeness."

SUSQUEHANNA UNIVERSITY

Financial Aid: 570-372-4450 • E-Mail: suadmiss@susqu.edu • Website: www.susqu.edu

THE PRINCETON REVIEW SAYS

Admissions

The school reports that its standardized testing policy for use in admission for Fall 2024 is Test Optional. It is unknown at this time if the 2024 testing policy will be permanent. The Princeton Review suggests that interested applicants consult with the school for the most up-to-date standardized testing policies. *Very important factors considered include:* rigor of secondary school record, academic GPA. *Important factors considered include:* class rank, standardized test scores, application essay, recommendation(s), interview, extracurricular activities, talent/ability, character/personal qualities, alumni/ae relation, racial/ethnic status, volunteer work, work experience, level of applicant' *Other factors considered include:* first generation, geographical residence, state residency. High school diploma is required and GED is accepted. *Academic units recommended:* 4 English, 4 math, 4 science, 2 science labs, 2 social studies, 1 history, 3 academic electives.

Financial Aid

Students should submit: FAFSA; State aid form. Priority filing deadline is 12/1. The Princeton Review suggests that all financial aid forms be submitted as soon as possible (see page 5 for a note on the FAFSA). *Need-based scholarships/grants offered:* College/university scholarship or grant aid from institutional funds; Federal Pell; Private scholarships; SEOG; State scholarships/grants. *Loan aid offered:* Direct PLUS loans; Direct Subsidized Loans; Direct Unsubsidized Loans; College/university loans from institutional funds; State Loans. Admitted students will be notified of awards on a rolling basis. Federal Work-Study Program available. Institutional employment available.

The Inside Word

Admissions officers at Susquehanna aim to understand the candidate behind the numbers. They want students who demonstrate intellect, creativity and leadership. The university also realizes that standardized test scores aren't always representative of a student's abilities. That's why the school is Test Optional. Finally, Susquehanna operates on a rolling admissions policy.

THE SCHOOL SAYS "..."

From the Admissions Office

"As a graduate from Susquehanna your career will ascend from your broad academic foundation, intercultural competence and other skills that you'll gain—critical thinking, writing, teamwork and communication. The median of our grads' earnings six years after graduation is $54,100—that's 64% higher than the national figure.

"Susquehanna faculty members care about your success. Nearly all of our students participate in internships, hands-on practicum and/or undergraduate research—resulting in 96% of new graduates employed or in graduate school within six months. Faculty will advise you about career strategies and support you with letters of recommendation. Many professors stay connected and follow their students' careers after graduation.

"Choose from more than 100 majors and minors in arts, humanities and sciences, or our preprofessional and engineering programs. Our business school guarantees international internships and is AACSB accredited—placing it among the top 5% worldwide.

"By completing a cross-cultural experience for at least two weeks in the U.S. or abroad through our nationally recognized Global Opportunities program, you'll broaden your perspective and professional options.

"You will enjoy exceptional learning, living, and health facilities on our beautiful residential campus with 300+ acres, much of it run on solar power. Make friends through 150+ student organizations, 23 NCAA Division III intercollegiate sports, fraternities, sororities, and affinity and service groups. Easy access to metropolitan hubs allows you to network with alumni, engage in professional development, and explore infinite options!"

SELECTIVITY

Admissions Rating	83
# of applicants	4,594
% of applicants accepted	87
% of acceptees attending	14
# of early decision applicants	61
% accepted early decision	82

FIRST-YEAR PROFILE

Testing policy	Test Optional
Range SAT composite	1070–1230
Range SAT EBRW	540–630
Range SAT math	530–610
Range ACT composite	22–28
# submitting SAT scores	475
% submitting SAT scores	83
# submitting ACT scores	85
% submitting ACT scores	15
Average HS GPA	3.6
% frosh submitting high school GPA	99
% graduated top 10% of class	23
% graduated top 25% of class	53
% graduated top 50% of class	84

DEADLINES

Early decision	
Deadline	11/15
Notification	12/1
Early action	
Deadline	11/1
Notification	12/1
Regular	
Notification	Rolling, 10/1
Nonfall registration?	Yes

APPLICANTS ALSO LOOK AT

Dickinson College; Elizabethtown College; Gettysburg College; Ithaca College; Juniata College; Penn State University Park

FINANCIAL FACTS

Financial Aid Rating	86
Annual tuition	$52,380
Room and board	$14,350
Required fees	$680
Books and supplies	$1,200
Average frosh need-based scholarship	$36,416
Average UG need-based scholarship	$36,533
% needy frosh rec. need-based scholarship or grant aid	100
% needy UG rec. need-based scholarship or grant aid	100
% needy frosh rec. non-need-based scholarship or grant aid	32
% needy UG rec. non-need-based scholarship or grant aid	23
% needy frosh rec. need-based self-help aid	67
% needy UG rec. need-based self-help aid	75
% frosh rec. any financial aid	99
% UG rec. any financial aid	100
% UG borrow to pay for school	86
Average cumulative indebtedness	$43,366
% frosh need fully met	36
% ugrads need fully met	27
Average % of frosh need met	86
Average % of ugrad need met	85

SWARTHMORE COLLEGE

500 College Avenue, Swarthmore, PA 19081 • Admissions: 610-328-8300

CAMPUS LIFE

Quality of Life Rating	72
Fire Safety Rating	91
Green Rating	96
Type of school	Private
Affiliation	No Affiliation
Environment	Village

STUDENTS

Total undergrad enrollment	1,619
% male/female/another gender	49/51/NR
% from out of state	88
% frosh from public high school	59
% frosh live on campus	100
% ugrads live on campus	96
# of fraternities	0
# of sororities	0
% African American	9
% Asian	18
% White	32
% Hispanic	14
% Native American	<1
% Pacific Islander	<1
% Two or more races	10
% Race and/or ethnicity unknown	3
% international	14
# of countries represented	53

SURVEY SAYS . . .

Lots of liberal students
Class discussions encouraged
Great financial aid
Students environmentally aware

ACADEMICS

Academic Rating	81
% students returning for sophomore year	96
% students graduating within 4 years	90
% students graduating within 6 years	94
Calendar	Semester
Student/faculty ratio	8:1
Profs interesting rating	90
Profs accessible rating	86

Most classes have 10–19 students.
Most lab/discussion sessions have 10–19 students.

MOST POPULAR MAJORS

Economics; Computer Science; Mathematics

STUDENTS SAY "..."

Academics

Swarthmore College "has a lovely campus, the people are almost unbelievably friendly, it's a safe environment, and it's really, really challenging academically," and "although it's not one of the most well-known schools, those who do know of it also know of its wonderful reputation. It's where to go for a real education—for learning for the sake of truly learning, rather than just for grades." Swarthmore can be "stressful," but students note that it teaches "not only about classes but about life, and though it may be extremely, almost unbearably difficult sometimes, it's totally worth it." Undergrads also note that "there are tons of resources to help you—professors, academic mentors, writing associates (who are really helpful to talk to when you have major papers), residential assistants, psychological counseling, multicultural support groups, queer/trans support groups—basically, whenever you need help with something, there's someone you can talk to." Swatties also love how "Swarthmore is amazingly flexible. The requirements are very limited, allowing you to explore whatever you are interested in and change your mind millions of times about your major and career path. If they don't offer a major you want, you can design your own with ease."

Campus Life

The Swarthmore community is "a family of students who are engaged in academics, learning, politics, activism, and civic responsibility, with a work hard, play hard, intense mentality, who don't get enough sleep because they're too busy doing all they want to do in their time here, and who (this is kind of cheesy, but true) when you really think about it are really just smart students who care about the world and want to make it better." There "is a misconception that Swarthmore students do nothing but study, [but] while we certainly do a lot of it, we still find many ways to have fun." Not so much in hometown Swarthmore—"there isn't a lot to do right in the area"—but "with a train station on campus, Philly is very accessible." Additionally, "there are so many organizations and clubs on campus that you'd be pressed to find none of the activities interesting. Even then, you can start your own club, so that takes care of it." The small size of the school means that "opportunities to participate in many different programs" are usually available. On-campus activities "are varied, and there is almost always something to do on the weekend. There are student musical performances, drama performances, movies, speakers, and comedy shows," as well as "several parties every weekend, with and without alcohol, and a lot of pre-partying with friends." One student sums up, "While it is tough to generalize on the life of a Swarthmore student, one word definitely applies to us all: busy. All of us are either working on extracurriculars, studying, or fighting sleep to do more work."

Student Body

Students are "not sure if there is a typical Swattie" but suspect that "the defining feature among us is that each person is brilliant at something: maybe dance, maybe quantum physics, maybe philosophy. Each person here has at least one thing that [he or she does] extraordinarily well." A Swattie "is [typically] liberal, involved in some kind of activism group or multicultural group, talks about classes all the time, was labeled a nerd by people in high school, and is really smart—one of those people where you just have to wonder, how do they get all their homework done and manage their extracurriculars and still have time for parties?" The campus "is very diverse racially but not in terms of thought—in other words, pretty much everyone's liberal, you don't get many different points of view. Multicultural and queer issues are big here, but you don't have to be involved in that to enjoy Swarthmore. You just have to accept it."

SWARTHMORE COLLEGE

Financial Aid: 610-328-8358 • E-Mail: admissions@swarthmore.edu • Website: www.swarthmore.edu

THE PRINCETON REVIEW SAYS

Admissions

The school reports that its standardized testing policy for use in admission for Fall 2024 is Test Optional. It is unknown at this time if the 2024 testing policy will be permanent. The Princeton Review suggests that interested applicants consult with the school for the most up-to-date standardized testing policies. *Very important factors considered include:* rigor of secondary school record, class rank, academic GPA, application essay, recommendation(s), character/personal qualities. *Other factors considered include:* standardized test scores, interview, extracurricular activities, talent/ability, first generation, alumni/ae relation, geographical residence, state residency, religious affiliation/commitment, racial/ethnic status, volunteer work, work experience. High school diploma or equivalent is not required. *Academic units recommended:* 4 English, 3 math, 3 science, 3 foreign language, 3 social studies, 3 history.

Financial Aid

Students should submit: CSS/Financial Aid Profile; FAFSA; Noncustodial Profile; State aid form; parent tax and other income documentation. Priority filing deadline is 1/4. The Princeton Review suggests that all financial aid forms be submitted as soon as possible (see page 5 for a note on the FAFSA). *Need-based scholarships/grants offered:* College/university scholarship or grant aid from institutional funds; Federal Pell; Private scholarships; SEOG; State scholarships/grants. *Loan aid offered:* Direct PLUS loans; Direct Subsidized Loans; Direct Unsubsidized Loans; State Loans. Admitted students will be notified of awards on or about 4/1. Federal Work-Study Program available. Institutional employment available.

The Inside Word

Competition for admission to Swarthmore remains fierce, as the school consistently receives applications from top students across the country. Applicants should understand that Swarthmore receives more than enough applications from well-qualified students to fill its classrooms. The SAT and ACT are currently optional, and the Writing portion is not required for the ACT if students are choosing to submit. Admissions officers comb applications carefully for evidence of intellectually curious, highly motivated, and creative-minded candidates.

THE SCHOOL SAYS ". . ."

From the Admissions Office

"Swarthmore College is a highly selective college of liberal arts and engineering located twenty-five minutes outside of Philadelphia. The college empowers students to intertwine academic curiosity with social responsibility and a sense of purpose. The campus community fully supports this mission, from world-class professors who engage directly with students in meaningful ways, to staff in the dining hall and libraries who can come to feel like friends. Close relationships fuel life at Swarthmore. Many students collaborate with professors on joint research projects, and the exchange of intellectual ideas is facilitated by small class sizes. The Honors Program extends the depth of free and critical discussion of ideas via small-group seminars. One trademark of a "Swattie" is the passion they devote to their many interests. Swatties can be astrophysicists who write poetry, economists who love to code, and athletes with a passion for choreography. Almost half of students enjoy playing sports, at the Division III level or in club and intramural teams. The College's Quaker roots emphasize the concept of access regardless of income; nearly everything is included in the annual activity fee, so things like movie nights, laundry, printing, and athletic events are free to all students. Additionally, as part of the Textbook Affordability Program, each student receives an annual $790 credit at the Swarthmore Campus and Community Store (the bookstore) for required course materials. Swarthmore's financial aid program ensures affordability—without loans. Fifty-two percent of the Class of 2026 received aid in 2022–2023, with an average aid award of $64,491. Swarthmore makes admissions decisions for U.S. citizens, permanent residents, and undocumented or DACA-eligible students graduating from U.S. high schools without considering a family's ability to pay. International applicants are admitted on a need-aware basis and are eligible for financial aid."

SELECTIVITY

Admissions Rating	98
# of applicants	14,707
% of applicants accepted	7
% of acceptees attending	42
# of early decision applicants	1,158
% accepted early decision	19

FIRST-YEAR PROFILE

Testing policy	Test Optional
Range SAT composite	1455–1540
Range SAT EBRW	710–770
Range SAT math	730–790
Range ACT composite	32–35
# submitting SAT scores	180
% submitting SAT scores	42
# submitting ACT scores	82
% submitting ACT scores	19
% graduated top 10% of class	89
% graduated top 25% of class	100
% graduated top 50% of class	100

DEADLINES

Early decision	
Deadline	11/15
Notification	12/15
Other ED deadline	1/4
Other ED notification	2/15
Regular	
Deadline	1/4
Notification	4/1
Nonfall registration?	No

FINANCIAL FACTS

Financial Aid Rating	98
Annual tuition	$61,992
Room and board	$18,964
Required fees	$420
Books and supplies	$760
Average frosh need-based scholarship	$62,988
Average UG need-based scholarship	$60,877
% needy frosh rec. need-based scholarship or grant aid	100
% needy UG rec. need-based scholarship or grant aid	100
% needy frosh rec. non-need-based scholarship or grant aid	0
% needy UG rec. non-need-based scholarship or grant aid	0
% needy frosh rec. need-based self-help aid	96
% needy UG rec. need-based self-help aid	96
% frosh rec. any financial aid	
% UG rec. any financial aid	52
% UG borrow to pay for school	21
Average cumulative indebtedness	$25,795
% frosh need fully met	100
% ugrads need fully met	100
Average % of frosh need met	100
Average % of ugrad need met	100

SYRACUSE UNIVERSITY

900 South Crouse Ave., Syracuse, NY 13244 • Admissions: 315-443-1870 • Fax: 315-443-4226

STUDENTS SAY "..."

Academics

The Orange of Syracuse University love their school and want the world to know it. Those who brave the northern winters are rewarded with a choice of around 200 majors and 100 minors, and "the distinct tracks students can take within each of the professional schools" is one of the university's greatest strengths. "There is so much to do with your education and it can be as specific or broad as you would like," says one student. "If you put in the work…it can make a world of a difference to your college experience." The school does a good job of being cohesive for its size, and "there is a sense of connection between all years of study." Alumni form an "everlasting network between Syracuse students" and the school has a "big reach" for a relatively tucked away school: "There is somebody from Syracuse everywhere you look." On top of the alumni, the school provides "ample amounts of resources in regard to finding jobs or applying to graduate programs," which "makes looking for that next step easy and not so intimidating."

Professors are "very intelligent and qualified individuals who have a strong base in what they teach," and are here "as a tool to enhance your knowledge and to help in any way possible." In general education classes, professors are "attentive and aware that students of varying interests and backgrounds are enrolled in the 101-level class and adjust teaching strategies accordingly." They are "quick to respond to emails," and "always open to meeting with you if you need help with anything, academic or personal." Professors typically "do justice to both sides of various arguments" and classroom discussions don't feel biased.

Campus Life

The atmosphere of Syracuse is "always electric, with something going on at all times." Student life can revolve around athletics, and campus is "the most fun place on the planet when the basketball team is doing well, but could be very dreary if they're not and the weather is bad." Students are especially eager to don their orange apparel and "tailgate until the wee hours," but they "always get studying done first." Greek life is popular for many students and "once the sun goes down, you will find a lot of the students all gathering at the fraternities and the bars on Marshall street," though 'Cuse still offers alternative activities, including the Orange After Dark program, "bowling, shopping, whitewater rafting, day trips to NYC, [and] movie nights" for students who have no interest in parties. The gym is always thumping: "it's a social thing here."

As this is Central NY, life takes a little hit when winter comes, and indoor socializing is more prominent. "Floors become close" and "movies and video games" are popular distractions. Syracuse has been quick to respond to student feedback about food, and has renovated to offer more dining options and a more flexible meal plan. That said, students note that off-campus has plenty of dining options at Destiny USA (one of the country's largest malls) and Armory Square.

Student Body

School spirit "runs rampant" here, and this "energized" group can be found "seeking the fun out of every opportunity thrown at them." Syracuse is "not as diverse as a city school but still pretty diverse nonetheless," with most students hailing from the northeast. No matter their background, students "very quickly find a home" whether it's with a sports team, club, organization, or Greek life, and everyone is active in the community. There is "very little competition" among this "practical student body…that doesn't take flack or do unnecessary work," and if there is any divide, it is between the driven students and those just here for a degree. Students "love to party, especially on game days, but also understand that they are here for academics."

SYRACUSE UNIVERSITY

Financial Aid: 315-443-1513 • E-Mail: orange@syr.edu • Website: www.syracuse.edu

THE PRINCETON REVIEW SAYS

Admissions

The school reports that its standardized testing policy for use in admission for Fall 2024 is Test Optional. It is unknown at this time if the 2024 testing policy will be permanent. The Princeton Review suggests that interested applicants consult with the school for the most up-to-date standardized testing policies. *Very important factors considered include:* rigor of secondary school record, class rank, academic GPA, application essay, recommendation(s), interview, extracurricular activities, talent/ability, character/personal qualities, volunteer work, level of applicant's interest. *Other factors considered include:* standardized test scores, first generation, alumni/ae relation, geographical residence, state residency, racial/ethnic status, work experience. High school diploma is required and GED is accepted. *Academic units recommended:* 4 English, 4 math, 4 science, 4 science labs, 4 foreign language, 4 social studies, 4 history.

Financial Aid

Students should submit: CSS/Financial Aid Profile; FAFSA; Noncustodial Profile. The Princeton Review suggests that all financial aid forms be submitted as soon as possible (see page 5 for a note on the FAFSA). *Need-based scholarships/grants offered:* College/university scholarship or grant aid from institutional funds; Federal Pell; Private scholarships; SEOG; State scholarships/grants. *Loan aid offered:* Direct PLUS loans; Direct Subsidized Loans; Direct Unsubsidized Loans. Admitted students will be notified of awards on or about 3/15. Federal Work-Study Program available. Institutional employment available.

The Inside Word

Syracuse's admissions process is competitive. Successful candidates will have strong GPAs and solid test scores. It's also important to note that students interested in applying to any fine or performing arts or architecture programs will need to audition and/or submit a portfolio. Finally, applicants who strongly feel that Syracuse is their first choice are highly encouraged to apply early decision.

THE SCHOOL SAYS "..."

From the Admissions Office

"In a world undergoing extraordinary transformation, leadership and innovation are more critical than ever. As a Carnegie classification Research 1 university, our students work alongside leading scholars and have access to hands-on research and learning opportunities—all of which prepare them to shape their communities and become the change-makers of tomorrow. From a rich array of degree programs and extracurricular activities that ignite their passions, to integrated health and wellness offerings that empower them to embrace the college experience with a sense of well-being—Syracuse University goes beyond the classroom to fuel discovery and drive positive impact.

"With 13 schools and colleges, 200 customizable majors and 100 minors, and online degrees and certificates, Syracuse University provides limitless educational pathways. New interdisciplinary areas ranging from social justice and artificial intelligence to energy and environment provide hands-on research experiences that broaden perspectives and prepare students for the careers of tomorrow. Syracuse University has five award-winning study abroad centers and international programs in 60 countries, where our students gain global perspectives that last a lifetime.

"The university is dedicated to being the best university for veterans and military-connected students, who make up more than five percent of the student body. The National Veterans Resource Center, opened in 2020, is located in the Daniel and Gayle D'Aniello Building. This state-of-the-art, fully-accessible facility is home to Syracuse University's innovative academic, government and community collaborations positioned to empower those who have or will serve in defense of the nation."

SELECTIVITY

Admissions Rating	91
# of applicants	41,489
% of applicants accepted	52
% of acceptees attending	19
# offered a place on the wait list	12,638
% accepting a place on wait list	32
% admitted from wait list	8

FIRST-YEAR PROFILE

Testing policy	Test Optional
Range SAT composite	1260–1410
Range SAT EBRW	630–710
Range SAT math	620–720
Range ACT composite	28–32
# submitting SAT scores	1,158
% submitting SAT scores	28
# submitting ACT scores	471
% submitting ACT scores	12
Average HS GPA	3.8
% frosh submitting high school GPA	100
% graduated top 10% of class	33
% graduated top 25% of class	67
% graduated top 50% of class	92

DEADLINES

Early decision	
Deadline	11/15
Other ED deadline	1/5
Regular	
Priority	11/15
Deadline	1/5
Nonfall registration?	Yes

FINANCIAL FACTS

Financial Aid Rating	90
Annual tuition	$58,440
Room and board	$17,170
Required fees	$1,695
Books and supplies	$1,690
Average frosh need-based scholarship	$39,480
Average UG need-based scholarship	$41,818
% needy frosh rec. need-based scholarship or grant aid	96
% needy UG rec. need-based scholarship or grant aid	97
% needy frosh rec. non-need-based scholarship or grant aid	18
% needy UG rec. non-need-based scholarship or grant aid	16
% needy frosh rec. need-based self-help aid	88
% needy UG rec. need-based self-help aid	89
% frosh rec. any financial aid	84
% UG rec. any financial aid	82
% UG borrow to pay for school	49
Average cumulative indebtedness	$39,319
% frosh need fully met	57
% ugrads need fully met	59
Average % of frosh need met	97
Average % of ugrad need met	96

TEMPLE UNIVERSITY

1801 North Broad Street, Philadelphia, PA 19122 • Admissions: 215-204-7000 • Fax: 215-204-5694

STUDENTS SAY "..."

Academics

Temple University, Philadelphia's largest university, is constantly growing, and not just in size. Currently, the 24,000+ undergraduates have more than 160 majors to choose from. But the school is also "constantly improving and upgrading its resources," which means that students always have access to something new, most recently a library that features "one of the world's first robot book fetchers." It also means that "career opportunities are plentiful and are available for all students" or as another respondent puts it, "Attending such a large school allows limitless internship, scholarship, academic, and social opportunities." There's even a nod to how the "Gen Ed courses are a great help to discover your interests." The university as a whole "is very well-rounded, and you are going to receive a really good education no matter what major you choose."

Such achievements wouldn't be nearly as effective if not for the faculty, and accordingly, professors are praised as being "extremely accessible," "highly skilled at relaying information and teaching," and providing "many opportunities outside of the classroom for students." It's not just about relaying information as it is about facilitating interactions and collaborations. Professors "genuinely care about how well you learn the material and try as hard as they can to get you as excited to learn as they are to teach," which is why classes involve "lots of discussion-based lectures and ways of challenging students to think outside the box." You're never alone at Temple either: "For example, for Calculus help I could go to the tutoring center, the student success center, MCC (Mathematics Counseling Center), or I could attend PASS (Peer Assisted Study Sessions) sessions offered for group tutoring before the exam."

Campus Life

The Temple campus is described as "a major highlight," one that "sits right in Philadelphia but maintains a distinct campus-like feel." Students rejoice in the freedom this offers: "Living in a city allows people largely to exist as they wish," which means students don't have to choose between "just their academic life or their partying life" and "are not confined to campus and can venture out into the major city." That said, those who choose to remain local will find "plenty of clubs and organizations to join as well as Greek life organizations," and "people enjoy going to sports games either for Temple teams or Philadelphia teams." Physical activities in particular are referenced by undergrads, with attention called to the campus's five gyms, and a "recreation center open on Wednesday and Friday nights for net sports."

Student Body

This is "a very likable campus" where everyone "respects everyone and who they choose to be and they celebrate it." Many at Temple are "engaged in public service" and the school "has amazing diversity, which is what Temple strives to have and support." A lot of students here "are commuters and spend their days in class or at the library/tech center," while many others "either live on campus or off campus close by in an apartment and work when not in class." There are also "lots of international students from many different countries." Students here "have their lives together...but also know how to have a good time."

TEMPLE UNIVERSITY

Financial Aid: 215-204-2244 • E-Mail: askanowl@temple.edu • Website: www.temple.edu

THE PRINCETON REVIEW SAYS

Admissions

The school reports that its standardized testing policy for use in admission for Fall 2024 is Test Optional. The 2024 testing policy will be permanent. The Princeton Review suggests that interested applicants consult with the school for the most up-to-date standardized testing policies. *Very important factors considered include:* rigor of secondary school record, academic GPA. *Other factors considered include:* standardized test scores, application essay, recommendation(s), extracurricular activities, talent/ability, character/personal qualities, first generation, alumni/ae relation, geographical residence, state residency, volunteer work, work experience, level of applicant's interest. High school diploma is required and GED is accepted. *Academic units required:* 4 English, 3 math, 2 science, 1 science lab, 2 foreign language, 2 social studies, 1 history, 1 visual/performing arts, 1 academic elective. *Academic units recommended:* 4 English, 4 math, 3 science, 2 science labs, 2 foreign language, 2 social studies, 1 history, 1 visual/performing arts, 3 academic electives.

Financial Aid

Students should submit: FAFSA; State aid form. Priority filing deadline is 2/1. The Princeton Review suggests that all financial aid forms be submitted as soon as possible (see page 5 for a note on the FAFSA). *Need-based scholarships/grants offered:* College/university scholarship or grant aid from institutional funds; Federal Nursing Scholarships; Federal Pell; Private scholarships; SEOG; State scholarships/grants; United Negro College Fund. *Loan aid offered:* Direct PLUS loans; Direct Subsidized Loans; Direct Unsubsidized Loans; Federal Nursing Loans; State Loans. Admitted students will be notified of awards on a rolling basis beginning in October. Federal Work-Study Program available. Institutional employment available.

The Inside Word

Gaining admission to Temple is competitive and a solid academic record is a must. Students need to have earned at least a minimum of a B-minus average or a 3.0 GPA in college prep courses to be considered serious contenders, and should demonstrate a well-rounded academic background and course distribution. Submitting SAT or ACT scores is optional.

THE SCHOOL SAYS "..."

From the Admissions Office

"Temple University attracts some of the most diverse, driven and motivated minds from across the nation and around the world. These students and faculty bring the university to life and move Temple forward and upward in academics, athletics, research and the arts. Powering Temple's ascent are innovative approaches to admissions and affordability; a campus transformation; plentiful creative and research opportunities; rigorous academic programs and real-world opportunities; an indelible bond with the city of Philadelphia; and groundbreaking work in science, research and technology. Temple is home to more than 33,000 students; is among the 45 largest public, four-year institutions in the U.S.; and offers more than 600 academic programs in 17 schools and colleges, on eight campuses, including locations in Japan and Italy. More than 3,600 distinguished faculty members, five professional schools and dozens of renowned programs make Temple an academic powerhouse. Academic programs not only help students gain valuable knowledge and experience during their time here, but they also prepare students for lifelong learning and success after graduation. Students enjoy the advantages and atmosphere of a large urban, public research university with the individualized attention that comes from a 12-1 student-faculty ratio. The majority of first-year students live on campus, where they are steps away from classes; the state-of-the-art Charles Library; the TECH Center; fitness and recreation facilities; dining options such as cafés, dining halls and food trucks; and the many arts, cultural, sports and scholarly events that happen daily at Temple and throughout the city. By living and learning in an urban environment, Temple students are well-prepared for the world. Employers laud Owls for their tenacity, teamwork and talent. Students also have access to an immense alumni network 362,000 strong for guidance, job opportunities and mentoring."

SELECTIVITY

Admissions Rating	85
# of applicants	38,666
% of applicants accepted	80
% of acceptees attending	15
# offered a place on the wait list	3,813
% accepting a place on wait list	20
% admitted from wait list	81

FIRST-YEAR PROFILE

Testing policy	Test Optional
Range SAT composite	1130–1360
Range SAT EBRW	570–690
Range SAT math	550–680
Range ACT composite	24–31
# submitting SAT scores	1,262
% submitting SAT scores	27
# submitting ACT scores	178
% submitting ACT scores	4
Average HS GPA	3.4
% frosh submitting high school GPA	98

DEADLINES

Early action	
Deadline	11/1
Notification	1/10
Regular	
Priority	11/1
Deadline	2/1
Nonfall registration?	Yes

APPLICANTS OFTEN PREFER
Drexel University; Penn State University Park; Rutgers University—New Brunswick

APPLICANTS SOMETIMES PREFER
University of Delaware; University of Maryland, College Park; University of Pittsburgh—Pittsburgh Campus; West Chester University of Pennsylvania

APPLICANTS RARELY PREFER
Howard University; Thomas Jefferson University; Towson University

FINANCIAL FACTS

Financial Aid Rating	79
Annual in-state tuition	$20,171
Annual out-of-state tuition	$35,032
Room and board	$13,612
Required fees	$924
Books and supplies	$1,526
Average frosh need-based scholarship	$12,023
Average UG need-based scholarship	$11,027
% needy frosh rec. need-based scholarship or grant aid	98
% needy UG rec. need-based scholarship or grant aid	96
% needy frosh rec. non-need-based scholarship or grant aid	74
% needy UG rec. non-need-based scholarship or grant aid	59
% needy frosh rec. need-based self-help aid	75
% needy UG rec. need-based self-help aid	78
% frosh rec. any financial aid	93
% UG rec. any financial aid	85
% UG borrow to pay for school	74
Average cumulative indebtedness	$39,869
% frosh need fully met	6
% ugrads need fully met	5
Average % of frosh need met	63
Average % of ugrad need met	62

Texas A&M University—College Station

Texas A&M University—College Station, College Station, TX 77843 • Admissions: 979-845-3211 • Fax: 979-845-8737

STUDENTS SAY ". . ."

Academics

The "untold spirit at Texas A&M" lies in its tradition, which is "the underlying pulse of Aggieland." This large research school has "deep-rooted values" and "runs as a tight-knit family despite the numerous population." This strong family dynamic makes the school an "open, friendly place to learn and grow," and the incredibly strong engineering and life science programs certainly don't hurt. The academics can be "difficult," but "the goal is to set [students] apart from the rest, so [they] can excel." The "wonderful" professors "do their best to bring the topics from pages to the real world." They "all have life experiences working with the topics that they teach, making them the perfect resource for information." These "top-notch" professors (well, aside from a very few who are "extremely dry") come back to A&M after working in powerful industry positions "because they love the atmosphere and the students." "I have never skipped a class because I thoroughly enjoy going," says one student. Particularly with the sciences, professors offer students the opportunity to participate in "world-changing research," and all such experiences "have had something useful to add to the material," which helps students when they go out into the real world. The "Aggie network" is something to behold; it reaches far across the nation ("Aggie alumni are loyal to their school forever") and "is good for getting jobs after graduation." The sense of pride here motivates students to do well "because they're part of something bigger than themselves." There is "great support" from both the faculty and staff together. "The mindset they have is to effectively prepare students for world-class challenges," says one student. "At Texas A&M, you learn to be a well-rounded, moral, and ethical person."

Campus Life

Student organizations positively abound at Texas A&M (there are more than 1,000), and they are a huge social outlet for students looking to find those with similar interests. "Get involved in something you're passionate about; there is a club for just about *everything*," says a student. Off-campus, there are "four-dollar movies, many dancehalls, endless restaurants to eat at, and a large mall," as well as "an ice-skating rink, bowling alley, and miniature golf place." Students at Texas A&M are "loyal to one another and are always willing to support their fellow Aggies." "Tradition and chivalry run the school," and students all "work hard during the week so we can party hard on the weekends," usually at Northgate, the "bar street." "Texas A&M is kind of like a cult—a really happy cult," explains a student. The "immense school spirit" is derived from the many "time-honored traditions," including the Big Event, which is the largest one-day, student-run service project in the nation. That's not even to mention the football: "Saturdays in the fall are owned by football." "Although the school is very large, whenever the…Aggies at Kyle Field are belting the war hymn and linking arms, I feel like I am part of a huge family." As one student cryptically sums up his school's mythology, "From the outside looking in, you can't understand it. From the inside looking out, you can't explain it."

Student Body

A typical student is "white," "conservative," "involved in at least one club, spends a fair amount of time studying, and learns to two-step for Thursday nights." This being Texas, "some wear cowboy boots, a flannel shirt, a cowboy hat/baseball cap, and jeans." There is also a strong faction of members of the Corps of Cadets, as well as religious folk (the school has "the largest Bible study in the world"). Though lacking cultural diversity, interests and hobbies run the gamut, and "students from other races and classes fit in just fine and are able to make friends just like anybody else." While it's a big school, "a lot of classes are pretty small, so it's easy to make friends in class." There are "no pretenses" among Aggies, and "everyone shows who they are." "Most of the people I have met here are truly genuine individuals," says a student.

TEXAS A&M UNIVERSITY—COLLEGE STATION

Financial Aid: 979-845-3236 • E-Mail: admissions@tamu.edu • Website: www.tamu.edu

THE PRINCETON REVIEW SAYS

Admissions

The school reports that its standardized testing policy for use in admission for Fall 2024 is Test Optional. It is unknown at this time if the 2024 testing policy will be permanent. The Princeton Review suggests that interested applicants consult with the school for the most up-to-date standardized testing policies. *Very important factors considered include:* rigor of secondary school record, class rank, academic GPA, standardized test scores, extracurricular activities, talent/ability. *Important factors considered include:* application essay, first generation, geographical residence, state residency, volunteer work, work experience. *Other factors considered include:* recommendation(s), character/personal qualities, level of applicant's interest. High school diploma is required and GED is accepted. *Academic units required:* 4 English, 3 math, 3 science, 1 science lab, 2 foreign language, 3 social studies, 1 visual/performing arts, 5 academic electives. *Academic units recommended:* 4 English, 4 math, 4 science, 2 science labs, 2 foreign language, 3 social studies, 1 visual/performing arts, 7 academic electives.

Financial Aid

Students should submit: FAFSA. Priority filing deadline is 1/15. The Princeton Review suggests that all financial aid forms be submitted as soon as possible (see page 5 for a note on the FAFSA). *Need-based scholarships/grants offered:* College/university scholarship or grant aid from institutional funds; Federal Pell; Private scholarships; SEOG; State scholarships/grants. *Loan aid offered:* Direct PLUS loans; Direct Subsidized Loans; Direct Unsubsidized Loans; College/university loans from institutional funds; Federal Nursing Loans; State Loans. Admitted students will be notified of awards on a rolling basis beginning 1/25. Federal Work-Study Program available. Institutional employment available.

The Inside Word

Texas A&M uses some cut-and-dried admissions criteria: students graduating in the top 10 percent of a recognized public or private high school in the state of Texas are automatically in; all they have to do is get their applications in on time. Students who land in the top 25 percent of their class can qualify for admissions under the State of Texas Uniform Admission Policy through coursework or test scores. All other applications are deemed "Review Admits" to be sorted through by the admissions committee.

THE SCHOOL SAYS "..."

From the Admissions Office

"Established in 1876 as the first public college in the state, Texas A&M University has become a world leader in teaching, research, and public service. Located in College Station in the heart of Texas, it is centrally situated among three of the country's ten largest cities: Dallas, Houston, and San Antonio. Texas A&M is ranked nationally in these four areas: enrollment, enrollment of top students, value of research, and endowment."

SELECTIVITY

Admissions Rating	90
# of applicants	44,110
% of applicants accepted	64
% of acceptees attending	44

FIRST-YEAR PROFILE

Testing policy	Test Optional
Range SAT composite	1160–1370
Range SAT EBRW	570–680
Range SAT math	570–700
Range ACT composite	25–31
# submitting SAT scores	7,371
% submitting SAT scores	68
# submitting ACT scores	3,442
% submitting ACT scores	32
% graduated top 10% of class	66
% graduated top 25% of class	92
% graduated top 50% of class	99

DEADLINES

Early action	
Deadline	10/15
Regular	
Deadline	12/1
Notification	Rolling, 12/15
Nonfall registration?	Yes

FINANCIAL FACTS

Financial Aid Rating	80
Annual in-state tuition	$9,208
Annual out-of-state tuition	$36,117
Room and board	$11,400
Required fees	$3,970
Books and supplies	$1,000
Average frosh need-based scholarship	$12,901
Average UG need-based scholarship	$11,231
% needy frosh rec. need-based scholarship or grant aid	90
% needy UG rec. need-based scholarship or grant aid	86
% needy frosh rec. non-need-based scholarship or grant aid	10
% needy UG rec. non-need-based scholarship or grant aid	6
% needy frosh rec. need-based self-help aid	43
% needy UG rec. need-based self-help aid	50
% frosh rec. any financial aid	69
% UG rec. any financial aid	65
% UG borrow to pay for school	41
Average cumulative indebtedness	$24,207
% frosh need fully met	22
% ugrads need fully met	17
Average % of frosh need met	69
Average % of ugrad need met	65

TEXAS CHRISTIAN UNIVERSITY

Texas Christian University, Fort Worth, TX 76129 • Admissions: 817-257-7490 • Fax: 817-257-7268

STUDENTS SAY "..."

Academics

Texas Christian University (TCU), a private liberal arts college in Fort Worth, was founded to provide classical education that would develop character. According to respondents, that's still very much the case, given an "emphasis on academics and broader thinking rather than just having us memorize information." Access to over 115 undergraduate programs ensures a broad-based education that can develop both intellect and integrity, whether that's in the familiar English or business management or less common courses like fashion merchandising and human-animal relationships. Students also take a minimum of one class involving religion, whether that's a look at Buddhism or a historical view of Early Christianity. In further accordance with the school's liberal arts ideals, students also cite the thoughtful discussions in their courses: "Our small class sizes are one of our greatest strengths." Students speak glowingly of their professors, praising their excellent teaching but also describing strong feelings of camaraderie, especially in the way they feel "they all will know your name and really get to know you."

Campus Life

The atmosphere on Texas Christian University's picturesque suburban campus is most commonly described as upbeat and animated: "Every day there is something new and my peers create a community that is unbeatable." As one junior put it "There is a lovely lively feeling to the campus, always bubbling with excitement for events or games!" Varsity team sports are an important part of life at the school, for the spectators as well as the athletes. Hundreds of boisterous "Frogs" (named for the school's intrepid horned frog mascot) can be seen enthusiastically cheering their football, baseball, and basketball teams. Greek life is also popular, as are the innumerable clubs and student organizations. TCU students can choose from over 275 groups, ranging from Arabic culture to student ministry to chess to meditation. In keeping with philanthropic values and the TCU heritage, many give their time freely to volunteer in the outside community or pursue charity work. Students might be seen caring for patients at a nearby Fort Worth hospital, playing Bingo in the park with people who are homeless, or providing music therapy for local children in need. In essence, "I was first drawn to TCU because everyone was smiling when I visited the campus, and now I'm one of those smiling students that prospective students see on their tour."

Student Body

"The often-celebrated 'Frog Family' is real: no matter who you are, you're welcomed and cared for." TCU students describe one another as gracious, helpful, and fiercely loyal to their peers and school. "I think TCU has one of the kindest and caring student bodies I have seen," one senior remarks. "Walking across campus you will see many, many students in TCU gear and I think that is representative of the love the student body has at this university." Another senior simply states "I would do anything for a Frog." Approximately 60% of TCU undergraduates are women and many are Christian, but as one junior puts it, "The 'C' in TCU can be as large or small as you want it to be." Students frequently note that diversity of all types has increased in recent years and that the community readily welcomes people of all faiths and creeds. There's an even mix of commuters and on-campus residents, with both groups reporting high levels of extracurricular participation and school pride: "I feel so blessed to go to a school where everyone is happy to be here and loving life."

TEXAS CHRISTIAN UNIVERSITY

Financial Aid: 817-257-7858 • E-Mail: frogmail@tcu.edu • Website: www.tcu.edu

THE PRINCETON REVIEW SAYS

Admissions

The school reports that its standardized testing policy for use in admission for Fall 2024 is Test Optional. The 2024 testing policy will be temporary. The Princeton Review suggests that interested applicants consult with the school for the most up-to-date standardized testing policies. *Very important factors considered include:* rigor of secondary school record, academic GPA. *Important factors considered include:* application essay, extracurricular activities, character/personal qualities, first generation, volunteer work, work experience. *Other factors considered include:* class rank, standardized test scores, recommendation(s), talent/ability, alumni/ae relation, geographical residence, state residency, religious affiliation/commitment, racial/ethnic status, level of applicant's interest. High school diploma is required and GED is not accepted. *Academic units required:* 4 English, 3 math, 3 science, 1 science lab, 2 language other than English (LOTE), 3 social studies, 2 academic electives. *Academic units recommended:* 4 English, 4 math, 4 science, 1 science lab, 4 (LOTE), 4 social studies.

Financial Aid

Students should submit: CSS Profile; FAFSA. Priority filing deadline is 2/1. The Princeton Review suggests that all financial aid forms be submitted as soon as possible (see page 5 for a note on the FAFSA). *Need-based scholarships/grants offered:* College/university scholarship or grant aid from institutional funds; Federal Pell; Private scholarships; SEOG; State scholarships/grants. *Loan aid offered:* Direct PLUS loans; Direct Subsidized Loans; Direct Unsubsidized Loans; Federal Nursing Loans; State Loans. Admitted students will be notified of awards on a rolling basis beginning 12/1. Federal Work-Study Program available. Institutional employment available.

The Inside Word

Admissions officers at Texas Christian University make it a priority to find applicants who will enrich the TCU community. The school does not maintain strict minimums for GPA or test scores. Admitted applicants are typically in the top 13 percent of their graduating class, with a roster of challenging courses behind them. Evaluations, essays, and activities will all be closely evaluated. Interviews and standardized tests are optional.

THE SCHOOL SAYS "..."

From the Admissions Office

"TCU is a major teaching and research university with the feel of a small college. The TCU academic experience includes small classes with top faculty; cutting-edge technology; a liberal arts and sciences core curriculum; and real-life application through faculty-directed research, group projects, and internships. While TCU faculty members are recognized for research, their main focus is on teaching and mentoring students. The friendly campus community welcomes new students at Frog Camp before classes begin, where students find three days of fun meeting new friends, learning campus traditions, and serving the community. Campus life includes 275 clubs and organizations and a spirited NCAA Division I athletics program in the Big 12 Conference. More than half of the students participate in a wide array of intramural sports, and about 40 percent are involved in Greek organizations, including ones emphasizing ethnic diversity as well as the Christian faith. The historic relationship to the Christian Church (Disciples of Christ) encourages a balance of faith and reason and a spirit for social justice and inclusiveness that's rooted in respect for one another. The university's mission—to educate individuals to think and act as ethical leaders and responsible citizens in a global community—influences everything from course work to study abroad to the way Horned Frogs act and interact. TCU attracts and serves students who are learning to change the world.

"TCU is Test Optional through 2024 and will accept either the SAT or the ACT (with or without the writing component) in admission and scholarship processes."

SELECTIVITY

Admissions Rating	**90**
# of applicants	16,197
% of applicants accepted	56
% of acceptees attending	27
# offered a place on the wait list	1,733
% accepting a place on wait list	31
% admitted from wait list	<1
# of early decision applicants	872
% accepted early decision	70

FIRST-YEAR PROFILE

Testing policy	Test Optional
Range SAT composite	1220–1370
Range SAT EBRW	600–680
Range SAT math	580–690
Range ACT composite	26–31
# submitting SAT scores	458
% submitting SAT scores	18
# submitting ACT scores	505
% submitting ACT scores	20
% frosh submitting high school GPA	97
% graduated top 10% of class	47
% graduated top 25% of class	77
% graduated top 50% of class	95

DEADLINES

Early decision	
Deadline	11/1
Notification	12/1
Other ED deadline	2/1
Other ED notification	3/15
Early action	
Deadline	11/1
Notification	12/15
Regular	
Deadline	2/1
Notification	4/1
Nonfall registration?	Yes

APPLICANTS OFTEN PREFER
University of Southern California; Vanderbilt University

APPLICANTS SOMETIMES PREFER
Baylor University; Clemson University; Gonzaga University; Miami University; Santa Clara University; Southern Methodist University; Texas A&M University—College Station; The University of Alabama—Tuscaloosa; The University of Texas at Austin; Trinity Univ

FINANCIAL FACTS

Financial Aid Rating	**84**
Annual tuition	$57,130
Room and board	$14,800
Required fees	$90
Books and supplies	$800
Average frosh need-based scholarship	$40,747
Average UG need-based scholarship	$37,342
% needy frosh rec. need-based scholarship or grant aid	97
% needy UG rec. need-based scholarship or grant aid	96
% needy frosh rec. non-need-based scholarship or grant aid	92
% needy UG rec. non-need-based scholarship or grant aid	88
% needy frosh rec. need-based self-help aid	65
% needy UG rec. need-based self-help aid	66
% frosh rec. any financial aid	86
% UG rec. any financial aid	84
% UG borrow to pay for school	33
Average cumulative indebtedness	$44,580
% frosh need fully met	49
% ugrads need fully met	32
Average % of frosh need met	82
Average % of ugrad need met	72

TEXAS STATE UNIVERSITY

601 University Drive, San Marcos, TX 78666 • Admissions: 512-245-2111 • Fax: 512-245-8044

STUDENTS SAY " . . ."

Academic

Students are drawn to Texas State University based on the quality and opportunity of its many offerings, in particular the "very strong STEM program," the "top of the line" education program, and for those studying chemistry, biology, and human health, "exceptional" research programs. Faculty are also admired on a personal level as they're "not only skilled, but care deeply about their students' success." One student enthuses: "I can't emphasize how much I love my professors and coursework. Honestly, school has felt like a hobby these past years that I have thoroughly enjoyed." Given that Texas State caters to over 33,000 undergraduates and offers more than 200 degree programs, students admit that there are a number of large-class lectures. But the general high satisfaction of students speaks to the quality of classes, and the "wonderful professors that ignite [their] academic passions." There's talk of a science course that had students "playing with Play-Doh to learn structures of meiosis" and taking a "New York fashion trip to learn about popular businesses." Marketing students enthusiastically speak of the actual campaigns they had to put together for class: "We actually demonstrated our knowledge when we implemented it in our project." As one student puts it: "I have loved all of my professors so far, they really are passionate about their work and their research, and they are also wonderful people to talk to. My overall experience has been amazing."

Campus Life

Texas State is an "absolutely beautiful" campus that is "surrounded by trees and wildlife" and marked by the "gorgeous river that runs through it." It's no surprise that river-based activities such as tubing, kayaking, and "the moonlight paddle board" are extremely popular. It's also fitting that students also make the most of opportunities to preserve that beauty "in the community, helping to conserve the San Marcos river and organize clean ups for the area." Other "outdoor opportunities," such as hiking, camping, or hanging out nearby Sewell Park, are favorite ways for Bobcats to "ease their worries." As one fourth-year student puts it, "you won't be bored." Some undergraduates "come to Texas State thinking it's party hard, which it can be and is, but you also have to work hard." It's an all-in sort of attitude, one that's best evoked by sports, shows, and Greek life: "I believe my school's spirit is our biggest trait."

Student Body

"The community of peers I have built at Texas State University is something I have always dreamed of," confides one senior. That's a common refrain, given there are over 350 student groups to choose from: "I am involved with TXST Trainwreck (ultimate frisbee) which has let me meet my closest friends on campus and future roommates!" Academically, "students at Texas State actively seek support through one another during class and outside." Students describe their peers as "knowledgeable and passionate for their studies," and given the school's demographics, are appreciative of the "strong female presence overall."

With a majority of students hailing originally from the Lone Star State, the vibe on campus is "very homey and welcoming." But don't be fooled, as "Texas State is a really diverse school in many aspects (race, national origin, gender/sexuality, etc.)." Moreover, "the curriculum is oriented toward inclusivity." The result, say students, is "a welcoming environment where the student body feels that they can be their true selves here without any judgment." All in all, "there's a place for everyone here."

TEXAS STATE UNIVERSITY

Financial Aid: 512-245-2315 • E-Mail: admissions@txstate.edu • Website: www.txst.edu

THE PRINCETON REVIEW SAYS

Admissions

The school reports that its standardized testing policy for use in admission for Fall 2024 is Test Optional. Students in last quarter of their high school class are required to submit test scores, others are encouraged for scholarship purposes. The Princeton Review suggests that interested applicants consult with the school for the most up-to-date standardized testing policies. *Very important factors considered include:* class rank, standardized test scores. *Other factors considered include:* rigor of secondary school record, application essay, extracurricular activities, talent/ability, first generation, volunteer work. High school diploma is required and GED is accepted. *Academic units required:* 4 English, 4 math, 4 science, 2 science labs, 2 foreign language, 2 social studies, 2 history, 1 visual/performing arts, 6 academic electives.

Financial Aid

Students should submit: FAFSA. Priority filing deadline is 1/15. The Princeton Review suggests that all financial aid forms be submitted as soon as possible (see page 5 for a note on the FAFSA). *Need-based scholarships/grants offered:* College/university scholarship or grant aid from institutional funds; Federal Pell; Private scholarships; SEOG; State scholarships/grants. *Loan aid offered:* Direct PLUS loans; Direct Subsidized Loans; Direct Unsubsidized Loans; College/university loans from institutional funds; State Loans. Admitted students will be notified of awards on a rolling basis beginning 5/1. Federal Work-Study Program available. Institutional employment available.

The Inside Word

Competition to become a Bobcat is fierce; first-year applicants should have four years of math, science, and English; three years of social studies; and two years of a foreign language, among other requirements. The state of Texas requires that all students meet specific college readiness standards, and assured admission is granted to all students with certain diploma types who meet specific test score and class ranking standards—students should visit the school's website in order to see if they qualify. Even if a student does not meet assured admission requirements, their application will be holistically reviewed by the school.

SELECTIVITY

Admissions Rating	83
# of applicants	28,908
% of applicants accepted	88
% of acceptees attending	30

FIRST-YEAR PROFILE

Testing policy	Test Optional
Range SAT composite	990–1170
Range SAT EBRW	500–600
Range SAT math	480–580
Range ACT composite	19–26
# submitting SAT scores	3,706
% submitting SAT scores	49
# submitting ACT scores	620
% submitting ACT scores	8
% graduated top 10% of class	13
% graduated top 25% of class	41
% graduated top 50% of class	79

DEADLINES

Regular	
Priority	12/1
Deadline	7/15
Notification	Rolling, 9/1
Nonfall registration?	Yes

APPLICANTS OFTEN PREFER
The University of Texas at Austin

APPLICANTS SOMETIMES PREFER
Texas A&M University—College Station

APPLICANTS RARELY PREFER
Texas Tech University; The University of Texas at San Antonio; University of Houston

FINANCIAL FACTS

Financial Aid Rating	80
Annual in-state tuition	$9,221
Annual out-of-state tuition	$21,461
Room and board	$11,516
Required fees	$2,986
Books and supplies	$790
Average frosh need-based scholarship	$10,924
Average UG need-based scholarship	$8,914
% needy frosh rec. need-based scholarship or grant aid	90
% needy UG rec. need-based scholarship or grant aid	82
% needy frosh rec. non-need-based scholarship or grant aid	29
% needy UG rec. non-need-based scholarship or grant aid	12
% needy frosh rec. need-based self-help aid	63
% needy UG rec. need-based self-help aid	69
% frosh rec. any financial aid	90
% UG rec. any financial aid	73
% UG borrow to pay for school	63
Average cumulative indebtedness	$24,875
% frosh need fully met	31
% ugrads need fully met	14
Average % of frosh need met	78
Average % of ugrad need met	62

THOMAS AQUINAS COLLEGE (CA)

10,000 Ojai Road, Santa Paula, CA 93060 • Admissions: 805-525-4417 • Fax: 805-525-9342

CAMPUS LIFE

Quality of Life Rating	95
Fire Safety Rating	97
Green Rating	60*
Type of school	Private
Affiliation	Roman Catholic
Environment	Town

STUDENTS

Total undergrad enrollment	355
% male/female/another gender	48/52/NR
% from out of state	57
% frosh from public high school	16
% frosh live on campus	100
% ugrads live on campus	100
# of fraternities	0
# of sororities	0
% Asian	2
% White	61
% Hispanic	22
% Pacific Islander	<1
% Two or more races	6
% Race and/or ethnicity unknown	4
% international	4
# of countries represented	9

SURVEY SAYS . . .

Lots of conservative students
Students are happy
Classroom facilities are great
Great library
Class discussions encouraged
Great financial aid
No one cheats
Students are friendly
Diverse student types interact on campus
Students are very religious
Dorms are like palaces
Easy to get around campus
Theater is popular

ACADEMICS

Academic Rating	92
% students returning for sophomore year	93
% students graduating within 4 years	81
% students graduating within 6 years	83
Calendar	Semester
Student/faculty ratio	11:1
Profs interesting rating	99
Profs accessible rating	98
Most classes have 10–19 students.	

MOST POPULAR MAJORS
Liberal Arts and Sciences/Liberal Studies

Note: The data and survey responses provided for Thomas Aquinas College apply only to the California campus.

STUDENTS SAY ". . ."

Academics

Thomas Aquinas College is a small, private Roman Catholic-affiliated liberal arts school located in Southern California. Students have a wide spectrum of terms with which to describe their unique education: "difficult, mind blowing, extremely enjoyable, and intensely interesting." Instead of taking the standard mix of general education requirements, electives, and coursework for majors and minors, TAC has a set curriculum for all first-years, sophomores, juniors, and seniors that is comprised entirely of reading and discussing the great books of Western civilization with the goal of "grappling with the greatest thinkers directly instead of…through a secondary text." Students say professors are excellent at facilitating discussions, "always accessible outside of their class hours," and "strong role models and mentors." With class sizes of "just over a dozen students," they typically rely on the Socratic Method with little to no lecturing. Students say the combination of curriculum and pedagogy allows them to "find the truth themselves," hone their critical thinking skills, and, by senior year, grasp essential "core ideas of the highest nature such as relativity, time, space and being." Some do note that courses could focus more on developing writing skills by assigning "more essays and papers" in addition to the heavy reading. By contrast, some students feel that while a classical education "may not prepare one for a specific job, it prepares one to be a good man [or woman]." One student sums the academic experience up by saying, "You have to work very hard, but…you see [it] pay off instantly in class."

Campus Life

During the week, Thomas Aquinas College students focus on preparing for class and on their work-study jobs, if they've taken one on. When they're looking for a break, they often find it in the college's intramural sports, which are "open to all students regardless of skill." Sports like basketball, ultimate Frisbee, tennis, soccer, baseball, or volleyball "bring the community together without taking over" campus life. Outside of athletics, students would like more variety in school sponsored extracurricular activities, but this outdoorsy student body has a plethora of options in their backyard. The campus is "a mile walk from the Los Padres National Forest, which is a beautiful location for hiking and mountain biking," and the local beach in Ventura is a popular swimming and surfing destination.

Campus rules "strongly reflect [TAC's] Catholic identity" and include a dress code and curfew. For some, this conservative culture "does not feel like college life but high school life," while others say it creates a peaceful environment where it's easy to prioritize coursework. Instead of traditional campus nightlife, there are frequent "small, informal waltz or swing nights." (Drinking isn't tolerated on campus, so those looking for such activities must head off campus.) Classes take turns hosting monthly themed dances, which are "often highlights of everyone's year." When they're not busy with this wide array of options, students simply "sit around and talk in the commons," play board games, read poetry, make music and movies, sing in the choir, knit, and hang out in the coffee shop.

Student Body

With a student body of about 400 undergrads, "each individual is a relevant member of the community." TAC students take pride in the "culture of casual kindnesses," where everyone "is friendly and comfortable with each other" and is "always willing to have a good conversation." Additionally, students describe their peers as "kind," "quirky," "genuine," and united by "a desire for [pursuing] knowledge for its own sake." This sense of community is bolstered by a "wide range of backgrounds and cultures," primarily from a traditional Catholic or Christian background—"most students attend mass daily." One student sums it up: "There are the athletic students, the studious students, the party-goers, and the introverted students," although "we joke that…everyone falls under the common category of nerd."

THOMAS AQUINAS COLLEGE (CA)

Financial Aid: 800-634-9797 • E-Mail: admissions@thomasaquinas.edu • Website: www.thomasaquinas.edu

THE PRINCETON REVIEW SAYS

Admissions

The school reports that its standardized testing policy for use in admission for Fall 2024 requires applicants to submit the SAT, ACT, or CLT. The Princeton Review suggests that interested applicants consult with the school for the most up-to-date standardized testing policies. *Very important factors considered include:* rigor of secondary school record, standardized test scores, application essay, recommendation(s), character/personal qualities, level of applicant's interest. *Important factors considered include:* academic GPA. *Other factors considered include:* class rank, interview, extracurricular activities, talent/ability, religious affiliation/commitment, volunteer work, work experience. High school diploma is required and GED is accepted. *Academic units required:* 4 English, 3 math, 2 science, 2 foreign language, 2 history. *Academic units recommended:* 4 English, 4 math, 3 science, 2 science labs, 2 history, 3 academic electives.

Financial Aid

Students should submit: CSS/Financial Aid Profile; FAFSA; Institution's own financial aid form; Noncustodial Profile; State aid form. The Princeton Review suggests that all financial aid forms be submitted as soon as possible (see page 5 for a note on the FAFSA). *Need-based scholarships/grants offered:* College/university scholarship or grant aid from institutional funds; Federal Pell; Private scholarships; State scholarships/grants. *Loan aid offered:* Direct PLUS loans; Direct Subsidized Loans; Direct Unsubsidized Loans; College/university loans from institutional funds. Admitted students will be notified of awards on a rolling basis beginning 2/1. Institutional employment available.

The Inside Word

A unique academic institution, Thomas Aquinas College thoroughly analyzes applicants to ensure accepted students will be a good fit on campus. Therefore, academic prowess is a must, and candidates should also demonstrate intellectual curiosity. Because of their holistic approach, admissions officers pay close attention to the application essays. The college operates on a rolling admissions schedule and, if interested, you should apply as early as possible. If you're thinking about attending the new western Massachusetts campus, note that you can only apply for admission at one location.

THE SCHOOL SAYS "..."

From the Admissions Office

"In 2019 Thomas Aquinas College launched a second campus on the beautiful former site of a preparatory school in Northfield, Massachusetts. Students can now choose between two locations to pursue the College's unique program of Catholic liberal education. California boasts year-round sunshine, mission architecture, and nearby beaches; New England claims four seasons, historic colonial buildings, and the majestic Connecticut River Valley. But both campuses offer the same comprehensive and unified academic program, taught under the light of faith.

"The College's curriculum includes no textbooks or lecture classes. In every subject—from philosophy, theology, mathematics, and science to language, music, literature, and history—students read the greatest written works in those disciplines, both ancient and modern: Homer, Plato, Aristotle, Augustine, Aquinas, Newton, Maxwell, Einstein, the Founding Fathers of the American Republic, Shakespeare, and T. S. Eliot, to name just a few. Instead of attending lecture classes, students gather in small tutorials, seminars, and laboratories for Socratic-style discussions.

"One mark of the program's success is the variety of professions and careers that graduates enter. Many attend graduate and professional schools in a wide array of disciplines; among them, theology, law, business, literature, medicine, and the sciences are most often chosen.

"High school juniors who are interested in learning more about the academic, spiritual, and social life of Thomas Aquinas College are strongly encouraged to participate in TAC's two-week Great Books Summer Program, offered both in California and New England. See thomasaquinas.edu/summer."

SELECTIVITY

Admissions Rating	88
# of applicants	163
% of applicants accepted	84
% of acceptees attending	67

FIRST-YEAR PROFILE

Testing policy	SAT, ACT, or CLT required
Range SAT composite	1220–1390
Range SAT EBRW	620–730
Range SAT math	580–680
Range ACT composite	28–32
# submitting SAT scores	43
% submitting SAT scores	43
# submitting ACT scores	15
% submitting ACT scores	15
Average HS GPA	3.8
% frosh submitting high school GPA	85

DEADLINES

Regular	
Notification	Rolling, 10/1
Nonfall registration?	No

APPLICANTS ALSO LOOK AT

Benedictine College; Christendom College; Franciscan University of Steubenville; Thomas More College of Liberal Arts; University of Dallas

FINANCIAL FACTS

Financial Aid Rating	96
Annual tuition	$28,700
Room and board	$10,700
Required fees	$0
Average frosh need-based scholarship	$16,099
Average UG need-based scholarship	$15,283
% needy frosh rec. need-based scholarship or grant aid	90
% needy UG rec. need-based scholarship or grant aid	89
% needy frosh rec. non-need-based scholarship or grant aid	8
% needy UG rec. non-need-based scholarship or grant aid	6
% needy frosh rec. need-based self-help aid	100
% needy UG rec. need-based self-help aid	98
% frosh rec. any financial aid	74
% UG rec. any financial aid	74
% UG borrow to pay for school	84
Average cumulative indebtedness	$18,581
% frosh need fully met	100
% ugrads need fully met	100
Average % of frosh need met	100
Average % of ugrad need met	100

TRANSYLVANIA UNIVERSITY

300 North Broadway, Lexington, KY 40508-1797 • Admissions: 859-233-8300 • Fax: 859-281-3649

STUDENTS SAY "..."

Academics

For many thrilled students, Transylvania University in Lexington, Kentucky feels "like home" from the minute they set foot on campus. This is due in large part to its "small size," which allows "Transy" to maintain a very "supportive" environment. When it comes to academics, undergrads at Transylvania savor the breadth of courses that are available. And they rush to highlight the "inclusive fine arts program," which lets non-majors still actively participate in "music or theatre." Many also note student success with graduate school, boasting of a "95 percent" acceptance rate to medical school and a whopping "100 percent" acceptance rate to law school. Much of this can be attributed to "rigorous" classes that "require you to think deeply and critically." Transy's "brilliant faculty" is owed some credit as well. They are "highly dedicated" instructors who continually demonstrate "interest...in [their] students' lives and ambitions." Even better, "they all have open office hours multiple days a week and often will meet with students other times as well." And one incredulous student interjects, "I am close enough with my professors to join them for department dinners or [non-alcoholic] drinks with guest lecturers. It is a one-of-a-kind situation that I wouldn't trade for the world."

Campus Life

It is pretty easy to lead a fun and robust life at Transylvania. While academics take top priority, there are also "many opportunities to get involved on campus." For example, "there are frequently guest speakers and movie nights that students can attend for fun and for class credit." The university hosts "a lot of theater productions and music concerts" as well. Most "people are involved with school-affiliated organizations, like the school's "environmental conservation group" and the "Student Activities Board." Athletics are a big draw too and you can often find undergrads playing "volleyball, basketball, soccer," and "intramurals." Those looking for instant community will be happy to hear that "Greek life is extremely popular." When students are itching to get a break from campus life, downtown Lexington offers a plethora of great options including "a ton of neat places within walking distance, such as... the Central Bank Center, Triangle Park, the Mary Todd Lincoln House, and the Lexington Opera House." All in all, there's "so much to do, and there's always something new to discover."

Student Body

Transylvania manages to foster a "very safe and accepting" atmosphere. Much of that can be attributed to the "incredibly welcoming and friendly" student body. And though the university is set in Kentucky, we're told you find a nice "mix of classic south[ern] and northern attitudes." You're also likely to discover both "liberal" and "conservative" students. Unfortunately, some undergrads do caution that Transylvania is "not very diverse." But many people insist that their peers "seem willing and curious to learn about different cultures and perspectives." As one undergrad shares, "The majority of students on campus are open-minded, creative people, and incredibly accepting of others no matter their gender, race, sexual/gender orientation, or socioeconomic status. They do not hesitate to band together to aid another student in need." Students also love that their peers are "goal oriented" and "take their education seriously." They "push to excel academically, socially, and athletically." And they all enjoy being "extremely involved on campus." Of course, the best aspect of Transy's student body is the fact that "anywhere you go you can always find a friend or at least some people that are easy to talk to."

TRANSYLVANIA UNIVERSITY

Financial Aid: 859-233-8239 • E-Mail: admissions@transy.edu • Website: www.transy.edu

THE PRINCETON REVIEW SAYS

Admissions

The school reports that its standardized testing policy for use in admission for Fall 2024 is Test Optional. The 2024 testing policy will be permanent. The Princeton Review suggests that interested applicants consult with the school for the most up-to-date standardized testing policies. *Very important factors considered include:* rigor of secondary school record, academic GPA, standardized test scores, application essay. *Important factors considered include:* recommendation(s), extracurricular activities, talent/ability, character/personal qualities. *Other factors considered include:* class rank, interview, first generation, alumni/ae relation, geographical residence, racial/ethnic status, volunteer work, work experience. High school diploma is required and GED is accepted. *Academic units required:* 4 English, 3 math, 3 science, 2 science labs, 2 foreign language, 2 social studies, 2 academic electives. *Academic units recommended:* 4 English, 4 math, 4 science, 3 science labs, 2 foreign language, 2 social studies, 1 history, 2 academic electives.

Financial Aid

Students should submit: FAFSA. Priority filing deadline is 10/15. The Princeton Review suggests that all financial aid forms be submitted as soon as possible (see page 5 for a note on the FAFSA). *Need-based scholarships/grants offered:* College/university scholarship or grant aid from institutional funds; Federal Pell; Private scholarships; SEOG; State scholarships/grants. *Loan aid offered:* Direct PLUS loans; Direct Subsidized Loans; Direct Unsubsidized Loans. Admitted students will be notified of awards on a rolling basis. Federal Work-Study Program available. Institutional employment available.

The Inside Word

Admissions officers at Transylvania realize that students are more than the mere sum of their GPA and test scores. And they strive to get a clear picture of the entire applicant. Therefore, while high school transcripts hold the most weight, the committee also closely considers your personal statement, extracurricular activities, and recommendations. And applicants wary of the SATs and ACTs can breathe a sigh of relief; Transylvania is a Test Optional school. You will not be at a disadvantage if you choose not to submit your scores.

THE SCHOOL SAYS "..."

From the Admissions Office

"At Transylvania, the 16th-oldest institution of higher learning in the U.S., students receive the skills they need to pursue bold paths toward personal fulfillment and professional success in any field. It's a unique journey built on making connections with professors, classmates, research and interests. Faculty get to know their students personally, helping them find opportunities that will allow them to reach their academic and career goals. There are no teaching assistants—just expert faculty who include students in research, help them find jobs and internships and work with them on an academic plan that meets their needs, including the option to design their own major. The liberal arts curriculum gives students broad experience and deep subject training, while developing their skills in communication, problem-solving and adaptability, which is why nearly all students find a job or graduate school placement within six months of graduation. Transylvania's campus in downtown Lexington, Kentucky, a thriving city of 300,000 people, is small enough for students to stand out, but with the amenities of one of the best college cities in America. Students have access to modern facilities and comprehensive student services, with more than 50 student clubs and organizations that let them pursue their interests and develop their leadership skills. A member of the NCAA Division III, Transy has 27 men's and women's intercollegiate athletic teams.

"Transylvania is a Test Optional school and does not require that students submit standardized test scores as part of the admission process. Read more at www.transy.edu/optional."

SELECTIVITY

Admissions Rating	83
# of applicants	1,781
% of applicants accepted	91
% of acceptees attending	17

FIRST-YEAR PROFILE

Testing policy	Test Optional
Range SAT composite	1120–1360
Range SAT EBRW	580–700
Range SAT math	540–660
Range ACT composite	23–29
# submitting SAT scores	24
% submitting SAT scores	9
# submitting ACT scores	189
% submitting ACT scores	67
Average HS GPA	3.7
% frosh submitting high school GPA	99
% graduated top 10% of class	33
% graduated top 25% of class	59
% graduated top 50% of class	85

DEADLINES

Regular	
Priority	11/1
Notification	Rolling, 11/1
Nonfall registration?	Yes

APPLICANTS OFTEN PREFER
Centre College; University of Kentucky

APPLICANTS SOMETIMES PREFER
Bellarmine University; Eastern Kentucky University; Georgetown College; Hanover College; University of Louisville; Western Kentucky University

APPLICANTS RARELY PREFER
Butler University; DePauw University; Morehead State University; Northern Kentucky University; University of Cincinnati; University of Tennessee—Knoxville

FINANCIAL FACTS

Financial Aid Rating	85
Annual tuition	$43,160
Room and board	$13,270
Required fees	$1,820
Books and supplies	$1,000
Average frosh need-based scholarship	$31,594
Average UG need-based scholarship	$31,674
% needy frosh rec. need-based scholarship or grant aid	100
% needy UG rec. need-based scholarship or grant aid	100
% needy frosh rec. non-need-based scholarship or grant aid	27
% needy UG rec. non-need-based scholarship or grant aid	22
% needy frosh rec. need-based self-help aid	62
% needy UG rec. need-based self-help aid	65
% frosh rec. any financial aid	99
% UG rec. any financial aid	98
% UG borrow to pay for school	68
Average cumulative indebtedness	$34,548
% frosh need fully met	33
% ugrads need fully met	30
Average % of frosh need met	82
Average % of ugrad need met	82

TRINITY COLLEGE (CT)

300 Summit Street, Hartford, CT 06106 • Admissions: 860-297-2180 • Fax: 860-297-2287

STUDENTS SAY "..."

Academics

Trinity College is a selective institution, but enrollees explain that once in, it is easy to flourish academically. Students are fans of having "small class sizes" be the norm, as well as the "plentiful" internships/research opportunities. They also note that the college provides "many resources to help support you in careers" as well "many different kinds of learning opportunities and…many levels of support." More specifically, undergrads can participate in "community-based learning" courses that seamlessly integrate hometown Hartford "into the classroom experience, either through research, excursions, or community partnerships." In turn, this allows "students to directly apply the theory from class to real-world problems." For example, one undergrad explains that their experiential "tax clinic class license[d] students to do…the taxes of Hartford residents."

Classes are only taught by professors, so students spend their time learning directly from "true experts in their field." Many students suggest that their academic experience is fantastic due to professors who routinely prove themselves to be "kind, enthusiastic, and extremely knowledgeable." As this student shares, "They spend time getting to know me personally, helping me grow as a student, and deliver[ing] compelling lectures." Students also want it on the record that the faculty really "push us to think beyond what we know and work towards gaining a deep understanding of the course material." Perhaps best of all, given that Trinity is "a small liberal arts college, professors are solely here to teach undergraduates and do not have ulterior agendas (research, climbing the academic ladder, etc.)."

Campus Life

Life at Trinity can be equally frenzied and fulfilling: "I have an internship, work on campus, dance, sing in an a cappella group, [and] am in a professional development organization, in addition to classes." Indeed, it's common for days to be "a mix of classes, homework, work, and athletics" and "at the end of the day, most people are able to wind down with friends or roommates or at least grab a meal or coffee with them." The pace stems from the bounty of extracurricular options, from a student investment fund to a mock trial team and more. "There is also an on-campus movie theater that my friends and I really enjoy going to." Fraternities and sororities are popular, as is the "rather large party scene on campus," though some undergrads note that "there is no pressure to involve yourself if you choose not to." Finally, when students need a respite from campus life, they can explore all Hartford has to offer. "There is a huge Caribbean, Latinx, and Turkish population so the food is great," as is the overall culture, especially for those who appreciate art and music.

Student Body

Trinity College's population is at a crossroads, with some feeling "divided profoundly by race and class," while others note that whereas they thought they might "face a lot of isolation and not feel like I fit in at all, the community is great and everyone is extremely connected." Respondents give the impression that the school is moving away from its past as "predominantly white, from the East Coast, and…financially comfortable" and actively "trying to diversify its student body ideologically, racially, and ethnically." The result is that Trinity "does feel quite international."

Students are far more apt to talk about the commonalities of this "tight-knit community" than the differences, however: "My peers are energetic, passionate about their education… and excited to engage in school activities." Indeed, "you can walk around campus and see numerous friendly faces that you have interacted with in classroom settings, at sporting events, or in extracurricular[s]." In turn, it's highly evident that "no one is stuck in one place or area of interests—everyone intersects and enjoys growing in all facets together."

TRINITY COLLEGE (CT)

Financial Aid: 860-297-2046 • E-Mail: admissions.office@trincoll.edu • Website: www.trincoll.edu/

THE PRINCETON REVIEW SAYS

Admissions

The school reports that its standardized testing policy for use in admission for Fall 2024 will remain Test Optional, as it has been since 2015. *Very important factors considered include:* rigor of secondary school record, academic GPA, character/personal qualities. *Important factors considered include:* class rank, application essay, recommendation(s), extra-curricular activities, talent/ability, level of applicant's interest. *Other factors considered include:* standardized test scores, interview, first generation, alumni/ae relation, geographical residence, state residency, racial/ethnic status, volunteer work, work experience. High school diploma is required and GED is accepted. *Academic units required:* 4 English, 3 math, 2 science, 2 science labs, 3 foreign language, 2 history.

Financial Aid

Students should submit: CSS/Financial Aid Profile; FAFSA; Noncustodial Profile. Priority filing deadline is 1/15. The Princeton Review suggests that all financial aid forms be submitted as soon as possible (see page 5 for a note on the FAFSA). *Need-based scholarships/grants offered:* College/university scholarship or grant aid from institutional funds; Federal Pell; Private scholarships; SEOG; State scholarships/grants. *Loan aid offered:* Direct PLUS loans; Direct Subsidized Loans; Direct Unsubsidized Loans; College/university loans from institutional funds; State Loans. Admitted students will be notified of awards on or about 4/1. Federal Work-Study Program available. Institutional employment available.

The Inside Word

Trinity College is seeking a wide range of individuals, and as such, there are many avenues for applicants to consider, especially those from low-income, first-generation, or student-of-color backgrounds. Admission is competitive, so finding ways to distinguish yourself, either by submitting optional standardized test scores or with an accomplished, rigorous academic transcript can take you far.

THE SCHOOL SAYS "..."

From the Admissions Office

"At Trinity College, we're known for getting things done—and for doing them in a way that creates lasting meaning. Students come to Trinity to engage in a challenging liberal arts education, live as part of a tenacious community, explore what's possible, and find answers to the challenges of tomorrow.

"When you become a Trinity Bantam, you will build a foundation of critical thinking that will prepare you to ask the right questions and seek the best solutions. Our small classes and 8:1 student-faculty ratio mean that professors will know you and take a personal interest in your success.

"On our 100-acre campus, you will join a vibrant community of peers from all over the world, engage with like-minded students in over 150 student clubs and organizations, and compete in the storied New England Small College Athletic Conference (NESCAC).

"Living in the heart of Connecticut's state capital, you can take advantage of all that Hartford has to offer, including diverse perspectives, experiential learning, and an energetic cultural life. You will gain experience in our thriving city through academic internships, including our Legislative Internship and Health Fellows programs, and a variety of community service and civic engagement opportunities.

"After graduating, you will join a distinguished, 200-year-old alumni network, including Fulbright and Watson scholars, MacArthur Fellows, and five Pulitzer Prize winners.

"At Trinity College, we are committed to making higher education accessible to more students and families. We offer generous financial aid and grant packages and meet the full calculated need for admitted students. Please visit us in Hartford to learn more about the Trinity experience."

SELECTIVITY

Admissions Rating	94
# of applicants	6,220
% of applicants accepted	36
% of acceptees attending	25
# of early decision applicants	530
% accepted early decision	60

FIRST-YEAR PROFILE

Testing policy	Test Optional
Range SAT composite	1300–1470
Range SAT EBRW	660–720
Range SAT math	640–750
Range ACT composite	30–32
# submitting SAT scores	81
% submitting SAT scores	14
# submitting ACT scores	26
% submitting ACT scores	5
% graduated top 10% of class	48
% graduated top 25% of class	74
% graduated top 50% of class	94

DEADLINES

Early decision	
Deadline	11/15
Notification	12/15
Other ED deadline	1/17
Other ED notification	2/15
Regular	
Deadline	1/17
Notification	4/1
Nonfall registration?	Yes

FINANCIAL FACTS

Financial Aid Rating	97
Annual tuition	$64,430
Room and board	$17,990
Required fees	$2,990
Books and supplies	$1,000
Average frosh need-based scholarship	$46,237
Average UG need-based scholarship	$48,268
% needy frosh rec. need-based scholarship or grant aid	97
% needy UG rec. need-based scholarship or grant aid	98
% needy frosh rec. non-need-based scholarship or grant aid	5
% needy UG rec. non-need-based scholarship or grant aid	3
% needy frosh rec. need-based self-help aid	59
% needy UG rec. need-based self-help aid	58
% frosh rec. any financial aid	49
% UG rec. any financial aid	45
% UG borrow to pay for school	45
Average cumulative indebtedness	$32,743
% frosh need fully met	100
% ugrads need fully met	100
Average % of frosh need met	100
Average % of ugrad need met	100

TRINITY UNIVERSITY

One Trinity Place, San Antonio, TX 78212-7200 • Admissions: 210-999-8483 • Fax: 210-999-8164

STUDENTS SAY "..."

Academics

Located in San Antonio, Trinity University is a small liberal arts college that offers substantial financial aid and encourages the exploration of academic interests and personal goals. Strong science programs and research opportunities abound, and students are interested in many different branches of academia and extracurricular life: "It's rare to find a student with one major and no minor." The Dean and President "have steady communication with the student body," and "they're open to criticism and willing to change the school's policy in order to advocate for the students' needs." The "highly intelligent" faculty "know their stuff and love what they do"; they are "very self-aware and are constantly trying to improve themselves and their students." The most distinguishable trait about Trinity professors is "the deeply-ingrained willingness to connect with and help their students," which is possible due to Trinity's small class sizes. Academics here are rigorous, and professors "expect their students to treat the class...as if it was the only class students have." Luckily, they will "bend over backwards to help you understand and complete material," and some professors even hold extra study sessions on Sundays (one-on-one attention from professors is common, as the university does not have TAs).

Above all else, Trinity University encourages students to take a wide range of classes and pursue a wide variety of interests, and a fair number of students choose to study abroad their junior year. The school "focuses on building a community based on the individual" and "fosters a space for the easy transfer of knowledge between faculty and students as well as the creation of new knowledge in research."

Campus Life

Most students at Trinity live on campus (and it's "hard to get off campus and do things if you don't have a car"), so there are always campus-wide events happening. Most people here are "happily overcommitted" and the "lovely campus" is big enough for all sorts of people to find their niche, but small enough "that you can connect with others who share similar interests as you within and without your major." Intramural sports and Greek life are popular, and "there's no tension between Greeks and non-Greeks." A healthy mix of activities complements the healthy mix of academic areas, and some people go out to parties on weekends, other people get ahead on studies, other people sleep." For those looking for some city culture, downtown San Antonio is ten minutes away, Austin is just a 90-minute drive, and "there are tons of restaurants and historical monuments and museums" nearby. Cowboys, the local country dance club ("only in Texas"), gets a lot of Trinity students visiting on weekends, and many people here "enjoy outdoor pursuits." Laid back, casual fun is the name of the game at Trinity, and students are perfectly happy to "catch a movie at the nearby theater, go to the local farmers' market, go to Spurs' games...or just hang out on campus."

Student Body

There is an "open-minded open-to-all mindset" that is readily seen on campus: "At Trinity, you're cool if you competitively roller skate, are an amateur baker, play a competitive sport, are freaky good at laser tag (ninja status), or anything else you can do well and makes you happy," says a student. Though most are "pretty middle- to upper middle-class," the school "encourages interactions with others from all walks of life." For the most part, everyone is "smart, committed, and involved," and an "overarching friendliness" pervades the entire student population.

TRINITY UNIVERSITY

Financial Aid: 210-999-8898 • E-Mail: admissions@trinity.edu • Website: www.trinity.edu

THE PRINCETON REVIEW SAYS

Admissions

The school reports that its standardized testing policy for use in admission for Fall 2024 is Test Flexible. It is unknown at this time if the 2024 testing policy will be permanent. The Princeton Review suggests that interested applicants consult with the school for the most up-to-date standardized testing policies. *Very important factors considered include:* rigor of secondary school record, class rank, academic GPA. *Important factors considered include:* application essay, recommendation(s), interview, extracurricular activities, talent/ability, character/personal qualities. *Other factors considered include:* standardized test scores, first generation, alumni/ae relation, geographical residence, volunteer work, work experience, level of applicant's interest. High school diploma is required and GED is accepted. *Academic units required:* 4 English, 3 math, 3 science, 2 science labs, 2 foreign language, 3 social studies.

Financial Aid

Students should submit: CSS/Financial Aid Profile; FAFSA. Priority filing deadline is 2/15. The Princeton Review suggests that all financial aid forms be submitted as soon as possible (see page 5 for a note on the FAFSA). *Need-based scholarships/grants offered:* College/university scholarship or grant aid from institutional funds; Federal Pell; Private scholarships; SEOG; State scholarships/grants. *Loan aid offered:* Direct PLUS loans; Direct Subsidized Loans; Direct Unsubsidized Loans; College/university loans from institutional funds; State Loans. Admitted students will be notified of awards on or about 3/15. Federal Work-Study Program available. Institutional employment available.

The Inside Word

As Trinity embraces a small, close-knit community of students, admissions officers are looking for the complete package: bright, capable, motivated students who are ready to take advantage of all the school has to offer. While academic performance is the factor considered most heavily on each application, recommendations, extracurricular activities, and standardized test scores should all be very strong as well.

THE SCHOOL SAYS ". . ."

From the Admissions Office

"Three qualities separate Trinity University from other selective, academically challenging institutions around the country. First, Trinity is unusual in the quality and quantity of resources devoted almost exclusively to its undergraduate students. Those resources give rise to a second distinctive aspect of Trinity—its emphasis on undergraduate research. Our students prefer being involved over observing. With superior laboratory facilities and strong, dedicated faculty, our undergraduates fill many of the roles formerly reserved for graduate students, and our professors often go to their undergraduates for help with their research. Other experiential learning opportunities including internships, study abroad, and service projects are also available to students. Finally, Trinity stands apart for the attitude of its students. In an atmosphere of academic camaraderie, our students work together to stretch their minds and broaden their horizons across academic disciplines. For quality of resources, for dedication to undergraduate research, and for the disposition of its student body, Trinity University holds a unique position in American higher education."

SELECTIVITY

Admissions Rating	94
# of applicants	11,463
% of applicants accepted	31
% of acceptees attending	19
# offered a place on the wait list	1,505
% accepting a place on wait list	40
% admitted from wait list	8
# of early decision applicants	206
% accepted early decision	57

FIRST-YEAR PROFILE

Testing policy	Test Flexible
Range SAT composite	1310–1450
Range SAT EBRW	660–730
Range SAT math	650–740
Range ACT composite	29–33
# submitting SAT scores	275
% submitting SAT scores	42
# submitting ACT scores	140
% submitting ACT scores	21
Average HS GPA	3.8
% frosh submitting high school GPA	100
% graduated top 10% of class	54
% graduated top 25% of class	29
% graduated top 50% of class	15

DEADLINES

Early decision	
Deadline	11/1
Notification	12/15
Other ED deadline	1/15
Other ED notification	2/1
Early action	
Deadline	11/1
Notification	12/15
Regular	
Deadline	1/15
Notification	3/15
Nonfall registration?	Yes

APPLICANTS ALSO LOOK AT

Baylor University; Southern Methodist University; Southwestern University; Texas A&M University—College Station; Texas Christian University; The University of Texas at Austin; The University of Texas at Dallas

FINANCIAL FACTS

Financial Aid Rating	90
Annual tuition	$48,648
Room and board	$14,134
Required fees	$616
Books and supplies	$1,000
Average frosh need-based scholarship	$38,597
Average UG need-based scholarship	$37,665
% needy frosh rec. need-based scholarship or grant aid	100
% needy UG rec. need-based scholarship or grant aid	100
% needy frosh rec. non-need-based scholarship or grant aid	37
% needy UG rec. non-need-based scholarship or grant aid	23
% needy frosh rec. need-based self-help aid	62
% needy UG rec. need-based self-help aid	57
% frosh rec. any financial aid	99
% UG rec. any financial aid	97
% UG borrow to pay for school	46
Average cumulative indebtedness	$40,141
% frosh need fully met	68
% ugrads need fully met	47
Average % of frosh need met	98
Average % of ugrad need met	95

TRUMAN STATE UNIVERSITY

100 E. Normal Ave., Kirksville, MO 63501 • Admissions: 660-785-4000 • Fax: 660-785-7456

STUDENTS SAY "..."

Academics

Located in northeast Missouri, Truman State University is a public university that combines the fundamentals of a liberal arts education with specialized programming and hands-on learning, offering "an amazing education at a great price." There are 52 majors available, with all students completing a core curriculum (called the Dialogues) that ensures they develop proficiencies in areas such as writing, speaking, and social perspectives. Truman undergrads also take part in the Truman Symposium, an educational endeavor in which they participate in projects and shared experiences that benefit the students, the university, and the Kirksville community.

This is "a very academically rigorous and challenging school" with "interesting classes galore," and "if you plan to attend any form of graduate school, this school definitely prepares you."

Every student "has to actually attend classes in order to get something out of the experience," but "the workload is manageable." To keep students involved and engaged, many classes are discussion-based and include projects called Facilitations, where students lead the class in a discussion related to a specific topic. Students appreciate the just-right size of the university and say "student-professor relationships are great for mentoring purposes and for future networking opportunities." Many professors have daily office hours "and even more answer emails outside of normal hours or even give students their personal contact info"; they "truly care about individual students, but in a tough love sort of way."

Campus Life

"Making your own fun is a real thing" in the small town of Kirksville, but "students here know how to make the most out of it." And because "Truman offers so many clubs and activities, that between those and classes and homework, you'll probably never get truly bored." In fact, Truman has well over 230 clubs and organizations, so it makes sense that "student organizations are the main source of socialization here." The Student Activities Board also provides events and entertainment for the students, including a Mario Kart tournament, entertainers like Josh Peck, and even bringing hot air balloons on campus. The university promotes school spirit with weekly events like Purple Friday, when faculty, students, and staff are encouraged to wear school colors, and there are activities and events in the student union and on the Mall. Not all entertainment is school-related; students also note that there is a "great Greek life" for those that want to partake.

When students need some downtime, there is "a state park close to Kirksville where you can go hiking and go to the lake," and "when the weather is nice it's such a mental health support being able to just sit on the Quad." There are various housing options for students, including the Living Learning Communities for students that want to share living space with others with similar academic interests. Kirksville is a college town, so every year the school has a community service day called The Big Event, and students show their appreciation of the surrounding community by performing volunteer services such as cleanup and maintenance tasks.

Student Body

Motivated students will do well here as Truman is "a collective place for ambitious individuals." The "majority of students here are focused on their academic studies" and are "driven, smart individuals who also value community." Although the school "is not racially diverse," there are "quite a few international students," as the overall population comes from a variety of socioeconomic backgrounds. "Many work a required campus job necessary for scholarships, along with taking heavy class loads, and being involved in multiple extracurriculars." Whether you're one of the "mainly liberal students" the atmosphere seems to be one where we are "all in this together."

TRUMAN STATE UNIVERSITY

Financial Aid: 660-785-4130 • E-Mail: admissions@truman.edu • Website: www.truman.edu

THE PRINCETON REVIEW SAYS

Admissions

The school reports that its standardized testing policy for use in admission for Fall 2024 is Test Optional. It is unknown at this time if the 2024 testing policy will be permanent. The Princeton Review suggests that interested applicants consult with the school for the most up-to-date standardized testing policies. *Very important factors considered include:* rigor of secondary school record, class rank, academic GPA. *Important factors considered include:* application essay. *Other factors considered include:* standardized test scores, recommendation(s), extracurricular activities, talent/ability, character/personal qualities, first generation, alumni/ae relation, geographical residence, state residency, racial/ethnic status, volunteer work, work experience, level of applicant's interest. High school diploma is required and GED is accepted. *Academic units required:* 4 English, 3 math, 3 science, 2 science labs, 2 foreign language, 2 social studies, 1 history, 1 visual/performing arts, 5 academic electives. *Academic units recommended:* 4 English, 4 math, 3 science, 2 science labs, 2 foreign language, 2 social studies, 1 history, 1 visual/performing arts, 5 academic electives.

Financial Aid

Students should submit: FAFSA. Priority filing deadline is 2/1. The Princeton Review suggests that all financial aid forms be submitted as soon as possible (see page 5 for a note on the FAFSA). *Need-based scholarships/grants offered:* College/university scholarship or grant aid from institutional funds; Federal Pell; Private scholarships; SEOG; State scholarships/grants. *Loan aid offered:* Direct PLUS loans; Direct Subsidized Loans; Direct Unsubsidized Loans; College/university loans from institutional funds; Federal Nursing Loans. Admitted students will be notified of awards on a rolling basis beginning 1/1. Federal Work-Study Program available. Institutional employment available.

The Inside Word

Truman State prides itself on taking a well-rounded approach to the admissions process. The university truly believes that students are more than just the sum of their grades and test scores. Therefore, expect that all application facets, from transcripts to extracurricular participation, will be heavily scrutinized. We do want to note that intended music majors will have to sit for an audition in addition to the regular application. And nursing candidates will need to be admitted to both the university overall as well as the specific nursing program.

THE SCHOOL SAYS "..."

From the Admissions Office

"Truman's talented student body enjoys small classes where undergraduate research and personal interaction with professors are the norm. Our outstanding internship and study abroad opportunities allow students to attend top graduate schools and graduate with strong job prospects. We are recognized consistently as one of the nation's 'Best Values' in higher education. Because we offer a variety of competitive scholarships but not a separate application for them, students are strongly encouraged to apply for admission by December 1st and submit an activities list or resume along with an essay for best consideration.

"Students applying to Truman State University can submit scores from both the ACT and the SAT. Their superscore from either test will be considered in admission and scholarship selection along with the student's weighted GPA. The ACT's writing section is not required.

"We believe a quality college experience starts in the classroom and travels with you past its doors. A sense of scholarship and discovery permeates our campus, offering opportunities that entertain, pique students' interest, and invite them deeper into their learning with practical experiences. Your time in college is about making great friends, getting involved in one of over 230 student organizations, exploring the areas you can influence in our world, and creating memories that will last a lifetime. Ours is a university that transforms lives. As one of the nation's premier public liberal arts and sciences institutions, our successes can be traced to one guiding principle: an unwavering devotion to the pursuit of knowledge, wherever your journey leads you."

SELECTIVITY
Admissions Rating	92
# of applicants	4,896
% of applicants accepted	45
% of acceptees attending	32

FIRST-YEAR PROFILE
Testing policy	Test Optional
Range SAT composite	1110–1325
Range SAT EBRW	510–650
Range SAT math	560–680
Range ACT composite	23–29
# submitting SAT scores	71
% submitting SAT scores	10
# submitting ACT scores	536
% submitting ACT scores	77
Average HS GPA	3.8
% frosh submitting high school GPA	87
% graduated top 10% of class	56
% graduated top 25% of class	80
% graduated top 50% of class	95

DEADLINES
Regular	
Priority	12/1
Notification	Rolling, 9/1
Nonfall registration?	Yes

APPLICANTS OFTEN PREFER
Missouri State University; Saint Louis University; University of Missouri

APPLICANTS SOMETIMES PREFER
Washington University in St. Louis

FINANCIAL FACTS
Financial Aid Rating	88
Annual in-state tuition	$8,690
Annual out-of-state tuition	$16,712
Room and board	$9,935
Required fees	$324
Required fees (first-year)	$674
Books and supplies	$1,000
Average frosh need-based scholarship	$9,576
Average UG need-based scholarship	$9,039
% needy frosh rec. need-based scholarship or grant aid	100
% needy UG rec. need-based scholarship or grant aid	96
% needy frosh rec. non-need-based scholarship or grant aid	99
% needy UG rec. non-need-based scholarship or grant aid	87
% needy frosh rec. need-based self-help aid	69
% needy UG rec. need-based self-help aid	74
% frosh rec. any financial aid	100
% UG rec. any financial aid	77
% UG borrow to pay for school	49
Average cumulative indebtedness	$25,451
% frosh need fully met	36
% ugrads need fully met	33
Average % of frosh need met	87
Average % of ugrad need met	83

TUFTS UNIVERSITY

2 The Green, Medford, MA 02155 • Admissions: 617-627-3170 • Fax: 617-627-3860

STUDENTS SAY ". . ."

Academics

The campus culture at Tufts University in Massachusetts is "thriving and alive," and as such it really encourages students to merge their academic and social interests and "pursue both in a passionate way." This is a place where, through active discussion and a student body with a zest for life, "passion meets reality." The academic experience here is marked by "small classes with knowledgeable and interesting professors." "I have had the opportunity to explore a huge amount of academic subjects and really challenge myself," says a student. If students actively seek out their "highly accessible and prompt" professors, they will be rewarded with "a better learning experience and with incomparable relationships with brilliant (yet down to earth) professors." "Whenever I ask them a question that they might not know the answer to, they do research on it immediately and return quickly with a detailed response." The academic curriculum is a "perfect mix of liberal arts and university," and the professors are actively concerned with making sure that students leave with a true understanding of the course material, "not just a book list under their arms." These "global minded, ambitious" students rise to the challenge and beyond, as "most every student focuses on life beyond their education" and seeks out a well-rounded life. "It is far easier to succeed here than to fail, as long as you are committed to getting as strong an education as possible," advises a student. "I've literally been offered a research position by asking questions multiple times," says another. The international relations program at this globally-aware school is particularly strong (as are study abroad options), but activism spills over into the entirety of the student body. "Change is easily made here," and "if you have a problem with something, you can easily address it." A lot of effort is put into ensuring that every student transitions well into college and succeeds. A strong alumni network and excellent internship opportunities also "open up a world of opportunities after graduation."

Campus Life

Though the campus itself is gorgeous, "the true beauty of the school is in the unique and quirky nature of its student body." Generally, there are "always a lot of events going on around campus that attract students every weekend" and the variety of clubs and activities available is "amazing." "Almost everything here is run by clubs and student organizations," and the Tufts Dance Collective and Quadball clubs are some of the most popular and fun options, as is a cappella. Public transportation "makes everything accessible," and on the weekends, students often go into Boston or Davis Square and spend the day shopping and "eating non-dining hall food," and at night "there are usually good parties to go to." "There is more to do in this city than anyone can possibly do in four years," says a student.

People here are "always thinking about politics" and all have a lot of spirit for Tufts, and "it's really nice to walk around campus knowing that you're in a place where almost everyone is excited to be there." "This is a great place to share knowledge you have, because everyone wants to hear it and share their own experiences and thoughts," says a student.

Student Body

This is a group of go-getters, so here "everyone has the same passion for excellence" and "is engaged in so many activities on campus." Tufts is "a quirky (yet normal) compilation of a bunch of young adults with not only big dreams for the world, but with dedication and motivation to complete them." "It's like a competition to be the "most interesting [person] in the world," says a senior. Even better, "being nerdy is cool!" "We here embrace weirdness. If talking to new people in daily life is awkward, we know it and we revel in it," says a sophomore. There is "no discrimination whatsoever," though "it can actually get frustrating how politically correct everyone is." From "dancing and singing to teaching and tutoring to international community service," students here are "stunningly busy and happy to be so."

TUFTS UNIVERSITY

Financial Aid: 617-627-2000 • E-Mail: undergraduate.admissions@tufts.edu • Website: www.tufts.edu

THE PRINCETON REVIEW SAYS

Admissions

The school reports that its standardized testing policy for use in admission for Fall 2024 is Test Optional. The 2024 testing policy will be temporary. The Princeton Review suggests that interested applicants consult with the school for the most up-to-date standardized testing policies. *Very important factors considered include:* rigor of secondary school record, class rank, academic GPA, application essay, recommendation(s), character/personal qualities. *Important factors considered include:* extracurricular activities, talent/ability. *Other factors considered include:* standardized test scores, interview, first generation, alumni/ae relation, geographical residence, racial/ethnic status, volunteer work, work experience, level of applicant's interest. High school diploma is required and GED is accepted. *Academic units required:* 4 English, 3 math, 3 science, 3 foreign language, 3 social studies. *Academic units recommended:* 4 math, 4 science, 4 foreign language, 4 social studies.

Financial Aid

Students should submit: CSS/Financial Aid Profile; FAFSA; Noncustodial Profile. The Princeton Review suggests that all financial aid forms be submitted as soon as possible (see page 5 for a note on the FAFSA). *Need-based scholarships/grants offered:* College/university scholarship or grant aid from institutional funds; Federal Pell; Private scholarships; SEOG; State scholarships/grants. *Loan aid offered:* Direct PLUS loans; Direct Subsidized Loans; Direct Unsubsidized Loans; College/university loans from institutional funds. Admitted students will be notified of awards on or about 4/1. Federal Work-Study Program available. Institutional employment available.

The Inside Word

Admission at Tufts is competitive. You'll need a stellar transcript to get accepted here, rounded out with strong recommendations and extracurriculars that reflect substantive engagement with your school or community. The Common App with Tufts' own writing supplement is required.

THE SCHOOL SAYS "..."

From the Admissions Office

"Tufts is a medium-sized liberal arts university with a focus on faculty relationships, research, and celebrating diverse experiences. Our 6,000+ undergraduate students pursue majors in one of three schools: the School of Arts and Sciences, the School of Engineering, or the School of the Museum of Fine Arts (SMFA). As part of a tier one research university, our students delve into world-class research easily and early, exploring fields from soft-bodied robotics to the rebirth of urban democracy, microbial communities to musical theater. Tufts offers the chance to join a close-knit community that supports intellectual risk-taking and a global outlook, all in a beautiful campus setting just five miles from downtown Boston.

"You can't fit Tufts students into a box. They are intellectually powerful, down-to-earth, driven, and civic-minded. At Tufts, they learn how to make a measurable difference and then start making it—even as undergraduates. On campus, the Tisch College of Civic Life leads the way, allowing students to take curricular courses in social change or even enroll in the Tufts Civic Semester. Whether they are engineers, studio artists, environment advocates, or poets, our students graduate from Tufts ready to enact positive change in the communities they join."

SELECTIVITY

Admissions Rating	98
# of applicants	34,881
% of applicants accepted	10
% of acceptees attending	50
# offered a place on the wait list	2,664
% accepting a place on wait list	50
% admitted from wait list	14

FIRST-YEAR PROFILE

Testing policy	Test Optional
Range SAT composite	1460–1540
Range SAT EBRW	710–760
Range SAT math	740–790
Range ACT composite	33–35
# submitting SAT scores	631
% submitting SAT scores	37
# submitting ACT scores	315
% submitting ACT scores	19
% graduated top 10% of class	87
% graduated top 25% of class	97
% graduated top 50% of class	99

DEADLINES

Early decision	
Deadline	11/1
Notification	12/15
Other ED deadline	1/1
Other ED notification	2/15
Regular	
Deadline	1/1
Notification	4/1
Nonfall registration?	No

APPLICANTS OFTEN PREFER

Brown University; Georgetown University; Harvard College; University of Pennsylvania

APPLICANTS SOMETIMES PREFER

Cornell University; Dartmouth College; Johns Hopkins University; Northwestern University; The University of Chicago; Washington University in St. Louis

FINANCIAL FACTS

Financial Aid Rating	96
Annual tuition	$59,560
Room and board	$15,630
Required fees	$1,302
Books and supplies	$1,000
Average frosh need-based scholarship	$55,283
Average UG need-based scholarship	$54,264
% needy frosh rec. need-based scholarship or grant aid	93
% needy UG rec. need-based scholarship or grant aid	93
% needy frosh rec. non-need-based scholarship or grant aid	4
% needy UG rec. non-need-based scholarship or grant aid	2
% needy frosh rec. need-based self-help aid	85
% needy UG rec. need-based self-help aid	87
% frosh rec. any financial aid	39
% UG rec. any financial aid	35
% UG borrow to pay for school	25
Average cumulative indebtedness	$24,468
% frosh need fully met	96
% ugrads need fully met	98
Average % of frosh need met	100
Average % of ugrad need met	100

TULANE UNIVERSITY

6823 St. Charles Avenue, New Orleans, LA 70118 • Admissions: 504-865-5000 • Fax: 504-862-8715

STUDENTS SAY "..."

Academics

There are many reasons to get excited about Tulane University in New Orleans, like its prized research opportunities, or the way in which "artistic excellence is the norm," but the biggest refrain from students is the way in which this "competitive school" manages to be "accommodating at the same time." Enrollees emphasize a "great academic flexibility that allows students to major across schools" on Tulane's campuses. Equally important, they point to "countless resources" including a frequent willingness "to step in to cover costs so that students don't miss out on opportunities." Students are also provided with "success coaching, supplemental instruction sessions, [and] quickly available advising." But don't be fooled—Tulane is also known for its academic rigor. As one student confides: "My courses were ALL challenging! Nothing was given; it was earned."

Tulane also works its "city like no other" location into the curriculum. All first-year students are immersed into local history and culture through the Tulane Interdisciplinary Experience Seminar (TIDES). One student's course used *Dungeons & Dragons* as a template for learning about "the campus, New Orleans, and each other; we are all now best friends and help each other on a daily basis." And then there's just the enrichment of the arts: Tulane "does shows with some of the best jazz musicians in the world" and dance classes offer "live drummers, which allows students to really explore and experience new and unique things."

Campus Life

"It doesn't get better than New Orleans!" exclaims one student, encapsulating the overall vibe. "It's a gift" or "a dream" for those who spend their free time watching sunsets by the river in Butterfly Park, "shopping at boutiques on Magazine Street," "eating at Cafe Beignet by Bourbon Street," and exploring "popular attractions like the French Quarter." One student lists a handful of festivals, from the well-known Mardi Gras to the Mac N Cheese Fest, and another just estimates that "there are more festivals in New Orleans than there are days of the year." Overall, "living in a city so cool and rich in history is a gift."

Of course, students don't have to leave "the sprawling campus" to have a good time—there's "a good balance of fun and academics" on site. "When it's light and warm out (which is very often), so many people will be out on the quads sunbathing." If the range of activities like WTUL, the on-campus radio station, or TUSTEP, a program for training service dogs, doesn't catch your eye, "starting clubs [and] joining clubs is straightforward."

Student Body

There are "lots of ambitious, bright young people" at Tulane: "Everyone is interested in working hard and doing well, as well as going out and experiencing New Orleans." The campus is "very progressive" as well as "predominantly white and very wealthy" and features "clubs celebrating Middle Eastern, Israeli, and Latin American culture." Students from all walks are united by a friendly camaraderie: "I have never not been able to find a study group, and often the entire class is willing to work together. The only competition is with ourselves, not against each other." One student is impressed by "how genuinely happy everyone is to be here! The warmth of the students and faculty is unlike anything I have ever seen." Many would agree: "Tulane is unique because everyone has a strong work ethic, but also knows how to enjoy themselves on the weekend."

Financial Aid: 504-865-5723 • E-Mail: undergrad.admission@tulane.edu • Website: www.tulane.edu

THE PRINCETON REVIEW SAYS

Admissions

The school reports that its standardized testing policy for use in admission for Fall 2024 is Test Optional. It is unknown at this time if the 2024 testing policy will be permanent. The Princeton Review suggests that interested applicants consult with the school for the most up-to-date standardized testing policies. *Very important factors considered include:* rigor of secondary school record, class rank, academic GPA, standardized test scores. *Important factors considered include:* application essay, recommendation(s), character/personal qualities, volunteer work, level of applicant's interest. *Other factors considered include:* extracurricular activities, talent/ability, first generation, alumni/ae relation, geographical residence, state residency, racial/ethnic status, work experience. High school diploma is required and GED is not accepted. *Academic units recommended:* 4 English, 4 math, 4 science, 4 science labs, 4 foreign language, 4 social studies.

Financial Aid

Students should submit: CSS/Financial Aid Profile; FAFSA; Noncustodial Profile. Priority filing deadline is 2/15. The Princeton Review suggests that all financial aid forms be submitted as soon as possible (see page 5 for a note on the FAFSA). *Need-based scholarships/grants offered:* College/university scholarship or grant aid from institutional funds; Federal Pell; Private scholarships; SEOG; State scholarships/grants. *Loan aid offered:* Direct PLUS loans; Direct Subsidized Loans; Direct Unsubsidized Loans. Admitted students will be notified of awards on a rolling basis beginning 12/15. Federal Work-Study Program available. Institutional employment available.

The Inside Word

When it comes to evaluating applicants, Tulane takes a fairly straight-forward approach. Expect admissions officers to closely consider your high school transcript and standardized test scores. Moreover, be aware that the most successful candidates will have taken a rigorous course load; load up on those honors and AP classes if possible! You should also know that extracurricular activities will be of secondary importance. Finally, if you're a budding architecture student, it's highly recommended that you submit a portfolio.

THE SCHOOL SAYS "..."

From the Admissions Office

"Tulane is one of the very few universities where students do not apply directly to a school or college and instead have immediate access to all academic programs upon admission. In addition, as the only major research university in America with a public service requirement for graduation, Tulane students are wholly committed to giving back to their communities. The opportunities for students to be involved in the rebirth of New Orleans offer an experience unavailable at any other place, at any other time.

"Tulane is committed to undergraduate education. Senior faculty members teach most introductory and lower-level courses, and most classes have twenty-five or fewer students. The close student-teacher relationship pays off. Tulane graduates are among the most likely to be selected for several prestigious fellowships that support graduate study abroad. Founded in 1834 and reorganized as Tulane University in 1884, Tulane is one of the major private research universities in the South.

"As previously mentioned, Tulane students highly value balance, and most of all they're happy with their choice and love the school."

SELECTIVITY

Admissions Rating	**97**
# of applicants	31,615
% of applicants accepted	11
% of acceptees attending	51
# offered a place on the wait list	6,232
% accepting a place on wait list	36
% admitted from wait list	0
# of early decision applicants	1,853
% accepted early decision	68

FIRST-YEAR PROFILE

Testing policy	Test Optional
Range SAT composite	1400–1500
Range SAT EBRW	680–750
Range SAT math	690–760
Range ACT composite	31–33
# submitting SAT scores	293
% submitting SAT scores	16
# submitting ACT scores	620
% submitting ACT scores	34
Average HS GPA	3.7
% frosh submitting high school GPA	100
% graduated top 10% of class	52
% graduated top 25% of class	80
% graduated top 50% of class	94

DEADLINES

Early decision	
Deadline	11/1
Notification	12/15
Other ED deadline	1/13
Other ED notification	1/31
Early action	
Deadline	11/15
Notification	1/15
Regular	
Priority	11/1
Deadline	1/15
Notification	4/1
Nonfall registration?	Yes

APPLICANTS SOMETIMES PREFER

University of Miami; University of Michigan—Ann Arbor; University of Southern California; University of Texas at Austin; University of Virginia; Vanderbilt University

FINANCIAL FACTS

Financial Aid Rating	**89**
Annual tuition	$58,666
Room and board	$17,346
Required fees	$4,178
Books and supplies	$1,200
Average frosh need-based scholarship	$43,039
Average UG need-based scholarship	$42,292
% needy frosh rec. need-based scholarship or grant aid	95
% needy UG rec. need-based scholarship or grant aid	95
% needy frosh rec. non-need-based scholarship or grant aid	29
% needy UG rec. non-need-based scholarship or grant aid	27
% needy frosh rec. need-based self-help aid	60
% needy UG rec. need-based self-help aid	66
% frosh rec. any financial aid	72
% UG rec. any financial aid	68
% UG borrow to pay for school	27
Average cumulative indebtedness	$29,234
% frosh need fully met	48
% ugrads need fully met	50
Average % of frosh need met	92
Average % of ugrad need met	91

TUSKEGEE UNIVERSITY

Kresge Center, Tuskegee, AL 36088 • Admissions: 334-727-8011 • Fax: 334-727-5750

CAMPUS LIFE

Quality of Life Rating	70
Fire Safety Rating	97
Green Rating	60*
Type of school	Private
Affiliation	No Affiliation
Environment	Rural

STUDENTS

Total undergrad enrollment	2,480
% male/female/another gender	39/61/0
% from out of state	70
% frosh from public high school	88
% frosh live on campus	98
% ugrads live on campus	55
# of fraternities (% join)	5 (6)
# of sororities (% join)	6 (5)
% African American	78
% Asian	1
% White	0
% Hispanic	1
% Native American	<1
% Pacific Islander	0
% Two or more races	0
% Race and/or ethnicity unknown	21
% international	1
# of countries represented	19

SURVEY SAYS . . .

Lots of liberal students
Students are very religious
Frats and sororities are popular

ACADEMICS

Academic Rating	75
% students returning for sophomore year	73
Calendar	Semester
Student/faculty ratio	14:1
Profs interesting rating	81
Profs accessible rating	88
Most classes have 10–19 students.	

MOST POPULAR MAJORS

Electrical and Electronics Engineering

STUDENTS SAY "..."

Academics

For the past 132 years, Tuskegee University has striven to continue the legacy of higher learning created by Booker T. Washington and upheld by its other notable presidents and benefactors. The "rich history" of the school has always been about "achieving the...highest level of performance" in all areas of service, leadership, and academics, and everyone in the community works to ensure that "the Tuskegee Experience is like none other." The veterinary and engineering schools are standouts here, but the school can transform any individual into a leader. "Tuskegee, figuratively speaking, is often given coal, and it *always* produces diamonds," says one student. Academics are "a top priority" for Tuskegee, and the classes and structure are designed to "effectively nurture students' academic, social, and professional potentials and produce great leaders in society." "School is about gaining independence and responsibility so that you will be able to grow and compete in the real world." Small classes and personal interaction with professors help further this process along, and the school aims for "excellence within every aspect of education offered at the institution." "My professors don't teach because it's their job; they do it because they care and want you to learn and succeed. It's very obvious," says one student. Though the alumni network is positively rock solid, and fundraising isn't a problem, some students question the allocation of funds. Many agree that "the development of new facilities/buildings around the campus" is a sore spot, and though the administration is in the process of updating some, "there is a lot of work to be done," particularly in the student housing arena.

Campus Life

The heritage of Tuskegee is felt in every step; "We literally walk on historic grounds," says a student of going to school on the only college or university campus in the nation to be designated a National Historic Site by Congress. The traditional festivities the school usually hosts are "quite enjoyable," and the school is in a "very quaint" town, which "allows for constant interaction among students on campus to occur." When there is nothing to do in Tuskegee, students usually go to Auburn, Montgomery, or even Atlanta. TU is for "academically inclined individuals," but when the books do shut, most people "go to the local clubs (The Soul Inn or Club Extreme)," or hang out at houses off campus. "Home football and basketball games are usually really fun" as well. "Even though people are serious about their work and classes, we all know how to have fun," says one student. "We're a school of weekend warriors." "It can be raining cats and dogs...and you will still see people going to class, or if it's the weekend you will see students going to a party."

Student Body

At this go-getter university, the typical student here is "someone who is driven to becoming successful in the future through studious methods." Though this HBCU is naturally predominantly Black, there is much diversity in that "people from all across the country come to school in this small city in Alabama." Most students here are "very outspoken and easy to work with" and "open to meeting and interacting with new people"; with students from all over the world, "the diverse environment helps keep the campus from getting too dull."

TUSKEGEE UNIVERSITY

Financial Aid: 334-727-8088 • E-Mail: admissions@mytu.tuskegee.edu • Website: www.tuskegee.edu

THE PRINCETON REVIEW SAYS

Admissions

The school reports that its standardized testing policy for use in admission for Fall 2024 requires applicants to submit either the SAT or ACT. It is unknown at this time if the 2024 testing policy will be permanent. The Princeton Review suggests that interested applicants consult with the school for the most up-to-date standardized testing policies. *Very important factors considered include:* rigor of secondary school record, class rank, academic GPA, standardized test scores, recommendation(s), talent/ability. *Important factors considered include:* character/personal qualities, alumni/ae relation. *Other factors considered include:* application essay, interview, extracurricular activities, first generation, geographical residence, state residency, volunteer work, work experience. High school diploma is required and GED is accepted. *Academic units required:* 4 English, 3 math, 2 science, 3 social studies, 4 academic electives.

Financial Aid

Students should submit: CSS/Financial Aid Profile; FAFSA; Institution's own financial aid form. Priority filing deadline is 3/31. The Princeton Review suggests that all financial aid forms be submitted as soon as possible (see page 5 for a note on the FAFSA). *Need-based scholarships/grants offered:* College/university scholarship or grant aid from institutional funds; Federal Nursing Scholarships; Federal Pell; Private scholarships; SEOG; State scholarships/grants; United Negro College Fund. *Loan aid offered:* Direct PLUS loans; Direct Subsidized Loans; Direct Unsubsidized Loans; College/university loans from institutional funds; Federal Nursing Loans; State Loans. Federal Work-Study Program available. Institutional employment available.

The Inside Word

Tuskegee presents its students with a myriad of opportunities for discovery and research. Therefore, Tuskegee seeks applicants who have proven themselves successful in the classroom. Admissions counselors consider each application holistically and individually. What they really like to see, though, is a GPA of at least 3.0 and a composite ACT score of 21 or better. Note also that requirements for the nursing and engineering programs are more stringent. For example, you'll probably need four years of high school math if you want to major in engineering here. Prospective students interested in either field should investigate the specific criteria.

THE SCHOOL SAYS "..."

From the Admissions Office

"Tuskegee University, located in south central Alabama, was founded in 1881 under the dynamic and creative leadership of Booker T. Washington. As a state-related, independent institution, Tuskegee offers undergraduate and graduate degrees through five colleges and two schools: the College of Agriculture, Environment and Nutrition Sciences; the Brimmer College of Business and Information Sciences; the College of Engineering; the College of Veterinary Medicine, Nursing and Allied Health; the Taylor School of Architecture and Construction Science; and the School of Education. Substantial research and service programs make Tuskegee University an effective comprehensive institution geared toward preparing tomorrow's leaders today.

"First-year applicants must take the SAT or ACT; the SAT is preferred. International applicants must complete the TOEFL. Nursing applicants must complete the National Nursing exam."

SELECTIVITY

Admissions Rating	86
# of applicants	7,529
% of applicants accepted	53
% of acceptees attending	15

FIRST-YEAR PROFILE

Testing policy	SAT or ACT required
Range SAT EBRW	440–510
Range SAT math	420–520
Range ACT composite	18–23
# submitting SAT scores	262
% submitting SAT scores	44
# submitting ACT scores	434
% submitting ACT scores	73
Average HS GPA	3.2
% frosh submitting high school GPA	100
% graduated top 10% of class	20
% graduated top 25% of class	60
% graduated top 50% of class	100

DEADLINES

Early action	
Deadline	8/31
Notification	10/1
Regular	
Priority	3/31
Deadline	7/15
Notification	Rolling, 3/1
Nonfall registration?	Yes

APPLICANTS ALSO LOOK AT

Alabama AandM University; Alabama State University; Florida Agriculture and Mechanical University; Jackson State University

FINANCIAL FACTS

Financial Aid Rating	80
Annual tuition	$18,100
Room and board	$8,510
Required fees	$3,525
Books and supplies	$1,282
Average frosh need-based scholarship	$1,500
Average UG need-based scholarship	$1,500
% needy frosh rec. need-based scholarship or grant aid	100
% needy UG rec. need-based scholarship or grant aid	100
% needy frosh rec. non-need-based scholarship or grant aid	17
% needy UG rec. non-need-based scholarship or grant aid	22
% needy frosh rec. need-based self-help aid	100
% needy UG rec. need-based self-help aid	68
% frosh rec. any financial aid	90
% UG rec. any financial aid	92
% UG borrow to pay for school	49
Average cumulative indebtedness	$18,100
% frosh need fully met	0
% ugrads need fully met	0
Average % of frosh need met	70
Average % of ugrad need met	70

UNION COLLEGE (NY)

807 Union Street, Schenectady, NY 12308 • Admissions: 518-388-6112

STUDENTS SAY "..."

Academics

Founded in 1795 as the first unified campus in the United States, Union College in upstate New York offers a rigorous education that integrates STEM and liberal arts. Around 2,000 undergraduates study on a trimester system, which means "you ultimately make your days how you want them to be, and you also make your own schedule." As one student says: "I love this structure...[and] I don't ever feel pushed back against the wall with work because I am able to manage my time correctly." That independence leads more than half of all students to study abroad for at least a partial term and is encouraging to those who want to do original research: roughly 80 percent do so. Benefits like the "internship courses that count as credit" and career center "[provide] students with a vast array of tools to help student break into the industry that interests them," and post-graduation, there's a "huge emphasis on alumni connections."

Overall, "the availability of undergraduate research makes it easy to get hands-on experience early," especially since there's a 9:1 student-to-faculty ratio that undergrads find "very helpful in learning." Professors are specifically highlighted for the way they "work tooth and nail to give us as much as they can" while also providing "very interesting" material that will "make you want to learn more and beyond the course material." This atmosphere, filled with "an ample amount of resources," leads students to say that they feel encouraged "to explore other disciplines."

Campus Life

The vast majority of students—90%—live on campus either in residence halls, one of 13 student-run theme houses, or across the street in campus-managed apartments. In addition, every student is sorted into one of seven Minerva Houses, which act as hubs for academic, social, and residential activities. Between the close quarters of their homes or houses, the school's ACE (Association for Campus Events) hosts "spectacular events every weekend," including "escape rooms, magicians, comedians, [and] painting events," though students also plan plenty of their own varied excursions, like "ski and hiking trips, movie nights, and Frisbee golf."

Since students only take three classes a term, they "have lots of free time each week," a much-appreciated boon that allows them to "study or do homework during the day and participate in clubs or activity events during lunch or in the late afternoons and evenings." This does mean that Greek life "plays a very large role in students' social lives," and "anyone who wants to be involved...can be," but it's worth noting that "you are still welcome" whether you go Greek or not.

Student Body

People at Union "take their educational experiences and opportunities seriously" but "also know how to spend time productively outside of class." Because Union isn't an overwhelmingly large school, students fondly describe both a sense of privacy and a relative ease in which to meet up with friends across "different majors and paths" to at least grab a bite to eat. As one puts it, people here "very genuinely care about each other in all directions." Many students are athletes, which makes for "a very active campus [where] the gyms are always busy." That said, the overall atmosphere "is highly collaborative and supportive, not competitive," and "the fact that Union is a liberal arts school with engineering means you get a really good well-rounded education and you are always interacting with those outside of your major."

UNION COLLEGE (NY)

Financial Aid: 518-388-6123 • E-Mail: admissions@union.edu • Website: www.union.edu

THE PRINCETON REVIEW SAYS

Admissions

The school reports that its standardized testing policy for use in admission for Fall 2024 will remain Test Optional, as it has been since 2014. The Princeton Review suggests that interested applicants consult with the school for the most up-to-date standardized testing policies. *Very important factors considered include:* rigor of secondary school record, class rank, academic GPA. *Important factors considered include:* standardized test scores, application essay, recommendation(s), extracurricular activities, talent/ability, character/personal qualities, volunteer work, work experience. *Other factors considered include:* interview, first generation, alumni/ae relation, geographical residence, state residency, racial/ethnic status, level of applicant's interest. High school diploma is required and GED is not accepted. *Academic units required:* 4 English, 3 math, 2 science, 2 foreign language, 2 social studies. *Academic units recommended:* 4 English, 4 math, 3 science, 3 foreign language, 2 social studies, 2 history, 1 visual/performing arts.

Financial Aid

Students should submit: CSS/Financial Aid Profile; FAFSA; Noncustodial Profile; State aid form. Priority filing deadline is 1/15. The Princeton Review suggests that all financial aid forms be submitted as soon as possible (see page 5 for a note on the FAFSA). *Need-based scholarships/grants offered:* College/university scholarship or grant aid from institutional funds; Federal Pell; Private scholarships; SEOG; State scholarships/grants. *Loan aid offered:* Direct PLUS loans; Direct Subsidized Loans; Direct Unsubsidized Loans; College/university loans from institutional funds. Admitted students will be notified of awards by 3/25. Federal Work-Study Program available. Institutional employment available.

The Inside Word

Union College is a Test Optional college. Students may simply indicate on their application if they would like the admissions committee to consider their test scores or not. However, applicants to the Leadership in Medicine Program (an eight-year MD/MBA program with Albany Medical College and Clarkson University Capital Region Campus), the Law and Public Policy program (a combined BA and JD with Albany Law School), and home-schooled students must submit test scores for consideration. For students who know that Union is their first choice, the school offers two early decision deadlines.

THE SCHOOL SAYS "..."

From the Admissions Office

"The Union academic program is characterized by breadth and flexibility across a range of disciplines and interdisciplinary programs in the liberal arts, sciences, and engineering. With nearly 1,000 courses to choose from, Union students may major in a single field, combine work in two or more departments, or create their own major. Opportunities for research are robust and give students a chance to work closely with professors year-round, take part in conferences, and use sophisticated scientific equipment. More than half of Union's students take advantage of the college's extensive international study program, and the College places students in internships with more than 500 companies and organizations. A rich array of service learning programs and strong athletic, cultural, and social activities also enhance the overall Union experience. Union's Scholars Program is a rigorous academic program offered to a select group of approximately 60 incoming students each year. Union's seven student-run Minerva Houses are lively hubs for intellectual and social activities. They bring together students, faculty and staff for hundreds of events, from lectures to live bands.

"The Union community welcomes talented and diverse students, and we work closely with each one to help identify and cultivate their passions. Admission to the college is based on excellent academic credentials (transcript, courses, recommendations) and essays. Personal interviews are recommended. All candidates who apply to Union receive a thorough and thoughtful review of their application. Submission of SAT and ACT scores is optional except for the law and medicine programs. Union College is one of the very few colleges and universities in the country (fewer than 5%) that commits to meeting 100% of demonstrated financial need of all admitted students."

SELECTIVITY

Admissions Rating	94
# of applicants	8,458
% of applicants accepted	47
% of acceptees attending	15
# offered a place on the wait list	582
% accepting a place on wait list	40
% admitted from wait list	4
# of early decision applicants	259
% accepted early decision	69

FIRST-YEAR PROFILE

Testing policy	Test Optional
Range SAT composite	1310–1490
Range SAT EBRW	650–730
Range SAT math	660–760
Range ACT composite	29–33
# submitting SAT scores	219
% submitting SAT scores	38
# submitting ACT scores	97
% submitting ACT scores	17
Average HS GPA	3.5
% frosh submitting high school GPA	100
% graduated top 10% of class	62
% graduated top 25% of class	85
% graduated top 50% of class	94

DEADLINES

Early decision	
Deadline	11/1
Notification	12/15
Other ED deadline	1/15
Other ED notification	2/8
Early action	
Deadline	11/1
Notification	12/21
Regular	
Deadline	1/15
Notification	4/1
Nonfall registration?	Yes

APPLICANTS OFTEN PREFER
Colgate University; Cornell University; Tufts University

APPLICANTS SOMETIMES PREFER
Hamilton College; Lafayette College; University of Rochester

APPLICANTS RARELY PREFER
University of Vermont

FINANCIAL FACTS

Financial Aid Rating	98
Annual tuition	$66,105
Room and board	$16,389
Required fees	$351
Average frosh need-based scholarship	$49,020
Average UG need-based scholarship	$47,100
% needy frosh rec. need-based scholarship or grant aid	99
% needy UG rec. need-based scholarship or grant aid	100
% needy frosh rec. non-need-based scholarship or grant aid	1
% needy UG rec. non-need-based scholarship or grant aid	1
% needy frosh rec. need-based self-help aid	87
% needy UG rec. need-based self-help aid	91
% frosh rec. any financial aid	92
% UG rec. any financial aid	87
% UG borrow to pay for school	57
Average cumulative indebtedness	$37,284
% frosh need fully met	100
% ugrads need fully met	100
Average % of frosh need met	100
Average % of ugrad need met	100

UNITED STATES AIR FORCE ACADEMY

2304 Cadet Drive, USAF Academy, CO 80840 • Admissions: 800-443-9266 • Fax: 719-333-3012

STUDENTS SAY ". . ."

Academics

Students who seek out a United States Air Force Academy education note their satisfaction in how "values of integrity, service, and excellence...are actually the norm." This esteemed institution not only promotes a "culture of excellence" that molds students into "leaders of character," but also offers "prestige in both the military and private sector." It does so, incidentally, while offering free tuition and a "guaranteed job" following graduation. Of course, if you decide to attend, be prepared to "be challenged physically and mentally" and held "to a higher standard" than at your average college. In return, however, students suggest you'll also get "incredible opportunities" not found elsewhere. These opportunities can range from taking "trips around the world" or "operating a real DoD satellite" to "jumping out of planes [and] getting a secret clearance." Additionally, undergrads benefit from "extremely small" class sizes. As one cadet shares, "the biggest class I've had in four years was 24 students." The faculty itself is a nice "mix of military and civilian" instructors who "tend to make class interesting" and often excel at "bring[ing] their life experiences into the classroom." The majority also do their utmost to ensure that they are "accessible for extra instruction, exam review, etc." Many students also feel that their professors "really seem to care about your performance and work with you on a one-on-one basis." As one cadet frames it, "Their only focus is supporting us."

Campus Life

As you might have suspected, life at the Air Force Academy is rather regimented and cadets "don't have much free time." Students "go to class from 0730 to 1530 [and] freshmen have physical training multiple times a week after[wards]." Additionally, everyone "participate[s] in an athletic activity [whether] it be NCAA athletics, club sports, or intramurals." And on the weekends it's quite common to "have the Cadet Wing marching" or to have to perform "other military duties." Students also make a point of mentioning that "once every semester we have mandatory fitness tests, and throughout the semester [there are] random mandatory military briefs in the evenings." Even with a schedule packed with academic obligations and military training, one individual notes that there are "various clubs and activities for different interests, as well as religious services, all [of] which take [place] intermittently throughout the week." And if they do have a moment to relax, cadets will typically kick back with "Netflix or video games." Of course, when students really want to have fun, they generally leave "USAFA and [go] out into CO Springs or Denver" or they will "take advantage of outdoor areas for hiking, fishing, etc."

Student Body

Air Force Academy cadets seem to agree that the school attracts a number of "type A personalities" and "hard working" individuals who are "much more motivated than many other normal college students." They are also united in their deep desire "to serve [the] country" and are often "team oriented" as well. Further, cadets pride themselves on being "more fit than the general population," and cadets at USAFA "come from all over the nation, territories included, and from allied partner nations." While there may be a "healthy diversity of thought" at the academy, students do acknowledge a disparity in gender. A few individuals also grumble that some of their peers can be "very cynical." Thankfully, students view themselves as "one brotherhood and sisterhood looking out for each other." One cadet delves deeper adding, "We hold each other to an honor code the best we can and feel very close as a student body because we all live on campus and spend a majority of our time together." All in all, "there is a definite culture of helping out fellow cadets and of striving to bring peers up that helps people to perform at their best."

UNITED STATES AIR FORCE ACADEMY

E-Mail: rr_admissions@usafa.edu • Website: www.usafa.edu/

THE PRINCETON REVIEW SAYS

Admissions

The school reports that its standardized testing policy for use in admission for Fall 2024 requires applicants to submit either the SAT or ACT. It is unknown at this time if the 2024 testing policy will be permanent. The Princeton Review suggests that interested applicants consult with the school for the most up-to-date standardized testing policies. *Very important factors considered include:* rigor of secondary school record, class rank, academic GPA, standardized test scores, application essay, recommendation(s), interview, extracurricular activities, character/personal qualities, geographical residence, level of applicant's interest. *Important factors considered include:* talent/ability, volunteer work. *Other factors considered include:* first generation, alumni/ae relation, racial/ethnic status, work experience. High school diploma is required and GED is accepted. *Academic units required:* 4 English, 3 math, 3 science, 3 social studies, 1 history. *Academic units recommended:* 4 English, 4 math, 4 science, 2 science labs, 2 foreign language, 2 social studies, 2 history, 1 computer science.

Financial Aid

Aside from the free tuition, room, and board, students receive a nominal monthly stipend. Each cadet will owe at least five years of service as an active duty officer upon graduation, though additional programs (such as attending higher education or becoming a pilot) can add to the commitment.

The Inside Word

Earning admission to the United States Air Force Academy is no easy feat. The process is extraordinarily competitive, and you'll need a very high GPA and class rank to be in contention. Beyond strong academics, your teacher evaluations and letters of recommendation will be extremely important. The school uses them to assess your moral character and leadership capabilities. Additionally, cadet life is physically demanding, and you'll have to meet specific fitness requirements. Finally, you must be a U.S. citizen in order to apply.

THE SCHOOL SAYS "..."

From the Admissions Office

"The United States Air Force Academy offers one of the most prestigious and respected undergraduate programs available. With twenty-seven majors and four minors offered at the Academy, there are programs of study for every interest. The academic challenges and expectations are high—but so are the rewards. You will emerge from the Academy with a well-rounded knowledge in many fields, an intimate knowledge in your major area of study, and the ability to serve our nation as a Second Lieutenant in the world's greatest air, space, and cyberspace force.

"At the United States Air Force Academy, every cadet is an athlete. Our extensive athletic program includes twenty-nine men's and women's NCAA Division I intercollegiate teams, intramural sports, physical education courses, and physical fitness tests tailored to prepare you for Air Force leadership by building confidence, physical courage, and the ability to perform under pressure.

"The Academy experience requires cadets to become active participants in leadership roles and opportunities that give a sense of honor and duty. The Air Force Academy's mission is to educate, train, and inspire men and women to become officers of character motivated to lead the United States Air Force in service to our nation. If you choose to accept the challenges, you will be rewarded with unique experiences and opportunities incomparable to any other college experience and the honor of serving your country in the United States Air Force."

SELECTIVITY

Admissions Rating	98
# of applicants	11,666
% of applicants accepted	12
% of acceptees attending	77

FIRST-YEAR PROFILE

Testing policy	SAT or ACT required
Range SAT composite	1190–1473
Range SAT EBRW	590–730
Range SAT math	618–760
Range ACT composite	29–34
# submitting SAT scores	377
% submitting SAT scores	35
# submitting ACT scores	231
% submitting ACT scores	21
Average HS GPA	3.8
% frosh submitting high school GPA	100
% graduated top 10% of class	53
% graduated top 25% of class	81
% graduated top 50% of class	97

DEADLINES

Regular	
Deadline	12/31
Notification	Rolling, 10/15
Nonfall registration?	No

APPLICANTS ALSO LOOK AT

United States Coast Guard Academy; United States Merchant Marine Academy; United States Military Academy; United States Naval Academy

FINANCIAL FACTS

Annual tuition	$0

UNITED STATES COAST GUARD ACADEMY

15 Mohegan Avenue, New London, CT 06320-8103 • Admissions: 866-435-7196 • Fax: 860-701-6700

CAMPUS LIFE

Quality of Life Rating	77
Fire Safety Rating	91
Green Rating	70
Type of school	Public
Environment	City

STUDENTS

Total undergrad enrollment	1,037
% male/female/another gender	59/41/0
% from out of state	94
% frosh from public high school	76
% frosh live on campus	100
% ugrads live on campus	100
# of fraternities	0
# of sororities	0
% African American	3
% Asian	7
% White	63
% Hispanic	11
% Native American	<1
% Pacific Islander	<1
% Two or more races	12
% Race and/or ethnicity unknown	1
% international	3
# of countries represented	12

SURVEY SAYS . . .

Students always studying
School is well run
Great financial aid
No one cheats
Diverse student types interact on campus
Everyone loves the Bears
Intramural sports are popular
Alumni active on campus

ACADEMICS

Academic Rating	87
% students returning for sophomore year	96
% students graduating within 4 years	84
% students graduating within 6 years	87
Calendar	Semester
Student/faculty ratio	7:1
Profs interesting rating	87
Profs accessible rating	98

Most classes have 10–19 students.
Most lab/discussion sessions have fewer than 10 students.

MOST POPULAR MAJORS

Business Administration and Management, General; Oceanography, Chemical and Physical; Political Science and Government, General

STUDENTS SAY ". . ."

Academics

Students at the United States Coast Guard Academy recommend their school as "highly demanding, immensely rewarding, professionally oriented, and the best choice to make the best friends you are ever going to have." Many appreciate the "regimented environment," which, according to one management major, "Gives me a standard to live up to and hold myself to, even when I am away from here." Cadets are "pushed to [the] limits" "academically, emotionally, and physically," and they wouldn't have it any other way. Importantly, "the academy fosters camaraderie amongst the Corps of Cadets that can't be found anywhere else. With a student body numbering a little less than 1,000, the Coast Guard Academy is truly unique in its ability to provide an environment where classmates become shipmates, friends, and eventually family." Though there are a number of excellent programs, cadets call the most attention to the strong engineering department. The academics are "challenging but rewarding." Professors challenge cadets "to reach farther, expand their horizons, and to develop outside the classroom as much as inside of it." An electrical engineering major expounds, "The most surprising and excellent trait that all teachers have is that they are always willing to help outside of the class rooms. Always." Some students contend "the best part about my school is the summer training programs." Students have traveled "across the Atlantic Ocean" stopping "in London, Iceland, and Nova Scotia." Others have been to "Bermuda, St. Pierre France, Guantanamo Bay, and St. Petersburg Florida since coming to the Academy, which is absolutely amazing."

Campus Life

"Life at USCGA is unique. Only way to put it," says one junior. Day-to-day life at the Coast Guard Academy is "orderly and predictable." During the week, it's difficult for people to do anything "outside of their military, athletic, and academic obligations." As one honest marine and environmental science major reveals, "Every moment of every day is planned out." Required sports credits "keep people active and involved either intercollegiate or intramurals." Of course, life at the Academy isn't 100 percent work and stress. Free time is at a premium on weekdays, but "weekends are the time to explore New England, New York City, and the downtown New London area." A senior shares, cadets "go to the beach, head up to Vermont for some hiking or skiing.... There is a lot to do if you look for it." While "students aren't allowed off campus during the week," unless participating in an academy sanctioned activity, "most try and get away for the weekend." Another senior elaborates, "Underage students tend to go to the movies or the local mall. Of-age students usually spend their time off drinking at the bars downtown." Life at USCGA can be "very challenging and demanding at times, but the goal of becoming an officer makes it worth it." A "guaranteed job upon graduation" is pretty persuasive as well.

Student Body

While in past, USGCA has been described as homogeneous; "the academy has been stressing diversity in its admissions and has had a good deal of success." Luckily, a civil engineering major assures us, "Those students of different backgrounds easily fit in with everyone else." In fact, one cadet goes so far to say "sometimes, I don't think that cadets recognize diversity because we all wear the same uniforms, take the same classes, and are going through the same experiences." Not surprisingly, the academy seems to attract "highly motivated [people] with a strong desire to serve in the Coast Guard." Certainly, another hallmark of Coast Guard cadets is that they're "hard working, smart, motivated, and in great shape." A naval architecture and marine engineering major adds, "Type-A personalities are most common among the Corps." A senior describes student as "very close with each other and for the most part, everyone has a group of friends that they fit in quite well with." This sophomore cheekily sums up his peers, "A typical student here is just like a typical student anywhere else but works harder, follows stricter rules, is in better shape, and is owned by the federal government."

UNITED STATES COAST GUARD ACADEMY

E-Mail: USCGA.Admissions@uscga.edu • Website: www.uscga.edu

THE PRINCETON REVIEW SAYS

Admissions

The school reports that its standardized testing policy for use in admission for Fall 2024 requires applicants to submit either the SAT or ACT. It is unknown at this time if the 2024 testing policy will be permanent. The Princeton Review suggests that interested applicants consult with the school for the most up-to-date standardized testing policies. *Very important factors considered include:* rigor of secondary school record, academic GPA, application essay, extracurricular activities, talent/ability, character/personal qualities. *Important factors considered include:* class rank, recommendation(s), level of applicant's interest. *Other factors considered include:* standardized test scores, interview, first generation, alumni/ae relation, geographical residence, state residency, religious affiliation/commitment, racial/ethnic status, volunteer work, work experience. High school diploma is required and GED is accepted. *Academic units required:* 4 English, 3 math, 3 science, 2 science labs, 2 social studies, 1 history, 7 academic electives. *Academic units recommended:* 4 English, 4 math, 4 science, 3 science labs, 2 foreign language, 2 social studies, 1 history, 7 academic electives.

Financial Aid

There is no cost for tuition, room, or board to attend the Coast Guard Academy. All cadets are paid a salary while attending the Coast Guard Academy.

The Inside Word

Gaining acceptance into the Coast Guard Academy is a highly competitive process. The admissions committee is looking not only for outstanding academic achievement but also for applicants who demonstrate leadership ability and strong moral character. In addition, unlike other colleges, you'll also need a physical fitness examination and evaluation.

THE SCHOOL SAYS ". . ."

From the Admissions Office

"Established in 1876, the Coast Guard Academy educates, trains, and inspires Cadets to serve their country and humanity. Leadership and character development are emphasized in academic life, athletic pursuits, and military training. Commitment to helping those in need is a personal quality shared by every student selected to attend the Coast Guard Academy. High levels of personal accountability are expected of Cadets and graduates.

"Fourth Class (freshmen) arrive in June to begin a strenuous seven week training program (Swab Summer) that prepares them to join the Corps of Cadets in August. Swab Summer culminates with a week at sea aboard America's only active tall ship, the EAGLE.

"The Corps of Cadets is comprised of talented Cadets from all fifty states and about twenty other nations. The Academy is diverse: Women and students of color, as groups, each comprise over 30 percent of the student body. Most Cadets are athletes—over 60 percent play on at least one NCAA Division III team. The opportunity to play is nearly unmatched in college athletics.

"The Academy's value proposition is also tough to beat. This is the only small, highly selective four year college in the U.S. that is free of charge to attend. This is possible because Academy grads go straight to a position of responsibility as a commissioned officer in the Coast Guard. All are obligated to serve for five years, and most make it a career. Aside from the satisfaction of saving lives and protecting others, the opportunity to fly is exceptional. And, about 85 percent of officers also earn a graduate degree at Coast Guard expense.

"If you are smart, adventuresome, physically fit, and want to achieve a higher purpose in your life, the U.S. Coast Guard Academy may be for you!"

SELECTIVITY

Admissions Rating	98
# of applicants	1,894
% of applicants accepted	15
% of acceptees attending	96
# offered a place on the wait list	36
% accepting a place on wait list	100
% admitted from wait list	75

FIRST-YEAR PROFILE

Testing policy	SAT or ACT required
Range SAT composite	1160–1365
Range SAT EBRW	580–680
Range SAT math	580–685
Range ACT composite	26–31
# submitting SAT scores	189
% submitting SAT scores	65
# submitting ACT scores	105
% submitting ACT scores	36
Average HS GPA	3.8
% frosh submitting high school GPA	100
% graduated top 10% of class	47
% graduated top 25% of class	85
% graduated top 50% of class	100

DEADLINES

Early action	
Deadline	11/15
Notification	2/1
Regular	
Priority	11/15
Deadline	1/15
Notification	4/15
Nonfall registration?	No

FINANCIAL FACTS

Annual tuition	$0

UNITED STATES MERCHANT MARINE ACADEMY

300 Steamboat Road, Kings Point, NY 11024-1699 • Admissions: 516-726-5800 • Fax: 516-773-5390

STUDENTS SAY "..."

Academics

Tucked away on Long Island, the United States Merchant Marine Academy offers students the chance to pursue a prestigious though rigorous and regimented education. Further, it allows undergrads to join "a group of elite students who work hard and [are] honest and patriotic." Students here caution that the academics are "extremely difficult," especially given the "fast-paced classroom environment." Additionally, when asked about their professors, students dole out mixed reviews. Though most assert that their teachers are "very intelligent," some bemoan a "lack of enthusiasm." While some professors are described as "fair, approachable, and extremely helpful," other professors come across as "heartless and condescending." Regardless of which classes you enroll in, the Merchant Marine Academy is "a school that requires plenty of effort on behalf of the student." As one midshipman proudly sums up, "The opportunities afforded by this Academy are unparalleled by any other college I have come across. Despite the immense sacrifices and hardships of this school, it is completely worth it for the right person."

Campus Life

Undergrads at the Merchant Marine Academy don't mince words about life at their school. Indeed, the majority seem to be in agreement that because "it is a military academy; fun is generally limited." As one straightforward student explains, "We are restricted to the campus grounds during the week until senior year. Life is pretty drab, dull, and boring [with] most time spent either in class, studying, or working out." Moreover, undergrads are "restricted by the regiment and disciplinary system." Of course, even these hardworking midshipmen get to kick back every now and again. Another undergrad cheerfully shares, "When the spring comes, everyone gets out to play rec sports (Ultimate Frisbee, tag football, soccer, swim, or bike ride) and goes to the park to BBQ." A fellow student chimes in, "We have a good time, and usually, it is the little things that make us happy. We enjoy hanging out on weekends and doing things that normal college students would do. Recently a few friends and I had a Nerf gun battle, which was pretty fun." When they are allowed, midshipmen rush to get off campus. Indeed, students here love to take advantage of the fact that they are "only twenty minutes from downtown NYC." As this wise midshipman concludes, "New York City in uniform boils down to cheap food, movies, plays, concerts, easy way to meet girls, you name it.... We work hard all week, but when it comes time, we get to play hard as well."

Student Body

At first glance, the average Merchant Marine Academy midshipman could be described as "a white, conservative male." Of course, there's definitely more to these students than race, gender, and political views. Certainly, undergrads can also be depicted as "respectful," "athletic," and "outgoing." They can also be categorized as "those that want to work in the maritime industry and those that want to join the military." Moreover, many are "hardworking and serious." As one undergrad explains, "If you aren't willing to work, you won't be here long." Another student continues, "The typical student has tons on his plate, whether it's regimental duties or academic ones. [However], no matter what, if you need help with something, somebody will be there for you." A fellow midshipman concurs, summing up, "The students here are all a family. Each one of us here at the Merchant Marine Academy [has] experienced the same rigorous training and tough treatment plebe year. We all work together in everything we do, and without one another it is almost impossible to succeed at the Academy." Actually, the U.S. Merchant Marine Academy is increasing the diversity of its student body every year.

UNITED STATES MERCHANT MARINE ACADEMY

Financial Aid: 516-773-5295 • E-Mail: admissions@usmma.edu • Website: www.usmma.edu

THE PRINCETON REVIEW SAYS

Admissions

The school reports that its standardized testing policy for use in admission for Fall 2024 requires applicants to submit either the SAT or ACT. It is unknown at this time if the 2024 testing policy will be permanent. The Princeton Review suggests that interested applicants consult with the school for the most up-to-date standardized testing policies. *Very important factors considered include:* rigor of secondary school record, class rank, standardized test scores, extracurricular activities, character/personal qualities. *Important factors considered include:* academic GPA, application essay, recommendation(s), talent/ability, level of applicant's interest. *Other factors considered include:* interview, first generation, geographical residence, state residency, racial/ethnic status, volunteer work, work experience. High school diploma is required and GED is accepted. *Academic units required:* 3 English, 3 math, 1 science, 1 science lab, 8 academic electives. *Academic units recommended:* 4 English, 4 math, 3 science, 2 science labs, 2 foreign language.

Financial Aid

Students should submit: FAFSA. The Princeton Review suggests that all financial aid forms be submitted as soon as possible (see page 5 for a note on the FAFSA). *Need-based scholarships/grants offered:* Federal Pell; Private scholarships; State scholarships/grants. *Loan aid offered:* Direct PLUS loans; Direct Subsidized Loans; Direct Unsubsidized Loans. Admitted students will be notified of awards on a rolling basis beginning 5/1.

The Inside Word

Securing admittance to the Merchant Marine Academy is no easy feat. The admissions committee is looking for stellar candidates who have the intelligence, fortitude, and leadership capabilities to survive (and thrive) at this institution. In addition to your transcripts and test scores, the admissions crew will closely assess your letters of recommendation. Moreover, unlike traditional colleges, you'll also have to pass a fitness requirement and secure a nomination from a U.S. representative or senator.

THE SCHOOL SAYS "..."

From the Admissions Office

"The U. S. Merchant Marine Academy (USMMA) at Kings Point, New York, is a federal service academy with the mission to educate and graduate licensed Merchant Marine Officers of exemplary character who serve America's marine transportation and defense needs in peace and war. The Academy's four-year program is a demanding academic schedule that includes hands on experience. In addition, each cadet participates in Sea Year, during which cadets acquire more hands-on experience working aboard commercial and military vessels sailing around the world. Due to the Academy's unique mission, its graduates have civilian and military career choices that are unmatched by any other federal or maritime academy.

"Kings Point graduates earn (1) a Bachelor of Science degree, (2) an unlimited U.S. Coast Guard license (Deck or Engine), as well as (3) an officer's commission in one of the U.S. Armed Forces. Graduates are obligated to serve as a licensed officer in the U.S. Merchant Marine for five years, and as a commissioned officer in one of the U.S. Armed Forces reserves for eight years following graduation. Alternatively, graduating midshipmen can apply for an active duty commission in any branch of the U.S Armed Forces or the National Oceanic and Atmospheric Administration (NOAA) Corps.

"USMMA graduates are highly sought after as officers in the military and the U.S. Merchant Marine. Further, according to recent reports from the Department of Education and others, Kings Point graduates earn some of the highest salaries of college graduates in the United States."

SELECTIVITY

Admissions Rating	96
# of applicants	1,855
% of applicants accepted	22
% of acceptees attending	68
# offered a place on the wait list	204
% accepting a place on wait list	100
% admitted from wait list	65

FIRST-YEAR PROFILE

Testing policy	SAT or ACT required
Range SAT EBRW	570–660
Range SAT math	630–660
% submitting SAT scores	66
% submitting ACT scores	75
% frosh submitting high school GPA	100
% graduated top 10% of class	22
% graduated top 25% of class	64
% graduated top 50% of class	96

DEADLINES

Regular	
Deadline	3/1
Notification	Rolling, 4/1
Nonfall registration?	No

FINANCIAL FACTS

Annual in-state tuition	$0
Annual out-of-state tuition	$0
Room and board	$0
Required fees	$1,050
Books and supplies	$2,880
% frosh rec. any financial aid	33
% UG rec. any financial aid	30

UNITED STATES MILITARY ACADEMY

646 Swift Road, West Point, NY 10996-1905 • Admissions: 845-938-4011 • Fax: 845-938-3021

STUDENTS SAY ". . ."

Academics

Throughout its 221 year history, the United States Military Academy at West Point, New York has produced United States presidents, NASA astronauts, notable generals, business leaders, and many medal of honor recipients. So it is no wonder that cadets say the academy's "leadership training is second to none." Cadets praise the school for "helping the students succeed not only in the classroom, but also outside in our daily lives as people and as leaders" by pairing "academic vigor" with "[experiences] which enrich your character and ultimately make you a better person." The academy extends its holistic education "with countless academic enrichment activities," like "scuba diving with NASA" or parachuting lessons. The United States Military Academy also "sends cadets all over the world for study abroad" and gives students practical experience to apply what they learn in the classroom through academic internships, such as working at "government research facilities during the summer doing relevant and cutting edge research." Professors are universally admired as "amazing," "very accessible and devoted" to their students. Students say this contributes an environment where everyone "cares about academics." It's a rigorous program, but professors "bend over backwards to accommodate" the busy schedules of West Point cadets, so any student can "succeed if you're willing to ask" for help.

Campus Life

To put it mildly, "life is extremely busy" at West Point. "Time management is one of the biggest things that you [will] learn" one cadet advises. Most days start with "formation in the morning before 7:30 A.M. classes" and cadets "are either [doing schoolwork], in class, or exercising for most of the day. After classes are over at 4:00 P.M.," time is divided between activities and studies. Moreover, fitness is mandatory: "Every cadet is required to play a sport." While most admit that they "live a regimented lifestyle," cadets still nonetheless find ways to relax and socialize: "until Taps, when everyone must be in their rooms. We play video games, go to clubs, play instruments, and go to NYC on the weekends for fun." The academic schedules of first- and second-year students are pre-selected "but junior and senior classes are chosen on your own depending on your major." Students praise the system because "you don't have to worry about a class filling up," and cadets "can study ANY major they want because we are all guaranteed a great job after graduation." And like any old institution there are "a lot of silly traditions that we hold on to long after we're gone."

Student Body

The Academy requires that applicants receive a nomination from their congressional representative, senator, the vice president of the united states, or have a military service connected nomination, so cadets assure us that they "never cease to be impressed with [their] peers," who are some "of the smartest sons and daughters of America." Cadets provide a litany of praise for their peers: "People are courteous, respectful, honest, honorable, and simply amazing at West Point." Cadets say that their "shared hardships foster an environment of camaraderie unparalleled anywhere else in the world." Students stress the importance of teamwork, cooperation, and leadership, explaining that "by the time you become a senior, you may be responsible for 120 other people." Cadets say the student body is geographically diverse with "students from every state in the US" represented as well as "some students from other countries like, Nigeria, Qatar, and France."

UNITED STATES MILITARY ACADEMY

E-Mail: admissions@westpoint.edu • Website: www.westpoint.edu

THE PRINCETON REVIEW SAYS

Admissions

The school reports that its standardized testing policy for use in admission for Fall 2024 requires applicants to submit the PSAT, SAT, or ACT. It is unknown at this time if the 2024 testing policy will be permanent. The Princeton Review suggests that interested applicants consult with the school for the most up-to-date standardized testing policies. *Very important factors considered include:* rigor of secondary school record, academic GPA, standardized test scores, interview, extracurricular activities, character/personal qualities. *Important factors considered include:* application essay, recommendation(s), talent/ability, level of applicant's interest. *Other factors considered include:* class rank, first generation, racial/ethnic status, volunteer work, work experience. High school diploma is required and GED is accepted. *Academic units recommended:* 4 English, 4 math, 2 science, 2 science labs, 2 foreign language, 1 social studies, 1 history, 2 academic electives.

Financial Aid

Every Cadet receives a fully funded education, including tuition, books, room and board, medical and dental care, and a student stipend for personal expenses.

The Inside Word

The fact that you must request to be nominated in order to apply to West Point tells you all you need to know about the school's selectivity. Successful candidates must demonstrate excellence in academics, physical conditioning, extracurricular involvement, and leadership. They must also be willing to commit to five years of active duty and three years of reserve duty upon graduation. The rigorous requirements and demanding commitments of a West Point education hardly dissuade applicants.

THE SCHOOL SAYS "..."

From the Admissions Office

"West Point is searching for applicants who possess the leadership skills, cultural sensibilities, and the moral fiber to handle the volatile, uncertain, complex, and ambiguous contemporary operating environment of today's world as a future U.S. Army Officer. As the preeminent leader development institute, we are looking for critical thinkers who have the sound judgment and drive to become leaders of character upon graduation.

"To assess your ability and preparation, admissions looks at more than your GPA or standardized test scores. The applications of almost 13,000 students are evaluated based on academic, physical, and leadership potential to find approximately 1,150 candidates who are ready to overcome the challenges they will face as members of the Corps of Cadets. With an amazingly high offer-acceptance rate, only the most dedicated, enthusiastic applicants make it to the finish line and report for duty each June.

"If you accept the challenge, you will be immersed in a military training program that ranges from marksmanship to orienteering, an academic program that offers over 36 majors ranging from electrical engineering to philosophy, and a physical program that finds every cadet participating in an intercollegiate, club, or intramural-level sport. The fully funded, four-year college education includes tuition, room, board, full medical and dental care, and a stipend for personal expenses. In return, you will graduate with a Bachelor of Science degree and be commissioned as a U.S. Army Officer with an active duty service obligation of five years active and three years reserve. Complete admissions guidance found online."

SELECTIVITY

Admissions Rating	98
# of applicants	12,559
% of applicants accepted	12
% of acceptees attending	78

FIRST-YEAR PROFILE

Testing policy	PSAT, SAT, or ACT required
Range SAT composite	1230–1430
Range SAT EBRW	610–710
Range SAT math	610–740
Range ACT composite	27–33
# submitting SAT scores	731
% submitting SAT scores	62
# submitting ACT scores	442
% submitting ACT scores	38
Average HS GPA	4.0
% frosh submitting high school GPA	100
% graduated top 10% of class	43
% graduated top 25% of class	69
% graduated top 50% of class	92

DEADLINES

Regular	
Deadline	1/31
Notification	Rolling, 11/1
Nonfall registration?	No

APPLICANTS SOMETIMES PREFER

United States Air Force Academy; United States Coast Guard Academy; United States Naval Academy

FINANCIAL FACTS

Annual tuition	$0

UNITED STATES NAVAL ACADEMY

121 Blake Road, Annapolis, MD 21402 • Admissions: 410-293-1000 • Fax: 410-293-4348

STUDENTS SAY ". . ."

Academics

It should come as no surprise that a United States Naval Academy education is all about "developing leaders" and fostering "a strong sense of honor and morals." The school—which is free to attend—is certainly successful in this mission. As one midshipman explains, "I seldom hear of a graduate that, following their naval service, does not excel in the civilian workforce and successfully lead their teams to excellence." An obvious explanation for this is in the way students are surrounded by "excellent people who genuinely care about your development" as well as "extensive study abroad opportunities and internships, relevant and respected guest speakers…hands-on learning on ships and other military platforms, [and] trips to nearby museums or other relevant locations." Additionally, as you'd expect given the military component, "many classes go beyond the normal style of lectures. For example, seamanship classes can involve piloting actual watercraft at sea."

Students find that their coursework is generally "challenging but definitely doable…You can tell that there are so many people that want to help you succeed." Midshipmen also happily report that their "professors are very knowledgeable and easy to learn from" and make themselves "always available for meetings and extra instruction," including their own—some note that "super open and extremely receptive to feedback on teaching style." In all, "My overall academic experience has been extremely positive and worthwhile due to a great work environment."

Campus Life

Life at the Naval Academy is fairly structured, with students out of bed by 6:30 (if not 5:30 for morning workouts) and pretty much in formation or class until 3:30 (with breaks for breakfast and lunch). Afternoons are then taken up with "sports/extracurriculars, and then any extra briefs or meetings." It's a packed schedule, but then again, "no one can leave [campus] on weekdays except for select upperclassmen." Given all the possible athletics—scuba to ultimate frisbee to pickleball and everything in between—students don't seem to mind. Students also highlight the arts—"outstanding music programs" that are "extremely worthwhile and staffed by experienced instructors"—and Navy Spirit events, "such as concerts from famous artists (like Pitbull) at the end of every school year, or food trucks for us to try, or little contests around our campus (finding a hidden stuffed mascot for prizes)." Of course, when the weekend rolls around, there's a little more opportunity for students to let loose. As this midshipmen explains, "Some go to parties at UMD while others hike, golf, fish…hang out with friends or go to the local bars in Annapolis."

Student Body

Without question, the Naval Academy seems to attract individuals who are "extremely driven, capable, and intelligent." As one student puts it, "Everyone here is the best where they come from and so it's a school full of academic and physical studs." Given the Academy's demanding nature, it's common for midshipmen to develop "strong bonds with one another." The knowledge that "we will be fighting side by side one day" brings a special sense of selflessness, and some even see their classmates as siblings. They aren't, according to students, homogenous: "My peers are all quite different. Some are nerdy. Some are more of the jock sort of variant." And since the Academy "pulls individuals from across the country" you're bound to meet people "from all walks of life and backgrounds." Nevertheless, "each one of them dreams unimaginably big, deeply cares for others, and has the safety of the American people on the forefront of their mind." Therefore, it's entirely understandable when this student simply states, "The caliber of people you meet here is unmatched."

UNITED STATES NAVAL ACADEMY

E-Mail: inquire@usna.edu • Website: www.usna.edu

THE PRINCETON REVIEW SAYS

Admissions

The school reports that its standardized testing policy for use in admission for Fall 2024 requires applicants to submit either the SAT or ACT. It is unknown at this time if the 2024 testing policy will be permanent. The Princeton Review suggests that interested applicants consult with the school for the most up-to-date standardized testing policies. *Very important factors considered include:* rigor of secondary school record, class rank, academic GPA, application essay, recommendation(s), interview, extracurricular activities, talent/ability, work experience, level of applicant's interest. *Important factors considered include:* standardized test scores. *Other factors considered include:* character/personal qualities, first generation, alumni/ae relation, geographical residence, religious affiliation/commitment, racial/ethnic status, volunteer work. High school diploma or equivalent is not required. *Academic units required: Academic units recommended:* 4 English, 4 math, 2 science, 1 science lab, 2 foreign language, 2 history, 2 computer science.

Financial Aid

The Navy pays 100 percent of the tuition, room and board, medical, and dental care costs of Naval Academy midshipmen. This means all students who attend the Naval Academy do so on a full scholarship in return for five years of active duty service upon graduation. Additionally, students also enjoy regular active-duty benefits including access to military commissaries and exchanges, commercial transportation and lodging discounts, and the ability to fly space-available in military aircraft around the world. Midshipmen pay is $1,185.00 monthly, from which laundry, barber, cobbler, activities fees, yearbook, and other service charges are deducted. Actual cash pay is $125 per month in the first year, which increases each year thereafter.

The Inside Word

Securing admission to the Naval Academy is no easy feat. To begin with, a top-notch academic record is a must. In addition to strong GPA and test scores, applicants also have to secure an official nomination (typically granted by a U.S. representative, U.S. senator, or the Vice President). Further, candidates need to prove physical fitness, be an unmarried U.S. citizen between the ages of seventeen and twenty-three with no dependents. And, perhaps most importantly, applicants should also demonstrate strong moral character. Finally, the earlier you apply the better.

THE SCHOOL SAYS "..."

From the Admissions Office

"The finest young men and women in the country come to the Naval Academy to develop into leaders to serve the nation; USNA is the school of admirals, presidents, Nobel Prize winners, astronauts, jet pilots and CEOs. At USNA, you will have the opportunity to pursue a four-year degree program that develops you mentally, morally, and physically as no civilian college can. As you might expect, this program is demanding, but the opportunities are limitless and more than worth the effort.

"Upon throwing the iconic Midshipmen hat into the air at graduation, you will serve your country in one of dozens of professional fields—primarily aviation, submarines, ships, or the Marine Corps, but with additional limited options for the SEALs, medical, and other communities."

SELECTIVITY

Admissions Rating	98
# of applicants	12,927
% of applicants accepted	11
% of acceptees attending	85
# offered a place on the wait list	233
% accepting a place on wait list	73
% admitted from wait list	36

FIRST-YEAR PROFILE

Testing policy	SAT or ACT required
Range SAT composite	1210–1310
Range SAT EBRW	600–720
Range SAT math	600–720
Range ACT composite	25–32
# submitting SAT scores	828
% submitting SAT scores	71
# submitting ACT scores	536
% submitting ACT scores	46
% graduated top 10% of class	62
% graduated top 25% of class	84
% graduated top 50% of class	97

DEADLINES

Regular	
Deadline	1/31
Notification	4/15
Nonfall registration?	No

APPLICANTS ALSO LOOK AT

United States Air Force Academy; United States Military Academy

FINANCIAL FACTS

Annual tuition	$0

THE UNIVERSITY OF ALABAMA AT BIRMINGHAM

1720 2nd Ave S, Birmingham, AL 35294 • Admissions: 205-934-4011 • Fax: 205-975-7114

CAMPUS LIFE

Quality of Life Rating	84
Fire Safety Rating	95
Green Rating	74
Type of school	Public
Environment	Metropolis

STUDENTS

Total undergrad enrollment	12,776
% male/female/another gender	38/62/NR
% from out of state	14
% frosh live on campus	80
% ugrads live on campus	25
# of fraternities (% join)	13 (6)
# of sororities (% join)	12 (8)
% African American	25
% Asian	8
% White	51
% Hispanic	7
% Native American	<1
% Pacific Islander	<1
% Two or more races	5
% Race and/or ethnicity unknown	1
% international	2
# of countries represented	60

SURVEY SAYS . . .

Lab facilities are great
Great library
Internships are widely available
Diverse student types interact on campus
Students are very religious
Recreation facilities are great
Alumni active on campus

ACADEMICS

Academic Rating	81
% students returning for sophomore year	82
% students graduating within 4 years	44
% students graduating within 6 years	64
Calendar	Semester
Student/faculty ratio	18:1
Profs interesting rating	88
Profs accessible rating	93

Most classes have 10–19 students.
Most lab/discussion sessions have
10–19 students.

MOST POPULAR MAJORS

Biology/Biological Sciences, General; Psychology,
General; Registered Nursing/Registered Nurse

STUDENTS SAY ". . ."

Academics

At The University of Alabama at Birmingham, professors and administrators "care about you." "For many of the professors, it's not just about a grade in a class that you are taking. Rather it's an experience and preparation for any of our further endeavors." The professors here are "experts in their fields," they're "accessible and exciting," and "they're down-to-earth enough to give students a real view of what it's like to enter the world of academia." Despite the fact that this is a large university, there are "small class sizes in even the 100-level classes," and "many professors are available for help outside the classroom and care about teaching their subjects to the students." Of particular note, students say professors in the science departments "are great. They do a great job with interactive learning, and they really put forth every effort to make sure that those who want help get it." Academically, students feel that the workload is rigorous, but "certainly worth the challenge." As one student notes, a graduate tends to feel like "a better person for having experienced the challenge of UAB as well as the diversity." With a biannual student forum, "the faculty and administration are very close with students and actively look to pursuing perfection and improving the collegiate experience."

Campus Life

"Campus life is vibrant and exciting," boasts the student body. Students "love the size of the school," finding it "like a small town in a big city." The impression is that "the campus is large enough that [you] meet and see new faces daily, but small enough to where [you] have personal relationships with teachers and the administration." Additionally, "there is a genuine interest among students in learning about the other cultures and religions represented on campus and in other cultures around the world." UAB "strongly encourages their students to get involved on campus in some shape or form," presenting the student body with such opportunities as "the widely used Campus Recreation Center where students can take free U-Fit Classes (kickboxing, krunk/hip-hop class, yoga, spin, etc.), swim in the wave pool, climb the rock wall, or play intramurals (flag football, dodgeball, soccer, volleyball, slow pitch softball, etc.)." In addition, the surrounding city of Birmingham has a list of attractions that "goes on and on," such that "students can dine or shop at the many malls located throughout the city. There are also many museums, art shows, concerts, dance clubs, [and] movie theaters to choose from." As one student puts it, "the problem [is] having to narrow down opportunities, rather than having to find something to do."

Student Body

"Everyone is so diverse that there is...something for everyone to get involved in." With more than 250 campus organizations, students say you'd "have to choose to not become involved." Many students love "how no one looks down on anyone," and how "everyone is so down to earth!" Most feel that they all come "from modest households." Regarding potential changes that could be made, "the meal plan situation could use some serious help." At UAB students feel, "it is easy to find a place where you fit in," although the student body will insist that "there is no typical student!" In general, students are "hard-working and serious," while doing their best to always "enjoy weekend fun with friends."

THE UNIVERSITY OF ALABAMA AT BIRMINGHAM

Financial Aid: 205-934-8223 • E-Mail: chooseuab@uab.edu • Website: www.uab.edu

THE PRINCETON REVIEW SAYS

Admissions

The school reports that its standardized testing policy for use in admission for Fall 2024 is Test Optional. The 2024 testing policy will be temporary. The Princeton Review suggests that interested applicants consult with the school for the most up-to-date standardized testing policies. *Very important factors considered include:* rigor of secondary school record, academic GPA, standardized test scores. *Other factors considered include:* High school diploma is required and GED is accepted. *Academic units required:* 4 English, 3 math, 3 science, 2 science labs, 1 foreign language, 3 social studies, 3 academic electives.

Financial Aid

Students should submit: FAFSA. Priority filing deadline is 12/1. The Princeton Review suggests that all financial aid forms be submitted as soon as possible (see page 5 for a note on the FAFSA). *Need-based scholarships/grants offered:* College/university scholarship or grant aid from institutional funds; Federal Pell; Private scholarships; SEOG; State scholarships/grants; United Negro College Fund. *Loan aid offered:* Direct PLUS loans; Direct Subsidized Loans; Direct Unsubsidized Loans; College/university loans from institutional funds; Federal Nursing Loans; State Loans. Admitted students will be notified of awards on a rolling basis beginning 12/1. Federal Work-Study Program available. Institutional employment available.

The Inside Word

UAB's incoming class tends to have an average GPA of 3.8, and that's the most important factor for admission. Administrators here are looking to admit a student body that's friendly, diverse, and intelligent with students who strive to be active in the community.

THE SCHOOL SAYS "..."

From the Admissions Office

"The University of Alabama at Birmingham (UAB) is a young, dynamic teaching and research university that has—in just four decades—won international renown for our collaborative and interdisciplinary culture. Our academic programs afford students unrivaled, hands-on experience in research and scholarship as UAB is first in the nation among public universities of federal research dollars per freshman. With over 120 areas of study, UAB attracts the best and brightest students from Alabama, the nation, and 109 countries around the globe.

"UAB students learn from—and work alongside—some of the world's top researchers, scholars, performers, and experts. Programs from the sciences and engineering to the arts and humanities give students the benefit of globally recognized faculty, exciting academic challenges, and experiences that will prepare them for a future in the job market.

"At UAB, we understand that having a fulfilling student life experience is as important as having a fulfilling academic experience. UAB has a rich mix of academic organizations, honor clubs, social fraternities and sororities, volunteer groups, and activities ranging from intramural sports and SGA to program-related clubs and supporting Blazer athletics. With 250 campus organizations to keep students involved, UAB offers the chance to make lifelong friendships while assisting in the development of skills essential to leadership and teamwork."

SELECTIVITY

Admissions Rating	85
# of applicants	9,947
% of applicants accepted	87
% of acceptees attending	26

FIRST-YEAR PROFILE

Testing policy	Test Optional
Range SAT composite	1200–1410
Range SAT EBRW	610–690
Range SAT math	590–720
Range ACT composite	23–30
# submitting SAT scores	145
% submitting SAT scores	7
# submitting ACT scores	1,081
% submitting ACT scores	49
Average HS GPA	3.8
% frosh submitting high school GPA	100
% graduated top 10% of class	24
% graduated top 25% of class	52
% graduated top 50% of class	80

DEADLINES

Regular	
Priority	6/1
Notification	Rolling, 8/1
Nonfall registration?	Yes

FINANCIAL FACTS

Financial Aid Rating	77
Annual in-state tuition	$11,040
Annual out-of-state tuition	$26,520
Room and board	$12,160
Required fees	$0
Books and supplies	$1,200
Average frosh need-based scholarship	$6,167
Average UG need-based scholarship	$6,249
% needy frosh rec. need-based scholarship or grant aid	62
% needy UG rec. need-based scholarship or grant aid	63
% needy frosh rec. non-need-based scholarship or grant aid	77
% needy UG rec. non-need-based scholarship or grant aid	58
% needy frosh rec. need-based self-help aid	59
% needy UG rec. need-based self-help aid	61
% frosh rec. any financial aid	
% UG rec. any financial aid	
% UG borrow to pay for school	56
Average cumulative indebtedness	$28,048
% frosh need fully met	20
% ugrads need fully met	15
Average % of frosh need met	60
Average % of ugrad need met	53

THE UNIVERSITY OF ALABAMA—TUSCALOOSA

719 University Blvd, Tuscaloosa, AL 35487-0100 • Admissions: 205-348-6010 • Fax: 205-348-9046

STUDENTS SAY "..."

Academics

Founded in 1831, University of Alabama—Tuscaloosa offers an educational experience ripe with "significant academic resources and infrastructure." Students can take advantage of "strong academic programs that rank highly," and while there is a range of difficulty across different fields of study, many classes "provide the opportunities for deep, sustained, and interesting engagement with the course material." The undergrad experience is elevated by "many outstanding, passionate, and brilliant professors" who "teach from a real-world perspective" and provide "extensive research opportunities." Instructors are known for putting "a ton of strategy and preparation into their lectures," and many faculty members are "amazing and care deeply about teaching." There are "opportunities to be challenged academically through honors classes and higher-level courses," which can mean everything from "[interviewing] prominent people from the Civil Rights Movement" to studying "the science of baking." Non-traditional subjects are popular, and "Many students take a class that allows you to make a book from the paper to the binding."

Campus Life

Outside the classroom, "There is so much to get involved in" at the University of Alabama. UA's Crimson Tide athletics give the school "a well-known name" and "are such a fun part" of undergrad culture. As one student puts it, "Saturdays in the fall are 100% dedicated to game day." This strong sense of school spirit also allows individuals "to unite with students of varying backgrounds on game day." Greek life is a major part of Alabama life, with organizations "unlike anywhere else in the country" that create connections across the entire student body: "Even those not involved still support [Greek life's] philanthropy and service events."

Tuscaloosa's warm climate provides plenty of opportunity for getting outdoors, and "There is a strong campus culture of keeping active and enjoying time outside." Exploring nature tops the list of students' favorite activities, with many taking advantage of the "good hiking spots near campus" and "adventuring through the surrounding wilderness of Alabama." On campus, students "[play] sports on the quad or sand volleyball at the courts," and "The club sports have lots of funding," making them as accessible as they are enjoyable.

Student Body

"Most students are here to have fun and learn at the same time" and have "no shortage of enthusiasm for the school." Undergrads agree that "One of the greatest strengths of UA is the strong community," as demonstrated by the way enrollees are known to "stand up for things they believe in." They truly create an atmosphere where "everyone is willing to help everyone." The University of Alabama campus is full of "smiling faces" and students "eager to learn from one another." It's an environment where "People always ask how you are doing even if you've never seen them before." With "such a large student body, there are so many different skills and talents present," providing undergrads the opportunity to make "friends of all sorts of ethnicities, backgrounds, and personalities." Students come from all around the world and "The out-of-state population brings different perspectives and backgrounds to the school."

THE UNIVERSITY OF ALABAMA—TUSCALOOSA

Financial Aid: 205-348-7949 • E-Mail: admissions@ua.edu • Website: www.ua.edu

THE PRINCETON REVIEW SAYS

Admissions

The school reports that its standardized testing policy for use in admission for Fall 2024 is Test Optional. It is unknown at this time if the 2024 testing policy will be permanent. The Princeton Review suggests that interested applicants consult with the school for the most up-to-date standardized testing policies. *Very important factors considered include:* rigor of secondary school record, academic GPA, standardized test scores. *Important factors considered include:* class rank, extracurricular activities, volunteer work. *Other factors considered include:* application essay, recommendation(s), interview, talent/ability, character/personal qualities, first generation, alumni/ae relation, work experience. High school diploma is required and GED is accepted. *Academic units required:* 4 English, 3 math, 3 science, 2 science labs, 1 foreign language, 4 social studies, 5 academic electives. *Academic units recommended:* 4 English, 3 math, 3 science, 2 science labs, 2 foreign language, 4 social studies, 5 academic electives.

Financial Aid

Students should submit: FAFSA and Application for Academic Scholarships. Priority filing deadline is 12/1. The Princeton Review suggests that all financial aid forms be submitted as soon as possible (see page 5 for a note on the FAFSA). *Need-based scholarships/grants offered:* College/university scholarship or grant aid from institutional funds; Federal Nursing Scholarships; Federal Pell; Private scholarships; SEOG; State scholarships/grants. *Loan aid offered:* Direct PLUS loans; Direct Subsidized Loans; Direct Unsubsidized Loans; College/university loans from institutional funds. Admitted students will be notified of awards on a rolling basis beginning 1/1. Federal Work-Study Program available. Institutional employment available.

The Inside Word

The best candidates for admission at Alabama are successful students who have big ambitions and the drive to make their dreams a reality. Students should possess a good GPA, impressive coursework, and solid test scores. Additionally, Alabama also takes your after-school activities, like employment, volunteer work, and clubs into consideration. Applicants who want priority consideration for competitive scholarships should make sure to apply early to make the cut off deadline.

THE SCHOOL SAYS "..."

From the Admissions Office

"Since its founding in 1831 as the first public university in the state, the University of Alabama has been committed to providing the best, most complete education possible for its students. Our commitment to that goal means that as times change, we sharpen our focus and methods to keep our graduates competitive in their fields. By offering outstanding teaching in a solid core curriculum enhanced by multimedia classrooms and campus-wide computer labs, the University of Alabama keeps its focus on the future while maintaining a traditional college atmosphere. Extensive international study opportunities, internship programs, and cooperative education placements help our students prepare for successful futures. Consisting of eleven colleges and schools offering 193 degrees in more than 100 fields of study, the university gives its students a wide range of choices and offers courses of study at the bachelor's, master's, specialist, and doctoral levels. The university emphasizes quality and breadth of academic opportunities and challenging programs for well-prepared students through its Honors College, including the University Honors Program, International Honors Program, and Computer-Based Honors Programs and Blount Undergraduate Initiative (liberal arts program). Thirty-one percent of undergraduates are from out of state, providing an enriching social and cultural environment.

"Applicants may submit either the SAT or the ACT. The ACT's writing component is accepted but not required for admission."

SELECTIVITY

Admissions Rating	86
# of applicants	54,072
% of applicants accepted	80
% of acceptees attending	19

FIRST-YEAR PROFILE

Testing policy	Test Optional
Range SAT composite	1090–1370
Range SAT EBRW	550–680
Range SAT math	530–690
Range ACT composite	22–31
# submitting SAT scores	1,668
% submitting SAT scores	21
# submitting ACT scores	4,431
% submitting ACT scores	55
Average HS GPA	3.8
% frosh submitting high school GPA	99
% graduated top 10% of class	49
% graduated top 25% of class	64
% graduated top 50% of class	84

DEADLINES

Regular	
Priority	2/1
Notification	Rolling, 7/15
Nonfall registration?	Yes

APPLICANTS OFTEN PREFER

Florida State University; University of Georgia; University of Tennessee—Knoxville

APPLICANTS SOMETIMES PREFER

Auburn University; The University of Alabama—Birmingham; University of Florida

FINANCIAL FACTS

Financial Aid Rating	80
Annual in-state tuition	$11,100
Annual out-of-state tuition	$31,460
Room and board	$12,296
Required fees	$840
Books and supplies	$800
Average frosh need-based scholarship	$15,166
Average UG need-based scholarship	$13,064
% needy frosh rec. need-based scholarship or grant aid	85
% needy UG rec. need-based scholarship or grant aid	78
% needy frosh rec. non-need-based scholarship or grant aid	75
% needy UG rec. non-need-based scholarship or grant aid	64
% needy frosh rec. need-based self-help aid	56
% needy UG rec. need-based self-help aid	66
% frosh rec. any financial aid	86
% UG rec. any financial aid	79
% UG borrow to pay for school	48
Average cumulative indebtedness	$38,615
% frosh need fully met	26
% ugrads need fully met	24
Average % of frosh need met	60
Average % of ugrad need met	57

UNIVERSITY OF ARIZONA

1200 E University Blvd, Tucson, AZ 85721-0066 • Admissions: 520-621-2211 • Fax: 520-621-9799

STUDENTS SAY "..."

Academics

The University of Arizona is a public university that blends a deep history with innovative, cutting edge research. The school offers its 40,000 undergraduates more than 150 majors spread across 20 colleges (and even more specialized schools within), and students "can choose from a variety of majors and minors and structure your own studies" in any way they see fit. The school highly emphasizes "communicating with its students and keeping up to date with student life," a service that extends to graduates as well, thanks to a "supportive and large alumni network." Current enrollees looking for additional support will find tons of resources, whether that's free tutoring in most introductory level subjects or "Supplemental Instruction sessions, which are like bonus discussion sections if you want more practice."

Professors here run the gamut in terms of passion and presentation, but for the most part, they "really [care] about the material; [have] funny, interesting, or engaging lectures; and [are] extremely willing to meet outside class." Some professors use a "flipped classroom" approach, "which really [helps] create an active learning environment," and the sciences offer lab-based classes with "many hands-on activities that teach what presentations [alone] could not." Many professors "bring in guest lectors or have guest presentations," and "classrooms are often set up in a manner in which group discussion is encouraged."

Campus Life

"Amazing weather and a beautiful campus" make for a happy, sunny time that is "full of life and fun." This is "a very active community [that uses] the gyms regularly," though there's plenty of exercise simply in traversing the sprawling campus via bike or foot. Arizona is "full of spirit" and sporting events (especially football and basketball) are popular; students describe hanging out in the raucous "ZonaZoo" to show support for their teams. Thanks to the centralized Mall, it's easy to find people to hang out with during the day, and clearly posted events speak to all types of nighttime entertainment, since "Some people love to party, some people love to study." The campus "has an extremely open, comfortable atmosphere," and because "some dorms cater to a certain audience with the in-hall communities," it's remarkably easy to find your niche. The community feel is a real bonus for students, who love that "it's a massive university, yet everyone knows everyone."

Student Body

Around 60 percent of students hail from Arizona in this diverse population that is "very passionate about what it means to Wildcat and [the] excessive amounts of school pride" that come with it. The university's sheer size means there are "people from all over the world studying hundreds of different things" and hence "there is a club, frat, sorority, [or] group to join for everyone to feel a part of something greater and get encouragement." An Arizona student "knows the importance of both studies and life experiences for a well-rounded college experience" and takes studying as seriously as the relaxing: "We all know that at the end of the day we're all here to get that degree, despite the fun we all have."

UNIVERSITY OF ARIZONA

Financial Aid: 520-621-1858 • E-Mail: admissions@arizona.edu • Website: www.arizona.edu

THE PRINCETON REVIEW SAYS

Admissions

The school reports that its standardized testing policy for use in admission for Fall 2024 is Test Optional. The 2024 testing policy will be permanent. The Princeton Review suggests that interested applicants consult with the school for the most up-to-date standardized testing policies. *Very important factors considered include:* rigor of secondary school record, academic GPA. *Important factors considered include:* extracurricular activities, talent/ ability, character/personal qualities, level of applicant's interest. *Other factors considered include:* class rank, standardized test scores, application essay, recommendation(s), volunteer work, work experience. High school diploma is required and GED is accepted. *Academic units required:* 4 English, 4 math, 3 science, 3 science labs, 2 foreign language, 2 social studies, 1 fine arts or career and technical education.

Financial Aid

Students should submit: FAFSA; Institution's own financial aid form. Priority filing deadline is 4/1. The Princeton Review suggests that all financial aid forms be submitted as soon as possible (see page 5 for a note on the FAFSA). *Need-based scholarships/grants offered:* College/ university scholarship or grant aid from institutional funds; Federal Pell; Private scholarships; SEOG; State scholarships/grants. *Loan aid offered:* Direct PLUS loans; Direct Subsidized Loans; Direct Unsubsidized Loans; College/university loans from institutional funds; Federal Nursing Loans; State Loans. Admitted students will be notified of awards on a rolling basis beginning 2/1. Federal Work-Study Program available. Institutional employment available.

The Inside Word

Admission to the University of Arizona is competitive, and you'll need to demonstrate achievement in college prep courses. Candidates applying from within the state who graduate in the top 25 percent of their class or have a minimum unweighted GPA of 3.0 in core competencies and meet all course requirements gain automatic acceptance through the assured admission program. Applicants should also recognize that some programs, such as the College of Engineering, College of Nursing, and College of Fine Arts, mandate additional materials and requirements.

THE SCHOOL SAYS "..."

From the Admissions Office

"From day one, University of Arizona students step into an unrivaled mix of academics, student life, and experiential learning enhanced with opportunities that only a top research institution can offer. A sunny campus, welcoming atmosphere, and diverse student body offer a place for everyone to pursue their passions. Students spend their days learning from a world-class faculty of Pulitzer and Nobel Prize winners, participating in countless recreation activities, and being valued members of a close-knit, active community. Through services like Student Engagement and Career Development, the university connects students with education-enhancing experiences like internships, research, or volunteering. The recently completed Student Success District in the heart of campus tremendously elevates student support in areas like academics, career, and health and wellness. Thanks to the knowledge and experience they gain here, Wildcats are often sought after by top employers because they graduate with a diverse set of knowledge and skills that can apply to the workplace. As the network of more than 300,000 global alumni can attest to, an Arizona education pays you back for a lifetime—one of the many reasons why Arizona is repeatedly recognized for its outstanding academics and exceptional value. From groundbreaking research to a bustling student life with 400+ student clubs, cultural centers, and unrivaled school spirit with winning athletics programs, the University of Arizona offers an ideal college experience."

SELECTIVITY

Admissions Rating	85
# of applicants	48,200
% of applicants accepted	87
% of acceptees attending	21

FIRST-YEAR PROFILE

Testing policy	Test Optional
Range SAT composite	1140–1360
Range SAT EBRW	560–680
Range SAT math	560–690
Range ACT composite	21–29
# submitting SAT scores	1,040
% submitting SAT scores	12
# submitting ACT scores	1,564
% submitting ACT scores	18
Average HS GPA	3.5
% frosh submitting high school GPA	100
% graduated top 10% of class	39
% graduated top 25% of class	66
% graduated top 50% of class	88

DEADLINES

Regular	
Deadline	5/2
Notification	Rolling, 8/15
Nonfall registration?	Yes

APPLICANTS ALSO LOOK AT

Arizona State University; University of Colorado Boulder; University of Oregon

FINANCIAL FACTS

Financial Aid Rating	81
Annual in-state tuition	$10,990
Annual in-state tuition (first-year)	$11,299
Annual out-of-state tuition	$33,739
Annual out-of-state tuition (first-year)	$35,821
Room and board	$13,450
Required fees	$1,414
Required fees (first-year)	$1,437
Books and supplies	$900
Average frosh need-based scholarship	$14,165
Average UG need-based scholarship	$12,906
% needy frosh rec. need-based scholarship or grant aid	96
% needy UG rec. need-based scholarship or grant aid	92
% needy frosh rec. non-need-based scholarship or grant aid	20
% needy UG rec. non-need-based scholarship or grant aid	13
% needy frosh rec. need-based self-help aid	32
% needy UG rec. need-based self-help aid	45
% frosh rec. any financial aid	95
% UG rec. any financial aid	82
% UG borrow to pay for school	44
Average cumulative indebtedness	$25,224
% frosh need fully met	22
% ugrads need fully met	16
Average % of frosh need met	66
Average % of ugrad need met	63

UNIVERSITY OF ARKANSAS—FAYETTEVILLE

University of Arkansas—Fayetteville, Fayetteville, AR 72701 • Admissions: 479-575-2000 • Fax: 479-575-7515

STUDENTS SAY "..."

Academics
The University of Arkansas—Fayetteville "is a large university with a community feel. It's big enough to have a lot of great opportunities, but small enough you see people you know on campus." With Fayetteville's outdoorsy culture, some students "would describe [the school] as a weird cross between Southern and hippie." Research opportunities abound, and prospective students are drawn to both the Honors College and the Sam Walton School of Business. Students also single out U of A's "strong engineering program, with the depth and diversity in every discipline from mechanical to computer science [and] biomedical." Even with the relaxed atmosphere—one student coins it as "Fayettechill"—students say that there are "tough programs that really make you work for your grade so you can be sure you are worth your degree." Professors are hit or miss; while some students say, "Most of my professors are extremely helpful," others lament that while "I enjoy most of my professors, but I do sometimes get the impression that they don't care about my individual success." Students in the larger majors say they often lack individualized attention. As one student points out: "My major is located in a smaller department so I know my professors very well. However, in larger classes and departments it is easy to 'get lost' or go unnoticed."

Campus Life
Football (this is Razorback country) and Greek activities are prevalent on campus, though some students say, "The school is very centered around Greek life, so for some students it is harder for them to find their place outside of Greek life." The school's location in the Ozark Mountains gives students ample opportunities for "hiking, kayaking, [and] rock climbing" on the weekends. Popular destinations "nearby to take daytrips with your friends [include] Devil's Den or Crystal Bridges." Students say, "The pace of life is comfortably slow, but still full of fun opportunities," and Fayetteville "is an incredibly vibrant city because it is a refreshing combination of elements of the old South and collegiate culture." One popular destination is Dickson Street, "home to a plethora of bars and restaurants." On campus, when the Razorbacks are playing, "The whole state turns up to 'Call the Hogs' on to victory." For those who aren't as interested in athletics, luckily, a "school this big has enough people of diverse interests to create a club or event almost incredibly tailored to you."

Student Body
Students describe their peers as "friendly" and living "relaxed lifestyles" but are quick to point out that this doesn't mean "they are not high-achieving students." In general, students say they're an "adventurous, fun loving, welcoming, genuine, [and] creative" bunch. While some say the school is "very diverse for a Southern university," others lament the lack of diversity and say that the campus is "very much white, upper-middle class" students from Arkansas and the surrounding states, noting that more could be done in "advocating for marginalized groups." But despite the lack of diversity, students say that their peers are "accepting" and "kind," and that "the campus has a very warm feeling to it."

UNIVERSITY OF ARKANSAS—FAYETTEVILLE

Financial Aid: 479-575-3806 • E-Mail: uofa@uark.edu • Website: www.uark.edu

THE PRINCETON REVIEW SAYS

Admissions

The school reports that its standardized testing policy for use in admission for Fall 2024 will remain Test Free, as it has been since 2022. *Very important factors considered include:* academic GPA. *Important factors considered include:* standardized test scores. *Other factors considered include:* rigor of secondary school record, class rank, application essay, recommendation(s), extracurricular activities, talent/ability, character/personal qualities, first generation, alumni/ae relation, geographical residence, state residency, volunteer work, work experience. High school diploma is required and GED is accepted. *Academic units required:* 4 English, 4 math, 3 science, 1 science lab, 1 social studies, 2 history, 2 academic electives. *Academic units recommended:* 4 English, 4 math, 3 science, 1 science lab, 2 foreign language, 1 social studies, 2 history, 2 academic electives.

Financial Aid

Students should submit: FAFSA. Priority filing deadline is 3/15. The Princeton Review suggests that all financial aid forms be submitted as soon as possible (see page 5 for a note on the FAFSA). *Need-based scholarships/grants offered:* College/university scholarship or grant aid from institutional funds; Federal Pell; Private scholarships; SEOG; State scholarships/grants. *Loan aid offered:* Direct PLUS loans; Direct Subsidized Loans; Direct Unsubsidized Loans; State Loans. Admitted students will be notified of awards on a rolling basis beginning 4/1. Federal Work-Study Program available. Institutional employment available.

The Inside Word

Please note that test scores may still be required for placement purposes and for state reporting, and must be submitted by all students by May 1. University of Arkansas has a rolling admissions policy, with the process beginning on September 15 for admission next fall. It's always in a prospective student's best interest to apply as early as possible.

THE SCHOOL SAYS "..."

From the Admissions Office

"The University of Arkansas is located in Fayetteville, a town consistently listed among the nation's top five best places to live. The university promotes undergraduate research in nearly every discipline and provides affordable higher education with competitively priced tuition and generous financial aid. Founded in 1871 as a land-grant institution, the U of A is the flagship campus of the UA System, home to 10 colleges and schools offering nearly 270 academic programs, the most in the state. Though more than 30,000 enroll at the U of A, students benefit from a low student-to-faculty ratio—currently 20:1—that prioritizes personal attention and guidance from professors who are passionate about teaching. Likewise, the Carnegie Foundation recognizes the U of A among the top U.S. universities with the highest levels of research activity, and undergraduates regularly win national honors, including some of the nation's top scholarships. The U of A has produced 11 Rhodes Scholars; 60 Goldwater Scholars; 155 National Science Foundation Graduate Research Fellows; 8 Marshall Scholars; 25 Truman Scholars; and 99 Fulbright Students, among others. Students have access to opportunities and amenities throughout Northwest Arkansas, a hub for business and research innovation and home to multiple Fortune 500 companies—including Walmart, Tyson Foods, and J.B. Hunt Transport Services—and a thriving art scene that are all steps away from outdoor adventure in one of the most beautiful areas in the country."

SELECTIVITY

Admissions Rating	85
# of applicants	26,210
% of applicants accepted	79
% of acceptees attending	34
# offered a place on the wait list	343
% accepting a place on wait list	57
% admitted from wait list	8

FIRST-YEAR PROFILE

Testing policy	Test Optional
Range SAT composite	1040–1210
Range SAT EBRW	520–610
Range SAT math	510–610
Range ACT composite	21–28
# submitting SAT scores	2,179
% submitting SAT scores	31
# submitting ACT scores	5,315
% submitting ACT scores	75
Average HS GPA	3.8
% frosh submitting high school GPA	100
% graduated top 10% of class	25
% graduated top 25% of class	54
% graduated top 50% of class	86

DEADLINES

Early action	
Deadline	11/1
Notification	12/15
Regular	
Priority	11/1
Deadline	8/1
Notification	Rolling, 10/1
Nonfall registration?	Yes

APPLICANTS ALSO LOOK AT

Baylor University; Oklahoma State University; Texas A&M University—College Station; Texas Christian University; Texas State University; Texas Tech University; The University of Texas at Austin; University of Oklahoma

FINANCIAL FACTS

Financial Aid Rating	79
Annual in-state tuition	$7,666
Annual out-of-state tuition	$25,420
Room and board	$12,368
Required fees	$1,990
Books and supplies	$1,100
Average frosh need-based scholarship	$8,116
Average UG need-based scholarship	$8,439
% needy frosh rec. need-based scholarship or grant aid	79
% needy UG rec. need-based scholarship or grant aid	76
% needy frosh rec. non-need-based scholarship or grant aid	12
% needy UG rec. non-need-based scholarship or grant aid	10
% needy frosh rec. need-based self-help aid	62
% needy UG rec. need-based self-help aid	62
% frosh rec. any financial aid	76
% UG rec. any financial aid	68
% UG borrow to pay for school	47
Average cumulative indebtedness	$29,001
% frosh need fully met	15
% ugrads need fully met	14
Average % of frosh need met	56
Average % of ugrad need met	56

UNIVERSITY OF CALIFORNIA—BERKELEY

110 Sproul Hall, Berkeley, CA 94720-5800 • Admissions: 510-642-6000

STUDENTS SAY "..."

Academics

The flagship campus of the University of California school system with a "highly respectable name," UC Berkeley "has great faculty, great research, great classes, and everyone knows it." The school "really encourages us to go out and learn, both inside and outside the classroom," and there is a real commitment to "a well- rounded, diverse education" that permeates the curriculum. "Berkeley is defined by its open, liberal education and culture for independent and collaborative thinking across all fields," sums up a senior molecular toxicology major.

Professors here are "fantastic," "the best in their fields," and each "offers a diverse perspective" toward the academic experience. There are some complaints that larger freshman courses can be "somewhat terrible" and "experience from professors can range widely" (though graduate student instructors "are very accessible and helpful"), but it is universally agreed that "after getting through lower division prerequisite classes, [the] academic experience has significantly improved." All faculty "have full command of their subjects and are determined to find an answer to anything they don't know, within their discipline."

UC Berkeley is known for having "some of the best engineering programs across the board among colleges," and it doesn't hurt that the school's Silicon Valley home is the "best location in the country for entrepreneurship and innovation." "Top-notch" research abounds, and there are "plenty of opportunities for undergrads to engage in it." "Berkeley will offer you all the opportunity you can handle, it's up to you to take hold of it," says a student.

Campus Life

There's "a constant buzz of student activity that drives everyday life" at Cal, where "academics are a priority" and "every single person has something that they are very passionate about and talking to them for five minutes about it makes you wonder if you should change your major." Students also really appreciate all of the tradition present at Cal. "It's a great choice for students who want the feeling of a big state school but want to also be pushed to their limits," says one. Berkeley is "very hard so free time isn't like it is at other places," but an "amazing community" of student-run organizations and "clubs, sports, student-run classes, seminars, [and] research opportunities" are among the "many different venues for people to find their passion." There's a lot to do off-campus in the downtown Berkeley area, and using the BART is "really convenient and time-saving to go to San Francisco." On campus, there is everything "from frat houses to coffee shop discussions, hiking the fire trails to studying for finals." In those moments that studying abates (a particular rarity for engineers), a lot of students enjoy going to football games, restaurant hopping, or (especially during welcome week) party hopping. Many people here do like to party and drink, but "if that's not your style, there are plenty of others to spend time with."

Student Body

Berkeley is a large school, so clusters naturally form along lines such as major or dorm, but all "mix among each other easily." "From clubs to DeCal courses, there is no way a student will not make a group of friends while here at Cal," says a junior. Most Berkeley students are generally "politically liberal, nonreligious, and pretty independent," and there is a large Asian student contingent here. One of the defining characteristics of a Cal student is "the ability to hold high-level conversation about basically anything." Everyone is accepted in here, "regardless of their sexual orientation, religion, or political beliefs."

UNIVERSITY OF CALIFORNIA—BERKELEY

Website: www.berkeley.edu

THE PRINCETON REVIEW SAYS

Admissions

The school reports that its standardized testing policy for use in admission for Fall 2024 is Test Free. It is unknown at this time if the 2024 testing policy will be permanent. The Princeton Review suggests that interested applicants consult with the school for the most up-to-date standardized testing policies. *Very important factors considered include:* rigor of secondary school record, academic GPA, application essay. *Important factors considered include:* extracurricular activities, character/personal qualities, volunteer work, work experience. *Other factors considered include:* standardized test scores, recommendation(s), talent/ability, first generation, state residency. High school diploma is required and GED is accepted. *Academic units required:* 4 English, 3 math, 2 science, 2 science labs, 2 foreign language, 2 history, 1 visual/performing arts, 1 academic elective. *Academic units recommended:* 4 English, 4 math, 3 science, 3 science labs, 3 foreign language, 2 history, 1 visual/performing arts, 1 academic elective.

Financial Aid

Students should submit: FAFSA; State aid form. Priority filing deadline is 3/2. The Princeton Review suggests that all financial aid forms be submitted as soon as possible (see page 5 for a note on the FAFSA). *Need-based scholarships/grants offered:* College/university scholarship or grant aid from institutional funds; Federal Pell; Private scholarships; SEOG; State scholarships/grants. *Loan aid offered:* Direct PLUS loans; Direct Subsidized Loans; Direct Unsubsidized Loans; College/university loans from institutional funds; State Loans. Admitted students will be notified of awards on or about 3/31. Federal Work-Study Program available. Institutional employment available.

The Inside Word

UC Berkeley is a top-notch public university with a well-regarded English and Literature department. Importance is placed on the totality of a student's application with a joint focus on the personal statement and academic excellence as noted by a student's GPA. Class rank isn't considered. The school is home to an incredible amount of students with as wide a range of interests. Successful applicants here are generally stellar both academically and personally. Applications, especially the personal statement, should create a picture of a unique candidate with a diversity of skills to offer this active community.

THE SCHOOL SAYS "..."

From the Admissions Office

"One of the top public universities in the nation and the world, the University of California—Berkeley offers a vast range of courses and a full menu of extracurricular activities. We challenge the status quo and make discoveries that reshape the future. As the birthplace of the Free Speech Movement, our students develop their own voices and stand up for what they believe. They find community in a place where diversity of all kinds is celebrated, nurtured, and valued. Berkeley's academic programs are internationally recognized for their excellence, and undergraduates can choose from over 100 majors. Students have access to twenty-three specialized libraries on campus and distinguished museums of anthropology, paleontology, and science. Many work directly with renowned faculty through the Undergraduate Research Apprentice Program, initiate their own research project, or join dozens of programs across campus. While here, we encourage our students to discover, connect, engage and reflect."

SELECTIVITY

Admissions Rating	92
# of applicants	128,226
% of applicants accepted	11
% of acceptees attending	46
# offered a place on the wait list	8,456
% accepting a place on wait list	55
% admitted from wait list	1

FIRST-YEAR PROFILE

Testing policy	Test Free
Average HS GPA	3.9
% frosh submitting high school GPA	100

DEADLINES

Regular	
Deadline	11/30
Notification	3/31
Nonfall registration?	Yes

FINANCIAL FACTS

Financial Aid Rating	83
Annual in-state tuition	$11,928
Annual out-of-state tuition	$42,954
Room and board	$21,168
Required fees	$3,244
Required fees (first-year)	$3,292
Books and supplies	$1,140
Average frosh need-based scholarship	$23,837
Average UG need-based scholarship	$23,585
% needy frosh rec. need-based scholarship or grant aid	90
% needy UG rec. need-based scholarship or grant aid	95
% needy frosh rec. non-need-based scholarship or grant aid	3
% needy UG rec. non-need-based scholarship or grant aid	2
% needy frosh rec. need-based self-help aid	60
% needy UG rec. need-based self-help aid	58
% frosh rec. any financial aid	50
% UG rec. any financial aid	52
% UG borrow to pay for school	28
Average cumulative indebtedness	$17,511
% frosh need fully met	23
% ugrads need fully met	27
Average % of frosh need met	76
Average % of ugrad need met	79

UNIVERSITY OF CALIFORNIA—DAVIS

One Shields Ave, Davis, CA 95616 • Admissions: 530-752-1011 • Fax: 530-752-1280

CAMPUS LIFE

Quality of Life Rating	86
Fire Safety Rating	96
Green Rating	97
Type of school	Public
Environment	Town

STUDENTS

Total undergrad enrollment	31,162
% male/female/another gender	39/61/0
% from out of state	5
% frosh from public high school	84
% frosh live on campus	28
% ugrads live on campus	15
# of fraternities (% join)	28 (5)
# of sororities (% join)	21 (7)
% African American	2
% Asian	28
% White	21
% Hispanic	24
% Native American	<1
% Pacific Islander	<1
% Two or more races	6
% Race and/or ethnicity unknown	2
% international	16
# of countries represented	121

SURVEY SAYS . . .

Students are happy
Students environmentally aware
Students love Davis, CA

ACADEMICS

Academic Rating	77
% students returning for sophomore year	92
% students graduating within 4 years	63
% students graduating within 6 years	87
Calendar	Quarter
Student/faculty ratio	20:1
Profs interesting rating	85
Profs accessible rating	89

Most classes have 20–29 students.
Most lab/discussion sessions have
  20–29 students.

MOST POPULAR MAJORS

Economics, General; Biology/Biological Sciences,
General; Psychology, General

STUDENTS SAY ". . ."

Academics

Situated on a "large campus [with] lots of land" in northern California, the University of California Davis is "a prestigious research university with great professors and brilliant students." With a longtime "focus on the agriculture and biological science," Davis has cultivated a "strong science-based education." Students also praise its "other great programs such as engineering and political science," as well as the "large variety of majors and [programs] offered" by the university. "Davis does have a fast-paced quarter system," but the "resources available to assist students" help them "feel at ease with their quarters." Beyond the "abundant research, internship, and job opportunities," Davis students rave about the support they receive from "tutoring and advising resources, opportunities to have a focus within each major, study abroad opportunities," and "all the counselors who can answer every question." "Professors here are true experts," and they have generated "a great research legacy in the animal, ag, environmental, health, and food sciences." "Top researchers are clearly going to get a place at UC Davis," which means that "classes are full of challenging, hands-on experiences." Students benefit from "passionate and devoted" scholars who "have their own research projects going on, and apply what they are teaching to their work." Students point out that "research skills do not translate into teaching skills," so some professors who "are pioneers," "superb at research," "and enthusiastic about their field of study" "might not be too good at teaching." But even when professors "seem to be more focused on research," "teaching assistants who want to help students" and "are also really great and amazing people" provide support. These stellar "TAs have a HUGE impact on classes" and contribute to the "very supportive campus community." Overall, UC Davis students agree that "the majority of my professors [care] very deeply about teaching" and provide a "challenging, but rewarding and successful academic experience."

Campus Life

UC Davis students boast about belonging to a "green school" that "promotes sustainability." Many students gravitate toward "outdoor activities to fill their time," like "pick-up soccer, slack lining," visiting the local farmers market or "reading at the arboretum." Students tell us that "even if you don't have a car," the "bike paths make it really easy to get around the city and campus" and the "free convenient bus systems" ensure there are "plenty of transportation options" available to students. Many say that Davis owes its "relaxed vibe" to the "close-knit" campus community where "everyone is very supportive of each other" and to the surrounding town that "supports the school." But many students point out that "despite the friendly community, we can still be educationally competitive." The "fast paced quarter system" keeps students busy, but students still say they maintain a good "balance between school life and their social life because of all the opportunities and activities to do on campus." With "700+ clubs on campus including seventy-one Greek organizations," many students spend their weeknights at club events. The downtown Davis nightlife is "mostly low-key," but students can enjoy "good food, open mic night, trivia night," "local shows, line dancing, and just about everything in between." And because it is near "Tahoe, San Francisco, [and] Napa," Davis is "a great location for day trips or weekend trips."

Student Body

Davis is a "pretty diverse community" where most students are "very friendly and thoughtful" and "few are quick to judge." As one undergrad notes, "Most students spend their days biking furiously from class to class," but "everyone is very nice and welcoming." "Anyone can ask any student for directions and the student will gladly stop biking to help out." While Davis "is a top university, you don't feel like everyone is competing against you" and "help from your peers" is easy to find. And while Davis students "are academically rigorous," they are "quirky and [creative]" too, creating "the perfect mixture of serious about studying and down to earth and fun." They like to make the most of the "beautiful campus," and "on sunny days, the quad is always filled with students lying down or sleeping in the hammocks." "Most people get involved in one of the clubs or athletics" groups, and "most are also very open to making new friends or trying something new."

UNIVERSITY OF CALIFORNIA—DAVIS

Financial Aid: 530-752-2396 • E-Mail: undergraduateadmissions@ucdavis.edu • Website: www.ucdavis.edu

THE PRINCETON REVIEW SAYS

Admissions

The school reports that its standardized testing policy for use in admission for Fall 2024 is Test Free. It is unknown at this time if the 2024 testing policy will be permanent. The Princeton Review suggests that interested applicants consult with the school for the most up-to-date standardized testing policies. *Very important factors considered include:* rigor of secondary school record, academic GPA, application essay. *Important factors considered include:* extracurricular activities, talent/ability, character/personal qualities, volunteer work. *Other factors considered include:* standardized test scores, first generation, state residency, work experience. High school diploma is required and GED is accepted. *Academic units required:* 4 English, 3 math, 2 science, 2 science labs, 2 foreign language, 1 social studies, 1 history, 1 visual/performing arts, 1 academic elective. *Academic units recommended:* 4 English, 4 math, 3 science, 3 science labs, 3 foreign language, 1 social studies, 1 history, 1 visual/performing arts, 1 academic elective.

Financial Aid

Students should submit: FAFSA; State aid form. Priority filing deadline is 3/2. The Princeton Review suggests that all financial aid forms be submitted as soon as possible (see page 5 for a note on the FAFSA). *Need-based scholarships/grants offered:* College/university scholarship or grant aid from institutional funds; Federal Pell; Private scholarships; SEOG; State scholarships/grants. *Loan aid offered:* Direct PLUS loans; Direct Subsidized Loans; Direct Unsubsidized Loans; College/university loans from institutional funds; State Loans. Admitted students will be notified of awards on a rolling basis beginning 3/12. Federal Work-Study Program available. Institutional employment available.

The Inside Word

Admission to UC Davis is not as competitive as, say, admission to Berkeley. Nevertheless, every school in the UC system is world-class, and the UC system in general is geared toward the best and brightest of not only California's high school and community college students but the nation and the globe.

THE SCHOOL SAYS "..."

From the Admissions Office

"UC Davis is one of the world's top public research universities, providing undergraduates with a wealth of research opportunities and challenging academics in more than 100 majors. Collegiality is a hallmark of the UC Davis experience, encouraging students to ask questions, explore new avenues of study, and work alongside faculty members engaged in solving the critical issues facing society today. UC Davis Aggies embrace a culture where what's considered different is the norm, challenging expectations and putting those ideas to the test through capstone projects, internships, studying abroad, and volunteering in programs like our student-run community clinics.

"UC Davis students are part of an active, diverse student community immersed in the arts and sciences. Aggies enjoy world-class cultural programs at the Robert and Margrit Mondavi Center for the Performing Arts, cheer on our 25 NCAA Division I sports teams, ride at the only Equestrian Center in the UC system, and stay fit at the Activities and Recreation Center. The friendly, supportive nature of our campus and surrounding community welcomes exploration of all kinds: learning about new cultures at a cultural celebration, connecting with students at a residence hall living-learning community, meeting new friends through our more than 800 student-run organizations, or building a career network through internships and research opportunities.

"UC Davis is a place for students who see a future that's not yet been conceived, and who thrive when challenged. This spirit is reflected in the income potential and career successes of our graduates. Join us and apply this fall."

SELECTIVITY

Admissions Rating	91
# of applicants	76,225
% of applicants accepted	46
% of acceptees attending	17
# offered a place on the wait list	13,092
% accepting a place on wait list	38
% admitted from wait list	79

FIRST-YEAR PROFILE

Testing policy	Test Free
Range SAT composite	1160–1370
Range SAT EBRW	560–670
Range SAT math	580–730
Range ACT composite	25–31
# submitting SAT scores	4,787
% submitting SAT scores	78
# submitting ACT scores	1,326
% submitting ACT scores	22
Average HS GPA	4.0
% frosh submitting high school GPA	100

DEADLINES

Regular	
Deadline	11/30
Notification	3/31
Nonfall registration?	No

FINANCIAL FACTS

Financial Aid Rating	81
Annual in-state tuition	$11,442
Annual out-of-state tuition	$41,196
Required fees	$3,212
Books and supplies	$1,197
Average frosh need-based scholarship	$19,830
Average UG need-based scholarship	$19,383
% needy frosh rec. need-based scholarship or grant aid	96
% needy UG rec. need-based scholarship or grant aid	97
% needy frosh rec. non-need-based scholarship or grant aid	3
% needy UG rec. non-need-based scholarship or grant aid	2
% needy frosh rec. need-based self-help aid	42
% needy UG rec. need-based self-help aid	41
% frosh rec. any financial aid	67
% UG rec. any financial aid	71
% UG borrow to pay for school	45
Average cumulative indebtedness	$17,736
% frosh need fully met	20
% ugrads need fully met	19
Average % of frosh need met	80
Average % of ugrad need met	79

UNIVERSITY OF CALIFORNIA—IRVINE

University of California-Irvine, Irvine, CA 92697 • Admissions: 949-824-5011 • Fax: 949-824-2951

STUDENTS SAY ". . ."

Academics

Though the University of California—Irvine was only recently founded in 1965; as a public research university in the California system, it already offers 87 bachelor's degrees to nearly 30,000 students. The proximity to Los Angeles "gives students a lot of educational opportunities" but also feels set apart enough to promote on-campus collaboration in "a beautiful and constructive atmosphere." Any student willing to work hard—the "academic standard is…super high at UC Irvine, which encourages students to excel and try their hardest in their studies"—will find a place to follow their dreams here.

Students emphasize that the classrooms here are active: "We get to talk about what we learn during class instead of passively learning" and there's a "learning of the material through hands-on experiences and participation." It works, because "professors are well-educated and knowledgeable [and] helpful when students have questions" and "do an excellent job of bringing lecture material into applicable daily life situations." The atmosphere also encourages students to utilize the "many undergraduate research opportunities," with equally "many resources both provided by the school and the professors." As far as administration goes, the school "strives to understand each student's unique situation (personal, family, financial, and academic) and accommodate their needs." And the school's tutoring center, which "definitely helps with intuition and deeper understanding" helps to keep students on track.

Campus Life

One of UCI's greatest strengths is that "everyone can find some form of community on campus or people willing to help them out with their needs." There are "clubs and activities for everyone whether or not you may think you fit in." One student notes that the ARC (Anteater Recreation Center) has "lots of different options, like badminton, ping pong, and rock climbing" and that you can play pool in the main lobbies of some dorms. Students also note that there's a global range to activities: "boba tea and anime are extremely popular" and "there are many local restaurants that are known for good food." The "campus and surrounding area is very safe" and "the community is also quite involved," with plenty of chances to take part in service volunteering. There is a "really nice park in the middle of campus" and the "peaceful and big campus…never feels boring or restricting." Though the social scene can be somewhat quiet, there are always people "eating on campus or studying together," and "travel becomes much easier if you have friends willing to go with you."

Student Body

UCI comprises "a diverse group of ambitious youths from all walks of life"—students note the "significant population of commuters and international students"—who come from "a variety of racial, ethnic, and cultural backgrounds." Though the university is competitive, "it is not cutthroat and students really strive to see the well-being of their fellow peers," and everyone is "driven and willing to work toward what they want." There "is an air of open friendliness" that is "very inclusive and promotes a safe and welcoming atmosphere for students." UCI also has a large "number of first-generation students who seem to have built a special community amongst themselves," but as a whole it "feels as though everyone is connected and on the same page."

UNIVERSITY OF CALIFORNIA—IRVINE

Financial Aid: 949-824-5337 • E-Mail: admissions@uci.edu • Website: www.uci.edu

THE PRINCETON REVIEW SAYS

Admissions

The school reports that its standardized testing policy for use in admission for Fall 2024 is Test Free. It is unknown at this time if the 2024 testing policy will be permanent. The Princeton Review suggests that interested applicants consult with the school for the most up-to-date standardized testing policies. *Very important factors considered include:* rigor of secondary school record, academic GPA, application essay, extracurricular activities, talent/ability, volunteer work, work experience. *Important factors considered include:* character/personal qualities. *Other factors considered include:* first generation, geographical residence, state residency. High school diploma is required and GED is accepted. *Academic units required:* 4 English, 3 math, 2 science, 2 science labs, 2 foreign language, 2 history, 1 visual/performing arts, 1 academic elective. *Academic units recommended:* 4 English, 4 math, 3 science, 3 science labs, 3 foreign language, 2 history, 1 visual/performing arts, 1 academic elective.

Financial Aid

Students should submit: FAFSA; State aid form. Priority filing deadline is 3/2. The Princeton Review suggests that all financial aid forms be submitted as soon as possible (see page 5 for a note on the FAFSA). *Need-based scholarships/grants offered:* College/university scholarship or grant aid from institutional funds; Federal Pell; Private scholarships; SEOG; State scholarships/grants. *Loan aid offered:* Direct PLUS loans; Direct Subsidized Loans; Direct Unsubsidized Loans; College/university loans from institutional funds; Federal Nursing Loans. Admitted students will be notified of awards on a rolling basis beginning 4/1. Federal Work-Study Program available. Institutional employment available.

The Inside Word

University of California—Irvine is considered one of the top ten public universities in the country, and application numbers are expectedly high. Over 100,000 vie for a position here, so while the school is large, only 30% of those are accepted. As a part of the University of California system, UCI is Test Free, meaning that standardized tests won't be reviewed, and letters of recommendation are not accepted. It's no surprise, then, that the majority of those accepted are in at least the top 10% of their class; if you think you're on the bubble, review the California system's method of evaluating your GPA.

THE SCHOOL SAYS "..."

From the Admissions Office

"We like that you do things differently. So do we.

"At UCI, we believe in the infinitely curious. Our students are the tinkerers, the dreamers, and the courageous of thought. They are inspiring, motivated, and they care about the world around them. And they aren't afraid to go where others won't.

"No other college or university nurtures fearless, independent thought like UCI. We take you beyond the classroom to see possibility where others only see the impossible.

"One of the top public universities in the country, UCI offers more than 85 undergraduate degree programs and the opportunity to work alongside internationally renowned faculty producing groundbreaking work. In fact, by the time you are a senior, 73 percent of your graduating class will have participated in undergraduate research.

"Once you become an Anteater, you become part of a supportive, tight-knit family for the rest of your life. And it begins as soon as you step on campus."

SELECTIVITY

Admissions Rating	94
# of applicants	119,199
% of applicants accepted	21
% of acceptees attending	22
# offered a place on the wait list	15,829
% accepting a place on wait list	35
% admitted from wait list	87

FIRST-YEAR PROFILE

Testing policy	Test Free
% graduated top 10% of class	98
% graduated top 25% of class	100
% graduated top 50% of class	100

DEADLINES

Regular	
Deadline	11/30
Notification	3/31
Nonfall registration?	No

FINANCIAL FACTS

Financial Aid Rating	82
Annual in-state tuition	$11,442
Annual out-of-state tuition	$41,196
Room and board	$16,135
Required fees	$2,285
Books and supplies	$1,390
Average frosh need-based scholarship	$22,257
Average UG need-based scholarship	$21,133
% needy frosh rec. need-based scholarship or grant aid	92
% needy UG rec. need-based scholarship or grant aid	95
% needy frosh rec. non-need-based scholarship or grant aid	2
% needy UG rec. non-need-based scholarship or grant aid	2
% needy frosh rec. need-based self-help aid	54
% needy UG rec. need-based self-help aid	45
% frosh rec. any financial aid	99
% UG rec. any financial aid	98
% UG borrow to pay for school	44
Average cumulative indebtedness	$17,472
% frosh need fully met	27
% ugrads need fully met	17
Average % of frosh need met	84
Average % of ugrad need met	79

UNIVERSITY OF CALIFORNIA—LOS ANGELES

405 Hilgard Avenue, Los Angeles, CA 90095-1405 • Admissions: 310-825-4321

STUDENTS SAY ". . ."

Academics
Undergrads at this esteemed university don't mince words when boasting about all that UCLA has to offer. As a geography and environmental science double-major proudly declares, "There's nothing that can't be accomplished at UCLA. The possibilities are endless, and the resources are unparalleled." Moreover, students appreciate the "ideal" location as well as the "pride of going to a Division I school with more NCAA championships than any other college/university." Perhaps more notable, "UCLA is the kind of school that pushes you to work hard academically but reminds you that interaction with people outside of the classroom is just as important." Students are continually impressed by their professors who are "leaders in their field." Indeed, most consider it "a privilege to study under them." While some undergrads caution that you might encounter some teachers simply "in it for the research," others insist, "Most professors care about their students." A political science major interjects, saying that professors "are willing to work extra hours with students and help us with anything we need." An English major concurs, sharing, "I have never had a professor that I did not feel comfortable approaching, which has made my academic experience incredibly more beneficial." As this grateful junior succinctly explains, "UCLA is the campus. The people, the weather, the academics, the sports; it has absolutely everything I could ever want."

Campus Life
There's so much "hustle and bustle" at UCLA that it would be virtually "impossible to [be] bored." While nearly everyone's "main focus is on school," most students also know how to "play hard." Indeed, "whether it be in Greek life, a club or organization, everybody has somewhere they can go to relax and have some fun. The apartments are close to campus, so nearly everybody lives in a small area with close proximity." Sports "are extremely popular here, and conversations about the Bruins are common." There are also "tons of movie showings on campus, recreation centers, pools, activities, [and] events." Additionally, students love being located in Los Angeles. A happy senior reveals, "You can take a five-minute drive and you'll be soaking in the Pacific Ocean, or take an hour drive where you can be hitting the slopes in Big Bear. You can walk down to the theater and run into Jennifer Lopez. The possibilities are endless here, with or without money."

Student Body
UCLA "is the mold that fits you." More than 30,000 undergraduates and more than 1,000 student groups virtually assure that "there is no 'typical' student" to be found at UCLA. This wide range of individuals and activities guarantees that "everyone has their niche." Certainly, the Bruin community is a "vibrant" one, and "the unmatched diversity broadens students' horizons culturally and socially." Of course, undergrads here do tread some common ground. Many define their peers as "very hardworking and ambitious," and they typically "strive for success and to do their absolute best." They "know how to have a good time, but they also know when it is time to study." Further, it's an active student body, and it often "seems like everyone is in at least one club or organization." Friendliness is another trademark of UCLA undergrads as a physiology major assures us, "It is very easy to talk to and meet new people and make new friends." Fortunately, most people are "laid-back," and while "academically invested,…[they're] not outright competitive with other students." This bio major sums up his peers easily by saying, "Everyone comes from different backgrounds with varied interests. The only common denominator is truly an appetite for excellence."

UNIVERSITY OF CALIFORNIA—LOS ANGELES

Financial Aid: 310-206-0400 • Website: www.ucla.edu

THE PRINCETON REVIEW SAYS

Admissions

The school reports that its standardized testing policy for use in admission for Fall 2024 is Test Free. The 2024 testing policy will be permanent. The Princeton Review suggests that interested applicants consult with the school for the most up-to-date standardized testing policies. *Very important factors considered include:* rigor of secondary school record, academic GPA, application essay. *Important factors considered include:* extracurricular activities, talent/ability, character/personal qualities, volunteer work, work experience. *Other factors considered include:* first generation, geographical residence, state residency. High school diploma is required and GED is accepted. *Academic units required:* 4 English, 3 math, 2 science, 2 science labs, 2 foreign language, 2 history, 1 visual/performing arts, 1 academic elective. *Academic units recommended:* 4 English, 4 math, 3 science, 3 science labs, 3 foreign language, 2 history, 1 visual/performing arts, 1 academic elective.

Financial Aid

Students should submit: FAFSA; State aid form. Priority filing deadline is 3/2. The Princeton Review suggests that all financial aid forms be submitted as soon as possible after October 1. *Need-based scholarships/grants offered:* College/university scholarship or grant aid from institutional funds; Federal Pell; Private scholarships; SEOG; State scholarships/grants. *Loan aid offered:* Direct PLUS loans; Direct Subsidized Loans; Direct Unsubsidized Loans; College/university loans from institutional funds; State Loans. Admitted students will be notified of awards on or about 3/31. Federal Work-Study Program available. Institutional employment available.

The Inside Word

Competition is fierce to secure admittance to one of the nation's top public universities. Academic success is paramount, and your GPA factors heavily into admissions decisions. You'll want to load up on challenging courses in high school. Indeed, taking advanced placement, IB, or honors classes is a must. Of course, UCLA also wants students who will actively contribute to their community, and it's also important to demonstrate commitment to extracurricular activities.

THE SCHOOL SAYS "..."

From the Admissions Office

"Undergraduates arrive at UCLA from throughout California and around the world with exceptional levels of academic preparation. They are attracted by our acclaimed degree programs, distinguished faculty, and the beauty of a park-like campus set amid the dynamism of the nation's second-largest city. UCLA's highly ranked undergraduate programs incorporate cutting-edge technology and teaching techniques that hone the critical-thinking skills and the global perspectives necessary for success in our rapidly changing world. The diversity of these programs draws strength from a student body that mirrors the cultural and ethnic vibrancy of Los Angeles. Generally ranked among the nation's top half-dozen universities, UCLA is at once distinguished and dynamic, academically rigorous, and responsive."

SELECTIVITY

Admissions Rating	92
# of applicants	149,815
% of applicants accepted	9
% of acceptees attending	50
# offered a place on the wait list	16,979
% accepting a place on wait list	66
% admitted from wait list	3

FIRST-YEAR PROFILE

Testing policy	Test Free
Average HS GPA	3.9
% frosh submitting high school GPA	99

DEADLINES

Regular	
Deadline	11/30
Notification	3/31
Nonfall registration?	No

FINANCIAL FACTS

Financial Aid Rating	84
Annual in-state tuition	$12,522
Annual out-of-state tuition	$45,096
Room and board	$17,148
Required fees	$1,230
Books and supplies	$1,574
Average frosh need-based scholarship	$24,289
Average UG need-based scholarship	$23,600
% needy frosh rec. need-based scholarship or grant aid	9
% needy UG rec. need-based scholarship or grant aid	97
% needy frosh rec. non-need-based scholarship or grant aid	4
% needy UG rec. non-need-based scholarship or grant aid	3
% needy frosh rec. need-based self-help aid	42
% needy UG rec. need-based self-help aid	43
% frosh rec. any financial aid	46
% UG rec. any financial aid	47
% UG borrow to pay for school	33
Average cumulative indebtedness	$17,920
% frosh need fully met	28
% ugrads need fully met	29
Average % of frosh need met	85
Average % of ugrad need met	84

UNIVERSITY OF CALIFORNIA—MERCED

5200 North Lake Road, Merced, CA 95343 • Admissions: 209-228-4400 • Fax: 209-228-4244

STUDENTS SAY "..."

Academic

The University of California—Merced's 2005 opening greatly expanded the access of the public California system to students of the San Joaquin Valley and created a research hub for the region. In the short time since, specialized institutes like the Health Sciences Research Institute and Center of Excellence on Health Disparities have made ground-breaking discoveries, and the students of this environmentally focused school have learned a lot. The "emphasis the school has on teaching information as it relates to sustainability is amazing" and there are "good student employment opportunities" as well as research and internship positions.

Students find this modern school to be fresh and forward-thinking, "with progressive lectures that are outstanding," and professors willing to "change up their teaching methods based on the particular class they are teaching," and to incorporate innovative pedagogy "such as rap battles to convince audience members of their research thesis." Both faculty and staff here are "warm and kind and understanding, yet challenging," and "you'll find yourself supported by the school, peers and the staff." Research is a huge part of a UCM education; as one student puts it, "getting hands-on experience...and designing our own experiments was a key tool." Additionally, the Learning Assistant initiative is a unique form of support where one "attends lecture with other students with the purpose of helping...fellow academics in their studies."

Campus Life

If you've got a car, Merced is "in the middle of California, [so] every attraction site is available to students" from nearby national parks to San Francisco and Santa Cruz. As for within the quiet and "quite peaceful" town itself, public bus transportation is available, but accessibility depends on your location. Luckily, students find Merced to be an "extremely clean campus, kept in pristine condition all the time." It's the sort of place that naturally leads to athletics, and indeed there is "a solid group of skaters on campus" and "a lot of students hit the gym" or play pickup soccer and basketball; many are "young and athletic." The school has more than 200 student organizations and "the student government hosts tons of events throughout the year," so "life as a student here is never repetitive." Attendees also note that the "student-hosted workshops we have throughout the year are quite helpful," and there are nice communal lounge areas for gaming or "where anyone can hang out and talk."

Student Body

Almost 100 percent of undergraduates hail from California, and the school leads the UC system in its proportion of students from underrepresented ethnic groups, low-income families, and first-generation attendees. "The diversity and inclusivity that UC Merced provides for students, staff, and faculty is really nice to be a part of," says a student. "Everyone comes from all over California and the vibes are good, everyone is just friendly and understanding," says a student. These are some of "the most hardworking, culturally diverse, and most of all helpful people" in the region, and "most of the students are focused on their work and being successful." Due to the size of the school (about 8,800 students in all), "it's so much easier to collaborate with other students and nothing really feels like a competition." There is "a lot of school pride and it is easy to meet new people and connect with others in your classes," and students "really have school spirit when it comes down to any school event."

UNIVERSITY OF CALIFORNIA—MERCED

Financial Aid: 209-228-7178 • E-Mail: admissions@ucmerced.edu • Website: www.ucmerced.edu

THE PRINCETON REVIEW SAYS

Admissions

The school reports that its standardized testing policy for use in admission for Fall 2024 is Test Free. The 2024 testing policy will be permanent. The Princeton Review suggests that interested applicants consult with the school for the most up-to-date standardized testing policies. *Very important factors considered include:* rigor of secondary school record, academic GPA, standardized test scores, application essay. *Important factors considered include:* extracurricular activities, talent/ability. *Other factors considered include:* recommendation(s), character/personal qualities, first generation, geographical residence, state residency, volunteer work, work experience. High school diploma is required and GED is accepted. *Academic units required:* 4 English, 3 math, 2 science, 2 science labs, 2 foreign language, 2 history, 1 visual/performing arts, 1 academic elective. *Academic units recommended:* 4 math, 3 science, 3 science labs, 3 foreign language.

Financial Aid

Students should submit: FAFSA. The Princeton Review suggests that all financial aid forms be submitted as soon as possible (see page 5 for a note on the FAFSA). *Need-based scholarships/grants offered:* Federal Pell; SEOG; State scholarships/grants. *Loan aid offered:* Direct PLUS loans; Direct Subsidized Loans; Direct Unsubsidized Loans. Admitted students will be notified of awards on a rolling basis beginning 4/1. Federal Work-Study Program available. Institutional employment available.

The Inside Word

Perhaps because it's still a newer school, Merced isn't quite as competitive as some of the other UC schools—more than 85% of applicants get in. That said, the school's emphasis on research and sustainability may create a more self-selecting group, so make sure you make the most out of your application to demonstrate Bobcat pride for peers and the world. It also helps your chances if you're coming from in-state—your GPA doesn't need to be quite as high as a 3.5 in that case, and your tuition will be substantially less as well.

THE SCHOOL SAYS "..."

From the Admissions Office

"UC Merced has earned widespread acclaim for building social mobility among first-generation and historically underrepresented young people, while advancing a research agenda that is creating new knowledge in sustainability, engineering, the sciences, humanities and more. The youngest research facility ever to earn Carnegie R2 research classification, UC Merced has five tenets that focus its institutional and intellectual priorities: educational opportunity; health care; economic revitalization; sustainability; and building civic capacity. The campus location provides a unique opportunity for research and stewardship crucial to the Central Valley and the state of California.

"Sustainability is in UC Merced's DNA. It is the only U.S. campus with every building LEED-certified and has received a platinum rating—the highest rating possible—by the Association for the Advancement of Sustainability in Higher Education. It is the first public research university in the country to achieve carbon neutrality, two years ahead of its goal. A strong relationship with Yosemite National Park enables important studies in climate change, water and biological diversity at longtime field stations, while also educating the park leaders of the future through the Yosemite Leadership Program. To accommodate its rapid growth, UC Merced recently doubled the square footage of the campus with the ambitious Merced 2020 Project, a $1.2 billion public-private partnership (P3). The first of its kind, the project is the largest P3 social infrastructure project completed in U.S. history and has received numerous awards for its design and infrastructure."

SELECTIVITY

Admissions Rating	83
# of applicants	27,795
% of applicants accepted	87
% of acceptees attending	10

FIRST-YEAR PROFILE

Testing policy	Test Free
Average HS GPA	3.5
% frosh submitting high school GPA	95
% graduated top 10% of class	13

DEADLINES

Regular	
Deadline	11/30
Notification	Rolling, 3/1
Nonfall registration?	Yes

APPLICANTS ALSO LOOK AT

University of California—Berkeley; University of California—Davis; University of California-Irvine; University of California—Los Angeles; University of California—Riverside; University of California—San Diego; University of California—Santa Barbara; University of California—Santa Cruz

FINANCIAL FACTS

Financial Aid Rating	82
Annual in-state tuition	$11,442
Annual out-of-state tuition	$41,196
Room and board	$18,887
Required fees	$2,123
Books and supplies	$1,073
Average frosh need-based scholarship	$21,558
Average UG need-based scholarship	$21,127
% needy frosh rec. need-based scholarship or grant aid	99
% needy UG rec. need-based scholarship or grant aid	99
% needy frosh rec. non-need-based scholarship or grant aid	1
% needy UG rec. non-need-based scholarship or grant aid	1
% needy frosh rec. need-based self-help aid	37
% needy UG rec. need-based self-help aid	41
% frosh rec. any financial aid	90
% UG rec. any financial aid	89
% UG borrow to pay for school	67
Average cumulative indebtedness	$17,413
% frosh need fully met	9
% ugrads need fully met	12
Average % of frosh need met	77
Average % of ugrad need met	78

UNIVERSITY OF CALIFORNIA—RIVERSIDE

900 University Ave., Riverside, CA 92521 • Admissions: 951-827-1012 • Fax: 951-827-6344

CAMPUS LIFE

Quality of Life Rating	87
Fire Safety Rating	93
Green Rating	97
Type of school	Public
Environment	City

STUDENTS

Total undergrad enrollment	22,847
% male/female/another gender	48/51/>1
% from out of state	1
% frosh from public high school	90
% frosh live on campus	68
% ugrads live on campus	35
# of fraternities (% join)	13 (2)
# of sororities (% join)	17 (4)
% African American	3
% Asian	37
% White	11
% Hispanic	39
% Native American	<1
% Pacific Islander	<1
% Two or more races	5
% Race and/or ethnicity unknown	1
% international	4
# of countries represented	93

SURVEY SAYS . . .

Recreation facilities are great
Diverse student types interact on campus
Frats and sororities are popular
Campus newspaper is popular

ACADEMICS

Academic Rating	77
% students returning for sophomore year	87
% students graduating within 4 years	62
% students graduating within 6 years	76
Calendar	Quarter
Student/faculty ratio	24:1
Profs interesting rating	85
Profs accessible rating	89

Most classes have 20–29 students.
Most lab/discussion sessions have 20–29 students.

MOST POPULAR MAJORS

Psychology, General; Business Administration and Management, General; Biology/Biological Sciences, General

STUDENTS SAY ". . ."

Academics

Undergraduates at the University of California—Riverside have the opportunity to get "a great education while also having fun." The university goes to great lengths to ensure that "everyone feels welcome and wanted on campus" and that's palpable to the students. Undergrads here also greatly benefit from all the research being conducted at Riverside. As one giddy student explains, "There are so many different projects happening in [a variety of] fields" and the opportunities to participate are quite "generous." Additionally, UCR undergrads appreciate that "there are so many programs to help student[s] stay on track academically and even more to help student[s] in academic recovery." Students have an abundance of courses and majors from which to choose; highlights include the "very prestigious entomology and agriculture departments." In general, students report that professors are "very helpful and friendly." They tend to be "passionate and engaged" as well as "knowledgeable." And they make it abundantly clear that "they love their field, their job, and their students." As one amazed student reveals, "I have not yet met a professor that wasn't happy to rearrange their plans, so they could help a student in need."

Campus Life

Boredom is virtually non-existent at UC Riverside. After all, "there is always something to do on campus throughout the day." For example, "Every week there is a mini-concert in the middle of campus to showcase a local group (small band or DJ)." There are also a number of "career workshops, movie screenings, [and] cultural events" of which to take advantage. Additionally, students have the opportunity to participate in "over 400 clubs on campus, many of which organize their own activities and will often go on excursions or trips." A number of undergrads also report that the "party scene is decent," though it's often relegated to the weekend. Outdoor enthusiasts love that UCR is adjacent to the Box Spring Mountains. Hence, there are "a plethora of trails for hiking." Plenty of students can also be found hanging at the Hub which has "a game room where you can play pool, board games or watch TV." Even more enticing, "the recreation center has a hot tub and a recreational pool with vortex current as well as lap pool. It's also possible to play volleyball, basketball, badminton, racquetball, and other games [as well as use] the rock climbing wall." But the best aspect of the rec center? It "provides free massages twice a week."

Student Body

Individuals greatly interested in UC Riverside will be delighted to learn that the school maintains a "very diverse" student body. In turn, this allows all undergrads to truly "feel welcome." Of course, the fact that most students here are "extremely friendly and supportive" also helps. One proud undergrad agrees sharing, "It is easy to approach most people and start a conversation." Beyond their general openness, Riverside students also describe their classmates as "liberal and politically-engaged." Additionally, the vast majority seem to have "an appetite to learn and discover." Perhaps more importantly, undergrads readily assert that their fellow students "are committed to the success of the [Riverside] community as a whole." Indeed, they empathize "with those who are struggling and they seek to be involved both on and off campus." And while they are certainly "passionate about what they believe in," they're also "respectful of…[the] opinions [of others]." Overall, as this grateful undergrad explains, "My peers at the University of California, Riverside make my college experience a great one. They make college feel safe, fun, and exciting." And this fellow student wholeheartedly agrees exclaiming, "College life is stressful but it is easier with the right people surrounding you. And that's what I have here at UCR."

UNIVERSITY OF CALIFORNIA—RIVERSIDE

Financial Aid: 951-827-3878 • E-Mail: admissions@ucr.edu • Website: www.ucr.edu

THE PRINCETON REVIEW SAYS

Admissions

The school reports that its standardized testing policy for use in admission for Fall 2024 is Test Free. The 2024 testing policy will be permanent. The Princeton Review suggests that interested applicants consult with the school for the most up-to-date standardized testing policies. *Very important factors considered include:* academic GPA, application essay. *Important factors considered include:* rigor of secondary school record. *Other factors considered include:* talent/ability, first generation, state residency. High school diploma is required and GED is accepted. *Academic units required:* 4 English, 3 math, 2 science, 2 science labs, 2 foreign language, 2 history, 1 visual/performing arts, 1 academic elective. *Academic units recommended:* 4 English, 4 math, 3 science, 3 science labs, 3 foreign language, 2 history, 1 visual/performing arts, 1 academic elective.

Financial Aid

Students should submit: FAFSA; State aid form. Priority filing deadline is 3/2. The Princeton Review suggests that all financial aid forms be submitted as soon as possible (see page 5 for a note on the FAFSA). *Need-based scholarships/grants offered:* College/university scholarship or grant aid from institutional funds; Federal Pell; Private scholarships; SEOG; State scholarships/grants. *Loan aid offered:* Direct PLUS loans; Direct Subsidized Loans; Direct Unsubsidized Loans; College/university loans from institutional funds. Admitted students will be notified of awards on a rolling basis beginning 3/1. Federal Work-Study Program available. Institutional employment available.

The Inside Word

As one of the top ranking universities within the California system, the admissions process at UC Riverside is certainly competitive. To determine who earns a coveted acceptance letter, the school closely evaluates each student's GPA. Successful applicants typically have a minimum 3.0 GPA (3.4 for non-residents). Admissions officers are also on the lookout for students who have earned a C or higher in AP/IB courses. Lastly, extra consideration is given to both first generation and low income applicants.

THE SCHOOL SAYS "..."

From the Admissions Office

"The University of California Riverside offers the quality, rigor, and facilities of a world-class research institution, while assuring its undergraduates personal attention and a welcoming campus community. Academic programs, teaching, advising and student services all reflect the supportive attitudes that characterize the campus. Exceptional opportunities include undergraduate research, University Honors, and the Thomas Haider Program (up to 24 spots to the UCR School of Medicine are guaranteed to UCR undergraduates each year). UCR's largest undergraduate program is biology, and it offers the only Bachelor of Arts in Creative Writing in the UC system.

"Students are actively involved in campus life—thanks to a variety of athletic and cultural events, ethnic and gender programs, community service opportunities, and more than 450 student organizations."

SELECTIVITY

Admissions Rating	85
# of applicants	53,787
% of applicants accepted	69
% of acceptees attending	15
# offered a place on the wait list	11,882
% accepting a place on wait list	49
% admitted from wait list	40

FIRST-YEAR PROFILE

Testing policy	Test Free
Average HS GPA	3.9
% frosh submitting high school GPA	100

DEADLINES

Regular	
Deadline	11/30
Notification	3/31
Nonfall registration?	No

FINANCIAL FACTS

Financial Aid Rating	85
Annual in-state tuition	$11,928
Annual out-of-state tuition	$42,954
Room and board	$17,333
Required fees	$2,513
Books and supplies	$1,566
Average frosh need-based scholarship	$22,547
Average UG need-based scholarship	$19,951
% needy frosh rec. need-based scholarship or grant aid	96
% needy UG rec. need-based scholarship or grant aid	96
% needy frosh rec. non-need-based scholarship or grant aid	2
% needy UG rec. non-need-based scholarship or grant aid	2
% needy frosh rec. need-based self-help aid	77
% needy UG rec. need-based self-help aid	72
% frosh rec. any financial aid	84
% UG rec. any financial aid	82
% UG borrow to pay for school	55
Average cumulative indebtedness	$18,960
% frosh need fully met	25
% ugrads need fully met	22
Average % of frosh need met	89
Average % of ugrad need met	86

THE BEST 389 COLLEGES ■ 619

UNIVERSITY OF CALIFORNIA—SAN DIEGO

9500 Gilman Drive, La Jolla, CA 92093 • Admissions: 858-534-4831 • Fax: 858-534-5723

STUDENTS SAY "..."

Academics

UC San Diego is widely regarded by students as "one of the top science universities in the United States." As a result, the school attracts bright students—and not just in the sciences—who desire/look for (or similar) "access to cutting edge technology and theories" and "great opportunities for undergraduates to do research." Professors "are incredibly knowledgeable about their material, and many of them are actively doing research in their field." Research opportunities are widely available to undergraduates across disciplines. The university is home to eight colleges, a system that students say is "a great way to not feel like a small fish in a huge ocean." Whereas it might seem like some science professors "are more interested in research than teaching," students say, "Humanities professors tend to be more accessible and more interested in their students as well as what they are teaching." Overall, however, "professors are very helpful and willing to take extra time to help students understand material." Given the fact that this is a large public university, students say, "Professors are extremely willing to help and mentor students if you seek them out." Another major benefit to attending a large university is that "there are a lot of resources, and there is always a faculty member or organization that will help you achieve what you want." Students say, "This university will undoubtedly set the new standard of what it means to be an elite public university in the years to come."

Campus Life

Students love to take advantage of UC San Diego's "unbeatable location," 10 minutes from the beach and a quick ride away from downtown San Diego. It is easy to enjoy "all the nature around the campus by hiking, biking, [and] camping," or taking surf lessons, which "are offered on campus for a modest fee." It is also "super easy to get to San Diego proper for a fun night out." There is a perception that social life is somewhat lacking on the campus itself, which may be the result of UC San Diego being such a large, academically intensive school. While some students have trouble fitting a social life into their busy study schedules, others say that, in fact, there are "tons of resources and ways to get involved" on campus; students "just have to actively seek them." Plenty of people "play sports or participate in clubs." "Lots of people enjoy...small parties but the party scene isn't too big here." In the spring, the Sun God Festival is "always a popular event" that brings the entire campus together. There "is not really a huge emphasis on the athletics department," but that may be changing given that UC San Diego recently became a member of the Big West Conference in NCAA Division I. However, students who make the most of their experience here maintain, "There is always an event going on and so many clubs to be involved in. From the Greek life, to the intramural sports, to the variety of clubs, there is literally a place for everyone."

Student Body

The typical student at UC San Diego "is a little nerdy and studies a lot." "Doing well academically at UC San Diego is an extreme priority, even to students who are not good students. Most of the students are geared toward extended education or professional school." However, "there are plenty of students who balance academics with other things, like sports or clubs." The student body "has such a diverse range of personalities" that almost anyone "can fit in here because it's such a big school, and there are so many different organizations and places where you can find people that enjoy the same things as you." Students say that the population of students in the humanities has been growing "rapidly" in recent years, but some still see room for improvement among the diversity of the student body. There are those who would love "to see more students become socially conscious" to enhance the overall student body experience on campus.

UNIVERSITY OF CALIFORNIA—SAN DIEGO

Financial Aid: 858-534-4480 • E-Mail: admissionsreply@ucsd.edu • Website: www.ucsd.edu

THE PRINCETON REVIEW SAYS

Admissions

The school reports that its standardized testing policy for use in admission for Fall 2024 is Test Free. The 2024 testing policy will be permanent. The Princeton Review suggests that interested applicants consult with the school for the most up-to-date standardized testing policies. *Very important factors considered include:* rigor of secondary school record, academic GPA, Personal Insight Questions or PIQs. *Important factors considered include:* extracurricular activities, talent/ability, character/personal qualities, state residency, volunteer work. *Other factors considered include:* first generation, geographical residence, work experience. High school diploma is required and GED is accepted. *Academic units required:* 4 English, 3 math, 2 science, 2 science labs, 2 foreign language, 2 history, 1 visual/performing arts, 1 academic elective. *Academic units recommended:* 4 English, 4 math, 3 science, 3 science labs, 3 foreign language, 2 history, 1 visual/performing arts, 1 academic elective.

Financial Aid

Students should submit: FAFSA or California Dream Act Application; State aid form. Priority filing deadline is 3/2. The Princeton Review suggests that all financial aid forms be submitted as soon as possible (see page 5 for a note on the FAFSA). *Need-based scholarships/grants offered:* College/university scholarship or grant aid from institutional funds; Federal Pell; Private scholarships; SEOG; State scholarships/grants. *Loan aid offered:* Direct PLUS loans; Direct Subsidized Loans; Direct Unsubsidized Loans; College/university loans from institutional funds. Admitted students will be notified of awards on a rolling basis beginning 3/15. Federal Work-Study Program available. Institutional employment available.

The Inside Word

UC San Diego is rapidly earning its place as one of the gems of the UC system, and admission is competitive. Applications are reviewed thoroughly by at least two readers. Applicants will need excellent grades in the rigorous college preparatory courses offered at their institution, and demonstrate personal qualities like leadership, tenacity, compassion, and independence.

THE SCHOOL SAYS "..."

From the Admissions Office

"UC San Diego is recognized for the exceptional quality of its academic programs in the arts, humanities, social sciences, biological and physical sciences, and engineering. With annual research funding topping $1.64 billion, UC San Diego is the top undergraduate campus in the University of California system for research spending and sixth in the nation for research and development expenditures. UC San Diego also offers a unique college system, which assigns undergraduates to one of the university's colleges, each with its own residential neighborhood, general education curriculum, support services, and distinctive traditions. This system allows students to thrive in a smaller neighborhood setting and enjoy a more personalized experience in utilizing college resources.

"UC San Diego's interdisciplinary approach to learning allows students to push the boundaries of their chosen fields of study. Students in any major can explore artistic ventures at the Craft Center or through the on-campus theater district, develop groundbreaking projects and inventions in the EnVision Arts and Engineering Maker Studio, or even gain hands-on experience as student researchers in their first year on campus. The campus also helps to connect students to real-world job and internship opportunities in the greater San Diego area, with trolley stops right on campus making such opportunities more accessible than ever."

SELECTIVITY

Admissions Rating	94
# of applicants	131,254
% of applicants accepted	24
% of acceptees attending	21
# offered a place on the wait list	51,350
% accepting a place on wait list	70
% admitted from wait list	7

FIRST-YEAR PROFILE

Testing policy	Test Free
Average HS GPA	4.2
% frosh submitting high school GPA	95
% graduated top 10% of class	100
% graduated top 25% of class	100
% graduated top 50% of class	100

DEADLINES

Regular	
Deadline	11/30
Notification	mid-March
Nonfall registration?	No

APPLICANTS OFTEN PREFER

Stanford University; University of California—Berkeley; University of California—Los Angeles

APPLICANTS SOMETIMES PREFER

University of California-Irvine; University of California—Santa Barbara; University of Southern California

FINANCIAL FACTS

Financial Aid Rating	85
Annual in-state tuition	$11,928
Annual out-of-state tuition	$42,954
Room and board	$16,713
Required fees	$5,401
Required fees (first-year)	$5,566
Books and supplies	$1,179
Average frosh need-based scholarship	$21,339
Average UG need-based scholarship	$21,607
% needy frosh rec. need-based scholarship or grant aid	92
% needy UG rec. need-based scholarship or grant aid	95
% needy frosh rec. non-need-based scholarship or grant aid	4
% needy UG rec. non-need-based scholarship or grant aid	2
% needy frosh rec. need-based self-help aid	63
% needy UG rec. need-based self-help aid	62
% frosh rec. any financial aid	83
% UG rec. any financial aid	73
% UG borrow to pay for school	77
Average cumulative indebtedness	$19,357
% frosh need fully met	33
% ugrads need fully met	31
Average % of frosh need met	83
Average % of ugrad need met	84

UNIVERSITY OF CALIFORNIA—SANTA BARBARA

552 University Road, Santa Barbara, CA 93106 • Admissions: 805-893-8000 • Fax: 805-893-2676

STUDENTS SAY ". . ."

Academics

It's easy to be dazzled by this University of California's "incredible location" in stunning Santa Barbara, but UCSB is much more than a "safe and beautiful campus." "It has one of the top chemical engineering departments in the country," a "highly ranked" mechanical engineering program, and is generally "strong in the sciences." Outstanding students can enroll in the College of Creative Studies, essentially a graduate school for undergraduates, which requires a supplemental application: CCS students report that it "allows me to pursue my academic interests with maximum freedom." While they love the "laid-back" atmosphere, students regard their course work in any school as both "academically challenging" and "down to earth": "Every other college on my list seemed locked in an ivory tower. UCSB was the exception with both the warm, sun-kissed charm of a beach town and excellent academics." "I would challenge any Ivy school to match" the quality of professors at UCSB, asserts one student, and another says the "outstanding professors" "are definitely an important source of inspiration for me." Some students comment on the "wide range of professors," and point out that "many of [the] professors are Nobel Prize winners or well-known in their field; however, these individuals are not necessarily the best teachers." Overall, though, UBSB undergrads name the "accessibility and knowledge of the professors" as one of the university's strengths. If you're seeking a dynamic college experience with choices within and outside the classroom, UCSB could be for you: "UCSB is the perfect blend of academics and social life. I get to study at a renowned research university and work closely with professors, while living on the beach and making lifelong friendships."

Campus Life

No matter the activity, UCSB students love to be involved: "85 percent of our student body is in at least one extracurricular activity—and I've met the smartest people of my life here." Outdoor pastimes like "rock climbing, beach volleyball," "surfing, hiking," "bik[ing], and skateboard[ing]," figure prominently in students' favorite ways to spend free time wholesomely. After the sun goes down, "a lot of people party at UCSB. What do you expect, we live on a beach? But don't be fooled. I've met some of the smartest, most hard-working people at UCSB." Social life at UCSB is as "varied" as you want it to be: "People think of UCSB exclusively as a party school but it's what you make of it." The party scene "is totally avoidable if you want," but "UCSB is famous for its party life" for a reason. Students looking to avoid drinking and drug culture entirely might be best advised to look elsewhere, and insiders say that "substance abuse is somewhat common off campus and not as much on campus; campus alcohol and drug policies are typically enforced strictly." At the end of the day, "everything is give and take here. You spend your week busting your butt in your internship and churning out research papers, and finish everything up in time to go indulge in some of the debauchery that is DP on a Friday night."

Student Body

To find your place at a big school, get ready to get out and do something: "The typical student is active and involved. Whether it be with sports, or in a community service or environmental club, rock climbing, politics, the list goes on. Students fit in by finding a good group of friends in the dorms and by getting involved in extracurricular activities." Because the university is accessible to so many different types of students, "there is a great sense of community among the students, and those with all sorts of socio-economic backgrounds feel at home here." UCSB undergrads care about more than partying, and are "intelligent, sociable, engaging" as well as "very motivated and driven to succeed academically." People are "laid-back but hard-working," at least partially because "the sunny weather keeps people happy." UCSB is "extremely diverse personality wise": "We've got the hippies, the sorority girls, the surfer dudes, the Jesus-lovers, the anarchists, the school-oriented folk and everything in between. Everyone finds their niche here."

UNIVERSITY OF CALIFORNIA—SANTA BARBARA

Financial Aid: 805-893-2432 • E-Mail: admissions@sa.ucsb.edu • Website: www.ucsb.edu

THE PRINCETON REVIEW SAYS

Admissions

The school reports that its standardized testing policy for use in admission for Fall 2024 is Test Free. It is unknown at this time if the 2024 testing policy will be permanent. The Princeton Review suggests that interested applicants consult with the school for the most up-to-date standardized testing policies. *Very important factors considered include:* academic GPA, application essay. *Important factors considered include:* rigor of secondary school record. *Other factors considered include:* extracurricular activities, talent/ability, character/personal qualities, first generation, geographical residence, state residency, volunteer work, work experience. High school diploma is required and GED is accepted. *Academic units required:* 4 English, 3 math, 2 science, 2 science labs, 2 foreign language, 2 history, 1 visual/performing arts, 1 academic elective. *Academic units recommended:* 4 English, 4 math, 3 science, 3 science labs, 3 foreign language, 2 history, 1 visual/performing arts, 1 academic elective.

Financial Aid

Students should submit: FAFSA or California Dream Act Application. The Princeton Review suggests that all financial aid forms be submitted as soon as possible (see page 5 for a note on the FAFSA). *Need-based scholarships/grants offered:* College/university scholarship or grant aid from institutional funds; Federal Pell; Private scholarships; SEOG; State scholarships/grants. *Loan aid offered:* Direct PLUS loans; Direct Subsidized Loans; Direct Unsubsidized Loans; College/university loans from institutional funds. Federal Work-Study Program available. Institutional employment available.

The Inside Word

UCSB uses a "minimum eligibility" index as a formula to calculate a student's viability for admission; other standards, including high school course load, are synthesized with a 3.0 minimum GPA for California students and a 3.4 for out-of-state applicants. Weakness in one area may be balanced out by strength in another, but don't be fooled by the fact that it's a state school: UCSB is competitive.

THE SCHOOL SAYS "..."

From the Admissions Office

"The University of California, Santa Barbara, is a leading research institution that also provides a comprehensive liberal arts learning experience. Teaching and research go hand-in-hand at UC Santa Barbara, and a majority of students are involved in the research process during their undergraduate studies. UCSB's academic community of faculty, students, and staff is characterized by a collaborative, dynamic atmosphere. Students at UCSB can choose from 90 majors, 40 minors, and honors programs for top students across three undergraduate colleges. Located on the edge of the Pacific Ocean, students have access to a stunning living-learning environment with excellent weather and outdoor recreation. The local Santa Barbara community enhances the on-campus experience by offering cultural outlets and access to a variety of job and internship opportunities in local schools, law offices, hospitals and clinics, and more.

"All applicants must complete the University of California application. UCSB uses eligibility requirements and selection criteria to admit its next class of first-time freshmen and junior-level transfers each year. UCSB does not use SAT/ACT scores in the admission decision or scholarship selection process."

SELECTIVITY

Admissions Rating	94
# of applicants	111,006
% of applicants accepted	26
% of acceptees attending	17
# offered a place on the wait list	16,340
% accepting a place on wait list	62
% admitted from wait list	27

FIRST-YEAR PROFILE

Testing policy	Test Free
Average HS GPA	4.3
% frosh submitting high school GPA	97
% graduated top 10% of class	100
% graduated top 25% of class	100
% graduated top 50% of class	100

DEADLINES

Regular	
Deadline	11/30
Notification	3/31
Nonfall registration?	No

APPLICANTS OFTEN PREFER

University of California—Berkeley; University of California—Los Angeles

APPLICANTS SOMETIMES PREFER

University of California—Davis; University of California-Irvine

APPLICANTS RARELY PREFER

California Polytechnic State University; University of California—Santa Cruz

FINANCIAL FACTS

Financial Aid Rating	83
Annual in-state tuition	$11,834
Annual in-state tuition (first-year)	$12,522
Annual out-of-state tuition	$42,611
Annual out-of-state tuition (first-year)	$45,096
Required fees	$1,166
Required fees (first-year)	$1,230
Books and supplies	$1,343
Average frosh need-based scholarship	$24,178
Average UG need-based scholarship	$22,834
% needy frosh rec. need-based scholarship or grant aid	93
% needy UG rec. need-based scholarship or grant aid	96
% needy frosh rec. non-need-based scholarship or grant aid	3
% needy UG rec. non-need-based scholarship or grant aid	2
% needy frosh rec. need-based self-help aid	47
% needy UG rec. need-based self-help aid	42
% frosh rec. any financial aid	61
% UG rec. any financial aid	59
% UG borrow to pay for school	40
Average cumulative indebtedness	$17,242
% frosh need fully met	23
% ugrads need fully met	20
Average % of frosh need met	84
Average % of ugrad need met	83

UNIVERSITY OF CALIFORNIA—SANTA CRUZ

1156 High Street, Santa Cruz, CA 95064 • Admissions: 831-459-0111 • Fax: 831-459-4452

STUDENTS SAY "..."

Academics

Nestled among California's coastal redwoods, UC Santa Cruz's campus "is one of the most unique, beautiful ecosystems I've ever seen," beams an environmental science major, noting that it's "a great resource for internship and job opportunities." It's also a boon for professors, who can "take time to teach students the importance of being outside and how it can impact their learning." It's not unusual for courses to include "taking class hikes and nature journaling trips," while also offering "extensive labs" and "rich discussions." Whether outdoors or in, UCSC presents "guest lectures and activities that allow for further engagement in many different areas of learning." As for academic support, "tutoring is widely available on campus no matter the class, and there are online tutoring options available that make it very accessible to those that may live off-campus or with transportation issues."

For all the support systems, as well as a number of professors who offer a much appreciated series of "low stakes tests and essays instead of a big final and midterm," students emphasize that "UCSC is a very academically competitive school," particularly in the prized technical fields. Students who actively pursue and value STEM research enjoy "internships that I can do hands-on work with and earn credit for." Interdisciplinary teaching is also enjoyed, like the "amazing" resources of the Coastal Science Campus and the agroecology department's farm.

Campus Life

"My college experience in the redwoods is magical," marvels one student. "The school is gorgeous and the coastline that surrounds us is second to none." This "beautiful forest setting," ideally located "between the mountains and the beach" means that many students "are active in outdoor hobbies including surfing, rock climbing, backpacking, and mountain biking." Students are equally interested in preserving the environment they so enjoy: "Everyone here cares about nature and the environment," and the UCSC Climate Coalition is "amazing." Others appreciate culturally based organizations such as Hillel and the Chinese Student Association. "It can be difficult to meet people without joining a club or group simply due to the nature of being a larger school."

Like many in California, UCSC has been affected by a housing shortage, and students wish for "more affordable and guaranteed student housing." Nevertheless, the school grounds provide "the perfect getaway when things get stressful" as well as the setting for plenty of college fun. "I enjoy the forest raves as well as the arts and crafts activities," says one student. "The Adventure Rec provides amazing programs for students to gain outdoor skills and experiences." As for off-campus experiences, students "love to go downtown and hang around, go to the beach at Sunny Cove or the boardwalk. They love to just bask in the California sun."

Student Body

The University of California—Santa Cruz isn't defined by any one thing, except for perhaps the way it's "extremely open and welcoming" such that there's the freedom to be anything." (Okay, and maybe an environment that is "perfect for outdoorsy folk.") You can see this uniqueness in the way students "express themselves through clothes, gender, hairstyle, [and] speech. There is a very laid-back and accepting mentality that all of us share." And yet, for all the different communities on campus, there's a sense that those at UCSC "help each other and stand with each other in times of need." That extends to the body's activism "in social justice and climate change cause" and "student clubs and organizations that promote social justice as well as inclusivity." As one student jokingly puts it, UCSC feels like "leftist Twitter, but real," a group of "very carefree, very creative, and very caring people with an anti-establishment lean and strong sustainability goals."

UNIVERSITY OF CALIFORNIA—SANTA CRUZ

Financial Aid: 831-459-2963 • E-Mail: admissions@ucsc.edu • Website: www.ucsc.edu

THE PRINCETON REVIEW SAYS

Admissions

The school reports that its standardized testing policy for use in admission for Fall 2024 is Test Free. It is unknown at this time if the 2024 testing policy will be permanent. The Princeton Review suggests that interested applicants consult with the school for the most up-to-date standardized testing policies. *Very important factors considered include:* rigor of secondary school record, academic GPA, application essay, state residency. *Important factors considered include:* extracurricular activities, talent/ability, character/personal qualities, first generation, geographical residence. *Other factors considered include:* volunteer work, work experience. High school diploma is required and GED is accepted. *Academic units required:* 4 English, 3 math, 2 science, 2 science labs, 2 foreign language, 1 social studies, 1 history, 1 visual/performing arts, 1 academic elective. *Academic units recommended:* 4 English, 4 math, 3 science, 3 science labs, 3 foreign language, 1 social studies, 1 history, 1 visual/performing arts, 1 academic elective.

Financial Aid

Students should submit: FAFSA; State aid form. The Princeton Review suggests that all financial aid forms be submitted as soon as possible (see page 5 for a note on the FAFSA). *Need-based scholarships/grants offered:* College/university scholarship or grant aid from institutional funds; Federal Pell; Private scholarships; SEOG; State scholarships/grants. *Loan aid offered:* Direct PLUS loans; Direct Subsidized Loans; Direct Unsubsidized Loans. Admitted students will be notified of awards on a rolling basis beginning 4/1. Federal Work-Study Program available. Institutional employment available.

The Inside Word

Professionally-trained Admissions readers conduct an in-depth review of your academic and personal achievements in light of the opportunities available to you and your demonstrated capacity to contribute to the intellectual and cultural life at UCSC. UCSC's acceptance rate belies the high caliber of applicants it regularly receives.

THE SCHOOL SAYS "..."

From the Admissions Office

"UC—Santa Cruz students, faculty, and researchers are working together to make a world of difference. Within our extraordinary educational community, students participate in the creation of new knowledge, new technologies, and new forms of expressing and understanding cultures. From helping teachers improve their skills to building more efficient solar cells and working to save endangered sea turtles, our focus is on improving our planet and the lives of all its inhabitants. The academic programs at UCSC are challenging and rigorous, and many of them are in newer fields that focus on interdisciplinary thinking. At UCSC, undergraduates conduct and publish research, working closely with faculty on leading-edge projects. Taking advantage of the campus' proximity to centers of industry and innovation such as the Monterey Bay National Marine Sanctuary and Silicon Valley, many students at UC—Santa Cruz take part in fieldwork and internships that complement their studies and provide practical experience in their fields."

SELECTIVITY

Admissions Rating	87
# of applicants	66,033
% of applicants accepted	47
% of acceptees attending	12
# offered a place on the wait list	18,099
% accepting a place on wait list	66
% admitted from wait list	13

FIRST-YEAR PROFILE

Testing policy	Test Free
Average HS GPA	4.0
% frosh submitting high school GPA	99

DEADLINES

Regular	
Deadline	11/30
Notification	3/31
Nonfall registration?	No

FINANCIAL FACTS

Financial Aid Rating	81
Annual in-state tuition	$13,104
Annual out-of-state tuition	$44,130
Room and board	$18,186
Required fees	$1,521
Books and supplies	$1,203
Average frosh need-based scholarship	$19,899
Average UG need-based scholarship	$20,744
% needy frosh rec. need-based scholarship or grant aid	94
% needy UG rec. need-based scholarship or grant aid	94
% needy frosh rec. non-need-based scholarship or grant aid	2
% needy UG rec. non-need-based scholarship or grant aid	2
% needy frosh rec. need-based self-help aid	51
% needy UG rec. need-based self-help aid	50
% frosh rec. any financial aid	53
% UG rec. any financial aid	52
% UG borrow to pay for school	53
Average cumulative indebtedness	$21,189
% frosh need fully met	12
% ugrads need fully met	16
Average % of frosh need met	75
Average % of ugrad need met	78

UNIVERSITY OF CENTRAL FLORIDA

P.O. Box 160111, Orlando, FL 32816-0111 • Admissions: 407-823-3000 • Fax: 407-823-5625

This narrative, like all others in this book, is based on student responses and data collected prior to the 2023–2024 academic school year. While these profiles strive to be an accurate depiction of what to expect for the upcoming year, recent developments in the Florida state system may change the academic offerings and overall atmosphere at colleges in the system. Students should check the free online tools for this book (see page vi) for any late-breaking administrative news and they should voice any concerns or questions with the colleges directly.

STUDENTS SAY ". . ."

Academics
To match "having one of the largest student bodies in the country," the University of Central Florida features "nearly every class or degree imaginable." Students speak fondly of that size, especially when it comes to registration, where they say "it's easy to get the classes you want." They also appreciate the location, as "there are many opportunities with big companies and corporations for … jobs and internships." Examples in action include the aeronautics department partnering "with NASA on new space-projects" and courses in 3D design that have led students "to start directly working with Universal Studios."

One of the ways in which UCF accommodates so many students is with a mix of in-person and remote learning options. Some obvious favorites, like Wines of the World and a scuba class, require a physical presence for wine tastings and diving, but for most classes, students note "the experience online is just as robust" and the "classes are structured in a way that keeps students engaged." Regardless of how the class is organized, "most professors are interested and dedicated to their craft, and it shows in their teaching." As one student tells us: "If you need help, just ask and someone will jump through hoops to make sure you get what you need to succeed."

Campus Life
If there's any doubt about school spirit for the University of Central Florida's Knights, just look "all around campus at all events…[for] the massive amounts of crowds (students and non-students) that come together." It helps that "athletics tickets are free for students" and "it's very popular to tailgate in Memory Mall before football games." Other popular hang-out highlights are the on-campus arcade and the "rock climbing wall in the gym." UCF also features "a huge arboretum with trails; I am able to go for a short hike between my classes." Students are even enthusiastic about the parking garage, which is also used for band practices that can be enjoyed across campus: "My favorite memory here is going to a rooftop rock concert, the crowd was amazing, everyone participated and would help anyone that fell in the mosh pit."

With 650 student clubs and a thriving Greek scene, there are plenty of on-campus social events at any given time. Orlando itself also provides "big city energy" and is a great option for those who want to go "exploring new places" or visiting the familiar attractions of nearby Disney World and Universal. Those wanting a less-structured outdoors experience appreciate that "beaches and wildlife habitats" are just a 30-minute drive away.

Student Body
"My university is one of the largest in the nation and with that comes … a mix of cultures, personalities, and traditions that allow for everyone at UCF to feel at home." Benefits of this "vast and diverse" student body extend throughout campus life, so you'll hear "many different ideas in the classroom." The only drawback for some is that the school's size "makes it difficult to make connections on a deeper level. You will see thousands of different faces everyday." That's why students swear by the importance of clubs in forming relationships: "I was part of a club specifically for Latinos in the medical field, which made me feel included and seen on campus." While Knights hail from "all ethnic, religious, and social backgrounds," one student describes the "students at UCF" as "young and full of energy." Another student agrees: "Mostly everyone I've met since coming to UCF has been warm and welcoming." One student sums up their experience by saying, "I have studied with some of the brightest and best."

UNIVERSITY OF CENTRAL FLORIDA

Financial Aid: 407-823-2827 • E-Mail: admission@ucf.edu • Website: www.ucf.edu

THE PRINCETON REVIEW SAYS

Admissions

The school reports that its standardized testing policy for use in admission for Fall 2024 is SAT or ACT Required. The 2024 testing policy will be permanent. The Princeton Review suggests that interested applicants consult with the school for the most up-to-date standardized testing policies. *Very important factors considered include:* rigor of secondary school record, academic GPA, standardized test scores. *Important factors considered include:* application essay. *Other factors considered include:* class rank, extracurricular activities, talent/ability, character/personal qualities, first generation, alumni/ae relation, geographical residence, state residency, volunteer work, work experience, level of applicant's interest. High school diploma is required and GED is accepted. *Academic units required:* 4 English, 4 math, 3 science, 2 science labs, 2 foreign language, 3 social studies, 2 academic electives.

Financial Aid

Students should submit: FAFSA. Priority filing deadline is 12/1. The Princeton Review suggests that all financial aid forms be submitted as soon as possible (see page 5 for a note on the FAFSA). *Need-based scholarships/grants offered:* College/university scholarship or grant aid from institutional funds; Federal Pell; Private scholarships; SEOG; State scholarships/grants. *Loan aid offered:* Direct PLUS loans; Direct Subsidized Loans; Direct Unsubsidized Loans; Federal Nursing Loans. Admitted students will be notified of awards on a rolling basis beginning 3/15. Federal Work-Study Program available. Institutional employment available.

The Inside Word

Like many state schools, earning admission to UCF is primarily a numbers game, meaning that the college largely considers your GPA and standardized test scores. We should also mention that grades earned in honors, IB, advanced placement, AICE and/or dual enrollment classes will be given greater weight. UCF does not require applicants to submit a personal statement, however, you are likely to give your candidacy a modest boost if you include one. Finally, we should note that students graduating from a Florida high school in the top 10 percent of their class (or with a recalculated academic core 3.9 GPA if their high school does not rank) and minimum test scores (1100 SAT or 22 ACT) will be guaranteed admission to the fall, summer, or spring semester.

THE SCHOOL SAYS "..."

From the Admissions Office

"The University of Central Florida offers competitive advantages to its student body. We're committed to teaching, providing advisement, and academic support services for all students. Our undergraduates have access to state-of-the-art wireless buildings, high-tech classrooms, research labs, web-based classes, and an undergraduate research and mentoring program.

"Our Career Services professionals help students gain practical experiences at NASA, schools, hospitals, high-tech companies, local municipalities, and the entertainment industry. With an international focus to our curricula and research programs, we enroll international students from 140 nations. Our study abroad programs and other study and research opportunities include agreements with ninety-eight institutions and thirty-six countries.

"UCF's 1,420-acre campus provides a safe and serene setting for learning, with natural lakes and woodlands. The bustle of Orlando lies a short distance away: the pro sport teams, the Kennedy Space Center, film studios, Walt Disney World, Universal Orlando, Sea World, and sandy beaches are all nearby.

"UCF is proud to be designated as a Hispanic Serving Institution (HSI) with a 27 percent Hispanic population (46 percent are students of color)."

SELECTIVITY

Admissions Rating	93
# of applicants	54,977
% of applicants accepted	41
% of acceptees attending	33
# offered a place on the wait list	6,410
% accepting a place on wait list	62
% admitted from wait list	0

FIRST-YEAR PROFILE

Testing policy	SAT or ACT Required
Range SAT EBRW	610–680
Range SAT math	590–680
Range ACT composite	25–29
# submitting SAT scores	5,367
% submitting SAT scores	71
# submitting ACT scores	2,145
% submitting ACT scores	29
Average HS GPA	4.2
% frosh submitting high school GPA	100
% graduated top 10% of class	35
% graduated top 25% of class	72
% graduated top 50% of class	96

DEADLINES

Regular	
Deadline	5/1
Notification	Rolling, 9/1
Nonfall registration?	Yes

FINANCIAL FACTS

Financial Aid Rating	79
Annual in-state tuition	$6,368
Annual out-of-state tuition	$22,467
Room and board	$10,000
Required fees	$0
Books and supplies	$1,200
Average frosh need-based scholarship	$7,245
Average UG need-based scholarship	$7,467
% needy frosh rec. need-based scholarship or grant aid	67
% needy UG rec. need-based scholarship or grant aid	75
% needy frosh rec. non-need-based scholarship or grant aid	85
% needy UG rec. non-need-based scholarship or grant aid	51
% needy frosh rec. need-based self-help aid	26
% needy UG rec. need-based self-help aid	36
% frosh rec. any financial aid	91
% UG rec. any financial aid	85
% UG borrow to pay for school	39
Average cumulative indebtedness	$21,727
% frosh need fully met	26
% ugrads need fully met	14
Average % of frosh need met	71
Average % of ugrad need met	63

THE UNIVERSITY OF CHICAGO

5801 South Ellis Avenue, Chicago, IL 60637 • Admissions: 773-702-1234 • Fax: 773-702-4199

CAMPUS LIFE

Quality of Life Rating	85
Fire Safety Rating	97
Green Rating	90
Type of school	Private
Affiliation	No Affiliation
Environment	Metropolis

STUDENTS

Total undergrad enrollment	7,459
% male/female/another gender	53/47/0
% from out of state	81
% frosh live on campus	100
% ugrads live on campus	61
% African American	7
% Asian	20
% White	32
% Hispanic	16
% Native American	<1
% Pacific Islander	<1
% Two or more races	7
% Race and/or ethnicity unknown	2
% international	16
# of countries represented	125

SURVEY SAYS . . .

Students always studying
Students are happy
Classroom facilities are great
Lab facilities are great
Great library
Career services are great
Internships are widely available
Great financial aid
Students love Chicago, IL
Dorms are like palaces
Easy to get around campus
Theater is popular

ACADEMICS

Academic Rating	98
% students returning for sophomore year	99
% students graduating within 4 years	89
% students graduating within 6 years	96
Calendar	Quarter
Student/faculty ratio	5:1
Profs interesting rating	90
Profs accessible rating	93

Most classes have fewer than 10 students.
Most lab/discussion sessions have
10–19 students.

MOST POPULAR MAJORS

Biology/Biological Sciences, General;
Mathematics, General; Econometrics and
Quantitative Economics

STUDENTS SAY " . . ."

Academics

The University of Chicago is known among students for its rigorous academics—and well-celebrated for that deep commitment, which is designed to help students not only learn but also to think, challenge, and question. The distinctive core curriculum is a series of sequences (including Humanities, Social Sciences, Physical Sciences, and Civilization) that make up an interdisciplinary framework that is then fleshed out with a vast number of electives, summer sessions, and research and internship opportunities. The academic calendar runs on a quarter system that "allows you to try so much, not just academically but outside of class," so that students "can be in a play one quarter, work for the newspaper another quarter, [and] work with a professor on research another quarter." Undergrads devoted to the pursuit of learning find that the hard work required by the school is excellent preparation for the workplace, or as one puts it: "So many recruiters comment that they love UChicago kids because we know how to put in the time."

Teachers also put in the time to provide what students describe as a "transformative education." Classes are regularly described as unique, with the note that "it is clear that teachers here are able to create courses that are their most specific passions." And while those classes come with high expectations, professors are people first, which means that they "uphold the rigorous academic standard while simultaneously being flexible, accommodating, and understanding."

Campus Life

Academic exploration is the reason people come here, and "students work almost twice as hard at their academics than they do on their personal/social life." Still, "everyone at UChicago has a deep inner life and is doing something interesting with their time," and there exists "a vibrant community for pretty much any interest you could have in a club," ranging from "being a part of the emergency medical service to pro-bono consulting groups to doing research with a Nobel Laureate in economics." There is a constant flow in and out of the libraries, but not many complaints about the workload: "We're all very busy, but we make it work."

The school's residential House system creates small communities with distinct traditions, competitions, and events, both within and between houses, which means that it's easy to find something to do with one's downtime: there are "bound to be several people in the house lounge playing video games, board games, just chilling." For those wanting to get out, it's notably "pretty easy to navigate Chicago," and students can often be found "walking to the Point, going to Chinatown, or going to various museums and bookstores downtown."

Student Body

Students at UChicago are both "incredibly diverse" and also consistently "intellectual and quirky," which speaks to a commonality of differences that hinges on learning: "everyone loves to learn and talk about what each other is learning." If you're one of those who is "genuinely driven to learn for the sake of learning, and love being challenged by their classes," undergrads say it'll be easy to find like-minded individuals "who are pursuing the most fascinating careers and studying interesting topics." There's a reason so many students here like to talk: it's only by diving deep into conversation with someone that you realize "they're double majoring astrophysics and English."

THE UNIVERSITY OF CHICAGO

Financial Aid: 773-702-8666 • E-Mail: collegeadmissions@uchicago.edu • Website: uchicago.edu

THE PRINCETON REVIEW SAYS

Admissions

The school reports that its standardized testing policy for use in admission for Fall 2024 is Test Optional. The 2024 testing policy will be permanent. The Princeton Review suggests that interested applicants consult with the school for the most up-to-date standardized testing policies. *Very important factors considered include:* rigor of secondary school record, application essay, recommendation(s), extracurricular activities, talent/ability, character/personal qualities. *Other factors considered include:* class rank, academic GPA, standardized test scores, first generation, alumni/ae relation, geographical residence, state residency, religious affiliation/commitment, racial/ethnic status, volunteer work, work experience. High school diploma is required and GED is accepted.

Financial Aid

Students should submit: FAFSA; Institution's own financial aid form. Priority filing deadline is 2/15. The Princeton Review suggests that all financial aid forms be submitted as soon as possible (see page 5 for a note on the FAFSA). *Need-based scholarships/grants offered:* College/university scholarship or grant aid from institutional funds; Federal Pell; Private scholarships; SEOG; State scholarships/grants. *Loan aid offered:* Direct PLUS loans; Direct Subsidized Loans; Direct Unsubsidized Loans. Admitted students will be notified of awards on or about 3/15. Federal Work-Study Program available. Institutional employment available.

The Inside Word

Students at the University of Chicago dwell on deep thoughts and big ideas. In your application, you'll need to demonstrate outstanding grades in tough courses and that you will fit in with a bunch of big thinkers. Although the University of Chicago uses the Common Application, essay topics remain "uncommon" and thought-provoking.

THE SCHOOL SAYS "..."

From the Admissions Office

"Chartered in 1890, the University of Chicago is universally recognized for its devotion to open and rigorous inquiry. The University has over 7,000 undergraduates from 50 states and 100+ countries that comprise a community of exceptional student scholars who chose UChicago for its rigorous liberal arts curriculum, small discussion-style seminars, and 5:1 student-faculty ratio. UChicago also prepares students for challenging careers and competitive graduate schools through professional and recreational opportunities on campus and in Chicago.

"Focused on careful reading, analytical writing, and critical thinking, UChicago's Core Curriculum is the perfect foundation for any major—and for all future endeavors. With over 50 majors and minors, students can double-major, create their own major, or explore interdisciplinary opportunities. Our newest interdisciplinary majors include Urban Environmental Studies, Data Science, and Media Arts & Design. Undergraduates choose electives from the 3,000+ courses offered each year and more than 40% of our students study abroad through 60 faculty-designed and taught programs.

"UChicago sponsors a wealth of undergraduate research opportunities in programs ranging from Economics and Cinema Studies to Astrophysics and Sociology. More than 160 institutes and centers provide sites for groundbreaking research. UChicago's Pritzker School of Molecular Engineering offers a unique opportunity to pursue molecular-level science in both an academic and research context.

"Undergraduates actively participate in 450+ student organizations encompassing athletics, the arts, community service, and Greek life. Varsity teams compete at the NCAA Division III level, and more than 70% of the student body participates in UChicago's extensive intramural and club sports programs."

SELECTIVITY

Admissions Rating	99
# of applicants	37,522
% of applicants accepted	5
% of acceptees attending	85

FIRST-YEAR PROFILE

Testing policy	Test Optional
Range SAT composite	1510–1560
Range SAT EBRW	740–780
Range SAT math	760–800
Range ACT composite	34–35
# submitting SAT scores	891
% submitting SAT scores	52
# submitting ACT scores	546
% submitting ACT scores	32
Average HS GPA	4.4
% frosh submitting high school GPA	60
% graduated top 10% of class	99
% graduated top 25% of class	100
% graduated top 50% of class	100

DEADLINES

Early decision	
Deadline	11/1
Notification	12/22
Other ED deadline	1/2
Other ED notification	2/15
Early action	
Deadline	11/1
Notification	12/22
Regular	
Deadline	1/2
Notification	3/15
Nonfall registration?	No

APPLICANTS ALSO LOOK AT

Columbia University; Harvard College; Northwestern University; Stanford University; University of Pennsylvania; Yale University

FINANCIAL FACTS

Financial Aid Rating	97
Annual tuition	$61,179
Room and board	$18,396
Required fees	$1,761
Books and supplies	$1,800
Average frosh need-based scholarship	$65,176
Average UG need-based scholarship	$61,561
% needy frosh rec. need-based scholarship or grant aid	98
% needy UG rec. need-based scholarship or grant aid	98
% needy frosh rec. non-need-based scholarship or grant aid	0
% needy UG rec. non-need-based scholarship or grant aid	0
% needy frosh rec. need-based self-help aid	38
% needy UG rec. need-based self-help aid	46
% frosh rec. any financial aid	46
% UG rec. any financial aid	49
% UG borrow to pay for school	14
Average cumulative indebtedness	$28,068
% frosh need fully met	99
% ugrads need fully met	98
Average % of frosh need met	100
Average % of ugrad need met	100

UNIVERSITY OF CINCINNATI

2600 Clifton Avenue, Cincinnati, OH 45221-0063 • Admissions: 513-556-6000 • Fax: 513-556-1105

STUDENTS SAY "...

Academics

At the University of Cincinnati, professors emphasize "the importance of gaining professional experience while [still] in school" and students are often encouraged "out of [their] comfort zones to go to networking events." Students mention "experiential learning the university provides through internships and co-ops," and many call it a "catalyst in [personal] growth." Students point to cross-disciplinary and pre-professional training in the university's co-op program, which while generally considered to be "a great program," has been said by some to "need a little bit of tweaking." With the Design, Architecture, Art, and Planning School (DAAP), a highly-ranked program with "studios [that] allow cross-collaboration with peers," "students are always tackling projects from different perspectives...and [appreciating] different learning styles." Many DAAP students love that they "are on a first-name basis" with their professors, who are "very passionate about what they are teaching." But other DAAP students mention that the demands are "too stress-inducing...and [that] the curriculum does not regard the well-being of the students." In contrast, students in other UC programs emphasize that their professors encourage them to "seek help at every turn, to lead healthy lives, and study in more effective ways." There is "plenty of opportunity for study outside of class including Supplemental Instruction (SI) sessions, office hours, and tutoring."

Campus Life

"We're so lucky to be right in the center of Cincinnati," says one student. And indeed, UC students "take full advantage of the restaurants, bars, museums, concerts, and local festivals in the city." This includes student tickets to Bengals and Reds games, free concerts, and farmers markets. Plus, "Oktoberfest is always popular," adds another Bearcat. Downtown Cincinnati also holds "many other interesting places to eat, drink, and socialize." Students de-stress on campus at the recreational facilities, which include an indoor track, a lazy river, and a hot tub, which one student stresses is "*super* nice." On the weekends, students go out to bars and restaurants near campus. They also "hang out in the student center, outdoors, or in the library between and after classes," and they often "attend the free sporting events or club meetings after." If you're hungry, head over to the Tangeman Center where you will find "many restaurants to choose from" or you can grab food at On the Green, the newest "super nice and...healthy" food court. Some find UC to be "fairly landlocked," with a "large number of students in a fairly small radius." They comment that this makes it "feel like a college city."

Student Body

The student body at the University of Cincinnati is "a fairly diverse community, with cultures from all across Ohio, the United States, and...the entire globe." "First-generation and minority students are well-represented and encouraged through programs such as Emerging Ethnic Engineers," says a student. Students describe themselves and each other as "motivated," "experienced," and "real-world-ready." "In addition to their academic prowess," students take on "numerous activities like intramural athletics, student government, [and] mental health initiatives." One Bearcat attributes the school's strengths to school spirit, saying, "[It] binds us." Another student says that everyone has "a different story and reason for being here, but all [share] a same liking of the institution."

UNIVERSITY OF CINCINNATI

Financial Aid: 513-556-1000 • E-Mail: admissions@uc.edu • Website: www.uc.edu

THE PRINCETON REVIEW SAYS

Admissions

The school reports that its standardized testing policy for use in admission for Fall 2024 is Test Optional. The 2024 testing policy will be temporary. The Princeton Review suggests that interested applicants consult with the school for the most up-to-date standardized testing policies. *Very important factors considered include:* academic GPA. *Important factors considered include:* rigor of secondary school record, application essay, talent/ability. *Other factors considered include:* class rank, standardized test scores, recommendation(s), extracurricular activities, character/personal qualities, first generation, geographical residence, state residency, racial/ethnic status, volunteer work, work experience. High school diploma is required and GED is accepted. *Academic units required:* 4 English, 4 math, 3 science, 3 social studies, 5 academic electives.

Financial Aid

Students should submit: FAFSA. Priority filing deadline is 12/1. The Princeton Review suggests that all financial aid forms be submitted as soon as possible (see page 5 for a note on the FAFSA). *Need-based scholarships/grants offered:* College/university scholarship or grant aid from institutional funds; Federal Pell; Private scholarships; SEOG; State scholarships/grants; United Negro College Fund. *Loan aid offered:* Direct PLUS loans; Direct Subsidized Loans; Direct Unsubsidized Loans; College/university loans from institutional funds; Federal Nursing Loans; State Loans. Admitted students will be notified of awards on a rolling basis beginning 2/15. Federal Work-Study Program available. Institutional employment available.

The Inside Word

The University of Cincinnati admissions officers advise students that they are looking for those who have been academically successful in past coursework, who show drive and a willingness to challenge themselves, and who are passionate about leaving a positive mark on the world. Essay prompts should be chosen with the goal of showing your authentic self in order to reveal something that wouldn't otherwise be apparent from other application material. All aspects of each student's application—from GPA to personal statements—are considered when making an admission decision. A letter of recommendation is optional for first-year applicants, although one is highly encouraged.

THE SCHOOL SAYS "..."

From the Admissions Office

"The University of Cincinnati provides a unique learning experience to students from around the globe. All students hone their skills outside the classroom through the university's nationally top-ranked co-op and internship program where students collectively earn $75 million annually. Other experiential-learning options include clinicals, undergraduate research, study abroad, service-learning, performances, or other approved activities. This focus on experience-based learning not only builds a student's resume, but allows students to network and build confidence within their chosen field. When combined with top academic programs, location, diversity, scope of majors and programs, and campus setting, the University of Cincinnati stands out among the top research universities in the country. Students and counselors agree:

"Heidi Clark-Smitley, the Director of Guidance and College Counseling at Catholic Central High School (Grand Rapids, MI) writes, 'I fell in love with the University of Cincinnati during an afternoon visit a few years ago. Cincinnati is one of the few out-of-state institutions I STRONGLY recommend for our students to consider.'

"Hannah, an architecture major, writes 'I knew the co-op program would allow me to have numerous professional experiences working in the design field and the university setting appealed to me more than a small art school. I am involved in several organizations and attend sporting events—which are both possible because DAAP is part of a larger university.'

"Come visit and find out how Cincinnati can benefit you both inside and outside the classroom: admissions.uc.edu/visit."

SELECTIVITY

Admissions Rating	84
# of applicants	29,024
% of applicants accepted	86
% of acceptees attending	25

FIRST-YEAR PROFILE

Testing policy	Test Optional
Range SAT composite	1170–1350
Range SAT EBRW	580–670
Range SAT math	580–690
Range ACT composite	24–29
# submitting SAT scores	662
% submitting SAT scores	10
# submitting ACT scores	2,634
% submitting ACT scores	41
Average HS GPA	3.7
% frosh submitting high school GPA	100
% graduated top 10% of class	23
% graduated top 25% of class	50
% graduated top 50% of class	83

DEADLINES

Regular	
Priority	12/1
Deadline	3/1
Notification	January
Nonfall registration?	Yes

FINANCIAL FACTS

Financial Aid Rating	74
Annual in-state tuition	$9,723
Annual in-state tuition (first-year)	$10,460
Annual out-of-state tuition	$25,057
Annual out-of-state tuition (first-year)	$25,794
Room and board	$10,054
Required fees	$1,678
Books and supplies	$1,200
Average frosh need-based scholarship	$9,349
Average UG need-based scholarship	$8,693
% needy frosh rec. need-based scholarship or grant aid	78
% needy UG rec. need-based scholarship or grant aid	76
% needy frosh rec. non-need-based scholarship or grant aid	8
% needy UG rec. non-need-based scholarship or grant aid	6
% needy frosh rec. need-based self-help aid	64
% needy UG rec. need-based self-help aid	64
% frosh rec. any financial aid	
% UG rec. any financial aid	
% UG borrow to pay for school	57
Average cumulative indebtedness	$24,936
% frosh need fully met	10
% ugrads need fully met	9
Average % of frosh need met	49
Average % of ugrad need met	46

UNIVERSITY OF COLORADO BOULDER

Office of Admissions, CO 80309-0552 • Admissions: 303-492-1411

STUDENTS SAY ". . ."

Academics

Located in the Rocky Mountain region, the University of Colorado Boulder is a "comprehensive public research university" boasting "five Nobel laureates and more than 50 members of prestigious academic academies." It "provides a modern, research-based education that focuses on creating aware citizens to go on to change the world (while having fun)." Students call it a "strong school academically with all the perks of a big state university" including "excellent diversity in subjects and courses, school spirit, packed sports games, and a fun, beautiful college town." Students get to enjoy a "beautiful campus with outdoor-oriented people" in addition to "a great research university," notes an international affairs major. Boulder offers a wide variety of degree programs, but students praise the "top-notch leadership program," "great business program," and "strong physics reputation" in particular. CU Boulder also offers a "strong environmental program" with opportunities for "both on- and off-campus" study. Students say the professors are "amazing," "approachable," "interested in students personally," and "will treat you as an adult." Professors are "consistently excellent across the wide variety of subjects I have taken courses in, from geography to astronomy and economics to literature," notes one student. "In my four years as an undergrad," says an environmental studies major, "I have traveled places and learned things that I never imagined I would or could experience." In addition, "the price for an education of this caliber is phenomenal," a creative writing major notes. "I was going to a private college for two years and can safely say that this education is significantly better, while the cost is relatively minimal." CU Boulder is a perfect fit for students who want to be in a "college town surrounded by other young intellectuals."

Campus Life

"Boulder is the best college town in the U.S.," raves one student. With the foothills of the Rockies as their home, "being active and outdoors is a staple for students." "Regardless of the time of day, students can be seen outside relaxing, exercising, or just hanging out with friends," according to one marketing major. Students "go hiking when the weather is nice" and many "go skiing in the mountains on days that [they] don't have classes." Snowboarding is also "extremely popular." And there is also a "prominent night life at the bars," including a music scene that is "diverse and active." Students "go shopping and eat out on Pearl Street" in "downtown Boulder" and "Farrand Field is always busy on nice days with students playing Frisbee, football, soccer, and tanning." It's a "fun college town," and many students "[like] to go out and party on the weekends."

Student Body

CU Boulder students consider themselves a diverse bunch from "diverse backgrounds" with "diverse passions." "There isn't really a typical student, which is awesome," notes a marketing major. But an international affairs major says, "Students are mostly upper-middle class white kids from Colorado, California, Texas, or Illinois." Typical CU Boulder students are "kind," "genuine," "smart," and "athletic." They are "outdoorsy, outgoing, and always up for anything." They "love to be outside and often will spend their weekends in the mountains." And though "partying is big," "most take school very seriously and are irritated by [its] depiction as a 'party school'" in the "media." "The school is so large that everyone fits into a group, no matter what your interests are," says an environmental studies major. In addition to those attracted to Greek life, there are "hippy concert going types and everything in between." An architecture major says, those "who make an effort to meet new people and try new things, will be very happy, and have a great time at CU Boulder." As one student notes: "When I stepped foot on CU's campus, I immediately felt at home." She adds: "Everyone is so friendly and welcoming. It's such a community atmosphere. Everyone watches out for each other and has each other's backs, even strangers."

UNIVERSITY OF COLORADO BOULDER

Financial Aid: 303-492-5091 • E-Mail: admissions@colorado.edu • Website: www.colorado.edu/

THE PRINCETON REVIEW SAYS

Admissions

The school reports that its standardized testing policy for use in admission for Fall 2024 is Test Optional. It is unknown at this time if the 2024 testing policy will be permanent. The Princeton Review suggests that interested applicants consult with the school for the most up-to-date standardized testing policies. *Very important factors considered include:* rigor of secondary school record, academic GPA. *Important factors considered include:* application essay, recommendation(s), extracurricular activities, talent/ability, character/personal qualities. *Other factors considered include:* class rank, first generation, standardized test scores, geographical residence, state residency, racial/ethnic status, volunteer work, work experience. High school diploma is required and GED is accepted. *Academic units required:* 4 English, 4 math, 3 science, 2 science labs, 1 foreign language, 3 social studies, 1 history.

Financial Aid

Students should submit: FAFSA. Priority filing deadline is 2/15. The Princeton Review suggests that all financial aid forms be submitted as soon as possible (see page 5 for a note on the FAFSA). *Need-based scholarships/grants offered:* College/university scholarship or grant aid from institutional funds; Federal Pell; Private scholarships; SEOG; State scholarships/grants. *Loan aid offered:* Direct PLUS loans; Direct Subsidized Loans; Direct Unsubsidized Loans. Admitted students will be notified of awards on a rolling basis beginning 3/1. Federal Work-Study Program available. Institutional employment available.

The Inside Word

Applicants must apply to a specific school within CU Boulder. Some programs are more competitive than others. Engineering and Applied Science and the Leeds School of Business are the most competitive. Those who apply to a competitive school within CU Boulder and are not selected will be automatically entered into consideration for admission to the College of Arts and Sciences.

THE SCHOOL SAYS "..."

From the Admissions Office

"Located at the foot of the Rocky Mountains, the University of Colorado Boulder has a breathtaking view from campus. But don't just come for the view. CU Boulder and its nationally and internationally ranked faculty have built a global reputation for outstanding teaching, research and creative work across more than 150 academic fields. Our innovative academic programs, hands-on opportunities, and rigorous coursework will prepare you for a complex global society. While working with faculty, you'll develop a broad understanding of the world, strong leadership skills and an enhanced ability to think critically.

"Within CU Boulder's inclusive community, you'll find many ways to get involved and make lifelong friends. We have one of the most active college campuses in the nation, where recreation, sports and student groups play a key role in the unique CU Boulder experience. We don't claim that we can change the world. Instead, we teach, inspire and encourage our students, faculty and researchers. So they can change the world. Live in spectacular surroundings and learn in a campus environment of extraordinary opportunities.

"Come to CU Boulder and discover what you can be.

"To find out if CU Boulder is the place for you, we encourage you to learn more. Check out our website, visit campus or take a virtual tour online.

"Be inspired. Be unique. Be driven.

"Be Boulder."

SELECTIVITY

Admissions Rating	85
# of applicants	54,861
% of applicants accepted	79
% of acceptees attending	16
# offered a place on the wait list	6,570
% accepting a place on wait list	39
% admitted from wait list	4

FIRST-YEAR PROFILE

Testing policy	Test Optional
Range SAT composite	1170–1380
Range SAT EBRW	590–690
Range SAT math	570–700
Range ACT composite	26–31
# submitting SAT scores	2,234
% submitting SAT scores	31
# submitting ACT scores	964
% submitting ACT scores	14
Average HS GPA	3.7
% frosh submitting high school GPA	99
% graduated top 10% of class	26
% graduated top 25% of class	54
% graduated top 50% of class	85

DEADLINES

Early action	
Deadline	11/15
Notification	2/1
Regular	
Priority	11/15
Deadline	1/15
Notification	4/1
Nonfall registration?	Yes

APPLICANTS ALSO LOOK AT

Arizona State University; California Polytechnic State University; Colorado School of Mines; Colorado State University; Indiana University—Bloomington; Penn State University Park; San Diego State University; University of Colorado at Denver; University of Utah; University of Wisconsin—Madison

FINANCIAL FACTS

Financial Aid Rating	82
Annual in-state tuition	$11,040
Annual in-state tuition (first-year)	$11,520
Annual out-of-state tuition	$37,642
Annual out-of-state tuition (first-year)	$38,770
Room and board	$16,146
Required fees	$1,586
Books and supplies	$1,200
Average frosh need-based scholarship	$14,314
Average UG need-based scholarship	$13,657
% needy frosh rec. need-based scholarship or grant aid	77
% needy UG rec. need-based scholarship or grant aid	79
% needy frosh rec. non-need-based scholarship or grant aid	6
% needy UG rec. non-need-based scholarship or grant aid	4
% needy frosh rec. need-based self-help aid	75
% needy UG rec. need-based self-help aid	76
% frosh rec. any financial aid	77
% UG rec. any financial aid	66
% UG borrow to pay for school	36
Average cumulative indebtedness	$29,719
% frosh need fully met	32
% ugrads need fully met	33
Average % of frosh need met	72
Average % of ugrad need met	74

UNIVERSITY OF CONNECTICUT

University of Connecticut, Storrs, CT 06269 • Admissions: 860-486-2000 • Fax: 860-486-1476

CAMPUS LIFE

Quality of Life Rating	87
Fire Safety Rating	93
Green Rating	99
Type of school	Public
Environment	Town

STUDENTS

Total undergrad enrollment	19,030
% male/female/another gender	50/50/0
% from out of state	22
% frosh from public high school	88
% frosh live on campus	97
% ugrads live on campus	67
# of fraternities (% join)	23 (12)
# of sororities (% join)	13 (17)
% African American	6
% Asian	11
% White	60
% Hispanic	10
% Native American	<1
% Pacific Islander	<1
% Two or more races	3
% Race and/or ethnicity unknown	5
% international	6
# of countries represented	71

SURVEY SAYS . . .

Everyone loves the Huskies
Students are happy
Great off-campus food

ACADEMICS

Academic Rating	78
% students returning for sophomore year	92
% students graduating within 4 years	70
% students graduating within 6 years	82
Calendar	Semester
Student/faculty ratio	16:1
Profs interesting rating	83
Profs accessible rating	88

Most classes have 10–19 students.
Most lab/discussion sessions have 10–19 students.

MOST POPULAR MAJORS

Economics, General; Communication, General; Psychology, General

STUDENTS SAY "..."

Academics

The University of Connecticut may be "known for our amazing athletics," but it's also "one of the top research universities and state schools," a "university [that] truly cares about their students." As one political science major puts it, UConn is "unique because it is comprised of all different types of students both in backgrounds and ethnicities. What makes us different than other universities is our cohesiveness despite these differences. We all go to one school, we all cheer on the same team, and we all bleed blue." While "basketball games are like religion," students say that, "UConn is focused on academic achievement." For one student, the school's main appeal is that it is a "large, public university [with] a variety of programs and diversity on campus." As the "flagship state school," UConn provides "research opportunities for undergrads" and "every student is supported in order to be the most successful student possible; UConn cares." When it comes to professors, the "performance level [varies], more so during the first couple years when the students are required to take general education requirements." Students say that in more advanced, major-specific courses, "the professors tend to be more interested in the topics of the course and thus more engaging." Those professors are "truly amazing, inspiring, and add so much to my academics," but the general consensus is that "UConn is a really big university, so professors can be hit or miss."

Campus Life

"Since it's a big school, there is always something going on on-campus, whether it's free movies, lectures, concerts, food, or more." For students who want to experience nature, "There's always the opportunity to go outdoors and walk to Horsebarn Hill, go on runs around campus or go on hikes in the UConn forest." Even though the campus a little off the beaten path—one transfer student laments "the nickname for Storrs is Snores"—students say "the downtown area has developed into its own mini city" with restaurants and cafés. As one student puts it, "I am never bored on the weekend between the many shows and concerts, movies and other activities offered by the university." Greek life plays a significant role on campus—some say that "Greek life dominates many aspects of social scene," while others say only that there are "frat parties if you're into that kind of scene." The school's reputation for top notch athletics is legendary; as one student puts it, "the celebrations after victories are unlike anything I've ever experienced elsewhere." Some students are frustrated that "athletics sometimes overshadows academic achievements in funding," but others underscore the rigorousness of UConn's academics, saying "UConn is a research school so classes are difficult and professors will not go out of their way to ensure you get a good grade." When it comes to kicking back after a long week, one student succinctly sums up the alcohol culture at the school: "UConn doesn't seem to be a party school, it is a drinking school—there is a difference."

Student Body

UConn students are typically "very diverse due to the large student body"—you can find "students who love to go out every weekend at the bar [and] you can find students whose hobby is knitting or [to] go to ComiCONN...there really is a peer group for everyone." The students, "the majority of which are from Connecticut," are "uniquely passionate and spirited." As one student puts it, the school is composed of "many small communities based on academics, sports, clubs, and interests, that come together to form a large community connected by a mutual love of UConn." Some pinpoint the average student as "white, upper middle class and wears L.L. Bean boots, North Face coats," but others stress that "it's a big school, so there is no one word to describe my peers." With "more happening on campus than you expect," there are "athletic teams and Greek life" but also "human rights organizations, activists, and volunteers."

UNIVERSITY OF CONNECTICUT

Financial Aid: 860-486-2819 • E-Mail: beahusky@uconn.edu • Website: www.uconn.edu

THE PRINCETON REVIEW SAYS

Admissions

The school reports that its standardized testing policy for use in admission for Fall 2024 is SAT or ACT Required. It is unknown at this time if the 2024 testing policy will be permanent. The Princeton Review suggests that interested applicants consult with the school for the most up-to-date standardized testing policies. *Very important factors considered include:* rigor of secondary school record, class rank, academic GPA, standardized test scores. *Important factors considered include:* application essay, recommendation(s), extracurricular activities, talent/ability, character/personal qualities, first generation, volunteer work. *Other factors considered include:* alumni/ae relation, geographical residence, state residency, racial/ethnic status, work experience, level of applicant's interest. High school diploma is required and GED is accepted. *Academic units required:* 4 English, 3 math, 2 science, 2 science labs, 2 foreign language, 2 social studies, 3 academic electives. *Academic units recommended:* 3 foreign language.

Financial Aid

Students should submit: FAFSA. Priority filing deadline is 3/1. The Princeton Review suggests that all financial aid forms be submitted as soon as possible (see page 5 for a note on the FAFSA). *Need-based scholarships/grants offered:* College/university scholarship or grant aid from institutional funds; Federal Pell; Private scholarships; SEOG; State scholarships/grants. *Loan aid offered:* Direct PLUS loans; Direct Subsidized Loans; Direct Unsubsidized Loans; Federal Nursing Loans. Admitted students will be notified of awards on a rolling basis beginning 3/1. Federal Work-Study Program available. Institutional employment available.

The Inside Word

The UConn admissions committee looks at every aspect of a prospective first year's application, taking everything from GPA, class rank, extracurricular activities, standardized test scores (if submitted), a required essay, and two letters of recommendation into consideration. The university is a very selective school—college preparatory coursework in high school is required, with additional requirements for School of Engineering and School of Nursing applicants—and students should be sure that all aspects of their application pass muster.

THE SCHOOL SAYS "..."

From the Admissions Office

"Founded in 1881, the University of Connecticut is ranked as one of the best public universities in the United States. With a combination of dynamic faculty, strong athletic pride and an extraordinary sense of community, UConn is a university like no other. Offering over 110 majors and the ability to create a major of your own, a broad range of academic choices is provided. Faculty members are top experts in their fields, and serve as mentors and advisors to students. Distinctive research opportunities pair undergraduate students with faculty in every academic discipline offered. The main campus in Storrs is located in a safe New England town midway between New York City and Boston. With one of the highest percentages of students living on campus of any public university in the United States, UConn is its own community within a thriving rural town. With on-campus museums and performances, and newly released movies right inside the Student Union's theater, UConn students work hard and play hard. Over 650 student clubs and organizations allow students to pursue their passions outside the classroom. School spirit permeates the campus. Students can cheer on one of our twenty-four Division I teams, or join one of our intramural or club sports teams. No matter how students are involved, they exemplify the Husky Spirit.

"Interested in learning more about what UConn can offer you? For details on the admissions process or to schedule a campus tour, visit admissions.uconn.edu."

SELECTIVITY

Admissions Rating	91
# of applicants	35,980
% of applicants accepted	49
% of acceptees attending	22
# offered a place on the wait list	3,386
% accepting a place on wait list	53
% admitted from wait list	8

FIRST-YEAR PROFILE

Testing policy	SAT or ACT Required
Range SAT EBRW	600–680
Range SAT math	610–710
Range ACT composite	26–31
# submitting SAT scores	3,011
% submitting SAT scores	82
# submitting ACT scores	1,233
% submitting ACT scores	33
% frosh submitting high school GPA	89
% graduated top 10% of class	51
% graduated top 25% of class	84
% graduated top 50% of class	98

DEADLINES

Regular	
Deadline	1/15
Notification	Rolling, 3/1
Nonfall registration?	Yes

FINANCIAL FACTS

Financial Aid Rating	77
Annual in-state tuition	$13,798
Annual out-of-state tuition	$36,466
Room and board	$13,258
Required fees	$3,428
Books and supplies	$950
Average frosh need-based scholarship	$14,041
Average UG need-based scholarship	$13,049
% needy frosh rec. need-based scholarship or grant aid	67
% needy UG rec. need-based scholarship or grant aid	71
% needy frosh rec. non-need-based scholarship or grant aid	40
% needy UG rec. non-need-based scholarship or grant aid	33
% needy frosh rec. need-based self-help aid	62
% needy UG rec. need-based self-help aid	72
% frosh rec. any financial aid	49
% UG rec. any financial aid	48
% UG borrow to pay for school	59
Average cumulative indebtedness	$28,028
% frosh need fully met	15
% ugrads need fully met	12
Average % of frosh need met	58
Average % of ugrad need met	57

UNIVERSITY OF DALLAS

1845 East Northgate Drive, Irving, TX 75062 • Admissions: 972-721-5000

STUDENTS SAY "..."

Academics

The University of Dallas is a great option for students looking to join a deeply intellectual and spiritual community. After all, the school "offers an incredible liberal arts education, an authentically Catholic community, an active and lively campus atmosphere, and a fantastic Rome study abroad program." UD prides itself on a core curriculum that introduces undergrads to "the great works of Western Civilization" and "gives all the students on campus a shared experience and a wide variety of subjects in which they have a foundational understanding." According to enrollees, this coursework is "good at making the students think independently." Students also appreciate that it is "rigorous but thorough,…[preparing] students to succeed after graduation." And while classes tend to be traditional, students emphasize that they're "done to the point of excellence." For example, a history discussion that weaves together "art, politics, music, literature, and philosophy."

That excellence may stem from the professors, described as "not only great teachers but great role models." They continually demonstrate that they "care about educating the entire person and are often willing to talk with students about broader life questions as well as course specific questions." And while they "expect students to work hard and grade accordingly," they're also "more than fair, and are always willing to go above and beyond to help any student who desires it." Even better, UD professors "truly engage the class and inspire learning through their own joy in the subject.." Indeed, "they do everything in their power to bring to life the content and help each student grow."

Campus Life

"There are so many things to do that I often find myself struggling to decide how to fit them all in!" That's a great "problem" to have, and one that showcases that "while students spend substantial time during the week on coursework, they are also quite creative when it comes to relaxing and having fun." All interests are on the table, whether that's fencing, knitting, or "societies dedicated to Tocqueville and Alexander Hamilton." For those seeking additional intellectual stimulation, there are "many lectures, debates, and discussions given by our professors throughout the year." For those wanting something different, there are activities like "bonfires, musical jam sessions, intramural sports, events in Dallas and Fort Worth, road trips, camping, hiking, etc."

Student Body

The University of Dallas has cultivated a "very lively and friendly" student body that's "bright and highly driven." They're "always asking the deeper questions and very passionate about the truth." Indeed, undergrads here love to "engage in spontaneous conversation" and it's quite common to "find students in and out of class discussing the classics as if they were common knowledge to everyone." UD students also "tend to value tradition, family, and faith." This isn't too surprising given that "a majority of the students are Christian, and of those, most are Catholic." Another undergrad elaborates, "More than anywhere else I've been, my peers also have a genuine interest in being faithful people and growing in their spiritual lives." A few individuals caution that the university's culture is "catered to very conservative white Catholics," but the majority assert that "the small student body allows for genuine connections and positive interactions to take place daily—at the campus cappuccino bar, school events, and even walking down the mall between classes." As one contented undergrad shares, "I haven't walked away from a conversation without smiling."

UNIVERSITY OF DALLAS

Financial Aid: 972-721-5266 • Website: www.udallas.edu

THE PRINCETON REVIEW SAYS

Admissions

The school reports that its standardized testing policy for use in admission for Fall 2024 is SAT or ACT Required. The 2024 testing policy will be permanent. The Princeton Review suggests that interested applicants consult with the school for the most up-to-date standardized testing policies. *Very important factors considered include:* rigor of secondary school record, academic GPA, standardized test scores, application essay, recommendation(s), character/personal qualities. *Important factors considered include:* class rank, talent/ability. *Other factors considered include:* interview, extracurricular activities, first generation, alumni/ae relation, volunteer work, work experience, level of applicant's interest. High school diploma is required and GED is accepted. *Academic units required:* 4 English, 3 math, 3 science, 2 foreign language, 3 social studies, 3 history, 1 visual/performing arts, 3 academic electives. *Academic units recommended:* 4 English, 4 math, 3 science, 3 science labs, 3 foreign language, 4 social studies, 4 history, 2 visual/performing arts, 4 academic electives.

Financial Aid

Students should submit: FAFSA. Priority filing deadline is 1/15. The Princeton Review suggests that all financial aid forms be submitted as soon as possible (see page 5 for a note on the FAFSA). *Need-based scholarships/grants offered:* College/university scholarship or grant aid from institutional funds; Federal Pell; Private scholarships; SEOG; State scholarships/grants. *Loan aid offered:* Direct PLUS loans; Direct Subsidized Loans; Direct Unsubsidized Loans; State Loans. Admitted students will be notified of awards on a rolling basis beginning 12/1. Federal Work-Study Program available. Institutional employment available.

The Inside Word

Because of University of Dallas's distinction as a Catholic liberal arts school, its applicant pool is frequently small but self-selective. As such, don't be fooled by its relatively high acceptance rate—strong academic performance and test scores are closely considered, as are students who demonstrate moral and ethical commitment in addition to intellectual curiosity.

THE SCHOOL SAYS "..."

From the Admissions Office

"Undergraduates at UD, whether they choose to major in art history, business, pastoral ministry, or one of 30 other programs, all share the formative experience of the Core Curriculum. 'The Core,' which consists of courses in humanities, sciences, and fine arts, provides a common cross-disciplinary foundation that students carry forth into their various majors. This curriculum roots all further studies in the great deeds and works of Western civilization and inspires an ongoing dialogue with the past that helps in understanding the present. The common Core fuels robust discussion both inside and outside of the classroom, even more so when students travel to Rome for a semester as part of our renowned Rome Program, where all classes are part of the Core. While there, students can experience firsthand much of what they have learned about in class. We believe that education is more than just a means to an end, so our curriculum is designed to provide students with wisdom, knowledge, and skills that can be applied to all areas of life—intellectual, professional, spiritual and personal. As students develop life skills, such as independent and critical thinking, UD also offers them the support and encouragement of a dedicated faith community that enables them to engage the world beyond graduation as people of faith. All in all, the undergraduate UD experience is an inquiry into the fundamental aspects of being and our relationship with God, nature, and our fellow human beings, all while pursuing wisdom, truth, and virtue as the proper and primary ends of education."

SELECTIVITY

Admissions Rating	89
# of applicants	4,307
% of applicants accepted	59
% of acceptees attending	16

FIRST-YEAR PROFILE

Testing policy	SAT or ACT Required
Range SAT composite	1190–1390
Range SAT EBRW	590–720
Range SAT math	580–680
Range ACT composite	24–31
# submitting SAT scores	122
% submitting SAT scores	30
# submitting ACT scores	72
% submitting ACT scores	18
Average HS GPA	4.0
% frosh submitting high school GPA	98
% graduated top 10% of class	18
% graduated top 25% of class	44
% graduated top 50% of class	65

DEADLINES

Early action	
Deadline	12/1
Notification	1/15
Regular	
Priority	12/1
Deadline	8/1
Notification	Rolling, 9/15
Nonfall registration?	Yes

APPLICANTS ALSO LOOK AT

Baylor University; Benedictine College; Franciscan University of Steubenville; Hillsdale College; Texas A&M University—College Station; Texas Tech University; The Catholic University of America; Trinity University; University of Houston; University of North Texas

FINANCIAL FACTS

Financial Aid Rating	85
Annual tuition	$47,300
Room and board	$14,360
Required fees	$3,580
Books and supplies	$1,500
Average frosh need-based scholarship	$38,946
Average UG need-based scholarship	$36,268
% needy frosh rec. need-based scholarship or grant aid	99
% needy UG rec. need-based scholarship or grant aid	61
% needy frosh rec. non-need-based scholarship or grant aid	11
% needy UG rec. non-need-based scholarship or grant aid	16
% needy frosh rec. need-based self-help aid	68
% needy UG rec. need-based self-help aid	40
% frosh rec. any financial aid	100
% UG rec. any financial aid	98
% UG borrow to pay for school	60
Average cumulative indebtedness	$28,706
% frosh need fully met	15
% ugrads need fully met	11
Average % of frosh need met	81
Average % of ugrad need met	77

UNIVERSITY OF DAYTON

300 College Park, Dayton, OH 45469 • Admissions: 937-229-1000 • Fax: 937-229-4729

STUDENTS SAY "..."

Academics

There are many reasons to attend the University of Dayton, but the one mentioned above all is its experiential learning. "We have opportunities for real world experience in every major" (and sometimes even further independent expertises by department), like "the Sophomore Experience Entrepreneurship Program that gives students a $5,000 grant to run their own microbusiness." Engineers have space, time, and resources to build rigs and run experiments, "the music program is phenomenal," and minicourses in subjects like microeconomics utilize the Dayton area to show "the interaction between economics and the environment through outdoor excursions that were often very informative." All of this is backstopped by the professors, whom students give high marks. "Most of my professors have been extremely nice, approachable, and engaging." They "challenge you but also really want you to succeed, especially if you participate in discussions and provide quality work on assignments and exams." Indeed, "they want to show each student that they have potential to be great, but they have to unlock it."

Campus Life

At the University of Dayton, learning and excitement extend far beyond the classroom: "there are activities going on everywhere, on-campus jobs to partake in, as well as a variety of organizations and clubs." As one undergrad elaborates, "I've been in Bella Voce (the women's choral ensembles), Opera Workshop (a musical theater class)...and Javanese Gamelan ensemble (a percussion tradition from Indonesia)." Additionally, "intramural sports are very active on campus...[along with] professional organizations that align with your major, ethnicity, or gender." Of course, there's plenty of casual fun to be had as well; students mention sledding in winter, hanging out at Kennedy Union and "[playing] pool or [going] bowling at the Hangar." And eating is a serious activity at Dayton, given that "the food is awesome." Some students describe "a lot of partying" on the weekends, but also suggest that "people do not pressure you into drinking if you don't want to."

Student Body

Undergrads at the University of Dayton overwhelmingly agree that their peers are "very sweet," and "super welcoming and approachable" people who foster a strong sense of community and school spirit. Given the "relatively small class sizes, it's easy to get to know a lot of people in your major" and others more simply describe it as common to see "strangers quickly become friends and friends become like family." As for finding a balance between school work and social lives: "we aren't just book worms, and we are not just party animals. We are both." The student body remains "predominantly white," though "there are [now] more POC and LGBTQ+ students than there have ever been before." Moreover, students feel strongly about inclusion, noting that "students never need to be told to work together to create a safe and inclusive campus, they just do."

UNIVERSITY OF DAYTON

Financial Aid: 800-427-5029 • E-Mail: admission@udayton.edu • Website: www.udayton.edu

THE PRINCETON REVIEW SAYS

Admissions

The school reports that its standardized testing policy for use in admission for Fall 2024 is Test Optional. The 2024 testing policy will be permanent. The Princeton Review suggests that interested applicants consult with the school for the most up-to-date standardized testing policies. *Very important factors considered include:* rigor of secondary school record, class rank, academic GPA, application essay. *Important factors considered include:* recommendation(s), extracurricular activities, character/personal qualities, alumni/ae relation, level of applicant's interest. *Other factors considered include:* standardized test scores, talent/ability, first generation, racial/ethnic status, volunteer work, work experience. High school diploma is required and GED is accepted. *Academic units recommended:* 4 English, 4 math, 4 science, 1 science lab, 2 foreign language, 4 social studies, 4 history, 4 computer science, 4 visual/performing arts.

Financial Aid

Students should submit: FAFSA. Priority filing deadline is 2/1. The Princeton Review suggests that all financial aid forms be submitted as soon as possible (see page 5 for a note on the FAFSA). *Need-based scholarships/grants offered:* College/university scholarship or grant aid from institutional funds; Federal Pell; Private scholarships; State scholarships/grants. *Loan aid offered:* Direct PLUS loans; Direct Subsidized Loans; Direct Unsubsidized Loans; College/university loans from institutional funds. Admitted students will be notified of awards on a rolling basis. Federal Work-Study Program available. Institutional employment available.

The Inside Word

When it comes to the admissions process at the University of Dayton, academics take top priority. Indeed, the committee pays close attention to both your GPA and grade pattern throughout your high school tenure, course selection, and class rank. UD is Test Optional. To a lesser extent, the university considers factors such as letters of recommendation. Demonstrating genuine, strong interest in the university helps.

THE SCHOOL SAYS "..."

From the Admissions Office

"The University of Dayton is a top-tier national Catholic research university, committed to a diverse, inclusive environment. Founded in 1850 by the Society of Mary (Marianists), UD is distinguished by our academics, research, and commitment to the common good. Our students don't just learn by doing—they learn by doing good in the world. We offer more than 80 undergraduate and 50 graduate and doctoral programs, as well as bachelor plus masters programs, and we provide credit for college-level courses and exams. Our students can work alongside GE Aviation and Emerson professionals in on-campus research facilities or study abroad at locations around the world. Academic programs are offered in the College of Arts and Sciences and the Schools of Business Administration, Education and Health Sciences, Engineering, and Law. Classes are small, which is just one reason nearly all of our students find success within six months of graduation. We're also a strong research institution; UD performed nearly $221 million in sponsored research last year, and our faculty are committed to teaching undergraduate students and involving them in their research projects. Dedicated to transparent affordability, we provide locked-in net tuition all four years, with no fees. We also offer scholarships for textbooks and studying abroad. Since we launched this innovative tuition plan, our students have reduced borrowing significantly, and our graduation rate is 81.5%, compared to an average 68% for four-year private universities. A strong sense of community is core to the UD experience; eighty-five percent of our students live on campus all four years, either in our residence halls or our unique, porch-clad student neighborhood. And through organizations like our Multi-Ethnic Education and Engagement Center, we build a community spirit that celebrates inclusivity and the Marianist values of learning, service, leadership, and community."

UNIVERSITY OF DELAWARE

University of Delaware, Newark, DE 19716 • Admissions: 302-831-2000 • Fax: 302-831-6905

CAMPUS LIFE

Quality of Life Rating	84
Fire Safety Rating	99
Green Rating	78
Type of school	Public
Environment	Town

STUDENTS

Total undergrad enrollment	17,968
% male/female/another gender	41/59/0
% from out of state	62
% frosh from public high school	80
% frosh live on campus	93
% ugrads live on campus	38
# of fraternities (% join)	24 (15)
# of sororities (% join)	19 (22)
% African American	6
% Asian	5
% White	69
% Hispanic	9
% Native American	<1
% Pacific Islander	<1
% Two or more races	4
% Race and/or ethnicity unknown	2
% international	5
# of countries represented	81

SURVEY SAYS . . .

Frats and sororities are popular
Students are happy
Great library
Great off-campus food

ACADEMICS

Academic Rating	76
% students returning for sophomore year	92
% students graduating within 4 years	73
% students graduating within 6 years	84
Calendar	4/1/4
Student/faculty ratio	12:1
Profs interesting rating	84
Profs accessible rating	88

Most classes have 20–29 students.
Most lab/discussion sessions have
20–29 students.

MOST POPULAR MAJORS

Registered Nursing/Registered Nurse; Biology/
Biological Sciences, General; Finance, General

STUDENTS SAY ". . ."

Academics

The University of Delaware is one of the country's oldest universities, providing its more than 18,000 undergraduates with access to 150 majors and minors and outstanding research opportunities thanks new "research labs in different areas" that are "being started each year" and "connections to local Delaware institutions." A STEM major says: "We have clinical rotations at hospitals built into our curriculum, which is great for real world experience, and even getting job offers from the hospitals that like you." Students also point to their World Scholars program, which pairs international study with "campus global engagement and internships" as proof that the school's "study abroad programs are some of the best you will find at any university." All in all, "the amount of resources for students is endless, whether it comes to advising, tutoring, career-oriented, or physical and mental health services."

Professors "are passionate about educating their students" and students are "allowed to debate and discuss…instead of just listening to the teacher tell us what we were supposed to think." Some "try using a reverse classroom (where you are exposed to the content before the lecture) and discussion-based classes," and others still "allow us to partake in field experiences starting in our [first] year." Faculty look to keep things fresh and engaging, whether that's "making a creative art project the final instead of a paper" or "bring[ing] in local companies and guest speakers from industry/academia often."

Campus Life

Students say that the University of Delaware is "a big school" but not overwhelmingly so, as "you will always see familiar faces," especially if you partake in the "many events during the week [for] school pride." To put it another way, it's a very "connected campus" with "a space or group for almost anything a student could possibly want to do, from creating music, to cooking, to playing video games, to woodworking." There are "a lot of hands-on activities clubs and student activities" for people to take part in, and many value the "club and intramural sports teams to join, as well as supporting our D1 sports teams." It's also a very maintained campus with "up-to-date and very nice" resources, like the beloved gym "where there is a swimming pool and a rock wall open to all students." The surrounding area's Main Street is a "super popular" venue, with "an abundant amount of restaurants that let you sit, talk, and/or do work." Location matters, but at this school, socializing comes first: "Anywhere from dining halls to student areas, everyone interacts with each other at all times."

Student Body

This is a group of "driven individuals who aren't afraid to push boundaries and know what they want for themselves," and are "hardworking and intelligent, but also easygoing and fun." As a larger school, there is a wide range of "different backgrounds, experiences, and other factors that lead to enlightening discussions and new perspectives," and students feel "there is a space somewhere on campus for everyone where they would feel comfortable and at home." UD is also home to "a massive community dedicated to their health and wanting to better themselves mentally and physically." According to respondents, "almost every person is involved in one way or another" whether that's with Greek life, dancing, sports, or work, so "it is easy to find the group of people that best match your personality and interests." To sum things up, "In general, my peers are very inclusive and enthusiastic about their time at UD."

UNIVERSITY OF DELAWARE

Financial Aid: 302-831-0520 • E-Mail: admissions@udel.edu • Website: www.udel.edu/

THE PRINCETON REVIEW SAYS

Admissions

The school reports that its standardized testing policy for use in admission for Fall 2024 is SAT or ACT Required. It is unknown at this time if the 2024 testing policy will be permanent. The Princeton Review suggests that interested applicants consult with the school for the most up-to-date standardized testing policies. *Very important factors considered include:* rigor of secondary school record, academic GPA, state residency. *Important factors considered include:* standardized test scores, application essay, recommendation(s), extracurricular activities, talent/ability, character/personal qualities, volunteer work, work experience. *Other factors considered include:* class rank, interview, first generation, alumni/ae relation, geographical residence, racial/ethnic status, level of applicant's interest. High school diploma is required and GED is accepted. *Academic units required:* 4 English, 3 math, 3 science, 2 science labs, 2 foreign language, 2 social studies, 2 history, 2 academic electives. *Academic units recommended:* 4 English, 4 math, 4 science, 3 science labs, 4 foreign language, 2 social studies, 2 history, 2 academic electives.

Financial Aid

Students should submit: FAFSA. Priority filing deadline is 1/15. The Princeton Review suggests that all financial aid forms be submitted as soon as possible (see page 5 for a note on the FAFSA). *Need-based scholarships/grants offered:* College/university scholarship or grant aid from institutional funds; Federal Pell; Private scholarships; SEOG; State scholarships/grants. *Loan aid offered:* Direct PLUS loans; Direct Subsidized Loans; Direct Unsubsidized Loans; Federal Nursing Loans. Admitted students will be notified of awards on a rolling basis beginning 2/1. Federal Work-Study Program available. Institutional employment available.

The Inside Word

UD is state assisted but privately governed. Out-of-state students also benefit from the school's academic and social offerings at a reasonable tuition. Even so, the school is expressly committed to supporting Delawarean students, who compose about 34 percent of each incoming class. More details and samples of qualifying high school curricula are available on the admissions department website. In all admissions decisions, UD considers the entirety of a student's application; there are no minimum test scores or GPAs.

THE SCHOOL SAYS "..."

From the Admissions Office

"The University of Delaware was chartered in 1743 and is located in Newark, DE, a vibrant college town midway between New York City and Washington, D.C. At UD, you can go from a concert in our music halls to a lecture on bioengineering to a tour of the ancient world in our study abroad program. For each of our 17,000 undergraduate students, we foster connections: connections to ideas, to professors and to alumni, connections that can be cultivated into assets for the future. In each of our 150+ majors, our broad academic selections and our priority for hands-on research is designed to stimulate a passion for learning, curiosity and a connection with the larger world.

"Our distinguished faculty includes internationally known authors, scientists, business professionals and artists. State-of-the-art facilities support UD's academic, research and service activities. You'll find campus life is welcoming, enriched by distinguished speakers from various fields, NCAA Division I intercollegiate athletics, 400-plus student organizations, and a host of cultural activities."

SELECTIVITY

Admissions Rating	87
# of applicants	33,965
% of applicants accepted	70
% of acceptees attending	18
# offered a place on the wait list	1,861
% accepting a place on wait list	11
% admitted from wait list	38

FIRST-YEAR PROFILE

Testing policy	SAT or ACT Required
Range SAT EBRW	590–670
Range SAT math	580–680
Range ACT composite	26–31
# submitting SAT scores	1,338
% submitting SAT scores	60
# submitting ACT scores	253
% submitting ACT scores	11
Average HS GPA	3.9
% frosh submitting high school GPA	98
% graduated top 10% of class	32
% graduated top 25% of class	65
% graduated top 50% of class	93

DEADLINES

Early action	
Deadline	11/1
Notification	1/31
Regular	
Priority	1/15
Deadline	1/15
Notification	Rolling, 11/1
Nonfall registration?	Yes

APPLICANTS OFTEN PREFER

Penn State University Park; University of Maryland, College Park

APPLICANTS SOMETIMES PREFER

James Madison University; University of Connecticut

FINANCIAL FACTS

Financial Aid Rating	79
Annual in-state tuition	$13,370
Annual out-of-state tuition	$35,890
Room and board	$14,234
Required fees	$2,040
Books and supplies	$1,000
Average frosh need-based scholarship	$13,169
Average UG need-based scholarship	$11,412
% needy frosh rec. need-based scholarship or grant aid	95
% needy UG rec. need-based scholarship or grant aid	89
% needy frosh rec. non-need-based scholarship or grant aid	13
% needy UG rec. non-need-based scholarship or grant aid	8
% needy frosh rec. need-based self-help aid	66
% needy UG rec. need-based self-help aid	75
% frosh rec. any financial aid	83
% UG rec. any financial aid	76
% UG borrow to pay for school	61
Average cumulative indebtedness	$39,841
% frosh need fully met	16
% ugrads need fully met	11
Average % of frosh need met	62
Average % of ugrad need met	55

UNIVERSITY OF DENVER

2199 South University Boulevard, Denver, CO 80208 • Admissions: 303-871-2036 • Fax: 303-871-2201

CAMPUS LIFE

Quality of Life Rating	91
Fire Safety Rating	82
Green Rating	93
Type of school	Private
Affiliation	No Affiliation
Environment	Metropolis

STUDENTS

Total undergrad enrollment	5,987
% male/female/another gender	45/55/NR
% from out of state	70
% frosh live on campus	95
% ugrads live on campus	51
% join fraternities	16
% join sororities	20
% African American	3
% Asian	4
% White	69
% Hispanic	13
% Native American	<1
% Pacific Islander	<1
% Two or more races	6
% Race and/or ethnicity unknown	2
% international	3
# of countries represented	51

SURVEY SAYS . . .

Lots of conservative students
Students are happy
Classroom facilities are great
Great library
Career services are great
Students are friendly
Students love Denver, CO
Easy to get around campus
Recreation facilities are great
Intramural sports are popular
Students get along with local community
Students environmentally aware
Great off-campus food
Everyone loves the Pioneers
Frats and sororities are popular
Active student government

ACADEMICS

Academic Rating	85
% students returning for sophomore year	88
% students graduating within 4 years	70
% students graduating within 6 years	77
Calendar	Quarter
Student/faculty ratio	8:1
Profs interesting rating	91
Profs accessible rating	94

Most classes have 10–19 students.
Most lab/discussion sessions have
20–29 students.

MOST POPULAR MAJORS

Psychology, General; Finance, General; Marketing/
Marketing Management, General

STUDENTS SAY "..."

Academics

At the University of Denver—the oldest private university in the Rocky Mountain region—the faculty and staff are "extremely dedicated to ensuring that the students receive a high-quality, worthwhile education." The business and accountancy programs are the standouts of the "plethora of classes to choose from," but the school is all about "a global view and interdisciplinary courses" and so has one of the best study abroad programs in the nation, giving students the option to do so without straying from their majors or incurring additional expense, and offering international travel interterm courses to students.

The "lively, passionate" professors teach with hands-on, real-life examples that "prompt students to critically think and apply what is learned in the classroom to our future careers and life." Teachers usually allow students to dictate speed and amount of discussion on a topic as the class allows, and take a vested interest in each student's success: They "care more about how you do in the long run than how you may perform in individual classes." "If you try hard, they will engage with you and truly become your friends." "The face-to-face time you get with them is a big reason why I feel so connected to my school," says another student.

Networking here "happens almost without effort; it is ingrained in every aspect of most classes and activities" and there is a "good connection with [the] Denver business community." DU has "basically every resource on campus for advising, counseling, health, and assistance with school work," an "awesome" library, and "there are a lot of 'green' initiatives...it feels quite progressive." Though the common curriculum isn't universally beloved, students appreciate that DU runs on a quarterly system, so people "can take more credits than other semester schools...if you don't like a particular class,...you are done within ten weeks and you can move on with classes you enjoy."

Campus Life

DU is close enough to the city of Denver that it is possible for students to head downtown whenever they feel like it (the light rail stops on campus and is free for students), but "far enough away that I still get the 'campus' feel." "The nightlife is great around the DU area (for students of age) and downtown has amazing bars and restaurants." The residential living communities and programs get high marks, and "there is never a dull moment on campus." "Everyone is so active and there is so much going on that you almost feel bad if you're not doing anything," says a student. "Microbrews! Pub Quizzes! Poetry Slams! Sleep! Reading! Concerts!" sums up another.

If there's one trait that DU students share, it's "outdoorsy." Many students spend their weekends being active, active, active and enjoy meeting people through the Alpine Club, which "sponsors trips to nearby mountains, deserts, and parks for outdoor activities like skiing, hiking, biking, and backpacking." "Find a friend who comes from one of the ski towns, and see if you can bum a ride from them for a weekend on the slopes," suggests a student. About one-quarter of the student population goes Greek, and intramurals and hockey are huge. Denver also has an amazing music scene; "Red Rocks Amphitheatre is—no exaggeration—the best music venue on the globe."

Student Body

DU has a wide variety of people (the majority being "white and middle to upper class") who are "pretty driven," while still "[knowing] how to make time to do something outdoorsy on the weekends." Everybody "respects themselves and the people around them, especially in the learning environment." Obviously, everyone here "loves to ski" and social lives are a huge part of the DU campus culture, so "many join club sports, student orgs, or student alliances" through which they "are able to easily find people to relate to."

UNIVERSITY OF DENVER

Financial Aid: 303-871-4020 • E-Mail: admission@du.edu • Website: www.du.edu

THE PRINCETON REVIEW SAYS

Admissions

The school reports that its standardized testing policy for use in admission for Fall 2024 is Test Optional. The 2024 testing policy will be permanent. The Princeton Review suggests that interested applicants consult with the school for the most up-to-date standardized testing policies. *Very important factors considered include:* rigor of secondary school record, academic GPA. *Important factors considered include:* standardized test scores, application essay, recommendation(s), extracurricular activities, talent/ability, character/personal qualities. *Other factors considered include:* first generation, alumni/ae relation, geographical residence, racial/ethnic status, volunteer work, work experience, level of applicant's interest. High school diploma is required and GED is accepted. *Academic units recommended:* 4 English, 4 math, 4 science, 2 science labs, 4 foreign language, 4 social studies.

Financial Aid

Students should submit: CSS/Financial Aid Profile; FAFSA; Noncustodial Profile. Priority filing deadline is 2/15. The Princeton Review suggests that all financial aid forms be submitted as soon as possible (see page 5 for a note on the FAFSA). *Need-based scholarships/ grants offered:* College/university scholarship or grant aid from institutional funds; Federal Pell; Private scholarships; SEOG; State scholarships/grants. *Loan aid offered:* Direct PLUS loans; Direct Subsidized Loans; Direct Unsubsidized Loans; College/university loans from institutional funds. Admitted students will be notified of awards on or about 3/1. Federal Work-Study Program available. Institutional employment available.

The Inside Word

Admission officers at University of Denver take a holistic approach to the application process. Therefore, they strive to look beyond quantitative factors and will also review your essay, recommendations, and extracurricular activities. The average high school GPA has been steadily rising each year, and is now up to a 3.8, so stay on top of your classes.

THE SCHOOL SAYS "..."

From the Admissions Office

"At the University of Denver—in our setting of great natural beauty, cultural richness, and intellectual energy—you'll experience meaningful interaction with professors who set you on paths toward personal discovery, paths that can change the course of your future. Our diverse student body, engaged faculty, and prime location provide a culture of opportunity that is unique and unrivaled. DU is continually developing educational initiatives that help students prepare for an ever-changing world. Our Living and Learning Communities and Pioneer Leadership Program provide extracurricular and co-curricular programming in specialized areas; the Partners in Scholarship (PinS) program funds undergraduate research for students wishing to pursue a topic of personal interest in greater depth; and nearly 80 percent of our students are taking advantage of invaluable internship opportunities in laboratories, corporate offices, government agencies, and cultural settings. One of the university's signature offerings is the Cherrington Global Scholars program, which allows students to study abroad at the same cost of a quarter spent on campus at DU. Over 70 percent of our students study abroad, which ranks DU fourth in the nation among doctoral and research institutions for percentage of students participating. Outside the classroom, DU students put ideas and ideals into action. They are active members of our community and they take advantage of the numerous recreational opportunities available to them, including club, intramural, and 17 Division I sports. Whatever their majors and interests, DU students are inspired by Denver's Rocky Mountain spirit of exploration and openness, and are encouraged to engage in and personalize their educational journey."

SELECTIVITY

Admissions Rating	87
# of applicants	19,342
% of applicants accepted	78
% of acceptees attending	11
# offered a place on the wait list	500
% accepting a place on wait list	40
% admitted from wait list	2
# of early decision applicants	224
% accepted early decision	62

FIRST-YEAR PROFILE

Testing policy	Test Optional
Range SAT composite	1240–1390
Range SAT EBRW	620–710
Range SAT math	600–690
Range ACT composite	28–32
# submitting SAT scores	444
% submitting SAT scores	27
# submitting ACT scores	378
% submitting ACT scores	23
Average HS GPA	3.8
% frosh submitting high school GPA	74
% graduated top 10% of class	41
% graduated top 25% of class	68
% graduated top 50% of class	94

DEADLINES

Early decision	
Deadline	11/1
Notification	12/15
Other ED deadline	1/15
Other ED notification	2/20
Early action	
Deadline	11/1
Notification	1/15
Regular	
Deadline	1/15
Notification	3/15
Nonfall registration?	Yes

APPLICANTS OFTEN PREFER

Colorado College; Colorado State University; University of Colorado Boulder

APPLICANTS SOMETIMES PREFER

Boston University; Santa Clara University; Southern Methodist University; The George Washington University; University of Puget Sound; University of Southern California; University of Vermont

FINANCIAL FACTS

Financial Aid Rating	86
Annual tuition	$58,032
Room and board	$17,049
Required fees	$1,179
Books and supplies	$1,000
Average frosh need-based scholarship	$40,912
Average UG need-based scholarship	$40,501
% needy frosh rec. need-based scholarship or grant aid	100
% needy UG rec. need-based scholarship or grant aid	99
% needy frosh rec. non-need-based scholarship or grant aid	26
% needy UG rec. non-need-based scholarship or grant aid	26
% needy frosh rec. need-based self-help aid	65
% needy UG rec. need-based self-help aid	63
% frosh rec. any financial aid	96
% UG rec. any financial aid	93
% UG borrow to pay for school	44
Average cumulative indebtedness	$31,313
% frosh need fully met	33
% ugrads need fully met	33
Average % of frosh need met	85
Average % of ugrad need met	83

UNIVERSITY OF FLORIDA

University of Florida, Gainesville, FL 32611 • Admissions: 352-392-3261 • Fax: 352-392-2115

This narrative, like all others in this book, is based on student responses and data collected prior to the 2023–2024 academic school year. While these profiles strive to be an accurate depiction of what to expect for the upcoming year, recent developments in the Florida state system may change the academic offerings and overall atmosphere at colleges in the system. Students should check the free online tools for this book (see page vi) for any late-breaking administrative news and they should voice any concerns or questions with the colleges directly.

STUDENTS SAY "..."

Academics

Located in the heart of the "Gator Nation," the University of Florida offers "one of the best educations in the nation." Students are proud that UF is "the best state school in Florida" and "one of the top public universities in the nation"; they also love that it's "a great school with a large alumni network," that there's plenty of "intellectual stimulation" to be found there, and that UF's "research opportunities are abundant." Though the school has "strong academic standards" across the board, programs in Business and Journalism are particularly "highly ranked." Students say that the university's size doesn't sacrifice individuals' ability to focus on their course of study: "Classes for your major are hard, but they prepare you for more than easier classes would. They better prepare you for your career." Moreover, "as a research university with nearly every graduate program imaginable, the opportunities are endless." Students praise the "truly incredible faculty and staff" and appreciate that "one of the greatest strengths of UF is the fact there is always someone to turn to for help." Class structure is still impacted by the school's size in that "lectures are 80–90 percent of class activities," but conversely, students love "having experts in my field teaching all of my classes for my major." If "breadth of opportunities" for a value price is a priority for you, "The Gator Nation is one where anyone can build a future for themselves."

Campus Life

Students with "tons of school spirit" will fit right in at the University of Florida, as "a lot of UF culture is based around sports." There's also a healthy share of party culture, with students stating that "Bars are the big scene" in town and that "there is a really intense nightlife," and noting that Greek life "is a big deal in both the social and extracurricular scene." Those seeking other options will find them, however, as "There is literally a club for everyone at UF" as well as volunteer opportunities, like "at the hospital located on campus." Ultimately, you "make it what you want. You can party every day or you can study every day."

Student Body

While "everyone is different," "fraternity and sorority participation...dominates the student culture." Students are "hard working and interested in getting ahead," and "even though UF is considered a party school, it is full of people who put their future careers first." "Students fit in by taking part in and participating in the various things our campus offers" and are often "busy and focused usually on one subject matter or area of interest to be involved in through extracurricular activities." Even though it's a large campus, one student remarks on the sense of community: "We're students? I thought we were all part of one big family!" They find each other "mostly accepting and friendly," but as a whole "hard to define. Gators are religious and non-religious, Greek and non-Greek, obsessed with athletics and some couldn't care less." Overall, the typical UF student "knows how to balance their school work and still have a good time."

UNIVERSITY OF FLORIDA

Financial Aid: 352-294-3226 • Website: www.ufl.edu

THE PRINCETON REVIEW SAYS

Admissions

The school reports that its standardized testing policy for use in admission for Fall 2024 is SAT or ACT Required. It is unknown at this time if the 2024 testing policy will be permanent. The Princeton Review suggests that interested applicants consult with the school for the most up-to-date standardized testing policies. *Very important factors considered include:* rigor of secondary school record, academic GPA, application essay, extracurricular activities, talent/ability, character/personal qualities. *Important factors considered include:* standardized test scores, first generation, volunteer work, work experience. *Other factors considered include:* class rank, geographical residence, state residency. High school diploma is required and GED is accepted. *Academic units required:* 4 English, 4 math, 3 science, 2 science labs, 2 foreign language *Academic units recommended:* 4 English, 4 math, 4 science, 4 foreign language.

Financial Aid

Students should submit: FAFSA. Priority filing deadline is 12/15. The Princeton Review suggests that all financial aid forms be submitted as soon as possible (see page 5 for a note on the FAFSA). *Need-based scholarships/grants offered:* College/university scholarship or grant aid from institutional funds; Federal Pell; Private scholarships; SEOG; State scholarships/grants; United Negro College Fund. *Loan aid offered:* Direct PLUS loans; Direct Subsidized Loans; Direct Unsubsidized Loans; College/university loans from institutional funds. Federal Work-Study Program available. Institutional employment available.

The Inside Word

Unlike many state universities, UF doesn't publish an admissions formula, saying rather that they use a "holistic review" process to determine candidates' eligibility. Their application's short-answer and essay questions are emphasized in factors considered, and first-generation college students from low-income backgrounds should take note of the Florida Opportunity Scholars program, which covers four years of tuition in full.

THE SCHOOL SAYS "..."

From the Admissions Office

"Thirty-two percent of the student body is composed of graduate students. Within the undergraduate population, approximately 1,739 African-American students, 8,293 Hispanic students, and 3,812 Asian-American students attend UF. Ninety percent of the entering freshmen rank above the national mean of scores on standard entrance exams. UF consistently ranks near the top among public universities in the number of new National Merit and Achievement scholars in attendance.

"Students must submit the SAT or the ACT with or without the writing section. UF considers your highest section scores across all SAT test dates."

SELECTIVITY

Admissions Rating	96
# of applicants	64,473
% of applicants accepted	23
% of acceptees attending	44

FIRST-YEAR PROFILE

Testing policy	SAT or ACT Required
Range SAT composite	1320–1470
Range SAT EBRW	650–730
Range SAT math	650–760
Range ACT composite	28–33
# submitting SAT scores	5,358
% submitting SAT scores	81
# submitting ACT scores	2,729
% submitting ACT scores	41
Average HS GPA	3.9
% frosh submitting high school GPA	96
% graduated top 10% of class	84
% graduated top 25% of class	98
% graduated top 50% of class	100

DEADLINES

Regular	
Priority	11/1
Deadline	3/1
Nonfall registration?	Yes

APPLICANTS ALSO LOOK AT

Florida State University; Georgia Institute of Technology; The University of Texas at Austin; University of Central Florida; University of Georgia; University of Miami; University of Michigan—Ann Arbor; University of North Carolina—Chapel Hill; University of South Florida; University of Virginia

FINANCIAL FACTS

Financial Aid Rating	82
Annual in-state tuition	$6,381
Annual out-of-state tuition	$28,658
Room and board	$10,400
Books and supplies	$810
Average frosh need-based scholarship	$9,083
Average UG need-based scholarship	$8,476
% frosh rec. any financial aid	93
% UG rec. any financial aid	88
% UG borrow to pay for school	38
Average cumulative indebtedness	$21,800

UNIVERSITY OF GEORGIA

Administration Building, Athens, GA 30602 • Admissions: 706-542-3000

STUDENTS SAY "..."

Academics

As at many large universities, UGA has a "mixed bag of professors," but there are "more good teachers" than bad. Though students don't love the core curriculum classes due to their large size and the prevalence of TAs, "once [you're] in your particular program, the teachers are outstanding and easy to reach." "The professors really do want to see you at office hours if you have questions," and they "want to share their love of learning with you." "My major-related classes are very small, and each student receives individual attention." The honors program also receives raves: "Many of my best classes and favorite teachers have come from the honors program, but non-honors classes are generally good as well." "The study spaces are well-equipped and quiet," but "the school of social work is still housed in an old dorm." "Administration is a pain (not the people, only the requirements), but I think that describes academia in general." In general, students "feel that the administration can be very accommodating at times, but at other times it can seem like it is full of red tape." Registration technology "needs to be brought out of the 1980s and into the 21st century." "The administration [can] seem like a bunch of penny-pinchers, but they must be to run a major research facility."

Campus Life

Life at UGA seems to be a good mix of the two different worlds of sports and arts: football, frats, and tailgating on campus come together nicely with the coffee shops and music scene in downtown Athens. "On Saturday afternoons in the fall, nearly everyone on campus is at the football game. It's a way of life here." "Everybody really gets behind the team, and Saturdays in Athens feel like mini vacations." Fraternities and sororities dominate the party scene, but "there is definitely plenty to do, even if you don't go Greek." Students love to brag about the high number of bars per capita in Athens, but there's plenty more to boast about. "The Athens music and art scene is very inspiring, and there are tons of opportunities for creativity here." "Downtown Athens is fabulous! Whether you drink or don't drink, all are welcome and all congregate there." Campus life offers plenty of activity too. "Fun is a part of daily life…with a dozen intramural sports each semester…and many community activities (multiple movie theaters, bowling allies, golf course)." "Ultimate Frisbee, walks around the multiple parks, days lounging on North Campus, and spending *lots* of time downtown are a couple ways I like to have fun at school." "There are so many organizations that everyone can find a place that will feel like home or find a place to meet new people." "It's no secret that UGA knows how to party. However, most of the students know how to manage social and academic time."

Student Body

"Students are generally white, upper-middle-class, smart, [and] involved, and [they] have a good time," "seem to be predominantly conservative," and "are usually involved in at least one organization whether it be Greek, a club, or sports." "The typical student at UGA is one who knows how and when to study but allows himself or herself to have a very active social life." The majority are southerners, with many students from within Georgia. "The stereotype is Southern, Republican, football-loving, and beer-drinking. While many, many of UGA's students do not fit this description, there is no lack of the above," and "there is a social scene for everyone in Athens." "There are a great number of atypical students in the liberal arts," which "creates a unique and exciting student body with greatly contrasting opinions."

UNIVERSITY OF GEORGIA

Financial Aid: 706-542-6147 • E-Mail: adm-info@uga.edu • Website: www.uga.edu

THE PRINCETON REVIEW SAYS

Admissions

The school reports that its standardized testing policy for use in admission for Fall 2024 is Requires applicants to submit either the SAT or ACT. The 2024 testing policy will be permanent. The Princeton Review suggests that interested applicants consult with the school for the most up-to-date standardized testing policies. *Very important factors considered include:* rigor of secondary school record, academic GPA. *Important factors considered include:* standardized test scores. *Other factors considered include:* application essay, recommendation(s), extracurricular activities, talent/ability, character/personal qualities, first generation, volunteer work, work experience. High school diploma is required and GED is accepted. *Academic units required:* 4 English, 4 math, 4 science, 2 science labs, 2 foreign language, 3 social studies. *Academic units recommended:* 4 English, 4 math, 4 science, 2 science labs, 3 foreign language, 3 social studies, 1 academic elective.

Financial Aid

Students should submit: FAFSA. Priority filing deadline is 12/15. The Princeton Review suggests that all financial aid forms be submitted as soon as possible (see page 5 for a note on the FAFSA). *Need-based scholarships/grants offered:* College/university scholarship or grant aid from institutional funds; Federal Pell; Private scholarships; SEOG; State scholarships/grants. *Loan aid offered:* Direct PLUS loans; Direct Subsidized Loans; Direct Unsubsidized Loans; College/university loans from institutional funds; State Loans. Admitted students will be notified of awards on a rolling basis beginning 12/15. Federal Work-Study Program available. Institutional employment available.

The Inside Word

A school as large as UGA must start winnowing applicants by the numbers. If you fail to meet certain baseline curricular, GPA, and standardized-test-score floors, only exceptional talent elsewhere (a gift for the arts or, better still, throwing a football) will get you past the first cut. Some students here are Georgia residents reaping the benefits of the state's HOPE/Zell Miller scholarship programs, which pay tuition and most school-related fees for state residents who earn at least a 3.7 GPA in high school, a 1200 SAT or 26 ACT score, and maintain a 3.3 in college. Georgia state residents who earn at least a 3.0 in high school will also have a large portion of their tuition paid.

THE SCHOOL SAYS "..."

From the Admissions Office

"The University of Georgia offers students the advantages and resources of a top public research university, including a wide range of majors and exceptional academic facilities such as the 260,000 square-foot Miller Learning Center. At the same time, UGA provides opportunities more common to smaller, private schools, such as first-year seminars led by distinguished faculty and learning communities that connect students with similar academic interests. The university is committed to challenging its academically superior students in the classroom and beyond, with increased emphasis on undergraduate research, service-learning, and study abroad. UGA students taking advantage of such offerings find themselves well positioned to compete with the best undergraduates in the country, as evidenced by their recent string of successes in winning Rhodes, Marshall, Truman, and other major scholarships. The UGA campus, considered one of the most beautiful in the nation, adjoins vibrant downtown Athens. While Athens is renowned for its local music scene, UGA also houses the Performing Arts Center, the Hugh Hodgson School of Music, the Lamar Dodd School of Art, and the Georgia Museum of Art. Sports—from football to gymnastics—are also a major attraction, with UGA teams perennially ranked among the best in the country. To experience the excitement of UGA, most prospective students visit campus, a ninety-minute drive northeast of the Atlanta airport. See the admissions website to sign up for a tour with the Visitors Center, view the weekday schedule of admissions information sessions, and find application details. Applicants for first-year admission will be required to submit either the SAT or ACT. Students submitting only the ACT must also submit the optional ACT Writing Test."

SELECTIVITY

Admissions Rating	94
# of applicants	39,354
% of applicants accepted	43
% of acceptees attending	37
# offered a place on the wait list	3,022
% accepting a place on wait list	51
% admitted from wait list	2

FIRST-YEAR PROFILE

Testing policy	SAT or ACT Required
Range SAT composite	1220–1400
Range SAT EBRW	620–710
Range SAT math	600–720
Range ACT composite	26–32
# submitting SAT scores	4,270
% submitting SAT scores	68
# submitting ACT scores	3,024
% submitting ACT scores	48
Average HS GPA	4.1
% frosh submitting high school GPA	99
% graduated top 10% of class	65
% graduated top 25% of class	93
% graduated top 50% of class	98

DEADLINES

Early action	
Deadline	10/15
Notification	12/1
Regular	
Priority	10/15
Deadline	1/1
Nonfall registration?	Yes

FINANCIAL FACTS

Financial Aid Rating	84
Annual in-state tuition	$9,790
Annual out-of-state tuition	$28,830
Room and board	$10,940
Required fees	$1,390
Books and supplies	$888
Average frosh need-based scholarship	$11,478
Average UG need-based scholarship	$10,659
% needy frosh rec. need-based scholarship or grant aid	91
% needy UG rec. need-based scholarship or grant aid	92
% needy frosh rec. non-need-based scholarship or grant aid	25
% needy UG rec. non-need-based scholarship or grant aid	20
% needy frosh rec. need-based self-help aid	31
% needy UG rec. need-based self-help aid	35
% frosh rec. any financial aid	91
% UG rec. any financial aid	89
% UG borrow to pay for school	36
Average cumulative indebtedness	$22,532
% frosh need fully met	30
% ugrads need fully met	26
Average % of frosh need met	78
Average % of ugrad need met	76

University of Hawai'i-Mānoa

2500 Campus Road, Honolulu, HI 96822-2301 • Admissions: 808-956-8111 • Fax: 808-956-4148

STUDENTS SAY "..."

Academics

This flagship school of the University of Hawai'i system offers more than 100 bachelor's programs to the 13,000 or so students who call the O'ahu campus home during the school year. Nearly 250 degree programs across 15 schools are available to students, but no matter the course of study, Hawai'i plays TA. "When someone goes to UH Mānoa, they aren't expecting to receive an education grounded in a Native Hawaiian place of learning but that is exactly what they get. Whether they are learning the Hawaiian language, Hawaiian culture, or about the Hawaiian ecosystem, there is a lot for everyone that goes along with their major," says a student. "UH really incorporates how important Hawai'i really is."

Sciences are particularly strong here, and the language offerings are incredibly diverse (think Ilocano and Samoan). Teachers are "always willing to go the extra mile to help students by offering office hours" and many professors challenge students while simultaneously "letting us know what content will be useful in our future careers and/or graduate-level exams." However, the real gold here is in the added resources for extra help in classes. There is "free one-on-one tutoring" and review sessions through the learning center, a writing center, a learning emporium for certain subjects, and "[you] can even walk into the library where librarians will help to find sources for papers and guide students in a great direction."

Campus Life

UH Mānoa is on an island that offers a bit of everything. Here you can find "the city, the country, the surf, the mountains, the malls, and so on and so on. Oahu has something to fit my every mood and need," says a student. There are always cultural festivals and activities, and Hawai'i is made for active people who "like to get lost in nature's beauty." Whether you're "running up Koko Head, swimming with dolphins on the west side, catching some rays between classes on the Waikiki strip, or jumping off rocks on the north shore, there's no way to escape the beauty that is Hawai'i." On the weekend, many local students travel home so the campus can get very quiet, but students do use their IDs for free bus transportation to explore the relatively small island and student services and student affairs are "excellent." As is common with college students, "many of us do not have enough money to enjoy the nightlife; therefore we enjoy our free time at the beach." Still, students "have work that we can't just blow off for a swim or something." People like to use the grill that the school has set up, and there are "always people walking from place to place until late at night, hanging out with friends in the courtyards, skateboarding, or cooking out."

Student Body

This group—mainly from the Asia-Pacific region and mainland USA, with the occasional European or South American throw in—is a "huge melting pot" that is just "filled with Aloha." An "incredible amount of culture is exhibited here," most of all the Hawaiian cool: "I have never been on another college campus where it is completely normal to ride your skateboard barefoot or walk around with your surfboard." This is good news for the plenty of exchange students from Asia are here "trying to have an American campus experience"; ROTC also has a "very large" presence. On the whole, this is a "very relaxed and cool" bunch of students with whom "you can strike up friendly conversations with strangers in the cafeteria, or while waiting to cross the street, or while ordering food."

UNIVERSITY OF HAWAI'I-MĀNOA

Financial Aid: 808-956-7251 • E-Mail: manoa.admissions@hawaii.edu • Website: manoa.hawaii.edu

THE PRINCETON REVIEW SAYS

Admissions

The school reports that its standardized testing policy for use in admission for Fall 2024 is Test Optional. It is unknown at this time if the 2024 testing policy will be permanent. The Princeton Review suggests that interested applicants consult with the school for the most up-to-date standardized testing policies. *Very important factors considered include:* rigor of secondary school record, academic GPA. *Important factors considered include:* state residency. *Other factors considered include:* class rank, standardized test scores, application essay, recommendation(s), extracurricular activities, talent/ability, geographical residence. High school diploma is required and GED is accepted. *Academic units required:* 4 English, 3 math, 3 science, 3 social studies, 5 academic electives.

Financial Aid

Students should submit: FAFSA. Priority filing deadline is 2/1. The Princeton Review suggests that all financial aid forms be submitted as soon as possible (see page 5 for a note on the FAFSA). *Need-based scholarships/grants offered:* College/university scholarship or grant aid from institutional funds; Federal Pell; Private scholarships; SEOG; State scholarships/grants. *Loan aid offered:* Direct PLUS loans; Direct Subsidized Loans; Direct Unsubsidized Loans; State Loans. Admitted students will be notified of awards on a rolling basis beginning 3/1. Federal Work-Study Program available. Institutional employment available.

The Inside Word

All students must have a minimum GPA of 2.8 and be in the top 40 percent of their high school class. All applicants are encouraged to apply by the priority consideration deadline of January 5, as this deadline increases your chance of receiving financial aid and student housing. Certain programs (nursing, social work, education, and others) may have earlier admission deadlines.

THE SCHOOL SAYS "..."

From the Admissions Office

"Aloha and welcome to UH Mānoa, the largest campus in the University of Hawai'i System. We are located on the island of O'ahu, in Honolulu's lush Mānoa valley. With over 100 undergraduate majors, over 200 student organizations, and a variety of Division I and intramural sports to choose from, you will agree that UH Mānoa is a great place for you to realize your academic, professional, and personal dreams.

"UH Mānoa is one of only a handful of institutions to hold the distinction of being a land-, sea-, sun-, and space-grant research institution. Classified by the Carnegie Foundation as having 'very high research activity,' UH Mānoa is known for its pioneering research in such fields as oceanography, astronomy, Pacific Islands and Asian area studies, linguistics, cancer research, and genetics.

"Applicants to UH Mānoa are expected to have completed a college preparatory high school curriculum. All applicants are encouraged to apply for priority consideration. Applying by this deadline (January 5 for fall admission, September 1 for spring) increases your chance of receiving financial aid and student housing.

"Experience the University of Hawai'i at Mānoa first hand. We welcome you to tour our Mānoa campus guided by our very own Rainbow Warrior students. Experience a campus tour by calling (808) 956-7137 or email visituhm@hawaii.edu."

SELECTIVITY

Admissions Rating	80
# of applicants	18,974
% of applicants accepted	73
% of acceptees attending	23

FIRST-YEAR PROFILE

Testing policy	Test Optional
Average HS GPA	3.7
% frosh submitting high school GPA	79
% graduated top 10% of class	30
% graduated top 25% of class	54
% graduated top 50% of class	87

DEADLINES

Regular	
Priority	1/5
Deadline	3/1
Notification	Rolling, 9/1
Nonfall registration?	Yes

FINANCIAL FACTS

Financial Aid Rating	83
Annual in-state tuition	$11,304
Annual out-of-state tuition	$33,336
Room and board	$11,235
Required fees	$882
Books and supplies	$1,350
Average frosh need-based scholarship	$11,656
Average UG need-based scholarship	$11,118
% needy frosh rec. need-based scholarship or grant aid	97
% needy UG rec. need-based scholarship or grant aid	97
% needy frosh rec. non-need-based scholarship or grant aid	26
% needy UG rec. non-need-based scholarship or grant aid	26
% needy frosh rec. need-based self-help aid	42
% needy UG rec. need-based self-help aid	46
% frosh rec. any financial aid	74
% UG rec. any financial aid	72
% UG borrow to pay for school	42
Average cumulative indebtedness	$23,479
% frosh need fully met	33
% ugrads need fully met	32
Average % of frosh need met	74
Average % of ugrad need met	72

UNIVERSITY OF HOUSTON

4302 University Drive, Houston, TX 77204 • Admissions: 713-743-1000 • Fax: 713-743-7542

CAMPUS LIFE

Quality of Life Rating	82
Fire Safety Rating	93
Green Rating	91
Type of school	Public
Environment	Metropolis

STUDENTS

Total undergrad enrollment	37,282
% male/female/another gender	48/52/0
% from out of state	2
% frosh from public high school	94
% frosh live on campus	42
% ugrads live on campus	18
# of fraternities (% join)	20 (3)
# of sororities (% join)	19 (3)
% African American	11
% Asian	24
% White	18
% Hispanic	37
% Native American	<1
% Pacific Islander	<1
% Two or more races	3
% Race and/or ethnicity unknown	1
% international	5
# of countries represented	111

SURVEY SAYS . . .

Students love Houston, TX
Intramural sports are popular
Recreation facilities are great
Students are happy
Students are friendly
Diverse student types interact on campus
Students get along with local community
Active student government

ACADEMICS

Academic Rating	75
% students returning for sophomore year	85
% students graduating within 4 years	39
% students graduating within 6 years	63
Calendar	Semester
Student/faculty ratio	21:1
Profs interesting rating	82
Profs accessible rating	87

Most classes have 10–19 students.
Most lab/discussion sessions have
20–29 students.

MOST POPULAR MAJORS

Computer and Information Sciences, General;
Biology/Biological Sciences, General; Health and
Wellness, General

STUDENTS SAY "..."

Academics

Those who attend the University of Houston tap into a wealth of resources: a long list of majors, plentiful student organizations, and an extensive alumni network. The "diversity of programs" brings with it "a lot of super hands-on programs," and in that, "the university provides many different ways to get ahead." This is evidenced by the "high job placement" students cite. To that benefit, there are "plenty of opportunities to volunteer within the college" and to get your foot in the door—the school is near the epicenter of a number of different fields, including healthcare, oil and gas, and many Fortune 500 companies. With all of that, one student says, "It really seems my future is cared for and cultivated here."

That cultivation wouldn't be possible without the instructors at UH. However, students admit that professors can be "a mixed bag" in terms of their teaching efficacy. Don't let that worry you too much, though—there are "some real hidden gems at this school" and most of the faculty "put effort into teaching the student on the fundamentals of the course." That's often done with "fun and engaging class projects, such as a Shark Tank simulation," "discussion-based exams," or TED Talks. They're also fairly accessible outside of class: "Making appointments with advisors is not very difficult," says one student. And given that it's a Tier One research university, there are opportunities for "nearly one-on-one researching" with faculty.

Campus Life

This is a "very organized and…active student body," the sort of place where you'll find that students "go to the rec [center] to work out before or after classes." Everyone is "very social"—between classes, "there are always clusters of people, and the school does a good job of providing a lot of group space" for collaboration. However, if you need some time to yourself, the campus also has plenty of "individual spaces when you need" them. Those attending campus events will find they "always have games [and] free food," which is great for the students who also "enjoy walking around campus and trying out the different food trucks" when there aren't events going on. Student organizations are also "very involved on campus…and try to help students do better or to provide opportunities for [growth]." Even with all of the options presented to them, for the most part "people are very focused on their studies." And since so many people here commute, "most students try to pack all their classes into two days," tending to "fill their day on campus with classes and studying/socializing in public places," such as the "really beautiful fountains and park-like areas around campus that are great for relaxing when it's warm out."

Student Body

The University is "extremely diverse both racially and culturally." As one student explains: "No two students sitting next to each other are the same." This diversity "makes for an environment that is collectively considerate about the circumstances of others." Even better, students are "approachable and just overall easy to talk to on campus" and "amazing with school spirit," particularly during athletic events. And while "many commute from home" and don't necessarily stick around to show that school spirit, "if you choose to get involved, you will meet some interesting and exciting people."

UNIVERSITY OF HOUSTON

Financial Aid: 713-743-1010 • E-Mail: admissions@uh.edu • Website: www.uh.edu

THE PRINCETON REVIEW SAYS

Admissions

The school's standardized testing policy for use in Fall 2023 was Test Optional, but by our print date, an announcement had not yet been made for Fall 2024. The Princeton Review suggests that interested applicants consult with the school for the most up-to-date standardized testing policies. *Very important factors considered include:* rigor of secondary school record, class rank, academic GPA. *Other factors considered include:* standardized test scores, application essay, recommendation(s), extracurricular activities, talent/ability, first generation, volunteer work, work experience. High school diploma is required and GED is accepted. *Academic units required:* 4 English, 3 math, 3 science, 2 science labs, 3 social studies. *Academic units recommended:* 4 math, 4 science, 2 foreign language, 1 history, 1 visual/performing arts.

Financial Aid

Students should submit: FAFSA. Priority filing deadline is 1/15. The Princeton Review suggests that all financial aid forms be submitted as soon as possible (see page 5 for a note on the FAFSA). *Need-based scholarships/grants offered:* College/university scholarship or grant aid from institutional funds; Federal Pell; Private scholarships; SEOG; State scholarships/grants; United Negro College Fund. *Loan aid offered:* Direct PLUS loans; Direct Subsidized Loans; Direct Unsubsidized Loans; State Loans. Admitted students will be notified of awards on a rolling basis beginning 3/1. Federal Work-Study Program available. Institutional employment available.

The Inside Word

The school's large size means that acceptance is easier to achieve than at some smaller schools. Students who meet the State of Texas Uniform Admissions Policy and satisfy a certain scale of requirements for class ranking or SAT or ACT scores are assured admission. But even if your grades aren't seemingly up to par, the admissions committee will consider students individually based on a holistic review of certain aspects, such as first-generation, socioeconomic background, rigor of high school curriculum, family responsibilities, special talents, public service, and strong letters of recommendation or a persuasive statement explaining your special circumstances.

THE SCHOOL SAYS "..."

From the Admissions Office

"The University of Houston is a public research university recognized throughout the world as a leader in energy and health research, law, business, and environmental education. Located in America's fourth-largest city, the University of Houston is one of the most ethnically diverse metropolitan research universities in the United States. Its 47,000 students hail from 111 countries.

"In addition to preparing its students to succeed in today's global economy, the University of Houston also is a catalyst within its own community—changing lives through health, education, and outreach projects that help build a future for children in Houston, in Texas, and in the world.

"Other distinctive merits of the University of Houston include the establishment of a Phi Beta Kappa chapter, which indicates a strong foundation for undergraduate education and academic achievement, a historic Division I athletic program, with premier facilities, top-level arts programs, and an internationally recognized faculty including winners of the National Medal of Science, Pulitzer, and Tony awards; and members of prestigious National Academies. The Princeton Review has chosen the University of Houston for inclusion in its guidebook of the nation's best colleges.

"Discover the greatness of the University of Houston's dynamic campus of more than 895 acres—nestled just minutes from Houston's bustling theater and museum districts—where innovative teaching, revolutionary research, and nationally recognized and motivated students work together to create a globally competitive educational environment."

SELECTIVITY

Admissions Rating	88
# of applicants	29,783
% of applicants accepted	66
% of acceptees attending	28

FIRST-YEAR PROFILE

Testing policy	Test Optional
Range SAT composite	1170–1330
Range SAT EBRW	580–660
Range SAT math	580–670
Range ACT composite	23–29
# submitting SAT scores	2,869
% submitting SAT scores	52
# submitting ACT scores	473
% submitting ACT scores	9
Average HS GPA	3.5
% frosh submitting high school GPA	95
% graduated top 10% of class	34
% graduated top 25% of class	69
% graduated top 50% of class	92

DEADLINES

Regular	
Priority	11/1
Deadline	5/1
Nonfall registration?	Yes

APPLICANTS ALSO LOOK AT

Texas A&M University—College Station; The University of Texas at Austin; The University of Texas at Dallas

FINANCIAL FACTS

Financial Aid Rating	79
Annual in-state tuition	$10,856
Annual out-of-state tuition	$26,096
Room and board	$10,418
Required fees	$1,014
Books and supplies	$1,434
Average frosh need-based scholarship	$11,258
Average UG need-based scholarship	$10,122
% needy frosh rec. need-based scholarship or grant aid	90
% needy UG rec. need-based scholarship or grant aid	86
% needy frosh rec. non-need-based scholarship or grant aid	5
% needy UG rec. non-need-based scholarship or grant aid	4
% needy frosh rec. need-based self-help aid	70
% needy UG rec. need-based self-help aid	76
% frosh rec. any financial aid	89
% UG rec. any financial aid	80
% UG borrow to pay for school	43
Average cumulative indebtedness	$21,553
% frosh need fully met	16
% ugrads need fully met	15
Average % of frosh need met	65
Average % of ugrad need met	66

UNIVERSITY OF IDAHO

875 Perimeter Drive MS 2282, Moscow, ID 83844-2282 • Admissions: 208-885-6111 • Fax: 208-885-9119

STUDENTS SAY "..."

Academics

University of Idaho is truly a school that invests in its students. Despite its large size, the university manages to create a "personalized learning experience" for all undergrads. Idaho also provides numerous "networking opportunities" for their students. One lucky beneficiary explains, "Being here at UI, I've had the chance to meet many people in industry, which helped me land an internship at NASA JPL this past summer." Academically, Idaho offers students a wide range of stellar departments. However, undergrads especially like to tout the fantastic "engineering, agriculture, business, and law programs." Fortunately, no matter what you choose to study, the university is "incredible at creating an environment [in which] to build great relationships between professors and students." Though it's certainly helped by the fact that "the faculty here really cares about the students and genuinely wants to see them succeed." Undergrads also value that their professors "don't want students who [simply] suck up information and then vomit it back on a test." Instead, they're hoping to form "well-educated students with the ability to think." They're also happy to "host study sessions [in preparation] for exams and quizzes, and they are willing to answer all of your questions." And, best of all, Idaho professors "are very interesting and really bring their lectures to life."

Campus Life

Undergrads at Idaho happily report that "there are always a lot of activities going on around campus." For starters, the student recreation center is often a big draw where students can "work out, play a variety of indoor sports, take classes, climb the rock wall, or just hang out." Students also love to explore the "two arboretums on campus." Idaho also has "a very involved Greek system that is always holding a philanthropic event somewhere on campus or in the community." The university sponsors a number of great cultural affairs including "an amazing Jazz Festival, Native American celebrations, African American celebrations, and many many more throughout the year." In fact, "on the weekends there is almost always [an] event to attend that is hosted by an organization at the university, whether it is just for fun or to raise money for a cause." Finally, students also love taking advantage of everything hometown Moscow has to offer. As one pleased Vandal elaborates, "There is usually something going on every night, be it trivia nights at local restaurants, local musicians playing at a coffee shop, or a book signing at Book People."

Student Body

On the surface, the student body at University of Idaho might appear a bit homogenous. After all, "most people are white," and it often feels like the vast majority hail from "Idaho, Washington, or Oregon." Nevertheless, the "population is slowly becoming more and more diverse." This is partially thanks to a "surprising number of international students." In turn, "this creates a unique opportunity to learn from people of different cultures." Undergrads also take great solace in the fact that their peers are "all very, very friendly" and united in their "kindness." Simply stroll across campus and you'll notice that "everyone smiles and says hi." An ecstatic student rushes to add, "My peers are the most supportive and uplifting people I've ever been surrounded by.... It's not uncommon to see students giving directions to lost tours or inviting perfect strangers to something like the farmers market or a film downtown." A lot of these Idaho Vandals also find common ground in their love of the outdoors, with many students looking to "take advantage of Moscow Mountain nearby for hiking, mountain biking, or snowshoeing." Finally, when it comes to political leanings, we're told that Idaho has an "unusually large number of libertarian-minded students here." Thankfully, most undergrads "are very respectful, even when they strongly disagree." As one contemplative student states, "We rarely talk about tolerance here, but we act on it daily."

UNIVERSITY OF IDAHO

Financial Aid: 208-885-6312 • E-Mail: admissions@uidaho.edu • Website: www.uidaho.edu/

THE PRINCETON REVIEW SAYS

Admissions

The school reports that its standardized testing policy for use in admission for Fall 2024 is Test Optional. The 2024 testing policy will be temporary. The Princeton Review suggests that interested applicants consult with the school for the most up-to-date standardized testing policies. *Very important factors considered include:* academic GPA, standardized test scores. *Other factors considered include:* High school diploma is required and GED is accepted. *Academic units required:* 4 English, 3 math, 3 science, 1 science lab, 3 social studies, 1 history, 2 visual/performing arts.

Financial Aid

Students should submit: FAFSA. Priority filing deadline is 12/1. The Princeton Review suggests that all financial aid forms be submitted as soon as possible (see page 5 for a note on the FAFSA). *Need-based scholarships/grants offered:* College/university scholarship or grant aid from institutional funds; Federal Pell; Private scholarships; SEOG; State scholarships/grants. *Loan aid offered:* Direct PLUS loans; Direct Subsidized Loans; Direct Unsubsidized Loans; College/university loans from institutional funds. Admitted students will be notified of awards on a rolling basis beginning 2/1. Federal Work-Study Program available. Institutional employment available.

The Inside Word

The admissions process at University of Idaho is fairly by the book. Indeed, officers closely consider each applicant's GPA. They also check to make sure that every candidate has completed their core requirements. Both homeschooled and GED students will have to submit three letters of recommendation attesting to their academic abilities. They'll also be expected to draft a written statement that discusses their educational goals and professional objectives.

THE SCHOOL SAYS "..."

From the Admissions Office

"A leading public research university in the West, the University of Idaho offers a traditional residential campus experience in a spectacular natural setting. It provides more than 100 undergraduate degree options and graduate degrees in sixty five discipline areas, which helps provide unprecedented undergraduate research opportunities. Idaho has become known for its academic excellence, student-centered, experiential learning, and an exceptional student living environment that coupled with dedicated faculty, world-class facilities, and renowned research has produced a proven track record of high-achieving graduates. The student population of 13,000 includes first-generation college students and ethnically diverse scholars, who select from hands-on learning experiences in the colleges of Agricultural and Life Sciences; Art and Architecture; Business and Economics; Education; Engineering; Law; Letters, Arts, and Social Sciences; Natural Resources; and Science. The university also provides medical education for the state through the WWAMI program. Increasingly its interdisciplinary teams involved in environmental, sustainability, engagement, and resource management have gained national recognition. Idaho combines the strength of a large, land grant university with the intimacy of a small learning community to help students succeed and become leaders. It is home to the Vandals and competes in the Big Sky Conference."

SELECTIVITY

Admissions Rating	85
# of applicants	13,393
% of applicants accepted	74
% of acceptees attending	20

FIRST-YEAR PROFILE

Testing policy	Test Optional
Range SAT composite	1000–1240
Range SAT EBRW	500–630
Range SAT math	490–620
Range ACT composite	20–27
# submitting SAT scores	1,261
% submitting SAT scores	65
# submitting ACT scores	170
% submitting ACT scores	9
Average HS GPA	3.5
% frosh submitting high school GPA	83
% graduated top 10% of class	17
% graduated top 25% of class	40
% graduated top 50% of class	70

DEADLINES

Regular	
Priority	2/1 (Fall)
Deadline	Rolling
Notification	Rolling
Nonfall registration?	Yes

FINANCIAL FACTS

Financial Aid Rating	82
Annual in-state tuition	$6,182
Annual out-of-state tuition	$25,418
Room and board	$9,898
Required fees	$2,214
Books and supplies	$1,232
Average frosh need-based scholarship	$5,277
Average UG need-based scholarship	$5,378
% needy frosh rec. need-based scholarship or grant aid	56
% needy UG rec. need-based scholarship or grant aid	64
% needy frosh rec. non-need-based scholarship or grant aid	81
% needy UG rec. non-need-based scholarship or grant aid	70
% needy frosh rec. need-based self-help aid	56
% needy UG rec. need-based self-help aid	61
% frosh rec. any financial aid	
% UG rec. any financial aid	
% UG borrow to pay for school	52
Average cumulative indebtedness	$20,587
% frosh need fully met	40
% ugrads need fully met	34
Average % of frosh need met	84
Average % of ugrad need met	79

UNIVERSITY OF ILLINOIS AT URBANA-CHAMPAIGN

601 E. John St., Champaign, IL 61820-5711 • Admissions: 217-333-1000 • Fax: 217-244-4614

STUDENTS SAY "..."

Academics

The University of Illinois' massive size means "opportunities, lots of classes, lots of student groups," and "an incredibly lively campus." "The research support is phenomenal on campus" and "there are a lot of resources to supplement your studies." Students find the university's "fantastic library system" and "phenomenal advisors" to be "such a benefit for research projects," and "countless on-campus resources such as the Career Center, Writers Workshop, Office of Minority Student Affairs, free tutoring services, and the Study Abroad Office" also support students' academic experiences. They praise their professors as "wonderful," "not just good at research but also instructing and mentoring," and "very approachable," and students thrive on the emphasis on experiences outside the classroom: "The field work (tons of field work) that they make us do really helped in getting used to the field." "Most professors here are devoted to teaching, not researching." Classes can be big—"As an underclassman, many classes I've taken have been with very large classes"—but "the professors are engaging and know how to keep a class of 700-plus entertained." U of I's programs in business and engineering have long been recognized as among the best, and one student says, "I liked the breadth of the engineering program and the opportunities associated with it." Even if you're not sure what you want to study yet, its undergrads feel that the university has "an amazing reputation and strong programs in many different majors, and that if I needed to change majors (which I ended up doing) I would still be getting a great degree."

Campus Life

In terms of location, "campus is located perfectly between Chicago, Indianapolis, and St. Louis, providing a unique atmosphere in town but close access to other urban areas for a change of pace." Students call social life "very exciting," and say, "The bars in downtown Champaign are great and super relaxed, plus there is an awesome music scene that most people don't expect from a college town." "People here like to party, but there are a lot of other fun things to do," whether it's "going to the Krannert Center to see plays or concerts" or the "movie theater and mall...on Saturday afternoons. Champaign-Urbana seems small to city kids, but to me it's the land of opportunity." Students relish the "nineteen-year-old bar age," and U of I also has "one of the largest Greek communities in the country." The combination of these facts does mean that "drinking culture is huge here" but "there's also tons to do beyond the bars." The range of social opportunities is nearly limitless: "There are 40,000 students, thousands of clubs, two gyms and several sport facilities, and array of establishments to explore on Green Street." As a whole, students report happily that "life is busy, but rewarding."

Student Body

"The diversity of the students here is astounding. Race, religion, major, you've got it all." Because in-state tuition is a major draw, "a majority of the students that you meet here will be from the Chicago suburbs," but the school also attracts "a wide variety of students from all across the world." "University of Illinois houses so many different types of students that the only way we are alike is our dedication to getting an education and our loyalty to UIUC." Undergrads feel that their peers "really know how to be academically successful," and shed state-school stereotypes like so many dirty socks: "It obviously takes a lot to get into this school so students aren't ready to throw it all away to sleep in every day." Social life changes as you find your "niche": "The typical student starts out going to a school of 40,000 students and is lucky if they know a handful of people. Within one week, life as that freshman student grows. There are so many opportunities to get involved on the floor of your residence hall, in organizations, in your classes, that it's hard not to make friends and close relationships."

UNIVERSITY OF ILLINOIS AT URBANA-CHAMPAIGN

Financial Aid: 217-333-0100 • Website: illinois.edu

THE PRINCETON REVIEW SAYS

Admissions

The school reports that its standardized testing policy for use in admission for Fall 2024 is Test Optional. It is unknown at this time if the 2024 testing policy will be permanent. The Princeton Review suggests that interested applicants consult with the school for the most up-to-date standardized testing policies. *Very important factors considered include:* rigor of secondary school record, academic GPA. *Important factors considered include:* standardized test scores, application essay, extracurricular activities, talent/ability. *Other factors considered include:* class rank, character/personal qualities, first generation, geographical residence, state residency, racial/ethnic status, volunteer work, work experience. High school diploma is required and GED is accepted. *Academic units required:* 4 English, 3 math, 2 science, 2 science labs, 2 foreign language, 2 social studies, 2 academic electives. *Academic units recommended:* 4 English, 4 math, 4 science, 4 science labs, 4 foreign language, 4 social studies, 4 academic electives.

Financial Aid

Students should submit: FAFSA. Priority filing deadline is 3/15. The Princeton Review suggests that all financial aid forms be submitted as soon as possible (see page 5 for a note on the FAFSA). *Need-based scholarships/grants offered:* College/university scholarship or grant aid from institutional funds; Federal Pell; Private scholarships; SEOG; State scholarships/grants; United Negro College Fund. *Loan aid offered:* Direct PLUS loans; Direct Subsidized Loans; Direct Unsubsidized Loans; College/university loans from institutional funds. Admitted students will be notified of awards on a rolling basis beginning 3/10. Federal Work-Study Program available. Institutional employment available.

The Inside Word

The University of Illinois' application review process distinguishes itself from that of many state schools in that every application is considered individually—no small feat for a campus of about 30,000 students. Don't be fooled by the university's high acceptance rate: U of I's applicant pool tends to be self-selective, and those without sufficient qualifications won't make the cut.

THE SCHOOL SAYS "..."

From the Admissions Office

"The campus has been aptly described as a collection of neighborhoods constituting a diverse and vibrant city. The neighborhoods are of many types: students and faculty within a department; people sharing a room or house; the members of a professional organization, a service club, or an intramural team; or simply people who, starting out as strangers sharing a class or a study lounge or a fondness for a weekly film series, have become friends. The city of this description is the university itself—a rich cosmopolitan environment constructed by students and faculty to meet their educational and personal goals. The quality of intellectual life parallels that of other great universities, and many faculty and students who have their choice of top institutions select Illinois over its peers. While such choices are based often on the quality of individual programs of study, another crucial factor is the 'tone' of the campus life that is linked with the virtues of Midwestern culture. There is an informality and a near-absence of pretension, which, coupled with a tradition of commitment to excellence, creates an atmosphere that is unique among the finest institutions."

SELECTIVITY

Admissions Rating	91
# of applicants	38,093
% of applicants accepted	60
% of acceptees attending	33
# offered a place on the wait list	2,846
% accepting a place on wait list	74
% admitted from wait list	17

FIRST-YEAR PROFILE

Testing policy	Test Optional
Range SAT EBRW	580–690
Range SAT math	700–790
Range ACT composite	26–32
# submitting SAT scores	1,564
% submitting SAT scores	21
# submitting ACT scores	6,422
% submitting ACT scores	85
% graduated top 10% of class	49
% graduated top 25% of class	82
% graduated top 50% of class	99

DEADLINES

Early action	
Deadline	11/15
Notification	2/15
Regular	
Deadline	1/5
Nonfall registration?	No

APPLICANTS ALSO LOOK AT

Georgia Institute of Technology; Indiana University—Bloomington; Loyola University of Chicago; New York University; Northwestern University; Purdue University—West Lafayette; University of California—Berkeley; University of California—Davis; University of California—Los Angeles; University of Michigan—Ann Arbor; University of Wisconsin—Madison

FINANCIAL FACTS

Financial Aid Rating	77
Annual in-state tuition	$12,036
Annual out-of-state tuition	$27,658
Annual out-of-state tuition (first-year)	$28,156
Room and board	$11,308
Required fees	$3,832
Books and supplies	$1,200
Average frosh need-based scholarship	$14,652
Average UG need-based scholarship	$14,244
% needy frosh rec. need-based scholarship or grant aid	81
% needy UG rec. need-based scholarship or grant aid	64
% needy frosh rec. non-need-based scholarship or grant aid	17
% needy UG rec. non-need-based scholarship or grant aid	8
% needy frosh rec. need-based self-help aid	74
% needy UG rec. need-based self-help aid	60
% UG borrow to pay for school	47
Average cumulative indebtedness	$25,222
% frosh need fully met	13
% ugrads need fully met	9
Average % of frosh need met	67
Average % of ugrad need met	65

UNIVERSITY OF IOWA

101 Jessup Hall, Iowa City, IA 52242-1396 • Admissions: 319-335-3500 • Fax: 319-333-1535

STUDENTS SAY "..."

Academics

The University of Iowa manages to pull off an amazing feat: It's a "Big Ten university full of exciting opportunities," yet it's still able to maintain "a small-college feel." Moreover, as the state's flagship school, Iowa provides a "great education" at a "reasonable price." Additionally, students here welcome the fact that "requirements are minimal." In turn, this truly encourages undergrads to "make [their] education [their] own." While there are certainly a "[wide] range of degree programs" from which to choose, students here are especially impressed with Iowa's journalism, pre-med, writing, nursing, and engineering departments. Though professors certainly run the gamut from "amazing" to "boring," the majority of them are "very engaged with students and are always helpful to any student looking to push their learning beyond the classroom." A fellow student concurs, adding that her professors are "passionate, encouraging, and invested in the success of their students both inside and outside of academia." Undergrads at Iowa also appreciate that their teachers really "do a nice job of balancing lectures with real-world applications of the material." Finally, as this pleased undergrad summarizes her school, "The University of Iowa is a platform to launch yourself to the top of your field at an affordable price."

Campus Life

If there's one thing that undergrads tend to agree on, it's that "life is pretty fun at The University of Iowa." To begin with, sports culture is definitely big here. As one student relays, "During football season, Saturdays get crazy. There is just a sea of black and gold swarming toward the stadium. Nothing can really compare to 70,000 Hawkeye fans in one place." Additionally, students love the new rec center, which frequently runs trips "to go rock-climbing, camping, hiking, or kayaking." Of course, the university also sponsors a number of other events outside of athletics. For example, "there are always concerts and comedians on campus, [and] many [of these shows] are even free to students. There are also free movies shown at the Iowa Memorial Union." Students also stress that the university has a lively drinking scene. Indeed, "there is always a party going on here at Iowa." Lastly, undergrads also love hometown Iowa City, which offers a "vibrant downtown" that's "literally across the street from campus." Students happily take advantage of the city's "unique places to eat, shop, or go out." As this undergrad poetically concludes, "When a man is tired of Iowa City, he is tired of life."

Student Body

With such a large student body, undergrads here all posit that there is no "typical" student. One pleased undergrad elaborates, "Everyone is unique and has a different story, but that's one thing that makes life here so great. You have the ability to meet people from around the country and around the world, and we all get to share the experience of college together." Indeed, students feel very fortunate to be surrounded by such diversity. "We have a strong LGBTQA presence on campus, [along with] different religious places near campus. [In addition,] there are many different organizations for minorities, religions, and everything else here on campus. I couldn't imagine someone coming here and not being able to find a student organization that is for them." Of course, if pressed to generalize, students will describe their fellow Hawkeyes as "friendly, hardworking, and studious" but also "laid-back" and "very social." However, what ultimately unites this student body is the fact that most undergrads have "their season football tickets by June."

UNIVERSITY OF IOWA

Financial Aid: 319-335-1450 • E-Mail: admissions@uiowa.edu • Website: www.uiowa.edu

THE PRINCETON REVIEW SAYS

Admissions

The school reports that its standardized testing policy for use in admission for Fall 2024 is Test Flexible. It is unknown at this time if the 2024 testing policy will be permanent. The Princeton Review suggests that interested applicants consult with the school for the most up-to-date standardized testing policies. *Very important factors considered include:* rigor of secondary school record, class rank, academic GPA, standardized test scores. *Other factors considered include:* recommendation(s), talent/ability, character/personal qualities, state residency. High school diploma is required and GED is accepted. *Academic units required:* 4 English, 3 math, 3 science, 2 foreign language, 3 social studies. *Academic units recommended:* 4 math.

Financial Aid

Students should submit: FAFSA. Priority filing deadline is 12/1. The Princeton Review suggests that all financial aid forms be submitted as soon as possible (see page 5 for a note on the FAFSA). *Need-based scholarships/grants offered:* College/university scholarship or grant aid from institutional funds; Federal Pell; Private scholarships; SEOG; State scholarships/grants. *Loan aid offered:* Direct PLUS loans; Direct Subsidized Loans; Direct Unsubsidized Loans; College/university loans from institutional funds; Federal Nursing Loans. Admitted students will be notified of awards on a rolling basis beginning 2/7. Federal Work-Study Program available. Institutional employment available.

The Inside Word

Like many large public universities, admissions officers at the University of Iowa rely heavily on quantitative factors when determining an applicant's status. Therefore, GPA and standardized test scores will likely hold the most weight. It should also be noted that the majority of applicants are admitted to the College of Liberal Arts & Sciences or the College of Engineering. Students interested in other programs (say within the College of Business or Nursing) often apply after they have enrolled in the university.

THE SCHOOL SAYS "..."

From the Admissions Office

"The University of Iowa offers all of the opportunities and resources of a large, research university, while putting a strong emphasis on the undergraduate student experience. As the first public university to enroll men and women on an equal basis, Iowa is proud of its history in providing a world-class education to students from all backgrounds. Today, the University of Iowa offers nationally ranked academic programs, strong pre-professional programs in the health sciences and law, and access to world-renowned faculty. With an emphasis on small class sizes, students interact with faculty both inside and outside the classroom. Located in one of the top college towns in America, Iowa City's vibrant downtown seamlessly blends with the heart of campus, making it easy to access academic resources and belong to a larger, welcoming community."

SELECTIVITY

Admissions Rating	84
# of applicants	22,434
% of applicants accepted	86
% of acceptees attending	23
# offered a place on the wait list	252
% accepting a place on wait list	100
% admitted from wait list	25

FIRST-YEAR PROFILE

Testing policy	Test Flexible
Range SAT composite	1140–1330
Range SAT EBRW	570–680
Range SAT math	560–670
Range ACT composite	22–29
# submitting SAT scores	800
% submitting SAT scores	18
# submitting ACT scores	2,944
% submitting ACT scores	65
Average HS GPA	3.8
% frosh submitting high school GPA	99
% graduated top 10% of class	33
% graduated top 25% of class	64
% graduated top 50% of class	92

DEADLINES

Regular	
Deadline	5/1
Notification	Rolling, 8/1
Nonfall registration?	Yes

APPLICANTS ALSO LOOK AT

Illinois State University; Indiana University—Bloomington; Iowa State University; Loyola University of Chicago; Marquette University; Miami University; Michigan State University; Purdue University—West Lafayette; The Ohio State University—Columbus; University of Illinois at Chicago; University of Illinois—Urbana-Champaign; University of Minnesota—Twin Cities; University of Missouri; University of Northern Iowa

FINANCIAL FACTS

Financial Aid Rating	79
Annual in-state tuition	$8,356
Annual out-of-state tuition	$30,319
Room and board	$11,780
Required fees	$1,533
Books and supplies	$950
Average frosh need-based scholarship	$11,854
Average UG need-based scholarship	$9,814
% needy frosh rec. need-based scholarship or grant aid	86
% needy UG rec. need-based scholarship or grant aid	81
% needy frosh rec. non-need-based scholarship or grant aid	13
% needy UG rec. non-need-based scholarship or grant aid	9
% needy frosh rec. need-based self-help aid	70
% needy UG rec. need-based self-help aid	75
% frosh rec. any financial aid	92
% UG rec. any financial aid	80
% UG borrow to pay for school	43
Average cumulative indebtedness	$15,441
% frosh need fully met	16
% ugrads need fully met	12
Average % of frosh need met	58
Average % of ugrad need met	54

UNIVERSITY OF KANSAS

1502 Iowa Street, Lawrence, KS 66045 • Admissions: 785-864-2700

CAMPUS LIFE

Quality of Life Rating	87
Fire Safety Rating	96
Green Rating	78
Type of school	Public
Environment	City

STUDENTS

Total undergrad enrollment	18,539
% male/female/another gender	46/54/NR
% from out of state	32
% frosh live on campus	72
% ugrads live on campus	25
# of fraternities (% join)	25 (18)
# of sororities (% join)	17 (25)
% African American	4
% Asian	6
% White	69
% Hispanic	10
% Native American	<1
% Pacific Islander	<1
% Two or more races	6
% Race and/or ethnicity unknown	1
% international	4
# of countries represented	93

SURVEY SAYS . . .

Students are happy
Great library
Career services are great
Students get along with local community
Students love Lawrence, KS
Great off-campus food
Recreation facilities are great
Everyone loves the Jayhawks
Campus newspaper is popular
Alumni active on campus

ACADEMICS

Academic Rating	79
% students returning for sophomore year	85
% students graduating within 4 years	53
% students graduating within 6 years	67
Calendar	Semester
Student/faculty ratio	17:1
Profs interesting rating	85
Profs accessible rating	93

Most classes have 10–19 students.
Most lab/discussion sessions have 10–19 students.

MOST POPULAR MAJORS

Journalism; Psychology, General; Finance, General

STUDENTS SAY "..."

Academics

Located in the heartland's quintessential college town, University of Kansas's flagship campus is a "place of tradition" as well as opportunity, combining "stimulating academics with a community that is passionate about the school." Most of KU's 2,800 faculty members are "actively engaged in research in their particular field," but there is nonetheless a real emphasis on undergraduate teaching. Here, "the faculty is obviously willing to do what it takes to help," and "teachers are always urging students to contact them with questions or visit their office hours." An undergrad details, "The personalities and teaching styles of KU's professors vary widely, but all of the instructors I have had are fully engaged in teaching and truly enjoy helping students learn." That said, "there are a lot of giant lecture halls your freshmen and sophomore year," which some students find "overwhelming." On the flip side, the big-school setting proffers "abundant resources," including "research opportunities" for undergraduates and "one of the best study abroad programs in the nation." In fact, many say, "The experience outside of the classroom is what sets you up for success after college." Speaking of life after graduation, KU's "career center is committed to getting students hired," and "there are many job opportunities" in nearby Topeka and Kansas City. To make the deal sweeter, KU graduates aren't strapped with insurmountable debt: "In-state tuition is very affordable."

Campus Life

In the pursuit of an "incredible college experience," KU undergrads definitely keep busy: "The typical student probably volunteers in the community, has a part time job, [and] has some special hobby (from rock climbing to tightrope walking)." Incoming freshman will find more than 500 student groups in which to participate, ranging from "Quidditch to chess club to the arts," and "there is never a dull night" on campus, where "Student Union Activities brings in comedians, authors, and movies on a regular basis." During the winter months, "KU basketball is our religion, and Allen Fieldhouse is our church." An undergrad admits, "I schedule everything in my life around the KU men's basketball schedule, as does much of the student population." Described as "the perfect college town," "Lawrence has a great live music scene, cool coffee shops, and eclectic stores," as well as bars and nightclubs popular with students. "People in Lawrence are also very outdoorsy," and, when the weather is nice, "you can rent camping equipment from the rec for a weekend out at the lake" or "go rock climbing" nearby. For a more cosmopolitan outing, "being close to Kansas City provides a lot of entertainment from museums and art shows to music and dining."

Students

Students say you'd be surprised by the diversity on this friendly Midwestern campus, lauding the KU's "ability to unite 30,000 people of different values and backgrounds." There are "students from every county in Kansas, every state, and over 100 countries," with noticeable representations from out-of-state cities like St. Louis and Denver mixing into the large in-state crowd. "KU students find a great balance in work and play," with some undergrads tipping the scales in one direction or the other: "You have your 'here for a good time' types, absolutely rock-star scholars, and dedicated students who balance their GPA and their social calendar." In terms of making friends and fitting in, getting involved is the best way to mitigate the campus's size: "There are so many opportunities at KU that it can seem a bit overwhelming, but students really find their niche and run with it." Of particular note, "there is definitely a big Greek life presence" on campus, which some say causes a "schism" in the undergraduate community. In counterpoint, a student reassures us, "The Greek community does intermingle frequently with non-Greeks. I'm not Greek, but I see it a lot and have a lot of Greek friends."

UNIVERSITY OF KANSAS

Financial Aid: 785-864-4700 • E-Mail: adm@ku.edu • Website: www.ku.edu/

THE PRINCETON REVIEW SAYS

Admissions

The school reports that its standardized testing policy for use in admission for Fall 2024 is Test Optional. The 2024 testing policy will be permanent. The Princeton Review suggests that interested applicants consult with the school for the most up-to-date standardized testing policies. *Very important factors considered include:* academic GPA. *Other factors considered include:* standardized test scores. High school diploma is required and GED is accepted. *Academic units recommended:* 4 English, 4 math, 3 science, 2 foreign language, 2 social studies, 1 history.

Financial Aid

Students should submit: FAFSA. Priority filing deadline is 12/1. The Princeton Review suggests that all financial aid forms be submitted as soon as possible (see page 5 for a note on the FAFSA). *Need-based scholarships/grants offered:* College/university scholarship or grant aid from institutional funds; Federal Nursing Scholarships; Federal Pell; Private scholarships; SEOG; State scholarships/grants. *Loan aid offered:* Direct PLUS loans; Direct Subsidized Loans; Direct Unsubsidized Loans; College/university loans from institutional funds; Federal Nursing Loans. Admitted students will be notified of awards on a rolling basis beginning in mid-February. Federal Work-Study Program available. Institutional employment available.

The Inside Word

KU has a great program for assured admission! The standards for 2022 are: A 3.25 GPA on a 4.0 scale, no test scores required or regardless of test score submitted, OR an ACT score of at least 21 or an SAT score of at least 1060 plus a GPA of at least 2.0. Professional schools have different standards. The University of Kansas is Test Optional for both admissions and scholarships.

THE SCHOOL SAYS "..."

From the Admissions Office

"The University of Kansas has a tradition of academic excellence. The mission of KU is to lift students and society by educating leaders, building healthy communities, and making discoveries that will change the world. Outstanding students from around the world attend KU for its outstanding academics, challenging opportunities, the Jayhawk community, and incredible value including four-year renewable scholarships. KU provides students exceptional opportunities in the University Honors Program, experiential learning, undergraduate research, internships, study abroad, and more than 600 clubs and organizations. The university is located in Lawrence (forty minutes from Kansas City), a vibrant community of 93,000 consistently recognized as one of the nation's top ten college towns.

"All students are encouraged to apply. KU does an individual review of each application. We consider many factors that are provided on the application such as cumulative high school GPA, ACT or SAT scores, GPA in the core curriculum, and strength of courses. We may also ask you to respond to short essay questions that will provide additional information to support your application."

SELECTIVITY

Admissions Rating	84
# of applicants	16,204
% of applicants accepted	88
% of acceptees attending	31

FIRST-YEAR PROFILE

Testing policy	Test Optional
Range SAT composite	1090–1320
Range SAT EBRW	550–670
Range SAT math	540–670
Range ACT composite	21–28
# submitting SAT scores	539
% submitting SAT scores	12
# submitting ACT scores	3,241
% submitting ACT scores	73
Average HS GPA	3.7
% frosh submitting high school GPA	99
% graduated top 10% of class	26
% graduated top 25% of class	53
% graduated top 50% of class	81

DEADLINES

Early action	
Deadline	11/1
Notification	11/15
Regular	
Priority	12/1
Notification	Rolling, 7/1
Nonfall registration?	Yes

APPLICANTS ALSO LOOK AT

Johnson County Community College; Kansas State University; Metropolitan Community College (Missouri); University of Missouri; Wichita State University

FINANCIAL FACTS

Financial Aid Rating	84
Annual in-state tuition	$10,092
Annual out-of-state tuition	$26,960
Room and board	$10,136
Required fees	$1,075
Books and supplies	$1,224
Average frosh need-based scholarship	$10,537
Average UG need-based scholarship	$9,455
% needy frosh rec. need-based scholarship or grant aid	90
% needy UG rec. need-based scholarship or grant aid	84
% needy frosh rec. non-need-based scholarship or grant aid	17
% needy UG rec. non-need-based scholarship or grant aid	12
% needy frosh rec. need-based self-help aid	56
% needy UG rec. need-based self-help aid	59
% frosh rec. any financial aid	89
% UG rec. any financial aid	78
% UG borrow to pay for school	50
Average cumulative indebtedness	$28,493
% frosh need fully met	42
% ugrads need fully met	39
Average % of frosh need met	77
Average % of ugrad need met	76

UNIVERSITY OF KENTUCKY

101 Main Building, Lexington, KY 40506 • Admissions: 859-257-9000 • Fax: 859-257-3823

STUDENTS SAY "..."

Academics

Founded in 1865, the University of Kentucky in Lexington offers more than 200 academic programs to its 22,000 undergraduate students. It is one of only eight institutions in the country with the full set of liberal arts, engineering, professional, agricultural and medical colleges. With a "great variety in majors and classes" available, many undergraduates find UK has "available opportunities for students in all fields of study." Enrollees find support outside their standard classroom work with "so many study abroad options" and the chance to "become involved in undergraduate research." Many courses also incorporate "active technology learning classrooms," and some degree programs have hybrid classes. From classroom to campus, Kentucky makes sure that "everything is there to help the students—all of the resources you could need."

Undergrads say the faculty is "passionate about giving us more than just degrees" and most have "a great base of knowledge, enthusiasm, and accessibility." Students enthusiastically recommend registering for courses with seasoned teachers who have industry experience because they "are the best at their job," and "are able to answer questions from personal experience more so than just textbook knowledge." But regardless of if you're learning from a TA or a tenured faculty member, undergrads appreciate the fact that their instructors "do their best to make the material interesting and engaging." Many enrollees also value "the availability of professors and their willingness to help" after class and during offices hours. "They are more than professors; they are mentors for me and networking connections for the field," says a student.

Campus Life

The University of Kentucky has made great efforts at "transforming itself into a more modern and thriving university city." "There is so much to do" at UK, and the "campus is close to downtown, so people will go out to eat or attend events happening there." The university is also located in "horse country and in a wonderful proximity to good hiking, so a lot of time is spent outdoors." During the week, you'll find students "[sitting] in common areas around campus to hang out and relax before the next class." After class, they will "usually study at the library or go to work" (UK has "a lot of opportunities for student employment"), but weekends are a time to let loose. "Sporting events are always popular," and students are "filled to the brim with pride." Home to a multitude of active Greek chapters, "Sorority/fraternity life is huge," as "Greek life is really important on campus." Beyond the Greek scene, "there are a lot of clubs that are very diverse and a lot of intramural sports," as well as opportunities to volunteer in Lexington and on campus.

Student Body

Many students express "a love for [their] school" and the "very friendly" community that comes with it. As one undergrad notes, "Big Blue Nation makes everyone feel a part of the school pride here at the University of Kentucky." The culture of being a Kentucky Wildcat unifies enrollees in many aspects of their college career. "Students of every major and discipline find commonality in a variety of things," including "great pride about the state of Kentucky and its values." And while the student body is diverse with "a healthy number of in-state and out-of-state students," as well as "many international students and nontraditional students," walking around campus, "there is a comfortable atmosphere," which "helps each student to learn how to communicate with people from many different backgrounds." "There isn't a sense of elitism here," but "students still value academia." In the end, "all of UK's students contribute to a very diverse atmosphere that creates its unique environment." As one student explains, "It's one big community, and people are so happy to engage in it."

UNIVERSITY OF KENTUCKY

Financial Aid: 859-257-3172 • E-Mail: recruitment@uky.edu • Website: www.uky.edu

THE PRINCETON REVIEW SAYS

Admissions

The school reports that its standardized testing policy for use in admission for Fall 2024 is Test Optional. It is unknown at this time if the 2024 testing policy will be permanent. The Princeton Review suggests that interested applicants consult with the school for the most up-to-date standardized testing policies. *Very important factors considered include:* rigor of secondary school record, academic GPA, standardized test scores, application essay. *Other factors considered include:* class rank, recommendation(s), interview, extracurricular activities, talent/ability, character/personal qualities, first generation, geographical residence, state residency, volunteer work, work experience. High school diploma is required and GED is accepted. *Academic units required:* 4 English, 3 math, 3 science, 1 science lab, 2 foreign language, 3 social studies, 1 visual/performing arts, 7 academic electives. *Academic units recommended:* 1 computer science.

Financial Aid

Students should submit: FAFSA. Priority filing deadline is 12/1. The Princeton Review suggests that all financial aid forms be submitted as soon as possible (see page 5 for a note on the FAFSA). *Need-based scholarships/grants offered:* College/university scholarship or grant aid from institutional funds; Federal Pell; Private scholarships; SEOG; State scholarships/grants. *Loan aid offered:* Direct PLUS loans; Direct Subsidized Loans; Direct Unsubsidized Loans; College/university loans from institutional funds; State Loans. Admitted students will be notified of awards on a rolling basis beginning 3/1. Federal Work-Study Program available.

The Inside Word

The University of Kentucky's admissions team is about as objective as they come. If you have the GPA, class rank, and test scores, you'll in all likelihood be welcomed into the Wildcat community. The university is continually looking to improve its selectivity, so hitting the books is a must if you want to be a serious contender. First-year applicants who have completed the pre-college curriculum, but do not have the requisite GPA, test scores or both, may be placed on a wait list.

THE SCHOOL SAYS "..."

From the Admissions Office

"The University of Kentucky has 16 degree-granting colleges, including the Lewis Honors College and the Graduate School. Only two percent of all colleges and universities in the country are comprehensive research-intensive institutions like UK.

"UK has invested more than $3.7 billion since July 2011 to transform the University of Kentucky campus. In addition to housing and dining revitalization accomplished through public private partnerships, UK has prioritized other student quality-of-life projects, including the new Gatton Student Center, Jacobs Science Building, the Gatton College of Business and Economics, campus recreation and athletics facilities among others.

"In the fall 2022, the university launched UK Invests, a first-of-its-kind holistic wellness program anchored in financial education and aimed at helping students secure a strong financial future.

"The university has a close connection with the city of Lexington, a vibrant, growing community with a culture students describe as close-knit, opportunity-rich and supportive of all things local. Students get the best of both worlds—urban bustle adjacent to campus and beautiful rolling hills, immaculate horse farms and wilderness adventures just a short drive out of town."

SELECTIVITY

Admissions Rating	83
# of applicants	22,109
% of applicants accepted	95
% of acceptees attending	29

FIRST-YEAR PROFILE

Testing policy	Test Optional
Range SAT composite	1080–1280
Range SAT EBRW	540–650
Range SAT math	530–640
Range ACT composite	21–28
# submitting SAT scores	531
% submitting SAT scores	9
# submitting ACT scores	3,666
% submitting ACT scores	61
Average HS GPA	3.6
% frosh submitting high school GPA	100
% graduated top 10% of class	31
% graduated top 25% of class	59
% graduated top 50% of class	86

DEADLINES

Early action	
Deadline	12/1
Notification	1/15
Regular	
Priority	2/15
Deadline	2/15
Nonfall registration?	Yes

FINANCIAL FACTS

Financial Aid Rating	75
Annual in-state tuition	$11,496
Annual out-of-state tuition	$30,913
Room and board	$14,438
Required fees	$1,363
Books and supplies	$1,200
Average frosh need-based scholarship	$7,329
Average UG need-based scholarship	$7,084
% needy frosh rec. need-based scholarship or grant aid	43
% needy UG rec. need-based scholarship or grant aid	45
% needy frosh rec. non-need-based scholarship or grant aid	96
% needy UG rec. non-need-based scholarship or grant aid	87
% needy frosh rec. need-based self-help aid	50
% needy UG rec. need-based self-help aid	55
% UG borrow to pay for school	49
Average cumulative indebtedness	$33,788
% frosh need fully met	21
% ugrads need fully met	17
Average % of frosh need met	65
Average % of ugrad need met	57

UNIVERSITY OF LOUISIANA AT LAFAYETTE

104 University Circle, Lafayette, LA 70504-1008 • Admissions: 337-482-1000 • Fax: 337-482-1112

STUDENTS SAY "..."

Academics

With a "beautiful campus" and "friendly atmosphere," it's quite easy to understand how students could be drawn to University of Louisiana at Lafayette. This public research university strives to provide undergrads with an affordable education and offers an "abundance [of] scholarship opportunities." Undergrads also appreciate the breadth of fantastic academic departments, from the "wonderful" nursing program and the "exceptional biology program" to the "good architecture program" and "phenomenal art [department]." And, since it's "smaller than most state schools," undergrads here are really able to interact with their professors and receive "quality in-class instruction." Indeed, students seem to thoroughly enjoy their courses. This can definitely be attributed to "amazing faculty." As an English major explains, "Most of the professors I've had have been very passionate about their subjects, which in turn makes the student interested in the class. They're all very open to questions and discussions." A fellow English student agrees, "My professors have been helpful and knowledgeable, and they are always willing to help their students succeed." Perhaps this pre-med student best sums up the experience here: "UL is all about melding creativity, spicy Cajun culture, and academia into a gumbo-pot of successful scholars!"

Campus Life

Students who attend University of Louisiana at Lafayette will likely never be bored. There's always something of which to take advantage. To begin with, we're told that "a lot of the buzz around campus [surrounds] sports." An English major confirms, "Football is a major thing in South Louisiana. I think we're the second biggest 'sports fan base' behind LSU, of course." Come game day, many people "tailgate and there is a big community of RVs and tents from [both] out-of-towners and [those who reside] on campus." Students also report that "the Ragin Cajun Catholics and Christian community is awesome and dynamic!" Many undergrads can also be found "working out in the gym." And a large number participate in Greek life as well. Lastly, students love the area surrounding UL. A biology major happily shares, "Throughout the year, there are tons of festivals unique to Lafayette, all of which are free to attend, such as Festivale Acadiens, which celebrates Cajun culture, as well as Festivale Internationale, which is the largest free world-music festival in the world."

Student Body

Undergrads at UL steadfastly insist that "there is no typical...student." Those who enroll here will discover all types, "from quiet students [and] outgoing students [to] sporty students [and] artsy students." A biology major explains, "We have students of all ethnicities, races, religions, and styles. There are very few social boundaries and mostly everyone is accepting of our diverse student body." Of course, when pressed, one journalism major admits that there is a typical UL Lafayette undergrad, one that "reflects Lafayette's culture: creative, friendly, and food-loving." Many are also "involved in Greek life, and therefore [frequently participate] in community service and [embody] school spirit." By and large, undergrads also report that their peers are "dedicated and determined to succeed." Finally, an art education major encapsulates her fellow students by simply stating, "Everyone accepts one another for who they are. There are friends for everyone." And "as long as you make it a point to get out of your dorm once in a while, you will have close knit circle of friends in no time."

UNIVERSITY OF LOUISIANA AT LAFAYETTE

Financial Aid: 337-482-6506 • E-Mail: enroll@louisiana.edu • Website: www.louisiana.edu

THE PRINCETON REVIEW SAYS

Admissions

The school reports that its standardized testing policy for use in admission for Fall 2024 is SAT or ACT Required. It is unknown at this time if the 2024 testing policy will be permanent. The Princeton Review suggests that interested applicants consult with the school for the most up-to-date standardized testing policies. *Very important factors considered include:* rigor of secondary school record, class rank, academic GPA, standardized test scores. *Other factors considered include:* state residency. High school diploma is required and GED is accepted. *Academic units required:* 4 English, 4 math, 3 science, 2 foreign language, 1 social studies, 2 history, 1 visual/performing arts.

Financial Aid

Students should submit: FAFSA. Priority filing deadline is 5/1. The Princeton Review suggests that all financial aid forms be submitted as soon as possible (see page 5 for a note on the FAFSA). *Need-based scholarships/grants offered:* College/university scholarship or grant aid from institutional funds; Federal Nursing Scholarships; Federal Pell; Private scholarships; SEOG; State scholarships/grants. *Loan aid offered:* Federal Nursing Loans. Admitted students will be notified of awards on a rolling basis beginning 4/1. Federal Work-Study Program available. Institutional employment available.

The Inside Word

Students hoping to attend the University of Louisiana at Lafayette must make sure they take a solid college prep curriculum in high school. Applicants need to complete 4 units of English, 4 units of math, 3 units of social studies, 3 units of science, 2 units of foreign language and 1 unit within the arts in order to qualify. Students must have a minimum overall GPA of 2.0 (on a 4 point scale), a composite ACT score of 23 and/or SAT score of 1050 to gain admission. Finally, any candidate requiring remedial classes should complete that coursework prior to enrolling at UL.

THE SCHOOL SAYS "..."

From the Admissions Office

"The University of Louisiana at Lafayette offers students from throughout the United States and more than ninety countries strong academic training and personal enrichment opportunities in a friendly, comfortable, student-centered environment. UL Lafayette students are taught, mentored, and advised by some of the brightest and most accomplished faculty members in the United States. Although UL Lafayette offers more than 100 programs of study and the research opportunities, internship possibilities, and facilities of a major research-intensive university, average class size is approximately the same as that at many high schools and smaller higher education institutions. UL students receive a good deal of individual attention and support—both personal and academic—from faculty and staff.

"A wide range of cultural, recreational, and social activities are available on and off campus, including more than 150 campus organizations and clubs, NCAA Division I and intramural athletics, a state-of-the-art recreation and aquatic center, a thriving arts scene, a wide range of live music venues, shopping, a great variety of excellent restaurants, theaters, the second largest Mardi Gras in the nation, and an international music festival. In fact, *Utne Reader* magazine selected the city of Lafayette as Louisiana's 'Most Enlightened Town.' Recently, Lafayette was also listed as one of America's most optimistic cities.

"Our generous financial aid and scholarship programs, including an out-of-state tuition waiver for qualified students, make UL Lafayette one of the most affordable universities in the nation. Students who have completed the required college preparatory core curriculum in high school may qualify for admission on the basis of a combination of their high school cumulative grade point average and ACT or SAT scores."

SELECTIVITY

Admissions Rating	85
# of applicants	10,409
% of applicants accepted	78
% of acceptees attending	33

FIRST-YEAR PROFILE

Testing policy	SAT or ACT Required
Range SAT composite	1028–1183
Range SAT EBRW	510–610
Range SAT math	513–588
Range ACT composite	19–24
# submitting SAT scores	110
% submitting SAT scores	4
# submitting ACT scores	2,591
% submitting ACT scores	96
Average HS GPA	3.4
% frosh submitting high school GPA	100
% graduated top 10% of class	16
% graduated top 25% of class	38
% graduated top 50% of class	70

DEADLINES

Regular	
Priority	7/20
Nonfall registration?	Yes

FINANCIAL FACTS

Financial Aid Rating	79
Annual in-state tuition	$5,407
Annual out-of-state tuition	$19,135
Room and board	$10,708
Required fees	$4,939
Books and supplies	$1,300
Average frosh need-based scholarship	$7,180
Average UG need-based scholarship	$6,558
% needy frosh rec. need-based scholarship or grant aid	96
% needy UG rec. need-based scholarship or grant aid	88
% needy frosh rec. non-need-based scholarship or grant aid	15
% needy UG rec. non-need-based scholarship or grant aid	9
% needy frosh rec. need-based self-help aid	48
% needy UG rec. need-based self-help aid	59
% frosh rec. any financial aid	87
% UG rec. any financial aid	72
% frosh need fully met	15
% ugrads need fully met	9
Average % of frosh need met	61
Average % of ugrad need met	52

UNIVERSITY OF LOUISVILLE

2301 South Third Street, Louisville, KY 40292-0001 • Admissions: 502-852-6531 • Fax: 502-852-4776

CAMPUS LIFE

Quality of Life Rating	79
Fire Safety Rating	94
Green Rating	96
Type of school	Public
Environment	Metropolis

STUDENTS

Total undergrad enrollment	13,822
% male/female/another gender	45/55/NR
% from out of state	22
% frosh from public high school	89
% frosh live on campus	65
% ugrads live on campus	35
# of fraternities (% join)	14 (14)
# of sororities (% join)	20 (11)
% African American	15
% Asian	5
% White	65
% Hispanic	7
% Native American	<1
% Pacific Islander	<1
% Two or more races	6
% Race and/or ethnicity unknown	1
% international	1
# of countries represented	49

SURVEY SAYS . . .

Recreation facilities are great
Everyone loves the Cardinals
Students love Louisville, KY

ACADEMICS

Academic Rating	75
% students returning for sophomore year	78
% students graduating within 4 years	42
% students graduating within 6 years	62
Calendar	Semester
Student/faculty ratio	13:1
Profs interesting rating	82
Profs accessible rating	88

Most classes have 20–29 students.

MOST POPULAR MAJORS

Sport and Fitness Administration/Management;
Psychology, General; Registered Nursing/
Registered Nurse

STUDENTS SAY ". . ."

Academics

University of Louisville is an institution that affords undergraduates "endless opportunities." Certainly, as one of Kentucky's premiere public universities, a Louisville education means students are getting a "great value" and an affordable price tag. And when you combine those attributes with a "beautiful" campus that's "easy to navigate," well it's understandable why students eagerly exclaim that Louisville "feels...like home." With regards to academics, undergrads truly appreciate the university's "[emphasis on] critical thinking" as well as the "personalized" attention they receive. Therefore, it's no surprise to hear that Louisville professors "generally [seem to] care about student success [both] in[side] and outside the classroom." As one satisfied biology student further explains, "They are willing to go above and beyond to help you gain a better understanding of course material and obtain supplementary experience outside of the classroom using their own collaborations and affiliations in the field." However, some students do find cause to mention that professors in "higher up courses...are better than professors who teach gen-ed courses." Fortunately, students are pleased to discover that, for the most part, "U of L is about immersing yourself in a diverse community where you have the chance to grow academically, socially, spiritually, and in whatever other ways you choose."

Campus Life

As one excited junior quickly exclaims, life at University of Louisville is "always lively." Indeed, "there is always something going on both on and off campus and numerous ways to get involved and have a great time." To begin with, Greek life is "fairly prominent." And, naturally, there's a small party scene to go with it. Fortunately, we're assured that "things never get out of hand; it's just students trying to wind down and have a good time." Sporting events are extremely popular as well and these undergrads generate a lot of Cardinal pride. As one music education major boasts, "We have several conference championships already this year." Additionally, Louisville students like to give back and community service is a common activity here. An impressed junior reveals, "People are pretty conscientious. They volunteer a lot and there are a million and one volunteer groups throughout the city. Same goes for environmental groups." Of course Louisville itself is a vibrant city and one of which undergrads love to take advantage. For example, students flock to "4th Street Live!, a popular hangout." And they also "enjoy Churchill Downs and going to horse races as well as the eclectic Highlands area of Bardstown Road."

Student Body

Undergrads at University of Louisville really value the amount of diversity found among their student body. As a highly content nursing student immediately chimes in, "We have so many people with different backgrounds, religions, and interests that no matter where you come from or what you are interested in, you will fit in." This sentiment is bolstered by a peer who states, "We have a little bit of everyone, from sorority girls to hippies to those who study all the time. You will not have trouble finding friends here." Certainly, there are also plenty of similarities to be found across the student body as well. After all, many undergrads hail from "the Louisville area" and hold "moderate political views." Students also say that "the majority of [individuals] are extremely nice and easy to get along with." And they are more than "willing to help" their peers whenever they're in need. Then again that's not terribly surprising given that, as this music education major eloquently states, "We are all Cardinals."

664 ■ FOR MORE FREE CONTENT, VISIT PRINCETONREVIEW.COM

UNIVERSITY OF LOUISVILLE

Financial Aid: 502-852-5511 • E-Mail: admitme@louisville.edu • Website: www.louisville.edu

THE PRINCETON REVIEW SAYS

Admissions

The school reports that its standardized testing policy for use in admission for Fall 2024 is Test Optional. It is unknown at this time if the 2024 testing policy will be permanent. The Princeton Review suggests that interested applicants consult with the school for the most up-to-date standardized testing policies. *Very important factors considered include:* rigor of secondary school record, academic GPA. *Important factors considered include:* standardized test scores. *Other factors considered include:* class rank, application essay, recommendation(s), extracurricular activities, talent/ability, state residency, volunteer work, work experience. High school diploma is required and GED is accepted. *Academic units required:* 4 English, 3 math, 3 science, 1 science lab, 2 foreign language, 3 social studies, 1 visual/performing arts, 5 academic electives. *Academic units recommended:* 3 math, 4 science.

Financial Aid

Students should submit: FAFSA. Priority filing deadline is 2/15. The Princeton Review suggests that all financial aid forms be submitted as soon as possible (see page 5 for a note on the FAFSA). *Need-based scholarships/grants offered:* College/university scholarship or grant aid from institutional funds; Federal Nursing Scholarships; Federal Pell; Private scholarships; SEOG; State scholarships/grants. *Loan aid offered:* Direct PLUS loans; Direct Subsidized Loans; Direct Unsubsidized Loans; Federal Nursing Loans. Admitted students will be notified of awards on a rolling basis beginning 4/1. Federal Work-Study Program available. Institutional employment available.

The Inside Word

By and large, admissions decisions at University of Louisville are highly dependent on quantitative data. This means that each applicant's class rank, GPA and standardized test scores (if submitted) will be of utmost importance. Attention will also be paid to course selection; a strong college prep curriculum should be a given. Requirements will vary depending on the specific school to which a candidate is applying. For example, applicants interested in the School of Music must also pass an audition. And nursing students face a two-part process; applying for the lower-level division in freshman year and then applying for the upper-level division in junior year.

THE SCHOOL SAYS "..."

From the Admissions Office

"The University of Louisville (UofL) has transformed into a premier metropolitan research university—and it keeps getting better. It is a tight knit community with the feel of a small college where you can walk anywhere on campus in only 10 minutes. Over the past ten years, it has dramatically improved its on-campus environment with the addition of new residence halls, new apartments near campus, a new state-of-the-art student recreation center, and restaurants and shopping near campus with the right mix of local flavor. Located in a vibrant city that is known worldwide for the Kentucky Derby, students quickly learn to navigate its great parks, discover local restaurants and explore a revitalized downtown and neighborhoods with an eclectic environment.

"With over 50 percent of our entering freshmen beginning their studies with college credit, UofL is a strong academic environment with opportunities inside and outside the classroom to prepare you for professional school or your first job. The city and UofL are closely linked, providing opportunities for internships, coops, part-time jobs and service learning experiences. Our commitment to diversity has created a culture with support for LGBTQ+ students and students of all socioeconomic and ethnic backgrounds.

"Although widely known for our engineering, business and medical programs, we offer over 200 academic programs and in recent years have added undergraduate programs in Public Health, Social Work, Asian Studies and Latin American and Latino Studies, demonstrating a desire to prepare students for the 21st-century needs of our city, region and beyond."

SELECTIVITY

Admissions Rating	84
# of applicants	15,462
% of applicants accepted	82
% of acceptees attending	23

FIRST-YEAR PROFILE

Testing policy	Test Optional
Range SAT composite	1055–1245
Range SAT EBRW	540–640
Range SAT math	530–630
Range ACT composite	19–27
# submitting SAT scores	368
% submitting SAT scores	13
# submitting ACT scores	2,486
% submitting ACT scores	85
Average HS GPA	3.6
% frosh submitting high school GPA	100

DEADLINES

Regular	
Priority	2/15
Deadline	8/1
Nonfall registration?	Yes

APPLICANTS ALSO LOOK AT
University of Kentucky

FINANCIAL FACTS

Financial Aid Rating	81
Annual in-state tuition	$12,324
Annual out-of-state tuition	$28,670
Room and board	$9,852
Required fees	$196
Books and supplies	$1,200
Average frosh need-based scholarship	$13,902
Average UG need-based scholarship	$12,692
% needy frosh rec. need-based scholarship or grant aid	99
% needy UG rec. need-based scholarship or grant aid	92
% needy frosh rec. non-need-based scholarship or grant aid	13
% needy UG rec. non-need-based scholarship or grant aid	12
% needy frosh rec. need-based self-help aid	46
% needy UG rec. need-based self-help aid	50
% UG borrow to pay for school	50
Average cumulative indebtedness	$26,252
% frosh need fully met	19
% ugrads need fully met	18
Average % of frosh need met	64
Average % of ugrad need met	61

UNIVERSITY OF LYNCHBURG

1501 Lakeside Drive, Lynchburg, VA 24501 • Admissions: 434-544-8100

STUDENTS SAY "..."

Academics

Beneath the Blue Ridge mountains in Lynchburg, Virginia, the University of Lynchburg students experience an "academic environment [that] is the perfect level of challenge and excitement." Lynchburg is "huge on community service" and opportunities on and around campus make it easy for students to "get out there and get involved in the local community." Students enjoy a "friendly environment" among peers who are "willing to help you out when needed." Students say that the academic environment is convivial, classes are "very discussion based and allow for conversation." Students appreciate that "class sizes are so small" and explain that this means "participation is necessary" from everyone. A low student-to-faculty ratio also means that it is "very easy to ask questions during class and meet with your professors" outside of class hours. One student in Lynchburg's well-regarded nursing program tells us "we have incredible faculty members who are caring, compassionate, and experienced. They go above and beyond for us each day to make us the best nurses possible." Lynchburg boasts "other amazing programs such as Exercise Physiology, Biology, Teaching, [and] Business," all of which "are backed by the liberal arts education that allows us to expand our thinking and look at the world in a broader view." "I have been given nothing but support and encouragement throughout my time in the program," one student tells us. This nurturing atmosphere helps students become "the best version of ourselves." It isn't uncommon to hear students say, "I wasn't very successful academically in high school but I have done extremely well in college. I would attribute that to the professors" who offer plenty of office hours to get in contact with them, as well as most classes having a class tutor with weekly study sessions to help you along with the class."

Campus Life

There is plenty going on around the University of Lynchburg campus to keep students busy. During the week "most people go to class and then have meetings for clubs," which are well attended at Lynchburg. "Very often, students are involved in at least two campus organizations," and it is a great way for them to get involved in the community: "Students spend a great deal of their out-of-class time working on planning events, service, and projects for these organizations." Athletics are popular on campus and "nearly 1 in 5 students is involved in Greek life." Students say they can "always fill any free time...exploring the city of Lynchburg," where they can check out "a movie, trampoline parks, skating rinks" or catch a bite downtown where "the restaurants and bars...are absolutely amazing." Outside the city, students can explore the foothills of the Blue Ridge Mountains where there are "lots of opportunities for hiking, cave diving, and rafting."

Student Body

Students at Lynchburg are described as "friendly and willing to work together and help each other out." Students agree that "the majority of students from Virginia or neighboring states" and tend to be "primarily Caucasian," but observe that the university is "beginning to have more cultural diversity." Lynchburg students are "open to ideas and accepting to others" while extending their welcoming Southern hospitality. Students will "hold the door for you and give you a sincere smile as you walk by them on the way to class." As one student puts it, "Everyone is very helping. If someone is not able to help you with a homework question or a project, then they will find you someone that can. It does feel like one giant family here."

UNIVERSITY OF LYNCHBURG

Financial Aid: 434-544-8228 • E-mail: admissions@lynchburg.edu • Website: www.lynchburg.edu

THE PRINCETON REVIEW SAYS

Admissions

The school reports that its standardized testing policy for use in admission for Fall 2024 is Test Optional. The 2024 testing policy will be temporary. The Princeton Review suggests that interested applicants consult with the school for the most up-to-date standardized testing policies. *Very important factors considered include:* rigor of secondary school record, academic GPA. *Important factors considered include:* interview. *Other factors considered include:* standardized test scores, application essay, recommendation(s), extracurricular activities, talent/ability, character/personal qualities, volunteer work, work experience, level of applicant's interest. High school diploma is required and GED is accepted. *Academic units required:* 4 English, 3 math, 3 science, 2 science labs, 2 foreign language, 2 social studies, 2 history. *Academic units recommended:* 4 English, 4 math, 4 science, 2 science labs, 3 foreign language, 2 social studies, 2 history, 1 academic elective.

Financial Aid

Students should submit: FAFSA; State aid form. Priority filing deadline is 11/1. The Princeton Review suggests that all financial aid forms be submitted as soon as possible (see page 5 for a note on the FAFSA). *Need-based scholarships/grants offered:* College/university scholarship or grant aid from institutional funds; Federal Pell; SEOG. *Loan aid offered:* Direct PLUS loans; Direct Subsidized Loans; Direct Unsubsidized Loans. Admitted students will be notified of awards on a rolling basis beginning 12/1. Federal Work-Study Program available. Institutional employment available.

The Inside Word

Lynchburg uses rolling admission, as well as Early Decision, so students can apply any time after their junior year of high school, and they recommend that students apply by the fall of their senior year. You only need to submit transcripts, but they highly recommend including a letter of recommendation from a teacher or counselor and a writing sample. The writing sample can be an essay on a topic of your choice or a graded essay from a class. Accepted students are automatically considered for academic scholarship based on their application materials.

THE SCHOOL SAYS "..."

From the Admissions Office

"The University of Lynchburg offers over 100 academic programs and offers degrees at the undergraduate, masters, and doctoral levels. Throughout their years at Lynchburg, students discover new things about themselves and their interests. Lynchburg provides an engaging and challenging curriculum of liberal arts, sciences, and professional programs that develops broad-based understanding and specialized knowledge, leading to fulfilling careers.

"Lynchburg students make many new connections starting with their first days on campus. They benefit from personal interaction with expert faculty. A vibrant campus life helps students forge meaningful connections with each other and with alumni who have excelled in countless career paths.

"Lynchburg students and alumni achieve excellence in the classroom, where they consistently earn places in competitive graduate programs; athletics, including multiple national and conference championships; and in the global workforce. Lynchburg students express high satisfaction with their school, giving it high marks in all five benchmarks of the National Survey of Student Engagement, which measures how colleges engage their students in activities related to learning and personal development. These areas include student-faculty interaction, supportive campus environment, level of academic challenge, active and collaborative learning, and enriching education experiences.

"From the moment prospective students step onto this beautiful campus, they begin to appreciate the Lynchburg experience. Students and families are invited to attend one of the many visit events throughout the year."

SELECTIVITY
Admissions Rating	80
# of applicants	3,230
% of applicants accepted	96
% of acceptees attending	13
# of early decision applicants	155
% accepted early decision	81

FIRST-YEAR PROFILE
Testing policy	Test Optional
Range SAT composite	1000–1220
Range SAT EBRW	500–620
Range SAT math	500–610
Range ACT composite	21–28
# submitting SAT scores	96
% submitting SAT scores	23
# submitting ACT scores	10
% submitting ACT scores	2
Average HS GPA	3.5
% frosh submitting high school GPA	100
% graduated top 10% of class	16
% graduated top 25% of class	42
% graduated top 50% of class	69

DEADLINES
Early decision	
Deadline	11/15
Notification	12/1
Regular	
Deadline	8/1
Notification	Rolling, 9/1
Nonfall registration?	Yes

APPLICANTS ALSO LOOK AT
James Madison University; Longwood University; Old Dominion University; Radford University; Virginia Commonwealth University; Virginia Tech

FINANCIAL FACTS
Financial Aid Rating	85
Annual tuition	$35,540
Room and board	$13,250
Required fees	
Books and supplies	$1,000
Average frosh need-based scholarship	$25,683
Average UG need-based scholarship	$23,804
% needy frosh rec. need-based scholarship or grant aid	89
% needy UG rec. need-based scholarship or grant aid	96
% needy frosh rec. non-need-based scholarship or grant aid	20
% needy UG rec. non-need-based scholarship or grant aid	21
% needy frosh rec. need-based self-help aid	59
% needy UG rec. need-based self-help aid	65
% frosh rec. any financial aid	99
% UG rec. any financial aid	98
% UG borrow to pay for school	87
Average cumulative indebtedness	$25,414
% frosh need fully met	25
% ugrads need fully met	28
Average % of frosh need met	71
Average % of ugrad need met	76

UNIVERSITY OF MAINE

168 College Ave, Orono, ME 04469 • Admissions: 207-581-1865 • Fax: 207-581-1213

CAMPUS LIFE

Quality of Life Rating	83
Fire Safety Rating	99
Green Rating	97
Type of school	Public
Environment	Village

STUDENTS

Total undergrad enrollment	8,374
% male/female/another gender	53/47/0
% from out of state	38
% frosh live on campus	90
% ugrads live on campus	38
# of fraternities	16
# of sororities	8
% African American	2
% Asian	2
% White	83
% Hispanic	5
% Native American	<1
% Pacific Islander	<1
% Two or more races	4
% Race and/or ethnicity unknown	2
% international	2
# of countries represented	57

SURVEY SAYS . . .

Intramural sports are popular
Recreation facilities are great
Great library

ACADEMICS

Academic Rating	76
% students returning for sophomore year	75
% students graduating within 4 years	42
% students graduating within 6 years	57
Calendar	Semester
Student/faculty ratio	15:1
Profs interesting rating	83
Profs accessible rating	88

Most classes have 10–19 students.
Most lab/discussion sessions have 10–19 students.

MOST POPULAR MAJORS

Mechanical Engineering; Psychology, General; Business Administration and Management, General

STUDENTS SAY "..."

Academics

Up in the Northeast corner of the United States, the University of Maine is a public research university with "all the opportunities of a large state school, while having the atmosphere of a small school." Students majoring in Business, Engineering, Marine Sciences, Forestry, Animal Science, Music, and Education majors all rave about their departments, but they also say that with nearly 100 majors, minors and degree programs, "the class choices are amazing." The great value is another draw: "UMaine provides one of the most affordable university educations in the area" with "great scholarships if you have decent high school grades [and] SAT scores." As for the classes themselves, undergrads caution that "the courses are rather challenging," but there's a sense of "camaraderie and willingness to...help—not just in professors but in your peers as well." Professors are generally "passionate, helpful, and actually want to see you at their office hours," and also bring "real-world experience into their classrooms." Juniors and seniors advise that "building a relationship with faculty is key" to success both at UMaine and beyond as they "are eager to recruit students to help with their [own] research" and provide connections to outside jobs and research positions in their fields. Other hands-on learning opportunities abound at UMaine, with some examples including "drilling through the ice to collect sediment samples" on a frozen lake and caring for "horses and dairy cows" on the university farm. Students also find "well-established connections outside of college" in the form of hospital internships to placements at local primary schools. Because of this, students seeking "opportunity and a sense of community" find this campus to "feel like home."

Campus Life

UMaine Black Bears are a very active bunch, and "sports, especially hockey, [are] a huge part of the...culture." At games, "the student section goes crazy (in the best way)" and "the school spirit is...incredible." Additionally, the school is situated in "such a unique place" that is "super green in the summer and pure white in the winter," providing this outdoorsy student body with miles of "trails for running and biking and a river [where] people often go paddling, kayaking, swimming, and fishing." (Yes, there's an on-campus canoe rental.) Both coastal Arcadia National Park and remote Baxter State Park, where "the Appalachian Trail ends...[atop] pristine Mount Katahdin," are just an hour's drive away. The winter season is popular for cross-country and alpine skiing, snowboarding, and other sports. Other forms of physical activity are available in UMaine's recreation center, which students boast is the "best in New England" and features "tons of equipment and...classes for people of all experience levels." For those who would rather stay inside during the winter, the campus puts on free movies, "drag shows, trivia nights, [and] amazing Collins Center performances." As for nightlife, while there are plenty of parties and drinking at downtown bars on weekends, there is little pressure to partake—students say their peers are "chill and accepting of whatever you do and do not do." While the school may be in a rural environment, that doesn't mean the students are bored or lonely. As one undergrad puts it: "When everyone's in the middle of nowhere, no one is."

Student Body

UMaine's "campus is filled with very welcoming people" who are "down to earth," "helpful," "hardworking," and, as one undergrad phrases it, "wicked friendly." The student body hails "mostly from the state of Maine or the surrounding New England area" and is predominantly white. Yet students emphasize that the campus is diverse, maintaining a "significant LGBT+ presence on campus" and a mix of social classes, religions, and political affiliations. Whatever the background, most students "share the love and passion of the outdoors." Additionally, one student tells us, "Everyone has their own different quirks and no one is judged for that." That acceptance also goes for nontraditional students. For example, the "veteran community is fantastic" and there are "many people with military partners [or] family members." Another student sums it up: "There is a unique sense of Maine here, and we are quite united under the Black Bear banner."

UNIVERSITY OF MAINE

Financial Aid: 207-581-1324 • E-Mail: umaineadmissions@maine.edu • Website: www.umaine.edu

THE PRINCETON REVIEW SAYS

Admissions

The school reports that its standardized testing policy for use in admission for Fall 2024 is Test Optional. The 2024 testing policy will be permanent. The Princeton Review suggests that interested applicants consult with the school for the most up-to-date standardized testing policies. *Very important factors considered include:* rigor of secondary school record, class rank, academic GPA, application essay, recommendation(s). *Other factors considered include:* standardized test scores, interview, extracurricular activities, talent/ability, character/personal qualities, volunteer work, work experience. High school diploma is required and GED is accepted. *Academic units required:* 4 English, 3 math, 2 science, 2 science labs, 2 social studies, 4 academic electives. *Academic units recommended:* 4 English, 4 math, 4 science, 3 science labs, 2 foreign language, 2 social studies, 1 history, 4 academic electives.

Financial Aid

Students should submit: FAFSA. Priority filing deadline is 3/1. The Princeton Review suggests that all financial aid forms be submitted as soon as possible (see page 5 for a note on the FAFSA). *Need-based scholarships/grants offered:* College/university scholarship or grant aid from institutional funds; Federal Pell; Private scholarships; SEOG; State scholarships/grants. *Loan aid offered:* Direct PLUS loans; Direct Subsidized Loans; Direct Unsubsidized Loans; College/university loans from institutional funds; State Loans. Admitted students will be notified of awards on a rolling basis beginning 1/1. Federal Work-Study Program available. Institutional employment available.

The Inside Word

Find ways—like campus visits—to stand out among local UMaine applicants. Admission is rolling, but apply earlier to optimize housing and financial aid prospects.

THE SCHOOL SAYS "..."

From the Admissions Office

"Maine's Flagship and Public Research University is at the forefront of national and international research, student engagement, innovation and collaboration. With experiential learning at its core, UMaine offers celebrated academics, student research opportunities and a close-knit community that strives for diversity, inclusion and excellence. UMaine offers more than one hundred undergraduate programs, and more than 140 programs through which students can earn graduate certificates, master's, C.A.S., Ed.S., and doctoral degrees. Top students are invited to join UMaine's Honors College, one of the country's oldest and most accomplished. The National Science Foundation ranks UMaine among the top third of public institutions engaged in research. Classified as a 'High Research Activity Institution' by the Carnegie Foundation for the Advancement of Teaching, its sixteen major research centers include The Laboratory for Surface Science and Technology, a hub for cutting-edge sensor and nanotechnology research, and the Advanced Structures and Composites Center, a global leader in deep water offshore wind energy development.

"Maine boasts a 15:1 student-to-faculty ratio, where faculty and administration members are known for having an open-door policy. Our students work alongside some of the most renowned scholars and scientists in their fields, whether they're talking civil engineering over lunch or traversing an Antarctic ice sheet with climate researchers.

"UMaine students gain real-world experience to prepare them for their professional careers after college. SPIFFY, our student investment club, manages a $3.2 million real-money portfolio. Wildlife ecology majors learn about bear behavior by going out and tagging cubs. Engineering majors take advantage of internships that often lead to employment after graduation. Marine science undergrads spend a semester by the sea at our internationally renowned Darling Marine Center."

SELECTIVITY

Admissions Rating	82
# of applicants	14,447
% of applicants accepted	94
% of acceptees attending	14

FIRST-YEAR PROFILE

Testing policy	Test Optional
Range SAT composite	1080–1320
Range SAT EBRW	550–670
Range SAT math	530–670
Range ACT composite	24–30
# submitting SAT scores	495
% submitting SAT scores	26
# submitting ACT scores	46
% submitting ACT scores	2
Average HS GPA	3.4
% frosh submitting high school GPA	98
% graduated top 10% of class	20
% graduated top 25% of class	28
% graduated top 50% of class	78

DEADLINES

Early action	
Deadline	12/1
Notification	1/15
Regular	
Priority	2/1
Notification	Rolling, 12/2
Nonfall registration?	Yes

APPLICANTS OFTEN PREFER
University of Massachusetts Amherst; University of New Hampshire

APPLICANTS SOMETIMES PREFER
Husson University; University of New England; University of Rhode Island; University of Southern Maine; University of Vermont

APPLICANTS RARELY PREFER
Southern Maine Community College; University of Connecticut; University of Massachusetts Lowell

FINANCIAL FACTS

Financial Aid Rating	83
Annual in-state tuition	$11,640
Annual out-of-state tuition	$33,240
Room and board	$12,050
Required fees	$496
Books and supplies	$1,000
Average frosh need-based scholarship	$11,498
Average UG need-based scholarship	$10,768
% needy frosh rec. need-based scholarship or grant aid	97
% needy UG rec. need-based scholarship or grant aid	95
% needy frosh rec. non-need-based scholarship or grant aid	22
% needy UG rec. non-need-based scholarship or grant aid	17
% needy frosh rec. need-based self-help aid	71
% needy UG rec. need-based self-help aid	74
% frosh rec. any financial aid	99
% UG rec. any financial aid	99
% UG borrow to pay for school	69
Average cumulative indebtedness	$36,656
% frosh need fully met	29
% ugrads need fully met	26
Average % of frosh need met	75
Average % of ugrad need met	74

UNIVERSITY OF MARY WASHINGTON

1301 College Avenue, Fredericksburg, VA 22401 • Admissions: 540-654-1000 • Fax: 540-654-1857

STUDENTS SAY "..."

Academics

Virginia's University of Mary Washington is a public liberal arts and sciences university offering a range of both disciplinary and interdisciplinary programs and "a small community with plenty of individualized attention for students." Students speak highly of those levels of support: "No matter what my problem is, personal or academic, there is a service on campus to help me if I want to reach out." There's also appreciation for "non-traditional class formats that are more flexible and convenient for full-time working adults to return to college."

Students add that they feel they "can form strong relationships with each other and professors." It goes both ways, too: enrollees emphasize how teachers "make every effort possible to have one-on-one time with every single student" and "reach out to individuals with opportunities as well as to check on them." This leads some to happily declare that: "I am able to participate in graduate-level research and projects in my majors." In short, faculty "want you to succeed and outline their classes in such a way that success is easy if you stay caught up with assignments" and participate, and they "devote plenty of class time to discussions around real topics and situations to help ensure we come out prepared."

Campus Life

Whether you're into athletics or academics, activities at Mary Washington have you covered. Students particularly note how clubs related to existing majors help students find "more people that share similar interests and have similar backgrounds" and go a long way toward "knowing your department as well." The same's true for the environment, which encourages students to get "outside or in some of our cool places to study," or to take a break: "On some really nice days in spring, kids will head down to the Rappahannock River to go swimming and play games like spike ball or frisbee on the beach." The school itself also maintains this balance, with "fun events planned for a lot of nights such as bingo and karaoke" right alongside "a nice range from keynote speakers to panels to participant discussions" at the James Farmer Multicultural Center. And even though students spend a lot of time studying, on-campus activities "like club carnival, drag shows, concerts, bonfires...typically have a large turnout." On the weekends, "most people either go home or go downtown to shop, eat, [or] visit an art gallery," and "downtown Fredericksburg is a popular place for young adults to get together and have social time." At the end of the day, "spending time with friends or diving into community events are the most popular ways to have fun."

Student Body

"Every student at Mary Washington has a different background and a different perspective to offer... which makes things in the classroom ten times more interesting and engaging." With this group being able to "contribute unique viewpoints in class discussions and come from all walks of life," it follows that "everyone has personality." Students say that "kindness is widespread, and when you are trusted and respected in the community, many students embrace you as a peer." Mary Washington has "strong school spirit and sense of community," and "everyone is kind and friendly and willing to go out of their way for a stranger." There is "a high LGBTQ+ community population, and by and large it feels like an accepting and welcoming community"; people are "outstandingly supportive of one another in all that we do...and encourage each other to step outside our comfort zones to meet people and gain new experiences." A student sums up: "It's the kind of place where no one ever has to eat alone if they don't want to. Every single person is genuinely kind and looking out for each other."

UNIVERSITY OF MARY WASHINGTON

Financial Aid: 540-654-1682 • E-Mail: admit@umw.edu • Website: www.umw.edu

THE PRINCETON REVIEW SAYS

Admissions

The school reports that its standardized testing policy for use in admission for Fall 2024 will remain Test Optional, as it has been since 2016. The Princeton Review suggests that interested applicants consult with the school for the most up-to-date standardized testing policies. *Very important factors considered include:* rigor of secondary school record, academic GPA. *Important factors considered include:* class rank, application essay, recommendation(s). *Other factors considered include:* standardized test scores, interview, extracurricular activities, talent/ability, character/personal qualities, first generation, alumni/ae relation, geographical residence, state residency, racial/ethnic status, volunteer work, work experience, level of applicant's interest. High school diploma is required and GED is accepted. *Academic units required:* 4 English, 3 math, 3 science, 3 science labs, 3 foreign language, 3 social studies. *Academic units recommended:* 4 English, 4 math, 4 science, 4 science labs, 4 foreign language, 2 social studies.

Financial Aid

Students should submit: FAFSA. Priority filing deadline is 2/1. The Princeton Review suggests that all financial aid forms be submitted as soon as possible (see page 5 for a note on the FAFSA). *Need-based scholarships/grants offered:* College/university scholarship or grant aid from institutional funds; Federal Pell; Private scholarships; SEOG; State scholarships/grants. *Loan aid offered:* Direct PLUS loans; Direct Subsidized Loans; Direct Unsubsidized Loans; College/university loans from institutional funds. Admitted students will be notified of awards on a rolling basis beginning 12/1. Federal Work-Study Program available. Institutional employment available.

The Inside Word

When considering candidates for admissions, University of Mary Washington does not subscribe to any particular formula. Indeed, the committee simply strives to create a diverse and well-rounded incoming class. Therefore, all aspects of your application will hold some weight. Of course, strong emphasis is placed on the quality and rigor of your high school curriculum: successful students tend to have a handful of honors, advanced placement, and/or IB classes.

THE SCHOOL SAYS "..."

From the Admissions Office

"The University of Mary Washington is for students who are serious about academics, committed to an inclusive community, and eager to contribute to the greater good. At UMW, we focus on what matters. We are here to create meaningful connections and powerful experiences.

"As a public liberal arts and sciences university, we stand for bold knowledge-building. Our three colleges (Arts & Sciences, Business, and Education) approach learning by giving your mind room to roam, go on adventures, take risks, seek out intersections, chase answers, and create fresh insight. We prepare students to think around corners and solve problems they've never imagined, let alone studied. Our small classes buzz with inquiry and exploration. Deep thinking and doing happen daily here. We go for collaboration over competition. Students work with professors who double as mentors. They'll help tap into students' strengths and talents.

"Distinctive to UMW is one of the nation's leading historic preservation programs, as well as strong creative writing and debate programs. Other top majors include political science and international affairs, computer science and cybersecurity, communication and digital studies, English, biology, psychology, earth and environmental science, visual and performing arts, theatre, economics and business.

"We see students—their potential, their purpose, their future. Conveniently located between Washington, D.C. and Richmond, VA and with over 90+ majors, minors, and programs, UMW is committed to connecting students to internships, study abroad, over 150 student organizations and clubs, NCAA Division III Athletics, research projects, community service, and job opportunities—the experiences that will take you to the next level."

SELECTIVITY

Admissions Rating	84
# of applicants	4,709
% of applicants accepted	86
% of acceptees attending	19
# of early decision applicants	95
% accepted early decision	80

FIRST-YEAR PROFILE

Testing policy	Test Optional
Range SAT composite	1170–1330
Range SAT EBRW	610–690
Range SAT math	560–650
Range ACT composite	25–30
# submitting SAT scores	193
% submitting SAT scores	26
# submitting ACT scores	31
% submitting ACT scores	4
Average HS GPA	3.7
% frosh submitting high school GPA	98
% graduated top 10% of class	11
% graduated top 25% of class	40
% graduated top 50% of class	72

DEADLINES

Early decision	
Deadline	11/1
Notification	12/10
Early action	
Deadline	12/1
Notification	1/31
Regular	
Priority	2/1
Notification	4/1
Nonfall registration?	Yes

APPLICANTS SOMETIMES PREFER
University of Virginia; Virginia Tech; William & Mary

APPLICANTS RARELY PREFER
George Mason University; Longwood University; Virginia Commonwealth University

FINANCIAL FACTS

Financial Aid Rating	75
Annual in-state tuition	$8,938
Annual out-of-state tuition	$25,858
Room and board	$12,090
Required fees	$5,296
Books and supplies	$1,200
Average frosh need-based scholarship	$4,294
Average UG need-based scholarship	$3,992
% needy frosh rec. need-based scholarship or grant aid	63
% needy UG rec. need-based scholarship or grant aid	67
% needy frosh rec. non-need-based scholarship or grant aid	83
% needy UG rec. non-need-based scholarship or grant aid	61
% needy frosh rec. need-based self-help aid	49
% needy UG rec. need-based self-help aid	59
% frosh rec. any financial aid	100
% UG rec. any financial aid	78
% UG borrow to pay for school	54
Average cumulative indebtedness	$32,352
% frosh need fully met	19
% ugrads need fully met	11
Average % of frosh need met	42
Average % of ugrad need met	44

UNIVERSITY OF MARYLAND, BALTIMORE COUNTY

1000 Hilltop Circle, Baltimore, MD 21250 • Admissions: 410-455-1000 • Fax: 410-455-1094

STUDENTS SAY ". . ."

Academics

The University of Maryland, Baltimore County, is a fitting choice for students who "want some research opportunities, but may also want more personal attention from professor. At this top-tier public research university, the STEM programs get a significant amount of the glory—the science labs are "gorgeous, state-of-the-art facilities," and many students "come out of school working for Boeing and the NSA" or, in the case of one scientist, developing the Moderna COVID-19 vaccine. But UMBC has strengths outside of science. As one student says, "I have had superb instruction in modern languages…including fantastic German translation and modern French literature courses." In fact, UMBC "has greatly expanded its support to the fine arts"—one can earn a Bachelor of Fine Arts in Acting and Studio Art, and one student describes a "really close-knit Arts department that feels like a second family." Overall, the feeling toward the faculty is very positive, and students feel that "professors are able to gain a better and closer professor-student relationship than those at large academic institutions." One student remarks, "They helped me see my true potential as a student, and also helped me find my passions," and another insists, "They really make the school shine."

Campus Life

"Life at UMBC is never dull," and the "small and cozy" campus feels like a connected community: "Most people gather with their friends in the library to study together, then… grab food together in [the] Commons." It takes no time to get from the pond outside the library to the "highly impressive" lab facilities: "Anything is within a 10–15 [minute] walk. It's quite convenient," especially since there are "ample opportunities for students to engage on campus." For instance, students enjoy competition with tournaments of paintball or ping-pong, as well as putting their mental acuity to the test: "We do also have a thriving intellectual sports scene including chess, mock trial, and ethics bowl." Clubs range from cultural to sports to career-building: "My favorite one is the video game development club, as it combines my interests of programming and video games into an opportunity to showcase my work in a way that could lead to a future career." Students also delight in events hosted by the University, "like Homecoming…[where it is] so much fun to watch the Bonfire, attend the Carnival and even see the puppy parade!"

Student Body

UMBC students are proud to call themselves "nerdy, but like the cool nerds," declaring: "Most students love studying," and "we're an Honors school, not a party school." A number of students are commuters, so the weekends can be quiet, but that doesn't stop them from forming the close bonds of "a community that could be found on a campus half of our size." Says one student, "I've met some of the most tenacious, dedicated, brilliant people in my four years here than ever before," while another delivers the ultimate compliment: "The community is amazing. I came here thinking I'd transfer after the first semester ends but ended [up] falling in love with the school."

The abundance of "cultures and backgrounds are celebrated," as is evidenced by the dozens of student-run cultural organizations and the echoed sentiment: "That's what makes UMBC so unique: the students are diverse and are not restricted by their appearances, personalities, religions, cultures, identities, etc. whatsoever." One student finds that the freedom to be oneself lays the foundation to thrive: "I feel as though it's a safe space and judgment-free zone. I've never been in an environment where people are themselves out loud the way they are at UMBC."

UNIVERSITY OF MARYLAND, BALTIMORE COUNTY

Financial Aid: 410-455-1517 • E-Mail: admissions@umbc.edu • Website: www.umbc.edu

THE PRINCETON REVIEW SAYS

Admissions

The school reports that its standardized testing policy for use in admission for Fall 2024 is Test Optional. The 2024 testing policy will be temporary. The Princeton Review suggests that interested applicants consult with the school for the most up-to-date standardized testing policies. *Very important factors considered include:* rigor of secondary school record, academic GPA, application essay, recommendation(s). *Important factors considered include:* class rank, talent/ability. *Other factors considered include:* standardized test scores, extracurricular activities, character/personal qualities, first generation, volunteer work, work experience. High school diploma is required and GED is accepted. *Academic units required:* 4 English, 4 math, 3 science, 2 foreign language, 3 history. *Academic units recommended:* 3 history.

Financial Aid

Students should submit: FAFSA. Priority filing deadline is 3/1. The Princeton Review suggests that all financial aid forms be submitted as soon as possible (see page 5 for a note on the FAFSA). *Need-based scholarships/grants offered:* College/university scholarship or grant aid from institutional funds; Federal Pell; Private scholarships; SEOG; State scholarships/grants; United Negro College Fund. *Loan aid offered:* Direct PLUS loans; Direct Subsidized Loans; Direct Unsubsidized Loans. Admitted students will be notified of awards on a rolling basis beginning 3/25. Federal Work-Study Program available. Institutional employment available.

The Inside Word

UMBC offers a large number of admissions events, online chats, a virtual tour, and other opportunities for prospective students to connect with the admissions team. The admissions committee considers the strength of your secondary school curriculum and class rank in combination with traditional factors, such as GPA, test scores, and essay when making an acceptance decision. Additionally, it's suggested that at least one letter of recommendation be written by a teacher.

THE SCHOOL SAYS "..."

From the Admissions Office

"UMBC is a university where highly motivated students are taught and mentored by faculty who have been consistently recognized for their commitment to undergraduate teaching. Innovative approaches to learning take place in world-class facilities—such as the Howard Hughes Medical Institute at UMBC and the world-class Performing Arts and Humanities building. UMBC celebrates undergraduate research and creative achievement, which means even first-year students are involved in research with their classmates and professors. The location of UMBC is just right—nestled just outside of Baltimore, in a quiet, green setting. UMBC is also a short commute to D.C., an advantage for jobs, internships, and networking opportunities. About 82 percent of the UMBC class of 2020 are in prestigious graduate programs and careers within six months of graduation. Student life is abundant at UMBC. With more students living on campus each year (over 70 percent of freshman), Division 1 sports, the Chesapeake Employers Insurance Arena, and more than 200 student organizations, students are creating experiences and friendships that will last a lifetime."

SELECTIVITY

Admissions Rating	85
# of applicants	11,534
% of applicants accepted	81
% of acceptees attending	23
# offered a place on the wait list	1,116
% accepting a place on wait list	100
% admitted from wait list	88

FIRST-YEAR PROFILE

Testing policy	Test Optional
Range SAT EBRW	610–690
Range SAT math	600–700
Range ACT composite	23–29
# submitting SAT scores	657
% submitting SAT scores	31
# submitting ACT scores	75
% submitting ACT scores	4
Average HS GPA	4.0
% frosh submitting high school GPA	100
% graduated top 10% of class	25
% graduated top 25% of class	54
% graduated top 50% of class	87

DEADLINES

Early action	
Deadline	11/1
Notification	12/15
Regular	
Priority	11/1
Deadline	2/1
Notification	Rolling, 2/1

APPLICANTS ALSO LOOK AT

Delaware State University; Johns Hopkins University; Pennsylvania State University - McKeesport Campus; Towson University; University of Maryland, College Park; Virginia Tech

FINANCIAL FACTS

Financial Aid Rating	78
Annual in-state tuition	$12,606
Annual out-of-state tuition	$29,370
Room and board	$13,378
Books and supplies	$1,600
Average frosh need-based scholarship	$12,865
Average UG need-based scholarship	$10,972
% needy frosh rec. need-based scholarship or grant aid	88
% needy UG rec. need-based scholarship or grant aid	81
% needy frosh rec. non-need-based scholarship or grant aid	40
% needy UG rec. non-need-based scholarship or grant aid	20
% needy frosh rec. need-based self-help aid	36
% needy UG rec. need-based self-help aid	45
% frosh rec. any financial aid	93
% UG rec. any financial aid	81
% UG borrow to pay for school	41
Average cumulative indebtedness	$23,350
% frosh need fully met	18
% ugrads need fully met	12
Average % of frosh need met	67
Average % of ugrad need met	60

UNIVERSITY OF MARYLAND, COLLEGE PARK

University of Maryland, College Park, College Park, MD 20742 • Admissions: 301-405-1000 • Fax: 301-314-9693

STUDENTS SAY ". . ."

Academics

The University of Maryland, College Park, is a grand mix of "twenty-minute walks to class across one of the country's most beautiful campuses, [an introduction] to high-level courses taught by the nation's top researchers, [and] a motivated 'green' campus" as well as "crowded, smelly frat parties, [and] living-learning communities that can make the gigantic campus much smaller." Students are quick to boast about sports, too, especially the men's and women's basketball teams. In short, it's a quintessential large university, offering "a great experience with a variety of opportunities that are what you make of them." Students crow about Maryland's "nationally recognized business program," a "top-ranked criminology program," a solid engineering school, a great political science department that capitalizes on the school's proximity to Washington, D.C., and the "top-notch honors program." Most of all, they love the "great price. This school gives you a great education for a really cheap price." Low cost doesn't translate to budget accommodations. On the contrary, "the administration shows a desire to always upgrade facilities, as can be witnessed by the tremendous business school and the brand new engineering building." In conclusion, students applaud "the widely diverse opportunities available at UMD. You can never get bored because there is always something to do."

Campus Life

"Life at UMD is awesome," with "a good mix of fun activities" including "school-sponsored parties, games," a "campus recreation center that has virtually everything you could wish for, including pools, an extensive gym, a rock wall, squash courts, an indoor track," and a student union "loaded with fun places like the arcade area, bowling alley," and "tons of places to eat as well." In addition, "there are always open games of soccer, football, or ultimate Frisbee being played on the mall and elsewhere." There are bars close to campus, and "students are always having parties," especially along College Park's raucous Frat Row. Terrapin sports are a passion for many. If all that isn't enough, "the proximity to D.C. makes clubbing, nights out on the town, and general visits to D.C. frequent." With all this going on, no wonder students say that "the social life at UMD is unsurpassed." Some warn the surrounding area is dicey; "It's pretty annoying and scary to get crime alerts from the police informing us of incidents close to campus," one student explains. Undergrads also warn that parking regulations are brutal. "Bus transportation around campus provided by the university is great, but for students and visitors with cars, it's a huge hassle. Permits are expensive, and free parking for visitors is impossible to find. School officials are strict with violations, and tickets are $75. They are hard to refute and very costly."

Student Body

"The University of Maryland is a very large school," so "there is no 'typical' student here. Everyone will find that they can fit in somewhere." Better still, "different groups are very accepting of other groups. Students in Greek life are just as accepting of students in non-Greek life. Athletes blend in with non-athletes. UMD provides a great environment for students to meet people they would normally not know and helps to provide great connections with these people." UMD is "an especially diverse school," and this makes people "more tolerant and accepting of people from different backgrounds and cultures." A student from New Jersey explains it this way: "Coming from a very diverse area, I thought it was going to be hard to find a school that had that same representation of minority and atypical students until I found Maryland. I don't think I have ever learned so much about different religions, cultures, orientations, or lifestyles. All of them are accepted and even celebrated" at UMD.

UNIVERSITY OF MARYLAND, COLLEGE PARK

Financial Aid: 1-888-313-2404 • E-Mail: ApplyMaryland@umd.edu • Website: www.umd.edu

THE PRINCETON REVIEW SAYS

Admissions

The school reports that its standardized testing policy for use in admission for Fall 2024 is Test Optional. It is unknown at this time if the 2024 testing policy will be permanent. The Princeton Review suggests that interested applicants consult with the school for the most up-to-date standardized testing policies. *Very important factors considered include:* rigor of secondary school record, academic GPA. *Important factors considered include:* class rank, application essay, recommendation(s), talent/ability, first generation, state residency. *Other factors considered include:* standardized test scores, extracurricular activities, character/personal qualities, alumni/ae relation, geographical residence, racial/ethnic status, volunteer work, work experience. High school diploma is required and GED is accepted. *Academic units required:* 4 English, 4 math, 3 science, 2 science labs, 2 foreign language, 3 social studies.

Financial Aid

Students should submit: FAFSA. Priority filing deadline is 1/1. The Princeton Review suggests that all financial aid forms be submitted as soon as possible (see page 5 for a note on the FAFSA). *Need-based scholarships/grants offered:* College/university scholarship or grant aid from institutional funds; Federal Pell; Private scholarships; SEOG; State scholarships/grants. *Loan aid offered:* Direct PLUS loans; Direct Subsidized Loans; Direct Unsubsidized Loans. Admitted students will be notified of awards on a rolling basis beginning 3/1. Federal Work-Study Program available. Institutional employment available.

The Inside Word

Maryland admissions officers don't simply crunch numbers and apply a formula. The school considers no fewer than 25 factors when determining who's in and who's out. Essays, recommendations, extracurricular activities, talents and skills, and demographic factors all figure into the mix along with high school transcript and standardized test scores. Give all aspects of your application your utmost attention; admissions is very competitive.

THE SCHOOL SAYS "..."

From the Admissions Office

"The University of Maryland (UMD) is a top-ranked flagship public research university, located within minutes from Washington, D.C. Students have opportunities to learn, explore and succeed through interaction with outstanding faculty that include Nobel Prize, Pulitzer Prize, Emmy and Tony winners. The beautifully landscaped 1,335-acre campus's proximity to major East Coast cities allows students to extend their education beyond the classroom through education abroad programs, and internships at U.S. federal agencies, research labs, global think tanks, major media outlets, world-class museums, and thriving companies. The university strongly encourages innovation, entrepreneurship and creativity by assisting students to launch startups, and serves as a model of cultural excellence through its arts programming. The University of Maryland also thrives on diversity, inclusion and engagement to prepare graduates to become excellent leaders in their communities and careers."

SELECTIVITY

Admissions Rating	94
# of applicants	56,637
% of applicants accepted	44
% of acceptees attending	23
# offered a place on the wait list	300
% accepting a place on wait list	100
% admitted from wait list	0

FIRST-YEAR PROFILE

Testing policy	Test Optional
Range SAT composite	1370–1510
Range SAT EBRW	670–740
Range SAT math	690–780
Range ACT composite	31–34
# submitting SAT scores	2,720
% submitting SAT scores	47
# submitting ACT scores	442
% submitting ACT scores	8
Average HS GPA	4.4
% frosh submitting high school GPA	97
% graduated top 10% of class	66
% graduated top 25% of class	90
% graduated top 50% of class	99

DEADLINES

Early action	
Deadline	11/1
Notification	2/1
Regular	
Priority	11/1
Deadline	1/20
Notification	Rolling, 4/1
Nonfall registration?	Yes

FINANCIAL FACTS

Financial Aid Rating	78
Annual in-state tuition	$9,695
Annual out-of-state tuition	$37,931
Room and board	$14,896
Required fees	$1,538
Books and supplies	$1,250
Average frosh need-based scholarship	$13,098
Average UG need-based scholarship	$12,559
% needy frosh rec. need-based scholarship or grant aid	75
% needy UG rec. need-based scholarship or grant aid	77
% needy frosh rec. non-need-based scholarship or grant aid	11
% needy UG rec. non-need-based scholarship or grant aid	6
% needy frosh rec. need-based self-help aid	77
% needy UG rec. need-based self-help aid	84
% frosh rec. any financial aid	88
% UG rec. any financial aid	71
% UG borrow to pay for school	36
Average cumulative indebtedness	$30,420
% frosh need fully met	20
% ugrads need fully met	16
Average % of frosh need met	65
Average % of ugrad need met	65

UNIVERSITY OF MASSACHUSETTS-AMHERST

181 Presidents Dr, Amherst, MA 01003 • Admissions: 413-545-0222 • Fax: 413-545-4312

STUDENTS SAY ". . ."

Academics

The University of Massachusetts-Amherst is a large university with all the perks: "so much opportunity and so many different people to meet... both socially and academically." Its status as the flagship of the UM system is well-earned: it's not just the largest public research university in New England but also "a great institute... [with] an amazing faculty that wants to help you." The 24,000 undergraduates (and 100+ majors) are also served by UMass being a part of the Five College Consortium, which allows access to a broader array of courses, academic resources, facilities, and libraries across five campuses in the Pioneer Valley. This scale means that some general education classes are very large, but students note that even here, they feel able to interact and network with professors, and they cite innovative approaches to keep things fresh ("Team-Based Learning classes where a large portion of the class is working with other students to solve problems") or to help support students ("recording lectures and automatically transcribing them").

The "teachers foster good learning environments" wherein they "try and connect with us on a personal level to make us feel more a part of the class." A student says: "My architecture classes have built-in work times where my professors stay and give feedback during the process." Faculty are "very aware of the world and how things connect" and provide a gateway to plenty of "internship opportunities and service learning courses." Some professors "are very good at engaging students by using anecdotes and demonstrations," and there are "wonderful opportunities and resources available to enhance learning."

Campus Life

The school features a "great mix of social and academic life" and has the facilities to support both. The rec center offers classes that students admire, the Student Union provides plenty of opportunities for "volunteering in different events," we're told that "people love to go to the gym," and many simply like to "hang with friends on my floor." Intramurals and "lots of outdoor activities" are quite popular, from "sports such as flag football, softball and basketball, plus the LUG ice hockey league." In short, as with the academics, there are "lots of resources, and lots of advertising of those resources" on the part of the school, and "so many options in regard to clubs, classes, and especially food." No wonder, then, that students say they "mainly fill their days with classes and friendships."

Student Body

The University of Massachusetts-Amherst is a collaborative environment where people "are extremely dedicated and hard-working students" and "everyone truly wants you to succeed with them." Students suggest that the majority of students are in-state, but still "a diverse group that comes together to pursue their different goals." One commonality, however, is "there are a lot of outgoing people here," or as one student puts it: "everyone is very nice and it's definitely a good community to be in." In essence, it's a "large student body so you meet a lot of people, but still small enough communities that you can make really good friend groups." This "unique and smart" bunch is "open, kind, [and] welcoming" and "love to share who they are with everyone." UMass students are also "very involved in campus and active members of the community" and "everyone is so willing to learn and cooperate in classes as much as possible."

UNIVERSITY OF MASSACHUSETTS-AMHERST

Financial Aid: 413-545-0801 • E-Mail: mail@admissions.umass.edu • Website: www.umass.edu

THE PRINCETON REVIEW SAYS

Admissions

The school reports that its standardized testing policy for use in admission for Fall 2024 is Test Optional. The Princeton Review suggests that interested applicants consult with the school for the most up-to-date standardized testing policies. *Very important factors considered include:* rigor of secondary school record, academic GPA. *Important factors considered include:* class rank, application essay, recommendation(s), extracurricular activities, talent/ability, character/personal qualities, first generation, work experience. *Other factors considered include:* standardized test scores (if submitted), state residency, racial/ethnic status, volunteer work. High school diploma is required and GED is accepted. *Academic units required:* 4 English, 4 math, 3 science, 3 science labs, 2 foreign language, 1 social studies, 1 history, 2 academic electives.

Financial Aid

Students should submit: FAFSA. Priority filing deadline is 3/1. The Princeton Review suggests that all financial aid forms be submitted as soon as possible (see page 5 for a note on the FAFSA). *Need-based scholarships/grants offered:* College/university scholarship or grant aid from institutional funds; Federal Pell; Private scholarships; SEOG; State scholarships/grants. *Loan aid offered:* Direct PLUS loans; Direct Subsidized Loans; Direct Unsubsidized Loans; Federal Nursing Loans. Admitted students will be notified of awards on a rolling basis beginning 1/1. Federal Work-Study Program available. Institutional employment available.

The Inside Word

UMass Amherst uses a holistic review process to carefully consider applicants in an individualized context. In addition to academic achievements (grade trends, course selection, major-related grades), the school is interested in a student's behavior and attitude. Applicants to the Architecture, Art, Dance, and Music majors are encouraged to contact the appropriate department and apply as early as possible to allow enough time for an audition or portfolio review. For all applicants, a strong senior year schedule is also strongly considered. The university is forward-thinking and socially conscious and therefore invites applications from and encourages the enrollment of undocumented students and students granted Deferred Action for Childhood Arrivals (DACA).

THE SCHOOL SAYS "..."

From the Admissions Office

"The University of Massachusetts-Amherst is the flagship campus of the Commonwealth and the largest public university in New England, offering its students an almost limitless variety of academic programs and activities. The Commonwealth Honors College is a national model and welcomes students who seek additional academic challenge and meet the requirements for acceptance. The school takes a holistic view of the student's application package and considers test scores (SAT or ACT) as only part of the evaluation criteria, if a student chooses to submit them. Greater weight in the selection process is placed on the student's performance in a rigorous curriculum. Increased applications in recent years have made admission more selective. Over one hundred majors are offered, including a unique program called Bachelor's Degree with Individual Concentration (BDIC) in which students create their own program of study. First-year students participate in the Residential First-Year Experience with opportunities to explore every possible interest through residential life. The extensive library system is the largest at any public institution in the Northeast. The campus competes in NCAA Division I sports for men and women, with teams garnering national recognition. About 6,500 students a year participate in the intramural sports program. The town of Amherst is consistently ranked one of the top college towns in the country. Through the Five College Consortium, students enroll in classes at nearby Amherst, Hampshire, Mount Holyoke, and Smith Colleges at no extra charge. A free bus system connects these five campuses, allowing students to participate in a wide array of social and cultural events."

SELECTIVITY

Admissions Rating	89
# of applicants	45,451
% of applicants accepted	64
% of acceptees attending	19
# offered a place on the wait list	8,531
% accepting a place on wait list	43
% admitted from wait list	2

FIRST-YEAR PROFILE

Testing policy	Test Optional
Range SAT composite	1280–1450
Range SAT EBRW	630–720
Range SAT math	630–760
Range ACT composite	29–33
# submitting SAT scores	1,656
% submitting SAT scores	30
# submitting ACT scores	294
% submitting ACT scores	5
Average HS GPA	4.0
% frosh submitting high school GPA	100
% graduated top 10% of class	29
% graduated top 25% of class	66
% graduated top 50% of class	94

DEADLINES

Early action	
Deadline	11/5
Regular	
Deadline	1/15
Nonfall registration?	Yes

APPLICANTS OFTEN PREFER
Boston College; Boston University; Northeastern University

APPLICANTS SOMETIMES PREFER
Syracuse University; University of Connecticut; Worcester Polytechnic Institute

APPLICANTS RARELY PREFER
Penn State University Park; University of Massachusetts Lowell; University of New Hampshire; University of Vermont

FINANCIAL FACTS

Financial Aid Rating	81
Annual in-state tuition	$16,186
Annual out-of-state tuition	$37,405
Room and board	$14,776
Required fees	$766
Books and supplies	$1,000
Average frosh need-based scholarship	$14,239
Average UG need-based scholarship	$13,269
% needy frosh rec. need-based scholarship or grant aid	93
% needy UG rec. need-based scholarship or grant aid	90
% needy frosh rec. non-need-based scholarship or grant aid	11
% needy UG rec. non-need-based scholarship or grant aid	9
% needy frosh rec. need-based self-help aid	86
% needy UG rec. need-based self-help aid	89
% frosh rec. any financial aid	88
% UG rec. any financial aid	91
% UG borrow to pay for school	60
Average cumulative indebtedness	$31,480
% frosh need fully met	17
% ugrads need fully met	17
Average % of frosh need met	83
Average % of ugrad need met	84

UNIVERSITY OF MIAMI

P.O. Box 248025, Coral Gables, FL 33124 • Admissions: 305-284-2211 • Fax: 305-284-2507

STUDENTS SAY "..."

Academics

"Gorgeous" University of Miami offers an "incredible range" of courses of study, chief among them "great programs in the sciences, engineering [and] music." Class sizes are small and internship opportunities are plentiful. Students here feel that they're getting a "well-rounded education," and "making connections" that they can capitalize on in the future. Though many undergrads report that their "courses are difficult," they also find them incredibly "rewarding." Inside the classroom, Miami students are delighted to find the majority of their professors are "easily approachable" and "incredibly knowledgeable." They clearly want "their students to learn and succeed." Indeed, "they are always there for you and open to helping in any way they can." Moreover, professors here are "well informed on the topic and are [typically] accessible after class." As one grateful student sums up, "I have had great academic success at UM largely because of my supportive and helpful professors. They deserve a lot more credit than they receive."

Campus Life

"There is always something going on" at the University of Miami. The campus is frequently abuzz with a multitude of fun events like the "farmers market, patio jams...and random activities [such as] laser tag, corn hole, food trucks [and] Frisbee game[s]." "The majority of students are involved in more than one campus club or activity" and a number of undergrads seek out volunteer opportunities. As one student explains, "We also have special service days that get good turnouts including Gandhi Day, Orientation Outreach, and MLK Day of Service." And plenty of undergrads spend their time "poolside, beachside, tailgating, anything they can find to have a good time." University of Miami also has a "very active/sporty population" with many students participating in both "club sports [and] intramural sports." Additionally, "Greek life is relatively popular, though the community is very welcoming and non-exclusive." And students also love "Canes After Dark [which often sponsors] cool activities like movies by the pool or snowball fights." Finally, nearby Miami "provides a lot of opportunity for adventure." Indeed, it has a "vibrant night life," a "wide array of cuisine," world-class museums, and beautiful beaches. You couldn't ask for anything more!

Student Body

Many undergrads at University of Miami proudly report that their peers are "very diverse." Indeed, you'll find that "there are people here from all over the world with different cultures, different experiences, and different likes and dislikes." As one amazed student shares, "You can hear so many different languages being spoken on campus." Nevertheless, while you might encounter people from around the country and the globe, a handful of undergrads insist that a number of their fellow students are "frat bros and girls that [simply] want to have fun." Additionally, a lot of students appear to come from "very affluent" families, and "luxury cars and going out to clubs on South Beach aren't out of the ordinary." However, others are quick to describe the culture as "very inclusive and understanding." And many assert that University of Miami students are "always willing to help out and assist you in finding your way." Another undergrad bolsters this claim by sharing, "I was lost on the first day of my first semester and an upperclassman pointed me in the direction of my class without being asked! It really made my day." Perhaps most importantly, we've been assured that "everyone can find their own social group here."

UNIVERSITY OF MIAMI

Financial Aid: 305-284-2270 • E-Mail: admission@miami.edu • Website: www.miami.edu

THE PRINCETON REVIEW SAYS

Admissions

The school reports that its standardized testing policy for use in admission for Fall 2024 is Test Optional. It is unknown at this time if the 2024 testing policy will be permanent. The Princeton Review suggests that interested applicants consult with the school for the most up-to-date standardized testing policies. *Very important factors considered include:* rigor of secondary school record, class rank, academic GPA, standardized test scores, application essay, extracurricular activities. *Important factors considered include:* talent/ability, character/personal qualities, volunteer work, work experience. *Other factors considered include:* recommendation(s), first generation, alumni/ae relation, geographical residence, state residency, racial/ethnic status, level of applicant's interest. High school diploma is required and GED is accepted. *Academic units recommended:* 4 English, 4 math, 4 science, 2 science labs, 4 foreign language, 4 social studies.

Financial Aid

Students should submit: Business/Farm Supplement; CSS/Financial Aid Profile; FAFSA; Noncustodial Profile. Priority filing deadline is 1/1. The Princeton Review suggests that all financial aid forms be submitted as soon as possible (see page 5 for a note on the FAFSA). *Need-based scholarships/grants offered:* College/university scholarship or grant aid from institutional funds; Federal Pell; Private scholarships; SEOG; State scholarships/grants. *Loan aid offered:* Direct PLUS loans; Direct Subsidized Loans; Direct Unsubsidized Loans; Federal Nursing Loans. Admitted students will be notified of awards on a rolling basis beginning 12/10. Federal Work-Study Program available. Institutional employment available.

The Inside Word

Interested candidates should be aware that the admissions process at University of Miami is competitive. Fortunately, the committee does its utmost to consider the whole candidate. Therefore, everything from your academic GPA and the strength of your high school curriculum and standardized test scores (if submitted) to extracurricular activities and awards earned will be reviewed thoroughly. Ultimately, the university is looking for intellectually curious students who will be leaders both inside and outside the classroom.

THE SCHOOL SAYS "..."

From the Admissions Office

"At the University of Miami, we educate leaders, problem solvers, and change makers. With the flexibility to choose from more than 180 majors and programs across 11 schools and colleges, students design their education based on the topics that excite them most. Here, coursework integrates academic rigor and theory with hands-on experience so students are able to convert knowledge into fulfilling achievements. As early as the first year of undergrad, students collaborate with award-winning faculty on projects that make meaningful contributions beyond the classroom. Projects range from volunteer experiences to cutting-edge research in topics such as climate change, public health, and privacy in the age of social media.

"With 10,000 undergraduate students, our close-knit campus combines the personal attention of a small college with the academic opportunity of a large research university. Our international location, just seven miles from downtown Miami, provides students with meaningful opportunities for experiential learning locally and in countries around the world. On campus, we are united in our diversity and working to cultivate a culture of belonging.

"Our students are passionate about learning, driven to contribute to their community, and encouraged to innovate. Whether you seek to make your mark in science, service, or the arts, the University of Miami will help you develop the skills needed to carve your own path to success."

SELECTIVITY

Admissions Rating	96
# of applicants	49,167
% of applicants accepted	19
% of acceptees attending	25
# offered a place on the wait list	20,206
% accepting a place on wait list	42
% admitted from wait list	1
# of early decision applicants	1,716
% accepted early decision	57

FIRST-YEAR PROFILE

Testing policy	Test Optional
Range SAT composite	1330–1450
Range SAT EBRW	650–730
Range SAT math	660–750
Range ACT composite	30–33
# submitting SAT scores	838
% submitting SAT scores	35
# submitting ACT scores	520
% submitting ACT scores	22
Average HS GPA	3.8
% frosh submitting high school GPA	100

DEADLINES

Early decision	
Deadline	11/1
Notification	12/15
Other ED deadline	1/1
Other ED notification	2/28
Early action	
Deadline	11/1
Notification	1/31
Regular	
Deadline	1/1
Notification	4/1
Nonfall registration?	Yes

APPLICANTS ALSO LOOK AT

Boston University; Cornell University; Drexel University; Duke University; Florida International University; Florida State University; Fordham University; New York University; Northeastern University; Penn State University Park

FINANCIAL FACTS

Financial Aid Rating	90
Annual tuition	$58,102
Room and board	$22,064
Required fees	$1,838
Books and supplies	$1,328
Average frosh need-based scholarship	$30,822
Average UG need-based scholarship	$36,105
% needy frosh rec. need-based scholarship or grant aid	62
% needy UG rec. need-based scholarship or grant aid	76
% needy frosh rec. non-need-based scholarship or grant aid	80
% needy UG rec. non-need-based scholarship or grant aid	46
% needy frosh rec. need-based self-help aid	71
% needy UG rec. need-based self-help aid	74
% frosh rec. any financial aid	69
% UG rec. any financial aid	69
% UG borrow to pay for school	33
Average cumulative indebtedness	$20,000
% frosh need fully met	99
% ugrads need fully met	76
Average % of frosh need met	100
Average % of ugrad need met	96

UNIVERSITY OF MICHIGAN—ANN ARBOR

500 S. State St., Ann Arbor, MI 48109,• Admissions: 734-764-1817 • Fax: 734-936-0740

STUDENTS SAY "..."

Academics

Among the many allures of the University of Michigan—Ann Arbor is that the school offers "a great environment both academically and socially." One student explains, "It has the social, fun atmosphere of any Big Ten university, but most people are still incredibly focused on their studies. It's great to be at a place where there is always something to do, but your friends completely understand when you have to stay in and get work done." With "an amazing honors program," a "wide range of travel-abroad opportunities," and "research strength" all available "at a low cost," it's no wonder students tell us that UM "provides every kind of opportunity at all times to all people." Academically, Michigan "is very competitive, and the professors have high academic standards for all the students." In fact, some here insist that "Michigan is as good as Ivy League schools in many disciplines." Standout offerings include business ("We have access to some of the brightest leaders" in the business world, students report), a "great engineering program," and "a good undergraduate program for medical school preparation." Those seeking add-on academic experiences here will find "a vast amount of resources. Internships, career opportunities, tutoring, community service projects, a plethora of student organizations, and a wealth of other resources" are all available, but "you need to make the first move" because no one "will seek you out."

Campus Life

Michigan is a huge university, meaning that students have endless extracurricular options here. One explains: "If you seek it out, you can find organizations for *any* interest. There are always people out there who share your interests. That's part of the benefit of 50,000-plus students!" There is a robust party scene. Students tell us that "most students go to house parties [or] hit the bars." There's also a vigorous social scene for the non-drinking crowd, with "great programs like UMix...phenomenal cultural opportunities in Ann Arbor especially music and movies," and "the hugely popular football Saturdays. The sense of school spirit here is impressive." Michigan students tend to be both academically serious and socially outgoing, which "is great because you can have a stimulating conversation with someone one day, and, the next day, be watching a silly movie or playing video games with this person."

Student Body

The Michigan student body "is hugely diverse," which "is one of the things Michigan prides itself on." "If you participate in extracurricular activities and make an effort to get to know other students in class and elsewhere, you'll definitely end up with a pretty diverse group of friends," undergrads assure us. Although varied, students tend to be similar in that they "are social but very academically driven." A number of students "are on the cutting edge of both research and progressive thinking," and there is a decided liberal tilt to campus politics. Even so, there's a place for everyone here, because "there are hundreds of mini-communities within the campus, made of everything from service fraternities to political organizations to dance groups. If you have an interest, you can find a group of people who enjoy the same thing."

UNIVERSITY OF MICHIGAN—ANN ARBOR

Financial Aid: 734-763-6600 • Website: umich.edu

THE PRINCETON REVIEW SAYS

Admissions

The school reports that its standardized testing policy for use in admission for Fall 2024 is Test Optional. Decided year-by-year. The Princeton Review suggests that interested applicants consult with the school for the most up-to-date standardized testing policies. *Very important factors considered include:* rigor of secondary school record, academic GPA. *Important factors considered include:* standardized test scores, application essay, recommendation(s), character/personal qualities, first generation. *Other factors considered include:* extracurricular activities, talent/ability, geographical residence, state residency, volunteer work, work experience, level of applicant's interest. High school diploma is required and GED is accepted. *Academic units required:* 4 English, 3 math, 3 science, 1 science lab, 2 foreign language, 1 social studies, 3 history. *Academic units recommended:* 4 English, 4 math, 4 science, 1 science lab, 4 foreign language, 1 social studies, 3 history, 1 computer science, 2 visual/performing arts.

Financial Aid

Students should submit: CSS/Financial Aid Profile; FAFSA. Priority filing deadline is 12/15. The Princeton Review suggests that all financial aid forms be submitted as soon as possible (see page 5 for a note on the FAFSA). *Need-based scholarships/grants offered:* College/university scholarship or grant aid from institutional funds; Federal Pell; Private scholarships; SEOG; State scholarships/grants. *Loan aid offered:* Direct PLUS loans; Direct Subsidized Loans; Direct Unsubsidized Loans; College/university loans from institutional funds; Federal Nursing Loans. Admitted students will be notified of awards on a rolling basis beginning 1/31. Federal Work-Study Program available. Institutional employment available.

The Inside Word

Michigan admissions are extremely competitive, so you will need high test scores, exemplary grades in challenging courses, and strong teacher recommendations to make the cut here. Though Michigan receives over 84,000 applications, each one is read at least twice. Use your extracurricular activities to demonstrate leadership and originality to stand out from the crowd.

THE SCHOOL SAYS "..."

From the Admissions Office

"The University of Michigan is one of the great public research universities in the U.S. and the world, located in vibrant Ann Arbor. Since 1817, U-M has been a global model of a diverse, comprehensive academic institution committed to the public good. Nineteen schools and colleges offer over 280 degree programs, featuring tremendous academic breadth and opportunity for discovery. Our thriving innovation ecosystem cultivates the ingenuity and entrepreneurial spirit of students across campus. Students study in an immersive, cross-disciplinary environment that encourages inquiry in the classroom and in undergraduate research, with a 15:1 student/faculty ratio and more than 1,500 students participating in undergraduate research partnerships with more than 800 research advisors. Students cultivate new interests and learn from peers with differing backgrounds in more than 1,400 registered student organizations. Numerous service learning programs link academics with volunteerism, such as Semester in Detroit. U-M is the fourth-largest all-time producer of Peace Corps volunteers. First-year students can find a sense of community and belonging in on-campus housing, which offers Living-Learning Programs for those interested in getting to know others with similar interests. With access to top-ranked programs and distinguished faculty, students have the resources and support they need to reach their full potential, to find their true voice, and to make a positive impact on the world. And with more than 640,000 living alumni around the world, new graduates can easily make personal and professional connections to other Michigan grads."

SELECTIVITY

Admissions Rating	97
# of applicants	84,289
% of applicants accepted	18
% of acceptees attending	47
# offered a place on the wait list	21,078
% accepting a place on wait list	72
% admitted from wait list	1

FIRST-YEAR PROFILE

Testing policy	Test Optional
Range SAT composite	1350–1530
Range SAT EBRW	670–750
Range SAT math	680–780
Range ACT composite	31–34
# submitting SAT scores	3,829
% submitting SAT scores	54
# submitting ACT scores	1,692
% submitting ACT scores	24
Average HS GPA	3.9
% frosh submitting high school GPA	93

DEADLINES

Early action	
Deadline	11/1
Notification	1/31
Regular	
Priority	11/1
Deadline	2/1
Nonfall registration?	Yes

FINANCIAL FACTS

Financial Aid Rating	87
Annual in-state tuition	$17,454
Annual in-state tuition (first-year)	$16,404
Annual out-of-state tuition	$56,941
Annual out-of-state tuition (first-year)	$55,002
Room and board	$13,171
Required fees	$332
Books and supplies	$1,092
Average frosh need-based scholarship	$19,514
Average UG need-based scholarship	$22,887
% needy frosh rec. need-based scholarship or grant aid	80
% needy UG rec. need-based scholarship or grant aid	82
% needy frosh rec. non-need-based scholarship or grant aid	69
% needy UG rec. non-need-based scholarship or grant aid	64
% needy frosh rec. need-based self-help aid	52
% needy UG rec. need-based self-help aid	60
% frosh rec. any financial aid	66
% UG rec. any financial aid	59
% UG borrow to pay for school	35
Average cumulative indebtedness	$28,487
% frosh need fully met	62
% ugrads need fully met	68
Average % of frosh need met	87
Average % of ugrad need met	90

UNIVERSITY OF MINNESOTA—TWIN CITIES

100 Church St. S.E., Minneapolis, MN 55455-0213 • Admissions: 612-625-2008 • Fax: 612-626-1693

CAMPUS LIFE

Quality of Life Rating	83
Fire Safety Rating	89
Green Rating	96
Type of school	Public
Environment	Metropolis

STUDENTS

Total undergrad enrollment	30,734
% male/female/another gender	46/54/0
% from out of state	25
% frosh live on campus	90
% ugrads live on campus	23
% African American	8
% Asian	14
% White	63
% Hispanic	5
% Native American	1
% Pacific Islander	<1
% Two or more races	5
% Race and/or ethnicity unknown	2
% international	6
# of countries represented	151

SURVEY SAYS . . .

Students are happy
Great library
Students love Minneapolis, MN
Recreation facilities are great
Everyone loves the Golden Gophers
Intramural sports are popular

ACADEMICS

Academic Rating	81
% students returning for sophomore year	90
% students graduating within 4 years	75
% students graduating within 6 years	84
Calendar	Semester
Student/faculty ratio	17:1
Profs interesting rating	85
Profs accessible rating	89

Most classes have 10–19 students.
Most lab/discussion sessions have 20–29 students.

MOST POPULAR MAJORS

Computer Science; Psychology, General; Finance and Financial Management Services, Other

STUDENTS SAY "..."

Academics

"Great research opportunities," and "phenomenal engineering programs" among other fantastic departments, attract students to the University of Minnesota, Twin Cities. "A top-ranked university in a beautiful city that has a lot of great job opportunities"—how could you resist? And, given its "large" size, it's a virtual guarantee that "anyone can find what they want to do." Even better, the university really makes an effort to "help students discover themselves." An impressed psych major explains, "Our school pushes us to expand our horizons, to go outside of our comfort zones, and to try things that we never would have considered trying before." And Minnesota deftly maintains "a small school feeling" amidst "an urban setting," something many undergrads here value. By and large, Minnesota professors tend to be "approachable and are more than willing to take time out of their day to ensure you understand the material." They are also "very knowledgeable" and "strive to make [the subject matter] exciting." In short, "the University of Minnesota is a place with endless opportunity for those willing to discover their passions."

Campus Life

Attending the University of Minnesota means that your life is likely to be "full of variety." Indeed, from "biking [and] outdoor games [to] reading in the park, going to the farmers market, attending events at Coffman or TCF Bank Stadium, or taking the green line down town to explore," undergrads here "can get involved in almost anything." UMN also "hosts a lot of lectures and discussions with prominent figures." Further, as a member of the Big Ten conference, it's no surprise that "sporting events are widely popular, even if we aren't doing very well." As if that wasn't enough, "the Coffman building always has something going on—movies, book signings—and there are a ton of student groups to join, no experience necessary." There is also a "thriving" Greek population on campus, and a social scene that also involves a handful of "house parties," which typically feature "alcohol and lots of dancing." And, of course, the Twin Cities themselves have "a lot going on!" As a political science student succinctly puts it, "If you're bored on a weekend, then you're not looking hard enough."

Student Body

Given the university's large undergraduate population, it's rather difficult to put "[students] into one category." Indeed, Minnesota truly manages to net "a wide variety of people." A dental hygiene student confirms this stating, "We have so much diversity here, that it is hard to pinpoint a general student type." And a mechanical engineering major quickly follows up, "Due to its size, everyone can find their niche and be free to express who they are." That being said, undergrads report that most of their peers are "generally quite friendly and outgoing." And everyone is "pretty willing to go out of their way for others, we are Minnesota nice after all." Further, many "students are driven to succeed and to make the most of the vast opportunities offered by the UMN." And a political science major matter-of-factly asserts that a large number of students are "white, middle to upper middle-class Midwesterner[s], most likely hailing from Minnesota, Wisconsin, or the Dakotas." Of course, at the very least, nearly all Minnesota undergrads can "fit in by bonding over how much [they] hate winter."

UNIVERSITY OF MINNESOTA—TWIN CITIES

Financial Aid: 612-624-1111 • Website: twin-cities.umn.edu/

THE PRINCETON REVIEW SAYS

Admissions

The school reports that its standardized testing policy for use in admission for Fall 2024 is Test Optional. It is unknown at this time if the 2024 testing policy will be permanent. The Princeton Review suggests that interested applicants consult with the school for the most up-to-date standardized testing policies. *Very important factors considered include:* rigor of secondary school record, class rank, academic GPA. *Other factors considered include:* standardized test scores, application essay, recommendation(s), extracurricular activities, talent/ability, character/personal qualities, first generation, alumni/ae relation, geographical residence, state residency, religious affiliation/commitment, racial/ethnic status, volunteer work, work experience. High school diploma is required and GED is accepted. *Academic units required:* 4 English, 4 math, 3 science, 1 science lab, 2 foreign language, 3 social studies, 1 visual/performing arts.

Financial Aid

Students should submit: FAFSA; Institution's own financial aid form. Priority filing deadline is 3/1. The Princeton Review suggests that all financial aid forms be submitted as soon as possible (see page 5 for a note on the FAFSA). *Need-based scholarships/grants offered:* College/university scholarship or grant aid from institutional funds; Federal Nursing Scholarships; Federal Pell; Private scholarships; SEOG; State scholarships/grants. *Loan aid offered:* Direct PLUS loans; Direct Subsidized Loans; Direct Unsubsidized Loans; College/university loans from institutional funds; Federal Nursing Loans; State Loans. Admitted students will be notified of awards on a rolling basis beginning 3/1. Federal Work-Study Program available. Institutional employment available.

The Inside Word

University of Minnesota, Twin Cities is a well-regarded institution and gaining admission is no easy feat. Academic preparation and performance are of primary concern. Therefore, course selection, GPA, and class rank will hold the most weight.

THE SCHOOL SAYS "..."

From the Admissions Office

"The University of Minnesota is one of the nation's top public research universities. That means your college experience will be enhanced by world-renowned faculty, state-of-the-art learning facilities, and an unprecedented variety of options (such as 150 majors). Eighty-one percent of our classes have fewer than fifty students, and our caring advisers will help you find opportunities that are right for you. Hands-on courses, volunteer opportunities, internships, study abroad, and undergraduate research are part of the U of M experience. Students benefit from programs and traditions designed to support their success, like Welcome Week, where freshmen explore campus, meet their classmates, and connect with faculty and staff before the school year begins. Our classic Big Ten campus is located in the heart of the vibrant Twin Cities. Just minutes away, intern at a Fortune 500 company, volunteer at a major hospital, or relax at the beautiful Chain of Lakes. With a wealth of cultural, career, and recreational opportunities, there's no better place to earn your degree. Last year, we awarded over $30 million in four-year scholarship packages. Residents of Minnesota benefit from in-state tuition and income-based benefits: those under $50,000 qualify for a new tuition-guarantee program, while those under $120,000 may get for tuition aid through the Promise Scholarship. Residents of North Dakota, South Dakota, Wisconsin, or Manitoba qualify for special reciprocity tuition rates.

"The University of Minnesota has been named a 'Best Value in Public Colleges' by multiple ranking organizations. As a U of M student, you will experience this value first-hand: you will step into a thriving academic community with some of the world's most renowned researchers. With direct access to these incredible resources, you will get a great education and a prestigious degree that helps you achieve your dreams."

SELECTIVITY

Admissions Rating	88
# of applicants	38,050
% of applicants accepted	73
% of acceptees attending	24

FIRST-YEAR PROFILE

Testing policy	Test Optional
Range SAT composite	1330–1500
Range SAT EBRW	630–730
Range SAT math	630–770
Range ACT composite	25–31
# submitting SAT scores	564
% submitting SAT scores	6
# submitting ACT scores	3,693
% submitting ACT scores	39
% graduated top 10% of class	41
% graduated top 25% of class	76
% graduated top 50% of class	98

DEADLINES

Early action	
Deadline	11/1
Notification	1/31
Other EA deadline	12/1
Other EA notification	2/15
Regular	
Priority	1/1
Nonfall registration?	Yes

FINANCIAL FACTS

Financial Aid Rating	84
Annual in-state tuition	$15,254
Annual out-of-state tuition	$33,818
Room and board	$11,894
Required fees	$1,721
Books and supplies	$1,000
Average frosh need-based scholarship	$14,002
Average UG need-based scholarship	$13,570
% needy frosh rec. need-based scholarship or grant aid	88
% needy UG rec. need-based scholarship or grant aid	88
% needy frosh rec. non-need-based scholarship or grant aid	9
% needy UG rec. non-need-based scholarship or grant aid	9
% needy frosh rec. need-based self-help aid	78
% needy UG rec. need-based self-help aid	77
% frosh rec. any financial aid	50
% UG rec. any financial aid	45
% UG borrow to pay for school	51
Average cumulative indebtedness	$26,576
% frosh need fully met	27
% ugrads need fully met	27
Average % of frosh need met	77
Average % of ugrad need met	77

THE BEST 389 COLLEGES ■ 683

UNIVERSITY OF MISSISSIPPI

PO Box 1848, University, MS 38677 • Admissions: 662-915-7211 • Fax: 662-915-5869

CAMPUS LIFE

Quality of Life Rating	**86**
Fire Safety Rating	**98**
Green Rating	**60***
Type of school	Public
Environment	Village

STUDENTS

Total undergrad enrollment	17,157
% male/female/another gender	43/57/0
% from out of state	48
% frosh live on campus	98
% ugrads live on campus	30
# of fraternities (% join)	20 (40)
# of sororities (% join)	15 (54)
% African American	11
% Asian	2
% White	78
% Hispanic	5
% Native American	<1
% Pacific Islander	<1
% Two or more races	2
% Race and/or ethnicity unknown	<1
% international	1

SURVEY SAYS . . .

Students are very religious
Everyone loves the Ole Miss Rebels
Frats and sororities are popular
Alumni active on campus

ACADEMICS

Academic Rating	**79**
% students returning for sophomore year	89
% students graduating within 4 years	54
% students graduating within 6 years	68
Calendar	Semester
Student/faculty ratio	16:1
Profs interesting rating	88
Profs accessible rating	94

Most classes have 10–19 students.
Most lab/discussion sessions have
20–29 students.

MOST POPULAR MAJORS

Accounting; Marketing/Marketing Management,
General

STUDENTS SAY "..."

Academics

Ole Miss is a prime example of Southern hospitality combined with the opportunity for greatness. Founded in 1848, the legendary university offers "'big-time' SEC athletics in the safe, quaint, and picturesque town of Oxford." Many of the school's services "are cheap if not free," and the school "puts on many programs that bring together lots of different people of different backgrounds." "It has a togetherness about it…there is something for a person with any interest here," says a student. There is also "a highly academic side to Ole Miss that many outsiders do not see." Business and international studies are programs of note, and the Honors College is a particular standout here, as it provides "unparalleled academic opportunities, such as beginning research as a freshman."

Most of the professors "hit the ball out of the park" when it comes to teaching, being available, and helping students acquire internships. Professors constantly organize discussion groups, dinner events, and other gatherings in order to "develop our ability to speak academically in a non-academic setting." Going to class is "critical"; professors "add much more than the textbook has to offer." Classes are designed to be "informative but also engaging and dynamic," and there is a deep understanding that individuals have an effect on the whole. "The teachers care, the university cares, [and] the students all care about the school and what it stands for."

It can be said again and again, but even beyond the "world-class programs and faculty," what students at Ole Miss value are the traditions and legacy of this school. People "are proud to have graduated from Ole Miss," and the tremendous amount of alumni support "gives Ole Miss a lot of confidence."

Campus Life

An Ole Miss existence is "always super busy." There is "a lot of work to be done" as "school and grades are a very important aspect of life," but there are also "a lot of opportunities for fun." "During football season, the Grove consumes our weekends. It's an amazing experience!" says a student. As a school that most admit is "known for its Greek life, beautiful women, and great parties," it's a common misconception that "most people's minds revolve around drinking, college football, and church on Sunday." If you take a closer look, you'll find that there is a huge literary scene "with Thacker Mountain Radio on Thursdays and poetry readings monthly at Proud Larry's," and students here also "really want to be active in making changes in the world."

The closeness of the community makes it easy to feel part of the University. "You'll hear the term the 'Ole Miss family,' and it won't seem forced or strange," explains a student. Oxford is also very appealing due to its "small, hometown feel," and the rich history you see everywhere you go (the Square is the center of town life, and most students can be found there at some point in a week). Basically, "there is never a dull moment, especially on the weekends."

Student Body

Ole Miss is a fairly diverse campus, with most students possessing "decent grades and an extravagant social life." One-third of the student body "belongs to either a fraternity or sorority, fancying the appropriate attire of a Polo shirt and loafers or baggy T-shirts and Nike shorts." The divide between Greek and non-Greek is stark here, though the two groups are not necessarily always adverse toward each other; this is a group of "open minds" in "a small-town" setting, with "a blend of Southern charm and laid-back manners" thrown in, after all. "Studying for your next exam over a glass of sweet tea is a common practice." As there are a lot of different groups on campus, "you can find a group of friends without much effort."

UNIVERSITY OF MISSISSIPPI

Financial Aid: 800-891-4596 • E-Mail: admissions@olemiss.edu • Website: www.olemiss.edu

THE PRINCETON REVIEW SAYS

Admissions

The school reports that its standardized testing policy for use in admission for Fall 2024 is SAT or ACT Required. It is unknown at this time if the 2024 testing policy will be permanent. The Princeton Review suggests that interested applicants consult with the school for the most up-to-date standardized testing policies. *Important factors considered include:* academic GPA. *Other factors considered include:* rigor of secondary school record, class rank, standardized test scores. High school diploma is required and GED is accepted. *Academic units required:* 4 English, 4 math, 3 science, 2 science labs, 3 social studies, 1 computer science, 1 visual/performing arts. *Academic units recommended:* 4 English, 4 math, 4 science, 2 science labs, 4 social studies, 1 computer science, 1 visual/performing arts.

Financial Aid

Students should submit: FAFSA. The Princeton Review suggests that all financial aid forms be submitted as soon as possible (see page 5 for a note on the FAFSA). *Need-based scholarships/grants offered:* College/university scholarship or grant aid from institutional funds; Federal Pell; Private scholarships; SEOG; State scholarships/grants. *Loan aid offered:* Direct PLUS loans; Direct Subsidized Loans; Direct Unsubsidized Loans; College/university loans from institutional funds. Admitted students will be notified of awards on a rolling basis beginning 4/1. Federal Work-Study Program available. Institutional employment available.

The Inside Word

Ole Miss offers students tremendous educational opportunities and its admissions policies are designed to help in-state students attain a college degree. In-state applicants must have a 3.2 GPA or greater, or a 2.5 GPA and a 16 on the ACT or 880 on the SAT.

THE SCHOOL SAYS "..."

From the Admissions Office

"The state's flagship university, affectionately known as Ole Miss, offers extraordinary opportunities through more than 120 areas of study from medicine and law to creative writing and accountancy. Its acclaimed offerings include the Sally McDonnell Barksdale Honors College, the Croft Institute for International Studies and the Center for Manufacturing Excellence, which incorporates coursework from schools of engineering, accountancy and business into its curriculum. Its Patterson School of Accountancy is nationally ranked for undergraduate and graduate education, the School of Law is a national leader in the fields of air and space law and sports law, and nearly 100 percent of School of Pharmacy graduates pass the national licensure exam on their first try. It was the state's first public university to shelter a chapter of the nation's oldest and most prestigious honor society, Phi Beta Kappa. Strong academic programs and a rich and varied campus life have helped Ole Miss produce twenty-six Rhodes Scholars and fifteen Truman Scholars. Since 1998 alone, UM has produced ten Goldwater Scholars, nineteen Fulbright Scholars, and twenty-one Boren Scholars.

"The campuses are diverse; 43 percent come from out of state, with all fifty states and ninety foreign countries represented, and 12 percent are Black. Recent significant campus improvements include several new residence halls and a totally renovated and expanded dining facility. Ole Miss is home to twenty research and education centers, including the National Center for Justice and the Rule of Law, which provides training on investigating and prosecuting cybercrime; the National Center for Physical Acoustics, which is helping to quiet jet engines and use infrasound to detect tornadoes; and the National Center for Natural Products Research, where scientists are working to find new drugs to treat cancer, AIDS, fungal infections, and more. Students submitting the ACT are not required to take the writing section."

SELECTIVITY

Admissions Rating	82
# of applicants	22,311
% of applicants accepted	97
% of acceptees attending	21

FIRST-YEAR PROFILE

Testing policy	SAT or ACT Required
Range SAT composite	1040–1220
Range SAT EBRW	520–620
Range SAT math	510–600
Range ACT composite	22–29
# submitting SAT scores	849
% submitting SAT scores	19
# submitting ACT scores	3,116
% submitting ACT scores	70
Average HS GPA	3.6
% frosh submitting high school GPA	100
% graduated top 10% of class	24
% graduated top 25% of class	48
% graduated top 50% of class	76

DEADLINES

Regular	
Priority	4/1
Notification	Rolling, 9/15
Nonfall registration?	Yes

FINANCIAL FACTS

Financial Aid Rating	83
Annual in-state tuition	$9,072
Annual out-of-state tuition	$26,292
Room and board	$11,490
Required fees	$148
Books and supplies	$1,200
Average frosh need-based scholarship	$12,931
Average UG need-based scholarship	$11,876
% needy frosh rec. need-based scholarship or grant aid	87
% needy UG rec. need-based scholarship or grant aid	89
% needy frosh rec. non-need-based scholarship or grant aid	18
% needy UG rec. non-need-based scholarship or grant aid	14
% needy frosh rec. need-based self-help aid	52
% needy UG rec. need-based self-help aid	55
% UG borrow to pay for school	47
Average cumulative indebtedness	$33,582
% frosh need fully met	21
% ugrads need fully met	17
Average % of frosh need met	79
Average % of ugrad need met	74

UNIVERSITY OF MISSOURI

230 Jesse Hall, Columbia, MO 65211 • Admissions: 573-882-2121 • Fax: 573-882-7887

STUDENTS SAY "..."

Academics

The "gorgeous campus" at the University of Missouri is filled with "a diverse group of students who are eager to learn and a staff that is eager to teach them." The school is all about "learning while networking," and the administration always has an ear to the students. "When we say there is a problem, it gets fixed," one student says. Mizzou takes pride in tradition, which is to be found "in all aspects that involve the University name," which makes for "a campus full of pride and spirit." There is a "constant focus on beautification, which makes for a great campus," and "top-of-the-line facilities" are available to all. One of the university's greatest strengths is its dependability: "From mass emails to mass texts, if there is an issue anywhere on campus you will know about it."

Professors teach "comprehensive courses" and "are always available to answer a question"; "even with large classes they are very attentive to individuals." "I've always had professors who have had a million ways to explain any given theory, problem, or question," says a student. The school boasts one of the country's best and most "intense" journalism schools (nursing is also a strong suit), and there are tons of "participation opportunities" for whatever area you choose to study. Classes may be hard, but "good grades are attainable." In addition to the "quality" academics, the advising system is "great," and Mizzou sets itself as a real model for its students: "It is always striving to achieve better, and not in just one specific category or area, but all around." "I came into college undecided and wanted to have plenty of options and opportunities to decide on a major," says a student of her reasoning for choosing Mizzou.

Campus Life

"There is never a dull moment to be had" at the University of Missouri. All athletic events are "heavily attended," especially football and basketball. Everyone walks or bikes everywhere in Columbia "because it's such a pedestrian friendly place," and "there are plenty of opportunities to chill out downtown." It is "the perfect mixture of small town and big city," and local attractions include a mall, small shops, micro-breweries, and tons of parks and hiking trails. If you're used to bigger cities, then it also happens to be located between Kansas City and St. Louis. "Best of both worlds!" says a student. The school has "a huge Greek life," and "it's a pretty close community." "Students enjoy going to off-campus parties or the bars downtown." "A lot of students spend their time in class, but every night of the week there is a party to go to," explains a student.

Student Body

The school has a giant spectrum of diversity, meaning "everyone is different. Anyone could fit in and find a group here." If a typical student has to be defined, most here are "friendly, outgoing, social, [and] very involved." Most of all, they are "proud to be Tiger[s]." "We all fit in because we have this in common," says a student. "It's pretty great company." "Classes have always felt like big families," and the majority of students find friends "by joining one of our million organizations," which is a common pastime among this "on-the-go" group. As everyone is "pretty easygoing and easy to get along with," "fitting in is easy; you just act like yourself!"

UNIVERSITY OF MISSOURI

Financial Aid: 573-882-7506 • E-Mail: MU4U@missouri.edu • Website: www.missouri.edu

THE PRINCETON REVIEW SAYS

Admissions

The school reports that its standardized testing policy for use in admission for Fall 2024 is Test Optional. It is unknown at this time if the 2024 testing policy will be permanent. The Princeton Review suggests that interested applicants consult with the school for the most up-to-date standardized testing policies. *Very important factors considered include:* class rank, academic GPA, standardized test scores. *Other factors considered include:* rigor of secondary school record, application essay, recommendation(s), talent/ability. High school diploma is required and GED is accepted. *Academic units required:* 4 English, 4 math, 3 science, 1 science lab, 2 foreign language, 3 social studies.

Financial Aid

Students should submit: FAFSA. Priority filing deadline is 1/10. The Princeton Review suggests that all financial aid forms be submitted as soon as possible (see page 5 for a note on the FAFSA). *Need-based scholarships/grants offered:* College/university scholarship or grant aid from institutional funds; Federal Nursing Scholarships; Federal Pell; Private scholarships; SEOG; State scholarships/grants. *Loan aid offered:* Direct PLUS loans; Direct Subsidized Loans; Direct Unsubsidized Loans; College/university loans from institutional funds; Federal Nursing Loans. Admitted students will be notified of awards on a rolling basis beginning 3/1. Federal Work-Study Program available. Institutional employment available.

The Inside Word

If your application suggests that you can handle the workload here, the school will find a place for you. Average test scores in conjunction with a college-prep high school curriculum should be all it takes. Even those who don't meet these criteria have a chance; admissions officers consider essays, recommendations, and special talents in the cases of borderline candidates.

THE SCHOOL SAYS "..."

From the Admissions Office

"Founded in 1839 as the first public university west of the Mississippi River, Mizzou is a member of the Association of American Universities, the nation's most prestigious group of research institutions. Mizzou is one of only thirty-eight public universities in the AAU. The National Science Foundation has recognized Mizzou as one of the top ten universities in the country for integrating research into undergraduate education, and Mizzou offers twelve major undergraduate research programs, some with freshmen participants.

"Mizzou is nestled in the heart of downtown Columbia, Missouri. Galleries, concert halls, theaters, shops, festivals, and restaurants are all just steps from campus, making it hard to tell where campus ends and downtown begins.

"Students get right into the mix at Mizzou with the Missouri Method. This hands-on learning methodology is central to students' learning experiences. They'll be reporting news live on the local NBC TV station, making ice cream, healing animals, trading stocks, and teaching kindergartners.

"Mizzou's Freshman Interest Groups (FIGs) program places freshmen in residence halls alongside students with similar interests. Freshmen take courses and participate in activities with the fellow FIG members, creating a sense of community and leading to academic success.

"There are more than 600 student organizations to belong to, and more than 300 degree programs for students to choose from. If a degree program doesn't quite meet a student's needs, they have the option of *creating their own.*

"Students can find admissions requirements at admissions.missouri.edu. The application takes about fifteen minutes to complete."

SELECTIVITY

Admissions Rating	86
# of applicants	19,966
% of applicants accepted	77
% of acceptees attending	32

FIRST-YEAR PROFILE

Testing policy	Test Optional
Range SAT EBRW	570–680
Range SAT math	560–670
Range ACT composite	23–30
# submitting SAT scores	342
% submitting SAT scores	7
# submitting ACT scores	3,468
% submitting ACT scores	72
% graduated top 10% of class	33
% graduated top 25% of class	64
% graduated top 50% of class	91

DEADLINES

Regular	
Notification	Rolling, 8/1
Nonfall registration?	Yes

FINANCIAL FACTS

Financial Aid Rating	80
Annual in-state tuition	$10,020
Annual out-of-state tuition	$29,400
Room and board	$11,520
Required fees	$1,529
Books and supplies	$1,000
Average frosh need-based scholarship	$12,822
Average UG need-based scholarship	$12,667
% needy frosh rec. need-based scholarship or grant aid	93
% needy UG rec. need-based scholarship or grant aid	90
% needy frosh rec. non-need-based scholarship or grant aid	12
% needy UG rec. non-need-based scholarship or grant aid	8
% needy frosh rec. need-based self-help aid	57
% needy UG rec. need-based self-help aid	53
% frosh rec. any financial aid	93
% UG borrow to pay for school	51
Average cumulative indebtedness	$26,231
% frosh need fully met	18
% ugrads need fully met	18
Average % of frosh need met	64
Average % of ugrad need met	64

THE UNIVERSITY OF MONTANA—MISSOULA

32 Campus Drive, Missoula, MT 59812 • Admissions: 406-243-0211 • Fax: 406-243-5711

CAMPUS LIFE

Quality of Life Rating	80
Fire Safety Rating	89
Green Rating	95
Type of school	Public
Environment	City

STUDENTS

Total undergrad enrollment	7,515
% male/female/another gender	44/56/0
% from out of state	30
% frosh live on campus	76
% ugrads live on campus	37
# of fraternities (% join)	6 (6)
# of sororities (% join)	4 (6)
% African American	1
% Asian	1
% White	78
% Hispanic	5
% Native American	3
% Pacific Islander	<1
% Two or more races	5
% Race and/or ethnicity unknown	5
% international	1
# of countries represented	43

SURVEY SAYS . . .

Recreation facilities are great
Everyone loves the Grizzlies
Students are happy
Students love Missoula, MT

ACADEMICS

Academic Rating	77
% students returning for sophomore year	71
% students graduating within 4 years	30
% students graduating within 6 years	49
Calendar	Semester
Student/faculty ratio	16:1
Profs interesting rating	87
Profs accessible rating	89

Most classes have 10–19 students.
Most lab/discussion sessions have
10–19 students.

MOST POPULAR MAJORS

Business Administration and Management,
General; Forest Management/Forest Resources
Management; Psychology, General

STUDENTS SAY "..."

Academics

Nestled in beautiful Missoula, The University of Montana is "a great place to live, work, and study." Indeed, Montana's awesome location and solid reputation coupled with low in-state tuition make it "hard to beat." Moreover, while it has a substantial number of students, we're assured that you're never "just a number" here. Undergrads also appreciate the university's focus on "environmental sustainability…and social justice" along with the fact that the University of Montana strives to develop "creative thinkers and engaged citizens." While the university maintains a fantastic liberal arts program, students especially laud the wildlife biology, forestry, physical therapy, and forensic anthropology departments. Moreover, undergrads at Montana are highly complementary of their teachers who are generally "helpful, engaging, and accessible." One thrilled student claims that the professors are "amazing! Math and science has never come easy for me, and my professors have taught in a way I completely understand the material." Another enthusiastic student summarizes her experience by stating, "The professors here are very knowledgeable and passionate about what they are teaching, because of this, the learning experience is always interesting and inviting. I truly appreciate all the effort that is put forward to help students succeed and prepare for the next steps in their life."

Campus Life

Undergrads seem to truly enjoy life at U of M. Indeed, the campus is often buzzing with activity. As one student happily shares, "When it's not snowing in the fall or spring, you can find people playing Frisbee, walking their dogs, catching footballs, and even playing with lightsabers." Additionally, there are "many music concerts and dance parties" one can attend. "Football is [also] really big here," and games are often packed with students. Beyond the campus, Montana offers a myriad of options for the outdoor enthusiast. As one ecstatic undergrad tells us, "Western Montana is a divine place for hiking, hunting, fishing, camping, snowshoeing, swimming, huckleberry picking, going to hot springs, mushroom picking, antler collecting, and just being immersed in nature. Near where I live there is access to the Rattlesnake Wilderness, mountains surround the valley, and the Clark Fork River runs right through town." Those with a more adventurous spirit can delight in "skiing and skydiving, hand gliding and parasailing, mountain climbing and repelling, caving and biking." As this pleased undergrad summarizes, "There is always something to do no matter what your interests are and great people to do them with."

Student Body

The University of Montana attracts a student body that's "pretty laid-back and easygoing." Many are "outdoorsy" and self-described as "hippies." Indeed, there are "quite a few granola kids" and "Carhartt-sporting, plaid-proud, future biologists" types. Though many students hail from within the state, one undergrad assures us that "increasing diversity efforts have begun to show in the past three years." Fortunately, for the most part, everyone is "accepting, friendly, and very involved in college and community life." Another student expands on this idea, stating, "People here do not seem to judge others or hold stereotypes against each other. If you're lost or need to ask a question you can ask anyone, and they're willing to give you the best answer they know in order to help you out even if they don't know you." A fellow undergrad agrees softly, sharing, "I feel like I've stepped into a melting pot of all beliefs and ideals. You can be yourself, and never be looked down on for that at this school."

THE UNIVERSITY OF MONTANA—MISSOULA

Financial Aid: 406-243-5373 • E-Mail: admiss@umontana.edu • Website: www.umt.edu

THE PRINCETON REVIEW SAYS

Admissions

The school reports that its standardized testing policy for use in admission for Fall 2024 is Test Optional. It is unknown at this time if the 2024 testing policy will be permanent. The Princeton Review suggests that interested applicants consult with the school for the most up-to-date standardized testing policies. *Very important factors considered include:* rigor of secondary school record, class rank, academic GPA, standardized test scores. *Important factors considered include:* extracurricular activities, talent/ability. *Other factors considered include:* High school diploma is required and GED is accepted. *Academic units required:* 4 English, 3 math, 2 science, 2 science labs, 3 social studies, 2 history. *Academic units recommended:* 2 foreign language, 2 computer science, 2 visual/performing arts.

Financial Aid

Students should submit: FAFSA. Priority filing deadline is 12/1. The Princeton Review suggests that all financial aid forms be submitted as soon as possible (see page 5 for a note on the FAFSA). *Need-based scholarships/grants offered:* College/university scholarship or grant aid from institutional funds; Federal Pell; Private scholarships; SEOG; State scholarships/grants. *Loan aid offered:* Direct PLUS loans; Direct Subsidized Loans; Direct Unsubsidized Loans. Admitted students will be notified of awards on a rolling basis beginning 3/16. Federal Work-Study Program available. Institutional employment available.

The Inside Word

The admissions game at the University of Montana is fairly straightforward. Officers here rely heavily on quantitative data. Applicants who meet standardized test and GPA minimums and are in the top half of their graduating class generally receive an acceptance letter. Those who did not meet the minimum requirements can often enroll on a conditional basis.

THE SCHOOL SAYS "..."

From the Admissions Office

"There's something special about this place. It's something different for each person. For some, it's the blend of academic quality and outdoor recreation. The University of Montana ranks fifth in the nation among public institutions for producing Rhodes scholars, and *Outside* Magazine lists Missoula in its 'Top Ten Amazing Places for Outdoor Recreation.' For others, it's size—not too big, not too small. The University of Montana is a midsized university in the heart of the Rocky Mountains—accessible in both admission and tuition bills—that produces graduates considered among the best and brightest in the world. It is located in a community that could pass for a cozy college town or a bustling big city, depending on your point of view. There's a lot happening, but you won't get lost. People are friendly and diverse. They come from all over the world to study and learn and to live a good life. They come to a place to be inspired, a place where they feel comfortable yet challenged. Some never leave. Most never want to."

SELECTIVITY

Admissions Rating	83
# of applicants	4,910
% of applicants accepted	94
% of acceptees attending	32

FIRST-YEAR PROFILE

Testing policy	Test Optional
Range SAT EBRW	535–635
Range SAT math	520–610
Range ACT composite	20–26
# submitting SAT scores	454
% submitting SAT scores	39
# submitting ACT scores	820
% submitting ACT scores	71
Average HS GPA	3.4
% frosh submitting high school GPA	97
% graduated top 10% of class	16
% graduated top 25% of class	40
% graduated top 50% of class	73

DEADLINES

Regular	
Priority	3/1
Notification	Rolling, 6/15
Nonfall registration?	Yes

FINANCIAL FACTS

Financial Aid Rating	77
Annual in-state tuition	$5,352
Annual out-of-state tuition	$24,144
Room and board	$9,966
Required fees	$2,002
Books and supplies	$1,100
Average frosh need-based scholarship	$5,168
Average UG need-based scholarship	$4,991
% needy frosh rec. need-based scholarship or grant aid	56
% needy UG rec. need-based scholarship or grant aid	61
% needy frosh rec. non-need-based scholarship or grant aid	80
% needy UG rec. non-need-based scholarship or grant aid	52
% needy frosh rec. need-based self-help aid	95
% needy UG rec. need-based self-help aid	91
% frosh rec. any financial aid	74
% UG rec. any financial aid	63
% UG borrow to pay for school	58
Average cumulative indebtedness	$27,132
% frosh need fully met	12
% ugrads need fully met	11
Average % of frosh need met	69
Average % of ugrad need met	61

University of Nebraska—Lincoln

1400 R St, Lincoln, NE 68588-0419 • Admissions: 402-472-7211 • Fax: 402-472-0670

STUDENTS SAY ". . ."

Academics

The University of Nebraska–Lincoln is situated in a great spot—Nebraska's capital city—to make "connections with companies in Lincoln, Omaha, and surrounding areas," and provides "tons of undergraduate research opportunities," "amazing internships," and "leadership opportunities." Students find the university to pair this practical focus on "job placement," which is aided by "career coaches and employer-in residences, and partnerships with "local businesses," with the recognition and prestige of a Big Ten, "rigorous" research institution. Students also praise "phenomenal advisors," especially for pre-health students, "great study abroad programs," and other specific schools and programs such as the business school, the honors academy, and Raikes School of Computer Science and Management. Professors are "passionate," and Nebraska being a research institution, can teach from "real world examples." After their first year, students typically begin "moving toward…project based courses where you…are paired with a company or using a real world example" instead of textbooks to do homework. Faculty is known to be accessible and generous with students, offering "personal advice," orienting students and "introducing campus resources," and sometimes even "welcoming [students] to their home." Nebraska is also known to have a "fantastic financial aid and scholarship program that makes it very affordable to attend," offering "great scholarships, especially to out-of-state students" who would have a higher tuition bill.

Campus Life

Nebraska is the "smallest Big Ten public school," so students say their "beautiful campus" is "great if you're looking for a prestigious school, but a bit smaller." Students overwhelmingly name the Division I football team ("Go Big Red!") as being a generator of school spirit that spreads into the "incredible college town." "Since this is the only football team here in Nebraska, many people are very excited for game days here in Lincoln," one student reports. Intramural sports are also popular: "there are always pick-up games of soccer, ultimate Frisbee, football" and so on "on the outdoor Astroturf fields, as well as the indoor practice facilities, which includes an "indoor football field for students…[donated] by the Athletic Department and the Husker Football Team."

About "20 percent of students are in Greek life," and "the whole campus is always attending their philanthropy events." And with over 600 clubs, students need not leave campus to pack their schedules with activities outside of studying. However, campus is right next to downtown, so the campus isn't isolated; students are "part of the Lincoln community," which offers a "small town feel with big town amenities." In the city, students "catch a movie at the downtown movie theater," "take swing dancing classes at the Pla Mor ballroom," go "ice skating," and "jogging" or "shop in the Haymarket area."

Student Body

University of Nebraska–Lincoln's student body is made up of an "array of students from small town Nebraska, the big cities of Lincoln and Omaha" as well as a number of "out-of-state and international students." "Kindness permeates interactions across campus," and the "passion that the students have for their institution is palpable." Students are by and large "friendly but conservative," a "mixture of rural and city kids." "The mix of cultures works really well" reflecting "Midwestern manners of kind, friendly people." Students are studious but interconnected, especially through their identification with "Husker power." "Sports aren't my main concern," says another, "but it is super awesome attending a Big Ten university" because of the "pride" and "positive and outgoing" Lincoln community.

UNIVERSITY OF NEBRASKA—LINCOLN

Financial Aid: 402-472-2030 • E-Mail: admissions@unl.edu • Website: www.unl.edu

THE PRINCETON REVIEW SAYS

Admissions

The school reports that its standardized testing policy for use in admission for Fall 2024 is Test Optional. The 2024 testing policy will be permanent. The Princeton Review suggests that interested applicants consult with the school for the most up-to-date standardized testing policies. *Important factors considered include:* rigor of secondary school record, class rank, academic GPA, standardized test scores. *Other factors considered include:* High school diploma is required and GED is accepted. *Academic units required:* 4 English, 4 math, 3 science, 1 science lab, 2 foreign language, 1 social studies, 2 history.

Financial Aid

Students should submit: FAFSA. Priority filing deadline is 4/1. The Princeton Review suggests that all financial aid forms be submitted as soon as possible (see page 5 for a note on the FAFSA). *Need-based scholarships/grants offered:* Federal Pell; Private scholarships; SEOG; State scholarships/grants. *Loan aid offered:* Direct PLUS loans; Direct Subsidized Loans; Direct Unsubsidized Loans. Admitted students will be notified of awards on a rolling basis beginning 12/15. Federal Work-Study Program available. Institutional employment available.

The Inside Word

Nebraska offers more than 150 majors. All applications will be weighed on the combined strength of course work, GPAs, and test scores. Applicants interested in applying to a specific school within the university should take into account those school's specialized requirements as they may include additional high school course work than what is required by the university's general studies program. To be considered for leadership and diversity scholarships, you must write a 500-word (maximum) scholarship statement that focuses on leadership, career goals, and community service.

THE SCHOOL SAYS "..."

From the Admissions Office

"We are Nebraska. We believe in the power of every person. We don't rest on our strengths—we stretch them. Sweat them. Combine them. Growing flexible, nimble, and strong minds. That's how we do big things. Our faculty and researchers work hard to help students succeed and to solve real-world issues. Students can quickly access the programs they desire, get involved in the university community and build their skills—all elements that will help them create the future they want. Nebraska has a low student-to-faculty ratio, a substantial out-of-state scholarship program and one of the nation's leading undergraduate research programs.

"The university is the heart of Lincoln, a growing, thriving contemporary city. Tech startups are flocking to Lincoln to recruit talent from the university and get involved with our cutting-edge Innovation Campus. The city's downtown is steps away from campus and home to a rich arts and music scene. Campus upgrades to the student union and rec centers, plus several building projects, contribute to a vibrant and dynamic culture. More than 200,000 alumni from the University of Nebraska–Lincoln's 150-year history have made a difference in the world and opened doors for those who've followed."

SELECTIVITY

Admissions Rating	86
# of applicants	19,102
% of applicants accepted	79
% of acceptees attending	31

FIRST-YEAR PROFILE

Testing policy	Test Optional
Range SAT composite	1100–1330
Range SAT EBRW	560–670
Range SAT math	550–670
Range ACT composite	22–28
# submitting SAT scores	391
% submitting SAT scores	8
# submitting ACT scores	4,014
% submitting ACT scores	87
Average HS GPA	3.7
% frosh submitting high school GPA	69
% graduated top 10% of class	30
% graduated top 25% of class	58
% graduated top 50% of class	86

DEADLINES

Regular	
Priority	3/1
Deadline	5/1
Notification	Rolling, 8/1
Nonfall registration?	Yes

APPLICANTS OFTEN PREFER
Creighton University; University of Nebraska at Kearney; University of Nebraska at Omaha; Wayne State College

APPLICANTS SOMETIMES PREFER
Iowa State University; Kansas State University; Nebraska Wesleyan University; University of Kansas

APPLICANTS RARELY PREFER
Concordia University, Nebraska; Doane University; Hastings College; Midland Lutheran College; Northwest Missouri State University; South Dakota State University; The University of South Dakota; University of Iowa; University of Minnesota—Twin Cities

FINANCIAL FACTS

Financial Aid Rating	81
Annual in-state tuition	$7,770
Annual out-of-state tuition	$24,900
Room and board	$11,928
Required fees	$2,084
Books and supplies	$1,200
Average frosh need-based scholarship	$9,862
Average UG need-based scholarship	$9,406
% needy frosh rec. need-based scholarship or grant aid	94
% needy UG rec. need-based scholarship or grant aid	89
% needy frosh rec. non-need-based scholarship or grant aid	14
% needy UG rec. non-need-based scholarship or grant aid	11
% needy frosh rec. need-based self-help aid	52
% needy UG rec. need-based self-help aid	52
% frosh rec. any financial aid	85
% UG rec. any financial aid	87
% UG borrow to pay for school	54
Average cumulative indebtedness	$24,811
% frosh need fully met	22
% ugrads need fully met	18
Average % of frosh need met	74
Average % of ugrad need met	68

UNIVERSITY OF NEW ENGLAND

11 Hills Beach Road, Biddeford, ME 04005-9599 • Admissions: 207-602-2847 • Fax: 207-602-5900

CAMPUS LIFE

Quality of Life Rating	81
Fire Safety Rating	94
Green Rating	95
Type of school	Private
Affiliation	No Affiliation
Environment	Town

STUDENTS

Total undergrad enrollment	2,272
% male/female/another gender	32/68/NR
% from out of state	76
% frosh live on campus	97
% ugrads live on campus	67
# of fraternities	0
# of sororities	0
% African American	1
% Asian	3
% White	86
% Hispanic	3
% Native American	<1
% Pacific Islander	<1
% Two or more races	3
% Race and/or ethnicity unknown	2
% international	1
# of countries represented	4

SURVEY SAYS . . .
Intramural sports are popular
Everyone loves the Nor'Easters
Students are happy
Students aren't religious
Students environmentally aware

ACADEMICS

Academic Rating	76
% students returning for sophomore year	70
% students graduating within 4 years	55
% students graduating within 6 years	62
Calendar	Semester
Student/faculty ratio	12:1
Profs interesting rating	85
Profs accessible rating	89

Most classes have 10–19 students.
Most lab/discussion sessions have
10–19 students.

MOST POPULAR MAJORS
Biomedical Sciences, General; Registered Nursing/
Registered Nurse; Marine Biology and Biological
Oceanography

STUDENTS SAY "..."

Academics
The University of New England boasts scenic coastal campuses on both sides of the Atlantic. Its motto, "Innovation for a healthier planet," is demonstrated through rigorous and research-driven programs in Marine Life and Medicine, like "semester long research projects with my classmates using zebrafish" or a VR patient-treating simulator available to Nursing students. It's a "dedicated student body, most of which (plan to continue) on to graduate school," and popular pre-dental, pre-medicine, and other pre-health programs offer a "GradVantage" track that allows promising students to combine UNE undergraduate admission with a potential graduate track.

When it comes to professors, students say, "UNE finds experts in their field to teach," a policy that opens the door for many undergraduate students to do graduate-level research and publish articles. And despite being the largest private university in Maine, many students still enjoy small class sizes and "build personal relationships with their professors, which in turn can lead to research opportunities." It can be a struggle, though, which is why it's nice that many professors know their students by name and are "always there to help us when needed" and that the Student Academic Success Center provides tutors to assist in everything "from writing papers to website building to math class."

Campus Life
Life at UNE is all about enjoying the outdoors. "Students spend a lot of time in the natural preserves and wildlife near campus," like the UNE Nature Trail and East Point Bird Sanctuary. The nearby beach is a popular respite "no matter the weather." When the weather shifts, students don't give up on outdoor activities: they make use of the school's "discounted ski passes."

Those who prefer indoor activities will also find much to do. On the scholarly side, there's the "innovative" Makerspace, a "fully equipped laboratory for creating and building," where students from all disciplines come to realize their ideas. There's also fun trivia or "Wicked Big Bingo." There's even a mix of both inside and outside participation for things like bird watching, where avid participants can either take to the forest or relax by spotting species "from the second floor of the commons."

UNE is "definitely not a party school"—in fact, the dining hall and library are referred to as "the heart of the campus."

There are, however, weekend gatherings on campus and "things to do in Biddeford; you don't have to drive to Portland." School spirit is also notably high for hockey—so much so that you might not be able to find parking!

Student Body
Education is what bonds the student body at UNE. "Most students here came for the academics and are focused on developing an education for a great future." Many are Pre-Health and Marine Science majors, and while friend groups often form within the fields, some students find they "strangely all get along in one form or another." Where women in science are underrepresented in the workforce, at UNE, "the average student is a woman in STEM," creating a rare opportunity for women to find like minds within their studies. The school is still working to be more diverse, "but as one of the few POC on campus, I really do feel the love and acceptance UNE and my peers offer." So far as "political standings, religion, sexual orientation, [and] gender identity" go, students welcome the opportunity to collaborate from different perspectives. Many students find common ground in their studies and building a better tomorrow: "I wouldn't be surprised if nearly every student said they hope to make the world better in some sort of way."

UNIVERSITY OF NEW ENGLAND

Financial Aid: 207-602-2342 • E-Mail: admissions@une.edu • Website: www.une.edu

THE PRINCETON REVIEW SAYS

Admissions

The school reports that its standardized testing policy for use in admission for Fall 2024 is Test Free. The 2024 testing policy will be permanent. The Princeton Review suggests that interested applicants consult with the school for the most up-to-date standardized testing policies. *Very important factors considered include:* rigor of secondary school record, academic GPA. *Important factors considered include:* application essay, extracurricular activities. *Other factors considered include:* class rank, recommendation(s), talent/ability, character/personal qualities, first generation, alumni/ae relation, volunteer work, work experience. High school diploma is required and GED is accepted. *Academic units recommended:* 4 English, 3 math, 2 science, 2 science labs, 2 social studies.

Financial Aid

Students should submit: FAFSA. The Princeton Review suggests that all financial aid forms be submitted as soon as possible (see page 5 for a note on the FAFSA). *Need-based scholarships/grants offered:* College/university scholarship or grant aid from institutional funds; Federal Pell; Private scholarships; SEOG; State scholarships/grants. *Loan aid offered:* Direct PLUS loans; Direct Subsidized Loans; Direct Unsubsidized Loans; State Loans. Admitted students will be notified of awards on a rolling basis beginning 12/15. Federal Work-Study Program available. Institutional employment available.

The Inside Word

A strong high school transcript is the best way to get the attention of the admissions department at University of New England. The average high school GPA for admitted students is 3.4. Since the school is so heavily focused in the sciences, students with a rigorous math and science course load in high school will likely do well. For those students who apply with set career aspirations, the GradVantage program is intended to allow talented undergraduate applicants the opportunity to combine their UNE undergraduate admission with a potential track into one of the school's graduate programs. Any student who wants an admissions answer sooner rather than later should consider applying Early Action—it's non-binding.

THE SCHOOL SAYS "..."

From the Admissions Office

"University of New England (UNE) uses a test-blind admissions policy. UNE is a private top-ranked university offering flagship programs in the health and life sciences as well as degrees in business, education, the social sciences and the liberal arts. UNE's three beautiful campuses in Biddeford and Portland, Maine, and Tangier, Morocco, are home to an active and close-knit student community engaged in rigorous academic experiences. With over 40 undergraduate degree programs, UNE students have plenty of opportunities for extensive fieldwork, clinical experiences, research, internships, and global experiences. Qualified UNE students can pursue UNE graduate or professional degrees through GradVantage in applied nutrition, dental medicine, education, health informatics, occupational therapy, osteopathic medicine, pharmacy, physical therapy, physician assistant, public health, and social work.

"UNE's Student Academic Success Center provides academic support services to help students attain their personal education goals. The Career Services Office provides academic and career exploration assistance, guidance in applying to graduate schools, self-assessment, résumé help, and information and access to job listings and job fairs.

"UNE's campuses offer a variety of cultural and social events and students are encouraged to become involved in activities, clubs, and sports. Popular interests include scuba diving, skiing, hiking, biking, surfing, music, theater, community service, and student leadership programs. UNE's Department of Athletics operates an NCAA Division III varsity athletics program. Varsity sports for men are basketball, cross country, football, golf, ice-hockey, lacrosse, and soccer. Varsity sports for women are basketball, cross country, field hockey, ice hockey, lacrosse, rugby, soccer, softball, swimming, track and field, and volleyball."

SELECTIVITY
Admissions Rating	76
# of applicants	4,941
% of applicants accepted	96
% of acceptees attending	16

FIRST-YEAR PROFILE
Testing policy	Test Free
Average HS GPA	3.4
% frosh submitting high school GPA	100

DEADLINES
Early action	
Deadline	11/15
Regular	
Deadline	2/15
Nonfall registration?	Yes

APPLICANTS ALSO LOOK AT
University of Maine; University of New Hampshire; University of Rhode Island; University of Southern Maine; University of Vermont

FINANCIAL FACTS
Financial Aid Rating	71
Annual tuition	$39,510
Room and board	$16,100
Required fees	$1,440
Books and supplies	$1,400
Average frosh need-based scholarship	$8,655
Average UG need-based scholarship	$9,273
% needy frosh rec. need-based scholarship or grant aid	78
% needy UG rec. need-based scholarship or grant aid	77
% needy frosh rec. non-need-based scholarship or grant aid	100
% needy UG rec. non-need-based scholarship or grant aid	100
% needy frosh rec. need-based self-help aid	85
% needy UG rec. need-based self-help aid	87
% UG borrow to pay for school	82
Average cumulative indebtedness	$54,956
% frosh need fully met	0
% ugrads need fully met	0

UNIVERSITY OF NEW HAMPSHIRE

University of New Hampshire, Durham, NH 03824 • Admissions: 603-862-1234 • Fax: 603-862-0077

STUDENTS SAY "…"

Academics

The University of New Hampshire is about connections, whether that's what a "state school offers… to local community" or the way in which it "makes use of their outdoors … and gets students involved in hands-on services and experiences." The students of its 100+ majors (and eleven schools and colleges) get lifelong support from the office of Career and Professional Success, which leaves students feeling that they can "learn whatever you want." It helps that UNH "is especially good at providing information and resources. There are millions of flyers all around campus, including in lecture halls and dorms, informing you of what is going on on campus and where you can go or who you can contact if you need help."

Professors are commended not just for being "very good lecturers" but for the way they are "happy to help in their area of expertise and genuinely interested in doing so." This may involve allowing students to "separate themselves in order to learn when necessary" during class and being "willing to spend time individually to explain material and offer learning resources outside of the classroom." Students also list a variety of teaching methods, including "small groups, large groups, class conversations, personal work, and all other manner of work in class, as well as a flipped classroom." Now add in "a constantly improving curriculum," "plenty of internships," "a plethora of research opportunities," and science labs that "have really taken the material to a whole other level of learning." As one student notes, "there is so much to do which prepares students for life after graduation that it's hard to list it all."

Campus Life

A student's standard routine is to "attend their classes, do work for a few hours, and hang out a lot with each other at night." Students do mention "a very active night life with dorm competitions and socials, countless intramural sports teams, and welcoming parties across the campus," as well as events like trivia and concerts. They also refer to the campus itself being "very pretty and easy to walk, making it have a more calming environment overall," and with a great location in Durham that provides "a safe rural environment while still being close to the ocean, activities, and cities like Boston." The winter gets a particular shout out because students can (and do) "go skiing or even just sledding around campus and there are always great trails to go hiking." Ultimately, with more than two hundred student clubs and organizations, including "student-run groups for various backgrounds, lifestyles and viewpoints, from political groups to hobby groups," students feel confident that there's something for everyone.

Student Body

Many students love the school's size of 14,000 students, which "is big enough to get lost in and small enough to find people who will become forever friends." People "tend to be very social" and many "are active and value physical activities, part of why the campus is so pristinely kept." Most students "are from New England in New Hampshire and Massachusetts," and although the school is "not very diverse, we have a lot of programs and are very accepting for our minority communities." Those who attend UNH are "generally driven, with a good sense of community and collaboration among the more difficult classes and majors," and "each student has a passion or goal that they want to achieve in life," so the university "is a great place to really expand your horizons and become who you've always wanted to be." There is "lots of pride in the school and events going on, so a lot of people are excited and energetic," and a student says that "whether it is presenting my research at our undergraduate research conference, or simply talking to somebody in the Dunkin line in the MUB [student center], the student body at UNH is overall friendly and approachable."

UNIVERSITY OF NEW HAMPSHIRE

Financial Aid: 603-862-3600 • E-Mail: admissions@unh.edu • Website: www.unh.edu

THE PRINCETON REVIEW SAYS

Admissions

The school reports that its standardized testing policy for use in admission for Fall 2024 is Test Optional. The 2024 testing policy will be permanent. The Princeton Review suggests that interested applicants consult with the school for the most up-to-date standardized testing policies. *Very important factors considered include:* rigor of secondary school record, academic GPA. *Important factors considered include:* recommendation(s). *Other factors considered include:* class rank, application essay, extracurricular activities, talent/ability, character/personal qualities, first generation, alumni/ae relation, geographical residence, state residency, volunteer work, work experience. High school diploma is required and high school equivalency such as GED/HiSET is accepted. *Academic units required:* 4 English, 3 math (including Algebra I & II and Geometry), 2 science labs, 2 social studies, 4 additional full-year college preparatory courses. *Academic units recommended:* 4 English, 3 math (including Algebra I & II and Geometry), 3 science labs, 2 world language, 2 social studies, 2 additional full-year college preparatory courses. *Some programs may have additional requirements.

Financial Aid

Students should submit: FAFSA. Priority filing deadline is 3/1. The Princeton Review suggests that all financial aid forms be submitted as soon as possible (see page 5 for a note on the FAFSA). *Need-based scholarships/grants offered:* College/university scholarship or grant aid from institutional funds; Federal Pell; Private scholarships; SEOG; State scholarships/grants. *Loan aid offered:* Direct PLUS loans; Direct Subsidized Loans; Direct Unsubsidized Loans. Admitted students will be notified of awards on a rolling basis. Federal Work-Study Program available. Institutional employment available.

The Inside Word

UNH's emphasis on academic accomplishment in the admissions process makes it clear that the admissions committee is looking for students who have taken high school seriously. Standardized tests take as much of a backseat here as is possible at a large, public university.

THE SCHOOL SAYS "..."

From the Admissions Office

"At the University of New Hampshire, we are limitless in everything we do. As an R1 Carnegie research university, we are a community of changemakers and trailblazers solving urgent challenges and building a better world through top-tier research and a nation-leading commitment to sustainability. With endless opportunities, our community knows relationships matter. With 100+ majors, we transcend boundaries by reaching higher and dreaming bigger, leading with innovation and creativity, and uniting disciplines. You will discover that what you learn, the friends you make, the adventures you have, and the passions you explore will be relevant and rewarding throughout your life.

"Located in the heart of New England, on New Hampshire's vibrant seacoast, UNH has a safe and inclusive campus where students are encouraged to step outside their comfort zone, reach their potential, and become the best version of themselves. Our limitless location offers a tight knit campus community, an Amtrak station on campus, and close proximity to Boston, the Atlantic Ocean, and the White Mountains. Students who are willing to engage in a high-quality academic community in meaningful ways, who have genuine interest in discovering or developing new ideas, and who believe in each person's obligation to improve the community they live in typify the most successful students at UNH. Undergraduate students practice these values in a variety of ways: by undertaking their own independent research projects; by collaborating in faculty research; and by participating in study abroad, residential communities, community service, and other cultural programs."

SELECTIVITY

Admissions Rating	83
# of applicants	21,016
% of applicants accepted	87
% of acceptees attending	16

FIRST-YEAR PROFILE

Testing policy	Test Optional
Range SAT composite	1130–1310
Range SAT EBRW	570–660
Range SAT math	550–660
Range ACT composite	26–31
# submitting SAT scores	1,155
% submitting SAT scores	39
# submitting ACT scores	79
% submitting ACT scores	3
Average HS GPA	3.6
% frosh submitting high school GPA	100
% graduated top 10% of class	23
% graduated top 25% of class	52
% graduated top 50% of class	87

DEADLINES

Early action	
Deadline	11/15
Notification	1/31
Regular	
Deadline	2/1
Notification	3/31, Rolling
Nonfall registration?	Yes

APPLICANTS ALSO LOOK AT

University of Connecticut; University of Maine; University of Massachusetts Amherst; University of Rhode Island; University of Vermont

FINANCIAL FACTS

Financial Aid Rating	80
Annual in-state tuition	$15,520
Annual out-of-state tuition	$35,290
Room and board	$12,992
Required fees	$3,592
Books and supplies	$1,000
Average frosh need-based scholarship	$9,847
Average UG need-based scholarship	$9,560
% needy frosh rec. need-based scholarship or grant aid	86
% needy UG rec. need-based scholarship or grant aid	90
% needy frosh rec. non-need-based scholarship or grant aid	33
% needy UG rec. non-need-based scholarship or grant aid	19
% needy frosh rec. need-based self-help aid	90
% needy UG rec. need-based self-help aid	92
% frosh rec. any financial aid	95
% UG rec. any financial aid	89
% UG borrow to pay for school	74
Average cumulative indebtedness	$44,341
% frosh need fully met	13
% ugrads need fully met	13
Average % of frosh need met	69
Average % of ugrad need met	68

UNIVERSITY OF NEW HAVEN

300 Boston Post Road, West Haven, CT 06516 • Admissions: 203-932-7000 Fax: 203-931-6093

STUDENTS SAY " . . ."

Academics

Interdisciplinary study is the highlight of an education from the University of New Haven, where students take courses from across the five colleges and schools and engage in project-based learning to build out a practical, personalized degree. The lauded criminal justice program, for instance, has "a lot of opportunities…and different pathways offered for those going into law," and "academics, especially the legal studies department, are out of this world." Because at least one component of experiential education is required for graduation, the school works to ensure that students get internships or service learning, whether that's in a booming field like cybersecurity or international business, or an up-and-coming degree in Fire Science or Esports and Gaming. "Most students choose this school due to their specific major," notes one student, and another points out that New Haven "has a lot of amazing programs you cannot attend anywhere else." Several students point to the renowned Henry C. Lee Institute of Forensic Science, "a great strength in this school."

Faculty "have resumes that are incredibly proficient, in some cases to the point where they are overqualified to teach," and bring this experience to the classroom via case studies, examples, and "real world stories as well as hands-on events and exercises." Also, because "class sizes tend to stay small [we can form] better relationships with our professors." Those seeking further support outside class will find "flexible office hours for professors," a "writing center [that] helps with papers," and Centers for Academic Success and Advising. Overall, "the learning style here feels very hands-on," with burn rooms and a crime scene house that students can investigate and "unique equipment, materials, and procedures." As one student puts it, "I've taken a number of labs and field trips in my classes that have really prepared me to use equipment and methods I'll need in my field."

Campus Life

Slightly more than half of the students live on campus, enjoying the "wonderful facilities for a school of our size" and because first-years can choose their Enhanced Learning Community by interest, things like "watching movies in the lounges and playing poker, dominoes, or cards are always fun every night." The weekdays, however, are "usually packed with school time" and activities with the 150 clubs and organizations (like Greek life), many of which support the different majors, like the Forensic Science club, or which set about "taking part in public service opportunities." As for the weekends, athletics are a big part of this Division II school, and both intramurals and intercollegiate games "always can bring out a good crowd," while New Haven itself features plenty of "cool places and restaurants" to explore.

Student Body

At New Haven you'll find "a large number of like-minded people who are motivated by the course work and offered programs." There are "people of different race, religion, and all other kinds of backgrounds" here, and "it is easy to find people you fit in with because the campus is so diverse." Students and faculty "are very protective over making sure everyone gets along and doesn't feel out of place," and people here are "very welcoming, always open to helping one another and supportive of people who want to learn more" regardless of their major, as well as "caring and considerate." Students say that "even though it's a small campus, there are still tons of people to meet," and "you don't have to run into or see anyone you don't want to see, unless they live on your floor."

UNIVERSITY OF NEW HAVEN

Financial Aid: 203-932-7315 • E-Mail: admissions@newhaven.edu • Website: www.newhaven.edu

THE PRINCETON REVIEW SAYS

Admissions

The school reports that its standardized testing policy for use in admission for Fall 2024 is Test Optional for most programs and populations. It is unknown at this time if the 2024 testing policy will be permanent. The Princeton Review suggests that interested applicants consult with the school for the most up-to-date standardized testing policies. *Very important factors considered include:* academic GPA. *Important factors considered include:* application essay, recommendation(s). *Other factors considered include:* rigor of secondary school record, class rank, standardized test scores, interview, extracurricular activities, character/personal qualities, volunteer work, work experience, level of applicant's interest. High school diploma is required and GED is accepted. *Academic units recommended:* 4 English, 3 math, 3 science, 2 science labs, 2 foreign language, 3 social studies.

Financial Aid

Students should submit: FAFSA. Priority filing deadline is 3/1. The Princeton Review suggests that all financial aid forms be submitted as soon as possible (see page 5 for a note on the FAFSA). *Need-based scholarships/grants offered:* College/university scholarship or grant aid from institutional funds; Federal Pell; Private scholarships; SEOG; State scholarships/grants. *Loan aid offered:* Direct PLUS loans; Direct Subsidized Loans; Direct Unsubsidized Loans. Admitted students will be notified of awards on a rolling basis. Federal Work-Study Program available. Institutional employment available.

The Inside Word

The University of New Haven is a rather welcoming institution. Don't feel rushed to apply for early decision (unless you want to have a personal interview). If you're in the top 50% of your class—standardized test scores aren't required, nor is a personal essay—you're in good shape, although it wouldn't hurt to demonstrate your interest or have a few AP-level courses to help you stand out.

THE SCHOOL SAYS "..."

From the Admissions Office

"The University of New Haven is a national leader in experiential education, offering several unique and innovative majors across the College of Arts & Sciences, AACSB-accredited Pompea College of Business, Tagliatela College of Engineering (ABET-accredited), Henry C. Lee College of Criminal Justice and Forensic Sciences, and the School of Health Sciences.

"In the last decade, the University has completed more than $300 million in major capital projects while launching 26 new academic programs. Exciting facilities on campus include our crime-simulation center, a state-of-the-art communication & media center, digital and analog recording studios, hospital room simulation labs, a dedicated business campus in Orange, Conn., dental center, and our two newest buildings: the Bergami Center for Science, Technology & Innovation and the Peterson Performance Center for student-athletes.

"We pride ourselves on providing students with great experiences and opportunities through Faculty-Mentored Student Research, Internships and Co-Ops, Academic Service Learning & Community Service, and Study Abroad. Our satellite campus in Prato, Italy, is popular as well as our Study Away Program in Nashville with Blackbird Studio and our two-week intensive study abroad programs where students can earn six credits.

"Some of our newest academic offerings include undergraduate degrees in Game Development & Interactive Media, Interdisciplinary Studies, Music Technology & Innovation, Intelligence Analysis, Public Health, Health Sciences, Medical Laboratory Sciences, Actuarial Science, Business Analytics, Cybersecurity, Paramedicine, International Affairs, Homeland Security & Emergency Management, and Esports & Gaming.

"NCAA Division II athletics, a 275-member marching band, student-run 88.7 FM radio station (WNHU), an amazing theater production company, Model United Nations team, and popular on-campus cafe managed entirely by our students are just a few more of the great things you can get involved with at the University of New Haven."

SELECTIVITY

Admissions Rating	82
# of applicants	10,277
% of applicants accepted	94
% of acceptees attending	13
# offered a place on the wait list	426
% accepting a place on wait list	99
% admitted from wait list	40
# of early decision applicants	52
% accepted early decision	98

FIRST-YEAR PROFILE

Testing policy	Test Optional
Range SAT composite	1110–1270
Range SAT EBRW	560–650
Range SAT math	550–630
# submitting SAT scores	322
% submitting SAT scores	26
# submitting ACT scores	35
% submitting ACT scores	3
Average HS GPA	3.5
% frosh submitting high school GPA	100
% graduated top 10% of class	18
% graduated top 25% of class	43
% graduated top 50% of class	76

DEADLINES

Early decision	
Deadline	12/1
Notification	12/15
Early action	
Deadline	12/15
Notification	1/15
EA II deadline	2/15
EA II notification	Rolling
Regular	
Deadline	3/1
Notification	Rolling
Nonfall registration?	Yes

APPLICANTS OFTEN PREFER

Central Connecticut State University; Southern Connecticut State University; University of Connecticut

APPLICANTS SOMETIMES PREFER

City University of New York - John Jay College of Criminal Justice; Sacred Heart University; University of Hartford; University of Rhode Island

FINANCIAL FACTS

Financial Aid Rating	81
Annual tuition	$42,610
Room and board	$17,778
Required fees	$1,574
Books and supplies	$1,000
Average frosh need-based scholarship	$27,491
Average UG need-based scholarship	$24,476
% needy frosh rec. need-based scholarship or grant aid	100
% needy UG rec. need-based scholarship or grant aid	99
% needy frosh rec. non-need-based scholarship or grant aid	14
% needy UG rec. non-need-based scholarship or grant aid	14
% needy frosh rec. need-based self-help aid	77
% needy UG rec. need-based self-help aid	77
% UG borrow to pay for school	83
Average cumulative indebtedness	$51,332
% frosh need fully met	14
% ugrads need fully met	17
Average % of frosh need met	67
Average % of ugrad need met	64

UNIVERSITY OF NEW MEXICO

1 University of New Mexico, Albuquerque, NM 86131-0001 • Admissions: 505-277-0111 • Fax: 505-277-6686

STUDENTS SAY "..."

Academics

Offering a "solid education" in a beautiful setting, the University of New Mexico offers "academic excellence…through some of the best teachers and tough classes." Students also cited affordability and excellent scholarships awarded to both in-state and out-of-state applicants as a decisive factor in attending UNM. The affordability also extends to "amazing opportunities to travel abroad." At UNM, "there is something here for everyone." The education program and variety of science programs—including Earth and planetary sciences, biology, and the premed and nursing programs—also attract students. Some students express frustration with it at times being "difficult to work your way around the student services system," but the "very knowledgeable" teaching faculty are roundly praised as "teachers who care." UNM students also agree that "professors are helpful [and] genuinely interested in your personal success." Professors are approachable both in class and out and "talk to and with you and not just at you." "It's very easy to come to instructors outside of class with questions," and "most professors are willing to meet with you at your convenience." As for UNM's greatest strengths, students cite both the "research-oriented staff" and "the research opportunities available. Oftentimes the research can be done with top-of-the-line equipment" nearby at Sandia National Labs, Los Alamos National Labs, and other well-known research institutes. In UNM's collaborative environment, students also often work together and "are eager to form study groups." Also, students who need additional help can rely on academic support with "tutoring, study groups, and supplemental instruction for most courses."

Campus Life

With "ways for everyone to get involved," UNM offers "hundreds of great student organizations" providing "opportunities for fun events." There is a student group "that will fit everyone," and at UNM, "everyone seems to find their niche." Offering another opportunity to become more involved on campus, the Greek community "makes up a lot of the senate and other extracurricular activities" and "with them, any activity has fun attached." UNM students are divided in their support of the school's athletics program. With some thinking "this school should concentrate less on sports and more on academics," other students feel "attending games is a must." Students enjoy spending time at the Student Union Building (SUB), because "there is always something going on." Even with a dry campus, "a lot of people drink, just like at any college." Students often leave campus for Albuquerque and its "excellent nightlife." UNM students also mention attending concerts and art shows for fun. Students also go to the weekly free movies at The Cellar, and to stay active, students frequent the Johnson Gym. Students say that "hanging out at the duck pond is a great way to pass time between classes in warmer months," and "during the winter season, there are numerous ski resorts and places to go snowboarding that are not far away."

Student Body

Time and time again, students select UNM's "diversity" as its greatest strength, and one student even stated "no one will ever feel ethnically alone since there are so many different kinds of people." This also means at UNM, "people never get boring," and "you meet someone different every day." In addition to the diversity, the prevailing atmosphere is a friendly one where "people get along regardless of origin," but "like any school there are cliques…but that does not mean they do not interact with each other." One student reserved special praise for the university, "UNM is sensitive and very engaged with its diverse population of students…concerned with facilitating in-depth inquiry and learning," and more than one student observed that at UNM, "everyone brings something to the table."

UNIVERSITY OF NEW MEXICO

Financial Aid: 505-277-8900 • E-Mail: apply@unm.edu • Website: www.unm.edu

THE PRINCETON REVIEW SAYS

Admissions

The school reports that its standardized testing policy for use in admission for Fall 2024 is Test Optional. It is unknown at this time if the 2024 testing policy will be permanent. The Princeton Review suggests that interested applicants consult with the school for the most up-to-date standardized testing policies.

Financial Aid

Students should submit: FAFSA. *Need based scholarships/grants offered:* College/university scholarship or grant aid from institutional funds; Federal; Federal Pell; Private scholarships; SEOG; State scholarships/grants. *Loan aid offered:* Direct PLUS loans; Direct Subsidized Loans; Direct Unsubsidized Loans. Federal Work-Study Program available. Institutional employment available.

The Inside Word

UNM offers online applications through its website, and you will also find specific scholastic standards for traditional and nontraditional students interested in applying to UNM. Traditional applicants should have completed core coursework and have an average or above-average GPA if they would like to be considered for admission at UNM.

THE SCHOOL SAYS "..."

From the Admissions Office

"The University of New Mexico is a major research institution nestled in the heart of multicultural Albuquerque on one of the nation's most beautiful and unique campuses. Students learn in an environment graced by distinctive Southwestern architecture, beautiful plazas and fountains, spectacular art and a national arboretum...all within view of the 10,000-foot Sandia Mountains. At UNM, diversity is a way of learning with education enriched by a lively mix of students being taught by a world-class research faculty that includes a Nobel laureate, a MacArthur Fellow, and members of several national academies. UNM offers more than 200 degree programs and majors and has earned national recognition in dozens of disciplines, ranging from primary care medicine and clinical law to engineering, photography, Latin American history, and intercultural communications. Research and the quest for new knowledge fuels the university's commitment to an undergraduate education where students work side-by-side with many of the finest scholars in their fields."

SELECTIVITY

Admissions Rating	88
# of applicants	13,676
% of applicants accepted	81
% of acceptees attending	14

FIRST-YEAR PROFILE

Testing policy	Test Optional
Range ACT composite	20–26
# submitting SAT scores	11
% submitting SAT scores	1
# submitting ACT scores	783
% submitting ACT scores	22
Average HS GPA	3.4
% frosh submitting high school GPA	74

DEADLINES

Regular	
Priority	12/1
Deadline	Rolling
Notification	Rolling
Nonfall registration?	Yes

FINANCIAL FACTS

Financial Aid Rating	74
Annual in-state tuition	$10,860
Annual out-of-state tuition	$27,166
Room and board	$10,916
Books and supplies	$1,253
Average frosh need-based scholarship	$9,079
Average UG need-based scholarship	$9,597
% needy frosh rec. need-based scholarship or grant aid	97
% needy UG rec. need-based scholarship or grant aid	92
% needy frosh rec. non-need-based scholarship or grant aid	1
% needy UG rec. non-need-based scholarship or grant aid	2
% needy frosh rec. need-based self-help aid	31
% needy UG rec. need-based self-help aid	35
% UG borrow to pay for school	40
Average cumulative indebtedness	$22.375
% frosh need fully met	14
% ugrads need fully met	17

UNIVERSITY OF NORTH CAROLINA ASHEVILLE

One University Heights, Asheville, NC 28804-8510 • Admissions: 828-251-6600 • Fax: 828-251-6482

CAMPUS LIFE

Quality of Life Rating	91
Fire Safety Rating	97
Green Rating	99
Type of school	Public
Environment	City

STUDENTS

Total undergrad enrollment	2,914
% male/female/another gender	42/58/NR
% from out of state	12
% frosh from public high school	85
% frosh live on campus	95
% ugrads live on campus	48
# of fraternities (% join)	2 (2)
# of sororities (% join)	1 (1)
% African American	5
% Asian	2
% White	75
% Hispanic	8
% Native American	<1
% Pacific Islander	<1
% Two or more races	5
% Race and/or ethnicity unknown	4
% international	1
# of countries represented	19

SURVEY SAYS . . .

Lots of liberal students
Students are happy
Great library
No one cheats
Students aren't religious
Students get along with local community
Students environmentally aware
Students are friendly
Students love Asheville, NC
Great off-campus food
Active student government
Diverse student types interact on campus
Active minority support groups
Students involved in community service
Easy to get around campus

ACADEMICS

Academic Rating	85
% students returning for sophomore year	69
% students graduating within 4 years	44
% students graduating within 6 years	59
Calendar	Semester
Student/faculty ratio	11:1
Profs interesting rating	93
Profs accessible rating	93

Most classes have 10–19 students.
Most lab/discussion sessions have
10–19 students.

MOST POPULAR MAJORS
Environmental Studies; Psychology, General;
Biology/Biological Sciences, General

STUDENTS SAY "..."

Academics

Nestled in the Blue Ridge Mountains, the University of North Carolina Asheville strives to exist at the intersection of curiosity and critical thinking. "Strong STEM and liberal arts programs" provide plenty of opportunity for different educational tracks, and "Small class sizes means more individual attention from professors" who are willing "to work with your needs and limits." The strength of the faculty is valued among enrollees, with one student saying, "My professors are the best educators that I have ever had in my entire academic career." Especially "if you're willing to put in the work," professors can "create an amazing, welcoming environment," culminating in an education that's "nothing short of phenomenal." In terms of the classroom experience, "First-year seminars provided at UNCA are really great courses for exceptional discussions," and undergrads tout the benefits of the many "entirely discussion-based" courses that "allow students to experience a leadership role." Learning is not limited to traditional lectures, with many courses taught outside and opportunities for coursework that's "entirely based around extracurricular involvement and action outside of the classroom."

Campus Life

The undergrad experience at University of North Carolina Asheville is rooted in students' passion for the world around them. Cause-driven activities like food distribution events and zero waste contests give undergrads the opportunity to interact with like-minded peers. Additionally, getting outdoors is a popular pastime. On any given day, you can find UNC Asheville students spending time outside. "Daily walks when the weather is nice is a must," and "dorm balconies, the quad, and the botanical gardens are wonderful spaces to spend time in nature by yourself or with friends." Even "during the summer there are always people out on the campus playing frisbee or hanging around in hammocks."

Venturing off-campus, there are "many national forests around UNCA" where students "go hiking a lot," and enjoy activities like swimming, kayaking, fishing, and rock climbing. For those looking for a more urban escape, downtown Asheville provides "a lot of things to do," with students heading there to "see small bands play" and "look at different art and stores." Additionally, "Many [businesses] are locally owned which brings a big sense of community" to the Asheville experience. At its core, the campus and surrounding area is "very welcoming and enjoyable and in a great location."

Student Body

The vibe on UNC Asheville campus "Feels extremely friendly," and as one student puts it, "I'm very proud to be a Bulldog and serve and interact with this empathetic, driven, and creative community." The student body is made up of "quality students" who have a "wide variety of life experiences and perspectives." People are "conscientious when it comes to social, political, and environmental" issues, with many working to "make positive changes to the campus culture and society at large." While most would consider themselves liberal, individuals are "tolerant of different groups" and they "embrace and celebrate our unique student body." Although some feel that the university could improve at "Being more inclusive for BIPOC, LGBT+, and religious minority students," others see "Inclusivity of all people" and "bringing awareness to social civil situations" as some of UNCA's greatest strengths. Ultimately, students agree that "A lot of attention" is dedicated to figuring out how to "best uphold our values and respect for each other, the greater world, and the environment."

University of North Carolina Asheville

Financial Aid: 828-251-6535 • E-Mail: admissions@unca.edu • Website: www.unca.edu

THE PRINCETON REVIEW SAYS

Admissions

The school reports that its standardized testing policy for use in admission for Fall 2024 is Test Optional. It is unknown at this time if the 2024 testing policy will be permanent. The Princeton Review suggests that interested applicants consult with the school for the most up-to-date standardized testing policies. *Very important factors considered include:* rigor of secondary school record, class rank, academic GPA, standardized test scores, application essay, recommendation(s). *Important factors considered include:* extracurricular activities, talent/ability, character/personal qualities. *Other factors considered include:* first generation, alumni/ae relation, geographical residence, state residency, racial/ethnic status, volunteer work, work experience, level of applicant's interest. High school diploma is required and GED is not accepted. *Academic units required:* 4 English, 4 math, 3 science, 1 science lab, 2 foreign language, 2 social studies.

Financial Aid

Students should submit: FAFSA. Priority filing deadline is 3/1. The Princeton Review suggests that all financial aid forms be submitted as soon as possible (see page 5 for a note on the FAFSA). *Need-based scholarships/grants offered:* College/university scholarship or grant aid from institutional funds; Federal Pell; Private scholarships; SEOG; State scholarships/grants. *Loan aid offered:* Direct PLUS loans; Direct Subsidized Loans; Direct Unsubsidized Loans. Admitted students will be notified of awards on a rolling basis beginning 2/15. Federal Work-Study Program available. Institutional employment available.

The Inside Word

The admissions team at UNCA seeks applicants who are open to new experiences, have original ideas, and want to embrace the opportunities before them. While high school classes, academic performance, and test scores (though optional), are important, UNC Asheville uses a holistic model to determine a students' acceptance status. Applicants should carefully review their application essay and make sure to showcase their activities, leadership roles, and other talents as well.

THE SCHOOL SAYS "..."

From the Admissions Office

"With a focus on collaborative, interdisciplinary education, UNC Asheville prepares students to be innovative critical thinkers, giving them the tools they need to thrive as experts in their area of study and beyond. Over thirty majors prepare students to understand and define their place in our ever-changing world. UNC Asheville students ask important questions and pursue answers across disciplines with a commitment to making an impact and building community. The result is a competitive advantage, not only for graduates but also for the organizations they work for, where the convergence of art and science leads the way in today's dynamic economy.

"UNC Asheville offers both Early Action and Regular Decision plans."

SELECTIVITY

Admissions Rating	86
# of applicants	4,278
% of applicants accepted	74
% of acceptees attending	16
# offered a place on the wait list	403
% accepting a place on wait list	24
% admitted from wait list	27
# of early decision applicants	264
% accepted early decision	78

FIRST-YEAR PROFILE

Testing policy	Test Optional
Range SAT composite	1160–1340
Range SAT EBRW	600–680
Range SAT math	540–650
Range ACT composite	21–28
# submitting SAT scores	81
% submitting SAT scores	16
# submitting ACT scores	121
% submitting ACT scores	24
Average HS GPA	3.5
% frosh submitting high school GPA	86
% graduated top 10% of class	16
% graduated top 25% of class	43
% graduated top 50% of class	78

DEADLINES

Early decision	
Deadline	11/15
Notification	12/15
Other ED deadline	1/15
Other ED notification	2/1
Early action	
Deadline	11/15
Notification	Rolling
Regular	
Priority	2/1
Deadline	7/31
Notification	Rolling, 12/15
Nonfall registration?	Yes

APPLICANTS ALSO LOOK AT

Appalachian State University; University Of North Carolina Charlotte; North Carolina State University; University Of North Carolina Greensboro; East Carolina University; University Of North Carolina at Chapel Hill; Western Carolina University; University Of North Carolina Wilmington; Asheville-Buncombe Technical Community College; Wake Technical Community College; Central Piedmont Community College; Pitt Community College

FINANCIAL FACTS

Financial Aid Rating	82
Annual in-state tuition	$4,122
Annual out-of-state tuition	$21,470
Room and board	$10,556
Required fees	$3,258
Required fees (first-year)	$3,408
Books and supplies	$1,200
Average frosh need-based scholarship	$8,518
Average UG need-based scholarship	$8,708
% needy frosh rec. need-based scholarship or grant aid	100
% needy UG rec. need-based scholarship or grant aid	96
% needy frosh rec. non-need-based scholarship or grant aid	9
% needy UG rec. non-need-based scholarship or grant aid	6
% needy frosh rec. need-based self-help aid	63
% needy UG rec. need-based self-help aid	64
% frosh rec. any financial aid	91
% UG rec. any financial aid	86
% UG borrow to pay for school	58
Average cumulative indebtedness	$23,246
% frosh need fully met	10
% ugrads need fully met	6
Average % of frosh need met	69
Average % of ugrad need met	66

UNIVERSITY OF NORTH CAROLINA AT CHAPEL HILL

University of North Carolina at Chapel Hill, Chapel Hill, NC 27599-9100 • Admissions: 919-962-2211 • Fax: 919-962-3045

STUDENTS SAY "..."

Academics

Citing "academic prestige" and "affordability," the "beautiful," "historic" setting, and "world-renowned" faculty, students take pride in "being a Tar Heel" at the University of North Carolina at Chapel Hill. The professors at UNC-Chapel Hill are "top-notch, many of them being academic celebrities," but "like the students, are never flashy" and remain "humble." Students find that their professors frequently stress that they are here to "learn from you all as much as you are here to learn from me." UNC offers undergrads "bountiful resources" as "one of the top public research universities in the nation," and students have the opportunity to participate in this research by applying for "generous academic grants." Academics are "rigorous," but the "quality of teaching makes the material intellectually stimulating." The college is fairly large, so students will likely attend "large lecture-hall style classes," yet students stress that as they advance, "class sizes are smaller," and this leads to "the opportunity to build more personal relationships with professors." UNC's "reputation and ranking in STEM programs," along with its well-regarded business school, are among its greatest strengths. Said one transfer student, "I visited countless top universities," but UNC was the only one that had a "population...both economically and ethnically diverse."

Campus Life

UNC offers its "more than 19,000 undergrads" a host of opportunities to socialize, relax, and pack themselves all together at the Dean E. Smith Center to cheer on the men's basketball team. Carolina has strong athletics, including opportunities for "potential student-athletes." For non-athletes, it's a great school to be a fan, "as basketball games especially create a special campus atmosphere that nothing can recreate." Despite the university's size, life on campus generally moves at a "slow pace"—in a good way. The campus is full of "gorgeous old buildings, towering oak trees, and ubiquitous birds, squirrels, and chipmunks," and students "love walking through the upper quad," a "beautiful green area with lots of old trees." Raleigh is "only 30 minutes away" and "Durham only 15," so students will head out there on weekends, and if they need to unwind during the week, they go "out to bars on Franklin Street." There's "always a party going on at UNC," but there are also "plenty of ways to have fun if you're not into the party scene." There are several "day hikes somewhat close to campus," and Carrboro is "within walking distance," providing a "hip space for social life including a farmers market, concert venue[s], and many bars and restaurants."

Student Body

The student body is "as helpful as it is inquisitive, and as creative as it is caring." For every "get-to-know-you question someone asks you," there is a "student happy to direct you to your classes." Everyone at Carolina is "fun, energetic, and passionate about something." The students "are smart, but they aren't haughty and ostentatious about it." Students are "generally liberal, but there is a vocal religious/conservative presence on campus as well." Ultimately, UNC is "unified unlike any other school I have encountered," says one student, "whether it's in the common support of a sports team, music group, or simply the pride in saying you are a Tar Heel." Another student agrees, "Donning Carolina blue almost constantly, we all just really love our school!"

UNIVERSITY OF NORTH CAROLINA AT CHAPEL HILL

Financial Aid: 919-962-8396 • E-Mail: unchelp@admissions.unc.edu • Website: www.unc.edu

THE PRINCETON REVIEW SAYS

Admissions

The school reports that its standardized testing policy for use in admission for Fall 2024 is Test Optional. The 2024 testing policy will be temporary. The Princeton Review suggests that interested applicants consult with the school for the most up-to-date standardized testing policies. *Very important factors considered include:* rigor of secondary school record, application essay, recommendation(s), extracurricular activities, talent/ability, character/personal qualities, state residency. *Important factors considered include:* class rank, academic GPA, volunteer work, work experience. *Other factors considered include:* standardized test scores, first generation, alumni/ae relation, racial/ethnic status. High school diploma is required and GED is not accepted. *Academic units required:* 4 English, 4 math, 3 science, 1 science lab, 2 foreign language, 1 social studies, 1 history, 1 academic elective.

Financial Aid

Students should submit: CSS/Financial Aid Profile; FAFSA. Priority filing deadline is 3/1. The Princeton Review suggests that all financial aid forms be submitted as soon as possible (see page 5 for a note on the FAFSA). *Need-based scholarships/grants offered:* College/university scholarship or grant aid from institutional funds; Federal Pell; Private scholarships; SEOG; State scholarships/grants. *Loan aid offered:* Direct PLUS loans; Direct Subsidized Loans; Direct Unsubsidized Loans; College/university loans from institutional funds; State Loans. Admitted students will be notified of awards on a rolling basis beginning 1/31. Federal Work-Study Program available. Institutional employment available.

The Inside Word

UNC's admissions process is highly selective. North Carolina students compete against other students from across the state for 82 percent of all spaces available in the freshman class; out-of-state students compete for the remaining 18 percent of the spaces. State residents will find the admissions standards high, and out-of-state applicants will find that it's one of the hardest offers of admission to come by in the country. While there's no formula, a fact UNC is proud of, students should expect to offer a compelling portrait to the admissions committee of their talents and achievements.

THE SCHOOL SAYS "..."

From the Admissions Office

"Carolina is proudly public and has earned a reputation as one of the best universities in the world, preparing its students for a lifetime of leadership and service. Carolina is best known for having one of the strongest and most diverse student bodies in the nation. Carolina's most recently admitted class includes students who will be the first in their families to graduate from college (18 percent of the class), are high school valedictorians or salutatorians (12 percent of the class), and are committed to serving their communities (74 percent volunteered during high school). Carolina offers academic opportunities that prepare students to empower themselves and their communities; even during the pandemic, 93 percent of graduates earned jobs, entered graduate school, joined the military, or committed to volunteering within six months of graduation.

"Admission to Carolina is competitive, but we are dedicated to making it fair and considerate. We don't use formulas or cutoffs; instead, we know that students travel many roads to Carolina, and we celebrate the variety of interests, backgrounds, and aspirations they bring. We actively seek excellence in academics, arts, athletics, leadership, service, citizenship, and character. This list isn't exhaustive or prescriptive. When we read an application, we're interested in what a student has done, what they care about, and the difference they will make as a member of Carolina's community. We're committed to ensuring that every student who earns a place at Carolina can afford to attend, and our financial aid program meets full need and enables qualified low-income students to graduate debt-free through the Carolina Covenant."

SELECTIVITY

Admissions Rating	97
# of applicants	57,221
% of applicants accepted	17
% of acceptees attending	46
# offered a place on the wait list	7,258
% accepting a place on wait list	74
% admitted from wait list	7

FIRST-YEAR PROFILE

Testing policy	Test Optional
Range SAT composite	1350–1510
Range SAT EBRW	670–750
Range SAT math	670–780
Range ACT composite	28–33
# submitting SAT scores	1,414
% submitting SAT scores	15
# submitting ACT scores	1,888
% submitting ACT scores	60
Average HS GPA	4.5
% frosh submitting high school GPA	91
% graduated top 10% of class	74
% graduated top 25% of class	95
% graduated top 50% of class	100

DEADLINES

Early action	
Deadline	10/15
Notification	1/31
Regular	
Priority	10/15
Deadline	1/15
Notification	3/31
Nonfall registration?	No

APPLICANTS SOMETIMES PREFER

Duke University; North Carolina State University; University of Pennsylvania; University of Virginia; Vanderbilt University

APPLICANTS RARELY PREFER

Appalachian State University; East Carolina University

FINANCIAL FACTS

Financial Aid Rating	92
Annual in-state tuition	$7,020
Annual out-of-state tuition	$37,360
Room and board	$13,016
Required fees	$1,978
Books and supplies	$1,290
Average frosh need-based scholarship	$15,704
Average UG need-based scholarship	$17,336
% needy frosh rec. need-based scholarship or grant aid	93
% needy UG rec. need-based scholarship or grant aid	92
% needy frosh rec. non-need-based scholarship or grant aid	12
% needy UG rec. non-need-based scholarship or grant aid	8
% needy frosh rec. need-based self-help aid	43
% needy UG rec. need-based self-help aid	49
% frosh rec. any financial aid	58
% UG rec. any financial aid	60
% UG borrow to pay for school	33
Average cumulative indebtedness	$20,680
% frosh need fully met	71
% ugrads need fully met	68
Average % of frosh need met	100
Average % of ugrad need met	100

UNIVERSITY OF NORTH CAROLINA AT GREENSBORO

1400 Spring Garden St, Greensboro, NC 27402 • Admissions: 336-334-5000

CAMPUS LIFE

Quality of Life Rating	**87**
Fire Safety Rating	**99**
Green Rating	**94**
Type of school	Public
Environment	City

STUDENTS

Total undergrad enrollment	13,862
% male/female/another gender	34/66/NR
% from out of state	4
% frosh from public high school	97
% frosh live on campus	79
% ugrads live on campus	36
# of fraternities (% join)	12 (1)
# of sororities (% join)	12 (1)
% African American	30
% Asian	6
% White	40
% Hispanic	16
% Native American	<1
% Pacific Islander	<1
% Two or more races	5
% Race and/or ethnicity unknown	1
% international	1
# of countries represented	60

SURVEY SAYS . . .

Students love Greensboro, NC
Recreation facilities are great
Frats and sororities are popular

ACADEMICS

Academic Rating	**77**
% students returning for sophomore year	73
% students graduating within 4 years	36
% students graduating within 6 years	57
Calendar	Semester
Student/faculty ratio	17:1
Profs interesting rating	86
Profs accessible rating	89
Most classes have 20–29 students.	
Most lab/discussion sessions have fewer than 10 students.	

MOST POPULAR MAJORS

Biology/Biological Sciences, General; Psychology, General; Business Administration and Management, General

STUDENTS SAY "..."

Academics

The University of North Carolina at Greensboro is a big school yet students "[don't] feel like a number." They find their professors are often "incredibly personable" and that they give advice "about finding internships and other opportunities to network." They're a great resource for getting "all the information and guidance [students] need to succeed." The Lloyd International Honors College "has an emphasis on…experiential learning," including visits to nearby Guilford forest where students "[learn] about the important points of the Underground Railroad." As standout offerings, students comment on the "superb online programs" offered by the school as well as the "great art, [music], and science programs." "Many programs are oriented toward student help and health" to make sure students don't fall behind. "I think the greatest strength of UNCG is that they are very good at [pointing] students in the right direction," says a student. They continue: "For example, [if] you approach your advisors…with a problem, they will show up with a big list of possible solutions."

Campus Life

"There is always something to do on this beautiful campus," boasts a student of UNCG. During their study time, plenty sit in the "Salad Bowl, [which is] a huge garden space with really huge trees canopying over top." Some get "geeky, fun, and athletic" with the Quidditch Club, which a student calls "the highlight of UNCG." Also praised is the recreation center, which has "a pool, lazy river, and sauna along with all of the athletic equipment…and group fitness classes." "People eat on Tate Street, [which has] very popular off-campus eateries," and take "day trips to Piney Lake for paddle boarding." Located in the center of North Carolina, "just a few hours east or west [of the school] will take you to the coast or the mountains if you need a change of scenery." On weekends, "many people go to clubs like Limelight or Arizona Pete's," and "there is a jazz night at Tate Street Coffee House,…which is a really fun thing."

Student Body

The student body at UNC Greensboro is "racially, economically, [and] ideologically diverse." "The political viewpoint…is [majorly] liberal," says a student. "What makes UNCG unique is our strong acceptance of the others of society," the student continues. Students note that the school's integrated programs "get all levels of students working together." The student body here is one with a "huge music/theater concentration but also a mix of athletes and fraternity/sorority members." As a "minority-serving institution,… the culture is rich and eclectic," and students say that it's "one of the most LGBTQ+ friendly campuses." One student puts it this way: "It is rare that I walk into a class of students [who] look like myself." They don't see this as a drawback, though, and say that it makes the campus feel "lively" and "diverse in many ways."

UNIVERSITY OF NORTH CAROLINA AT GREENSBORO

Financial Aid: 336-334-5702 • E-Mail: admissions@uncg.edu • Website: www.uncg.edu

THE PRINCETON REVIEW SAYS

Admissions

The school reports that its standardized testing policy for use in admission for Fall 2024 is Test Optional. It is unknown at this time if the 2024 testing policy will be permanent. The Princeton Review suggests that interested applicants consult with the school for the most up-to-date standardized testing policies. *Very important factors considered include:* rigor of secondary school record, academic GPA. *Important factors considered include:* standardized test scores. *Other factors considered include:* class rank, application essay, recommendation(s), extracurricular activities, volunteer work. High school diploma is required and GED is accepted. *Academic units required:* 4 English, 4 math, 3 science, 1 science lab, 2 foreign language, 2 social studies.

Financial Aid

Students should submit: FAFSA. Priority filing deadline is 1/15. The Princeton Review suggests that all financial aid forms be submitted as soon as possible (see page 5 for a note on the FAFSA). *Need-based scholarships/grants offered:* College/university scholarship or grant aid from institutional funds; Federal Pell; Private scholarships; SEOG; State scholarships/grants. *Loan aid offered:* Direct PLUS loans; Direct Subsidized Loans; Direct Unsubsidized Loans; College/university loans from institutional funds; State Loans. Admitted students will be notified of awards on a rolling basis beginning 3/15. Federal Work-Study Program available. Institutional employment available.

The Inside Word

UNCG emphasizes GPA and test scores (if submitting) in the admissions process. However, they also consider high school course selection and progression, Senior class schedule, all test scores (where submitted), and community standards concerns. First year applicants are encouraged to apply by the Early Action I deadline December 1 to receive a decision in January. Students may also apply to Early Action II on January 15 to receive a decision in February. March 1 is the regular deadline, and applications after this date are only reviewed on a space-available basis.

THE SCHOOL SAYS "..."

From the Admissions Office

"Founded in 1891, UNC Greensboro is one of the original three institutions in the UNC System. Today, UNCG is 1 of only 40 doctoral institutions in the world classified by the Carnegie Foundation for both higher research activity and community engagement. With 20,000 students, 17 Division I athletic teams, 125+ undergraduate areas of study, and over 300 student-led clubs, UNC Greensboro is consistently recognized nationally among the top universities for academic excellence and value.

"UNCG is committed to transforming its students through challenging academics and enriching extracurricular opportunities. Undergraduates can choose from more than 125 degree programs including familiar degrees like business, education, and nursing, and unique options like fashion and retail, interior architecture, sign language interpreting, and data science.

"One common factor that drives UNCG students is a passion for making an impact. In fact, the University is listed among the top three North Carolina public universities based on contribution to the public good. Faculty here are engaged in life-changing research and community work, and they give students ample opportunities to participate. Experiences like supervised research and service learning make students' time in school more meaningful and help them stand out in the job market.

"The rich diversity of UNCG's student body creates a welcoming campus environment and brings a dynamic energy to class discussions and campus events. Empowered by the encouragement of their peers, students here take an active role in campus leadership, learning soft skills and building deep relationships that last far beyond graduation."

SELECTIVITY
Admissions Rating	83
# of applicants	11,515
% of applicants accepted	92
% of acceptees attending	22

FIRST-YEAR PROFILE
Testing policy	Test Optional
Range SAT composite	1110–1280
Range SAT EBRW	570–660
Range SAT math	540–620
Range ACT composite	22–27
# submitting SAT scores	123
% submitting SAT scores	5
# submitting ACT scores	186
% submitting ACT scores	8
Average HS GPA	3.6
% frosh submitting high school GPA	100
% graduated top 10% of class	<1
% graduated top 25% of class	6
% graduated top 50% of class	31

DEADLINES
Early action	
Deadline	11/1
Notification	12/15
Regular	
Priority	11/1
Deadline	3/1
Notification	Rolling, 11/1
Nonfall registration?	Yes

FINANCIAL FACTS
Financial Aid Rating	79
Annual in-state tuition	$4,422
Annual out-of-state tuition	$19,582
Room and board	$9,924
Required fees	$2,957
Required fees (first-year)	$3,076
Books and supplies	$850
Average frosh need-based scholarship	$8,831
Average UG need-based scholarship	$8,819
% needy frosh rec. need-based scholarship or grant aid	95
% needy UG rec. need-based scholarship or grant aid	88
% needy frosh rec. non-need-based scholarship or grant aid	14
% needy UG rec. non-need-based scholarship or grant aid	12
% needy frosh rec. need-based self-help aid	58
% needy UG rec. need-based self-help aid	59
% frosh rec. any financial aid	78
% UG rec. any financial aid	76
% UG borrow to pay for school	69
Average cumulative indebtedness	$25,477
% frosh need fully met	6
% ugrads need fully met	4
Average % of frosh need met	67
Average % of ugrad need met	67

UNIVERSITY OF NORTH DAKOTA

3501 University Avenue Stop 8357, Grand Forks, ND 58202 • Admissions: 701-777-3000 • Fax: 701-777-2721

CAMPUS LIFE

Quality of Life Rating	86
Fire Safety Rating	84
Green Rating	89
Type of school	Public
Environment	Town

STUDENTS

Total undergrad enrollment	9,928
% male/female/another gender	55/45/NR
% from out of state	64
% frosh from public high school	97
% frosh live on campus	89
% ugrads live on campus	24
# of fraternities (% join)	13 (12)
# of sororities (% join)	7 (10)
% African American	2
% Asian	3
% White	77
% Hispanic	5
% Native American	1
% Pacific Islander	<1
% Two or more races	5
% Race and/or ethnicity unknown	3
% international	4
# of countries represented	80

SURVEY SAYS . . .

Lots of conservative students
Recreation facilities are great
Everyone loves the Fighting Hawks
Intramural sports are popular
Frats and sororities are popular

ACADEMICS

Academic Rating	76
% students returning for sophomore year	79
% students graduating within 4 years	42
% students graduating within 6 years	63
Calendar	Semester
Student/faculty ratio	17:1
Profs interesting rating	84
Profs accessible rating	88

Most classes have 20–29 students.
Most lab/discussion sessions have
20–29 students.

MOST POPULAR MAJORS

Psychology, General; Aviation/Airway Management
and Operations; Registered Nursing/Registered
Nurse

STUDENTS SAY "..."

Academics

If you love hockey, want to study at the nation's foremost aerospace and aviation school, and you're not afraid of the cold temperatures, the University of North Dakota in Grand Forks wants you on their team. The largest university in the state, UND is internationally recognized in the aviation industry for its aerospace program, which offers "the highest level of flight training," thanks to "incredible professors" who "know the industry." Other schools including the college of business and public administration, the college of engineering and mines, and the school of medicine and health sciences are praised for their "innovation and intelligence." UND also benefits from its "strong and active alumni network." Students have mixed experiences with the quality of advisement and experiences with faculty seeming to vary depending on the students' interests. "General education teachers are very hit or miss," one student says. But another offers, "Every single professor that I've had has been engaging, [and] interested in my learning...and have also given me opportunities for success by introducing me to internships or jobs that I should apply for, as well as being willing to write recommendation letters or talk during their office hours whenever possible." UND offers "great on-campus resources for its students, including "counseling, student health, LGBTQ+ office, International Center, Student Government, and *The Dakota Student,* the student newspaper." Small class sizes "make for a more personalized learning experience," and "tuition costs are still reasonable compared to other schools and states," proving "bang for your buck." And there are "numerous resources and organizations available for students on campus to help them succeed...academically, socially, and mentally"—including a "strategic plan recently implemented that focuses more on the student experience and being a leader in action."

Campus Life

Students love the "tight-knit community support," and say "everyone in Grand Forks wants the students at UND to succeed." School spirit "is very strong...which makes it extremely fun to attend basketball, football, volleyball, or hockey games." Emphasis on the hockey games: "There is nothing that brings us together more than hockey." The Ralph Engelstad Arena "nearly sells out at any home game" and "many people begin lining up in the cold as early as 8:00 A.M. on some game days." The city has a lot of outdoor skating rinks. The "greenway is great in the warmer months." The "beautiful campus" is "relatively compact in size," so traveling to and from classes is easy and "convenient." There is "support for Greek organizations and other organizations that support leadership opportunities," and the "attitude of all people, staff, and workers is always uplifting." Most students' days are "filled with studying and homework," but in between classes students visit the "local coffee shop, Archives," or visit the Wellness Center, which "is always busy, either with individual workouts, group exercise classes, intramural or pick-up games, or cooking classes."

Student Body

The "conservative" student body "is mostly comprised of Midwestern students," a "large majority from Minnesota and North Dakota," with the aviation program bringing in "a decent amount of diversity from around the U.S. and the world." Students also note the quality of their classmates: "It takes a special kind of person to be able to suffer through the long, dark, and extremely cold winters." Those who land on campus are more than "willing to lend a helping hand" and that's true "not only for the campus but for the community as well."

UNIVERSITY OF NORTH DAKOTA

Financial Aid: 701-777-1234 • E-Mail: admissions@UND.edu • Website: http://und.edu

THE PRINCETON REVIEW SAYS

Admissions

The school reports that its standardized testing policy for use in admission for Fall 2024 is Test Free. The 2024 testing policy will be permanent. The Princeton Review suggests that interested applicants consult with the school for the most up-to-date standardized testing policies. *Very important factors considered include:* academic GPA. *Important factors considered include:* rigor of secondary school record. *Other factors considered include:* recommendation(s). High school diploma is required and GED is accepted. *Academic units required:* 4 English, 3 math, 3 science, 2 science labs, 3 social studies.

Financial Aid

Students should submit: FAFSA. The Princeton Review suggests that all financial aid forms be submitted as soon as possible (see page 5 for a note on the FAFSA). *Need-based scholarships/grants offered:* College/university scholarship or grant aid from institutional funds; Federal Pell; Private scholarships; SEOG; State scholarships/grants. *Loan aid offered:* Direct PLUS loans; Direct Subsidized Loans; Direct Unsubsidized Loans; Federal Nursing Loans; State Loans. Federal Work-Study Program available. Institutional employment available.

The Inside Word

As a potential incoming student, you will find that the University of North Dakota is ready and willing to help you apply. The website has applications broken down by student type, and you'll also find admissions guidelines to help you see if you would be accepted for admission. However, the school says that everyone should apply for admission, even if you don't meet these standards, since your application will be reviewed by a committee that may make the decision based on other factors or recommend you for its LAUNCH program. If you're 25 plus years old on the first day of class OR you've completed 24 (including in progress) transferable college credits after graduating high school, you're not required to submit ACT or SAT test scores. However, if you've taken the ACT or SAT, it's highly recommended that you submit your official scores to UND for proper placement into English and math courses, as well as for scholarship purposes.

THE SCHOOL SAYS "..."

From the Admissions Office

"Founded in 1883, UND offers more than 225 fields of study, including aerospace, nursing, education, engineering, business, medicine, law, the arts and more. With so many options, you can explore all of your interests to discover your passion. You'll get the experience you need to succeed through internships, hands-on learning and real world projects, such as building a hydrogen-powered car, writing and producing a magazine, running a capitalist venture fund, or simulating a mission to Mars. And you'll graduate with the skills that will get you hired by today's employers.

"Nestled in a classic college town of 65,000, UND offers the atmosphere of a small college campus while giving you opportunities found only at large universities. You can do what you love by joining one of 250+ student organizations—ranging from Swing Dance Club to Robotics Club to the Photography Society. And, if you're up for an adventure, you can study abroad in more than 40 countries around the world.

"Like to work out? You'll be at home in one of the best campus Wellness Centers in the nation. Love sports? Whether you're an athlete or a fan, you can get in the game with our Fighting Hawks NCAA Division I athletic teams and 20+ intramural and club sports. And did we mention that our 8-time national men's hockey champions play in the finest collegiate hockey venue in the world? After all, there's a reason Grand Forks has been named as America's Best Hockey Town—five years in a row!"

SELECTIVITY

Admissions Rating	84
# of applicants	6,957
% of applicants accepted	83
% of acceptees attending	32

FIRST-YEAR PROFILE

Testing policy	Test Free
Range SAT composite	1100–1280
Range SAT EBRW	540–640
Range SAT math	550–640
Range ACT composite	20–26
# submitting SAT scores	89
% submitting SAT scores	5
# submitting ACT scores	819
% submitting ACT scores	47
Average HS GPA	3.6
% frosh submitting high school GPA	98
% graduated top 10% of class	23
% graduated top 25% of class	49
% graduated top 50% of class	78

DEADLINES

Regular	
Priority	2/1
Deadline	8/15
Notification	Rolling, 8/1
Nonfall registration?	Yes

APPLICANTS OFTEN PREFER

North Dakota State University; University of Minnesota Duluth

APPLICANTS SOMETIMES PREFER

Concordia College (Moorhead, MN); Minnesota State University Moorhead; South Dakota School of Mines and Technology; The University of South Dakota; University of Minnesota—Twin Cities

FINANCIAL FACTS

Financial Aid Rating	81
Annual in-state tuition	$9,237
Annual out-of-state tuition	$13,856
Room and board	$10,170
Required fees	$1,714
Books and supplies	$800
Average frosh need-based scholarship	$6,739
Average UG need-based scholarship	$6,407
% needy frosh rec. need-based scholarship or grant aid	88
% needy UG rec. need-based scholarship or grant aid	80
% needy frosh rec. non-need-based scholarship or grant aid	15
% needy UG rec. non-need-based scholarship or grant aid	10
% needy frosh rec. need-based self-help aid	70
% needy UG rec. need-based self-help aid	73
% frosh rec. any financial aid	92
% UG rec. any financial aid	76
% UG borrow to pay for school	71
Average cumulative indebtedness	
% frosh need fully met	47
% ugrads need fully met	37
Average % of frosh need met	52
Average % of ugrad need met	41

UNIVERSITY OF NOTRE DAME

University of Notre Dame, Notre Dame, IN 46556 • Admissions: 574-631-5000 • Fax: 574-631-8865

STUDENTS SAY " . . ."

Academics

Notre Dame has many traditions, including a "devotion to undergraduate education" you might not expect from a school with such an athletic reputation. Professors here are, by all accounts, "wonderful": "Not only are they invested in their students," they're "genuinely passionate about their fields of study," "enthusiastic and animated in lectures," and "always willing to meet outside of class to give extra help." Wary that distance might breed academic disengagement, professors ensure "large lectures are broken down into smaller discussion groups once a week to help with class material and…give the class a personal touch." For its part, "the administration tries its best to stay on top of the students' wants and needs." They make it "extremely easy to get in touch with anyone." Like the professors, administrators try to make personal connections with students. For example, "our president (a priest), as well as both of our presidents emeritus, make it a point to interact with the students in a variety of ways—teaching a class, saying mass in the dorms, etc." Overall, "while classes are difficult," "students are competitive against one another," and "it's necessary to study hard and often, there's also time to do other things."

Campus Life

Life at Notre Dame is centered around two things—"residential life" and "sports." The "dorms on campus provide the social structure" and supply undergrads with tons of opportunities to get involved and have fun. "During the school week," students "study a lot, but on the weekends everyone seems to make up for the lack of partying during the week." The school "does not have any fraternities or sororities, but campus is not dry, and drinking/partying is permitted within the residence halls." The administration reportedly tries "to keep the parties on campus due to the fact that campus is such a safe place and they truly do care about our safety." In addition to parties the dorms are really competitive in the Interhall Sport System, and "virtually every student plays some kind of sport [in] his/her residence hall." Intercollegiate sports, "are huge" (to put it mildly): "If someone is not interested in sports upon arrival, he or she will be by the time he or she leaves." To put it another way, "Everybody goes to the football games, and it's common to see 1,000 students at a home soccer game." Beyond residential life and sports, "religious activities," volunteering, "campus publications, student government, and academic clubs round out the rest of ND life."

Student Body

Undergrads at Notre Dame report "the vast majority" of their peers are "very smart" "white kids from upper- to middle-class backgrounds from all over the country, especially the Midwest and Northeast." The typical student "is a type-A personality that studies a lot, yet is athletic and involved in the community. They are usually the outstanding seniors in their high schools," the "sort of people who can talk about the BCS rankings and Derrida in the same breath." Additionally, something like "85 percent of Notre Dame students earned a varsity letter in high school." Students note that many, but not all, students are Catholic, but overall, undergrads seem to "have some sort of spirituality present in their daily lives." So far as diversity goes, ND is reported to be improving when it comes to "economic backgrounds, with the university's policy to meet all demonstrate financial need." And while students are working to help everyone fit in, they note that those who don't still "hang out in their own groups."

UNIVERSITY OF NOTRE DAME

Financial Aid: 574-631-6436 • E-Mail: admissions@nd.edu • Website: www.nd.edu

THE PRINCETON REVIEW SAYS

Admissions

The school reports that its standardized testing policy for use in admission for Fall 2024 is Test Optional. It is unknown at this time if the 2024 testing policy will be permanent. The Princeton Review suggests that interested applicants consult with the school for the most up-to-date standardized testing policies. *Very important factors considered include:* rigor of secondary school record, character/personal qualities. *Important factors considered include:* class rank, academic GPA, application essay, recommendation(s), interview, extracurricular activities, talent/ability, first generation, racial/ethnic status, volunteer work. *Other factors considered include:* standardized test scores, alumni/ae relation, religious affiliation/commitment, work experience, level of applicant's interest. High school diploma is required and GED is accepted. *Academic units required:* 4 English, 3 math, 2 science, 2 science labs, 2 foreign language, 2 history, 3 academic electives. *Academic units recommended:* 4 English, 4 math, 4 science, 2 science labs, 4 foreign language, 4 history.

Financial Aid

Students should submit: CSS/Financial Aid Profile; FAFSA; Noncustodial Profile. Priority filing deadline is 11/1. The Princeton Review suggests that all financial aid forms be submitted as soon as possible (see page 5 for a note on the FAFSA). *Need-based scholarships/grants offered:* College/university scholarship or grant aid from institutional funds; Federal Pell; Private scholarships; SEOG; State scholarships/grants. *Loan aid offered:* Direct PLUS loans; Direct Subsidized Loans; Direct Unsubsidized Loans; College/university loans from institutional funds. Admitted students will be notified of awards on a rolling basis beginning 2/15. Federal Work-Study Program available. Institutional employment available.

The Inside Word

Notre Dame is one of the most selective colleges in the country. Almost everyone who enrolls is in the top 10 percent of their graduating class and possesses test scores in the highest percentiles. But, as the student respondents suggest, strong academic ability isn't enough to get you in here. The school looks for students with other talents, and seems to have a predilection for athletic achievement. Legacy students get a leg up but are by no means assured of admission.

THE SCHOOL SAYS "..."

From the Admissions Office

"Notre Dame is a Catholic university, which means it offers unique opportunities for academic, ethical, spiritual, and social service development. The First Year of Studies program provides special assistance to our students as they make the adjustment from high school to college. The first-year curriculum includes many core requirements, while allowing students to explore several areas of possible future study. Each residence hall is home to students from all classes; most will live in the same hall for all their years on campus. An average of 93 percent of entering students will graduate within five years."

SELECTIVITY

Admissions Rating	98
# of applicants	26,509
% of applicants accepted	13
% of acceptees attending	60

FIRST-YEAR PROFILE

Testing policy	Test Optional
Range SAT EBRW	700–760
Range SAT math	720–790
Range ACT composite	32–35
# submitting SAT scores	731
% submitting SAT scores	54
# submitting ACT scores	628
% submitting ACT scores	46
% graduated top 10% of class	91
% graduated top 25% of class	97
% graduated top 50% of class	100

DEADLINES

Early action	
Deadline	11/1
Notification	12/15
Regular	
Deadline	1/1
Notification	4/1
Nonfall registration?	Yes

APPLICANTS ALSO LOOK AT

Duke University; Harvard College; Northwestern University; Princeton University; University of Pennsylvania

FINANCIAL FACTS

Financial Aid Rating	95
Annual tuition	$59,794
Room and board	$16,710
Required fees	$507
Books and supplies	$1,250
Average frosh need-based scholarship	$52,218
Average UG need-based scholarship	$50,894
% needy frosh rec. need-based scholarship or grant aid	99
% needy UG rec. need-based scholarship or grant aid	99
% needy frosh rec. non-need-based scholarship or grant aid	30
% needy UG rec. non-need-based scholarship or grant aid	28
% needy frosh rec. need-based self-help aid	79
% needy UG rec. need-based self-help aid	82
% frosh rec. any financial aid	63
% UG rec. any financial aid	75
% UG borrow to pay for school	36
Average cumulative indebtedness	$28,625
% frosh need fully met	100
% ugrads need fully met	99
Average % of frosh need met	100
Average % of ugrad need met	100

UNIVERSITY OF OKLAHOMA

660 Parrington Oval, Norman, OK 73019-0390 • Admissions: 405-325-0311 • Fax: 405-325-7124

CAMPUS LIFE

Quality of Life Rating	91
Fire Safety Rating	97
Green Rating	95
Type of school	Public
Environment	City

STUDENTS

Total undergrad enrollment	20,842
% male/female/another gender	49/51/NR
% from out of state	39
% frosh live on campus	89
% ugrads live on campus	32
# of fraternities (% join)	29 (28)
# of sororities (% join)	24 (32)
% African American	5
% Asian	7
% White	58
% Hispanic	13
% Native American	3
% Pacific Islander	<1
% Two or more races	10
% Race and/or ethnicity unknown	1
% international	3
# of countries represented	126

SURVEY SAYS . . .

Students are happy
Great library
Career services are great
Internships are widely available
School is well run
Students are friendly
Students are very religious
Students get along with local community
Students love Norman, OK
Great food on campus
Great off-campus food
Recreation facilities are great
Everyone loves the Sooners
Intramural sports are popular
Frats and sororities are popular
Theater is popular
Alumni active on campus

ACADEMICS

Academic Rating	82
% students returning for sophomore year	88
% students graduating within 4 years	53
% students graduating within 6 years	76
Calendar	Semester
Student/faculty ratio	16:1
Profs interesting rating	88
Profs accessible rating	94

Most classes have 10–19 students.
Most lab/discussion sessions have 20–29 students.

MOST POPULAR MAJORS

Zoology/Animal Biology; Psychology, General; Finance, General

STUDENTS SAY ". . ."

Academics

The University of Oklahoma (OU), located in Norman, OK, outranks all other public and private universities in National Merit Scholars, and boasts 134 undergraduate degree programs. It is an "intellectually fertile, opportunity-laden public research institution" with a "rich tradition of community" that offers "an Ivy League quality education within a public university." OU has over 30,000 students, but still manages to have a "small town feel" that is "very comfortable and welcoming." Students call OU "not just a school," but "a place to meet others in the OU family, be a part of long-standing traditions," and "receive a quality education from challenging courses." Home of the Sooners football team, which won seven national championships, it's no wonder OU's school spirit is strong. The University also holds 39 overall NCAA National Championships, and a host of other athletic championships and accolades. Though OU "might be known for its athletic program," students say "academics don't suffer from it." OU has "fantastic," "engaging," "encouraging" "professors that truly care for the well-being of the students." "The professors here don't feel like your average teachers," notes a Psychology and Economics major, "but exceptional instructors who relate on a personal basis and actually help you comprehend the material." OU gives "tons of opportunities to its students," including "jobs, networking, study abroad" programs and more. The university combines "tradition with advancement to encourage you to become the best version of yourself possible" says an Elementary Education major. Student after student noted the sense of "family" everyone has at OU, as well as the importance of "tradition, unity, and togetherness."

Campus Life

OU is home to a host of strong athletic teams and students frequent "football games and other athletic events for fun." During the fall, "most students attend at least one football game." "Greek life" is also "very important." Some complain that "if you're not in a fraternity or sorority, there's not a lot to do on campus on the weekends." Others, though, say "there are many opportunities to be involved on campus," including "free movie nights and pool." There is always "something going on, and whether it be a sports event or a fine arts event, the quality is always excellent." Students can visit the world-renowned art in the Fred Jones Jr. Museum of Art or the 26-foot tall dinosaur (an Apatosaurus!) at OU's Sam Noble Museum of Natural History. There is also "Campus Corner," which has "restaurants, bars and boutiques." And it's also "an easy drive to the movies, a nice restaurant, or night life." Students note that the "social atmosphere is very alive most of the time." But it's not all about football and parties. "People are very considerate of one another and make efforts to support each other during rough times," notes a Psychology and Mathematics major. That extends beyond campus as well, and students take advantage of "all kinds of volunteering opportunities." In fact, "every year everyone on campus drops what they're doing for one weekend to spend all day volunteering in the local Norman and Oklahoma City communities." Students value their commitment to community service. "We genuinely care for one another and are very passionate about the university," says one student. "I cannot imagine there being a happier campus than OU anywhere in the country." Or, as another says: "Life is great."

Student Body

A typical OU student is "friendly," "down to earth," "aware," and "motivated." They have a "nice balance" between their "academic and social lives" and are committed to "volunteering," "sports" and "Greek life." Many students join a fraternity or sorority. Incoming students are most likely to "fit in" by "being involved on campus" and joining "lots of organizations." Students describe their classmates as primarily "white, upper-middle class, and Christian," but "with a broad mix of international and minority students."

UNIVERSITY OF OKLAHOMA

Financial Aid: 405-325-5505 • E-Mail: admissions@ou.edu • Website: www.ou.edu

THE PRINCETON REVIEW SAYS

Admissions

The school reports that its standardized testing policy for use in admission for Fall 2024 is Test Optional. The 2024 testing policy will be temporary. The Princeton Review suggests that interested applicants consult with the school for the most up-to-date standardized testing policies. *Very important factors considered include:* rigor of secondary school record, academic GPA, standardized test scores. *Important factors considered include:* class rank, application essay, recommendation(s). *Other factors considered include:* interview, extracurricular activities, talent/ability, character/personal qualities, first generation, alumni/ae relation, geographical residence, state residency, volunteer work, work experience, level of applicant's interest. High school diploma is required and GED is accepted. *Academic units required:* 4 English, 3 math, 3 science, 3 science labs, 1 social studies, 2 history, 2 academic electives. *Academic units recommended:* 4 math, 4 science, 2 foreign language, 1 computer science.

Financial Aid

Students should submit: FAFSA. Priority filing deadline is 3/1. The Princeton Review suggests that all financial aid forms be submitted as soon as possible (see page 5 for a note on the FAFSA). *Need-based scholarships/grants offered:* College/university scholarship or grant aid from institutional funds; Federal Pell; Private scholarships; SEOG; State scholarships/grants; United Negro College Fund. *Loan aid offered:* Direct PLUS loans; Direct Subsidized Loans; Direct Unsubsidized Loans; College/university loans from institutional funds. Admitted students will be notified of awards on a rolling basis beginning 12/15. Federal Work-Study Program available. Institutional employment available.

The Inside Word

Accepted students at OU graduated from high school with an average GPA of 3.7. But while academic grades and standardized test scores (if submitted) are very important to the admissions process at OU, they also place importance on community service, leadership, and extracurricular activities. In fact, the applicant's "engagement" accounts for one-quarter of their decision.

THE SCHOOL SAYS "..."

From the Admissions Office

"Ask yourself some significant questions. What are your ambitions, goals, and dreams? Do you desire opportunity, and are you ready to accept challenge? What do you hope to gain from your educational experience? Are you looking for a university that will provide you with the tools, resources, and motivation to convert ambitions, opportunities, and challenges into meaningful achievement? To effectively answer these questions you must carefully seek out your options, look for direction, and make the right choice. The University of Oklahoma combines a unique mixture of academic excellence, varied social cultures, and a variety of campus activities to make your educational experience complete. At OU, comprehensive learning is our goal for your life. Not only do you receive a valuable classroom learning experience, but OU is also one of the finest research institutions in the United States. This allows OU students the opportunity to be a part of technology in progress. It's not just learning, it's discovery, invention, and dynamic creativity, a hands-on experience that allows you to be on the cutting edge of knowledge. Make the right choice and consider the University of Oklahoma!"

SELECTIVITY

Admissions Rating	87
# of applicants	21,548
% of applicants accepted	73
% of acceptees attending	30
# offered a place on the wait list	2,646
% accepting a place on wait list	100
% admitted from wait list	6

FIRST-YEAR PROFILE

Testing policy	Test Optional
Range SAT composite	1130–1320
Range SAT EBRW	570–670
Range SAT math	560–660
Range ACT composite	23–29
# submitting SAT scores	1,233
% submitting SAT scores	34
# submitting ACT scores	2,430
% submitting ACT scores	66
Average HS GPA	3.7
% frosh submitting high school GPA	100
% graduated top 10% of class	33
% graduated top 25% of class	62
% graduated top 50% of class	91

DEADLINES

Early action	
Deadline	11/1
Regular	
Priority	11/1
Deadline	2/1
Notification	Rolling, 9/1
Nonfall registration?	Yes

APPLICANTS ALSO LOOK AT

Baylor University; Oklahoma State University; Southern Methodist University; Texas A&M University—College Station; Texas Christian University; Texas Tech University; The University of Alabama—Tuscaloosa; The University of Texas at Austin; University of Ar

FINANCIAL FACTS

Financial Aid Rating	86
Annual in-state tuition	$4,920
Annual out-of-state tuition	$21,488
Room and board	$12,200
Required fees	$4,392
Books and supplies	$800
Average frosh need-based scholarship	$3,759
Average UG need-based scholarship	$3,596
% needy frosh rec. need-based scholarship or grant aid	38
% needy UG rec. need-based scholarship or grant aid	42
% needy frosh rec. non-need-based scholarship or grant aid	66
% needy UG rec. non-need-based scholarship or grant aid	52
% needy frosh rec. need-based self-help aid	59
% needy UG rec. need-based self-help aid	59
% frosh rec. any financial aid	90
% UG rec. any financial aid	79
% UG borrow to pay for school	45
Average cumulative indebtedness	$31,768
% frosh need fully met	79
% ugrads need fully met	83
Average % of frosh need met	80
Average % of ugrad need met	84

UNIVERSITY OF OREGON

1226 University of Oregon, Eugene, OR 97403-1226 • Admissions: 541-346-1000 • Fax: 541-346-5815

CAMPUS LIFE

Quality of Life Rating	78
Fire Safety Rating	93
Green Rating	98
Type of school	Public
Environment	City

STUDENTS

Total undergrad enrollment	19,443
% male/female/another gender	44/55/<1
% from out of state	49
% frosh live on campus	93
% ugrads live on campus	29
# of fraternities (% join)	18 (16)
# of sororities (% join)	15 (17)
% African American	3
% Asian	7
% White	62
% Hispanic	15
% Native American	<1
% Pacific Islander	<1
% Two or more races	9
% Race and/or ethnicity unknown	1
% international	2
# of countries represented	61

SURVEY SAYS . . .

Students environmentally aware
Recreation facilities are great
Everyone loves the Ducks

ACADEMICS

Academic Rating	78
% students returning for sophomore year	86
% students graduating within 4 years	61
% students graduating within 6 years	73
Calendar	Quarter
Student/faculty ratio	19:1
Profs interesting rating	86
Profs accessible rating	90

Most classes have 10–19 students.
Most lab/discussion sessions have
  20–29 students.

MOST POPULAR MAJORS

Physiology, General; Psychology, General;
Business/Commerce, General

STUDENTS SAY "..."

Academics

If the University of Oregon excels at anything, it is in providing students with a wealth of academic opportunities. Indeed, students feel it is "a perfect place for someone seeking a well-rounded liberal arts secondary education," a school that has "all of the creative perks of a small learning environment with all of the excitement of a big school." Sports are a big deal here, "but there is also an emphasis on rigorous academics." Business, architecture, ecology, journalism, international studies, and political science all win accolades. If there is a chink in UO's armor, it is the "inability for some students to get the classes they need." With such a wide array of fields of study available, some students find that essential classes are only available at difficult hours. Students also give mixed grades to the professors, who range from "remarkable" and "really passionate" educators who "are invested in their students" to a few "quite terrible" teachers who "are not dedicated to the students." Those attending UO should be self-motivating, since "the weight falls on the students to create relationships with professors." It is worth the effort, though, as "doing so can open many doors." When it all clicks—and many students report that once they were focused on their major things began to fall into place—students have enjoyed an education that "deeply altered the way I see things."

Campus Life

Eugene, Oregon is not going to give the nation's big cities a run for their money, but students here like it that way. When the weather is nice, students can be found outside "playing Frisbee, football, soccer, or just lounging in the grass," and when the rainy weather of the Pacific Northwest forces people indoors, "you find students in coffee shops on campus and off, studying, visiting, or relaxing." Music, hiking, and other outdoor activities are also popular pastimes. Indeed, the scenery proves a draw for many. "The coast is an hour away, hiking trails and mountains are everywhere, and you can even drive or take a bus up to Portland to get some city life." Greek life is growing on campus but does not dominate the school, and despite prohibitions on drinking in the dorms, students manage it anyway. With the gorgeous scenery and wealth of things to do, it's no wonder students think that "life at school is pretty great."

Student Body

What kind of student attends the University of Oregon? The typical answer is that there is no typical answer. "You have your hipsters, hippies, jocks, athletes, drunks, nerds, and every other cliché you can think of"—students from "dreadlocked hippies to straight-laced conservatives, and everything else in between." That diversity in the student body means, "if you're willing to put forth any sort of effort into meeting people, you'll find a group" who will click with you. "No matter who you are," another student agrees, "there are programs and clubs on campus to take part in." Greek or non-Greek does make a difference. Students say there is a "huge divide between Greek life and the rest of the student body." But overall, University of Oregon students are "friendly, open-minded, and generally environmentally/socially conscious." In other words, "there are all sorts of students at Oregon, and it is pretty diverse."

UNIVERSITY OF OREGON

Financial Aid: 541-346-3221 • E-Mail: admissions@uoregon.edu • Website: www.uoregon.edu

THE PRINCETON REVIEW SAYS

Admissions

The school reports that its standardized testing policy for use in admission for Fall 2024 is Test Optional. The 2024 testing policy will be permanent. The Princeton Review suggests that interested applicants consult with the school for the most up-to-date standardized testing policies. *Very important factors considered include:* rigor of secondary school record, academic GPA. *Important factors considered include:* application essay. *Other factors considered include:* class rank, standardized test scores, recommendation(s), extracurricular activities, talent/ability, character/personal qualities, first generation, geographical residence, state residency, racial/ethnic status, volunteer work, work experience. High school diploma is required and GED is accepted. *Academic units required:* 4 English, 3 math, 3 science, 2 foreign language, 3 social studies. *Academic units recommended:* 1 science lab.

Financial Aid

Students should submit: FAFSA. Priority filing deadline is 3/1. The Princeton Review suggests that all financial aid forms be submitted as soon as possible (see page 5 for a note on the FAFSA). *Need-based scholarships/grants offered:* College/university scholarship or grant aid from institutional funds; Federal Pell; Private scholarships; SEOG; State scholarships/grants. *Loan aid offered:* Direct PLUS loans; Direct Subsidized Loans; Direct Unsubsidized Loans. Admitted students will be notified of awards on a rolling basis beginning 4/1. Federal Work-Study Program available. Institutional employment available.

The Inside Word

Your ticket to UO is a strong GPA in challenging college prep courses, although you may consider optionally submitting your standardized test scores if they're particularly good. If your high school grades dropped due to personal circumstances, or indicate an upward trajectory due to personal growth, consider addressing that in your personal statement.

THE SCHOOL SAYS "..."

From the Admissions Office

"At the UO, you'll be part of a community dedicated to making a difference in the world and you'll find the inspiration and resources you'll need to succeed. You'll attend classes alongside students from all fifty states and more than 90 countries, and learn from people whose cultural, ethnic, political, and religious perspectives differ from your own. You'll have opportunities to participate in cutting-edge research and study with renowned faculty. You'll graduate with the critical thinking skills and professional preparation necessary to succeed in an increasingly global job market. Set in a 295-acre arboretum, the UO is literally green. Academic and outdoor programs will bring you into forests, mountains, rivers, and lakes. The state-of-the-art Lewis Integrative Science Building earned a 'platinum' certification from the U.S. Green Building Council's Leadership in Energy and Environmental Design program; the new student union and recreation center are both on track for the same distinction. You'll have access to nationally recognized programs in sustainable architecture, psychology, geography, economics, education, and business. With a student/teacher ratio of nineteen to one and median class size of 20 students, you'll find a campus that meets your individual needs. You'll also have the benefits of a premier research university: more than 300 academic programs, excellent academic facilities, and more than 250 student organizations. To be eligible for freshman admission, submit your official high school transcript, graduate from an accredited high school, and write an essay, SAT or ACT scores are optional, and alternative admission students are welcome (GED, homeschooled, etc.)."

SELECTIVITY

Admissions Rating	84
# of applicants	37,154
% of applicants accepted	86
% of acceptees attending	17
# offered a place on the wait list	1,111
% accepting a place on wait list	39
% admitted from wait list	54

FIRST-YEAR PROFILE

Testing policy	Test Optional
Range SAT composite	1140–1370
Range SAT EBRW	580–690
Range SAT math	560–680
Range ACT composite	24–30
# submitting SAT scores	564
% submitting SAT scores	11
# submitting ACT scores	332
% submitting ACT scores	6
Average HS GPA	3.8
% frosh submitting high school GPA	100

DEADLINES

Early action	
Deadline	11/1
Notification	12/15
Regular	
Deadline	1/15
Notification	4/1
Nonfall registration?	Yes

FINANCIAL FACTS

Financial Aid Rating	77
Annual in-state tuition	$11,674
Annual in-state tuition (first-year)	$12,512
Annual out-of-state tuition	$37,363
Annual out-of-state tuition (first-year)	$39,158
Room and board	$14,640
Required fees	$2,438
Required fees (first-year)	$2,542
Books and supplies	$1,227
Average frosh need-based scholarship	$11,137
Average UG need-based scholarship	$11,207
% needy frosh rec. need-based scholarship or grant aid	89
% needy UG rec. need-based scholarship or grant aid	82
% needy frosh rec. non-need-based scholarship or grant aid	52
% needy UG rec. non-need-based scholarship or grant aid	29
% needy frosh rec. need-based self-help aid	79
% needy UG rec. need-based self-help aid	77
% frosh rec. any financial aid	71
% UG rec. any financial aid	68
% UG borrow to pay for school	42
Average cumulative indebtedness	$24,823
% frosh need fully met	7
% ugrads need fully met	6
Average % of frosh need met	47
Average % of ugrad need met	51

UNIVERSITY OF PENNSYLVANIA

1 College Hall, Room 100, Philadelphia, PA 19104-6228 • Admissions: 215-898-5000 • Fax: 215-898-7507

CAMPUS LIFE

Quality of Life Rating	81
Fire Safety Rating	83
Green Rating	98
Type of school	Private
Affiliation	No Affiliation
Environment	Metropolis

STUDENTS

Total undergrad enrollment	9,760
% male/female	46/54
% from out of state	81
% frosh live on campus	100
% ugrads live on campus	60
# of fraternities (% join)	36 (20)
# of sororities (% join)	13 (21)
% African American	8
% Asian	28
% White	31
% Hispanic	10
% Native American	<1
% Pacific Islander	<1
% Two or more races	5
% Race and/or ethnicity unknown	5
% international	13
# of countries represented	126

SURVEY SAYS . . .

Internships are widely available
Great financial aid
Campus newspaper is popular
Alumni active on campus

ACADEMICS

Academic Rating	86
% students returning for sophomore year	98
% students graduating within 4 years	88
% students graduating within 6 years	96
Calendar	Semester
Student/faculty ratio	8:1
Profs interesting rating	85
Profs accessible rating	90
Most classes have 10–19 students.	

MOST POPULAR MAJORS

Economics, General; Registered Nursing/
Registered Nurse; Finance, General

STUDENTS SAY ". . ."

Academics

At the University of Pennsylvania, students share an intellectual curiosity and top-notch resources but don't "buy into the stigma of being an Ivy League school." Students here are "very passionate about what they do outside the classroom" and the "flexible core requirements." The university is composed of four undergraduate schools (and "a library for pretty much any topic"). "You can take courses in any of the schools, including graduate-level courses." Luckily, there's a vast variety of disciplines available to students: "I can take a course in old Icelandic and even another one about the politics of food," says a student. Wharton, Penn's highly regarded, "highly competitive undergraduate business school" attracts "career-oriented" students who don't mind a "strenuous course load." There are "more than enough" resources, funding, and opportunity here for any student to take advantage of, and "Penn encourages students to truly take advantage of it all!" Professors can "sometimes seem to be caught up more in their research than their classes," but all "are incredibly well-versed in their subject (as well as their audience)." If you're willing to put in the time and effort, your professors "will be happy to reciprocate." In general, the instructors here are "very challenging academically" and are "always willing to offer their more than relevant life experience in class discussion."

Campus Life

Penn students don't mind getting into intellectual conversations during dinner—"Politics and religion come up often, but so does baseball, types of wine, and restaurants"—but some "partying is a much higher priority here than it is at other Ivy League schools." "Campus is split between the downtown club scene and the frat/bar scene, depending on your preference." However, when it comes down to midterms and finals, "people get really serious and…buckle down and study." There's easy access to downtown Philadelphia, yet "still the comfortable feeling of having our own campus," giving students plenty of access to restaurants (BYO restaurants in Philly are "a huge hit"), shopping, concerts, and sports games, as well as plain old "hanging out with hallmates playing Mario Kart." "It's the perfect mix between an urban setting a traditional college campus." The school provides plenty of guest speakers, cultural events, clubs, and organizations for students to channel their energies (all of which "makes the campus feel smaller"), and seniors can even attend "Feb Club" in the month of February, which is essentially an event every night. The weekend buses to/from New York and D.C. "are always packed." It's a busy life at Penn, and "people are constantly trying to think about how they can balance getting good grades academically and their weekend plans."

Student Body

This "determined" bunch "is either focused on one specific interest, or very well-rounded." Pretty much everyone "was an overachiever ('that kid') in high school," and some students "are off-the-charts brilliant," making everyone here "sort of fascinated by everyone else." Everyone has "a strong sense of personal style and his or her own credo," but no group deviates too far from the more mainstream stereotypes. There's a definite lack of "emos" and hippies. There's "the career-driven Wharton kid who will stab you in the back to get your interview slot" and "the nursing kid who's practically nonexistent," but on the whole, there's tremendous school diversity, with "people from all over the world of all kinds of experiences of all perspectives."

UNIVERSITY OF PENNSYLVANIA

Financial Aid: 215-898-1988 • E-Mail: info@admissions.upenn.edu • Website: www.upenn.edu

THE PRINCETON REVIEW SAYS

Admissions

The school reports that its standardized testing policy for use in admission for Fall 2024 is Test Optional. It is unknown at this time if the 2024 testing policy will be permanent. The Princeton Review suggests that interested applicants consult with the school for the most up-to-date standardized testing policies. *Very important factors considered include:* rigor of secondary school record, academic GPA, standardized test scores, application essay, recommendation(s), character/personal qualities. *Important factors considered include:* class rank, interview, extracurricular activities, talent/ability. *Other factors considered include:* first generation, alumni/ae relation, geographical residence, state residency, racial/ethnic status, volunteer work, work experience, level of applicant's interest. High school diploma or equivalent is not required. *Academic units recommended:* 4 English, 4 math, 3 science, 3 science labs, 4 foreign language, 2 social studies, 3 history.

Financial Aid

Students should submit: Business/Farm Supplement; CSS/Financial Aid Profile; FAFSA; Institution's own financial aid form; Noncustodial Profile. Priority filing deadline is 2/15. The Princeton Review suggests that all financial aid forms be submitted as soon as possible (see page 5 for a note on the FAFSA). *Need-based scholarships/grants offered:* College/university scholarship or grant aid from institutional funds; Federal Pell; Private scholarships; SEOG; State scholarships/grants. *Loan aid offered:* Direct PLUS loans; Direct Subsidized Loans; Direct Unsubsidized Loans; College/university loans from institutional funds; Federal Nursing Loans. Admitted students will be notified of awards on or about 4/1. Federal Work-Study Program available. Institutional employment available.

The Inside Word

The competition in the applicant pool is formidable. Applicants can safely assume that they need to be one of the strongest students in their graduating class in order to be successful.

THE SCHOOL SAYS "..."

From the Admissions Office

"Founded by Benjamin Franklin in 1740 to push the frontiers of knowledge and to benefit society, Penn continues to nurture a sense of public mindedness in its students, inspiring them to make vital contributions as they become engaged citizens in an evolving world. Penn's students and faculty work toward the shared goal of enacting change by questioning, thinking, and doing—often across traditional academic disciplines. The integration of knowledge and learning spans four undergraduate schools: the College of Arts & Sciences, the School of Engineering & Applied Science, the Wharton School of Business, and the School of Nursing. Penn offers more than ninety majors, eighty minors, and the ability to earn more than one degree in four years.

"The Penn community thrives on the open exchange of ideas and shared learning experiences, made possible by the faculty and students of all four undergraduate and twelve graduate schools who coexist and collaborate on one beautiful 300 acre campus in Philadelphia. Students regularly conduct research with faculty and actively participate in over 500 clubs and organizations. Education through engagement is made possible by Penn's extensive partnerships around the world and close to our Philadelphia campus, ranging from over 150 Academically-Based Community Service courses to internships in twenty-two foreign countries.

"Penn understands that the best minds should have access to the finest education, regardless of their families' ability to pay. To achieve this, Penn practices need-blind admissions for applicants who are citizens and permanent residents of the United States, Canada, and Mexico, meets 100 percent of demonstrated financial need, and provides an all-grant aid package for all undergraduates receiving financial aid. Our goal is to allow students to pursue their aspirations without assuming a burden of debt."

SELECTIVITY

Admissions Rating	99
# of applicants	54,588
% of applicants accepted	7
% of acceptees attending	68
# offered a place on the wait list	3,351
% accepting a place on wait list	75
% admitted from wait list	6

FIRST-YEAR PROFILE

Testing policy	Test Optional
Range SAT EBRW	730–770
Range SAT math	770–800
Range ACT composite	34–35
# submitting SAT scores	1,153
% submitting SAT scores	48
# submitting ACT scores	545
% submitting ACT scores	23
Average HS GPA	3.0
% frosh submitting high school GPA	96
% graduated top 10% of class	93
% graduated top 25% of class	98
% graduated top 50% of class	100

DEADLINES

Early decision	
Deadline	11/1
Notification	12/15
Regular	
Deadline	1/5
Notification	Rolling, 4/1
Nonfall registration?	No

FINANCIAL FACTS

Financial Aid Rating	96
Annual tuition	$58,620
Room and board	$18,496
Required fees	$7,484
Books and supplies	$1,358
Average frosh need-based scholarship	$59,883
Average UG need-based scholarship	$58,232
% needy frosh rec. need-based scholarship or grant aid	99
% needy UG rec. need-based scholarship or grant aid	99
% needy frosh rec. non-need-based scholarship or grant aid	0
% needy UG rec. non-need-based scholarship or grant aid	0
% needy frosh rec. need-based self-help aid	100
% needy UG rec. need-based self-help aid	100
% UG borrow to pay for school	18
Average cumulative indebtedness	$27,705
% frosh need fully met	100
% ugrads need fully met	100
Average % of frosh need met	100
Average % of ugrad need met	100

UNIVERSITY OF PITTSBURGH—PITTSBURGH CAMPUS

4200 Fifth Avenue, Pittsburgh, PA 15260 • Admissions: 412-624-4141 • Fax: 412-624-4138

CAMPUS LIFE

Quality of Life Rating	85
Fire Safety Rating	90
Green Rating	94
Type of school	Public
Environment	Metropolis

STUDENTS

Total undergrad enrollment	19,803
% male/female/another gender	43/57/NR
% from out of state	36
% frosh live on campus	96
% ugrads live on campus	42
# of fraternities (% join)	25 (11)
# of sororities (% join)	20 (14)
% African American	5
% Asian	14
% White	63
% Hispanic	7
% Native American	<1
% Pacific Islander	<1
% Two or more races	5
% Race and/or ethnicity unknown	2
% international	5
# of countries represented	56

SURVEY SAYS . . .

Students are happy
Lab facilities are great
Students love Pittsburgh, PA
Everyone loves the Panthers
Great off-campus food

ACADEMICS

Academic Rating	79
% students returning for sophomore year	93
% students graduating within 4 years	69
% students graduating within 6 years	84
Calendar	Semester
Student/faculty ratio	13:1
Profs interesting rating	84
Profs accessible rating	88

Most classes have 10–19 students.
Most lab/discussion sessions have 20–29 students.

MOST POPULAR MAJORS

Research and Experimental Psychology, Other; Registered Nursing/Registered Nurse; Biology/Biological Sciences, General

STUDENTS SAY ". . ."

Academics

There's a good reason students clamor to attend the University of Pittsburgh every year. After all, the school provides "an amazing balance between an urban and traditional college experience," along with a "large student body [that manages to] feel small and super connected." It's also an institution teeming with resources and opportunities, from scholarships and study abroad to internships and undergraduate research. Student success is a priority, and undergrads have easy access to both career development assistance and tutoring services.

When it comes to academics, some students suggest that there's "a strong lean toward the STEM fields as it is a research university with a medical school." However, others are quick to highlight the sheer breadth of courses available, "including the history of jazz, love in France, the origins of fashion, Led Zeppelin, and vampires." Regardless of the class or department, students can expect challenging coursework that will prepare them for their career paths. Much of this can be attributed to "knowledgeable" and "engaging" professors who "know [their] material very well." And plenty praise their instructors for their accessibility, noting that they truly "make an effort to get to know their students." As this impressed undergrad sums up, "almost every single one of my professors across all departments has bent over backward to satisfy their students."

Campus Life

There is definitely life beyond the classroom at Pitt. To begin with, the university "is always hosting some form of campus-wide program to motivate student engagement." This can be anything from various dances or bingo nights to flower arranging classes. Additionally, Pitt students are an active lot, and the school's numerous club sports and intramural leagues tend to draw lots of participants because there are so many options. Students can find everything from club figure skating to volleyball; there's even a recreational climbing team and a Quidditch team. Don't sweat it if you're not into athletics. Pitt also sponsors and organizes plenty of programs such as movie screenings, open mic nights, and art workshops throughout the year.

Students note that there's also "a very healthy…Greek [scene] here" for those interested, but there are many other social opportunities too. Finally, undergrads love to venture beyond the confines of the campus and explore the city of Pittsburgh. This is easy to do since students can ride the Port Authority buses for free. Therefore, it's common to find students heading to the city to try a new restaurant, go shopping, or visit a museum.

Student Body

Given that it's a large public university, it shouldn't be too surprising to learn that Pitt has a "student body that's diverse." Indeed, the school is a "melting pot of every different type of student you can find." Though some do argue that it can often feel like most undergraduates hail "from PA, NY, NJ, and OH," regardless of where they're from, Pitt students manage to foster "a very encouraging community where everyone wants each other to succeed." Another undergrad wholeheartedly agrees, adding, "I have been able to meet a lot of incredibly supportive people and surround myself with exceptional student leaders that inspire me to be a better student, friend, and person."

Many students also bond over the fact that they're "academically driven" and "enjoy learning." Additionally, the majority seem to identify as "very socially and politically progressive." And nearly all of them seem to have tons of "pride in their university." We'll give the last word to this undergrad who proudly sums up, "My peers are the smartest, kindest, involved, and motivated people I've ever met, and I have all the faith in the world that they will make the world a better place."

UNIVERSITY OF PITTSBURGH—PITTSBURGH CAMPUS

Financial Aid: 412-624-7488 • E-Mail: pitt.admissions@pitt.edu • Website: www.pitt.edu

THE PRINCETON REVIEW SAYS

Admissions

The school reports that its standardized testing policy for use in admission for Fall 2024 is Test Optional. The test optional program has been extended through Fall 2025. The Princeton Review suggests that interested applicants consult with the school for the most up-to-date standardized testing policies. *Very important factors considered include:* rigor of secondary school record, academic GPA, application essay. *Important factors considered include:* talent/ability, character/personal qualities, volunteer work, work experience, level of applicant's interest. *Other factors considered include:* class rank, standardized test scores, recommendation(s), extracurricular activities, first generation, geographical residence, state residency, religious affiliation/commitment, racial/ethnic status. High school diploma is required and GED is accepted. *Academic units required:* 4 English, 3 math, 3 science, 2 foreign language, 2 social studies, 2 history, 3 academic electives. *Academic units recommended:* 3 foreign language, 3 social studies, 3 history, 5 academic electives.

Financial Aid

Students should submit: FAFSA; State aid form. The Princeton Review suggests that all financial aid forms be submitted as soon as possible (see page 5 for a note on the FAFSA). *Need-based scholarships/grants offered:* College/university scholarship or grant aid from institutional funds; Federal Pell; Private scholarships; SEOG; State scholarships/grants. *Loan aid offered:* Direct PLUS loans; Direct Subsidized Loans; Direct Unsubsidized Loans; College/university loans from institutional funds; Federal Nursing Loans. Admitted students will be notified of awards on a rolling basis. Federal Work-Study Program available. Institutional employment available.

The Inside Word

University of Pittsburgh operates on a rolling admission policy and although there is no specific deadline to apply for admission, your chances are better if you apply on the earlier side. Pitt reviews applications for the School of Medicine Guaranteed Admissions Application through November 1, and the Academic Scholarships Priority Review Application through December 1. Pitt offers extensive need- and merit-based financial aid, including the prestigious Chancellor's Scholarship. While SAT/ACT scores and the Short Answer Questions section of the Pitt application is optional, both are highly recommended.

THE SCHOOL SAYS "..."

From the Admissions Office

"The University of Pittsburgh, a public research university, is a member of the Association of American Universities. Home to sixteen undergraduate, graduate, and professional schools, including an internationally renowned health sciences educational and research complex, Pitt is also affiliated with the University of Pittsburgh Medical Center. Its five-campus system offers more than 480 degree programs, and awards academic merit scholarships and guaranteed admission to graduate and professional programs. Pitt faculty have pioneered major medical advances including the Salk polio vaccine, multiple-organ transplantation, and CPR. Pitt alumni have won the Nobel Peace prize, the Nobel Prize in Medicine, the Pulitzer Prize, the National Medal of Science, Olympic gold medals, Academy Awards, and Super Bowl championships. University Honors College students have a proven track record of earning prestigious honors including Rhodes, Marshall, Goldwater, Truman, Udall Scholarships, Humanity in Action Scholarship, as well as a Gates Cambridge Scholarship; Pitt educates the whole student through a unique Outside the Classroom Curriculum program that helps students develop holistically; University Center for International Studies certificate programs; and Engineering Co-Op program; study abroad just about anywhere in the world; and more. There are 694 student organizations and student-athletes participate in Division I college athletics, supported by one of the most recognizable student-led fan bases in the nation. Encouraging students to take advantage of the city as their campus, Pitt grants fare-free access to city buses and discounted tickets to cultural events, opening them to the full experiences of a city that has been cited as the most livable in the U.S."

SELECTIVITY

Admissions Rating	92
# of applicants	53,072
% of applicants accepted	49
# offered a place on the wait list	6,905
% accepting a place on wait list	55
% admitted from wait list	44

FIRST-YEAR PROFILE

Testing policy	Test Optional
Range SAT EBRW	640–720
Range SAT math	640–750
Range ACT composite	29–33
# submitting SAT scores	2,072
% submitting SAT scores	47
# submitting ACT scores	689
% submitting ACT scores	16
Average HS GPA	4.2
% frosh submitting high school GPA	100
% graduated top 10% of class	56
% graduated top 25% of class	89
% graduated top 50% of class	99

DEADLINES

Regular	
Notification	Rolling, 9/1
Nonfall registration?	Yes

APPLICANTS OFTEN PREFER
Boston University; Carnegie Mellon University; New York University; University of Michigan—Ann Arbor; University of Pennsylvania; University of Virginia

APPLICANTS SOMETIMES PREFER
Case Western Reserve University; Northeastern University; Penn State University Park; Rochester Institute of Technology; Rutgers University–Camden; Syracuse University; Temple University; The Ohio State University—Columbus; University of Delaware; University Maryland—College Park; Virginia Tech

APPLICANTS RARELY PREFER
Drexel University

FINANCIAL FACTS

Financial Aid Rating	77
Annual in-state tuition	$19,760
Annual out-of-state tuition	$36,000
Room and board	$12,360
Required fees	$1,320
Books and supplies	$716
Average frosh need-based scholarship	$15,557
Average UG need-based scholarship	$14,700
% needy frosh rec. need-based scholarship or grant aid	81
% needy UG rec. need-based scholarship or grant aid	78
% needy frosh rec. non-need-based scholarship or grant aid	9
% needy UG rec. non-need-based scholarship or grant aid	8
% needy frosh rec. need-based self-help aid	72
% needy UG rec. need-based self-help aid	72
% frosh rec. any financial aid	62
% UG rec. any financial aid	53
% UG borrow to pay for school	59
Average cumulative indebtedness	$38,460
% frosh need fully met	9
% ugrads need fully met	9
Average % of frosh need met	56
Average % of ugrad need met	56

UNIVERSITY OF PORTLAND

5000 N. Willamette Boulevard, Portland, OR 97203 • Admissions: 503-943-7147

CAMPUS LIFE

Quality of Life Rating	84
Fire Safety Rating	60*
Green Rating	60*
Type of school	Private
Affiliation	Roman Catholic
Environment	Metropolis

STUDENTS

Total undergrad enrollment	3,352
% male/female/another gender	36/64/NR
% from out of state	70
% frosh live on campus	87
% ugrads live on campus	46
# of fraternities	0
# of sororities	0
% African American	2
% Asian	20
% White	45
% Hispanic	17
% Native American	<1
% Pacific Islander	1
% Two or more races	10
% Race and/or ethnicity unknown	1
% international	3
# of countries represented	38

SURVEY SAYS . . .

Great library
Students are happy
Student love Portland, OR
Great off-campus food
Easy to get around campus

ACADEMICS

Academic Rating	82
% students returning for sophomore year	86
% students graduating within 4 years	70
% students graduating within 6 years	79
Calendar	Semester
Student/faculty ratio	11:1
Profs interesting rating	90
Profs accessible rating	93

Most classes have 20–29 students.
Most lab/discussion sessions have 10–19 students.

MOST POPULAR MAJORS

Registered Nursing, Nursing Administration, Nursing Research and Clinical Nursing; Biology/Biological Sciences, General; Psychology, General

STUDENTS SAY "..."

Academics

Students can't stop raving about the quality of professors at the University of Portland: "phenomenal—no question about it," puts one, while another elaborates that students are "always able to get something out of every lecture" because of how "clear, brilliant, and genuinely enjoyable" the teachers are. This boils down to two things: First, the smaller class sizes mean establish a "super strong community" in which "the professors get the chance to get to know each and every one of their students personally and are able to help them in a way that is customized to them." Second, the faculty "are all incredibly knowledgeable and interested in both the course content and their students." As an education major puts it about their department, having professors who "were teachers themselves" is a huge perk that makes this undergrad "feel very confident about my ability to find a teaching job and thrive in my own classroom." Instructors also don't hesitate to take learning off campus. One senior boasts that as part of their capstone class they are "part of a racing team where we are developing an electric go-kart to race in an upcoming collegiate competition."

It seems that at UP, students do indeed go up, up, and away, with business students emphasizing the school's "connections at Nike, Adidas, Intel, and most companies based in Portland." Others value the "etiquette dinner for business students to network with alumni and learn proper manners." The University of Portland also boasts a highly valued nursing program. "I'm very thankful and grateful for the professors I've had during my college experience," says one nursing student, "I feel better prepared for the beginning of my post-grad life working as an RN thanks to them."

Campus Life

Affectionately known as "The Bluff," the UP campus offers a lifestyle "like no other." Dorms offer a strong "'lobby culture' so there's always people in the lobby doing homework, or playing a game with a friend, or just relaxing." There's an equally strong religious culture—true to the school's Holy Cross roots—in that each dorm has its own chapel. "There is always a way to grow stronger in your faith here." And while students emphasize all the fun there is to be had with sports and dances and the weekly Pilots After Dark pub-style event ("Sometimes there is trivia, drag performances, [or] seasonal activities"), UP is "overall not a party school." Instead of discussing drinking, students speak of how "The Bluff is a beautiful place, and just walking around campus is so relaxing," and revel in the "outdoor opportunities available in the Pacific Northwest," like kayaking, camping, and skiing. There's an Outdoor Pursuits Program that "offers students the ability to learn the basics and exposes people to the outdoors."

Student Body

"The sense of community here is unmatched," enthuses one student—as long as you're willing to get involved. In short, "while students are focused on their academics...there is still a social scene and atmosphere if you want it." To put it another way: "Almost everyone I know is involved in a club or organization, and it is where I have met almost all of my friends."

The student body includes "students with different identities, cultures, [and] passions." One student describes their peers as "mostly PNW-style, [and] outdoorsy...either non-religious or progressive religious," and others value the "diverse set of minds" and "very unique people" they're surrounded by on campus. Students also note that "the University of Portland has been growing with more diverse students, but more importantly more diverse professors." The University of Portland also has "a large amount of students from other nations, which really enriches the culture and connectedness between one another." Students are "very outspoken, they are not scared to speak up," and are known for their willingness to "uplift each student's uniqueness."

UNIVERSITY OF PORTLAND

Financial Aid: 503-943-7311 • E-Mail: admissions@up.edu • Website: www.up.edu

THE PRINCETON REVIEW SAYS

Admissions

The school reports that its standardized testing policy for use in admission for Fall 2024 is Test Optional. The Princeton Review suggests that interested applicants consult with the school for the most up-to-date standardized testing policies. *Very important factors considered include:* rigor of secondary school record, academic GPA. *Important factors considered include:* class rank, application essay, recommendation(s), extracurricular activities, talent/ability, volunteer work, work experience. *Other factors considered include:* standardized test scores, interview, character/personal qualities, first generation, alumni/ae relation, geographical residence, religious affiliation/commitment, racial/ethnic status, level of applicant's interest. High school diploma is required and GED is accepted. *Academic units required:* 4 English, 3 math, 3 science, 2 foreign language, 3 social studies, 2 history, 7 academic electives. *Academic units recommended:* 4 English, 4 math, 4 science, 3 foreign language, 4 social studies, 4 history, 7 academic electives.

Financial Aid

Students should submit: FAFSA. Priority filing deadline is 1/15. The Princeton Review suggests that all financial aid forms be submitted as soon as possible (see page 5 for a note on the FAFSA). *Need-based scholarships/grants offered:* College/university scholarship or grant aid from institutional funds; Federal Nursing Scholarships; Federal Pell; Private scholarships; SEOG; State scholarships/grants. *Loan aid offered:* Direct PLUS loans; Direct Subsidized Loans; Direct Unsubsidized Loans; College/university loans from institutional funds; Federal Nursing Loans. Admitted students will be notified of awards on a rolling basis beginning 11/15. Federal Work-Study Program available. Institutional employment available.

The Inside Word

The University of Portland is a well-rounded college that welcomes all students. To make applying easier for students, standardized testing is optional, and they're equally accepting of both their own application and the Common App. That said, this means the admissions committee will be carefully looking at whatever you chose to submit, so it behooves you to have things like a thoughtful letter of recommendation and a solid transcript. Note that admission to the Honors Program is considered separately, so complete your general forms early if you're going this route.

SELECTIVITY

Admissions Rating	83
# of applicants	10,122
% of applicants accepted	93
% of acceptees attending	9
# offered a place on the wait list	408
% accepting a place on wait list	38
% admitted from wait list	39

FIRST-YEAR PROFILE

Testing policy	Test Optional
Range SAT EBRW	610–690
Range SAT math	610–720
Range ACT composite	27–31
# submitting SAT scores	104
% submitting SAT scores	13
# submitting ACT scores	46
% submitting ACT scores	6
Average HS GPA	3.4
% frosh submitting high school GPA	100

DEADLINES

Regular	
Priority	11/15
Deadline	1/15
Notification	Rolling, 10/1
Nonfall registration?	Yes

APPLICANTS ALSO LOOK AT

Gonzaga University; Oregon State University; Seattle University; University of Oregon; University of Washington

FINANCIAL FACTS

Financial Aid Rating	79
Annual tuition	$51,352
Room and board	$17,172
Required fees	$460
Books and supplies	$780
Average frosh need-based scholarship	$37,475
Average UG need-based scholarship	$34,220
% needy frosh rec. need-based scholarship or grant aid	81
% needy UG rec. need-based scholarship or grant aid	76
% needy frosh rec. non-need-based scholarship or grant aid	97
% needy UG rec. non-need-based scholarship or grant aid	95
% needy frosh rec. need-based self-help aid	71
% needy UG rec. need-based self-help aid	69
% frosh rec. any financial aid	99
% UG rec. any financial aid	99
% UG borrow to pay for school	55
Average cumulative indebtedness	$31,865
% frosh need fully met	14
% ugrads need fully met	11
Average % of frosh need met	77
Average % of ugrad need met	77

UNIVERSITY OF PUGET SOUND

1500 North Warner Street, Tacoma, WA 98416-1062 • Admissions: 253-879-3100 • Fax: 253-879-3993

CAMPUS LIFE
Quality of Life Rating	91
Fire Safety Rating	91
Green Rating	86
Type of school	Private
Affiliation	No Affiliation
Environment	City

STUDENTS
Total undergrad enrollment	1,712
% male/female/another gender	42/58/0
% from out of state	71
% frosh from public high school	77
% frosh live on campus	99
% ugrads live on campus	64
# of fraternities (% join)	4 (25)
# of sororities (% join)	5 (18)
% African American	3
% Asian	7
% White	66
% Hispanic	12
% Native American	<1
% Pacific Islander	<1
% Two or more races	9
% Race and/or ethnicity unknown	3
% international	1
# of countries represented	12

SURVEY SAYS . . .
Lots of liberal students
Lab facilities are great
Great library
Students aren't religious
Students environmentally aware
Easy to get around campus
Recreation facilities are great
College radio is popular
Active minority support groups

ACADEMICS
Academic Rating	87
% students returning for sophomore year	79
% students graduating within 4 years	70
% students graduating within 6 years	76
Calendar	Semester
Student/faculty ratio	9:1
Profs interesting rating	92
Profs accessible rating	95

Most classes have 10–19 students.
Most lab/discussion sessions have 10–19 students.

MOST POPULAR MAJORS
Biology/Biological Sciences, General; Psychology, General; Business Administration and Management, General

STUDENTS SAY " . . ."

Academics

Featuring a "beautiful campus" and "excellent academics," the University of Puget Sound is a great option for anyone hoping to study in the Pacific Northwest. The school provides students with "an amazing support system" and truly strives to "help them [meet] their goal[s] in whatever capacity necessary." Academically, undergrads here are especially quick to highlight Puget Sound's "great arts programs, whether [in] English, music, or theater." They also applaud the fact that there are ample "project-based learning opportunities such as relevant work study [and] summer research for all majors and interests." Additionally, students benefit from small class sizes, which lead to plenty of "open discussion and interactive engagement with the course material." This also allows undergrads to develop "close student-professor relationships." And speaking of professors, they work hard to ensure their classes are "challenging" yet "accessible." Importantly, "they have open office hours that all students are encouraged to attend, and there is no shame in [doing so]." As one grateful student sums up, "Professors are genuinely excited to make time for students in their schedule for advice, homework help, or even just sharing a coffee. The level of concern of the professors for undergraduate education is almost unmatched."

Campus Life

It's no secret that undergrads at Puget Sound are "very dedicated to their studies." In fact, "most students have a fun time studying in [the] three different cafés on campus." Of course, even these dedicated scholars need to kick back, so they frequently take advantage of the various "performances, talks, or events going on almost every week." Additionally, many students flock to "the athletic center to get in a workout, attend a dance class, or rock climb." A good number also participate in "at least one club or are [involved] in Greek life." Puget Sound undergrads report that "on any given Friday night you can find a party" to attend. No need to worry if that's not your scene. Students here are an "outdoorsy" lot, and when the weekend rolls around, many of them can be found "hiking, skiing, kayaking" or "[taking] camping trips to the Olympic Peninsula or out to Eastern Washington." People are also just as happy to stay local and explore all that the surrounding area has to offer including "the Bridge of Glass, Point Defiance park, and the Puget Sound waterfront."

Student Body

At first glance, the University of Puget Sound's student body appears "fairly homogenous." After all, most undergrads come from "white middle-class families along the West Coast." However, the school is making strides to become "more diverse," especially "in terms of gender expression and sexuality." What's more, Puget Sound students are "not afraid to voice their [opinions or] their views [on] everything from political to social issues." In turn, students also caution that "more conservative views can [either] fall on deaf ears [or] can be met with a strong argument." However, others quickly assert that no matter your background or leanings, Puget Sound students are "open and welcoming to all." As one undergrad shares, "[Students are] not just nice in passing, but they have depth and consideration; when you run into someone in a café and [make] small talk, it doesn't feel surface level." This makes for a "general vibe…[that is] laid back." Students also tend to describe their classmates as "unique," "adventurous," and "passionate" people who maintain a strong "desire for new experiences." Of course, if you're looking to easily pinpoint these undergrads, you'd simply say that the "typical [Puget Sound] student loves the outdoors, is a critical thinker, and knows what makes a good raincoat."

UNIVERSITY OF PUGET SOUND

Financial Aid: 253-879-3214 • E-Mail: admission@pugetsound.edu • Website: www.pugetsound.edu

THE PRINCETON REVIEW SAYS

Admissions

The school reports that its standardized testing policy for use in admission for Fall 2024 is Test Optional. The 2024 testing policy will be permanent. The Princeton Review suggests that interested applicants consult with the school for the most up-to-date standardized testing policies. *Very important factors considered include:* rigor of secondary school record, academic GPA, application essay, character/personal qualities. *Important factors considered include:* recommendation(s), extracurricular activities, talent/ability, volunteer work, work experience. *Other factors considered include:* class rank, standardized test scores, interview, first generation, racial/ethnic status, alumni/ae relation, level of applicant's interest. High school diploma is required and GED is accepted. *Academic units recommended:* 4 English, 3 math, 3 science, 3 science labs, 2 foreign language, 3 social studies, 3 history, 1 visual/performing arts.

Financial Aid

Students should submit: FAFSA. Priority filing deadline is 11/1. The Princeton Review suggests that all financial aid forms be submitted as soon as possible (see page 5 for a note on the FAFSA). *Need-based scholarships/grants offered:* College/university scholarship or grant aid from institutional funds; Federal Pell; Private scholarships; SEOG; State scholarships/grants. *Loan aid offered:* Direct PLUS loans; Direct Subsidized Loans; Direct Unsubsidized Loans. Admitted students will be notified of awards on or about 3/1. Federal Work-Study Program available. Institutional employment available.

The Inside Word

University of Puget Sound is a selective school, so gaining admission is certainly competitive. The college is eager to build a diverse student body that actively contributes to campus life. Thus, you can expect the admissions committee to take a holistic approach; everything from GPA to personal statements to extracurricular involvement will be closely considered. Nevertheless, the rigor of your high school curriculum will be of the utmost importance. It is also highly recommended that you sit for an interview, although it is not required.

THE SCHOOL SAYS "..."

From the Admissions Office

"We're a classic, forward-thinking and entrepreneurial liberal arts college with a renowned School of Music and an innovative business and leadership program. Our 2,000 undergraduate students are proudly unclassifiable and universally kind. Our professors win a metric ton of teaching awards and do research with students that pushes the figurative envelope. We're ambitious and modest. We're collaborative and independent minded. We're rooted in the innovative Pacific Northwest and in love with the world. None of these things are contradictions. All of them make sense. They add up to an education that is perfectly suited to this vast, brave, unclassifiable world. We award a variety of scholarships including: Academic Merit Scholarships; Talent Scholarships in Music, Theater, Debate, & Art, Full-Ride Leadership and Research Scholarships."

SELECTIVITY

Admissions Rating	85
# of applicants	5,345
% of applicants accepted	83
% of acceptees attending	9
# offered a place on the wait list	21
% accepting a place on wait list	14
% admitted from wait list	0
# of early decision applicants	89
% accepted early decision	52

FIRST-YEAR PROFILE

Testing policy	Test Optional
Range SAT composite	1190–1370
Range SAT EBRW	600–700
Range SAT math	570–690
Range ACT composite	27–32
# submitting SAT scores	136
% submitting SAT scores	34
# submitting ACT scores	55
% submitting ACT scores	14
Average HS GPA	3.6
% frosh submitting high school GPA	99
% graduated top 10% of class	29
% graduated top 25% of class	54
% graduated top 50% of class	87

DEADLINES

Early decision	
Deadline	11/1
Notification	12/15
Early action	
Deadline	11/1
Notification	1/15
Regular	
Priority	1/15
Notification	3/15
Nonfall registration?	Yes

APPLICANTS ALSO LOOK AT

Lewis & Clark College; Pacific Lutheran University; Seattle University; University of California—Davis; University of Oregon; University of Washington; Western Washington University; Whitman College; Willamette University

FINANCIAL FACTS

Financial Aid Rating	85
Annual tuition	$57,330
Room and board	$14,430
Required fees	$296
Books and supplies	$1,000
Average frosh need-based scholarship	$38,898
Average UG need-based scholarship	$38,210
% needy frosh rec. need-based scholarship or grant aid	100
% needy UG rec. need-based scholarship or grant aid	99
% needy frosh rec. non-need-based scholarship or grant aid	16
% needy UG rec. non-need-based scholarship or grant aid	14
% needy frosh rec. need-based self-help aid	75
% needy UG rec. need-based self-help aid	75
% frosh rec. any financial aid	100
% UG rec. any financial aid	98
% UG borrow to pay for school	50
Average cumulative indebtedness	$28,069
% frosh need fully met	23
% ugrads need fully met	22
Average % of frosh need met	82
Average % of ugrad need met	83

UNIVERSITY OF REDLANDS

1200 East Colton Avenue, Redlands, CA 92373-0999 • Admissions: 909-793-2121 Fax: 909-335-4089

STUDENTS SAY "..."

Academics

A small institution in Redlands, California, offering both liberal arts and professional studies, the University of Redlands is passionate about "helping students find what they are interested in," and about "allowing them to pursue avenues that will make them successful throughout life." Boasting a small student-to-faculty ratio (13:1), and more than 40 programs of study, this stunning West Coast university provides a "warm, friendly, and inspirational environment inside and outside classes." Most seniors complete a research capstone, and because Redlands is a liberal arts college, students "get a well-rounded education and can easily befriend students in other disciplines." Students love that Redlands is "not a super competitive nor a high-stress environment," and "the size of our classrooms (approximately 18 students) ensures that we reach our full potential." The administration and professors "really care about the success students acquire," and the system is structured in a way that "caters to students off all mindsets." No matter how you learn, the University of Redlands "will cultivate and inspire you to be the better version of yourself."

Professors are "thoughtful, engaging, enthusiastic," "very personable," and "love [us] to use their first name and get to know each student individually." Instructors are "extremely knowledgeable in their field of study" and make an effort "to engage their students in discussions during class time rather than lecture." Almost all the professors are easily accessible either after class or during their office hours. This "intimate learning environment" caters to each person differently, and faculty remain "very attentive to [students'] needs." Although certain courses aren't offered every semester, they happen "often enough for students to take them," and some classes are split into two, allowing for "more variety."

Campus Life

The University of Redlands "absolutely gorgeous" campus has "the classic feel of a small liberal arts university with the California vibe," with outdoor programs that give students "the opportunity to experience California." Academics fill the weekdays, but many people also find time to "work out, go sit outside on the Quad, go hiking, study in the library, or grab food with friends." Students also find it fun to go downtown, "especially on Thursdays for Market Night," and on weekends they can often be found nearby at the "beach, the mountains, Disneyland, or Los Angeles." ("Everything is about an hour away" from campus). Though there is a shuttle downtown, "one needs a car here to go do fun things," but "thankfully, parking is free." There are also "on-campus parties, outdoor program trips, and activities" provided through the school. Greek life and sports are big here, and "attendance at sports events is pretty impressive." Even during the week, "the student body tends to fill a majority of the student section at basketball games."

Student Body

This is a "truly inclusive," "ecologically-minded," student body, with the majority being "open-minded with liberal inclinations." Since this is a small campus, everyone is "really close," and "there is a niche for all types of people." "You can't go anywhere on campus without running into someone you know," says a student. It is easy to get involved on campus, and "there is a good dynamic between students and professors." There tends to be a bit of a divide between the 200 or so students living and studying in the Johnston Center for Integrative Studies (who are more on the "creative" side) and the College of Arts and Sciences: "a weird dynamic, not a bad or troubling one."

UNIVERSITY OF REDLANDS

Financial Aid: 909-748-8047 • E-Mail: admissions@redlands.edu • Website: www.redlands.edu

THE PRINCETON REVIEW SAYS

Admissions

The school reports that its standardized testing policy for use in admission for Fall 2024 is Test Optional. It is unknown at this time if the 2024 testing policy will be permanent. The Princeton Review suggests that interested applicants consult with the school for the most up-to-date standardized testing policies. *Very important factors considered include:* academic GPA. *Important factors considered include:* rigor of secondary school record, standardized test scores, application essay, recommendation(s). *Other factors considered include:* class rank, interview, extracurricular activities, talent/ability, character/personal qualities, first generation, alumni/ae relation, geographical residence, racial/ethnic status, volunteer work, work experience. High school diploma is required and GED is accepted. *Academic units required:* 4 English, 3 math, 2 science, 2 science labs, 2 foreign language, 2 social studies. *Academic units recommended:* 3 science, 3 foreign language, 3 social studies.

Financial Aid

Students should submit: FAFSA. Priority filing deadline is 11/15. The Princeton Review suggests that all financial aid forms be submitted as soon as possible (see page 5 for a note on the FAFSA). *Need-based scholarships/grants offered:* College/university scholarship or grant aid from institutional funds; Federal Pell; Private scholarships; SEOG; State scholarships/grants. *Loan aid offered:* Direct PLUS loans; Direct Subsidized Loans; Direct Unsubsidized Loans; College/university loans from institutional funds; State Loans. Admitted students will be notified of awards on a rolling basis beginning 2/17. Federal Work-Study Program available.

The Inside Word

The admit rate at the University of Redlands is 83 percent, and students with above-average high school records should consider the school a target. Candidates who are interested in pursuing the self-designed programs available through the Johnston Center for Integrative Studies will find the admissions process to be distinctly more personal. Note, though, that you have to be admitted as a regular student in the College of Arts and Sciences first.

THE SCHOOL SAYS "..."

From the Admissions Office

"We've created an unusually blended curriculum of the liberal arts and pre-professional study because we think education is about learning how to think and learning how to do. For example, our environmental studies students have synthesized their study of sociology, biology, and economics to develop an actual resource management plan for the local mountain communities. Our creative writing program encourages internships with publishing or television production companies. We educate managers, poets, environmental scientists, teachers, musicians, and speech therapists to be reflective about culture and society so that they can better understand and improve the world they'll enter upon graduation.

"International students for whom English is not their first language may meet our English proficiency requirement through the SAT, ACT, Duolingo, TOEFL, or IELTS. Please check our website for score requirements.

"More than 90% of our students receive some form of financial assistance."

SELECTIVITY

Admissions Rating	84
# of applicants	4,562
% of applicants accepted	75
% of acceptees attending	17
# offered a place on the wait list	40
% accepting a place on wait list	40
% admitted from wait list	100

FIRST-YEAR PROFILE

Testing policy	Test Optional
Range SAT EBRW	490–590
Range SAT math	490–600
Range ACT composite	22–27
# submitting SAT scores	428
% submitting SAT scores	72
# submitting ACT scores	290
% submitting ACT scores	49
Average HS GPA	3.5
% frosh submitting high school GPA	100
% graduated top 10% of class	22
% graduated top 25% of class	55
% graduated top 50% of class	88

DEADLINES

Early action	
Deadline	11/15
Notification	1/15
Regular	
Priority	11/15
Deadline	1/15
Notification	Rolling, 1/10
Nonfall registration?	Yes

FINANCIAL FACTS

Financial Aid Rating	85
Annual tuition	$53,716
Required fees	$350
Required fees (first-year)	$500
Books and supplies	$1,850
Average frosh need-based scholarship	$29,047
Average UG need-based scholarship	$28,598
% needy frosh rec. need-based scholarship or grant aid	100
% needy UG rec. need-based scholarship or grant aid	99
% needy frosh rec. non-need-based scholarship or grant aid	23
% needy UG rec. non-need-based scholarship or grant aid	21
% needy frosh rec. need-based self-help aid	81
% needy UG rec. need-based self-help aid	82
% frosh rec. any financial aid	94
% UG rec. any financial aid	94
% UG borrow to pay for school	68
Average cumulative indebtedness	$32,662
% frosh need fully met	27
% ugrads need fully met	25
Average % of frosh need met	84
Average % of ugrad need met	84

UNIVERSITY OF RHODE ISLAND

University of Rhode Island, Kingston, RI 02881 • Admissions: 401-874-1000

STUDENTS SAY ". . ."

Academics

Located in the village of Kingston in the southern part of the state, The University of Rhode Island is a public research institution known for having "excellent science programs," including a "marine biology program [that] is one of the best in the Northeast." URI is a school that challenges me to think big and outside the box," says one student. Other stand-out majors include "nursing, pharmacy," which students feel is "excellent—one of the top in the country," and engineering." Students feel that "all professors have a unique style of teaching. Most are very willing to adapt their style to fit students' needs though" and many "are able to share stories from their experiences that make the material more accessible and interesting." Another student observes that the staff is also "great at helping freshmen transferring from home to college, and there are lots of different programs offered to help students excel academically." Overall, URI is known to have a solid liberal ideology with "openness to creative and critical exploration." This engineering major finds the environment to be rather "forward-thinking [with an] emphasis on today's global workforce."

Campus Life

The school's proximity to the beach and to other major cities like Providence and Boston make it appealing to students from all over the Northeast. One student reports that "driving to one of the nearby beaches to just clear your mind and relax is one of the many benefits of URI's location." Students are said to have a "two brain track" in terms of serious attention to study followed by equal attention to "relaxing and having a good time." If fine dining is meaningful to your quality of life, it's worth noting that URI's dining hall has "won a national award the past two years in a row." And, while there are complaints about the dry campus, one senior notes that this is a surmountable obstacle, in that "people usually live in the surrounding neighborhoods, so you can travel to your friends' houses and party." Others say that students who live nearby still choose to stay on campus during weekends, since this is where their social life is centered. Life isn't all about "getting wasted," chides one sophomore. "Sometimes we get together [to] make dinner and just have a movie night inside our apartment."

Student Body

URI, as an affordable state school, naturally attracts a large percentage of Rhode Islanders. Rumor has it that this group "sticks to their friends from high school," yet one undergrad observes, "Rhody-borns are so afraid of college turning into another four years of high school that we go searching for new people to meet." The typical URI student "is involved in at least one student organization, but many are involved in more than one. They usually go out about once a week on average and study about an hour a day." There are "many students...involved in at least one type of extracurricular activity," "then there are students who are not involved at all." Campus diversity is strong, and most groups intermingle without issue.

UNIVERSITY OF RHODE ISLAND

Financial Aid: 401-874-7530 • E-Mail: admission@uri.edu • Website: www.uri.edu

THE PRINCETON REVIEW SAYS

Admissions

The school reports that its standardized testing policy for use in admission for Fall 2024 is Test Optional. The Princeton Review suggests that interested applicants consult with the school for the most up-to-date standardized testing policies. *Very important factors considered include:* rigor of secondary school record, academic GPA. *Important factors considered include:* application essay, recommendation(s). *Other factors considered include:* class rank, standardized test scores, extracurricular activities, talent/ability, character/personal qualities, first generation, alumni/ae relation, geographical residence, state residency, racial/ethnic status, volunteer work, work experience, level of applicant's interest. High school diploma is required and GED is accepted. *Academic units required:* 4 English, 3 math, 2 science, 1 science lab, 2 foreign language, 2 social studies, 5 academic electives.

Financial Aid

Students should submit: FAFSA. Priority filing deadline is 3/1. The Princeton Review suggests that all financial aid forms be submitted as soon as possible (see page 5 for a note on the FAFSA). *Need-based scholarships/grants offered:* College/university scholarship or grant aid from institutional funds; Federal Pell; Private scholarships; SEOG; State scholarships/grants. *Loan aid offered:* Direct PLUS loans; Direct Subsidized Loans; Direct Unsubsidized Loans; College/university loans from institutional funds; Federal Nursing Loans. Admitted students will be notified of awards on a rolling basis. Federal Work-Study Program available. Institutional employment available.

The Inside Word

Applications here are evaluated on the basis of course selection, academic performance, standardized test scores (if submitted), and unique talents. Don't forget to apply to URI's merit-based scholarships, which are open to international students as well. Remember if you're a resident of another New England state (besides Rhode Island) you may be eligible, depending on your major, for discounted tuition.

THE SCHOOL SAYS "..."

From the Admissions Office

"One only needs to visit this beautiful school to know that it is a university on the move. In the past twelve years, URI has invested over $900 million in new facilities and improvements. The most recent two are the new $150 million engineering complex and a new 500-bed residence hall. Couple these enhancements with the hiring of 346 new faculty members in the last eight years, one can see the transformation of this university.

"The University of Rhode Island is competitively priced, especially for out-of-state students. The University offers a range of merit scholarships to students who have demonstrated academic success in a challenging college preparatory curriculum. You may be eligible for these awards if you have earned a recalculated GPA of 3.2 on a 4.0 scale at the end of your junior year and have demonstrated leadership and involvement in your school and/or community. All applicants are considered for these scholarships by submitting a complete application by February 1. There is no separate scholarship application. Please note that merit scholarships for first-year students are awarded only to students enrolling in the fall semester. To be considered for our highest scholarships, we recommend that you apply by our December 1 Early Action deadline. We also strongly recommend that students interested in engineering, nursing, and the doctorate in pharmacy apply by December 1 as spaces are limited in these programs."

SELECTIVITY

Admissions Rating	85
# of applicants	25,481
% of applicants accepted	76
% of acceptees attending	17
# offered a place on the wait list	850
% accepting a place on wait list	94
% admitted from wait list	0

FIRST-YEAR PROFILE

Testing policy	Test Optional
Range SAT composite	1140–1300
Range SAT EBRW	530–640
Range SAT math	520–630
Range ACT composite	25–30
# submitting SAT scores	987
% submitting SAT scores	29
# submitting ACT scores	74
% submitting ACT scores	2
Average HS GPA	3.6
% frosh submitting high school GPA	99
% graduated top 10% of class	18
% graduated top 25% of class	49
% graduated top 50% of class	86

DEADLINES

Early action	
Deadline	12/1
Notification	12/15
Regular	
Deadline	2/1
Notification	3/31
Nonfall registration?	Yes

APPLICANTS ALSO LOOK AT

Boston University; Northeastern University; University of Connecticut; University of Massachusetts—Boston; University of New Hampshire; University of Vermont

FINANCIAL FACTS

Financial Aid Rating	82
Annual in-state tuition	$13,586
Annual out-of-state tuition	$32,068
Room and board	$13,584
Required fees	$2,294
Books and supplies	$1,250
Average frosh need-based scholarship	$13,130
Average UG need-based scholarship	$11,450
% needy frosh rec. need-based scholarship or grant aid	97
% needy UG rec. need-based scholarship or grant aid	91
% needy frosh rec. non-need-based scholarship or grant aid	8
% needy UG rec. non-need-based scholarship or grant aid	6
% needy frosh rec. need-based self-help aid	65
% needy UG rec. need-based self-help aid	52
% frosh rec. any financial aid	97
% UG rec. any financial aid	84
% UG borrow to pay for school	73
Average cumulative indebtedness	$38,164
% frosh need fully met	37
% ugrads need fully met	27
Average % of frosh need met	63
Average % of ugrad need met	57

UNIVERSITY OF RICHMOND

410 Westhampton Way, University of Richmond, VA 23173 • Admissions: 804-289-8640 • Fax: 804-287-6003

CAMPUS LIFE

Quality of Life Rating	95
Fire Safety Rating	95
Green Rating	98
Type of school	Private
Affiliation	No Affiliation
Environment	City

STUDENTS

Total undergrad enrollment	3,069
% male/female/another gender	46/54/0
% from out of state	77
% frosh from public high school	55
% frosh live on campus	99
% ugrads live on campus	86
# of fraternities (% join)	6 (26)
# of sororities (% join)	8 (18)
% African American	6
% Asian	7
% White	60
% Hispanic	10
% Native American	<1
% Pacific Islander	<1
% Two or more races	4
% Race and/or ethnicity unknown	2
% international	10
# of countries represented	73

SURVEY SAYS . . .

Students always studying
Students are happy
Classroom facilities are great
Lab facilities are great
Great library
Career services are great
Internships are widely available
Class discussions encouraged
School is well run
Students love Richmond, VA
Great food on campus
Great off-campus food
Easy to get around campus
Recreation facilities are great
Frats and sororities are popular
Active student government
Intramural sports are popular
Dorms are like palaces

ACADEMICS

Academic Rating	95
% students returning for sophomore year	91
% students graduating within 4 years	83
% students graduating within 6 years	88
Calendar	Semester
Student/faculty ratio	8:1
Profs interesting rating	95
Profs accessible rating	97

Most classes have 10–19 students.
Most lab/discussion sessions have
10–19 students.

MOST POPULAR MAJORS

Biology/Biological Sciences, General; Business
Administration and Management, General;
Organizational Behavior Studies

STUDENTS SAY "..."

Academics

At the University of Richmond, students "like to enjoy themselves but most have their priorities straight," and they know that "school comes first." As one student puts it, "There is a good balance of work and play here, and students are competitive, but to a healthy extent. The expectations for students here really push you to be involved, get at least two internships or research opportunities, and secure a good job by graduation." Students praise the University of Richmond's "unparalleled resources," particularly the "high number of research, internship, and study abroad opportunities available." As one business administration major gushes, at the University of Richmond "we combine the resources of a major research institution, the breadth of development of a liberal arts education, and amplifying effect of out of classroom opportunities (speakers, programs, student activities) to deliver an undergraduate experience that is both unique to every student and universally top notch." One key resource available is that they'll pay $5,000 so that "students [can] participate in an internship, research opportunity, or project." This allows all students "an opportunity to have meaningful, career-oriented experiences." Professors at the University of Richmond earn generally high marks, with one student admitting, "My professors showed me how to love to learn again." Another echoes that "the entire University of Richmond staff treats everyone like an individual and not just another student circling through the system." "The schoolwork is difficult, but manageable," and "Richmond is incredibly generous with not only need-based but merit-based aid, which is unusual for liberal arts colleges of a similar caliber."

Campus Life

"The student body is academic but also enjoys having a social life," and students note that much of "the social scene is generally dominated by events thrown by Greek life." Students disagree on how open those events are, but do suggest that "There's also plenty to get involved with, so you would have a hard time finding a student who is not involved with some sport, artistic group, club, or organization." As one student puts it, "Everyone is doing some sort of juggling act," but "students are also academically driven, and because classes are difficult and demanding, people will find themselves doing a lot of academic work throughout the week." Weekends are a time to kick back and enjoy what Richmond has to offer in the way of "clubs downtown," "the Virginia Museum of Fine Arts, over 900 restaurants, Carytown (a hipster area with boutiques and unique restaurants), various festivals and events, and athletic competitions."

Student Body

Students describe the typical student as one who cares about "performing extremely well in class and extracurriculars." Beyond that, "everyone dresses how they want, without judgment." This stems, in part, from the way in which the University of Richmond is moving toward a more inclusive population that sees students as "diverse, from their backgrounds, races, religions, and ethnicity," and away from a homogeneity of "New England prepsters and Old South heirs/heiresses." They also note that there is less "competition to do better than your peers when it comes to grades—students are laid back in the sense that they are happy to see their peers do well." Students stress the friendliness of their fellow Spiders, saying, "Everyone that I have met has been super helpful and kind—even as a first-year."

UNIVERSITY OF RICHMOND

Financial Aid: 804-289-8438 • E-Mail: admission@richmond.edu • Website: www.richmond.edu

THE PRINCETON REVIEW SAYS

Admissions

The school reports that its standardized testing policy for use in admission for Fall 2024 is Test Optional. The 2024 testing policy will be temporary. The Princeton Review suggests that interested applicants consult with the school for the most up-to-date standardized testing policies. *Very important factors considered include:* rigor of secondary school record, academic GPA. *Important factors considered include:* class rank, standardized test scores, application essay, recommendation(s), extracurricular activities, talent/ability, character/personal qualities. *Other factors considered include:* first generation, alumni/ae relation, geographical residence, state residency, life experience, volunteer work, work experience. High school diploma is required and GED is accepted. *Academic units required:* 4 English, 3 math, 2 science, 2 science labs, 2 second language, 2 history. *Academic units recommended:* 4 English, 4 math, 4 science, 4 science labs, 4 second language, 4 history.

Financial Aid

Students should submit: CSS/Financial Aid Profile; FAFSA; Noncustodial Profile. The Princeton Review suggests that all financial aid forms be submitted as soon as possible (see page 5 for a note on the FAFSA). *Need-based scholarships/grants offered:* College/university scholarship or grant aid from institutional funds; Federal Pell; Private scholarships; SEOG; State scholarships/grants; United Negro College Fund. *Loan aid offered:* Direct PLUS loans; Direct Subsidized Loans; Direct Unsubsidized Loans. Admitted students will be notified of awards on or about 4/1. Federal Work-Study Program available. Institutional employment available.

The Inside Word

University of Richmond office of admission takes a holistic view toward applications, and demonstration of character, leadership, and independence is evaluated alongside academic record. That said, applicants will need strong transcripts and high test scores to compete in this applicant pool. The school offers generous merit-based scholarships to those who demonstrate exemplary academic achievement.

THE SCHOOL SAYS "..."

From the Admissions Office

"University of Richmond is one of very few colleges that is need blind in admission and meets 100 percent of demonstrated financial need for U.S. citizens and permanent residents. University of Richmond combines the characteristics of a well-resourced college with the dynamics and resources of a large university to provide extraordinary experiences for students. Our unique size, beautiful suburban campus and outstanding facilities offer students opportunities for intellectual achievement and personal growth. While faculty-student interaction and dialogue are at the forefront of the academic experience, research, internships and international experiences are important components of students' lives. Richmond is committed to providing students with rigorous academics and experiential learning. The university offers funding for undergraduate research, summer fellowships and internships. Our global approach to education shines through our many study-abroad programs. We are committed to diversity and believe in leveraging its benefits in all aspects of college life. The student body is composed of scholars from a variety of backgrounds. Nearly one in four undergraduates is a domestic student of color; one in seven is the first in his or her family to attend college; one in eleven is an international student; and 77 percent hail from outside of Virginia."

SELECTIVITY

Admissions Rating	95
# of applicants	14,364
% of applicants accepted	24
% of acceptees attending	24
# offered a place on the wait list	3,903
% accepting a place on wait list	17
% admitted from wait list	0
# of early decision applicants	865
% accepted early decision	44

FIRST-YEAR PROFILE

Testing policy	Test Optional
Range SAT composite	1410–1500
Range SAT EBRW	690–750
Range SAT math	710–780
Range ACT composite	32–34
# submitting SAT scores	190
% submitting SAT scores	22
# submitting ACT scores	151
% submitting ACT scores	18
Average HS GPA	3.8
% frosh submitting high school GPA	100
% graduated top 10% of class	56
% graduated top 25% of class	86
% graduated top 50% of class	98

DEADLINES

Early decision	
Deadline	11/1
Notification	12/15
Other ED deadline	1/1
Other ED notification	2/15
Early action	
Deadline	11/1
Notification	1/20
Regular	
Deadline	1/1
Notification	4/1
Nonfall registration?	No

APPLICANTS ALSO LOOK AT

University of Virginia; College of William & Mary; University of North Carolina-Chapel Hill; Boston College; Bucknell University; Villanova University; Davidson College; Colgate University; Williams College; Bowdoin College

APPLICANTS OFTEN PREFER

Boston College; Wake Forest University; University of Virginia; William & Mary

FINANCIAL FACTS

Financial Aid Rating	85
Annual tuition	$62,600
Room and board	$15,790
Books and supplies	$1,000
Average frosh need-based scholarship	$49,405
Average UG need-based scholarship	$51,209
% needy frosh rec. need-based scholarship or grant aid	99
% needy UG rec. need-based scholarship or grant aid	99
% needy frosh rec. non-need-based scholarship or grant aid	28
% needy UG rec. non-need-based scholarship or grant aid	20
% needy frosh rec. need-based self-help aid	71
% needy UG rec. need-based self-help aid	77
% frosh rec. any financial aid	60
% UG rec. any financial aid	68
% UG borrow to pay for school	37
Average cumulative indebtedness	$27,352
% frosh need fully met	89
% ugrads need fully met	84
Average % of frosh need met	100
Average % of ugrad need met	99

UNIVERSITY OF ROCHESTER

300 Wilson Boulevard, Rochester, NY 14627-0251 • Admissions: 585-275-2121 • Fax: 585-461-4595

CAMPUS LIFE

Quality of Life Rating	**86**
Fire Safety Rating	**93**
Green Rating	**91**
Type of school	Private
Affiliation	No affiliation
Environment	City

STUDENTS

Total undergrad enrollment	6,570
% male/female/another gender	49/50/2
% from out of state	58
% frosh from public high school	67
% frosh live on campus	98
% ugrads live on campus	70
# of fraternities (% join)	18 (13)
# of sororities (% join)	11 (12)
% African American	5
% Asian	16
% White	40
% Hispanic	8
% Native American	<1
% Pacific Islander	<1
% Two or more races	4
% Race and/or ethnicity unknown	3
% international	24
# of countries represented	87

SURVEY SAYS . . .

Great library
Great financial aid
Lab facilities are great
Recreation facilities are great

ACADEMICS

Academic Rating	**84**
% students returning for sophomore year	92
% students graduating within 4 years	82
% students graduating within 6 years	90
Calendar	Semester
Student/faculty ratio	9:1
Profs interesting rating	87
Profs accessible rating	89
Most classes have fewer than 10 students.	

MOST POPULAR MAJORS
Computer Science; Biology/Biological Sciences, General; Psychology, General

STUDENTS SAY "..."

Academics

The University of Rochester is a private research university in western New York. The school's programs are rigorous, but students appreciate the freedom to create their own paths. Rochester "does not require general education classes, but instead encourages students to pursue their passions through the cluster system," which groups classes together in divisions of Humanities, Social Sciences, and Natural Sciences and Engineering. While the programs offer flexibility, the academic requirements are demanding, but regardless of field of study, "tutoring services, [the] University Counseling Center, and staff [who] focus on creating a supportive environment" are always available. "Most people...spend all of their time studying," says one student. But the intellectual efforts come with benefits: the combination of motivated peers and academics "makes...a better student and learner." Faculty also play an important role here with professors who are "really knowledgeable and passionate" about what they're teaching. One student comments that professors "keep material interesting, [are] approachable, and [are] very fair." And class structures are varied so as to "incorporate design thinking" or to feature "more interactive problems." Added benefits to that structure include "small class sizes and individual attention," and "so many opportunities...[are] offered to students both inside and outside of class."

Campus Life

University of Rochester is "very much an academically driven institution," and course work is the top priority. But as one student says, "The weekend [is] when most people fill their days with different activities." One such activity that many students rave about is movie night: "School movie nights are [the] best school-provided weekend activity." Athletics are, of course, present, but as one student notes, "Rochester varsity sports are not very competitive, [however]...a lot of people...do club sports." Other students mention weekend hikes, dance groups, plays and recitals. One thing to contend with at Rochester is the long winter; as some students put it, it's "winter 90 percent of the time." Both the school and students have adapted, and one student offers assurances that Rochester has "established a tunnel system which provides convenience." Dining halls on campus also provide comfort, and anyone looking for a tasty bite to eat can rest easy: "There are a bunch of places to eat on campus." Another way to socialize on campus is through Greek life, but even that is "not as fratty" as you'd expect. As for parties? "There is not a huge party scene on campus, but it's there if you want it," claims one Yellowjacket. Off-campus activities are plentiful, "if you have a car." Otherwise, students rely on the shuttle system. Overall, "there is always something to do on the weekend for entertainment" if students need a study break.

Student Body

Diversity is key at UR, "both [in] background and academic interests." As one student states, "In my class alone, 46 percent of us are international students." Those different backgrounds branch into an even wider range of activities. "Some [students] are filmmakers, some are dancers, some love sailing, some love art. Everyone has their own passions," another student describes. The variety is a benefit, with students claiming "the best thing about the UR community is that nobody can be put into a box." Undergrads describe their peers as "charmingly nerdy" or "chill nerds" who are "very down to have interesting and academic conversations." While most students are "academically focused" and "really care about what they do here," they are for the most part "more collaborative than competitive." "People range from passionate to apathetic, party animals to total nerds." However, amidst all the diversity is a strong sense of camaraderie, and "everyone holds each other accountable in terms of pursuing their absolute best."

UNIVERSITY OF ROCHESTER

Financial Aid: 585-275-3226 • E-Mail: admit@admissions.rochester.edu • Website: www.rochester.edu

THE PRINCETON REVIEW SAYS

Admissions

The school reports that its standardized testing policy for use in admission for Fall 2024 is Test Optional. The 2024 testing policy will be permanent. The Princeton Review suggests that interested applicants consult with the school for the most up-to-date standardized testing policies. *Very important factors considered include:* rigor of secondary school record, academic GPA, application essay, extracurricular activities, character/personal qualities. *Important factors considered include:* recommendation(s), interview, level of applicant's interest. *Other factors considered include:* class rank, standardized test scores, talent/ability, first generation, geographical residence, cultural context, leadership, volunteer work, work experience. High school diploma is required and GED is accepted.

Financial Aid

Students should submit: CSS/Financial Aid Profile; FAFSA; Noncustodial Profile; State aid form. Priority filing deadline is 2/15. The Princeton Review suggests that all financial aid forms be submitted as soon as possible (see page 5 for a note on the FAFSA). *Need-based scholarships/grants offered:* College/university scholarship or grant aid from institutional funds; Federal Pell; Private scholarships; SEOG; State scholarships/grants. *Loan aid offered:* Direct PLUS loans; Direct Subsidized Loans; Direct Unsubsidized Loans. Admitted students will be notified of awards on or about 3/15. Federal Work-Study Program available. Institutional employment available.

The Inside Word

The University of Rochester's academic reputation is supported by its competitive 39 percent acceptance rate. Rochester is Test Optional, it considers a variety of academic records, including SAT, ACT, AP, IB, A-Level, and many international exams. Currently, admissions officers take a holistic approach, seeking applicants from around the world who have demonstrated intellectual curiosity, extracurricular engagement, and ethical character.

THE SCHOOL SAYS "..."

From the Admissions Office

"Rochester students customize their academic experience from the outset. With no general education requirements, every student in every class wants to be there and is highly engaged. Right away, entering students can delve into specific academic areas, while other Exploratory students who haven't chosen a major begin an intellectual adventure with the help of advisors and professors. Many students explore interdisciplinary studies or carry multiple majors.

"Learning here takes place on a personal scale. Rochester offers smaller classes and meaningful collaborations with faculty, with all the amenities of a top research university—a rare combination in higher education. Students undertake research projects, internships, and shadowing experiences in Rochester's nationally ranked schools of engineering, medicine, nursing, music, education, and business. Rochester faculty are world-renowned experts who attract more than $438 Million in research funding annually and recognize that tomorrow's breakthroughs in knowledge and creativity will occur by collaborating across academic disciplines.

"Students live up to Rochester's motto, 'Meliora' (ever better), preparing to lead the future of industry, education, and culture. Navigating through world-renowned facilities and resources, a day in the life of two Rochester students, or any two days in the life of a single student, are never the same.

"Rochester offers academic merit scholarships and meets 100% of demonstrated need for admitted students. Rochester's holistic Test Optional admissions process assesses academic excellence but also asks: What are your values? How have you made yourself and your community better? How will you make the world better?"

SELECTIVITY

Admissions Rating	89
# of applicants	19,170
% of applicants accepted	39
% of acceptees attending	20
# offered a place on the wait list	2,138
% accepting a place on wait list	56
% admitted from wait list	1
# of early decision applicants	1,437
% accepted early decision	43

FIRST-YEAR PROFILE

Testing policy	Test Optional
Range SAT composite	1410–1520
Range SAT EBRW	680–750
Range SAT math	710–790
Range ACT composite	31/34
# submitting SAT scores	435
% submitting SAT scores	29
# submitting ACT scores	170
% submitting ACT scores	11
Average HS GPA	3.8
% frosh submitting high school GPA	99
% graduated top 10% of class	62
% graduated top 25% of class	90
% graduated top 50% of class	98

DEADLINES

Early decision	
Deadline	11/1
Notification	12/15
Other ED deadline	1/5
Other ED notification	2/7
Regular	
Priority	12/1
Deadline	1/5
Notification	4/1
Nonfall registration?	Yes

APPLICANTS ALSO LOOK AT

Boston College; Boston University; Brown University; Case Western Reserve University; Cornell University; New York University; Northeastern University; Syracuse University, Tufts University, University of Pittsburgh

FINANCIAL FACTS

Financial Aid Rating	95
Annual tuition	$63,150
Room and board	$18,784
Required fees	$1,172
Books and supplies	$1,310
Average frosh need-based scholarship	$53,997
Average UG need-based scholarship	$50,333
% needy frosh rec. need-based scholarship or grant aid	100
% needy UG rec. need-based scholarship or grant aid	99
% needy frosh rec. non-need-based scholarship or grant aid	14
% needy UG rec. non-need-based scholarship or grant aid	14
% needy frosh rec. need-based self-help aid	83
% needy UG rec. need-based self-help aid	82
% frosh rec. any financial aid	73
% UG rec. any financial aid	73
% UG borrow to pay for school	47
Average cumulative indebtedness	$29,386
% frosh need fully met	93
% ugrads need fully met	92
Average % of frosh need met	98
Average % of ugrad need met	97

UNIVERSITY OF ST. THOMAS (MN)

2115 Summit Avenue, St. Paul, MN 55105 • Admissions: 651-962-5000 • Fax: 651-962-6160

CAMPUS LIFE

Quality of Life Rating	89
Fire Safety Rating	60*
Green Rating	95
Type of school	Private
Affiliation	Roman Catholic
Environment	Metropolis

STUDENTS

Total undergrad enrollment	5,942
% male/female/another gender	51/49/0
% from out of state	19
% frosh from public high school	73
% frosh live on campus	93
% ugrads live on campus	48
# of fraternities	1
# of sororities	0
% African American	6
% Asian	5
% White	69
% Hispanic	8
% Native American	<1
% Pacific Islander	<1
% Two or more races	4
% Race and/or ethnicity unknown	4
% international	4
# of countries represented	71

SURVEY SAYS . . .

Students are happy
Classroom facilities are great
Great library
School is well run
Students love St. Paul, MN
Easy to get around campus
Recreation facilities are great
Students environmentally aware

ACADEMICS

Academic Rating	82
% students returning for sophomore year	86
% students graduating within 4 years	70
% students graduating within 6 years	80
Calendar	4/1/4
Student/faculty ratio	13:1
Profs interesting rating	90
Profs accessible rating	92

Most classes have 20–29 students.
Most lab/discussion sessions have
10–19 students.

STUDENTS SAY "..."

Academics

University of St. Thomas is Minnesota's largest private university. The Catholic institution "[holds] a high standard of academic excellence," and in turn, "[offers a] myriad of resources for each student to take advantage of." Students have the opportunity to participate in honors classes that are "more discussion-based." Many students appreciate the chances to participate in non-traditional learning, citing activities such as "going" down to the Mississippi River to do research for geology class" or "attending the Nobel Peace Prize Conference," and "listening in on court cases."

Professors have the ability to "make or break the experience," and many faculty members prioritize "intellectual curiosity" and "get excited when you want to dive deeper into course material outside of the classroom." The modest student-to-faculty ratio makes it "easy to connect in the classroom, which then makes it easier to succeed in a class." Plus, many love that there are "professors who actively help find internships and jobs that expand learning and experience." And the relationships go beyond just the academic: "The faculty at St. Thomas [serves] as teachers, guidance counselors, career advisors, and even friends."

Campus Life

"The greatest strengths of St. Thomas would be [its] dedication to making students feel at home" through an "impactful focus on building community" among undergrads. As one transfer student puts it, "As soon as I moved in I felt like I found my home." In their free time, St. Thomas enrollees—affectionately known as "Tommies"—can be found working out at the gym, exploring "neighborhood bars and restaurants" and "[taking] advantage of our numerous coffee shops on campus and off." The school "offers free transportation to locations all around the Twin Cities," making it easy to get off campus even without access to a car. In the warmer months, people leverage the "many open grassy areas that allow students to hang out, hammock, play causal games, and even study," and they're "able to rent out yard games and other activity supplies either at a low cost or for free." If organized fun is more your style, "There are a lot of school-sponsored events" featuring "free goodies around campus (such as crafts, T-shirts, [and] food)." Truly, "You'd have to be actively trying to be bored" at St. Thomas.

Student Body

People at University of St. Thomas are first and foremost "friendly and nice" and "very respectful of each other." Here, your peers want you to succeed and are "eager to help each other out." In fact, some even say their student body is one of their "biggest motiving factors." For many, the student body "energy is very supportive and comforting."

Despite a lack of diversity on campus, students are focused on "always making connections." Most feel "there are lots of opportunities...for supporting underrepresented identities and magnifying those voices." Many students are "passionate advocates for inclusivity and representation," and in recent years, "creating a culture of love and kindness toward one another has been effective at changing the culture on campus and helping everyone feel more included." Even with the current advancements, some students would like to see further improvement in "diversity and outreach to underrepresented populations," but still acknowledge that it "is getting better."

UNIVERSITY OF ST. THOMAS (MN)

Financial Aid: 651-962-6550 • E-Mail: admissions@stthomas.edu • Website: www.stthomas.edu

THE PRINCETON REVIEW SAYS

Admissions

The school reports that its standardized testing policy for use in admission for Fall 2024 is Test Optional. It is unknown at this time if the 2024 testing policy will be permanent. The Princeton Review suggests that interested applicants consult with the school for the most up-to-date standardized testing policies. *Very important factors considered include:* rigor of secondary school record, academic GPA. *Important factors considered include:* application essay. *Other factors considered include:* class rank, standardized test scores, recommendation(s), extracurricular activities, talent/ability, character/personal qualities, first generation, alumni/ae relation, geographical residence, state residency, racial/ethnic status, volunteer work, work experience. High school diploma is required and GED is accepted. 3 math. *Academic units recommended:* 4 English, 4 math, 3 science, 4 foreign language.

Financial Aid

Students should submit: FAFSA. The Princeton Review suggests that all financial aid forms be submitted as soon as possible (see page 5 for a note on the FAFSA). *Need-based scholarships/grants offered:* College/university scholarship or grant aid from institutional funds; Federal Pell; Private scholarships; SEOG; State scholarships/grants. *Loan aid offered:* Direct PLUS loans; Direct Subsidized Loans; Direct Unsubsidized Loans; State Loans. Admitted students will be notified of awards on a rolling basis beginning 1/15. Federal Work-Study Program available. Institutional employment available.

Inside Word

There is no application fee at St. Thomas. The school evaluates each application holistically, and consideration is given both to academic performance and accomplishments outside the classroom. However, students should note the average GPA of admitted students is 3.7. Applicants should make sure their transcripts demonstrate a diverse and challenging academics, good GPA trends, and a solid class rank.

THE SCHOOL SAYS "..."

From the Admissions Office

"Nationally recognized as a top 20 Catholic university, the University of St. Thomas educates students to be morally responsible leaders who think critically, act wisely and work skillfully to advance the common good. St. Thomas is big enough to offer more than 150 undergraduate majors and minors, yet small enough for professors to know every student's name. We emphasize practical skills and hands-on experience that prepare students for today's workplace, while also preparing them for long-term success by building timeless qualities including leadership, creativity and ethical decision-making. Students have opportunities to conduct research alongside faculty in fields ranging from engineering and environmental science to English. The university's partnerships (with Fortune 500 companies and its 110,000+ alumni) connect students to internships and job opportunities – 71 percent of undergraduates complete at least one internship. Ninety-five percent of students are employed or enrolled in graduate school within one year of graduation. Campus life means getting involved. Now NCAA Division I athletics, St. Thomas has plenty of varsity sports to play or cheer on. Students widely participate in the 100+ academic and recreational clubs, and can live in learning communities with students who share their affinities."

SELECTIVITY

Admissions Rating	86
# of applicants	9,154
% of applicants accepted	78
% of acceptees attending	21

FIRST-YEAR PROFILE

Testing policy	Test Optional
Range SAT composite	1140–1320
Range SAT EBRW	550–670
Range SAT math	570–680
Range ACT composite	22–28
# submitting SAT scores	51
% submitting SAT scores	3
# submitting ACT scores	777
% submitting ACT scores	53
Average HS GPA	3.7
% frosh submitting high school GPA	94
% graduated top 10% of class	18
% graduated top 25% of class	49
% graduated top 50% of class	86

DEADLINES

Early action	
Deadline	11/1
Notification	12/15
Regular	
Deadline	1/15
Notification	2/15
Nonfall registration?	Yes

FINANCIAL FACTS

Financial Aid Rating	85
Annual tuition	$48,930
Room and board	$12,260
Required fees	$1,436
Books and supplies	$1,500
Average frosh need-based scholarship	$29,785
Average UG need-based scholarship	$27,099
% needy frosh rec. need-based scholarship or grant aid	97
% needy UG rec. need-based scholarship or grant aid	97
% needy frosh rec. non-need-based scholarship or grant aid	24
% needy UG rec. non-need-based scholarship or grant aid	23
% needy frosh rec. need-based self-help aid	67
% needy UG rec. need-based self-help aid	69
% UG rec. any financial aid	94
% UG borrow to pay for school	59
Average cumulative indebtedness	$43,219
% frosh need fully met	34
% ugrads need fully met	33
Average % of frosh need met	71
Average % of ugrad need met	69

UNIVERSITY OF SAN DIEGO

5998 Alcala Park, San Diego, CA 92110-2492 • Admissions: 619-260-4600 • Fax: 619-260-6836

STUDENTS SAY "..."

Academics

The University of San Diego is a private Catholic institution that prides itself on its status as a "Changemaker," which represents its dedication to creating sustainable solutions locally and afar. In fact, 50 percent of students take advantage of the school's vast study abroad network, which includes programs and internships in 44 countries. "USD encourages its students to apply what they learn in the world to make positive, impactful, sustainable change," says one. Strong curricula and academic advising help students construct four-year plans and create enjoyable schedules, and "projects, seminars, field trips, study abroad programs, and team-taught courses are some of the ways the university gets students engaged." "My class took a trip to the U.S.–Mexico border and talked to border patrol agents, and then we went to an immigrant safe house facility to talk to people who help immigrants with their visa/citizenship status," says one student.

Professors "are eager to share" their passion for their subject with students and offer "personalized one-on-one learning through office hours." They "communicate directly with the students on what material they find to be important." Most "adapt to the new research that has come out on how students learn best" and "bring in speakers to show how [students] can implement Changemaking into...future classrooms." That also extends into "many informative meetings about research opportunities and internships." Speaking of which, the "Career Center [is] very helpful with landing students jobs."

Campus Life

The "weather is so perfect and the campus so beautiful [that] most students spend time outside" at USD, which is "ten minutes away from both the beach and city." Here it's easy for students to take their pick of a litany of activities—they can "lay out on the lawn, take in the sun, skateboard, surf, [or] go out in the town or beach." "San Diego [is] such a large city that there is so much to do and see," and weekends tend to be devoted to exploring; however, there are plenty of social activities and clubs to join on campus. The "Torero Program Board makes sure there is always something for the students to do." One student comments on the "very accepting Greek life system," citing their motto: "These hands don't haze." Of all first-year students, 95 percent live on campus, and all first years (and transfers) participate in a Living Learning Community, which "puts people from the same general living area in a class together focused on a general theme" such as innovation or advocacy. USD is a place where students "can thrive because [their] physical and mental wellness is cared for alongside [their] education."

Student Body

This is "truly...a campus of Changemakers" and "people passionate about causes [where] everyone is hard working yet still socially engaged." USD "does a great job of making sure that students feel like they have a home," and the school has worked to make common areas where students feel comfortable and seen. Because of the "sunny, more relaxed environment" students enjoy on this California campus, they lean "toward casual" in their attire—"balanced and stylish," as one student describes. Many here come from a "strong religious background and greatly utilize the ministry services on campus," and everyone is "welcoming and enjoyable to be around."

UNIVERSITY OF SAN DIEGO

Financial Aid: 619-260-2700 • E-Mail: admissions@sandiego.edu • Website: www.sandiego.edu

THE PRINCETON REVIEW SAYS

Admissions

The school reports that its standardized testing policy for use in admission for Fall 2024 is Test Free. It is unknown at this time if the 2024 testing policy will be permanent. The Princeton Review suggests that interested applicants consult with the school for the most up-to-date standardized testing policies. *Very important factors considered include:* rigor of secondary school record, academic GPA. *Important factors considered include:* class rank, application essay, recommendation(s), extracurricular activities, talent/ability, character/personal qualities, volunteer work. *Other factors considered include:* interview, first generation, geographical residence, religious affiliation/commitment, racial/ethnic status, work experience, level of applicant's interest. High school diploma is required and GED is accepted. *Academic units required:* 4 English, 3 math, 3 science, 2 science labs, 3 foreign language, 2 social studies. *Academic units recommended:* 4 English, 4 math, 4 science, 3 science labs, 4 foreign language, 3 social studies.

Financial Aid

Students should submit: FAFSA. The Princeton Review suggests that all financial aid forms be submitted as soon as possible (see page 5 for a note on the FAFSA). *Need-based scholarships/grants offered:* College/university scholarship or grant aid from institutional funds; Federal Nursing Scholarships; Federal Pell; Private scholarships; SEOG; State scholarships/grants. *Loan aid offered:* Direct PLUS loans; Direct Subsidized Loans; Direct Unsubsidized Loans; College/university loans from institutional funds. Admitted students will be notified of awards on a rolling basis beginning 3/1. Federal Work-Study Program available. Institutional employment available.

The Inside Word

Admissions officers at University of San Diego really aim to take a well-rounded approach to the application process. Hence, they thoroughly evaluate all aspects of a candidate's application, from academic achievements to personal statements and recommendations. Of course, since gaining admission to the university is competitive (each year USD admits around half of those who apply), a strong academic showing is a must, and the school calculates a weighted GPA that awards credit for any honors, AP, or IB classes that have been completed. Admissions officers really keep an eye out for students who demonstrate leadership and community engagement or who show genuine interest in sustainability and global perspective.

THE SCHOOL SAYS "..."

From the Admissions Office

"The University of San Diego has received many local, regional, and national honors in its short, seventy four year history. We are known around the world for our beautiful campus, our outstanding faculty, our sustainability efforts, study abroad programs and the community service work done by our students. Perhaps most significantly, USD has been selected as a "changemaker" campus, one of only 41 in the world so designated by the Ashoka Foundation. It is this honor that captures the spirit of USD and ties together all the others. In addition to strengthening our campus community through service learning and civic engagement, USD is making strides to empower its students to create a socially just and inclusive community by working to become a designated Hispanic Serving Institution by 2026.

"We believe that the world's problems can be solved. We believe that the solution to these problems will not be found through a single discipline or focus. Instead, we know that the world's problems will be solved through innovation, collaboration, and compassion. USD was founded seven decades ago with the principles of Catholic social teaching, a living tradition to work for socially just and peaceful societies and a mission to prepare generations of people changing the world for the better.

"We seek students who also believe in social innovation and change. Students at USD are bright, as our rapidly-growing student profile attests. But they also bring a passion for learning and making a difference. Through our strong liberal arts curriculum, international experiences, faculty and programs, we take that passion and turn it into a lifetime of making the world a better place."

SELECTIVITY

Admissions Rating	83
# of applicants	14,334
% of applicants accepted	53
% of acceptees attending	16
# offered a place on the wait list	3,072
% accepting a place on wait list	44
% admitted from wait list	3

FIRST-YEAR PROFILE

Testing policy	Test Free
Average HS GPA	4.0
% frosh submitting high school GPA	100
% graduated top 10% of class	30
% graduated top 25% of class	68
% graduated top 50% of class	96

DEADLINES

Regular	
Deadline	12/1
Notification	Rolling, 3/1
Nonfall registration?	Yes

APPLICANTS OFTEN PREFER

California Polytechnic State University; University of California—Los Angeles; University of California—San Diego

APPLICANTS SOMETIMES PREFER

Loyola Marymount University; Santa Clara University; University of California—Berkeley; University of Southern California

APPLICANTS RARELY PREFER

Gonzaga University; Pepperdine University; University of San Francisco

FINANCIAL FACTS

Financial Aid Rating	84
Annual tuition	$55,690
Room and board	$18,084
Required fees	$754
Books and supplies	$938
Average frosh need-based scholarship	$40,274
Average UG need-based scholarship	$38,027
% needy frosh rec. need-based scholarship or grant aid	99
% needy UG rec. need-based scholarship or grant aid	98
% needy frosh rec. non-need-based scholarship or grant aid	69
% needy UG rec. non-need-based scholarship or grant aid	58
% needy frosh rec. need-based self-help aid	63
% needy UG rec. need-based self-help aid	66
% frosh rec. any financial aid	84
% UG rec. any financial aid	78
% UG borrow to pay for school	51
Average cumulative indebtedness	$25,208
% frosh need fully met	15
% ugrads need fully met	16
Average % of frosh need met	83
Average % of ugrad need met	78

UNIVERSITY OF SAN FRANCISCO

2130 Fulton Street, San Francisco, CA 94117 • Admissions: 415-422-5555 • Fax: 415-422-2217

STUDENTS SAY "..."

Academics

Students find the quality of University of San Francisco's location to be inseparable from the school's "small-ish private liberal arts college" appeal: "San Francisco is a global city with a wealth of opportunity." However, it's not just the "diverse education in an even more diverse setting" that makes USF stand out so much as its "dedication to social justice." The school's Jesuit roots "is outstanding for students who care about their community and the world beyond themselves," and that shows in the school's approach to "philanthropy and a relatively left and liberal style of teaching." Undergrads love USF's "small class sizes, good work opportunities in the city," and "comprehensive core curriculum." In short, "USF is interested in developing the individual into a strong leader with a particular emphasis on the forces of self-reflection and self-awareness."

Holding true to its mission to students to "change the world from here," a USF education empowers students to make "an impact in the world in an area that you are passionate about." The "extremely talented, well-educated, hard-working, and passionate professors" are "well qualified and deeply care for my education," facilitating "fun and learning combined" in "interesting, engaging classes that are small." In class, students find "the opportunity to discuss, to ask questions, and to give feedback. It was not the professor's classroom, where the professor was controlling the classroom, it was our classroom, all of us together." Students are encouraged to think for themselves in an intellectual atmosphere that "emphasizes acceptance, diversity, and critical thinking." That said, the university offers plenty of support: "We have academic success advisers who help make sure we are on track with graduation, help with major changes, and choosing class schedules." USF's "very prestigious nursing program" and a "five-year program for obtaining a Master's in Education" stand out as major attractions, as do its financial aid resources.

Campus Life

To many students, USF is all about "getting to know each other academically, socially and morally while allowing ourselves to get distracted by the city of San Francisco." One can't help but note that the campus is "in a beautiful location" that's "the ultimate city to be in as a young person," and "USF is located near the Haight, which means that there's always something to do even near the campus." Thanks to "the Muni bus pass that USF gives you," it's easy to get around the city ("public transportation becomes your best friend"), and "students very often go off-campus on weekends to visit tourist attractions, go hiking, explore new food places, go shopping," "hit the nightclubs and bars around the city," and enjoy "concerts and trips to various museums, shows, and performances." There's something for everyone, "whether you enjoy hiking and nature (Golden Gate Park) or enjoy small coffee shops for a nice read." USF tends not to "care for Greek life/sports," and on "weekends campus is barren because everyone is out exploring," but campus is still a "welcoming, second home for all of its students."

Student Body

At USF, students combine in "in one of the best cities in the world" to form what they perceive as "a culturally diverse community that teaches respect, dignity, and honor for all individuals." They describe themselves and their peers as "artistic, smart, morally sound," "quirky and interesting." True to San Francisco's long history as a home for immigrants and trailblazers, at USF, students will find a "very LGBT friendly environment" where it may even be "more normal to be diverse and weird or queer." Students "care about the community and believe in taking action to demonstrate their beliefs," and "the average student may be working for an NGO or volunteering regularly at one of the many non-profits in San Francisco." They "come from all over the world," as well as from many "different cultural backgrounds and hobbies and interests," but hold a common interest of being "committed to their education" and, for the most part, "everyone gets along very well."

UNIVERSITY OF SAN FRANCISCO

Financial Aid: 415-422-3387 • E-Mail: admission@usfca.edu • Website: www.usfca.edu

THE PRINCETON REVIEW SAYS

Admissions

The school reports that its standardized testing policy for use in admission for Fall 2024 is Test Optional. The 2024 testing policy will be permanent. The Princeton Review suggests that interested applicants consult with the school for the most up-to-date standardized testing policies. *Very important factors considered include:* rigor of secondary school record, academic GPA. *Important factors considered include:* application essay, character/personal qualities, volunteer work. *Other factors considered include:* class rank, standardized test scores, recommendation(s), interview, extracurricular activities, talent/ability, first generation, alumni/ae relation, racial/ethnic status, work experience, level of applicant's interest. High school diploma is required and GED is accepted. *Academic units required:* 4 English, 3 math, 2 science, 2 science labs, 2 foreign language, 3 social studies, 6 academic electives.

Financial Aid

Students should submit: FAFSA; State aid form. The Princeton Review suggests that all financial aid forms be submitted as soon as possible (see page 5 for a note on the FAFSA). *Need-based scholarships/grants offered:* College/university scholarship or grant aid from institutional funds; Federal Pell; Private scholarships; SEOG; State scholarships/grants. *Loan aid offered:* Direct PLUS loans; Direct Subsidized Loans; Direct Unsubsidized Loans; Federal Nursing Loans. Admitted students will be notified of awards on a rolling basis beginning 12/15. Federal Work-Study Program available. Institutional employment available.

The Inside Word

USF offers attractive financial aid packages in a gorgeous city, but getting in isn't purely a competitive numbers game: successful applications show genuine intellectual and moral curiosity. Make sure there's real heart in your essay and recommendations. Also, interested students are encouraged to check out USF's early action and decision options and their multicultural recruitment.

THE SCHOOL SAYS "..."

From the Admissions Office

"The University of San Francisco has experienced a significant increase in applications for admission over the past five years. We select applicants with strong academic credentials who will make the most of the university's academic opportunities, location in San Francisco, and its mission to change the world from here. Community outreach and service to others, along with academic excellence, are characteristics that help distinguish those offered admission.

"SAT and ACT tests are optional."

SELECTIVITY

Admissions Rating	87
# of applicants	23,103
% of applicants accepted	71
% of acceptees attending	9
# offered a place on the wait list	1,863
% accepting a place on wait list	38
% admitted from wait list	10
# of early decision applicants	146
% accepted early decision	62

FIRST-YEAR PROFILE

Testing policy	Test Optional
Range SAT composite	1230–1390
Range SAT EBRW	610–700
Range SAT math	600–710
Range ACT composite	27–31
# submitting SAT scores	269
% submitting SAT scores	17
# submitting ACT scores	123
% submitting ACT scores	8
Average HS GPA	3.7
% frosh submitting high school GPA	100
% graduated top 10% of class	30
% graduated top 25% of class	68
% graduated top 50% of class	95

DEADLINES

Early decision	
Deadline	11/1
Notification	12/1
Early action	
Deadline	11/1
Notification	12/14
Regular	
Priority	1/15
Deadline	1/15
Notification	Rolling, 3/15
Nonfall registration?	Yes

APPLICANTS ALSO LOOK AT

University of California—Berkeley; University of California—Davis; University of California-Irvine; University of California—Los Angeles; University of California—Santa Barbara

FINANCIAL FACTS

Financial Aid Rating	81
Annual tuition	$57,670
Room and board	$19,536
Required fees	$552
Books and supplies	$1,152
Average frosh need-based scholarship	$37,074
Average UG need-based scholarship	$32,176
% needy frosh rec. need-based scholarship or grant aid	99
% needy UG rec. need-based scholarship or grant aid	98
% needy frosh rec. non-need-based scholarship or grant aid	10
% needy UG rec. non-need-based scholarship or grant aid	8
% needy frosh rec. need-based self-help aid	71
% needy UG rec. need-based self-help aid	70
% frosh rec. any financial aid	87
% UG rec. any financial aid	87
% UG borrow to pay for school	53
Average cumulative indebtedness	$34,000
% frosh need fully met	12
% ugrads need fully met	10
Average % of frosh need met	73
Average % of ugrad need met	67

THE UNIVERSITY OF SCRANTON

800 Linden Street, Scranton, PA 18510 • Admissions: 570-941-7400 • Fax: 570-941-5928

STUDENTS SAY "..."

Academics

Whether the 3,500 undergraduates at The University of Scranton enroll in the Kania School of Management, Panuska College of Professional Studies, or College of Arts and Sciences, they're likely to end up in at least one nationally recognized program across the nearly 70 bachelor's degrees offered. They'll also get firsthand experience with the school's Jesuit ideals, which are designed to help students graduate with a "strong commitment to…ethics." Alumni can be counted on to keep looking out for their Scranton successors, which helps explain the high 99% job-placement rate: as the school puts it, "more than 1,000 Scranton alumni are CEOs of their company or organization." Things are blooming on the STEM side as well: "This university has a very strong and [well-]known science department." Students also mention the recent improvements Scranton has been making, from laboratories and simulation spaces that impart vital firsthand experiences to "the gorgeous glass study rooms in the Loyola Science Center" and the cadaver lab to "academic buildings [that] are the greatest strength of the school because most have nice classrooms and places to study that foster learning."

Of course, those buildings owe much to the teachers within them, and students are quick to point out that "professors try to create an environment that isn't just them talking at us. They try to engage and get us thinking," which in turn leads to "student-run discussions or even projects that allow you to work with fellow students and get to know one another." Classes, capped at around 35 students, ensure that "the professor [is] able to know your name and take an investment in each individual." Many students describe them as being "very easy to reach" and "truly [caring] about their students," and the bottom line, per one enrollee, is that "I honestly do not think I would have been as successful in attaining my aspirations if it were not for the faculty within my major's department and those from outside."

Campus Life

Students frequently describe The University of Scranton as lovely, and not just because of the scenery. "Everyone knows each other here and support is easy to find…. I love just walking around campus because of how beautiful it is and how many people I stop and say hello to." To put it simply, the school's greatest strength is its ability to "foster a sense of community amongst everyone, faculty and students alike. You feel yourself…getting excited to go to campus." Many students speak fondly of just throwing a Frisbee around Dionne Green (the free-play lawn area) or, "on cold days people go to the nearby mountain for [discounted] skiing and snowboarding." Those seeking to be more competitive can join intramural sports, which "are so incredibly well-run and enjoyable that anyone of any athletic ability can participate and have a blast." There is no Greek life on campus, and students report that "though partying is pretty popular," that's not a big part of the culture. Instead, many students walk into nearby Scranton: "There are a couple of restaurants near campus that I will go to with my friends," check out the programming board's "late-night events every weekend…[which] are usually interesting and draw in a large crowd," check out sporting events, or take part in clubs, many of which happen to be service-oriented, like Beading Hope, which "provides bracelets to the local mental hospital." Says one athlete, "I'm so happy to be part of such a positive environment."

Student Body

Some students refer to The University of Scranton as "Disney World in PA" because "everyone is so friendly and helpful," and note that "even the novice Jesuits who come to visit Scranton always comment on the feeling of community." Diversity seems to be the one area that's still being worked on—the "majority is a richer upper-class white population" of conservatives that has "a growing number of Hispanic students"—but students do report "many different cultural events and support groups, alliances, and clubs for diverse populations." The clubs and organizations are seen as a major driver of change: "Campus ministries and the center for social justice are strong entities on our campus," and undergraduates are "bright and genuinely wanting to better themselves and others."

THE UNIVERSITY OF SCRANTON

Financial Aid: 570-941-7701 • E-Mail: admissions@scranton.edu • Website: www.scranton.edu

THE PRINCETON REVIEW SAYS

Admissions

The school reports that its standardized testing policy for use in admission for Fall 2024 is Test Optional. The Princeton Review suggests that interested applicants consult with the school for the most up-to-date standardized testing policies. *Very important factors considered include:* rigor of secondary school record, class rank, academic GPA, standardized test scores (if submitted). *Important factors considered include:* extracurricular activities. *Other factors considered include:* application essay, recommendation(s), interview, talent/ability, character/personal qualities, alumni/ae relation, volunteer work, work experience, level of applicant's interest. High school diploma is required and GED is accepted. *Academic units required:* 4 English, 3 math, 1 science, 2 foreign language, 2 history. *Academic units recommended:* 4 English, 4 math, 2 science, 2 foreign language, 3 history.

Financial Aid

Students should submit: FAFSA; State aid form. Priority filing deadline is 2/15. The Princeton Review suggests that all financial aid forms be submitted as soon as possible (see page 5 for a note on the FAFSA). *Need-based scholarships/grants offered:* College/university scholarship or grant aid from institutional funds; Federal Pell; Private scholarships; SEOG; State scholarships/grants. *Loan aid offered:* Direct PLUS loans; Direct Subsidized Loans; Direct Unsubsidized Loans; Federal Nursing Loans. Admitted students will be notified of awards on a rolling basis beginning 1/15. Federal Work-Study Program available. Institutional employment available.

The Inside Word

The University of Scranton claims to have "the keys to your success," and that much is certainly true for its easily unlocked Common Application process. That said, the school holistically reviews candidates, so they will consider whatever you include. Note that while the school's overall acceptance numbers are high—more than 80% of those who apply get in—certain programs are highly competitive, and the school encourages you to apply as early as possible for them.

THE SCHOOL SAYS "..."

From the Admissions Office

"The University of Scranton is a premier Catholic and Jesuit university that provides rigorous academics grounded in the liberal arts. Our 58-acre campus offers the best of both worlds—the city and the mountains. We are in the heart of the city of Scranton, in Pennsylvania's Pocono Northeast, just two hours from New York City and Philadelphia. In recent years, we have invested more than $295 million in campus improvements, including new residence halls, an athletics campus, a science center and the state-of-the-art Leahy Hall, which houses our physical therapy, occupational therapy and health and human performance departments.

"This university is more than a respected institution; we are also a caring, nurturing community whose graduates are known for their devotion to the welfare of others and by their special commitment to social justice.

"We offer 69 majors, more than 80 clubs and organizations, and 23 Division III athletic teams to the 3,500 undergraduate students in attendance.

"Scranton develops leaders in every sense through rigorous preparation in students' chosen fields coupled with a commitment to educating the whole person. Students extend their academic experience through participation in honors programs, internships, faculty-student research and study abroad, and the university provides excellent preparation for medical and other health professions doctoral programs, law school, graduate school, and post-graduate fellowships and scholarships. Our AACSB-accredited Kania School of Management has received national recognition for our business programs.

"Students can apply online for free at scranton.edu/apply, or schedule a visit online at scranton.edu/visit or by calling us at 1-888-SCRANTON."

SELECTIVITY

Admissions Rating	85
# of applicants	9,236
% of applicants accepted	83
% of acceptees attending	11
# offered a place on the wait list	1,061
% accepting a place on wait list	17
% admitted from wait list	82

FIRST-YEAR PROFILE

Testing policy	Test Optional
Range SAT composite	1140–1310
Range SAT EBRW	580–660
Range SAT math	560–660
Range ACT composite	27–32
# submitting SAT scores	336
% submitting SAT scores	40
# submitting ACT scores	49
% submitting ACT scores	6
Average HS GPA	3.6
% frosh submitting high school GPA	100
% graduated top 10% of class	28
% graduated top 25% of class	59
% graduated top 50% of class	87

DEADLINES

Early action	
Deadline	11/15
Notification	12/15
Regular	
Priority	11/15
Deadline	3/1
Nonfall registration?	Yes

APPLICANTS OFTEN PREFER

Fairfield University; Penn State University Park; Sacred Heart University; Saint Joseph's University (PA); Temple University; University of Delaware; West Chester University of Pennsylvania

APPLICANTS SOMETIMES PREFER

Loyola University Maryland; Marist College; Quinnipiac University; Rutgers University—New Brunswick; Seton Hall University; State University of New York—Binghamton University; The College of New Jersey; University of Pittsburgh—Pittsburgh Campus

FINANCIAL FACTS

Financial Aid Rating	81
Annual tuition	$44,132
Room and board	$15,182
Required fees	$400
Books and supplies	$1,300
Average frosh need-based scholarship	$16,286
Average UG need-based scholarship	$16,503
% needy frosh rec. need-based scholarship or grant aid	83
% needy UG rec. need-based scholarship or grant aid	83
% needy frosh rec. non-need-based scholarship or grant aid	89
% needy UG rec. non-need-based scholarship or grant aid	81
% needy frosh rec. need-based self-help aid	71
% needy UG rec. need-based self-help aid	75
% frosh rec. any financial aid	99
% UG rec. any financial aid	93
% UG borrow to pay for school	73
Average cumulative indebtedness	$45,439
% frosh need fully met	21
% ugrads need fully met	21
Average % of frosh need met	71
Average % of ugrad need met	71

THE UNIVERSITY OF THE SOUTH

735 University Avenue, Sewanee, TN 37383-1000 • Admissions: 931-598-1000 • Fax: 931-538-3248

STUDENTS SAY "..."

Academics

The unique mountaintop Tennessee location allows the University of the South, known as Sewanee, to utilize "our beautiful campus not only as a classroom but also as a tool for learning itself." Whether you are studying the humanities—being treated to "a good amount of instruction...outdoors"—or studying the hard sciences the "natural biodiversity of the campus" is appreciated. As the school is predominantly an undergraduate institution, students report that "all of the research opportunities professors have go to us, which rocks." And for teachers who don't naturally have research, the "incredible" small class sizes\ and low student-teacher ratio means there's ample time to make "connections and [get] excellent letters of recommendation for graduate school."

Courses on campus are primarily discussion based, so students are constantly "encouraged to participate and voice their ideas." They also provide a lauded flexibility: "I don't think I've had a stereotypical final exam in my entire time at Sewanee. Most of the time, we are actively applying our studies or content to real-world problems or something that will help us in our field." One first-year student particularly loved "a final project that was both chemistry and art based, joining the two subjects together in a lab setting with the creation of cyanotypes."

Campus Life

Sewanee's 13,000 acre campus, The Domain, "is unbeatable." One student emphasizes that "being on the secluded mountain with your classmates, peers, and most of your professors brings the community closer together." The on-campus farm provides another opportunity for students to enjoy the outdoors: "We get to hang out with animals whenever, make our own food and food for the community, and spend some quality time with our peers outdoors while still getting to work hard to take care of our community."

"The social scene is driven by Greek Life; however, all parties are open to the entire community." There's also the incredibly popular Sewanee Outing Program, which has events that "are always cool" and then there's plenty of celebrated canoeing, mountain biking, running, climbing, and spelunking throughout the Domain, while others love just "looking at the stars with friends."

Student Body

"People don't choose to come here just because of the academics. They choose to come here because of the strong community." They also come for the setting, which means you'll find a lot of "nature lovers, the type of people who write songs about a view and sit outside when they study" as well as "athletes, outdoorsy kids, pre-professional kids who are really focused on their studies, and many more groups." Regardless of background, the consensus is that "everyone meshes well together," though some note that the "environment definitely caters to more extroverted people" and that it's "no secret that Sewanee students love to party." Overall, students are united by a "genuine passion amongst our student body for social justice and community service." This sentiment is visible on campus daily as "people at Sewanee smile at strangers when they walk by, even if it feels awkward, out of the innate belief that they might be a friend later or maybe just that it'll brighten someone's day."

THE UNIVERSITY OF THE SOUTH

Financial Aid: 931-598-1312 • E-Mail: admiss@sewanee.edu • Website: www.sewanee.edu

THE PRINCETON REVIEW SAYS

Admissions

The school reports that its standardized testing policy for use in admission for Fall 2024 is Test Optional. The 2024 testing policy will be permanent. The Princeton Review suggests that interested applicants consult with the school for the most up-to-date standardized testing policies. *Very important factors considered include:* rigor of secondary school record, academic GPA, recommendation(s). *Important factors considered include:* application essay, extracurricular activities, character/personal qualities, volunteer work, work experience. *Other factors considered include:* class rank, standardized test scores, interview, first generation, alumni/ae relation, level of applicant's interest. High school diploma is required and GED is not accepted. *Academic units required:* 4 English, 3 math, 2 science, 2 science labs, 2 foreign language, 1 social studies, 1 history. *Academic units recommended:* 4 English, 4 math, 4 science, 3 science labs, 4 foreign language, 2 social studies, 2 history.

Financial Aid

Students should submit: CSS/Financial Aid Profile; FAFSA. The Princeton Review suggests that all financial aid forms be submitted as soon as possible (see page 5 for a note on the FAFSA). *Need-based scholarships/grants offered:* College/university scholarship or grant aid from institutional funds; Federal Pell; Private scholarships; SEOG; State scholarships/grants. *Loan aid offered:* Direct PLUS loans; Direct Subsidized Loans; Direct Unsubsidized Loans. Admitted students will be notified of awards on or about in early March. Federal Work-Study Program available. Institutional employment available.

The Inside Word

The admissions office at The University of the South is very personable and accessible to students. Its staff includes some of the most well-respected admissions professionals in the South, and that shows in the way they work with students. Despite a fairly high acceptance rate, candidates who take the admissions process here lightly may find themselves disappointed. Applicant evaluation is too personal for a lackadaisical approach to yield success. A demonstrated interest in attending, evidenced by campus visits or reaching out to the admissions office, is advised.

THE SCHOOL SAYS " . . . "

From the Admissions Office

"The University of the South is consistently ranked among the top tier of national liberal arts universities. Sewanee is committed to a rigorous academic curriculum that focuses on the liberal arts as the most valuable form of undergraduate education. It offers a wide range of majors, minors, and pre-professional programs including business, medicine, law, and engineering.

"Sewanee is a small residential college located on a 13,000-acre campus atop Tennessee's Cumberland Plateau between Chattanooga and Nashville. Largely forested, rich in biodiversity, the campus is a distinctive asset offering an unparalleled outdoor laboratory and boundless recreational opportunities.

"The university has an impressive record of academic achievement—27 Rhodes Scholars and 34 NCAA postgraduate scholarship recipients have graduated from Sewanee. Four recent Tennessee Professors of the Year have been members of Sewanee's faculty. Professors are leading scholars and researchers with a commitment to teaching, and in Sewanee's close community they develop rich and lasting relationships with their students.

"Since 2009, prospective students have had the option of choosing whether or not to submit standardized test scores. Test scores are considered to be purely supplementary in the admission process and students who choose not to submit the will be given equal consideration to those who do. To ensure that students get the most value out of their time at Sewanee, we make the Sewanee Pledge: we will help students secure good jobs or spots in graduate programs by providing funding for a summer internship or research opportunity; we will provide students with access to a semester-long study abroad program at no additional tuition cost; and we guarantee that you will graduate (with one major) in four consecutive years or the fifth is on us."

SELECTIVITY

Admissions Rating	90
# of applicants	4,578
% of applicants accepted	52
% of acceptees attending	17
# offered a place on the wait list	321
% accepting a place on wait list	46
% admitted from wait list	7
# of early decision applicants	202
% accepted early decision	60

FIRST-YEAR PROFILE

Testing policy	Test Optional
Range SAT composite	1190–1358
Range SAT EBRW	620–708
Range SAT math	570–668
Range ACT composite	26–31
# submitting SAT scores	98
% submitting SAT scores	24
# submitting ACT scores	171
% submitting ACT scores	41
% graduated top 10% of class	32
% graduated top 25% of class	66
% graduated top 50% of class	91

DEADLINES

Early decision	
Deadline	11/15
Notification	12/15
Other ED deadline	1/15
Other ED notification	1/31
Early action	
Deadline	12/1
Notification	1/31
Regular	
Deadline	2/1
Notification	3/1
Nonfall registration?	Yes

FINANCIAL FACTS

Financial Aid Rating	88
Annual tuition	$53,418
Room and board	$15,338
Required fees	$286
Books and supplies	$1,200
Average frosh need-based scholarship	$36,856
Average UG need-based scholarship	$38,677
% needy frosh rec. need-based scholarship or grant aid	99
% needy UG rec. need-based scholarship or grant aid	99
% needy frosh rec. non-need-based scholarship or grant aid	27
% needy UG rec. non-need-based scholarship or grant aid	19
% needy frosh rec. need-based self-help aid	73
% needy UG rec. need-based self-help aid	71
% frosh rec. any financial aid	97
% UG rec. any financial aid	96
% UG borrow to pay for school	36
Average cumulative indebtedness	$33,670
% frosh need fully met	41
% ugrads need fully met	36
Average % of frosh need met	92
Average % of ugrad need met	90

UNIVERSITY OF SOUTH CAROLINA—COLUMBIA

University of South Carolina—Columbia, Columbia, SC 29208 • Admissions: 803-777-7000 • Fax: 803-777-0101

STUDENTS SAY "..."

Academics

More than 200 years of southern traditions and academic leadership provide the foundation for the University of South Carolina—Columbia, a historic institution that is "constantly working on being the absolute best university it can be for its students" and "open to any suggestions." The school provides "a wealth of opportunities for undergraduate research, study abroad, service learning, and unique organizations," and advisors and the Student Success Center are "always looking to help" students find post-graduation plans. "The University of South Carolina is about what you make it, as the university provides opportunities for everyone to make the absolute most of their time here," says one student.

Those who teach here are "intent on getting their students involved outside of the classroom," and "able to relate their in-class lectures to the real world." "I've had a ton of professors present me with opportunities for research, internship, or part-time employment on campus which has all developed me into being a very employable prospect upon graduation," says one student. While classes "can sometimes be very difficult," there are tutors and supplemental instructors through the university ("for free!") who "will always fill in the gaps that you are missing." UofSC's size "lends itself to interdisciplinary degree programs and individual projects," and faculty fosters academic exploration in asking for student opinions and "[encouraging] us to argue and consider other students' opinions."

Campus Life

The students at the University of South Carolina are "extraordinarily social:" "From tailgates to intramural sports to Greek life, there is always something to do." Saturday football games are such a tradition that "traffic patterns are altered because it is such a huge deal." Traditions are "highly important" to the school, and events such as Tiger Burn and Homecoming are dotted throughout the year. Greene Street (the main street on campus) is closed off to traffic 24/7, which allows students to walk freely between classes and also allows organizations and activities such as Hip Hop Wednesdays and a farmer's market to take place. The weather is usually beautiful, and many students can be found "sitting on the horseshoe between classes or grabbing a bite to eat" or availing themselves of the "ton of outdoor recreation activities run through the university."

On the weekends, many upperclassmen spend time in Five Points, a "very student-friendly bar district beside campus," and Columbia's central location "grants shorter distances to the beach as well as the mountains"; the town itself is very easy to get around on foot and "very artsy." There is "literally a club for everything," from "skydiving to Latin dance to language," and service opportunities are also very popular. Additionally, the amenities that UofSC provides are "phenomenal," and include everything from "free athletic tickets to twelve free counseling sessions a year." UofSC really cares about the well-being and safety of its students, and "offers so many things to help the students here to succeed."

Student Body

This medium-sized, genteel Southern institution is "all about being a family and feeling like the University of South Carolina is your home away from home." There is a "good mix" of people of different ethnicity, genders, and personalities, and a lot of the student body is "relatively laid-back in dress and attitude." There is "certainly that southern charm, especially because of the large Greek population" on campus, and this is "a unified student body in relation to each other and between students and faculty and staff." "The university welcomes everyone with open arms to make everyone feel included in the Gamecock experience," says a student.

UNIVERSITY OF SOUTH CAROLINA—COLUMBIA

Financial Aid: 803-777-8134 • E-Mail: admissions-ugrad@sc.edu • Website: www.sc.edu

THE PRINCETON REVIEW SAYS

Admissions

The school reports that its standardized testing policy for use in admission for Fall 2024 is Test Optional. It is unknown at this time if the 2024 testing policy will be permanent. The Princeton Review suggests that interested applicants consult with the school for the most up-to-date standardized testing policies. *Very important factors considered include:* academic GPA. *Important factors considered include:* rigor of secondary school record, class rank, standardized test scores. *Other factors considered include:* application essay, recommendation(s), extracurricular activities, talent/ability, state residency, volunteer work, work experience. High school diploma is required and GED is accepted. *Academic units required:* 4 English, 4 math, 3 science, 3 science labs, 2 foreign language, 2 social studies, 1 history, 1 visual/performing arts, 2 academic electives.

Financial Aid

Students should submit: FAFSA. Priority filing deadline is 4/1. The Princeton Review suggests that all financial aid forms be submitted as soon as possible (see page 5 for a note on the FAFSA). *Need-based scholarships/grants offered:* College/university scholarship or grant aid from institutional funds; Federal Nursing Scholarships; Federal Pell; Private scholarships; SEOG; State scholarships/grants; United Negro College Fund. *Loan aid offered:* Direct PLUS loans; Direct Subsidized Loans; Direct Unsubsidized Loans; Federal Nursing Loans. Admitted students will be notified of awards on a rolling basis beginning 4/1. Federal Work-Study Program available. Institutional employment available.

The Inside Word

At University of South Carolina, as at most large schools, admissions decisions are based almost entirely on a prospective student's grades, test scores, and high school curriculum. A personal statement is required. Applicants with an A-minus average and a combined SAT score in the 1150–1280 range (or an ACT composite of 25–30) often get in. Higher standardized scores can offset a lower GPA, and vice versa.

THE SCHOOL SAYS "..."

From the Admissions Office

"The University of South Carolina is a destination of choice for students from all fifty states and more than 100 countries. UofSC is one of only forty public research institutions to earn both the top-tier research classification and the community service classification from the Carnegie Foundation. As early as their freshman year, undergraduates are encouraged to compete for research grants. As South Carolina's flagship institution, UofSC offers more than 300 degree programs. More than 35,000 students seek baccalaureate, masters, or doctoral degrees. UofSC is known for its top-ranked academic programs, including its international business and exercise science programs—both rated number one nationally. Other notable programs include chemical and nuclear engineering; health education; hotel, restaurant, and tourism; marine science; law; medicine; nursing; and psychology, among others. UofSC is recognized for its pioneering efforts in freshman outreach, and the South Carolina Honors College is ranked number one in the country compared to all other honors colleges in public university settings. UofSC offers student support in such areas as career development, leadership training, research grants, pre-professional planning, and study abroad. On campus, students enjoy a state-of-the-art fitness center, an 18,000-seat arena, an 80,000-seat stadium, and more than 400 student organizations. Off campus, South Carolina's world-famous beaches and the Blue Ridge Mountains are each less than a three-hour drive away. The University of South Carolina is located in the state's capital city, making it a great place for internships and job opportunities."

SELECTIVITY

Admissions Rating	80
# of applicants	42,188
% of applicants accepted	64
% of acceptees attending	24
# offered a place on the wait list	5,847
% accepting a place on wait list	38
% admitted from wait list	1

FIRST-YEAR PROFILE

Testing policy	Test Optional
Range SAT composite	1200–1380
Range SAT EBRW	600–690
Range SAT math	580–690
Range ACT composite	27–32
# submitting SAT scores	2,182
% submitting SAT scores	33
# submitting ACT scores	1,124
% submitting ACT scores	17
Average HS GPA	3.7
% frosh submitting high school GPA	97
% graduated top 10% of class	26
% graduated top 25% of class	58
% graduated top 50% of class	91

DEADLINES

Early action	
Deadline	10/15
Notification	12/15
Regular	
Deadline	12/1
Notification	3/15
Nonfall registration?	Yes

FINANCIAL FACTS

Financial Aid Rating	78
Annual in-state tuition	$12,228
Annual out-of-state tuition	$33,528
Room and board	$11,780
Required fees	$400
Books and supplies	$1,312
Average frosh need-based scholarship	$8,042
Average UG need-based scholarship	$7,467
% needy frosh rec. need-based scholarship or grant aid	44
% needy UG rec. need-based scholarship or grant aid	49
% needy frosh rec. non-need-based scholarship or grant aid	92
% needy UG rec. non-need-based scholarship or grant aid	75
% needy frosh rec. need-based self-help aid	68
% needy UG rec. need-based self-help aid	71
% UG borrow to pay for school	53
Average cumulative indebtedness	$31,695
% frosh need fully met	29
% ugrads need fully met	28
Average % of frosh need met	71
Average % of ugrad need met	76

THE UNIVERSITY OF SOUTH DAKOTA

414 East Clark St., Vermillion, SD 57069 • Admissions: 877-269-6837 • Fax: 605-677-6323

STUDENTS SAY "..."

Academics

With an honors program that is "the best-kept secret in the country" and professors who are "nearly always willing to go the extra mile for students," the University of South Dakota offers a "great student to faculty communicative experience at a reasonable price." Numerous departments garner praise from students, and the University boasts winners "almost every year for big scholarships like the Goldwater and Truman, competing with big, Ivy League, private colleges that charge quadruple the amount for the same education." While the nursing school is the most frequently praised, the "business, biology, premed, law, and psychology classes are very solid," and the "dental hygiene, music, and journalism schools" also stand out, with the most copious laurels heaped on the music department's professors who are "some of the best." All told, the wide selection of quality academics "gives students many options as far as majors go," and for students willing to throw themselves into their studies, "the odds of getting into a professional or graduate program are good."

Campus Life

"We work hard, so we can play hard," sums up the undergraduate philosophy at USD. "Although there is a lot of partying that happens, the students keep themselves occupied with school work, intramural sports, and hanging out with their friends." Vermillion's small size seems to be a double-edged sword; some insist that "the size of the town means no one is more than a 10-minute walk/bike ride away!" and that "since it is a smaller campus, students have more opportunities to be involved in internships and various other activities." But the fact remains that "many of the upperclassmen live in the larger cities to the north and south." In general, "students have to make their own fun, which often involves partying or taking small road trips to other cities in the area." For those planning to roam further afield, "Vermillion is located very close to Yankton, Sioux City (IA), and Sioux Falls (all within an hour). They are bigger cities and offer everything a person would want to do (shopping, movies, entertainment)."

Student Body

A typical USD student "would be a conservative Midwesterner. He or she would be Caucasian" and would most likely have originated in "small towns in South Dakota, Iowa, and Nebraska." "Many people join a Greek system or are athletes or musicians. Those who do not fit into these three main groups seem to focus on their academics" and "[fit] in fine with the majority because of the open mindedness of most students." For example, "gay students are able to get along with the rest of student population." There's no denying that "partying is a definite part of the culture, though many of the 'smart' kids both party and work hard." Student organizations call out to many, and "it seems like every person on campus is part of at least one of them. It is a great way to meet new people and [to participate in] activities."

THE UNIVERSITY OF SOUTH DAKOTA

E-Mail: admissions@usd.edu • Website: www.usd.edu

THE PRINCETON REVIEW SAYS

Admissions

The school reports that its standardized testing policy for use in admission for Fall 2024 is Test Optional. It is unknown at this time if the 2024 testing policy will be permanent. The Princeton Review suggests that interested applicants consult with the school for the most up-to-date standardized testing policies. *Very important factors considered include:* rigor of secondary school record, class rank, academic GPA, standardized test scores. *Other factors considered include:* application essay, recommendation(s). High school diploma is required and GED is accepted. *Academic units required:* 4 English, 3 math, 3 science, 3 science labs, 3 social studies, 1 visual/performing arts. *Academic units recommended:* 4 English, 4 math, 4 science, 3 science labs, 2 foreign language, 3 social studies, 1 visual/performing arts.

Financial Aid

Students should submit: FAFSA. Priority filing deadline is 4/1. The Princeton Review suggests that all financial aid forms be submitted as soon as possible (see page 5 for a note on the FAFSA). *Need-based scholarships/grants offered:* College/university scholarship or grant aid from institutional funds; Federal Pell; Private scholarships; SEOG; State scholarships/grants; United Negro College Fund. *Loan aid offered:* Direct PLUS loans; Direct Subsidized Loans; Direct Unsubsidized Loans. Admitted students will be notified of awards on a rolling basis beginning 5/1. Federal Work-Study Program available. Institutional employment available.

The Inside Word

To be a candidate for general admission to USD, you must meet one of three general requirements: rank in the top 50 percent of your graduating class, obtain an ACT/SAT composite score of 21/990 or higher, or have a minimum grade point average of at least 2.6 on a 4.0 scale in all high school courses. An applicant's high school curricula must also meet certain minimum requirements.

THE SCHOOL SAYS "..."

From the Admissions Office

"The University of South Dakota is the perfect fit for students looking for a smart educational investment. USD is South Dakota's only designated liberal arts university and is consistently rated among the top doctoral institutions in the country. Annually, USD awards $7.2 million in scholarships. More than 80 percent of USD students receive financial aid through grants, loans and work-study jobs.

"USD students earn the nation's most prestigious scholarships. Our quality of teaching and research prepares students to pursue their passions all over the world, at institutions such as Columbia, Princeton, John Hopkins, Harvard Medical School, Massachusetts Institute of Technology, The University of Chicago and beyond. One hundred and three students have been awarded prestigious Fulbright, Rhodes, National Science Foundation, Boren, Truman, Udall, Gilman and Goldwater scholarships and grants for graduate study. Personal attention from our award-winning faculty and our welcoming environment makes students feel right at home.

"As the flagship liberal arts institution in South Dakota, USD—founded in 1862—has long been regarded as a leader in the state and the region. Notable undergraduate and postgraduate alumni include author and former news anchor Tom Brokaw, U.S. Senator Tim Johnson, U.S. Representative Kevin Brady, *USA Today* founder Al Neuharth and U.S. Senator John Thune.

"Though it is currently optional, USD recommends taking the ACT over the SAT. Students who wish to send their SAT scores will have their scores converted to ACT scores for placement and scholarship consideration."

SELECTIVITY

Admissions Rating	82
# of applicants	4,480
% of applicants accepted	99
% of acceptees attending	30

FIRST-YEAR PROFILE

Testing policy	Test Optional
Range SAT composite	1050–1260
Range SAT EBRW	500–640
Range SAT math	520–660
Range ACT composite	19–25
# submitting SAT scores	38
% submitting SAT scores	3
# submitting ACT scores	1,007
% submitting ACT scores	76
Average HS GPA	3.5
% frosh submitting high school GPA	98
% graduated top 10% of class	16
% graduated top 25% of class	41
% graduated top 50% of class	75

DEADLINES

Regular	
Notification	Rolling, 8/1
Nonfall registration?	Yes

FINANCIAL FACTS

Financial Aid Rating	76
Annual in-state tuition	$7,773
Annual out-of-state tuition	$11,283
Room and board	$8,604
Required fees	$1,659
Books and supplies	$1,200
Average frosh need-based scholarship	$5,583
Average UG need-based scholarship	$5,516
% needy frosh rec. need-based scholarship or grant aid	47
% needy UG rec. need-based scholarship or grant aid	49
% needy frosh rec. non-need-based scholarship or grant aid	73
% needy UG rec. non-need-based scholarship or grant aid	63
% needy frosh rec. need-based self-help aid	86
% needy UG rec. need-based self-help aid	89
% frosh rec. any financial aid	
% UG rec. any financial aid	
% UG borrow to pay for school	70
Average cumulative indebtedness	$28,354
% frosh need fully met	16
% ugrads need fully met	16
Average % of frosh need met	55
Average % of ugrad need met	58

UNIVERSITY OF SOUTH FLORIDA

4202 East Fowler Avenue, Tampa, FL 33620-9951 • Admissions: 813-974-2011 • Fax: 813-974-9689

This narrative, like all others in this book, is based on student responses and data collected prior to the 2023–2024 academic school year. While these profiles strive to be an accurate depiction of what to expect for the upcoming year, recent developments in the Florida state system may change the academic offerings and overall atmosphere at colleges in the system. Students should check the free online tools for this book (see page vi) for any late-breaking administrative news and they should voice any concerns or questions with the colleges directly.

STUDENTS SAY ". . ."

Academics
The University of South Florida provides undergraduates with a "beautiful campus," a strong "sense of community," and "great financial aid," so it's easy to understand why students clamor to attend. From the moment you step onto the grounds, it's clear that the university is "committed to [your] success and [that] there are countless opportunities and support programs" available. This is showcased everywhere from the "many unique study abroad programs" to "tutoring [resources] for a variety of subjects." Academically, students are quick to highlight USF's "strong STEM programs" and note the abundance of "nursing/medical opportunities," which are courtesy of the university partnering with the "incredible [number] of hospitals in the vicinity." However, undergrads here have decidedly mixed reviews for their teachers. Indeed, they generally witness "less enthusiasm from [general education] professors." Fortunately, when it comes to their core major classes, students happily report that instructors are truly "passionate about what they teach." As one eager undergrad shares, "[Professors] go above and beyond to make their class lectures interesting and understandable." Students also enjoy the "blend of lecture and discussion" in courses. Another thrilled undergrad simply concludes, "My professors are the best [because they] encourage me not only with my work…but also…in my overall life."

Campus Life
Admittedly, the University of South Florida has "a lot of commuters," but that doesn't mean the campus transforms into a ghost town once classes are finished! In fact, there are numerous activities and events of which to take advantage. For example, you can always find students enjoying "movies on the lawn, international fairs, [and] artistic presentations." Every Wednesday is "Bull Market, [which consists of] a collection of various student orgs and off-campus vendors…giving away freebies…or selling baked goods or raffle tickets to raise money." Need something a little more active? Well then you will be delighted to learn that "USF recreation…has its own park where you can rent kayaks and go down the Hillsborough river." Of course, many undergrads simply love "lounging in a campus hammock" or kicking back in "the student commons [with some] foosball, video games, or pool." And when you need a respite from collegiate life, downtown Tampa also offers a good deal of excitement. There's a wide array of bars and restaurants as well as Busch Gardens, which is only "five minutes from campus…[and] a popular hangout." The pristine beaches of St. Pete's and Walt Disney World are within driving distance as well.

Student Body
Undergrads at USF proudly proclaim that their school is "very diverse" and "like a mini-city." Indeed, you'll find "many cultures and…tons of international students." "I have met such a variety of people from different ethnic backgrounds, religions, abilities, talents, ideologies, sexual orientations, gender expressions, interests, and life experiences," says a student. The age of students also varies widely on-campus, with one undergrad sharing, "I've seen students with grey hair, students who look fresh out of high school, and everything in between." Importantly, it's not hard for these Bulls to find common ground. That's because USF students are all typically "helpful, accommodating, and kind." Another student further explains, "My peers are very personable, smart, and caring. Everyone I met has helped me in some way and has been very pleasant to be around." And a fellow undergrad concurs by stating, "Everyone has an aura about them that makes you feel comfortable and welcomed."

UNIVERSITY OF SOUTH FLORIDA

Financial Aid: 813-974-3039 • E-Mail: admissions@usf.edu • Website: www.usf.edu

THE PRINCETON REVIEW SAYS

Admissions

The school reports that its standardized testing policy for use in admission for Fall 2024 is Requires applicants to submit either the SAT or ACT. The 2024 testing policy will be permanent. The Princeton Review suggests that interested applicants consult with the school for the most up-to-date standardized testing policies. *Very important factors considered include:* rigor of secondary school record, academic GPA, standardized test scores. *Other factors considered include:* class rank, talent/ability, first generation. High school diploma is required and GED is accepted. *Academic units required:* 4 English, 4 math, 3 science, 2 science labs, 2 foreign language, 3 social studies, 2 academic electives. *Academic units recommended:* 4 English, 4 math, 4 science, 2 science labs, 2 foreign language, 3 social studies, 2 academic electives.

Financial Aid

Students should submit: FAFSA. Priority filing deadline is 1/1. The Princeton Review suggests that all financial aid forms be submitted as soon as possible (see page 5 for a note on the FAFSA). *Need-based scholarships/grants offered:* College/university scholarship or grant aid from institutional funds; Federal Pell; Private scholarships; SEOG; State scholarships/grants; United Negro College Fund. *Loan aid offered:* Direct PLUS loans; Direct Subsidized Loans; Direct Unsubsidized Loans; College/university loans from institutional funds; Federal Nursing Loans. Admitted students will be notified of awards on a rolling basis. Federal Work-Study Program available. Institutional employment available.

The Inside Word

USF keeps the admissions process streamlined and simplified. In other words, the university takes a fairly quantitative and objective approach, so expect that your GPA and standardized test scores will hold the most weight. The admissions committee will also consider the rigor of your coursework, which means applicants who have taken multiple AP, IB, honors, or AICE courses are at a definite advantage. Finally, grade trends also matter; don't panic if your high school career began inauspiciously as long as your grades steadily improved. If they declined over time, you may have to make up for that elsewhere in your application.

THE SCHOOL SAYS "..."

From the Admissions Office

"Located in the Tampa Bay metropolitan area, USF is recognized as a top-fifty public research university. USF takes great pride in its global faculty. Professors in all academic areas are responsible for discovering new solutions to existing and emerging problems. As an undergraduate at USF, you can participate actively in the creation of the knowledge that will be taught on other college campuses for decades to come. The faculty at USF is diverse as well.

"As students begin the application process, they should become familiar with USF's admission requirements. USF used extensive institutional research to validate that the high school GPA coupled with grade trends and the rigor of student's curriculum in high school are the most critical factors in student academic success at USF. Preference in admission, therefore, is given to students who complete at least three AP or IB courses, at least two college-level courses through dual enrollment, and additional coursework in math, science or foreign language beyond minimum requirements. SAT and ACT scores, while important, are less critical in USF's admission decisions when the high school GPA and rigor of curriculum are both strong. USF does use the ACT English/writing components to make decisions, as a score of 24 is an additional indicator of potential for academic success. USF also takes into account special talents in and outside of the classroom as well as whether a student would be in the first generation of the family to attend college. With some of the best weather in the country, it's always a great time to visit USF. Campus tours, information sessions and tours of the residence halls are offered on weekdays throughout the year and on most Saturday mornings from September through April. Reservations are strongly encouraged."

SELECTIVITY

Admissions Rating	92
# of applicants	65,567
% of applicants accepted	44
% of acceptees attending	24

FIRST-YEAR PROFILE

Testing policy	SAT or ACT Required
Range SAT composite	1240–1370
Range SAT EBRW	610–690
Range SAT math	610–700
Range ACT composite	27–30
# submitting SAT scores	5,157
% submitting SAT scores	76
# submitting ACT scores	1,643
% submitting ACT scores	24
Average HS GPA	4.1
% frosh submitting high school GPA	100
% graduated top 10% of class	29
% graduated top 25% of class	65
% graduated top 50% of class	91

DEADLINES

Regular	
Priority	11/1
Deadline	3/1
Notification	5/1
Nonfall registration?	Yes

APPLICANTS ALSO LOOK AT

Florida International University; Florida State University; The University of Tampa; University of Central Florida; University of Florida

FINANCIAL FACTS

Financial Aid Rating	82
Annual in-state tuition	$4,559
Annual out-of-state tuition	$15,473
Room and board	$12,622
Required fees	$1,851
Books and supplies	$770
Average frosh need-based scholarship	$12,035
Average UG need-based scholarship	$10,309
% needy frosh rec. need-based scholarship or grant aid	90
% needy UG rec. need-based scholarship or grant aid	88
% needy frosh rec. non-need-based scholarship or grant aid	12
% needy UG rec. non-need-based scholarship or grant aid	8
% needy frosh rec. need-based self-help aid	33
% needy UG rec. need-based self-help aid	39
% UG borrow to pay for school	37
Average cumulative indebtedness	$19,949
% frosh need fully met	18
% ugrads need fully met	13
Average % of frosh need met	69
Average % of ugrad need met	64

UNIVERSITY OF SOUTHERN CALIFORNIA

University Park, Los Angeles, CA 90089 • Admissions: 213-740-2311 • Fax: 213-821-0200

CAMPUS LIFE

Quality of Life Rating	75
Fire Safety Rating	97
Green Rating	93
Type of school	Private
Affiliation	No Affiliation
Environment	Metropolis

STUDENTS

Total undergrad enrollment	20,619
% male/female/another gender	48/52/0
% from out of state	39
% frosh from public high school	54
% frosh live on campus	98
% ugrads live on campus	35
# of fraternities (% join)	32 (10)
# of sororities (% join)	26 (12)
% African American	6
% Asian	24
% White	32
% Hispanic	17
% Native American	<1
% Pacific Islander	<1
% Two or more races	6
% Race and/or ethnicity unknown	2
% international	12
# of countries represented	114

SURVEY SAYS . . .

Everyone loves the Trojans
Theater is popular
Alumni active on campus

ACADEMICS

Academic Rating	80
% students returning for sophomore year	96
% students graduating within 4 years	79
% students graduating within 6 years	92
Calendar	Semester
Student/faculty ratio	9:1
Profs interesting rating	83
Profs accessible rating	88

Most classes have 10–19 students.
Most lab/discussion sessions have
10–19 students.

MOST POPULAR MAJORS

Visual and Performing Arts, General; Business
Administration and Management, General; Social
Sciences, General

STUDENTS SAY ". . ."

Academics

The University of Southern California boasts "a dynamic and culturally diverse campus located in a world-class city which is equally dynamic and culturally diverse." Everything related to cinema is "top notch." Among the other 150 or so majors here, programs in journalism, business, engineering, and architecture are particularly notable. The honors programs are "very good" too. One of the best perks about USC is its "large and enthusiastic alumni network." Becoming "part of the Trojan Family" is a great way to jumpstart your career because USC graduates love to hire other USC graduates. "Almost everyone talks about getting job offers based solely on going to USC." "The school seems to run very smoothly, with few administrative issues ever being problematic enough to reach the awareness of the USC student community," says an international relations major. The top brass "is a bit mysterious and heavy handed," though. Also, "they milk every dime they can get from you." Academically, some students call the general education courses "a complete waste of time." There are a few "real narcissists" on the faculty as well as some professors "who seem to just be there because they want to do research." Overall, though, students report professors "make the subject matter come alive" and make themselves "very available" outside the classroom. "My academic experience at USC is fabulous," gushes an aerospace engineering major. "I would not choose any other school."

Campus Life

On campus, life is "vibrant." There are more than 850 student organizations. Theatrical and musical productions are "excellent." School spirit is "extreme" and "infectious." "Football games are huge." "There is absolutely nothing that can top watching our unbelievable football team throttle the competition," says a merciless sophomore. "Drinking is a big part of the social scene" as well. "We definitely have some of the sickest parties ever," claims an impressed freshman. "Greek life is very big" and, on the weekends, a strong contingent of students "religiously" visits "The Row, the street lined with all the fraternity and sorority houses." Students also have "the sprawling city of Los Angeles as their playground." It's an "eclectic place with both high and low culture and some of the best shopping in the world." "Hollywood clubs and downtown bars" are popular destinations. Art exhibits, concerts, and "hip restaurants" are everywhere. However, "you need a car." Los Angeles traffic may be "a buzz kill," but students report that it's considerably preferable to the "absolutely terrible" public transportation system.

Student Body

The one thing that unites everyone here is "tons of Trojan pride." USC students are also "intensely ambitious" and, while there are some "complete slackers," many students hit the books "harder than they let on." Otherwise, students insist that, "contrary to popular belief, USC has immense diversity." "The stereotypical USC student is a surfer fraternity bro or a tan, trendy sorority girl from the O.C." You'll find plenty of those. Many students are also "extremely good looking." "No one cares what your orientation is," says a first-year student. There are "prissy Los Angeles types" and "spoiled" kids. In some circles, "family income and the brands of clothes you wear definitely matter." However, "though there are quite a few who come from mega wealth, there are also many who are here on a great deal of financial aid." There are "lots of nerds," too, and a smattering of "band geeks and film freaks."

UNIVERSITY OF SOUTHERN CALIFORNIA

Financial Aid: 213-740-4444 • E-Mail: admitusc@usc.edu • Website: www.usc.edu

THE PRINCETON REVIEW SAYS

Admissions

The school reports that its standardized testing policy for use in admission for Fall 2024 is Requires applicants to submit either the SAT or ACT. It is unknown at this time if the 2024 testing policy will be permanent. The Princeton Review suggests that interested applicants consult with the school for the most up-to-date standardized testing policies. *Very important factors considered include:* rigor of secondary school record, academic GPA, standardized test scores, application essay, recommendation(s). *Important factors considered include:* extracurricular activities, talent/ability, character/personal qualities. *Other factors considered include:* first generation, alumni/ae relation, racial/ethnic status, volunteer work, work experience. High school diploma is required and GED is not accepted. *Academic units required:* 4 English, 3 math, 2 science, 2 science labs, 2 foreign language, 2 social studies, 3 academic electives. *Academic units recommended:* 4 English, 4 math, 3 science, 3 science labs, 3 foreign language, 3 social studies, 3 academic electives.

Financial Aid

Students should submit: Business/Farm Supplement; CSS/Financial Aid Profile; FAFSA; Noncustodial Profile. Priority filing deadline is 2/17. The Princeton Review suggests that all financial aid forms be submitted as soon as possible (see page 5 for a note on the FAFSA). *Need-based scholarships/grants offered:* College/university scholarship or grant aid from institutional funds; Federal Pell; Private scholarships; SEOG; State scholarships/grants. *Loan aid offered:* Direct PLUS loans; Direct Subsidized Loans; Direct Unsubsidized Loans; College/university loans from institutional funds. Admitted students will be notified of awards on or about 4/1. Federal Work-Study Program available. Institutional employment available.

The Inside Word

USC doesn't have the toughest admissions standards in California, but it's up there. Your grades and test scores need to be outstanding to compete. Even if you are a borderline candidate, though, USC is certainly worth a shot. Few schools on the planet have a better alumni network and the "Trojan Family" really does create all kinds of opportunities for its members upon graduation.

THE SCHOOL SAYS "..."

From the Admissions Office

"One of the best ways to discover if USC is right for you is to walk around campus, talk to students, and get a feel for the area both as a place to study and a place to live. If you can't visit, we hold admission information programs around the country. Watch your mailbox for an invitation, or send us an e-mail if you're interested."

SELECTIVITY

Admissions Rating	97
# of applicants	71,031
% of applicants accepted	13
% of acceptees attending	41

FIRST-YEAR PROFILE

Testing policy	SAT or ACT Required
Range SAT composite	1330–1520
Range SAT EBRW	650–740
Range SAT math	670–780
Range ACT composite	30–34
# submitting SAT scores	1,709
% submitting SAT scores	47
# submitting ACT scores	962
% submitting ACT scores	26
Average HS GPA	3.8
% frosh submitting high school GPA	98
% graduated top 10% of class	80
% graduated top 25% of class	95
% graduated top 50% of class	99

DEADLINES

Regular	
Priority	12/1
Deadline	1/15
Notification	4/1
Nonfall registration?	Yes

FINANCIAL FACTS

Financial Aid Rating	94
Annual tuition	$60,446
Room and board	$16,732
Required fees	$1,057
Required fees (first-year)	$1,507
Books and supplies	$1,200
Average frosh need-based scholarship	$45,003
Average UG need-based scholarship	$42,905
% needy frosh rec. need-based scholarship or grant aid	92
% needy UG rec. need-based scholarship or grant aid	92
% needy frosh rec. non-need-based scholarship or grant aid	68
% needy UG rec. non-need-based scholarship or grant aid	61
% needy frosh rec. need-based self-help aid	73
% needy UG rec. need-based self-help aid	87
% frosh rec. any financial aid	68
% UG rec. any financial aid	65
% UG borrow to pay for school	32
Average cumulative indebtedness	$27,413
% frosh need fully met	95
% ugrads need fully met	97
Average % of frosh need met	106
Average % of ugrad need met	107

THE UNIVERSITY OF TAMPA

401 West Kennedy Boulevard, Tampa, FL 33606-1490 • Admissions: 813-253-3333 • Fax: 813-258-7398

CAMPUS LIFE

Quality of Life Rating	88
Fire Safety Rating	95
Green Rating	71
Type of school	Private
Affiliation	No Affiliation
Environment	Metropolis

STUDENTS

Total undergrad enrollment	9,593
% male/female/another gender	41/59/NR
% from out of state	73
% frosh from public high school	66
% frosh live on campus	94
% ugrads live on campus	43
# of fraternities (% join)	13 (15)
# of sororities (% join)	14 (25)
% African American	3
% Asian	2
% White	69
% Hispanic	12
% Native American	<1
% Pacific Islander	<1
% Two or more races	3
% Race and/or ethnicity unknown	6
% international	5
# of countries represented	130

SURVEY SAYS . . .

Students love Tampa, FL
Easy to get around campus
Recreation facilities are great

ACADEMICS

Academic Rating	79
% students returning for sophomore year	81
% students graduating within 4 years	57
% students graduating within 6 years	66
Calendar	Semester
Student/faculty ratio	17:1
Profs interesting rating	86
Profs accessible rating	90

Most classes have 20–29 students.
Most lab/discussion sessions have
10–19 students.

MOST POPULAR MAJORS

Criminology; Finance, General; Marketing/
Marketing Management, General

STUDENTS SAY "..."

Academics

The University of Tampa is a sunny, growing, global university that affords its undergraduates the choice of more than 200 areas of study, as well as "many resources and opportunities…[that provide] hands-on and experiential learning." Students rarely feel overwhelmed, and they find they "have a lot of support from staff and peers." Everyone is "eager to help and provide opportunities to make up any missed work or [to] obtain extra credit." The business and the science programs here are "amazing and what UT's forefront is about," and the campus location near downtown means "job opportunities are everywhere." The school hosts "seminars going on all the time about…jobs, social skills, law school, [and] medical school."

"Professors are very personal with students" and "are very much available for extra help or extra explanations both during and outside of class." Faculty members are often also researchers, which gives students "the opportunity to create and carry out experiments," and additionally, there are "many internship and career opportunities that are available while you are still in college." Classes often take on a non-traditional format, featuring guest lectures from professionals or graduate professors. The experiential learning offered at UT means that "undergraduate time is not wasted and is truly going to prepare students for post-graduate [life]."

Campus Life

A typical day for students "is always planned around knowing it's going to be a sunny day." The university's campus "feels like summer every day," and it's within walking distance of downtown as well as "within a five-minute drive from Hyde Park, Ybor, and Soho, which all offer a wide variety of activities." The nearby theme parks are also a fun getaway. "A lot of students come [to UT] for the warm weather, the nice campus, and the city life," says one. Many students study by the river or walk around campus with others; "hammocks are super popular" (there's even a Hammock Club), and "renting bikes and biking the Riverwalk is also a fun way to pass time." Although students typically start partying on Thursday nights, some point out that "nothing is crazy" in that regard. "Many people are involved in Greek life," and others enjoy extracurricular clubs. Of course, students are always happy to head to the beach. "There is just so much to do so that every day is not exactly the same," one student says.

Student Body

The University of Tampa is "very diverse in that people from all different cultures make up the community." There is a large international student population and the majority of students are from out of state, and "many are very outgoing and will go out of their way to be there for other students." "I've met people from Sweden, Bermuda, Nigeria, and many other nations…. The diversity among the…cultures [at] UT is something," says a student. There is much promotion of diversity among students, so they are introduced to "a large variety of beliefs, backgrounds, ethnicities, and ideologies." Many who go here "are in athletics or just use the gym regularly," but they are "motivated to do well in their field of study" at the same time.

THE UNIVERSITY OF TAMPA

Financial Aid: 813-253-6219 • E-Mail: admissions@ut.edu • Website: www.ut.edu

THE PRINCETON REVIEW SAYS

Admissions

The school reports that its standardized testing policy for use in admission for Fall 2024 is Test Optional. The 2024 testing policy will be permanent. The Princeton Review suggests that interested applicants consult with the school for the most up-to-date standardized testing policies. *Very important factors considered include:* rigor of secondary school record, academic GPA. *Important factors considered include:* application essay, recommendation(s), talent/ability. *Other factors considered include:* class rank, interview, extracurricular activities, character/personal qualities, first generation, alumni/ae relation, volunteer work, work experience, level of applicant's interest. High school diploma is required and GED is accepted. *Academic units required:* 4 English, 3 math, 3 science, 2 science labs, 2 foreign language, 3 social studies, 3 academic electives.

Financial Aid

Students should submit: FAFSA. Priority filing deadline is 5/1. The Princeton Review suggests that all financial aid forms be submitted as soon as possible (see page 5 for a note on the FAFSA). *Need-based scholarships/grants offered:* College/university scholarship or grant aid from institutional funds; Federal Pell; Private scholarships; SEOG; State scholarships/grants. *Loan aid offered:* Direct PLUS loans; Direct Subsidized Loans; Direct Unsubsidized Loans. Admitted students will be notified of awards on a rolling basis beginning 11/1. Federal Work-Study Program available. Institutional employment available.

The Inside Word

The University of Tampa accepts either the Common Application, Coalition Application, or its own application, and admissions officers look for applicants with high standardized test scores and an average high school GPA of 3.5. A rigorous high school course load is encouraged, as are extracurricular activities such as participation in sports, internship experience, and volunteer work. Early Action applications are due by November 15.

THE SCHOOL SAYS "..."

From the Admissions Office

"The University of Tampa is a diverse and dynamic community of students from all 50 states and over 130 countries. Situated on a beautiful 110-acre campus along the Hillsborough river, the University's location within downtown Tampa is unmatched, providing students walking access to hundreds of internship, job, and research opportunities. UT's medium size overall population couple (10,500) with its smaller average class size (21) provides a unique balance for students looking to have the best of both worlds professionally, socially, and academically.

"Admission is competitive, and students are encouraged to apply early. Completed applications must include a student's official high school transcript and personal essay. A letter of recommendation is not required, but strongly encouraged. A college preparatory curriculum is required, including a minimum of eighteen academic units: four English courses, three sciences (two must be laboratory sciences), three mathematics, three social studies, two foreign languages and three academic electives. Certain majors require separate departmental applications and/or requirements.

"Applications are reviewed holistically, examining the entire student application file, the whole person, and the context of the student's environment. While academic accomplishment plays a strong role in evaluation, we are particularly interested student character, leadership, and community service.

"Applicants are automatically considered for invitation to the University's Honors Program, as well as merit-based scholarships. Academic challenge (number of AP, IB, AICE, or dual enrollment courses attempted) and leadership are considered in these reviews. Admitted students are eligible to apply for additional departmental and specialized scholarships after receiving their acceptance notice."

SELECTIVITY

Admissions Rating	93
# of applicants	40,286
% of applicants accepted	26
% of acceptees attending	18
# offered a place on the wait list	6,055
% accepting a place on wait list	9
% admitted from wait list	0

FIRST-YEAR PROFILE

Testing policy	Test Optional
Range SAT composite	1100–1260
Range SAT EBRW	540–640
Range SAT math	540–640
Range ACT composite	22–28
# submitting SAT scores	429
% submitting SAT scores	23
# submitting ACT scores	231
% submitting ACT scores	12
Average HS GPA	3.5
% frosh submitting high school GPA	100
% graduated top 10% of class	15
% graduated top 25% of class	40
% graduated top 50% of class	77

DEADLINES

Early decision	
Deadline	11/1
Early action	
Deadline	11/15
Notification	12/15
Regular	
Priority	11/15
Notification	Rolling, 10/1
Nonfall registration?	Yes

FINANCIAL FACTS

Financial Aid Rating	82
Annual tuition	$31,162
Room and board	$12,676
Required fees	$2,262
Books and supplies	$1,500
Average frosh need-based scholarship	$14,764
Average UG need-based scholarship	$13,714
% needy frosh rec. need-based scholarship or grant aid	99
% needy UG rec. need-based scholarship or grant aid	97
% needy frosh rec. non-need-based scholarship or grant aid	17
% needy UG rec. non-need-based scholarship or grant aid	14
% needy frosh rec. need-based self-help aid	82
% needy UG rec. need-based self-help aid	84
% frosh rec. any financial aid	100
% UG rec. any financial aid	99
% UG borrow to pay for school	63
Average cumulative indebtedness	$38,959
% frosh need fully met	21
% ugrads need fully met	18
Average % of frosh need met	70
Average % of ugrad need met	67

UNIVERSITY OF TENNESSEE—KNOXVILLE

527 Andy Holt Tower, Knoxville, TN 37996-0230 • Admissions: 865-974-1000

STUDENTS SAY ". . ."

Academics

At the flagship University of Tennessee—Knoxville, students can test the variables of their education and explore the unknowns. Local affiliations, as with the Oak Ridge National Laboratory, are just one example of the "extensive opportunities for undergraduate research" that let students—especially those in engineering and life sciences—actively experiment with "really cool resources" and this availability is UTK's "biggest hidden treasure." Students also appreciate how UTK helps them zero in on their interests; though it's a moderately large school, "it is easy to make it a small school by focusing on a certain field" in which they can get all the attention they crave.

These strong academics owe a lot to the "outstanding, passionate, intelligent" professors, who are "compelling and excited to teach," though a few students note this depends on your department and recommend the school's honors program. Ultimately, students describe how professors " have helped me get published, navigate my academic program, and get experiences that I otherwise may not have had." As a backstop, there are also "countless centers to help students succeed and feel at home," like the Academic Success Center, which provides coaching and leadership workshops, academic strategies, and "true feedback" that "made me want to broaden my education." Whether inspiration is found in the woods, lab, or seminar, students know their "creativity is encouraged and rewarded."

Campus Life

UTK students contend that their "school spirit is unmatched." Decked in orange, they cheer with pride for their football team on game day: "The energy the stadiums and teams bring to campus is unparalleled," and the prestigious Pride of the Southland Marching Band dazzles fans at half-time. Even those that are "not a huge fan of sports" find, "You can truly feel the energy not just in the stadiums but also just walking through campus on a normal day."

Participation is high in clubs and intramural sports, and there are "constantly free events for students that exceed expectations," like shows and guest lectures. The campus is "quite walkable," so there's no reason not to partake in the various activities, whether that's hanging on the lawns, heading to the Student Union, or utilizing the rock climbing, tennis, and yoga of the athletic facilities. Those willing to go a bit further can sign up for the Outdoor Pursuits program or venture across the Tennessee river to hike the many trails at Urban Wilderness. Despite being a dry campus, students do note that there is a "Knoxville party scene" and Greek life, as well as a contingent of those who like "exploring downtown or having a nice night in."

Student Body

"The UTK student body is a diverse group of people waiting to be friends with you." Self-described as outgoing and "remarkably kind," students seek out "stimulating conversations" with peers whose backgrounds contrast in culture, birthplace, sexual orientation and religious beliefs. While a number of students find pride in being a "progressive" University—asserting that "UTK is one of the most liberal schools in the South"—a few find things "very Southern, Christian, and conservative." Still, the spirit of UTK is strong; Vols take seriously their commitment to improving their community— volunteering for local organizations like Habitat for Humanity—and working actively to understand and support their classmates: "I feel it is vital to learn the perspectives of my peers," and to "always [be] willing to lend a helping hand." Above all, students describe the importance of safe spaces in queer, cultural, and religious organizations: "We look out for each other." With nearly 25,000 undergraduates, students can find the company that "does their best to make you feel like you belong."

UNIVERSITY OF TENNESSEE—KNOXVILLE

Financial Aid: 865-974-1111 • E-Mail: admissions@utk.edu • Website: www.utk.edu

THE PRINCETON REVIEW SAYS

Admissions

The school reports that its standardized testing policy for use in admission for Fall 2024 is requires applicants to submit either the SAT or ACT. The 2024 testing policy will be permanent. The Princeton Review suggests that interested applicants consult with the school for the most up-to-date standardized testing policies. *Very important factors considered include:* rigor of secondary school record, academic GPA. *Important factors considered include:* standardized test scores, application essay, extracurricular activities, talent/ability, character/personal qualities. *Other factors considered include:* recommendation(s), geographical residence, state residency, volunteer work, work experience. High school diploma is required and GED is accepted. *Academic units recommended:* 4 English, 4 math, 3 science, 1 science lab, 2 foreign language, 1 social studies, 1 history, 1 visual/performing arts.

Financial Aid

Students should submit: FAFSA. Priority filing deadline is 2/15. The Princeton Review suggests that all financial aid forms be submitted as soon as possible (see page 5 for a note on the FAFSA). *Need-based scholarships/grants offered:* College/university scholarship or grant aid from institutional funds; Federal Pell; Private scholarships; SEOG; State scholarships/grants. *Loan aid offered:* Direct PLUS loans; Direct Subsidized Loans; Direct Unsubsidized Loans; College/university loans from institutional funds; State Loans. Admitted students will be notified of awards on a rolling basis beginning 2/15. Federal Work-Study Program available.

The Inside Word

The University of Tennessee—Knoxville is looking for bright, competitive students to join the school's ranks. To find them, the school takes a holistic approach to the admissions process. UT considers everything from standardized test scores, rigor of high school curriculum, and overall GPA to personal statements and community engagement and leadership. Finally, certain colleges within the university have specific requirements. For example, applicants must audition for the UT School of Music, and applicants to the Tickle College of Engineering must meet minimum academic requirements in Math and Science either through coursework or standardized test scores.

THE SCHOOL SAYS "..."

From the Admissions Office

"The University of Tennessee, Knoxville, offers students the great program diversity of a major university, opportunities for research or original creative work in every degree program, and a welcoming campus environment. Nine colleges offer more than 360 undergraduate programs of study to students from all fifty states and 100 foreign countries, Honors and Scholars Programs provide students with dynamic experiences through unique academic opportunities, interactive and interdisciplinary seminars, and hands-on activities. Students from all majors enjoy an intimate college experience that integrates academic achievement and student life within a culture of intellectual and civic engagement. More than 500 clubs and organizations on campus allow students to further individualize their college experience in service, recreation, academics, and professional development. UT blends more than 225 years of history, tradition, and 'Volunteer Spirit' with the latest technology and innovation."

SELECTIVITY

Admissions Rating	87
# of applicants	36,290
% of applicants accepted	68
% of acceptees attending	28
# offered a place on the wait list	2,198
% accepting a place on wait list	42
% admitted from wait list	15

FIRST-YEAR PROFILE

Testing policy	SAT or ACT Required
Range SAT composite	1180–1320
Range SAT EBRW	590–660
Range SAT math	580–670
Range ACT composite	25–31
# submitting SAT scores	1,454
% submitting SAT scores	21
# submitting ACT scores	4,014
% submitting ACT scores	59
Average HS GPA	4.1
% frosh submitting high school GPA	100
% graduated top 10% of class	34
% graduated top 25% of class	64
% graduated top 50% of class	92

DEADLINES

Early action	
Deadline	11/1
Notification	12/1
Regular	
Priority	11/1
Notification	Rolling, 12/1
Nonfall registration?	Yes

APPLICANTS ALSO LOOK AT

Middle Tennessee State University; The University of Alabama—Tuscaloosa; University of Georgia; University of South Carolina—Columbia

FINANCIAL FACTS

Financial Aid Rating	80
Annual in-state tuition	$11,332
Annual out-of-state tuition	$29,522
Room and board	$12,150
Required fees	$1,912
Books and supplies	$1,598
Average frosh need-based scholarship	$12,544
Average UG need-based scholarship	$11,336
% needy frosh rec. need-based scholarship or grant aid	92
% needy UG rec. need-based scholarship or grant aid	84
% needy frosh rec. non-need-based scholarship or grant aid	0
% needy UG rec. non-need-based scholarship or grant aid	0
% needy frosh rec. need-based self-help aid	47
% needy UG rec. need-based self-help aid	49
% UG borrow to pay for school	49
Average cumulative indebtedness	$27,949
% frosh need fully met	20
% ugrads need fully met	17
Average % of frosh need met	54
Average % of ugrad need met	52

UNIVERSITY OF TEXAS AT AUSTIN

University of Texas at Austin, Austin, TX 78705 • Admissions: 512-471-3434 • Fax: 512-475-7478

CAMPUS LIFE

Quality of Life Rating	82
Fire Safety Rating	84
Green Rating	96
Type of school	Public
Environment	Metropolis

STUDENTS

Total undergrad enrollment	40,980
% male/female/another gender	43/57/NR
% from out of state	5
% frosh live on campus	63
% ugrads live on campus	18
# of fraternities (% join)	33 (10)
# of sororities (% join)	31 (11)
% African American	5
% Asian	24
% White	33
% Hispanic	28
% Native American	<1
% Pacific Islander	<1
% Two or more races	4
% Race and/or ethnicity unknown	1
% international	4
# of countries represented	103

SURVEY SAYS . . .

Great library
Internships are widely available
Students environmentally aware
Students love Austin, TX
Recreation facilities are great
Everyone loves the Longhorns
Intramural sports are popular
Alumni active on campus

ACADEMICS

Academic Rating	80
% students returning for sophomore year	97
% students graduating within 4 years	72
% students graduating within 6 years	88
Calendar	Semester
Student/faculty ratio	18:1
Profs interesting rating	86
Profs accessible rating	88

Most classes have 10–19 students.
Most lab/discussion sessions have
10–19 students.

MOST POPULAR MAJORS

Biology/Biological Sciences, General; Business
Administration and Management, General;
Experimental Psychology

STUDENTS SAY "..."

Academics

Students insist that the University of Texas at Austin has "everything you want in a college: academics, athletics, social life, location," and it's hard to argue with them. UT is "a huge school and has a lot to offer," meaning students have "an infinite number of possibilities open to them and can use them in their own way to figure out what they want for their lives." As one student tells us about arriving on campus, "I did not realize how much was available to me just as an enrolled student. There is free tutoring, gym membership, professional counseling, doctor visits, legal help, career advising, and many distinguished outside speakers. The campus is crawling with experts in every field you can imagine." Standout academic departments are numerous: from the sciences to the humanities to creative arts, UT makes a strong bid for the much-sought-after mantle of "Harvard of the South." Also, the school does a surprisingly good job of avoiding the factory-like feel of many large schools. One student observes: "coming to a large university, there was a prejudgment that the huge classes will make it impossible to know your professor, and vice versa. The university has dispelled that myth with professors who want to know you and [who] provide opportunities to get to know them." While professors "can vary greatly across a spectrum from 'I'm smarter than him' to 'I want to follow in his footsteps,'" "the class offerings at UT are generally vast and diverse, and students can often avoid taking the less-qualified professors with a little research."

Campus Life

Life at UT Austin is "very relaxed.... Students usually wear shorts and a T-shirt to class. When the weather gets cold, you might find students wearing the same shorts and T-shirt with a sweatshirt. Students and faculty frequently picnic all over campus. There are plenty of outdoor tables and grassy areas to sit." Undergrads "are often found throwing a Frisbee outside the tower or taking a nap under a tree. It's truly what you see in one of those cheesy brochures with everyone studying and smiling. Of course, the smiles aren't so bright during finals. We switch to an over-caffeinated, glazed-eye look instead." Hometown Austin "provides a social education that a college student newly out on his own would not find anywhere else," with "festivals or fairs of some kind going on downtown all the time" and "the infamous 6th Street with nightlife that dies down only after the bars close." Campus and the surrounding area offer "many hike-and-bike trails and fitness organizations. It's possible for students to train for marathons, half marathons, and triathlons while in school. Barton Springs pool is a natural spring that is very popular year-round. On any given Saturday you will find students throwing a football, going for a run, biking through the hills, kayaking in the river, having a late lunch at one of Austin's great restaurants, or just sleeping in."

Student Body

"Because of the huge Greek life at UT, a 'typical student' would be a sorority girl or fraternity boy," but—and it's a big but—such students "are hardly the majority, since UT is actually made of more 'atypical' people than most other schools. Everyone here has his own niche, and I could not think of any type of individual who would not be able to find one of his own." Indeed, "everyone at Texas is different! When you walk across campus, you see every type of ethnicity. There are a lot of minorities at Texas. Also, I see many disabled people, whom the school accommodates well. Everyone seems to get along. The different types of students just blend in together." Especially by Texas standards, "Austin is known for being 'weird.' If you see someone dressed in a way you've never seen before, you just shrug it off and say 'That's Austin!'"

UNIVERSITY OF TEXAS AT AUSTIN

Financial Aid: (512) 232-6988 • E-Mail: admissions@austin.utexas.edu • Website: www.utexas.edu

THE PRINCETON REVIEW SAYS

Admissions

The school reports that its standardized testing policy for use in admission for Fall 2024 is Test Optional. The 2024 testing policy will be temporary. The Princeton Review suggests that interested applicants consult with the school for the most up-to-date standardized testing policies. *Other factors considered include:* rigor of secondary school record, class rank, academic GPA, standardized test scores, application essay, recommendation(s), interview, extracurricular activities, talent/ability, character/personal qualities, first generation, geographical residence, state residency, religious affiliation/commitment, racial/ethnic status, volunteer work, work experience. High school diploma is required and GED is accepted. *Academic units required:* 4 English, 3 math, 2 science, 2 foreign language, 3 social studies. *Academic units recommended:* 4 math, 4 science, 4 social studies, 6 academic electives.

Financial Aid

Students should submit: FAFSA; Institution's own financial aid form. Priority filing deadline is 1/15. The Princeton Review suggests that all financial aid forms be submitted as soon as possible (see page 5 for a note on the FAFSA). *Need-based scholarships/grants offered:* College/university scholarship or grant aid from institutional funds; Federal Pell; Private scholarships; SEOG; State scholarships/grants. *Loan aid offered:* Direct PLUS loans; Direct Subsidized Loans; Direct Unsubsidized Loans; College/university loans from institutional funds; Federal Nursing Loans; State Loans. Admitted students will be notified of awards on a rolling basis beginning 3/15. Federal Work-Study Program available. Institutional employment available.

The Inside Word

The university is required to automatically admit enough Texas applicants to fill 75 percent of available spaces set aside for students from Texas. As a result, Texan students in the top 6 percent of their high school class applying for Summer/Fall 2023 or Spring 2024 are guaranteed admission. All students, including those eligible for automatic admission, should submit the strongest possible application to increase the likelihood of admission to the university and to their requested major. Admissions are quite competitive. Space for out-of-state students is limited, meaning they'll have even higher hurdles to clear.

THE SCHOOL SAYS "..."

From the Admissions Office

"Like the state it calls home, The University of Texas at Austin is a bold, ambitious leader committed to innovative learning and research, and encourages creativity, analysis, and critical thinking. Ranked among the top research universities in the country, UT Austin is home to more than 51,000 students and 3,000 teaching faculty. Through more than 170 undergraduate fields of study across 13 colleges and schools (and hundreds of study abroad programs, comprehensive student services, exceptional cultural centers, and more than 1,100 student organizations), you will find an engaging, diverse, multi-dimensional experience that will unlock your future potential and prepare you to make an impact on the world. Our students enjoy a vibrant college experience on our urban campus in the heart of the city of Austin—consistently recognized as the nation's best place to live—and an HQ for creatives and entrepreneurs. Longhorns are part of a strong community, and inherit a storied history and rich tradition of success that's as evident in our Big 12 athletics as it is in the classroom or laboratory. Almost half a million alumni lead worldwide industries from technology to politics to entertainment, and provide a robust network of UT connections around the world and in every field. Together, we're working to make the world a better place, united by the belief that creating and sharing knowledge can transform society. It's why we say 'What starts here changes the world.'"

SELECTIVITY

Admissions Rating	93
# of applicants	59,767
% of applicants accepted	31
% of acceptees attending	48

FIRST-YEAR PROFILE

Testing policy	Test Optional

DEADLINES

Regular	
Priority	11/1
Deadline	12/1
Nonfall registration?	Yes

FINANCIAL FACTS

Financial Aid Rating	81
Annual in-state tuition	$11,758
Annual out-of-state tuition	$41,070
Room and board	$13,058
Books and supplies	$724
Average frosh need-based scholarship	$15,233
Average UG need-based scholarship	$13,616
% needy frosh rec. need-based scholarship or grant aid	93
% needy UG rec. need-based scholarship or grant aid	93
% needy frosh rec. non-need-based scholarship or grant aid	10
% needy UG rec. non-need-based scholarship or grant aid	8
% needy frosh rec. need-based self-help aid	56
% needy UG rec. need-based self-help aid	53
% frosh rec. any financial aid	86
% UG rec. any financial aid	76
% UG borrow to pay for school	41
Average cumulative indebtedness	$21,633
% frosh need fully met	18
% ugrads need fully met	16
Average % of frosh need met	81
Average % of ugrad need met	77

THE UNIVERSITY OF TEXAS AT DALLAS

800 West Campbell Road, Richardson, TX 75080 • Admissions: 972-883-2111 • Fax: 972-883-2599

CAMPUS LIFE

Quality of Life Rating	**84**
Fire Safety Rating	**91**
Green Rating	**89**
Type of school	Public
Environment	Metropolis

STUDENTS

Total undergrad enrollment	21,311
% male/female/another gender	56/44/0
% from out of state	6
% frosh from public high school	93
% frosh live on campus	52
% ugrads live on campus	23
# of fraternities (% join)	12 (3)
# of sororities (% join)	14 (5)
% African American	5
% Asian	41
% White	24
% Hispanic	18
% Native American	<1
% Pacific Islander	<1
% Two or more races	4
% Race and/or ethnicity unknown	3
% international	4
# of countries represented	50

SURVEY SAYS . . .

Classroom facilities are great
Lab facilities are great
Career services are great

ACADEMICS

Academic Rating	**73**
% students returning for sophomore year	87
% students graduating within 4 years	56
% students graduating within 6 years	74
Calendar	Semester
Student/faculty ratio	26:1
Profs interesting rating	87
Profs accessible rating	89

Most classes have 50-59 students.
Most lab/discussion sessions have
20–29 students.

MOST POPULAR MAJORS

Computer and Information Sciences, General;
Mechanical Engineering; Biology/Biological
Sciences, General

STUDENTS SAY ". . ."

Academics

The University of Texas at Dallas is a large public university offering its 21,000 undergraduates 56 majors across seven schools. "Great academics and amazingly qualified professors and research opportunities" are just some of the many resources offered to help students succeed. STEM and business programs are popular here, with research opportunities right out of the gate for first-years who are interested. More than 50 years on, UTD shows no signs of slowing down and if anything has been taking even more "great measures to make sure that students know that they are supported academically, emotionally, and mentally." The professional development and "great guidance surrounding pre-professional careers" extends to services like the Student Success Center, which provides free tutoring, and the Testing Center, a 300-seat computer lab that undergrads can use as a secure and comfortable testing environment for any tests, exams, or assessments.

The school "is excellent at preparing students for their future careers and offering many opportunities to prepare them to do so," and the "diverse learning culture" gives everyone a chance to expand their horizons outside of their major. Classes take a hands-on approach, and students "are often confronted with exciting project prompts" both in and out of class: "There's always a research team, project, or development happening in the departments." Professors "give all required resources to students in order to excel," and "the coursework, projects and tests are challenging and prepare us for post-graduation."

Campus Life

Students here "spend many hours on their lectures or doing homework," but after the day is done, they enjoy kicking back with friends, "going out to eat somewhere close to campus or going to take photos for Instagram somewhere in Dallas," or just taking part in low-key casual activities like "sand volleyball, walks around campus with friends, [and] basketball." Even though there is already "so much space to study or do whatever you need to," the campus is in the midst of a growth spurt: there are plans for "a DART station and a whole second part of campus." If all the options for "tons of random activities" sounds a bit chaotic, know that there are also plenty of student organizations, "career-focused and community service clubs," and student volunteering opportunities.

Student Body

Most students define Comets as "hardworking, nerdy, and tech savvy," where "school spirit thrives the most in meme culture" and everyone "probably enjoys games and anime." People take academics seriously but know how to relax, or as one student describes it, "everyone is also just trying to have a good time while giving enough time to their textbooks." There's a "limited amount" of jock culture and traditional sports on campus, but "you can have any type of life you want because there is every type of group of people at UTD." That is, "you can really find or make your group here, you just have to seek it out."

THE UNIVERSITY OF TEXAS AT DALLAS

Financial Aid: 972-883-2941 • E-Mail: admission@utdallas.edu • Website: www.utdallas.edu

THE PRINCETON REVIEW SAYS

Admissions

The school reports that its standardized testing policy for use in admission for Fall 2024 is Test Optional. The Princeton Review suggests that interested applicants consult with the school for the most up-to-date standardized testing policies. *Very important factors considered include:* rigor of secondary school record, class rank, academic GPA, preparation for intended major. *Important factors considered include:* application essay, extracurricular activities. *Other factors considered include:* recommendation(s), talent/ability, character/personal qualities, volunteer work, work experience, level of applicant's interest. High school diploma is required and GED is accepted. *Academic units required:* 4 English, 4 math, 4 science, 3 science labs, 2 foreign language, 3 social studies, 1 visual/performing arts. *Academic units recommended:* 4 English, 4 math, 4 science, 3 science labs, 3 foreign language, 4 social studies, 1 computer science, 1 visual/performing arts, 5 academic electives.

Financial Aid

Students should submit: FAFSA. Priority filing deadline is 1/15. The Princeton Review suggests that all financial aid forms be submitted as soon as possible (see page 5 for a note on the FAFSA). *Need-based scholarships/grants offered:* College/university scholarship or grant aid from institutional funds; Federal Pell; Private scholarships; SEOG; State scholarships/grants. *Loan aid offered:* Direct PLUS loans; Direct Subsidized Loans; Direct Unsubsidized Loans; College/university loans from institutional funds; State Loans. Admitted students will be notified of awards on a rolling basis beginning in January. Federal Work-Study Program available. Institutional employment available.

The Inside Word

UT Dallas is one of those by-the-numbers schools for the majority of its admitted students. Texas law requires that prospective students are automatically admitted to the university as first-years if they graduate in the top 10% of their class from an accredited Texas high school and successfully earn the Distinguished Level of Achievement. Students outside of the top 10 percent are subject to a more holistic review based on individual strengths.

THE SCHOOL SAYS "..."

From the Admissions Office

"The University of Texas at Dallas is a leading research institution in Texas. It provides some of the state's most-lauded business, engineering and science programs, as well as innovative and traditional programs in the liberal arts, and offers diverse educational paths through 147 academic programs across seven schools.

"UTD's trajectory as one of the fastest-growing public universities in the U.S. is fueled by its bright students, faculty, staff, alumni and the stature of its programs. Designated as an "R1" institution—a classification reserved for doctoral universities with "very high research activity" by the Carnegie Commission on Higher Education, UTD is part of The University of Texas System and is aligned strategically with other institutions, corporations and nonprofits, including UT Southwestern Medical Center and prestigious universities worldwide.

"UTD is home to over 31,000 students, including 6,900 international students from about 100 countries. This diverse student body benefits from a residential campus known for academic rigor, career focus and social opportunities.

"In addition to an array of nationally ranked programs, UTD is a campus enriched by prestigious art collections, service-learning opportunities, and NCAA Division III athletics. Its students have access to over 400 student organizations, various intramural sports, and nearly 30 club sports.

"At graduation, UTD students walk the stage ready for the next phase of life. Programs like UTDesign, UTDsolv, UTDiscovery, UTeach Dallas, and the Teacher Development Center provide students with the opportunity to stretch their creativity and work on projects with companies and other organizations before they leave the university."

SELECTIVITY

Admissions Rating	85
# of applicants	21,500
% of applicants accepted	85
% of acceptees attending	23

FIRST-YEAR PROFILE

Testing policy	Test Optional
Range SAT composite	1180–1410
Range SAT EBRW	580–700
Range SAT math	590–730
Range ACT composite	24–32
# submitting SAT scores	3,320
% submitting SAT scores	79
# submitting ACT scores	793
% submitting ACT scores	19
% graduated top 10% of class	36
% graduated top 25% of class	66
% graduated top 50% of class	94

DEADLINES

Regular	
Priority	12/1
Deadline	5/1
Nonfall registration?	No

APPLICANTS OFTEN PREFER

Texas A&M University—College Station; The University of Texas at Austin; University of Houston

APPLICANTS SOMETIMES PREFER

Texas Tech University; Texas Woman's University; The University of Texas at Arlington; University of North Texas; University of Oklahoma

APPLICANTS RARELY PREFER

Baylor University; University of Arkansas—Fayetteville

FINANCIAL FACTS

Financial Aid Rating	81
Annual in-state tuition	$16,412
Annual out-of-state tuition	$44,812
Room and board	$12,142
Books and supplies	$1,200
Average frosh need-based scholarship	$12,976
Average UG need-based scholarship	$11,149
% needy frosh rec. need-based scholarship or grant aid	84
% needy UG rec. need-based scholarship or grant aid	87
% needy frosh rec. non-need-based scholarship or grant aid	7
% needy UG rec. non-need-based scholarship or grant aid	5
% needy frosh rec. need-based self-help aid	89
% needy UG rec. need-based self-help aid	90
% frosh rec. any financial aid	70
% UG rec. any financial aid	70
% UG borrow to pay for school	29
Average cumulative indebtedness	$23,403
% frosh need fully met	15
% ugrads need fully met	13
Average % of frosh need met	67
Average % of ugrad need met	63

THE UNIVERSITY OF TULSA

800 South Tucker Drive, Tulsa, OK 74104 • Admissions: 918-631-2307 • Fax: 918-631-5003

STUDENTS SAY ". . ."

Academics

The many students at The University of Tulsa, a small private research university, find it to be the total package. After all, it combines "the friendly environment of a smaller university and the academic, employment, extracurricular, and service opportunities of a larger university." It also does a tremendous job of fostering an atmosphere that's "conducive to collaboration and growth." In general, students describe the academics as "challenging." And a number of undergrads emphasize TU's "strong engineering school," which thoroughly prepares students for "work[ing] in the industry, especially [within the] energy [sector]." All undergraduates, no matter their major, benefit from "small class sizes." In turn, this affords students the opportunity to build "close relationships...with [the] faculty," full of professors who "are great resources for [both] internships and real-world advice." Aside from being great contacts, Tulsa professors are "very knowledgeable and passionate about their subjects." They also "make their students a priority" and they're "very accessible outside of class." As one student expounds, "Many of my professors frequently invite students to their office hours and remind us of their availability.... [It's clear they] care about my academic experience, career readiness, and about me as a person."

Campus Life

While University of Tulsa undergrads say that "a good portion of [their] time is...spent studying," there's still plenty of fun to be had outside the confines of the library and/or classroom. For example, "there are a ton of active student organizations" and you can always find "an event to attend or free food to eat." Popular options include "homecoming...dog petting days, bowling, [and] carnivals." One excited student adds, "TU is good about providing events bi-weekly, like S'mores at the Student Union, an outdoor movie, or a play." If the Greek scene interests you, you'll be happy to learn that "the fraternities on campus...usually [host] events Thursday through Saturday." A number of undergrads also love to take advantage of the "many [beautiful] lawns" on the TU campus. And you're sure to find a handful of students playing any number of games, from "baseball [and] football [to] Capture the Flag." If you prefer your athletics to be a little more structured, there's also a "very popular... intramural sports [program]." As for hometown Tulsa, "there's a great food, music, and art culture in downtown Tulsa so you can always find something to do." And we're told that "the restaurants here are awesome, small and large concert venues attract all types of artists, and there all festivals of all types throughout the year."

Student Body

The student body at The University of Tulsa is comprised of "friendly" and "inclusive" individuals. Of course, it probably helps that the school is home to "a diverse group of students from various economic, academic, religious, political, and ethnic backgrounds." Indeed, "Division I athletes, international students, military veterans, sorority sisters, petroleum engineering majors, and piano performance majors represent a few of the many groups woven together on TU's campus." Undergrads are "committed to doing well in school." As one student explains, "We are all here to do well, but we are here to do well together." Undergrads also describe their classmates as "smart," "engaging," and "extremely focused on their studies." And most "are incredibly involved at TU, whether it be in Greek life, athletics, music, [or] research." Additionally, a lot of "TU students look for opportunities to challenge themselves and impact their community." One thrilled undergrad sums up the campus experience: "TU honestly feels like a small town community. Everyone is so friendly and kind, and it's like having one giant family."

THE UNIVERSITY OF TULSA

Financial Aid: 918-631-2526 • E-Mail: admission@utulsa.edu • Website: utulsa.edu

THE PRINCETON REVIEW SAYS

Admissions

The school reports that its standardized testing policy for use in admission for Fall 2024 is Test Optional. It is unknown at this time if the 2024 testing policy will be permanent. The Princeton Review suggests that interested applicants consult with the school for the most up-to-date standardized testing policies. *Very important factors considered include:* rigor of secondary school record, academic GPA, standardized test scores. *Important factors considered include:* class rank, application essay, recommendation(s), interview, level of applicant's interest. *Other factors considered include:* extracurricular activities, talent/ability, character/personal qualities, first generation, alumni/ae relation, racial/ethnic status, volunteer work, work experience. High school diploma is required and GED is accepted. *Academic units recommended:* 4 English, 4 math, 3 science, 3 science labs, 2 foreign language, 3 social studies.

Financial Aid

Students should submit: FAFSA. Priority filing deadline is 2/1. The Princeton Review suggests that all financial aid forms be submitted as soon as possible (see page 5 for a note on the FAFSA). *Need-based scholarships/grants offered:* College/university scholarship or grant aid from institutional funds; Federal Pell; Private scholarships; SEOG; State scholarships/grants. *Loan aid offered:* Direct PLUS loans; Direct Subsidized Loans; Direct Unsubsidized Loans. Admitted students will be notified of awards on a rolling basis beginning 2/1. Federal Work-Study Program available. Institutional employment available.

The Inside Word

The admissions process at TU is fairly straightforward. For starters, the school closely evaluates high school transcripts and standardized test scores (if submitted). Candidates are strongly encouraged to sit for an admissions interview, as well. It's also important to note that The University of Tulsa evaluates applications on a rolling basis. The earlier you apply, the more slots will be available. In fact, it's recommended that students submit their applications by January 15 for full consideration for scholarships.

THE SCHOOL SAYS "..."

From the Admissions Office

"The University of Tulsa is a private university with a comprehensive scope. Students choose from more than fifty majors offered through four undergraduate colleges—Kendall College of Arts and Sciences, Collins College of Business, Oxley College of Health Sciences, and the College of Engineering and Natural Sciences. Curricula can be customized with collaborative and interdisciplinary research, joint undergraduate and graduate programs, the Global Scholars program and an honors program. Professors are equally committed to teaching undergraduates and to scholarly research. This results in extraordinary individual achievement, resulting in the nationally competitive scholarships students have won since 1995: sixty-five Goldwaters, seventy National Science Foundation scholars, twelve Trumans, nine Department of Defense scholars, twenty-two Fulbrights, eleven Phi Kappa Phi, nine Udalls, five British Marshalls, and three Rhodes Scholars, including one in 2017. In the past decade, over 1,000,000 square feet of facilities have been added. These include athletic venues, additional apartments, fitness center, Legal Information Center, library expansion and renovation, two new engineering buildings and a new performing arts center. Over 200 registered clubs and interest groups, including intramural and recreational sports teams exist along with seven fraternities and nine sororities. The 8,300 seat Reynolds Center is home to the men's and women's basketball teams, campus events, and concerts. A forty-acre sports complex includes the fitness center and indoor tennis center. An outdoor freshman orientation program launches an entire first-year experience dedicated to developing students' full potential.

"Due to the COVID-19 global pandemic, applicants are not currently required to submit an official ACT or SAT test score for admission."

SELECTIVITY

Admissions Rating	86
# of applicants	12,042
% of applicants accepted	69
% of acceptees attending	8

FIRST-YEAR PROFILE

Testing policy	Test Optional
Range SAT composite	1060–1360
Range SAT EBRW	540–680
Range SAT math	538–670
Range ACT composite	21–30
# submitting SAT scores	164
% submitting SAT scores	25
# submitting ACT scores	338
% submitting ACT scores	52
Average HS GPA	3.6
% frosh submitting high school GPA	99

DEADLINES

Regular	
Notification	Rolling, 1/15
Nonfall registration?	Yes

APPLICANTS OFTEN PREFER

Rice University; Texas A&M University—College Station; The University of Texas at Austin; Washington University in St. Louis

APPLICANTS SOMETIMES PREFER

Baylor University; Colorado School of Mines; Oklahoma State University; Southern Methodist University; Texas Christian University; Trinity University; University of Arkansas—Fayetteville; University of Oklahoma

APPLICANTS RARELY PREFER

Creighton University; University of Kansas; University of Missouri

FINANCIAL FACTS

Financial Aid Rating	83
Annual tuition	$46,932
Required fees	$1,170
Average frosh need-based scholarship	$31,086
Average UG need-based scholarship	$30,840
% needy frosh rec. need-based scholarship or grant aid	92
% needy UG rec. need-based scholarship or grant aid	94
% needy frosh rec. non-need-based scholarship or grant aid	89
% needy UG rec. non-need-based scholarship or grant aid	52
% needy frosh rec. need-based self-help aid	60
% needy UG rec. need-based self-help aid	62
% UG borrow to pay for school	40
Average cumulative indebtedness	$25,789
% frosh need fully met	28
% ugrads need fully met	27
Average % of frosh need met	64
Average % of ugrad need met	63

UNIVERSITY OF UTAH

University of Utah, Salt Lake City, UT 84112 • Admissions: 801-581-7200 • Fax: 801-585-7864

STUDENTS SAY "..."

Academics

Nestled amid Salt Lake City's snowcapped mountains, the University of Utah is a large public school that offers extensive academic programs, ample research opportunities, and a surprisingly student-friendly atmosphere. No matter what your interests, you'll find like minds at The U. "I have studied everything from [the] Tai Chi/Yoga movement and stage combat to differential equations and linear algebra," says a junior. "The one thing that has remained consistent throughout is the appreciation and dedication the people have for the topic they are involved in." The U is a research university that actually takes teaching seriously, and "every teacher...shows incredible knowledge in their area, as well as personality and wit." "Classes are informative, challenging, and genuinely enjoyable." As is the case in many larger universities, students note that many "general education courses are taught by grad students," whose teaching abilities can range from great to below average. "Ninety percent of my professors are fantastic; the ones that aren't are usually grad students," explains a junior. On this large campus, students have little contact with the school's administration and "there's definitely no hand-holding at The U. If you're unsure of your major or career plans, it's easy to slip through the cracks." However, students assure us, "The administration puts student interests first whenever possible with a focus on keeping tuition low, creating a diverse environment, and providing opportunities and experience in order to prepare students to be productive citizens."

Campus Life

While a large percentage of the undergraduate community at the University of Utah commutes to campus, there are still plenty of activities for the school's 4,000 resident students. There are many people "active in politics, environmental issues, and international issues," and, after hours, "the school holds different events throughout the year, such as Crimson Nights that feature activities such as bowling, crafts, games, food, and music." Socially, "Greek life is not as large as at other schools but is definitely a lot of fun and the best way to get to know more people your age." In addition, "during football season there are great tailgate parties with friends, drinks, and food." Right off campus, there are a range of great restaurants, and "the nightlife is hard to keep up with." There's always something good going on—whether it's at the bars and clubs downtown, or at small music venues." For outdoorsy types, The U is a paradise. "We have all four seasons and some of the best outdoors in the nation," explains one student. "Killer snow, amazing hills, mountains, lakes, and streams." In this natural wonderland, "hiking, biking, boating, snow-skiing, and snowboarding are just a few of the hundreds of activities available to students."

Student Body

Located in Salt Lake City, The U has "plenty of social niches to fall into, and none of them are rigidly exclusive." One student notes that part of the student body is "the typical Utah Mormon, and [the rest] is a mix of everything. The two [groups] usually stay separate but they get along." University of Utah students agree that "there is more diversity here than in any other part of the state." However, out-of-state students are not as common, and "those of us not from Utah are definitely in the minority." While there are a number of residential students, a very large percentage of students also choose to commute to school while living with their parents or family. In addition, "there are a lot of older students and a lot of married students." Academically, however, U undergraduates are "independent, smart, and come to class ready to discuss ideas."

University of Utah

Financial Aid: 801-581-6211 • E-Mail: admissions@utah.edu • Website: www.utah.edu

THE PRINCETON REVIEW SAYS

Admissions

The school reports that its standardized testing policy for use in admission for Fall 2024 is Test Optional. It is unknown at this time if the 2024 testing policy will be permanent. The Princeton Review suggests that interested applicants consult with the school for the most up-to-date standardized testing policies. *Very important factors considered include:* rigor of secondary school record, academic GPA. *Other factors considered include:* class rank, standardized test scores, application essay, recommendation(s), extracurricular activities, talent/ability, character/personal qualities, volunteer work, work experience. High school diploma is required and GED is accepted.

Financial Aid

Students should submit: FAFSA. Priority filing deadline is 2/1. The Princeton Review suggests that all financial aid forms be submitted as soon as possible (see page 5 for a note on the FAFSA). *Need-based scholarships/grants offered:* College/university scholarship or grant aid from institutional funds; Federal Nursing Scholarships; Federal Pell; Private scholarships; SEOG; State scholarships/grants. *Loan aid offered:* Direct PLUS loans; Direct Subsidized Loans; Direct Unsubsidized Loans; College/university loans from institutional funds; Federal Nursing Loans; State Loans. Admitted students will be notified of awards on a rolling basis beginning 3/1. Federal Work-Study Program available. Institutional employment available.

The Inside Word

Admission is based primarily on the big three: Course selection, grades, and test scores. If you have a 3.0 GPA or better and average test scores, you're close to a sure bet for admission.

THE SCHOOL SAYS "..."

From the Admissions Office

"Salt Lake is the U's 'college city,' pairing outdoor adventure—including world-class skiing and five national parks (plus low-cost campus equipment rentals and outings to help students explore)—with sophisticated urban offerings from Utah Jazz NBA games to Broadway shows.

"However, students don't have to leave campus to experience outstanding music, theater, and dance performances. Talented students and faculty create and perform hundreds of shows each year, and the student government has hosted concerts featuring such artists as B.o.B and Icona Pop. Recent speakers have included former U.S. Vice President (and now President) Joe Biden and the creator of Humans of New York.

"Salt Lake City is top in the nation for diversity of jobs, according to LinkUp, which means there is an abundance of companies providing internship and employment opportunities. And, when students land that job downtown, their transportation is covered. U students have access to public transportation to, from, and around campus and the Salt Lake Valley for no additional cost.

"The U offers an affordable investment in a high-quality and high-value degree by having one of the lowest out-of-state cost of attendances in the Pac-12, along with the opportunity to meet requirements for in-state tuition after just one year.

"As a leader in global research and innovation, the U provides students with exciting ways to discover and nurture their interests. From Lassonde Studios (an on-campus entrepreneurial center) to its international campus in Incheon, South Korea, to its hundreds of undergrad research opportunities, the possibilities are only limited by the imagination."

SELECTIVITY

Admissions Rating	85
# of applicants	21,072
% of applicants accepted	89
% of acceptees attending	29

FIRST-YEAR PROFILE

Testing policy	Test Optional
Range SAT composite	1200–1380
Range SAT EBRW	600–690
Range SAT math	590–700
Range ACT composite	22–29
# submitting SAT scores	643
% submitting SAT scores	12
# submitting ACT scores	2,651
% submitting ACT scores	48
Average HS GPA	3.7
% frosh submitting high school GPA	95

DEADLINES

Early action	
Deadline	12/1
Notification	1/15
Regular	
Priority	12/1
Deadline	4/1
Nonfall registration?	Yes

APPLICANTS ALSO LOOK AT

Brigham Young University (UT); Salt Lake Community College; University of Colorado Boulder; Utah State University

FINANCIAL FACTS

Financial Aid Rating	80
Annual in-state tuition	$8,628
Annual out-of-state tuition	$30,201
Room and board	$10,662
Required fees	$1,188
Books and supplies	$1,036
Average frosh need-based scholarship	$2,832
Average UG need-based scholarship	$3,071
% needy frosh rec. need-based scholarship or grant aid	95
% needy UG rec. need-based scholarship or grant aid	87
% needy frosh rec. non-need-based scholarship or grant aid	71
% needy UG rec. non-need-based scholarship or grant aid	51
% needy frosh rec. need-based self-help aid	95
% needy UG rec. need-based self-help aid	87
% frosh rec. any financial aid	95
% UG rec. any financial aid	54
% UG borrow to pay for school	38
Average cumulative indebtedness	$6,962
% frosh need fully met	13
% ugrads need fully met	11
Average % of frosh need met	72
Average % of ugrad need met	66

UNIVERSITY OF VERMONT

South Prospect Street, Burlington, VT 05405-0160 • Admissions: 802-656-3370

STUDENTS SAY ". . ."

Academics

A public research university in Burlington, the University of Vermont offers the complete package: "great academics…in a great area [with] lots to do while getting a great education." This is bolstered by professors who are "engaging and clearly very passionate about what they teach." One student says, "[Professors] have opened my eyes to new interests, new ways of thinking, new skills, and new innovations." While some students voice concerns of "too many general education requirements" and the need for "access to quality counseling, advising, and therapists," they overall appreciate the variety of "rigorous yet interesting" programs. The pre-med programs benefit from the school's proximity to the UVM Medical Center, and students also note strong environmental, social justice, and STEM programs. Plus, the opportunity to study across departments and colleges "allows and encourages students to take a variety of classes outside of their major requirements." As one student says, "I was able to pick which college I wanted to be in and had a wide array of classes to choose from."

Campus Life

While being considered "absolutely…academically rigorous," there's also a strong focus on extracurriculars, and there are plentiful opportunities to get involved: "UVM offers lots of clubs to participate in, and if you don't see something you want, you can start your own club." In addition to clubs, the school is "always putting on different events," and on top of those options, many are drawn to the recreation the nearby terrain offers as well. One student says, "It is simply an outdoorsy school. Hiking, fishing, boating, skiing, snowboarding, [and] running…are all extremely popular." Off campus, "Students go downtown to cafés, restaurants, galleries, and shops." Many students are drawn to the "chill, small town atmosphere" of Burlington and its "amenities of urban life," and the "small community feel" of the school itself complements that. One student remarks, "I cannot walk across campus…without seeing at least eight to ten friends." An enthusiastic peer states that it's one of "the best places to live as a college student on the East Coast."

Student Body

UVM undergrads think highly of each other, saying things like: "All of my peers are intelligent, hardworking, cooperative, and all around good people." They also note a range of personalities on campus—"there is no one stereotype that UVM students conform to"—claiming that "there is truly a place for everyone, whether you're a sorority girl or a member of our woodsmen team." However, there is still a common thread that holds them all together: "exceptional passion for what they do, whether in the classroom or out." Some would like to see the school improve its "racial/ethnic/religious diversity, which the school is aware of but needs to make great strides to achieve." Overall, UVM students are "friendly, passionate, and involved" and they "care about cultural, societal, and political situations both locally and globally."

UNIVERSITY OF VERMONT

Financial Aid: 802-656-5700 • E-Mail: admissions@uvm.edu • Website: www.uvm.edu

THE PRINCETON REVIEW SAYS

Admissions

The school reports that its standardized testing policy for use in admission for Fall 2024 is Test Optional as a pilot program in effect through Spring 2027. The Princeton Review suggests that interested applicants consult with the school for the most up-to-date standardized testing policies. *Very important factors considered include:* rigor of secondary school record. *Important factors considered include:* academic GPA, application essay, character/personal qualities, state residency. *Other factors considered include:* standardized test scores, recommendation(s), extracurricular activities, talent/ability, first generation, alumni/ae relation, geographical residence, racial/ethnic status, volunteer work, work experience, level of applicant's interest. High school diploma is required and GED is accepted. *Academic units required:* 4 English, 3 math, 3 science, 1 science lab, 2 foreign language, 3 social studies.

Financial Aid

Students should submit: FAFSA. Priority filing deadline is 2/1. The Princeton Review suggests that all financial aid forms be submitted as soon as possible (see page 5 for a note on the FAFSA). *Need-based scholarships/grants offered:* College/university scholarship or grant aid from institutional funds; Federal Pell; Private scholarships; SEOG; State scholarships/grants. *Loan aid offered:* Direct PLUS loans; Direct Subsidized Loans; Direct Unsubsidized Loans; College/university loans from institutional funds; Federal Nursing Loans. Admitted students will be notified of awards on a rolling basis beginning 3/1. Federal Work-Study Program available. Institutional employment available.

The Inside Word

Admissions officers take a broad view of an applicant's academic program, class standing, grades, standardized test results, and trends in performance. Though tests are currently optional, they're still a good metric by which to assess your chances. Students who get in tend to have high GPAs and test scores. Applicants must select one of seven undergraduate schools based on their desired major. Early action is an option. Be aware of deadline variations for first-year, transfer, and international applicants.

THE SCHOOL SAYS "..."

From the Admissions Office

"Since 1791, the University of Vermont has been a leader in higher education and research advancing human and global health. Students come to UVM from around the country and globe, drawn to the breadth of UVM's programs; ready access to top faculty conducting national research; and outstanding facilities supporting discoveries in health and medicine, engineering, environmental science, and other fields.

"Students find an inclusive community on campus and throughout Burlington, one of the nation's favorite small cities surrounded by mountains on Lake Champlain. This compelling landscape also attracts innovative businesses—including many start-ups that are now international brands. For UVM students, this means career-building internships near and far.

"Learning with experience underscores a UVM education; 92 percent of students report having internships, doing mentored research, and other experience-based learning promoting success. A three-year average of the classes of 2020–22 shows 94% of UVM grads have jobs or are continuing their education within six months of graduating.

"Global perspective is highly valued at UVM and enriched by students from nearly 40 countries. Students interested in study abroad have 700 programs in 70 countries to choose from, including options for students on engineering and health science tracks. Several clubs engage in international service, as well as competition; UVM's proximity to French-speaking Quebec further expands horizons.

"Every UVM student completes the Catamount Core Curriculum, comprising coursework in quantitative and data literacy, sustainability, liberal arts, diversity and global citizenship—a foundation for lifelong learning and valuable contributions to local and global communities."

SELECTIVITY

Admissions Rating	90
# of applicants	30,231
% of applicants accepted	60
% of acceptees attending	17
# offered a place on the wait list	7,348
% accepting a place on wait list	39
% admitted from wait list	<1

FIRST-YEAR PROFILE

Testing policy	Test Optional
Range SAT composite	1280–1420
Range SAT EBRW	640–720
Range SAT math	620–710
Range ACT composite	28–32
# submitting SAT scores	1,126
% submitting SAT scores	38
# submitting ACT scores	431
% submitting ACT scores	14
Average HS GPA	3.8
% frosh submitting high school GPA	45
% graduated top 10% of class	41
% graduated top 25% of class	77
% graduated top 50% of class	98

DEADLINES

Early action	
Deadline	11/1
Notification	12/16
Regular	
Deadline	1/15
Notification	3/31
Nonfall registration?	Yes

APPLICANTS ALSO LOOK AT

St. Lawrence University; State University of New York—Binghamton University; Syracuse University; University of Colorado Boulder; University of Connecticut; University of Massachusetts Amherst; University of New Hampshire

FINANCIAL FACTS

Financial Aid Rating	82
Annual in-state tuition	$16,280
Annual out-of-state tuition	$41,280
Room and board	$13,354
Required fees	$2,610
Books and supplies	$1,200
Average frosh need-based scholarship	$20,922
Average UG need-based scholarship	$19,403
% needy frosh rec. need-based scholarship or grant aid	100
% needy UG rec. need-based scholarship or grant aid	98
% needy frosh rec. non-need-based scholarship or grant aid	19
% needy UG rec. non-need-based scholarship or grant aid	15
% needy frosh rec. need-based self-help aid	58
% needy UG rec. need-based self-help aid	59
% frosh rec. any financial aid	98
% UG rec. any financial aid	92
% UG borrow to pay for school	59
Average cumulative indebtedness	$35,533
% frosh need fully met	23
% ugrads need fully met	19
Average % of frosh need met	74
Average % of ugrad need met	69

UNIVERSITY OF VIRGINIA

University of Virginia, Charlottesville, VA 22904 • Admissions: 434-982-3200 • Fax: 434-924-3587

STUDENTS SAY ". . ."

Academics

For over 200 years, the University of Virginia has been an anchor of the state, now serving 17,000 undergraduates and with almost 10,000 full-time faculty and staff. One of many "rigorous but rewarding" academic experience is the J term, a set of January classes based around field experiences and unusual topics such as "impact investing in Appalachia... which involves visiting various local businesses and VC firms." Other approaches lauded for "allow[ing] us to collaborate and think creatively" include worksheet-based classes, where students work and "the professor only teaches when the whole class gets stuck," and "class discussions, where material is studied beforehand, and learning mostly done in classroom through talking." These courses "are difficult, but in a way that will ensure a bright future for all students and helps guarantee careers upon graduation."

Overall, students are left happily fascinated by the available courses and "highly encouraged" study abroad opportunities. They also find professors to be helpful in all regards: "very accessible outside of class and want[ing] their students to thrive; grading is fair; the workload is appropriate." There are "a lot of support resources for all areas of growth," and students say they "[have] never met someone unwilling to share their expertise with students." When it comes to crunch time, faculty "are also great about making sure you can succeed if you don't come to class all the time by posting their lectures."

Campus Life

UVA has "beautiful and historic grounds, which add to the unique character of the university." It's the sort of picturesque college setting wherein "the libraries are always full, the lawn and rotunda are frequently filled with friends hanging out," and "many students go to fitness centers often to fill their days and remain active." As you might expect from that setting, "during the week, UVA students can often be found studying with their friends, meeting with peers for group projects, and studying alone in the many quiet spaces grounds has to offer," like how "dorms and living spaces are used quite frequently for relaxing nights and study sessions." As for downtime and weekends, peers "are very engaged with social events that are hosted by the college or student organizations where there may be food or activities to do with friends."

Student Body

Students at the University of Virginia describe themselves and their peers as "kind and compassionate," the sort of "driven, empathetic, action-orientated, proactive leaders who know how to work across lines of difference and create a diverse yet cohesive community." This is due in part to trickle-down support, as the "environment here for learning and growing connections is exceptionally strong due to the eagerness of upperclassmen to help their younger peers." As one undergrad puts it, "there seems to be every kind of person here," and that's supported by an inclusive attitude that makes room for them. That said, the average student is a self-starter, in short the type "who want to be here, want to learn, and want to have a rounded college experience." According to one undergrad, "you won't find anyone who's not involved in at least one club or group outside of their classes, and it's more common to find people who fill their schedules with 4-5 groups and clubs." Posting extracurricular numbers like those means many are "involved in a really unexpected cross section of interests," and "there is a very strong esprit de corps." It also means that UVA is "a well-sized school where it feels like you can find anything you may be looking for, but also not so big you get overwhelmed."

UNIVERSITY OF VIRGINIA

Financial Aid: 434-982-6000 • E-Mail: undergradadmission@virginia.edu • Website: www.virginia.edu

THE PRINCETON REVIEW SAYS

Admissions

The school reports that its standardized testing policy for use in admission for Fall 2024 is Test Optional. The 2024 testing policy will be temporary. The Princeton Review suggests that interested applicants consult with the school for the most up-to-date standardized testing policies. *Very important factors considered include:* rigor of secondary school record, class rank, academic GPA, character/personal qualities, state residency. *Important factors considered include:* application essay, recommendation(s), extracurricular activities, talent/ability. *Other factors considered include:* standardized test scores (if submitted), first generation, alumni/ae relation, geographical residence, race or ethnicity (if and as permitted by law), volunteer work, work experience. High school diploma is required and GED is accepted. *Academic units required:* 4 English, 4 math, 2 science, 2 foreign language, 1 social studies. *Academic units recommended:* 4 English, 4 math, 4 science, 4 foreign language, 3 social studies.

Financial Aid

Students should submit: CSS/Financial Aid Profile; FAFSA. Priority filing deadline is 3/1. The Princeton Review suggests that all financial aid forms be submitted as soon as possible (see page 5 for a note on the FAFSA). *Need-based scholarships/grants offered:* College/university scholarship or grant aid from institutional funds; Federal Nursing Scholarships; Federal Pell; Private scholarships; SEOG; State scholarships/grants. *Loan aid offered:* Direct PLUS loans; Direct Subsidized Loans; Direct Unsubsidized Loans. Admitted students will be notified of awards on or about 4/1. Federal Work-Study Program available. Institutional employment available.

The Inside Word

Unlike many public universities, UVA does not use a formula or minimum scores in its admission process, but applicants must have stellar academic records and demonstrate willingness to rise to the school's academic challenges. The most important parts of the application are academic performance, rigor of high school curriculum, and recommendations. Admission here is competitive, particularly for students from out of state.

THE SCHOOL SAYS "..."

From the Admissions Office

"UVA aspires to cultivate the most vibrant community in higher education, in order to prepare our students to be servant-leaders in a diverse and globally connected world. We welcome talented students from all walks of life. Because we're a public university, outstanding Virginians who take at least five challenging academic courses each year and earn excellent grades generally enjoy great success when they apply. For other students, UVA looks not only for excellence in academics but also for information about their lived experience and evidence that they will contribute outside the classroom as caring and engaged members of the UVA community.

"We've extended our current test-optional practice for two years. If you're applying for admission for Fall 2024 or Fall 2025, you'll have the choice of sharing or not sharing results from the SAT and ACT. Whichever path you choose, we'll consider your application with care and respect, and you won't be disadvantaged because of the choice you've made. Regardless of whether you think you'll share your scores, we encourage you to take either or both exams, at least once. Although you're more than any one test can ever say, either of these tests may help you identify strengths you can build on as you get ready for college. And whether you choose UVA or some other school, we want you to be ready for the challenges and the opportunities that await you."

SELECTIVITY

Admissions Rating	96
# of applicants	50,926
% of applicants accepted	19
% of acceptees attending	42
# offered a place on the wait list	8,368
% accepting a place on wait list	59
% admitted from wait list	<1
# of early decision applicants	2,462
% accepted early decision	45

FIRST-YEAR PROFILE

Testing policy	Test Optional
Range SAT composite	1400–1540
Range SAT EBRW	690–750
Range SAT math	710–790
Range ACT composite	32–34
# submitting SAT scores	2,200
% submitting SAT scores	54
# submitting ACT scores	720
% submitting ACT scores	17
% graduated top 10% of class	85
% graduated top 25% of class	96
% graduated top 50% of class	99

DEADLINES

Early decision	
Deadline	11/1
Notification	1/31
Early action	
Deadline	11/1
Notification	2/15
Regular	
Deadline	1/5
Notification	4/1
Nonfall registration?	No

APPLICANTS ALSO LOOK AT

Cornell University; Duke University; New York University; University of Pennsylvania; Vanderbilt University; Virginia Tech; William & Mary

FINANCIAL FACTS

Financial Aid Rating	94
Annual in-state tuition	$19,023
Annual in-state tuition (first-year)	$17,627
Annual out-of-state tuition	$55,483
Annual out-of-state tuition (first-year)	$53,836
Room and board	$13,600
Required fees	$4,183
Required fees (first-year)	$4,178
Books and supplies	$1,400
Average frosh need-based scholarship	$29,216
Average UG need-based scholarship	$30,695
% needy frosh rec. need-based scholarship or grant aid	88
% needy UG rec. need-based scholarship or grant aid	86
% needy frosh rec. non-need-based scholarship or grant aid	14
% needy UG rec. non-need-based scholarship or grant aid	10
% needy frosh rec. need-based self-help aid	44
% needy UG rec. need-based self-help aid	50
% UG borrow to pay for school	32
Average cumulative indebtedness	$26,211
% frosh need fully met	100
% ugrads need fully met	100
Average % of frosh need met	100
Average % of ugrad need met	100

UNIVERSITY OF WASHINGTON

1410 NE Campus Parkway, Seattle, WA 98195 • Admissions: 206-543-9198 • Fax: 206-685-3655

CAMPUS LIFE

Quality of Life Rating	81
Fire Safety Rating	88
Green Rating	98
Type of school	Public
Environment	Metropolis

STUDENTS

Total undergrad enrollment	31,578
% male/female/another gender	43/57/0
% from out of state	23
% frosh live on campus	63
% ugrads live on campus	29
# of fraternities	33
# of sororities	28
% African American	4
% Asian	27
% White	35
% Hispanic	10
% Native American	<1
% Pacific Islander	<1
% Two or more races	8
% Race and/or ethnicity unknown	3
% international	14
# of countries represented	79

SURVEY SAYS . . .
Great library
Internships are widely available
No one cheats
Students environmentally aware
Students love Seattle, WA
Recreation facilities are great
Everyone loves the Huskies

ACADEMICS

Academic Rating	82
% students returning for sophomore year	94
% students graduating within 4 years	71
% students graduating within 6 years	84
Calendar	Quarter
Student/faculty ratio	21:1
Profs interesting rating	85
Profs accessible rating	90

Most classes have 20–29 students.
Most lab/discussion sessions have 20–29 students.

STUDENTS SAY "..."

Academics

Students find "a great combination of high-powered academics, an excellent social life, and a wide variety of courses, all in the midst of the exciting Seattle life" at the University of Washington, the state's flagship institution of higher learning. UW offers "a lot of really stellar programs and the best bang for the buck, especially for in-state students or those in the sciences." Indeed, science programs "are incredible. The research going on here is cutting-edge and the leaders of biomedical sciences, stem cell research, etc. are accessible to students." Undergrads warn, however, that science programs are extremely competitive, "high pressure," and "challenging," with "core classes taught in lectures that seat more than 500 people," creating the sense that "professors don't seem to care too much whether you succeed." Pre-professional programs in business, law, nursing, medicine, and engineering all earn high marks, although again with the caveat that the workload is tough and the hand-holding nominal. As one student puts it, "The University of Washington provides every resource and opportunity for its students to succeed. You just have to take advantage of them. No one will do it for you." For those fortunate enough to get in, the Honors Program "creates a smaller community of highly motivated students.... It puts this school on top."

Campus Life

UW students typically "have a good balance in their lives of education and fun." They "generally study hard and work in the libraries, but once the nighttime hits, they look forward to enjoying the night with their friends." Between the large university community and the surrounding city of Seattle, undergrads have a near-limitless selection of extracurricular choices. As one student explains, "There are tons of options for fun in Seattle. Going down to Pike's Market on a Saturday and eating your way through is always popular. There are tons of places to eat on 'The Ave,'" the shopping district that abuts campus, "and the UVillage shopping mall is a five-minute walk from campus with chain-store comfort available. Intramural sports are big for activities, and going to undergraduate theater productions is never a disappointing experience. During autumn or spring, renting a canoe and paddling around lake Washington down by the stadium is fun." Husky football games "are amazing," and the Greek community "is very big" without dominating campus social life. In short, "UW has anything you could want to do in your free time."

Student Body

"At such a large university, there is no 'typical' student," undergrads tell us, observing "one can find just about any demographic here and there is a huge variety in personalities." There "are quite a lot of yuppies, but then again, it's Seattle," and by and large "the campus is ultraliberal. Most students care about the environment, are not religious, and are generally accepting of other diverse individuals." Otherwise, "you've got your stereotypes: the Greeks, the street fashion pioneers, the various ethnic communities, the Oxford-looking grad students, etc." In terms of demographics, "the typical student at UW is white, middle-class, and is from the Seattle area," but "there are a lot of African American students and a very large number of Asian students." All groups "seem to socialize with each other."

UNIVERSITY OF WASHINGTON

Financial Aid: 206-543-6101 • Website: www.washington.edu

THE PRINCETON REVIEW SAYS

Admissions

The school reports that its standardized testing policy for use in admission for Fall 2024 is Test Free. The 2024 testing policy will be permanent. The Princeton Review suggests that interested applicants consult with the school for the most up-to-date standardized testing policies. *Very important factors considered include:* rigor of secondary school record, academic GPA, application essay. *Important factors considered include:* extracurricular activities, talent/ability, first generation, volunteer work, work experience. *Other factors considered include:* character/personal qualities, state residency. High school diploma or equivalent is not required. *Academic units required:* 4 English, 3 math, 3 science, 2 science labs, 2 foreign language, 3 social studies, 1 visual/performing arts, 1 academic elective.

Financial Aid

Students should submit: FAFSA. Priority filing deadline is 1/15. The Princeton Review suggests that all financial aid forms be submitted as soon as possible (see page 5 for a note on the FAFSA). *Need-based scholarships/grants offered:* College/university scholarship or grant aid from institutional funds; Federal Pell; Private scholarships; SEOG; State scholarships/grants. *Loan aid offered:* Direct PLUS loans; Direct Subsidized Loans; Direct Unsubsidized Loans; College/university loans from institutional funds; Federal Nursing Loans. Admitted students will be notified of awards on or about 4/1. Federal Work-Study Program available. Institutional employment available.

The Inside Word

UW performs a thorough review of all freshman applications. Its holistic approach allows admissions officers to take into account a student's background, the degree to which he or she has overcome personal adversity, and such intangibles as leadership quality and special skills. The result has been an increased racial and socioeconomic diversity on campus.

THE SCHOOL SAYS "..."

From the Admissions Office

"Do you want to be an artist, adventurer, entrepreneur—or all the above? The University of Washington in Seattle can help make it happen. Nestled among two mountain ranges, old-growth forests, Lake Washington and the Pacific Ocean, Seattle is a vibrant, multicultural city with career, arts, sports, and outdoor opportunities for everyone.

"At the UW, we aim to be the greatest public university in the world—as measured by our impact. That's why we're devoted to advancing a culture of diversity, inclusion, and belonging. We honor the relationships between people and our planet. We strive to create an equitable, just, and sustainable future.

"The UW offers a breadth of academic programs with more than 180 majors, many of which are ranked among the best in the country. With top-rated faculty and endless ways to feed your interests outside the classroom, no matter which challenges and curiosities you want to pursue, the UW will help you find them.

"Our graduates can start their careers anywhere, but many begin at well-known institutions right here in the Pacific Northwest. Rich in talent and capital, Seattle is a hotbed for innovators and entrepreneurs. Huskies can get hands-on experience through research, mentorships, and internships with some of the most groundbreaking visionaries in the world.

"Beyond grades, we consider an applicant's academic achievements (rigor of curriculum, academic preparation) and personal history, including community service, leadership, and accomplishments. We do this because we believe that what you care about can change the world. Are you ready?"

SELECTIVITY
Admissions Rating	93
# of applicants	52,488
% of applicants accepted	48
% of acceptees attending	30
# offered a place on the wait list	9,450
% accepting a place on wait list	58
% admitted from wait list	2

FIRST-YEAR PROFILE
Testing policy	Test Free
Range SAT composite	1320–1500
Range SAT EBRW	640–740
Range SAT math	660–780
Range ACT composite	29–34
# submitting SAT scores	1,297
% submitting SAT scores	17
# submitting ACT scores	491
% submitting ACT scores	7
Average HS GPA	3.8
% frosh submitting high school GPA	100

DEADLINES
Regular	
Deadline	11/15
Notification	3/15
Nonfall registration?	No

APPLICANTS ALSO LOOK AT
California Polytechnic State University; New York University; University of California—Berkeley; University of California—Davis; University of California—Los Angeles; University of California—San Diego; University of California—Santa Barbara; University of Wisconsin-Madison

FINANCIAL FACTS
Financial Aid Rating	81
Annual in-state tuition	$11,189
Annual out-of-state tuition	$39,687
Room and board	$16,068
Required fees	$1,053
Books and supplies	$900
Average frosh need-based scholarship	$16,997
Average UG need-based scholarship	$18,188
% needy frosh rec. need-based scholarship or grant aid	86
% needy UG rec. need-based scholarship or grant aid	88
% needy frosh rec. non-need-based scholarship or grant aid	4
% needy UG rec. non-need-based scholarship or grant aid	3
% needy frosh rec. need-based self-help aid	37
% needy UG rec. need-based self-help aid	38
% frosh rec. any financial aid	37
% UG rec. any financial aid	37
% UG borrow to pay for school	28
Average cumulative indebtedness	$18,136
% frosh need fully met	10
% ugrads need fully met	10
Average % of frosh need met	73
Average % of ugrad need met	74

UNIVERSITY OF WISCONSIN-MADISON

161 Bascom Hall, Madison, WI 53706 • Admissions: 608-262-1234 • Fax: 608-262-7706

STUDENTS SAY "..."

Academics

The University of Wisconsin—Madison is a large research campus sitting on an isthmus between two lakes that lets more than 31,000 undergraduates avail themselves of 4,700 courses, 129 majors, and "an abundance of research opportunities in all fields." Resources abound here: students have "access to state-of-the-art technology" and "lots of programs and opportunities to go abroad." First-years "can easily work in a lab, and…there is potential for publication" if they spend enough time there. The school "provides amazing opportunities to its students and is extremely accommodating." As one student describes, "Academic tutoring happens around campus for almost every single class and mental health resources are available 24/7."

Professors "know that the university culture involves lots of interaction and mentoring of students" and therefore "are truly about teaching and learning." "Tests are generally fair and…outlined well," says a student. Another notes that some courses are styled as "active learning classes," in which "students watch short lecture videos" and work out homework with the assistance of the professor and TAs during class time. There are "multiple avenues to gain research experience on campus" thanks to the great many labs offered. Since "there is very little downtime here," the academic curriculum "does not occupy your time with busy work." Though students admit that there are a few faculty members with areas for improvement, they say "Wisconsin does a pretty good job of keeping professors who don't like to teach" out of the classroom.

Campus Life

Even during cold weather "people spend a lot of time outside" and students can often be found "by the beautiful lakes [and hanging] out in the city, student unions, or parks." The "bus system is excellent" and "makes getting around campus very easy," which is useful as the campus sits on 936 acres. It "is part of a city environment," so students can go "to State Street to grab food or coffee," and "there are several concert venues around that attract pretty intriguing acts." Additionally, the school itself hosts "lots of free activities like concerts and art events and food events and speakers" that are "always well-attended." Several of the dorms "are top-notch" and the "dorm food is usually very good."

"It's never hard to find a party" here, but even though "students may go out and be social at night, the library is full by 9 A.M. the next morning." "The average student…parties a lot, and studies even more," says one. But regardless of what you like to do, students are confident that even "if you do not drink, you will find other people" to hang out with.

Student Body

Most students here "are from around the Midwest, especially Wisconsin," and "midwestern kindness prevails" among this "fun and intellectually diverse student body," which is "not too big or too small." Students are "extremely active in extracurriculars," and they take full advantage of the more than one thousand student organizations on offer. "Everyone gets so excited about sports," particularly during football and basketball season ("athletic games are sacred places for [the] Badger teams"). "Everyone is genuinely thrilled to be at this school, whether it be on a football Saturday or just another day of class," says a student. Most here "care about preparing for their future, but don't get too competitive about grades," and "it's easy to pick up new study partners in any class by introducing yourself on the first day."

UNIVERSITY OF WISCONSIN-MADISON

Financial Aid: 608-262-3060 • E-Mail: onwisconsin@admissions.wisc.edu • Website: www.wisc.edu

THE PRINCETON REVIEW SAYS

Admissions

The school reports that its standardized testing policy for use in admission for Fall 2024 is Test Optional. It is unknown at this time if the 2024 testing policy will be permanent. The Princeton Review suggests that interested applicants consult with the school for the most up-to-date standardized testing policies. *Very important factors considered include:* rigor of secondary school record, application essay. *Important factors considered include:* academic GPA, state residency. *Other factors considered include:* class rank, standardized test scores, recommendation(s), extracurricular activities, talent/ability, character/personal qualities, first generation, racial/ethnic status, volunteer work, work experience, level of applicant's interest. High school diploma is required and GED is accepted. *Academic units required:* 4 English, 4 math, 3 science, 3 foreign language, 3 social studies. *Academic units recommended:* 4 English, 4 math, 4 science, 2 science labs, 4 foreign language, 4 social studies.

Financial Aid

Students should submit: FAFSA. Priority filing deadline is 12/1. The Princeton Review suggests that all financial aid forms be submitted as soon as possible (see page 5 for a note on the FAFSA). *Need-based scholarships/grants offered:* College/university scholarship or grant aid from institutional funds; Federal Pell; Private scholarships; SEOG; State scholarships/grants. *Loan aid offered:* Direct PLUS loans; Direct Subsidized Loans; Direct Unsubsidized Loans; Federal Nursing Loans. Admitted students will be notified of awards on a rolling basis beginning 3/1. Federal Work-Study Program available. Institutional employment available.

The Inside Word

Though UW—Madison is a large state school, it still manages to take a holistic approach to the admissions game. Indeed, there are no minimum GPAs, class ranks, or test scores required. That said, a strong academic record is paramount. Looking beyond your transcript, Wisconsin wants candidates who will actively contribute to campus life. And it also seeks diversity in both background and personal experience. Finally, students who intend to major in either dance or music must schedule an audition as well as submit a regular application.

THE SCHOOL SAYS "..."

From the Admissions Office

"UW-Madison is the university of choice for some of the best students from around the world. First-year students have high standardized test scores and GPAs and are ranked toward the top of their high-school classes.

"These factors combine to make admission to UW-Madison both competitive and selective. We consider academic record, strength of curriculum (honors, AP, IB, etc.), grade trend, class rank, results of the ACT/SAT, and non-academic factors. There is no prescribed minimum test score, GPA, or class rank criteria. Rather, we admit the best and most well-prepared students—students who have challenged themselves and who will contribute to Wisconsin's strength and diversity—for the limited space available. "Each application is personally reviewed by our admission counselors. All freshman applications completed by February 1 receive full and equal consideration. We offer two decision plans for freshman applicants. To receive a decision during the Early Action period, you must complete the application by November 1 and submit all required materials (application fee, official transcript(s), official test scores, personal essays, and one required academic letter of recommendation) by our materials deadline. Early Action period applicants will receive a decision by the end of January. All students who complete their application during the Regular Decision period (after November 1 but before the February 1 deadline) will receive a decision by the end of March. UW-Madison has a commitment to a holistic, competitive, and selective admission process for all applicants."

SELECTIVITY

Admissions Rating	91
# of applicants	53,829
% of applicants accepted	60
% of acceptees attending	26
# offered a place on the wait list	8,128
% accepting a place on wait list	53
% admitted from wait list	0

FIRST-YEAR PROFILE

Testing policy	Test Optional
Range SAT composite	1350–1480
Range SAT EBRW	650–730
Range SAT math	690–780
Range ACT composite	28–32
# submitting SAT scores	1,258
% submitting SAT scores	15
# submitting ACT scores	3,864
% submitting ACT scores	46
Average HS GPA	3.9
% frosh submitting high school GPA	90
% graduated top 10% of class	49
% graduated top 25% of class	86
% graduated top 50% of class	99

DEADLINES

Early action	
Deadline	11/1
Notification	1/31
Regular	
Deadline	2/1
Notification	3/31
Nonfall registration?	Yes

APPLICANTS ALSO LOOK AT

Indiana University—Bloomington; Purdue University—West Lafayette; University of Illinois—Urbana-Champaign; University of Michigan—Ann Arbor; University of Minnesota—Twin Cities

FINANCIAL FACTS

Financial Aid Rating	85
Annual in-state tuition	$10,722
Annual out-of-state tuition	$39,354
Room and board	$12,894
Books and supplies	$1,150
Average frosh need-based scholarship	$16,739
Average UG need-based scholarship	$17,444
% needy frosh rec. need-based scholarship or grant aid	74
% needy UG rec. need-based scholarship or grant aid	76
% needy frosh rec. non-need-based scholarship or grant aid	8
% needy UG rec. non-need-based scholarship or grant aid	8
% needy frosh rec. need-based self-help aid	70
% needy UG rec. need-based self-help aid	70
% UG borrow to pay for school	41
Average cumulative indebtedness	$27,323
% frosh need fully met	49
% ugrads need fully met	49
Average % of frosh need met	77
Average % of ugrad need met	80

UNIVERSITY OF WYOMING

1000 E. University Ave, Laramie, WY 82071 • Admissions: 307-766-5160 • Fax: 307-766-4042

CAMPUS LIFE
Quality of Life Rating	**87**
Fire Safety Rating	**71**
Green Rating	**81**
Type of school	Public
Environment	Town

STUDENTS
Total undergrad enrollment	8,363
% male/female/another gender	47/53/0
% from out of state	33
% frosh live on campus	82
% ugrads live on campus	26
# of fraternities	10
# of sororities	6
% African American	1
% Asian	1
% White	78
% Hispanic	8
% Native American	<1
% Pacific Islander	<1
% Two or more races	4
% Race and/or ethnicity unknown	5
% international	2
# of countries represented	49

SURVEY SAYS . . .
Lots of conservative students
Recreation facilities are great
Students are happy

ACADEMICS
Academic Rating	**78**
% students returning for sophomore year	75
% students graduating within 4 years	39
% students graduating within 6 years	61
Calendar	Semester
Student/faculty ratio	13:1
Profs interesting rating	84
Profs accessible rating	89
Most classes have 10–19 students.	
Most lab/discussion sessions have 20–29 students.	

MOST POPULAR MAJORS
Psychology, General; Exercise Science and Kinesiology; Mechanical Engineering

STUDENTS SAY "..."

Academics

The only four-year university in the state, University of Wyoming has a lot to offer students with its large campus and small class sizes that give students the best of both worlds, and teachers "work hard for the students," "care about the material they are teaching and make it interesting," and are "knowledgeable and supportive." Doors are always open, and professors are "always happy to talk to you about experiences with work or research or school." Student Support resources are similarly very helpful; though there have been complaints of recent budget cuts, "there are a lot of options for academic help as well as personal help if you are going through a rough time." In that vein, school advisors "really get to know you and try to find the best options for you." Professors actually teach the classes instead of relying on TAs, and "eager to clarify any topics both in the classroom as well as in office hours." These dedicated instructors often assist with club programs, and are happy to help students in those clubs make connections with working professionals to improve their chances of finding future employment. The variety of courses available to students is a huge draw (there are more than 80 undergraduate majors to choose from), with a lot of niche classes and "some engineering programs that aren't found in many other universities." Students support one another and "although some programs are competitive, it is not very cutthroat." On top of the quality education available right on campus, the school also has "great study abroad programs." The university also offers research to undergraduate students as early as their first semester, for those that want to begin padding their academic résumé.

Campus Life

Wyoming is "known for how untouched by civilization it is," and the small town of Laramie is almost entirely college-oriented. Lots of people go swing dancing, hike, fish, and ski, and "hunting is common." The outdoors is very important to the majority of the student body, and "Yes, it gets cold and snowy, but that just means the snow sculptures students make last longer!" University of Wyoming athletics are "always enjoyable to watch" and the newest addition to the campus is "a huge gym." Despite the great wide open that characterizes the state of Wyoming, the campus itself is condensed into "a smallish area" so students can walk to class from any building and be there in under ten minutes.

Outside of Laramie, it's easy enough to travel to Cheyenne or Fort Collins for shopping or other activities. The university sponsors plenty of events to keep students occupied, such as "movie nights, musical productions, [and other] de-stressors," and on Thursdays there is always live music in the student union, as well as some event usually scheduled for Friday evening.

Student Body

The University of Wyoming student body "is not full of the stereotypical cowboys" that many would expect; this is a young (mostly white) university composed of "a strong mix of western blue collar cowboy culture mixed with the more liberal ideas of bordering Colorado," all of which "combines to create a very libertarian atmosphere." There are quite a few veterans and international students here, and a simple stroll through campus lets one "see the wide range of personal expression that makes our campus a fun place." School pride is the best at UW and "there is always a sea of gold on Saturdays. We bleed brown and gold and aren't afraid to show it." To wit, "everyone here is in support of the WHOLE state, not just our region."

UNIVERSITY OF WYOMING

Financial Aid: 307-766-2116 • E-Mail: admissions@uwyo.edu • Website: www.uwyo.edu

THE PRINCETON REVIEW SAYS

Admissions

The school reports that its standardized testing policy for use in admission for Fall 2024 is Test Optional. The policy is in effect through Fall 2025. The Princeton Review suggests that interested applicants consult with the school for the most up-to-date standardized testing policies. *Very important factors considered include:* rigor of secondary school record, academic GPA. *Other factors considered include:* application essay. High school diploma is required and GED is accepted. *Academic units required:* 4 English, 4 math, 4 science, 3 science labs, 3 social studies.

Financial Aid

Students should submit: FAFSA. Priority filing deadline is 2/1. The Princeton Review suggests that all financial aid forms be submitted as soon as possible (see page 5 for a note on the FAFSA). *Need-based scholarships/grants offered:* College/university scholarship or grant aid from institutional funds; Federal Pell; Private scholarships; SEOG; State scholarships/grants. *Loan aid offered:* Direct PLUS loans; Direct Subsidized Loans; Direct Unsubsidized Loans; College/university loans from institutional funds; Federal Nursing Loans; State Loans. Admitted students will be notified of awards on a rolling basis beginning 1/27. Federal Work-Study Program available. Institutional employment available.

The Inside Word

The admissions process at University of Wyoming is formula-driven. An unweighted high school GPA of 3.0 in a traditional college prep curriculum combined with some solid test scores will open the door to this university.

THE SCHOOL SAYS "..."

From the Admissions Office

"The University of Wyoming offers a personalized education for a fraction of the cost of other public universities. Located in Laramie, UW is regularly recognized as one of the nation's best college values. This comes as no surprise, as UW is a national research university offering countless academic opportunities.

"Explore 200+ programs of study through seven colleges and three specialized schools. From Engineering to Business, Performing Arts to Geology and Agricultural Economics to Nursing, we are sure you will find your program at UW.

"Over the past seven years, the UW campus has experienced incredible growth. 750 million dollars have been invested in new facilities including a new Business building, Creative Arts facility, UW Library and most recently the introduction of the NCAR supercomputer. The NCAR computer is a joint partnership between UW and the National Center for Atmospheric Research. Undergraduate students have access to all these facilities for instruction, internships and research.

"Set at 7,200 feet above sea level, UW and Laramie are in a pristine location to attend school and enjoy the outdoors. UW was recently recognized by *Outside* magazine as the fifteenth best college campus in the country for outdoor adventure. Just thirty miles from campus is over two million acres of national forest with peaks climbing over 12,000 feet. Campus life is exciting with 200+ student clubs and organizations as well as NCAA Division I-A sports in the Mountain West conference."

SELECTIVITY

Admissions Rating	82
# of applicants	5,732
% of applicants accepted	96
% of acceptees attending	30

FIRST-YEAR PROFILE

Testing policy	Test Optional
Range SAT composite	1030–1230
Range SAT EBRW	510–620
Range SAT math	520–620
Range ACT composite	20–27
# submitting SAT scores	295
% submitting SAT scores	18
# submitting ACT scores	1,093
% submitting ACT scores	67
Average HS GPA	3.5
% frosh submitting high school GPA	99
% graduated top 10% of class	21
% graduated top 25% of class	47
% graduated top 50% of class	79

DEADLINES

Regular	
Deadline	8/10
Notification	Rolling
Nonfall registration?	Yes

APPLICANTS ALSO LOOK AT

Colorado State University; Laramie County Community College; Montana State University; Northern Wyoming Community College—Gillette Campus; University of Colorado Boulder

FINANCIAL FACTS

Financial Aid Rating	78
Annual in-state tuition	$4,800
Annual out-of-state tuition	$19,950
Room and board	$11,610
Required fees	$1,821
Books and supplies	$1,400
Average frosh need-based scholarship	$6,081
Average UG need-based scholarship	$6,036
% needy frosh rec. need-based scholarship or grant aid	77
% needy UG rec. need-based scholarship or grant aid	69
% needy frosh rec. non-need-based scholarship or grant aid	84
% needy UG rec. non-need-based scholarship or grant aid	69
% needy frosh rec. need-based self-help aid	42
% needy UG rec. need-based self-help aid	46
% frosh rec. any financial aid	93
% UG rec. any financial aid	86
% UG borrow to pay for school	41
Average cumulative indebtedness	$24,661
% frosh need fully met	21
% ugrads need fully met	15
Average % of frosh need met	62
Average % of ugrad need met	55

URSINUS COLLEGE

601 East Main Street, Collegeville, PA 19426 • Admissions: 610-409-3200 • Fax: 610-409-3197

STUDENTS SAY "..."

Academics

Located just outside of Philadelphia, Ursinus College has done a remarkable job of building a "close-knit community" dedicated to helping students succeed with strong academics and "plenty of opportunities for leadership involvement through clubs, student jobs, and internships." The "liberal arts curricula [encourages undergrads] to explore different fields" and potentially uncover new academic areas of interest. Even better, there's a tremendous "focus on research." Students also rush to highlight the "science and pre-health prep program[s]," duly noting Ursinus's "high medical school acceptance rate." Some of that success can likely be attributed to "small" classes, which are a staple here. As one first-year student brags, "My smallest class size is seven and my largest is twenty-one." She continues, "I receive...[so much] attention that [it] makes it feel as though I have a seal team of PhDs looking out for me, and that is truly amazing." Indeed, professors here are "very supportive, intelligent, and passionate about the subjects they are teaching." And they work hard to make sure they're accessible. As one student shares, "Their office hours are incredibly flexible (at certain times and by appointment as well). I've gone into some professors' office hours three times a week for the entirety of the semester, I've had professors come in on Sundays to help, and I've been to their houses for dinner...I've grown substantially...with their help."

Campus Life

We've been assured that "there's never a dull moment" at Ursinus. After all, the college "offer[s] so many activities [with which] to get involved." Extracurricular clubs range from a "premedicine help group...to a nerf club where [members] battle on the weekends in academic buildings." Community service is also pretty popular here too. For example, "on Saturdays, groups of people will generally wake up and volunteer at the soup kitchen or go to the local nursing home and either visit or sing songs to them." Once the weekend rolls around, you can certainly find "a lot of parties." Then again, that's probably a given considering that "many students are [involved] in Greek life." However, if you aren't down for drinking, it's not a problem. There "are always people who will just hang out and watch movies or play silly board games." Students who love to laugh will be delighted to learn that Ursinus sponsors a number of "comedy events," either "hosted by the UC improv club or...a guest comedian [brought in by the school.]" Finally, the "Campus Activities Board also puts on events multiple times a month that can be anything from trivia to Pinterest nights." It's virtually impossible not to have fun here!

Student Body

Students at Ursinus speak enthusiastically about their classmates. Of course, it's difficult to say something negative about people who "are always smiling" and "very welcoming." Undergrads do admit that the majority of their peers are "white [and] middle class": "While the college is homogeneous...in ethnic terms, it is ideologically very heterogeneous." As one undergrad explains, "I have encountered many ideas and beliefs that have challenged my own...[which] I very much appreciate." Students also stress that their classmates are "hardworking" and "down to earth." Moreover, as you might expect with college students, these undergrads also "tend to be curious." Indeed, "Everyone has something they really want to know more about." Interests and passions seem to run the gamut at Ursinus; you'll find everyone from "athletes [and] bio nerds [to] theatre kids" along with "prep[s and] hipsters." You "truly get a bit of everything here." Another happy student concludes, "Ursinus is a school where everyone fits in and you are encouraged to be yourself no matter how weird you may be. [It's a place that] appreciates people with different backgrounds, interests, and abilities."

Ursinus College

Financial Aid: 610-409-3600 • E-Mail: admission@ursinus.edu • Website: www.ursinus.edu

THE PRINCETON REVIEW SAYS

Admissions

The school reports that its standardized testing policy for use in admission for Fall 2024 is Test Optional. The 2024 testing policy will be permanent. The Princeton Review suggests that interested applicants consult with the school for the most up-to-date standardized testing policies. *Very important factors considered include:* rigor of secondary school record, academic GPA, character/personal qualities. *Important factors considered include:* class rank, application essay, recommendation(s), interview, extracurricular activities, talent/ability. *Other factors considered include:* standardized test scores, first generation, alumni/ae relation, geographical residence, state residency, racial/ethnic status, volunteer work, work experience, level of applicant's interest. High school diploma is required and GED is accepted. *Academic units required:* 4 English, 3 math, 1 science, 1 science lab, 2 foreign language, 1 social studies, 5 academic electives. *Academic units recommended:* 4 English, 4 math, 4 science, 3 science labs, 3 foreign language, 4 social studies.

Financial Aid

Students should submit: FAFSA; State aid form. Priority filing deadline is 2/1. The Princeton Review suggests that all financial aid forms be submitted as soon as possible (see page 5 for a note on the FAFSA). *Need-based scholarships/grants offered:* College/university scholarship or grant aid from institutional funds; Federal Pell; Private scholarships; SEOG; State scholarships/grants. *Loan aid offered:* Direct PLUS loans; Direct Subsidized Loans; Direct Unsubsidized Loans. Admitted students will be notified of awards on or about 3/15. Federal Work-Study Program available. Institutional employment available.

The Inside Word

Admissions officers at Ursinus are looking for motivated students who demonstrate intellectual curiosity. They want applicants who have pushed themselves academically in high school, beyond basic college prep courses. Students who have filled their schedules with some advanced placement or IB classes might find they have a leg up. Ursinus is Test Optional. Those students who choose to submit can use either the SAT or ACT. Finally, to be considered for all possible scholarships, it's best to apply either Early Action or Early Decision.

THE SCHOOL SAYS "..."

From the Admissions Office

"Located in suburban Philadelphia, the college boasts a beautiful 170-acre campus that features a highly individualized academic experience; the nationally recognized Common Intellectual Experience first-year seminar, which is a component of the Quest: Open Questions Open Minds core curriculum; residential village housing for students; the Floy Lewis Bakes Athletic Center with an indoor track and fieldhouse; the Berman Museum of Art; The Kaleidoscope performing arts center; the state-of-the-art interdisciplinary Innovation and Discovery Center; and the new Schellhase Commons, a student hub and admission welcome center. Ursinus is a member of the Centennial Conference along with Dickinson, Franklin & Marshall, Gettysburg, Muhlenberg, and Swarthmore. The academic environment is enhanced by a chapter of Phi Beta Kappa; a direct admission partnership with Saint Joseph's University (MBA program); dual-degree engineering agreements with Columbia University and Case Western Reserve; an affiliation agreement with the Villanova University M. Louise Fitzpatrick College of Nursing (accelerated BSN); international study abroad; and three centers: the Center for Science and the Common Good, the U-Imagine Center for Integrative and Entrepreneurial Studies, and the Melrose Center for Global Civic Engagement. The college offers student research carried out with one-on-one faculty attention and extensive internship opportunities. Financial aid and scholarships are generous with special awards for outstanding academics; distinguished creative writing; music, dance and theater auditions; and Bonner leadership in service. Intercollegiate and intramural sports are very popular on campus. The Ursinus admission application requires strong and consistent performance in a college preparatory curriculum. Submission of standardized test scores is optional."

SELECTIVITY

Admissions Rating	85
# of applicants	3,237
% of applicants accepted	82
% of acceptees attending	14
# offered a place on the wait list	192
% accepting a place on wait list	11
% admitted from wait list	73
# of early decision applicants	50
% accepted early decision	98

FIRST-YEAR PROFILE

Testing policy	Test Optional
Range SAT composite	1200–1370
Range SAT EBRW	600–690
Range SAT math	580–690
Range ACT composite	28–32
# submitting SAT scores	139
% submitting SAT scores	36
# submitting ACT scores	21
% submitting ACT scores	6
Average HS GPA	3.6
% frosh submitting high school GPA	100
% graduated top 10% of class	24
% graduated top 25% of class	47
% graduated top 50% of class	83

DEADLINES

Early decision	
Deadline	12/1
Notification	12/15
Other ED deadline	2/1
Early action	
Deadline	11/1
Notification	12/15
Regular	
Priority	2/1
Deadline	5/1
Nonfall registration?	Yes

APPLICANTS ALSO LOOK AT

Penn State University Park; Saint Joseph's University (PA); Temple University; University of Delaware; West Chester University of Pennsylvania

FINANCIAL FACTS

Financial Aid Rating	86
Annual tuition	$59,176
Room and board	$15,064
Required fees	$0
Books and supplies	$1,000
Average frosh need-based scholarship	$42,219
Average UG need-based scholarship	$40,236
% needy frosh rec. need-based scholarship or grant aid	99
% needy UG rec. need-based scholarship or grant aid	100
% needy frosh rec. non-need-based scholarship or grant aid	25
% needy UG rec. non-need-based scholarship or grant aid	22
% needy frosh rec. need-based self-help aid	70
% needy UG rec. need-based self-help aid	73
% frosh rec. any financial aid	100
% UG rec. any financial aid	99
% UG borrow to pay for school	75
Average cumulative indebtedness	$45,929
% frosh need fully met	36
% ugrads need fully met	30
Average % of frosh need met	85
Average % of ugrad need met	83

VANDERBILT UNIVERSITY

Vanderbilt University, Nashville, TN 37240 • Admissions: 615-322-7311 • Fax: 615-343-7765

STUDENTS SAY "..."

Academics

Vanderbilt University's courses "are rigorous and meant to challenge you"—and also one of the school's "greatest strengths." That's because students have all "the resources and support they need to succeed, including access to world-class libraries, technology, and career services." Those high standards reflect well upon career-oriented students, especially those seeking "numerous opportunities to engage in research projects and pursue their academic interests." Speaking on "behalf of pre-meds," one student relates that "it feels like a majority of us are in research labs and shadow doctors at the Vanderbilt hospital." Another student reports: "My electronics lab actually helped me get a summer internship offer from an electronics company!"

Professors value "honest discourse" with students "because they want you to succeed." (For that same reason, the administration is "very responsive to students who reach out to them.") Additionally, the faculty seem to "really strive to make personal connections with their students and get to know them as people outside of their classes." One student particularly appreciates that "the small class sizes help students build a stronger connection," especially valuable when it comes to, say, "a professional pianist who personally knows many artists, like Sheryl Crow and members of the Rolling Stones," or business professors with loads of experience. "The thing that I think I have enjoyed most about my professors at Vandy," concludes one student, "is that I feel like they are real people. They talk with my classes about our subject matter in a real way, relating it back to real human experience."

Campus Life

"There is a huge emphasis on building community here at Vanderbilt," explains one student, "Students are greatly encouraged to join many clubs and organizations. The university doesn't expect students to spend all of their time studying." Many tout the music clubs on campus, like the Spirit of Gold Marching Band and the Vanderbilt Commodore Orchestra, a "great community" for "non-music majors." One member describes the South Asian Cultural Exchange as "the largest and most impactful student organization on campus." Others enjoy service-oriented and athletic groups on campus: "My favorite extracurricular activities at Vanderbilt University include working with Vanderbilt's Habitat for Humanity organization and running with Vanderbilt's Run Club. Habitat for Humanity in Vanderbilt allows great volunteer service to be done easily." Students note that "a surprisingly large proportion of the student body takes part in Greek Life events to some extent." They also take pride in their football being part of the "best sports conferences, the SEC!" Students also brag that Vanderbilt's "location is ideal," loving that "Nashville has an amazing food scene as well as lots of live music."

Student Body

The most important takeaway for those at Vanderbilt University is that "the students here are going to support you." Overwhelmingly, students agree that their school offers a "collaborative environment of people from different backgrounds who are happy to engage with each other." Moreover, "students at Vanderbilt are very driven, but in a ... non-competitive manner that cultivates a challenging but enjoyable learning experience." One student playfully describes the student body as "sociable nerds—academics are important to us but we also love to party and have fun." Others attest that students are "very intelligent" with a "work-hard-play-hard kind of attitude. The same kid you see out on Broadway at 3:00 A.M. is the same one who will wreck the curve on your final exam." One student affirms that "everyone has their niche, and because of the school's breadth of programs, often those niches are unique. Artists, scientists, musicians, engineers, and teachers all can come together to hang out and enjoy college life together."

VANDERBILT UNIVERSITY

Financial Aid: 800-288-0204 • E-Mail: admissions@vanderbilt.edu • Website: www.vanderbilt.edu

THE PRINCETON REVIEW SAYS

Admissions

The school reports that its standardized testing policy for use in admission for Fall 2024 is Test Optional. The Princeton Review suggests that interested applicants consult with the school for the most up-to-date standardized testing policies. *Very important factors considered include:* rigor of secondary school record, class rank, academic GPA, standardized test scores (if submitted), application essay, extracurricular engagement, character/personal qualities. *Important factors considered include:* recommendation(s), talent/ability. *Other factors considered include:* interview, first generation, alumni/ae relation, geographical residence, racial/ethnic status, volunteer work, work experience. *Academic units recommended:* 4 English, 4 math, 4 science, 2 foreign language, 2 social studies/humanities, and 4 units of additional course work in these areas or in other academic areas.

Financial Aid

Students should submit: CSS/Financial Aid Profile; FAFSA. Priority filing deadline is 2/1. The Princeton Review suggests that all financial aid forms be submitted as soon as possible (see page 5 for a note on the FAFSA). *Need-based scholarships/grants offered:* College/university scholarship or grant aid from institutional funds; Federal Pell; Private scholarships; SEOG; State scholarships/grants; United Negro College Fund. *Loan aid offered:* Direct PLUS loans; Direct Subsidized Loans; Direct Unsubsidized Loans; Federal Nursing Loans. Admitted students will be notified of awards on or about 4/1. Federal Work-Study Program available. Institutional employment available.

The Inside Word

Vanderbilt deliberately keeps its incoming first-year class small at roughly 1,600 students and admission to this Nashville institution continues to be highly selective. With the admission committee's holistic approach to reviewing candidates, interested students should take stock of more than just their GPAs. Many students take the early decision route—Vanderbilt has two early decision deadlines. A final note: Most successful candidates present the equivalent of 5 academic subjects each year for 4 years of high school.

THE SCHOOL SAYS "..."

From the Admissions Office

"The Vanderbilt undergraduate experience is often described as uniquely balanced. Within the context of an outstanding academic landscape, students are encouraged to participate in a broad spectrum of campus organizations among a highly diverse population. Many students take classes in all four undergraduate schools, stretching their intellectual experience far beyond that of their declared major. Students typically live on campus all four years, beginning in a living and learning residential community for first-year students. Three new residential colleges have expanded living-learning opportunities for upperclass students. Students take full advantage of Nashville, participating in internships and cultural offerings from a city that *Travel + Leisure* ranked as one of the 15 Best Cities in the United States.

"The university makes three commitments to financial aid: (1) to be need-blind for all U.S. citizens and eligible non-citizens, (2) to meet 100 percent of a family's demonstrated financial need, (3) to avoid loans, instead providing grant assistance and reasonable work-study.

"The admissions process is holistic—Vanderbilt does not employ cutoffs for standardized testing or grade point averages. Students admitted to Vanderbilt typically show exceptional academic accomplishment and are highly engaged in their communities, often serving in leadership roles. The prescreening video and audition are of primary importance for students applying to the Blair School of Music."

SELECTIVITY

Admissions Rating	98
# of applicants	46,377
% of applicants accepted	7
% of acceptees attending	52
# of early decision applicants	5,044
% accepted early decision	18

FIRST-YEAR PROFILE

Testing policy	Test Optional
Range SAT composite	1490–1530
Range SAT EBRW	730–770
Range SAT math	760–800
Range ACT composite	34–35
# submitting SAT scores	468
% submitting SAT scores	29
# submitting ACT scores	519
% submitting ACT scores	32
Average HS GPA	3.9
% frosh submitting high school GPA	100
% graduated top 10% of class	91
% graduated top 25% of class	96
% graduated top 50% of class	99

DEADLINES

Early decision	
Deadline	11/1
Notification	12/15
Other ED deadline	1/1
Other ED notification	2/15
Regular	
Priority	1/1
Deadline	1/1
Notification	4/1
Nonfall registration?	No

APPLICANTS ALSO LOOK AT

Brown University; Columbia University; Cornell University; Dartmouth College; Duke University; Harvard College; Johns Hopkins University; Northwestern University; Princeton University; Rice University

FINANCIAL FACTS

Financial Aid Rating	98
Annual tuition	$58,130
Room and board	$19,862
Required fees	$1,480
Required fees (first-year)	$2,423
Books and supplies	$1,194
Average frosh need-based scholarship	$66,031
Average UG need-based scholarship	$63,479
% needy frosh rec. need-based scholarship or grant aid	100
% needy UG rec. need-based scholarship or grant aid	99
% needy frosh rec. non-need-based scholarship or grant aid	8
% needy UG rec. non-need-based scholarship or grant aid	5
% needy frosh rec. need-based self-help aid	60
% needy UG rec. need-based self-help aid	67
% UG borrow to pay for school	18
Average cumulative indebtedness	$30,364
% frosh need fully met	100
% ugrads need fully met	100
Average % of frosh need met	100
Average % of ugrad need met	100

VASSAR COLLEGE

124 Raymond Avenue, Poughkeepsie, NY 12604 • Admissions: 845-437-7000

STUDENTS SAY ". . ."

Academics

Vassar College is a small "academically challenging" school that offers a "perfect liberal arts feel" and seeks to broaden students' perspectives. The "strong sense of community" is apparent both in and out of the classroom, where the school drums home the idea that "it's all about being unique and letting your quirky characteristics shine." "We're asked to critically think about the world we live in and how our privilege plays into these systems," says a student. This freedom of character is a main reason why everyone here is "excited to be with each other, which creates this school spirit that isn't necessarily based on sports."

The lack of core requirements is "a great opportunity for students to explore anything they want before settling into a major." "Amazing" professors are "super accessible" and "fully engaged in the total Vassar community." "They are willing to meet you outside their office hours if they don't work for you," says a student. "My professors are...spectacular at illuminating difficult material," says a junior psychology major. Classes are all small and "most are very discussion-based"; students are "not competitive with each other, but with themselves," which creates a more relaxed environment despite the very high academics. Many do admit that there could stand to be "more sections of the most popular classes so that the most amount of people can be happy with their course selections."

Opportunities are there for students' voices to be heard, and "the administration is very willing to work with the student organization to accomplish goals," such as a ban on bottled water from dining services as a result of an initiative by the environmental group on campus. "Vassar students will do things in any way but the traditional way," says a sophomore. "No problem goes undiscussed." "Incredible" study abroad opportunities and a "beautiful campus" don't hurt, either.

Campus Life

"When you get here it starts to feel like home very quickly," says a student of the "stunning" campus. "The vibe of the whole school is so chill," but does not hamper a "vibrant extracurricular scene." Vassar is "bursting at the seams with orgs": there are "a ton of intramural sports teams," nine a cappella groups, plenty of political organizations, a large performing arts contingent, and "basically anything else you can think of." "Close-knit dormitory communities" and an emphasis on being "hyper-socially aware" lead students to be "very politically conscious and deeply involved in volunteerism and activism."

New York City isn't far, so some people take advantage of that, and "there are always parties you can go to if you want to," but "there is nothing wrong with staying in and watching a movie or chatting with friends." There is no Greek life; intellectual conversations abound at all hours, and students spend "significant time thinking about the state of the world and what's going on within the campus community." There are always a decent amount of weekend activities such as "concerts, comedy shows, plays, dances, etc." Be warned: "transportation is limited to get off campus unless you own a car."

Student Body

The "left wing, artsy, intelligent," and "open-minded" individuals that make up the "eclectic" student body "thrive" in the "welcoming" environs of Vassar. The "very generous" amount of need-based financial aid that is awarded "allows for wide socioeconomic diversity," and "Freshman Orientation is a great way for people to make friends here." Many here are philosophically minded and "strive to be as politically correct as possible," and there is "a good amount of hipsters." "You can definitely find at least one other student for every obscure interest you have," assures a student.

VASSAR COLLEGE

Financial Aid: 845-437-5320 • Website: www.vassar.edu

THE PRINCETON REVIEW SAYS

Admissions

The school reports that its standardized testing policy for use in admission for Fall 2024 is SAT or ACT Required. It is unknown at this time if the 2024 testing policy will be permanent. The Princeton Review suggests that interested applicants consult with the school for the most up-to-date standardized testing policies. *Very important factors considered include:* rigor of secondary school record, academic GPA, application essay, recommendation(s), extracurricular activities, talent/ability, character/personal qualities. *Important factors considered include:* class rank, volunteer work, work experience. *Other factors considered include:* standardized test scores, interview, first generation, alumni/ae relation, geographical residence, religious affiliation/commitment, racial/ethnic status. High school diploma is required and GED is accepted. *Academic units recommended:* 4 English, 4 math, 4 science, 4 foreign language, 4 social studies.

Financial Aid

Students should submit: CSS/Financial Aid Profile; FAFSA; Noncustodial Profile. Priority filing deadline is 3/30. The Princeton Review suggests that all financial aid forms be submitted as soon as possible (see page 5 for a note on the FAFSA). *Need-based scholarships/ grants offered:* College/university scholarship or grant aid from institutional funds; Federal Pell; Private scholarships; SEOG; State scholarships/grants. *Loan aid offered:* Direct PLUS loans; Direct Subsidized Loans; Direct Unsubsidized Loans; College/university loans from institutional funds. Federal Work-Study Program available. Institutional employment available.

The Inside Word

With acceptance rates hitting record lows, stellar academic credentials are a must for any serious Vassar candidate. Once admissions officers see you meet their rigorous scholastic standards, they'll closely assess your personal essay, recommendations, and extracurricular activities. The college prides itself on selecting students who will add to the vitality of the campus. Demonstrating an intellectual curiosity that extends outside the classroom is as important as success within it.

THE SCHOOL SAYS "..."

From the Admissions Office

"Vassar presents a rich variety of social and cultural activities, clubs, living arrangements, and regional attractions. Vassar also fields 23 Varsity sports plus 4 intercollegiate club teams, and more than 23 percent of students participate. Vassar is a vital, residential college community recognized for its respect for the rights and individuality of others."

SELECTIVITY

Admissions Rating	96
# of applicants	11,412
% of applicants accepted	19
% of acceptees attending	32
# offered a place on the wait list	1,336
% accepting a place on wait list	48
% admitted from wait list	5
# of early decision applicants	940
% accepted early decision	39

FIRST-YEAR PROFILE

Testing policy	SAT or ACT Required
Range SAT composite	1440–1510
Range SAT EBRW	720–760
Range SAT math	710–775
Range ACT composite	32–34
# submitting SAT scores	227
% submitting SAT scores	33
# submitting ACT scores	120
% submitting ACT scores	18
% graduated top 10% of class	77
% graduated top 25% of class	94
% graduated top 50% of class	99

DEADLINES

Early decision	
Deadline	11/15
Notification	12/15
Other ED deadline	1/1
Other ED notification	2/1
Regular	
Deadline	11/15
Notification	4/1
Nonfall registration?	No

APPLICANTS SOMETIMES PREFER

Brown University; Tufts University; Wesleyan University; Yale University

FINANCIAL FACTS

Financial Aid Rating	99
Annual tuition	$63,840
Room and board	$16,560
Required fees	$960
Books and supplies	$2,250
Average frosh need-based scholarship	$58,722
Average UG need-based scholarship	$55,413
% needy frosh rec. need-based scholarship or grant aid	99
% needy UG rec. need-based scholarship or grant aid	99
% needy frosh rec. non-need-based scholarship or grant aid	0
% needy UG rec. non-need-based scholarship or grant aid	0
% needy frosh rec. need-based self-help aid	96
% needy UG rec. need-based self-help aid	96
% frosh rec. any financial aid	64
% UG rec. any financial aid	66
% UG borrow to pay for school	45
Average cumulative indebtedness	$24,138
% frosh need fully met	100
% ugrads need fully met	100
Average % of frosh need met	100
Average % of ugrad need met	100

VILLANOVA UNIVERSITY

800 E. Lancaster Avenue, Villanova, PA 19085 • Admissions: 610-519-4500 • Fax: 610-519-6450

CAMPUS LIFE
Quality of Life Rating	83
Fire Safety Rating	60*
Green Rating	94
Type of school	Private
Affiliation	Roman Catholic
Environment	Village

STUDENTS
Total undergrad enrollment	6,989
% male/female/another gender	46/54/0
% from out of state	78
% frosh live on campus	99
% ugrads live on campus	83
% of fraternities (% join)	11 (17)
% of sororities (% join)	12 (19)
% African American	6
% Asian	7
% White	68
% Hispanic	11
% Native American	<1
% Pacific Islander	<1
% Two or more races	4
% Race and/or ethnicity unknown	2
% international	2

SURVEY SAYS . . .
Career services are great
Internships are widely available
School is well run
Students are very religious
Recreation facilities are great
Intramural sports are popular

ACADEMICS
Academic Rating	88
% students returning for sophomore year	96
% students graduating within 4 years	88
% students graduating within 6 years	91
Calendar	Semester
Student/faculty ratio	10:1
Profs interesting rating	92
Profs accessible rating	96

Most classes have 20–29 students.
Most lab/discussion sessions have 10–19 students.

STUDENTS SAY "..."

Academics
Known for being a basketball powerhouse, Villanova University (located in Pennsylvania) has developed an equally impressive reputation for academics. The school's admissions standards have continued to rise, and there is a "great support system" in place to help students achieve, between professors, advisors, tutors, research librarians, as well as a writing, math, and language learning center. Nova's career center and internship offices focus on getting students into jobs after college, and "the opportunities outside of the classroom really complement your education." "Villanova is full of resources for my success now, as a student, and will continue to be after I graduate as an alum," says a student. There is a real sense of community here, "stemming from service, school spirit around the basketball team, and everyone actively pursuing their own area of academic interest." The "passionate" professors are "true teachers and scholars," and they "go above and beyond their office hours." They are "easily accessible," and though some will seek you out, "it is mostly up to you to take advantage of them as a resource." "If you want to succeed, the community will do everything in its power to make sure you can do so," says a student. In addition to superior classroom quality (the faculty gets "fired up about what they teach"), there are "a lot of projects across majors that have real-world applications and are designed to help students in the long run." Classes are often a mixture of "lecture, discussion, individual/group projects, [and] fieldtrips." Villanova's "emphasis on service" is a point of praise for the student body, and everyone here embraces a sense of duty to make the world a better place. "We are the Nova Nation, built upon an unbreakable foundation of community," says a student.

Campus Life
Many buildings are new or have been recently renovated, and "most residence halls are really impressive and kept up very well." Most of campus "has a focused atmosphere during the week," but come Thursday afternoon, "you can feel campus relax and people are more likely to go out," mainly off campus. During basketball season, "people get their work done early to flock to the [Pavilion] for games." Almost everyone is involved in at least one (but probably more) extracurricular activities and clubs, and "a ton of students get involved with intramurals or club sports teams, as well." The Campus Activity Team puts on different events over the weekend, including "a cinema that is always showing a movie," and the school also offers great service experiences, whether "week-long service break experiences all over the world, cheering on the athletes at Special Olympics Fall Festival, or driving into Philly to play with kids and help them with their studies." Formals are also "a big deal" on campus. For those who want to take a break from college life, the massive King of Prussia Mall is found nearby (with a free weekend shuttle), and it is "an easy short train ride to go to Philadelphia."

Student Body
This "outstanding community" is built on "a lot of mutual respect." People are "well-rounded," "very friendly," and "proud of Villanova," and almost everyone here "dresses well" and is "extremely affable, professional, and an achiever." "Sometimes I think of Villanova as a school full of all the high school superstars," says one student. Balance is a skill that all Villanovans possess, and most are involved in some sort of volunteer activity; many also "party on the weekends, and show up ready to all of their classes." One can find a "very attractive student body" here as well.

VILLANOVA UNIVERSITY

Financial Aid: 610-519-4010 • E-Mail: gotovu@villanova.edu • Website: www.villanova.edu

THE PRINCETON REVIEW SAYS

Admissions

The school reports that its standardized testing policy for use in admission for Fall 2024 is Test Optional. It is unknown at this time if the 2024 testing policy will be permanent. The Princeton Review suggests that interested applicants consult with the school for the most up-to-date standardized testing policies. *Very important factors considered include:* rigor of secondary school record, academic GPA. *Important factors considered include:* application essay, recommendation(s), extracurricular activities, talent/ability, character/personal qualities, volunteer work. *Other factors considered include:* class rank, standardized test scores, first generation, alumni/ae relation, geographical residence, state residency, racial/ethnic status, level of applicant's interest. High school diploma is required and GED is accepted. *Academic units required:* 4 English, 4 math, 4 science, 2 science labs, 3 foreign language, 2 academic electives. *Academic units recommended:* 4 English, 4 math, 4 science, 3 science labs, 4 foreign language, 2 academic electives.

Financial Aid

Students should submit: CSS/Financial Aid Profile; FAFSA; Noncustodial Profile. Priority filing deadline is 1/15. The Princeton Review suggests that all financial aid forms be submitted as soon as possible (see page 5 for a note on the FAFSA). *Need-based scholarships/grants offered:* College/university scholarship or grant aid from institutional funds; Federal Pell; Private scholarships; SEOG; State scholarships/grants. *Loan aid offered:* Direct PLUS loans; Direct Subsidized Loans; Direct Unsubsidized Loans; Federal Nursing Loans. Admitted students will be notified of awards on or about 4/1. Federal Work-Study Program available. Institutional employment available.

The Inside Word

Villanova's growing academic reputation means its application process is growing more competitive as well: 93 percent of the most recent admitted freshman class ranked in the top 20 percent of their high school graduating class. Although academic achievement is important, the university looks at the whole package when considering applicants and expects candidates to be well rounded. As a private university, Villanova is not exactly cheap, but the school offers a wide variety of scholarships and aid to qualifying students.

THE SCHOOL SAYS "..."

From the Admissions Office

"Villanova is the oldest and largest Catholic university in Pennsylvania, founded in 1842 by the Order of Saint Augustine. Students of all faiths are welcome. The university tends to attract students who are interested in volunteerism. Villanovans provide more than 249,000 hours of service annually and host the largest student-run Special Olympics in the nation. Villanova's scenic campus is located twelve miles west of Philadelphia. The university offers programs through four undergraduate colleges: the College of Liberal Arts and Sciences, the College of Engineering, the M. Louise Fitzpatrick College of Nursing, and the Villanova School of Business. There are 265 student organizations and thirty-six National Honor Societies at Villanova. Incoming freshmen can opt to be part of a Learning Community, through which student groups live together in specially-designated residence halls and learn together in courses and co-curricular programs. The university offers Naval and Marine Reserve Officers Training Corps (ROTC) programs and hundreds of options for studying abroad. Nova's alumni body is comprised of more than 135,000 people. Some prominent grads include: Bert Jacobs, co-founder, Life Is Good Co.; Dr. Jill Biden, First Lady of the United States of America; and James C. Davis, chairman, Allegis Group.

"If you're looking to join Nova Nation, be prepared: The competition for admission is getting tougher every year."

SELECTIVITY

Admissions Rating.	96
# of applicants	23,835
% of applicants accepted	23
% of acceptees attending	32
# offered a place on the wait list	3,355
% accepting a place on wait list	54
% admitted from wait list	1
# of early decision applicants	1,467
% accepted early decision	56

FIRST-YEAR PROFILE

Testing policy	Test Optional
Range SAT EBRW	678–730
Range SAT math	700–770
Range ACT composite	32–34
# submitting SAT scores	492
% submitting SAT scores	28
# submitting ACT scores	265
% submitting ACT scores	15
Average HS GPA	3.9
% frosh submitting high school GPA	18

DEADLINES

Early decision	
Deadline	11/1
Notification	12/15
Other ED deadline	1/15
Other ED notification	3/1
Regular	
Deadline	1/15
Notification	Rolling, 4/1

FINANCIAL FACTS

Financial Aid Rating	83
Annual tuition	$63,806
Room and board	$16,896
Required fees	$1,156
Books and supplies	$1,100
Average frosh need-based scholarship	$40,829
Average UG need-based scholarship	$40,453
% needy frosh rec. need-based scholarship or grant aid	87
% needy UG rec. need-based scholarship or grant aid	89
% needy frosh rec. non-need-based scholarship or grant aid	28
% needy UG rec. non-need-based scholarship or grant aid	38
% needy frosh rec. need-based self-help aid	93
% needy UG rec. need-based self-help aid	92
% UG borrow to pay for school	37
Average cumulative indebtedness	$38,870
% frosh need fully met	19
% ugrads need fully met	19
Average % of frosh need met	80
Average % of ugrad need met	80

VIRGINIA TECH

800 Drillfield Drive, Blacksburg, VA 24061 • Admissions: 540-231-6000 • Fax: 540-231-3242

STUDENTS SAY ". . ."

Academics

Virginia Tech is a school with a reputation as big as its campus. Known for its "beautiful campus, amazing community feel, top-notch engineering field," and as a "good value"—not to mention its renowned athletics—Virginia Tech offers "a perfect blend of challenging and fun, encompassed in an unparalleled community feel." That community feel is a big part of the attraction to this top-ranked school, with students saying they feel "more comfortable here than anywhere in the world." Students are here, of course, for an education at a well-respected research university. At Virginia Tech, that education is provided by "passionate professors who bring real-life examples and cases into their teachings." The school's size and correspondingly large teaching staff mean that at times "professors are hit-or-miss," with "a few who just see it as another job." Most, however, "are really there to help you know as much as you can," a group who are "are extremely helpful and devoted to their students." The best of this school's professors "really makes students eager to learn." One student enthuses, "My professors here have changed the way I look at the world and have become some of my biggest heroes." But maybe another student sums it up best: "I would definitely say that my academic experience has been outstanding and that it has opened my eyes to even more possibilities.

Campus Life

Living "in the middle of nowhere" may seem like a recipe for boredom, but members of VT's Hokie Nation make the most of this "perfect college town." After all, when "there are 30,000 people around you that are the same age as you, you find stuff to do." When not consumed with Virginia Tech football—you'll see more maroon and orange in a single day here than most people will see in a lifetime—students here do, well, a little bit of everything. "School-related and Greek-life functions are the main sources of weekend activities," students say, but deceptively quiet Blacksburg and the surrounding area offer plenty of other options. On weekends, students "go out to parties or downtown with friends, we go out to eat, we play tennis, lay out on the Drillfield, play in the snow when we have some, go on hikes, and go to the river." That's just a start. Students find "there is always something fun going on to do with your friends," including "bowling, movies, club sports, video games," and more. If you can't find it in Blacksburg, it's ten minutes away in Christiansburg. Students enjoy relaxing, getting into discussions, or having outdoor adventures in a pastoral setting. When autumn arrives, "football games dominate the social scene."

Student Body

Better be ready to be part of the Hokie Nation, because the "typical student is someone who has a love for all things Virginia Tech." Those who attend VT "are proud of our school," and "A typical student here wears Virginia Tech clothes practically every day." Indeed, "you will find them at every VT football game." But the student body is about more than cheering for the maroon and orange. These "middle-class" students study hard "but play harder." Education matters here, but maybe not as much as living life. "The typical student is serious about schoolwork," students say, "but also knows how to have a good time." A majority of students are "white and from Virginia or North Carolina," but students prefer to describe their peers as "smart, approachable, and kind" and note that "we have every personality type and quirk you could ever imagine." If you are "well-rounded, involved, and [have] lots of school spirit," you are likely to fit in at VT.

VIRGINIA TECH

Financial Aid: 540-231-5179 • E-Mail: admissions@vt.edu • Website: www.vt.edu

THE PRINCETON REVIEW SAYS

Admissions

The school reports that its standardized testing policy for use in admission for Fall 2024 is Test Optional and will remain so for students entering through fall 2025. The Princeton Review suggests that interested applicants consult with the school for the most up-to-date standardized testing policies. *Very important factors considered include:* rigor of secondary school record, academic GPA, application essay, first generation, geographical residence, state residency, racial/ethnic status. *Other factors considered include:* standardized test scores, extracurricular activities, talent/ability, character/personal qualities, alumni/ae relation, volunteer work, work experience. High school diploma is required and GED is not accepted. *Academic units required:* 4 English, 3 math, 2 laboratory science, 2 social science, 3 additional academic units, 4 elective units.

Financial Aid

Students should submit: FAFSA. Priority filing deadline is 3/1. The Princeton Review suggests that all financial aid forms be submitted as soon as possible (see page 5 for a note on the FAFSA). *Need-based scholarships/grants offered:* College/university scholarship or grant aid from institutional funds; Federal Pell; Private scholarships; SEOG; State scholarships/grants; United Negro College Fund. *Loan aid offered:* Direct PLUS loans; Direct Subsidized Loans; Direct Unsubsidized Loans; College/university loans from institutional funds. Admitted students will be notified of awards on or about 3/5. Federal Work-Study Program available. Institutional employment available.

The Inside Word

With over 45,000 applications pouring into the admissions office each year, it's no wonder that the game here is all about numbers, numbers, numbers. Your high school grades will be top priority, so maintain strong grades. Most solid performers will find that acceptance comes with few problems, though the school's competitive disciplines—engineering and architecture, for example—will demand a higher caliber of student.

THE SCHOOL SAYS "..."

From the Admissions Office

"Virginia Tech offers the best of both worlds—everything a large university can provide and a small-town atmosphere. Undergraduates choose from more than 150 majors in eight colleges, including nationally ranked architecture, business, forestry, and engineering schools, as well as excellent computer science, biology, and communication studies. Technology is a key focus, both in classes and in general. Faculty incorporate a wide variety of technology into class, utilizing chat rooms, online lecture notes, and multimedia presentations. The university offers cutting-edge facilities for classes and research, abundant opportunities for advanced study in the Honors College, undergraduate research opportunities, study abroad, internships, and cooperative education. Students enjoy nearly 800 organizations which offer something for everyone. Students living on campus can join one of the more than 20 living-learning communities that allow them to live among students with similar interests, areas of study, or population groups such as first-generation students."

SELECTIVITY

Admissions Rating	91
# of applicants	45,321
% of applicants accepted	57
% of acceptees attending	28
# offered a place on the wait list	2,458
% accepting a place on wait list	24
% admitted from wait list	100
# of early decision applicants	2,796
% accepted early decision	50

FIRST-YEAR PROFILE

Testing policy	Test Optional
Range SAT EBRW	610–700
Range SAT math	610–720
Range ACT composite	26–32
# submitting SAT scores	3,369
% submitting SAT scores	47
# submitting ACT scores	788
% submitting ACT scores	11
Average HS GPA	4.0
% frosh submitting high school GPA	98

DEADLINES

Early decision	
Deadline	11/1
Early action	
Deadline	12/1
Notification	2/22
Regular	
Priority	12/1
Deadline	3/15
Notification	3/1
Nonfall registration?	Yes

FINANCIAL FACTS

Financial Aid Rating	78
Annual in-state tuition	$12,104
Annual out-of-state tuition	$31,754
Room and board	$14,490
Required fees	$2,482
Books and supplies	$1,100
Average frosh need-based scholarship	$8,274
Average UG need-based scholarship	$8,153
% needy frosh rec. need-based scholarship or grant aid	76
% needy UG rec. need-based scholarship or grant aid	76
% needy frosh rec. non-need-based scholarship or grant aid	53
% needy UG rec. non-need-based scholarship or grant aid	42
% needy frosh rec. need-based self-help aid	64
% needy UG rec. need-based self-help aid	64
% UG borrow to pay for school	46
Average cumulative indebtedness	$32,376
% frosh need fully met	14
% ugrads need fully met	13
Average % of frosh need met	51
Average % of ugrad need met	54

VIRGINIA WESLEYAN UNIVERSITY

5817 Wesleyan Drive, Virginia Beach, VA 23455 • Admissions: 757-455-3200 • Fax: 757-461-5238

CAMPUS LIFE

Quality of Life Rating	81
Fire Safety Rating	79
Green Rating	89
Type of school	Private
Affiliation	Methodist
Environment	Town

STUDENTS

Total undergrad enrollment	1,190
% male/female/another gender	39/61/0
% from out of state	27
% frosh live on campus	89
% ugrads live on campus	77
# of fraternities	4
# of sororities	5
% African American	26
% Asian	2
% White	52
% Hispanic	9
% Native American	<1
% Pacific Islander	<1
% Two or more races	6
% Race and/or ethnicity unknown	3
% international	1
# of countries represented	8

SURVEY SAYS . . .

Students are happy
Internships are widely available
Everyone loves the Blue Marlins
Campus newspaper is popular

ACADEMICS

Academic Rating	82
% students returning for sophomore year	66
% students graduating within 4 years	44
% students graduating within 6 years	47
Calendar	4/1/4
Student/faculty ratio	11:1
Profs interesting rating	90
Profs accessible rating	94
Most classes have 10–19 students.	

MOST POPULAR MAJORS

Criminal Justice/Safety Studies; Social Sciences, General; Business Administration and Management, General

STUDENTS SAY "..."

Academics

Virginia Wesleyan is the quintessential small liberal arts university, providing undergraduates with "a close-knit community" where one "can easily build strong relationship[s]." Indeed, you're guaranteed to be "more than a number" on this Virginia Beach campus of 1,500 undergrads. "Small classes" are a hallmark of a Virginia Wesleyan education with many being "discussion- or interaction-based." And students love the fact that they are "always taught by...professors"—no teaching assistants here! Speaking of professors, VWU undergrads are full of praise for theirs. They seem to "genuinely care about their students and are approachable outside the classroom." A current student agrees, "I have never met a faculty so invested in my own personal success." And an earth and environmental studies student excitedly interjects, "I have never experienced [a] learning environment like this one. Professors not only care about their students, but they go above and beyond to ensure that every student understands the material. Professors make lifelong connections with students." All in all, Virginia Wesleyan offers individuals a college experience that's "all about making every single student feel as though this is their second home and that every person they come into contact with is looking out for the student's best interest."

Campus Life

Despite students reporting that "the food could be better," by and large undergrads seem to enjoy life at Virginia Wesleyan. To begin with, there are plenty of activities with which to get involved, be it "Greek life, music, arts, religion, sciences, business, etc." Indeed, there's truly something for everyone! Students also like taking advantage of various campus amenities such as "the pool, the rock wall, the indoor track, the gymnasium, and the pool table in the student center." Of course, similar to many undergraduate institutions, "social gatherings are huge here." Students "love inviting [their] friends and teammates over to get over a stressful week of studying and homework." However, these get-togethers don't tend to get too raucous. As an English major tells us, "Although fun is encouraged, we are often reminded of how to keep everyone safe. Underage drinking is NOT tolerated, and we take it seriously when rules are broken." Finally, when the weather permits, these undergrads flock to nearby Chick's Beach. And many can be found sampling the "delicious restaurants around Norfolk" and Virginia Beach.

Student Body

Undergrads at Virginia Wesleyan speak very highly of their peers. Granted, this isn't surprising given that the student body is comprised of "friendly and outgoing" individuals who are typically "laid back." A psychology major provides a little more insight by stating, "Students are generally pretty spirited and helpful, and most [people] seem to genuinely care about their academics." By and large, undergrads here are "open to new things." They also tend to be "very busy" since it's quite typical for students to be "involved in several different clubs and community service groups." Of course, though many VWU undergrads "join one of the [eight] Greek organizations available" or become "a member of a sports team" to "fit in," we're also told that it's by no means a necessity. A chemistry major assures us, "Whatever you are interested in, you can easily find a group of people that connect with you. Our school is so inviting that it's hard to not fit in somewhere." Finally, another psychology major boasts, "I feel like my school is extremely accepting, and we have events for all cultures, beliefs, and extracurricular [activities] all the time."

VIRGINIA WESLEYAN UNIVERSITY

Financial Aid: 757-455-3345 • E-Mail: admissions@vwu.edu • Website: www.vwu.edu

THE PRINCETON REVIEW SAYS

Admissions

The school reports that its standardized testing policy for use in admission for Fall 2024 is Test Optional. The 2024 testing policy will be temporary. The Princeton Review suggests that interested applicants consult with the school for the most up-to-date standardized testing policies. *Very important factors considered include:* rigor of secondary school record, academic GPA, standardized test scores, level of applicant's interest. *Important factors considered include:* extracurricular activities. *Other factors considered include:* recommendation(s), interview, talent/ability, character/personal qualities, first generation, alumni/ae relation, volunteer work, work experience. High school diploma is required and GED is accepted. *Academic units required:* 4 English, 3 math, 2 science, 2 science labs, 2 foreign language, 1 history, 1 computer science. *Academic units recommended:* 4 English, 3 math, 2 science, 2 science labs, 2 foreign language, 1 history, 1 computer science, 4 academic electives.

Financial Aid

Students should submit: FAFSA; State aid form. Priority filing deadline is 3/1. The Princeton Review suggests that all financial aid forms be submitted as soon as possible (see page 5 for a note on the FAFSA). *Need-based scholarships/grants offered:* College/university scholarship or grant aid from institutional funds; Federal Pell; Private scholarships; SEOG; State scholarships/grants. *Loan aid offered:* Direct PLUS loans; Direct Subsidized Loans; Direct Unsubsidized Loans. Admitted students will be notified of awards on a rolling basis beginning 10/15. Federal Work-Study Program available. Institutional employment available.

The Inside Word

As Virginia Wesleyan's profile rises, so too does the number of applications it receives. And each year, competition for admission increases. Therefore, to receive a coveted acceptance letter, applicants need to have earned strong grades in college prep courses. Additionally, given the college's small size, admissions officers are on the lookout for students who will contribute to campus life. Therefore, active and sustained participation in a handful of extracurricular activities helps candidates appear more attractive to the admissions committee.

THE SCHOOL SAYS "..."

From the Admissions Office

"Virginia Wesleyan University seeks to enroll qualified students from diverse social, religious, racial, economic, and geographic backgrounds. Admission is based solely on the applicant's academic and personal qualifications. Factors considered include grades, recommendations, standardized test scores, and extracurricular activities. Virginia Wesleyan is using a Test Optional admissions process, but we will accept SAT or ACT scores for use in placement and advising. A high school diploma is required (GED accepted) and proof of English proficiency is required for all international applicants. Virginia Wesleyan considers applications on a rolling admissions basis. Applicants can typically expect notification within two to three weeks after we receive your completed application and supporting documents. Prospective students are encouraged to visit our beautiful 300-acre wooded campus for a tour and to meet with an enrollment counselor. Learn more about admissions at www.vwu.edu."

SELECTIVITY

Admissions Rating	80
# of applicants	2,076
% of applicants accepted	86
% of acceptees attending	19

FIRST-YEAR PROFILE

Testing policy	Test Optional
# submitting SAT scores	44
% submitting SAT scores	13
# submitting ACT scores	15
% submitting ACT scores	4
Average HS GPA	3.4
% frosh submitting high school GPA	99
% graduated top 10% of class	15
% graduated top 25% of class	36
% graduated top 50% of class	66

DEADLINES

Regular	
Priority	3/1
Notification	Rolling, 9/15
Nonfall registration?	Yes

APPLICANTS OFTEN PREFER
Old Dominion University

FINANCIAL FACTS

Financial Aid Rating	83
Annual tuition	$36,010
Room and board	$11,513
Required fees	$950
Books and supplies	$1,500
Average frosh need-based scholarship	$3,192
Average UG need-based scholarship	$4,256
% needy frosh rec. need-based scholarship or grant aid	63
% needy UG rec. need-based scholarship or grant aid	51
% needy frosh rec. non-need-based scholarship or grant aid	99
% needy UG rec. non-need-based scholarship or grant aid	97
% needy frosh rec. need-based self-help aid	67
% needy UG rec. need-based self-help aid	73
% frosh rec. any financial aid	98
% UG rec. any financial aid	91
% UG borrow to pay for school	83
Average cumulative indebtedness	$35,685
% frosh need fully met	19
% ugrads need fully met	20
Average % of frosh need met	67
Average % of ugrad need met	66

WABASH COLLEGE

410 West Wabash Avenue, Crawfordsville, IN 47933-0352 • Admissions: 765-361-6100 • Fax: 765-361-6437

STUDENTS SAY ". . ."

Academics

Students live by "the Gentleman's Rule" at the all-male Wabash College in Crawfordsville, Indiana. Backed by an "exceptional" academic reputation and preparation for graduate professional schools ("Wabash's medical school acceptance rates are above 80 percent"), Wabash is "truly an A school for B students." As one student puts it, Wabash "opened the world up to me and changed the arc of my life." The school has a "great alumni base" and "does a great job of making opportunity for students in the Rust Belt." Professors come highly recommended, described as both "outstanding" and "down to earth" and not only "always have their doors open for questions," but sometimes also open their homes as well for "dinner and discussion about an assignment or topic that is bothering you." The "classes are tough but rewarding" and require "lots of reading…and critical thinking." There is plenty of "opportunity for students to take leadership positions on campus," with students having "a lot of control over their budget," as one example. Students also praise Wabash's office of "career services" and "immersion learning." And not for nothing, students feel respected and heard: "I think that our school does a great job of…engaging with the students and allowing their voices to be heard equally with that of the professor in order to progress the narrative and enhance the learning process, rather than just dismissing student perspectives as background noise."

Campus Life

"Our school spirit and tradition-oriented culture is second to none!" exclaims one student. Wabash is an "academically rigorous school," with classes running until around 4:00 P.M. and the remaining weekdays "devoted to studying." That said, "extracurriculars are easy to come by" and many students "compete in intramural sports." Students also tend to be "very involved with extracurricular organizations," which include "jazz band, "dance marathon, "German club," and "College Mentors for Kids." The "surrounding area is very rural, so life is centered around the campus." Greek life is also big, as "over half of the campus is in a fraternity," and on weekends, "a fraternity is almost always holding a party on Friday and Saturday nights." There are "campus unity tours (otherwise called TGIF)" where students "go to each fraternity house and living unit and socialize for fifteen minutes or so," a "great way to get to know people." The Wabash "brotherhood" also "love to support athletic teams." The football home section is "almost always sold out." About "half of the student body plays a sport," and the vast majority of the student body is "in a school-sponsored club or organization." On weekends, students are also down to take a "quick trip to Lafayette or Indianapolis to experience the bigger-city life."

Student Body

This "800-odd all male campus in rural western Indiana is more than just a brotherhood." Students generally hold each other in high esteem: "When I go out into the world, if I find another Wabash man, the connection we have is instantaneous," one student says. "Our experiences, while different, are rooted in the same traditions and ideals, and thus, we can share a bond, despite the other man being 10, 20, 30, 40, or even 50 years older." An "openly gay" student observes that the "overall atmosphere…is a welcoming and accepting one; I feared attending a small campus in Indiana, but, entering my last semester, I realize it is incredibly easy to find a loving group of individuals. I truly believe a great majority of Wabash's students embody the Gentleman's Rule and act accordingly." The student body is a "diverse melting pot of all kinds of students." From "rural Midwestern towns to rough inner city neighborhoods in Philly and Chicago, to affluent suburbs and many foreign countries, the student body at Wabash is home to a breathtakingly wide array of perspectives and beliefs." This amount of diversity "poses a positive challenge to Wabash men, as it gives us the ability to open our eyes to new ways of thinking and living…and also teaches how to go into a new and changing world."

WABASH COLLEGE

Financial Aid: 765-361-6375 • E-Mail: admissions@wabash.edu • Website: www.wabash.edu

THE PRINCETON REVIEW SAYS

Admissions

The school reports that its standardized testing policy for use in admission for Fall 2024 is Test Optional. The 2024 testing policy will be permanent. The Princeton Review suggests that interested applicants consult with the school for the most up-to-date standardized testing policies. *Very important factors considered include:* rigor of secondary school record, class rank, unweighted academic GPA, level of applicant's interest. *Important factors considered include:* recommendation(s), interview, extracurricular activities, talent/ability. *Other factors considered include:* standardized test scores, application essay, character/personal qualities, first generation, alumni/ae relation, geographical residence, racial/ethnic status, volunteer work, work experience. High school diploma is required and GED is accepted. *Academic units recommended:* 4 English, 4 math, 2 science, 2 science labs, 2 foreign language, 2 social studies, 2 history, 2 academic electives.

Financial Aid

Students should submit: FAFSA. Priority filing deadline is 1/15. The Princeton Review suggests that all financial aid forms be submitted as soon as possible (see page 5 for a note on the FAFSA). *Need-based scholarships/grants offered:* College/university scholarship or grant aid from institutional funds; Federal Pell; Private scholarships; SEOG; State scholarships/grants; United Negro College Fund. *Loan aid offered:* Direct PLUS loans; Direct Subsidized Loans; Direct Unsubsidized Loans. Admitted students will be notified of awards on a rolling basis beginning 12/15. Federal Work-Study Program available. Institutional employment available.

The Inside Word

Because Wabash is so specific and unique, it self-selects a small but strong applicant pool. Don't let its relatively high acceptance rate deceive you: admitted students are in for four years of academic rigor, so don't apply if you're not ready to apply serious intellectual muscle and work ethic. Although not a requirement, an applicant may also submit their SAT/ACT scores and/or a written statement to include additional details about himself for consideration during the application review.

THE SCHOOL SAYS "..."

From the Admissions Office

"Wabash College is different—and distinctive—from other liberal arts colleges. Different in that Wabash is an outstanding college for men only. Distinctive in the quality and character of the faculty, in the demanding nature of the academic program, in the seriousness and maturity of the men who enroll, and in the richness of the traditions that have evolved throughout its 190 years. Wabash is preeminently a teaching institution and the Princeton Review annually lauds the accessibility of the faculty and the classroom experience. Faculty and students talk to each other with mutual respect for the expression of informed opinion. Students who collaborate with faculty on research projects are considered their peers in the research—an esteem not usually extended to undergraduates—and are honored annually in a celebration of undergraduate research. Wabash also earns national recognition for its alumni network, internship program, and career services, all of which are critical to our graduates' success in every walk of life. But perhaps the single most striking aspect of student life at Wabash is personal freedom. The College has only one rule: 'The student is expected to conduct himself at all times, both on and off the campus, as a gentleman and a responsible citizen.' Wabash College treats students as adults, and such treatment attracts responsible freshmen and fosters their independence and maturity. For students seeking admission, Wabash places emphasis on high school GPA and difficulty of subjects, and is currently Test Optional."

SELECTIVITY

Admissions Rating	88
# of applicants	1,914
% of applicants accepted	61
% of acceptees attending	22
# of early decision applicants	68
% accepted early decision	85

FIRST-YEAR PROFILE

Testing policy	Test Optional
Range SAT composite	1140–1320
Range SAT EBRW	560–650
Range SAT math	562–670
Range ACT composite	22–30
# submitting SAT scores	134
% submitting SAT scores	52
# submitting ACT scores	34
% submitting ACT scores	13
Average HS GPA	3.6
% frosh submitting high school GPA	91
% graduated top 10% of class	33
% graduated top 25% of class	64
% graduated top 50% of class	92

DEADLINES

Early decision	
Deadline	11/15
Notification	12/5
Early action	
Deadline	12/1
Notification	12/31
Regular	
Priority	12/1
Notification	Rolling, 1/18
Nonfall registration?	Yes

APPLICANTS SOMETIMES PREFER
DePauw University; Indiana University—Bloomington; Purdue University—West Lafayette

FINANCIAL FACTS

Financial Aid Rating	92
Annual tuition	$48,200
Room and board	$13,300
Required fees	$925
Books and supplies	$1,250
Average frosh need-based scholarship	$39,107
Average UG need-based scholarship	$37,419
% needy frosh rec. need-based scholarship or grant aid	98
% needy UG rec. need-based scholarship or grant aid	98
% needy frosh rec. non-need-based scholarship or grant aid	25
% needy UG rec. non-need-based scholarship or grant aid	21
% needy frosh rec. need-based self-help aid	70
% needy UG rec. need-based self-help aid	75
% frosh rec. any financial aid	100
% UG rec. any financial aid	100
% UG borrow to pay for school	73
Average cumulative indebtedness	$33,285
% frosh need fully met	70
% ugrads need fully met	68
Average % of frosh need met	95
Average % of ugrad need met	93

WAGNER COLLEGE

One Campus Road, Staten Island, NY 10301 • Admissions: 718-390-3100 • Fax: 718-390-3105

CAMPUS LIFE

Quality of Life Rating	79
Fire Safety Rating	99
Green Rating	60*
Type of school	Private
Affiliation	No Affiliation
Environment	Metropolis

STUDENTS

Total undergrad enrollment	1,576
% male/female/another gender	38/62/NR
% from out of state	40
% frosh from public high school	67
% frosh live on campus	57
% ugrads live on campus	45
# of fraternities (% join)	5 (6)
# of sororities (% join)	4 (13)
% African American	7
% Asian	5
% White	59
% Hispanic	14
% Native American	<1
% Pacific Islander	<1
% Two or more races	3
% Race and/or ethnicity unknown	5
% international	7
# of countries represented	47

SURVEY SAYS . . .

Class discussions encouraged
Theater is popular
Everyone loves the Seahawks

ACADEMICS

Academic Rating	80
% students returning for sophomore year	82
% students graduating within 4 years	64
% students graduating within 6 years	71
Calendar	Semester
Student/faculty ratio	10:1
Profs interesting rating	86
Profs accessible rating	88

Most classes have 10–19 students.
Most lab/discussion sessions have 20–29 students.

MOST POPULAR MAJORS

Visual and Performing Arts, General; Nursing Science; Business/Commerce, General

STUDENTS SAY "..."

Academics

Wagner College, located on Staten Island, is a "tight-knit and fun, yet academically challenging," liberal arts school that operates under the Wagner Plan, combining a solid foundation in the liberal arts with practical and applied experiences like internships, with a commitment to service learning and community. The school is "in the perfect location with a surplus of unique resources" and is composed of "an excellent and vibrant community that supports its students every step of the way." The "commitment of the faculty and staff have for the student body is outstanding." The school's curriculum is lauded: "Even though I am a biology major, I have the wonderful opportunity to explore interdisciplinary topics in the humanities and social sciences throughout my undergraduate career," says one student. The college's unique first-year program consists of a set of three classes with the same 28 students, which "helps transition us from high school to college by progressively learning how to write college-level pieces as well as by engaging in a mandatory thirty-hour community service requirement." This "small, beautiful learning community" is guided by an "extremely attentive and competent" faculty. The professors "ask you to do your best and to push your limitations away" and are "extremely accessible outside of class." "The first time I was nervous about registration, my advisor sat down had lunch, and we registered together," says a student. "It is comforting that I can go to my professors whenever I need assistance with work." The school's science and physicians' assistant programs are notably strong, as are the "fantastic" theater and musical programs. Students all universally agree that Wagner "lets you experience all different types of subjects by following the concept: learning by doing."

Campus Life

At Wagner, students are "mostly concerned about their careers, whether they want to make it on Broadway or find the cure for cancer." There's plenty of school-run activities "through co-curricular programs and various clubs," so there are "countless things to do." Beyond all doubt, "the best thing to do…is to take advantage of New York City." The campus is just "a ferry ride away from Manhattan," and the majority of people takes the Wagner shuttle to the S.I. ferry ("all for free!") and goes to the city, whether to shop, eat, or go to a Broadway show. On weekends, there are "parties run by organizations from time to time" or in dorm rooms, since "there is no off-campus housing." Every year, the school has an event called Wagner Stock, where a famous musician or group comes to play. Food is a huge pain point here: students want "more access to the dining hall in the late hours of the night," "more food options," and just better food in general.

Student Body

The student body here celebrates its "diverse" makeup, but Division I athletics and the "great theater program" are very visible in this "small close community." But a student not in either of these programs can find their group through clubs and the major that they are in." Many students have "one major and a minor," and "half of them might study abroad for a semester and or have one or two internships before they graduate." Everyone basically goes about their own business, but "is very approachable." No one seems to have any trouble finding their own crowd, but even once that occurs, "different crowds frequently mingle and almost everyone gets along." "People just talk to everyone," says a student.

WAGNER COLLEGE

Financial Aid: 718-390-3183 • E-Mail: admissions@wagner.edu • Website: www.wagner.edu

THE PRINCETON REVIEW SAYS

Admissions

The school reports that its standardized testing policy for use in admission for Fall 2024 is Test Optional. The 2024 testing policy will be permanent. The Princeton Review suggests that interested applicants consult with the school for the most up-to-date standardized testing policies. *Very important factors considered include:* rigor of secondary school record. *Important factors considered include:* class rank, academic GPA, application essay, recommendation(s), interview, extracurricular activities, talent/ability, character/personal qualities. *Other factors considered include:* standardized test scores, volunteer work, work experience, level of applicant's interest. High school diploma is required and GED is accepted. *Academic units required:* 4 English, 3 math, 2 science, 1 science lab, 2 foreign language, 3 history, 7 academic electives.

Financial Aid

Students should submit: FAFSA. Priority filing deadline is 1/15. The Princeton Review suggests that all financial aid forms be submitted as soon as possible (see page 5 for a note on the FAFSA). *Need-based scholarships/grants offered:* College/university scholarship or grant aid from institutional funds; Federal Pell; Private scholarships; SEOG; State scholarships/grants. *Loan aid offered:* Direct PLUS loans; Direct Subsidized Loans; Direct Unsubsidized Loans; Federal Nursing Loans. Admitted students will be notified of awards on a rolling basis. Federal Work-Study Program available. Institutional employment available.

The Inside Word

As far as grades and test scores, the profile of the average freshman class at Wagner is solid. Standardized tests are optional, and there is more value placed on the strength of your course work and your grades in those classes. The admissions staff here is dedicated to finding the right students for their school. Wagner is looking for students who like to be involved in community events, so make sure your application reflects your extracurriculars. An interview bodes well for serious applicants.

THE SCHOOL SAYS "..."

From the Admissions Office

"At Wagner College, we attract and develop active learners and future leaders. Wagner College has received national acclaim (*Time* magazine, American Association of Colleges and Universities) for its innovative curriculum, The Wagner Plan for the Practical Liberal Arts. At Wagner, we capitalize on our unique geography; we are a traditional, scenic, residential campus, which happens to sit atop a hill on an island overlooking lower Manhattan. Our location allows us to offer a program that couples required off-campus experiences (experiential learning), with 'learning community' clusters of courses. This program begins in the first semester and continues through the senior capstone experience in the major. Fieldwork and internships, writing-intensive reflective tutorials, connected learning, 'reading, writing, and doing': At Wagner College our students truly discover 'the practical liberal arts in New York City.'"

SELECTIVITY

Admissions Rating	87
# of applicants	2,645
% of applicants accepted	69
% of acceptees attending	22
# offered a place on the wait list	44
% accepting a place on wait list	77
% admitted from wait list	29

FIRST-YEAR PROFILE

Testing policy	Test Optional
Range SAT composite	1100–1260
Range SAT EBRW	550–640
Range SAT math	540–650
Range ACT composite	24–29
# submitting SAT scores	96
% submitting SAT scores	24
# submitting ACT scores	24
% submitting ACT scores	6
Average HS GPA	3.6
% frosh submitting high school GPA	100
% graduated top 10% of class	26
% graduated top 25% of class	48
% graduated top 50% of class	78

DEADLINES

Early action	
Deadline	12/1
Notification	1/5
Regular	
Priority	12/1
Deadline	2/15
Notification	Rolling, 1/5
Nonfall registration?	Yes

APPLICANTS OFTEN PREFER
Fordham University; New York University

APPLICANTS SOMETIMES PREFER
Fairfield University; Ithaca College; Pace University

APPLICANTS RARELY PREFER
Drew University; Manhattan College; Marist College; Quinnipiac University

FINANCIAL FACTS

Financial Aid Rating	83
Annual tuition	$50,200
Room and board	$16,012
Required fees	$1,800
Books and supplies	$1,034
Average frosh need-based scholarship	$23,387
Average UG need-based scholarship	$27,807
% needy frosh rec. need-based scholarship or grant aid	100
% needy UG rec. need-based scholarship or grant aid	100
% needy frosh rec. non-need-based scholarship or grant aid	0
% needy UG rec. non-need-based scholarship or grant aid	0
% needy frosh rec. need-based self-help aid	69
% needy UG rec. need-based self-help aid	73
% frosh rec. any financial aid	99
% UG rec. any financial aid	93
% frosh need fully met	27
% ugrads need fully met	28
Average % of frosh need met	75
Average % of ugrad need met	75

WAKE FOREST UNIVERSITY

1834 Wake Forest Road, Winston Salem, NC 27109 • Admissions: 336-758-5201 • Fax: 336-758-4324

STUDENTS SAY "..."

Academics

North Carolina's own Wake Forest University prepares students to lead lives that matter and has a reputation for quality that affords its students "excellent placement into jobs and graduate schools." Students come to Wake Forest for an education of the entire person, and the school "practices intentional interactions between professors and students, students with each other, and students and their larger community." This grand scale plan for well-rounded development includes "opportunities to serve, to become a leader, and to become part of initiatives that are larger than you." Professors "demand a lot of work but love teaching" and "ensure that students are comfortable with voicing their opinions." Classes "are not easy and good grades are tough to come by." Fortunately, faculty "are extremely helpful" and it's worth noting that many students receive academic credit for faculty-directed research. "Overall I've had a fantastic academic experience with professors that have helped me discover my intellectual passions and have had a vested interest in my success," says a junior.

Some students note that "the greatest aspects of Wake Forest" are the small school atmosphere but large school resources, as well as the high levels of support. "I feel that I could ask any professor I've had at Wake for a letter of recommendation, and they would know me personally enough to do so," says a student. There is a similarly "strong vision and support" from the administration and the alumni network, who back "opportunities that meld ideas and people that just don't happen at other colleges."

Campus Life

Wake Forest students work extremely hard on weekdays, often spending hours in the library to complete work, but "absolutely let loose on weekends." The school's "vibrant social scene" and a schedule that is "always bustling with extracurricular activities" keep the candle burning at both ends, and "parties, going to bars downtown, concerts, game nights, and chill hang outs at friends' houses" are other methods of fun. The Division I athletics—perhaps you've heard of them?—lend Wake Forest a "big-school sports feel at a small school"; and many students play intramural sports or exercise fairly regularly as "people are very conscious of their image" at this health-conscious university. While Greek life is highly visible here, there are also organizations like the Student Union that "promote other fun aspects of campus life (i.e., movie nights, guest speakers, campus carnivals)." Students take part in "lots of great traditions at Wake Forest, like our annual Shag on the Mag dance in the spring," "rolling the quad after a big athletic win," and dinner at the on-campus restaurant Shorty's. Philanthropy is a "HUGE part of the WFU experience," and there are several extremely large community service events that happen throughout the year, including the Project Pumpkin Halloween festival, the Hit the Bricks race to support cancer research, and many others.

Student Body

The university is steeped in Southern traditions and hospitality that "most students fit into or learn to adhere to in their tenure as Wake Students," but the school "is also home to students from around the country and the world." In this "tight-knit, supportive community" nearly everybody is "intelligent, ambitious, [and] highly involved." Some even describe the experience as "a living J. Crew magazine" in which many students are "preppy, involved in Greek life, [and] from the East Coast." But thanks to a strong foundation of friendliness and acceptance among the student body, "people generally don't have any trouble fitting in here, and can usually easily find groups of people who share their interests." WFU students come from 49 states and more than 40 countries.

WAKE FOREST UNIVERSITY

Financial Aid: 336-758-5154 • E-Mail: admissions@wfu.edu • Website: www.wfu.edu

THE PRINCETON REVIEW SAYS

Admissions

The school reports that its standardized testing policy for use in admission for Fall 2024 is Test Optional. It is unknown at this time if the 2024 testing policy will be permanent. The Princeton Review suggests that interested applicants consult with the school for the most up-to-date standardized testing policies. *Very important factors considered include:* rigor of secondary school record, class rank, academic GPA, application essay, character/personal qualities. *Important factors considered include:* recommendation(s), interview, extracurricular activities, talent/ability. *Other factors considered include:* standardized test scores, first generation, alumni/ae relation, geographical residence, state residency, religious affiliation/commitment, racial/ethnic status, volunteer work, level of applicant's interest. High school diploma is required and GED is accepted. *Academic units required:* 4 English, 3 math, 1 science, 2 foreign language, 2 social studies. *Academic units recommended:* 4 English, 4 math, 4 science, 4 foreign language, 4 social studies.

Financial Aid

Students should submit: CSS/Financial Aid Profile; FAFSA; Noncustodial Profile; State aid form. Priority filing deadline is 1/1. The Princeton Review suggests that all financial aid forms be submitted as soon as possible (see page 5 for a note on the FAFSA). *Need-based scholarships/grants offered:* College/university scholarship or grant aid from institutional funds; Federal Pell; Private scholarships; SEOG; State scholarships/grants; United Negro College Fund. *Loan aid offered:* Direct PLUS loans; Direct Subsidized Loans; Direct Unsubsidized Loans; College/university loans from institutional funds; State Loans. Admitted students will be notified of awards on a rolling basis beginning 4/1. Federal Work-Study Program available. Institutional employment available.

The Inside Word

Wake Forest's considerable application numbers afford admissions officers the opportunity to be rather selective. In particular, admissions officers remain diligent in their matchmaking efforts—finding students who are good fits for the school—and their hard work is rewarded by a high graduation rate. Candidates will need to be impressive in all areas to gain admission, since all areas of their applications are considered carefully. A relatively large number of qualified students find themselves on Wake Forest's wait list.

THE SCHOOL SAYS "..."

From the Admissions Office

"Wake Forest University has been dedicated to the liberal arts for over a century and a half; this means education in the fundamental fields of human knowledge and achievement. It seeks to encourage habits of mind that ask why, that evaluate evidence, that are open to new ideas, that attempt to understand and appreciate the perspective of others, that accept complexity and grapple with it, that admit error, and that pursue truth. Wake Forest is among a small, elite group of American colleges and universities recognized for their outstanding academic quality. It offers small classes taught by full-time faculty—not graduate assistants—and a commitment to student interaction with those professors. Wake Forest balances the personal attention of a liberal arts college with the academic vitality and broad opportunities of a research university. Students are admitted based on the unique qualities they bring to our community. Wake Forest's generous financial aid program allows deserving students to enroll regardless of their financial circumstances.

"Wake Forest is the first top thirty national university in the United States to make standardized tests such as the SAT and ACT with writing optional in the admissions process. If applicants feel that their SAT or ACT with writing scores are a good indicator of their abilities, they may submit them and they will be considered in the admissions decision. If, however, a prospective student does not feel that their scores accurately represent their academic abilities, they do not need to submit them until after they have been accepted and choose to enroll. Wake Forest takes a holistic look at each applicant."

SELECTIVITY

Admissions Rating	95
# of applicants	16,857
% of applicants accepted	21
% of acceptees attending	38

FIRST-YEAR PROFILE

Testing policy	Test Optional
Range SAT composite	1400–1500
Range SAT EBRW	680–740
Range SAT math	700–770
Range ACT composite	31–34
# submitting SAT scores	384
% submitting SAT scores	28
# submitting ACT scores	395
% submitting ACT scores	29
% graduated top 10% of class	74
% graduated top 25% of class	93
% graduated top 50% of class	98

DEADLINES

Early decision	
Deadline	11/15
Notification	Rolling
Other ED deadline	1/1
Other ED notification	2/15
Regular	
Deadline	1/1
Notification	4/1

FINANCIAL FACTS

Financial Aid Rating	96
Annual tuition	$58,708
Room and board	$18,014
Required fees	$1,062
Books and supplies	$1,500
Average frosh need-based scholarship	$57,633
Average UG need-based scholarship	$52,881
% needy frosh rec. need-based scholarship or grant aid	96
% needy UG rec. need-based scholarship or grant aid	97
% needy frosh rec. non-need-based scholarship or grant aid	82
% needy UG rec. non-need-based scholarship or grant aid	63
% needy frosh rec. need-based self-help aid	87
% needy UG rec. need-based self-help aid	91
% frosh rec. any financial aid	39
% UG rec. any financial aid	34
% UG borrow to pay for school	30
Average cumulative indebtedness	$36,016
% frosh need fully met	98
% ugrads need fully met	99
Average % of frosh need met	100
Average % of ugrad need met	100

WARREN WILSON COLLEGE

701 Warren Wilson College Road, Asheville, NC 28815-9000 • Admissions: 828-771-2000 • Fax: 828-771-2073

STUDENTS SAY " . . ."

Academics

Everything at Warren Wilson College, a small liberal arts school outside Asheville, North Carolina, can be attributed to its unique approach to learning, where academics are combined with "work and service." As one student describes the College, it's "work for the hands, service for the heart, learning for the mind." Outside the classroom, students "are also required to fulfill a certain amount of community service work in coordination with one of many community partners." The "work program at Warren Wilson is one of the main reasons I chose the school," says one environmental science major, and another student adds that the "work program is [what's] truly interesting about this school. We run our own little country here basically." That doesn't mean academics get short shrift—as one history major points out, "We take as many credits as other college students and we work 8–16 hours a week." Professors at Warren Wilson earn mostly high praise from students: "They are great at both lectures and discussion, and are able to teach nuanced, complex ideas and concepts in interesting and concise ways." With the small size and strong sense of community, the faculty here is very involved and very accessible.

Campus Life

With class work, community service, and time spent on one of the numerous campus work crews, students say "days are easily filled" and "weekdays tend to be very busy." When it's time to relax, "plenty of students spend as much time outside as possible hiking, swimming, skating, exploring the city of Asheville, and partying." "It's a very outdoorsy campus environment because we are in the middle of Appalachia" and "we have miles and miles of hiking trails that are campus property." Beyond the outdoors, "creative writing and coffee culture are a big part of Warren Wilson's culture," along with live music and "contra dancing on Thursdays." Some students say that the work crews are the closest thing the school has to fraternities and some of the more popular pastimes are "activities related to the crews—like blacksmithing workshops, beekeeping workshops, fabric workshops." With the school's appreciation of music, the "cafe is usually hosting shows that are a huge draw." In one student's estimation, "Everyone at the school loves the outdoors and has a healthy appreciation for taking an afternoon off to explore the river or trails." Warren Wilson is a place where politically-, socially-, and environmentally-focused "discussions are ubiquitous in and out of the classroom."

Student Body

"The student body at [Warren Wilson] is sustainable, eclectic, earthy, hard-working, and very community oriented." As one photography major puts it, "If you're looking for someplace different, this is it." The school's former motto was "We're not for everyone, but maybe you're not everyone," and some students find that still holds true, though others note that "limited racial diversity" "does not create a welcoming environment to racial and ethnic minorities on the campus." At the same time, vocal students stress the school's accepting nature, underscoring that Warren Wilson "has a strong LGBTQ community that [faces] a far lesser level of discrimination at this school than at most colleges and universities." As an environmental science major puts it, "The environment and proximity to Asheville attract the typical tree-hugging hippie crowd, but there's really a place for everyone at the college" and nearly everyone is "actively engaged in issues of social justice." In short, Warren Wilson students are "fantastically talented, hardworking, and willing to think outside the box."

WARREN WILSON COLLEGE

Financial Aid: 828-771-2081 • E-Mail: admit@warren-wilson.edu • Website: www.warren-wilson.edu

THE PRINCETON REVIEW SAYS

Admissions

The school reports that its standardized testing policy for use in admission for Fall 2024 is Test Optional. The 2024 testing policy will be permanent. The Princeton Review suggests that interested applicants consult with the school for the most up-to-date standardized testing policies. *Very important factors considered include:* rigor of secondary school record, academic GPA. *Important factors considered include:* class rank, application essay, recommendation(s). *Other factors considered include:* standardized test scores, interview, extracurricular activities, talent/ability, character/personal qualities, first generation, racial/ethnic status, volunteer work, work experience. High school diploma is required and GED is accepted. *Academic units required:* 4 English, 3 math, 2 science, 1 social studies, 2 history. *Academic units recommended:* 2 foreign language, 2 academic electives.

Financial Aid

Students should submit: FAFSA; State aid form. The Princeton Review suggests that all financial aid forms be submitted as soon as possible (see page 5 for a note on the FAFSA). *Need-based scholarships/grants offered:* College/university scholarship or grant aid from institutional funds; Federal Pell; Private scholarships; SEOG; State scholarships/grants. *Loan aid offered:* Direct PLUS loans; Direct Subsidized Loans; Direct Unsubsidized Loans. Admitted students will be notified of awards on a rolling basis beginning 3/1. Federal Work-Study Program available. Institutional employment available.

The Inside Word

In keeping with Warren Wilson College's mission of combining academics, work, and community service, prospective students should be aware that their efforts outside the classroom are as important as their performance in it. The admissions committee looks for signs of maturity, integrity, and a commitment to the mission of the college in each applicant. Warren Wilson accepts the Common Application, with their own writing supplement (not required, but strongly recommended), and standardized test scores are optional.

THE SCHOOL SAYS "..."

From the Admissions Office

"Warren Wilson College is for people who want an active educational and intellectual experience. And with our deep, proven commitment to a just, equitable, and sustainable world, we're for people who see learning as a way to be a better human being.

"Our experiential academic program gives you breadth through a time-honored liberal arts core and depth through specialization. And with over a thousand acres of farm, forests, mountains, and streams right here on campus, your classrooms, studios, and laboratories are not limited to those with walls.

"As one of only nine Work Colleges nationally and as a top-ranked service-learning college, Warren Wilson College builds on academic experiences by fully integrating on-campus work and community engagement into every student's learning. Your work experience sets you apart when you're applying for jobs—you'll already have a resume full of accomplishments. And community engagement gives you more than just marketable skills—you are empowered to advocate for causes you care about and improve your community.

"Our students can and do change the world. When you graduate, you won't say you learned how to do it. You will say you've done it.

"Warren Wilson College is also committed to affordability. Every student receives financial aid, including over $6,000 per year in work scholarships and grants, and our two free tuition programs provide even greater access for students who qualify. Our Financial Aid Office works with you to ensure that a Warren Wilson education is accessible."

SELECTIVITY

Admissions Rating	82
# of applicants	905
% of applicants accepted	84
% of acceptees attending	25
# of early decision applicants	14
% accepted early decision	79

FIRST-YEAR PROFILE

Testing policy	Test Optional
Range ACT composite	25–31
# submitting SAT scores	1
% submitting SAT scores	1
# submitting ACT scores	30
% submitting ACT scores	16
Average HS GPA	3.6
% frosh submitting high school GPA	100
% graduated top 10% of class	14
% graduated top 25% of class	38
% graduated top 50% of class	72

DEADLINES

Early decision	
Deadline	11/1
Notification	12/1
Early action	
Deadline	11/15
Notification	12/15
Regular	
Priority	2/1
Deadline	7/1
Notification	Rolling, 12/1
Nonfall registration?	Yes

FINANCIAL FACTS

Financial Aid Rating	84
Annual tuition	$39,300
Room and board	$12,610
Required fees	$990
Average frosh need-based scholarship	$26,406
Average UG need-based scholarship	$26,787
% needy frosh rec. need-based scholarship or grant aid	100
% needy UG rec. need-based scholarship or grant aid	100
% needy frosh rec. non-need-based scholarship or grant aid	17
% needy UG rec. non-need-based scholarship or grant aid	15
% needy frosh rec. need-based self-help aid	82
% needy UG rec. need-based self-help aid	84
% frosh rec. any financial aid	99
% UG rec. any financial aid	99
% UG borrow to pay for school	67
Average cumulative indebtedness	$30,597
% frosh need fully met	20
% ugrads need fully met	18
Average % of frosh need met	78
Average % of ugrad need met	79

WASHINGTON COLLEGE

300 Washington Avenue, Chestertown, MD 21620 • Admissions: 410-778-2800 • Fax: 410-778-7287

CAMPUS LIFE

Quality of Life Rating	82
Fire Safety Rating	90
Green Rating	82
Type of school	Private
Affiliation	No Affiliation
Environment	Rural

STUDENTS

Total undergrad enrollment	935
% male/female/another gender	42/58/0
% from out of state	56
% frosh live on campus	98
% ugrads live on campus	85
# of fraternities (% join)	2 (4)
# of sororities (% join)	3 (6)
% African American	12
% Asian	3
% White	64
% Hispanic	9
% Native American	<1
% Pacific Islander	<1
% Two or more races	0
% Race and/or ethnicity unknown	8
% international	3
# of countries represented	16

SURVEY SAYS . . .

Students are happy
Lab facilities are great
Career services are great
Internships are widely available
Class discussions encouraged
Easy to get around campus
Recreation facilities are great
Everyone loves the Sho'men & Sho'women
Theater is popular
Students aren't religious

ACADEMICS

Academic Rating	88
% students returning for sophomore year	83
% students graduating within 4 years	67
% students graduating within 6 years	71
Calendar	Semester
Student/faculty ratio	9:1
Profs interesting rating	95
Profs accessible rating	96

Most classes have fewer than 10 students.
Most lab/discussion sessions have
10–19 students.

MOST POPULAR MAJORS

Biology/Biological Sciences, General; Psychology, General; Business Administration and Management, General

STUDENTS SAY " . . ."

Academics

Washington College in Chestertown, Maryland is "a really beautiful environment to learn in." The academic experience is "rigorous and rewarding," with small class sizes that allow students to "feel incredibly connected to your professors." The faculty is "incredibly kind, empathetic, and passionate" and "challenge students and push them to give their best work." Many say "The professors are the greatest strength" of Washington College. "They are always accessible, very understanding, and happy to help in pursuing your goals outside of class through letters of recommendations, internship searches, and graduate school research." Students feel "the courses are always engaging," noting specifically that the "English program is impeccable," with "many academic resources and opportunities for professional development," such as "field work, faculty-assisted studies, publication opportunities," and access to the renowned Rose O'Neill Literary House.

Campus Life

Some may worry that living in a small town while attending Washington College might be difficult, but rest assured "if you make friends and get involved, it's engaging and fun." The Student Events Board "does a lot of work to give everyone options and fun things to do," and offer involvement opportunities like "varsity sports, intramurals, [and] Greek life." Intramural sports, like dodgeball and ultimate Frisbee, are fun ways "to compete and make new friends," and for those in Greek life, "there's no competition or animosity between chapters." Organized events are plentiful, where "Theatre productions are somewhat significant events," as are "poetry readings and author discussions" at the Literary House. On evenings and weekends, "There's a party culture," one student admits, but it's "pretty safe and tame."

Students trying to get off-campus enjoy visiting the boathouse on the nearby Chester River, where they can kayak and paddleboard for free, or simply "take a step back from [their] busy life around school and enjoy the scenery on the water." Nearby Chestertown "is a really lovable town and the surrounding area is also incredibly pretty." Many feel that "The town is a great place for a walk," and "going to the farmer's market on Saturday mornings is popular." Beyond Chestertown, "going to Annapolis, MD or Middletown, DE [a]re the two major outings students take."

Student Body

At Washington College, "there is a connected feel throughout the student body," which is a product of the small campus size. "[E]veryone knows each other in some sort of fashion," and "it's quite the treat to walk around and only see familiar faces." Even though "everyone tends to stay in their groups," most "belong to multiple categories of social life," and "there is no animosity between any of the groups." As one undergrad notes, "By and at large, students are respectful and caring toward each other, and there's a broad friendliness to the community." Students describe their peers as "diverse, opinionated, and intelligent" people who "want to be actively involved in their institution and have their voices heard."

At Washington College, "there is a wide range of intellect, ability, and personality that come together to make an interesting campus atmosphere." Although there's "a diverse political background" among its student body, "it's still a predominantly white institution." Students say "addressing racial bias on campus is an ongoing process," but that the school and community have "taken ample steps" in addressing this. "For example, in my Human Right and Social Justice class, my group and I are working within the town and the college to create a plan of racial reconciliation that includes meetings with advocacy groups and the local community as well as with those from our institution," one student says. All in all, undergrads can confidently say that there are "plenty of nice and accepting students."

WASHINGTON COLLEGE

Financial Aid: 410-778-7214 • E-Mail: wc_admissions@washcoll.edu • Website: www.washcoll.edu

THE PRINCETON REVIEW SAYS

Admissions

The school reports that its standardized testing policy for use in admission for Fall 2024 is Test Optional. The 2024 testing policy will be permanent. The Princeton Review suggests that interested applicants consult with the school for the most up-to-date standardized testing policies. *Very important factors considered include:* rigor of secondary school record, academic GPA, level of applicant's interest. *Important factors considered include:* class rank, application essay, recommendation(s), interview. *Other factors considered include:* standardized test scores, extracurricular activities, talent/ability, character/personal qualities, first generation, alumni/ae relation, geographical residence, state residency, racial/ethnic status, volunteer work, work experience. High school diploma is required and GED is accepted. *Academic units required:* 4 English, 3 math, 3 science, 2 science labs, 2 foreign language, 2 social studies, 2 history. *Academic units recommended:* 4 English, 4 math, 4 science, 3 science labs, 4 foreign language, 2 social studies, 2 history.

Financial Aid

Students should submit: FAFSA. Priority filing deadline is 3/1. The Princeton Review suggests that all financial aid forms be submitted as soon as possible (see page 5 for a note on the FAFSA). *Need-based scholarships/grants offered:* College/university scholarship or grant aid from institutional funds; Federal Pell; Private scholarships; SEOG; State scholarships/grants. *Loan aid offered:* Direct PLUS loans; Direct Subsidized Loans; Direct Unsubsidized Loans. Admitted students will be notified of awards on a rolling basis beginning 2/1. Federal Work-Study Program available. Institutional employment available.

Inside Word

Washington College is interested in student potential inside the classroom and beyond, and therefore evaluate them based on a series of factors including academic performance, character, and extracurricular involvement. The most promising candidates possess high GPAs and have challenged themselves with APs, honors, or IB courses, but also perform well during their interview and in their essay by illustrating ways in which they've been involved with their school or community and steps they've taken to pursue their passions and goals. As of Fall 2022, the college is Test Optional.

THE SCHOOL SAYS "..."

From the Admissions Office

"Washington College is one of the top liberal arts institutions in the nation. Students engage in a challenging academic experience with outstanding opportunities that have a valuable impact on our students after graduation. From internships and research to study abroad and civic engagement, our students take advantage of wide array or opportunities that move their classroom learning into the real world and gives graduates an advantage in careers or graduate and professional degree programs.

"A Washington College education affords students unmatched opportunities to work closely with an exceptional faculty on projects they are passionate about. Whether they study the sciences or the liberal arts, our students have access to top-notch facilities and programs. Run experiments in our state-of-the-art Toll Science Center, print a book of poetry on our working antique letterpresses in the Rose O'Neill Literary House, or trek out to our 4,700-acre River and Field Campus to band birds or scan the Chester River on one of our research vessels.

"We believe that a diverse liberal arts education is both academically rewarding and the most effective way to prepare for a future in anything you want to do. Our students are driven to explore their interests, examine different perspectives, and challenge old ways of thinking. There is no one-size-fits-all education at Washington College: from double-majoring to internships to study abroad and semester-long interdisciplinary programs, students at Washington College get the chance to shape a college experience that is right for them.

"Admission to Washington College is selective; decisions are based primarily on a student's record of academic achievement. We strongly recommend visiting campus."

SELECTIVITY

Admissions Rating	87
# of applicants	2,554
% of applicants accepted	75
% of acceptees attending	12
# of early decision applicants	65
% accepted early decision	98

FIRST-YEAR PROFILE

Testing policy	Test Optional
Range SAT composite	1200–1370
Range SAT EBRW	620–710
Range SAT math	570–680
Range ACT composite	25–29
# submitting SAT scores	66
% submitting SAT scores	29
# submitting ACT scores	18
% submitting ACT scores	8
Average HS GPA	3.7
% frosh submitting high school GPA	100
% graduated top 10% of class	31
% graduated top 25% of class	62
% graduated top 50% of class	86

DEADLINES

Early decision	
Deadline	11/15
Notification	12/15
Early action	
Deadline	12/1
Notification	1/15
Regular	
Deadline	2/15
Notification	Rolling, 11/15
Nonfall registration?	Yes

APPLICANTS OFTEN PREFER

Goucher College; McDaniel College; Salisbury University; St. Mary's College of Maryland; Towson University; University of Delaware; University of Maryland, College Park

APPLICANTS SOMETIMES PREFER

Dickinson College; Gettysburg College; Loyola University Maryland; Stevenson University

FINANCIAL FACTS

Financial Aid Rating	81
Annual tuition	$52,146
Room and board	$15,814
Required fees	$1,630
Required fees (first-year)	$2,120
Books and supplies	$900
Average frosh need-based scholarship	$7,563
Average UG need-based scholarship	$14,428
% needy frosh rec. need-based scholarship or grant aid	38
% needy UG rec. need-based scholarship or grant aid	55
% needy frosh rec. non-need-based scholarship or grant aid	100
% needy UG rec. non-need-based scholarship or grant aid	100
% needy frosh rec. need-based self-help aid	48
% needy UG rec. need-based self-help aid	62
% frosh rec. any financial aid	99
% UG rec. any financial aid	96
% UG borrow to pay for school	74
Average cumulative indebtedness	$28,922
% frosh need fully met	41
% ugrads need fully met	35
Average % of frosh need met	80
Average % of ugrad need met	84

WASHINGTON & JEFFERSON COLLEGE

60 South Lincoln Street, Washington, PA 15301 • Admissions: 724-222-4400 • Fax: 724-223-6534

STUDENTS SAY "..."

Academics

Founded in 1781, Washington & Jefferson College is a top-notch liberal arts college that offers an integrative education to 1,100 students, preparing students "for life after graduation, whether that be continuing education or getting a job." There is "a long and deep history that involves a lot of traditions," such as the college's signature Magellan Project, which provides funding for students to pursue internships and research to open their eyes to the possibilities that lie beyond the classroom, or the JayTerm that "allows students to take a class abroad with a professor" (88 percent of students take part in at least one real-world experience while at W&J). "First-Year Seminars also include trips off campus" such as "attending a concert by the Pittsburgh Symphony Orchestra," and "many professors are willing to hold class outside." There is "a lot of potential for opportunities and employment networking," and "small class sizes and activities outside of the classroom [allow students] to create trusting and productive networks with the faculty at the college."

A 10:1 student-to-faculty ratio "is just right and most professors are eager to interact with their students on a one-on-one basis," creating an environment where they "walk the line of friend and professor...in the best ways possible." It's not unusual that "each [professor] knows your name and little details about you," or comes to "support [you] at sporting events," and that connection helps to enhance the discussion-based classes, in that there's "a space where we can share our ideas without feeling insecure about it." Of course, that's also due to professors being "passionate about what they teach," that each class "is designed remarkably well and prepares each student for their respective majors and future careers," and that instructors "make sure that all the students understand the concepts and are thoroughly set for the exams."

Campus Life

"Most students are constantly doing work for school or a job," but on weekends they "spend time on and off campus, hanging with friends or doing events." Foodies will rejoice to know there "are a high number of chain restaurants and local restaurants" within a five-minute drive, and for those who want to explore, the Pittsburgh Pipeline shuttle offers free trips into the city. "Leadership on campus is really strong among student organizations" and there's "a weekly calendar of different events that are happening, ranging from concerts to escape rooms." Everyone "is very involved on campus" and there is "a lot of school spirit [so] you'll always see people in the student section supporting their classmates at sports games." Students "fill their free time with studying, athletic practices, and club meetings in the evening," and "volunteering with professors for service activities like creek clean-ups."

Student Body

Washington & Jefferson is "a positive environment that draws in students from all over the nation and world." The majority of the student body "is white, but our school is trying to grow and focus on diversity," and students often challenge each other "to have productive conversations" about their differences. Everyone "knows everyone because of how small our student body is," forming a "tight-knit community of people with a lot of different interests, whether that be primarily in academics, arts, sports, or other extracurriculars." While everyone is motivated, there "is a mixture of people who are more driven and people who are more laid-back."

Washington & Jefferson College

Financial Aid: 724-503-1001 x3353 • E-Mail: admission@washjeff.edu • Website: www.washjeff.edu

THE PRINCETON REVIEW SAYS

Admissions

The school reports that its standardized testing policy for use in admission for Fall 2024 is Test Free. The 2024 testing policy will be permanent. The Princeton Review suggests that interested applicants consult with the school for the most up-to-date standardized testing policies. *Very important factors considered include:* academic GPA. *Other factors considered include:* rigor of secondary school record, class rank, application essay, recommendation(s), interview, extracurricular activities, talent/ability, character/personal qualities, volunteer work, work experience, level of applicant's interest. High school diploma is required and GED is accepted. *Academic units required:* 4 English, 3 math, 1 science, 1 science lab, 2 foreign language, 1 social studies, 4 academic electives.

Financial Aid

Students should submit: FAFSA; Institution's own financial aid form; State aid form. The Princeton Review suggests that all financial aid forms be submitted as soon as possible (see page 5 for a note on the FAFSA). *Need-based scholarships/grants offered:* College/university scholarship or grant aid from institutional funds; Federal Pell; Private scholarships; SEOG; State scholarships/grants. *Loan aid offered:* Direct PLUS loans; Direct Subsidized Loans; Direct Unsubsidized Loans. Admitted students will be notified of awards on a rolling basis. Federal Work-Study Program available. Institutional employment available.

The Inside Word

Solid students with co-curricular involvement should have no trouble gaining admission to W&J, where admitted students have an average GPA of 3.5. Many of the admissions requirements (such as a personal essay or letter of recommendation) are optional, but should be submitted as the school evaluates applicants holistically. One hundred percent of students receive some type of scholarship or grant, and the college offers an "on-time" guarantee that all students who meet academic expectations will graduate in four years (98 percent of all students do so).

THE SCHOOL SAYS "..."

From the Admissions Office

"For two and a half centuries, Washington & Jefferson College has provided an unsurpassed liberal arts education that is both broad and practical, preparing students as ethical leaders poised for professional success. Located just south of Pittsburgh, Pa., W&J is proud to foster a supportive and diverse environment where students sharpen their intellectual capabilities, pursue their passions, and discover their true potential.

"The W&J experience stands apart by emphasizing continuous professional preparation and the development of leaders committed to a standard of uncommon integrity. The Centers for Ethical Leadership and Professional Pathways ensure that students learn to lead and make a difference for others—both personally and professionally—in our complex and rapidly changing world.

"W&J is recognized nationally for providing a superb education at a cost families can afford—an exceptional value that is further enhanced as students connect to real-world networks of professional mentors. Our Faculty and Professional Pathway advisors provide guidance for practical experiences to ensure professional readiness through opportunities that may include conducting research with scholars on campus or at world-leading universities, developing professional skills through high-quality internships, or traveling individually to destinations around the world through our unique Magellan Project funded by generous W&J alumni. All W&J students choose not one, but two primary areas of study and graduate with the intellectual acumen and hands-on knowledge that leading employers and top graduate schools are seeking.

"At W&J, generations of students have found that lifelong success is *Founded Here.*"

SELECTIVITY

Admissions Rating	82
# of applicants	3,414
% of applicants accepted	88
% of acceptees attending	12
# of early decision applicants	51
% accepted early decision	31

FIRST-YEAR PROFILE

Testing policy	Test Free
Range SAT composite	1020–1250
Range SAT EBRW	510–630
Range SAT math	500–620
Range ACT composite	19–28
# submitting SAT scores	146
% submitting SAT scores	42
# submitting ACT scores	48
% submitting ACT scores	14
Average HS GPA	3.5
% frosh submitting high school GPA	100
% graduated top 10% of class	23
% graduated top 25% of class	50
% graduated top 50% of class	81

DEADLINES

Early decision	
Deadline	12/15
Notification	1/15
Regular	
Priority	4/1
Notification	Rolling, 8/15
Nonfall registration?	Yes

APPLICANTS OFTEN PREFER

Duquesne University; Penn State University Park; University of Pittsburgh—Pittsburgh Campus; Westminster College (PA)

APPLICANTS SOMETIMES PREFER

Edinboro University of Pennsylvania

FINANCIAL FACTS

Financial Aid Rating	85
Annual tuition	$27,605
Room and board	$13,910
Required fees	$580
Books and supplies	$1,000
Average frosh need-based scholarship	$35,201
Average UG need-based scholarship	$34,147
% needy frosh rec. need-based scholarship or grant aid	100
% needy UG rec. need-based scholarship or grant aid	100
% needy frosh rec. non-need-based scholarship or grant aid	21
% needy UG rec. non-need-based scholarship or grant aid	4
% needy frosh rec. need-based self-help aid	67
% needy UG rec. need-based self-help aid	70
% frosh rec. any financial aid	100
% UG rec. any financial aid	100
% UG borrow to pay for school	83
Average cumulative indebtedness	$44,051
% frosh need fully met	29
% ugrads need fully met	25
Average % of frosh need met	83
Average % of ugrad need met	80

WASHINGTON STATE UNIVERSITY

PO Box 645910, Pullman, WA 99164-5910 • Admissions: 509-335-3564 • Fax: 509-335-4902

CAMPUS LIFE

Quality of Life Rating	95
Fire Safety Rating	92
Green Rating	98
Type of school	Public
Environment	Town

STUDENTS

Total undergrad enrollment	22,256
% male/female/another gender	47/53/NR
% from out of state	15
% frosh live on campus	81
% ugrads live on campus	23
# of fraternities (% join)	24 (21)
# of sororities (% join)	14 (23)
% African American	3
% Asian	7
% White	60
% Hispanic	16
% Native American	<1
% Pacific Islander	<1
% Two or more races	8
% Race and/or ethnicity unknown	2
% international	3
# of countries represented	94

SURVEY SAYS . . .

Students are happy
Great library
Career services are great
Internships are widely available
Students are friendly
Recreation facilities are great
Everyone loves the Cougars
Intramural sports are popular
Frats and sororities are popular
Campus newspaper is popular
College radio is popular
Alumni active on campus
Active student government
Active minority support groups
Diverse student types interact on campus
Students get along with local community
Students involved in community service
Students love Pullman, WA
Dorms are like palaces

ACADEMICS

Academic Rating	79
% students returning for sophomore year	81
% students graduating within 4 years	41
% students graduating within 6 years	62
Calendar	Semester
Student/faculty ratio	14:1
Profs interesting rating	86
Profs accessible rating	92
Most classes have 20–29 students.	

Note: Washington State University is a multi-campus system that is also located in Spokane, the Tri-Cities, Vancouver, Everett, and online. The data reflects those collective totals, but the rankings and the following narrative is based entirely on feedback from students at the Pullman campus, which is the only one with a residential component.

STUDENTS SAY ". . ."

Academics

With six campuses across the state and $358 million in annual research expenditures, Washington State University is a public-school powerhouse, offering 95 majors and study abroad opportunities in 70 countries, and a library that's one of the largest in the entire Pacific Northwest. Here, there are "ample opportunities to explore interests" and research opportunities and associated funding are available at all levels. The state-of-the-art classrooms have "all-inclusive presentation screens for everyone to see," and The Spark (on the main Pullman campus) is an "academic innovation hub" that uses formal and informal learning to encourage collaboration between faculty and students. The administration also "provides some amazing resources and prioritizes mental health," and "makes students feel included and provide a great education."

The school's creativity and compassion extends to the professors, who provide ways to "learn in different forms" and bring in "guest speakers from the industry" to shake things up. Moreover, the "smaller student-to-faculty ratio has increased the amount of in-class discussion we do rather than sitting and listening." It also yields professors who are "extremely approachable and…always trying to help [us] find research opportunities." Those extra steps of encouragement, of teachers "eager to help students participate and build their resume" are what lead students to declare things like "More than a university, WSU is a community," says a student.

Campus Life

"There is never a day that an event is not happening" at WSU, and "people find things to do on campus constantly." Whether students have a good old-fashioned "hang with friends" or get involved with the 350 clubs and student organizations, "there are so many ways to explore interests and find opportunities." The Student Entertainment Board is always putting on "up-all-night events or concerts," and "skiing, backpacking, [and] hiking" are common activities here, as are the wildly popular intramural programs ("The gym is also very accessible"). Greek life and multicultural organizations are big on campus, and students also enjoy taking part in "local community projects" and completing meaningful work.

Student Body

Students at WSU "come from everywhere," are "intelligent and creative," and "ask inquisitive questions and engage in class." The school's numerous extracurriculars give this "wide variety of students from various backgrounds" ample opportunity to show off their "many unique hobbies and values," and ultimately, "everyone is able to find a place where they feel they belong." An oft-spoken motto at WSU is "Cougs help Cougs," meaning "the student body supports and uplifts each other both academically and socially." As one student says: "Whenever I wear my WSU gear in public, whether at the airport or even at a beach in Hawaii, people will say 'Go Cougs.'" This is a group that is "like-minded in pursuing success and professional and academic development" all "with the desire to connect with others and learn from each other."

WASHINGTON STATE UNIVERSITY

Financial Aid: 509-335-9711 • E-Mail: admissions@wsu.edu • Website: www.wsu.edu

THE PRINCETON REVIEW SAYS

Admissions

The school reports that its standardized testing policy for use in admission for Fall 2024 is Test Free. The 2024 testing policy will be permanent. The Princeton Review suggests that interested applicants consult with the school for the most up-to-date standardized testing policies. *Very important factors considered include:* academic GPA. *Important factors considered include:* rigor of secondary school record, class rank. *Other factors considered include:* application essay, recommendation(s), extracurricular activities, talent/ability, character/personal qualities, volunteer work, work experience. High school diploma is required and GED is accepted. *Academic units required:* 4 English, 3 math, 2 science, 2 foreign language, 3 social studies, 1 visual/performing arts. *Academic units recommended:* 4 English, 4 math, 2 science, 2 foreign language, 3 social studies, 1 visual/performing arts.

Financial Aid

Students should submit: FAFSA; State aid form. Priority filing deadline is 1/31. The Princeton Review suggests that all financial aid forms be submitted as soon as possible (see page 5 for a note on the FAFSA). *Need-based scholarships/grants offered:* College/university scholarship or grant aid from institutional funds; Federal Pell; Private scholarships; SEOG; State scholarships/grants. *Loan aid offered:* Direct PLUS loans; Direct Subsidized Loans; Direct Unsubsidized Loans; Federal Nursing Loans. Admitted students will be notified of awards on a rolling basis beginning 4/15. Federal Work-Study Program available. Institutional employment available.

The Inside Word

Washington State's offerings are appealing enough to draw students from all fifty states, so applicants should have a competitive resume if they want to attend—in fact, the school automatically accepts students in the top ten percent of their graduating class, or with an unweighted GPA of 3.6 or higher. Just know that because WSU is Test Free, it won't look at your SAT or ACT scores, so you'll have to find other highlights with which to make a case for admission.

THE SCHOOL SAYS "..."

From the Admissions Office

"One of America's leading public research institutions, Washington State University unlocks possibilities for eager minds to make an impact on the world. Graduates benefit from an outstanding education, delivered affordably, with exceptionally high return on investment.

"As a student, you'll explore your interests with guidance from nationally recognized faculty. Academic programs are so strong that graduates become a top pick for employers in every sector: high-tech, healthcare, news media, energy, finance, and more. A worldwide network of alumni supports your transition to a career.

"For more than 130 years, WSU has championed the greater good. Its research targets critical challenges: resource sustainability, human/animal health, opportunity and equity, smart systems, and national security. WSU Health Sciences colleges educate healthcare professionals to serve communities where they are needed most.

"WSU locations make degree programs accessible to all. Campuses in Pullman, Spokane, the Tri-Cities, Vancouver, Everett, and online (Global Campus) enroll undergraduate, graduate, and professional students from every state and 94 countries.

"The Global Campus shares its vast expertise in online teaching methods with faculty university-wide to deliver compelling academic experiences.

"To be considered for admission, complete the high school core curriculum. If you apply by the designated date and are among the top 10 percent of your high school class or have at least a 3.6 cumulative GPA on a 4.0 scale, you are assured admission. (Note that this GPA requirement may change for Fall 2024.) For priority dates and deadlines for admission, financial aid, and scholarship applications, check apply.wsu.edu."

SELECTIVITY

Admissions Rating	83
# of applicants	19,401
% of applicants accepted	83
% of acceptees attending	25

FIRST-YEAR PROFILE

Testing policy	Test Free
Range SAT composite	1020–1260
Range SAT EBRW	510–640
Range SAT math	500–630
Range ACT composite	20–28
# submitting SAT scores	350
% submitting SAT scores	9
# submitting ACT scores	98
% submitting ACT scores	2
Average HS GPA	3.5
% frosh submitting high school GPA	99

DEADLINES

Regular	
Priority	1/31
Notification	Rolling, 11/1
Nonfall registration?	Yes

APPLICANTS OFTEN PREFER

Central Washington University; Eastern Washington University; University of Washington; Western Washington University

APPLICANTS SOMETIMES PREFER

Gonzaga University; Oregon State University; Seattle University; University of Idaho; University of Oregon

APPLICANTS RARELY PREFER

Arizona State University; Pacific Lutheran University; Seattle Pacific University

FINANCIAL FACTS

Financial Aid Rating	81
Annual in-state tuition	$10,708
Annual out-of-state tuition	$26,392
Room and board	$12,396
Required fees	$1,993
Books and supplies	$960
Average frosh need-based scholarship	$12,735
Average UG need-based scholarship	$12,504
% needy frosh rec. need-based scholarship or grant aid	95
% needy UG rec. need-based scholarship or grant aid	91
% needy frosh rec. non-need-based scholarship or grant aid	9
% needy UG rec. non-need-based scholarship or grant aid	6
% needy frosh rec. need-based self-help aid	51
% needy UG rec. need-based self-help aid	52
% frosh rec. any financial aid	84
% UG rec. any financial aid	72
% UG borrow to pay for school	50
Average cumulative indebtedness	$25,559
% frosh need fully met	18
% ugrads need fully met	14
Average % of frosh need met	72
Average % of ugrad need met	70

WASHINGTON UNIVERSITY IN ST. LOUIS

MSC 1089-105-05, St. Louis, MO 63130-4899 • Admissions: 314-935-5000 • Fax: 314-696-0562

STUDENTS SAY "..."

Academics

Washington University in St. Louis is a private research institution committed to being at the forefront of discovery, teaching, and making real-world contributions. Interdisciplinary study and global awareness are tenets of the WashU mission, and 80% of students opt for multiple majors or minors, while 30% of students study abroad. There is an "amazing and robust research scene." Even during the summer, research opportunities are plentiful, with positions in several of the school's centers and institutes and throughout each of WashU's seven schools. And WashU is especially good for students who appreciate teamwork. "Collaboration is definitely pushed throughout every corner of WashU"—there are even "interactive study groups to help apply the material." Students also have academic options such as the Beyond Boundaries program—a series of "interdisciplinary classes which follow a curriculum unlike your normal lecture classes," and after the first year in the program students can transition into any course of study while remaining connected to the program.

A 7:1 student-to-faculty ratio provides incredible support across 100 fields of study and more than 1,500 "very rigorous and challenging" classes, including "some really interesting and unique courses that provide great opportunities for students to explore their interests experientially." Professors "are so dedicated and truly invested in learning," and the school "has the best resources out there." Students remark that advisors and instructors are there for students and are "always willing to help." People appreciate that "there are a ton of projects built into...classes"; for example, business courses "include a component where we get to work with a real company/non-profit on a project related to the course material." Many classes are also discussion-based or involve interactive and flipped classrooms where students watch the lecture videos before class and apply the concepts during class.

Campus Life

This "very pretty place" has more than 460 student groups, so one can "get involved in just about anything." And there is plenty of "free food from student organizations and free event tickets," such as the honey tasting events courtesy of the Beekeeper's Club in the spring. When students want some time off campus, they can take an "easy train ride to restaurants and shopping." Students here "definitely have fun, but that comes second after getting your responsibilities done," and "students really care about their classes and their future careers, and prioritize their life based on these activities." Greek life was once prominent on campus but has become much less so, and much of the social scene "has shifted to off-campus bars/clubs and parties at off-campus apartments."

Student Body

Ninety percent of students are from out of state at WashU, yet everyone is "Midwest nice," making for a collaborative environment where "everyone is willing to help each other out or study together." They "are all very intelligent and very driven people who are willing to go to great lengths to do good." Students are also "very eager to learn and excited about school," and they get "involved in many activities." The student body "is generally pretty socially and politically progressive," but people are "always willing to help and talk about whatever they are interested in." Acceptance and inclusivity are found here, with people "always celebrating different cultures."

WASHINGTON UNIVERSITY IN ST. LOUIS

Financial Aid: 888-547-6670 • E-Mail: admissions@wustl.edu • Website: wustl.edu

THE PRINCETON REVIEW SAYS

Admissions

The school reports that its standardized testing policy for use in admission for Fall 2024 is Test Optional. The 2024 testing policy will be temporary. The Princeton Review suggests that interested applicants consult with the school for the most up-to-date standardized testing policies. *Very important factors considered include:* rigor of secondary school record, class rank, academic GPA, standardized test scores, application essay, recommendation(s), talent/ability, character/personal qualities. *Important factors considered include:* extracurricular activities, first generation, volunteer work, work experience. *Other factors considered include:* interview, alumni/ae relation, geographical residence, racial/ethnic status. High school diploma is required and GED is accepted. *Academic units required:* 4 English, 3 math, 3 science, 2 science labs, 2 foreign language, 2 social studies, 2 history. *Academic units recommended:* 4 English, 4 math, 4 science, 4 science labs, 4 foreign language, 4 social studies, 4 history.

Financial Aid

Students should submit: CSS/Financial Aid Profile; FAFSA; Noncustodial Profile. The Princeton Review suggests that all financial aid forms be submitted as soon as possible (see page 5 for a note on the FAFSA). *Need-based scholarships/grants offered:* College/university scholarship or grant aid from institutional funds; Federal Pell; Private scholarships; SEOG; State scholarships/grants; United Negro College Fund. *Loan aid offered:* Direct PLUS loans; Direct Subsidized Loans; Direct Unsubsidized Loans; College/university loans from institutional funds; State Loans. Admitted students will be notified of financial aid offers at the time of admission. Federal Work-Study Program available. Institutional employment available.

The Inside Word

Washington University is highly selective, and competition for admission is fierce. A strong transcript and course selection will also be important. For example, it's highly recommended that business candidates take calculus, and all STEM candidates take calculus, chemistry, and physics. Finally, students applying to the College of Architecture are highly encouraged to submit a portfolio. Portfolios are required for applicants to the College of Art.

THE SCHOOL SAYS "..."

From the Admissions Office

"Nestled in the heart of St. Louis, Washington University offers a nurturing, yet intellectually rigorous, environment where students from all identities and backgrounds thrive. WashU's state-of-the-art buildings, laboratories, classrooms, and libraries foster a sense of community, creativity, and collaboration. On campus and across the world, you'll find talented, inspiring students and faculty developing big ideas and tackling challenging problems.

"WashU's undergraduate program is comprised of four undergraduate schools: the Sam Fox School of Design & Visual Arts, which houses both the College of Architecture and College of Art, College of Arts & Sciences, Olin Business School, and McKelvey School of Engineering. Offering more than 100 areas of study and 1,500 courses, students have the flexibility to explore multiple interests.

"Students can choose to join one of WashU's 460+ clubs and organizations, get involved in the St. Louis community, and have the opportunity to participate in cutting-edge research alongside professors who are leaders in their fields.

"WashU accepts Common Application and Coalition Application in Early Decision I, Early Decision II, and Regular Decision rounds. In an effort to make WashU accessible to every qualified student, each applicant is reviewed individually and with a holistic perspective. WashU doesn't consider the financial situation or ability to pay when making admissions decisions for first-year, domestic applicants. Additionally, we commit to meeting 100 percent of demonstrated financial need, and counselors from Student Financial Services work with students and their families to ensure that a WashU education is not out of reach."

SELECTIVITY

Admissions Rating	98
# of applicants	33,214
% of applicants accepted	11
% of acceptees attending	48
% admitted from wait list	5
# of early decision applicants	4,175
% accepted early decision	27

FIRST-YEAR PROFILE

Testing policy	Test Optional
Range SAT composite	1500–1570
Range SAT EBRW	730–770
Range SAT math	770–800
Range ACT composite	33–35
# submitting SAT scores	492
% submitting SAT scores	27
# submitting ACT scores	597
% submitting ACT scores	33
Average HS GPA	4.2
% frosh submitting high school GPA	89
% graduated top 10% of class	90
% graduated top 25% of class	99
% graduated top 50% of class	100

DEADLINES

Early decision	
Deadline	11/1
Notification	12/15
Other ED deadline	1/3
Other ED notification	2/16
Regular	
Deadline	1/3
Notification	4/1
Nonfall registration?	No

APPLICANTS OFTEN PREFER
Brown University; Columbia University; Harvard College; Johns Hopkins University; Princeton University; Stanford University; University of Pennsylvania; Yale University

APPLICANTS SOMETIMES PREFER
Cornell University; Duke University; Northwestern University; Rice University; University of California—Los Angeles; University of Michigan—Ann Arbor; University of Southern California; Vanderbilt University

FINANCIAL FACTS

Financial Aid Rating	98
Annual tuition	$61,750
Room and board	$20,778
Required fees	$1,232
Books and supplies	$1,264
Average frosh need-based scholarship	$62,849
Average UG need-based scholarship	$58,197
% needy frosh rec. need-based scholarship or grant aid	99
% needy UG rec. need-based scholarship or grant aid	98
% needy frosh rec. non-need-based scholarship or grant aid	35
% needy UG rec. non-need-based scholarship or grant aid	17
% needy frosh rec. need-based self-help aid	71
% needy UG rec. need-based self-help aid	63
% frosh rec. any financial aid	47
% UG rec. any financial aid	46
% UG borrow to pay for school	23
Average cumulative indebtedness	$21,932
% frosh need fully met	100
% ugrads need fully met	100
Average % of frosh need met	100
Average % of ugrad need met	100

WEBB INSTITUTE

298 Crescent Beach Road, Glen Cove, NY 11542-1398 • Admissions: 516-671-8355 • Fax: 516-674-9838

STUDENTS SAY ". . ."

Academics
All 100 students at Webb Institute are driven by two loves: engineering and ships. That's to be expected of this Long Island institution, the oldest school devoted to naval architecture and marine engineering in the United States. It's "a very niche school [that] is very good at what it does," and each student graduates with a dual degree in the school's two subjects. The academic calendar runs on semesters, and also adds a highly unique Winter Work Term, which takes place during Winter break and "tremendously augments learning and professional development" by letting students complete a paid internship in the maritime industry, whether that's yacht design or time on a cruise ship or Antarctic icebreaker. Needless to say, the hands-on learning opportunities are extremely interesting, and include "assembling and disassembling engines, visiting the Merchant Marine Academy's lab spaces, attending boat shows, [and] going on board ships for field trips." All students also attend a Monday Lecture Series, "where industry leaders come to campus and give lectures on leading-edge topics like environmental science and new technologies."

The two subjects taught at Webb have been "honed to excellence through the exhaustive course of study" and the invested professors "seek to support students both academically and personally." (Says one student, "it is normal to see several students talking with professors while waiting in line for lunch.") The small student body also naturally lends itself to close-knit bonds, both in terms of the present ("so many people collaborate on homework") and the future (warm relations with alumni "results in donations and job opportunities for Webb"). Brought and bonded together by their academic focus from the start of the first year, and students "know exactly what [they] are going to accomplish from the outset." In order "to cope with the stress students normally feel, Webb employs a psychologist," and there is a remediation program so that students can still get credit for a class if they do other work over the Winter Work or summer break.

Campus Life
"Time has to be utilized very effectively at Webb" to keep stress levels down, and if students work diligently, they "typically can have a day off on the weekend." All students live on campus, and since Webb is so small, there's opportunity to jump in on any activity, even sports. "Anyone can play anything even if they are not athletic or have never played the sport in their life." New York is only about 45 minutes away, and when the weather is nice, students "often take study breaks after class to go swimming or boating from the beach." There is a student-run pub on campus for those over 21, and "for the outdoorsy types, there's always sailing, hiking, kayaking, wakeboarding," and the nature preserve next door.

Student Body
"At Webb, you are one percent of the school," which means "everyone goes through so much together" and it follows that everyone is "very independent and trustworthy." The student body "relies heavily on having each other around, both socially and academically," and there is "an environment of accountability and responsibility" that extends beyond the classroom and the school's respected Honor Code. There are "many musical members…many Eagle scouts, and fishing enthusiasts," and "water sports, disk golf, music, and video games" are some of the most popular hobbies. The "diversity itself at Webb is not the greatest" (more than 80 percent of the student body is white), but at least "everyone has their own specific interests such as cruise ships, submarines, tankers, and private yachts," and everyone is accepting of absolutely everything: "We love our school and each other."

WEBB INSTITUTE

Financial Aid: 516-403-5928 • E-Mail: admissions@webb.edu • Website: www.webb.edu

THE PRINCETON REVIEW SAYS

Admissions

The school reports that its standardized testing policy for use in admission for Fall 2024 is SAT or ACT Required. It is unknown at this time if the 2024 testing policy will be permanent. The Princeton Review suggests that interested applicants consult with the school for the most up-to-date standardized testing policies. *Very important factors considered include:* rigor of secondary school record, class rank, academic GPA, standardized test scores, application essay, recommendation(s), interview, character/personal qualities, level of applicant's interest. *Important factors considered include:* extracurricular activities, talent/ability. *Other factors considered include:* volunteer work, work experience. High school diploma is required and GED is not accepted. *Academic units required:* 4 English, 4 math, 2 science, 2 science labs, 2 social studies, 4 academic electives.

Financial Aid

Students should submit: Business/Farm Supplement; FAFSA. Priority filing deadline is 4/1. The Princeton Review suggests that all financial aid forms be submitted as soon as possible (see page 5 for a note on the FAFSA). *Need-based scholarships/grants offered:* College/university scholarship or grant aid from institutional funds; Federal Pell; Private scholarships; SEOG; State scholarships/grants. *Loan aid offered:* Direct PLUS loans; Direct Subsidized Loans; Direct Unsubsidized Loans. Admitted students will be notified of awards on a rolling basis.

The Inside Word

Although the applicant pool is highly self-selecting, fewer than 30 open slots each year means admission to Webb is ultra-tough. (The fact that every enrolled student who is a U.S. citizen or permanent resident gets a full-tuition scholarship also draws a fair share of applicants.) The admissions committee is dedicated to finding students who will excel in the school's rigorous program. To apply, prospective students must submit high-school transcripts indicating rank in class, two letters of recommendation, and SAT or ACT scores.

THE SCHOOL SAYS "..."

From the Admissions Office

"Webb, the only college in the country that specializes in the engineering field of naval architecture and marine engineering, seeks young men and women of all races from all over the country who are interested in receiving an excellent engineering education with a full-tuition scholarship. Students don't have to know anything about ships, they just have to be motivated to study how mechanical, civil, structural, and electrical engineering come together with the design elements that make up a ship and all its systems. Being small and private has its major advantages. Every applicant is special and the President as well as a faculty member will interview all entering students personally. The student/faculty ratio is nine to one, and since there are no teaching assistants, interaction with the faculty occurs daily in class and labs at a level not found at most other colleges. The entire campus operates under the Student Organization's honor system that allows unsupervised exams and twenty-four-hour access to the library, every classroom and laboratory, and the shop and gymnasium. Despite a total enrollment of approximately one hundred students and a demanding workload, Webb manages to field five intercollegiate teams. Currently more than 60 percent of the members of the student body play on one or more intercollegiate teams. Work hard, play hard and the payoff is a job for every student upon graduation. The placement record of the college is 100 percent every year.

"First-year applicants must take the SAT or ACT."

SELECTIVITY

Admissions Rating	98
# of applicants	176
% of applicants accepted	20
% of acceptees attending	72
# offered a place on the wait list	16
% accepting a place on wait list	100
% admitted from wait list	19
# of early decision applicants	48
% accepted early decision	19

FIRST-YEAR PROFILE

Testing policy	SAT or ACT Required
Range SAT composite	1400–1500
Range SAT EBRW	670–720
Range SAT math	720–770
Range ACT composite	31–35
# submitting SAT scores	13
% submitting SAT scores	50
# submitting ACT scores	18
% submitting ACT scores	31
Average HS GPA	4.0
% frosh submitting high school GPA	88
% graduated top 10% of class	20
% graduated top 25% of class	80

DEADLINES

Early decision	
Deadline	10/15
Notification	12/15
Regular	
Priority	10/15
Deadline	1/15
Notification	Rolling, 3/15
Nonfall registration?	No

APPLICANTS SOMETIMES PREFER

Massachusetts Institute of Technology; United States Naval Academy; University of Michigan—Ann Arbor

FINANCIAL FACTS

Annual tuition	$55,075
Room and board	$13,990
Required fees	$3,075
Required fees (first-year)	$6,475
Books and supplies	$800
Average frosh need-based scholarship	$57,465
Average UG need-based scholarship	$57,465
% needy frosh rec. need-based scholarship or grant aid	100
% needy UG rec. need-based scholarship or grant aid	100
% needy frosh rec. non-need-based scholarship or grant aid	100
% needy UG rec. non-need-based scholarship or grant aid	100
% needy frosh rec. need-based self-help aid	100
% needy UG rec. need-based self-help aid	100
% frosh rec. any financial aid	100
% UG rec. any financial aid	100
% UG borrow to pay for school	32
Average cumulative indebtedness	$5,270
% frosh need fully met	100
% ugrads need fully met	72
Average % of frosh need met	100
Average % of ugrad need met	72

WELLESLEY COLLEGE

106 Central Street, Wellesley, MA 02481 • Admissions: 781-283-1000 Fax: 781-283-3678

STUDENTS SAY ". . ."

Academics

For more than 150 years, Wellesley College has given ambitious young women an education in the liberal arts with a global perspective by offering more than 50 majors and hundreds of funded internships around the world. The school's financial support allows "students to pursue internships and research [opportunities] that they would otherwise not take because they are unpaid." The school stresses leadership, service, and the idea of Wellesley students contributing to the world both now and after graduation. To enhance that education even further, enrollees are able to cross-register (or even dual degree) with other nearby colleges. Students are "pushed to explore different departments through the distribution requirements, providing them with a liberal arts education that shapes their personhood and education." And each department is "provided with ample resources and handpicked professors" who "truly value building relationships with their students." It's not uncommon for faculty "to take their class out to a restaurant, or even invite students to their home for a meal." The First-Year Experience at Wellesley further helps ease students into college, including mentor groups, a required writing class, and First-Year Seminars where new students "have the chance to dive deep into a specific topic without feeling the pressure of having [senior students] dominate the conversation."

Academic opportunities extend beyond the classroom: the school's reputation and alumnae network "open so many doors for you in the future," and students can "take part from the moment [they] accept the enrollment offer, and for as long afterwards as [they] wish." Wellesley works to create an environment "where students can naturally progress through leadership positions on campus, whether that be through research, residential life, or student-run organizations." There are also "vast opportunities [for] study abroad programs in so many locations."

Campus Life

While the average Wellesley "workload is not for the faint of heart," students find balance "with extracurricular activities, social life, and self-care." One student explains, "Even when classes are stressful, there is a beautiful·campus that sparks happiness at random moments." That joy is apparent because almost everyone here is passionate about their extracurriculars, and "each organization at Wellesley is full of members who intensely love what they do." Outside of clubs or organizations, tons of students engage in "the weekly Thursday pub night" on campus, and Wellesley "usually has some cultural shows or lectures going on in the afternoon" which are well-attended. When they need a change of scenery, people often head to "neighboring universities to have fun on weekends" and "there is a bus that provides easy transportation" into Boston; many also "take advantage of [the] proximity to other east coast cities and states and take weekend trips." One student sums up the campus life at Wellesley: "Going to a party is just as acceptable as staying in and watching a movie or playing board games," and the school is "very much a choose your own adventure" environment.

Student Body

Among this "study-focused group of diverse people who hail from many countries and backgrounds," students "can be who [they] want and explore different identities." Thanks to that aspect of the student body, everyone is "exposed to countless cultures and viewpoints." These "intellectual, driven, [and] inclusive scholars" are "uplifting and kind to each other both in class and outside of class," and part of the campus culture "is the 'Why not?' attitude that we all share." There's also a "large feminist culture and LGBT population" on campus and overall, students suggest that their peers are "nonjudgmental." Another student sums up the campus environment, saying Wellesley makes a huge effort "to cultivate and facilitate a strong support network for all."

WELLESLEY COLLEGE

Financial Aid: 781-283-2360 • E-Mail: admission@wellesley.edu • Website: www.wellesley.edu

THE PRINCETON REVIEW SAYS

Admissions

The school reports that its standardized testing policy for use in admission for Fall 2024 is Test Optional. It is unknown at this time if the 2024 testing policy will be permanent. The Princeton Review suggests that interested applicants consult with the school for the most up-to-date standardized testing policies. *Very important factors considered include:* rigor of secondary school record, academic GPA, recommendation(s), character/personal qualities. *Important factors considered include:* class rank, application essay, extracurricular activities, talent/ability. *Other factors considered include:* standardized test scores, first generation, alumni/ae relation, geographical residence, state residency, racial/ethnic status, volunteer work, work experience, level of applicant's interest. High school diploma or equivalent is not required. *Academic units recommended:* 4 English, 4 math, 3 science, 2 science labs, 4 foreign language, 4 social studies.

Financial Aid

Students should submit: CSS/Financial Aid Profile; FAFSA; Noncustodial Profile. Priority filing deadline is 1/15. The Princeton Review suggests that all financial aid forms be submitted as soon as possible (see page 5 for a note on the FAFSA). *Need-based scholarships/ grants offered:* College/university scholarship or grant aid from institutional funds; Federal Pell; Private scholarships; SEOG; State scholarships/grants; United Negro College Fund. *Loan aid offered:* Direct PLUS loans; Direct Subsidized Loans; Direct Unsubsidized Loans; College/university loans from institutional funds. Admitted students will be notified of awards on or about 4/1. Federal Work-Study Program available. Institutional employment available.

The Inside Word

When making an admissions decision, Wellesley considers a broad range of factors, including a student's academic record, the difficulty of her high school curriculum, participation in extracurricular activities, class rank, recommendations, personal essay, standardized test scores, leadership, and special talents (students may submit an art, music, or theater supplements along with their applications if they have a special talent in those areas).

THE SCHOOL SAYS "..."

From the Admissions Office

"Widely acknowledged as the nation's best women's college, Wellesley College provides students with numerous opportunities on campus and beyond. With a long-standing commitment to and established reputation for academic excellence, Wellesley offers more than 1,000 courses in more than fifty departmental and interdepartmental majors and supports more than 160 clubs, organizations, and activities for its students. The College is easily accessible to Boston, a great city in which to meet other college students and to experience theater, art, sports, and entertainment. Considered one of the most diverse colleges in the nation, Wellesley students hail from over eighty countries and all fifty states.

"As a community, we are looking for students who possess intellectual curiosity: the ability to think independently, ask challenging questions, and grapple with answers. Strong candidates demonstrate both academic achievement and an excitement for learning. They also display leadership, an appreciation for diverse perspectives, and an understanding of the College's mission to educate women who will make a difference in the world.

"There's no typical Wellesley student (we know: every college says that; and yet!), but they tend to be people who know that they don't know everything; who have a strong voice but listen to other voices; who have big plans but are totally open to changing them; who have taken risks, failed, and figured out a better way. They believe in connection."

SELECTIVITY

Admissions Rating	97
# of applicants	8,491
% of applicants accepted	13
% of acceptees attending	50
# offered a place on the wait list	2,578
% accepting a place on wait list	50
% admitted from wait list	3
# of early decision applicants	887
% accepted early decision	29

FIRST-YEAR PROFILE

Testing policy	Test Optional
Range SAT composite	1440–1540
Range SAT EBRW	720–770
Range SAT math	710–780
Range ACT composite	33–35
# submitting SAT scores	234
% submitting SAT scores	40
# submitting ACT scores	122
% submitting ACT scores	21
% graduated top 10% of class	89
% graduated top 25% of class	98
% graduated top 50% of class	100

DEADLINES

Early decision	
Deadline	11/1
Notification	12/15
Other ED deadline	1/1
Other ED notification	2/15
Regular	
Deadline	1/8
Notification	3/15
Nonfall registration?	No

APPLICANTS ALSO LOOK AT

Barnard College; Brown University; Harvard College; Smith College; University of California—Berkeley; University of California—Los Angeles; Yale University

FINANCIAL FACTS

Financial Aid Rating	97
Annual tuition	$64,000
Room and board	$19,920
Required fees	$320
Books and supplies	$800
Average frosh need-based scholarship	$62,395
Average UG need-based scholarship	$62,132
% needy frosh rec. need-based scholarship or grant aid	97
% needy UG rec. need-based scholarship or grant aid	96
% needy frosh rec. non-need-based scholarship or grant aid	0
% needy UG rec. non-need-based scholarship or grant aid	1
% needy frosh rec. need-based self-help aid	96
% needy UG rec. need-based self-help aid	92
% frosh rec. any financial aid	52
% UG rec. any financial aid	54
% UG borrow to pay for school	41
Average cumulative indebtedness	$18,512
% frosh need fully met	100
% ugrads need fully met	100
Average % of frosh need met	100
Average % of ugrad need met	100

WESLEYAN UNIVERSITY

70 Wyllys Avenue, Middletown, CT 06459 • Admissions: 860-685-3000 • Fax: 860-685-3001

CAMPUS LIFE

Quality of Life Rating	87
Fire Safety Rating	92
Green Rating	60*
Type of school	Private
Affiliation	No Affiliation
Environment	Town

STUDENTS

Total undergrad enrollment	3,006
% male/female/another gender	46/54/0
% from out of state	91
% frosh from public high school	50
% frosh live on campus	100
% ugrads live on campus	99
# of fraternities (% join)	4 (1)
# of sororities	0
% African American	5
% Asian	9
% White	54
% Hispanic	11
% Native American	<1
% Pacific Islander	<1
% Two or more races	7
% Race and/or ethnicity unknown	3
% international	10
# of countries represented	63

SURVEY SAYS . . .

Lots of liberal students
Students are happy
Classroom facilities are great
Great library
Great financial aid
Students aren't religious
Students environmentally aware
Great food on campus
Theater is popular
Campus newspaper is popular
Active student government
Active minority support groups
Easy to get around campus

ACADEMICS

Academic Rating	87
% students returning for sophomore year	95
% students graduating within 4 years	89
% students graduating within 6 years	93
Calendar	Semester
Student/faculty ratio	7:1
Profs interesting rating	91
Profs accessible rating	93

Most classes have 10–19 students.
Most lab/discussion sessions have
10–19 students.

MOST POPULAR MAJORS
Psychology, General; Econometrics and
Quantitative Economics; Political Science and
Government, General

STUDENTS SAY "..."

Academics

Nestled in the middle of Connecticut is Wesleyan University, a historic private liberal arts university that prides itself on an open curriculum that lets students explore interests and activities outside of their major. The school does have general education expectations, which help illustrate pathways through the curriculum; it also offers a flexible framework of four competencies that provide suggestions as to skills and capabilities that students should acquire in their course choices, which is useful with more than 1,000 courses on offer. A 7:1 student-to-faculty ratio means small class sizes, which creates an "enjoyable work environment that promotes learning, questioning, debate, and just overall fun"; this includes interactive learning, "excellent introductory STEM labs, field trips, ample research opportunities, and unique in-class projects." This experiential philosophy even translates to larger formats: "I've had lecture classes that are so open to student questions that they begin to seem more like seminars," says a student. Seniors are also allowed to "teach student forums on topics they are passionate about and provide a space for current events."

Inclusivity is a priority, and the school offers courses like Queer Studies and African American Studies. Along with inclusivity, Wesleyan stresses the importance of faculty as teachers and mentors. Professors are "intentional and thoughtful about every aspect of the course" and "patient and understanding when it comes to students needing extensions." They "embrace students from majors outside their field and encourage academic exploration," As one student notes, "Every class I've taken has made me want to learn more." In addition, faculty "research is significant, and they use it to compliment the classes," and they all have "workable office hours and [are] exceptionally accommodating." The alumni network is similarly willing to assist students: "Whether that is through mentoring us or hiring us as interns, they have been incredibly helpful."

Campus Life

While many admit that "there is a lot of studying during the week," they say "it's easy to find groups to study with" through tutors, study groups, or class-sponsored activities. And students here definitely find time to have fun. Because Wesleyan "is not in a big city, most of the social life is on campus," and "on the weekends, that can look like parties and performances," or taking advantage of the "strong arts and music scene," including "lots of fun concerts, films, comedy shows, or dance performances." Weekend trips to New Haven or Boston are not out of the question, but most stay local, and "people love to go thrifting at the closest places [and] eat food in Middletown" for their trips off-campus.

Outdoor activities such as hiking are widely undertaken (ultimate Frisbee is very popular here!), and many students join multiple groups and teams. In the winter there's plenty of snow, "so people like to sled on Foss Hill and have big snowball fights." Snowball fights aside, "the best days are when it's nice out in the spring, and everyone sits and eats outside," and "everyone says hi to everyone."

Student Body

Wesleyan students are "eclectic, artsy, liberal," diverse, and inclusive. There are many different personalities at Wesleyan, but the one common denominator is that they are accepting. Everyone here "has their 'thing' that they are eager to share with others." One student adds, "No two students share exactly the same combination of interests, which makes Wesleyan a very fun place to make friends."

Though this "incredibly academically motivated" group is "talented, active, and open-minded," they "don't tend to be obsessive about academics," and "there's a good balance between work and life." Students say that "it feels like everyone at Wes does a million things, so for many, clubs and other extracurriculars [that] are just as meaningful as classes."

Students do say that as far as sports go, "there are the athletes and non-athletes with very few individuals crossing battle lines." Still, there is "a strong culture of social acceptance and progressiveness," and people "come from all over the world and always have such amazing anecdotes to share."

WESLEYAN UNIVERSITY

Financial Aid: 860-685-2800 • E-Mail: admission@wesleyan.edu • Website: www.wesleyan.edu

THE PRINCETON REVIEW SAYS

Admissions

The school reports that its standardized testing policy for use in admission for Fall 2024 is Test Optional. The 2024 testing policy will be permanent. The Princeton Review suggests that interested applicants consult with the school for the most up-to-date standardized testing policies. *Very important factors considered include:* rigor of secondary school record. *Important factors considered include:* class rank, academic GPA, application essay, recommendation(s), talent/ability, character/personal qualities, first generation, racial/ethnic status. *Other factors considered include:* standardized test scores, extracurricular activities, alumni/ae relation, geographical residence, volunteer work, work experience. High school diploma is required and GED is accepted. *Academic units recommended:* 4 English, 4 math, 4 science, 3 science labs, 4 foreign language, 4 social studies, 4 history.

Financial Aid

Students should submit: CSS/Financial Aid Profile; FAFSA; Noncustodial Profile. Priority filing deadline is 1/15. The Princeton Review suggests that all financial aid forms be submitted as soon as possible (see page 5 for a note on the FAFSA). *Need-based scholarships/grants offered:* College/university scholarship or grant aid from institutional funds; Federal Pell; Private scholarships; SEOG; State scholarships/grants. *Loan aid offered:* Direct PLUS loans; Direct Subsidized Loans; Direct Unsubsidized Loans; College/university loans from institutional funds. Admitted students will be notified of awards on or about 4/1. Federal Work-Study Program available. Institutional employment available.

The Inside Word

Tuition, fees, residential comprehensive fee, and estimated cost for books, supplies, and miscellaneous expenses for 2022–23 totaled $85,172 for first-year students, $84,872 for sophomores, and $85,598 for juniors and seniors; 39 percent of students received need-based scholarship awards averaging nearly $60,143. Beginning with students entering in the 2021–22 academic year and beyond, the school makes it so that if a student's annual family income is less than $120,000, their financial aid package includes only scholarships, grants, and work-study, not loans. A three-year curriculum is offered for students who opt to also take summer courses, which saves about 20 percent of the total cost of a Wesleyan education.

THE SCHOOL SAYS "..."

From the Admissions Office

"Wesleyan faculty believe in an education that is flexible and affords individual freedom and that a strong liberal arts education is the best foundation for success in any endeavor. The broad curriculum provides a rigorous education that values putting ideas into practice. Students have the opportunity to discover what they love to do, work at the highest level, and apply their knowledge in meaningful ways. As a result, Wesleyan students achieve a very personalized but broad education. Wesleyan's Vice President and Dean of Admission and Financial Aid, Amin Abdul-Malik Gonzalez, describes the qualities Wesleyan seeks in its students: 'Our holistic process, which carefully considers candidates in their respective contexts, aims to select high-achieving, intellectually engaged, broadly talented, and socially conscious students who will thrive in Wesleyan's vibrant academic environment. At Wesleyan, we value character and personal promise as much as impressive credentials and accomplishments. We seek students who will leverage our outstanding resources, realize their personal potentials, and make meaningful contributions to both our dynamically diverse community and wider world.'"

SELECTIVITY

Admissions Rating	96
# of applicants	14,521
% of applicants accepted	14
% of acceptees attending	35
# offered a place on the wait list	2,754
% accepting a place on wait list	57
% admitted from wait list	5
# of early decision applicants	1,047
% accepted early decision	40

FIRST-YEAR PROFILE

Testing policy	Test Optional
Range SAT composite	1310–1505
Range SAT EBRW	660–750
Range SAT math	660–760
Range ACT composite	31–34
# submitting SAT scores	384
% submitting SAT scores	52
# submitting ACT scores	176
% submitting ACT scores	24
% graduated top 10% of class	79
% graduated top 50% of class	99

DEADLINES

Early decision	
Deadline	11/15
Notification	12/15
Other ED deadline	1/1
Other ED notification	2/15
Regular	
Deadline	1/1
Notification	4/1
Nonfall registration?	No

APPLICANTS ALSO LOOK AT

Brown University; Columbia University; Harvard College; Princeton University; Tufts University; University of California—Berkeley; University of California—Los Angeles; University of Pennsylvania; Williams College; Yale University

FINANCIAL FACTS

Financial Aid Rating	95
Annual tuition	$63,722
Room and board	$18,180
Required fees	$300
Books and supplies	$1,200
Average frosh need-based scholarship	$64,308
Average UG need-based scholarship	$62,338
% needy frosh rec. need-based scholarship or grant aid	99
% needy UG rec. need-based scholarship or grant aid	98
% needy frosh rec. non-need-based scholarship or grant aid	4
% needy UG rec. non-need-based scholarship or grant aid	2
% needy frosh rec. need-based self-help aid	95
% needy UG rec. need-based self-help aid	96
% frosh rec. any financial aid	38
% UG rec. any financial aid	39
% UG borrow to pay for school	28
Average cumulative indebtedness	$25,283
% frosh need fully met	100
% ugrads need fully met	100
Average % of frosh need met	100
Average % of ugrad need met	100

WEST VIRGINIA UNIVERSITY

Presidents Office, Morgantown, WV 26506-6201 • Admissions: 304-293-0111 • Fax: 304-293-3080

CAMPUS LIFE

Quality of Life Rating	79
Fire Safety Rating	98
Green Rating	89
Type of school	Public
Environment	Town

STUDENTS

Total undergrad enrollment	20,499
% male/female/another gender	52/48/0
% from out of state	48
% frosh live on campus	92
% ugrads live on campus	22
# of fraternities	9
# of sororities	8
% African American	4
% Asian	2
% White	80
% Hispanic	4
% Native American	<1
% Pacific Islander	<1
% Two or more races	4
% Race and/or ethnicity unknown	1
% international	6
# of countries represented	75

SURVEY SAYS . . .
Great library
Recreation facilities are great
Everyone loves the Mountaineers

ACADEMICS

Academic Rating	77
% students returning for sophomore year	76
% students graduating within 4 years	35
% students graduating within 6 years	58
Calendar	Semester
Student/faculty ratio	18:1
Profs interesting rating	86
Profs accessible rating	91

Most classes have 20–29 students.
Most lab/discussion sessions have
20–29 students.

MOST POPULAR MAJORS
Engineering, General; Business Administration
and Management, General; Journalism

STUDENTS SAY ". . ."

Academics

One student reports that West Virginia University boasts "a relaxed, social, and extremely school-spirited environment," and that WVU's academics "challenge students in the classroom" and prepare them "to be successful in the next step of life after college." Another student praises the engineering program, which offers "many opportunities for seniors looking for jobs. I also like the fact that it is a big university, but being in Morgantown gives it a homey feel." Students find a happy medium that combines studying and socializing. "The school is all about connecting academics and leadership with incredible enthusiasm for school activities." "A wonderful experience with a good balance of academics and fun opportunities." "Great academic experience wrapped up in a fun college atmosphere." For in-state undergraduates, affordability is the key to choosing WVU. Many students are drawn to the "diversity of programs" offered at West Virginia University. With this variety of programs comes a "diversified faculty who bring a wide range of knowledge and experiences." Some students would prefer smaller classes because, as one student put it, "The large classes make it difficult to form solid teacher-student relationships." But another student offers a different perspective, "If you put forth any type of effort, you'll get to know your professors at WVU. Of course, with some of the bigger classes, you can sit in the back and go unnoticed, but that's a personal choice."

Campus Life

There is no escaping the "pride" West Virginia University students feel for their school, many of whom say they were "born to be a Mountaineer." Whether it's describing their majors, the marching band, alumni, or the football and basketball teams, it seems unanimous that the "spirit of the university is outstanding." As one student states, "West Virginia University is all about combining such high academic standards with the atmosphere of Mountaineer pride, only something you can feel at a football game singing 'Country Roads' with 50,000 of your closest friends." "Fun" seems to best describe student life at WVU. Whether on campus at the "amazing student recreational center," which is "complete with weight room, indoor swimming pool, hot tubs, indoor track, indoor basketball and racquetball courts, ping-pong tables, and boxing equipment," at the Mountainlair student union watching free movies, or off campus exploring Morgantown, everyone seems to be having a good time. "One of the best things about Morgantown is downtown High Street. People always ask, 'you goin downtown tonight?'" This is referring to the very wide selection of bars, clubs, lounges, and restaurants that are located downtown, most concentrated along High Street. High Street starts at the south end of downtown and travels all the way up through the downtown campus. Some students would like to see an improvement in both parking and transportation, but the beauty of the area and the level of student assistance "outside the classroom with learning centers, free tutors, [and] group work areas" all get high marks.

Student Body

Students describe themselves as "outgoing" as well as "relaxed and social." School spirit is evident. "The typical student always has some piece of WVU apparel on, and that's usually sweatpants." "Students are very involved on campus with academics and various clubs and organizations. It is a very lively campus and there is always something going on. Although one student reports, "A lot of people here drink quite often," students also say that there is plenty to do on campus that doesn't include alcohol.

WEST VIRGINIA UNIVERSITY

Financial Aid: 304-293-5242 • E-Mail: go2wvu@mail.wvu.edu • Website: www.wvu.edu

THE PRINCETON REVIEW SAYS

Admissions

The school reports that its standardized testing policy for use in admission for Fall 2024 is SAT or ACT Required. It is unknown at this time if the 2024 testing policy will be permanent. The Princeton Review suggests that interested applicants consult with the school for the most up-to-date standardized testing policies. *Very important factors considered include:* academic GPA, standardized test scores. *Important factors considered include:* rigor of secondary school record, state residency. *Other factors considered include:* extracurricular activities, talent/ability. High school diploma is required and GED is accepted. *Academic units required:* 4 English, 4 math, 3 science, 3 science labs, 2 foreign language, 3 social studies, 1 visual/performing arts.

Financial Aid

Students should submit: FAFSA. Priority filing deadline is 3/1. The Princeton Review suggests that all financial aid forms be submitted as soon as possible (see page 5 for a note on the FAFSA). *Need-based scholarships/grants offered:* College/university scholarship or grant aid from institutional funds; Federal Nursing Scholarships; Federal Pell; Private scholarships; SEOG. *Loan aid offered:* Direct PLUS loans; Direct Subsidized Loans; Direct Unsubsidized Loans; College/university loans from institutional funds; Federal Nursing Loans; State Loans. Admitted students will be notified of awards on a rolling basis beginning 12/1. Federal Work-Study Program available. Institutional employment available.

The Inside Word

While standards for general admission to WVU aren't especially rigorous, you'll find admission to its premier programs to be quite competitive. Admission to the College of Business and Economics, for example, requires a high school GPA of at least 3.75. Programs in computer science, education, engineering, fine arts, forensics, journalism, medicine, and nursing all require fairly impressive credentials. If you're not admitted to the program of your choice, you may be able to transfer to it later if your grades are good enough, but it won't be easy.

THE SCHOOL SAYS "..."

From the Admissions Office

"From quality academic programs and outstanding, caring faculty, to incredible new facilities and a campus environment that focuses on students' needs, WVU is a place where dreams can come true. Our tradition of academic excellence attracts some of the region's best high school seniors. WVU has produced twenty-four Rhodes Scholars, thirty-five Goldwater Scholars, twenty-two Truman Scholars, six members of the *USA Today*'s All-USA College Academic First Team, and two Udall Scholarship winners. Whether your goal is to be an aerospace engineer, reporter, physicist, athletic trainer, opera singer, forensic investigator, pharmacist, or CEO, WVU's 191 degree choices can make it happen. Unique student-centered initiatives help students experience true education beyond the classroom. The Mountaineer parents club connects more than 20,000 families, and a parents' helpline (800-WVU-0096) leads to a full-time parent advocate. A Student Recreation Center includes athletic courts, pools, weight/fitness equipment, and a fifty-foot indoor climbing wall. A major building program is creating new classrooms, labs, health-care facilities, an art museum, and a student wellness center. With programs for studying abroad, a Center from Black Culture and Research, and Office of Disability Services, and a student body that comes from every WV county, fifty states, and 108 different countries, WVU encourages diversity. WVU research funding has topped $174 million for the second consecutive year, making WVU a major research institution where undergraduates can participate."

SELECTIVITY

Admissions Rating	84
# of applicants	18,639
% of applicants accepted	82
% of acceptees attending	31

FIRST-YEAR PROFILE

Testing policy	SAT or ACT Required
Range SAT EBRW	530–620
Range SAT math	520–620
Range ACT composite	21–27
# submitting SAT scores	2,688
% submitting SAT scores	57
# submitting ACT scores	3,088
% submitting ACT scores	65
Average HS GPA	3.5
% frosh submitting high school GPA	100
% graduated top 10% of class	23
% graduated top 25% of class	48
% graduated top 50% of class	78

DEADLINES

Regular	
Priority	3/1
Deadline	8/1
Notification	Rolling, 9/15
Nonfall registration?	Yes

APPLICANTS OFTEN PREFER
Penn State University Park; University of Maryland, College Park; Virginia Tech

APPLICANTS SOMETIMES PREFER
James Madison University; Towson University; University of Pittsburgh–Pittsburgh Campus

APPLICANTS RARELY PREFER
Fairmont State University, including Pierpont Community & Technical College

FINANCIAL FACTS

Financial Aid Rating	72
Annual in-state tuition	$8,976
Annual out-of-state tuition	$25,320
Books and supplies	$950
Average frosh need-based scholarship	$6,190
Average UG need-based scholarship	$5,812
% needy frosh rec. need-based scholarship or grant aid	81
% needy UG rec. need-based scholarship or grant aid	74
% needy frosh rec. non-need-based scholarship or grant aid	46
% needy UG rec. non-need-based scholarship or grant aid	39
% needy frosh rec. need-based self-help aid	69
% needy UG rec. need-based self-help aid	77
% frosh rec. any financial aid	72
% UG rec. any financial aid	75
% UG borrow to pay for school	61
Average cumulative indebtedness	$32,541
% frosh need fully met	13
% ugrads need fully met	11

WESTMINSTER COLLEGE OF SALT LAKE CITY

1840 South 1300 East, Salt Lake City, UT 84105 • Admissions: 801-484-7651 • Fax: 801-832-3101

CAMPUS LIFE

Quality of Life Rating	90
Fire Safety Rating	95
Green Rating	86
Type of school	Private
Affiliation	No Affiliation
Environment	Metropolis

STUDENTS

Total undergrad enrollment	1,153
% male/female/another gender	36/64/0
% from out of state	36
% frosh live on campus	81
% ugrads live on campus	29
# of fraternities	0
# of sororities	0
% African American	2
% Asian	2
% White	71
% Hispanic	13
% Native American	<1
% Pacific Islander	<1
% Two or more races	4
% Race and/or ethnicity unknown	3
% international	4
# of countries represented	26

SURVEY SAYS . . .

Class discussions encouraged
Students environmentally aware
Students love Salt Lake City, UT
Easy to get around campus

ACADEMICS

Academic Rating	86
% students returning for sophomore year	85
% students graduating within 4 years	50
% students graduating within 6 years	63
Calendar	Other
Student/faculty ratio	8:1
Profs interesting rating	91
Profs accessible rating	93

Most classes have fewer than 10 students.
Most lab/discussion sessions have
10–19 students.

STUDENTS SAY "..."

Academics

Set amidst the spectacular peaks of the Wasatch Mountains, Westminster College is a quaint liberal arts college in a small neighborhood of Salt Lake City. Undergrads praise "a very rigorous academic load" and "a community that doesn't center around academic competition, but academic empowerment." This collaborative culture includes faculty that is "attentive and understanding." One undergrad says, "Professors are very accessible,... [and] if office hours don't work for you, they will make other times to meet." Students generally agree that professors are "experts in their fields [and] extremely knowledgeable." There are complaints, however, about adjunct professors who "seem to be less committed." The small campus and class sizes allow students "to communicate one-on-one with professors [and give students] the opportunity to get to know...classmates better." Despite the size of Westminster, "resources are abundant at the college," and students have access to hands-on research opportunities, internships, study abroad programs, and conferences. Frequently mentioned majors include "a great nursing program," biology, and theater.

Campus Life

Outdoor activities are a big draw to students at Westminster. And with six ski resorts within a half-hour drive, "a lot of people look forward to snowboarding and skiing." In fact, one student says that "Westminster has a core of people who like to ski and that is often all they do"—Griffins love their slopes! Others clarify that "there is more [to] Westminster than just skiing and snowboarding." Sure, "winter sports are popular here, but most of us are more concerned with our academics than the ski hill." A happy medium would be the on-campus clubs available to students, which "always try to provide activities or events." Something students are unanimous on is the food options, from on-campus student centers that "are great stops for a quick meal or coffee to recharge" to the restaurants in Salt Lake City, which has the added benefit of being "a very cool city."

Student Body

"The culture is welcoming and socially relaxed" at Westminster College. "There is a general mix of artistic and intellectual students who are driven by learning." Additionally, there is also an awareness of social issues, and "it's easy to strike up a conversation about gender bias or cultural inequality because our students are well educated and always up for challenging their thought process to make positive change happen," one undergrad reports. That said, some take issue with the common "liberal ideology." Moreover, while students may have a "diversity of interests," some find that "there is not much diversity in terms of race, gender, sexual orientation, and ability." The student body is predominantly "white and at least upper middle class." But while it might seem like a fairly uniform campus, "everyone you meet is open to every walk of life [and] accepting of differences."

WESTMINSTER COLLEGE OF SALT LAKE CITY

Financial Aid: 801-832-2502 • E-Mail: admission@westminstercollege.edu • Website: www.westminstercollege.edu

THE PRINCETON REVIEW SAYS

Admissions

The school reports that its standardized testing policy for use in admission for Fall 2024 is Test Optional. The 2024 testing policy will be permanent. The Princeton Review suggests that interested applicants consult with the school for the most up-to-date standardized testing policies. *Very important factors considered include:* rigor of secondary school record. *Important factors considered include:* academic GPA. *Other factors considered include:* class rank, standardized test scores, application essay, recommendation(s), interview, extracurricular activities, talent/ability, character/personal qualities, first generation, alumni/ae relation, racial/ethnic status, volunteer work, work experience, level of applicant's interest. High school diploma is required and GED is accepted. *Academic units recommended:* 3 English, 3 math, 3 science, 2 foreign language, 3 social studies, 1 visual/performing arts.

Financial Aid

Students should submit: FAFSA. Priority filing deadline is 12/1. The Princeton Review suggests that all financial aid forms be submitted as soon as possible (see page 5 for a note on the FAFSA). *Need-based scholarships/grants offered:* College/university scholarship or grant aid from institutional funds; Federal Pell; Private scholarships; SEOG; State scholarships/grants. *Loan aid offered:* Direct PLUS loans; Direct Subsidized Loans; Direct Unsubsidized Loans. Admitted students will be notified of awards on a rolling basis beginning 12/1. Federal Work-Study Program available. Institutional employment available.

The Inside Word

A strong academic record isn't the top priority at Westminster. With a 76 percent acceptance rate, considerations mainly include the rigor of a student's high school transcript although test scores will also be considered if submitted. Admitted students have average SAT scores of between 1215–1355 or an average ACT score of 23–29. A strong personal statement plays an important role in the admission decision and gives admissions officers an opportunity to get to know the person behind the transcript. A campus interview is encouraged, and admissions are rolling.

THE SCHOOL SAYS "..."

From the Admissions Office

"At Westminster, you'll spend less time with your nose in a textbook and more time engaged in lively discussion with your classmates. You'll be challenged to apply your knowledge in interesting, innovative ways, while learning from professors who are passionate about what they do. And with an average class size of 17, your teachers won't just know you by name, they'll know what drives you.

"Our new general education program, WCore, gives you the opportunity to explore new subjects through small, interdisciplinary courses, where you'll spend time engaging in and challenging ideas, rather than just memorizing facts. With specialized offerings like our Honors College, dedicated faculty mentors, and internship and professional connections throughout the community, you'll graduate prepared to take on whatever's next.

"Each application is read and reviewed individually by an admission committee that takes into account both level of challenge in coursework and grades received. Either the SAT or ACT is accepted. Westminster College has a rolling application deadline and will accept applications until the class is filled. To be eligible for the widest array of financial aid—more than 98 percent of first-year students receive scholarship or financial aid—April 15 is the priority consideration deadline for fall semester, and May 15 is the priority deadline for on-campus housing applications."

SELECTIVITY

Admissions Rating	85
# of applicants	1,945
% of applicants accepted	76
% of acceptees attending	11

FIRST-YEAR PROFILE

Testing policy	Test Optional
Range SAT composite	1215–1355
Range SAT EBRW	635–695
Range SAT math	555–680
Range ACT composite	23–29
# submitting SAT scores	13
% submitting SAT scores	8
# submitting ACT scores	34
% submitting ACT scores	20
Average HS GPA	3.6
% frosh submitting high school GPA	100
% graduated top 10% of class	27
% graduated top 25% of class	50
% graduated top 50% of class	80

DEADLINES

Early action	
Deadline	12/1
Notification	12/1
Regular	
Priority	12/1
Notification	Rolling, 12/1
Nonfall registration?	Yes

APPLICANTS OFTEN PREFER
University of Utah; Utah State University

APPLICANTS SOMETIMES PREFER
Brigham Young University (UT); Southern Utah University; Weber State University

APPLICANTS RARELY PREFER
Boise State University; Idaho State University; Montana State University; Northern Arizona University

FINANCIAL FACTS

Financial Aid Rating	86
Annual tuition	$39,312
Room and board	$11,814
Required fees	$520
Required fees (first-year)	$820
Books and supplies	$1,000
Average frosh need-based scholarship	$30,618
Average UG need-based scholarship	$27,372
% needy frosh rec. need-based scholarship or grant aid	100
% needy UG rec. need-based scholarship or grant aid	99
% needy frosh rec. non-need-based scholarship or grant aid	28
% needy UG rec. non-need-based scholarship or grant aid	16
% needy frosh rec. need-based self-help aid	74
% needy UG rec. need-based self-help aid	85
% frosh rec. any financial aid	100
% UG rec. any financial aid	99
% UG borrow to pay for school	60
Average cumulative indebtedness	$26,187
% frosh need fully met	42
% ugrads need fully met	33
Average % of frosh need met	92
Average % of ugrad need met	85

WHEATON COLLEGE (IL)

501 College Avenue, Wheaton, IL 60187 • Admissions: 630-752-5000 • Fax: 630-752-5285

STUDENTS SAY "..."

Academics

Wheaton College, located just outside of Chicago, Illinois, is a great option for students who want a school with a "phenomenal" sense of community and "exceptional liberal arts program." It's also an evangelical institution and undergrads here value "the college's commitment to providing a rigorous academic experience through a Christian worldview." As one undergrad explains, "I wanted to come to a school where my faith would be challenged and grown by those around me." Beyond religion, students love that class sizes are "relatively small," which "make it easier to develop relationships with professors and peers." The classroom experience consists of "uniformly fantastic" professors who care deeply and "genuinely want to know about their students' lives." Another incredulous undergrad shares, "They invest time and energy into their students and all are always available for office hours or meals." Wheaton professors also actively look to "involve students in research or mentoring." Just as crucial, they are "super knowledgeable and enthusiastic about the subject they teach." And they're "always open to questions/challenges and at the same time are willing to challenge and encourage students in a way that maximizes learning." It is truly evident that Wheaton professors "want their students to succeed."

Campus Life

It's rather easy to lead a fun and fulfilling life at Wheaton. For starters, students have "chapel services every other day during the week, with worship and guest speakers who are simply amazing." Many people also "like to attend events put on by Wheaton's music conservatory." Additionally, the majority of students are rather "active" and a large number "participat[e] in intramural sports." Even if sports aren't your strong suit, the athletic program "encourages non-athletic people to get involved." Wheaton students are also quite adept at finding "creative ways to have fun." For example, "geocaching" is pretty popular. Once the weekend rolls around, lots of undergrads participate in "game night," "movie night," or "college events such as lip syncing competitions or an interactive art festival." It's also rather common for people to attend both "church and brunch." Of course, when students want a break from campus life, they can easily "take the train to Chicago to enjoy the sights and the lights." A student concludes, "There is never a dull moment here on campus, whether I'm studying or having fun with friends or attending special lectures, concerts, services, or just class. I love life at Wheaton!"

Student Body

Unsurprisingly, undergrads at Wheaton are "uniformly Christian" and "devoted to serving Christ and His Kingdom." The student body is also "predominantly white" though many individuals insist, "diversity is a big part of the campus conversation." Thankfully, beyond these two facets, you'll find a variety of "background[s], opinion[s], and interests around Wheaton." As one student interjects, "Wheaton gets a bad rap for being really conservative, but that doesn't mean there's not a diversity of political and theological thought." What's more, students say that their peers comprise of a "caring group of individuals who have fun while living an upright lifestyle." The vast majority are also "hardworking" and "very, very driven." And they're fairly worldly since a good number "have traveled to participate in some type of missions or humanitarian work." Wheaton undergrads are impressed by their fellow students' intellect as well, reporting that they "are exceptionally versatile, excelling in music, art, athletics, and oftentimes speaking multiple languages." Finally, another student praises, "I am consistently blown away by the high intellectual capacity the students of Wheaton College possess, as well as their resolve to live selflessly, and use their education to create a better world."

WHEATON COLLEGE (IL)

Financial Aid: 630-752-5021 • E-Mail: admissions@wheaton.edu • Website: www.wheaton.edu

THE PRINCETON REVIEW SAYS

Admissions

The school reports that its standardized testing policy for use in admission for Fall 2024 is Test Optional. It is unknown at this time if the 2024 testing policy will be permanent. The Princeton Review suggests that interested applicants consult with the school for the most up-to-date standardized testing policies. *Very important factors considered include:* rigor of secondary school record, academic GPA, application essay, recommendation(s), character/personal qualities, religious affiliation/commitment. *Important factors considered include:* interview, extracurricular activities, talent/ability, volunteer work. *Other factors considered include:* class rank, standardized test scores, first generation, alumni/ae relation, geographical residence, state residency, racial/ethnic status, work experience, level of applicant's interest. High school diploma is required and GED is accepted. *Academic units required:* 4 English, 3 math, 3 science, 2 foreign language, 3 social studies. *Academic units recommended:* 4 English, 4 math, 3 science, 3 foreign language, 4 social studies.

Financial Aid

Students should submit: FAFSA. Priority filing deadline is 11/10. The Princeton Review suggests that all financial aid forms be submitted as soon as possible (see page 5 for a note on the FAFSA). *Need-based scholarships/grants offered:* College/university scholarship or grant aid from institutional funds; Federal Pell; Private scholarships; SEOG; State scholarships/grants. *Loan aid offered:* Direct PLUS loans; Direct Subsidized Loans; Direct Unsubsidized Loans; College/university loans from institutional funds. Admitted students will be notified of awards on a rolling basis beginning 12/20. Federal Work-Study Program available. Institutional employment available.

The Inside Word

Wheaton College is looking for applicants who display a thirst for knowledge. Therefore, admissions officers tend to favor students who have taken at least a handful of honors, advanced placement or IB classes. Given the school's evangelical association, students must also demonstrate a commitment to their faith. To that end, all applicants are required to submit a Christian faith reference in the form of an interview or a Christian mentor recommendation letter. It's also important to note that candidates can apply to either the College of Arts and Sciences or the Conservatory of Music, but not both.

THE SCHOOL SAYS ". . ."

From the Admissions Office

"Here at Wheaton College, you can deepen your faith as you learn alongside like-hearted peers and distinguished faculty who are true mentors and guides. Across-the-board high standards mean that all our 150+ majors, minors, and certificates are top-notch, cultivating your gifts and passions. Wheaton—the home of integrated faith and learning—is a place of curiosity and conviction, wisdom and growth, hands-on and collaborative learning, beauty and belonging, and grace and truth.

"Every applicant to Wheaton is considered holistically for academic scholarships ranging from $10,000–$16,000 renewed annually, based on unweighted GPA, academic rigor of curriculum including number of advanced level courses, and standardized test scores. Students who qualify will receive their scholarship offer with their acceptance letter.

"Wheaton will not make you choose between intellectual rigor and deep faith centered on Jesus. At Wheaton, we believe it's possible. We believe you will find it here."

SELECTIVITY

Admissions Rating	88
# of applicants	1,872
% of applicants accepted	89
% of acceptees attending	30
# offered a place on the wait list	47
% accepting a place on wait list	77
% admitted from wait list	14

FIRST-YEAR PROFILE

Testing policy	Test Optional
Range SAT composite	1260–1420
Range SAT EBRW	610–710
Range SAT math	640–720
Range ACT composite	28–33
# submitting SAT scores	191
% submitting SAT scores	38
# submitting ACT scores	117
% submitting ACT scores	23
Average HS GPA	3.8
% frosh submitting high school GPA	98
% graduated top 10% of class	48
% graduated top 25% of class	75
% graduated top 50% of class	90

DEADLINES

Early action	
Deadline	11/15
Notification	12/31
Regular	
Priority	2/15
Deadline	8/1
Notification	4/1
Nonfall registration?	Yes

APPLICANTS SOMETIMES PREFER
Calvin University; Taylor University

APPLICANTS RARELY PREFER
Baylor University; Biola University; Covenant College; Gordon College; Grove City College; Hope College

FINANCIAL FACTS

Financial Aid Rating	82
Annual tuition	$43,670
Room and board	$13,512
Required fees	$260
Books and supplies	$700
Average frosh need-based scholarship	$18,833
Average UG need-based scholarship	$18,689
% needy frosh rec. need-based scholarship or grant aid	81
% needy UG rec. need-based scholarship or grant aid	84
% needy frosh rec. non-need-based scholarship or grant aid	83
% needy UG rec. non-need-based scholarship or grant aid	76
% needy frosh rec. need-based self-help aid	58
% needy UG rec. need-based self-help aid	63
% frosh rec. any financial aid	92
% UG rec. any financial aid	86
% UG borrow to pay for school	57
Average cumulative indebtedness	$27,569
% frosh need fully met	17
% ugrads need fully met	16
Average % of frosh need met	75
Average % of ugrad need met	76

WHEATON COLLEGE (MA)

26 East Main Street, Norton, MA 02766 • Admissions: 508-286-8200 • Fax: 508-286-8271

STUDENTS SAY ". . ."

Academics

Set at a "gorgeous" campus in Norton, Massachusetts, that boasts a "community" feel, Wheaton College aims to provide an "interdisciplinary" liberal arts education that "fosters appreciation for critical thinking, diversity, and civic engagement." Undergrads here particularly love that their school champions "diversity and multiculturalism." And, in doing so, Wheaton has created a "very progressive and forward-thinking environment." Students also greatly appreciate that their classes are chockfull of "active learning." Indeed, professors "encourage you to ask questions instead of quietly sitting in the back of the classroom." It also helps that instructors are "incredibly knowledgeable in their fields." More importantly, it's quite evident that professors "work really hard to put the student interests first." For example, "they love to discuss their areas of study with students and are accessible outside of class time." A junior explains, "I have made extremely close ties to many professors here at Wheaton. My art history professors have helped me get internships over the summer, given me research opportunities, and helped me with my transition to college. I honestly couldn't ask for a better support system." All in all, it is "obvious that everyone who works at Wheaton is passionate about the institution and care[s] about the student body."

Campus Life

There's no denying that Wheaton undergrads love to stay busy. As such, they are "very committed to extracurricular activities." To begin with, "student musical groups are big on campus as well as other performing arts groups." Many Wheaton undergraduates are "involved in community service" as well. People frequently gather at the Lyons Den, a student-run coffee shop that's "open late and hosts open mics on Wednesdays." Once the weekend rolls around, you'll discover that "there are numerous events scheduled. Anything from a movie in one of the auditoriums to food trucks to dance and music performances." Wheaton also sponsors "special treats from time to time." During a recent exam week, students were able to enjoy and de-stress with "a little animal petting farm." As if that wasn't enough, "cupcakes were brought in [too]!" Additionally, plenty of students can also be found attending parties on "Thursday, Friday, and Saturday" at different theme houses, though there "is a definite sober population on campus." Unfortunately, there "is not much to do in Norton." But if students are looking for off-campus excitement, they can easily head into Providence or Boston (20 minutes and 40 minutes away, respectively).

Student Body

Undergraduates at Wheaton seem to agree that their peers are "creative, energetic, and have a love for academics." They also continually prove themselves to be "kind," "respectful," and "interested in being…genuinely good [people]." Moreover, students here do an admirable job of making sure they're conscious about what's happening "outside the Wheaton bubble." To that end, many are "very liberally minded and outspoken with those views." Undergrads also applaud the fact that their college "is home to a wide array of culturally-diverse and open-minded individuals." Indeed, "everybody is very welcoming and very willing to learn about new cultures and experiences." That's probably due in large part to the fact that Wheaton has "students from all over the country as well as the world, a prominent LGBTQ community, [and] students from all walks of life." Further, since the college "is able to offer financial aid to many [individuals], Wheaton students are not all just upper-class suburban kids like at other private colleges around the country." All of this helps to foster a "sense of community [that] runs deep throughout the student body." As one thankful student summarizes, "Unity is a trait that shines here…[and] something that we are all extremely proud of."

WHEATON COLLEGE (MA)

Financial Aid: 508-286-8232 • E-Mail: admission@wheatoncollege.edu • Website: www.wheatoncollege.edu

THE PRINCETON REVIEW SAYS

Admissions

The school reports that its standardized testing policy for use in admission for Fall 2024 is Test Optional. It is unknown at this time if the 2024 testing policy will be permanent. The Princeton Review suggests that interested applicants consult with the school for the most up-to-date standardized testing policies. *Very important factors considered include:* rigor of secondary school record, academic GPA, application essay, recommendation(s), character/personal qualities. *Important factors considered include:* extracurricular activities, talent/ability, level of applicant's interest. *Other factors considered include:* class rank, standardized test scores, interview, alumni/ae relation, geographical residence, state residency, racial/ethnic status, volunteer work, work experience. High school diploma is required and GED is accepted. *Academic units required:* 4 English. *Academic units recommended:* 4 math, 4 science, 4 foreign language, 4 social studies, 4 history.

Financial Aid

Students should submit: Business/Farm Supplement; CSS/Financial Aid Profile; FAFSA; Noncustodial Profile. The Princeton Review suggests that all financial aid forms be submitted as soon as possible (see page 5 for a note on the FAFSA). *Need-based scholarships/grants offered:* College/university scholarship or grant aid from institutional funds; Federal Pell; Private scholarships; SEOG; State scholarships/grants. *Loan aid offered:* Direct PLUS loans; Direct Subsidized Loans; Direct Unsubsidized Loans; College/university loans from institutional funds. Admitted students will be notified of awards on or about 3/15. Federal Work-Study Program available. Institutional employment available.

The Inside Word

Wheaton is a selective college so gaining admission won't be a cakewalk. The school takes a holistic approach when evaluating applicants meaning everything from the difficulty of your high school curriculum to your writing ability and extracurricular involvement will be considered. And if you're standardized test-averse, take heart; Wheaton is Test Optional. Finally, if you're confident that Wheaton is your first choice, the college highly recommends that you apply Early Decision.

THE SCHOOL SAYS "..."

From the Admissions Office

"We have been described as a place sparking possibilities and world-changing ideas. Our students come from all over the world, and they definitely stand out from the crowd. Since 2000, more than 250 Wheaton students have won national and international scholarships, including the Rhodes, Marshall, Fulbright, Truman, and Watson awards. Our faculty are world-class researchers, scholars, artists, teachers, and advisors, as well as involved and connected community members. They engage their students in original research and scholarship projects and build relationships that sustain and last a lifetime. Our Filene Center for Academic Advising and Career Services invests about $1.2 million in stipends annually as part of The Wheaton Edge, which provides access to funding for an internship or other experiential learning opportunity to every student before the start of their senior year. We also get our students connected to our passionate, worldwide alumni network, who advise graduates on career choices, internships and getting acclimated to their first jobs. The value of a Wheaton education is undeniable and success for Wheaton graduates starts early, with 97 percent of respondents to our First Destination survey over the past five years finding employment, graduate education or social change opportunities within six months after leaving our picturesque New England campus."

SELECTIVITY

Admissions Rating	86
# of applicants	4,004
% of applicants accepted	80
% of acceptees attending	15

FIRST-YEAR PROFILE

Testing policy	Test Optional
Range SAT EBRW	630–700
Range SAT math	630–690
Range ACT composite	27–33
# submitting SAT scores	122
# submitting ACT scores	23

DEADLINES

Early decision	
Deadline	11/15
Notification	12/20
Other ED deadline	1/15
Other ED notification	2/1
Early action	
Deadline	11/15
Notification	12/20
Regular	
Priority	11/15
Deadline	1/15
Nonfall registration?	Yes

FINANCIAL FACTS

Financial Aid Rating	87
Annual tuition	$61,600
Room and board	$15,430
Required fees	$480
Books and supplies	$940
Average frosh need-based scholarship	$42,146
Average UG need-based scholarship	$38,800
% needy frosh rec. need-based scholarship or grant aid	100
% needy UG rec. need-based scholarship or grant aid	100
% needy frosh rec. non-need-based scholarship or grant aid	12
% needy UG rec. non-need-based scholarship or grant aid	8
% needy frosh rec. need-based self-help aid	76
% needy UG rec. need-based self-help aid	83
% frosh rec. any financial aid	99
% UG rec. any financial aid	97
% UG borrow to pay for school	66
Average cumulative indebtedness	$34,530
% frosh need fully met	53
% ugrads need fully met	41
Average % of frosh need met	91
Average % of ugrad need met	87

WHITMAN COLLEGE

345 Boyer Avenue, Walla Walla, WA 99362 • Admissions: 509-527-5111 • Fax: 509-527-4967

STUDENTS SAY ". . ."

Academics

If learning can be both rigorous and laid-back at the same time, it happens at Whitman College in Walla Walla, WA. The "challenging" academics here are coupled with a "relaxed attitude" in order to give students "the best education possible without sacrificing all the fun one expects of college." Populated mainly by "intelligent, ambitious liberals with far-reaching goals," this somewhat idealistic school seeks to build critical-thinking skills through "an earnest discourse about 'life, the universe, and everything.'" So no one starts off with a blank slate, all first-year students are required to take a course referred to as "Encounters," which is a two-semester introduction to the liberal arts and the academic construction of knowledge. Distribution requirements ensure that all students get a breadth of courses, and a lack of TAs ensures that they get all the attention they need. Although there's always a dud or two in the mix, professors are "genuinely brilliant and interesting people" and "love to spend time with students outside of class," whether it be for academic help or just conversation. "It is not uncommon to have potlucks, classes, or movie night over at your professor's house with your class," says one student.

On the administrative side of things, bureaucracy and red tape are kept to a minimum in this chill environment through "effortless use of the 'system'" and the administration gets raves all around for its devotion to "maintaining quality student life," which is something of a rarity. "I have never heard of *any* college being as supportive as this place has been to me in just the past two years," says a student. As one can imagine, all these things come together to form a student body that's "happy, well-balanced, and well-cared-for."

Campus Life

Most people stay on campus for their fun, "especially first-years," and throughout this "bubble" the "sense of closeness and comradeship is very evident through attendance at student-run concerts, art shows, etc." Everything is within ten minutes' walking distance. Academics take precedence for almost everyone, but "most students find time to party on the weekends," due to a "lenient and fair" alcohol policy. Thanks to the campus activities board, "there's almost always something fun going on, whether or not a person chooses to drink," such as Drive-In Movie Night and Casino Night. With "four beautiful seasons," outdoor activities are also very popular, thanks to "a great gear rental program that gets people outside hiking, biking, kayaking, and rock-climbing," and "Frisbees are everywhere when it's warm." In fact, there's so much going on "if someone says they are bored, students laugh and wish they could relate."

Student Body

It's a sociable bunch at Whitman, where most students "are interested in trying new things and meeting new people" and "everyone seems to have a weird interest or talent or passion." The quirky Whitties "usually have a strong opinion about *something*," and one freshman refers to her classmates as "cool nerds." Diversity has risen steadily over the past several years, as the school has made an effort to recruit beyond the typical "mid- to upper-class and white" contingent. Everyone here is pretty outdoorsy and environmentally aware ("to the point where you almost feel guilty for printing an assignment"), and a significant number of students have won fellowships and scholarships such as the Fulbright, Watson, Truman, and Udall.

WHITMAN COLLEGE

Financial Aid: 509-527-5178 • E-Mail: admission@whitman.edu • Website: www.whitman.edu

THE PRINCETON REVIEW SAYS

Admissions

The school reports that its standardized testing policy for use in admission for Fall 2024 is Test Optional. The 2024 testing policy will be permanent. The Princeton Review suggests that interested applicants consult with the school for the most up-to-date standardized testing policies. *Very important factors considered include:* rigor of secondary school record, academic GPA, application essay. *Important factors considered include:* recommendation(s), extracurricular activities, talent/ability, character/personal qualities. *Other factors considered include:* class rank, standardized test scores, interview, first generation, alumni/ae relation, geographical residence, state residency, religious affiliation/commitment, racial/ethnic status, volunteer work, work experience, level of applicant's interest. High school diploma is required and GED is accepted. *Academic units recommended:* 4 English, 4 math, 3 science, 3 science labs, 2 foreign language, 2 social studies, 2 history, 1 visual/performing arts.

Financial Aid

Students should submit: CSS/Financial Aid Profile; FAFSA; Noncustodial Profile. Priority filing deadline is 11/15. The Princeton Review suggests that all financial aid forms be submitted as soon as possible (see page 5 for a note on the FAFSA). *Need-based scholarships/grants offered:* College/university scholarship or grant aid from institutional funds; Federal Pell; Private scholarships; SEOG; State scholarships/grants. *Loan aid offered:* Direct PLUS loans; Direct Subsidized Loans; Direct Unsubsidized Loans. Admitted students will be notified of awards on or about 3/1. Federal Work-Study Program available. Institutional employment available.

The Inside Word

Whitman's admissions committee emphasizes essays and extracurriculars more than standardized test scores, which are optional here. The college cares much more about who you are and what you have to offer if you enroll than it does about what your numbers will do for the freshman academic profile. Whitman is a mega-sleeper. Educators all over the country know it as an excellent institution, and the college's alums support it at one of the highest rates of giving at any college in the nation. Students seeking a top-quality liberal arts college owe it to themselves to take a look.

THE SCHOOL SAYS "..."

From the Admissions Office

"Whitman College offers a rigorous but collaborative academic environment, a down-to-earth Northwest culture, and a vibrant campus life. Whitman is also distinguished by the following:

- Capstone written and oral assessments in one's major field of study
- Numerous winners of Fulbright, Watson, Goldwater, National Science Foundation, Rhodes, Truman, Beinecke, and Udall fellowships and scholarships
- A Student Engagement Center which oversees internship and community service opportunities as well as graduate school and employment planning
- Science departments that have been recognized by the National Science Foundation as among the top fifty colleges per capita producing graduates who earn PhD's in science and engineering
- Eighty-eight off-campus study opportunities
- State of the art facilities including a library, computer labs and a health center open 24/7
- The Harper Joy Theatre, which hosts 8 productions a year open to all students
- An annual undergraduate research conference with over 200 students presenting their original research to the Whitman community
- Strong intramural, club and NCAA Division III sports programs
- A nationally renowned Outdoor Program
- Semester in the West, an experiential, on-the-road study of economic, cultural and environmental issues
- A 94 percent retention rate, 87 percent graduation rate, and a 70 percent graduate school rate."

SELECTIVITY

Admissions Rating	89
# of applicants	5,155
% of applicants accepted	69
% of acceptees attending	13
# offered a place on the wait list	39
% accepting a place on wait list	18
% admitted from wait list	0
# of early decision applicants	256
% accepted early decision	60

FIRST-YEAR PROFILE

Testing policy	Test Optional
Range SAT composite	1275–1415
Range SAT EBRW	645–725
Range SAT math	620–730
Range ACT composite	29–33
# submitting SAT scores	102
% submitting SAT scores	21
# submitting ACT scores	93
% submitting ACT scores	19
Average HS GPA	3.7
% frosh submitting high school GPA	81
% graduated top 10% of class	43
% graduated top 25% of class	75
% graduated top 50% of class	97

DEADLINES

Early decision	
Deadline	11/15
Notification	12/20
Other ED deadline	1/10
Other ED notification	2/1
Regular	
Priority	11/15
Deadline	1/15
Notification	3/1
Nonfall registration?	No

APPLICANTS OFTEN PREFER
Bowdoin College; Brown University; Carleton College; Macalester College; Middlebury College; Pomona College; Stanford University; University of California—Berkeley

APPLICANTS SOMETIMES PREFER
Colorado College; Reed College; University of California—Davis; University of Puget Sound; University of Washington; Western Washington University

FINANCIAL FACTS

Financial Aid Rating	85
Annual tuition	$55,560
Room and board	$13,800
Required fees	$422
Books and supplies	$1,400
Average frosh need-based scholarship	$43,745
Average UG need-based scholarship	$43,599
% needy frosh rec. need-based scholarship or grant aid	100
% needy UG rec. need-based scholarship or grant aid	100
% needy frosh rec. non-need-based scholarship or grant aid	8
% needy UG rec. non-need-based scholarship or grant aid	8
% needy frosh rec. need-based self-help aid	100
% needy UG rec. need-based self-help aid	100
% frosh rec. any financial aid	97
% UG rec. any financial aid	92
% UG borrow to pay for school	40
Average cumulative indebtedness	$19,204
% frosh need fully met	37
% ugrads need fully met	38
Average % of frosh need met	89
Average % of ugrad need met	88

WHITTIER COLLEGE

13406 Philadelphia Street, Whittier, CA 90608-0634 • Admissions: 562-907-4200 • Fax: 562-907-4870

STUDENTS SAY "..."

Academics

This tiny pearl of a liberal arts school is home to around 1,600 undergrads and focuses on an interdisciplinary education for all. Considering the small population, Whittier offers a relatively good breadth in classes and "is a great school for those who are trying to figure out what they want to do or those who want to create their own major." One-on-one interaction is quite prevalent among teachers and students, and everyone here is "passionate about the subject that they teach." It should be unsurprising that a school whose mascot is Johnny Poet provides "a nuanced literary foundation" for all students.

The faculty brings real-world and work experience to their various courses: "they're not just lifelong academics; most of them have had successful professional careers outside of teaching" and they "really make [Whittier] worthwhile." These professors are "engaged, love what they do," and "truly care about the success of their students, both academically and personally." Discussions are highly encouraged and interesting debates fostered, and assigned papers "always force you to stretch your knowledge." Teachers sometimes challenge the class's knowledge by "presenting a topic that can have pros and cons and by asking to prove where the idea came from." Classes are small, so professors "know your strengths and weaknesses and try their best to help you out."

Campus Life

The campus is small, so "it's easy to make friends" and there are typically "lots of events (academic or recreational) to go to." Different clubs run the gamut from Anime Club to Fun Night Club to a larping group, but marauders beware: "RAs are required to put on events such as Assassins." "There was once a Beowulf reading at night where you got a free dinner in addition," says a student. Whittier's version of Greek life comes in the form of the school's 11 "societies," and a majority of students have some form of involvement in a society or a sport. The school's size naturally leaves enough time to for extracurriculars and outside interests, as "it is difficult not to get involved when everyone is."

Whitter is relatively close to LA and the beach, so the weather is "mostly very nice" and students often "lounge around outside under trees and on the grass to do homework and socialize," "play Frisbee, walk on slack lines, and play soccer for fun in the courtyards." The pool facility is brand new and many "hang out on the decks to tan and cool off in the heat," and there are hills behind the campus that are good for hiking or running. There "is always something going on on-campus and that makes students even more involved."

Student Body

This is a "diverse community" that includes a sizable number of non-Californians, and most people are "very friendly, respectful of others' different identities, and comfortable with people of different backgrounds." There is "a good meshing" of all the students regardless of what their involvements are, and a real "community-based feeling" abounds. Whittier sees a higher transfer rate than many similar schools, so "it is very easy to know at least ten or more students who transfer after a year or two." The majority of people here are involved in some form of sport, but are not looking to go beyond the collegiate or intramural level.

WHITTIER COLLEGE

Financial Aid: 562-907-4285 • E-Mail: admissions@whittier.edu • Website: www.whittier.edu

THE PRINCETON REVIEW SAYS

Admissions

The school reports that its standardized testing policy for use in admission for Fall 2024 is Test Optional. It is unknown at this time if the 2024 testing policy will be permanent. The Princeton Review suggests that interested applicants consult with the school for the most up-to-date standardized testing policies. *Very important factors considered include:* rigor of secondary school record, academic GPA, application essay, recommendation(s), character/personal qualities. *Important factors considered include:* interview, extracurricular activities, talent/ability, volunteer work. *Other factors considered include:* class rank, standardized test scores, first generation, alumni/ae relation, geographical residence, state residency, racial/ethnic status, work experience. High school diploma is required and GED is accepted. *Academic units required:* 3 English, 2 math, 1 science, 1 science lab, 2 foreign language, 1 social studies. *Academic units recommended:* 4 English, 3 math, 2 science, 3 foreign language, 2 social studies.

Financial Aid

Students should submit: FAFSA. Priority filing deadline is 3/1. The Princeton Review suggests that all financial aid forms be submitted as soon as possible (see page 5 for a note on the FAFSA). *Need-based scholarships/grants offered:* College/university scholarship or grant aid from institutional funds; Federal Pell; Private scholarships; SEOG; State scholarships/grants. *Loan aid offered:* Direct PLUS loans; Direct Subsidized Loans; Direct Unsubsidized Loans; College/university loans from institutional funds. Admitted students will be notified of awards on a rolling basis beginning 2/15. Federal Work-Study Program available.

The Inside Word

Whittier is looking for well-rounded students, and so activities and recommendations are just as important as scores and grades—the admissions office hates to focus just on numbers. In fact, test scores are optional for students with a GPA of 3.0 or higher. Though 65 percent of students hail from California, no preference is given to state of origin. Through the Whittier Scholars program, students may construct a personalized major that fits academic and career goals.

THE SCHOOL SAYS "..."

From the Admissions Office

"Faculty and students at Whittier share a love of learning and delight in the life of the mind. They join in understanding the value of the intellectual quest, the use of reason, and a respect for values. They seek knowledge of their own culture and the informed appreciation of other traditions, and they explore the interrelatedness of knowledge and the connections among disciplines. An extraordinary community emerges from teachers and students representing a variety of academic pursuits, individuals who have come together at Whittier in the belief that study within the liberal arts forms the best foundation for rewarding endeavor throughout a lifetime.

"Whittier College is a vibrant, residential, four-year liberal arts institution where intellectual inquiry and experiential learning are fostered in a community that promotes respect for diversity of thought and culture. A Whittier College education produces enthusiastic, independent thinkers who flourish in graduate studies, the evolving global workplace, and life."

SELECTIVITY

Admissions Rating	85
# of applicants	3,014
% of applicants accepted	75
% of acceptees attending	11

FIRST-YEAR PROFILE

Testing policy	Test Optional
Range SAT EBRW	550–650
Range SAT math	590–690
Range ACT composite	24–30
# submitting SAT scores	22
% submitting SAT scores	8
# submitting ACT scores	13
% submitting ACT scores	5

DEADLINES

Early action	
Deadline	11/15
Notification	12/15
Regular	
Priority	2/1
Notification	Rolling, 12/15
Nonfall registration?	Yes

APPLICANTS OFTEN PREFER

Occidental College; University of Redlands

APPLICANTS SOMETIMES PREFER

Loyola Marymount University; Pitzer College

APPLICANTS RARELY PREFER

Chapman University; Claremont McKenna College

FINANCIAL FACTS

Financial Aid Rating	83
Annual tuition	$48,924
Room and board	$15,272
Required fees	$590
Books and supplies	$1,000
Average frosh need-based scholarship	$38,039
Average UG need-based scholarship	$36,009
% needy frosh rec. need-based scholarship or grant aid	86
% needy UG rec. need-based scholarship or grant aid	89
% needy frosh rec. non-need-based scholarship or grant aid	14
% needy UG rec. non-need-based scholarship or grant aid	11
% needy frosh rec. need-based self-help aid	81
% needy UG rec. need-based self-help aid	82
% frosh rec. any financial aid	92
% UG rec. any financial aid	89
% UG borrow to pay for school	77
Average cumulative indebtedness	$32,167
% frosh need fully met	19
% ugrads need fully met	15
Average % of frosh need met	79
Average % of ugrad need met	77

WILLIAM & MARY

P.O. Box 8795, Williamsburg, VA 23187-8795 • Admissions: 757-221-4000 • Fax: 757-221-1241

CAMPUS LIFE

Quality of Life Rating	91
Fire Safety Rating	92
Green Rating	72
Type of school	Public
Environment	Town

STUDENTS

Total undergrad enrollment	6,778
% male/female/another gender	42/58/NR
% from out of state	32
% frosh from public high school	71
% frosh live on campus	99
% ugrads live on campus	66
# of fraternities (% join)	18
# of sororities (% join)	14
% African American	6
% Asian	11
% White	60
% Hispanic	9
% Native American	<1
% Pacific Islander	<1
% Two or more races	7
% Race and/or ethnicity unknown	3
% international	4
# of countries represented	39

SURVEY SAYS . . .

Students are happy
Lab facilities are great
Great library
Career services are great
Internships are widely available
No one cheats
Students are friendly
Diverse student types interact on campus
Students involved in community service
Students environmentally aware
Easy to get around campus
Frats and sororities are popular
Theater is popular
Active student government
Active minority support groups
Active student-run political groups
Campus newspaper is popular

ACADEMICS

Academic Rating	87
% students returning for sophomore year	95
% students graduating within 4 years	86
% students graduating within 6 years	91
Calendar	Semester
Student/faculty ratio	13:1
Profs interesting rating	93
Profs accessible rating	94

Most classes have 10–19 students.
Most lab/discussion sessions have
10–19 students.

MOST POPULAR MAJORS
Biology/Biological Sciences, General; Psychology,
General; Political Science and Government,
General

STUDENTS SAY "..."

Academics

Chartered in 1693, William & Mary is one of the nation's first and most selective public universities, seeking to bring its extremely rigorous, interdisciplinary academics to curious, accomplished students who want to learn beyond a textbook. Hands-on research is a fundamental aspect of a William & Mary education for humanities, STEM, and computational field majors alike, and "the administration supports student involvement" at every level. That's not just a matter of studying abroad, which 60 percent of students take advantage of in over 50 countries, but also doing faculty-student research and having the opportunity for authorship and conference presentations. Students can "mix and match so many different aspects of majors to customize and find the perfect fit for yourself" and the end goal seems to be not just for picking up specific course material, but learning "how to study and learn more efficiently."

Professors are "happy to work with students" and welcome the chance for collaboration, which means they "tend to be very excited at the chance to get to know as many students as possible, even for the large lecture classes." They match the passion levels found in the classroom, and "love when students attend office hours to dive deeper into the subject." Teachers also "go above and beyond to find interesting guest speakers and create really interesting courses" that bring the material to life, such as in the way history professors use the surrounding landmarks "to provide students with a tangible experience of history."

Campus Life

There are "so many different clubs and activities," including pre-professional organizations, community service-oriented activities, and club sports, and the 6,800 undergraduates see these as opportunities to "spend so much of their time on making others' experiences better." The school hosts guest lectures each semester that "are tailored to a majority of students' interests and are done by experts in their fields," and since William & Mary is filled with "lots of people who take their studies seriously" but remain committed to their social lives, "people often gather in the library to do homework together and to talk as they do it." Regular old pleasures such as "meeting with friends for meals, working out, doing homework, baking, and reading for fun" help students relax, and "many people spend lots of times outdoors, on the trails or on the Sunken Garden." Nearby Colonial Williamsburg "is a fun place to explore and get lunch with your friends," and students also head to the beach just a short drive away.

Student Body

Hailing from all over the country and world, this group of unique individuals "has very diverse passions," but they're all "extremely motivated to perform and excel in their given field." This energy, of students who are all "excited about their involvements, however niche their interests may be," bubbles over into the social fabric of the school, where most everyone is "open to being friends with anyone," students and faculty included. "I had a professor take care of my fish over a break," shares one undergrad. As for the campus's size, it is "large enough that you can meet someone new each day, but small enough that you'll likely run into a friend every day on campus." In true Goldilocks fashion, this "really intimate and positive campus" is just right.

WILLIAM & MARY

Financial Aid: 757-221-2420 • E-Mail: admission@wm.edu • Website: www.wm.edu

THE PRINCETON REVIEW SAYS

Admissions

The school reports that its standardized testing policy for use in admission for Fall 2024 is Test Optional. The 2024 testing policy will be permanent. The Princeton Review suggests that interested applicants consult with the school for the most up-to-date standardized testing policies. *Very important factors considered include:* rigor of secondary school record, class rank, academic GPA, standardized test scores, application essay, recommendation(s), extracurricular activities, talent/ability, character/personal qualities, state residency, volunteer work, work experience. *Other factors considered include:* interview, first generation, alumni/ae relation, geographical residence, racial/ethnic status, level of applicant's interest. High school diploma or equivalent is not required. *Academic units recommended:* 4 English, 4 math, 4 science, 3 science labs, 4 foreign language, 4 social studies.

Financial Aid

Students should submit: CSS/Financial Aid Profile; FAFSA. Priority filing deadline is 3/1. The Princeton Review suggests that all financial aid forms be submitted as soon as possible (see page 5 for a note on the FAFSA). *Need-based scholarships/grants offered:* College/university scholarship or grant aid from institutional funds; Federal Pell; Private scholarships; SEOG; State scholarships/grants. *Loan aid offered:* Direct PLUS loans; Direct Subsidized Loans; Direct Unsubsidized Loans. Admitted students will be notified of awards on or about 3/15. Federal Work-Study Program available. Institutional employment available.

The Inside Word

The volume of applications at William & Mary is extremely high; thus, admission is ultracompetitive, and only very strong students should apply (more than three-quarters of freshmen are in the top 10% of their class). The large applicant pool necessitates a labor-intensive evaluation process; each application is read twice, and each admissions officer reads roughly 150 application folders per week during the peak review season. But this is one admissions committee that moves fast without sacrificing a thorough holistic review. There probably isn't a tougher public college admission committee in the country.

THE SCHOOL SAYS "..."

From the Admissions Office

"For more than 330 years, William & Mary has convened great hearts and minds who continue to write history as innovative thinkers and creators. Located in Williamsburg, Virginia, W&M brings together the award-winning faculty and global opportunities of a larger research university with the close-knit and personalized education of a liberal arts and sciences institution. As a W&M student, you'll learn to apply the theory you study in class to advance the knowledge that can help society tackle complex issues and challenges.

"Our mission at William & Mary is to help every student fulfill their greatest academic potential. We offer a 13:1 student-to-faculty ratio and over 115 majors and minors with more than a third in STEM and computational-related fields. With more than 450 campus clubs and organizations and a Division I athletics program, W&M students have no shortage of opportunities to explore their passions and have fun.

"Our graduates include former U.S. presidents, executives, and innovators at Hulu, Netflix, and Apple, Super Bowl and World Cup-winning head coaches, Emmy award-winning actors, leaders of the FBI and CIA, NASA's chief scientists, and groundbreaking producers in gaming.

"In short, William & Mary provides a top-rated educational experience while being consistently recognized as one of the best values in the nation. If you are an academically strong, involved student looking for a challenge in a globally minded community, W&M may well be the place for you. Come learn for yourself what makes W&M so powerfully unique."

SELECTIVITY

Admissions Rating	95
# of applicants	18,087
% of applicants accepted	33
% of acceptees attending	27
# offered a place on the wait list	4,004
% accepting a place on wait list	51
% admitted from wait list	0
# of early decision applicants	1,247
% accepted early decision	50

FIRST-YEAR PROFILE

Testing policy	Test Optional
Range SAT composite	1375–1520
Range SAT EBRW	695–750
Range SAT math	680–770
Range ACT composite	32–34
# submitting SAT scores	860
% submitting SAT scores	52
# submitting ACT scores	300
% submitting ACT scores	18
Average HS GPA	4.3
% frosh submitting high school GPA	87
% graduated top 10% of class	77
% graduated top 25% of class	95
% graduated top 50% of class	99

DEADLINES

Early decision	
Deadline	11/1
Notification	12/15
Other ED deadline	1/1
Other ED notification	2/1
Regular	
Deadline	1/1
Notification	4/1
Nonfall registration?	No

APPLICANTS ALSO LOOK AT

Boston College; Cornell University; Duke University; Georgetown University; Princeton University; University of North Carolina—Chapel Hill; University of Richmond; University of Virginia; Vanderbilt University; Virginia Tech

FINANCIAL FACTS

Financial Aid Rating	82
Annual in-state tuition	$17,434
Annual out-of-state tuition	$40,089
Room and board	$13,534
Required fees	$6,536
Books and supplies	$1,080
Average frosh need-based scholarship	$20,857
Average UG need-based scholarship	$20,449
% needy frosh rec. need-based scholarship or grant aid	87
% needy UG rec. need-based scholarship or grant aid	90
% needy frosh rec. non-need-based scholarship or grant aid	39
% needy UG rec. non-need-based scholarship or grant aid	37
% needy frosh rec. need-based self-help aid	45
% needy UG rec. need-based self-help aid	50
% frosh rec. any financial aid	73
% UG rec. any financial aid	52
% UG borrow to pay for school	33
Average cumulative indebtedness	$27,866
% frosh need fully met	29
% ugrads need fully met	27
Average % of frosh need met	82
Average % of ugrad need met	82

WILLIAM JEWELL COLLEGE

500 College Hill, Liberty, MO 64068 • Admissions: 816-415-7511 • Fax: 816-415-5040

CAMPUS LIFE
Quality of Life Rating	83
Fire Safety Rating	88
Green Rating	60*
Type of school	Private
Affiliation	No Affiliation
Environment	Town

STUDENTS
Total undergrad enrollment	824
% male/female/another gender	52/49/0
% from out of state	41
% frosh from public high school	90
% frosh live on campus	99
% ugrads live on campus	89
# of fraternities (% join)	3 (37)
# of sororities (% join)	3 (48)
% African American	8
% Asian	2
% White	67
% Hispanic	11
% Native American	<1
% Pacific Islander	<1
% Two or more races	6
% Race and/or ethnicity unknown	2
% international	3
# of countries represented	20

SURVEY SAYS . . .
Students are happy
Internships are widely available
Class discussions encouraged
Students are friendly
Students are very religious
Students get along with local community

ACADEMICS
Academic Rating	89
% students returning for sophomore year	74
% students graduating within 4 years	59
% students graduating within 6 years	61
Calendar	Semester
Student/faculty ratio	10:1
Profs interesting rating	93
Profs accessible rating	96

Most classes have 2–9 students.
Most lab/discussion sessions have
fewer than 10 students.

MOST POPULAR MAJORS
Biology/Biological Sciences, General; Registered
Nursing/Registered Nurse; Business
Administration and Management, General

STUDENTS SAY "..."

Academics

The minute students step onto campus at William Jewell, they are welcomed into an "amazing community" replete with "top-notch academics." As one senior gushes, "Everyone on campus makes you feel at home and the faculty and staff are some of the most genuine people you will ever meet." Moreover, as a small liberal arts college, William Jewell "provides a superb education" that many undergrads here feel is "unmatched in the Midwest." After all, the college endeavors to transform undergrads into "critical thinkers" who are bound to achieve "success and find [their] passion." This is no doubt due in large part to the fact that "William Jewell provides a well-rounded education for its students and challenges them to step outside of their own perspectives." Though the college has many fantastic majors from which to choose, undergrads are especially quick to highlight "the strong science and pre-med program" along with the "well established" non-profit program. The nursing program also has a "great reputation." On the whole, undergrads speak very highly of their "amazingly dedicated" professors. Impressively, teachers here tend to be "great lecturers…who [also] excel in discussion formatted classes." Another senior adds, "The professors at William Jewell are very personable and willing to go the extra step to build a connection with each and every student. They are always finding the best way to reach out to their students and provide each student with the best chance of success." Overall, William Jewell offers a "rigorous set of programs that push you to the limits of your ability."

Campus Life

Students here agree that "life at Jewell is a busy one." As one knowledgeable senior happily shares, "There are always campus activities going on whether that be sporting events or resident hall gatherings or even the occasional fraternity/sorority party." A junior specifies, "Student organizations often sponsor events like CU-At-the-Movies, Skate Night, [and] Bowling Night where we get discounted prices to go out and have fun. Additionally, "a number of students…are active in Greek life." Fortunately, we're assured that there's no pressure to join, and independent students still feel included. Undergrads here also love to take advantage of the "Harriman-Jewell series, [which] offers free tickets to students, and brings world-class arts and culture such as pianists (Emanuel Ax) and dance (Mark Morris Dance Group) to Kansas City." Speaking of KC, William Jewell is only a "twenty-minute drive away" from the heart of the city. As another senior brags, "Once downtown, you can do just about anything. There is the Power & Light District with the T-Mobile Center, the Kaufman Center and just a few miles south you get into Westport where you can find numerous college/young adult students at any given time."

Student Body

Undergrads at William Jewell are a "laid back but focused" lot. Indeed, students are quick to define their peers as "driven" and "intelligent" people who are "committed to their education and community." Of course, some see the typical Jewell student as "a white, Protestant, upper-middle class, girl who loves Pinterest." Although a junior cautions that, "the population isn't as diverse as other schools I have been to," he also counters that, "everyone is pretty open and accepting of just about anyone." Fortunately, many find that "students fit in very easily." Overall, "no one really is ever left out of anything as long as they're putting the effort in to have friends and be a part of an organization as well as the Jewell community as a whole." Another junior adds that, "While most [undergrads] attend college straight out of high school, there is a growing number of non-traditional students especially in the nursing program." Finally, as one satisfied political science student succinctly states, "We have a high retention rate, which tells me that students fit in well."

WILLIAM JEWELL COLLEGE

Financial Aid: 816-415-5975 • E-Mail: admission@william.jewell.edu • Website: www.jewell.edu

THE PRINCETON REVIEW SAYS

Admissions

The school reports that its standardized testing policy for use in admission for Fall 2024 is Test Optional. The 2024 testing policy will be permanent. The Princeton Review suggests that interested applicants consult with the school for the most up-to-date standardized testing policies. *Very important factors considered include:* rigor of secondary school record, academic GPA. *Important factors considered include:* class rank, recommendation(s), extracurricular activities, talent/ability, character/personal qualities, level of applicant's interest. *Other factors considered include:* standardized test scores, application essay, interview, first generation, alumni/ae relation, volunteer work, work experience. High school diploma is required and GED is accepted. *Academic units required:* 4 English, 3 math, 3 science, 1 science lab, 2 foreign language, 3 social studies. *Academic units recommended:* 4 math, 3 foreign language, 2 academic electives.

Financial Aid

Students should submit: FAFSA. Priority filing deadline is 2/1. The Princeton Review suggests that all financial aid forms be submitted as soon as possible (see page 5 for a note on the FAFSA). *Need-based scholarships/grants offered:* College/university scholarship or grant aid from institutional funds; Federal Pell; Private scholarships; SEOG; State scholarships/grants; United Negro College Fund. *Loan aid offered:* Direct PLUS loans; Direct Subsidized Loans; Direct Unsubsidized Loans; Federal Nursing Loans. Admitted students will be notified of awards on a rolling basis beginning 11/1. Federal Work-Study Program available. Institutional employment available.

The Inside Word

Competition for admission is strong and candidates must demonstrate success with a rigorous course load. Of course, similar to most small colleges, Jewell is also looking for applicants who will complement the campus. Therefore, you can be assured that personal statements and recommendations will be closely assessed.

THE SCHOOL SAYS "..."

From the Admissions Office

"William Jewell College is a four-year, private liberal arts college in Liberty, Missouri. Jewell's commitment to cultivating critical thinkers in pursuit of meaningful lives is woven into the living and learning community and is the basis of the Critical Thought and Inquiry Core Curriculum. Our 30-plus majors include nursing, civil engineering, data science, business, music, psychological science and nonprofit leadership, with 98.8% of students employed or in graduate school within six months of graduation. Jewell's one to ten faculty-student ratio allows a personalized experience through numerous distinctive programs. The Oxbridge Honors Program, supported by the Hall Family Foundation, combines British tutorial methods of instruction with a year of study in Oxford, England. Students have traveled to 59 countries with their Journey Grants, a $2,000 minimum grant available for academic enrichment, leadership and service. Our Pryor Leadership Program is open to students from all disciplines, featuring an Outward Bound experience in the Florida Everglades and culminating in a class legacy project. Jewell's national award-winning Concert Choir has produced two CDs, and members go on a triennial concert tour in England and Scotland. A national champion debate team, the Harriman-Jewell premier performing arts series and the Idea Exchange Innovation Lab also demonstrate the depth of opportunities available to students."

SELECTIVITY

Admissions Rating	91
# of applicants	1,671
% of applicants accepted	41
% of acceptees attending	36

FIRST-YEAR PROFILE

Testing policy	Test Optional
Range SAT composite	1090–1290
Range SAT EBRW	560–650
Range SAT math	530–620
Range ACT composite	21–27
% submitting SAT scores	4
% submitting ACT scores	70
Average HS GPA	3.6
% frosh submitting high school GPA	99
% graduated top 10% of class	24
% graduated top 25% of class	53
% graduated top 50% of class	91

DEADLINES

Regular	
Notification	Rolling, 9/15
Nonfall registration?	Yes

APPLICANTS OFTEN PREFER

University of Missouri; University of Missouri--Kansas City

APPLICANTS SOMETIMES PREFER

Truman State University; University of Kansas

APPLICANTS RARELY PREFER

Missouri State University; Rockhurst University

FINANCIAL FACTS

Financial Aid Rating	82
Annual tuition	$18,360
Room and board	$10,130
Required fees	$1,250
Books and supplies	$800
Average frosh need-based scholarship	$30,230
Average UG need-based scholarship	$27,554
% needy frosh rec. need-based scholarship or grant aid	100
% needy UG rec. need-based scholarship or grant aid	92
% needy frosh rec. non-need-based scholarship or grant aid	22
% needy UG rec. non-need-based scholarship or grant aid	20
% needy frosh rec. need-based self-help aid	68
% needy UG rec. need-based self-help aid	69
% frosh need fully met	22
% ugrads need fully met	30
Average % of frosh need met	88
Average % of ugrad need met	62

WILLIAMS COLLEGE

995 Main St., Williamstown, MA 01267 • Admissions: 413-597-3131 • Fax: 413-597-4052

CAMPUS LIFE

Quality of Life Rating	**92**
Fire Safety Rating	**60***
Green Rating	**99**
Type of school	Private
Affiliation	No Affiliation
Environment	Village

STUDENTS

Total undergrad enrollment	2,129
% male/female/another gender	47/52/2
% from out of state	84
% frosh from public high school	50
% frosh live on campus	100
% ugrads live on campus	93
# of fraternities	0
# of sororities	0
% African American	5
% Asian	14
% White	48
% Hispanic	13
% Native American	0
% Pacific Islander	<1
% Two or more races	8
% Race and/or ethnicity unknown	4
% international	9
# of countries represented	59

SURVEY SAYS . . .

Students always studying
Students are happy
Classroom facilities are great
Lab facilities are great
Great library
Internships are widely available
Great financial aid
No one cheats
Students aren't religious
Students environmentally aware
Dorms are like palaces
Easy to get around campus
Everyone loves the Ephs
Theater is popular
Campus newspaper is popular
Alumni active on campus
Active minority support groups
Students are friendly

ACADEMICS

Academic Rating	**99**
% students returning for sophomore year	97
% students graduating within 4 years	88
% students graduating within 6 years	95
Calendar	4/1/4
Student/faculty ratio	7:1
Profs interesting rating	95
Profs accessible rating	99

Most classes have fewer than 10 students.
Most lab/discussion sessions have
10–19 students.

MOST POPULAR MAJORS

Biology/Biological Sciences, General; Mathematics, General; Econometrics and Quantitative Economics

STUDENTS SAY "..."

Academics

Tucked away in western Massachusetts, Williams College is a "top-notch" liberal arts college that is "committed to making all students' dreams a reality." Indeed, this highly-selective institution is an ideal place for people "who truly love to learn and explore new academic passions." And it offers the "perfect combination of...liberal arts and research opportunities; neither one has to be sacrificed here." Moreover, undergrads report that "the courses offered are diverse and interesting, while the divisional requirements mean that classes are more open to non-majors than at other schools." Of course, no matter what classes they take, students can rest assured that they'll be taught "how to think critically." Further, Williams' "small" size, with an enrollment of 2,121, also allows for "individualized attention." Undergrads also proudly proclaim that their professors are "the best in the nation, if not the world." Not only is each instructor "an expert in his or her field" but the vast majority have proven themselves to be "gifted teacher[s] as well." Even better, "they all make sure to be readily accessible and try to get to know every single student, even in a larger lecture class." And while they maintain "high expectations," courses are often "highly rewarding." What more could you hope for?

Campus Life

Undergrads at Williams are "always busy, always a little bit stressed." This comes as no surprise given that there are so many activities hosted on campus. To begin with, "the college makes sure to offer a ton of lectures, performances, art exhibits, movie screenings, fun activities, etc. so that people feel fulfilled staying on campus." There are also numerous "student-led events." As one content undergrad explains, "On Wednesday nights, my friends and I [go] to Stressbusters where you get free treats and the student-run coffee bar has an open tab." Additionally, Williams undergrads are always game for sporting events. After all, "35 percent of the school are varsity athletes [and] almost everyone else either is on a club sport, plays intramural, or goes to the gym regularly." There are also plenty of "opportunities to explore the outdoors [including] hiking, skiing, running, biking, [and] swimming." And once the weekend hits, you can find "lots of different kinds of parties... all-campus parties that the college puts on, big parties sponsored by different clubs, smaller parties, and people just hanging out in dorms." Lastly, though Williamstown is pretty "rural" and "remote," there are "amazing art offerings in the area at the Clark Art Institute, Massachusetts Museum of Contemporary Art, and the Williams College Museum of Art." Overall, you're bound to find something that will pique your interest and keep you entertained at Williams.

Student Body

The student body at Williams College is comprised of "driven," "quirky," and "mostly type-A" individuals. Across the board, undergrads here stress that their peers are incredibly "intelligent." As one impressed student shares, "Williams is great because you never feel like the smartest one in the room, and you genuinely feel as though your classmates have valuable input in all scenarios." In addition, Williams students are "dedicated to pursuing their passions, which cover a diverse spectrum and often fall outside of what is typical." Indeed, "it's not unusual to find a football player who is deeply interested in experimental theatre or a computer science major who is also one of the friendliest people you know." While many Williams students categorize each other as "white, athlet[ic and] preppy," lots of undergrads assure us that "so many people fall outside of [these boxes]" as well. However, some do caution that "the average student is very socially and politically liberal, and conservative ideas (particularly socially conservative ideas) aren't welcome on campus." Nevertheless, most agree that the "sense of community is overwhelmingly strong and welcoming." After all, the students here "want to be surrounded by each other and learn from each other—otherwise they wouldn't have chosen to go to a school together in the middle of nowhere!"

WILLIAMS COLLEGE

Financial Aid: 413-597-4181 • E-Mail: admission@williams.edu • Website: www.williams.edu

THE PRINCETON REVIEW SAYS

Admissions

All students applying for entry through the fall of 2025 may choose whether to submit SAT/ACT exam results. This policy applies to all applicants—first-year and transfer, domestic and international. *Very important factors considered include:* rigor of secondary school record, class rank, academic GPA, recommendation(s), character/personal qualities. *Important factors considered include:* application essay, extracurricular activities, talent/ability, first generation, racial/ethnic status, volunteer work, work experience. *Other factors considered include:* standardized test scores, alumni/ae relation, geographical residence, religious affiliation/commitment. High school diploma or equivalent is not required. *Academic units recommended:* 4 English, 4 math, 4 science, 3 science labs, 4 foreign language, 4 social studies.

Financial Aid

Students should submit: CSS/Financial Aid Profile; FAFSA; Noncustodial Profile. The Princeton Review suggests that all financial aid forms be submitted as soon as possible (see page 5 for a note on the FAFSA). *Need-based scholarships/grants offered:* College/university scholarship or grant aid from institutional funds; Federal Pell; SEOG; State scholarships/grants. *Loan aid offered:* Direct PLUS loans; Direct Subsidized Loans; Direct Unsubsidized Loans. Admitted students will be notified of awards on or about 4/1. Federal Work-Study Program available. Institutional employment available.

The Inside Word

Williams College is incredibly selective and earning a coveted acceptance letter will not be easy. Certainly, applicants will need to have earned top grades in a rigorous high school curriculum; advanced placement, honors and/or IB courses are a must. Beyond academic accolades, admissions officers are looking for students who demonstrate themselves to be creative thinkers and individuals who will bring diverse perspectives to campus life. To that end, personal statements, extracurricular involvement, and letters of recommendation also hold substantial weight.

THE SCHOOL SAYS "..."

From the Admissions Office

"In addition to all the things that make liberal arts colleges the gold standard—small classes, attentive faculty, close-knit community—Williams offers unique opportunities like the renowned tutorial program, where students (in pairs) research and defend ideas and engage in weekly discussion with a professor. Half of Williams' students study abroad, with 26 juniors spending a year at Oxford annually. Four weeks of Winter Study each January provide time for individualized projects, research, and novel fields of study. The college receives several million dollars annually for undergraduate science research and is a leader in preparing students for graduate study. Students compete on 34 Division III athletic teams, perform in 25 musical groups, stage 10 theatrical productions, and volunteer in 350 local organizations. The local community offers three distinguished art museums, the Williams College Museum of Art, the Clark Art Institute, the Massachusetts Museum of Contemporary Art, and 2,200 forest acres—complete with a treetop canopy walkway—for environmental research and recreation.

"Students applying for entry through Fall 2025 may choose whether to submit SAT or ACT results. Regardless, all applications will continue to be reviewed in a student-centered, holistic admission process. As announced in Spring 2022, Williams is the first college in the nation to eliminate loans, as well as required campus and summer jobs from its financial aid packages. The components will be replaced with equivalent grant funds, dollar for dollar. Additionally, Williams guarantees free textbooks, health insurance, summer storage, optional funding for travel courses and internships, and more, for aid recipients."

SELECTIVITY

Admissions Rating	98
# of applicants	15,321
% of applicants accepted	8
% of acceptees attending	44
# offered a place on the wait list	2,241
% accepting a place on wait list	38
% admitted from wait list	0
# of early decision applicants	814
% accepted early decision	31

FIRST-YEAR PROFILE

Testing policy	Test Optional
Range SAT composite	1490–1550
Range SAT EBRW	730–780
Range SAT math	750–790
Range ACT composite	34–35
# submitting SAT scores	235
% submitting SAT scores	41
# submitting ACT scores	120
% submitting ACT scores	21
% frosh submitting high school GPA	73
% graduated top 10% of class	86
% graduated top 25% of class	100
% graduated top 50% of class	100

DEADLINES

Early decision	
Deadline	11/15
Notification	12/15
Regular	
Deadline	1/9
Notification	4/1
Nonfall registration?	No

APPLICANTS OFTEN PREFER
Brown University; Columbia University; Harvard College; Princeton University; Stanford University; Yale University

APPLICANTS SOMETIMES PREFER
Cornell University; Dartmouth College; Duke University; Northwestern University; The University of Chicago; University of Pennsylvania

FINANCIAL FACTS

Financial Aid Rating	99
Annual tuition	$61,450
Room and board	$15,530
Required fees	$320
Books and supplies	$1,000
Average frosh need-based scholarship	$65,134
Average UG need-based scholarship	$66,083
% needy frosh rec. need-based scholarship or grant aid	100
% needy UG rec. need-based scholarship or grant aid	100
% needy frosh rec. non-need-based scholarship or grant aid	0
% needy UG rec. non-need-based scholarship or grant aid	0
% needy frosh rec. need-based self-help aid	0
% needy UG rec. need-based self-help aid	0
% frosh rec. any financial aid	58
% UG rec. any financial aid	51
% UG borrow to pay for school	32
Average cumulative indebtedness	$13,341
% frosh need fully met	100
% ugrads need fully met	100
Average % of frosh need met	100
Average % of ugrad need met	100

WITTENBERG UNIVERSITY

P.O. Box 720, Springfield, OH 45501 • Admissions: 937-327-6321 • Fax: 937-327-6379

STUDENTS SAY "..."

Academics

Located in Springfield, Ohio, Wittenberg combines a "small school atmosphere" with "a wide horizon of learning opportunities." The school offers "high academic standards and a dedication to research" that makes "an environment where students can excel in the classroom and out." This "friendly, athletic campus" offers a close-knit community where professors and students build professional and personal relationships." The school's motto is "Having Light, We Pass It On To Others." This is taken seriously by the "extremely engaging" professors who are "committed to helping students both in and out of the classroom." The "fabulous" teachers at Wittenberg are "always accessible and willing to help" and really get to know students "on a personal level." "I feel like I am learning from my best friends," one happy student reports. An environmental science student agrees, saying, "I have become very close to a few of my professors and have really come to enjoy my classroom experience." Some students say that "communication with the student body" and "upper level administration" "is not always the best." Still, a communications major lavishes praise on the entire staff, "not only just teachers, but I would go as far to say even down to the maintenance and janitor crew." Part of the reason students love classes at Wittenberg is the small class sizes. This "means excellent attention paid to students." "The class sizes and student-teacher ratio makes it an ideal place to develop professional relationships," and this situation "really elevates the learning environment and makes classes far more interesting than large schools." The "open-minded and encouraging" faculty really pushes "students to build our own ideas and projects." All in all, "the people, the faculty and students are a very happy, connected, and welcoming community." This, combined with the "gorgeous campus" might explain the "high morale among the students." As a psychology major explains, "Wittenberg is a place where students can develop themselves as a whole person—academically, professionally, and socially."

Campus Life

Students are typically busy and even "often over-involved" at Wittenberg. Your average student might be "involved and overcommitted in at least two clubs and a sport or Greek life." "With over 100 student clubs and organizations, it is easy to find things to get involved in," one student explains. "Witt students generally know how to work hard and play hard" and "party every day." One student says that partying is so pervasive that "if you do not drink, then you have no chance of fitting in." "The typical student is one who drinks constantly, and rarely ever gets in trouble for it," since, students say, the University is lax on enforcing drug and alcohol rules. Still, there are plenty of other activities to do on campus from "just hang[ing] out and spend[ing] time with each other" to "Witt Wednesday" in which "comedians or musicians come to entertain." "What don't we do?" one student says. One novel part of campus life has to do with the crows. "Our crow-deterrent alarms, which are mounted on the roofs of every building, are triggered by students walking by," one student explains. "It's downright uncanny at night to hear crow death screams played from the rooftops as you walk back to your dorm." Students who love nature will enjoy "a reservoir to swim in, two playgrounds/parks, and three national parks for hiking."

Student Body

This "beautiful school" is filled with "friendly," "outgoing," and "quirky people." "It is hard to describe a typical student because we are very diverse, but with that diversity we all are able to get in," an environmental science student says. If you had to generalize, most students are "white, from Ohio, [and] middle class," but "Wittenberg has a wonderful variety of students." Students tend to be "fun personalities, engaged, curious and eager to learn, smart." "All types of students here are welcomed in with ease" and everyone can "find at least one friend group." One student elaborates that these groups "are like amoebas that are constantly shifting, made up of many different people." Overall Wittenberg is a "tight-knit community" where all you have to do to make a friend is "step out and say hello!"

WITTENBERG UNIVERSITY

Financial Aid: 937-327-7318 • E-Mail: admission@wittenberg.edu • Website: www.wittenberg.edu

THE PRINCETON REVIEW SAYS

Admissions

The school reports that its standardized testing policy for use in admission for Fall 2024 is Test Optional. The 2024 testing policy will be permanent. The Princeton Review suggests that interested applicants consult with the school for the most up-to-date standardized testing policies. *Very important factors considered include:* rigor of secondary school record, academic GPA. *Important factors considered include:* class rank, application essay, recommendation(s), extracurricular activities, talent/ability, character/personal qualities, volunteer work. *Other factors considered include:* standardized test scores, interview, first generation, alumni/ae relation, work experience, level of applicant's interest. High school diploma is required and GED is accepted. *Academic units required:* 4 English, 3 math, 3 science, 2 science labs, 2 foreign language, 2 history. *Academic units recommended:* 4 English, 4 math, 5 science, 2 science labs, 3 foreign language, 3 history.

Financial Aid

Students should submit: FAFSA. Priority filing deadline is 3/1. The Princeton Review suggests that all financial aid forms be submitted as soon as possible (see page 5 for a note on the FAFSA). *Need-based scholarships/grants offered:* College/university scholarship or grant aid from institutional funds; Federal Pell; Private scholarships; SEOG; State scholarships/grants; United Negro College Fund. *Loan aid offered:* Direct PLUS loans; Direct Subsidized Loans; Direct Unsubsidized Loans; College/university loans from institutional funds. Admitted students will be notified of awards on a rolling basis beginning 2/1. Federal Work-Study Program available. Institutional employment available.

The Inside Word

Wittenberg accepts both its own application and the Common Application, and the application fee is waived if you apply online. The university only requires a short personal statement instead of the traditional formal essay. Wittenberg has a fairly high acceptance rate, but students will still want to make sure all parts of their application are the best they can be.

THE SCHOOL SAYS "..."

From the Admissions Office

"At Wittenberg, you will experience an active and engaged learning environment, a setting where you can refine your definition of self yet gain exposure to the varied kinds of knowledge, people, views, activities, options, and ideas that add richness to our lives. Wittenberg is a university where students are able to thrive in a small campus environment with many opportunities for intellectual and personal growth in and out of the classroom. Campus life is as diverse as the interests of our students. Wittenberg attracts students from all over the United States and from many other countries. Historically, the university has been committed to geographical, educational, cultural, and religious diversity. With their varied backgrounds and interests, Wittenberg students have helped initiate many of the more than 125 student organizations that are active on campus. The students will be the first to tell you there's never a lack of things to do on or near the campus any day of the week, if you're willing to get involved.

"Wittenberg University is Test Optional. Freshman applicants can choose to submit either ACT (with or without writing component) or SAT scores."

SELECTIVITY

Admissions Rating	81
# of applicants	2,998
% of applicants accepted	94
% of acceptees attending	14
# of early decision applicants	39
% accepted early decision	97

FIRST-YEAR PROFILE

Testing policy	Test Optional
Range SAT composite	1000–1310
Range SAT EBRW	510–678
Range SAT math	510–638
Range ACT composite	20–27
# submitting SAT scores	45
% submitting SAT scores	11
# submitting ACT scores	165
% submitting ACT scores	41
Average HS GPA	3.6
% frosh submitting high school GPA	100
% graduated top 10% of class	11
% graduated top 25% of class	24
% graduated top 50% of class	88

DEADLINES

Early decision	
Deadline	11/1
Notification	12/1
Other ED deadline	12/1
Other ED notification	1/1
Early action	
Deadline	12/1
Notification	1/1
Nonfall registration?	Yes

APPLICANTS SOMETIMES PREFER

Capital University; Miami University; Ohio University—Athens; Ohio Wesleyan University; Otterbein College; The Ohio State University—Columbus; University of Cincinnati; University of Dayton; Wright State University; Xavier University (OH)

FINANCIAL FACTS

Financial Aid Rating	85
Annual tuition	$42,260
Room and board	$11,280
Required fees	$846
Books and supplies	$1,000
Average frosh need-based scholarship	$10,490
Average UG need-based scholarship	$10,170
% needy frosh rec. need-based scholarship or grant aid	80
% needy UG rec. need-based scholarship or grant aid	85
% needy frosh rec. non-need-based scholarship or grant aid	100
% needy UG rec. non-need-based scholarship or grant aid	100
% needy frosh rec. need-based self-help aid	76
% needy UG rec. need-based self-help aid	76
% frosh rec. any financial aid	83
% UG rec. any financial aid	76
% UG borrow to pay for school	97
Average cumulative indebtedness	$29,217
% frosh need fully met	28
% ugrads need fully met	29
Average % of frosh need met	87
Average % of ugrad need met	87

WOFFORD COLLEGE

429 North Church Street, Spartanburg, SC 29303-3663 • Admissions: 864-597-4100 • Fax: 864-597-4147

STUDENTS SAY "..."

Academics

With a "family atmosphere and close-knit community," Wofford College in Spartanburg, South Carolina, is a fantastic option for students seeking a "rigorous" liberal arts experience. It also helps that the "campus is beautiful" and "the facilities are clean and up to date." More impressively, undergrads here have the opportunity to "network with highly influential people" and participate in "an outstanding study abroad program." And thanks to Wofford's "small" size, students are truly able to receive "an individualized education and personal attention." While coursework is "challenging," undergrads are appreciative, noting that their college "specializes in preparing students for graduate or professional school." For the most part, they also give their professors high marks. After all, Wofford instructors tend to be "extremely passionate about their fields and are very well educated." And they "frequently hold review sessions and are always available by email if they are not in their offices." Best of all, "each person, whether in the dining hall or the classroom, is there for your success. Knowing that we have these amazing adults there for us no matter what is something that allows us to thrive and become the best personal versions of ourselves."

Campus Life

At Wofford College, dull moments are few and far between. Sure, students "work hard during the week," but they also manage to carve out time for some fun. For example, many undergrads "spend a lot of time at the gym, either working out, playing games, or participating in classes such as yoga or Afro beat." Students also "love to hang out at Burwell, our main cafeteria, and grab a bite to eat." Once the weekend hits, you will find lots of undergrads "playing sand volleyball and dancing at the Greek Village with their friends to the live bands." Indeed, the college maintains six fraternities, four sororities, two historically African-American fraternities, and a multicultural house at the Greek Village and much of the social life revolves around them. However, there's still plenty to enjoy if Greek life isn't your scene. After all, Wofford sponsors a number of great events like "trivia nights," "cultural events" and concerts. Further, outdoor enthusiasts will be thrilled to learn that there are "countless hiking trails near campus, including those at Glendale Shoals," where Wofford's Goodall Environmental Studies Center with its vineyard garden and amphitheater is located. Lastly, though some individuals complain that the city of Spartanburg doesn't offer much to do for fun, heading "off-campus" for activities like "bowling, shopping, or movies are common."

Student Body

Wofford undergrads are "kind," "friendly" and often embody "Southern hospitality." They tend to view their peers as "family" rather than simply fellow students. And while people certainly "have friend groups that they commonly hang out with, [there are] no strict cliques like in high school." Just as critical, Wofford students are "hardworking" and "driven" and they "all take pride in their academic success." Undergrads do acknowledge, however, that the college is "predominantly white." Though they also insist "diversity has increased." And a handful of individuals argue that Wofford yields "many international students from various countries as well as American students from all across the country from all financial backgrounds." Regardless of where they come from, undergrads say it is very "easy to connect with most other students" and that everyone is "respectful and kind toward one another." After all, it is "a very open school and everyone says 'Hi' because you've most likely had a class with them before." One student points out, "you may not know everyone's name, but everyone has some common ground...no one feels left out."

WOFFORD COLLEGE

Financial Aid: 864-597-4160 • E-Mail: admissions@wofford.edu • Website: www.wofford.edu

THE PRINCETON REVIEW SAYS

Admissions

The school reports that its standardized testing policy for use in admission for Fall 2024 is Test Optional. The 2024 testing policy will be permanent. The Princeton Review suggests that interested applicants consult with the school for the most up-to-date standardized testing policies. *Very important factors considered include:* rigor of secondary school record, academic GPA. *Important factors considered include:* class rank, application essay, extracurricular activities, talent/ability, character/personal qualities. *Other factors considered include:* standardized test scores, recommendation(s), interview, first generation, alumni/ae relation, geographical residence, state residency, religious affiliation/commitment, racial/ethnic status, volunteer work, work experience, level of applicant's interest. High school diploma is required and GED is accepted. *Academic units required:* 4 English, 4 math, 3 science, 3 science labs, 3 foreign language, 3 social studies. *Academic units recommended:* 4 English, 4 math, 3 science, 3 science labs, 3 foreign language, 3 social studies, 1 history, 1 computer science, 1 visual/performing arts, 1 academic elective.

Financial Aid

Students should submit: FAFSA. Priority filing deadline is 1/1. The Princeton Review suggests that all financial aid forms be submitted as soon as possible (see page 5 for a note on the FAFSA). *Need-based scholarships/grants offered:* College/university scholarship or grant aid from institutional funds; Federal Pell; Private scholarships; SEOG; State scholarships/grants. *Loan aid offered:* Direct PLUS loans; Direct Subsidized Loans; Direct Unsubsidized Loans. Admitted students will be notified of awards on or about 2/15. Federal Work-Study Program available. Institutional employment available.

The Inside Word

Wofford College aims to take a holistic approach to the admissions process. Therefore, students can expect all facets of their application will be closely scrutinized. Successful candidates typically have completed a rigorous high school curriculum, replete with a few honors or AP courses. They also present thoughtful personal statements and are active in their school and community. It's important to mention that Wofford is a Test Optional school. Students should only submit their scores if they feel that they adequately represent their academic abilities.

THE SCHOOL SAYS "..."

From the Admissions Office

"A century ago, Wofford College athletics teams chose the Boston Terrier as the mascot. The small but tenacious and fierce dog is full of intelligence and energy making it an ideal mascot for the 1,823 undergraduates who call Wofford home. Nationally known for the strength of its academic program, outstanding faculty, study abroad participation, and successful graduates, Wofford scores among the best in the country on the National Survey of Student Engagement, which measures high-impact, transformative learning experiences, and the college was ranked seventh in the nation by Open Doors (2021) for the percentage of students who study abroad for credit. In 2021, Wofford received a $150 million gift to its endowment from alumnus Jerry Richardson to support scholarships and experiential learning for students with financial need, provide an increase in the minimum wage on campus for Wofford staff, and fund for the repair and maintenance of buildings named after the Richardson family. Wofford students, faculty, and staff, as well as the upstate South Carolina community, are enjoying five new buildings that have been erected on campus within the past five years. The Chandler Center for Environmental Studies, Rosalind Sallenger Richardson Center for the Arts, Jerome Johnson Richardson Hall, and the Jerry Richardson Indoor Stadium, along with the new Stewart H. Johnson Greek Village, are game changers, offering exciting and diverse opportunities for academic and social enrichment."

SELECTIVITY

Admissions Rating	89
# of applicants	4,425
% of applicants accepted	60
% of acceptees attending	19
# offered a place on the wait list	811
% accepting a place on wait list	32
% admitted from wait list	13
# of early decision applicants	153
% accepted early decision	84

FIRST-YEAR PROFILE

Testing policy	Test Optional
Range SAT composite	1210–1340
Range SAT EBRW	610–680
Range SAT math	590–673
Range ACT composite	27–31
# submitting SAT scores	152
% submitting SAT scores	30
# submitting ACT scores	124
% submitting ACT scores	24
Average HS GPA	3.7
% frosh submitting high school GPA	100
% graduated top 10% of class	31
% graduated top 25% of class	63
% graduated top 50% of class	90

DEADLINES

Early decision	
Deadline	11/1
Notification	12/1
Early action	
Deadline	11/15
Notification	2/1
Regular	
Deadline	1/15
Notification	3/1
Nonfall registration?	Yes

APPLICANTS SOMETIMES PREFER

Furman University

FINANCIAL FACTS

Financial Aid Rating	89
Annual tuition	$51,750
Room and board	$15,015
Required fees	$2,350
Books and supplies	$1,200
Average frosh need-based scholarship	$40,896
Average UG need-based scholarship	$39,669
% needy frosh rec. need-based scholarship or grant aid	100
% needy UG rec. need-based scholarship or grant aid	100
% needy frosh rec. non-need-based scholarship or grant aid	39
% needy UG rec. non-need-based scholarship or grant aid	37
% needy frosh rec. need-based self-help aid	47
% needy UG rec. need-based self-help aid	48
% frosh rec. any financial aid	98
% UG rec. any financial aid	96
% UG borrow to pay for school	54
Average cumulative indebtedness	$34,925
% frosh need fully met	48
% ugrads need fully met	46
Average % of frosh need met	92
Average % of ugrad need met	89

WORCESTER POLYTECHNIC INSTITUTE

100 Institute Road, Worcester, MA 01609 • Admissions: 508-831-5000 • Fax: 508-831-5875

CAMPUS LIFE

Quality of Life Rating	87
Fire Safety Rating	84
Green Rating	94
Type of school	Private
Affiliation	No Affiliation
Environment	City

STUDENTS

Total undergrad enrollment	5,146
% male/female/another gender	63/37/NR
% from out of state	52
% frosh live on campus	97
% ugrads live on campus	53
# of fraternities (% join)	13 (25)
# of sororities (% join)	7 (27)
% African American	3
% Asian	12
% White	65
% Hispanic	9
% Native American	<1
% Pacific Islander	<1
% Two or more races	4
% Race and/or ethnicity unknown	1
% international	7
# of countries represented	61

SURVEY SAYS . . .

Students always studying
Students are happy
Classroom facilities are great
Lab facilities are great
Great library
Career services are great
School is well run
Students are friendly
Diverse student types interact on campus
Easy to get around campus
Intramural sports are popular
Frats and sororities are popular
Alumni active on campus
Students environmentally aware
Active student government

ACADEMICS

Academic Rating	83
% students returning for sophomore year	91
% students graduating within 4 years	82
% students graduating within 6 years	89
Calendar	Other
Student/faculty ratio	13:1
Profs interesting rating	86
Profs accessible rating	92

Most lab/discussion sessions have
20–29 students.

MOST POPULAR MAJORS

Computer Science; Bioengineering and Biomedical
Engineering; Mechanical Engineering

STUDENTS SAY ". . ."

Academics

Sometimes it can be challenging to understand how to apply your college coursework to your future career. But for the approximately 5,000 undergrads at Massachusetts' Worcester Polytechnic Institute, there's no doubt that their global, project-based STEM education gives them "a lot of necessary tools" to succeed. From the very first day of class, many students say the "unique quarter system" and "projects that are related to the real world" are foundational to their success. This program, known as the WPI Plan, is split into seven-week terms, each of which has three classes. A two-term Great Problems Seminar serves to ease students into university-level research, and subsequent classes continue to emphasize the "learn by doing" method. Once settled into the WPI academic structure, many students take advantage of the "excellent resources for academics and future aspirations" by actively pursuing "personal engineering projects" and "opportunities for study abroad, co-ops, [and] internships." Of course, as an interdisciplinary and global institution with over 50 project centers around the world, most students rave about the "research opportunities...available for students who wish to have a larger role in the subject they enjoy." At the end of their academic career with WPI, not only do all students end up completing the equivalent of a minor in Humanities & Arts, but they know that their "hands-on learning, group work, and cool projects where you actually get to make something" are exactly what "employers love best about [them]."

Project-based learning is central to the academic experience at WPI, which involves an "incredibly supportive and collaborative" environment between students and faculty. A project often incorporates real world problems and "allows [students] to actually utilize the theoretical knowledge [they] are learning" via "lots of hands-on learning [where] students steer most projects themselves." There are "a plethora of projects...that reflect what can actually happen in the workplace." These ventures range from managing an "independent software startup" to completing a software engineering class that is "run like an internship." Many students say that for both their larger capstone projects and regular coursework, "professors are always available for office hours and meetings" to help. Instructors also "work hard to engage students in course material," so expect them to support all types of learners with lectures "reinforced with some kind of lab, project, practice, or interactive activity." Working closely with such "interested and engaged" educators has had a long-term impact on some undergrads. As one student notes, "My chemistry professor has inspired me to pursue a masters or PhD in renewable energy after I graduate from WPI."

Campus Life

Academics are time-consuming, and everyone runs on a "very intense schedule," but students enjoy taking breaks with "school-sponsored events such as karaoke, Just Dance, and trivia" and there's "always time for socializing on the quad when it is nice out." Schedules "are filled to the brim with club involvements [and] sports." Activities range from "a lot of... intramural sports" to "theater and performance groups," and even an active "Greek life [that] is run very well and makes a large impact on the community." As one undergrad puts it, "We live by our Outlook calendars, and they fill up quickly with club meetings and sports." And if students are looking to get off campus, the hopping town of Worcester is just down the hill, filled with "so many good places to eat." Even with all the exciting activities on and off campus, "students manage their time extremely well and remain positive about their school life."

Student Body

WPI undergrads are "well-rounded students" who "are very involved on campus and live the campus life to the fullest." Many enrollees note that people are "extremely interested in their respective STEM fields but also have incredibly diverse extracurricular interests," which contributes to the "specific vibe" at WPI. That is, when you get on the WPI wavelength, "you feel as if you finally belong somewhere." Everyone "is so warm and inviting to anyone new" and "the sense of community is extremely strong, and students are very supportive and welcoming." And if you find yourself struggling, fellow students "are super willing to help you if you have a tough class." One student captures the spirit of the institution, saying, "The student body at WPI feels like a community of like-minded peers. It is exciting to see what other people achieve, both inside and outside the classroom. Even if you don't know someone, it feels like they're your friend because you know how much hard work they put in to reach their achievements."

WORCESTER POLYTECHNIC INSTITUTE

Financial Aid: 508-831-5469 • E-Mail: admissions@wpi.edu • Website: www.wpi.edu

THE PRINCETON REVIEW SAYS

Admissions

The school reports that its standardized testing policy for use in admission for Fall 2024 is Test Free. The Princeton Review suggests that interested applicants consult with the school for the most up-to-date standardized testing policies. *Very important factors considered include:* rigor of secondary school record, academic GPA. *Important factors considered include:* class rank, recommendation(s), extracurricular activities, character/personal qualities. *Other factors considered include:* application essay, talent/ability, first generation, alumni/ae relation, geographical residence, racial/ethnic status, volunteer work, work experience, level of applicant's interest. High school diploma is required and GED is accepted. *Academic units required:* 4 English, 4 math, 2 science, 2 science labs. *Academic units recommended:* 4 science, 2 foreign language, 2 social studies, 1 history, 1 computer science.

Financial Aid

Students should submit: CSS/Financial Aid Profile; FAFSA; Noncustodial Profile. Priority filing deadline is 2/15. The Princeton Review suggests that all financial aid forms be submitted as soon as possible (see page 5 for a note on the FAFSA). *Need-based scholarships/grants offered:* College/university scholarship or grant aid from institutional funds; Federal Pell; Private scholarships; SEOG; State scholarships/grants. *Loan aid offered:* Direct PLUS loans; Direct Subsidized Loans; Direct Unsubsidized Loans; College/university loans from institutional funds; State Loans. Admitted students will be notified of awards on a rolling basis beginning 12/15. Federal Work-Study Program available. Institutional employment available.

The Inside Word

The WPI applicant pool is both self-selective and competitive, due to its focused curriculum and solid reputation. Admissions officers tend to prioritize those interested in STEM fields and who show a fit with the campus vibe, but they are also looking for students who have interests that go beyond science and math. Consequently, it would be wise to emphasize your extracurricular passions on your applications along with your academic record. WPI is Test Free.

THE SCHOOL SAYS "..."

From the Admissions Office

"WPI is a research university distinguished by an innovative project-based curriculum converting classroom concepts to real-world impact, empowering students to pursue their passions in solving critical problems and developing skills employers seek. By pairing together theory and practice, students receive a high-caliber education fused with hands-on solving of issues in the world.

"WPI's return on investment enables students to receive a strong starting salary and to ascend to high-income brackets over their lives. Students call WPI's project-based, global approach "life-changing." WPI works with more than 400 companies, government agencies, and private organizations each year, providing opportunities to work in real, professional settings. WPI also receives acclaim for professors who engage their students in research.

"WPI consistently achieves high rankings for academic reputation and student satisfaction. A majority of students travel to over 50 global project centers as part of their project work, leading to ranking No. 1 for the best study-abroad program in the nation (*Princeton Review*). WPI offers every student a Global Scholarship of up to $5,000 to help with travel costs."

SELECTIVITY

Admissions Rating	86
# of applicants	11,599
% of applicants accepted	57
% of acceptees attending	20
# offered a place on the wait list	3,109
% accepting a place on wait list	43
% admitted from wait list	43
# of early decision applicants	254
% accepted early decision	74

FIRST-YEAR PROFILE

Testing policy	Test Free
Average HS GPA	3.9
% frosh submitting high school GPA	82
% graduated top 10% of class	62
% graduated top 25% of class	89
% graduated top 50% of class	99

DEADLINES

Early decision	
Deadline	11/1
Notification	12/15
Other ED deadline	1/15
Other ED notification	2/15
Early action	
Deadline	11/1
Notification	1/15
Regular	
Deadline	2/15
Notification	4/1
Nonfall registration?	No

APPLICANTS ALSO LOOK AT

Boston University; Carnegie Mellon University; Case Western Reserve University; Georgia Institute of Technology; Massachusetts Institute of Technology; Northeastern University; Purdue University—West Lafayette; Rensselaer Polytechnic Institute; Rochester Institute of Technology; Stevens Institute of Technology; University of Connecticut; University of Massachusetts Amherst; University of Massachusetts Lowell; Virginia Tech

FINANCIAL FACTS

Financial Aid Rating	84
Annual tuition	$56,000
Room and board	$16,688
Required fees	$896
Required fees (first-year)	$1,096
Books and supplies	$1,200
Average frosh need-based scholarship	$28,657
Average UG need-based scholarship	$28,952
% needy frosh rec. need-based scholarship or grant aid	100
% needy UG rec. need-based scholarship or grant aid	100
% needy frosh rec. non-need-based scholarship or grant aid	29
% needy UG rec. non-need-based scholarship or grant aid	21
% needy frosh rec. need-based self-help aid	67
% needy UG rec. need-based self-help aid	72
% frosh rec. any financial aid	100
% UG rec. any financial aid	97
% frosh need fully met	31
% ugrads need fully met	24
Average % of frosh need met	74
Average % of ugrad need met	70

XAVIER UNIVERSITY OF LOUISIANA

One Drexel Drive, New Orleans, LA 70125 • Admissions: 504-486-7411 • Fax: 504-520-7941

CAMPUS LIFE

Quality of Life Rating	79
Fire Safety Rating	99
Green Rating	60*
Type of school	Private
Affiliation	Roman Catholic
Environment	Metropolis

STUDENTS

Total undergrad enrollment	2,696
% male/female/another gender	22/78/<1
% from out of state	71
% frosh live on campus	87
% ugrads live on campus	62
# of fraternities (% join)	4 (1)
# of sororities (% join)	4 (5)
% African American	86
% Asian	2
% White	1
% Hispanic	4
% Native American	<1
% Pacific Islander	<1
% Two or more races	4
% Race and/or ethnicity unknown	1
% international	2
# of countries represented	19

SURVEY SAYS . . .

Lots of liberal students
Students involved in community service
Lab facilities are great
Frats and sororities are popular
Campus newspaper is popular
Active minority support groups

ACADEMICS

Academic Rating	76
% students returning for sophomore year	68
% students graduating within 4 years	38
% students graduating within 6 years	48
Calendar	Semester
Student/faculty ratio	13:1
Profs interesting rating	82
Profs accessible rating	88

Most classes have 20–29 students.
Most lab/discussion sessions have
20–29 students.

MOST POPULAR MAJORS

Psychology, General; Pre-Medicine/Pre-Medical
Studies; Pre-Pharmacy Studies

STUDENTS SAY ". . ."

Academics

Recognized for its "challenging classes" and "academic resources," Xavier University of Louisiana is a Catholic and historically Black university that stresses a well-rounded curriculum within a nurturing learning environment. Students here can "be whoever they want to be," which is why the school's support extends beyond programs in STEM and health sciences to a required 40-hour credit core curriculum that focuses on Catholic tradition and contemporary learning. For many students, attending this "extremely academically focused" university pays off. Several undergrads cite that the university is "known for having successful graduates go on to complete medical and graduate school."

But don't let Xavier's strenuous curriculum intimidate you. Many students agree, "[Our] school's greatest strength is our sense of togetherness. We all want to see each other succeed and are willing to help each other along the way," professors included. Most students describe their professors as "kind, understanding and always willing to work with you to achieve a goal." Faculty at the university "value [their students'] education," as observed by students who find that their instructors go above and beyond conventional teaching methods and try to incorporate pedagogical innovation into classes: "Instead of a final exam, my professor is making us do a podcast project in the style of a Vanderbilt professor." Additionally, as a school that challenges its students to be their best, "there is always a resource center or a teacher offering their services" to offer additional guidance. Overall, students agree that Xavier "truly prepares students for experiences after they graduate."

Campus Life

It's a life of books at this rigorously academic university, so "literally most of us are in the library most of the day if not in class," though you will find that "students congregate in their dorm rooms or in the lobby area of the cafeteria." A life of books, at least, until the weekend, at which point the bustle of the nearby city calls out: "There's always something to do in New Orleans." As far as clubs and organizations go, there is "something for everyone, and you even have the opportunity to start clubs of your own." Many enrollees enjoy the Peer Dean Association, which has select members "provide a family space for incoming students" and help them acclimate to life on campus." Student ambassadors "are seen as the faces of Xavier" and offer tours and host events for prospective undergrads. Additionally, basketball games are wildly popular, and there are some events thrown on campus, such as "live music [on] Fridays," which "includes free food, dancing, and fun."

Student Body

"Though Xavier University of Louisiana is a historically Black university, the student body is very diverse," with notably "well-rounded" and "community-minded" individuals. Several students identify that "even though this is a small campus, the people can be so different." Since Xavierites come from so many different backgrounds and regions, "they bring unique elements such as regional dances, phrases, mannerisms, and recipes." Though some might worry about feeling isolated, Xavier is "one big family" where "no one feels unreachable or untouchable." Additionally, it's clear that Xavier students recognize how hard their classmates work and make the effort to lift one another up. As one student puts it best, "No one will allow you to fail," but they will "[give] you challenges to push yourself forward."

XAVIER UNIVERSITY OF LOUISIANA

Financial Aid: 504-520-7835 • E-Mail: apply@xula.edu • Website: www.xula.edu

THE PRINCETON REVIEW SAYS

Admissions

The school reports that its standardized testing policy for use in admission for Fall 2024 is Test Optional. It is unknown at this time if the 2024 testing policy will be permanent. The Princeton Review suggests that interested applicants consult with the school for the most up-to-date standardized testing policies. *Very important factors considered include:* rigor of secondary school record, academic GPA, standardized test scores, recommendation(s). *Important factors considered include:* class rank, application essay. *Other factors considered include:* interview, extracurricular activities, talent/ability, character/personal qualities, alumni/ae relation, volunteer work, work experience, level of applicant's interest. High school diploma is required and GED is accepted. *Academic units required:* 4 English, 2 math, 2 science, 1 social studies, 7 academic electives. *Academic units recommended:* 4 math, 3 science, 1 foreign language, 1 history.

Financial Aid

Students should submit: FAFSA. Priority filing deadline is 1/1. The Princeton Review suggests that all financial aid forms be submitted as soon as possible (see page 5 for a note on the FAFSA). *Need-based scholarships/grants offered:* College/university scholarship or grant aid from institutional funds; Federal Pell; Private scholarships; SEOG; State scholarships/grants; United Negro College Fund. *Loan aid offered:* Direct PLUS loans; Direct Subsidized Loans; Direct Unsubsidized Loans. Admitted students will be notified of awards on a rolling basis beginning 4/1. Federal Work-Study Program available. Institutional employment available.

The Inside Word

Gaining admission to Xavier University of Louisiana is competitive. Fortunately, admissions officers make every effort to take a holistic approach and strive to get to know each candidate as best as possible. To that end, the university considers everything from high school transcripts and standardized test scores to recommendations and extracurricular involvement. Xavier also makes a point of noting that it does not consider gender, race, religion, creed, color, national origin, or handicap when deciding who to admit.

THE SCHOOL SAYS " . . ."

From the Admissions Office

"You have made a great decision in planning to go to college. You will make another important decision when you select Xavier University of Louisiana for your college education. With a mission to 'seek a more just and humane society,' Xavier attracts students from all over the world who desire to be change agents. For almost 100 years, Xavier has continued to create enriching experiences and foster relationships between faculty and students who go on to make a global impact. With a strong STEM representation, we offer numerous research opportunities through our Center for Undergraduate Research and Graduate Opportunity (CURGO). In the health professions, Xavier is a national leader in providing graduates for schools of medicine and dentistry. The College of Pharmacy continues to make an impact with graduates serving widely in the pharmaceutical industry, in hospitals and in neighborhoods often located or central to underserved communities. Students studying the humanities receive one-on-one contact with professors as they strengthen their skill set, stretching their reach across various art performance stages, community-based organizations, national publications, network television and more. Xavier graduates have heeded the call of providing enlightened leadership in city government; Xavier graduates have served as mayors, headed municipal agencies, donned judicial robes and served in state and national legislatures. Xavier-taught educators are in all levels of classrooms. They also serve as system presidents, superintendents, and principals. Business graduates from Xavier rise quickly in the world of business and industry. Students who leave Xavier, leave ready. We stand ready to motivate scholars through activism, elevate minds via a rigorous curriculum and educate students on how to merge their passion to influence the greater good. You can join the ranks of our notable alumni by joining the Xavier family today."

SELECTIVITY

Admissions Rating	82
# of applicants	8,803
% of applicants accepted	95
% of acceptees attending	10

FIRST-YEAR PROFILE

Testing policy	Test Optional
Range SAT composite	1000–1190
Range SAT EBRW	510–580
Range SAT math	490–580
Range ACT composite	20–25
# submitting SAT scores	281
% submitting SAT scores	34
# submitting ACT scores	390
% submitting ACT scores	47
Average HS GPA	3.8
% frosh submitting high school GPA	98
% graduated top 10% of class	33
% graduated top 25% of class	56
% graduated top 50% of class	85

DEADLINES

Regular	
Priority	3/1
Deadline	7/1
Nonfall registration?	Yes

FINANCIAL FACTS

Financial Aid Rating	83
Annual tuition	$24,836
Room and board	$10,946
Required fees	$3,034
Books and supplies	$1,300
Average frosh need-based scholarship	$11,699
Average UG need-based scholarship	$10,580
% needy frosh rec. need-based scholarship or grant aid	100
% needy UG rec. need-based scholarship or grant aid	97
% needy frosh rec. non-need-based scholarship or grant aid	0
% needy UG rec. non-need-based scholarship or grant aid	0
% needy frosh rec. need-based self-help aid	94
% needy UG rec. need-based self-help aid	91
% frosh rec. any financial aid	100
% UG rec. any financial aid	99
% UG borrow to pay for school	99
Average cumulative indebtedness	$21,992
% frosh need fully met	15
% ugrads need fully met	26
Average % of frosh need met	65
Average % of ugrad need met	60

XAVIER UNIVERSITY (OH)

3800 Victory Parkway, Cincinnati, OH 45207-5311 • Admissions: 877-982-3648 • Fax: 513-745-4319

STUDENTS SAY "..."

Academics

Xavier University is a Catholic college that prides itself on being a small community driven by Jesuit ideals, making "[all students] feel comfortable in every aspect over their four years." The school "focuses on how to make [its students] better people," and the school's connections throughout the city and state provide "post-graduate opportunities that involve careers [and] volunteer work," as well as access to the sprawling Jesuit alumni network. Study abroad, field work, and internship opportunities are plentiful, and many students also volunteer on campus, which brings to the school "an amazing atmosphere for any student regardless of...age, religion, or culture."

"Professors are more than enthusiastic about their students' success," says a student. Faculty members utilize their skills and resources to "challenge the minds of students in the best possible way," truly preparing them for the future "especially when it comes to critical thinking." Classes incorporate guest speakers who "share experiences and tips," projects utilize programs that are relevant to real world practices, such as Qualtrics and Nielsen, and many core classes are seminars where students "solely discuss as a class and engage with each other" rather than a traditional lecture. Although "exams can be difficult depending on the class," most professors will offer the opportunity "to earn points back or redo parts of [an] exam," and "smaller class sizes make it easy to get to know your professors and create a bond with many of them."

Campus Life

At Xavier, students tend to be "very devoted to studying," at least during the weekdays. "There is more time to go out and roam around off-campus [and] the Cincinnati area on the weekends," which is when social gatherings usually take place. That said, this is a social bunch that "truly likes to be around others, since everyone is so nice," and when not studying, many students fill their time with clubs, activities, sports, or just "go grab coffee at Gallagher Student Center or hang out on the lawn if the weather is good." The campus is, after all, "gorgeous and well-maintained," even if some students feel it "could use more on-campus dining options." Overall, the university's size lends itself to a beloved "general feel"—which is to say that it's "very easy to see the same people each and every day" and, in turn, "easy and fun" to make friends. Students are also described as having "so much school spirit" and some note that "Basketball season is the best time of year."

Student Body

"Xavier students are well-rounded and highly involved individuals," which means "the campus feels like family." The small, tight-knit community here "brings a sense of intimacy." As one student explains, "If you're struggling with something, there will be someone to help you." People tend to be "laid-back and welcoming but are also a somewhat homogenous group," though everyone is "inclusive and supportive of different faiths [and] political views." Students note that the school is in the act of "becoming more diverse," which allows "for more discussion to learn new perspectives and...in turn to understand each other more deeply."

XAVIER UNIVERSITY (OH)

Financial Aid: 513-745-3302 • E-Mail: xuadmit@xavier.edu • Website: www.xavier.edu

THE PRINCETON REVIEW SAYS

Admissions
The school reports that its standardized testing policy for use in admission for Fall 2024 is Test Optional. The 2024 testing policy will be permanent. The Princeton Review suggests that interested applicants consult with the school for the most up-to-date standardized testing policies. *Very important factors considered include:* rigor of secondary school record, academic GPA. *Important factors considered include:* application essay, recommendation(s), extracurricular activities, character/personal qualities. *Other factors considered include:* class rank, standardized test scores, talent/ability, volunteer work, work experience, level of applicant's interest. High school diploma is required and GED is accepted. *Academic units recommended:* 4 English, 3 math, 3 science, 2 foreign language, 3 social studies, 5 academic electives.

Financial Aid
Students should submit: FAFSA. Priority filing deadline is 2/15. The Princeton Review suggests that all financial aid forms be submitted as soon as possible (see page 5 for a note on the FAFSA). *Need-based scholarships/grants offered:* College/university scholarship or grant aid from institutional funds; Federal Pell; Private scholarships; SEOG; State scholarships/grants; United Negro College Fund. *Loan aid offered:* Direct PLUS loans; Direct Subsidized Loans; Direct Unsubsidized Loans; College/university loans from institutional funds; Federal Nursing Loans. Admitted students will be notified of awards on a rolling basis beginning 12/15. Federal Work-Study Program available. Institutional employment available.

The Inside Word
There will be no major hurdles for above-average students when it comes to gaining admission to Xavier. For select schools within Xavier, it will take a little more legwork; Music and Theatre students must audition, and Nursing students must indicate their intent to enroll in the nursing school on the initial application. Look to provide credible demonstrations of commitment to academics and Jesuit ideals of service if you want to win over admissions officers.

THE SCHOOL SAYS "..."

From the Admissions Office
"Founded in 1831, Xavier University is the fourth oldest of the twenty-seven Jesuit colleges and universities in the United States. The Jesuit tradition is evident in the university's core curriculum, degree programs, and involvement opportunities. Xavier is home to approximately 7,000 total students, including 5,200 degree-seeking undergraduates. The student population represents more than forty-five states and thirty foreign countries. Xavier offers more than ninety undergraduate academic majors and more than eighty minors in the College of Arts and Sciences, Williams College of Business, College of Nursing, and the College of Professional Sciences. Most popular majors include business, natural sciences, nursing, liberal arts, education, psychology, biology, and pre-professional study. Other programs of note include University Scholars; Honors AB; Philosophy, Politics, and the Public; Data Science Honors Program; Smith Scholars program; study abroad; service and community-engaged learning. There are more than 100 academic clubs, social and service organizations, and recreational sports activities on campus. Students participate in groups such as student government, campus ministry, performing arts, and intramural sports as well as one of the largest service-oriented Alternative Break clubs in the country. Xavier is a member of the Division I Big East Conference and fields teams in men's and women's basketball, cross-country, track, golf, soccer, swimming, and tennis, as well as men's baseball and women's volleyball. Xavier is situated on more than 180 acres in a residential area of Cincinnati, Ohio. Xavier University offers Test Optional admission."

SELECTIVITY
Admissions Rating	83
# of applicants	14,836
% of applicants accepted	85
% of acceptees attending	9
# offered a place on the wait list	696
% admitted from wait list	63

FIRST-YEAR PROFILE
Testing policy	Test Optional
SAT Composite range	1140–1300
SAT EBRW	570–660
SAT Math	550–650
ACT Composite range	23–30
# submitting SAT	179
% submitting SAT	15
# submitting ACT	437
% submitting ACT	37
Average HS GPA	3.7
% frosh submitting high school GPA	100
% graduated top 10% of class	24
% graduated top 25% of class	53
% graduated top 50% of class	84

DEADLINES
Regular	
Priority	12/1
Notification	Rolling, 10/1
Nonfall registration?	Yes

APPLICANTS ALSO LOOK AT
Indiana University—Bloomington; Marquette University; Miami University; Miami University - Hamilton Campus; Miami University - Middletown Campus; Ohio University—Athens; Purdue University—West Lafayette; Saint Louis University; The Ohio State University—Columbus; University of Cincinnati; University of Dayton; University of Kentucky

FINANCIAL FACTS
Financial Aid Rating	80
Annual tuition	$47,896
Room and board	$13,820
Required fees	$230
Books and supplies	$1,300
Average frosh need-based scholarship	$30,263
Average UG need-based scholarship	$26,620
% needy frosh rec. need-based scholarship or grant aid	54
% needy UG rec. need-based scholarship or grant aid	62
% needy frosh rec. non-need-based scholarship or grant aid	47
% needy UG rec. non-need-based scholarship or grant aid	63
% needy frosh rec. need-based self-help aid	43
% needy UG rec. need-based self-help aid	78
% frosh rec. any financial aid	100
% UG rec. any financial aid	100
% UG borrow to pay for school	50
Average cumulative indebtedness	$11,115
% frosh need fully met	11
% ugrads need fully met	15
Average % of frosh need met	75
Average % of ugrad need met	70

YALE UNIVERSITY

Yale University, New Haven, CT 06520 • Admissions: 203-432-4771 • Fax: 203-432-9392

STUDENTS SAY "..."

Academics

Listening to Yale students wax rhapsodic about their school, one can be forgiven for wondering whether they aren't actually describing the platonic form of the university. By their own account, students here benefit not only from "amazing academics and extensive resources" that provide "phenomenal in- and out-of-class education," but also from participation in "a student body that is committed to learning and to each other." Unlike some other prestigious, prominent research universities, Yale "places unparalleled focus on undergraduate education," requiring all professors to teach at least one undergraduate course each year. "[You know] the professors actually love teaching, because if they just wanted to do their research, they could have easily gone elsewhere." A residential college system further personalizes the experience. Each residential college "has a Dean and a [Head], each of which is only responsible for 300 to 500 students, so administrative attention is highly specialized and widely available." Students further enjoy access to "a seemingly never-ending supply of resources (they really just love throwing money at us)" that includes "the [13.8] million volumes in our libraries." In short, "the opportunities are truly endless." "The experiences you have here and the people that you meet will change your life and strengthen your dreams," says one student. Looking for the flip side to all this? "If the weather were a bit nicer, that would be excellent," one student offers. Guess that will have to do.

Campus Life

Yale is, of course, extremely challenging academically, but students assure us that "aside from the stress of midterms and finals, life at Yale is relatively carefree." Work doesn't keep undergrads from participating in "a huge variety of activities for fun. There are more than 400 student groups, including singing, dancing, juggling fire, theater…the list goes on. Because of all of these groups, there are shows on-campus all the time, which are a lot of fun and usually free or less than five dollars. On top of that, there are parties and events on campus and off campus, as well as many subsidized trips to New York City and Boston." Many here "are politically active (or at least politically aware)" and "a very large number of students either volunteer or try to get involved in some sort of organization to make a difference in the world." When the weekend comes around, "there are always parties to go to, whether at the frats or in rooms, but there's definitely no pressure to drink if you don't want to. A good friend of mine pledged a frat without drinking and that's definitely not unheard of (but still not common)." The relationship between Yale and the city of New Haven "sometimes leaves a little to be desired, but overall it's a great place to be for four years."

Student Body

A typical Yalie is "tough to define because so much of what makes Yale special is the unique convergence of different students to form one cohesive entity. Nonetheless, the one common characteristic of Yale students is passion—each Yalie is driven and dedicated to what he or she loves most, and it creates a palpable atmosphere of enthusiasm on campus." True enough, the student body represents a wide variety of ethnic, religious, economic, and academic backgrounds, but they all "thrive on learning, whether in a class, from a book, or from a conversation with a new friend." Students here also "tend to do a lot." "Everyone has many activities that they are a part of, which in turn fosters the closely connected feel of the campus." Undergrads tend to lean to the left politically, but for "those whose political views aren't as liberal as the rest of the campus…there are several campus organizations that cater to them."

YALE UNIVERSITY

Financial Aid: 203-432-2700 • E-Mail: student.questions@yale.edu • Website: www.yale.edu

THE PRINCETON REVIEW SAYS

Admissions

The school reports that its standardized testing policy for use in admission for Fall 2024 is Test Optional. It is unknown at this time if the 2024 testing policy will be permanent. The Princeton Review suggests that interested applicants consult with the school for the most up-to-date standardized testing policies. *Very important factors considered include:* rigor of secondary school record, class rank, academic GPA, application essay, recommendation(s), extracurricular activities, talent/ability, character/personal qualities. *Other factors considered include:* standardized test scores, interview, first generation, alumni/ae relation, geographical residence, state residency, racial/ethnic status, volunteer work, work experience. High school diploma is required and GED is accepted.

Financial Aid

Students should submit: CSS/Financial Aid Profile; FAFSA; Institution's own financial aid form; Noncustodial Profile. Priority filing deadline is 3/1. The Princeton Review suggests that all financial aid forms be submitted as soon as possible (see page 5 for a note on the FAFSA). *Need-based scholarships/grants offered:* College/university scholarship or grant aid from institutional funds; Federal Pell; Private scholarships; SEOG; State scholarships/grants; United Negro College Fund. *Loan aid offered:* Direct PLUS loans; Direct Subsidized Loans; Direct Unsubsidized Loans; College/university loans from institutional funds; Federal Nursing Loans; State Loans. Admitted students will be notified of awards on or about 4/1. Institutional employment available.

The Inside Word

Yale estimates that over three-quarters of all its applicants are qualified to attend the university, but less than 10 percent get in. That adds up to a lot of broken hearts among kids who, if admitted, could probably handle the academic program. With so many qualified applicants to choose from, Yale can winnow to build an incoming class that is balanced in terms of income level, racial/ethnic background, geographic origin, and academic interest. Legacies (descendants of Yale grads) gain some advantage—although they still need exceptionally strong credentials.

THE SCHOOL SAYS "..."

From the Admissions Office

"The most important questions the admissions committee must resolve are 'Who is likely to make the most of Yale's resources?' and 'Who will contribute significantly to the Yale community?' These questions suggest an approach to evaluating applicants that is more complex than whether Yale would rather admit well-rounded people or those with specialized talents. In selecting a class of 1,550 from roughly 50,000 applicants, the admissions committee looks for academic ability and achievement combined with such personal characteristics as motivation, curiosity, energy, and leadership ability. The nature of these qualities is such that there is no simple profile of grades, scores, interests, and activities that will assure admission. Diversity within the student population is important, and the admissions committee selects a class of able and contributing individuals from a variety of backgrounds and with a broad range of interests and skills."

SELECTIVITY

Admissions Rating	99
# of applicants	50,060
% of applicants accepted	5
% of acceptees attending	68
# offered a place on the wait list	1,000
% accepting a place on wait list	78
% admitted from wait list	1

FIRST-YEAR PROFILE

Testing policy	Test Optional
Range SAT composite	1470–1560
Range SAT EBRW	740–780
Range SAT math	760–800
Range ACT composite	33–35
# submitting SAT scores	913
% submitting SAT scores	59
# submitting ACT scores	455
% submitting ACT scores	29
% graduated top 10% of class	97
% graduated top 25% of class	99
% graduated top 50% of class	100

DEADLINES

Early action	
Deadline	11/1
Notification	12/15
Regular	
Deadline	1/2
Notification	4/1
Nonfall registration?	No

FINANCIAL FACTS

Financial Aid Rating	99
Annual tuition	$64,700
Room and board	$19,180
Books and supplies	$3,700
Average frosh need-based scholarship	$61,067
Average UG need-based scholarship	$59,150
% needy frosh rec. need-based scholarship or grant aid	100
% needy UG rec. need-based scholarship or grant aid	100
% needy frosh rec. non-need-based scholarship or grant aid	0
% needy UG rec. non-need-based scholarship or grant aid	0
% needy frosh rec. need-based self-help aid	72
% needy UG rec. need-based self-help aid	83
% frosh rec. any financial aid	51
% UG rec. any financial aid	52
% UG borrow to pay for school	15
Average cumulative indebtedness	$15,379
% frosh need fully met	100
% ugrads need fully met	100
Average % of frosh need met	100
Average % of ugrad need met	100

2024 BEST REGIONAL COLLEGES

In addition to the 389 schools in this book, we salute the following 245 schools that we consider academically outstanding and well worth consideration in your college search. For more information on these schools, visit PrincetonReview.com to find admissions information, costs, and more.

MID-ATLANTIC

Maryland
Hood College
Maryland Institute College of Art
Towson University

Pennsylvania
Albright College
Arcadia University
California University of Pennsylvania
Chatham University
Chestnut Hill College
Delaware Valley University
Elizabethtown College
King's College (PA)
Kutztown University of Pennsylvania
La Roche University
Lebanon Valley College
Messiah University
Misericordia University
Neumann University
Robert Morris University
Seton Hill University
Slippery Rock University of Pennsylvania
University of Pittsburgh at Bradford
Westminster College (PA)
Wilkes University
York College of Pennsylvania

Virginia
Averett University
Bridgewater College
Mary Baldwin University
Old Dominion University
Radford University
Sweet Briar College

West Virginia
Concord University
Shepherd University
University of Charleston
West Virginia Wesleyan College

MIDWEST

Illinois
Augustana College (IL)
Dominican University
Elmhurst University
Illinois College
Lewis University
Millikin University
Monmouth College
North Central College

Principia College
Rockford University
Southern Illinois University–Carbondale
University of St. Francis (IL)
Western Illinois University

Indiana
Anderson University (IN)
Ball State University
Grace College and Seminary
Huntington University
Indiana State University
Manchester University
Saint Mary's College (IN)
Taylor University
Trine University
Valparaiso University

Iowa
Briar Cliff University
Drake University
Graceland University
Luther College
Morningside College
Northwestern College (IA)
St. Ambrose University
University of Northern Iowa
Wartburg College

Kansas
Baker University
Emporia State University
Pittsburg State University
Sterling College
University of Saint Mary (KS)

Michigan
Alma College
Grand Valley State University
Hope College
University of Michigan-Flint
Western Michigan University

Minnesota
Gustavus Adolphus College
Saint Mary's University of Minnesota
St. Catherine University
The College of Saint Scholastica
University of Minnesota, Crookston
Winona State University

Missouri
Columbia College (MO)
Southeast Missouri State University
Stephens College

University of Central Missouri
University of Missouri—Kansas City
Westminster College (MO)

Nebraska
Doane University
University of Nebraska at Omaha

North Dakota
Mayville State University
University of Jamestown

Ohio
Ashland University
Baldwin Wallace University
Cedarville University
Cleveland Institute of Art
Hiram College
Lourdes University
The University of Akron
The University of Findlay
Wright State University

South Dakota
Augustana University

Wisconsin
Carthage College
Edgewood College
Milwaukee School of Engineering
Northland College
St. Norbert College
University of Wisconsin—Eau Claire
University of Wisconsin—Milwaukee
University of Wisconsin—River Falls

NORTHEAST

Connecticut
Central Connecticut State University
Eastern Connecticut State University
Trinity College (CT)

Maine
University of Maine—Fort Kent

Massachusetts
Bard College at Simon's Rock
Hampshire College
Hult International Business School
Merrimack College
Nichols College
University of Massachusetts—Boston
Wentworth Institute of Technology
Worcester State University

New Hampshire
Keene State College

New Jersey
Ramapo College of New Jersey
Stockton University

New York
Adelphi University
Hartwick College
Houghton College
Iona College

LIM College
Long Island University
Molloy College
Niagara University
Parsons School of Design at The New School
Pratt Institute
Roberts Wesleyan College
St. John Fisher College
State University of New York—Alfred State College
State University of New York—Brockport
State University of New York—Cortland
State University of New York—Fredonia
State University of New York—Maritime College
State University of New York—New Paltz
State University of New York—Oswego
State University of New York—University at Albany
State University of New York—University at Buffalo
Wells College

Rhode Island
Roger Williams University

SOUTH

Alabama
Auburn University at Montgomery
Huntingdon College
Samford University
Talladega College
Troy University—Troy

Arkansas
Arkansas State University
Harding University
Hendrix College
Lyon College

Florida
Florida A&M University
Florida Atlantic University
Florida Gulf Coast University
Palm Beach Atlantic University
University of North Florida
University of West Florida

Georgia
Brenau University
Clark Atlanta University
Covenant College
Georgia College & State University
Oglethorpe University
Savannah College of Art and Design
Shorter University
University of West Georgia
Wesleyan College

Kentucky
Kentucky State University
Kentucky Wesleyan College

Louisiana
Centenary College of Louisiana
University of New Orleans

North Carolina
Barton College
Campbell University
Catawba College

Guilford College
Meredith College
University of North Carolina—Charlotte
University of North Carolina—Wilmington

South Carolina
Anderson University (SC)
Coker University
Winthrop University

Tennessee
Belmont University
Carson-Newman University
Christian Brothers University
East Tennessee State University
Fisk University
King University
Lee University
Lipscomb University
Tennessee Technological University
Union University
University of Tennessee at Martin

SOUTHWEST

Arizona
Prescott College

Colorado
Fort Lewis College

New Mexico
New Mexico Institute of Mining and Technology
Santa Fe University of Art and Design

Oklahoma
Oklahoma Baptist University
Oklahoma City University
Oklahoma State University
Oral Roberts University

Texas
Abilene Christian University
Hardin-Simmons University
Schreiner University
St. Edward's University
Texas Lutheran University
Texas Tech University
The University of Texas at Arlington
University of North Texas
University of St. Thomas (Texas)

WEST

Alaska
University of Alaska Fairbanks

California
Azusa Pacific University
Biola University
California Institute of the Arts
California State Polytechnic University, Pomona
California State University, East Bay
California State University, Long Beach
California State University, San Bernardino
Humboldt State University
Menlo College
Otis College of Art and Design
University of La Verne
University of the Pacific

Hawaii
Hawai'i Pacific University

Idaho
Northwest Nazarene University
The College of Idaho

Oregon
George Fox University
Linfield University
University of Portland
Willamette University

Utah
Southern Utah University
Utah State University
Weber State University

Washington
Pacific Lutheran University
Seattle Pacific University
University of Washington—Bothell
Whitworth University

INTERNATIONAL

Canada
University of Toronto
McGill University

Ireland
Maynooth University
Trinity College Dublin

PART 4

Indexes

INDEX OF SCHOOLS BY LOCATION

Virginia

Washington

West Virginia

Wisconsin

Wyoming

INDEX OF SCHOOLS BY TUITION

Price categories are based on figures the schools reported to us in early spring 2023 for tuition and required fees (in-state tuition for public schools) and do not include room, board, transportation, or other expenses.

No Tuition

Less than $9,999

$10,000–$19,999

Marquette University	372	Goucher College	274
McDaniel College	376	Hampden-Sydney College	282
Millsaps College	390	Harvard College	288
Monmouth University (NJ)	394	Hofstra University	300
Moravian University	398	Illinois Institute of Technology	306
Pace University	432	Illinois Wesleyan University	308
Randolph-Macon College	454	Johns Hopkins University	324
Rider University	464	Juniata College	326
Rochester Institute of Technology	470	Kalamazoo College	328
Sacred Heart University	480	Knox College	336
Saint Anselm College	482	Lafayette College	338
St. John's University (NY)	490	Lake Forest College	340
Salve Regina University	508	Lawrence University	344
Seton Hall University	520	Lewis & Clark College	350
Siena College	522	Loyola Marymount University	354
Simmons University	524	Loyola University Maryland	358
Suffolk University	556	Massachusetts Institute of Technology	374
Transylvania University	574	New York University	410
Trinity University	578	Ohio Wesleyan University	428
University of Dayton	638	Quinnipiac University	450
University of New England	692	Rhodes College	460
University of New Haven	696	Rice University	462
The University of Scranton	736	Ripon College	466
The University of Tulsa	756	Rollins College	472
Wabash College	782	Rose-Hulman Institute of Technology	474
Warren Wilson College	788	Saint Joseph's University (PA)	492
Wheaton College (IL)	808	Saint Louis University	496
Whittier College	814	Saint Mary's College of California	498
Wittenberg University	822	Saint Michael's College	502
Xavier University (OH)	830	St. Olaf College	504
		Sarah Lawrence College	514

$50,000–$59,999

		Seattle University	518
Albion College	58	Smith College	528
Allegheny College	62	Southwestern University	534
American University	64	Stanford University	538
Babson College	80	Stetson University	550
Bard College	82	Stevens Institute of Technology	552
Barnard College	84	Stonehill College	554
Bates College	86	Susquehanna University	558
Baylor University	88	Swarthmore College	560
Beloit College	92	Texas Christian University	568
Bentley University	96	University of Dallas	636
Brandeis University	110	University of Denver	642
Bryant University	116	University of Miami	678
Bryn Mawr College	118	University of Portland	718
The Catholic University of America	136	University of Puget Sound	720
Clarkson University	158	University of Redlands	722
Clark University	160	University of St. Thomas (MN)	730
College of Saint Benedict/Saint John's University	174	University of San Diego	732
College of the Holy Cross	178	University of San Francisco	734
The College of Wooster	182	The University of the South	738
Cornell College	194	Ursinus College	770
Davidson College	202	Vanderbilt University	772
DePauw University	210	Villanova University	776
Drexel University	216	Wagner College	784
Duke University	220	Wake Forest University	786
Emerson College	234	Washington College	790
Emory University	236	Wesleyan University	802
Eugene Lang College of Liberal Arts at The New School	238	Whitman College	812
Fairfield University	242	Wofford College	824
Fordham University	252	Worcester Polytechnic Institute	826
Franklin W. Olin College of Engineering	256		
Furman University	258	**OVER $60,000**	
Georgetown University	262	Amherst College	66
George Washington University	264	Bennington College	94
Gonzaga University	270	Boston College	102

Boston University	104	Northwestern University	416
Bowdoin College	106	Oberlin College	418
Brown University	114	Occidental College	420
Bucknell University	120	Pepperdine University	436
California Institute of Technology	124	Pitzer College	438
Carleton College	130	Pomona College	440
Carnegie Mellon University	132	Princeton University	444
Case Western Reserve University	134	Providence College	446
Chapman University	142	Reed College	456
Claremont McKenna College	156	Rensselaer Polytechnic Institute	458
Colby College	166	St. Lawrence University	494
Colgate University	168	Santa Clara University	512
Colorado College	184	Scripps College	516
Columbia University	188	Skidmore College	526
Connecticut College	190	Southern Methodist University	532
Cornell University	196	Syracuse University	562
Dartmouth College	200	Trinity College (CT)	576
Denison University	206	Tufts University	582
Dickinson College	212	Tulane University	584
Franklin & Marshall College	254	Union College (NY)	588
Gettysburg College	268	The University of Chicago	628
Grinnell College	276	University of Notre Dame	708
Hamilton College	280	University of Pennsylvania	714
Harvey Mudd College	290	University of Richmond	726
Haverford College	292	University of Rochester	728
Hobart and William Smith Colleges	298	University of Southern California	746
Kenyon College	332	Vassar College	774
Lehigh University	346	Washington University in St. Louis	796
Macalester College	364	Wellesley College	800
Middlebury College	386	Wheaton College (MA)	810
Mount Holyoke College	400	Williams College	820
Muhlenberg College	402	Yale University	832
Northeastern University	414		

THE PRINCETON REVIEW NATIONAL COLLEGE COUNSELOR ADVISORY BOARD, 2023–2024

We thank the members of this board for their careful and considered input.

Michael Acquilano, Director of College Guidance, Staten Island Academy, Staten Island, NY

Casey Barneson, College Counselor, Beverly Hills High School, Beverly Hills, CA

Lee Bierer, Weekly College Advice and Timely Tips Syndicated Columnist and Independent College Counselor, Bierer College Consulting, Charlotte, NC

Nick Bucci, Director of Student Personnel Services, Passaic County Technical-Vocational Schools, Wayne, NJ

Ellen O'Neill Deitrich, Assistant Head of School for Academics and Dean of College Counseling, St. Mary's Hall, San Antonio, TX

Henry DelAngelo, School Counselor, Joel Barlow High School, Redding, CT

Meghan Farley, Director of College Counseling, Cape Cod Academy, Osterville, MA

Anne Gregory, College & Career Counselor at Mountain Lakes High School, Mountain Lakes, NJ

Nancy Griesemer, Independent Educational Consultant and Co-author of Admission Matters, 5th Edition, College Explorations LLC, Oakton, VA

Troy B. Hammond, Director of University Counseling & Student Services Department Head, Bayview Glen Independent School, Toronto, Ontario (Canada)

Jodi Hester, Associate Director of College Counseling, Woodward Academy, College Park, GA

William Hirt, College Counselor, Professional Children's School, New York, NY

Nikki Lugo Hostnik, Director of College Counseling, Saint Louis Priory School, St. Louis, MO

Marilyn J. Kaufman, M.Ed., Certified College Counselor and Educational Consultant, President, College Admission Consultants, Dallas, TX

Joanne Levy-Prewitt; Co-Founder, Get Going Workshops; Moraga, CA

Earl R. Macam, Ed.D., College Counselor, Mary Institute and St. Louis Country Day School, St. Louis, MO

Susan Marrs; Director, College Counseling; Seven Hills School, Cincinnati, OH

Erin McElligott, Director of College & School Counseling, Prospect Hill Academy Charter School, Cambridge, MA

Nancy Ortiz, School Counselor, Innovation High School, Jersey City, NJ

Elizabeth A. Roper, Director of College Counseling, AP Coordinator, Soccer Coach, Mount Saint Mary Academy, Watchung, NJ

Mary Russell, College and Career Programs Coordinator, Corona Del Mar High School, Newport Beach, CA

Kimberly Simpson, Independent Educational Consultant, Collegiate Admissions Consulting Services, LLC, Covington, LA

Ed Stone, College & Career Specialist, Freehold Regional High School District, Englishtown, NJ

Theresa Urist, Global Director of University Counseling, The Aga Khan Academies, and Educational Consultant, Cambridge, MA.

Toby Walker, Vice President, BASIS Independent Schools, Redmond, WA

Michael Wilner, Educational Consultant and Founder, Wilner Education, Putney, VT

SCHOOL SAYS . . .

In this section you'll find advertisements directly from colleges with information they'd like you to consider about their schools. The editorial in these pages is written by the schools, which pay a fee to offset the cost of printing their advertisements in this section.

The Princeton Review does not charge schools for inclusion in the School Profiles (pp 55–833) section in this book. The company has never required colleges, universities, or any institutions to pay a fee for their profiles or inclusions in our books.

For information about how we selected the 389 outstanding schools in this book, see page 18, "How We Produce This Book."

SEE YOURSELF HERE.

KNOW ANYTHING IS POSSIBLE.

You are wonderfully unique. Your education should be equally so.

HERE, you will be guided by trusted mentors who understand your goals and dreams, connect you with life-changing opportunities and consider your well-being as important as their own.

(Come see what's possible when people walking different paths come together with common purpose.)

FLORIDA INTERNATIONAL UNIVERSITY

FORWARD-THINKING
INNOVATIVE
UNSTOPPABLE

#32
National University
Washington Monthly

TOP 50
Entrepreneurship Undergrad program
Princeton Review

#72
Public University Rankings
U.S. News & World Report, 2023

STUDENT SUCCESS

TOP 5
Social Mobility
U.S. News & World Report

TOP 10
Economic ROI in a college degree
Degree Choices

#1
in the nation awarding
bachelor's degrees to minorities

RESEARCH & INNOVATION

$1 Billion
Research expenditures
in the last five years

TOP 15
Most Innovative Public Universities
U.S. News & World Report

TOP 20
Utility Patents Public Universities
Intellectual Property Owners Association

Miami's Carnegie R1 Research University

Learn more at

FIND YOUR PURPOSE.
BUILD YOUR FUTURE.

Dive in to the waters of Tampa Bay and research stone crabs. Learn to trade through our student-run investment fund. Intern on Capitol Hill.

Hands-on, real-world experiences ensure you graduate with the know-how employers and graduate schools demand.

WHATEVER IS NEXT

Everyone wonders what's next.
For Grand Valley students, next
is opportunity and innovation.
Next is global, connecting and
uniting us. It's local, shaping the
spaces in which we work and live.
It's a commitment to progress.
Next is where minds are free to
imagine what could be. At GVSU,
next is now. And whatever's next
for you, we will help you get there.

gvsu.edu/next

Explore.
Build experiences.
DISCOVER
WHAT IS
POSSIBLE.

LEARN MORE AT **NAZ.EDU**

NAZARETH COLLEGE

DISCOVER SAINT ANSELM

A nationally ranked, best value liberal arts college by *U.S. News & World Report*, *Kiplinger*, and Payscale.

by the numbers

100%
of first-year students receive some type of gift or grant aid

89%
retention rate

99%
of 2021 graduates were employed, in graduate school, or engaged in service within 6 months of graduation

18
average class size

11:1
student to faculty ratio

SAINT ANSELM 1889

find your reason

SAINT ANSELM

Set Your Success in Motion at Salisbury University

Academic Excellence
Offering over 60 majors and graduate programs, SU is one of those rare universities that celebrates your individual talents and encourages big ideas.

National Recognition
SU ranks among the nation's top colleges and best values in *U.S. News & World Report* and Princeton Review. The Sea Gulls have won 22 NCAA Division III team national championships.

Accomplished Alumni
Over 60,000 graduates are taking the lead in the boardroom, the lab, the legislature and on Broadway. Professors are deeply invested in their students, nurturing graduate school and career possibilities.

Beautiful Campus
Home to over 7,100 students, state-of-the-art facilities and a national arboretum, SU is between the Atlantic Ocean and Chesapeake Bay – the perfect place to chart your future.

Make Tomorrow Yours
Go to salisbury.edu/visit

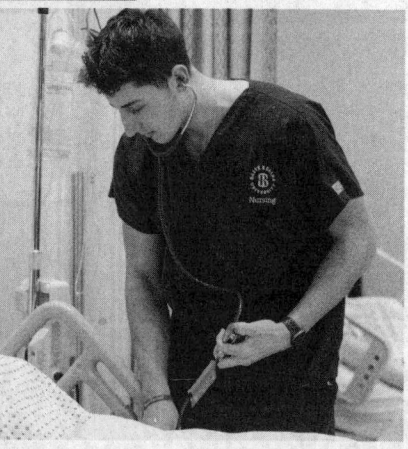

WHAT GREAT MINDS CAN DO

"I felt so confident having Seton Hall on my resume because I know it stands for excellence, and employers know it too. My internships and leadership experiences at Seton Hall helped me get my job at CBS."

Darryl Sessoms
Marketing major
Union, New Jersey

SETON HALL
UNIVERSITY
1 8 5 6

Ranked a
TOP 5
University
for internships

#1
leadership
program

98%
employment
rate

98%
students receiving
financial aid

TOP 25
NATIONAL RANKING
for graduates who
received the
highest paid jobs

(973) 313-6146 • **thehall@shu.edu** • **admissions.shu.edu**

REDEFINE
POSSIBLE

At Thomas Jefferson University we dare to ask bold questions, like **Can an industrial designer get a surfer back on his board?** and **Can the future of architecture empower global sustainability?**

But asking tough questions isn't enough — we need to answer them. So, we are converging people, ideas and perspectives to find leading-edge solutions for real-world problems. We focus on our craft to drive progress and growth in architecture, business, design, engineering, fashion & textiles, health, medicine, nursing, science and social science.

Built for a future that has yet to be defined, Jefferson is crossing disciplines to bring unrivaled innovation and discovery to higher education and to answer the questions that will redefine possible.

Jefferson
Thomas Jefferson University
HOME OF SIDNEY KIMMEL MEDICAL COLLEGE

ARCHITECTURE • BUSINESS • DESIGN • ENGINEERING • FASHION & TEXTILES • HEALTH • MEDICINE • NURSING • SCIENCE • SOCIAL SCI

RIGHT HERE. RIGHT NOW.
WRIGHT STATE

Get excellent, affordable education and one of the highest returns on investment (ROI) of any public university in Ohio.*

Learn more:
wright.edu/now

WRIGHT STATE UNIVERSITY

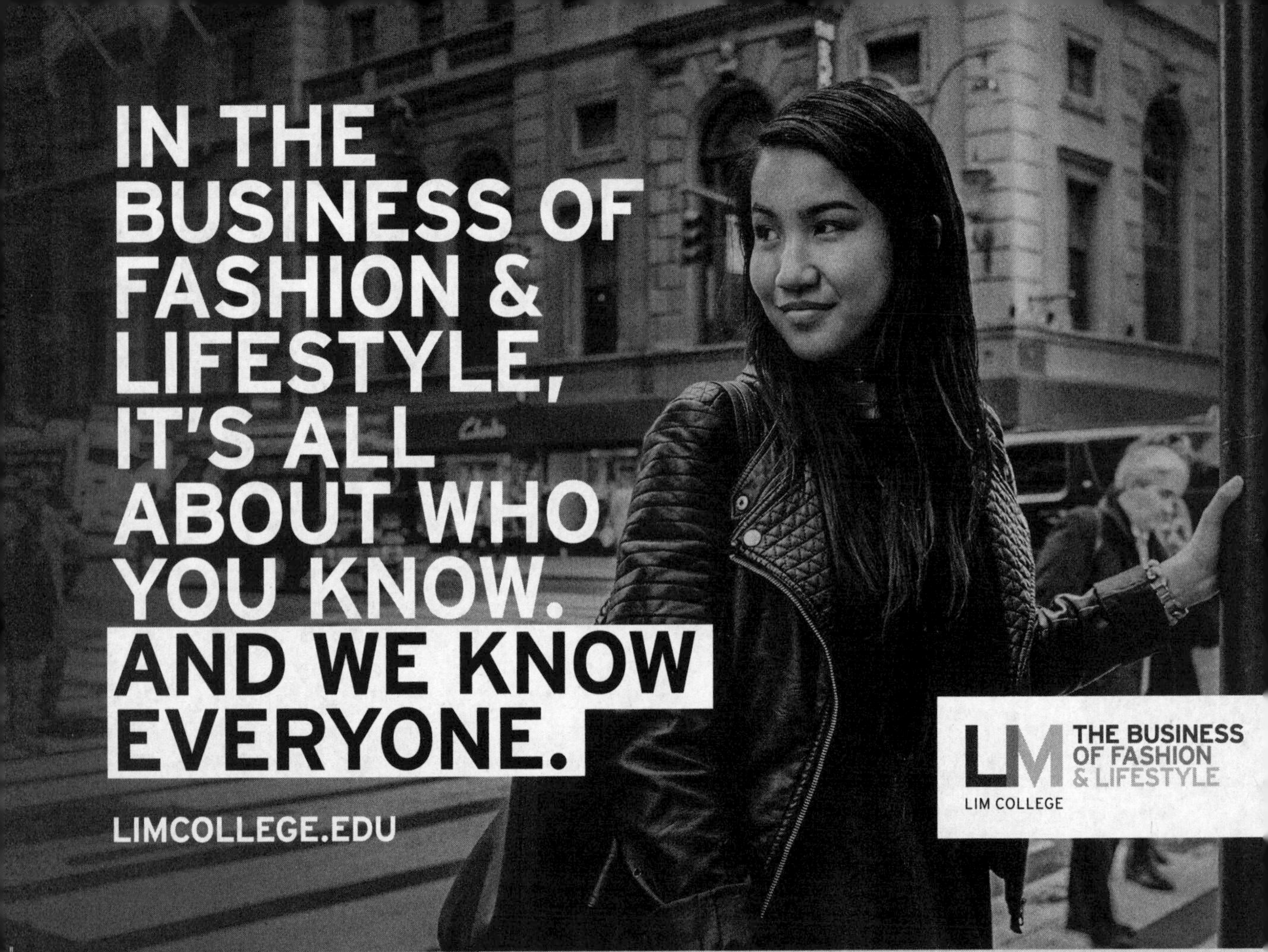

College Hopes & Worries Survey 2024

Mail to The Princeton Review, 2024 College Hopes & Worries Survey, c/o Robert Franek, The Princeton Review, 110 E. 42nd Street, 7th Fl., New York, NY 10017 (mailed entries must be received by February 24, 2024) or fill out online (online entries can be submitted between January 19 and February 29, 2024) at www.Princeton-Review.com/go/survey.

TAKE 3 MINUTES FOR A CHANCE TO WIN OUR $3,500 SCHOLARSHIP!

Name

Address (optional) _____

City / State / ZIP _____

Daytime phone _____

E-mail address _____

I am a:

- ○ student applying to college
- ○ parent of a student applying to college

What year will you (your child) begin college?

- ○ 2023
- ○ 2024
- ○ 2025
- ○ 2026
- ○ Other (please specify) _____

1. **What would be your "dream" college? What college would you most like to attend (or see your child attend) if chance of being accepted or cost were not an issue? (Please write complete name of the school, e.g., "University of Oklahoma," not initials such as "OU" which could also be the abbreviation for Ohio University.)**

   _____

2. **How many colleges will you (your child) apply to?**

   - ○ 1 to 4
   - ○ 5 to 8
   - ○ 9 to 12
   - ○ 13 or more

3. **Which of the following do you think will be the most important part of your (your child's) college application?**

   ○ Class rank

   ○ High school transcript, grades and GPA

   ○ SAT®/ACT® scores

   ○ Extracurriculars

   ○ Essay

   ○ Recommendations

4. **What is/will be the toughest part of your (your child's) college application experience?**

   ○ Researching colleges

   ○ Taking SAT, ACT, or AP® Exams

   ○ Completing applications for admission and financial aid

   ○ Waiting for the decision letters and choosing which college to attend

5. **Which college admission exam(s) have you (has your child) taken or plan to take?**

   ○ ACT

   ○ SAT

   ○ Both tests

   ○ Neither test

6. **Over the past two years, many colleges have announced they are "test optional" (i.e., no longer require applicants to submit SAT or ACT scores). While some schools still require these scores, and others may return to requiring them, which of the following best characterizes your (your child's) current perspective on the test optional movement?**

   ○ I (my child) is more likely to apply to a college that is test optional.

   ○ I (my child) is less likely to apply to a college that is test optional.

   ○ Admission test policies don't affect my (my child's) application decisions.

7. **As most test optional colleges will still consider SAT or ACT scores (only a low percentage say they are "test blind" and won't consider the scores), are you (your child) planning to take the SAT or ACT to be able to submit scores to such schools? If so — what is the key reason? (Note: If you (your child) is not planning to do this, skip this question.)**

   ○ Scores are considered in scholarship and financial aid award decisions.

   ○ Scores can enhance and distinguish my (my child's) application in a pool of others admission officers are receiving.

   ○ I (my child) want to have the scores "on hand" in case they are needed for application(s) ahead.

8. **The SAT is going digital. It will become a computer adaptive test in spring 2023 at international test centers and spring 2024 at U.S. test centers. What is your opinion of this big change ahead? (Need more information? Check our website: https://survey.vovici.com/se/5985395322055B14.)**

   ○ I think it will be a better test for me (my child).

   ○ I am concerned it may be a more difficult test for me (my child).

   ○ I (my child) will likely take the (still!) paper-and-pencil ACT instead.

   ○ I (my child) will not take either the SAT or the ACT.

9. **Have colleges' SAT/ACT test optional policies affected your (your child's) decisions with respect to taking AP courses (if available) and / or AP exams?**

   ○ Yes: More likely to take AP courses and/or exams.

   ○ No: Not more likely to take AP courses and/or exams.

10. **What do you estimate your (or your child's) college degree will cost, including four years of tuition, room & board, fees, books and other expenses?**

    ○ More than $100,000

    ○ $75,000 to $100,000

    ○ $50,000 to $75,000

    ○ $25,000 to $50,000

    ○ More than $25,000

11. **How necessary will financial aid—education loans, scholarships or grants—be to pay for your (your child's) college education?**

    ○ Extremely

    ○ Very

    ○ Somewhat

    ○ Not at all

12. **What's your biggest concern about your (your child's) college applications?**

   ○ Won't get into first-choice college

   ○ Will get into first-choice college but won't be able to afford to attend

   ○ Level of debt I (my child) will take on to pay for the degree

   ○ Will attend a college I (my child) may regret

13. **How would you gauge your stress level about the college application process?**

   ○ Very High

   ○ High

   ○ Average

   ○ Low

   ○ Very Low

14. **Ideally, how far from home would you like the college you (your child) attend(s) to be?**

   ○ Fewer than 250 miles

   ○ 250 to 500 miles

   ○ 500 to 1,000 miles

   ○ More than 1,000 miles

15. **When it comes to choosing the college you (your child) will attend, which of the following do you think it is most likely to be?**

   ○ College with best academic reputation

   ○ College that will be the most affordable

   ○ College with best program for my (my child's) career interests

   ○ College that will be the best overall fit

16. **If you (your child) had a way to compare colleges based on their reputation with regard to their career services offerings, how much would this contribute to your (your child's) decision to apply to or attend a school?**

   ○ Strongly

   ○ Very much

   ○ Somewhat

   ○ Not much

   ○ Not at all

17. **If you (your child) had a way to compare colleges based on their commitment to the environment (e.g., practices concerning energy use; recycling and sustainability; availability of "green" majors and course offerings), how much would this contribute to your (your child's) decision to apply to or attend a school?**

- ○ Strongly
- ○ Very much
- ○ Somewhat
- ○ Not much
- ○ Not at all

18. **If you (your child) had a way to compare colleges based on their health and wellness center services (e.g., counseling, fitness facilities, and other resources promoting students' mental and physical health), how much would this contribute to your (your child's) decision to apply to or attend a school?**

- ○ Strongly
- ○ Very much
- ○ Somewhat
- ○ Not much
- ○ Not at all

19. **What will be the biggest benefit of your (your child) getting a college degree?**

- ○ The education overall
- ○ The exposure to new ideas, places, people
- ○ The potentially better job and higher income

20. **On the whole, do you believe college will be "worth it" for you (your child)?**

- ○ Yes
- ○ No

What advice would you give to college applicants or parents of applicants going through this experience next year?

_____

_____

_____

_____

_____

_____

_____

_____

ABOUT THE AUTHORS

Robert Franek, Editor-in-Chief at The Princeton Review, is the company's chief expert on education and college issues. Over his 29-year career, he has served as a college admissions administrator, test prep teacher, author, and lecturer. Rob visits more than 50 colleges a year and oversees the company's line of 150 titles from best-selling test-prep guides to college- and graduate school-related books. He is also the host of 125 videos on The Princeton Review's YouTube channel. In three series—COVID-19 News and Updates, Key Concepts for AP Exams, and the College Admission 101 Learning Playlist—his videos provide timely advice for students and parents on current education topics. Collectively, they have received nearly 1,000,000 views. Prior to joining The Princeton Review in 1999, Rob served as a college admissions administrator at Wagner College (New York City) for six years. He earned his BA at Drew University in Political Science and History. Follow him on Twitter: @RobFranek.

David Soto, Senior Director of Data Operations, is a graduate of the Walter Cronkite School of Journalism at Arizona State University. He creates content on various aspects of the admissions process, including college, graduate school, and career-related topics, as well as the company website which serves more than half of all college-bound students. Prior to joining The Princeton Review in 2001, David worked as a photojournalist at The Arizona Republic (Phoenix). He lives in Brooklyn, NY, with his wife and two sons.

Stephen Koch, Senior Manager, Data Operations, received a BA from Wesleyan University in Middletown, Connecticut. He has been a member of The Princeton Review admissions content team since 2011. Stephen gathers and synthesizes all types of data The Princeton Review uses to create our guidebooks and website content. He lives in Brooklyn, NY.

Aaron Riccio, Senior Editor, earned a BA from Binghamton University in 2005. Since then, he has been working in various capacities within educational services, and has been with The Princeton Review's editorial department as of 2013, where he works to develop test-prep and guidebook titles.

Laura Rose, Editor, is a graduate of American University in Washington, D.C. Prior to joining The Princeton Review in 2021, Laura was the editorial director at Metromedia, Inc.